D0931387

The Famine Immigrants

Lists of Irish Immigrants Arriving at the Port of New York, 1846-1851

Illustrated London News

Emigrants Embarking from Waterloo Docks, Liverpool, 1850

THE FAMINE IMMIGRANTS

Lists of Irish Immigrants Arriving at the Port of New York, 1846 - 1851

Ira A. Glazier
Editor
Michael Tepper
Associate Editor

Volume IV
April 1849- September 1849

Baltimore
GENEALOGICAL PUBLISHING CO., INC.
1984

Library of Congress Catalogue Card Number 83-80078
International Standard Book Number 0-8063-1084-7
Made in the United States of America

FOREWORD

Like the preceding volumes in the series, the fourth volume of *The Famine Immigrants* contains a chronological list of Irish passengers who arrived at the port of New York during the period of the great Potato Famine. Spanning the six months from April to September 1849, it affords evidence of an unprecedented leap in the number of Irishmen reaching port, with more than 80,000 immigrants disembarking amidst the hurly-burly of a port which even yet had no central landing depot, twice as many as in the previous six months.

In Ireland itself the floodgates were open full, for with the second total failure of the potato crop the year before, the bankruptcy of the Poor Law Unions in the south and southwest, and the perversity of the British government in its new relief measures and in its fanatical adherence to the economic doctrine of *laissez-faire,* there was now little reason to believe that salvation lay in any path but emigration.

In numbers alone, this volume provides evidence of the failure of British policies and the limited alternatives to emigration remaining to the Irish peasant. Here then is an index of the despair that gripped the Irish nation at the very height of the Famine period — an enumeration of thousands of wretched souls compelled to take part in the historic exodus from Ireland.

M.H.T.

KEY

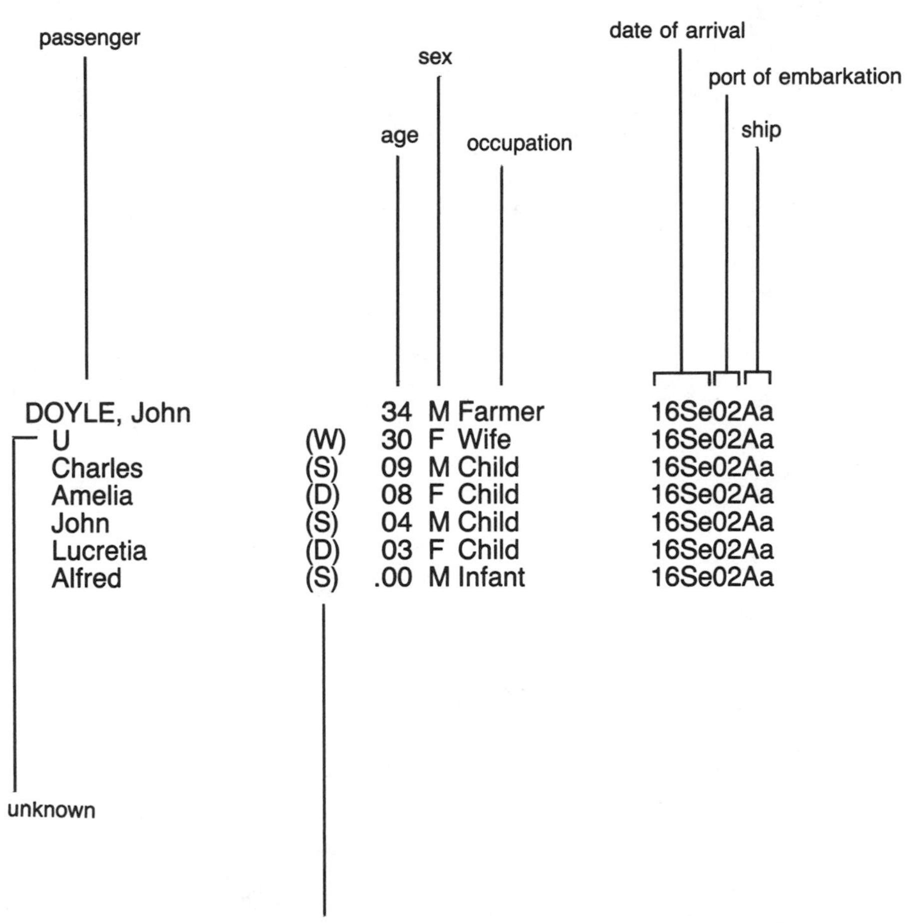

Also *A* aunt; *B* brother; *C* cousin; *F* stepdaughter; *G* stepson; *H* husband; *L* in-law; *M* mother; *N* niece/nephew; *O* widow/widower; *P* father; *R* relative; *T* sister; *Y* grandparent; *Z* grandchild.

LIST OF SHIPS
With Code Letters

AA WISCONSIN
AB CANTON
AC KEYING
AD CORONET
AE ELIZABETH-HAMILTON
AF CALEDONIA
AG NEW-ZEALAND
AH EMPEROR
AI SARAH
AJ BROOKSBY
AK MONTAUK
AL JAVA
AM WILLIAM-SPRAGUE
AN MARY-FLORENCE
AO QUEEN-OF-THE-WEST
AP GENERAL-GREENE
AQ GEORGE-BROWN
AR GREAT-BRITAIN
AS PRINCE-ALBERT
AT JUDSON
AU ELSINOR
AV HIGGINSON
AW METOKA
AX NEW-YORK
AY GEORGE-EVANS
AZ GLEN
BA SARAH-AND-LOUISA
BB L.Z.
BC ARTHUR
BD WESTMINSTER
BE WM.JARVIS
BF ARABELLA
BG ANNIE
BH ST.LAWRENCE
BI CRESCENT-CITY
BJ LADY-CONSTABLE
BK ELIZABETH
BL BETHEL
BM ARKANSAS
BN CALIFORNIA
BO HYNDEFORD
BP WARREN
BQ PROBUS
BR ATALANTA
BS SIR-COLIN-CAMPBELL
BT DOWNES
BU AYRSHIRE
BV RAINBOW
BW CAMILLUS
BX SHERIDAN
BY JOHN-J.D.WOLF
BZ JOHN-C.CALHOUN
CA MONTEZUMA
CB CAROLINA
CC INDUSTRY
CD HURON
CE WALTRON
CF ADMIRAL
CG CHINA
CH ALARM
CI BURLINGTON
CJ JOSEPH-MEIGS
CK EUROPA
CL VICTORIA
CM HUDSON
CN MESSENGER
CO HENRY-CLAY
CP DROMAHARN
CQ LYARA
CR ACADIAN
CS MARGARET
CT CAROLINE-READ
CU MT.STEW.ELPHINSTON
CV SEA-BIRD
CW MARMION
CX SWAN
CY HARVARD
CZ INDEPENDENCE
DA ABBEY-LAND
DB ARABIAN
DC COSMO
DD HOME
DE COLONY
DF WASHINGTON
DG DANIEL
DH DEVON
DI URANIA
DJ E.BENTLEY
DK FANNY
DL JAMES-FAGAN
DM SARAH-SANDS
DN SILAS-GRIMSHAW
DO OXFORD
DP CONSTITUTION
DQ TYPHIS
DR ROYAL-WILLIAM
DS NORTHUMBERLAND
DT WARRIOR
DU ANDREW-FOSTER
DV DANUBE
DW CASHMERE
DX CHESTER
DY WM.MILES
DZ WAVE
EA M.MELLON
EB AMERICA
EC NOEMIE
ED THREE-SISTERS
EE TERE-FOGO
EF C.MCLAUGHLIN
EG CELESTE
EH CUTHBERT
EI JOHN-R.SKIDDY
EJ CALEB-GRIMSHAW
EK GERTRUDE
EL NORWAY
EM WISSAHICKON
EN ORIENTAL
EO LINDEN
EP CARACTACUS
EQ EMMA-SEARLE
ER DUNBRODY
ES EL-DORADO
ET SILAS-GREENMAN
EU AFFGHAN
EV DINA-CARMALELY
EW BLANCHARD
EX H.H.BOODY
EY HONOR
EZ NUMA
FA HEATHER-BELL
FB ARAB
FC JANET
FD ALBANIA
FE SAMUEL
FF MOZAMBIQUE
FG MCDONNELL
FH LA-RUE
FI AUGUSTA
FJ HAYTI
FK SCOTIA
FL JUNIPER
FM HINDOSTAN
FN HANNAH-KERR
FO EDWARD
FP ARAMENTA
FQ JAMES
FR ALBERT
FS TRIUMPH
FT WENHAM
FU INFANTA
FV E.E.PERKINS
FW MARCHIONESS-OF-CLYSDALE
FX BOREAS
FY CANADA
FZ THAMES
GA ENTERPRISE
GB ORINOCO
GC MARY-MITCHELL
GD N.H.WOLFE
GE J.Z.
GF LIBERTY
GG MIDWAY
GH SIBSON
GI BOLTON-ABBEY
GJ AMBASSADRESS
GK CAMBRIDGE
GL STANDARD
GM BERIL
GN JAMES-HALL
GO HIBERNIA
GP LADY-HARVEY
GQ MARY-AND-MARTHA
GR RICHARD-N.PARKER
GS ELIJAH-SWIFT
GT JAMES-REDDIN
GU ABERDEEN
GV LEMUEL-DYER
GW NERO
GX VELOCITY
GY ROSETTA
GZ WILLIAM-D.SEWALL
HA ST.PATRICK
HB EFFINGHAM
HC FINGAL
HD BROTHERS
HE UNICORN
HF SERAPHINE
HG NEW-WORLD
HH GARRICK
HI CONRAD
HJ ANN-HARLEY
HK SILAS-RICHARDS
HL WEST-POINT
HM BRITANNIA
HN CATHERINE
HO WOLFVILLE
HP DEFENSE
HQ OSCEOLA
HR GALENA
HS YORKTOWN
HT CHIEFTAIN
HU HELEN-THOMPSON
HV THOS.TROWBRIDGE
HW BRITISH-QUEEN
HX MILICETE
HY ANN-MCLESTER
HZ CHARLOTTE-HARRISON
IA SEA
IB JANE

IC FIDELIA
ID SHANNON
IE MALABER
IF WARD-CHIPMAN
IG NIAGARA
IH JAMES-PENNELL
II HEBE
IJ TYRINGHAM
IK ASHLAND
IL COLUMBIA
IM MARY
IN LAWRENCE-FORESTAL
IO GOLDEN-SPRING
IP A.Z.
IQ REINZI
IR SENATOR
IS EARL-OF-DURHAM
IT BERLIN
IU ADELINE
IV MANILA
IW BREWER
IX HEROINE
IY KENT
IZ GREAT-WESTERN
JA TWO-SISTERS
JB BARBARA
JC QUEBEC-PACKET
JD CLARE
JE HOTTINGER
JF JAMESTOWN
JG CHRISTIAN
JH JULIET
JI MARY-HARRINGTON
JJ CAMBRIA
JK HARMONIA
JL ROSCIUS
JM PURSUIT
JN CORNELIA
JO JAMES-H.SHEPHERD
JP GOV.HINCKLEY
JQ MARIA
JR MORTIMER-LIVINGSTON
JS AGNES
JT JOHN-HANCOCK
JU LONDON
JV DE-WITT-CLINTON
JW SARDINIA
JX COLUMBINE
JY COLUMBUS
JZ METEOR
KA THETIS
KB OREGON
KC M.HAWES
KD FALCON
KE MGT.EVANS
KF E.FORESTAL
KG CLUTHA
KH JOSEPHINE
KI ANN-CARR
KJ TADMOR
KK DAVID-CARMON
KL KATE
KM ISAAC-WRIGHT
KN CHATHAM
KO LAING
KP JNO.COLBY
KQ TRANSIT
KR SHELTON
KS PROGRESS
KT HYPERION
KU WILBERFORCE
KV COLONIST
KW AEOLUS
KX DEVONIA
KY E.Z.
KZ HERALD
LA HERMES
LB ELIZA-CAROLINE
LC GUY-MANNERING
LD PELTONA
LE ASHBURTON
LF ARGYLE
LG RICHARD-ALSOP
LH MONTREAL-OF-NY
LI CONSTELLATION
LJ MARTHA-J.WARD
LL FOREST-KING
LM THOMAS-BAKER
LN ESCORT
LO CHENANGO
LP SATELLITE
LQ CENTURION
LR W.H.HARBECK
LS HENRY-POTTINGER
LT NAOMI
LU CHARLES-SAUNDERS
LV VIRGINIA
LW IVANHOE
LX ALEXINA
LY MARIANE
LZ YORKSHIRE
MA CAROLINE-NESMITH
MB ABEONA
MC EUGENIA
MD ANN-DASHWOOD
ME JUNIATA
MF AYOFF
MG CARLOTTA
MH Z.RING
MI NICOLAI-AND-JOVAN
MJ ASIA
MK RAPPAHANNOCK
ML LADY-MILTON
MM CYNTHIA
MN BRYAN-ABBS
MO PREDRAGA
MP ST.JOHN
MQ MECCA
MR GLENLYON
MS SALACIA
MT CUSHLAMACHREE
MU FEROZEPORE
MV QUEBEC
MW KATE-HUNTER
MX ORION
MY GERMANIA
MZ MARIA-BRENNAN
NA ST.GEORGE
NB MARY-ANN-HENRY
NC CHARLOTTE
ND LIVERPOOL
NE KOREA
NF FAVORITE
NG SIDDONS
NH CORA-LINN
NI HELEN
NJ SUPERB
NK NAPOLEON
NL ALLICE-WILSON
NM EMERALD
NN VANDALIA
NO BRITISH-OAK
NP BERKENHEAD
NQ DUKE-OF-WELLINGTON
NR MARY-MORRIS
NS BACHE-MCEVERS
NT DEVONSHIRE
NU LADY-OF-THE-LAKE
NV JULIA-HOWARD
NW JNO.KERR
NX ATLAS
NY CREMONA
NZ INDIANA
OA JOHN-BARING
OB LIVELY
OC SUSAN
OD HUNTRESS
OE PRINCETON
OF WATERLOO
OG PILGRIM
OH PIONEER
OI CALLENDAR
OJ SIR-WILLIAM-MOLESWORTH
OK JESSICA
OL HERO
OM GROWLER
ON GUILFORD
OO AMERICAN-EAGLE
OP MARCHIONESS-OF-BUTE
OQ HARRIET-AND-AUGUSTA
OR ODESSA
OS BOADICEA
OT SHEPHERDESS
OU HARTFORD
OV LAUREL
OW JOHN-FULDEN
OX MONUMENT
OY HUMPHREY-PURINTON
OZ WM.HITCHCOCK
PA SOLON
PB LOODIANAH
PC R.A.PARK
PD HUGUENOT
PE BOMBAY
PF POLANDER
PG JERSEY
PH ROSALINDA
PI NEW-HAMPSHIRE
PJ RICHARD-COBDEN
PK HALCYON
PL ERIN-GO-BRAGH
PM FANCHON
PN ABBY-PRATT
PO REPUBLIC
PP KINGSTON
PQ CLARENCE
PR LAURA
PS JENNY-LIND
PT HOLYOKE
PU PRINCE-OF-WALES
PV TERRA-NOVA
PW OHIO
PX MINERVA
PY JESSORE
PZ FAIRFIELD
QA WM.CHASE
QB SIR-HARRY-SMITH
QC ROLLA
QD OLYMPUS
QE EMPIRE-STATE
QF SCHOODIAC
QG CALCUTTA
QH ELVIRA
QI WYANDOTTE

PORTS OF EMBARKATION
With Code Numbers

00 UNKNOWN
01 LONDONDERRY
02 LIVERPOOL
03 QUEENSTOWN
04 GLASGOW
05 BELFAST
06 GALWAY
07 NEWFOUNDLAND
08 CORK
09 DEMERARA
10 BRISTOL
11 NEWRY
12 DUBLIN
13 LONDON
14 CARDIFF
15 WATERFORD
16 WEXFORD
17 BERBICE
18 NEWCASTLE
19 ST.MARTINS
20 PENZANCE
21 SLIGO
22 HULL
23 CANTON
24 MAYAQUEZ
25 NEW ROSS
26 CARNARVON
27 CHAGRAS, SAN JUAN, HAVANA
28 YOUGHAL
29 BERMUDA
30 DROGHEDA
31 NEWPORT
32 TRALEE
33 GREENOCK
34 DONEGAL
35 LIMERICK
36 SUNDERLAND
37 SANTIAGO
38 KILLIBEGS
39 ST.CROIX
40 MATANZAS
41 SYDNEY,CAPE BRETON
42 ARICHAT
43 HALIFAX
44 PORT-AU-PRINCE
45 NUEVITAS
46 PORTSMOUTH
47 BERMUDA AND ST.THOMAS
48 MARANHAM
49 LIVERPOOL AND HALIFAX
50 NORTH SHIELDS
51 HARTLEPOOL
52 MATANZAS
53 DEMERARA AND ST.THOMAS
54 LONDON AND PLYMOUTH
55 WINDSOR
56 ST. JOHNS, N.F.
57 JERSEY
58 CHAGRES AND JAMAICA
59 FORTUNE ISLAND
60 HAMILTON, BERMUDA
61 ST.JOHNS,N.B.
62 PICTOU,N.S.
63 LONDON AND PORTSMOUTH
64 BUENOS AIRES
65 LANZARATA
66 PONCE
67 TURKS ISLAND
68 LIVERPOOL AND CORK
69 LIVORNO
70 NASSAU
71 VERA CRUZ
72 TORTOLA
73 TOBAGO

LIST OF OCCUPATIONS
With Code Letters

AGRC	AGRICULTURALIST
AGRT	AGRICULTURIST
BLR	BOILER MAKER
BOMKR	BONNET MAKER
BRF	BRASS FOUNDER
BRFHR	BRASS FINISHER
BRWKR	BRASS WORKER
BTNM	BUTTON MAKER
BTTBYR	BUTTER BUYER
BXMRFY	FANCY BOX MAKER
CBTMKR	CABINET MAKER
CHPTR	COACH PAINTER
CK-LAD	COOK-LAUNDRESS
CKASST	COOK'S ASSISTANT
CLCP	CALICO PRINTER
CLDRS	CLOTH DRESSER
CLRWKR	COLLAR WORKER
CMAGT	COMMISSION AGENT
CNF	CONFECTIONER
CPT	CAPTAIN OR SHIPMASTER
CPTR-APDST	CARPENTER APPRENTICE
CRPW	CARPET WEAVER
CTNSP	COTTON SPINNER
CTNTW	COTTON TWISTER
CVER	CIVIL ENGINEER
CVR-GLDR	CARVER-GILDER
DIASTER	DIAMOND SETTER
FEFNDR	IRON FOUNDER
FLABR	FARM LABORER
FLAXDR	FLAX DRESSER
FLMFT	FLANNEL MANUFACTURER
FLXSP	FLAX SPINNER
FSVNT	FARM SERVANT
GCR-AGR	GROCER-AGRICULTURIST
GDNR	GARDENER/GROWER
GLSBR	GLASS BLOWER
GLSCTR	GLASS CUTTER
HPNTR	HOUSE PAINTER
HRSM	HARNESS MAKER
LAD	LAUNDRY WORKER
LNWVR	LINEN WEAVER
LRDRS	LEATHER DRESSER
MAT	MATTRESS MAKER
MCHTCL	MERCHANT'S CLERK
MNFTR	MANUFACTURER
MNTL	MANTLE MAKER
MTMKR	MANTEAU MAKER
NGTWTCH	NIGHT WATCHMAN
NVOF	NAVY OFFICER
OAT	OATMEAL MANUFACTURER
OLMCHT	OIL MERCHANT
PMFR	PAINT MANUFACTURER
PNTR-GZR	PAINTER-GLAZIER
PPSTR	PAPER STAINER
PVMT	PROVISION MERCHANT
PWLWVR	POWERLOOM WEAVER
RLST	RAIL STRAIGHTENER
RP	REPORTING PRINTER
SCHM	SCHOOL MASTER
SCHMS	SCHOOL MISTRESS
SGINMKR	SURGICAL INSTRUMENT MAKER
STCTR	STONE CUTTER
STCWKR	STUCCO WORKER
SUGPL	SUGAR PLANTER
TCHR-SVNT	TEACHER-SERVANT
TCHRL	TEACHER OF LANGUAGES
TIPWKR	TINPLATE WORKER
VSGN	VET. SURGEON
W-FMR	WIFE OF FARMER
W-LABR	WIFE OF LABORER
W-MECH	WIFE OF MECHANIC
W-MNR	WIFE OF MINER
WDMCHT	WOOD MERCHANT
WI	WIDOW/WIDOWER
WLMCHT	WOOL MERCHANT
WLNMCHT	WOOLEN MERCHANT
WWSH	WHITE WASHER

THE FAMINE IMMIGRANTS

Lists of Irish Immigrants
Arriving at the Port of New York,
1846-1851

WISCONSIN 01 APRIL 1849

From Liverpool

NAMES OF PASSENGERS	AGE	SEX	OCCUPATIONS	DATE PORT SHIP
HUGHES, Edwd.	00	M	Unknown	01Ap02Aa
MCKENNA, Mary	45	F	Unknown	01Ap02Aa
Mary	13	F	Unknown	01Ap02Aa
HOUGH, Joseph	33	M	Laborer	01Ap02Aa
Ann	38	F	Unknown	01Ap02Aa
Elzth.	10	F	Unknown	01Ap02Aa
Saml.	04	M	Child	01Ap02Aa
Charlotte	.00	F	Infant	01Ap02Aa
RYAN, John	15	M	Unknown	01Ap02Aa
ALSOP, John	52	M	Miner	01Ap02Aa
Ann	52	F	Unknown	01Ap02Aa
SPILLANE, Jas.	30	M	Farmer	01Ap02Aa
LAHY, John	22	M	Cooper	01Ap02Aa
HANLON, John	50	M	Weaver	01Ap02Aa
Mary	45	F	Unknown	01Ap02Aa
Johanna	18	F	Servant	01Ap02Aa
Michl.	20	M	Laborer	01Ap02Aa
LANE, Dennis	05	M	Child	01Ap02Aa
BRAYFINER, Henry	24	M	Farmer	01Ap02Aa
SMITH, Jas.	34	M	Tinker	01Ap02Aa
U (W)	26	F	Unknown	01Ap02Aa
SHEA, Michl.	28	M	Unknown	01Ap02Aa
WALLS, Jerh.	22	M	Blacksmith	01Ap02Aa
ROE, Peter-H.	21	M	Blacksmith	01Ap02Aa
SHARPE, Henry	31	M	Unknown	01Ap02Aa
SMITH, George	30	M	Unknown	01Ap02Aa
GILLING, George	30	M	Farmer	01Ap02Aa
Elzth.	30	F	Unknown	01Ap02Aa
HAGAE, Wm.	26	M	Locksmith	01Ap02Aa
Martha	22	F	Unknown	01Ap02Aa
Ann	01	F	Child	01Ap02Aa
FARRADAY, John	40	M	Brick Maker	01Ap02Aa
Pat	18	M	Unknown	01Ap02Aa
Ann	16	F	Unknown	01Ap02Aa
Margt.	15	F	Unknown	01Ap02Aa
SMITH, Pat	12	M	Unknown	01Ap02Aa
DONLY, John	39	M	Laborer	01Ap02Aa
Elzth.	40	F	Unknown	01Ap02Aa
KIERNAN, John	29	M	Laborer	01Ap02Aa
ANDERSON, John	23	M	Laborer	01Ap02Aa
SMITH, Cath.	18	F	Laborer	01Ap02Aa
Jas.	15	F	Laborer	01Ap02Aa
CARMEY, Owen	16	F	Laborer	01Ap02Aa
Winefred	29	F	Servant	01Ap02Aa
Honora	07	F	Child	01Ap02Aa
Bridget	03	F	Child	01Ap02Aa
ALLEN, Mary-A.	18	F	Servant	01Ap02Aa
Jane	19	F	Servant	01Ap02Aa
CALLAGHAN, Mary	26	F	Servant	01Ap02Aa
DEVLIN, Mary	24	F	Servant	01Ap02Aa
Michl.	16	M	Servant	01Ap02Aa
Pat	14	M	Servant	01Ap02Aa
MORRISON, Alex.	21	M	Servant	01Ap02Aa
MCKAGNE, John	21	M	Servant	01Ap02Aa
THORNBURY, Jas.	18	M	Servant	01Ap02Aa
SMITH, U-Mrs.	34	F	Servant	01Ap02Aa
REILLY, Mic.	19	M	Servant	01Ap02Aa
MALONE, Chas.	22	M	Laborer	01Ap02Aa
TATE, Joseph	27	M	Farmer	01Ap02Aa
Caroline	27	F	Farmer	01Ap02Aa
John	04	M	Child	01Ap02Aa
Mary	02	F	Child	01Ap02Aa
Thos.	.00	M	Infant	01Ap02Aa
GILES, Thos.	50	M	Farmer	01Ap02Aa
MANNING, Peter	24	M	Farmer	01Ap02Aa

NAMES OF PASSENGERS	AGE	SEX	OCCUPATIONS	DATE PORT SHIP
CONWAY, Peter	23	M	Farmer	01Ap02Aa
LYNCH, John	18	M	Farmer	01Ap02Aa
Danl.	14	M	Farmer	01Ap02Aa
MOONEY, Matt	25	M	Farmer	01Ap02Aa
KIERNAN, Cath.	21	F	Servant	01Ap02Aa
DONOVAN, Cath.	28	F	Servant	01Ap02Aa
VAUGHAN, Edwd.	28	M	Groom	01Ap02Aa
FLYNN, Winnefred	16	F	Bell Hanger	01Ap02Aa
SMITH, John	30	M	Bell Hanger	01Ap02Aa
MCKENNA, Owen	22	M	Bell Hanger	01Ap02Aa
DONNELLY, Hugh	19	M	Bell Hanger	01Ap02Aa
DUFFY, Hugh	20	M	Bell Hanger	01Ap02Aa
Bridget	09	F	Child	01Ap02Aa
KIERNAN, Phillip	27	M	Bell Hanger	01Ap02Aa
Bernd.	25	M	Bell Hanger	01Ap02Aa
Mary	20	F	Bell Hanger	01Ap02Aa
CONLY, Pat	40	M	Bell Hanger	01Ap02Aa
RIELLY, Chas.	30	M	Farmer	01Ap02Aa
Honor	28	F	Farmer	01Ap02Aa
Harriet	20	F	Farmer	01Ap02Aa
MCMANUS, Felix	15	M	Farmer	01Ap02Aa
COOK, Ann	15	M	Farmer	01Ap02Aa
COYLE, Hugh	15	M	Farmer	01Ap02Aa
BROADY, Ann	20	F	Farmer	01Ap02Aa
TIERNEY, Norah	18	F	Servant	01Ap02Aa
QUINN, Norah	16	F	Unknown	01Ap02Aa
ODONNELL, John	19	M	Cooper	01Ap02Aa
Sarah	17	F	Servant	01Ap02Aa
Cath.	21	F	Servant	01Ap02Aa
THATCHER, Saml.	30	M	Weaver	01Ap02Aa
U-Mrs.	29	F	Unknown	01Ap02Aa
STONE, John	19	M	Tailor	01Ap02Aa
BANKS, Mary	18	F	Tailor	01Ap02Aa
Betsey	17	F	Tailor	01Ap02Aa
Rose	12	F	Tailor	01Ap02Aa
KELLY, Thos.	21	M	Tailor	01Ap02Aa
FITZPATRICK, Rose	20	F	Tailor	01Ap02Aa
GROGAN, Jane	20	F	Tailor	01Ap02Aa
MCBRIDE, Rose	20	F	Tailor	01Ap02Aa
RONAYNE, David	34	M	Tailor	01Ap02Aa
FITZGIBBON, Michl.	40	M	Tailor	01Ap02Aa
BENNETT, John	19	M	Tailor	01Ap02Aa
KENNEDY, John	30	M	Tailor	01Ap02Aa
MEHAN, Thos.	19	M	Tailor	01Ap02Aa
FITZGERALD, Wm.	32	M	Groom	01Ap02Aa
ROURK, Jas.	26	M	Unknown	01Ap02Aa
Michl.	.00	M	Infant	01Ap02Aa
CASICK, Pat	34	M	Fiddler	01Ap02Aa
SMITH, Pat	24	M	Fiddler	01Ap02Aa
Mary	09	F	Child	01Ap02Aa
KEOUGH, Gerald	16	M	Farmer	01Ap02Aa
SMITH, Pat	27	M	Fiddler	01Ap02Aa
FEE, Elzth.	22	F	Fiddler	01Ap02Aa
DABBIN, John	24	M	Fiddler	01Ap02Aa
MCGOWLEY, Thos.	21	M	Fiddler	01Ap02Aa
RUDICON, Mary	25	F	Fiddler	01Ap02Aa
MCCAFFREY, Mary	18	F	Servant	01Ap02Aa
REILLY, Ann	40	F	Servant	01Ap02Aa
FOX, John	19	M	Servant	01Ap02Aa
GLASSY, Jas.	27	M	Servant	01Ap02Aa
KENNEDY, Ellen	20	F	Servant	01Ap02Aa
Celia	18	F	Servant	01Ap02Aa
John	14	M	Servant	01Ap02Aa
CLIFFORD, Pat	30	M	Servant	01Ap02Aa
Jas.	28	M	Servant	01Ap02Aa
CANDEN, Mary	14	F	Servant	01Ap02Aa
Ellen	12	F	Servant	01Ap02Aa
BRASSETT, Honor	30	F	Servant	01Ap02Aa
NIXON, Thos.	22	M	Servant	01Ap02Aa
GILPIN, William	19	M	Saddler	01Ap02Aa
Rebecca	18	F	Saddler	01Ap02Aa
Mary	16	F	Saddler	01Ap02Aa
WATSON, W.	26	M	Saddler	01Ap02Aa
PYE, Jabez	26	M	Saddler	01Ap02Aa
MURRY, John	35	M	Saddler	01Ap02Aa

NAMES OF PASSENGERS	AGE	SEX	OCCUPATIONS	DATE PORT SHIP
MURRY, Mary	35	F	Saddler	01Ap02Aa
Terence	10	M	Saddler	01Ap02Aa
Cath.	05	F	Child	01Ap02Aa
Pat	02	M	Child	01Ap02Aa
TOWNE, Thos.	16	M	Saddler	01Ap02Aa
MURRAY, Jas.	.00	M	Infant	01Ap02Aa
MARTIN, Ellen	30	F	Saddler	01Ap02Aa
Owen	03	M	Child	01Ap02Aa
MCQUEENY, Bridget	22	F	Servant	01Ap02Aa
Peter	04	M	Child	01Ap02Aa
Margt.	02	F	Child	01Ap02Aa
CLARKE, Alfred	25	M	Unknown	01Ap02Aa
U (W)	24	F	Unknown	01Ap02Aa
DOUGHERTY, Pat	24	M	Unknown	01Ap02Aa
FINNEGAN, Thos.	20	M	Unknown	01Ap02Aa
MULGREW, John	25	M	Unknown	01Ap02Aa
GARRETT, Thos.	30	M	Unknown	01Ap02Aa
Jane	30	F	Servant	01Ap02Aa
GETTING, Ann	20	F	Servant	01Ap02Aa
GARRETT, Hannah	06	F	Child	01Ap02Aa
Jane	04	F	Child	01Ap02Aa
Thos.H.	02	M	Child	01Ap02Aa
Caesar	20	M	Farmer	01Ap02Aa
GILL, John	16	M	Farmer	01Ap02Aa
CREER, Evan	24	M	Farmer	01Ap02Aa
CROW, Thos.	23	M	Farmer	01Ap02Aa
QUILLIAM, John	34	M	Tinker	01Ap02Aa
Jane	18	F	Unknown	01Ap02Aa
KIRK, Eliza	40	F	Carpenter	01Ap02Aa
CHICK, Esther	14	F	Carpenter	01Ap02Aa
QUILLIAM, Ann	08	F	Child	01Ap02Aa
Richd.	06	M	Child	01Ap02Aa
John	04	M	Child	01Ap02Aa
Ellen	01	F	Child	01Ap02Aa
MCKENNA, John	40	M	Carpenter	01Ap02Aa
Mary-Anne	13	F	Unknown	01Ap02Aa
Michl.	11	M	Unknown	01Ap02Aa
Cath.	10	F	Unknown	01Ap02Aa
John	07	M	Child	01Ap02Aa
Pat	20	M	Laborer	01Ap02Aa
CORRIGAN, Cath.	00	F	Laborer	01Ap02Aa
Jane	00	F	Laborer	01Ap02Aa
GOODMAN, Jas.	50	M	Laborer	01Ap02Aa
Mary	60	F	Laborer	01Ap02Aa
Edwd.	00	M	Laborer	01Ap02Aa
James	00	M	Laborer	01Ap02Aa
MCELROY, Susan	19	F	Laborer	01Ap02Aa
JOHNSTON, Pat	20	M	Laborer	01Ap02Aa
TRAINER, Pat	25	M	Laborer	01Ap02Aa
GALLAGHER, Chas.	00	M	Laborer	01Ap02Aa
MCMENOMY, Danl.	25	M	Farmer	01Ap02Aa
TUBMAN, Mary	22	F	Servant	01Ap02Aa
YOUNG, Thos.	21	M	Servant	01Ap02Aa
Wm.	32	M	Servant	01Ap02Aa
Saml.	24	M	Servant	01Ap02Aa
LABRON, Thos.	30	M	Servant	01Ap02Aa
PRICE, Henry	40	M	Servant	01Ap02Aa
WILSON, Jas.	22	M	Servant	01Ap02Aa
DENNIS, Jas.	25	M	Servant	01Ap02Aa
Mary	20	F	Servant	01Ap02Aa
MCKENNA, Jas.	18	M	Servant	01Ap02Aa
WARD, Jane	20	F	Servant	01Ap02Aa
GALVEN, Anty.	40	F	Servant	01Ap02Aa
Anty.	02	F	Child	01Ap02Aa
Thos.	.00	M	Infant	01Ap02Aa
MATHER, Nancy	40	F	Unknown	01Ap02Aa
Maria	18	F	Servant	01Ap02Aa
BALL, Wm.	25	M	Farmer	01Ap02Aa
MCGINN, Sally	20	F	Servant	01Ap02Aa
TRAINER, Chas.	23	M	Unknown	01Ap02Aa
MCNAMARA, Robt.	20	M	Unknown	01Ap02Aa
Rose	19	F	Unknown	01Ap02Aa
FLYNN, Gilbert	28	M	Shoemaker	01Ap02Aa
Mary	30	F	Servant	01Ap02Aa
Bridget	.00	F	Infant	01Ap02Aa

NAMES OF PASSENGERS	AGE	SEX	OCCUPATIONS	DATE PORT SHIP
WALL, Johanna	27	F	Infant	01Ap02Aa
GAHAN, Michl.	07	M	Child	01Ap02Aa
Wm.	05	M	Child	01Ap02Aa
Pat	.00	M	Infant	01Ap02Aa
ATCHESON, Eliza	30	F	Servant	01Ap02Aa
Sarah-Ann	04	F	Child	01Ap02Aa
Jas.	02	M	Child	01Ap02Aa
Wm.	.00	M	Infant	01Ap02Aa
LYNCH, Pat	30	M	Smith	01Ap02Aa
BRADY, Peter	20	M	Smith	01Ap02Aa
DOUGALL, Mary-A.	17	F	Unknown	01Ap02Aa
ATCHISON, Rich.	30	M	Unknown	01Ap02Aa
COGERTY, Jas.	36	M	Weaver	01Ap02Aa
LYONS, Bernd.	18	M	Cooper	01Ap02Aa
WHITE, Richd.	25	M	Cooper	01Ap02Aa
BELL, Jas.	25	M	Cooper	01Ap02Aa
Mary	22	F	Unknown	01Ap02Aa
Esther	50	F	Unknown	01Ap02Aa
FOSTER, Martha	18	F	Servant	01Ap02Aa
Andrew	.00	M	Infant	01Ap02Aa
BRADY, Barney	22	M	Laborer	01Ap02Aa
Ann	45	F	Unknown	01Ap02Aa
MONAGHAN, Pat	20	M	Laborer	01Ap02Aa
BRANASALL, Geo.	25	M	Laborer	01Ap02Aa
SMITH, Jas.	26	M	Laborer	01Ap02Aa
MCGUIRK, Peter	22	M	Laborer	01Ap02Aa
Alice	20	F	Unknown	01Ap02Aa
RAGAN, Jane	18	F	Servant	01Ap02Aa
OHARA, Mary	18	F	Servant	01Ap02Aa
GITTLAND, Pat	50	M	Farmer	01Ap02Aa
Mary	50	F	Farmer	01Ap02Aa
Fras.	19	M	Farmer	01Ap02Aa
Margt.	20	F	Farmer	01Ap02Aa
Michl.	19	M	Farmer	01Ap02Aa
Danl.	16	M	Farmer	01Ap02Aa
Jos.	04	M	Child	01Ap02Aa
George	06	M	Child	01Ap02Aa
QUINN, Thos.	19	M	Laborer	01Ap02Aa

CANTON 02 APRIL 1849

From Cork

NAMES OF PASSENGERS	AGE	SEX	OCCUPATIONS	DATE PORT SHIP
ROBERTS, Mary	24	F	Unknown	02Ap08Ab
John	4	M	Child	02Ap08Ab
GARDS, John	25	M	Unknown	02Ap08Ab
ROE, James	25	M	Unknown	02Ap08Ab
HODDER, George	7	M	Child	02Ap08Ab
John	9	M	Child	02Ap08Ab
HANNON, Rich.	35	M	Unknown	02Ap08Ab
BUCKLEY, John	28	M	Unknown	02Ap08Ab
CRENIN, Mary	30	F	Unknown	02Ap08Ab
MCDONNELL, Eliza	22	F	Unknown	02Ap08Ab
CAREY, Frank	47	M	Unknown	02Ap08Ab
Fanny	34	F	Unknown	02Ap08Ab
TOBIN, Ned	20	M	Unknown	02Ap08Ab
CREEDEN, Mary	19	F	Unknown	02Ap08Ab
BUTLER, John	22	M	Unknown	02Ap08Ab
ARPEN, George	36	M	Unknown	02Ap08Ab
Wm.	13	M	Unknown	02Ap08Ab
SHEEHAN, Danl.	35	M	Unknown	02Ap08Ab
Norry	35	F	Unknown	02Ap08Ab
Wm.	13	M	Unknown	02Ap08Ab
Cath.	9	F	Child	02Ap08Ab
COWMANE, Tead	30	M	Unknown	02Ap08Ab
GREGG, Michl.	20	M	Unknown	02Ap08Ab
Margt.	14	F	Unknown	02Ap08Ab
WALSH, Michl.	20	M	Unknown	02Ap08Ab
DOWNEY, Jerry	24	M	Unknown	02Ap08Ab

NAMES OF PASSENGERS	AGE	SEX	OCCUPATIONS	DATE PORT SHIP
DONOVAN, Wm.	20	M	Unknown	02Ap08Ab
SULLIVAN, Tom	35	M	Unknown	02Ap08Ab
BOWEN, Lawrence	26	M	Unknown	02Ap08Ab
CONNELL, Norry	20	F	Unknown	02Ap08Ab
MCCARTHY, David	20	M	Unknown	02Ap08Ab
ENGLISH, Patt	35	M	Unknown	02Ap08Ab
Wm.	20	M	Unknown	02Ap08Ab
Eliza	20	F	Unknown	02Ap08Ab
Johanna	21	F	Unknown	02Ap08Ab
Patk.	21	M	Unknown	02Ap08Ab
Mary	20	F	Unknown	02Ap08Ab
Peggy	22	F	Unknown	02Ap08Ab
TOBIN, Wm.	35	M	Unknown	02Ap08Ab
MERRICK, Latres	36	U	Unknown	02Ap08Ab
Judith	25	F	Unknown	02Ap08Ab
Matilda	6	F	Child	02Ap08Ab
Rosabella	5	F	Child	02Ap08Ab
Obel	.08	U	Infant	02Ap08Ab
CRAWFORD, David	25	M	Unknown	02Ap08Ab
Charles	20	M	Unknown	02Ap08Ab
COSGRAVE, John	19	M	Unknown	02Ap08Ab
DONOVAN, Matt.	25	M	Unknown	02Ap08Ab
Bess	20	F	Unknown	02Ap08Ab
MURPHY, Danl.	20	M	Unknown	02Ap08Ab
MCDONNELL, Batt.	30	U	Unknown	02Ap08Ab
Mary	30	F	Unknown	02Ap08Ab
Patt	.10	M	Infant	02Ap08Ab
DRISCOLL, Jerry	20	M	Unknown	02Ap08Ab
Johanna	17	F	Unknown	02Ap08Ab
MEARA, James	20	M	Unknown	02Ap08Ab
MURPHY, Maurice	24	M	Unknown	02Ap08Ab
Cath.	23	F	Unknown	02Ap08Ab
Johanna	11	F	Unknown	02Ap08Ab
Bridget	9	F	Child	02Ap08Ab
James	2	M	Child	02Ap08Ab
JERRY, Charles	22	M	Unknown	02Ap08Ab
CRONIN, William	25	M	Unknown	02Ap08Ab
BOURKE, John	25	M	Unknown	02Ap08Ab
Bridget	25	F	Unknown	02Ap08Ab
Cathn.	22	F	Unknown	02Ap08Ab
SCULLY, Johanna	20	F	Unknown	02Ap08Ab
Jim	22	M	Unknown	02Ap08Ab
John	20	M	Unknown	02Ap08Ab
HURLEY, John	22	M	Unknown	02Ap08Ab
ADAMS, Hannah	20	F	Unknown	02Ap08Ab
HARTNETT, Margt.	35	F	Unknown	02Ap08Ab
John	40	M	Unknown	02Ap08Ab
Mary	18	F	Unknown	02Ap08Ab
Danl.	12	M	Unknown	02Ap08Ab
HAWKES, Johanna	40	F	Unknown	02Ap08Ab
James	18	M	Unknown	02Ap08Ab
Michl.	16	M	Unknown	02Ap08Ab
Johanna	13	F	Unknown	02Ap08Ab
MAGUIRE, Mary	30	F	Unknown	02Ap08Ab
HAYES, Fanny	28	F	Unknown	02Ap08Ab
HICKEY, Andy	30	M	Unknown	02Ap08Ab
DOWLING, Willm.	30	M	Unknown	02Ap08Ab
BUTLER, Mary	28	F	Unknown	02Ap08Ab
CRONIN, Mary	24	F	Unknown	02Ap08Ab
REGAN, Mary	18	F	Unknown	02Ap08Ab
HAYES, Honora	18	F	Unknown	02Ap08Ab
CRONIN, Wm.	5	M	Child	02Ap08Ab
DESMOND, Mary	40	F	Unknown	02Ap08Ab
WHITE, Ellen	40	F	Unknown	02Ap08Ab
HOULAHAN, Danl.	30	M	Unknown	02Ap08Ab
FOLEY, James	28	M	Unknown	02Ap08Ab
WHITE, Paul	30	M	Unknown	02Ap08Ab
Patt	28	M	Unknown	02Ap08Ab
OBRIEN, Mary	30	F	Unknown	02Ap08Ab
Ellen	20	F	Unknown	02Ap08Ab
LYSGATH, James	18	M	Unknown	02Ap08Ab
John	20	M	Unknown	02Ap08Ab
Mary	12	F	Unknown	02Ap08Ab
SWAYNE, U	20	U	Unknown	02Ap08Ab
BOURKE, James	26	M	Unknown	02Ap08Ab
MALVEY, Matt	40	M	Unknown	02Ap08Ab
Johanna	40	F	Unknown	02Ap08Ab
LYNCH, John	20	M	Unknown	02Ap08Ab
LUDDY, Thos.	25	M	Unknown	02Ap08Ab
MAHONY, Mary	24	F	Unknown	02Ap08Ab
MCDONNELL, Betty	40	F	Unknown	02Ap08Ab
Danl.	22	M	Unknown	02Ap08Ab
Denis	20	M	Unknown	02Ap08Ab
Judy	16	F	Unknown	02Ap08Ab
Judy	16	F	Unknown	02Ap08Ab
Timothy	14	M	Unknown	02Ap08Ab
MURPHY, James	30	M	Unknown	02Ap08Ab
Ellen	32	F	Unknown	02Ap08Ab
Denis	23	M	Unknown	02Ap08Ab
FETHERSTON, Edmd.	30	M	Unknown	02Ap08Ab
NEAGLE, James	40	M	Unknown	02Ap08Ab
FRANKLIN, John	40	M	Unknown	02Ap08Ab
Thos.	30	M	Unknown	02Ap08Ab
Wm.	20	M	Unknown	02Ap08Ab
NEIL, Michl.	20	M	Unknown	02Ap08Ab
GARVIN, James	25	M	Unknown	02Ap08Ab
HAYES, Margt.	23	F	Unknown	02Ap08Ab
KEILY, John	35	M	Unknown	02Ap08Ab
SULLIVAN, Ellen	30	F	Unknown	02Ap08Ab
WALSH, Mary	20	F	Unknown	02Ap08Ab
SMITH, U-Mrs.	30	F	Unknown	02Ap08Ab
HORAGAN, Bridget	50	F	Unknown	02Ap08Ab
Ellen	20	F	Unknown	02Ap08Ab
CALAHAN, Denis	30	M	Unknown	02Ap08Ab
BORMEHAN, Johanna	24	F	Unknown	02Ap08Ab
COLLINS, Jerh.	26	M	Unknown	02Ap08Ab
Mary	20	F	Unknown	02Ap08Ab
KELLEHER, James	20	M	Unknown	02Ap08Ab
HANLON, Bill	30	M	Unknown	02Ap08Ab
John	18	M	Unknown	02Ap08Ab
SHEEHAN, Timothy	30	M	Unknown	02Ap08Ab
Ellen	30	M	Unknown	02Ap08Ab
Mary	11	F	Unknown	02Ap08Ab
Thomas	9	M	Child	02Ap08Ab
Margt.	3	F	Child	02Ap08Ab
Ellen	.02	F	Infant	02Ap08Ab
SULLIVAN, Jeremiah	20	M	Unknown	02Ap08Ab
Ellen	40	F	Unknown	02Ap08Ab
MANNING, Michl.	25	M	Unknown	02Ap08Ab
LINEHAN, Danl.	20	M	Unknown	02Ap08Ab
Jane	22	F	Unknown	02Ap08Ab
MEHEGAN, Eugene	20	M	Unknown	02Ap08Ab
FLAHERTY, Timothy	20	M	Unknown	02Ap08Ab
FALVEY, Denis	18	M	Unknown	02Ap08Ab
HANNON, Mary	18	F	Unknown	02Ap08Ab
MURPHY, Eugene	14	M	Unknown	02Ap08Ab
LEARY, Timothy	35	M	Unknown	02Ap08Ab
Mary	35	F	Unknown	02Ap08Ab
Danl.	13	M	Unknown	02Ap08Ab
Timothy	10	M	Unknown	02Ap08Ab
Mary	7	F	Child	02Ap08Ab
John	5	M	Child	02Ap08Ab
WILLIAMS, Griffiths	28	M	Unknown	02Ap08Ab
Anne	25	F	Unknown	02Ap08Ab
FITZGERALD, Margt.	30	F	Unknown	02Ap08Ab
HIBBS, Cathe.	30	F	Unknown	02Ap08Ab
Henry	14	M	Unknown	02Ap08Ab
Isabella	3	F	Child	02Ap08Ab
BROWNE, Margt.	24	F	Unknown	02Ap08Ab
BRODER, John	35	M	Unknown	02Ap08Ab
HURLEY, John	22	M	Unknown	02Ap08Ab
SHEA, Jerh.	20	M	Unknown	02Ap08Ab
SULLIVAN, Denis	21	M	Unknown	02Ap08Ab
Johanna	23	F	Unknown	02Ap08Ab
Died-At-Sea				
FITZGERALD, John	36	M	Unknown	02Ap08Ab
Jane	18	F	Unknown	02Ap08Ab
CALAHAN, Norry	26	M	Unknown	02Ap08Ab
MCCARTHY, Julia	30	F	Unknown	02Ap08Ab
John	1	M	Child	02Ap08Ab

NAMES OF PASSENGERS	AGE	SEX	OCCUPATIONS	DATE PORT SHIP
HARRINGTON, Danl.	22	M	Unknown	02Ap08Ab
CROWLEY, Cath.	20	F	Unknown	02Ap08Ab
SHEA, John	22	M	Unknown	02Ap08Ab
MCCARTHY, Owen	33	M	Unknown	02Ap08Ab
FINNEGAN, W.W.	43	M	Merchant	02Ap08Ab
BYARD, T.Capt.	30	M	Mariner	02Ap08Ab
BARRY, John	27	M	Merchant	02Ap08Ab
Edw.	18	M	Unknown	02Ap08Ab
Edmond	12	M	Unknown	02Ap08Ab
Henry	13	M	Unknown	02Ap08Ab
DESMOND, Anne	30	F	Lady	02Ap08Ab
ELTON, Hannah	28	F	Lady	02Ap08Ab

KEYING 02 APRIL 1849

From Cardiff

NAMES OF PASSENGERS	AGE	SEX	OCCUPATIONS	DATE PORT SHIP
REGEN, James	25	M	Laborer	02Ap14Ac
BURRY, Patrick	27	M	Laborer	02Ap14Ac
HOWARD, Mortimer	22	M	Carpenter	02Ap14Ac
FORREST, Morris	31	M	Laborer	02Ap14Ac
GRIFFIN, Thomas	24	M	Carpenter	02Ap14Ac
Johannah	22	F	Servant	02Ap14Ac

CORONET 02 APRIL 1849

From Dublin

NAMES OF PASSENGERS	AGE	SEX	OCCUPATIONS	DATE PORT SHIP
FINNANE, Thos.	30	M	Farmer	02Ap12Ad
Margt.	28	F	Unknown	02Ap12Ad
SHANNON, Wm.	30	M	Unknown	02Ap12Ad
GRIFFITH, John	16	M	Unknown	02Ap12Ad
RYAN, Eliza	21	F	Unknown	02Ap12Ad
GALVIN, Matt	20	M	Unknown	02Ap12Ad
Margt.	18	F	Unknown	02Ap12Ad
BUCKLEY, John	28	M	Unknown	02Ap12Ad
Esther	26	F	Unknown	02Ap12Ad
MCQUINN, Thos.	40	M	Unknown	02Ap12Ad
Cath.	20	F	Unknown	02Ap12Ad
DIVINE, John	21	M	Unknown	02Ap12Ad
Bridget	45	F	Unknown	02Ap12Ad
SWEENY, Nichels	50	M	Unknown	02Ap12Ad
GORMAN, Moses	18	M	Unknown	02Ap12Ad
MOAKES, Patt	21	M	Unknown	02Ap12Ad
LAMBERT, Miles	26	M	Unknown	02Ap12Ad
DUFFY, Mary	24	F	Unknown	02Ap12Ad
ENIS, Bridget	30	F	Unknown	02Ap12Ad
CAHIL, James	40	M	Unknown	02Ap12Ad
Rose	29	F	Unknown	02Ap12Ad
Mary	30	F	Unknown	02Ap12Ad
KIRWAN, Mary	28	F	Unknown	02Ap12Ad
WHITE, Ellen	19	F	Unknown	02Ap12Ad
KIRWAN, John	21	M	Unknown	02Ap12Ad
FARRINGTON, Jas.	40	M	Unknown	02Ap12Ad
KELLY, Michl.	39	M	Unknown	02Ap12Ad
FORD, Mary	40	F	Unknown	02Ap12Ad
Emily	10	F	Unknown	02Ap12Ad
Wm.	8	M	Child	02Ap12Ad
Andrew	6	M	Child	02Ap12Ad
Garret	.00	M	Infant	02Ap12Ad
MULLEN, John	28	M	Unknown	02Ap12Ad
Thomas	25	M	Unknown	02Ap12Ad
REDMOND, John	30	M	Unknown	02Ap12Ad
DALEY, Jas.	45	M	Unknown	02Ap12Ad
RAFFERTY, James	38	M	Farmer	02Ap12Ad
Mary	35	F	Farmer	02Ap12Ad
Mary	12	F	Farmer	02Ap12Ad
Bridget	8	F	Child	02Ap12Ad
Eliza	4	F	Child	02Ap12Ad
Sally	.00	F	Infant	02Ap12Ad
MAHER, Eliza	36	F	Unknown	02Ap12Ad
FLANAGAN, Bryan	37	M	Unknown	02Ap12Ad
Elisa	40	F	Unknown	02Ap12Ad
DUANE, Mary	26	F	Unknown	02Ap12Ad
DOWNEY, John	50	M	Unknown	02Ap12Ad
Joseph	45	M	Unknown	02Ap12Ad
FREEMAN, Henry	60	M	Unknown	02Ap12Ad
RAFERTY, Daniel	29	M	Unknown	02Ap12Ad
Betsy	25	F	Unknown	02Ap12Ad
Paddy	.00	M	Infant	02Ap12Ad
CORCORAN, Peggy	50	F	Unknown	02Ap12Ad
BROWN, John	40	M	Unknown	02Ap12Ad
LOKER, Martin	41	M	Unknown	02Ap12Ad
MAGUIRE, Bridget	39	F	Unknown	02Ap12Ad
BURNS, Mary	19	F	Unknown	02Ap12Ad
DORAN, Ellen	16	F	Unknown	02Ap12Ad
WHITE, Wm.	27	M	Unknown	02Ap12Ad
BREMAN, John	30	M	Unknown	02Ap12Ad
HOLT, Garret	27	M	Unknown	02Ap12Ad
Mary	25	F	Unknown	02Ap12Ad
John	3	M	Child	02Ap12Ad
Margt.	.00	F	Infant	02Ap12Ad
CANNON, Bridget	60	F	Unknown	02Ap12Ad
SMITH, Ann	30	F	Unknown	02Ap12Ad
CANNON, Mary	26	F	Unknown	02Ap12Ad
MCLAMMON, Mary-A.	19	F	Unknown	02Ap12Ad
FITZPATRICK, Michl.	21	M	Unknown	02Ap12Ad
Maria	19	F	Unknown	02Ap12Ad
DRUSE, John-M.A.	30	M	Unknown	02Ap12Ad
PENNY, Jas.	60	M	Unknown	02Ap12Ad
Christopher	35	M	Unknown	02Ap12Ad
Bridget	28	F	Unknown	02Ap12Ad
Cath.	2	F	Child	02Ap12Ad
Margt.	.00	F	Infant	02Ap12Ad
CAIN, John	50	M	Unknown	02Ap12Ad
Margt.	19	F	Unknown	02Ap12Ad
Matt	28	M	Unknown	02Ap12Ad
Mary-Ann	40	F	Unknown	02Ap12Ad
Anne	30	F	Unknown	02Ap12Ad
Maria	21	F	Unknown	02Ap12Ad
Bridget	12	F	Unknown	02Ap12Ad
John	6	M	Child	02Ap12Ad
Rose	3	F	Child	02Ap12Ad
Cath.	.00	F	Infant	02Ap12Ad
REILLY, Thomas	50	M	Unknown	02Ap12Ad
Jane	45	F	Unknown	02Ap12Ad
Thos.	22	M	Unknown	02Ap12Ad
Patrick	18	M	Unknown	02Ap12Ad
Bridget	14	F	Unknown	02Ap12Ad
Anne	10	F	Unknown	02Ap12Ad
Margt.	6	F	Child	02Ap12Ad
CAVANAGH, Owen	60	M	Unknown	02Ap12Ad
Ellen	52	F	Unknown	02Ap12Ad
Michl.	22	M	Unknown	02Ap12Ad
Jas.	19	M	Unknown	02Ap12Ad
Mary	19	F	Unknown	02Ap12Ad
Ellen	15	F	Unknown	02Ap12Ad
CALLAGHAN, John	32	M	Unknown	02Ap12Ad
Mary	30	F	Unknown	02Ap12Ad
Mary-Ann	8	F	Child	02Ap12Ad
Rose	4	F	Child	02Ap12Ad
REILLY, Hugh	52	M	Unknown	02Ap12Ad
Ann	49	F	Unknown	02Ap12Ad
John	23	M	Unknown	02Ap12Ad
Thomas	18	M	Unknown	02Ap12Ad
Patk.	12	M	Unknown	02Ap12Ad
Hugh	9	M	Child	02Ap12Ad
Matt	8	M	Child	02Ap12Ad

NAMES OF PASSENGERS	AGE	SEX	OCCUPATIONS	DATE PORT SHIP
REILLY, Christopher	4	M	Child	02Ap12Ad
Mary	2	F	Child	02Ap12Ad
Ann	.00	F	Infant	02Ap12Ad
KELLY, James	54	M	Unknown	02Ap12Ad
Mary	48	F	Unknown	02Ap12Ad
Mary	23	F	Unknown	02Ap12Ad
Cath.	20	F	Unknown	02Ap12Ad
Cath.	15	F	Unknown	02Ap12Ad
Bridget	8	F	Child	02Ap12Ad
Patk.	5	M	Child	02Ap12Ad
John	3	M	Child	02Ap12Ad
Rose	.00	F	Infant	02Ap12Ad
HIGGINS, John	40	M	Unknown	02Ap12Ad
Bridget	38	F	Unknown	02Ap12Ad
Michl.	6	M	Child	02Ap12Ad
DOWLING, Francis	30	M	Unknown	02Ap12Ad
DUFFY, Luke	21	M	Unknown	02Ap12Ad
Mary	20	F	Unknown	02Ap12Ad
Cath.	17	F	Unknown	02Ap12Ad
CORAN, Mary	30	F	Unknown	02Ap12Ad
Cath.	29	F	Unknown	02Ap12Ad
MONAGHAN, Ann	60	F	Unknown	02Ap12Ad
BURNS, Ann	43	F	Unknown	02Ap12Ad
Cath.	21	F	Unknown	02Ap12Ad
KENNEDY, Mary	19	F	Unknown	02Ap12Ad
Anne	19	F	Unknown	02Ap12Ad
LAMB, Elisa	20	F	Unknown	02Ap12Ad
MEANIE, Michl.	25	M	Unknown	02Ap12Ad
MEAGHER, Michl.	38	M	Unknown	02Ap12Ad
KENNEDY, Dennis	18	M	Unknown	02Ap12Ad
Margt.	15	F	Unknown	02Ap12Ad
Ann	37	F	Unknown	02Ap12Ad
WALSH, Johanna	27	F	Unknown	02Ap12Ad
OBRIEN, Daniel	50	M	Unknown	02Ap12Ad
Timothy	39	M	Unknown	02Ap12Ad
CASSIDY, Jas.	50	M	Unknown	02Ap12Ad
Cath.	42	F	Unknown	02Ap12Ad
John	15	M	Unknown	02Ap12Ad
MOLONNEY, Matthew	23	M	Unknown	02Ap12Ad
Michl.	26	M	Unknown	02Ap12Ad
Julia	22	F	Unknown	02Ap12Ad
Cath.	.00	F	Infant	02Ap12Ad
ROLLINS, Michl.	45	M	Unknown	02Ap12Ad
Bridget	42	F	Unknown	02Ap12Ad
Ann	23	F	Unknown	02Ap12Ad
Thos.	15	M	Unknown	02Ap12Ad
Mary	9	F	Child	02Ap12Ad
James	5	M	Child	02Ap12Ad
John	3	M	Child	02Ap12Ad
Ann	.00	F	Infant	02Ap12Ad
MORRIS, John	30	M	Unknown	02Ap12Ad
Patrick	27	M	Unknown	02Ap12Ad
Daniel	18	M	Unknown	02Ap12Ad
LUTE, Michl.	30	M	Unknown	02Ap12Ad
Robt.	28	M	Unknown	02Ap12Ad
Cath.	19	F	Unknown	02Ap12Ad
Ellen	17	F	Unknown	02Ap12Ad
REED, Margt.	30	F	Unknown	02Ap12Ad
DUFF, Julia	29	F	Unknown	02Ap12Ad
MURTAGH, Johanna	40	F	Unknown	02Ap12Ad
Bridget	49	F	Unknown	02Ap12Ad
MOONEY, Thos.	40	M	Unknown	02Ap12Ad
Ann	18	F	Unknown	02Ap12Ad
James	45	M	Unknown	02Ap12Ad
Thomas	21	M	Unknown	02Ap12Ad
Maria	4	F	Child	02Ap12Ad
Ann	.00	F	Infant	02Ap12Ad
COLEMAN, John	42	M	Unknown	02Ap12Ad
Bridget	40	F	Unknown	02Ap12Ad
Ann	15	F	Unknown	02Ap12Ad
Patk.	13	M	Unknown	02Ap12Ad
Mary-Ann	10	F	Unknown	02Ap12Ad
Margt.	8	F	Child	02Ap12Ad
Cath.	6	F	Child	02Ap12Ad
John	.00	M	Infant	02Ap12Ad
HINES, Patt	25	M	Unknown	02Ap12Ad
Connor	44	M	Unknown	02Ap12Ad
James	23	M	Unknown	02Ap12Ad
John	19	M	Unknown	02Ap12Ad
Bridget	15	F	Unknown	02Ap12Ad
Ann	12	F	Unknown	02Ap12Ad
Julia	10	F	Unknown	02Ap12Ad
Connor	8	M	Child	02Ap12Ad
Mary	.00	F	Infant	02Ap12Ad
HEALY, Lawrence	50	M	Unknown	02Ap12Ad
Mary	45	F	Unknown	02Ap12Ad
Mary	20	F	Unknown	02Ap12Ad
Ann	18	F	Unknown	02Ap12Ad
Bridget	16	F	Unknown	02Ap12Ad
Patk.	13	M	Unknown	02Ap12Ad
Madge	11	F	Unknown	02Ap12Ad
Peter	8	M	Child	02Ap12Ad
DOYLE, Michl.	30	M	Unknown	02Ap12Ad
Ann	26	F	Unknown	02Ap12Ad
Ellen	7	F	Child	02Ap12Ad
Cath.	6	F	Child	02Ap12Ad
Michl.	4	M	Child	02Ap12Ad
MILEY, Edwd.	24	M	Unknown	02Ap12Ad
KEARNS, Michl.	60	M	Unknown	02Ap12Ad
FARRINGTON, John	23	M	Unknown	02Ap12Ad
REILLY, John	38	M	Unknown	02Ap12Ad
COX, Patk.	50	M	Unknown	02Ap12Ad
WALSH, Patt	39	M	Unknown	02Ap12Ad
MEAGHEN, Patt	29	M	Unknown	02Ap12Ad
FARRINGTON, Bryan	50	M	Unknown	02Ap12Ad
Mary	48	F	Unknown	02Ap12Ad
Mary	24	F	Unknown	02Ap12Ad
Andrew	21	M	Unknown	02Ap12Ad
Bridget	19	F	Unknown	02Ap12Ad
John	14	M	Unknown	02Ap12Ad
James	10	M	Unknown	02Ap12Ad
Cath.	6	F	Child	02Ap12Ad
Margt.	2	F	Child	02Ap12Ad
Ann	1	F	Child	02Ap12Ad
Elisa	.00	F	Infant	02Ap12Ad
DIGNAN, Andrew	35	M	Unknown	02Ap12Ad
John	36	M	Unknown	02Ap12Ad
Ann	8	F	Child	02Ap12Ad
Mary	5	F	Child	02Ap12Ad
Christopher	3	M	Child	02Ap12Ad
CONNERTON, Jas.	30	M	Unknown	02Ap12Ad
Bridget	27	F	Unknown	02Ap12Ad
HAIGNER, Patt	38	M	Unknown	02Ap12Ad
WARD, Edwd.	40	M	Unknown	02Ap12Ad
HOWARD, Patt	18	M	Unknown	02Ap12Ad
POWER, Patt	21	M	Unknown	02Ap12Ad
PERRICK, Patt	60	M	Unknown	02Ap12Ad
Margt.	40	F	Unknown	02Ap12Ad
Margt.	11	F	Unknown	02Ap12Ad
Thos.	5	M	Child	02Ap12Ad
Bridget	3	F	Child	02Ap12Ad
Mary	.00	F	Infant	02Ap12Ad
BURKE, Mary	40	F	Unknown	02Ap12Ad
Julia	37	F	Unknown	02Ap12Ad
Wm.	15	M	Unknown	02Ap12Ad
Barney	12	M	Unknown	02Ap12Ad
Tobias	9	M	Child	02Ap12Ad
Cath.	6	F	Child	02Ap12Ad
GAFFNEY, Dave	4	M	Child	02Ap12Ad
Cath.	40	F	Unknown	02Ap12Ad
Mary	28	F	Unknown	02Ap12Ad
DICKSON, Patt	40	M	Unknown	02Ap12Ad
FARRELL, Susan	38	F	Unknown	02Ap12Ad
Jane	25	F	Unknown	02Ap12Ad
CORRIGAN, Wm.	38	M	Unknown	02Ap12Ad
Ann	30	F	Unknown	02Ap12Ad
Ellen	8	F	Child	02Ap12Ad
Thos.	5	M	Child	02Ap12Ad
Patt	.00	M	Infant	02Ap12Ad
GAFFNEY, Daniel	45	M	Unknown	02Ap12Ad

NAMES OF PASSENGERS	AGE	SEX	OCCUPATIONS	DATE PORT SHIP
GAFFNEY, Jane	41	F	Unknown	02Ap12Ad
Mary	20	F	Unknown	02Ap12Ad
Cath.	18	F	Unknown	02Ap12Ad
Michl.	12	M	Unknown	02Ap12Ad
Lawrence	9	M	Child	02Ap12Ad
James	7	M	Child	02Ap12Ad
Daniel	4	M	Child	02Ap12Ad
GIBNEY, Thomas	50	M	Unknown	02Ap12Ad
Henry	47	M	Unknown	02Ap12Ad
Thos.	25	M	Unknown	02Ap12Ad
Osben	23	M	Unknown	02Ap12Ad
Thos.	15	M	Unknown	02Ap12Ad
Bridget	9	F	Child	02Ap12Ad
Mary	6	F	Child	02Ap12Ad
Julia	3	F	Child	02Ap12Ad
Mary	.00	F	Infant	02Ap12Ad
MORRIS, Thomas	60	M	Unknown	02Ap12Ad
MALONE, Jas.	66	M	Unknown	02Ap12Ad
Mary	62	F	Unknown	02Ap12Ad
Jane	30	F	Unknown	02Ap12Ad
Ann	24	F	Unknown	02Ap12Ad
Mary	25	F	Unknown	02Ap12Ad
Julia	23	F	Unknown	02Ap12Ad
Thomas	19	M	Unknown	02Ap12Ad
Michl.	16	M	Unknown	02Ap12Ad
Ellen	8	F	Child	02Ap12Ad
Bridget	4	F	Child	02Ap12Ad
SHERLOCK, Ned	40	M	Unknown	02Ap12Ad
CAIN, Patt	38	M	Unknown	02Ap12Ad
Ann	20	F	Unknown	02Ap12Ad
MURPHY, Patt	30	M	Unknown	02Ap12Ad
Ann	24	F	Unknown	02Ap12Ad
Mary	12	F	Unknown	02Ap12Ad
Michl.	9	M	Child	02Ap12Ad
Elisa	7	F	Child	02Ap12Ad
Jane	6	F	Child	02Ap12Ad
Jos.	3	M	Child	02Ap12Ad
Margt.	.00	F	Infant	02Ap12Ad
POLLICK, U	00	M	Unknown	02Ap12Ad
U	00	F	Unknown	02Ap12Ad
Catharine	00	F	Unknown	02Ap12Ad
Mary-William	00	F	Unknown	02Ap12Ad
Sampson	00	M	Unknown	02Ap12Ad
John	00	M	Unknown	02Ap12Ad
SOLLEN, U-Mrs.	00	F	Unknown	02Ap12Ad
William	00	M	Unknown	02Ap12Ad
CARBETT, M.	00	M	Unknown	02Ap12Ad
DONOVAN, U-Miss	00	F	Unknown	02Ap12Ad

ELIZABETH-HAMILTON 02 APRIL 1849

From Liverpool

NAMES OF PASSENGERS	AGE	SEX	OCCUPATIONS	DATE PORT SHIP
KELLY, James	28	M	Laborer	02Ap02Ae
HALPIN, Mary	36	F	Unknown	02Ap02Ae
Lawrence	08	M	Child	02Ap02Ae
Charlotte	06	F	Child	02Ap02Ae
Mary	04	F	Child	02Ap02Ae
STEPHENS, William-A.	24	M	Farmer	02Ap02Ae
VANN, Walter	26	M	Farmer	02Ap02Ae
FITZHENRY, Maud	30	F	Unknown	02Ap02Ae
Sarah	12	F	Unknown	02Ap02Ae
William	09	M	Child	02Ap02Ae
Mary	08	F	Child	02Ap02Ae
Jane	06	F	Child	02Ap02Ae
Ann	04	F	Child	02Ap02Ae
Thomas	.00	M	Infant	02Ap02Ae
RYAN, John	49	M	Farmer	02Ap02Ae
Mick.	13	M	Farmer	02Ap02Ae
RYAN, John	12	M	Farmer	02Ap02Ae
Alice	16	F	Farmer	02Ap02Ae
BURKE, Edward	22	M	Laborer	02Ap02Ae
Mary	28	F	Unknown	02Ap02Ae
GRAY, Martin	28	M	Laborer	02Ap02Ae
PADDEN, George	17	M	Laborer	02Ap02Ae
LOOBY, Thomas	50	M	Laborer	02Ap02Ae
Mick.	22	M	Farmer	02Ap02Ae
MCENTYRE, John	24	M	Laborer	02Ap02Ae
Bridget	22	F	Unknown	02Ap02Ae
ROCKFORD, Martin	25	M	Laborer	02Ap02Ae
BIGNALL, James	21	M	Laborer	02Ap02Ae
COLLERY, William	20	M	Laborer	02Ap02Ae
LANURET, Edward	22	M	Laborer	02Ap02Ae
ORNSLEY, Eleanor	20	F	Laborer	02Ap02Ae
THOMPSON, Winney	20	F	Laborer	02Ap02Ae
COLLERY, Mick.	28	M	Laborer	02Ap02Ae
Mary	26	F	Unknown	02Ap02Ae
Bridget	04	F	Child	02Ap02Ae
Mick.	02	M	Child	02Ap02Ae
KEOGH, Mick.	20	M	Laborer	02Ap02Ae
DOYLE, William	22	M	Laborer	02Ap02Ae
NEALE, William	25	M	Laborer	02Ap02Ae
WILLIAMSON, William	21	M	Laborer	02Ap02Ae
Sarah	21	F	Unknown	02Ap02Ae
Gordon	19	M	Unknown	02Ap02Ae
MULHADY, Philip	24	M	Laborer	02Ap02Ae
MALONE, John	28	M	Laborer	02Ap02Ae
MCCORMICK, Denis	29	M	Farmer	02Ap02Ae
DAGNAN, John	30	M	Farmer	02Ap02Ae
Barney	13	M	Farmer	02Ap02Ae
Catherine	16	F	Unknown	02Ap02Ae
NORTON, Pat	20	M	Laborer	02Ap02Ae
Mary	15	F	Unknown	02Ap02Ae
Matty	13	F	Unknown	02Ap02Ae
Bridget	11	F	Unknown	02Ap02Ae
CUSHLAND, Bridget	11	F	Unknown	02Ap02Ae
BYRNES, Mick	24	M	Laborer	02Ap02Ae
NOLAND, Thomas	30	M	Laborer	02Ap02Ae
HARTIGAN, Daniel	45	M	Laborer	02Ap02Ae
Daniel	09	M	Child	02Ap02Ae
MARSHALL, Andrew	26	M	Laborer	02Ap02Ae
ELLIS, John	19	M	Laborer	02Ap02Ae
WRENN, Lawrence	40	M	Laborer	02Ap02Ae
HUGHES, James	14	M	Laborer	02Ap02Ae
Winefrida	13	F	Unknown	02Ap02Ae
Mary	10	F	Unknown	02Ap02Ae
NOLAN, Pat	21	M	Laborer	02Ap02Ae
CAMEAN, James	15	M	Laborer	02Ap02Ae
GOUGH, Pat	23	M	Laborer	02Ap02Ae
GRADY, Anthony	40	M	Farmer	02Ap02Ae
Ann	13	F	Unknown	02Ap02Ae
GIBBIN, Pat	25	M	Farmer	02Ap02Ae
Mary	25	F	Unknown	02Ap02Ae
Biddy	13	F	Unknown	02Ap02Ae
Mary	.00	F	Infant	02Ap02Ae
FLINN, Martin	40	M	Farmer	02Ap02Ae
U (W)	36	F	Unknown	02Ap02Ae
Richard	18	M	Unknown	02Ap02Ae
Martin	16	M	Unknown	02Ap02Ae
Nicholas	13	M	Unknown	02Ap02Ae
Magt.	12	F	Unknown	02Ap02Ae
Anne	11	F	Unknown	02Ap02Ae
Joseph	03	M	Child	02Ap02Ae
HUTCHISON, Eliza	23	F	Unknown	02Ap02Ae
Peggy-Jane	20	F	Unknown	02Ap02Ae
JONES, Thos.	50	M	Farmer	02Ap02Ae
Christopher	19	M	Unknown	02Ap02Ae
Patrick	17	M	Unknown	02Ap02Ae
George	15	M	Unknown	02Ap02Ae
Mary	13	F	Unknown	02Ap02Ae
LENNON, Michl.	30	M	Laborer	02Ap02Ae
TEAMON, Lawrence	40	M	Farmer	02Ap02Ae
U (W)	40	F	Unknown	02Ap02Ae
John	18	M	Unknown	02Ap02Ae

NAMES OF PASSENGERS	AGE	SEX	OCCUPATIONS	DATE PORT SHIP
TEAMON, Martin	16	M	Unknown	02Ap02Ae
James	10	M	Unknown	02Ap02Ae
Cath.	08	F	Child	02Ap02Ae
BIGGET, Henry	49	M	Farmer	02Ap02Ae
U (W)	49	F	Unknown	02Ap02Ae
Martin	10	M	Unknown	02Ap02Ae
DONCLAN, Tim	08	M	Child	02Ap02Ae
BEGET, Patt	20	M	Laborer	02Ap02Ae
CARNEY, Bridget	18	F	Unknown	02Ap02Ae
MORGAN, Bridget	15	F	Unknown	02Ap02Ae
YOUNG, William	26	M	Laborer	02Ap02Ae
MCCARTY, Furtan	20	M	Unknown	02Ap02Ae
Judy	12	F	Unknown	02Ap02Ae
KILCUMESS, Daniel	18	M	Unknown	02Ap02Ae
WALLACE, Michl.	15	M	Unknown	02Ap02Ae
MULLEN, Winny	15	F	Unknown	02Ap02Ae
GRIFFIN, Thos.	16	M	Unknown	02Ap02Ae
MILLER, U-Mrs.	30	F	Unknown	02Ap02Ae
Mary	07	F	Child	02Ap02Ae
Eliza	04	F	Child	02Ap02Ae
FLEMING, Mary	16	F	Unknown	02Ap02Ae
NOBLE, Robt.	25	M	Farmer	02Ap02Ae
U (W)	25	F	Unknown	02Ap02Ae
MEEHAN, David	25	M	Laborer	02Ap02Ae
Francis	.00	M	Infant	02Ap02Ae
SMITHY, Edwd.	36	M	Farmer	02Ap02Ae
SMITH, W.H.	12	M	Unknown	02Ap02Ae
DUFFY, Thos.	28	M	Laborer	02Ap02Ae
DALY, John	32	M	Laborer	02Ap02Ae
Sarah	28	F	Unknown	02Ap02Ae
DUFFY, Mary	18	F	Unknown	02Ap02Ae
MCCABE, Susan	18	F	Unknown	02Ap02Ae
KEENAN, Bard.	18	M	Laborer	02Ap02Ae
MARRON, James	26	M	Laborer	02Ap02Ae
CONNELLY, Alice	20	F	Unknown	02Ap02Ae
WARD, Judy	50	F	Unknown	02Ap02Ae
John	18	M	Unknown	02Ap02Ae
Biddy	16	F	Unknown	02Ap02Ae
Rosey	28	F	Unknown	02Ap02Ae
WARNING, Edwd.	40	M	Farmer	02Ap02Ae
CONNER, Moses	40	M	Laborer	02Ap02Ae
LYNN, Michl.	40	M	Laborer	02Ap02Ae
COSTELLO, Batt.	50	M	Farmer	02Ap02Ae
John	16	M	Unknown	02Ap02Ae
Mary	18	F	Unknown	02Ap02Ae
GALLAVAN, Jerry	24	M	Laborer	02Ap02Ae
BEST, James	58	M	Laborer	02Ap02Ae
Anne	40	F	Unknown	02Ap02Ae
Robt.	24	M	Laborer	02Ap02Ae
MCDONALD, Bard.	18	M	Laborer	02Ap02Ae
HANNES, James	26	M	Laborer	02Ap02Ae
FOLY, John	28	M	Laborer	02Ap02Ae
KELLY, Thos.	25	M	Laborer	02Ap02Ae
KEFF, William	25	M	Laborer	02Ap02Ae
BENT, James	36	M	Laborer	02Ap02Ae
GREEN, Pat	36	M	Laborer	02Ap02Ae
MCCASKER, Rose	19	F	Unknown	02Ap02Ae
REARDON, James	25	M	Laborer	02Ap02Ae
GALLAVEN, William	22	M	Laborer	02Ap02Ae
CONNER, Anne	20	F	Laborer	02Ap02Ae
ANDERSON, William	26	M	Laborer	02Ap02Ae
THOMPSON, Francis	22	M	Laborer	02Ap02Ae
LYNCH, Patt	30	M	Laborer	02Ap02Ae
CASH, John	30	M	Laborer	02Ap02Ae
U (W)	30	F	Unknown	02Ap02Ae
YOUNG, Patt	24	M	Mason	02Ap02Ae
Thos.	21	M	Mason	02Ap02Ae
HORAN, John	28	M	Carpenter	02Ap02Ae
GRAY, Luke	19	M	Laborer	02Ap02Ae
KILPATRICK, Magt.	33	F	Unknown	02Ap02Ae
Thos.	26	M	Laborer	02Ap02Ae
ROSS, William	23	M	Laborer	02Ap02Ae
WALSH, Magt.	19	F	Unknown	02Ap02Ae
NARY, Patt	30	M	Blacksmith	02Ap02Ae
BOLAND, Michl.	46	M	Laborer	02Ap02Ae
CLARKE, Magt.	18	F	Unknown	02Ap02Ae
WHITE, Cath.	16	F	Unknown	02Ap02Ae
MCDONAGH, Chas.	26	M	Laborer	02Ap02Ae
Ellen	50	F	Unknown	02Ap02Ae
Honora	19	F	Unknown	02Ap02Ae
BOLAND, Mary	21	F	Unknown	02Ap02Ae
Ellen	18	F	Unknown	02Ap02Ae
SMITH, Mary	25	F	Unknown	02Ap02Ae
BATTLE, Winefred	26	F	Unknown	02Ap02Ae
MCCANN, Cath.	22	F	Unknown	02Ap02Ae
FLINN, Bridget	18	F	Unknown	02Ap02Ae
MULLEN, Pat	22	M	Laborer	02Ap02Ae
WINN, Domnick	22	M	Laborer	02Ap02Ae
BOWLES, Luke	22	M	Laborer	02Ap02Ae
KILLEGAN, Michl.	40	M	Laborer	02Ap02Ae
Thos.	21	M	Laborer	02Ap02Ae
GILLIGAN, James	20	M	Laborer	02Ap02Ae
BEANNON, Patt	23	M	Laborer	02Ap02Ae
FOLY, Thos.	22	M	Laborer	02Ap02Ae
FARRELL, Michl.	22	M	Laborer	02Ap02Ae
HALROYD, James	30	M	Laborer	02Ap02Ae
DOYLE, James	22	M	Laborer	02Ap02Ae
Anthony	18	M	Laborer	02Ap02Ae
Patt	20	M	Laborer	02Ap02Ae
JOHNSTON, George	26	M	Laborer	02Ap02Ae
RUTLEDGE, John	22	M	Laborer	02Ap02Ae
DONOHUE, John	24	M	Laborer	02Ap02Ae
MORAN, Pat	32	M	Laborer	02Ap02Ae
Michl.	40	M	Laborer	02Ap02Ae
CONNOR, Joseph	20	M	Laborer	02Ap02Ae
Bridget	22	F	Unknown	02Ap02Ae
FARRELL, Mark	27	M	Laborer	02Ap02Ae
DAILY, Pat	30	M	Laborer	02Ap02Ae
HOWE, James	23	M	Laborer	02Ap02Ae
RICH, Edmond	32	M	Laborer	02Ap02Ae
WALLS, Thos.	23	M	Laborer	02Ap02Ae
REWIN, Martin	25	M	Laborer	02Ap02Ae
Biddy	13	F	Unknown	02Ap02Ae
BURKE, Matt	27	M	Laborer	02Ap02Ae
Mary	26	F	Unknown	02Ap02Ae
DUFF, John	23	M	Laborer	02Ap02Ae
ROONEY, Christopher	22	M	Laborer	02Ap02Ae
BRANNIGAN, Nath.	50	M	Laborer	02Ap02Ae
Bridget	12	F	Unknown	02Ap02Ae
Ellen	10	F	Unknown	02Ap02Ae
COLLINS, Thomas	20	M	Unknown	02Ap02Ae
GRANT, Bernard	22	M	Unknown	02Ap02Ae
KILLALA, Lawrence	24	M	Laborer	02Ap02Ae
THURLY, Pat	22	M	Laborer	02Ap02Ae
STANNTON, Martin	18	M	Laborer	02Ap02Ae
BYRNE, David	16	M	Laborer	02Ap02Ae
NOWLAN, Charles	27	M	Farmer	02Ap02Ae
GAFFIGAN, Thomas	16	M	Farmer	02Ap02Ae
Julia	18	F	Unknown	02Ap02Ae
BRADIGAN, U-Mrs.	18	F	Unknown	02Ap02Ae
WALSH, Mary	19	F	Unknown	02Ap02Ae
TIER, James	20	M	Laborer	02Ap02Ae
KIBBIN, Pat	20	M	Laborer	02Ap02Ae
Bridget	20	F	Unknown	02Ap02Ae
CREBNA, John	35	M	Farmer	02Ap02Ae
Margaret	08	F	Child	02Ap02Ae
Mary	.00	F	Infant	02Ap02Ae
COONAL, Thomas	50	M	Farmer	02Ap02Ae
Catherine	50	F	Unknown	02Ap02Ae
Mary	10	F	Unknown	02Ap02Ae
John	08	M	Child	02Ap02Ae
Michael	06	M	Child	02Ap02Ae
Thomas	03	M	Child	02Ap02Ae
Rose	.00	F	Infant	02Ap02Ae
CORBETT, Thomas	26	M	Laborer	02Ap02Ae
Pat	24	M	Laborer	02Ap02Ae
DUFFY, David	24	M	Laborer	02Ap02Ae
SHAW, Edmond	30	M	Laborer	02Ap02Ae
OKEEFF, John	22	M	Laborer	02Ap02Ae
DAILY, Pat	35	M	Laborer	02Ap02Ae

NAMES OF PASSENGERS	AGE	SEX	OCCUPATIONS	DATE PORT SHIP
DAILY, Mary	20	F	Unknown	02Ap02Ae
TROY, Catherine	20	F	Unknown	02Ap02Ae
DAILY, Thomas	08	M	Child	02Ap02Ae
Honora	.00	F	Infant	02Ap02Ae
HALLORAN, Thomas	25	M	Laborer	02Ap02Ae
Ann	20	F	Unknown	02Ap02Ae
HEALY, Michael	28	M	Laborer	02Ap02Ae
Nancy	26	F	Unknown	02Ap02Ae
Pat	.00	M	Infant	02Ap02Ae
GORMAN, Thomas	28	M	Laborer	02Ap02Ae
CLACKIN, Michael	24	M	Laborer	02Ap02Ae
MULRAY, Thomas	20	M	Laborer	02Ap02Ae
RIELLY, Michael	28	M	Laborer	02Ap02Ae
LYONS, John	24	M	Laborer	02Ap02Ae
CONNOR, Ellen	23	F	Unknown	02Ap02Ae
DIGNAN, John	30	M	Farmer	02Ap02Ae
REYNOLDS, Thomas	25	M	Farmer	02Ap02Ae
HALEY, John	31	M	Farmer	02Ap02Ae
Margaret	30	F	Unknown	02Ap02Ae
Maurice	05	M	Child	02Ap02Ae
Ellen	03	F	Child	02Ap02Ae
Margaret	02	F	Child	02Ap02Ae
Ann	.00	F	Infant	02Ap02Ae
MAHONEY, Ellen	20	F	Unknown	02Ap02Ae

CALEDONIA 02 APRIL 1849

From Liverpool

NAMES OF PASSENGERS	AGE	SEX	OCCUPATIONS	DATE PORT SHIP
NEILE, Andy	40	M	Laborer	02Ap02Af
Biddy	40	F	Unknown	02Ap02Af
Ellen	.00	F	Infant	02Ap02Af
Judy	13	F	Unknown	02Ap02Af
Peter	12	M	Unknown	02Ap02Af
Ann	08	F	Child	02Ap02Af
Margaretta	07	F	Child	02Ap02Af
LATIMER, Jane	20	F	Unknown	02Ap02Af
CREW, John	26	M	Laborer	02Ap02Af
Peter	20	M	Laborer	02Ap02Af
REDER, Edward	24	M	Laborer	02Ap02Af
FINN, James	22	M	Laborer	02Ap02Af
MCGOWEN, Margaret	21	M	Laborer	02Ap02Af
DAVITT, Bridget	24	M	Laborer	02Ap02Af
Ann	21	M	Laborer	02Ap02Af
FLOOD, John	25	M	Laborer	02Ap02Af
SHANNON, Matthew	21	M	Laborer	02Ap02Af
CANNON, Anthony	21	M	Laborer	02Ap02Af
BENNETT, John	22	M	Laborer	02Ap02Af
MCGRATH, John	21	M	Laborer	02Ap02Af
Celia	20	F	Unknown	02Ap02Af
MANNON, Mary	20	F	Unknown	02Ap02Af
MURRAY, Mary	20	F	Unknown	02Ap02Af
LEONARD, James	30	M	Laborer	02Ap02Af
KENNON, John	30	M	Laborer	02Ap02Af
LYNCH, John	30	M	Laborer	02Ap02Af
U, Jas.	00	M	Laborer	02Ap02Af
REISTON, Wm.	26	M	Laborer	02Ap02Af
REILSTON, Isaac	22	M	Laborer	02Ap02Af
MCCLUSKEY, Mary	20	F	Laborer	02Ap02Af
Mary	14	F	Laborer	02Ap02Af
Jno.	09	M	Child	02Ap02Af
Francis	07	M	Child	02Ap02Af
Gell.	15	M	Unknown	02Ap02Af
DALY, Wm.	31	M	Laborer	02Ap02Af
MANSON, Owen-M.	11	M	Laborer	02Ap02Af
FITZPATRICK, Thos.	24	M	Laborer	02Ap02Af
CAIN, Geo.	45	M	Laborer	02Ap02Af
Jane	43	F	Laborer	02Ap02Af
Abel	17	M	Unknown	02Ap02Af

NAMES OF PASSENGERS	AGE	SEX	OCCUPATIONS	DATE PORT SHIP
CAIN, Henry	16	M	Unknown	02Ap02Af
Emma	10	F	Unknown	02Ap02Af
George	08	M	Child	02Ap02Af
Charlotte	04	F	Child	02Ap02Af
Manon	01	F	Child	02Ap02Af
Wm.	.00	M	Infant	02Ap02Af
CORIGAN, Michael	40	M	Unknown	02Ap02Af
James	38	M	Unknown	02Ap02Af
Eliza	20	F	Unknown	02Ap02Af
QUE, Michael	20	M	Unknown	02Ap02Af
Bessy	18	F	Unknown	02Ap02Af
MELIE, Jno.	34	M	Laborer	02Ap02Af
Mary	19	F	Unknown	02Ap02Af
CAIN, Patrick	30	M	Laborer	02Ap02Af
DEONSE, Dennis	21	M	Laborer	02Ap02Af
Martin	20	M	Laborer	02Ap02Af
GOLDEN, Patrick	50	M	Laborer	02Ap02Af
Peggy	27	F	Unknown	02Ap02Af
John	21	M	Laborer	02Ap02Af
MEAR, Judy	25	F	Unknown	02Ap02Af
REGNEY, Mary	26	F	Unknown	02Ap02Af
MOONEY, Thomas	29	M	Laborer	02Ap02Af
CARDON, U-Mrs.	26	F	Unknown	02Ap02Af
HEALEY, Hugh	18	M	Laborer	02Ap02Af
HIGNETT, Jno.	32	M	Laborer	02Ap02Af
CANNON, Thos.	30	M	Laborer	02Ap02Af
U (W)	16	F	Unknown	02Ap02Af
Mary	02	F	Child	02Ap02Af
Dennis	.00	M	Infant	02Ap02Af
Bridget	10	F	Unknown	02Ap02Af
MELIA, Patt	50	M	Laborer	02Ap02Af
U (W)	50	F	Unknown	02Ap02Af
Ann	.00	F	Infant	02Ap02Af
Patrick	10	M	Unknown	02Ap02Af
BRADY, Catharine	26	F	Laborer	02Ap02Af
BUTLER, Dennis	40	M	Laborer	02Ap02Af
Mary	30	F	Laborer	02Ap02Af
Henry	18	M	Laborer	02Ap02Af
Ellen	14	F	Laborer	02Ap02Af
Mary	05	F	Child	02Ap02Af
DILLON, John	25	M	Laborer	02Ap02Af
DOUINER, John	30	M	Laborer	02Ap02Af
ADAMS, James	27	M	Laborer	02Ap02Af
Margt.	27	F	Unknown	02Ap02Af
LAUGHLIN, Dennis	30	M	Laborer	02Ap02Af
Thomas	06	M	Child	02Ap02Af
Michael	21	M	Servant	02Ap02Af
CARLEY, Wm.	21	M	Servant	02Ap02Af
HOGAN, John	24	M	Laborer	02Ap02Af
MULVILLE, Margt.	19	F	Unknown	02Ap02Af
RYAN, Mary	19	F	Unknown	02Ap02Af
GLEESON, Johanna	19	F	Unknown	02Ap02Af
PRICE, Thomas	40	M	Farmer	02Ap02Af
Eliza	36	F	Unknown	02Ap02Af
Richard	21	M	Laborer	02Ap02Af
DALY, Matthew	26	M	Laborer	02Ap02Af
MAMETT, Thomas	27	M	Laborer	02Ap02Af
RYAN, Ann	30	F	Unknown	02Ap02Af
NOLAN, George	36	M	Farmer	02Ap02Af
Jno.	11	M	Farmer	02Ap02Af
HASTON, William	35	M	Unknown	02Ap02Af
Mary	34	F	Unknown	02Ap02Af
Jno.	05	M	Child	02Ap02Af
Elizabeth	03	F	Child	02Ap02Af
Thomas	.00	M	Infant	02Ap02Af
NORTON, Biddy	24	F	Unknown	02Ap02Af
LYDON, Michael	24	M	Laborer	02Ap02Af
Patrick	22	M	Laborer	02Ap02Af
BARRY, Thomas	55	M	Laborer	02Ap02Af
OCORMAN, Charles	28	M	Laborer	02Ap02Af
NASH, Jno.	19	M	Laborer	02Ap02Af
FARREL, Michael	18	M	Laborer	02Ap02Af
RUBY, Mary	18	F	Unknown	02Ap02Af
MCCARE, Jno.	40	M	Farmer	02Ap02Af
Susan	16	F	Unknown	02Ap02Af

NAMES OF PASSENGERS	AGE	SEX	OCCUPATIONS	DATE PORT SHIP
MEAN, Patt	29	M	Laborer	02Ap02Af
Peter	05	M	Child	02Ap02Af
OMEARA, Robert	20	M	Laborer	02Ap02Af
LAWLESS, Patrick	21	M	Laborer	02Ap02Af
TROY, Mary	12	F	Unknown	02Ap02Af
Milles	30	F	Unknown	02Ap02Af
Richard	11	M	Unknown	02Ap02Af
MCGENA, Patrick	22	M	Farmer	02Ap02Af
MEGAN, Joseph	30	M	Farmer	02Ap02Af
Jas.	32	M	Laborer	02Ap02Af
Cathe.	20	F	Unknown	02Ap02Af
Peter	23	M	Laborer	02Ap02Af
Owen	16	M	Laborer	02Ap02Af
NASH, Mary	28	F	Unknown	02Ap02Af
MCFARREL, Bridget	25	F	Unknown	02Ap02Af
MEIGAN, Mary	40	F	Unknown	02Ap02Af
Law.	30	M	Unknown	02Ap02Af
Sally	13	F	Unknown	02Ap02Af
Alley	11	F	Unknown	02Ap02Af
Died-At-Sea				
James	09	M	Child	02Ap02Af
Catharine	06	F	Child	02Ap02Af
Died-At-Sea				
Thomas	.00	M	Infant	02Ap02Af
Mary	.00	F	Infant	02Ap02Af
HANNON, James	.00	M	Infant	02Ap02Af
REAL, Thomas	18	M	Unknown	02Ap02Af
FITZGERALD, Mannie	40	F	Unknown	02Ap02Af
ENGLISH, Michael	20	M	Laborer	02Ap02Af
MULONEY, Mary	25	F	Unknown	02Ap02Af
MCLEON, Andrew	21	M	Laborer	02Ap02Af
Margt.	25	F	Unknown	02Ap02Af
MORRISON, M.A.	22	F	Unknown	02Ap02Af
HIGGINS, Patrick	40	M	Laborer	02Ap02Af
Eliza	27	F	Unknown	02Ap02Af
Catharine	22	F	Unknown	02Ap02Af
Garret	.00	M	Infant	02Ap02Af
Died-At-Sea				
NOLAN, Jno.	24	M	Laborer	02Ap02Af
BYRNE, Thos.	20	M	Laborer	02Ap02Af
Cathe.	30	F	Unknown	02Ap02Af
Jno.	10	M	Unknown	02Ap02Af
Hugh	07	M	Child	02Ap02Af
Biddy	04	F	Child	02Ap02Af
Jos.	.00	M	Infant	02Ap02Af
STAFFORD, Ann	20	F	Unknown	02Ap02Af
WELDEN, Patrick	29	M	Laborer	02Ap02Af
GARRON, Patrick	22	M	Laborer	02Ap02Af
FALLON, Jno.	22	M	Laborer	02Ap02Af
OHARA, Wm.	40	M	Laborer	02Ap02Af
Sally	17	F	Unknown	02Ap02Af
Ellen	10	F	Unknown	02Ap02Af
Mary	20	F	Unknown	02Ap02Af
MCCOOKE, John	37	M	Laborer	02Ap02Af
NEAGLE, Patrick	20	M	Farmer	02Ap02Af
SEFTEN, Michael	20	M	Farmer	02Ap02Af
James	20	M	Farmer	02Ap02Af
MCCABE, Martin	20	M	Farmer	02Ap02Af
LUFFERS, Mary	20	F	Unknown	02Ap02Af
NORTON, Thos.	35	M	Farmer	02Ap02Af
Betty	18	M	Unknown	02Ap02Af
DALY, Eliza	40	F	Unknown	02Ap02Af
ELLIOTT, Ann	00	F	Unknown	02Ap02Af
MORTON, Jas.	30	M	Laborer	02Ap02Af
DONNELE, Jno.	37	M	Laborer	02Ap02Af
COLLINS, David	21	M	Laborer	02Ap02Af
MURPHY, James	20	M	Laborer	02Ap02Af
Ann	18	F	Unknown	02Ap02Af
LAMB, James	20	M	Laborer	02Ap02Af
QUINTON, Henry	21	M	Laborer	02Ap02Af
LAMB, Peter	15	M	Laborer	02Ap02Af
NOONE, Thomas	21	M	Laborer	02Ap02Af
MALONEY, Biddy	20	F	Unknown	02Ap02Af
MCGUIRE, Biddy	20	F	Unknown	02Ap02Af
DARCY, Ann	20	F	Unknown	02Ap02Af
FLYNNE, Jno.	17	M	Unknown	02Ap02Af
Mary	19	F	Unknown	02Ap02Af
CLOONE, John	20	M	Laborer	02Ap02Af
FAHEY, Thomas	30	M	Laborer	02Ap02Af
DOYNE, Biddy	20	F	Unknown	02Ap02Af
BYRNE, Jno.	24	M	Laborer	02Ap02Af
Catherine	23	F	Laborer	02Ap02Af
Patrick	02	M	Child	02Ap02Af
Edward	.00	M	Infant	02Ap02Af
COLLINS, Jno.	22	M	Laborer	02Ap02Af
Ann	20	F	Unknown	02Ap02Af
Jno.	.00	M	Infant	02Ap02Af
Died-At-Sea				
Mary	22	F	Unknown	02Ap02Af
HANLEY, Jeremiah	25	M	Laborer	02Ap02Af
FINNEGAN, Wm.	26	M	Laborer	02Ap02Af
MEMBRAN, James	18	M	Laborer	02Ap02Af
GEASLEY, James	23	M	Laborer	02Ap02Af
Winefred	18	F	Unknown	02Ap02Af
HERMAN, Ann	18	F	Unknown	02Ap02Af
MUSTEN, Patrick	18	M	Laborer	02Ap02Af
Biddy	45	F	Unknown	02Ap02Af
Betty	22	F	Unknown	02Ap02Af
Judy	09	F	Child	02Ap02Af
Mary	11	F	Unknown	02Ap02Af
James	10	M	Unknown	02Ap02Af
MCPARLEN, James	30	M	Laborer	02Ap02Af
SIMSON, John	40	M	Farmer	02Ap02Af
MEENE, Patrick	22	M	Farmer	02Ap02Af
MCGARTY, James	20	M	Farmer	02Ap02Af
GOLDBOUGH, Jacob	27	M	Farmer	02Ap02Af
MURPHY, John	40	M	Farmer	02Ap02Af
CUNNINGHAM, Thomas	20	M	Farmer	02Ap02Af
Ellen	18	F	Farmer	02Ap02Af
MCELROY, Peter	20	M	Farmer	02Ap02Af
MCNALLY, James	20	M	Farmer	02Ap02Af
MURPHY, Mary	12	F	Farmer	02Ap02Af
COLEMAN, Daniel	52	M	Farmer	02Ap02Af
DOYLE, Fanny	20	F	Farmer	02Ap02Af
HALL, David	37	M	Farmer	02Ap02Af
HULCHEN, Isaac	22	M	Laborer	02Ap02Af
MCCALL, Peter	20	M	Laborer	02Ap02Af
MCCABE, Judy	21	F	Unknown	02Ap02Af
RYAN, Mary	23	F	Unknown	02Ap02Af
MCCANTER, Mary	28	F	Unknown	02Ap02Af
LYNCH, Jno.	21	M	Laborer	02Ap02Af
SAXTON, Jno.	00	M	Laborer	02Ap02Af
Alexander	00	M	Laborer	02Ap02Af
WILLSON, James	00	M	Laborer	02Ap02Af

NEW-ZEALAND 02 APRIL 1849

From Newry

NAMES OF PASSENGERS	AGE	SEX	OCCUPATIONS	DATE PORT SHIP
DAVIDSON, William	24	M	Farmer	02Ap11Ag
WARBUNTER, James	22	M	Servant	02Ap11Ag
MURPHY, Peter	26	M	Cooper	02Ap11Ag
Rose	30	F	Wife	02Ap11Ag
MCKINLEY, Margaret	20	F	Servant	02Ap11Ag
Mary	18	F	Nurse	02Ap11Ag
SAVAGE, Eliza	20	F	Servant	02Ap11Ag
MCCONVILLE, John	32	M	Laborer	02Ap11Ag
MOORE, Robert	24	M	Laborer	02Ap11Ag
Martha	23	F	Servant	02Ap11Ag
ROBINSON, Margaret	18	F	Spinster	02Ap11Ag
GORDEN, John	17	M	Farmer	02Ap11Ag
James	12	M	Unknown	02Ap11Ag
Samuel	35	M	Unknown	02Ap11Ag
Margaret	34	F	Unknown	02Ap11Ag

NAMES OF PASSENGERS	AGE	SEX	OCCUPATIONS	DATE PORT SHIP
GORDEN, Mary	60	F	Unknown	02Ap11Ag
Jane	06	F	Child	02Ap11Ag
DINLEY, Patrick	18	M	Laborer	02Ap11Ag
ROONEY, Biddy	22	F	Spinster	02Ap11Ag
HILL, Jane	24	F	Nurse	02Ap11Ag
BERRY, Mary	17	F	Servant	02Ap11Ag
MOORE, William	20	M	Laborer	02Ap11Ag
DAVIDSON, Agnes	24	F	House Maid	02Ap11Ag
HUGHES, Bernard	21	M	Farmer	02Ap11Ag
Mary	20	F	Servant	02Ap11Ag
Margaret	44	F	Spinster	02Ap11Ag
MULLIN, Nancy	26	F	Bomkr	02Ap11Ag
BURNS, John	22	M	Shoemaker	02Ap11Ag
MCDONALD, Susan	20	F	Spinster	02Ap11Ag
SLINT, Stephen	32	M	Laborer	02Ap11Ag
Sicily	27	F	Wife	02Ap11Ag
HAGGAN, Biddy	25	F	Bomkr	02Ap11Ag
TRAINER, Catharine	18	F	Servant	02Ap11Ag
DAVIDSON, Thomas	20	M	Painter	02Ap11Ag
WATSON, Robert	35	M	Baker	02Ap11Ag
COLLINS, Mary	23	F	House Maid	02Ap11Ag
MORGAN, Hugh	24	M	Fisherman	02Ap11Ag
Mary	20	F	Servant	02Ap11Ag
Bridget	27	F	Spinster	02Ap11Ag
BOYLE, Catharine	26	F	Servant	02Ap11Ag
MAJANISS, James	20	M	Ploughman	02Ap11Ag
Mary	18	F	Wife	02Ap11Ag
Catharine	16	F	Spinster	02Ap11Ag
WATERS, Alice	21	F	Seamstress	02Ap11Ag
MCKEOWN, Annie	23	F	Spinster	02Ap11Ag
SLOAN, Thomas	26	M	Ploughman	02Ap11Ag
Biddy	24	F	Wife	02Ap11Ag
John	.06	M	Infant	02Ap11Ag
MADDEN, John	23	M	Ploughman	02Ap11Ag
HUGHES, Ellen	30	F	Seamstress	02Ap11Ag
PASSMORE, Theresa	10	F	Spinster	02Ap11Ag
HUGHES, Mary	20	F	Seamstress	02Ap11Ag
FANELL, Cathaerine	21	F	Seamstress	02Ap11Ag
Joseph	19	M	Servant	02Ap11Ag
Annie	24	F	Spinster	02Ap11Ag
SOMMERVILLE, A.J.	30	M	Stone Layer	02Ap11Ag
MCBURNEY, Eliza	24	F	Spinster	02Ap11Ag
MURPHY, Patrick	26	M	Planter	02Ap11Ag
TRACEY, Biddy	25	F	Nurse	02Ap11Ag
MCSHANE, Mary	20	F	Servant	02Ap11Ag
HOGAN, Jane	19	F	Nurse	02Ap11Ag
STEVENSON, Elizabeth	45	F	Stone Layer	02Ap11Ag
Samuel	21	M	Stone Layer	02Ap11Ag
James	20	M	Stone Layer	02Ap11Ag
Eliza	16	F	Stone Layer	02Ap11Ag
William	14	M	Stone Layer	02Ap11Ag
Isabella	12	F	Stone Layer	02Ap11Ag
OHARE, Henry	26	M	Farmer	02Ap11Ag
Bridget	14	F	Spinster	02Ap11Ag
MCKENNA, John	25	M	Laborer	02Ap11Ag
SMYTH, Michl.	24	M	Builder	02Ap11Ag
MCKEOWN, Peter	20	M	Mason	02Ap11Ag
MCANNLTY, Anne	18	F	Spinster	02Ap11Ag
Ellen	16	F	Spinster	02Ap11Ag
BOYLE, Betty	24	F	Spinster	02Ap11Ag
GARLAND, John	27	M	Tailor	02Ap11Ag
MURPHY, Thomas	24	M	Farmer	02Ap11Ag
SLOAN, Biddy	36	F	Wife	02Ap11Ag
Owen	11	M	Relative	02Ap11Ag
Thomas	09	M	Child	02Ap11Ag
Mary	06	F	Child	02Ap11Ag
TRAINER, Thomas	40	M	Farmer	02Ap11Ag
Mary	40	F	Wife	02Ap11Ag
Jennie	06	F	Child	02Ap11Ag
James	04	M	Child	02Ap11Ag
John	.06	M	Infant	02Ap11Ag
BURNS, Mary	18	F	Servant	02Ap11Ag
DONNELLY, Ellen	18	F	Spinster	02Ap11Ag
OHARA, Thomas	23	M	Printer	02Ap11Ag
MCGUINNESS, John	24	M	Engraver	02Ap11Ag
CUNNINGHAM, John	32	M	Nailer	02Ap11Ag
KEENAN, Patrick	21	M	Farmer	02Ap11Ag
CLAPHAM, William	25	M	Ploughman	02Ap11Ag
MCSHANE, Danl.	20	M	Servant	02Ap11Ag
HARVEY, Danl.	32	M	Laborer	02Ap11Ag
CULLEN, Patrick	54	M	Shoemaker	02Ap11Ag
HARVEY, Anne	28	F	Spinster	02Ap11Ag
MURPHY, Anne	26	F	Servant	02Ap11Ag
QUINN, Felix	24	M	Ploughman	02Ap11Ag
SLOAN, Peter	21	M	Farmer	02Ap11Ag
FEGAN, Anne	18	F	Nurse	02Ap11Ag
DYER, Jane	18	F	House Maid	02Ap11Ag
MULRAINE, Bernard	20	M	Laborer	02Ap11Ag
MCGUINNESS, Mary	20	F	Seamstress	02Ap11Ag
MCKEOWN, Rose	20	F	Servant	02Ap11Ag
Mary	28	F	Bomkr	02Ap11Ag
GARTLAND, Patrick	27	M	Baker	02Ap11Ag
RODGERS, Mary	21	F	Servant	02Ap11Ag
MAGEE, Edward	20	M	Farmer	02Ap11Ag
Alice	27	F	Relative	02Ap11Ag
John	04	M	Child	02Ap11Ag
Biddy	02	F	Child	02Ap11Ag
Patrick	.03	M	Infant	02Ap11Ag
PASSMORE, Jane	20	F	Nurse	02Ap11Ag
SOMMERVILLE, Archd.J.	11	M	Stone Layer	02Ap11Ag
IRWIN, Sarah	19	F	Servant	02Ap11Ag
DIXON, Anne	26	F	Spinster	02Ap11Ag
MILLER, Henry	32	M	Farmer	02Ap11Ag
Sarah	20	F	Wife	02Ap11Ag
John	.04	M	Infant	02Ap11Ag
OCONNOR, Bernard	13	M	Servant	02Ap11Ag
Ellen	16	F	Spinster	02Ap11Ag
John	40	M	Farmer	02Ap11Ag
MCDONNELL, Catherine	40	F	Wife	02Ap11Ag
Elizabeth	18	F	Spinster	02Ap11Ag
Lucinda	16	F	Spinster	02Ap11Ag
Matilda	14	F	Mtmkr	02Ap11Ag
FARRELLY, Thomas	40	M	Wdmcht	02Ap11Ag
Daniel	10	M	Relative	02Ap11Ag
Owen	08	M	Child	02Ap11Ag
Biddy	06	F	Child	02Ap11Ag
QUINN, Mary	22	F	Spinster	02Ap11Ag
HAUGHY, John	19	M	Servant	02Ap11Ag
MURPHY, John	34	M	Laborer	02Ap11Ag
CUNNINGHAM, John	38	M	Stone Layer	02Ap11Ag
Jane	35	F	Wife	02Ap11Ag
George	07	M	Child	02Ap11Ag
Arabella	04	F	Child	02Ap11Ag
John	02	M	Child	02Ap11Ag
BOYD, Robert	32	M	Carpenter	02Ap11Ag
Sarah	21	F	Wife	02Ap11Ag
Robert	.09	M	Infant	02Ap11Ag
MCPARLANE, Ambrose	30	M	Laborer	02Ap11Ag
MCMULLIN, James	47	M	Farmer	02Ap11Ag
Biddy	40	F	Wife	02Ap11Ag
James	12	M	Servant	02Ap11Ag
MARKEY, James	24	M	Tailor	02Ap11Ag
DEVLIN, Bernard	27	M	Tailor	02Ap11Ag
SMITH, Elizabeth	20	F	Spinster	02Ap11Ag
RICE, Eleanor	24	F	House Maid	02Ap11Ag
DONNELLY, Felix	28	M	Ploughman	02Ap11Ag
MCDONALD, John	30	M	Cooper	02Ap11Ag
QUIN, Charles	22	M	Baker	02Ap11Ag
HUGHES, Elizabeth	35	F	Bomkr	02Ap11Ag
Sarah	18	F	Bomkr	02Ap11Ag
Margaret	15	F	Bomkr	02Ap11Ag
MCKEOWN, Catherine	30	F	Servant	02Ap11Ag
HUGHES, James	18	M	Servant	02Ap11Ag
John	13	M	Servant	02Ap11Ag
Nicholas	09	M	Child	02Ap11Ag
Patrick	11	M	Servant	02Ap11Ag
DIAS, Joseph	39	M	Gdnr	02Ap11Ag
SHONBOE, Mary	26	F	Spinster	02Ap11Ag
BRADLEY, Ellen	13	F	Seamstress	02Ap11Ag
MCCOURT, Bridget	40	F	Spinster	02Ap11Ag

NAMES OF PASSENGERS	AGE	SEX	OCCUPATIONS	DATE PORT SHIP
MCCOURT, Bridget	07	F	Child	02Ap11Ag
HUNTER, Margt.	20	F	Servant	02Ap11Ag
MCCAHEY, James	20	M	Ploughman	02Ap11Ag
MCCANN, Margt.	14	F	Servant	02Ap11Ag
FREEBURN, Samel.	22	M	Gdnr	02Ap11Ag
KEARNEY, Stephen	30	M	Laborer	02Ap11Ag
LARKEN, Nelson	35	M	Tinsmith	02Ap11Ag
DAVIDSON, Rachel	12	F	Servant	02Ap11Ag
LATHIN, U	25	M	Ploughman	02Ap11Ag
Eliza	20	F	Spinster	02Ap11Ag
Rebecca	.05	F	Infant	02Ap11Ag
DORAN, Thomas	21	M	Farmer	02Ap11Ag
ORR, Wm.	30	M	Sailor	02Ap11Ag
MAGGEE, Patt.	18	M	Laborer	02Ap11Ag
CARVAN, Peter	27	M	Servant	02Ap11Ag
TURNER, Betty	18	F	Spinster	02Ap11Ag
HANSATLY, Catherine	03	F	Child	02Ap11Ag
Mary	.02	F	Infant	02Ap11Ag
DENCHY, Barth.	40	M	Boatman	02Ap11Ag
BOWLEN, John	29	M	Boatman	02Ap11Ag
Mary	25	F	Wife	02Ap11Ag
Ellen	.08	F	Infant	02Ap11Ag
CALLAGHAN, Florence	13	F	Laborer	02Ap11Ag
HANSATLY, Hugh	30	M	Laborer	02Ap11Ag
COLLINS, Mary	.06	F	Infant	02Ap11Ag
LINDEN, Thomas	25	M	Preceptor	02Ap11Ag
DONNELLY, John	22	M	Laborer	02Ap11Ag
BURNS, Patrick	24	M	Farmer	02Ap11Ag
MAGEE, John	27	M	Farmer	02Ap11Ag
Mary	35	F	Relative	02Ap11Ag
Mary	19	F	Relative	02Ap11Ag
SHAT, Mary	20	F	Spinster	02Ap11Ag
MOORE, Mary	20	F	Spinster	02Ap11Ag
HENRATLY, Biddy	12	F	Seamstress	02Ap11Ag
BOWLAN, Mary	11	F	Seamstress	02Ap11Ag
BERRY, Bridget	20	F	Seamstress	02Ap11Ag

EMPEROR 02 APRIL 1849

From Liverpool

NAMES OF PASSENGERS	AGE	SEX	OCCUPATIONS	DATE PORT SHIP
DUNNE, Mary	50	F	Unknown	02Ap02Ah
Peter	36	M	Laborer	02Ap02Ah
Patt	26	M	Unknown	02Ap02Ah
Jane	21	F	Unknown	02Ap02Ah
Ann	20	F	Unknown	02Ap02Ah
CAREY, James	34	M	Unknown	02Ap02Ah
Bridget	32	F	Unknown	02Ap02Ah
Thomas	17	M	Unknown	02Ap02Ah
KELLEY, Jos.	25	M	Unknown	02Ap02Ah
FARRELLY, Cornl.	35	M	Unknown	02Ap02Ah
SHEARON, Ant.	26	M	Unknown	02Ap02Ah
James	21	M	Unknown	02Ap02Ah
CLEARY, Ellen	40	F	Unknown	02Ap02Ah
Jhn.	20	M	Unknown	02Ap02Ah
Peter	15	M	Unknown	02Ap02Ah
Mary	16	F	Unknown	02Ap02Ah
FLANAGAN, Lc.	20	M	Unknown	02Ap02Ah
HOODS, Patt	30	M	Unknown	02Ap02Ah
Bridget	50	F	Unknown	02Ap02Ah
Edward	23	M	Unknown	02Ap02Ah
Jhn.	19	M	Unknown	02Ap02Ah
Bridget	17	F	Unknown	02Ap02Ah
Julia	12	F	Unknown	02Ap02Ah
BRERMAN, Catharine	28	F	Unknown	02Ap02Ah
Thomas	26	M	Unknown	02Ap02Ah
Thos.	06	M	Child	02Ap02Ah
Bridget	04	F	Child	02Ap02Ah
Mithcl.	01	M	Child	02Ap02Ah
RYAN, Ann	21	F	Unknown	02Ap02Ah
ROYDEN, George	22	M	Unknown	02Ap02Ah
HOLMES, Wm.	19	M	Unknown	02Ap02Ah
RILEY, Peter	30	M	Unknown	02Ap02Ah
KELCHER, Peter	50	M	Unknown	02Ap02Ah
REYNOLDS, Bernd.	30	M	Unknown	02Ap02Ah
MURPHY, James	30	M	Unknown	02Ap02Ah
Mary	14	F	Unknown	02Ap02Ah
DILLON, James	30	M	Unknown	02Ap02Ah
Rose	20	F	Unknown	02Ap02Ah
BURKE, John	28	M	Unknown	02Ap02Ah
Elisa	07	F	Child	02Ap02Ah
Died-At-Sea				
Tobias	03	M	Child	02Ap02Ah
KENNEY, Patt	30	M	Unknown	02Ap02Ah
Ann	26	F	Unknown	02Ap02Ah
Died-At-Sea				
Patt	04	M	Child	02Ap02Ah
Mary	02	F	Child	02Ap02Ah
Died-At-Sea				
CORBETT, Pat	26	M	Unknown	02Ap02Ah
RILLEY, Wm.	21	M	Unknown	02Ap02Ah
CATRILL, Ellen	30	F	Unknown	02Ap02Ah
Thos.	01	M	Child	02Ap02Ah
CASSEY, Mary	20	F	Unknown	02Ap02Ah
Betsey	16	F	Unknown	02Ap02Ah
MCKENNA, Wm.	24	M	Unknown	02Ap02Ah
Ellen	25	F	Unknown	02Ap02Ah
Fanny	21	F	Unknown	02Ap02Ah
Arthur	24	M	Unknown	02Ap02Ah
MONAGHAN, Nancy	35	F	Unknown	02Ap02Ah
KELLY, James	17	M	Unknown	02Ap02Ah
DONNELLY, Mil.	20	M	Unknown	02Ap02Ah
MULLEN, Nancy	45	F	Unknown	02Ap02Ah
RYAN, Martin	42	M	Unknown	02Ap02Ah
James	10	M	Unknown	02Ap02Ah
BRYAN, Michl.	42	M	Unknown	02Ap02Ah
James	21	M	Unknown	02Ap02Ah
Ellen	25	F	Unknown	02Ap02Ah
SHEA, Patt	42	M	Unknown	02Ap02Ah
COCERAN, James	25	M	Unknown	02Ap02Ah
Martin	20	M	Unknown	02Ap02Ah
MYLER, Thos.	30	M	Unknown	02Ap02Ah
WARREN, Henry	30	M	Unknown	02Ap02Ah
MCCORMICK, Mary	16	F	Unknown	02Ap02Ah
CULLEN, Danl.	23	M	Unknown	02Ap02Ah
HAYDEN, John	24	M	Unknown	02Ap02Ah
Mary	22	F	Unknown	02Ap02Ah
Ellen	01	F	Child	02Ap02Ah
NEALE, Christy	19	M	Unknown	02Ap02Ah
CAVANAGH, Wm.	20	M	Unknown	02Ap02Ah
HARRISON, Edwd.	24	M	Unknown	02Ap02Ah
BURNESS, Michl.	26	M	Unknown	02Ap02Ah
HOWE, Michl.	24	M	Unknown	02Ap02Ah
John	21	M	Unknown	02Ap02Ah
CONNERFORD, Richd.	20	M	Unknown	02Ap02Ah
LERMON, Thos.	26	M	Unknown	02Ap02Ah
SCULLY, James	22	M	Unknown	02Ap02Ah
MCGURIN, Mary	26	F	Unknown	02Ap02Ah
BYRONE, Robert	20	M	Unknown	02Ap02Ah
Cath.	16	F	Unknown	02Ap02Ah
Mames	15	M	Unknown	02Ap02Ah
GOLLIGHE, Michl.	20	M	Unknown	02Ap02Ah
HARROLL, Patt	40	M	Unknown	02Ap02Ah
GALLIGHER, Mary	25	F	Unknown	02Ap02Ah
DUGGAN, Terran	24	M	Unknown	02Ap02Ah
LEA, James	24	M	Unknown	02Ap02Ah
GASON, Jm.	20	M	Unknown	02Ap02Ah
CONNELL, Thos.	22	M	Unknown	02Ap02Ah
CRIBBONS, James	30	M	Unknown	02Ap02Ah
SLOSAN, James	26	M	Unknown	02Ap02Ah
CARROLL, Elisa	20	F	Unknown	02Ap02Ah
FITZGIBBON, Jane	20	F	Unknown	02Ap02Ah
BURKE, James	28	M	Unknown	02Ap02Ah
Honora	24	F	Unknown	02Ap02Ah

NAMES OF PASSENGERS	AGE	SEX	OCCUPATIONS	DATE PORT SHIP
BURKE, Honora	03	F	Child	02Ap02Ah
COLEMAN, Mary	25	F	Unknown	02Ap02Ah
Johanna	22	F	Unknown	02Ap02Ah
GLOVER, James	38	M	Unknown	02Ap02Ah
CARROLL, Hugh	25	M	Unknown	02Ap02Ah
DAFFAY, Patty	20	F	Unknown	02Ap02Ah
CAVANAGH, Francis	21	M	Unknown	02Ap02Ah
MOONEY, James	22	M	Unknown	02Ap02Ah
CAVANAGH, Sarah	18	F	Unknown	02Ap02Ah
LEDRUDGE, Wm.	35	M	Unknown	02Ap02Ah
U-Mrs.	30	F	Unknown	02Ap02Ah
Wm.	05	M	Child	02Ap02Ah
James	04	M	Child	02Ap02Ah
Died-At-Sea				
Mary-Ann	01	F	Child	02Ap02Ah
Died-At-Sea				
COSGOWN, Honora	28	F	Unknown	02Ap02Ah
DONEGAN, Owen	24	M	Unknown	02Ap02Ah
CLINTON, Jno.	21	M	Unknown	02Ap02Ah
HANLEY, James	28	M	Unknown	02Ap02Ah
Bridget	26	F	Unknown	02Ap02Ah
WALLACE, Jon.	25	M	Unknown	02Ap02Ah
HUGHES, Richd.	21	M	Unknown	02Ap02Ah
OBRIEN, Saml.	25	M	Unknown	02Ap02Ah
Esther	21	F	Unknown	02Ap02Ah
DOWLING, John	19	M	Unknown	02Ap02Ah
CONNELL, James	21	M	Unknown	02Ap02Ah
DAILEY, Jos.	24	M	Unknown	02Ap02Ah
Susan	15	F	Unknown	02Ap02Ah
DOWD, James	24	M	Unknown	02Ap02Ah
NIGHTINGALE, Richd.	40	M	Unknown	02Ap02Ah
Died-At-Sea				
OBRIEN, Simone	30	M	Unknown	02Ap02Ah
James	20	M	Unknown	02Ap02Ah
Peter	18	M	Unknown	02Ap02Ah
Jerome	16	M	Unknown	02Ap02Ah
Bridget	14	F	Unknown	02Ap02Ah
Edwd.	12	M	Unknown	02Ap02Ah
FINNEGAN, Michl.	18	M	Unknown	02Ap02Ah
CONNELL, Thos.	25	M	Unknown	02Ap02Ah
James	17	M	Unknown	02Ap02Ah
Bridget	18	F	Unknown	02Ap02Ah
MCKEOWN, Cathe.	20	F	Unknown	02Ap02Ah
COMERFORD, Pattk.	70	M	Unknown	02Ap02Ah
Cath.	50	F	Unknown	02Ap02Ah
James	24	M	Unknown	02Ap02Ah
Biddy	20	F	Unknown	02Ap02Ah
Ann	18	F	Unknown	02Ap02Ah
Cath.	17	F	Unknown	02Ap02Ah
Biddy	03	F	Child	02Ap02Ah
HOLORAN, James	25	M	Unknown	02Ap02Ah
MURPHY, Mary	24	F	Unknown	02Ap02Ah
FARRELLY, Julia	30	F	Unknown	02Ap02Ah
Mary	11	F	Unknown	02Ap02Ah
James	06	M	Child	02Ap02Ah
Ellen	04	F	Child	02Ap02Ah
WHITE, Mary	17	F	Unknown	02Ap02Ah
KERWIN, Mary	19	F	Unknown	02Ap02Ah
KELLY, Bridget	32	F	Unknown	02Ap02Ah
Died-At-Sea				
Pattk.	14	M	Unknown	02Ap02Ah
Corns.	10	M	Unknown	02Ap02Ah
Thos.	09	M	Child	02Ap02Ah
Hugh	05	M	Child	02Ap02Ah
Mary	03	F	Child	02Ap02Ah
BURKE, Phillip	24	M	Unknown	02Ap02Ah
MULLIGAN, Nobby	20	M	Unknown	02Ap02Ah
FLYMAN, Cath.	30	F	Unknown	02Ap02Ah
Dennis	12	M	Unknown	02Ap02Ah
Charles	10	M	Unknown	02Ap02Ah
William	08	M	Child	02Ap02Ah
Patk.	06	M	Child	02Ap02Ah
Francis	04	M	Child	02Ap02Ah
QUILLIGHAN, Dasby	18	F	Unknown	02Ap02Ah
QUIGLEY, Mich.	22	F	Unknown	02Ap02Ah

NAMES OF PASSENGERS	AGE	SEX	OCCUPATIONS	DATE PORT SHIP
GARRON, M.	21	F	Unknown	02Ap02Ah
RYAN, Mary	21	F	Unknown	02Ap02Ah
COGLIN, John	20	M	Unknown	02Ap02Ah
CONEGAN, Joseph	20	M	Unknown	02Ap02Ah
GLYNON, Mich.	20	M	Unknown	02Ap02Ah
BURR, Mary	26	F	Unknown	02Ap02Ah
DIXON, Adam	45	M	Unknown	02Ap02Ah
James	11	M	Unknown	02Ap02Ah

SARAH 02 APRIL 1849

From Dublin

NAMES OF PASSENGERS	AGE	SEX	OCCUPATIONS	DATE PORT SHIP
DELANTY, Patrick	20	M	Unknown	02Ap12Al
Ann	19	F	Unknown	02Ap12Al
CLARKE, Kitty	20	F	Unknown	02Ap12Al
Judy	19	F	Unknown	02Ap12Al
Malechai	22	M	Unknown	02Ap12Al
HART, Thomas	22	M	Unknown	02Ap12Al
Margaret	20	F	Unknown	02Ap12Al
BEGGS, Michael	21	M	Unknown	02Ap12Al
GILMORE, James	20	M	Unknown	02Ap12Al
DIGNAM, Patk.	25	M	Unknown	02Ap12Al
MCGANN, Ann	28	F	Unknown	02Ap12Al
Margaret	10	F	Unknown	02Ap12Al
Mary	08	F	Child	02Ap12Al
Susan	06	F	Child	02Ap12Al
CULLEN, James	22	M	Unknown	02Ap12Al
BRADY, Mary	40	F	Unknown	02Ap12Al
DUNNE, John	22	M	Unknown	02Ap12Al
BROWN, Jeremiah	22	M	Unknown	02Ap12Al
Margaret	20	F	Unknown	02Ap12Al
HOLLAND, John	20	M	Unknown	02Ap12Al
MCMAHON, Patk.	25	M	Unknown	02Ap12Al
U-Mrs.	26	F	Unknown	02Ap12Al
WHITE, Patk.	28	M	Unknown	02Ap12Al
U-Mrs.	24	F	Unknown	02Ap12Al
ARMSTRONG, Thos.	21	M	Unknown	02Ap12Al
U (W)	40	F	Unknown	02Ap12Al
Mary	19	F	Unknown	02Ap12Al
GALLIGAN, Mary	19	F	Unknown	02Ap12Al
DOYLE, Ignatius	22	M	Unknown	02Ap12Al
FREELY, Patk.	27	M	Unknown	02Ap12Al
Cath.	24	F	Unknown	02Ap12Al
MURPHY, Robert	28	M	Unknown	02Ap12Al
Jane	26	F	Unknown	02Ap12Al
Mary	45	F	Unknown	02Ap12Al
Martin	09	M	Child	02Ap12Al
MAHON, Edward	35	M	Unknown	02Ap12Al
Mary	30	F	Unknown	02Ap12Al
Mary	05	F	Child	02Ap12Al
Peter	.00	M	Infant	02Ap12Al
SHERRY, John	22	M	Unknown	02Ap12Al
KERRY, Ann	20	F	Unknown	02Ap12Al
BRENNAN, U-Mrs.	35	F	Unknown	02Ap12Al
Patt	13	M	Unknown	02Ap12Al
Michael	13	M	Unknown	02Ap12Al
MCKEON, Mary	20	F	Unknown	02Ap12Al
HAND, James	20	M	Unknown	02Ap12Al
MAHON, Ellen	10	F	Unknown	02Ap12Al
LOWE, George	23	M	Unknown	02Ap12Al
U-Mrs.	20	F	Unknown	02Ap12Al
FLEMMING, George	22	M	Unknown	02Ap12Al
MAHON, Peter	55	M	Unknown	02Ap12Al
Ellen	40	F	Unknown	02Ap12Al
Michael	20	M	Unknown	02Ap12Al
Biddy	18	F	Unknown	02Ap12Al
Ellen	16	F	Unknown	02Ap12Al
COFFEE, Lawrence	24	M	Unknown	02Ap12Al

NAMES OF PASSENGERS	AGE	SEX	OCCUPATIONS	DATE PORT SHIP
COFFEE, Anne	26	F	Unknown	02Ap12Al
U-Mrs.	28	F	Unknown	02Ap12Al
Thomas	09	M	Child	02Ap12Al
Margaret	07	F	Child	02Ap12Al
Bessy	06	F	Child	02Ap12Al
William	05	M	Child	02Ap12Al
STEELE, Ann	20	F	Unknown	02Ap12Al
CORMACK, Robt.	30	M	Unknown	02Ap12Al
Sarah	26	F	Unknown	02Ap12Al
John	06	M	Child	02Ap12Al
GAFFNEY, Thos.	21	M	Unknown	02Ap12Al
MORAN, James	21	M	Unknown	02Ap12Al
CONNER, Lawrence	21	M	Unknown	02Ap12Al
FOY, Charles	18	M	Unknown	02Ap12Al
HYLAND, William	20	M	Unknown	02Ap12Al
MCMURRAGH, Jas.	21	M	Unknown	02Ap12Al
DORAN, Charles	20	M	Unknown	02Ap12Al
SMITH, George	23	M	Unknown	02Ap12Al
U-Mrs.	20	F	Unknown	02Ap12Al
CARNEY, Thos.	22	M	Unknown	02Ap12Al
U-Mrs.	20	F	Unknown	02Ap12Al
GOODWIN, James	35	M	Unknown	02Ap12Al
REILLY, John	25	M	Unknown	02Ap12Al
SULLIVAN, John	30	M	Unknown	02Ap12Al
WHITE, John	30	M	Unknown	02Ap12Al
GAITY, Henry	30	M	Unknown	02Ap12Al
Mary	26	F	Unknown	02Ap12Al
Michael	00	M	Unknown	02Ap12Al
MURRAY, Edward	20	M	Unknown	02Ap12Al
SHEA, Richard	20	M	Unknown	02Ap12Al
KELLY, Edward	21	M	Unknown	02Ap12Al
FROTHER, John	21	M	Unknown	02Ap12Al
BEAMISH, Thos.	20	M	Unknown	02Ap12Al
KEMAN, Mathw.	18	M	Unknown	02Ap12Al
ENNIS, Mathw.	30	M	Unknown	02Ap12Al
COSGRAVE, Mary	20	F	Unknown	02Ap12Al
JOHNSTON, Thomas	30	M	Unknown	02Ap12Al
DUGAN, Cath.	40	F	Unknown	02Ap12Al
Patk.	22	M	Unknown	02Ap12Al
Margt.	18	F	Unknown	02Ap12Al
CARROLL, Margt.	40	F	Unknown	02Ap12Al
Daniel	16	M	Unknown	02Ap12Al
Mary	11	F	Unknown	02Ap12Al
Judy	09	F	Child	02Ap12Al
Bridget	07	F	Child	02Ap12Al
Anne	05	F	Child	02Ap12Al
James	.00	M	Infant	02Ap12Al
CANTON, William	21	M	Unknown	02Ap12Al
LAVEN, Patk.	24	M	Unknown	02Ap12Al
DUNNE, Eliza	18	F	Unknown	02Ap12Al
Mary	16	F	Unknown	02Ap12Al
BRUTON, William	44	M	Unknown	02Ap12Al
Harriett	40	F	Unknown	02Ap12Al
Mary	21	F	Unknown	02Ap12Al
William	20	M	Unknown	02Ap12Al
John	17	M	Unknown	02Ap12Al
Kitty	13	F	Unknown	02Ap12Al
Fanny	11	F	Unknown	02Ap12Al
Robert	07	M	Child	02Ap12Al
James	03	M	Child	02Ap12Al
FARRELL, James	20	M	Unknown	02Ap12Al
MCCORMICK, Patk.	30	M	Unknown	02Ap12Al
Margaret	30	F	Unknown	02Ap12Al
Mary	06	F	Child	02Ap12Al
Patrick	03	M	Child	02Ap12Al
James	30	M	Unknown	02Ap12Al
Rachael	30	F	Unknown	02Ap12Al
Catherine	08	F	Child	02Ap12Al
Biddy	.00	F	Infant	02Ap12Al
DRISCOLL, Mark	35	M	Unknown	02Ap12Al
Patk.	32	M	Unknown	02Ap12Al
James	30	M	Unknown	02Ap12Al
Arthur	11	M	Unknown	02Ap12Al
Catherine	.00	F	Infant	02Ap12Al
Patrick	05	M	Child	02Ap12Al
CURTAIN, Mary	20	F	Unknown	02Ap12Al
NEILL, Mary	20	F	Unknown	02Ap12Al
ROONEY, Luke	20	M	Unknown	02Ap12Al
PLUNKETT, Michl.	46	M	Unknown	02Ap12Al
Mary	45	F	Unknown	02Ap12Al
Mary	23	F	Unknown	02Ap12Al
Patrick	21	M	Unknown	02Ap12Al
Catherine	18	F	Unknown	02Ap12Al
Judy	15	F	Unknown	02Ap12Al
Bridget	13	F	Unknown	02Ap12Al
Rose	11	F	Unknown	02Ap12Al
Michael	09	M	Child	02Ap12Al
John	05	M	Child	02Ap12Al
Margaret	03	M	Child	02Ap12Al
EGGLINTON, Ann	52	M	Unknown	02Ap12Al
Patk.	26	M	Unknown	02Ap12Al
Edmond	23	M	Unknown	02Ap12Al
Mary	20	F	Unknown	02Ap12Al
Catherine	17	F	Unknown	02Ap12Al
Anne	14	F	Unknown	02Ap12Al
Ellen	24	F	Unknown	02Ap12Al
HEALY, Patk.	35	M	Unknown	02Ap12Al
Bridget	32	F	Unknown	02Ap12Al
Ann	10	F	Unknown	02Ap12Al
Eliza	04	F	Child	02Ap12Al
John	.00	M	Infant	02Ap12Al
FAGEN, Thos.	52	M	Unknown	02Ap12Al
Mary	52	F	Unknown	02Ap12Al
Eliza	22	F	Unknown	02Ap12Al
Rose	20	F	Unknown	02Ap12Al
James	16	M	Unknown	02Ap12Al
Mary	13	F	Unknown	02Ap12Al
NEWNAY, Thos.	45	M	Unknown	02Ap12Al
Anne	45	F	Unknown	02Ap12Al
Mary	25	F	Unknown	02Ap12Al
Mary	20	F	Unknown	02Ap12Al
Patk.	14	M	Unknown	02Ap12Al
William	.00	M	Infant	02Ap12Al
CAROLAN, Michl.	26	M	Unknown	02Ap12Al
Ann	26	F	Unknown	02Ap12Al
MARTIN, James	45	M	Unknown	02Ap12Al
Bridget	35	F	Unknown	02Ap12Al
Jane	20	F	Unknown	02Ap12Al
Mary	18	F	Unknown	02Ap12Al
Anne	13	F	Unknown	02Ap12Al
Christo.	11	M	Unknown	02Ap12Al
James	.00	M	Infant	02Ap12Al
REILLY, William	50	M	Unknown	02Ap12Al
Margt.	45	F	Unknown	02Ap12Al
James	20	M	Unknown	02Ap12Al
Lawrence	18	M	Unknown	02Ap12Al
Mary	40	F	Unknown	02Ap12Al
SMITH, James	40	M	Unknown	02Ap12Al
Mary	35	F	Unknown	02Ap12Al
Mathew	14	M	Unknown	02Ap12Al
Eliza	12	F	Unknown	02Ap12Al
Mary	10	F	Unknown	02Ap12Al
Catherine	08	F	Child	02Ap12Al
Bridget	06	F	Child	02Ap12Al
Ann	.00	F	Infant	02Ap12Al
HANNERY, Widow	60	F	Unknown	02Ap12Al
Philip	27	M	Unknown	02Ap12Al
Michael	25	M	Unknown	02Ap12Al
Mary	22	F	Unknown	02Ap12Al
Mary	25	F	Unknown	02Ap12Al
Patrick	.00	M	Infant	02Ap12Al
Phillip	.00	M	Infant	02Ap12Al
Michael	.00	M	Infant	02Ap12Al
KANE, Owen	60	M	Unknown	02Ap12Al
Ellen	50	F	Unknown	02Ap12Al
Rose	27	F	Unknown	02Ap12Al
Anne	30	F	Unknown	02Ap12Al
Owen	20	M	Unknown	02Ap12Al
Michael	16	M	Unknown	02Ap12Al
John	14	M	Unknown	02Ap12Al

NAMES OF PASSENGERS	AGE	SEX	OCCUPATIONS	DATE PORT SHIP
WALKER, John	22	M	Unknown	02Ap12Ai
Mary	19	F	Unknown	02Ap12Ai
Michael	13	M	Unknown	02Ap12Ai
CORMICK, Peter	50	M	Unknown	02Ap12Ai
Margt.	48	F	Unknown	02Ap12Ai
James	20	M	Unknown	02Ap12Ai
John	18	M	Unknown	02Ap12Ai
Rose	16	F	Unknown	02Ap12Ai
Mary	00	F	Unknown	02Ap12Ai
Margaret	00	F	Unknown	02Ap12Ai
Lawrence	.00	M	Infant	02Ap12Ai
MULLEN, Owen	27	M	Unknown	02Ap12Ai
James	25	M	Unknown	02Ap12Ai
Mary	19	F	Unknown	02Ap12Ai
Ellen	14	F	Unknown	02Ap12Ai
Eliza	12	F	Unknown	02Ap12Ai
Lawrence	09	M	Child	02Ap12Ai
LEONARD, Patk.	70	M	Unknown	02Ap12Ai
Mary	60	F	Unknown	02Ap12Ai
Thomas	30	M	Unknown	02Ap12Ai
Mary	29	F	Unknown	02Ap12Ai
Margaret	27	F	Unknown	02Ap12Ai
Patrick	25	M	Unknown	02Ap12Ai
John	23	M	Unknown	02Ap12Ai
Ann	21	F	Unknown	02Ap12Ai
Cath.	19	F	Unknown	02Ap12Ai
GILLOCK, Cath.	22	F	Unknown	02Ap12Ai
Ann	17	F	Unknown	02Ap12Ai
Judy	05	F	Child	02Ap12Ai
Rose	07	F	Child	02Ap12Ai
MCDONALD, U-Widow	47	F	Unknown	02Ap12Ai
Margt.	22	F	Unknown	02Ap12Ai
Eliza	20	F	Unknown	02Ap12Ai
Edward	17	M	Unknown	02Ap12Ai
Maria	15	F	Unknown	02Ap12Ai
Judy	13	F	Unknown	02Ap12Ai
Ann	11	F	Unknown	02Ap12Ai
Sarah	08	F	Child	02Ap12Ai
Catherine	06	F	Child	02Ap12Ai
John	04	M	Child	02Ap12Ai
James	.00	M	Infant	02Ap12Ai
HARRINGTON, Biddy	46	F	Unknown	02Ap12Ai
Ellen	24	F	Unknown	02Ap12Ai
Margaret	.00	F	Infant	02Ap12Ai
COLLINS, Margaret	18	F	Unknown	02Ap12Ai
Sarah	15	F	Unknown	02Ap12Ai
RICHARDS, Wm.	30	M	Unknown	02Ap12Ai
MUNROE, Wm.	21	M	Unknown	02Ap12Ai
HARFORD, John	22	M	Unknown	02Ap12Ai
HENRY, William	20	M	Unknown	02Ap12Ai
KELLY, John	00	M	Unknown	02Ap12Ai
GINNISS, James	40	M	Unknown	02Ap12Ai
BRADY, Patrick	18	M	Unknown	02Ap12Ai
WHITNEY, Stephen	22	M	Unknown	02Ap12Ai
BRADY, William	21	M	Unknown	02Ap12Ai
ELLEN, Saml.	30	M	Unknown	02Ap12Ai

BROOKSBY 02 APRIL 1849

From Glasgow

NAMES OF PASSENGERS	AGE	SEX	OCCUPATIONS	DATE PORT SHIP
MCCABE, Henry	54	M	Farmer	02Ap04Aj
REID, Geo.	46	M	Farmer	02Ap04Aj
MCDONALD, John	24	M	Farmer	02Ap04Aj
MCELINE, Donald	24	M	Farmer	02Ap04Aj
CHRISTIE, Jane	19	F	Farmer	02Ap04Aj
MCLELAND, John	18	M	Farmer	02Ap04Aj
KEON, Mary	19	F	Farmer	02Ap04Aj
DONAGH, William	13	M	Farmer	02Ap04Aj
QUINN, Edward	19	M	Laborer	02Ap04Aj
GORDON, John	40	M	Farmer	02Ap04Aj
DAILY, Miachael	29	M	Ctnsp	02Ap04Aj
ODONELL, Edward	30	M	Unknown	02Ap04Aj
GALLACHER, Domonick	22	M	Unknown	02Ap04Aj
Rose	25	F	Unknown	02Ap04Aj
BEGGEM, John	20	M	Unknown	02Ap04Aj
James	22	M	Mill Worker	02Ap04Aj
MCANALLY, Wm.	22	M	Mill Worker	02Ap04Aj
Michael	21	M	Mill Worker	02Ap04Aj
DALTON, James	25	M	Ctnsp	02Ap04Aj
MCNAULIS, Michael	26	M	Ctnsp	02Ap04Aj
SMITH, Robt.	15	M	Ctnsp	02Ap04Aj
SWEENEY, Margt.	18	F	Ctnsp	02Ap04Aj
MULLRINS, Andw.	31	M	Ctnsp	02Ap04Aj
COSTELLO, John	38	M	Farmer	02Ap04Aj
Elizabeth	36	F	Unknown	02Ap04Aj
MORGAN, James	50	M	Wheelwright	02Ap04Aj
ONEIL, John	24	M	Wheelwright	02Ap04Aj
DONNOR, John	37	M	Engineer	02Ap04Aj
Rosey	62	F	Engineer	02Ap04Aj
MCGOWAN, James	21	M	Engineer	02Ap04Aj
WOODS, Sarah	30	F	W-Fmr	02Ap04Aj
Mary	30	F	W-Fmr	02Ap04Aj
Joseph	13	M	Unknown	02Ap04Aj
Sarah	09	F	Child	02Ap04Aj
Died-At-Sea				
Owen	06	M	Child	02Ap04Aj
Mary	04	F	Child	02Ap04Aj
James	02	M	Child	02Ap04Aj
NUGENT, Mary	15	F	Miner	02Ap04Aj
Catharine	18	F	Miner	02Ap04Aj
BROWN, Robt.	40	M	Miner	02Ap04Aj
OCONNER, John	21	M	Farmer	02Ap04Aj
MCSHERRY, James	48	M	Farmer	02Ap04Aj
MCCADDON, Peter	30	M	Laborer	02Ap04Aj
BLACK, Daniel	19	M	Laborer	02Ap04Aj
RITCHMOND, Wm.	25	M	Laborer	02Ap04Aj
MCDONALD, John	28	M	Laborer	02Ap04Aj
BRADEY, Danil.	20	M	Laborer	02Ap04Aj
DIAMOND, Edmond	17	M	Farmer	02Ap04Aj
CARDWELL, Wm.	26	M	Farmer	02Ap04Aj
Catharine	26	F	Farmer	02Ap04Aj
Ann	13	F	Farmer	02Ap04Aj
QUIGGLEY, Mathw.	13	M	Laborer	02Ap04Aj
MCCADDIN, Francis	18	M	Laborer	02Ap04Aj
MCCULLOCK, John	50	M	Laborer	02Ap04Aj
Jane	17	F	Laborer	02Ap04Aj
ASHBORN, John	21	M	Laborer	02Ap04Aj
MCCENOTT, Patrick	24	M	Laborer	02Ap04Aj
MULLHOLONE, Mary-Jane	20	F	Laborer	02Ap04Aj
WILSON, James	40	M	Farmer	02Ap04Aj
Died-At-Sea				
James	12	M	Shoemaker	02Ap04Aj
Robert	08	M	Child	02Ap04Aj
Died-At-Sea				
Hugh	03	M	Child	02Ap04Aj
NEWELL, James	30	M	Farmer	02Ap04Aj
COLLONS, James	17	M	Farmer	02Ap04Aj
DAREY, Silias	22	M	Farmer	02Ap04Aj
CAMPBELL, Ann	20	F	Farmer	02Ap04Aj
MCCARDLE, Samul	35	M	Laborer	02Ap04Aj
CHEMLUS, Thos.	30	M	Weaver	02Ap04Aj
MCMICHAEL, Alexr.	57	M	Unknown	02Ap04Aj
Ann	42	F	W-Fmr	02Ap04Aj
Catharine	12	F	Unknown	02Ap04Aj
Elizabeth	06	F	Child	02Ap04Aj
Alexander	.10	M	Infant	02Ap04Aj
CANE, Hugh	19	M	Cooper	02Ap04Aj
KELLEY, Rose	30	F	Cooper	02Ap04Aj
HEWS, Patrick	25	M	Cooper	02Ap04Aj
TRAINNER, John	25	M	Cooper	02Ap04Aj
Margrit	20	F	Unknown	02Ap04Aj

JAVA 03 APRIL 1849

From Liverpool

NAMES OF PASSENGERS	AGE	SEX	OCCUPATIONS	DATE PORT SHIP
BOWEN, Richard	40	M	Unknown	03Ap02AI
Thomas	21	M	Unknown	03Ap02AI
Michl.	13	M	Unknown	03Ap02AI
Mary	15	F	Unknown	03Ap02AI
BUTTON, James	30	M	Unknown	03Ap02AI
Susan	30	F	Unknown	03Ap02AI
Eliza-Jane	07	F	Child	03Ap02AI
James	06	M	Child	03Ap02AI
Robert	03	M	Child	03Ap02AI
WADE, Francis	36	M	Unknown	03Ap02AI
Catharine	30	F	Unknown	03Ap02AI
GARRET, James	36	M	Unknown	03Ap02AI
RODY, Mark	22	M	Unknown	03Ap02AI
CALDWELL, Cath.	20	F	Unknown	03Ap02AI
BOND, Thomas	22	M	Unknown	03Ap02AI
MURPHY, Ann	20	F	Unknown	03Ap02AI
Cath.	22	F	Unknown	03Ap02AI
CULLEN, Patk.	20	M	Unknown	03Ap02AI
Bridget	20	F	Unknown	03Ap02AI
CONLAN, Ann	20	F	Unknown	03Ap02AI
FLEMING, John	27	M	Unknown	03Ap02AI
Johanna	20	F	Unknown	03Ap02AI
SILK, Eliza	30	F	Unknown	03Ap02AI
James	27	M	Unknown	03Ap02AI
Michael	10	M	Unknown	03Ap02AI
Martin	08	M	Child	03Ap02AI
Patrick	06	M	Child	03Ap02AI
Mary	04	F	Child	03Ap02AI
Cath.	03	F	Child	03Ap02AI
Edmund	02	M	Child	03Ap02AI
TULLY, Mary	20	F	Unknown	03Ap02AI
CEEP, Mary	18	F	Unknown	03Ap02AI
James	17	M	Unknown	03Ap02AI
CASEY, Jane	16	F	Unknown	03Ap02AI
Margaret	17	F	Unknown	03Ap02AI
KEENAN, John	20	M	Unknown	03Ap02AI
John	50	M	Unknown	03Ap02AI
Bridget	17	F	Unknown	03Ap02AI
Mary	17	F	Unknown	03Ap02AI
BANNON, Patrick	20	M	Unknown	03Ap02AI
DEGNAN, John	18	M	Unknown	03Ap02AI
George	20	M	Unknown	03Ap02AI
EGAN, James	24	M	Unknown	03Ap02AI
Thomas	17	M	Unknown	03Ap02AI
Bridget	11	F	Unknown	03Ap02AI
Margt.	47	F	Unknown	03Ap02AI
TOSS, Mick	40	M	Unknown	03Ap02AI
U-Mrs.	40	F	Unknown	03Ap02AI
LYONS, Mick	23	M	Unknown	03Ap02AI
Maria	20	F	Unknown	03Ap02AI
CASULL, John	36	M	Unknown	03Ap02AI
Eliza	36	F	Unknown	03Ap02AI
U	.00	U	Infant	03Ap02AI
Mick.	11	M	Unknown	03Ap02AI
Mary	10	F	Unknown	03Ap02AI
Patrick	05	M	Child	03Ap02AI
Martin	04	M	Child	03Ap02AI
CLEIMENT, Keam	27	U	Unknown	03Ap02AI
BEST, John	40	M	Unknown	03Ap02AI
ESTRANGE, Martin	24	M	Unknown	03Ap02AI
MCCABE, Pat	20	M	Unknown	03Ap02AI
LAFFERTY, Cath.	18	F	Unknown	03Ap02AI
Mary	16	F	Unknown	03Ap02AI
MULLAN, John	44	M	Unknown	03Ap02AI
Mick	20	M	Unknown	03Ap02AI

NAMES OF PASSENGERS	AGE	SEX	OCCUPATIONS	DATE PORT SHIP
NAUGHTEN, John	24	M	Unknown	03Ap02AI
MITCHELL, Thomas	30	M	Unknown	03Ap02AI
Bridget	27	F	Unknown	03Ap02AI
Ann	04	F	Child	03Ap02AI
TIVERROW, Bridget	08	F	Child	03Ap02AI
KILLEN, Patrick	24	M	Unknown	03Ap02AI
KELLY, Patrick	20	M	Unknown	03Ap02AI
HEALY, Maria	20	F	Unknown	03Ap02AI
NEWLAN, Ann	20	F	Unknown	03Ap02AI
MCNEALIE, Eliza	20	F	Unknown	03Ap02AI
BRADY, James	21	M	Unknown	03Ap02AI
Bessy	21	F	Unknown	03Ap02AI
RILEY, Teresa	10	F	Unknown	03Ap02AI
Rose	12	F	Unknown	03Ap02AI
CONELLY, James	47	M	Unknown	03Ap02AI
Jane	20	F	Unknown	03Ap02AI
Cath.	17	F	Unknown	03Ap02AI
Ann	16	F	Unknown	03Ap02AI
KELLY, Mary	50	F	Unknown	03Ap02AI
Patrick	12	M	Unknown	03Ap02AI
Margt.	08	F	Child	03Ap02AI
Mary	04	F	Child	03Ap02AI
Mary	13	F	Unknown	03Ap02AI
CONOLLY, Eliza	29	F	Unknown	03Ap02AI
TOBIN, John	22	M	Unknown	03Ap02AI
CASLIN, Pat	30	M	Unknown	03Ap02AI
Rose	30	F	Unknown	03Ap02AI
Thomas	04	M	Child	03Ap02AI
BIGLOW, John	16	M	Unknown	03Ap02AI
COVENTRY, Charles	15	M	Unknown	03Ap02AI
Rose	12	F	Unknown	03Ap02AI
MCMAHON, M.	20	U	Unknown	03Ap02AI
CASLINAHAN, C.	17	U	Unknown	03Ap02AI
HEAVNEY, Julia	24	F	Unknown	03Ap02AI
Wm.	20	M	Unknown	03Ap02AI
GASNAN, Thomas	45	M	Unknown	03Ap02AI
MARKAN, Mick	24	M	Unknown	03Ap02AI
Thomas	16	M	Unknown	03Ap02AI
FARRELL, Mick	20	M	Unknown	03Ap02AI
HAVWELL, T.	22	U	Unknown	03Ap02AI
HARK, Pat	00	M	Unknown	03Ap02AI
MUSTAGH, Ann	22	F	Unknown	03Ap02AI
FARRELL, James	30	M	Unknown	03Ap02AI
Elizer	30	M	Unknown	03Ap02AI
Thomas	12	M	Unknown	03Ap02AI
Maria	11	F	Unknown	03Ap02AI
Berry	10	M	Unknown	03Ap02AI
Ann	08	F	Child	03Ap02AI
Charly	06	M	Child	03Ap02AI
Bridget	03	F	Child	03Ap02AI
REED, Bridget	20	F	Unknown	03Ap02AI
Ann	18	F	Unknown	03Ap02AI
DONLAN, James	50	M	Unknown	03Ap02AI
U-Mrs.	40	F	Unknown	03Ap02AI
James	18	M	Unknown	03Ap02AI
Mick	12	M	Unknown	03Ap02AI
Bridget	11	F	Unknown	03Ap02AI
Peggy	09	F	Child	03Ap02AI
Mavalla	07	U	Child	03Ap02AI
POWER, Richard	24	M	Unknown	03Ap02AI
James	20	M	Unknown	03Ap02AI
Julia	19	F	Unknown	03Ap02AI
ONEIL, James	25	M	Unknown	03Ap02AI
MCCONNGHY, James	00	M	Unknown	03Ap02AI
Mary	00	F	Unknown	03Ap02AI
MORGAN, James	20	M	Unknown	03Ap02AI
Maralla	20	U	Unknown	03Ap02AI
BRADY, Edwd.	20	M	Unknown	03Ap02AI
FITZSIMMONS, Wm.	20	M	Unknown	03Ap02AI
BYRNES, James	30	M	Unknown	03Ap02AI
RILEY, Ann	20	F	Unknown	03Ap02AI
FARALLY, Mary	20	F	Unknown	03Ap02AI
HEALY, Cath.	16	F	Unknown	03Ap02AI
Margt.	19	F	Unknown	03Ap02AI
MCGEE, M.	21	U	Unknown	03Ap02AI

NAMES OF PASSENGERS	AGE	SEX	OCCUPATIONS	DATE PORT SHIP
DONLAN, O.	22	U	Unknown	03Ap02Al
KALAHAN, John	22	M	Unknown	03Ap02Al
TOWERY, Pat	22	M	Unknown	03Ap02Al
MCGEE, Kelly	18	U	Unknown	03Ap02Al
Ellen	17	F	Unknown	03Ap02Al
GIVERN, A.	20	U	Unknown	03Ap02Al
REEHAN, M.	30	U	Unknown	03Ap02Al
Mary	30	F	Unknown	03Ap02Al
U	.00	U	Infant	03Ap02Al
ONEIL, J.	25	U	Unknown	03Ap02Al
CORNAY, P.	18	U	Unknown	03Ap02Al
CRAWFORD, H.	36	U	Unknown	03Ap02Al
Jane	30	F	Unknown	03Ap02Al
Sarah	03	F	Child	03Ap02Al
Catharine	01	F	Child	03Ap02Al
CAFFERY, Pat	16	M	Unknown	03Ap02Al
THOMAS, Peter	24	M	Unknown	03Ap02Al
DEAN, James	50	M	Unknown	03Ap02Al
CALLAGHAN, James	50	M	Unknown	03Ap02Al
Rose	50	F	Unknown	03Ap02Al
Mick	18	M	Unknown	03Ap02Al
Mary	15	F	Unknown	03Ap02Al
James	11	M	Unknown	03Ap02Al
DONNELLY, Rose	09	F	Child	03Ap02Al
Pat	11	M	Unknown	03Ap02Al
SMITH, O.	21	U	Unknown	03Ap02Al
FITZPATRICK, Thomas	30	M	Unknown	03Ap02Al
MCARDLE, Cath.	50	F	Unknown	03Ap02Al
Peter	20	M	Unknown	03Ap02Al
Cath.	14	F	Unknown	03Ap02Al
MCELROY, E.	12	U	Unknown	03Ap02Al
DUFFY, P.	35	U	Unknown	03Ap02Al
C.	40	U	Unknown	03Ap02Al
MEEHAN, Rose	14	F	Unknown	03Ap02Al
HUGHES, Mary	17	F	Unknown	03Ap02Al
HARRISON, A.	20	U	Unknown	03Ap02Al
SMITH, M.	17	U	Unknown	03Ap02Al
TOHER, Wm.	28	M	Unknown	03Ap02Al
TAYLOR, E.	24	U	Unknown	03Ap02Al
SPILLMAN, J.	24	U	Unknown	03Ap02Al
J.	20	U	Unknown	03Ap02Al
Mary	20	F	Unknown	03Ap02Al
LIND, Owen	34	M	Unknown	03Ap02Al
LEAVY, M.	28	U	Unknown	03Ap02Al
MORGAN, T.	25	U	Unknown	03Ap02Al
T.	22	U	Unknown	03Ap02Al
CONNER, Biddy	24	F	Unknown	03Ap02Al
Mary	08	F	Child	03Ap02Al
HUSSY, Jane	20	F	Unknown	03Ap02Al
POWER, B.	20	U	Unknown	03Ap02Al
DOYLE, Ann	28	F	Unknown	03Ap02Al
MULLIN, John	20	M	Unknown	03Ap02Al
BIERMAN, Bridget	18	F	Unknown	03Ap02Al
TOBIN, John	22	M	Unknown	03Ap02Al
CUSHION, Pat	30	M	Unknown	03Ap02Al
KIERHAN, Martin	30	M	Unknown	03Ap02Al
PRICE, Bridget	20	F	Unknown	03Ap02Al
MURTHER, Ann	22	F	Unknown	03Ap02Al
WILDE, Owen	24	M	Unknown	03Ap02Al
WALSH, Thos.	20	M	Unknown	03Ap02Al
ODONNELL, Wm.	28	M	Unknown	03Ap02Al
MALONEY, Honora	20	F	Unknown	03Ap02Al
MANILL, Edwd.	25	M	Unknown	03Ap02Al
GRIFFIN, Ellen	40	F	Unknown	03Ap02Al
Wm.	50	M	Unknown	03Ap02Al
Michael	30	M	Unknown	03Ap02Al
John	17	M	Unknown	03Ap02Al
Catherin	09	F	Child	03Ap02Al
FINNEGAN, Thos.	21	M	Unknown	03Ap02Al
Mary	21	F	Unknown	03Ap02Al
HUSEY, Micahel	21	M	Unknown	03Ap02Al
Edwd.	21	M	Unknown	03Ap02Al

WILLIAM-SPRAGUE 03 APRIL 1849

From Liverpool

NAMES OF PASSENGERS	AGE	SEX	OCCUPATIONS	DATE PORT SHIP
BRAMMILL, Benj.	18	M	Laborer	03Ap02Am
PALEY, Mick	17	M	Laborer	03Ap02Am
GALVAN, Edw.	30	M	Laborer	03Ap02Am
Biddy	30	F	Servant	03Ap02Am
Mary	07	F	Child	03Ap02Am
John	05	M	Child	03Ap02Am
James	.00	M	Infant	03Ap02Am
Died-At-Sea				
COSTELLOE, Biddy	21	F	Servant	03Ap02Am
Biddy	.00	F	Infant	03Ap02Am
Thos.	48	M	Farmer	03Ap02Am
FLYNN, John	25	M	Laborer	03Ap02Am
COSTOLOR, Ellen	20	F	Servant	03Ap02Am
LYNCH, Pat	16	M	Laborer	03Ap02Am
MURRAY, Berd.	18	M	Laborer	03Ap02Am
Thos.	13	M	Laborer	03Ap02Am
Ellen	09	F	Child	03Ap02Am
CONNELL, Patrick	40	M	Farmer	03Ap02Am
Mary	38	F	Farmer	03Ap02Am
Cath.	18	F	Servant	03Ap02Am
Anne	16	F	Servant	03Ap02Am
Philip	13	M	Laborer	03Ap02Am
Mary	09	F	Child	03Ap02Am
James	03	M	Child	03Ap02Am
Pat	.00	M	Infant	03Ap02Am
DIVINE, Alice	21	F	Servant	03Ap02Am
GILLSHERRAN, Jane	40	F	Seamstress	03Ap02Am
Mary	20	F	Seamstress	03Ap02Am
Rose	18	F	Seamstress	03Ap02Am
Edward	16	M	Laborer	03Ap02Am
WARD, Michael	50	M	Farmer	03Ap02Am
Mary	17	F	Seamstress	03Ap02Am
Bridget	15	F	Seamstress	03Ap02Am
Cath.	11	F	Seamstress	03Ap02Am
GIBBON, John	32	M	Farmer	03Ap02Am
Mary	28	F	Unknown	03Ap02Am
Michael	07	M	Child	03Ap02Am
Mary	05	F	Child	03Ap02Am
Ellinor	.00	F	Infant	03Ap02Am
BARRY, Jody	28	M	Farmer	03Ap02Am
NAUGHTON, Sally	26	F	Servant	03Ap02Am
NOONAN, Mick	25	F	Baker	03Ap02Am
BINK, George	30	F	Laborer	03Ap02Am
Margt.	17	F	Servant	03Ap02Am
SMITH, Michl.	30	M	Farmer	03Ap02Am
Mary	25	F	Unknown	03Ap02Am
James	.00	M	Infant	03Ap02Am
MCCORMICK, Cath.	30	F	Servant	03Ap02Am
Pat	20	M	Laborer	03Ap02Am
Martin	05	M	Child	03Ap02Am
Cath.	19	F	Servant	03Ap02Am
Mgt.	06	F	Child	03Ap02Am
SHERIDAN, Bridget	45	F	Servant	03Ap02Am
Pat	23	M	Farmer	03Ap02Am
Ann	26	F	Servant	03Ap02Am
WALSH, Thos.	40	M	Laborer	03Ap02Am
SHEVLIN, James	34	M	Farmer	03Ap02Am
Dan.	24	M	Laborer	03Ap02Am
COSTIGAN, Lawrence	34	M	Baker	03Ap02Am
CRAWFORD, James	42	M	Weaver	03Ap02Am
TARPHEY, Mick	30	M	Farmer	03Ap02Am
LEHIN, Michl.	20	M	Farmer	03Ap02Am
COLLINS, John	26	M	Laborer	03Ap02Am
MURPHY, Mary	20	F	Servant	03Ap02Am
HOORAHAN, Dan.	21	M	Laborer	03Ap02Am

NAMES OF PASSENGERS	AGE	SEX	OCCUPATIONS	DATE PORT SHIP
HOORAHAN, Pat	32	M	Laborer	03Ap02Am
Mary	20	F	Servant	03Ap02Am
CARROLL, Jerry	24	M	Shoemaker	03Ap02Am
Michl.	13	M	Shoemaker	03Ap02Am
WADE, John	15	M	Laborer	03Ap02Am
MAHOR, Thos.	30	M	Farmer	03Ap02Am
CONNOLLY, John	30	M	Farmer	03Ap02Am
James	22	M	Farmer	03Ap02Am
TOBIN, Wm.	36	M	Laborer	03Ap02Am
Pat	30	M	Laborer	03Ap02Am
HOGAN, Pat	40	M	Carpenter	03Ap02Am
READ, Wm.	28	M	Tailor	03Ap02Am
KING, Thos.	21	M	Laborer	03Ap02Am
Owen	20	M	Laborer	03Ap02Am
DOWD, Michl.	19	M	Laborer	03Ap02Am
BOYLE, Mary	22	F	Servant	03Ap02Am
James	.00	M	Infant	03Ap02Am
MCMANUS, John	24	M	Laborer	03Ap02Am
GALVIN, John	17	M	Laborer	03Ap02Am
NUTLY, Martin	20	M	Laborer	03Ap02Am
JAMES, Pat	20	M	Laborer	03Ap02Am
RYAN, Pat	11	M	Laborer	03Ap02Am
CASEY, Pat	18	M	Laborer	03Ap02Am
DAVY, Michl.	21	M	Laborer	03Ap02Am
MCMAHON, Thos.	50	M	Farmer	03Ap02Am
James	22	M	Farmer	03Ap02Am
Ann	24	F	Servant	03Ap02Am
BYRNES, Henry	25	M	Laborer	03Ap02Am
GORATTY, Michl.	21	M	Farmer	03Ap02Am
Owen	18	M	Farmer	03Ap02Am
GANNON, Mary	21	F	Servant	03Ap02Am
Alice	18	F	Servant	03Ap02Am
GIBBONS, Thos.	17	M	Laborer	03Ap02Am
Winifred	15	F	Servant	03Ap02Am
RABBIT, Michl.	26	M	Laborer	03Ap02Am
Wm.	20	M	Laborer	03Ap02Am
Alice	22	F	Servant	03Ap02Am
MCFEAGE, Michl.	15	M	Laborer	03Ap02Am
Mary	14	F	Servant	03Ap02Am
REILLY, John	45	M	Farmer	03Ap02Am
DUFFEY, Thos.	49	M	Farmer	03Ap02Am
Mary	21	F	Servant	03Ap02Am
Nancy	21	F	Servant	03Ap02Am
Bryan	19	M	Laborer	03Ap02Am
Thos.	17	M	Laborer	03Ap02Am
PHEELEY, Bridget	19	F	Servant	03Ap02Am
FAVALE, John	21	M	Laborer	03Ap02Am
James	22	M	Laborer	03Ap02Am
COLEMAN, Bridget	22	F	Servant	03Ap02Am
TYRULL, Thos.	50	M	Mason	03Ap02Am
Jane	45	F	Unknown	03Ap02Am
Bridget	35	F	Servant	03Ap02Am
Betty	19	F	Servant	03Ap02Am
Joseph	12	M	Mason	03Ap02Am
MCCASH, Dan	19	M	Laborer	03Ap02Am
Mary	20	F	Servant	03Ap02Am
HAVORIN, Martin	30	M	Farmer	03Ap02Am
John	24	M	Farmer	03Ap02Am
MCKENNA, John	20	M	Trade Man	03Ap02Am
DUNN, Ellen	20	F	Servant	03Ap02Am
NOLAN, Michl.	40	M	Farmer	03Ap02Am
MCDONNOTT, Edwd.	20	M	Laborer	03Ap02Am
Cath.	24	F	Servant	03Ap02Am
MATHEWS, Harry	20	M	Laborer	03Ap02Am
ADAMS, Alex.	24	M	Laborer	03Ap02Am
MILLER, Andrew	20	M	Laborer	03Ap02Am
DAVY, Peter	52	M	Farmer	03Ap02Am
Ellen	52	F	Unknown	03Ap02Am
Peter	20	M	Farmer	03Ap02Am
Edmund	07	M	Child	03Ap02Am
Ann	16	F	Servant	03Ap02Am
DOWNEY, Wm.	30	M	Laborer	03Ap02Am
Ellen	30	F	Unknown	03Ap02Am
James	28	M	Laborer	03Ap02Am
JEFFREY, Wm.	05	M	Child	03Ap02Am

NAMES OF PASSENGERS	AGE	SEX	OCCUPATIONS	DATE PORT SHIP
MOORAY, Peter	26	M	Farmer	03Ap02Am
WHALAN, Edward	40	M	Farmer	03Ap02Am
Johanna	40	F	Unknown	03Ap02Am
Wm.	19	M	Farmer	03Ap02Am
Ann	16	F	Unknown	03Ap02Am
Biddy	14	F	Farmer	03Ap02Am
Mary	08	F	Child	03Ap02Am
QUINLAN, Thos.	30	M	Farmer	03Ap02Am
Keeran	25	M	Farmer	03Ap02Am
GRANT, James	35	M	Farmer	03Ap02Am
James	05	M	Child	03Ap02Am
KELLY, Edwd.	25	M	Farmer	03Ap02Am
DULLARD, Pat	23	M	Farmer	03Ap02Am
Ann	18	F	Servant	03Ap02Am
KAY, John	20	M	Laborer	03Ap02Am
Mary	18	F	Servant	03Ap02Am
WHEELING, Mary	20	F	Servant	03Ap02Am
DOHORTY, Betsey	20	F	Servant	03Ap02Am
Margt.	18	F	Servant	03Ap02Am
CAMBODY, Joseph	29	M	Farmer	03Ap02Am
LEESON, Andrew	20	M	Farmer	03Ap02Am
CARROLL, John	21	M	Laborer	03Ap02Am
BRADY, Pat	21	M	Laborer	03Ap02Am
MANNINGS, Fanny	20	F	Servant	03Ap02Am
ANDERSON, Mary	15	F	Servant	03Ap02Am
KELLY, Patrick	26	M	Laborer	03Ap02Am
SLAVIN, Thos.	24	M	Laborer	03Ap02Am
TULLY, Cath.	19	F	Servant	03Ap02Am
MCCORMICK, Betsy	20	F	Servant	03Ap02Am
MURTAGH, George	20	M	Mason	03Ap02Am
John	18	M	Mason	03Ap02Am
FAY, John	18	M	Mason	03Ap02Am
HANARY, John	23	M	Mason	03Ap02Am
HENALY, Martin	20	M	Mason	03Ap02Am
TIGHE, John	45	M	Mason	03Ap02Am
Bridget	45	F	Unknown	03Ap02Am
John	17	M	Laborer	03Ap02Am
Mary	20	F	Servant	03Ap02Am
Cath.	09	F	Child	03Ap02Am
Bridget	06	F	Child	03Ap02Am
Mary	04	F	Child	03Ap02Am
MCGRATH, Sally	20	F	Servant	03Ap02Am
Bridget	19	F	Servant	03Ap02Am
ROONEY, Wm.	19	M	Laborer	03Ap02Am
Bridget	20	F	Servant	03Ap02Am
Cath.	19	F	Servant	03Ap02Am
FANGHAN, Patt	29	M	Laborer	03Ap02Am
CLARY, Michael	24	M	Shoemaker	03Ap02Am
RAFTON, James	26	M	Farmer	03Ap02Am
DUNN, Martin	23	M	Carpenter	03Ap02Am
Ann	21	F	Servant	03Ap02Am
BRYAN, Ellen	48	F	Farmer	03Ap02Am
Mary	25	F	Farmer	03Ap02Am
James	21	M	Farmer	03Ap02Am
Mgt.	19	F	Farmer	03Ap02Am
Honora	17	F	Unknown	03Ap02Am
Judy	15	F	Unknown	03Ap02Am
TULLY, Patt	20	M	Laborer	03Ap02Am
SMYTH, Lawrence	20	M	Farmer	03Ap02Am
Patt	15	M	Unknown	03Ap02Am
Bridget	12	F	Unknown	03Ap02Am
Thos.	09	M	Child	03Ap02Am
Mary	07	F	Child	03Ap02Am
CLIRLLY, Thos.	13	M	Laborer	03Ap02Am
REYNOLDS, Mary	22	F	Servant	03Ap02Am
DAVIDGE, Henry-Guy	18	M	Unknown	03Ap02Am
HEARNE, Fogus-Farrill	32	M	Unknown	03Ap02Am
CARMICHAEL, John	26	M	Unknown	03Ap02Am

MARY-FLORENCE 05 APRIL 1849

From Liverpool

NAMES OF PASSENGERS	AGE	SEX	OCCUPATIONS	DATE PORT SHIP
DAREY, Pat	24	M	Bootmaker	05Ap02An
Mary	21	F	Unknown	05Ap02An
GILLENLANE, Pat	25	M	Farmer	05Ap02An
HUKEY, Jas.	23	M	Farmer	05Ap02An
MYERS, Michl.	21	M	Farmer	05Ap02An
BRENNAN, Pat	20	M	Laborer	05Ap02An
CURRAN, Jas.	20	M	Laborer	05Ap02An
CUNNINGHAM, John	16	M	Unknown	05Ap02An
MILLANANCE, John	18	M	Unknown	05Ap02An
MCINTYRE, Mary	30	F	Servant	05Ap02An
WANES, Robt.	30	M	Blacksmith	05Ap02An
Margt.	30	F	Unknown	05Ap02An
Charlotte	10	F	Unknown	05Ap02An
DUYNAN, Bridget	19	F	Unknown	05Ap02An
SWEENEY, Mary	30	F	Unknown	05Ap02An
SHERIDAN, Bridget	50	F	Servant	05Ap02An
LYNCH, Owen	30	M	Unknown	05Ap02An
BUTLER, Joshua	22	M	Smith	05Ap02An
DOLAN, Elzth.	18	F	Servant	05Ap02An
CLANCY, Ellen	18	F	Servant	05Ap02An
JOHNSTEN, Jas.	25	M	Laborer	05Ap02An
SHELLY, Cath.	18	F	Servant	05Ap02An
Pat	13	M	Unknown	05Ap02An
MCELHALTEN, Mary	20	F	Unknown	05Ap02An
WISTON, Andrew	50	M	Farmer	05Ap02An
HART, Thos.	50	M	Butcher	05Ap02An
GRAGHTY, Jas.	24	M	Butcher	05Ap02An
MAINE, Winny	24	F	Unknown	05Ap02An
Michl.	26	M	Unknown	05Ap02An
REILLY, Jas.	27	M	Unknown	05Ap02An
MCKEONGH, Edw.	21	M	Smith	05Ap02An
S----, Ellen	00	F	Unknown	05Ap02An
DONOHOE, Jas.	28	M	Unknown	05Ap02An
GIBNEY, John	50	M	Cooper	05Ap02An
SCUIPE, Wm.	25	M	Cooper	05Ap02An
FIROGART, John	25	M	Weaver	05Ap02An
Wm.	20	F	Servant	05Ap02An
BENNETT, Thos.	45	M	Farmer	05Ap02An
TEDDY, Bridgt.	19	F	Unknown	05Ap02An
BARRY, Mary	50	F	Unknown	05Ap02An
DOHIS, Owen	28	M	Unknown	05Ap02An
HIBBERT, Elzth.	24	F	Servant	05Ap02An
BRIDGE, Mary-A.	19	F	Servant	05Ap02An
LARKIN, John	42	M	Farmer	05Ap02An
MCBRENN, Felix	06	M	Child	05Ap02An
SERLE, John	20	M	Unknown	05Ap02An
CAHILL, Bridget	18	F	Servant	05Ap02An
CUDDIHY, Edw.	21	M	Farmer	05Ap02An
SCALLY, Edw.	45	M	Farmer	05Ap02An
Mary	40	F	Farmer	05Ap02An
Mary	11	F	Farmer	05Ap02An
Thos.	10	M	Unknown	05Ap02An
Pat	08	M	Child	05Ap02An
MCAVIDDY, Wm.	22	M	Laborer	05Ap02An
DUNCAN, Owen	20	M	Laborer	05Ap02An
DUNNELLAN, Thos.	16	M	Laborer	05Ap02An
HENCHAN, Jas.	18	M	Laborer	05Ap02An
GLENNAN, Bridget	18	F	Servant	05Ap02An
MCBRIAN, Pat	17	M	Unknown	05Ap02An
PERWIN, Ellen	20	F	Butcher	05Ap02An
BLIGH, Ann	08	F	Child	05Ap02An
KILKENNY, Jane	50	F	Unknown	05Ap02An
Jane	04	F	Child	05Ap02An
Ellen	.00	F	Infant	05Ap02An
JOHNSTON, Mary	30	F	Unknown	05Ap02An
JOHNSTON, Alice	06	F	Child	05Ap02An
LEUDY, Anaren	21	M	Laborer	05Ap02An
FITZPATRICK, John	33	M	Laborer	05Ap02An
BRYAN, Jane	30	F	Servant	05Ap02An
Mary	12	F	Servant	05Ap02An
SHEA, Darby	40	M	Farmer	05Ap02An
Marty	11	M	Unknown	05Ap02An
CONDEN, Wm.	22	M	Unknown	05Ap02An
FLEMMING, Mary	25	F	Servant	05Ap02An
CONNELL, Mary	50	F	Servant	05Ap02An
Cath.	12	F	Servant	05Ap02An
THOMAS, John	22	M	Servant	05Ap02An
MCVEY, Betty	14	F	Servant	05Ap02An
BENNETT, Wm.	31	M	Weaver	05Ap02An
Edw.	18	M	Weaver	05Ap02An
Ellen	30	F	Weaver	05Ap02An
Elzth.	05	F	Child	05Ap02An
NEWELL, Harriet	03	F	Child	05Ap02An
COUGHLIN, John	40	M	Cooper	05Ap02An
John	23	M	Cooper	05Ap02An
KEEFE, Michl.	10	M	Cooper	05Ap02An
FLYNN, Michl.	16	M	Cooper	05Ap02An
REILLY, Pat	20	M	Cooper	05Ap02An
MORAN, Bridget	18	F	Servant	05Ap02An
ONEAL, Bridget	15	F	Servant	05Ap02An
FLYNN, Jane	18	F	Servant	05Ap02An
CAVANAGH, Cath.	50	F	Servant	05Ap02An
Cath.	11	F	Unknown	05Ap02An
DOOLY, Michl.	25	M	Smith	05Ap02An
LYON, Margt.	35	F	Servant	05Ap02An
James	13	M	Servant	05Ap02An
Ann	09	F	Child	05Ap02An
John	08	M	Child	05Ap02An
Michl.	07	M	Child	05Ap02An
DWYER, Eliza	22	F	Servant	05Ap02An
MALONE, Margt.	17	F	Servant	05Ap02An
CARREN, Bess	20	F	Servant	05Ap02An
CARROLL, Michl.	30	M	Butcher	05Ap02An
DONOHOE, Margt.	15	F	Unknown	05Ap02An
Margt.	10	F	Unknown	05Ap02An
Bridget	08	F	Child	05Ap02An
KENNY, Mary	21	F	Servant	05Ap02An
John	16	M	Unknown	05Ap02An
Ra.	11	M	Unknown	05Ap02An
QUINN, Hugh	21	M	Baker	05Ap02An
LOUGHLY, Thos.	40	M	Farmer	05Ap02An
Honor	40	F	Unknown	05Ap02An
Michl.	08	M	Child	05Ap02An
Mary	06	F	Child	05Ap02An
Thos.	04	M	Child	05Ap02An
Martin	02	M	Child	05Ap02An
Matthew	.00	M	Infant	05Ap02An
JOHNENS, Mary	19	F	Servant	05Ap02An
KILKENNY, Mary	19	F	Servant	05Ap02An
MCGEOUGHY, John	20	M	Millwright	05Ap02An
Mary	16	F	Unknown	05Ap02An
CARROLL, Elzth.	11	F	Unknown	05Ap02An
MCDOWELL, Robt.	21	M	Bricklayer	05Ap02An
HERNES, Elzth.	16	F	Bricklayer	05Ap02An
CARPENTER, Betty	50	F	Bricklayer	05Ap02An
Mary	15	F	Bricklayer	05Ap02An
John	03	M	Child	05Ap02An
Thos.	09	M	Child	05Ap02An
Pat	06	M	Child	05Ap02An
Ann	.00	F	Infant	05Ap02An
LYONS, Sarah	30	F	Servant	05Ap02An
Jane	10	F	Servant	05Ap02An
Mary	03	F	Child	05Ap02An
Margt.	01	F	Child	05Ap02An
Died-At-Sea				
CARROLL, Pat	20	M	Unknown	05Ap02An
MCGOVERN, Rose	22	F	Servant	05Ap02An
GEOUGHAN, Ann	20	F	Servant	05Ap02An
Ellen	17	F	Servant	05Ap02An
GREGG, John	30	M	Farmer	05Ap02An

NAMES OF PASSENGERS	AGE	SEX	OCCUPATIONS	DATE PORT SHIP
MCGEOUGH, Mary	24	F	Servant	05Ap02An
MADDEN, John	27	M	Smith	05Ap02An
QUINN, Elzth.	22	F	Servant	05Ap02An
MCCORMICK, Jas.	24	M	Farmer	05Ap02An
TRACY, Pat	13	M	Farmer	05Ap02An
BATLER, Thos.	20	M	Farmer	05Ap02An
Fras.	22	M	Farmer	05Ap02An
HARRINGTON, Cath.	24	F	Servant	05Ap02An
Mary	22	F	Servant	05Ap02An
DRAKE, John	15	M	Servant	05Ap02An
MARTIN, Pat	28	M	Servant	05Ap02An
FORD, Cath.	10	F	Servant	05Ap02An
Margt.	09	F	Child	05Ap02An
DONOHUE, Ellen	50	F	Unknown	05Ap02An
Ellen	09	F	Child	05Ap02An
Honor	07	F	Child	05Ap02An
LEFFER, Michl.	14	M	Unknown	05Ap02An
COALES, Mark	27	M	Cooper	05Ap02An
Ann	26	F	Unknown	05Ap02An
Wm.	04	M	Child	05Ap02An
CAVAN, Pat	26	M	Bricklayer	05Ap02An
JONES, John	25	M	Bricklayer	05Ap02An
FLYNN, Wm.	30	M	Unknown	05Ap02An
BARDEN, Ann	21	F	Unknown	05Ap02An
GREENE, John	33	M	Farmer	05Ap02An
TITLEY, Remington	22	M	Farmer	05Ap02An
U-Mrs.	21	F	Unknown	05Ap02An
KELLY, John	23	M	Unknown	05Ap02An
PICKLES, Robert	26	M	Unknown	05Ap02An
BOYLE, Tom	20	M	Laborer	05Ap02An
MCPHERSON, Saml.	22	M	Unknown	05Ap02An
BOYLE, Christ	27	M	Unknown	05Ap02An
DAYLY, John	35	M	Unknown	05Ap02An
Elizbethe	30	F	Unknown	05Ap02An
Edwd.	05	M	Child	05Ap02An
BIRD, Michael	35	M	Unknown	05Ap02An
Biddy	28	F	Unknown	05Ap02An
Cath.	07	F	Child	05Ap02An
Pat	03	M	Child	05Ap02An
MULROY, John	20	M	Unknown	05Ap02An
MCALLISTER, Jno. Died-At-Sea	26	M	Unknown	05Ap02An
John	35	M	Unknown	05Ap02An
Matilda	30	F	Unknown	05Ap02An
LATCLIFF, Whitaker	30	M	Unknown	05Ap02An
SHANE, William	25	M	Seaman	05Ap02An

QUEEN-OF-THE-WEST 05 APRIL 1849

From Liverpool

NAMES OF PASSENGERS	AGE	SEX	OCCUPATIONS	DATE PORT SHIP
CAHILL, Pat	35	M	Laborer	05Ap02Ao
SMITH, Mathew	21	M	Laborer	05Ap02Ao
DIXON, Honor	20	F	Unknown	05Ap02Ao
KELLY, Ally	19	F	Unknown	05Ap02Ao
GALLAGHAN, John	33	M	Laborer	05Ap02Ao
KELLY, Pat	20	M	Laborer	05Ap02Ao
LATTIN, John	20	M	Laborer	05Ap02Ao
OREGAN, Corns.	49	M	Mason	05Ap02Ao
WALL, Mary	21	F	Unknown	05Ap02Ao
Brigt.	19	F	Unknown	05Ap02Ao
CONNELL, Rich.	20	M	Unknown	05Ap02Ao
Johana	24	F	Unknown	05Ap02Ao
RYAN, Danir	.00	M	Infant	05Ap02Ao
FIELEY, Morriss	30	M	Laborer	05Ap02Ao
Mich.	37	M	Laborer	05Ap02Ao
BROOMFIELD, Cath.	16	F	Laborer	05Ap02Ao
MCCORD, Eliza	23	F	Weaver	05Ap02Ao
PATERSON, James	25	M	Weaver	05Ap02Ao
STATTERY, Mick	22	M	Laborer	05Ap02Ao
DALTON, Mick	20	M	Laborer	05Ap02Ao
BURNE, Peter	20	M	Laborer	05Ap02Ao
FARY, Eliza	24	F	Unknown	05Ap02Ao
MCLOUGHLIN, Mich	21	M	Laborer	05Ap02Ao
LAMB, Eliza	25	F	Unknown	05Ap02Ao
Ellen	20	F	Unknown	05Ap02Ao
BOWE, Judy	17	F	Unknown	05Ap02Ao
HENDERSON, James	21	M	Weaver	05Ap02Ao
MCCOURT, Thoms.	20	M	Weaver	05Ap02Ao
MCCANN, Thoms.	21	M	Weaver	05Ap02Ao
STAPLETON, Mary	50	F	Unknown	05Ap02Ao
HOLCHAN, Mary	10	F	Unknown	05Ap02Ao
BRANWICK, Win.	18	F	Unknown	05Ap02Ao
MULLIGAN, Tim.	50	M	Unknown	05Ap02Ao
Mary	40	F	Unknown	05Ap02Ao
Bessy	20	F	Farmer	05Ap02Ao
Agnes	19	F	Unknown	05Ap02Ao
Phil.	16	M	Unknown	05Ap02Ao
GORMAN, John	22	M	Laborer	05Ap02Ao
CROSBY, Peter	20	M	Laborer	05Ap02Ao
CROWLEY, Margt.	20	F	Laborer	05Ap02Ao
TOORING, Ann	30	F	Laborer	05Ap02Ao
GAVIN, Esther	20	F	Laborer	05Ap02Ao
HANLEY, Eliza	17	F	Laborer	05Ap02Ao
BROTHER, Judy	28	F	Laborer	05Ap02Ao
COLLIN, Ann	20	F	Laborer	05Ap02Ao
RUSSELL, Cath.	20	F	Laborer	05Ap02Ao
Brid.	19	F	Laborer	05Ap02Ao
Judy	18	F	Laborer	05Ap02Ao
COSTELLO, John	20	M	Laborer	05Ap02Ao
Fanny	18	F	Unknown	05Ap02Ao
LYNCH, Mary	40	F	Unknown	05Ap02Ao
Ann	15	F	Unknown	05Ap02Ao
Margt.	12	F	Unknown	05Ap02Ao
Betsey	09	F	Child	05Ap02Ao
Mich.	07	M	Child	05Ap02Ao
John	06	M	Child	05Ap02Ao
Cath.	04	F	Child	05Ap02Ao
Owen	.00	M	Infant	05Ap02Ao
MCMANUS, Pat	24	M	Laborer	05Ap02Ao
RILEY, John	20	M	Laborer	05Ap02Ao
SHEEHAN, Mick	23	M	Laborer	05Ap02Ao
BURNS, Eliza	20	F	Unknown	05Ap02Ao
MEMAGRAN, James	18	M	Unknown	05Ap02Ao
PINKERTON, Mary	20	F	Unknown	05Ap02Ao
BOWERS, Chas.	20	M	Watchmaker	05Ap02Ao
Esther	15	F	Unknown	05Ap02Ao
MCAVOY, Agnes	25	F	Unknown	05Ap02Ao
ONEAL, James	20	M	Unknown	05Ap02Ao
Margt.	17	F	Laborer	05Ap02Ao
Cath.	09	F	Child	05Ap02Ao
SHERIDAN, Ann	20	F	Unknown	05Ap02Ao
WATERS, Cath.	20	F	Unknown	05Ap02Ao
COOK, Owen	32	M	Unknown	05Ap02Ao
Mich.	05	M	Child	05Ap02Ao
MCADAMS, Pat	56	M	Unknown	05Ap02Ao
John	26	M	Unknown	05Ap02Ao
Pat	16	M	Laborer	05Ap02Ao
Ann	18	F	Unknown	05Ap02Ao
MCGRATH, Rose	18	F	Unknown	05Ap02Ao
COX, William	25	M	Laborer	05Ap02Ao
MCCORMICK, Pat	21	M	Laborer	05Ap02Ao
BUTLER, Pat	21	M	Laborer	05Ap02Ao
Cath.	18	F	Unknown	05Ap02Ao
FOLEY, Pat	30	M	Unknown	05Ap02Ao
WINER, Mich.	18	M	Unknown	05Ap02Ao
KEANE, Morris	20	M	Unknown	05Ap02Ao
KERWAN, Mary	20	F	Unknown	05Ap02Ao
OBRIEN, Maurice	22	F	Unknown	05Ap02Ao
LANE, Pat	21	M	Unknown	05Ap02Ao
DUME, John	30	M	Unknown	05Ap02Ao
CORN, Pat	30	M	Laborer	05Ap02Ao
Brid.	22	F	Unknown	05Ap02Ao
WALKER, Wm.	16	M	Unknown	05Ap02Ao

NAMES OF PASSENGERS	AGE	SEX	OCCUPATIONS	DATE PORT SHIP
MCNEALY, Domk.	26	M	Laborer	05Ap02Ao
MCNAMARA, Cath.	20	F	Unknown	05Ap02Ao
Anty.	18	F	Unknown	05Ap02Ao
Mary	12	F	Unknown	05Ap02Ao
HUGHES, John	23	M	Laborer	05Ap02Ao
Chris.	20	U	Laborer	05Ap02Ao
DUFFY, Ann	20	F	Laborer	05Ap02Ao
HOBAN, Pat	25	M	Laborer	05Ap02Ao
WEST, Mary	28	F	Unknown	05Ap02Ao
Mary	09	F	Child	05Ap02Ao
Jos.	.00	M	Infant	05Ap02Ao
IRWIN, D.	22	M	Unknown	05Ap02Ao
MAHONEY, Cath.	20	F	Unknown	05Ap02Ao
REED, Mary	17	F	Unknown	05Ap02Ao
MCCARTY, James	30	M	Unknown	05Ap02Ao
John	12	M	Unknown	05Ap02Ao
ONAGAN, Tim.	24	M	Unknown	05Ap02Ao
CALAHAN, Ann	23	F	Unknown	05Ap02Ao
Mick.	20	M	Laborer	05Ap02Ao
COSTELLO, Thoms.	23	M	Laborer	05Ap02Ao
KELLY, Wm.	25	M	Laborer	05Ap02Ao
KERSBY, Rich.	24	M	Unknown	05Ap02Ao
MURPHY, Margt.	22	F	Unknown	05Ap02Ao
DOYLE, Wm.	22	M	Unknown	05Ap02Ao
MCNAMARA, Mick	20	M	Laborer	05Ap02Ao
FOLEY, Andrew	22	M	Unknown	05Ap02Ao
Cath.	20	F	Unknown	05Ap02Ao
WINTERS, Jos.	22	M	Unknown	05Ap02Ao
DERMOVY, Cath.	40	F	Unknown	05Ap02Ao
Bessy	16	F	Unknown	05Ap02Ao
Brid.	16	F	Unknown	05Ap02Ao
CONWAY, Margt.	30	F	Unknown	05Ap02Ao
Mary	10	F	Unknown	05Ap02Ao
Thoms.	05	M	Child	05Ap02Ao
Cath.	.00	F	Infant	05Ap02Ao
MCGORNEY, Cath.	19	F	Unknown	05Ap02Ao
MCDORMOTT, Pat	20	M	Unknown	05Ap02Ao
RUSTER, Mary	20	F	Laborer	05Ap02Ao
OCONNER, Pat	26	M	Laborer	05Ap02Ao
EGAN, Thoms.	40	M	Laborer	05Ap02Ao
DOOLING, Pat	35	M	Laborer	05Ap02Ao
TYREN, John	26	M	Laborer	05Ap02Ao
BARRY, Edwin	25	M	Laborer	05Ap02Ao
FLYNN, Mary	30	F	Unknown	05Ap02Ao
MARTIN, John	30	M	Unknown	05Ap02Ao
KEENAN, Cath.	24	F	Unknown	05Ap02Ao
MADDEN, Margt.A.	20	F	Unknown	05Ap02Ao
MCKINLEY, John	15	M	Laborer	05Ap02Ao
WATSON, M.A.	20	F	Unknown	05Ap02Ao
HENRY, M.J.	04	F	Child	05Ap02Ao
WALDEN, Margt.	20	F	Unknown	05Ap02Ao
MULRAY, Nick	18	M	Laborer	05Ap02Ao
RIELLY, Ann	20	F	Unknown	05Ap02Ao
WALLACE, Sarah	21	F	Unknown	05Ap02Ao
LYNCH, Mich.	24	M	Laborer	05Ap02Ao
MOOD, Margt.	25	F	Unknown	05Ap02Ao
BOYD, Sandy	21	M	Blacksmith	05Ap02Ao
MCALANEY, Peter	20	M	Blacksmith	05Ap02Ao
SMALLFIELD, Brid.	20	F	Unknown	05Ap02Ao
KELLY, Hugh	48	M	Unknown	05Ap02Ao
Eliza	40	F	Mason	05Ap02Ao
MURRAY, Margt.	26	F	Unknown	05Ap02Ao
STAPLETON, Thoms.	25	M	Unknown	05Ap02Ao
Judy	20	F	Laborer	05Ap02Ao
COSTRICK, Daniel	50	M	Unknown	05Ap02Ao
Cavan	20	F	Laborer	05Ap02Ao
MCAVOY, Mary	18	F	Laborer	05Ap02Ao
KENNEDY, Pat	25	M	Laborer	05Ap02Ao
MCMANUS, James	25	M	Laborer	05Ap02Ao
HINCKLEY, Mich.	40	M	Laborer	05Ap02Ao
NELSON, J.D.	18	M	Clerk	05Ap02Ao
RICE, Pat	26	M	Laborer	05Ap02Ao
BRENNAN, Mary	26	F	Smith	05Ap02Ao
MCLOUGHLIN, Mary	22	F	Smith	05Ap02Ao
GORMAN, Pat	20	M	Laborer	05Ap02Ao
SANDERS, James	20	M	Laborer	05Ap02Ao
MCCUTCHEONE, Eliza	30	F	Laborer	05Ap02Ao
WHALAN, Betty	18	F	Unknown	05Ap02Ao
TAYLOR, James	27	M	Unknown	05Ap02Ao
MULDOWY, Edward	24	M	Laborer	05Ap02Ao
MCCOLL, John	20	M	Laborer	05Ap02Ao
HENDERSON, Francis	40	M	Laborer	05Ap02Ao
U-Mrs.	38	F	Unknown	05Ap02Ao
David	14	M	Unknown	05Ap02Ao
Wm.	12	M	Unknown	05Ap02Ao
Sarah	10	F	Editor	05Ap02Ao
James	08	M	Child	05Ap02Ao
Cath.	.00	F	Infant	05Ap02Ao
John	06	M	Child	05Ap02Ao
GOODFELLOW, Eliza	17	F	Unknown	05Ap02Ao
GINGHAM, Terence	17	M	Unknown	05Ap02Ao
MCGOLD, Peter	18	M	Unknown	05Ap02Ao
VEACK, Sarah-A.	60	F	Laborer	05Ap02Ao
Aliciee	20	F	Laborer	05Ap02Ao
Mary	23	F	Laborer	05Ap02Ao
Billson	26	M	Painter	05Ap02Ao
CONNER, Andrew	18	M	Painter	05Ap02Ao
BLEASDALE, R.P.	22	M	Painter	05Ap02Ao
DEOLINE, Philip	30	M	Farmer	05Ap02Ao
BREOWN, Cath.	19	F	Unknown	05Ap02Ao
BROGAN, John	20	M	Farmer	05Ap02Ao
NOWLAN, Jane	20	F	Unknown	05Ap02Ao
HANLIN, Rose	18	F	Unknown	05Ap02Ao
Kate	12	F	Unknown	05Ap02Ao
DUNN, Mich.	21	M	Unknown	05Ap02Ao
NOWLAN, Mat.	35	M	Unknown	05Ap02Ao
U-Mrs.	32	F	Unknown	05Ap02Ao
Pat	11	M	Farmer	05Ap02Ao
Ellen	09	F	Child	05Ap02Ao
Jos.	07	M	Child	05Ap02Ao
Wm.	03	M	Child	05Ap02Ao
Michael	.00	M	Infant	05Ap02Ao
DAILY, Margt.	21	F	None	05Ap02Ao
JOHNSON, Mick.	20	M	Founder	05Ap02Ao
LANCY, Thoms.	20	M	Laborer	05Ap02Ao
KILLAND, Mick.	20	M	Laborer	05Ap02Ao
FITZGERALD, Jas.	30	M	Trade Man	05Ap02Ao
CONNEL, Mat.	20	M	Trade Man	05Ap02Ao
RILEY, Chas.	20	M	Laborer	05Ap02Ao
KAVAN, Mat	20	M	Laborer	05Ap02Ao
KILLIGRO, Mich.	24	M	Gdnr	05Ap02Ao
Ally	20	M	Gdnr	05Ap02Ao
CHER, Biddy	10	F	Printer	05Ap02Ao
BURNS, Daniel	40	M	Printer	05Ap02Ao
BELTLY, John	18	M	Draper	05Ap02Ao
Jane	16	F	Unknown	05Ap02Ao
ROGERS, Mary	19	F	Unknown	05Ap02Ao
COLONEL, Ellen	16	F	Unknown	05Ap02Ao
MURREY, Thoms.	20	M	Laborer	05Ap02Ao
WALSH, James	26	M	Laborer	05Ap02Ao
JORDAN, James	24	M	Laborer	05Ap02Ao
DALENTY, Cath.	18	F	Laborer	05Ap02Ao
Julia	18	F	Laborer	05Ap02Ao
OGRADY, Henry	27	M	None	05Ap02Ao
Mary	25	F	None	05Ap02Ao
REYNOLDS, Mary	17	F	None	05Ap02Ao
CONNELLY, Chris	18	M	Laborer	05Ap02Ao
LENNON, James	18	M	Laborer	05Ap02Ao
DOLAN, John	20	M	Laborer	05Ap02Ao
NIXON, Mary	18	F	Laborer	05Ap02Ao
MENGMAN, Thoms.	20	M	Laborer	05Ap02Ao
John	18	M	Laborer	05Ap02Ao
Ann	20	F	Unknown	05Ap02Ao
PAGAN, Mick	20	M	Unknown	05Ap02Ao
OHARA, Wm.	30	M	Unknown	05Ap02Ao
GANNON, Mary	40	F	Unknown	05Ap02Ao
Peggy	18	F	Unknown	05Ap02Ao
Mary	15	F	Unknown	05Ap02Ao
Brid.	12	F	Unknown	05Ap02Ao
Rich.	10	M	Unknown	05Ap02Ao

NAMES OF PASSENGERS	AGE	SEX	OCCUPATIONS	DATE PORT SHIP
GANNON, James	09	M	Child	05Ap02Ao
Wm.	07	M	Child	05Ap02Ao
Daniel	05	M	Child	05Ap02Ao
Judy	04	F	Child	05Ap02Ao
Anty	.00	F	Infant	05Ap02Ao
KERWIN, Mick	20	M	Unknown	05Ap02Ao
TRAVIS, Nick	20	M	Unknown	05Ap02Ao
Mary	15	F	Unknown	05Ap02Ao
BROPHY, Cath.	11	F	Unknown	05Ap02Ao
KING, Oney	19	M	Laborer	05Ap02Ao
MAMRY, Judy	17	F	Laborer	05Ap02Ao
BROPHY, Brid.	23	F	Laborer	05Ap02Ao
Mary	30	F	Laborer	05Ap02Ao
Ellen	24	F	Laborer	05Ap02Ao
Peter	04	M	Child	05Ap02Ao
TRAVIS, Margt.	20	F	Laborer	05Ap02Ao
KAVANAGH, Martin	24	M	Laborer	05Ap02Ao
W.	24	M	Laborer	05Ap02Ao
DOOLY, Maurice	18	M	Laborer	05Ap02Ao
SWEENEY, James	18	M	Laborer	05Ap02Ao
Bessy	20	F	Laborer	05Ap02Ao
FARLEY, John	24	M	Carpenter	05Ap02Ao
RAY, John	40	M	Laborer	05Ap02Ao
Alice	38	F	Laborer	05Ap02Ao
Mary	09	F	Child	05Ap02Ao
Alice	06	F	Child	05Ap02Ao
Law.	.00	M	Infant	05Ap02Ao
LEATON, Wm.	25	M	Laborer	05Ap02Ao
PEARCE, Francis	17	M	Laborer	05Ap02Ao
Michl.	20	M	Laborer	05Ap02Ao
KEOUGH, John	29	M	Laborer	05Ap02Ao
DORAN, Pat	30	M	Farmer	05Ap02Ao
DONNAN, John	30	M	Farmer	05Ap02Ao
LEARE, Mick	21	M	Farmer	05Ap02Ao
CARROL, Cath.	18	F	Farmer	05Ap02Ao
CANINES, Thomas	40	M	Farmer	05Ap02Ao
TURNER, W.C.	20	M	None	05Ap02Ao
WARD, W.	19	M	Carpenter	05Ap02Ao
DOONAN, Andrew	40	M	Laborer	05Ap02Ao
Abby	40	F	Laborer	05Ap02Ao
Pat	19	M	Laborer	05Ap02Ao
Thoms.	17	M	Laborer	05Ap02Ao
Peter	15	M	Laborer	05Ap02Ao
Ann	10	F	Laborer	05Ap02Ao
Honora	20	F	Laborer	05Ap02Ao
Hugh	10	M	Laborer	05Ap02Ao
Mary	08	F	Child	05Ap02Ao
DONAGAN, Patt	30	M	Laborer	05Ap02Ao
Mary	30	F	Laborer	05Ap02Ao
FLYNN, Andrew	15	M	Laborer	05Ap02Ao
KIRWAN, Honor	20	F	Laborer	05Ap02Ao
ROWAN, Eliza	23	F	Laborer	05Ap02Ao
BURKE, Cath.	25	F	Laborer	05Ap02Ao
KIRWAN, Margt.	21	F	Laborer	05Ap02Ao
FLYNNN, Thoms.	22	M	Laborer	05Ap02Ao
FALY, James	18	M	Laborer	05Ap02Ao
FITZGERALD, Mary	20	F	Laborer	05Ap02Ao
NOWLAN, Willm.	35	M	Laborer	05Ap02Ao
James	30	M	Laborer	05Ap02Ao
SULLIVAN, Jno.	26	M	Laborer	05Ap02Ao
GRACE, Anty.	18	F	Laborer	05Ap02Ao
SHERRY, Dan.	20	M	Laborer	05Ap02Ao
HUGHES, Jno.	31	M	Laborer	05Ap02Ao
SHERRY, Ann	20	F	Laborer	05Ap02Ao
MURPHY, Marg.	22	F	Laborer	05Ap02Ao
BRIEN, James	16	M	Laborer	05Ap02Ao
Molly	24	F	Laborer	05Ap02Ao
HOLLAND, Margt.	20	F	Laborer	05Ap02Ao
SHERRY, Margt.	19	F	Laborer	05Ap02Ao
HUGHES, Mary	20	F	Laborer	05Ap02Ao
MCMANUS, Peter	20	M	Laborer	05Ap02Ao
BRADLEY, W.P.	18	M	Engineer	05Ap02Ao
MCGUIRE, John	24	M	Laborer	05Ap02Ao
DALEY, Ann	40	F	Laborer	05Ap02Ao
ANDREWS, John	19	M	Laborer	05Ap02Ao
FLYNN, Chas.	32	M	Laborer	05Ap02Ao
CARDIN, Edward	44	M	Laborer	05Ap02Ao
RAYN, John	21	M	Laborer	05Ap02Ao
MCDONNELL, Wm.	26	M	Laborer	05Ap02Ao
FITZSIMMONS, Brid.	22	F	Miner	05Ap02Ao
Ellen	19	F	Miner	05Ap02Ao
CAVANAGH, Ellen	20	F	Miner	05Ap02Ao
BRYAN, Jno.	28	M	Laborer	05Ap02Ao
Ellen	29	F	Laborer	05Ap02Ao
HATTIGAN, John	23	M	Laborer	05Ap02Ao
Ellen	16	F	Farmer	05Ap02Ao
DELANY, James	26	M	Farmer	05Ap02Ao
BURKE, Pat	27	M	Farmer	05Ap02Ao
CASSETT, Denis	30	M	Farmer	05Ap02Ao
Cath.	18	F	Unknown	05Ap02Ao
MURPHY, Lawrance	24	F	Unknown	05Ap02Ao
Mary	22	F	Farmer	05Ap02Ao
DUNKERN, Andw.	40	F	Farmer	05Ap02Ao
Thoms.	20	F	Farmer	05Ap02Ao
Wm.	15	F	Farmer	05Ap02Ao
IRWIN, John	40	F	Farmer	05Ap02Ao
DWYER, Pat	30	F	Laborer	05Ap02Ao
DONNALLY, John	40	F	Laborer	05Ap02Ao
Margt.	42	F	Laborer	05Ap02Ao
MOORE, Thoms.	42	F	Laborer	05Ap02Ao
KEAGH, John	40	M	Laborer	05Ap02Ao
MORAN, Ann	31	F	Laborer	05Ap02Ao
JAMON, Lle.	22	M	Laborer	05Ap02Ao
Jno.	20	M	Laborer	05Ap02Ao
FOX, Peter	24	M	Laborer	05Ap02Ao
DEIMENTY, Cath.	22	F	Laborer	05Ap02Ao
MURPHY, Martin	30	M	Shoemaker	05Ap02Ao
Margt.	25	F	Shoemaker	05Ap02Ao
DAILY, James	24	M	Laborer	05Ap02Ao
HORGAN, John	20	M	Laborer	05Ap02Ao
LEEHAN, Ellen	18	F	Unknown	05Ap02Ao
MORDAN, Thoms.	20	M	Unknown	05Ap02Ao
CAVENAGH, John	22	M	Laborer	05Ap02Ao
MANSFIELD, Mich.	35	M	Weaver	05Ap02Ao
NAIL, Cath.	20	F	Unknown	05Ap02Ao
CARTY, Cath.	20	F	Unknown	05Ap02Ao
TRANCE, John	40	M	Unknown	05Ap02Ao
U-Mrs.	40	F	Unknown	05Ap02Ao
Mary	14	F	Unknown	05Ap02Ao
John	05	M	Child	05Ap02Ao
Pat	.00	M	Infant	05Ap02Ao
CURRAN, Mary	22	F	Unknown	05Ap02Ao
RENSHAW, Thoms.	20	M	Laborer	05Ap02Ao
SCHOLE, Wm.	24	M	Miner	05Ap02Ao
MCANULTY, F.	20	M	Miner	05Ap02Ao
JONNAN, Margt.	20	F	Unknown	05Ap02Ao
CORRIGAN, John	21	M	Laborer	05Ap02Ao
GRIFFIN, John	22	M	Laborer	05Ap02Ao
Bid.	24	F	Laborer	05Ap02Ao
MCGANN, Ann	20	F	Laborer	05Ap02Ao
TIERNEY, Thoms.	25	M	Cbtmkr	05Ap02Ao
CONNER, Wm.	60	M	Dealer	05Ap02Ao
MCDONNELL, Mick.	27	M	Butcher	05Ap02Ao
EVANS, M.	27	M	Merchant	05Ap02Ao
MCJAHEN, Mary	11	F	Unknown	05Ap02Ao
SEYMOUR, U-Mrs.	47	F	Unknown	05Ap02Ao
NORCOTT, D.	48	U	Unknown	05Ap02Ao
WELDON, U	49	F	Unknown	05Ap02Ao
CALLEGHEN, Jno.C.	50	M	Unknown	05Ap02Ao
LOWNDES, F.	52	F	Unknown	05Ap02Ao
CASSON, U	54	M	Unknown	05Ap02Ao
U-Mrs.	55	F	Unknown	05Ap02Ao
LOWNERS, U-Mrs.	56	F	Unknown	05Ap02Ao

GENERAL-GREENE 05 APRIL 1849

From Dublin

NAMES OF PASSENGERS	AGE	SEX	OCCUPATIONS	DATE PORT SHIP
DUME, Peter	30	M	Blacksmith	05Ap12Ap
Anne	20	F	Blacksmith	05Ap12Ap
MOLLOY, Aliza	20	F	Servant	05Ap12Ap
DONAN, Sarah	22	F	Servant	05Ap12Ap
Died-At-Sea				
Michl.	06	M	Child	05Ap12Ap
MULLALY, Anne	20	F	Unknown	05Ap12Ap
STAPLETON, John	33	M	Carpenter	05Ap12Ap
Ellen	30	F	Carpenter	05Ap12Ap
Johanna	05	F	Child	05Ap12Ap
John	04	M	Child	05Ap12Ap
Bridget	.11	F	Infant	05Ap12Ap
FORELS, Anne	20	F	Servant	05Ap12Ap
ELEAN, Wm.	50	M	Tailor	05Ap12Ap
Eliza	45	F	Tailor	05Ap12Ap
Ellen	18	F	Tailor	05Ap12Ap
Mary	13	F	Tailor	05Ap12Ap
Johanna	11	F	Tailor	05Ap12Ap
Catharine	09	F	Child	05Ap12Ap
Michl.	07	M	Child	05Ap12Ap
Matilda	05	F	Child	05Ap12Ap
John	03	M	Child	05Ap12Ap
Wm.	.10	M	Infant	05Ap12Ap
FELTIHER, Bridget	45	F	Unknown	05Ap12Ap
Catherine	21	F	Unknown	05Ap12Ap
Johanna	19	F	Unknown	05Ap12Ap
John	17	M	Unknown	05Ap12Ap
Thos.	15	M	Unknown	05Ap12Ap
Wm.	44	M	Unknown	05Ap12Ap
Patt	12	M	Unknown	05Ap12Ap
Eliza	11	F	Unknown	05Ap12Ap
Mary	10	F	Unknown	05Ap12Ap
Anne	07	F	Child	05Ap12Ap
Bridget	05	F	Child	05Ap12Ap
ATKINSON, U-Mrs.	40	F	Tailor	05Ap12Ap
Thos.	19	M	Tailor	05Ap12Ap
Anne	17	F	Tailor	05Ap12Ap
BRADY, John	20	M	Mechanic	05Ap12Ap
MAHER, Margt.	20	F	Mechanic	05Ap12Ap
BYRNE, U	20	F	Servant	05Ap12Ap
HYLAND, John	22	M	Mechanic	05Ap12Ap
James	20	M	Mechanic	05Ap12Ap
Rose	19	F	Mechanic	05Ap12Ap
Anne	17	F	Mechanic	05Ap12Ap
COLLEGAN, James	27	M	Farmer	05Ap12Ap
WALSH, Patt	20	M	Farmer	05Ap12Ap
BUSSELL, U	21	F	Milliner	05Ap12Ap
CHAMPION, James	48	M	Farmer	05Ap12Ap
Bridget	46	F	Farmer	05Ap12Ap
Anne	17	F	Farmer	05Ap12Ap
James	13	M	Farmer	05Ap12Ap
Daniel	12	M	Farmer	05Ap12Ap
Lot	10	M	Farmer	05Ap12Ap
CORRIGAN, Michl.	37	M	Farmer	05Ap12Ap
Judy	35	F	Farmer	05Ap12Ap
John	10	M	Farmer	05Ap12Ap
Daniel	08	M	Child	05Ap12Ap
Michl.	06	M	Child	05Ap12Ap
Anne	.09	F	Infant	05Ap12Ap
FORDS, Patt	11	M	Unknown	05Ap12Ap
MARKENS, Mary	20	F	Domestic	05Ap12Ap
HANDY, Eliza	20	F	Domestic	05Ap12Ap
WALSH, James	24	M	Carpenter	05Ap12Ap
CATHER, Robert	24	M	Carpenter	05Ap12Ap
NERVIN, Bridget	40	F	Carpenter	05Ap12Ap
NERVIN, Mary	20	F	Carpenter	05Ap12Ap
Catherine	13	F	Carpenter	05Ap12Ap
MARKSMAN, Dora	11	F	Carpenter	05Ap12Ap
SCULLY, James	16	M	Carpenter	05Ap12Ap
VEREY, Patt	22	M	Tailor	05Ap12Ap
KANE, Martin	23	M	Tailor	05Ap12Ap
ZEATIE, James	20	M	Tailor	05Ap12Ap
WRIGHT, U	20	F	Tailor	05Ap12Ap
CORRIGAN, John	30	M	Farmer	05Ap12Ap
Ellena.	30	F	Farmer	05Ap12Ap
Mary	06	F	Child	05Ap12Ap
MORGAN, Bridget	18	F	Farmer	05Ap12Ap
Mary	16	F	Farmer	05Ap12Ap
DROODY, Thos.	30	M	Farmer	05Ap12Ap
Mary	30	F	Farmer	05Ap12Ap
Martin	06	M	Child	05Ap12Ap
MULOONY, Margt.	32	F	Farmer	05Ap12Ap
Catherine	12	F	Farmer	05Ap12Ap
KELLY, Mary	20	F	Farmer	05Ap12Ap
KENEDY, Peter	30	M	Farmer	05Ap12Ap
Biddy	12	F	Farmer	05Ap12Ap
Winny	10	F	Farmer	05Ap12Ap
Patt	08	M	Child	05Ap12Ap
SHANNON, Patt	30	M	Farmer	05Ap12Ap
Biddy	30	F	Farmer	05Ap12Ap
Patt	07	M	Child	05Ap12Ap
Michl.	.11	M	Infant	05Ap12Ap
EGAN, John	30	M	Farmer	05Ap12Ap
Mary	30	F	Farmer	05Ap12Ap
Peter	12	M	Farmer	05Ap12Ap
Harry	09	M	Child	05Ap12Ap
Michl.	06	M	Child	05Ap12Ap
Edward	04	M	Child	05Ap12Ap
Anne	.10	F	Infant	05Ap12Ap
MUMPLY, Mary	21	F	Laborer	05Ap12Ap
DONOLSON, Thos.	18	M	Laborer	05Ap12Ap
NEAL, Bartle	30	M	Laborer	05Ap12Ap
MOVIE, James	20	M	Laborer	05Ap12Ap
LANG, Mamby	30	M	Laborer	05Ap12Ap
MCGIBBINS, Andre	40	M	Laborer	05Ap12Ap
John	18	M	Laborer	05Ap12Ap
Mary	13	F	Laborer	05Ap12Ap
CONNOLY, Judith	40	F	Laborer	05Ap12Ap
John	07	M	Child	05Ap12Ap
SPUID, James	30	M	Laborer	05Ap12Ap
U-Mrs.	30	F	Laborer	05Ap12Ap
Sutton	25	M	Laborer	05Ap12Ap
John	06	M	Child	05Ap12Ap
James	03	M	Child	05Ap12Ap
Patt	02	M	Child	05Ap12Ap
STOWE, John	40	M	Farmer	05Ap12Ap
CURRALL, James	50	M	Farmer	05Ap12Ap
Anne	40	F	Farmer	05Ap12Ap
Bessy	04	F	Child	05Ap12Ap
Mary	17	F	Laborer	05Ap12Ap
LEVY, Bessy	18	F	Laborer	05Ap12Ap

GREAT-BRITAIN 05 APRIL 1849

From Liverpool

NAMES OF PASSENGERS	AGE	SEX	OCCUPATIONS	DATE PORT SHIP
GANIGAN, John	27	M	Laborer	05Ap02Ar
Judy	27	F	Unknown	05Ap02Ar
Owen	21	M	Laborer	05Ap02Ar
Mary	17	F	Unknown	05Ap02Ar
Felix	12	M	Unknown	05Ap02Ar
Kitty	.00	F	Infant	05Ap02Ar
Patrick	03	M	Child	05Ap02Ar
FORSYTHE, George	50	M	Laborer	05Ap02Ar

NAMES OF PASSENGERS	AGE	SEX	OCCUPATIONS	DATE PORT SHIP
FORSYTHE, Catherine	50	F	Unknown	05Ap02Ar
Sarah	15	F	Unknown	05Ap02Ar
Catherine	13	F	Unknown	05Ap02Ar
Mary	12	F	Unknown	05Ap02Ar
Patrick	10	M	Unknown	05Ap02Ar
George	09	M	Child	05Ap02Ar
Bridget	06	F	Child	05Ap02Ar
FARLEY, Patrick	21	M	Laborer	05Ap02Ar
RONS, Peter	18	M	Laborer	05Ap02Ar
RICE, William	26	M	Tailor	05Ap02Ar
Catherine	24	F	Unknown	05Ap02Ar
Edward	05	M	Child	05Ap02Ar
Catherine	.00	F	Infant	05Ap02Ar
BRODRICK, John	55	M	Laborer	05Ap02Ar
Anty.	32	F	Unknown	05Ap02Ar
Mary	13	F	Unknown	05Ap02Ar
Margaret	10	F	Unknown	05Ap02Ar
Catherine	08	F	Child	05Ap02Ar
WALSH, John	25	M	Laborer	05Ap02Ar
CRAIG, Mathew	20	M	Laborer	05Ap02Ar
Eliza	22	F	Unknown	05Ap02Ar
SULLIVAN, Peter	30	M	Laborer	05Ap02Ar
MCANDREW, William	09	M	Child	05Ap02Ar
MCKEOWEN, Lucy	40	F	Unknown	05Ap02Ar
GRAHAM, Ann	30	F	Unknown	05Ap02Ar
Pat	.00	M	Infant	05Ap02Ar
OWENS, Margaret	19	F	Unknown	05Ap02Ar
HONEYMAN, Pat	16	M	Laborer	05Ap02Ar
RADDIGAN, Mary	19	F	Unknown	05Ap02Ar
CAFFRY, Owen	25	M	Laborer	05Ap02Ar
FILTSON, William	06	M	Child	05Ap02Ar
Robert	04	M	Child	05Ap02Ar
Pheobe	08	F	Child	05Ap02Ar
FARLEY, Mary	50	F	Unknown	05Ap02Ar
Bridget	20	F	Unknown	05Ap02Ar
Thomas	14	M	Unknown	05Ap02Ar
Catherine	13	F	Unknown	05Ap02Ar
FILTSON, James	35	M	Laborer	05Ap02Ar
Mary	35	F	Unknown	05Ap02Ar
Humphry	.00	M	Infant	05Ap02Ar
Joseph	50	M	Laborer	05Ap02Ar
ROURKE, Thomas	40	M	Laborer	05Ap02Ar
Catherine	15	F	Unknown	05Ap02Ar
Patsey	14	M	Unknown	05Ap02Ar
James	08	M	Child	05Ap02Ar
Mary	.00	F	Infant	05Ap02Ar
DELANEY, Catherine	20	F	Unknown	05Ap02Ar
BRYAN, James	28	M	Laborer	05Ap02Ar
SMITH, Thomas	26	M	Laborer	05Ap02Ar
Judith	26	F	Unknown	05Ap02Ar
LARNEY, Thomas	30	M	Laborer	05Ap02Ar
James	17	M	Laborer	05Ap02Ar
BURKE, Margaret	21	F	Unknown	05Ap02Ar
COIN, Honer	22	F	Unknown	05Ap02Ar
MCNALLY, Pat	35	M	Laborer	05Ap02Ar
Margaret	25	F	Unknown	05Ap02Ar
Mary	.00	F	Infant	05Ap02Ar
KILLDIGAN, Michael	20	M	Laborer	05Ap02Ar
GORMAN, Pat	20	M	Laborer	05Ap02Ar
MCNALLY, Walter	13	M	Unknown	05Ap02Ar
Pat	11	M	Unknown	05Ap02Ar
Michael	50	M	Unknown	05Ap02Ar
Catherine	40	F	Unknown	05Ap02Ar
Bridget	09	F	Child	05Ap02Ar
John	06	M	Child	05Ap02Ar
Michael	04	M	Child	05Ap02Ar
NIHILL, Michael	29	M	Laborer	05Ap02Ar
Mary-Ann	21	F	Unknown	05Ap02Ar
John	27	M	Shoemaker	05Ap02Ar
DOLAN, Thomas	20	M	Cooper	05Ap02Ar
OHARA, James	30	M	Laborer	05Ap02Ar
Felix	16	M	Laborer	05Ap02Ar
RODGERS, William	21	M	Laborer	05Ap02Ar
BRADY, Tim	26	M	Laborer	05Ap02Ar
OHARA, Thomas	35	M	Laborer	05Ap02Ar

NAMES OF PASSENGERS	AGE	SEX	OCCUPATIONS	DATE PORT SHIP
OHARA, Catherine	29	F	Unknown	05Ap02Ar
MCPARTLEN, Margaret	20	F	Unknown	05Ap02Ar
OHARA, Bridget	.00	F	Infant	05Ap02Ar
TALLY, Peter	14	M	Laborer	05Ap02Ar
MCINTYER, James	14	M	Laborer	05Ap02Ar
DAY, John	29	M	Laborer	05Ap02Ar
Catherine	25	F	Unknown	05Ap02Ar
Michael	.00	M	Infant	05Ap02Ar
COLLINS, John	16	M	Laborer	05Ap02Ar
KIEGAN, Daniel	11	M	Unknown	05Ap02Ar
PRUNTY, Peter	21	M	Laborer	05Ap02Ar
QUIRK, Patrick	20	M	Laborer	05Ap02Ar
COMMINS, James	26	M	Miller	05Ap02Ar
William	24	M	Laborer	05Ap02Ar
Peter	18	M	Laborer	05Ap02Ar
Michael	12	M	Unknown	05Ap02Ar
Margaret	11	F	Unknown	05Ap02Ar
QUIRK, Bridget	19	F	Unknown	05Ap02Ar
DOOLEY, Ann	19	F	Unknown	05Ap02Ar
CONNOLY, Patrick	26	M	Laborer	05Ap02Ar
COMMINS, John	30	M	Laborer	05Ap02Ar
Mary	18	F	Unknown	05Ap02Ar
MCHALE, Thomas	26	M	Laborer	05Ap02Ar
Mary	26	F	Unknown	05Ap02Ar
MCVADY, Bridget	20	F	Unknown	05Ap02Ar
Mary	22	F	Unknown	05Ap02Ar
RYAN, Bridget	20	F	Unknown	05Ap02Ar
HYDE, Alice	22	F	Unknown	05Ap02Ar
Catherine	20	F	Unknown	05Ap02Ar
Bridget	12	F	Unknown	05Ap02Ar
MULLIN, Catherine	10	F	Unknown	05Ap02Ar
James	34	M	Carpenter	05Ap02Ar
Mary	31	F	Unknown	05Ap02Ar
John	15	M	Unknown	05Ap02Ar
Thomas	12	M	Unknown	05Ap02Ar
Michael	08	M	Child	05Ap02Ar
James	05	M	Child	05Ap02Ar
Mary	.00	F	Infant	05Ap02Ar
Patsey	.00	M	Infant	05Ap02Ar
CONNOR, Thomas	20	M	Laborer	05Ap02Ar
Andrew	18	M	Laborer	05Ap02Ar
LAVIN, Peter	45	M	Laborer	05Ap02Ar
Bridget	36	F	Unknown	05Ap02Ar
BALL, John	19	M	Laborer	05Ap02Ar
MANSFIELD, John	36	M	Laborer	05Ap02Ar
CLARK, Patrick	25	M	Laborer	05Ap02Ar
Michael	20	M	Laborer	05Ap02Ar
CONNORS, Murty	30	M	Laborer	05Ap02Ar
HICKEY, Martin	30	M	Laborer	05Ap02Ar
SHANAGHEY, Pat	22	M	Laborer	05Ap02Ar
LAVIN, John	21	M	Laborer	05Ap02Ar
BENY, Ann	21	F	Unknown	05Ap02Ar
HENON, John	25	M	Laborer	05Ap02Ar
KANE, James	20	M	Clerk	05Ap02Ar
Ellen	22	F	Unknown	05Ap02Ar
KENEN, Alice	30	F	Unknown	05Ap02Ar
HIGGINS, James	30	M	Laborer	05Ap02Ar
Martin	37	M	Laborer	05Ap02Ar
Catherine	30	F	Unknown	05Ap02Ar
WALSH, Anthony	60	M	Laborer	05Ap02Ar
Catherine	18	F	Unknown	05Ap02Ar
MITCHAEL, Patrick	40	M	Laborer	05Ap02Ar
KERIGAN, Patrick	19	M	Laborer	05Ap02Ar
SMALL, William	21	M	Laborer	05Ap02Ar
DWYER, Thomas	22	M	Laborer	05Ap02Ar
GOOLD, Pat	22	M	Laborer	05Ap02Ar
BURKE, William	22	M	Laborer	05Ap02Ar
RYAN, Timothy	22	M	Laborer	05Ap02Ar
Edmond	50	M	Laborer	05Ap02Ar
Margaret	50	F	Unknown	05Ap02Ar
Ellen	16	F	Unknown	05Ap02Ar
Margaret	.00	F	Infant	05Ap02Ar
MCGRATH, Alice	21	F	Unknown	05Ap02Ar
BURKE, Nancy	20	F	Unknown	05Ap02Ar
RYAN, Mary	09	F	Child	05Ap02Ar

NAMES OF PASSENGERS	AGE	SEX	OCCUPATIONS	DATE PORT SHIP
RYAN, Michael	11	M	Laborer	05Ap02Ar
John	06	M	Child	05Ap02Ar
CONWAY, Pat	20	M	Laborer	05Ap02Ar
MELVIN, Michael	18	M	Laborer	05Ap02Ar
Mary	19	F	Unknown	05Ap02Ar
Catherine	17	F	Unknown	05Ap02Ar
KILLCULLEN, Catherine	11	F	Unknown	05Ap02Ar
WALSH, Catherine	22	F	Unknown	05Ap02Ar
Michael	40	M	Laborer	05Ap02Ar
CAULLY, Martin	21	M	Laborer	05Ap02Ar
CUNARD, Thomas	18	M	Laborer	05Ap02Ar
CAULLY, Pat	20	M	Laborer	05Ap02Ar
Bridget	12	F	Unknown	05Ap02Ar
Catherine	09	F	Child	05Ap02Ar
CARTY, James	08	M	Child	05Ap02Ar
CALELLY, Thomas	19	M	Unknown	05Ap02Ar
MCGLENN, Catherine	20	F	Unknown	05Ap02Ar
SMITH, Andrew	24	M	Laborer	05Ap02Ar
BRADY, Charles	23	M	Laborer	05Ap02Ar
KINSILLE, Michael	40	M	Miner	05Ap02Ar
MURRAY, Elizabeth	14	F	Unknown	05Ap02Ar
FARRELL, John	17	M	Laborer	05Ap02Ar
CUMISKE, Catherine	30	F	Unknown	05Ap02Ar
Mary	07	F	Child	05Ap02Ar
Catherine	.00	F	Infant	05Ap02Ar
RYAN, James	45	M	Laborer	05Ap02Ar
Ellen	27	F	Unknown	05Ap02Ar
Judy	18	F	Unknown	05Ap02Ar
Kearin	.00	F	Infant	05Ap02Ar
Mary	.00	F	Infant	05Ap02Ar
CONLIN, Pat	40	M	Laborer	05Ap02Ar
Bridget	30	F	Unknown	05Ap02Ar
Elenor	15	F	Unknown	05Ap02Ar
Bridget	07	F	Child	05Ap02Ar
Ann	05	F	Child	05Ap02Ar
Bryan	03	M	Child	05Ap02Ar
Pat	.00	M	Infant	05Ap02Ar
TIVNEN, Thomas	20	M	Shoemaker	05Ap02Ar
Catherine	30	F	Unknown	05Ap02Ar
Thomas	06	M	Child	05Ap02Ar
Domnick	.00	M	Infant	05Ap02Ar
Owen	09	M	Child	05Ap02Ar
FLYNN, Paddy	26	M	Laborer	05Ap02Ar
FREINER, Owen	28	M	Laborer	05Ap02Ar
RICE, Catherine	45	F	Unknown	05Ap02Ar
WALSH, Mary	32	F	Unknown	05Ap02Ar
Michael	12	M	Unknown	05Ap02Ar
James	10	M	Unknown	05Ap02Ar
Nicholas	08	M	Child	05Ap02Ar
Margaret	04	F	Child	05Ap02Ar
FEHERY, Rosa	53	F	Unknown	05Ap02Ar
DELANY, Bridget	13	F	Unknown	05Ap02Ar
CROKE, Richard	29	M	Laborer	05Ap02Ar
CONNELL, Patrick	30	M	Laborer	05Ap02Ar
WALSH, Patrick	20	M	Laborer	05Ap02Ar
KINNANE, James	53	M	Laborer	05Ap02Ar
Margaret	47	F	Unknown	05Ap02Ar
John	20	M	Laborer	05Ap02Ar
Mary	18	F	Unknown	05Ap02Ar
HONAGHAN, Bridget	10	F	Unknown	05Ap02Ar
Johanna	19	F	Unknown	05Ap02Ar
Mary	15	F	Unknown	05Ap02Ar
LONG, Mary	20	F	Unknown	05Ap02Ar
FLYNN, Mary	13	F	Unknown	05Ap02Ar
Johanna	11	F	Unknown	05Ap02Ar
Joseph	45	M	Laborer	05Ap02Ar
Margaret	35	F	Unknown	05Ap02Ar
Daglin	40	M	Laborer	05Ap02Ar
MURRAY, Martin	35	M	Laborer	05Ap02Ar
CAMPBELL, James	20	M	Laborer	05Ap02Ar
MULLIN, James	25	M	Laborer	05Ap02Ar
MELLON, Margaret	20	F	Unknown	05Ap02Ar
OCONNOR, Nancy	21	F	Unknown	05Ap02Ar
MONAGHAN, John	30	M	Laborer	05Ap02Ar
FENERTHY, Pat	45	M	Laborer	05Ap02Ar
MACKIN, Pat	33	M	Laborer	05Ap02Ar
Ellen	32	F	Laborer	05Ap02Ar
Margaret	11	F	Unknown	05Ap02Ar
Mary	06	F	Child	05Ap02Ar
Michael	04	M	Child	05Ap02Ar
James	.00	M	Infant	05Ap02Ar
KELLY, John	25	M	Laborer	05Ap02Ar
SMITH, Terrance	25	M	Laborer	05Ap02Ar
John	08	M	Child	05Ap02Ar
MCQUADY, John	30	M	Child	05Ap02Ar
Margaret	26	F	Unknown	05Ap02Ar
Ann	.00	F	Infant	05Ap02Ar
FLAHERTY, Martin	26	M	Baker	05Ap02Ar
MEANY, Bridget	23	F	Unknown	05Ap02Ar
HUGHS, Thomas	50	M	Laborer	05Ap02Ar
Judy	40	F	Unknown	05Ap02Ar
John	14	M	Laborer	05Ap02Ar
Catherine	12	F	Unknown	05Ap02Ar
Bridget	11	F	Unknown	05Ap02Ar
Mary	04	F	Child	05Ap02Ar
Paddy	.00	M	Infant	05Ap02Ar
BRANNON, Charles	29	M	Laborer	05Ap02Ar
HEADE, John	40	M	Laborer	05Ap02Ar
Ann	40	F	Unknown	05Ap02Ar
Mary	42	F	Unknown	05Ap02Ar
Ann	.00	F	Infant	05Ap02Ar
WILKINSON, James	25	M	Laborer	05Ap02Ar
GARRETY, Mary	25	F	Unknown	05Ap02Ar
PATTON, Bridget	18	F	Unknown	05Ap02Ar
MURRAY, John	22	M	Laborer	05Ap02Ar
Michael	24	M	Laborer	05Ap02Ar
James	30	M	Laborer	05Ap02Ar
GUGNAN, Bernard	26	M	Laborer	05Ap02Ar
CAIN, Pat	40	M	Laborer	05Ap02Ar
Martin	11	M	Unknown	05Ap02Ar
Mary	13	F	Unknown	05Ap02Ar
WALLIS, Thomas	22	M	Laborer	05Ap02Ar
Bridget	19	F	Unknown	05Ap02Ar
RIELLY, Ann	24	F	Unknown	05Ap02Ar
COWEN, John	24	M	Laborer	05Ap02Ar
KILLBRIDE, Mary	49	F	Unknown	05Ap02Ar
James	16	M	Laborer	05Ap02Ar
CAINE, Thomas	30	M	Laborer	05Ap02Ar
Catherine	30	F	Unknown	05Ap02Ar
Catherine	20	F	Unknown	05Ap02Ar
Thomas	04	M	Child	05Ap02Ar
DOOLEY, Edward	40	M	Laborer	05Ap02Ar
Bridget	47	F	Unknown	05Ap02Ar
Bridget	15	F	Unknown	05Ap02Ar
Ann	10	F	Unknown	05Ap02Ar
MCKINSON, Thomas	27	M	Laborer	05Ap02Ar
Hugh	05	M	Child	05Ap02Ar
HOLAHEN, Thomas	17	M	Laborer	05Ap02Ar
BLISSING, Bridget	20	F	Unknown	05Ap02Ar
CLIFFORD, Bernard	22	M	Laborer	05Ap02Ar
OBRIEN, Patrick	30	M	Carpenter	05Ap02Ar
ROURKE, Patrick	23	M	Laborer	05Ap02Ar
Mary	24	F	Unknown	05Ap02Ar
WOODS, Christain	20	F	Unknown	05Ap02Ar
THOMSON, James	30	M	Laborer	05Ap02Ar
MCGUIRE, Francis	24	M	Laborer	05Ap02Ar
BIRNEY, James	20	M	Laborer	05Ap02Ar
Pat	23	M	Laborer	05Ap02Ar
BARRETT, John	26	M	Laborer	05Ap02Ar
FOX, John	30	M	Shoemaker	05Ap02Ar
PLUNKETT, John	40	M	Laborer	05Ap02Ar
CAVANAGH, Bryan	32	M	Laborer	05Ap02Ar
Ann	30	F	Unknown	05Ap02Ar
Mary	.00	F	Infant	05Ap02Ar
ROURKE, Ann	18	F	Unknown	05Ap02Ar
PLUNKETT, Ann	17	F	Unknown	05Ap02Ar
MCFARLANE, Michael	32	M	Laborer	05Ap02Ar
Mary-Ann	20	F	Unknown	05Ap02Ar
Catherine	.00	F	Infant	05Ap02Ar
MCQUE, Thomas	26	M	Laborer	05Ap02Ar

NAMES OF PASSENGERS	AGE	SEX	OCCUPATIONS	DATE PORT SHIP
MCQUE, Bridget	22	F	Unknown	05Ap02Ar
Michael	05	M	Child	05Ap02Ar
Miles	.00	M	Infant	05Ap02Ar
DOLAN, Anne	20	F	Laborer	05Ap02Ar
NONAN, Patrick	20	M	Laborer	05Ap02Ar
TRACEY, William	24	M	Laborer	05Ap02Ar
BURNS, Bridget	21	F	Laborer	05Ap02Ar
REILLY, Jane	19	F	Laborer	05Ap02Ar
HANRATY, Mary-Ann	.00	F	Infant	05Ap02Ar
TRAINER, Rosanna	19	F	Unknown	05Ap02Ar
HORAN, Michael	24	M	Laborer	05Ap02Ar

ELSINOR 05 APRIL 1849

From Liverpool

NAMES OF PASSENGERS	AGE	SEX	OCCUPATIONS	DATE PORT SHIP
MADDEN, Biddy	20	F	Servant	05Ap02Au
MCHUGH, Pat	20	M	Laborer	05Ap02Au
FLYNN, James	24	M	Laborer	05Ap02Au
FAILEY, James	18	M	Laborer	05Ap02Au
BRYAN, John	26	M	Laborer	05Ap02Au
MURRY, Pat	18	M	Laborer	05Ap02Au
QUINN, Mic.	18	M	Laborer	05Ap02Au
CALLERY, Thos.	26	M	Laborer	05Ap02Au
LOKEN, Betsey	50	F	Servant	05Ap02Au
DOLAN, Mic.	24	M	Laborer	05Ap02Au
Margt.	24	F	Servant	05Ap02Au
Teresa	.03	F	Infant	05Ap02Au
MURRIN, Betsey	30	F	Servant	05Ap02Au
Pat	31	M	Laborer	05Ap02Au
PEARSLEY, Rett	20	M	Laborer	05Ap02Au
BRADY, Mary	19	F	Servant	05Ap02Au
Mary	17	F	Servant	05Ap02Au
ROWE, Pat	20	M	Laborer	05Ap02Au
Mary	19	F	Servant	05Ap02Au
MCANERNY, Wm.	23	M	Laborer	05Ap02Au
SCHAENY, Edmond	21	M	Laborer	05Ap02Au
HEFFON, Mic.	22	M	Laborer	05Ap02Au
BROPHY, John	24	M	Laborer	05Ap02Au
ROE, Mary	30	F	Servant	05Ap02Au
Pat	08	M	Child	05Ap02Au
Mary	10	F	Servant	05Ap02Au
GIBBONS, Bridget	18	F	Servant	05Ap02Au
GORMAN, Mary	20	F	Servant	05Ap02Au
FITZPATRICK, Eliza	15	F	Servant	05Ap02Au
SAVAGE, Robt.	29	M	Laborer	05Ap02Au
Edw.	27	M	Laborer	05Ap02Au
Mary	23	F	Servant	05Ap02Au
Thos.	.04	M	Infant	05Ap02Au
Died-At-Sea				
Richard	28	M	Laborer	05Ap02Au
Mary	26	F	Servant	05Ap02Au
Susan	06	F	Child	05Ap02Au
Mary	04	F	Child	05Ap02Au
Catherin	02	F	Child	05Ap02Au
Mary	.06	F	Infant	05Ap02Au
Ann	26	F	Servant	05Ap02Au
Francis	27	F	Servant	05Ap02Au
Sarah	21	F	Servant	05Ap02Au
MCGRATH, Ellen	21	F	Servant	05Ap02Au
Rose	19	F	Servant	05Ap02Au
Mary	17	F	Servant	05Ap02Au
KELLY, Bessy	15	F	Servant	05Ap02Au
ROWNE, Rose	45	F	Servant	05Ap02Au
Marg.	22	F	Servant	05Ap02Au
James	20	M	Servant	05Ap02Au
STEAMY, Marg.	40	M	Laborer	05Ap02Au
MCCASTEN, James	18	M	Laborer	05Ap02Au
KARNES, Junr.	56	M	Laborer	05Ap02Au
KARNES, James	16	M	Laborer	05Ap02Au
Josiah	24	M	Laborer	05Ap02Au
STERNES, George	35	M	Laborer	05Ap02Au
U-Mrs.	26	F	Servant	05Ap02Au
WILLIAM, Thos.	45	M	Laborer	05Ap02Au
Mary	40	F	Servant	05Ap02Au
Died-At-Sea				
Bridget	17	F	Servant	05Ap02Au
SHEARAN, Judy	20	F	Servant	05Ap02Au
CASEY, Cath.	18	F	Servant	05Ap02Au
CONNOLLY, Alex.	24	M	Laborer	05Ap02Au
Mary	20	F	Servant	05Ap02Au
MERMICK, James	24	M	Laborer	05Ap02Au
Wm.	40	M	Laborer	05Ap02Au
HAPPEN, Mic.	21	M	Laborer	05Ap02Au
HYNES, Mary	21	F	Servant	05Ap02Au
KELLY, Pat	20	M	Mason	05Ap02Au
WALSH, James	22	M	Mason	05Ap02Au
HURLEY, Wm.	13	M	Laborer	05Ap02Au
KEARNES, Pat	18	M	Laborer	05Ap02Au
JONES, Wm.	50	M	Laborer	05Ap02Au
EGAN, Maurice	25	M	Laborer	05Ap02Au
Bridget	25	F	Servant	05Ap02Au
MCCANN, Pat	20	M	Laborer	05Ap02Au
GRIMSHAW, George	30	M	Laborer	05Ap02Au
FLYNN, James	21	M	Laborer	05Ap02Au
CARROLL, Mic.	19	M	Laborer	05Ap02Au
HUXLEY, Mic.	20	M	Laborer	05Ap02Au
DREA, Ellen	20	F	Servant	05Ap02Au
HURLEY, Ellen	20	F	Servant	05Ap02Au
KENNEDEY, John	26	M	Laborer	05Ap02Au
KELAPHE, Wm.	21	M	Laborer	05Ap02Au
Mary	16	F	Servant	05Ap02Au
Biddy	45	F	Servant	05Ap02Au
PATER, Robert	35	M	Laborer	05Ap02Au
Elizabeth	40	F	Servant	05Ap02Au
Eliza	18	F	Servant	05Ap02Au
William	16	M	Laborer	05Ap02Au
James	12	M	Laborer	05Ap02Au
Sally	10	F	Servant	05Ap02Au
Martin	08	M	Child	05Ap02Au
Ann	06	F	Child	05Ap02Au
Jane	05	F	Child	05Ap02Au
Lydia	03	F	Child	05Ap02Au
TIMNEY, Charles	37	M	Laborer	05Ap02Au
MEEK, Cath.	20	F	Unknown	05Ap02Au
DONNELLY, Mary	21	F	Unknown	05Ap02Au
HEALY, Mathew	22	M	Laborer	05Ap02Au
Thomas	20	M	Laborer	05Ap02Au
DONOHUE, Martin	20	M	Laborer	05Ap02Au
Ann	18	F	Servant	05Ap02Au
MULHALE, Edw.	26	M	Laborer	05Ap02Au
Mary	30	F	Servant	05Ap02Au
ROLANDS, Robert	26	M	Laborer	05Ap02Au
FIELD, Owen	25	M	Laborer	05Ap02Au
BRIEN, Mary	30	F	Servant	05Ap02Au
Mary	.04	F	Infant	05Ap02Au
REDDY, John	28	M	Laborer	05Ap02Au
DONIGHAN, Mic.	28	M	Laborer	05Ap02Au
JONES, Thomas	29	M	Laborer	05Ap02Au
Catherin	18	F	Servant	05Ap02Au
Ann	25	F	Servant	05Ap02Au
Rose-Ann	.02	F	Infant	05Ap02Au
John	.06	M	Infant	05Ap02Au
MORAN, Dennis	32	M	Laborer	05Ap02Au
MCSEAN, Malcolm	45	M	Laborer	05Ap02Au
ALWORTH, Jos.	26	M	Laborer	05Ap02Au
BRIEN, Daniel	15	M	Laborer	05Ap02Au
KELLY, Mary	20	F	Servant	05Ap02Au
MCGANN, Mary	18	F	Servant	05Ap02Au
PHILLIPS, Mary	18	F	Servant	05Ap02Au
Mary	17	F	Servant	05Ap02Au
MURPHY, Judith	26	F	Servant	05Ap02Au
WYANN, Mary	18	F	Servant	05Ap02Au
REGNEY, John	28	M	Laborer	05Ap02Au

NAMES OF PASSENGERS	AGE	SEX	OCCUPATIONS	DATE PORT SHIP
REGNEY, Biddy	60	F	Servant	05Ap02Au
SEIN, Cath.	28	F	Servant	05Ap02Au
RIELLY, Cath.	17	F	Servant	05Ap02Au
HOOKS, Martin	21	M	Laborer	05Ap02Au
RYAN, Timothy	40	M	Laborer	05Ap02Au
MALONEY, Daniel	32	M	Laborer	05Ap02Au
John	27	M	Laborer	05Ap02Au
Martin	32	M	Laborer	05Ap02Au
Judy	27	F	Laborer	05Ap02Au
DOYLE, William	17	M	Laborer	05Ap02Au
HENNESSEY, James	23	M	Laborer	05Ap02Au
WELCH, Samuel	35	M	Laborer	05Ap02Au
Honor	34	F	Laborer	05Ap02Au
James	09	M	Child	05Ap02Au
Rob.	07	M	Child	05Ap02Au
Mary	03	F	Servant	05Ap02Au
CONOLLY, Mary	04	F	Child	05Ap02Au
PHEPOE, Henry	24	M	Laborer	05Ap02Au
WYMAN, Andrew	22	M	Laborer	05Ap02Au
Pat	20	M	Laborer	05Ap02Au
Bryan	21	M	Laborer	05Ap02Au
PADDON, Anne	21	F	Servant	05Ap02Au
TUNGESON, Thomas	47	M	Laborer	05Ap02Au
Anne	45	F	Servant	05Ap02Au
CUFFNEY, Terence	30	M	Laborer	05Ap02Au
MURPHY, Peirce	30	M	Laborer	05Ap02Au
FURLAN, James	34	M	Laborer	05Ap02Au
BYRNE, Charles	26	M	Laborer	05Ap02Au
PENDERGAST, Jno.	24	M	Laborer	05Ap02Au
MURPHY, James	26	M	Laborer	05Ap02Au
Judy	24	F	Laborer	05Ap02Au
John	.06	M	Infant	05Ap02Au
DOYLE, Biddy	37	F	Servant	05Ap02Au
Pat	18	M	Laborer	05Ap02Au
BULGAR, John	24	M	Laborer	05Ap02Au
Elgin	20	F	Servant	05Ap02Au
Mary	38	F	Servant	05Ap02Au
MURPHY, Johanna	19	F	Servant	05Ap02Au
MORRESSEY, Mic.	40	M	Laborer	05Ap02Au
Cath.	38	F	Servant	05Ap02Au
Mary	09	F	Child	05Ap02Au
Biddy	.03	F	Infant	05Ap02Au
MURPHY, Pat	38	M	Laborer	05Ap02Au
Judy	35	M	Laborer	05Ap02Au
Thomas	17	F	Servant	05Ap02Au
John	14	M	Laborer	05Ap02Au
Martin	13	M	Laborer	05Ap02Au
Cath.	09	F	Child	05Ap02Au
Steven	08	M	Child	05Ap02Au
GREENMAN, James	18	M	Laborer	05Ap02Au
MURPHY, Hugh	18	M	Laborer	05Ap02Au
BLANCHFIELD, Mic.	17	M	Laborer	05Ap02Au
DORAN, Cath.	18	F	Servant	05Ap02Au
QUINN, Biddy	20	F	Servant	05Ap02Au
Johanna	21	F	Servant	05Ap02Au
MURRY, Daniel	45	M	Laborer	05Ap02Au
Biddy	40	F	Servant	05Ap02Au
John	17	M	Servant	05Ap02Au
Catherine	11	F	Servant	05Ap02Au
Thomas	07	M	Child	05Ap02Au
Ellen	03	F	Child	05Ap02Au
James	.04	M	Infant	05Ap02Au
WALSH, Mic.	28	M	Laborer	05Ap02Au
MURRY, John	17	M	Laborer	05Ap02Au
POWER, Cath.	22	F	Servant	05Ap02Au
WALSH, Mic.	21	M	Laborer	05Ap02Au
MURRY, John	25	M	Laborer	05Ap02Au
DALTON, Luke	50	M	Laborer	05Ap02Au
Luke	18	M	Laborer	05Ap02Au
Cath.	60	F	Servant	05Ap02Au
HANNAGAN, Marg.	24	F	Servant	05Ap02Au
OCONNOR, John	30	M	Laborer	05Ap02Au
DALY, John	40	M	Laborer	05Ap02Au
CURRAN, John	37	M	Laborer	05Ap02Au
POWER, James	26	M	Laborer	05Ap02Au

NAMES OF PASSENGERS	AGE	SEX	OCCUPATIONS	DATE PORT SHIP
FARRELL, Dennis	50	M	Laborer	05Ap02Au
Biddy	30	F	Servant	05Ap02Au
Mary	13	F	Servant	05Ap02Au
Johanna	10	F	Servant	05Ap02Au
Daniel	09	M	Child	05Ap02Au
WASSETT, John	11	M	Laborer	05Ap02Au
KENNEDY, Pat	40	M	Laborer	05Ap02Au
Judy	30	F	Laborer	05Ap02Au
Pat	12	M	Laborer	05Ap02Au
Mic.	11	M	Laborer	05Ap02Au
James	02	M	Child	05Ap02Au
Mary	.06	F	Infant	05Ap02Au
MACNAMARA, John	30	M	Laborer	05Ap02Au
Cathrine	23	F	Servant	05Ap02Au
John	.04	M	Infant	05Ap02Au
HALLORAN, John	30	M	Laborer	05Ap02Au
Pen	30	M	Laborer	05Ap02Au
Pat	07	M	Child	05Ap02Au
Maria	04	F	Child	05Ap02Au
Dennis	.07	M	Infant	05Ap02Au
SANDY, Alice	50	F	Laborer	05Ap02Au
FIELD, Pat	21	M	Laborer	05Ap02Au
SANDY, Marg.	16	F	Servant	05Ap02Au
Ann	13	F	Servant	05Ap02Au
Mary	11	F	Servant	05Ap02Au
POWDERLEY, Thomas	37	M	Laborer	05Ap02Au
Mary	25	F	Laborer	05Ap02Au
Mic.	07	M	Child	05Ap02Au
Pat	04	M	Child	05Ap02Au
POWDERLY, John	33	M	Laborer	05Ap02Au
Edward	.03	M	Infant	05Ap02Au
MOIN, Francis	25	M	Laborer	05Ap02Au
Mary	28	F	Servant	05Ap02Au
DALY, John	38	M	Laborer	05Ap02Au
MURPHY, Thomas	26	M	Laborer	05Ap02Au
BUCKLEY, Corny.	24	M	Laborer	05Ap02Au
CRONAN, Mary	20	F	Servant	05Ap02Au
ONIEL, Ellen	26	F	Servant	05Ap02Au
MULLIN, Neal	24	M	Laborer	05Ap02Au
BERNUM, Thomas	10	M	Laborer	05Ap02Au
GUY, Biddy	20	F	Servant	05Ap02Au
U Born-At-Sea	.00	U	Infant	05Ap02Au

HIGGINSON 05 APRIL 1849

From Carnarvon

(A list of Welsh passengers, this was noticed too late to be dropped from the print-out)

NAMES OF PASSENGERS	AGE	SEX	OCCUPATIONS	DATE PORT SHIP
WILLIAMS, Griffith	20	M	Laborer	05Ap26Av
EVANS, William	18	M	Laborer	05Ap26Av
David	19	M	Laborer	05Ap26Av
REED, Evan	21	M	Laborer	05Ap26Av
JONES, Richard	25	M	Laborer	05Ap26Av
RICHARDS, Robert	25	M	Smith	05Ap26Av
DAVIES, John	23	M	Unknown	05Ap26Av
OWEN, Richard	30	M	Laborer	05Ap26Av
EVANS, Evan	30	M	Laborer	05Ap26Av
ROWLANDS, William	22	M	Laborer	05Ap26Av
ROBERTS, Thomas	18	M	Laborer	05Ap26Av
ROWLANDS, Owen	24	M	Sawer	05Ap26Av
John	20	M	Laborer	05Ap26Av
JONES, John	21	M	Laborer	05Ap26Av
DAVIES, Griffith	40	M	Quarryman	05Ap26Av
Catharine	38	F	Relative	05Ap26Av
Griffith	13	M	Relative	05Ap26Av
John	09	M	Child	05Ap26Av
Jane	07	F	Child	05Ap26Av
Morris	02	M	Child	05Ap26Av
William	.00	M	Infant	05Ap26Av

NAMES OF PASSENGERS	AGE	SEX	OCCUPATIONS	DATE PORT SHIP
DAVIES, Evan	25	M	Laborer	05Ap26Av
PRICHARD, John	26	M	Quarryman	05Ap26Av
LEWIS, Saml.	23	M	Laborer	05Ap26Av
WILLIAMS, William	42	M	Laborer	05Ap26Av
Margaret	37	F	Relative	05Ap26Av
Anne	08	F	Child	05Ap26Av
Cathrine	06	F	Child	05Ap26Av
OWEN, John	18	M	Quarryman	05Ap26Av
WILLIAMS, Peter	20	M	Tailor	05Ap26Av
EVANS, John	28	M	Laborer	05Ap26Av
JONES, John	27	M	Quarryman	05Ap26Av
Ellen	28	F	Relative	05Ap26Av
William	13	M	Relative	05Ap26Av
Ellen	08	F	Child	05Ap26Av
Robert	06	M	Child	05Ap26Av
Mary	.00	F	Infant	05Ap26Av
ROBERTS, John	30	M	Quarryman	05Ap26Av
Cathrine	26	F	Relative	05Ap26Av
John	08	M	Child	05Ap26Av
William	.00	M	Infant	05Ap26Av
EVANS, John	30	M	Laborer	05Ap26Av
MORRIS, William	28	M	Laborer	05Ap26Av
WILLIAMS, William	26	M	Laborer	05Ap26Av
JONES, William	30	M	Laborer	05Ap26Av
HUGHES, Evan	47	M	Tailor	05Ap26Av
Mary	45	F	Wife	05Ap26Av
Mary	22	F	Relative	05Ap26Av
Grace	20	F	Relative	05Ap26Av
Sarah	17	F	Relative	05Ap26Av
Evan	13	M	Relative	05Ap26Av
Cathrine	10	F	Relative	05Ap26Av
William	08	M	Child	05Ap26Av
Thomas	07	M	Child	05Ap26Av
John	05	M	Child	05Ap26Av
Ellen	.00	F	Infant	05Ap26Av
PRICHARD, Hugh	54	M	Farmer	05Ap26Av
Mary	52	F	Wife	05Ap26Av
Thomas	30	M	Laborer	05Ap26Av
STREET, John	30	M	Brick Maker	05Ap26Av
Cathrine	27	F	Relative	05Ap26Av
Hugh	04	M	Child	05Ap26Av
William	.00	M	Infant	05Ap26Av
HUGHES, Margret	27	F	Wife	05Ap26Av
JONES, Elias	25	M	Laborer	05Ap26Av
Robert	30	M	Laborer	05Ap26Av
Thomas	25	M	Laborer	05Ap26Av
Griffith	23	M	Laborer	05Ap26Av
HUGHES, Robert	21	M	Stone Mason	05Ap26Av
JONES, John	19	M	Laborer	05Ap26Av
ROBERTS, Griffith	30	M	Quarryman	05Ap26Av
Mary	29	F	Relative	05Ap26Av
Elizabeth	11	F	Relative	05Ap26Av
Gwen	.00	F	Infant	05Ap26Av
PARRY, William	24	M	Laborer	05Ap26Av
Jane	23	F	Relative	05Ap26Av
William	.00	M	Infant	05Ap26Av
WILLIAMS, Thomas	30	M	Smith	05Ap26Av
Diana	27	F	Relative	05Ap26Av
Jane	11	F	Relative	05Ap26Av
William	07	M	Child	05Ap26Av
Elizabeth	.00	F	Infant	05Ap26Av
JONES, Thomas	24	M	Laborer	05Ap26Av
Robert	22	M	Laborer	05Ap26Av
ROBERTS, John	28	M	Laborer	05Ap26Av
Margaret	26	F	Relative	05Ap26Av
Thomas	.00	M	Infant	05Ap26Av
EDWARDS, John	19	M	Laborer	05Ap26Av
JONES, Robert	27	M	Laborer	05Ap26Av
Rowland	25	M	Laborer	05Ap26Av
PARRY, Henry	27	M	Laborer	05Ap26Av
John	22	M	Laborer	05Ap26Av
MORRIS, John	21	M	Smith	05Ap26Av
ROBERTS, Thomas	28	M	Laborer	05Ap26Av
Margret	35	F	Relative	05Ap26Av
Margret	20	F	Relative	05Ap26Av
ROBERTS, Robert	17	M	Relative	05Ap26Av
Moses	14	M	Relative	05Ap26Av
John	11	M	Relative	05Ap26Av
JONES, Daniel	24	M	Laborer	05Ap26Av
William	26	M	Laborer	05Ap26Av
David	28	M	Laborer	05Ap26Av
Elizabeth	24	F	Wife	05Ap26Av
John	.00	M	Infant	05Ap26Av
WILLIAMS, Thomas	22	M	Carpenter	05Ap26Av
JONES, David	27	M	Farmer	05Ap26Av
ROBERTS, Roger	25	M	Miner	05Ap26Av
PARRY, Hugh	19	M	Smith	05Ap26Av
THOMAS, John	40	M	Quarryman	05Ap26Av
Jane	38	F	Relative	05Ap26Av
Elizabeth	19	F	Relative	05Ap26Av
Gwen	13	F	Relative	05Ap26Av
Mary	07	F	Child	05Ap26Av
John	.00	M	Infant	05Ap26Av
MORRIS, Richard	24	M	Laborer	05Ap26Av
HUGHES, Richard	27	M	Laborer	05Ap26Av
DAVIES, William	22	M	Laborer	05Ap26Av
HUMPHREY, Mary	21	F	Spinster	05Ap26Av
HUGHES, Michael	30	M	Farmer	05Ap26Av
PARRY, Owen	35	M	Laborer	05Ap26Av
Elizabeth	32	F	Wife	05Ap26Av
HUGHES, William	30	M	Quarryman	05Ap26Av
WILLIAMS, Robert	23	M	Quarryman	05Ap26Av
EVANS, Richard	25	M	Laborer	05Ap26Av
DAVIES, Henry	22	M	Laborer	05Ap26Av
EDWARDS, William	28	M	Farmer	05Ap26Av
Susannah	36	F	Unknown	05Ap26Av
Edward	13	M	Relative	05Ap26Av
Gwen	12	F	Relative	05Ap26Av
John	10	M	Relative	05Ap26Av
William	07	M	Child	05Ap26Av
Robert Died-At-Sea	01	M	Child	05Ap26Av
JONES, James	29	M	Laborer	05Ap26Av
Ellen	27	F	Relative	05Ap26Av
Jane	.00	F	Infant	05Ap26Av
WILLIAMS, Cathrine	30	F	Farmer	05Ap26Av
Anne	09	F	Child	05Ap26Av
Jane	.00	F	Infant	05Ap26Av
HUGHES, John	28	M	Tailor	05Ap26Av
JONES, Jane	22	F	Spinster	05Ap26Av
OWEN, Robert	25	M	Laborer	05Ap26Av
POOL, Jane	27	F	Relative	05Ap26Av
OWEN, Ellen	24	F	Spinster	05Ap26Av
DAVIES, Margret	27	F	Spinster	05Ap26Av
EVANS, Jane	25	F	Wi	05Ap26Av
GRIFFITH, Sidney	19	F	Spinster	05Ap26Av
William	07	M	Child	05Ap26Av
ROBERTS, Ann	27	F	Spinster	05Ap26Av

METOKA 05 APRIL 1849

From Liverpool

NAMES OF PASSENGERS	AGE	SEX	OCCUPATIONS	DATE PORT SHIP
LIDDY, Aaron	26	M	Laborer	05Ap02Aw
Cattie	08	F	Child	05Ap02Aw
Mary	06	F	Child	05Ap02Aw
Ann	03	F	Child	05Ap02Aw
Peter	.05	M	Infant	05Ap02Aw
KIMDECK, Thos.	36	M	Laborer	05Ap02Aw
Rose	30	F	Unknown	05Ap02Aw
James	08	M	Child	05Ap02Aw
Mary	06	F	Child	05Ap02Aw
John	03	M	Child	05Ap02Aw
Ann	.05	F	Infant	05Ap02Aw

NAMES OF PASSENGERS	AGE	SEX	OCCUPATIONS	DATE PORT SHIP
KILEY, John	24	M	Laborer	05Ap02Aw
James	20	M	Laborer	05Ap02Aw
DONAHUE, John	23	M	Laborer	05Ap02Aw
FLYNN, Pat	24	M	Laborer	05Ap02Aw
MULLEN, Francis	20	M	Laborer	05Ap02Aw
Rose	.05	F	Infant	05Ap02Aw
KILEY, Phil.	26	M	Laborer	05Ap02Aw
Cattie	24	F	Unknown	05Ap02Aw
COYLE, Ellen	30	F	Unknown	05Ap02Aw
GAFFNEY, Bernard	50	M	Laborer	05Ap02Aw
James	20	M	Laborer	05Ap02Aw
Bridget	18	F	Unknown	05Ap02Aw
DOWNEY, Owen	18	M	Laborer	05Ap02Aw
DULLY, Michael	20	M	Laborer	05Ap02Aw
FLINN, Bridget	30	F	Unknown	05Ap02Aw
LEE, John	18	M	Laborer	05Ap02Aw
COLLINS, Pat	25	M	Laborer	05Ap02Aw
Joc.	26	M	Laborer	05Ap02Aw
Mary	20	F	Unknown	05Ap02Aw
GARRIGAN, Bridget	20	F	Unknown	05Ap02Aw
SHERIDAN, John	38	M	Laborer	05Ap02Aw
Ann	35	F	Unknown	05Ap02Aw
Bernard	06	M	Child	05Ap02Aw
Pat	04	M	Child	05Ap02Aw
Morgan	.05	M	Infant	05Ap02Aw
FLOOD, Catherine	20	F	Unknown	05Ap02Aw
LIDDY, Peter	35	M	Laborer	05Ap02Aw
MCNAMARRA, Michael	25	M	Laborer	05Ap02Aw
FITZGIBBON, David	27	M	Laborer	05Ap02Aw
COFFY, Pat	27	M	Laborer	05Ap02Aw
DOYLE, John	25	M	Laborer	05Ap02Aw
BRADY, Michael	20	M	Farmer	05Ap02Aw
SHARKEY, Pat	55	M	Farmer	05Ap02Aw
John	04	M	Child	05Ap02Aw
CONNOR, Michael	28	M	Farmer	05Ap02Aw
TIERNEY, Pat	20	M	Farmer	05Ap02Aw
HARSTON, Philip	20	M	Farmer	05Ap02Aw
DENNAN, Pat	20	M	Farmer	05Ap02Aw
SHIELD, Mary	20	F	Unknown	05Ap02Aw
FITZPATRICK, Ellen	22	F	Unknown	05Ap02Aw
Mary	18	F	Unknown	05Ap02Aw
SHIELDS, Rose	20	F	Unknown	05Ap02Aw
SHERIDAN, Ann	28	F	Unknown	05Ap02Aw
John	05	M	Child	05Ap02Aw
Pat	03	M	Child	05Ap02Aw
Bernard	02	M	Child	05Ap02Aw
Philip	.06	M	Infant	05Ap02Aw
SHARKEY, James	20	M	Farmer	05Ap02Aw
KEENAN, Nicholas	40	M	Farmer	05Ap02Aw
CONNOR, Pat	40	M	Farmer	05Ap02Aw
CANN, Thomas	20	M	Farmer	05Ap02Aw
Pat	18	M	Farmer	05Ap02Aw
Doran	14	M	Farmer	05Ap02Aw
Cathe.	12	F	Unknown	05Ap02Aw
Ellen	10	F	Unknown	05Ap02Aw
NICHOLS, John	20	M	Farmer	05Ap02Aw
Pat	18	M	Farmer	05Ap02Aw
PURCELL, Thomas	25	M	Farmer	05Ap02Aw
James	20	M	Farmer	05Ap02Aw
Stephen	17	M	Farmer	05Ap02Aw
Winifred	34	M	Farmer	05Ap02Aw
BORAN, Pat	20	M	Farmer	05Ap02Aw
PURCELL, Cathe.	24	F	Unknown	05Ap02Aw
Mary	20	F	Unknown	05Ap02Aw
Austey	14	F	Unknown	05Ap02Aw
Bridget	13	F	Unknown	05Ap02Aw
RYAN, Timothy	21	M	Farmer	05Ap02Aw
Wm.	18	M	Farmer	05Ap02Aw
Cathe.	25	F	Unknown	05Ap02Aw
BRYATH, Judy	24	F	Unknown	05Ap02Aw
BURKE, Thomas	18	M	Farmer	05Ap02Aw
SMITH, James	22	M	Farmer	05Ap02Aw
GARRIGAN, Edward	49	M	Farmer	05Ap02Aw
Ann	42	F	Unknown	05Ap02Aw
Simon	17	M	Farmer	05Ap02Aw
GARRIGAN, Ellen	15	F	Unknown	05Ap02Aw
Bridget	13	F	Unknown	05Ap02Aw
Mary	12	F	Unknown	05Ap02Aw
James	09	M	Child	05Ap02Aw
Michl.	06	M	Child	05Ap02Aw
Ann	04	F	Child	05Ap02Aw
Edward	02	M	Child	05Ap02Aw
FAGAN, Pat	24	M	Farmer	05Ap02Aw
GIBBONS, Benjm.	21	M	Farmer	05Ap02Aw
SIMCOX, Joseph	26	M	Farmer	05Ap02Aw
GUNNING, John	25	M	Farmer	05Ap02Aw
MEHAN, U-Mrs.	40	F	Unknown	05Ap02Aw
CANNON, Dominick	40	M	Farmer	05Ap02Aw
U-Mrs.	40	F	Unknown	05Ap02Aw
NOON, Daniel	27	M	Farmer	05Ap02Aw
FARREL, James	20	M	Farmer	05Ap02Aw
POLLON, Lawrence	20	M	Farmer	05Ap02Aw
PLUNKETT, John	30	M	Farmer	05Ap02Aw
Mary	18	F	Unknown	05Ap02Aw
COYLE, Mary	18	F	Unknown	05Ap02Aw
SOVELY, Michael	40	M	Farmer	05Ap02Aw
MCDERMOT, Ellen	50	F	Unknown	05Ap02Aw
DUNN, John	27	M	Farmer	05Ap02Aw
SMITH, James	21	M	Farmer	05Ap02Aw
Margt.	40	F	Unknown	05Ap02Aw
MCKAY, Nancy	18	F	Unknown	05Ap02Aw
DELMER, John	40	M	Farmer	05Ap02Aw
Mary	40	F	Unknown	05Ap02Aw
John	10	M	Farmer	05Ap02Aw
Thos.	05	M	Child	05Ap02Aw
Bridget	07	F	Child	05Ap02Aw
Cathe.	.06	F	Infant	05Ap02Aw
WARD, Ann	33	F	Unknown	05Ap02Aw
NEWELL, John	20	M	Farmer	05Ap02Aw
WARD, Thomas	09	M	Child	05Ap02Aw
John	07	M	Child	05Ap02Aw
James	05	M	Child	05Ap02Aw
Emma	.06	F	Infant	05Ap02Aw
MCGRATH, Thos.	25	M	Laborer	05Ap02Aw
Pat	24	M	Laborer	05Ap02Aw
James	18	M	Laborer	05Ap02Aw
Margt.	11	F	Unknown	05Ap02Aw
Dennis	14	M	Farmer	05Ap02Aw
KENNEY, Nancy	18	F	Unknown	05Ap02Aw
LYNCH, Wm.	20	F	Unknown	05Ap02Aw
DUFFY, Rose	27	F	Unknown	05Ap02Aw
COLLINS, Pat	18	M	Farmer	05Ap02Aw
TIERNEY, John	25	M	Farmer	05Ap02Aw
DONELLY, Michael	40	M	Farmer	05Ap02Aw
Jane	22	F	Unknown	05Ap02Aw
FITZSIMMONS, Jane	24	F	Unknown	05Ap02Aw
KENAN, James	24	M	Farmer	05Ap02Aw
MALAY, Cathe.	30	F	Unknown	05Ap02Aw
MCDERMOTT, Michael	24	M	Farmer	05Ap02Aw
Anne	18	F	Unknown	05Ap02Aw
Mary	18	F	Unknown	05Ap02Aw
Thomas	12	M	Farmer	05Ap02Aw
Henry	10	M	Farmer	05Ap02Aw
Elisa	08	F	Child	05Ap02Aw
CONNOR, Cathe.	14	F	Unknown	05Ap02Aw
DARELLY, Elisa	20	F	Unknown	05Ap02Aw
MORAN, Thos.	27	M	Farmer	05Ap02Aw
FITZSIMMONS, Henry	20	M	Farmer	05Ap02Aw
Elisa	15	F	Unknown	05Ap02Aw
Mary	10	F	Unknown	05Ap02Aw
CANNON, Michael	20	M	Farmer	05Ap02Aw
MULROLL, Thos.	20	M	Farmer	05Ap02Aw
MCDERMOTT, Mary	20	F	Unknown	05Ap02Aw
RILEY, Bridget	18	F	Unknown	05Ap02Aw
WHITE, Francis	19	M	Farmer	05Ap02Aw
LINCH, Pat	19	M	Farmer	05Ap02Aw
NUGENT, Pat	18	M	Farmer	05Ap02Aw
DOYLE, Tim	24	M	Farmer	05Ap02Aw
MULLOY, Cathe.	15	F	Unknown	05Ap02Aw
Michl.	12	M	Laborer	05Ap02Aw

NAMES OF PASSENGERS	AGE	SEX	OCCUPATIONS	DATE PORT SHIP
GRAY, Thos.	20	M	Laborer	05Ap02Aw
SHEENAN, Cathe.	16	F	Unknown	05Ap02Aw
HARRINGTON, Thos.	16	F	Unknown	05Ap02Aw
MULLOY, John	20	F	Unknown	05Ap02Aw
OBRIAN, Michl.	26	F	Farmer	05Ap02Aw
CONNELLY, James	20	F	Farmer	05Ap02Aw
DOURGAN, Michael	20	F	Farmer	05Ap02Aw
HICKEY, Sally	16	F	Unknown	05Ap02Aw
NASON, John	20	M	Farmer	05Ap02Aw
SPOTTS, John	35	M	Farmer	05Ap02Aw
Barthy	11	M	Farmer	05Ap02Aw
RILROY, Mary	07	F	Child	05Ap02Aw
LOWE, Mary	50	F	Unknown	05Ap02Aw
Martin	21	M	Farmer	05Ap02Aw
GREY, Thos.	18	M	Farmer	05Ap02Aw
Margt.	04	F	Child	05Ap02Aw
HUNTER, David	24	M	Farmer	05Ap02Aw
MALIUM, Wm.	25	M	Farmer	05Ap02Aw
GOWAN, Michael	20	M	Farmer	05Ap02Aw
KELLY, Thos.	40	M	Farmer	05Ap02Aw
GREY, John	20	M	Farmer	05Ap02Aw
KELLY, Ellen	18	F	Unknown	05Ap02Aw
COOK, John	30	M	Unknown	05Ap02Aw
Elisa	20	F	Unknown	05Ap02Aw
SLOAN, Jane	18	F	Unknown	05Ap02Aw
HYNES, Bernard	25	M	Laborer	05Ap02Aw
Margt.	22	F	Unknown	05Ap02Aw
Wm.	20	M	Farmer	05Ap02Aw
PARKER, W.	21	M	Farmer	05Ap02Aw
Margt.	21	F	Unknown	05Ap02Aw
Elisa	.06	F	Infant	05Ap02Aw
BYRNE, John	37	M	Farmer	05Ap02Aw
FREENAY, John	40	M	Farmer	05Ap02Aw
Pat	05	M	Child	05Ap02Aw
SMALL, Pat	22	M	Farmer	05Ap02Aw
SCOTT, Owen	18	M	Farmer	05Ap02Aw
LARKIN, Pat	18	M	Farmer	05Ap02Aw
WHITE, Mary	36	F	Unknown	05Ap02Aw
Thos.	11	M	Farmer	05Ap02Aw
Margt.	09	F	Child	05Ap02Aw
John	07	M	Child	05Ap02Aw
Morris	02	M	Child	05Ap02Aw
ELLIS, Michael	20	M	Farmer	05Ap02Aw
GARVIN, Rosanna	17	F	Unknown	05Ap02Aw
Joseph	22	M	Farmer	05Ap02Aw
HACKET, Pat	27	M	Laborer	05Ap02Aw
U-Mrs.	20	F	Unknown	05Ap02Aw
FOORD, Farrel	28	M	Laborer	05Ap02Aw
MARTIN, Mary	14	F	Unknown	05Ap02Aw
MALONE, Abraham	21	M	Laborer	05Ap02Aw
Darby	50	M	Laborer	05Ap02Aw
Mary	18	F	Unknown	05Ap02Aw
Ellen	40	F	Unknown	05Ap02Aw
Francis	13	M	Laborer	05Ap02Aw
PADIN, Catherine	30	F	Unknown	05Ap02Aw
GANNON, Mary	20	F	Unknown	05Ap02Aw
QUINN, Mary	18	F	Unknown	05Ap02Aw
LEE, Margaret	18	F	Unknown	05Ap02Aw
LAUGHLIN, Pat	20	M	Laborer	05Ap02Aw
MCNAMARA, Daniel	25	M	Laborer	05Ap02Aw
MORAN, Martin	13	M	Laborer	05Ap02Aw
HANLEY, Thos.	30	M	Laborer	05Ap02Aw
Ann	30	F	Unknown	05Ap02Aw
MORAN, Paddy	40	M	Laborer	05Ap02Aw
LAUGHLIN, Pat	30	M	Laborer	05Ap02Aw
MAHONEY, Cathe.	20	F	Unknown	05Ap02Aw
HIGGINS, Pater	30	M	Laborer	05Ap02Aw
NOWRANS, Nelly	40	F	Unknown	05Ap02Aw
MURPHY, Jane	27	F	Unknown	05Ap02Aw
BRIAN, Pat	20	M	Laborer	05Ap02Aw
LENNOL, Mary	18	F	Unknown	05Ap02Aw
FINN, Ellen	30	F	Unknown	05Ap02Aw
Michl.	12	M	Laborer	05Ap02Aw
John	06	M	Child	05Ap02Aw
REYNOLDS, James	27	M	Laborer	05Ap02Aw

NAMES OF PASSENGERS	AGE	SEX	OCCUPATIONS	DATE PORT SHIP
REYNOLDS, U-Mrs.	24	F	Unknown	05Ap02Aw
Wm.	02	M	Child	05Ap02Aw
Elisa	.06	F	Infant	05Ap02Aw
SULLIVAN, Dennis	40	M	Laborer	05Ap02Aw
GREEN, Charles	27	M	Laborer	05Ap02Aw
MURRAY, Philip	30	M	Laborer	05Ap02Aw
MULONEY, Rose	40	F	Unknown	05Ap02Aw
PURCELL, Pat	12	M	Farmer	05Ap02Aw
OSHAUGHNESSEY, Hugh	18	M	Farmer	05Ap02Aw
Mary	17	F	Unknown	05Ap02Aw
Michl.	18	M	Laborer	05Ap02Aw
John	19	M	Laborer	05Ap02Aw
CASEY, Cathe.	45	F	Unknown	05Ap02Aw
James	22	M	Farmer	05Ap02Aw
Bridget	19	F	Unknown	05Ap02Aw
John	14	M	Farmer	05Ap02Aw
Michael	09	M	Child	05Ap02Aw
Ann	07	F	Child	05Ap02Aw
Peter	.06	M	Infant	05Ap02Aw
DWYER, Ellen	09	F	Child	05Ap02Aw
Bridget	20	F	Unknown	05Ap02Aw
BURKE, Pat	35	M	Farmer	05Ap02Aw
Michael	28	M	Farmer	05Ap02Aw
CAREY, John	20	M	Farmer	05Ap02Aw
Margt.	20	F	Unknown	05Ap02Aw
Cathe.	16	F	Unknown	05Ap02Aw
HOLTON, Mary	40	F	Unknown	05Ap02Aw
Margt.	19	F	Unknown	05Ap02Aw
Cathe.	17	F	Unknown	05Ap02Aw
Edward	24	M	Farmer	05Ap02Aw
GALLGHER, Bess	30	F	Unknown	05Ap02Aw
WHEATLEY, Ann	30	F	Unknown	05Ap02Aw
LANGAN, Thos.	32	M	Farmer	05Ap02Aw
HOLLAN, Elizabeth	19	F	Unknown	05Ap02Aw
John	08	M	Child	05Ap02Aw
Wm.	02	M	Child	05Ap02Aw
James	06	M	Child	05Ap02Aw
MURPHY, Bridget	18	F	Unknown	05Ap02Aw
Philip	19	M	Farmer	05Ap02Aw
HOGAN, Pat	30	M	Farmer	05Ap02Aw
MCTULLER, Thos.	21	M	Farmer	05Ap02Aw
COMASKEY, John	23	M	Farmer	05Ap02Aw
SMITH, James	15	M	Farmer	05Ap02Aw
OLDEN, Martin	25	M	Farmer	05Ap02Aw
MORRISON, Mary	32	F	Unknown	05Ap02Aw
ROBERTS, Bridget	23	F	Unknown	05Ap02Aw
TULLY, Rose	30	F	Unknown	05Ap02Aw
HANLEY, Bridget	12	F	Unknown	05Ap02Aw
KELLEY, Ann	40	F	Unknown	05Ap02Aw
Margt.	19	F	Unknown	05Ap02Aw
FREENERY, Margt.	30	F	Unknown	05Ap02Aw
CENNAN, Cathe.	09	F	Child	05Ap02Aw
PLUNKETT, James	24	M	Laborer	05Ap02Aw
SHARKEY, Thomas	17	M	Farmer	05Ap02Aw
Pat	50	M	Farmer	05Ap02Aw
Margt.	43	F	Unknown	05Ap02Aw
Pat	21	M	Unknown	05Ap02Aw
MALONE, Michael	50	M	Farmer	05Ap02Aw

NEW-YORK 06 APRIL 1849

From Liverpool

NAMES OF PASSENGERS	AGE	SEX	OCCUPATIONS	DATE PORT SHIP
CLEBURN, Jos.	36	M	Surgeon	06Ap02Ax
MCGUIRE, Rose	21	F	Laborer	06Ap02Ax
KENNEDY, Thadeus	21	M	Laborer	06Ap02Ax
DONNELSON, Margaret	18	F	Laborer	06Ap02Ax
BOYD, Nancy	29	F	Laborer	06Ap02Ax
U	.06	F	Infant	06Ap02Ax

NAMES OF PASSENGERS	AGE	SEX	OCCUPATIONS	DATE PORT SHIP
BOYD, Thomas	06	M	Child	06Ap02Ax
Margaret	05	F	Child	06Ap02Ax
John	02	M	Child	06Ap02Ax
KEENAN, Stephen	18	M	Laborer	06Ap02Ax
MORRIS, Catherine	20	F	Laborer	06Ap02Ax
DELANEY, Patrick	26	M	Laborer	06Ap02Ax
GILLOOLY, Euphemia	28	F	Laborer	06Ap02Ax
Charles	01	M	Child	06Ap02Ax
CLARKEN, Patrick	18	M	Laborer	06Ap02Ax
Mary	16	F	Laborer	06Ap02Ax
MCCABE, John	21	M	Laborer	06Ap02Ax
CARLIS, Mary	17	F	Laborer	06Ap02Ax
BURGEN, James	22	M	Laborer	06Ap02Ax
CROSSEN, Hugh	38	M	Laborer	06Ap02Ax
Bridget	30	F	Laborer	06Ap02Ax
Jane	07	F	Child	06Ap02Ax
Mary	07	F	Child	06Ap02Ax
Kitty	03	F	Child	06Ap02Ax
MCGRATH, Dennis	30	M	Laborer	06Ap02Ax
GILLEN, Patrick	24	M	Laborer	06Ap02Ax
MURPHY, Edward	28	M	Laborer	06Ap02Ax
Johanna	24	F	Laborer	06Ap02Ax
CARRIGAN, Murly	25	M	Laborer	06Ap02Ax
CORBITT, Ann	26	F	Laborer	06Ap02Ax
REILLY, Michael	18	M	Laborer	06Ap02Ax
PURCELL, Bridget	20	F	Laborer	06Ap02Ax
OHARE, Margaret	20	F	Laborer	06Ap02Ax
FLAHERTY, Ellen	24	F	Laborer	06Ap02Ax
MCGUIRE, John	14	M	Laborer	06Ap02Ax
HAYES, Thos.	22	M	Laborer	06Ap02Ax
Honora	25	F	Laborer	06Ap02Ax
LOONAN, Winefred	17	F	Laborer	06Ap02Ax
DOHERTY, Barnard	18	M	Laborer	06Ap02Ax
ROCK, Patrick	30	M	Laborer	06Ap02Ax
CONNOR, Daniel	24	M	Laborer	06Ap02Ax
BRIEN, Patrick	19	M	Laborer	06Ap02Ax
BYRNES, Mary	18	F	Laborer	06Ap02Ax
WHITE, Essy	18	F	Laborer	06Ap02Ax
MCGUIRE, Mary	50	F	Laborer	06Ap02Ax
William	50	M	Laborer	06Ap02Ax
Michael	16	M	Laborer	06Ap02Ax
Bridget	14	F	Laborer	06Ap02Ax
Catherine	10	F	Laborer	06Ap02Ax
Hugh	07	M	Child	06Ap02Ax
CORNAY, James	20	M	Laborer	06Ap02Ax
Bessy	19	F	Laborer	06Ap02Ax
ELLIOTT, U-Mrs.	29	F	Laborer	06Ap02Ax
U	.03	F	Infant	06Ap02Ax
COX, Timothy	20	M	Laborer	06Ap02Ax
DELAHANTY, Ellen	15	F	Laborer	06Ap02Ax
SWEENY, Thomas	15	M	Laborer	06Ap02Ax
MCCABE, Mary	18	F	Laborer	06Ap02Ax
GREEHEN, U	40	F	Wi	06Ap02Ax
Barney	17	M	Laborer	06Ap02Ax
Ellen	13	F	Laborer	06Ap02Ax
Bartley	11	M	Laborer	06Ap02Ax
DONOUGH, John	21	M	Laborer	06Ap02Ax
BURNS, William	18	M	Laborer	06Ap02Ax
DUNCAN, Mary-Ann	18	F	Laborer	06Ap02Ax
REYNOLDS, Thomas	20	M	Laborer	06Ap02Ax
LEAVER, Thomas	21	M	Laborer	06Ap02Ax
FEGAN, John	20	M	Laborer	06Ap02Ax
COWLEY, John	50	M	Laborer	06Ap02Ax
Patrick	22	M	Laborer	06Ap02Ax
MCKAY, Walter	18	M	Laborer	06Ap02Ax
MARK, Mary	44	F	Laborer	06Ap02Ax
SHEA, Patrick	37	M	Laborer	06Ap02Ax
Ellen	40	F	Laborer	06Ap02Ax
Thos.	11	M	Laborer	06Ap02Ax
Dennis	09	M	Child	06Ap02Ax
Johanna	04	F	Child	06Ap02Ax
DOWNES, Michael	24	M	Laborer	06Ap02Ax
KELLY, Margaret	20	F	Laborer	06Ap02Ax
Bridget	19	F	Laborer	06Ap02Ax
GORDON, Jane	17	F	Laborer	06Ap02Ax
SEARY, Thos.	30	M	Laborer	06Ap02Ax
COFFEE, Catherine	08	F	Child	06Ap02Ax
GEARY, Michael	38	M	Laborer	06Ap02Ax
Michael	04	M	Child	06Ap02Ax
CAVANNAH, Stephen	21	M	Laborer	06Ap02Ax
KENNALLY, Mary	17	F	Laborer	06Ap02Ax
DOWNEY, Margaret	16	F	Laborer	06Ap02Ax
TOOMEY, Eliza	04	F	Child	06Ap02Ax
Mary	06	F	Child	06Ap02Ax
Bridget	08	F	Child	06Ap02Ax
DAWSON, Maria	20	F	Laborer	06Ap02Ax
SMITH, Thomas	03	M	Child	06Ap02Ax
CROAKE, Ellen	25	F	Laborer	06Ap02Ax
HART, Julia	40	F	Laborer	06Ap02Ax
John	11	M	Laborer	06Ap02Ax
Anne	05	F	Child	06Ap02Ax
TINDALL, Lawrence	24	M	Laborer	06Ap02Ax
John	22	M	Laborer	06Ap02Ax
Mary	21	F	Laborer	06Ap02Ax
MOORE, Mathew	22	M	Laborer	06Ap02Ax
Mary-Ann	14	F	Laborer	06Ap02Ax
TORMING, Hugh	20	M	Laborer	06Ap02Ax
FANIGAN, U-Mrs.	30	F	Laborer	06Ap02Ax
Ann	27	F	Laborer	06Ap02Ax
Eliza	03	F	Child	06Ap02Ax
MICK, Bridget	02	F	Child	06Ap02Ax
MCAVENEY, Mary	59	F	Laborer	06Ap02Ax
Terance	62	M	Laborer	06Ap02Ax
MCCUSKER, Catherine	20	F	Laborer	06Ap02Ax
MCGUIRE, John	20	M	Laborer	06Ap02Ax
KEIRNAN, Alice	18	F	Laborer	06Ap02Ax
Elizabeth	20	F	Laborer	06Ap02Ax
Ellen	21	F	Laborer	06Ap02Ax
HUTCHINSON, Thomas	25	M	Laborer	06Ap02Ax
Isabella	22	F	Laborer	06Ap02Ax
U	.02	F	Infant	06Ap02Ax
Edward	05	M	Child	06Ap02Ax
MCCORMICK, Francis	31	M	Laborer	06Ap02Ax
KEARDON, Michael	21	M	Laborer	06Ap02Ax
GORMAN, John	21	M	Laborer	06Ap02Ax
THORPE, Bridget	21	F	Laborer	06Ap02Ax
BARRET, James	11	M	Laborer	06Ap02Ax
DILLON, Anne	30	F	Laborer	06Ap02Ax
Anne	02	F	Child	06Ap02Ax
U	.00	U	Infant	06Ap02Ax
Born-At-Sea				
COSTELLO, John	18	M	Laborer	06Ap02Ax
COFFEE, Bridget	04	F	Child	06Ap02Ax
RICHARDS, Michael	22	M	Laborer	06Ap02Ax
LAMB, John	30	M	Laborer	06Ap02Ax
TIERNAN, Michael	23	M	Laborer	06Ap02Ax
KELLY, James	22	M	Laborer	06Ap02Ax
GILLOOLY, Mary	16	F	Laborer	06Ap02Ax
Patrick	12	M	Laborer	06Ap02Ax
Michael	10	M	Laborer	06Ap02Ax
FLYNNE, Pat	17	M	Laborer	06Ap02Ax
PARTLAN, William	28	M	Laborer	06Ap02Ax
Anne	28	F	Laborer	06Ap02Ax
REILLY, Bernard	15	M	Laborer	06Ap02Ax
MURPHY, Bridget	20	F	Laborer	06Ap02Ax
PHILLIPS, Judith	16	F	Laborer	06Ap02Ax
Judith	14	F	Laborer	06Ap02Ax
Bridget	11	F	Laborer	06Ap02Ax
Mary	06	F	Child	06Ap02Ax
OHARE, Anne	12	F	Laborer	06Ap02Ax
FAGAN, Mary	20	F	Laborer	06Ap02Ax
REILLY, Julia	30	F	Laborer	06Ap02Ax
James	02	M	Child	06Ap02Ax
CASSIDAY, Maria	14	F	Laborer	06Ap02Ax
COSTELLO, Maryanne	20	F	Laborer	06Ap02Ax
DONALDSON, Mary	20	F	Laborer	06Ap02Ax
PERRYMAN, Ellen	20	F	Laborer	06Ap02Ax
JAMES, Mary	19	F	Laborer	06Ap02Ax
REYNOLDS, Mary	30	F	Laborer	06Ap02Ax
DOWNEY, Daniel	29	M	Laborer	06Ap02Ax

NAMES OF PASSENGERS	AGE	SEX	OCCUPATIONS	DATE PORT SHIP
DALY, Michael	27	M	Laborer	06Ap02Ax
Mary	29	F	Laborer	06Ap02Ax
FALLON, Patrick	17	M	Laborer	06Ap02Ax
HAUGH, Patrick	27	M	Laborer	06Ap02Ax
CONLAN, Anne	40	F	Laborer	06Ap02Ax
Allen	08	M	Child	06Ap02Ax
John	10	M	Laborer	06Ap02Ax
FANNCAN, Thomas	22	M	Laborer	06Ap02Ax
DENMEY, James	17	M	Laborer	06Ap02Ax
CARROLL, Anne	17	F	Laborer	06Ap02Ax
Bridget	17	F	Laborer	06Ap02Ax
SMITH, Patrick	26	M	Laborer	06Ap02Ax
LOWED, Cormac	36	M	Laborer	06Ap02Ax
CARROLINE, Hugh	18	M	Laborer	06Ap02Ax
MALOWNEY, Mick	35	M	Laborer	06Ap02Ax
CONCIDINE, Mick	18	M	Laborer	06Ap02Ax
HAYES, William	44	M	Laborer	06Ap02Ax
BRADY, James	30	M	Laborer	06Ap02Ax
FEENAN, Thomas	20	M	Laborer	06Ap02Ax
CUDDY, Darby	30	M	Laborer	06Ap02Ax
RYAN, Patrick	22	M	Laborer	06Ap02Ax
CARMODY, John	20	M	Laborer	06Ap02Ax
CUMMES, Michael	27	M	Laborer	06Ap02Ax
WATERS, Patrick	27	M	Laborer	06Ap02Ax
MIDNEY, James	25	M	Laborer	06Ap02Ax
BRYAN, James	40	M	Laborer	06Ap02Ax
SHEA, Ellen	39	F	Laborer	06Ap02Ax
DOWNEY, Thos.	25	M	Laborer	06Ap02Ax
Mary	50	F	Laborer	06Ap02Ax
Johanna	18	F	Laborer	06Ap02Ax
John	14	M	Laborer	06Ap02Ax
LINDSAY, Esther-A.	20	F	Laborer	06Ap02Ax
Margaret	18	F	Laborer	06Ap02Ax
STAPLETON, Margaret	18	F	Laborer	06Ap02Ax
MCEWING, Bridget	40	F	Laborer	06Ap02Ax
TOMENING, Owen	36	M	Laborer	06Ap02Ax
MULLOY, James	41	M	Laborer	06Ap02Ax
COUISINS, Patrick	19	M	Laborer	06Ap02Ax
MURPHY, Thomas	20	M	Laborer	06Ap02Ax
LEYNARD, Peter	20	M	Laborer	06Ap02Ax
KEEFFEE, Patrick	20	M	Laborer	06Ap02Ax
FORD, Thomas	20	M	Laborer	06Ap02Ax
FAMIN, Martin	35	M	Laborer	06Ap02Ax
Sarah	27	F	Laborer	06Ap02Ax
U	.06	F	Infant	06Ap02Ax
Rose	09	F	Child	06Ap02Ax
FORD, Catherine	30	F	Laborer	06Ap02Ax
COLLINS, George	30	M	Laborer	06Ap02Ax
U-Mrs.	30	F	Laborer	06Ap02Ax
U	.04	M	Infant	06Ap02Ax
James	02	M	Child	06Ap02Ax
KELLY, Thomas	20	M	Laborer	06Ap02Ax
James	19	M	Laborer	06Ap02Ax
FORAN, Edward	24	M	Laborer	06Ap02Ax
FLOOD, Nicholas	20	M	Laborer	06Ap02Ax
BRENNAN, Catherine	20	F	Laborer	06Ap02Ax
GREENWOOD, Redmond	34	M	Laborer	06Ap02Ax
Anne	27	F	Laborer	06Ap02Ax
TOOLE, John	20	M	Laborer	06Ap02Ax
BYRNE, Patrick	24	M	Laborer	06Ap02Ax
FINNE, Thos.	20	M	Laborer	06Ap02Ax
FITZPATRICK, John	34	M	Laborer	06Ap02Ax
William	22	M	Laborer	06Ap02Ax
KENADY, Thomas	22	M	Laborer	06Ap02Ax
FORREST, Mary-Jane	20	F	Laborer	06Ap02Ax
MEGAHAN, Barny	23	M	Laborer	06Ap02Ax
JOHNSON, Barney	30	M	Laborer	06Ap02Ax
MCDONNAL, Thos.	20	M	Laborer	06Ap02Ax
LAWLER, John	20	M	Laborer	06Ap02Ax
DALY, Bridget	25	F	Laborer	06Ap02Ax
Bridget	24	F	Laborer	06Ap02Ax
Bryan	15	M	Laborer	06Ap02Ax
REID, Patrick	24	M	Laborer	06Ap02Ax
ELLIOTT, William	24	M	Laborer	06Ap02Ax
Joseph	17	M	Laborer	06Ap02Ax
HISLOP, Christy	27	M	Laborer	06Ap02Ax
BROWN, Fred	27	M	Laborer	06Ap02Ax
LEESON, Henry	21	M	Laborer	06Ap02Ax
COSTELLO, James	50	M	Laborer	06Ap02Ax
HENRY, Patrick	48	M	Laborer	06Ap02Ax
U (W)	47	F	Laborer	06Ap02Ax
John	30	M	Laborer	06Ap02Ax
James	20	M	Laborer	06Ap02Ax
Francis	19	M	Laborer	06Ap02Ax
Peter	17	M	Laborer	06Ap02Ax
HEYDON, John	46	M	Laborer	06Ap02Ax
Anne	40	F	Laborer	06Ap02Ax
Catherine	12	F	Laborer	06Ap02Ax
MCDERMOTT, John	09	M	Child	06Ap02Ax
HICKEY, William	34	M	Laborer	06Ap02Ax
WALSH, Catherine	34	F	Laborer	06Ap02Ax
TEVIN, James	19	M	Laborer	06Ap02Ax
William	17	M	Laborer	06Ap02Ax
KELLY, John	20	M	Laborer	06Ap02Ax
DAWSON, John	19	M	Laborer	06Ap02Ax
COYLE, Bryan	40	M	Laborer	06Ap02Ax
HALSTON, Anne	16	F	Laborer	06Ap02Ax
SWEENEY, Bridget	15	F	Laborer	06Ap02Ax
MCKAY, Edward	25	M	Laborer	06Ap02Ax
LONG, James	22	M	Laborer	06Ap02Ax
Richard	24	M	Laborer	06Ap02Ax
MCKAY, Betty	38	F	Laborer	06Ap02Ax
COSTELLO, Margaret	20	F	Laborer	06Ap02Ax
MURPHY, William	22	M	Laborer	06Ap02Ax
Ellen	22	F	Laborer	06Ap02Ax
Ellen	21	F	Laborer	06Ap02Ax
MONAGHAN, Ellen	21	F	Laborer	06Ap02Ax
LOGAN, Patrick	18	M	Laborer	06Ap02Ax
FARRELL, John	18	M	Laborer	06Ap02Ax
MCARDLE, Mick	18	M	Laborer	06Ap02Ax
SMITH, John	21	M	Laborer	06Ap02Ax
BANE, James	28	M	Laborer	06Ap02Ax
MCARDLE, Margaret	16	F	Laborer	06Ap02Ax
DOYLE, Daniel	21	M	Laborer	06Ap02Ax
MARKEY, Margaret	21	F	Laborer	06Ap02Ax
ARMSTRONG, George	49	M	Laborer	06Ap02Ax
HACKET, James	33	M	Laborer	06Ap02Ax
BUCKLEY, Thomas	38	M	Laborer	06Ap02Ax
SWEENEY, Patrick	32	M	Laborer	06Ap02Ax
TUCKER, Jamies	26	M	Laborer	06Ap02Ax
RYAN, Bridget	50	F	Laborer	06Ap02Ax
Catherine	25	F	Laborer	06Ap02Ax
CONROY, John	13	M	Laborer	06Ap02Ax
MCENERTRAY, Margaret	20	F	Laborer	06Ap02Ax
BEVIN, Bridget	23	M	Laborer	06Ap02Ax
HOWARD, Bridget	23	F	Laborer	06Ap02Ax
BURNE, Catherine	22	F	Laborer	06Ap02Ax
PAGE, Thos.	25	M	Laborer	06Ap02Ax
BROWN, Peter	25	M	Laborer	06Ap02Ax
CONROY, Mick	28	M	Laborer	06Ap02Ax
MAHONY, Ellen	20	F	Laborer	06Ap02Ax
BAMFIELD, Eliza	40	F	Laborer	06Ap02Ax
Anne	20	F	Laborer	06Ap02Ax
Margret	18	F	Laborer	06Ap02Ax
James	16	M	Laborer	06Ap02Ax
Eliza	14	F	Laborer	06Ap02Ax
CRATON, Dennis	30	M	Laborer	06Ap02Ax
CONDINE, Mick	51	M	Laborer	06Ap02Ax
MURRAY, James	47	M	Laborer	06Ap02Ax
CULL, James	25	M	Laborer	06Ap02Ax
BELL, Samuel	24	M	Laborer	06Ap02Ax
U (W)	24	F	Laborer	06Ap02Ax
SUNDERLAND, Ernest	28	M	Laborer	06Ap02Ax
WAKELEY, John	27	M	Laborer	06Ap02Ax
FITZPATRICK, Ellen	30	F	Laborer	06Ap02Ax
U	.07	F	Infant	06Ap02Ax
MCPARLANE, Patrick	40	M	Laborer	06Ap02Ax
BRADY, Patrick	27	M	Laborer	06Ap02Ax
Margaret	18	F	Laborer	06Ap02Ax
MCSHERRY, Thos.	30	M	Laborer	06Ap02Ax

NAMES OF PASSENGERS	AGE	SEX	OCCUPATIONS	DATE PORT SHIP
CLARK, Joseph	35	M	Laborer	06Ap02Ax
MURTAGH, William	46	M	Laborer	06Ap02Ax
Michael	20	M	Laborer	06Ap02Ax
Mick	18	M	Laborer	06Ap02Ax
Mary	44	F	Laborer	06Ap02Ax
BROPHY, Michael	18	M	Laborer	06Ap02Ax
Margaret	21	F	Laborer	06Ap02Ax
ROCKS, Mary	40	F	Laborer	06Ap02Ax
Dennis	17	M	Laborer	06Ap02Ax
Margaret	15	F	Laborer	06Ap02Ax
Anne	13	F	Laborer	06Ap02Ax
MCKINNA, Betty	30	F	Laborer	06Ap02Ax
U	.01	F	Infant	06Ap02Ax
Ellen	03	F	Child	06Ap02Ax
Anne	01	F	Child	06Ap02Ax
FARRELL, Martin	20	M	Laborer	06Ap02Ax
BURN, John	02	M	Child	06Ap02Ax
CUNNINGHAM, Mick	20	M	Laborer	06Ap02Ax
NANGLE, Peter	25	F	Laborer	06Ap02Ax
MURPHY, Thomas	25	F	Laborer	06Ap02Ax
U (W)	20	F	Laborer	06Ap02Ax
TEVIN, U-Mrs.	46	F	Laborer	06Ap02Ax
Anne	30	F	Laborer	06Ap02Ax
Martin	28	M	Laborer	06Ap02Ax
WILLIAMS, Samuel	36	M	Laborer	06Ap02Ax
FAGAN, Peter	24	M	Laborer	06Ap02Ax
TOOMY, Thos.	24	M	Laborer	06Ap02Ax
Anne	23	F	Laborer	06Ap02Ax
John	20	M	Laborer	06Ap02Ax
FAGAN, Anthony	22	M	Laborer	06Ap02Ax
ROONEY, Mary	23	F	Laborer	06Ap02Ax
CAHILL, James	23	M	Laborer	06Ap02Ax
BAKER, John	25	M	Laborer	06Ap02Ax

GEORGE-EVANS 06 APRIL 1849

From Liverpool

NAMES OF PASSENGERS	AGE	SEX	OCCUPATIONS	DATE PORT SHIP
HORDAN, Wm.	40	M	Farmer	06Ap02Ay
Jane	40	F	Unknown	06Ap02Ay
Wm.	11	M	Unknown	06Ap02Ay
Margt.	24	F	Unknown	06Ap02Ay
WALSH, Wm.	18	M	Unknown	06Ap02Ay
ANDRAHAM, Peggy	20	F	Unknown	06Ap02Ay
GROTTY, Ellen	22	F	Unknown	06Ap02Ay
MCGRATH, Cath.	20	F	Unknown	06Ap02Ay
DOOLEY, Jno.	20	M	Unknown	06Ap02Ay
U (W)	28	F	Unknown	06Ap02Ay
FARREL, Martin	20	M	Farmer	06Ap02Ay
PURCELL, Michl.	22	M	Farmer	06Ap02Ay
Pat	20	M	Unknown	06Ap02Ay
Mary	18	F	Unknown	06Ap02Ay
HERAGHAM, Pat	18	M	Unknown	06Ap02Ay
AMMAN, Margt.	20	F	Unknown	06Ap02Ay
KILFOYLE, Cath.	20	F	Unknown	06Ap02Ay
BROPHY, Margt.	20	F	Unknown	06Ap02Ay
MULLAN, Pat	25	M	Unknown	06Ap02Ay
Cath.	25	F	Unknown	06Ap02Ay
Jas.	.00	M	Infant	06Ap02Ay
MULLONEY, Edwd.	30	M	Laborer	06Ap02Ay
Mary	23	F	Laborer	06Ap02Ay
Julia	00	F	Child	06Ap02Ay
Dan	.00	M	Infant	06Ap02Ay
SALLOGHER, Mary	18	F	Unknown	06Ap02Ay
MCCARTY, Danl.	19	M	Farmer	06Ap02Ay
MADDEN, Jno.	26	M	Farmer	06Ap02Ay
DUFFY, Pat	18	M	Farmer	06Ap02Ay
KEEGAN, Jno.	26	M	Farmer	06Ap02Ay
MULLONEY, Eliza	18	F	Farmer	06Ap02Ay

NAMES OF PASSENGERS	AGE	SEX	OCCUPATIONS	DATE PORT SHIP
DOYLE, Betty	18	F	Farmer	06Ap02Ay
COLLINS, Cath.	04	F	Child	06Ap02Ay
Jno.	02	M	Child	06Ap02Ay
Jno.	.00	M	Infant	06Ap02Ay
MULLEN, James	35	M	Farmer	06Ap02Ay
Peggy	30	F	Farmer	06Ap02Ay
Mary	20	F	Farmer	06Ap02Ay
Pat	.00	M	Infant	06Ap02Ay
POWLER, Wm.	33	M	Tailor	06Ap02Ay
ATKINS, Richd.	24	M	Farmer	06Ap02Ay
ALLISON, Ann	60	F	Unknown	06Ap02Ay
WALSH, Robt.	35	M	Farmer	06Ap02Ay
PYNE, John	22	M	Farmer	06Ap02Ay
FOLEY, Margt.	20	F	Farmer	06Ap02Ay
Ellen	18	F	Farmer	06Ap02Ay
CARR, John	21	M	Weaver	06Ap02Ay
MCGRATH, Ben	21	M	Weaver	06Ap02Ay
SLOAN, Mary	20	F	Unknown	06Ap02Ay
KING, John	21	M	Farmer	06Ap02Ay
Mary	13	F	Farmer	06Ap02Ay
Ann	11	F	Farmer	06Ap02Ay
MURPHY, Mary	20	F	Farmer	06Ap02Ay
LYONS, Dan	20	M	Carpenter	06Ap02Ay
Ann	18	F	Unknown	06Ap02Ay
BRENNAN, Bridgt.	18	F	Unknown	06Ap02Ay
MCKERNAN, Cahat	25	F	Unknown	06Ap02Ay
Edwd.	19	M	Farmer	06Ap02Ay
RODDY, Mary	18	F	Unknown	06Ap02Ay
LEE, William	40	M	Farmer	06Ap02Ay
KELLY, John	25	M	Farmer	06Ap02Ay
Sarah	25	F	Unknown	06Ap02Ay
Law.	07	U	Child	06Ap02Ay
MCLOUGHLIN, Tom	25	M	Farmer	06Ap02Ay
NEVILL, Mick	30	M	Farmer	06Ap02Ay
BOYERS, Mick	30	M	Farmer	06Ap02Ay
Mary	34	F	Unknown	06Ap02Ay
SMITH, Martha	30	F	Unknown	06Ap02Ay
CARPENTER, Ann	40	F	Bomkr	06Ap02Ay
CRONAN, David	23	M	Blacksmith	06Ap02Ay
Ellen	25	F	Unknown	06Ap02Ay
COLLINS, Wm.	28	M	Farmer	06Ap02Ay
James	24	M	Farmer	06Ap02Ay
FERNSIDE, Nancy	23	F	Unknown	06Ap02Ay
Selia	19	F	Unknown	06Ap02Ay
James	08	M	Child	06Ap02Ay
Betset	43	F	Unknown	06Ap02Ay
Susan	.00	F	Infant	06Ap02Ay
SWAN, Pat	40	M	Farmer	06Ap02Ay
Biddy	16	F	Farmer	06Ap02Ay
MURRY, Mick	20	M	Farmer	06Ap02Ay
GORMAN, Mary	45	F	Unknown	06Ap02Ay
Cath.	16	F	Unknown	06Ap02Ay
Mick	20	M	Weaver	06Ap02Ay
Tiernan	12	M	Unknown	06Ap02Ay
Patt	.00	M	Infant	06Ap02Ay
HOWRAKER, Patt	25	M	Weaver	06Ap02Ay
VALE, Jno.	09	M	Child	06Ap02Ay
Cath.	04	F	Child	06Ap02Ay
BERRY, Jno.	20	M	Weaver	06Ap02Ay
HOWELL, Jno.	22	M	Farmer	06Ap02Ay
FOLEY, Pat	25	M	Farmer	06Ap02Ay
Tim	40	M	Farmer	06Ap02Ay
LACEY, Dan	30	M	Farmer	06Ap02Ay
SHANAGHER, John	50	M	Farmer	06Ap02Ay
James	26	M	Farmer	06Ap02Ay
CONNAR, James	06	M	Child	06Ap02Ay
SHANLEY, Mary-A.	16	F	Unknown	06Ap02Ay
STANFORD, Pat	20	M	Farmer	06Ap02Ay
Eliza	18	F	Unknown	06Ap02Ay
Brid.	12	F	Unknown	06Ap02Ay
MULLIGAN, Cath.	11	F	Unknown	06Ap02Ay
Ann	09	F	Child	06Ap02Ay
Pat	.00	M	Infant	06Ap02Ay
MADDEN, Bernard	16	M	Peddler	06Ap02Ay
DEVINE, Jno.	30	M	Farmer	06Ap02Ay

NAMES OF PASSENGERS	AGE	SEX	OCCUPATIONS	DATE PORT SHIP	NAMES OF PASSENGERS	AGE	SEX	OCCUPATIONS	DATE PORT SHIP
DEVINE, Margt.	25	F	Unknown	06Ap02Ay	CRONIN, John	10	M	Unknown	06Ap02Ay
CARROL, John	13	M	Farmer	06Ap02Ay	Michl.	08	M	Child	06Ap02Ay
COAKLEY, Dan	40	M	Farmer	06Ap02Ay	FERAGHTY, Mary	20	F	Unknown	06Ap02Ay
JOHNSTON, James	50	M	Farmer	06Ap02Ay	EGAN, Peter	09	M	Child	06Ap02Ay
KEEGAN, Mick	40	M	Farmer	06Ap02Ay	KENNEDY, Pat	30	M	Farmer	06Ap02Ay
STANTON, Mary	30	F	Farmer	06Ap02Ay	LOGAN, Michl.	28	M	Farmer	06Ap02Ay
LEPPARD, Thomas	28	M	Farmer	06Ap02Ay	Mary	27	F	Unknown	06Ap02Ay
BOYD, Jane	17	F	Farmer	06Ap02Ay	Eliza	03	F	Child	06Ap02Ay
MCANDREWS, John	20	M	Farmer	06Ap02Ay	WHALEN, Pat.O.	40	M	Farmer	06Ap02Ay
WALSH, Pat	15	M	Farmer	06Ap02Ay	WOODS, James	26	M	Farmer	06Ap02Ay
MOONEY, Pat	19	M	Farmer	06Ap02Ay	COCKS, Pat	40	M	Farmer	06Ap02Ay
Lucy	17	F	Unknown	06Ap02Ay	Pat	16	M	Farmer	06Ap02Ay
JORDAN, Thomas	18	M	Farmer	06Ap02Ay	Mary	18	F	Unknown	06Ap02Ay
NORA, Brid.	16	F	Farmer	06Ap02Ay	Cath.	11	F	Unknown	06Ap02Ay
CLARK, Owen	17	M	Farmer	06Ap02Ay	Margt.	09	F	Child	06Ap02Ay
Peter	16	M	Farmer	06Ap02Ay	Mary-A.	01	F	Child	06Ap02Ay
SARVAN, Mary	25	F	Unknown	06Ap02Ay	LENNAN, Brian	28	M	Blacksmith	06Ap02Ay
SMALL, Peter	23	M	Unknown	06Ap02Ay	DEVLIN, Michl.	24	M	Unknown	06Ap02Ay
GILLESPIE, Rebecca	30	F	Unknown	06Ap02Ay	Cath.	23	F	Unknown	06Ap02Ay
James	07	M	Child	06Ap02Ay	CARNAN, Peter	20	M	Tailor	06Ap02Ay
Peggy	05	F	Child	06Ap02Ay	GORAGAN, Eannl.	20	U	Unknown	06Ap02Ay
John	.00	M	Infant	06Ap02Ay	BRADDEN, Neil	26	M	Plasterer	06Ap02Ay
GOODWIN, James	18	M	Farmer	06Ap02Ay	MCGILL, Susan	00	F	Unknown	06Ap02Ay
JENNINGS, Catharine	20	F	Unknown	06Ap02Ay	HANNAN, James	30	M	Farmer	06Ap02Ay
HARRIS, John	20	M	Unknown	06Ap02Ay	MCGILL, Pat	35	M	Farmer	06Ap02Ay
MCCABE, Anne	34	F	Unknown	06Ap02Ay	HANNESLY, Michl.	23	M	Farmer	06Ap02Ay
Mary	36	F	Unknown	06Ap02Ay	BRISLEN, John	22	M	Farmer	06Ap02Ay
James	16	M	Farmer	06Ap02Ay	BLATE, Henry	25	M	Farmer	06Ap02Ay
Anne	12	F	Unknown	06Ap02Ay	U (W)	30	F	Unknown	06Ap02Ay
Bernd.	11	M	Unknown	06Ap02Ay	U	.00	U	Infant	06Ap02Ay
Mary	08	F	Child	06Ap02Ay	MCMANRA, Dennis	27	M	Farmer	06Ap02Ay
John	06	M	Child	06Ap02Ay	U (W)	20	F	Unknown	06Ap02Ay
Thomas	01	M	Child	06Ap02Ay	FLINN, Michl.	20	M	Farmer	06Ap02Ay
KENNEDY, James	17	M	Unknown	06Ap02Ay	John	.00	M	infant	06Ap02Ay
CROYRSUILE, Wm.	12	M	Unknown	06Ap02Ay	MOORE, David	35	M	Farmer	06Ap02Ay
BRADLEY, Name	18	U	Unknown	06Ap02Ay	U (W)	25	F	Unknown	06Ap02Ay
MULVESHALA, Julia	20	F	Unknown	06Ap02Ay	SLOAN, James	35	M	Farmer	06Ap02Ay
John	06	M	Child	06Ap02Ay	HAMILTON, James	30	M	Farmer	06Ap02Ay
DILLEN, Thomas	20	M	Weaver	06Ap02Ay	FLANICAN, Edwd.	16	M	Farmer	06Ap02Ay
Ann	17	F	Weaver	06Ap02Ay	Mary	25	F	Unknown	06Ap02Ay
COLLINS, Mick	00	M	Unknown	06Ap02Ay	Thomas	03	M	Child	06Ap02Ay
Mary	24	F	Unknown	06Ap02Ay	LEARY, Mary	20	F	Unknown	06Ap02Ay
LOWE, Saml.	16	M	Weaver	06Ap02Ay	MCMANNUS, Lucy	20	F	Unknown	06Ap02Ay
LEERY, Brid.	40	F	Carpenter	06Ap02Ay	MARTIN, Brigt.	20	F	Unknown	06Ap02Ay
MILLEN, Richd.	30	M	Tailor	06Ap02Ay	STANFORD, James	22	M	Unknown	06Ap02Ay
Michl.	25	M	Tailor	06Ap02Ay	FLINN, Julia	22	F	Unknown	06Ap02Ay
CONNELL, Dennis	20	M	Farmer	06Ap02Ay	CRAWFORD, Eliza	18	F	Unknown	06Ap02Ay
BURKE, Florence	20	F	Farmer	06Ap02Ay	GERAGHTY, Wm.	24	M	Unknown	06Ap02Ay
Mick	18	M	Farmer	06Ap02Ay	SPIELMAN, John	26	M	Unknown	06Ap02Ay
CARRIGAN, Wm.	22	M	Farmer	06Ap02Ay	Mary	26	F	Unknown	06Ap02Ay
Jas.	13	M	Farmer	06Ap02Ay	Peter	.00	M	Infant	06Ap02Ay
KELLY, Brigt.	26	F	Unknown	06Ap02Ay	CARBURY, Margt.	40	F	Unknown	06Ap02Ay
Pat	05	M	Child	06Ap02Ay	Betty	18	F	Unknown	06Ap02Ay
Maria	24	F	Unknown	06Ap02Ay	Lucy	14	F	Unknown	06Ap02Ay
SMITH, Michl.	18	M	Unknown	06Ap02Ay	Biddy	08	F	Child	06Ap02Ay
CANFIELD, Pat	36	M	Farmer	06Ap02Ay	RILEY, Mata.	37	U	Unknown	06Ap02Ay
Barney	13	M	Farmer	06Ap02Ay	MADDEN, Fergus	33	M	Unknown	06Ap02Ay
BIRNARD, Mary	37	F	Farmer	06Ap02Ay	BRYAN, John	50	M	Unknown	06Ap02Ay
Thomas	35	M	Unknown	06Ap02Ay	Cath.	58	F	Unknown	06Ap02Ay
Ellin	09	F	Child	06Ap02Ay	Michl.	22	M	Unknown	06Ap02Ay
Mary	06	F	Child	06Ap02Ay	Mary	12	F	Unknown	06Ap02Ay
MULLAN, Nancy	20	F	Schms	06Ap02Ay	Cath.	06	F	Child	06Ap02Ay
Alice	11	F	Unknown	06Ap02Ay	DESMOND, Pat	03	M	Child	06Ap02Ay
Rose	08	F	Child	06Ap02Ay	FOGARTY, Eliza	24	F	Unknown	06Ap02Ay
Jno.	05	M	Child	06Ap02Ay	KELLY, Edwd.	20	M	Unknown	06Ap02Ay
Bridgt.	03	F	Child	06Ap02Ay	DEMPSEY, Mary	16	F	Unknown	06Ap02Ay
MCGRATH, Alice	21	F	Unknown	06Ap02Ay	DELANEY, Margt.	30	F	Unknown	06Ap02Ay
CONNER, Pat	20	M	Nailer	06Ap02Ay	Brigt.	12	F	Unknown	06Ap02Ay
HAY, Mary	20	F	Unknown	06Ap02Ay	Brigt.	20	F	Unknown	06Ap02Ay
MURRAY, Brid.	60	F	Unknown	06Ap02Ay	BRYAN, Mary	26	F	Unknown	06Ap02Ay
Mary	23	F	Unknown	06Ap02Ay	KINNIS, Anne	22	F	Unknown	06Ap02Ay
Brid.	.00	F	Infant	06Ap02Ay	James	.00	M	Infant	06Ap02Ay
SMYTH, Mick	20	M	Unknown	06Ap02Ay	LEONARD, John	26	M	Unknown	06Ap02Ay
CONNOUGHTON, Pat	20	M	Farmer	06Ap02Ay	Mary	21	F	Unknown	06Ap02Ay
CRONIN, Brid.	12	F	Farmer	06Ap02Ay	HERROD, Thomas	30	M	Unknown	06Ap02Ay

GLEN 06 APRIL 1849

From Sligo

NAMES OF PASSENGERS	AGE	SEX	OCCUPATIONS	DATE PORT SHIP
HARAGHTY, P.	40	M	Farmer	06Ap21Az
CONNELL, O.	24	M	Unknown	06Ap21Az
FLYNN, Bgt.	26	F	Unknown	06Ap21Az
BARRETT, P.	19	U	Unknown	06Ap21Az
BARNES, M.	28	U	Unknown	06Ap21Az
GILMARTIN, J.	28	U	Unknown	06Ap21Az
Cath.	01	F	Child	06Ap21Az
Ann	13	F	None	06Ap21Az
WARREN, J.	43	M	Unknown	06Ap21Az
Cath.	11	F	None	06Ap21Az
Jane	09	F	Child	06Ap21Az
FEENY, J.	30	M	Unknown	06Ap21Az
KEEGHEAM, J.	30	M	Unknown	06Ap21Az
ROTCHFORT, Mgt.	23	F	None	06Ap21Az
FEELY, My.	28	F	None	06Ap21Az
GLEER, Ann-M.	30	F	None	06Ap21Az
ROVER, Bessy	19	F	None	06Ap21Az
GILGAN, L.	20	M	Unknown	06Ap21Az
GREEN, T.	19	M	Unknown	06Ap21Az
MCNIFF, M.	22	M	Unknown	06Ap21Az
Ann	19	F	None	06Ap21Az
MONAGHAN, J.	20	M	Unknown	06Ap21Az
HORAN, T.	19	M	Unknown	06Ap21Az
MCMANY, M.	22	M	Unknown	06Ap21Az
Peter	20	M	Unknown	06Ap21Az
GILGAN, P.	20	M	Unknown	06Ap21Az
DARCY, Cath.	20	F	None	06Ap21Az
HART, M.	23	M	Unknown	06Ap21Az
STEPHEN, M.	23	M	Unknown	06Ap21Az
BATTLE, Besse	17	F	None	06Ap21Az
My.	15	F	None	06Ap21Az
Thos.	12	M	None	06Ap21Az
John	16	M	Unknown	06Ap21Az
HART, Mgt.	13	F	None	06Ap21Az
Cath.	11	F	None	06Ap21Az
Domnick	09	M	Child	06Ap21Az
Ann	07	F	Child	06Ap21Az
OATS, P.	21	M	Unknown	06Ap21Az
WYNN, My.	15	F	None	06Ap21Az
LYNN, Bgt.	17	F	None	06Ap21Az
MONAGHAN, Bgt.	26	F	None	06Ap21Az
GALAGHER, J.	22	M	Unknown	06Ap21Az
Bgt.	20	F	None	06Ap21Az
Thos.	01	M	Child	06Ap21Az
MCPADDEN, D.	22	M	Laborer	06Ap21Az
GALLAGHER, My.	15	F	None	06Ap21Az
CLARKE, Sah.	18	F	None	06Ap21Az
SCANLAN, F.	28	M	Unknown	06Ap21Az
SLANE, D.	17	M	Unknown	06Ap21Az
Cath.	20	F	None	06Ap21Az
Eleanor	18	F	None	06Ap21Az
Prolok--, Bgt.	47	F	None	06Ap21Az
Anne	12	F	None	06Ap21Az
John	19	M	Unknown	06Ap21Az
BENENT, P.	20	M	Unknown	06Ap21Az
My.	24	F	None	06Ap21Az
Bgt.	18	F	None	06Ap21Az
Thos.	02	M	Child	06Ap21Az
MCKEE, W.	18	M	Unknown	06Ap21Az
COSSAN, Cath.	19	F	None	06Ap21Az
SMITH, Bgt.	18	F	None	06Ap21Az
ATKINSON, Mgt.	20	F	None	06Ap21Az
COLEMAN, Mgt.	15	F	None	06Ap21Az
John	22	M	Unknown	06Ap21Az
WALSH, B.	36	M	Unknown	06Ap21Az
PRESTON, J.	35	M	Unknown	06Ap21Az
KENNY, W.	17	M	Unknown	06Ap21Az
IRWIN, A.	25	M	Unknown	06Ap21Az
SAVAGE, Rose	20	F	None	06Ap21Az
Roger	30	M	Unknown	06Ap21Az
MULLONY, My.	30	F	None	06Ap21Az
CAWLY, M.	21	M	Unknown	06Ap21Az
DEMPSEY, M.	21	M	Unknown	06Ap21Az
Pat	20	M	Unknown	06Ap21Az
CAWLY, Bgt.	18	F	None	06Ap21Az
DEMPSEY, My.	24	F	None	06Ap21Az
MELVIN, T.	26	M	Unknown	06Ap21Az
Bgt.	26	F	None	06Ap21Az
Mich.	03	M	Child	06Ap21Az
My.	01	F	Child	06Ap21Az
HILL, C.	25	M	Unknown	06Ap21Az
Mgt.	18	F	None	06Ap21Az
FEENEY, Bgt.	24	F	None	06Ap21Az
OHARA, J.	40	M	Laborer	06Ap21Az
CALLEN, J.	30	M	Laborer	06Ap21Az
GALLAGHER, A.	35	M	Laborer	06Ap21Az
My.	16	F	None	06Ap21Az
Bgt.	11	F	None	06Ap21Az
CASSIDY, B.	24	M	Unknown	06Ap21Az
HENGER, Lucy	20	F	None	06Ap21Az
Cath.	24	F	None	06Ap21Az
CAREY, D.	23	M	Unknown	06Ap21Az
MCGRATH, M.	25	M	Unknown	06Ap21Az
MORON, P.	20	M	Unknown	06Ap21Az
Judith	18	F	None	06Ap21Az
GALLAGHER, Elen	16	F	None	06Ap21Az
MANN, M.	01	F	None	06Ap21Az
MCGAN, Eleanor	30	F	None	06Ap21Az
KENNY, J.	35	M	Unknown	06Ap21Az
OBEIRNE, T.	24	M	Unknown	06Ap21Az
Bgt.	43	F	None	06Ap21Az
COARE, P.	27	M	Unknown	06Ap21Az
My.	27	F	None	06Ap21Az
Mich.	03	M	Child	06Ap21Az
MCGRATH, Bgt.	17	F	None	06Ap21Az
MCGLEEN, W.	33	M	Unknown	06Ap21Az
FLYNN, J.	28	M	Unknown	06Ap21Az
Bgt.	20	F	None	06Ap21Az
Bgt.	01	F	Child	06Ap21Az
MCGLEEN, Rose	16	F	None	06Ap21Az
DONLAN, M.	19	M	Unknown	06Ap21Az
Luke	18	M	Unknown	06Ap21Az
Mgt.	17	F	None	06Ap21Az
HOWE, R.	23	M	Unknown	06Ap21Az
My.	23	F	None	06Ap21Az
Wm.	01	M	Child	06Ap21Az
OHARA, J.	24	M	Unknown	06Ap21Az
ATKINSON, J.	22	M	Unknown	06Ap21Az
FLYNN, T.	20	M	Unknown	06Ap21Az
FRANCES, Mgt.	25	F	None	06Ap21Az
CONLAN, J.	30	M	Unknown	06Ap21Az
Mgt.	25	F	None	06Ap21Az
BLACK, J.	55	M	Unknown	06Ap21Az
Jane	52	F	None	06Ap21Az
R.	22	M	Laborer	06Ap21Az
Jane	18	F	None	06Ap21Az
Thos.	14	M	Unknown	06Ap21Az
Mgt.	10	F	None	06Ap21Az
Wm.	09	M	Child	06Ap21Az
Gustavus	07	M	Child	06Ap21Az
John	20	M	Unknown	06Ap21Az
OBRIEN, My.	20	F	None	06Ap21Az
FLYNN, J.	34	M	Unknown	06Ap21Az
GANTY, P.	30	M	Unknown	06Ap21Az
FADDEN, J.	29	M	Unknown	06Ap21Az
Emma	29	F	None	06Ap21Az
HENDERSON, J.	18	M	Unknown	06Ap21Az
Anna	15	F	None	06Ap21Az
KELLES, Cath.	20	F	Unknown	06Ap21Az
SMITH, Sarah	14	F	Unknown	06Ap21Az

NAMES OF PASSENGERS	AGE	SEX	OCCUPATIONS	DATE PORT SHIP
BYRNE, Thomas	5	M	Child	06Ap02Ba
Margt.	6	F	Child	06Ap02Ba
CANERTY, Patrick	48	M	Laborer	06Ap02Ba
FITZGERALD, John	28	M	Farmer	06Ap02Ba
CANNAN, John	40	M	Laborer	06Ap02Ba
SULIVAN, Thomas	35	M	Laborer	06Ap02Ba
CANNAN, Margaret	28	F	Dairymaid	06Ap02Ba
BREAN, Kitty	24	F	Dressmaker	06Ap02Ba
MCCARTY, James	30	M	Laborer	06Ap02Ba
HENEBURY, John	23	M	Bricklayer	06Ap02Ba

SARAH-AND-LOUISA 06 APRIL 1849

From Liverpool

NAMES OF PASSENGERS	AGE	SEX	OCCUPATIONS	DATE PORT SHIP
HASSETT, John	30	M	Laborer	06Ap02Ba
U-Mrs.	25	F	Housekeeper	06Ap02Ba
Mary	4	F	Child	06Ap02Ba
Patrick	3	M	Child	06Ap02Ba
Ellen	2	F	Child	06Ap02Ba
KILMARTIN, Patrick	30	M	Laborer	06Ap02Ba
CARRIGG, Elizy	23	F	Dressmaker	06Ap02Ba
CORNELL, Wm.	22	M	Laborer	06Ap02Ba
HUBBARD, John	63	M	Laborer	06Ap02Ba
Catherine	32	F	Housekeeper	06Ap02Ba
Ellen	21	F	Housekeeper	06Ap02Ba
Catherine	15	F	Housekeeper	06Ap02Ba
GALVIN, Patrick	3	M	Child	06Ap02Ba
Johanna	26	F	Lady'S Maid	06Ap02Ba
MARTIN, Mary	36	F	Lad	06Ap02Ba
James	2	M	Child	06Ap02Ba
Ellen	4	F	Child	06Ap02Ba
Michael	6	M	Child	06Ap02Ba
DONOHUE, Philip	52	M	Farmer	06Ap02Ba
Mary	53	F	Lad	06Ap02Ba
Patrick	20	M	Laborer	06Ap02Ba
Rose	12	F	House Maid	06Ap02Ba
Ann	10	F	House Maid	06Ap02Ba
KANE, Thomas	72	M	Laborer	06Ap02Ba
Andrew	19	M	Laborer	06Ap02Ba
LARKIN, John	50	M	Laborer	06Ap02Ba
Mary	60	F	Lad	06Ap02Ba
James	20	M	Laborer	06Ap02Ba
Philip	12	M	Laborer	06Ap02Ba
GRAHAM, Patrick	33	M	Baker	06Ap02Ba
TULLY, Andrew	20	M	Laborer	06Ap02Ba
Wm.	17	M	Laborer	06Ap02Ba
Patrick	16	M	Laborer	06Ap02Ba
Margt.	14	F	Knitter	06Ap02Ba
CAFFREY, Maria	20	F	House Maid	06Ap02Ba
MCATEE, Edward	40	M	Laborer	06Ap02Ba
Mary	7	F	Laborer	06Ap02Ba
CUNNIFF, Winny	14	F	Domestic	06Ap02Ba
MCMULLAN, Danl.	54	M	Laborer	06Ap02Ba
CARTON, John	22	M	Laborer	06Ap02Ba
John	22	M	Laborer	06Ap02Ba
WELCH, Bridget	50	F	Housekeeper	06Ap02Ba
FANNING, Thomas	35	M	Servant	06Ap02Ba
MAKER, Eliza	25	F	Dressmaker	06Ap02Ba
HANEGAN, Thomas	33	M	Laborer	06Ap02Ba
Mary	28	F	Housekeeper	06Ap02Ba
NEAL, Peggy	25	F	Housekeeper	06Ap02Ba
COSTELLO, Dennis	40	M	Laborer	06Ap02Ba
Ellen	30	F	Housekeeper	06Ap02Ba
Dennis	5	M	Child	06Ap02Ba
Mary	3	F	Child	06Ap02Ba
John	.10	M	Infant	06Ap02Ba
CARY, Patrick	30	M	Laborer	06Ap02Ba
Ellen	25	F	Lad	06Ap02Ba
Ellen	.08	F	Infant	06Ap02Ba
POWER, Deglan	25	M	Laborer	06Ap02Ba
BRYAN, Ellen	25	F	House Maid	06Ap02Ba
CREAVY, John	20	M	Laborer	06Ap02Ba
HAYES, Michael	20	M	Laborer	06Ap02Ba
HUBERT, Catherine	24	F	House Maid	06Ap02Ba
MOONEY, James	30	M	Laborer	06Ap02Ba
KEAN, Patrick	24	M	Farmer	06Ap02Ba
Johanna	22	F	Housekeeper	06Ap02Ba
BYRNE, Michael	40	M	Farmer	06Ap02Ba
Biddy	30	F	Housekeeper	06Ap02Ba
KEAN, Wm.	40	M	Farmer	06Ap02Ba
Julia	16	F	Servant	06Ap02Ba
Mary	15	F	Servant	06Ap02Ba
CAHALIN, Mary	20	F	Dairymaid	06Ap02Ba
MCKERNAN, Thomas	22	M	Schm	06Ap02Ba
DONOHUE, Judy	12	F	Servant	06Ap02Ba
WELCH, Thomas	30	M	Laborer	06Ap02Ba
Nelly	30	F	Tailor	06Ap02Ba
MERRICKS, Mary	27	F	Housekeeper	06Ap02Ba
GLENN, Patrick	25	M	Laborer	06Ap02Ba
DOYLE, John	23	M	Servant	06Ap02Ba
HOGARTY, Peter	24	M	Laborer	06Ap02Ba
Died-At-Sea				
DONOHUE, Thomas	24	M	Laborer	06Ap02Ba
KELLY, Edward	30	M	Farmer	06Ap02Ba
POWER, Thomas	30	M	Laborer	06Ap02Ba
BYRNE, Wm.	27	M	Laborer	06Ap02Ba
CUNNAN, Patrick	19	M	Laborer	06Ap02Ba
TAVILAN, Catherine	20	F	Housekeeper	06Ap02Ba
MORAN, John	24	M	Flaxdr	06Ap02Ba
Michael	23	M	Laborer	06Ap02Ba
Brien	20	M	Laborer	06Ap02Ba
OBRIEN, John	20	M	Farmer	06Ap02Ba
John	23	M	Farmer	06Ap02Ba
Terence	20	M	Farmer	06Ap02Ba
BLAIN, Oliver	31	M	Farmer	06Ap02Ba
FLEMING, U-Mrs.	26	F	Housekeeper	06Ap02Ba
James	30	M	Laborer	06Ap02Ba
Michael	.09	M	Infant	06Ap02Ba
BEDDIN, Maurice	30	M	Farmer	06Ap02Ba
Eliza	30	F	Housekeeper	06Ap02Ba
MORRICY, John	25	M	Laborer	06Ap02Ba
HARRINGTON, James	21	M	Laborer	06Ap02Ba
LAWTON, John	50	M	Laborer	06Ap02Ba
Margaret	50	F	Housekeeper	06Ap02Ba
Thomas	20	M	Laborer	06Ap02Ba
Margt.	16	F	Servant	06Ap02Ba
Mary	13	F	Servant	06Ap02Ba
Eliza	9	F	Servant	06Ap02Ba
SIGNON, Robt.	22	M	Stctr	06Ap02Ba
Sarah	21	F	Dressmaker	06Ap02Ba
ANGLIN, Margt.	20	F	House Maid	06Ap02Ba
HOGAN, Margt.	16	F	House Maid	06Ap02Ba
CRANN, Pierce	20	M	Ploughman	06Ap02Ba
Bridget	14	F	Servant	06Ap02Ba
Michael	30	M	Grocer	06Ap02Ba
Edward	27	M	Servant	06Ap02Ba
Alice	25	F	Servant	06Ap02Ba
LUCY, Julia	17	F	Servant	06Ap02Ba
Ellen	30	F	Servant	06Ap02Ba
CALLAGAN, Michael	32	M	Laborer	06Ap02Ba
Johanna	26	F	Servant	06Ap02Ba
LYNCH, Mary	19	F	Servant	06Ap02Ba
HOBBARD, John	12	M	Servant	06Ap02Ba
PIERSON, Ellen	20	F	Servant	06Ap02Ba
PLUNKET, Mary	40	F	Dressmaker	06Ap02Ba
NELSON, James	22	M	Laborer	06Ap02Ba
Mary	18	F	Servant	06Ap02Ba
WADE, Brien	36	M	Laborer	06Ap02Ba
Mary	16	F	Servant	06Ap02Ba
FITZGERALD, John	34	M	Farmer	06Ap02Ba
Catherine	27	F	Housekeeper	06Ap02Ba
Bridget	.06	F	Infant	06Ap02Ba
DOHERTY, Edward	35	M	Laborer	06Ap02Ba
Bridget	24	F	Housekeeper	06Ap02Ba

NAMES OF PASSENGERS	AGE	SEX	OCCUPATIONS	DATE PORT SHIP
DOHERTY, Mary	.00	F	Infant	06Ap02Ba
SHELLY, Thomas	23	M	Laborer	06Ap02Ba
Mary	30	F	Dairymaid	06Ap02Ba
Margt.	.08	F	Infant	06Ap02Ba
Mary	20	F	Dairymaid	06Ap02Ba
FOY, Judy	26	F	Housekeeper	06Ap02Ba
DOHERTY, John	27	M	Shoemaker	06Ap02Ba
FERRIGAN, Patrick	26	M	Laborer	06Ap02Ba
U-Mrs.	21	F	House Maid	06Ap02Ba
CROWLEY, Eliza	22	F	House Maid	06Ap02Ba
COMMERFER, Bridget	20	F	House Maid	06Ap02Ba
MCCOWLEY, Lawrence	23	M	Stone Mason	06Ap02Ba
HOGAN, Thomas	30	M	Stone Mason	06Ap02Ba
RYAN, Lawrence	27	M	Laborer	06Ap02Ba
FERRELL, Catherine	60	F	Housekeeper	06Ap02Ba
CONOWAY, Ester	19	F	Housekeeper	06Ap02Ba
BURKE, Michael	22	M	Laborer	06Ap02Ba
Patrick	20	M	Laborer	06Ap02Ba
CRAWFORD, Mary	18	F	House Maid	06Ap02Ba
HICKEY, Mary	18	F	House Maid	06Ap02Ba
GILLMON, John	48	M	Farmer	06Ap02Ba
FERRELL, Catherine	17	F	Servant	06Ap02Ba
KELLY, Thomas	18	M	Laborer	06Ap02Ba
John	2	M	Laborer	06Ap02Ba
BRADY, Hugh	27	M	Laborer	06Ap02Ba
U-Mrs.	30	F	Housekeeper	06Ap02Ba
Margt.	19	F	House Maid	06Ap02Ba
James	8	M	Child	06Ap02Ba
Mary	5	F	Child	06Ap02Ba
Died-At-Sea				
Owen	3	M	Child	06Ap02Ba
Died-At-Sea				
Ann	.00	F	Infant	06Ap02Ba
MORAN, John	40	M	Flaxdr	06Ap02Ba
WHALEN, Margaret	19	F	Dressmaker	06Ap02Ba
KELLEY, John	30	M	Farmer	06Ap02Ba
U-Mrs.	31	F	Housekeeper	06Ap02Ba
Christopher	2	M	Child	06Ap02Ba
BRIEN, John	29	M	Farmer	06Ap02Ba
GILLESPY, Margaret	40	F	Housekeeper	06Ap02Ba
Hugh	17	M	Laborer	06Ap02Ba
Michael	16	M	Laborer	06Ap02Ba
Bridget	13	F	Servant	06Ap02Ba
Ellen	9	F	Servant	06Ap02Ba
MCCURLAN, Margt.	20	F	Housekeeper	06Ap02Ba
Honour-Emily	19	F	Housekeeper	06Ap02Ba
PHILIPS, James	28	M	Laborer	06Ap02Ba
JORDAN, John	26	M	Laborer	06Ap02Ba
FOY, Patrick	30	M	Laborer	06Ap02Ba
HURDLEY, Peter	20	M	Laborer	06Ap02Ba
MCDONALD, Michael	19	M	Laborer	06Ap02Ba
MURPHY, Michael	18	M	Laborer	06Ap02Ba
MORAN, Mary	17	F	Servant	06Ap02Ba
GLINS, Patrick	40	M	Laborer	06Ap02Ba
Michael	20	M	Laborer	06Ap02Ba
BRADY, Danl.	20	M	Laborer	06Ap02Ba
William	20	M	Laborer	06Ap02Ba
HAYS, Alexander	29	M	Farmer	06Ap02Ba
Ann	29	F	House Maid	06Ap02Ba
Mary-Jane	6	F	Child	06Ap02Ba
Harriet	.06	F	Infant	06Ap02Ba
HOGAN, Betty	27	F	Servant	06Ap02Ba
KERWAN, James	24	M	Laborer	06Ap02Ba
HAGARTY, Thomas	24	M	Laborer	06Ap02Ba
Wm.	44	M	Laborer	06Ap02Ba
FERNEY, U-Mrs.	30	F	Housekeeper	06Ap02Ba
Wm.	30	M	Laborer	06Ap02Ba
Bridget	6	F	Child	06Ap02Ba
Thomas	5	M	Child	06Ap02Ba
John	2	M	Child	06Ap02Ba
Catherine	.00	F	Infant	06Ap02Ba
HICKEY, John	27	M	Laborer	06Ap02Ba
CALAGAN, Michael	28	M	Laborer	06Ap02Ba
John	22	M	Laborer	06Ap02Ba
FLING, Brien	20	M	Unknown	06Ap02Ba

L.Z. 06 APRIL 1849

From Liverpool

NAMES OF PASSENGERS	AGE	SEX	OCCUPATIONS	DATE PORT SHIP
FLANARY, Pat	21	M	Laborer	06Ap02Bb
EARLY, Pat	20	M	Laborer	06Ap02Bb
KILERIN, William	30	M	Laborer	06Ap02Bb
Pat	17	M	Laborer	06Ap02Bb
Martha	11	F	Laborer	06Ap02Bb
NANGLE, Edward	26	M	Cbtmkr	06Ap02Bb
MCDERMOTT, Michael	26	M	Cbtmkr	06Ap02Bb
CARROLL, Patrick	40	M	Laborer	06Ap02Bb
James	10	M	Laborer	06Ap02Bb
CUMMINGS, Thomas	20	M	Laborer	06Ap02Bb
RILEY, Owen	20	M	Laborer	06Ap02Bb
DARLEY, Mary	22	F	Servant	06Ap02Bb
Alice	19	F	Servant	06Ap02Bb
FARRELLY, Phillip	30	M	Laborer	06Ap02Bb
Catharine	26	F	Servant	06Ap02Bb
Catharine	.06	F	Infant	06Ap02Bb
TENNELL, Catharine	25	F	Servant	06Ap02Bb
RYAN, Pat	35	M	Laborer	06Ap02Bb
Nicholas	21	M	Laborer	06Ap02Bb
CASEY, Margarett	15	F	Servant	06Ap02Bb
Ann	13	F	Servant	06Ap02Bb
Bridget	13	F	Servant	06Ap02Bb
Mary	12	F	Servant	06Ap02Bb
William	7	M	Child	06Ap02Bb
GOLAHER, Mary	22	F	Laborer	06Ap02Bb
Pat	19	M	Laborer	06Ap02Bb
William	10	M	Laborer	06Ap02Bb
WILLIAMS, Pat	25	M	Tanner	06Ap02Bb
LEGGITT, Ann	24	F	Servant	06Ap02Bb
MADDAN, Bridget	29	F	Servant	06Ap02Bb
LAWLESS, Catherine	14	F	Servant	06Ap02Bb
Honora	14	F	Servant	06Ap02Bb
MCCUE, Thomas	25	M	Laborer	06Ap02Bb
FARRELL, Feargus	21	M	Farmer	06Ap02Bb
Margt.	16	F	Servant	06Ap02Bb
REYNOLDS, Maria	16	F	Servant	06Ap02Bb
MONAHAN, Pat	30	M	Laborer	06Ap02Bb
MCALOONS, Wm.	21	M	Laborer	06Ap02Bb
SMITH, Pat	19	M	Laborer	06Ap02Bb
GARRIGAN, Mary	26	F	Servant	06Ap02Bb
TUITE, Alice	22	F	Servant	06Ap02Bb
Mary	30	F	Servant	06Ap02Bb
SMITH, Ann	18	F	Servant	06Ap02Bb
Elizabeth	00	F	Servant	06Ap02Bb
RILLY, James	00	M	Laborer	06Ap02Bb
FOX, Bridget	6	F	Child	06Ap02Bb
James	2	M	Child	06Ap02Bb
Catharine	.02	F	Infant	06Ap02Bb
RILLEY, Margt.	20	F	Servant	06Ap02Bb
KUGHLAHER, Catharine	20	F	Servant	06Ap02Bb
MURTAGH, Peter	25	M	Laborer	06Ap02Bb
Elizabeth	23	F	Servant	06Ap02Bb
MURRAY, Honora	30	F	Servant	06Ap02Bb
FINEGAN, James	25	M	Laborer	06Ap02Bb
Simon	45	M	Laborer	06Ap02Bb
BRIEN, Pat	45	M	Laborer	06Ap02Bb
MCGRATH, Pat	28	M	Farmer	06Ap02Bb
CRONAN, Denis	21	M	Farmer	06Ap02Bb
HOOLEHAN, Pat	22	M	Farmer	06Ap02Bb
RILLEY, Michael	22	M	Farmer	06Ap02Bb
HAGAN, James	24	M	Farmer	06Ap02Bb
John	22	M	Farmer	06Ap02Bb
MCGUNN, Pat	21	M	Laborer	06Ap02Bb
SHANNON, William	26	M	Laborer	06Ap02Bb
Susan	24	F	Servant	06Ap02Bb

NAMES OF PASSENGERS	AGE	SEX	OCCUPATIONS	DATE PORT SHIP
HUGHES, Biddy	19	F	Servant	06Ap02Bb
MORETON, Delia	13	F	Servant	06Ap02Bb
MAHON, Honora	20	F	Servant	06Ap02Bb
Ann	22	F	Servant	06Ap02Bb
MCDONNELL, Michael	14	M	Laborer	06Ap02Bb
LYNCH, Ann	20	F	Servant	06Ap02Bb
Margt.	21	F	Servant	06Ap02Bb
MURPHY, Michael	24	M	Laborer	06Ap02Bb
DOULAN, James	40	M	Laborer	06Ap02Bb
Ellen	20	F	Seamstress	06Ap02Bb
Michael	3	M	Child	06Ap02Bb
MASTERSON, Mary	17	F	Servant	06Ap02Bb
DUNNE, Mary	25	F	Servant	06Ap02Bb
URELL, Pat	20	M	Laborer	06Ap02Bb
HOY, Judy	25	F	Servant	06Ap02Bb
FARRELLY, Ann	20	F	Servant	06Ap02Bb
TYGHE, Condy	30	M	Laborer	06Ap02Bb
DAGHERTY, Pat	35	M	Laborer	06Ap02Bb
FIELDING, Ann	34	F	Servant	06Ap02Bb
MERRY, John	35	M	Farmer	06Ap02Bb
Mary	30	F	Seamstress	06Ap02Bb
Catharine	12	F	Seamstress	06Ap02Bb
Mary	9	F	Child	06Ap02Bb
Patrick	7	M	Child	06Ap02Bb
Honora	3	F	Child	06Ap02Bb
Alice	2	F	Child	06Ap02Bb
Eustacia	13	U	Laborer	06Ap02Bb
Bridget	.09	F	Infant	06Ap02Bb
HOULEHAN, Magt.	25	F	Servant	06Ap02Bb
KAYE, Robert	30	M	Laborer	06Ap02Bb
TINNELLY, Pat	24	M	Farmer	06Ap02Bb
FAHEY, Thomas	21	M	Farmer	06Ap02Bb
LEONARD, Hugh	21	M	Farmer	06Ap02Bb
Cathe.	21	F	Dressmaker	06Ap02Bb
MCGUIRE, Mary	21	F	Dressmaker	06Ap02Bb
MCBURNEY, James	18	M	Farmer	06Ap02Bb
STANFIELDS, William	16	M	Farmer	06Ap02Bb
HAUGH, Sarah	26	F	Dressmaker	06Ap02Bb
KAY, Richard	20	M	Servant	06Ap02Bb
BOYD, Lettie	20	F	Servant	06Ap02Bb
MORGAN, Rose	24	F	Servant	06Ap02Bb
ROONEY, Mary	24	F	Servant	06Ap02Bb
MARTIN, Mary-Jane	22	F	Bomkr	06Ap02Bb
MCQUADE, John	22	M	Farmer	06Ap02Bb
Pat	40	M	Farmer	06Ap02Bb
MCCORMICK, Pat	40	M	Farmer	06Ap02Bb
KANE, Cathe.	21	F	Servant	06Ap02Bb
RILLEY, Cathe.	40	F	Seamstress	06Ap02Bb
MCGOWAN, Magat.	18	F	Servant	06Ap02Bb
GANNON, Mary	20	F	Servant	06Ap02Bb
MCGUINESS, Bridget	19	F	Laborer	06Ap02Bb
MARKEY, Ann	22	F	Servant	06Ap02Bb
KERN, Pierce	43	M	Laborer	06Ap02Bb
KEENAN, Grace	43	F	Servant	06Ap02Bb
DORAN, Thomas	34	M	Laborer	06Ap02Bb
KEEVANS, Mary	15	F	Servant	06Ap02Bb
TOOHILL, Johanna	21	F	Servant	06Ap02Bb
OBRIEN, Daniel	26	M	Laborer	06Ap02Bb
ROURKE, Mary	10	F	Servant	06Ap02Bb
MCCARTHY, Charles	14	M	Clerk	06Ap02Bb
BRADY, Margt.	16	F	Servant	06Ap02Bb
FLANARY, Pat	21	M	Laborer	06Ap02Bb
EARLY, Pat	20	M	Laborer	06Ap02Bb
KILERIE, William	30	M	Laborer	06Ap02Bb
Pat	17	M	Laborer	06Ap02Bb
Martha	11	F	Laborer	06Ap02Bb
NAUGLE, Edward	26	M	Cbtmkr	06Ap02Bb
MCDOMIOTT, Michael	26	M	Cbtmkr	06Ap02Bb
CARROLL, Patrick	40	M	Laborer	06Ap02Bb
James	10	M	Laborer	06Ap02Bb
CUMMINGS, Thomas	20	M	Laborer	06Ap02Bb
RILEY, Owen	20	M	Laborer	06Ap02Bb
DARLEY, Mary	22	F	Servant	06Ap02Bb
Alice	19	F	Servant	06Ap02Bb
FARRELLY, Phillip	30	M	Laborer	06Ap02Bb
FARRELLY, Catharine	26	F	Servant	06Ap02Bb
Catharine	.06	F	Infant	06Ap02Bb
TENNELL, Catharine	25	F	Servant	06Ap02Bb
RYAN, Pat	35	M	Laborer	06Ap02Bb
Nicholas	21	M	Laborer	06Ap02Bb
CASEY, Margarette	15	F	Servant	06Ap02Bb
Ann	13	F	Servant	06Ap02Bb
Bridget	13	F	Servant	06Ap02Bb
Mary	12	F	Servant	06Ap02Bb
William	07	M	Child	06Ap02Bb
GOLAHER, Mary	22	F	Laborer	06Ap02Bb
Pat	19	M	Laborer	06Ap02Bb
William	10	M	Laborer	06Ap02Bb
WILLIAMS, Pat	25	M	Tanner	06Ap02Bb
LEGITT, Ann	24	F	Servant	06Ap02Bb
MADDAN, Bridget	29	F	Servant	06Ap02Bb
LAWBELL, Catherine	19	F	Servant	06Ap02Bb
Honora	14	F	Servant	06Ap02Bb
MCCUE, Thomas	25	M	Laborer	06Ap02Bb
FARRELL, Feargus	21	M	Farmer	06Ap02Bb
Margt.	16	F	Servant	06Ap02Bb
REYNOLDS, Maria	16	F	Servant	06Ap02Bb
MONAHAN, Pat	30	M	Laborer	06Ap02Bb
MCALOOUS, Wm.	21	M	Laborer	06Ap02Bb
SMITH, Pat	19	M	Laborer	06Ap02Bb
GARIGAN, Mary	26	F	Servant	06Ap02Bb
TUITE, Alice	22	F	Servant	06Ap02Bb
Mary	30	F	Servant	06Ap02Bb
SMITH, Ann	18	F	Servant	06Ap02Bb
Elizabeth	00	F	Servant	06Ap02Bb
RILLY, James	00	M	Laborer	06Ap02Bb
FOX, Bridget	06	F	Child	06Ap02Bb
James	02	M	Child	06Ap02Bb
Catharine	.02	F	Infant	06Ap02Bb
RILLEY, Magt.	20	F	Servant	06Ap02Bb
BRADY, Magt.	16	F	Servant	06Ap02Bb
KUGHLAHER, Catharine	20	F	Servant	06Ap02Bb
MURTAGH, Peter	25	M	Laborer	06Ap02Bb
Elizabeth	23	F	Servant	06Ap02Bb
MURRAY, Honora	30	F	Servant	06Ap02Bb
FINEGAN, James	25	M	Laborer	06Ap02Bb
Simon	45	M	Laborer	06Ap02Bb
BRIEN, Pat	45	M	Laborer	06Ap02Bb
MCGRATH, Pat	28	M	Farmer	06Ap02Bb
CRONAN, Denis	21	M	Farmer	06Ap02Bb
HOOLEHAN, Pat	22	M	Farmer	06Ap02Bb
RILEEY, Michael	22	M	Farmer	06Ap02Bb
HUGAN, James	24	M	Farmer	06Ap02Bb
John	22	M	Farmer	06Ap02Bb
MCGAUN, Pat	21	M	Laborer	06Ap02Bb
SHAMON, William	26	M	Laborer	06Ap02Bb
Susan	24	F	Servant	06Ap02Bb
HUGHES, Biddy	19	F	Servant	06Ap02Bb
MORETON, Delia	13	F	Servant	06Ap02Bb
MAHON, Honora	20	F	Servant	06Ap02Bb
Ann	22	F	Servant	06Ap02Bb
MCDONNELL, Michael	14	M	Laborer	06Ap02Bb
LYNCH, Ann	20	F	Servant	06Ap02Bb
Magt.	21	F	Servant	06Ap02Bb
MURPHY, Michael	24	M	Laborer	06Ap02Bb
DOULAN, James	40	M	Laborer	06Ap02Bb
Ellen	30	F	Seamstress	06Ap02Bb
Michael	03	M	Child	06Ap02Bb
MASTERSON, Mary	17	F	Servant	06Ap02Bb
DUNNE, Mary	25	F	Servant	06Ap02Bb
WRELL, Pat	20	M	Laborer	06Ap02Bb
HOY, Judy	25	F	Servant	06Ap02Bb
FARRELLY, Ann	20	F	Servant	06Ap02Bb
TYGHE, Condy	30	M	Laborer	06Ap02Bb
DAGHERTY, Pat	35	M	Laborer	06Ap02Bb
FIELDING, Ann	34	F	Servant	06Ap02Bb
MERRY, John	35	M	Farmer	06Ap02Bb
Mary	30	F	Seamstress	06Ap02Bb
Catharine	12	F	Seamstress	06Ap02Bb
Mary	09	F	Child	06Ap02Bb

NAMES OF PASSENGERS	AGE	SEX	OCCUPATIONS	DATE PORT SHIP
MERRY, Patrick	07	M	Child	06Ap02Bb
Honora	03	F	Child	06Ap02Bb
Alice	02	F	Child	06Ap02Bb
Austacia	13	F	Laborer	06Ap02Bb
Bridget	.09	F	Infant	06Ap02Bb
HOULEHAN, Magt.	25	F	Servant	06Ap02Bb
KAYS, Robert	30	M	Laborer	06Ap02Bb
TRINELLY, Pat	24	M	Farmer	06Ap02Bb
FAHEY, Thomas	21	M	Farmer	06Ap02Bb
LEONARDS, Hugh	21	M	Farmer	06Ap02Bb
Cathe.	21	F	Dressmaker	06Ap02Bb
MCGUIRE, Mary	21	F	Dressmaker	06Ap02Bb
MCBURNEY, James	18	M	Farmer	06Ap02Bb
STANFIELDS, William	16	M	Farmer	06Ap02Bb
HAUGH, Sarah	26	F	Dressmaker	06Ap02Bb
RAY, Richard	20	M	Servant	06Ap02Bb
BOYD, Lettie	20	F	Servant	06Ap02Bb
MORGAN, Rose	24	F	Servant	06Ap02Bb
ROONEY, Mary	24	F	Servant	06Ap02Bb
MARTIN, Mary-Jane	22	F	Bomkr	06Ap02Bb
MCQUADE, John	22	M	Farmer	06Ap02Bb
Pat	40	M	Farmer	06Ap02Bb
MCCORMICK, Pat	40	M	Farmer	06Ap02Bb
KANE, Cathe.	21	F	Servant	06Ap02Bb
RILLEY, Cathe.	40	F	Seamstress	06Ap02Bb
MCGOWAN, Magt.	18	F	Servant	06Ap02Bb
GANNON, Mary	20	F	Servant	06Ap02Bb
MCGUINESS, Bridget	19	F	Laborer	06Ap02Bb
MARKEY, Ann	00	F	Servant	06Ap02Bb
U, Puree	00	M	Laborer	06Ap02Bb
KEENAN, Grace	43	F	Servant	06Ap02Bb
DORAN, Thomas	34	M	Laborer	06Ap02Bb
KEEVANS, Mary	15	F	Servant	06Ap02Bb
TOOHILL, Johana	21	F	Servant	06Ap02Bb
OBRIEN, Daniel	26	M	Laborer	06Ap02Bb
ROURKE, Mary	10	F	Servant	06Ap02Bb
MCCARTHY, Charles	14	M	Clerk	06Ap02Bb

ARTHUR 06 APRIL 1849

From Liverpool

NAMES OF PASSENGERS	AGE	SEX	OCCUPATIONS	DATE PORT SHIP
BRAIDON, Rose	30	F	None	06Ap02Bc
CASSEDY, John	11	M	None	06Ap02Bc
CASSADY, Ann	07	F	Child	06Ap02Bc
DAVEY, Peter	40	M	Laborer	06Ap02Bc
Peter	03	M	Child	06Ap02Bc
OBRIEN, Catherine	20	F	None	06Ap02Bc
Amris	04	F	Child	06Ap02Bc
ROACK, Peter	13	M	None	06Ap02Bc
CARR, James	17	M	None	06Ap02Bc
AADAHAR, Ann	20	F	None	06Ap02Bc
OBARRY, Jane	20	F	None	06Ap02Bc
BOMCABEMT, Brid.	20	F	None	06Ap02Bc
CARNEY, Mary	20	F	None	06Ap02Bc
Nicholas	04	M	Child	06Ap02Bc
GALLAGHER, Franciss	25	M	Laborer	06Ap02Bc
Sarah	21	F	None	06Ap02Bc
DONENY, Thomas	21	M	None	06Ap02Bc
DEMPSEY, Daniel	21	M	Mason	06Ap02Bc
DENT, James	23	M	Shoemaker	06Ap02Bc
Bridget-Jox.	24	F	None	06Ap02Bc
KELLY, Daniel	60	M	Laborer	06Ap02Bc
John	13	M	None	06Ap02Bc
Hannah	16	F	None	06Ap02Bc
Sarah	17	F	None	06Ap02Bc
GILBRAITH, Sally	20	F	None	06Ap02Bc
Cathern.	18	F	None	06Ap02Bc
BOYLE, Philip	40	M	Laborer	06Ap02Bc
BOYLE, Cecily	40	F	None	06Ap02Bc
Hugh	15	M	None	06Ap02Bc
Mary	12	F	None	06Ap02Bc
Biddy	10	F	None	06Ap02Bc
Charles	08	M	Child	06Ap02Bc
Daniel	06	M	Child	06Ap02Bc
James	04	M	Child	06Ap02Bc
TRACEY, Mary	40	F	None	06Ap02Bc
Tereca	09	F	Child	06Ap02Bc
Patric	07	M	Child	06Ap02Bc
BRADELY, Robert	19	M	Laborer	06Ap02Bc
Edward	11	M	Laborer	06Ap02Bc
John	14	M	Laborer	06Ap02Bc
EGAN, Mick	35	M	Laborer	06Ap02Bc
KANE, Elen	20	F	None	06Ap02Bc
MCILRANE, Robert	20	M	Laborer	06Ap02Bc
HERAN, Patric	23	M	Laborer	06Ap02Bc
FLYNN, Pat	20	M	Laborer	06Ap02Bc
DEVLIN, Alice	20	F	Laborer	06Ap02Bc
MCHUGH, Pat	20	M	Laborer	06Ap02Bc
BUTLER, Thomas	24	M	Unknown	06Ap02Bc
DONNELLY, Peter	50	M	Laborer	06Ap02Bc
RICE, Peter	26	M	Laborer	06Ap02Bc
Hannah	18	F	None	06Ap02Bc
MAHER, William	28	M	Laborer	06Ap02Bc
John	21	M	Laborer	06Ap02Bc
HANLEY, Tim	26	M	Laborer	06Ap02Bc
MURREY, Thomas	24	M	Laborer	06Ap02Bc
DEMPSEY, Thomas	20	M	Laborer	06Ap02Bc
CRAWFORD, Margeret	25	F	None	06Ap02Bc
BRADY, Thomas	36	M	Laborer	06Ap02Bc
MCLANGHIN, Mary	20	F	Lad	06Ap02Bc
MCLANGIN, Elen	33	F	None	06Ap02Bc
Michal	21	M	Laborer	06Ap02Bc
Ann	19	F	None	06Ap02Bc
SOLAN, Thomas	22	M	Laborer	06Ap02Bc
Anthony	20	M	Laborer	06Ap02Bc
John	20	M	Laborer	06Ap02Bc
ALLEN, William	40	M	Laborer	06Ap02Bc
Mary	35	F	None	06Ap02Bc
Michal	17	M	None	06Ap02Bc
Bernard	14	M	None	06Ap02Bc
William	10	M	None	06Ap02Bc
Mary	09	F	Child	06Ap02Bc
Cathrn.	04	F	Child	06Ap02Bc
Ann	02	F	Child	06Ap02Bc
James	.00	M	Infant	06Ap02Bc
MCKARTHER, Andrew	24	M	Laborer	06Ap02Bc
Cathern.	50	F	None	06Ap02Bc
TRACY, Cathern.	21	F	Dressmaker	06Ap02Bc
Michal	19	M	Laborer	06Ap02Bc
Jos.	33	M	Laborer	06Ap02Bc
RILEY, John	38	M	Laborer	06Ap02Bc
William	38	M	Laborer	06Ap02Bc
KELLY, Martin	21	M	Laborer	06Ap02Bc
DOYLE, Mick	40	M	Laborer	06Ap02Bc
FARRELL, John	30	M	Laborer	06Ap02Bc
Marcella	30	F	None	06Ap02Bc
John	12	M	None	06Ap02Bc
William	10	M	None	06Ap02Bc
Mary	09	F	Child	06Ap02Bc
Edward	03	M	Child	06Ap02Bc
Cathern.	.00	F	Infant	06Ap02Bc
Died-At-Sea				
Ellen	20	F	None	06Ap02Bc
MORAN, James	20	M	Laborer	06Ap02Bc
Jane	22	F	None	06Ap02Bc
EGAN, Mary	20	F	None	06Ap02Bc
MURPHY, Mick	40	M	Bricklayer	06Ap02Bc
Ann	35	F	None	06Ap02Bc
Kate	11	F	None	06Ap02Bc
Mary	07	F	Child	06Ap02Bc
Christiana	04	F	Child	06Ap02Bc
Ellen	.00	F	Infant	06Ap02Bc
MCDONNELL, James	25	M	None	06Ap02Bc

NAMES OF PASSENGERS	AGE	SEX	OCCUPATIONS	DATE PORT SHIP
HANLOR, Pat	35	M	Bricklayer	06Ap02Bc
Jane	30	F	None	06Ap02Bc
Bernard	02	M	Child	06Ap02Bc
Kate	.00	F	Infant	06Ap02Bc
MCAOVY, Pat	32	M	Bricklayer	06Ap02Bc
LEDWIRTH, Mick	20	M	Laborer	06Ap02Bc
Margeret	19	F	Laborer	06Ap02Bc
FALLEN, William	18	M	Laborer	06Ap02Bc
BOYD, Robert	20	M	Laborer	06Ap02Bc
BRADAN, Ann	20	F	None	06Ap02Bc
BAYLE, Cathern.	20	F	None	06Ap02Bc
GALLAGHER, John	30	M	Laborer	06Ap02Bc
DEMPSEY, Martin	40	M	Laborer	06Ap02Bc
Sally	12	F	None	06Ap02Bc
FITZGERALD, Mick	35	M	Laborer	06Ap02Bc
WELSH, Thomas	21	M	Laborer	06Ap02Bc
EGAN, Mick	25	M	Laborer	06Ap02Bc
Dennis	22	M	Laborer	06Ap02Bc
GAVAN, Patrick	30	M	Laborer	06Ap02Bc
U	30	F	None	06Ap02Bc
Pat	03	M	Child	06Ap02Bc
Cathern.	16	F	None	06Ap02Bc
Mick	18	M	Laborer	06Ap02Bc
Pat	20	M	Laborer	06Ap02Bc
GILL, John	26	M	Shoemaker	06Ap02Bc
FOREMAN, Letitia	20	F	Dressmaker	06Ap02Bc
Mary	18	F	Dressmaker	06Ap02Bc
MITCHELL, Charles	20	M	Clerk	06Ap02Bc
DRAGAN, William	19	M	Laborer	06Ap02Bc
MORGAN, Peter	18	M	Laborer	06Ap02Bc
EGAN, Pat	19	M	Tailor	06Ap02Bc
SILLY, Ann	40	F	None	06Ap02Bc
MEEHAN, Pat	28	M	Laborer	06Ap02Bc
ODONNELL, Bridget	18	F	Servant	06Ap02Bc
REANIS, Thomas	04	M	Child	06Ap02Bc
Cathern.	02	F	Child	06Ap02Bc
THAMPHSEN, Ann	18	F	None	06Ap02Bc
CARROLL, Thomas	20	M	Laborer	06Ap02Bc
GILLEN, Thomas	17	M	Laborer	06Ap02Bc
KEANE, Pat	40	M	Laborer	06Ap02Bc
ROAK, Margeret	20	F	None	06Ap02Bc
PALIN, Calab.	20	M	Laborer	06Ap02Bc
TULLY, John	30	M	Laborer	06Ap02Bc
BUTLER, John	18	M	Laborer	06Ap02Bc
WATSON, Arthur	22	M	Laborer	06Ap02Bc
HADFORD, John	22	M	Baker	06Ap02Bc
BERRY, Bessy	20	F	None	06Ap02Bc
HART, Pat	50	M	Farmer	06Ap02Bc
Bridget	48	F	None	06Ap02Bc
MULLARTY, William	18	M	Laborer	06Ap02Bc
MCGUIRE, Ann	21	F	None	06Ap02Bc
WRIGHT, Hannah	40	F	Unknown	06Ap02Bc
Ellen	17	F	Unknown	06Ap02Bc
William	16	M	Unknown	06Ap02Bc
Mary	13	F	Unknown	06Ap02Bc
John	10	M	Unknown	06Ap02Bc
Cathern.	08	F	Child	06Ap02Bc
LAUTEN, John	26	M	Laborer	06Ap02Bc
LINCHAN, Johannah	30	F	None	06Ap02Bc
STANTEN, William	20	M	Laborer	06Ap02Bc
SEXTEN, Thomas	40	M	Laborer	06Ap02Bc
LINCHAN, Pat	37	M	Laborer	06Ap02Bc
HUTCHISEN, John	18	M	Laborer	06Ap02Bc
MURRY, William	40	M	Laborer	06Ap02Bc
BROWN, William	26	M	Laborer	06Ap02Bc
CALLOW, Rise	18	F	None	06Ap02Bc
FITZGERALD, Ellen	20	F	None	06Ap02Bc
MCGEE, Jane	20	F	None	06Ap02Bc
WELSH, Pat	37	M	Laborer	06Ap02Bc

WESTMINSTER 06 APRIL 1849

From London

NAMES OF PASSENGERS	AGE	SEX	OCCUPATIONS	DATE PORT SHIP
DUGGAN, George	35	M	Cver	06Ap13Bd
Harriett	25	M	Cver	06Ap13Bd
Jno.	.00	M	Infant	06Ap13Bd
SULLIVAN, Ann	17	F	None	06Ap13Bd
Kate	20	F	None	06Ap13Bd
HENSSY, Ann	26	F	Unknown	06Ap13Bd
MILLINS, Jno.	38	M	Laborer	06Ap13Bd
Mary	00	F	Unknown	06Ap13Bd
CAREY, Samuel	23	M	Laborer	06Ap13Bd

WM.JARVIS 06 APRIL 1849

From Liverpool

NAMES OF PASSENGERS	AGE	SEX	OCCUPATIONS	DATE PORT SHIP
QUIN, Darby	50	M	Farmer	06Ap02Be
Margaret	45	F	Farmer	06Ap02Be
Thomas	21	M	Farmer	06Ap02Be
Mary	25	F	Farmer	06Ap02Be
Margaret	13	F	Farmer	06Ap02Be
Sally	10	F	Farmer	06Ap02Be
KEELAN, Margaret	35	F	Housekeeper	06Ap02Be
Ann	17	F	Housekeeper	06Ap02Be
Thomas	28	M	Housekeeper	06Ap02Be
Bridget	22	F	Servant	06Ap02Be
BURKE, Bridget	20	F	Housekeeper	06Ap02Be
DONAHUE, John	21	M	Farmer	06Ap02Be
MCGOWAN, Patrick	40	M	Laborer	06Ap02Be
Pat	17	M	Laborer	06Ap02Be
BECKET, George	22	M	Laborer	06Ap02Be
WALSH, Patrick	27	M	Farmer	06Ap02Be
Michael	22	M	Laborer	06Ap02Be
POWER, John	23	M	Farmer	06Ap02Be
Bridget	35	F	Servant	06Ap02Be
Elizabeth	10	F	Servant	06Ap02Be
James	06	M	Child	06Ap02Be
Ellen	03	F	Child	06Ap02Be
David	.00	M	Infant	06Ap02Be
GILLELAN, Matilda	20	F	Servant	06Ap02Be
BROPHEY, Michael	26	M	Shoemaker	06Ap02Be
CANTUCLE, Joseph	19	M	Shoemaker	06Ap02Be
CONNOR, Michael	21	M	Laborer	06Ap02Be
Thomas	23	M	Laborer	06Ap02Be
SMITH, Charles	22	M	Farmer	06Ap02Be
NELIGAR, Deniel	40	M	Farmer	06Ap02Be
ROSS, Mary	55	F	Nurse	06Ap02Be
Elizabeth	23	F	Seamstress	06Ap02Be
John	22	M	Carpenter	06Ap02Be
Matilda	19	F	House Maid	06Ap02Be
MCKINNEY, Joseph	20	M	Farmer	06Ap02Be
Martha	19	F	House Maid	06Ap02Be
HONARD, John	67	M	Smith	06Ap02Be
Honora	53	F	House Maid	06Ap02Be
John	23	M	Smith	06Ap02Be
Thomas	09	M	Child	06Ap02Be
Jane	32	F	Mtmkr	06Ap02Be
Catherine	18	F	Mtmkr	06Ap02Be
SULLEVAN, Timothy	21	M	Laborer	06Ap02Be
DRISCOL, Eliza	22	F	Dressmaker	06Ap02Be
FLYNNE, Thomas	28	M	Plasterer	06Ap02Be

NAMES OF PASSENGERS	AGE	SEX	OCCUPATIONS	DATE PORT SHIP
CARR, Mary	18	F	House Maid	06Ap02Be
MCGARRY, Margaret	20	F	House Maid	06Ap02Be
HAFFEY, Wm.	26	M	Laborer	06Ap02Be
Judy	21	F	Housekeeper	06Ap02Be
GALLAHER, Martin	25	M	Laborer	06Ap02Be
MYRON, Honora	00	F	Bomkr	06Ap02Be
CONNOR, Danl.	42	M	Farmer	06Ap02Be
DAVIS, Thomas	19	M	Servant	06Ap02Be
YATES, John	25	M	Farmer	06Ap02Be
Mary	23	F	Dressmaker	06Ap02Be
George	21	M	Farmer	06Ap02Be
Thomas	18	M	Carpenter	06Ap02Be
Wm.	56	M	Farmer	06Ap02Be
NEAL, Wm.	22	M	Shoemaker	06Ap02Be
Gabriel	24	M	Draper	06Ap02Be
WIGINGS, Jane	20	F	Unknown	06Ap02Be
STANKARD, Thomas	26	M	Laborer	06Ap02Be
Edward	18	M	Laborer	06Ap02Be
HUME, John	26	M	Laborer	06Ap02Be
CLARRY, Nicolas	28	M	Laborer	06Ap02Be
Sally	28	F	House Maid	06Ap02Be
PHHILAR, Denis	56	M	Farmer	06Ap02Be
Mary	50	F	Housekeeper	06Ap02Be
Fanny	28	F	House Maid	06Ap02Be
John	22	M	Farmer	06Ap02Be
Denis	18	M	Farmer	06Ap02Be
Anthony	15	M	Farmer	06Ap02Be
Rhodey	25	M	Grocer	06Ap02Be
CAHALAN, John	18	M	Farmer	06Ap02Be
BROTHER, Michael	22	M	Laborer	06Ap02Be
MARTIN, James	23	M	Farmer	06Ap02Be
Catherine	18	F	House Maid	06Ap02Be
Winifred	16	F	House Maid	06Ap02Be
John	14	M	Farmer	06Ap02Be
ORR, Richard	28	M	Tailor	06Ap02Be
RIELEY, Ann	16	F	Dressmaker	06Ap02Be
Rose	18	F	Dressmaker	06Ap02Be
Mary	17	F	Housekeeper	06Ap02Be
LITTLE, Thomas	46	M	Laborer	06Ap02Be
HOVEY, Thomas	18	M	Gdnr	06Ap02Be
Richard	21	M	Gdnr	06Ap02Be
SHERIDAN, Farel	20	M	Laborer	06Ap02Be
BROGAN, John	18	M	Laborer	06Ap02Be
Ann	38	F	Housekeeper	06Ap02Be
RILEY, Mary	28	F	House Maid	06Ap02Be
DANIEL, Bridget	38	F	Dressmaker	06Ap02Be
IVORY, Edward	36	M	Laborer	06Ap02Be
HUSLEY, John	42	M	Farmer	06Ap02Be
Catherine	38	F	Housekeeper	06Ap02Be
Mary	04	F	Child	06Ap02Be
John	07	M	Child	06Ap02Be
Wm.	10	M	Unknown	06Ap02Be
Thomas	09	M	Child	06Ap02Be
MELONEY, Timothy	40	M	Farmer	06Ap02Be
Wm.	20	M	Farmer	06Ap02Be
Mary	17	F	Housekeeper	06Ap02Be
Bridget	15	F	Housekeeper	06Ap02Be
John	13	M	Farmer	06Ap02Be
Margaret	09	F	Child	06Ap02Be
STACKPOOL, Mary	40	F	Dressmaker	06Ap02Be
James	11	M	None	06Ap02Be
Bridget	08	F	Child	06Ap02Be
Alicia	07	F	Child	06Ap02Be
BRISCOL, James	35	M	Laborer	06Ap02Be
Mary	33	F	Dressmaker	06Ap02Be
Mary	04	F	Child	06Ap02Be
Catherine	02	F	Child	06Ap02Be
MELONY, Patrick	60	M	Farmer	06Ap02Be
Catherine	50	F	Housekeeper	06Ap02Be
STACRA, Ann	24	F	Dressmaker	06Ap02Be
Eliza	22	F	Dressmaker	06Ap02Be
Honora	26	F	Dressmaker	06Ap02Be
Margaret	18	F	Dressmaker	06Ap02Be
Bridget	12	F	None	06Ap02Be
James	14	M	None	06Ap02Be
IVORY, Margaret	46	F	Housekeeper	06Ap02Be
Alicia	18	F	Servant	06Ap02Be
John	13	M	None	06Ap02Be
Judy	06	F	Child	06Ap02Be
PATTER, Mary	48	F	House Maid	06Ap02Be
CASS, Mary	26	F	Unknown	06Ap02Be
FREHAW, John	14	M	Servant	06Ap02Be
CASS, Wm.	28	M	Servant	06Ap02Be
U-Mrs.	38	F	Servant	06Ap02Be
CASHETT, Bridget	28	F	Servant	06Ap02Be
DITCHANTY, Wm.	17	M	Laborer	06Ap02Be
HARTY, Pat	19	M	Laborer	06Ap02Be
TERLIN, Mary	24	F	Dressmaker	06Ap02Be
CLARK, Margaret	18	F	House Maid	06Ap02Be
WALSH, James	28	M	Shopman	06Ap02Be
CARWEN, James	27	M	Farmer	06Ap02Be
BREMIN, Martin	24	M	Laborer	06Ap02Be
JOIRE, James	18	M	Farmer	06Ap02Be
CUTTY, Timothy	21	M	Miller	06Ap02Be
OBRIEN, Danl.	32	M	Laborer	06Ap02Be
BRIEN, Michael	28	M	Farmer	06Ap02Be
PHILAN, Philip	23	M	Farmer	06Ap02Be
BRIEN, Michael	30	M	Laborer	06Ap02Be
MCGRATH, Miles	40	M	Laborer	06Ap02Be
DALZ, Richard	50	M	Laborer	06Ap02Be
Johanna	40	F	Housekeeper	06Ap02Be
Ellen	.00	F	Infant	06Ap02Be
John	03	M	Child	06Ap02Be
Honora	06	F	Child	06Ap02Be
Thomas	07	M	Child	06Ap02Be
SLANE, Peter	48	M	Baker	06Ap02Be
DOWNY, Bessey	24	F	Servant	06Ap02Be
SULLIVAN, Michael	48	M	Gdnr	06Ap02Be
MURRY, Michael	28	M	Laborer	06Ap02Be
RILEY, Pat	46	M	Laborer	06Ap02Be
Bridget	35	F	Housekeeper	06Ap02Be
Michael	04	M	Child	06Ap02Be
Mary	.06	F	Infant	06Ap02Be
CONNEL, Thomas	22	M	Laborer	06Ap02Be
COONEY, Johanna	25	F	Servant	06Ap02Be
CONELEY, Edward	32	M	Cbtmkr	06Ap02Be
Mary	25	F	Dressmaker	06Ap02Be
SWENEY, Dennis	24	M	Gdnr	06Ap02Be
Bridget	24	F	Servant	06Ap02Be
BARRY, James	21	M	Mason	06Ap02Be
HAMEVAN, Wm.	25	M	Servant	06Ap02Be
NEAGLE, U-Mrs.	48	F	Housekeeper	06Ap02Be
U-Ms.	17	F	Dressmaker	06Ap02Be
ROSMAN, U-Mrs.	25	F	Dressmaker	06Ap02Be
HASLEM, Mary-A.	20	F	Seamstress	06Ap02Be
MARRESEY, B.	21	M	Laborer	06Ap02Be
Mary	18	F	Servant	06Ap02Be
MEEHIN, Michael	46	M	Weaver	06Ap02Be
MCCARTER, Denis	23	M	Hpntr	06Ap02Be
COLLINS, John	28	M	Laborer	06Ap02Be
HASHMAN, Dennis	32	M	Chptr	06Ap02Be
SHARKIN, Timothy	24	M	Wheelwright	06Ap02Be
LOW, Nathanl.	26	M	Laborer	06Ap02Be
Robt.	22	M	Unknown	06Ap02Be
Margaret	18	F	Unknown	06Ap02Be
Eliza	16	F	Unknown	06Ap02Be
Alicia	11	F	Unknown	06Ap02Be
LEONARD, Peter	26	M	Laborer	06Ap02Be
DURSY, Patrick	26	M	Laborer	06Ap02Be
BURKE, Edward	03	M	Child	06Ap02Be
Pat	10	M	None	06Ap02Be
SMITH, Bridget	20	F	Servant	06Ap02Be
Michael	02	M	Child	06Ap02Be
MCDONNAL, Edward	60	M	Farmer	06Ap02Be
GILLELAN, James	19	M	Farmer	06Ap02Be
DORETY, Margaret	37	F	Servant	06Ap02Be
CAULLIN, Thomas	43	M	Laborer	06Ap02Be
Pat	28	M	Laborer	06Ap02Be
DUFFEY, Honora	22	F	Dressmaker	06Ap02Be
Bridget	24	F	Dressmaker	06Ap02Be

ANNIE 07 APRIL 1849

From Belfast

NAMES OF PASSENGERS	AGE	SEX	OCCUPATIONS	DATE PORT SHIP
CHAMBERS, John	24	M	Laborer	07Ap05Bg
MCHUGH, Edwd.	35	M	Laborer	07Ap05Bg
WEBSTER, Wm.	21	M	Laborer	07Ap05Bg
Ann	13	F	Laborer	07Ap05Bg
GORDON, Patt	24	M	Laborer	07Ap05Bg
Sarah	24	F	Laborer	07Ap05Bg
Patt	04	M	Child	07Ap05Bg
James	03	M	Child	07Ap05Bg
Michael	.00	M	Infant	07Ap05Bg
HAYES, Saml.	21	M	Laborer	07Ap05Bg
FALOON, John	20	M	Laborer	07Ap05Bg
DOURNOODY, Ch.	26	M	Laborer	07Ap05Bg
BOYD, Alex	62	M	Laborer	07Ap05Bg
Margt.	60	F	Laborer	07Ap05Bg
Ann	40	F	Laborer	07Ap05Bg
Rachel	20	F	Laborer	07Ap05Bg
James	08	M	Child	07Ap05Bg
Alex	05	M	Child	07Ap05Bg
Hugh	03	M	Child	07Ap05Bg
Jane	.00	F	Infant	07Ap05Bg
MACCRELIS, Jane	35	F	Laborer	07Ap05Bg
Mary	17	F	Laborer	07Ap05Bg
John	15	M	Laborer	07Ap05Bg
Deonil	12	M	Laborer	07Ap05Bg
Margt.	09	F	Child	07Ap05Bg
Arch.	05	M	Child	07Ap05Bg
Jane	02	F	Child	07Ap05Bg
SMYTH, Sam	25	M	Laborer	07Ap05Bg
MULLAN, Francis	25	M	Laborer	07Ap05Bg
Jane	30	F	Laborer	07Ap05Bg
Mary	20	F	Laborer	07Ap05Bg
Cath.	14	F	Laborer	07Ap05Bg
MACILROY, Ed.	20	M	Laborer	07Ap05Bg
WALLAGH, Wm.	30	M	Laborer	07Ap05Bg
DUNCAN, Jane	30	F	Laborer	07Ap05Bg
Hannah	28	F	Laborer	07Ap05Bg
WALLAGH, Margt.	26	F	Laborer	07Ap05Bg
BRIDGET, Nancy	27	F	Laborer	07Ap05Bg
WALLAGH, James	06	M	Child	07Ap05Bg
Elizabeth	05	F	Child	07Ap05Bg
John	04	M	Child	07Ap05Bg
Robert	.00	M	Infant	07Ap05Bg
GEDDIS, Arch.	60	M	Laborer	07Ap05Bg
Ann	60	F	Laborer	07Ap05Bg
Andrew	28	M	Laborer	07Ap05Bg
Charlotte	24	F	Laborer	07Ap05Bg
Margt.	20	F	Laborer	07Ap05Bg
SMITH, George	21	M	Laborer	07Ap05Bg
WILSON, Mary-A.	21	F	Laborer	07Ap05Bg
HESLOSS, Sarah	30	F	Laborer	07Ap05Bg
LUCAS, Mary	20	F	Laborer	07Ap05Bg
Eliza	17	F	Laborer	07Ap05Bg
MCKEON, Joseph	26	M	Laborer	07Ap05Bg
Mary	24	F	Laborer	07Ap05Bg
Margt.	18	F	Laborer	07Ap05Bg
Anna	02	F	Child	07Ap05Bg
Eliza-Jane	.00	F	Infant	07Ap05Bg
WITTEN, John-W.	13	M	Laborer	07Ap05Bg
Wm.	60	M	Laborer	07Ap05Bg
MCILROY, Cath.	10	F	Laborer	07Ap05Bg
Eliza	.00	F	Infant	07Ap05Bg
JAMISON, Hugh	23	M	Laborer	07Ap05Bg
DALLON, John	31	M	Laborer	07Ap05Bg
DRAKE, Christopher	22	M	Laborer	07Ap05Bg
Ann	22	F	Laborer	07Ap05Bg
CASEMENT, Mary	20	F	Laborer	07Ap05Bg
ORR, Arthur	18	M	Laborer	07Ap05Bg
MCILROY, John	17	M	Laborer	07Ap05Bg
MCLAUGHLIN, Alice	40	F	Laborer	07Ap05Bg
Mary-Jane	31	F	Laborer	07Ap05Bg
Thomas	19	M	Laborer	07Ap05Bg
Debriel	17	M	Laborer	07Ap05Bg
Margt.	16	F	Laborer	07Ap05Bg
Maria	14	F	Laborer	07Ap05Bg
John	13	M	Laborer	07Ap05Bg
Wm.	10	M	Laborer	07Ap05Bg
MACPADAN, Jas.	42	M	Laborer	07Ap05Bg
Mary	40	F	Laborer	07Ap05Bg
Mary-Jane	16	F	Laborer	07Ap05Bg
Mathew	11	M	Laborer	07Ap05Bg
CLARKE, Anne	00	F	Laborer	07Ap05Bg
JAMISON, John	28	M	Laborer	07Ap05Bg
Mary-Jane	26	F	Laborer	07Ap05Bg
Wm.	.00	M	Infant	07Ap05Bg
DUFFIN, Saml.	30	M	Laborer	07Ap05Bg
Jane	24	F	Laborer	07Ap05Bg
Ann	10	F	Laborer	07Ap05Bg
Jane	08	F	Child	07Ap05Bg
Henry	06	M	Child	07Ap05Bg
John	04	M	Child	07Ap05Bg
Mary	02	F	Child	07Ap05Bg
NEILL, Jane	50	F	Laborer	07Ap05Bg
Elizabeth	30	F	Laborer	07Ap05Bg
MIBRIN, Grace	20	F	Laborer	07Ap05Bg
WERNER, Hugh	19	M	Laborer	07Ap05Bg
REID, Jane	36	F	Laborer	07Ap05Bg
GUNNING, Wm.	20	M	Laborer	07Ap05Bg
DORAN, Wm.	18	M	Laborer	07Ap05Bg
GOUGHT, Joseph	40	M	Laborer	07Ap05Bg
Sarah	35	F	Laborer	07Ap05Bg
Wm.	20	M	Laborer	07Ap05Bg
ENGLISH, Jane	17	F	Laborer	07Ap05Bg
Mary-Ann	15	F	Laborer	07Ap05Bg
Sarah	13	F	Laborer	07Ap05Bg
James	11	M	Laborer	07Ap05Bg
Alex	07	M	Child	07Ap05Bg
Agnes	05	F	Child	07Ap05Bg
Joseph	03	M	Child	07Ap05Bg
DOWNEY, Matilda	24	F	Laborer	07Ap05Bg
Mary-Jane	20	F	Laborer	07Ap05Bg
CREE, Wm.	22	M	Laborer	07Ap05Bg
MURRAY, Maria	15	F	Laborer	07Ap05Bg
MORRISON, Patt	21	M	Laborer	07Ap05Bg
ROWAN, Hamilton	23	M	Laborer	07Ap05Bg
YOUNG, James	24	M	Laborer	07Ap05Bg
MCMEGH, Margt.	22	F	Laborer	07Ap05Bg
Patt.	21	M	Laborer	07Ap05Bg
DRAKE, Cath.	22	F	Laborer	07Ap05Bg
OGLE, John	30	M	Laborer	07Ap05Bg
Eliza	30	F	Laborer	07Ap05Bg
Mary	70	F	Laborer	07Ap05Bg
Hugh	02	M	Child	07Ap05Bg
MCCULLOUGH, Mary	30	F	Laborer	07Ap05Bg
Hugh	06	M	Child	07Ap05Bg
BROWN, Matilda	30	F	Laborer	07Ap05Bg
Joseph	05	M	Child	07Ap05Bg
MULHOLLAND, Debby	25	F	Laborer	07Ap05Bg
BROWN, James	20	M	Laborer	07Ap05Bg
MCCONEL, Cath.	30	F	Laborer	07Ap05Bg
Hanna	30	F	Laborer	07Ap05Bg
MORRISON, Joseph	21	M	Laborer	07Ap05Bg
TIERNEY, Margt.	40	F	Laborer	07Ap05Bg
Mary	15	F	Laborer	07Ap05Bg
Ellen	14	F	Laborer	07Ap05Bg
CAMPBELL, Chs.	16	M	Laborer	07Ap05Bg
BLANE, James	44	M	Laborer	07Ap05Bg
Mary	44	F	Laborer	07Ap05Bg
James	18	M	Laborer	07Ap05Bg
Isabella	15	F	Laborer	07Ap05Bg
John	11	M	Laborer	07Ap05Bg

NAMES OF PASSENGERS	AGE	SEX	OCCUPATIONS	DATE PORT SHIP
BLANE, James	11	M	Laborer	07Ap05Bg
Alex	08	M	Child	07Ap05Bg
BOWERS, Wm.	30	M	Laborer	07Ap05Bg
BURNEL, Hugh	21	M	Laborer	07Ap05Bg
Robert	30	M	Laborer	07Ap05Bg
MORRISON, Mary	40	F	Laborer	07Ap05Bg
UTUMAN, Saml.	30	M	Laborer	07Ap05Bg
Rebecca	30	F	Laborer	07Ap05Bg
David	06	M	Child	07Ap05Bg
Saml.	35	M	Laborer	07Ap05Bg
NEIL, Wm.	22	M	Laborer	07Ap05Bg
KIETH, John	28	M	Laborer	07Ap05Bg
HENDERSON, James	35	M	Laborer	07Ap05Bg
CAMPBELL, John	17	M	Laborer	07Ap05Bg
IRVIN, Wm.	23	M	Laborer	07Ap05Bg
MCNIGH, Ed.	15	M	Laborer	07Ap05Bg
CRAWFORD, John	25	M	Laborer	07Ap05Bg
RIPLEY, Lina	30	F	Laborer	07Ap05Bg
MCGRATH, James	22	M	Laborer	07Ap05Bg
OHAYNE, Michl.	20	M	Laborer	07Ap05Bg
MCQUIN, Mary	20	F	Laborer	07Ap05Bg
BROMLEY, Mgt.	40	F	Laborer	07Ap05Bg
OGLE, Rose	.00	F	Infant	07Ap05Bg
James	30	M	Laborer	07Ap05Bg
Margt.	30	F	Laborer	07Ap05Bg
Wm.	14	M	Laborer	07Ap05Bg
Sarah	13	F	Laborer	07Ap05Bg
Mary-Ann	11	F	Laborer	07Ap05Bg
MCWHEIR, Thos.	30	M	Laborer	07Ap05Bg
JOHNSTON, David	19	M	Laborer	07Ap05Bg
GALWIN, Hugh	19	M	Laborer	07Ap05Bg
DOGHERTY, Wm.	50	M	Laborer	07Ap05Bg
Wm.	18	M	Laborer	07Ap05Bg
John	21	M	Laborer	07Ap05Bg
Margt.	17	F	Laborer	07Ap05Bg
Robert	13	M	Laborer	07Ap05Bg
LUNDY, Margt-Ann	17	F	Laborer	07Ap05Bg
DANREY, Sarah	11	F	Laborer	07Ap05Bg
MORAN, James	25	M	Laborer	07Ap05Bg
Patte	24	M	Laborer	07Ap05Bg
Isabella	50	F	Laborer	07Ap05Bg
Maria	22	F	Laborer	07Ap05Bg
Isabella	25	F	Laborer	07Ap05Bg
NURM, Patt	25	M	Laborer	07Ap05Bg
Mary	20	F	Laborer	07Ap05Bg
STEWART, Martha	29	F	Laborer	07Ap05Bg
WELSH, John	25	M	Laborer	07Ap05Bg
Mathew	23	M	Laborer	07Ap05Bg
Nicholas	25	M	Laborer	07Ap05Bg
Patt	27	M	Laborer	07Ap05Bg
Mary	23	F	Laborer	07Ap05Bg
Ann	17	F	Laborer	07Ap05Bg
MCQUINNERY, Bernard	20	M	Laborer	07Ap05Bg
BROWN, John	24	M	Laborer	07Ap05Bg
KYLE, Wm.	15	M	Laborer	07Ap05Bg
Esther	13	F	Laborer	07Ap05Bg
CLARKE, James	21	M	Laborer	07Ap05Bg
THOMSON, Martha	22	F	Laborer	07Ap05Bg
MCCULLOUGH, Margt.	30	F	Laborer	07Ap05Bg
LAVENDER, Joseph	22	M	Laborer	07Ap05Bg
Sarah	22	F	Laborer	07Ap05Bg
DRAKE, John	31	M	Laborer	07Ap05Bg
Mary	31	F	Laborer	07Ap05Bg
Susanne	16	F	Laborer	07Ap05Bg
Eliza	11	F	Laborer	07Ap05Bg
Kitty	20	F	Laborer	07Ap05Bg
James	06	M	Child	07Ap05Bg
Isabella	.00	F	Infant	07Ap05Bg
Sarah	.00	F	Infant	07Ap05Bg
MCVEIGH, Hugh	22	M	Laborer	07Ap05Bg
Patt	55	M	Laborer	07Ap05Bg
Jane	50	F	Laborer	07Ap05Bg
MOURIA, Patt	22	M	Laborer	07Ap05Bg
Mary	22	F	Laborer	07Ap05Bg
MCNAGH, Patt	19	M	Laborer	07Ap05Bg
MCNAGH, Edward	13	M	Laborer	07Ap05Bg
Jane	10	F	Laborer	07Ap05Bg
Margt	09	F	Child	07Ap05Bg
Patt	09	M	Child	07Ap05Bg
MONIN, Edw.	21	M	Laborer	07Ap05Bg
Mary	21	F	Laborer	07Ap05Bg
MCMANUS, John	21	M	Laborer	07Ap05Bg
MCMORRIN, Wm.	19	M	Laborer	07Ap05Bg
TRINNEY, Pat	19	M	Laborer	07Ap05Bg
ROONEY, Michl.	19	M	Laborer	07Ap05Bg
DUNN, Wm.	19	M	Laborer	07Ap05Bg
MCMAN, Bernard	19	M	Laborer	07Ap05Bg
TAYLOR, Anthony	21	M	Laborer	07Ap05Bg
NESBITT, Henry	20	M	Laborer	07Ap05Bg
PATTERSON, J.	44	M	Laborer	07Ap05Bg
Sarah	21	F	Laborer	07Ap05Bg
Margt	19	F	Laborer	07Ap05Bg
Marianne	15	F	Laborer	07Ap05Bg
June	12	F	Laborer	07Ap05Bg
Saml.	09	M	Child	07Ap05Bg
John	07	M	Child	07Ap05Bg
Eliza	04	F	Child	07Ap05Bg
JOHNSON, Robt.	12	M	Laborer	07Ap05Bg
COULAND, John	40	M	Laborer	07Ap05Bg
Cath.	35	F	Laborer	07Ap05Bg
Joseph	11	M	Laborer	07Ap05Bg
Thos.	16	M	Laborer	07Ap05Bg
Patt	13	M	Laborer	07Ap05Bg
Mary	12	F	Laborer	07Ap05Bg
Jane	09	F	Child	07Ap05Bg
Ann	06	F	Child	07Ap05Bg
John	02	M	Child	07Ap05Bg
FANNOR, Betty	45	F	Laborer	07Ap05Bg
BROUNLER, Patt	45	M	Laborer	07Ap05Bg

ST.LAWRENCE 07 APRIL 1849

From Cork

NAMES OF PASSENGERS	AGE	SEX	OCCUPATIONS	DATE PORT SHIP
DARLING, Ned	22	M	Laborer	07Ap08Bh
CRONIN, Jerry	30	M	Laborer	07Ap08Bh
TAGNEY, John	30	M	Laborer	07Ap08Bh
BOYLE, Danl.	20	M	Laborer	07Ap08Bh
Michl.	23	M	Laborer	07Ap08Bh
DEE, Pat	20	M	Laborer	07Ap08Bh
FOLEY, Pat	30	M	Laborer	07Ap08Bh
CROLEY, John	20	M	Laborer	07Ap08Bh
SWEENEY, Edw.	20	M	Laborer	07Ap08Bh
BARRETT, Nancy	20	F	Laborer	07Ap08Bh
CROWE, Richd.	25	M	Laborer	07Ap08Bh
CONNORS, Ann	20	F	Laborer	07Ap08Bh
MARTIN, Sally	18	F	Laborer	07Ap08Bh
MURPHY, Michl.	24	M	Laborer	07Ap08Bh
SULLIVAN, G.	24	M	Laborer	07Ap08Bh
CARROLL, Johanna	20	F	Laborer	07Ap08Bh
BOYLE, James	40	M	Laborer	07Ap08Bh
WHITE, John	24	M	Laborer	07Ap08Bh
LYONS, Michl.	20	M	Laborer	07Ap08Bh
Jerry	30	M	Laborer	07Ap08Bh
Jerry	20	M	Laborer	07Ap08Bh
Mary	25	F	Laborer	07Ap08Bh
HAGARTHY, Pat	18	M	Laborer	07Ap08Bh
Mary	20	F	Laborer	07Ap08Bh
BARRY, John	25	M	Laborer	07Ap08Bh
MARTIN, Ann	20	F	Laborer	07Ap08Bh
MOHER, Michl.	24	M	Laborer	07Ap08Bh
SULLIVAN, John	26	M	Laborer	07Ap08Bh
Daniel	24	M	Laborer	07Ap08Bh
COLLINS, John	28	M	Laborer	07Ap08Bh

NAMES OF PASSENGERS	A G E	S E X	OCCUPATIONS	DATE PORT SHIP
SULLIVAN, Hannora	30	F	Laborer	07Ap08Bh
Ellen	02	F	Child	07Ap08Bh
Johanna	.03	F	Infant	07Ap08Bh
HARRINGTON, Timothy	25	M	Laborer	07Ap08Bh
COLEMAN, Ellen	20	F	Laborer	07Ap08Bh
HIGGINS, Richd.	20	M	Laborer	07Ap08Bh
MCNAMARA, John	32	M	Laborer	07Ap08Bh
ODONNELL, Patt	25	M	Laborer	07Ap08Bh
HERLEHEY, Con	25	M	Laborer	07Ap08Bh
Mary	23	F	Laborer	07Ap08Bh
BARREY, Anne	30	F	Laborer	07Ap08Bh
RIORDAN, James	30	M	Laborer	07Ap08Bh
CONNERS, Mauria	30	F	Laborer	07Ap08Bh
CORBETT, Wm.	20	M	Laborer	07Ap08Bh
CONNORS, Mary	26	F	Laborer	07Ap08Bh
MADDEN, Bess	20	F	Laborer	07Ap08Bh
CONNORS, Mary	.09	F	Infant	07Ap08Bh
DONOVAN, John	20	M	Laborer	07Ap08Bh
MINEHAN, Biddy	26	F	Laborer	07Ap08Bh
John	40	M	Laborer	07Ap08Bh
Jean	13	M	Laborer	07Ap08Bh
Nancy	11	F	Laborer	07Ap08Bh
Maurice	06	M	Child	07Ap08Bh
COLEMAN, D.	30	M	Laborer	07Ap08Bh
Cath.	30	F	Laborer	07Ap08Bh
John	13	M	Laborer	07Ap08Bh
Anne	09	F	Child	07Ap08Bh
Margt.	06	F	Child	07Ap08Bh
Dennis	04	M	Child	07Ap08Bh
Michl.	01	M	Child	07Ap08Bh
Ellen	23	F	Laborer	07Ap08Bh
Mary	15	F	Laborer	07Ap08Bh
DALY, Thos.	24	M	Laborer	07Ap08Bh
BUCKLEY, Ellen	20	F	Laborer	07Ap08Bh
CALEY, Wm.	20	M	Laborer	07Ap08Bh
BYRNE, Cathe.	20	F	Laborer	07Ap08Bh
DRADDY, Patt	25	M	Laborer	07Ap08Bh
NOONAN, David	30	M	Laborer	07Ap08Bh
GALAVIN, Michl.	20	M	Laborer	07Ap08Bh
QUINN, Maurice	30	M	Laborer	07Ap08Bh
BRIEN, Ally	40	M	Laborer	07Ap08Bh
Richd.	17	M	Laborer	07Ap08Bh
Mich.	13	M	Laborer	07Ap08Bh
James	11	M	Laborer	07Ap08Bh
Ellen	07	F	Child	07Ap08Bh
DALEY, Julia	25	F	Laborer	07Ap08Bh
MURPHY, Peggy	20	F	Laborer	07Ap08Bh
CALAGHAN, Patt	20	M	Laborer	07Ap08Bh
CONNOR, Patt	20	M	Laborer	07Ap08Bh
Cath.	18	F	Laborer	07Ap08Bh
GRIFFEN, Patt	25	M	Laborer	07Ap08Bh
BOWLEY, Ellen	20	F	Laborer	07Ap08Bh
DUCKET, Henry	18	M	Laborer	07Ap08Bh
Mary	20	F	Laborer	07Ap08Bh
GODLOW, Peggy	26	F	Laborer	07Ap08Bh
MURPHY, Johanna	26	F	Laborer	07Ap08Bh
Mary	13	F	Laborer	07Ap08Bh
Peggy	12	F	Laborer	07Ap08Bh
Ellen	09	F	Child	07Ap08Bh
Bridget	07	F	Child	07Ap08Bh
Hannora	06	F	Child	07Ap08Bh
John	04	M	Child	07Ap08Bh
James	02	M	Child	07Ap08Bh
Cath.	.02	F	Infant	07Ap08Bh
KENNEDY, John	40	M	Laborer	07Ap08Bh
Julia	30	F	Laborer	07Ap08Bh
MURPHY, Jerh.	20	M	Laborer	07Ap08Bh
WELDEN, John	30	M	Laborer	07Ap08Bh
GILMAN, James	20	M	Laborer	07Ap08Bh
FLAHERTY, H.	26	M	Unknown	07Ap08Bh
HARTLAND, Wm.	39	M	Unknown	07Ap08Bh

CRESCENT-CITY 07 APRIL 1849

From CHAGRAS, San JUAN, Havana

NAMES OF PASSENGERS	A G E	S E X	OCCUPATIONS	DATE PORT SHIP
SULLIVAN, J.	35	M	Butcher	07Ap27Bi

LADY-CONSTABLE 07 APRIL 1849

From New Ross

NAMES OF PASSENGERS	A G E	S E X	OCCUPATIONS	DATE PORT SHIP
NEEHAM, Andrew	40	M	Laborer	07Ap25Bj
WING, Thomas	35	M	Laborer	07Ap25Bj
CASEY, Pat	32	M	Laborer	07Ap25Bj
CAMFIELD, J.	20	F	Laborer	07Ap25Bj
Thom.	16	M	Laborer	07Ap25Bj
LEARY, Martin	20	M	Laborer	07Ap25Bj
BRENNEN, John	25	M	Laborer	07Ap25Bj
FITZGERALD, John	26	M	Laborer	07Ap25Bj
FARMER, Thomas	26	M	Laborer	07Ap25Bj
James	20	M	Laborer	07Ap25Bj
CONALEY, Eliza	22	F	Laborer	07Ap25Bj
WALSH, Pat	22	M	Laborer	07Ap25Bj
MURRAY, Thom.	23	M	Laborer	07Ap25Bj
HANROCK, Lawrence	24	M	Laborer	07Ap25Bj
SHEA, Rich	26	M	Laborer	07Ap25Bj
HURT, Francis	27	M	Laborer	07Ap25Bj
WATERS, James	00	M	Laborer	07Ap25Bj
DOYLE, James	26	M	Laborer	07Ap25Bj
MURPHY, Thomas	24	M	Laborer	07Ap25Bj
WALSH, James	27	M	Laborer	07Ap25Bj
HANAGAN, Cornelius	29	M	Laborer	07Ap25Bj
MURPHY, James	27	M	Laborer	07Ap25Bj
BRUEN, Michl.	33	M	Laborer	07Ap25Bj
Cath.	29	F	Laborer	07Ap25Bj
WALSH, Pat	27	M	Laborer	07Ap25Bj
DELANEY, Mic	28	M	Laborer	07Ap25Bj
MURPHY, Michl.	40	M	Laborer	07Ap25Bj
SHERWOOD, Rich.N.	39	M	Laborer	07Ap25Bj
Hariet	39	M	Laborer	07Ap25Bj
HARE, Elenor-H.	20	F	Laborer	07Ap25Bj
NIXON, Rich-Jr.	29	M	Laborer	07Ap25Bj
George	19	M	Laborer	07Ap25Bj
Elizabeth	00	F	Laborer	07Ap25Bj
William-R.	16	M	Laborer	07Ap25Bj
CULLEN, Pierce	40	M	Laborer	07Ap25Bj
KENNEDY, Mathew	42	M	Laborer	07Ap25Bj
Mary	40	F	Laborer	07Ap25Bj
U	.00	U	Infant	07Ap25Bj
DATTON, Mary	30	F	Laborer	07Ap25Bj
Redmond	29	M	Laborer	07Ap25Bj
NEIL, Patrick	27	M	Laborer	07Ap25Bj
Mary	25	F	Laborer	07Ap25Bj
NOWLAN, Patt	25	M	Laborer	07Ap25Bj
MULLOY, Unity	26	F	Laborer	07Ap25Bj
RYAN, Edward	28	M	Laborer	07Ap25Bj
KAVANAGH, Mick	30	M	Laborer	07Ap25Bj
ROURKE, Pat	31	M	Laborer	07Ap25Bj
SHEA, Pat	30	M	Laborer	07Ap25Bj
KEHOE, Johanna	40	F	Laborer	07Ap25Bj
Margt	39	F	Laborer	07Ap25Bj
Edward	20	M	Laborer	07Ap25Bj
Mary	18	F	Laborer	07Ap25Bj
Catherine	16	F	Laborer	07Ap25Bj

NAMES OF PASSENGERS	AGE	SEX	OCCUPATIONS	DATE PORT SHIP
KEHOE, Johanna	14	F	Laborer	07Ap25Bj
Thomas	12	M	Laborer	07Ap25Bj
HENRY, Pat	30	M	Laborer	07Ap25Bj
NEIL, Mick	31	M	Laborer	07Ap25Bj
PENDERGAST, John	32	M	Laborer	07Ap25Bj
FLEMING, Peter	34	M	Laborer	07Ap25Bj
WALSH, Nathan	37	M	Laborer	07Ap25Bj
FURLONG, Eliza	28	F	Laborer	07Ap25Bj
HEARE, Bridget	30	F	Laborer	07Ap25Bj
ALWOOD, Michl	31	M	Laborer	07Ap25Bj
LAMBERT, Pat	32	M	Laborer	07Ap25Bj
Catherine	30	F	Laborer	07Ap25Bj
U	.00	U	Infant	07Ap25Bj
TOBIN, Phil	40	M	Laborer	07Ap25Bj
Bridget	39	F	Laborer	07Ap25Bj
U	.00	U	Infant	07Ap25Bj
James	00	M	Laborer	07Ap25Bj
BOOKILL, Michl.	35	M	Laborer	07Ap25Bj
John	33	M	Laborer	07Ap25Bj
Jude	04	M	Child	07Ap25Bj
NOLAN, John	25	M	Laborer	07Ap25Bj
Mary	23	F	Laborer	07Ap25Bj
CAVANOUGH, John	35	M	Laborer	07Ap25Bj
CULEN, Wm.	33	M	Laborer	07Ap25Bj
DEMPSEY, Margt.	33	M	Laborer	07Ap25Bj
KELLY, James	31	M	Laborer	07Ap25Bj
CULLEN, Rich	40	M	Laborer	07Ap25Bj
Mary	38	F	Laborer	07Ap25Bj
U	.00	U	Infant	07Ap25Bj
Martin	18	M	Laborer	07Ap25Bj
Mary	16	F	Laborer	07Ap25Bj
Anne	14	F	Laborer	07Ap25Bj
Anty	12	F	Laborer	07Ap25Bj
Anne	10	F	Laborer	07Ap25Bj
Nancy	08	F	Child	07Ap25Bj
Martin	06	M	Child	07Ap25Bj
Michael	04	M	Child	07Ap25Bj
WHELAN, Thomas	40	M	Laborer	07Ap25Bj
James	18	M	Laborer	07Ap25Bj
Catherine	16	F	Laborer	07Ap25Bj
Bridget	15	F	Laborer	07Ap25Bj
Moses	10	M	Laborer	07Ap25Bj
Nicholas	08	M	Child	07Ap25Bj
James	06	M	Child	07Ap25Bj
Catherine	04	F	Child	07Ap25Bj
NUSEY, Patt	35	M	Laborer	07Ap25Bj
Peter	22	M	Laborer	07Ap25Bj
Abbey	18	F	Laborer	07Ap25Bj
Mary	16	F	Laborer	07Ap25Bj
MURPHY, John	30	M	Laborer	07Ap25Bj
Lawrence	28	M	Laborer	07Ap25Bj
RIESSAN, Phil	30	M	Laborer	07Ap25Bj
GILLIAN, Mary	34	F	Laborer	07Ap25Bj
FLEMING, Charles	37	M	Laborer	07Ap25Bj
Mary	35	F	Laborer	07Ap25Bj
BRYNE, Margt.	31	F	Laborer	07Ap25Bj
DOYLE, John	22	M	Laborer	07Ap25Bj
WALSH, Margt.	35	F	Laborer	07Ap25Bj
MURPHY, Ann	26	F	Laborer	07Ap25Bj
CUNNINGHAM, Rich	27	M	Laborer	07Ap25Bj
GULL, Rich	28	M	Laborer	07Ap25Bj
MILENS, John	31	M	Laborer	07Ap25Bj
TOBIN, Nancy	33	F	Laborer	07Ap25Bj
CADIM, Dan	33	M	Laborer	07Ap25Bj
DOYLE, Phil	34	M	Laborer	07Ap25Bj
Elizth	22	F	Laborer	07Ap25Bj
CORCORAN, Pat	34	M	Laborer	07Ap25Bj
FOGARTY, James	27	M	Laborer	07Ap25Bj
Lawrence	28	M	Laborer	07Ap25Bj
SHERMAN, Pat	30	M	Laborer	07Ap25Bj
Anne	28	F	Laborer	07Ap25Bj
DARLING, Rich	29	M	Laborer	07Ap25Bj
JASON, Wm.	31	M	Laborer	07Ap25Bj
Michl	29	M	Laborer	07Ap25Bj
Mary	12	F	Laborer	07Ap25Bj
JASON, Ellen	10	F	Laborer	07Ap25Bj
FURSTED, Cath.	14	F	Laborer	07Ap25Bj
MCNAMARA, John	20	M	Laborer	07Ap25Bj
CHISM, John	25	M	Laborer	07Ap25Bj
REILLY, Andy	27	M	Laborer	07Ap25Bj
Mary	25	F	Laborer	07Ap25Bj
NEIL, Rich	40	M	Laborer	07Ap25Bj
WALSH, James	38	M	Laborer	07Ap25Bj
DUNN, John	29	M	Laborer	07Ap25Bj
Luke	27	M	Laborer	07Ap25Bj
Mary	06	F	Child	07Ap25Bj
Anne	25	F	Laborer	07Ap25Bj
U	.00	U	Infant	07Ap25Bj
CALIGHAN, John	24	M	Laborer	07Ap25Bj
MURPHY, James	26	M	Laborer	07Ap25Bj
TILIAN, Thomas	27	M	Laborer	07Ap25Bj
SWORDS, Margt.	29	F	Laborer	07Ap25Bj
TUGBY, Johanna	27	F	Laborer	07Ap25Bj
MURPHY, Nora	23	F	Laborer	07Ap25Bj
LARY, Garret	27	M	Laborer	07Ap25Bj
Mary	25	F	Laborer	07Ap25Bj
FOLEY, Phil	40	M	Laborer	07Ap25Bj
BRENNEN, Martin	28	M	Laborer	07Ap25Bj
NAUGHTON, Thos.	27	M	Laborer	07Ap25Bj
SHOUGHIERY, Lar	33	M	Laborer	07Ap25Bj
NEKASEY, Ann	24	F	Laborer	07Ap25Bj
Mary	22	F	Laborer	07Ap25Bj
BYRNE, Thos.	39	M	Laborer	07Ap25Bj
CULLEN, James	32	M	Laborer	07Ap25Bj
LAPHAM, Mathew	32	M	Laborer	07Ap25Bj
MURPHY, Dan	21	M	Laborer	07Ap25Bj
KEALY, Charles	30	M	Laborer	07Ap25Bj
TAYLOR, Geo.	25	M	Laborer	07Ap25Bj
MURPHY, Mich	27	M	Laborer	07Ap25Bj
BALYER, Owen	43	M	Laborer	07Ap25Bj
Anty	33	F	Laborer	07Ap25Bj
U	.00	U	Infant	07Ap25Bj
Wineford	18	F	Laborer	07Ap25Bj
Mary	16	F	Laborer	07Ap25Bj
Michl.	17	M	Laborer	07Ap25Bj
SMITH, James	40	M	Laborer	07Ap25Bj
Ann	38	F	Laborer	07Ap25Bj
ROURKE, Ann	27	F	Laborer	07Ap25Bj
MCDAVIE, Bridget	30	F	Laborer	07Ap25Bj
Judy	16	F	Laborer	07Ap25Bj
Ellen	14	F	Laborer	07Ap25Bj
Stephen	11	M	Laborer	07Ap25Bj
John	04	M	Child	07Ap25Bj
DOYLE, Ann	00	F	Unknown	07Ap25Bj
U	.00	U	Infant	07Ap25Bj
FITZGERALD, Mary	27	F	Laborer	07Ap25Bj
John	16	M	Laborer	07Ap25Bj
NEIL, Kitty	14	F	Laborer	07Ap25Bj
MCCUSSY, Mary	22	F	Laborer	07Ap25Bj
NOLAN, Mary	22	F	Laborer	07Ap25Bj
DUNN, Ellen	24	F	Laborer	07Ap25Bj
DOYLE, Mary	23	F	Laborer	07Ap25Bj
CLOREN, Mary	22	F	Laborer	07Ap25Bj
CORCORAN, James	30	M	Laborer	07Ap25Bj
Mary	28	F	Laborer	07Ap25Bj
Michl.	04	M	Child	07Ap25Bj
Nancy	02	F	Child	07Ap25Bj
NOLAN, James	24	M	Laborer	07Ap25Bj
Mary	22	F	Laborer	07Ap25Bj
DOYLE, Anthony	27	M	Laborer	07Ap25Bj
Eliza	25	F	Laborer	07Ap25Bj
KINSALLA, Pat	23	M	Laborer	07Ap25Bj
BURGESS, Mary	00	F	Laborer	07Ap25Bj
GREEN, Thomas	24	M	Laborer	07Ap25Bj
Ann	22	F	Laborer	07Ap25Bj
MORGAN, James	30	M	Laborer	07Ap25Bj
WALSH, Anthony	26	M	Laborer	07Ap25Bj
DOYLE, Betsy	22	F	Laborer	07Ap25Bj
COADEY, Cath.	22	F	Laborer	07Ap25Bj
TRACY, Pat	00	M	Laborer	07Ap25Bj

NAMES OF PASSENGERS	AGE	SEX	OCCUPATIONS	DATE PORT SHIP
SMITH, John	00	M	Laborer	07Ap25Bj
THOMPSON, James	00	M	Laborer	07Ap25Bj
MELVANEY, John	00	M	Laborer	07Ap25Bj
COONEY, William	00	M	Laborer	07Ap25Bj
FLAHERTY, William	00	M	Laborer	07Ap25Bj
MCNAMARA, John	00	M	Laborer	07Ap25Bj
CASSIER, John	00	M	Laborer	07Ap25Bj
CONNOLLY, Pat	00	M	Laborer	07Ap25Bj

ELIZABETH 09 APRIL 1849

From Liverpool

NAMES OF PASSENGERS	AGE	SEX	OCCUPATIONS	DATE PORT SHIP
GRAHAM, James	19	M	Flaxdr	09Ap02Bk
COYLE, Francis	19	M	Laborer	09Ap02Bk
GAIRY, Daniel	20	M	Laborer	09Ap02Bk
CONNALD, Daniel	20	M	Carpenter	09Ap02Bk
KELLY, Michael	19	M	Laborer	09Ap02Bk
FLYNN, Patrick	19	M	Laborer	09Ap02Bk
HART, James	22	M	Laborer	09Ap02Bk
DORHY, Michael	21	M	Laborer	09Ap02Bk
CREMEN, John	45	M	Laborer	09Ap02Bk
MORNATHY, Michael	40	M	Laborer	09Ap02Bk
LEARY, Daniel	20	M	Laborer	09Ap02Bk
HART, Mary	19	F	Seamstress	09Ap02Bk
MCCASKER, Mary	18	F	Spinster	09Ap02Bk
MORRISON, Bridget	24	F	House Woman	09Ap02Bk
MADIGAN, Thomas	32	M	Laborer	09Ap02Bk
MARLAN, Michael	20	M	Laborer	09Ap02Bk
RYAN, Mary	20	F	Servant	09Ap02Bk
FLOYD, Elizabeth	14	F	Spinster	09Ap02Bk
MACGEE, James	17	M	Laborer	09Ap02Bk
John	19	M	Laborer	09Ap02Bk
MACQUINAY, Ellen	20	F	Spinster	09Ap02Bk
Sarah	19	F	Spinster	09Ap02Bk
MACKOEN, Catherine	18	F	Spinster	09Ap02Bk
TACKENY, Mary	28	F	Servant	09Ap02Bk
MACGEE, Mary	14	F	Spinster	09Ap02Bk
DOGHORTY, U	30	F	Spinster	09Ap02Bk
MCINERNEY, Dennis	30	M	Laborer	09Ap02Bk
MACMANARA, Dennis	30	M	Laborer	09Ap02Bk
GRIFFIN, Matthew	30	M	Laborer	09Ap02Bk
TIMMORS, William	35	M	Laborer	09Ap02Bk
TACKNEY, Michael	32	M	Laborer	09Ap02Bk
DOGHORTY, Felix	25	M	Laborer	09Ap02Bk
FARLEY, Michael	20	M	Laborer	09Ap02Bk
MURPHY, James	22	M	Laborer	09Ap02Bk
DRISCOL, Daniel	20	M	Laborer	09Ap02Bk
DAY, James	30	M	Carpenter	09Ap02Bk
LEARY, Patrick	20	M	Laborer	09Ap02Bk
CAHILL, Barthw.	27	M	Laborer	09Ap02Bk
Lawrence	35	M	Laborer	09Ap02Bk
SHAR, John	23	M	Laborer	09Ap02Bk
MACNAMARA, Thomas	30	M	Laborer	09Ap02Bk
MAHONY, Edmund	30	M	Laborer	09Ap02Bk
MULLOHANN, John	14	M	Laborer	09Ap02Bk
MACCARTY, Martin	23	M	Laborer	09Ap02Bk
ENGLAND, James	27	M	Laborer	09Ap02Bk
MAMARA, Bridget	32	F	Servant	09Ap02Bk
HARVEY, Ellen	18	F	Seamstress	09Ap02Bk
MURPHY, Nora	24	F	House Woman	09Ap02Bk
Daniel	02	M	Child	09Ap02Bk
MALONE, Daniel	20	M	Laborer	09Ap02Bk
Bridget	21	F	Spinster	09Ap02Bk
OBRIEN, Thomas	24	M	Laborer	09Ap02Bk
Mary	24	F	House Woman	09Ap02Bk
KELLEN, Paul	21	M	Stone Mason	09Ap02Bk
FANNON, John	26	M	Weaver	09Ap02Bk
CARTHEY, Patrick	21	M	Laborer	09Ap02Bk
CARTHEY, Timothy	60	M	Laborer	09Ap02Bk
FANNON, Margaret	23	F	Pwlwvr	09Ap02Bk
CARTHY, Catherine	21	F	Spinster	09Ap02Bk
MACDONALD, Sarah	25	F	Spinster	09Ap02Bk
HUNT, Elizabeth	40	F	House Woman	09Ap02Bk
DUGGON, John	13	M	Unknown	09Ap02Bk
Patrick	40	M	Laborer	09Ap02Bk
GALLUGHER, Margery	24	F	House Woman	09Ap02Bk
Neeil	20	M	Laborer	09Ap02Bk
Rosa	22	F	Seamstress	09Ap02Bk
Bryant	03	M	Child	09Ap02Bk
FRRANINA, James	32	M	Laborer	09Ap02Bk
John	24	M	Laborer	09Ap02Bk
Patrick	21	M	Laborer	09Ap02Bk
COURTNEY, Michael	25	M	Laborer	09Ap02Bk
JENNINGS, Michael	20	M	Weaver	09Ap02Bk
FAHAY, James	18	M	Cord Winder	09Ap02Bk
NOWLAND, Thomas	20	M	Laborer	09Ap02Bk
MULROY, Thomas	20	M	Laborer	09Ap02Bk
MOORE, Daniel	55	M	Laborer	09Ap02Bk
Catherine	48	F	House Woman	09Ap02Bk
William	17	M	Laborer	09Ap02Bk
Mary	11	F	Unknown	09Ap02Bk
Daniel	14	M	Unknown	09Ap02Bk
MORAN, Anne	25	F	Servant	09Ap02Bk
MOORE, Anne	15	F	Servant	09Ap02Bk
BENNY, Caroline	14	F	Spinster	09Ap02Bk
WELSH, Ann	16	F	Spinster	09Ap02Bk
GAFFERY, Mary	20	F	Spinster	09Ap02Bk
COYNE, Patrick	30	M	Grocer	09Ap02Bk
DOLAN, Thomas	08	M	Child	09Ap02Bk
MORLAN, John	30	M	Laborer	09Ap02Bk
NUGENT, James	24	M	Laborer	09Ap02Bk
CHEEKY, Catherine	16	F	Spinster	09Ap02Bk
BYRNE, Margaret	25	F	Servant	09Ap02Bk
CANTWELL, Mary	25	F	Spinster	09Ap02Bk
CREMER, Ann	20	F	Spinster	09Ap02Bk
CHEEKY, Patrick	18	M	Laborer	09Ap02Bk
MAY, Michael	20	M	Laborer	09Ap02Bk
BYRNE, Patrick	27	M	Laborer	09Ap02Bk
MULLIGAN, John	18	M	Laborer	09Ap02Bk
GRAHAM, Thomas	06	M	Child	09Ap02Bk
Edmund	11	M	Unknown	09Ap02Bk
James	13	M	Unknown	09Ap02Bk
SHEPPARD, James	68	M	Mason	09Ap02Bk
Margaret	68	F	Housewife	09Ap02Bk
GRAHAM, Thomas	50	M	Laborer	09Ap02Bk
Joannah	50	F	Housewife	09Ap02Bk
DALTON, Patrick	30	M	Carpenter	09Ap02Bk
Patrick	40	M	Laborer	09Ap02Bk
CRAWLEY, Thomas	25	M	Laborer	09Ap02Bk
CUMMINS, Andrew	24	M	Laborer	09Ap02Bk
SHEA, Catherine	26	F	Spinster	09Ap02Bk
GRAHAM, Jane	16	F	Spinster	09Ap02Bk
SHEA, Ellen	24	F	Housewife	09Ap02Bk
SHIRLEY, Thomas	26	M	Laborer	09Ap02Bk
FLOYD, James	14	M	Laborer	09Ap02Bk
MACGONAN, Patrick	60	M	Cord Winder	09Ap02Bk
GILLAND, James	35	M	Lnwvr	09Ap02Bk
HADDOCK, Richard	30	M	Tailor	09Ap02Bk
SIMPSON, Anne	20	F	Seamstress	09Ap02Bk
MACCOMB, Mary	20	F	Seamstress	09Ap02Bk
ROACH, Richard	26	M	Laborer	09Ap02Bk
HAFFRON, David	35	M	Laborer	09Ap02Bk
CROWLEY, Patrick	25	M	Tin Maker	09Ap02Bk
POPE, Mary	22	F	Spinster	09Ap02Bk
MONARTHY, Ellen	20	F	Spinster	09Ap02Bk
CRONIA, Johanna	20	F	Spinster	09Ap02Bk
MAHAR, Mary	23	F	Housewife	09Ap02Bk
U	.00	U	Infant	09Ap02Bk
Mary-Anne	06	F	Child	09Ap02Bk
Ellen	04	F	Child	09Ap02Bk
TALLIS, Richard	21	M	Laborer	09Ap02Bk
SINNETT, Thomas	20	M	Carpenter	09Ap02Bk
IRELAND, Richard	40	M	Carpenter	09Ap02Bk

NAMES OF PASSENGERS	AGE	SEX	OCCUPATIONS	DATE PORT SHIP
CONERY, Thomas	35	M	Accountant	09Ap02Bk
Patrick	20	M	Laborer	09Ap02Bk
CROAKE, Patrick	21	M	Laborer	09Ap02Bk
CARROL, Mary	60	F	Housewife	09Ap02Bk
RYAN, Timothy	08	M	Child	09Ap02Bk
Patrick	04	M	Child	09Ap02Bk
Dennis	31	M	Laborer	09Ap02Bk
Bridget	28	F	Housewife	09Ap02Bk
U	.00	U	Infant	09Ap02Bk
Michael	02	M	Child	09Ap02Bk
CROAK, Ellen	20	F	Milliner	09Ap02Bk
SHANNON, Ellen	19	F	Seamstress	09Ap02Bk
GLEESON, Anne	18	F	Seamstress	09Ap02Bk
FLYNN, James	40	M	Laborer	09Ap02Bk
Dennis	30	M	Laborer	09Ap02Bk
Michael	18	M	Tailor	09Ap02Bk
Ellen	12	M	Unknown	09Ap02Bk
HANARY, Andrw	17	M	Laborer	09Ap02Bk
GLEESON, Thomas	26	M	Laborer	09Ap02Bk
LONG, Martin	30	M	Laborer	09Ap02Bk
COYLE, Barnard	50	M	Laborer	09Ap02Bk
OHARE, Edward	40	M	Laborer	09Ap02Bk
AGNEW, Mary	11	F	Unknown	09Ap02Bk
Barney	06	M	Child	09Ap02Bk
COYLE, Judith	20	F	Servant	09Ap02Bk
SMITH, Mary	25	F	Housewife	09Ap02Bk
U	.00	U	Infant	09Ap02Bk
Catherine	07	F	Child	09Ap02Bk
ROACH, Morris	25	M	Laborer	09Ap02Bk
FIELD, Charles	30	M	Accountant	09Ap02Bk
MACGORLOCK, Bridget	35	F	Housewife	09Ap02Bk
Michael	03	M	Child	09Ap02Bk
Anne	07	F	Child	09Ap02Bk
Bridget	05	F	Child	09Ap02Bk
Patrick	10	M	Unknown	09Ap02Bk
Mary	18	F	Spinster	09Ap02Bk
DONLEY, Ann	14	F	Spinster	09Ap02Bk
ONEIL, Fanny	16	F	Spinster	09Ap02Bk
FLOOD, Patrick	23	M	Laborer	09Ap02Bk
ONEIL, Joseph	20	M	Joiner	09Ap02Bk
William	15	M	Joiner	09Ap02Bk
DORAN, James	28	M	Laborer	09Ap02Bk
Patrick	12	M	Unknown	09Ap02Bk
Francis	14	M	Unknown	09Ap02Bk
Bridget	16	F	Servant	09Ap02Bk
John	50	M	Laborer	09Ap02Bk
Bridget	50	F	Housewife	09Ap02Bk
Julia	03	F	Child	09Ap02Bk
John	25	M	Mason	09Ap02Bk
MURRAY, Hugh	35	M	Laborer	09Ap02Bk
LEE, John	26	M	Enginesmith	09Ap02Bk
HALLY, Michael	20	M	Laborer	09Ap02Bk
MADDON, Anne	35	F	Spinster	09Ap02Bk
Bridget	24	F	Dressmaker	09Ap02Bk
Catherine	20	F	Spinster	09Ap02Bk
COFFY, Michael	40	M	Laborer	09Ap02Bk
DWYEN, Philip	30	M	Laborer	09Ap02Bk
BRANNON, John	24	M	Laborer	09Ap02Bk
COFFY, Mary	11	F	Unknown	09Ap02Bk
John	12	M	Unknown	09Ap02Bk
FOGARTY, Mry	25	F	Servant	09Ap02Bk
MAGGUIRE, Owen	18	M	Laborer	09Ap02Bk
AGNEW, James	25	M	Laborer	09Ap02Bk
GULLIAM, Michael	30	M	Laborer	09Ap02Bk
DIVET, William	18	M	Cord Winder	09Ap02Bk
MAGGUIRE, Susan	50	F	Housewife	09Ap02Bk
Mary	22	F	Seamstress	09Ap02Bk
DIVIT, Olevie	19	F	Servant	09Ap02Bk
KEENAN, John	25	M	Accountant	09Ap02Bk
FLYNN, Peter	50	M	Laborer	09Ap02Bk
Margaret	15	F	Spinster	09Ap02Bk
FITZPATRICK, James	30	M	Laborer	09Ap02Bk
LAWLIN, Phil	18	M	Laborer	09Ap02Bk
REHARTY, Michael	20	M	Laborer	09Ap02Bk
DWYN, Andrew	25	M	Accountant	09Ap02Bk
DWYN, Thomas	22	M	Laborer	09Ap02Bk
REHARTY, Catherine	14	F	Spinster	09Ap02Bk
ALLEN, Elizabeth	20	F	Spinster	09Ap02Bk
KELLY, Mary-Anne	23	F	Spinster	09Ap02Bk
WHITE, Mary	20	F	Spinster	09Ap02Bk
ROACH, Elizabeth	20	F	Housewife	09Ap02Bk
HOGAN, Ellen	20	F	Spinster	09Ap02Bk
LOW, Michael	21	M	Laborer	09Ap02Bk
TYNG, John	40	M	Laborer	09Ap02Bk
Mary	10	F	Unknown	09Ap02Bk
RYAN, Patrick	24	F	Laborer	09Ap02Bk
KENNADY, Simon	20	F	Laborer	09Ap02Bk
WALKER, Mary	40	F	Housewife	09Ap02Bk
U	.00	U	Infant	09Ap02Bk
Catherine	03	F	Child	09Ap02Bk

BETHEL 09 APRIL 1849

From Limerick

NAMES OF PASSENGERS	AGE	SEX	OCCUPATIONS	DATE PORT SHIP
HAYES, Edward	40	M	Farmer	09Ap35Bl
Ellen	18	F	Servant	09Ap35Bl
RYAN, Mary	24	F	Servant	09Ap35Bl
ROURKE, Bryan	20	M	Laborer	09Ap35Bl
LENAHAN, Lawrence	30	M	Laborer	09Ap35Bl
Mary	24	F	Servant	09Ap35Bl
HALPIN, Cathe.	18	F	Servant	09Ap35Bl
CARROLL, Michael	25	M	Farmer	09Ap35Bl
BOURKE, Patt	55	M	Farmer	09Ap35Bl
U (W)	50	F	Farmer	09Ap35Bl
Patt	22	M	Farmer	09Ap35Bl
Edward	20	M	Farmer	09Ap35Bl
John	18	M	Farmer	09Ap35Bl
Daniel	13	M	Farmer	09Ap35Bl
Mary	16	F	Farmer	09Ap35Bl
Nancy	11	F	Farmer	09Ap35Bl
Honorah	09	F	Child	09Ap35Bl
FITZGIBBON, John	40	M	Laborer	09Ap35Bl
HIGGINS, Aliche	33	M	Farmer	09Ap35Bl
Mary	32	F	Wife	09Ap35Bl
Rodger	07	M	Child	09Ap35Bl
Eliza	04	F	Child	09Ap35Bl
John	02	M	Child	09Ap35Bl
HYNES, Anne	48	F	Laborer	09Ap35B
HARTIGAN, John	25	M	Laborer	09Ap35B
NEALTY, Michael	30	M	Farmer	09Ap35B
Ellen	21	F	Farmer	09Ap35B
Honorah	09	F	Child	09Ap35B
MCNAMARA, Martin	30	M	Laborer	09Ap35B
NELSON, Patt	45	M	Laborer	09Ap35B
James	10	M	Laborer	09Ap35B
FRAWLEY, Michael	25	M	Farmer	09Ap35B
NINETER, Maurice	36	M	Farmer	09Ap35B
Margaret	25	F	Wife	09Ap35B
Catherine	10	F	Farmer	09Ap35B
Margaret	08	F	Child	09Ap35B
Anne	06	F	Child	09Ap35B
MCDERMOTT, John	36	M	Farmer	09Ap35B
Mary-Anne	34	F	Wife	09Ap35B
Francis	13	M	Farmer	09Ap35B
Catherine	06	F	Child	09Ap35B
Mary-Anne	.10	F	Infant	09Ap35B
HALPIN, Margaret	20	F	Servant	09Ap35B
MULLANE, Thomas	30	M	Laborer	09Ap35B
GILTMAN, Thomas	20	M	Laborer	09Ap35B
NEALTY, Mary	25	F	Servant	09Ap35B
BOURKE, Michl.	25	M	Laborer	09Ap35B
MADIGAN, Mary	19	F	Servant	09Ap35B
BOURKE, Michl.	18	M	Farmer	09Ap35B

NAMES OF PASSENGERS		AGE	SEX	OCCUPATIONS	DATE PORT SHIP
HAYES, Mary		20	F	Servant	09Ap35BI
QUINLIVAR, Danl.		20	M	Laborer	09Ap35BI
MCGRATH, John		20	M	Laborer	09Ap35BI
NAUGHTON, Bridget		24	F	Servant	09Ap35BI
Catherine		16	F	Unknown	09Ap35BI
CURTIN, James		20	M	Laborer	09Ap35BI
OSULLIVAN, John		25	M	Laborer	09Ap35BI
Catherine		30	F	Wife	09Ap35BI
MCNAMARA, Anne		20	F	Servant	09Ap35BI
KEOGH, James		21	M	Laborer	09Ap35BI
Mary	(W)	20	F	Wife	09Ap35BI
Bridget	(T)	16	F	Relative	09Ap35BI
NELSON, Mary		30	F	Servant	09Ap35BI
Michael	(S)	06	M	Child	09Ap35BI
Mary	(D)	03	F	Child	09Ap35BI
John	(S)	.00	M	Infant	09Ap35BI
HYNES, Thomas		25	M	Laborer	09Ap35BI
HENNESSY, James		20	M	Laborer	09Ap35BI
PAUL, Eliza		17	F	Servant	09Ap35BI
Ellen		50	F	Servant	09Ap35BI
MCGRATH, John		38	M	Farmer	09Ap35BI
OBRIEN, John		17	M	Farmer	09Ap35BI
Terence		10	M	Farmer	09Ap35BI
MASON, John		30	M	Laborer	09Ap35BI
HAGARTY, Wm.		20	M	Laborer	09Ap35BI
Bridget	(T)	25	F	Relative	09Ap35BI
CONNELL, Thomas		24	M	Laborer	09Ap35BI
HICKEY, Bridget		03	F	Child	09Ap35BI
Mary		.09	F	Infant	09Ap35BI
MOYLAN, Mary		09	F	Child	09Ap35BI
Wm.		12	M	Relative	09Ap35BI
MARONEY, Patt		12	M	Farmer	09Ap35BI
Mary		10	F	Wife	09Ap35BI
Michael		08	M	Child	09Ap35BI
Margaret		06	F	Child	09Ap35BI
John		04	M	Child	09Ap35BI
DONOLAN, Bridget		20	F	Servant	09Ap35BI
Mary		18	F	Relative	09Ap35BI
HALLORAN, John		20	M	Farmer	09Ap35BI
Mary		18	F	Relative	09Ap35BI
ROUGHAN, Bridget		19	F	Servant	09Ap35BI
Mary		18	F	Relative	09Ap35BI
MOYLAN, Patt		40	M	Farmer	09Ap35BI
Hanorah		40	F	Farmer	09Ap35BI
Mary	(D)	22	F	Relative	09Ap35BI
Bridget		18	F	Relative	09Ap35BI
HICKEY, Michael		30	M	Laborer	09Ap35BI
Bridget		28	F	Wife	09Ap35BI
MCNAMARA, Patt		20	M	Farmer	09Ap35BI
Mary		11	F	Farmer	09Ap35BI
MOYLAN, Mary		18	F	Servant	09Ap35BI
Margaret		11	F	Servant	09Ap35BI
MORONEY, Michael		40	M	Farmer	09Ap35BI
Margaret		35	F	Wife	09Ap35BI
ANGLEM, John		20	M	Laborer	09Ap35BI
Cath.		20	F	Wife	09Ap35BI
LYNCH, Cath.		20	F	Servant	09Ap35BI
Margt.		18	F	Servant	09Ap35BI
MCNAMARA, Michael		40	M	Farmer	09Ap35BI
Patt	(S)	17	M	Relative	09Ap35BI
HALLORAN, Patt		40	M	Laborer	09Ap35BI
LONG, John		30	M	Laborer	09Ap35BI
James		20	M	Laborer	09Ap35BI
John		23	M	Laborer	09Ap35BI
MCNAMARA, John		35	M	Farmer	09Ap35BI
Daniel		20	M	Relative	09Ap35BI
NEHILL, Ellee		40	F	Relative	09Ap35BI
Michael		14	M	Relative	09Ap35BI
WHITE, John		20	M	Farmer	09Ap35BI
NEHILL, Thomas		10	M	Child	09Ap35BI
CARMODY, Mary		28	F	Servant	09Ap35BI
ODONNELL, John		25	M	Servant	09Ap35BI
MCNAMARA, Dennis		22	M	Laborer	09Ap35BI
KELLY, Martin		20	M	Laborer	09Ap35BI
GYLES, Eliza		19	F	Laborer	09Ap35BI
GYLES, Mary		17	F	Laborer	09Ap35BI
MURPHY, Edmond		21	M	Laborer	09Ap35BI
Ellen		18	F	Laborer	09Ap35BI
GALLIVAN, Dennis		32	M	Laborer	09Ap35BI
Catherine		25	F	Laborer	09Ap35BI
STOKES, Patrick		30	M	Laborer	09Ap35BI
ROURKE, Francis		20	M	Laborer	09Ap35BI
MCCARTHY, Michael		48	M	Laborer	09Ap35BI
Cornelius		29	M	Laborer	09Ap35BI
Dennis		21	M	Laborer	09Ap35BI
BROWN, Michael		33	M	Laborer	09Ap35BI
MCELLIGOTT, Maurice		36	M	Laborer	09Ap35BI
SCANLON, Thos.		30	M	Laborer	09Ap35BI
WALSH, Wm.		34	M	Laborer	09Ap35BI
CONNELL, John		30	M	Laborer	09Ap35BI
HENNESSEY, Winfred		26	M	Laborer	09Ap35BI
BROWN, James		20	M	Laborer	09Ap35BI
FLYNN, Patrick		30	M	Laborer	09Ap35BI
ODONNELL, James		20	M	Laborer	09Ap35BI
KELLEHAN, Michael		32	M	Laborer	09Ap35BI
LONG, Mary		28	F	Laborer	09Ap35BI
COLLINS, Johannah		30	F	Laborer	09Ap35BI
TWOPEY, Jeremiah		33	M	Laborer	09Ap35BI
CONVERS, Martin		28	M	Laborer	09Ap35BI
SWEENEY, Patt		20	M	Laborer	09Ap35BI
NEALON, U-Mrs.		40	F	Laborer	09Ap35BI
John		13	M	Laborer	09Ap35BI
Patrick		07	M	Child	09Ap35BI
William		03	M	Child	09Ap35BI
Ellen		10	F	Child	09Ap35BI
Honorah		00	F	Unknown	09Ap35BI
U, U		.00	U	Infant	09Ap35BI
Born-At-Sea					
U		.00	U	Infant	09Ap35BI
Born-At-Sea					

ARKANSAS 09 APRIL 1849

From Dublin

NAMES OF PASSENGERS		AGE	SEX	OCCUPATIONS	DATE PORT SHIP
HENNESSY, Patt		40	M	Smith	09Ap12Bm
Margaret		40	F	Seamstress	09Ap12Bm
FORTUNE, Julia		22	F	Seamstress	09Ap12Bm
Jane		20	F	Seamstress	09Ap12Bm
FARRELL, Ignatious		21	M	Carpenter	09Ap12Bm
CAVANAGH, James		30	M	Stctr	09Ap12Bm
PERCY, Sam		23	M	Carpenter	09Ap12Bm
FULLAM, Thomas		50	M	Farmer	09Ap12Bm
Catherine		45	F	Farmer	09Ap12Bm
Henrietta		27	F	Farmer	09Ap12Bm
John		22	M	Farmer	09Ap12Bm
Martin		20	M	Farmer	09Ap12Bm
Henry		18	M	Farmer	09Ap12Bm
Thomas		12	M	Farmer	09Ap12Bm
MCCANN, Thomas		40	M	Gdnr	09Ap12Bm
SHERLOCK, Rose		20	F	Seamstress	09Ap12Bm
By---, Mary		22	F	Servant	09Ap12Bm
Lucy		18	F	Servant	09Ap12Bm
HAWKINS, Wm.		30	M	Shoemaker	09Ap12Bm
George		28	M	Shoemaker	09Ap12Bm
Mary		25	F	Shoemaker	09Ap12Bm
Eliza		04	F	Child	09Ap12Bm
Samuel		06	M	Child	09Ap12Bm
Wm.		02	M	Child	09Ap12Bm
NOWLAN, Wm.		35	M	Farmer	09Ap12Bm
U	(W)	32	F	Farmer	09Ap12Bm
Eliza		27	F	Farmer	09Ap12Bm
Margaret		20	F	Farmer	09Ap12Bm
Wm.		22	M	Farmer	09Ap12Bm

NAMES OF PASSENGERS	AGE	SEX	OCCUPATIONS	DATE PORT SHIP
NOWLAN, Richard	18	M	Farmer	09Ap12Bm
John	16	M	Farmer	09Ap12Bm
GORMAN, John	22	M	Laborer	09Ap12Bm
Bridget	28	F	Servant	09Ap12Bm
MAHON, Cath.	30	F	Servant	09Ap12Bm
Philipp	04	M	Child	09Ap12Bm
TYRILL, Edward	38	M	Farmer	09Ap12Bm
Richard	03	M	Child	09Ap12Bm
Thomas	.00	M	Infant	09Ap12Bm
Betty	34	F	Farmer	09Ap12Bm
Anne	02	F	Child	09Ap12Bm
BYRNE, John	55	M	Farmer	09Ap12Bm
Patt	21	M	Farmer	09Ap12Bm
James	17	M	Farmer	09Ap12Bm
Mary	23	F	Farmer	09Ap12Bm
Anne	13	F	Farmer	09Ap12Bm
FITZSIMMONS, Margaret	20	F	Servant	09Ap12Bm
Michael	21	M	Laborer	09Ap12Bm
WALSH, Michael	22	M	Laborer	09Ap12Bm
KERNON, Patt	20	M	Laborer	09Ap12Bm
FLANAGAN, Dennis	20	M	Laborer	09Ap12Bm
GRAHAM, Wm.	40	M	Laborer	09Ap12Bm
Wm.	20	M	Laborer	09Ap12Bm
HARROLD, John	35	M	Store Clerk	09Ap12Bm
Mary	35	F	Store Clerk	09Ap12Bm
Eliza	10	F	Store Clerk	09Ap12Bm
Sarah	08	F	Child	09Ap12Bm
John	.00	M	Infant	09Ap12Bm
James	05	M	Child	09Ap12Bm
SERVANT, Balia	25	F	Unknown	09Ap12Bm
PENROSE, Sarah	18	F	Servant	09Ap12Bm
LAWLESS, Patt	20	M	Laborer	09Ap12Bm
BLAKE, Janus	20	M	Laborer	09Ap12Bm
CASGROVE, Patt	20	M	Laborer	09Ap12Bm
BRYNE, Christy	21	M	Laborer	09Ap12Bm
Maria	20	F	Servant	09Ap12Bm
DOWNEY, Thomas	25	M	Mason	09Ap12Bm
SWEENY, William	20	M	Laborer	09Ap12Bm
KINSELLA, Patt	21	M	Laborer	09Ap12Bm
MOLOY, Mariss	20	F	Servant	09Ap12Bm
DOWNEY, Ellin	20	F	Nurse	09Ap12Bm
KENNEDY, Bridget	18	F	Servant	09Ap12Bm
DOOLEY, Joseph	32	M	Mechanic	09Ap12Bm
Catherine	30	F	Mechanic	09Ap12Bm
Mary	03	F	Child	09Ap12Bm
Judy	.00	F	Infant	09Ap12Bm
DUNCAN, Wm.	24	M	Blacksmith	09Ap12Bm
U-Mrs.	24	F	Blacksmith	09Ap12Bm
Catherine	.00	F	Infant	09Ap12Bm
MULLIGAN, Bridget	25	F	Servant	09Ap12Bm
DONAHUE, Mary	45	F	Nurse	09Ap12Bm
Biddy	20	F	Nurse	09Ap12Bm
SCALLAN, U	17	M	Laborer	09Ap12Bm
DONAHUE, James	17	M	Laborer	09Ap12Bm
TAYLOR, Wm.	24	M	Laborer	09Ap12Bm
KENNEDY, John	25	M	Laborer	09Ap12Bm
CAGMINS, Margaret	55	F	Farmer	09Ap12Bm
Mary	22	F	Farmer	09Ap12Bm
Catherine	20	F	Farmer	09Ap12Bm
Betty	19	F	Farmer	09Ap12Bm
Margaret	17	F	Farmer	09Ap12Bm
Michael	28	M	Farmer	09Ap12Bm
Lawrence	24	M	Farmer	09Ap12Bm
KEERNON, John	36	M	Farmer	09Ap12Bm
Anne	30	F	Farmer	09Ap12Bm
Catherine	11	F	Farmer	09Ap12Bm
Thomas	04	M	Child	09Ap12Bm
KEOGH, John	20	M	Laborer	09Ap12Bm
Eliza	19	F	Laborer	09Ap12Bm
KEANE, Mary	00	F	Dressmaker	09Ap12Bm
CAHITT, Ellen	20	F	Servant	09Ap12Bm
KENNA, James	24	M	Laborer	09Ap12Bm
CARTER, Alice	50	F	Farmer	09Ap12Bm
Catherine	24	F	Farmer	09Ap12Bm
Johana	19	F	Farmer	09Ap12Bm
CARTER, Mary	18	F	Farmer	09Ap12Bm
Margaret	12	F	Farmer	09Ap12Bm
Michael	30	M	Farmer	09Ap12Bm
Daniel	28	M	Farmer	09Ap12Bm
William	20	M	Farmer	09Ap12Bm
Thomas	16	M	Farmer	09Ap12Bm
Luke	14	M	Farmer	09Ap12Bm
Doyl-, Thomas	24	M	Table Maker	09Ap12Bm
MCCORMACK, Edward	27	M	Laborer	09Ap12Bm
SULLIVAN, Daniel	32	M	Musician	09Ap12Bm
REYNOLDS, Francis	20	M	Laborer	09Ap12Bm
HURLEY, Wm.	18	M	Brush Maker	09Ap12Bm
MCEVOY, Wm.	20	M	Laborer	09Ap12Bm
NOLAN, Bridget	32	F	Nurse	09Ap12Bm
John	12	M	Unknown	09Ap12Bm
SPOLLEN, James	45	M	Laborer	09Ap12Bm
SNOWLAN, Patt	18	M	Unknown	09Ap12Bm
Margaret	25	F	Unknown	09Ap12Bm
Anne	19	F	Unknown	09Ap12Bm
Catherine	17	F	Unknown	09Ap12Bm
Bridget	40	F	Unknown	09Ap12Bm
BERRY, Thomas	36	M	Laborer	09Ap12Bm
James	08	M	Child	09Ap12Bm
John	02	M	Child	09Ap12Bm
U (W)	34	F	Unknown	09Ap12Bm
Catharine	09	F	Child	09Ap12Bm
Rose	15	F	Laborer	09Ap12Bm
Mary	.00	F	Infant	09Ap12Bm
Edward	20	M	Laborer	09Ap12Bm
KENNAN, Chas.	50	M	Farmer	09Ap12Bm
Thomas	22	M	Farmer	09Ap12Bm
Ellen	20	F	Farmer	09Ap12Bm
Mary	14	F	Farmer	09Ap12Bm
BERRY, Mary	20	F	Servant	09Ap12Bm
DOYLE, Wi	40	F	Nurse	09Ap12Bm
Margaret	20	F	Nurse	09Ap12Bm
SCOTT, Wi	22	F	Servant	09Ap12Bm
CARMAN, Patt	22	M	Laborer	09Ap12Bm
U (W)	20	F	Laborer	09Ap12Bm
John	.00	M	Infant	09Ap12Bm
CARTON, Winny	20	M	Servant	09Ap12Bm
QUINN, Anthony	25	M	Laborer	09Ap12Bm
GREY, Patt	32	M	Farmer	09Ap12Bm
U	30	M	Farmer	09Ap12Bm
LABOR, Tim	35	M	Farmer	09Ap12Bm
Anne	30	F	Farmer	09Ap12Bm
Kate	13	F	Farmer	09Ap12Bm
Charles	12	M	Farmer	09Ap12Bm
Thomas	11	M	Farmer	09Ap12Bm
James	09	M	Child	09Ap12Bm
William	10	M	Farmer	09Ap12Bm
Tim	06	M	Child	09Ap12Bm
Patt	.00	M	Infant	09Ap12Bm
POWER, Bridget	20	F	Servant	09Ap12Bm
NOLAN, Margaret	20	F	Servant	09Ap12Bm
KEATY, Catherine	20	F	Servant	09Ap12Bm
MORTON, Thomas	21	M	Laborer	09Ap12Bm
John	18	M	Laborer	09Ap12Bm
Htomas	04	M	Child	09Ap12Bm
Catherine	15	F	Laborer	09Ap12Bm
LABOR, Michael	20	M	Baker	09Ap12Bm
LAWGHLAN, Patt	22	M	Tailor	09Ap12Bm
BOULGER, Richard	20	M	Laborer	09Ap12Bm
BONN, John	20	M	Mason	09Ap12Bm
James	21	M	Mason	09Ap12Bm
Anne	24	F	Seamstress	09Ap12Bm
Judith	24	F	Seamstress	09Ap12Bm
Eliza	20	F	Seamstress	09Ap12Bm
NEAL, Patt	25	M	Laborer	09Ap12Bm
ROACH, Tom	19	M	Laborer	09Ap12Bm
HANLEN, Lan	22	M	Laborer	09Ap12Bm
FRONT, John	20	M	Laborer	09Ap12Bm
CASTILLO, Michael	40	M	Farmer	09Ap12Bm
LYNCH, John	40	M	Farmer	09Ap12Bm
U (W)	30	F	Farmer	09Ap12Bm

NAMES OF PASSENGERS	AGE	SEX	OCCUPATIONS	DATE PORT SHIP
LAFFY, Coner	40	M	Farmer	09Ap12Bm
MCMANNAS, Ellen	27	F	Servant	09Ap12Bm
Mary	07	F	Child	09Ap12Bm
Michael	05	M	Child	09Ap12Bm
SEXTON, Warren	20	M	Servant	09Ap12Bm
MORGAN, Biddy	20	F	Servant	09Ap12Bm
ANDREWS, James-A	28	M	Agrt	09Ap12Bm
MASON, Kendrick	24	M	Draftsman	09Ap12Bm
COLLINS, Patt	30	M	Clerk	09Ap12Bm
BRYNE, Catherine	21	F	Hat Trimmer	09Ap12Bm
CASSELLS, Francis	22	M	Mason	09Ap12Bm
MANNING, Edward-T.	30	M	Farmer	09Ap12Bm
Ann-M.	30	F	Farmer	09Ap12Bm
ROONEY, Maria	25	F	Milliner	09Ap12Bm
SMITH, Abraham	30	M	Farmer	09Ap12Bm
Enoch	28	M	Farmer	09Ap12Bm
CARROLL, John	22	M	Tailor	09Ap12Bm

CALIFORNIA 10 APRIL 1849

From Dublin

NAMES OF PASSENGERS	AGE	SEX	OCCUPATIONS	DATE PORT SHIP
BRUTON, Patt	35	M	Unknown	10Ap12Bn
Ann	30	F	Unknown	10Ap12Bn
Robert	11	M	Unknown	10Ap12Bn
Julia	10	F	Unknown	10Ap12Bn
Bridget	03	F	Child	10Ap12Bn
John	06	M	Child	10Ap12Bn
Chuty	.00	M	Infant	10Ap12Bn
U	.00	F	Infant	10Ap12Bn
Michael	30	M	Unknown	10Ap12Bn
Margaret	28	F	Unknown	10Ap12Bn
Robert	09	M	Child	10Ap12Bn
Christy	07	M	Child	10Ap12Bn
Bridget	03	F	Child	10Ap12Bn
Patrick	02	M	Child	10Ap12Bn
MCGUIRE, James	24	M	Unknown	10Ap12Bn
Ann	26	F	Unknown	10Ap12Bn
REYNOLDS, Bridget	18	F	Unknown	10Ap12Bn
Catherine	18	F	Unknown	10Ap12Bn
FLYNN, Betty	19	F	Unknown	10Ap12Bn
MCHUGH, Ann	22	F	Unknown	10Ap12Bn
WALKER, Charles	30	M	Unknown	10Ap12Bn
Jane	30	F	Unknown	10Ap12Bn
SHAW, Eliza	22	F	Unknown	10Ap12Bn
DOWE, U	23	F	Unknown	10Ap12Bn
MANNING, Patt	24	M	Unknown	10Ap12Bn
Joseph	22	M	Unknown	10Ap12Bn
Kate	20	F	Unknown	10Ap12Bn
BOYLE, Kate	30	F	Unknown	10Ap12Bn
GOLDING, Richard	21	M	Unknown	10Ap12Bn
HARTY, Wm.	21	M	Unknown	10Ap12Bn
JOB, David	18	M	Unknown	10Ap12Bn
HAYS, Pleehan	16	M	Unknown	10Ap12Bn
REYNOLDS, John	30	M	Unknown	10Ap12Bn
Mary	24	F	Unknown	10Ap12Bn
Joseph	.00	M	Infant	10Ap12Bn
MCGOWEN, Mary	20	F	Unknown	10Ap12Bn
ENGLISH, Ellen	22	F	Unknown	10Ap12Bn
Catherine	04	F	Child	10Ap12Bn
MAHON, Honor	22	F	Unknown	10Ap12Bn
EARLEY, Margaret	20	F	Unknown	10Ap12Bn
William	10	M	Unknown	10Ap12Bn
Mary	07	F	Child	10Ap12Bn
NUGENT, Patt	25	M	Unknown	10Ap12Bn
Biddy	24	F	Unknown	10Ap12Bn
Patrick	.00	M	Infant	10Ap12Bn
MURPHY, Mary-Ann	20	F	Unknown	10Ap12Bn
FITZWILLIAM, John	26	M	Unknown	10Ap12Bn
FITZWILLIAM, Sarah	25	F	Unknown	10Ap12Bn
Rich	.00	M	Infant	10Ap12Bn
JONES, Bernard	24	M	Unknown	10Ap12Bn
BREAN, James	35	M	Unknown	10Ap12Bn
Rose	35	F	Unknown	10Ap12Bn
James	19	M	Unknown	10Ap12Bn
CLOONEY, George	30	M	Unknown	10Ap12Bn
Margaret	30	F	Unknown	10Ap12Bn
Georginia	15	F	Unknown	10Ap12Bn
Charlotte	08	F	Child	10Ap12Bn
Eliza	06	F	Child	10Ap12Bn
Benjamin	02	M	Child	10Ap12Bn
Joseph	.00	M	Infant	10Ap12Bn
MURPHY, Martin	25	M	Unknown	10Ap12Bn
RODGERS, James	22	M	Unknown	10Ap12Bn
Thomas	20	M	Unknown	10Ap12Bn
CUNNIGHAM, Mary	25	F	Unknown	10Ap12Bn
LEE, Christopher	23	M	Unknown	10Ap12Bn
Cath.	20	F	Unknown	10Ap12Bn
DUNN, Ann	50	F	Unknown	10Ap12Bn
Thomas	28	M	Unknown	10Ap12Bn
COSGRAVE, Ann	24	F	Unknown	10Ap12Bn
PURCAL, Peter	22	M	Unknown	10Ap12Bn
Margaret	18	F	Unknown	10Ap12Bn
KERWAN, James	21	M	Unknown	10Ap12Bn
STEVANS, John	40	M	Unknown	10Ap12Bn
BOLIN, Daniel	49	M	Unknown	10Ap12Bn
Mary	48	F	Unknown	10Ap12Bn
Kitty	22	F	Unknown	10Ap12Bn
Mary	16	F	Unknown	10Ap12Bn
Biddy	14	F	Unknown	10Ap12Bn
Jane	09	F	Child	10Ap12Bn
Mary	07	F	Child	10Ap12Bn
Patt	03	M	Child	10Ap12Bn
Thos.	.00	M	Infant	10Ap12Bn
HALLERAN, Thomas	25	M	Unknown	10Ap12Bn
Joe	23	M	Unknown	10Ap12Bn
BOWE, John	25	M	Unknown	10Ap12Bn
DOLIN, George	20	M	Unknown	10Ap12Bn
CRANSEEN, James	30	M	Unknown	10Ap12Bn
FEYAN, James	25	M	Unknown	10Ap12Bn
Mary	20	F	Unknown	10Ap12Bn
BUTTERLY, Francis	20	M	Unknown	10Ap12Bn
RUTLEDGE, Brien	22	M	Unknown	10Ap12Bn
COGHLAN, Jane	20	F	Unknown	10Ap12Bn
HAGERTY, Christy	50	M	Unknown	10Ap12Bn
Catherine	50	F	Unknown	10Ap12Bn
Mary	21	F	Unknown	10Ap12Bn
Ann	19	F	Unknown	10Ap12Bn
John	17	M	Unknown	10Ap12Bn
William	15	M	Unknown	10Ap12Bn
Catherine	11	F	Unknown	10Ap12Bn
Thomas	09	M	Child	10Ap12Bn
Patrick	07	M	Child	10Ap12Bn
Christy	05	M	Child	10Ap12Bn
Nicholas	03	M	Child	10Ap12Bn
U	.00	F	Infant	10Ap12Bn
FOLIER, Peter	25	M	Unknown	10Ap12Bn
Peter	.00	M	Infant	10Ap12Bn
FITZPATRICK, Phillip	25	M	Unknown	10Ap12Bn
MULLOY, Kate	21	F	Unknown	10Ap12Bn
HORAN, Eliza	25	F	Unknown	10Ap12Bn
MCHUGH, Francis	22	M	Unknown	10Ap12Bn
REYNOLDS, Francis	25	M	Unknown	10Ap12Bn
Ann	25	F	Unknown	10Ap12Bn
ENGLISH, John	25	U	Unknown	10Ap12Bn
Eliza	22	F	Unknown	10Ap12Bn
SMITH, Mary	25	F	Unknown	10Ap12Bn
WHELAN, Stephen	24	M	Unknown	10Ap12Bn
DUFFEY, Patt	21	M	Unknown	10Ap12Bn
KENDRICK, William	22	M	Unknown	10Ap12Bn
SHERIDAN, John	22	M	Unknown	10Ap12Bn
Michael	18	M	Unknown	10Ap12Bn
Phillip	12	M	Unknown	10Ap12Bn
Mary	19	F	Unknown	10Ap12Bn

NAMES OF PASSENGERS	AGE	SEX	OCCUPATIONS	DATE PORT SHIP
SHERIDAN, Catherine	10	F	Unknown	10Ap12Bn
MCKEOUGH, Patt	20	M	Unknown	10Ap12Bn
MAX, John	25	M	Unknown	10Ap12Bn
SHERWICK, John	24	M	Unknown	10Ap12Bn
HUSSEY, Peter	20	M	Unknown	10Ap12Bn
MULDOON, Peter	25	M	Unknown	10Ap12Bn
TALOR, Michael	30	M	Unknown	10Ap12Bn
Mary	30	F	Unknown	10Ap12Bn
James	05	M	Child	10Ap12Bn
Michael	03	M	Child	10Ap12Bn
Patrick	01	M	Child	10Ap12Bn
U	.00	F	Infant	10Ap12Bn
CONLAN, Tim	40	M	Unknown	10Ap12Bn
Margaret	35	F	Unknown	10Ap12Bn
Rose	13	F	Unknown	10Ap12Bn
Peter	11	M	Unknown	10Ap12Bn
Kate	09	F	Child	10Ap12Bn
MURRAY, Francis	22	M	Unknown	10Ap12Bn
CAHILL, Mary	22	F	Unknown	10Ap12Bn
Ann	18	F	Unknown	10Ap12Bn
U	.00	M	Infant	10Ap12Bn
DONLIN, James	50	M	Unknown	10Ap12Bn
Patt	30	M	Unknown	10Ap12Bn
Mary	30	F	Unknown	10Ap12Bn
William	06	M	Child	10Ap12Bn
Peter	04	M	Child	10Ap12Bn
U	.00	F	Infant	10Ap12Bn
LYNCH, Patrick	30	M	Unknown	10Ap12Bn
Jane	30	F	Unknown	10Ap12Bn
Michael	17	M	Unknown	10Ap12Bn
Bridget	19	F	Unknown	10Ap12Bn
Thomas	08	M	Child	10Ap12Bn
Patrick	06	M	Child	10Ap12Bn
U	.00	F	Infant	10Ap12Bn
RINGWOOD, William	30	M	Unknown	10Ap12Bn
QUIGHLY, Patrick	24	M	Unknown	10Ap12Bn
SAVAGE, William	20	M	Unknown	10Ap12Bn
Phillip	19	M	Unknown	10Ap12Bn
MCGARAHAN, Balla	20	F	Unknown	10Ap12Bn
BIRAN, Ann	18	M	Unknown	10Ap12Bn
MALINE, Michael	20	M	Unknown	10Ap12Bn
RUSSELL, Patt	26	M	Unknown	10Ap12Bn
Margaret	24	F	Unknown	10Ap12Bn
Catherine	02	F	Child	10Ap12Bn
U	.00	M	Infant	10Ap12Bn
ODONNELL, Margaret	60	F	Unknown	10Ap12Bn
FITZGERALD, John	26	M	Unknown	10Ap12Bn
Michael	23	M	Unknown	10Ap12Bn
SHEA, Tim	24	M	Unknown	10Ap12Bn
Margaret	20	F	Unknown	10Ap12Bn
BAKER, Ural	21	M	Unknown	10Ap12Bn
FLANIGAN, Eliza	40	F	Unknown	10Ap12Bn
Bridget	09	F	Child	10Ap12Bn
FITZPATRICK, John	30	M	Unknown	10Ap12Bn
Bridget	26	F	Unknown	10Ap12Bn
Bernard	18	M	Unknown	10Ap12Bn
Maryann	05	F	Child	10Ap12Bn
Bridget	03	F	Child	10Ap12Bn
U	.00	F	Infant	10Ap12Bn
QUINN, Bridget	40	F	Unknown	10Ap12Bn
Thomas	20	M	Unknown	10Ap12Bn
FEAHY, Mary	20	F	Unknown	10Ap12Bn
HOLLERAN, Bridget	40	F	Unknown	10Ap12Bn
Thomas	18	M	Unknown	10Ap12Bn
Denis	10	M	Unknown	10Ap12Bn
Michael	07	M	Child	10Ap12Bn
CREAMER, Daniel	21	M	Unknown	10Ap12Bn
WALSH, William	24	M	Unknown	10Ap12Bn
Bridget	22	F	Unknown	10Ap12Bn
Maurice	03	M	Child	10Ap12Bn
Mary	02	F	Child	10Ap12Bn
U	.00	F	Infant	10Ap12Bn
Mary	25	F	Unknown	10Ap12Bn
Catharine	20	F	Unknown	10Ap12Bn
OGLE, Joseph	20	M	Unknown	10Ap12Bn
DUNN, Janes	25	M	Unknown	10Ap12Bn
Betty	19	F	Unknown	10Ap12Bn
HEFFERNAN, Margaret	20	F	Unknown	10Ap12Bn
Eliza	18	F	Unknown	10Ap12Bn
ROGERSON, Ellen	24	F	Unknown	10Ap12Bn
KENMAN, Patrick	27	M	Unknown	10Ap12Bn
KING, John	35	M	Unknown	10Ap12Bn
John	18	M	Unknown	10Ap12Bn
Ann	16	F	Unknown	10Ap12Bn
Michael	12	M	Unknown	10Ap12Bn
William	08	M	Child	10Ap12Bn
FLOOD, Michael	21	M	Unknown	10Ap12Bn
GERAGTY, Jol.	22	M	Unknown	10Ap12Bn
LONG, John	30	M	Unknown	10Ap12Bn
Margaret	30	F	Unknown	10Ap12Bn
Patrick	04	M	Child	10Ap12Bn
Jane	02	F	Child	10Ap12Bn
HEFFERMAN, Ellen	19	F	Unknown	10Ap12Bn
QUIGHEY, Mary	20	F	Unknown	10Ap12Bn
LEE, Mary	20	F	Unknown	10Ap12Bn
DOYLE, Mary	20	F	Unknown	10Ap12Bn
MEVORE, Patrick	25	M	Unknown	10Ap12Bn
FEGAN, John	25	M	Unknown	10Ap12Bn
QUIRKE, Tim	20	M	Unknown	10Ap12Bn
OROURKE, Patt	20	M	Unknown	10Ap12Bn
BERGEN, Lawrence	20	M	Unknown	10Ap12Bn
MONAGHAN, James	20	M	Unknown	10Ap12Bn
WHELAN, Mary	30	F	Unknown	10Ap12Bn
James	06	M	Child	10Ap12Bn
MCAFFREY, Patt	30	M	Unknown	10Ap12Bn
FARLEY, Patt	20	M	Unknown	10Ap12Bn
ELLIS, Edward	28	M	Unknown	10Ap12Bn
Eliza	28	F	Unknown	10Ap12Bn
William	12	M	Unknown	10Ap12Bn
Edward	06	M	Child	10Ap12Bn
BOLAND, Daniel	20	M	Unknown	10Ap12Bn
MULLIGAN, Mary	20	F	Unknown	10Ap12Bn
BRULEN, Jane	20	F	Unknown	10Ap12Bn
GOLDEN, Christopher	26	M	Unknown	10Ap12Bn
MCCARROLL, Eliza	22	F	Unknown	10Ap12Bn
Mary	20	F	Unknown	10Ap12Bn
DUGGUMORE, Stanhope	25	M	Unknown	10Ap12Bn
WILHAM, W.H.	20	U	Unknown	10Ap12Bn
SWYED, Thos.	23	M	Unknown	10Ap12Bn
BURKE, Valentine	20	U	Unknown	10Ap12Bn
LANGAN, Patrick	27	M	Unknown	10Ap12Bn
GALBRAITH, James	25	M	Unknown	10Ap12Bn
HERAN, Patrick	25	M	Unknown	10Ap12Bn
Matilda	27	F	Unknown	10Ap12Bn
GRANCE, Maria	20	F	Unknown	10Ap12Bn
Henry	03	M	Child	10Ap12Bn

HYNDEFORD 10 APRIL 1849

From Glasgow

NAMES OF PASSENGERS		AGE	SEX	OCCUPATIONS	DATE PORT SHIP
SOMMERHILL, Farquhar		23	M	Laborer	10Ap04Bo
SEENAN, Jas.		28	M	Laborer	10Ap04Bo
FLANNAGHAN, Jno.		27	M	Laborer	10Ap04Bo
MILLER, Wm.		48	M	Laborer	10Ap04Bo
Catherine	(W)	48	F	Wife	10Ap04Bo
James		9	M	Relative	10Ap04Bo
William		7	M	Relative	10Ap04Bo
John		5	M	Relative	10Ap04Bo
Nathaniel		3	M	Relative	10Ap04Bo
Jonathan		.10	M	Infant	10Ap04Bo
ONEIL, Bernard		20	M	Laborer	10Ap04Bo
BLAIR, Hugh		21	M	Laborer	10Ap04Bo
Jane	(W)	20	F	Wife	10Ap04Bo

NAMES OF PASSENGERS		AGE	SEX	OCCUPATIONS	DATE PORT SHIP
SHARKEY, Isabella		20	F	Wife	10Ap04Bo
LLOYD, James		20	M	Laborer	10Ap04Bo
STEVENSON, Mary		18	F	Servant	10Ap04Bo
Margt.		10	F	Servant	10Ap04Bo
MCCAGHEY, Bernard		45	M	Laborer	10Ap04Bo
DONNELLY, Jas.		22	M	Laborer	10Ap04Bo
MCDERMOTT, Ann		18	F	Servant	10Ap04Bo
HENRY, Thos.		18	M	Laborer	10Ap04Bo
CRAWFORD, Jno.		49	M	Laborer	10Ap04Bo
GALLAGHER, Manus		24	M	Laborer	10Ap04Bo
Mary		20	F	Servant	10Ap04Bo
WILLLIS, Margt.		19	F	Servant	10Ap04Bo
GRAHAM, Jas.		40	M	Farmer	10Ap04Bo
Jane	(W)	30	F	Wife	10Ap04Bo
FERGUSON, Jno.		13	M	Laborer	10Ap04Bo
SNEDDEN, Jas.		33	M	Laborer	10Ap04Bo
MONTGOMERY, Jno.		31	M	Laborer	10Ap04Bo
Charlotte	(W)	30	F	Wife	10Ap04Bo
Henry		20	M	Relative	10Ap04Bo
Jane		9	F	Relative	10Ap04Bo
Thomas		7	M	Relative	10Ap04Bo
John		5	M	Relative	10Ap04Bo
RAVEY, Ann		30	F	Spinster	10Ap04Bo
BRUCE, Eliza		18	F	Servant	10Ap04Bo
MCCANN, Jane		18	F	Wife	10Ap04Bo
CONWAY, Helen		19	F	Wife	10Ap04Bo
Joseph		.10	M	Infant	10Ap04Bo
GREBBIN, Jas.		23	M	Laborer	10Ap04Bo
Mary		20	F	Servant	10Ap04Bo
SHEED, Daniel		30	M	Laborer	10Ap04Bo
WALKER, Margt.		22	F	Wife	10Ap04Bo
Ellen		.10	F	Infant	10Ap04Bo
MARTIN, Robt.		27	M	Laborer	10Ap04Bo
U	(W)	21	F	Wife	10Ap04Bo
John		5	M	Relative	10Ap04Bo
MCGAW, Saml.		40	M	Laborer	10Ap04Bo
Mary	(W)	35	F	Wife	10Ap04Bo
Matilda		22	F	Relative	10Ap04Bo
Thomas		19	M	Relative	10Ap04Bo
Eliza		14	F	Relative	10Ap04Bo
James		10	M	Relative	10Ap04Bo
Stewart		7	M	Relative	10Ap04Bo
Robert		4	M	Relative	10Ap04Bo
MCTEER, Patk.		25	M	Laborer	10Ap04Bo
Hannah	(W)	20	F	Wife	10Ap04Bo
CALDWELL, Eliza		19	F	Servant	10Ap04Bo
Jane		20	F	Servant	10Ap04Bo
James		21	M	Laborer	10Ap04Bo
MONAGHAN, Mary		20	F	Servant	10Ap04Bo
MCKEARNY, Mary		19	F	Servant	10Ap04Bo
Ann		14	F	Servant	10Ap04Bo
Bridget		18	F	Servant	10Ap04Bo
MCMULLEN, Saml.		22	M	Laborer	10Ap04Bo

PROBUS 10 APRIL 1849

From Liverpool

NAMES OF PASSENGERS	AGE	SEX	OCCUPATIONS	DATE PORT SHIP
CONNOR, Michl.	30	M	Farmer	10Ap02Bq
Margt.	30	F	Fsvnt	10Ap02Bq
Catherine	10	F	Unknown	10Ap02Bq
SULLIVAN, Jerry	35	M	Farmer	10Ap02Bq
Mary	35	F	Servant	10Ap02Bq
CONNOR, Con	24	M	Servant	10Ap02Bq
WHITESIDE, Elen	18	F	Dressmaker	10Ap02Bq
Ruth	17	F	Dressmaker	10Ap02Bq
CUNNINGHAM, Sarah	36	F	Servant	10Ap02Bq
Margaret	9	F	Child	10Ap02Bq
MCMAHON, Jas.	24	M	Rlst	10Ap02Bq
WHELAN, Jas.	50	M	Farmer	10Ap02Bq
Roger	16	M	Farmer	10Ap02Bq
Judy	11	F	Unknown	10Ap02Bq
CARRIGAN, Jas.	24	M	Laborer	10Ap02Bq
RYAN, Mary	40	F	Servant	10Ap02Bq
Bridget	14	F	Servant	10Ap02Bq
Judith	12	F	Unknown	10Ap02Bq
Mary	10	F	Unknown	10Ap02Bq
Wm.	16	M	Servant	10Ap02Bq
ONEILL, Jerry	18	M	Servant	10Ap02Bq
MORRISSON, Jno.	19	M	Servant	10Ap02Bq
Martha	40	F	Fsvnt	10Ap02Bq
Mary	17	F	Fsvnt	10Ap02Bq
Sarah-Eliza	11	F	Unknown	10Ap02Bq
Margt.	19	F	Servant	10Ap02Bq
Jno.	40	M	Servant	10Ap02Bq
LOGAN, Jas.	20	M	Servant	10Ap02Bq
CURRAN, Mary	20	F	Servant	10Ap02Bq
HORAN, Thos.	27	M	Laborer	10Ap02Bq
FALEY, Jno.	19	M	Laborer	10Ap02Bq
HAYES, Dan	40	M	Laborer	10Ap02Bq
Catherine	40	F	None	10Ap02Bq
Margt	11	F	None	10Ap02Bq
Jno.	9	M	Child	10Ap02Bq
Dan	7	M	Child	10Ap02Bq
Bridget	5	F	Child	10Ap02Bq
DILLON, Pat	25	M	Farmer	10Ap02Bq
Margt	25	F	Fsvnt	10Ap02Bq
EVATT, Sophia-Mrs.	30	F	None	10Ap02Bq
Eliz.	17	F	None	10Ap02Bq
Sophia	15	F	None	10Ap02Bq
Carolina	10	F	None	10Ap02Bq
Chas.	13	M	None	10Ap02Bq
Evelyn	10	M	None	10Ap02Bq
Clayton-Bayly	9	M	Child	10Ap02Bq
Augusta	7	F	Child	10Ap02Bq
DORAN, Anne	20	F	Servant	10Ap02Bq
BAYLY, Clayton	40	M	Nvof	10Ap02Bq
CORRIGAN, Jas.	30	M	Farmer	10Ap02Bq
GAFNEY, Phil	30	M	Farmer	10Ap02Bq
BRANEY, Mary	36	F	Shoemaker	10Ap02Bq
RIDGE, Jno.	20	M	Shop Boy	10Ap02Bq
KENNEDY, Jno.	20	M	Shop Boy	10Ap02Bq
BUTLER, Jno.	23	M	Policeman	10Ap02Bq
LYNCH, Jas.	36	M	Farmer	10Ap02Bq
Margt.	34	F	None	10Ap02Bq
Barnard	10	M	None	10Ap02Bq
Owen	.00	M	Infant	10Ap02Bq
GAFNEY, Thos.	3	M	Child	10Ap02Bq
MORGAN, Jno.	30	M	Broker	10Ap02Bq
CONDON, Thos.	20	M	Farmer	10Ap02Bq
David	22	M	Farmer	10Ap02Bq
Ellen	30	F	Servant	10Ap02Bq
Bridget	25	F	Servant	10Ap02Bq
Margret	26	F	Servant	10Ap02Bq
Mary	20	F	Servant	10Ap02Bq
Jno.	5	M	Child	10Ap02Bq
Peggy	1	F	Child	10Ap02Bq
MAHER, Thos.	22	M	Farmer	10Ap02Bq
KEATING, Mary	17	F	Servant	10Ap02Bq
ROWNAN, Jno.	20	M	Trader	10Ap02Bq
PHELAN, Pat	24	M	Wheelwright	10Ap02Bq
Bridget	30	F	Dairymaid	10Ap02Bq
BURKE, Thos.	24	M	Trader	10Ap02Bq
NAUGHTEN, Mary	30	F	None	10Ap02Bq
RUBRY, Edwd.	35	M	Cooper	10Ap02Bq
FARLEY, Pat	20	M	Farmer	10Ap02Bq
Mary	18	F	Seamstress	10Ap02Bq
Catherine	13	F	Seamstress	10Ap02Bq
CLERKIN, Jno.	40	M	Farmer	10Ap02Bq
HICKEY, Wm.	38	M	Farmer	10Ap02Bq
BURN, Thos.	38	M	Farmer	10Ap02Bq
ROCHE, Mary	22	F	Servant	10Ap02Bq
MCDERMOTT, Thos.	20	M	Farmer	10Ap02Bq
FARRELLEY, Anne	20	F	None	10Ap02Bq

NAMES OF PASSENGERS	AGE	SEX	OCCUPATIONS	DATE PORT SHIP
MCKENNA, Mary	20	F	None	10Ap02Bq
MCALLEER, Henry	20	M	None	10Ap02Bq
FRYERS, Wm.	26	M	Flxsp	10Ap02Bq
RAFTER, Jno.	28	M	Farmer	10Ap02Bq
HIGHLAND, Owen	25	M	Farmer	10Ap02Bq
CONNOR, Dennis	27	M	Laborer	10Ap02Bq
PHITZSIMMONS, Phillip	40	M	Weaver	10Ap02Bq
Pat	10	M	None	10Ap02Bq
Phil	7	M	Child	10Ap02Bq
FARRELL, Lawrence	40	M	Laborer	10Ap02Bq
BRADEY, Jno.	24	M	Laborer	10Ap02Bq
FARRELLEY, Jas.	37	M	Laborer	10Ap02Bq
SMITH, Phil	40	M	Laborer	10Ap02Bq
Mary	36	F	None	10Ap02Bq
Michl.	12	M	None	10Ap02Bq
Mary	21	F	None	10Ap02Bq
Anne	10	F	None	10Ap02Bq
Mary	8	F	Child	10Ap02Bq
Bessy	5	F	Child	10Ap02Bq
Joseph	2	M	Child	10Ap02Bq
Stephen	.00	M	Infant	10Ap02Bq
GAFNEY, Thos.	25	M	Laborer	10Ap02Bq
CONNOR, Anne	21	F	Servant	10Ap02Bq
SIMSON, Mary	46	F	None	10Ap02Bq
ROCK, Jno.	26	M	Laborer	10Ap02Bq
Mary	16	F	None	10Ap02Bq
DURKIN, Anne	16	F	None	10Ap02Bq
DONLIN, Mary	17	F	None	10Ap02Bq
TIERNAN, Michl.	19	M	Carpenter	10Ap02Bq
DALLON, Jno.	20	M	Shoemaker	10Ap02Bq
Mary	23	F	None	10Ap02Bq
MULLANEY, Pat	27	M	Farmer	10Ap02Bq
Mary	26	F	None	10Ap02Bq
Pat	12	M	None	10Ap02Bq
Thos.	10	M	None	10Ap02Bq
Jas.	9	M	Child	10Ap02Bq
Mary	7	F	Child	10Ap02Bq
ROSS, Thos.	30	M	Farmer	10Ap02Bq
DEVINE, Geo.	20	M	Farmer	10Ap02Bq
MCBRIDE, Pat	22	M	Farmer	10Ap02Bq
Rose	18	F	None	10Ap02Bq
MCCULLAH, Jno.	20	M	Farmer	10Ap02Bq
Pat	18	M	Farmer	10Ap02Bq
CUGGEY, Thos.	24	M	Laborer	10Ap02Bq
FARRELL, Pat	24	M	Laborer	10Ap02Bq
DUGGAN, Jno.	20	M	Laborer	10Ap02Bq
FARRELL, Jno.	20	M	Laborer	10Ap02Bq
MCGEOGHE, Margt.	20	F	Servant	10Ap02Bq
DOWDE, Mary	30	F	None	10Ap02Bq
Barney	11	M	None	10Ap02Bq
Mary	8	F	Child	10Ap02Bq
CROWLEY, Jerry	48	M	Laborer	10Ap02Bq
Michl.	13	M	None	10Ap02Bq
Mary	11	F	None	10Ap02Bq
Jas.	7	M	Child	10Ap02Bq
GARVEY, Martin	20	M	Laborer	10Ap02Bq
CROWLEY, Richd.	40	M	Laborer	10Ap02Bq
MCLOUGHLIN, Michl.	32	M	Laborer	10Ap02Bq
FLYNN, Margt.	30	F	Servant	10Ap02Bq
KENAHAN, Jno.	40	M	Farmer	10Ap02Bq
KEOGH, Margt.	26	F	Servant	10Ap02Bq
Margt.	50	F	None	10Ap02Bq
Pat	3	M	Child	10Ap02Bq
BAUNAHER, Jas.	20	M	Laborer	10Ap02Bq
MCSHANE, Felix	30	M	Baker	10Ap02Bq
Henry	24	M	Baker	10Ap02Bq
BROWN, Mchl.	26	M	Laborer	10Ap02Bq
Anne	40	F	Servant	10Ap02Bq
CONNAUGHTEN, Thos.	30	M	Laborer	10Ap02Bq
Pat	33	M	Laborer	10Ap02Bq
Margt.	30	F	Servant	10Ap02Bq
WALSH, Mary	25	F	Servant	10Ap02Bq
FLEMMING, Jno.	27	M	Laborer	10Ap02Bq
FITZHENNERY, Thos.	30	M	Laborer	10Ap02Bq
FLEMMING, Johannah	20	F	Servant	10Ap02Bq
NURNEY, Luke	35	M	Farmer	10Ap02Bq
Ellen	30	F	None	10Ap02Bq
RYAN, Jas.	50	M	Farmer	10Ap02Bq
Biddy	50	F	None	10Ap02Bq
Mchl.	18	M	Servant	10Ap02Bq
Ellen	20	F	None	10Ap02Bq
MCSURLEY, Pat	22	M	Laborer	10Ap02Bq
Allice	19	F	Servant	10Ap02Bq
RILEY, Rose-Anne	32	F	None	10Ap02Bq
FITZSIMMONS, Allice	18	F	Servant	10Ap02Bq
RILEY, Thos.	14	M	None	10Ap02Bq
Geo.	7	M	Child	10Ap02Bq
Wm.	5	M	Child	10Ap02Bq
Richd.	4	M	Child	10Ap02Bq
Rose-Anne	2	F	Child	10Ap02Bq
Matthew	.00	M	Infant	10Ap02Bq
BARR, David	21	M	Weaver	10Ap02Bq
Margt.	22	F	Nurse	10Ap02Bq
Alex.	.00	M	Infant	10Ap02Bq
LAMONT, Joha.	22	F	Servant	10Ap02Bq
MCARTHUR, Alex.	60	M	Farmer	10Ap02Bq
Margt.	22	F	None	10Ap02Bq
Jane	17	F	None	10Ap02Bq
MORRIS, Mchl.	20	M	Laborer	10Ap02Bq
MCALLEER, Anne	18	F	Servant	10Ap02Bq
MCCULLAH, Anne	23	F	Servant	10Ap02Bq
Frank	21	M	Laborer	10Ap02Bq
MURPHY, Lawrence	43	M	Carpenter	10Ap02Bq
Mary	35	F	None	10Ap02Bq
Jno.	8	M	Child	10Ap02Bq
Ellen	6	F	Child	10Ap02Bq
Thos.	4	M	Child	10Ap02Bq
Margt.	3	F	Child	10Ap02Bq
Mary	2	F	Child	10Ap02Bq
Anne	.00	F	Infant	10Ap02Bq
KEEFE, Hugh	50	M	Farmer	10Ap02Bq
Mary	45	F	None	10Ap02Bq
Rose	22	F	None	10Ap02Bq
Thos.	18	M	None	10Ap02Bq
Mchl.	13	M	None	10Ap02Bq
Mary	11	F	None	10Ap02Bq
Margt.	9	F	None	10Ap02Bq
Francis	4	M	None	10Ap02Bq
Margt.	.00	F	Infant	10Ap02Bq
WALSH, Pat	40	M	Laborer	10Ap02Bq
Julia	40	F	None	10Ap02Bq
Jas.	13	M	None	10Ap02Bq
Catherine	7	F	Child	10Ap02Bq
MCHUGH, Peggy	26	F	Servant	10Ap02Bq
HORAHO, Bridget	18	F	Servant	10Ap02Bq
MASTERSON, Mchl.	42	M	Farmer	10Ap02Bq
KEARNEY, Felix	46	M	Farmer	10Ap02Bq
KELLY, Thos.	22	M	Laborer	10Ap02Bq
Anne	20	F	None	10Ap02Bq
Margt.	18	F	None	10Ap02Bq
DONNEGAN, Mchl.	25	M	Laborer	10Ap02Bq
WEIR, Thos.	26	M	Laborer	10Ap02Bq
HELEY, Martin	25	M	Laborer	10Ap02Bq
Biddy	26	F	Servant	10Ap02Bq
Bridget	24	F	Servant	10Ap02Bq
FLANNEGAN, Biddy	26	F	Servant	10Ap02Bq
MORRIS, Mary	24	F	Servant	10Ap02Bq
OWENS, Mary	24	F	Servant	10Ap02Bq
WEIR, Margt.	21	F	Servant	10Ap02Bq
HANLEY, Catherine	22	F	Servant	10Ap02Bq
POWER, Jno.	20	M	Laborer	10Ap02Bq
KILROY, Mary	17	F	Servant	10Ap02Bq
DISNEY, Jas.	21	M	Saddler	10Ap02Bq
HANLEY, Andrw.	20	M	Shoemaker	10Ap02Bq
GLEEN, Jno.	20	M	Shoemaker	10Ap02Bq
ABRAHAM, Thos.	20	M	Mason	10Ap02Bq
LYNCH, Jno.	22	M	Servant	10Ap02Bq
NEILSON, Jas.	26	M	Servant	10Ap02Bq
Anne	26	F	Servant	10Ap02Bq
HAGAN, Owen	38	M	Farmer	10Ap02Bq

NAMES OF PASSENGERS	AGE	SEX	OCCUPATIONS	DATE PORT SHIP
HAGAN, Biddy	22	F	None	10Ap02Bq
Pat	6	M	Child	10Ap02Bq
Jno.	4	M	Child	10Ap02Bq
Peter	3	M	Child	10Ap02Bq
TRAINER, Eliza	16	F	Servant	10Ap02Bq
MCGOWAN, Biddy	16	F	Servant	10Ap02Bq
SEEREY, Pat	19	M	Servant	10Ap02Bq
Peggy	18	F	Servant	10Ap02Bq
MCALROY, Jane	22	F	Dressmaker	10Ap02Bq
MCCULLOUGH, Jas.	23	M	Laborer	10Ap02Bq
MCPHILLIPS, Barney	30	M	Laborer	10Ap02Bq
DONEGAN, Peggy	20	F	None	10Ap02Bq

ATALANTA 10 APRIL 1849

From Wexford

NAMES OF PASSENGERS	AGE	SEX	OCCUPATIONS	DATE PORT SHIP
BRYAN, Patrick	32	M	Laborer	10Ap16Br
John	34	M	Laborer	10Ap16Br
MURPHY, Richard	18	M	Laborer	10Ap16Br
Michael	25	M	Carpenter	10Ap16Br
CONNORS, Thos.	25	M	Laborer	10Ap16Br
CLIFFORD, Michael	25	M	Carpenter	10Ap16Br
BREERS, Marten	22	M	Laborer	10Ap16Br
BULGER, James	22	M	Laborer	10Ap16Br
DOYLE, Patrick	23	M	Laborer	10Ap16Br
MALONE, Patrick	25	M	Laborer	10Ap16Br
BENT, Ellen	21	F	Servant	10Ap16Br
CORMORS, Margaret	21	F	Servant	10Ap16Br
DEALEY, Patrick	24	M	Laborer	10Ap16Br
LACEY, Anastasia	21	F	Servant	10Ap16Br
BRIEN, William	18	M	Laborer	10Ap16Br
FOLEY, Patrick	24	M	Laborer	10Ap16Br
Margaret	27	F	Servant	10Ap16Br
DOYLE, Margaret	26	F	Servant	10Ap16Br
BENT, Eliza	23	F	Servant	10Ap16Br
FITZSIMMONS, James	18	M	Laborer	10Ap16Br
MURPHY, Catherine	22	F	Servant	10Ap16Br
WAFER, Michael	21	M	Mechanic	10Ap16Br
MURPHY, Arthur	34	M	Laborer	10Ap16Br
TESTON, Norah	20	F	Servant	10Ap16Br
BYRNE, Marten	51	M	Laborer	10Ap16Br
Betsey	20	F	Servant	10Ap16Br
QUIRK, Michael	40	M	Laborer	10Ap16Br
ROACH, Thos.	34	M	Laborer	10Ap16Br
LEARY, John	22	M	Laborer	10Ap16Br
DOYLE, Bridget	50	F	Servant	10Ap16Br
BOWMAN, Jacob	23	M	Laborer	10Ap16Br
MURPHY, James	20	M	Laborer	10Ap16Br
REDMOND, Edward	17	M	Laborer	10Ap16Br
BYRNE, Stephen	39	M	Laborer	10Ap16Br
Mary	50	F	Servant	10Ap16Br
SINNOTT, Margaret	19	F	Servant	10Ap16Br
Ellen	20	F	Servant	10Ap16Br
BYRNE, Martin	13	M	Laborer	10Ap16Br
Moses	11	M	Laborer	10Ap16Br
Ellen	9	F	Child	10Ap16Br
LACEY, George	30	M	Laborer	10Ap16Br
BYRNE, James	50	M	Laborer	10Ap16Br
Ann	35	F	Servant	10Ap16Br
Mary-Ann	3	F	Child	10Ap16Br
DUNNE, James	30	M	Laborer	10Ap16Br
Anne	16	F	Servant	10Ap16Br
DEMPSEY, Robt.	16	M	Laborer	10Ap16Br
AITKEN, John	20	M	Laborer	10Ap16Br
CARTY, Daniel	26	M	Laborer	10Ap16Br
MURPHY, Mary	21	F	Servant	10Ap16Br
ROCHE, Peter	27	M	Laborer	10Ap16Br
HOWLIN, James	27	M	Laborer	10Ap16Br

NAMES OF PASSENGERS	AGE	SEX	OCCUPATIONS	DATE PORT SHIP
BOWDEN, Richard	26	M	Laborer	10Ap16Br
LEARY, Mary	35	F	Servant	10Ap16Br
Eliza	23	F	Servant	10Ap16Br
Johanna	20	F	Servant	10Ap16Br
ROCHE, Nicholas	22	M	Laborer	10Ap16Br
CLENCEY, John	27	M	Laborer	10Ap16Br
DOYLE, Margaret	27	F	Servant	10Ap16Br
PEIRCE, Mathew	24	M	Laborer	10Ap16Br
MURPHY, Margaret	22	F	Servant	10Ap16Br
BYRNE, Michl.	50	M	Laborer	10Ap16Br
SINNOTT, Patrick	19	M	Laborer	10Ap16Br
CONNOR, Michael	30	M	Laborer	10Ap16Br
Mary	39	F	Servant	10Ap16Br
James	.00	M	Infant	10Ap16Br
DELANCEY, Catherine	26	F	Servant	10Ap16Br
CALLEN, Edward	25	M	Laborer	10Ap16Br
NOWLAN, James	40	M	Laborer	10Ap16Br
FURLONG, George	21	M	Laborer	10Ap16Br
Ellen	25	F	Servant	10Ap16Br
MCDONALD, John	46	M	Laborer	10Ap16Br
Ellen	46	F	Servant	10Ap16Br
Michael	22	M	Laborer	10Ap16Br
Ellen	15	F	Servant	10Ap16Br
Martha	12	F	Servant	10Ap16Br
Elizabeth	9	F	Child	10Ap16Br
Bridget	7	F	Child	10Ap16Br
BUTLER, Elloner	30	F	Servant	10Ap16Br
HANRAHAN, John	25	M	Farmer	10Ap16Br
Thomas	22	M	Farmer	10Ap16Br
ROURKE, Edward	22	M	Laborer	10Ap16Br
KEATING, Margaret	33	F	Servant	10Ap16Br
Elizabeth	25	F	Servant	10Ap16Br
KAVAGHAN, Thos.	40	M	Farmer	10Ap16Br
KAVANAGH, Martha	40	F	Wife	10Ap16Br
Ellen	15	F	None	10Ap16Br
Mathew	13	M	None	10Ap16Br
Margaret	11	F	None	10Ap16Br
Michael	7	M	Child	10Ap16Br
Bridget	5	F	Child	10Ap16Br
Mary	.00	F	Infant	10Ap16Br
CARTER, Morris	36	M	Carpenter	10Ap16Br
MURPHY, Patrick	33	M	Laborer	10Ap16Br
MYTHEN, John	28	M	Laborer	10Ap16Br
MURPHY, Anty.	26	F	Servant	10Ap16Br
James	23	M	Laborer	10Ap16Br
MEYLER, Richard	20	M	Laborer	10Ap16Br
WALSH, Francis	33	M	Laborer	10Ap16Br
DEMPSEY, Catherine	26	F	Servant	10Ap16Br
MURPHY, Thomas	32	M	Laborer	10Ap16Br
Bridget	25	F	Servant	10Ap16Br
Peter	23	M	Laborer	10Ap16Br
RINSHELD, Richard	25	M	Laborer	10Ap16Br
THORNTON, John	19	M	Laborer	10Ap16Br
KEATING, Patrick	18	M	Laborer	10Ap16Br
LACEY, Catherine	23	F	Servant	10Ap16Br
MURPHY, James	33	M	Laborer	10Ap16Br
CULLEN, James	26	M	Laborer	10Ap16Br
Elizabeth	24	F	Servant	10Ap16Br
ROACH, Morris	27	M	Laborer	10Ap16Br
WICKHAM, Julia	23	F	Servant	10Ap16Br
Margaret	21	F	Servant	10Ap16Br
MALONE, Jas.	21	M	Laborer	10Ap16Br
NEAL, Catherine	20	F	Servant	10Ap16Br
Margaret	18	F	Servant	10Ap16Br
John	15	M	Laborer	10Ap16Br
CONNOR, John	20	M	Laborer	10Ap16Br
MURPHY, Thos.	28	M	Laborer	10Ap16Br
PINDER, Thos.	39	M	Laborer	10Ap16Br
GOSLER, John	25	M	Laborer	10Ap16Br
BYRNE, Francis	23	M	Laborer	10Ap16Br
BURKE, John	27	M	Laborer	10Ap16Br
MONOHON, John	25	M	Laborer	10Ap16Br
LACEY, Joseph	30	M	Laborer	10Ap16Br
Thos.	13	M	None	10Ap16Br
CACEY, Robt.	21	M	Laborer	10Ap16Br

NAMES OF PASSENGERS	AGE	SEX	OCCUPATIONS	DATE PORT SHIP
BYRNE, Margaret	9	F	Child	10Ap16Br
CARTY, Margaret	.00	F	Infant	10Ap16Br
Margaret	30	F	Servant	10Ap16Br
DEMPSEY, Donald	25	M	Laborer	10Ap16Br
DUFF, Andrew	19	M	Laborer	10Ap16Br
SINNOTT, Michl.	26	M	Laborer	10Ap16Br

SIR-COLIN-CAMPBELL 11 APRIL 1849

From Belfast

NAMES OF PASSENGERS	AGE	SEX	OCCUPATIONS	DATE PORT SHIP
LORIMER, John	27	M	Farmer	11Ap05Bs
Eliza	26	F	Farmer	11Ap05Bs
John	3	M	Child	11Ap05Bs
HEFFERN, James	29	M	Farmer	11Ap05Bs
MCFALL, John	20	M	Farmer	11Ap05Bs
MCNELLY, Wm.	56	M	Farmer	11Ap05Bs
Anne	53	F	Farmer	11Ap05Bs
John	35	M	Farmer	11Ap05Bs
Hugh	27	M	Farmer	11Ap05Bs
Margt.	25	F	Farmer	11Ap05Bs
Hannah	35	F	Farmer	11Ap05Bs
Wm.	7	M	Child	11Ap05Bs
MCGOVERNEY, Wm.	36	M	Farmer	11Ap05Bs
Ellen	26	F	Farmer	11Ap05Bs
Thos.	4	M	Child	11Ap05Bs
Ellen	2	F	Child	11Ap05Bs
MADDEN, John	13	M	Farmer	11Ap05Bs
PURDY, Jane	4	F	Child	11Ap05Bs
FEY, Sarah	20	F	Farmer	11Ap05Bs
REED, Wm.	25	M	Farmer	11Ap05Bs
James	22	M	Farmer	11Ap05Bs
Eliza	20	F	Farmer	11Ap05Bs
Eliza	10	F	Farmer	11Ap05Bs
Thos.	.00	M	Infant	11Ap05Bs
STEELE, Wm.	30	M	Farmer	11Ap05Bs
Mary	26	F	Farmer	11Ap05Bs
Eliza	2	F	Child	11Ap05Bs
David	.00	M	Infant	11Ap05Bs
WILSON, Chs.	25	M	Farmer	11Ap05Bs
Mary	23	F	Farmer	11Ap05Bs
MALAVELLE, James	30	M	Farmer	11Ap05Bs
Julia	28	F	Farmer	11Ap05Bs
James	5	M	Child	11Ap05Bs
Robt.	.00	M	Infant	11Ap05Bs
GRAHAM, James	19	M	Farmer	11Ap05Bs
FARE, James	29	M	Farmer	11Ap05Bs
KIRK, Wm.	20	M	Farmer	11Ap05Bs
MCQUOID, John	29	M	Farmer	11Ap05Bs
HALL, Abraham	25	M	Farmer	11Ap05Bs
ANDERSON, Saml.	21	M	Farmer	11Ap05Bs
Ann	18	F	Farmer	11Ap05Bs
Isabella	20	F	Farmer	11Ap05Bs
Alexander	25	M	Farmer	11Ap05Bs
John	45	M	Farmer	11Ap05Bs
JOHNSTON, Wm.	30	M	Farmer	11Ap05Bs
Margt.	30	F	Farmer	11Ap05Bs
MCNEILL, Bell	22	F	Farmer	11Ap05Bs
JOHNSTON, John	9	M	Child	11Ap05Bs
Henry	7	M	Child	11Ap05Bs
Hugh	5	M	Child	11Ap05Bs
Margt.	2	F	Child	11Ap05Bs
DOUGLAS, Jane	50	F	Farmer	11Ap05Bs
Hugh	20	M	Farmer	11Ap05Bs
Barbara	12	F	Farmer	11Ap05Bs
WILDE, Margt.	14	F	Farmer	11Ap05Bs
Isabella	22	F	Farmer	11Ap05Bs
Nancy	20	F	Farmer	11Ap05Bs
James	22	M	Farmer	11Ap05Bs
MCCLUSKY, James	20	M	Farmer	11Ap05Bs
MURPHY, John	20	M	Farmer	11Ap05Bs
SMITH, John	25	M	Farmer	11Ap05Bs
Jane	20	F	Farmer	11Ap05Bs
ESLER, Eliza	20	F	Farmer	11Ap05Bs
ARMSTRONG, Thos.	24	M	Farmer	11Ap05Bs
MCCOLLOUGH, Wm.	60	M	Farmer	11Ap05Bs
Archy	19	M	Farmer	11Ap05Bs
Alex	18	M	Farmer	11Ap05Bs
MCDERMOND, John	22	M	Farmer	11Ap05Bs
MCAULEY, John	20	M	Farmer	11Ap05Bs
Denis	18	M	Farmer	11Ap05Bs
JAMISON, Chs.	19	M	Farmer	11Ap05Bs
SMITH, Robt.	20	M	Farmer	11Ap05Bs
WILSON, James	21	M	Farmer	11Ap05Bs
PINKERTON, Robt.	22	M	Farmer	11Ap05Bs
LOUGHLIN, Wm.	18	M	Farmer	11Ap05Bs
CAMPBELL, Margt.	18	F	Farmer	11Ap05Bs
COCHRANE, Mary	5	F	Child	11Ap05Bs
Nancy	3	F	Child	11Ap05Bs
MCLELLEND, John	30	M	Farmer	11Ap05Bs
Eliza	20	F	Farmer	11Ap05Bs
HAMILTON, Isaac	24	M	Farmer	11Ap05Bs
Eliza	20	F	Farmer	11Ap05Bs
ESLER, James	18	M	Farmer	11Ap05Bs
MAGRAW, Rose	20	F	Farmer	11Ap05Bs
FINLEY, Margt.	20	F	Farmer	11Ap05Bs
BAIN, John	28	M	Farmer	11Ap05Bs
Margt.	26	F	Farmer	11Ap05Bs
COURTNEY, Francis	28	M	Farmer	11Ap05Bs
COOPER, John	22	M	Farmer	11Ap05Bs
HENRY, John	22	M	Farmer	11Ap05Bs
BROWN, Charlotte	20	F	Farmer	11Ap05Bs
RODGERS, Eliza	27	F	Farmer	11Ap05Bs
Esther	6	F	Child	11Ap05Bs
DENNIS, John	29	M	Farmer	11Ap05Bs
Anne	29	F	Farmer	11Ap05Bs
MARTIN, Wm.	21	M	Farmer	11Ap05Bs
NICHOLL, Andrew	21	M	Farmer	11Ap05Bs
Jane	20	F	Farmer	11Ap05Bs
HARPER, Mary	30	F	Farmer	11Ap05Bs
Peggy	13	F	Farmer	11Ap05Bs
Eliza	9	F	Child	11Ap05Bs
Mary	5	F	Child	11Ap05Bs
Ellen	2	F	Child	11Ap05Bs
Wilm.	.00	M	Infant	11Ap05Bs
KERR, Matthew	18	M	Farmer	11Ap05Bs
RODGER, John	21	M	Farmer	11Ap05Bs
RUSSELL, Robt.	20	M	Farmer	11Ap05Bs
RODGERS, Mary	21	F	Farmer	11Ap05Bs
EWART, Helen	19	F	Farmer	11Ap05Bs
BROWN, Wm.	20	M	Farmer	11Ap05Bs
CORAS, Danl.	20	M	Farmer	11Ap05Bs
MCCREDY, James	30	M	Farmer	11Ap05Bs
ONEIL, Chs.	20	M	Farmer	11Ap05Bs
MEENAN, Thos.	25	M	Farmer	11Ap05Bs
GRILLEY, Nancy	18	F	Farmer	11Ap05Bs
DICKSON, Sarah	60	F	Farmer	11Ap05Bs
Robt.	27	M	Farmer	11Ap05Bs
Mary	25	F	Farmer	11Ap05Bs
Anne	28	F	Farmer	11Ap05Bs
Mary	26	F	Farmer	11Ap05Bs
Anne	24	F	Farmer	11Ap05Bs
Hamilton	18	M	Farmer	11Ap05Bs
LYLE, John	50	M	Farmer	11Ap05Bs
Hanna	45	F	Farmer	11Ap05Bs
Margt.	18	F	Farmer	11Ap05Bs
Jane	10	F	Farmer	11Ap05Bs
ONEIL, Hanna	50	F	Farmer	11Ap05Bs
John	20	M	Farmer	11Ap05Bs
Cath.	18	F	Farmer	11Ap05Bs
Chs.	12	M	Farmer	11Ap05Bs
Margt.	10	F	Farmer	11Ap05Bs
Joseph	8	M	Child	11Ap05Bs
MULHOLLAND, Mary	18	F	Farmer	11Ap05Bs

NAMES OF PASSENGERS	AGE	SEX	OCCUPATIONS	DATE PORT SHIP
WILEY, David	30	M	Farmer	11Ap05Bs
HOOD, John	30	M	Farmer	11Ap05Bs
BOGUE, Wm.	21	M	Farmer	11Ap05Bs
OSBORNE, Hamilton	21	M	Farmer	11Ap05Bs
CARMICHAEL, Wm.	26	M	Farmer	11Ap05Bs
ARMOUR, Mary	21	F	Farmer	11Ap05Bs
MCMULLEN, Adam	18	M	Farmer	11Ap05Bs
MACGOLDRICK, James	21	M	Farmer	11Ap05Bs
ONEIL, Neil	21	M	Farmer	11Ap05Bs
CAMPBELL, Margt.	23	F	Farmer	11Ap05Bs
MACDOWELL, Alex	20	M	Farmer	11Ap05Bs
MACGOWAN, John	28	M	Farmer	11Ap05Bs
GRAY, Saml.	25	M	Farmer	11Ap05Bs
MACCLEAN, James	25	M	Farmer	11Ap05Bs
Mary	25	F	Farmer	11Ap05Bs
Wm.	.00	M	Infant	11Ap05Bs
BOYD, Eliza	25	F	Farmer	11Ap05Bs
GILLEN, Rose	20	F	Farmer	11Ap05Bs
MCMAHON, Bernard	20	M	Farmer	11Ap05Bs
KANE, Mary	20	F	Farmer	11Ap05Bs
Cath.	15	F	Farmer	11Ap05Bs
CAMPBELL, Mary	28	F	Farmer	11Ap05Bs
Robt.	28	M	Farmer	11Ap05Bs
COULTER, James	20	M	Farmer	11Ap05Bs
Thos.	18	M	Farmer	11Ap05Bs
LIDDY, Sarah	20	F	Farmer	11Ap05Bs
LOUGHRIDGE, Margt.	20	F	Farmer	11Ap05Bs
MOYNE, John	25	M	Farmer	11Ap05Bs
MILFORD, Robt.	22	M	Farmer	11Ap05Bs
Mary	22	F	Farmer	11Ap05Bs
John	.09	M	Infant	11Ap05Bs
HAROLD, John	28	M	Farmer	11Ap05Bs
KELLEN, Mary-L.	20	F	Farmer	11Ap05Bs
SIMPSON, James	21	M	Farmer	11Ap05Bs
MACKELVEY, Edwd.	45	M	Farmer	11Ap05Bs
Eliza	30	F	Farmer	11Ap05Bs
NEVILLE, Wm.	20	M	Farmer	11Ap05Bs
MOORE, John	30	M	Farmer	11Ap05Bs
MCCLAVERTY, Robt.	19	M	Farmer	11Ap05Bs
REA, George	29	M	Farmer	11Ap05Bs
Agnes	27	F	Farmer	11Ap05Bs
Margt.	.09	F	Infant	11Ap05Bs
JUNTH, Creighton	22	M	Farmer	11Ap05Bs
Thos.	20	M	Farmer	11Ap05Bs
James	18	M	Farmer	11Ap05Bs
SKILLEN, John	24	M	Farmer	11Ap05Bs
HANNA, Hugh	30	M	Farmer	11Ap05Bs
Eliza	30	F	Farmer	11Ap05Bs
Louisa	11	F	Farmer	11Ap05Bs
Lessy	9	F	Child	11Ap05Bs
Wm.	7	M	Child	11Ap05Bs
Anne	5	F	Child	11Ap05Bs
Mary	3	F	Child	11Ap05Bs
John	.09	M	Infant	11Ap05Bs
MCCRAIG, Ann	20	F	Farmer	11Ap05Bs
FLINN, Rose-A.	28	F	Farmer	11Ap05Bs
KENNEDY, Henry	28	M	Farmer	11Ap05Bs
HEFFERN, Mary-A.	29	F	Farmer	11Ap05Bs
ADAMS, Robt.	20	M	Farmer	11Ap05Bs
ONEIL, Chs.	20	M	Farmer	11Ap05Bs
MACCAFFERTY, Ann	40	F	Farmer	11Ap05Bs
JENNINGS, Wm.	21	M	Farmer	11Ap05Bs
MAGEE, John	21	M	Farmer	11Ap05Bs
IRVANE, Jane	26	F	Farmer	11Ap05Bs
Bessy	13	F	Farmer	11Ap05Bs
Charlotte	11	F	Farmer	11Ap05Bs
Hugh	9	M	Child	11Ap05Bs
Wm.	3	M	Child	11Ap05Bs
Margt.	3	F	Child	11Ap05Bs
MCCORMICK, Thos.	26	M	Farmer	11Ap05Bs
JAMISON, Mary	24	F	Farmer	11Ap05Bs
DONEGAN, Ann	24	F	Farmer	11Ap05Bs
Danl.	24	M	Farmer	11Ap05Bs
Eliza	22	F	Farmer	11Ap05Bs
LENNON, Alex	21	M	Farmer	11Ap05Bs
HALL, James	22	M	Farmer	11Ap05Bs
MAY, Nancy	19	F	Farmer	11Ap05Bs
PEAK, Mary-A.	21	F	Farmer	11Ap05Bs
MCMULLEN, Patt	27	M	Farmer	11Ap05Bs
BRADLEY, Michl.	60	M	Farmer	11Ap05Bs
Rose	40	F	Farmer	11Ap05Bs
Dominick	20	M	Farmer	11Ap05Bs
WALSH, David	20	M	Farmer	11Ap05Bs
KIRKPATRICK, J.	24	M	Farmer	11Ap05Bs
RAFFERTY, Rose	21	F	Farmer	11Ap05Bs
MACILROY, Mary	20	F	Farmer	11Ap05Bs
CUNNINGHAM, James	24	M	Farmer	11Ap05Bs

DOWNES 11 APRIL 1849

From Waterford

NAMES OF PASSENGERS	AGE	SEX	OCCUPATIONS	DATE PORT SHIP
DONAVAN, W.	21	M	Laborer	11Ap15Bt
GALLAGHAN, P.	22	M	Laborer	11Ap15Bt
CAHILL, J.	25	M	Laborer	11Ap15Bt
Mary	25	F	Spinster	11Ap15Bt
TRACY, Mary	21	F	Spinster	11Ap15Bt
BREAN, John	38	M	Laborer	11Ap15Bt
Eliza	30	F	Spinster	11Ap15Bt
POWER, W.	20	M	Student	11Ap15Bt
DOYLE, H.	19	M	Laborer	11Ap15Bt
SINNATT, P.	24	M	Laborer	11Ap15Bt
WALSH, T.	19	M	Laborer	11Ap15Bt
NOWLAN, T.	20	M	Laborer	11Ap15Bt
Ann	21	F	Spinster	11Ap15Bt
COMMENS, R.	33	M	Laborer	11Ap15Bt
QUIN, R.	34	M	Laborer	11Ap15Bt
COMMENS, R.Jr.	28	M	Laborer	11Ap15Bt
John	25	M	Laborer	11Ap15Bt
BROWN, A.	40	M	Farmer	11Ap15Bt
Mary	36	F	Wife	11Ap15Bt
Moses	15	M	Laborer	11Ap15Bt
James	14	M	None	11Ap15Bt
Sarah	13	F	None	11Ap15Bt
Jane	12	F	None	11Ap15Bt
Mary	10	F	None	11Ap15Bt
Alex	9	M	Child	11Ap15Bt
Susannah	3	F	Child	11Ap15Bt
CHRISTIAN, G.	40	M	Laborer	11Ap15Bt
Bridgitte	35	F	Spinster	11Ap15Bt
Dennis	22	M	Laborer	11Ap15Bt
Mary	18	F	Spinster	11Ap15Bt
Ellen	16	F	Spinster	11Ap15Bt
Henry	13	M	Unknown	11Ap15Bt
Bridgitte	7	F	Child	11Ap15Bt
Mich.	5	M	Child	11Ap15Bt
SULLIVAN, Ellen	20	F	Spinster	11Ap15Bt
GRIDDY, T.	21	M	Laborer	11Ap15Bt
Daniel	30	M	Laborer	11Ap15Bt
BARRY, Mich.	21	M	Laborer	11Ap15Bt
FURLONG, James	40	M	Laborer	11Ap15Bt
BEHAN, N.	20	M	Laborer	11Ap15Bt
HURLEY, Mary	20	F	Spinster	11Ap15Bt
CONNORS, Mich.	42	M	Laborer	11Ap15Bt
Cath.	38	F	Spinster	11Ap15Bt
Patrick	25	M	Laborer	11Ap15Bt
Mich.	19	M	Laborer	11Ap15Bt
Brigitte	15	F	Spinster	11Ap15Bt
Anty.	12	M	Laborer	11Ap15Bt
GLESSEN, Cath.	26	F	Spinster	11Ap15Bt
Alice	7	F	Child	11Ap15Bt
Ths.	5	M	Child	11Ap15Bt
W.	4	M	Child	11Ap15Bt
HARRINGTON, E.	22	M	Laborer	11Ap15Bt

NAMES OF PASSENGERS	AGE	SEX	OCCUPATIONS	DATE PORT SHIP
HARRINGTON, Mary	16	F	Spinster	11Ap15Bt
Marg.	20	F	Spinster	11Ap15Bt
EGAN, J.	23	M	Laborer	11Ap15Bt
COGHLAN, M.	28	M	Laborer	11Ap15Bt
BURLAND, J.	25	M	Laborer	11Ap15Bt
Johannah	23	F	Spinster	11Ap15Bt
MOORE, Catherine	22	F	Spinster	11Ap15Bt
SANFIELD, Cath.	18	F	Spinster	11Ap15Bt
POWER, Mary	30	F	Spinster	11Ap15Bt
KEFFE, John	24	M	Laborer	11Ap15Bt
Mary	23	F	Wife	11Ap15Bt
KEHOE, Wm.	40	M	Laborer	11Ap15Bt
MAHER, J.	30	M	Laborer	11Ap15Bt
PLUNKETT, J.	23	M	Tailor	11Ap15Bt
SHAY, J.	20	M	Laborer	11Ap15Bt
CONNORS, Mary	20	F	Spinster	11Ap15Bt
CALLAGHAN, Ellen	22	F	Spinster	11Ap15Bt
ROCHE, John	20	M	Laborer	11Ap15Bt
KEFFE, Wm.	26	M	Laborer	11Ap15Bt
DOODY, Mary	26	F	Spinster	11Ap15Bt
HABELIN, A.	29	M	Laborer	11Ap15Bt
HEALEY, P.	29	M	Laborer	11Ap15Bt
SLINEY, T.	25	M	Laborer	11Ap15Bt
Mary	23	F	Wife	11Ap15Bt
TOBIN, James	26	M	Laborer	11Ap15Bt
DUNN, James	21	M	Laborer	11Ap15Bt
SALMON, Mich.	22	M	Laborer	11Ap15Bt
FENNESY, Mich.	23	M	Laborer	11Ap15Bt
Ths.	24	M	Laborer	11Ap15Bt
HAMMILL, E.	25	M	Laborer	11Ap15Bt
CURRINE, T.	28	M	Laborer	11Ap15Bt
LYNCH, Johannah	24	F	Spinster	11Ap15Bt
WALSH, Bridgitt	19	F	Spinster	11Ap15Bt
BRYANT, John	22	M	Laborer	11Ap15Bt
Cath.	20	F	Spinster	11Ap15Bt
Bridgitt	22	F	Spinster	11Ap15Bt
HANRAHAN, Margaret	33	F	Spinster	11Ap15Bt
William	3	M	Child	11Ap15Bt
WOLFE, John	23	M	Laborer	11Ap15Bt
Mary	21	F	Spinster	11Ap15Bt
DOYLE, D.	20	M	Laborer	11Ap15Bt
RYAN, James	20	M	Laborer	11Ap15Bt
Peter	24	M	Laborer	11Ap15Bt
CONOLLY, R.	29	M	Laborer	11Ap15Bt
EGGINS, W.	21	M	Laborer	11Ap15Bt
Ellen	20	F	Spinster	11Ap15Bt

JOHN-C.CALHOUN 11 APRIL 1849

From Liverpool

NAMES OF PASSENGERS	AGE	SEX	OCCUPATIONS	DATE PORT SHIP
COCKS, John	25	M	Blacksmith	11Ap02Bz
MAXWELL, Saml.	40	M	Blacksmith	11Ap02Bz
GROMLEY, James	35	M	Farmer	11Ap02Bz
SALE, Wm.	20	M	Farmer	11Ap02Bz
GOMERLY, Martin	20	M	Farmer	11Ap02Bz
GILRICK, Patrick	20	M	Farmer	11Ap02Bz
LYNCH, Bridget	20	F	Daughter	11Ap02Bz
MCCABE, Bridget	18	F	Servant	11Ap02Bz
DAWSON, Jno.	30	M	Farmer	11Ap02Bz
Hannah	3	F	Child	11Ap02Bz
Jane	25	F	Farmer	11Ap02Bz
Eliza	.03	F	Infant	11Ap02Bz
MEREDITH, Charlotte	28	F	Farmer	11Ap02Bz
METCALF, Jno.	26	M	Mechanic	11Ap02Bz
Alexander	22	M	Mechanic	11Ap02Bz
NEWILL, Matilda	23	F	Unknown	11Ap02Bz
MASON, James	25	M	Farmer	11Ap02Bz
Michael	27	M	Farmer	11Ap02Bz
CARROLL, Edward	21	M	Farmer	11Ap02Bz
BRYAN, Ellen	40	F	Servant	11Ap02Bz
DWIER, Edward	24	M	Farmer	11Ap02Bz
Mary	20	F	Unknown	11Ap02Bz
FLEMING, Nicholas	22	M	Unknown	11Ap02Bz
SMITH, James	22	M	Unknown	11Ap02Bz
CARIGAN, Edward	30	M	Laborer	11Ap02Bz
Mary	27	F	Unknown	11Ap02Bz
BRYAN, James	9	M	Child	11Ap02Bz
Thomas	6	M	Child	11Ap02Bz
Daniel	5	M	Child	11Ap02Bz
CARRIGAN, Wm.	24	M	Laborer	11Ap02Bz
WALL, Edwd.M.	40	M	Farmer	11Ap02Bz
MORAN, Bridget	20	F	Farmer	11Ap02Bz
DUFFEY, Pat.	22	M	Laborer	11Ap02Bz
CALDUN, Ellen	30	F	Unknown	11Ap02Bz
Margt.	10	F	Unknown	11Ap02Bz
CARPENTER, Saml.	60	M	Unknown	11Ap02Bz
Edwd.	40	M	Unknown	11Ap02Bz
Johannah	4	F	Child	11Ap02Bz
BRYAN, Margt.	30	F	Servant	11Ap02Bz
KIRVING, Johannah	18	F	Unknown	11Ap02Bz
CRITCHLEY, James	28	M	Bookbinder	11Ap02Bz
Mary	24	F	Unknown	11Ap02Bz
David	3	M	Child	11Ap02Bz
Mary	2	F	Child	11Ap02Bz
SMITH, John	15	M	Apprentice	11Ap02Bz
BROONAN, Edwd.	21	M	Grocer	11Ap02Bz
MCDANIEL, Jno.	24	M	Farmer	11Ap02Bz
CAULEY, Jno.	40	M	Farmer	11Ap02Bz
WALL, Samuel	37	M	Farmer	11Ap02Bz
POWELL, Nicholas	24	M	Shoemaker	11Ap02Bz
Honorah	23	F	Unknown	11Ap02Bz
Margt.	21	F	Unknown	11Ap02Bz
John	22	M	Unknown	11Ap02Bz
John	8	M	Child	11Ap02Bz
Mary-Ann	10	F	Unknown	11Ap02Bz
Patrick	12	M	Unknown	11Ap02Bz
MORISON, Bridget	32	F	Unknown	11Ap02Bz
POWER, Margt.	50	F	Unknown	11Ap02Bz
BAGG, Edwd.	35	M	Shoemaker	11Ap02Bz
GIFNEY, Jno.	20	M	Farmer	11Ap02Bz
FLINN, Henry	20	M	Laborer	11Ap02Bz
DORAN, Thomas	20	M	Laborer	11Ap02Bz
WHALAN, Patrick	19	M	Farmer	11Ap02Bz
WALSH, Mary	25	F	Unknown	11Ap02Bz
GIFFNEY, Mary	20	F	Servant	11Ap02Bz
TOBIN, Phillip	34	M	Laborer	11Ap02Bz
DANFOLEY, Elizabeth	20	F	Unknown	11Ap02Bz
TOBIN, Ellen	32	F	Unknown	11Ap02Bz
Cath.	8	F	Child	11Ap02Bz
John	6	M	Child	11Ap02Bz
James	4	M	Child	11Ap02Bz
Anthony	2	M	Child	11Ap02Bz
DWEYER, Mick	19	M	Clerk	11Ap02Bz
BROWN, Pat.	22	M	Laborer	11Ap02Bz
HEFFRON, Mary	45	F	Servant	11Ap02Bz
John	12	M	Unknown	11Ap02Bz
DUMER, Mary	36	F	Unknown	11Ap02Bz
Pat	8	M	Child	11Ap02Bz
Mary	6	F	Child	11Ap02Bz
Sally	.00	F	Infant	11Ap02Bz
MCLOUGHLIN, Mick	24	M	Farmer	11Ap02Bz
CONLAN, David	50	M	Unknown	11Ap02Bz
HANLEY, Edmund	34	M	Unknown	11Ap02Bz
Rebecca	33	F	Unknown	11Ap02Bz
Price	5	M	Child	11Ap02Bz
Wm.	.00	M	Infant	11Ap02Bz
Jno.	35	M	Unknown	11Ap02Bz
STAPLETON, Edmund	32	M	Laborer	11Ap02Bz
DOOLING, Owen	23	M	Unknown	11Ap02Bz
Michael	19	M	Unknown	11Ap02Bz
CASTELER, Pat.	36	M	Carpenter	11Ap02Bz
Bridget	12	F	Unknown	11Ap02Bz
GORE, Mary	15	F	Unknown	11Ap02Bz

NAMES OF PASSENGERS	AGE	SEX	OCCUPATIONS	DATE PORT SHIP
GORE, Margt.	12	F	Unknown	11Ap02Bz
CONLAY, James	30	M	Laborer	11Ap02Bz
CALLING, Owen	22	M	Farmer	11Ap02Bz
MOORE, Thomas	16	M	Unknown	11Ap02Bz
HAND, John-B.	40	M	Gdnr	11Ap02Bz
Ellen	36	F	Unknown	11Ap02Bz
JOHNSON, Henry	37	M	Cutler	11Ap02Bz
SHOOLIN, James	30	M	Farmer	11Ap02Bz
Died-At-Sea				
George	10	M	Unknown	11Ap02Bz
James	12	M	Unknown	11Ap02Bz
SMITH, Jno.	23	M	Engineer	11Ap02Bz
MOSSISS, Thomas	23	M	Farmer	11Ap02Bz
George	19	M	Farmer	11Ap02Bz
MARTIN, Jno.	28	M	Farmer	11Ap02Bz
HEGLAND, Joseph	27	M	Unknown	11Ap02Bz
HEALEY, Pat	21	M	Unknown	11Ap02Bz
DOOLAN, Mick	32	M	Unknown	11Ap02Bz
CUMMINGS, Jno.	25	M	Unknown	11Ap02Bz
MURRAY, Martin	27	M	Unknown	11Ap02Bz
CUDDY, Wm.	26	M	Unknown	11Ap02Bz
DOONEY, Cath.	22	F	Unknown	11Ap02Bz
CASTIGAN, Mary	22	F	Unknown	11Ap02Bz
MCGEE, Mary	21	F	Unknown	11Ap02Bz
GALLAGHER, James	28	M	Unknown	11Ap02Bz
Cath.	25	F	Unknown	11Ap02Bz
Mary	.00	F	Infant	11Ap02Bz
MCMAHON, Mary	19	F	Servant	11Ap02Bz
RAFTER, Thomas	30	M	Farmer	11Ap02Bz
KINVIN, Tim	42	M	Unknown	11Ap02Bz
Elizabeth	30	F	Unknown	11Ap02Bz
Rody	15	M	Unknown	11Ap02Bz
Margt.	12	F	Unknown	11Ap02Bz
Jno.	10	M	Unknown	11Ap02Bz
Thomas	1	M	Child	11Ap02Bz
Died-At-Sea				
Elizabeth	.00	F	Infant	11Ap02Bz
Died-At-Sea				
Pat	21	M	Unknown	11Ap02Bz
Died-At-Sea				
HEALEY, Cath.	40	F	Unknown	11Ap02Bz
Thomas	19	M	Laborer	11Ap02Bz
Winfred	17	M	Laborer	11Ap02Bz
Biddy	15	F	Laborer	11Ap02Bz
Ann	14	F	Laborer	11Ap02Bz
Jno.	8	M	Child	11Ap02Bz
BYRNE, Betty	20	F	Unknown	11Ap02Bz
SMITH, Mary	13	F	Servant	11Ap02Bz
MORTAGH, Thomas	20	M	Farmer	11Ap02Bz
Bridget	20	F	Unknown	11Ap02Bz
CASEY, Lawrence	32	M	Unknown	11Ap02Bz
ROBINSON, Richard	26	M	Laborer	11Ap02Bz
James	20	M	Unknown	11Ap02Bz
CLANTY, James	19	M	Servant	11Ap02Bz
SMITH, James	22	M	Servant	11Ap02Bz
WALSH, James	21	M	Servant	11Ap02Bz
CONWAY, Dennis	25	M	Laborer	11Ap02Bz
JOHNSTON, John	24	M	Farmer	11Ap02Bz
DANIEL, Michael	24	M	Laborer	11Ap02Bz
Mary	24	F	Unknown	11Ap02Bz
TUHAN, Bridget	23	F	Unknown	11Ap02Bz
PRATT, Wm.	29	M	Unknown	11Ap02Bz
CONDIN, Pat.	25	M	Laborer	11Ap02Bz
HALLINAN, Michl.	25	M	Unknown	11Ap02Bz
POWER, Edmund	32	M	Unknown	11Ap02Bz
Cath.	22	F	Unknown	11Ap02Bz
Patrick	.00	M	Infant	11Ap02Bz
BRYAN, Michal	29	M	Farmer	11Ap02Bz
HARTIGAN, Martin	25	M	Laborer	11Ap02Bz
NEVIN, Wm.	27	M	Servant	11Ap02Bz
DWIER, Thomas	22	M	Farmer	11Ap02Bz
GLEESON, Bryan	27	M	Farmer	11Ap02Bz
CONNOLLY, Jno.	25	M	Clerk	11Ap02Bz
Mick	35	M	Farmer	11Ap02Bz
FLEMING, John	40	M	Unknown	11Ap02Bz

NAMES OF PASSENGERS	AGE	SEX	OCCUPATIONS	DATE PORT SHIP
FLEMING, Eliza	30	F	Unknown	11Ap02Bz
REYNOLDS, Cath.	17	F	Unknown	11Ap02Bz
Died-At-Sea				
FLEMING, Dennis	11	M	Unknown	11Ap02Bz
Richard	9	M	Child	11Ap02Bz
Died-At-Sea				
Ellen	3	F	Child	11Ap02Bz
Died-At-Sea				
Johanna	2	F	Child	11Ap02Bz
Died-At-Sea				
SHEA, John	35	M	Unknown	11Ap02Bz
Andy	24	M	Unknown	11Ap02Bz
Daniel	30	M	Unknown	11Ap02Bz
David	30	M	Unknown	11Ap02Bz
DOWLEY, James	30	M	Unknown	11Ap02Bz
Cath.	28	F	Unknown	11Ap02Bz
FOY, Jno.	35	M	Unknown	11Ap02Bz
KILCHAN, Hugh	28	M	Unknown	11Ap02Bz
WALSH, Pat	30	M	Laborer	11Ap02Bz
Mary	25	F	Unknown	11Ap02Bz
Died-At-Sea				
Jno.	.00	M	Infant	11Ap02Bz
Died-At-Sea				
Cath.	19	F	Unknown	11Ap02Bz
HURLEY, James	26	M	Unknown	11Ap02Bz
FLANIGAN, Margt.	30	F	Servant	11Ap02Bz
Ellen	23	F	Unknown	11Ap02Bz
COLLINS, Mary	33	F	Unknown	11Ap02Bz
Mary	17	F	Unknown	11Ap02Bz
Cath.	16	F	Unknown	11Ap02Bz
Anthony	5	M	Child	11Ap02Bz
Pat	4	M	Child	11Ap02Bz
SINCLAIR, Timothy	30	M	Laborer	11Ap02Bz
WHITE, Wm.	25	M	Unknown	11Ap02Bz
Died-At-Sea				
LANE, Dennis	25	M	Unknown	11Ap02Bz
MURPHY, Pat.	25	M	Unknown	11Ap02Bz
SULLIVAN, Jno.	30	M	Unknown	11Ap02Bz
LAW, Cath.	27	F	Unknown	11Ap02Bz
Mary	19	F	Unknown	11Ap02Bz
Kate	.00	F	Infant	11Ap02Bz
BARRY, Edward	36	M	Unknown	11Ap02Bz
DOONEY, Edward	19	M	Clerk	11Ap02Bz
SCUSE, Edward	22	M	Laborer	11Ap02Bz
KING, Mary	25	F	Servant	11Ap02Bz
COLTON, Anne	18	F	Unknown	11Ap02Bz
DENIGER, Johanna	24	F	Unknown	11Ap02Bz
HARRINGTON, Darby	40	M	Laborer	11Ap02Bz
CONDON, James	45	M	Unknown	11Ap02Bz
Mary	10	F	Unknown	11Ap02Bz
Died-At-Sea				
Thomas	8	M	Child	11Ap02Bz
BOWLER, Wm.	32	M	Unknown	11Ap02Bz
Lawrence	22	M	Unknown	11Ap02Bz
LAWLESS, Patrick	28	M	Carpenter	11Ap02Bz
GRIFFIN, Mick	26	M	Laborer	11Ap02Bz
MORRIS, James	22	M	Carpenter	11Ap02Bz
DOWNING, Julia	19	F	Unknown	11Ap02Bz
Margt.	17	F	Unknown	11Ap02Bz
LYNCH, Pat.	22	M	Laborer	11Ap02Bz
CRONIN, Barry	42	M	Gdnr	11Ap02Bz
Bridget	12	F	Unknown	11Ap02Bz
SHEEHAN, Daniel	26	M	Laborer	11Ap02Bz
CAVANAGH, Henry	40	M	Weaver	11Ap02Bz
Daniel	.00	M	Infant	11Ap02Bz
Died-At-Sea				
SHEEHAN, Bridget	26	F	Unknown	11Ap02Bz
Died-At-Sea				
FLYNN, Mick	27	M	Laborer	11Ap02Bz
HENLY, Jerry	40	M	Unknown	11Ap02Bz
Died-At-Sea				
Nelly	30	F	Unknown	11Ap02Bz
Died-At-Sea				
DIVINE, Wm.	25	M	Unknown	11Ap02Bz
Martin	23	M	Unknown	11Ap02Bz

NAMES OF PASSENGERS	AGE	SEX	OCCUPATIONS	DATE PORT SHIP
DIVINE, Mick	22	M	Unknown	11Ap02Bz
Hannah	27	F	Unknown	11Ap02Bz
MYERS, John	45	M	Carpenter	11Ap02Bz
Billy	9	M	Child	11Ap02Bz
Died-At-Sea				
Ellen	40	F	Unknown	11Ap02Bz
Jno.	35	M	Unknown	11Ap02Bz
Peggy	28	F	Unknown	11Ap02Bz
Ellen	24	F	Unknown	11Ap02Bz
LOUTY, Edwd.	25	M	Laborer	11Ap02Bz
Cath.	21	F	Unknown	11Ap02Bz
MORAN, Jno.	24	M	Farmer	11Ap02Bz
Margt.	25	F	Unknown	11Ap02Bz
SHEEHAN, Jno.	23	M	Laborer	11Ap02Bz
LASEY, Eliza	24	F	Unknown	11Ap02Bz
MCQUINN, Dennis	35	M	Unknown	11Ap02Bz
Margt.	30	F	Unknown	11Ap02Bz
Died-At-Sea				
Mary	3	F	Child	11Ap02Bz
Thomas	.00	M	Infant	11Ap02Bz
Died-At-Sea				
KENNEDY, John	30	M	Unknown	11Ap02Bz
DOWD, Michael	47	M	Unknown	11Ap02Bz
OBRIEN, Margt.	37	F	Unknown	11Ap02Bz
AHIN, Pat.	30	M	Unknown	11Ap02Bz
HENNELY, Mich.	28	M	Unknown	11Ap02Bz
Margt.	28	F	Unknown	11Ap02Bz
FISHER, John	25	M	Unknown	11Ap02Bz
LANE, Margt.	34	F	Servant	11Ap02Bz
CONOLY, Pat	35	M	Laborer	11Ap02Bz
Jno.	35	M	Unknown	11Ap02Bz
HOGAN, Margt.	30	F	Servant	11Ap02Bz
MCCARTNEY, Mick	9	M	Child	11Ap02Bz
Ellen	18	F	Unknown	11Ap02Bz
Johanna	7	F	Child	11Ap02Bz
Died-At-Sea				
Michael	40	M	Unknown	11Ap02Bz
SHEAR, Dennis	40	M	Carpenter	11Ap02Bz
SLATERY, Mathew	30	M	Priest	11Ap02Bz
DOWNIG, Wm.	20	M	Unknown	11Ap02Bz
DORRETY, Patrick	.00	M	Infant	11Ap02Bz

CAROLINA 12 APRIL 1849

From Glasgow

NAMES OF PASSENGERS	AGE	SEX	OCCUPATIONS	DATE PORT SHIP
BARNET, Wm.	60	M	Laborer	12Ap04Cb
Peter	22	M	Laborer	12Ap04Cb
Isabella	33	F	Unknown	12Ap04Cb
KENNON, Patrick-J.	24	M	Schm	12Ap04Cb
Mary	24	F	Unknown	12Ap04Cb
Thomas	.11	M	Infant	12Ap04Cb
WHILLICHAN, Samuel	27	M	Laborer	12Ap04Cb
MOFFAT, Agnes	18	F	Unknown	12Ap04Cb

MONTEZUMA 12 APRIL 1849

From Liverpool

NAMES OF PASSENGERS	AGE	SEX	OCCUPATIONS	DATE PORT SHIP
SHEPARD, Joseph	42	M	Gentleman	12Ap02Ca
Emily-Mrs.	27	F	Unknown	12Ap02Ca
Letitia	8	F	Child	12Ap02Ca
Emily	7	F	Child	12Ap02Ca
SHEPARD, William	5	M	Child	12Ap02Ca
Joseph	3	M	Child	12Ap02Ca
MCARDLE, Bridget	18	F	Servant	12Ap02Ca
SYMONS, Robert	18	M	Laborer	12Ap02Ca
MOSS, George	27	M	Laborer	12Ap02Ca
Eliza	30	F	Unknown	12Ap02Ca
U	.00	U	Infant	12Ap02Ca
George	2	M	Child	12Ap02Ca
HALFPENNY, John	30	M	Shoemaker	12Ap02Ca
WATERS, Francis	20	M	Shoemaker	12Ap02Ca
HUGHES, Owen	22	M	Unknown	12Ap02Ca
WATERS, Catherine	18	F	Servant	12Ap02Ca
MOLLOY, Bella	40	F	Unknown	12Ap02Ca
MOLLOGHAN, Ann	27	F	Servant	12Ap02Ca
FULLANE, Thomas	24	M	Servant	12Ap02Ca
Patrick	14	M	Unknown	12Ap02Ca
TRACY, Edward	18	M	Unknown	12Ap02Ca
CONOLLY, James	20	M	Laborer	12Ap02Ca
CASSIDY, Bridget	18	F	Unknown	12Ap02Ca
COPLEY, John	40	M	Farmer	12Ap02Ca
NUGENT, William	34	M	Laborer	12Ap02Ca
U-Mrs.	26	F	Laborer	12Ap02Ca
U	.00	U	Infant	12Ap02Ca
Catherine	4	F	Child	12Ap02Ca
Michael	3	M	Child	12Ap02Ca
MCGERAGHTY, Philip	25	M	Laborer	12Ap02Ca
U-Mrs.	22	F	Unknown	12Ap02Ca
U	.00	U	Infant	12Ap02Ca
KELLY, Mary	18	F	Servant	12Ap02Ca
HAGARTY, Ellen	19	F	Servant	12Ap02Ca
WALSH, Ellen-Mrs.	26	F	Servant	12Ap02Ca
John	3	M	Child	12Ap02Ca
JENKINS, William	22	M	Laborer	12Ap02Ca
ROURKE, Hugh	56	M	Laborer	12Ap02Ca
Died-At-Sea				
Mathew	28	M	Laborer	12Ap02Ca
John	22	M	Laborer	12Ap02Ca
Philip	18	M	Laborer	12Ap02Ca
Hugh	10	M	Laborer	12Ap02Ca
Mary	24	F	Laborer	12Ap02Ca
U-Mrs.	50	F	Laborer	12Ap02Ca
CARROLL, Patrick	19	M	Laborer	12Ap02Ca
BELL, Biddy	16	F	Unknown	12Ap02Ca
Mary	13	F	Unknown	12Ap02Ca
HANSON, Margaret	13	F	Laborer	12Ap02Ca
DERLIN, Sarah	20	F	Servant	12Ap02Ca
BRENNAN, Honora	21	F	Servant	12Ap02Ca
LELLIS, Mary	40	F	Servant	12Ap02Ca
GRIFFIN, Thomas	35	M	Servant	12Ap02Ca
DELOWNEY, John	22	M	Servant	12Ap02Ca
Patrick	25	M	Servant	12Ap02Ca
HANAHAN, John	22	M	Servant	12Ap02Ca
PARCY, Michael	22	M	Servant	12Ap02Ca
LYNCH, Catherine	20	F	Servant	12Ap02Ca
RILEY, Cornelius	21	M	Servant	12Ap02Ca
CLARK, John	18	M	Servant	12Ap02Ca
FERRALTY, Thomas	17	M	Servant	12Ap02Ca
SMITH, Patrick	21	M	Servant	12Ap02Ca
DUNN, Mary	18	F	Servant	12Ap02Ca
Ann	16	F	Servant	12Ap02Ca
FERRALTY, Bridget	8	F	Child	12Ap02Ca
DUNN, John	22	M	Laborer	12Ap02Ca
GARRY, Michael	22	M	Laborer	12Ap02Ca
LYNCH, Bridget	20	F	Laborer	12Ap02Ca
MCDONNELL, Margaret	20	F	Laborer	12Ap02Ca
GOLDIN, Susan	20	F	Laborer	12Ap02Ca
Died-At-Sea				
BOYLE, Eliza	21	F	Laborer	12Ap02Ca
MCMAHON, Catherine	16	F	Laborer	12Ap02Ca
GILL, William	21	M	Laborer	12Ap02Ca
Died-At-Sea				
BYRNE, Patrick	40	M	Laborer	12Ap02Ca
Mary	40	F	Laborer	12Ap02Ca
U	.00	U	Infant	12Ap02Ca
Margaret	2	F	Child	12Ap02Ca

NAMES OF PASSENGERS	AGE	SEX	OCCUPATIONS	DATE PORT SHIP	NAMES OF PASSENGERS	AGE	SEX	OCCUPATIONS	DATE PORT SHIP
MCGUINESS, Rose	20	F	Servant	12Ap02Ca	MITCHELL, Anne	18	F	Servant	12Ap02Ca
CARLAN, Thomas	21	M	Servant	12Ap02Ca	GORDAN, Sarah	20	F	Unknown	12Ap02Ca
BARNE, Michael	22	M	Servant	12Ap02Ca	DEMPSEY, Anne	44	F	Servant	12Ap02Ca
COPPALL, C.L.	48	U	Servant	12Ap02Ca	Michael	13	M	Unknown	12Ap02Ca
FLANAGAN, Francis	38	M	Laborer	12Ap02Ca	Anne	7	F	Child	12Ap02Ca
Margaret	40	F	Unknown	12Ap02Ca	KILLIEVE, Thomas	24	M	Laborer	12Ap02Ca
Thomas	11	M	Unknown	12Ap02Ca	CAVANAGH, John	16	M	Laborer	12Ap02Ca
James	8	M	Child	12Ap02Ca	Owen	14	M	Laborer	12Ap02Ca
GOLDING, Ann	21	F	Servant	12Ap02Ca	KEATING, Catherine	45	F	Servant	12Ap02Ca
MADDEN, Margaret	30	F	Servant	12Ap02Ca	Dennis	22	M	Servant	12Ap02Ca
SULLIVAN, Mary	20	F	Servant	12Ap02Ca	Margaret	20	F	Servant	12Ap02Ca
SHERIDAN, Eliza	18	F	Servant	12Ap02Ca	Edmund	18	M	Servant	12Ap02Ca
Ellen	19	F	Servant	12Ap02Ca	Patrick	15	M	Servant	12Ap02Ca
CAHILL, Thomas	22	M	Laborer	12Ap02Ca	MCPHILLIPS, Ann	40	F	Servant	12Ap02Ca
U-Mrs.	22	F	Laborer	12Ap02Ca	MCQUILLAN, Ann	14	F	Servant	12Ap02Ca
AHERAN, Ann	22	F	Laborer	12Ap02Ca	MANIVIEX, Thomas	40	M	Servant	12Ap02Ca
MCKEY, Thomas	20	M	Laborer	12Ap02Ca	DALY, Catherine	22	F	Servant	12Ap02Ca
MCCABE, Patrick	48	M	Laborer	12Ap02Ca	CODY, Mary-Ann	22	F	Servant	12Ap02Ca
ONEILL, Mary	20	F	Laborer	12Ap02Ca	COCHLAN, Ann	23	F	Servant	12Ap02Ca
MITCHELL, Ann	6	F	Child	12Ap02Ca	Donnell	2	U	Child	12Ap02Ca
MORAN, Dennis	20	M	Laborer	12Ap02Ca	COLLINS, Ellen	21	F	Unknown	12Ap02Ca
REIDON, Henry	23	M	Laborer	12Ap02Ca	CONLAN, William	18	M	Unknown	12Ap02Ca
BANNIERS, Thomas	25	M	Laborer	12Ap02Ca	Sarah	30	F	Servant	12Ap02Ca
BATTE, Thady	21	M	Laborer	12Ap02Ca	SHANNON, Peter	37	M	Laborer	12Ap02Ca
MCGLONE, Patrick	21	M	Laborer	12Ap02Ca	ROGERS, Bernard	18	M	Laborer	12Ap02Ca
Edward	19	M	Laborer	12Ap02Ca	DARNEY, Owen	26	M	Laborer	12Ap02Ca
Betty	12	F	Laborer	12Ap02Ca	DALEY, Peter	18	M	Laborer	12Ap02Ca
MCDERMOTT, James	24	M	Laborer	12Ap02Ca	LILLIS, Eliza	57	F	Unknown	12Ap02Ca
FITZPATRICK, Joseph	24	M	Laborer	12Ap02Ca	REGAN, Margaret	30	F	Unknown	12Ap02Ca
LEYDEN, Thomas	40	M	Laborer	12Ap02Ca	John	30	M	Laborer	12Ap02Ca
Patrick	10	M	Laborer	12Ap02Ca	Patrick	27	M	Laborer	12Ap02Ca
MCDONNELL, John	32	M	Laborer	12Ap02Ca	Honora	20	F	Servant	12Ap02Ca
GLERMON, Patrick	26	M	Laborer	12Ap02Ca	NEW, Julia	22	F	Servant	12Ap02Ca
LYNCH, Mary	20	F	Servant	12Ap02Ca	BEGLEY, U	30	F	Wi	12Ap02Ca
FARRELL, Michael	16	M	Servant	12Ap02Ca	Ellen	11	F	Unknown	12Ap02Ca
Margaret	18	F	Servant	12Ap02Ca	Margaret	9	F	Child	12Ap02Ca
CORDIAL, Michael	26	M	Laborer	12Ap02Ca	KEANE, Catherine	22	F	Servant	12Ap02Ca
BARTLEY, Ann	30	F	Laborer	12Ap02Ca	KELLY, Martin	28	M	Laborer	12Ap02Ca
U	.00	U	Infant	12Ap02Ca	Mary	18	F	Unknown	12Ap02Ca
MURPHY, Michael	28	M	Laborer	12Ap02Ca	CONWAY, Mary	46	F	Servant	12Ap02Ca
QUINN, Martha	30	F	Servant	12Ap02Ca	DWYER, John	28	M	Laborer	12Ap02Ca
Bridget	9	F	Child	12Ap02Ca	ONEILL, Mary	20	F	Unknown	12Ap02Ca
Lawrence	6	M	Child	12Ap02Ca	SEALLY, Catherine	33	F	Servant	12Ap02Ca
Patrick	4	M	Child	12Ap02Ca	REYNOLDS, Eliza	20	F	Unknown	12Ap02Ca
GERRATY, Mathew	20	M	Servant	12Ap02Ca	THOMPSON, Bernand	28	M	Unknown	12Ap02Ca
FLYNN, John	18	M	Servant	12Ap02Ca	DONOHUE, John	18	M	Unknown	12Ap02Ca
LYNCH, Lawrence	13	M	Servant	12Ap02Ca	KELLY, Ann	18	M	Unknown	12Ap02Ca
Patrick	40	M	Laborer	12Ap02Ca	FITZGERALD, Margaret	14	F	Unknown	12Ap02Ca
HAILEY, Edward	28	M	Shoemaker	12Ap02Ca	MCCABE, Patrick	32	M	Laborer	12Ap02Ca
LIMMINS, Ellen	18	F	Unknown	12Ap02Ca	COMISKEY, Mary	48	F	Unknown	12Ap02Ca
COSGROVE, Catherine	11	F	Unknown	12Ap02Ca	Eliza	18	F	Unknown	12Ap02Ca
BYRNE, Nicholas	24	M	Shoemaker	12Ap02Ca	MURPHY, Ann	20	F	Unknown	12Ap02Ca
Mary	15	F	Unknown	12Ap02Ca	FINNIGAN, Dennis	32	M	Unknown	12Ap02Ca
CAMPLE, James	00	M	Unknown	12Ap02Ca	LYNCH, Mary	18	F	Unknown	12Ap02Ca
DONOVAN, Thomas	20	M	Unknown	12Ap02Ca	HALAHAN, U-Mrs.	25	F	Unknown	12Ap02Ca
CARMODY, John	24	M	Shoemaker	12Ap02Ca	James	2	M	Child	12Ap02Ca
Patrick	24	M	Shoemaker	12Ap02Ca	COWELL, Margt.	25	F	Unknown	12Ap02Ca
Died-At-Sea					U	.00	U	Infant	12Ap02Ca
CROWE, Michael	24	M	Shoemaker	12Ap02Ca	George	12	M	Unknown	12Ap02Ca
HOFF, Martin	24	M	Shoemaker	12Ap02Ca	Margaret	10	F	Unknown	12Ap02Ca
Margaret	23	F	Servant	12Ap02Ca	Robert	7	M	Child	12Ap02Ca
CONNORS, John	24	M	Laborer	12Ap02Ca	SCOLLAN, John	30	M	Laborer	12Ap02Ca
GAWEY, Bridget	27	F	Servant	12Ap02Ca	Rose	25	F	Servant	12Ap02Ca
Catherine	25	F	Servant	12Ap02Ca	MCGUIRE, Bridget	20	F	Servant	12Ap02Ca
CLARK, Bridget	25	F	Unknown	12Ap02Ca	SPELLANE, Joseph	21	M	Servant	12Ap02Ca
U	.00	U	Infant	12Ap02Ca	FULLANE, William	25	M	Laborer	12Ap02Ca
SMITH, Terence	21	M	Servant	12Ap02Ca	Ellen	12	F	Laborer	12Ap02Ca
Rose	12	F	Unknown	12Ap02Ca	Owen	9	M	Child	12Ap02Ca
KIRWIN, Judy	25	F	Servant	12Ap02Ca	KELLY, John	26	M	Unknown	12Ap02Ca
Martin	6	M	Child	12Ap02Ca	REILLY, Edward	20	M	Unknown	12Ap02Ca
CONNORS, Nancy	16	F	Unknown	12Ap02Ca	SCOTT, James	24	M	Laborer	12Ap02Ca
ENNIS, Michael	24	M	Servant	12Ap02Ca	Jane	24	F	Unknown	12Ap02Ca
BRADLEY, Margaret	20	F	Servant	12Ap02Ca	William	9	M	Child	12Ap02Ca
HOFF, Jane	20	F	Servant	12Ap02Ca	Martha	7	F	Child	12Ap02Ca
KELLY, Mary	25	F	Servant	12Ap02Ca	James	5	M	Child	12Ap02Ca

NAMES OF PASSENGERS	AGE	SEX	OCCUPATIONS	DATE PORT SHIP
SCOTT, John	3	M	Child	12Ap02Ca
GEREHELY, James	20	M	Laborer	12Ap02Ca
CORBETT, Margaret	20	F	Unknown	12Ap02Ca
MAGADON, Michael	24	M	Laborer	12Ap02Ca
Died-At-Sea				
KELLY, Bridget	8	F	Child	12Ap02Ca
Ann	7	F	Child	12Ap02Ca
FLANAGAN, Margaret	20	F	Unknown	12Ap02Ca
MAHONEY, David	18	M	Unknown	12Ap02Ca
Bridget	20	F	Unknown	12Ap02Ca
NEALON, Ellen	20	F	Unknown	12Ap02Ca
MCBRYAN, Peter	14	M	Unknown	12Ap02Ca
KING, Mary	10	F	Unknown	12Ap02Ca
HENRY, Ann	30	F	Servant	12Ap02Ca
DEMPSEY, Ellen	30	F	Servant	12Ap02Ca
Mary-Ann	8	F	Child	12Ap02Ca
Ellen	5	F	Child	12Ap02Ca
LAWLEY, Margaret	20	F	Unknown	12Ap02Ca
REILLY, Lawrence	25	M	Laborer	12Ap02Ca
CAHILL, Martin	25	M	Laborer	12Ap02Ca
CONNORS, Catherine	24	F	Servant	12Ap02Ca
MEAGHER, William	26	M	Unknown	12Ap02Ca
NOLAN, Bridget	20	F	Unknown	12Ap02Ca
CAHILL, Bridget	26	F	Servant	12Ap02Ca
Bridget	7	F	Child	12Ap02Ca
SAMONS, Michael	22	M	Unknown	12Ap02Ca
Thomas	16	M	Unknown	12Ap02Ca
CUFFE, James	30	M	Laborer	12Ap02Ca
KEOGAN, Mary	20	F	Unknown	12Ap02Ca
James	10	M	Unknown	12Ap02Ca
CONAGHTON, Thomas	6	M	Child	12Ap02Ca
Mary	7	F	Child	12Ap02Ca
CAREY, Michael	21	M	Unknown	12Ap02Ca
DORAN, Bridget	22	F	Unknown	12Ap02Ca
Catherine	18	F	Unknown	12Ap02Ca
DWYER, Essy	22	F	Unknown	12Ap02Ca
PIGOTT, Thomas	24	M	Unknown	12Ap02Ca
Johannah	24	F	Unknown	12Ap02Ca
John	6	M	Child	12Ap02Ca
William	4	M	Child	12Ap02Ca
Michael	.00	M	Infant	12Ap02Ca
HALPIN, Thomas	23	M	Laborer	12Ap02Ca
REILLY, Margaret	18	F	Unknown	12Ap02Ca
MOORE, James	20	M	Laborer	12Ap02Ca
HANEY, Thomas	20	M	Laborer	12Ap02Ca
MCCABE, Ann	24	F	Servant	12Ap02Ca
DUFF, Margaret	20	F	Servant	12Ap02Ca
MORAN, Margaret	20	F	Servant	12Ap02Ca
MEELEN, Samuel	22	M	Servant	12Ap02Ca
Anne	20	F	Unknown	12Ap02Ca
LYNCH, Terence	14	M	Unknown	12Ap02Ca
Anne	16	F	Unknown	12Ap02Ca
BANKS, Margaret	18	F	Unknown	12Ap02Ca
BROMLEY, Mary	21	F	Unknown	12Ap02Ca
Jonathan	8	M	Child	12Ap02Ca
EUSTACE, Bridget	19	F	Unknown	12Ap02Ca
NOLAN, Martin	11	M	Unknown	12Ap02Ca
Patrick	5	M	Child	12Ap02Ca
MURRAY, John	24	M	Laborer	12Ap02Ca
MCCORMICK, Mathew	26	M	Laborer	12Ap02Ca
GALLIGAN, Patrick	22	M	Unknown	12Ap02Ca
John	18	M	Unknown	12Ap02Ca
HYLAND, Mary	40	F	Unknown	12Ap02Ca
May	4	F	Child	12Ap02Ca
RHOOL, Edward	15	M	Unknown	12Ap02Ca
John	12	M	Unknown	12Ap02Ca
Owen	10	M	Unknown	12Ap02Ca
BRENNAN, Michael	30	M	Laborer	12Ap02Ca
May	30	F	Unknown	12Ap02Ca
Pat	7	M	Child	12Ap02Ca
Jane	5	F	Child	12Ap02Ca
Edward	2	M	Child	12Ap02Ca
REILLY, James	30	M	Laborer	12Ap02Ca
BOTTOM, Lawrence	20	M	Unknown	12Ap02Ca
FINIGAN, Thomas	31	M	Laborer	12Ap02Ca

NAMES OF PASSENGERS	AGE	SEX	OCCUPATIONS	DATE PORT SHIP
FINIGAN, Pat	10	M	Unknown	12Ap02Ca
Rose	5	F	Child	12Ap02Ca
BRADY, Bernard	30	M	Unknown	12Ap02Ca
BOYLE, Patrick	20	M	Unknown	12Ap02Ca
Lawrence	15	M	Unknown	12Ap02Ca
GREHAN, John	40	M	Unknown	12Ap02Ca
SCULLY, Bridget	9	F	Child	12Ap02Ca
Hugh	7	M	Child	12Ap02Ca
REILLY, Jane	20	F	Unknown	12Ap02Ca
Hugh	14	M	Unknown	12Ap02Ca
ENNIS, Jane	26	F	Unknown	12Ap02Ca
CALDWELL, Mary	19	F	Unknown	12Ap02Ca
HAND, Anne	30	F	Unknown	12Ap02Ca
James	3	M	Child	12Ap02Ca
Michael	2	M	Child	12Ap02Ca
MALONE, Patrick	26	M	Unknown	12Ap02Ca
RAUL, Patrick	20	M	Unknown	12Ap02Ca
SMITH, Anne	25	F	Unknown	12Ap02Ca
GARRIGAN, Judith	21	F	Unknown	12Ap02Ca
STEWART, Owen	26	M	Unknown	12Ap02Ca
HUGHES, John	31	M	Unknown	12Ap02Ca
GILHOOLY, Ellen	20	F	Unknown	12Ap02Ca
Michael	11	M	None	12Ap02Ca
MCCORMICK, James	24	M	Unknown	12Ap02Ca
CONROLY, Ann	18	F	Unknown	12Ap02Ca
COX, Ann	17	F	Unknown	12Ap02Ca
U, U	00	U	Unknown	12Ap02Ca
Died-At-Sea				

INDUSTRY 12 APRIL 1849

From Cork

NAMES OF PASSENGERS	AGE	SEX	OCCUPATIONS	DATE PORT SHIP
MURPHY, Darby	60	M	Laborer	12Ap08Cc
Ellen	50	F	Unknown	12Ap08Cc
Ellen	21	F	Unknown	12Ap08Cc
Jeremiah	17	M	Laborer	12Ap08Cc
DUANE, Margt.	20	F	Unknown	12Ap08Cc
BOURK, Michl.	30	M	Laborer	12Ap08Cc
Bridget	25	F	Unknown	12Ap08Cc
KENEPICK, Dennis	30	M	Laborer	12Ap08Cc
REGAN, David	20	M	Laborer	12Ap08Cc
Margt.	18	F	Unknown	12Ap08Cc
MADDEN, Robt.	33	M	Laborer	12Ap08Cc
Margt.	30	F	Unknown	12Ap08Cc
Michl.	.00	M	Infant	12Ap08Cc
BOHEN, Danl.	30	M	Laborer	12Ap08Cc
Mary	26	F	Unknown	12Ap08Cc
Johannah	.00	F	Infant	12Ap08Cc
MCCARTHY, Patk.	24	M	Laborer	12Ap08Cc
CROWLEY, John	35	M	Laborer	12Ap08Cc
Mary	24	F	Unknown	12Ap08Cc
Julia	13	F	Unknown	12Ap08Cc
LUCEY, Denis	29	M	Laborer	12Ap08Cc
EVANS, Andrew	30	M	Laborer	12Ap08Cc
Cath.	8	F	Child	12Ap08Cc
WALSH, Pierce	27	M	Laborer	12Ap08Cc
Cath.	22	F	Unknown	12Ap08Cc
James	6	M	Child	12Ap08Cc
Julia	4	F	Child	12Ap08Cc
John	2	M	Child	12Ap08Cc
Edmond	.00	M	Infant	12Ap08Cc
OBRIEN, Valentine	23	M	Laborer	12Ap08Cc
MCCARTHY, Michael	25	M	Laborer	12Ap08Cc
CADEGAN, Mary	22	F	Unknown	12Ap08Cc
GREENEY, Denis	40	M	Laborer	12Ap08Cc
BARRETT, Wm.	40	M	Laborer	12Ap08Cc
Wm.	14	M	Laborer	12Ap08Cc
MEAD, Jane	28	F	Unknown	12Ap08Cc

NAMES OF PASSENGERS	AGE	SEX	OCCUPATIONS	DATE PORT SHIP
SCANNEL, Michl.	28	M	Laborer	12Ap08Cc
WALSH, Thos.	20	M	Laborer	12Ap08Cc
CADEGAN, Maurice	20	M	Laborer	12Ap08Cc
FLYN, John	18	M	Laborer	12Ap08Cc
HOGAN, Margt.	20	F	Unknown	12Ap08Cc
RONAN, David	40	M	Laborer	12Ap08Cc
Patk.	12	M	Laborer	12Ap08Cc
Wm.	10	M	Laborer	12Ap08Cc
John	8	M	Child	12Ap08Cc
JOYCE, Thos.	30	M	Laborer	12Ap08Cc
Mary	25	F	Unknown	12Ap08Cc
Bridget	.00	F	Infant	12Ap08Cc
HICKEY, John	30	M	Laborer	12Ap08Cc
Mary	27	F	Unknown	12Ap08Cc
WALSH, Wm.	30	M	Laborer	12Ap08Cc
FOLEY, Bridget	30	F	Unknown	12Ap08Cc
COTTER, Mary	24	F	Unknown	12Ap08Cc
DONOGHUE, Batt	24	M	Laborer	12Ap08Cc
Michl.	38	M	Laborer	12Ap08Cc
Cath.	18	F	Laborer	12Ap08Cc
RAHILLY, Martin	20	M	Laborer	12Ap08Cc
DALY, Thos.	28	M	Laborer	12Ap08Cc
RINESY, Betty	26	F	Unknown	12Ap08Cc
STACK, Edmond	20	M	Laborer	12Ap08Cc
LUCEY, Johannah	20	F	Unknown	12Ap08Cc
NOONAN, Timothy	34	M	Laborer	12Ap08Cc
Cath.	26	F	Unknown	12Ap08Cc
Timothy	.00	M	Infant	12Ap08Cc
LUCY, Timothy	27	M	Laborer	12Ap08Cc
Margt.	24	F	Unknown	12Ap08Cc
CALLAGHER, Jerry	20	M	Laborer	12Ap08Cc
HOUREGAN, Cath.	20	F	Unknown	12Ap08Cc
CLANCY, James	25	M	Laborer	12Ap08Cc
KEEFFE, Cors.	21	M	Laborer	12Ap08Cc
HALLAHAN, John	23	M	Laborer	12Ap08Cc
SCANLON, John	24	M	Laborer	12Ap08Cc
LEANEY, Thos.	22	M	Laborer	12Ap08Cc
Mary	20	F	Unknown	12Ap08Cc
MORRISSY, Patk.	20	M	Laborer	12Ap08Cc
COGHLAN, Margt.	23	F	Unknown	12Ap08Cc

HURON 13 APRIL 1849

From Belfast

NAMES OF PASSENGERS	AGE	SEX	OCCUPATIONS	DATE PORT SHIP
HARRY, P.	45	M	Laborer	13Ap05Cd
Cath.	45	F	Unknown	13Ap05Cd
Elzt.	18	F	Unknown	13Ap05Cd
Jane	16	F	Unknown	13Ap05Cd
My.	13	F	Unknown	13Ap05Cd
DAISEY, J.	32	M	Laborer	13Ap05Cd
John	30	M	Laborer	13Ap05Cd
Ann	30	F	Unknown	13Ap05Cd
Sarah	30	F	Unknown	13Ap05Cd
Teresa	18	F	Unknown	13Ap05Cd
Sarah	14	F	Unknown	13Ap05Cd
Jas.	21	M	Laborer	13Ap05Cd
ELLISON, Ro.	19	F	Unknown	13Ap05Cd
MCAULEY, A.	30	M	Laborer	13Ap05Cd
MCCLUSKY, A.	55	M	Laborer	13Ap05Cd
FORSYTH, G.	45	M	Laborer	13Ap05Cd
Alex.	16	M	Laborer	13Ap05Cd
Elza.	18	F	Unknown	13Ap05Cd
MCCAUGHLIN, D.	45	M	Laborer	13Ap05Cd
Betty	40	F	Unknown	13Ap05Cd
Jno.	13	M	Unknown	13Ap05Cd
Ann	11	F	Unknown	13Ap05Cd
Peter	9	M	Child	13Ap05Cd
John	8	M	Child	13Ap05Cd
MCCAUGHLIN, Cath.	45	F	Unknown	13Ap05Cd
My.	22	F	Unknown	13Ap05Cd
Owen	20	M	Laborer	13Ap05Cd
John	8	M	Child	13Ap05Cd
Ja--, J.	25	M	Laborer	13Ap05Cd
My.	22	F	Unknown	13Ap05Cd
TOONY, J.	22	M	Laborer	13Ap05Cd
Cath.	20	F	Unknown	13Ap05Cd
MULHOLLAND, C.	60	M	Laborer	13Ap05Cd
Felix	23	M	Laborer	13Ap05Cd
Ellen	18	F	Unknown	13Ap05Cd
Cath.	60	F	Unknown	13Ap05Cd
BARKER, W.	31	M	Laborer	13Ap05Cd
My.	30	F	Unknown	13Ap05Cd
Fanny	7	F	Child	13Ap05Cd
Richd.	5	M	Child	13Ap05Cd
My.	2	F	Child	13Ap05Cd
U, Am.	1	U	Child	13Ap05Cd
DUFFEY, U	36	M	Laborer	13Ap05Cd
Susan	13	F	Unknown	13Ap05Cd
CLEFFERTY, P.	19	M	Laborer	13Ap05Cd
F.	20	M	Laborer	13Ap05Cd
GILES, J.	24	M	Laborer	13Ap05Cd
MILLER, J.	20	M	Laborer	13Ap05Cd
OBRIEN, H.	24	M	Laborer	13Ap05Cd
DONALD, J.W.	50	M	Laborer	13Ap05Cd
ADAMS, F.	10	M	Laborer	13Ap05Cd
BYOD, M.	10	F	Unknown	13Ap05Cd
BARKER, U	25	F	Unknown	13Ap05Cd
Re--Er--, L.	20	M	Laborer	13Ap05Cd
DOROHY, G.	20	M	Laborer	13Ap05Cd
Caroline	20	F	Unknown	13Ap05Cd
MCCLUSKY, Sah.	27	F	Unknown	13Ap05Cd
HANLON, J.	25	M	Laborer	13Ap05Cd
My.	21	F	Unknown	13Ap05Cd
BAILEY, J.	19	M	Laborer	13Ap05Cd
Mgt.	11	F	Unknown	13Ap05Cd
HENSEY, U	27	F	Unknown	13Ap05Cd
MCARDLE, Cath.	19	F	Unknown	13Ap05Cd
MEEHAN, M.	14	M	Laborer	13Ap05Cd
MCCONELL, W.	50	M	Laborer	13Ap05Cd
BOYLIN, My.	11	F	Unknown	13Ap05Cd
BURKE, J.	30	M	Laborer	13Ap05Cd
DAVIS, M.A.	40	F	Unknown	13Ap05Cd
Mich.	4	M	Child	13Ap05Cd
Cath.	1	F	Child	13Ap05Cd
Pat	25	M	Laborer	13Ap05Cd
DOYLE, J.	40	M	Laborer	13Ap05Cd
GORMAN, E.	30	M	Laborer	13Ap05Cd
C--T--, G.	20	M	Laborer	13Ap05Cd
Pa--P--, A.	16	M	Laborer	13Ap05Cd
Robt.	22	M	Laborer	13Ap05Cd
M.	20	M	Laborer	13Ap05Cd
WEGINS, R.	25	M	Laborer	13Ap05Cd
DALY, U	35	M	Laborer	13Ap05Cd
SINCLAIR, D.	40	M	Laborer	13Ap05Cd
SCHOLES, J.	40	M	Laborer	13Ap05Cd
Rose	16	F	Unknown	13Ap05Cd
Thos.	13	M	Unknown	13Ap05Cd
Rose	13	F	Unknown	13Ap05Cd
John	11	M	Unknown	13Ap05Cd
Pat	9	M	Child	13Ap05Cd
Jas.	5	M	Child	13Ap05Cd
F.	1	M	Child	13Ap05Cd
Jane	19	F	Unknown	13Ap05Cd
U	1	M	Child	13Ap05Cd
GUBBIN, Rose	20	F	Unknown	13Ap05Cd
DAVESON, W.	30	M	Laborer	13Ap05Cd
DONNELLY, Ellen	30	F	Unknown	13Ap05Cd
U	1	F	Child	13Ap05Cd
HEARN, N.	19	F	Unknown	13Ap05Cd
MCQUADE, U	25	M	Laborer	13Ap05Cd
Pete	22	M	Laborer	13Ap05Cd
TAEHE, My.	22	F	Unknown	13Ap05Cd
DONAGH, E.	20	M	Laborer	13Ap05Cd

NAMES OF PASSENGERS	AGE	SEX	OCCUPATIONS	DATE PORT SHIP
DONAGH, U	18	F	Unknown	13Ap05Cd
GRAHAM, J.	25	M	Laborer	13Ap05Cd
Well--Y, U	22	F	Unknown	13Ap05Cd
MCCANN, P.	30	M	Laborer	13Ap05Cd
DOUGHTY, G.	20	M	Laborer	13Ap05Cd
MENTY, W.	20	M	Laborer	13Ap05Cd
MCGLINN, A.	20	F	Unknown	13Ap05Cd
SHEFFINGTON, A.	20	M	Laborer	13Ap05Cd
ROBINSON, F.	20	M	Laborer	13Ap05Cd
LOVE, J.	58	M	Laborer	13Ap05Cd
Elza.	45	F	Unknown	13Ap05Cd
Elza.	22	F	Unknown	13Ap05Cd
Jas.	19	M	Laborer	13Ap05Cd
Joseph	13	M	Unknown	13Ap05Cd
John	11	M	Unknown	13Ap05Cd
Mgt.	8	F	Child	13Ap05Cd
Jane	6	F	Child	13Ap05Cd
Wm.	3	M	Child	13Ap05Cd
Saml.	1	M	Child	13Ap05Cd
CRAWFORD, J.	26	M	Laborer	13Ap05Cd
Isabella	25	F	Unknown	13Ap05Cd
Mgt.	6	F	Child	13Ap05Cd
Andrew	4	M	Child	13Ap05Cd
Jas.	2	M	Child	13Ap05Cd
Elza.	1	F	Child	13Ap05Cd
W.	22	M	Laborer	13Ap05Cd
Andrew	19	M	Laborer	13Ap05Cd
BIGBY, Cath.	15	F	Unknown	13Ap05Cd
MAHER, Biddy	17	F	Unknown	13Ap05Cd
DERROH, B.	26	M	Laborer	13Ap05Cd
DONNELY, F.	40	M	Laborer	13Ap05Cd
EVANS, P.	22	M	Laborer	13Ap05Cd
MCGOWAN, C.	26	M	Laborer	13Ap05Cd
CAHOON, J.	21	M	Laborer	13Ap05Cd
LOVE, Joh.	50	F	Unknown	13Ap05Cd
Ann	20	F	Unknown	13Ap05Cd
Thos.	13	M	Unknown	13Ap05Cd
Wm.	11	M	Unknown	13Ap05Cd
Edwd.	6	M	Child	13Ap05Cd
BAY, Isa.	18	F	Unknown	13Ap05Cd
LOVE, Jane	30	F	Unknown	13Ap05Cd
DEEROR, Chat.	21	F	Unknown	13Ap05Cd
FETTURGE, R.	20	M	Laborer	13Ap05Cd
GODFREY, Isa.	45	F	Unknown	13Ap05Cd
U	16	M	Laborer	13Ap05Cd
Isa.	12	F	Unknown	13Ap05Cd
George	9	M	Child	13Ap05Cd
Chr.	7	M	Child	13Ap05Cd
BROWN, Jane	20	F	Unknown	13Ap05Cd
MESSATH, Mgt.	20	F	Unknown	13Ap05Cd
KELY, J.	25	M	Laborer	13Ap05Cd
M.	20	F	Unknown	13Ap05Cd
Matilda	18	F	Unknown	13Ap05Cd
MCKEFFY, W.	16	M	Laborer	13Ap05Cd
YOUNG, Isa.	57	F	Unknown	13Ap05Cd
Isa.	15	F	Unknown	13Ap05Cd
Rich.	12	M	Unknown	13Ap05Cd
U	10	M	Unknown	13Ap05Cd
Sarah	8	F	Unknown	13Ap05Cd
DONELLY, J.	17	M	Laborer	13Ap05Cd
FORSYTH, C.	21	M	Laborer	13Ap05Cd
JEAGER, W.	21	M	Laborer	13Ap05Cd
STEARNS, J.	40	M	Laborer	13Ap05Cd
NEWELL, W.	30	M	Laborer	13Ap05Cd
IRVINE, Sa.	21	F	Unknown	13Ap05Cd
MCKEOWN, J.	24	M	Unknown	13Ap05Cd
Biddy	22	F	Unknown	13Ap05Cd
SUGRU, Biddy	19	F	Unknown	13Ap05Cd
MURPHY, Ann	20	F	Unknown	13Ap05Cd
GORHAM, Elza.	21	F	Unknown	13Ap05Cd
George	19	M	Laborer	13Ap05Cd
CONNER, J.	25	M	Laborer	13Ap05Cd
Me--S, Jane	25	F	Unknown	13Ap05Cd
CULLY, P.	20	M	Laborer	13Ap05Cd
TORHILL, J.	18	M	Laborer	13Ap05Cd
PEDLOW, Jane	20	F	Unknown	13Ap05Cd
MCKEOWN, U	21	F	Unknown	13Ap05Cd
CASSIDY, T.	24	M	Laborer	13Ap05Cd
CHRISTY, J.	30	M	Laborer	13Ap05Cd
Mgt.	21	F	Unknown	13Ap05Cd
E.	19	F	Unknown	13Ap05Cd
DAVIDSON, Ann	30	F	Unknown	13Ap05Cd
Ann	3	F	Child	13Ap05Cd
HAY, Mgt.	22	F	Unknown	13Ap05Cd

WALTRON 13 APRIL 1849

From Belfast

NAMES OF PASSENGERS	AGE	SEX	OCCUPATIONS	DATE PORT SHIP
LOUGHRAN, Henry	16	M	Laborer	13Ap05Ce
ARMOUR, Jane	16	F	Spinster	13Ap05Ce
WAUGH, David	25	M	Farmer	13Ap05Ce
Robert	19	M	Farmer	13Ap05Ce
TOWMAN, Daniel	28	M	Farmer	13Ap05Ce
Mary	28	F	Wife	13Ap05Ce
LINDSLEY, Nancy	43	F	Wi	13Ap05Ce
Thomas	18	M	Farmer	13Ap05Ce
William	15	M	Farmer	13Ap05Ce
Andrew	11	M	None	13Ap05Ce
Margaret	8	F	Child	13Ap05Ce
George	6	M	Child	13Ap05Ce
James	3	M	Child	13Ap05Ce
HEILL, Margaret	18	F	Spinster	13Ap05Ce
JOHNSTON, Thos.	21	M	Farmer	13Ap05Ce
Elizabeth	23	F	Wife	13Ap05Ce
MCKAY, Thos.	25	M	Laborer	13Ap05Ce
RAINEY, William	21	M	Farmer	13Ap05Ce
ROSS, Thos.	42	M	Farmer	13Ap05Ce
Margaret	37	F	Wife	13Ap05Ce
Jane	13	F	None	13Ap05Ce
Agnes	11	F	None	13Ap05Ce
Susan	9	F	Child	13Ap05Ce
Eliza	7	F	Child	13Ap05Ce
Ezekial	5	M	Child	13Ap05Ce
Thos.	3	M	Child	13Ap05Ce
Nathan	.00	M	Infant	13Ap05Ce
MINIS, Thomas	22	M	Laborer	13Ap05Ce
Sarah	18	F	Wife	13Ap05Ce
Mary-Ann	13	F	None	13Ap05Ce
LAND, Agnes	15	F	Spinster	13Ap05Ce
MCCONNELL, Eliza	19	F	Spinster	13Ap05Ce
Susan	17	F	Spinster	13Ap05Ce
MCCOLTER, Jane	26	F	Spinster	13Ap05Ce
MCDOWELL, Mary	25	F	Wife	13Ap05Ce
James	4	M	Child	13Ap05Ce
Thos.	3	M	Child	13Ap05Ce
Ann	.00	F	Infant	13Ap05Ce
OHAIR, Peter	22	M	Laborer	13Ap05Ce
HOLLAND, Mary	40	F	Wi	13Ap05Ce
Catharine	19	F	Spinster	13Ap05Ce
Felix	17	M	Laborer	13Ap05Ce
Bridget	12	F	None	13Ap05Ce
Mary	8	F	Child	13Ap05Ce
Rose	6	F	Child	13Ap05Ce
Ann	6	F	Child	13Ap05Ce
Margaret	5	F	Child	13Ap05Ce
Sarah	3	F	Child	13Ap05Ce
Ellen	.00	F	Infant	13Ap05Ce
GILLELAND, Jane	30	F	Spinster	13Ap05Ce
MCFARLAND, Robt.	22	M	Laborer	13Ap05Ce
Jane	20	F	Wife	13Ap05Ce
Wm.	.00	M	Infant	13Ap05Ce
CARSON, Mary-Ann	20	F	Spinster	13Ap05Ce
HAMILTON, Rose	20	F	Spinster	13Ap05Ce

NAMES OF PASSENGERS	AGE	SEX	OCCUPATIONS	DATE PORT SHIP
BOLE, Andrew	24	M	Laborer	13Ap05Ce
Sarah	24	F	Wife	13Ap05Ce
OLIVER, James	34	M	Laborer	13Ap05Ce
STEWART, Betty	31	F	Wi	13Ap05Ce
Jane	15	F	Spinster	13Ap05Ce
Mary	13	F	None	13Ap05Ce
Catharine	11	F	None	13Ap05Ce
Hugh	9	M	Child	13Ap05Ce
Alexander	7	M	Child	13Ap05Ce
Rose	5	F	Child	13Ap05Ce
Daniel	2	M	Child	13Ap05Ce
NULLY, Alexander	24	M	Laborer	13Ap05Ce
James	22	M	Laborer	13Ap05Ce
OLIVER, Thos.	34	M	Laborer	13Ap05Ce
FREEMAN, James	17	M	Laborer	13Ap05Ce
H--EWCE, Thomas	20	M	Laborer	13Ap05Ce
HAMILTON, James	21	M	Laborer	13Ap05Ce
Stewart	27	M	Laborer	13Ap05Ce
Isaiah	25	M	Laborer	13Ap05Ce
James	5	M	Child	13Ap05Ce
Eliza	2	F	Child	13Ap05Ce
Isabella	.00	F	Infant	13Ap05Ce
MCCURRY, John	24	M	Laborer	13Ap05Ce
MEGRATH, Mary	9	F	Child	13Ap05Ce
James	10	M	None	13Ap05Ce
STEWARD, Thomas	21	M	Unknown	13Ap05Ce
MAINE, James	21	M	Laborer	13Ap05Ce
James	.00	M	Infant	13Ap05Ce

SHERIDAN 14 APRIL 1849

From Liverpool

NAMES OF PASSENGERS	AGE	SEX	OCCUPATIONS	DATE PORT SHIP
COOK, Joseph-Henry	23	M	Gentleman	14Ap02Bx
LABERT, Edwd.	19	M	Gentleman	14Ap02Bx
ONEIL, Henry	21	M	Gentleman	14Ap02Bx
HOWE, Julia	22	F	Servant	14Ap02Bx
SHANNON, J.B.	24	U	Servant	14Ap02Bx
MARKS, Wm.	24	M	Laborer	14Ap02Bx
Rose	21	F	Laborer	14Ap02Bx
DONELAN, Robert	21	M	Laborer	14Ap02Bx
HANNAH, Ann	20	F	Laborer	14Ap02Bx
COWIN, Edwd.	25	M	Laborer	14Ap02Bx
DAVINE, Wm.	23	M	Laborer	14Ap02Bx
U-Mrs.	21	F	Laborer	14Ap02Bx
FARRELL, John	25	M	Laborer	14Ap02Bx
DIGNAN, John	25	M	Laborer	14Ap02Bx
GALLIGAN, B.	18	U	Laborer	14Ap02Bx
Rosey	15	F	Laborer	14Ap02Bx
FARLEY, Ellen	20	F	Laborer	14Ap02Bx
CROONAN, Jas.	40	F	Laborer	14Ap02Bx
CASEY, Ann	20	F	Laborer	14Ap02Bx
Patt.	30	M	Laborer	14Ap02Bx
Mary	20	F	Laborer	14Ap02Bx
MURRANON, John	25	M	Laborer	14Ap02Bx
MCDERMOTT, John	20	M	Laborer	14Ap02Bx
CARTY, John	26	M	Laborer	14Ap02Bx
MCDONNELL, Colin	20	M	Laborer	14Ap02Bx
GIBNEY, Mary	20	F	Servant	14Ap02Bx
MCCANN, Patt	26	M	Laborer	14Ap02Bx
CARROLL, Cathn.	20	F	Unknown	14Ap02Bx
MCCAFFREY, Alice	20	F	Servant	14Ap02Bx
CARRIGAN, John	20	M	Servant	14Ap02Bx
KEEGAN, Mary	20	F	Servant	14Ap02Bx
CARROLL, Patt	30	M	Servant	14Ap02Bx
SILVA, William	21	M	Servant	14Ap02Bx
CROSNAN, Ellen	30	F	Servant	14Ap02Bx
Cathn.	18	F	Servant	14Ap02Bx
FANNON, Patt	40	M	Servant	14Ap02Bx
FANNON, Alice	10	F	Servant	14Ap02Bx
John	08	M	Child	14Ap02Bx
CONROY, Cathn.	20	F	Servant	14Ap02Bx
LAKE, James	24	M	Laborer	14Ap02Bx
FARRELL, Mary	36	F	Laborer	14Ap02Bx
B.	18	U	Laborer	14Ap02Bx
FLINN, Patt	26	M	Laborer	14Ap02Bx
FLYNN, Bridt.	20	F	Laborer	14Ap02Bx
CONNOR, Bridt.	26	F	Laborer	14Ap02Bx
Domk.	.00	M	Infant	14Ap02Bx
FITZGERALD, William	50	M	Unknown	14Ap02Bx
KILGROVE, Peggy	20	F	Unknown	14Ap02Bx
HOWE, Ellen	22	F	Unknown	14Ap02Bx
HUNTER, G.W.	22	M	Weaver	14Ap02Bx
QUADE, John	20	M	Unknown	14Ap02Bx
MCKEE, Robt.	20	M	Laborer	14Ap02Bx
Jemima	28	F	Laborer	14Ap02Bx
KELLY, John	26	M	Laborer	14Ap02Bx
MCQUADE, Cathn.	17	F	Laborer	14Ap02Bx
BOHANNA, Bridt.	18	F	Laborer	14Ap02Bx
MCKENNA, Jas.	22	M	Laborer	14Ap02Bx
Cathn.	18	F	Laborer	14Ap02Bx
SPANE, John	50	M	Laborer	14Ap02Bx
Ann	50	F	Laborer	14Ap02Bx
Mary	18	F	Laborer	14Ap02Bx
Cathn.	11	F	Laborer	14Ap02Bx
DOYLE, Michl.	12	M	Laborer	14Ap02Bx
BERGN, Cathn.	11	F	Laborer	14Ap02Bx
QUINN, Mary	22	F	Laborer	14Ap02Bx
MCINERNEY, Mary	27	F	Laborer	14Ap02Bx
BOYLE, Bridt.	20	F	Laborer	14Ap02Bx
FOOLEY, Margt.	18	F	Servant	14Ap02Bx
SWEENEY, John	30	M	Laborer	14Ap02Bx
Ann	10	F	Laborer	14Ap02Bx
LIDDY, Patt	20	M	Laborer	14Ap02Bx
RILEY, John	19	M	Laborer	14Ap02Bx
SMITH, Patt	27	M	Laborer	14Ap02Bx
Margt.	27	F	Laborer	14Ap02Bx
Jas.	04	M	Child	14Ap02Bx
ARCHESON, Frans.	20	M	Laborer	14Ap02Bx
CLARKE, John	17	M	Baker	14Ap02Bx
HENRY, Margt.	40	F	Servant	14Ap02Bx
Saml.	13	M	Servant	14Ap02Bx
Eliza	10	F	Servant	14Ap02Bx
BRADY, Cathn.	16	F	Servant	14Ap02Bx
Mary	14	F	Servant	14Ap02Bx
MONAGHAN, Christopher	24	M	Laborer	14Ap02Bx
CORR, Mary	21	F	Laborer	14Ap02Bx
MCQUADE, Jane	20	F	Laborer	14Ap02Bx
MCDEVITT, D.	20	U	Laborer	14Ap02Bx
KELLY, Ellen	20	F	Laborer	14Ap02Bx
Hugh	16	M	Butcher	14Ap02Bx
BARRATT, Thos.	58	M	Laborer	14Ap02Bx
Bridt.	58	F	Laborer	14Ap02Bx
Michl.	30	M	Laborer	14Ap02Bx
Bridt.	20	F	Laborer	14Ap02Bx
QUIGLEY, Bridt.	60	F	Servant	14Ap02Bx
OHARA, Bridt.	40	F	Servant	14Ap02Bx
Mary	06	F	Child	14Ap02Bx
Thos.	04	M	Child	14Ap02Bx
FLANIGAN, Cathn.	60	M	Servant	14Ap02Bx
OCONNOR, Jas.	25	M	Servant	14Ap02Bx
LUMRY, Mary	16	F	Servant	14Ap02Bx
OBRIEN, Cathn.	20	F	Servant	14Ap02Bx
DWYER, Johan	22	M	Laborer	14Ap02Bx
John	20	M	Unknown	14Ap02Bx
Cathn.	18	F	Unknown	14Ap02Bx
ACKERMAN, M.	10	U	Tailor	14Ap02Bx
Wm.	06	M	Child	14Ap02Bx
GILROY, Thos.	30	M	Laborer	14Ap02Bx
GALLAGHER, Danl.	23	M	Laborer	14Ap02Bx
PARSONS, Jane	18	F	Laborer	14Ap02Bx
Ann	16	F	Laborer	14Ap02Bx
MONLE, Ann	20	F	Laborer	14Ap02Bx
Sevina	16	F	Laborer	14Ap02Bx

NAMES OF PASSENGERS	AGE	SEX	OCCUPATIONS	DATE PORT SHIP
MCGOVERN, Patt	16	M	Laborer	14Ap02Bx
Mary	17	F	Laborer	14Ap02Bx
Michl.	20	M	Laborer	14Ap02Bx
MARTIN, Michl.	50	M	Laborer	14Ap02Bx
MCKEOWN, Patt	20	M	Laborer	14Ap02Bx
WARD, Ellen	22	F	Laborer	14Ap02Bx
KELLY, Ellen	20	F	Laborer	14Ap02Bx
REILEY, Patt	20	M	Laborer	14Ap02Bx
ROBERTS, Agnes	22	F	Laborer	14Ap02Bx
DELANY, Jas.	25	M	Laborer	14Ap02Bx
BIRD, Dan	25	M	Farmer	14Ap02Bx
Margt.	20	F	Farmer	14Ap02Bx
Michl.	23	M	Farmer	14Ap02Bx
GILSHELA, Patt	40	M	Farmer	14Ap02Bx
WELSH, Cathn.	13	F	Farmer	14Ap02Bx
MCHEGGAN, Michl.	30	M	Farmer	14Ap02Bx
MCCARTY, Bart.	21	M	Laborer	14Ap02Bx
KYLE, Mary	18	F	Laborer	14Ap02Bx
CALLAGAN, Bridt.	24	F	Laborer	14Ap02Bx
MURPHEY, Quinn	30	M	Laborer	14Ap02Bx
CONGLIN, John	25	M	Laborer	14Ap02Bx
CALLAGHAN, Pat	50	M	Farmer	14Ap02Bx
Betsey	13	F	Farmer	14Ap02Bx
Rose	11	F	Farmer	14Ap02Bx
KELLY, Ann	18	F	Farmer	14Ap02Bx
COONEY, Thos.	12	M	Farmer	14Ap02Bx
MURRY, Patt	20	M	Farmer	14Ap02Bx
DOOLIN, Ann	19	F	Farmer	14Ap02Bx
KENNA, Michl.	20	M	Farmer	14Ap02Bx
WALLACE, Wm.	18	M	Farmer	14Ap02Bx
CROONEN, Wm.	13	M	Farmer	14Ap02Bx
Michl.	10	M	Farmer	14Ap02Bx
SHEEN, Con	30	M	Farmer	14Ap02Bx
MALONY, U	22	U	Farmer	14Ap02Bx
Jas.	20	M	Farmer	14Ap02Bx
RICHARDSON, Alexander	60	M	Farmer	14Ap02Bx
Eliza	14	F	Farmer	14Ap02Bx
Mary-Jane	18	F	Farmer	14Ap02Bx
Alexr.	12	M	Farmer	14Ap02Bx
STEWART, Robert	18	M	Farmer	14Ap02Bx
Mary	50	F	Farmer	14Ap02Bx
Susannah	13	F	Farmer	14Ap02Bx
Cathn.	11	F	Farmer	14Ap02Bx
DIRAIN, Mary	17	F	Farmer	14Ap02Bx
SMITH, Patk.	24	M	Servant	14Ap02Bx
RYAN, Michl.	34	M	Laborer	14Ap02Bx
DONOLAN, Cathn.	18	F	Laborer	14Ap02Bx
IRUM, Sarah	19	F	Laborer	14Ap02Bx
DELANY, Martha	24	F	Laborer	14Ap02Bx
BARRY, Jannet	32	F	Laborer	14Ap02Bx
Jno.	30	M	Laborer	14Ap02Bx
KELLY, Patk.	24	M	Laborer	14Ap02Bx
LYNCH, Cathn.	18	F	Laborer	14Ap02Bx
CONN, Ally	19	F	Laborer	14Ap02Bx
CRAIG, Elizabeth	20	F	Laborer	14Ap02Bx
Martha	18	F	Laborer	14Ap02Bx
Ellen	24	F	Laborer	14Ap02Bx
CAMPBELL, James	40	M	Weaver	14Ap02Bx
Ann	22	F	Weaver	14Ap02Bx
Hugh	19	M	Weaver	14Ap02Bx
Jane	16	F	Weaver	14Ap02Bx
William	13	M	Weaver	14Ap02Bx
John	09	M	Child	14Ap02Bx
Cathn.	06	F	Child	14Ap02Bx
Robert	48	M	Weaver	14Ap02Bx
Agnes	38	F	Weaver	14Ap02Bx
Agnes	09	F	Child	14Ap02Bx
David	07	M	Child	14Ap02Bx
William	05	M	Child	14Ap02Bx
Elizabeth	03	F	Child	14Ap02Bx
DOLAN, William	28	M	Weaver	14Ap02Bx
Cathn.	20	F	Servant	14Ap02Bx
CAMPBELL, Jane	48	F	Servant	14Ap02Bx
Cathn.	15	F	Servant	14Ap02Bx
Mary	11	F	Servant	14Ap02Bx
CAMPBELL, Margt.	13	F	Servant	14Ap02Bx
William	09	M	Child	14Ap02Bx
Thomas	01	M	Child	14Ap02Bx
CASHAM, John	17	M	Shoemaker	14Ap02Bx
MCCANN, Cathn.	17	F	Servant	14Ap02Bx
FLEMING, Michl.	21	M	Laborer	14Ap02Bx
CARROLL, Jgt.	20	U	Unknown	14Ap02Bx
Mary	20	F	Unknown	14Ap02Bx
WYNN, Timothy	25	M	Tailor	14Ap02Bx
KELLY, Cathn.	16	F	Servant	14Ap02Bx
COFFREY, Patk.	24	M	Laborer	14Ap02Bx
Mary	55	F	Unknown	14Ap02Bx
CANN, Cathn.	04	F	Child	14Ap02Bx
CANNAN, Ellen	12	F	Unknown	14Ap02Bx
DERMOTT, Thos.	35	M	Unknown	14Ap02Bx
U-Mrs.	30	F	Unknown	14Ap02Bx
MURRY, Patt	36	M	Unknown	14Ap02Bx
Betty	17	F	Unknown	14Ap02Bx
SPOLTEEN, John	18	M	Unknown	14Ap02Bx
MCCABE, John	16	M	Laborer	14Ap02Bx
CARNEY, Alley	16	F	Unknown	14Ap02Bx
HALES, Mary-Mrs.	50	F	Unknown	14Ap02Bx
Mary	19	F	Unknown	14Ap02Bx
COATES, Geo.	20	M	Laborer	14Ap02Bx
Patt	18	M	Laborer	14Ap02Bx
MAHON, Mathew	21	M	Laborer	14Ap02Bx
DARCEY, Thos.	21	M	Laborer	14Ap02Bx
ROUKE, Philip	23	M	Laborer	14Ap02Bx
MURPHY, James	23	M	Laborer	14Ap02Bx
CORKER, James	45	M	Laborer	14Ap02Bx
Betty	45	F	Laborer	14Ap02Bx
Hannah	17	F	Laborer	14Ap02Bx
Emelia	13	F	Laborer	14Ap02Bx
Jas.	11	M	Laborer	14Ap02Bx
Miles	09	M	Child	14Ap02Bx
Sarah	06	F	Child	14Ap02Bx
Elizabeth	03	F	Child	14Ap02Bx
Edwd.	33	M	Laborer	14Ap02Bx
GARSIDE, James	23	M	Farmer	14Ap02Bx
Elizabeth	23	F	Unknown	14Ap02Bx
COAN, Andrew	28	M	Laborer	14Ap02Bx
Mary	30	F	Laborer	14Ap02Bx
GRIFFIN, Patk.	22	M	Laborer	14Ap02Bx
NICKLE, Joseph	30	M	Laborer	14Ap02Bx
Martha	06	F	Child	14Ap02Bx
MCCOOLE, Mary-Ann	25	F	Laborer	14Ap02Bx
Thos.	.00	M	Infant	14Ap02Bx
MCLAUGHLIN, James	25	M	Laborer	14Ap02Bx
AUSTON, Andrew	28	M	Laborer	14Ap02Bx
John	22	M	Laborer	14Ap02Bx
MCCALL, James	24	M	Laborer	14Ap02Bx
DEANES, Geo.	20	M	Laborer	14Ap02Bx
QUINN, Bernard	24	M	Farmer	14Ap02Bx
MCGORRY, Peter	20	M	Unknown	14Ap02Bx
ONEIL, Hugh	35	M	Shoemaker	14Ap02Bx
Mary	20	F	Unknown	14Ap02Bx
Alice	.00	F	Infant	14Ap02Bx
MCGUIRE, Peter	20	M	Shoemaker	14Ap02Bx
MCHANNA, Allice	20	F	Shoemaker	14Ap02Bx
DALEY, Thos.	30	M	Laborer	14Ap02Bx
MCCABE, Michl.	30	M	Laborer	14Ap02Bx
Biddy	14	F	Laborer	14Ap02Bx
MCBRIDE, James	14	M	Laborer	14Ap02Bx
MURRAY, James	20	M	Laborer	14Ap02Bx
LED, James	40	M	Laborer	14Ap02Bx
MOONEY, David	32	M	Laborer	14Ap02Bx
Margt.	27	F	Laborer	14Ap02Bx
CONNER, Mary	38	F	Laborer	14Ap02Bx
MCCANN, Edwd.	40	M	Blacksmith	14Ap02Bx
NOLAN, U-Mrs.	38	F	Blacksmith	14Ap02Bx
HANLEY, U-Mrs.	30	F	Blacksmith	14Ap02Bx
John	05	M	Child	14Ap02Bx
Elizabeth	09	F	Child	14Ap02Bx
Charles	.00	M	Infant	14Ap02Bx
MOONEY, Riglo	03	M	Child	14Ap02Bx

NAMES OF PASSENGERS	AGE	SEX	OCCUPATIONS	DATE PORT SHIP
MOONEY, John	.00	M	Infant	14Ap02Bx
RICE, Margt.	30	F	Servant	14Ap02Bx
REILEY, Laurence	21	M	Laborer	14Ap02Bx
PETITT, John	12	M	Laborer	14Ap02Bx
DONAHOE, Rose	18	F	Laborer	14Ap02Bx
NUGENT, James	24	M	Laborer	14Ap02Bx
SMYTH, John	25	M	Laborer	14Ap02Bx
William	23	M	Laborer	14Ap02Bx
HIGGINS, Michl.	19	M	Laborer	14Ap02Bx
GREGORY, Thos.	24	M	Laborer	14Ap02Bx
MURRY, Edwd.	30	M	Laborer	14Ap02Bx
DOYLE, Matilda	16	F	Laborer	14Ap02Bx
MOONEY, Cathn.	18	F	Laborer	14Ap02Bx
KENNEDY, Michl.	24	M	Laborer	14Ap02Bx
KERNIN, Ona	21	F	Unknown	14Ap02Bx
BRIAN, Mary	08	F	Child	14Ap02Bx
RILEY, Ann	21	F	Unknown	14Ap02Bx
IRWIN, Eliza	22	F	Unknown	14Ap02Bx
PHILIPS, William	36	M	Carpenter	14Ap02Bx
James	26	M	Unknown	14Ap02Bx
GAYNOR, John	24	M	Laborer	14Ap02Bx
LOFTUS, Michl.	22	M	Laborer	14Ap02Bx
JOHNSTON, Ann	50	M	Laborer	14Ap02Bx
Ann	22	M	Laborer	14Ap02Bx
MITCHIN, Mary	25	M	Laborer	14Ap02Bx
Elizabeth	.00	F	Infant	14Ap02Bx
DALEY, Patk.	25	M	Laborer	14Ap02Bx
Mary	23	F	Laborer	14Ap02Bx
Cathn.	21	F	Laborer	14Ap02Bx
MURRAY, John	24	M	Laborer	14Ap02Bx
GAFNEY, Ralph	30	M	Laborer	14Ap02Bx
Ann	30	F	Laborer	14Ap02Bx
CAREY, Christopher	40	M	Laborer	14Ap02Bx
Alice	40	F	Laborer	14Ap02Bx
Christopher	18	M	Laborer	14Ap02Bx
William	13	M	Laborer	14Ap02Bx
Peter	11	M	Laborer	14Ap02Bx
Hugh	06	M	Child	14Ap02Bx
MAHER, John	24	M	Laborer	14Ap02Bx
HARNAN, James	26	M	Laborer	14Ap02Bx
SHERIDAN, William	26	M	Laborer	14Ap02Bx
Anna	22	F	Laborer	14Ap02Bx
MCHAND, John	30	M	Laborer	14Ap02Bx
Mary	22	F	Laborer	14Ap02Bx
TOOLE, Margt.	18	F	Laborer	14Ap02Bx
PURCELL, Stephen	21	M	Laborer	14Ap02Bx
Mary-Ann	15	F	Laborer	14Ap02Bx
BARRY, Richd.	30	M	Laborer	14Ap02Bx
Caroline	25	F	Laborer	14Ap02Bx
Caroline	.00	F	Infant	14Ap02Bx
HURLEY, Thos.	28	M	Laborer	14Ap02Bx
Cathn.	22	F	Laborer	14Ap02Bx
HAGERTY, Cathn.	21	F	Servant	14Ap02Bx
MARTIN, Bornet	35	M	Laborer	14Ap02Bx
Bornet	20	M	Laborer	14Ap02Bx
DAVIES, David	21	M	Laborer	14Ap02Bx

JOHN-J.D.WOLF 16 APRIL 1849

From Liverpool

NAMES OF PASSENGERS	AGE	SEX	OCCUPATIONS	DATE PORT SHIP
CUNNINGHAM, Peter	23	M	Tailor	16Ap02By
HYNES, Wm.	24	M	Laborer	16Ap02By
RILEY, John	26	M	Laborer	16Ap02By
Died-At-Sea				
TRACEY, Thomas	34	M	Mechanic	16Ap02By
FARRAGAN, Tury.	18	M	Laborer	16Ap02By
MITCHELL, Pat.	23	M	Laborer	16Ap02By
CAMPBELL, Pat.	26	M	Laborer	16Ap02By
HEALY, Michl.	19	M	Laborer	16Ap02By
FEENY, Martin	20	M	Laborer	16Ap02By
Died-At-Sea				
DONNOTHY, Pat	20	M	Laborer	16Ap02By
HIGGINS, Michl.	30	M	Laborer	16Ap02By
FLANNAGAN, Pat	30	M	Laborer	16Ap02By
GOGGIN, Cath.	21	F	Spinster	16Ap02By
QUINN, Ellen	20	F	Spinster	16Ap02By
FARRELL, Rose	30	F	Spinster	16Ap02By
LYNCH, Wm.	45	M	Laborer	16Ap02By
C.	12	F	Spinster	16Ap02By
PENLON, Edwd.	25	M	Laborer	16Ap02By
Died-At-Sea				
GRIMES, Wm.	26	M	Laborer	16Ap02By
CONNOLLY, John	24	M	Laborer	16Ap02By
MCKEOGH, Jas.	20	M	Laborer	16Ap02By
Eliz. (W)	38	F	Wife	16Ap02By
Died-At-Sea				
MCDERMOTT, John	25	M	Laborer	16Ap02By
MCKEON, Mary	20	F	Spinster	16Ap02By
Cath.	07	F	Child	16Ap02By
Died-At-Sea				
JOHNSTON, Thos.	24	M	Laborer	16Ap02By
SMITH, Pat.	24	M	Laborer	16Ap02By
FOX, John	18	M	Laborer	16Ap02By
FLINN, James	24	M	Laborer	16Ap02By
MCFERREN, John	25	M	Laborer	16Ap02By
Died-At-Sea				
Mary	20	F	Spinster	16Ap02By
Chas.	.08	M	Infant	16Ap02By
CALEY, James	21	M	Laborer	16Ap02By
KILHEAY, Mary	20	F	Spinster	16Ap02By
STACK, Bryan	40	M	Laborer	16Ap02By
QUINN, James	25	M	Laborer	16Ap02By
Nancy	24	F	Spinster	16Ap02By
BYRNE, Pat.	20	M	Laborer	16Ap02By
COONEY, James	20	M	Laborer	16Ap02By
MCFERNEN, Cath.	20	F	Spinster	16Ap02By
BRADY, Danl.	40	M	Servant	16Ap02By
DOYLE, Ned	35	M	Laborer	16Ap02By
Died-At-Sea				
Bridg. (W)	30	F	Wife	16Ap02By
David	06	M	Child	16Ap02By
Died-At-Sea				
Stephen	04	M	Child	16Ap02By
Died-At-Sea				
Mary	03	F	Child	16Ap02By
Died-At-Sea				
Pat	.09	M	Infant	16Ap02By
Died-At-Sea				
DOOLEY, Ellen	20	F	Spinster	16Ap02By
SLARAN, U-Mrs.	40	F	Spinster	16Ap02By
Died-At-Sea				
Bridgt.	16	F	Spinster	16Ap02By
Kitty	14	F	Spinster	16Ap02By
Martin	10	M	Unknown	16Ap02By
Mary	05	F	Child	16Ap02By
John	03	M	Child	16Ap02By
Ann	.09	F	Infant	16Ap02By
Died-At-Sea				
Honora	15	F	Spinster	16Ap02By
RATCHGAN, J.	30	M	Laborer	16Ap02By
U (W)	30	F	Wife	16Ap02By
Mat.	.08	M	Infant	16Ap02By
John	04	M	Child	16Ap02By
Mary	08	F	Child	16Ap02By
WALSH, Thos.	25	M	Laborer	16Ap02By
U (W)	25	F	Wife	16Ap02By
Died-At-Sea				
FERAX, James	20	M	Seaman	16Ap02By
MORRIS, Kitty	20	F	Spinster	16Ap02By
MCALAIR, John	24	M	Shoemaker	16Ap02By
NARY, Michl.	41	M	Laborer	16Ap02By
RAHAN, James	20	M	Mechanic	16Ap02By
SHEEHAN, Owen	20	M	Laborer	16Ap02By

NAMES OF PASSENGERS		AGE	SEX	OCCUPATIONS	DATE PORT SHIP
SHEEHAN, James		18	M	Laborer	16Ap02By
WALSH, Margt.		18	F	Spinster	16Ap02By
GLYNN, Bridgt.		18	F	Spinster	16Ap02By
WALSH, Mary		16	F	Spinster	16Ap02By
CURLEY, Mat.		34	M	Laborer	16Ap02By
BRITT, Michl.		21	M	Laborer	16Ap02By
HOLLAND, Pat		18	M	Laborer	16Ap02By
MCANALLY, Pat		25	M	Laborer	16Ap02By
Mary	(W)	20	F	Wife	16Ap02By
HOLAND, Cath.		18	F	Spinster	16Ap02By
BERRY, Pat		29	M	Laborer	16Ap02By
REILEY, John		27	M	Laborer	16Ap02By
GLYNN, Cath.		25	M	Laborer	16Ap02By
DUNN, Barny		40	M	Laborer	16Ap02By
U	(W)	40	F	Wife	16Ap02By
Peter		05	M	Child	16Ap02By
BRENNAN, James		50	M	Farmer	16Ap02By
Ann	(W)	50	F	Wife	16Ap02By
Died-At-Sea					
Edwd.		20	M	Farmer	16Ap02By
Rose		20	F	Spinster	16Ap02By
Mary		.06	F	Infant	16Ap02By
FARRELL, John		24	M	Mechanic	16Ap02By
Cath.	(W)	24	F	Wife	16Ap02By
Cath.		.08	F	Infant	16Ap02By
BRENNAN, James		25	M	Farmer	16Ap02By
HANLON, Ellen		20	F	Spinster	16Ap02By
BRENNAN, J.		18	M	Farmer	16Ap02By
Margt.		18	F	Spinster	16Ap02By
HOGAN, Pat		33	M	Merchant	16Ap02By
NOWLAN, Mary		20	F	Spinster	16Ap02By
FINAN, Ann		20	F	Spinster	16Ap02By
MCGOVERN, Mary		25	F	Spinster	16Ap02By
Mary		20	F	Spinster	16Ap02By
KILBY, Bridgt.		18	F	Spinster	16Ap02By
MCFADDEN, Gavan		18	M	Laborer	16Ap02By
MCGOVERN, Felix		20	M	Laborer	16Ap02By
Phil		20	M	Laborer	16Ap02By
MCCARTHY, Michl.		22	M	Laborer	16Ap02By
PRYOR, Cath.		20	F	Spinster	16Ap02By
MCGOWAN, Beth		18	F	Spinster	16Ap02By
Mary		18	F	Spinster	16Ap02By
MCCARTHY, Mary		19	F	Spinster	16Ap02By
Ann		20	F	Spinster	16Ap02By
Ca.		09	F	Child	16Ap02By
SANCE, Richd.		30	M	Laborer	16Ap02By
KARNE, John		18	M	Laborer	16Ap02By
SANCE, John		13	M	Laborer	16Ap02By
Michl.		11	M	Laborer	16Ap02By
CRANE, Thos.		20	M	Laborer	16Ap02By
HARRIGAN, Mary		25	F	Spinster	16Ap02By
MURRAY, Wm.		04	M	Child	16Ap02By
Died-At-Sea					
MCGOVERN, Mary		50	F	Wi	16Ap02By
Ann		10	F	Spinster	16Ap02By
TIERNEY, Henry		19	M	Laborer	16Ap02By
DONOHUE, Ann		20	F	Spinster	16Ap02By
MANNING, Jos.		30	M	Mechanic	16Ap02By
Mary	(W)	28	F	Wife	16Ap02By
Died-At-Sea					
Edwd.		04	M	Child	16Ap02By
Judy		02	F	Child	16Ap02By
Died-At-Sea					
Peter		.06	M	Infant	16Ap02By
Died-At-Sea					
Jas.		20	M	Laborer	16Ap02By
KEEFE, Mary		20	F	Spinster	16Ap02By
CURTIS, E.		20	F	Spinster	16Ap02By
FERMEDY, Mary		18	F	Spinster	16Ap02By
COSGROVE, James		24	M	Mechanic	16Ap02By
Mary	(W)	21	F	Wife	16Ap02By
BERRY, Mary		21	F	Spinster	16Ap02By
CARROLL, Ann		20	F	Spinster	16Ap02By
Died-At-Sea					
MCMANUS, Wm.		26	M	Laborer	16Ap02By

NAMES OF PASSENGERS		AGE	SEX	OCCUPATIONS	DATE PORT SHIP
TEARNEY, Peter		24	M	Laborer	16Ap02By
A., Danl.		20	M	Laborer	16Ap02By
RYAN, James		28	M	Laborer	16Ap02By
A--Y		26	M	Laborer	16Ap02By
KEEFE, Mary		13	F	Unknown	16Ap02By
Died-At-Sea					
GALLAGHER, Bridgt.		12	F	Spinster	16Ap02By
DAVINY, James		40	M	Laborer	16Ap02By
Ellen	(W)	40	F	Wife	16Ap02By
Owen		24	M	Laborer	16Ap02By
Jas.		20	M	Laborer	16Ap02By
Ellen		24	F	Wife	16Ap02By
Chas.		18	M	Laborer	16Ap02By
Hugh		16	M	Laborer	16Ap02By
Died-At-Sea					
MURRAY, Pat		40	M	Laborer	16Ap02By
LAMBERT, Cath.		31	F	Spinster	16Ap02By
Isabella		14	F	Spinster	16Ap02By
MCKEE, Pat		26	M	Cldrs	16Ap02By
Peter		24	M	Cldrs	16Ap02By
CASSENGER, Pat.		20	M	Laborer	16Ap02By
Peter		18	M	Laborer	16Ap02By
LYNCH, Philip		40	M	Laborer	16Ap02By
Bridgt.	(W)	40	F	Wife	16Ap02By
Pat		18	M	Laborer	16Ap02By
E.		16	M	Laborer	16Ap02By
R.		12	M	Laborer	16Ap02By
DOOLY, James		20	M	Laborer	16Ap02By
GORMLEY, Bridgt.		20	F	Spinster	16Ap02By
MURRAY, John		27	M	Mechanic	16Ap02By
Johanna	(W)	27	F	Wife	16Ap02By
Wm.		.06	M	Infant	16Ap02By
Died-At-Sea					
KENNY, Bridgt.		40	F	Spinster	16Ap02By
Martin		12	M	Unknown	16Ap02By
John		10	M	Unknown	16Ap02By
Died-At-Sea					
Margt.		06	F	Child	16Ap02By
Died-At-Sea					
ROWAN, James		19	M	Laborer	16Ap02By
Bessy		25	F	Spinster	16Ap02By
CARNALL, John		14	M	Laborer	16Ap02By
CARNEY, John		14	M	Laborer	16Ap02By
Bridgt.		09	F	Child	16Ap02By
Died-At-Sea					
MCHUGH, Thos.		18	M	Laborer	16Ap02By
LINDSAY, Cath.		30	F	Spinster	16Ap02By
LYNDSAY, John		02	M	Child	16Ap02By
LINDSAY, Mary		.08	F	Infant	16Ap02By
BLACK, Margt.		40	F	Wi	16Ap02By
Hugh		16	M	Laborer	16Ap02By
John		12	M	Laborer	16Ap02By
James		10	M	Laborer	16Ap02By
Margt.		08	F	Child	16Ap02By
Bernard		06	M	Child	16Ap02By
KIRBY, Andw.		36	M	Laborer	16Ap02By
MCCORMICK, Michl.		22	M	Laborer	16Ap02By
Mary	(W)	20	F	Wife	16Ap02By
James		21	M	Laborer	16Ap02By
HEATING, Wm.		21	M	Laborer	16Ap02By
MCGROGHAY, John		21	M	Laborer	16Ap02By
LEATHAM, U		21	M	Laborer	16Ap02By
RYAN, Pat.		21	M	Laborer	16Ap02By
PHILAM, Mary		21	F	Wife	16Ap02By
J.		20	M	Laborer	16Ap02By
DERRICK, John		00	M	Unknown	16Ap02By
MCTIERNY, Danl.		00	M	Unknown	16Ap02By
BREENAN, Jas.		00	M	Unknown	16Ap02By

NAMES OF PASSENGERS		AGE	SEX	OCCUPATIONS	DATE PORT SHIP

AYRSHIRE 17 APRIL 1849

From Newry

NAMES OF PASSENGERS		AGE	SEX	OCCUPATIONS	DATE PORT SHIP
HAMILTON, James		36	M	Clerk	17Ap11Bu
Jane	(W)	32	F	Wife	17Ap11Bu
Mary		06	F	Child	17Ap11Bu
John		03	M	Child	17Ap11Bu
OHANLON, Thos.		55	M	Farmer	17Ap11Bu
Mary	(W)	47	F	Wife	17Ap11Bu
Thomas		09	M	Child	17Ap11Bu
Mary		20	F	Relative	17Ap11Bu
Margaret		13	F	Relative	17Ap11Bu
CONNOLLY, Stephen		20	M	Laborer	17Ap11Bu
DORAN, Danl.		22	M	Laborer	17Ap11Bu
MCCONVILL, John		40	M	Laborer	17Ap11Bu
Danl.		18	M	Laborer	17Ap11Bu
FAIRM, Laurence		17	M	Laborer	17Ap11Bu
DALY, Patrick		23	M	Laborer	17Ap11Bu
Nicholas		22	M	Laborer	17Ap11Bu
KEARY, Peter		40	M	Laborer	17Ap11Bu
MCCONVILL, James		50	M	Laborer	17Ap11Bu
John		30	M	Laborer	17Ap11Bu
Mary		28	F	Spinster	17Ap11Bu
Anne		19	F	Spinster	17Ap11Bu
CHRISTY, William		16	M	Laborer	17Ap11Bu
GRIBBEN, Patrick		13	M	Unknown	17Ap11Bu
Bridget		10	F	Unknown	17Ap11Bu
CAMPBELL, John		25	M	Blacksmith	17Ap11Bu
HANLON, Patrick		60	M	Laborer	17Ap11Bu
DONNELLY, Hugh		22	M	Laborer	17Ap11Bu
CLARKE, Michael		18	M	Laborer	17Ap11Bu
MCGRAHAM, Andrew		60	M	Laborer	17Ap11Bu
Mary	(W)	25	F	Wife	17Ap11Bu
Margaret		18	F	Spinster	17Ap11Bu
Bridget		13	F	Spinster	17Ap11Bu
HANLON, Hugh		50	M	Farmer	17Ap11Bu
Patrick		22	M	Farmer	17Ap11Bu
Catherine		23	F	Relative	17Ap11Bu
Anne		20	F	Relative	17Ap11Bu
Loughlin		16	M	Relative	17Ap11Bu
Mary		13	F	Relative	17Ap11Bu
Alice		11	F	Relative	17Ap11Bu
Hugh		10	M	Relative	17Ap11Bu
DELANY, James		27	M	Laborer	17Ap11Bu
FINNEGAN, John		32	M	Laborer	17Ap11Bu
Mary		25	F	Relative	17Ap11Bu
Patrick		03	M	Child	17Ap11Bu
Thomas		.00	M	Infant	17Ap11Bu
ROONEY, Hugh		60	M	Farmer	17Ap11Bu
Nancy	(W)	57	F	Wife	17Ap11Bu
Peter		17	M	Relative	17Ap11Bu
John		16	M	Relative	17Ap11Bu
Patrick		12	M	Relative	17Ap11Bu
Michael		11	M	Relative	17Ap11Bu
James		10	M	Relative	17Ap11Bu
Margaret		.06	F	Infant	17Ap11Bu
MURPHY, James		24	M	Laborer	17Ap11Bu
Mary	(W)	22	F	Wife	17Ap11Bu
ROCKS, Anne		24	F	Spinster	17Ap11Bu
Patt.		21	M	Laborer	17Ap11Bu
SARVEY, John		55	M	Farmer	17Ap11Bu
Mary		50	F	Relative	17Ap11Bu
Ally		22	F	Relative	17Ap11Bu
James		20	M	Relative	17Ap11Bu
Honor		11	F	Relative	17Ap11Bu
Rose		09	F	Child	17Ap11Bu
Patrick		.08	M	Infant	17Ap11Bu
KELLY, Margaret		26	F	Spinster	17Ap11Bu
MCBRIDE, John		25	M	Laborer	17Ap11Bu
TALLON, William		24	M	Laborer	17Ap11Bu
CANNAHAN, John		30	M	Laborer	17Ap11Bu
MCPARTLAN, Stephen		16	M	Laborer	17Ap11Bu
Michael		24	M	Laborer	17Ap11Bu
MCCARTEN, Hugh		27	M	Laborer	17Ap11Bu
ALLEN, Nancy		35	F	Spinster	17Ap11Bu
CARROLL, Bess		32	F	Spinster	17Ap11Bu
MONROE, Henry		25	M	Laborer	17Ap11Bu
Eliza		22	F	Spinster	17Ap11Bu
MCMANUS, Margt.		24	F	Spinster	17Ap11Bu
MCGEARY, Mary-Ann		28	F	Spinster	17Ap11Bu
AKENS, John		23	M	Laborer	17Ap11Bu
Jane	(T)	12	F	Sister	17Ap11Bu
JOHNSTON, John		29	M	Laborer	17Ap11Bu
Thomas		24	M	Laborer	17Ap11Bu
CALTER, Biddy		26	F	Spinster	17Ap11Bu
MALONE, Mary		17	F	Spinster	17Ap11Bu
Sarah		12	F	Spinster	17Ap11Bu
MULLEN, Arthur		45	M	Laborer	17Ap11Bu
Ellen		39	F	Relative	17Ap11Bu
Owen		09	M	Child	17Ap11Bu
Mary		.03	F	Infant	17Ap11Bu
MCCABE, Mary		25	F	Spinster	17Ap11Bu
CAHERTY, Edwd.		24	M	Laborer	17Ap11Bu
HUGHES, James		26	M	Laborer	17Ap11Bu
Margt.		19	F	Spinster	17Ap11Bu
KEENAN, Sarah		20	F	Spinster	17Ap11Bu
MALLOW, Patk.		50	M	Farmer	17Ap11Bu
Neal		48	M	Relative	17Ap11Bu
Owen		46	M	Relative	17Ap11Bu
Betty		38	F	Relative	17Ap11Bu
WARD, Peter		24	M	Farmer	17Ap11Bu
Cath.		22	F	Relative	17Ap11Bu
Rose		11	F	Relative	17Ap11Bu
Michael		08	M	Child	17Ap11Bu
Mary		.05	F	Infant	17Ap11Bu
CUNNINGHAM, Wardy		55	M	Farmer	17Ap11Bu
Rose	(W)	50	F	Wife	17Ap11Bu
John		22	M	Relative	17Ap11Bu
Biddy		25	F	Relative	17Ap11Bu
Margaret		24	F	Relative	17Ap11Bu
Eliza		18	F	Relative	17Ap11Bu
Mary		16	F	Relative	17Ap11Bu
Isabella		.07	F	Infant	17Ap11Bu
Edward		11	M	Relative	17Ap11Bu
HALY, Patrick		35	M	Laborer	17Ap11Bu
BENNETT, Hugh		23	M	Laborer	17Ap11Bu
TRENN, Margt.		40	F	Spinster	17Ap11Bu
WHITTEN, James		24	M	Laborer	17Ap11Bu
ROGER, Patt		29	M	Laborer	17Ap11Bu
MCNAMEE, Thos.		32	M	Tailor	17Ap11Bu
NUGENT, Arthur		40	M	Laborer	17Ap11Bu
CARLAN, Mary		24	F	Spinster	17Ap11Bu
ROOKE, Owen		23	M	Laborer	17Ap11Bu
Mary		22	F	Spinster	17Ap11Bu
John		.02	M	Infant	17Ap11Bu
Alice		15	F	Relative	17Ap11Bu
ONEILL, Arthur		30	M	Laborer	17Ap11Bu
Mary		28	F	Spinster	17Ap11Bu
Anne		22	F	Spinster	17Ap11Bu
TAYLOR, George		25	M	Laborer	17Ap11Bu
OHEAR, John		29	M	Laborer	17Ap11Bu
Mary	(W)	28	F	Wife	17Ap11Bu
MCDERMOTT, Sally		50	F	Wi	17Ap11Bu
Bernard		19	M	Relative	17Ap11Bu
Mary		13	F	Relative	17Ap11Bu
Bridget		12	F	Relative	17Ap11Bu
Laurence		.09	M	Infant	17Ap11Bu
MURPHY, Margt.		13	F	Spinster	17Ap11Bu
FLINN, Mary-Ann		18	F	Spinster	17Ap11Bu
Elizabeth		12	F	Spinster	17Ap11Bu
MORGAN, James		40	M	Farmer	17Ap11Bu
Catherine		35	F	Relative	17Ap11Bu
Bernard		13	M	Relative	17Ap11Bu

NAMES OF PASSENGERS		AGE	SEX	OCCUPATIONS	DATE PORT SHIP
MORGAN, Thomas		12	M	Relative	17Ap11Bu
Anne		.11	F	Infant	17Ap11Bu
KEENAN, James		21	M	Laborer	17Ap11Bu
Rose	(W)	19	F	Wife	17Ap11Bu
GRAHAM, Jeremiah		30	M	Laborer	17Ap11Bu
RUSH, Patrick		60	M	Farmer	17Ap11Bu
Alice	(W)	50	F	Wife	17Ap11Bu
Biddy		13	F	Relative	17Ap11Bu
Anne		12	F	Relative	17Ap11Bu
Margt.		11	F	Relative	17Ap11Bu
Mary		09	F	Child	17Ap11Bu
Alice		.07	F	Infant	17Ap11Bu
BOYLE, Thomas		30	M	Laborer	17Ap11Bu
MASON, Robert		50	M	Laborer	17Ap11Bu
Mary-Ann		45	F	Relative	17Ap11Bu
Anne		13	F	Relative	17Ap11Bu
Sarah		.08	F	Infant	17Ap11Bu
GILBERT, Jonathan		18	M	Laborer	17Ap11Bu
CLARKE, James		25	M	Laborer	17Ap11Bu
BOYLE, Joseph		45	M	Laborer	17Ap11Bu
FEGAN, Henry		30	M	Laborer	17Ap11Bu
KENEDY, William		23	M	Laborer	17Ap11Bu
MOGAN, Joseph		25	M	Laborer	17Ap11Bu
MCIDARRAH, Owen		30	M	Laborer	17Ap11Bu
GRILLS, James		22	M	Carpenter	17Ap11Bu
Mary	(T)	19	F	Sister	17Ap11Bu
YOUNG, Fanny		29	F	Spinster	17Ap11Bu
John		22	M	Laborer	17Ap11Bu
James		17	M	Laborer	17Ap11Bu
MCPARTLAND, Bridget		17	F	Spinster	17Ap11Bu
MCGEARY, Anne		17	F	Spinster	17Ap11Bu
MCCONVILLE, Patt		40	M	Laborer	17Ap11Bu
MCCALLIN, Margt.		28	F	Spinster	17Ap11Bu
DONNELLY, Bridget		25	F	Spinster	17Ap11Bu
MULHOLLAND, Danl.		55	M	Farmer	17Ap11Bu
Ellen	(W)	50	F	Wife	17Ap11Bu
Owen		22	M	Relative	17Ap11Bu
Mary		13	F	Relative	17Ap11Bu
Catherine		12	F	Relative	17Ap11Bu
James		10	M	Relative	17Ap11Bu
Ellen		09	F	Child	17Ap11Bu
Anne		07	F	Child	17Ap11Bu
Danl.		.05	M	Infant	17Ap11Bu
CUNNINGHAM, John		35	M	Laborer	17Ap11Bu
Margt.	(T)	22	F	Sister	17Ap11Bu
Danl.		23	M	Laborer	17Ap11Bu
MAGILL, Robert		22	M	Blacksmith	17Ap11Bu
John		24	M	Blacksmith	17Ap11Bu
MCNEAGH, Bernard		37	M	Blacksmith	17Ap11Bu
OHANLON, Patrick		22	M	Laborer	17Ap11Bu
Nancy	(W)	20	F	Wife	17Ap11Bu
Bridget		.04	F	Infant	17Ap11Bu
JORDAN, Mary		25	F	Spinster	17Ap11Bu
FINLAY, Samuel		26	M	Farmer	17Ap11Bu
CANAHAN, Mary		29	F	Spinster	17Ap11Bu
MCDERMOTT, Henry		37	M	Laborer	17Ap11Bu
REYNOLDS, Mary		29	F	Spinster	17Ap11Bu
OHANLON, Margt.		13	F	Spinster	17Ap11Bu
WHITE, Mary		16	F	Spinster	17Ap11Bu
OHANLON, Loughlin		10	M	Relative	17Ap11Bu
Thomas		09	M	Child	17Ap11Bu
John		08	M	Child	17Ap11Bu
MURPHY, Betty		12	F	Spinster	17Ap11Bu
MCKENNA, John		26	M	Laborer	17Ap11Bu
FEGAN, John		65	M	Laborer	17Ap11Bu
Sheby		60	F	Spinster	17Ap11Bu
Margt.		27	F	Spinster	17Ap11Bu
Susan		24	F	Spinster	17Ap11Bu
Catharine		17	F	Spinster	17Ap11Bu
MARTEN, John		21	M	Laborer	17Ap11Bu
DEVLIN, John		47	M	Laborer	17Ap11Bu
Ellen		37	F	Relative	17Ap11Bu
Mary		12	F	Relative	17Ap11Bu
Anne		09	F	Child	17Ap11Bu

RAINBOW 17 APRIL 1849

From Liverpool

NAMES OF PASSENGERS	AGE	SEX	OCCUPATIONS	DATE PORT SHIP
DERRY, Valentine	25	M	Laborer	17Ap02Bv
Edward	20	M	Tailor	17Ap02Bv
HAYBURN, George	20	M	Blacksmith	17Ap02Bv
Mary	18	F	Dressmaker	17Ap02Bv
HIGGINS, Mary	18	F	Bomkr	17Ap02Bv
MCQUADE, Hugh	26	M	Laborer	17Ap02Bv
Catherine	20	F	Spinster	17Ap02Bv
MCCANN, Michael	16	M	Laborer	17Ap02Bv
ROONEY, Daniel	20	M	Servant	17Ap02Bv
CASEY, Joseph	22	M	Miller	17Ap02Bv
Matilda	20	F	Spinster	17Ap02Bv
LAPPAN, Peter	22	M	Painter	17Ap02Bv
GLOGHAN, Michael	20	M	Laborer	17Ap02Bv
Patrick	22	M	Laborer	17Ap02Bv
Mary-Ann	24	F	Spinster	17Ap02Bv
LOWRY, William	20	M	Flaxdr	17Ap02Bv
James	19	M	Carpenter	17Ap02Bv
Mary	17	F	Spinster	17Ap02Bv
MCCARROL, James	25	M	Laborer	17Ap02Bv
PEARNS, John	30	M	Laborer	17Ap02Bv
Robert	18	M	Laborer	17Ap02Bv
CONLAN, Terance	20	M	Laborer	17Ap02Bv
KANE, Daniel	35	M	Laborer	17Ap02Bv
DUNN, William-John	12	M	Unknown	17Ap02Bv
Hiram	10	M	Unknown	17Ap02Bv
Mary	08	F	Child	17Ap02Bv
Stewart	06	M	Child	17Ap02Bv
James	04	M	Child	17Ap02Bv
Elizabeth	03	F	Child	17Ap02Bv
BELL, Mary	26	F	Spinster	17Ap02Bv
Mary-Jane	02	F	Child	17Ap02Bv
Jane	24	F	Spinster	17Ap02Bv
MCCANN, Michael	29	M	Weaver	17Ap02Bv
Biddy	27	F	Spinster	17Ap02Bv
LAIRD, Alexander	20	M	Laborer	17Ap02Bv
Edward	18	M	Laborer	17Ap02Bv
BROWN, John	36	M	Laborer	17Ap02Bv
Ann	28	F	Spinster	17Ap02Bv
William	07	M	Child	17Ap02Bv
John	.00	M	Infant	17Ap02Bv
KENNEDY, John	18	M	Laborer	17Ap02Bv
Ross	22	M	Laborer	17Ap02Bv
MCCANN, Thomas	45	M	Laborer	17Ap02Bv
Eliza	40	F	Spinster	17Ap02Bv
William	15	M	Potter	17Ap02Bv
Ann	14	F	Spinster	17Ap02Bv
MCILMEAL, John	35	M	Laborer	17Ap02Bv
Biddy	42	F	Spinster	17Ap02Bv
THOMPSON, Biddy	30	F	Spinster	17Ap02Bv
MCNAMARA, Daniel	40	M	Laborer	17Ap02Bv
Maryann	36	F	Spinster	17Ap02Bv
JAMISON, John	32	M	Laborer	17Ap02Bv
GREEN, James	32	M	Trader	17Ap02Bv
MCCOURT, Patrick	23	M	Blacksmith	17Ap02Bv
Margret	17	F	Spinster	17Ap02Bv
NIXON, William	42	M	Flaxdr	17Ap02Bv
COURTNEY, Hugh	38	M	Shoemaker	17Ap02Bv
MCCONVEY, James	20	M	Laborer	17Ap02Bv
Richard	18	M	Laborer	17Ap02Bv
Mary	52	F	Spinster	17Ap02Bv
SMITH, John	45	M	Carpenter	17Ap02Bv
Daniel	14	M	Unknown	17Ap02Bv
MEABON, John	26	M	Laborer	17Ap02Bv
HOY, Samuel	20	M	Laborer	17Ap02Bv
CAVANAGH, Margret	46	F	Servant	17Ap02Bv

NAMES OF PASSENGERS	AGE	SEX	OCCUPATIONS	DATE PORT SHIP
CAVANAGH, Michael	17	M	Laborer	17Ap02Bv
ONEIL, Sarah	25	F	Milliner	17Ap02Bv
MCCANNA, Bridget	20	F	Spinster	17Ap02Bv
ERAT, Lucinda	22	F	Dressmaker	17Ap02Bv
CRANGLE, Francis	30	M	Stone Mason	17Ap02Bv
MCMULLIN, Michael	12	M	Unknown	17Ap02Bv
Thomas	25	M	Laborer	17Ap02Bv
WARRICK, Samuel	26	M	Shoemaker	17Ap02Bv
Nancy-Jane	30	F	Dressmaker	17Ap02Bv
MONTGOMERY, James	65	M	Weaver	17Ap02Bv
Mary	54	F	Spinster	17Ap02Bv
John	20	M	Carpenter	17Ap02Bv
Ann	47	F	Spinster	17Ap02Bv
Matthew	12	M	Unknown	17Ap02Bv
CURRY, John	20	M	Laborer	17Ap02Bv
DUNN, Stewart	40	M	Laborer	17Ap02Bv
Mary	35	F	Spinster	17Ap02Bv
MCLEUGHLIN, Daniel	30	M	Seaman	17Ap02Bv
DOYLE, Maria	40	F	Spinster	17Ap02Bv
Michael	30	M	Seaman	17Ap02Bv
BENNISTON, Eliza	36	F	Spinster	17Ap02Bv
Mary	08	F	Child	17Ap02Bv
Eliza	06	F	Child	17Ap02Bv
Sarah-Ann	04	F	Child	17Ap02Bv
CRAWFORD, Hugh	40	M	Laborer	17Ap02Bv
Eliza	38	F	Spinster	17Ap02Bv
Thomas	19	M	Laborer	17Ap02Bv
Hugh	14	M	Laborer	17Ap02Bv
Andrew	05	M	Child	17Ap02Bv
HALL, Charles	38	M	Merchant	17Ap02Bv
MOAN, Ann	18	F	Spinster	17Ap02Bv
MCPHILLIPS, Margret	19	F	Spinster	17Ap02Bv
LOY, Ann	60	F	Spinster	17Ap02Bv
John	16	M	Unknown	17Ap02Bv
James	14	M	Unknown	17Ap02Bv
ROSS, Ann	38	F	Spinster	17Ap02Bv
CLARKE, Lendrum	26	M	Gentleman	17Ap02Bv
HOLLYWOOD, Eliza	25	F	Spinster	17Ap02Bv
Patrick	.00	M	Infant	17Ap02Bv
Samuel	.00	M	Infant	17Ap02Bv
GRAHAM, Mary	18	F	Spinster	17Ap02Bv
Jane	16	F	Spinster	17Ap02Bv
MCKEE, David	30	M	Laborer	17Ap02Bv
SIMMS, James	28	M	Farmer	17Ap02Bv
Isabella	26	F	Dressmaker	17Ap02Bv
Mille	04	F	Child	17Ap02Bv
Isabella	02	F	Child	17Ap02Bv
HEARST, George	35	M	Laborer	17Ap02Bv
TUMBLETY, Biddy	20	F	Dressmaker	17Ap02Bv
SMITH, Catherine	30	F	Spinster	17Ap02Bv
BRYSON, Thomas	24	M	Shoemaker	17Ap02Bv
Jane	24	F	Spinster	17Ap02Bv
Elizabeth	03	F	Child	17Ap02Bv
James	.00	M	Infant	17Ap02Bv
Robert	21	M	Laborer	17Ap02Bv
MCAFEE, Willialm	40	M	Laborer	17Ap02Bv
MCCULLOGH, Jane	18	F	Spinster	17Ap02Bv
BOYLAN, Elizabeth	40	F	Spinster	17Ap02Bv
Ellen	18	F	Spinster	17Ap02Bv
John	14	M	Unknown	17Ap02Bv
Mary	10	F	Unknown	17Ap02Bv
Eliza	.00	F	Infant	17Ap02Bv
MULHOLLAND, Arthur	27	M	Tanner	17Ap02Bv
MCALEER, Ann	30	F	Spinster	17Ap02Bv
MAGUIRE, Betty	27	F	Spinster	17Ap02Bv
TREANOR, James	36	M	Laborer	17Ap02Bv
Catherine	30	F	Spinster	17Ap02Bv
Biddy	25	F	Spinster	17Ap02Bv
Ann	23	F	Spinster	17Ap02Bv
CONLAN, Catherine	17	F	Spinster	17Ap02Bv
DONNELLY, Daniel	20	M	Baker	17Ap02Bv
QUINN, Bernard	20	M	Surveyor	17Ap02Bv
KANE, James	27	M	Laborer	17Ap02Bv
RAFFERTY, Ann	17	F	Spinster	17Ap02Bv
BODLE, John	40	M	Laborer	17Ap02Bv
MCPEAK, Sarah	22	F	Spinster	17Ap02Bv
LARUM, Margret-Jane	25	F	Spinster	17Ap02Bv
ALLCOCK, William	28	M	Seaman	17Ap02Bv

CAMILLUS 17 APRIL 1849

From Liverpool

NAMES OF PASSENGERS	AGE	SEX	OCCUPATIONS	DATE PORT SHIP
MCCARTHY, Ellen	28	F	Laborer	17Ap02Bw
GREEN, Jas.	42	M	Laborer	17Ap02Bw
BURNS, Pat	23	M	Laborer	17Ap02Bw
HIGGINS, Andrew	25	M	Laborer	17Ap02Bw
REILLY, Pat	20	M	Laborer	17Ap02Bw
Ann	16	F	Laborer	17Ap02Bw
KENNEDY, Margt.	18	F	Laborer	17Ap02Bw
REDMAN, John	35	M	Laborer	17Ap02Bw
Bess	33	F	Laborer	17Ap02Bw
BOYLAND, Thos.	18	M	Laborer	17Ap02Bw
BELLAMY, Thos.	35	M	Laborer	17Ap02Bw
U (W)	30	F	Laborer	17Ap02Bw
Robert	02	M	Child	17Ap02Bw
Charles	.00	M	Infant	17Ap02Bw
RYAN, Michael	22	M	Laborer	17Ap02Bw
KELLY, Pat	30	M	Laborer	17Ap02Bw
WINTERS, Chas.	22	M	Laborer	17Ap02Bw
MATHEWS, Isaac	39	M	Laborer	17Ap02Bw
WALLACE, Jas.	30	M	Laborer	17Ap02Bw
Rose	26	F	Laborer	17Ap02Bw
LISCHANGE, Thos.	20	M	Laborer	17Ap02Bw
REGAN, Michael	20	M	Laborer	17Ap02Bw
Catherine	25	F	Laborer	17Ap02Bw
GELLARD, John	28	M	Laborer	17Ap02Bw
Mary-Ann	28	F	Laborer	17Ap02Bw
MACCURDY, Jas.	25	M	Laborer	17Ap02Bw
MCKEY, Frank	26	M	Laborer	17Ap02Bw
MCMULLEN, Alex	23	M	Laborer	17Ap02Bw
KILLPATRICK, C.	20	M	Laborer	17Ap02Bw
STEWART, Ed.	20	M	Laborer	17Ap02Bw
CUNNINGHAM, Sam.	21	M	Laborer	17Ap02Bw
MCBRIDE, Ths.	23	M	Laborer	17Ap02Bw
CASSIDY, Bernd.	18	M	Laborer	17Ap02Bw
MULLIGHAN, Owen	29	M	Laborer	17Ap02Bw
U (W)	28	F	Laborer	17Ap02Bw
FRITZPATRICK, Ewd.	31	M	Laborer	17Ap02Bw
Pat	20	M	Laborer	17Ap02Bw
DOLAN, Mike	20	M	Laborer	17Ap02Bw
FAIRHURST, Wm.	20	M	Laborer	17Ap02Bw
BAYNTON, Wm.	21	M	Clerk	17Ap02Bw
DARKIN, Ths.	40	M	Laborer	17Ap02Bw
SMITH, Jno.	30	M	Joiner	17Ap02Bw
Julia	18	F	Unknown	17Ap02Bw
MORONEY, Pat	28	M	Laborer	17Ap02Bw
Briget	22	F	Laborer	17Ap02Bw
Hannah	18	F	Laborer	17Ap02Bw
Jno.	17	M	Laborer	17Ap02Bw
Catharine	08	F	Child	17Ap02Bw
Mary	03	F	Child	17Ap02Bw
Bridget	.00	F	Infant	17Ap02Bw
CAVANAH, Jno.	20	M	Laborer	17Ap02Bw
DONOVAN, Dennis	46	M	Laborer	17Ap02Bw
Johanna	30	F	Laborer	17Ap02Bw
Wm.	08	M	Child	17Ap02Bw
POWER, Patk.	32	M	Laborer	17Ap02Bw
MCGRATH, Rodger	30	M	Laborer	17Ap02Bw
SULLIVAN, Mike	30	M	Laborer	17Ap02Bw
Michael	20	M	Laborer	17Ap02Bw
GRIFFIN, Con	20	M	Laborer	17Ap02Bw
CAIN, Cath.	20	F	Laborer	17Ap02Bw
Mary	19	F	Laborer	17Ap02Bw

NAMES OF PASSENGERS	AGE	SEX	OCCUPATIONS	DATE PORT SHIP
KEEFE, Pat	20	M	Laborer	17Ap02Bw
LEVY, Julia	20	F	Laborer	17Ap02Bw
COY, Mary	20	F	Laborer	17Ap02Bw
U, Ann	24	F	Laborer	17Ap02Bw
SHEEDY, Ths.	25	M	Laborer	17Ap02Bw
FOX, Mary	18	F	Laborer	17Ap02Bw
HONE, Ben-A.	40	M	Laborer	17Ap02Bw
KALLIGHAN, Dan	18	M	Laborer	17Ap02Bw
Mary	20	F	Laborer	17Ap02Bw
VAUGHAN, Brid	20	F	Laborer	17Ap02Bw
CARSON, Jno.	30	M	Laborer	17Ap02Bw
Julia	25	F	Laborer	17Ap02Bw
BOWEN, Mary	20	F	Laborer	17Ap02Bw
DONEL, Charles	17	M	Laborer	17Ap02Bw
FADDEN, Ths.	25	M	Laborer	17Ap02Bw
MACKEEFER, M.	20	F	Laborer	17Ap02Bw
FARRELL, E.	40	F	Laborer	17Ap02Bw
HENERAN, Edwd.	18	M	Laborer	17Ap02Bw
MCDADE, Cath.	20	F	Laborer	17Ap02Bw
CANREY, Peter	20	M	Laborer	17Ap02Bw
Ellen	16	F	Laborer	17Ap02Bw
MADE, Pat	30	M	Laborer	17Ap02Bw
CAREY, Pat	32	M	Laborer	17Ap02Bw
FURLONG, Ellen	30	F	Laborer	17Ap02Bw
Margt.	19	F	Laborer	17Ap02Bw
MCLOUGHLIN, Corn.	19	M	Laborer	17Ap02Bw
SCULLY, Jerh.	22	M	Laborer	17Ap02Bw
SHANE, Cat.	17	F	Laborer	17Ap02Bw
MURPHY, Timy.	35	M	Laborer	17Ap02Bw
Bridgt.	30	F	Laborer	17Ap02Bw
Mary	06	F	Child	17Ap02Bw
DONOHOE, Honora	60	F	Laborer	17Ap02Bw
Cath.	27	F	Laborer	17Ap02Bw
MCKENEDY, Ths.	32	M	Laborer	17Ap02Bw
Donald	00	M	Laborer	17Ap02Bw
MCAVOY, Pat	36	M	Laborer	17Ap02Bw
NAUGHTEN, Jas.	21	M	Laborer	17Ap02Bw
DONOLY, My.	50	F	Laborer	17Ap02Bw
GALLAGHER, Dennis	22	M	Laborer	17Ap02Bw
KENNAY, Frs.	20	M	Laborer	17Ap02Bw
KERNAN, Andw.	16	F	Laborer	17Ap02Bw
Mary	17	F	Laborer	17Ap02Bw
AHURN, Brid.	22	F	Laborer	17Ap02Bw
CAVANAH, Sarah	22	F	Laborer	17Ap02Bw
MURPHY, Pat	28	M	Laborer	17Ap02Bw
Betsy	24	F	Laborer	17Ap02Bw
DOLAN, Brid.	18	F	Laborer	17Ap02Bw
REYNOLDS, Ths.	27	M	Laborer	17Ap02Bw
Jos.	20	M	Laborer	17Ap02Bw
KELLY, Jno.	60	M	Laborer	17Ap02Bw
QUINEY, Pat	30	M	Laborer	17Ap02Bw
QUINN, Pat	20	M	Laborer	17Ap02Bw
SMITH, E.	17	M	Laborer	17Ap02Bw
CASSIDY, E.	13	M	Laborer	17Ap02Bw
CALLAGRES, Jno.	30	M	Laborer	17Ap02Bw
KILLMARTIN, Pat	32	M	Laborer	17Ap02Bw
KINNAN, H.	21	M	Laborer	17Ap02Bw
Ann	20	F	Laborer	17Ap02Bw
Pat	08	M	Child	17Ap02Bw
SMITH, Eliz.	18	F	Laborer	17Ap02Bw
REYNOLDS, Mike	18	M	Laborer	17Ap02Bw
FARRELL, Owen	18	M	Laborer	17Ap02Bw
COX, Bridget	04	F	Child	17Ap02Bw
CHALLE, Darby	50	M	Laborer	17Ap02Bw
Brid.	40	F	Laborer	17Ap02Bw
Jeremh.	17	M	Laborer	17Ap02Bw
Norris	13	M	Laborer	17Ap02Bw
Kitty	10	F	Laborer	17Ap02Bw
Neddy	06	F	Child	17Ap02Bw
Jno.	05	M	Child	17Ap02Bw
Margt.	05	F	Child	17Ap02Bw
Bridget	02	F	Child	17Ap02Bw
Edwd.	30	M	Laborer	17Ap02Bw
MCGRATH, Daniel	31	M	Laborer	17Ap02Bw
KEEF, Tim	17	M	Laborer	17Ap02Bw
RYAN, Norry	20	F	Laborer	17Ap02Bw
Michael	36	M	Laborer	17Ap02Bw
Judy	32	F	Laborer	17Ap02Bw
Jno.	03	M	Child	17Ap02Bw
Bridget	.00	F	Infant	17Ap02Bw
JENKINS, Jno.	30	M	Laborer	17Ap02Bw
Joseph	22	M	Laborer	17Ap02Bw
MARLAM, Wm.	30	M	Laborer	17Ap02Bw
Mary	33	F	Laborer	17Ap02Bw
Richard	20	M	Laborer	17Ap02Bw
Ann	04	F	Child	17Ap02Bw
DONOVAN, Jno.	25	M	Laborer	17Ap02Bw
COLEMAN, Richd.	30	M	Laborer	17Ap02Bw
Judith	20	F	Laborer	17Ap02Bw
PHEELAM, Jerry	25	M	Laborer	17Ap02Bw
Cath.	20	F	Laborer	17Ap02Bw
BURKE, Joseph	13	M	Laborer	17Ap02Bw
QUINLAM, Wm.	24	M	Laborer	17Ap02Bw
BOWES, Lawerance	26	M	Laborer	17Ap02Bw
DOWNEY, Richd.	26	M	Laborer	17Ap02Bw
KENNY, Nancy	22	F	Laborer	17Ap02Bw
DONAN, Nancy	15	F	Laborer	17Ap02Bw
WHEELAN, Nelly	15	F	Laborer	17Ap02Bw
BROUGHTON, Jno.	18	M	Laborer	17Ap02Bw
MCGAHAN, Jno.	30	M	Laborer	17Ap02Bw
Rosa	30	F	Laborer	17Ap02Bw
MARLOW, Jane	18	F	Laborer	17Ap02Bw
Mary	.00	F	Infant	17Ap02Bw
DUN, Bridgt.	20	F	Laborer	17Ap02Bw
MULVEY, Margt.	11	F	Laborer	17Ap02Bw
DAGNAN, Cath.	18	F	Laborer	17Ap02Bw
CRAWFORD, Martin	20	M	Laborer	17Ap02Bw
ONEIL, Edwd.	25	M	Laborer	17Ap02Bw
Mike	16	M	Laborer	17Ap02Bw
David	09	M	Child	17Ap02Bw
Edwd.	07	M	Child	17Ap02Bw
BRADY, Cathe.	20	F	Laborer	17Ap02Bw
KEELAN, Margt.	20	F	Laborer	17Ap02Bw
MCDURMOT, Henry	18	M	Laborer	17Ap02Bw
HAMRALT, Alex	20	M	Laborer	17Ap02Bw
Eliz.	21	F	Laborer	17Ap02Bw
DEVLIN, Felix	20	M	Laborer	17Ap02Bw
MCCARRON, Jas.	20	M	Laborer	17Ap02Bw
KAIN, Mike	30	M	Laborer	17Ap02Bw
MORRISON, M.A.	26	F	Laborer	17Ap02Bw
HAILES, Jane	21	F	Laborer	17Ap02Bw
MCGERITY, Maria	68	F	Laborer	17Ap02Bw
KELLY, Margt.	20	F	Laborer	17Ap02Bw
SWEENEY, Sarah	40	F	Laborer	17Ap02Bw
Nick	18	M	Laborer	17Ap02Bw
WALLACE, Chs.	30	M	Laborer	17Ap02Bw
HEARN, Charles	39	M	Laborer	17Ap02Bw
Catherine	40	F	Laborer	17Ap02Bw
Charles	15	M	Laborer	17Ap02Bw
Pat	11	M	Laborer	17Ap02Bw
Ann	12	F	Laborer	17Ap02Bw
HENDERSON, Alex	20	M	Laborer	17Ap02Bw
HARRIGAN, Isabella	17	F	Laborer	17Ap02Bw
MAGUIRE, Margt.	22	F	Laborer	17Ap02Bw
DOLAN, Eleanor	20	F	Laborer	17Ap02Bw
MADDEN, Betsy	17	F	Laborer	17Ap02Bw
MITCHELL, Owen	50	M	Laborer	17Ap02Bw
Margt.	24	F	Laborer	17Ap02Bw
CAVANAGH, Martin	15	M	Laborer	17Ap02Bw
CONBEE, Daniel	26	M	Laborer	17Ap02Bw
Johannah	25	F	Laborer	17Ap02Bw
Ellen	21	F	Laborer	17Ap02Bw
CHANEHAN, Margt.	26	F	Laborer	17Ap02Bw
KEENAN, Bryan	24	M	Laborer	17Ap02Bw
SWEENEY, Briget	20	F	Laborer	17Ap02Bw
MAGUIRE, Jno.	25	M	Laborer	17Ap02Bw
U (W)	23	F	Laborer	17Ap02Bw
BOYLE, Wm.	24	M	Laborer	17Ap02Bw
ROONEY, Mary-A.	18	F	Laborer	17Ap02Bw
GARDEN, Jos.	46	M	Laborer	17Ap02Bw

NAMES OF PASSENGERS	AGE	SEX	OCCUPATIONS	DATE PORT SHIP
CASSIDY, Frs.	20	F	Laborer	17Ap02Bw
DUGGIN, David	25	M	Laborer	17Ap02Bw
CONOLY, Henry	22	M	Laborer	17Ap02Bw
BRANNIN, Ellen	18	F	Laborer	17Ap02Bw
HAGAN, Jane	19	F	Laborer	17Ap02Bw
MORESSEY, Pat	34	M	Laborer	17Ap02Bw
HOBBINS, Jno.	30	M	Laborer	17Ap02Bw
WILSON, Wm.	26	M	Laborer	17Ap02Bw
DOHERTY, Hugh	26	M	Laborer	17Ap02Bw
REARDON, Pat	32	M	Laborer	17Ap02Bw
WILSON, Dpraim	45	M	Surgeon	17Ap02Bw

ADMIRAL 18 APRIL 1849

From Londonderry

NAMES OF PASSENGERS	AGE	SEX	OCCUPATIONS	DATE PORT SHIP
LAGAN, Betty	22	F	Servant	18Ap01Cf
Sophia	21	F	Servant	18Ap01Cf
BAILLEY, Patrick	20	M	Farmer	18Ap01Cf
MORAN, Patrick	24	M	Laborer	18Ap01Cf
Ann	22	F	Servant	18Ap01Cf
MCGLADE, Mary	26	F	Servant	18Ap01Cf
ODONNELL, Betty	40	F	Servant	18Ap01Cf
Mary	16	F	Servant	18Ap01Cf
BOYLE, Owen	16	M	Servant	18Ap01Cf
MCSORLEY, Mary	18	F	Servant	18Ap01Cf
MCGUIGAN, Margaret	17	F	Servant	18Ap01Cf
PEOPLES, George	20	M	Laborer	18Ap01Cf
MULLANE, Marcus	26	M	Gdnr	18Ap01Cf
WALKER, John	44	M	Laborer	18Ap01Cf
WARD, James	20	M	Laborer	18Ap01Cf
WILSON, Ann-Jane	26	F	Wife	18Ap01Cf
CREIGHTON, Martha	38	F	Wife	18Ap01Cf
Hannah	15	F	None	18Ap01Cf
Alexander	13	M	None	18Ap01Cf
James	11	M	None	18Ap01Cf
John	17	M	Blacksmith	18Ap01Cf
Thomas	6	M	Child	18Ap01Cf
Rebecca	2	F	Child	18Ap01Cf
KANE, Michael	17	M	Servant	18Ap01Cf
MCHENRY, Morriss	49	M	Farmer	18Ap01Cf
Biddy	53	F	Wife	18Ap01Cf
Francis	22	M	Farmer	18Ap01Cf
Bridget	20	F	Seamstress	18Ap01Cf
Nancy	18	F	Seamstress	18Ap01Cf
Morriss	15	M	Farmer	18Ap01Cf
George	12	M	None	18Ap01Cf
Mary	10	F	Seamstress	18Ap01Cf
Rose	8	F	Child	18Ap01Cf
HASSAN, Patrick	20	M	Laborer	18Ap01Cf
KANE, Ann	17	F	Servant	18Ap01Cf
CONNORS, Peggy	20	F	Servant	18Ap01Cf
CONNERY, John	24	M	Laborer	18Ap01Cf
MCDOUGAL, Nancy	22	F	Seamstress	18Ap01Cf
SMITH, Nancy	19	F	Seamstress	18Ap01Cf
SLOAN, Mary	22	F	Servant	18Ap01Cf
Ann	17	F	Servant	18Ap01Cf
REED, Eliza-Jane	19	F	Seamstress	18Ap01Cf
Sarah	17	F	Seamstress	18Ap01Cf
MCCLARY, Alick	21	M	Laborer	18Ap01Cf
MCSHANE, Brian	60	M	Laborer	18Ap01Cf
Biddy	50	F	Wife	18Ap01Cf
Andrew	10	M	None	18Ap01Cf
BRYSON, Ellen	21	F	Servant	18Ap01Cf
LOVE, James	19	M	Shoemaker	18Ap01Cf
SMITH, John	23	M	Porter	18Ap01Cf
MCSHANE, Sarah	10	F	None	18Ap01Cf
MCCAFFERTY, Edward	23	M	Carter	18Ap01Cf
John	21	M	Shoemaker	18Ap01Cf
MCCAFFERTY, Mary	19	F	Seamstress	18Ap01Cf
Catherine	22	F	Seamstress	18Ap01Cf
MEHAN, James	21	M	Laborer	18Ap01Cf
DOHERTY, Anthony	20	M	Laborer	18Ap01Cf
MCCLUNIN, Francis	26	M	Laborer	18Ap01Cf
STEWART, Hugh	15	M	None	18Ap01Cf
KELLY, Michael	14	M	None	18Ap01Cf
ELLIOTT, Eliza	20	F	Servant	18Ap01Cf
Sarah-Jane	19	F	Seamstress	18Ap01Cf
MOREHEAD, John	23	M	Farmer	18Ap01Cf
MAXWELL, Thomas	40	M	Farmer	18Ap01Cf
Martha	40	F	Wife	18Ap01Cf
Elizabeth	18	F	Seamstress	18Ap01Cf
Martha	14	F	Seamstress	18Ap01Cf
Margeret	12	F	Seamstress	18Ap01Cf
Robert	10	M	None	18Ap01Cf
Samuel	6	M	Child	18Ap01Cf
Martha-Jane	4	F	Child	18Ap01Cf
Thomas	8	M	Child	18Ap01Cf
SMITH, Susan	21	F	Seamstress	18Ap01Cf
BRADLEY, John	45	M	Farmer	18Ap01Cf
Catherine	21	F	Seamstress	18Ap01Cf
Patrick	15	M	None	18Ap01Cf
MARSHALL, James	21	M	Farmer	18Ap01Cf
Mary	23	F	Housekeeper	18Ap01Cf
MULLAN, Matilda	22	F	Housekeeper	18Ap01Cf
JOHNSTON, Margeret	15	F	Servant	18Ap01Cf
Susan	18	F	Servant	18Ap01Cf
CLARKE, James	19	M	Shoemaker	18Ap01Cf
Matilda	32	F	Lad	18Ap01Cf
FOREMAN, Arthur	17	M	Farmer	18Ap01Cf
MILLAN, Wm.	47	M	Farmer	18Ap01Cf
Sam.	19	M	Farmer	18Ap01Cf
TOSH, Robert	32	M	Laborer	18Ap01Cf
Eliza-Jane	13	F	Servant	18Ap01Cf
REID, John	21	M	Farmer	18Ap01Cf
Saml.	17	M	Farmer	18Ap01Cf
TOSH, Isaac	17	M	None	18Ap01Cf
QUIGLEY, Wm.	19	M	None	18Ap01Cf
DOHERTY, James	19	M	Farmer	18Ap01Cf
Margaret	17	F	None	18Ap01Cf
ROSS, David	19	M	Laborer	18Ap01Cf
FINLEY, Mary-Ann	17	F	Seamstress	18Ap01Cf
MCNALL, John	39	M	Laborer	18Ap01Cf
MCTEAGUE, John	26	M	Laborer	18Ap01Cf
Mary	23	F	Wife	18Ap01Cf
MCCANDLASS, Eliza-Jane	18	F	Servant	18Ap01Cf
STERLING, Mary-Ann	20	F	Servant	18Ap01Cf
SMITH, James	17	M	Laborer	18Ap01Cf
DOHERTY, Edward	23	M	Bricklayer	18Ap01Cf
Jane	21	F	Wife	18Ap01Cf
Catherine	.03	F	Infant	18Ap01Cf
Daniel	25	M	Laborer	18Ap01Cf
MCNICOLL, Patrick	66	M	Bleacher	18Ap01Cf
Mary	60	F	Wife	18Ap01Cf
Thomas	25	M	Carpenter	18Ap01Cf
Sarah	15	F	Seamstress	18Ap01Cf
Rose	13	F	None	18Ap01Cf
Catherine	22	F	Seamstress	18Ap01Cf
James-Wm.	4	M	Child	18Ap01Cf
Mary-Ann	2	F	Child	18Ap01Cf
KING, Hyland	21	M	Millwright	18Ap01Cf
LYNCH, Catherine	17	F	Seamstress	18Ap01Cf
DALE, John	56	M	Farmer	18Ap01Cf
Mathy	56	F	Wife	18Ap01Cf
Samuel	22	M	Farmer	18Ap01Cf
Sarah	18	F	Seamstress	18Ap01Cf
Mary-Ann	16	F	None	18Ap01Cf
THOMPSON, Alexander	19	M	Miller	18Ap01Cf
DONEGHY, George	30	M	Farmer	18Ap01Cf
CONLAN, James	29	M	Farmer	18Ap01Cf
NEAL, Mary-A.	23	F	Servant	18Ap01Cf
JAMIESON, John	20	M	Weaver	18Ap01Cf
CONWELL, Charles	42	M	Overseer	18Ap01Cf
KANE, Margaret	25	F	Seamstress	18Ap01Cf

NAMES OF PASSENGERS	AGE	SEX	OCCUPATIONS	DATE PORT SHIP
MCGONIGLE, Charles	36	M	Laborer	18Ap01Cf
MCLOUGHLIN, Hannah	32	F	Housekeeper	18Ap01Cf
HUTCHISON, Samuel	21	M	Laborer	18Ap01Cf
Matilda	21	F	Wife	18Ap01Cf
WALLACE, Robert	25	M	Weaver	18Ap01Cf
Peggy	25	F	Wife	18Ap01Cf
MCIVOR, John	24	M	Laborer	18Ap01Cf
Ellen	22	F	Wife	18Ap01Cf
MCCANN, Jane	19	F	Seamstress	18Ap01Cf
MCKEEVER, Denis	18	M	Laborer	18Ap01Cf
MCMORROUGH, Dan	24	M	Laborer	18Ap01Cf
MCKEE, Wm.	18	M	Farmer	18Ap01Cf
THOMPSON, Robert	20	M	Laborer	18Ap01Cf
ORR, Joseph	30	M	Farmer	18Ap01Cf
ONEILL, Betty	35	F	Housekeeper	18Ap01Cf
MILLER, David	20	M	Engineer	18Ap01Cf
MCLOUGHLIN, Ann	18	F	Housekeeper	18Ap01Cf
Mary	24	F	Housekeeper	18Ap01Cf
TEAS, Wm.	23	M	Farmer	18Ap01Cf
Mary-Jane	22	F	Wife	18Ap01Cf
John	.04	M	Infant	18Ap01Cf
WILSON, James	27	M	Laborer	18Ap01Cf
Jane	17	F	Wife	18Ap01Cf
LYNCH, Philip	19	M	Fisherman	18Ap01Cf
Peggy	17	F	Servant	18Ap01Cf
MCFEELY, Wm.	18	M	Weaver	18Ap01Cf
ROGERS, Livia	28	F	Housekeeper	18Ap01Cf
Robert	20	M	Laborer	18Ap01Cf
MCCUTCHEON, Fred.	18	M	Blacksmith	18Ap01Cf
ALGO, Saml.	20	M	Saddler	18Ap01Cf
CUNNINGHAM, Eliza	19	F	Dressmaker	18Ap01Cf
MAXWELL, John	19	M	Laborer	18Ap01Cf
BURKE, Patrick	21	M	Laborer	18Ap01Cf
ONEILL, Thomas	28	M	Laborer	18Ap01Cf
CONRONY, Denis	32	M	Farmer	18Ap01Cf
WILLIAMSON, James	28	M	Farmer	18Ap01Cf
STINGHAM, Adam	44	M	Farmer	18Ap01Cf
Jane	16	F	Seamstress	18Ap01Cf
MEHAN, Pat.	20	M	Laborer	18Ap01Cf
Mary	18	F	Seamstress	18Ap01Cf
GILLESPIE, Catherine	20	F	Servant	18Ap01Cf
SIKIN, Catherine	19	F	Lad	18Ap01Cf
Alexander	16	M	None	18Ap01Cf
CURRY, Laurence	25	M	Butler	18Ap01Cf
Sarah	25	F	Cook	18Ap01Cf
LEONARD, James	20	M	Servant	18Ap01Cf
DUFFERY, Neal	18	M	Laborer	18Ap01Cf
Nancy	40	F	Housekeeper	18Ap01Cf
MCKENELL, Danl.	54	M	Farmer	18Ap01Cf
Rosanna	26	F	Wife	18Ap01Cf
Ellen	49	F	Housekeeper	18Ap01Cf
Daniel	3	M	Child	18Ap01Cf
Mary	.11	F	Infant	18Ap01Cf
ONEILL, John	19	M	Servant	18Ap01Cf
Eliza	22	F	Housekeeper	18Ap01Cf
MCCLOSKEY, Henry	45	M	Farmer	18Ap01Cf
Pat.	20	M	Farmer	18Ap01Cf
MURRIONS, Thomas	29	M	Farmer	18Ap01Cf
MCGARRY, James	24	M	Groom	18Ap01Cf
GILLESPIE, Charles	45	M	Laborer	18Ap01Cf
CONNOLLY, Teddy	23	M	Laborer	18Ap01Cf
John	17	M	Laborer	18Ap01Cf
MCNULTY, Michael	25	M	Laborer	18Ap01Cf
MCGOWAN, Denis	26	M	Laborer	18Ap01Cf
LOGAN, George	18	M	Weaver	18Ap01Cf
Mary	22	F	Servant	18Ap01Cf
DOUGHERTY, Wm.	19	M	Servant	18Ap01Cf
CRAWFORD, Margaret	20	F	Seamstress	18Ap01Cf
CLARKE, Jno.	22	M	Farmer	18Ap01Cf
MOORE, Jno.	21	M	Farmer	18Ap01Cf
Ann	19	F	Housekeeper	18Ap01Cf
HEGARTY, Mary	30	F	Wife	18Ap01Cf
LEPIN, Joseph	28	M	Farmer	18Ap01Cf
Isabella	26	F	Wife	18Ap01Cf
RAY, Margaret	19	F	Servant	18Ap01Cf
ASKEW, John	64	M	Farmer	18Ap01Cf
SHERIN, James	28	M	Farmer	18Ap01Cf
HUNTER, Wm.	28	M	Draper	18Ap01Cf
Henry	14	M	Student	18Ap01Cf
ROGERS, Saml.	22	M	Wool Draper	18Ap01Cf
BOYLE, Bernard	20	M	Farmer	18Ap01Cf
Hugh	20	M	Farmer	18Ap01Cf
CALL, Catherine	20	F	Servant	18Ap01Cf
GAULAGHER, U	45	F	Pawn Broker	18Ap01Cf
Hugh	18	M	Scholar	18Ap01Cf
Mary-Ann	12	F	None	18Ap01Cf
Ellen-Jane	8	F	Child	18Ap01Cf
John	10	M	Student	18Ap01Cf
MCMULLAN, Catherine	28	F	Upholsterer	18Ap01Cf
GREGG, Wm.	21	M	Weaver	18Ap01Cf
Mary	22	F	Servant	18Ap01Cf
MCMATHEWS, Sarah	32	F	Wife	18Ap01Cf
MCILWORTH, Jane	18	F	Housekeeper	18Ap01Cf
MATHEWS, Mary-Ann	8	F	Child	18Ap01Cf
MCCROMY, Bridget	18	F	Seamstress	18Ap01Cf
ROBINSON, Marshall	26	M	Farmer	18Ap01Cf
MOONEY, John	20	M	Farmer	18Ap01Cf
James	20	M	Farmer	18Ap01Cf
HASSAN, Wm.	17	M	Laborer	18Ap01Cf
POLLOCK, Jane	21	F	Servant	18Ap01Cf
MULCAHEMY, Pat	18	M	Farmer	18Ap01Cf
Catherine	16	F	Seamstress	18Ap01Cf
ROGERS, M.	22	F	Seamstress	18Ap01Cf
MARTIN, Robert	17	M	Student	18Ap01Cf
DEVAN, Bernard	19	M	Maltster	18Ap01Cf
Sarah	17	F	Seamstress	18Ap01Cf
TRAVERS, John	24	M	Servant	18Ap01Cf
Anthony	26	M	Servant	18Ap01Cf
MCNALTY, Wm.	30	M	Servant	18Ap01Cf
BURR, Wm.	28	M	Farmer	18Ap01Cf
MCMINERRY, Bernard	16	M	Student	18Ap01Cf
SHEIL, Charles	20	M	Farmer	18Ap01Cf
GINN, John	64	M	Weaver	18Ap01Cf
WORNSLEY, James	32	M	Ploughman	18Ap01Cf
Ann	12	F	None	18Ap01Cf
Edward	2	M	Child	18Ap01Cf
Mary	35	F	Wife	18Ap01Cf
JOHNSTONE, Fanny	21	F	Seamstress	18Ap01Cf
FARREN, James	23	M	Farmer	18Ap01Cf
MCMULLAN, Wm.	25	M	Farmer	18Ap01Cf
Peggy	25	F	Dressmaker	18Ap01Cf
Robert	2	M	Child	18Ap01Cf
Wm.	8	M	Child	18Ap01Cf
GALLEN, Michael	40	M	Laborer	18Ap01Cf
CARLTON, Hugh	20	M	Laborer	18Ap01Cf
Mary	20	F	House Maid	18Ap01Cf
Ann	19	F	Seamstress	18Ap01Cf
DEVAN, Hugh	25	M	Laborer	18Ap01Cf
MCCULLOUGH, Hugh	30	M	Laborer	18Ap01Cf
YOUNG, Thomas	21	M	Engineer	18Ap01Cf
MACARTNEY, U	00	F	Lady	18Ap01Cf
CARLISLE, Samuel	22	M	Preacher	18Ap01Cf

CHINA 19 APRIL 1849

From Liverpool

NAMES OF PASSENGERS	AGE	SEX	OCCUPATIONS	DATE PORT SHIP
EMERSON, George	13	M	Unknown	19Ap02Cg
TOWERS, James	38	M	Unknown	19Ap02Cg
Alice	38	F	Unknown	19Ap02Cg
Lucy	15	F	Unknown	19Ap02Cg
John	13	M	Unknown	19Ap02Cg
Mary	10	F	Unknown	19Ap02Cg
Ann	8	F	Child	19Ap02Cg

NAMES OF PASSENGERS	AGE	SEX	OCCUPATIONS	DATE PORT SHIP
TOWERS, George	4	M	Child	19Ap02Cg
Emma	2	F	Child	19Ap02Cg
HOLMES, John	26	M	Laborer	19Ap02Cg
HEVEY, James	22	M	Laborer	19Ap02Cg
Catherine	23	F	Unknown	19Ap02Cg
SULLIVAN, Betsey	24	F	Servant	19Ap02Cg
MCDONALD, Margt.	20	F	Milliner	19Ap02Cg
NELSON, Edward	30	M	Joiner	19Ap02Cg
HANLEY, P.K.	20	M	Laborer	19Ap02Cg
CAREY, Margaret	20	F	Servant	19Ap02Cg
GILDENEN, F.	30	M	Laborer	19Ap02Cg
H.	.07	M	Infant	19Ap02Cg
GALLACHER, Owen	20	M	Laborer	19Ap02Cg
BROOKS, Robt.	24	M	Tailor	19Ap02Cg
Catherine	23	F	Unknown	19Ap02Cg
James	4	M	Child	19Ap02Cg
Martha	.10	F	Infant	19Ap02Cg
SALT, Thomas	33	M	Laborer	19Ap02Cg
Mary	33	F	Unknown	19Ap02Cg
John	7	M	Child	19Ap02Cg
Ann	5	F	Child	19Ap02Cg
John	30	M	Laborer	19Ap02Cg
FINN, Fergus	21	M	Laborer	19Ap02Cg
John	20	M	Laborer	19Ap02Cg
Winefred	30	M	Laborer	19Ap02Cg
SHEEKY, Thomas	35	M	Laborer	19Ap02Cg
Catherine	32	F	Unknown	19Ap02Cg
Michael	12	M	Unknown	19Ap02Cg
John	10	M	Unknown	19Ap02Cg
Patrick	5	M	Child	19Ap02Cg
Bridget	7	F	Child	19Ap02Cg
MCMANNUS, James	22	M	Laborer	19Ap02Cg
MCKINNEY, Mary	19	F	Dressmaker	19Ap02Cg
GILDENEN, Margt.	30	F	Unknown	19Ap02Cg
REYNOLDS, Catherine	40	F	Unknown	19Ap02Cg
John	7	M	Child	19Ap02Cg
CHURCH, Jane	30	F	Unknown	19Ap02Cg
Hugh	9	M	Child	19Ap02Cg
PATTERSON, Mary	22	F	Servant	19Ap02Cg
FITZGERALD, Michael	26	M	Laborer	19Ap02Cg
SPEAR, Thomas	21	M	Laborer	19Ap02Cg
HAMILTON, William	20	M	Painter	19Ap02Cg
BARRYGIND, Andrew	19	M	Grocer	19Ap02Cg
EAGAN, James	50	M	Laborer	19Ap02Cg
Thomas	20	M	Laborer	19Ap02Cg
John	13	M	Laborer	19Ap02Cg
Patrick	40	M	Laborer	19Ap02Cg
MCDONOGH, Bridget	40	F	Servant	19Ap02Cg
Rose	8	F	Child	19Ap02Cg
Anne	7	F	Child	19Ap02Cg
Michael	5	M	Child	19Ap02Cg
Mary	3	F	Child	19Ap02Cg
RYAN, Patrick	24	M	Laborer	19Ap02Cg
Died-At-Sea				
GARVIE, Daniel	32	M	Laborer	19Ap02Cg
MURPHY, Peter	30	M	Laborer	19Ap02Cg
CALLAGHAN, Thomas	35	M	Laborer	19Ap02Cg
REDGEONT, Thomas	26	M	Laborer	19Ap02Cg
Mary	29	F	Unknown	19Ap02Cg
Betsey	.10	F	Infant	19Ap02Cg
FRENCH, Jacob	42	M	Unknown	19Ap02Cg
Mary-Anne	32	F	Unknown	19Ap02Cg
Samuel	9	M	Child	19Ap02Cg
Julia	7	F	Child	19Ap02Cg
Henrietta	5	F	Child	19Ap02Cg
Jessy	3	F	Child	19Ap02Cg
Mary	.10	F	Infant	19Ap02Cg
Died-At-Sea				
MCMANUS, James	55	M	Unknown	19Ap02Cg
U-Mrs.	50	F	Unknown	19Ap02Cg
John	20	M	Unknown	19Ap02Cg
Anne	17	F	Unknown	19Ap02Cg
Daniel	15	M	Unknown	19Ap02Cg
Thomas	6	M	Child	19Ap02Cg
Michael	22	M	Unknown	19Ap02Cg
CONNOR, Daniel	35	M	Unknown	19Ap02Cg
Patrick	24	M	Unknown	19Ap02Cg
CORBET, Catherine	22	F	Unknown	19Ap02Cg
CASSIDY, Bridget	22	F	Unknown	19Ap02Cg
CROPPER, James	28	M	Unknown	19Ap02Cg
BALL, Thomas	30	M	Unknown	19Ap02Cg
GIBNEY, Mary	22	F	Unknown	19Ap02Cg
MCDONALD, John	29	M	Unknown	19Ap02Cg
Bridget	26	F	Unknown	19Ap02Cg
Bridget	.10	F	Infant	19Ap02Cg
DOYLE, Margaret	26	F	Unknown	19Ap02Cg
MAGUIRE, Michael	30	M	Unknown	19Ap02Cg
HORAN, Timothy	36	M	Unknown	19Ap02Cg
FOLLY, Thades	34	M	Unknown	19Ap02Cg
NALLY, Thomas	36	M	Unknown	19Ap02Cg
U-Mrs.	30	F	Unknown	19Ap02Cg
Julia	.11	F	Infant	19Ap02Cg
Died-At-Sea				
DUGGAN, Mary	36	F	Unknown	19Ap02Cg
RATCHFORD, John	50	M	Unknown	19Ap02Cg
Wm.	24	M	Unknown	19Ap02Cg
U	22	M	Unknown	19Ap02Cg
Mary	17	F	Unknown	19Ap02Cg
MANDERS, S.	25	M	Unknown	19Ap02Cg
JAMES, Elias	30	M	Unknown	19Ap02Cg
Cairon	23	M	Unknown	19Ap02Cg
William	18	M	Unknown	19Ap02Cg
CHILDS, James	23	M	Unknown	19Ap02Cg
Hannah	21	F	Unknown	19Ap02Cg
OCONNELL, John	35	M	Unknown	19Ap02Cg
QUIN, Frederick	15	M	Unknown	19Ap02Cg
CLARKE, Philip	17	M	Unknown	19Ap02Cg
MOORE, Thomas	19	M	Unknown	19Ap02Cg
COMMONS, Michael	20	M	Unknown	19Ap02Cg
KERRIN, Michael	30	M	Unknown	19Ap02Cg
Catherine	22	F	Unknown	19Ap02Cg
OLOUGHLAM, Johanna	18	F	Unknown	19Ap02Cg
DUFFY, Bridget	35	F	Unknown	19Ap02Cg
OLOUGHLAM, Arthur	35	M	Unknown	19Ap02Cg
Catherine	13	F	Unknown	19Ap02Cg
MAGEE, Mary	25	F	Unknown	19Ap02Cg
PARKHILL, Sarah	22	F	Unknown	19Ap02Cg
Rachel	20	F	Unknown	19Ap02Cg
COMMONS, Timothy	45	M	Unknown	19Ap02Cg
John	36	M	Unknown	19Ap02Cg
John	34	M	Unknown	19Ap02Cg
Bridget	20	F	Unknown	19Ap02Cg
Honora	24	F	Unknown	19Ap02Cg
Catherine	19	F	Unknown	19Ap02Cg
DWYER, Con.	21	M	Unknown	19Ap02Cg
CLARY, W.	21	M	Unknown	19Ap02Cg
ADAMS, Robt.	20	M	Unknown	19Ap02Cg
HOOKEY, Catherine	20	F	Unknown	19Ap02Cg
LOONY, Margaret	17	F	Unknown	19Ap02Cg
COCHINGTON, Judith	20	F	Unknown	19Ap02Cg
DUGGAN, Martin	40	M	Unknown	19Ap02Cg
DOOLEY, Malachi	48	M	Unknown	19Ap02Cg
Catherine	25	F	Unknown	19Ap02Cg
DUGGAN, Jeremiah	27	M	Unknown	19Ap02Cg
RYAN, Michael	20	M	Unknown	19Ap02Cg
SULLIVAN, Jeremiah	38	M	Unknown	19Ap02Cg
GABIN, Thomas	50	M	Unknown	19Ap02Cg
Bridget	50	F	Unknown	19Ap02Cg
Bridget	20	F	Unknown	19Ap02Cg
James	24	M	Unknown	19Ap02Cg
CASEY, Mary	26	F	Unknown	19Ap02Cg
James	24	M	Unknown	19Ap02Cg
GAHAN, John	22	M	Unknown	19Ap02Cg
WARD, John	30	M	Unknown	19Ap02Cg
PIGEON, Ellen	20	F	Unknown	19Ap02Cg
HARRISON, Philip	26	M	Unknown	19Ap02Cg
TUMORS, John	24	M	Unknown	19Ap02Cg
BANNON, Dennis	27	M	Unknown	19Ap02Cg
CORBIT, Mary	26	F	Unknown	19Ap02Cg
LANEGAN, M.	22	M	Unknown	19Ap02Cg

NAMES OF PASSENGERS	AGE	SEX	OCCUPATIONS	DATE PORT SHIP
WYDE, W.	13	M	Unknown	19Ap02Cg
HAND, John	38	M	Unknown	19Ap02Cg
Bridget	35	F	Unknown	19Ap02Cg
Bridget	.09	F	Infant	19Ap02Cg
MAHON, Pat.	20	M	Unknown	19Ap02Cg
ECCLESFORD, R.	25	M	Unknown	19Ap02Cg
SWANSEA, Thomas	29	M	Unknown	19Ap02Cg
U-Mrs.	29	F	Unknown	19Ap02Cg
Wm.	.06	M	Infant	19Ap02Cg
MACHINE, Philip	20	M	Unknown	19Ap02Cg
RYAN, Wm.	36	M	Unknown	19Ap02Cg
DUFFY, Ellen	30	F	Unknown	19Ap02Cg
HOPKINS, Hugh	45	M	Unknown	19Ap02Cg
OBRIAN, N.	26	M	Unknown	19Ap02Cg
LOOSKIN, M.	30	M	Unknown	19Ap02Cg
MCCRONE, J.	30	M	Unknown	19Ap02Cg
LOOSKIN, M.	28	M	Unknown	19Ap02Cg
P.	30	M	Unknown	19Ap02Cg
Catherine	28	F	Unknown	19Ap02Cg
MCQUIRK, Ann	17	F	Unknown	19Ap02Cg
MCCRONE, Mary	29	F	Unknown	19Ap02Cg
GRIFFIN, Cecilia	21	F	Unknown	19Ap02Cg
LOOSKIN, Nancy	20	F	Unknown	19Ap02Cg
M.	.11	M	Infant	19Ap02Cg
KELLY, Martha	17	F	Unknown	19Ap02Cg
NICHOLSON, A.	30	M	Unknown	19Ap02Cg
KELLY, Biddy	40	F	Unknown	19Ap02Cg
DILLON, Biddy	18	F	Unknown	19Ap02Cg
REILLY, Mary	6	F	Child	19Ap02Cg
BEGBIE, Daniel	26	M	Unknown	19Ap02Cg
MURPHY, R.	56	M	Unknown	19Ap02Cg
Honora	50	F	Unknown	19Ap02Cg
Catherine	18	F	Unknown	19Ap02Cg
M.	12	M	Unknown	19Ap02Cg
A.	10	M	Unknown	19Ap02Cg
LANGAN, John	20	M	Unknown	19Ap02Cg
Edward	13	M	Unknown	19Ap02Cg
WYER, E.	40	M	Unknown	19Ap02Cg
MCGAR, Barney	30	M	Unknown	19Ap02Cg
PARR, Joseph	30	M	Unknown	19Ap02Cg
RONDERTY, John	20	M	Unknown	19Ap02Cg
RIDGE, John	9	M	Child	19Ap02Cg
Sarah	.11	F	Infant	19Ap02Cg
SUTHERLAND, John	24	M	Unknown	19Ap02Cg
C.	26	F	Unknown	19Ap02Cg
TUMULTY, P.	26	M	Unknown	19Ap02Cg
Mary	26	F	Unknown	19Ap02Cg
WALKER, John	30	M	Unknown	19Ap02Cg
MCGUIRL, Anne	20	F	Unknown	19Ap02Cg
HARKIN, P.	30	M	Unknown	19Ap02Cg
P.	11	M	Unknown	19Ap02Cg
FULTON, H.	30	M	Unknown	19Ap02Cg
FLANIKIN, J.	32	M	Unknown	19Ap02Cg
RENWICK, Eliza	11	F	Unknown	19Ap02Cg
MCLEARY, Mary	20	F	Unknown	19Ap02Cg
DUFFY, M.	30	M	Unknown	19Ap02Cg
FARRELL, Thomas	35	M	Unknown	19Ap02Cg
Thomas	2	M	Child	19Ap02Cg
HEFFASON, Eliza	20	F	Unknown	19Ap02Cg
MCCABE, Joseph	17	M	Unknown	19Ap02Cg
CAMPBELL, Pat	22	M	Unknown	19Ap02Cg
STEPHENSON, Leonard	36	M	Unknown	19Ap02Cg
Anne	38	F	Unknown	19Ap02Cg
John	11	M	Unknown	19Ap02Cg
Mary-Anne	9	F	Child	19Ap02Cg
Leonard	8	M	Child	19Ap02Cg
Thomas	6	M	Child	19Ap02Cg
Susanna	4	F	Child	19Ap02Cg
Robt.	2	M	Child	19Ap02Cg
TINKLER, William	7	M	Child	19Ap02Cg
MCDONALD, James	25	M	Unknown	19Ap02Cg
SMITH, Wm.	18	M	Joiner	19Ap02Cg
CARROLL, Owen	23	M	Unknown	19Ap02Cg
Patrick	19	M	Unknown	19Ap02Cg
ROGERS, Thomas	20	M	Unknown	19Ap02Cg

NAMES OF PASSENGERS	AGE	SEX	OCCUPATIONS	DATE PORT SHIP
LAVERLY, P.	20	M	Unknown	19Ap02Cg
COLEMAN, Bridget	12	F	Unknown	19Ap02Cg
MCIVOR, Ellen	22	F	Servant	19Ap02Cg
MURPHY, Bridget	36	F	Servant	19Ap02Cg
SIMPSON, Charles	27	M	Laborer	19Ap02Cg
DYER, Patrick	18	M	Laborer	19Ap02Cg
ATTERIDGE, Agnes	26	F	Unknown	19Ap02Cg

ALARM 20 APRIL 1849

From Cork

NAMES OF PASSENGERS	AGE	SEX	OCCUPATIONS	DATE PORT SHIP
SULLIVAN, James	00	M	Farmer	20Ap08Ch
OBRIEN, Mick	25	M	Farmer	20Ap08Ch
FITZGERALD, Rich	45	M	Farmer	20Ap08Ch
Hannah	.00	F	Infant	20Ap08Ch
CALLAGHAN, Catha.	10	F	None	20Ap08Ch
BRIEN, Darby	34	M	Farmer	20Ap08Ch
REGAN, Mich.	40	M	Farmer	20Ap08Ch
Jeremiah	23	M	Farmer	20Ap08Ch
DONOVAN, James	23	M	Farmer	20Ap08Ch
Patrick	.00	M	Infant	20Ap08Ch
REGAN, Hannah	40	F	Farmer	20Ap08Ch
Mary	20	F	Farmer	20Ap08Ch
HEALEY, Honora	2	F	Child	20Ap08Ch
Michael	.00	M	Infant	20Ap08Ch
OLEARY, Caharles	20	M	Farmer	20Ap08Ch
Catherine	22	F	Farmer	20Ap08Ch
MANNING, James	40	M	Farmer	20Ap08Ch
FITZGERALD, Thomas	20	M	Farmer	20Ap08Ch
GEHIN, Patrick	20	M	Farmer	20Ap08Ch
SULLIVAN, Johanna	17	F	Farmer	20Ap08Ch
MCDONNELL, Mary	30	F	Farmer	20Ap08Ch
SHEA, Pegga	22	F	Farmer	20Ap08Ch
GILBECK, Mathew	50	M	Farmer	20Ap08Ch
John	24	M	Farmer	20Ap08Ch
Mathew	22	M	Farmer	20Ap08Ch
Thomas	21	M	Farmer	20Ap08Ch
GILBERT, James	15	M	Farmer	20Ap08Ch
My.	18	F	Farmer	20Ap08Ch
Samuel	14	M	Farmer	20Ap08Ch
George	11	M	Farmer	20Ap08Ch
Eliza	9	F	Child	20Ap08Ch
Richard	18	M	Farmer	20Ap08Ch
HEIVANE, John	20	M	Farmer	20Ap08Ch
Johanna	24	F	Farmer	20Ap08Ch
Denis	24	M	Farmer	20Ap08Ch
BOWLER, John	40	M	Farmer	20Ap08Ch
LOVELL, John	19	M	Farmer	20Ap08Ch
Edmund	19	M	Farmer	20Ap08Ch
CAHOLANE, Mary	20	F	Farmer	20Ap08Ch
MCCARTHY, Terence	20	M	Farmer	20Ap08Ch
Mary	40	F	Farmer	20Ap08Ch
FITZGERALD, John	10	M	Farmer	20Ap08Ch
Honora	24	F	Farmer	20Ap08Ch
DALTERAN, Catherine	21	F	Farmer	20Ap08Ch
COGHLAN, Cath.	30	F	Farmer	20Ap08Ch
DONOGHUE, Edu.	20	M	Farmer	20Ap08Ch
TALVEY, Cath.	23	F	Farmer	20Ap08Ch
CAHOLANE, John	28	M	Farmer	20Ap08Ch
QUINN, John	26	M	Farmer	20Ap08Ch
DRISCOLE, Daniel	30	M	Farmer	20Ap08Ch
Catherine	32	F	Farmer	20Ap08Ch
Margaret	22	F	Farmer	20Ap08Ch
OBRIEN, Ellen	50	F	Farmer	20Ap08Ch
MURPHY, John	28	M	Farmer	20Ap08Ch
LANGTEN, Augusta	21	F	Farmer	20Ap08Ch
DUMNY, Patrick	21	M	Farmer	20Ap08Ch
KELLY, Margaret	21	F	Farmer	20Ap08Ch

NAMES OF PASSENGERS	AGE	SEX	OCCUPATIONS	DATE PORT SHIP
HENESSEY, William	30	M	Farmer	20Ap08Ch
Bridget	35	F	Farmer	20Ap08Ch
William	3	M	Child	20Ap08Ch
Mary	.00	F	Infant	20Ap08Ch
KENNEDY, John	21	M	Farmer	20Ap08Ch
CROWLEY, Ellen	20	F	Farmer	20Ap08Ch
BROWNE, Richard	19	M	Farmer	20Ap08Ch
HURLEY, Catherine	16	F	Farmer	20Ap08Ch
Constantine	14	M	Farmer	20Ap08Ch
Garrett	11	M	Farmer	20Ap08Ch
MURPHY, Daniel	25	M	Farmer	20Ap08Ch
NOLTER, John	40	M	Farmer	20Ap08Ch
Richard	10	M	Farmer	20Ap08Ch
HEGARTY, Daniel	21	M	Farmer	20Ap08Ch
DALIA, Edward	16	M	Farmer	20Ap08Ch
WARREN, Teresa	19	F	Farmer	20Ap08Ch
HALMAN, Merto	21	M	Farmer	20Ap08Ch
CASEY, Denis	50	M	Farmer	20Ap08Ch
John	18	M	Farmer	20Ap08Ch
DANIEL, Henry	21	M	Farmer	20Ap08Ch
MANNING, John	25	M	Farmer	20Ap08Ch
GLEESEN, Judy	21	F	Farmer	20Ap08Ch

EUROPA 20 APRIL 1849

From Liverpool

NAMES OF PASSENGERS	AGE	SEX	OCCUPATIONS	DATE PORT SHIP
MOOREHEAD, Jno.	58	M	Merchant	20Ap02Ck
KEOGH, D.P.	26	M	Gentleman	20Ap02Ck
SMITH, U	25	F	Unknown	20Ap02Ck
GRAYDON, S.	33	M	Farmer	20Ap02Ck
U (W)	28	F	Unknown	20Ap02Ck
FRORD, U	30	M	Farmer	20Ap02Ck
LONG, U	20	M	Farmer	20Ap02Ck
H.	19	M	Farmer	20Ap02Ck

BURLINGTON 23 APRIL 1849

From Liverpool

NAMES OF PASSENGERS	AGE	SEX	OCCUPATIONS	DATE PORT SHIP
INNIGAN, Philip	20	M	Carpenter	23Ap02Ci
Bridget	21	F	None	23Ap02Ci
ICGOVERN, Mary	18	F	Servant	23Ap02Ci
ARREL, Cath.	17	F	Servant	23Ap02Ci
Thos.	45	M	Laborer	23Ap02Ci
Ann	40	F	Unknown	23Ap02Ci
John	21	M	Unknown	23Ap02Ci
Jas.	18	M	Unknown	23Ap02Ci
Margt.	15	F	Unknown	23Ap02Ci
Nicholas	13	M	Unknown	23Ap02Ci
Biddy	5	F	Child	23Ap02Ci
Thos.	7	M	Child	23Ap02Ci
Cath.	11	M	None	23Ap02Ci
Wm.	00	M	None	23Ap02Ci
Ellen	9	F	Child	23Ap02Ci
ALLAGHER, Ann	18	F	Servant	23Ap02Ci
Mary	16	F	Unknown	23Ap02Ci
ANIGAN, Ellen	19	F	Unknown	23Ap02Ci
ARGAN, Philip	24	M	Laborer	23Ap02Ci
Margaret	21	F	Unknown	23Ap02Ci
NIS, James	26	M	Unknown	23Ap02Ci
Mary	24	F	Unknown	23Ap02Ci
ARRALLY, Pat	23	M	Laborer	23Ap02Ci
FARRALLY, Bess	22	F	Unknown	23Ap02Ci
GARGAN, Phil.	20	M	Laborer	23Ap02Ci
COFFEE, James	26	M	Cooper	23Ap02Ci
Rose	26	F	Unknown	23Ap02Ci
Mary	.00	F	Infant	23Ap02Ci
M--HALY, Walter	30	M	Laborer	23Ap02Ci
Bridget	30	F	Unknown	23Ap02Ci
Julia	7	F	Child	23Ap02Ci
Thos.	5	M	Child	23Ap02Ci
Pat	20	M	Unknown	23Ap02Ci
Mat	20	M	Unknown	23Ap02Ci
Pat	.00	M	Infant	23Ap02Ci
MCINTOSH, Henry	25	M	Laborer	23Ap02Ci
FARREL, Richard	25	M	Laborer	23Ap02Ci
U, Michl.	23	M	Unknown	23Ap02Ci
Bridget	21	F	Unknown	23Ap02Ci
HAYES, Anthony	23	M	Unknown	23Ap02Ci
HOLOHAN, Daniel	29	M	Unknown	23Ap02Ci
SHANLEY, Wm.	22	M	Unknown	23Ap02Ci
CONNOR, John	25	M	Unknown	23Ap02Ci
BIGGERS, Sarah	22	F	Servant	23Ap02Ci
DALY, Mary-A.	17	F	Unknown	23Ap02Ci
MCGUIRE, Pat	46	M	Seaman	23Ap02Ci
U-Mrs.	35	F	Unknown	23Ap02Ci
Michl.	9	M	Child	23Ap02Ci
Pat	7	M	Child	23Ap02Ci
William	14	M	None	23Ap02Ci
BARROW, Mary	20	F	Servant	23Ap02Ci
BEER, Mary	22	F	Servant	23Ap02Ci
U	.00	U	Infant	23Ap02Ci
Born-At-Sea				
MOFFAT, Thos.	28	M	Laborer	23Ap02Ci
CARR, Francis	20	M	Farmer	23Ap02Ci
William	16	M	Farmer	23Ap02Ci
Ann	12	F	Farmer	23Ap02Ci
ROGERS, Susan	40	F	Unknown	23Ap02Ci
Biddy	14	F	None	23Ap02Ci
John	.00	M	Infant	23Ap02Ci
Mary	9	F	Child	23Ap02Ci
Michl.	7	M	Child	23Ap02Ci
HEARNS, Dennis	56	M	Farmer	23Ap02Ci
Michl.	24	M	Unknown	23Ap02Ci
Patt	16	M	Unknown	23Ap02Ci
DELANEY, Mich.	25	M	Laborer	23Ap02Ci
MORAN, Thos.	23	M	Unknown	23Ap02Ci
DALY, Peter	28	M	Unknown	23Ap02Ci
CONLON, Margaret	21	F	Seamstress	23Ap02Ci
DUNN, Eliza	20	F	Unknown	23Ap02Ci
SURLEY, Mich.	23	M	Laborer	23Ap02Ci
Mary	20	F	Unknown	23Ap02Ci
SHAUGHNESSY, Edmund	45	M	Laborer	23Ap02Ci
EAGAN, Henry	25	M	Laborer	23Ap02Ci
MCKENNA, Owen	40	M	Laborer	23Ap02Ci
Eliza	17	F	Servant	23Ap02Ci
MCGUIRE, Michl.	50	M	Farmer	23Ap02Ci
Ellen	50	F	Farmer	23Ap02Ci
John	20	M	Farmer	23Ap02Ci
Julia	13	F	None	23Ap02Ci
Margt.	15	F	None	23Ap02Ci
Rose	11	F	None	23Ap02Ci
Thos.	9	M	Child	23Ap02Ci
Michl.	3	M	Child	23Ap02Ci
QUINN, Patrick	25	M	Laborer	23Ap02Ci
Rose	20	F	Wife	23Ap02Ci
TRAINER, James	25	M	Laborer	23Ap02Ci
HADDEN, Robert	15	M	Shop Boy	23Ap02Ci
Jane	20	F	Spinster	23Ap02Ci
Sarah	17	F	Spinster	23Ap02Ci
MEAGHAN, Cath.	20	F	Spinster	23Ap02Ci
SHEEDER, Wm.	23	M	Clerk	23Ap02Ci
FOGG, Samuel	24	M	Carpenter	23Ap02Ci
SULLIVAN, John	25	M	Laborer	23Ap02Ci
DIGNAN, James	28	M	Farmer	23Ap02Ci
Elizabeth	26	F	Wife	23Ap02Ci
MURPHY, William	20	M	Laborer	23Ap02Ci

NAMES OF PASSENGERS	AGE	SEX	OCCUPATIONS	DATE PORT SHIP
MURPHY, Anty	19	F	Spinster	23Ap02Ci
WOODBURN, John	21	M	Laborer	23Ap02Ci
NOONAN, Timothy	18	M	Laborer	23Ap02Ci
Thos.	12	M	None	23Ap02Ci
COTTOR, William	30	M	Farmer	23Ap02Ci
HURLEY, Cath.	34	F	None	23Ap02Ci
Johanna	3	F	Child	23Ap02Ci
Ellen	.00	F	Infant	23Ap02Ci
GUINNAN, Thos.	18	M	Cook	23Ap02Ci
DUNN, George	20	M	Laborer	23Ap02Ci
KELLY, James	20	M	Laborer	23Ap02Ci
GORMON, Mary	25	F	House Woman	23Ap02Ci
Anne	5	F	Child	23Ap02Ci
Eliza	.00	F	Infant	23Ap02Ci
POWER, Patk.	25	M	Carpenter	23Ap02Ci
Michl.	24	M	Carpenter	23Ap02Ci
Mary	22	F	Wife	23Ap02Ci
Martin	.00	M	Infant	23Ap02Ci
PHELAN, James	45	M	Farmer	23Ap02Ci
Mary	23	F	Wife	23Ap02Ci
Niel	26	M	None	23Ap02Ci
Ellen	11	F	None	23Ap02Ci
Wile	20	M	Laborer	23Ap02Ci
Lawre	22	M	Laborer	23Ap02Ci
John	13	M	None	23Ap02Ci
COFFE, John	32	M	Farmer	23Ap02Ci
PINDAR, James	18	M	Laborer	23Ap02Ci
HUGHES, Felix	25	M	Laborer	23Ap02Ci
Alice	25	F	Wife	23Ap02Ci
James	.00	M	Infant	23Ap02Ci
GOLAGLEY, John	21	M	Laborer	23Ap02Ci
Cath.	21	F	Servant	23Ap02Ci
Mary	.00	F	Infant	23Ap02Ci
HUGHES, Patk.	25	M	Laborer	23Ap02Ci
Cath.	23	F	Wife	23Ap02Ci
Patk.	.00	M	Infant	23Ap02Ci
COLBERT, Patk.	25	M	Laborer	23Ap02Ci
John	19	M	Laborer	23Ap02Ci
Mary	21	F	Servant	23Ap02Ci
BOYLE, James	22	M	Laborer	23Ap02Ci
MCCAHY, Pat	19	M	Laborer	23Ap02Ci
MEAGHAN, Henry	26	M	Laborer	23Ap02Ci
LYNCH, Honora	25	F	Servant	23Ap02Ci
MILES, Bridget	22	F	Servant	23Ap02Ci
COTTOR, Margt.	27	F	Servant	23Ap02Ci
BOYLE, Sarah	18	F	Servant	23Ap02Ci
ODONOVAN, John	19	M	Shoemaker	23Ap02Ci
COLLINS, Daniel	22	M	Laborer	23Ap02Ci
MURPHY, Jeremiah	20	M	Laborer	23Ap02Ci
SHEEHAN, John	24	M	Laborer	23Ap02Ci
CONDON, Michl.	26	M	Laborer	23Ap02Ci
CONNORS, Thos.	23	M	Laborer	23Ap02Ci
POWER, Edmund	26	M	Carpenter	23Ap02Ci
Maria	24	F	Wife	23Ap02Ci
MCKEOWN, Bridget	26	F	Wife	23Ap02Ci
Pat	5	M	Child	23Ap02Ci
Mick	3	M	Child	23Ap02Ci
Hugh	2	M	Child	23Ap02Ci
WOOLFOOT, Margt.	24	F	Unknown	23Ap02Ci
HOLMES, John	36	M	Shoemaker	23Ap02Ci
Maria	36	F	Wife	23Ap02Ci
Susan	11	F	None	23Ap02Ci
Thos.	.00	M	Infant	23Ap02Ci
Wm.	2	M	Child	23Ap02Ci
George	9	M	Child	23Ap02Ci
REYNOLDS, Patk.	25	M	Laborer	23Ap02Ci
James	21	M	Laborer	23Ap02Ci
HOLBINS, Mich.	20	M	Laborer	23Ap02Ci
HEANY, John	25	M	Laborer	23Ap02Ci
WELSH, Wm.	34	M	Farmer	23Ap02Ci
Margt.	34	F	Wife	23Ap02Ci
Margt.	12	F	None	23Ap02Ci
Morris	9	M	Child	23Ap02Ci
John	.00	M	Infant	23Ap02Ci
HAGGERTY, Mary	21	F	None	23Ap02Ci

NAMES OF PASSENGERS	AGE	SEX	OCCUPATIONS	DATE PORT SHIP
DONOVAN, Mary	20	F	None	23Ap02Ci
HAWES, Pat	21	M	Laborer	23Ap02Ci
LAW, Benj.	25	M	Laborer	23Ap02Ci
MCGOWAN, Frank	19	M	Laborer	23Ap02Ci
FOLEY, Ann	21	F	Servant	23Ap02Ci
Ellen	17	F	Servant	23Ap02Ci
BRADY, Mary-A.	18	F	Servant	23Ap02Ci
COLLINS, Ellen	18	F	Servant	23Ap02Ci
BOYLAN, James	19	M	Farmer	23Ap02Ci
Patk.	7	M	Child	23Ap02Ci
SHERRY, Peter	21	M	Laborer	23Ap02Ci
GRANT, Jane	18	F	None	23Ap02Ci
Margt.	15	F	None	23Ap02Ci
MCNEMARA, Mic.	24	M	Laborer	23Ap02Ci
FOLEY, James	21	M	Laborer	23Ap02Ci
GRANT, Thos.	22	M	Laborer	23Ap02Ci

JOSEPH-MEIGS 23 APRIL 1849

From Londonderry

NAMES OF PASSENGERS	AGE	SEX	OCCUPATIONS	DATE PORT SHIP
BRANNON, Jas.	34	M	Farmer	23Ap01Cj
Mary	32	F	Matron	23Ap01Cj
Cath.	3	F	Child	23Ap01Cj
DUNBAR, Jas.	50	M	Farmer	23Ap01Cj
BRANNON, Jas.	.04	M	Infant	23Ap01Cj
DUNBAR, Margt.	45	F	Matron	23Ap01Cj
David	14	M	Unknown	23Ap01Cj
Thos.	12	M	Unknown	23Ap01Cj
Rachael	8	F	Child	23Ap01Cj
Elisa	6	F	Child	23Ap01Cj
Jas.	3	M	Child	23Ap01Cj
Margt.	16	F	Unknown	23Ap01Cj
HUNTER, Robt.	30	M	Farmer	23Ap01Cj
KILPATRICK, Jno.	20	M	Farmer	23Ap01Cj
MCGRATH, Jas.	22	M	Farmer	23Ap01Cj
HAGERTY, Corn.	20	M	Farmer	23Ap01Cj
THOMPSON, Margt.	21	F	Spinster	23Ap01Cj
DUGGAN, Mary	24	F	Spinster	23Ap01Cj
GREER, Isabell	18	F	Spinster	23Ap01Cj
MCCOLOSEY, Bridget	20	F	Spinster	23Ap01Cj
BOYLE, Mary	18	F	Spinster	23Ap01Cj
LINDSEY, Ellen	17	F	Spinster	23Ap01Cj
STEWART, John	17	M	Farmer	23Ap01C
KILDARE, Rodger	20	M	Farmer	23Ap01C
BURNS, Elenor	22	F	Spinster	23Ap01C
FRIEL, Jas.	19	M	Farmer	23Ap01C
LAND, Edmd.	22	M	Farmer	23Ap01C
MCMULLEN, Hugh	28	M	Farmer	23Ap01C
MCKELVEY, Barney	28	M	Farmer	23Ap01C
MCGONAGLE, Jas.	20	M	Farmer	23Ap01C
Ann	18	F	Spinster	23Ap01C
Jno.	5	M	Child	23Ap01C
MCDERMOTH, Mary	20	F	Spinster	23Ap01C
RODDY, Bridgt.	16	F	Spinster	23Ap01C
CASIDY, Cath.	18	F	Spinster	23Ap01C
Mary	16	F	Spinster	23Ap01C
SMITH, Cath.	19	F	Spinster	23Ap01C
ORR, Edwin	20	M	Farmer	23Ap01C
MCGONIGALL, Nell	21	F	Spinster	23Ap01C
CARLIN, Wm.	18	M	Farmer	23Ap01C
DERMOUTH, Chas.	21	M	Farmer	23Ap01C
CANNING, Manus	21	M	Farmer	23Ap01C
CARLEN, Jno.	21	M	Farmer	23Ap01C
BONNER, Jno.	20	M	Farmer	23Ap01C
CANE, Patk.	33	M	Farmer	23Ap01C
MCCREDER, Wm.	20	M	Farmer	23Ap01C
DOHERTY, Danl.	21	M	Farmer	23Ap01C
MCGONAGLE, Hugh	23	M	Farmer	23Ap01C

NAMES OF PASSENGERS	AGE	SEX	OCCUPATIONS	DATE PORT SHIP
IRWIN, Robt.	20	M	Farmer	23Ap01Cj
TERRY, Jno.	37	M	Farmer	23Ap01Cj
MCCAIN, Jno.	20	M	Farmer	23Ap01Cj
Betty	18	F	Spinster	23Ap01Cj
GILL, Owen	30	M	Farmer	23Ap01Cj
HAMMELL, Jas.	24	M	Farmer	23Ap01Cj
CASIDY, Mary	19	F	Spinster	23Ap01Cj
Nancy	20	F	Spinster	23Ap01Cj
MCKANNAH, Grace	.04	F	Infant	23Ap01Cj
DERMOUTH, Betsey	18	F	Spinster	23Ap01Cj
HAGERTY, Wm.	25	M	Farmer	23Ap01Cj
Margt.	25	F	Spinster	23Ap01Cj
MCNALLY, Mary	19	F	Spinster	23Ap01Cj
SWEENY, Rose	20	F	Spinster	23Ap01Cj
MCGRATH, Jas.	19	M	Farmer	23Ap01Cj
Michl.	17	M	Farmer	23Ap01Cj
HOUSTON, Henry	20	M	Farmer	23Ap01Cj
HORN, Hugh	20	M	Farmer	23Ap01Cj
SCANLEN, Betsey	18	F	Spinster	23Ap01Cj
COOK, Matty	30	F	Spinster	23Ap01Cj
GILLON, Ellen	18	F	Spinster	23Ap01Cj
Bridgt.	14	F	Spinster	23Ap01Cj
BATES, Jas.	19	M	Farmer	23Ap01Cj
Robt.	15	M	Farmer	23Ap01Cj
Jane	17	F	Spinster	23Ap01Cj
BOYLE, Andrew	19	M	Farmer	23Ap01Cj
WILLOCK, Jos.	25	M	Farmer	23Ap01Cj
BRUCE, Wm.	19	M	Farmer	23Ap01Cj
BENSLOW, Thos.	36	M	Farmer	23Ap01Cj
MCGEE, Patk.	36	M	Farmer	23Ap01Cj
Dennis	21	M	Farmer	23Ap01Cj
Betsey	18	F	Spinster	23Ap01Cj
DIVERS, Michl.	24	M	Farmer	23Ap01Cj
Margt.	18	F	Farmer	23Ap01Cj
CANNING, Jas.	70	M	Farmer	23Ap01Cj
Jas.	24	M	Farmer	23Ap01Cj
DUFFY, Mary	25	F	Spinster	23Ap01Cj
HENDERSON, Mary	18	F	Spinster	23Ap01Cj
Ann	13	F	Unknown	23Ap01Cj
Elisa	14	F	Unknown	23Ap01Cj
Isabel	11	F	Unknown	23Ap01Cj
Saml.	9	M	Child	23Ap01Cj
PINKERTON, Elisa	20	F	Spinster	23Ap01Cj
DONAHEW, Rose	22	F	Spinster	23Ap01Cj
EARLEY, Cath.	22	F	Spinster	23Ap01Cj
DEVLIN, Mary	20	F	Spinster	23Ap01Cj
MCGILLON, Patk.	19	M	Farmer	23Ap01Cj
GORMLEY, Wm.	30	M	Farmer	23Ap01Cj
Margt.	28	F	Matron	23Ap01Cj
Ann	.06	F	Infant	23Ap01Cj
MCCUTCHEON, Robt.	21	M	Farmer	23Ap01Cj
MCELVENNY, Andrew	30	M	Tailor	23Ap01Cj
Wm.	25	M	Tailor	23Ap01Cj
DONNALD, Ellen	34	F	Matron	23Ap01Cj
Conner	13	M	Unknown	23Ap01Cj
Margt.	11	F	Unknown	23Ap01Cj
Mary	9	F	Child	23Ap01Cj
Patk.	7	M	Child	23Ap01Cj
Bridget	6	F	Child	23Ap01Cj
Sally	3	F	Child	23Ap01Cj
GALAHER, Danl.	20	M	Farmer	23Ap01Cj
Jas.	23	M	Farmer	23Ap01Cj
CANAGAN, Barney	22	M	Farmer	23Ap01Cj
KERR, John	19	M	Farmer	23Ap01Cj
John	16	M	Farmer	23Ap01Cj
Jos.	14	M	Farmer	23Ap01Cj
BUTLER, Wm.	20	M	Farmer	23Ap01Cj
MCCAFFREY, Patk.	25	M	Farmer	23Ap01Cj
Jas.	17	M	Farmer	23Ap01Cj
HUSTON, Jas.	22	M	Farmer	23Ap01Cj
MCLAUGHLEN, Dennis	23	M	Farmer	23Ap01Cj
Margt.	21	F	Spinster	23Ap01Cj
ARMSTRONG, Robt.	35	M	Farmer	23Ap01Cj
GALLAGER, Felix	50	M	Farmer	23Ap01Cj
BRENNAN, Patk.	35	M	Farmer	23Ap01Cj
MAIGHER, Wm.	32	M	Farmer	23Ap01Cj
CROSBY, Edwd.	50	M	Farmer	23Ap01Cj
MCCUIGGEN, Patk.	50	M	Farmer	23Ap01Cj
Ann	40	F	Matron	23Ap01Cj
Sarah	19	F	Unknown	23Ap01Cj
Betsey	17	F	Unknown	23Ap01Cj
Thos.	16	M	Unknown	23Ap01Cj
Michl.	14	M	Unknown	23Ap01Cj
Susan	12	F	Unknown	23Ap01Cj
Ellen	10	F	Unknown	23Ap01Cj
Mary	8	F	Child	23Ap01Cj
Danl.	6	M	Child	23Ap01Cj
James	4	M	Child	23Ap01Cj
Patk.	2	M	Child	23Ap01Cj
Bernard	.06	F	Infant	23Ap01Cj
PHILIPS, Danl.	13	M	Unknown	23Ap01Cj
DOHERTY, Elisa	17	F	Spinster	23Ap01Cj
GILL, Jas.	19	M	Farmer	23Ap01Cj

VICTORIA 23 APRIL 1849

From Liverpool

NAMES OF PASSENGERS	AGE	SEX	OCCUPATIONS	DATE PORT SHIP
FLYNN, Pat	20	M	Laborer	23Ap02Cl
PECK, Chas.	18	M	Laborer	23Ap02Cl
HEAVY, Jas.	21	M	Laborer	23Ap02Cl
HOPKINS, Ant.	24	M	Laborer	23Ap02Cl
LEARY, Mary	20	F	Unknown	23Ap02Cl
CUMANGHAM, Michael	40	M	Laborer	23Ap02Cl
Mary	40	F	Unknown	23Ap02Cl
Danl.	15	M	Laborer	23Ap02Cl
Thos.	15	M	Laborer	23Ap02Cl
Rose	15	F	Unknown	23Ap02Cl
COUFELY, Matth.	40	M	Laborer	23Ap02Cl
MAXWELL, Jas.	14	M	Laborer	23Ap02Cl
Jas.	4	M	Child	23Ap02Cl
LEAHY, Owen	30	M	Laborer	23Ap02Cl
Mary	24	F	Unknown	23Ap02Cl
ROWLEY, Bridget	22	F	Unknown	23Ap02Cl
Le--, U	30	M	Laborer	23Ap02Cl
Mary	12	F	Unknown	23Ap02Cl
MURPHY, Mary	20	F	Unknown	23Ap02Cl
MCDONALD, Jas.	18	M	Laborer	23Ap02Cl
Chas.	16	M	Laborer	23Ap02Cl
JOHNSTON, Jane	30	F	Unknown	23Ap02Cl
ROBINSON, Cath.	25	F	Unknown	23Ap02Cl
Cath.	1	F	Child	23Ap02Cl
HOSLAN, James	19	M	Laborer	23Ap02Cl
DOUGHERTY, Harvey	19	M	Laborer	23Ap02Cl
GIVNY, Mary	22	F	Unknown	23Ap02Cl
Pat	5	M	Child	23Ap02Cl
DARCEY, Cath.	50	F	Unknown	23Ap02Cl
STEWART, Ellen	26	F	Unknown	23Ap02Cl
Jane	18	F	Unknown	23Ap02Cl
Thos.	8	M	Child	23Ap02Cl
Wm.J.	5	M	Child	23Ap02Cl
HEANY, Mad.B.	70	F	Unknown	23Ap02Cl
Died-At-Sea				
Luke	7	M	Child	23Ap02Cl
HEGAN, Cath.	18	F	Unknown	23Ap02Cl
GUNSHENAN, Ann	20	F	Unknown	23Ap02Cl
MCKENNA, Eleanor	20	F	Unknown	23Ap02Cl
HEMLY, Brid.	17	F	Unknown	23Ap02Cl
RATHER, Marella	12	F	Unknown	23Ap02Cl
MCMULLEN, Bernard	44	M	Laborer	23Ap02Cl
Sarah	35	F	Unknown	23Ap02Cl
James	30	M	Laborer	23Ap02Cl
Eliza	15	F	Unknown	23Ap02Cl
Ann	6	F	Child	23Ap02Cl

NAMES OF PASSENGERS	AGE	SEX	OCCUPATIONS	DATE PORT SHIP
MCMULLEN, Mary	4	F	Child	23Ap02CI
SWEENEY, Hugh	20	M	Laborer	23Ap02CI
Cath.	25	F	Unknown	23Ap02CI
MCDERMOTT, Bernard	20	F	Unknown	23Ap02CI
DONOHUE, Brid.	20	F	Unknown	23Ap02CI
MANUS, Bessy	23	F	Unknown	23Ap02CI
DORAN, Val.	23	F	Unknown	23Ap02CI
MCCAHANY, Pat	25	M	Laborer	23Ap02CI
MANUS, Magt.	16	F	Unknown	23Ap02CI
FERSUTH, Thos.	45	M	Laborer	23Ap02CI
CUNNINGHAM, Peter	24	M	Laborer	23Ap02CI
Pat	16	M	Laborer	23Ap02CI
Ann	19	F	Unknown	23Ap02CI
WHITE, May	30	F	Unknown	23Ap02CI
SWEENEY, Jane	10	F	Unknown	23Ap02CI
Jane	12	F	Unknown	23Ap02CI
Pat	30	M	Laborer	23Ap02CI
WALSH, La.	45	M	Laborer	23Ap02CI
Eliza	9	F	Child	23Ap02CI
Julia	3	F	Child	23Ap02CI
ROGERS, John	45	M	Laborer	23Ap02CI
Eliza	11	F	Unknown	23Ap02CI
MCHEALE, Denis	20	M	Laborer	23Ap02CI
DOOGAN, Brid.	30	F	Unknown	23Ap02CI
BRIGLEY, Marg.	5	F	Child	23Ap02CI
John	36	M	Laborer	23Ap02CI
RYAN, Pat	35	M	Laborer	23Ap02CI
Honora	00	F	Unknown	23Ap02CI
Nick	9	M	Child	23Ap02CI
Judy	7	F	Child	23Ap02CI
Teddy	5	M	Child	23Ap02CI
Roda	3	F	Child	23Ap02CI
Pat	.00	M	Infant	23Ap02CI
CASEY, Bridget	21	F	Unknown	23Ap02CI
CASSIDY, James	25	M	Laborer	23Ap02CI
CUNNINGHAM, Wm.	44	M	Laborer	23Ap02CI
Cath.	32	F	Unknown	23Ap02CI
Fred.	10	M	Laborer	23Ap02CI
John	6	M	Child	23Ap02CI
Mary	2	F	Child	23Ap02CI
CONALLY, Cath.	40	F	Unknown	23Ap02CI
Hugh	16	M	Laborer	23Ap02CI
Cath.	3	F	Child	23Ap02CI
Died-At-Sea				
Jno.	1	M	Child	23Ap02CI
MEHAN, Edwd.	24	M	Laborer	23Ap02CI
OBRIEN, Jos.	20	M	Laborer	23Ap02CI
REILLY, Jno.	11	M	Laborer	23Ap02CI
Cath.	4	F	Child	23Ap02CI
MORAN, Ellen	16	F	Unknown	23Ap02CI
Bid.	15	F	Unknown	23Ap02CI
TAYLOR, Ann	24	F	Unknown	23Ap02CI
Thos.	4	M	Child	23Ap02CI
Rose	.00	F	Infant	23Ap02CI
GUNSHEIMER, Ann	20	F	Unknown	23Ap02CI
MCGUINNESS, Mary	21	F	Unknown	23Ap02CI
CLARKE, Bid.	20	M	Laborer	23Ap02CI
MAHON, Pat	22	M	Laborer	23Ap02CI
KELLY, Tim.	17	M	Laborer	23Ap02CI
MCCARTY, Ellen	23	F	Unknown	23Ap02CI
FARRELL, Balth.	45	M	Laborer	23Ap02CI
CUNNINGHAM, Ellen	20	F	Unknown	23Ap02CI
CONWAY, Thos.	12	M	Laborer	23Ap02CI
Margt.	10	F	Unknown	23Ap02CI
Cath.	8	F	Child	23Ap02CI
SHEEHY, Julia	20	F	Unknown	23Ap02CI
PLANT, Ellen	20	F	Unknown	23Ap02CI
KELLEY, Michael	22	M	Laborer	23Ap02CI
FOREST, Wm.	26	M	Laborer	23Ap02CI
Ellen	10	F	Unknown	23Ap02CI
COHEN, Brid.	20	F	Unknown	23Ap02CI
BOYD, Mary	12	F	Unknown	23Ap02CI
KEELEN, Honora	20	F	Unknown	23Ap02CI
KENNELLY, Honor	20	F	Unknown	23Ap02CI
MCCANN, Laughlin	21	M	Laborer	23Ap02CI
CALLAGHAN, Jas.	23	M	Laborer	23Ap02CI
KELLY, Mich.	22	M	Laborer	23Ap02CI
FINLEY, Jane	16	F	Unknown	23Ap02CI
James	20	M	Laborer	23Ap02CI
SULLIVAN, Matth.	25	M	Laborer	23Ap02CI
LOFTUS, Ellen	20	F	Unknown	23Ap02CI
RYAN, Thos.	20	M	Laborer	23Ap02CI
CASEY, Bid.	18	M	Laborer	23Ap02CI
MAUNDER, Jno.	15	M	Laborer	23Ap02CI
MORAN, Winefd.	11	F	Unknown	23Ap02CI
FINEGAN, Hugh	18	M	Laborer	23Ap02CI
MCAULEY, Ann	20	F	Unknown	23Ap02CI
LYNCH, John	30	M	Laborer	23Ap02CI
KELLY, Peter	20	M	Laborer	23Ap02CI
TROPEN, Saml.	20	M	Laborer	23Ap02CI
TAYLOR, Fran.	22	M	Laborer	23Ap02CI
MALONEY, Rose	62	F	Unknown	23Ap02CI
YORK, Pat	35	M	Laborer	23Ap02CI
MANN, Peggy	33	F	Unknown	23Ap02CI
MALONY, Peggy	24	F	Unknown	23Ap02CI
DUNLAN, Bryan	10	M	Laborer	23Ap02CI
MOREAN, Owen	21	M	Laborer	23Ap02CI
Margt.	21	F	Unknown	23Ap02CI
Cath.	18	F	Unknown	23Ap02CI
GAY, Ellen	30	F	Unknown	23Ap02CI
John	.00	M	Infant	23Ap02CI
LEAHY, Margt.	40	F	Unknown	23Ap02CI
RYAN, Cath.	24	F	Unknown	23Ap02CI
GRAY, David	18	M	Laborer	23Ap02CI
NEILAN, Mary	18	F	Unknown	23Ap02CI
MCCABE, Mary	19	F	Unknown	23Ap02CI
DALEY, Wm.	40	M	Laborer	23Ap02CI
DELLAN, Mary	22	F	Unknown	23Ap02CI
RYAN, Leo	36	M	Laborer	23Ap02CI
John	2	M	Child	23Ap02CI
LEAHY, Thos.	20	M	Laborer	23Ap02CI
FAIR, Thos.	20	M	Laborer	23Ap02CI
MCGUIRE, Pat	20	M	Laborer	23Ap02CI
HENNESSY, Jno.	30	M	Laborer	23Ap02CI
Brid.	30	F	Unknown	23Ap02CI
RYAN, Dan.	25	M	Laborer	23Ap02CI
DUNN, Mich.	20	M	Laborer	23Ap02CI
BRIEN, Mary	20	F	Unknown	23Ap02CI
DOYLE, Luke	26	M	Laborer	23Ap02CI
KELLY, Edw.	20	M	Laborer	23Ap02CI
BUTLER, James	20	M	Laborer	23Ap02CI
Marg.	18	F	Unknown	23Ap02CI
BURNS, Tim.	20	M	Laborer	23Ap02CI
DONOVAN, Thos.	20	M	Laborer	23Ap02CI
John	20	M	Laborer	23Ap02CI
DALEY, Julia	18	F	Unknown	23Ap02CI
KEEGAN, John	26	M	Laborer	23Ap02CI
MCGUIRE, Jno.	21	M	Laborer	23Ap02CI
WALSH, Mich.	14	M	Laborer	23Ap02CI
OBRIEN, Mich.	27	M	Laborer	23Ap02CI
GOHAGAN, Pat	20	M	Laborer	23Ap02CI
WARREN, Richd.	30	M	Laborer	23Ap02CI
Du--RY, Pat	20	M	Laborer	23Ap02CI
KEEFE, David	28	M	Laborer	23Ap02C
RYAN, Lew.	30	M	Laborer	23Ap02C
NUGANT, Jos.	26	M	Laborer	23Ap02C
Ellen	20	F	Unknown	23Ap02C
FARLEY, Bryan	35	M	Laborer	23Ap02C
Jane	30	F	Unknown	23Ap02C
Edwd.	45	M	Laborer	23Ap02C
Cormich	2	F	Child	23Ap02C
Pat	.00	M	Infant	23Ap02C
Collr--, Jno.	28	M	Laborer	23Ap02C
LERENY, Thos.	28	M	Laborer	23Ap02C
WALSH, Pat	22	M	Laborer	23Ap02C
Edwd.	20	M	Laborer	23Ap02C
QUINLAN, John	28	M	Laborer	23Ap02C
MCPARLIN, Peter	30	M	Laborer	23Ap02C
JOHNSTON, Peter	28	M	Laborer	23Ap02C
DOGHERTY, James	25	M	Laborer	23Ap02C

NAMES OF PASSENGERS	AGE	SEX	OCCUPATIONS	DATE PORT SHIP
HANLY, Cath.	20	F	Unknown	23Ap02CI
Mara.	3	F	Child	23Ap02CI
KEETING, Edw.	30	M	Laborer	23Ap02CI
CORNBLUM, Jno.	28	M	Laborer	23Ap02CI
HERENY, Thos.	28	M	Laborer	23Ap02CI
WALSH, Pat	22	M	Laborer	23Ap02CI
Edwd.	21	M	Laborer	23Ap02CI
QUINLAN, Jno.	28	M	Laborer	23Ap02CI
DULANTY, Jno.	23	M	Laborer	23Ap02CI
HANLY, John	24	M	Laborer	23Ap02CI
NEWLIN, Ann	21	F	Unknown	23Ap02CI
ROBINSON, Geo.	25	M	Laborer	23Ap02CI
NEEDAN, Th.	20	M	Laborer	23Ap02CI
JOHNSTON, Wm.	24	M	Laborer	23Ap02CI
ENGLISH, Jno.	21	M	Laborer	23Ap02CI
RYAN, Pat	19	M	Laborer	23Ap02CI
CASEY, Brid.	15	F	Unknown	23Ap02CI
GILLEN, Ann	25	F	Unknown	23Ap02CI
RICHAM, Wm.	18	M	Laborer	23Ap02CI
RICHARDS, Hannah	22	F	Unknown	23Ap02CI
LARGHAM, Fanny	21	F	Unknown	23Ap02CI
Eliza	20	F	Unknown	23Ap02CI
HEGARTY, Hugh	22	M	Laborer	23Ap02CI
DRAVER, Pat	27	M	Laborer	23Ap02CI
Jno.	20	M	Laborer	23Ap02CI
HANLY, Cath.	20	F	Unknown	23Ap02CI
Maria	3	F	Child	23Ap02CI
REILY, Ellen	11	F	Unknown	23Ap02CI
DOWD, Bridgt.	6	F	Child	23Ap02CI
DOOLIN, James	40	M	Laborer	23Ap02CI
Margt.	16	F	Unknown	23Ap02CI
Ra--, S.	30	F	Unknown	23Ap02CI
BRIDGER, Jno.	26	M	Laborer	23Ap02CI
KENNY, T.	20	M	Laborer	23Ap02CI
HOVY, Cath.	30	F	Unknown	23Ap02CI
Cath.	2	F	Child	23Ap02CI
MCDONALD, J.	26	M	Laborer	23Ap02CI
REILLY, Mary	30	F	Unknown	23Ap02CI
MCDONNELL, Dan.	22	M	Laborer	23Ap02CI
MCMALLEN, Cath.	20	F	Unknown	23Ap02CI
MCCAFFERY, Cath.	20	F	Unknown	23Ap02CI
LAFFERTY, Rose	20	F	Unknown	23Ap02CI
CASHET, Pat	20	M	Laborer	23Ap02CI
NEALON, James	28	M	Laborer	23Ap02CI
Magt.	28	F	Unknown	23Ap02CI
James	2	M	Child	23Ap02CI
NOONE, Cath.	16	F	Unknown	23Ap02CI
HAGAN, Ba.	17	M	Laborer	23Ap02CI
TEAGUE, Jno.	21	M	Laborer	23Ap02CI
Jane	17	F	Unknown	23Ap02CI
BULKLEY, Jno.	25	F	Unknown	23Ap02CI
MALONEY, Pat	30	M	Laborer	23Ap02CI
GALVIN, Bridget	60	F	Unknown	23Ap02CI
Bridget	15	F	Unknown	23Ap02CI
MURRY, John	26	M	Laborer	23Ap02CI
Ann	18	F	Unknown	23Ap02CI
MADEN, F.	33	M	Laborer	23Ap02CI
TATE, Mchl.	40	M	Laborer	23Ap02CI
BRADY, Rose	24	F	Unknown	23Ap02CI
Bessy	11	F	Unknown	23Ap02CI
Mchl.	8	M	Child	23Ap02CI
KEHERY, Bridt.	20	F	Unknown	23Ap02CI
BRENNAN, Luke	28	M	Laborer	23Ap02CI
Mar.	15	F	Unknown	23Ap02CI
DARREN, Ann	20	F	Unknown	23Ap02CI
TULLY, Ma.	16	F	Unknown	23Ap02CI
Mgt.	14	F	Unknown	23Ap02CI
PALMER, Geo.	40	M	Laborer	23Ap02CI
LEHMAN, Coleman-O.	20	M	Laborer	23Ap02CI

HUDSON 23 APRIL 1849

From Glasgow

NAMES OF PASSENGERS	AGE	SEX	OCCUPATIONS	DATE PORT SHIP
COLLINS, John	25	M	None	23Ap04Cm
Patt.	28	M	None	23Ap04Cm
DOLAN, Peter	33	M	None	23Ap04Cm
FITZPATRICK, Patt.	30	M	None	23Ap04Cm
Jannet	24	F	None	23Ap04Cm
U, U	.00	U	Infant	23Ap04Cm

MESSENGER 24 APRIL 1849

From Galway

NAMES OF PASSENGERS	AGE	SEX	OCCUPATIONS	DATE PORT SHIP
KING, Michl.	36	M	Laborer	24Ap06Cn
JOYCE, Martin	28	M	Laborer	24Ap06Cn
COMMINS, Daniel	19	M	Laborer	24Ap06Cn
FEENEY, Mary	38	F	Unknown	24Ap06Cn
Bartly	40	M	Laborer	24Ap06Cn
COMMINS, Bridget	26	F	Unknown	24Ap06Cn
COLEMAN, Patt	32	M	Laborer	24Ap06Cn
Biddy	.00	F	Infant	24Ap06Cn
BURKE, Mary	28	F	Unknown	24Ap06Cn
REGAN, Dabby	40	M	Laborer	24Ap06Cn
Ann	30	F	Unknown	24Ap06Cn
Mary	12	F	Unknown	24Ap06Cn
Catherine	10	F	Unknown	24Ap06Cn
John	.00	M	Infant	24Ap06Cn
ROCK, Biddy	40	F	Unknown	24Ap06Cn
MURPHY, Patt	32	M	Laborer	24Ap06Cn
HANBURY, Thos.	28	M	Laborer	24Ap06Cn
DONOGHUE, Thos.	40	M	Laborer	24Ap06Cn
RAFFERTY, John	18	M	Laborer	24Ap06Cn
DONOGHUE, Ann	19	F	Unknown	24Ap06Cn
Biddy	26	F	Unknown	24Ap06Cn
FAHEY, Margaret	30	F	Unknown	24Ap06Cn
Nancy	29	F	Unknown	24Ap06Cn
WARD, Mathew	40	M	Laborer	24Ap06Cn
Henry	38	M	Laborer	24Ap06Cn
COMMINS, Paul	27	M	Laborer	24Ap06Cn
DUFFEY, John	30	M	Laborer	24Ap06Cn
ODEA, Edmund	60	M	Laborer	24Ap06Cn
Ned	57	M	Laborer	24Ap06Cn
Dennis	22	M	Laborer	24Ap06Cn
Bridget	20	F	Unknown	24Ap06Cn
Catharine	10	F	Unknown	24Ap06Cn
Bridget	.00	F	Infant	24Ap06Cn
FINIGAN, Mich.	29	M	Laborer	24Ap06Cn
WALSH, William	28	M	Laborer	24Ap06Cn
GREANEY, William	30	M	Laborer	24Ap06Cn
U	29	M	Laborer	24Ap06Cn
Judy	10	F	Unknown	24Ap06Cn
WARD, Thos.	19	M	Laborer	24Ap06Cn
LYNCH, John	30	M	Laborer	24Ap06Cn
WARD, Nancy	27	F	Laborer	24Ap06Cn
CONNELLY, Owen	60	M	Laborer	24Ap06Cn
WALSH, Arthur	48	M	Laborer	24Ap06Cn
NAUGHTEN, Mary	23	F	Unknown	24Ap06Cn
CAULFIELD, Michl.	30	M	Laborer	24Ap06Cn
Maria	28	F	Unknown	24Ap06Cn
PICKER, Michl.	27	M	Laborer	24Ap06Cn
Mary	29	F	Unknown	24Ap06Cn

NAMES OF PASSENGERS	AGE	SEX	OCCUPATIONS	DATE PORT SHIP
LYONS, Patt	44	M	Laborer	24Ap06Cn
LARDIN, John	40	M	Laborer	24Ap06Cn
Mary	36	F	Unknown	24Ap06Cn
DINSLAN, William	33	M	Laborer	24Ap06Cn
FAHEY, Patt	28	M	Laborer	24Ap06Cn
FOLAN, Patt	40	M	Laborer	24Ap06Cn
Barbara	51	F	Unknown	24Ap06Cn
CAULFIELD, Winifred	30	F	Unknown	24Ap06Cn
Catharine	27	F	Unknown	24Ap06Cn
MILLET, Daniel	40	M	Laborer	24Ap06Cn
Mary	42	F	Unknown	24Ap06Cn
KENNA, Brady	21	M	Laborer	24Ap06Cn
FLAHERTY, Biddy	20	F	Unknown	24Ap06Cn
CONNELLY, Biddy	40	F	Unknown	24Ap06Cn
Catharine	39	F	Unknown	24Ap06Cn
COSTELLO, Michl.	60	M	Laborer	24Ap06Cn
MCLAUGHLIN, John	40	M	Laborer	24Ap06Cn
Mary	38	F	Unknown	24Ap06Cn
SILVER, Kitty	21	F	Unknown	24Ap06Cn
HYNES, Mary	23	F	Unknown	24Ap06Cn
MORAN, Kitty	19	F	Unknown	24Ap06Cn
KEAN, William	17	M	Laborer	24Ap06Cn
GEAGEN, Patt	18	M	Laborer	24Ap06Cn
COLEMAN, Michl.	34	M	Laborer	24Ap06Cn
CALMER, Thos.	40	M	Laborer	24Ap06Cn
CLASBY, Honoria	19	F	Unknown	24Ap06Cn
MULLIN, Timothy	50	M	Laborer	24Ap06Cn
NOLAN, Michl.	49	M	Laborer	24Ap06Cn
GILL, Hines	30	F	Unknown	24Ap06Cn
CONLAN, Patt	29	M	Laborer	24Ap06Cn
SMITH, Patt	36	M	Laborer	24Ap06Cn
Mary	30	F	Unknown	24Ap06Cn
FAHEY, Biddy	21	F	Unknown	24Ap06Cn
Margaret	10	F	Unknown	24Ap06Cn
SMITH, Patt	7	M	Child	24Ap06Cn
John	5	M	Child	24Ap06Cn
KING, Matthew	30	M	Laborer	24Ap06Cn
Barbara	21	F	Unknown	24Ap06Cn
OBRIEN, Thos.	40	M	Laborer	24Ap06Cn
FLANIGAN, Matthew	38	M	Laborer	24Ap06Cn
OBRIEN, Mary	32	F	Unknown	24Ap06Cn
MCHUGO, John	40	M	Laborer	24Ap06Cn
SWEENEY, Patt	28	M	Laborer	24Ap06Cn
NOLAN, John	19	M	Laborer	24Ap06Cn
KING, Martin	30	M	Laborer	24Ap06Cn
Mick.	32	M	Laborer	24Ap06Cn
Catharine	6	F	Child	24Ap06Cn
MULIGAN, Michl.	29	M	Laborer	24Ap06Cn
BROWN, Mary	30	F	Unknown	24Ap06Cn
KING, Martin	42	M	Laborer	24Ap06Cn
MOLLOY, Martin	20	M	Laborer	24Ap06Cn
John	19	M	Laborer	24Ap06Cn
COX, Fanny	32	F	Unknown	24Ap06Cn
DUGGAN, Patt	41	M	Laborer	24Ap06Cn
Daniel	45	M	Laborer	24Ap06Cn
DAVIS, Mick	42	M	Laborer	24Ap06Cn
William	19	M	Laborer	24Ap06Cn
Sally	40	F	Unknown	24Ap06Cn
Biddy	12	F	Unknown	24Ap06Cn
Mary	9	F	Child	24Ap06Cn
Biddy	.00	F	Infant	24Ap06Cn
CAVANAGH, John	32	M	Laborer	24Ap06Cn
TOOLE, Barbara	18	F	Unknown	24Ap06Cn
FARRELL, John	22	M	Laborer	24Ap06Cn
HYNES, Edward	33	M	Laborer	24Ap06Cn
WALSH, Cath.	40	F	Unknown	24Ap06Cn
GORMAN, Peter	20	M	Laborer	24Ap06Cn
Mary	18	F	Unknown	24Ap06Cn
CANNON, Andrew	40	M	Laborer	24Ap06Cn
LYNCH, Patt	39	M	Laborer	24Ap06Cn
VAIL, Thos.	28	M	Laborer	24Ap06Cn
DAVIS, Bartly	42	F	Unknown	24Ap06Cn
DALEY, John	19	M	Laborer	24Ap06Cn
CONNELLY, Mary	41	F	Unknown	24Ap06Cn
MCHUGH, Mary-Ann	23	F	Unknown	24Ap06Cn

NAMES OF PASSENGERS	AGE	SEX	OCCUPATIONS	DATE PORT SHIP
BURKE, Thos.	20	M	Laborer	24Ap06Cn
James	19	M	Laborer	24Ap06Cn
BODKIN, Biddy	26	F	Unknown	24Ap06Cn
MELANY, Bidilia	00	U	Unknown	24Ap06Cn
James	00	M	Unknown	24Ap06Cn
GERATHY, Maria	00	F	Unknown	24Ap06Cn
HALLORAN, Mary	00	F	Unknown	24Ap06Cn

HENRY-CLAY 25 APRIL 1849

From Liverpool

NAMES OF PASSENGERS	AGE	SEX	OCCUPATIONS	DATE PORT SHIP
HAID, Patk.	28	M	Surveyor	25Ap02Co
Jane	25	F	Unknown	25Ap02Co
MCEWAN, John	21	M	Farmer	25Ap02Co
Saml.	26	M	Farmer	25Ap02Co
ELLIOTT, Richd.	36	M	Farmer	25Ap02Co
MURPHY, James	28	M	Farmer	25Ap02Co
NUGENT, John	26	M	Farmer	25Ap02Co
RIELLY, Patk.	24	M	Farmer	25Ap02Co
QUINN, Thos.	25	M	Clerk	25Ap02Co
WARD, Patk.	28	M	Farmer	25Ap02Co
CASEY, John	24	M	Farmer	25Ap02Co
OKEEFE, Michael	27	M	Farmer	25Ap02Co
SPILLANE, Thimothy	30	M	Clerk	25Ap02Co
Jane	32	F	Unknown	25Ap02Co
Ann	16	F	Unknown	25Ap02Co
MULLINS, Honora	24	F	Unknown	25Ap02Co
PAGAN, Peter	28	M	Farmer	25Ap02Co
Kate	24	F	Unknown	25Ap02Co
Ellen	.08	F	Infant	25Ap02Co
ORR, John	32	M	Farmer	25Ap02Co
Agnes	28	F	Farmer	25Ap02Co
Margt.	.08	F	Infant	25Ap02Co
Mary	18	F	Unknown	25Ap02Co
BOYD, Wm.	27	M	Farmer	25Ap02Co
CHARLES, John-W.	22	M	Farmer	25Ap02Co
Andrew	21	M	Farmer	25Ap02Co
CROMA, James	20	M	Farmer	25Ap02Co
WALLACE, Robert	26	M	Farmer	25Ap02Co
Thomas	22	M	Mechanic	25Ap02Co
SMITH, James	26	M	Clerk	25Ap02Co
HARRISON, Thomas	16	M	Unknown	25Ap02Co
TERNINER, Patrick	27	M	Mechanic	25Ap02Co
CORMACK, Patrick	24	M	Mechanic	25Ap02Co
SPILLANE, John	29	M	Mechanic	25Ap02Co
JOHNSTONE, Thos.	21	M	Mechanic	25Ap02Co
MCCABE, Luke	22	M	Mechanic	25Ap02Co
Bridget	20	F	Mechanic	25Ap02Co
HANLAN, Jane	20	F	Mechanic	25Ap02Co
FLANAGAN, Ed.	26	M	Farmer	25Ap02Co
MONK, Thomas	27	M	Mechanic	25Ap02Co
Elizabeth	22	F	Unknown	25Ap02Co
CAMPBELL, Brien	25	M	Farmer	25Ap02Co
CRAVEN, Patrick	21	M	Farmer	25Ap02Co
Mathew	20	M	Farmer	25Ap02Co
DYER, Owen	11	M	Tailor	25Ap02Co
Margt.	40	F	Unknown	25Ap02Co
John	22	M	Tailor	25Ap02Co
Kate	14	F	Unknown	25Ap02Co
Margt.	8	F	Child	25Ap02Co
Bridget	6	F	Child	25Ap02Co
DORRAN, John	26	M	Farmer	25Ap02Co
NUGENT, Margt.	20	F	Unknown	25Ap02Co
CASSIDY, Margt.	17	F	Unknown	25Ap02Co
BURN, Patk.	21	M	Farmer	25Ap02Co
KIDD, Wm.	22	M	Farmer	25Ap02Co
CONAGHAN, Lawrence	22	M	Farmer	25Ap02Co
MALOY, John	23	M	Mechanic	25Ap02Co

NAMES OF PASSENGERS	AGE	SEX	OCCUPATIONS	DATE PORT SHIP
REYNOLDS, James	28	M	Farmer	25Ap02Co
FADIGAN, Mary	26	F	Unknown	25Ap02Co
James	2	M	Child	25Ap02Co
Cathrine	.09	F	Infant	25Ap02Co
HOBBIE, John	22	M	Farmer	25Ap02Co
Patk.	18	M	Farmer	25Ap02Co
Bridget	20	F	Farmer	25Ap02Co
RYAN, Thomas	30	M	Farmer	25Ap02Co
FARREN, Patrick	18	M	Farmer	25Ap02Co
LEHANNIE, Mary	20	F	Unknown	25Ap02Co
GRADY, John	26	M	Farmer	25Ap02Co
Mary	16	F	Unknown	25Ap02Co
CHAPLIN, Wm.	53	M	Mechanic	25Ap02Co
MORRISON, John	20	M	Mechanic	25Ap02Co
DUNIGAN, Cathrine	16	F	Unknown	25Ap02Co
Bridget	11	F	Unknown	25Ap02Co
Thomas	14	M	Mechanic	25Ap02Co
TAYLOR, Alexr.	22	M	Mechanic	25Ap02Co
BARRON, Richd.	27	M	Farmer	25Ap02Co
John	30	M	Farmer	25Ap02Co
RIELLY, Edward	21	M	Farmer	25Ap02Co
LOGAN, Hanora	20	F	Farmer	25Ap02Co
LAWLYER, Ellen	10	F	Unknown	25Ap02Co
Thomas	4	M	Child	25Ap02Co
CARBERRY, James	20	M	Farmer	25Ap02Co
FIELDING, Thomas	20	M	Farmer	25Ap02Co
CANWORTH, Michael	21	M	Farmer	25Ap02Co
COYLE, Patrick	38	M	Farmer	25Ap02Co
FIELDING, Mary	20	F	Farmer	25Ap02Co
DOOLEY, Mary	20	F	Farmer	25Ap02Co
KENNY, John	30	M	Farmer	25Ap02Co
DILLON, Thomas	22	M	Farmer	25Ap02Co
MALONE, John	28	M	Farmer	25Ap02Co
KELLY, Patrick	20	M	Farmer	25Ap02Co
GAVGAN, Anthony	28	M	Farmer	25Ap02Co
MCCORMACK, John	27	M	Farmer	25Ap02Co
CONSTON, Patrick	20	M	Farmer	25Ap02Co
MURPHY, Micheal	26	M	Farmer	25Ap02Co
James	24	M	Farmer	25Ap02Co
Margt.	20	F	Unknown	25Ap02Co
MAHAN, Ellis	20	F	Farmer	25Ap02Co
LYLE, James	22	M	Farmer	25Ap02Co
WOODSIDE, John	26	M	Farmer	25Ap02Co
THOMSON, Robert	26	M	Farmer	25Ap02Co
RIELLY, Robert	21	M	Mechanic	25Ap02Co
MCALLISTER, Mary	21	F	Unknown	25Ap02Co
MCANANL, Ann	21	F	Unknown	25Ap02Co
DARGIN, Martin	27	M	Mechanic	25Ap02Co
Margt.	26	F	Mechanic	25Ap02Co
BURKE, Thomas	40	M	Farmer	25Ap02Co
Thomas-Jr.	15	M	Farmer	25Ap02Co
Thomas	20	M	Farmer	25Ap02Co
BAIN, Thimothy	11	M	Farmer	25Ap02Co
SMITH, Hellen	21	F	Unknown	25Ap02Co
Wm.	19	M	Farmer	25Ap02Co
CORLAN, Mick.	20	M	Farmer	25Ap02Co
SMITH, Wm.	25	M	Farmer	25Ap02Co
GARRITY, Peter	26	M	Farmer	25Ap02Co
SORRAHAN, James	21	M	Farmer	25Ap02Co
MOONEY, Mary	21	F	Farmer	25Ap02Co
FARDEN, Francis	15	F	Farmer	25Ap02Co
GALLAGHER, Mary	18	F	Unknown	25Ap02Co
JODROAN, Mary	10	F	Unknown	25Ap02Co
JOHNSTONE, John	23	M	Mechanic	25Ap02Co
DEMPSEY, Patk.	20	M	Farmer	25Ap02Co
HICKEY, John	45	M	Farmer	25Ap02Co
FIELD, Margt.	14	F	Unknown	25Ap02Co
DAVIS, Margt.	30	F	Unknown	25Ap02Co
Michael	30	M	Farmer	25Ap02Co
CASSELAY, Michael	30	M	Farmer	25Ap02Co
MALONE, Patk.	27	M	Farmer	25Ap02Co
DUFF, John	27	M	Farmer	25Ap02Co
DOWLIN, Thomas	23	M	Farmer	25Ap02Co
THALLON, James	46	M	Farmer	25Ap02Co
DOCHERTY, Henry	40	M	Farmer	25Ap02Co
SHERWOOD, Thos.	39	M	Farmer	25Ap02Co
BROWN, Mick.	20	M	Farmer	25Ap02Co
HAGAN, Jas.	20	M	Farmer	25Ap02Co
Jas.Jr.	21	M	Farmer	25Ap02Co
DONALD, Thomas	20	M	Farmer	25Ap02Co
CURRAN, Rose	20	F	Unknown	25Ap02Co
HAGAN, Eliza	18	F	Mechanic	25Ap02Co
Thomas	10	M	Unknown	25Ap02Co
John	9	M	Child	25Ap02Co
HIBE, Thos.	11	M	Unknown	25Ap02Co
HAGAN, James	44	M	Mechanic	25Ap02Co
Sophia	40	F	Unknown	25Ap02Co
Margret	7	F	Child	25Ap02Co
Alexr.	3	M	Child	25Ap02Co
MCLAUGHLAN, John	50	M	Farmer	25Ap02Co
THOMAS, Mary	48	F	Unknown	25Ap02Co
MCLAUGHLAN, Patrick	22	M	Farmer	25Ap02Co
Thomas	20	M	Farmer	25Ap02Co
Morris	14	M	Farmer	25Ap02Co
Ann	10	F	Unknown	25Ap02Co
FINN, Jeremiah	54	M	Farmer	25Ap02Co
Ellen	50	F	Unknown	25Ap02Co
John	22	M	Farmer	25Ap02Co
Ellen	20	F	Unknown	25Ap02Co
Died-At-Sea				
James	17	M	Farmer	25Ap02Co
Jeremiah	15	M	Farmer	25Ap02Co
Mary	14	F	Unknown	25Ap02Co
Elizabeth	11	F	Unknown	25Ap02Co
ROACH, David	25	M	Farmer	25Ap02Co
Ellen	28	F	Unknown	25Ap02Co
CONNOR, Danl.	25	M	Farmer	25Ap02Co
CONNELL, Danl.	40	M	Farmer	25Ap02Co
MCLOUAGHLIN, Cony.	28	M	Farmer	25Ap02Co
DONOHUE, Patk.	25	M	Farmer	25Ap02Co
HICKEY, Owen	25	M	Farmer	25Ap02Co
Ellen	22	F	Unknown	25Ap02Co
FINN, Daniel	30	M	Farmer	25Ap02Co
Mary	30	F	Unknown	25Ap02Co
John	2	M	Child	25Ap02Co
David	1	M	Child	25Ap02Co
NEWMAN, Mary	20	F	Unknown	25Ap02Co
HENDERSON, Isaac	25	M	Farmer	25Ap02Co
BROGAN, John	26	M	Mechanic	25Ap02Co
Mary	18	F	Unknown	25Ap02Co
Rose	16	F	Unknown	25Ap02Co
MCDONALD, Mary	18	F	Unknown	25Ap02Co
SMITH, James	28	M	Farmer	25Ap02Co
MCNAMARA, Ellen	36	F	Unknown	25Ap02Co
Ed	15	M	Farmer	25Ap02Co
Mary	9	F	Child	25Ap02Co
Kate	11	F	Unknown	25Ap02Co
BRANNAN, Thomas	22	M	Farmer	25Ap02Co
MORRISON, Micheal	23	M	Farmer	25Ap02Co
CARNEY, Micheal	20	M	Farmer	25Ap02Co
COY, Mary	50	F	Unknown	25Ap02Co
CLARK, John	3	M	Child	25Ap02Co
Margt.	5	F	Child	25Ap02Co
HARRISON, Ann	20	F	Unknown	25Ap02Co
DOLLAN, Ellen	20	F	Unknown	25Ap02Co
BRANNAN, Mary	20	F	Unknown	25Ap02Co
DOLLAN, Andrew	24	M	Farmer	25Ap02Co
FIELDING, Willm.	35	M	Farmer	25Ap02Co
BARTHY, Owen	40	M	Farmer	25Ap02Co
Thos.	20	M	Farmer	25Ap02Co
GORMAN, John	11	M	Mechanic	25Ap02Co
MURPHY, Mick	17	M	Mechanic	25Ap02Co
BRIEN, Patk.	18	M	Mechanic	25Ap02Co
GORMAN, Cathrine	18	F	Unknown	25Ap02Co
MCEWAN, Mary	31	F	Unknown	25Ap02Co
BAILEY, Joseph	31	M	Mechanic	25Ap02Co
Eliza	25	F	Unknown	25Ap02Co
MCCANN, Patk.	26	M	Farmer	25Ap02Co
DUFF, Thomas	21	M	Farmer	25Ap02Co
ROGERS, Edward	26	M	Farmer	25Ap02Co

NAMES OF PASSENGERS	AGE	SEX	OCCUPATIONS	DATE PORT SHIP
FITZPATRICK, Michael	22	M	Farmer	25Ap02Co
BOFFY, Micheal	36	M	Farmer	25Ap02Co
BROFFY, Kate	30	F	Unknown	25Ap02Co
GREEK, James	20	M	Farmer	25Ap02Co
Anna	21	F	Unknown	25Ap02Co
Ann	17	F	Unknown	25Ap02Co
BRAY, Kit	26	M	Farmer	25Ap02Co
Mary	30	F	Unknown	25Ap02Co
Winey	3	F	Child	25Ap02Co
Martin	.06	M	Infant	25Ap02Co
DRURY, U-Mrs.	34	F	Unknown	25Ap02Co
HEWITT, Mary	22	F	Unknown	25Ap02Co
HEFFERNAN, Danl.	27	M	Farmer	25Ap02Co
MURPHY, Patk.	36	M	Unknown	25Ap02Co
TIGHE, Wm.	32	M	Unknown	25Ap02Co
TWIST, Mary	65	F	Unknown	25Ap02Co
GILLIGAN, Patk.	15	M	Mechanic	25Ap02Co
Bridget	10	F	Unknown	25Ap02Co
CARRAGHAN, Mary	17	F	Unknown	25Ap02Co
MOONEY, Kate	18	F	Unknown	25Ap02Co
DARBY, Ann	20	F	Unknown	25Ap02Co
KELLY, Kate	20	F	Unknown	25Ap02Co
DEVINE, Anna	18	F	Unknown	25Ap02Co
RIELLY, Lewis	50	M	Farmer	25Ap02Co
MALONE, Sally	20	F	Unknown	25Ap02Co
DORRAN, Archd.	24	M	Farmer	25Ap02Co
EAGLE, Patk.	22	M	Farmer	25Ap02Co
MURPHY, Richd.	27	M	Farmer	25Ap02Co
HOPKINS, Simon	28	M	Farmer	25Ap02Co
Margt.	27	F	Unknown	25Ap02Co
John	.02	M	Infant	25Ap02Co
SWEENIE, Margt.	60	F	Unknown	25Ap02Co
LONGHRAN, John	14	M	Farmer	25Ap02Co
CONNELL, John	27	M	Farmer	25Ap02Co
KELLY, Thos.	3	M	Child	25Ap02Co
REILLY, Kit	28	M	Unknown	25Ap02Co
Judith	27	F	Unknown	25Ap02Co
GOLDTHORP, Wm.	26	M	Farmer	25Ap02Co
DOWNEY, Donald	40	M	Unknown	25Ap02Co
LYNCH, Mick	22	M	Unknown	25Ap02Co
MCPARLAND, Charles	40	M	Unknown	25Ap02Co
WELSH, Honora	60	F	Unknown	25Ap02Co
Wm.	20	M	Farmer	25Ap02Co
Ed.	18	M	Farmer	25Ap02Co
THALLON, James	18	M	Unknown	25Ap02Co
Kate	42	F	Unknown	25Ap02Co
John	15	M	Farmer	25Ap02Co
Patk.	13	M	Farmer	25Ap02Co
Thomas	6	M	Child	25Ap02Co
Mick.	11	M	Unknown	25Ap02Co
James	2	M	Child	25Ap02Co
Cathrine	.01	F	Infant	25Ap02Co
CALLAGAN, Thomas	26	M	Farmer	25Ap02Co
CARTERRY, Hugh	24	M	Farmer	25Ap02Co
Terry	20	M	Farmer	25Ap02Co
CALLAGAN, Thos.	60	M	Farmer	25Ap02Co
LYNCH, Mary	19	F	Unknown	25Ap02Co
GARRITY, Mary	2	F	Child	25Ap02Co
GRUMLEY, Margt.	19	F	Unknown	25Ap02Co
RIELLY, Nancy	20	F	Unknown	25Ap02Co
FAIRLEY, Thomas	26	M	Farmer	25Ap02Co
HANNULL, Thomas	21	M	Farmer	25Ap02Co
HODGSON, Thomas	20	M	Farmer	25Ap02Co
DRUNN, Jerry	50	M	Farmer	25Ap02Co
CONRAGHAN, Margt.	60	F	Unknown	25Ap02Co
LONRAGHAN, Mary	21	F	Unknown	25Ap02Co
Hanora	21	F	Unknown	25Ap02Co
Thomas	18	M	Farmer	25Ap02Co
Eliza	14	F	Unknown	25Ap02Co
DESKIN, Thomas	18	M	Farmer	25Ap02Co
WHELLAN, Micheal	25	M	Farmer	25Ap02Co
FLINN, Morries	26	M	Farmer	25Ap02Co
HAYS, Mick	18	M	Farmer	25Ap02Co
ROBERTS, Biddy	19	F	Farmer	25Ap02Co
HAYS, Mary	18	F	Unknown	25Ap02Co

NAMES OF PASSENGERS	AGE	SEX	OCCUPATIONS	DATE PORT SHIP
HAMMELL, Jane	18	F	Unknown	25Ap02Co
LYNCH, James	19	M	Farmer	25Ap02Co
BRADY, John	21	M	Farmer	25Ap02Co
BURN, John	14	M	Farmer	25Ap02Co
CONLAN, Esther	30	F	Unknown	25Ap02Co
Mary	11	F	Unknown	25Ap02Co
Fanny	8	F	Child	25Ap02Co
Thos.	7	M	Child	25Ap02Co
John	3	M	Child	25Ap02Co
KILROY, Anna	22	F	Unknown	25Ap02Co
WARD, Mary	24	F	Unknown	25Ap02Co
CURTIS, Judith	14	F	Unknown	25Ap02Co
CONAGHAN, Mary	14	F	Unknown	25Ap02Co
CUITH, Mary	23	F	Unknown	25Ap02Co
HANKETT, Bridget	23	F	Unknown	25Ap02Co
ALLEN, Rebecca	28	F	Unknown	25Ap02Co
MALOY, Anna	23	F	Unknown	25Ap02Co
YOUNG, Godfrey	22	M	Unknown	25Ap02Co
Charles	26	M	Unknown	25Ap02Co

MARGARET 25 APRIL 1849

From Glasgow

NAMES OF PASSENGERS	AGE	SEX	OCCUPATIONS	DATE PORT SHIP
MCALLISTER, Catherine	45	F	Unknown	25Ap04Cs
Mary	8	F	Child	25Ap04Cs
Daniel	6	M	Child	25Ap04Cs
Angus	2	M	Child	25Ap04Cs
LOWRIE, Francis	34	M	Miner	25Ap04Cs
Jean	33	F	Unknown	25Ap04Cs
Jean	11	F	Unknown	25Ap04Cs
Mary	9	F	Child	25Ap04Cs
William	8	M	Child	25Ap04Cs
David	5	M	Child	25Ap04Cs
Andrew	3	M	Child	25Ap04Cs
Jessie	2	M	Child	25Ap04Cs
FULTON, John	33	M	Blacksmith	25Ap04Cs
Isabella	27	F	Unknown	25Ap04Cs
Joie	9	F	Child	25Ap04Cs
Jeanie	6	F	Child	25Ap04Cs
Margaret	5	F	Child	25Ap04Cs
Catherine	2	F	Child	25Ap04Cs
BROWNLIE, James	35	M	Blacksmith	25Ap04Cs
William	32	M	Unknown	25Ap04Cs
MCROSSAN, Hugh	26	M	Grocer	25Ap04Cs
Mary	26	F	Unknown	25Ap04Cs
Mary	2	F	Child	25Ap04Cs
Helen	.07	F	Infant	25Ap04Cs
Joseph	24	M	Cbtmkr	25Ap04Cs
Agnes	24	F	Unknown	25Ap04Cs
John	35	M	Laborer	25Ap04Cs
Helen	28	F	Unknown	25Ap04Cs
Thomas	8	M	Child	25Ap04Cs
Christina	6	F	Child	25Ap04Cs
LINDSAY, Donald	27	M	Forgeman	25Ap04Cs
Jean	26	F	Unknown	25Ap04Cs
GILCHRIST, John	35	M	Contractor	25Ap04Cs
Charles	23	M	Servant	25Ap04Cs
Thomas	10	M	None	25Ap04Cs
Jannet	18	F	None	25Ap04Cs
CAMERON, Archd.	34	M	Laborer	25Ap04Cs
CHARLISTON, George	30	M	Weaver	25Ap04Cs
Mary	30	F	Unknown	25Ap04Cs
SMITH, Mark	30	M	Smith	25Ap04Cs
Isabella	30	F	Unknown	25Ap04Cs
SEMPLETON, Mary	16	F	Servant	25Ap04Cs
SIMPSON, Thomas	26	M	Laborer	25Ap04Cs
HISLOP, John	24	M	Laborer	25Ap04Cs
LAWRIE, Robert	13	M	None	25Ap04Cs

NAMES OF PASSENGERS	AGE	SEX	OCCUPATIONS	DATE PORT SHIP
BUCHAN, William	22	M	Smith	25Ap04Cs
RODEY, Mary	18	F	Servant	25Ap04Cs
OWENS, Ann-Jean	16	F	Servant	25Ap04Cs
Daniel	8	M	Child	25Ap04Cs
Peter	5	M	Child	25Ap04Cs
MAXWELL, James	30	M	Joiner	25Ap04Cs
Margaret	24	F	Unknown	25Ap04Cs
FREELY, Betsey	19	F	Servant	25Ap04Cs
MAXWELL, Susan	10	F	None	25Ap04Cs
GRAHAM, William	30	M	Upholsterer	25Ap04Cs
JOHNSTON, Peter	24	M	Shoemaker	25Ap04Cs
GILCHRIST, Dora	48	F	Unknown	25Ap04Cs
William	25	M	Miner	25Ap04Cs
Marion	25	F	Servant	25Ap04Cs
PARK, George	24	M	Laborer	25Ap04Cs
Agnes	23	F	Unknown	25Ap04Cs
RONALD, Robert	42	M	Farmer	25Ap04Cs
FEE, Alexander	21	M	Seaman	25Ap04Cs
FOTHERINGHAM, Jane	44	F	Unknown	25Ap04Cs
William	21	M	Laborer	25Ap04Cs
Alexander	19	M	Laborer	25Ap04Cs
Margaret	15	F	Servant	25Ap04Cs
Jean	9	F	Child	25Ap04Cs
Mary	7	F	Child	25Ap04Cs
Ann	7	F	Child	25Ap04Cs
TAYLOR, William	40	M	Joiner	25Ap04Cs
Anne	38	F	Unknown	25Ap04Cs
COWAN, James	19	M	Mercer	25Ap04Cs
WATSON, Alexander	25	M	Cbtmkr	25Ap04Cs
EVANS, Joseph	30	M	Merchant	25Ap04Cs
MILLEN, Robert	23	M	Clerk	25Ap04Cs
BURTON, Jos.S.	30	M	Joiner	25Ap04Cs
MILLER, David	28	M	Joiner	25Ap04Cs
CAIRNS, Robert	26	M	Joiner	25Ap04Cs
David	24	M	Joiner	25Ap04Cs
BREMNER, James	37	M	Joiner	25Ap04Cs
TORRANCE, John	65	M	Joiner	25Ap04Cs
FAULDS, Margaret	25	F	Unknown	25Ap04Cs
Jannet	5	F	Child	25Ap04Cs
Euphemia	1	F	Child	25Ap04Cs
RAMSEY, James	50	M	Gdnr	25Ap04Cs
Ellen	48	F	Unknown	25Ap04Cs
James	12	M	None	25Ap04Cs
Ellen	11	F	None	25Ap04Cs
LESLIE, William	23	M	Currier	25Ap04Cs
Agnes	22	F	Unknown	25Ap04Cs
Christina	2	F	Child	25Ap04Cs
MCINTYRE, Dennis	30	M	Laborer	25Ap04Cs
REID, James	22	M	Farmer	25Ap04Cs
THORBURN, James	50	M	Farmer	25Ap04Cs
Mary	55	F	Unknown	25Ap04Cs
SOMERVILLE, William	28	M	Farmer	25Ap04Cs
Mary	26	F	Unknown	25Ap04Cs
James	2	M	Child	25Ap04Cs
Christina	2	F	Child	25Ap04Cs
Thomas	28	M	Farmer	25Ap04Cs
MILNE, George	22	M	Farmer	25Ap04Cs
CALDER, James	24	M	Joiner	25Ap04Cs
WIER, John	21	M	Miner	25Ap04Cs
MCPHAIL, Charles	21	M	Hatter	25Ap04Cs
Mary	21	F	Unknown	25Ap04Cs
Robert	30	M	Hatter	25Ap04Cs
Jonathan	3	M	Child	25Ap04Cs
James	1	M	Child	25Ap04Cs
DEWAN, John	27	M	Mason	25Ap04Cs
Mary	27	F	Unknown	25Ap04Cs
George	4	M	Child	25Ap04Cs
Ellen	3	F	Child	25Ap04Cs
William	2	M	Child	25Ap04Cs
RUSSEL, Alexander	27	M	Miner	25Ap04Cs
Jane	27	F	Unknown	25Ap04Cs
Mary	4	F	Child	25Ap04Cs
Ellen	10	F	None	25Ap04Cs
Thomas	22	M	Miner	25Ap04Cs
[illegible]ASTON, James	22	M	Miner	25Ap04Cs

NAMES OF PASSENGERS	AGE	SEX	OCCUPATIONS	DATE PORT SHIP
MCEWAN, George	22	M	Hatter	25Ap04Cs
WHITE, John	26	M	Stctr	25Ap04Cs
MITCHELL, Robert	26	M	Stctr	25Ap04Cs
STEWARD, Edward	27	M	Currier	25Ap04Cs
Helen	27	F	Unknown	25Ap04Cs
GALLAGHER, Susan	19	F	Servant	25Ap04Cs
BROUGHTON, John	25	M	Blacksmith	25Ap04Cs
Mary	25	F	Unknown	25Ap04Cs
Yenk.	.06	F	Infant	25Ap04Cs
MCEWEN, John	26	M	Miner	25Ap04Cs
RIDD, Thomas	24	M	Smith	25Ap04Cs
MATHUSON, John	26	M	Tailor	25Ap04Cs
WILSON, John	22	M	Tailor	25Ap04Cs
KIDSTOW, Alexander	29	M	Engineer	25Ap04Cs
WILSON, John	28	M	Engineer	25Ap04Cs
MUTRIE, John	18	M	Bxmrfy	25Ap04Cs
Hugh	16	M	Unknown	25Ap04Cs
Thomas	21	M	Blacksmith	25Ap04Cs
NIELSON, Jannet	20	F	Weaver	25Ap04Cs
Mary	17	F	Servant	25Ap04Cs
James	13	M	None	25Ap04Cs
Thomas	7	M	Child	25Ap04Cs
Gaven	5	M	Child	25Ap04Cs
Margaret	3	F	Child	25Ap04Cs
William	1	M	Child	25Ap04Cs
Jane	40	F	Unknown	25Ap04Cs
DUNBAR, William	31	M	Laborer	25Ap04Cs
KING, Marion	30	F	Servant	25Ap04Cs
STEELE, Mathew	7	M	Child	25Ap04Cs
MCLAUGHLIN, John	20	M	Mechanic	25Ap04Cs
Thaddeus	22	M	Mechanic	25Ap04Cs
MARTIN, William	25	M	Joiner	25Ap04Cs
DEWAN, James	23	M	Joiner	25Ap04Cs
Thomas	24	M	Joiner	25Ap04Cs
MCDONALD, Jas.	30	M	Potter	25Ap04Cs
INGLIS, George	34	M	Potter	25Ap04Cs
DAVIDSON, William	24	M	Flaxdr	25Ap04Cs
GILCHRIST, David	7	M	Child	25Ap04Cs
PARK, Agnes	8	F	Child	25Ap04Cs
STEWARD, James	3	M	Child	25Ap04Cs
BOYCE, Francis	30	M	Weaver	25Ap04Cs
BARTON, James	25	M	Cooper	25Ap04Cs
PARKER, Agnes	17	F	Servant	25Ap04Cs
KELLY, Edward	22	M	Laborer	25Ap04Cs
DERR, Michael	23	M	Laborer	25Ap04Cs
BANNIGAN, Patrick	18	M	Laborer	25Ap04Cs
James	15	M	Laborer	25Ap04Cs
BLACK, David	24	M	Joiner	25Ap04Cs
BONIE, William	27	M	Laborer	25Ap04Cs
Mary	26	F	Unknown	25Ap04Cs
Agnes	5	F	Child	25Ap04Cs
RUSHERFORD, A.	24	M	Cooper	25Ap04Cs
GORDON, George-A.	24	M	Clerk	25Ap04Cs
KIDD, Jane-A.	30	F	Servant	25Ap04Cs
HAMILTON, John	45	M	Farmer	25Ap04Cs
KIDD, Ann	2	F	Child	25Ap04Cs
LIDDELE, Andrew	30	M	Surgeon	25Ap04Cs
DENHAM, George	1	M	Child	25Ap04Cs
WILLIAMS, George	30	M	Laborer	25Ap04Cs
DENHAM, Mary	24	F	Servant	25Ap04Cs

DROMAHARN 25 APRIL 1849

From Sligo

NAMES OF PASSENGERS	AGE	SEX	OCCUPATIONS	DATE PORT SHIP
GILGAN, Mary	45	F	Unknown	25Ap21Cp
Bridget	17	F	Unknown	25Ap21Cp
Matthew	14	M	Unknown	25Ap21Cp
SCALLEY, Bernard	25	M	Unknown	25Ap21Cp

NAMES OF PASSENGERS	AGE	SEX	OCCUPATIONS	DATE PORT SHIP
OBRIEN, James	40	M	Laborer	25Ap21Cp
MCCOY, Mary	22	F	Unknown	25Ap21Cp
SEXTON, Patrick	22	M	Laborer	25Ap21Cp
Cathe.	17	F	Unknown	25Ap21Cp
KIOLHAN, Bridget	18	F	Unknown	25Ap21Cp
JUDGE, John	30	M	Carpenter	25Ap21Cp
Cathr.	30	F	Unknown	25Ap21Cp
John	3	M	Child	25Ap21Cp
Mary	.00	F	Infant	25Ap21Cp
MORAIN, John	30	M	Farmer	25Ap21Cp
Bridget	20	F	Unknown	25Ap21Cp
Mary	.00	F	Infant	25Ap21Cp
WATERS, Mary	20	F	Unknown	25Ap21Cp
CAVENY, Mary	20	F	Unknown	25Ap21Cp
Ellen	22	F	Unknown	25Ap21Cp
MIGHAN, James	30	M	Farmer	25Ap21Cp
MCCORMICK, Bryan	22	M	Laborer	25Ap21Cp
MCCARROLL, John	18	M	Laborer	25Ap21Cp
GILLAN, Cath.	20	F	Unknown	25Ap21Cp
Eliza	17	F	Unknown	25Ap21Cp
FONLEY, Doley	25	M	Laborer	25Ap21Cp
CAMPBELL, Margt.	20	F	Unknown	25Ap21Cp
Anne	.00	F	Infant	25Ap21Cp
DOWNES, Ellen	18	F	Unknown	25Ap21Cp
MARAHEN, Timothy	30	M	Farmer	25Ap21Cp
Mary	22	F	Unknown	25Ap21Cp
Bridget	.00	F	Infant	25Ap21Cp
REYNOLDS, John	20	M	Unknown	25Ap21Cp
MONAHAN, John	19	M	Farmer	25Ap21Cp
MCGOWAN, Thos.	40	M	Farmer	25Ap21Cp
Edwd.	40	M	Farmer	25Ap21Cp
BREHANY, Thos.	30	M	Farmer	25Ap21Cp
Bridget	30	F	Unknown	25Ap21Cp
CROWN, Martin	23	M	Laborer	25Ap21Cp
GRUNNING, George	20	M	Unknown	25Ap21Cp
CONWAY, Mary	25	F	Unknown	25Ap21Cp
JUDGE, Edward	5	M	Child	25Ap21Cp
MEHAN, Darby	35	M	Laborer	25Ap21Cp
DOWD, Mich.	50	M	Laborer	25Ap21Cp
Anne	50	F	Unknown	25Ap21Cp
Anne	23	F	Unknown	25Ap21Cp
John	22	M	Laborer	25Ap21Cp
Patrick	20	M	Laborer	25Ap21Cp
Hugh	28	M	Laborer	25Ap21Cp
FINNENN, James	26	M	Laborer	25Ap21Cp
Bridget	24	F	Unknown	25Ap21Cp
ANDERSON, Bridget	18	F	Unknown	25Ap21Cp
CROWN, Mary	26	F	Unknown	25Ap21Cp
Anne	27	F	Unknown	25Ap21Cp
FIRNAN, Thomas	22	M	Laborer	25Ap21Cp
MULHERIN, John	40	M	Farmer	25Ap21Cp
FLANAGAN, Thomas	24	M	Farmer	25Ap21Cp
Bridget	22	F	Unknown	25Ap21Cp
Mary	4	F	Child	25Ap21Cp
Catherine	2	F	Child	25Ap21Cp
Bridget	.00	F	Infant	25Ap21Cp
BOLAND, John	20	M	Laborer	25Ap21Cp
TUCKER, Catherine	17	F	Unknown	25Ap21Cp
HOPPER, Cathe.	20	F	Unknown	25Ap21Cp
FOLEY, Ellen	18	F	Unknown	25Ap21Cp
MCGARRY, James	20	M	Laborer	25Ap21Cp
Bridget	17	F	Unknown	25Ap21Cp
MCMANUS, James	20	M	Laborer	25Ap21Cp
FOX, John	28	M	Laborer	25Ap21Cp
MCGUIRE, James	50	M	Farmer	25Ap21Cp
MCGUINESS, John	20	M	Farmer	25Ap21Cp
Sarah	16	F	Unknown	25Ap21Cp
ROUSE, Cath.	40	F	Unknown	25Ap21Cp
Patrick	4	M	Child	25Ap21Cp
MCGOVERN, James	15	M	Laborer	25Ap21Cp
LYNN, Michael	18	M	Laborer	25Ap21Cp
CULLEN, Lazarus	30	M	Laborer	25Ap21Cp
RORKE, Patrick	30	M	Laborer	25Ap21Cp
KENNY, Hugh	35	M	Upholsterer	25Ap21Cp
FOY, Winifred	35	F	Unknown	25Ap21Cp
MORAHAN, John	35	M	Laborer	25Ap21Cp
REGAN, Farrell	19	M	Laborer	25Ap21Cp
BEGLY, James	63	M	Laborer	25Ap21Cp
Mary	20	F	Unknown	25Ap21Cp
CARTHY, John	37	M	Surveyor	25Ap21Cp
Mary	35	F	Unknown	25Ap21Cp
John	.00	M	Infant	25Ap21Cp
COONEY, Ellen	20	F	Unknown	25Ap21Cp
HIGGINS, Ann	20	F	Unknown	25Ap21Cp
HUGHES, James	26	M	Farmer	25Ap21Cp
KELLY, Charles	25	M	Laborer	25Ap21Cp
Sarah	60	F	Unknown	25Ap21Cp
Sarah	50	F	Unknown	25Ap21Cp
REGAN, Mary	8	F	Child	25Ap21Cp
DEAN, Bridget	20	F	Child	25Ap21Cp
MELANY, Hugh	35	M	Laborer	25Ap21Cp
Mary	30	F	Unknown	25Ap21Cp
Owen	13	M	Laborer	25Ap21Cp
Hugh	8	M	Child	25Ap21Cp
HEALY, Marcus	21	M	Laborer	25Ap21Cp
LEVENS, Patrick	23	M	Laborer	25Ap21Cp
BARTLEY, Miles	40	M	Laborer	25Ap21Cp
Bridget	35	F	Unknown	25Ap21Cp
Patrick	9	M	Child	25Ap21Cp
Michael	7	M	Child	25Ap21Cp
Mary	.00	F	Infant	25Ap21Cp
DEVANY, John	23	M	Farmer	25Ap21Cp
FAHY, John	28	M	Farmer	25Ap21Cp
Mary	28	F	Unknown	25Ap21Cp
Ann	.00	F	Infant	25Ap21Cp
HUNT, James	23	M	Laborer	25Ap21Cp
Cathn.	21	F	Unknown	25Ap21Cp
TIGHE, Michael	53	M	Laborer	25Ap21Cp
Cathn.	30	F	Unknown	25Ap21Cp
Kelly	17	M	Unknown	25Ap21Cp
John	12	M	Unknown	25Ap21Cp
Winifred	13	F	Unknown	25Ap21Cp
Dominick	6	M	Child	25Ap21Cp
Bridget	3	F	Child	25Ap21Cp
Michael	1	M	Child	25Ap21Cp
Died-At-Sea				
MCSHANEY, Mich.	20	M	Farmer	25Ap21Cp
CONWAY, James	45	M	Farmer	25Ap21Cp
Jane	40	F	Unknown	25Ap21Cp
Patrick	22	M	Farmer	25Ap21Cp
James	16	M	Laborer	25Ap21Cp
Jane	15	F	Laborer	25Ap21Cp
Mary	21	F	Laborer	25Ap21Cp
Sarah	14	F	Unknown	25Ap21Cp
John	12	M	Laborer	25Ap21Cp
Cathn.	4	F	Child	25Ap21Cp
HARAN, Patrick	40	M	Farmer	25Ap21Cp
Ann	35	F	Unknown	25Ap21Cp
Patrick	12	M	Unknown	25Ap21Cp
Mary	10	F	Unknown	25Ap21Cp
Bridget	8	F	Child	25Ap21Cp
Thomas	6	M	Child	25Ap21Cp
Margaret	4	F	Child	25Ap21Cp
Hugh	.00	M	Infant	25Ap21Cp
Died-At-Sea				
MCDONAGH, Mary	30	F	Unknown	25Ap21Cp
BROWN, Margaret	25	F	Unknown	25Ap21Cp
MCYANAGHAN, Wm.	22	M	Merchant	25Ap21Cp
POWELL, Jane	36	F	Unknown	25Ap21Cp
Mary	24	F	Unknown	25Ap21Cp
Susan	27	F	Unknown	25Ap21Cp
Julia	6	F	Child	25Ap21Cp
Margt.	4	F	Child	25Ap21Cp
Fanny	2	F	Child	25Ap21Cp
WOODLAND, Isabella	22	F	Unknown	25Ap21Cp
DUNCAN, Patrick	16	M	Farmer	25Ap21Cp
DOLAN, John	25	M	Farmer	25Ap21Cp
DEVANY, Michl.	30	M	Farmer	25Ap21Cp
CARROLL, Jane	25	F	Farmer	25Ap21Cp
CASCADDON, John	20	M	Farmer	25Ap21Cp

NAMES OF PASSENGERS	AGE	SEX	OCCUPATIONS	DATE PORT SHIP
CASCADDON, Mary-Anne	20	F	Unknown	25Ap21Cp
CALLAGHAN, Mary	20	F	Unknown	25Ap21Cp
Laura	25	F	Unknown	25Ap21Cp
OHARRA, John	30	M	Tailor	25Ap21Cp
DOLAN, Winifred	36	F	Unknown	25Ap21Cp
FOLEY, Turner	20	M	Merchant	25Ap21Cp
KEVINS, Andrew	29	M	Unknown	25Ap21Cp
MOONEY, Patrick	35	M	Farmer	25Ap21Cp

CAROLINE-READ 25 APRIL 1849

From Liverpool

NAMES OF PASSENGERS	AGE	SEX	OCCUPATIONS	DATE PORT SHIP
FAGAN, Pat	15	M	Laborer	25Ap02Ct
CRATON, William	36	M	Laborer	25Ap02Ct
Thomas	14	M	Laborer	25Ap02Ct
KENNEY, Joseph	52	M	Hatter	25Ap02Ct
DONNELLY, Edward	40	M	Laborer	25Ap02Ct
MCGUIRE, James	30	M	Farmer	25Ap02Ct
C.	28	M	Laborer	25Ap02Ct
Elenor	16	F	Laborer	25Ap02Ct
QUIN, Andrew	20	M	Laborer	25Ap02Ct
Catherin	17	F	Laborer	25Ap02Ct
FLANAGEN, Mary	12	F	Laborer	25Ap02Ct
BRENNEN, Michael	24	M	Laborer	25Ap02Ct
William	24	M	Laborer	25Ap02Ct
Margaret	20	F	Laborer	25Ap02Ct
John	11	M	Laborer	25Ap02Ct
FARREL, John	20	M	Laborer	25Ap02Ct
CONSIDINE, Michael	24	M	Laborer	25Ap02Ct
KELLY, Thomas	20	M	Laborer	25Ap02Ct
Bridget	22	F	Laborer	25Ap02Ct
BIRD, Michael	18	M	Laborer	25Ap02Ct
GAFNEY, Pat	45	M	Laborer	25Ap02Ct
MCGUNY, Mary	20	F	Laborer	25Ap02Ct
FLANAGEN, Mary	20	F	Laborer	25Ap02Ct
BRANNAN, Ellen	20	F	Laborer	25Ap02Ct
UFFY, Jane	40	F	Laborer	25Ap02Ct
Pat	30	M	Laborer	25Ap02Ct
Dan	16	M	Laborer	25Ap02Ct
Edward	12	M	Laborer	25Ap02Ct
Thos.	9	M	Child	25Ap02Ct
Eliza	7	F	Child	25Ap02Ct
Peter	.00	M	Infant	25Ap02Ct
NGEL, Maria	15	F	Laborer	25Ap02Ct
ORTIS, Sarah	17	F	Laborer	25Ap02Ct
AHAGAN, Lucy	24	F	Laborer	25Ap02Ct
YONS, Thos.	28	M	Laborer	25Ap02Ct
Julia	20	F	Laborer	25Ap02Ct
OWE, Bridget	20	F	Laborer	25Ap02Ct
ENNEY, Isabel	20	F	Laborer	25Ap02Ct
ONAGHAN, Michael	24	M	Laborer	25Ap02Ct
ALLAGHER, Amelia	28	F	Laborer	25Ap02Ct
Ellen	.00	F	Infant	25Ap02Ct
HRISTY, George	16	M	Laborer	25Ap02Ct
HORTY, Mary	12	F	Laborer	25Ap02Ct
CKAGEN, Michel	18	M	Laborer	25Ap02Ct
EHOE, Jo	19	M	Tailor	25Ap02Ct
AGRA, Bridget	20	F	Laborer	25Ap02Ct
Micahel	24	M	Laborer	25Ap02Ct
RENNAN, Mary	20	F	Laborer	25Ap02Ct
HERIDAN, Edward	22	M	Laborer	25Ap02Ct
Margaret	20	F	Laborer	25Ap02Ct
ANAN, John	21	M	Laborer	25Ap02Ct
Ann	18	F	Laborer	25Ap02Ct
DEVITT, Thomas	15	M	Blacksmith	25Ap02Ct
Alexander	13	M	Laborer	25Ap02Ct
LEY, Margaret	20	F	Laborer	25Ap02Ct
YNCH, Thomas	21	M	Laborer	25Ap02Ct
LYNCH, Bridget	40	F	Laborer	25Ap02Ct
ARMSTRONG, James	24	M	Joiner	25Ap02Ct
Eliza	.00	F	Infant	25Ap02Ct
Mary	29	F	Laborer	25Ap02Ct
MAGNELL, Robert	28	M	Laborer	25Ap02Ct
MOELICK, James	22	M	Laborer	25Ap02Ct
Michael	12	M	Laborer	25Ap02Ct
IRENE, Joseph	23	M	Laborer	25Ap02Ct
Thomas	17	M	Laborer	25Ap02Ct
MAHER, Josef	30	M	Laborer	25Ap02Ct
Josef	17	M	Laborer	25Ap02Ct
Mary	23	F	Laborer	25Ap02Ct
OBRIEN, Thomas	22	M	Farmer	25Ap02Ct
Margaret	30	F	Farmer	25Ap02Ct
JACKSON, John	22	M	Farmer	25Ap02Ct
BERGAN, Mary	24	F	Laborer	25Ap02Ct
Margaret	22	F	Laborer	25Ap02Ct
LENTHAN, William	22	M	Farmer	25Ap02Ct
CORMACK, Mary	20	F	Farmer	25Ap02Ct
John	35	M	Farmer	25Ap02Ct
Ellen	11	F	Farmer	25Ap02Ct
John	9	M	Child	25Ap02Ct
Mary	7	F	Child	25Ap02Ct
Thomas	5	M	Child	25Ap02Ct
Margaret	2	F	Child	25Ap02Ct
Johanna	.00	F	Infant	25Ap02Ct
MORRIS, John	22	M	Farmer	25Ap02Ct
James	20	M	Joiner	25Ap02Ct
Mary	42	F	Laborer	25Ap02Ct
MURPHY, Michael	22	M	Laborer	25Ap02Ct
QUIGLEY, James	22	M	Farmer	25Ap02Ct
COMMOND, James	22	M	Farmer	25Ap02Ct
GRAHAM, Pat	28	M	Farmer	25Ap02Ct
Mary	28	F	Farmer	25Ap02Ct
Liney	19	F	Farmer	25Ap02Ct
GILROY, Thos.	17	M	Farmer	25Ap02Ct
Mary	4	F	Child	25Ap02Ct
Margaret	22	F	Farmer	25Ap02Ct
Thos.	.00	M	Infant	25Ap02Ct
GARSHAM, William	25	M	Farmer	25Ap02Ct
REILY, Margaret	23	F	Farmer	25Ap02Ct
MOORE, Andrew	35	M	Laborer	25Ap02Ct
Mary	11	F	Laborer	25Ap02Ct
Hana	13	F	Laborer	25Ap02Ct
Pat	6	M	Child	25Ap02Ct
Catherin	3	F	Child	25Ap02Ct
DOOLAN, Bridget	16	F	Laborer	25Ap02Ct
GROGAN, Mary	12	F	Laborer	25Ap02Ct
JERVITT, William	30	M	Laborer	25Ap02Ct
BRADAY, Peter	21	M	Surveyor	25Ap02Ct
FARRELL, Pat	22	M	Surveyor	25Ap02Ct
CHESTNUT, Pat	28	M	Laborer	25Ap02Ct
BYRN, Pat	30	M	Laborer	25Ap02Ct
FURLEY, Hugh	20	M	Laborer	25Ap02Ct
BYRN, Thos.	16	M	Laborer	25Ap02Ct
CASEY, Pat	27	M	Laborer	25Ap02Ct
Jack	28	M	Laborer	25Ap02Ct
MCGURY, Mary	18	F	Laborer	25Ap02Ct
REYNOLDS, Elen	30	F	Laborer	25Ap02Ct
DUNE, Judy	20	F	Laborer	25Ap02Ct
Michael	18	M	Laborer	25Ap02Ct
Pat	12	M	Laborer	25Ap02Ct
MARTERON, Owen	40	M	Laborer	25Ap02Ct
Law.	18	M	Laborer	25Ap02Ct
Julia	16	F	Laborer	25Ap02Ct
KERNAN, Condy	20	M	Laborer	25Ap02Ct
REYNOLDS, Elen	25	F	Laborer	25Ap02Ct
Margaret	20	F	Laborer	25Ap02Ct
KENNY, Robert	18	M	Joiner	25Ap02Ct
HODSON, Wm.	26	M	Laborer	25Ap02Ct
MCKENNY, John	24	M	Laborer	25Ap02Ct
RYAN, Pat	20	M	Laborer	25Ap02Ct
DELNY, Pat	22	M	Carpenter	25Ap02Ct
BENSON, Pat	40	M	Weaver	25Ap02Ct
STEWART, Hugh	29	M	Weaver	25Ap02Ct

NAMES OF PASSENGERS	AGE	SEX	OCCUPATIONS	DATE PORT SHIP
KILKENNY, Thomas	24	M	Farmer	25Ap02Ct
KENEDY, Michael	40	M	Laborer	25Ap02Ct
LONG, Thomas	31	M	Farmer	25Ap02Ct
DUNN, Edward	28	M	Painter	25Ap02Ct
Jack	15	M	Laborer	25Ap02Ct
DOOLEY, Dan	33	M	Laborer	25Ap02Ct
KELLY, John	32	M	Laborer	25Ap02Ct
FLYN, Richard	26	M	Farmer	25Ap02Ct
Michael	15	M	Farmer	25Ap02Ct
Dan	14	M	Farmer	25Ap02Ct
Ann	50	F	Farmer	25Ap02Ct
Ann	18	F	Farmer	25Ap02Ct
Catherine	10	F	Farmer	25Ap02Ct
Elen	6	F	Child	25Ap02Ct
HINDS, William	26	M	Carpenter	25Ap02Ct
Mary	22	F	Laborer	25Ap02Ct
Ann	.00	F	Infant	25Ap02Ct
MOONY, Mary	14	F	Laborer	25Ap02Ct
Bety	3	F	Child	25Ap02Ct
MAYLAND, Jack	28	M	Laborer	25Ap02Ct
Margaret	28	F	Laborer	25Ap02Ct
LOUGHLIN, John	15	M	Laborer	25Ap02Ct
CANNY, Mary	25	F	Laborer	25Ap02Ct
FIRGON, Thomas	24	M	Laborer	25Ap02Ct
James	19	M	Laborer	25Ap02Ct
COBURN, Jack	46	M	Laborer	25Ap02Ct
Maria	13	F	Laborer	25Ap02Ct
James	10	M	Laborer	25Ap02Ct
GASKELL, Pat	20	M	Laborer	25Ap02Ct
MURLEY, Hugh	50	M	Farmer	25Ap02Ct
Sarah	20	F	Farmer	25Ap02Ct
REYNOLDS, Catherine	22	F	Farmer	25Ap02Ct
GROSGROVE, Ann	20	F	Farmer	25Ap02Ct
HICKNEY, Pat	25	M	Farmer	25Ap02Ct
JENKINS, Bessy	18	F	Farmer	25Ap02Ct
MCGREGER, Peter	36	M	Laborer	25Ap02Ct
Catherine	36	F	Laborer	25Ap02Ct
Maria	11	F	Laborer	25Ap02Ct
SMITH, Thos.	20	M	Laborer	25Ap02Ct
Bartley	21	M	Laborer	25Ap02Ct
BAXTER, John	46	M	Brick Maker	25Ap02Ct
HASKINS, James	25	M	Laborer	25Ap02Ct
DOUGHERTY, Francis	22	M	Laborer	25Ap02Ct
Cony	20	M	Fisherman	25Ap02Ct
LINK, Pat	18	M	Fisherman	25Ap02Ct
MCGUIRE, Pat	21	M	Ctnsp	25Ap02Ct
KNOTT, Moses	40	M	Ctnsp	25Ap02Ct
Ann	31	F	Ctnsp	25Ap02Ct
Jas.	4	M	Child	25Ap02Ct
MARTIN, Catherine	16	F	Farmer	25Ap02Ct
ONEIL, Pat	54	M	Laborer	25Ap02Ct
CONNOLEY, Bridget	54	F	Laborer	25Ap02Ct
CAMBIL, Bridget	26	F	Laborer	25Ap02Ct
SMITH, Barney	22	M	Laborer	25Ap02Ct
REYNOLDS, Bridget	22	F	Laborer	25Ap02Ct
QUINN, Catherine	20	F	Laborer	25Ap02Ct
BRAY, Michael	20	M	Laborer	25Ap02Ct
GRIMES, Jno.	20	M	Cooper	25Ap02Ct
MCGURKIN, Owen	19	M	Laborer	25Ap02Ct
DERMODY, Margaret	45	F	Laborer	25Ap02Ct
Pat	10	M	Laborer	25Ap02Ct
HUTCKINSON, Chris	30	M	Weaver	25Ap02Ct
BROWN, Mary	50	F	Farmer	25Ap02Ct
John	20	M	Farmer	25Ap02Ct
Mary	16	F	Farmer	25Ap02Ct
Bridget	9	F	Child	25Ap02Ct
Michael	12	M	Farmer	25Ap02Ct
SULLIVAN, Catherine	26	F	Farmer	25Ap02Ct
COMER, Wm.	18	M	Tailor	25Ap02Ct
ORYAN, Pat	33	M	Tailor	25Ap02Ct
John	8	M	Child	25Ap02Ct
LYNCH, Peter	21	M	Farmer	25Ap02Ct
GAGIN, Mary	27	F	Farmer	25Ap02Ct
HIGGINS, Betsey	5	F	Child	25Ap02Ct
WHELON, Mary	46	F	Farmer	25Ap02Ct

NAMES OF PASSENGERS	AGE	SEX	OCCUPATIONS	DATE PORT SHIP
WHELON, Thos.	16	M	Farmer	25Ap02Ct
Catherine	3	F	Child	25Ap02Ct
MARLEY, Michael	35	M	Bricklayer	25Ap02Ct
WARD, Hugh	30	M	Laborer	25Ap02Ct
MCDERMOTT, John	30	M	Laborer	25Ap02Ct
DOYHER, John	30	M	Laborer	25Ap02Ct
QUINN, Catherine	14	F	Laborer	25Ap02Ct
Sarah	10	F	Laborer	25Ap02Ct
Jack	8	M	Child	25Ap02Ct
KEAN, Pat	17	M	Laborer	25Ap02Ct
WARD, Elias	20	M	Farmer	25Ap02Ct
AMEY, Andrew	25	M	Farmer	25Ap02Ct
SMITH, William	30	M	Farmer	25Ap02Ct
BOSHWELL, John	40	M	Farmer	25Ap02Ct
PHOLOPHLAN, Betsey	40	F	Farmer	25Ap02Ct
ASHTON, John	20	M	Farmer	25Ap02Ct
MULIN, Jack	2	M	Child	25Ap02Ct
BERNAN, Andrew	18	M	Farmer	25Ap02Ct
MCKENNEY, Edward	42	M	Clergyman	25Ap02Ct

LYARA 26 APRIL 1849

From Dublin

NAMES OF PASSENGERS	AGE	SEX	OCCUPATIONS	DATE PORT SHIP
ROARK, James	25	M	Laborer	26Ap12Cq
CROSBY, Mary	24	F	Unknown	26Ap12Cq
FAGAN, Patt	22	M	Unknown	26Ap12Cq
Thomas	21	M	Unknown	26Ap12Cq
Biddy	20	F	Unknown	26Ap12Cq
KEEGAN, Jane	60	F	Unknown	26Ap12Cq
Michael	30	M	Unknown	26Ap12Cq
Bess	28	F	Unknown	26Ap12Cq
Margaret	24	F	Unknown	26Ap12Cq
MCGOVERN, Michl.	60	M	Unknown	26Ap12Cq
Margaret	24	F	Unknown	26Ap12Cq
John	22	M	Unknown	26Ap12Cq
Bessy	20	F	Unknown	26Ap12Cq
BAIL, Edward	30	M	Unknown	26Ap12Cq
U-Mrs.	30	F	Unknown	26Ap12Cq
Catharine	13	F	Unknown	26Ap12Cq
Margaret	11	F	Unknown	26Ap12Cq
John	8	M	Child	26Ap12Cq
Mary	4	F	Child	26Ap12Cq
Biddy	.00	F	Infant	26Ap12Cq
FLAHERTY, James	24	M	Unknown	26Ap12Cq
MCDONALD, Pat	56	M	Unknown	26Ap12Cq
Ally	40	F	Unknown	26Ap12Cq
Ann	16	F	Unknown	26Ap12Cq
Owen	13	M	Unknown	26Ap12Cq
Catharine	11	F	Unknown	26Ap12Cq
MCDENNELL, Mary	4	F	Child	26Ap12Cq
Rose	.00	F	Infant	26Ap12Cq
HART, Peter	50	M	Unknown	26Ap12Cq
John	17	M	Unknown	26Ap12Cq
Susan	15	F	Unknown	26Ap12Cq
Margaret	13	F	Unknown	26Ap12Cq
Patrick	11	M	Unknown	26Ap12Cq
Conner	7	M	Child	26Ap12Cq
Maryann	3	F	Child	26Ap12Cq
Michael	.00	M	Infant	26Ap12Cq
Patrick	46	M	Unknown	26Ap12Cq
Patrick	15	M	Unknown	26Ap12Cq
John	13	M	Unknown	26Ap12Cq
Peter	11	M	Unknown	26Ap12Cq
Phillip	7	M	Child	26Ap12Cq
Conner	3	M	Child	26Ap12Cq
Charles	.00	M	Infant	26Ap12Cq
SMITH, James	35	M	Unknown	26Ap12C
Mary	34	F	Unknown	26Ap12C

NAMES OF PASSENGERS	AGE	SEX	OCCUPATIONS	DATE PORT SHIP
SMITH, Patt	13	M	Unknown	26Ap12Cq
Charles	4	M	Child	26Ap12Cq
Jane	.00	F	Infant	26Ap12Cq
SEDWITH, Patt	20	M	Unknown	26Ap12Cq
Mary	18	F	Unknown	26Ap12Cq
GARRY, Thomas	40	M	Unknown	26Ap12Cq
Margaret	40	F	Unknown	26Ap12Cq
James	9	M	Child	26Ap12Cq
Thomas	6	M	Child	26Ap12Cq
Patrick	3	M	Child	26Ap12Cq
Ann	.00	F	Infant	26Ap12Cq
BRAN, Andrew	25	M	Unknown	26Ap12Cq
Mary	20	F	Unknown	26Ap12Cq
CAVANAGH, Thomas	50	M	Unknown	26Ap12Cq
U-Mrs.	50	F	Unknown	26Ap12Cq
Catharine	17	F	Unknown	26Ap12Cq
Patrick	15	M	Unknown	26Ap12Cq
William	13	M	Unknown	26Ap12Cq
Mary	11	F	Unknown	26Ap12Cq
Margaret	10	F	Unknown	26Ap12Cq
Thomas	9	M	Child	26Ap12Cq
Ann	7	F	Child	26Ap12Cq
Michael	4	M	Child	26Ap12Cq
Edward	.00	M	Infant	26Ap12Cq
William	40	M	Unknown	26Ap12Cq
U-Mrs.	38	F	Unknown	26Ap12Cq
Edward	15	M	Unknown	26Ap12Cq
Bridget	13	F	Unknown	26Ap12Cq
Patrick	10	M	Unknown	26Ap12Cq
Dudley	6	M	Child	26Ap12Cq
Jerry	3	M	Child	26Ap12Cq
BRENNAN, Michl.	26	M	Unknown	26Ap12Cq
Murtagh	23	M	Unknown	26Ap12Cq
Margaret	20	F	Unknown	26Ap12Cq
John	40	M	Unknown	26Ap12Cq
Betty	30	F	Unknown	26Ap12Cq
Margaret	.00	F	Infant	26Ap12Cq
WALL, Mary	40	F	Unknown	26Ap12Cq
Larry	60	M	Unknown	26Ap12Cq
MACKEY, Mary	19	F	Unknown	26Ap12Cq
Patt	16	M	Unknown	26Ap12Cq
Catharine	16	F	Unknown	26Ap12Cq
WALL, Mary	6	F	Child	26Ap12Cq
KELLY, Michl.	40	M	Unknown	26Ap12Cq
Mary	40	F	Unknown	26Ap12Cq
Catharine	20	F	Unknown	26Ap12Cq
Larry	20	M	Unknown	26Ap12Cq
William	19	M	Unknown	26Ap12Cq
Denny	8	M	Child	26Ap12Cq
John	12	M	Unknown	26Ap12Cq
Molly	9	F	Child	26Ap12Cq
Nanny	10	F	Unknown	26Ap12Cq
Betty	3	F	Child	26Ap12Cq
MURPHY, Patrick	27	M	Unknown	26Ap12Cq
Ann	19	F	Unknown	26Ap12Cq
John	18	M	Unknown	26Ap12Cq
Betty	16	F	Unknown	26Ap12Cq
KEEFE, Wm.	40	M	Unknown	26Ap12Cq
U-Mrs.	38	F	Unknown	26Ap12Cq
Patrick	15	M	Unknown	26Ap12Cq
Margaret	13	F	Unknown	26Ap12Cq
Mary-Ann	11	F	Unknown	26Ap12Cq
Biddy	9	F	Child	26Ap12Cq
Catharine	5	F	Child	26Ap12Cq
Hugh	.00	M	Infant	26Ap12Cq
LIVER, U-Mrs.	28	F	Unknown	26Ap12Cq
William	3	M	Child	26Ap12Cq
Kate	.00	F	Infant	26Ap12Cq
HELAN, Michl.	45	M	Unknown	26Ap12Cq
Bridget	40	F	Unknown	26Ap12Cq
Judy	20	F	Unknown	26Ap12Cq
Margaret	18	F	Unknown	26Ap12Cq
Biddy	15	F	Unknown	26Ap12Cq
Ann	13	F	Unknown	26Ap12Cq
William	9	M	Child	26Ap12Cq

NAMES OF PASSENGERS	AGE	SEX	OCCUPATIONS	DATE PORT SHIP
WHELAN, Joseph	5	M	Child	26Ap12Cq
DUNN, John	40	M	Unknown	26Ap12Cq
Bridget	40	F	Unknown	26Ap12Cq
Margaret	18	F	Unknown	26Ap12Cq
Catharine	16	F	Unknown	26Ap12Cq
Ellen	14	F	Unknown	26Ap12Cq
Patrick	6	M	Child	26Ap12Cq
Margaret	.00	F	Infant	26Ap12Cq
BENNINGHAM, Thos.	30	M	Unknown	26Ap12Cq
U-Mrs.	30	F	Unknown	26Ap12Cq
Thomas	.00	M	Infant	26Ap12Cq
GRENNAN, Mary	35	F	Unknown	26Ap12Cq
Ann	16	F	Unknown	26Ap12Cq
William	14	M	Unknown	26Ap12Cq
John	10	M	Unknown	26Ap12Cq
CASEY, U	40	M	Unknown	26Ap12Cq
Mary	13	F	Unknown	26Ap12Cq
WILSEN, Widow	40	F	Unknown	26Ap12Cq
Isabella	18	F	Unknown	26Ap12Cq
DAGNER, Edward	25	M	Unknown	26Ap12Cq
CASEY, Tom	14	M	Unknown	26Ap12Cq
CAVANAGH, Richard	.00	M	Infant	26Ap12Cq

ELIZABETH 28 APRIL 1849

From Bristol

NAMES OF PASSENGERS	AGE	SEX	OCCUPATIONS	DATE PORT SHIP
BRUNT, John	38	M	Farmer	28Ap10Bk
WHITE, James	40	M	Farmer	28Ap10Bk
Susannah	17	F	Farmer	28Ap10Bk
David	12	M	Farmer	28Ap10Bk
Mary-Ann	10	F	Farmer	28Ap10Bk
William	7	M	Child	28Ap10Bk
STOKES, Phoebe	32	F	Farmer	28Ap10Bk
Jane	4	F	Child	28Ap10Bk
WHITE, Norah	19	F	Farmer	28Ap10Bk
STOKES, John	9	M	Child	28Ap10Bk
Ann	11	F	Farmer	28Ap10Bk
Mary	6	F	Child	28Ap10Bk
David	.00	M	Infant	28Ap10Bk
WILLIAMS, H.	26	M	Farmer	28Ap10Bk
CLARK, James	23	M	Farmer	28Ap10Bk
Elizabeth	22	F	Farmer	28Ap10Bk
MOSS, William	19	M	Farmer	28Ap10Bk
BRUNT, Elizabeth	40	F	Servant	28Ap10Bk
Thos.	11	M	Unknown	28Ap10Bk
Eliza	10	F	Unknown	28Ap10Bk
Silvester	8	M	Child	28Ap10Bk
Henry	6	M	Child	28Ap10Bk
Sarah	2	F	Child	28Ap10Bk
Louisa	.00	F	Infant	28Ap10Bk
SMITH, Richard	24	M	Farmer	28Ap10Bk
GULLIVER, Wm.	30	M	Farmer	28Ap10Bk
PERKINS, Edward	31	M	Farmer	28Ap10Bk
BLICK, Wm.	24	M	Clothier	28Ap10Bk
DOWDING, Thos.	50	M	Agrt	28Ap10Bk
FUDGE, George	32	M	Agrt	28Ap10Bk
HAMMOND, Robt.	40	M	Agrt	28Ap10Bk
WATTS, S.	22	M	Agrt	28Ap10Bk
WARREN, Clement	35	M	Agrt	28Ap10Bk
RICKETTS, J.	25	M	Agrt	28Ap10Bk
NORMAN, Nic	21	M	Agrt	28Ap10Bk
PINCH, Ann	30	F	Agrt	28Ap10Bk
John	4	M	Child	28Ap10Bk
Ann	2	F	Child	28Ap10Bk
Wm.	.00	M	Infant	28Ap10Bk
EVANS, Caroline	28	F	Unknown	28Ap10Bk
W.	26	M	Unknown	28Ap10Bk
Maria	24	F	Unknown	28Ap10Bk

NAMES OF PASSENGERS	AGE	SEX	OCCUPATIONS	DATE PORT SHIP
EVANS, J.	5	M	Child	28Ap10Bk
Sarah	3	F	Child	28Ap10Bk
G.	.00	M	Infant	28Ap10Bk
PINCH, S.	32	M	Agrt	28Ap10Bk
Saml.	37	M	Agrt	28Ap10Bk
Mary	8	F	Child	28Ap10Bk
E.	3	F	Child	28Ap10Bk
TANNER, Chas.	24	M	Agrt	28Ap10Bk
BAKER, Thos.	20	M	Agrt	28Ap10Bk
ROBERTS, S.	43	M	Agrt	28Ap10Bk
Linora	11	F	Agrt	28Ap10Bk
COPLE, John	45	M	Agrt	28Ap10Bk
Died-At-Sea				
Jas.	55	M	Agrt	28Ap10Bk
Martha	57	F	Seamstress	28Ap10Bk
Jane	23	F	Seamstress	28Ap10Bk
Martha	16	F	Seamstress	28Ap10Bk
Sarah	30	F	Seamstress	28Ap10Bk
Charlotte	12	F	Seamstress	28Ap10Bk
Henry	7	M	Child	28Ap10Bk
Maria	5	F	Child	28Ap10Bk
Alfred	3	M	Child	28Ap10Bk
John	.00	M	Infant	28Ap10Bk
WALL, Geo.	25	M	Farmer	28Ap10Bk
LOVELACE, Ann	23	F	Servant	28Ap10Bk
ROSSITER, John	20	M	Mechanic	28Ap10Bk
Mary	30	F	Unknown	28Ap10Bk
FILER, J.	21	M	Laborer	28Ap10Bk
BAKER, Saml.	18	M	Laborer	28Ap10Bk
DONNELLY, James	19	M	Laborer	28Ap10Bk
ROBERTS, Harriet	10	F	Laborer	28Ap10Bk
HART, Jas.	40	M	Laborer	28Ap10Bk
COURT, Rob.	34	M	Laborer	28Ap10Bk
WILLIAMS, W.	26	M	Farmer	28Ap10Bk
WEBBER, Rob.	22	M	Artist	28Ap10Bk
COOMBS, Geo.	43	M	Artist	28Ap10Bk
HIBBARD, Geo.	23	M	Farmer	28Ap10Bk
DOWDING, Sol.	20	M	Trade Man	28Ap10Bk
SLOTTARD, Edwd.	17	M	Trade Man	28Ap10Bk
HARTSHAM, Emanuel	38	M	Farmer	28Ap10Bk
LEWIS, W.	28	M	Farmer	28Ap10Bk
GILLINGHAM, J.	19	M	Farmer	28Ap10Bk
MORGAN, Catharine	21	F	Spinster	28Ap10Bk
SHORT, Jane	28	F	Unknown	28Ap10Bk
Chas.	5	M	Child	28Ap10Bk
Matthew	.00	M	Infant	28Ap10Bk
LEWIS, Ann	28	F	Unknown	28Ap10Bk
Emma	5	F	Child	28Ap10Bk
Jane	.00	F	Infant	28Ap10Bk
Chas.	50	M	Agrt	28Ap10Bk
Hester	55	F	Unknown	28Ap10Bk
BALL, Sarah	35	F	Unknown	28Ap10Bk
Mary	5	F	Child	28Ap10Bk
RICKETTS, Geo.	21	M	Unknown	28Ap10Bk
WATTS, Sarah	22	F	Unknown	28Ap10Bk
YOUNG, Daniel	30	M	Laborer	28Ap10Bk
PAGINTON, W.	22	M	Laborer	28Ap10Bk
BURTON, B.	33	M	Unknown	28Ap10Bk
BUTLER, Jane	2	F	Child	28Ap10Bk
Mary-Ann	6	F	Child	28Ap10Bk
MARSHMAN, Walter	30	M	Agrt	28Ap10Bk
PORK, R.	17	M	Agrt	28Ap10Bk
WOODFORD, Jas.	40	M	Agrt	28Ap10Bk
Elizabeth	32	F	Unknown	28Ap10Bk
James	14	M	Agrt	28Ap10Bk
W.	11	M	Unknown	28Ap10Bk
Elizabeth	9	F	Child	28Ap10Bk
HAWKINS, R.	31	M	Unknown	28Ap10Bk
TANNER, Chas.	23	M	Laborer	28Ap10Bk
Caroline	30	F	Unknown	28Ap10Bk
DAY, John	20	M	Artist	28Ap10Bk
REED, James	30	M	Artist	28Ap10Bk
Elizabeth	60	F	Unknown	28Ap10Bk
Joseph	40	M	Unknown	28Ap10Bk
Jones	19	M	Unknown	28Ap10Bk
COURTENAY, E.	47	M	Agrt	28Ap10Bk
Mary	40	F	Agrt	28Ap10Bk
Danl.	3	M	Child	28Ap10Bk
MORGAN, Jenney	32	M	Child	28Ap10Bk
MOORE, Cushing	19	F	Unknown	28Ap10Bk
SEAMEN, Henry	45	M	Unknown	28Ap10Bk
Harriet	44	F	Agrt	28Ap10Bk
Jas.	19	M	Agrt	28Ap10Bk
Elizabeth	16	F	Agrt	28Ap10Bk
Geo.	11	M	Unknown	28Ap10Bk
Jane	.00	F	Infant	28Ap10Bk
SIMMONDS, Thos.	30	M	Laborer	28Ap10Bk
Charlotte	28	F	Unknown	28Ap10Bk
John	9	M	Child	28Ap10Bk
Harriet	6	F	Child	28Ap10Bk
Henry	2	M	Child	28Ap10Bk
Mary	.00	F	Infant	28Ap10Bk
MAME, Jane	50	F	Unknown	28Ap10Bk
GULLIVER, Sarah	30	F	Unknown	28Ap10Bk
TOOLE, James	40	M	Upholsterer	28Ap10Bk
Caroline	42	F	Upholsterer	28Ap10Bk
JAMES, Anne	26	F	Surgeon	28Ap10Bk
DONNE, Geo.	40	M	Unknown	28Ap10Bk
MARDON, T.W.	21	M	Unknown	28Ap10Bk
WATTS, Henry	40	M	Farmer	28Ap10Bk
Thos.	50	M	Farmer	28Ap10Bk
JOYCE, John	50	M	Farmer	28Ap10Bk
WHITE, Hannah	40	F	Farmer	28Ap10Bk

MT.STEW.ELPHINSTON 28 APRIL 1849

From Glasgow

NAMES OF PASSENGERS		AGE	SEX	OCCUPATIONS	DATE PORT SHIP
NEEDHAM, John		30	M	Weaver	28Ap04Cu
ROGAN, Agnes		34	F	Wife	28Ap04Cu
BOURKE, William		23	M	Farmer	28Ap04Cu
DIGMAN, Hugh		30	M	Laborer	28Ap04Cu
Mary	(W)	24	F	Wife	28Ap04Cu
John	(S)	.01	M	Infant	28Ap04Cu
FINNIGAN, Thomas		18	M	Laborer	28Ap04Cu
KANE, Else		47	F	None	28Ap04Cu
Francis	(S)	10	M	None	28Ap04Cu
Paul	(S)	8	M	Child	28Ap04C
ARMSTRONG, John		18	M	Fsvnt	28Ap04C
CLERAN, Edward		40	M	Laborer	28Ap04C
MCKNIGHT, Samuel		21	M	Fsvnt	28Ap04C
KIRK, James		30	M	Laborer	28Ap04C
DAWSON, Andrew		36	M	Servant	28Ap04C
HETHERINGTON, James		40	M	Farmer	28Ap04C
Isabella	(T)	28	F	Sister	28Ap04C
DONALD, Francis		22	M	Laborer	28Ap04C
COLLINS, Robert		33	M	Laborer	28Ap04C
Catherine	(W)	28	F	Wife	28Ap04C
Mary-Jane	(D)	8	F	Child	28Ap04C
John	(S)	.03	M	Infant	28Ap04C
Robert	(S)	.03	M	Infant	28Ap04C
MITCHELL, Matilda		21	F	None	28Ap04C

SEA-BIRD 28 APRIL 1849

From Galway

NAMES OF PASSENGERS	AGE	SEX	OCCUPATIONS	DATE PORT SHIP
ROONAN, John	21	M	Laborer	28Ap06Cv
NOONE, Danl.	22	M	Laborer	28Ap06Cv
TOLAN, Michael	35	M	Laborer	28Ap06Cv
CLAGHERTY, Jno.	25	M	Laborer	28Ap06Cv
DRIEN, Wm.	20	M	Laborer	28Ap06Cv
TALMON, John	20	M	Laborer	28Ap06Cv
MORISSY, Edwd.	20	M	Laborer	28Ap06Cv
FOSTER, James	18	M	Laborer	28Ap06Cv
GILLIGAN, Mary	23	F	Spinster	28Ap06Cv
WALSH, Thos.	33	M	Laborer	28Ap06Cv
CONNELL, John	29	M	Laborer	28Ap06Cv
KILKELLY, John	29	M	Laborer	28Ap06Cv
LINNANE, Brdiget	20	F	Spinster	28Ap06Cv
CARLER, Michael	25	M	Laborer	28Ap06Cv
NILAND, Bridget	20	F	Spinster	28Ap06Cv
Martin	16	M	Laborer	28Ap06Cv
DONLAN, Mary	22	F	Spinster	28Ap06Cv
DONELLY, Pat	25	M	Laborer	28Ap06Cv
HOLLERAN, Michael	26	M	Laborer	28Ap06Cv
Anne	23	F	Spinster	28Ap06Cv
DEGIDEN, Bridget	20	F	Spinster	28Ap06Cv
MCTEAGUE, Pat	40	M	Laborer	28Ap06Cv
GILL, Mary	18	F	Spinster	28Ap06Cv
COSTELLO, Michael	18	M	Laborer	28Ap06Cv
Mary	50	F	Spinster	28Ap06Cv
Pat	12	M	Laborer	28Ap06Cv
Honor	6	F	Child	28Ap06Cv
LACY, Martin	22	M	Laborer	28Ap06Cv
TADE, Michael	20	M	Laborer	28Ap06Cv
TOLAN, Michael	21	M	Laborer	28Ap06Cv
FREEMAN, Charles	32	M	Laborer	28Ap06Cv
MURPHY, Mary	14	F	Spinster	28Ap06Cv
FREEMAN, Bridget	40	F	Spinster	28Ap06Cv
MURPHY, Ned	13	M	Laborer	28Ap06Cv
CURRY, Honor	22	F	Spinster	28Ap06Cv
DONOHOE, Michael Died-At-Sea	30	M	Laborer	28Ap06Cv
Honor	30	F	Spinster	28Ap06Cv
CONOR, John	25	M	Laborer	28Ap06Cv
Michael	20	M	Laborer	28Ap06Cv
Bridget	30	F	Spinster	28Ap06Cv
Mary	20	F	Spinster	28Ap06Cv
NOLAND, Mary	21	F	Spinster	28Ap06Cv
.EE, Michael	30	M	Laborer	28Ap06Cv
Kitty	30	F	Spinster	28Ap06Cv
CONNOR, Pat	22	M	Laborer	28Ap06Cv
Kitty	20	F	Spinster	28Ap06Cv
LANEY, Barthw.	35	M	Laborer	28Ap06Cv
ARR, Martin	36	M	Laborer	28Ap06Cv
LINNANE, Michl.	18	M	Laborer	28Ap06Cv
CDOUGH, Peter	25	M	Laborer	28Ap06Cv
ONAGHAN, Peter	22	M	Laborer	28Ap06Cv
YDON, James	25	M	Laborer	28Ap06Cv
Judy	22	F	Spinster	28Ap06Cv
ONNELLY, Pat	30	M	Laborer	28Ap06Cv
YDON, Judy	8	F	Child	28Ap06Cv
ONNELLY, Sally	26	F	Spinster	28Ap06Cv
TANTON, John	17	M	Laborer	28Ap06Cv
OONE, Thos.	18	M	Laborer	28Ap06Cv
ELLY, Andrew	30	M	Laborer	28Ap06Cv
EMPSEY, John	26	M	Laborer	28Ap06Cv
Michael	22	M	Laborer	28Ap06Cv
James	19	M	Laborer	28Ap06Cv
ASE, Cathe.	20	F	Spinster	28Ap06Cv
JINE, Richd.	35	M	Laborer	28Ap06Cv
QUINE, Mary	23	F	Spinster	28Ap06Cv
BRETT, Thos.	20	M	Laborer	28Ap06Cv
GADIN, James	26	M	Laborer	28Ap06Cv
MEALY, Luke	30	M	Laborer	28Ap06Cv
QUINE, Mary	20	F	Spinster	28Ap06Cv
U	.00	U	Infant	28Ap06Cv
MAYER, John	21	M	Laborer	28Ap06Cv
Bridget	18	F	Spinster	28Ap06Cv
MALOWNEY, Owen	20	M	Laborer	28Ap06Cv
SILK, Thos.	40	M	Laborer	28Ap06Cv
Margt.	40	F	Spinster	28Ap06Cv
Wm.	13	M	Laborer	28Ap06Cv
Mary	14	F	Spinster	28Ap06Cv
Sally	11	F	Spinster	28Ap06Cv
Winny	8	F	Child	28Ap06Cv
TOLAN, John	40	M	Laborer	28Ap06Cv
LYDAN, Ferty	20	M	Laborer	28Ap06Cv
KELLY, Tady	50	M	Laborer	28Ap06Cv
LYON, Biddy	19	F	Spinster	28Ap06Cv
SULLIVAN, James	40	M	Laborer	28Ap06Cv
Mary	30	F	Spinster	28Ap06Cv
Patk.	8	M	Child	28Ap06Cv
Cath.	6	F	Child	28Ap06Cv
U, U	.06	U	Infant	28Ap06Cv
FAHY, Thomas	27	M	Laborer	28Ap06Cv
KEADY, Mark	23	M	Laborer	28Ap06Cv
MCDONAGH, Pat	25	M	Laborer	28Ap06Cv
MORRISS, Martin	26	M	Laborer	28Ap06Cv
CLANCEY, Biddy	13	F	Spinster	28Ap06Cv
FORD, Barthw.	20	M	Laborer	28Ap06Cv
Honor	18	F	Spinster	28Ap06Cv
MAYAR, Martin	18	M	Laborer	28Ap06Cv
CLANCEY, Ellen	30	F	Spinster	28Ap06Cv
HANROY, Michl.	21	M	Laborer	28Ap06Cv
Margt.	21	F	Spinster	28Ap06Cv
LYON, Dudley	30	M	Laborer	28Ap06Cv
NEVILLE, Michael	25	M	Laborer	28Ap06Cv
WOOLY, Thos.	19	M	Laborer	28Ap06Cv
KYNE, Michael	19	M	Laborer	28Ap06Cv
KAFTERTY, Anne	30	F	Spinster	28Ap06Cv
Michael	10	M	Laborer	28Ap06Cv
Biddy	7	F	Child	28Ap06Cv
U	.06	U	Infant	28Ap06Cv
LYDEN, Pat	30	M	Laborer	28Ap06Cv
Ann	26	F	Spinster	28Ap06Cv
U	.02	U	Infant	28Ap06Cv
BURKE, Martin	27	M	Laborer	28Ap06Cv
Mary	29	F	Spinster	28Ap06Cv
HEALY, John	27	M	Laborer	28Ap06Cv
Ellen	27	F	Spinster	28Ap06Cv
DEVENNY, James	28	M	Laborer	28Ap06Cv
Peggy	28	F	Spinster	28Ap06Cv
WHEALON, John	30	M	Laborer	28Ap06Cv
FAHEY, John	30	M	Laborer	28Ap06Cv
KEAREY, Thos.	20	M	Laborer	28Ap06Cv
FEERY, Pat	23	M	Laborer	28Ap06Cv
CONNELLY, Barthlw.	24	M	Laborer	28Ap06Cv
HENREE, Pat	24	M	Laborer	28Ap06Cv
ENGLISH, Pat	22	M	Laborer	28Ap06Cv
COYNE, A.	24	M	Laborer	28Ap06Cv
ENGLISH, Michael	23	M	Laborer	28Ap06Cv
THOMPSON, John	20	M	Laborer	28Ap06Cv
WARD, Bessy	25	F	Spinster	28Ap06Cv
THOMPSON, Bessy	20	F	Spinster	28Ap06Cv
FALLEN, Ellen	21	F	Spinster	28Ap06Cv
FAHEY, Andrew	35	M	Laborer	28Ap06Cv
KILDAY, Bridget	20	F	Spinster	28Ap06Cv
FAHEY, Mary	30	F	Spinster	28Ap06Cv
HICKEY, Cath.	20	F	Spinster	28Ap06Cv
SULLLIVAN, Thos.	22	M	Laborer	28Ap06Cv
FAHEY, John	40	M	Laborer	28Ap06Cv
Ellen	30	F	Spinster	28Ap06Cv
MAHER, James	25	M	Laborer	28Ap06Cv
NEE, Pat	30	M	Laborer	28Ap06Cv
John	30	M	Laborer	28Ap06Cv

NAMES OF PASSENGERS	AGE	SEX	OCCUPATIONS	DATE PORT SHIP
RYAN, Thos.	25	M	Laborer	28Ap06Cv
NAUGHTON, Bridget	25	F	Spinster	28Ap06Cv
MCCNAMARA, Pat	40	M	Laborer	28Ap06Cv
GREANEY, Mary	17	F	Spinster	28Ap06Cv
HIGGINS, Biddy	55	F	Spinster	28Ap06Cv
GREANEY, Pat	17	M	Laborer	28Ap06Cv
MCDONAGH, Hugh	20	M	Laborer	28Ap06Cv
MORISSEY, John	20	M	Laborer	28Ap06Cv
TIERNEY, John	21	M	Laborer	28Ap06Cv
FAHEY, Winny	3	F	Child	28Ap06Cv
CONNER, Mary	21	F	Spinster	28Ap06Cv
PHEN, James	23	M	Laborer	28Ap06Cv
MURRAY, Martin	21	M	Laborer	28Ap06Cv
BRAZIE, Anthony	20	M	Laborer	28Ap06Cv
RUTLEDGE, Edwd.	22	M	Laborer	28Ap06Cv
COEN, Pat	20	M	Laborer	28Ap06Cv
FAHEY, Pat	21	M	Laborer	28Ap06Cv
LARKIN, Martin	22	M	Laborer	28Ap06Cv
CUMY, John	21	M	Laborer	28Ap06Cv
WHEALON, Pat	21	M	Laborer	28Ap06Cv
FAHERTY, Pat	23	M	Laborer	28Ap06Cv
Bessy	19	F	Spinster	28Ap06Cv
FORD, James	25	M	Laborer	28Ap06Cv
MOORE, Honor	16	F	Spinster	28Ap06Cv
KILLALLY, Selia	16	F	Spinster	28Ap06Cv
MULLIN, Cathe.	13	F	Spinster	28Ap06Cv
KILLALLY, John	19	M	Laborer	28Ap06Cv
CROSBY, Barthw.	18	M	Laborer	28Ap06Cv
Mary	20	F	Spinster	28Ap06Cv
Bridget	13	F	Spinster	28Ap06Cv
LARKIN, Cathe.	45	F	Spinster	28Ap06Cv
Mary	18	F	Spinster	28Ap06Cv
Michael	13	M	Laborer	28Ap06Cv
Biddy	12	F	Spinster	28Ap06Cv
FENNICK, John	35	M	Laborer	28Ap06Cv
Mary	9	F	Child	28Ap06Cv
Cathe.	8	F	Child	28Ap06Cv
John	7	M	Child	28Ap06Cv
U, U	.06	U	Infant	28Ap06Cv
DONNELLY, James	24	M	Laborer	28Ap06Cv
WALSH, Michael	35	M	Laborer	28Ap06Cv
DUANE, John	33	M	Laborer	28Ap06Cv
Biddy	30	F	Spinster	28Ap06Cv
HYNES, John	32	M	Laborer	28Ap06Cv
DUANE, James	20	M	Laborer	28Ap06Cv
GORDON, George	40	M	Laborer	28Ap06Cv
Jane	25	F	Spinster	28Ap06Cv
Ellen	3	F	Child	28Ap06Cv
KILLEA, Martin	23	M	Laborer	28Ap06Cv
DUANE, Miche.	50	M	Laborer	28Ap06Cv
Bridget	48	F	Spinster	28Ap06Cv
Bridget	18	F	Spinster	28Ap06Cv
CONNELLY, Bridget	24	F	Spinster	28Ap06Cv
Mary	20	F	Spinster	28Ap06Cv
Biddy	6	F	Child	28Ap06Cv
DONOHOE, Pat	24	M	Laborer	28Ap06Cv
KEADY, Miche.	26	M	Laborer	28Ap06Cv
Honor	20	F	Spinster	28Ap06Cv
KING, Miche.	21	M	Laborer	28Ap06Cv
Bridget	19	F	Spinster	28Ap06Cv
DALY, Pat	19	M	Laborer	28Ap06Cv
Margt.	20	F	Spinster	28Ap06Cv
HAWKINS, Kitty	20	F	Spinster	28Ap06Cv
Honor	30	F	Spinster	28Ap06Cv
MITCHELL, Honor	20	F	Spinster	28Ap06Cv
RAFTERY, Michl.	47	M	Laborer	28Ap06Cv
JOYCE, Michl.	22	M	Laborer	28Ap06Cv
SULLIVAN, Michl.	70	M	Laborer	28Ap06Cv
Ellen	70	F	Spinster	28Ap06Cv
Cathe.	23	F	Spinster	28Ap06Cv
Mary	36	F	Spinster	28Ap06Cv
MCGRATH, James	12	M	Laborer	28Ap06Cv
John	10	M	Laborer	28Ap06Cv
Selia	8	F	Child	28Ap06Cv
MCHUGH, U	00	M	Unknown	28Ap06Cv
MCHUGH, Kate	00	F	Unknown	28Ap06Cv
CULLINANE, Margt.	00	F	Unknown	28Ap06Cv
KELLY, W.	00	M	Clergyman	28Ap06Cv
CROSBY, Barth.	00	M	Unknown	28Ap06Cv
Mary	00	F	Unknown	28Ap06Cv
Bridget	00	F	Unknown	28Ap06Cv
MCDEMIOTT, Edwd.	00	M	Unknown	28Ap06Cv
Eliza	00	F	Unknown	28Ap06Cv
BARRETT, Ann	00	F	Unknown	28Ap06Cv
WARD, Jane	00	F	Unknown	28Ap06Cv
KELLY, Margt.	00	F	Unknown	28Ap06Cv
Ellen	00	F	Unknown	28Ap06Cv
FINCOSA, U	00	M	Unknown	28Ap06Cv
MCDERMOTT, U	00	M	Unknown	28Ap06Cv
U	00	M	Unknown	28Ap06Cv

ACADIAN 28 APRIL 1849

From Newry

NAMES OF PASSENGERS	AGE	SEX	OCCUPATIONS	DATE PORT SHIP
MCGUNN, Mary	35	F	Spinster	28Ap11Cr
MCCARVER, Biddy	60	F	Spinster	28Ap11Cr
Mary	20	F	Spinster	28Ap11Cr
OHEAR, Rose	24	F	Seamstress	28Ap11Cr
James	21	M	Ploughman	28Ap11Cr
MCCANN, Hugh	17	M	Weaver	28Ap11Cr
ROLSTEN, Hannah	40	F	Spinster	28Ap11Cr
Sarah-Jane	14	F	Spinster	28Ap11Cr
Mary-Ann	12	F	Relative	28Ap11Cr
Hugh	10	M	Relative	28Ap11Cr
Essey	7	F	Child	28Ap11Cr
Margaret	4	F	Child	28Ap11Cr
GEDDES, William	14	M	Servant	28Ap11Cr
Mary-Ann	12	F	Servant	28Ap11Cr
MCKEORAGHAN, Francis	50	M	Farmer	28Ap11Cr
Peter	25	M	Farmer	28Ap11Cr
Margaret	23	F	Relative	28Ap11Cr
Bridget	20	F	Relative	28Ap11Cr
Bridget	8	F	Child	28Ap11Cr
Francis	.00	M	Infant	28Ap11Cr
GORMLEY, Mary	18	F	Hatter	28Ap11Cr
OHARE, Owen	17	M	Laborer	28Ap11Cr
HENRY, Michael	25	M	Ploughman	28Ap11Cr
HAUGHEY, Patt	25	M	Shoemaker	28Ap11Cr
HALL, Mary	40	F	Spinster	28Ap11Cr
Charles	21	M	Relative	28Ap11Cr
James	17	M	Relative	28Ap11Cr
Mary	13	F	Relative	28Ap11Cr
Samuel	10	M	Relative	28Ap11Cr
John	8	M	Relative	28Ap11Cr
DUFFY, Bernard	14	M	Ploughman	28Ap11Cr
Nancy	40	F	Wife	28Ap11Cr
DALY, Mary	20	F	Spinster	28Ap11Cr
Patt	18	M	Servant	28Ap11Cr
Alice	13	F	Relative	28Ap11Cr
Rose	11	F	Relative	28Ap11Cr
Ann	6	F	Relative	28Ap11Cr
BOYLAN, Elizabeth	40	F	Spinster	28Ap11Cr
John	25	M	Gdnr	28Ap11Cr
Mary	21	F	Servant	28Ap11Cr
KELLY, Anne	41	F	Servant	28Ap11Cr
KILPATRICK, Andrew	19	M	Clerk	28Ap11Cr
TATE, John	30	M	Weaver	28Ap11Cr
RUSSELL, Jane	30	F	House Maid	28Ap11Cr
James	.00	M	Infant	28Ap11Cr
DAVY, Bridget	18	F	Spinster	28Ap11Cr
SMITH, James	25	M	Wood Man	28Ap11Cr
Mary (W)	23	F	Wife	28Ap11Cr
Patk. (S)	.00	M	Infant	28Ap11C

NAMES OF PASSENGERS		AGE	SEX	OCCUPATIONS	DATE PORT SHIP
LINDEN, Margaret		19	F	Spinster	28Ap11Cr
MURPHY, Bridget		20	F	Seamstress	28Ap11Cr
Ellen		30	F	Seamstress	28Ap11Cr
Lawrence		21	M	Servant	28Ap11Cr
MCCREADY, Hugh		20	M	Gdnr	28Ap11Cr
GOOSE, Owen		25	M	Laborer	28Ap11Cr
Mary	(W)	26	F	Wife	28Ap11Cr
TREANOR, John		30	M	Fisherman	28Ap11Cr
Mary	(W)	26	F	Wife	28Ap11Cr
MCBRIDE, Sarah		20	F	Spinster	28Ap11Cr
MCGIVERNS, Bridget		20	F	Servant	28Ap11Cr
PINDEY, Sarah		20	F	Servant	28Ap11Cr
SMITH, Biddy		20	F	Seamstress	28Ap11Cr
MCMAHON, Mary		25	F	Bomkr	28Ap11Cr
NEILL, Susan		40	F	Dressmaker	28Ap11Cr
Margaret		11	F	Relative	28Ap11Cr
Hugh		9	M	Relative	28Ap11Cr
FINEGAN, Biddy		40	F	Spinster	28Ap11Cr
MULLEN, Jane	(W)	22	F	Wife	28Ap11Cr
Edward	(H)	23	M	Husband	28Ap11Cr
MARSHALL, Hannah		19	F	House Maid	28Ap11Cr
GALLAGHER, Francis		23	M	Laborer	28Ap11Cr
HARVEY, John		23	M	Baker	28Ap11Cr
DONAGHY, Thos.		21	M	Servant	28Ap11Cr
SONNOR, Catherine		18	F	Spinster	28Ap11Cr
HARVEY, William		33	M	Laborer	28Ap11Cr
RUDDOCK, Robert		20	M	Servant	28Ap11Cr
LONG, Anne		40	F	Spinster	28Ap11Cr
QUINN, Peter		30	M	Servant	28Ap11Cr
LONG, John		25	M	Farmer	28Ap11Cr
Mary	(W)	20	F	Wife	28Ap11Cr
MOONEY, James		25	M	Gdnr	28Ap11Cr
Ellen	(W)	22	F	Wife	28Ap11Cr
CANNEN, James		20	M	Hrstnr	28Ap11Cr
DEVLIN, Francis		22	M	Servant	28Ap11Cr
KIERANS, Francis		25	M	Farmer	28Ap11Cr
Mary		25	F	Relative	28Ap11Cr
Margaret		.00	F	Infant	28Ap11Cr
CONNOR, Patrick		38	M	Laborer	28Ap11Cr
MURPHY, Michael		26	M	Ploughman	28Ap11Cr
MCCOURT, James		20	M	Servant	28Ap11Cr
MAMON, Owen		22	M	Laborer	28Ap11Cr
WARD, Ann		19	F	Spinster	28Ap11Cr
John		14	M	Tailor	28Ap11Cr
CUNNINGHAM, Mary		21	F	Spinster	28Ap11Cr
COLGAN, Anne		21	F	Spinster	28Ap11Cr
GRANT, Peter		18	M	Baker	28Ap11Cr
WHITE, Catherine		20	F	Spinster	28Ap11Cr
Margaret		20	F	House Maid	28Ap11Cr
FEARN, Daniel		28	M	Boatman	28Ap11Cr
Rose	(W)	25	F	Wife	28Ap11Cr
MARTIN, Michael		45	M	Farmer	28Ap11Cr
James		30	M	Ploughman	28Ap11Cr
Bernard		19	M	Relative	28Ap11Cr
Patt		17	M	Relative	28Ap11Cr
Mary		14	F	Relative	28Ap11Cr
Ellen		40	F	Relative	28Ap11Cr
CUNNINGHAM, Henry		35	M	Farmer	28Ap11Cr
Mary		35	F	Relative	28Ap11Cr
Owen		12	M	Relative	28Ap11Cr
Patrick		10	M	Relative	28Ap11Cr
Ellen		8	F	Relative	28Ap11Cr
Mary		3	F	Relative	28Ap11Cr
MARTIN, Catharine		22	F	Spinster	28Ap11Cr
Biddy		20	F	Relative	28Ap11Cr
Ellen		18	F	Relative	28Ap11Cr
Rose		16	F	Relative	28Ap11Cr
Patt		13	M	Relative	28Ap11Cr
James		11	M	Relative	28Ap11Cr
Owen		45	M	Farmer	28Ap11Cr
Bridget		34	F	Relative	28Ap11Cr
Mary		13	F	Relative	28Ap11Cr
Michael		10	M	Relative	28Ap11Cr
Patrick		8	M	Relative	28Ap11Cr
Francis		3	M	Relative	28Ap11Cr

NAMES OF PASSENGERS		AGE	SEX	OCCUPATIONS	DATE PORT SHIP
MCMAHON, Patrick		55	M	Farmer	28Ap11Cr
Elizabeth		45	F	Relative	28Ap11Cr
Edward		19	M	Relative	28Ap11Cr
Thomas		17	M	Relative	28Ap11Cr
Mary		12	F	Relative	28Ap11Cr
Owen		10	M	Relative	28Ap11Cr
Catharine		8	F	Relative	28Ap11Cr
Elizabeth		6	F	Relative	28Ap11Cr
Anne		3	F	Relative	28Ap11Cr
TREANOR, Mary		18	F	Spinster	28Ap11Cr
FINNEGAN, Rose		54	F	Spinster	28Ap11Cr
Mary		22	F	Servant	28Ap11Cr
Rose		20	F	Servant	28Ap11Cr
CASSIDY, Biddy		36	F	Spinster	28Ap11Cr
Judy		7	F	Child	28Ap11Cr
Margaret		5	F	Child	28Ap11Cr
MCGRATH, John		27	M	Laborer	28Ap11Cr
CONNOR, Hugh		16	M	Laborer	28Ap11Cr
MONAGHAN, John		35	M	Mariner	28Ap11Cr
Martha	(W)	20	F	Wife	28Ap11Cr
Henry	(S)	.00	M	Infant	28Ap11Cr
MCGEARY, Alice		55	F	Spinster	28Ap11Cr
Catharine		20	F	Spinster	28Ap11Cr
ROURKE, Margaret		20	F	Seamstress	28Ap11Cr
GOOSE, Betty		.00	F	Infant	28Ap11Cr
CASSIDY, Matthew		3	M	Child	28Ap11Cr
MCCLORY, Henry		24	M	Preceptor	28Ap11Cr

MARMION 30 APRIL 1849

From Liverpool

NAMES OF PASSENGERS		AGE	SEX	OCCUPATIONS	DATE PORT SHIP
CLOWEY, Ann		34	F	Servant	30Ap02Cw
Mary		30	F	Servant	30Ap02Cw
Patrick		29	M	Laborer	30Ap02Cw
NOWLAN, Lawrence		29	M	Laborer	30Ap02Cw
Daniel		24	M	Laborer	30Ap02Cw
CONNOR, Mary		24	F	Servant	30Ap02Cw
POWELL, John		28	M	Laborer	30Ap02Cw
KANE, James		26	M	Laborer	30Ap02Cw
Richard		24	M	Laborer	30Ap02Cw
Isabella		23	F	Unknown	30Ap02Cw
DALZELL, William		22	M	Laborer	30Ap02Cw
Elizabeth		24	F	Unknown	30Ap02Cw
FARRELLY, Phillip		20	M	Laborer	30Ap02Cw
MCCORMICK, James		30	M	Laborer	30Ap02Cw
WILLIAMS, James		23	M	Laborer	30Ap02Cw
FOGARTY, Michael		24	M	Laborer	30Ap02Cw
Johanna		24	F	Unknown	30Ap02Cw
William		3	M	Child	30Ap02Cw
Dennis		2	M	Child	30Ap02Cw
Michael		.00	M	Infant	30Ap02Cw
HARTIGAN, Timothy		24	M	Laborer	30Ap02Cw
HENESSY, James		30	M	Laborer	30Ap02Cw
CLANCY, William		26	M	Laborer	30Ap02Cw
FARRELL, Richard		40	M	Laborer	30Ap02Cw
Ann		40	F	Unknown	30Ap02Cw
Matthew		18	M	Unknown	30Ap02Cw
Edward		16	M	Unknown	30Ap02Cw
Mary		9	F	Child	30Ap02Cw
Richard		7	M	Child	30Ap02Cw
Christopher		5	M	Child	30Ap02Cw
KING, Michael		17	M	Miller	30Ap02Cw
MCGOVERN, Luke		22	M	Clerk	30Ap02Cw
DEVLIN, Anthony		24	M	Laborer	30Ap02Cw
DOWD, Martin		30	M	Laborer	30Ap02Cw
LAVIN, Jane		20	F	Servant	30Ap02Cw
Celia		17	F	Servant	30Ap02Cw
DOWD, Ann		20	F	Servant	30Ap02Cw

NAMES OF PASSENGERS	AGE	SEX	OCCUPATIONS	DATE PORT SHIP
DONOHUE, John	18	M	Laborer	30Ap02Cw
MURRAY, John	30	M	Laborer	30Ap02Cw
Ann	30	F	Unknown	30Ap02Cw
Mary	7	F	Child	30Ap02Cw
Ann	3	F	Child	30Ap02Cw
Daniel	.00	M	Infant	30Ap02Cw
CASEY, William	25	M	Joiner	30Ap02Cw
Charlotte	26	F	Unknown	30Ap02Cw
CROTTY, John	29	M	Laborer	30Ap02Cw
POTTER, Thomas	22	M	Plasterer	30Ap02Cw
GREENLAND, James	30	M	Plasterer	30Ap02Cw
TAINSBURG, Joshua	22	M	Plasterer	30Ap02Cw
SOMERS, William	27	M	Carpenter	30Ap02Cw
HERBERT, Bridget	21	F	Servant	30Ap02Cw
GREENAN, Michael	23	M	Laborer	30Ap02Cw
CRITTERDON, Matthew	21	M	Laborer	30Ap02Cw
CAIRNS, Peter	20	M	Shoemaker	30Ap02Cw
PINDON, Ann	15	F	Servant	30Ap02Cw
CORCERY, John	23	M	Laborer	30Ap02Cw
William	14	M	Laborer	30Ap02Cw
HOGAN, Daniel	22	M	Laborer	30Ap02Cw
MCDONNELL, Edwd.	28	M	Student	30Ap02Cw
WALSH, Patrick	20	M	Laborer	30Ap02Cw
COURTNEY, Andrew	26	M	Laborer	30Ap02Cw
KNOX, William	22	M	Laborer	30Ap02Cw
Mary	22	F	Unknown	30Ap02Cw
Ellen	40	F	Unknown	30Ap02Cw
Mary	13	F	Unknown	30Ap02Cw
Richard	11	M	Unknown	30Ap02Cw
DALTON, Margaret	16	F	Servant	30Ap02Cw
HYLAND, Kearn	30	M	Laborer	30Ap02Cw
Mary	30	F	Unknown	30Ap02Cw
Patrick	2	M	Child	30Ap02Cw
Mary	.00	F	Infant	30Ap02Cw
Michael	25	M	Laborer	30Ap02Cw
DELANY, Martin	25	M	Laborer	30Ap02Cw
Anty	22	F	Unknown	30Ap02Cw
BROPHY, Catherine	21	F	Dressmaker	30Ap02Cw
FORSYTH, Douglass	21	M	Laborer	30Ap02Cw
LYNCH, John	28	M	Laborer	30Ap02Cw
MANGAN, John	35	M	Laborer	30Ap02Cw
FOLEY, Maurice	30	M	Laborer	30Ap02Cw
OCONNOR, Mary	18	F	Servant	30Ap02Cw
DALTON, Honora	20	F	Servant	30Ap02Cw
Mary	19	F	Servant	30Ap02Cw
SHANAHAN, Margaret	19	F	Servant	30Ap02Cw
DALHUNTY, Wm.	27	M	Millwright	30Ap02Cw
Johanna	22	F	Unknown	30Ap02Cw
SOLMON, Jane	22	F	Unknown	30Ap02Cw
WHITE, Michael	32	M	Laborer	30Ap02Cw
Mary	28	F	Unknown	30Ap02Cw
Margaret	18	F	Unknown	30Ap02Cw
MAHER, Mary	20	F	Servant	30Ap02Cw
KEENAN, Edward	25	M	Laborer	30Ap02Cw
HUTCHINSON, Jane	21	F	Servant	30Ap02Cw
Eliza	30	F	Servant	30Ap02Cw
KENNEDY, Ellen	22	F	Servant	30Ap02Cw
CREGAN, Thomas	22	M	Laborer	30Ap02Cw
Ann	22	F	Servant	30Ap02Cw
OHARE, Hugh	40	M	Laborer	30Ap02Cw
MYLAND, Patrick	36	M	Laborer	30Ap02Cw
LYONS, Bernard	21	M	Laborer	30Ap02Cw
SCINION, Mark	36	M	Laborer	30Ap02Cw
Bernard	34	M	Laborer	30Ap02Cw
ROURKE, John	25	M	Laborer	30Ap02Cw
FLANNAGAN, Mary	20	F	Servant	30Ap02Cw
WILLIAMS, Jeremiah	22	M	Laborer	30Ap02Cw
FLYNN, James	24	M	Laborer	30Ap02Cw
Ellen	20	F	Unknown	30Ap02Cw
LYNCH, Phillip	24	M	Laborer	30Ap02Cw
Ann	23	F	Unknown	30Ap02Cw
Ann	2	F	Child	30Ap02Cw
DOWDELL, Thomas	24	M	Baker	30Ap02Cw
MURPHY, Pat	30	M	Laborer	30Ap02Cw
KEARY, Wm.	20	M	Laborer	30Ap02Cw
KEARY, Martin	15	M	Laborer	30Ap02Cw
ONEILL, Thos.	16	M	Nailer	30Ap02Cw
BYRNE, Ellen	20	F	Servant	30Ap02Cw
COSTELLO, John	28	M	Laborer	30Ap02Cw
TRACEY, Thos.	28	M	Laborer	30Ap02Cw
ROURKE, Frederick	25	M	Laborer	30Ap02Cw
NOLAN, James	20	M	Laborer	30Ap02Cw
PHORTEL, Michael	21	M	Laborer	30Ap02Cw
BRIEN, Lucy	20	F	Servant	30Ap02Cw
Margaret	20	F	Servant	30Ap02Cw
SHIELS, Robert	30	M	Miller	30Ap02Cw
GILLIES, Nancy	26	F	Servant	30Ap02Cw
HACKETT, Patt	18	M	Servant	30Ap02Cw
John	16	M	Servant	30Ap02Cw
MOORE, Ellen	22	F	Servant	30Ap02Cw
SYKES, Lawrence	22	M	Laborer	30Ap02Cw
WALSH, Thomas	20	M	Laborer	30Ap02Cw
Michael	19	M	Laborer	30Ap02Cw
POWER, Thomas	23	M	Laborer	30Ap02Cw
FITZPATRICK, Mary	50	F	Unknown	30Ap02Cw
KAYES, James	18	M	Clerk	30Ap02Cw
KENNEDY, Thomas	24	M	Tailor	30Ap02Cw
Edward	40	M	Tailor	30Ap02Cw
GILTINANE, John	30	M	Farmer	30Ap02Cw
SEXTON, John	20	M	Laborer	30Ap02Cw
STOKES, John	24	M	Laborer	30Ap02Cw
Mary	20	F	Unknown	30Ap02Cw
Patrick	.00	M	Infant	30Ap02Cw
PRENDERGRAST, Mary	40	F	Unknown	30Ap02Cw
HENESSY, Catherine	40	F	Unknown	30Ap02Cw
COLLINS, Mary	20	F	Unknown	30Ap02Cw
PRENDERGAST, Mary	13	F	Unknown	30Ap02Cw
Ellen	8	F	Child	30Ap02Cw
DUGAN, Patrick	35	M	Laborer	30Ap02Cw
Honoria	30	F	Unknown	30Ap02Cw
Margaret	2	F	Child	30Ap02Cw
John	.00	M	Infant	30Ap02Cw
MCCARTHY, John	40	M	Laborer	30Ap02Cw
Catherine	30	F	Unknown	30Ap02Cw
Cornelius	8	M	Child	30Ap02Cw
Nancy	8	M	Child	30Ap02Cw
SCULLY, Honoria	22	F	Unknown	30Ap02Cw
CUMMINGS, Matthew	21	M	Laborer	30Ap02Cw
Bridget	29	F	Servant	30Ap02Cw
William	15	M	None	30Ap02Cw
THOMPSON, Eleanor	16	F	Servant	30Ap02Cw
MCCONNELL, Brian	22	M	Carpenter	30Ap02Cw
Julia	17	F	Servant	30Ap02Cw
MCNAMARA, Hugh	21	M	Laborer	30Ap02Cw
DOYLE, Catherine	20	F	Servant	30Ap02Cw
TRACEY, Celia	22	F	Servant	30Ap02Cw
CARROLL, Ann	20	F	Servant	30Ap02Cw
MITCHELL, Patrick	24	M	Laborer	30Ap02Cw
LYNCH, Bridget	19	F	Servant	30Ap02Cw
BRODERICK, Ann	18	F	Servant	30Ap02Cw

SWAN 30 APRIL 1849

From Cork

NAMES OF PASSENGERS	AGE	SEX	OCCUPATIONS	DATE PORT SHIP
CONNELL, Garrett	11	M	Laborer	30Ap08Cx
KIRK, William	22	M	Laborer	30Ap08Cx
COLE, John	23	M	Laborer	30Ap08Cx
KIELY, Biddy	23	F	Unknown	30Ap08Cx
CASEY, William	22	M	Laborer	30Ap08Cx
LOONEY, Michael	18	M	Laborer	30Ap08Cx
CASEY, Bridget	25	F	Unknown	30Ap08Cx
DUGGAN, James	20	M	Laborer	30Ap08Cx
PENDERGAST, Jas.	24	M	Laborer	30Ap08Cx

NAMES OF PASSENGERS	AGE	SEX	OCCUPATIONS	DATE PORT SHIP
DALY, Catherine	20	F	Laborer	30Ap08Cx
CUNNINGHAM, Catherine	20	F	Laborer	30Ap08Cx
SOTTY, Mary	22	F	Laborer	30Ap08Cx
DONOGHUE, Anne	21	F	Laborer	30Ap08Cx
LOOMEY, Michl.	23	M	Laborer	30Ap08Cx
MEADE, Danl.	24	M	Laborer	30Ap08Cx
NOWLAN, Richd.	51	M	Laborer	30Ap08Cx
Betty	50	F	Laborer	30Ap08Cx
John	26	M	Laborer	30Ap08Cx
Abby	24	F	Laborer	30Ap08Cx
James	22	M	Laborer	30Ap08Cx
Margt.	20	F	Laborer	30Ap08Cx
Richard	16	M	Laborer	30Ap08Cx
SHANAHAN, Ellen	28	F	Laborer	30Ap08Cx
BARRY, John	24	M	Laborer	30Ap08Cx
NOWLAN, Mary	12	F	Laborer	30Ap08Cx
Michael	11	M	Laborer	30Ap08Cx
KEEFE, Nancy	17	F	Laborer	30Ap08Cx
OBRIEN, Michael	26	M	Laborer	30Ap08Cx
Margt.	24	F	Laborer	30Ap08Cx
CROWLEY, Timothy	30	M	Laborer	30Ap08Cx
BRIEN, Jerry	2	M	Laborer	30Ap08Cx
Ellen	25	F	Laborer	30Ap08Cx
Mary	50	F	Laborer	30Ap08Cx
MAHONEY, Michael	28	M	Laborer	30Ap08Cx
KIELY, Jerry	30	M	Laborer	30Ap08Cx
FANT, Margt.	22	F	Laborer	30Ap08Cx
Barth.	22	M	Laborer	30Ap08Cx
BARRETT, John	24	M	Laborer	30Ap08Cx
CAREY, John	50	M	Laborer	30Ap08Cx
Johanna	50	F	Laborer	30Ap08Cx
HENNESSY, Maurice	20	M	Laborer	30Ap08Cx
Mary	20	F	Laborer	30Ap08Cx
CAREY, John	10	M	None	30Ap08Cx
GRIFFIN, Michael	30	M	Laborer	30Ap08Cx
HARTY, John	20	M	Laborer	30Ap08Cx
CARTY, David	20	M	Laborer	30Ap08Cx
DINAN, Michael	26	M	Laborer	30Ap08Cx
MURRAY, Kate	25	F	Laborer	30Ap08Cx
Biddy	23	F	Laborer	30Ap08Cx
TOMMEY, Margt.	26	F	Laborer	30Ap08Cx
NANGLE, Richard	26	M	Laborer	30Ap08Cx
FORREST, John	28	M	Laborer	30Ap08Cx
LEAHY, Betty	25	F	Laborer	30Ap08Cx
TOOMEY, Denis	20	M	Laborer	30Ap08Cx
KIRBY, Denis	20	M	Laborer	30Ap08Cx
Jerry	24	M	Laborer	30Ap08Cx
MCGRATH, Jerry	35	M	Laborer	30Ap08Cx
Margt.	30	F	Laborer	30Ap08Cx
TOOMEY, Margt.	20	F	Laborer	30Ap08Cx
BARRY, Nancy	20	F	Laborer	30Ap08Cx
GOGGIN, John	26	M	Laborer	30Ap08Cx
CONNOR, Michael	22	M	Laborer	30Ap08Cx
GARSFIELD, John	26	M	Laborer	30Ap08Cx
ENGLISH, Ellen	28	F	Laborer	30Ap08Cx
WHEELAN, Maurice	25	M	Laborer	30Ap08Cx
CARTY, John	26	M	Laborer	30Ap08Cx
Patt	28	M	Laborer	30Ap08Cx
FENTON, Thomas	25	M	Laborer	30Ap08Cx
GRIFFIN, Michael	30	M	Laborer	30Ap08Cx
WIGMORE, John	25	M	Laborer	30Ap08Cx
Michael	20	M	Laborer	30Ap08Cx
CURTIN, Patrick	35	M	Laborer	30Ap08Cx
Margt.	33	F	Laborer	30Ap08Cx
LINEHAM, Denis	26	M	Laborer	30Ap08Cx
KEMP, Thomas	28	M	Laborer	30Ap08Cx
AHEARN, Martha	26	F	Laborer	30Ap08Cx
Johanna	.00	F	Infant	30Ap08Cx
MULCHAHY, John	26	M	Laborer	30Ap08Cx
GLINY, Mary	20	F	Laborer	30Ap08Cx
DRISCOLL, Thomas	30	M	Laborer	30Ap08Cx
U, Ansty	18	U	Laborer	30Ap08Cx
CARTY, Tim	35	M	Laborer	30Ap08Cx
BARRETT, Tim	21	M	Laborer	30Ap08Cx
DRISCOLL, Mary	20	F	Laborer	30Ap08Cx
HYDE, James	22	M	Laborer	30Ap08Cx
LEARY, Catherine	26	F	Laborer	30Ap08Cx
HYDE, Wm.	24	M	Laborer	30Ap08Cx
MURPHY, John	28	M	Laborer	30Ap08Cx
FENTON, Catherine	26	F	Laborer	30Ap08Cx
MCCARTY, Danl.	30	M	Laborer	30Ap08Cx
Margt.	28	F	Laborer	30Ap08Cx
WIGMORE, Cath.	22	F	Laborer	30Ap08Cx
CONNOR, George	20	M	Laborer	30Ap08Cx
MAHONEY, Catherine	25	F	Laborer	30Ap08Cx
CASEY, John	30	M	Laborer	30Ap08Cx
HAYS, James	28	M	Laborer	30Ap08Cx
MCCARTHY, William	18	M	Laborer	30Ap08Cx
Fanny	21	F	Laborer	30Ap08Cx
CONNOR, Andy	21	U	Unknown	30Ap08Cx
KEEFE, Mary	20	F	Unknown	30Ap08Cx
HEGARTHY, Jeremiah	20	M	Laborer	30Ap08Cx
HURLY, James	22	M	Laborer	30Ap08Cx

HARVARD 30 APRIL 1849

From Liverpool

NAMES OF PASSENGERS	AGE	SEX	OCCUPATIONS	DATE PORT SHIP
DONNELY, Pat	17	M	Farmer	30Ap02Cy
John	9	M	Child	30Ap02Cy
Ann	5	F	Child	30Ap02Cy
James	3	M	Child	30Ap02Cy
KELLY, Pat	30	M	Farmer	30Ap02Cy
Ann	25	F	Farmer	30Ap02Cy
James	4	M	Child	30Ap02Cy
Mary	.00	F	Infant	30Ap02Cy
HEGARTY, Catharine	28	F	Farmer	30Ap02Cy
Pat	.00	M	Infant	30Ap02Cy
MOORE, Pat	30	M	Farmer	30Ap02Cy
Catharine	28	F	Farmer	30Ap02Cy
Daniel	11	M	Farmer	30Ap02Cy
James	.00	M	Infant	30Ap02Cy
Daniel	27	M	Farmer	30Ap02Cy
MURRAY, Pat	25	M	Farmer	30Ap02Cy
Ann	.00	F	Infant	30Ap02Cy
Biddy	48	F	Farmer	30Ap02Cy
LAMB, Pat	50	M	Stone Mason	30Ap02Cy
Elizth.	22	F	Unknown	30Ap02Cy
Benj.	22	M	Stone Mason	30Ap02Cy
James	14	M	Stone Mason	30Ap02Cy
FURRY, William	20	M	Farmer	30Ap02Cy
James	30	M	Farmer	30Ap02Cy
Catharine	18	F	Farmer	30Ap02Cy
HEGAN, Dennis	20	M	Farmer	30Ap02Cy
BURNS, Pat	23	M	Farmer	30Ap02Cy
Honora	25	F	Farmer	30Ap02Cy
LAWLER, Mary	25	F	Farmer	30Ap02Cy
HENNESSY, Dennis	50	M	Farmer	30Ap02Cy
Mary	50	F	Farmer	30Ap02Cy
Wm.	22	M	Carpenter	30Ap02Cy
Pat	17	M	Carpenter	30Ap02Cy
Sarah	12	F	Unknown	30Ap02Cy
Ann	11	F	Unknown	30Ap02Cy
Mary	10	F	Unknown	30Ap02Cy
SHEENY, Daniel	55	M	Farmer	30Ap02Cy
Daniel	20	M	Farmer	30Ap02Cy
BUCKLEY, Tim	30	M	Farmer	30Ap02Cy
DAVIS, George	20	M	Farmer	30Ap02Cy
Wm.	20	M	Farmer	30Ap02Cy
GILMARTIN, Michl.	10	M	Farmer	30Ap02Cy
Mary	.00	F	Infant	30Ap02Cy
QUINLAND, Sally	12	F	Unknown	30Ap02Cy
RYAN, Michl.	30	M	Farmer	30Ap02Cy
James	24	M	Farmer	30Ap02Cy

NAMES OF PASSENGERS	AGE	SEX	OCCUPATIONS	DATE PORT SHIP
QUINN, Wm.	20	M	Farmer	30Ap02Cy
Mary-Ann	17	F	Farmer	30Ap02Cy
Margaret	13	F	Farmer	30Ap02Cy
Nicholas	6	M	Child	30Ap02Cy
RANKIN, Mary	17	F	Farmer	30Ap02Cy
MURPHY, Margt.	25	F	Farmer	30Ap02Cy
SMITH, John	20	M	Farmer	30Ap02Cy
BURNS, Anty	23	F	Farmer	30Ap02Cy
Cathe.	25	F	Farmer	30Ap02Cy
BURKE, John	35	M	Farmer	30Ap02Cy
KENNEDY, Daniel	50	M	Farmer	30Ap02Cy
WHITE, Ann	25	F	Farmer	30Ap02Cy
FEW, John	43	M	Carpenter	30Ap02Cy
Rebecca	42	F	Unknown	30Ap02Cy
John-Thompson	21	M	Carpenter	30Ap02Cy
Edwd.Crow	11	M	Carpenter	30Ap02Cy
Mary-Ann	8	F	Child	30Ap02Cy
Robert-Henry	4	M	Child	30Ap02Cy
Eliza-Emma	3	F	Child	30Ap02Cy
Sarah-Shelling	.00	F	Infant	30Ap02Cy
HIGGINS, Thomas	26	M	Farmer	30Ap02Cy
Nelly	22	F	Farmer	30Ap02Cy
Libby	20	F	Farmer	30Ap02Cy
MCCARTNEY, Michl.	33	M	Farmer	30Ap02Cy
Mary	27	F	Farmer	30Ap02Cy
Cath.	3	F	Child	30Ap02Cy
John	2	M	Child	30Ap02Cy
Ellen	21	F	Farmer	30Ap02Cy
RAHAN, Cathe.	21	F	Farmer	30Ap02Cy
DALTON, Mary	22	F	Farmer	30Ap02Cy
HAMER, John	27	M	Plasterer	30Ap02Cy
HAMMOND, Thos.	25	M	Farmer	30Ap02Cy
MOONEY, Wm.	30	M	Farmer	30Ap02Cy
MCDONALD, Thos.	17	M	Farmer	30Ap02Cy
TOONEY, Cathe.	17	F	Farmer	30Ap02Cy
DORSEY, Juedah	24	F	Farmer	30Ap02Cy
HERN, James	30	M	Farmer	30Ap02Cy
Mary	23	F	Servant	30Ap02Cy
MAHAN, Dennis	30	M	Servant	30Ap02Cy
KENYAN, Thos.	20	M	Servant	30Ap02Cy
Jane	12	F	Servant	30Ap02Cy
DOYLE, Ody	12	F	Servant	30Ap02Cy
Bridget	20	F	Servant	30Ap02Cy
COCKRAN, Mick	25	M	Servant	30Ap02Cy
RAFFERTY, Margt.	20	F	Servant	30Ap02Cy
James	18	M	Servant	30Ap02Cy
COCKRAN, Ann	20	F	Servant	30Ap02Cy
CROSSLEY, Thos.	20	M	Servant	30Ap02Cy
WALLSEY, Mick	40	M	Farmer	30Ap02Cy
BLANEY, Samuel	9	M	Child	30Ap02Cy
FINNEGAN, Francis	23	M	Farmer	30Ap02Cy
Alice	33	F	Farmer	30Ap02Cy
Pat	5	M	Child	30Ap02Cy
WARDLE, Matthew	29	M	Farmer	30Ap02Cy
MAHAN, Renall	7	M	Child	30Ap02Cy
Cath.	13	F	Farmer	30Ap02Cy
HENDERSON, John	14	M	Farmer	30Ap02Cy
CUNNINGHAM, Pat	20	M	Farmer	30Ap02Cy
HUSEY, James	30	M	Farmer	30Ap02Cy
Bridget	25	F	Farmer	30Ap02Cy
James	.00	M	Infant	30Ap02Cy
BRYLAN, Cath.	20	F	Farmer	30Ap02Cy
THOMAS, Henry	20	M	Molder	30Ap02Cy
James	20	M	Molder	30Ap02Cy
JOICE, Bridget	16	F	Molder	30Ap02Cy
KEYLAN, Francis	3	M	Child	30Ap02Cy
John	20	M	Carpenter	30Ap02Cy
MILLER, John-Alex	28	M	Carpenter	30Ap02Cy
MAHAN, Wm.	33	M	Carpenter	30Ap02Cy
GRAHAM, Hugh	46	M	Trader	30Ap02Cy
ENNIS, Wm.	18	M	Trader	30Ap02Cy
BRIDGAN, Susan	40	F	Trader	30Ap02Cy
DOWNING, Mary-Jane	8	F	Child	30Ap02Cy
FARRELL, John	30	M	Trader	30Ap02Cy
Ellen	20	F	Trader	30Ap02Cy
DWYER, Pat	22	M	Trader	30Ap02Cy
John	30	M	Trader	30Ap02Cy
Peggy	20	F	Trader	30Ap02Cy
Thomas	6	M	Child	30Ap02Cy
James	4	M	Child	30Ap02Cy
COFFEE, Thos.	28	M	Carpenter	30Ap02Cy
Cathe.	18	F	Unknown	30Ap02Cy
LYNCH, Pat	23	M	Carpenter	30Ap02Cy
KALLEYHAN, Jas.	18	M	Laborer	30Ap02Cy
Ann	18	F	Laborer	30Ap02Cy
FARELL, Pat	20	M	Laborer	30Ap02Cy
Thos.	18	M	Laborer	30Ap02Cy
Mary	17	F	Laborer	30Ap02Cy
WALLESE, James	20	M	Laborer	30Ap02Cy
REGAN, Pat	25	M	Laborer	30Ap02Cy
Mars.	20	F	Laborer	30Ap02Cy
Ned	.00	M	Infant	30Ap02Cy
FEENY, Cath.	18	F	Laborer	30Ap02Cy
Emma	17	F	Laborer	30Ap02Cy
DENNISON, John	25	M	Laborer	30Ap02Cy
Bridget	20	F	Laborer	30Ap02Cy
Cathe.	18	F	Laborer	30Ap02Cy
DALTON, Thos.	30	M	Laborer	30Ap02Cy
LYNAS, Michl.	14	M	Laborer	30Ap02Cy
Chrs.	8	M	Child	30Ap02Cy
WALSH, Michl.	22	M	Laborer	30Ap02Cy
Ann	30	F	Laborer	30Ap02Cy
John	.00	M	Infant	30Ap02Cy
Norry	4	F	Child	30Ap02Cy
WILSON, James	20	M	Laborer	30Ap02Cy
BRADY, John	18	M	Laborer	30Ap02Cy
Charles	18	M	Laborer	30Ap02Cy
RILEY, Bridget	20	F	Laborer	30Ap02Cy
SMITH, John	20	M	Laborer	30Ap02Cy
WINTER, Charles	30	M	Laborer	30Ap02Cy
ENNIS, Pat	37	M	Laborer	30Ap02Cy
Pat	5	M	Child	30Ap02Cy
LYNCH, Dan	24	M	Farmer	30Ap02Cy
John	7	M	Child	30Ap02Cy
PETER, Mick	18	M	Farmer	30Ap02Cy
COLLIER, James	18	M	Farmer	30Ap02Cy
BURKE, Richd.	40	M	Farmer	30Ap02Cy
Edwd.	17	M	Farmer	30Ap02Cy
John	21	M	Farmer	30Ap02Cy
TRACEY, John	24	M	Farmer	30Ap02Cy
James	18	M	Farmer	30Ap02Cy
Edwd.	13	M	Farmer	30Ap02Cy
MELDEN, Wm.	28	M	Farmer	30Ap02Cy
WRIGHT, George	24	M	Farmer	30Ap02Cy
Mary	23	F	Farmer	30Ap02Cy
Sarah	22	F	Farmer	30Ap02Cy
Robert	30	M	Farmer	30Ap02Cy
Edwd.	28	M	Farmer	30Ap02Cy
Wm.	7	M	Child	30Ap02Cy
CAMPBELL, David	22	M	Farmer	30Ap02Cy
JANEY, Mick	22	M	Laborer	30Ap02Cy
SULLIVAN, Jerry	32	M	Laborer	30Ap02Cy
OLEY, Janet	22	F	Laborer	30Ap02Cy
DOWNING, Doly	21	F	Laborer	30Ap02Cy
DALEY, James	19	M	Laborer	30Ap02Cy
RILEY, Pat	31	M	Laborer	30Ap02Cy
HEATON, James	25	M	Laborer	30Ap02Cy
James	.00	M	Infant	30Ap02Cy
BRADOW, Martin	28	M	Laborer	30Ap02Cy
CHILD, John	20	M	Laborer	30Ap02Cy
MCKAY, John	24	M	Laborer	30Ap02Cy
SANDERSON, John	22	M	Farmer	30Ap02Cy
CORNISH, Ann	18	F	Farmer	30Ap02Cy
SMITH, Ann	18	F	Farmer	30Ap02Cy
OKEIAN, Jamy	19	M	Farmer	30Ap02Cy
Mick	45	M	Farmer	30Ap02Cy
Mary	43	F	Farmer	30Ap02Cy
Mick	11	M	Farmer	30Ap02Cy
Richd.	.00	M	Infant	30Ap02Cy
Died-At-Sea				

NAMES OF PASSENGERS	AGE	SEX	OCCUPATIONS	DATE PORT SHIP
FITZGERALD, Joana	30	F	Farmer	30Ap02Cy
ALLEN, Thos.	48	M	Farmer	30Ap02Cy
John	12	M	Farmer	30Ap02Cy
NICHOLSON. Pat	25	M	Farmer	30Ap02Cy
Mary	24	F	Farmer	30Ap02Cy
John	9	M	Child	30Ap02Cy
Ann	2	F	Child	30Ap02Cy
MANING, John	20	M	Farmer	30Ap02Cy
DALEY, James	44	M	Farmer	30Ap02Cy
John	19	M	Farmer	30Ap02Cy
JOHNSON. Thos.	33	M	Farmer	30Ap02Cy
KUNK, John	22	M	Farmer	30Ap02Cy
FARRELL, John	23	M	Farmer	30Ap02Cy
TRACEY, Mary	35	F	Farmer	30Ap02Cy
Michl.	5	M	Child	30Ap02Cy
Edwd.	2	M	Child	30Ap02Cy

INDEPENDENCE 30 APRIL 1849

From London

NAMES OF PASSENGERS	AGE	SEX	OCCUPATIONS	DATE PORT SHIP
CRAWLEY, William	28	M	Laborer	30Ap13Cz
Patrick	24	M	Laborer	30Ap13Cz

ABBEY-LAND 01 MAY 1849

From Liverpool

NAMES OF PASSENGERS	AGE	SEX	OCCUPATIONS	DATE PORT SHIP
ARNOLD, John	28	M	Farmer	01Ma02Da
Eliza	25	F	Unknown	01Ma02Da
Mary	10	F	Unknown	01Ma02Da
Anne	8	F	Child	01Ma02Da
John	3	M	Child	01Ma02Da
Ellen	4	F	Child	01Ma02Da
Margt.	2	F	Child	01Ma02Da
BILLINS. Henry	22	M	Laborer	01Ma02Da
REST, Frances	20	F	Laborer	01Ma02Da
COSTELLO. Thos.	30	M	Farmer	01Ma02Da
Anne	28	F	Unknown	01Ma02Da
Kate	8	F	Child	01Ma02Da
William	6	M	Child	01Ma02Da
Louisa	2	F	Child	01Ma02Da
Jane	.00	F	Infant	01Ma02Da
RICHARDS. George	21	M	Mason	01Ma02Da
ENGLISH, Antonie	18	M	Mason	01Ma02Da
HENRICH. Christiana	22	F	Farmer	01Ma02Da
LYNCH. James	50	M	Laborer	01Ma02Da
U-Mrs.	40	F	Unknown	01Ma02Da
Peter	21	M	Laborer	01Ma02Da
Margt.	15	F	Unknown	01Ma02Da
John	13	M	Unknown	01Ma02Da
BRADY, Thos.	48	M	Carpenter	01Ma02Da
U-Mrs.	40	F	Unknown	01Ma02Da
Rose	14	F	Unknown	01Ma02Da
Mary	11	F	Unknown	01Ma02Da
Matthew	9	M	Child	01Ma02Da
Michl.	7	M	Child	01Ma02Da
Cath.	5	F	Child	01Ma02Da
Thomas	2	M	Child	01Ma02Da
MARTIN. Patrick	31	M	Laborer	01Ma02Da
Bridget	25	F	Unknown	01Ma02Da
MCDONAGH. Matthew	20	M	Laborer	01Ma02Da
READ, Thomas	52	M	Laborer	01Ma02Da
READ, Margt.	56	F	Unknown	01Ma02Da
John	23	M	Laborer	01Ma02Da
CAMPBELL, Chris	23	M	Laborer	01Ma02Da
Phoebe	21	F	Unknown	01Ma02Da
Elizabeth	.00	F	Infant	01Ma02Da
BRAITHWAITE, Wm.	24	M	Mason	01Ma02Da
Hodgen	22	M	Mason	01Ma02Da
SIGERSON, George	21	M	Mason	01Ma02Da
AYER, John	20	M	Mason	01Ma02Da
BEDDY, John	31	M	Laborer	01Ma02Da
U-Mrs.	20	F	Unknown	01Ma02Da
PAESTON, U-Miss	20	F	Unknown	01Ma02Da
DUFFY, Mary	21	F	Unknown	01Ma02Da
YULE, Wm.	23	M	Laborer	01Ma02Da
BRADLY, Mary-A.	25	F	Unknown	01Ma02Da
GASH, Wm.	20	M	Unknown	01Ma02Da
KANE, Danl.	20	M	Farmer	01Ma02Da
PATSH, Edwd.	23	M	Farmer	01Ma02Da
JACKSON, John	25	M	Farmer	01Ma02Da
Susan	20	F	Unknown	01Ma02Da
Sarah	20	F	Unknown	01Ma02Da
Alice	18	F	Unknown	01Ma02Da
GARRATT, Thos.	26	M	Mason	01Ma02Da
Mary-Ann	24	F	Unknown	01Ma02Da
John	.00	M	Infant	01Ma02Da
Anne	22	F	Unknown	01Ma02Da
KELLY, Edwd.	21	M	Mason	01Ma02Da
BRENNAN, Edwd.	26	M	Mason	01Ma02Da
ORAUL, Jerh.	18	M	Laborer	01Ma02Da
HENAHAY, Joe	26	M	Laborer	01Ma02Da
Martin	23	M	Laborer	01Ma02Da
Cath.	20	F	Unknown	01Ma02Da
GATHAN, James	29	M	Mason	01Ma02Da
Cath.	25	F	Unknown	01Ma02Da
James	2	M	Child	01Ma02Da
Celia	.00	F	Infant	01Ma02Da
DOYLE, Martha	50	F	Unknown	01Ma02Da
Pat	22	M	Mason	01Ma02Da
MCGLAGHAN, Will	45	M	Farmer	01Ma02Da
Wm.	19	M	Farmer	01Ma02Da
FINNEGAN, Lany	35	F	Farmer	01Ma02Da
MURPHY, Miles	21	M	Farmer	01Ma02Da
MCDEVITT, Bridget	18	F	Farmer	01Ma02Da
WALSH, Michl.	41	M	Laborer	01Ma02Da
Nancy	40	F	Farmer	01Ma02Da
Nancy	15	F	Unknown	01Ma02Da
Lawrence	11	M	Unknown	01Ma02Da
Martin	9	M	Child	01Ma02Da
Mary	7	F	Child	01Ma02Da
Oliver	5	M	Child	01Ma02Da
James	3	M	Child	01Ma02Da
Michl.	1	M	Child	01Ma02Da
PURCELL, James	25	M	Laborer	01Ma02Da
CODY, Patt	25	M	Laborer	01Ma02Da
CAMPION, John	20	M	Laborer	01Ma02Da
FITZPATRICK, Biddy	18	F	Laborer	01Ma02Da
BROPHY, Margt.	20	F	Laborer	01Ma02Da
Cathe.	18	F	Laborer	01Ma02Da
WHELAN, John	35	M	Farmer	01Ma02Da
Margt.	30	F	Unknown	01Ma02Da
Michl.	1	M	Child	01Ma02Da
GARTRIDE, Sam	25	M	Laborer	01Ma02Da
LESTER, Joseph	36	M	Laborer	01Ma02Da
MONTGOMERY, Jas.	19	M	Laborer	01Ma02Da
BARLON, Sam	29	M	Laborer	01Ma02Da
STOKES, Benj.	35	M	Laborer	01Ma02Da
PEIRCE. Wm.	30	M	Laborer	01Ma02Da
WARD, Harvey	16	M	Laborer	01Ma02Da
SUTTON, Wm.	20	M	Laborer	01Ma02Da
QUINN, Eliza	16	F	Unknown	01Ma02Da
Ellen	12	F	Unknown	01Ma02Da
Rose	9	F	Child	01Ma02Da
MAGUIRE. John	24	M	Laborer	01Ma02Da
JOHNSTON, George	41	M	Laborer	01Ma02Da
Mary	20	F	Unknown	01Ma02Da

NAMES OF PASSENGERS	AGE	SEX	OCCUPATIONS	DATE PORT SHIP
FITZGIBBON, John	27	M	Mason	01Ma02Da
Mary	26	F	Unknown	01Ma02Da
Cath.	21	F	Unknown	01Ma02Da
Mick	12	M	Laborer	01Ma02Da
John	26	M	Laborer	01Ma02Da
HOGAN. John	25	M	Laborer	01Ma02Da
RYAN, Edwd.	28	M	Laborer	01Ma02Da
Cath.	28	F	Unknown	01Ma02Da
Cath.	3	F	Child	01Ma02Da
James	.00	M	Infant	01Ma02Da
MAHER. Wm.	23	M	Laborer	01Ma02Da
KNIGHT, Fredk.	24	M	Laborer	01Ma02Da
STOWE. Richd.	31	M	Laborer	01Ma02Da
CONNELLY, Bryan	21	M	Laborer	01Ma02Da
Bridget	18	F	Unknown	01Ma02Da
MARTIN, Cath.	23	F	Unknown	01Ma02Da
MCMAHON. John	16	M	Laborer	01Ma02Da
Mary	2	F	Child	01Ma02Da
KAYE. Susan	40	F	Unknown	01Ma02Da
CARTER. Gilbert	28	M	Laborer	01Ma02Da
BARBER. James	43	M	Mason	01Ma02Da
Sarah	63	F	Unknown	01Ma02Da
Mary	20	F	Unknown	01Ma02Da
WARD, Anne	18	F	Unknown	01Ma02Da
David	22	M	Laborer	01Ma02Da
GOMMERSAL, Aaron	16	M	Laborer	01Ma02Da
BARBER. John	12	M	Laborer	01Ma02Da
Jane	8	F	Child	01Ma02Da
Hannah	6	F	Child	01Ma02Da
Eliza	2	F	Child	01Ma02Da
STEEL, John	20	M	Farmer	01Ma02Da
Anne	20	F	Unknown	01Ma02Da
Sarah	1	F	Child	01Ma02Da
U	.00	F	Infant	01Ma02Da
BLAKELY, John	26	M	Laborer	01Ma02Da
Harriott	26	F	Unknown	01Ma02Da
THACKINS, Wm.	20	M	Mason	01Ma02Da
BAINES, James	19	M	Laborer	01Ma02Da
ELLY, John	40	M	Laborer	01Ma02Da
LACY, Wm.	20	M	Laborer	01Ma02Da
POWELL, Henry	28	M	Laborer	01Ma02Da
Martha	20	F	Unknown	01Ma02Da
SMITH, Jane	25	F	Unknown	01Ma02Da
BILLINGTON. John	22	M	Carpenter	01Ma02Da
Anne	20	F	Unknown	01Ma02Da
U-Mrs.	50	F	Unknown	01Ma02Da
DYSON, Joseph	27	M	Laborer	01Ma02Da
RICHARDSON, Wm.	24	M	Laborer	01Ma02Da
CHAMBERS, Thos.	30	M	Laborer	01Ma02Da
CUMMINS, Joseph	22	M	Laborer	01Ma02Da
MULLEN, John	25	M	Laborer	01Ma02Da
ROBERTS, Thos.	45	M	Laborer	01Ma02Da
Anne	22	F	Unknown	01Ma02Da
MCENTYRE, Hugh	45	M	Laborer	01Ma02Da
James	12	M	Laborer	01Ma02Da
ANNERSON. Elizabeth	40	F	Unknown	01Ma02Da
George	24	M	Unknown	01Ma02Da
ABRAHAM, Wm.	26	M	Laborer	01Ma02Da
RICHARDSON, John	25	M	Laborer	01Ma02Da
MCCONNELL, Margt.	17	F	Unknown	01Ma02Da
Eliza	15	F	Unknown	01Ma02Da
Cath.	14	F	Unknown	01Ma02Da
CASSEDY, Bridget	18	F	Unknown	01Ma02Da
Pat	20	M	Laborer	01Ma02Da

ARABIAN 01 MAY 1849

From Liverpool

NAMES OF PASSENGERS	AGE	SEX	OCCUPATIONS	DATE PORT SHIP
MCGRAW, James	24	M	Farmer	01Ma02Db
KELLY, Bridget	25	F	Farmer	01Ma02Db
MULLALL, Elizabeth	20	F	Farmer	01Ma02Db
DUFFEY, Bridget	23	F	Farmer	01Ma02Db
CRENNARD, Laughlin	20	M	Farmer	01Ma02Db
Bridget	11	F	Farmer	01Ma02Db
FOSTER, William	17	M	Farmer	01Ma02Db
Eliza	15	F	Farmer	01Ma02Db
HARRIS, Lanty	20	M	Farmer	01Ma02Db
CASSIDY, Hugh	17	M	Farmer	01Ma02Db
MCDERMOTT. Hugh	20	M	Farmer	01Ma02Db
QUINN, John	18	M	Farmer	01Ma02Db
Bridget	20	F	Farmer	01Ma02Db
STEVENS, James	20	M	Farmer	01Ma02Db
CULLANANE, Michl.	14	M	Farmer	01Ma02Db
Mary	18	F	Farmer	01Ma02Db
DANLAN, Thomas	16	M	Farmer	01Ma02Db
HOPKINS, John	30	M	Farmer	01Ma02Db
STEEL, Wm.	30	M	Farmer	01Ma02Db
CARNEY, James	19	M	Farmer	01Ma02Db
KELLY, Michl.	35	M	Farmer	01Ma02Db
U	30	F	Farmer	01Ma02Db
Thomas	2	M	Child	01Ma02Db
Mary	.00	F	Infant	01Ma02Db
GEORGE. John	49	M	Farmer	01Ma02Db
JONES, George	19	M	Farmer	01Ma02Db
DELANEY, Thomas	24	M	Farmer	01Ma02Db
MURPHY, Maria	26	F	Farmer	01Ma02Db
Eliza	26	F	Farmer	01Ma02Db
NOWLAN, Maria	23	F	Farmer	01Ma02Db
WALSH, David	23	M	Farmer	01Ma02Db
Michael	18	M	Farmer	01Ma02Db
ROBINSON, Kirkwood	25	M	Farmer	01Ma02Db
U (W)	25	F	Farmer	01Ma02Db
Kirkwood	18	M	Farmer	01Ma02Db
CONNOR, Tom	28	M	Farmer	01Ma02Db
MCCANNON, Charles	19	M	Farmer	01Ma02Db
COOK, Henry	40	M	Farmer	01Ma02Db
CONGERS, Pat	20	M	Farmer	01Ma02Db
HILAND, Maria	26	F	Farmer	01Ma02Db
CARNEY, John	28	M	Farmer	01Ma02Db
U (W)	28	F	Farmer	01Ma02Db
Bridget	26	F	Farmer	01Ma02Db
HILAND, Hugh	18	M	Farmer	01Ma02Db
Rose	16	F	Farmer	01Ma02Db
MURPHY, John	22	M	Farmer	01Ma02Db
Winifred	20	F	Farmer	01Ma02Db
MCNASH, Wm.	28	M	Farmer	01Ma02Db
U (W)	21	F	Farmer	01Ma02Db
MILLER, John	23	M	Farmer	01Ma02Db
Patt	26	M	Farmer	01Ma02Db
Mary	18	F	Farmer	01Ma02Db
GRADY, Honora	16	F	Farmer	01Ma02Db
Matthew	22	M	Farmer	01Ma02Db
Bridget	20	F	Farmer	01Ma02Db
MILLAT, John	28	M	Farmer	01Ma02Db
CUFF, M.	21	M	Farmer	01Ma02Db
MCGRATH, Thomas	23	M	Farmer	01Ma02Db
Martin	18	M	Farmer	01Ma02Db
Mary	20	F	Farmer	01Ma02Db
Bridget	29	F	Farmer	01Ma02Db
James	6	M	Child	01Ma02Db
HOOPER, Henry	19	M	Farmer	01Ma02Db
RUSSELL, William	18	M	Farmer	01Ma02Db
PORTER. James	40	M	Farmer	01Ma02Db

NAMES OF PASSENGERS	AGE	SEX	OCCUPATIONS	DATE PORT SHIP
PORTER. U	25	F	Farmer	01Ma02Db
Henrietta	9	F	Child	01Ma02Db
Mary	6	F	Child	01Ma02Db
Clara	3	F	Child	01Ma02Db
Eliza	.00	F	Infant	01Ma02Db
CONNOLLY, Bridget	30	F	Farmer	01Ma02Db
Thomas	8	M	Child	01Ma02Db
Maria	3	F	Child	01Ma02Db
Ann	6	F	Child	01Ma02Db
WALLACE. Patt	18	M	Farmer	01Ma02Db
CAFFREY, Phillip	30	M	Farmer	01Ma02Db
Rose	13	F	Farmer	01Ma02Db
MCNEILL, Andrew	20	M	Farmer	01Ma02Db
Hannah	20	F	Farmer	01Ma02Db
PINDER, Edwd.	25	M	Farmer	01Ma02Db
CARROLL, Mary	25	F	Farmer	01Ma02Db
FALLON, James	41	M	Farmer	01Ma02Db
BRANNON. James	26	M	Farmer	01Ma02Db
WARD, John	40	M	Farmer	01Ma02Db
MCINTIRE, Mary	22	F	Farmer	01Ma02Db
Catherine	16	F	Farmer	01Ma02Db
Susan	10	F	Farmer	01Ma02Db
Ann	8	F	Child	01Ma02Db
MCKADE, Hugh	28	M	Farmer	01Ma02Db
DIXON. Cath.	37	F	Farmer	01Ma02Db
MASON. William	35	M	Farmer	01Ma02Db
COONEY, Patt	20	M	Farmer	01Ma02Db
HADLEY, Mary	20	F	Farmer	01Ma02Db
MCELARNEY, Thomas	20	M	Farmer	01Ma02Db
MITCHELL, J.	20	M	Farmer	01Ma02Db
MCNULTY, J.	20	M	Farmer	01Ma02Db
KERRIGAN, Mark	23	M	Farmer	01Ma02Db
U-Mrs.	23	F	Farmer	01Ma02Db
Patrick	.00	M	Infant	01Ma02Db
ARMSTRONG, Ann	25	F	Farmer	01Ma02Db
CONNOR. Martha	50	F	Farmer	01Ma02Db
U-Mrs.	50	F	Farmer	01Ma02Db
Catharine	15	F	Farmer	01Ma02Db
Thomas	.00	M	Infant	01Ma02Db
DONLIN. Judith	12	F	Farmer	01Ma02Db
FLEMING, Francis	20	M	Farmer	01Ma02Db
HIGGINS. Morris	20	M	Farmer	01Ma02Db
RANKIN. M.	42	M	Farmer	01Ma02Db
MCGOMEREY, Jas.	27	M	Farmer	01Ma02Db
U (W)	24	F	Farmer	01Ma02Db
James	2	M	Child	01Ma02Db
Michael	.00	M	Infant	01Ma02Db
John	26	M	Farmer	01Ma02Db
MULROONEY, Patt	30	M	Farmer	01Ma02Db
FAGAN. Patt	30	M	Farmer	01Ma02Db
KEOUGH, Matt	25	M	Farmer	01Ma02Db
BRICE, Thomas	18	M	Farmer	01Ma02Db
William	38	M	Farmer	01Ma02Db
HANARTY, Barnd.	35	M	Farmer	01Ma02Db
MCGRATH, Michl.	50	M	Farmer	01Ma02Db
U-Mrs.	50	F	Farmer	01Ma02Db
COYNE, Eliza	22	F	Farmer	01Ma02Db
Michael	.00	M	Infant	01Ma02Db
DONEGAN. Patt	20	M	Farmer	01Ma02Db
DALEY, Ellen	20	F	Farmer	01Ma02Db
GRIFFEN, Cath.	20	F	Farmer	01Ma02Db
JULIAN, John	30	M	Farmer	01Ma02Db
ELLIOTT, John	35	M	Farmer	01Ma02Db
JACKSON. Margt.	21	F	Farmer	01Ma02Db
Mary	20	F	Farmer	01Ma02Db
WALSH, Margaret	20	F	Farmer	01Ma02Db
MCELROY, Michl.	20	M	Farmer	01Ma02Db
CROUCHE. George	20	M	Farmer	01Ma02Db
U-Mrs.	20	F	Farmer	01Ma02Db
BAKER. John	20	M	Farmer	01Ma02Db
CASSIDEY, John	20	M	Farmer	01Ma02Db
Mary	30	F	Farmer	01Ma02Db
Elizabeth	4	F	Child	01Ma02Db
Catharine	2	F	Child	01Ma02Db
Maria	.00	F	Infant	01Ma02Db
CONNOR, Dan	25	M	Farmer	01Ma02Db
U (W)	25	F	Farmer	01Ma02Db
Ellen	3	F	Child	01Ma02Db
Michael	.00	M	Infant	01Ma02Db
MCFADDEN, Daniel	22	M	Farmer	01Ma02Db
Michl.	25	M	Farmer	01Ma02Db
SWEENEY, Cath.	18	F	Farmer	01Ma02Db
LONGHLEY, John	20	M	Farmer	01Ma02Db
SWEENEY, Patt	30	M	Farmer	01Ma02Db
MCKENSEY, Ann	50	F	Farmer	01Ma02Db
Kate	20	F	Farmer	01Ma02Db
Flora	14	F	Farmer	01Ma02Db
TRACEY, Edward	40	M	Farmer	01Ma02Db
MCKENNA, Margaret	15	F	Farmer	01Ma02Db
MATHEWS, James	20	M	Farmer	01Ma02Db
FAIRLEY, John	20	M	Farmer	01Ma02Db
ELIZA, Ann	18	F	Farmer	01Ma02Db
HAWKINS, Wm.	40	M	Farmer	01Ma02Db
LUCK, Thomas	27	M	Farmer	01Ma02Db
CAMDEN, William	30	M	Farmer	01Ma02Db
Charles	6	M	Child	01Ma02Db
KIMBERLEY, Isaiah	25	M	Farmer	01Ma02Db
John	32	M	Farmer	01Ma02Db
JACKSON, Robert	30	M	Farmer	01Ma02Db
MULKIAN, Thomas	30	M	Farmer	01Ma02Db
RYAN, Ann	30	F	Farmer	01Ma02Db
LANG, U-Mrs.	30	F	Farmer	01Ma02Db
HALL, U-Mrs.	30	F	Farmer	01Ma02Db
FARLEY, Samuel	50	M	Farmer	01Ma02Db
MURPHY, John	20	M	Farmer	01Ma02Db
GRANE, John	53	M	Farmer	01Ma02Db
Patt	21	M	Farmer	01Ma02Db
Margaret	33	F	Farmer	01Ma02Db
Maria	26	F	Farmer	01Ma02Db
Bridget	21	F	Farmer	01Ma02Db
Margaret	26	F	Farmer	01Ma02Db
Michael	32	M	Farmer	01Ma02Db
OBRIEN, Patt	26	M	Farmer	01Ma02Db
GEAREY, Patt	25	M	Farmer	01Ma02Db
HOSKINS, John	40	M	Farmer	01Ma02Db
James	17	M	Farmer	01Ma02Db
DWYER, Honora	16	F	Farmer	01Ma02Db
WALSH, Ellen	14	F	Farmer	01Ma02Db
Ellen	40	F	Farmer	01Ma02Db
John	13	M	Farmer	01Ma02Db
James	11	M	Farmer	01Ma02Db
Margaret	6	F	Child	01Ma02Db
Bridget	2	F	Child	01Ma02Db
MCNAMARA. Patt	25	M	Farmer	01Ma02Db
KEATING, Morris	30	M	Farmer	01Ma02Db
HOLLAND, James	21	M	Farmer	01Ma02Db
WOOD, Henry	24	M	Farmer	01Ma02Db
MURPHY, Daniel	38	M	Farmer	01Ma02Db
Mary	25	F	Farmer	01Ma02Db
Margaret	16	F	Farmer	01Ma02Db
William	13	M	Farmer	01Ma02Db
Patt	11	M	Farmer	01Ma02Db
Michael	8	M	Child	01Ma02Db
Mary-Ann	9	F	Child	01Ma02Db
Catharine	.00	F	Infant	01Ma02Db
RYAN, John	21	M	Farmer	01Ma02Db
Biddy	20	F	Farmer	01Ma02Db
DWYRE, Patt	18	M	Farmer	01Ma02Db
ROCK, Patt	25	M	Farmer	01Ma02Db

MARCHIONESS-OF-CLYSDALE 01 MAY 1849

From Londonderry

NAMES OF PASSENGERS	AGE	SEX	OCCUPATIONS	DATE PORT SHIP
MCGINNIS. Betty	27	F	Spinster	01Ma01Fw
DORION. Thos.	16	M	Laborer	01Ma01Fw
MCGIVEGAN. Ellen	12	F	Spinster	01Ma01Fw
HAGAN. James	50	M	Laborer	01Ma01Fw
Sarah	45	F	Spinster	01Ma01Fw
Michael	15	M	Laborer	01Ma01Fw
Mary	12	F	Spinster	01Ma01Fw
Cath.	10	F	Unknown	01Ma01Fw
Bridget	6	F	Child	01Ma01Fw
Sarah	8	F	Child	01Ma01Fw
ONEILL, Susan	12	F	Unknown	01Ma01Fw
TOLAND, Owen	45	M	Laborer	01Ma01Fw
BEGLEY, John	28	M	Laborer	01Ma01Fw
HOUSTON. Mary	18	F	Spinster	01Ma01Fw
PARKER. James	25	M	Laborer	01Ma01Fw
LINDSAY, Sonan	17	M	Laborer	01Ma01Fw
PARKER, James	22	M	Laborer	01Ma01Fw
HARKIN, Maggy	20	F	Spinster	01Ma01Fw
MCTAGART, Margaret	19	F	Spinster	01Ma01Fw
COLLER, Jane	10	F	Spinster	01Ma01Fw
John	12	M	Unknown	01Ma01Fw
HENRY, John	13	M	Unknown	01Ma01Fw
DEVER, Nancy	49	F	Spinster	01Ma01Fw
John	17	M	Laborer	01Ma01Fw
Thos.	15	M	Laborer	01Ma01Fw
Hugh	13	M	Laborer	01Ma01Fw
Danl.	11	M	Laborer	01Ma01Fw
Pat	5	M	Child	01Ma01Fw
BRADY, Ellen	60	F	Spinster	01Ma01Fw
BEGLEY, Cath.	30	F	Spinster	01Ma01Fw
ONEILL, Pat	20	M	Laborer	01Ma01Fw
KELLY, Rosey	23	F	Spinster	01Ma01Fw
ADAMS. Sally	18	F	Spinster	01Ma01Fw
FRIZZLE. Amelia	20	F	Spinster	01Ma01Fw
FINLEY, John	20	M	Laborer	01Ma01Fw
FRIZZLE. Rose	19	F	Spinster	01Ma01Fw
CONNORS. Pat	20	M	Laborer	01Ma01Fw
Margaret	17	F	Spinster	01Ma01Fw
MURPHY, John	36	M	Laborer	01Ma01Fw
Rosey	25	F	Spinster	01Ma01Fw
James	.00	M	Infant	01Ma01Fw
LEECH. Rosanna	16	F	Spinster	01Ma01Fw
JEMMISON. Isaac	27	M	Laborer	01Ma01Fw
Jane	21	F	Spinster	01Ma01Fw
QUIGLEY, John	19	M	Laborer	01Ma01Fw
MCKINNEY, Sarah	17	F	Spinster	01Ma01Fw
BELL, James	23	M	Laborer	01Ma01Fw
BRUSTER. Robert	23	M	Laborer	01Ma01Fw
PARKHILL, James	18	M	Laborer	01Ma01Fw
KINKADE. Sarah	34	F	Spinster	01Ma01Fw
SCOTT, Daniel	24	M	Laborer	01Ma01Fw
TOLAND, Ann	40	F	Spinster	01Ma01Fw
Peggy	14	F	Spinster	01Ma01Fw
Pat	12	M	Laborer	01Ma01Fw
Ellenor	8	F	Child	01Ma01Fw
Dennis	5	M	Child	01Ma01Fw
Daniel	6	M	Child	01Ma01Fw
MCCANDY, Margret	18	F	Spinster	01Ma01Fw
TRACY, Hanah	55	F	Spinster	01Ma01Fw
Cath.	17	F	Spinster	01Ma01Fw
GALLAGHER, James	24	M	Laborer	01Ma01Fw
Mary	23	F	Spinster	01Ma01Fw
TERNEY, John	25	M	Laborer	01Ma01Fw
CAMPBELL, Ann	18	F	Spinster	01Ma01Fw
GILLAND, John	16	M	Laborer	01Ma01Fw

NAMES OF PASSENGERS	AGE	SEX	OCCUPATIONS	DATE PORT SHIP
GOURLEY, James	18	M	Laborer	01Ma01Fw
BOYD, Jane	44	F	Spinster	01Ma01Fw
MCLAUGHLIN. James	20	M	Laborer	01Ma01Fw
BRADLEY, Mary	30	F	Spinster	01Ma01Fw
MCHARKIN, Cath.	18	F	Spinster	01Ma01Fw
OBRIEN, James	18	M	Laborer	01Ma01Fw
KEARNEY, Michial	16	M	Laborer	01Ma01Fw
DOUGHERTY, Dudely	22	M	Laborer	01Ma01Fw
HUNTER, William	20	M	Laborer	01Ma01Fw
Eliza	20	F	Spinster	01Ma01Fw
BRYSON, Charles	22	M	Laborer	01Ma01Fw
MCGOWEN, Connell	18	M	Laborer	01Ma01Fw
MCLAUGHLIN, William	20	M	Laborer	01Ma01Fw
GANAGH, Chas.	25	M	Laborer	01Ma01Fw
ODONNELL, John	23	M	Laborer	01Ma01Fw
BOYLE, Edward	24	M	Laborer	01Ma01Fw
MCLAUGHLIN, Patrick	30	M	Laborer	01Ma01Fw
MCGROREY, James	18	M	Laborer	01Ma01Fw
KINCADE, Sarah	53	F	Spinster	01Ma01Fw
KERLIN, Susan	40	F	Spinster	01Ma01Fw
GENTLES, Eliza	15	F	Spinster	01Ma01Fw
COONEY, Isabella	17	F	Spinster	01Ma01Fw
MAHON, Mary	18	F	Spinster	01Ma01Fw
Margret	16	F	Spinster	01Ma01Fw
Martha	14	F	Spinster	01Ma01Fw
DEVIN, Mary-Ann	20	F	Spinster	01Ma01Fw
PARKER, U	24	F	Spinster	01Ma01Fw
DONNELL, John	24	M	Laborer	01Ma01Fw
SUNDAY, Thos.	30	M	Laborer	01Ma01Fw
GLASS, Margret	29	F	Spinster	01Ma01Fw
William	28	M	Laborer	01Ma01Fw
CAMPBELL, Robert	26	M	Laborer	01Ma01Fw
MCELHENY, Eliza	19	F	Spinster	01Ma01Fw
MCLAUGHLIN, Ann	20	F	Spinster	01Ma01Fw
STEWERT. Margret	20	F	Spinster	01Ma01Fw
EMBERSON, Mary	25	F	Spinster	01Ma01Fw
Rebecca	22	F	Spinster	01Ma01Fw
CALWELL, Ann	28	F	Spinster	01Ma01Fw
MCLAUGHLIN, Bety	21	F	Spinster	01Ma01Fw
MCCLUGHAN, James	25	M	Laborer	01Ma01Fw
KEY, Marth.	20	F	Spinster	01Ma01Fw
Ann.J.	.00	F	Infant	01Ma01Fw
MCMICHAEL, Walter	65	M	Laborer	01Ma01Fw
Stewart	21	M	Laborer	01Ma01Fw
Archey	18	M	Laborer	01Ma01Fw
James	5	M	Child	01Ma01Fw
HALL, James	20	M	Laborer	01Ma01Fw
DOUGHERTY, Cath.	48	F	Spinster	01Ma01Fw
Jas.	17	M	Laborer	01Ma01Fw
Hugh	12	M	Laborer	01Ma01Fw
Wm.	10	M	Laborer	01Ma01Fw
John	8	M	Child	01Ma01Fw
MCCLINTON, Peter	18	M	Laborer	01Ma01Fw
MCKINNA, Cath.	20	F	Spinster	01Ma01Fw
BRADLEY, Margret	19	F	Spinster	01Ma01Fw
BRANNAN, Peter	28	M	Laborer	01Ma01Fw
Biddy	29	F	Spinster	01Ma01Fw
FORRIST, Jane	22	F	Spinster	01Ma01Fw
DOUGHERTY, Geo.	21	M	Laborer	01Ma01Fw
Eliza	42	F	Spinster	01Ma01Fw
Mary	18	F	Spinster	01Ma01Fw
HARKIN, Pat	28	M	Laborer	01Ma01Fw
MCDADE, John	25	M	Laborer	01Ma01Fw
GILL, Rodger	24	M	Laborer	01Ma01Fw
DOHERTY, Daniel	21	M	Laborer	01Ma01Fw
Michael	23	M	Laborer	01Ma01Fw
CARR, Philip	24	M	Laborer	01Ma01Fw
DEVER, Mary	20	F	Spinster	01Ma01Fw
DOHERTY, Fanny	17	F	Spinster	01Ma01Fw
MCDADE, Daniel	27	M	Laborer	01Ma01Fw
GIBBON, Pat	19	M	Laborer	01Ma01Fw
MCDADE, James	40	M	Laborer	01Ma01Fw
DOUGHERTY, John	26	M	Laborer	01Ma01Fw
BOYLE, Margret	25	F	Spinster	01Ma01Fw
DEVIN, Cath.	19	F	Spinster	01Ma01Fw

NAMES OF PASSENGERS	AGE	SEX	OCCUPATIONS	DATE PORT SHIP
BOYLE, Wm.	24	M	Laborer	01Ma01Fw
MCFADDEN, Ann	28	F	Spinster	01Ma01Fw
John	32	M	Laborer	01Ma01Fw
Margret	20	F	Spinster	01Ma01Fw
MCBRIDE, Stepen	40	M	Laborer	01Ma01Fw
DOUGHERTY, Jane	25	F	Spinster	01Ma01Fw
Susan	5	F	Child	01Ma01Fw
Edward	10	M	Laborer	01Ma01Fw
CAMPBELL, Geo.	16	M	Laborer	01Ma01Fw
Mary-A.	15	F	Spinster	01Ma01Fw
MARTIN. Eliza	17	F	Spinster	01Ma01Fw
MCCAFFERTY, Pat.	35	M	Laborer	01Ma01Fw
GALLAUGHER, Henry	30	M	Laborer	01Ma01Fw
DOUGHERTY, Geo.	27	M	Spinster	01Ma01Fw
LANNEY, Margrt.	17	F	Spinster	01Ma01Fw
Rebecca	19	F	Spinster	01Ma01Fw
MCFEGAN. James	24	M	Laborer	01Ma01Fw
ODONNELL, Rodger	22	M	Laborer	01Ma01Fw
ARMSTRONG, Thos.	25	M	Laborer	01Ma01Fw
Daniel	22	M	Laborer	01Ma01Fw
LYNCH. Pegy	17	F	Spinster	01Ma01Fw
ONEILL, Pat	21	M	Laborer	01Ma01Fw
DONNELLY, Owen	22	M	Laborer	01Ma01Fw
Ann	18	F	Spinster	01Ma01Fw
Sarah	16	F	Spinster	01Ma01Fw
Biddy	7	F	Child	01Ma01Fw
GALLAGHER, John	29	M	Laborer	01Ma01Fw
MCLAUGHLIN, Ann	21	F	Spinster	01Ma01Fw
KEOGH, Mary	18	F	Spinster	01Ma01Fw
Cath.	20	F	Spinster	01Ma01Fw
FERRY, Miles	14	M	Laborer	01Ma01Fw
ROBINSON. Ann	50	F	Spinster	01Ma01Fw
MARSHELL, Robt.	30	M	Laborer	01Ma01Fw
MCCLOSKEY, John	24	M	Laborer	01Ma01Fw
WILSON, John	22	M	Laborer	01Ma01Fw
DOHERTY, Robert	18	M	Laborer	01Ma01Fw
Edward	16	M	Laborer	01Ma01Fw
FERNS. Isabella	25	F	Spinster	01Ma01Fw
Alexander	.00	M	Infant	01Ma01Fw
Isabella	3	F	Child	01Ma01Fw
Rosana	28	F	Spinster	01Ma01Fw
DEVELIN. Michael	16	M	Laborer	01Ma01Fw
BRANNAN. Edward	48	M	Laborer	01Ma01Fw
FLETCHER, Stewart	40	M	Laborer	01Ma01Fw
STERLING, William	22	M	Laborer	01Ma01Fw
MORROW, Mary	30	F	Spinster	01Ma01Fw
James	25	M	Laborer	01Ma01Fw
MCALTON, Thos.	22	M	Laborer	01Ma01Fw
Eliza	22	F	Spinster	01Ma01Fw
Mary	.00	F	Infant	01Ma01Fw
KERR. Rodger	19	M	Laborer	01Ma01Fw
Hugh	21	M	Laborer	01Ma01Fw
GAMBLE. Ann	50	F	Spinster	01Ma01Fw
Mathew	18	M	Laborer	01Ma01Fw
Doritha	16	F	Spinster	01Ma01Fw
WHITE, Martha	50	F	Spinster	01Ma01Fw
Margret	23	F	Spinster	01Ma01Fw
MCMICHAEL, Hanah	60	F	Spinster	01Ma01Fw

HOME 01 MAY 1849

From Liverpool

NAMES OF PASSENGERS	AGE	SEX	OCCUPATIONS	DATE PORT SHIP
MOLLOY, Michl.	21	M	Laborer	01Ma02Dd
HIGGINS. John	18	M	Laborer	01Ma02Dd
BERRIN. Pat	37	M	Laborer	01Ma02Dd
CONNOR. Margt.	38	F	Laborer	01Ma02Dd
Mary	17	F	Laborer	01Ma02Dd
Thomas	13	M	Laborer	01Ma02Dd
CONNOR, Dennis	6	M	Child	01Ma02Dd
Arthur	5	M	Child	01Ma02Dd
John	.00	M	Infant	01Ma02Dd
BYRNES, Margt.	26	F	Laborer	01Ma02Dd
Pat	28	M	Laborer	01Ma02Dd
CONNELL, John	17	M	Laborer	01Ma02Dd
COOK, Wm.	27	M	Laborer	01Ma02Dd
SELLMAN, Josiah	30	M	Laborer	01Ma02Dd
PIPER, George	28	M	Laborer	01Ma02Dd
OHARA, Rose	40	F	Laborer	01Ma02Dd
REILLY, Rose	20	F	Laborer	01Ma02Dd
CONORD, Mary	20	F	Laborer	01Ma02Dd
LAWLESS, Peter	18	M	Laborer	01Ma02Dd
James	14	M	Laborer	01Ma02Dd
RYAN, James	12	M	Laborer	01Ma02Dd
GUNN, Phillip	40	M	Laborer	01Ma02Dd
Edwd.	14	M	Laborer	01Ma02Dd
Bernd.	12	M	Laborer	01Ma02Dd
JONES, Thomas	45	M	Laborer	01Ma02Dd
Thomas	17	M	Laborer	01Ma02Dd
QUINN, Wm.	40	M	Laborer	01Ma02Dd
COSGROVE, Susan	20	F	Laborer	01Ma02Dd
CUNNINGHAM, Betsey	22	F	Laborer	01Ma02Dd
HANES, Sarah	22	F	Laborer	01Ma02Dd
TRACEY, James	26	M	Laborer	01Ma02Dd
ELLIOTT. Willm.	22	M	Laborer	01Ma02Dd
KELLY, Martin	30	M	Laborer	01Ma02Dd
CUNNINGHAM, John	22	M	Laborer	01Ma02Dd
HAYES, Sarah	22	F	Laborer	01Ma02Dd
SMITH, Ellen	18	F	Laborer	01Ma02Dd
Patk.	6	M	Child	01Ma02Dd
MCCARROLL, Owen	21	M	Laborer	01Ma02Dd
ROBINSON, Robt.	36	M	Laborer	01Ma02Dd
FLOCKHART, Jas.	27	M	Laborer	01Ma02Dd
GARLAND, Barney	25	M	Laborer	01Ma02Dd
FLOOD, Betsey	27	F	Laborer	01Ma02Dd
Thomas	33	M	Laborer	01Ma02Dd
LYNCH, Edwd.	23	M	Laborer	01Ma02Dd
FLOOD, Betsey	.00	F	Infant	01Ma02Dd
SHAW, John	30	M	Laborer	01Ma02Dd
BROWN, Jacob	30	M	Laborer	01Ma02Dd
MCCADDON, Patk.	28	M	Laborer	01Ma02Dd
LAWLESS, Thos.	50	M	Laborer	01Ma02Dd
Jane	20	F	Laborer	01Ma02Dd
Rose	8	F	Child	01Ma02Dd
Pat	7	M	Child	01Ma02Dd
Betsey	2	F	Child	01Ma02Dd
Cath.	16	F	Laborer	01Ma02Dd
Bridget	9	F	Child	01Ma02Dd
Thomas	6	M	Child	01Ma02Dd
Margt.	50	F	Laborer	01Ma02Dd
Michl.	.00	M	Infant	01Ma02Dd
MCCOURT. Bridget	16	F	Laborer	01Ma02Dd
BATES, Eliza	30	F	Laborer	01Ma02Dd
BOWES, Cath.	28	F	Laborer	01Ma02Dd
CASEY, Mary	26	F	Laborer	01Ma02Dd
MOONEY, Ann	30	F	Laborer	01Ma02Dd
James	30	M	Laborer	01Ma02Dd
HICKEY, Edwd.	38	M	Laborer	01Ma02Dd
MOONEY, Danl.	.00	M	Infant	01Ma02Dd
CASEY, Richd.	25	M	Laborer	01Ma02Dd
BURNS, Thos.	21	M	Laborer	01Ma02Dd
BARKLEY, Ellen	21	F	Laborer	01Ma02Dd
MARHER, Ann	20	F	Laborer	01Ma02Dd
Constance	21	F	Laborer	01Ma02Dd
HORN. Edwd.	24	M	Laborer	01Ma02Dd
MARHER, Patk.	25	M	Laborer	01Ma02Dd
CAHAEL, Mary	21	F	Laborer	01Ma02Dd
RYAN, Lucy	17	F	Laborer	01Ma02Dd
MARHER, Thomas	28	M	Laborer	01Ma02Dd
Michl.	27	M	Laborer	01Ma02Dd
James	23	M	Laborer	01Ma02Dd
MCCORMICK, Michl.	25	M	Laborer	01Ma02Dd
NICHOLL, Robert	43	M	Laborer	01Ma02Dd
HARELL, Geo.	50	M	Laborer	01Ma02Dd

NAMES OF PASSENGERS	AGE	SEX	OCCUPATIONS	DATE PORT SHIP
HARELL, James	9	M	Child	01Ma02Dd
DEGNAN, Thomas	40	M	Laborer	01Ma02Dd
Betsey	40	F	Laborer	01Ma02Dd
Patk.	6	M	Child	01Ma02Dd
Rose	9	F	Child	01Ma02Dd
PATTERSON. Michl.	35	M	Laborer	01Ma02Dd
SMITH. Patrick	20	M	Laborer	01Ma02Dd
PATTERSON. Matthw.	14	M	Laborer	01Ma02Dd
Mary	15	F	Laborer	01Ma02Dd
RYAN. Mary	19	F	Laborer	01Ma02Dd
MCCORMICK, John	25	M	Laborer	01Ma02Dd
HOWE. Richd.	25	M	Laborer	01Ma02Dd
CROWLEY, Michl.	25	M	Laborer	01Ma02Dd
Mary	24	F	Wife	01Ma02Dd
CARROLL, Edwd.	40	M	Laborer	01Ma02Dd
Ann	30	F	Laborer	01Ma02Dd
KIHOE, Cath.	17	F	Laborer	01Ma02Dd
MANYON, Mary	17	F	Laborer	01Ma02Dd
Cath.	18	F	Laborer	01Ma02Dd
RADIAN, Owen	20	M	Laborer	01Ma02Dd
LANHEEN. James	22	M	Laborer	01Ma02Dd
MANYON. James	21	M	Laborer	01Ma02Dd
Wm.	20	M	Laborer	01Ma02Dd
KIHOE, Wm.	20	M	Laborer	01Ma02Dd
GARTLAND, Eliza	20	F	Laborer	01Ma02Dd
Bridget	15	F	Laborer	01Ma02Dd
Cath.	16	F	Laborer	01Ma02Dd
Bartlett	17	M	Laborer	01Ma02Dd
DEE, Patrick	42	M	Laborer	01Ma02Dd
Michl.	12	M	Laborer	01Ma02Dd
Judith	34	F	Laborer	01Ma02Dd
DEGNAN, John	2	M	Child	01Ma02Dd
DEE, Mary	17	F	Laborer	01Ma02Dd
John	8	M	Child	01Ma02Dd
PHALAN, Mary	50	F	Laborer	01Ma02Dd
Patk.	26	M	Laborer	01Ma02Dd
Honora	18	F	Laborer	01Ma02Dd
POWER, Johanna	40	F	Laborer	01Ma02Dd
Margt.	9	F	Child	01Ma02Dd
Patrick	3	M	Child	01Ma02Dd
GATHNEY, Jane	18	F	Spinster	01Ma02Dd
CONLY, Mary	18	F	Spinster	01Ma02Dd
WALLACE, Edwd.	36	M	Laborer	01Ma02Dd
Anty	36	M	Laborer	01Ma02Dd
Kate	7	F	Child	01Ma02Dd
Joseph	6	M	Child	01Ma02Dd
FINLEY, Margt.	50	F	Laborer	01Ma02Dd
Bridgt.	18	F	Laborer	01Ma02Dd
James	25	M	Laborer	01Ma02Dd
DWYER. Phillip	25	M	Laborer	01Ma02Dd
Michl.	24	M	Laborer	01Ma02Dd
John	23	M	Laborer	01Ma02Dd
Mary	26	F	Laborer	01Ma02Dd
Johanna	24	F	Laborer	01Ma02Dd
Judith	50	F	Laborer	01Ma02Dd
FITZGERALD, Wm.	22	M	Laborer	01Ma02Dd
KELLY, Wm.	20	M	Laborer	01Ma02Dd
FINTON, Cathe.	17	F	Laborer	01Ma02Dd
Mary	15	F	Laborer	01Ma02Dd
FITZGERALD, James	29	M	Laborer	01Ma02Dd
Edwd.	20	M	Laborer	01Ma02Dd
MCATEER. Hugh	35	M	Laborer	01Ma02Dd
CONNOR. John	30	M	Laborer	01Ma02Dd
JACKSON. John	18	M	Laborer	01Ma02Dd
CALLAHAN. John	50	M	Laborer	01Ma02Dd
BURNS. Patk.	45	M	Laborer	01Ma02Dd
John	16	M	Laborer	01Ma02Dd
Thos.	14	M	Laborer	01Ma02Dd
Robt.	8	M	Child	01Ma02Dd
Elizth.	44	F	Child	01Ma02Dd
Grace	5	F	Child	01Ma02Dd
CONNOR. Cath.	28	F	Laborer	01Ma02Dd
Margt.	.00	F	Infant	01Ma02Dd
PHELAN. James	20	M	Laborer	01Ma02Dd
HART, Peter	18	M	Laborer	01Ma02Dd
TULLY, Moses	35	M	Laborer	01Ma02Dd
WALSH, Patk.	19	M	Laborer	01Ma02Dd
HICKEY, Danl.	20	M	Laborer	01Ma02Dd
BRADY, Sarah	17	F	Laborer	01Ma02Dd
Veronee	16	F	Laborer	01Ma02Dd
Eliza	20	F	Laborer	01Ma02Dd
MADDON, Michl.	24	M	Laborer	01Ma02Dd
GIBSON, James	20	M	Laborer	01Ma02Dd
HENNESSY, Thomas	18	M	Laborer	01Ma02Dd
HARKEN, Johanna	18	F	Laborer	01Ma02Dd
SHANDLEY, Mary	17	F	Laborer	01Ma02Dd
DUFFY, James	30	M	Laborer	01Ma02Dd
Mary	35	F	Laborer	01Ma02Dd
James	.00	M	Infant	01Ma02Dd
CONNOR, Patk.	17	M	Laborer	01Ma02Dd
HARRINGTON, Patk.	26	M	Laborer	01Ma02Dd
DONAHER. Thos.	18	M	Laborer	01Ma02Dd
MANES, Donald	18	M	Laborer	01Ma02Dd
Roger	14	M	Laborer	01Ma02Dd
Robert	5	M	Child	01Ma02Dd
Cath.	40	F	Laborer	01Ma02Dd
Janette	.00	F	Infant	01Ma02Dd
GLEN, Henry	30	M	Laborer	01Ma02Dd
CAVERS, Betsey	16	F	Laborer	01Ma02Dd
NAUGHTON, Betsey	16	F	Laborer	01Ma02Dd
MANES, Mary	16	F	Laborer	01Ma02Dd
Cathe.	11	F	Laborer	01Ma02Dd
Rebecca	7	F	Child	01Ma02Dd
Jemina	3	F	Child	01Ma02Dd
MCDONALD, Pat	40	M	Laborer	01Ma02Dd
Bridgt.	18	F	Laborer	01Ma02Dd
Fergus	18	M	Laborer	01Ma02Dd
DONALD, Joseph	16	M	Laborer	01Ma02Dd
DWYER, James	24	M	Laborer	01Ma02Dd
MACKNAMARA, John	24	M	Laborer	01Ma02Dd
Thos.	24	M	Laborer	01Ma02Dd
RYAN, John	40	M	Laborer	01Ma02Dd
Cath.	30	F	Laborer	01Ma02Dd
SEXTON, Mary	36	F	Laborer	01Ma02Dd
FITZPATRICK, Phillip	60	M	Laborer	01Ma02Dd
John	25	M	Laborer	01Ma02Dd
HUGHES, Charles	20	M	Laborer	01Ma02Dd
MANOHAN, Ellen	26	F	Laborer	01Ma02Dd
Mary	.00	F	Infant	01Ma02Dd
FITZPATRICK, Bridgt.	21	F	Laborer	01Ma02Dd
HALL, Bridgt.	20	F	Laborer	01Ma02Dd
RYLEY, Mary	4	F	Child	01Ma02Dd
FITZPATRICK, Mary	40	F	Laborer	01Ma02Dd
REYLEY, Bridget	29	F	Laborer	01Ma02Dd
Phillip	2	M	Child	01Ma02Dd
KELLY, Michl.	37	M	Laborer	01Ma02Dd
Judith	35	F	Laborer	01Ma02Dd
Mary	11	F	Laborer	01Ma02Dd
Pat	5	M	Child	01Ma02Dd
Danl.	8	M	Child	01Ma02Dd
Bridget	6	F	Child	01Ma02Dd
TOLES, Richard	28	M	Laborer	01Ma02Dd
KELLY, Jas.	.00	M	Infant	01Ma02Dd
BOWLES, John	25	M	Laborer	01Ma02Dd
NIRMAN, Thos.	12	M	Laborer	01Ma02Dd
James	8	M	Child	01Ma02Dd
Richard	46	M	Laborer	01Ma02Dd
Mary	16	F	Laborer	01Ma02Dd
DEVINE, Margt.	40	F	Laborer	01Ma02Dd
SMITH, James	37	M	Laborer	01Ma02Dd
BROWN, James	22	M	Laborer	01Ma02Dd
MAHAAN, Thomas	20	M	Laborer	01Ma02Dd
SMITH, James	40	M	Laborer	01Ma02Dd
Wm.	16	M	Laborer	01Ma02Dd
CHALTON, Wm.	33	M	Laborer	01Ma02Dd
Mathw.	31	M	Laborer	01Ma02Dd
Jane	21	F	Laborer	01Ma02Dd
GOREL, Peter	33	M	Laborer	01Ma02Dd
DUGAN, Patk.	32	M	Laborer	01Ma02Dd
Abigail	30	F	Laborer	01Ma02Dd

NAMES OF PASSENGERS	AGE	SEX	OCCUPATIONS	DATE PORT SHIP
U, Mary	5	F	Child	01Ma02Dd
Elizth.	3	F	Child	01Ma02Dd
Mary	.00	F	Infant	01Ma02Dd
BEAVANS. John	35	M	Laborer	01Ma02Dd
HAYES, James	26	M	Laborer	01Ma02Dd
GORARD, Michl.	50	M	Laborer	01Ma02Dd
John	16	M	Laborer	01Ma02Dd
Bridget	30	F	Laborer	01Ma02Dd
COOK, Michl.	26	M	Laborer	01Ma02Dd
SHEA, Wm.	24	M	Laborer	01Ma02Dd
CONNOR. Michl.	21	M	Laborer	01Ma02Dd
RYAN, John	10	M	Laborer	01Ma02Dd
OCONNOR. Thos.	28	M	Laborer	01Ma02Dd
Cathe.	21	F	Laborer	01Ma02Dd
Mary	.00	F	Infant	01Ma02Dd
CAVANAGH, Margt.	22	F	Laborer	01Ma02Dd
MAHER. Ellen	17	F	Laborer	01Ma02Dd
WILSON. James	30	M	Laborer	01Ma02Dd
Margt.	24	F	Laborer	01Ma02Dd
James	2	M	Child	01Ma02Dd
Margt.	.00	F	Infant	01Ma02Dd
Died-At-Sea				
GREY, Elizth.	14	F	Laborer	01Ma02Dd
REYLEY, John	20	M	Laborer	01Ma02Dd
MCFALLAN, Chas.	18	M	Laborer	01Ma02Dd
DONOHOE, Barney	19	M	Laborer	01Ma02Dd
CROSSWELL, James	50	M	Laborer	01Ma02Dd
DOHERTY, Thomas	45	M	Laborer	01Ma02Dd
MCCLOSKEY, James	21	M	Laborer	01Ma02Dd
HERRON. John	24	M	Laborer	01Ma02Dd
Maurice	18	M	Laborer	01Ma02Dd
CUNNINGHAM, Pat	22	M	Laborer	01Ma02Dd
FORD, Jerh.	20	M	Laborer	01Ma02Dd
GINEAN, John	32	M	Laborer	01Ma02Dd
ROACH, Thomas	26	M	Laborer	01Ma02Dd
GALOAN, Jas.	3	M	Child	01Ma02Dd
MCCLUSKEY, Mary	17	F	Laborer	01Ma02Dd
WHITEHEAD, Sarah	37	F	Laborer	01Ma02Dd
Elizth.	16	F	Laborer	01Ma02Dd
Sarah-Ann	12	F	Laborer	01Ma02Dd
Francis	10	M	Laborer	01Ma02Dd
Charles	8	M	Child	01Ma02Dd
Fredk.	6	M	Child	01Ma02Dd
Edward	3	M	Child	01Ma02Dd
Isaac	.00	M	Infant	01Ma02Dd
HAY, Henry	23	M	Laborer	01Ma02Dd
Mary-Ann	21	F	Laborer	01Ma02Dd
RENNY, John	27	M	Laborer	01Ma02Dd
Caroline	24	F	Laborer	01Ma02Dd
Mary-Ann	2	F	Child	01Ma02Dd
John	.00	M	Infant	01Ma02Dd
MANES. Robert	38	M	Laborer	01Ma02Dd

COLONY 01 MAY 1849

From Liverpool

NAMES OF PASSENGERS	AGE	SEX	OCCUPATIONS	DATE PORT SHIP
COLEMAN, James	21	M	Laborer	01Ma02De
GATENNY, Catherine	24	F	Laborer	01Ma02De
Mary	21	F	Laborer	01Ma02De
KELLY, Patrick	27	M	Laborer	01Ma02De
Mary	24	F	Laborer	01Ma02De
COLEMAN, John	21	M	Laborer	01Ma02De
BREADY, James	24	M	Laborer	01Ma02De
NEILL, Michael	24	M	Laborer	01Ma02De
John	22	M	Laborer	01Ma02De
BAYLAHER, James	50	M	Laborer	01Ma02De
John	26	M	Laborer	01Ma02De
Thomas	24	M	Laborer	01Ma02De
BAYLAHER, William	22	M	Laborer	01Ma02De
Catherine	22	F	Laborer	01Ma02De
Rose	20	F	Laborer	01Ma02De
MARTIN, Edwd.	27	M	Laborer	01Ma02De
Bernard	50	M	Laborer	01Ma02De
John	26	M	Laborer	01Ma02De
VAUGHAN, John	24	M	Laborer	01Ma02De
DUGGAN, Wm.	22	M	Laborer	01Ma02De
Catherine	50	F	Laborer	01Ma02De
Peggy	20	F	Laborer	01Ma02De
Mary	18	F	Laborer	01Ma02De
William	16	M	Laborer	01Ma02De
Mary	9	F	Child	01Ma02De
NOLAN, Garret	25	M	Laborer	01Ma02De
SMITH, Ann	20	F	Laborer	01Ma02De
CONNOR, Ann	20	F	Laborer	01Ma02De
HOGAN, James	29	M	Laborer	01Ma02De
Catherine	30	F	Laborer	01Ma02De
U	.00	M	Infant	01Ma02De
GURGAN, Matthew	29	M	Laborer	01Ma02De
Jane	29	F	Laborer	01Ma02De
U	.00	M	Infant	01Ma02De
Jane	.00	F	Infant	01Ma02De
MULGAN, James	40	M	Laborer	01Ma02De
HOPKINS, Patrick	23	M	Laborer	01Ma02De
DELANEY, Jno.	20	M	Laborer	01Ma02De
BUTLER, Wm.	21	M	Laborer	01Ma02De
FITZGERALD, Michl.	20	M	Laborer	01Ma02De
MANSADE, Catherine	29	F	Laborer	01Ma02De
MULVEY, Michael	30	M	Laborer	01Ma02De
RYAN, Bernard	29	M	Laborer	01Ma02De
Isabell	20	F	Laborer	01Ma02De
HORNER, Sarah	20	F	Laborer	01Ma02De
DAVIES, Elizabeth	20	F	Laborer	01Ma02De
STEWARD, A.	17	M	Laborer	01Ma02De
Jas.	25	M	Laborer	01Ma02De
ARMSTRONG, Wm.	21	M	Laborer	01Ma02De
CARFORD, Elizabeth	20	F	Laborer	01Ma02De
CULLEN, Michl.	24	M	Laborer	01Ma02De
Mary	50	F	Laborer	01Ma02De
MADDEN, James	22	M	Laborer	01Ma02De
HART, John	19	M	Laborer	01Ma02De
MURPHY, Maria	22	F	Laborer	01Ma02De
LYNNAUGH, Patt	29	M	Laborer	01Ma02De
Bridget	32	F	Laborer	01Ma02De
Margaret	.00	F	Infant	01Ma02De
Mary	.00	F	Infant	01Ma02De
PHILLIPS, Patrick	30	M	Laborer	01Ma02De
HOMLLY, John	20	M	Laborer	01Ma02De
GALE, Edwd.	21	M	Laborer	01Ma02De
Ralph	22	M	Laborer	01Ma02De
Bernard	20	M	Laborer	01Ma02De
Wm.	21	M	Laborer	01Ma02De
James	23	M	Laborer	01Ma02De
Alley	22	M	Laborer	01Ma02De
James	24	M	Laborer	01Ma02De
Thomas	.00	M	Infant	01Ma02De
MEANY, Michael	24	M	Laborer	01Ma02De
MEALY, Michael	40	M	Laborer	01Ma02De
Richd.	12	M	Laborer	01Ma02De
MURPHY, John	40	M	Laborer	01Ma02De
Ann	30	F	Laborer	01Ma02De
John	8	M	Child	01Ma02De
Patrick	6	M	Child	01Ma02De
PALMER, John	37	M	Laborer	01Ma02De
BLACKBURN, Thomas	45	M	Laborer	01Ma02De
Henry	50	M	Laborer	01Ma02De
Susan	43	F	Laborer	01Ma02De
Jane	16	F	Laborer	01Ma02De
Ann	10	F	Laborer	01Ma02De
Alice	8	F	Child	01Ma02De
John	6	M	Child	01Ma02De
Fanny	4	F	Child	01Ma02De
William	.00	M	Infant	01Ma02De
PATLY, Ada	20	F	Laborer	01Ma02De

NAMES OF PASSENGERS	AGE	SEX	OCCUPATIONS	DATE PORT SHIP
FEENAN. Ann	20	F	Laborer	01Ma02De
THOMPSON. Ann	20	F	Laborer	01Ma02De
EAGAN. Mary	20	F	Laborer	01Ma02De
Denis	24	M	Laborer	01Ma02De
GRABBLE, Thomas	19	M	Laborer	01Ma02De
Catherine	17	F	Laborer	01Ma02De
PRIEST, Ann	30	F	Laborer	01Ma02De
NORMAN. Thomas	16	M	Laborer	01Ma02De
MEEHAN, Patrick	20	M	Laborer	01Ma02De
L.	12	M	Laborer	01Ma02De
U-Mrs.	20	F	Laborer	01Ma02De
MULGAN. Margaret	36	F	Laborer	01Ma02De
Maria	9	F	Child	01Ma02De
Patrick	5	M	Child	01Ma02De
Michael	20	M	Laborer	01Ma02De
U	.00	F	Infant	01Ma02De
HOGAN. Ellen	29	F	Laborer	01Ma02De
John	23	M	Laborer	01Ma02De
Edwd.	21	M	Laborer	01Ma02De
DOYLE. Mary	41	F	Laborer	01Ma02De
JORDAN, James	21	M	Laborer	01Ma02De
GATY, Lawrence	21	M	Laborer	01Ma02De
Margaret	21	F	Laborer	01Ma02De
EGAN. William	35	M	Laborer	01Ma02De
U-Mrs.	33	F	Laborer	01Ma02De
Charles	10	M	Laborer	01Ma02De
PARKER. James	42	M	Laborer	01Ma02De
Richd.	13	M	Laborer	01Ma02De
TURNCROSS. John	22	M	Laborer	01Ma02De
U-Mrs.	22	F	Laborer	01Ma02De
PHELAN, John	21	F	Laborer	01Ma02De
Eliza	20	F	Laborer	01Ma02De
CONFREY, John	26	M	Laborer	01Ma02De
MCKEON. Peter	24	M	Laborer	01Ma02De
LAWLE. Robert	22	M	Laborer	01Ma02De
RAFFERTY, Catherine	40	F	Laborer	01Ma02De
Ann	7	F	Child	01Ma02De
Mary	7	F	Child	01Ma02De
Catherine	.00	F	Infant	01Ma02De
Ellen	.00	F	Infant	01Ma02De
PROHY, Catherine	25	F	Laborer	01Ma02De
Mary	4	F	Child	01Ma02De
Caroline	.00	F	Infant	01Ma02De
HOLLY, Denis	26	M	Laborer	01Ma02De
SEDGWICK, Joseph	30	M	Laborer	01Ma02De
LEE, Terence	40	M	Laborer	01Ma02De
James	17	M	Laborer	01Ma02De
John	11	M	Laborer	01Ma02De
Alexander	7	M	Child	01Ma02De
FEE, Maragaret	20	F	Laborer	01Ma02De
MARTIN. Maragaret	20	F	Laborer	01Ma02De
REILY, James	30	M	Laborer	01Ma02De
Patrick	5	M	Child	01Ma02De
HART, Edwd.	25	M	Laborer	01Ma02De
MCKENNY, Patrick	24	M	Laborer	01Ma02De
Catherine	20	F	Laborer	01Ma02De
KENNEDY, John	18	M	Laborer	01Ma02De
MURPHY, Jerh.	30	M	Laborer	01Ma02De
LANNON. David	20	M	Laborer	01Ma02De
MALONE, Patrick	26	M	Laborer	01Ma02De
SHORT, John	26	M	Laborer	01Ma02De
MORAN. Barney	25	M	Laborer	01Ma02De
Jane	20	F	Laborer	01Ma02De
WEST. Geo.	20	M	Laborer	01Ma02De
Elizabeth	25	F	Laborer	01Ma02De
CONNELL, Michl.	30	M	Laborer	01Ma02De
CASEY, Cath.	20	F	Laborer	01Ma02De
WALSH, Ellen	17	F	Laborer	01Ma02De
Margt.	20	F	Laborer	01Ma02De
SHEELY, John	26	M	Laborer	01Ma02De
TULLY, Phillip	35	M	Laborer	01Ma02De
DOYLE. Thomas	26	M	Laborer	01Ma02De
KENEDY, Lawrence	30	M	Laborer	01Ma02De
Eleanor	26	F	Laborer	01Ma02De
DOYLE, Ann	26	F	Laborer	01Ma02De
GILHARTY, Patrick	30	M	Laborer	01Ma02De
Mary	28	F	Laborer	01Ma02De
Bessy	5	F	Child	01Ma02De
Catherine	4	F	Child	01Ma02De
Judy	17	F	Laborer	01Ma02De
MCCALE. Edwd.	40	M	Laborer	01Ma02De
Elizabeth	35	F	Laborer	01Ma02De
Sarah-Jane	12	F	Laborer	01Ma02De
Ann	10	F	Laborer	01Ma02De
Eugene	7	M	Child	01Ma02De
FAIR, Isabella	18	F	Laborer	01Ma02De
REA, Martin-Ann	25	F	Laborer	01Ma02De
Emily	.00	F	Infant	01Ma02De
DOHERTY, Mary	20	F	Laborer	01Ma02De
BRYAN, John	27	M	Laborer	01Ma02De
MCCABE. Nancy	30	F	Laborer	01Ma02De
Owen	20	M	Laborer	01Ma02De
FINNEGAN, Darby	30	M	Laborer	01Ma02De
U-Mrs.	30	F	Laborer	01Ma02De
Biddy	11	F	Laborer	01Ma02De
Michl.	9	M	Child	01Ma02De
Martin	9	M	Child	01Ma02De
Patrick	.00	M	Infant	01Ma02De
KEENAN, Jane	26	F	Laborer	01Ma02De
SHUTTLEWORTH, Wm.	23	M	Laborer	01Ma02De
HARROP, Robert	20	M	Laborer	01Ma02De
MYANS, Margaret	50	F	Laborer	01Ma02De
Christy	17	M	Laborer	01Ma02De
James	15	M	Laborer	01Ma02De
Rose	12	F	Laborer	01Ma02De
John	10	M	Laborer	01Ma02De
REILLY, Rose	14	F	Laborer	01Ma02De

WASHINGTON 01 MAY 1849

From Liverpool

NAMES OF PASSENGERS	AGE	SEX	OCCUPATIONS	DATE PORT SHIP
HARDERY, J.B.	50	M	Unknown	01Ma02Df
DAVIS, Thomas	21	M	Unknown	01Ma02Df
GIBLIN. Robert	28	M	Unknown	01Ma02Df
FARRELL, Chas.	58	M	Unknown	01Ma02Df
U-Mrs.	18	F	Unknown	01Ma02Df
Mary	10	F	Unknown	01Ma02Df
James	12	M	Unknown	01Ma02Df
Francis	8	M	Child	01Ma02Df
Eliza	20	F	Unknown	01Ma02Df
Bridget	21	F	Unknown	01Ma02Df
BERRY, Eliza	25	F	Unknown	01Ma02Df
GOUCHEN, Henry	19	M	Unknown	01Ma02Df
CAVANAGH, John	24	M	Unknown	01Ma02Df
U (W)	24	F	Unknown	01Ma02Df
HARRY, John	24	M	Unknown	01Ma02Df
U (W)	22	F	Unknown	01Ma02Df
Thomas	9	M	Child	01Ma02Df
LEONARD, Eliza	20	F	Unknown	01Ma02Df
GURLAND, Ellen	50	F	Unknown	01Ma02Df
Mary	24	F	Unknown	01Ma02Df
Michael	20	M	Unknown	01Ma02Df
Ellen	18	F	Unknown	01Ma02Df
Patt	15	M	Unknown	01Ma02Df
Catherine	11	F	Unknown	01Ma02Df
Bridget	7	F	Child	01Ma02Df
MAHER, John	56	M	Unknown	01Ma02Df
Bernard	27	M	Unknown	01Ma02Df
Edward	25	M	Unknown	01Ma02Df
James	23	M	Unknown	01Ma02Df
Julia	18	F	Unknown	01Ma02Df
Bridget	16	F	Unknown	01Ma02Df
Ann	13	F	Unknown	01Ma02Df

NAMES OF PASSENGERS		AGE	SEX	OCCUPATIONS	DATE PORT SHIP
MAHER, Catherine		20	F	Unknown	01Ma02Df
DUNCAN, Ann		32	F	Unknown	01Ma02Df
Anne		.00	F	Infant	01Ma02Df
Marty		3	M	Child	01Ma02Df
GARLAND, Martin		40	M	Unknown	01Ma02Df
Elizabeth		39	F	Unknown	01Ma02Df
Peter		15	M	Unknown	01Ma02Df
Michl.		13	M	Unknown	01Ma02Df
Jullia		11	F	Unknown	01Ma02Df
Bridget		9	F	Child	01Ma02Df
Mary		3	F	Child	01Ma02Df
CONNOR. Mary		25	F	Unknown	01Ma02Df
WHELAN. Susan		21	F	Unknown	01Ma02Df
Robt.		19	M	Unknown	01Ma02Df
Martin		17	M	Unknown	01Ma02Df
LYNAN, U		45	M	Unknown	01Ma02Df
U	(W)	40	F	Unknown	01Ma02Df
BRENNAN, U		40	M	Unknown	01Ma02Df
Cath.		28	F	Unknown	01Ma02Df
James		5	M	Child	01Ma02Df
John		.00	M	Infant	01Ma02Df
Maria		9	F	Child	01Ma02Df
DUFFY, Michl.		40	M	Unknown	01Ma02Df
CUNNINGHAM, Michl.		40	M	Unknown	01Ma02Df
U	(W)	40	F	Unknown	01Ma02Df
Michl.		19	M	Unknown	01Ma02Df
John		17	M	Unknown	01Ma02Df
Mary		13	F	Unknown	01Ma02Df
Cath.		12	F	Unknown	01Ma02Df
Bernard		11	M	Unknown	01Ma02Df
Patt		9	M	Child	01Ma02Df
Julia		25	F	Unknown	01Ma02Df
HAVY, John		25	M	Unknown	01Ma02Df
BROWN, Eliza		20	F	Unknown	01Ma02Df
GANNON, Margt.		20	F	Unknown	01Ma02Df
Bess		30	F	Unknown	01Ma02Df
MORTON, U		25	M	Unknown	01Ma02Df
U	(W)	25	F	Unknown	01Ma02Df
John		5	M	Child	01Ma02Df
Henry		.00	M	Infant	01Ma02Df
GIBSON, U-Miss		25	F	Unknown	01Ma02Df
CAVANAGH, John		25	M	Unknown	01Ma02Df
Ann		20	F	Unknown	01Ma02Df
WHITE. John		20	M	Unknown	01Ma02Df
DEVINE, Michal		20	M	Unknown	01Ma02Df
LAWLOR. Patt		40	M	Unknown	01Ma02Df
Alice		30	F	Unknown	01Ma02Df
Margaret-Ann		8	F	Child	01Ma02Df
Alice		6	F	Child	01Ma02Df
Catherine		4	F	Child	01Ma02Df
Michal		.00	M	Infant	01Ma02Df
Eliza		9	F	Child	01Ma02Df
KILLMURRY, John		20	M	Unknown	01Ma02Df
RYAN, Patt		22	M	Unknown	01Ma02Df
SHAW, John		30	M	Unknown	01Ma02Df
HOEY, John		30	M	Unknown	01Ma02Df
CAREEY, Patt		20	M	Unknown	01Ma02Df
SMITH. Richard		35	M	Unknown	01Ma02Df
U	(W)	30	F	Unknown	01Ma02Df
HACKET, Joseph		24	M	Unknown	01Ma02Df
BAGNELL, John		24	M	Unknown	01Ma02Df
LOUREY, Patt		25	M	Unknown	01Ma02Df
Stephan		22	M	Unknown	01Ma02Df
CAREY, M.		21	F	Single	01Ma02Df
WATRAN. U		30	M	Unknown	01Ma02Df
U	(W)	27	F	Unknown	01Ma02Df
John	(W)	.00	M	Infant	01Ma02Df
WHITE, U-Mrs.		50	F	Unknown	01Ma02Df
CATELY, Catherine		35	F	Unknown	01Ma02Df
KANE, Edward		35	M	Unknown	01Ma02Df
BRADY, Thomas		17	M	Unknown	01Ma02Df
DUNGAN. Owen		35	M	Unknown	01Ma02Df
CANE. James		50	M	Unknown	01Ma02Df
Pat		24	M	Unknown	01Ma02Df
Kate		19	F	Unknown	01Ma02Df
CANE. Richard		17	M	Unknown	01Ma02Df
Barney		15	M	Unknown	01Ma02Df
James		.00	M	Infant	01Ma02Df
Julia		9	F	Child	01Ma02Df
CONCANNON, Wm.		24	M	Unknown	01Ma02Df
BIDDEL, William		17	M	Unknown	01Ma02Df
BYRNES, Margaret		28	F	Unknown	01Ma02Df
Margaret		00	F	Unknown	01Ma02Df
Maria		.00	F	Infant	01Ma02Df
FLOOD, Hugh		20	F	Unknown	01Ma02Df
RIELLY, Pat		20	F	Unknown	01Ma02Df
Ann		25	F	Unknown	01Ma02Df
Mary		21	F	Unknown	01Ma02Df
MURPHY, M.		28	U	Unknown	01Ma02Df
Thomas		.00	M	Infant	01Ma02Df
GRENNAN, James		9	M	Child	01Ma02Df
FAGAN, Edward		20	M	Unknown	01Ma02Df
MCDONNELL, Joh.		9	U	Child	01Ma02Df
WHITE, Patt		20	M	Unknown	01Ma02Df
GRADEY, John		25	M	Unknown	01Ma02Df
TODD, Ann		22	F	Unknown	01Ma02Df
James		20	M	Unknown	01Ma02Df
Thomas		20	M	Unknown	01Ma02Df
BYRNE, Sophia		18	F	Unknown	01Ma02Df
Kate		23	F	Unknown	01Ma02Df
NUGENT, Jane		20	F	Unknown	01Ma02Df
SHERIDAN, Thos.		.00	M	Infant	01Ma02Df
MURPHY, Alick		7	M	Child	01Ma02Df
My.		20	F	Unknown	01Ma02Df
ARMSTRONG, Jane		20	F	Unknown	01Ma02Df
Margaret		20	F	Unknown	01Ma02Df
BUDD, William		40	M	Unknown	01Ma02Df
Lucy		16	F	Unknown	01Ma02Df
Johanna		3	F	Child	01Ma02Df
Robert		7	M	Child	01Ma02Df
BLANCHE, Mary		20	F	Unknown	01Ma02Df
BOLAND, Betty		20	F	Unknown	01Ma02Df
BOWAN, Mary		20	F	Unknown	01Ma02Df
DALTON, Widow		40	F	Unknown	01Ma02Df
John		16	M	Unknown	01Ma02Df
Mary		11	F	Unknown	01Ma02Df
Ellen		9	F	Child	01Ma02Df
MARTIN, Christopher		30	M	Unknown	01Ma02Df
Mary		30	F	Unknown	01Ma02Df
John		10	M	Unknown	01Ma02Df
Ann		8	F	Child	01Ma02Df
Mary		16	F	Unknown	01Ma02Df
MORAN, Mary		17	F	Unknown	01Ma02Df

E.BENTLEY 01 MAY 1849

From Liverpool

NAMES OF PASSENGERS	AGE	SEX	OCCUPATIONS	DATE PORT SHIP
FLANEGAN, Phillip	50	M	Laborer	01Ma02Dj
Janett	50	F	Laborer	01Ma02Dj
Ann	24	F	Laborer	01Ma02Dj
James	18	M	Laborer	01Ma02Dj
Mary	13	F	Laborer	01Ma02Dj
Jane	12	F	Laborer	01Ma02Dj
Danl.	8	M	Child	01Ma02Dj
FARRELL, Edwd.	20	M	Laborer	01Ma02Dj
Elizth.	40	F	Laborer	01Ma02Dj
Cath.	24	F	Laborer	01Ma02Dj
Ann	22	F	Laborer	01Ma02Dj
Bridget	34	F	Laborer	01Ma02Dj
Ellen	17	F	Laborer	01Ma02Dj
REILLY, Michl.	7	M	Child	01Ma02Dj
WAUSHTLESS, Thos.	40	M	Laborer	01Ma02Dj
Pat	25	M	Laborer	01Ma02Dj

NAMES OF PASSENGERS	AGE	SEX	OCCUPATIONS	DATE PORT SHIP
WAUSHTLESS, U-Mrs.	25	F	Laborer	01Ma02Dj
MOONEY, Pat	24	M	Laborer	01Ma02Dj
MCDONNELL, Wm.	27	M	Laborer	01Ma02Dj
FLEMMING, James	21	M	Laborer	01Ma02Dj
MOONEY, James	29	M	Laborer	01Ma02Dj
FLYNN. Jas.	20	M	Laborer	01Ma02Dj
Mary	22	F	Laborer	01Ma02Dj
REED, Phillip	30	M	Laborer	01Ma02Dj
LANAGAN, Wm.	25	M	Laborer	01Ma02Dj
HURST, Julia	24	F	Laborer	01Ma02Dj
SMITH, Michl.	24	M	Laborer	01Ma02Dj
Ann	20	F	Laborer	01Ma02Dj
COX, Pat	25	M	Laborer	01Ma02Dj
Mary	25	F	Laborer	01Ma02Dj
MCLOUGHLAN. Michl.	25	M	Laborer	01Ma02Dj
MURPHY, Dennis	20	M	Laborer	01Ma02Dj
DEVEREAUX, Margt.	24	F	Laborer	01Ma02Dj
Alex.	20	M	Laborer	01Ma02Dj
MURPHY, Thomas	23	M	Laborer	01Ma02Dj
Pat	35	M	Laborer	01Ma02Dj
DOUGLAS. Pat	21	M	Laborer	01Ma02Dj
Martin	24	M	Laborer	01Ma02Dj
LYNCH. Michl.	24	M	Laborer	01Ma02Dj
Betty	20	F	Laborer	01Ma02Dj
Ann	18	F	Laborer	01Ma02Dj
AUGHLEY, James	24	M	Laborer	01Ma02Dj
Mary	20	F	Laborer	01Ma02Dj
SHIRLEY, Bridget	20	F	Laborer	01Ma02Dj
MITCHELL, Margt.	30	F	Laborer	01Ma02Dj
George	4	M	Child	01Ma02Dj
WILSON. Sarah	20	F	Laborer	01Ma02Dj
CUMMINS. James	50	M	Laborer	01Ma02Dj
Died-At-Sea				
Mary	50	F	Laborer	01Ma02Dj
Died-At-Sea				
Andrew	10	M	Laborer	01Ma02Dj
HEALY, Martin	50	M	Laborer	01Ma02Dj
MCCONNOR. Cath.	18	F	Laborer	01Ma02Dj
James	26	M	Laborer	01Ma02Dj
Cath.	19	F	Laborer	01Ma02Dj
Rose	9	F	Child	01Ma02Dj
James	.00	M	Infant	01Ma02Dj
MCKEARN. James	35	M	Laborer	01Ma02Dj
Rose	21	F	Laborer	01Ma02Dj
Bridget	22	F	Laborer	01Ma02Dj
GORLIN. Michael	21	M	Laborer	01Ma02Dj
Mary	21	F	Laborer	01Ma02Dj
Ann	19	F	Laborer	01Ma02Dj
RANAGAN, John	30	M	Laborer	01Ma02Dj
U-Mrs.	24	F	Laborer	01Ma02Dj
GAYNOR. Cath.	30	F	Laborer	01Ma02Dj
OAKNER, Cath.	29	F	Laborer	01Ma02Dj
Mary	14	F	Laborer	01Ma02Dj
Bridgt.	.00	F	Infant	01Ma02Dj
MCKENNY, Robert	20	M	Laborer	01Ma02Dj
BRINEN, Pat	40	M	Laborer	01Ma02Dj
HEALY, Eliza	23	F	Laborer	01Ma02Dj
MULLEN, John	24	M	Laborer	01Ma02Dj
U-Mrs.	22	F	Laborer	01Ma02Dj
Edward	10	M	Laborer	01Ma02Dj
Pat	8	M	Child	01Ma02Dj
CASSON. Margt.	19	F	Laborer	01Ma02Dj
GARVEY, Mary	19	F	Laborer	01Ma02Dj
MELLON. Margt.	40	F	Laborer	01Ma02Dj
Mary	6	F	Child	01Ma02Dj
Samuel	4	M	Child	01Ma02Dj
CONWAY, Mary	50	F	Laborer	01Ma02Dj
John	30	M	Laborer	01Ma02Dj
Mary	9	F	Child	01Ma02Dj
Cath.	8	F	Child	01Ma02Dj
KEAN. Michl.	26	M	Laborer	01Ma02Dj
CASEY, James	50	M	Laborer	01Ma02Dj
Margt.	30	F	Laborer	01Ma02Dj
Michl.	12	M	Laborer	01Ma02Dj
SMITH, Thomas	50	M	Laborer	01Ma02Dj
SMITH, John	12	M	Laborer	01Ma02Dj
CANNON, Ellen	25	F	Laborer	01Ma02Dj
Cath.	23	F	Laborer	01Ma02Dj
MCMANUS, James	18	M	Laborer	01Ma02Dj
KEANE, Michl.	26	M	Laborer	01Ma02Dj
Maria	25	F	Laborer	01Ma02Dj
KEELY, Pat	29	M	Laborer	01Ma02Dj
Cath.	24	F	Laborer	01Ma02Dj
DALEY, Pat	60	M	Laborer	01Ma02Dj
Pat	20	M	Laborer	01Ma02Dj
Bridget	18	F	Laborer	01Ma02Dj
HACKETT, Cath.	20	F	Laborer	01Ma02Dj
DALEY, Edwd.	40	M	Laborer	01Ma02Dj
BURNS. Thos.	60	M	Laborer	01Ma02Dj
U-Mrs.	30	F	Laborer	01Ma02Dj
John	20	M	Laborer	01Ma02Dj
Thos.	12	M	Laborer	01Ma02Dj
William	10	M	Laborer	01Ma02Dj
Robert	9	M	Child	01Ma02Dj
Elizth.	7	F	Child	01Ma02Dj
Charles	.00	M	Infant	01Ma02Dj
Sarah	13	F	Laborer	01Ma02Dj
Hannah	11	F	Laborer	01Ma02Dj
MANNY, Martin	36	M	Laborer	01Ma02Dj
Michl.	30	M	Laborer	01Ma02Dj
Mary	36	F	Laborer	01Ma02Dj
Mary	8	F	Child	01Ma02Dj
Ned	6	M	Child	01Ma02Dj
Mary	5	F	Child	01Ma02Dj
Luke	.00	M	Infant	01Ma02Dj
Bridget	2	F	Child	01Ma02Dj
SULLIVAN, Owen	60	M	Laborer	01Ma02Dj
Denis	20	M	Laborer	01Ma02Dj
BRIEN, Patk.	25	M	Laborer	01Ma02Dj
MCDERMOTT, Patk.	36	M	Laborer	01Ma02Dj
John	34	M	Laborer	01Ma02Dj
Ellen	50	F	Laborer	01Ma02Dj
Michl.	21	M	Laborer	01Ma02Dj
Ann	29	F	Laborer	01Ma02Dj
GALLAGHER, Michl.	20	M	Laborer	01Ma02Dj
Chas.	24	M	Laborer	01Ma02Dj
MALONEY, John	24	M	Laborer	01Ma02Dj
Margt.	50	F	Laborer	01Ma02Dj
Eliza	26	F	Laborer	01Ma02Dj
MCSORLEY, Chas.	20	M	Laborer	01Ma02Dj
Ellen	23	F	Laborer	01Ma02Dj
HOWARD, Thos.	50	M	Laborer	01Ma02Dj
Elizth.	48	F	Laborer	01Ma02Dj
Mary-Ann	16	F	Laborer	01Ma02Dj
WHELAN, Thos.	35	M	Laborer	01Ma02Dj
John	24	M	Laborer	01Ma02Dj
Edward	22	M	Laborer	01Ma02Dj
Michl.	12	M	Laborer	01Ma02Dj
GALLAHER, Michl.	24	M	Laborer	01Ma02Dj
MCGANLEY, Richard	25	M	Laborer	01Ma02Dj
COLOUGH, Thos.	40	M	Laborer	01Ma02Dj
CONNELL, John	20	M	Laborer	01Ma02Dj
Ann	23	F	Laborer	01Ma02Dj
Bridget	17	F	Laborer	01Ma02Dj
LENAN, James	20	M	Laborer	01Ma02Dj
COLOR, Ann	21	F	Laborer	01Ma02Dj
CONNOLLY, Peter	50	M	Laborer	01Ma02Dj
WOOD, James	35	M	Laborer	01Ma02Dj
BROWN, Patrick	81	M	Laborer	01Ma02Dj
PROCTOR. Timy.	50	M	Laborer	01Ma02Dj
U-Mrs.	50	F	Laborer	01Ma02Dj
LYNE, Thomas	25	M	Laborer	01Ma02Dj
HALL, Wm.	25	M	Laborer	01Ma02Dj
U-Mrs.	30	F	Laborer	01Ma02Dj
Ann	.00	F	Infant	01Ma02Dj
ROOKS, Henry	45	M	Laborer	01Ma02Dj
John	25	M	Laborer	01Ma02Dj
U-Mrs.	25	F	Laborer	01Ma02Dj
MORRIS, Rosa	20	F	Laborer	01Ma02Dj
MCCURRIN, Ellen	24	F	Laborer	01Ma02Dj

NAMES OF PASSENGERS	AGE	SEX	OCCUPATIONS	DATE PORT SHIP
MANNA, Cath.	20	F	Laborer	01Ma02Dj
ELLIS, Alex.	40	M	Laborer	01Ma02Dj
MCMULLEN, Francis	50	M	Laborer	01Ma02Dj
ELIS, Sally	12	F	Laborer	01Ma02Dj
Margt.Ann	12	F	Laborer	01Ma02Dj
RUFT, Michl.	20	M	Laborer	01Ma02Dj
CLARE, Judah	40	F	Laborer	01Ma02Dj
Mary	11	F	Laborer	01Ma02Dj
MCGOWAN, Pat	50	M	Laborer	01Ma02Dj
Mary	50	F	Laborer	01Ma02Dj
Mary-Ann	23	F	Laborer	01Ma02Dj
James	26	M	Laborer	01Ma02Dj
Patrick	16	M	Laborer	01Ma02Dj
Thomas	13	M	Laborer	01Ma02Dj
HENSON. Edward	24	M	Laborer	01Ma02Dj
Cath.	18	F	Laborer	01Ma02Dj
Bernard	4	M	Child	01Ma02Dj
Pat	.00	M	Infant	01Ma02Dj
GREWER. Mary	20	F	Laborer	01Ma02Dj
JACKSON. Loucia	30	F	Laborer	01Ma02Dj
MADDOCKS, John	23	M	Laborer	01Ma02Dj
U-Mrs.	23	F	Laborer	01Ma02Dj
CLEARY, Thomas	25	M	Laborer	01Ma02Dj
SLAVIN, Martin	25	M	Laborer	01Ma02Dj
Ann	23	F	Laborer	01Ma02Dj
Patrick	21	M	Laborer	01Ma02Dj
Bridget	12	F	Laborer	01Ma02Dj
Michael	28	M	Laborer	01Ma02Dj
COFFIN, U-Mrs.	25	F	Laborer	01Ma02Dj
MARTIN, Jas.	35	M	Laborer	01Ma02Dj
U-Mrs.	30	F	Laborer	01Ma02Dj
Thos.	3	M	Child	01Ma02Dj
Cath.	.00	F	Infant	01Ma02Dj
DOWNEY, Thomas	38	M	Laborer	01Ma02Dj
PALMER. Ann	27	F	Laborer	01Ma02Dj
Janett	.00	F	Infant	01Ma02Dj
HEASSY, William	26	M	Laborer	01Ma02Dj
ROGERS. James	26	M	Laborer	01Ma02Dj
Mary	22	F	Laborer	01Ma02Dj
Francis	19	M	Laborer	01Ma02Dj
Thomas	14	M	Laborer	01Ma02Dj
John	25	M	Laborer	01Ma02Dj
JOHNSON. John	50	M	Laborer	01Ma02Dj
Ellen	21	F	Laborer	01Ma02Dj
SCHARKEY, Thos.	30	M	Laborer	01Ma02Dj
Margt.	25	F	Laborer	01Ma02Dj
Patrick	27	M	Laborer	01Ma02Dj
Mary	.00	F	Infant	01Ma02Dj
MAGNIS. Jas.	40	M	Laborer	01Ma02Dj
MORRIS. George	41	M	Laborer	01Ma02Dj
CONNORS. Margt.	40	F	Laborer	01Ma02Dj
WOODS. Margt.	20	F	Laborer	01Ma02Dj
CARTWRIGHT, Ann	18	F	Laborer	01Ma02Dj
William	6	M	Child	01Ma02Dj
NAILOR. James	25	M	Laborer	01Ma02Dj
Harriet	23	F	Laborer	01Ma02Dj
Hasten	25	M	Laborer	01Ma02Dj
ROBINSON. Josiah	24	M	Laborer	01Ma02Dj
ELLOCK, Ellis	3	M	Child	01Ma02Dj
William	50	M	Laborer	01Ma02Dj
Ellen	46	F	Laborer	01Ma02Dj
Eliza	15	F	Laborer	01Ma02Dj
Cath.	13	F	Laborer	01Ma02Dj
WHITE. James	33	M	Laborer	01Ma02Dj
Ann	8	F	Child	01Ma02Dj
GRIWSAL, Edwd.	42	M	Laborer	01Ma02Dj
Ann	40	F	Laborer	01Ma02Dj
Joseph	7	M	Child	01Ma02Dj
ARMSTRONG, John	25	M	Laborer	01Ma02Dj
Ann	18	F	Laborer	01Ma02Dj
STAFFORD, Patk.	25	M	Laborer	01Ma02Dj
MURPHY, Denis	19	M	Laborer	01Ma02Dj
ROLLINS. James	22	M	Laborer	01Ma02Dj
BRENNAN, Thomas	20	M	Laborer	01Ma02Dj
FINNEGAN. Michl.	38	M	Laborer	01Ma02Dj

NAMES OF PASSENGERS	AGE	SEX	OCCUPATIONS	DATE PORT SHIP
MARTIN. James	40	M	Laborer	01Ma02Dj
MAYOR. Philip	38	M	Laborer	01Ma02Dj
Bridget	35	F	Laborer	01Ma02Dj
Ned	11	M	Laborer	01Ma02Dj
Mary	6	F	Child	01Ma02Dj
James	16	M	Laborer	01Ma02Dj
John	8	M	Child	01Ma02Dj
MCCLANY, Fanny	20	F	Laborer	01Ma02Dj
VILLIAS, William	30	M	Laborer	01Ma02Dj
GREEN. John	21	M	Laborer	01Ma02Dj
ROSE. William	45	M	Laborer	01Ma02Dj
Ann	32	F	Laborer	01Ma02Dj
James	11	M	Laborer	01Ma02Dj
Robt.	10	M	Laborer	01Ma02Dj
Ellen	7	F	Child	01Ma02Dj
SMITH, Robt.	28	M	Laborer	01Ma02Dj
Janett	23	F	Laborer	01Ma02Dj
Francis	9	M	Child	01Ma02Dj
Edwd.	7	M	Child	01Ma02Dj
Nelly	5	F	Child	01Ma02Dj
Patk.	.00	M	Infant	01Ma02Dj
CONNOLLY, Robert	18	M	Laborer	01Ma02Dj
BYRON. Bartw.	25	M	Laborer	01Ma02Dj
JONES. John	46	M	Laborer	01Ma02Dj
U-Mrs.	44	F	Laborer	01Ma02Dj
John	20	M	Laborer	01Ma02Dj
William	18	M	Laborer	01Ma02Dj
Sarah	10	F	Laborer	01Ma02Dj
George	10	M	Laborer	01Ma02Dj
Alfred	7	M	Child	01Ma02Dj
Julia	5	F	Child	01Ma02Dj
Henry	.00	M	Infant	01Ma02Dj
Died-At-Sea				
Fredk.	4	M	Child	01Ma02Dj
KELLY, William	20	M	Laborer	01Ma02Dj
U-Mrs.	20	F	Laborer	01Ma02Dj
MURRY, Philip	27	M	Laborer	01Ma02Dj
Bridget	30	F	Laborer	01Ma02Dj
DOHERTY, Menis	25	F	Laborer	01Ma02Dj
MAHONE, Edwd.	24	M	Laborer	01Ma02Dj
Ann	23	F	Laborer	01Ma02Dj
Mary	7	F	Child	01Ma02Dj
Bridget	.00	F	Infant	01Ma02Dj
DOWNEY, Thomas	28	M	Laborer	01Ma02Dj
Betsy	26	F	Laborer	01Ma02Dj
Thomas	3	M	Child	01Ma02Dj
Mary	2	F	Child	01Ma02Dj
Philip	.00	M	Infant	01Ma02Dj
BURKE, Thomas	16	M	Laborer	01Ma02Dj
BLAKE, William	50	M	Laborer	01Ma02Dj
SHERIDAN, Michl.	25	M	Laborer	01Ma02Dj
LEDGER, Wm.	29	M	Laborer	01Ma02Dj
SMITH, John	19	M	Laborer	01Ma02Dj
DALEY, Danl.	24	M	Laborer	01Ma02Dj
CALINANE, Michl.	30	M	Laborer	01Ma02Dj
U-Mrs.	30	F	Laborer	01Ma02Dj
BYRNE. Ann	20	F	Laborer	01Ma02Dj
Ann	60	F	Laborer	01Ma02Dj
ALLEN, Alex.	25	M	Laborer	01Ma02Dj
MARTIN. Lawr.	23	M	Laborer	01Ma02Dj
FARRELL, Michl.	30	M	Laborer	01Ma02Dj
DAVIS, William	40	M	Laborer	01Ma02Dj
Died-At-Sea				
Edwd.	14	M	Laborer	01Ma02Dj
Mary-Ann	19	F	Laborer	01Ma02Dj
William	8	M	Child	01Ma02Dj
John	10	M	Laborer	01Ma02Dj
MOCKLAN, John	37	M	Laborer	01Ma02Dj
U-Mrs.	35	F	Laborer	01Ma02Dj
Peggy	8	F	Child	01Ma02Dj
Mary	1	F	Child	01Ma02Dj
Ann	.00	F	Infant	01Ma02Dj
GENNY, Martin	25	M	Laborer	01Ma02Dj
DEVINE. Owen	25	M	Laborer	01Ma02Dj
MILLER, Chas.	30	M	Laborer	01Ma02Dj

NAMES OF PASSENGERS	AGE	SEX	OCCUPATIONS	DATE PORT SHIP
MILLER, U-Mrs.	27	F	Laborer	01Ma02Dj
Chas.	7	M	Child	01Ma02Dj
William	6	M	Child	01Ma02Dj
Mary	.00	F	Infant	01Ma02Dj
HARVEY, George	23	M	Laborer	01Ma02Dj
Ann	37	F	Laborer	01Ma02Dj
Sarah	13	F	Laborer	01Ma02Dj
Richard	7	M	Child	01Ma02Dj
David	37	M	Laborer	01Ma02Dj
Emma	12	F	Laborer	01Ma02Dj
John	7	M	Child	01Ma02Dj
LARNER. Richd.	65	M	Laborer	01Ma02Dj
Mary	65	F	Laborer	01Ma02Dj
NICHOLS, Martin	22	M	Laborer	01Ma02Dj
RANDOLL, John	24	M	Laborer	01Ma02Dj
BRICK, James	32	M	Laborer	01Ma02Dj
COOPER. George	23	M	Laborer	01Ma02Dj
WILKES. Geo.	20	M	Laborer	01Ma02Dj
FLETCHER, Edwd.	30	M	Laborer	01Ma02Dj
MULLIN. John	40	M	Laborer	01Ma02Dj
Margt.	35	F	Laborer	01Ma02Dj
Peggy	8	F	Child	01Ma02Dj
Mary	.00	F	Infant	01Ma02Dj
HEWBITT, Henry	25	M	Laborer	01Ma02Dj
WRIGHT. Robt.	22	M	Laborer	01Ma02Dj
CAHILL, John	21	M	Laborer	01Ma02Dj
PERKINS. Thomas	40	M	Laborer	01Ma02Dj
U-Mrs.	35	F	Laborer	01Ma02Dj
Ann	.00	F	Infant	01Ma02Dj
TRAYNOR. Hugh	42	M	Laborer	01Ma02Dj
U-Mrs.	30	F	Laborer	01Ma02Dj
Betty	.00	F	Infant	01Ma02Dj
Died-At-Sea				
BLANC, Charles	23	M	Laborer	01Ma02Dj
U-Mrs.	23	F	Laborer	01Ma02Dj
John	.00	M	Infant	01Ma02Dj
HOWE. Thomas	00	M	Unknown	01Ma02Dj
PROCTOR. Andrew	25	M	Laborer	01Ma02Dj
Joseph	23	M	Laborer	01Ma02Dj
RODGERS. Ellen	.00	F	Infant	01Ma02Dj
DAVIS. U-Mrs.	40	F	Laborer	01Ma02Dj
BROOKES, Wm.	30	M	Unknown	01Ma02Dj
U-Mrs.	27	F	Unknown	01Ma02Dj
SHRABY, Robt.	30	M	Unknown	01Ma02Dj
DAVIES. Thomas	28	M	Unknown	01Ma02Dj
SMITH. James	25	M	Unknown	01Ma02Dj
U-Mrs.	22	F	Unknown	01Ma02Dj
LEECH, Joseph	25	M	Laborer	01Ma02Dj
U-Mrs.	25	F	Laborer	01Ma02Dj
ALLEN, James	25	M	Laborer	01Ma02Dj
LARNER, Ann	20	F	Laborer	01Ma02Dj

FANNY 01 MAY 1849

From Londonderry

NAMES OF PASSENGERS	AGE	SEX	OCCUPATIONS	DATE PORT SHIP
MCBREARTY, Biddy	17	F	Servant	01Ma01Dk
HART, Biddy	22	F	Servant	01Ma01Dk
MCCLINTICK, Mary	20	F	Servant	01Ma01Dk
HAVLIN, James	30	M	Laborer	01Ma01Dk
HILLIARD, John	25	M	Laborer	01Ma01Dk
MCCLINTICK, George	25	M	Laborer	01Ma01Dk
FRIEL, Giley	30	F	Servant	01Ma01Dk
MCCANN. Biddy	19	F	Servant	01Ma01Dk
DOGHERTY, Pat	21	M	Laborer	01Ma01Dk
MCFEELY, Charles	21	M	Laborer	01Ma01Dk
MCGORIGLE. Ann	25	F	Servant	01Ma01Dk
MCLYNCHY, Michael	19	M	Laborer	01Ma01Dk
LYNCH, Daniel	40	M	Laborer	01Ma01Dk
LYNCH. Edward	15	M	Laborer	01Ma01Dk
DOGHERTY, Philip	20	M	Laborer	01Ma01Dk
FRIEL, James	19	M	Laborer	01Ma01Dk
Henry	17	M	Laborer	01Ma01Dk
ELWEE, Biddy	20	F	Servant	01Ma01Dk
Danl.	25	M	Laborer	01Ma01Dk
MCBRIDE. Catherine	24	F	Servant	01Ma01Dk
MCGRORY, Patrick	20	M	Laborer	01Ma01Dk
HAGAN. Philip	20	M	Laborer	01Ma01Dk
HASLET, Charles	25	M	Laborer	01Ma01Dk
Martha	20	F	Servant	01Ma01Dk
HUNTER. William	25	M	Laborer	01Ma01Dk
Mary	20	F	Servant	01Ma01Dk
CASKIE, Leslie	21	M	Laborer	01Ma01Dk
NEWTON. Alexander	20	M	Tailor	01Ma01Dk
MCNAIR, Margt.	18	F	Tchr-Svnt	01Ma01Dk
DOGHERTY, Sarah	30	F	Servant	01Ma01Dk
MICHAN, James	24	M	Laborer	01Ma01Dk
MCCOLGAN, Michael	25	M	Laborer	01Ma01Dk
GRAHAM, Mary	21	F	Servant	01Ma01Dk
DOGHERTY, James	20	M	Laborer	01Ma01Dk
MCCOLGAN, Philip	24	M	Laborer	01Ma01Dk
MCFEELY, Mary	18	F	Servant	01Ma01Dk
MCSHEAFRY, Biddy	18	F	Servant	01Ma01Dk
FALKENTER. Charles	21	M	Laborer	01Ma01Dk
HUNTER. David	25	M	Laborer	01Ma01Dk
MCGONIGLE, Biddy	19	F	Servant	01Ma01Dk
FULLERTON, Mary	20	F	Servant	01Ma01Dk
HAGAN, Ann	17	F	Servant	01Ma01Dk
MCGRORY, Margaret	18	F	Servant	01Ma01Dk
MCCARROL, Rose	21	F	Servant	01Ma01Dk
FLEMMING, Fanny	26	F	Servant	01Ma01Dk
SMYTH, Edward	18	M	Laborer	01Ma01Dk
William	14	M	Laborer	01Ma01Dk
MCBRIEN, Ann	19	F	Servant	01Ma01Dk
DOHERTY, Corry	26	M	Laborer	01Ma01Dk
Mary	21	F	Servant	01Ma01Dk
MCABOY, Morgan	26	M	Currier	01Ma01Dk
Eleanor	23	F	Glover	01Ma01Dk
MCLAUGHLIN, Dennis	35	M	Laborer	01Ma01Dk
DUFFY, Ellen	24	F	Servant	01Ma01Dk
MURONY, Sally	35	F	Seamstress	01Ma01Dk
CONAGHAN, William	24	M	Laborer	01Ma01Dk
QUIGLEY, Rose-Ann	19	F	Servant	01Ma01Dk
Jane	20	F	Servant	01Ma01Dk
FOX, Mary	18	F	Servant	01Ma01Dk
HANNIGAN, David	18	M	Mason	01Ma01Dk
FRIEL, Catherine	18	F	Servant	01Ma01Dk
BOYLE. Margaret	18	F	Servant	01Ma01Dk
BROWN, Margaret	17	F	Servant	01Ma01Dk
MCGINNISS, Grace	20	F	Servant	01Ma01Dk
FARRIN, John	23	M	Laborer	01Ma01Dk
KEARNY, Peggy	23	F	Servant	01Ma01Dk
ODONNELL, Belle	28	F	Servant	01Ma01Dk
DUGAN, John	17	M	Laborer	01Ma01Dk
CARNEY, John	27	M	Laborer	01Ma01Dk
GALASBY, James	24	M	Laborer	01Ma01Dk
GALLAGHER, Neil	25	M	Laborer	01Ma01Dk
GILLIN, Nancy	20	F	Servant	01Ma01Dk
Mary	18	F	Servant	01Ma01Dk
DOGHERTY, Nancy	16	F	Servant	01Ma01Dk
RODON. Peggy	17	F	Servant	01Ma01Dk
MCGARRIGLE. John	21	M	Farmer	01Ma01Dk
CONNOR. Ellen	22	F	Seamstress	01Ma01Dk
FARREN, Mary	19	F	Servant	01Ma01Dk
CARNEY, Margaret	20	F	Servant	01Ma01Dk
MCDERMOT, Sally	23	F	Servant	01Ma01Dk
MCGINNIS, Grace	20	F	Servant	01Ma01Dk
BAR, Anne	15	F	Servant	01Ma01Dk
MEEHAN, Ellen	15	F	Servant	01Ma01Dk
DOGHERTY, Agnes	15	F	Servant	01Ma01Dk
LYNCH, Hugh	27	M	Mason	01Ma01Dk
MCALLENY, Ellen	30	F	Servant	01Ma01Dk
Hugh	9	M	Child	01Ma01Dk
Mary	7	F	Child	01Ma01Dk

NAMES OF PASSENGERS		AGE	SEX	OCCUPATIONS	DATE PORT SHIP
CLARK, Catherine		17	F	Servant	01Ma01Dk
ODONNELL, Catherine		14	F	Servant	01Ma01Dk
MCCALLY, Hugh		28	M	Farmer	01Ma01Dk
FARREN. Neil		11	M	None	01Ma01Dk
MCFEELY, John		23	M	Farmer	01Ma01Dk
MCGEGHAN, Anne		15	F	Milkmaid	01Ma01Dk
MCDERMOT, Grace		20	F	Servant	01Ma01Dk
MCLOUGHLIN. Edward		24	M	Laborer	01Ma01Dk
Neil		20	M	Laborer	01Ma01Dk
MCDERMOT, Sarah		23	F	Servant	01Ma01Dk
DOGHERTY, Magy		18	F	Servant	01Ma01Dk
HART, James		15	M	Laborer	01Ma01Dk
MCMULLEN. James		20	M	Farmer	01Ma01Dk
Jane	(W)	25	F	Wife	01Ma01Dk
CASSETY, Edward		40	M	Laborer	01Ma01Dk
DERRY, John		25	M	Mason	01Ma01Dk
GOLLIGER, Forgle		19	M	Shoemaker	01Ma01Dk
MCLOUGHLIN, Daniel		23	M	Laborer	01Ma01Dk
BAR, Margt.		21	F	Servant	01Ma01Dk
MCINTERE. Samuel		20	M	Farmer	01Ma01Dk
MARTIN. John		40	M	Farmer	01Ma01Dk
Mary	(W)	40	F	Wife	01Ma01Dk
James	(S)	7	M	Child	01Ma01Dk
LOGAN. John		31	M	Farmer	01Ma01Dk
Catherine	(W)	31	F	Wife	01Ma01Dk
John	(S)	10	M	Child	01Ma01Dk
DOGHERTY, Alexr.		22	M	Laborer	01Ma01Dk
CAREY, John		30	M	Servant	01Ma01Dk
PROOKINS. Nancy		22	F	Servant	01Ma01Dk
Sarah		24	F	Servant	01Ma01Dk
CLARK, William		49	M	Farmer	01Ma01Dk
CAGHAN. Bernard		26	M	Laborer	01Ma01Dk
BARREN. Edward		20	M	Laborer	01Ma01Dk
COLLINS. Rebecca		24	F	Servant	01Ma01Dk
John		27	M	Laborer	01Ma01Dk
William		21	M	Laborer	01Ma01Dk
DOGHERTY, Michael		12	M	None	01Ma01Dk
Daniel		10	M	None	01Ma01Dk
DEVENREY, Patrick		38	M	Farmer	01Ma01Dk
Sarah	(W)	38	F	Wife	01Ma01Dk
Michael	(S)	12	M	None	01Ma01Dk
William	(S)	10	M	None	01Ma01Dk
Margaret	(D)	8	F	Child	01Ma01Dk
Patrick	(S)	5	M	Child	01Ma01Dk
Mary	(D)	2	F	Child	01Ma01Dk
MCLOUGHLIN, Margaret		22	F	Servant	01Ma01Dk
DOGHERTY, William		22	M	Servant	01Ma01Dk
QUIGLEY, James		19	M	Farmer	01Ma01Dk
MCADOO, James		30	M	Farmer	01Ma01Dk
BRADLEY, Charles		25	M	Farmer	01Ma01Dk
John		16	M	Farmer	01Ma01Dk
Rebecca		18	F	Servant	01Ma01Dk
Mary		21	F	Servant	01Ma01Dk
MCCUGH, Arthur		17	M	Bleacher	01Ma01Dk
SWEENY, William		17	M	Joiner	01Ma01Dk
Edward		29	M	Laborer	01Ma01Dk
CARNEY, Mary		20	F	Dressmaker	01Ma01Dk
Fanny		19	F	Dressmaker	01Ma01Dk
Ellen		17	F	Dressmaker	01Ma01Dk
OGAN. Ellen		24	F	Dressmaker	01Ma01Dk
Sarah		26	F	Dressmaker	01Ma01Dk
MCCONNALOGUE. Margaret		34	F	Servant	01Ma01Dk
CCARTY, Jane		38	F	Seamstress	01Ma01Dk
John		12	M	Child	01Ma01Dk
Jane		5	F	Child	01Ma01Dk
CDERMOT, Alesia		18	F	Servant	01Ma01Dk
CLOUGHLIN. Mary		17	F	Servant	01Ma01Dk
EW, Bridget		37	F	Servant	01Ma01Dk
CGEGHAN, Edward		37	M	Servant	01Ma01Dk
ILLESPIE. Jas.		17	M	Fisherman	01Ma01Dk

JAMES-FAGAN 01 MAY 1849

From Dublin

NAMES OF PASSENGERS	AGE	SEX	OCCUPATIONS	DATE PORT SHIP
MORAN, Thomas	50	M	Farmer	01Ma12DI
Joseph	25	M	Farmer	01Ma12DI
John	23	M	Farmer	01Ma12DI
Michael	21	M	Laborer	01Ma12DI
Cathe.	21	F	Spinster	01Ma12DI
William	14	M	Carpenter	01Ma12DI
Bridget	11	F	Child	01Ma12DI
LEE, Bridget	45	F	Matron	01Ma12DI
Bridget	10	F	Child	01Ma12DI
Catharine	7	F	Child	01Ma12DI
BRENNAN, Miles	60	M	Farmer	01Ma12DI
Mary	40	F	Matron	01Ma12DI
Edward	28	M	Painter	01Ma12DI
James	24	M	Painter	01Ma12DI
GLEESON. Cornelius	6	M	Child	01Ma12DI
Mary	4	F	Child	01Ma12DI
DEMPSEY. Jane	24	F	Matron	01Ma12DI
Patrick	.00	M	Infant	01Ma12DI
STAPLETON. Timothy	26	M	Clerk	01Ma12DI
John	20	M	Shoemaker	01Ma12DI
Cathe.	20	F	Spinster	01Ma12DI
Judith	16	F	Spinster	01Ma12DI
William	30	M	Shoemaker	01Ma12DI
COWLEY, Patrick	29	M	Painter	01Ma12DI
U	.00	M	Infant	01Ma12DI
CONWAY, Thos.	40	M	Farmer	01Ma12DI
Mary	43	F	Matron	01Ma12DI
Patrick	7	M	Child	01Ma12DI
RICE, Abraham	22	M	Laborer	01Ma12DI
GALLAGHER, John	21	M	Laborer	01Ma12DI
KEEFFE, Patrick	30	M	Laborer	01Ma12DI
SWEETMAN, Christopher	50	M	Farmer	01Ma12DI
Mary	59	F	Matron	01Ma12DI
Lawrence	27	M	Laborer	01Ma12DI
Math.	26	M	Farmer	01Ma12DI
Richd.	23	M	Farmer	01Ma12DI
William	21	M	Farmer	01Ma12DI
Thos.	16	M	Farmer	01Ma12DI
Mary	16	F	Spinster	01Ma12DI
Christopher	11	M	Child	01Ma12DI
Cathe.	8	F	Child	01Ma12DI
GALLAGHER. Patrick	22	M	Laborer	01Ma12DI
MOAN, Bridget	27	F	Spinster	01Ma12DI
Mary	.00	F	Infant	01Ma12DI
BRIEN, Jas.	20	M	Painter	01Ma12DI
FITZSIMMONS. P.	20	M	Laborer	01Ma12DI
DONOUGH, John	20	M	Gdnr	01Ma12DI
Francis	26	M	Baker	01Ma12DI
Bridget	20	F	Matron	01Ma12DI
MURPHY, Bridget	46	F	Matron	01Ma12DI
John	20	M	Shoemaker	01Ma12DI
SHERIDAN, Thos.	18	M	Shoemaker	01Ma12DI
Cathe.	18	F	Spinster	01Ma12DI
DELANY, Danl.	29	M	Laborer	01Ma12DI
Mary-Ann	24	F	Matron	01Ma12DI
LARKIN, Mark	16	M	Carpenter	01Ma12DI
DELANY, Henry	3	M	Child	01Ma12DI
U	.00	U	Infant	01Ma12DI
DERENZEY, Edwd.	25	M	Painter	01Ma12DI
LAMBERT. Thos.	25	M	Painter	01Ma12DI
MOLLOY, James	55	M	Painter	01Ma12DI
Bridget	60	F	Matron	01Ma12DI
Chas.	21	M	Laborer	01Ma12DI
Thos.	20	M	Laborer	01Ma12DI
Bridget	14	F	Laborer	01Ma12DI

NAMES OF PASSENGERS	AGE	SEX	OCCUPATIONS	DATE PORT SHIP
MOLLOY, Edwd.	11	M	Child	01Ma12DI
GRAYDEN. E.Miss	24	F	Spinster	01Ma12DI
BRIEN. Patrick	18	M	Farmer	01Ma12DI
TYRRELL, Eliza	40	F	Matron	01Ma12DI
Garret	19	M	Plasterer	01Ma12DI
Jas.	15	M	Plasterer	01Ma12DI
BRYAN. Mary	25	F	Spinster	01Ma12DI
CONWAY, Thos.	45	M	Farmer	01Ma12DI
GERRAGHTY, Arthur	40	M	Farmer	01Ma12DI
Eliza	40	F	Matron	01Ma12DI
Mary	20	F	Matron	01Ma12DI
James	16	M	Rope Maker	01Ma12DI
Michael	15	M	Goldbeater	01Ma12DI
MCBRIDE. Bernard	18	M	Clerk	01Ma12DI
QUINN. Miles	25	M	Carpenter	01Ma12DI
MCCAMMON. Eliza	26	F	Spinster	01Ma12DI
WRIGHT. Patrick	23	M	Laborer	01Ma12DI
Mary	20	F	Matron	01Ma12DI
FITZACKREY, Lawrence	26	M	Laborer	01Ma12DI
CULLINEL, Ellen	28	F	Spinster	01Ma12DI
Ellen	60	F	Matron	01Ma12DI
LYNCH, William	21	M	Farmer	01Ma12DI
Bridget	21	F	Matron	01Ma12DI
KENNA, Thos.	21	M	Mason	01Ma12DI
Bridget	.06	F	Infant	01Ma12DI
TAYLOR. Michl.	18	M	Engineer	01Ma12DI
MATHEWS. Edwd.	18	M	Engineer	01Ma12DI
KELLY, William	24	M	Engineer	01Ma12DI
DONNELLY, Michl.	30	M	Engineer	01Ma12DI
MOONEY, Patrick	30	M	Engineer	01Ma12DI
CULINANE. Jas.	20	M	Carpenter	01Ma12DI
BYRNE, William	26	M	Carpenter	01Ma12DI
THORPE. Chas.	30	M	Carpenter	01Ma12DI
BRIERTON. Michl.	35	M	Laborer	01Ma12DI
HAGARTY, Edwd.	20	M	Bricklayer	01Ma12DI
DONNELLY, Edwd.	30	M	Mason	01Ma12DI
LONG, Thos.	25	M	Farmer	01Ma12DI
REDMOND, Peter	40	M	Farmer	01Ma12DI
Chas.T.	14	M	Clerk	01Ma12DI
RUSSELL, Sarah	20	F	Spinster	01Ma12DI
MOOREHOUSE. Mary	20	F	Matron	01Ma12DI
U	.00	U	Infant	01Ma12DI
BRIEN, Jas.	20	M	Unknown	01Ma12DI
GLEESON. Cathe.	25	F	Spinster	01Ma12DI
HOGAN, William	23	M	Laborer	01Ma12DI
Danl.	21	M	Laborer	01Ma12DI
Bridget	20	F	Spinster	01Ma12DI
William	19	M	Laborer	01Ma12DI
Stephen	18	M	Laborer	01Ma12DI
MURPHY, Patrick	26	M	Laborer	01Ma12DI
Margt.	20	F	Spinster	01Ma12DI
DUNLAVY, Thos.	33	M	Laborer	01Ma12DI
BRIEN. Henry	20	M	Gdnr	01Ma12DI
Rosanna	18	F	Matron	01Ma12DI
COYLE. U-Miss	24	F	Spinster	01Ma12DI
MCDONNELL, Bridget	23	F	Spinster	01Ma12DI
Matthew	21	M	Laborer	01Ma12DI
CALLAGHAR, Patt	21	M	Laborer	01Ma12DI
SMITH. William	30	M	Laborer	01Ma12DI
U-Mrs.	26	F	Spinster	01Ma12DI
BULGAR. Mary	20	F	Spinster	01Ma12DI
HICK, James	20	M	Laborer	01Ma12DI
SMITH. William	26	M	Laborer	01Ma12DI
QUINLAN. James	16	M	Laborer	01Ma12DI
DUNN. Mary	32	F	Spinster	01Ma12DI
MAGAW, Bridget	40	F	Spinster	01Ma12DI
HALT, William	34	M	Carpenter	01Ma12DI
MCGUIRE. John	18	M	Carpenter	01Ma12DI
MURPHY, Thos.	20	M	Carpenter	01Ma12DI
WHITE, Thos.	18	M	Carpenter	01Ma12DI
FARRELL, John	23	M	Carpenter	01Ma12DI
SIMPSON. James	25	M	Carpenter	01Ma12DI
MUNHUNAN. John	23	M	Carpenter	01Ma12DI
BRIERTON. Ann	23	F	Carpenter	01Ma12DI
WARREN. Francis	31	M	Clerk	01Ma12DI
WARREN, Cathe.	23	F	Spinster	01Ma12DI
CAMNEN, Mary	36	F	Spinster	01Ma12DI
GRIFFITH, John	20	M	Carpenter	01Ma12DI
GIBBON, Ann	23	F	Spinster	01Ma12DI
DALY, Peter	17	M	Carpenter	01Ma12DI
REILLY, Chas.	20	M	Carpenter	01Ma12DI
Thos.	24	M	Carpenter	01Ma12DI
BERTHY, Jas.	50	M	Carpenter	01Ma12DI
Ann	50	F	Matron	01Ma12DI
Patrick	27	M	Carpenter	01Ma12DI
Jas.	28	M	Carpenter	01Ma12DI
William	18	M	Carpenter	01Ma12DI
Cathe.	15	F	Spinster	01Ma12DI
Biddy	22	F	Spinster	01Ma12DI
Ann	20	F	Spinster	01Ma12DI
ALEXANDER, William	31	M	Carpenter	01Ma12DI
CERNAN, Mary	23	F	Matron	01Ma12DI
ELLIS, John	23	M	Gdnr	01Ma12DI
MURPHY, John	24	M	Gdnr	01Ma12DI
RUTH, John	30	M	Gdnr	01Ma12DI
Mary	30	F	Matron	01Ma12DI
HOGAN, Michl.	25	M	Laborer	01Ma12DI
Thos.	20	M	Laborer	01Ma12DI
HAMILTON. Cathe.	27	F	Spinster	01Ma12DI
HANLON. Mark	18	M	Mason	01Ma12DI
MURAY, Mick	16	M	Mason	01Ma12DI
MCCANN. Patt	31	M	Mason	01Ma12DI
John	30	M	Mason	01Ma12DI
WATERS. Ann	20	F	Spinster	01Ma12DI
RYAN, James	20	M	Carpenter	01Ma12DI
Betsey	20	F	Carpenter	01Ma12DI
CASTELLAN, Jas.	28	M	Farmer	01Ma12DI
Peter	27	M	Farmer	01Ma12DI
GEARY, James	23	M	Farmer	01Ma12DI
HYNES, Thos.	28	M	Mason	01Ma12DI
QUINLAN, Johanna	50	F	Spinster	01Ma12DI
Martin	18	M	Carpenter	01Ma12DI
Johanna	16	F	Spinster	01Ma12DI
MOONEY, Denis	26	M	Laborer	01Ma12DI
ENNIS, Ann	48	F	Spinster	01Ma12DI
BOYLE, John	25	M	Laborer	01Ma12DI
MACK, Henry	19	M	Laborer	01Ma12DI
DRAKE. Edwd.	17	M	Laborer	01Ma12DI
BRADY, Mcihl.	20	M	Laborer	01Ma12DI
SULLIVAN, Patrick	31	M	Laborer	01Ma12DI
MCTERNAN, Patk.	21	M	Laborer	01Ma12DI
DALY, Lawrence	30	M	Laborer	01Ma12DI
RYE. Thos.	20	M	Laborer	01Ma12DI
LEMING, Rose	18	F	Spinster	01Ma12DI
CALLON. Richd.	14	M	Mason	01Ma12DI
MANNY, Patt	35	M	Mason	01Ma12DI
MCGEE. Patt	30	M	Mason	01Ma12DI
MATHEWS, Patt	20	M	Mason	01Ma12DI
BERTHY, Frances	20	F	Spinster	01Ma12D
CULLIN, William	20	M	Clerk	01Ma12D
GILLIN, Andrew	27	M	Clerk	01Ma12D
DUNLAVY, Richd.	20	M	Clerk	01Ma12D
FOX, Maria	20	F	Spinster	01Ma12D
CAHILL, Joseph	20	M	Laborer	01Ma12D
STAPLETON, Mary	25	F	Spinster	01Ma12D
KEATING, Edwd.	32	M	Laborer	01Ma12D
U-Mrs.	23	F	Matron	01Ma12D
RYAN, Thos.	20	M	Carpenter	01Ma12D
CROWLEY, Mary	40	F	Matron	01Ma12D
RYAN, Ellen	25	F	Matron	01Ma12D
HICK, Mary	26	F	Matron	01Ma12D
GRAYDEN, William	15	M	Mason	01Ma12D
MITCHELL, Patt	20	M	Mason	01Ma12D
MCGILL, Bridget	28	F	Spinster	01Ma12D
LAWLESS. Mick	21	M	Carpenter	01Ma12D
HEWITT, John	50	M	Tailor	01Ma12D
FERRY, Saml.	35	M	Farmer	01Ma12D
M.Mrs.	30	F	Matron	01Ma12D
Chas.	17	M	Clerk	01Ma12D
John-F.	15	M	Clerk	01Ma12D

NAMES OF PASSENGERS	AGE	SEX	OCCUPATIONS	DATE PORT SHIP
KAVANAGH, Ann-Mrs.	20	F	Spinster	01Ma12DI

DEVON 01 MAY 1849

From Liverpool

NAMES OF PASSENGERS	AGE	SEX	OCCUPATIONS	DATE PORT SHIP
CAMBELL, John	25	M	Servant	01Ma02Dh
DEVLIN. Catherine	40	F	Servant	01Ma02Dh
Ellen	18	F	Servant	01Ma02Dh
BOHEN. Francis	22	M	Laborer	01Ma02Dh
MEDES. Joseph	50	M	Laborer	01Ma02Dh
U (W)	50	F	Unknown	01Ma02Dh
Wm.	20	M	Blacksmith	01Ma02Dh
Sarah	17	F	None	01Ma02Dh
PRESTON. Thomas	26	M	Laborer	01Ma02Dh
U (W)	26	F	Unknown	01Ma02Dh
MCGRENNY, Margaret	25	F	Servant	01Ma02Dh
CARVILLE. William	20	M	Farmer	01Ma02Dh
COLAMAN. Pat	23	M	Laborer	01Ma02Dh
MCKEY, Lawrence	32	M	Farmer	01Ma02Dh
U (W)	26	F	Unknown	01Ma02Dh
OBRIEN. Pat	40	M	Blacksmith	01Ma02Dh
U (W)	36	F	Unknown	01Ma02Dh
John	22	M	Blacksmith	01Ma02Dh
Bridget	22	F	Unknown	01Ma02Dh
Pat	14	M	None	01Ma02Dh
Mary-Ann	12	F	None	01Ma02Dh
ALY, Margt.	25	F	Governess	01Ma02Dh
UTTERA, John	28	M	Farmer	01Ma02Dh
Julia	25	F	Unknown	01Ma02Dh
U	.00	U	Infant	01Ma02Dh
ERBEY, Hannah	25	F	Unknown	01Ma02Dh
MARD, Peter	21	M	Laborer	01Ma02Dh
HITE, Tim	40	M	Farmer	01Ma02Dh
Mary	40	F	Unknown	01Ma02Dh
Mary	.00	F	Infant	01Ma02Dh
UGENT, Arthur	40	M	Sawer	01Ma02Dh
Ellen	34	F	Unknown	01Ma02Dh
ULLIVAN. Thed	35	M	Laborer	01Ma02Dh
HITE, Wm.	45	M	Farmer	01Ma02Dh
Mary	30	F	Unknown	01Ma02Dh
Pat	5	M	Child	01Ma02Dh
John	3	M	Child	01Ma02Dh
Catherine	.00	F	Infant	01Ma02Dh
EVLIN. Giffy	30	M	Farmer	01Ma02Dh
Giffy	25	M	Farmer	01Ma02Dh
RPHY, Charles	40	M	Farmer	01Ma02Dh
Bridget	36	F	None	01Ma02Dh
Daniel	6	M	Child	01Ma02Dh
Corl.	.00	U	Infant	01Ma02Dh
Catherine	18	F	None	01Ma02Dh
LIGAN. Wm.	28	M	Farmer	01Ma02Dh
Eliza	25	F	None	01Ma02Dh
Michael	22	M	Laborer	01Ma02Dh
RNER, John	20	M	Farmer	01Ma02Dh
OWLY, Thos.	24	M	Farmer	01Ma02Dh
Judy	24	F	Unknown	01Ma02Dh
Johanna	24	F	Unknown	01Ma02Dh
Mary	.00	F	Infant	01Ma02Dh
GLE. Richard	56	M	Farmer	01Ma02Dh
Edward	28	M	Farmer	01Ma02Dh
Richard	25	M	Farmer	01Ma02Dh
William	20	M	Farmer	01Ma02Dh
Hannah	22	F	None	01Ma02Dh
TON. Thomas	40	M	Farmer	01Ma02Dh
Y, Thos.	30	M	Laborer	01Ma02Dh
ANE. Johanna	24	F	Unknown	01Ma02Dh
LIVAN. Dennis	21	M	Laborer	01Ma02Dh
CARTHY, Dan	21	M	Laborer	01Ma02Dh
GALLAGHER, Dan	30	M	Laborer	01Ma02Dh
HARRINGTON. Dan	27	M	Laborer	01Ma02Dh
SULLIVAN, Dennis	22	M	Laborer	01Ma02Dh
Bess	22	F	None	01Ma02Dh
Norris	20	F	Servant	01Ma02Dh
Mary	60	F	Unknown	01Ma02Dh
DOODY, John	40	M	Farmer	01Ma02Dh
BYRNES. Bess	20	F	Servant	01Ma02Dh
Honora	20	F	Servant	01Ma02Dh
FAHY, Ellen	20	F	Servant	01Ma02Dh
BYRNES. Francis	30	M	Farmer	01Ma02Dh
Mary-Anne	22	F	None	01Ma02Dh
HANLY, Anne	20	F	None	01Ma02Dh
James	20	M	Mason	01Ma02Dh
Jane	17	F	None	01Ma02Dh
Anne	16	F	None	01Ma02Dh
ERIN, Margt.	17	F	Unknown	01Ma02Dh
FRENN. Margt.	20	F	Unknown	01Ma02Dh
Bridget	20	F	Unknown	01Ma02Dh
REILLY, Pat	20	M	Laborer	01Ma02Dh
COFFEE, Pat	26	M	Laborer	01Ma02Dh
DOOLAN, Bridget	18	F	Unknown	01Ma02Dh
EGAN, Edward	20	M	Laborer	01Ma02Dh
SCULLY, Pat	25	M	Laborer	01Ma02Dh
Mary	13	F	None	01Ma02Dh
Margaret	18	F	None	01Ma02Dh
BULGER, William	16	M	Laborer	01Ma02Dh
CLARKIN, Ann	20	F	Servant	01Ma02Dh
Anne	21	F	Servant	01Ma02Dh
Sally	25	F	Servant	01Ma02Dh
MCMANNES. Ann	20	F	None	01Ma02Dh
George	.00	M	Infant	01Ma02Dh
CONMICK, John	25	M	Clerk	01Ma02Dh
U (W)	25	F	None	01Ma02Dh
MORRIS. James	20	M	Unknown	01Ma02Dh
BAILY, Pat	25	M	Weaver	01Ma02Dh
OBRIEN, Catherine	18	F	Unknown	01Ma02Dh
BANNON. Thomas	19	M	Laborer	01Ma02Dh
Mary	16	F	Laborer	01Ma02Dh
KENNEDY, John	40	M	Baker	01Ma02Dh
Bridget	40	F	None	01Ma02Dh
John	14	M	None	01Ma02Dh
Thomas	10	M	None	01Ma02Dh
Mike	9	M	Child	01Ma02Dh
James	4	M	Child	01Ma02Dh
Celia	1	F	Child	01Ma02Dh
Mat	.00	M	Infant	01Ma02Dh
HAND, John	15	M	Groom	01Ma02Dh
KEARNEY, Mary	15	F	Dressmaker	01Ma02Dh
READY, Pat	38	M	Laborer	01Ma02Dh
GOWIN, Anthony	30	M	Groom	01Ma02Dh
JOHNSTON. George	41	M	Groom	01Ma02Dh
Mary	30	F	None	01Ma02Dh
MALONE, Larry	23	M	Farmer	01Ma02Dh
DAVIS, Kate	28	F	Unknown	01Ma02Dh
TRAINOR. Owen	17	M	Farmer	01Ma02Dh
BRENNAN, Mike	26	M	Laborer	01Ma02Dh
GILFOIL, Danl.	22	M	Laborer	01Ma02Dh
FLYNN, Danl.	22	M	Laborer	01Ma02Dh
KERNIG, Richard	20	M	Baker	01Ma02Dh
SMITH, Honora	18	F	Unknown	01Ma02Dh
MARRON. Margaret	22	F	Unknown	01Ma02Dh
CONROY, John	23	M	Laborer	01Ma02Dh
MULANE, Dennis	28	M	Laborer	01Ma02Dh
Margt.	24	F	None	01Ma02Dh
Johanna	.00	F	Infant	01Ma02Dh
SULLIVAN, Dennis	35	M	Farmer	01Ma02Dh
Margt.	35	F	None	01Ma02Dh
Eugene	5	M	Child	01Ma02Dh
Justine	4	F	Child	01Ma02Dh
THORNTON, Margaret	26	F	Servant	01Ma02Dh
PITCHAN, William	20	M	Gdnr	01Ma02Dh
WALSH, William	30	M	Miller	01Ma02Dh
James	25	M	Laborer	01Ma02Dh
WHELAN, James	26	M	Laborer	01Ma02Dh

NAMES OF PASSENGERS		AGE	SEX	OCCUPATIONS	DATE PORT SHIP
WHELAN. Peter		24	M	Laborer	01Ma02Dh
MCGATTIN. Mary-Anne		22	F	Servant	01Ma02Dh
MCCLUSKY, Bridget		20	F	Servant	01Ma02Dh
HOY, John		24	M	Groom	01Ma02Dh
Rosey		23	F	None	01Ma02Dh
CONNELLY, Ann		19	F	Servant	01Ma02Dh
Patrick		21	M	Laborer	01Ma02Dh
Ellen		19	F	Unknown	01Ma02Dh
Anne		13	F	Unknown	01Ma02Dh
HOY, Judy		21	F	Unknown	01Ma02Dh
BYSON. Barney		25	M	Laborer	01Ma02Dh
U	(W)	25	F	None	01Ma02Dh
BRADY, Martin		40	M	Laborer	01Ma02Dh
U	(W)	40	F	None	01Ma02Dh
Thomas		13	M	None	01Ma02Dh
Michael		11	M	None	01Ma02Dh
William		9	M	Child	01Ma02Dh
John		7	M	Child	01Ma02Dh
Mary-Anne		5	F	Child	01Ma02Dh
James		2	M	Child	01Ma02Dh
Jane		.00	F	Infant	01Ma02Dh
TREATH. Andrew		23	M	Weaver	01Ma02Dh
MURPHY, Corn		50	M	Farmer	01Ma02Dh
Eliza		50	F	None	01Ma02Dh
Patrick		22	M	Farmer	01Ma02Dh
Daniel		18	M	Farmer	01Ma02Dh
John		13	M	Farmer	01Ma02Dh
William		11	M	None	01Ma02Dh
DALY, James		36	M	Farmer	01Ma02Dh
Patrick		7	M	Child	01Ma02Dh
Johanna		9	F	Child	01Ma02Dh
John		6	M	Child	01Ma02Dh
John		34	M	Farmer	01Ma02Dh
Mary		28	F	None	01Ma02Dh
Johanna		8	F	Child	01Ma02Dh
Mary		4	F	Child	01Ma02Dh
Patrick		.00	M	Infant	01Ma02Dh
CONNELL, Owen		33	M	Farmer	01Ma02Dh
Johanna		27	F	None	01Ma02Dh
Ellen		4	F	Child	01Ma02Dh
MOLYNEUX, Mary		30	F	Unknown	01Ma02Dh
Michael		22	M	Laborer	01Ma02Dh
Patrick		34	M	Laborer	01Ma02Dh
Ellen		21	F	Unknown	01Ma02Dh
FLAHERTY, John		40	M	Laborer	01Ma02Dh
DOLAN. James		18	M	Laborer	01Ma02Dh
KEEF, Michael		25	M	Laborer	01Ma02Dh
PIPES. Thomas		20	M	Miller	01Ma02Dh
ANDERSON, Jim		20	M	Block Maker	01Ma02Dh

DANIEL 02 MAY 1849

From St.Croix

NAMES OF PASSENGERS	AGE	SEX	OCCUPATIONS	DATE PORT SHIP
GILMORE, Alexander	23	M	Gentleman	02Ma39Dg
Eliza	27	F	Lady	02Ma39Dg

URANIA 02 MAY 1849

From Youghal

NAMES OF PASSENGERS	AGE	SEX	OCCUPATIONS	DATE PORT SHIP
POWER. Bridget	24	F	Fsvnt	02Ma28Di
CONRY, Catherine	32	F	Fsvnt	02Ma28Di
CONRY, Patrick	13	M	None	02Ma28D
Wm.	12	M	None	02Ma28D
Mary	8	F	Child	02Ma28D
DAY, Honora	42	F	Servant	02Ma28D
HUMPHRY, Eliza	8	F	Child	02Ma28D
JOYCE, Julia	28	F	None	02Ma28D
Julia	3	F	Child	02Ma28D
SAVAGE, Michael	28	M	Fsvnt	02Ma28D
MEARA, John	25	M	Fsvnt	02Ma28D
CONNOLLY, James	30	M	Fsvnt	02Ma28D
Mary	25	F	Fsvnt	02Ma28D
Catherine	19	F	Fsvnt	02Ma28D
DRISCOLL, Mary	20	F	Fsvnt	02Ma28D
MALEY, Bridget	26	F	Fsvnt	02Ma28D
AHERN, Patrick	22	M	Fsvnt	02Ma28D
SPLANE, Mary	23	F	Fsvnt	02Ma28D
MURRAY, Charles	60	M	Farmer	02Ma28D
Elizabeth	52	F	Farmer	02Ma28D
Michael	22	M	Farmer	02Ma28D
Wm.	17	M	Farmer	02Ma28D
James	15	M	Farmer	02Ma28D
Mary	13	F	Farmer	02Ma28D
Susana	11	F	Farmer	02Ma28D
CURTIN, Margaret	35	F	Servant	02Ma28D
MURRAY, Michael	27	M	Servant	02Ma28D
MALONE, Margaret	26	F	Servant	02Ma28D
MACCARTY, John	29	M	Farmer	02Ma28D
Anne	29	F	Farmer	02Ma28D
John	3	M	Child	02Ma28D
Thos.	.08	M	Infant	02Ma28D
COCKRAN, Mary	18	F	Servant	02Ma28D
MCCARTY, Thos.	45	M	Carpenter	02Ma28D
GEIRY, Mic	21	M	Fisherman	02Ma28D
KELLY, Daniel	22	M	Servant	02Ma28D
FOLLY, Patrick	32	M	Farmer	02Ma28D
Nancy	35	F	Farmer	02Ma28D
KEANE, Martin	13	M	None	02Ma28D
Philip	12	M	None	02Ma28D
Michael	9	M	Child	02Ma28D
U, Nancy	5	F	Child	02Ma28D
DEVENE, James	49	M	Servant	02Ma28D
CURTIN, Nancy	40	F	Servant	02Ma28D
CONRY, John	18	M	Servant	02Ma28
Ellen	20	F	Servant	02Ma28
KENEFIRK, Patrick	33	M	Farmer	02Ma28
Ellen	33	F	Farmer	02Ma28
Margaret	3	F	Child	02Ma28
Ellen	.06	F	Infant	02Ma28
QUIRK, Ellen	19	F	Servant	02Ma28
COLEBORT, Mary	30	F	Servant	02Ma28
DUGGAN, Wm.	20	M	Servant	02Ma28
CAREW, Wm.	40	M	Fisherman	02Ma28
Mary	35	F	None	02Ma28
Patrick	8	M	Child	02Ma28
Margaret	3	F	Child	02Ma28
James	28	M	Laborer	02Ma28
PICKET, Wm.	25	M	Servant	02Ma28
WHALEN, Brien	18	M	Servant	02Ma28
Thos.	16	M	Servant	02Ma28
Wm.	14	M	Servant	02Ma28
TERRY, Jas.	30	M	Servant	02Ma28
CAREW, Lawrence	30	M	Servant	02Ma28
FITZGERALD, Redmond	19	M	Miller	02Ma28
Wm.	24	M	Joiner	02Ma28
Michael	22	M	Miller	02Ma28
HAYES, John	33	M	Servant	02Ma28
POWER, Patrick	50	M	Farmer	02Ma28
James	14	M	None	02Ma28
David	8	M	Child	02Ma28
Norry	20	F	Servant	02Ma28
DEE, Ellen	30	F	Servant	02Ma28
KELLY, John	28	M	Servant	02Ma28
FLYNN. John	27	M	Servant	02Ma2
OBRIEN, Kennedy	35	M	Currier	02Ma2
Margaret	20	F	None	02Ma2

NAMES OF PASSENGERS	AGE	SEX	OCCUPATIONS	DATE PORT SHIP
OBRIEN. Jeremiah	12	M	None	02Ma28Di
WELSH. Mary-Ellen	12	F	None	02Ma28Di
CLEARY, Patrick	35	M	Laborer	02Ma28Di
SPRATT. James	18	M	Laborer	02Ma28Di
FITZGERALD. Maurice	30	M	Laborer	02Ma28Di
SHEA. Michael	26	M	Clerk	02Ma28Di
CAHILL. Elizabeth	30	F	Servant	02Ma28Di
CONRY. Owen	50	M	Sawer	02Ma28Di
Bridget	40	F	None	02Ma28Di
John	14	M	None	02Ma28Di
Johanna	12	F	None	02Ma28Di
Mary-Ann	11	F	None	02Ma28Di
Thos.	9	M	Child	02Ma28Di
James	7	M	Child	02Ma28Di
Ellen	5	F	Child	02Ma28Di
SHIEL, Thomas	20	M	Unknown	02Ma28Di

SARAH-SANDS 02 MAY 1849

From Liverpool

NAMES OF PASSENGERS	AGE	SEX	OCCUPATIONS	DATE PORT SHIP
COTTER. John-Bukley	49	M	Navy	02Ma02Dm
BILBROUGH, S.E.	25	M	Gentleman	02Ma02Dm
COPELAND, Maria	18	F	Spinster	02Ma02Dm
WITHERS. Sophia (N)	11	F	Niece	02Ma02Dm
SHERRARD, Joseph	17	M	Gentleman	02Ma02Dm
WELLS. Edwd.E.	24	M	Bookseller	02Ma02Dm
Margaret	23	F	Bookseller	02Ma02Dm
WHITE. Marshall-M.	25	M	Clergyman	02Ma02Dm
Eliza-J. (W)	24	F	Wife	02Ma02Dm
MOORE. George	15	M	Gentleman	02Ma02Dm
MAHONY, Cornelius-R.	29	M	Gentleman	02Ma02Dm
WHITE. James	26	M	Grocer	02Ma02Dm
MCELDANY. Robert	19	M	Grocer	02Ma02Dm
ORILEY. Catherine	28	F	None	02Ma02Dm
OHAGAN. Ann	30	F	None	02Ma02Dm
ORILEY, Mary	18	F	None	02Ma02Dm
ELLIOT. John	30	M	Laborer	02Ma02Dm
Jane	28	F	Laborer	02Ma02Dm
Thomas	10	M	None	02Ma02Dm
James	3	M	Child	02Ma02Dm
OBRIEN. Michael	42	M	Laborer	02Ma02Dm
MAHAFFY, Alexander	23	M	Farmer	02Ma02Dm
Mary	23	F	Farmer	02Ma02Dm
BRYON. Bartholomew	25	M	Laborer	02Ma02Dm
GARTLAND, Patrick	26	M	Tailor	02Ma02Dm
MCKENNA. Philip	25	M	Carpenter	02Ma02Dm
MCGILL. Alexander	19	M	Carpenter	02Ma02Dm
Rose	20	F	None	02Ma02Dm
COULON. Catherine	20	F	None	02Ma02Dm
GIBSON, William	18	M	Tailor	02Ma02Dm
ANKES. Henry	21	M	Painter	02Ma02Dm
DAWSON. Daniel	23	M	Farmer	02Ma02Dm
FITZGIBBON, James	19	M	Farmer	02Ma02Dm
Bridget	22	F	None	02Ma02Dm
MCMAHON. John	19	M	Farmer	02Ma02Dm
LYNN. William	26	M	Farmer	02Ma02Dm

SILAS-GRIMSHAW 02 MAY 1849

From Liverpool

NAMES OF PASSENGERS	AGE	SEX	OCCUPATIONS	DATE PORT SHIP
LOSTY, Edward	27	M	Laborer	02Ma02Dn
BRADY. Pat	26	M	Laborer	02Ma02Dn
DUNNE. Dominic	25	M	Laborer	02Ma02Dn
ROURKE. Joseph	25	M	Laborer	02Ma02Dn
MCARDEL, U	56	M	Shopkeeper	02Ma02Dn
U	56	F	Shopkeeper	02Ma02Dn
Mary	16	F	None	02Ma02Dn
Terence	12	M	None	02Ma02Dn
John	11	M	None	02Ma02Dn
Felix	8	M	Child	02Ma02Dn
Anna	5	F	Child	02Ma02Dn
MALONE. Thos.	25	M	Laborer	02Ma02Dn
Patrick	24	M	Laborer	02Ma02Dn
GLYNNE. James	26	M	Laborer	02Ma02Dn
Marcella	20	F	None	02Ma02Dn
Margaret	.00	F	Infant	02Ma02Dn
MCGUINNES. Bridget	18	F	Servant	02Ma02Dn
CASSIDY, Peter	24	M	Laborer	02Ma02Dn
MORAN. Willm.	27	M	Laborer	02Ma02Dn
Michl.	21	M	Laborer	02Ma02Dn
BRADY. Phil	30	M	Farmer	02Ma02Dn
Rose	30	F	None	02Ma02Dn
John	8	M	Child	02Ma02Dn
Bernard	5	M	Child	02Ma02Dn
Cath.	2	F	Child	02Ma02Dn
Julia	.00	F	Infant	02Ma02Dn
REILLY. Bridget	18	F	Servant	02Ma02Dn
SMITH, Mary	18	F	Servant	02Ma02Dn
ELLIOTT. Fanny	23	F	Servant	02Ma02Dn
KELLY. James	40	M	Laborer	02Ma02Dn
U-Mrs.	35	F	None	02Ma02Dn
Patrick	13	M	None	02Ma02Dn
Mary	11	F	None	02Ma02Dn
Margaret	9	F	Child	02Ma02Dn
Peter	7	M	Child	02Ma02Dn
Thomas	5	M	Child	02Ma02Dn
DONNELLY. Anne	21	F	Laborer	02Ma02Dn
QUIRK. John	28	M	Laborer	02Ma02Dn
U-Mrs.	24	F	None	02Ma02Dn
Mary	4	F	Child	02Ma02Dn
Julia	2	F	Child	02Ma02Dn
William	.00	M	Infant	02Ma02Dn
KENNEY, Willm.	38	M	Farmer	02Ma02Dn
Patrick	32	M	None	02Ma02Dn
Martin	36	M	None	02Ma02Dn
Dennis	37	M	None	02Ma02Dn
CARRICK. John	16	M	None	02Ma02Dn
KENNEY. Fanne	16	F	None	02Ma02Dn
Bridget	18	F	None	02Ma02Dn
Cath.	10	F	None	02Ma02Dn
HOMER. Cath.	22	F	None	02Ma02Dn
CURRIN, John	24	M	Farmer	02Ma02Dn
Margt.	22	F	Farmer	02Ma02Dn
KENNY. Michael	25	M	Farmer	02Ma02Dn
John	20	M	Farmer	02Ma02Dn
NAUGHTON. Peter	20	M	Farmer	02Ma02Dn
MCCORMICK. Patt	22	M	Joiner	02Ma02Dn
Anne	20	F	Joiner	02Ma02Dn
TRENOR. Joseph	21	M	Joiner	02Ma02Dn
MOLLY, Robert	24	M	Joiner	02Ma02Dn
MCCUE. Patk.	26	M	Unknown	02Ma02Dn
PURCELL, Richd. Died-At-Sea	24	M	Unknown	02Ma02Dn
WILSON. Robt.	35	M	Farmer	02Ma02Dn
Ellen	13	F	None	02Ma02Dn

NAMES OF PASSENGERS	AGE	SEX	OCCUPATIONS	DATE PORT SHIP
BURNETT. Geo.	21	M	Farmer	02Ma02Dn
KILBY, Geo.	23	M	Farmer	02Ma02Dn
MILLS. Susan	20	F	None	02Ma02Dn
RYDER. Richd.	35	M	Farmer	02Ma02Dn
CRAWFORD. Fanny	16	F	None	02Ma02Dn
REILLY, Michl.	21	M	Farmer	02Ma02Dn
KILBRIDE. Bernd.	21	M	Farmer	02Ma02Dn
Patk.	22	M	Farmer	02Ma02Dn
Peter	20	M	Farmer	02Ma02Dn
MCGUIRE. Patt	24	M	Farmer	02Ma02Dn
Cath.	21	F	None	02Ma02Dn
KILBRIDE. Margt.	24	F	None	02Ma02Dn
MCGOVERN. Biddy	18	F	None	02Ma02Dn
KEATING, David	27	M	Farmer	02Ma02Dn
RYAN, John	28	M	Farmer	02Ma02Dn
CARTY. Andrew	36	M	Farmer	02Ma02Dn
PRENDERGHAST. Garret	26	M	Farmer	02Ma02Dn
HICKEY. James	20	M	Farmer	02Ma02Dn
GRADY, Timothy	22	M	Farmer	02Ma02Dn
FOY, Owen	40	M	Farmer	02Ma02Dn
Biddy	35	F	Farmer	02Ma02Dn
Patrick	12	M	None	02Ma02Dn
James	10	M	None	02Ma02Dn
Bridget	8	F	Child	02Ma02Dn
Paul	6	M	Child	02Ma02Dn
Owen	4	M	Child	02Ma02Dn
Peter	.00	M	Infant	02Ma02Dn
Anne	50	F	None	02Ma02Dn
Died-At-Sea				
Betty	21	F	None	02Ma02Dn
FARRFLLY, Patt	26	M	Farmer	02Ma02Dn
CAROLAN. Peter	25	M	Farmer	02Ma02Dn
MORAN. Thomas	23	M	Farmer	02Ma02Dn
Edwd.	12	M	Farmer	02Ma02Dn
Margt.	22	F	None	02Ma02Dn
RYAN. Owen	45	M	Farmer	02Ma02Dn
Died-At-Sea				
Willm.	22	M	Farmer	02Ma02Dn
DUFFY, Patk.	26	M	Farmer	02Ma02Dn
BLAKE. Mathw.	40	M	Farmer	02Ma02Dn
Elizabeth	35	F	None	02Ma02Dn
Robert	16	M	None	02Ma02Dn
Thomas	13	M	None	02Ma02Dn
Grace-Anne	11	F	None	02Ma02Dn
Eliza	10	F	None	02Ma02Dn
Susannah	7	F	Child	02Ma02Dn
Willm.	4	M	Child	02Ma02Dn
Nathl.	.00	M	Infant	02Ma02Dn
Died-At-Sea				
PIERCE. Edward	35	M	Farmer	02Ma02Dn
Mary	32	F	None	02Ma02Dn
Thomas	10	M	None	02Ma02Dn
Henry	9	M	Child	02Ma02Dn
Edward	7	M	Child	02Ma02Dn
John	5	M	Child	02Ma02Dn
Willm.	4	M	Child	02Ma02Dn
Nathl.	2	M	Child	02Ma02Dn
BRADLEY. John	16	M	None	02Ma02Dn
FELTAS. Fanny	16	F	Servant	02Ma02Dn
FEGAN, James	24	M	Laborer	02Ma02Dn
BRADY, Cath.	22	F	Laborer	02Ma02Dn
MCGAHEN. Mary	40	F	Laborer	02Ma02Dn
MARRIN, Nancy	26	F	Laborer	02Ma02Dn
DUFFY, Owen	24	M	Laborer	02Ma02Dn
BYRNES. Alice	22	F	None	02Ma02Dn
Mary	20	F	None	02Ma02Dn
LAMB, Nichl.	18	M	Laborer	02Ma02Dn
REILLY, Cathe.	16	F	None	02Ma02Dn
LAMB, Cathe.	18	F	None	02Ma02Dn
DUFFY, John	.00	M	Infant	02Ma02Dn
SULLIVAN. John	50	M	Laborer	02Ma02Dn
Mary	24	F	None	02Ma02Dn
Bridget	22	F	None	02Ma02Dn
Michael	20	M	None	02Ma02Dn
Patrick	12	M	None	02Ma02Dn

NAMES OF PASSENGERS	AGE	SEX	OCCUPATIONS	DATE PORT SHIP
SULLIVAN, John	10	M	None	02Ma02Dr
WALSH, John	36	M	Laborer	02Ma02Dr
U-Mrs.	34	F	None	02Ma02Dr
TELHALY. Thos.	34	M	Laborer	02Ma02Dr
BARRY. Margt.	24	F	None	02Ma02Dr
MADAGAN, Mary	28	F	None	02Ma02Dr
HOGAN, Daniel	20	M	Laborer	02Ma02Dr
DIVERIN, James	20	M	Laborer	02Ma02Dr
BAILEY. Henry-Wm.	12	M	Laborer	02Ma02Dr
ELLIOTT. John	24	M	Laborer	02Ma02Dr
GRANT. Anne	24	F	Farmer	02Ma02Dr
Eliza	21	F	None	02Ma02Dr
Mary	18	F	None	02Ma02Dr
Anne	14	F	None	02Ma02Dr
John	13	M	None	02Ma02Dr
Michael	13	M	None	02Ma02Dr
Catherine	11	F	None	02Ma02Dr
Richard	9	M	Child	02Ma02Dr
Tedy	9	M	Child	02Ma02Dr
LAWLESS. Thomas	21	M	Blacksmith	02Ma02Dr
MORAN, Patk.	21	M	Laborer	02Ma02Dr
BEARY. Patk.	48	M	Laborer	02Ma02Dr
BRENNAN. Thos.	26	M	Laborer	02Ma02Dr
Alice	24	F	None	02Ma02Dr
Michael	.00	M	Infant	02Ma02D
DELANEY. Cathe.	18	F	Servant	02Ma02Dr
MAYE. Patk.	20	M	Laborer	02Ma02Dr
KILACCY. Edwd.	21	M	None	02Ma02Dr
MCGUINNESS. Bridget	21	F	None	02Ma02D
LANDON. Anne	21	F	None	02Ma02Dr
CULLEN, Nics.	40	M	Laborer	02Ma02D
CAROLAN, Thomas	40	M	Laborer	02Ma02D
MCCARTY, John	24	M	Laborer	02Ma02D
KIERNAN, Anne	26	F	Lace Maker	02Ma02D
Edward	7	M	Child	02Ma02D
Peter	6	M	Child	02Ma02D
ARDELL, George	25	M	Shopman	02Ma02D
MCKENNA, Patt	24	M	Laborer	02Ma02D
Alexr.	22	M	Laborer	02Ma02D
John	22	M	Laborer	02Ma02D
Mary	20	F	None	02Ma02D
MURPHY. John	30	M	Laborer	02Ma02D
Anne	30	F	None	02Ma02D
Cathe.	18	F	None	02Ma02D
Nichls.	16	M	None	02Ma02D
Mary	13	F	None	02Ma02D
Patrick	11	M	None	02Ma02D
Michl.	3	M	Child	02Ma02D
Denis	.00	M	Infant	02Ma02D
LOWRY, Thomas	48	M	Farmer	02Ma02D
Mary	45	F	None	02Ma02D
James	15	M	None	02Ma02D
Mary	13	F	None	02Ma02D
Biddy	9	F	Child	02Ma02D
Kate	5	F	Child	02Ma02D
DALY, Patt	28	M	Farmer	02Ma02D
Cathe.	24	F	None	02Ma02D
MCKENNA. Wm.	35	M	Laborer	02Ma02D
Mary	30	F	None	02Ma02
Margt.	.00	F	Infant	02Ma02
DONOHAN, Danl.	26	M	Farmer	02Ma02
HORAN. John	35	M	Farmer	02Ma02
STUART. John	20	M	Farmer	02Ma02
JOHNSON. Moses	30	M	Laborer	02Ma02
CARROLL. Patk.	26	M	Laborer	02Ma02
LAVIN, Mary	30	F	Servant	02Ma02
MARSHALL, Thomas	20	M	Servant	02Ma02
TAYLOR. Willm.	23	M	None	02Ma02
CARLISLE, Michael	24	M	None	02Ma02
MCGRATH, Thomas	20	M	None	02Ma02
Mary	18	F	None	02Ma02
FITZPATRICK. Edward	21	M	None	02Ma02
Cathe.	20	F	None	02Ma02
PURCELL. Patk.	21	M	None	02Ma02
KEIGHER. Patk.	46	M	Laborer	02Ma02

NAMES OF PASSENGERS	AGE	SEX	OCCUPATIONS	DATE PORT SHIP
KEIGHER. Cathe.	40	F	None	02Ma02Dn
Michael	18	M	Laborer	02Ma02Dn
James	8	M	Child	02Ma02Dn
Mary	12	F	None	02Ma02Dn
Mary	26	F	None	02Ma02Dn
John	5	M	Child	02Ma02Dn
HANLEY. Cathe.	20	F	Servant	02Ma02Dn
Cathe.	21	F	Servant	02Ma02Dn
PETIT. Cathe.	22	F	Servant	02Ma02Dn
BRADY, Ellen	20	F	None	02Ma02Dn
MULHEIRN. Mary	22	F	None	02Ma02Dn
HILL, Willm.	22	M	None	02Ma02Dn
PIERCE. John	30	M	None	02Ma02Dn
HOARTY, James	35	M	Laborer	02Ma02Dn
Michl.	27	M	Laborer	02Ma02Dn
BURKE. Jno.	25	M	None	02Ma02Dn
Cathe.	21	F	None	02Ma02Dn
CAHILL, Michl.	22	M	None	02Ma02Dn
FAHEY, John	28	M	None	02Ma02Dn
MANTON. Michl.	26	M	None	02Ma02Dn
COAN. Martin	25	M	None	02Ma02Dn
SHAUGHNESSY, Jno.	20	M	None	02Ma02Dn
Mary	18	F	None	02Ma02Dn
HOARTY. Thomas	35	M	None	02Ma02Dn
Mary	30	F	None	02Ma02Dn
BUTLER. Michl.	18	M	None	02Ma02Dn
KEAN. Judy	21	F	None	02Ma02Dn
KELLY, John	32	M	None	02Ma02Dn
BRADY, Philip	30	M	Laborer	02Ma02Dn
MCKENNA. Owen	22	M	Laborer	02Ma02Dn
FOLEY. George	22	M	Laborer	02Ma02Dn
DATE. James	21	M	Laborer	02Ma02Dn
KEATING, Eliza	30	F	Bomkr	02Ma02Dn
Edward	22	M	None	02Ma02Dn
BEST. Ellen	22	F	None	02Ma02Dn
Susannah	21	F	None	02Ma02Dn
MCCABE. Anne	20	F	None	02Ma02Dn
FLANAGAN. Anne	40	F	None	02Ma02Dn
Thomas	19	M	None	02Ma02Dn
John	15	M	None	02Ma02Dn
Andrew	12	M	None	02Ma02Dn
MCGOVERN. Geo.	20	M	None	02Ma02Dn
Mary	18	F	Dressmaker	02Ma02Dn
MCMANUS. Michl.	22	M	Laborer	02Ma02Dn
Mary	20	F	None	02Ma02Dn
MCNALLY, Andrw.	40	M	None	02Ma02Dn
Mary	40	F	None	02Ma02Dn
John	20	M	None	02Ma02Dn
Anne	17	F	None	02Ma02Dn
ICARDLE. James	25	M	None	02Ma02Dn
Mary	20	F	None	02Ma02Dn
ICGUINNESS. Peter	17	M	None	02Ma02Dn
CARNEY. James	21	M	None	02Ma02Dn
ICDERMOTT. Jno.	45	M	Blacksmith	02Ma02Dn
Michl.	13	M	None	02Ma02Dn
Anne	27	F	None	02Ma02Dn
ANE. Will.	40	M	Laborer	02Ma02Dn
Mary	28	F	None	02Ma02Dn
OUGH. Michl.	25	M	None	02Ma02Dn
Margt.	25	M	None	02Ma02Dn
LSELY. Isaac	26	M	None	02Ma02Dn
AMB, James	23	M	Unknown	02Ma02Dn
Bridget	20	F	Unknown	02Ma02Dn
James	1	M	Child	02Ma02Dn
LLEN. John	24	M	Farmer	02Ma02Dn
U (W)	24	F	None	02Ma02Dn
John	6	M	Child	02Ma02Dn
Edward	4	M	Child	02Ma02Dn
Elizth.	2	F	Child	02Ma02Dn
ONELLY, Margt.	15	F	Servant	02Ma02Dn
JNBAR. Dominick	22	M	Laborer	02Ma02Dn
ILLOONY, Anne	20	F	None	02Ma02Dn
ARTIN. Bryan	18	M	Laborer	02Ma02Dn
IERIDAN. Mary	20	F	None	02Ma02Dn
Bridget	18	F	None	02Ma02Dn

NAMES OF PASSENGERS	AGE	SEX	OCCUPATIONS	DATE PORT SHIP
SHERIDAN, Patrick	15	M	Laborer	02Ma02Dn
Teresa	10	F	Laborer	02Ma02Dn
MCCORMICK. Patt	24	M	Seaman	02Ma02Dn
MONAHAN. Patt	22	M	Shoemaker	02Ma02Dn
FARRELL. Dominick	20	M	Shoemaker	02Ma02Dn
Margt.	18	F	None	02Ma02Dn
CUMAGAN. Edward	20	M	None	02Ma02Dn
RYAN, Patt	30	M	None	02Ma02Dn
U (W)	29	F	None	02Ma02Dn
Mary	.00	F	Infant	02Ma02Dn
BOWES. Patt	40	M	None	02Ma02Dn
QUINLAN. Danl.	24	M	None	02Ma02Dn
Ellen	21	F	None	02Ma02Dn
RAVILLE. George	30	M	None	02Ma02Dn
U (W)	26	F	None	02Ma02Dn
MCPARTLAND. Alex	00	M	None	02Ma02Dn
BRENNAN, Robert	23	M	None	02Ma02Dn
WARD. Thos.	24	M	None	02Ma02Dn
BURKE. Patk.	25	M	None	02Ma02Dn
MARA. Ellen	21	F	None	02Ma02Dn
MILLAN, Thos.	40	M	Shopkeeper	02Ma02Dn
RING, Andrw.	26	M	None	02Ma02Dn
Ellen (W)	22	F	None	02Ma02Dn
COUGHLIN, Dennis	34	M	None	02Ma02Dn
GARVIN, James	25	M	None	02Ma02Dn
CONNOR. Patk.	23	M	Grocer	02Ma02Dn
U (W)	20	F	None	02Ma02Dn
Maria	.00	F	Infant	02Ma02Dn
BAMBRICK. Thomas	24	M	Policeman	02Ma02Dn
FALKNER. Patk.	60	M	None	02Ma02Dn
Bridget	40	F	None	02Ma02Dn
Michl.	13	M	None	02Ma02Dn
Peter	10	M	None	02Ma02Dn
Anne	8	F	Child	02Ma02Dn
CARROLL. Cathe.	10	F	Servant	02Ma02Dn
KENNEDY. Patk.	20	M	Laborer	02Ma02Dn
MCCONNELL. Thos.	19	M	Laborer	02Ma02Dn
MCGOVERN. Margt.	35	F	None	02Ma02Dn
FARRELL, Mary	22	F	None	02Ma02Dn
TULLY. Patk.	23	M	None	02Ma02Dn
MCGUIRE. Michl.	26	M	None	02Ma02Dn
MELGAN. James	26	M	None	02Ma02Dn
MAXWELL. Christe.	20	F	None	02Ma02Dn
Jane	17	F	None	02Ma02Dn
U, U	21	F	None	02Ma02Dn
MCCABE. Honora	20	F	None	02Ma02Dn
THOMPSON. Eleanor	16	F	None	02Ma02Dn
FALLON. Cathe.	20	F	None	02Ma02Dn
CATHCART. Elizth.	17	F	None	02Ma02Dn
BRUNDER. Mary	22	F	None	02Ma02Dn

CONSTITUTION 09* MAY 1849

From Liverpool

NAMES OF PASSENGERS	AGE	SEX	OCCUPATIONS	DATE PORT SHIP
JULLOCH, James	45	M	Officer	09Ma02Dp
Ann	36	F	None	09Ma02Dp
ROBLEY. Ann	64	F	None	09Ma02Dp
Ann	40	F	None	09Ma02Dp
HANLEY. Joseph	40	M	Gentleman	09Ma02Dp
OBRAIKE. John	21	M	Gentleman	09Ma02Dp
THALE, Samuel	24	M	Gentleman	09Ma02Dp
WILSON. William	22	M	Gentleman	09Ma02Dp
JACKSON. Alfred	23	M	Gentleman	09Ma02Dp
BARROW, John	38	M	Engineer	09Ma02Dp
PECK, Charles	21	M	Gentleman	09Ma02Dp
John	24	M	Gentleman	09Ma02Dp
GALE, Jeanetta	28	F	Lady	09Ma02Dp
CARROLL. Ann	16	F	Spinster	09Ma02Dp

*should be 02 May

NAMES OF PASSENGERS	AGE	SEX	OCCUPATIONS	DATE PORT SHIP
DUFFY, James	50	M	Laborer	09Ma02Dp
James	20	M	Laborer	09Ma02Dp
Fanny	14	F	Spinster	09Ma02Dp
Edward	12	M	Unknown	09Ma02Dp
Christian	10	M	Child	09Ma02Dp
WALKER, James	10	M	Farmer	09Ma02Dp
RILEY, Daniel	16	M	Farmer	09Ma02Dp
GANNON, Owen	17	M	Farmer	09Ma02Dp
CRODAM, Thomas	32	M	Farmer	09Ma02Dp
WELCH, Michel	30	M	Farmer	09Ma02Dp
LYNCH, Philip	18	M	Farmer	09Ma02Dp
DOYLE, Darby	36	M	Laborer	09Ma02Dp
RUNEY, Patt	50	M	Laborer	09Ma02Dp
Thomas	16	M	Laborer	09Ma02Dp
DOONAN, James	22	M	Laborer	09Ma02Dp
EGAN, Michael	18	M	Laborer	09Ma02Dp
Daniel	20	M	Laborer	09Ma02Dp
NOONAN, Patt	21	M	Laborer	09Ma02Dp
SAVAGE, Thos.	40	M	Laborer	09Ma02Dp
Alie	12	F	None	09Ma02Dp
Patt	10	M	Child	09Ma02Dp
Wm.	8	M	Child	09Ma02Dp
MURPHY, Tim	30	M	Weaver	09Ma02Dp
Patt	20	M	Weaver	09Ma02Dp
KELLEY, Margret	25	F	Spinster	09Ma02Dp
DONNELL, Ellen	20	F	Spinster	09Ma02Dp
HENESEY, Ellen	21	F	Spinster	09Ma02Dp
SULLIVAN, Catherine	20	F	Spinster	09Ma02Dp
MCGOVERN, Thos.	17	M	Laborer	09Ma02Dp
Michael	10	M	Child	09Ma02Dp
CLAREY, James	13	M	Unknown	09Ma02Dp
CORIGAN, Ann	25	F	Spinster	09Ma02Dp
RYAN, Hugh	22	M	Laborer	09Ma02Dp
FARLEY, Ann	18	F	Servant	09Ma02Dp
Sus.	16	F	Servant	09Ma02Dp
CARTER, Patt	25	M	Laborer	09Ma02Dp
John	50	M	Laborer	09Ma02Dp
MCDERMOTT, Eliza	18	F	Spinster	09Ma02Dp
MCKENNA, Philip	19	M	Laborer	09Ma02Dp
Mary	16	F	Spinster	09Ma02Dp
LAUGHLAN, Thomas	20	M	Laborer	09Ma02Dp
Isabella	18	F	Spinster	09Ma02Dp
TALLEY, Nancy	16	F	Spinster	09Ma02Dp
Bridget	14	F	Spinster	09Ma02Dp
RICER, Ellen	20	F	Spinster	09Ma02Dp
KELLY, Mary	8	F	Child	09Ma02Dp
ROGERS, Thomas	45	M	Laborer	09Ma02Dp
Margaret	45	F	Spinster	09Ma02Dp
Mary	18	F	Spinster	09Ma02Dp
Margaret	9	F	Child	09Ma02Dp
Patt	8	M	Child	09Ma02Dp
COWOPLY, Patt	35	M	Laborer	09Ma02Dp
Mary	30	F	Servant	09Ma02Dp
ROACH, Ann	16	F	Servant	09Ma02Dp
LEREY, John	18	M	Laborer	09Ma02Dp
Jane	16	F	Spinster	09Ma02Dp
TOURNEY, Marcella	17	F	Spinster	09Ma02Dp
DAULTON, Mary	17	F	Spinster	09Ma02Dp
FITZSIMMONS, Bernard	17	M	Laborer	09Ma02Dp
Thomas	15	M	Laborer	09Ma02Dp
CLARK, Owen	16	M	Laborer	09Ma02Dp
ROCK, Catherine	21	F	Servant	09Ma02Dp
Eliza	20	F	Servant	09Ma02Dp
MEHAN, John	25	M	Servant	09Ma02Dp
JOHNSTON, Mary	20	F	Servant	09Ma02Dp
DUNNIGAN, John	35	M	Laborer	09Ma02Dp
BURNE, Alice	30	F	Spinster	09Ma02Dp
TREMAN, Jane	17	F	Spinster	09Ma02Dp
Margret	40	F	Spinster	09Ma02Dp
Thomas	9	M	Child	09Ma02Dp
Rose	7	F	Child	09Ma02Dp
Ann	5	F	Child	09Ma02Dp
MARTINSON, Tim.	20	M	Laborer	09Ma02Dp
John	5	M	Child	09Ma02Dp
CONOLEY, Michael	20	M	Unknown	09Ma02Dp
AGNEW, Rachel	20	F	Spinster	09Ma02Dp
MCCULLOCH, Wm.	19	M	Laborer	09Ma02Dp
MULHOLLAND, John	20	M	Laborer	09Ma02Dp
HALL, M.J.	20	M	Laborer	09Ma02Dp
GOODMAN, Patt	16	M	Laborer	09Ma02Dp
Mary	18	F	Spinster	09Ma02Dp
MULHALLAN, Eliza	18	F	Spinster	09Ma02Dp
HOGAN, Thomas	50	M	Laborer	09Ma02Dp
Mary	50	F	Spinster	09Ma02Dp
Mich.	14	M	Laborer	09Ma02Dp
Bridget	16	F	Spinster	09Ma02Dp
Catherine	16	F	Spinster	09Ma02Dp
BRINNINGHAM, Cahterine	11	F	None	09Ma02Dp
MINOGUE, Catherine	10	F	Child	09Ma02Dp
ARMSTRONG, Matilda	20	F	Spinster	09Ma02Dp
CANNING, William	20	M	Laborer	09Ma02Dp
CARTEY, Thomas	28	M	Laborer	09Ma02Dp
MARTIN, Michael	20	M	Laborer	09Ma02Dp
KERNAN, Owen	24	M	Laborer	09Ma02Dp
James	22	M	Laborer	09Ma02Dp
LANNON, Patt	19	M	Laborer	09Ma02Dp
BYRN, Ann	18	F	Servant	09Ma02Dp
MATHEWS, Judy	17	F	Servant	09Ma02Dp
DAILEY, John	29	M	Shoemaker	09Ma02Dp
FRANKS, Henry	23	M	Laborer	09Ma02Dp
LANGMERE, James	26	M	Laborer	09Ma02Dp
Mary	26	F	Spinster	09Ma02Dp
Hanna	3	F	Child	09Ma02Dp
TURNEY, Francis	21	M	Laborer	09Ma02Dp
BRODRICK, Franc.	30	M	Farmer	09Ma02Dp
HUGINS, Charles	17	M	Laborer	09Ma02Dp
ELLGIRE, Patt	28	M	Laborer	09Ma02Dp
CRANAN, Richd.	22	M	Joiner	09Ma02Dp
GRAY, Amelia	42	F	Servant	09Ma02Dp
Isabella	15	F	Servant	09Ma02Dp
P.C.	42	M	Mason	09Ma02Dp
David	12	M	Mason	09Ma02Dp
John	7	M	Child	09Ma02Dp
SANDERSON, Walter	32	M	Carpenter	09Ma02Dp
MUIR, Fanny	32	F	Spinster	09Ma02Dp
PETHER, Wm.	48	M	Laborer	09Ma02Dp
Robt.	11	M	Laborer	09Ma02Dp
WILSON, Robt.	30	M	Carpenter	09Ma02Dp
CHRISTIE, Robt.	28	M	Carpenter	09Ma02Dp
FARRELL, Patt	40	M	Laborer	09Ma02Dp
Tom	30	M	Laborer	09Ma02Dp
Mary	25	F	Servant	09Ma02Dp
Alice	4	F	Child	09Ma02Dp
John	2	M	Child	09Ma02Dp
ROONEY, Mary	25	F	Servant	09Ma02Dp
MCGINNEYS, Jane	50	F	Servant	09Ma02Dp
Thomas	6	M	Child	09Ma02Dp
Alice	3	F	Child	09Ma02Dp
NEAL, James	30	M	Laborer	09Ma02Dp
ROGIN, John	37	M	Laborer	09Ma02Dp
MOORE, Wm.	40	M	Laborer	09Ma02Dp
SMITH, Thomas	35	M	Laborer	09Ma02Dp
RILEY, John	30	M	Laborer	09Ma02Dp
GOODFELLOW, Ann	21	F	Spinster	09Ma02Dp
Sarah	22	F	Spinster	09Ma02Dp
POLLOCK, Marshall	23	F	Spinster	09Ma02Dp
Eliza	24	F	Spinster	09Ma02Dp
CASSIDY, Owen	30	M	Laborer	09Ma02Dp
John	40	M	Laborer	09Ma02Dp
Julia	60	F	Spinster	09Ma02Dp
BROWN, John	22	M	Laborer	09Ma02Dp
WILLIAMSON, Ruth	22	F	Spinster	09Ma02Dp
CHUSTIN, Ann	25	F	Spinster	09Ma02Dp
SAILIN, Mary	18	F	Spinster	09Ma02Dp
SAVAGE, Thomas	38	M	Laborer	09Ma02Dp
Catherine	37	F	Servant	09Ma02Dp
Margaret	25	F	Servant	09Ma02Dp
MOORE, Tim	24	M	Laborer	09Ma02Dp
CONNER, Mary	22	F	Spinster	09Ma02Dp
Betty	22	F	Spinster	09Ma02D

NAMES OF PASSENGERS	AGE	SEX	OCCUPATIONS	DATE PORT SHIP
HANGEE. Pat	22	F	Spinster	09Ma02Dp
BERRY, Betty	24	F	Spinster	09Ma02Dp
MCGILL. Patt	35	M	Laborer	09Ma02Dp
HAGERTY. Margaret	20	F	Servant	09Ma02Dp
COUSINS. Wm.	25	M	Laborer	09Ma02Dp
Margaret	24	F	None	09Ma02Dp
DOWLING, Thomas	22	M	Laborer	09Ma02Dp
HANNA. John	25	M	Laborer	09Ma02Dp
LARAN. John	18	M	Laborer	09Ma02Dp
JOHNSTEN. Richd.	22	M	Carpenter	09Ma02Dp
RILEY. John	20	M	Carpenter	09Ma02Dp
DUGAN. Jerm.	24	M	Laborer	09Ma02Dp
Catherine	17	F	Spinster	09Ma02Dp
MAHEN. Michael	20	M	Laborer	09Ma02Dp
Dan	24	M	Laborer	09Ma02Dp
HOGAN Michael	23	M	Laborer	09Ma02Dp
GLEESON. Margaret	23	F	Servant	09Ma02Dp
SEXTON. Ellen	23	F	Servant	09Ma02Dp
PINNEY. Mary	20	F	Spinster	09Ma02Dp
CLANCEY. Michael	24	M	Laborer	09Ma02Dp
Bridget	23	F	Servant	09Ma02Dp
KELLY, Wm.	18	M	Servant	09Ma02Dp
Sophia	15	F	Servant	09Ma02Dp
DAVIS. James	25	M	Laborer	09Ma02Dp
ROIRE. Daniel	24	M	Laborer	09Ma02Dp
GOODMAN. Judy	21	F	Servant	09Ma02Dp
WELCH. Peter	25	M	Laborer	09Ma02Dp
Rose	22	F	Servant	09Ma02Dp
DAVIS. Mary	25	F	Spinster	09Ma02Dp
SMITH. Honor	25	F	Servant	09Ma02Dp
RAMSBOTTOM. William	25	M	Farmer	09Ma02Dp
HOLDEN. Thomas	25	M	Farmer	09Ma02Dp
MUHANEY, Bridget	18	F	Servant	09Ma02Dp
GARITZ. Martin	28	M	Servant	09Ma02Dp
TALLON. Michael	18	M	Servant	09Ma02Dp
CONELY, Michael	18	M	Servant	09Ma02Dp
FLOTHEN. Robt.	23	M	Servant	09Ma02Dp
RAY, John	19	M	Servant	09Ma02Dp
HAYS. Thomas	30	M	Farmer	09Ma02Dp
Jane	50	F	Spinster	09Ma02Dp
BROWN. J.B.	26	M	Laborer	09Ma02Dp
HUNT. John	26	M	Laborer	09Ma02Dp
Margaret	25	F	Servant	09Ma02Dp
Margaret	25	F	Servant	09Ma02Dp
ARMSTRONG, M.Jane	24	F	Dressmaker	09Ma02Dp
SULIVAN Ann	35	F	Dressmaker	09Ma02Dp
LYNCH. Hanah	25	F	Servant	09Ma02Dp
DUGAN. John	30	M	Servant	09Ma02Dp
MILTHORP. Ellen	27	F	Servant	09Ma02Dp
DALLEY. Thomas	21	M	Laborer	09Ma02Dp
John	18	M	Laborer	09Ma02Dp
Margaret	10	F	Laborer	09Ma02Dp
DANES. James	20	M	Laborer	09Ma02Dp
Fanny	20	F	Servant	09Ma02Dp
BREEN. John	20	M	Servant	09Ma02Dp
WHALIN. Tim	20	M	Servant	09Ma02Dp
WHATON. M	30	M	Laborer	09Ma02Dp
CONDER. Wm.	30	M	Laborer	09Ma02Dp
WHALEN. Catherine	30	F	Spinster	09Ma02Dp
Johanna	22	F	Spinster	09Ma02Dp
MURRY, Margaret	45	F	Spinster	09Ma02Dp
Mary	45	F	Spinster	09Ma02Dp
John	21	M	Laborer	09Ma02Dp
KIDNEY, John	19	M	Laborer	09Ma02Dp
TAYLOR. Margaret	21	F	Spinster	09Ma02Dp
RILEY. Owen	18	M	Laborer	09Ma02Dp
Thomas	16	M	Laborer	09Ma02Dp
DOUGHERTY, Daniel	24	M	Servant	09Ma02Dp
STEEL, Michel	22	M	Servant	09Ma02Dp
DONAHUE. John	23	M	Servant	09Ma02Dp
DEGAN. Eliza	24	F	Servant	09Ma02Dp
HAGGERTY. Eliza	20	F	Servant	09Ma02Dp
WICKER. Philip	30	M	Laborer	09Ma02Dp
Mary	50	F	Spinster	09Ma02Dp
Ellen	21	F	Spinster	09Ma02Dp
WICKER. Margaret	19	F	Spinster	09Ma02Dp
Mary	17	F	Spinster	09Ma02Dp
Pearce	15	M	Unknown	09Ma02Dp
Dennis	12	M	Unknown	09Ma02Dp
John	20	F	Spinster	09Ma02Dp
Catherine	9	F	Child	09Ma02Dp
Wm.	7	M	Child	09Ma02Dp
Johanna	5	F	Child	09Ma02Dp
James	2	M	Child	09Ma02Dp
SHARP, Wm.	15	M	Servant	09Ma02Dp
DAILEY. Frank	20	M	Servant	09Ma02Dp
PEARCE, William	20	M	Servant	09Ma02Dp
TODD. William	36	M	Servant	09Ma02Dp
REYNOLDS. William	36	M	Servant	09Ma02Dp
COONAN, John	20	M	Servant	09Ma02Dp
SEASON. John	18	M	Servant	09Ma02Dp
HUGHES. Wm.	23	M	Servant	09Ma02Dp
LENAHAN, John	26	M	Laborer	09Ma02Dp
MAINON. James	21	M	Laborer	09Ma02Dp
Patt	20	M	Laborer	09Ma02Dp
Robt.	22	M	Laborer	09Ma02Dp
Margt.	16	F	Unknown	09Ma02Dp
Mathew	15	M	Laborer	09Ma02Dp
Sarah	10	F	Child	09Ma02Dp
Mary	50	F	Spinster	09Ma02Dp
Martha	20	F	Spinster	09Ma02Dp
STRONG, John	22	M	Laborer	09Ma02Dp
ARCHIBALD. James	38	M	Laborer	09Ma02Dp
BRENNAN, Mary	24	F	Servant	09Ma02Dp
CASEY. Patt	14	M	Servant	09Ma02Dp
Susan	14	F	Servant	09Ma02Dp
LAWRENCE. W.	40	M	Laborer	09Ma02Dp
CASSIDY. Patt	28	M	Laborer	09Ma02Dp
CRONAN. Bridget	40	F	Spinster	09Ma02Dp
Thomas	22	M	Laborer	09Ma02Dp
DAVIS. Thomas	48	M	Laborer	09Ma02Dp
LERESEY. Thomas	48	M	Laborer	09Ma02Dp
KENNY. Robt.	50	M	Laborer	09Ma02Dp
John	21	M	Laborer	09Ma02Dp
Mary	19	F	Laborer	09Ma02Dp
Margt.	17	F	Laborer	09Ma02Dp
Philip	11	M	Laborer	09Ma02Dp
Michel	9	M	Child	09Ma02Dp
JONES. Martha	40	M	Spinster	09Ma02Dp
William	21	M	Carpenter	09Ma02Dp
Henry	18	M	Carpenter	09Ma02Dp
George	11	M	None	09Ma02Dp
John	9	M	Child	09Ma02Dp
Susan	8	F	Child	09Ma02Dp
Martha	14	F	Servant	09Ma02Dp
Lucy	7	F	Child	09Ma02Dp
DARIN, Michael	20	M	Laborer	09Ma02Dp
BRENNAN, John	28	M	Laborer	09Ma02Dp
ANDERSON. William	30	M	Laborer	09Ma02Dp
Martha	27	F	Servant	09Ma02Dp
Rechel	5	F	Child	09Ma02Dp
Ann	3	F	Child	09Ma02Dp
WILLIAMS, Isaac	24	M	Carpenter	09Ma02Dp
Eliza	23	F	Spinster	09Ma02Dp
ALLOHIN, William	24	M	Laborer	09Ma02Dp
BURK, Prudence	30	F	Servant	09Ma02Dp
Ann	8	F	Child	09Ma02Dp
Thomas	5	F	Child	09Ma02Dp
John	3	M	Child	09Ma02Dp
REEDIN. John	20	M	Farmer	09Ma02Dp
ROBINSON. J.J.	23	M	Farmer	09Ma02Dp
CONNELL. Robt.	21	M	Farmer	09Ma02Dp
DONNELY. Patt	20	M	Farmer	09Ma02Dp
CHARS. Reilly	25	M	Farmer	09Ma02Dp
LINTON. James	35	M	Farmer	09Ma02Dp

ANDREW-FOSTER 02 MAY 1849

From Liverpool

NAMES OF PASSENGERS	AGE	SEX	OCCUPATIONS	DATE PORT SHIP
MOCLAIR. Mary	40	F	Unknown	02Ma02Du
Anna-M	16	F	Unknown	02Ma02Du
Eliz.	10	F	Unknown	02Ma02Du
NEVIN. Revd.John	35	M	Clergyman	02Ma02Du
GLOVER. John	23	M	Gentleman	02Ma02Du
Eliz.C.	23	F	Unknown	02Ma02Du
OBRIEN. James	24	M	Surgeon	02Ma02Du
YAREY, Bridget	18	F	Servant	02Ma02Du
MURPHY, Mary	20	F	Servant	02Ma02Du
MACARTHY, Patrick	21	M	Servant	02Ma02Du
BRENNAN. James	30	M	Unknown	02Ma02Du
NOWLAN. Michael	20	M	Laborer	02Ma02Du
RYAN John	19	M	Laborer	02Ma02Du
SHEA, James	27	M	Laborer	02Ma02Du
MCCRIE. Mary	18	F	Unknown	02Ma02Du
COONEY, David	33	M	Unknown	02Ma02Du
CARNEY, William	40	M	Farmer	02Ma02Du
Elizabeth	40	F	Unknown	02Ma02Du
REILLY, Philip	19	M	Laborer	02Ma02Du
DONOHUE. Farrell	35	M	Farmer	02Ma02Du
Mary	30	F	Unknown	02Ma02Du
Mary	.07	F	Infant	02Ma02Du
WHELAM, William	30	F	Laborer	02Ma02Du
MCAVOY, Stephan	18	M	Laborer	02Ma02Du
HYLAND, Michael	35	M	Farmer	02Ma02Du
Mary	30	F	Unknown	02Ma02Du
Michael	.06	M	Infant	02Ma02Du
NEALE. Ellen	44	F	Unknown	02Ma02Du
Michael	24	M	Unknown	02Ma02Du
John	24	M	Unknown	02Ma02Du
Mary	22	F	Unknown	02Ma02Du
Anne	20	F	Unknown	02Ma02Du
Bridget	18	F	Unknown	02Ma02Du
James	16	M	Unknown	02Ma02Du
Thomas	14	M	Unknown	02Ma02Du
William	12	M	Unknown	02Ma02Du
Philip	10	M	Unknown	02Ma02Du
Owen	8	M	Child	02Ma02Du
Ellen	4	F	Child	02Ma02Du
CULLIGAN Dennis	27	M	Farmer	02Ma02Du
Margaret	25	F	Unknown	02Ma02Du
Dennis	.10	M	Infant	02Ma02Du
James	4	M	Child	02Ma02Du
Mary	3	F	Child	02Ma02Du
LEARY, Cornelius	28	M	Laborer	02Ma02Du
TYREMAN. Thomas	24	M	Laborer	02Ma02Du
BESTON. William	24	M	Laborer	02Ma02Du
EGAN. Patrick	24	M	Farmer	02Ma02Du
FANEY, John	24	M	Farmer	02Ma02Du
LOOBY, Michael	24	M	Laborer	02Ma02Du
FEENEY, Patrick	24	M	Painter	02Ma02Du
TIERMAN. Luke	20	M	Laborer	02Ma02Du
HUNT. Andy	20	M	Laborer	02Ma02Du
CASEY, John	20	M	Laborer	02Ma02Du
Mary	20	F	Unknown	02Ma02Du
EGAN. Margaret	20	F	Unknown	02Ma02Du
CASEY, Mary	21	F	Unknown	02Ma02Du
LANNAN. Mary	19	F	Unknown	02Ma02Du
MCDERMOTT, Patrick	20	M	Laborer	02Ma02Du
COUGAN. Mathew	27	M	Laborer	02Ma02Du
FITZSIMMONS. Bessy	30	F	Unknown	02Ma02Du
KIERNAN. Peter	24	M	Laborer	02Ma02Du
Mary	20	F	Unknown	02Ma02Du
MCAVOY, Eliza	18	F	Unknown	02Ma02Du
CONNOR Cornelius	24	M	Laborer	02Ma02Du
CUSKELY, Michael	24	M	Laborer	02Ma02Du
DUNN. Edward	24	M	Laborer	02Ma02Du
DEVLIN, John	38	M	Laborer	02Ma02Du
ONEALE. Catherine	34	F	Unknown	02Ma02Du
DONAGHEY. Bridget	34	F	Unknown	02Ma02Du
DOORASS. Rose	16	F	Unknown	02Ma02Du
MULDOON. James	10	F	Unknown	02Ma02Du
MCCLEAN. Christopher	20	M	Farmer	02Ma02Du
Bridget	22	F	Unknown	02Ma02Du
Christopher	.00	M	Infant	02Ma02Du
James	3	M	Child	02Ma02Du
MURPHY, John	30	M	Laborer	02Ma02Du
DONELLY, Richard	28	M	Farmer	02Ma02Du
Mary	24	F	Unknown	02Ma02Du
Francis	46	M	Unknown	02Ma02Du
CORCORAN, Michael	18	M	Unknown	02Ma02Du
Thomas	20	M	Unknown	02Ma02Du
FURLONG, George	23	M	Mechanic	02Ma02Du
William	23	M	Mechanic	02Ma02Du
NEALE. John	28	M	Mechanic	02Ma02Du
MCDONNELL, Patrick	22	M	Laborer	02Ma02Du
MCGRATH, Michael	20	M	Laborer	02Ma02Du
MURPHY. Michael	22	M	Laborer	02Ma02Du
James	19	M	Laborer	02Ma02Du
Honora	22	F	Unknown	02Ma02Du
James	.06	M	Infant	02Ma02Du
Mary	18	F	Unknown	02Ma02Du
BURKE. Mary	20	F	Unknown	02Ma02Du
Margaret	18	F	Unknown	02Ma02Du
DUGGAN. Michael	30	M	Farmer	02Ma02Du
Betty	39	F	Unknown	02Ma02Du
Michael	.05	M	Infant	02Ma02Du
CAVANAGH, Patrick	30	M	Laborer	02Ma02Du
WELSH. James	30	M	Laborer	02Ma02Du
CAVANAGH, Catherine	20	F	Unknown	02Ma02Du
BURKE. Bridget	20	F	Unknown	02Ma02Du
RICE. Biddy	25	F	Unknown	02Ma02Du
MCBRIDE. Mary	25	F	Unknown	02Ma02Du
DONELLY, Bernard	25	M	Laborer	02Ma02Du
BRADLEY. Michael	25	M	Laborer	02Ma02Du
MORAN. Mary	22	F	Unknown	02Ma02Du
John	25	M	Laborer	02Ma02Du
HOGAN. Francis	24	M	Laborer	02Ma02Du
CONNELLY. Edward	21	M	Laborer	02Ma02Du
CHRISTIAN. Andrew	20	M	Laborer	02Ma02Du
MORAN, John	20	M	Laborer	02Ma02Du
MONAHAN, Susan	21	F	Unknown	02Ma02Du
HARRISSON. James	26	M	Laborer	02Ma02Du
GRIMES. John	27	M	Laborer	02Ma02Du
Thomas	30	M	Laborer	02Ma02Du
Johanna	23	F	Unknown	02Ma02Du
GORMAN. Nancy	11	F	None	02Ma02Du
Ally	8	F	Child	02Ma02Du
Patrick	7	M	Child	02Ma02Du
Died-At-Sea				
Daniel	7	M	Child	02Ma02Du
ROUCHE. William	19	M	Unknown	02Ma02Du
KING, Bryan	21	M	Mechanic	02Ma02Du
Daniel	22	M	Mechanic	02Ma02Du
BRESMAN. Timothy	21	M	Unknown	02Ma02Du
Jeremiah	22	M	Farmer	02Ma02Du
John	23	M	Unknown	02Ma02Du
Catherine	18	F	Unknown	02Ma02Du
DOLAN, Patrick	40	M	Farmer	02Ma02Du
Thomas	18	M	Unknown	02Ma02Du
MCKEOUGH, Edward	22	M	Unknown	02Ma02Du
MOORE. James	23	M	Unknown	02Ma02Du
CURWEN, Thomas	30	M	Farmer	02Ma02Du
CHERNOCK, Luke	20	M	Blacksmith	02Ma02D
WILSON. James	33	M	Farmer	02Ma02Du
Eliza	30	F	Unknown	02Ma02Du
GARRAGHER. Hugh	30	M	Laborer	02Ma02Du
POWER. James	25	M	Laborer	02Ma02D
CONWAY. Mary	30	F	Unknown	02Ma02Du
MANNING, Margaret	55	F	Unknown	02Ma02D

NAMES OF PASSENGERS	A G E	S E X	OCCUPATIONS	DATE PORT SHIP
CONWAY, Mary	.07	F	Infant	02Ma02Du
FARROLL. Richard	14	M	None	02Ma02Du
Michael	20	M	Unknown	02Ma02Du
DUNN. Bridget	21	F	Unknown	02Ma02Du
Joannet	11	F	Unknown	02Ma02Du
Patrick	9	M	Child	02Ma02Du
Mary	7	F	Child	02Ma02Du
Rose	5	F	Child	02Ma02Du
Anne	3	F	Child	02Ma02Du
Terence	2	M	Child	02Ma02Du
ROURKE. John	20	M	Unknown	02Ma02Du
SMITH. Patrick	20	M	Unknown	02Ma02Du
MULLIGAN. Mary	18	F	Unknown	02Ma02Du
ROCHE. James	18	M	Unknown	02Ma02Du
John	15	M	Unknown	02Ma02Du
RAFFERTY. John	55	M	Unknown	02Ma02Du
Mary	50	F	Unknown	02Ma02Du
Patrick	18	M	Unknown	02Ma02Du
LAUGH. Joseph	22	M	Unknown	02Ma02Du
Sarah	20	F	Unknown	02Ma02Du
COLLINS. David	29	M	Unknown	02Ma02Du
DRAKE. Isaac	29	M	Unknown	02Ma02Du
RAFFERTY, Mary	16	F	Unknown	02Ma02Du
MORRIS. Betty	44	F	Unknown	02Ma02Du
NOONE. Catherine	15	F	Unknown	02Ma02Du
Mary	11	F	None	02Ma02Du
John	5	M	Child	02Ma02Du
LYNCH. John	15	M	Unknown	02Ma02Du
Anne	13	F	Unknown	02Ma02Du
KING, Thomas	16	M	Unknown	02Ma02Du
Mary	16	F	Unknown	02Ma02Du
FARLEY, Margaret	18	F	Unknown	02Ma02Du
NOLAN. Catherine	25	F	Unknown	02Ma02Du
CONDALON. Margaret	16	F	Unknown	02Ma02Du
SULLIVAN. Nancy	20	F	Unknown	02Ma02Du
Catherine	18	F	Unknown	02Ma02Du
OGRADY, Bridget	50	F	Unknown	02Ma02Du
Johannah	26	F	Unknown	02Ma02Du
Mary	20	F	Unknown	02Ma02Du
Jeremiah	19	M	Unknown	02Ma02Du
Thomas	28	M	Unknown	02Ma02Du
SANDERSON. Hannah	26	F	Unknown	02Ma02Du
Emily	.09	F	Infant	02Ma02Du
Richard	2	M	Child	02Ma02Du
HUNTER. James	21	M	Unknown	02Ma02Du
KELLY, Eliza	20	F	Unknown	02Ma02Du
BENNETT. Bridget	24	F	Unknown	02Ma02Du
Eliza	20	F	Unknown	02Ma02Du
COYNE. Catherine	19	F	Unknown	02Ma02Du
FRALEY, James	22	M	Unknown	02Ma02Du
MALOWNEY, Ellen	18	F	Unknown	02Ma02Du
MILCHAN. John	18	M	Unknown	02Ma02Du
Annie	13	F	Unknown	02Ma02Du
MURPHY, Mathew	24	M	Unknown	02Ma02Du
Bridget	30	F	Unknown	02Ma02Du
RESPIN. Catherine	17	F	Unknown	02Ma02Du
MATHEWS, Anne	30	F	Unknown	02Ma02Du
CONNERS. Bridget	18	F	Unknown	02Ma02Du
HURLEY, Michael	30	M	Unknown	02Ma02Du
CAHILL, William	17	M	Unknown	02Ma02Du
Bridget	20	F	Unknown	02Ma02Du
MCQUIRKE. Jane	20	F	Unknown	02Ma02Du
MADDEN. Bridget	20	F	Unknown	02Ma02Du
KELLY, Catherine	9	F	Child	02Ma02Du
TIERNEY, Michael	25	M	Unknown	02Ma02Du
NOLAN. Philip	40	M	Unknown	02Ma02Du
Sarah	30	F	Unknown	02Ma02Du
Catherine	20	F	Unknown	02Ma02Du
HUGHES. Elizabeth	6	F	Child	02Ma02Du
NOLAN. James	.06	M	Infant	02Ma02Du
HUGHES. Ellen	4	F	Child	02Ma02Du
Sarah	2	F	Child	02Ma02Du
James	.10	M	Infant	02Ma02Du
CRISTY, John	22	M	Unknown	02Ma02Du
BERCY, Ann	18	F	Unknown	02Ma02Du

NAMES OF PASSENGERS	A G E	S E X	OCCUPATIONS	DATE PORT SHIP
MCGARCY. Betty	22	F	Unknown	02Ma02Du
RUDDY, Thomas	23	M	Unknown	02Ma02Du
Mary-Ann	20	F	Unknown	02Ma02Du
MASTERSON. Patrick	20	M	Unknown	02Ma02Du
FITZPATRICK, Ann	15	F	Unknown	02Ma02Du
GRAY. Jane	23	F	Unknown	02Ma02Du
Sarah	24	F	Unknown	02Ma02Du
WINDERHAM, Elizabeth	50	F	Unknown	02Ma02Du
HENRY, Elizabeth	20	F	Unknown	02Ma02Du
DRAFZAN, Sarah	14	F	Unknown	02Ma02Du
CRAWFORD, Sarah	21	F	Unknown	02Ma02Du
Isabella	26	F	Unknown	02Ma02Du
MAHON. Patrick	30	M	Unknown	02Ma02Du
WHITE. John	25	M	Unknown	02Ma02Du
MORAHAN, William	20	M	Unknown	02Ma02Du
WISE. Margaret	22	F	Unknown	02Ma02Du
GAUGHRAN, Bridget	20	F	Unknown	02Ma02Du
ARMSTRONG, Mary-Ann	21	F	Unknown	02Ma02Du
MARTIN. Thomas	30	M	Unknown	02Ma02Du
Mary	28	F	Unknown	02Ma02Du
Patrick	2	M	Child	02Ma02Du
GRADY. Daniel	25	M	Unknown	02Ma02Du
CASHAN. Michael	25	M	Unknown	02Ma02Du
CAHILL. Michael	25	M	Unknown	02Ma02Du
GREY. Elizabeth	7	F	Child	02Ma02Du
MOODY. Robert	60	M	Unknown	02Ma02Du
Betty	52	F	Unknown	02Ma02Du
Samuel	19	M	Unknown	02Ma02Du
William	15	M	Unknown	02Ma02Du
Sarah	13	F	Unknown	02Ma02Du
Matilda	11	F	Unknown	02Ma02Du
HUGHES. Mary	60	F	Unknown	02Ma02Du
BURNS. Lawrence	32	M	Unknown	02Ma02Du
Margaret	23	F	Unknown	02Ma02Du
SCHAEL, Ann	24	F	Unknown	02Ma02Du
HESLIN. James	26	M	Unknown	02Ma02Du
DOOLON. Edward	18	M	Unknown	02Ma02Du
LUNCH. Thos.	21	M	Unknown	02Ma02Du
MADDEN. Bridget	50	F	Unknown	02Ma02Du

OXFORD 02 MAY 1849

From Liverpool

NAMES OF PASSENGERS	A G E	S E X	OCCUPATIONS	DATE PORT SHIP
HANSEN. John	65	M	Carpenter	02Ma02Do
Mary	65	F	None	02Ma02Do
DUNBAR, William	50	M	Farmer	02Ma02Do
Jane	21	F	Farmer	02Ma02Do
Eliza	17	F	Farmer	02Ma02Do
Betta	14	F	Farmer	02Ma02Do
Phebe	16	F	Farmer	02Ma02Do
Mark	11	M	Farmer	02Ma02Do
Rose	11	F	Farmer	02Ma02Do
Phebe	40	F	Farmer	02Ma02Do
KELLY. Edward	27	M	Laborer	02Ma02Do
RILEY. Ann	18	F	Servant	02Ma02Do
U	.00	U	Infant	02Ma02Do
NEWMAN. John	24	M	Laborer	02Ma02Do
Mary	24	F	Servant	02Ma02Do
ODONOVAN. James	19	M	Farmer	02Ma02Do
RIGNEY. James	30	M	Farmer	02Ma02Do
SMITH. Philip	25	M	Laborer	02Ma02Do
Betty	30	F	Servant	02Ma02Do
Mary	.00	F	Infant	02Ma02Do
Margaret	10	F	Servant	02Ma02Do
Betsy	23	F	Servant	02Ma02Do
NAULTY. Matthew	25	M	Laborer	02Ma02Do
Mary	30	F	Servant	02Ma02Do
U	.00	U	Infant	02Ma02Do

NAMES OF PASSENGERS	AGE	SEX	OCCUPATIONS	DATE PORT SHIP
MULLIGAN. John	25	M	Laborer	02Ma02Do
Michael	30	M	Laborer	02Ma02Do
FAGAN, John	28	M	Laborer	02Ma02Do
CLAREN. Michael	20	M	Laborer	02Ma02Do
MCELHANEY, Rose	35	F	Servant	02Ma02Do
LAMB, Michael	30	M	Laborer	02Ma02Do
MANNERS. Jane	17	F	Servant	02Ma02Do
MARSDEN. Brien	26	M	Laborer	02Ma02Do
TOBIN. Catherine	20	F	Servant	02Ma02Do
BRANNAN. Ann	45	F	Servant	02Ma02Do
Patrick	20	M	Carpenter	02Ma02Do
SMITH. Philip	30	M	Laborer	02Ma02Do
ONEIL, Sarah	20	F	Servant	02Ma02Do
MCKENNON. James	35	M	Farmer	02Ma02Do
James	8	M	Child	02Ma02Do
MINIS. Robert	21	M	Laborer	02Ma02Do
MULHOLL. Michael	20	M	Laborer	02Ma02Do
CALLAGHAN. Jerry	28	M	Carpenter	02Ma02Do
CROWLEY. Michael	45	M	Laborer	02Ma02Do
MORAN. Michael	20	M	Laborer	02Ma02Do
KELLY, Mary	18	F	Servant	02Ma02Do
MCKENNA. Joseph	18	M	Laborer	02Ma02Do
John	25	M	Laborer	02Ma02Do
CONOLLEY, Mary-Ann	20	F	Servant	02Ma02Do
Rose	15	F	Servant	02Ma02Do
OBRIEN. Mary	21	F	Servant	02Ma02Do
Michael	14	M	Laborer	02Ma02Do
CARLEY. Dennis	38	M	Laborer	02Ma02Do
LITTLE William	30	M	Laborer	02Ma02Do
SMITH. James	27	M	Plumber	02Ma02Do
BUTLER. James	17	M	Plumber	02Ma02Do
MCTANNEY. James	25	M	Laborer	02Ma02Do
Margaret	3	F	Child	02Ma02Do
Mary	20	F	Servant	02Ma02Do
WARD, Patrick	24	M	Laborer	02Ma02Do
Ann	16	F	Servant	02Ma02Do
HARWOOD, Mary	19	F	Servant	02Ma02Do
HANNEGAN. Margaret	18	F	Servant	02Ma02Do
HARRISON. Samuel	14	M	Laborer	02Ma02Do
Isabellia	8	F	Servant	02Ma02Do
CARTY, Patrick	18	M	Laborer	02Ma02Do
John	18	M	Laborer	02Ma02Do
Catherine	20	F	Servant	02Ma02Do
TURNER. Catherine	21	F	Servant	02Ma02Do
BURNS. Pat	35	M	Laborer	02Ma02Do
MCGRATH. Mary	20	F	Servant	02Ma02Do
John	8	M	Laborer	02Ma02Do
Ellen	5	F	Servant	02Ma02Do
Catherine	1	F	Child	02Ma02Do
COWRAN, Mary	25	F	Servant	02Ma02Do
SMITH, Mary	25	F	Servant	02Ma02Do
MCALEY, John	20	M	Laborer	02Ma02Do
NELSON. William	20	M	Laborer	02Ma02Do
COSGROVE. Patrick	26	M	Laborer	02Ma02Do
MARTIN. Ellen	25	F	Servant	02Ma02Do
GELLIC, Cath.	25	F	Servant	02Ma02Do
LANTRY, Margaret	18	F	Servant	02Ma02Do
HUGHES. Samuel	25	M	Laborer	02Ma02Do
RIGNEY, Bridget	20	F	Servant	02Ma02Do
HUGHES. Cath.	24	F	Servant	02Ma02Do
KELLY, Hannah	20	F	Servant	02Ma02Do
KENNY, Ann	20	F	Servant	02Ma02Do
SMITH. Bridget	20	F	Servant	02Ma02Do
MCGRANN. Edwd.	30	M	Laborer	02Ma02Do
RILEY, Ellen	25	F	Servant	02Ma02Do
Patrick	4	M	Child	02Ma02Do
TIGHE. Patrick	30	M	Laborer	02Ma02Do
MOORE. Cath.	18	F	Servant	02Ma02Do
DWYER. Pat	30	M	Laborer	02Ma02Do
Owen	18	M	Laborer	02Ma02Do
Peter	10	M	Laborer	02Ma02Do
OWEN. James	18	M	Laborer	02Ma02Do
SMITH, Peter	25	M	Laborer	02Ma02Do
John	22	M	Laborer	02Ma02Do
Died-At-Sea				
GRAMMAN. Lawrence	20	M	Laborer	02Ma02Do
CULLAN, Mary-T.	40	F	Servant	02Ma02Do
MCKEON. James	35	M	Weaver	02Ma02Do
Robert	14	M	Weaver	02Ma02Do
William	11	M	Weaver	02Ma02Do
Eliza	30	F	Weaver	02Ma02Do
Henry	9	M	Child	02Ma02Do
John	7	M	Child	02Ma02Do
James	8	M	Child	02Ma02Do
OBRIEN. John	16	M	Weaver	02Ma02Do
Ann	17	F	Servant	02Ma02Do
BOYLE. Margaret	18	F	Servant	02Ma02Do
MORAN. Roger	26	M	Laborer	02Ma02Do
Mary	26	F	Servant	02Ma02Do
ONEIL, Bridget	30	F	Servant	02Ma02Do
Mary	10	F	Servant	02Ma02Do
Michael	6	M	Child	02Ma02Do
Patrick	2	M	Child	02Ma02Do
MURDY. James	22	M	Laborer	02Ma02Do
KINSLEY. James	40	M	Laborer	02Ma02Do
Margaret	14	F	Servant	02Ma02Do
Michael	11	M	Laborer	02Ma02Do
Patrick	8	M	Child	02Ma02Do
John	4	M	Child	02Ma02Do
Thomas	4	M	Child	02Ma02Do
MCKENN. Ellen	18	F	Servant	02Ma02Do
JOHNSON. Margaret	15	F	Servant	02Ma02Do
Sarah	14	F	Servant	02Ma02Do
MCKEON. Mary	14	F	Servant	02Ma02Do
ONEIL, John	13	M	Laborer	02Ma02Do
RILEY. Rose	21	F	Servant	02Ma02Do
DOYLE. Martin	21	M	Laborer	02Ma02Do
Bridget	18	F	Servant	02Ma02Do
BURNS. Thomas	13	M	Laborer	02Ma02Do
WOODS. Pat	20	M	Laborer	02Ma02Do
MCKANNA. James	21	M	Laborer	02Ma02Do
Sarah	20	F	Servant	02Ma02Do
SMITH. Margaret	18	F	Servant	02Ma02Do
MCGREON. John	19	M	Laborer	02Ma02Do
James	18	M	Laborer	02Ma02Do
MCELHANNA. Rose	20	F	Servant	02Ma02Do
KARNEY. Susan	22	F	Servant	02Ma02Do
HUNTER. Mary	22	F	Servant	02Ma02Do
BRADY, Mary	28	F	Servant	02Ma02Do
U	.00	U	Infant	02Ma02Do
BANNAN, William	40	M	Laborer	02Ma02Do
DALEY. John	25	M	Laborer	02Ma02Do
Cath.	18	F	Servant	02Ma02Do
MULLIGAN. Mary	25	F	Servant	02Ma02Do
DALEY. Thomas	11	M	Servant	02Ma02Do
FAGAN. John	5	M	Child	02Ma02Do
Thomas	3	M	Child	02Ma02Do
WOOD, Rosanna	45	F	Servant	02Ma02Do
WEEAVER. Patrick	40	M	Weaver	02Ma02Do
KING, Cath.	16	F	Servant	02Ma02Do
COFFEE. William	18	M	Laborer	02Ma02Do
NAULTY. Richard	26	M	Servant	02Ma02Do
Mary	10	F	Servant	02Ma02Do
Margaret	8	F	Child	02Ma02Do
Cath.	6	F	Child	02Ma02Do
Bridget	3	F	Child	02Ma02Do
CARTY. John	14	M	Laborer	02Ma02Do
Catherine	15	F	Servant	02Ma02Do
CALLAGHER. Ann	14	F	Servant	02Ma02Do
KELLET. Patrick	16	M	Laborer	02Ma02Do
BOYLE. Thomas	28	M	Blacksmith	02Ma02Do
MCGARLIC. Rose	21	F	Servant	02Ma02Do
MCCANNA. Elizabeth	22	F	Servant	02Ma02Do
HENNESSY. Mich	20	M	Laborer	02Ma02Do
KELLY. Mich	22	M	Laborer	02Ma02Do
COOLGALL. Margt.	40	F	Servant	02Ma02Do
Daniel	10	M	Servant	02Ma02Do
NEWMAN. Ellen	57	F	Servant	02Ma02Do
KELLEY. John	18	M	Laborer	02Ma02Do
GLENNON. John	22	M	Shoemaker	02Ma02Do

NAMES OF PASSENGERS	AGE	SEX	OCCUPATIONS	DATE PORT SHIP
NAUGHTON. Mary	41	F	Servant	02Ma02Do
Margaret	10	F	Servant	02Ma02Do
Cath.	24	F	Servant	02Ma02Do
U	.00	U	Infant	02Ma02Do
Patrick	8	M	Child	02Ma02Do
Edwd.	6	M	Child	02Ma02Do
GENNIS, Margaret	40	F	Servant	02Ma02Do
COX, Patrick	21	M	Laborer	02Ma02Do
Catherine	25	F	Servant	02Ma02Do
BRADLEY, Mich	25	M	Laborer	02Ma02Do
SHERIDAN, James	40	M	Laborer	02Ma02Do
RILEY, Ellenor	25	F	Servant	02Ma02Do
KILLBURY, John-B.	5	M	Laborer	02Ma02Do
Hugh	3	M	Laborer	02Ma02Do
BRADY, Cath.	13	F	Servant	02Ma02Do
SMITH, Sydney	26	M	Servant	02Ma02Do
CLARK, James	27	M	Laborer	02Ma02Do
Mary	13	F	Servant	02Ma02Do
LEDWORTH, Bridget	50	F	Servant	02Ma02Do
MCLELLAN, Christ.	15	M	Laborer	02Ma02Do
CUNNIFFE. Cath.	19	F	Servant	02Ma02Do
KING, Patrick	19	M	Laborer	02Ma02Do
MURPHY, Julia	46	F	Servant	02Ma02Do
Mary	15	F	Servant	02Ma02Do
RUDDER. Ann	40	F	Servant	02Ma02Do
Cath.	15	F	Servant	02Ma02Do
CONNOR. Dennis	30	M	Laborer	02Ma02Do
BENNETT. John	16	M	Laborer	02Ma02Do
MCKERNEY, Joseph	25	M	Laborer	02Ma02Do
HENNESSEY, Mary	21	F	Servant	02Ma02Do

DANUBE 02 MAY 1849

From Liverpool

NAMES OF PASSENGERS	AGE	SEX	OCCUPATIONS	DATE PORT SHIP
HARRISON. Henry	24	M	Engineer	02Ma02Dv
BURTON. Richard	26	M	Weaver	02Ma02Dv
FARRISON. John	19	M	Unknown	02Ma02Dv
CUBBIN. John	27	M	Engineer	02Ma02Dv
U-Mrs.	26	F	Wife	02Ma02Dv
Kate	4	F	Child	02Ma02Dv
MCGUINESS. Hugh	55	M	Laborer	02Ma02Dv
Arthur	32	M	Laborer	02Ma02Dv
SLOAN. Pat	28	M	Laborer	02Ma02Dv
MCCANA. Tom	45	M	Laborer	02Ma02Dv
Mary	20	F	Unknown	02Ma02Dv
Pat.	1	M	Child	02Ma02Dv
ROURKE. John	30	M	Laborer	02Ma02Dv
MCANDREWS, Martin	19	M	Laborer	02Ma02Dv
DALTON. John	50	M	Laborer	02Ma02Dv
Anty	45	F	Unknown	02Ma02Dv
William	20	M	Unknown	02Ma02Dv
Anty	17	F	Unknown	02Ma02Dv
Kitty	12	F	Unknown	02Ma02Dv
WALKER. William	21	M	Unknown	02Ma02Dv
SHEENAN, E.Mrs.	19	F	Unknown	02Ma02Dv
GREENE. Thos.	24	M	Maltster	02Ma02Dv
HUFF, John	24	M	Butcher	02Ma02Dv
FURNAN, William	25	M	Engineer	02Ma02Dv
STOKES. John	45	M	Unknown	02Ma02Dv
KELLY, Edward-S.	23	M	Shoemaker	02Ma02Dv
FARLEY, Frank	16	M	Shoemaker	02Ma02Dv
CONNOR. Margaret	27	F	Spinster	02Ma02Dv
MANNING, Catherine	13	F	Spinster	02Ma02Dv
ONEILL, Mary	22	F	Spinster	02Ma02Dv
MURPHY, Ann	17	F	Spinster	02Ma02Dv
Catherine	14	F	Spinster	02Ma02Dv
DUFFEY, Ellen	16	F	Spinster	02Ma02Dv
GORMLEY, James	22	M	Shoemaker	02Ma02Dv
GORMLEY, U	20	M	Laborer	02Ma02Dv
Biddy	18	F	Laborer	02Ma02Dv
ROGERS. Alley	25	F	Spinster	02Ma02Dv
MCKENNA, Terry	24	M	Laborer	02Ma02Dv
AGNEW, Alex.	24	M	Laborer	02Ma02Dv
MCGUIRE, Jas.	20	M	Laborer	02Ma02Dv
Richard	22	M	Shoemaker	02Ma02Dv
MCGEE, Peter	24	M	Laborer	02Ma02Dv
CARTNEY, Jane	30	F	Unknown	02Ma02Dv
PETERS. John	21	M	Shoemaker	02Ma02Dv
BARRAY, John	18	M	Laborer	02Ma02Dv
James	21	M	Laborer	02Ma02Dv
MCCARTNEY, John	20	M	Laborer	02Ma02Dv
KERIGAN, Jerome	21	M	Laborer	02Ma02Dv
Garret	24	M	Laborer	02Ma02Dv
AHERN. Mary	35	F	Unknown	02Ma02Dv
HORRIGAN, John	24	M	Laborer	02Ma02Dv
CONNOR. James	24	M	Laborer	02Ma02Dv
John	30	M	Laborer	02Ma02Dv
WALSH, John	30	M	Laborer	02Ma02Dv
FLEMING, Richard	30	M	Laborer	02Ma02Dv
CONNER, Edmund	11	M	Laborer	02Ma02Dv
FREEMAN, Dan	45	M	Farmer	02Ma02Dv
U-Mrs.	40	F	Wife	02Ma02Dv
Ann	30	F	Farmer	02Ma02Dv
Maria	12	F	Unknown	02Ma02Dv
Catherine	11	F	Unknown	02Ma02Dv
John	9	M	Child	02Ma02Dv
David	2	M	Child	02Ma02Dv
CONNERY, U-Mrs.	30	F	Unknown	02Ma02Dv
REYNOLDS, Thos.	40	M	Shoemaker	02Ma02Dv
FLEMING, Margt.	60	F	Unknown	02Ma02Dv
Catherine	23	F	Unknown	02Ma02Dv
James	39	M	Unknown	02Ma02Dv
Jas.Wm.	12	M	Unknown	02Ma02Dv
Jane	6	F	Child	02Ma02Dv
Catherine	.00	F	Infant	02Ma02Dv
CANTRELL, U-Mrs.	40	F	Unknown	02Ma02Dv
ADAMS, Sarah-J.	23	F	Unknown	02Ma02Dv
Stewart	2	M	Child	02Ma02Dv
Mary-Ann	.00	F	Infant	02Ma02Dv
MCCARTY, Ewd.	21	M	Draper	02Ma02Dv
DELANY, Wm.	33	M	Laborer	02Ma02Dv
Margt.	30	F	Unknown	02Ma02Dv
Pat	3	M	Child	02Ma02Dv
Mary	.00	F	Infant	02Ma02Dv
TAYLOR, Chas.	22	M	Gdnr	02Ma02Dv
THOMPSON. Augustus	22	M	Laborer	02Ma02Dv
FURLY, Pat	40	M	Stone Mason	02Ma02Dv
John	20	M	Unknown	02Ma02Dv
Peter	12	M	Unknown	02Ma02Dv
PURDY, Hugh	28	M	Laborer	02Ma02Dv
Margt.	26	F	Unknown	02Ma02Dv
Sarah-Jane	2	F	Child	02Ma02Dv
John	1	M	Child	02Ma02Dv
POOLE, Francis	21	M	Unknown	02Ma02Dv
HEASE, Jos.	18	M	Unknown	02Ma02Dv
HENRY, Jno.	20	M	Unknown	02Ma02Dv
DEMPSEY, Fred	28	M	Clerk	02Ma02Dv
Jos.	16	M	Unknown	02Ma02Dv
MOLLOY, Peter	20	M	Unknown	02Ma02Dv
DINMORE, Pat	22	M	Laborer	02Ma02Dv
Ellen	17	F	Unknown	02Ma02Dv
JOHNSTON. Caroline	43	F	Servant	02Ma02Dv
Janett	19	F	Unknown	02Ma02Dv
Wm.	17	M	Unknown	02Ma02Dv
Caroline	14	F	Unknown	02Ma02Dv
BRANGOR. Thos.	11	M	Unknown	02Ma02Dv
MCKIERNAN, Mich.	22	M	Laborer	02Ma02Dv
KELLY, Ann	19	F	Spinster	02Ma02Dv
DALY, Law.	30	M	Carpenter	02Ma02Dv
Mich.	20	M	Laborer	02Ma02Dv
CONLAN, Bridget	19	F	Unknown	02Ma02Dv
MCBURISSE, Thos.	25	M	Laborer	02Ma02Dv
PARLAND, Patrick	22	M	Gdnr	02Ma02Dv

NAMES OF PASSENGERS	AGE	SEX	OCCUPATIONS	DATE PORT SHIP
CORBETT, Will.	23	M	Miller	02Ma02Dv
FOGARTY, John	21	M	Laborer	02Ma02Dv
CASSIDY, Owen	26	M	Laborer	02Ma02Dv
Ann	24	F	Unknown	02Ma02Dv
SMITH, Robt.	25	M	Farmer	02Ma02Dv
U-Mrs.	23	F	Unknown	02Ma02Dv
John	3	M	Child	02Ma02Dv
Will.	.00	M	Infant	02Ma02Dv
GREENE, Will.	26	M	Farmer	02Ma02Dv
BENELECK, Stephen	25	M	Farmer	02Ma02Dv
LONGHMAN, John	40	M	Laborer	02Ma02Dv
OREGAN. Patrick	20	M	Draper	02Ma02Dv
Jeremiah	19	M	Hrsm	02Ma02Dv
KEAN, James	24	M	Couchman	02Ma02Dv
ARTHUR. John	26	M	Laborer	02Ma02Dv
U-Mrs.	23	F	Unknown	02Ma02Dv
MCDONNELL, Cath.	20	F	Spinster	02Ma02Dv
PHILLIPS, Ellen	25	F	Spinster	02Ma02Dv
KNAGGS, John	45	M	Farmer	02Ma02Dv
William	43	M	Farmer	02Ma02Dv
HARNETT, Wm.	26	M	Engineer	02Ma02Dv
HOLWRIGHT. John	27	M	Laborer	02Ma02Dv
Mary	23	F	Laborer	02Ma02Dv
Richard	.00	M	Infant	02Ma02Dv
SIMPSON. James	24	M	Joiner	02Ma02Dv
Thos.	22	M	Bricklayer	02Ma02Dv
HUTTON, John	24	M	Farmer	02Ma02Dv
THOMPSON, John	24	M	Farmer	02Ma02Dv
CUTTS. John	40	M	Farmer	02Ma02Dv
Jonathan	22	M	Farmer	02Ma02Dv
SAMUEL, Elizabeth	27	F	Unknown	02Ma02Dv
Ellen	1	F	Child	02Ma02Dv
MOLLOW, Fred	25	M	Laborer	02Ma02Dv
John	22	M	Farmer	02Ma02Dv
HEASCHEL, Fred	27	M	Tailor	02Ma02Dv
HUTTON. Wm.	30	M	Laborer	02Ma02Dv
MULLIGAN. Eliza	21	F	Unknown	02Ma02Dv
SCULLY, Pat	20	M	Laborer	02Ma02Dv
LONG, Pat	21	M	Laborer	02Ma02Dv
WALSH. John	23	M	Carpenter	02Ma02Dv
BENNETT, Willm.	24	M	Hatter	02Ma02Dv
STROUD, George	38	M	Butcher	02Ma02Dv
GREGORY, Henry	27	M	Clerk	02Ma02Dv
KANE, Mich.	16	M	Unknown	02Ma02Dv
Pat	14	M	Unknown	02Ma02Dv
James	11	M	Unknown	02Ma02Dv
BYRNE, Pat	17	M	Unknown	02Ma02Dv
ROE, George	22	M	Miller	02Ma02Dv
CASH. John	23	M	Clerk	02Ma02Dv
REILLY, Mich.	20	M	Farmer	02Ma02Dv
SMITH. Mary	20	F	Farmer	02Ma02Dv
Bessy	18	F	Farmer	02Ma02Dv
FISHER, Mathew	40	M	Block Maker	02Ma02Dv
Henry	20	M	Blacksmith	02Ma02Dv
DOYLE, Thos.	24	M	Couchman	02Ma02Dv
Rosanna	20	F	Unknown	02Ma02Dv
SOMERS. Morgan	26	M	Clerk	02Ma02Dv
BRENNER. M.	25	M	Locksmith	02Ma02Dv
MAYER. Wm.	24	M	Locksmith	02Ma02Dv
DALTON. Edward	20	M	Joiner	02Ma02Dv
SHIPMAN. George	37	M	Baker	02Ma02Dv
FRAZER, Margaret	20	F	Spinster	02Ma02Dv
ERWIN. Sam.	17	M	Clerk	02Ma02Dv
KENNEDY, Bertha	20	F	Blacksmith	02Ma02Dv
CORRY, James	27	M	Farmer	02Ma02Dv
JOYCE. U-Mrs.	36	F	Unknown	02Ma02Dv
Mary	11	F	Unknown	02Ma02Dv
Elizabeth	9	F	Child	02Ma02Dv
Clement	7	M	Child	02Ma02Dv
John	6	M	Child	02Ma02Dv
Louisa	2	F	Child	02Ma02Dv
JORDAN, Robt.	21	M	Laborer	02Ma02Dv
CLARKE. Henry	24	M	Musician	02Ma02Dv
WATSON. George	25	M	Farmer	02Ma02Dv
MULLEN. Edward	20	M	Tailor	02Ma02Dv
MULLEN, John	8	M	Child	02Ma02Dv
FOX, Mary	22	F	Unknown	02Ma02Dv
COLTON. Catherine	19	F	Unknown	02Ma02Dv
DAVIS, Thos.	24	M	Laborer	02Ma02Dv
TEALE. Willm.	22	M	Laborer	02Ma02Dv
Mary-Ann	20	F	Unknown	02Ma02Dv
DUNN, Willm.	24	M	Laborer	02Ma02Dv
Margaret	22	F	Unknown	02Ma02Dv
Anne	27	F	Unknown	02Ma02Dv
QUIG, John	22	M	Laborer	02Ma02Dv
Francis	20	M	Laborer	02Ma02Dv
GLASS, Mathew	23	M	Laborer	02Ma02Dv
CAIN, John	21	M	Laborer	02Ma02Dv
MURPHY, Stephen	20	M	Laborer	02Ma02Dv
CULLIGHAN, Bernard	45	M	Farmer	02Ma02Dv
U-Mrs.	45	F	Wife	02Ma02Dv
Margaret	20	F	Unknown	02Ma02Dv
John	14	M	Unknown	02Ma02Dv
SHARKEY, Peter	20	M	Farmer	02Ma02Dv
Anne	20	F	Unknown	02Ma02Dv
GREENE, Edward-D.	20	M	Butcher	02Ma02Dv
HERBERT, Samuel	21	M	Unknown	02Ma02Dv
MAHONEY, Edward	20	M	Carpenter	02Ma02Dv
John	19	M	Laborer	02Ma02Dv
FITZGERALD, James	60	M	Farmer	02Ma02Dv
U-Mrs.	50	F	Wife	02Ma02Dv
James	25	M	Farmer	02Ma02Dv
John	22	M	Farmer	02Ma02Dv
Mary	20	F	Unknown	02Ma02Dv
Richard	18	M	Unknown	02Ma02Dv
Debora	16	F	Unknown	02Ma02Dv
Catherine	20	F	Unknown	02Ma02Dv
FLYNN. Garret	29	M	Farmer	02Ma02Dv
U-Mrs.	50	F	Unknown	02Ma02Dv
SHEADY, Mary	19	F	Unknown	02Ma02Dv
DEVLIN, Margaret	19	F	Unknown	02Ma02Dv
CORKERS. Corn.	28	M	Laborer	02Ma02Dv
SHEEHAN, Willm.	38	M	Laborer	02Ma02Dv
NOONAN, Mich.	40	M	Farmer	02Ma02Dv
BUCKLEY, Corn.	38	M	Laborer	02Ma02Dv
Ellen	34	F	Unknown	02Ma02Dv
Mathew	2	M	Child	02Ma02Dv
Patrick	.00	M	Infant	02Ma02Dv
SHEEHAN, John	30	M	Laborer	02Ma02Dv
Daniel	20	M	Laborer	02Ma02Dv
HUDNER, Willm.	26	M	Laborer	02Ma02Dv
Francis	23	M	Laborer	02Ma02Dv
Marie	21	F	Laborer	02Ma02Dv
CARTER. Michl.	23	M	Laborer	02Ma02Dv
QUINLAN, Cath.	22	F	Spinster	02Ma02Dv
RAHSEY, Pat	22	M	Laborer	02Ma02Dv
SMALL, John	25	M	Laborer	02Ma02Dv
LYNCH, John	40	M	Farmer	02Ma02Dv
U-Mrs.	40	F	Farmer	02Ma02Dv
Jane	34	F	Unknown	02Ma02Dv
Richard	15	M	Unknown	02Ma02Dv
Margaret	12	F	Unknown	02Ma02Dv
Lucy	9	F	Child	02Ma02Dv
Jane	7	F	Child	02Ma02Dv
Willm.	.00	M	Infant	02Ma02Dv
BOLSTER. Eliza	30	F	Unknown	02Ma02Dv
SULLIVAN, Willm.	40	M	Laborer	02Ma02Dv
NOONAN, Cath.	20	F	Unknown	02Ma02Dv
FLANAGAN, Mich.	18	M	Unknown	02Ma02Dv
CALLAHAN, Willm.	20	M	Unknown	02Ma02Dv
DONAHY, Ellen	30	F	Unknown	02Ma02Dv
Cath.	26	F	Unknown	02Ma02Dv
John	20	M	Unknown	02Ma02Dv
Bridget	17	F	Unknown	02Ma02Dv
WHITE. Mary	22	F	Dressmaker	02Ma02Dv
KEEFE. Ellen	20	F	Cnf	02Ma02Dv
LYNCH, Pat	22	M	Laborer	02Ma02Dv
FITZPATRICK, Mary	22	F	Cnf	02Ma02Dv
NEALE. Patrick	28	M	Chandler	02Ma02Dv
AHEARN. Ben	20	M	Dyer	02Ma02Dv

NAMES OF PASSENGERS	AGE	SEX	OCCUPATIONS	DATE PORT SHIP
CAHILL, Cath.	20	F	Spinster	02Ma02Dv
BUCKLEY, Julia	30	F	Spinster	02Ma02Dv
Nancy	20	F	Spinster	02Ma02Dv
Mary	18	F	Spinster	02Ma02Dv
DEE, Bridget	40	F	Spinster	02Ma02Dv
Patrick	17	M	Spinster	02Ma02Dv
MCQUIN, Mary	20	F	Spinster	02Ma02Dv
Patrick	16	M	Unknown	02Ma02Dv
MCMAHON, Roger	50	M	Farmer	02Ma02Dv
Hester	50	M	Unknown	02Ma02Dv
Ann	11	F	Unknown	02Ma02Dv
John	9	M	Child	02Ma02Dv
HORNER. Mich.	31	M	Unknown	02Ma02Dv
DEVINE. Mary	20	F	Unknown	02Ma02Dv
KENNEDY, Maria	30	F	Unknown	02Ma02Dv
CULLEN. Mary	30	F	Unknown	02Ma02Dv
MCCABE. John	00	M	Unknown	02Ma02Dv
MACKIE, U-Mr.	00	M	Unknown	02Ma02Dv
U-Mrs.	00	F	Unknown	02Ma02Dv
U	00	U	Child	02Ma02Dv
U	00	U	Child	02Ma02Dv
U	00	U	Child	02Ma02Dv
U, U	00	U	Servant	02Ma02Dv
DAWSON. U-Mr.	00	M	Unknown	02Ma02Dv
MCMURRAY, U-Miss	00	F	Unknown	02Ma02Dv
FITZPATRICK, Mary	40	F	Cnf	02Ma02Dv

WARRIOR 02 MAY 1849

From Newry

NAMES OF PASSENGERS	AGE	SEX	OCCUPATIONS	DATE PORT SHIP
MCCRARAN. Peter	24	M	Unknown	02Ma11Dt
MCCAMBRY, James	27	M	Unknown	02Ma11Dt
Margaret	25	F	Unknown	02Ma11Dt
Thomas	17	M	Unknown	02Ma11Dt
James	16	M	Unknown	02Ma11Dt
Margaret-Jane	14	F	Unknown	02Ma11Dt
Bess	12	F	Unknown	02Ma11Dt
Daniel	11	M	Unknown	02Ma11Dt
Mary	10	F	Unknown	02Ma11Dt
Henry	8	M	Child	02Ma11Dt
Fanny	.00	F	Infant	02Ma11Dt
SANDS. Patrick	22	M	Unknown	02Ma11Dt
HANDCOCK, James	25	M	Unknown	02Ma11Dt
PRAY, Betty	40	F	Unknown	02Ma11Dt
Alice	35	F	Unknown	02Ma11Dt
HAWTHORNE. Hugh	40	M	Unknown	02Ma11Dt
MCKINLEY, John	27	M	Unknown	02Ma11Dt
Jane	25	F	Unknown	02Ma11Dt
Elizabeth	12	F	Unknown	02Ma11Dt
CONN, Sarah	29	F	Unknown	02Ma11Dt
JONES, Terrance	22	M	Unknown	02Ma11Dt
Ceciely	20	F	Unknown	02Ma11Dt
Peter	14	M	Unknown	02Ma11Dt
Mary	12	F	Unknown	02Ma11Dt
PERIE. Robert	25	M	Unknown	02Ma11Dt
JONES, Patrick	40	M	Unknown	02Ma11Dt
Biddy	39	F	Unknown	02Ma11Dt
Owen	17	M	Unknown	02Ma11Dt
Terence	16	M	Unknown	02Ma11Dt
Patrick	14	M	Unknown	02Ma11Dt
Mary	13	F	Unknown	02Ma11Dt
Mary	12	F	Unknown	02Ma11Dt
Biddy	.00	F	Infant	02Ma11Dt
OHARE, Patrick	25	M	Unknown	02Ma11Dt
Ellen	20	F	Unknown	02Ma11Dt
Mary-Ann	14	F	Unknown	02Ma11Dt
Margaret	12	F	Unknown	02Ma11Dt
Teresa	.00	F	Infant	02Ma11Dt
CARR, Mary	29	F	Unknown	02Ma11Dt
KEENAN, Betty	33	F	Unknown	02Ma11Dt
MCKENNA, Terance	35	M	Unknown	02Ma11Dt
Margaret	30	F	Unknown	02Ma11Dt
HINDEN, Bridget-M.	27	F	Unknown	02Ma11Dt
OHEAR. Arthur	24	M	Unknown	02Ma11Dt
ROBINSON. William	39	M	Unknown	02Ma11Dt
MCCANN. George	44	M	Unknown	02Ma11Dt
COUWGAN, Bridget	20	F	Unknown	02Ma11Dt
TURAN, Patrick	22	M	Unknown	02Ma11Dt
TURANY, Ann	45	F	Unknown	02Ma11Dt
John	39	M	Unknown	02Ma11Dt
MCCANN, Peter	18	M	Unknown	02Ma11Dt
Ann	15	F	Unknown	02Ma11Dt
Owen	12	M	Unknown	02Ma11Dt
ONET, Margaret	42	F	Unknown	02Ma11Dt
CONWAY, Margaret	37	F	Unknown	02Ma11Dt
DONAGH, Maria	27	F	Unknown	02Ma11Dt
TONER. John	22	M	Unknown	02Ma11Dt
Mary	19	F	Unknown	02Ma11Dt
CONWAY, Bridget	22	F	Unknown	02Ma11Dt
MCCOUB, James	27	M	Unknown	02Ma11Dt
MCCOUL, Elizabeth	.00	F	Infant	02Ma11Dt
JONES. Mary-Jane	15	F	Unknown	02Ma11Dt
BENNETT. John	40	M	Unknown	02Ma11Dt
MURRAY, Hugh	45	M	Unknown	02Ma11Dt
MCCAFFREY. Eliza-Jane	40	F	Unknown	02Ma11Dt
HAWITT. Debora	40	F	Unknown	02Ma11Dt
U	.00	U	Infant	02Ma11Dt
MCSHANE, Patrick	25	M	Unknown	02Ma11Dt
James	22	M	Unknown	02Ma11Dt
OURIH, Judith	20	F	Unknown	02Ma11Dt
HUGHES, Frances	19	U	Unknown	02Ma11Dt
RUSSELL, James	22	M	Unknown	02Ma11Dt
MCCAUL, Ann	29	F	Unknown	02Ma11Dt
MCKEBLAN, Mary-Ann	17	F	Unknown	02Ma11Dt
HANNIGAN, James	40	M	Unknown	02Ma11Dt
Margaret	38	F	Unknown	02Ma11Dt
RAFFERTY, Mary-A.	22	F	Unknown	02Ma11Dt
HAGAN, Hugh	41	M	Unknown	02Ma11Dt
Mary	39	F	Unknown	02Ma11Dt
Ellen	19	F	Unknown	02Ma11Dt
Eliza	17	F	Unknown	02Ma11Dt
Patrick	.00	M	Infant	02Ma11Dt
JONES. Patrick	42	M	Unknown	02Ma11Dt
Peter	40	M	Unknown	02Ma11Dt
BARTON. John	17	M	Unknown	02Ma11Dt
Catherine	15	F	Unknown	02Ma11Dt
COPLAN, Rose	42	F	Unknown	02Ma11Dt
Robert	27	M	Unknown	02Ma11Dt
MCKEE, James	40	M	Unknown	02Ma11Dt
James	39	M	Unknown	02Ma11Dt
Mary-Jane	42	F	Unknown	02Ma11Dt
Sarah	39	F	Unknown	02Ma11Dt
CUNNINGHAM, Thomas	22	M	Unknown	02Ma11Dt
BLAKE. William	40	M	Unknown	02Ma11Dt
Ellen	34	F	Unknown	02Ma11Dt
Christ.	14	M	Unknown	02Ma11Dt
Mathw.	.00	M	Infant	02Ma11Dt
MYHL, James	21	M	Unknown	02Ma11Dt
John	19	M	Unknown	02Ma11Dt

CASHMERE 02 MAY 1849

From Galway

NAMES OF PASSENGERS	AGE	SEX	OCCUPATIONS	DATE PORT SHIP
NAUGHTON. Mary	21	F	Laborer	02Ma06Dw
FRANCIS, James	20	M	Laborer	02Ma06Dw
BEDDIN, U-Mrs.	46	F	Spinster	02Ma06Dw

NAMES OF PASSENGERS	AGE	SEX	OCCUPATIONS	DATE PORT SHIP
BEDDIN, Patt	18	M	Laborer	02Ma06Dw
REDDIN. Honor	26	F	Spinster	02Ma06Dw
Eliza	8	F	Child	02Ma06Dw
CONNOR. Patt	21	M	Laborer	02Ma06Dw
KAIN, John	40	M	Laborer	02Ma06Dw
MURRAY, Peter	30	M	Laborer	02Ma06Dw
Peter	30	M	Carpenter	02Ma06Dw
NOON. John	17	M	Carpenter	02Ma06Dw
MITCHELL, Mary	20	F	Spinster	02Ma06Dw
CALNAN, Michl.	26	M	Laborer	02Ma06Dw
GLEESON, Joseph	18	M	Laborer	02Ma06Dw
COLEMAN, Winny	22	F	Spinster	02Ma06Dw
CALNANE, Bedilia	19	F	Spinster	02Ma06Dw
CUNNINGHAM, Michael	19	M	Laborer	02Ma06Dw
KINVAN, Patt	30	M	Laborer	02Ma06Dw
CARTY, Denis	24	M	Laborer	02Ma06Dw
HAVERTY, Peter	24	M	Laborer	02Ma06Dw
FYNN. John	21	M	Laborer	02Ma06Dw
MARA, Patt	24	M	Laborer	02Ma06Dw
KENELLY, John	24	M	Laborer	02Ma06Dw
MADIGAN. Honor	46	F	Spinster	02Ma06Dw
REEDY, Bridget	18	F	Spinster	02Ma06Dw
CULLAMY, Timothy	8	M	Child	02Ma06Dw
DAVERN. Mary	28	F	Spinster	02Ma06Dw
Margaret	40	F	Spinster	02Ma06Dw
Honor	20	F	Spinster	02Ma06Dw
Mary	25	F	Spinster	02Ma06Dw
GORDON. Mary	18	F	Spinster	02Ma06Dw
MOONEY, Ellen	18	F	Spinster	02Ma06Dw
Patt	24	M	Laborer	02Ma06Dw
CANNELL, Martin	30	M	Laborer	02Ma06Dw
FALL, Patt	21	M	Laborer	02Ma06Dw
DALY, Andrew	27	M	Laborer	02Ma06Dw
Dennis	40	M	Laborer	02Ma06Dw
Dennis	18	M	Laborer	02Ma06Dw
William	24	M	Laborer	02Ma06Dw
Sally	18	F	Spinster	02Ma06Dw
Biddy	48	F	Spinster	02Ma06Dw
Bridget	4	F	Child	02Ma06Dw
DALLY, Patt	4	M	Child	02Ma06Dw
WARD, Winny	18	F	Spinster	02Ma06Dw
KAIN. Michael	30	M	Laborer	02Ma06Dw
Mary	28	F	Spinster	02Ma06Dw
SWEENEY, Margaret	24	F	Spinster	02Ma06Dw
CONWAY, Michael	24	M	Carpenter	02Ma06Dw
Bidget (W)	24	F	Wife	02Ma06Dw
CURTAIN. Margaret	20	F	Spinster	02Ma06Dw
Judy	18	F	Spinster	02Ma06Dw
SCANLAN, Patt	48	M	Laborer	02Ma06Dw
Mary	36	F	Laborer	02Ma06Dw
CUNNINGHAM, Denis	48	M	Laborer	02Ma06Dw
Bridget	24	F	Spinster	02Ma06Dw
Denis	9	M	Child	02Ma06Dw
Patt	3	M	Child	02Ma06Dw
John	1	M	Child	02Ma06Dw
FAHY, Stephen	40	M	Laborer	02Ma06Dw
Sally	40	F	Spinster	02Ma06Dw
Michael	20	M	Laborer	02Ma06Dw
John	14	M	Laborer	02Ma06Dw
CULLINANE, Patt	30	M	Laborer	02Ma06Dw
NEILAND, John	20	M	Laborer	02Ma06Dw
CUMMINGS, Mary	37	F	Spinster	02Ma06Dw
Margaret	16	F	Spinster	02Ma06Dw
CUNNISS. Patt	30	M	Laborer	02Ma06Dw
CANNON. Ann	20	F	Spinster	02Ma06Dw
HORETY, Biddy	20	F	Spinster	02Ma06Dw
COONEY, Thomas	18	M	Laborer	02Ma06Dw
FAMMINGTON. Mary	16	F	Spinster	02Ma06Dw
NELLY, Bridget	20	F	Spinster	02Ma06Dw
GARVER. Catherine	27	F	Spinster	02Ma06Dw
GARVEY, Bridget	10	F	Unknown	02Ma06Dw
QUINN. James	21	M	Laborer	02Ma06Dw
KEHELAN. Martin	21	M	Laborer	02Ma06Dw
QUINN. Peggy	40	F	Matron	02Ma06Dw
WARD, Michael	24	M	Carpenter	02Ma06Dw

NAMES OF PASSENGERS	AGE	SEX	OCCUPATIONS	DATE PORT SHIP
FLAHERTY, Patt	21	M	Laborer	02Ma06Dw
HALAN, Martin	21	M	Laborer	02Ma06Dw
NEIL, Mary	30	F	Spinster	02Ma06Dw
HIELAND, Bridget	21	F	Spinster	02Ma06Dw
GANON. Martin	24	M	Laborer	02Ma06Dw
MCGUINESS. Patt	27	M	Laborer	02Ma06Dw
Mary	22	F	Spinster	02Ma06Dw
KEARNS. Stephen	30	M	Laborer	02Ma06Dw
CONEAR. Patt	25	M	Laborer	02Ma06Dw
TARPY, Mary	18	F	Spinster	02Ma06Dw
GLYNN. Thomas	32	M	Laborer	02Ma06Dw
Mary	21	F	Spinster	02Ma06Dw
James	14	M	Laborer	02Ma06Dw
Maria	.00	F	Infant	02Ma06Dw
NEIL, Martin	36	M	Laborer	02Ma06Dw
May	18	F	Spinster	02Ma06Dw
KAIN, John	29	M	Laborer	02Ma06Dw
Kate	23	F	Spinster	02Ma06Dw
FALY, John	22	M	Laborer	02Ma06Dw
MORAN, John	26	M	Laborer	02Ma06Dw
LAMBERT, Mary	29	F	Spinster	02Ma06Dw
BURKE, Patt	40	M	Laborer	02Ma06Dw
Kate	.00	F	Infant	02Ma06Dw
Patt	6	M	Child	02Ma06Dw
REEDY, Michael	24	M	Laborer	02Ma06Dw
Kate	24	F	Spinster	02Ma06Dw
MOORE. Timothy	24	M	Laborer	02Ma06Dw
Biddy	26	F	Spinster	02Ma06Dw
GRIFFY, Patt	30	M	Laborer	02Ma06Dw
CUSACK, Michael	28	M	Laborer	02Ma06Dw
FLAHERTY, Martin	24	M	Laborer	02Ma06Dw
KAIN, Catherine	24	F	Spinster	02Ma06Dw
HALLORAN, Michael	24	M	Laborer	02Ma06Dw
CAULFIELD, Thomas	29	M	Laborer	02Ma06Dw
COSGRAVE, Timothy	20	M	Laborer	02Ma06Dw
MARA, John	50	M	Laborer	02Ma06Dw
MANA. Lucy	45	F	Spinster	02Ma06Dw
WARD, Maria	19	F	Spinster	02Ma06Dw
Patt	17	M	Laborer	02Ma06Dw
Margaret	14	F	Spinster	02Ma06Dw
John	10	M	Unknown	02Ma06Dw
William	9	M	Child	02Ma06Dw
Lucinda	6	F	Child	02Ma06Dw
Eleanor	4	F	Child	02Ma06Dw
MURRAY, Patt	26	M	Carpenter	02Ma06Dw
ROBERTS, William	25	M	Laborer	02Ma06Dw
Ann	12	F	Spinster	02Ma06Dw
CONNELLY, Biddy	24	F	Spinster	02Ma06Dw
KAIN. Thomas	28	M	Laborer	02Ma06Dw
Honor	20	F	Spinster	02Ma06Dw
Patt	29	M	Laborer	02Ma06Dw
Sally	21	F	Spinster	02Ma06Dw
CORLESS, Mary	20	F	Spinster	02Ma06Dw
KEENAN, Bartly	23	M	Laborer	02Ma06Dw
KENNITT, Patt-S.	28	M	Laborer	02Ma06Dw
SWEENY, Martin	00	M	Laborer	02Ma06Dw
BIRMINGHAM, Martin	21	M	Laborer	02Ma06Dw
MITCHELL, Patt	21	M	Laborer	02Ma06Dw
BURKE. Mary	34	F	Spinster	02Ma06Dw
Mary	12	F	Spinster	02Ma06Dw
Margaret	10	F	Spinster	02Ma06Dw
EGAN, Garrett	50	M	Tailor	02Ma06Dw
Mary	15	F	Spinster	02Ma06Dw
U-Mrs.	47	F	Matron	02Ma06Dw
Garrett	17	M	Clerk	02Ma06Dw
Honor	13	F	Unknown	02Ma06Dw
Michael	7	M	Child	02Ma06Dw
Denis	41	M	Carpenter	02Ma06Dw
CANCY, Eliza	25	F	Spinster	02Ma06Dw
COONEY, Charles	9	M	Child	02Ma06Dw
QUINN, Andrew	27	M	Mason	02Ma06Dw
FARRELL, Mary	20	F	Spinster	02Ma06Dw
TREACY, Mary	20	F	Spinster	02Ma06Dw
LYON, Margaret	30	F	Matron	02Ma06Dw

CHESTER 02 MAY 1849

From Dublin

NAMES OF PASSENGERS	AGE	SEX	OCCUPATIONS	DATE PORT SHIP
ROBASIN, Margt.	7	F	Child	02Ma12Dx
Mary-A.	3	F	Child	02Ma12Dx
Harriett	.00	F	Infant	02Ma12Dx
FERRILL, U-Miss	20	F	Unknown	02Ma12Dx
TRACEY, Andrew	21	M	Unknown	02Ma12Dx
GRAHAM, Thomas	21	M	Unknown	02Ma12Dx
PROPLEY, Peter	25	M	Unknown	02Ma12Dx
Ann	22	F	Unknown	02Ma12Dx
MERAN. Wm.	20	M	Unknown	02Ma12Dx
HYLAND, Pat	22	M	Unknown	02Ma12Dx
Bridget	22	F	Unknown	02Ma12Dx
SALER, Daniel	21	M	Unknown	02Ma12Dx
Mary	20	F	Unknown	02Ma12Dx
DOYLE. James	40	M	Unknown	02Ma12Dx
MCCORMICK, Pat	13	M	Unknown	02Ma12Dx
Thomas	11	M	Unknown	02Ma12Dx
Biddy	9	F	Child	02Ma12Dx
Catharine	7	F	Child	02Ma12Dx
MOYLETT, John	28	M	Unknown	02Ma12Dx
Bernard	24	M	Unknown	02Ma12Dx
Bridget	20	F	Unknown	02Ma12Dx
COSTELLO. Biddy	20	F	Unknown	02Ma12Dx
LYONS. Patrick	20	M	Unknown	02Ma12Dx
BRACHEY, Edward	20	M	Unknown	02Ma12Dx
KENNEDY, Samuel	40	M	Unknown	02Ma12Dx
Martha	5	F	Child	02Ma12Dx
Susan	3	F	Child	02Ma12Dx
Samuel	.00	M	Infant	02Ma12Dx
DESMODY, Pat	25	M	Unknown	02Ma12Dx
MCDOWELL, Thomas	25	M	Unknown	02Ma12Dx
HEAVY, Bessy	21	F	Unknown	02Ma12Dx
SMITH. Luke	20	M	Unknown	02Ma12Dx
FITZSIMMONS. Thomas	20	M	Unknown	02Ma12Dx
DUGGAN, John	20	M	Unknown	02Ma12Dx
MCQUADE. Peter	25	M	Unknown	02Ma12Dx
LANGAN. Pat.	22	M	Unknown	02Ma12Dx
James	20	M	Unknown	02Ma12Dx
Kate	13	F	Unknown	02Ma12Dx
HOWARD, Matt	20	M	Unknown	02Ma12Dx
MURPHY, John	20	M	Unknown	02Ma12Dx
KELLY, Michael	32	M	Unknown	02Ma12Dx
U-Mrs.	28	F	Unknown	02Ma12Dx
Mary	6	F	Child	02Ma12Dx
John	4	M	Child	02Ma12Dx
Margaret	2	F	Child	02Ma12Dx
Catharine	.00	F	Infant	02Ma12Dx
Patrick	21	M	Unknown	02Ma12Dx
Edward	18	M	Unknown	02Ma12Dx
Mary	45	F	Unknown	02Ma12Dx
GUINNESS. Hugh	45	M	Unknown	02Ma12Dx
EAGAN. John	25	M	Unknown	02Ma12Dx
Catharine	22	F	Unknown	02Ma12Dx
Catharine	.00	F	Infant	02Ma12Dx
RUSSELL, William	24	M	Unknown	02Ma12Dx
DONOHUE, Patrick	22	M	Unknown	02Ma12Dx
DALTON. Martin	21	M	Unknown	02Ma12Dx
IRELAND, Thomas	21	M	Unknown	02Ma12Dx
DONOHUE, Catharine	19	F	Unknown	02Ma12Dx
PRENDERGAST, Cath.	18	F	Unknown	02Ma12Dx
RYAN. Phillip	28	M	Unknown	02Ma12Dx
MCGUIRK, Mat.	40	M	Unknown	02Ma12Dx
REARDON. M.	24	M	Unknown	02Ma12Dx
KELLY, M.J.	25	M	Unknown	02Ma12Dx
BERRY, Edward	21	M	Unknown	02Ma12Dx
MCDERMOTT, Michael	55	M	Unknown	02Ma12Dx
WARREN, Joseph	13	M	Unknown	02Ma12Dx
DOYLE. M.	24	M	Unknown	02Ma12Dx
CAVANAGH, Bartly	25	M	Unknown	02Ma12Dx
TASELBERRY, Robert	23	M	Unknown	02Ma12Dx
COLLIGAN, Beivin	45	M	Unknown	02Ma12Dx
Biddy	20	F	Unknown	02Ma12Dx
Andrew	16	M	Unknown	02Ma12Dx
Peter	13	M	Unknown	02Ma12Dx
CONWAY, James	30	M	Unknown	02Ma12Dx
U-Mrs.	25	F	Unknown	02Ma12Dx
John	.00	M	Infant	02Ma12Dx
Lawrence	20	M	Unknown	02Ma12Dx
KENNY, Michael	20	M	Unknown	02Ma12Dx
BYRNE, Patrick	45	M	Unknown	02Ma12Dx
Michael	40	M	Unknown	02Ma12Dx
Hugh	21	M	Unknown	02Ma12Dx
John	18	M	Unknown	02Ma12Dx
Margaret	.00	F	Infant	02Ma12Dx
Christy	21	M	Unknown	02Ma12Dx
CAREY, Patrick	21	M	Unknown	02Ma12Dx
WHELAN, Mary	20	F	Unknown	02Ma12Dx
MORTEN. Ellen	20	F	Unknown	02Ma12Dx
SWORDS. Pall	24	M	Unknown	02Ma12Dx
MULAVEY, James	30	M	Unknown	02Ma12Dx
CARROL, James	21	M	Unknown	02Ma12Dx
DARCY, U-Miss	20	F	Unknown	02Ma12Dx
MAHEN, Ellen	20	F	Unknown	02Ma12Dx
FARROLL, Christy	25	M	Unknown	02Ma12Dx
GIBSEN, John	20	M	Unknown	02Ma12Dx
WAREY, Michael	30	M	Unknown	02Ma12Dx
HARRINGTON. Thomas	25	M	Unknown	02Ma12Dx
OCONNER. James	28	M	Unknown	02Ma12Dx
U-Miss	21	F	Unknown	02Ma12Dx
MATHEWS, U-Mrs.	24	F	Unknown	02Ma12Dx
James	.00	M	Infant	02Ma12Dx
Jane	20	F	Unknown	02Ma12Dx
HARPER, Christy	20	M	Unknown	02Ma12Dx
CONNOR. Rose	28	F	Unknown	02Ma12Dx
HEALEY, James	26	M	Unknown	02Ma12Dx
MCMANUS. Thomas	20	M	Unknown	02Ma12Dx
Onay	40	M	Unknown	02Ma12Dx
RILLEY, M.	20	M	Unknown	02Ma12Dx
CARROLL. John	18	M	Unknown	02Ma12Dx
CUSHLIN, Michael	20	M	Unknown	02Ma12Dx
Catharine	20	F	Unknown	02Ma12Dx
MACKEN, Pall	55	M	Unknown	02Ma12Dx
DUFFEY, John	19	M	Unknown	02Ma12Dx
Patt	19	M	Unknown	02Ma12Dx
ROURKE. William	30	M	Unknown	02Ma12Dx
Margaret	20	F	Unknown	02Ma12Dx
CHRISTIAN, Ann	.00	F	Infant	02Ma12Dx
DEMPSEY, Peter	28	M	Unknown	02Ma12Dx
WALSH. Robert	30	M	Unknown	02Ma12Dx
Catharine	15	F	Unknown	02Ma12Dx
MOORE. Thomas	18	M	Unknown	02Ma12Dx
Samuel	25	M	Unknown	02Ma12Dx
HAYDEN, William	22	M	Unknown	02Ma12Dx
HARTNELL, William	45	M	Unknown	02Ma12Dx
Margaret	40	F	Unknown	02Ma12Dx
Timothy	25	M	Unknown	02Ma12Dx
Mary	13	F	Unknown	02Ma12Dx
Johanna	11	F	Unknown	02Ma12Dx
David	9	M	Child	02Ma12Dx
William	7	M	Child	02Ma12Dx
CASSIDY, Thomas	21	M	Unknown	02Ma12Dx
ROACHE, James	50	M	Unknown	02Ma12Dx
Johanna	40	F	Unknown	02Ma12Dx
David	19	M	Unknown	02Ma12Dx
John	17	M	Unknown	02Ma12Dx
Margaret	15	F	Unknown	02Ma12Dx
Michael	12	M	Unknown	02Ma12Dx
James	7	M	Child	02Ma12Dx
Honora	3	F	Child	02Ma12Dx
Mary	.00	F	Infant	02Ma12Dx
Michael	27	M	Unknown	02Ma12Dx

NAMES OF PASSENGERS	AGE	SEX	OCCUPATIONS	DATE PORT SHIP
ROACHE, Margaret	27	F	Unknown	02Ma12Dx
Edward	6	M	Child	02Ma12Dx
Michael	4	M	Child	02Ma12Dx
James	.00	M	Infant	02Ma12Dx
LYNCH, U-Mrs.	35	F	Unknown	02Ma12Dx
Martha	8	F	Child	02Ma12Dx
CARBERRY, Patrick	16	M	Unknown	02Ma12Dx
NUTTY, Mat.	22	M	Unknown	02Ma12Dx
DUNN, Stephen	26	M	Unknown	02Ma12Dx
Rolly	18	M	Unknown	02Ma12Dx
HANELL, James	20	M	Unknown	02Ma12Dx
ROACHE, James	30	M	Unknown	02Ma12Dx
MCNEARY, James	20	M	Unknown	02Ma12Dx
ROACHE. Margaret	20	F	Unknown	02Ma12Dx
HORAN, Winnia	28	F	Unknown	02Ma12Dx
MCKEIMAN, Richard	13	M	Unknown	02Ma12Dx
LANGAN. John	13	M	Unknown	02Ma12Dx
MALINE, U-Mrs.	50	F	Unknown	02Ma12Dx
Michael	35	M	Unknown	02Ma12Dx
Margaret	21	F	Unknown	02Ma12Dx
Ann	24	F	Unknown	02Ma12Dx
SWEENEY, Mary	45	F	Unknown	02Ma12Dx
Eliza	18	F	Unknown	02Ma12Dx
Biddy	13	F	Unknown	02Ma12Dx
CLARKE, Thomas	25	M	Unknown	02Ma12Dx
Bridget	24	F	Unknown	02Ma12Dx
Mary	20	F	Unknown	02Ma12Dx
Ann	18	F	Unknown	02Ma12Dx
Nora	11	F	Unknown	02Ma12Dx
JAMES, Pat	20	M	Unknown	02Ma12Dx
CONNOR, John	20	M	Unknown	02Ma12Dx
CALL, Denis	27	M	Unknown	02Ma12Dx
GAFFREY, Margaret	20	F	Unknown	02Ma12Dx
JAMES. John	30	M	Unknown	02Ma12Dx
Thomas	12	M	Unknown	02Ma12Dx
SHANLEY, William	27	M	Unknown	02Ma12Dx
JOHNSON. Richard	45	M	Unknown	02Ma12Dx
U-Mrs.	40	F	Unknown	02Ma12Dx
JOHNSEN. John	21	M	Unknown	02Ma12Dx
Robert	21	M	Unknown	02Ma12Dx
Mary-Ann	19	F	Unknown	02Ma12Dx
Sarah	17	F	Unknown	02Ma12Dx
Margaret	15	F	Unknown	02Ma12Dx
Kate	12	F	Unknown	02Ma12Dx
PURCELL, Edward	25	M	Unknown	02Ma12Dx
U-Mrs.	25	F	Unknown	02Ma12Dx
REVELL, James	46	M	Unknown	02Ma12Dx
U-Mrs.	41	F	Unknown	02Ma12Dx
John	17	M	Unknown	02Ma12Dx
James	16	M	Unknown	02Ma12Dx
Anna	14	F	Unknown	02Ma12Dx
Sidney	13	M	Unknown	02Ma12Dx
Marcella	11	F	Unknown	02Ma12Dx
Martha	12	F	Unknown	02Ma12Dx
William	7	M	Child	02Ma12Dx
Joseph	6	M	Child	02Ma12Dx
Thomas	3	M	Child	02Ma12Dx
Nathaniel	.00	M	Infant	02Ma12Dx
TOMLINSON. U-Miss	24	F	Unknown	02Ma12Dx
MALEVEY, John	25	M	Unknown	02Ma12Dx
Died-At-Sea				
Rosey	30	F	Unknown	02Ma12Dx
Died-At-Sea				
KENNEDY, Ann	30	F	Unknown	02Ma12Dx
Died-At-Sea				
Maria	.00	F	Infant	02Ma12Dx
Died-At-Sea				
BYRNE, U-Mrs.	40	F	Unknown	02Ma12Dx
Died-At-Sea				
Owen	7	M	Child	02Ma12Dx
Died-At-Sea				
Lawrence	.00	M	Infant	02Ma12Dx
Died-At-Sea				
BUNN. William	4	M	Child	02Ma12Dx
Died-At-Sea				

NAMES OF PASSENGERS	AGE	SEX	OCCUPATIONS	DATE PORT SHIP
BUNN. James	.00	M	Infant	02Ma12Dx
Died-At-Sea				
MCINTYN, Patrick	25	M	Unknown	02Ma12Dx
Died-At-Sea				
MCMANUS. Mary	19	F	Unknown	02Ma12Dx
Died-At-Sea				
Bridget	17	F	Unknown	02Ma12Dx
Died-At-Sea				
ROACHE, Patrick	.00	M	Infant	02Ma12Dx
Died-At-Sea				
KEYS, John	55	M	Unknown	02Ma12Dx
Died-At-Sea				
William	.00	M	Infant	02Ma12Dx
Died-At-Sea				
Michael	9	M	Child	02Ma12Dx
Died-At-Sea				
PHELIN, Thos.	27	M	Unknown	02Ma12Dx
Mary-Ann	13	F	Unknown	02Ma12Dx
CHRISTIE, Nicholas	25	M	Unknown	02Ma12Dx
Elizabeth	25	F	Unknown	02Ma12Dx
MCGEE, Cath.	30	F	Unknown	02Ma12Dx
CHRISTIE, Humas	.00	M	Infant	02Ma12Dx
CASEY, William	40	M	Unknown	02Ma12Dx
U-Mrs.	35	F	Unknown	02Ma12Dx
Peter	15	M	Unknown	02Ma12Dx
Ann	13	F	Unknown	02Ma12Dx
Margaret	10	F	Unknown	02Ma12Dx
Edward	7	M	Child	02Ma12Dx
Sarah	.00	F	Infant	02Ma12Dx
MCDERMOTT, Bernard	40	M	Unknown	02Ma12Dx
Mary	20	F	Unknown	02Ma12Dx
Margaret	18	F	Unknown	02Ma12Dx
DARCY, Denis	24	M	Unknown	02Ma12Dx
ONEILL, James	35	M	Unknown	02Ma12Dx
OCONNOR, U-Miss	20	F	Unknown	02Ma12Dx
Mary-Ann	18	F	Unknown	02Ma12Dx
Margaret	16	F	Unknown	02Ma12Dx
MCCULLOUGH, U-Miss	25	F	Unknown	02Ma12Dx
WOODMAN, Wm.	24	M	Unknown	02Ma12Dx
U-Mrs.	20	F	Unknown	02Ma12Dx
Bessy	.00	F	Infant	02Ma12Dx
WILLIAMS, Hannah	20	F	Unknown	02Ma12Dx
William	40	M	Unknown	02Ma12Dx
Alice	33	M	Unknown	02Ma12Dx
KELLY, Mary-A.	30	F	Unknown	02Ma12Dx
DEMPSEY, Biddy	20	F	Unknown	02Ma12Dx
WHELAN, Mary	18	F	Unknown	02Ma12Dx
SCULLY, James	21	M	Unknown	02Ma12Dx
Peter	25	M	Unknown	02Ma12Dx
Ann	19	F	Unknown	02Ma12Dx
Eliza	21	F	Unknown	02Ma12Dx
FURLONG, Patrick	16	M	Unknown	02Ma12Dx
DONNOLLY, Mary-J.	18	F	Unknown	02Ma12Dx
John-P.	.00	M	Infant	02Ma12Dx
BRABSEN, Wm.	43	M	Unknown	02Ma12Dx
U-Mrs.	43	F	Unknown	02Ma12Dx
Alicia	33	F	Unknown	02Ma12Dx
George	10	M	Unknown	02Ma12Dx
RULEDGE. R.O.	40	M	Unknown	02Ma12D
U-Mrs.	35	F	Unknown	02Ma12D
RIERMAN, S.N.	17	F	Unknown	02Ma12D
SEATON, Robt.	45	M	Unknown	02Ma12D
HOSKINS, C.	22	M	Unknown	02Ma12D
CAWELL, C.R.	28	M	Unknown	02Ma12D
ALTON, W.D.	23	M	Unknown	02Ma12D
LEON. John-M.	40	M	Unknown	02Ma12D
RIERNAN, U	16	F	Unknown	02Ma12D
SHEARN. R.	15	M	Unknown	02Ma12D

WM.MILES 03 MAY 1849

From Cork

NAMES OF PASSENGERS	AGE	SEX	OCCUPATIONS	DATE PORT SHIP
PENNY, John	20	M	Laborer	03Ma08Dy
KEATING, John	20	M	Laborer	03Ma08Dy
POWERS. Jeremiah	28	M	Laborer	03Ma08Dy
COLEMAN. John	23	M	Laborer	03Ma08Dy
LYNCH. Humphrey	40	M	Laborer	03Ma08Dy
FINN. Patrick	22	M	Laborer	03Ma08Dy
Johanna	20	F	Unknown	03Ma08Dy
MURPHY, Edward	25	M	Laborer	03Ma08Dy
Eliza	25	F	Spinster	03Ma08Dy
MALONEY, Thos.	25	M	Laborer	03Ma08Dy
COFF, Michl.	24	M	Laborer	03Ma08Dy
John	24	M	Laborer	03Ma08Dy
CONWAY, James	22	M	Laborer	03Ma08Dy
COLLINS. Jeremiah	32	M	Laborer	03Ma08Dy
John	26	M	Farmer	03Ma08Dy
Norry	26	M	Farmer	03Ma08Dy
MCCARTHY, Mary	30	F	Servant	03Ma08Dy
GEARY, Edmond	30	M	Laborer	03Ma08Dy
KEARNEY, Bridget	25	F	Unknown	03Ma08Dy
Jno.	30	M	Laborer	03Ma08Dy
Pat	18	M	Laborer	03Ma08Dy
COTTER. Wm.	18	M	Laborer	03Ma08Dy
ARUNDEL, Patrick	22	M	Laborer	03Ma08Dy
DUGGAN. Timothy	46	M	Carpenter	03Ma08Dy
Cath.	40	F	Unknown	03Ma08Dy
Ellen	17	F	Servant	03Ma08Dy
Patrick	15	M	Laborer	03Ma08Dy
Dennis	13	M	Laborer	03Ma08Dy
Catherine	12	F	Unknown	03Ma08Dy
Mary	10	F	Unknown	03Ma08Dy
Johanna	8	F	Child	03Ma08Dy
John	6	M	Child	03Ma08Dy
Margt.	4	F	Child	03Ma08Dy
RING, Joseph	46	M	Laborer	03Ma08Dy
Dorah	40	F	Unknown	03Ma08Dy
Richard	20	M	Unknown	03Ma08Dy
SWEENEY, James	16	M	Unknown	03Ma08Dy
QUINN, Tully	20	M	Unknown	03Ma08Dy
COFFEY, James	20	M	Unknown	03Ma08Dy
Mary	40	F	Unknown	03Ma08Dy
GRIFFIN, Patrick	35	M	Unknown	03Ma08Dy
LEHANE, Abby	20	F	Unknown	03Ma08Dy
BARRY, Eliza	25	F	Unknown	03Ma08Dy
MCAULIFF, Con	28	M	Laborer	03Ma08Dy
Cath.	32	F	Unknown	03Ma08Dy
Cath.	3	F	Child	03Ma08Dy
Mary	1	F	Child	03Ma08Dy
Patrick	.00	M	Infant	03Ma08Dy
DONOVAN, Julia	50	F	Unknown	03Ma08Dy
Patrick	25	M	Laborer	03Ma08Dy
Bridget	18	F	Unknown	03Ma08Dy
Julia	14	F	Unknown	03Ma08Dy
DOWNEY, Thos.	23	M	Laborer	03Ma08Dy
Johanna	18	F	Unknown	03Ma08Dy
MCSWENY, James	30	M	Laborer	03Ma08Dy
Ann	30	F	Unknown	03Ma08Dy
HEALEY, James	25	M	Laborer	03Ma08Dy
GAGGIN. Margt.	40	F	Unknown	03Ma08Dy
Nelly	30	F	Unknown	03Ma08Dy
CONDON. John	40	M	Laborer	03Ma08Dy
BAILEY, Sarah	25	F	Unknown	03Ma08Dy
Eliza	.00	F	Infant	03Ma08Dy
BURNS. Patrick	50	M	Laborer	03Ma08Dy
Johanna	36	F	Unknown	03Ma08Dy
Michl.	21	M	Laborer	03Ma08Dy

NAMES OF PASSENGERS	AGE	SEX	OCCUPATIONS	DATE PORT SHIP
BURNS, Bridget	20	F	Unknown	03Ma08Dy
Peter	12	M	Laborer	03Ma08Dy
Ellen	10	F	Unknown	03Ma08Dy
SWEENEY, Nelly	26	F	Spinster	03Ma08Dy
Mary	6	F	Child	03Ma08Dy
OGRADY, John-L.	29	M	Farmer	03Ma08Dy
Mary	26	F	Unknown	03Ma08Dy
Anne	7	F	Child	03Ma08Dy
Mary	5	F	Child	03Ma08Dy
LOCHLIN, James	30	M	Farmer	03Ma08Dy
Mary	28	F	Unknown	03Ma08Dy
Cath.	16	F	Farmer	03Ma08Dy
MILLER, Mary-Anne	23	F	Servant	03Ma08Dy
KELCHER, Wm.	20	M	Farmer	03Ma08Dy
HAGERTY, Ellen	40	F	Unknown	03Ma08Dy
FITZGERALD, Mathew	19	M	Farmer	03Ma08Dy
HENNESSY, Mary	19	F	Unknown	03Ma08Dy
Ellen	14	F	Unknown	03Ma08Dy
GRIFFIN, Ellen	40	F	Unknown	03Ma08Dy
COLLINS. Mary-Anne	20	F	Unknown	03Ma08Dy
BARRETT, Ellen	16	F	Unknown	03Ma08Dy
FINN, Wm.	3	M	Child	03Ma08Dy
Thos.	7	M	Child	03Ma08Dy
SHEA, Bat	23	M	Laborer	03Ma08Dy
DRISCOL, John	25	M	Laborer	03Ma08Dy
RICHARDSON. Frank	24	M	Laborer	03Ma08Dy
James	23	M	Laborer	03Ma08Dy
COLLINS. John	21	M	Laborer	03Ma08Dy
LOONEY, Edward	16	M	Laborer	03Ma08Dy
OREILLY, Maurice	20	M	Laborer	03Ma08Dy
OSULLIVAN, Patrick	20	M	Laborer	03Ma08Dy
Jerry	18	M	Laborer	03Ma08Dy
Danl.	20	M	Laborer	03Ma08Dy
LEHANE, Eliza	18	F	Spinster	03Ma08Dy
LOOTE. John	4	M	Child	03Ma08Dy
DELANEY, Wm.	34	M	Farmer	03Ma08Dy
OLEARY, Charles	19	M	Farmer	03Ma08Dy
Mary	26	F	Unknown	03Ma08Dy
GLEESON. John	25	M	Laborer	03Ma08Dy
MURRAY, Wm.	21	M	Laborer	03Ma08Dy
CAHALANE, James	21	M	Laborer	03Ma08Dy
HALLORAN, Mary	22	F	Spinster	03Ma08Dy
DONOVAN, Ellen	30	F	Spinster	03Ma08Dy
REGAN, Michl.	22	M	Laborer	03Ma08Dy
KESHANE, James	22	M	Laborer	03Ma08Dy
CONNOLLY, John	22	M	Laborer	03Ma08Dy
CROWLY, Lenny	30	M	Laborer	03Ma08Dy
COSTIGAN. Dennis	30	M	Laborer	03Ma08Dy
James	25	M	Laborer	03Ma08Dy
RIORDAN, Johanna	17	F	Unknown	03Ma08Dy
HAYES. Margt.	18	F	Unknown	03Ma08Dy
CONNORS. Owen	26	M	Laborer	03Ma08Dy
DESMOND, John	35	M	Laborer	03Ma08Dy
Margt.	30	F	Unknown	03Ma08Dy
Cornelius	12	M	Unknown	03Ma08Dy
Margt.	10	F	Unknown	03Ma08Dy
CREEN, Mary	17	F	Unknown	03Ma08Dy
NEAMAN, Mary	18	F	Unknown	03Ma08Dy
MADDEN, Johanna	20	F	Unknown	03Ma08Dy
Hannah	18	F	Unknown	03Ma08Dy
ROYCROFT. Thos.	34	M	Laborer	03Ma08Dy
KIRBY, Michl.	25	M	Farmer	03Ma08Dy
MURPHY, Bridget	16	F	Unknown	03Ma08Dy
OLEARY, John	30	M	Farmer	03Ma08Dy
Johanna	22	F	Unknown	03Ma08Dy
ONIEL, Darby	18	M	Farmer	03Ma08Dy
ALDRIDGE. John	14	M	Farmer	03Ma08Dy
RUSSELL, Margt.	30	F	Unknown	03Ma08Dy
REA, Michl.	45	M	Farmer	03Ma08Dy
Margt.	15	F	Unknown	03Ma08Dy
Mary	13	F	Unknown	03Ma08Dy
Mat	12	M	Farmer	03Ma08Dy
Eliza	1	F	Child	03Ma08Dy
LEA, John	40	M	Farmer	03Ma08Dy
Alice	40	F	Unknown	03Ma08Dy

NAMES OF PASSENGERS	AGE	SEX	OCCUPATIONS	DATE PORT SHIP
LEA, Thomas	17	M	Farmer	03Ma08Dy
Ellen	15	F	Unknown	03Ma08Dy
LEE, Bridget	12	F	Unknown	03Ma08Dy
Mary	11	F	Unknown	03Ma08Dy
Wm.	7	M	Child	03Ma08Dy
Patrick	5	M	Child	03Ma08Dy
PEGOT, Richard	25	M	Laborer	03Ma08Dy
MORRISSEY, Mary	20	F	Unknown	03Ma08Dy
CONDON, Patrick	18	M	Farmer	03Ma08Dy
Mary	14	F	Spinster	03Ma08Dy
CROWLEY, Johanna	35	F	Spinster	03Ma08Dy
BOISE, Bessy	20	F	Spinster	03Ma08Dy
FITZGIBBONS. James	5	M	Child	03Ma08Dy
CLEAR. Phoebe	50	F	Spinster	03Ma08Dy
ONEILL, Owen	25	M	Farmer	03Ma08Dy
GRANVILLE. John	20	M	Laborer	03Ma08Dy
James	19	M	Laborer	03Ma08Dy
SUGRUE. James	25	M	Laborer	03Ma08Dy
SHEA, Michael	25	M	Laborer	03Ma08Dy
LEE. Michael	25	M	Laborer	03Ma08Dy
BRENNAN. Michael	30	M	Laborer	03Ma08Dy
CASEY, Ellen	18	F	Spinster	03Ma08Dy
HART. James	45	M	Laborer	03Ma08Dy

WAVE 03 MAY 1849

From Dublin

NAMES OF PASSENGERS	AGE	SEX	OCCUPATIONS	DATE PORT SHIP
HART, John	25	M	Unknown	03Ma12Dz
MCALLESTER, Wm.	22	M	Unknown	03Ma12Dz
CUNNINGHAM, Patt	27	M	Unknown	03Ma12Dz
Mary	25	F	Unknown	03Ma12Dz
Judy	2	F	Child	03Ma12Dz
Catherine	.00	F	Infant	03Ma12Dz
MCDONALD, Michael	24	M	Unknown	03Ma12Dz
GOGARTY, Pat	21	M	Unknown	03Ma12Dz
U.-Mrs.	20	F	Unknown	03Ma12Dz
Casi---, Thomas	18	M	Unknown	03Ma12Dz
GUSSION, Rody	00	M	Unknown	03Ma12Dz
Margt.	50	F	Unknown	03Ma12Dz
Ellen	15	F	Unknown	03Ma12Dz
GULLIN. Langhlin	28	M	Unknown	03Ma12Dz
Ann	26	F	Unknown	03Ma12Dz
John	22	M	Unknown	03Ma12Dz
SHERIDAN, Ann	40	F	Unknown	03Ma12Dz
SHERLOCK, Mary	21	F	Unknown	03Ma12Dz
Ann	19	F	Unknown	03Ma12Dz
GALE. Pat	20	M	Unknown	03Ma12Dz
CORCORAN. C.-Mrs.	36	F	Unknown	03Ma12Dz
Cath	18	F	Unknown	03Ma12Dz
Teresa	16	F	Unknown	03Ma12Dz
Pat	13	M	Unknown	03Ma12Dz
Georgine	9	F	Child	03Ma12Dz
Alexander	5	M	Child	03Ma12Dz
Henry	.00	M	Infant	03Ma12Dz
BRYNE, Pat	45	M	Unknown	03Ma12Dz
U.-Mrs.	40	F	Unknown	03Ma12Dz
John	26	M	Unknown	03Ma12Dz
Thomas	21	M	Unknown	03Ma12Dz
Mary	19	F	Unknown	03Ma12Dz
Fanny	24	F	Unknown	03Ma12Dz
Patrick	4	M	Child	03Ma12Dz
Patrick	.00	M	Infant	03Ma12Dz
REYNOLDS. John	16	M	Unknown	03Ma12Dz
MORAN, Michl.	32	M	Unknown	03Ma12Dz
CLEMENTS, Thos.	28	M	Unknown	03Ma12Dz
BUCKSTONE. Michl.	20	M	Unknown	03Ma12Dz
CARMEN, Michl.	21	M	Unknown	03Ma12Dz
Michl.	40	M	Unknown	03Ma12Dz

NAMES OF PASSENGERS	AGE	SEX	OCCUPATIONS	DATE PORT SHIP
CARMEN, Cath.	40	F	Unknown	03Ma12Dz
Eliza	16	F	Unknown	03Ma12Dz
John	13	M	Unknown	03Ma12Dz
Lawrence	17	M	Unknown	03Ma12Dz
Pat	7	M	Child	03Ma12Dz
Catherine	9	F	Child	03Ma12Dz
Maria	.00	F	Infant	03Ma12Dz
MCDONNELL, William	22	M	Unknown	03Ma12Dz
U.-Mrs.	22	F	Unknown	03Ma12Dz
KELLY, Joseph	55	M	Unknown	03Ma12Dz
Francis	21	M	Unknown	03Ma12Dz
BRADY, Rose	20	F	Unknown	03Ma12Dz
ANDERSON, Sarah	20	F	Unknown	03Ma12Dz
DELAHANE, John	27	M	Unknown	03Ma12Dz
MAHONY, Pat	20	M	Unknown	03Ma12Dz
SMYTH, Rich	35	M	Unknown	03Ma12Dz
MARYING, Lawrence	40	M	Unknown	03Ma12Dz
U.-Mrs.	17	F	Unknown	03Ma12Dz
Martha	19	F	Unknown	03Ma12Dz
DEMPHINE, I.	35	U	Unknown	03Ma12Dz
GRAINGAN, John	16	M	Unknown	03Ma12Dz
Pat	13	M	Unknown	03Ma12Dz
GARIGAN, Thos.	10	M	Unknown	03Ma12Dz
Catherine	8	F	Child	03Ma12Dz
Bridget	.00	F	Infant	03Ma12Dz
BEGG, Joseph	19	M	Unknown	03Ma12Dz
MORRAN, Anne	40	F	Unknown	03Ma12Dz
Bernard	25	M	Unknown	03Ma12Dz
PARKER, Pat	27	M	Unknown	03Ma12Dz
FLYNN, Pat	24	M	Unknown	03Ma12Dz
RYAN, Pat	22	M	Unknown	03Ma12Dz
CULLEN, Pat	30	M	Unknown	03Ma12Dz
CUSLEY, Pat	27	M	Unknown	03Ma12Dz
HART, John	30	M	Unknown	03Ma12Dz
GRICE, Wm.	30	M	Unknown	03Ma12Dz
TOOLE, James	27	M	Unknown	03Ma12Dz
Michl.	20	M	Unknown	03Ma12Dz
CAUSACK, Thos.	24	M	Unknown	03Ma12Dz
SACUSY, Wm.	40	M	Unknown	03Ma12Dz
BROWN, Bessy	22	F	Unknown	03Ma12Dz
Sarah	22	F	Unknown	03Ma12Dz
FITZPATRICK, John	18	M	Unknown	03Ma12Dz
KEANY, William	50	M	Unknown	03Ma12Dz
James	18	M	Unknown	03Ma12Dz
Bridget	15	F	Unknown	03Ma12Dz
Thomas	13	M	Unknown	03Ma12Dz
Pat	11	M	Unknown	03Ma12Dz
Ann	9	F	Child	03Ma12Dz
William	7	M	Child	03Ma12Dz
Mary	.00	F	Infant	03Ma12Dz
QUIGKLEY, James	38	M	Unknown	03Ma12Dz
Margaret	34	F	Unknown	03Ma12Dz
Margaret	13	F	Unknown	03Ma12Dz
Joseph	11	M	Unknown	03Ma12Dz
Ellen	9	F	Child	03Ma12Dz
Charles	7	M	Child	03Ma12Dz
Mary	5	F	Child	03Ma12Dz
James	3	M	Child	03Ma12Dz
Doroty	.00	F	Infant	03Ma12Dz
Michael	19	M	Unknown	03Ma12Dz
DOMCA, Julia	20	F	Unknown	03Ma12Dz
Mary	18	F	Unknown	03Ma12Dz
Mary	16	F	Unknown	03Ma12Dz
BUNNA. Horence	37	M	Unknown	03Ma12Dz
Ann	34	F	Unknown	03Ma12Dz
Mary	6	F	Child	03Ma12Dz
James	.00	M	Infant	03Ma12Dz
GARLAM, Ellen	50	F	Unknown	03Ma12Dz
Mary	24	F	Unknown	03Ma12Dz
Michael	20	M	Unknown	03Ma12Dz
Ellen	18	F	Unknown	03Ma12Dz
Pat	15	M	Unknown	03Ma12Dz
Catherine	11	F	Unknown	03Ma12Dz
Bridget	.00	F	Infant	03Ma12Dz
MAHAN, Julia	56	F	Unknown	03Ma12Dz

NAMES OF PASSENGERS	AGE	SEX	OCCUPATIONS	DATE PORT SHIP
MAHAN, Brennan	27	U	Unknown	03Ma12Dz
Edward	25	M	Unknown	03Ma12Dz
James	23	M	Unknown	03Ma12Dz
Catherine	20	F	Unknown	03Ma12Dz
Julia	18	F	Unknown	03Ma12Dz
Bridget	15	F	Unknown	03Ma12Dz
Ann	13	F	Unknown	03Ma12Dz
GALIN, Pat	34	M	Unknown	03Ma12Dz
Ann	32	F	Unknown	03Ma12Dz
Mary	10	F	Unknown	03Ma12Dz
Bridget	8	F	Child	03Ma12Dz
Ann	.00	F	Infant	03Ma12Dz
GARLAN, Martin	40	M	Unknown	03Ma12Dz
Eliza	39	F	Unknown	03Ma12Dz
Peter	15	M	Unknown	03Ma12Dz
Catherine	.00	F	Infant	03Ma12Dz
FOLEY, William	21	M	Unknown	03Ma12Dz
SMITH, U.-Mr.	20	M	Unknown	03Ma12Dz
U.-Mrs.	20	F	Unknown	03Ma12Dz
LYNCH, Lawrence	13	M	Unknown	03Ma12Dz
ROGERS, Eliza	28	F	Unknown	03Ma12Dz
Jane	30	F	Unknown	03Ma12Dz
DONIGAN, John	21	M	Unknown	03Ma12Dz
FORCH, Thos.	22	M	Unknown	03Ma12Dz
SHEA, John	26	M	Unknown	03Ma12Dz
U.-Mrs.	21	F	Unknown	03Ma12Dz
James	.00	M	Infant	03Ma12Dz
MCCANN, Thos.	21	M	Unknown	03Ma12Dz
DRUME, John	34	M	Unknown	03Ma12Dz
BOYLAN, Edw.	30	M	Unknown	03Ma12Dz
LAWPESS, Michl.	31	M	Unknown	03Ma12Dz
BRADY, U.-Mrs.	28	F	Unknown	03Ma12Dz
Mary	.00	F	Infant	03Ma12Dz
KANE, Mary	21	F	Unknown	03Ma12Dz
GARIGAN, Michl.	40	M	Unknown	03Ma12Dz
Catherine	40	F	Unknown	03Ma12Dz
Philip	.00	M	Infant	03Ma12Dz
ALLEN, Thomas	35	M	Unknown	03Ma12Dz
U.-Mrs.	30	F	Unknown	03Ma12Dz
Anne	13	F	Unknown	03Ma12Dz
John	10	M	Child	03Ma12Dz
Robert	8	M	Child	03Ma12Dz
Peter	6	M	Child	03Ma12Dz
William	.00	M	Infant	03Ma12Dz
BARNEY, Daniel	25	M	Unknown	03Ma12Dz
U.-Mrs.	25	F	Unknown	03Ma12Dz
Daniel	3	M	Child	03Ma12Dz
Mary	.00	F	Infant	03Ma12Dz
WHELAN, Michl.	27	M	Unknown	03Ma12Dz
John	5	M	Child	03Ma12Dz
MASON, U.-Mr.	40	M	Unknown	03Ma12Dz
DUFFEY, James	21	M	Unknown	03Ma12Dz
RIDEN, U.-Mrs.	25	F	Unknown	03Ma12Dz
BRYNE, U.-Miss	20	F	Unknown	03Ma12Dz
WIAFSOME, Ann	20	F	Unknown	03Ma12Dz
NOLAN, U.-Mrs.	40	F	Unknown	03Ma12Dz
Teresa	17	F	Unknown	03Ma12Dz
Anna	15	F	Unknown	03Ma12Dz
Patrick	13	M	Unknown	03Ma12Dz
Peter	10	M	Unknown	03Ma12Dz
Alice	12	F	Unknown	03Ma12Dz
John	8	M	Child	03Ma12Dz
Michl.	4	M	Child	03Ma12Dz
Richard	.00	M	Infant	03Ma12Dz
MULLEN, Morris	27	M	Unknown	03Ma12Dz
LOWLOR, Michl.	21	M	Unknown	03Ma12Dz
YATES, Benjamin	21	M	Unknown	03Ma12Dz
HOGAN, John	30	M	Unknown	03Ma12Dz
HILMURRAY, John	20	M	Unknown	03Ma12Dz
DOYLE, Michl.	25	M	Unknown	03Ma12Dz
Margaret	23	F	Unknown	03Ma12Dz
John	3	M	Child	03Ma12Dz
MARTIN, Mary	20	F	Unknown	03Ma12Dz
Peter	.00	M	Infant	03Ma12Dz
KENNEY, John	21	M	Unknown	03Ma12Dz
KENNEY, Mary	25	F	Unknown	03Ma12Dz
TURNER, James	30	M	Unknown	03Ma12Dz
DOYLE, Joseph	00	M	Unknown	03Ma12Dz
RYAN, Mary	45	F	Unknown	03Ma12Dz
Mary	.00	F	Infant	03Ma12Dz
Lawrence	17	M	Unknown	03Ma12Dz
John	16	M	Unknown	03Ma12Dz
Margaret	11	F	Unknown	03Ma12Dz
Margaret	50	F	Unknown	03Ma12Dz
Henry	.00	M	Infant	03Ma12Dz
LAWLOR, Eliza	21	F	Unknown	03Ma12Dz
WILLIAMS, Wm.	30	M	Unknown	03Ma12Dz
U.-Mrs.	28	F	Unknown	03Ma12Dz
GARLAN, Margaret	13	F	Unknown	03Ma12Dz
Julia	11	F	Unknown	03Ma12Dz
Bridget	9	F	Child	03Ma12Dz
DONEAU, Ann	32	F	Unknown	03Ma12Dz
Ann	6	F	Child	03Ma12Dz
Marty	3	U	Child	03Ma12Dz
MOLLOY, Lawrence	32	M	Unknown	03Ma12Dz
Ann	30	F	Unknown	03Ma12Dz
Rose	9	F	Child	03Ma12Dz
Margaret	7	F	Child	03Ma12Dz
Pat	4	M	Child	03Ma12Dz
Julia	.00	F	Infant	03Ma12Dz
DARBY, Margaret	38	F	Unknown	03Ma12Dz
Hanna	36	F	Unknown	03Ma12Dz
Pat	12	M	Unknown	03Ma12Dz
John	8	M	Child	03Ma12Dz
Thomas	5	M	Child	03Ma12Dz
Mary	3	F	Child	03Ma12Dz
Ann	.00	F	Infant	03Ma12Dz

JOHN-R.SKIDDY 03 MAY 1849

From Liverpool

NAMES OF PASSENGERS	AGE	SEX	OCCUPATIONS	DATE PORT SHIP
GAYNOR, John-P.	23	M	Gentleman	03Ma02Ei
MOORE, James	30	M	Grocer	03Ma02Ei
BATTELLE, Michael-M.	31	M	Cmgent	03Ma02Ei
QUINLIVAN, Maria	23	F	Unknown	03Ma02Ei
Ellen	21	F	Unknown	03Ma02Ei
QUINLAN, James	24	M	Clerk	03Ma02Ei
Barbara	19	F	Unknown	03Ma02Ei
OHALLAN, John	19	M	Clerk	03Ma02Ei
BERRILE, John-H.	30	M	Mmrnr	03Ma02Ei
MCMILLAN, William-H.	19	M	Clerk	03Ma02Ei
MCNEIL, John	19	M	Clerk	03Ma02Ei
DEVINE, David	26	M	Dealer	03Ma02Ei
CLANCY, Cornelius	64	M	Farmer	03Ma02Ei
William	33	M	Farmer	03Ma02Ei
Daniel	23	M	Farmer	03Ma02Ei
Michael	21	M	Farmer	03Ma02Ei
Dennis	18	M	Farmer	03Ma02Ei
Matthew	16	M	Farmer	03Ma02Ei
Mark	10	M	Farmer	03Ma02Ei
Catherine	54	F	Unknown	03Ma02Ei
Ann	26	F	Unknown	03Ma02Ei
Mary	22	F	Unknown	03Ma02Ei
Eliza	14	F	Unknown	03Ma02Ei
MCGRATH, Catherine	20	F	Unknown	03Ma02Ei
DUGGAN, Peter	26	M	Farmer	03Ma02Ei
Margaret (W)	26	F	Unknown	03Ma02Ei
OLDREN, Mary-Ann	22	F	Unknown	03Ma02Ei
Alice	2	F	Child	03Ma02Ei
William	1	M	Child	03Ma02Ei
CLANAGAN, Stephen	23	M	Farmer	03Ma02Ei
Bridget	18	F	Unknown	03Ma02Ei
Kate	16	F	Unknown	03Ma02Ei

NAMES OF PASSENGERS		AGE	SEX	OCCUPATIONS	DATE PORT SHIP
DORAN, Peter		11	M	Farmer	03Ma02Ei
MCCANNE, Lawrence		21	M	Farmer	03Ma02Ei
Edward		23	M	Farmer	03Ma02Ei
MALONEY, Michael		24	M	Farmer	03Ma02Ei
Ann		27	F	Unknown	03Ma02Ei
BARRETT, Edward		48	M	Farmer	03Ma02Ei
Mary	(W)	47	F	Unknown	03Ma02Ei
Johannah		16	F	Unknown	03Ma02Ei
Patrick		12	M	Unknown	03Ma02Ei
John		6	M	Child	03Ma02Ei
Edward		4	M	Child	03Ma02Ei
HOGAN, John		30	M	Farmer	03Ma02Ei
Ellen	(W)	30	F	Unknown	03Ma02Ei
Patrick		12	M	Unknown	03Ma02Ei
Margaret		10	F	Unknown	03Ma02Ei
Ellen		8	F	Child	03Ma02Ei
Daniel		2	M	Child	03Ma02Ei
John		.00	M	Infant	03Ma02Ei
GUBBINS, Joseph		30	M	Farmer	03Ma02Ei
Johannah	(W)	30	F	Unknown	03Ma02Ei
Joseph		11	M	Unknown	03Ma02Ei
William		9	M	Child	03Ma02Ei
Honora		6	F	Child	03Ma02Ei
Maria		4	F	Child	03Ma02Ei
Robert		3	M	Child	03Ma02Ei
Eliza		1	F	Child	03Ma02Ei
Washington		.00	M	Infant	03Ma02Ei
CONNERY, Honora		20	F	Servant	03Ma02Ei
PRENDERGAST, Patrick		32	M	Farmer	03Ma02Ei
Allice	(W)	30	F	Unknown	03Ma02Ei
Ellen		3	F	Child	03Ma02Ei
Mary		.00	F	Infant	03Ma02Ei
HEFFERNAN, Thomas		38	M	Laborer	03Ma02Ei
AHERN, Cornelius		38	M	Laborer	03Ma02Ei
QUINN, James		23	M	Laborer	03Ma02Ei
Allice		25	F	Unknown	03Ma02Ei
FEORE, John		24	M	Shoemaker	03Ma02Ei
KENNA, Mrgaret		17	F	Unknown	03Ma02Ei
Ellen		20	F	Unknown	03Ma02Ei
MCGRATH, Michael		25	M	Laborer	03Ma02Ei
MANE, Johannah		20	F	Unknown	03Ma02Ei
ODONNEL, John		36	M	Laborer	03Ma02Ei
CLAHAN, Timothy		25	M	Laborer	03Ma02Ei
CARROL, John		25	M	Laborer	03Ma02Ei
HOGAN, Maurice		24	M	Laborer	03Ma02Ei
CASSIDY, William		22	M	Printer	03Ma02Ei
Charles		16	M	Printer	03Ma02Ei
KING, James		30	M	Laborer	03Ma02Ei
BARRY, Robert		23	M	Shoemaker	03Ma02Ei
RYAN, Matthew		25	M	Carpenter	03Ma02Ei
MANEY, George		35	M	Laborer	03Ma02Ei
LYNCH, John		40	M	Laborer	03Ma02Ei
BENNET, Bryan		30	M	Laborer	03Ma02Ei
EGLESON, Robert		40	M	Laborer	03Ma02Ei
LYNCH, Mary		20	F	Unknown	03Ma02Ei
EGLESON, Mary		30	F	Unknown	03Ma02Ei
RYAN, Bridget		28	F	Unknown	03Ma02Ei
DUNN, Joseph		40	M	Laborer	03Ma02Ei
Mary	(W)	25	F	Unknown	03Ma02Ei
Catherine		18	F	Unknown	03Ma02Ei
John		20	M	Laborer	03Ma02Ei
WOOD, Bridget		26	F	Unknown	03Ma02Ei
Rose		24	F	Unknown	03Ma02Ei
HUGHES, Catherine		25	F	Unknown	03Ma02Ei
COLTON, Bridget		20	F	Unknown	03Ma02Ei
TRAINER, Ellen		25	F	Unknown	03Ma02Ei
CASEY, James		25	M	Laborer	03Ma02Ei
DUFFY, Patrick		30	M	Laborer	03Ma02Ei
HUGHES, Patrick		24	M	Laborer	03Ma02Ei
JACKSON, William		25	M	Laborer	03Ma02Ei
MCCULLUM, Michael		21	M	Laborer	03Ma02Ei
Catherine	(W)	20	F	Unknown	03Ma02Ei
Margaret		1	F	Child	03Ma02Ei
CONROY, John		21	M	Laborer	03Ma02Ei
Patrick		20	M	Laborer	03Ma02Ei
LAMB, Thomas		50	M	Laborer	03Ma02Ei
CINEY, John		35	M	Laborer	03Ma02Ei
MAHONEY, Margaret		26	F	Unknown	03Ma02Ei
Mary		26	F	Unknown	03Ma02Ei
Catherine		14	F	Unknown	03Ma02Ei
RAIDERN, Thomas		22	M	Brf	03Ma02Ei
LYNCH, Thomas		22	M	Brf	03Ma02Ei
MAHONEY, Darby		60	M	Farmer	03Ma02Ei
Darby		7	M	Child	03Ma02Ei
SULLIVAN, Margaret		43	F	Unknown	03Ma02Ei
John		14	M	Unknown	03Ma02Ei
Margaret		7	F	Child	03Ma02Ei
DORAN, Mortimer		35	M	Laborer	03Ma02Ei
HONOHAN, James		22	M	Laborer	03Ma02Ei
Loughlan		26	M	Laborer	03Ma02Ei
Bridget	(W)	22	F	Unknown	03Ma02Ei
John	(W)	.00	M	Infant	03Ma02Ei
SHAW, John		20	M	Shoemaker	03Ma02Ei
WHITE, Hugh		24	M	Shoemaker	03Ma02Ei
CRAWFORD, Andrew		19	M	Farmer	03Ma02Ei
MURPHY, James		22	M	Farmer	03Ma02Ei
MARSHAL, John		25	M	Farmer	03Ma02Ei
RYAN, Peter		24	M	Tailor	03Ma02Ei
Kate		28	F	Unknown	03Ma02Ei
CARROL, Mary		16	F	Unknown	03Ma02Ei
KENNEDY, Bridget		18	F	Unknown	03Ma02Ei
DOWNS, Patrick		5	M	Child	03Ma02Ei
DOLAN, Miles		28	M	Stctr	03Ma02Ei
Bridget	(W)	19	F	Unknown	03Ma02Ei
WALSH, John		23	M	Laborer	03Ma02Ei
KELLY, John		28	M	Laborer	03Ma02Ei
HIGGINS, Maurice		28	M	Laborer	03Ma02Ei
MULLALLY, James		28	M	Laborer	03Ma02Ei
REEKILL, Bernard		36	M	Laborer	03Ma02Ei
DOHERTY, Mary		26	F	Unknown	03Ma02Ei
BOYLAN, Elizabeth		20	F	Unknown	03Ma02Ei
DONLAN, Bridget		28	F	Unknown	03Ma02Ei
KELLY, Bridget		26	F	Unknown	03Ma02Ei
ROE, Thomas		20	M	Clerk	03Ma02Ei
CROFT, Margaret		20	F	Laborer	03Ma02Ei
Martha		.00	F	Infant	03Ma02Ei
MCGRATH, Michael		28	M	Laborer	03Ma02Ei
MAURAN, Lawrence		28	M	Laborer	03Ma02Ei
HEALY, John		20	M	Laborer	03Ma02Ei
CARROL, John		12	M	Laborer	03Ma02Ei
FANNON, Thomas		26	M	Laborer	03Ma02Ei
Mary		20	F	Laborer	03Ma02Ei
JOHNSON, Patrick		20	M	Laborer	03Ma02Ei
Luke		18	M	Laborer	03Ma02Ei
KELLY, James		26	M	Clerk	03Ma02Ei
CARROL, Christopher		30	M	Laborer	03Ma02Ei
Catherine	(W)	50	F	Unknown	03Ma02Ei
KEERNAN, James		55	M	Laborer	03Ma02Ei
Elizabeth		52	F	Laborer	03Ma02Ei
DALE, Allice		18	F	Servant	03Ma02Ei
KEERNAN, Margaret		13	F	Servant	03Ma02Ei
DENNELLY, Mary		13	F	Servant	03Ma02Ei
REILLY, Catherine		20	F	Servant	03Ma02Ei
Rose		17	F	Servant	03Ma02Ei
REGAN, Mary		18	F	Servant	03Ma02Ei
MURRAY, Henry		63	M	Teacher	03Ma02Ei
MCDOUGAL, Patrick		24	M	Blacksmith	03Ma02Ei
SEALY, William		24	M	Laborer	03Ma02Ei
CARROL, John		32	M	Farmer	03Ma02Ei
MARTIN, James		25	M	Farmer	03Ma02Ei
COFFEE, Daniel		24	M	Farmer	03Ma02Ei
TREACY, William		18	M	Shoemaker	03Ma02Ei
MOORHOAN, John		13	M	Laborer	03Ma02Ei
TRAHER, Johannah		25	F	Servant	03Ma02Ei
Catherine		23	F	Servant	03Ma02Ei
COAKEY, Caleb		54	M	Wheelwright	03Ma02Ei
William		23	M	Wheelwright	03Ma02Ei
DEA, Thomas		24	M	Laborer	03Ma02Ei
TIERNEY, Matthew		36	M	Farmer	03Ma02Ei
MOGLAN, Catherine		20	F	Servant	03Ma02E

NAMES OF PASSENGERS	AGE	SEX	OCCUPATIONS	DATE PORT SHIP
RICE, Margaret	18	F	Servant	03Ma02Ei
BYRNE, Mary	26	F	Servant	03Ma02Ei
DOYLE, Margaret	27	F	Servant	03Ma02Ei
RAFTER, John	30	M	Laborer	03Ma02Ei
GARDNER, Ann	73	F	Unknown	03Ma02Ei
OBRIEN, Michael	50	M	Laborer	03Ma02Ei
Margaret (W)	44	F	Unknown	03Ma02Ei
Catherine	12	F	Unknown	03Ma02Ei
Bridget	22	F	Unknown	03Ma02Ei
Thomas	25	M	Laborer	03Ma02Ei
Mary	23	F	Unknown	03Ma02Ei
Ally	20	M	Laborer	03Ma02Ei
John	14	M	Laborer	03Ma02Ei
CLANCY, William	40	M	Farmer	03Ma02Ei
Mary (W)	40	F	Unknown	03Ma02Ei
Margaret	4	F	Child	03Ma02Ei
John	12	M	Unknown	03Ma02Ei
William	10	M	Unknown	03Ma02Ei
Johannah	8	F	Child	03Ma02Ei
COX, John	24	M	Laborer	03Ma02Ei
TALOR, Mary	20	F	Unknown	03Ma02Ei
CONNOR, Patrick	20	M	Laborer	03Ma02Ei
SMITH, Bernard	21	M	Laborer	03Ma02Ei
Ann	20	F	Unknown	03Ma02Ei
TRIMMER, Henry	26	M	Tailor	03Ma02Ei
KERRY, Patrick	25	M	Laborer	03Ma02Ei
GLISMAN, Jane	22	F	Servant	03Ma02Ei
Maria	21	F	Servant	03Ma02Ei
DOYLE, Thomas	30	F	Servant	03Ma02Ei
CONNEL, Miles	25	M	Carpenter	03Ma02Ei
CASHIN, Michael	22	M	Laborer	03Ma02Ei
COSGRAVE, Mary	23	F	Servant	03Ma02Ei
HINDES, Mary-Jane	22	F	Dressmaker	03Ma02Ei
ENGLISH, Sarah	20	F	Dressmaker	03Ma02Ei
KELLY, Bridget	15	F	Dressmaker	03Ma02Ei
TEANOR, Ann	20	F	Dressmaker	03Ma02Ei
FINNEGAN, Bernard	26	M	Laborer	03Ma02Ei
MCCABE, Terrence	26	M	Laborer	03Ma02Ei
FINNIGAN, Mary	20	F	Servant	03Ma02Ei
SHERIDAN, Mary	16	F	Servant	03Ma02Ei
RICE, Robert-W.	26	M	Clerk	03Ma02Ei
HILL, Margaret	36	F	Servant	03Ma02Ei
Ann	15	F	Servant	03Ma02Ei
MITCHEL, Catherine	44	F	Dressmaker	03Ma02Ei
Mary	17	F	Dressmaker	03Ma02Ei

C.MCLAUGHLIN 03 MAY 1849

From Dublin

NAMES OF PASSENGERS	AGE	SEX	OCCUPATIONS	DATE PORT SHIP
WALSH, Thomas	50	M	Laborer	03Ma12Ef
U-Mrs.	40	F	Unknown	03Ma12Ef
Mary	14	F	Unknown	03Ma12Ef
Ellen	13	F	Unknown	03Ma12Ef
Jona	10	M	Unknown	03Ma12Ef
Honor	8	F	Child	03Ma12Ef
Pat	6	M	Child	03Ma12Ef
Francis	4	M	Child	03Ma12Ef
Anthony	3	M	Child	03Ma12Ef
U	.09	U	Infant	03Ma12Ef
PRUSEN, U-Mr.	53	M	Laborer	03Ma12Ef
U-Mrs.	42	F	Unknown	03Ma12Ef
Edward	14	M	Unknown	03Ma12Ef
Frances-Ann	15	F	Unknown	03Ma12Ef
John	11	M	Unknown	03Ma12Ef
Henry-J.	7	M	Child	03Ma12Ef
MAHON, Mary	32	F	Unknown	03Ma12Ef
DARCY, Michael	40	M	Laborer	03Ma12Ef
Mary	35	F	Laborer	03Ma12Ef
DARCY, Frances	7	F	Child	03Ma12Ef
HENRY, William	39	M	Laborer	03Ma12Ef
Ann	32	F	Unknown	03Ma12Ef
Mary-Ann	6	F	Child	03Ma12Ef
John	.01	M	Infant	03Ma12Ef
LYNCH, Mary	26	F	Unknown	03Ma12Ef
HORY, Ellen	7	F	Child	03Ma12Ef
YOUNG, Mary-Ann	21	F	Unknown	03Ma12Ef
Jane	17	F	Unknown	03Ma12Ef
John	13	M	Unknown	03Ma12Ef
DUNN, Theresa	3	F	Child	03Ma12Ef
U	.11	U	Infant	03Ma12Ef
BAGGOTT, James	17	M	Laborer	03Ma12Ef
AGAN, Peter	45	M	Laborer	03Ma12Ef
DOOLAN, Pat	35	M	Laborer	03Ma12Ef
DOOLEY, Ellen	20	F	Unknown	03Ma12Ef
SHERLOCK, Ann	25	F	Unknown	03Ma12Ef
LEECH, Adam	40	M	Laborer	03Ma12Ef
Cath.	40	F	Unknown	03Ma12Ef
KIRBY, Mary	20	F	Unknown	03Ma12Ef
LEECH, Oliver	20	M	Laborer	03Ma12Ef
Francis	18	M	Laborer	03Ma12Ef
Eliza	19	F	Unknown	03Ma12Ef
John	7	M	Child	03Ma12Ef
U	.09	U	Infant	03Ma12Ef
DONOHUE, Thomas	30	M	Laborer	03Ma12Ef
FASTEEN, Mary	35	F	Unknown	03Ma12Ef
GUIGAN, Thomas	30	M	Laborer	03Ma12Ef
BOYLE, Pat	28	M	Laborer	03Ma12Ef
KENEDY, James	25	M	Laborer	03Ma12Ef
Dennis	21	M	Laborer	03Ma12Ef
Bridget	20	F	Unknown	03Ma12Ef
Edward	17	M	Laborer	03Ma12Ef
MAHON, Pat	25	M	Laborer	03Ma12Ef
MURRAY, Michl.	34	M	Laborer	03Ma12Ef
John	12	M	Laborer	03Ma12Ef
CLOONAN, John	35	M	Laborer	03Ma12Ef
BURNS, John	27	M	Laborer	03Ma12Ef
MCANTIFFE, Danl.	40	M	Laborer	03Ma12Ef
Mary	40	F	Unknown	03Ma12Ef
CASTOR, James	40	M	Laborer	03Ma12Ef
Johanna	40	F	Unknown	03Ma12Ef
Pat	12	M	Unknown	03Ma12Ef
John	10	M	Unknown	03Ma12Ef
Pat	8	M	Child	03Ma12Ef
Andrew	5	M	Child	03Ma12Ef
Margt.	.10	F	Infant	03Ma12Ef
DOVAN, William	35	M	Laborer	03Ma12Ef
LOCKLAW, James	30	M	Laborer	03Ma12Ef
TOOLE, James	29	M	Laborer	03Ma12Ef
CLANCEY, Michl.	36	M	Laborer	03Ma12Ef
Peter	21	M	Laborer	03Ma12Ef
TOOLE, James	27	M	Laborer	03Ma12Ef
GRAHAM, Francis	22	M	Laborer	03Ma12Ef
BRENNAN, Pat	35	M	Laborer	03Ma12Ef
RILEY, Pat	20	M	Laborer	03Ma12Ef
Thomas	20	M	Laborer	03Ma12Ef
DUGGAN, Michl.	40	M	Laborer	03Ma12Ef
Edward	30	M	Laborer	03Ma12Ef
ROBINSON, George	50	M	Laborer	03Ma12Ef
DOYLE, John	55	M	Laborer	03Ma12Ef
COOLIGAN, Pat	22	M	Laborer	03Ma12Ef
FORTUNE, Walter	26	M	Laborer	03Ma12Ef
Joshua	24	M	Laborer	03Ma12Ef
MOONEY, Pat	21	M	Laborer	03Ma12Ef
CLARK, Mary	26	F	Unknown	03Ma12Ef
HEALY, Christopher	22	M	Laborer	03Ma12Ef
MORAN, Christopher	30	M	Laborer	03Ma12Ef
RICHARDSON, William	22	M	Laborer	03Ma12Ef
MULLAN, Pat	25	M	Laborer	03Ma12Ef
CARTER, Bridget	6	F	Child	03Ma12Ef
BIDGWOOD, Samuel	22	M	Laborer	03Ma12Ef
Jane	20	F	Unknown	03Ma12Ef
STEPHANSON, Maria	20	F	Unknown	03Ma12Ef
WEST, William	50	M	Laborer	03Ma12Ef

NAMES OF PASSENGERS	AGE	SEX	OCCUPATIONS	DATE PORT SHIP
ELLEN, Mary	20	F	Unknown	03Ma12Ef
FORAN, Lucy	20	F	Unknown	03Ma12Ef
DOOLEY, Ellen	25	F	Unknown	03Ma12Ef
NOWLAN, Dennis	35	M	Laborer	03Ma12Ef
FLYNN, William	22	M	Laborer	03Ma12Ef
RYAN, Bridget	18	F	Unknown	03Ma12Ef
FLYNN, Thomas	35	M	Laborer	03Ma12Ef
WALSH, Pat	35	M	Laborer	03Ma12Ef
Sarah	30	F	Unknown	03Ma12Ef
FARRELL, Michl.	28	M	Laborer	03Ma12Ef
BROWN, William	46	M	Laborer	03Ma12Ef
U	40	M	Laborer	03Ma12Ef
Isabella	18	F	Unknown	03Ma12Ef
Margt.	10	F	Unknown	03Ma12Ef
Flora	7	F	Child	03Ma12Ef
U	.11	U	Infant	03Ma12Ef
DUNN, Darby	50	M	Laborer	03Ma12Ef
Winifred	35	M	Laborer	03Ma12Ef
John	35	M	Laborer	03Ma12Ef
Cath.	40	F	Unknown	03Ma12Ef
Mary	26	F	Unknown	03Ma12Ef
Mary-Ann	7	F	Child	03Ma12Ef
John	5	M	Child	03Ma12Ef
HEARNEY, Thomas	42	M	Laborer	03Ma12Ef

M.MELLON 03 MAY 1849

From Galway

NAMES OF PASSENGERS	AGE	SEX	OCCUPATIONS	DATE PORT SHIP
FLAHERTY, Ellen	20	F	Unknown	03Ma06Ea
LEE, John	30	M	Unknown	03Ma06Ea
KYRE, John	45	M	Unknown	03Ma06Ea
CONWELL, William	35	M	Unknown	03Ma06Ea
Mary	25	F	Unknown	03Ma06Ea
Winey	.00	U	Infant	03Ma06Ea
WALSH, William	30	M	Unknown	03Ma06Ea
CONWELL, James	4	M	Child	03Ma06Ea
HALLORAN, Patt	32	M	Unknown	03Ma06Ea
FORD, Thomas	19	M	Unknown	03Ma06Ea
MURRAY, Retty	24	U	Unknown	03Ma06Ea
FORD, Bridget	25	F	Unknown	03Ma06Ea
COYNE, Kelly	20	U	Unknown	03Ma06Ea
Sarah	22	F	Unknown	03Ma06Ea
MOLLOY, Martin	40	M	Unknown	03Ma06Ea
Mary	20	F	Unknown	03Ma06Ea
Ellen	18	F	Unknown	03Ma06Ea
Honnor	15	F	Unknown	03Ma06Ea
Biddy	12	F	Unknown	03Ma06Ea
Martin	8	M	Unknown	03Ma06Ea
HOWARD, Catherine	23	F	Unknown	03Ma06Ea
Mary	23	F	Unknown	03Ma06Ea
Kate	18	F	Unknown	03Ma06Ea
ROACH, John	26	M	Unknown	03Ma06Ea
Edward	24	M	Unknown	03Ma06Ea
Allice	17	F	Unknown	03Ma06Ea
VAUGHAN, Thomas	24	M	Unknown	03Ma06Ea
Patt	22	M	Unknown	03Ma06Ea
MCNENNY, John	22	M	Unknown	03Ma06Ea
VAUGHAN, Thomas	30	M	Unknown	03Ma06Ea
Bridget	22	F	Unknown	03Ma06Ea
Judy	32	F	Unknown	03Ma06Ea
LOYNS, Patt	32	M	Unknown	03Ma06Ea
READY, John	30	M	Unknown	03Ma06Ea
KELLANY, Martin	25	M	Unknown	03Ma06Ea
WALSH, Michael	20	M	Unknown	03Ma06Ea
Mary	7	F	Child	03Ma06Ea
BOYLE, Teddy	26	U	Unknown	03Ma06Ea
GLESON, Bridget	20	F	Unknown	03Ma06Ea
WALSH, Patt	20	M	Unknown	03Ma06Ea
LOYNS, Mary	28	F	Unknown	03Ma06Ea
LYONS, Patt	.00	M	Infant	03Ma06Ea
HIGGINS, Ellen	35	F	Unknown	03Ma06Ea
John	11	M	Unknown	03Ma06Ea
OBRIAN, John	32	M	Unknown	03Ma06Ea
MAHON, Michael	50	M	Unknown	03Ma06Ea
Ellen	18	F	Unknown	03Ma06Ea
Mary	16	F	Unknown	03Ma06Ea
WALSH, John	30	M	Unknown	03Ma06Ea
Mary	24	F	Unknown	03Ma06Ea
NOON, Patt	27	M	Unknown	03Ma06Ea
LUPHANS, Margt.	22	F	Unknown	03Ma06Ea
FATY, Biddy	22	F	Unknown	03Ma06Ea
FARNLAW, Thomas	18	M	Unknown	03Ma06Ea
CASTILLA, Thomas	21	M	Unknown	03Ma06Ea
Bridget	25	F	Unknown	03Ma06Ea
SHEAHAN, Patt	22	M	Unknown	03Ma06Ea
BURNS, Henry	25	M	Unknown	03Ma06Ea
JENNY, Patt	25	M	Unknown	03Ma06Ea
DONOHAN, Michael	20	M	Unknown	03Ma06Ea
DOOLY, Michael	30	M	Unknown	03Ma06Ea
CLANANG, Patt	25	M	Unknown	03Ma06Ea
MARTIN, Margaret	23	F	Unknown	03Ma06Ea
GLYNN, Jane	35	F	Unknown	03Ma06Ea
John	7	M	Child	03Ma06Ea
Bridget	.00	F	Infant	03Ma06Ea
LUDOW, Ralph	36	M	Unknown	03Ma06Ea
CEVLEHAN, John	20	M	Unknown	03Ma06Ea
COONERLY, Ned	20	M	Unknown	03Ma06Ea
HIGGANS, Michael	22	M	Unknown	03Ma06Ea
LOUGHLAN, Bridget	25	F	Unknown	03Ma06Ea
LYONS, Biddy	50	F	Unknown	03Ma06Ea
FAHY, George	20	M	Unknown	03Ma06Ea
Nancy	22	F	Unknown	03Ma06Ea
GEAGHAN, Mary	23	F	Unknown	03Ma06Ea
COLLINS, Patt	20	M	Unknown	03Ma06Ea
MAUCON, Patt	18	M	Unknown	03Ma06Ea
Margt.	22	F	Unknown	03Ma06Ea
EGAN, Michael	44	M	Unknown	03Ma06Ea
RONAHAN, Michael	19	M	Unknown	03Ma06Ea
BURKE, Michael	22	M	Unknown	03Ma06Ea
DURLY, Catherine	20	F	Unknown	03Ma06Ea
CULLIVAN, John	32	M	Unknown	03Ma06Ea
HYANS, Martha	40	F	Unknown	03Ma06Ea
Biddy	26	F	Unknown	03Ma06Ea
Patt	6	M	Child	03Ma06Ea
William	.00	M	Infant	03Ma06Ea
BRODERICK, Lawrence	18	M	Unknown	03Ma06Ea
ERALS, Mary	16	F	Unknown	03Ma06Ea
DOLLY, Mary	30	F	Unknown	03Ma06Ea
HESSINS, John	24	M	Unknown	03Ma06Ea
MCDONOUGH, Eliza	32	F	Unknown	03Ma06Ea
FAHY, Honora	25	F	Unknown	03Ma06Ea
MCDONOUGH, Patt	15	M	Unknown	03Ma06Ea
Ellen	10	F	Unknown	03Ma06Ea
Margaret	.00	F	Infant	03Ma06Ea
KEVIL, Patt	21	M	Unknown	03Ma06Ea
FLAHERTY, Honora	20	F	Unknown	03Ma06Ea
JENNY, Biddy	30	F	Unknown	03Ma06Ea
Mary	5	F	Child	03Ma06Ea
John	.00	M	Infant	03Ma06Ea
MARTIN, John	25	M	Unknown	03Ma06Ea
Honor	25	F	Unknown	03Ma06Ea
QUICK, Michael	22	M	Unknown	03Ma06Ea
HAWKINS, Laws.	50	M	Unknown	03Ma06Ea
Celia	40	F	Unknown	03Ma06Ea
Thomas	25	M	Unknown	03Ma06Ea
Patt	18	M	Unknown	03Ma06Ea
Michael	12	M	Unknown	03Ma06Ea
WALSH, Neil	20	M	Unknown	03Ma06E
KINNEGAN, Margaret	50	F	Unknown	03Ma06E
GLYNN, Patt	.00	M	Infant	03Ma06E
Margt.	.00	F	Infant	03Ma06E
WHELAN, Patt	50	M	Infant	03Ma06E
RYAN, Mary	30	F	Unknown	03Ma06E

NAMES OF PASSENGERS	AGE	SEX	OCCUPATIONS	DATE PORT SHIP
RYAN, Daniel	24	M	Unknown	03Ma06Ea
LEEDON, Mary	25	F	Unknown	03Ma06Ea
John	30	M	Unknown	03Ma06Ea
KELLY, Cornelius	30	M	Unknown	03Ma06Ea
John	37	M	Unknown	03Ma06Ea
LOBY, Biddy	22	F	Unknown	03Ma06Ea
MULKINS, Bridget	25	F	Unknown	03Ma06Ea
Ellen	23	F	Unknown	03Ma06Ea
LEDON, Mary	28	F	Unknown	03Ma06Ea
Wenny	.00	U	Infant	03Ma06Ea
PEGOT, Henry	30	M	Unknown	03Ma06Ea

AMERICA 03 MAY 1849

From Cork

NAMES OF PASSENGERS	AGE	SEX	OCCUPATIONS	DATE PORT SHIP
MCNAMARA, Bridget	20	F	Laborer	03Ma08Eb
WEBB, William	26	M	Laborer	03Ma08Eb
Rebecca	24	F	Unknown	03Ma08Eb
DESMOND, Margt.	24	F	Laborer	03Ma08Eb
Cath.	3	F	Child	03Ma08Eb
LANE, Michael	24	M	Laborer	03Ma08Eb
BARRY, Ellen	20	F	Unknown	03Ma08Eb
PUMPRN, Ellen	20	F	Unknown	03Ma08Eb
CAVANAGH, Maurice	20	M	Laborer	03Ma08Eb
Mary	20	F	Unknown	03Ma08Eb
LEAHY, Kate	18	F	Unknown	03Ma08Eb
CRONIN, Richard	30	M	Laborer	03Ma08Eb
OHARE, Geo.	26	M	Laborer	03Ma08Eb
MAHONY, Jas.	26	M	Carpenter	03Ma08Eb
BUCKLEY, Jas.	26	M	Laborer	03Ma08Eb
COLLINS, Johanna	20	F	Unknown	03Ma08Eb
GOOD, John	27	M	Laborer	03Ma08Eb
James	22	M	Laborer	03Ma08Eb
Rich.	19	M	Laborer	03Ma08Eb
Mary	55	F	Unknown	03Ma08Eb
Francis	24	M	Laborer	03Ma08Eb
SWEENEY, Anne	4	F	Child	03Ma08Eb
Rich.	25	M	Laborer	03Ma08Eb
CUNNINGHAM, John	19	M	Laborer	03Ma08Eb
U-Mrs.	28	F	Unknown	03Ma08Eb
ANNING, Daniel	24	M	Laborer	03Ma08Eb
ALSH, Daniel	50	M	Laborer	03Ma08Eb
Cath.	00	F	Unknown	03Ma08Eb
Wm.	9	M	Child	03Ma08Eb
ARRY, Mich.	29	M	Laborer	03Ma08Eb
ANE, John	25	M	Laborer	03Ma08Eb
RIDE, Thomas	26	M	Laborer	03Ma08Eb
URRAY, Jas.	23	M	Laborer	03Ma08Eb
AYSTAFF, John	16	M	Laborer	03Ma08Eb
Thos.	13	M	Laborer	03Ma08Eb
CCARTHY, Jas.	20	M	Laborer	03Ma08Eb
INELLY, Margt.	20	F	Unknown	03Ma08Eb
Ann	14	F	Unknown	03Ma08Eb
Eliza	12	F	Unknown	03Ma08Eb
John	7	M	Child	03Ma08Eb
ASEY, Nan.	14	F	Unknown	03Ma08Eb
INELLY, Cath.	11	F	Unknown	03Ma08Eb
JIRK, John	24	M	Laborer	03Ma08Eb
Danl.	25	M	Laborer	03Ma08Eb
YONS, Jas.	22	M	Laborer	03Ma08Eb
Hannah	20	F	Unknown	03Ma08Eb
NNELL, John	23	M	Laborer	03Ma08Eb
Margt.	32	F	Unknown	03Ma08Eb
Kate	48	F	Unknown	03Ma08Eb
Andy	18	M	Laborer	03Ma08Eb
John	13	M	Laborer	03Ma08Eb
LLY, Abby	20	F	Unknown	03Ma08Eb
EFE, Johanna	24	F	Unknown	03Ma08Eb
COTTER, Mary	24	F	Unknown	03Ma08Eb
COLBAITH, John	28	M	Laborer	03Ma08Eb
Mary	20	F	Unknown	03Ma08Eb
Jas.	.06	M	Infant	03Ma08Eb
WALSH, Robt.	20	M	Laborer	03Ma08Eb
CULIGAN, Johanna	18	F	Unknown	03Ma08Eb
KEELEY, Julia	12	F	Unknown	03Ma08Eb
SULLIVAN, Michael	40	M	Laborer	03Ma08Eb
COLBAITH, Wm.	28	M	Laborer	03Ma08Eb
Jas.	25	M	Laborer	03Ma08Eb
KEEFE, Danl.	45	M	Laborer	03Ma08Eb
Johanna	29	F	Unknown	03Ma08Eb
Owen	15	M	Laborer	03Ma08Eb
KELLEHER, Mary	25	F	Unknown	03Ma08Eb
MURRAY, Stephen	20	M	Laborer	03Ma08Eb
BARRY, David	21	M	Laborer	03Ma08Eb
JORDAN, Jn.	20	M	Laborer	03Ma08Eb
DELLANY, Pat	22	M	Laborer	03Ma08Eb
KELLY, Jas.	24	M	Laborer	03Ma08Eb
MURPHY, Jeremiah	50	M	Laborer	03Ma08Eb
Jas.	22	M	Laborer	03Ma08Eb
Margt.	13	F	Unknown	03Ma08Eb
Mary	12	F	Unknown	03Ma08Eb
TULLANY, Margt.	17	F	Unknown	03Ma08Eb
WALSH, Ellen	13	F	Unknown	03Ma08Eb
CREEDON, Pat	38	M	Laborer	03Ma08Eb
Honora	13	F	Unknown	03Ma08Eb
HEARN, Jas.	24	M	Laborer	03Ma08Eb
Mary	20	F	Unknown	03Ma08Eb
CROTTY, Eliza	21	F	Unknown	03Ma08Eb
NOONAN, Thos.	25	M	Laborer	03Ma08Eb
MORIARTY, Tim.	28	M	Laborer	03Ma08Eb
LYNCH, Eliza	26	F	Unknown	03Ma08Eb
MORIARTY, Cath.	22	F	Unknown	03Ma08Eb
DOWNEY, John	24	M	Laborer	03Ma08Eb
LANE, Thos.	32	M	Laborer	03Ma08Eb
Bridget	30	F	Unknown	03Ma08Eb
Tim	10	M	Unknown	03Ma08Eb
DUGGAN, Mary	24	F	Unknown	03Ma08Eb
MCENERY, Pat	20	M	Laborer	03Ma08Eb
Cornelius	17	M	Laborer	03Ma08Eb
CURTIN, Pat	30	M	Laborer	03Ma08Eb
Cath.	50	F	Unknown	03Ma08Eb
CASEY, John	20	M	Laborer	03Ma08Eb
LYONS, Mary	20	F	Unknown	03Ma08Eb
BARRY, Patrick	20	M	Unknown	03Ma08Eb
CARLTON, Thos.	40	M	Unknown	03Ma08Eb

TYPHIS 03 MAY 1849

From Jersey

NAMES OF PASSENGERS	AGE	SEX	OCCUPATIONS	DATE PORT SHIP
HAMON, Thos.	33	M	Mariner	03Ma57Dq
Caroline	30	F	None	03Ma57Dq
James	2	M	Child	03Ma57Dq
Thos.	.03	M	Infant	03Ma57Dq
SHALES, Saml.	36	M	Tailor	03Ma57Dq
Grace	30	F	None	03Ma57Dq
Matilda	1	F	Child	03Ma57Dq
COOPER, Cecilia	28	F	None	03Ma57Dq
PEARSON, Charlotte	20	F	None	03Ma57Dq
CONSTANCHE, Henry	22	M	Carpenter	03Ma57Dq

ROYAL-WILLIAM 03 MAY 1849

From Sunderland

NAMES OF PASSENGERS		AGE	SEX	OCCUPATIONS	DATE PORT SHIP
SHANK, John		50	M	Pitman	03Ma36Dr
HASWELL, Christr.		20	M	Pitman	03Ma36Dr
SPENCE, Elizabeth		30	F	Wife	03Ma36Dr
Mary		7	F	Child	03Ma36Dr
Thomas		6	M	Child	03Ma36Dr
Jane		3	F	Child	03Ma36Dr
ELLISON, Robert		32	M	Pitman	03Ma36Dr
Mary	(W)	35	F	Wife	03Ma36Dr
Elizth.Jane	(D)	5	F	Child	03Ma36Dr
Sarah	(D)	1	F	Child	03Ma36Dr
HUNTER, William		36	M	Pitman	03Ma36Dr
Jane	(W)	33	F	Wife	03Ma36Dr
Elizabeth		15	F	None	03Ma36Dr
Thomas		10	M	None	03Ma36Dr
Alexander		6	M	Child	03Ma36Dr
RAND, John		37	M	Pitman	03Ma36Dr
Hannah	(W)	35	F	Wife	03Ma36Dr
Margaret		12	F	None	03Ma36Dr
Hannah		7	F	Child	03Ma36Dr
BELL, Joseph		26	M	Pitman	03Ma36Dr
Ann	(W)	30	F	Wife	03Ma36Dr
GOLLICK, William		18	M	Pitman	03Ma36Dr
ANDERSON, John		30	M	Pitman	03Ma36Dr
FOSTER, George		31	M	Pitman	03Ma36Dr
HALL, James		32	M	Pitman	03Ma36Dr
LINSLEY, Robert		36	M	Pitman	03Ma36Dr
FOTHERINGELL, Joseph		38	M	Pitman	03Ma36Dr
DOCODING, Charles		49	M	Pitman	03Ma36Dr
Samuel		19	M	Pitman	03Ma36Dr
STANTON, George		36	M	Molder	03Ma36Dr
BOND, John		37	M	Molder	03Ma36Dr

CUTHBERT 03 MAY 1849

From Greenock

NAMES OF PASSENGERS	AGE	SEX	OCCUPATIONS	DATE PORT SHIP
CLOUGHAN, William	48	M	Miner	03Ma33Eh
CAMPBELL, John	45	M	Dresser	03Ma33Eh
U-Mrs.	44	F	None	03Ma33Eh
ANDERSON, Samuel	29	M	Laborer	03Ma33Eh
U-Mrs.	28	F	None	03Ma33Eh
SMITH, Catherine-Mrs.	30	F	None	03Ma33Eh
WARD, U-Mrs.	30	F	None	03Ma33Eh
CLEGHORN, Marie	20	F	Spinster	03Ma33Eh
MCCULLOW, Ann	18	F	Spinster	03Ma33Eh
KELLY, Denis	22	M	Laborer	03Ma33Eh
MCAVENIE, Philip	24	M	Gdnr	03Ma33Eh
Patrick	56	M	Laborer	03Ma33Eh
Ann	28	F	Spinster	03Ma33Eh
QUIN, James	24	M	Laborer	03Ma33Eh
Mathew	22	M	Laborer	03Ma33Eh
JOHNSTONE, Robert	17	M	Laborer	03Ma33Eh
CAMPBELL, U-Mrs.	27	F	None	03Ma33Eh
RUSSELL, George	27	M	Cbtmkr	03Ma33Eh
MCALVIE, Charles	22	M	Laborer	03Ma33Eh

CALEB-GRIMSHAW 03 MAY 1849

From Liverpool

NAMES OF PASSENGERS	AGE	SEX	OCCUPATIONS	DATE PORT SHIP
FARLEY, Pat	19	M	Bricklayer	03Ma02Ej
CARRAHER, Mary	00	F	Servant	03Ma02Ej
SHAUGHNESSY, John	18	M	Cooper	03Ma02Ej
SLAVIN, Felix	22	M	Cooper	03Ma02Ej
SHEERMAN, Richd.	39	M	Farmer	03Ma02Ej
Ann	37	F	Farmer	03Ma02Ej
Wm.	14	M	Farmer	03Ma02Ej
Mary	12	F	Farmer	03Ma02Ej
Anney	8	F	Child	03Ma02Ej
Isaac	6	M	Child	03Ma02Ej
Eliza	2	F	Child	03Ma02Ej
CAMPBELL, J.E.	20	M	Farmer	03Ma02Ej
LONKS, Thos.	23	M	Clothier	03Ma02Ej
GARDNER, Geo.	26	M	Farmer	03Ma02Ej
Sarah	25	F	Unknown	03Ma02Ej
LEE, John	20	M	Unknown	03Ma02Ej
MARRY, Timothy	36	M	Laborer	03Ma02Ej
RYAN, John	26	M	Laborer	03Ma02Ej
Cath.	22	F	Unknown	03Ma02Ej
DELANY, Edwd.	32	M	Laborer	03Ma02Ej
Pat	28	M	Laborer	03Ma02Ej
KANE, Martin	32	M	Farmer	03Ma02Ej
CUNNINGHAM, Honor	22	F	Servant	03Ma02Ej
REED, Mary	00	F	Servant	03Ma02Ej
FARLEY, Mary	14	F	Servant	03Ma02Ej
DOWD, John	22	M	Cooper	03Ma02Ej
Mary	12	F	Unknown	03Ma02Ej
KILLIGRAM, Jas.	20	M	Shoemaker	03Ma02Ej
KERMISTY, Thos.	23	M	Shoemaker	03Ma02E
BYRNES, Richd.	30	M	Shoemaker	03Ma02E
Cath.	28	F	Shoemaker	03Ma02E
DOLAN, Chas.	16	M	Shoemaker	03Ma02E
BRADY, Ellen	18	F	Shoemaker	03Ma02E
Pat	18	M	Shoemaker	03Ma02E
FRAISER, Thos.	30	M	Farmer	03Ma02E
MURPHY, John	26	M	Farmer	03Ma02E
CONWAY, John	20	M	Farmer	03Ma02E
Mary	14	F	Farmer	03Ma02E
Patt	11	M	Farmer	03Ma02E
Jas.	7	M	Child	03Ma02E
DOOHAN, Wm.	32	M	Farmer	03Ma02E
CASSIDY, Peter	19	M	Laborer	03Ma02E
MANYAN, Mary	20	F	Servant	03Ma02E
GIBB, Ann	20	F	Servant	03Ma02E
OLEARY, Michl.	19	M	Servant	03Ma02E
CARTHY, Jerry	46	M	Servant	03Ma02E
Margt.	40	F	Servant	03Ma02E
Dennis	20	M	Servant	03Ma02E
Mick	16	M	Servant	03Ma02E
Johannah	17	F	Servant	03Ma02E
Margt.	15	F	Servant	03Ma02E
CASTIGAN, Dennis	26	M	Servant	03Ma02E
Dennis	28	M	Servant	03Ma02
SANDERSEN, Arch.	20	M	Servant	03Ma02
HANNOVER, Rd.	27	M	Laborer	03Ma02
COLEMAN, Pat	14	M	Laborer	03Ma02
MCCARTY, Chas.	35	M	Laborer	03Ma02
SULLIVAN, Margt.	4	F	Child	03Ma02
CORBET, Ellen	18	F	Unknown	03Ma02
CASHIN, Pat	20	M	Laborer	03Ma02
FINNEGAN, Ann	13	F	Laborer	03Ma02
KELLY, Sally	28	F	Laborer	03Ma02
Ellen	2	F	Child	03Ma02
Bridget	.00	F	Infant	03Ma02
CAMPBELL, Mary	27	F	Laborer	03Ma02

NAMES OF PASSENGERS	AGE	SEX	OCCUPATIONS	DATE PORT SHIP
MCLEAR, Dennis	20	M	Laborer	03Ma02Ej
EVANS, Ric.	35	M	Laborer	03Ma02Ej
KIERNAN, Mary	19	F	Servant	03Ma02Ej
TIERNEY, Owen	20	M	Servant	03Ma02Ej
COOK, Jas.	30	M	Unknown	03Ma02Ej
Johanna	30	F	Unknown	03Ma02Ej
Ellen	7	F	Child	03Ma02Ej
Mary	4	F	Child	03Ma02Ej
Johannah	3	F	Child	03Ma02Ej
MULCALY, Bridget	20	F	Unknown	03Ma02Ej
Mary	18	F	Unknown	03Ma02Ej
MCCAWLEY, Margt.	15	F	Unknown	03Ma02Ej
MCCARNN, Nancy	25	F	Unknown	03Ma02Ej
BERRY, Michl.	22	M	Unknown	03Ma02Ej
RYAN, John	25	M	Unknown	03Ma02Ej
Winnifred	20	F	Unknown	03Ma02Ej
BAKER, Simon	26	M	Unknown	03Ma02Ej
HUMPHREY, Henry	19	M	Laborer	03Ma02Ej
JULIEN, T.H.	29	M	Laborer	03Ma02Ej
MURPHY, John	23	M	Laborer	03Ma02Ej
LINDEN, John	24	M	Laborer	03Ma02Ej
CONNALLY, Edw.	27	M	Laborer	03Ma02Ej
FITZGERALD, Mary	24	F	Servant	03Ma02Ej
Jas.	24	M	Servant	03Ma02Ej
DRISCOLE, Mary	26	F	Servant	03Ma02Ej
BAIKLY, Johannah	20	F	Servant	03Ma02Ej
HAYES, Alice	18	F	Servant	03Ma02Ej
SHEEHAN, Nancy	45	F	Servant	03Ma02Ej
Mary	18	F	Servant	03Ma02Ej
DRUM, Bridget	20	F	Servant	03Ma02Ej
CORLENE, Chas.	16	M	Servant	03Ma02Ej
LONGHAN, Cath.	13	F	Servant	03Ma02Ej
ROCKFORD, Wm.	22	M	Cooper	03Ma02Ej
PARKER, Thos.	26	M	Cooper	03Ma02Ej
BERRY, Elizth.	63	F	Unknown	03Ma02Ej
BARNAME, Josh.	20	M	Unknown	03Ma02Ej
PALMER, Wm.	18	M	Unknown	03Ma02Ej
CALLAGHAN, Cath.	16	M	Unknown	03Ma02Ej
STOTT, Jas.	37	M	Unknown	03Ma02Ej
HICKS, Richd.	40	M	Unknown	03Ma02Ej
U-Mrs.	40	F	Unknown	03Ma02Ej
Cath.	22	F	Unknown	03Ma02Ej
Wm.	16	M	Unknown	03Ma02Ej
John	13	M	Unknown	03Ma02Ej
Edw.	10	M	Unknown	03Ma02Ej
Alfred	6	M	Child	03Ma02Ej
ALLAN, Richd.	24	M	Laborer	03Ma02Ej
U-Mrs.	24	F	Unknown	03Ma02Ej
USNELL, Chas.	20	M	Laborer	03Ma02Ej
GLE, Thos.	18	M	Unknown	03Ma02Ej
AVAGE, Michl.	40	M	Laborer	03Ma02Ej
U-Mrs.	35	F	Unknown	03Ma02Ej
Letitia	7	F	Child	03Ma02Ej
Richd.	18	M	Unknown	03Ma02Ej
CCARSON, Betsey	30	F	Servant	03Ma02Ej
CCAFFREY, Hugh	34	M	Servant	03Ma02Ej
IDDLE, Wm.	28	M	Unknown	03Ma02Ej
Betsey	29	F	Unknown	03Ma02Ej
Wm.	6	M	Child	03Ma02Ej
Mry	5	F	Child	03Ma02Ej
George	3	F	Child	03Ma02Ej
Jona.	.00	M	Infant	03Ma02Ej
Betty	16	F	Unknown	03Ma02Ej
ULLIVAN, Ann	20	F	Unknown	03Ma02Ej
CHART, Wm.	21	M	Cooper	03Ma02Ej
THERS, Chas.	20	M	Cooper	03Ma02Ej
ALKINS, Wm.	24	M	Cooper	03Ma02Ej
VINGSTON, John	19	M	Cooper	03Ma02Ej
Mary-A.	17	F	Servant	03Ma02Ej
Thos.	20	M	Unknown	03Ma02Ej
RAN, John	32	M	Unknown	03Ma02Ej
NDERGAST, Edmund	25	M	Unknown	03Ma02Ej
LLEN, George	25	M	Unknown	03Ma02Ej
Maria	18	F	Unknown	03Ma02Ej
SH, Eliza	18	F	Unknown	03Ma02Ej

NAMES OF PASSENGERS	AGE	SEX	OCCUPATIONS	DATE PORT SHIP
MAHER, John	20	M	Laborer	03Ma02Ej
DEMPSEY, Richd.	21	M	Unknown	03Ma02Ej
KILLEIN, Mary	30	F	Unknown	03Ma02Ej
WRIGHT, Wm.	25	M	Unknown	03Ma02Ej
MARSH, Aaren	25	M	Unknown	03Ma02Ej
HEGAN, Margt.	40	M	Unknown	03Ma02Ej
FALLON, Thos.	30	M	Farmer	03Ma02Ej
MORN, Thos.	18	M	Farmer	03Ma02Ej
MONKS, Lawrence	24	M	Farmer	03Ma02Ej
MCCUE, Pat	18	M	Farmer	03Ma02Ej
DOYLE, Jas.	17	M	Farmer	03Ma02Ej
SMITH, Ellen	20	F	Unknown	03Ma02Ej
NEAL, Judith	20	F	Unknown	03Ma02Ej
HENNEYFELD, Thos.	22	M	Unknown	03Ma02Ej
KEYS, Michl.	18	M	Unknown	03Ma02Ej
DUMMERY, Jas.	20	M	Unknown	03Ma02Ej
MER, Thos.	20	M	Unknown	03Ma02Ej
TAYLER, Jas.	21	M	Unknown	03Ma02Ej
COOPER, Alex.	19	M	Unknown	03Ma02Ej
DEWCAR, Alice	18	F	Unknown	03Ma02Ej
CONNER, Mary	18	F	Unknown	03Ma02Ej
MULLIGAN, Owen	32	M	Laborer	03Ma02Ej
MARKINSON, John	20	M	Unknown	03Ma02Ej
DONOHOE, Mary	20	F	Unknown	03Ma02Ej
ROAH, Jas.	18	M	Unknown	03Ma02Ej
KENNEDY, Margt.	20	F	Unknown	03Ma02Ej
RYAN, Math.	28	M	Unknown	03Ma02Ej
MASTERSON, Cath.	30	F	Servant	03Ma02Ej
MORRISEY, Jas.	18	M	Servant	03Ma02Ej
MCCABE, Alex.	22	M	Servant	03Ma02Ej
MCCULLINAN, John	21	M	Servant	03Ma02Ej
Pat	22	M	Servant	03Ma02Ej
GARRITY, Brien	16	M	Servant	03Ma02Ej
Mary	13	F	Unknown	03Ma02Ej
GANNON, Brigt.	18	F	Servant	03Ma02Ej
GILL, Alice	36	F	Unknown	03Ma02Ej
DOGNAN, Pat	4	M	Child	03Ma02Ej
CAIN, Jas.	30	M	Unknown	03Ma02Ej
KEENAN, John	20	M	Laborer	03Ma02Ej
DWYER, Alice	20	M	Servant	03Ma02Ej
QUAILL, Donald	20	M	Servant	03Ma02Ej
SMITH, Peter	20	M	Servant	03Ma02Ej
Ann	24	F	Unknown	03Ma02Ej
Ellen	13	F	Unknown	03Ma02Ej
HUGHES, Jas.	32	M	Cooper	03Ma02Ej
POWER, John	28	M	Cooper	03Ma02Ej
Jas.	26	M	Cooper	03Ma02Ej
TOBIN, Mary	25	F	Servant	03Ma02Ej
CASS, Elizth.	26	F	Unknown	03Ma02Ej
HINNS, Jas.	30	F	Unknown	03Ma02Ej
MURPHY, Brien	22	M	Unknown	03Ma02Ej
NOWLAN, Jas.	24	M	Unknown	03Ma02Ej
CLINTON, Chris	44	M	Unknown	03Ma02Ej
Rose	44	F	Unknown	03Ma02Ej
BALL, Jas.	12	M	Unknown	03Ma02Ej
Cath.	11	F	Unknown	03Ma02Ej
Pat	9	M	Child	03Ma02Ej
Michl.	6	M	Child	03Ma02Ej
Edw.	4	M	Child	03Ma02Ej
LEARY, Conn.	22	M	Hatter	03Ma02Ej
NOBLE, Wm.	30	M	Hatter	03Ma02Ej
Elizth.	21	F	Servant	03Ma02Ej
BYRNE, Peter	65	M	Unknown	03Ma02Ej
John	27	M	Unknown	03Ma02Ej
Pat	30	M	Unknown	03Ma02Ej
Ann	18	F	Unknown	03Ma02Ej
REILLY, John	25	M	Unknown	03Ma02Ej
KELLY, Pat	20	M	Unknown	03Ma02Ej
LEONARD, Jas.	21	M	Unknown	03Ma02Ej
NEAL, John	30	M	Unknown	03Ma02Ej
KELLY, John	14	M	Unknown	03Ma02Ej
VESEY, John	00	M	Unknown	03Ma02Ej
WILKINSON, Geo.	00	M	Unknown	03Ma02Ej
PRITCHARD, Thos.	00	M	Unknown	03Ma02Ej
POWELL, Thos.	30	M	Unknown	03Ma02Ej

NAMES OF PASSENGERS	AGE	SEX	OCCUPATIONS	DATE PORT SHIP
HANNAHORN, Brien	20	M	Unknown	03Ma02Ej
MADDAGAN, Michl.	24	M	Unknown	03Ma02Ej
Red.	20	M	Unknown	03Ma02Ej
GURNON, Thos.	24	M	Unknown	03Ma02Ej
MADGAN, Honorah	26	F	Unknown	03Ma02Ej
HOLLINSHEAD, Thos.	35	M	Unknown	03Ma02Ej
Elzth.	35	M	Unknown	03Ma02Ej
BEEBY, Wm.	29	M	Unknown	03Ma02Ej
Mary	27	F	Unknown	03Ma02Ej
Hellen	2	F	Child	03Ma02Ej
Wm.	.00	M	Infant	03Ma02Ej
BRADMERK, Pat	35	M	Farmer	03Ma02Ej
DOYLE, Julia	30	F	Unknown	03Ma02Ej
Mary-J.	7	F	Child	03Ma02Ej
Johanna	.00	F	Infant	03Ma02Ej
MCDONALD, Boyd	27	M	Servant	03Ma02Ej
CRAWFORD, Saml.	20	M	Unknown	03Ma02Ej
NEVIN, John	22	M	Unknown	03Ma02Ej
LOGAN, Elenner	19	F	Unknown	03Ma02Ej
MCHESON, Elenner	23	F	Unknown	03Ma02Ej
SHELTON, Geo.	26	M	Unknown	03Ma02Ej
Sarah	27	F	Unknown	03Ma02Ej
HATHAM, Benj.	37	M	Unknown	03Ma02Ej
MILLER, Jos.	23	M	Miller	03Ma02Ej
BELL, John	30	M	Miller	03Ma02Ej
BUZZ, Albion	10	M	Unknown	03Ma02Ej
KIERNAN, Thos.	30	M	Unknown	03Ma02Ej
CONNELL, Wid.	40	F	Unknown	03Ma02Ej
Chris.	20	M	Unknown	03Ma02Ej
Bridget	16	F	Unknown	03Ma02Ej
WARD, John	30	M	Laborer	03Ma02Ej
CONNER, Thos.	27	M	Laborer	03Ma02Ej
Esther	22	F	Unknown	03Ma02Ej
WHELAHAN, Pat	45	M	Unknown	03Ma02Ej
CONNOR, Matt.	25	M	Unknown	03Ma02Ej
MOONEY, Mary	20	F	Unknown	03Ma02Ej
CONNERS, Ann	20	F	Unknown	03Ma02Ej
WHICKHAM, Jas.	28	M	Unknown	03Ma02Ej
Mary	20	F	Unknown	03Ma02Ej
KENNEDY, Pat	23	M	Farmer	03Ma02Ej
Cath.	21	F	Unknown	03Ma02Ej
Alice	16	F	Unknown	03Ma02Ej
SCANLON, Cath.	22	F	Unknown	03Ma02Ej
THOMPSON, Jas.	22	M	Unknown	03Ma02Ej
POLLACK, Robt.	19	M	Unknown	03Ma02Ej
MCGRATH, John	50	M	Unknown	03Ma02Ej
OBRIEN, Esther	30	F	Unknown	03Ma02Ej
RYAN, Wm.	15	M	Unknown	03Ma02Ej
MCCOLLUM, W.J.	37	M	Unknown	03Ma02Ej
Betsey	30	F	Unknown	03Ma02Ej
Elzth.	6	F	Child	03Ma02Ej
Jane	.00	F	Infant	03Ma02Ej
CUSHING, Mary	21	F	Unknown	03Ma02Ej
CAVANAGH, Chas.	28	M	Unknown	03Ma02Ej
OHARA, Ally	15	F	Unknown	03Ma02Ej
FEE, Cath.	20	F	Unknown	03Ma02Ej
CASEY, John	30	M	Unknown	03Ma02Ej
Ann	25	F	Unknown	03Ma02Ej
JOHNSTON, Elzth.	18	F	Unknown	03Ma02Ej
KEARNAN, John	30	M	Unknown	03Ma02Ej
Elzth.	24	F	Unknown	03Ma02Ej
COLLINS, Susan	32	F	Unknown	03Ma02Ej
Mary	10	F	Unknown	03Ma02Ej
Elzth.	9	F	Child	03Ma02Ej
Jas.	6	M	Child	03Ma02Ej
WARD, Michl.	30	M	Unknown	03Ma02Ej
DAVIES, Evan	26	M	Farmer	03Ma02Ej
Elzth.	20	F	Farmer	03Ma02Ej
David	2	M	Child	03Ma02Ej
Griffith	.00	M	Infant	03Ma02Ej
Jacob	46	M	Unknown	03Ma02Ej
MCKENNA, Susannah	60	F	Unknown	03Ma02Ej
MCELROY, Henry	18	M	Groom	03Ma02Ej
CONLY, Ellen	40	F	Servant	03Ma02Ej
MCCAFFRY, Owen	24	M	Unknown	03Ma02Ej

NAMES OF PASSENGERS	AGE	SEX	OCCUPATIONS	DATE PORT SHIP
GRINCE, Susan	17	F	Unknown	03Ma02Ej
BOYLEN, Maria	22	F	Unknown	03Ma02Ej
ROONEY, Hugh	13	M	Unknown	03Ma02Ej
KENNEDY, Mary	20	F	Servant	03Ma02Ej
GAFFNEY, Mary	40	F	Unknown	03Ma02Ej
KENNEDY, Martin	42	M	Unknown	03Ma02Ej
Nelly	30	F	Unknown	03Ma02Ej
WARD, Thos.	40	M	Unknown	03Ma02Ej
NESBIT, Sarah	21	F	Unknown	03Ma02Ej
BLANCH, Wm.	20	M	Unknown	03Ma02Ej
GREEN, Wm.	27	F	Unknown	03Ma02Ej
U-Mrs.	20	F	Unknown	03Ma02Ej
CORRIGAN, Michl.	24	M	Laborer	03Ma02Ej
FAIRHURST, Wm.	00	M	Laborer	03Ma02Ej
SHEA, Walter	26	M	Laborer	03Ma02Ej
DEADY, Chas.	27	M	Laborer	03Ma02Ej
GREEN, John	22	M	Laborer	03Ma02Ej
READ, John	21	M	Laborer	03Ma02Ej
KENNY, Margt.	21	F	Servant	03Ma02Ej
SMITH, Hannah	20	F	Servant	03Ma02Ej
CONNELL, Julia	20	F	Servant	03Ma02Ej
MURPHY, Jas.	27	F	Groom	03Ma02Ej
BRYAN, John	30	F	Cooper	03Ma02Ej
Kate	20	F	Unknown	03Ma02Ej
JUDGINGS, Danl.	22	M	Farmer	03Ma02Ej
OBRIEN, Cath.	17	F	Farmer	03Ma02Ej
DEVLIN, Ellen	40	F	Unknown	03Ma02Ej
Elicoha	10	F	Unknown	03Ma02Ej
DONLAN, Pat	28	M	Laborer	03Ma02Ej
FARRELL, Tony	28	M	Laborer	03Ma02Ej
BURN, Ann	20	F	Servant	03Ma02Ej
HUGHES, Mary	20	F	Servant	03Ma02Ej
NOWLAN, Ellen	20	F	Servant	03Ma02Ej
MILLER, Robt.	22	M	Unknown	03Ma02Ej
WILLIAMS, U	28	F	Unknown	03Ma02Ej
SMITH, Hugh	18	M	Unknown	03Ma02Ej
BRYAN, Mary	18	F	Unknown	03Ma02Ej
GORMAN, Margt.	20	F	Unknown	03Ma02Ej
COULTER, Chas.	38	M	Unknown	03Ma02Ej
NORTON, Ann	18	F	Unknown	03Ma02Ej
FERGUSON, U-Mrs.	29	F	Unknown	03Ma02Ej
MCCUSKER, Barney	32	M	Farmer	03Ma02Ej
BURKE, Pat	60	M	Farmer	03Ma02Ej
BYRNE, Peter	17	M	Farmer	03Ma02Ej
MCCOLLUM, Ann	.00	F	Infant	03Ma02Ej
STARR, John	24	M	Unknown	03Ma02Ej
Joseph	26	M	Unknown	03Ma02Ej
GRAYSON, Isaac	23	M	Unknown	03Ma02Ej
FERGUSON, U	25	F	Unknown	03Ma02Ej
OBRIEN, Mary	9	F	Child	03Ma02Ej
MACQUEEN, Mary	57	F	Lady	03Ma02Ej
Heilen	24	F	Lady	03Ma02Ej
Annie	13	F	None	03Ma02Ej

COSMO 03 MAY 1849

From Bristol

NAMES OF PASSENGERS	AGE	SEX	OCCUPATIONS	DATE PORT SHIP
LYNCH, Robt.	20	M	Carver	03Ma10D

THREE-SISTERS 03 MAY 1849

From Halifax

NAMES OF PASSENGERS		AGE	SEX	OCCUPATIONS	DATE PORT SHIP
JONES, James		21	M	Clerk	03Ma43Ed
IMESHAM, Timothy		20	M	Clerk	03Ma43Ed

MARGARET 03 MAY 1849

From New Ross

NAMES OF PASSENGERS		AGE	SEX	OCCUPATIONS	DATE PORT SHIP
BYRNE, John		56	M	Farmer	03Ma25Cs
Judith	(W)	54	F	Wife	03Ma25Cs
Patt		28	M	Laborer	03Ma25Cs
Died-At-Sea					
James		26	M	Laborer	03Ma25Cs
Edmond		30	M	Laborer	03Ma25Cs
John		22	M	Laborer	03Ma25Cs
Tom		7	M	Child	03Ma25Cs
Ellen		21	F	Spinster	03Ma25Cs
Mary		23	F	Spinster	03Ma25Cs
Catherine		24	F	Spinster	03Ma25Cs
Margaret		26	F	Spinster	03Ma25Cs
Anthy.		15	M	None	03Ma25Cs
Honor		18	F	None	03Ma25Cs
Bridget		20	F	None	03Ma25Cs
MEANEY, Margaret		23	F	Spinster	03Ma25Cs
Mary		20	F	Spinster	03Ma25Cs
FLING, Anne		19	F	Spinster	03Ma25Cs
Eliza		23	F	Spinster	03Ma25Cs
HICKEY, James		21	M	Laborer	03Ma25Cs
CORCORAN, Robin		27	M	Laborer	03Ma25Cs
HAY, James		28	M	Laborer	03Ma25Cs
KELLY, James		25	M	Servant	03Ma25Cs
FENELLY, Jno.		26	M	Laborer	03Ma25Cs
BROPHY, Jno.		30	M	Laborer	03Ma25Cs
Michl.		27	M	Laborer	03Ma25Cs
NEEFE, Ellen		21	F	Spinster	03Ma25Cs
ROCKFORD, Ellen		23	F	Spinster	03Ma25Cs
Margaret		18	F	Spinster	03Ma25Cs
WALSHE, Jno.		27	M	Laborer	03Ma25Cs
KOUGH, Anne		21	F	Spinster	03Ma25Cs
KAVANNAGH, Anne		23	F	Spinster	03Ma25Cs
KOUGH, Thos.		34	M	Laborer	03Ma25Cs
KENEHAM, Pat		23	M	Laborer	03Ma25Cs
MARTIN, Michael		21	M	Laborer	03Ma25Cs
Bridget		24	F	Spinster	03Ma25Cs
PHELAN, Thos.		50	M	Farmer	03Ma25Cs
Hannah	(W)	49	F	Wife	03Ma25Cs
Ellen		18	F	Spinster	03Ma25Cs
Eliza		20	F	Spinster	03Ma25Cs
William		12	M	Laborer	03Ma25Cs
Thomas		14	M	Laborer	03Ma25Cs
John		16	M	Laborer	03Ma25Cs
Died-At-Sea					
Peter		10	M	None	03Ma25Cs
James		9	M	Child	03Ma25Cs
ATE, Wm.		40	M	Farmer	03Ma25Cs
Susan	(W)	39	F	Wife	03Ma25Cs
James		9	M	Child	03Ma25Cs
Died-At-Sea					
YRNE, Michael		30	M	Laborer	03Ma25Cs
YDE, Wm.		56	M	Farmer	03Ma25Cs
HYDE, Margaret		28	F	Wife	03Ma25Cs
Anne		23	F	None	03Ma25Cs
Eliza		18	F	None	03Ma25Cs
Amelia		19	F	None	03Ma25Cs
BYRNE, James		26	M	Laborer	03Ma25Cs
MURPHY, Maurice		30	M	Laborer	03Ma25Cs
BYRNE, Pat		29	M	Laborer	03Ma25Cs
DOYLE, Mathew		27	M	Laborer	03Ma25Cs
NEILL, James		40	M	Laborer	03Ma25Cs
MURPHY, Andrew		36	M	Laborer	03Ma25Cs
DUNNE, David		20	M	Laborer	03Ma25Cs
Mary	(W)	25	F	Wife	03Ma25Cs
SWEENEY, James		40	M	Laborer	03Ma25Cs
Bridget	(W)	35	F	Wife	03Ma25Cs
COMERFORD, Lawrence		36	M	Farmer	03Ma25Cs
Mary	(W)	34	F	Wife	03Ma25Cs
Thomas		11	M	Laborer	03Ma25Cs
Wm.		13	M	Laborer	03Ma25Cs
KENNEDY, Catherine		19	F	Spinster	03Ma25Cs
KAVAHAM, Margaret		24	F	Spinster	03Ma25Cs
KENNEDY, Mary		23	F	Spinster	03Ma25Cs
BYRNE, Michael		18	M	Laborer	03Ma25Cs
WALSHE, Maurice		30	M	Laborer	03Ma25Cs
Anty		25	F	Spinster	03Ma25Cs
MOONEY, Robert		36	M	Farmer	03Ma25Cs
Mary	(W)	28	F	Wife	03Ma25Cs
WALSHE, Margaret		24	F	Spinster	03Ma25Cs
Bridget		26	F	Spinster	03Ma25Cs
WHITE, Hy.		17	M	Laborer	03Ma25Cs
CONNERS, James		19	M	Laborer	03Ma25Cs
FLAVIN, Patk.		20	M	Laborer	03Ma25Cs
HARVEY, Richd.		34	M	Laborer	03Ma25Cs
Cath.	(W)	23	F	Wife	03Ma25Cs
KEITH, Wm.		30	M	Laborer	03Ma25Cs
TOBIN, Jno.		36	M	Farmer	03Ma25Cs
Honor	(W)	34	F	Wife	03Ma25Cs
Bridget		13	F	Spinster	03Ma25Cs
Margt.		11	F	Spinster	03Ma25Cs
Margt.		11	F	Spinster	03Ma25Cs
Ellen		6	F	Child	03Ma25Cs
FLYNNE, Pat		19	M	Laborer	03Ma25Cs
MOONEY, Martin		23	M	Laborer	03Ma25Cs
Andrew		20	M	Laborer	03Ma25Cs
KEITH, John		23	M	Laborer	03Ma25Cs
ROACH, Edwd.		45	M	Laborer	03Ma25Cs
Mary		42	F	Spinster	03Ma25Cs
Cath.		15	F	Spinster	03Ma25Cs
Michl.		18	M	Laborer	03Ma25Cs
COMMIN, Anne		30	F	Spinster	03Ma25Cs
MURPHY, Martin		16	M	Laborer	03Ma25Cs
MADOGAN, James		40	M	Farmer	03Ma25Cs
Ellen		21	F	Wife	03Ma25Cs
PENDERGAST, David		23	M	Cooper	03Ma25Cs
DOYLE, Catherine		14	F	Spinster	03Ma25Cs
BYRNE, Mary		25	F	Spinster	03Ma25Cs
CALSHE, James-N.		22	M	Farmer	03Ma25Cs
STOKES, Margaret		19	F	Spinster	03Ma25Cs
DUREY, John		14	M	Laborer	03Ma25Cs
BYRNE, James		17	M	Laborer	03Ma25Cs
JOYCE, James		45	M	Farmer	03Ma25Cs
Margaret		19	F	None	03Ma25Cs
William		50	M	Laborer	03Ma25Cs
Died-At-Sea					
Thomas		48	M	Laborer	03Ma25Cs
Martin		23	M	Laborer	03Ma25Cs
Pat		24	M	Laborer	03Ma25Cs
Died-At-Sea					
Anty.	(W)	19	F	Wife	03Ma25Cs
Anty.		15	F	Spinster	03Ma25Cs
LAMBERT, Thomas		17	M	Laborer	03Ma25Cs
REDMORE, Denis		16	M	Farmer	03Ma25Cs
LAMBERT, Miles		23	M	Farmer	03Ma25Cs
CONNAY, Margaret		35	F	Spinster	03Ma25Cs
POWER, John		21	M	Farmer	03Ma25Cs
Bridget	(W)	15	F	Wife	03Ma25Cs

NAMES OF PASSENGERS		AGE	SEX	OCCUPATIONS	DATE PORT SHIP
POWER, Anne		19	F	Spinster	03Ma25Cs
BYRNE, James		22	M	Laborer	03Ma25Cs
LAMBERT, Thomas		15	M	Laborer	03Ma25Cs
Mary		19	F	Wife	03Ma25Cs
BOLGER, Martin		40	M	Farmer	03Ma25Cs
Jane	(W)	30	F	Wife	03Ma25Cs
SIMOTT, Michl.		15	M	Farmer	03Ma25Cs
Catherine	(W)	16	F	Wife	03Ma25Cs
David		40	M	Unknown	03Ma25Cs
David		38	M	Farmer	03Ma25Cs
Anne	(W)	32	F	Wife	03Ma25Cs
James		22	M	Unknown	03Ma25Cs
MURPHY, Bridget		23	F	Spinster	03Ma25Cs
Anty		12	F	Spinster	03Ma25Cs
FARRELL, Anne		19	F	Spinster	03Ma25Cs
DWYER, Judy		20	F	Spinster	03Ma25Cs
MURPHY, Margaret		12	F	Spinster	03Ma25Cs
GARVEY, Catherine		16	F	Spinster	03Ma25Cs
Patrick		14	M	Laborer	03Ma25Cs
Died-At-Sea					
CULLEN, John		15	M	Laborer	03Ma25Cs
GORMAN, James		14	M	Laborer	03Ma25Cs
HAYES, Patk.		23	M	Laborer	03Ma25Cs
CONNERS, Mary		25	F	Wife	03Ma25Cs
WALSHE, Lawrence		25	M	Unknown	03Ma25Cs
Anne		23	F	Unknown	03Ma25Cs
Eliza		15	F	Unknown	03Ma25Cs
James		36	M	Laborer	03Ma25Cs
John		33	M	Laborer	03Ma25Cs
Lawrence		14	M	None	03Ma25Cs
Margt.		12	F	None	03Ma25Cs
Anne		10	F	None	03Ma25Cs
MURPHY, James		8	M	Child	03Ma25Cs
Thomas		6	M	Child	03Ma25Cs
John		4	M	Child	03Ma25Cs
BRUDY, Thos.		21	M	Laborer	03Ma25Cs
TOBIN, Richard		20	M	Farmer	03Ma25Cs
Judy		00	F	Unknown	03Ma25Cs
Edwd.		18	M	Laborer	03Ma25Cs
Robt.		25	M	Laborer	03Ma25Cs
REDMOND, Daniel		23	M	Farmer	03Ma25Cs
Patrick		9	M	Farmer	03Ma25Cs
Michael		7	M	Farmer	03Ma25Cs
Ellen		33	F	Spinster	03Ma25Cs
Bridget		28	F	Spinster	03Ma25Cs
ROCHE, Patk.		20	M	Laborer	03Ma25Cs
RYAN, Thomas		18	M	Laborer	03Ma25Cs
John		14	M	Laborer	03Ma25Cs
Michael		12	M	Laborer	03Ma25Cs
POWER, John		21	M	Laborer	03Ma25Cs
BUTLER, Arthur		20	M	Laborer	03Ma25Cs
KELLY, P.		18	M	Laborer	03Ma25Cs
BURKE, Margt.		35	F	Spinster	03Ma25Cs
FOX, Patk.		46	M	Laborer	03Ma25Cs
SUMMERS, Patk.		20	M	Laborer	03Ma25Cs
LOUGHLAN, Anty.		14	F	Spinster	03Ma25Cs
COMMINS, Moses		35	M	Laborer	03Ma25Cs
BROWNER, James		16	M	Farmer	03Ma25Cs
Bridget		14	F	Spinster	03Ma25Cs
Thomas		42	M	Laborer	03Ma25Cs
John		40	M	Farmer	03Ma25Cs
James		20	M	Laborer	03Ma25Cs
CASEY, Ellen		18	F	Spinster	03Ma25Cs
FARDY, Bartlet		14	M	Laborer	03Ma25Cs
BROWNER, Thomas		23	M	Laborer	03Ma25Cs
CALPER, Thomas		20	M	Laborer	03Ma25Cs
RYAN, Wm.		20	M	Laborer	03Ma25Cs
BRENAN, Wm.		20	M	Laborer	03Ma25Cs
SHEEHAN, Richard		30	M	Laborer	03Ma25Cs
Died-At-Sea					
MURPHY, Richard		28	M	Laborer	03Ma25Cs
LOVETT, Bridget		12	F	Spinster	03Ma25Cs
FITZGERALD, James		18	M	Laborer	03Ma25Cs
Died-At-Sea					
LACY, Stephen		20	M	Laborer	03Ma25Cs

NAMES OF PASSENGERS		AGE	SEX	OCCUPATIONS	DATE PORT SHIP
GORMAN, Nicholas		20	M	Laborer	03Ma25Cs
COCKER, John		14	M	Laborer	03Ma25Cs
WILLIAMS, Edwd.		24	M	Laborer	03Ma25Cs
KEHOE, James		22	M	Laborer	03Ma25Cs
KAVANAGH, James		23	M	Laborer	03Ma25Cs
Bridget		00	F	Spinster	03Ma25Cs
FITZPATRICK, Patrick		00	M	Laborer	03Ma25Cs
KELLY, Margaret		00	F	Spinster	03Ma25Cs
KENNEDY, Moses		00	M	Farmer	03Ma25Cs
Bridget		21	F	Wife	03Ma25Cs
MASTERSON, Thomas		24	M	Laborer	03Ma25Cs
DUMPHY, Patk.		20	M	Laborer	03Ma25Cs
MEYLER, Michl.		18	M	Laborer	03Ma25Cs
KEEGHAN, Michl.		20	M	Laborer	03Ma25Cs
MOLLEN, John		19	M	Laborer	03Ma25Cs
Eliza		17	F	Spinster	03Ma25Cs
WELLS, Jno.		18	M	Farmer	03Ma25Cs
Pat		24	M	Farmer	03Ma25Cs
POWER, Morris		22	M	Laborer	03Ma25Cs
Bridget		20	F	Spinster	03Ma25Cs
CADEY, Thos.		18	M	Laborer	03Ma25Cs
HAYES, Margaret		40	F	Wife	03Ma25Cs
MALLOY, Pat		38	M	Laborer	03Ma25Cs
John		23	M	Laborer	03Ma25Cs
FOX, James		21	M	Unknown	03Ma25Cs
CAHILL, U		35	M	Unknown	03Ma25Cs
BURKE, U-Miss		19	F	Unknown	03Ma25Cs
GIBSON, Pat		00	M	Unknown	03Ma25Cs

SILAS-GREENMAN 03 MAY 1849

From Liverpool

NAMES OF PASSENGERS		AGE	SEX	OCCUPATIONS	DATE PORT SHIP
LOSTY, Edwd.		27	M	Laborer	03Ma02E
BRADY, Patt.		26	M	Laborer	03Ma02E
DUNNE, Dominick		25	M	Laborer	03Ma02E
ROURKE, Joseph		25	M	Laborer	03Ma02E
MCARDLE, John		56	M	Laborer	03Ma02E
U	(W)	56	F	None	03Ma02E
Mary		16	F	None	03Ma02E
Terence		12	M	Laborer	03Ma02E
John		11	M	Laborer	03Ma02E
Felix		8	M	Child	03Ma02E
Anna		5	F	Child	03Ma02E
MALONE, Thos.		25	M	Laborer	03Ma02E
Patrick		24	M	Laborer	03Ma02E
GLYNNE, James		26	M	Laborer	03Ma02E
Marcella		20	F	None	03Ma02
Margt.		.00	F	Infant	03Ma02
MCGUINNESS, Bridget		18	F	None	03Ma02
Mary		28	F	None	03Ma02
FIER, Richard		52	M	Laborer	03Ma02
Hannah		45	F	None	03Ma02
Robert		16	M	Laborer	03Ma02
Wm.		10	M	Laborer	03Ma02
Diana		5	F	Child	03Ma02
CASSIDY, Peter		24	M	Laborer	03Ma02
MORAN, Wm.		27	M	Laborer	03Ma02
Nichs.		21	M	Laborer	03Ma02
BRADY, Phil.		30	M	Laborer	03Ma02
Rose		30	F	None	03Ma02
John		8	M	Child	03Ma02
Bernard		5	M	Child	03Ma02
Cathr.		2	F	Child	03Ma02
Julia		.00	F	Infant	03Ma02
REILLY, Bridget		18	F	None	03Ma02
SMITH, Mary		18	F	None	03Ma02
ELLIOTT, Fanny		23	F	None	03Ma02
KELLY, James		40	M	Laborer	03Ma02

NAMES OF PASSENGERS		AGE	SEX	OCCUPATIONS	DATE PORT SHIP
KELLY, U	(W)	35	F	None	03Ma02Et
Patrick		13	M	Laborer	03Ma02Et
Mary		11	F	None	03Ma02Et
Margt.		9	F	Child	03Ma02Et
Peter		7	M	Child	03Ma02Et
Thos.		5	M	Child	03Ma02Et
DUNBAR, Dominick		22	M	Laborer	03Ma02Et
GILLOONY, Ann		20	F	None	03Ma02Et
THOMAS, G.		22	M	Laborer	03Ma02Et
U	(W)	20	F	None	03Ma02Et
MARTIN, Bryan		18	M	Laborer	03Ma02Et
SHERIDAN, Mary		20	F	None	03Ma02Et
Bridget		18	F	None	03Ma02Et
Patrick		15	M	Laborer	03Ma02Et
Teresa		10	F	None	03Ma02Et
MCCORMICK, Patt.		24	M	Laborer	03Ma02Et
MONAHAN, Patt.		22	M	Laborer	03Ma02Et
FARRELL, Dominick		20	M	Laborer	03Ma02Et
Margt.		18	F	None	03Ma02Et
CARRAGAN, Edwd.		20	M	Laborer	03Ma02Et
HOLDERNESS, Thos.		30	M	Laborer	03Ma02Et
Fanny		26	F	None	03Ma02Et
Samuel		5	M	Child	03Ma02Et
Eliza		3	F	Child	03Ma02Et
George		.00	M	Infant	03Ma02Et
Robert		31	M	Laborer	03Ma02Et
U	(W)	26	F	None	03Ma02Et
U		.00	U	Infant	03Ma02Et
KEOUGH, Wm.		25	M	Laborer	03Ma02Et
CHRIGHTON, Richd.		22	M	Laborer	03Ma02Et
COX, Charles		22	M	Laborer	03Ma02Et
YEATES, Thos.		30	M	Laborer	03Ma02Et
DAVISON, Thos.		23	M	Laborer	03Ma02Et
SCOTT, Thos.		48	M	Laborer	03Ma02Et
MCCLUSKEY, James		25	M	Laborer	03Ma02Et
RYAN, Patt.		30	M	Laborer	03Ma02Et
U	(W)	29	F	None	03Ma02Et
Mary		.00	F	Infant	03Ma02Et
BOWES, Pat.		40	M	Laborer	03Ma02Et
QUINLAN, Danl.		24	M	Laborer	03Ma02Et
Ellen		21	F	None	03Ma02Et
RANILLE, Geo.		30	M	Laborer	03Ma02Et
U	(W)	26	F	None	03Ma02Et
MCPARTLAND, Alexr.		30	M	Laborer	03Ma02Et
VOLLERTON, Thos.		30	M	Laborer	03Ma02Et
Ellen		26	F	None	03Ma02Et
Edmd.		4	F	Child	03Ma02Et
ARSONS, George		26	M	Laborer	03Ma02Et
U	(W)	24	F	None	03Ma02Et
MCMANUS, Michl.		22	M	Laborer	03Ma02Et
Mary		20	F	None	03Ma02Et
MCNALLY, Andrew		40	M	Laborer	03Ma02Et
Mary		40	F	None	03Ma02Et
John		20	M	Laborer	03Ma02Et
Anne		17	F	None	03Ma02Et
CARDLE, James		25	M	Laborer	03Ma02Et
Mary		20	F	None	03Ma02Et
CGUINNESS, Peter		17	M	Laborer	03Ma02Et
ARNEY, James		21	M	Laborer	03Ma02Et
NSTEY, Henry		21	M	Laborer	03Ma02Et
ALE, John		21	M	Laborer	03Ma02Et
ARRIS, Wm.		34	M	Laborer	03Ma02Et
ASS, George		30	M	Laborer	03Ma02Et
AYLOR, John		37	M	Laborer	03Ma02Et
OOMBES, James		46	M	Laborer	03Ma02Et
Mary		45	F	None	03Ma02Et
Amelia		24	F	None	03Ma02Et
Elizth.		21	F	None	03Ma02Et
Anna		18	F	None	03Ma02Et

CELESTE 04 MAY 1849

From Dublin

NAMES OF PASSENGERS	AGE	SEX	OCCUPATIONS	DATE PORT SHIP
BARTON, Frederick	26	M	Tailor	04Ma12Eg
SHEA, Michael	18	M	Tailor	04Ma12Eg
KEEGAN, John	20	M	Tailor	04Ma12Eg
DELANY, Isabella	10	F	Child	04Ma12Eg
FLEMMING, Jas.	50	M	Farmer	04Ma12Eg
Thomas	10	M	Child	04Ma12Eg
Daniel	8	M	Child	04Ma12Eg
Wm.	20	M	Mason	04Ma12Eg
John	23	M	Mason	04Ma12Eg
CONNOR, Cath.	24	F	Spinster	04Ma12Eg
FIELDING, Cath.	.00	F	Infant	04Ma12Eg
KEARNY, Robt.	18	M	Laborer	04Ma12Eg
BRYAN, Mary	28	F	Matron	04Ma12Eg
KAVANAGH, Eliza	16	F	Matron	04Ma12Eg
KENNEDY, Thomas	29	M	Mason	04Ma12Eg
NEILE, James	30	M	Mason	04Ma12Eg
REDMOND, Cath.	20	F	Unknown	04Ma12Eg
BRYNE, Michl.	.00	M	Infant	04Ma12Eg
BERINE, Mary	24	F	Spinster	04Ma12Eg
BRYNE, Louisa	28	F	Spinster	04Ma12Eg
HERDIN, Wm.	29	M	Laborer	04Ma12Eg
RYAN, Mary	30	F	Spinster	04Ma12Eg
Michl.	30	M	Mason	04Ma12Eg
U	4	M	Child	04Ma12Eg
U	.00	U	Infant	04Ma12Eg
KERLEY, Michl.	18	M	Mason	04Ma12Eg
Ellen	20	F	Wife	04Ma12Eg
ONEILL, Mark	38	M	Mason	04Ma12Eg
FENLON, John	30	M	Mason	04Ma12Eg
SMITH, Peter	28	M	Mason	04Ma12Eg
Mary	22	F	Spinster	04Ma12Eg
HANLON, James	51	M	Farmer	04Ma12Eg
Mary	49	F	Matron	04Ma12Eg
Mary-A.	20	F	Matron	04Ma12Eg
Jas.	18	M	Mason	04Ma12Eg
John	16	M	Mason	04Ma12Eg
Cath.	14	F	Unknown	04Ma12Eg
Stephen	12	M	Unknown	04Ma12Eg
Peter	6	M	Child	04Ma12Eg
Jas.	2	M	Child	04Ma12Eg
U	.00	U	Infant	04Ma12Eg
JOHNSON, Jas.	40	M	Mason	04Ma12Eg
U	.00	U	Infant	04Ma12Eg
CASSIDY, John	30	M	Mason	04Ma12Eg
CARTHY, Daniel	5	M	Child	04Ma12Eg
BRYNE, Pat	24	M	Mason	04Ma12Eg
ENNIS, Thomas	29	M	Mason	04Ma12Eg
DAILY, Patrick	6	M	Child	04Ma12Eg
HENSON, Wm.	20	M	Mason	04Ma12Eg
Mary	18	F	Spinster	04Ma12Eg
KENNA, Michl.	46	M	Farmer	04Ma12Eg
Eliza	40	F	Matron	04Ma12Eg
Jas.	20	M	Mason	04Ma12Eg
Rose	18	F	Spinster	04Ma12Eg
Michl.	10	M	Child	04Ma12Eg
John	8	M	Child	04Ma12Eg
Mary	.00	F	Infant	04Ma12Eg
KENSELLA, Mary	20	F	Spinster	04Ma12Eg
BRYNE, Michl.	18	M	Mason	04Ma12Eg
NEILE, Jas.	19	M	Mason	04Ma12Eg
SHEA, Michl.	28	M	Mason	04Ma12Eg
REDMOND, Cath.	24	F	Spinster	04Ma12Eg
REILLY, Cath.	18	F	Spinster	04Ma12Eg
MELLON, Cath.	20	F	Spinster	04Ma12Eg
LYNAN, Cath.	28	F	Spinster	04Ma12Eg

NAMES OF PASSENGERS	AGE	SEX	OCCUPATIONS	DATE PORT SHIP
MCQUIRK, Mary	9	F	Child	04Ma12Eg
DALY, Richard	39	M	Mason	04Ma12Eg
BRIDGE, Francis	24	M	Mason	04Ma12Eg
ROCHE, Bridget	18	F	Spinster	04Ma12Eg
BRYNE, Brian	28	M	Laborer	04Ma12Eg
MANAGHAN, Ann	28	F	Spinster	04Ma12Eg
MERTAGH, Daniel	18	M	Mason	04Ma12Eg
ZACHIAN, Biddy	4	F	Child	04Ma12Eg
MCMANNIS, John	30	M	Unknown	04Ma12Eg
MURPHY, Ann	6	F	Child	04Ma12Eg
Terry	31	M	Laborer	04Ma12Eg
SMITH, Mary	18	F	Spinster	04Ma12Eg
MURRAY, Cath.	34	F	Spinster	04Ma12Eg
Rose	30	F	Spinster	04Ma12Eg
Biddy	4	F	Child	04Ma12Eg
U	.00	U	Infant	04Ma12Eg
STEPHANSON, Stephan	25	M	Painter	04Ma12Eg
GAFFREY, Philip	8	M	Child	04Ma12Eg
John	23	M	Painter	04Ma12Eg
CONVOY, Ellen	24	F	Spinster	04Ma12Eg
DORAN, Mary	10	F	Unknown	04Ma12Eg
OSBOURNE, Ann	26	F	Spinster	04Ma12Eg
Rich.	8	M	Child	04Ma12Eg
Peter	.00	M	Infant	04Ma12Eg
DAVIS, Jane	18	F	Spinster	04Ma12Eg
BRIDGE, John	29	M	Mason	04Ma12Eg
COCHLAN, Cath.	19	F	Spinster	04Ma12Eg
CONLAN, Patrick	11	M	Child	04Ma12Eg
MALONEY, Patrick	28	M	Mason	04Ma12Eg
GLYNN, James	29	M	Mason	04Ma12Eg
Mary	29	F	Spinster	04Ma12Eg
Mary	3	F	Child	04Ma12Eg
Cath.	.00	F	Infant	04Ma12Eg
HAY, Christopher	20	M	Carpenter	04Ma12Eg
HAYLAND, Ellen	20	F	Spinster	04Ma12Eg
OSHEA, Margt.	30	F	Spinster	04Ma12Eg
OBRIEN, Ellen	12	F	Child	04Ma12Eg
GILFOYLE, Cath.	10	F	Child	04Ma12Eg
BOOTH, John	21	M	Clerk	04Ma12Eg
BURNEY, Patt	10	M	Child	04Ma12Eg
MURRAY, Daniel	8	M	Child	04Ma12Eg
MCCANE, Patt	6	M	Child	04Ma12Eg
KELLY, Jas.	29	M	Mason	04Ma12Eg
TORNEY, Jas.	10	M	Child	04Ma12Eg
POWER, Patt	19	M	Mason	04Ma12Eg
LAWLESS, John	28	M	Farmer	04Ma12Eg
OBRIEN, James	4	M	Child	04Ma12Eg
DUNN, Michl.	38	M	Farmer	04Ma12Eg
Patt	8	M	Child	04Ma12Eg
John	19	M	Mason	04Ma12Eg
Ann	16	F	Spinster	04Ma12Eg
Wm.	12	M	Child	04Ma12Eg
Mary	.00	F	Infant	04Ma12Eg
CONNOR, John	29	M	Mason	04Ma12Eg
ABBOTT, Mary	20	F	Spinster	04Ma12Eg
BULGER, Peggy	4	F	Child	04Ma12Eg
RYAN, Patt	24	M	Mason	04Ma12Eg
John	4	M	Child	04Ma12Eg

NORWAY 04 MAY 1849

From Liverpool

NAMES OF PASSENGERS	AGE	SEX	OCCUPATIONS	DATE PORT SHIP
LAVY, Thomas	40	M	Laborer	04Ma02El
Mary	38	F	Laborer	04Ma02El
Michl.	12	M	Laborer	04Ma02El
Catherine	25	F	Laborer	04Ma02El
John	.00	M	Infant	04Ma02El
SUTTON, John	40	M	Laborer	04Ma02El

NAMES OF PASSENGERS	AGE	SEX	OCCUPATIONS	DATE PORT SHIP
SUTTON, Jane	17	F	Laborer	04Ma02El
Thomas	13	M	Laborer	04Ma02El
Jeremiah	11	M	Laborer	04Ma02El
COMERS, James	20	M	Laborer	04Ma02El
HALONED, Henry-Joseph	40	M	Laborer	04Ma02El
KENNEY, Julia	32	F	Laborer	04Ma02El
Margret	18	F	Laborer	04Ma02El
Mary	12	F	Laborer	04Ma02El
Thomas	9	M	Child	04Ma02El
Catherine	7	F	Child	04Ma02El
Bridget	.00	F	Infant	04Ma02El
BOYLE, Cunningham	18	M	Laborer	04Ma02El
ZEESTER, Joseph	25	M	Laborer	04Ma02El
LEONARD, Thomas	21	M	Laborer	04Ma02El
CONNELL, Mary	25	F	Laborer	04Ma02El
HEALY, Bridt.	16	F	Laborer	04Ma02El
CONNERS, Bridt.	12	F	Laborer	04Ma02El
CLARKE, Peter	29	M	Laborer	04Ma02El
Margt.	29	F	Laborer	04Ma02El
Alice	.00	F	Infant	04Ma02El
BANNINGTON, John	35	M	Laborer	04Ma02El
Jane	30	F	Laborer	04Ma02El
William	10	M	Child	04Ma02El
Mary	8	F	Child	04Ma02El
Sarah	6	F	Child	04Ma02El
Ellen	.00	F	Infant	04Ma02El
MYERS, Fred.R.	29	M	Laborer	04Ma02El
SHELDERS, Eamus	20	M	Laborer	04Ma02El
BAUSKE, A.	30	M	Laborer	04Ma02El
ROBERTSON, Peter	22	M	Laborer	04Ma02El
COHEN, Lizea-W.	18	F	Laborer	04Ma02El
ZEMAN, Kitty	24	F	Laborer	04Ma02El
BRESHAMN, Perry	22	M	Laborer	04Ma02El
DUNN, Ann	20	F	Laborer	04Ma02El
KELLY, Pat	30	M	Laborer	04Ma02El
SMITH, Pat	23	M	Laborer	04Ma02El
MCNALLY, Cath.	40	F	Laborer	04Ma02E
Elizabeth	15	F	Laborer	04Ma02E
Matthew	18	M	Laborer	04Ma02E
George	19	M	Laborer	04Ma02E
Jane	13	F	Laborer	04Ma02E
Robt.	10	M	Laborer	04Ma02E
ALLEN, Michl.	45	M	Laborer	04Ma02E
Thomas	11	M	Laborer	04Ma02E
CRAIG, Charles	28	M	Laborer	04Ma02E
FARMUS, Thos.	25	M	Laborer	04Ma02E
KILCUS, Thos.	45	M	Laborer	04Ma02E
Catherine	40	F	Laborer	04Ma02E
Ann	18	F	Laborer	04Ma02E
Pat	15	M	Laborer	04Ma02E
Thomas	13	M	Laborer	04Ma02E
Mary	11	F	Laborer	04Ma02E
Catherine	8	F	Child	04Ma02E
Bridt.	6	F	Child	04Ma02E
James	4	M	Child	04Ma02E
Julia	.00	F	Infant	04Ma02
WALSH, Wm.	24	M	Laborer	04Ma02
FLYNN, Catherine	32	F	Laborer	04Ma02
FOLEY, Ellen	28	F	Laborer	04Ma02
Mary	10	F	Child	04Ma02
Daniel	6	M	Child	04Ma02
James	3	M	Child	04Ma02
John	.00	M	Infant	04Ma02
CATNEY, F.	18	M	Laborer	04Ma02
MILLS, Mary	40	F	Laborer	04Ma02
James	18	M	Laborer	04Ma02
Jane	12	F	Laborer	04Ma02
William	.00	M	Infant	04Ma02
SHEANY, Patrick	25	M	Laborer	04Ma02
DOWD, Judith	30	F	Laborer	04Ma02
Alley	25	F	Laborer	04Ma02
John	9	M	Child	04Ma02
BARBY, John	28	M	Laborer	04Ma0
FERMART, Wm.	29	M	Laborer	04Ma0
CANTWELL, John	25	M	Laborer	04Ma0

NAMES OF PASSENGERS	AGE	SEX	OCCUPATIONS	DATE PORT SHIP
FLANNY, Mary	21	F	Laborer	04Ma02El
CULLINS, Julia	20	F	Laborer	04Ma02El
FITZGERALD, James	29	M	Laborer	04Ma02El
Edward	20	M	Laborer	04Ma02El
CAMPBELL, Thomas	26	M	Laborer	04Ma02El
GILL, Cath.	18	F	Laborer	04Ma02El
MAHONS, Jude	20	F	Laborer	04Ma02El
MUNAN, Francis	20	M	Laborer	04Ma02El
MCGINLEY, Unity	17	F	Laborer	04Ma02El
KEEGAN, Pat	16	M	Laborer	04Ma02El
Bridt.	20	F	Laborer	04Ma02El
WHITE, N.	21	F	Laborer	04Ma02El
DWYER, Ann	22	F	Laborer	04Ma02El
HARTRUE, Mary	22	F	Laborer	04Ma02El
DOOLY, John	20	M	Laborer	04Ma02El
Mary	21	F	Laborer	04Ma02El
Pat	25	M	Laborer	04Ma02El
FEEHAN, Martin	17	M	Laborer	04Ma02El
DOOLY, Joseph	26	M	Laborer	04Ma02El
CASEY, Dennis	24	M	Laborer	04Ma02El
WALSH, Thos.	24	M	Laborer	04Ma02El
James	22	M	Laborer	04Ma02El
John	16	M	Laborer	04Ma02El
William	25	M	Laborer	04Ma02El
Ellen	18	F	Laborer	04Ma02El
MARTIN, Philip	30	M	Laborer	04Ma02El
Mary	30	F	Laborer	04Ma02El
Pat	3	M	Child	04Ma02El
Philip	.00	M	Infant	04Ma02El
Bridget	28	F	Laborer	04Ma02El
MCMAHON, Pat	47	M	Laborer	04Ma02El
Margt.	45	F	Laborer	04Ma02El
Owen	17	M	Laborer	04Ma02El
Ann	13	F	Laborer	04Ma02El
Peter	5	M	Child	04Ma02El
Betty	.00	F	Infant	04Ma02El
MCLAUGHLIN, C.	17	M	Laborer	04Ma02El
BYRNES, Pat	15	M	Laborer	04Ma02El
CUNNINGHAM, John	25	M	Laborer	04Ma02El
RIVEN, Anty	24	M	Laborer	04Ma02El
COLE, Ann	35	F	Laborer	04Ma02El
MOONEY, Jane	.00	F	Infant	04Ma02El
John	7	M	Child	04Ma02El
William	.00	M	Infant	04Ma02El
MCHALE, James	27	M	Laborer	04Ma02El
Walter	21	M	Laborer	04Ma02El
FLYNN, Ann	13	F	Laborer	04Ma02El
WILLIAMS, Thomas	21	M	Laborer	04Ma02El
FLYNN, Pat	30	M	Laborer	04Ma02El
MARSHALL, Eliza	45	F	Laborer	04Ma02El
Mary	45	F	Laborer	04Ma02El
George	3	M	Child	04Ma02El
EALEY, Bridget	19	F	Laborer	04Ma02El
OGAN, Jos.	26	M	Laborer	04Ma02El
Ann	23	F	Laborer	04Ma02El
HITE, Morris	25	M	Laborer	04Ma02El

LINDEN 04 MAY 1849

From Sligo

NAMES OF PASSENGERS	AGE	SEX	OCCUPATIONS	DATE PORT SHIP
NET, Patk.	30	M	Laborer	04Ma21Eo
RY, Mary	18	F	Spinster	04Ma21Eo
DERMOTT, Thos.	22	M	Laborer	04Ma21Eo
YTH, Mary-A.	24	F	Spinster	04Ma21Eo
WLY, John	25	M	Farmer	04Ma21Eo
NLAN, Owen	30	M	Clerk	04Ma21Eo
Michl.	18	M	Clerk	04Ma21Eo
WAN, Pat	26	M	Carter	04Ma21Eo
TOWLY, Margt.	18	F	Spinster	04Ma21Eo
GILGIN, Dennis	23	M	Laborer	04Ma21Eo
MCDERMOTT, Cath.	19	F	Spinster	04Ma21Eo
RYAN, Thady	24	M	Laborer	04Ma21Eo
OCONNOR, Mary	17	F	Spinster	04Ma21Eo
FERGUSON, Francis	25	M	Laborer	04Ma21Eo
MURRAY, Winefred	18	F	Spinster	04Ma21Eo
MCGOWAN, Mary	19	F	Spinster	04Ma21Eo
GORMAN, Eliza	24	F	Wife	04Ma21Eo
CONLAN, Thos.	21	M	Clerk	04Ma21Eo
ORORKE, Patk.	22	M	Farmer	04Ma21Eo
MISSETT, Robert	26	M	Laborer	04Ma21Eo
MCDONNELL, Anne	23	F	Spinster	04Ma21Eo
FARVEY, Margt.	25	F	Spinster	04Ma21Eo
MALONE, Thos.	27	M	Clerk	04Ma21Eo
FLYNN, Ann	17	F	Spinster	04Ma21Eo
SMYTH, Mary	28	F	Spinster	04Ma21Eo
MCDERMOTT, Mary	24	F	Spinster	04Ma21Eo
MALONE, J.R.	2	M	Child	04Ma21Eo
Ellen	24	F	Matron	04Ma21Eo
MCGUIRE, John	29	M	Laborer	04Ma21Eo
Margaret	26	F	Spinster	04Ma21Eo
MOORE, Jas.	14	M	Farmer	04Ma21Eo
GERATHY, Honora	24	F	Spinster	04Ma21Eo
ROONEY, Luke	30	M	Laborer	04Ma21Eo
CAFRY, John	24	M	Laborer	04Ma21Eo
DOHERTY, Michl.	19	M	Dealer	04Ma21Eo
MCCAULEY, Terence	25	M	Farmer	04Ma21Eo
LEONARD, Dennis	26	M	Farmer	04Ma21Eo
CONNOLY, John	40	M	Farmer	04Ma21Eo
Wm.	16	M	Farmer	04Ma21Eo
MCCAWLEY, John	30	M	Farmer	04Ma21Eo
Cath.	25	F	Matron	04Ma21Eo
Ann-J.	.00	F	Infant	04Ma21Eo
MCBLANNETT, Sarah-A.	16	F	Spinster	04Ma21Eo
KERRIGAN, Owen	24	M	Farmer	04Ma21Eo
Cath.	17	F	Wife	04Ma21Eo
GILLASPIE, Jas.	25	M	Farmer	04Ma21Eo
NOBLE, Bridget	23	F	Matron	04Ma21Eo
Edwd.	10	M	Child	04Ma21Eo
Mary	8	F	Child	04Ma21Eo
FINEGAN, Darby	21	M	Farmer	04Ma21Eo
GOLDEN, Bridget	20	F	Matron	04Ma21Eo
Mary	6	F	Child	04Ma21Eo
Bessy	3	F	Child	04Ma21Eo
Sarah	2	F	Child	04Ma21Eo
Cath.	7	F	Child	04Ma21Eo
ROONEY, Mary	19	F	None	04Ma21Eo
Michl.	21	M	Farmer	04Ma21Eo
Peter	7	M	Child	04Ma21Eo
LARKIN, John	20	M	Laborer	04Ma21Eo
Patk.	18	M	Laborer	04Ma21Eo
SPENCE, John	22	M	Laborer	04Ma21Eo
Jane	20	F	Matron	04Ma21Eo
Jane	.00	F	Infant	04Ma21Eo
DOLAN, Peter	32	M	Farmer	04Ma21Eo
KILPATRICK, John	24	M	Farmer	04Ma21Eo
FENTON, Michl.	26	M	Laborer	04Ma21Eo
BURKE, Cath.	24	F	Spinster	04Ma21Eo
Mary	33	F	Spinster	04Ma21Eo
SMYTH, George	24	M	Farmer	04Ma21Eo
ROONEY, Cormack	33	M	Farmer	04Ma21Eo
COGAN, Anthony	25	M	Laborer	04Ma21Eo
FEENEY, Mary	23	F	Spinster	04Ma21Eo
REILEY, Michl.	24	M	Laborer	04Ma21Eo
HEALEY, Martin	30	M	Laborer	04Ma21Eo
DURKIN, Cath.	20	F	Spinster	04Ma21Eo
Margt.	00	F	Spinster	04Ma21Eo
Bridget	26	F	Spinster	04Ma21Eo
Anne	23	F	Spinster	04Ma21Eo
Hugh	22	M	Farmer	04Ma21Eo
GAFFENEY, John	20	M	Laborer	04Ma21Eo
MCILROY, Thos.	23	M	Laborer	04Ma21Eo
REILEY, Bridget	22	F	Spinster	04Ma21Eo
MCLAUGHLIN, Thos.	24	M	Clerk	04Ma21Eo

NAMES OF PASSENGERS	AGE	SEX	OCCUPATIONS	DATE PORT SHIP
MULLARKY, John	19	M	Clerk	04Ma21Eo
ROONEY, Terence	22	M	Farmer	04Ma21Eo
MULLARKY, John	40	M	Doctor	04Ma21Eo
ROONEY, Mary	23	F	Spinster	04Ma21Eo
Cath.	21	F	Spinster	04Ma21Eo
LAUGHLIN, Mary	18	F	Spinster	04Ma21Eo
FLYNN, Wm.	36	M	Laborer	04Ma21Eo
Cath.	27	F	Spinster	04Ma21Eo
GLANCEY, Roger	29	M	Farmer	04Ma21Eo
FLYNN, Mary	22	F	Spinster	04Ma21Eo
GLANCEY, Ellen	24	F	Matron	04Ma21Eo
CLANCY, Mary	21	F	None	04Ma21Eo
CONLAN, Ann	20	F	Spinster	04Ma21Eo
FLYNN, Cath.	.00	F	Infant	04Ma21Eo
KELLY, Michl.	25	M	Farmer	04Ma21Eo
MORAN, Owen	30	M	Farmer	04Ma21Eo
Ellen	22	F	Farmer	04Ma21Eo
MIDDLETON, John	18	M	Unknown	04Ma21Eo
FENNERAN, Jas.	30	M	Farmer	04Ma21Eo
Winefred (W)	28	F	Wife	04Ma21Eo
Jas.Clinton	25	M	Laborer	04Ma21Eo
FARRELL, John	28	M	Laborer	04Ma21Eo
KERNEY, Andrew	27	M	Laborer	04Ma21Eo
Susan	22	F	Wife	04Ma21Eo
Patk.	24	M	Laborer	04Ma21Eo
MCGAVIN, John	21	M	Laborer	04Ma21Eo
OROURKE, Terence	18	M	Laborer	04Ma21Eo
Mary	20	F	Spinster	04Ma21Eo
Ann	7	F	Child	04Ma21Eo
MCDONOUGH, Peter	45	M	Farmer	04Ma21Eo
Cath.	50	F	Matron	04Ma21Eo
Bridget	14	F	Child	04Ma21Eo
Cath.	7	F	Child	04Ma21Eo
MULLANY, Cath.	20	F	Spinster	04Ma21Eo
MCDONOUGH, Bridget	41	F	Spinster	04Ma21Eo
CATTON, Ann	36	F	Wife	04Ma21Eo
Patk.	30	M	Farmer	04Ma21Eo
Cath.	7	F	Child	04Ma21Eo
KERR, Anthony	27	M	Farmer	04Ma21Eo
CULLEN, Thos.	10	M	Child	04Ma21Eo
James	7	M	Child	04Ma21Eo
MCDONOUGH, Mary	30	F	Matron	04Ma21Eo
GRADY, Winefred	32	F	Spinster	04Ma21Eo
COSGROVE, Mary	25	F	Matron	04Ma21Eo
Mary	20	F	None	04Ma21Eo
Barth	7	M	Child	04Ma21Eo
Bridget	6	F	Child	04Ma21Eo
MCDONOUGH, Bridget	4	F	Spinster	04Ma21Eo
Mary	21	F	Spinster	04Ma21Eo
KERR, Ann	30	F	Matron	04Ma21Eo
Ann	26	F	Matron	04Ma21Eo
DURKEN, Bridget	.00	F	Infant	04Ma21Eo
KERR, Patrick	.00	M	Infant	04Ma21Eo
BEATY, Robt.	18	M	Student	04Ma21Eo
BURKE, John	26	M	Law Clerk	04Ma21Eo

CARACTACUS 04 MAY 1849

From Galway

NAMES OF PASSENGERS	AGE	SEX	OCCUPATIONS	DATE PORT SHIP
MORGAN, James	26	M	Laborer	04Ma06Ep
LAWLESS, James	50	M	Laborer	04Ma06Ep
Rose	40	F	Spinster	04Ma06Ep
KEELY, John	33	M	Laborer	04Ma06Ep
MURPHY, Judy	40	F	Spinster	04Ma06Ep
Biddy	20	F	Spinster	04Ma06Ep
HIGGINS, Peter	30	M	Laborer	04Ma06Ep
Catherine	23	F	Spinster	04Ma06Ep
KING, Martin	21	M	Laborer	04Ma06Ep
KING, Mary	19	F	Spinster	04Ma06Ep
FURY, Honor	25	F	Spinster	04Ma06Ep
MORRIS, Michael	19	M	Carpenter	04Ma06Ep
MORRISSY, Thomas	19	M	Laborer	04Ma06Ep
CAHILL, Margaret	14	F	None	04Ma06Ep
Honor	10	F	None	04Ma06Ep
Catherine	7	F	Child	04Ma06Ep
TYNAN, Patrick	40	M	Mason	04Ma06Ep
SCULLY, Peter	18	M	Laborer	04Ma06Ep
TRACY, John	20	M	Laborer	04Ma06Ep
DONOHOE, Thomas	18	M	Laborer	04Ma06Ep
KILLEEN, Thomas	20	M	Laborer	04Ma06Ep
RIDGE, Dudley	21	M	Laborer	04Ma06Ep
DOLAN, Sabina	17	F	Spinster	04Ma06Ep
BURKE, John	5	M	Child	04Ma06Ep
KELLY, May	18	F	Spinster	04Ma06Ep
Catherine	16	F	Spinster	04Ma06Ep
BURKE, Judy	30	F	Spinster	04Ma06Ep
Mary	3	F	Child	04Ma06Ep
CUNNIFF, John	45	M	Laborer	04Ma06Ep
FEGAN, John	25	M	Laborer	04Ma06Ep
CONNORS, Biddy	19	F	Spinster	04Ma06Ep
NEILAND, Thomas	50	M	Laborer	04Ma06Ep
Died-At-Sea				
CONNORS, Nancy	50	F	Matron	04Ma06Ep
BRODIE, Biddy	17	F	Spinster	04Ma06Ep
Connor	20	M	Laborer	04Ma06Ep
BURKE, John	27	M	Laborer	04Ma06Ep
Catherine	24	F	Spinster	04Ma06Ep
NOLAN, James	22	M	Laborer	04Ma06Ep
CAHER, John	16	M	Laborer	04Ma06Ep
SHAUGHNESSY, James	18	M	Laborer	04Ma06Ep
Mich	19	M	Laborer	04Ma06Ep
Martin	18	M	Laborer	04Ma06Ep
JORDAN, Daniel	28	M	Laborer	04Ma06Ep
Mary	15	F	Spinster	04Ma06Ep
Died-At-Sea				
Catherine	14	F	None	04Ma06Ep
OBRIEN, Thomas	25	M	Laborer	04Ma06Ep
SHAUGHNESSY, Patt	32	M	Laborer	04Ma06Ep
Kitty	.11	F	Infant	04Ma06Ep
KING, John	22	M	Laborer	04Ma06Ep
Mary	21	F	Spinster	04Ma06Ep
Thomas	30	M	Laborer	04Ma06Ep
SHANY, Patrick	22	M	Laborer	04Ma06Ep
COLEMAN, Mark	26	M	Laborer	04Ma06Ep
KANE, Charles	17	M	Laborer	04Ma06Ep
KELLY, James	21	M	Laborer	04Ma06Ep
NOLAN, James	21	M	Laborer	04Ma06Ep
CONNELLY, Francis	26	M	Laborer	04Ma06Ep
DEVANNY, Biddy	28	F	Spinster	04Ma06Ep
GILL, Martin	4	M	Child	04Ma06Ep
Mark	4	M	Child	04Ma06Ep
MANNING, Mary	18	F	Spinster	04Ma06Ep
Catherine	15	F	Spinster	04Ma06Ep
CUNNIFFE, Bridget	40	F	Spinster	04Ma06Ep
ROLAN, Michael	20	M	Laborer	04Ma06Ep
CABBALL, John	17	M	Laborer	04Ma06Ep
WATERS, Nary	21	F	Spinster	04Ma06Ep
FLYNN, Thomas	30	M	Laborer	04Ma06Ep
Bridget	28	F	Spinster	04Ma06Ep
KAIN, Michael	24	M	Laborer	04Ma06Ep
FLYNN, Michael	.10	M	Infant	04Ma06Ep
FLANAGAN, Mary	17	F	Spinster	04Ma06Ep
JOYCE, John	22	M	Laborer	04Ma06Ep
DEVANY, Michael	30	M	Laborer	04Ma06Ep
Margaret	30	F	Spinster	04Ma06Ep
Martin	4	M	Child	04Ma06E
READY, John	50	M	Laborer	04Ma06E
Maria	45	F	Spinster	04Ma06E
CONNELLY, Stephen	23	M	Laborer	04Ma06E
Mary	16	F	Spinster	04Ma06E
Margaret	14	F	Spinster	04Ma06E
FINY, John	28	M	Laborer	04Ma06E
MAAN, Patrick	50	M	Laborer	04Ma06E

NAMES OF PASSENGERS	AGE	SEX	OCCUPATIONS	DATE PORT SHIP
MAAN, Bridget	50	F	Spinster	04Ma06Ep
MARIS, Thomas	18	M	Laborer	04Ma06Ep
MAAN, Patrick	21	M	Laborer	04Ma06Ep
COFFEE, Miles	22	M	Laborer	04Ma06Ep
KAINE, Stephen	20	M	Laborer	04Ma06Ep
CONNOR, Patrick	19	M	Laborer	04Ma06Ep
EDWARDS, William	24	M	Laborer	04Ma06Ep
WILSON, Mary	26	F	Spinster	04Ma06Ep
FOLAN, Michael	20	M	Laborer	04Ma06Ep
HESSIAN, John	20	M	Laborer	04Ma06Ep
FURY, William	20	M	Laborer	04Ma06Ep
MITCHELL, Honor	25	F	Spinster	04Ma06Ep
SCOVAN, Kate	20	F	Spinster	04Ma06Ep
MARIS, James	19	M	Laborer	04Ma06Ep
Michael	18	M	Laborer	04Ma06Ep
BURNES, Michael	27	M	Laborer	04Ma06Ep
HOLLAND, Patrick	22	M	Laborer	04Ma06Ep
ONEIL, James	30	M	Laborer	04Ma06Ep
Margaret	21	F	Spinster	04Ma06Ep
Ann	5	F	Child	04Ma06Ep
KELLY, John	30	M	Laborer	04Ma06Ep
CAMICAN, John	26	M	Laborer	04Ma06Ep
Patrick	19	M	Laborer	04Ma06Ep
HYNES, Michael	21	M	Laborer	04Ma06Ep
Died-At-Sea				
CALAMAN, John	18	M	Laborer	04Ma06Ep
Thomas	20	M	Laborer	04Ma06Ep
CONROY, Judy	35	F	Spinster	04Ma06Ep
WELSH, Patrick	28	M	Laborer	04Ma06Ep
COSTELLO, Thomas	35	M	Laborer	04Ma06Ep
LEAHY, John	25	M	Laborer	04Ma06Ep
FAHY, Michael	31	M	Laborer	04Ma06Ep
Margaret	25	F	Spinster	04Ma06Ep
James	20	M	Laborer	04Ma06Ep
Fidelia	3	F	Child	04Ma06Ep
Martin	.10	M	Infant	04Ma06Ep
PRICE, Patrick	50	M	Laborer	04Ma06Ep
William	20	M	Laborer	04Ma06Ep
John	18	M	Laborer	04Ma06Ep
Mary	14	F	None	04Ma06Ep
Fidelia	10	F	None	04Ma06Ep
CARY, Ellen	38	F	Spinster	04Ma06Ep
ONEIL, John	30	M	Laborer	04Ma06Ep
Honor	20	F	Spinster	04Ma06Ep
HART, William	17	M	Laborer	04Ma06Ep
DEVANY, John	3	M	Child	04Ma06Ep
LOFTUS, Mary	20	F	Spinster	04Ma06Ep
MATRONE, Mary	20	F	Spinster	04Ma06Ep
WINTON, John	25	M	Laborer	04Ma06Ep
GREEN, Eliza	19	F	Spinster	04Ma06Ep
TULLY, James	20	M	Laborer	04Ma06Ep
NAGLE, Patt	24	M	Laborer	04Ma06Ep
FOLAN, Thomas	29	M	Laborer	04Ma06Ep
MATMINE, Ellen	20	F	Spinster	04Ma06Ep
MCDONOGH, Ellen	20	F	Spinster	04Ma06Ep
MAAN, Ann	19	F	Spinster	04Ma06Ep
Bridget	16	F	Spinster	04Ma06Ep
CONNOR, Thomas	25	M	Laborer	04Ma06Ep
Ann	25	F	Spinster	04Ma06Ep
NOWLAN, Ellen	20	F	Spinster	04Ma06Ep
MAAN, James	23	M	Laborer	04Ma06Ep

WISSAHICKON 04 MAY 1849

From St.Croix

NAMES OF PASSENGERS	AGE	SEX	OCCUPATIONS	DATE PORT SHIP
MCADAMS, Henry	36	M	Sugpl	04Ma39Em

DINA-CARMALELY 04 MAY 1849

From Limerick

NAMES OF PASSENGERS		AGE	SEX	OCCUPATIONS	DATE PORT SHIP
LYDDY, Matt		25	M	Farmer	04Ma35Ev
CLANCEY, Daniel		25	M	Farmer	04Ma35Ev
Anne	(W)	25	F	Wife	04Ma35Ev
HANNAH, John		40	M	Farmer	04Ma35Ev
ROWHAN, James		18	M	Farmer	04Ma35Ev
GALLIGAN, Patt		36	M	Farmer	04Ma35Ev
MEEHAN, William		16	M	Farmer	04Ma35Ev
Patt		18	M	Farmer	04Ma35Ev
WALSH, Ellen		35	F	Servant	04Ma35Ev
KEANE, Thomas		35	M	Farmer	04Ma35Ev
Catherine	(T)	22	F	None	04Ma35Ev
Margaret	(T)	16	F	None	04Ma35Ev
John	(S)	4	M	Child	04Ma35Ev
Nancy	(T)	17	F	None	04Ma35Ev
LARKIN, Patt		25	M	Farmer	04Ma35Ev
BARRY, Ellen		40	F	Wi	04Ma35Ev
John	(S)	18	M	None	04Ma35Ev
Honorah	(D)	20	F	None	04Ma35Ev
SHANAHAN, Michael		22	M	Farmer	04Ma35Ev
Anne	(W)	22	F	Wife	04Ma35Ev
Anne	(D)	.03	F	Infant	04Ma35Ev
SETTLETON, Patt		30	M	Laborer	04Ma35Ev
Nancy	(W)	30	F	Wife	04Ma35Ev
Patt	(S)	.02	M	Infant	04Ma35Ev
COSTELLO, Mary		23	F	Servant	04Ma35Ev
CARROLL, Mary		35	F	Wi	04Ma35Ev
Martin	(S)	15	M	None	04Ma35Ev
Margaret	(D)	13	F	None	04Ma35Ev
John	(S)	6	M	Child	04Ma35Ev
Michael	(S)	5	M	Child	04Ma35Ev
GORGON, John		25	M	Laborer	04Ma35Ev
CARROLL, Thomas		2	M	Son	04Ma35Ev
MARATTY, Catherine		22	F	Servant	04Ma35Ev
QUIN, Michael		35	M	Laborer	04Ma35Ev
BRAZIL, Edward		25	M	Laborer	04Ma35Ev
FARRELL, Tim		30	M	Laborer	04Ma35Ev
MOLONEY, Honorah		24	F	Servant	04Ma35Ev
HOUGH, Tom		35	M	Farmer	04Ma35Ev
MOLONEY, Michael		18	M	Farmer	04Ma35Ev
BRAZIL, Michael		30	M	Farmer	04Ma35Ev
LYNCH, John		30	M	Farmer	04Ma35Ev
HOUGH, Bridget		25	F	Farmer	04Ma35Ev
Margaret		.06	F	Infant	04Ma35Ev
SLATTERY, John		23	M	Farmer	04Ma35Ev
MCNAMARA, Batt		27	M	Farmer	04Ma35Ev
Margaret		00	F	Farmer	04Ma35Ev
LOW, Henry		22	M	Farmer	04Ma35Ev
NASH, Mary		22	F	Farmer	04Ma35Ev
Ellen		20	F	Farmer	04Ma35Ev
RYAN, Bridget		45	F	Farmer	04Ma35Ev
James		24	M	Farmer	04Ma35Ev
Margaret		21	F	Farmer	04Ma35Ev
Catherine		13	F	Farmer	04Ma35Ev
Bridget		12	F	Farmer	04Ma35Ev
Patt		11	M	Farmer	04Ma35Ev
GARVEN, John		24	M	Farmer	04Ma35Ev
DALEY, Michael		30	M	Farmer	04Ma35Ev
HAGAN, Patt		33	M	Farmer	04Ma35Ev
Mary		31	F	Farmer	04Ma35Ev
MURPHY, Patt		21	M	Farmer	04Ma35Ev
HYNES, Michael		20	M	Farmer	04Ma35Ev
Edward		14	M	Farmer	04Ma35Ev
Ellen		10	F	Farmer	04Ma35Ev
Anne		8	F	Child	04Ma35Ev
MOLONEY, Dan		21	M	Farmer	04Ma35Ev

NAMES OF PASSENGERS	AGE	SEX	OCCUPATIONS	DATE PORT SHIP
MOLONEY, James	19	M	Farmer	04Ma35Ev
QUELAN, John	30	M	Farmer	04Ma35Ev
RYAN, Matt	24	M	Farmer	04Ma35Ev
John	22	M	Farmer	04Ma35Ev
MCINNERY, John	28	M	Farmer	04Ma35Ev
BOURKE, Jeffrey	60	M	Farmer	04Ma35Ev
Catherine	51	F	Farmer	04Ma35Ev
Johannah	17	F	Farmer	04Ma35Ev
Bridget	14	F	Farmer	04Ma35Ev
Honorah	12	F	Farmer	04Ma35Ev
Jeffrey	10	M	Farmer	04Ma35Ev
DYAN, James	58	M	Farmer	04Ma35Ev
Thomas	17	M	Farmer	04Ma35Ev
Ellen	15	F	Farmer	04Ma35Ev
Johannah	13	F	Farmer	04Ma35Ev
CASEY, Tim	22	M	Farmer	04Ma35Ev
KEANE, Michael	22	M	Farmer	04Ma35Ev
NUNAN, John	27	M	Farmer	04Ma35Ev
DIJAN, Michael	27	M	Farmer	04Ma35Ev
MCAULIFFE, John	20	M	Farmer	04Ma35Ev
CARMOODY, John	20	M	Farmer	04Ma35Ev
BLAKE, John	20	M	Farmer	04Ma35Ev
CROWE, Antony	20	M	Farmer	04Ma35Ev
KEANE, Michael	20	M	Farmer	04Ma35Ev
MANNIX, John	35	M	Farmer	04Ma35Ev
FITZPATRICK, James	22	M	Farmer	04Ma35Ev
NUNAN, Patrick	27	M	Farmer	04Ma35Ev
CASEY, Thomas	25	M	Farmer	04Ma35Ev
ONEIL, Patt	25	M	Farmer	04Ma35Ev
CAHILL, James	23	M	Farmer	04Ma35Ev
AUSTIN, George	35	M	Farmer	04Ma35Ev
Nancy	25	F	Farmer	04Ma35Ev
John	32	M	Farmer	04Ma35Ev
BECHAN, Austin	30	M	Farmer	04Ma35Ev
MURRAY, John	30	M	Farmer	04Ma35Ev
MOHANEY, John	35	M	Farmer	04Ma35Ev
Mary	00	F	Unknown	04Ma35Ev
DOLOHORY, Thomas	37	M	Farmer	04Ma35Ev
ONEILL, James	20	M	Farmer	04Ma35Ev
GARVEY, Francis	16	M	Farmer	04Ma35Ev
Patt	23	M	Farmer	04Ma35Ev
LYNCH, James	23	M	Farmer	04Ma35Ev
Patt	50	M	Farmer	04Ma35Ev
KEATING, Bridget	22	F	Farmer	04Ma35Ev
WALSH, Patt	19	M	Farmer	04Ma35Ev
GRIFFIN, John	40	M	Farmer	04Ma35Ev
Mary	24	F	Farmer	04Ma35Ev
KEANE, Johannah	16	F	Farmer	04Ma35Ev
Margaret	20	F	Farmer	04Ma35Ev
COLLINS, John	28	M	Farmer	04Ma35Ev
Johannah	20	F	Farmer	04Ma35Ev
BREW, John	22	M	Farmer	04Ma35Ev
Catherine	35	F	Farmer	04Ma35Ev
Mary	15	F	Farmer	04Ma35Ev
HINLEY, John	40	M	Farmer	04Ma35Ev
Mary	40	F	Farmer	04Ma35Ev
Patt	13	M	Farmer	04Ma35Ev
DOWNEY, Tim	40	M	Farmer	04Ma35Ev
LYDDY, Patrick	14	M	Farmer	04Ma35Ev

H.H.BOODY 04 MAY 1849

From Liverpool

NAMES OF PASSENGERS	AGE	SEX	OCCUPATIONS	DATE PORT SHIP
DOWNS, Thomas	24	M	Tailor	04Ma02Ex
DOWNES, U-Mrs.	26	F	Unknown	04Ma02Ex
U	.00	U	Infant	04Ma02Ex
William	5	M	Child	04Ma02Ex
MCCRASKER, Hugh	36	M	Laborer	04Ma02Ex
GALLAGHER, Mary	26	F	Unknown	04Ma02Ex
Betsy	2	F	Child	04Ma02Ex
DWYER, John	29	M	Clerk	04Ma02Ex
Ellen	29	F	Unknown	04Ma02Ex
Patrick	24	M	Clerk	04Ma02Ex
Thomas	13	M	Unknown	04Ma02Ex
GALLIGAN, Bartley	41	M	Laborer	04Ma02Ex
U-Mrs.	30	F	Unknown	04Ma02Ex
Thomas	20	M	Unknown	04Ma02Ex
Ann	15	F	Unknown	04Ma02Ex
Catharine	11	F	Unknown	04Ma02Ex
Farrell	46	M	Laborer	04Ma02Ex
U-Mrs.	40	F	Laborer	04Ma02Ex
Owen	18	M	Laborer	04Ma02Ex
Charles	12	M	Laborer	04Ma02Ex
Mary	16	F	Laborer	04Ma02Ex
COYLE, Thomas	22	M	Laborer	04Ma02Ex
SMITH, Thomas	40	M	Laborer	04Ma02Ex
Mary	14	F	Laborer	04Ma02Ex
Thomas	13	M	Unknown	04Ma02Ex
MCGIVNEY, Patrick	20	M	Laborer	04Ma02Ex
GALLIGAN, Mary	18	F	Unknown	04Ma02Ex
DOBSON, Rose	17	F	Unknown	04Ma02Ex
GALLIGAN, William	30	M	Laborer	04Ma02Ex
U-Mrs.	28	F	Unknown	04Ma02Ex
U	.00	U	Infant	04Ma02Ex
Patrick	3	M	Child	04Ma02Ex
Farrel	2	M	Child	04Ma02Ex
HYLAND, Catharine	16	F	Unknown	04Ma02Ex
GALLIGAN, Farrel	20	M	Laborer	04Ma02Ex
Mary	28	F	Unknown	04Ma02Ex
HUTCHISON, Thomas	17	M	Laborer	04Ma02Ex
HIGGINS, Walter	21	M	Laborer	04Ma02Ex
KEARNEY, Thomas	27	M	Laborer	04Ma02Ex
Catherine	19	F	Unknown	04Ma02Ex
BARRY, Mary	26	F	Servant	04Ma02Ex
WELDEN, Timothy	40	M	Laborer	04Ma02Ex
U-Mrs.	36	F	Unknown	04Ma02Ex
Bridget	10	F	Unknown	04Ma02Ex
Dan	8	M	Child	04Ma02Ex
Mary	6	F	Child	04Ma02Ex
MULVEY, Mary	18	F	Servant	04Ma02Ex
HAYES, William	21	M	Laborer	04Ma02E
James	23	M	Laborer	04Ma02E
HARLEHEY, Catherine	23	F	Servant	04Ma02E
Ellen	17	F	Servant	04Ma02E
MOFFATT, Thomas	22	M	Laborer	04Ma02E
Ann	20	F	Unknown	04Ma02E
FAGAN, Patrick	40	M	Laborer	04Ma02E
DONOHUE, Anne	30	F	Servant	04Ma02E
MURRAY, Thomas	25	M	Carter	04Ma02E
COX, Martin	40	M	Weaver	04Ma02E
FAGAN, Bridget	20	F	Servant	04Ma02E
DERMOTT, Mary	17	F	Servant	04Ma02E
FAGAN, Bernard	10	M	Unknown	04Ma02E
FEAHAN, Daniel	30	M	Laborer	04Ma02E
MCDONAL, Betsey	18	F	Servant	04Ma02E
Catherine	17	F	Servant	04Ma02E
HAM, Ellen	18	F	Servant	04Ma02E
MCMANUS, Bridget	20	F	Unknown	04Ma02E
GROGAN, Honora	12	F	Unknown	04Ma02E
John	11	M	Unknown	04Ma02E
Mary	8	F	Child	04Ma02E
KEARNEY, John	35	M	Laborer	04Ma02
Edward	12	M	Unknown	04Ma02
LOFTUS, Bridget	20	F	Unknown	04Ma02
Thomas	18	M	Laborer	04Ma02
MCTEAGUE, Elly	30	U	Laborer	04Ma02
Margaret	20	F	Unknown	04Ma02
WARD, Jeremiah	27	M	Laborer	04Ma02
BURNS, Richard	24	M	Laborer	04Ma02
Margaret	16	F	Laborer	04Ma02
DONOHUE, Brian	20	M	Laborer	04Ma02
John	17	M	Laborer	04Ma02
SHERIDAN, John	24	M	Laborer	04Ma02

AMES OF PASSENGERS	AGE	SEX	OCCUPATIONS	DATE PORT SHIP	NAMES OF PASSENGERS	AGE	SEX	OCCUPATIONS	DATE PORT SHIP
KEIRNAN, Catherine	20	F	Spinster	04Ma02Ex	LANCASTER, Richard	27	M	Laborer	04Ma02Ex
SHERIDAN, Rose	18	F	Servant	04Ma02Ex	U-Mrs.	24	F	Laborer	04Ma02Ex
HIGGINS, John	20	M	Laborer	04Ma02Ex	DAVIDSON, Bella	20	F	Laborer	04Ma02Ex
MCCORMACK, Mary	18	F	Servant	04Ma02Ex	Nancy	20	F	Dressmaker	04Ma02Ex
CUSACK, Patrick	18	M	Servant	04Ma02Ex	HAW, Mary	21	F	Dressmaker	04Ma02Ex
MCGOVERN, Margaret	46	F	Servant	04Ma02Ex	Sally	19	F	Servant	04Ma02Ex
LYNCH, Jane	34	F	Servant	04Ma02Ex	COLLINS, Eliza	26	F	Unknown	04Ma02Ex
James	12	M	Servant	04Ma02Ex	CLARKE, Patrick	24	M	Butcher	04Ma02Ex
Peter	8	M	Child	04Ma02Ex	U-Mrs.	24	F	Unknown	04Ma02Ex
Rose	6	F	Child	04Ma02Ex	U	.00	U	Infant	04Ma02Ex
Bridget	3	F	Child	04Ma02Ex	John	3	M	Child	04Ma02Ex
FARRELL, Jane	20	F	Servant	04Ma02Ex	HUGHES, Mary	22	F	Servant	04Ma02Ex
LYNCH, Mary	35	F	Servant	04Ma02Ex	AMOOTY, John	29	M	Laborer	04Ma02Ex
Matthew	9	M	Child	04Ma02Ex	Mary	27	F	Unknown	04Ma02Ex
John	6	M	Child	04Ma02Ex	Peter	16	M	Unknown	04Ma02Ex
Catharine	3	F	Child	04Ma02Ex	TAYLOR, James	27	M	Navigator	04Ma02Ex
KELLY, Nancy	20	F	Servant	04Ma02Ex	POWER, Michael	28	M	Laborer	04Ma02Ex
Letitia	20	F	Servant	04Ma02Ex	TORMEY, Michael	25	M	Laborer	04Ma02Ex
STEWART, Eliza	24	F	Servant	04Ma02Ex	DONOVAN, Richard	20	M	Laborer	04Ma02Ex
MCKENNICK, Nancy	24	F	Servant	04Ma02Ex	Thomas	19	M	Laborer	04Ma02Ex
GILMORE, Eliza	24	F	Servant	04Ma02Ex	FITZGERALD, James	26	M	Laborer	04Ma02Ex
GORMSON, Catharine	24	F	Servant	04Ma02Ex	Ellen	19	F	Laborer	04Ma02Ex
SMITH, Mary	24	F	Unknown	04Ma02Ex	CASEY, John	29	M	Carpenter	04Ma02Ex
KEFFEE, Patrick	24	M	Laborer	04Ma02Ex	FLYNN, Ellen	26	F	Servant	04Ma02Ex
U-Mrs.	21	F	Unknown	04Ma02Ex	DONOVAN, John	36	M	Laborer	04Ma02Ex
Anne	20	F	Unknown	04Ma02Ex	Patrick	21	M	Laborer	04Ma02Ex
Eliza	12	F	Unknown	04Ma02Ex	COLLIN, John	27	M	Laborer	04Ma02Ex
HEPBURN, Patrick	20	M	Laborer	04Ma02Ex	STACK, Mary	26	F	Servant	04Ma02Ex
DWYER, Mary	20	F	Dressmaker	04Ma02Ex	COSTELLO, Edmund	34	M	Laborer	04Ma02Ex
COLEHURST, Francis	20	M	Laborer	04Ma02Ex	GALLIGAN, Michael	11	M	Laborer	04Ma02Ex
COOKE, Margaret	44	F	Servant	04Ma02Ex	Ellen	10	F	Unknown	04Ma02Ex
HEADEN, Ellen	22	F	Servant	04Ma02Ex	COSGROVE, Dan	28	M	Laborer	04Ma02Ex
DEVIT, Mary	10	F	Servant	04Ma02Ex	U-Mrs.	20	F	Unknown	04Ma02Ex
REILLY, Thomas	17	M	Laborer	04Ma02Ex	U	.00	U	Infant	04Ma02Ex
TEAGUE, Mary	30	F	Spinster	04Ma02Ex	GALIGAN, Michael	11	M	Unknown	04Ma02Ex
MCGRADY, Hugh	26	M	Laborer	04Ma02Ex	FINIGAN, Andrew	18	M	Laborer	04Ma02Ex
Anne	24	F	Unknown	04Ma02Ex	Ann	14	F	Unknown	04Ma02Ex
James	2	M	Child	04Ma02Ex	DONELLY, Ellen	20	F	Unknown	04Ma02Ex
ELLY, Mary	8	F	Child	04Ma02Ex	GALAGAN, Bryan	30	M	Laborer	04Ma02Ex
LEVIN, Anne	19	F	Servant	04Ma02Ex	Patrick	10	M	Unknown	04Ma02Ex
EELY, Margaret	16	F	Servant	04Ma02Ex	Anne	8	F	Child	04Ma02Ex
Julia	12	F	Unknown	04Ma02Ex	Andrew	18	M	Unknown	04Ma02Ex
UFFEY, Mary	30	F	Servant	04Ma02Ex	NULTY, Mathew	20	M	Dealer	04Ma02Ex
OUGHLIN, William	16	M	Laborer	04Ma02Ex	COSGROVE, Patrick	20	M	Laborer	04Ma02Ex
Maneleo	14	U	Laborer	04Ma02Ex	KEIRNAN, Thomas	18	M	Laborer	04Ma02Ex
OHNSON, Michael	20	M	Laborer	04Ma02Ex	James	19	M	Laborer	04Ma02Ex
John	19	M	Laborer	04Ma02Ex	MARTIN, Mary	20	F	Servant	04Ma02Ex
ALEY, Patrick	16	M	Laborer	04Ma02Ex	GOWY, James	20	M	Servant	04Ma02Ex
YRNE, John	24	M	Laborer	04Ma02Ex	WHELAN, Keirnan	18	M	Laborer	04Ma02Ex
Margaret	22	F	Unknown	04Ma02Ex	SANFORD, Patrick	19	M	Laborer	04Ma02Ex
EARDON, Edward	30	M	Laborer	04Ma02Ex	BYRNE, Mary	17	F	Unknown	04Ma02Ex
Catherine	25	F	Unknown	04Ma02Ex	HOLAHAN, Judith	24	F	Servant	04Ma02Ex
OLEY, Patrick	35	M	Laborer	04Ma02Ex	Mary	20	F	Servant	04Ma02Ex
NN, William	22	M	Laborer	04Ma02Ex	CURRAN, Kitty	19	F	Servant	04Ma02Ex
Mary	18	F	Laborer	04Ma02Ex	WALSH, Martin	20	M	Laborer	04Ma02Ex
YDEN, Maria	15	F	Servant	04Ma02Ex	MARTIN, James	20	M	Laborer	04Ma02Ex
AIN, Patrick	18	M	Laborer	04Ma02Ex	MCMANUS, John	24	M	Servant	04Ma02Ex
OLAN, Ann	18	F	Servant	04Ma02Ex	CONLAN, Anne	40	F	Servant	04Ma02Ex
GAN, Thomas	20	M	Laborer	04Ma02Ex	DEVLIN, Martha	20	F	Servant	04Ma02Ex
STERSON, Walter	18	M	Laborer	04Ma02Ex	DWYER, Catharine	18	F	Servant	04Ma02Ex
NAGAN, Bridget	18	F	Laborer	04Ma02Ex	MOORE, George	23	M	Shoemaker	04Ma02Ex
BLER, Thomas	11	F	Unknown	04Ma02Ex	U-Mrs.	23	F	Unknown	04Ma02Ex
LE, John	26	M	Laborer	04Ma02Ex	Eliza	2	F	Child	04Ma02Ex
RTLEY, Archibald	29	M	Laborer	04Ma02Ex	John	4	M	Child	04Ma02Ex
Mary	29	F	Laborer	04Ma02Ex	Mary-Anne	6	F	Child	04Ma02Ex
Mary	7	F	Child	04Ma02Ex	CANNON, Mary	24	F	Servant	04Ma02Ex
Ann	6	F	Child	04Ma02Ex	Daniel	20	M	Laborer	04Ma02Ex
ALLISTER, Samuel	25	M	Laborer	04Ma02Ex	KERR, John	20	M	Laborer	04Ma02Ex
DERSON, Jane	30	F	Laborer	04Ma02Ex	Susan	21	F	Dressmaker	04Ma02Ex
IGHTON, Richard	25	M	Laborer	04Ma02Ex	GRIER, Thomas	20	M	Laborer	04Ma02Ex
NNAN, Dominick	25	M	Laborer	04Ma02Ex	DALEY, Anne	30	F	Servant	04Ma02Ex
Betty	25	F	Laborer	04Ma02Ex	KEIRNAN, Luke	26	M	Laborer	04Ma02Ex
LLACE, John	25	M	Laborer	04Ma02Ex	MCDONNELL, Patrick	30	M	Laborer	04Ma02Ex
IGHER, James	25	M	Laborer	04Ma02Ex	Betty	18	F	Unknown	04Ma02Ex
CABE, Edward	25	M	Laborer	04Ma02Ex	HIGGINS, Margaret	18	F	Servant	04Ma02Ex

NAMES OF PASSENGERS	AGE	SEX	OCCUPATIONS	DATE PORT SHIP
REYNOLDS, Bryan	40	M	Laborer	04Ma02Ex
Margaret	20	F	Servant	04Ma02Ex
Eliza	6	F	Child	04Ma02Ex
GWINARY, Ann	12	F	Servant	04Ma02Ex
CONNAUGHT, William	22	M	Laborer	04Ma02Ex
DONOVAN, John	30	M	Laborer	04Ma02Ex
KELLEHER, Cornelius	30	M	Laborer	04Ma02Ex
Ellen	30	F	Unknown	04Ma02Ex
U	.00	U	Infant	04Ma02Ex
Margaret	10	F	Unknown	04Ma02Ex
James	8	M	Child	04Ma02Ex
Mary	6	F	Child	04Ma02Ex
Eliza	4	F	Child	04Ma02Ex
BARRY, Michael	30	M	Laborer	04Ma02Ex
U-Mrs.	30	F	Unknown	04Ma02Ex
U	.00	U	Infant	04Ma02Ex
BARY, Patrick	26	M	Laborer	04Ma02Ex
Mary	20	F	Unknown	04Ma02Ex
TOBIN, Edmund	30	M	Laborer	04Ma02Ex
Michael	9	M	Child	04Ma02Ex
SHERIDAN, Philip	46	M	Laborer	04Ma02Ex
GERRATY, Peter	40	M	Laborer	04Ma02Ex
Bridget	40	M	Laborer	04Ma02Ex
Ellen	5	F	Child	04Ma02Ex
Bridget	5	F	Child	04Ma02Ex

ELIZABETH 04 MAY 1849

From Belfast

NAMES OF PASSENGERS	AGE	SEX	OCCUPATIONS	DATE PORT SHIP
REID, John	26	M	Minister	04Ma05Bk
Agnes	20	F	Unknown	04Ma05Bk
STEVENSON, Jane	38	F	Unknown	04Ma05Bk
Ellen	16	F	Unknown	04Ma05Bk
BELL, Eliza	45	F	Unknown	04Ma05Bk
Jane	22	F	Unknown	04Ma05Bk
Anna	17	F	Unknown	04Ma05Bk
Wm.Robert	15	M	Unknown	04Ma05Bk
Thomas	13	M	Unknown	04Ma05Bk
Rebecca	11	F	Unknown	04Ma05Bk
Joseph	8	M	Child	04Ma05Bk
Georgina	6	F	Child	04Ma05Bk
Ann-Green	32	F	Unknown	04Ma05Bk
Jane	5	F	Child	04Ma05Bk
MCMENOMY, Dorothea	19	F	Unknown	04Ma05Bk
ALLEN, Adam	30	M	Farmer	04Ma05Bk
MCALISTER, Chas.	23	M	Unknown	04Ma05Bk
KELLY, John	26	M	Laborer	04Ma05Bk
BOYLE, Pat	21	M	Laborer	04Ma05Bk
DAWBY, Pat	18	M	Laborer	04Ma05Bk
THISTLE, Robert	25	M	Laborer	04Ma05Bk
WILEY, Abraham	26	M	Laborer	04Ma05Bk
Jane	24	F	Unknown	04Ma05Bk
Thomas	.00	M	Infant	04Ma05Bk
ALDER, Robert	25	M	Farmer	04Ma05Bk
William	23	M	Farmer	04Ma05Bk
BALLINGTINE, A.	23	M	Laborer	04Ma05Bk
Jane	18	F	Unknown	04Ma05Bk
MCALISTER, Mary	40	F	Unknown	04Ma05Bk
SHIELS, Pat	20	M	Laborer	04Ma05Bk
CAMPBELL, Mary	25	F	Unknown	04Ma05Bk
Jane	14	F	Unknown	04Ma05Bk
MCLENAGHAN, Bridget	16	F	Unknown	04Ma05Bk
SAYRS, Mary	18	F	Unknown	04Ma05Bk
ANDERSON, Cathn.	16	F	Unknown	04Ma05Bk
MCCLACKEY, Edwd.	20	M	Laborer	04Ma05Bk
Sarah	18	F	Unknown	04Ma05Bk
MCCLACKEREY, Mary	17	F	Unknown	04Ma05Bk
ONEILL, James	20	M	Laborer	04Ma05Bk

NAMES OF PASSENGERS	AGE	SEX	OCCUPATIONS	DATE PORT SHIP
ROBINSON, Jane	21	F	Unknown	04Ma05
Mary	21	F	Unknown	04Ma05
RODGERS, John	20	M	Laborer	04Ma05
NUGENT, Bridget	16	F	Unknown	04Ma05
Bridget	20	F	Unknown	04Ma05
KILE, Andrew	27	M	Laborer	04Ma05
Mary	30	F	Unknown	04Ma05
Margt.	21	F	Unknown	04Ma05
MACKIN, John	14	M	Farmer	04Ma05
ROGERS, Edwd.	16	M	Laborer	04Ma05
TIERNEY, Stephen	21	M	Laborer	04Ma05
MCCARR, Mary	17	F	Unknown	04Ma05
CRAWFORD, James	40	M	Farmer	04Ma05
Jane	11	F	Unknown	04Ma05
Mary	10	F	Unknown	04Ma05
James	4	M	Child	04Ma05
Daniel	6	M	Child	04Ma05
Nancy	5	F	Child	04Ma05
John	14	M	Unknown	04Ma05
PATTERSON, John	20	M	Laborer	04Ma05
POLAND, Jane	19	F	Unknown	04Ma05
HOWELL, Francis	42	F	Laborer	04Ma05
Elizabeth	12	F	Unknown	04Ma05
DURNING, John	40	M	Farmer	04Ma05
Ann	30	F	Unknown	04Ma05
Jane	4	F	Child	04Ma05
Rosetta	2	F	Child	04Ma05
CHESING, Hugh	26	M	Laborer	04Ma05
Saml.	20	M	Laborer	04Ma05
MOONEY, Mary	17	F	Unknown	04Ma05
Ely	16	F	Unknown	04Ma05
Martha	8	F	Child	04Ma05
DOGHERTY, Biddy	20	F	Unknown	04Ma05
MILLAR, Jane	20	F	Unknown	04Ma05
STEWART, John	25	M	Laborer	04Ma05
James	20	M	Laborer	04Ma05
BOYD, Alex.	21	M	Laborer	04Ma05
Ann-Jane	20	F	Unknown	04Ma05
Charles	.00	M	Infant	04Ma05
MCNEIL, James	22	M	Laborer	04Ma05
AGNEW, John	25	M	Laborer	04Ma05
COOPER, Lucinda	24	F	Unknown	04Ma05
HUGHES, Pat	20	M	Laborer	04Ma05
SOMERVILLE, Margt.	20	F	Unknown	04Ma05
JOHNSON, Joseph	20	M	Laborer	04Ma05
WILSON, Kennedy	21	M	Laborer	04Ma05
William	19	M	Laborer	04Ma05
MCKITTRICK, Eliza	18	F	Unknown	04Ma05
CULLIN, Peter	40	M	Farmer	04Ma0
Alice	35	M	Unknown	04Ma0
Jane	18	F	Unknown	04Ma0
Sarah	25	F	Unknown	04Ma0
FOX, John	45	M	Farmer	04Ma0
Mary	42	F	Unknown	04Ma0
Owen	19	M	Laborer	04Ma0
Patrick	16	M	Unknown	04Ma0
Margaret	13	F	Unknown	04Ma0
Ellen	11	F	Unknown	04Ma0
Peter	8	M	Child	04Ma0
Thomas	6	M	Child	04Ma0
Daniel	3	M	Child	04Ma0
VOGAN, Mary	35	F	Unknown	04Ma0
Sarah	12	F	Unknown	04Ma0
Mary	10	F	Unknown	04Ma0
Elena	7	F	Child	04Ma0
John	9	M	Child	04Ma0
Robert	4	M	Child	04Ma0
ONEIL, Michael	50	M	Farmer	04Ma0
Henry	48	M	Farmer	04Ma0
Sarah	42	F	Unknown	04Ma0
Mary	15	F	Unknown	04Ma
Elizabeth	10	F	Unknown	04Ma
LOUGHRAN, Danl.	60	M	Farmer	04Ma
Ellen	40	F	Unknown	04Ma
Bridget	15	F	Unknown	04Ma

NAMES OF PASSENGERS	AGE	SEX	OCCUPATIONS	DATE PORT SHIP
OUGHRAN, Michael	13	M	Unknown	04Ma05Bk
Catharine	11	F	Unknown	04Ma05Bk
Daniel	9	M	Child	04Ma05Bk
Peter	4	M	Child	04Ma05Bk
OVELY, Mary	46	F	Unknown	04Ma05Bk
Sarah	23	F	Unknown	04Ma05Bk
Andrew	14	M	Laborer	04Ma05Bk
Ellen	11	F	Unknown	04Ma05Bk
CCAUGHY, Pat	55	M	Farmer	04Ma05Bk
Cath.	42	F	Unknown	04Ma05Bk
Felix	20	M	Laborer	04Ma05Bk
Pat	16	M	Laborer	04Ma05Bk
John	11	M	Unknown	04Ma05Bk
Cathn.	7	F	Child	04Ma05Bk
CGUIGAN, Cath.	50	F	Unknown	04Ma05Bk
Ellen	46	F	Unknown	04Ma05Bk
Rose	44	F	Unknown	04Ma05Bk
ITZPATRICK, Cath.	60	F	Unknown	04Ma05Bk
Maryann	25	F	Unknown	04Ma05Bk
Cathn.	23	F	Unknown	04Ma05Bk
Eliza	20	F	Unknown	04Ma05Bk
OGHERTY, Eleanor	24	F	Unknown	04Ma05Bk
UGAN, Ann	24	F	Laborer	04Ma05Bk
EWITT, Wm.	23	M	Laborer	04Ma05Bk
ILSON, Edw.	23	M	Laborer	04Ma05Bk
ONES, Wm.	24	M	Laborer	04Ma05Bk
EWETT, Phoebe	18	F	Unknown	04Ma05Bk
Maria	20	F	Unknown	04Ma05Bk
RAZER, David	28	M	Laborer	04Ma05Bk
HORT, Daniel	26	M	Laborer	04Ma05Bk
Ann-J.	18	F	Unknown	04Ma05Bk
EGAN, Andrew	26	M	Laborer	04Ma05Bk
Elizabeth	24	F	Unknown	04Ma05Bk
LACK, Wm.	20	M	Laborer	04Ma05Bk
ORRISON, Mary	20	F	Unknown	04Ma05Bk
ARMICHAEL, Robert	40	M	Laborer	04Ma05Bk
ARK, Andrew	50	M	Laborer	04Ma05Bk
Margt.	14	F	Unknown	04Ma05Bk
NEILL, Ambrose	40	M	Farmer	04Ma05Bk
HARE, Rose	20	F	Unknown	04Ma05Bk
REY, James	16	M	Laborer	04Ma05Bk
TEWART, John	19	M	Laborer	04Ma05Bk
MPBELL, Mary	18	F	Unknown	04Ma05Bk
NSK, Mary	20	F	Unknown	04Ma05Bk
JGHES, Edwd.	18	M	Laborer	04Ma05Bk
RNES, Wm.	23	M	Laborer	04Ma05Bk
KIBBIN, Saml.	32	M	Laborer	04Ma05Bk
RDON, Alice	40	F	Unknown	04Ma05Bk
Lucy	30	F	Unknown	04Ma05Bk
INE, Chevalier	22	M	Laborer	04Ma05Bk
KANE, Margt.	22	F	Unknown	04Ma05Bk
Jane	20	F	Unknown	04Ma05Bk
William	20	M	Unknown	04Ma05Bk
James	20	M	Unknown	04Ma05Bk
CAULEY, Mary	20	F	Unknown	04Ma05Bk
VILAND, Hugh	25	M	Farmer	04Ma05Bk
Margt.	21	F	Unknown	04Ma05Bk
HNSON, Saml.	30	M	Farmer	04Ma05Bk
Jane	40	F	Unknown	04Ma05Bk
James	10	M	Farmer	04Ma05Bk
Ellen-Jane	3	F	Child	04Ma05Bk
TTEN, Ellener	21	F	Unknown	04Ma05Bk
VEY, John	21	M	Laborer	04Ma05Bk
KIBBIN, Jane	30	F	Unknown	04Ma05Bk
John	.00	M	Infant	04Ma05Bk
TEN, Mary-Ann	20	F	Unknown	04Ma05Bk
AN, Mary	24	F	Unknown	04Ma05Bk
EN, John-W.	20	M	Laborer	04Ma05Bk
TH, Sam.	20	M	Laborer	04Ma05Bk
UAID, Mary	50	F	Unknown	04Ma05Bk
ane	20	F	Unknown	04Ma05Bk
oseph	19	M	Farmer	04Ma05Bk
aryann	17	F	Unknown	04Ma05Bk
eter	15	M	Laborer	04Ma05Bk
athn.	13	F	Unknown	04Ma05Bk

NAMES OF PASSENGERS	AGE	SEX	OCCUPATIONS	DATE PORT SHIP
MCQUAID, Ellen	11	F	Unknown	04Ma05Bk
John	.00	M	Infant	04Ma05Bk
Hugh	9	M	Child	04Ma05Bk
Mary-Jane	.00	F	Infant	04Ma05Bk
MCQUILLAN, James	35	M	Farmer	04Ma05Bk
Cathn.	30	F	Unknown	04Ma05Bk
MCQUAID, Cath.	30	F	Unknown	04Ma05Bk
BLACK, Elizabeth	60	F	Unknown	04Ma05Bk
Sally	20	F	Unknown	04Ma05Bk
JOHNSON, Hugh	26	M	Laborer	04Ma05Bk
MCGRANEY, Edwd.	25	M	Laborer	04Ma05Bk
CASSIDY, Sarah-Ann	24	F	Unknown	04Ma05Bk
MCGARRY, Matilda	11	F	Unknown	04Ma05Bk
TOWER, Jemima	50	F	Unknown	04Ma05Bk
Robert	25	M	Laborer	04Ma05Bk
Abraham	21	M	Laborer	04Ma05Bk
Isaac	17	M	Laborer	04Ma05Bk
Jacob	15	M	Laborer	04Ma05Bk
DONLY, Alice	20	F	Unknown	04Ma05Bk
Daniel	5	M	Child	04Ma05Bk
DOWLEY, Edward	45	M	Laborer	04Ma05Bk
Martha	40	F	Unknown	04Ma05Bk
Patrick	13	M	Laborer	04Ma05Bk
Mary	11	F	Unknown	04Ma05Bk
Matilda	8	F	Child	04Ma05Bk
Sarah-Ann	6	F	Child	04Ma05Bk
Michael	47	M	Laborer	04Ma05Bk
Ellen	40	F	Unknown	04Ma05Bk
John	8	M	Child	04Ma05Bk
Ann	5	F	Child	04Ma05Bk
HUGHES, Peter	32	M	Laborer	04Ma05Bk
Alice	30	F	Unknown	04Ma05Bk
Peter	8	M	Child	04Ma05Bk
Jane	6	F	Child	04Ma05Bk
Frances	4	F	Child	04Ma05Bk
Maryann	.00	F	Infant	04Ma05Bk
AKIN, Lucy	35	F	Unknown	04Ma05Bk
Jane	15	F	Unknown	04Ma05Bk
John	12	M	Unknown	04Ma05Bk
Sarah	9	F	Child	04Ma05Bk
REID, Fanny	50	F	Unknown	04Ma05Bk
Maryann	16	F	Unknown	04Ma05Bk
MATINN, Michael	27	M	Laborer	04Ma05Bk
STEVENSON, Ellen	20	F	Unknown	04Ma05Bk
James	11	M	Laborer	04Ma05Bk
RODGERS, Ellen	19	F	Unknown	04Ma05Bk
COPLAND, Hugh	24	M	Laborer	04Ma05Bk
LOUGHLEN, James	24	M	Laborer	04Ma05Bk
Mary	18	F	Unknown	04Ma05Bk
HUGHES, Francis	34	F	Laborer	04Ma05Bk
CAUGHY, John	28	M	Laborer	04Ma05Bk
HEWETT, Fredk.	20	M	Laborer	04Ma05Bk
Sarah-Jane	19	F	Laborer	04Ma05Bk
HODGE, Rosetta	18	F	Unknown	04Ma05Bk
MCINTYRE, Wm.	20	M	Laborer	04Ma05Bk
MCQUAID, Joseph	25	M	Laborer	04Ma05Bk
MCCUSKEE, Edwd.	20	M	Laborer	04Ma05Bk
MCKOWEN, Thos.	20	M	Laborer	04Ma05Bk
THOMPSON, Fanny	22	F	Unknown	04Ma05Bk
CULLEN, Pat	20	M	Laborer	04Ma05Bk
Ann	20	F	Unknown	04Ma05Bk
HAMPTON, Mary	20	F	Unknown	04Ma05Bk
QUINCY, James	40	M	Farmer	04Ma05Bk
FERRYSMAN, Mary	23	F	Unknown	04Ma05Bk

MOZAMBIQUE 04 MAY 1849

From Sligo

NAMES OF PASSENGERS	AGE	SEX	OCCUPATIONS	DATE PORT SHIP
CONWAY, John	20	M	Farmer	04Ma21Ff
Pat	21	M	Farmer	04Ma21Ff
Cath.	19	F	Spinster	04Ma21Ff
BARBER, James	25	M	Laborer	04Ma21Ff
John	23	M	Laborer	04Ma21Ff
SCULLY, Thady	24	F	Spinster	04Ma21Ff
Anne	27	F	Spinster	04Ma21Ff
Mary	.06	F	Infant	04Ma21Ff
REGAN, Thos.	25	M	Farmer	04Ma21Ff
HINNIGAN, Math.	24	M	Butcher	04Ma21Ff
James	25	M	Farmer	04Ma21Ff
Michl.	21	M	Farmer	04Ma21Ff
Elenor	24	F	Spinster	04Ma21Ff
Bridgt.	30	F	Spinster	04Ma21Ff
Honor	27	F	Spinster	04Ma21Ff
Owen	29	M	Farmer	04Ma21Ff
Cath.	23	F	Spinster	04Ma21Ff
BRENAN, Pat	20	M	Farmer	04Ma21Ff
MCGOWN, Terence	21	M	Farmer	04Ma21Ff
Owen	25	M	Farmer	04Ma21Ff
GINHEIN, Magt.	23	F	Spinster	04Ma21Ff
MCGOWAN, Bartely	24	M	Farmer	04Ma21Ff
CLINTON, Mary	25	F	Spinster	04Ma21Ff
MCGOWAN, Mary	27	F	Spinster	04Ma21Ff
Pat	26	M	Farmer	04Ma21Ff
THORNTON, Thoms.	24	M	Farmer	04Ma21Ff
Mary	23	F	Spinster	04Ma21Ff
Nelly	20	F	Spinster	04Ma21Ff
Libby	25	F	Spinster	04Ma21Ff
Thoms.	.00	M	Infant	04Ma21Ff
SWEENY, Martin	30	M	Laborer	04Ma21Ff
MCHALE, John	34	M	Laborer	04Ma21Ff
QUINAN, Pat	21	M	Laborer	04Ma21Ff
CUMMINGS, Owen	30	M	Laborer	04Ma21Ff
Anne	31	F	Spinster	04Ma21Ff
John	22	M	Laborer	04Ma21Ff
Mary	24	F	Spinster	04Ma21Ff
CARTEY, Michl.	21	M	Laborer	04Ma21Ff
COGGINS, Patk.	27	M	Laborer	04Ma21Ff
CONANGHTON, Pat	28	M	Laborer	04Ma21Ff
CONNOR, John	27	M	Laborer	04Ma21Ff
Biddy	00	F	Spinner	04Ma21Ff
Charles	23	M	Laborer	04Ma21Ff
John	24	M	Laborer	04Ma21Ff
Mary	25	F	Spinster	04Ma21Ff
Pat	.07	M	Infant	04Ma21Ff
WELCH, Thoms.	3	M	Child	04Ma21Ff
GRIMES, Thoms.	31	M	Laborer	04Ma21Ff
Mary	31	F	Spinster	04Ma21Ff
Cath.	.03	F	Infant	04Ma21Ff
U	.03	U	Infant	04Ma21Ff
CUNNANE, Michl.	32	M	Laborer	04Ma21Ff
PADDEN, Magt.	29	F	Spinster	04Ma21Ff
ZUCCAN, Cath.	27	F	Spinster	04Ma21Ff
LYNCH, Mary	24	F	Spinster	04Ma21Ff
NAUGHTON, Michl.	21	M	Laborer	04Ma21Ff
TUFFY, Dennis	24	M	Laborer	04Ma21Ff
ROONEY, Bartley	27	M	Laborer	04Ma21Ff
FEEHLY, Michl.	40	M	Laborer	04Ma21Ff
FECKELY, Elenor	41	F	Spinster	04Ma21Ff
MCDERMOT, Thaddy	28	M	Laborer	04Ma21Ff
ATKINSON, Thoms.	27	M	Laborer	04Ma21Ff
Mary	24	F	Spinster	04Ma21Ff
Robt.	28	M	Laborer	04Ma21Ff
COWLEY, Pat	.09	M	Infant	04Ma21Ff

NAMES OF PASSENGERS	AGE	SEX	OCCUPATIONS	DATE PORT SHIP
COWLEY, Bridget	25	F	Spinster	04Ma21F
Pat	23	M	Laborer	04Ma21F
CARROL, Mary	25	F	Spinster	04Ma21F
KEAN, Ellen	26	F	Spinster	04Ma21F
FEE, Jane	27	F	Spinster	04Ma21F
BROWN, Cath.	25	F	Spinster	04Ma21F
FENARGHTY, Owen	24	M	Farmer	04Ma21F
Cath.	27	F	Spinster	04Ma21F
Ellen	25	F	Spinster	04Ma21F
William	10	M	Unknown	04Ma21F
GORDON, James	24	M	Farmer	04Ma21F
MAY, John	31	M	Farmer	04Ma21F
GROVE, Thoms.	30	M	Farmer	04Ma21F
FANSSELL, Robt.	35	M	Farmer	04Ma21F
BOWELS, Pat	35	M	Farmer	04Ma21F
BOWLEY, Cath.	34	F	Spinster	04Ma21F
HARRISON, Rebecca	37	F	Spinster	04Ma21F
James	27	M	Spinster	04Ma21F
Thomas	29	M	Farmer	04Ma21F
Robt.	31	M	Farmer	04Ma21F
Rebecca-Jane	30	F	Spinster	04Ma21F
FOLEY, Bridgt.	34	F	Spinster	04Ma21F
SMITH, Winfred.	25	M	Laborer	04Ma21F
LINCH, Bridgt.	27	F	Spinster	04Ma21F
Domnick	.08	M	Infant	04Ma21F
KOHENG, Thady	27	M	Laborer	04Ma21F
KILCULLER, Michl.	25	M	Laborer	04Ma21F
CAVANAGH, Ann	45	F	Spinster	04Ma21F
Bridget	29	F	Spinster	04Ma21F
KAHENY, John	17	M	Laborer	04Ma21F
John	25	M	Laborer	04Ma21F
HATICERY, Hugh	19	M	Laborer	04Ma21F
KAHENY, Letty	27	F	Spinster	04Ma21
GILGAN, Domnick	27	M	Laborer	04Ma21
SMITH, Wm.	18	M	Laborer	04Ma21
FENARGHTY, Thomas	25	M	Laborer	04Ma21
Cath.	24	F	Spinster	04Ma21
Mary	27	F	Spinster	04Ma21
DOUD, Winifred	30	F	Spinster	04Ma21
WATERS, Pat	31	M	Farmer	04Ma21
Mary	37	F	Spinster	04Ma21
RIELY, Pat	29	M	Farmer	04Ma21
GILLEN, Mary	24	F	Spinster	04Ma21
HENRY, James	27	M	Farmer	04Ma21
KILCORN, Mary	19	F	Spinster	04Ma21
GANNON, Thoms.	18	M	Farmer	04Ma21
Cath.	20	F	Spinster	04Ma21
Cath.	21	F	Spinster	04Ma21
Pat	35	M	Laborer	04Ma21
WYNINS, Pat	40	M	Laborer	04Ma2
Margt.	41	F	Spinster	04Ma2
Michl.	10	M	Unknown	04Ma2
COULTER, William	19	M	Farmer	04Ma2
Jane	18	F	Unknown	04Ma2
Mary	25	F	Spinster	04Ma2
CONNOLLY, Owen	24	M	Farmer	04Ma2
Cath.	27	F	Spinster	04Ma2
BOLAND, Thoms.	15	M	Unknown	04Ma2
Magt.	9	F	Child	04Ma2
JORDAN, Henry	21	M	Farmer	04Ma2
MITCHEL, Cath.	20	F	Spinster	04Ma2
SHERIDAN, Susan	24	F	Spinster	04Ma2
WALLACE, Bridgt.	21	F	Spinster	04Ma2
CAMARON, Thoms.	17	M	Farmer	04Ma2
Cath.	29	F	Spinster	04Ma2
FLYNN, Bridgt.	25	F	Spinster	04Ma2
GOLLICA, Patk.	24	M	Farmer	04Ma2
Patk.	43	M	Farmer	04Ma2
MAILEY, Patk.	25	M	Farmer	04Ma2
BOYD, James	19	M	Farmer	04Ma2
Bridgt.	19	F	Spinster	04Ma2
Thoms.	25	M	Laborer	04Ma2
Biddy	34	F	Spinster	04Ma2
Ann	.09	F	Infant	04Ma2
OCOUNSELL, Pat	27	M	Laborer	04Ma2

NAMES OF PASSENGERS	AGE	SEX	OCCUPATIONS	DATE PORT SHIP
OCONNOR, Ann	24	F	Spinster	04Ma21Ff
TENPANY, Thoms.	29	M	Farmer	04Ma21Ff
Mary	30	F	Spinster	04Ma21Ff
SMITH, Bernard	27	M	Farmer	04Ma21Ff
HURT, Willaim	29	M	Farmer	04Ma21Ff
HART, Sally	21	F	Spinster	04Ma21Ff
Margt.	15	F	Spinster	04Ma21Ff
Rodger	19	M	Farmer	04Ma21Ff
CONNERS, Biddy	24	F	Wife	04Ma21Ff
Peter	27	M	Farmer	04Ma21Ff
Hugh	29	M	Farmer	04Ma21Ff
Cath.	23	F	Wife	04Ma21Ff
CURNAN, Owen	24	M	Farmer	04Ma21Ff
Hugh	25	M	Farmer	04Ma21Ff
MASTINID, Pat	27	M	Farmer	04Ma21Ff
CALLAGHAN, John	29	M	Farmer	04Ma21Ff
Cath.	31	F	Wife	04Ma21Ff
GILLER, John	42	M	Farmer	04Ma21Ff
MULLEN, Susan	41	F	Spinster	04Ma21Ff
HURT, Mark	27	M	Farmer	04Ma21Ff
Martin	49	M	Farmer	04Ma21Ff
PEARY, Eliza	16	F	Unknown	04Ma21Ff
HINIGAN, John	25	M	Farmer	04Ma21Ff
JOHNSTON, Eliza	24	F	Spinster	04Ma21Ff
Eliza	27	F	Wife	04Ma21Ff
GALLAGHER, John	34	M	Farmer	04Ma21Ff
MCDERMOT, Margt.	21	F	Spinster	04Ma21Ff
MCGOWAN, Margt.	23	F	Spinster	04Ma21Ff
THACKERBERRY, Jane	18	F	Unknown	04Ma21Ff
KEIR, Ellen	20	F	Unknown	04Ma21Ff

MCDONNELL 04 MAY 1849

From Liverpool

NAMES OF PASSENGERS	AGE	SEX	OCCUPATIONS	DATE PORT SHIP
CUNIFFE, Matthew	45	M	Laborer	04Ma02Fg
Michal	45	M	Laborer	04Ma02Fg
John	18	M	Laborer	04Ma02Fg
Thomas	16	M	Laborer	04Ma02Fg
Bridget	13	F	Laborer	04Ma02Fg
Mat.	11	M	Laborer	04Ma02Fg
Charles	9	M	Child	04Ma02Fg
William	.00	M	Infant	04Ma02Fg
COUGHLAN, Pat	28	M	Unknown	04Ma02Fg
CLARK, John	35	M	Unknown	04Ma02Fg
PAGE, George	24	M	Unknown	04Ma02Fg
DOWNEY, John	27	M	Unknown	04Ma02Fg
Susan	21	F	Unknown	04Ma02Fg
William	26	M	Unknown	04Ma02Fg
MCPHILE, Michal	14	M	Unknown	04Ma02Fg
FLAGHERTY, Pat	21	M	Unknown	04Ma02Fg
WALSH, Edward	21	M	Unknown	04Ma02Fg
Arty.	16	M	Unknown	04Ma02Fg
FITZUALL, James	28	M	Unknown	04Ma02Fg
Ellen	39	F	Unknown	04Ma02Fg
Margret	.00	F	Infant	04Ma02Fg
RYAN, Thomas	25	M	Unknown	04Ma02Fg
Bridget	22	F	Unknown	04Ma02Fg
GRAY, Mary	23	F	Unknown	04Ma02Fg
CULHAN, Davey	40	M	Unknown	04Ma02Fg
Edward	40	M	Unknown	04Ma02Fg
Mary	12	F	Unknown	04Ma02Fg
Anty	10	M	Unknown	04Ma02Fg
Kelly	8	M	Child	04Ma02Fg
Pat	5	M	Child	04Ma02Fg
John	3	M	Child	04Ma02Fg
Biddy	.00	F	Infant	04Ma02Fg
OHN, Michal	35	M	Unknown	04Ma02Fg
UDAN, Mary	11	F	Unknown	04Ma02Fg
LUDAN, Thomas	7	M	Child	04Ma02Fg
William	.00	M	Infant	04Ma02Fg
James	30	M	Unknown	04Ma02Fg
CAINBELL, Tim	24	M	Unknown	04Ma02Fg
Cath.	27	F	Unknown	04Ma02Fg
KUSOP, James	20	M	Unknown	04Ma02Fg
FLYNN, Margret	40	F	Unknown	04Ma02Fg
Deboral	35	F	Unknown	04Ma02Fg
James	13	M	Unknown	04Ma02Fg
Isaac	11	M	Unknown	04Ma02Fg
Elizabeth	9	F	Child	04Ma02Fg
Thomas	6	M	Child	04Ma02Fg
John	4	M	Child	04Ma02Fg
Joseph	.00	M	Infant	04Ma02Fg
BALL, Penn.	25	M	Unknown	04Ma02Fg
BOYCE, James	28	M	Unknown	04Ma02Fg
Mary	24	F	Unknown	04Ma02Fg
Mary	5	F	Child	04Ma02Fg
Michal	.00	M	Infant	04Ma02Fg
WRIGHT, Robert	22	M	Unknown	04Ma02Fg
Elizabeth	50	F	Unknown	04Ma02Fg
Elizabeth	29	F	Unknown	04Ma02Fg
Henriette	22	F	Unknown	04Ma02Fg
Eliza	20	F	Unknown	04Ma02Fg
ALTENSWORTH, George	25	M	Unknown	04Ma02Fg
John	24	M	Unknown	04Ma02Fg
SCULLY, Wm.	25	M	Unknown	04Ma02Fg
Elisa	28	F	Unknown	04Ma02Fg
Mary-Anne	17	F	Unknown	04Ma02Fg
FLYNN, James	40	M	Unknown	04Ma02Fg
Cath.	38	F	Unknown	04Ma02Fg
Mary	19	F	Unknown	04Ma02Fg
Judy	16	F	Unknown	04Ma02Fg
John	12	M	Unknown	04Ma02Fg
Pat	8	M	Child	04Ma02Fg
HUGHES, Rose	40	F	Unknown	04Ma02Fg
Rose	.00	F	Infant	04Ma02Fg
WILLIAMSON, Alice	20	F	Unknown	04Ma02Fg
MULLOY, Connor	35	M	Unknown	04Ma02Fg
BRYANS, Ellen	42	F	Unknown	04Ma02Fg
Ellen	7	F	Child	04Ma02Fg
Tim	35	M	Unknown	04Ma02Fg
Cath.	15	F	Unknown	04Ma02Fg
RYAN, Tim	13	M	Unknown	04Ma02Fg
Lawrence	17	M	Unknown	04Ma02Fg
HENRYS, Mich.	17	M	Unknown	04Ma02Fg
TYNAN, Mary	24	F	Unknown	04Ma02Fg
CIVAN, John	19	M	Unknown	04Ma02Fg
FITZPATRICK, Robt.	22	M	Unknown	04Ma02Fg
Martin	50	M	Unknown	04Ma02Fg
Sarah	45	F	Unknown	04Ma02Fg
Julia	27	F	Unknown	04Ma02Fg
Bridget	16	F	Unknown	04Ma02Fg
Thomas	7	M	Child	04Ma02Fg
HARRISON, Richd.	24	M	Unknown	04Ma02Fg
KILLIEN, John	22	M	Unknown	04Ma02Fg
SMITH, David	34	M	Unknown	04Ma02Fg
Cath.	26	F	Unknown	04Ma02Fg
REYNOLDS, Peter	20	M	Unknown	04Ma02Fg
GORMLEY, Patt	20	M	Unknown	04Ma02Fg
FOLEY, Thomas	18	M	Unknown	04Ma02Fg
BARRY, James	18	M	Unknown	04Ma02Fg
Phillip	17	M	Unknown	04Ma02Fg
Ann	16	F	Unknown	04Ma02Fg
MURPHY, Michl.	20	M	Unknown	04Ma02Fg
BINNIS, Ann	20	F	Unknown	04Ma02Fg
TAYLOR, Wm.	19	M	Unknown	04Ma02Fg
BERGIN, Michl.	20	M	Unknown	04Ma02Fg
FOGHERY, Thos.	36	M	Unknown	04Ma02Fg
LEWIS, John	40	M	Unknown	04Ma02Fg
HAMMELL, Margt.	28	F	Unknown	04Ma02Fg
RUFF, Robt.	36	M	Unknown	04Ma02Fg
Sarah	30	F	Unknown	04Ma02Fg
Johanna	.00	F	Infant	04Ma02Fg
LAMBERS, George	20	M	Unknown	04Ma02Fg

NAMES OF PASSENGERS	AGE	SEX	OCCUPATIONS	DATE PORT SHIP
LANGAN, Phil.	24	M	Unknown	04Ma02Fg
ROBERTS, Joseph	24	M	Unknown	04Ma02Fg
DALTON, Jas.	25	M	Unknown	04Ma02Fg
Cath.	22	F	Unknown	04Ma02Fg
Michl.	.00	M	Infant	04Ma02Fg
HAWKSWATT, Matt	20	M	Unknown	04Ma02Fg
JESSOP, Jas.	31	M	Unknown	04Ma02Fg
Ann	30	F	Unknown	04Ma02Fg
Wm.	8	M	Child	04Ma02Fg
Thos.	3	M	Child	04Ma02Fg
James	.00	M	Infant	04Ma02Fg
John	28	M	Unknown	04Ma02Fg
HELLET, John	30	M	Unknown	04Ma02Fg
George	8	M	Child	04Ma02Fg
LANGAN, Phillip	24	M	Unknown	04Ma02Fg
MAXWELL, Cath.	22	F	Unknown	04Ma02Fg
KELLY, John	30	M	Unknown	04Ma02Fg
Cath.	27	F	Unknown	04Ma02Fg
Julia	25	F	Unknown	04Ma02Fg
Patt	.00	M	Infant	04Ma02Fg
MURRAY, John	25	M	Unknown	04Ma02Fg
Margt.	25	F	Unknown	04Ma02Fg
CHATWOOD, Wm.	35	M	Unknown	04Ma02Fg
Francis	37	M	Unknown	04Ma02Fg
Elisabeth	12	F	Unknown	04Ma02Fg
George	11	M	Unknown	04Ma02Fg
Emma	9	F	Child	04Ma02Fg
Thos.	5	M	Child	04Ma02Fg
Wm.	7	M	Child	04Ma02Fg
Ann	3	F	Child	04Ma02Fg
Fanny	.00	F	Infant	04Ma02Fg
HURST, Patt	30	M	Unknown	04Ma02Fg
REILLY, Michl.	30	M	Unknown	04Ma02Fg
MEEHAN, Darby	40	M	Unknown	04Ma02Fg
MCDONNELL, Thomas	25	M	Unknown	04Ma02Fg
BEIN, Jas.	16	M	Unknown	04Ma02Fg
OXFORD, Edwd.	29	M	Unknown	04Ma02Fg
CAMPBELL, John	40	M	Unknown	04Ma02Fg
Cicely	40	F	Unknown	04Ma02Fg
Mary	.00	F	Infant	04Ma02Fg
OGREAVER, George	18	M	Unknown	04Ma02Fg
WARD, Patt	42	M	Unknown	04Ma02Fg
GORRAN, Michl.	25	M	Unknown	04Ma02Fg
Pattk.	13	M	Unknown	04Ma02Fg
FITZGERALD, John	48	M	Unknown	04Ma02Fg
PRIESTLY, John	28	M	Unknown	04Ma02Fg
HOLKINS, Ennis	30	M	Unknown	04Ma02Fg
KENNICKS, Cath.	40	F	Unknown	04Ma02Fg
Mary	8	F	Child	04Ma02Fg
John	6	M	Child	04Ma02Fg
BROWN, Margt.	40	F	Unknown	04Ma02Fg
Margt.	20	F	Unknown	04Ma02Fg
Jane	18	F	Unknown	04Ma02Fg
Elisa	16	F	Unknown	04Ma02Fg
John	13	M	Unknown	04Ma02Fg
Cath.	20	F	Unknown	04Ma02Fg
HANLON, Danl.	28	M	Unknown	04Ma02Fg
Cath.	26	F	Unknown	04Ma02Fg
Keran	8	M	Child	04Ma02Fg
Johanna	.00	F	Infant	04Ma02Fg
Bridget	28	F	Unknown	04Ma02Fg
FARRELL, Thomas	24	M	Unknown	04Ma02Fg
James	22	M	Unknown	04Ma02Fg
KEOUGH, John	24	M	Unknown	04Ma02Fg
DUNN, Betsy	26	F	Unknown	04Ma02Fg
Mary	4	F	Child	04Ma02Fg
John	.00	M	Infant	04Ma02Fg
Thomas	.00	M	Infant	04Ma02Fg
BLAKE, Phillip	35	M	Unknown	04Ma02Fg
Mary	30	F	Unknown	04Ma02Fg
John	13	M	Unknown	04Ma02Fg
Mary-Anne	10	F	Unknown	04Ma02Fg
GORMAN, Michl.	30	M	Unknown	04Ma02Fg
Alice	24	F	Unknown	04Ma02Fg
John	2	M	Child	04Ma02Fg
GORMAN, David	.00	M	Infant	04Ma02Fg
CONLIN, Wm.	35	M	Unknown	04Ma02Fg
MEEHAN, Patt	30	M	Unknown	04Ma02Fg
Bridget	27	F	Unknown	04Ma02Fg
Bridget	25	F	Unknown	04Ma02Fg
BROWN, John	19	F	Unknown	04Ma02Fg
MAYERS, Mary	34	F	Unknown	04Ma02Fg
FEEHEY, Elisa	18	F	Unknown	04Ma02Fg
BROWN, John	35	M	Unknown	04Ma02Fg
CREEN, James	35	M	Unknown	04Ma02Fg
WALL, Nelly	30	F	Unknown	04Ma02Fg
DRISCOLL, Matt	30	M	Unknown	04Ma02Fg
FOLEY, Bridget	30	F	Unknown	04Ma02Fg
Michl.	30	M	Unknown	04Ma02Fg
John	34	M	Unknown	04Ma02Fg
Nelly	11	F	Unknown	04Ma02Fg
CUNIN, Thos.	20	M	Unknown	04Ma02Fg
PHELAN, Maurice	30	M	Unknown	04Ma02Fg
COLBERT, Johanna	26	F	Unknown	04Ma02Fg
PHELANS, Joseph	5	M	Child	04Ma02Fg
Thomas	3	M	Child	04Ma02Fg
Cath.	.00	F	Infant	04Ma02Fg
COLBERT, Thos.	28	M	Unknown	04Ma02Fg
Cath.	28	F	Unknown	04Ma02Fg
ALLENS, Johanna	60	F	Unknown	04Ma02Fg
COBERT, Patt	4	M	Child	04Ma02Fg
Thomas	3	M	Child	04Ma02Fg
Ellen	.00	F	Infant	04Ma02Fg
CANNY, John	25	M	Unknown	04Ma02Fg
LUDAN, Eliza	5	F	Child	04Ma02Fg

DUNBRODY 04 MAY 1849

From New Ross

NAMES OF PASSENGERS	AGE	SEX	OCCUPATIONS	DATE PORT SHIP
GAFFRY, Anthony	32	M	Laborer	04Ma25Er
MASON, Martin	20	M	Laborer	04Ma25Er
OCONNOR, Wm.	18	M	Laborer	04Ma25Er
MURPHY, Dennis	26	M	Laborer	04Ma25Er
EGAN, Mary	19	F	Spinster	04Ma25Er
DOYLE, Jno.	20	M	Laborer	04Ma25Er
ROACH, Mary	68	F	Wi	04Ma25Er
James	28	M	Laborer	04Ma25Er
Catherine	26	F	Wife	04Ma25Er
Nichls.	.11	M	Infant	04Ma25Er
LAWLON, Martha	26	F	Laborer	04Ma25Er
LAWLOR, Ellen	28	F	Laborer	04Ma25Er
Peter	25	M	Laborer	04Ma25Er
U	00	F	Laborer	04Ma25Er
Catherine	23	F	Laborer	04Ma25Er
Biddy	.11	F	Infant	04Ma25Er
Patk.	2	M	Child	04Ma25Er
WICKHAM, Jno.	29	M	Laborer	04Ma25Er
Ellen	26	F	Laborer	04Ma25Er
MACK, Tim	28	M	Laborer	04Ma25Er
WICKAN, Richard	25	M	Carpenter	04Ma25Er
KEANE, Martin	40	M	Carpenter	04Ma25Er
Patrick	17	M	Carpenter	04Ma25Er
MULLETT, Edwd.	27	M	Carpenter	04Ma25Er
CULLEN, Michl.	40	M	Carpenter	04Ma25Er
Anty (W)	40	F	Wife	04Ma25Er
Mary (D)	16	F	None	04Ma25Er
Catherine (D)	13	F	None	04Ma25Er
Margaret (D)	10	F	None	04Ma25Er
Jno. (S)	8	M	Child	04Ma25E
Richd. (S)	25	M	None	04Ma25E
FITZGERALD, Ellen	76	F	Wi	04Ma25E
KEOGH, Biddy	25	F	Spinster	04Ma25E
Catherine	20	F	Spinster	04Ma25E

NAMES OF PASSENGERS		AGE	SEX	OCCUPATIONS	DATE PORT SHIP
CULLEN, Ellen		5	F	Child	04Ma25Er
CONNOR, Ann		25	F	Milliner	04Ma25Er
EVOY, John		35	M	Farmer	04Ma25Er
Martha	(W)	30	F	Wife	04Ma25Er
CORGIONE, Ann		20	F	Milliner	04Ma25Er
WHITE, John		30	M	Laborer	04Ma25Er
REDMOND, Danl.		23	M	Shoemaker	04Ma25Er
Mary		20	F	Spinster	04Ma25Er
MURPHY, Anty		18	F	Spinster	04Ma25Er
HENERY, Pat		25	M	Mason	04Ma25Er
OCONNOR, Stephen		15	M	Servant	04Ma25Er
MAHER, Darby		58	M	Farmer	04Ma25Er
Mary	(W)	58	F	Wife	04Ma25Er
Margt.		20	F	Spinster	04Ma25Er
Bridget		19	F	Spinster	04Ma25Er
Jane		18	F	Spinster	04Ma25Er
Ann		15	F	Spinster	04Ma25Er
Patt		13	M	None	04Ma25Er
DOYLE, Peter		18	M	Baker	04Ma25Er
MURPHY, Jno.		25	M	Laborer	04Ma25Er
Dennis		28	M	Laborer	04Ma25Er
BYRNE, Pat		25	M	Gdnr	04Ma25Er
DAILY, Owen		26	M	Farmer	04Ma25Er
BYRNE, Margaret		28	F	Milliner	04Ma25Er
DAILY, Mary		25	F	Wife	04Ma25Er
HANLON, Maurice		19	M	Coachman	04Ma25Er
BRODERS, Anthy		19	M	Farmer	04Ma25Er
DORAN, Peter		50	M	Gdnr	04Ma25Er
FITZGERALD, Patk.		24	M	Farmer	04Ma25Er
RODGERS, Mary		19	F	Milliner	04Ma25Er
ROGERS, Bridget		17	F	Milliner	04Ma25Er
WHITTY, Jno.		21	M	Clerk	04Ma25Er
DUNN, Mary		20	F	Milliner	04Ma25Er
HANNON, John		37	M	Laborer	04Ma25Er
DOYLE, John		20	M	Laborer	04Ma25Er
KEATING, Andy		28	M	Laborer	04Ma25Er
Mary		28	F	Spinster	04Ma25Er
DILLON, Miles		25	M	Shoemaker	04Ma25Er
Mary		60	F	Wi	04Ma25Er
JORDON, Pat		23	M	Laborer	04Ma25Er
MURPHY, Dennis		25	M	Farmer	04Ma25Er
Thos.		26	M	Clerk	04Ma25Er
BYRNE, Wm.		28	M	Laborer	04Ma25Er
WHITE, Michl.		50	M	Farmer	04Ma25Er
Anty	(W)	50	F	Wife	04Ma25Er
Pat		17	M	None	04Ma25Er
Joanna		17	F	None	04Ma25Er
Moses		11	M	None	04Ma25Er
James		7	M	Child	04Ma25Er
COUSH, Philip		28	M	Blacksmith	04Ma25Er
MURPHY, Ellen		25	F	Spinster	04Ma25Er
MAHER, Tim		28	M	Laborer	04Ma25Er
OHEAN, James		30	M	Farmer	04Ma25Er
CALLSTON, John		28	M	Farmer	04Ma25Er
MORRISEY, Ann		25	F	Housekeeper	04Ma25Er
PHELAN, John		00	M	Unknown	04Ma25Er
GOAN, Catherine		21	F	Dairymaid	04Ma25Er
EAGAN, John		28	M	Farmer	04Ma25Er
Elizabeth	(W)	22	F	Wife	04Ma25Er
Patk.	(S)	.06	M	Infant	04Ma25Er
SHANNON, Dan		22	M	Mason	04Ma25Er
KERNAN, Patk.		26	M	Cooper	04Ma25Er
MAKASY, Larry		21	M	Farmer	04Ma25Er
Margt.		23	F	Spinster	04Ma25Er
Richard		15	M	None	04Ma25Er
KEAGAN, Catherine		20	F	Milliner	04Ma25Er
TOLLIS, Wm.		21	M	Laborer	04Ma25Er
MEAGHER, Michl.		28	M	Laborer	04Ma25Er
HENERY, Matthew		22	M	Laborer	04Ma25Er
DOYLE, Dennis		42	M	Farmer	04Ma25Er
Tom		20	M	Farmer	04Ma25Er
James		19	M	Farmer	04Ma25Er
Eliza		12	F	None	04Ma25Er
Patk.		11	M	None	04Ma25Er
RYAN, Phil		17	M	Carpenter	04Ma25Er
OCONNOR, Dan		16	M	None	04Ma25Er
DUNN, Mary		20	F	Milkmaid	04Ma25Er
RUTHFORD, Patk.		26	M	Farmer	04Ma25Er
BRIDGES, John		48	M	Farmer	04Ma25Er
Anty	(W)	46	F	Wife	04Ma25Er
Patk.		23	M	Farmer	04Ma25Er
Wm.		17	M	Farmer	04Ma25Er
Bridget		15	F	Spinster	04Ma25Er
Nichs.		12	M	None	04Ma25Er
John		6	M	Child	04Ma25Er
REDMOND, Jas.		26	M	Laborer	04Ma25Er
Sarah	(W)	32	F	Wife	04Ma25Er
Wm.	(S)	3	M	Child	04Ma25Er
Jno.	(S)	1	M	Child	04Ma25Er
DOOLEY, Thos.		28	M	Laborer	04Ma25Er
MURPHY, Thomas		46	M	Farmer	04Ma25Er
Catherine		17	F	Unknown	04Ma25Er
Anty		17	F	Spinster	04Ma25Er
John		14	M	None	04Ma25Er
Bridget		11	F	None	04Ma25Er
Mary		9	F	Child	04Ma25Er
Catherine		6	F	Child	04Ma25Er
James		4	M	Child	04Ma25Er
SHEA, Jno.		20	M	Farmer	04Ma25Er
RYAN, Pat		20	M	Farmer	04Ma25Er
Ann		18	F	Spinster	04Ma25Er
MURPHY, Simon		21	M	Laborer	04Ma25Er
COWMAN, Matthew		21	M	Laborer	04Ma25Er
CULLEN, John		16	M	Laborer	04Ma25Er
MURPHY, Pat		20	M	Laborer	04Ma25Er
Thos.		18	M	Laborer	04Ma25Er
POWER, Ellen		30	F	Wife	04Ma25Er
Philip		2	M	Child	04Ma25Er
MORRISY, Jno.		22	M	Laborer	04Ma25Er
CASHEN, Michl.		30	M	Laborer	04Ma25Er
QUINN, Simon		30	M	Laborer	04Ma25Er
JORDAN, Catherine		38	F	Wi	04Ma25Er
Margaret		13	F	None	04Ma25Er
Martin		10	M	None	04Ma25Er
Edward		6	M	Child	04Ma25Er
Ellen		3	F	Child	04Ma25Er
HERBERT, John		28	M	Saddler	04Ma25Er
CLARK, Richard		30	M	Mason	04Ma25Er
POWER, Edmond		24	M	Farmer	04Ma25Er
HOLDEN, Wm.		35	M	Laborer	04Ma25Er
SKENE, Thos.		20	M	Laborer	04Ma25Er
KEEFE, Patk.		30	M	Laborer	04Ma25Er
Cathe.	(W)	25	F	Wife	04Ma25Er
Mary	(D)	.02	F	Infant	04Ma25Er
MCDONALD, Margt.		27	F	Wife	04Ma25Er
Edwd.		.11	M	Infant	04Ma25Er
WHELAN, Thos.		25	M	Carpenter	04Ma25Er
BYRNE, Michl.		20	M	Carpenter	04Ma25Er
WELSH, Joe		26	M	Miller	04Ma25Er
MORAN, Philip		40	M	Laborer	04Ma25Er
Margt.	(W)	30	F	Wife	04Ma25Er
Mary		12	F	None	04Ma25Er
FURLONG, Michl.		22	M	Mason	04Ma25Er
MORAN, Margt.		10	F	None	04Ma25Er
Eliza		1	F	Child	04Ma25Er
HANNAN, Biddy		30	F	Wife	04Ma25Er
Michl.		4	M	Child	04Ma25Er
Wm.		2	M	Child	04Ma25Er
ROURKE, Mary		25	F	Stewardess	04Ma25Er
ROACH, Mich.		25	M	Tailor	04Ma25Er
KENT, Mary		18	F	Spinster	04Ma25Er
CULLEN, Eliza		19	F	Spinster	04Ma25Er

AUGUSTA 04 MAY 1849

From Glasgow

NAMES OF PASSENGERS	AGE	SEX	OCCUPATIONS	DATE PORT SHIP
SUTHERLAND, Donald	27	M	Optician	04Ma04Fi
John	24	M	Optician	04Ma04Fi
MCINTYRE, Pat	30	M	Laborer	04Ma04Fi
HERFORD, Conrad	40	M	Farmer	04Ma04Fi
MURPHY, Patrick	20	M	Laborer	04Ma04Fi

ALBANIA 04 MAY 1849

From Liverpool

NAMES OF PASSENGERS	AGE	SEX	OCCUPATIONS	DATE PORT SHIP
JONES, W.	24	M	Farmer	04Ma02Fd
M.	24	F	None	04Ma02Fd
Robert	1	M	Child	04Ma02Fd
Sarah-Ann	3	F	Child	04Ma02Fd
Benj.	6	M	Carpenter	04Ma02Fd
Maria	.00	F	Infant	04Ma02Fd
MITTERGE, George	40	M	Farmer	04Ma02Fd
U (W)	40	F	None	04Ma02Fd
George	17	M	Mechanic	04Ma02Fd
John	14	M	Mechanic	04Ma02Fd
Sarah	9	F	Child	04Ma02Fd
Margaret	6	F	Child	04Ma02Fd
Mary-Ann	3	F	Child	04Ma02Fd
Edwin	2	M	Child	04Ma02Fd
Ellen	.00	F	Infant	04Ma02Fd
WOOD, Adam	26	M	Mechanic	04Ma02Fd
U (W)	32	F	None	04Ma02Fd
CRAWFORD, Eliza	25	F	None	04Ma02Fd
STONY, Michael	67	M	Laborer	04Ma02Fd
Betty	30	F	Servant	04Ma02Fd
Daniel	34	M	Farmer	04Ma02Fd
Margarett	34	F	Servant	04Ma02Fd
Ellen	13	F	Servant	04Ma02Fd
Marcella	11	F	Servant	04Ma02Fd
Jane	9	F	Child	04Ma02Fd
Margaret	6	F	Child	04Ma02Fd
Ellen	4	F	Child	04Ma02Fd
Rose	2	F	Child	04Ma02Fd
Betsey	20	F	None	04Ma02Fd
Jane	20	F	Servant	04Ma02Fd
MCGEE, John	25	M	Farmer	04Ma02Fd
Bessey	14	F	Servant	04Ma02Fd
HUGHES, James	17	M	Servant	04Ma02Fd
CARNACK, James	40	M	Laborer	04Ma02Fd
ROWEN, Thomas	14	M	Laborer	04Ma02Fd
Margarett	21	F	Servant	04Ma02Fd
WRIGHT, H.	35	M	Mechanic	04Ma02Fd
Isabella	35	F	Servant	04Ma02Fd
David	.00	M	Infant	04Ma02Fd
LARK, David	16	M	Mechanic	04Ma02Fd
Thomas	14	M	Mechanic	04Ma02Fd
John	12	M	Mechanic	04Ma02Fd
THOMPSON, Henry	31	M	Laborer	04Ma02Fd
U (W)	31	F	Servant	04Ma02Fd
James	11	M	Farmer	04Ma02Fd
Anna	8	F	Child	04Ma02Fd
William	7	M	Child	04Ma02Fd
John	4	M	Child	04Ma02Fd
Henry	2	M	Child	04Ma02Fd

NAMES OF PASSENGERS	AGE	SEX	OCCUPATIONS	DATE PORT SHIP
THOMPSON, Betty	.00	F	Infant	04Ma02Fd
MAHON, James	30	M	Farmer	04Ma02Fd
WEBSTER, Mary	29	F	None	04Ma02Fd
FINEGAN, Mary	21	F	None	04Ma02Fd
HUGHES, Samuel	50	M	Servant	04Ma02Fd
Mary	45	F	Servant	04Ma02Fd
Samuel	27	M	Laborer	04Ma02Fd
Eliza-Jane	22	F	None	04Ma02Fd
Anna	20	F	Servant	04Ma02Fd
Joseph	18	M	Farmer	04Ma02Fd
John	14	M	Farmer	04Ma02Fd
Maria	6	F	Child	04Ma02Fd
Thomas	5	M	Child	04Ma02Fd
Flora	4	F	Child	04Ma02Fd
Robert	10	M	Laborer	04Ma02Fd
SEMAN, Alexander	24	M	Laborer	04Ma02Fd
HUGHES, James	20	M	Laborer	04Ma02Fd
GILBERT, James	24	M	Mechanic	04Ma02Fd
Ellen	29	F	Servant	04Ma02Fd
Emily	6	F	Child	04Ma02Fd
Frederick	4	M	Child	04Ma02Fd
William	2	M	Child	04Ma02Fd
George	.00	M	Infant	04Ma02Fd
Samuel	.00	M	Infant	04Ma02Fd
ABBENY, Julia	18	F	Servant	04Ma02Fd
GILBERT, Charles	56	M	Mechanic	04Ma02Fd
SEVENLAND, Joseph	38	M	Mechanic	04Ma02Fd
COLESON, Thomas	25	M	Mechanic	04Ma02Fd
JEFTCOCK, Osman	22	M	Farmer	04Ma02Fd
GLOSSOP, George	21	M	Farmer	04Ma02Fd
SHAW, John	20	M	Farmer	04Ma02Fd
WOODCOCK, Henry	32	M	Farmer	04Ma02Fd
Hannah	38	F	None	04Ma02Fd
Emma	.00	F	Infant	04Ma02Fd
FAIRBROW, James	18	M	Mechanic	04Ma02Fd
SMITH, Richard	16	M	Mechanic	04Ma02Fd
JONES, Robert	18	M	Farmer	04Ma02Fd
HILL, William	28	M	Farmer	04Ma02Fd
Clara	30	F	Servant	04Ma02Fd
RILEY, Bridget	30	F	Servant	04Ma02Fd
POWER, Thomas	20	M	Laborer	04Ma02Fd
HANLAN, John	24	M	Laborer	04Ma02Fd
FORREST, Benj.	29	M	Farmer	04Ma02Fd
Abbey	29	F	None	04Ma02Fd
Joseph	6	M	Child	04Ma02Fd
Caroline	2	F	Child	04Ma02Fd
Mary-Jane	.00	F	Infant	04Ma02Fd
NEWBORN, William	30	M	Laborer	04Ma02Fd
Mary-Ann	30	F	None	04Ma02Fd
BULLIVANT, John Died-At-Sea	30	M	Farmer	04Ma02Fd
Elisa	30	F	None	04Ma02Fd
George	3	M	Child	04Ma02Fd
Emma Died-At-Sea	.00	F	Infant	04Ma02Fd
JORDAN, Edward	20	M	Mechanic	04Ma02Fd
KILPATRICK, John	20	M	Mechanic	04Ma02Fd
MCKANE, William	20	M	Mechanic	04Ma02Fd
Mary-Jane	23	F	None	04Ma02Fd
FERRIS, Mary	18	F	Servant	04Ma02Fd
NERBERT, John	35	M	Laborer	04Ma02Fd
FORBES, George	40	M	Mechanic	04Ma02Fd
Sarah	40	F	None	04Ma02Fd
BULLOCK, William	21	M	Farmer	04Ma02Fd
MALONEY, Mary	18	F	None	04Ma02Fd
MCDERMOT, Catherine	16	F	None	04Ma02Fd
MCCANN, Hugh	26	M	Farmer	04Ma02Fd
BRANNAN, William	22	M	Farmer	04Ma02Fd
POWERS, John	20	M	Mechanic	04Ma02Fd
LONG, Batts	12	M	Mechanic	04Ma02F
John	10	M	Farmer	04Ma02F
KIRWAN, Ellen	30	F	None	04Ma02F
MURPHY, Martin	00	M	Mechanic	04Ma02F
Margaret	24	F	Unknown	04Ma02F
Annanias	25	M	Farmer	04Ma02F

NAMES OF PASSENGERS	AGE	SEX	OCCUPATIONS	DATE PORT SHIP
HAM, Thomas	28	M	Farmer	04Ma02Fd
NUGENT, Mick	20	M	Laborer	04Ma02Fd
HALSEY, Mary	18	F	Laborer	04Ma02Fd
SEYMOUR, Charles	12	M	Laborer	04Ma02Fd
Simeon	45	M	Laborer	04Ma02Fd
KELLEY, Bridget	45	F	None	04Ma02Fd
SEYMOUR, Charlotta	10	F	None	04Ma02Fd
John	9	M	Child	04Ma02Fd
Thomas	20	M	Farmer	04Ma02Fd
BURKE, Thomas	12	M	None	04Ma02Fd
KEEGAN, Pat	37	M	Farmer	04Ma02Fd
Michael	21	M	Farmer	04Ma02Fd
MURPHY, John	27	M	Farmer	04Ma02Fd
Jane	23	F	Servant	04Ma02Fd
Judith	1	F	Child	04Ma02Fd
Mary	.00	F	Infant	04Ma02Fd
ONIEL, James	30	M	Laborer	04Ma02Fd
John	3	M	Child	04Ma02Fd
Ann	1	F	Child	04Ma02Fd
John	30	M	Farmer	04Ma02Fd
POYNAN, Catherine	20	F	None	04Ma02Fd
CAMERON, John	24	M	Farmer	04Ma02Fd
Ann	24	F	None	04Ma02Fd
Margarett	9	F	Child	04Ma02Fd
Margarett	6	F	Child	04Ma02Fd
Thomas	3	M	Child	04Ma02Fd
James	4	M	Child	04Ma02Fd
JOHNSON, William	26	M	Mechanic	04Ma02Fd

SAMUEL 04 MAY 1849

From Liverpool

NAMES OF PASSENGERS	AGE	SEX	OCCUPATIONS	DATE PORT SHIP
SHANGLEY, Ann	18	F	Spinster	04Ma02Fe
FORAN, Dennis	20	M	Shoemaker	04Ma02Fe
Ellen	14	F	Unknown	04Ma02Fe
LOWE, Simon	50	M	Laborer	04Ma02Fe
Mary	52	F	Unknown	04Ma02Fe
Wm.	16	M	Blacksmith	04Ma02Fe
Geo.	22	M	Blacksmith	04Ma02Fe
Mary	12	F	Unknown	04Ma02Fe
Ann	8	F	Child	04Ma02Fe
LOONEY, Wm.	26	M	Laborer	04Ma02Fe
Honor	20	F	Spinster	04Ma02Fe
WALLACE, Eliza	14	F	Unknown	04Ma02Fe
OBRIEN, Patk.	50	M	Laborer	04Ma02Fe
MAHONEY, Margt.	50	F	Unknown	04Ma02Fe
Jno.	10	M	Unknown	04Ma02Fe
Eugene	8	M	Child	04Ma02Fe
Cathe.	12	F	Unknown	04Ma02Fe
KIRROVAN, Jno.	38	M	Unknown	04Ma02Fe
GODLEY, Johanna	22	F	Spinster	04Ma02Fe
BRESHNAHAN, Cathe.	17	F	Spinster	04Ma02Fe
DOYLE, Fanny	26	F	Spinster	04Ma02Fe
Wm.	5	M	Child	04Ma02Fe
Jno.	3	M	Child	04Ma02Fe
FENNEDY, Ann	29	F	Spinster	04Ma02Fe
FARRELL, Cathe.	53	F	Unknown	04Ma02Fe
COLLINS, Lawrence	21	M	Clerk	04Ma02Fe
STACKPOLE, Cathe.	16	F	Spinster	04Ma02Fe
MAURRICE, Kitty	22	F	Spinster	04Ma02Fe
MURRAY, Wm.	14	M	Laborer	04Ma02Fe
Edwd.	10	M	Unknown	04Ma02Fe
Jno.	50	M	Tailor	04Ma02Fe
Mary	50	F	Unknown	04Ma02Fe
DONOHUE, Jno.	22	M	Laborer	04Ma02Fe
Ann	17	F	Spinster	04Ma02Fe
Margt.	15	F	Spinster	04Ma02Fe
Rose	12	F	Spinster	04Ma02Fe
CONDON, Pat	55	M	Laborer	04Ma02Fe
Wm.	21	M	Laborer	04Ma02Fe
Thomas	19	M	Unknown	04Ma02Fe
Cathe.	19	F	Spinster	04Ma02Fe
Margt.	21	F	Spinster	04Ma02Fe
Mary	14	F	Spinster	04Ma02Fe
Ellen	22	F	Spinster	04Ma02Fe
Mary	24	F	Spinster	04Ma02Fe
Margt.	50	F	Unknown	04Ma02Fe
HENNESSY, Bridget	50	F	Wi	04Ma02Fe
Wm.	21	M	Laborer	04Ma02Fe
Bridget	19	F	Spinster	04Ma02Fe
Ellen	17	F	Spinster	04Ma02Fe
Margt.	15	F	Spinster	04Ma02Fe
Jno.	23	M	Laborer	04Ma02Fe
James	25	M	Laborer	04Ma02Fe
FRAHER, Edmund	40	M	Tailor	04Ma02Fe
MCCABE, Mary	32	F	Unknown	04Ma02Fe
COSTELLO, Michl.	31	M	Farmer	04Ma02Fe
MCCARTHY, Wm.	16	M	Laborer	04Ma02Fe
BARRY, Margt.	16	F	Dressmaker	04Ma02Fe
CONNORS, Mary	18	F	Spinster	04Ma02Fe
CARMODY, Julia	24	F	Spinster	04Ma02Fe
HANNOVAN, Dennis	24	M	Laborer	04Ma02Fe
LUMBARD, Patrick	26	M	Carpenter	04Ma02Fe
CURTIN, Wm.	30	M	Farmer	04Ma02Fe
Jeremiah	13	M	Unknown	04Ma02Fe
MCCARTY, Jno.	20	M	Laborer	04Ma02Fe
TOBIN, Jno.	24	M	Laborer	04Ma02Fe
Bridget	20	F	Spinster	04Ma02Fe
MAGUER, Margt.	24	F	Spinster	04Ma02Fe
WELCH, Wm.	30	M	Shoemaker	04Ma02Fe
Jas.	22	M	Shoemaker	04Ma02Fe
JOHNSON, John	14	M	Shoemaker	04Ma02Fe
CLARK, Jos.	9	M	Child	04Ma02Fe
CADY, John	18	M	Laborer	04Ma02Fe
DUFFY, Mary	7	F	Child	04Ma02Fe
MCVEY, Agnes	12	F	Unknown	04Ma02Fe
Eliza	5	F	Child	04Ma02Fe
YOUNG, Mary	20	F	Spinster	04Ma02Fe
MALLONEY, Ellen	17	F	Dressmaker	04Ma02Fe
PHALEN, Julia	16	F	Spinster	04Ma02Fe
Maria	14	F	Spinster	04Ma02Fe
MONAGHAN, Mary	20	F	Spinster	04Ma02Fe
DEMPSEY, Marly	46	M	Laborer	04Ma02Fe
MCCABE, Jno.	21	M	Laborer	04Ma02Fe
RYAN, Jno.	47	M	Farmer	04Ma02Fe
Mary	45	F	Unknown	04Ma02Fe
Rose	17	F	Spinster	04Ma02Fe
Judy	16	F	Spinster	04Ma02Fe
Margt.	11	F	Spinster	04Ma02Fe
Jno.	10	M	Unknown	04Ma02Fe
Cathe.	6	F	Child	04Ma02Fe
Mary	12	F	Unknown	04Ma02Fe
FAY, Jno.	21	M	Laborer	04Ma02Fe
MCGEE, Patk.	20	M	Laborer	04Ma02Fe
LILLY, Ann	21	F	Spinster	04Ma02Fe
CLARK, Jas.	40	M	Plasterer	04Ma02Fe
Jas.	9	M	Child	04Ma02Fe
GAENESS, Phillip	16	M	Laborer	04Ma02Fe
GEANESS, Ellen	15	F	Laborer	04Ma02Fe
JENKINS, Nora	60	F	Wi	04Ma02Fe
Wm.	28	M	Laborer	04Ma02Fe
QUINTON, Henry	18	M	Weaver	04Ma02Fe
MARTIN, Ann	30	F	Unknown	04Ma02Fe
DUFFEY, Ann	13	F	Unknown	04Ma02Fe
GERRAGHTY, Jno.	25	M	Laborer	04Ma02Fe
HEAGAN, Wm.	26	M	Laborer	04Ma02Fe
CARROCAN, Jas.	14	M	Laborer	04Ma02Fe
GILROY, Edwd.	23	M	Laborer	04Ma02Fe
MCMANUS, Ellen	20	F	Spinster	04Ma02Fe
GORDON, Bridget	17	F	Spinster	04Ma02Fe
CADY, Bridget	23	F	Spinster	04Ma02Fe
DALE, Frank	26	M	Laborer	04Ma02Fe
ROWAN, Cathe.	20	F	Spinster	04Ma02Fe

NAMES OF PASSENGERS	AGE	SEX	OCCUPATIONS	DATE PORT SHIP
DOWD, Chr.	30	M	Laborer	04Ma02Fe
MCMANUS, Cathe.	60	F	Wi	04Ma02Fe
Cathe.	10	F	Unknown	04Ma02Fe
GILANE, Cornelius	60	M	Shoemaker	04Ma02Fe
Jno.	28	M	Shoemaker	04Ma02Fe
Pat	22	M	Shoemaker	04Ma02Fe
Mary	16	F	Spinster	04Ma02Fe
LAWLER, Jno.	22	M	Laborer	04Ma02Fe
ALLAN, Jas.	28	M	Laborer	04Ma02Fe
Julia	27	F	Spinster	04Ma02Fe
Jno.	29	M	Laborer	04Ma02Fe
Edwd.	20	M	Laborer	04Ma02Fe
Cathe.	18	F	Spinster	04Ma02Fe
MCDOWLE, Jas.	35	M	Draper	04Ma02Fe
HARRIGAN, Norah	15	F	Spinster	04Ma02Fe
SHAWNESSY, Thos.	30	M	Farmer	04Ma02Fe
LENEHAN, Michl.	28	M	Farmer	04Ma02Fe
FERRY, Jno.	24	M	Laborer	04Ma02Fe
MAY, Matilda	16	F	Spinster	04Ma02Fe
COUGHLIN, John	30	M	Laborer	04Ma02Fe
LEAN, Darby	30	M	Unknown	04Ma02Fe
MCNULTY, Wm.	30	M	Laborer	04Ma02Fe
GILLIGAN, Margt.	15	F	Spinster	04Ma02Fe
MCHENEY, Bernard	22	M	Laborer	04Ma02Fe
ODONNELL, Lawrence	50	M	Laborer	04Ma02Fe
Ann	50	F	Unknown	04Ma02Fe
Mary	16	F	Spinster	04Ma02Fe
Henry	7	M	Child	04Ma02Fe
MCMANN, Rose	18	F	Spinster	04Ma02Fe
Barney	8	M	Child	04Ma02Fe
Sarah	3	F	Child	04Ma02Fe
BURN, Henry	20	M	Spinster	04Ma02Fe
DUFFEY, Michl.	5	M	Child	04Ma02Fe
HARVEY, Ann	21	F	Spinster	04Ma02Fe
Cathe.	4	F	Child	04Ma02Fe
Ellen	1	F	Child	04Ma02Fe
MCGRATH, Mary	16	F	Spinster	04Ma02Fe
WOODS, Patk.	26	M	Laborer	04Ma02Fe
GILROY, Ann	18	F	Spinster	04Ma02Fe
MADEN, Michl.	12	M	Laborer	04Ma02Fe
Francis	11	M	Unknown	04Ma02Fe
HORAN, Cathe.	14	F	Unknown	04Ma02Fe
Winey	24	U	Unknown	04Ma02Fe
CASEY, Bridget	27	F	Unknown	04Ma02Fe
Jno.	1	M	Child	04Ma02Fe
HUGHES, Ellen	22	F	Spinster	04Ma02Fe
STEWART, Jas.	19	M	Farmer	04Ma02Fe
Rob.	17	M	Unknown	04Ma02Fe
HUGHES, Mary-Ann	20	F	Dressmaker	04Ma02Fe
Nancy	17	F	Spinster	04Ma02Fe
CURREY, Cathe.	20	F	Spinster	04Ma02Fe
DIXON, Ann	21	F	Unknown	04Ma02Fe
Geo.	1	M	Child	04Ma02Fe
Eliza	3	F	Child	04Ma02Fe
MOFFATT, Margt.	22	F	Spinster	04Ma02Fe
Jane	21	F	Spinster	04Ma02Fe
WHITE, Margt.	30	F	Spinster	04Ma02Fe
FLAHERTY, Pat.	12	M	Unknown	04Ma02Fe
Michl.	9	M	Child	04Ma02Fe
Mary-Ann	6	F	Child	04Ma02Fe
FEENEY, Jno.	12	M	Unknown	04Ma02Fe
AMBERY, Maria	30	F	Unknown	04Ma02Fe
Lucy	2	F	Child	04Ma02Fe
Kate	1	F	Child	04Ma02Fe
MAHER, Lawrence	30	M	Miller	04Ma02Fe
REIDY, Michl.	24	M	Laborer	04Ma02Fe
RILEY, Jno.	27	M	Farmer	04Ma02Fe
ROURKE, Eliza	17	F	Spinster	04Ma02Fe
Mary	17	F	Spinster	04Ma02Fe
BYRNE, Ann	10	F	Unknown	04Ma02Fe
Lawrence	8	M	Child	04Ma02Fe
Elias	6	M	Child	04Ma02Fe
Cathe.	4	F	Child	04Ma02Fe
Margt.	42	F	Unknown	04Ma02Fe
NOLAN, Jno.	23	M	Laborer	04Ma02Fe

NAMES OF PASSENGERS	AGE	SEX	OCCUPATIONS	DATE PORT SHIP
MCGUIRE, Jno.	17	M	Laborer	04Ma02Fe
MULLEN, Jno.	40	M	Laborer	04Ma02Fe
RONAN, Cathe.	50	F	Wi	04Ma02Fe
Jno.	23	M	Dreiner	04Ma02Fe
Hanna	19	F	Dressmaker	04Ma02Fe
Mary	14	F	Spinster	04Ma02Fe
DAY, Margt.	49	F	Wi	04Ma02Fe
DEVAR, Ellen	18	F	Spinster	04Ma02Fe
BARRY, Wm.	37	M	Laborer	04Ma02Fe
Margt.	37	F	Unknown	04Ma02Fe
Pat	13	M	Unknown	04Ma02Fe
Wm.	1	M	Child	04Ma02Fe
MCGONAGLE, Bernard	14	M	Unknown	04Ma02Fe
GEAGHTON, Cathe.	15	F	Unknown	04Ma02Fe
KENNEDY, Ellen	36	F	Wi	04Ma02Fe
Ellen	12	F	Unknown	04Ma02Fe
KENAN, Ann	21	F	Spinster	04Ma02Fe
Handy	21	M	Laborer	04Ma02Fe
SMITH, Jno.	18	M	Unknown	04Ma02Fe
Rose	12	F	Spinster	04Ma02Fe
Thos.	24	M	Laborer	04Ma02Fe
FOLEY, Thos.	19	M	Unknown	04Ma02Fe
FLANNERY, Mary	20	F	Spinster	04Ma02Fe
MCDOWAL, Pat	25	M	Laborer	04Ma02Fe
HAYDEN, Anthony	82	M	Laborer	04Ma02Fe
Patk.	27	M	Unknown	04Ma02Fe
Mary	27	F	Unknown	04Ma02Fe
Wm.	.00	M	Infant	04Ma02Fe
CODY, Sally	14	F	Spinster	04Ma02Fe
Jas.	26	M	Laborer	04Ma02Fe
OHARE, Ann	26	F	Dressmaker	04Ma02Fe
ROAN, Jno.	20	M	Unknown	04Ma02Fe
FLYNN, Abby	18	F	Spinster	04Ma02Fe
NEIL, Felix	40	M	Farmer	04Ma02Fe
Maria	10	F	Unknown	04Ma02Fe
Jno.	7	M	Child	04Ma02Fe
Ann	76	F	Unknown	04Ma02Fe
MCMANUS, Francis	20	M	Mason	04Ma02Fe
MURRAY, Barney	20	M	Laborer	04Ma02Fe
BOURKE, Patk.	30	M	Laborer	04Ma02Fe
DARWIN, Thos.	23	M	Laborer	04Ma02Fe
MCANDREWS, Jas.	40	M	Laborer	04Ma02Fe
COYLE, Phelix	24	M	Laborer	04Ma02Fe
KELLY, Edwd.	20	M	Laborer	04Ma02Fe
BARRETT, David	42	M	Laborer	04Ma02Fe
MAHONEY, Jas.	27	M	Unknown	04Ma02Fe
SHOTTON, Thos.	35	M	Shoemaker	04Ma02Fe
Ann	36	F	Unknown	04M[illegible]2Fe
Rob.	6	U	Child	04Ma02Fe
MATHER, Edwd.H.	24	M	Miller	04Ma02Fe
Jane	22	F	Unknown	04Ma02Fe
ELLISON, Thos.	22	M	Builder	04Ma02Fe

EMMA-SEARLE 04 MAY 1849

From Belfast

NAMES OF PASSENGERS	AGE	SEX	OCCUPATIONS	DATE PORT SHIP
MCCLELLAND, Andrew	60	M	Laborer	04Ma05Eq
Sarah	55	F	Unknown	04Ma05Eq
Margt.	27	F	Unknown	04Ma05Eq
Richard	23	M	Unknown	04Ma05Ec
MCKNIGHT, Mary	60	F	Unknown	04Ma05Ec
William	22	M	Unknown	04Ma05Ec
Eliza-A.	21	F	Unknown	04Ma05Ec
Margt.	.00	F	Infant	04Ma05Ec
CLEGG, Thomas	35	M	Unknown	04Ma05Ec
Sarah	21	F	Unknown	04Ma05Ec
David	.00	M	Infant	04Ma05E
BOYD, Thomas	28	M	Unknown	04Ma05Ec

NAMES OF PASSENGERS	AGE	SEX	OCCUPATIONS	DATE PORT SHIP
BOYD, Margt.	26	F	Unknown	04Ma05Eq
ROGAN, John	24	M	Unknown	04Ma05Eq
Rose	25	F	Unknown	04Ma05Eq
BANNON, Patk.	56	M	Unknown	04Ma05Eq
Mary	40	F	Unknown	04Ma05Eq
Cecily	19	F	Unknown	04Ma05Eq
James	17	M	Unknown	04Ma05Eq
Mary	9	F	Child	04Ma05Eq
Betty	7	F	Child	04Ma05Eq
Anne	3	F	Child	04Ma05Eq
Catherine	.10	F	Infant	04Ma05Eq
Rosey	5	F	Child	04Ma05Eq
COMB, David	21	M	Unknown	04Ma05Eq
MCCOMB, John	26	M	Unknown	04Ma05Eq
James	24	M	Unknown	04Ma05Eq
MORLAND, John	29	M	Unknown	04Ma05Eq
Eliza	29	F	Unknown	04Ma05Eq
Thomas	.02	M	Infant	04Ma05Eq
BERGAN, William	25	M	Unknown	04Ma05Eq
Catherine	25	F	Unknown	04Ma05Eq
Margaret	3	F	Child	04Ma05Eq
Eliza	.00	F	Infant	04Ma05Eq
WALLACE, Francis	26	M	Unknown	04Ma05Eq
FOX, John	26	M	Unknown	04Ma05Eq
SALL, Bernard	24	M	Unknown	04Ma05Eq
Bridget	24	F	Unknown	04Ma05Eq
MCWILLIAMS, Saml.	23	M	Unknown	04Ma05Eq
HOLLAN, Henry	40	M	Unknown	04Ma05Eq
Eliza-J.	35	F	Unknown	04Ma05Eq
Sarah-J.	12	F	Unknown	04Ma05Eq
Eliza	3	F	Child	04Ma05Eq
HOGG, Rachel	17	F	Unknown	04Ma05Eq
Margt.	20	F	Unknown	04Ma05Eq
TAYLER, Eliza	20	F	Unknown	04Ma05Eq
DONAGHY, John	38	M	Unknown	04Ma05Eq
Jane	30	F	Unknown	04Ma05Eq
William	3	M	Child	04Ma05Eq
John	.00	M	Infant	04Ma05Eq
Died-At-Sea				
MURDOCK, Saml.	20	M	Unknown	04Ma05Eq
MCDONALD, Danl.	21	M	Unknown	04Ma05Eq
MCNALLY, Bernard	20	M	Unknown	04Ma05Eq
CANAVAN, Biddy	16	F	Unknown	04Ma05Eq
MCSHATTAN, Mary	19	F	Unknown	04Ma05Eq
BOYLE, William	20	M	Unknown	04Ma05Eq
HAMILTON, James	20	M	Unknown	04Ma05Eq
MCDONALD, Nancy	20	F	Unknown	04Ma05Eq
ANDERSON, Isabella	34	F	Unknown	04Ma05Eq
Isabella	14	F	Unknown	04Ma05Eq
Robert	11	M	Unknown	04Ma05Eq
Rebecca	7	F	Child	04Ma05Eq
William	5	M	Child	04Ma05Eq
DONLEY, John	24	M	Unknown	04Ma05Eq
Jane	22	F	Unknown	04Ma05Eq
MAGUIRE, Thomas	25	M	Unknown	04Ma05Eq
Mary	16	F	Unknown	04Ma05Eq
BELL, William	36	M	Unknown	04Ma05Eq
Jane	36	F	Unknown	04Ma05Eq
MORROW, John	18	M	Unknown	04Ma05Eq
MCNEILLY, Adam	22	M	Unknown	04Ma05Eq
GALLOWAY, John	25	M	Unknown	04Ma05Eq
Henrietta	20	F	Unknown	04Ma05Eq
MORRISON, James	56	M	Unknown	04Ma05Eq
Hugh	30	M	Unknown	04Ma05Eq
James	26	M	Unknown	04Ma05Eq
Mary-J.	21	F	Unknown	04Ma05Eq
Barbara	19	F	Unknown	04Ma05Eq
Ann	.00	F	Infant	04Ma05Eq
U	.00	F	Infant	04Ma05Eq
Eliza-J.	21	F	Unknown	04Ma05Eq
LONG, John	20	M	Unknown	04Ma05Eq
CARSON, Mary-J.	21	F	Unknown	04Ma05Eq
James	19	M	Unknown	04Ma05Eq
DAVIS, William	36	M	Unknown	04Ma05Eq
Mary	32	F	Unknown	04Ma05Eq
DAVIS, George-A.	9	M	Child	04Ma05Eq
Wm.	7	M	Child	04Ma05Eq
Ester	11	F	Unknown	04Ma05Eq
John-Charles	.00	M	Infant	04Ma05Eq
VAUGHAN, U	.00	U	Infant	04Ma05Eq
WOOD, James	30	M	Unknown	04Ma05Eq
Ann	20	F	Unknown	04Ma05Eq
MORROW, Joseph	38	M	Unknown	04Ma05Eq
HAMILTON, John	28	M	Unknown	04Ma05Eq
Jane	26	F	Unknown	04Ma05Eq
James	4	M	Child	04Ma05Eq
John	6	M	Child	04Ma05Eq
Patrick	.00	M	Infant	04Ma05Eq
Jane	.00	F	Infant	04Ma05Eq
SMITH, John	40	M	Unknown	04Ma05Eq
READE, John	20	M	Unknown	04Ma05Eq
CRAWFORD, Malcolm	60	M	Unknown	04Ma05Eq
Eliza	47	F	Unknown	04Ma05Eq
Eliza	25	F	Unknown	04Ma05Eq
Mary	16	F	Unknown	04Ma05Eq
Grace	14	F	Unknown	04Ma05Eq
Matilda	12	F	Unknown	04Ma05Eq
Rose-Ann	10	F	Unknown	04Ma05Eq
Wm.Robert	8	M	Child	04Ma05Eq
Susan	6	F	Child	04Ma05Eq
LAIRD, Malcolm	3	M	Child	04Ma05Eq
MCGINNIS, Martha	22	F	Unknown	04Ma05Eq
MCCONNELL, Malcolm	41	M	Unknown	04Ma05Eq
Margaret	21	F	Unknown	04Ma05Eq
Eliza-Margt.	.00	F	Infant	04Ma05Eq
Samuel	37	M	Unknown	04Ma05Eq
Mary	25	F	Unknown	04Ma05Eq
Grace	7	F	Child	04Ma05Eq
Malcolm	5	M	Child	04Ma05Eq
Mary	3	F	Child	04Ma05Eq
Samuel	.00	M	Infant	04Ma05Eq
GORMAN, Henry	45	M	Unknown	04Ma05Eq
Mary	44	F	Unknown	04Ma05Eq
Robert	17	M	Unknown	04Ma05Eq
Elizabeth	19	F	Unknown	04Ma05Eq
Mary	12	F	Unknown	04Ma05Eq
Thomas	9	M	Child	04Ma05Eq
Ann	7	F	Child	04Ma05Eq
Henry	6	M	Child	04Ma05Eq
William	4	M	Child	04Ma05Eq
Jane	.00	F	Infant	04Ma05Eq
MCCONNELL, John	21	M	Unknown	04Ma05Eq
MCCOMB, William	30	M	Unknown	04Ma05Eq
Elizabeth	28	F	Unknown	04Ma05Eq
MCKIBBIN, Jane	50	F	Unknown	04Ma05Eq
MCCOMB, Robert	13	M	Unknown	04Ma05Eq
Jane	13	F	Unknown	04Ma05Eq
TATE, Samuel	33	M	Unknown	04Ma05Eq
CAMPBELL, George	22	M	Unknown	04Ma05Eq
ROBINSON, Thomas	22	M	Unknown	04Ma05Eq
BOYLE, Martin	50	M	Unknown	04Ma05Eq
MCKEON, Edwd.	24	M	Unknown	04Ma05Eq
NALLELY, James	30	M	Unknown	04Ma05Eq
Ellen	30	F	Unknown	04Ma05Eq
Jane	.00	F	Infant	04Ma05Eq
Died-At-Sea				
MURPHY, Neil	20	M	Unknown	04Ma05Eq
KENNEDY, John	25	M	Unknown	04Ma05Eq
RUDDY, John	20	M	Unknown	04Ma05Eq
LOWRY, Nathaniel	18	M	Unknown	04Ma05Eq
SCANLAN, John	25	M	Unknown	04Ma05Eq
Margaret	22	F	Unknown	04Ma05Eq
Francis	19	M	Unknown	04Ma05Eq
SMITH, Biddy	21	F	Unknown	04Ma05Eq
CONLIN, Phoebe	24	F	Unknown	04Ma05Eq
KNOX, Mary-Ann	25	F	Unknown	04Ma05Eq
LIVINGSTON, John	18	M	Unknown	04Ma05Eq
MITCHEL, John	25	M	Unknown	04Ma05Eq
Jane	26	F	Unknown	04Ma05Eq
Ellen	24	F	Unknown	04Ma05Eq

NAMES OF PASSENGERS	AGE	SEX	OCCUPATIONS	DATE PORT SHIP
MITCHEL, Betty	22	F	Unknown	04Ma05Eq
HARBISON, William	23	M	Unknown	04Ma05Eq
PATTIESON, William	22	M	Unknown	04Ma05Eq
MCKENNA, Peter	25	M	Unknown	04Ma05Eq
Nancy	25	F	Unknown	04Ma05Eq
HARVEY, John	22	M	Unknown	04Ma05Eq
CAMPBELL, Rosan	40	F	Unknown	04Ma05Eq
MCGUIN, Mary	28	F	Unknown	04Ma05Eq
Ann	22	F	Unknown	04Ma05Eq
MCGEE, William	24	M	Unknown	04Ma05Eq
MALKIN, Henry	24	M	Unknown	04Ma05Eq
D--ND, William	19	M	Unknown	04Ma05Eq
Mary	22	F	Unknown	04Ma05Eq
STEWART, Ellen	23	F	Unknown	04Ma05Eq
MCKEEVER, Catherine	20	F	Unknown	04Ma05Eq
WARD, Thomas	25	M	Unknown	04Ma05Eq
Margaret	25	F	Unknown	04Ma05Eq
DUNCAN, Letitia	17	F	Unknown	04Ma05Eq
DUNLAP, Jackson	25	M	Unknown	04Ma05Eq
Thomas	20	M	Unknown	04Ma05Eq
Jackson	10	M	Unknown	04Ma05Eq
David	6	M	Child	04Ma05Eq
Robert	4	M	Child	04Ma05Eq
Margaret	.00	F	Infant	04Ma05Eq
Elizabeth	3	F	Child	04Ma05Eq
MCILROY, Alexander	50	M	Unknown	04Ma05Eq
Mary	20	F	Unknown	04Ma05Eq
THOMPSON, Sarah	20	F	Unknown	04Ma05Eq
COOPER, James	20	M	Unknown	04Ma05Eq
CUNNINGHAM, Teressa	15	F	Unknown	04Ma05Eq
GILLESPIE, William	30	M	Unknown	04Ma05Eq
Martha	30	F	Unknown	04Ma05Eq
William-John	8	M	Child	04Ma05Eq
Margaret	3	F	Child	04Ma05Eq
Martin	.00	M	Infant	04Ma05Eq
TOOL, Anne	40	F	Unknown	04Ma05Eq
Mary	13	F	Unknown	04Ma05Eq
WOOD, U	9	F	Child	04Ma05Eq
MCIREA, Mary	20	F	Unknown	04Ma05Eq
GIBSON, Margt.	24	F	Unknown	04Ma05Eq
Eliza	22	F	Unknown	04Ma05Eq
MCKENNA, James	30	M	Unknown	04Ma05Eq
MITCHELL, James	19	M	Unknown	04Ma05Eq
CONNELLY, Sarah	18	F	Unknown	04Ma05Eq
FINLAY, Eliza	18	F	Unknown	04Ma05Eq
CARR, George	40	M	Unknown	04Ma05Eq
Mary	30	F	Unknown	04Ma05Eq
Catherine	10	F	Unknown	04Ma05Eq
Patrick	.00	M	Infant	04Ma05Eq
CONNOLLY, Catherine	25	F	Unknown	04Ma05Eq
CASSIDY, Patrick	13	M	Unknown	04Ma05Eq
Bernard	8	M	Child	04Ma05Eq
Mary	10	F	Unknown	04Ma05Eq
U, U Born-At-Sea	.00	U	Infant	04Ma05Eq

HINDOSTAN 05 MAY 1849

From Unknown

NAMES OF PASSENGERS	AGE	SEX	OCCUPATIONS	DATE PORT SHIP
THOMAS, David	34	M	Agrc	05Ma00Fm
Mary	30	F	Unknown	05Ma00Fm
JONES, Emmeline	39	F	Unknown	05Ma00Fm
Sarah	16	F	Unknown	05Ma00Fm
Ann	10	F	Unknown	05Ma00Fm
Emily	6	F	Child	05Ma00Fm
Oliver	3	M	Child	05Ma00Fm
Mary	.08	F	Infant	05Ma00Fm
WEST, Sarah	41	F	Unknown	05Ma00Fm
WEST, Jane	11	F	Unknown	05Ma00Fm
Henry	9	M	Child	05Ma00Fm
Ann	7	F	Child	05Ma00Fm
ROGERS, Edwin	42	M	Farmer	05Ma00Fm
Rachel	38	F	Unknown	05Ma00Fm
James	18	M	Unknown	05Ma00Fm
Edwin	13	M	Unknown	05Ma00Fm
Mary	16	F	Unknown	05Ma00Fm
Ann	11	F	Unknown	05Ma00Fm
Charles	8	M	Child	05Ma00Fm
Oliver	6	M	Child	05Ma00Fm
GOODHIND, Esan	36	M	Shoemaker	05Ma00Fm
Mary	31	F	Unknown	05Ma00Fm
George	7	M	Child	05Ma00Fm
Sarah	4	F	Child	05Ma00Fm
Martha	2	F	Child	05Ma00Fm
Mary-Anne	4	F	Child	05Ma00Fm
VIMPANY, Thomas	45	M	Farmer	05Ma00Fm
Henry	12	M	Unknown	05Ma00Fm
HAGMAN, Henry	50	M	Unknown	05Ma00Fm
BLANDFORD, James	33	M	Farmer	05Ma00Fm
Mary-Anne	29	F	Unknown	05Ma00Fm
William	6	M	Child	05Ma00Fm
Isaac	4	M	Child	05Ma00Fm
James	69	M	Unknown	05Ma00Fm
FRICKEN, William	22	M	Unknown	05Ma00Fm
BARTLEY, Noah	26	M	Carpenter	05Ma00Fm
Job	23	M	Unknown	05Ma00Fm
HATHERBY, Sarah	25	F	Unknown	05Ma00Fm
William	3	M	Child	05Ma00Fm
Sarah-Jane	47	F	Unknown	05Ma00Fm
PARKER, Susan	26	F	Unknown	05Ma00Fm
HAMPTON, William	24	M	Cooper	05Ma00Fm
Jane	21	F	Unknown	05Ma00Fm
William	1	M	Child	05Ma00Fm
EVANS, Eliza	23	F	Unknown	05Ma00Fm
Ann	3	F	Child	05Ma00Fm
William	.07	M	Infant	05Ma00Fm
MORGAN, John	23	M	Cooper	05Ma00Fm
Ann	22	F	Unknown	05Ma00Fm
CLEMENTS, Hugh	48	F	Laborer	05Ma00Fm
PERRY, William	46	M	Joiner	05Ma00Fm
MAGNER, James	31	M	Unknown	05Ma00Fm
DIXON, William-Henry	36	M	Shipwright	05Ma00Fm
REEVES, George	23	M	Unknown	05Ma00Fm
BROWN, James	42	M	Joiner	05Ma00Fm
SMITH, Henry	27	M	Joiner	05Ma00Fm
Elizabeth	22	F	Unknown	05Ma00Fm
COX, John	17	M	Unknown	05Ma00Fm
COOK, Matthew	17	M	Unknown	05Ma00Fm
BATTEN, Wm.	16	M	Apprentice	05Ma00Fm
MATTHEWS, Thomas	27	M	Farmer	05Ma00Fm
GROGAN, Patrick	22	M	Laborer	05Ma00Fm
Nora	25	F	Unknown	05Ma00Fm
Patrick	.10	M	Infant	05Ma00Fm
FITZGERALD, Thomas	23	M	Farmer	05Ma00Fm
THORN, William	20	M	Farmer	05Ma00Fm
Sarah	20	F	Unknown	05Ma00Fm
WHELAN, Michael	37	M	Farmer	05Ma00Fm
PHILLIPS, John	32	M	Farmer	05Ma00Fm
BOYLES, Ann	16	F	Unknown	05Ma00Fm
GRIFFIN, John	23	M	Unknown	05Ma00Fm
Tabitha	19	F	Unknown	05Ma00Fm
NEWTON, Henry	15	M	Unknown	05Ma00Fm
SPRATT, John	22	M	Farmer	05Ma00Fm
WINSLOW, John	14	M	Farmer	05Ma00Fm
DAWSON, William	17	M	Farmer	05Ma00Fm
WHITE, Henry	31	M	Farmer	05Ma00Fm
HARLEY, Luke	29	M	Farmer	05Ma00Fm
Jane	26	F	Unknown	05Ma00Fm
Thomas	6	M	Child	05Ma00Fm
TAGLEY, William	41	M	Farmer	05Ma00Fm
MATTHEWS, John	23	M	Unknown	05Ma00Fm
Edward	21	M	Unknown	05Ma00F
GREEN, James	27	M	Laborer	05Ma00F

NAMES OF PASSENGERS	AGE	SEX	OCCUPATIONS	DATE PORT SHIP
GREEN, Ellen	24	F	Unknown	05Ma00Fm
HOOK, Abram	17	M	Butcher	05Ma00Fm
WILLIAMS, Richard-S.	29	M	Laborer	05Ma00Fm
PEARSE, John	18	M	Farmer	05Ma00Fm
SMITH, John	25	M	Farmer	05Ma00Fm
Ellen	26	F	Unknown	05Ma00Fm
Mary	4	F	Child	05Ma00Fm
Charles	1	M	Child	05Ma00Fm
ROW, Daniel	29	M	Tailor	05Ma00Fm
Ann	27	F	Unknown	05Ma00Fm
Selina	4	F	Child	05Ma00Fm
John-Henry	.11	M	Infant	05Ma00Fm
COURT, Edward	26	M	Unknown	05Ma00Fm
Hannah	23	F	Unknown	05Ma00Fm

EL-DORADO 05 MAY 1849

From Liverpool

NAMES OF PASSENGERS	AGE	SEX	OCCUPATIONS	DATE PORT SHIP
HOWE, John	35	M	Laborer	05Ma02Es
U-Mrs.	35	F	Unknown	05Ma02Es
Sarah	15	F	None	05Ma02Es
ROBERTS, Geo.	31	M	Laborer	05Ma02Es
U-Mrs.	31	F	Unknown	05Ma02Es
Ann	.00	F	Infant	05Ma02Es
ANLIFFE, Thos.	35	M	Laborer	05Ma02Es
U-Mrs.	35	F	Unknown	05Ma02Es
FLOWER, Geo.	19	M	Unknown	05Ma02Es
BETTINGTON, Edwd.	26	M	Unknown	05Ma02Es
U-Mrs.	26	F	Unknown	05Ma02Es
Eliza	.00	F	Infant	05Ma02Es
Thomas	.00	M	Infant	05Ma02Es
HOLLY, Thos.	45	M	Unknown	05Ma02Es
U-Mrs.	45	F	Unknown	05Ma02Es
Jane	22	F	Unknown	05Ma02Es
William	18	M	Unknown	05Ma02Es
Eliza	13	F	Unknown	05Ma02Es
Richd.	11	M	Unknown	05Ma02Es
George	22	M	Unknown	05Ma02Es
PENHURST, Wm.	25	M	Unknown	05Ma02Es
WRIGHT, John	50	M	Unknown	05Ma02Es
U-Mrs.	50	F	Unknown	05Ma02Es
Wm.	12	M	Unknown	05Ma02Es
DOUGHTON, U	11	U	Unknown	05Ma02Es
John	25	M	Unknown	05Ma02Es
U-Mrs.	25	F	Unknown	05Ma02Es
U	.00	U	Infant	05Ma02Es
CLARKE, Wm.	30	M	Unknown	05Ma02Es
U-Mrs.	30	F	Unknown	05Ma02Es
WATSON, Wm.	28	M	Unknown	05Ma02Es
U-Mrs.	28	F	Unknown	05Ma02Es
WRIGHT, Jas.	30	M	Unknown	05Ma02Es
U-Mrs.	30	F	Unknown	05Ma02Es
Kesia	2	U	Child	05Ma02Es
U	.00	F	Infant	05Ma02Es
Died-At-Sea				
COLE, Chas.	20	M	Unknown	05Ma02Es
CARLEY, John	24	M	Unknown	05Ma02Es
U-Mrs.	24	F	Unknown	05Ma02Es
Emily	.00	F	Infant	05Ma02Es
CAMBLE, John	36	M	Laborer	05Ma02Es
U-Mrs.	36	F	Unknown	05Ma02Es
Mary-Anne	.00	F	Infant	05Ma02Es
ACKSON, Wm.	30	M	Unknown	05Ma02Es
Jane	30	F	None	05Ma02Es
Joseph	6	M	Child	05Ma02Es
OLLY, Thomas	25	M	Laborer	05Ma02Es
BRIAN, Thos.	26	M	Laborer	05Ma02Es
Ellen	21	F	Laborer	05Ma02Es

NAMES OF PASSENGERS		AGE	SEX	OCCUPATIONS	DATE PORT SHIP
MONNEY, Jerm.		30	M	Laborer	05Ma02Es
BURKE, Wm.		30	M	Laborer	05Ma02Es
HOPE, James		25	M	Laborer	05Ma02Es
Michl.		20	M	Laborer	05Ma02Es
PARSON, Ellen		34	F	Laborer	05Ma02Es
Robt.		8	M	Child	05Ma02Es
Ellen		6	F	Child	05Ma02Es
Lucy		3	F	Child	05Ma02Es
Jane		.00	F	Infant	05Ma02Es
NOWLAN, Jas.		18	M	Laborer	05Ma02Es
Bridget		20	F	Laborer	05Ma02Es
FARRELL, Peggy		20	F	Laborer	05Ma02Es
DWYER, Nancy		20	F	Laborer	05Ma02Es
HOPSON, John		40	M	Laborer	05Ma02Es
FARRELL, Jas.		20	M	Laborer	05Ma02Es
FITZSIMONS, Jas.		20	M	Laborer	05Ma02Es
DUFF, Phil		16	M	Laborer	05Ma02Es
MCGOVERN, Bryan		30	M	Laborer	05Ma02Es
Honora	(W)	25	F	Wife	05Ma02Es
John	(S)	.00	M	Infant	05Ma02Es
Cornl.		18	M	Laborer	05Ma02Es
Mary		20	F	Wife	05Ma02Es
DIGNAN, Mary		20	F	Unknown	05Ma02Es
MCCURDAN, John		30	M	Laborer	05Ma02Es
U	(W)	30	F	None	05Ma02Es
William		3	M	Child	05Ma02Es
John		.00	M	Infant	05Ma02Es
PORTER, Jas.		27	M	Laborer	05Ma02Es
Wm.		17	M	Laborer	05Ma02Es
HOLLINER, Chas.		40	M	Laborer	05Ma02Es
U	(W)	40	F	None	05Ma02Es
John		13	M	None	05Ma02Es
Cath.		11	F	None	05Ma02Es
Jon.		9	U	Child	05Ma02Es
Mary		7	F	Child	05Ma02Es
Ann		5	F	Child	05Ma02Es
Bridget		3	F	Child	05Ma02Es
WILSON, Geo.		26	M	Laborer	05Ma02Es
COATSWORTH, Kate		19	F	Laborer	05Ma02Es
Jane		17	F	Laborer	05Ma02Es
MULLIGAN, U-Mrs.		45	F	Wife	05Ma02Es
Kate		18	F	None	05Ma02Es
Julia		16	F	None	05Ma02Es
CONNELL, Thos.		27	M	Laborer	05Ma02Es
U	(W)	27	F	None	05Ma02Es
U-Mrs.		45	F	None	05Ma02Es
Eliza		2	F	Child	05Ma02Es
John		.00	M	Infant	05Ma02Es
BEDFORD, John		30	M	Laborer	05Ma02Es
DWYER, Ann		00	F	Unknown	05Ma02Es
ODONNELL, Mary		45	F	Unknown	05Ma02Es
Berd.		15	M	Laborer	05Ma02Es
Danl.		11	M	None	05Ma02Es
John		9	M	Child	05Ma02Es
James		7	M	Child	05Ma02Es
COX, Wm.		30	M	Laborer	05Ma02Es
PEACOCK, Geo.		38	M	Laborer	05Ma02Es
HILL, Danl.		25	M	Laborer	05Ma02Es
KEOWN, Bridget		15	F	Spinster	05Ma02Es
Pat		13	M	None	05Ma02Es
Edmond		11	M	None	05Ma02Es
Ann		6	F	Child	05Ma02Es
Winifred		6	F	Child	05Ma02Es
Mary		9	F	Child	05Ma02Es
FENNOYLE, Pat		27	M	Laborer	05Ma02Es
Judith		24	F	Unknown	05Ma02Es
Honora		20	F	Unknown	05Ma02Es
BEATTY, Cath.		18	F	Unknown	05Ma02Es
MURPHY, Bernd.		53	M	Farmer	05Ma02Es
Betty		12	F	None	05Ma02Es
Pat		9	M	Child	05Ma02Es
Bridget		7	F	Child	05Ma02Es
Mat		4	M	Child	05Ma02Es
Mick		.00	M	Infant	05Ma02Es
Peter		40	M	Laborer	05Ma02Es

NAMES OF PASSENGERS		AGE	SEX	OCCUPATIONS	DATE PORT SHIP
MCLOUGHLIN, Biddy		18	F	Spinster	05Ma02Es
FEGAN, Cath.		18	F	Spinster	05Ma02Es
MCQUADE. Jas.		16	M	Laborer	05Ma02Es
HAGAN, Jno.		21	M	Laborer	05Ma02Es
COGHRAN, Mary		32	F	None	05Ma02Es
Margt.		6	F	Child	05Ma02Es
DUNN. Mary		28	F	Unknown	05Ma02Es
JUDE. Jas.		45	M	Laborer	05Ma02Es
BEILIAN. Mary		45	F	None	05Ma02Es
Bern.		18	M	Laborer	05Ma02Es
Pat		21	M	Laborer	05Ma02Es
ROURKE. Betty		21	F	Laborer	05Ma02Es
HIGGINS. Pat		23	M	Laborer	05Ma02Es
COFFEY, Ajs.		38	M	Laborer	05Ma02Es
Eliza		36	F	Laborer	05Ma02Es
QUADE. Penny		40	U	Unknown	05Ma02Es
Margt.		38	F	Wife	05Ma02Es
Mary		16	F	None	05Ma02Es
Bridget		12	F	None	05Ma02Es
Mick		10	M	None	05Ma02Es
COFFEY, Tom		13	M	None	05Ma02Es
John		11	M	None	05Ma02Es
Eliza		8	F	Child	05Ma02Es
CARNEY, Darby		70	M	Servant	05Ma02Es
Bridget	(W)	60	F	Wife	05Ma02Es
Darby		24	M	Laborer	05Ma02Es
Pat		19	M	Laborer	05Ma02Es
Winney		17	U	Laborer	05Ma02Es
LARKIN, Mary		20	F	Laborer	05Ma02Es
LANAN, Bridget		20	F	Laborer	05Ma02Es
MORAN. Pat		25	M	Laborer	05Ma02Es
Winney		18	U	Laborer	05Ma02Es
KING, Winney		18	U	Laborer	05Ma02Es
HEARY, James		25	M	Laborer	05Ma02Es
Jno.		23	M	Laborer	05Ma02Es
DAKROY, Bridget		20	F	Wife	05Ma02Es
CURROCK, Eliza		20	F	Unknown	05Ma02Es
Peggy		22	F	Unknown	05Ma02Es
MARK, Mary		21	F	Unknown	05Ma02Es
CARNEY, Hiram		24	M	Laborer	05Ma02Es
CUNNINGHAM, Pat		24	M	Laborer	05Ma02Es
DOYLE. Cath.		18	F	Unknown	05Ma02Es
Stephen		16	M	Unknown	05Ma02Es
Mary-Ann		11	F	None	05Ma02Es
CROSS. Thos.		30	M	Laborer	05Ma02Es
RONAY, Michael		21	M	Laborer	05Ma02Es
BURN. John		21	M	Laborer	05Ma02Es
MATESON, John		32	M	Laborer	05Ma02Es
Geo.		22	M	Laborer	05Ma02Es
WATERSON. Geo.		20	M	Laborer	05Ma02Es
HEYMINS. Roger		21	M	Laborer	05Ma02Es
MOSES. Saml.		24	M	Laborer	05Ma02Es
Eliza		23	F	Wife	05Ma02Es
FLETCHER, Harriet		18	F	Unknown	05Ma02Es
Ellen		.00	F	Infant	05Ma02Es
MCLEE. Hugh		30	M	Laborer	05Ma02Es
Rosanna		26	F	Laborer	05Ma02Es
CONERY, Mick		50	M	Laborer	05Ma02Es
Dolly		40	F	Laborer	05Ma02Es
BUTTERY, John		70	M	Laborer	05Ma02Es
Mary		54	F	Laborer	05Ma02Es
Fanny		24	F	Laborer	05Ma02Es
Fred		15	M	Laborer	05Ma02Es
Mary-Ann		13	F	Laborer	05Ma02Es
Wm.		23	M	Laborer	05Ma02Es
Henry		18	M	Laborer	05Ma02Es
WATSON. Thos.		21	M	Laborer	05Ma02Es
Eliza		21	F	Spinster	05Ma02Es
MARKLEY, Jacob		28	M	Laborer	05Ma02Es
SHERMAN. John		26	M	Laborer	05Ma02Es
HUDSON. Thos.		35	M	Laborer	05Ma02Es
KING, Stockley		26	M	Laborer	05Ma02Es
WYNN, Arthur		30	M	Laborer	05Ma02Es
HOPS, Edwd.		20	M	Laborer	05Ma02Es
MCKENNY, Danl.		20	M	Laborer	05Ma02Es
MCENTEE, Simon		22	M	Laborer	05Ma02E
NEWMAN, John		19	M	Laborer	05Ma02E
LOUGHRICK, Mary		23	F	Wife	05Ma02E
MCELROY, Jane		18	F	Unknown	05Ma02E
Mary		21	F	Unknown	05Ma02E
HALL, Grace		19	F	Unknown	05Ma02E
MCCOLLUM, John		35	M	Laborer	05Ma02E
Ann		21	F	Laborer	05Ma02E
KING, Hannah		25	F	Laborer	05Ma02E
PALMER, Ellen		25	F	Laborer	05Ma02E
HATTON. Martha		18	F	Laborer	05Ma02E
MCKENNY, Mary		20	F	Laborer	05Ma02E
SINGLETON, Fanny		50	F	Laborer	05Ma02E
John		21	M	Laborer	05Ma02E
Thomas		19	M	Laborer	05Ma02E
Fanny		14	F	Laborer	05Ma02E
WRIGHT, Mary-Ann		30	F	Dressmaker	05Ma02E
MORRILL, Ben		30	M	Laborer	05Ma02E
U	(W)	26	F	Laborer	05Ma02E
John		12	M	None	05Ma02E
Sarah		5	F	Child	05Ma02E
Mary		7	F	Child	05Ma02E
Eliza		4	F	Child	05Ma02E
Benj.		2	M	Child	05Ma02E
ELTON, Wm.		30	M	Laborer	05Ma02E
HARKIN, Jas.		20	M	Laborer	05Ma02E
SHAY, Walter		31	M	Laborer	05Ma02E
U	(W)	31	F	Unknown	05Ma02E
Eliza		7	F	Child	05Ma02E
Walt		5	M	Child	05Ma02E
Charles		.00	M	Infant	05Ma02E
John-Richd.		3	M	Child	05Ma02E
DONOHUE, Tom		30	M	Laborer	05Ma02E
MURPHY, John		25	M	Laborer	05Ma02E
WHELAN, John		20	M	Laborer	05Ma02E
LYSON, Tom		30	M	Laborer	05Ma02E
John		12	M	Laborer	05Ma02E
Mick		10	M	Laborer	05Ma02E
HANLEY, Sarah		55	F	Laborer	05Ma02E
Dinah		20	F	Laborer	05Ma02E
GRAVES, Wm.		20	M	Laborer	05Ma02E
SUTTON, John		20	M	Laborer	05Ma02E
ROBINSON, Henry		20	M	Laborer	05Ma02E
DARCEY, Pat		40	M	Laborer	05Ma02E
Mary		12	F	None	05Ma02E
WHELAN, Biddy		26	F	Wife	05Ma02E
Honora		20	F	Unknown	05Ma02E
BROPHY, Thos.		46	M	Farmer	05Ma02E
SMITH, Margt.		20	F	Servant	05Ma02E
MCCORMICK, Bridget		20	F	Servant	05Ma02E
MCDONALD, Jas.		18	M	Laborer	05Ma02E
Betsey		16	F	Spinster	05Ma02E
MCPHILIP, Henry		30	M	Laborer	05Ma02E
CLARK, Henry		22	M	Unknown	05Ma02E
CUPPAGE, Martha		35	F	Unknown	05Ma02E
Louisa		30	F	Wife	05Ma02E
EVANS, Bridget		24	F	Unknown	05Ma02E
ARMSTRONG, Alexr.		20	M	Laborer	05Ma02E
CROSHA, Thornton		42	M	Laborer	05Ma02E
U	(W)	42	F	Unknown	05Ma02E
Hercules		12	M	None	05Ma02E
Jacob		10	M	None	05Ma02E
ARNOLD, Jas.		42	M	Laborer	05Ma02
THORP, Jno.		23	M	Laborer	05Ma02
U	(W)	21	F	Wife	05Ma02
Ann		.00	F	Infant	05Ma02
LUNDY, Geo.		20	M	Laborer	05Ma02
Wm.		13	M	None	05Ma02
GUNNINGLE, Pat		50	M	Laborer	05Ma02
Pat		20	M	Laborer	05Ma02
Jas.		12	M	Laborer	05Ma02
SCOTT, Philip		40	M	Laborer	05Ma02
SCUTTON, Geo.		19	M	Laborer	05Ma02
Judith		16	F	Spinster	05Ma02
Joseph		13	M	None	05Ma02

AMES OF PASSENGERS		AGE	SEX	OCCUPATIONS	DATE PORT SHIP
SCUTTON, Michl.		11	M	None	05Ma02Es
MAHER, Judah		17	F	Unknown	05Ma02Es
DELAHUNTY, John		22	M	Farmer	05Ma02Es
Tim		19	M	Farmer	05Ma02Es
Julia		17	F	Spinster	05Ma02Es
Judith		13	F	Spinster	05Ma02Es
Cath.		12	F	Spinster	05Ma02Es
SYMONS, Wm.		60	M	Laborer	05Ma02Es
U	(W)	56	F	Wife	05Ma02Es
Jas.		28	M	Laborer	05Ma02Es
Joseph		22	M	Laborer	05Ma02Es
Sarah		30	F	Laborer	05Ma02Es
Jane		29	F	Laborer	05Ma02Es
Caroline		18	F	Laborer	05Ma02Es
WHITTY, John		27	M	Laborer	05Ma02Es
Anty		22	F	Laborer	05Ma02Es
EREBOUGH, Moses		31	M	Laborer	05Ma02Es
CLANCEY, Michl.		30	M	Laborer	05Ma02Es
ARNOLDS, Archd.		32	M	Laborer	05Ma02Es
ATANLY, Richd.		35	M	Laborer	05Ma02Es
KING, Margt.		18	F	Spinster	05Ma02Es
FARRELL, Rody		60	U	Unknown	05Ma02Es
Mary		60	F	Unknown	05Ma02Es
MADDEN, Bridget		20	F	Spinster	05Ma02Es
KEARNY, Dominick		40	M	Laborer	05Ma02Es
MADDEN, John		18	M	Laborer	05Ma02Es
CORTILL, John		20	M	Laborer	05Ma02Es
CONNOR, Jas.		28	M	Laborer	05Ma02Es
DAY, Tim		22	M	Laborer	05Ma02Es
HANLEY, Joseph		32	M	Laborer	05Ma02Es
Thos.		18	M	Laborer	05Ma02Es
KING, Richd.		30	M	Laborer	05Ma02Es
Alexr.		40	M	Laborer	05Ma02Es
Bridget		19	F	Spinster	05Ma02Es
BARON, Geo.		35	M	Laborer	05Ma02Es
REED, Mary		20	F	Unknown	05Ma02Es
HEFFERIN, John		20	M	Farmer	05Ma02Es
HAGAN, Cath.		20	F	Servant	05Ma02Es
EAGAN, Thos.		22	M	Laborer	05Ma02Es
U	(W)	22	F	Wife	05Ma02Es
FAY, Ellen		35	F	Unknown	05Ma02Es
EAGAN, Thos.		22	M	Laborer	05Ma02Es
U	(W)	22	F	Unknown	05Ma02Es
AY, Ellen		35	F	Unknown	05Ma02Es
LARKE, Ann		13	F	Unknown	05Ma02Es
Pat		11	M	None	05Ma02Es
ULLIVAN, Robt.		22	M	Unknown	05Ma02Es
U	(W)	20	F	Wife	05Ma02Es
Ann		.00	F	Infant	05Ma02Es
ALLAGHAN, Mary		20	F	Unknown	05Ma02Es
ILLON, John		25	M	Laborer	05Ma02Es
RADY, Wm.		35	M	Laborer	05Ma02Es
ITZPATRICK, Jas.		26	M	Laborer	05Ma02Es
EARCEY, Thos.		24	M	Laborer	05Ma02Es
ITZPATRICK, Margt.		22	F	Laborer	05Ma02Es
ACKSON, Eliza		3	F	Child	05Ma02Es
Cath.		5	F	Child	05Ma02Es
CDONALD, Jas.		18	M	Laborer	05Ma02Es
ILSON, John		26	M	None	05Ma02Es

HANNAH-KERR 05 MAY 1849

From Belfast

NAMES OF PASSENGERS	AGE	SEX	OCCUPATIONS	DATE PORT SHIP
UGLAS, Nancy	35	F	Unknown	05Ma05Fn
John	11	M	Unknown	05Ma05Fn
Francis	.00	M	Infant	05Ma05Fn
CANN, Mary	30	F	Unknown	05Ma05Fn
Michael	20	M	Unknown	05Ma05Fn
HANVEY, John	24	M	Unknown	05Ma05Fn
BOLE, William	20	M	Unknown	05Ma05Fn
BYERS, William	20	M	Unknown	05Ma05Fn
LUNDIE, Hugh	17	M	Unknown	05Ma05Fn
MARTIN, John	25	M	Unknown	05Ma05Fn
Eliza	25	F	Unknown	05Ma05Fn
KISSOCK, James	30	F	Unknown	05Ma05Fn
Matilda	28	F	Unknown	05Ma05Fn
John	7	M	Child	05Ma05Fn
Mary	5	F	Child	05Ma05Fn
Joseph	1	M	Child	05Ma05Fn
Eliza	.00	F	Infant	05Ma05Fn
BELL, John	30	M	Unknown	05Ma05Fn
Mary	32	F	Unknown	05Ma05Fn
Margaret	8	F	Child	05Ma05Fn
Nancy	6	F	Child	05Ma05Fn
Eliza	4	F	Child	05Ma05Fn
Sarah	.00	F	Infant	05Ma05Fn
SCOTT, Margaret	50	F	Unknown	05Ma05Fn
George	27	M	Unknown	05Ma05Fn
William	24	M	Unknown	05Ma05Fn
Eliza	21	F	Unknown	05Ma05Fn
Thomas	16	M	Unknown	05Ma05Fn
John	33	M	Unknown	05Ma05Fn
Sarah	27	F	Unknown	05Ma05Fn
James	4	M	Child	05Ma05Fn
Eliza	.00	F	Infant	05Ma05Fn
MOORE, Margaret	17	F	Unknown	05Ma05Fn
BELL, George	21	M	Unknown	05Ma05Fn
BARR, John	23	M	Unknown	05Ma05Fn
MCCANEL, William	21	M	Unknown	05Ma05Fn
ORR, Jane	25	M	Unknown	05Ma05Fn
HAMILTON, Agnes	20	F	Unknown	05Ma05Fn
JOHNSON, Henry	20	M	Unknown	05Ma05Fn
BRADLEY, Mary	20	F	Unknown	05Ma05Fn
MONAGHAN, Ann	20	F	Unknown	05Ma05Fn
MCKEOWN, Robert	20	F	Unknown	05Ma05Fn
Mary	20	F	Unknown	05Ma05Fn
ROBINSON, James	21	M	Unknown	05Ma05Fn
TREN, Thomas	16	M	Unknown	05Ma05Fn
SMITH, Hamilton	18	M	Unknown	05Ma05Fn
MORROW, James	19	M	Unknown	05Ma05Fn
STEWART, Robert	18	M	Unknown	05Ma05Fn
NEELY, David	18	M	Unknown	05Ma05Fn
Mary	16	F	Unknown	05Ma05Fn
MURRAY, Susan	40	F	Unknown	05Ma05Fn
Bernard	9	M	Child	05Ma05Fn
Susan	7	F	Child	05Ma05Fn
Mary	5	F	Child	05Ma05Fn
John	.00	M	Infant	05Ma05Fn
FARRIER, Fanny	18	F	Unknown	05Ma05Fn
MCCLUSKER, Mathew	18	M	Unknown	05Ma05Fn
BRADLEY, Edward	21	M	Unknown	05Ma05Fn
Biddy	16	F	Unknown	05Ma05Fn
MORAN, Michael	25	M	Unknown	05Ma05Fn
Mary	60	F	Unknown	05Ma05Fn
Biddy	20	F	Unknown	05Ma05Fn
Charles	18	M	Unknown	05Ma05Fn
LITTLE, Alexander	48	M	Unknown	05Ma05Fn
Margaret	40	F	Unknown	05Ma05Fn
John	19	M	Unknown	05Ma05Fn
William	16	M	Unknown	05Ma05Fn
Ann	14	F	Unknown	05Ma05Fn
Alexander	6	M	Child	05Ma05Fn
Rose	.00	F	Infant	05Ma05Fn
MOODEY, Jane	24	F	Unknown	05Ma05Fn
SHEELER, William	25	M	Unknown	05Ma05Fn
REGAN, Margt.	29	F	Unknown	05Ma05Fn
SINGLETON, John	20	M	Unknown	05Ma05Fn
BECK, John	25	M	Unknown	05Ma05Fn
MCCROOLEY, John	18	M	Unknown	05Ma05Fn
Rose	20	F	Unknown	05Ma05Fn
SIMPSON, Thomas	20	M	Unknown	05Ma05Fn
WALLACE, Francis	18	M	Unknown	05Ma05Fn
MCANALLY, Ann	20	F	Unknown	05Ma05Fn

NAMES OF PASSENGERS	AGE	SEX	OCCUPATIONS	DATE PORT SHIP
MCANALLY, Tool	18	U	Unknown	05Ma05Fn
Margarey	13	F	Unknown	05Ma05Fn
James	9	M	Child	05Ma05Fn
CUNY, Eliza	22	F	Unknown	05Ma05Fn
TONER, James	22	M	Unknown	05Ma05Fn
MITCHELL, Mary	22	F	Unknown	05Ma05Fn
HENRY, Mathew	17	M	Unknown	05Ma05Fn
WELSH, John	26	M	Unknown	05Ma05Fn
Rose	24	F	Unknown	05Ma05Fn
Arthur	.00	M	Infant	05Ma05Fn
Lewis	2	M	Child	05Ma05Fn
LINN, William	44	M	Unknown	05Ma05Fn
Mary	40	F	Unknown	05Ma05Fn
Ann	22	F	Unknown	05Ma05Fn
Margaret	19	F	Unknown	05Ma05Fn
Mary	17	F	Unknown	05Ma05Fn
Eliza	15	F	Unknown	05Ma05Fn
Jane	13	F	Unknown	05Ma05Fn
Matilda	11	F	Unknown	05Ma05Fn
Johanna	8	F	Child	05Ma05Fn
Isabella	5	F	Child	05Ma05Fn
John	4	M	Child	05Ma05Fn
Nancy	.00	F	Infant	05Ma05Fn
SEIMAN, Mary	65	F	Unknown	05Ma05Fn
William	25	M	Unknown	05Ma05Fn
John	23	M	Unknown	05Ma05Fn
Sarah	.00	F	Infant	05Ma05Fn
Martha	22	F	Unknown	05Ma05Fn
ELLIOTT, Adam	18	M	Unknown	05Ma05Fn
HAGAN, Alice	9	F	Child	05Ma05Fn
Eliza	7	F	Child	05Ma05Fn
HENRY, Catharine	24	F	Unknown	05Ma05Fn
TONER, John	20	M	Unknown	05Ma05Fn
Michael	24	M	Unknown	05Ma05Fn
WALKER, Charles	50	M	Unknown	05Ma05Fn
Christian	50	M	Unknown	05Ma05Fn
Robert	16	M	Unknown	05Ma05Fn
Eliza	15	F	Unknown	05Ma05Fn
Margaret	14	F	Unknown	05Ma05Fn
Charles	11	M	Unknown	05Ma05Fn
Herman	.00	M	Infant	05Ma05Fn
MCGUCKAN, John	25	M	Unknown	05Ma05Fn
MANCELY, James	25	M	Unknown	05Ma05Fn
MCCELLAND, Nelsen	25	M	Unknown	05Ma05Fn
WHITESIDE, Margaret	20	F	Unknown	05Ma05Fn
BROWN, Andrew	20	M	Unknown	05Ma05Fn
MCAULEY, James	22	M	Unknown	05Ma05Fn
Isabella	20	F	Unknown	05Ma05Fn
JUIERS, Ann	20	F	Unknown	05Ma05Fn
MCCANN, Margaret	20	F	Unknown	05Ma05Fn
FLINN, Christopher	16	M	Unknown	05Ma05Fn
Ann	13	F	Unknown	05Ma05Fn
LOWRY, Sarah	40	F	Unknown	05Ma05Fn
Flora	20	F	Unknown	05Ma05Fn
John	16	M	Unknown	05Ma05Fn
Robert	14	M	Unknown	05Ma05Fn
BLACK, Little	23	M	Unknown	05Ma05Fn
CARROLL, James	18	M	Unknown	05Ma05Fn
RACEY, Edward	20	M	Unknown	05Ma05Fn
JUNK, Eliza	20	F	Unknown	05Ma05Fn
MCALLISTER, Nancy	23	F	Unknown	05Ma05Fn
ANDANSEN, John	27	M	Unknown	05Ma05Fn
ROBINSEN, David	22	M	Unknown	05Ma05Fn
Mary	19	F	Unknown	05Ma05Fn
MCCRIERY, John	21	M	Unknown	05Ma05Fn
HEANEY, James	21	M	Unknown	05Ma05Fn
WILLIAMSEN, James	47	M	Unknown	05Ma05Fn
Patrick	30	M	Unknown	05Ma05Fn
Rose	25	F	Unknown	05Ma05Fn
James	.00	M	Infant	05Ma05Fn
Eliza	7	F	Child	05Ma05Fn
John	5	M	Child	05Ma05Fn
KANE, Sarah	15	F	Unknown	05Ma05Fn
STINGER, Sarah	19	F	Unknown	05Ma05Fn
Jane	12	F	Unknown	05Ma05Fn
STINGER, James	15	M	Unknown	05Ma05Fn
COLLINS, Eliza	18	M	Unknown	05Ma05Fn
SHEPPARD, John	20	M	Unknown	05Ma05Fn
MCMAHON, John	60	M	Unknown	05Ma05Fn
James	22	M	Unknown	05Ma05Fn
Fanny	20	F	Unknown	05Ma05Fn
Ann	15	F	Unknown	05Ma05Fn
ARMSTRONG, William	28	M	Unknown	05Ma05Fn
Ann	26	F	Unknown	05Ma05Fn
Andrew	3	M	Child	05Ma05Fn
Robert	.00	M	Infant	05Ma05Fn
MOORELAND, William	22	M	Unknown	05Ma05Fn
KIRKPATRICK, Auley	18	U	Unknown	05Ma05Fn
Mary	16	F	Unknown	05Ma05Fn
LOUGHLAN, William	25	F	Unknown	05Ma05Fn
CHEVEY, William	19	M	Unknown	05Ma05Fn
HACKET, Hugh	21	M	Unknown	05Ma05Fn
Eliza	19	F	Unknown	05Ma05Fn
CURRY, Ellen	19	F	Unknown	05Ma05Fn
WINCHESTER, David	21	M	Unknown	05Ma05Fn
SCOTT, George	21	M	Unknown	05Ma05Fn
HILL, David	21	M	Unknown	05Ma05Fn
WARNOCK, Robert	24	M	Unknown	05Ma05Fn
MCCUSKIN, Margaret	25	M	Unknown	05Ma05Fn
PURRIN, Minus	21	M	Unknown	05Ma05Fn
MCGLADE, Henry	20	M	Unknown	05Ma05Fn
MCCLARON, John	28	M	Unknown	05Ma05Fn
HALLIDAY, Francis	20	M	Unknown	05Ma05Fn
MCWILLIAMS, John	29	M	Unknown	05Ma05Fn
MCCANN, Mary	22	F	Unknown	05Ma05Fn
Mackay	16	F	Unknown	05Ma05Fn
John	24	F	Unknown	05Ma05Fn
HOUSTON, Sarah	50	M	Unknown	05Ma05Fn
John	30	M	Unknown	05Ma05Fn
Catharine	18	F	Unknown	05Ma05Fn
Elizabeth	14	F	Unknown	05Ma05Fn
REED, Thomas	30	M	Unknown	05Ma05Fn
William	.00	M	Infant	05Ma05Fn
MCKENNA, John	25	M	Unknown	05Ma05Fn
WELLS, Walter	21	M	Unknown	05Ma05Fn
MCGOWAN, John	30	M	Unknown	05Ma05Fn
Eliza	30	F	Unknown	05Ma05Fn
WELSH, John	24	M	Unknown	05Ma05Fn
WATT, Catharine	19	F	Unknown	05Ma05Fn
SCULLY, Eliza	20	F	Unknown	05Ma05Fn
FISHER, Neill	30	M	Unknown	05Ma05Fn
Mary-Jane	16	F	Unknown	05Ma05Fn
Ann	12	F	Unknown	05Ma05Fn
MCHENRY, James	20	M	Unknown	05Ma05Fn
Jane	18	F	Unknown	05Ma05Fn
OHARA, Luke	18	M	Unknown	05Ma05Fn
GRAHAM, Josias	19	M	Unknown	05Ma05Fn
Samuel	17	M	Unknown	05Ma05Fn
KENNY, James	30	M	Unknown	05Ma05Fn
Robert	20	M	Unknown	05Ma05Fn
MCCOULING, Margaret	30	F	Unknown	05Ma05Fn
John	10	M	Unknown	05Ma05Fn
Bridget	8	F	Child	05Ma05Fn
Isabella	4	F	Child	05Ma05Fn
MCGOVERN, Catharine	7	F	Child	05Ma05Fn
John	.00	M	Infant	05Ma05Fn
KEAN, Robert-M.	30	M	Unknown	05Ma05Fn
Margaret	20	F	Unknown	05Ma05Fn
MUTEN, William	22	M	Unknown	05Ma05Fn
MCCLURCAN, Mathew	21	M	Unknown	05Ma05Fn
REDMOND, Eliza	30	F	Unknown	05Ma05Fn
Mary-Anne	30	F	Unknown	05Ma05Fn
SEAL, Ellen	.00	F	Infant	05Ma05Fn
John	22	M	Unknown	05Ma05Fn
SCOTT, Sarah	46	F	Unknown	05Ma05Fn
Edward	22	M	Unknown	05Ma05Fn
Susanna	20	F	Unknown	05Ma05Fn
Thomas	18	M	Unknown	05Ma05Fn
Nelson	15	M	Unknown	05Ma05Fn
Robert	11	M	Unknown	05Ma05F

NAMES OF PASSENGERS	AGE	SEX	OCCUPATIONS	DATE PORT SHIP
SCOTT, Henry	9	M	Child	05Ma05Fn
WILKINSON, Esther	13	F	Unknown	05Ma05Fn
MCKEOWN, Alexander	24	M	Unknown	05Ma05Fn

GERTRUDE 05 MAY 1849

From Belfast

NAMES OF PASSENGERS	AGE	SEX	OCCUPATIONS	DATE PORT SHIP
MALLON, Jno.	20	M	Weaver	05Ma05Ek
BODEN, Jno.	21	M	Weaver	05Ma05Ek
MCELVENA, Wm.	40	M	Weaver	05Ma05Ek
Anne	35	F	Weaver	05Ma05Ek
Mary	26	F	Weaver	05Ma05Ek
Fanny	16	F	Weaver	05Ma05Ek
MAXWELL, Hugh	30	M	Weaver	05Ma05Ek
THOMPSON, Pat	20	M	Weaver	05Ma05Ek
MORRISON, Jno.	30	M	Weaver	05Ma05Ek
Margt.	30	F	Weaver	05Ma05Ek
Jas.	.00	M	Infant	05Ma05Ek
John	.00	M	Infant	05Ma05Ek
MAWHING, And.	50	M	Farmer	05Ma05Ek
Jas.	31	M	Farmer	05Ma05Ek
Jno.	30	M	Farmer	05Ma05Ek
Isabella	31	F	Farmer	05Ma05Ek
CURRAY, William	21	M	Farmer	05Ma05Ek
MCCRACKEN, Jas.	30	M	Farmer	05Ma05Ek
Eliza	30	F	Farmer	05Ma05Ek
Jno.	.00	M	Infant	05Ma05Ek
Agnes	.00	F	Infant	05Ma05Ek
MCKINSEY, Ellen	20	F	Spinster	05Ma05Ek
MCKEE, Maria	20	F	Spinster	05Ma05Ek
MCCLEARN, Jas.	27	M	Weaver	05Ma05Ek
Margt.	19	F	Weaver	05Ma05Ek
JOHNSON, Jas.	24	M	Weaver	05Ma05Ek
Jane	23	F	Weaver	05Ma05Ek
Mary	3	F	Child	05Ma05Ek
Agnes	.00	F	Infant	05Ma05Ek
BAILEY, Robt.	40	M	Weaver	05Ma05Ek
Jane	40	F	Weaver	05Ma05Ek
Jane	19	F	Weaver	05Ma05Ek
J.	17	M	Weaver	05Ma05Ek
U	10	F	Weaver	05Ma05Ek
MAWHUNG, Hugh	20	M	Weaver	05Ma05Ek
Mary	20	F	Weaver	05Ma05Ek
MCNUPIAN, And.	20	M	Weaver	05Ma05Ek
BOYCE, Anne	25	F	Weaver	05Ma05Ek
Mary	8	F	Child	05Ma05Ek
Ellen	6	F	Child	05Ma05Ek
Jane	.00	F	Infant	05Ma05Ek
MCCRACKEN, Alex.	26	M	Weaver	05Ma05Ek
Jno.	17	M	Weaver	05Ma05Ek
GRAHAM, Robt.	30	M	Weaver	05Ma05Ek
SHANNON, Robt.	30	M	Weaver	05Ma05Ek
Margt.	28	F	Weaver	05Ma05Ek
Margt.	5	F	Child	05Ma05Ek
Jas.	.00	M	Infant	05Ma05Ek
BLACK, William	23	M	Weaver	05Ma05Ek
MURPHY, Jas.	25	M	Weaver	05Ma05Ek
JOHNSTON, Hugh	25	M	Weaver	05Ma05Ek
J, Jno.	40	M	Weaver	05Ma05Ek
Catherine	40	F	Weaver	05Ma05Ek
Mary	22	F	Weaver	05Ma05Ek
Eliza	20	F	Weaver	05Ma05Ek
Hugh	18	M	Weaver	05Ma05Ek
Jas.	16	M	Weaver	05Ma05Ek
Jno.	13	M	Weaver	05Ma05Ek
Jane	.11	F	Infant	05Ma05Ek
William	9	M	Child	05Ma05Ek
Samuel	7	M	Child	05Ma05Ek

NAMES OF PASSENGERS	AGE	SEX	OCCUPATIONS	DATE PORT SHIP
U, Alexander	.00	M	Infant	05Ma05Ek
BROWN, Samuel	50	M	Weaver	05Ma05Ek
Jane	46	F	Weaver	05Ma05Ek
Thomas	13	M	Weaver	05Ma05Ek
James	10	M	Weaver	05Ma05Ek
Robt.	8	M	Child	05Ma05Ek
Jno.	.00	M	Infant	05Ma05Ek
Ellen	.00	F	Infant	05Ma05Ek
MCDOWELL, And.	29	M	Weaver	05Ma05Ek
BROWN, Margt.	15	F	Weaver	05Ma05Ek
CAMPBELL, Jane	21	F	Weaver	05Ma05Ek
FORSYTH, Robt.	21	M	Weaver	05Ma05Ek
DONAN, Thomas	45	M	Weaver	05Ma05Ek
Jno.	25	M	Weaver	05Ma05Ek
Eliza	45	F	Weaver	05Ma05Ek
CLELAND, Mathew	30	M	Weaver	05Ma05Ek
Jane	28	F	Weaver	05Ma05Ek
DOURAN, Jane	18	F	Weaver	05Ma05Ek
KINGAN, Jane	18	F	Weaver	05Ma05Ek
ENGLISH, David	22	M	Weaver	05Ma05Ek
RALSTON, Hugh	20	M	Weaver	05Ma05Ek
ADAIR, William	29	M	Weaver	05Ma05Ek
William	6	M	Child	05Ma05Ek
KENNEDY, Wm.	16	M	Weaver	05Ma05Ek
AGNEW, Wm.	27	M	Weaver	05Ma05Ek
MCKEE, David	29	M	Weaver	05Ma05Ek
MURRAY, Henry	22	M	Weaver	05Ma05Ek
SAVAGE, Patt	50	M	Weaver	05Ma05Ek
Jno.	26	M	Weaver	05Ma05Ek
Francis	20	M	Weaver	05Ma05Ek
HARVEY, Samuel	24	M	Weaver	05Ma05Ek
MORROW, Adam	28	M	Weaver	05Ma05Ek
Margt.	28	F	Weaver	05Ma05Ek
FISHER, James	22	M	Weaver	05Ma05Ek
MCWILLIAMS, Hugh	21	M	Weaver	05Ma05Ek
PELAN, Jas.	21	M	Weaver	05Ma05Ek
CAWLEY, Henry	21	M	Weaver	05Ma05Ek
CARLAN, James	21	M	Weaver	05Ma05Ek
HADDEN, Worthy	22	M	Weaver	05Ma05Ek
ROBERTS, Sarah	28	F	Weaver	05Ma05Ek
Catherine	18	F	Weaver	05Ma05Ek
Samuel	.00	M	Infant	05Ma05Ek
Sarah	4	F	Child	05Ma05Ek
BOYD, Jane	18	F	Weaver	05Ma05Ek
KIRK, Mary	20	F	Weaver	05Ma05Ek
FERGEY, Saml.	20	M	Weaver	05Ma05Ek
Robt.	18	M	Weaver	05Ma05Ek
MAWHUNG, Susan	22	F	Weaver	05Ma05Ek
DUNN, Alfred	22	M	Weaver	05Ma05Ek
STEPHENSON, Jas.	28	M	Weaver	05Ma05Ek
KIRK, Jas.	24	M	Weaver	05Ma05Ek
MCCORMACK, Jas.	44	M	Weaver	05Ma05Ek
Eliza	40	F	Weaver	05Ma05Ek
Sarah	7	F	Child	05Ma05Ek
Hercules	5	M	Child	05Ma05Ek
William	3	M	Child	05Ma05Ek
WARNOCK, Campbell	19	M	Weaver	05Ma05Ek
KELLY, Adam	24	M	Weaver	05Ma05Ek
MCELVENA, Jas.	24	M	Weaver	05Ma05Ek
GRACE, Eliza	30	F	Weaver	05Ma05Ek
MILLER, Mary	20	F	Weaver	05Ma05Ek
BOYD, Eliza	30	F	Weaver	05Ma05Ek
David	15	M	Weaver	05Ma05Ek
Mary	12	F	Weaver	05Ma05Ek
Nevin	10	M	Weaver	05Ma05Ek
MCCLURE, Jas.	24	M	Weaver	05Ma05Ek
ALEXANDER, And.	24	M	Weaver	05Ma05Ek
JOHNSON, Robt.	40	M	Weaver	05Ma05Ek
LOCK, David	23	M	Weaver	05Ma05Ek
Jas.	21	M	Weaver	05Ma05Ek
CRAIG, Jno.	19	M	Weaver	05Ma05Ek
Martha	19	F	Weaver	05Ma05Ek
MCWILLIAMS, Crawford	20	M	Weaver	05Ma05Ek
Fullerton	20	M	Weaver	05Ma05Ek
CARSE, Jno.	29	M	Weaver	05Ma05Ek

NAMES OF PASSENGERS	AGE	SEX	OCCUPATIONS	DATE PORT SHIP
JAMISON, Wm.	25	M	Weaver	05Ma05Ek
Johanna	18	F	Weaver	05Ma05Ek
WILEY, William	21	M	Weaver	05Ma05Ek
SHAW, Jos.	21	M	Weaver	05Ma05Ek
MCWILLIAMS, Mary	18	F	Weaver	05Ma05Ek
MCCRACKEN, Margt.	18	F	Weaver	05Ma05Ek
BOYD, Mary	20	F	Weaver	05Ma05Ek
George	18	M	Weaver	05Ma05Ek
Robt.	20	M	Weaver	05Ma05Ek
MOORE, Mary	20	F	Weaver	05Ma05Ek
MAWHING, Saml.	25	M	Weaver	05Ma05Ek
LOGAN, Martha	20	F	Weaver	05Ma05Ek
MCDOWELL, Jas.	19	M	Weaver	05Ma05Ek
Jane	17	F	Weaver	05Ma05Ek
MURPHY, Alexr.	21	M	Weaver	05Ma05Ek
STONES, Jos.	22	M	Weaver	05Ma05Ek
Agnes	22	F	Weaver	05Ma05Ek
STOCK, Ben	30	M	Weaver	05Ma05Ek
MACKEN, Redmond	22	M	Weaver	05Ma05Ek
MORRISON, Jas.	21	M	Weaver	05Ma05Ek
MCALISEE, Francis	21	M	Weaver	05Ma05Ek
MCCLUGGE, Robt.	21	M	Weaver	05Ma05Ek
MCROBERTS, Mathew	21	M	Weaver	05Ma05Ek
MAGILL, Mary	18	F	Weaver	05Ma05Ek
ROBINSON, Jas.	18	M	Weaver	05Ma05Ek
KIRKPATRICK, Robt.	21	M	Weaver	05Ma05Ek
MCNEILL, Saml.	.00	M	Infant	05Ma05Ek
WILSON, Jas.	24	M	Weaver	05Ma05Ek
SHARP, Jas.	20	M	Weaver	05Ma05Ek
Catherine	18	F	Weaver	05Ma05Ek
Mary	.00	F	Infant	05Ma05Ek
WILSON, Jas.	21	M	Weaver	05Ma05Ek
BLANEY, Chas.	21	M	Weaver	05Ma05Ek
Rose	20	F	Weaver	05Ma05Ek
MCCOLLUM, Molly	21	F	Weaver	05Ma05Ek
WILSON, Jno.	24	M	Weaver	05Ma05Ek
Margt.	20	F	Weaver	05Ma05Ek
KEEGAN, Mary	4	F	Child	05Ma05Ek
WILSON, Catherine	18	F	Weaver	05Ma05Ek
KEEGAN, Alex	30	M	Weaver	05Ma05Ek
Margt.	26	F	Weaver	05Ma05Ek
Catherine	.00	F	Infant	05Ma05Ek
Sally	.00	F	Infant	05Ma05Ek
MCCOLLUM, Danl.	24	M	Weaver	05Ma05Ek
Alexander	19	M	Weaver	05Ma05Ek
MCCORMACK, Dennis	29	M	Weaver	05Ma05Ek
DILLON, Jno.	20	M	Weaver	05Ma05Ek
Mary	20	F	Weaver	05Ma05Ek
Jane	20	F	Weaver	05Ma05Ek
Mary	12	F	Weaver	05Ma05Ek
Anne	10	F	Weaver	05Ma05Ek
Patt	8	M	Weaver	05Ma05Ek
LAFFERTY, Eneas	34	M	Weaver	05Ma05Ek
QUINN, Ann	20	F	Weaver	05Ma05Ek
LEWIS, Hugh	60	M	Weaver	05Ma05Ek
Margt.	58	F	Weaver	05Ma05Ek
Agnes	25	F	Weaver	05Ma05Ek
MCCOURT, Frank	29	M	Weaver	05Ma05Ek
Eliza	35	F	Weaver	05Ma05Ek
Mathew	3	M	Child	05Ma05Ek
Margt.	.00	F	Infant	05Ma05Ek
KIRK, Martin	27	M	Weaver	05Ma05Ek
HAMILTON, Jno.	19	M	Weaver	05Ma05Ek
And.	20	M	Weaver	05Ma05Ek
MCBRIAN, Jno.	28	M	Weaver	05Ma05Ek
OHARRA, Jno.	40	M	Weaver	05Ma05Ek
Chas.	6	M	Child	05Ma05Ek
MARSHALL, Wm.	60	M	Weaver	05Ma05Ek
Mary	60	F	Weaver	05Ma05Ek
Margt.	17	F	Weaver	05Ma05Ek
Mary	14	F	Weaver	05Ma05Ek
Jane	12	F	Weaver	05Ma05Ek
Nancy	9	F	Child	05Ma05Ek
William	7	M	Child	05Ma05Ek
James	5	M	Child	05Ma05Ek
MARSHALL, And.	.00	M	Infant	05Ma05Ek
PORTER, Mary	18	F	Weaver	05Ma05Ek
MCCLAWSON, Robt.	20	M	Weaver	05Ma05Ek
SMITH, Jas.	18	M	Weaver	05Ma05Ek
SAULTER, Sarah	21	F	Weaver	05Ma05Ek
RODGER, Hugh	21	M	Weaver	05Ma05Ek
BELL, Wm.S.	28	M	Weaver	05Ma05Ek
Eliza-S.	26	F	Weaver	05Ma05Ek
U	.00	U	Infant	05Ma05Ek
PEEL, Margt.	14	F	Weaver	05Ma05Ek
IRELAND, Jane	17	F	Weaver	05Ma05Ek
VINT, Wm.	23	M	Weaver	05Ma05Ek
CAMPBELL, Robt.	32	M	Weaver	05Ma05Ek
Elizabeth	28	F	Weaver	05Ma05Ek
Mary	8	F	Child	05Ma05Ek
Alex	4	M	Child	05Ma05Ek
Jas.	.00	M	Infant	05Ma05Ek
BOYD, Sarah	18	F	Weaver	05Ma05Ek
SHAW, Henry	18	M	Weaver	05Ma05Ek
CAMPBELL, Wm.Jno.	20	M	Weaver	05Ma05Ek
Geo.Jas.	25	M	Weaver	05Ma05Ek
CRANSTON, Saml.	25	M	Weaver	05Ma05Ek
NICHOLSON, Jas.	28	M	Weaver	05Ma05Ek
BOTHWELL, Jno.	21	M	Weaver	05Ma05Ek

BLANCHARD 05 MAY 1849

From Liverpool

NAMES OF PASSENGERS	AGE	SEX	OCCUPATIONS	DATE PORT SHIP
CODDINGTON, Morris	30	M	Merchant	05Ma02Ew
Hannah	20	F	None	05Ma02Ew
WHITE, James	26	M	Attorney	05Ma02Ew
HANNAY, William	20	M	Clerk	05Ma02Ew
MONOGHAN, Edward	24	M	Shepherd	05Ma02Ew
HORIGAN, Michael	30	M	Polisher	05Ma02Ew
SMITH, Thomas	18	M	Miller	05Ma02Ew
COOK, Thomas	20	M	Laborer	05Ma02Ew
RILEY, John	28	M	Polisher	05Ma02Ew
Jane	18	F	Polisher	05Ma02Ew
Bridget	17	F	Servant	05Ma02Ew
Margaret	16	F	Servant	05Ma02Ew
MCGEE, Mary	16	F	Servant	05Ma02Ew
ATEWELL, Mary	17	F	Servant	05Ma02Ew
CASEY, John	14	M	Laborer	05Ma02Ew
RILEY, Pat	25	M	Shoemaker	05Ma02Ew
MCDONNELL, William	26	M	Servant	05Ma02Ew
James	32	M	Laborer	05Ma02Ew
Catherine	27	F	Servant	05Ma02Ew
Ann	26	F	Servant	05Ma02Ew
Eliza	20	F	Dressmaker	05Ma02Ew
Francis	.00	M	Infant	05Ma02Ew
Robert	.00	M	Infant	05Ma02Ew
CARROL, Ann	20	F	Servant	05Ma02Ew
TAYLOR, James	40	M	Laborer	05Ma02Ew
FITZGERALD, William	27	M	Laborer	05Ma02Ew
MURRY, James	28	M	Farmer	05Ma02Ew
Ellen	28	F	Farmer	05Ma02Ew
James	35	M	Farmer	05Ma02Ew
Jeremiah	22	M	Farmer	05Ma02Ew
Catherine	.00	F	Infant	05Ma02Ew
BUCK, Michael	31	M	Farmer	05Ma02Ew
MCGRANE, Andrew	19	M	Laborer	05Ma02Ew
DONNAUGH, Anna	20	F	Lady'S Maid	05Ma02Ew
MORAN, Margaret	30	F	Lady'S Maid	05Ma02Ew
JENGHTON, Mariah	20	F	Lady'S Maid	05Ma02Ew
STEVENSON, Terrace	16	M	Plumber	05Ma02Ew
ELLIOTT, Thomas	27	M	Farmer	05Ma02Ew
MORRIS, Will	35	M	Laborer	05Ma02Ew
COOLAN, Rebecca	20	F	Servant	05Ma02Ew

NAMES OF PASSENGERS	AGE	SEX	OCCUPATIONS	DATE PORT SHIP
BUTLER, Ellen	24	F	Servant	05Ma02Ew
Laurence	25	M	Laborer	05Ma02Ew
HANTON, Richard	30	M	Carpenter	05Ma02Ew
QUALEY, Thomas	22	M	Laborer	05Ma02Ew
MOUN, John	33	M	Carpenter	05Ma02Ew
Mary	23	F	None	05Ma02Ew
Johanna	18	F	Dressmaker	05Ma02Ew
John	.00	M	Infant	05Ma02Ew
FLAHERTY, Thady	30	M	Farmer	05Ma02Ew
Sarah	30	F	Farmer	05Ma02Ew
MCELVOE, Mary	25	F	None	05Ma02Ew
BRIDE, Robert	18	M	Laborer	05Ma02Ew
MCCABE, Pat	20	M	Laborer	05Ma02Ew
NATERY, John	30	M	Laborer	05Ma02Ew
MALERHY, John	24	M	Laborer	05Ma02Ew
FRAZER, Robert	24	M	Bootmaker	05Ma02Ew
Ann	24	F	None	05Ma02Ew
Ann	.00	F	Infant	05Ma02Ew
KAVANAGH, Michael	25	M	Clerk	05Ma02Ew
Charlotte	25	F	None	05Ma02Ew
Edward	4	M	Child	05Ma02Ew
Pat	2	M	Child	05Ma02Ew
John	.00	M	Infant	05Ma02Ew
CARTER, James	33	M	Blacksmith	05Ma02Ew
Kitty	26	F	None	05Ma02Ew
MCINTRIE, Thomas	25	M	Laborer	05Ma02Ew
KELLY, Elizabeth	26	F	Dressmaker	05Ma02Ew
Edward	15	M	Servant	05Ma02Ew
Mary	10	F	Servant	05Ma02Ew
William	46	M	Farmer	05Ma02Ew
James	35	M	Farmer	05Ma02Ew
HUGHES, John	25	M	Farmer	05Ma02Ew
KEAN, Adam	43	M	Laborer	05Ma02Ew
MAHONY, Michael	28	M	Laborer	05Ma02Ew
LEARY, Arthur	55	M	Farmer	05Ma02Ew
Mary	25	F	None	05Ma02Ew
Bridget	25	F	None	05Ma02Ew
Arther	5	M	Child	05Ma02Ew
John	2	M	Child	05Ma02Ew
Dennis	33	M	Farmer	05Ma02Ew
MCCORMACK, John	35	M	Farmer	05Ma02Ew
DONERUAN, Pat	25	M	Laborer	05Ma02Ew
BARNEY, Honor	40	F	Servant	05Ma02Ew
CONNER, Daniel	15	M	Laborer	05Ma02Ew
Thomas	33	M	Laborer	05Ma02Ew
CALLISLEAN, Julia	16	F	Servant	05Ma02Ew
CONNER, William	3	M	Child	05Ma02Ew
HERK, Charles	50	M	Carpenter	05Ma02Ew
Charles	8	M	Child	05Ma02Ew
FOLEY, Dennis	25	M	Blacksmith	05Ma02Ew
BARNET, Ellen	30	F	Servant	05Ma02Ew
LONERGAN, Will	25	M	Laborer	05Ma02Ew
COFFEE, Cath.	25	F	Servant	05Ma02Ew
HEATEN, Betsey	25	F	Servant	05Ma02Ew
PARCELL, Julia	23	F	Servant	05Ma02Ew
MCDONNELL, John	55	M	Farmer	05Ma02Ew
Edward	13	M	Farmer	05Ma02Ew
Thomas	11	M	Farmer	05Ma02Ew
Cath.	12	F	Farmer	05Ma02Ew
ENGLISH, Nancy	28	F	Servant	05Ma02Ew
BARNETT, Richard	32	M	Laborer	05Ma02Ew
WHITE, Pat	30	M	Laborer	05Ma02Ew
Ann	30	F	Laborer	05Ma02Ew
LYONS, Mary	40	F	Dressmaker	05Ma02Ew
KAFFE, John	20	M	Laborer	05Ma02Ew
RALPH, Thomas	45	M	Farmer	05Ma02Ew
John	22	M	Farmer	05Ma02Ew
Thom	14	M	Farmer	05Ma02Ew
CARTORE, James	24	M	Farmer	05Ma02Ew
RALPH, Margaret	17	F	Farmer	05Ma02Ew
DAVIS, C.	21	F	Servant	05Ma02Ew
LYONS, Michael	20	M	Laborer	05Ma02Ew
CAVANAGH, Catherine	24	F	Servant	05Ma02Ew
LODGE, Honor	37	F	Fefndr	05Ma02Ew
CARY, Tom	28	M	Laborer	05Ma02Ew
CARY, Katy	32	F	None	05Ma02Ew
WALSH, Mary	12	F	None	05Ma02Ew
BRIGHEN, James	22	M	Servant	05Ma02Ew
GALLASPIE, Susan	28	F	Servant	05Ma02Ew
FITZPATRICK, Catherine	17	F	Servant	05Ma02Ew
BASLAND, And	30	M	Laborer	05Ma02Ew
CASSID, Edward	18	M	Shoemaker	05Ma02Ew
MCLEAN, Mary	18	F	Servant	05Ma02Ew
STACK, Honora	33	F	Servant	05Ma02Ew
LARGAN, Bride	24	F	Servant	05Ma02Ew
Mary	2	F	Child	05Ma02Ew
MCDONIGLE, Bessy	17	F	Servant	05Ma02Ew
MCGOVRE, Michael	57	M	Servant	05Ma02Ew
Died-At-Sea				
FORREST, Cath.	19	F	Servant	05Ma02Ew
Mary	17	F	Servant	05Ma02Ew
FITZSIMMONS, Ann	20	F	Servant	05Ma02Ew
MCDONNELL, Brid	19	F	Servant	05Ma02Ew
Cath	22	F	Servant	05Ma02Ew
GALLAGHER, Elizabeth	4	F	Child	05Ma02Ew
RILEY, James	16	M	Laborer	05Ma02Ew
KENEY, Mary	16	F	Servant	05Ma02Ew
HAGGART, Margaret	25	F	Servant	05Ma02Ew
DIVINS, Mary	4	F	Servant	05Ma02Ew
BRADY, Michael	28	M	Carter	05Ma02Ew
TUITT, Philip	50	M	Tailor	05Ma02Ew
Rose	50	F	Tailor	05Ma02Ew
Ann	11	F	None	05Ma02Ew
Rose	9	F	Child	05Ma02Ew
MORAN, Mary	30	F	Servant	05Ma02Ew
GORMAN, Mary-A.	10	F	Servant	05Ma02Ew
RIELL, Ellen	40	F	Servant	05Ma02Ew
Mary	10	F	Servant	05Ma02Ew
Bernard	8	M	Child	05Ma02Ew
Hugh	6	M	Child	05Ma02Ew
Ter.	3	U	Child	05Ma02Ew
Eliza	26	F	Servant	05Ma02Ew
COOLY, Bridget	14	F	Servant	05Ma02Ew
DWIRE, Mary	30	F	Servant	05Ma02Ew
MUCHALAND, Rose	20	F	Servant	05Ma02Ew
DENNEST, A.	40	M	Laborer	05Ma02Ew
CARY, Margaret	29	F	Servant	05Ma02Ew
NEAL, Margaret	18	F	Servant	05Ma02Ew

WENHAM 05 MAY 1849

From London

NAMES OF PASSENGERS	AGE	SEX	OCCUPATIONS	DATE PORT SHIP
WAKEFORD, Henry	20	M	Engineer	05Ma13Ft
Margeret	21	F	Unknown	05Ma13Ft
EAGLES, Samuel	25	M	Carpenter	05Ma13Ft
Jane	24	F	Unknown	05Ma13Ft
HOLSTON, William	40	M	Farmer	05Ma13Ft
Elizabeth	42	F	Unknown	05Ma13Ft
WELLS, John	20	M	Farmer	05Ma13Ft
HOLSTON, Fanny	18	F	Unknown	05Ma13Ft
Charlotte	15	F	Unknown	05Ma13Ft
Mary-Ann	13	F	Unknown	05Ma13Ft
William	9	M	Child	05Ma13Ft
GOER, James	32	M	Farmer	05Ma13Ft
Sarah	30	F	Unknown	05Ma13Ft
James	7	M	Child	05Ma13Ft
Mary-Ann	2	F	Child	05Ma13Ft
POTTER, Thomas	40	M	Farmer	05Ma13Ft
ELSON, William	50	M	Shoemaker	05Ma13Ft
John	12	M	Unknown	05Ma13Ft
NORTH, Stephen	19	M	Carver	05Ma13Ft
COOKE, James	33	M	Editor	05Ma13Ft
Amelia	30	F	Unknown	05Ma13Ft

NAMES OF PASSENGERS	AGE	SEX	OCCUPATIONS	DATE PORT SHIP
COOKE, Percy	2	M	Child	05Ma13Ft
BURLING, George	35	M	Shoemaker	05Ma13Ft
Edward	25	M	Shoemaker	05Ma13Ft
GREEN, William	33	M	Painter	05Ma13Ft
WELLS, John	25	M	Carpenter	05Ma13Ft
BELLINGHAM, Charles-Th	27	M	Farmer	05Ma13Ft
Martha	26	F	Unknown	05Ma13Ft
LONG, Henry	30	M	Farmer	05Ma13Ft
Jane	38	F	Unknown	05Ma13Ft
BELLINGHAM, Charles	1	M	Child	05Ma13Ft
BUSHELL, Thomas	26	M	Printer	05Ma13Ft
Sarah-Ann	26	F	Unknown	05Ma13Ft
BARBER, Thomas	28	M	Clerk	05Ma13Ft
PARKHOUSE, William	20	M	Carpenter	05Ma13Ft
SMITH, Charles	21	M	Carpenter	05Ma13Ft
BLACKBOURNE, John	26	M	Farmer	05Ma13Ft
DAVIS, John	31	M	Blacksmith	05Ma13Ft
MILEN, John	20	M	Brick Maker	05Ma13Ft
Robert	18	M	Brick Maker	05Ma13Ft
TURNER, John	20	M	Pawn Broker	05Ma13Ft
Elizabeth	18	F	Unknown	05Ma13Ft
HATCHER, George	34	M	Baker	05Ma13Ft
Meda	35	F	Unknown	05Ma13Ft
George	.05	M	Infant	05Ma13Ft
LAZARUS, Lewis	26	M	Engraver	05Ma13Ft
MARRIOTT, James	47	M	Laborer	05Ma13Ft
Rosamond	30	F	Unknown	05Ma13Ft
WASS, Sarah	36	F	Unknown	05Ma13Ft
Thomas	11	M	Unknown	05Ma13Ft
MOORE, Susanah	4	F	Child	05Ma13Ft
GRANDEN, Johana	23	F	Unknown	05Ma13Ft
SAUNDERS, George	40	M	Farmer	05Ma13Ft
Ann	46	F	Unknown	05Ma13Ft
WILLIAMS, John	46	M	Stationer	05Ma13Ft
Mary	45	F	Unknown	05Ma13Ft
Frederick	18	M	Unknown	05Ma13Ft
Helen	11	F	Unknown	05Ma13Ft
Richard	7	M	Child	05Ma13Ft
Louis	4	M	Child	05Ma13Ft
Edwin	.11	M	Infant	05Ma13Ft
TRESS, Charles	46	M	Storekeeper	05Ma13Ft
Charles	12	M	Unknown	05Ma13Ft
WALKER, Benjamin	33	M	Farmer	05Ma13Ft
Martha	31	F	Unknown	05Ma13Ft
Mary	7	F	Child	05Ma13Ft
WOOD, James	24	M	Blacksmith	05Ma13Ft
MURRAY, James	20	M	Stationer	05Ma13Ft
REGAN, Daniel	31	M	Laborer	05Ma13Ft
COGAN, Charles	22	M	Tailor	05Ma13Ft
GARY, Thomas	28	M	Laborer	05Ma13Ft
Bridget	28	F	Unknown	05Ma13Ft
Ellen	2	F	Child	05Ma13Ft
Mary	.08	F	Infant	05Ma13Ft
KNIGHT, John	34	M	Shoemaker	05Ma13Ft
Sarah	35	F	Unknown	05Ma13Ft
William	9	M	Child	05Ma13Ft
Emily	7	F	Child	05Ma13Ft
Henry	3	M	Child	05Ma13Ft
William	23	M	Wheelwright	05Ma13Ft
Thomas	.10	M	Infant	05Ma13Ft
GUNN, Thomas-B.	23	M	Artist	05Ma13Ft
BOLTON, George	23	M	Farmer	05Ma13Ft
GUNN, Richard	23	M	Farmer	05Ma13Ft
MANNING, Louis	22	M	Clerk	05Ma13Ft
Francis	25	M	Clerk	05Ma13Ft
SNEESBY, Robert	37	M	Laborer	05Ma13Ft
Elizabeth	35	F	Unknown	05Ma13Ft
Henry	6	M	Child	05Ma13Ft
Elizabeth	4	F	Child	05Ma13Ft
Henry	42	M	Laborer	05Ma13Ft
Susanah	29	F	Unknown	05Ma13Ft
Elizabeth	9	F	Child	05Ma13Ft
Henry	7	M	Child	05Ma13Ft
HALEY, Mary	30	F	Unknown	05Ma13Ft
ARTHUR, Justin	52	M	Artist	05Ma13Ft
ARTHUR, Margeret	44	F	Unknown	05Ma13Ft
Justinian	22	M	Pntr-Gzr	05Ma13Ft
John	13	M	Unknown	05Ma13Ft
Jane	12	F	Unknown	05Ma13Ft
Margeret	10	F	Unknown	05Ma13Ft
Thomas	8	M	Child	05Ma13Ft
George	5	M	Child	05Ma13Ft
PAGE, Edward	27	M	Engineer	05Ma13Ft
Sarah	23	F	Unknown	05Ma13Ft
Harriet	.03	F	Infant	05Ma13Ft
COWLEY, James	25	M	Farmer	05Ma13Ft
GRAY, William	26	M	Painter	05Ma13Ft
Samuel	27	M	Pawn Broker	05Ma13Ft
MORRIS, John	45	M	Painter	05Ma13Ft
Sarah	40	F	Unknown	05Ma13Ft
Robert	21	M	Painter	05Ma13Ft
Sarah	20	F	Unknown	05Ma13Ft
Magnus	17	M	Unknown	05Ma13Ft
Alice	8	F	Child	05Ma13Ft
Margeret	5	F	Child	05Ma13Ft
HIGGINS, Robert	45	M	Bookbinder	05Ma13Ft
MOORE, James	17	M	Weaver	05Ma13Ft
GORDON, John	30	M	Watchmaker	05Ma13Ft
Martha	22	F	Unknown	05Ma13Ft
Martha	2	F	Child	05Ma13Ft
William	.10	M	Infant	05Ma13Ft
WHITFIELD, William	40	M	Farmer	05Ma13Ft
WICKENS, Stephen	50	M	Farmer	05Ma13Ft
Charlotte	50	F	Unknown	05Ma13Ft
Charlotte	20	F	Unknown	05Ma13Ft
Elizabeth	18	F	Unknown	05Ma13Ft
Luke	12	M	Unknown	05Ma13Ft
Stephen	8	M	Child	05Ma13Ft
RAMPTON, John	20	M	Farmer	05Ma13Ft
NOYCE, Eliza	22	F	Unknown	05Ma13Ft
HEADLAND, Daniel	39	M	Farmer	05Ma13Ft
Francis	32	U	Unknown	05Ma13Ft
Sarah	8	F	Child	05Ma13Ft
Thomas	4	M	Child	05Ma13Ft
Fanny	.11	F	Infant	05Ma13Ft
GOLDING, John	47	M	Farmer	05Ma13Ft
William	9	M	Child	05Ma13Ft
Charles	7	M	Child	05Ma13Ft
CROFT, William	30	M	Carpenter	05Ma13Ft
CORNES, James	32	M	Carpenter	05Ma13Ft
Mary-Ann	31	M	Carpenter	05Ma13Ft
Edward	8	M	Child	05Ma13Ft
Charles	6	M	Child	05Ma13Ft
James	4	M	Child	05Ma13Ft
John	2	M	Child	05Ma13Ft
Mary-Ann	.09	F	Infant	05Ma13Ft
WAGHORN, Thomas	30	M	Butcher	05Ma13Ft
Mary	34	F	Unknown	05Ma13Ft
Jane	10	F	Unknown	05Ma13Ft
William	9	M	Child	05Ma13Ft
Thomas	6	M	Child	05Ma13Ft
Mary	3	F	Child	05Ma13Ft
BRUNGER, John	22	M	Laborer	05Ma13Ft
James	32	M	Laborer	05Ma13Ft
KEMP, Stephen	30	M	Laborer	05Ma13Ft
ATTAWAY, Charles	25	M	Laborer	05Ma13Ft
Mary-Ann	21	F	Unknown	05Ma13Ft
Charles	.00	M	Infant	05Ma13Ft
CLARK, Gilbert	20	M	Laborer	05Ma13Ft
Elizabeth	27	F	Unknown	05Ma13Ft
WOOD, Elizabeth	22	F	Unknown	05Ma13Ft
CLARK, Thomas	26	M	Laborer	05Ma13Ft
LEE, Richard	50	M	Cbtmkr	05Ma13Ft
HICKMOTT, Silas	28	M	Farmer	05Ma13Ft
BRIDGELAND, Daniel	22	M	Farmer	05Ma13Ft
HART, Elizabeth	35	F	Unknown	05Ma13Ft
COPPINGER, William-S.	25	M	Hairdresser	05Ma13Ft
PURSER, James	47	M	Lrdrs	05Ma13Ft
COYNE, William	38	M	Laborer	05Ma13Ft
Margeret	36	F	Unknown	05Ma13Ft

NAMES OF PASSENGERS	AGE	SEX	OCCUPATIONS	DATE PORT SHIP
LEWIS, Sarah	40	F	Unknown	05Ma13Ft
DADSON, James	22	M	Farmer	05Ma13Ft
George	22	M	Farmer	05Ma13Ft
Alfred	25	M	Farmer	05Ma13Ft
Sarah	24	F	Unknown	05Ma13Ft
CARDEN, Eliza	28	F	Unknown	05Ma13Ft
CRANE, William	45	M	Farmer	05Ma13Ft
John	19	M	Farmer	05Ma13Ft
HUGHES, Charles	23	M	Shoemaker	05Ma13Ft
David	56	M	Shoemaker	05Ma13Ft
DOWLING, James	34	M	Mason	05Ma13Ft
NORTH, Robert	30	M	Locksmith	05Ma13Ft
DAWSON, Elizabeth	20	F	Unknown	05Ma13Ft
SALMON, Elizabeth	30	F	Unknown	05Ma13Ft
William	11	M	Unknown	05Ma13Ft
George	8	M	Child	05Ma13Ft

HAYTI 05 MAY 1849

From Port-Au-Prince

NAMES OF PASSENGERS	AGE	SEX	OCCUPATIONS	DATE PORT SHIP
ORD, Edward	55	M	Merchant	05Ma44Fj
ARK, Wm.	40	M	Merchant	05Ma44Fj

HEATHER-BELL 05 MAY 1849

From Tralee

NAMES OF PASSENGERS	AGE	SEX	OCCUPATIONS	DATE PORT SHIP
ONNOR, James	33	M	Farmer	05Ma32Fa
Catherine	22	F	Wife	05Ma32Fa
Jeremiah	.10	M	Infant	05Ma32Fa
ROONEY, Francis	23	M	Laborer	05Ma32Fa
ONNOR, Honorah	20	F	Spinster	05Ma32Fa
AHER, John	50	M	Farmer	05Ma32Fa
Catherine (W)	50	F	Unknown	05Ma32Fa
Michael	19	M	Shoemaker	05Ma32Fa
Ellen	18	F	Spinster	05Ma32Fa
ONNANE, David	45	M	Laborer	05Ma32Fa
OCHRAN, John	50	M	Laborer	05Ma32Fa
Died-At-Sea				
REARY, James	40	M	Laborer	05Ma32Fa
REANING, Joseph	14	M	Laborer	05Ma32Fa
Ellen	13	F	Unknown	05Ma32Fa
OVETT, John	59	M	Laborer	05Ma32Fa
Catherine	20	F	Spinster	05Ma32Fa
EALY, Joseph	27	M	Laborer	05Ma32Fa
HEEHY, Pat	23	M	Tailor	05Ma32Fa
Mary	25	F	Matron	05Ma32Fa
AHER, Thomas	45	M	Carpenter	05Ma32Fa
EAL, Richard	40	M	Laborer	05Ma32Fa
ITZGERALD, Maurice	22	M	Laborer	05Ma32Fa
RICK, John	22	M	Laborer	05Ma32Fa
AHILL, John	40	M	Laborer	05Ma32Fa
Johannah (W)	35	F	Unknown	05Ma32Fa
Mary	13	F	Unknown	05Ma32Fa
Margaret	11	F	Unknown	05Ma32Fa
Catherine	7	F	Child	05Ma32Fa
Johannah	.11	F	Infant	05Ma32Fa
HEEHY, Thomas	50	M	Laborer	05Ma32Fa
NNOR, Michael	26	M	Laborer	05Ma32Fa
ALY, Elizabeth	22	F	Matron	05Ma32Fa
GHNANE, Johannah	23	F	Spinster	05Ma32Fa
HEEHAN, Timothy	28	M	Laborer	05Ma32Fa
SHEEHAN, John	22	M	Laborer	05Ma32Fa
Mary (W)	21	F	Unknown	05Ma32Fa
CUNANE, Denis	29	M	Laborer	05Ma32Fa
GALLAGHAN, Darby	26	M	Laborer	05Ma32Fa
SHEEHY, John	30	M	Laborer	05Ma32Fa
Mary (W)	30	F	Unknown	05Ma32Fa
ABBOTT, Ann	25	F	Spinster	05Ma32Fa
QUIRK, Patt	40	M	Laborer	05Ma32Fa
HOWARD, Catherine	60	F	Matron	05Ma32Fa
QUIRK, John	12	M	Unknown	05Ma32Fa
Mary	10	F	Unknown	05Ma32Fa
Patrick	3	M	Child	05Ma32Fa
Catherine	.09	F	Infant	05Ma32Fa
CORKERY, Patrick	40	M	Laborer	05Ma32Fa
Ellen (W)	32	F	Unknown	05Ma32Fa
John	.11	M	Infant	05Ma32Fa
Mary	3	F	Child	05Ma32Fa
SUGRA, John	21	M	Laborer	05Ma32Fa
ODONNELL, Ellen	19	F	Spinster	05Ma32Fa
CONNORS, John	40	M	Laborer	05Ma32Fa
Johannah	24	F	Spinster	05Ma32Fa
DONOGHUE, Matthew	20	M	Laborer	05Ma32Fa
CRANE, Eliza	00	F	Spinster	05Ma32Fa
MULOIHILL, Mary	20	F	Spinster	05Ma32Fa
MOYNIHAN, Timothy	23	M	Laborer	05Ma32Fa
Ellen	20	F	Spinster	05Ma32Fa
HEALY, Michael	26	M	Laborer	05Ma32Fa
THORNTON, Eliza	17	F	Spinster	05Ma32Fa
SHEAHAN, Mary	22	F	Spinster	05Ma32Fa
FINN, James	26	M	Laborer	05Ma32Fa
CONNORS, Timothy	21	M	Laborer	05Ma32Fa
Johannah	.10	F	Infant	05Ma32Fa
FORAN, Honora	25	F	Matron	05Ma32Fa
DRISCOLL, James	21	M	Laborer	05Ma32Fa
NELLIGAN, Mary	25	F	Matron	05Ma32Fa
John	.07	M	Infant	05Ma32Fa
GRIFFITH, Owen	19	M	Laborer	05Ma32Fa
OFLAGHERTY, Ellen	20	F	Spinster	05Ma32Fa
PRENDISALL, Garret	28	M	Laborer	05Ma32Fa
HORN, Bridget	22	F	Spinster	05Ma32Fa
OBRIEN, Timothy	22	M	Laborer	05Ma32Fa
CONNOR, Mary	19	F	Spinster	05Ma32Fa
HIXON, Christopher	27	M	Laborer	05Ma32Fa
DEADY, Johannah	40	F	Matron	05Ma32Fa
Eugene	9	M	Child	05Ma32Fa
Honora	3	F	Child	05Ma32Fa
Michael	.06	M	Infant	05Ma32Fa
CONNOR, Terence	25	M	Laborer	05Ma32Fa
CRINAN, Ellen	13	F	Unknown	05Ma32Fa
MURPHY, David	24	M	Laborer	05Ma32Fa
SULLIVAN, Mary	14	F	Unknown	05Ma32Fa
EARLY, Andrew	19	M	Laborer	05Ma32Fa
FITZGERALD, Edmond	36	M	Laborer	05Ma32Fa
SCAFF, Joseph	36	M	Painter	05Ma32Fa
Richard	32	M	Glover	05Ma32Fa
CRINAN, David	17	M	Painter	05Ma32Fa
SULLIVAN, Mary	25	F	Spinster	05Ma32Fa
PARKER, Robert	23	M	Laborer	05Ma32Fa
MCCLURE, Anthony	24	M	Laborer	05Ma32Fa
BOURKE, Patt	32	M	Laborer	05Ma32Fa
CONNOR, Mary	16	F	Spinster	05Ma32Fa
PEMBROKE, Christopher	35	M	Farmer	05Ma32Fa
Margaret (W)	35	F	Unknown	05Ma32Fa
Mary	5	F	Child	05Ma32Fa
Johannah	.00	F	Infant	05Ma32Fa
CONNELL, Patt	40	M	Laborer	05Ma32Fa
Mary (W)	40	F	Unknown	05Ma32Fa
CLANCY, John	34	M	Laborer	05Ma32Fa
FERRITER, Mary	25	F	Matron	05Ma32Fa
Catharine	12	F	Unknown	05Ma32Fa
DRISCOLL, Ellen	20	F	Spinster	05Ma32Fa
MURPHY, Thomas	18	M	Tailor	05Ma32Fa
OREILLY, Mary	20	F	Spinster	05Ma32Fa
MAHER, Catherine	3	F	Child	05Ma32Fa
POMANE, Mary	50	F	Matron	05Ma32Fa

NAMES OF PASSENGERS		AGE	SEX	OCCUPATIONS	DATE PORT SHIP
BRONAHAN, Mary		.11	F	Infant	05Ma32Fa
LINALIE, Thomas		18	M	Laborer	05Ma32Fa
CONNET, John		15	M	Laborer	05Ma32Fa
Patrick		14	M	Laborer	05Ma32Fa
GIBSON, Peter		48	M	Farmer	05Ma32Fa
Mary	(W)	36	F	Unknown	05Ma32Fa
Mary		15	F	Unknown	05Ma32Fa
John		13	M	Unknown	05Ma32Fa
Mary		11	F	Unknown	05Ma32Fa
Thomas		5	M	Child	05Ma32Fa
James		3	M	Child	05Ma32Fa
LINANE, Mary		14	F	Servant	05Ma32Fa
WALSH, Michael		20	M	Gentleman	05Ma32Fa

ARAMENTA 03* MAY 1849

From Belfast

NAMES OF PASSENGERS		AGE	SEX	OCCUPATIONS	DATE PORT SHIP
MURPHY, James		25	M	Laborer	03Ma05Fp
Sarah	(W)	22	F	Unknown	03Ma05Fp
DOWNING, Wm.		21	M	Laborer	03Ma05Fp
Barbara		15	F	Unknown	03Ma05Fp
Mary		13	F	Unknown	03Ma05Fp
Edward		10	M	Unknown	03Ma05Fp
DEGAN, Sarah		25	F	Spinster	03Ma05Fp
ROSS, Hugh		21	M	Laborer	03Ma05Fp
MOLES, R.M.		19	M	Laborer	03Ma05Fp
CONNELL, Alecia		30	F	Spinster	03Ma05Fp
REA, Edw.		27	M	Farmer	03Ma05Fp
Mary-Ann	(W)	27	F	Unknown	03Ma05Fp
Wm.		7	M	Child	03Ma05Fp
Ed.		5	M	Child	03Ma05Fp
Robt.		3	M	Child	03Ma05Fp
Ann-Jane		1	F	Child	03Ma05Fp
WELSHMAN, Alex.		21	M	Laborer	03Ma05Fp
SMITH, Mary-Ann		21	F	Spinster	03Ma05Fp
LONG, Wm.		45	M	Unknown	03Ma05Fp
Ann		40	F	Wife	03Ma05Fp
Ann-Jane		18	F	Spinster	03Ma05Fp
Elisa		15	F	Spinster	03Ma05Fp
Sarah		10	F	Unknown	03Ma05Fp
Mary		7	F	Child	03Ma05Fp
Isabella		5	F	Child	03Ma05Fp
Margt.		2	F	Child	03Ma05Fp
John		24	M	Laborer	03Ma05Fp
SMITH, John		16	M	Laborer	03Ma05Fp
Isabella		18	F	Spinster	03Ma05Fp
MULLER, Patk.		60	M	Farmer	03Ma05Fp
Hhenry		16	M	Laborer	03Ma05Fp
Mary		15	F	Unknown	03Ma05Fp
MAGEE, Saml.		24	M	Unknown	03Ma05Fp
BASSETT, Robt.		29	M	Laborer	03Ma05Fp
Ann	(W)	22	F	Unknown	03Ma05Fp
KING, Hugh		21	M	Laborer	03Ma05Fp
SMITH, James		25	M	Laborer	03Ma05Fp
JOHNSTON, Joseph		25	M	Laborer	03Ma05Fp
Letitia	(W)	25	F	Unknown	03Ma05Fp
WALLACE, Wm.		20	M	Laborer	03Ma05Fp
Jane		18	F	Spinster	03Ma05Fp
Susanna		16	F	Spinster	03Ma05Fp
ARMSTRONG, Thomas		35	M	Farmer	03Ma05Fp
Gabriel		34	M	Farmer	03Ma05Fp
Ann-Eliza		30	F	Spinster	03Ma05Fp
Wm.		14	M	Laborer	03Ma05Fp
Wm. Died-At-Sea		00	M	Unknown	03Ma05Fp
ROURKE, James		24	M	Farmer	03Ma05Fp
OLIVE, Joseph		23	M	Laborer	03Ma05Fp
ELLIOTT, Robt.		26	M	Laborer	03Ma05Fp
ELLIOTT, James		24	M	Laborer	03Ma05Fp
EMMERSON, Thomas		40	M	Laborer	03Ma05Fp
CAMPBELL, Cathe.		18	F	Spinster	03Ma05Fp
MCAVOY, John		43	M	Laborer	03Ma05Fp
Margt.	(W)	23	F	Unknown	03Ma05Fp
COATE, Thomas		30	M	Laborer	03Ma05Fp
DOWNES, Edward		22	M	Laborer	03Ma05Fp
BRIGGS, John		37	M	Laborer	03Ma05Fp
DUNLOP, Bernard		7	M	Child	03Ma05Fp
CONNORSEY, Mary		30	F	Spinster	03Ma05Fp
GRAY, Thomas		18	M	Laborer	03Ma05Fp
BLANEY, Charles		24	M	Laborer	03Ma05Fp
RANAGHAN, James		21	M	Laborer	03Ma05Fp
MCQUADE, Patk.		30	M	Laborer	03Ma05Fp
Margt.	(W)	30	F	Unknown	03Ma05Fp
Henry		.06	M	Infant	03Ma05Fp
MCKNIGHT, Mary-Ann		21	F	Spinster	03Ma05Fp
PARKER, John		16	M	Laborer	03Ma05Fp
PUNTON, Margt.		8	F	Child	03Ma05Fp
CAMPBELL, James		40	M	Farmer	03Ma05Fp
Mary	(W)	40	F	Unknown	03Ma05Fp
Charles		18	M	Unknown	03Ma05Fp
James		13	M	Unknown	03Ma05Fp
Daniel		9	M	Child	03Ma05Fp
MCQUADE, James		45	M	Laborer	03Ma05Fp
Susana		25	F	Unknown	03Ma05Fp
Alice		35	F	Unknown	03Ma05Fp
Alice		1	F	Child	03Ma05Fp
MCBRIDE, James		28	M	Laborer	03Ma05Fp
MCKEMIE, Owen		25	M	Laborer	03Ma05Fp
Rose	(W)	18	F	Unknown	03Ma05Fp
MCAVICKE, Mary		24	F	Spinster	03Ma05Fp
ROANEY, Margt.		18	F	Spinster	03Ma05Fp
MCCRACKEN, James		11	M	Unknown	03Ma05Fp
Elisa		9	F	Child	03Ma05Fp
Margt.		7	F	Child	03Ma05Fp
Arabella		12	F	Unknown	03Ma05Fp
WHISKER, David		13	M	Unknown	03Ma05Fp
MONTGOMERY, Alexr.		37	M	Laborer	03Ma05Fp
Stephen		23	M	Laborer	03Ma05Fp
LOVE, David		22	M	Laborer	03Ma05Fp
BYRNES, James		20	M	Laborer	03Ma05Fp
MCCORMICK, Margt.		20	F	Spinster	03Ma05Fp
CROOKS, Jane		20	F	Spinster	03Ma05Fp
QUINN, Eliza		22	F	Spinster	03Ma05Fp
MCCULLOGH, Letitia		25	F	Spinster	03Ma05Fp
SANDERSON, Elizth.		36	F	Spinster	03Ma05Fp
John		13	M	Unknown	03Ma05Fp
Ann-Jane		11	F	Unknown	03Ma05Fp
DODDS, Archd.		55	M	Farmer	03Ma05Fp
Elizth.	(W)	48	F	Unknown	03Ma05Fp
Robt.		19	M	Laborer	03Ma05Fp
Attchinson		17	M	Laborer	03Ma05Fp
Josiah		15	M	Laborer	03Ma05Fp
George		13	M	Unknown	03Ma05F
Wm.		11	M	Unknown	03Ma05F
AMER, Nancy		9	F	Child	03Ma05F
Eliza		7	F	Child	03Ma05F
Sarah-Jane		5	F	Child	03Ma05F
WINDRUM, Wm.		23	M	Laborer	03Ma05F
Agnes	(W)	33	F	Unknown	03Ma05F
Mary-Jane		4	F	Child	03Ma05F
John		1	M	Child	03Ma05F
KENNEAR, Wm.		16	M	Laborer	03Ma05F
CRANE, Mary		29	F	Spinster	03Ma05F
KELLEY, Anne		60	F	Spinster	03Ma05F
QUINN, Mary		15	F	Spinster	03Ma05F
Matthew		35	M	Laborer	03Ma05F
KELLY, James		16	M	Laborer	03Ma05F
MCARDLE, Cathr.		21	F	Spinster	03Ma05F
Bess		20	F	Spinster	03Ma05F
Patk.		23	M	Laborer	03Ma05F
DALEY, Thomas		40	M	Laborer	03Ma05F
Aley	(W)	30	F	Unknown	03Ma05F
Aley		.02	F	Infant	03Ma05F

*should be 05 May

NAMES OF PASSENGERS		AGE	SEX	OCCUPATIONS	DATE PORT SHIP
PRITCHARD, Elisa		35	F	Spinster	03Ma05Fp
Ed.		9	M	Child	03Ma05Fp
Wm.John		4	M	Child	03Ma05Fp
Margt.		.09	F	Infant	03Ma05Fp
ALLER, Moses		19	M	Laborer	03Ma05Fp
Alexr.		32	M	Laborer	03Ma05Fp
HASSAN, Margt.		38	F	Spinster	03Ma05Fp
Mary		18	F	Spinster	03Ma05Fp
Jane		16	F	Spinster	03Ma05Fp
Ellen		14	F	Spinster	03Ma05Fp
John		12	M	Unknown	03Ma05Fp
James		4	M	Child	03Ma05Fp
Margt.		2	F	Child	03Ma05Fp
CLOSE, John		52	M	Laborer	03Ma05Fp
Sally	(W)	50	F	Unknown	03Ma05Fp
BOOMER, Margt.		14	F	Unknown	03Ma05Fp
GRAHAM, Betty		9	F	Child	03Ma05Fp
WIGHTMAN, Wm.		22	M	Laborer	03Ma05Fp
MCCUNE, Wm.		22	M	Laborer	03Ma05Fp
Elisa		50	F	Wi	03Ma05Fp
Jane		25	F	Spinster	03Ma05Fp
Mary		26	F	Spinster	03Ma05Fp
Eliza		.09	F	Infant	03Ma05Fp
CARSONS, John		20	M	Laborer	03Ma05Fp
MUIR, Elizth.		30	F	Wife	03Ma05Fp
Eliza		4	F	Child	03Ma05Fp
Sarah		2	F	Child	03Ma05Fp
Wm.John		.10	M	Infant	03Ma05Fp
TAYLOR, John		26	M	Laborer	03Ma05Fp
Ann	(W)	22	F	Unknown	03Ma05Fp
Samuel		.06	M	Infant	03Ma05Fp
MOORE, Robert		54	M	Laborer	03Ma05Fp
Matilda	(W)	55	F	Unknown	03Ma05Fp
Thomas		22	M	Laborer	03Ma05Fp
Jane		19	F	Spinster	03Ma05Fp
Eliza		17	F	Spinster	03Ma05Fp
SLOAN, William		17	M	Laborer	03Ma05Fp
CANE, Andrew		21	M	Laborer	03Ma05Fp
HADDOCK, James		46	M	Laborer	03Ma05Fp
COOK, William		30	M	Laborer	03Ma05Fp
Jane		20	F	Spinster	03Ma05Fp
ROBINSON, Mary		30	F	Spinster	03Ma05Fp
RUSSELL, Thomas		36	M	Laborer	03Ma05Fp
Catharine	(W)	30	F	Unknown	03Ma05Fp
Nelson		25	M	Laborer	03Ma05Fp
WADE, Susanna		35	F	Spinster	03Ma05Fp
RUSSELL, John		1	M	Child	03Ma05Fp
MARLING, William		17	M	Laborer	03Ma05Fp
HUNTER, Sarah		20	F	Spinster	03Ma05Fp
JOHNSTON, Martha		40	F	Spinster	03Ma05Fp
Rober.		10	M	Unknown	03Ma05Fp
ILSTON, John		22	M	Laborer	03Ma05Fp
ESANY, Mary		20	F	Spinster	03Ma05Fp
MCCRACKEN, John		40	M	Farmer	03Ma05Fp
Jane	(W)	35	F	Unknown	03Ma05Fp
Samuel		18	M	Laborer	03Ma05Fp
Mary-Jane		16	F	Spinster	03Ma05Fp
William		13	M	Unknown	03Ma05Fp
RANE, Alexander		3	M	Child	03Ma05Fp
ACHNIMUL, Eline		20	F	Spinster	03Ma05Fp
Mary-Ann		17	F	Spinster	03Ma05Fp
Rosanna		13	F	Spinster	03Ma05Fp
John		15	M	Laborer	03Ma05Fp
ODGERS, Elizabeth		50	F	Wi	03Ma05Fp
Jane		26	F	Spinster	03Ma05Fp
Ann		20	F	Spinster	03Ma05Fp
JRPHY, Thomas		38	M	Farmer	03Ma05Fp
Mary-Ann	(W)	28	F	Unknown	03Ma05Fp
Died-At-Sea					
John		7	M	Child	03Ma05Fp
James		5	M	Child	03Ma05Fp
Andrew		3	M	Child	03Ma05Fp
INGAN, James		30	M	Laborer	03Ma05Fp
EDMOND, John		21	M	Laborer	03Ma05Fp
LSON, Samuel		24	M	Laborer	03Ma05Fp
GREGORY, Thos.		23	M	Laborer	03Ma05Fp
HUNTER, James		25	M	Laborer	03Ma05Fp
WILSON, William		18	M	Laborer	03Ma05Fp
GREGORY, Agnes		56	F	Wi	03Ma05Fp
Hannah		25	F	Spinster	03Ma05Fp
Robert		4	M	Child	03Ma05Fp
Samuel		2	M	Child	03Ma05Fp
JAMIESON, Eliza		18	F	Spinster	03Ma05Fp
CURLEY, Owen		21	M	Laborer	03Ma05Fp
GREEN, James		30	M	Laborer	03Ma05Fp
DONLEY, Patrick		30	M	Laborer	03Ma05Fp
MCGRIFFITH, William		20	M	Laborer	03Ma05Fp
DONNELLY, Mary		40	F	Spinster	03Ma05Fp
JUMMET, William		22	M	Laborer	03Ma05Fp
GARROW, James		21	M	Laborer	03Ma05Fp
DUNN, John		30	M	Farmer	03Ma05Fp
GLASS, Eliza		22	F	Spinster	03Ma05Fp
NAPIER, Mary-Jane		30	F	Wife	03Ma05Fp
U		00	M	Gentleman	03Ma05Fp
Matilda		26	F	Unknown	03Ma05Fp
John	(S)	19	M	Unknown	03Ma05Fp
MACKAY, John		18	M	Merchant	03Ma05Fp

INFANTA 05 MAY 1849

From Liverpool

NAMES OF PASSENGERS		AGE	SEX	OCCUPATIONS	DATE PORT SHIP
SHEATE, Ralph		29	M	Laborer	05Ma02Fu
HIBBERT, Jas.		30	M	Laborer	05Ma02Fu
Mary-Ann	(W)	32	F	Unknown	05Ma02Fu
SLATER, Jane		20	F	Spinster	05Ma02Fu
CONNOLLY, Elizabeth		25	F	Spinster	05Ma02Fu
MOONEY, Elizabeth		21	F	Spinster	05Ma02Fu
HALL, Henry		14	M	Laborer	05Ma02Fu
CONSTINE, John		26	M	Laborer	05Ma02Fu
MCEROY, Hugh		22	M	Laborer	05Ma02Fu
QUINN, Pat		15	M	Laborer	05Ma02Fu
Susan		15	F	Spinster	05Ma02Fu
Mary		20	F	Spinster	05Ma02Fu
ROONEY, Andw.		21	M	Laborer	05Ma02Fu
MCCABE, Rosann		22	F	Spinster	05Ma02Fu
PARSONS, James		21	M	Laborer	05Ma02Fu
FEE, Robert		29	M	Laborer	05Ma02Fu
MCGUINESS, Pat		29	M	Laborer	05Ma02Fu
Cath.	(W)	25	F	Unknown	05Ma02Fu
Mary		7	F	Child	05Ma02Fu
Margt.		5	F	Child	05Ma02Fu
Barnet		.06	M	Infant	05Ma02Fu
TOLSON, John		27	M	Farmer	05Ma02Fu
Harriet	(W)	27	F	Unknown	05Ma02Fu
Hannah		.08	F	Infant	05Ma02Fu
Martha		6	F	Child	05Ma02Fu
Henry		4	M	Child	05Ma02Fu
DONOHUE, Simon		26	M	Laborer	05Ma02Fu
Rose	(W)	24	F	Unknown	05Ma02Fu
COSGROVE, Mary-Ann		21	F	Spinster	05Ma02Fu
MCGUIRE, John		25	M	Laborer	05Ma02Fu
RUSSEL, Harry		28	M	Laborer	05Ma02Fu
MCGUIRE, Bernard		27	M	Laborer	05Ma02Fu
MORRIS, U		25	F	Wife	05Ma02Fu
QUINN, U		20	F	Spinster	05Ma02Fu
MORRIS, Ann		9	F	Child	05Ma02Fu
Obad.		8	M	Child	05Ma02Fu
Eliza		7	F	Child	05Ma02Fu
Grace		4	F	Child	05Ma02Fu
Louisa		.09	F	Infant	05Ma02Fu
PATRICK, Geo.		50	M	Farmer	05Ma02Fu
Sarah	(W)	50	F	Unknown	05Ma02Fu
Geo.		19	M	Farmer	05Ma02Fu

NAMES OF PASSENGERS		AGE	SEX	OCCUPATIONS	DATE PORT SHIP
PATRICK, Joseph		14	M	Farmer	05Ma02Fu
Fanny		13	F	Spinster	05Ma02Fu
Ann		10	F	Spinster	05Ma02Fu
WOODMESS, Mary		30	F	Wife	05Ma02Fu
Wm.		32	M	Farmer	05Ma02Fu
Elizabeth		6	F	Child	05Ma02Fu
Saml.		3	M	Child	05Ma02Fu
Jonathan		.10	M	Infant	05Ma02Fu
CASSICK, Edwd.		30	M	Laborer	05Ma02Fu
FOY, Barnes		30	M	Laborer	05Ma02Fu
DALEY, Barnes		40	M	Laborer	05Ma02Fu
Bridgt.	(W)	40	F	Unknown	05Ma02Fu
Patrick		2	M	Child	05Ma02Fu
Wm.		.06	M	Infant	05Ma02Fu
MORGAN, Geo.		28	M	Laborer	05Ma02Fu
JONES, James		30	M	Laborer	05Ma02Fu
Elizabeth	(W)	22	F	Unknown	05Ma02Fu
MORGAN, Mary		32	F	Wife	05Ma02Fu
Martha		.08	F	Infant	05Ma02Fu
Fell--, Christ.		30	M	Laborer	05Ma02Fu
BOLAN, Jas.		30	M	Laborer	05Ma02Fu
Patk.		20	M	Laborer	05Ma02Fu
GARRY, Michl.		25	M	Laborer	05Ma02Fu
DUGAN, Hugh		50	M	Laborer	05Ma02Fu
Matthew		50	M	Laborer	05Ma02Fu
Matt		19	M	Laborer	05Ma02Fu
Wm.		20	M	Laborer	05Ma02Fu
Cath.		30	F	Wife	05Ma02Fu
Eliza		14	F	Spinster	05Ma02Fu
FAHEY, John		24	M	Laborer	05Ma02Fu
FAHY, Thos.		17	M	Laborer	05Ma02Fu
MAHAR, James		20	M	Laborer	05Ma02Fu
WHITE, John		25	M	Laborer	05Ma02Fu
BURN, Michl.		20	M	Laborer	05Ma02Fu
CONNOR, James		27	M	Laborer	05Ma02Fu
John		30	M	Laborer	05Ma02Fu
Bridget		26	F	Wife	05Ma02Fu
Mary		.06	F	Infant	05Ma02Fu
LONDEGAN, John		22	M	Laborer	05Ma02Fu
POWER, Edwd.		27	M	Laborer	05Ma02Fu
KEOUGH, Wm.		28	M	Laborer	05Ma02Fu
Ann	(W)	26	F	Unknown	05Ma02Fu
Cath.		24	F	Spinster	05Ma02Fu
QUAIL, Wm.		25	M	Laborer	05Ma02Fu
CORBATE, Wm.H.		20	M	Laborer	05Ma02Fu
QUAIL, Thos.F.		17	M	Laborer	05Ma02Fu
COALMAN, Michl.		20	M	Laborer	05Ma02Fu
BRYAN, John		20	M	Laborer	05Ma02Fu
FLING, Thos.		27	M	Laborer	05Ma02Fu
LUSKE, James		50	M	Farmer	05Ma02Fu
Honora	(W)	49	F	Unknown	05Ma02Fu
Mary		30	F	Spinster	05Ma02Fu
Thomas		21	M	Farmer	05Ma02Fu
Biddy		19	F	Wife	05Ma02Fu
Judy		15	F	Spinster	05Ma02Fu
Michl.		11	M	Unknown	05Ma02Fu
Ann		9	F	Child	05Ma02Fu
GREEGAN, Edwd.		21	M	Laborer	05Ma02Fu
Michl.		19	M	Laborer	05Ma02Fu
Eliza		20	F	Wife	05Ma02Fu
Rose		24	F	Spinster	05Ma02Fu
HELAND, Ann		23	F	Spinster	05Ma02Fu
Arabella		21	F	Spinster	05Ma02Fu
WALSH, Wm.		40	M	Laborer	05Ma02Fu
TOLBERT, Thos.		31	M	Laborer	05Ma02Fu
Peggy	(W)	21	F	Unknown	05Ma02Fu
CARROLL, James		55	M	Laborer	05Ma02Fu
Anthy.		55	M	Laborer	05Ma02Fu
Michl.		30	M	Laborer	05Ma02Fu
Johanna	(W)	27	F	Unknown	05Ma02Fu
Betty		25	F	Spinster	05Ma02Fu
BROTHERS, Biddy		25	F	Spinster	05Ma02Fu
Pat		4	M	Child	05Ma02Fu
Anthy.		.08	M	Infant	05Ma02Fu
WALSH, Ml.		22	M	Laborer	05Ma02Fu

NAMES OF PASSENGERS		AGE	SEX	OCCUPATIONS	DATE PORT SHIP
CORCHERAN, Pat		28	M	Laborer	05Ma02Fu
Ann	(W)	24	F	Unknown	05Ma02Fu
BAILEY, Daniel		26	M	Laborer	05Ma02Fu
Fns.		30	M	Laborer	05Ma02Fu
WILSON, John		24	M	Laborer	05Ma02Fu
MCGRAUGH, Mary		23	F	Spinster	05Ma02Fu
CARNY, James		20	M	Laborer	05Ma02Fu
John		24	M	Laborer	05Ma02Fu
Eleanor		21	F	Wife	05Ma02Fu
Catharine		19	F	Spinster	05Ma02Fu
Susana		16	F	Spinster	05Ma02Fu
JOHNSTON, Biddy		21	F	Spinster	05Ma02Fu
LOGAN, Mary		21	F	Spinster	05Ma02Fu
CILMOY, Rose		20	F	Wife	05Ma02Fu
JOHNSTON, Margt.		26	F	Spinster	05Ma02Fu
WHITE, Edwd.		40	M	Farmer	05Ma02Fu
James		16	M	Farmer	05Ma02Fu
Amelia		13	F	Spinster	05Ma02Fu
Frs.		12	M	Laborer	05Ma02Fu
John		10	M	Laborer	05Ma02Fu
WALCH, Jas.		23	M	Laborer	05Ma02Fu
BUTLER, Thos.		51	M	Laborer	05Ma02Fu
Cath.		18	F	Spinster	05Ma02Fu
Peggy		45	F	Wife	05Ma02Fu
Sus.		17	F	Spinster	05Ma02Fu
John		16	M	Laborer	05Ma02Fu
Patrick		14	M	Laborer	05Ma02Fu
Thos.		9	M	Child	05Ma02Fu
Edwd.		6	M	Child	05Ma02Fu
Piers		3	M	Child	05Ma02Fu
QUINN, Mary		20	F	Spinster	05Ma02Fu
FELIN, Michl.		21	M	Farmer	05Ma02Fu
DUFFY, Patrick		26	M	Farmer	05Ma02Fu
Fany	(W)	25	F	Unknown	05Ma02Fu
James		2	M	Child	05Ma02Fu
Thomas		.06	M	Infant	05Ma02Fu
Ann		17	F	Spinster	05Ma02Fu
SHERIDAN, Jas.		25	M	Farmer	05Ma02Fu
Pritch		17	M	Laborer	05Ma02Fu
SULLIVAN, Andw.		25	M	Laborer	05Ma02Fu
SHERIDAN, Ann		49	F	Wi	05Ma02Fu
ORLEY, Patk.		24	M	Laborer	05Ma02Fu
MCCORMACK, Jas.		30	M	Laborer	05Ma02Fu
MCGOVERN, Chas.		29	M	Laborer	05Ma02Fu
CARTY, Ml.		30	M	Laborer	05Ma02F
Pat.		10	M	Laborer	05Ma02F
MCLACHLAN, Eliza		22	F	Spinster	05Ma02F
HICKEY, John		29	M	Laborer	05Ma02F
MCDONALD, Bernard		24	M	Laborer	05Ma02F
Alice	(W)	20	F	Unknown	05Ma02F
Pat.		.06	M	Infant	05Ma02F
APPLEFIELD, Jas.		22	M	Farmer	05Ma02F
LORAN, John		30	M	Farmer	05Ma02F
WILSON, John		20	M	Farmer	05Ma02F
Pat		20	M	Laborer	05Ma02F
MCMAN, John		29	M	Laborer	05Ma02F
Danl.		23	M	Laborer	05Ma02F
Pat		20	M	Laborer	05Ma02F
FITZGERALD, Garret		45	M	Laborer	05Ma02F
MOLY, John		20	M	Laborer	05Ma02F
SHERMAN, Mary		17	F	Spinster	05Ma02F
SMITH, Sidy		17	M	Laborer	05Ma02F
ENRIGHT, Mich.		28	M	Laborer	05Ma02F
BRESNER, Michl.		35	M	Farmer	05Ma02F
Jane		20	F	Spinster	05Ma02F
John		30	M	Farmer	05Ma02F
Mich.		30	M	Farmer	05Ma02F
Mat.		7	M	Child	05Ma02F
Thos.		5	M	Child	05Ma02F
Ellen		.08	F	Infant	05Ma02
Mary-Ann		14	F	Spinster	05Ma02
MCCARDELL, Wm.		20	M	Laborer	05Ma02
Henry		20	M	Laborer	05Ma02
ANDREWS, Pat.		40	M	Laborer	05Ma02
CONNORS, James		32	M	Laborer	05Ma02

NAMES OF PASSENGERS		AGE	SEX	OCCUPATIONS	DATE PORT SHIP
CONNORS, Mary	(W)	25	F	Unknown	05Ma02Fu

ST.LAWRENCE 06 MAY 1849

From Liverpool

NAMES OF PASSENGERS		AGE	SEX	OCCUPATIONS	DATE PORT SHIP
ASHTON, Thomas		21	M	Laborer	06Ma02Bh
DOOLAN, Thomas		34	M	Laborer	06Ma02Bh
REEGAN, John		34	M	Laborer	06Ma02Bh
MURPHY, Bridget		26	F	Servant	06Ma02Bh
RYAN, Edmund		20	M	Laborer	06Ma02Bh
RILEY, Patrick		18	M	Laborer	06Ma02Bh
DWYER, John		35	M	Laborer	06Ma02Bh
Norry	(W)	35	F	Wife	06Ma02Bh
RYAN, Tim		21	M	Blacksmith	06Ma02Bh
MOONEY, Mary		19	F	Servant	06Ma02Bh
ODEA, Ann		20	F	Servant	06Ma02Bh
ROCKAM, Bridget		12	F	Servant	06Ma02Bh
COYLE, Bridget		12	F	Servant	06Ma02Bh
WHELAN, Maurice		34	M	Laborer	06Ma02Bh
MAURISSEY, Lawrence		40	M	Laborer	06Ma02Bh
LEMAN, Patrick		26	M	Mason	06Ma02Bh
SHEIN, Thomas		35	M	Laborer	06Ma02Bh
CLAVERN, Owen		35	M	Laborer	06Ma02Bh
Betsy	(W)	26	F	Wife	06Ma02Bh
Pat		1	F	Child	06Ma02Bh
James		.00	M	Infant	06Ma02Bh
LYNCH, Peter		14	M	Laborer	06Ma02Bh
RYLEY, Ann		16	F	Servant	06Ma02Bh
MANOHAN, Mary		22	F	Servant	06Ma02Bh
SMITH, Honora		16	F	Servant	06Ma02Bh
Catherine		17	F	Servant	06Ma02Bh
Anne		15	F	Servant	06Ma02Bh
Mary		13	F	Servant	06Ma02Bh
Betsy		11	F	Servant	06Ma02Bh
KENNEY, Thomas		20	M	Laborer	06Ma02Bh
REGAN, Catherine		20	F	Servant	06Ma02Bh
MCGARR, John		34	M	Shoemaker	06Ma02Bh
CANNINGS, Patrick		16	M	Servant	06Ma02Bh
MARKEY, Margaret		30	F	Servant	06Ma02Bh
Rose		23	F	Servant	06Ma02Bh
Daniel		22	M	Servant	06Ma02Bh
SULLIVAN, Mathias		30	M	Servant	06Ma02Bh
FLYNN, Michael		25	M	Laborer	06Ma02Bh
HAYDEN, John		48	M	Laborer	06Ma02Bh
MANN, Mary		16	F	Servant	06Ma02Bh
QUINN, Mary		12	F	Servant	06Ma02Bh
RYLEY, Ann		22	F	Dressmaker	06Ma02Bh
FAGAN, Margaret		30	F	Dressmaker	06Ma02Bh
KENNEY, Richard		18	M	Servant	06Ma02Bh
MAHON, Catherine		14	F	Servant	06Ma02Bh
DWYER, Jeremiah		31	M	Servant	06Ma02Bh
Mary	(W)	31	F	Wife	06Ma02Bh
Pat		2	M	Child	06Ma02Bh
DAY, Patrick		32	M	Laborer	06Ma02Bh
MCFARLAN, Wm.		22	M	Plasterer	06Ma02Bh
DOOLAN, Paul		24	M	Laborer	06Ma02Bh
Ann		19	F	Servant	06Ma02Bh
WELSH, Ann		30	F	Servant	06Ma02Bh
LATTERY, Thos.		50	M	Butcher	06Ma02Bh
Mary	(W)	36	F	Wife	06Ma02Bh
Alice		23	F	Servant	06Ma02Bh
Patrick		20	M	Laborer	06Ma02Bh
John		8	M	Child	06Ma02Bh
ENEGRASS, Janat		30	M	Laborer	06Ma02Bh
YRNES, James		20	M	Servant	06Ma02Bh
IDAS, Eliza		25	F	Servant	06Ma02Bh
Ann		23	F	Servant	06Ma02Bh
YAN, Edward		40	M	Laborer	06Ma02Bh

NAMES OF PASSENGERS		AGE	SEX	OCCUPATIONS	DATE PORT SHIP
RYAN, Margaret	(W)	34	F	Wife	06Ma02Bh
John		30	M	Laborer	06Ma02Bh
James		12	M	Laborer	06Ma02Bh
Mary		9	F	Child	06Ma02Bh
Phillip Died-At-Sea		6	M	Child	06Ma02Bh
Patrick		2	M	Child	06Ma02Bh
CRONGHAN, Mary		25	F	Servant	06Ma02Bh
RYAN, Michael		40	M	Farmer	06Ma02Bh
Margaret	(W)	40	F	Wife	06Ma02Bh
Patrick	(S)	11	M	Son	06Ma02Bh
Mathew	(S)	9	M	Child	06Ma02Bh
Michael	(S)	6	M	Child	06Ma02Bh
Mary	(D)	2	F	Child	06Ma02Bh
Bridget	(D)	.00	F	Infant	06Ma02Bh
SMITH, Catherine		18	F	Servant	06Ma02Bh
Edward		16	M	Laborer	06Ma02Bh
ADAMSON, Thomas		50	M	Laborer	06Ma02Bh
MURRAY, James		25	M	Laborer	06Ma02Bh
Pat		12	M	Laborer	06Ma02Bh
Mary		50	F	Housekeeper	06Ma02Bh
BOOLAN, Mary		29	F	Servant	06Ma02Bh
MURREY, Nancy		22	F	Servant	06Ma02Bh
Margaret		20	F	Servant	06Ma02Bh
Judy		16	F	Servant	06Ma02Bh
RYAN, Daniel		23	M	Laborer	06Ma02Bh
Catherine		22	F	Servant	06Ma02Bh
MORRISON, Thomas		21	M	Weaver	06Ma02Bh
Mary		20	F	Weaver	06Ma02Bh
Sarah		17	F	Servant	06Ma02Bh
MCCANN, Henry		24	M	Laborer	06Ma02Bh
MAHON, James		17	M	Laborer	06Ma02Bh
BELL, Mathew		24	M	Laborer	06Ma02Bh
RILEY, Rose		18	F	Servant	06Ma02Bh
LARKEY, Patrick		40	M	Shoemaker	06Ma02Bh
Ann	(W)	40	F	Wife	06Ma02Bh
MURRY, Ann		20	F	Servant	06Ma02Bh
MAHON, Peter		42	M	Laborer	06Ma02Bh
Catherine		40	F	Servant	06Ma02Bh
MARTIN, James		22	M	Laborer	06Ma02Bh
REEGAN, Patrick		30	M	Laborer	06Ma02Bh
DARBY, Wm.		20	M	Brick Maker	06Ma02Bh
Bridget	(W)	18	F	Wife	06Ma02Bh
BAXTER, John		40	M	Laborer	06Ma02Bh
U	(W)	40	F	Wife	06Ma02Bh
Michael		20	M	Laborer	06Ma02Bh
Anne		16	F	Servant	06Ma02Bh
Catherine		12	F	Servant	06Ma02Bh
Mary		10	F	Servant	06Ma02Bh
Bridget		7	F	Child	06Ma02Bh
Patrick		4	M	Child	06Ma02Bh
Margaret		.00	F	Infant	06Ma02Bh
DONNELLY, John		26	M	Bricklayer	06Ma02Bh
BAGLAN, Thos.		21	M	Laborer	06Ma02Bh
Catherine		24	F	Servant	06Ma02Bh
CARLAN, Jesse		30	M	Laborer	06Ma02Bh
Betsy	(W)	25	F	Wife	06Ma02Bh
FARRELL, Francis		25	M	Weaver	06Ma02Bh
Betsy		22	F	Sister	06Ma02Bh
Mary		20	F	Servant	06Ma02Bh
BARNARD, Hugh		21	M	Laborer	06Ma02Bh
RYAN, Thomas		20	M	Laborer	06Ma02Bh
PETERS, Patrick		25	M	Laborer	06Ma02Bh
BOLEY, James		24	M	Laborer	06Ma02Bh
RYAN, Mathew		22	M	Laborer	06Ma02Bh
Anora		20	F	Servant	06Ma02Bh
HAYS, Mary		16	F	Servant	06Ma02Bh
BOYLE, Patrick		24	M	Laborer	06Ma02Bh
LINNEHEAN, Michael		21	M	Laborer	06Ma02Bh
WALLACE, Thos.		25	M	Laborer	06Ma02Bh
Theresa	(W)	24	F	Wife	06Ma02Bh
Mary		5	F	Child	06Ma02Bh
Margaret		.00	F	Infant	06Ma02Bh
KILFINN, Mary		14	F	Servant	06Ma02Bh
HARDY, Beverly		35	M	Farmer	06Ma02Bh

NAMES OF PASSENGERS	AGE	SEX	OCCUPATIONS	DATE PORT SHIP
MURRY, Patrick	26	M	Laborer	06Ma02Bh
KEARNEY, Patrick	26	M	Laborer	06Ma02Bh
Wm.	28	M	Laborer	06Ma02Bh
CUSWICK, Ann	21	F	Servant	06Ma02Bh
Alice	24	F	Servant	06Ma02Bh
FOSTER, John	30	M	Unknown	06Ma02Bh
BRIEN, John	24	M	Laborer	06Ma02Bh
MOONEY, Margaret	20	F	Servant	06Ma02Bh
RYAN, Mathew	26	M	Laborer	06Ma02Bh
PASCHOL, Andrew	30	M	Laborer	06Ma02Bh
HALL, George	18	M	Laborer	06Ma02Bh
Mary	20	F	Servant	06Ma02Bh
RYAN, Bridget	20	F	Servant	06Ma02Bh

JUNIPER 07 MAY 1849

From Londonderry

NAMES OF PASSENGERS	AGE	SEX	OCCUPATIONS	DATE PORT SHIP
MCKENNA, Patk.	20	M	Laborer	07Ma01Fl
MONTGOMERY, Thos.	20	M	Laborer	07Ma01Fl
Margaret	18	F	Spinster	07Ma01Fl
MCLUCAS, Eliza	20	F	Spinster	07Ma01Fl
BOYLAND, Anty	20	F	Spinster	07Ma01Fl
Hannah	17	F	Spinster	07Ma01Fl
BOYLE, Dennis	17	M	Unknown	07Ma01Fl
ARMOND, Thos.	32	M	Unknown	07Ma01Fl
Cath.	27	F	Wife	07Ma01Fl
MCLOUGHLIN, Danl.	28	M	Unknown	07Ma01Fl
GALLAGHER, Manasus	20	M	Unknown	07Ma01Fl
HEANY, John	20	M	Laborer	07Ma01Fl
GILLESPIE, Nancy	23	F	Unknown	07Ma01Fl
MEHAN, William	37	M	Unknown	07Ma01Fl
HARNE, Michael	24	M	Unknown	07Ma01Fl
TEANLIN, Michl.	20	M	Unknown	07Ma01Fl
IRVINE, Jas.	46	M	Unknown	07Ma01Fl
Ann (W)	44	F	Wife	07Ma01Fl
Mary-Jane	3	F	Child	07Ma01Fl
KANE, John	27	M	Farmer	07Ma01Fl
Margt.	30	F	Spinster	07Ma01Fl
Pat	.00	M	Infant	07Ma01Fl
BROGAN, Cormick	27	M	Unknown	07Ma01Fl
MCCLURE, Thos.	30	M	Laborer	07Ma01Fl
KANE, John	25	M	Laborer	07Ma01Fl
MCCAFFREY, Rose	22	F	Unknown	07Ma01Fl
KENNEDY, John	28	M	Unknown	07Ma01Fl
Elizabeth (W)	24	F	Wife	07Ma01Fl
Sarah	5	F	Child	07Ma01Fl
Mary	3	F	Child	07Ma01Fl
James	.00	M	Infant	07Ma01Fl
TOLAND, Mary	32	F	Unknown	07Ma01Fl
James	.00	M	Infant	07Ma01Fl
HAMILTON, Jas.	18	M	Laborer	07Ma01Fl
HEGARTY, John	20	M	Laborer	07Ma01Fl
BAILEY, Saml.	50	M	Laborer	07Ma01Fl
Mary	40	F	Unknown	07Ma01Fl
Robert	18	M	Laborer	07Ma01Fl
Eliza	15	F	Child	07Ma01Fl
Francis	11	M	Unknown	07Ma01Fl
Susan	9	F	Child	07Ma01Fl
DONNELLY, John	21	M	Laborer	07Ma01Fl
MCCANN, Nancy (W)	20	F	Wife	07Ma01Fl
GILLESPIE, Margt.	18	F	Unknown	07Ma01Fl
DOYLE, Pat	18	M	Laborer	07Ma01Fl
BROGAN, Jas.	17	M	Laborer	07Ma01Fl
GWYNE, Jas.	18	M	Laborer	07Ma01Fl
MCDADE, Rose	18	F	Spinster	07Ma01Fl
GALLAGHER, Bridget	17	F	Spinster	07Ma01Fl
BRIGLAND, Dennis	23	M	Laborer	07Ma01Fl
SEATON, Henry	21	M	Laborer	07Ma01Fl

NAMES OF PASSENGERS	AGE	SEX	OCCUPATIONS	DATE PORT SHIP
KELLY, Ann	17	F	Unknown	07Ma01Fl
John	60	M	Unknown	07Ma01Fl
BRENNAN, Frank	24	M	Unknown	07Ma01Fl
Wm.	21	M	Unknown	07Ma01Fl
FERRY, Jas.	18	M	Unknown	07Ma01Fl
WARD, Pat	23	M	Unknown	07Ma01Fl
Owen	23	M	Unknown	07Ma01Fl
Mary	20	F	Unknown	07Ma01Fl
SAYRES, Jas.	24	M	Laborer	07Ma01Fl
HANLON, Jas.	24	M	Laborer	07Ma01Fl
BEATTY, Mary	30	F	Wife	07Ma01Fl
John	2	M	Child	07Ma01Fl
MURREY, Sarah	21	F	Spinster	07Ma01Fl
GORMAN, Pat	27	M	Laborer	07Ma01Fl
DOHERTY, Wm.	26	M	Laborer	07Ma01Fl
MULLEN, Mary	34	F	Unknown	07Ma01Fl
Thos.	10	M	Unknown	07Ma01Fl
Pat	8	M	Child	07Ma01Fl
Cath.	5	F	Child	07Ma01Fl
Henry	.00	M	Infant	07Ma01Fl
KELLY, Margt.	18	F	Unknown	07Ma01Fl
MCCAFFREY, John	17	M	Servant	07Ma01Fl
Bridget	18	F	Spinster	07Ma01Fl
GALLAGHER, Mary	23	F	Spinster	07Ma01Fl
BEATLE, Eliza	40	F	Spinster	07Ma01Fl
Mary	17	F	Spinster	07Ma01Fl
Ellen	14	F	Spinster	07Ma01Fl
Ann	21	F	Spinster	07Ma01Fl
Susannah	.00	F	Infant	07Ma01Fl
FIELDS, Ralph	23	M	Laborer	07Ma01Fl
Sarah	19	F	Unknown	07Ma01Fl
GRACEN, Robt.	23	M	Unknown	07Ma01Fl
HARRINGTON, John	45	M	Laborer	07Ma01Fl
DEENEY, James	19	M	Laborer	07Ma01Fl
QUIGLEY, Hannah	19	F	Spinster	07Ma01Fl
MCCAFFREY, Bridget	17	F	Spinster	07Ma01Fl
Edw.	19	M	Unknown	07Ma01Fl
MCLOUGHLIN, Pat	35	M	Unknown	07Ma01Fl
MCGEE, John	36	M	Unknown	07Ma01Fl
MCMONAGH, Pat	35	M	Unknown	07Ma01F
KELLY, James	28	M	Unknown	07Ma01F
Bernd.	22	M	Unknown	07Ma01F
MCCAFFERTY, Rose	17	F	Spinster	07Ma01F
GALLAGHER, Margt.	18	F	Spinster	07Ma01F
MCCANN, Jane	18	F	Spinster	07Ma01F
PATTON, Betsey	45	F	Spinster	07Ma01F
MCKENNA, Jas.	20	M	Laborer	07Ma01F
Mary	18	F	Unknown	07Ma01F
GALLAGHER, Bridget	47	F	Unknown	07Ma01F
JORDAN, Mary	47	F	Unknown	07Ma01F
MOORE, Heather	00	F	Unknown	07Ma01F
BOYLE, Margt.	56	M	Unknown	07Ma01F
HARKING, Danl.	20	M	Unknown	07Ma01F
CONAGHAN, Manasus	30	M	Unknown	07Ma01F
Mary	25	F	Unknown	07Ma01F
Margery	23	F	Wife	07Ma01F
SWEENEY, Danl.	18	M	Unknown	07Ma01
DUGGAN, Pat	22	M	Farmer	07Ma01
BOYLE, Ann	16	F	Spinster	07Ma01
MCFADDEN, Biddy	16	F	Spinster	07Ma01
SIZE, Donato	13	M	Child	07Ma01
MCGAFFREY, Ann	15	F	Spinster	07Ma01
MCGEEHAN, Jas.	44	M	Laborer	07Ma01
Ellen	40	F	Unknown	07Ma01
John	17	M	Unknown	07Ma01
Biddy	14	F	Spinster	07Ma01
Jas.	12	M	Child	07Ma01
Nealy	10	F	Child	07Ma01
Hannah	6	F	Child	07Ma01
Mary	30	F	Unknown	07Ma01
KELLY, John	28	M	Laborer	07Ma01
PATTON, Wm.	23	M	Laborer	07Ma01
Wm.	45	M	Laborer	07Ma01
Giley	20	M	Laborer	07Ma01
GALLAGHER, Chas.	26	M	Laborer	07Ma01

NAMES OF PASSENGERS	AGE	SEX	OCCUPATIONS	DATE PORT SHIP
GALLAGHER, Ann	28	F	Wife	07Ma01Fl
Susan	.00	F	Infant	07Ma01Fl
MACKLIN, John	24	M	Laborer	07Ma01Fl
HARRITY, Margt.	20	F	Unknown	07Ma01Fl
DONNELLY, Jas.	21	M	Unknown	07Ma01Fl
MCCOLLMAN, Dennis	20	M	Unknown	07Ma01Fl
MCGINLEY, Jane	19	F	Laborer	07Ma01Fl
MULLIGAN, Cornl.	18	M	Laborer	07Ma01Fl
GALLAGHER, Biddy	30	F	Spinster	07Ma01Fl
PINKERTON, John	34	M	Laborer	07Ma01Fl
MCGEEHAN, Ellen	18	F	Unknown	07Ma01Fl
BOYLE, Danl.	27	M	Unknown	07Ma01Fl
Eliza	25	F	Unknown	07Ma01Fl
Mary-Ann	.00	F	Infant	07Ma01Fl
DEVELIN, Margt.	16	F	Unknown	07Ma01Fl
Fanny	15	F	Unknown	07Ma01Fl
CASEY, Celia	21	F	Unknown	07Ma01Fl
DEVLIN, Teresa	11	F	Unknown	07Ma01Fl
MOURAN, Mary	23	F	Unknown	07Ma01Fl
Peggy	25	F	Unknown	07Ma01Fl

E.E.PERKINS 07 MAY 1849

From Liverpool

NAMES OF PASSENGERS	AGE	SEX	OCCUPATIONS	DATE PORT SHIP
MONROE, John	20	M	Laborer	07Ma02Fv
DOWNS, Thomas	40	M	Laborer	07Ma02Fv
MCCORMICK, John	26	M	Laborer	07Ma02Fv
Maria	20	F	Laborer	07Ma02Fv
BOUGH, Joseph	20	M	Laborer	07Ma02Fv
Mary	18	F	Laborer	07Ma02Fv
FARLEY, Luke	32	M	Laborer	07Ma02Fv
TOBIN, Jas.	35	M	Laborer	07Ma02Fv
Ellen	35	F	Laborer	07Ma02Fv
Jos.	5	M	Child	07Ma02Fv
Betty	3	F	Child	07Ma02Fv
Judy	1	F	Child	07Ma02Fv
Mary	.00	F	Infant	07Ma02Fv
UGGAN, Phillip	28	M	Laborer	07Ma02Fv
CCARTEY, James	40	M	Laborer	07Ma02Fv
Honora	36	F	Laborer	07Ma02Fv
Bridget	60	F	Laborer	07Ma02Fv
Danl.	.00	M	Infant	07Ma02Fv
Bridget	11	F	Unknown	07Ma02Fv
YAN, Jno.	20	M	Laborer	07Ma02Fv
Michl.	20	M	Laborer	07Ma02Fv
Ann	17	F	Laborer	07Ma02Fv
IEVIERN, Ann	26	F	Laborer	07Ma02Fv
CLOUGHLIN, Frank	27	M	Laborer	07Ma02Fv
ILLEN, Cathe.	22	F	Laborer	07Ma02Fv
EENAN, Cathe.	30	F	Laborer	07Ma02Fv
X, Dennis	50	M	Laborer	07Ma02Fv
Mary	50	F	Laborer	07Ma02Fv
Margt.	13	F	Laborer	07Ma02Fv
Mary	9	F	Child	07Ma02Fv
Cathe.	6	F	Child	07Ma02Fv
James	21	M	Laborer	07Ma02Fv
Jos.	23	M	Laborer	07Ma02Fv
CKEY, Jno.	21	M	Laborer	07Ma02Fv
LFPENNY, Jno.	19	M	Laborer	07Ma02Fv
LLEN, Pat	40	M	Laborer	07Ma02Fv
Catherine	35	F	Laborer	07Ma02Fv
Pat	14	M	Laborer	07Ma02Fv
James	12	M	Laborer	07Ma02Fv
Ann	9	F	Child	07Ma02Fv
Rose	5	F	Child	07Ma02Fv
Pat	22	M	Laborer	07Ma02Fv
CARTY, Owen	35	M	Laborer	07Ma02Fv
LLINS, Eliza	20	F	Laborer	07Ma02Fv

NAMES OF PASSENGERS	AGE	SEX	OCCUPATIONS	DATE PORT SHIP
BALEY, Thos.	45	M	Laborer	07Ma02Fv
Margt.	32	F	Laborer	07Ma02Fv
Ellen	33	F	Laborer	07Ma02Fv
Geo.	10	M	Laborer	07Ma02Fv
Mary	5	F	Child	07Ma02Fv
Thos.	3	M	Child	07Ma02Fv
HALEY, Thos.	24	M	Laborer	07Ma02Fv
Cathe.	15	F	Laborer	07Ma02Fv
GREEN, Mary	25	F	Laborer	07Ma02Fv
KING, Margt.	40	F	Laborer	07Ma02Fv
HEREN, Betty	40	F	Laborer	07Ma02Fv
MULDOON, Michl.	40	M	Laborer	07Ma02Fv
FARRELL, Cathe.	18	F	Laborer	07Ma02Fv
PORTER, Belle	50	F	Laborer	07Ma02Fv
GAVINE, Mark	20	M	Laborer	07Ma02Fv
RILEY, Henry	25	M	Laborer	07Ma02Fv
Margt.	25	F	Laborer	07Ma02Fv
Michl.	5	M	Child	07Ma02Fv
Wm.	.00	M	Infant	07Ma02Fv
MCTIGHLEH, Nancy	25	F	Laborer	07Ma02Fv
FITZPATRICK, Hearn	40	U	Laborer	07Ma02Fv
FARRELL, Ann	60	F	Laborer	07Ma02Fv
Pat	25	M	Laborer	07Ma02Fv
Geo.	18	M	Laborer	07Ma02Fv
Wm.	15	M	Laborer	07Ma02Fv
TULLY, Ann	20	F	Laborer	07Ma02Fv
MCGLOUGHLIN, Thos.	22	M	Laborer	07Ma02Fv
Biddy	20	F	Laborer	07Ma02Fv
GRANT, Wm.	22	M	Laborer	07Ma02Fv
KELLY, Lucy	20	F	Laborer	07Ma02Fv
DOOGAN, Ann	20	F	Laborer	07Ma02Fv
CUNNINGHAM, Geo.	27	M	Laborer	07Ma02Fv
Mary	27	F	Laborer	07Ma02Fv
Bartley	2	M	Child	07Ma02Fv
Thos.	.00	M	Infant	07Ma02Fv
MANIGAN, Pat	25	M	Laborer	07Ma02Fv
LINNETT, Martha	30	F	Laborer	07Ma02Fv
Julia	25	F	Laborer	07Ma02Fv
Pat	2	M	Child	07Ma02Fv
James	.00	M	Infant	07Ma02Fv
POWERS, Morris	45	M	Baker	07Ma02Fv
Ellen	45	F	Unknown	07Ma02Fv
Richd.	28	M	Unknown	07Ma02Fv
Alley	26	F	Unknown	07Ma02Fv
Mary	24	F	Unknown	07Ma02Fv
Margt.	22	F	Unknown	07Ma02Fv
Anty.	20	M	Unknown	07Ma02Fv
Ellen	16	F	Unknown	07Ma02Fv
Cathe.	14	F	Unknown	07Ma02Fv
Wm.	2	M	Child	07Ma02Fv
BLAKE, Bridget	40	F	Unknown	07Ma02Fv
PLEBLEIN, Cathe.	14	F	Unknown	07Ma02Fv
BURNS, Peter	20	M	Laborer	07Ma02Fv
Mary	20	F	Laborer	07Ma02Fv
Pat	60	M	Laborer	07Ma02Fv
James	22	M	Laborer	07Ma02Fv
CULLIN, Peter	27	M	Laborer	07Ma02Fv
Cathe.	25	F	Laborer	07Ma02Fv
MALONE, James	21	M	Laborer	07Ma02Fv
BRADEN, Michl.	20	M	Laborer	07Ma02Fv
BRADY, Mary	20	F	Laborer	07Ma02Fv
CARROLL, Dennis	60	M	Laborer	07Ma02Fv
Bridget	22	F	Laborer	07Ma02Fv
QUINN, Cathe.	22	F	Laborer	07Ma02Fv
SEE, Francis	26	M	Laborer	07Ma02Fv
FATTEES, Geo.	26	M	Laborer	07Ma02Fv
FENNON, Michl.	28	M	Laborer	07Ma02Fv
Mary-Ann	20	F	Laborer	07Ma02Fv
COUGHLER, James	37	M	Laborer	07Ma02Fv
ROGERS, Richd.	30	M	Laborer	07Ma02Fv
Elizth.	30	F	Laborer	07Ma02Fv
Emma	9	F	Child	07Ma02Fv
Mary	7	F	Child	07Ma02Fv
Ann	5	F	Child	07Ma02Fv
Jane	2	F	Child	07Ma02Fv

NAMES OF PASSENGERS	AGE	SEX	OCCUPATIONS	DATE PORT SHIP
LOVELOCK, Honora	35	F	Unknown	07Ma02Fv
Pat	10	M	Unknown	07Ma02Fv
HOGAN, Mick.	40	M	Unknown	07Ma02Fv
HALEY, Mich.	21	M	Unknown	07Ma02Fv
HOGAN, Margt.	20	F	Unknown	07Ma02Fv
PRICE, James	27	M	Unknown	07Ma02Fv
Pat	30	M	Unknown	07Ma02Fv
MCANDREWS, James	30	M	Unknown	07Ma02Fv
Mary	25	F	Unknown	07Ma02Fv
Bridget	20	F	Unknown	07Ma02Fv
SCOVINGER, Miles	21	M	Unknown	07Ma02Fv
Pat	20	M	Unknown	07Ma02Fv
PAIN, Jno.	21	M	Unknown	07Ma02Fv
Danl.	25	M	Unknown	07Ma02Fv
FOGERTY, Cathe.	21	F	Unknown	07Ma02Fv
Mary	18	F	Unknown	07Ma02Fv
DULING, Howard	16	M	Unknown	07Ma02Fv
DOUGHERTY, Sarah	35	F	Unknown	07Ma02Fv
ROWE, Michl.	24	M	Unknown	07Ma02Fv
Sarah	22	F	Unknown	07Ma02Fv
CONLY, Mary	12	F	Spinster	07Ma02Fv
SCHOFIELD, Jno.	50	M	Laborer	07Ma02Fv
Mary	22	F	Laborer	07Ma02Fv
OLARY, Mary	24	F	Laborer	07Ma02Fv
HEFFEREN, Jas.	28	M	Laborer	07Ma02Fv
Biddy	21	F	Laborer	07Ma02Fv
MCCORMICK, Jas.	25	M	Laborer	07Ma02Fv
BANKS, Bridget	50	F	Unknown	07Ma02Fv
CLARK, Mary	20	F	Unknown	07Ma02Fv
LAWTON, Adam	33	M	Unknown	07Ma02Fv
Mary	30	F	Unknown	07Ma02Fv
Sarah-Ann	.00	F	Infant	07Ma02Fv
MANIN, Ann	22	F	Unknown	07Ma02Fv
LEES, Dave	50	M	Unknown	07Ma02Fv
COREY, Rleidades	17	M	Laborer	07Ma02Fv
BUTLER, Jno.	20	M	Laborer	07Ma02Fv
Geo.	16	M	Unknown	07Ma02Fv
Honora	16	U	Unknown	07Ma02Fv
Margt.	14	F	Unknown	07Ma02Fv
ODONNELL, Cathe.	20	F	Unknown	07Ma02Fv
SWEENEY, Cathe.	45	F	Unknown	07Ma02Fv
Mary	40	F	Unknown	07Ma02Fv
Margt.	7	F	Child	07Ma02Fv
James	5	M	Child	07Ma02Fv
Marcia	3	F	Child	07Ma02Fv
Danl.	.00	M	Infant	07Ma02Fv
DEVAN, Pat	22	M	Unknown	07Ma02Fv
FRASEY, Michl.	32	M	Unknown	07Ma02Fv
CLARKE, Margt.	25	F	Unknown	07Ma02Fv
ROUKLIN, Ann	25	F	Unknown	07Ma02Fv
HICKEY, Patk.	14	M	Unknown	07Ma02Fv

ALBERT 07 MAY 1849

From Liverpool

NAMES OF PASSENGERS	AGE	SEX	OCCUPATIONS	DATE PORT SHIP
CLARKE, Thomas	18	M	Laborer	07Ma02Fr
William	18	M	Laborer	07Ma02Fr
REYNOLDS, Hugh	20	M	Laborer	07Ma02Fr
NEIVMAN, Eliza	20	F	Unknown	07Ma02Fr
MCMANUS, Cath.	15	F	Unknown	07Ma02Fr
MUNCRIFF, Chas.	40	M	Unknown	07Ma02Fr
U-Mrs.	30	F	Unknown	07Ma02Fr
BRAKEN, U-Mr.	21	M	Unknown	07Ma02Fr
John	21	M	Unknown	07Ma02Fr
MCCANE, Ellen	20	F	Unknown	07Ma02Fr
BRID, Joseph	50	M	Unknown	07Ma02Fr
Elizabeth	24	F	Unknown	07Ma02Fr
Isaac	.00	M	Infant	07Ma02Fr
ALLYES, George	30	M	Farmer	07Ma02Fr
Charlotte	28	F	Farmer	07Ma02Fr
Mary	3	F	Child	07Ma02Fr
Ann	.00	F	Infant	07Ma02Fr
HITCHCOCK, Maria	19	F	Laborer	07Ma02Fr
MCCABE, Mary	30	F	Unknown	07Ma02Fr
CALLY, Thos.	30	M	Unknown	07Ma02Fr
U-Mrs.	30	F	Unknown	07Ma02Fr
MURPHY, Thos.	25	M	Unknown	07Ma02Fr
FLEMMING, Joe	20	M	Unknown	07Ma02Fr
FLYNN, Terrence	25	M	Unknown	07Ma02Fr
U-Mrs.	30	F	Unknown	07Ma02Fr
COGGINS, Jno.	13	M	Unknown	07Ma02Fr
BOLAN, Robt.	18	M	Unknown	07Ma02Fr
MCMANNUS, Robt.	27	M	Unknown	07Ma02Fr
MCKENEN, Michl.	24	M	Unknown	07Ma02Fr
DOWAN, Eliza	20	F	Unknown	07Ma02Fr
CHERAN, Wm.	20	M	Unknown	07Ma02Fr
PENKION, Fenton	18	M	Unknown	07Ma02Fr
COFFER, Thos.	25	M	Unknown	07Ma02Fr
JENNINGS, Mary	20	F	Unknown	07Ma02Fr
Jno.	6	M	Child	07Ma02Fr
Johanna	.00	F	Infant	07Ma02Fr
TOTEN, Thos.	29	M	Unknown	07Ma02Fr
HATELLMAN, Mark	30	M	Unknown	07Ma02Fr
MURPHY, Jno.	20	M	Unknown	07Ma02Fr
Cath.	20	F	Unknown	07Ma02Fr
Edward	.00	M	Infant	07Ma02Fr
Thos.	20	M	Unknown	07Ma02Fr
Mary	60	F	Unknown	07Ma02Fr
Michael	18	M	Unknown	07Ma02Fr
MCGOWAN, Michl.	20	M	Unknown	07Ma02Fr
MAHON, Michl.	16	M	Unknown	07Ma02Fr
FLYNNE, Margt.	35	F	Unknown	07Ma02Fr
Myles	12	M	Unknown	07Ma02Fr
Bridget	10	F	Unknown	07Ma02Fr
Frances	4	F	Child	07Ma02Fr
Edward	2	M	Child	07Ma02Fr
Cath.	.00	F	Infant	07Ma02Fr
DILLON, Richard	17	M	Unknown	07Ma02Fr
Jno.	14	M	Unknown	07Ma02Fr
ROURKE, Math.	22	M	Unknown	07Ma02Fr
Mary	25	F	Unknown	07Ma02Fr
Theresa	19	F	Unknown	07Ma02Fr
HEALY, Felix	30	M	Unknown	07Ma02Fr
MCKERNAN, Ellen	20	F	Unknown	07Ma02F
CANNON, Ellen	20	F	Unknown	07Ma02F
DONNELL, Danl.	10	M	Unknown	07Ma02F
ONEILL, James	35	M	Unknown	07Ma02F
Fanny	28	F	Unknown	07Ma02F
Maria	7	F	Child	07Ma02F
Martin	9	M	Child	07Ma02F
Jno.	5	M	Child	07Ma02F
Alice	3	F	Child	07Ma02F
Pat	.00	M	Infant	07Ma02F
KERNAN, Eliza	18	F	Unknown	07Ma02F
CONNOR, Pat	30	M	Unknown	07Ma02F
WOODCOCK, Jamison	29	M	Unknown	07Ma02F
BURKE, Richd.	40	M	Unknown	07Ma02F
Margt.	40	F	Unknown	07Ma02F
SMITH, Jno.	25	M	Unknown	07Ma02F
MCCLOSKEY, Jno.	20	M	Unknown	07Ma02F
CAIN, Jno.	20	M	Unknown	07Ma02F
LEGG, Jno.	40	M	Unknown	07Ma02F
DOLLON, Jno.	26	M	Unknown	07Ma02F
NOLAN, John	26	M	Unknown	07Ma02F
MOLLY, Ian	24	M	Unknown	07Ma02F
U-Mrs.	20	F	Unknown	07Ma02F
Jno.	3	M	Child	07Ma02F
Pat	3	M	Child	07Ma02F
KELLY, Owen	20	M	Unknown	07Ma02F
WHELAGAN, Keora	15	F	Unknown	07Ma02F
Robt.	16	M	Unknown	07Ma02F
LAROLES, James	20	M	Unknown	07Ma02
MCDONAGH, U-Mrs.	60	F	Unknown	07Ma02

NAMES OF PASSENGERS	AGE	SEX	OCCUPATIONS	DATE PORT SHIP
BURKE, Jno.	30	M	Unknown	07Ma02Fr
Judith	19	U	Unknown	07Ma02Fr
KELLY, Edw.	33	M	Unknown	07Ma02Fr
RUPERT, Pat.	25	M	Unknown	07Ma02Fr
James	20	M	Unknown	07Ma02Fr
Frank	18	M	Unknown	07Ma02Fr
William	16	M	Unknown	07Ma02Fr
Mary	14	F	Unknown	07Ma02Fr
Kitty	18	F	Unknown	07Ma02Fr
Edward	31	M	Unknown	07Ma02Fr
HUFFORD, Margaret	20	F	Unknown	07Ma02Fr
Cath.	19	F	Unknown	07Ma02Fr
DAYNE, Neil	25	M	Unknown	07Ma02Fr
MORGAN, James	20	M	Unknown	07Ma02Fr
PHILLIPS, Ann	20	F	Unknown	07Ma02Fr
MAKING, Jno.	20	M	Unknown	07Ma02Fr
FEICON, Pat	36	M	Unknown	07Ma02Fr
MURRAY, Pat	34	M	Unknown	07Ma02Fr
CONSTANTINE, M.	30	M	Unknown	07Ma02Fr
LYNCH, Philip	14	M	Unknown	07Ma02Fr
Thos.	12	M	Unknown	07Ma02Fr
MULLEN, Chas.	30	M	Unknown	07Ma02Fr
MCGOVERN, Mary	26	F	Unknown	07Ma02Fr
CONNELLY, Pat	22	M	Unknown	07Ma02Fr
Bridget	50	F	Unknown	07Ma02Fr
HEALY, Peter	40	M	Unknown	07Ma02Fr
Cath.	28	F	Unknown	07Ma02Fr
Ann	7	F	Child	07Ma02Fr
Sally	9	F	Child	07Ma02Fr
RYAN, Peter	60	M	Unknown	07Ma02Fr
MILLAY, John	22	M	Unknown	07Ma02Fr
Ellen	40	F	Unknown	07Ma02Fr
Jane	20	F	Unknown	07Ma02Fr
MURRAY, Michl.	31	M	Unknown	07Ma02Fr
ROWLEY, James	20	M	Unknown	07Ma02Fr
GALLAGHER, Neil	50	M	Unknown	07Ma02Fr
Judy	55	F	Unknown	07Ma02Fr
Margt.	16	F	Unknown	07Ma02Fr
Ann	15	F	Unknown	07Ma02Fr
Patt	12	M	Unknown	07Ma02Fr
Cath.	10	F	Unknown	07Ma02Fr
CARROLL, Johanna	27	F	Unknown	07Ma02Fr
BROWN, Ann	20	F	Unknown	07Ma02Fr
HANGAN, Pat	30	M	Unknown	07Ma02Fr
U-Mrs.	30	F	Unknown	07Ma02Fr
Jim	26	M	Unknown	07Ma02Fr
Thomas	15	M	Unknown	07Ma02Fr
Mary	17	F	Unknown	07Ma02Fr
MCDONALD, Pat	27	M	Unknown	07Ma02Fr
Pat	13	M	Unknown	07Ma02Fr
MURRAY, Margt.	40	F	Unknown	07Ma02Fr
MCDONALD, Tom	.00	M	Infant	07Ma02Fr
MURRAY, Thos.	30	M	Unknown	07Ma02Fr
MCCALLY, Pat	19	M	Unknown	07Ma02Fr
Thos.	23	M	Unknown	07Ma02Fr
WALSH, John	20	M	Unknown	07Ma02Fr
DEVINE, Neil	30	M	Unknown	07Ma02Fr
LUNDREGAN, James	36	M	Unknown	07Ma02Fr
Thos.	24	M	Unknown	07Ma02Fr
BELTON, Thos.	20	M	Unknown	07Ma02Fr
Cath.	20	F	Unknown	07Ma02Fr
Mary	20	F	Unknown	07Ma02Fr
Mary	21	F	Unknown	07Ma02Fr
FARLEY, Frank	15	M	Unknown	07Ma02Fr
SMITH, James	42	M	Unknown	07Ma02Fr
Maria	22	F	Unknown	07Ma02Fr
Died-At-Sea				
MCMAHON, Rae	30	M	Unknown	07Ma02Fr
Cath.	16	F	Unknown	07Ma02Fr
FINEY, Thos.	00	M	Unknown	07Ma02Fr
Pat	00	M	Unknown	07Ma02Fr
HARRIGAN, Rich	36	M	Unknown	07Ma02Fr
SCANLON, Edward	20	M	Unknown	07Ma02Fr
John	22	M	Unknown	07Ma02Fr
Thos.	20	M	Unknown	07Ma02Fr

NAMES OF PASSENGERS	AGE	SEX	OCCUPATIONS	DATE PORT SHIP
KELLON, James	26	M	Unknown	07Ma02Fr
JOICE, James	30	M	Unknown	07Ma02Fr
KEARNEY, Thos.	32	M	Unknown	07Ma02Fr
Mary	30	F	Unknown	07Ma02Fr
Pat	4	M	Child	07Ma02Fr
Honor	2	F	Child	07Ma02Fr
Rose	20	F	Unknown	07Ma02Fr
Peggy	21	F	Unknown	07Ma02Fr
KELLY, Thos.	26	M	Unknown	07Ma02Fr
LARKIN, Pat	20	M	Unknown	07Ma02Fr
KEARNEY, Pat	18	M	Unknown	07Ma02Fr
John	10	M	Unknown	07Ma02Fr
LALTON, Mary	26	F	Unknown	07Ma02Fr
CANLAN, Peter	40	M	Unknown	07Ma02Fr
Died-At-Sea				
GREENE, Thos.	21	M	Unknown	07Ma02Fr
PINDER, James	21	M	Unknown	07Ma02Fr
CAHILL, James	17	M	Unknown	07Ma02Fr
LEES, Peter	21	M	Unknown	07Ma02Fr
MCEVERAN, Biddy	21	F	Unknown	07Ma02Fr
Margt.	19	F	Unknown	07Ma02Fr
HALLOGAN, Michael	21	M	Unknown	07Ma02Fr
KEENAN, Margt.	20	F	Unknown	07Ma02Fr
MCGENSEGHER, Biddy	20	F	Unknown	07Ma02Fr
DONOHAN, Marion	26	F	Unknown	07Ma02Fr
Rose	24	F	Unknown	07Ma02Fr
LEORAN, Pat	20	M	Unknown	07Ma02Fr
BURKE, Wm.	27	M	Unknown	07Ma02Fr
MCVANY, Bridget	21	F	Unknown	07Ma02Fr
NUGENT, Edward	27	F	Unknown	07Ma02Fr
RIELLY, Bridget	22	F	Unknown	07Ma02Fr
MURPHY, Pat	21	M	Unknown	07Ma02Fr
FULTY, Bessy	20	F	Unknown	07Ma02Fr
RODGERS, Mary	20	F	Unknown	07Ma02Fr
GAHANAN, Bridget	20	F	Unknown	07Ma02Fr
SMITH, John	26	M	Unknown	07Ma02Fr
DONAGHER, Thos.	20	M	Unknown	07Ma02Fr
FLYNN, Thos.	22	M	Unknown	07Ma02Fr
Caroline	22	M	Unknown	07Ma02Fr
Margaret	27	F	Unknown	07Ma02Fr
CARLLETT, Roger	30	M	Unknown	07Ma02Fr
KAINE, John	40	M	Unknown	07Ma02Fr
HITCHCOCK, Sarah	16	F	Unknown	07Ma02Fr
GAVIN, Rose	00	F	Unknown	07Ma02Fr
GOOKLIN, Miles	00	M	Unknown	07Ma02Fr
ROWLEY, John	00	M	Unknown	07Ma02Fr
DOYLE, Eliza	00	F	Unknown	07Ma02Fr

TRIUMPH 07 MAY 1849

From Limerick

NAMES OF PASSENGERS	AGE	SEX	OCCUPATIONS	DATE PORT SHIP
RUDY, Johannah	30	F	Matron	07Ma35Fs
Patt	35	M	Unknown	07Ma35Fs
Daniel	.10	M	Infant	07Ma35Fs
Margt.	2	F	Child	07Ma35Fs
John	7	M	Child	07Ma35Fs
George	6	M	Child	07Ma35Fs
Died-At-Sea				
GLEESON, Andrew	20	M	Farmer	07Ma35Fs
Michael	28	M	Farmer	07Ma35Fs
Michael	28	M	Farmer	07Ma35Fs
TAYLOR, Robt.	50	M	Farmer	07Ma35Fs
CULLIHANE, John	22	M	Laborer	07Ma35Fs
Honora (W)	20	F	Wife	07Ma35Fs
Margt.	5	F	Child	07Ma35Fs
Michael	.06	M	Infant	07Ma35Fs
ENRIGHT, Cath.	20	F	Spinster	07Ma35Fs
CULLIHANE, Thos.	25	M	Farmer	07Ma35Fs

NAMES OF PASSENGERS	AGE	SEX	OCCUPATIONS	DATE PORT SHIP
CULLIHANE, Margaret (W)	22	F	Farmer	07Ma35Fs
Jas.	5	M	Child	07Ma35Fs
Mary	.09	F	Infant	07Ma35Fs
BIVINZIA, Barbara	20	F	Spinster	07Ma35Fs
HOGAN, Cath.	20	F	Spinster	07Ma35Fs
MULCAHY, Jas.	20	M	Farmer	07Ma35Fs
Timothy	12	M	Child	07Ma35Fs
Johannah	15	F	Child	07Ma35Fs
LEONARD, Jas.	30	M	Laborer	07Ma35Fs
DANAHAN, Timothy	40	M	Laborer	07Ma35Fs
DONOHUE, Mary (W)	35	F	Wife	07Ma35Fs
CROCKER, John	25	M	Laborer	07Ma35Fs
DANAHAN, Johannah	8	F	Child	07Ma35Fs
Ellen	6	F	Child	07Ma35Fs
David	4	M	Child	07Ma35Fs
Thos.	.06	M	Infant	07Ma35Fs
Died-At-Sea				
DWYER, Mary	40	F	Matron	07Ma35Fs
James	.10	M	Infant	07Ma35Fs
Cath.	15	F	Child	07Ma35Fs
MURPHY, Michl.	26	M	Farmer	07Ma35Fs
MORONY, Pat	26	M	Laborer	07Ma35Fs
GRENVILLE, Thos.	18	M	Slater	07Ma35Fs
REAKARDT, Robt.	22	M	Nailer	07Ma35Fs
MANGON, Michl.	25	M	Farmer	07Ma35Fs
Ellen (W)	20	F	Wife	07Ma35Fs
MCLAUGHLIN, Pat	20	M	Laborer	07Ma35Fs
FITZGERALD, Bridget	30	F	Spinster	07Ma35Fs
CONNOR, Michl.	20	M	Farmer	07Ma35Fs
MADIGAN, Dennis	20	M	Laborer	07Ma35Fs
FITZGERALD, Michl.	25	M	Farmer	07Ma35Fs
GALLIGAN, John	26	M	Farmer	07Ma35Fs
Richd.	22	M	Farmer	07Ma35Fs
KELLIHAN, Ellen	30	F	Matron	07Ma35Fs
Cath.	30	F	Matron	07Ma35Fs
Michl.	10	M	Child	07Ma35Fs
ARMITAGE, Joseph	40	M	Farmer	07Ma35Fs
MCGRATH, Michl.	20	M	Carpenter	07Ma35Fs
BRAZIL, Mary	26	F	Spinster	07Ma35Fs
DEVENICH, John	22	M	Clerk	07Ma35Fs
Mary	40	F	Matron	07Ma35Fs
ONEIL, Thos.	44	M	Farmer	07Ma35Fs
Mary (W)	21	F	Wife	07Ma35Fs
DOOLAN, Thos.	20	M	Laborer	07Ma35Fs
Peter	18	M	Laborer	07Ma35Fs
LENNIHAN, Dennis	24	M	Farmer	07Ma35Fs
Bridget (W)	20	M	Wife	07Ma35Fs
James	1	M	Child	07Ma35Fs
Ann	.00	F	Infant	07Ma35Fs
HAYES, Dennis	20	M	Laborer	07Ma35Fs
BURKE, Richd.	50	M	Farmer	07Ma35Fs
Pat	25	M	Farmer	07Ma35Fs
HURLEY, Michael	36	M	Farmer	07Ma35Fs
FLANIGAN, Margt.	20	M	Spinster	07Ma35Fs
HANAHAN, Margt.	20	M	Spinster	07Ma35Fs
MCNAMARA, Jeremiah	30	M	Farmer	07Ma35Fs
Matilda (W)	30	F	Wife	07Ma35Fs
Pat	4	M	Child	07Ma35Fs
Anne	3	F	Child	07Ma35Fs
Jeremiah	.10	M	Infant	07Ma35Fs
MADIGAN, Simon	40	M	Laborer	07Ma35Fs
MULQUICK, James	20	M	Laborer	07Ma35Fs
HADDEN, Gabriel	22	M	Laborer	07Ma35Fs
MALONE, Michl.	56	M	Laborer	07Ma35Fs
Betsey (W)	40	F	Wife	07Ma35Fs
Michl.	20	M	Unknown	07Ma35Fs
Bridget	18	F	Unknown	07Ma35Fs
Ellen	15	F	Unknown	07Ma35Fs
Pat	9	M	Child	07Ma35Fs
James	6	M	Child	07Ma35Fs
Matt	4	M	Child	07Ma35Fs
Died-At-Sea				
HOGAN, John	30	M	Laborer	07Ma35Fs
KELLIHAN, Danl.	25	M	Laborer	07Ma35Fs
CONNELL, John	25	M	Laborer	07Ma35Fs

NAMES OF PASSENGERS	AGE	SEX	OCCUPATIONS	DATE PORT SHIP
CONNELL, Mary (W)	20	F	Wife	07Ma35Fs
Thos.	.06	M	Infant	07Ma35Fs
MACKEY, Danl.	18	M	Farmer	07Ma35Fs
BROWN, Michl.	22	M	Farmer	07Ma35Fs
ODONNELL, Thos.	40	M	Farmer	07Ma35Fs
Cath. (W)	40	F	Wife	07Ma35Fs
LYNCH, Walter	23	M	Laborer	07Ma35Fs
Ellen (W)	18	F	Wife	07Ma35Fs
ODONNELL, Rich	5	M	Child	07Ma35Fs
Francis	2	M	Child	07Ma35Fs
MORAN, James	18	M	Laborer	07Ma35Fs
VAUGHAN, Darby	20	M	Laborer	07Ma35Fs
ELLIARD, Andrew	30	M	Gentleman	07Ma35Fs
STEWARD, Matilda	20	F	Unknown	07Ma35Fs
GRADY, Ellen	40	F	Unknown	07Ma35Fs
John	20	M	Unknown	07Ma35Fs
Ellen	18	F	Unknown	07Ma35Fs
Mary	16	F	Unknown	07Ma35Fs

ENTERPRISE 07 MAY 1849

From Dublin

NAMES OF PASSENGERS	AGE	SEX	OCCUPATIONS	DATE PORT SHIP
COSTELLO, U-Mrs.	40	F	Unknown	07Ma12Ga
U-Miss	20	F	Unknown	07Ma12Ga
Christy	.00	M	Infant	07Ma12Ga
Julia	20	F	Unknown	07Ma12Ga
SAVOY, Ml.	40	M	Laborer	07Ma12Ga
FRAZER, Wm.	20	M	Laborer	07Ma12Ga
Bessy	17	F	Unknown	07Ma12Ga
MORRISSON, Alice	13	F	Unknown	07Ma12Ga
Ann	10	F	Unknown	07Ma12Ga
Edward	8	M	Child	07Ma12Ga
MCGRATH, Ann	13	F	Unknown	07Ma12Ga
BYRNE, Phelix	50	M	Laborer	07Ma12Ga
Martin	25	M	Laborer	07Ma12Ga
Phelix	26	M	Laborer	07Ma12Ga
Bessy	23	F	Unknown	07Ma12Ga
Mary	21	F	Unknown	07Ma12Ga
MURPHY, Patt.	24	M	Laborer	07Ma12Ga
CONWAY, Matt	55	M	Laborer	07Ma12Ga
Bridget	55	F	Unknown	07Ma12Ga
Laughlin	27	M	Laborer	07Ma12Ga
Michael	25	M	Laborer	07Ma12Ga
William	13	M	Laborer	07Ma12Ga
James	11	M	Laborer	07Ma12Ga
Julia	20	F	Unknown	07Ma12Ga
Catharine	19	F	Unknown	07Ma12Ga
Ellen	12	F	Unknown	07Ma12Ga
Laughlin	30	M	Laborer	07Ma12Ga
BYRNE, Patt	50	M	Laborer	07Ma12Ga
Eliza	50	F	Unknown	07Ma12Ga
Denis	24	M	Laborer	07Ma12Ga
Robert	24	M	Laborer	07Ma12Ga
Jane	26	F	Unknown	07Ma12Ga
Catharine	30	F	Unknown	07Ma12Ga
Ellen	18	F	Unknown	07Ma12Ga
CULLEN, Mary	20	F	Unknown	07Ma12Ga
BYRNE, John	31	M	Laborer	07Ma12Ga
Mary	29	F	Unknown	07Ma12Ga
Ellen	5	F	Child	07Ma12Ga
Margaret	.00	F	Infant	07Ma12Ga
CAVANAGH, Patt.	28	M	Laborer	07Ma12Ga
Michael	24	M	Laborer	07Ma12Ga
ACKANSAN, Ml.	20	M	Laborer	07Ma12Ga
WHITE, John	22	M	Laborer	07Ma12Ga
Ellen	18	F	Unknown	07Ma12Ga
CAVANAGH, Patt.	27	M	Unknown	07Ma12Ga
Eliza	50	F	Unknown	07Ma12Ga

NAMES OF PASSENGERS		AGE	SEX	OCCUPATIONS	DATE PORT SHIP
CAVANAGH, Hugh		25	M	Unknown	07Ma12Ga
Maria		23	F	Unknown	07Ma12Ga
Thomas		13	M	Unknown	07Ma12Ga
John		11	M	Unknown	07Ma12Ga
Ann		18	F	Unknown	07Ma12Ga
Bridget		.00	F	Infant	07Ma12Ga
BUTTERFIELD, Patt.		24	M	Unknown	07Ma12Ga
MULVEHILL, Thomas		22	M	Unknown	07Ma12Ga
Lucy		.00	F	Infant	07Ma12Ga
MEHAN, Mary		13	F	Unknown	07Ma12Ga
KELLY, MI.		34	M	Unknown	07Ma12Ga
Eliza		15	F	Unknown	07Ma12Ga
DOYLE, Patt.		22	M	Unknown	07Ma12Ga
LEONARD, Ellen		20	F	Unknown	07Ma12Ga
RYAN, John		22	M	Unknown	07Ma12Ga
MAHAN, Jane		20	F	Unknown	07Ma12Ga
DUGLASS, Robert		22	M	Unknown	07Ma12Ga
Catharine		20	F	Unknown	07Ma12Ga
MANNY, Thomas		30	M	Unknown	07Ma12Ga
Robert		20	M	Unknown	07Ma12Ga
CARBERY, Alice		20	F	Unknown	07Ma12Ga
CARR, Mary		20	F	Unknown	07Ma12Ga
FLOOD, Mary		20	F	Unknown	07Ma12Ga
RYAN, Michael		20	M	Unknown	07Ma12Ga
Ellen		18	F	Unknown	07Ma12Ga
Ellen		.00	F	Infant	07Ma12Ga
NOLAN, Thomas		35	M	Unknown	07Ma12Ga
Patt.		30	M	Unknown	07Ma12Ga
ROTCHEFIELD, Martin		30	M	Unknown	07Ma12Ga
U	(W)	30	F	Unknown	07Ma12Ga
John		.00	M	Infant	07Ma12Ga
BRENNAN, Peter		50	M	Unknown	07Ma12Ga
U	(W)	40	F	Unknown	07Ma12Ga
John		8	M	Child	07Ma12Ga
Bridget		8	F	Child	07Ma12Ga
Edward		6	M	Child	07Ma12Ga
Patt.		5	M	Child	07Ma12Ga
Judy		4	F	Child	07Ma12Ga
May		2	F	Child	07Ma12Ga
Kitty		.00	F	Infant	07Ma12Ga
Catharine		45	F	Unknown	07Ma12Ga
HENESSY, Thomas		45	M	Unknown	07Ma12Ga
Patt.		15	M	Unknown	07Ma12Ga
Bridget		13	F	Unknown	07Ma12Ga
LEONARD, Michael		51	M	Unknown	07Ma12Ga
U	(W)	42	F	Unknown	07Ma12Ga
Denis		21	M	Unknown	07Ma12Ga
Mathew		17	M	Unknown	07Ma12Ga
Catharine		13	F	Unknown	07Ma12Ga
Bridget		13	F	Unknown	07Ma12Ga
Mary		10	F	Unknown	07Ma12Ga
Julia		7	F	Child	07Ma12Ga
RYAN, John		50	M	Unknown	07Ma12Ga
Margaret		25	F	Unknown	07Ma12Ga
James		23	M	Unknown	07Ma12Ga
MORRISSON, William		22	M	Unknown	07Ma12Ga
BUTLER, Thos.		50	M	Unknown	07Ma12Ga
U	(W)	50	F	Unknown	07Ma12Ga
John		24	M	Unknown	07Ma12Ga
Denis		20	M	Unknown	07Ma12Ga
James		18	M	Unknown	07Ma12Ga
Patrick		.00	M	Infant	07Ma12Ga
Michael		35	M	Unknown	07Ma12Ga
U	(W)	30	F	Unknown	07Ma12Ga
Thomas		6	M	Child	07Ma12Ga
John		4	M	Child	07Ma12Ga
Denis		2	M	Child	07Ma12Ga
James		.00	M	Infant	07Ma12Ga
LEONARD, Mathew		50	M	Unknown	07Ma12Ga
Mary		20	F	Unknown	07Ma12Ga
Patt.		18	M	Unknown	07Ma12Ga
Catharine		16	F	Unknown	07Ma12Ga
Margaret		13	F	Unknown	07Ma12Ga
Michael		12	M	Unknown	07Ma12Ga
Ann		9	F	Child	07Ma12Ga
MARNELL, Luke		30	M	Unknown	07Ma12Ga
U	(W)	26	F	Unknown	07Ma12Ga
DILLON, John		19	M	Unknown	07Ma12Ga
FARRELL, Mary		40	F	Unknown	07Ma12Ga
John		20	M	Unknown	07Ma12Ga
Ann		18	F	Unknown	07Ma12Ga
Biddy		16	F	Unknown	07Ma12Ga
Mary		12	F	Unknown	07Ma12Ga
MCNALLY, John		26	M	Unknown	07Ma12Ga
Patrick		24	M	Unknown	07Ma12Ga
BOULGER, Patt.		30	M	Unknown	07Ma12Ga
MURPHY, Thos.		45	M	Unknown	07Ma12Ga
SHEEHAN, Thomas		22	M	Unknown	07Ma12Ga
U	(W)	22	F	Unknown	07Ma12Ga
Ellen		5	F	Child	07Ma12Ga
Ann		.00	F	Infant	07Ma12Ga
James		22	M	Unknown	07Ma12Ga
Catharine		20	F	Unknown	07Ma12Ga
QUINN, John		22	M	Unknown	07Ma12Ga
MATHEWS, Bridget		40	F	Unknown	07Ma12Ga
Ann		20	F	Unknown	07Ma12Ga
PINANE, Mary		20	F	Unknown	07Ma12Ga
COLLIERS, Watt		24	M	Unknown	07Ma12Ga
DALEY, James		45	M	Unknown	07Ma12Ga
Judy		45	F	Unknown	07Ma12Ga
Mary		22	F	Unknown	07Ma12Ga
Marcella		20	F	Unknown	07Ma12Ga
Jane		19	F	Unknown	07Ma12Ga
John		17	M	Unknown	07Ma12Ga
Patt.		10	M	Unknown	07Ma12Ga
Bridget		8	F	Child	07Ma12Ga
John		4	M	Child	07Ma12Ga
Mary		2	F	Child	07Ma12Ga
William		.00	M	Infant	07Ma12Ga
COONEY, Patt.		30	M	Unknown	07Ma12Ga
Mary		20	F	Unknown	07Ma12Ga
Jane		.00	F	Infant	07Ma12Ga
William		3	M	Child	07Ma12Ga
PIERCE, Mary		40	F	Unknown	07Ma12Ga
Thomas		18	M	Unknown	07Ma12Ga
Mary		13	F	Unknown	07Ma12Ga
James		7	M	Child	07Ma12Ga
George		5	M	Child	07Ma12Ga
Patt.		.00	M	Infant	07Ma12Ga
MOONEY, Bridget		26	F	Unknown	07Ma12Ga
Mary		7	F	Child	07Ma12Ga
Patt.		5	M	Child	07Ma12Ga
GREHAN, Thomas		26	M	Unknown	07Ma12Ga
Michael		3	M	Child	07Ma12Ga
Luke		.00	M	Infant	07Ma12Ga
TEDD, Ann		28	F	Wife	07Ma12Ga
James		3	M	Child	07Ma12Ga
Thomas		2	M	Child	07Ma12Ga
Sophia		.00	F	Infant	07Ma12Ga
BYRNE, Kate		20	F	Unknown	07Ma12Ga
CUMPHAN, Bridget		20	F	Unknown	07Ma12Ga
REILLEY, John		27	M	Unknown	07Ma12Ga
KELLY, John		20	M	Unknown	07Ma12Ga
DOWLEY, John		20	M	Unknown	07Ma12Ga
SEPHRIN, U		36	M	Unknown	07Ma12Ga
U	(W)	36	F	Unknown	07Ma12Ga
Ann		12	F	Unknown	07Ma12Ga
James		10	M	Unknown	07Ma12Ga
John		9	M	Child	07Ma12Ga
William		7	M	Child	07Ma12Ga
Robert		5	M	Child	07Ma12Ga
Sarah		3	F	Child	07Ma12Ga
CARACY, John		22	M	Unknown	07Ma12Ga
LALOR, Wm.		24	M	Unknown	07Ma12Ga
DEVINE, Andrew		30	M	Unknown	07Ma12Ga
WILKS, Samuel		19	M	Unknown	07Ma12Ga
DAVIS, John		20	M	Unknown	07Ma12Ga
MUNSILL, Robt.		40	M	Unknown	07Ma12Ga
DONAL, Win.		20	F	Unknown	07Ma12Ga
Jane		18	F	Unknown	07Ma12Ga

NAMES OF PASSENGERS	AGE	SEX	OCCUPATIONS	DATE PORT SHIP
KELLY, Thos.	30	M	Unknown	07Ma12Ga
John	26	M	Unknown	07Ma12Ga
BOLIG, Wm.	19	M	Unknown	07Ma12Ga
HARLSSIN, Win.	22	F	Unknown	07Ma12Ga
CONNOR, Wm.	23	M	Unknown	07Ma12Ga

SCOTIA 07 MAY 1849

From Arichat

NAMES OF PASSENGERS	AGE	SEX	OCCUPATIONS	DATE PORT SHIP
DOYLE, Peter	27	M	Farmer	07Ma42Fk
LIVINGSTON, Alex	23	M	Farmer	07Ma42Fk

EDWARD 07 MAY 1849

From Limerick

NAMES OF PASSENGERS	AGE	SEX	OCCUPATIONS	DATE PORT SHIP
PURCELL, Mary	20	F	Laborer	07Ma35Fo
KEOGH, James	20	M	Unknown	07Ma35Fo
DOHERTY, Bridget	22	F	Unknown	07Ma35Fo
BROWNE, William	22	M	Unknown	07Ma35Fo
HEALEY, James	34	M	Unknown	07Ma35Fo
John	56	M	Unknown	07Ma35Fo
LYNCH, William	35	M	Unknown	07Ma35Fo
DOHERTY, Pat	30	M	Unknown	07Ma35Fo
FLYNN, Timothy	35	M	Unknown	07Ma35Fo
SHEA, Pat	30	M	Unknown	07Ma35Fo
Hannah	27	F	Unknown	07Ma35Fo
Danl.	20	M	Unknown	07Ma35Fo
FITZGERALD, Hannah	24	F	Unknown	07Ma35Fo
SULLIVAN, Michl.	35	M	Unknown	07Ma35Fo
KEANNEY, Thomas	35	M	Unknown	07Ma35Fo
MOLONY, David	35	M	Unknown	07Ma35Fo
LYONS, Jean	20	M	Unknown	07Ma35Fo
POWERS, Margaret	20	F	Unknown	07Ma35Fo
HEALEY, Patt	22	M	Unknown	07Ma35Fo
Georgiana	50	F	Unknown	07Ma35Fo
Ellen	16	F	Unknown	07Ma35Fo
HERLELY, Daniel	50	M	Unknown	07Ma35Fo
Mary	40	F	Unknown	07Ma35Fo
Cath.	22	F	Unknown	07Ma35Fo
Ellen	20	F	Unknown	07Ma35Fo
Honor	16	F	Unknown	07Ma35Fo
David	15	M	Unknown	07Ma35Fo
Patrick	12	M	Unknown	07Ma35Fo
Morgane	10	F	Unknown	07Ma35Fo
Betsy	8	F	Child	07Ma35Fo
Margery	6	F	Child	07Ma35Fo
Daniel	4	M	Child	07Ma35Fo
Richard	00	M	Unknown	07Ma35Fo
Frank	23	M	Unknown	07Ma35Fo
HIGGINS, Thomas	50	M	Unknown	07Ma35Fo
Margt.	45	F	Unknown	07Ma35Fo
Michl.	20	M	Unknown	07Ma35Fo
Margaret	18	F	Unknown	07Ma35Fo
Mary	11	F	Unknown	07Ma35Fo
John	13	M	Unknown	07Ma35Fo
Thomas	7	M	Child	07Ma35Fo
DANIEL, Bridget	20	F	Unknown	07Ma35Fo
DAVIES, George	22	M	Unknown	07Ma35Fo
HAYES, Dennis	23	M	Unknown	07Ma35Fo
OBRIEN, Michl.	20	M	Unknown	07Ma35Fo
SHEANNY, George	60	M	Unknown	07Ma35Fo

NAMES OF PASSENGERS	AGE	SEX	OCCUPATIONS	DATE PORT SHIP
BRESDAN, Thomas	35	M	Unknown	07Ma35Fo
Cath.	35	F	Unknown	07Ma35Fo
HOGAN, Michl.	8	M	Child	07Ma35Fo
Anne	6	F	Child	07Ma35Fo
RIVIDANE, Emelia	4	F	Child	07Ma35Fo
Cath.	2	F	Child	07Ma35Fo
James	.02	M	Infant	07Ma35Fo
DWYER, John	29	M	Unknown	07Ma35Fo
Honora	28	F	Unknown	07Ma35Fo
Mary	4	F	Child	07Ma35Fo
Dennis	1	M	Child	07Ma35Fo
Mary	.09	F	Infant	07Ma35Fo
OBRIEN, Bridget	20	F	Unknown	07Ma35Fo
DALY, John	35	M	Unknown	07Ma35Fo
Bridget	36	F	Unknown	07Ma35Fo
Mary	5	F	Child	07Ma35Fo
NEILL, Cath.	20	F	Unknown	07Ma35Fo
CORCORAN, Michl.	24	M	Unknown	07Ma35Fo
MCCORMANT, William	24	M	Unknown	07Ma35Fo
OBRIEN, John	40	M	Unknown	07Ma35Fo
Margt.	35	F	Unknown	07Ma35Fo
Bridget	20	F	Unknown	07Ma35Fo
Michl.	21	M	Unknown	07Ma35Fo
Margt.	13	F	Unknown	07Ma35Fo
Cath.	11	F	Unknown	07Ma35Fo
Patt	9	M	Child	07Ma35Fo
Daniel	7	M	Child	07Ma35Fo
ODEA, Thomas	25	M	Unknown	07Ma35Fo
WHEELAN, Thomas	38	M	Unknown	07Ma35Fo
STAPLETON, Michl.	40	M	Unknown	07Ma35Fo
GLEESON, Cath.	17	F	Unknown	07Ma35Fo
QUIN, John	34	M	Unknown	07Ma35Fo
LEARY, William	22	M	Unknown	07Ma35Fo
ODONNELL, Thomas	20	M	Unknown	07Ma35Fo
Richd.	18	M	Unknown	07Ma35Fo
KEATING, Margt.	24	F	Unknown	07Ma35Fo
Honorah	22	F	Unknown	07Ma35Fo
BREMEN, Stephen	50	M	Unknown	07Ma35Fo
Thom.	20	M	Unknown	07Ma35Fo
Margt.	18	F	Unknown	07Ma35Fo
BLAKE, Thomas	30	M	Unknown	07Ma35Fo
CONWAY, Margt.	22	F	Unknown	07Ma35Fo
KEANE, Mary	24	F	Unknown	07Ma35Fo
MCMAHON, Thomas	48	M	Unknown	07Ma35Fo
Bridget	40	F	Unknown	07Ma35Fo
Patt	18	M	Unknown	07Ma35Fo
ROCHE, John	20	M	Unknown	07Ma35Fo
James	18	M	Unknown	07Ma35Fo
SHANNON, Michl.	30	M	Unknown	07Ma35Fo
Timothy	22	M	Unknown	07Ma35Fo
BRENNAN, Martin	23	M	Unknown	07Ma35Fo
QUINHOAN, John	50	M	Unknown	07Ma35Fo
Mary	20	F	Unknown	07Ma35Fo
John	17	M	Unknown	07Ma35Fo
John	32	M	Laborer	07Ma35Fo
Dennis	28	M	Unknown	07Ma35Fo
MUNGOVAN, Thomas	25	M	Unknown	07Ma35Fo
CARTHY, John	35	M	Unknown	07Ma35Fo
Ellen	6	F	Child	07Ma35Fo
KEATING, Edmund	35	M	Unknown	07Ma35Fo
MCINERNY, John	32	M	Unknown	07Ma35Fo
LYNCH, Mary	40	F	Unknown	07Ma35Fo
Cath.	15	F	Unknown	07Ma35Fo
HALPIN, James	26	M	Unknown	07Ma35Fo
John	23	M	Unknown	07Ma35Fo
SHEEBY, Edward	00	M	Unknown	07Ma35Fo
Michl.	10	M	Unknown	07Ma35Fo
John	8	M	Child	07Ma35Fo
Mary	3	F	Child	07Ma35Fo
CREAGH, Michl.	47	M	Unknown	07Ma35Fo
FITZGERALD, Thomas	21	M	Unknown	07Ma35Fo
EVANS, Joseph	25	M	Unknown	07Ma35Fo
Ally	25	M	Unknown	07Ma35Fo
MORAN, Michl.	30	M	Unknown	07Ma35Fo
NICHOL, John	33	M	Unknown	07Ma35Fo

NAMES OF PASSENGERS	AGE	SEX	OCCUPATIONS	DATE PORT SHIP
DWYER, Margt.	30	F	Unknown	07Ma35Fo
FLYNN, Harriet	30	F	Unknown	07Ma35Fo
Margt.	2	F	Child	07Ma35Fo
HAYES, Anne	30	F	Unknown	07Ma35Fo
ODONNELL, David	26	M	Unknown	07Ma35Fo
Patrick	23	M	Unknown	07Ma35Fo
KEATING, John	35	M	Unknown	07Ma35Fo

ARAB 07 MAY 1849

From Belfast

NAMES OF PASSENGERS	AGE	SEX	OCCUPATIONS	DATE PORT SHIP
DEEN, Eliza	21	F	Laborer	07Ma05Fb
DONOHUE, Michael	42	M	Unknown	07Ma05Fb
Nancy	41	F	Unknown	07Ma05Fb
Nancy	13	F	Unknown	07Ma05Fb
Patrick	10	M	Unknown	07Ma05Fb
Francis	6	M	Child	07Ma05Fb
Mary	3	F	Child	07Ma05Fb
GREEN, Ann	22	F	Unknown	07Ma05Fb
Mary	23	F	Unknown	07Ma05Fb
John	48	M	Unknown	07Ma05Fb
TROTTEE, William	25	M	Unknown	07Ma05Fb
LEESE, Ann	20	F	Unknown	07Ma05Fb
Jane	18	F	Unknown	07Ma05Fb
HARVEY, John	34	M	Unknown	07Ma05Fb
Catherine	33	F	Unknown	07Ma05Fb
Mary	13	F	Unknown	07Ma05Fb
Eliza	11	F	Unknown	07Ma05Fb
Ellen	9	F	Child	07Ma05Fb
Thomas	7	M	Child	07Ma05Fb
Patrick	00	M	Unknown	07Ma05Fb
John	.00	M	Infant	07Ma05Fb
MCGEE, William	35	M	Unknown	07Ma05Fb
GROGAN, Peter	18	M	Unknown	07Ma05Fb
GRAHAM, Mary	23	F	Unknown	07Ma05Fb
MCCASKER, Peter	18	M	Unknown	07Ma05Fb
MCKENNA, Owen	40	M	Unknown	07Ma05Fb
KELLY, Hugh	22	M	Unknown	07Ma05Fb
MCHUILAY, Thomas	50	M	Unknown	07Ma05Fb
Thomas	17	M	Unknown	07Ma05Fb
CORBITT, William	24	M	Unknown	07Ma05Fb
James	36	M	Unknown	07Ma05Fb
Mary	16	F	Unknown	07Ma05Fb
Anna	13	F	Unknown	07Ma05Fb
John	10	M	Unknown	07Ma05Fb
James	8	M	Child	07Ma05Fb
MCCAIN, Patrick	40	M	Unknown	07Ma05Fb
CLARKE, Maxwell	45	M	Unknown	07Ma05Fb
Eliza	40	F	Unknown	07Ma05Fb
Mary-Ann	16	F	Unknown	07Ma05Fb
Eliza	13	F	Unknown	07Ma05Fb
Robt.	11	M	Unknown	07Ma05Fb
Agnes	9	F	Child	07Ma05Fb
Sarah	5	F	Child	07Ma05Fb
ROLL, Mathew	18	M	Unknown	07Ma05Fb
Bella	15	F	Unknown	07Ma05Fb
GORMAN, Michl.	26	M	Unknown	07Ma05Fb
MCGARRY, John	24	M	Unknown	07Ma05Fb
FEY, Robt.	20	M	Unknown	07Ma05Fb
MCALLISTER, Margt.	25	F	Unknown	07Ma05Fb
Ann	21	F	Unknown	07Ma05Fb
James	13	M	Unknown	07Ma05Fb
MURPHY, Alex.	21	M	Unknown	07Ma05Fb
MCCLOOGNE, Mary	13	F	Unknown	07Ma05Fb
JOHNSTON, Roger	40	M	Unknown	07Ma05Fb
Mary	37	F	Unknown	07Ma05Fb
Catherine	18	F	Unknown	07Ma05Fb
John	15	M	Unknown	07Ma05Fb
JOHNSTON, Mary	13	F	Unknown	07Ma05Fb
Edw.	12	M	Unknown	07Ma05Fb
Margt.	9	F	Child	07Ma05Fb
Patrick	7	M	Child	07Ma05Fb
Daniel	5	M	Child	07Ma05Fb
James	.00	M	Infant	07Ma05Fb
MULHANY, Robt.	30	M	Unknown	07Ma05Fb
Elizabeth	24	F	Unknown	07Ma05Fb
Jane	.00	F	Infant	07Ma05Fb
LESLIE, Hugh	25	F	Unknown	07Ma05Fb
Dorothy	21	F	Unknown	07Ma05Fb
Robt.	.00	M	Infant	07Ma05Fb
SUNDERLAND, Robt.	26	M	Unknown	07Ma05Fb
MCMANN, Henry	24	M	Unknown	07Ma05Fb
RAY, Patrick	20	M	Unknown	07Ma05Fb
Ellen	18	F	Unknown	07Ma05Fb
TAGGART, Margt.	20	F	Unknown	07Ma05Fb
MCCARTHY, John	20	M	Unknown	07Ma05Fb
Sally	20	F	Unknown	07Ma05Fb
FITZSIMMONS, Mary	20	F	Unknown	07Ma05Fb
LEMON, Rose	20	F	Unknown	07Ma05Fb
MCCARTIN, Nelly	20	F	Unknown	07Ma05Fb
FITZSIMMONS, Pat.	24	M	Unknown	07Ma05Fb
MCGREW, John	30	M	Unknown	07Ma05Fb
MCNAY, James	20	M	Unknown	07Ma05Fb
SMITH, Mary-Jane	20	F	Unknown	07Ma05Fb
MCHELLEY, Joseph	18	M	Unknown	07Ma05Fb
BOYNE, James	21	M	Unknown	07Ma05Fb
DUGGAN, Edw.	21	M	Unknown	07Ma05Fb
Hugh	18	M	Unknown	07Ma05Fb
COLEMAN, John	20	M	Unknown	07Ma05Fb
Bella	16	F	Unknown	07Ma05Fb
PRICE, George	30	M	Unknown	07Ma05Fb
Joseph	25	M	Unknown	07Ma05Fb
MCAVEY, John	19	M	Unknown	07Ma05Fb
Eliza	11	F	Unknown	07Ma05Fb
NEWBERRY, James	50	M	Unknown	07Ma05Fb
Jane	50	F	Unknown	07Ma05Fb
James	28	M	Unknown	07Ma05Fb
Eliza	12	F	Unknown	07Ma05Fb
ABRAHAM, Geo.	22	M	Unknown	07Ma05Fb
NICHOLSON, Jane	20	F	Unknown	07Ma05Fb
CAMERON, John	24	M	Unknown	07Ma05Fb
CRATHER, Saml.	21	M	Unknown	07Ma05Fb
Jane	18	F	Unknown	07Ma05Fb
MORRISON, David	20	M	Unknown	07Ma05Fb
Saml.	30	M	Unknown	07Ma05Fb
DICKEY, Nathaniel	24	M	Unknown	07Ma05Fb
MCCLELLAND, U	34	M	Unknown	07Ma05Fb
James	12	M	Unknown	07Ma05Fb
SANDERSON, James	45	M	Unknown	07Ma05Fb
James	12	M	Unknown	07Ma05Fb
James	10	M	Unknown	07Ma05Fb
James	4	M	Child	07Ma05Fb
MONOHAN, Brid.	22	F	Unknown	07Ma05Fb
MCDONNELL, Cath.	18	F	Unknown	07Ma05Fb
MULLEN, John	22	M	Unknown	07Ma05Fb
Susanna	18	F	Unknown	07Ma05Fb
BEATTY, James	40	M	Unknown	07Ma05Fb
BURNS, Patrick	30	M	Unknown	07Ma05Fb
Margt.	25	F	Unknown	07Ma05Fb
Daniel	17	M	Unknown	07Ma05Fb
MCROBERTS, Edw.	22	M	Unknown	07Ma05Fb
FALLON, Mary	21	F	Unknown	07Ma05Fb
Margt.	19	F	Unknown	07Ma05Fb
MCCHEYNE, James	24	M	Unknown	07Ma05Fb
John	16	M	Unknown	07Ma05Fb
MURRAY, Danl.	20	M	Unknown	07Ma05Fb
MCMANN, Joseph	32	M	Unknown	07Ma05Fb
Mary	32	F	Unknown	07Ma05Fb
CONNELL, Peter	40	M	Unknown	07Ma05Fb
Ann	35	F	Unknown	07Ma05Fb
MCKENNA, Ellen	20	F	Unknown	07Ma05Fb
CONNELL, Thos.	11	M	Unknown	07Ma05Fb
Mary	8	F	Child	07Ma05Fb

NAMES OF PASSENGERS	AGE	SEX	OCCUPATIONS	DATE PORT SHIP
CONNELL, Patk.	.00	M	Infant	07Ma05Fb
Peter	.00	M	Infant	07Ma05Fb
James	8	M	Child	07Ma05Fb
KELLY, Margt.	50	F	Unknown	07Ma05Fb
Henry	20	M	Unknown	07Ma05Fb
Cathe.	18	F	Unknown	07Ma05Fb
DONNELLY, John	20	M	Unknown	07Ma05Fb
MASON, Henry	20	M	Unknown	07Ma05Fb
MCGUINESS, Edw.	24	M	Unknown	07Ma05Fb
Sally	20	F	Unknown	07Ma05Fb
Mary-Ann	.00	F	Infant	07Ma05Fb

JANET 08 MAY 1849

From Liverpool

NAMES OF PASSENGERS	AGE	SEX	OCCUPATIONS	DATE PORT SHIP
U, Geo.	25	M	Watchmaker	08Ma02Fc
BARROW, Geo.	43	M	Laborer	08Ma02Fc
U-Mrs.	32	F	Unknown	08Ma02Fc
MELIA, Mary	40	F	Unknown	08Ma02Fc
BOYAN, Ellen	50	F	Unknown	08Ma02Fc
Edw.	21	M	Unknown	08Ma02Fc
James	17	M	Unknown	08Ma02Fc
Mary	20	F	Unknown	08Ma02Fc
Marcella	18	F	Unknown	08Ma02Fc
John	13	M	Unknown	08Ma02Fc
Thos.	.00	M	Infant	08Ma02Fc
DEE, David	18	M	Unknown	08Ma02Fc
Sally	20	F	Unknown	08Ma02Fc
WARREN, Henry	20	M	Unknown	08Ma02Fc
OBRIEN, Tim	26	M	Unknown	08Ma02Fc
Martin	25	M	Unknown	08Ma02Fc
CAVANAGH, Paul	20	M	Unknown	08Ma02Fc
MULEAHY, John	20	M	Unknown	08Ma02Fc
BURKE, Cath.	35	F	Unknown	08Ma02Fc
Cath.	35	F	Unknown	08Ma02Fc
Eliza	12	F	Unknown	08Ma02Fc
U	4	U	Child	08Ma02Fc
MAGUINE, Kate	.00	F	Infant	08Ma02Fc
MCCANN, Con.	22	M	Unknown	08Ma02Fc
Thos.	27	M	Unknown	08Ma02Fc
Inez	25	F	Unknown	08Ma02Fc
KEARNEY, Mary	20	F	Unknown	08Ma02Fc
LEONARD, John	25	M	Unknown	08Ma02Fc
CARRIGAN, Mat.	20	M	Unknown	08Ma02Fc
MCTIGH, Andrew.	25	M	Unknown	08Ma02Fc
MCNUTTY, Pat.	24	M	Unknown	08Ma02Fc
CAFFERTY, Pat.	26	M	Unknown	08Ma02Fc
SHANNON, Walter	38	M	Cooper	08Ma02Fc
John	4	M	Child	08Ma02Fc
Mary	.00	F	Infant	08Ma02Fc
FAGAN, Pat.	36	M	Laborer	08Ma02Fc
Bridget	25	F	Unknown	08Ma02Fc
CLARKE, James	36	M	Unknown	08Ma02Fc
Sarah	34	F	Unknown	08Ma02Fc
John	.00	M	Infant	08Ma02Fc
Pat	9	M	Child	08Ma02Fc
Cath.	3	F	Child	08Ma02Fc
MCGUIRE, John	32	M	Laborer	08Ma02Fc
SHANGHESSEY, Pat.	26	M	Unknown	08Ma02Fc
KELLY, Pat.	32	M	Unknown	08Ma02Fc
NAUGHTON, Dennis	26	M	Unknown	08Ma02Fc
SULLIVAN, Danl.	25	M	Unknown	08Ma02Fc
HALORAN, John	22	M	Unknown	08Ma02Fc
COLLON, Pat	22	M	Unknown	08Ma02Fc
MURPHY, Mary	20	F	Unknown	08Ma02Fc
BALDWIN, Mary	22	F	Unknown	08Ma02Fc
LEARY, John	30	M	Unknown	08Ma02Fc
Cath.	5	F	Child	08Ma02Fc

NAMES OF PASSENGERS	AGE	SEX	OCCUPATIONS	DATE PORT SHIP
REID, John	35	M	Unknown	08Ma02Fc
Mary	32	F	Unknown	08Ma02Fc
WARREN, U	45	U	Unknown	08Ma02Fc
REID, Nancy	.00	F	Infant	08Ma02Fc
BARRETT, Jas.	23	M	Unknown	08Ma02Fc
DUNN, Richard	30	M	Unknown	08Ma02Fc
DWYER, Wm.	25	M	Unknown	08Ma02Fc
DOLAN, Jas.	40	M	Unknown	08Ma02Fc
Pat	5	M	Child	08Ma02Fc
DIGNAN, Pat.	33	M	Unknown	08Ma02Fc
MURPHY, Hugh	27	M	Unknown	08Ma02Fc
MCNIFF, Pat	27	M	Unknown	08Ma02Fc
CRAMER, Pat	30	M	Unknown	08Ma02Fc
Bridget	30	F	Unknown	08Ma02Fc
Mary	10	F	Unknown	08Ma02Fc
Ann	5	F	Child	08Ma02Fc
GANOR, Thos.	23	M	Unknown	08Ma02Fc
Ellen	21	F	Unknown	08Ma02Fc
Cath.	.00	F	Infant	08Ma02Fc
MCTAGER, Honora	22	F	Unknown	08Ma02Fc
Mary	18	F	Unknown	08Ma02Fc
OBRIEN, Cath.	17	F	Unknown	08Ma02Fc
Jane	11	F	Unknown	08Ma02Fc
MURPHY, Wm.	17	M	Butcher	08Ma02Fc
CONNOR, Pat	26	M	Laborer	08Ma02Fc
ASH, Mat.	30	M	Unknown	08Ma02Fc
RYAN, Jyan	50	M	Unknown	08Ma02Fc
Johanna	30	F	Unknown	08Ma02Fc
Jn.	12	U	Unknown	08Ma02Fc
Eliza	.00	F	Infant	08Ma02Fc
WRICKSON, Dennis	24	M	Blacksmith	08Ma02Fc
Mary	24	F	Unknown	08Ma02Fc
CARTY, William	19	M	Laborer	08Ma02Fc
Alice	18	F	Unknown	08Ma02Fc
PIERSON, Cath.	20	F	Unknown	08Ma02Fc
LANE, Wm.	40	M	Unknown	08Ma02Fc
Danl.	35	M	Unknown	08Ma02Fc
KINNINGTON, Wm.	25	M	Unknown	08Ma02Fc
MASON, Jas.	28	M	Laborer	08Ma02Fc
Mary	25	F	Unknown	08Ma02Fc
Bridget	15	F	Unknown	08Ma02Fc
MCDONALD, Pat.	30	M	Unknown	08Ma02Fc
FLEMMING, John	24	M	Stctr	08Ma02Fc
LEONARD, Ellen	30	F	Unknown	08Ma02Fc
DOBBINS, Ann	15	F	Unknown	08Ma02F
GRADY, John	46	M	Laborer	08Ma02F
Mary	13	F	Laborer	08Ma02F
SCANLON, Pat	36	M	Unknown	08Ma02F
KELLY, Michl.	40	M	Unknown	08Ma02F
DONNELL, Pat	50	M	Unknown	08Ma02F
BRANNIGAN, Hannah	20	F	Unknown	08Ma02F
GEATLEY, Pat.	22	M	Unknown	08Ma02F
Michl.	19	M	Unknown	08Ma02F
John	50	M	Unknown	08Ma02F
Bridget	13	F	Unknown	08Ma02F
Mary	10	F	Unknown	08Ma02F
MURPHY, Rich.	27	M	Unknown	08Ma02F
Cath.	26	F	Unknown	08Ma02F
CONNOR, Michl.	22	M	Unknown	08Ma02F
SHEILDS, Michl.	20	M	Baker	08Ma02F
BRIEN, Edw.	20	M	Laborer	08Ma02F
BREWEN, Jno.	30	M	Unknown	08Ma02F
U-Mrs.	31	F	Unknown	08Ma02F
Henry	33	M	Unknown	08Ma02F
Eliza	9	F	Child	08Ma02F
Ann	6	F	Child	08Ma02F
Sarah	.00	F	Infant	08Ma02F
Henry	.00	M	Infant	08Ma02F
DOLAN, Ann	30	F	Unknown	08Ma02F
DONOVAN, Jerh.	25	M	Unknown	08Ma02F
DRISCOLL, Timy.	24	M	Unknown	08Ma02F
CASEY, Pat Died-At-Sea	30	M	Unknown	08Ma02F
MURPHY, Mary Died-At-Sea	18	F	Unknown	08Ma02F

NAMES OF PASSENGERS	AGE	SEX	OCCUPATIONS	DATE PORT SHIP
MCCANN, Dennis	21	M	Unknown	08Ma02Fc
Died-At-Sea				
CLARKE, Margt.	.00	F	Infant	08Ma02Fc
Died-At-Sea				
BREWEN, John	4	M	Child	08Ma02Fc
WRICKSON, Mary	.00	F	Infant	08Ma02Fc
Born-At-Sea				
BARROW, U	.00	F	Infant	08Ma02Fc
Born-At-Sea Died-At-Sea				
LEARY, Mary	3	F	Child	08Ma02Fc
MCCOOM, Joseph	28	M	Unknown	08Ma02Fc

STANDARD 08 MAY 1849

From Belfast

NAMES OF PASSENGERS	AGE	SEX	OCCUPATIONS	DATE PORT SHIP
KENNEDY, Hugh	19	M	Farmer	08Ma05GI
MORGAN, James	20	M	Farmer	08Ma05GI
MCCLATCHY, Nan	22	F	Unknown	08Ma05GI
STOPFORD, John	19	M	Unknown	08Ma05GI
FINLEY, James	24	M	Unknown	08Ma05GI
Susan	26	F	Unknown	08Ma05GI
U	.00	U	Infant	08Ma05GI
MOOREHEAD, James	20	M	Unknown	08Ma05GI
DUFFY, Patrick	20	M	Unknown	08Ma05GI
Mary	50	F	Unknown	08Ma05GI
Nancy	22	F	Unknown	08Ma05GI
ROGAN, Ester	18	F	Unknown	08Ma05GI
RICE, Robert	20	M	Unknown	08Ma05GI
Clare	19	F	Unknown	08Ma05GI
Elizabeth	28	F	Unknown	08Ma05GI
ROLSTON, Elizabeth	24	F	Unknown	08Ma05GI
OHAGEN, Elizabeth	30	F	Unknown	08Ma05GI
GRAHAM, Ellen	16	F	Unknown	08Ma05GI
MCAVEY, Hugh	33	M	Unknown	08Ma05GI
FORNAM, Richard	20	M	Unknown	08Ma05GI
MCKEE, James	20	M	Unknown	08Ma05GI
NELSON, John	21	M	Unknown	08Ma05GI
ARGAN, Eliza	30	F	Unknown	08Ma05GI
Charles	6	M	Child	08Ma05GI
William	4	M	Child	08Ma05GI
Francis	.00	M	Infant	08Ma05GI
IXON, Ellen	19	F	Unknown	08Ma05GI
Elizabeth	17	F	Unknown	08Ma05GI
ARKER, Samuel	20	M	Unknown	08Ma05GI
ANN, Margaret	24	F	Unknown	08Ma05GI
UDEY, Patrick	40	M	Unknown	08Ma05GI
Sarah	30	F	Unknown	08Ma05GI
Patrick	13	M	Unknown	08Ma05GI
J.	.00	M	Infant	08Ma05GI
OYER, Owen	22	M	Unknown	08Ma05GI
RINGLE, John	25	M	Unknown	08Ma05GI
OHNSON, John	50	M	Unknown	08Ma05GI
Jane	50	F	Unknown	08Ma05GI
Mary-Jane	18	F	Unknown	08Ma05GI
John	16	M	Unknown	08Ma05GI
Jane	.00	F	Infant	08Ma05GI
ENNEDY, Jane	15	F	Unknown	08Ma05GI
ILSON, Jane	20	F	Unknown	08Ma05GI
ACKARD, Patrick	26	M	Unknown	08Ma05GI
Allan	30	M	Unknown	08Ma05GI
U	.00	U	Infant	08Ma05GI
RADY, John	15	F	Unknown	08Ma05GI
ONNELL, Catharine	40	F	Unknown	08Ma05GI
RUCE, Charles	25	M	Unknown	08Ma05GI
Isabella	19	F	Unknown	08Ma05GI
RTY, Catherine	19	F	Unknown	08Ma05GI
ULKNER, William	22	M	Unknown	08Ma05GI
LLER, Robert	22	M	Unknown	08Ma05GI
MITCHEL, Thomas	20	M	Unknown	08Ma05GI
DICKERSON, James	30	M	Unknown	08Ma05GI
Francis	29	M	Unknown	08Ma05GI
Robert	24	M	Unknown	08Ma05GI
Eliza	21	F	Unknown	08Ma05GI
Robert	.00	M	Infant	08Ma05GI
SCOTT, Eliza	26	F	Unknown	08Ma05GI
DUGAN, Arthur	28	M	Unknown	08Ma05GI
Mary	16	F	Unknown	08Ma05GI
David	15	M	Unknown	08Ma05GI
MCCLELLAN, Adam	30	M	Unknown	08Ma05GI
Mary	20	F	Unknown	08Ma05GI
Jane	5	F	Child	08Ma05GI
James	2	M	Child	08Ma05GI
Robert	.00	M	Infant	08Ma05GI
SCAMPBEL, Robert	25	M	Unknown	08Ma05GI
MORRISON, Michal	20	M	Unknown	08Ma05GI
Jane	22	F	Unknown	08Ma05GI
Ann	25	F	Unknown	08Ma05GI
CRULY, James	20	M	Unknown	08Ma05GI
KERNAN, John	19	M	Unknown	08Ma05GI
Peter	20	M	Unknown	08Ma05GI
Mary	21	F	Unknown	08Ma05GI
KILION, James	30	M	Unknown	08Ma05GI
MCLANLEN, Robert	26	M	Unknown	08Ma05GI
GRUNN, John	40	M	Unknown	08Ma05GI
BRIAN, John	36	M	Unknown	08Ma05GI
Catherine	30	F	Unknown	08Ma05GI
CRENAN, J.	20	F	Unknown	08Ma05GI
KERNAN, James	20	M	Unknown	08Ma05GI
LITTLE, Robert	20	M	Unknown	08Ma05GI
MCCARTNY, J.G.H.	24	M	Unknown	08Ma05GI
Eliza	27	F	Unknown	08Ma05GI
KILLAN, John	24	M	Unknown	08Ma05GI
MULLON, Henry	24	M	Unknown	08Ma05GI
LYNCH, Mary	50	F	Unknown	08Ma05GI
John	20	M	Unknown	08Ma05GI
Frances	.00	F	Infant	08Ma05GI
COLVILLE, Alexander	37	M	Unknown	08Ma05GI
Alexander	25	M	Unknown	08Ma05GI
NOLELAN, Margret	29	F	Unknown	08Ma05GI
MATHEW, George	18	M	Unknown	08Ma05GI
DELZULE, Alexander	20	M	Unknown	08Ma05GI
CERR, Francis	35	M	Unknown	08Ma05GI
CUNNINGHAM, Charles	24	M	Unknown	08Ma05GI
BROWN, David	21	M	Unknown	08Ma05GI
WALLACE, Hugh	50	M	Unknown	08Ma05GI
Michal	50	F	Unknown	08Ma05GI
Joseph	20	M	Unknown	08Ma05GI
William	18	M	Unknown	08Ma05GI
Margaret	16	F	Unknown	08Ma05GI
John	14	M	Unknown	08Ma05GI
Hugh	12	M	Unknown	08Ma05GI
James	10	M	Unknown	08Ma05GI
David	8	M	Child	08Ma05GI
MCWHERRY, Jane	30	F	Unknown	08Ma05GI
MCSHAIN, James	46	M	Unknown	08Ma05GI
Margret	46	F	Unknown	08Ma05GI
Maria	12	F	Unknown	08Ma05GI
Sarah	10	F	Unknown	08Ma05GI
Mary	8	F	Child	08Ma05GI
Eliza	6	F	Child	08Ma05GI
John	3	M	Child	08Ma05GI
James	.00	M	Infant	08Ma05GI
AICKEN, John	50	M	Unknown	08Ma05GI
REECE, Eliza	44	F	Unknown	08Ma05GI
Hugh	19	M	Unknown	08Ma05GI
Robert	15	M	Unknown	08Ma05GI
MCCLURE, John	19	M	Unknown	08Ma05GI
NICHOLSON, Bridget	28	F	Unknown	08Ma05GI
William	3	M	Child	08Ma05GI
Felix	2	M	Child	08Ma05GI
Mary-Jane	.00	F	Infant	08Ma05GI
SCOTT, Jane	46	F	Unknown	08Ma05GI
Ann	26	F	Unknown	08Ma05GI

NAMES OF PASSENGERS	AGE	SEX	OCCUPATIONS	DATE PORT SHIP
SCOTT, Francis	24	M	Unknown	08Ma05GI
Jane	19	F	Unknown	08Ma05GI
Richard	15	M	Unknown	08Ma05GI
Blaney	13	M	Unknown	08Ma05GI
Fanny	2	F	Child	08Ma05GI
Ann	.00	F	Infant	08Ma05GI
NEILL, Francis	25	M	Unknown	08Ma05GI
GILBERT, U	30	M	Unknown	08Ma05GI
Carson	10	M	Unknown	08Ma05GI
DOUGHERY, James	50	M	Unknown	08Ma05GI
TAYLOR, James	45	M	Unknown	08Ma05GI
Ellen	30	F	Unknown	08Ma05GI
U	.00	U	Infant	08Ma05GI
ROSS, Henry	50	M	Unknown	08Ma05GI
U (W)	50	F	Unknown	08Ma05GI
Robert	25	M	Unknown	08Ma05GI
Isabella	21	F	Unknown	08Ma05GI
John	19	M	Unknown	08Ma05GI
William	17	M	Unknown	08Ma05GI
GEORGEAN, I.	18	U	Unknown	08Ma05GI
Isabella	22	F	Unknown	08Ma05GI
Fanny	20	F	Unknown	08Ma05GI
Richard	16	M	Unknown	08Ma05GI
Eliza	38	F	Unknown	08Ma05GI
Catharine	16	F	Unknown	08Ma05GI
TELSTON, John	22	M	Unknown	08Ma05GI
MCKILBER, Mary-Jane	20	F	Unknown	08Ma05GI
QUINN, Michal	35	U	Unknown	08Ma05GI
Hugh	15	M	Unknown	08Ma05GI
James	11	M	Unknown	08Ma05GI
Margret	9	F	Child	08Ma05GI
Michal	.00	U	Infant	08Ma05GI
MCKENGER, Richard	22	M	Unknown	08Ma05GI
Mary-Ann	20	F	Unknown	08Ma05GI
HAETER, William	20	M	Unknown	08Ma05GI
CELLOTT, Robert	40	M	Unknown	08Ma05GI
Jane	40	F	Unknown	08Ma05GI
John	38	M	Unknown	08Ma05GI
Margret	.00	F	Infant	08Ma05GI
STEWARD, Cab.	25	U	Unknown	08Ma05GI
MCGEE, Andrew	24	M	Unknown	08Ma05GI
Catherine	21	F	Unknown	08Ma05GI
MURPHY, James	35	M	Unknown	08Ma05GI
MCDERMOTT, Arthur	36	M	Unknown	08Ma05GI
Mary	30	F	Unknown	08Ma05GI
Eliza	10	F	Unknown	08Ma05GI
Rosey-Ann	7	F	Child	08Ma05GI
MCCONNEL, John	30	M	Unknown	08Ma05GI
MCARDLE, Peter	40	M	Unknown	08Ma05GI
Rose	30	F	Unknown	08Ma05GI
Pat	11	M	Unknown	08Ma05GI
Edward	9	M	Child	08Ma05GI
Bridget	7	F	Child	08Ma05GI
Mer.	5	U	Child	08Ma05GI
John	3	M	Child	08Ma05GI
James	.00	M	Infant	08Ma05GI
ROSS, Mary-A.	19	F	Unknown	08Ma05GI
RILCHER, Robert	00	M	Unknown	08Ma05GI

AMERICA 08 MAY 1849

From Liverpool And Halifax

NAMES OF PASSENGERS	AGE	SEX	OCCUPATIONS	DATE PORT SHIP
BATES, Joshua	58	M	Merchant	08Ma49Eb
Lucretia	40	F	Unknown	08Ma49Eb
ERICKSON, Charlotte	18	F	Unknown	08Ma49Eb
KERR, Thos.	29	M	Merchant	08Ma49Eb
THOMAS, U	15	F	Unknown	08Ma49Eb
Kate	17	F	Unknown	08Ma49Eb
LEVEY, Charles-E.	75	M	Merchant	08Ma49Eb
Jeremiah	20	F	Unknown	08Ma49Eb
MAY, Sophia	28	F	Unknown	08Ma49Eb
PEMBERTON, George	40	M	Unknown	08Ma49Eb
TOBY, G.	65	M	Gentleman	08Ma49Eb
TORRY, J.B.	48	M	Gentleman	08Ma49Eb
GREENSHEILD, W.G.	49	M	Gentleman	08Ma49Eb
CUVILLIER, A.	55	M	Gentleman	08Ma49Eb
MACKAY, Joseph	33	M	Merchant	08Ma49Eb
BEAMIN, Wm.J.C.	32	M	Merchant	08Ma49Eb
SMITH, John	24	M	Merchant	08Ma49Eb
LEWIS, D.	27	M	Merchant	08Ma49Eb
JOHNSTON, James	30	M	Merchant	08Ma49Eb
NICKEY, Edw.	45	M	Merchant	08Ma49Eb
WILDMAY, Humphrey	23	M	Merchant	08Ma49Eb
ARTHUR, Alex	35	M	Merchant	08Ma49Eb
WAINWRIGHT, Richard	40	M	Merchant	08Ma49Eb
STRICKLAND, Fred.	29	M	Merchant	08Ma49Eb
MCBLAIR, Henry	26	M	Merchant	08Ma49Eb
CONNOLLY, M.	50	M	Merchant	08Ma49Eb
REILLY, Richard	35	M	Merchant	08Ma49Eb
CHRISTIAN, Alex.	29	M	Gentleman	08Ma49Eb
CRAGGS, F.	40	M	Gentleman	08Ma49Eb
U-Mrs.	35	F	Gentleman	08Ma49Eb
MURPHY, Edw.J.	49	M	Engineer	08Ma49Eb
PATTERSON, U-Mrs.	22	F	Unknown	08Ma49Eb
PARKIN, J.	29	M	Gentleman	08Ma49Eb
DYKES, A.	26	M	Farmer	08Ma49Eb
GARGARD, W.	24	M	Laborer	08Ma49Eb
WILKINSON, E.	37	M	Laborer	08Ma49Eb
WARD, Wm.W.	16	M	Unknown	08Ma49Eb
STRICKLAND, Henry	28	M	Unknown	08Ma49Eb
LINN, Wm.	36	M	Merchant	08Ma49Eb
BRUYERE, O.B.	38	M	Merchant	08Ma49Eb
GLANNELL, Wm.	47	M	Merchant	08Ma49Eb
EDWARDS, Jas.A.	30	M	Jeweller	08Ma49Eb
GRAGG, Mary-Mrs.	35	F	Unknown	08Ma49Eb
LEWIS, Mary	23	F	Unknown	08Ma49Eb
PATTERSON, John	2	M	Child	08Ma49Eb
ROBERTS, Elizabeth	25	F	Unknown	08Ma49Eb

ORINOCO 08 MAY 1849

From Waterford

NAMES OF PASSENGERS	AGE	SEX	OCCUPATIONS	DATE PORT SHIP
HERLINGS, James	25	M	Unknown	08Ma15G
Catherine	23	F	Unknown	08Ma15G
FITZGERALD, Catherine	22	F	Unknown	08Ma15G
Margret	20	F	Unknown	08Ma15G
QUANE, William	30	M	Unknown	08Ma15G
BRIEN, Catherine	19	F	Unknown	08Ma15G
HAYS, Judea	21	U	Unknown	08Ma15G
MCDONNELL, John	40	M	Unknown	08Ma15G
Margret	38	F	Unknown	08Ma15G
MCNAMARA, Mary	21	F	Unknown	08Ma15G
HAYES, Janet	30	F	Unknown	08Ma15G
John	21	M	Unknown	08Ma15G
MALONEY, Patrick	25	M	Unknown	08Ma15G
Alice	23	F	Unknown	08Ma15G
Edward	19	M	Unknown	08Ma15G
John	17	M	Unknown	08Ma15G
Cathern	16	F	Unknown	08Ma15G
Patrick	15	M	Unknown	08Ma15G
Thomas	14	M	Unknown	08Ma15G
Joseph	13	M	Unknown	08Ma15G
Keryan	7	F	Child	08Ma15G
Margret	.00	F	Infant	08Ma15G
MCNAMARA, Patrick	21	M	Unknown	08Ma15G
MULHONEY, Thomas	32	M	Unknown	08Ma15G

NAMES OF PASSENGERS	AGE	SEX	OCCUPATIONS	DATE PORT SHIP
CODY, Margret	22	F	Unknown	08Ma15Gb
Mary	19	F	Unknown	08Ma15Gb
Judy	17	F	Unknown	08Ma15Gb
James	16	M	Unknown	08Ma15Gb
Patrick	12	M	Unknown	08Ma15Gb
William	.00	M	Infant	08Ma15Gb
CONIG, Perse	25	U	Unknown	08Ma15Gb
DUNNE, Ann	20	F	Unknown	08Ma15Gb
KAND, Margret	33	F	Unknown	08Ma15Gb
DOHERTY, Stephan	40	M	Unknown	08Ma15Gb
Richard	39	M	Unknown	08Ma15Gb
RYAN, Michal	19	M	Unknown	08Ma15Gb
MURPHY, James	49	M	Unknown	08Ma15Gb
Margret	47	F	Unknown	08Ma15Gb
HOWEL, Bridget	21	F	Unknown	08Ma15Gb
DOODY, Matthew	12	M	Unknown	08Ma15Gb
HENESSEY, Sylvester	21	M	Unknown	08Ma15Gb
KELLY, Michal	45	M	Unknown	08Ma15Gb
John	39	M	Unknown	08Ma15Gb
SPARK, Fiderick	42	M	Unknown	08Ma15Gb
WHITE, Wall	39	U	Unknown	08Ma15Gb
Benjamine	38	M	Unknown	08Ma15Gb
Deb.	7	F	Child	08Ma15Gb
Samuel	.00	M	Infant	08Ma15Gb
VILCH, George	40	M	Unknown	08Ma15Gb
Jane	38	F	Unknown	08Ma15Gb
ARDAGH, Kate	19	F	Unknown	08Ma15Gb
MCGRATH, Richard	17	M	Unknown	08Ma15Gb
DONNEDY, William	41	M	Unknown	08Ma15Gb
Margret	38	F	Unknown	08Ma15Gb
James	9	M	Child	08Ma15Gb
Margret	.00	F	Infant	08Ma15Gb
HAYES, John	33	M	Unknown	08Ma15Gb
Jane	30	F	Unknown	08Ma15Gb
FITZGERALD, Pierce	28	M	Unknown	08Ma15Gb
BRYAN, Thomas	42	M	Unknown	08Ma15Gb
BOLTON, Mary	21	F	Unknown	08Ma15Gb
Bridget	20	F	Unknown	08Ma15Gb
MARTIN, Edward	40	M	Unknown	08Ma15Gb
Jane	38	F	Unknown	08Ma15Gb
Janson	19	M	Unknown	08Ma15Gb
Mary	17	F	Unknown	08Ma15Gb
Sarah	15	F	Unknown	08Ma15Gb
Martha	13	F	Unknown	08Ma15Gb
Henry	.00	M	Infant	08Ma15Gb
POWER, William	40	M	Unknown	08Ma15Gb
Michal	38	M	Unknown	08Ma15Gb
ENNAN, Martin	25	M	Unknown	08Ma15Gb
OWLETT, Catherine	40	F	Unknown	08Ma15Gb
ALSH, Margret	49	F	Unknown	08Ma15Gb
Jane	40	F	Unknown	08Ma15Gb
Mary	19	F	Unknown	08Ma15Gb
Patrick	17	M	Unknown	08Ma15Gb
Catherine	16	F	Unknown	08Ma15Gb
Margret	.00	F	Infant	08Ma15Gb
TAGGARD, Catherine	40	F	Unknown	08Ma15Gb
Thomas	38	M	Unknown	08Ma15Gb
Edward	7	M	Child	08Ma15Gb
Margret	.00	F	Infant	08Ma15Gb
ROWNE, Catherine	42	F	Unknown	08Ma15Gb
TAFFORD, Ellen	34	F	Unknown	08Ma15Gb
ROTTY, Johanna	40	F	Unknown	08Ma15Gb
Bridget	32	F	Unknown	08Ma15Gb
OWER, Perse	42	U	Unknown	08Ma15Gb
YAN, Patrick	42	M	Unknown	08Ma15Gb
Johannah	40	F	Unknown	08Ma15Gb
Margret	.00	F	Infant	08Ma15Gb
OWER, Thomas	40	M	Unknown	08Ma15Gb
IRBY, Catherine	40	F	Unknown	08Ma15Gb
Nora	34	F	Unknown	08Ma15Gb
ALSH, William	39	M	Unknown	08Ma15Gb
RITT, John	40	M	Unknown	08Ma15Gb
ITE, Michal	39	M	Unknown	08Ma15Gb
James	37	M	Unknown	08Ma15Gb
NCTON, George	19	M	Unknown	08Ma15Gb
MCDONALD, Jane	40	F	Unknown	08Ma15Gb
Sarah	38	F	Unknown	08Ma15Gb
SPRING, Catherine	14	F	Unknown	08Ma15Gb
KEEFFY, Mara	30	F	Unknown	08Ma15Gb
DUMFALEX, Patrick	19	M	Unknown	08Ma15Gb
DENNAN, Michal	42	M	Unknown	08Ma15Gb
RAHES, Alice	19	F	Unknown	08Ma15Gb
Anty	17	F	Unknown	08Ma15Gb
DOLLARD, James	40	M	Unknown	08Ma15Gb
DEMPSY, Mary	47	F	Unknown	08Ma15Gb
SHANAHAN, John	40	M	Unknown	08Ma15Gb
Michal	30	M	Unknown	08Ma15Gb
CORCORAN, Mary	14	F	Unknown	08Ma15Gb
HANNAGAN, Thomas	24	M	Unknown	08Ma15Gb
John	20	M	Unknown	08Ma15Gb
MALLONEY, Nancy	42	F	Unknown	08Ma15Gb
CALBERT, Bridget	38	F	Unknown	08Ma15Gb
POWER, Bridget	17	F	Unknown	08Ma15Gb
Died-At-Sea				
Michal	15	M	Unknown	08Ma15Gb
WALSH, Thomas	29	M	Unknown	08Ma15Gb
John	27	M	Unknown	08Ma15Gb
PHELAN, Patrick	40	M	Unknown	08Ma15Gb
Jane	48	F	Unknown	08Ma15Gb
HANTORE, John	14	M	Unknown	08Ma15Gb
WALSH, Thomas	17	M	Unknown	08Ma15Gb
MCDONALD, John	17	M	Unknown	08Ma15Gb
BECKEY, John	14	M	Unknown	08Ma15Gb
POWER, John	42	M	Unknown	08Ma15Gb
WALMAN, Margret	40	F	Unknown	08Ma15Gb
Antios	38	U	Unknown	08Ma15Gb
James	.00	M	Infant	08Ma15Gb
SANOTT, James	41	M	Unknown	08Ma15Gb
Michal	38	M	Unknown	08Ma15Gb
POWAL, Patrick	19	M	Unknown	08Ma15Gb
HURLEY, William	45	M	Unknown	08Ma15Gb
POWER, Thomas	39	M	Unknown	08Ma15Gb
CONNELLY, Mary	19	F	Unknown	08Ma15Gb
TANNING, Martin	15	M	Unknown	08Ma15Gb
ROWE, Thomas	17	M	Unknown	08Ma15Gb
NADDAY, Edward	21	M	Unknown	08Ma15Gb
BERGAN, Mary	25	F	Unknown	08Ma15Gb
QUINN, James	42	M	Unknown	08Ma15Gb
COFFAY, Margret	44	F	Unknown	08Ma15Gb
MORAN, Mary	17	F	Unknown	08Ma15Gb
EGAN, James	42	M	Unknown	08Ma15Gb
MORAN, Ellen	14	F	Unknown	08Ma15Gb
DEMPSEY, Richard	25	M	Unknown	08Ma15Gb
CARROL, Nancy	42	F	Unknown	08Ma15Gb
ADAMS, John	29	M	Unknown	08Ma15Gb
Hana	.00	F	Infant	08Ma15Gb
HOGAN, Silvester	30	M	Unknown	08Ma15Gb
MORAN, Jane	20	F	Unknown	08Ma15Gb
PHELAN, Richard	21	M	Unknown	08Ma15Gb
CONNEY, Laurence	24	M	Unknown	08Ma15Gb
Norry	40	M	Unknown	08Ma15Gb
MALONE, James	21	M	Unknown	08Ma15Gb
BAYAN, Sarah	10	F	Unknown	08Ma15Gb
William	14	M	Unknown	08Ma15Gb
Margt.	25	F	Unknown	08Ma15Gb
STOKES, James	28	M	Unknown	08Ma15Gb
Bridget	20	F	Unknown	08Ma15Gb
SHANAHAN, Catherin	42	F	Unknown	08Ma15Gb
SENICA, John	16	M	Unknown	08Ma15Gb
MULLOONEY, Mary	18	F	Unknown	08Ma15Gb
HURM, William	40	M	Unknown	08Ma15Gb
BLAKE, Anty	41	F	Unknown	08Ma15Gb
Thomas	13	M	Unknown	08Ma15Gb
MANOGH, Nancy	18	F	Unknown	08Ma15Gb
Patrick	24	M	Unknown	08Ma15Gb
WALSH, Catherine	9	F	Child	08Ma15Gb
MAHER, Biddy	17	F	Unknown	08Ma15Gb
FAGAN, George	42	M	Unknown	08Ma15Gb
Mary	47	F	Unknown	08Ma15Gb
Thomas	19	M	Unknown	08Ma15Gb

NAMES OF PASSENGERS	AGE	SEX	OCCUPATIONS	DATE PORT SHIP
FAGAN, Bridget	18	F	Unknown	08Ma15Gb
Ann	40	F	Unknown	08Ma15Gb
Ambros	32	M	Unknown	08Ma15Gb
Mary	27	F	Unknown	08Ma15Gb
Biddy	.00	F	Infant	08Ma15Gb
WHITE, Walter	20	M	Unknown	08Ma15Gb
Thomas	12	M	Unknown	08Ma15Gb
WALSH, Richd.	50	M	Unknown	08Ma15Gb
DELANY, Thos.	25	M	Unknown	08Ma15Gb
KENNEDY, Edwd.	20	M	Unknown	08Ma15Gb

EMPEROR 08 MAY 1849

From Sunderland

NAMES OF PASSENGERS	AGE	SEX	OCCUPATIONS	DATE PORT SHIP
MURPHY, Peter	28	M	Laborer	08Ma36Ah
DONOVAN, James	27	M	Laborer	08Ma36Ah
MCGEE, Peter	23	M	Unknown	08Ma36Ah
FANNIGAN, Danl.	25	M	Unknown	08Ma36Ah
ARTSON, Thos.	20	M	Unknown	08Ma36Ah
LOFTUS, John	21	M	Unknown	08Ma36Ah
ROSS, Thos.	35	M	Unknown	08Ma36Ah

NUMA 08 MAY 1849

From Hartlepool

NAMES OF PASSENGERS	AGE	SEX	OCCUPATIONS	DATE PORT SHIP
HASSEL, John	29	M	Painter	08Ma51Ez
Margaret	20	F	Unknown	08Ma51Ez
Charles	7	M	Child	08Ma51Ez
PATTERSON, Thomas	39	M	Sawer	08Ma51Ez
Elizabeth	39	F	Unknown	08Ma51Ez
John	4	M	Child	08Ma51Ez
SMITH, Rawlins	39	M	Blacksmith	08Ma51Ez
Jane	54	F	Unknown	08Ma51Ez
Robert	14	M	Unknown	08Ma51Ez
GREATHEAD, Edward	26	M	Pitman	08Ma51Ez
Elizabeth	23	F	Unknown	08Ma51Ez
Elizabeth-Ann	3	F	Child	08Ma51Ez
FILLER, Martha	21	F	Unknown	08Ma51Ez
George	27	M	Pitman	08Ma51Ez
Mary-Ann	2	F	Child	08Ma51Ez
GULLICK, James	39	M	Pitman	08Ma51Ez
Clementina (W)	37	F	Wife	08Ma51Ez
Jane	7	F	Child	08Ma51Ez
James	5	M	Child	08Ma51Ez
Clementina	1	F	Child	08Ma51Ez

HONOR 08 MAY 1849

From Limerick

NAMES OF PASSENGERS	AGE	SEX	OCCUPATIONS	DATE PORT SHIP
BUTLER, Cath.	20	F	Matron	08Ma35Ey
Fanny	.11	F	Infant	08Ma35Ey
CORBETT, Cath.	25	F	Spinster	08Ma35Ey
James	30	M	Farmer	08Ma35Ey
LAKER, Marty	24	M	Unknown	08Ma35Ey
DUNDIN, Philip	23	M	Unknown	08Ma35Ey
Patt	18	M	Unknown	08Ma35Ey
Honora	20	F	Unknown	08Ma35Ey
MORAN, Margt.	20	F	Unknown	08Ma35Ey
RYAN, John	16	M	Unknown	08Ma35Ey
Ellen	19	F	Unknown	08Ma35Ey
CUNNEEN, Ellen	22	F	Unknown	08Ma35Ey
Patt	23	M	Unknown	08Ma35Ey
John	18	M	Unknown	08Ma35Ey
MURREY, John	60	M	Unknown	08Ma35Ey
John	20	M	Unknown	08Ma35Ey
David	18	M	Unknown	08Ma35Ey
Philip	13	M	Unknown	08Ma35Ey
Wm.	9	M	Child	08Ma35Ey
Edward	17	M	Unknown	08Ma35Ey
Mary	18	F	Unknown	08Ma35Ey
FITZGERALD, Michl.	20	M	Unknown	08Ma35Ey
Cath.	17	M	Unknown	08Ma35Ey
MALOON, Michl.	17	M	Unknown	08Ma35Ey
Biddy	19	F	Unknown	08Ma35Ey
SHEAHY, James	36	M	Unknown	08Ma35Ey
KELLY, Michl.	25	M	Unknown	08Ma35Ey
U, Patt	12	M	Unknown	08Ma35Ey
KEOGH, Patt	20	M	Unknown	08Ma35Ey
MULLINS, Michl.	26	M	Unknown	08Ma35Ey
Mary	26	F	Unknown	08Ma35Ey
BARRY, Patt	25	M	Unknown	08Ma35Ey
Mary	24	F	Unknown	08Ma35Ey
OBRIEN, Ellen	35	F	Unknown	08Ma35Ey
Patt	12	M	Unknown	08Ma35Ey
BARRY, Patt Died-At-Sea	20	M	Unknown	08Ma35Ey
Biddy	18	F	Unknown	08Ma35Ey
HAYES, Denis	20	M	Unknown	08Ma35Ey
Cath.	20	F	Unknown	08Ma35Ey
QUIN, James	26	M	Unknown	08Ma35Ey
SHEAHAN, Patt	25	M	Unknown	08Ma35Ey
MADDEN, Danl.	27	M	Unknown	08Ma35Ey
Biddy	20	F	Unknown	08Ma35Ey
QUAID, Pat	16	M	Unknown	08Ma35Ey
FITZGERALD, Michl.	17	M	Unknown	08Ma35Ey
CARRIDINE, Ellen	20	F	Unknown	08Ma35Ey
DONOHUE, Tom	24	M	Unknown	08Ma35Ey
Danl.	25	M	Unknown	08Ma35Ey
Cath.	23	F	Unknown	08Ma35Ey
COLLINS, Richard	24	M	Unknown	08Ma35Ey
KIEFFE, Thos.	24	M	Unknown	08Ma35Ey
Mary-Ann	24	F	Unknown	08Ma35Ey
DUNDON, James	25	M	Unknown	08Ma35Ey
Hannah	24	F	Unknown	08Ma35Ey
KELLY, Patt	25	M	Unknown	08Ma35Ey
Eliza	20	F	Unknown	08Ma35Ey
COMERFORD, Sally	20	F	Unknown	08Ma35Ey
Sarah	4	F	Child	08Ma35Ey
KELLY, Fanney	40	F	Unknown	08Ma35Ey
Eliza	18	F	Unknown	08Ma35Ey
Cath.	17	F	Unknown	08Ma35Ey
DONNELLY, Wm.	28	M	Unknown	08Ma35Ey
Margt.	28	F	Unknown	08Ma35Ey
Mary	6	F	Child	08Ma35Ey
Margt.	4	F	Child	08Ma35Ey
Wm. Died-At-Sea	2	M	Child	08Ma35Ey
Patt	1	M	Child	08Ma35Ey
CONNELL, Chs.	23	M	Unknown	08Ma35E
HELVER, Martin	23	M	Unknown	08Ma35E
GRIFFIN, Anne	27	F	Unknown	08Ma35E
DOOLEY, Pat	26	M	Unknown	08Ma35E
COSTELLOE, John Died-At-Sea	15	M	Unknown	08Ma35E
MURPHY, Margt.	24	F	Unknown	08Ma35E
KENNEDY, Michl.	24	M	Unknown	08Ma35E
John	19	M	Unknown	08Ma35E
FITZGERALD, Margt.	40	F	Unknown	08Ma35E
Biddy	25	F	Unknown	08Ma35E

NAMES OF PASSENGERS	A G E	S E X	OCCUPATIONS	DATE PORT SHIP
HEA, John	26	M	Unknown	08Ma35Ey
LANAGAN, James	25	M	Unknown	08Ma35Ey
OLLINS, John	16	M	Unknown	08Ma35Ey
UNGOVAN, Eliza	44	F	Unknown	08Ma35Ey
Michl.	18	M	Unknown	08Ma35Ey
James	9	M	Child	08Ma35Ey
Biddy	21	F	Unknown	08Ma35Ey
EYLAN, Martin	21	M	Unknown	08Ma35Ey
LANAGAN, Nancy	20	F	Unknown	08Ma35Ey
OUBLIAN, Michl.	28	M	Unknown	08Ma35Ey
John	23	M	Unknown	08Ma35Ey
Betty	20	F	Unknown	08Ma35Ey
MEAGHER, Patt.	14	M	Unknown	08Ma35Ey
CORRY, John	20	M	Unknown	08Ma35Ey
QUIGLY, Ann	24	F	Unknown	08Ma35Ey
MCDONNELL, John	20	M	Unknown	08Ma35Ey
HEALEY, Hannah	20	F	Unknown	08Ma35Ey
GALLAGHER, John	22	M	Unknown	08Ma35Ey
HANLY, Martin	36	M	Unknown	08Ma35Ey
Hannah	26	F	Unknown	08Ma35Ey
Thos.	8	M	Child	08Ma35Ey
Mary	5	F	Child	08Ma35Ey
Anne	1	F	Child	08Ma35Ey
CULLINAN, John	26	M	Unknown	08Ma35Ey
Eliza	21	F	Unknown	08Ma35Ey
Cath.	23	F	Unknown	08Ma35Ey
Danl.	14	M	Unknown	08Ma35Ey
Eliza	4	F	Child	08Ma35Ey
Ellen	.11	F	Infant	08Ma35Ey
DUNNAGAN, John	30	M	Unknown	08Ma35Ey
Mary	26	F	Unknown	08Ma35Ey
KENNEDY, Mary	30	F	Unknown	08Ma35Ey
KEANE, Wm.	40	M	Unknown	08Ma35Ey
Johanna	40	F	Unknown	08Ma35Ey
Margt.	21	F	Unknown	08Ma35Ey
Mary	19	F	Unknown	08Ma35Ey
John	13	M	Unknown	08Ma35Ey
Wm.	11	M	Unknown	08Ma35Ey
Edward	10	M	Unknown	08Ma35Ey
Johanna	7	F	Child	08Ma35Ey
Patt	5	M	Child	08Ma35Ey
Thos.	1	M	Child	08Ma35Ey
CARROLL, Cath.	25	F	Unknown	08Ma35Ey
HICKEY, Michl.	10	M	Unknown	08Ma35Ey
MOLONY, John	30	M	Unknown	08Ma35Ey
QUINNANE, Dennis	40	M	Unknown	08Ma35Ey
MURRAY, Margt.	25	F	Unknown	08Ma35Ey
HEIDERMAN, Dan	21	M	Unknown	08Ma35Ey
GORMAN, John	30	M	Unknown	08Ma35Ey
ODONNELL, Michl.	24	M	Unknown	08Ma35Ey
ROURKE, Wm.	24	M	Unknown	08Ma35Ey
TOAHY, Biddy	30	F	Unknown	08Ma35Ey
MCELONE, James	26	M	Unknown	08Ma35Ey
MARTIN, Jas.	20	M	Unknown	08Ma35Ey
Wm.	18	M	Unknown	08Ma35Ey
Mary	16	F	Unknown	08Ma35Ey
WHEATON, Ann	14	F	Unknown	08Ma35Ey
CAHILL, Mary	26	F	Unknown	08Ma35Ey
SHEAHAN, John	20	M	Unknown	08Ma35Ey

BOREAS 09 MAY 1849

From New Ross

NAMES OF PASSENGERS	A G E	S E X	OCCUPATIONS	DATE PORT SHIP
_ING, Joseph	28	M	Laborer	09Ma25Fx
NNIS, John	38	M	Laborer	09Ma25Fx
Mary	34	F	Housewife	09Ma25Fx
James	7	M	Child	09Ma25Fx
Bridget	5	F	Child	09Ma25Fx
ENNIS, Eliza	.08	F	Infant	09Ma25Fx
DOHERTY, John	28	M	Laborer	09Ma25Fx
WALSH, James	40	M	Baker	09Ma25Fx
Moses	24	M	Shepherd	09Ma25Fx
Margaret	20	F	Spinster	09Ma25Fx
FOWLER, James	30	M	Laborer	09Ma25Fx
DOYLE, Robert	34	M	Laborer	09Ma25Fx
ASPIL, Mary	25	F	Spinster	09Ma25Fx
John	29	M	Laborer	09Ma25Fx
BYREN, William	38	M	Laborer	09Ma25Fx
WARD, Michael	32	M	Laborer	09Ma25Fx
Anty.	30	F	Spinster	09Ma25Fx
MEANY, Bridget	24	F	Spinster	09Ma25Fx
HANBURY, Richard	28	M	Laborer	09Ma25Fx
MURPHY, Thomas	29	M	Laborer	09Ma25Fx
POWER, Michael	28	M	Laborer	09Ma25Fx
GRIFFIN, Michael	27	M	Laborer	09Ma25Fx
Mary	24	F	Spinster	09Ma25Fx
DOYLE, Mary	22	F	Spinster	09Ma25Fx
Died-At-Sea				
DIER, William	24	M	Laborer	09Ma25Fx
DOYLE, Joseph	30	M	Tailor	09Ma25Fx
BYRNE, Lawrence	38	M	Laborer	09Ma25Fx
Elizabeth	36	F	Housewife	09Ma25Fx
William	9	M	Child	09Ma25Fx
Luke	11	M	Unknown	09Ma25Fx
Tehara	3	F	Child	09Ma25Fx
Martin	.07	M	Infant	09Ma25Fx
Died-At-Sea				
BRENNAN, Columbus	35	M	Laborer	09Ma25Fx
Died-At-Sea				
Elizabeth	34	F	Housewife	09Ma25Fx
Margaret	13	F	Unknown	09Ma25Fx
Andrew	12	M	Unknown	09Ma25Fx
James	9	M	Child	09Ma25Fx
Mary	7	F	Child	09Ma25Fx
Honor	5	F	Child	09Ma25Fx
MYLER, Nicholas	26	M	Laborer	09Ma25Fx
HOWLAN, Micheal	28	M	Laborer	09Ma25Fx
MYLER, Catherine	24	F	Spinster	09Ma25Fx
Nancy	29	F	Spinster	09Ma25Fx
Bridget	20	F	Spinster	09Ma25Fx
Judith	22	F	Spinster	09Ma25Fx
WALSH, Dennis	24	M	Laborer	09Ma25Fx
NICOLE, Margaret	22	F	Spinster	09Ma25Fx
CONNICK, Thomas	40	M	Laborer	09Ma25Fx
Mary	36	F	Housewife	09Ma25Fx
SUMMERS, Edward	32	M	Gdnr	09Ma25Fx
BLANCH, James	20	M	Laborer	09Ma25Fx
DINN, Pat	44	M	Laborer	09Ma25Fx
LAWLER, Joseph	48	M	Laborer	09Ma25Fx
MAHON, Patt	26	M	Laborer	09Ma25Fx
NEAL, Henry	23	M	Laborer	09Ma25Fx
KENNEDY, John	44	M	Laborer	09Ma25Fx
MAHEN, Margaret	20	F	Spinster	09Ma25Fx
DUNN, Catherine	36	F	Housewife	09Ma25Fx
FINN, Pat	24	M	Laborer	09Ma25Fx
GUFFIN, Pat	42	M	Laborer	09Ma25Fx
Died-At-Sea				
Ellen	38	F	Housewife	09Ma25Fx
Bridget	18	F	Spinster	09Ma25Fx
Ellen	17	F	Spinster	09Ma25Fx
John	13	M	Unknown	09Ma25Fx
Alice	11	F	Unknown	09Ma25Fx
Lawrence	9	M	Child	09Ma25Fx
William	7	M	Child	09Ma25Fx
Died-At-Sea				
Patt	4	M	Child	09Ma25Fx
Thomas	.11	M	Infant	09Ma25Fx
POWER, Margaret	48	F	Housewife	09Ma25Fx
James	17	M	Laborer	09Ma25Fx
Micheal	13	M	Unknown	09Ma25Fx
FLING, Ann	28	F	Spinster	09Ma25Fx
LANDEFAN, Nicholas	30	M	Laborer	09Ma25Fx
NEAL, Moses	45	M	Laborer	09Ma25Fx

NAMES OF PASSENGERS	AGE	SEX	OCCUPATIONS	DATE PORT SHIP
NEAL, Catherine	40	F	Housewife	09Ma25Fx
Edward	16	M	Laborer	09Ma25Fx
NOLAN, James	38	M	Laborer	09Ma25Fx
KEYAN, William	20	M	Laborer	09Ma25Fx
MCEVERS, Michl.	36	M	Laborer	09Ma25Fx
BYRNE, Thomas	37	M	Laborer	09Ma25Fx
CLARK, Thomas	24	M	Laborer	09Ma25Fx
Wwilliam	22	M	Laborer	09Ma25Fx
Bridget	20	F	Spinster	09Ma25Fx
Mary	18	F	Spinster	09Ma25Fx
SHIELS, Margaret	22	F	Spinster	09Ma25Fx
DIER, William	19	M	Laborer	09Ma25Fx
BYRNE, John	28	M	Laborer	09Ma25Fx
ELLY, Thomas	24	M	Laborer	09Ma25Fx
CONNERS, Margaret	25	F	Wi	09Ma25Fx
ELLY, Anty	22	F	Spinster	09Ma25Fx
Mary-Ann	21	F	Housewife	09Ma25Fx
LONG, Pat	28	M	Laborer	09Ma25Fx
Died-At-Sea				
BYRNE, Lawrence	26	M	Laborer	09Ma25Fx
MURPHY, Sally	24	F	Spinster	09Ma25Fx
DOYLE, John	22	M	Laborer	09Ma25Fx
James	36	M	Laborer	09Ma25Fx
Margaret	34	F	Housewife	09Ma25Fx
John	11	M	Unknown	09Ma25Fx
Mary	9	F	Child	09Ma25Fx
Thomas	4	F	Child	09Ma25Fx
LONG, Pat	26	M	Laborer	09Ma25Fx
Died-At-Sea				
Bridget	23	F	Spinster	09Ma25Fx
Ellen	21	F	Spinster	09Ma25Fx
KELLY, Mary	18	F	Spinster	09Ma25Fx
TOBIN, Thomas	24	M	Laborer	09Ma25Fx
Mary	23	F	Spinster	09Ma25Fx
Margaret	21	F	Spinster	09Ma25Fx
TOLLIN, James	19	M	Laborer	09Ma25Fx
Judith	47	F	Spinster	09Ma25Fx
Stephen	12	M	Unknown	09Ma25Fx
DOOLEY, John	32	M	Laborer	09Ma25Fx
Judith	38	F	Housewife	09Ma25Fx
GLASCITT, Frank	17	M	Laborer	09Ma25Fx
Mary	13	F	Unknown	09Ma25Fx
TOLLIN, Patrick	34	M	Laborer	09Ma25Fx
SHANAHAN, Michl.	36	M	Laborer	09Ma25Fx
Judy	24	F	Housewife	09Ma25Fx
Mary	2	F	Child	09Ma25Fx
John	.00	M	Infant	09Ma25Fx
Died-At-Sea				
BRYAN, John	27	M	Laborer	09Ma25Fx
Johana	25	F	Spinster	09Ma25Fx
MORISEY, Micheal	24	M	Laborer	09Ma25Fx
DUNN, John	20	M	Laborer	09Ma25Fx
HEASE, Michl.	26	M	Laborer	09Ma25Fx
CASEY, James	26	M	Laborer	09Ma25Fx
Mary	22	F	Housewife	09Ma25Fx
DOOLEY, Pat	30	M	Laborer	09Ma25Fx
DOYLE, Betty	28	F	Spinster	09Ma25Fx
Died-At-Sea				
BUTTETIN, Thomas	26	M	Laborer	09Ma25Fx
COADY, Edward	36	M	Laborer	09Ma25Fx
James	34	M	Laborer	09Ma25Fx
RYAN, Patt	36	M	Laborer	09Ma25Fx
DINHARN, Simon	30	M	Laborer	09Ma25Fx
DOYLE, William	28	M	Laborer	09Ma25Fx
NOLAN, Margaret	24	F	Spinster	09Ma25Fx
Johana	22	F	Spinster	09Ma25Fx
NEAL, Birdget	24	F	Spinster	09Ma25Fx
BRUN, John	24	M	Laborer	09Ma25Fx
MCGRATH, Thomas	23	M	Laborer	09Ma25Fx
BYRNE, Mary	19	F	Housewife	09Ma25Fx
KUNFE, Edward	18	M	Laborer	09Ma25Fx
MURPHY, Edward	26	M	Servant	09Ma25Fx
JOYCE, Edward	21	M	Laborer	09Ma25Fx
GANNON, Thomas	24	M	Laborer	09Ma25Fx
NEAL, Edward	26	M	Laborer	09Ma25Fx

NAMES OF PASSENGERS	AGE	SEX	OCCUPATIONS	DATE PORT SHIP
DORAN, Anty	34	F	Spinster	09Ma25F
LOVETT, Mary	13	F	Spinster	09Ma25F
DINN, Mary	26	F	Unknown	09Ma25F
WALSH, Thomas	22	M	Laborer	09Ma25F
WHITE, James	28	M	Laborer	09Ma25F
Mary	7	F	Child	09Ma25F
Margaret	.07	F	Infant	09Ma25F
WELSH, Michl.	35	M	Unknown	09Ma25F
WALSHE, William	30	M	Unknown	09Ma25F
HANRAHAN, Thomas	24	M	Unknown	09Ma25F
POWER, Micheal	21	M	Unknown	09Ma25F

ELIZABETH 09 MAY 1849

From Newcastle

NAMES OF PASSENGERS	AGE	SEX	OCCUPATIONS	DATE PORT SHIP
LOSSEY, Joseph	27	M	Plasterer	09Ma18B
Fanny	25	F	Unknown	09Ma18B
Edwin	2	M	Child	09Ma18B
John	.07	M	Infant	09Ma18B
PATT, Richard	25	M	Joiner	09Ma18B
Ann	24	F	Unknown	09Ma18B
Wm.	1	M	Child	09Ma18B
HAMMALT, Allan	29	M	Plasterer	09Ma18B
GERRY, Wm.	22	M	Plasterer	09Ma18B

LA-RUE 10 MAY 1849

From Liverpool

NAMES OF PASSENGERS	AGE	SEX	OCCUPATIONS	DATE PORT SHIP
EARL, William	25	M	Laborer	10Ma02F
FITZPATRICK, John	40	M	Unknown	10Ma02F
MCCANN, Thomas	21	M	Unknown	10Ma02F
CLEARY, Christy	15	F	Unknown	10Ma02F
Eliza	29	F	Unknown	10Ma02F
MONTGOMERY, Mary	20	F	Unknown	10Ma02F
CARROLL, Cath.	52	F	Unknown	10Ma02F
Ellen	21	F	Unknown	10Ma02F
GEARY, Jerry	20	M	Unknown	10Ma02F
GAVIN, William	20	M	Unknown	10Ma02F
BURKE, Charley	50	M	Unknown	10Ma02F
William	13	M	Unknown	10Ma02F
Bridget	11	F	Unknown	10Ma02F
CANSY, Richard	13	M	Unknown	10Ma02F
Eliza	9	F	Child	10Ma02F
WALSH, Michl.	20	M	Unknown	10Ma02
Margt.	25	F	Unknown	10Ma02
Maurice	5	M	Child	10Ma02
Nancy	2	F	Child	10Ma02
FITZGIBBONS, Ellen	23	F	Child	10Ma02
CURNEY, Dennis	22	M	Unknown	10Ma02
Mary	30	F	Unknown	10Ma02
Dennis	22	M	Unknown	10Ma02
John	18	M	Unknown	10Ma02
Oliver	13	M	Unknown	10Ma02
Michael	8	M	Child	10Ma02
Comerley	6	M	Child	10Ma02
Margt.	4	F	Child	10Ma02
David	3	M	Child	10Ma02
Thomas	.00	M	Infant	10Ma02
REILLY, Thomas	26	M	Unknown	10Ma02
MCGOVERN, Bgt.	15	F	Unknown	10Ma02
REID, James	25	M	Unknown	10Ma02

NAMES OF PASSENGERS	AGE	SEX	OCCUPATIONS	DATE PORT SHIP
CHARLEY, Ann	16	F	Unknown	10Ma02Fh
FOLEN, Cath.	16	F	Unknown	10Ma02Fh
HIAM, Michael	20	M	Unknown	10Ma02Fh
QUIRCK, Pat	19	M	Unknown	10Ma02Fh
Jimmy	24	M	Unknown	10Ma02Fh
FLANINGAN, Mary	20	F	Unknown	10Ma02Fh
LEARY, James	19	M	Unknown	10Ma02Fh
FARRELL, John	22	M	Unknown	10Ma02Fh
MCGRATH, Margt.	28	F	Unknown	10Ma02Fh
LAWLESS, Pat	28	M	Unknown	10Ma02Fh
LAMBERT, Pat	18	M	Unknown	10Ma02Fh
BROWN, Jimmy	23	F	Unknown	10Ma02Fh
Margt.	21	F	Unknown	10Ma02Fh
NIGLERBY, Peter	25	M	Unknown	10Ma02Fh
BRADY, Joseph	15	M	Unknown	10Ma02Fh
Anne	17	F	Unknown	10Ma02Fh
WELL, James	24	M	Unknown	10Ma02Fh
KINSELLA, John	23	M	Unknown	10Ma02Fh
BYRNE, Margt.	15	F	Unknown	10Ma02Fh
KINGSBALLA, Batt	40	M	Unknown	10Ma02Fh
William	20	M	Unknown	10Ma02Fh
FITZPATRICK, John	18	M	Unknown	10Ma02Fh
MCQUADE, Peter	19	M	Unknown	10Ma02Fh
MCBRIDE, Hugh	20	M	Unknown	10Ma02Fh
BRIEN, Edwd.	25	M	Unknown	10Ma02Fh
REILLY, Kate	25	F	Unknown	10Ma02Fh
WALLACE, Pat	23	M	Unknown	10Ma02Fh
FLALANG, Thomas	20	M	Unknown	10Ma02Fh
MURPHY, Mary	45	F	Unknown	10Ma02Fh
CONWAY, Thomas	20	M	Unknown	10Ma02Fh
HENRY, Ellen	18	F	Unknown	10Ma02Fh
MCCALLAGH, James	31	M	Unknown	10Ma02Fh
MCIVES, Jos.	24	M	Unknown	10Ma02Fh
GOLAND, Michael	34	M	Unknown	10Ma02Fh
WATSON, Robt.	24	M	Unknown	10Ma02Fh
DEFTY, Michael	20	M	Unknown	10Ma02Fh
MCCORREA, Judith Died-At-Sea	10	F	Unknown	10Ma02Fh
LEONARD, Sarah	45	F	Unknown	10Ma02Fh
Anne	13	F	Unknown	10Ma02Fh
Margt.	9	F	Child	10Ma02Fh
Ellen	12	F	Unknown	10Ma02Fh
James	5	M	Child	10Ma02Fh
ULLIGAN, J.	7	M	Child	10Ma02Fh
ULLHALL, John	40	M	Unknown	10Ma02Fh
Bridget	35	F	Unknown	10Ma02Fh
Mary	12	F	Unknown	10Ma02Fh
Anne	9	F	Unknown	10Ma02Fh
Bridget	7	F	Unknown	10Ma02Fh
Jamy	5	M	Unknown	10Ma02Fh
OORE, James	60	M	Unknown	10Ma02Fh
William	22	M	Unknown	10Ma02Fh
Thomas	15	M	Unknown	10Ma02Fh
Mary	20	F	Unknown	10Ma02Fh
CCLELLAND, Saml.	22	M	Unknown	10Ma02Fh
Margt.	17	F	Unknown	10Ma02Fh
OLLY, Thomas	45	M	Unknown	10Ma02Fh
AHER, Chas.	21	M	Unknown	10Ma02Fh
OWD, Pat	21	M	Unknown	10Ma02Fh
UINN, Jno.	25	M	Unknown	10Ma02Fh
CDERMOTT, Peter	21	M	Unknown	10Ma02Fh
Cath.	23	F	Unknown	10Ma02Fh
EGAN, Cath.	16	F	Unknown	10Ma02Fh
AINES, Pat	25	M	Unknown	10Ma02Fh
Eliza	20	F	Unknown	10Ma02Fh
IERNS, John	40	M	Unknown	10Ma02Fh
EANE, Hannah	40	F	Unknown	10Ma02Fh
NCHAN, Michael	20	M	Unknown	10Ma02Fh
RISLANE, David	20	M	Unknown	10Ma02Fh
LLIVAN, Dennis	24	M	Unknown	10Ma02Fh
Dennis	24	M	Unknown	10Ma02Fh
OONEY, Pat	26	M	Unknown	10Ma02Fh
REARY, Michl.	24	M	Unknown	10Ma02Fh
ARTZ, Dennis	26	M	Unknown	10Ma02Fh
LLIVAN, Michl.	46	M	Unknown	10Ma02Fh
CREAN, Dennis	38	M	Unknown	10Ma02Fh
CONNOR, John	30	M	Unknown	10Ma02Fh
William	26	M	Unknown	10Ma02Fh
MORGAN, Biddy	22	F	Unknown	10Ma02Fh
Mary	2	F	Child	10Ma02Fh
Cath.	.00	F	Infant	10Ma02Fh
DEENAN, Margt.	25	F	Unknown	10Ma02Fh
RYAN, Johanna	20	F	Unknown	10Ma02Fh
GROLE, Jas.	19	M	Unknown	10Ma02Fh
Pat	20	M	Unknown	10Ma02Fh
HAYES, Edw.	31	M	Unknown	10Ma02Fh
CONNOR, Thos.	34	M	Unknown	10Ma02Fh
GLEASON, Mary	20	F	Unknown	10Ma02Fh
Biddy	18	F	Unknown	10Ma02Fh
KENNEDY, Pat	20	M	Unknown	10Ma02Fh
Honora	18	F	Unknown	10Ma02Fh
GLEESON, Edw.	23	M	Unknown	10Ma02Fh
MCKISSAN, Margt.	26	F	Unknown	10Ma02Fh
WOODCOCK, Joseph	43	M	Unknown	10Ma02Fh
PEARSON, Henry	25	M	Unknown	10Ma02Fh
HERTHER, Thos.	25	M	Unknown	10Ma02Fh
U-Mrs.	45	F	Unknown	10Ma02Fh
CARROLL, Pat	20	M	Unknown	10Ma02Fh
NOLE, Pat	20	M	Unknown	10Ma02Fh
Margt.	28	F	Unknown	10Ma02Fh
Margt.	8	F	Child	10Ma02Fh
Cath.	5	F	Child	10Ma02Fh
John	1	M	Child	10Ma02Fh
Pat	.00	M	Infant	10Ma02Fh
MURPHY, Cornelius	17	M	Unknown	10Ma02Fh
SMITH, Ann	21	F	Unknown	10Ma02Fh
HUNTER, John	20	M	Unknown	10Ma02Fh
SKILLAN, Jas.	20	M	Unknown	10Ma02Fh
LIDLEY, Rt.	19	M	Unknown	10Ma02Fh
BOYD, Thos.	20	M	Unknown	10Ma02Fh
HOWIE, Rt.	20	M	Unknown	10Ma02Fh
DAN, Fran.	34	F	Unknown	10Ma02Fh
Mary	30	F	Unknown	10Ma02Fh
Thomas	12	M	Unknown	10Ma02Fh
Ann	10	F	Unknown	10Ma02Fh
Rose	8	F	Child	10Ma02Fh
Edward	6	M	Child	10Ma02Fh
Cath.	2	F	Child	10Ma02Fh
Terence	.00	M	Infant	10Ma02Fh
COX, Peter	14	M	Unknown	10Ma02Fh
CUMMINS, Dennis	28	M	Unknown	10Ma02Fh
Richard	24	M	Unknown	10Ma02Fh
James	22	M	Unknown	10Ma02Fh
COLLINS, Thomas	28	M	Unknown	10Ma02Fh
Cath.	25	F	Unknown	10Ma02Fh
Ellen	.00	F	Infant	10Ma02Fh
MCSHAN, Wm.	30	M	Unknown	10Ma02Fh
Margt.	30	F	Unknown	10Ma02Fh
KENNA, Bridget	26	F	Unknown	10Ma02Fh
Kate	3	F	Child	10Ma02Fh
Pat	.00	M	Infant	10Ma02Fh
SULLIVAN, Batt	25	M	Unknown	10Ma02Fh
LAVELLE, Pat	24	M	Unknown	10Ma02Fh
Cath.	26	F	Unknown	10Ma02Fh
Ester	40	F	Unknown	10Ma02Fh
Mary	2	F	Child	10Ma02Fh
CADEJANO, John	30	M	Unknown	10Ma02Fh
BARRY, John	30	M	Unknown	10Ma02Fh
TRACEY, Mary	20	F	Unknown	10Ma02Fh
LAHEY, Mary	20	F	Unknown	10Ma02Fh
BRONARDEN, John	21	M	Unknown	10Ma02Fh
Michl.	24	M	Unknown	10Ma02Fh
MCBRIDE, Hugh	30	M	Unknown	10Ma02Fh
MCCORMICK, Michl.	35	M	Unknown	10Ma02Fh
Wm.	30	M	Unknown	10Ma02Fh
Cath.	10	F	Unknown	10Ma02Fh
Batt	8	M	Child	10Ma02Fh
Thomas	6	M	Child	10Ma02Fh
Simmons	2	M	Child	10Ma02Fh
Michael	.00	M	Infant	10Ma02Fh

NAMES OF PASSENGERS		AGE	SEX	OCCUPATIONS	DATE PORT SHIP
MCGOVERN, Rod		25	M	Unknown	10Ma02Fh
OBRIEN, Cath.		28	F	Unknown	10Ma02Fh
HYLAND, Cath.		14	F	Unknown	10Ma02Fh
CANNIFF, Thos.		25	M	Unknown	10Ma02Fh
REARDON, Dan		25	M	Unknown	10Ma02Fh
MCDERMOTT, Jno.		25	M	Unknown	10Ma02Fh
WOODS, James		30	M	Unknown	10Ma02Fh
Died-At-Sea					
WALSH, John		30	M	Unknown	10Ma02Fh
James		27	M	Unknown	10Ma02Fh
FARLEY, Mich.		50	M	Unknown	10Ma02Fh
Wm.		50	M	Unknown	10Ma02Fh
Ellen		20	F	Unknown	10Ma02Fh
Susan		18	F	Unknown	10Ma02Fh
Pat		17	M	Unknown	10Ma02Fh
Thos.		16	M	Unknown	10Ma02Fh
Mable		15	F	Unknown	10Ma02Fh
Mary		13	F	Unknown	10Ma02Fh
Mich.		11	M	Unknown	10Ma02Fh
DOOLEY, Mich.		20	M	Unknown	10Ma02Fh
MURPHY, John		28	M	Unknown	10Ma02Fh
SMITH, Wm.		30	M	Unknown	10Ma02Fh
Joseph		4	M	Child	10Ma02Fh
CAHILL, Mary		50	F	Unknown	10Ma02Fh
Thomas		21	M	Unknown	10Ma02Fh
John		28	M	Unknown	10Ma02Fh
James		12	M	Unknown	10Ma02Fh
KENNAHER, John		18	M	Unknown	10Ma02Fh
FARRELL, John		23	M	Unknown	10Ma02Fh
BRADY, Bridget		50	F	Unknown	10Ma02Fh
Died-At-Sea					
Rosanna		50	F	Unknown	10Ma02Fh
Mary		8	F	Child	10Ma02Fh
MCCORMICK, Celia		20	F	Unknown	10Ma02Fh
MORGAN, John		35	M	Laborer	10Ma02Fh
JENNINGS, John		20	M	Merchant	10Ma02Fh
HEALY, James		22	M	Merchant	10Ma02Fh
CUMMINS, Mary		20	F	Merchant	10Ma02Fh
U, U		.00	U	Infant	10Ma02Fh
Born-At-Sea					

JAMES 10 MAY 1849

From Newry

NAMES OF PASSENGERS		AGE	SEX	OCCUPATIONS	DATE PORT SHIP
VALLELY, Arthur		30	M	Farmer	10Ma11Fq
Margaret	(W)	28	F	Wife	10Ma11Fq
MCKEOWN, James		20	M	Laborer	10Ma11Fq
MCKENNA, Sally		20	F	Servant	10Ma11Fq
MEEHAN, Margaret		21	F	Servant	10Ma11Fq
ONEILL, Margaret		23	F	Servant	10Ma11Fq
Susan		19	F	Servant	10Ma11Fq
HARVEY, John		18	M	Laborer	10Ma11Fq
Pat		15	M	Laborer	10Ma11Fq
Bridget		11	F	Servant	10Ma11Fq
MCNALLY, Jane		19	F	Servant	10Ma11Fq
MCGEOUGH, Hugh		21	M	Laborer	10Ma11Fq
MCCARTON, Jane		19	F	Servant	10Ma11Fq
QUIN, Bridget		17	F	Servant	10Ma11Fq
FANNY, Mary		23	F	Servant	10Ma11Fq
MCGRORY, Mary		18	F	Servant	10Ma11Fq
MCELDUFF, Mary		24	F	Servant	10Ma11Fq
KYLE, Nancy		24	F	Servant	10Ma11Fq
MCGINTY, Mary		14	F	Servant	10Ma11Fq
CULLAN, Catherine		20	F	Servant	10Ma11Fq
HART, Catherine		30	F	Servant	10Ma11Fq
MCGEARY, John		24	M	Laborer	10Ma11Fq
Edward		30	M	Laborer	10Ma11Fq
DOOGAN, William		30	M	Shoemaker	10Ma11Fq
DOOGAN, Jane	(W)	25	F	Wife	10Ma11Fq
MCDERMOT, Anne		24	F	Servant	10Ma11Fq
MCCARTON, Mary		40	F	Wi	10Ma11Fq
Betty		22	F	Unknown	10Ma11Fq
Ann		18	F	Unknown	10Ma11Fq
Owen		14	M	Unknown	10Ma11Fq
Biddy		12	F	Unknown	10Ma11Fq
Mary		8	F	Child	10Ma11Fq
Hugh		5	M	Child	10Ma11Fq
CLARK, Christiana		20	F	Spinster	10Ma11Fq
WHITE, Roger		20	M	Laborer	10Ma11Fq
DOYLE, Susan		17	F	Servant	10Ma11Fq
ORR, Christiana		24	F	Servant	10Ma11Fq
ROGERS, Sarah		30	F	Wi	10Ma11Fq
Edward		12	M	Unknown	10Ma11Fq
Peter		9	M	Child	10Ma11Fq
Michael		6	M	Child	10Ma11Fq
TURBETT, David		50	M	Laborer	10Ma11Fq
FOW, Charles		33	M	Mechanic	10Ma11Fq
Jane	(W)	26	F	Wife	10Ma11Fq
William		5	M	Child	10Ma11Fq
James		3	M	Child	10Ma11Fq
Eliza		2	F	Child	10Ma11Fq
MAGILL, William		35	M	Mechanic	10Ma11Fq
Mary	(W)	28	F	Wife	10Ma11Fq
William		5	M	Child	10Ma11Fq
Catherine		3	F	Child	10Ma11Fq
James		1	M	Child	10Ma11Fq
BARRY, Ann		38	F	Lad	10Ma11Fq
Ann-Jane	(D)	10	F	Daughter	10Ma11Fq
NELSON, William		25	M	Gdnr	10Ma11Fq
QUIN, Nancy		20	F	Servant	10Ma11Fq
NESBITT, Joseph		28	M	Laborer	10Ma11Fq
MCGUIGAN, Hugh		35	M	Farmer	10Ma11Fq
Ann	(W)	26	F	Wife	10Ma11Fq
John	(S)	6	M	Child	10Ma11Fq
Peter	(S)	4	M	Child	10Ma11Fq
Bridget	(D)	8	F	Child	10Ma11Fq
Catherine	(D)	2	F	Child	10Ma11Fc
KERR, John		56	M	Farmer	10Ma11Fc
Edward		38	M	Farmer	10Ma11Fc
Mary	(W)	30	F	Wife	10Ma11Fc
John		11	M	Unknown	10Ma11Fc
Patrick		19	M	Unknown	10Ma11Fc
James		17	M	Unknown	10Ma11F
Ann		5	F	Child	10Ma11F
Edward		3	M	Child	10Ma11F
MCARDLE, Patrick		19	M	Laborer	10Ma11F
John		25	M	Laborer	10Ma11F
PINKERTON, John		30	M	Farmer	10Ma11F
MARGUAY, Owen		45	M	Farmer	10Ma11F
Betty		20	F	Unknown	10Ma11F
Rose		17	F	Unknown	10Ma11F
Biddy		14	F	Unknown	10Ma11F
CONNELLY, Biddy		18	F	Servant	10Ma11F
LOUGHRAN, Arthur		32	M	Laborer	10Ma11F
MCBENNETT, Sarah		40	F	Wife	10Ma11F
Edward		18	M	Unknown	10Ma11F
James		16	M	Unknown	10Ma11F
SHARY, Owen		32	M	Laborer	10Ma11F
MCALEARY, Peter		20	M	Laborer	10Ma11F
CUNNINGHAM, Ann		26	F	Servant	10Ma11F
BROWN, Arthur		32	M	Shoemaker	10Ma11F
STELLE, John		23	M	Mechanic	10Ma11F
MCARDLE, Michl.		22	M	Laborer	10Ma11F
ROGERS, Felix		3	M	Child	10Ma11F
VALLELY, Susan		.06	F	Infant	10Ma11F
DOOGAN, John		.07	M	Infant	10Ma11F
MCGUIGAN, Hugh		.06	M	Infant	10Ma11F

NAMES OF PASSENGERS	AGE	SEX	OCCUPATIONS	DATE PORT SHIP

TERE-FOGO 11 MAY 1849

From Maranham

NAMES OF PASSENGERS	AGE	SEX	OCCUPATIONS	DATE PORT SHIP
VIONNCE, John	28	M	Merchant	11Ma48Ee

THAMES 12 MAY 1849

From Bermuda

NAMES OF PASSENGERS	AGE	SEX	OCCUPATIONS	DATE PORT SHIP
MACRAE, U-Mr.	50	M	Gentleman	12Ma29Fz
TRISTRAM, U-Mr.	33	M	Clergyman	12Ma29Fz
DOWNES, U-Mr.	25	M	Army	12Ma29Fz
ELLIOT, U-Mrs.	40	F	Unknown	12Ma29Fz
Hugh	18	M	Unknown	12Ma29Fz
Emma	5	F	Child	12Ma29Fz
CAMERON, U-Mrs.	30	F	Unknown	12Ma29Fz
I.	1	M	Child	12Ma29Fz
ROSS, Wm.	40	M	Laborer	12Ma29Fz
Peter	7	M	Child	12Ma29Fz
JONES, Sarah	35	F	Nurse	12Ma29Fz
DITMAN, Louisa	30	F	Nurse	12Ma29Fz

LEMUEL-DYER 12 MAY 1849

From Liverpool

NAMES OF PASSENGERS	AGE	SEX	OCCUPATIONS	DATE PORT SHIP
MCGUIRE, Patrick	29	M	Laborer	12Ma02Gv
Mary	3	F	Child	12Ma02Gv
WALSH, James	30	M	Laborer	12Ma02Gv
William	20	M	Laborer	12Ma02Gv
GROGAN, Michl.	25	M	Laborer	12Ma02Gv
HAIGHER, John	36	M	Seaman	12Ma02Gv
Ellen	34	F	Unknown	12Ma02Gv
Thos.	23	M	Unknown	12Ma02Gv
John	18	M	Unknown	12Ma02Gv
Catherine	16	F	Unknown	12Ma02Gv
Jane	14	F	Unknown	12Ma02Gv
Ann	7	F	Child	12Ma02Gv
William	4	M	Child	12Ma02Gv
James	3	M	Child	12Ma02Gv
EACE, William	17	M	Fisherman	12Ma02Gv
ILLON, Robt.	32	M	Farmer	12Ma02Gv
Catherine (W)	30	F	Unknown	12Ma02Gv
EALE, William	14	M	Unknown	12Ma02Gv
Jane	4	F	Child	12Ma02Gv
Mary	.00	F	Infant	12Ma02Gv
UIRK, William	17	M	Farmer	12Ma02Gv
UAILL, Thos.	19	M	Farmer	12Ma02Gv
Robert	25	M	Mason	12Ma02Gv
REW, Daniel	22	M	Farmer	12Ma02Gv
Robt.	16	M	Farmer	12Ma02Gv
IEL, Charles	23	M	Farmer	12Ma02Gv
OLLETT, Henry	17	M	Farmer	12Ma02Gv
ELLEY, Patck.	28	M	Farmer	12Ma02Gv
AVIN, Danl.	22	M	Farmer	12Ma02Gv
AGGART, John	28	M	Laborer	12Ma02Gv
TAGGART, Catherine	29	F	Unknown	12Ma02Gv
CLARK, Betsey	22	F	Servant	12Ma02Gv
CORBETT, Danl.	50	M	Farmer	12Ma02Gv
Margt.	50	F	Unknown	12Ma02Gv
Catherine	20	F	Unknown	12Ma02Gv
GILL, James	25	M	Unknown	12Ma02Gv
NELSON, Richard	23	M	Parson	12Ma02Gv
MULLOY, William	28	M	Farmer	12Ma02Gv
QUAIL, Edwd.	21	M	Farmer	12Ma02Gv
DUNN, Michael	30	M	Steward	12Ma02Gv
LEHAN, William	18	M	Clerk	12Ma02Gv
BRENNAN, Cathne.	20	F	Servant	12Ma02Gv
DELANY, Mary	25	F	Servant	12Ma02Gv
FLOOD, Saml.	18	M	Farmer	12Ma02Gv
CLINCH, James	26	M	Farmer	12Ma02Gv
RYLIE, Peter	12	M	Farmer	12Ma02Gv
CLARK, James	20	M	Farmer	12Ma02Gv
GLEESON, James	25	M	Farmer	12Ma02Gv
Jere.	24	M	Farmer	12Ma02Gv
Died-At-Sea				
NOOLAN, John	23	M	Ostler	12Ma02Gv
Catherine	22	F	Servant	12Ma02Gv
RYAN, Bessey	18	F	Servant	12Ma02Gv
Mary	16	F	Servant	12Ma02Gv
GAINGAN, Philip	30	M	Laborer	12Ma02Gv
Catherine (W)	30	F	Unknown	12Ma02Gv
Chas.	16	M	Unknown	12Ma02Gv
Bud	10	M	Unknown	12Ma02Gv
SMITH, Chas.	18	M	Farmer	12Ma02Gv
CARTEN, Corns.	21	M	Laborer	12Ma02Gv
Cate	00	F	Laborer	12Ma02Gv
Ann	5	F	Child	12Ma02Gv
HEDLEY, Patck.	27	M	Carpenter	12Ma02Gv
RYAN, Michl.	27	M	Laborer	12Ma02Gv
MORONEY, Michl.	26	M	Laborer	12Ma02Gv
KENNEDY, John	25	M	Ostler	12Ma02Gv
Jas.	24	M	Ostler	12Ma02Gv
HOYNE, Patck.	24	M	Ostler	12Ma02Gv
COOLEY, Jas.	24	M	Laborer	12Ma02Gv
HEFFERAM, Jas.	24	M	Laborer	12Ma02Gv
ELLCOTT, Thos.	24	M	Laborer	12Ma02Gv
RYAN, Judy	21	F	Servant	12Ma02Gv
DRANNON, Mary	21	F	Servant	12Ma02Gv
COOLEY, Mary	21	F	Servant	12Ma02Gv
SHILLEY, Margt.	23	F	Servant	12Ma02Gv
MURPHEY, John	23	M	Servant	12Ma02Gv
Mary	23	F	Servant	12Ma02Gv
LOOLY, Catherine	22	F	Servant	12Ma02Gv
HANDLAN, Ellen	21	F	Servant	12Ma02Gv
GLEESON, Wm.	27	M	Ploughman	12Ma02Gv
KENNEDAY, Jas.	20	M	Laborer	12Ma02Gv
Judy	20	F	Unknown	12Ma02Gv
Thos.	21	M	Laborer	12Ma02Gv
Margt.	16	F	Laborer	12Ma02Gv
Nory	17	F	Unknown	12Ma02Gv
CAREY, Patck.	19	M	Laborer	12Ma02Gv
MULLOY, Thos.	20	M	Laborer	12Ma02Gv
Bud	20	M	Laborer	12Ma02Gv
MCALLY, Mary	30	F	Spinster	12Ma02Gv
BUCKLEY, John	44	M	Carpenter	12Ma02Gv
Margt.	44	F	Unknown	12Ma02Gv
Wm.	19	M	Carpenter	12Ma02Gv
Edwd.	17	M	Carpenter	12Ma02Gv
Honora	15	F	Unknown	12Ma02Gv
James	14	M	Carpenter	12Ma02Gv
Catherine	10	F	Unknown	12Ma02Gv
Thos.	8	M	Child	12Ma02Gv
Margt.	6	F	Child	12Ma02Gv
Mary	3	F	Child	12Ma02Gv
DOOLEY, Thos.	4	M	Child	12Ma02Gv
MATTHEWS, Bartley	24	M	Unknown	12Ma02Gv
BERRY, James	25	M	Unknown	12Ma02Gv
SULLIVAN, John	28	M	Laborer	12Ma02Gv
SANDERS, Adams	22	M	Shoemaker	12Ma02Gv
BLACKMOOR, Henry	21	M	Shoemaker	12Ma02Gv

NAMES OF PASSENGERS	AGE	SEX	OCCUPATIONS	DATE PORT SHIP
BLACKMOOR, Mary	19	F	Unknown	12Ma02Gv
Margt.	17	F	Unknown	12Ma02Gv
LEAHY, Bridget	20	F	Servant	12Ma02Gv
RYAN, Margt.	22	F	Servant	12Ma02Gv
GEE, Michl.	30	M	Clerk	12Ma02Gv
RYLIE, Patck.	25	M	Laborer	12Ma02Gv
CARTY, Edward	32	M	Laborer	12Ma02Gv
CUNNAN, John	30	M	Laborer	12Ma02Gv
RYLIE, Jas.	22	M	Laborer	12Ma02Gv
KEEFFE, John	45	M	Laborer	12Ma02Gv
Mary	30	F	Servant	12Ma02Gv
Michl.	35	M	Laborer	12Ma02Gv
CONNOLY, John	20	M	Laborer	12Ma02Gv
Johan	18	M	Servant	12Ma02Gv
FOGARTY, Thos.	25	M	Laborer	12Ma02Gv
AKERN, John	35	M	Laborer	12Ma02Gv
QUINLAN, James	40	M	Farmer	12Ma02Gv
John	00	M	Farmer	12Ma02Gv
MONTGOMERY, Thos.	00	M	Laborer	12Ma02Gv
Margt.	00	F	Servant	12Ma02Gv
GILL, Ann	20	F	Servant	12Ma02Gv
HANLAN, Chas.	20	M	Plumber	12Ma02Gv
DRENNAN, U	40	M	Farmer	12Ma02Gv
BRANNON, Edward	30	M	Farmer	12Ma02Gv
Mary	26	F	Farmer	12Ma02Gv
MCGEE, Patck.	20	M	Carpenter	12Ma02Gv
MCKIN, John	35	M	Carpenter	12Ma02Gv
CURTIS, Michl.	36	M	Laborer	12Ma02Gv
Mary	32	F	Unknown	12Ma02Gv
Thomas	6	M	Child	12Ma02Gv
MURPHEY, Rose	20	F	Servant	12Ma02Gv
BEGLAND, John	30	M	Laborer	12Ma02Gv
Ann	40	F	Unknown	12Ma02Gv
Cath.	18	F	Unknown	12Ma02Gv
CONNELLEN, Cath.	20	F	Unknown	12Ma02Gv
FITZPATRICK, Catherine	21	F	Unknown	12Ma02Gv
BRENAN, Edward	22	M	Farmer	12Ma02Gv
Thomas	24	M	Farmer	12Ma02Gv
Mary	17	F	Farmer	12Ma02Gv
SOUTHERLAND, Geo.	23	M	Draper	12Ma02Gv
COLLINS, John	30	M	Laborer	12Ma02Gv
Patck.	50	M	Laborer	12Ma02Gv
Ann	50	F	Unknown	12Ma02Gv
Martin	11	M	Unknown	12Ma02Gv
Stephen	9	M	Child	12Ma02Gv
Bridget	21	F	Unknown	12Ma02Gv
Owen	30	M	Laborer	12Ma02Gv
GAGIN, Thomas	30	M	Laborer	12Ma02Gv
Bridget	26	F	Servant	12Ma02Gv
Ann	.00	F	Infant	12Ma02Gv
HANLEY, Thomas	44	M	Farmer	12Ma02Gv
Margaret	40	F	Unknown	12Ma02Gv
Margaret	11	F	Unknown	12Ma02Gv
William	13	M	Unknown	12Ma02Gv
John	9	M	Child	12Ma02Gv
Mary	7	F	Child	12Ma02Gv
Michael	4	M	Child	12Ma02Gv
Thomas	.00	M	Infant	12Ma02Gv
GRONS, John	24	M	Laborer	12Ma02Gv
FREANY, John	21	M	Laborer	12Ma02Gv
RYAN, John	26	M	Laborer	12Ma02Gv
CARROLL, Richard	40	M	Laborer	12Ma02Gv
Mary	30	F	Unknown	12Ma02Gv
LAWLESS, Thos.	21	M	Laborer	12Ma02Gv
Michl.	30	M	Laborer	12Ma02Gv
Margeret	50	F	Unknown	12Ma02Gv
DALTON, Thomas	19	M	Unknown	12Ma02Gv
HEALEY, Mary	24	F	Unknown	12Ma02Gv
FITZGERALD, M.	32	M	Joiner	12Ma02Gv
POWER, Michl.	39	M	Weaver	12Ma02Gv
MANGAN, Patck.	20	M	Laborer	12Ma02Gv
MCDERMET, Thomas	20	M	Farmer	12Ma02Gv
TOOKEY, John	20	M	Laborer	12Ma02Gv
COSTELLO, Jas.	28	M	Farmer	12Ma02Gv
BYRNE, Peter	28	M	Farmer	12Ma02Gv

NAMES OF PASSENGERS	AGE	SEX	OCCUPATIONS	DATE PORT SHIP
BYRNE, Ann	18	F	Servant	12Ma02G
CLOFFY, Richard	18	M	Servant	12Ma02G
SMITH, Jane	17	F	Servant	12Ma02G
FITZSIMMONS, Sarah	30	F	Servant	12Ma02G
DELANEY, William	30	M	Carpenter	12Ma02G
CONNOLLY, Patck.	16	M	Laborer	12Ma02G
MCGUIRE, Mary	17	F	Servant	12Ma02G
HIGGINS, Patck.	18	M	Servant	12Ma02G
FREANY, Eliza	16	F	Servant	12Ma02G
MAHONEY, Thomas	30	M	Smith	12Ma02G
RYLIE, Owen	25	M	Laborer	12Ma02G
Catherine	30	F	Unknown	12Ma02G
QUINN, Richard	35	M	Shoemaker	12Ma02G
BYRNE, Thomas	24	M	Laborer	12Ma02G
DONNELLY, Patck.	35	M	Paper Maker	12Ma02G
CUDDAHY, Nancy	60	F	Unknown	12Ma02G
MCGRATH, Thos.	17	M	Laborer	12Ma02G
DOOLEY, John	30	M	Laborer	12Ma02G
John	10	M	Laborer	12Ma02G
Mary	7	F	Child	12Ma02G

SARAH 14 MAY 1849

From St. JOHNS, N.F.

NAMES OF PASSENGERS	AGE	SEX	OCCUPATIONS	DATE PORT SHIP
MARSHALL, John	29	M	Bricklayer	14Ma56A
Elizabeth	30	F	None	14Ma56A
Sarah	6	F	Child	14Ma56A
Frances	4	F	Child	14Ma56A
Elizabeth	2	F	Child	14Ma56A
U	.02	F	Infant	14Ma56A
BROWNING, Thomas	17	M	Mason	14Ma56A
MURPHY, Lawrence	30	M	Fisherman	14Ma56A
CUNNINGHAM, Alexander	32	M	Carpenter	14Ma56A
BYRNE, Michael	36	M	Fisherman	14Ma56A
WHALEN, Michael	55	M	Fisherman	14Ma56A
DOHENY, Patk.	36	M	Fisherman	14Ma56A
LANDY, Michael	35	M	Carpenter	14Ma56A
KENT, Thomas	26	M	Fisherman	14Ma56A
WILLIAMS, Patrick	28	M	Fisherman	14Ma56A
POPE, Henry	19	M	Blacksmith	14Ma56A
BRENAN, John	30	M	Tailor	14Ma56A
BARKER, George	20	M	Carpenter	14Ma56A
KUMBLE, Wm.	26	M	Seaman	14Ma56A
WALSH, Michael	41	M	Cooper	14Ma56A
CONDON, John	37	M	Fisherman	14Ma56A
BROWNING, Thomas	36	M	Carpenter	14Ma56A

MARY-MITCHELL 14 MAY 1849

From Cork

NAMES OF PASSENGERS	AGE	SEX	OCCUPATIONS	DATE PORT SHIP
ROONEY, William	24	M	Tailor	14Ma08
Alexander	23	M	Farmer	14Ma08
James	53	M	Tailor	14Ma08
James	.04	M	Infant	14Ma08
Ellen	23	F	Mntl	14Ma08
Margaret	56	F	Mntl	14Ma08
John	24	M	Mechanic	14Ma08
MOUGHAN, Catherine	22	F	Servant	14Ma08
CREITMAN, Margaret	24	F	Servant	14Ma08
Mary	20	F	Servant	14Ma08
MURPHY, John	27	M	Farmer	14Ma08

NAMES OF PASSENGERS	AGE	SEX	OCCUPATIONS	DATE PORT SHIP
MURPHY, Margaret	24	F	Mntl	14Ma08Gc
Timothy	2	M	Child	14Ma08Gc
Catherine	.01	F	Infant	14Ma08Gc
COWHIG, Daniel	25	M	Farmer	14Ma08Gc
BRYAN, Denis	24	M	Farmer	14Ma08Gc
HEFFEMAN, John	00	M	Unknown	14Ma08Gc
Margaret	26	F	Servant	14Ma08Gc
William	3	M	Child	14Ma08Gc
BRENNAN, Jeremiah	18	M	Farmer	14Ma08Gc
DRINNAN, Johanna	26	F	Servant	14Ma08Gc
KINNERRY, Michl.	22	M	Farmer	14Ma08Gc
CROWLEY, Michl.	20	M	Farmer	14Ma08Gc
Margaret	22	F	Servant	14Ma08Gc
DONOVAN, Michl.	20	M	Servant	14Ma08Gc
ONEIL, Pat	45	M	Laborer	14Ma08Gc
TOOMEY, Daniel	28	M	Laborer	14Ma08Gc
RIORDAN, Ellen	22	F	Servant	14Ma08Gc
Kitty	16	F	Servant	14Ma08Gc
LONERGAN, Mary	24	F	Servant	14Ma08Gc
CURTAIN, Timothy	30	M	Laborer	14Ma08Gc
Colman	20	M	Laborer	14Ma08Gc
Johanna	22	F	Servant	14Ma08Gc
BARRY, Mary	4	F	Child	14Ma08Gc
DEMPSEY, Tead	23	M	Farmer	14Ma08Gc
Mary	24	F	Servant	14Ma08Gc
DALY, Daniel	30	M	Farmer	14Ma08Gc
Julia	30	F	Seamstress	14Ma08Gc
Mary	10	F	Unknown	14Ma08Gc
John	7	M	Child	14Ma08Gc
Anne	4	F	Child	14Ma08Gc
Catherine	.10	F	Infant	14Ma08Gc
CALLAHAN, Margaret	12	F	Servant	14Ma08Gc
HALLAHAN, Margaret	18	F	Servant	14Ma08Gc
CROWLEY, Elizabeth	20	F	Servant	14Ma08Gc
RYAN, Ellen	30	F	Mntl	14Ma08Gc
MCCARTHY, Kate	35	F	Mntl	14Ma08Gc
Kate	1	F	Child	14Ma08Gc
SHEEHY, Pat	20	M	Farmer	14Ma08Gc
Bridget	23	F	Seamstress	14Ma08Gc
WALSH, John	27	M	Farmer	14Ma08Gc
Nanne	18	F	Seamstress	14Ma08Gc
BARRY, James	19	M	Laborer	14Ma08Gc
HANIFAN, Mary	18	F	Servant	14Ma08Gc
WALSH, John	24	M	Unknown	14Ma08Gc
TOOHIG, Paddy	30	M	Laborer	14Ma08Gc
NEINAN, Denis	26	M	Laborer	14Ma08Gc
RIORDON, Edmund	20	M	Laborer	14Ma08Gc
COLLINS, John	40	M	Farmer	14Ma08Gc
Eliza	40	F	Seamstress	14Ma08Gc
Johannan	11	F	Child	14Ma08Gc
SHEA, Honora	20	F	Servant	14Ma08Gc
DRISCOLL, John	20	M	Farmer	14Ma08Gc
Denis	21	M	Farmer	14Ma08Gc
Mary	63	F	Seamstress	14Ma08Gc
SPENCER, Robert	20	M	Bookkeeper	14Ma08Gc
SULLIVAN, Daniel	38	M	Farmer	14Ma08Gc
SPENCER, Richard	26	M	Bookkeeper	14Ma08Gc
SCANNELL, William	25	M	Farmer	14Ma08Gc
MURRAY, Julia	21	F	Farmer	14Ma08Gc
STACK, John	20	M	Bookkeeper	14Ma08Gc
MURPHY, Jerry	23	M	Laborer	14Ma08Gc
Biddy	20	F	Servant	14Ma08Gc
CONNORS, Mary	54	F	Servant	14Ma08Gc
FEHELY, Catherine	26	F	Servant	14Ma08Gc
MAHONEY, Andy	28	M	Farmer	14Ma08Gc
DONOVAN, James	55	M	Farmer	14Ma08Gc
Harriet	40	F	Seamstress	14Ma08Gc
Timothy	18	M	Farmer	14Ma08Gc
Ellen	13	F	Unknown	14Ma08Gc
Denis	11	M	Unknown	14Ma08Gc
Honora	3	F	Child	14Ma08Gc
CONNORS, Edmund	19	M	Farmer	14Ma08Gc
Abigal	24	F	Servant	14Ma08Gc
DONOVAN, Daniel	49	M	Farmer	14Ma08Gc
Kitty	30	F	Servant	14Ma08Gc

NAMES OF PASSENGERS	AGE	SEX	OCCUPATIONS	DATE PORT SHIP
DONOVAN, Denis	6	M	Child	14Ma08Gc
Honora	4	F	Child	14Ma08Gc
Ellen	.07	F	Infant	14Ma08Gc
SHEEHAN, David	28	M	Laborer	14Ma08Gc
CARROLL, Mary	50	F	Servant	14Ma08Gc
SHANAHAN, Denis	35	M	Laborer	14Ma08Gc
COTTER, Mary	20	F	Seamstress	14Ma08Gc
FLYNN, Norry	18	F	Servant	14Ma08Gc
CONNORS, John	25	M	Mechanic	14Ma08Gc
BARRY, Johannan	48	F	Seamstress	14Ma08Gc
Peggy	20	F	Seamstress	14Ma08Gc
Mary	8	F	Child	14Ma08Gc
MURPHY, Denis	26	M	Carpenter	14Ma08Gc
GLEE, Larry	30	M	Laborer	14Ma08Gc
FEEN, John	30	M	Laborer	14Ma08Gc
Daniel	30	M	Laborer	14Ma08Gc
Cornelius	18	M	Laborer	14Ma08Gc
SHEA, Ellen	14	F	Servant	14Ma08Gc
CASEY, Thomas	30	M	Servant	14Ma08Gc
FOLY, Ellen	20	F	Seamstress	14Ma08Gc
MAHONEY, Julia	20	F	Seamstress	14Ma08Gc
FRIEMAN, Esther	22	F	Seamstress	14Ma08Gc
GRANGER, Eliza	35	F	Seamstress	14Ma08Gc
COLLINS, James-Mrs.	28	F	Seamstress	14Ma08Gc
HYDE, Henry	26	M	Farmer	14Ma08Gc
Robert	24	M	Farmer	14Ma08Gc
William	22	M	Farmer	14Ma08Gc
MCQUIRE, Terence	50	M	Farmer	14Ma08Gc
DIVINE, Bridget	20	F	Farmer	14Ma08Gc
MCQUIRE, Peter	18	M	Farmer	14Ma08Gc
DIVINE, Julia	18	F	Farmer	14Ma08Gc
MURPHY, Hanah	32	F	Farmer	14Ma08Gc
FITZGERALD, Ellen	50	F	Seamstress	14Ma08Gc
Anne	18	F	Seamstress	14Ma08Gc
Sarah	16	F	Seamstress	14Ma08Gc
ANDERSON, Charles-F.	32	M	Architect	14Ma08Gc
U-Mrs.	28	F	Unknown	14Ma08Gc
Charles-F.	16	M	Unknown	14Ma08Gc
Robert	15	M	Unknown	14Ma08Gc
Lawrence	17	M	Unknown	14Ma08Gc
Pelham	12	M	Unknown	14Ma08Gc
Eliza	8	F	Child	14Ma08Gc
Francis	6	M	Child	14Ma08Gc
TERRY, Richard	40	M	Farmer	14Ma08Gc
MURPHY, Patrick	45	M	Carpenter	14Ma08Gc
LYONS, Mary	30	F	Seamstress	14Ma08Gc

N.H.WOLF 15 MAY 1849

From Liverpool

NAMES OF PASSENGERS	AGE	SEX	OCCUPATIONS	DATE PORT SHIP
BURILL, Jno.	58	M	Laborer	15Ma02Gd
Richard	28	M	Laborer	15Ma02Gd
Mary	10	F	Unknown	15Ma02Gd
MAID, Margt.	20	F	Spinster	15Ma02Gd
Mary	18	F	Spinster	15Ma02Gd
HEFFRON, Wm.	22	M	Trade Man	15Ma02Gd
Bridget	23	F	Trade Man	15Ma02Gd
CUNNUNGHAM, Johanna	19	F	Spinster	15Ma02Gd
CORRIGAN, Wm.	28	M	Laborer	15Ma02Gd
MISKILL, Thos.	20	M	Laborer	15Ma02Gd
OROURKE, Tim	26	M	Laborer	15Ma02Gd
Tim	24	M	Laborer	15Ma02Gd
LANDRIGAN, Edwd.	20	M	Laborer	15Ma02Gd
BURKE, Judy	22	F	Spinster	15Ma02Gd
FLINN, Alice	20	F	Spinster	15Ma02Gd
WARD, Mary	28	F	Spinster	15Ma02Gd
RYAN, Jno.	30	M	Trade Man	15Ma02Gd
DONOVAN, Mic	30	M	Laborer	15Ma02Gd

NAMES OF PASSENGERS	AGE	SEX	OCCUPATIONS	DATE PORT SHIP
PRICE, Wm.	30	M	Laborer	15Ma02Gd
Mary	55	F	Laborer	15Ma02Gd
Michl.	.00	M	Infant	15Ma02Gd
COLLINS, Mary-Ann	19	F	Spinster	15Ma02Gd
ODEMPSEY, Fred.Jas.	28	M	Laborer	15Ma02Gd
Jos.	16	M	Laborer	15Ma02Gd
MOSSOP, Peter	19	M	Laborer	15Ma02Gd
MCCAFFREY, Berd.	42	M	Laborer	15Ma02Gd
Bridget	40	F	Laborer	15Ma02Gd
James	13	M	Laborer	15Ma02Gd
Denis	4	M	Child	15Ma02Gd
Mary-Ann	.00	F	Infant	15Ma02Gd
James	22	M	Laborer	15Ma02Gd
Margt.	19	F	Spinster	15Ma02Gd
GENFIELD, Jas.	35	M	Laborer	15Ma02Gd
Susan	33	F	Unknown	15Ma02Gd
Thos.	5	M	Child	15Ma02Gd
Jas.	3	M	Child	15Ma02Gd
RICHARDSON, Jas.	25	M	Servant	15Ma02Gd
Susan	22	F	Servant	15Ma02Gd
HEADEN, Pat	27	M	Laborer	15Ma02Gd
Bridget	25	F	Servant	15Ma02Gd
Mgt.	22	F	Servant	15Ma02Gd
HEALEY, Mich.	30	M	Laborer	15Ma02Gd
HEADON, Dan	20	M	Laborer	15Ma02Gd
Jno.	11	M	Laborer	15Ma02Gd
Mary	9	F	Servant	15Ma02Gd
MURRAN, Tim.	60	M	Servant	15Ma02Gd
HEADON, Ann	20	F	Servant	15Ma02Gd
FOGARTY, Thos.	23	M	Laborer	15Ma02Gd
HINDS, Mgt.	48	F	Spinster	15Ma02Gd
Ellen	24	F	Spinster	15Ma02Gd
Johanna	20	F	Spinster	15Ma02Gd
Mgt.	4	F	Child	15Ma02Gd
GRAHAM, Wm.	28	M	Laborer	15Ma02Gd
Ellenor	25	F	Servant	15Ma02Gd
Jno.Jas.	3	M	Child	15Ma02Gd
Died-At-Sea				
Wm.Henry	.00	M	Infant	15Ma02Gd
Died-At-Sea				
MCCABE, Owen	37	M	Carpenter	15Ma02Gd
Judy	35	F	Servant	15Ma02Gd
Hugh	9	M	Child	15Ma02Gd
Jane	7	F	Child	15Ma02Gd
Pat	5	M	Child	15Ma02Gd
Peter	2	M	Child	15Ma02Gd
Pat	33	M	Laborer	15Ma02Gd
Cath.	31	F	Spinster	15Ma02Gd
Mary	3	F	Child	15Ma02Gd
FLANNINGAN, Bridget	24	F	Spinster	15Ma02Gd
Owen	18	M	Laborer	15Ma02Gd
BOYLE, Pat	31	M	Laborer	15Ma02Gd
Bridget	31	F	Servant	15Ma02Gd
Cath	4	F	Child	15Ma02Gd
Pat	1	M	Child	15Ma02Gd
PRICE, Jno.	27	M	Laborer	15Ma02Gd
David	25	M	Laborer	15Ma02Gd
KIRBY, Fred	34	M	Laborer	15Ma02Gd
Cath.	32	F	Spinster	15Ma02Gd
Jim	11	M	Laborer	15Ma02Gd
Fanny	6	F	Child	15Ma02Gd
Thos.	7	M	Child	15Ma02Gd
Phillip	4	M	Child	15Ma02Gd
Wm.	.00	M	Infant	15Ma02Gd
Esther	56	F	Servant	15Ma02Gd
Job	38	M	Laborer	15Ma02Gd
PILKINS, Chas.	38	M	Laborer	15Ma02Gd
Mary-Ann	32	F	Servant	15Ma02Gd
Eliza	5	F	Child	15Ma02Gd
KERSEY, Richard	28	M	Laborer	15Ma02Gd
Emma	26	F	Spinster	15Ma02Gd
Vincent	2	M	Child	15Ma02Gd
Thos.	.00	M	Infant	15Ma02Gd
COX, Henry	26	M	Laborer	15Ma02Gd
Maria	25	F	Servant	15Ma02Gd

NAMES OF PASSENGERS	AGE	SEX	OCCUPATIONS	DATE PORT SHIP
COX, Ruth	5	F	Child	15Ma02Gd
COLLINSON, Jno.	42	M	Laborer	15Ma02Gd
ROUSE, Jas.	24	M	Laborer	15Ma02Gd
PALL, Wm.	18	M	Laborer	15Ma02Gd
WALKIN, Enoch	18	M	Laborer	15Ma02Gd
ELLISTON, Geo.	23	M	Laborer	15Ma02Gd
ACROFT, Geo.	39	M	Laborer	15Ma02Gd
Ann	26	F	Servant	15Ma02Gd
Thos.	3	M	Child	15Ma02Gd
Jas.	5	M	Child	15Ma02Gd
MASON, Jas.	29	M	Laborer	15Ma02Gd
Mary	32	F	Spinster	15Ma02Gd
WRIGHT, Jno.	40	M	Laborer	15Ma02Gd
RYAN, Jno.	23	M	Laborer	15Ma02Gd
Mgt.	24	F	Servant	15Ma02Gd
Jas.	2	M	Child	15Ma02Gd
DWYER, Jim	22	M	Laborer	15Ma02Gd
MCCABE, Thos.	18	M	Laborer	15Ma02Gd
Rose	20	F	Servant	15Ma02Gd
KELLAN, Jas.	50	M	Laborer	15Ma02Gd
Mary	41	F	Spinster	15Ma02Gd
Mary	21	F	Spinster	15Ma02Gd
Ann	15	F	Spinster	15Ma02Gd
Peter	13	M	Laborer	15Ma02Gd
Bridget	11	F	Servant	15Ma02Gd
Eliz.	9	F	Child	15Ma02Gd
Thos.	7	M	Child	15Ma02Gd
Pat	4	M	Child	15Ma02Gd
HUDSON, Wm.	28	M	Laborer	15Ma02Gd
Ellen	23	F	Servant	15Ma02Gd
Hannah	3	F	Child	15Ma02Gd
Mary-Ann	.00	F	Infant	15Ma02Gd
ROBINSON, Jno.	45	M	Laborer	15Ma02Gd
BRIGGS, Thos.	31	M	Laborer	15Ma02Gd
Mary	30	F	Servant	15Ma02Gd
Thos.	6	M	Child	15Ma02Gd
Mary	2	F	Child	15Ma02Gd
Eliza	.00	F	Infant	15Ma02Gd
CARROLL, Pat	21	M	Laborer	15Ma02Gd
JAMESTON, Chas.	32	M	Laborer	15Ma02Gd
Ellen	25	F	Servant	15Ma02Gd
Ellen	5	F	Child	15Ma02Gd
DALEY, Mary	30	F	Servant	15Ma02Gd
HOAKS, Wm.	34	M	Laborer	15Ma02Gd
DUNNE, Wm.	30	M	Laborer	15Ma02Gd
MCCARTY, Chas.	11	M	Laborer	15Ma02Gd
KENNEDY, Robert	22	M	Laborer	15Ma02Gd
Andrew	16	M	Laborer	15Ma02Gd
REANEY, Wm.	18	M	Laborer	15Ma02Gd
MCDERMOTT, Edwd.	24	M	Laborer	15Ma02Gd
LLOYD, Mary	20	F	Servant	15Ma02Gd
CASEY, James	50	M	Servant	15Ma02Gd
ROAN, Darley	35	M	Servant	15Ma02Gd
COLGAN, James	30	M	Laborer	15Ma02Gd
Sarah	30	F	Servant	15Ma02Gd
Died-At-Sea				
Cath	18	F	Servant	15Ma02Gd
Wm.	25	M	Laborer	15Ma02Gd
CASSIDY, Mich	15	M	Laborer	15Ma02G
SHOAVAN, Jane	10	F	Servant	15Ma02G
DALTON, Jane	32	F	Servant	15Ma02G
AVERYARD, Sarah	28	F	Servant	15Ma02G
Eliza	.00	F	Infant	15Ma02G
BRYAN, Thos.	35	M	Laborer	15Ma02G
Cath	30	F	Servant	15Ma02G
COLGAN, Dan	28	M	Servant	15Ma02G
Norry	29	F	Servant	15Ma02G
Biddy	4	F	Child	15Ma02G
Mich.	1	M	Child	15Ma02G
GLEESON, Mary	24	F	Servant	15Ma02G
ROGAN, Jas.	13	M	Laborer	15Ma02G
BLUANEY, Pat	26	M	Laborer	15Ma02G
FLARETY, Jno.	26	M	Laborer	15Ma02G
SWENDERGEN, Jas.	22	M	Laborer	15Ma02G
CORCORAN, Jno	19	M	Laborer	15Ma02G

NAMES OF PASSENGERS	AGE	SEX	OCCUPATIONS	DATE PORT SHIP
CORCORAN, Cath.	20	F	Spinster	15Ma02Gd
HICKEY, Jno.	40	M	Laborer	15Ma02Gd
Mary	35	F	Servant	15Ma02Gd
Pat	13	M	Laborer	15Ma02Gd
Cath.	9	F	Child	15Ma02Gd
Jno.	5	M	Child	15Ma02Gd
Ellen	3	F	Child	15Ma02Gd
Cath.	2	F	Child	15Ma02Gd
MAHON, Judy	21	F	Spinster	15Ma02Gd
MONA, Richard	35	M	Laborer	15Ma02Gd
Anty	32	F	Spinster	15Ma02Gd
COGLAN, Jas.	25	M	Laborer	15Ma02Gd
HIGGINS, Jerry	36	M	Laborer	15Ma02Gd
MCQUADE, Edward	30	M	Laborer	15Ma02Gd
MCNAMARA, Thos.	24	M	Laborer	15Ma02Gd
MCGURNE, Owen	26	M	Laborer	15Ma02Gd
GRADY, Dan	22	M	Laborer	15Ma02Gd
Ellen	20	F	Servant	15Ma02Gd
KAYMAN, Rose	30	F	Servant	15Ma02Gd
WAID, Jno.	20	M	Laborer	15Ma02Gd
MITCHELL, Wm.	19	M	Laborer	15Ma02Gd
CONNELL, Rich.	35	M	Laborer	15Ma02Gd
Mary	30	F	Servant	15Ma02Gd
Pat	10	M	Servant	15Ma02Gd
Cath.	.00	F	Infant	15Ma02Gd
CLASEY, Jno.	35	M	Laborer	15Ma02Gd
MARTIN, Mary	20	F	Servant	15Ma02Gd
CREED, Bridget	20	F	Servant	15Ma02Gd
GRADY, Jas.	25	M	Servant	15Ma02Gd
MCMAHON, Owen	20	M	Servant	15Ma02Gd
Anne	18	F	Servant	15Ma02Gd
Cath.	15	F	Servant	15Ma02Gd
MACINTYRE, Pat	20	M	Laborer	15Ma02Gd
DENIS, Jno.	13	M	Laborer	15Ma02Gd
MACMAN, Ann	25	F	Spinster	15Ma02Gd
DYSEN, Anne	4	F	Child	15Ma02Gd
LLEEVIN, Mic.	45	M	Laborer	15Ma02Gd
Cath.	41	F	Servant	15Ma02Gd
Jane	10	F	Servant	15Ma02Gd
SMITH, Michl.	25	M	Laborer	15Ma02Gd
U-Mrs.	20	F	Spinster	15Ma02Gd
MCDONALD, Mick	24	M	Laborer	15Ma02Gd
JOICE, Bridget	35	F	Servant	15Ma02Gd
Mark	6	M	Child	15Ma02Gd

CANADA 17 MAY 1849

From Liverpool And Halifax

NAMES OF PASSENGERS	AGE	SEX	OCCUPATIONS	DATE PORT SHIP
WETHERELL, Alex.	26	M	Unknown	17Ma49Fy
Edwd.	24	M	Unknown	17Ma49Fy
CURRIE, L.D.H.	17	M	Army	17Ma49Fy
MILLER, R.T.	26	M	Merchant	17Ma49Fy
BROWN, Chas.	28	M	Merchant	17Ma49Fy
TAYLOR, T.T.	35	M	Merchant	17Ma49Fy
SIDNEY, Ggeo.	40	M	Merchant	17Ma49Fy
HOWAT, R.K.	19	M	Unknown	17Ma49Fy
HAYES, J.M.	56	M	Merchant	17Ma49Fy
CLAYTON, G.R.	26	M	Merchant	17Ma49Fy
PHILLIPS, E.	24	F	Unknown	17Ma49Fy
WATKINS, John	55	M	Merchant	17Ma49Fy
E.	37	F	Unknown	17Ma49Fy
WORTLEY, E.Stuart	30	F	Unknown	17Ma49Fy
U	12	F	Unknown	17Ma49Fy
OYTE, Ann	30	F	Unknown	17Ma49Fy
WILKINSON, M.A.	25	F	Unknown	17Ma49Fy
ARCLAY, A.C.	25	M	Merchant	17Ma49Fy
LLIOTT, W.	28	M	Unknown	17Ma49Fy
E.	28	F	Unknown	17Ma49Fy
ROBIN, T.V.	20	M	Unknown	17Ma49Fy
BELLHOUSE, A.	40	M	Merchant	17Ma49Fy
D.	18	M	Unknown	17Ma49Fy
KLOHS, U-Mrs.	23	F	Unknown	17Ma49Fy
HARVEY, Aaron	48	M	Farmer	17Ma49Fy
THORP, Robert	35	M	Merchant	17Ma49Fy
HESLOP, Geo.	37	M	Miller	17Ma49Fy
LUCAS, Thos.	32	M	Draper	17Ma49Fy
Agnes	27	F	Unknown	17Ma49Fy
Emma	1	F	Child	17Ma49Fy
LABRAY, Wm.	24	M	Unknown	17Ma49Fy
MIDDLETON, Wm.	22	M	Stationer	17Ma49Fy
ROBB, John	41	M	Merchant	17Ma49Fy
MCFARLAN, D.	40	M	Merchant	17Ma49Fy
BROWN, Thos.	53	M	Merchant	17Ma49Fy
SIMPSON, Saml.	27	M	Merchant	17Ma49Fy
SANDERSON, Wm.	21	M	Merchant	17Ma49Fy
HAMILTON, James	36	M	Farmer	17Ma49Fy

J.Z. 17 MAY 1849

From Liverpool

NAMES OF PASSENGERS	AGE	SEX	OCCUPATIONS	DATE PORT SHIP
WHELAN, Richard	12	M	Farmer	17Ma02Ge
Pat	13	M	Farmer	17Ma02Ge
John	40	M	Farmer	17Ma02Ge
Mich.	50	M	Farmer	17Ma02Ge
FORD, James	26	M	Farmer	17Ma02Ge
Robt.	28	M	Farmer	17Ma02Ge
Bridget	50	F	Farmer	17Ma02Ge
CLORAN, John	40	M	Baker	17Ma02Ge
Mich.	18	M	Baker	17Ma02Ge
Francis	16	F	Baker	17Ma02Ge
Mary	40	F	Baker	17Ma02Ge
John	7	M	Child	17Ma02Ge
Maria	4	F	Child	17Ma02Ge
Rose	19	F	Baker	17Ma02Ge
FAHEY, Mich.	35	M	Baker	17Ma02Ge
DEAN, John	22	M	Mason	17Ma02Ge
PARKERS, Mary	19	F	Laborer	17Ma02Ge
RYAN, Dan	23	M	Laborer	17Ma02Ge
MCDERMOTT, Pat	30	M	Laborer	17Ma02Ge
HINES, Edna	40	F	Laborer	17Ma02Ge
Edna	6	F	Child	17Ma02Ge
Mary	4	F	Child	17Ma02Ge
GARRATY, Hugh	25	M	Laborer	17Ma02Ge
MCEVER, Grace	50	F	Laborer	17Ma02Ge
Cath.	4	F	Child	17Ma02Ge
Anty	6	F	Child	17Ma02Ge
BRADLEY, Ellen	50	F	Laborer	17Ma02Ge
MCDERMOTT, John	30	M	Laborer	17Ma02Ge
COLLINS, Mary	16	F	Laborer	17Ma02Ge
BRANICAN, Brig.	50	F	Laborer	17Ma02Ge
LANTY, Mary	30	F	Laborer	17Ma02Ge
Matt	8	M	Child	17Ma02Ge
Ellen	6	F	Child	17Ma02Ge
Rose	5	F	Child	17Ma02Ge
Cath.	.08	F	Infant	17Ma02Ge
HARLEY, Owen	28	M	Laborer	17Ma02Ge
Martin	26	M	Laborer	17Ma02Ge
MACKERELL, S.	20	M	Laborer	17Ma02Ge
ORNSBEY, Wm.	26	M	Shoemaker	17Ma02Ge
COLEMAN, Thos.	58	M	Blacksmith	17Ma02Ge
Cath.	58	F	Blacksmith	17Ma02Ge
Rich.	16	M	Blacksmith	17Ma02Ge
Edw.	12	M	Blacksmith	17Ma02Ge
Cath.	11	F	Blacksmith	17Ma02Ge
Hones	10	F	Blacksmith	17Ma02Ge
Peggy	6	F	Child	17Ma02Ge

NAMES OF PASSENGERS	AGE	SEX	OCCUPATIONS	DATE PORT SHIP	NAMES OF PASSENGERS	AGE	SEX	OCCUPATIONS	DATE PORT SHIP
CAVANAGH, Mary	50	F	Lad	17Ma02Ge	MOLONEY, Dennis	22	M	Laborer	17Ma02Ge
Dan	10	M	Unknown	17Ma02Ge	CONELLY, Mich.	22	M	Laborer	17Ma02Ge
Mary	7	F	Child	17Ma02Ge	Mary	24	F	Laborer	17Ma02Ge
MCHALE, Brig.	60	F	Unknown	17Ma02Ge	Francis	30	F	Laborer	17Ma02Ge
Marg.	20	F	Unknown	17Ma02Ge	MCGUIRE, James	30	M	Shoemaker	17Ma02Ge
Celia	9	F	Child	17Ma02Ge	MCCABE, Ann	23	F	Unknown	17Ma02Ge
NAUGHTON, Bryan	50	M	Laborer	17Ma02Ge	MCCARLINE, John	25	M	Clerk	17Ma02Ge
Will	50	M	Laborer	17Ma02Ge	COGAN, Mich.	35	M	Farmer	17Ma02Ge
Died-At-Sea					Judy	30	F	Unknown	17Ma02Ge
Mary	11	F	Laborer	17Ma02Ge	SHANNON, James	38	M	Tailor	17Ma02Ge
John	10	M	Laborer	17Ma02Ge	Cath.	40	F	Tailor	17Ma02Ge
Anne	7	F	Child	17Ma02Ge	Margt.	5	F	Child	17Ma02Ge
Mich.	5	M	Child	17Ma02Ge	Ellen	.07	F	Infant	17Ma02Ge
Win.	3	F	Child	17Ma02Ge	JOHNSON, Wm.	24	M	Laborer	17Ma02Ge
Anne	9	F	Child	17Ma02Ge	RIGGS, Wm.	24	M	Laborer	17Ma02Ge
BURKE, Mary	20	F	Lad	17Ma02Ge	WORTHINGTON, Mark	25	M	Laborer	17Ma02Ge
FURRY, James	19	M	Laborer	17Ma02Ge	DONAGHUE, Will	20	M	Laborer	17Ma02Ge
BIGLEY, Thos.	20	M	Unknown	17Ma02Ge	COPLEY, John	28	M	Laborer	17Ma02Ge
BYRNE, John	25	M	Unknown	17Ma02Ge	CASH, Will.	50	M	Farmer	17Ma02Ge
Anne	20	F	Servant	17Ma02Ge	Ellen	48	F	Farmer	17Ma02Ge
SMITH, Phil.	50	M	Laborer	17Ma02Ge	Ann	20	F	Farmer	17Ma02Ge
Marg.	50	F	Laborer	17Ma02Ge	Mary	18	F	Farmer	17Ma02Ge
Pat	11	M	Laborer	17Ma02Ge	Bridget	16	F	Farmer	17Ma02Ge
Marg.	9	F	Child	17Ma02Ge	Will	12	M	Farmer	17Ma02Ge
Rose	7	F	Child	17Ma02Ge	Mic	5	M	Child	17Ma02Ge
Phil	5	M	Child	17Ma02Ge	Kate	8	F	Child	17Ma02Ge
BRENAN, Mary	17	F	Servant	17Ma02Ge	Judy	.10	F	Infant	17Ma02Ge
MCGARRY, Pat	10	M	Servant	17Ma02Ge	CLANCY, Thos.	20	M	Farmer	17Ma02Ge
LEWIS, Richd.	27	M	Laborer	17Ma02Ge	CONELLY, Thos.	20	M	Farmer	17Ma02Ge
DANAGH, Ellen	27	F	Laborer	17Ma02Ge	LAFRAN, Edw.	20	M	Farmer	17Ma02Ge
MURRY, Cath.	9	F	Child	17Ma02Ge	CALLAHAN, Thos.	20	M	Shoemaker	17Ma02Ge
Mich.	7	M	Child	17Ma02Ge	RYAN, Jer.	20	M	Shoemaker	17Ma02Ge
CLARK, John	17	M	Laborer	17Ma02Ge	Ellen	18	F	Shoemaker	17Ma02Ge
MCGARTY, Brid.	17	F	Servant	17Ma02Ge	CONLAN, Bart.	29	M	Cooper	17Ma02Ge
GURREY, Mary	40	F	Unknown	17Ma02Ge	LYONS, Mich.	30	M	Farmer	17Ma02Ge
James	17	M	Laborer	17Ma02Ge	Brid.	27	F	Farmer	17Ma02Ge
FLETCHER, Cath.	22	F	Servant	17Ma02Ge	Honora	.11	F	Infant	17Ma02Ge
SNEE, Cath.	29	F	Servant	17Ma02Ge	LYNON, Will	50	M	Miller	17Ma02Ge
KILLERLAN, Brig.	18	F	Servant	17Ma02Ge	DONOGHUE, Hugh	29	M	Farmer	17Ma02Ge
SMITH, Eliza	20	F	Servant	17Ma02Ge	MARTIN, Geo.	40	M	Weaver	17Ma02Ge
ASPOLS, Cath.	19	F	Servant	17Ma02Ge	KELLY, Pat	40	M	Laborer	17Ma02Ge
MCKEEVER, James	21	M	Laborer	17Ma02Ge	BOWDEN, Rich.	40	M	Porter	17Ma02Ge
HARLEY, Honora	45	F	Servant	17Ma02Ge	WHITE, Martin	32	M	Laborer	17Ma02Ge
STANLEY, Jane	20	F	Lad	17Ma02Ge	Mich.	37	M	Laborer	17Ma02Ge
HICKEY, Mary	20	F	Unknown	17Ma02Ge	RYAN, John	20	M	Laborer	17Ma02Ge
CONNELL, Rose	19	F	Unknown	17Ma02Ge	Amos	20	M	Laborer	17Ma02Ge
CAVAN, Thos.	24	M	Laborer	17Ma02Ge	Con.	21	M	Laborer	17Ma02Ge
BARRETT, John	20	M	Laborer	17Ma02Ge	Cath.	26	F	Laborer	17Ma02Ge
TOGHER, James	24	M	Laborer	17Ma02Ge	MAHER, Mary	19	F	Laborer	17Ma02Ge
ROLAND, Cath.	28	F	Laborer	17Ma02Ge	HALPIN, Mic.	20	M	Shoemaker	17Ma02Ge
Pat	6	M	Child	17Ma02Ge	BOLSTER, John	25	M	Shoemaker	17Ma02Ge
Mich.	3	M	Child	17Ma02Ge	Rich.	24	M	Laborer	17Ma02Ge
MURPHY, James	25	M	Laborer	17Ma02Ge	Brid.	30	F	Laborer	17Ma02Ge
BRENNAN, Marg.	25	F	Servant	17Ma02Ge	RYAN, Cath.	25	F	Laborer	17Ma02Ge
FLYNN, Johanna	20	F	Servant	17Ma02Ge	BURNS, Johanna	40	F	Laborer	17Ma02Ge
FIERY, Mary	25	F	Servant	17Ma02Ge	Mary	6	F	Child	17Ma02Ge
TIERNEY, Geo.	3	M	Child	17Ma02Ge	CONNOR, Pat	20	M	Laborer	17Ma02Ge
ALLEN, Ellen	30	F	Servant	17Ma02Ge	OBRIEN, Morgen	25	M	Laborer	17Ma02Ge
HAWKES, Will.	34	M	Laborer	17Ma02Ge	MACKEY, Will	34	M	Laborer	17Ma02Ge
COYNE, John	24	M	Unknown	17Ma02Ge	RYAN, John	30	M	Laborer	17Ma02Ge
CAREY, James	50	M	Farmer	17Ma02Ge	Mary	24	F	Laborer	17Ma02Ge
Pat	20	M	Farmer	17Ma02Ge	Honora	26	F	Laborer	17Ma02Ge
Esther	22	F	Farmer	17Ma02Ge	Will.	4	M	Child	17Ma02Ge
DORAN, Marg.	22	F	Farmer	17Ma02Ge	FRANKLIN, John	20	M	Child	17Ma02Ge
Brig.	23	F	Farmer	17Ma02Ge	John	.09	M	Infant	17Ma02Ge
CAROON, Cath.	23	F	Farmer	17Ma02Ge	WHOLEHAM, Ann	19	F	Servant	17Ma02Ge
GIBNEY, James	24	M	Farmer	17Ma02Ge	DOWDELL, Will.	28	M	Bricklayer	17Ma02Ge
FITZGERALD, And.	26	M	Carpenter	17Ma02Ge	U-Mrs.	33	F	Bricklayer	17Ma02Ge
Pat	20	M	Laborer	17Ma02Ge	BUSKLEY, Rich.	23	M	Seaman	17Ma02Ge
CRAWFORD, Sarah	32	F	Servant	17Ma02Ge	MINAGAN, Rich.	20	M	Farmer	17Ma02Ge
Mary	4	F	Child	17Ma02Ge	Brid.	20	F	Farmer	17Ma02Ge
FINLAN, Mich.	25	M	Servant	17Ma02Ge	John	2	M	Child	17Ma02Ge
U-Mrs.	25	F	Laborer	17Ma02Ge	Cath.	.11	F	Infant	17Ma02Ge
Mary	3	F	Child	17Ma02Ge	MAHON, John	25	M	Farmer	17Ma02Ge
Marg.	.10	F	Infant	17Ma02Ge	U-Mrs.	24	F	Farmer	17Ma02Ge

NAMES OF PASSENGERS	AGE	SEX	OCCUPATIONS	DATE PORT SHIP
LAHEY, Law.	28	M	Laborer	17Ma02Ge
NUGENT, Mic.	30	M	Laborer	17Ma02Ge
CUDDY, Dan.	32	M	Laborer	17Ma02Ge
HOGAN, Andw.	34	M	Laborer	17Ma02Ge
KING, Eliza	20	F	Dressmaker	17Ma02Ge
Margt.	21	F	Dressmaker	17Ma02Ge
ROGERS, Susan	20	F	Dressmaker	17Ma02Ge
LITTLE, Eliza	23	F	Servant	17Ma02Ge
Thos.	.10	M	Infant	17Ma02Ge
DONICAN, Pat	30	M	Coachman	17Ma02Ge
Ann	25	F	Coachman	17Ma02Ge
Robt.	4	M	Child	17Ma02Ge
Eliza	2	F	Child	17Ma02Ge
NOLAND, Mary	23	F	Dressmaker	17Ma02Ge
DUFFY, Mary	28	F	Servant	17Ma02Ge
Alice	18	F	Servant	17Ma02Ge
SHERRY, Thos.	25	M	Gdnr	17Ma02Ge
MURRAY, John	50	M	Laborer	17Ma02Ge
Thos.	30	M	Laborer	17Ma02Ge
CONNORS, Thos.	24	M	Laborer	17Ma02Ge
Tho.	20	M	Laborer	17Ma02Ge
Johanna	26	F	Laborer	17Ma02Ge
LITTLE, Will.	22	M	Servant	17Ma02Ge

LIBERTY 21 MAY 1849

From Liverpool

NAMES OF PASSENGERS	AGE	SEX	OCCUPATIONS	DATE PORT SHIP
MONAGHAN, Jas.	22	M	Laborer	21Ma02Gf
PILKEY, Wm.	40	M	Laborer	21Ma02Gf
Jane	36	F	Servant	21Ma02Gf
Jas.	8	M	Child	21Ma02Gf
Rebecca	4	F	Child	21Ma02Gf
Margt.	1	F	Child	21Ma02Gf
MCGLINCHY, Michl.	21	M	Laborer	21Ma02Gf
MCNAUGHT, Mary	45	F	Laborer	21Ma02Gf
Isabella	14	F	Laborer	21Ma02Gf
Wm.	12	M	Laborer	21Ma02Gf
Johnston	10	M	Laborer	21Ma02Gf
Thos.	8	M	Child	21Ma02Gf
Darin	3	M	Child	21Ma02Gf
MACKIN, John	60	M	Cooper	21Ma02Gf
Ann	23	F	Unknown	21Ma02Gf
JAMESON, Mary	20	F	Unknown	21Ma02Gf
MCCANON, Cath.	00	F	Unknown	21Ma02Gf
Thos.	20	M	Unknown	21Ma02Gf
Ann	7	F	Child	21Ma02Gf
Margt.	4	F	Child	21Ma02Gf
Died-At-Sea				
MCNAUGHT, Saml.	6	M	Child	21Ma02Gf
CRASSEN, Brid.	18	F	Fisherman	21Ma02Gf
RILEY, Brid.	18	F	Fisherman	21Ma02Gf
CRASSEN, Susan	56	F	Fisherman	21Ma02Gf
Edw.	18	M	Unknown	21Ma02Gf
HARKIN, Wm.	19	M	Brazier	21Ma02Gf
CONNALLY, John	25	M	Brazier	21Ma02Gf
FARQUAR, John	25	M	Brazier	21Ma02Gf
Darin	21	M	Brazier	21Ma02Gf
Martha	18	F	Brazier	21Ma02Gf
DOGHERTY, Immay	21	F	Brazier	21Ma02Gf
MCGOVERN, Michl.	24	M	Brazier	21Ma02Gf
FERGUSON, Andrew	25	M	Brazier	21Ma02Gf
WRIGHT, Geo.	21	M	Brazier	21Ma02Gf
CONNER, Margt.	30	F	Unknown	21Ma02Gf
HALLORAN, John	30	M	Unknown	21Ma02Gf
WALKINS, Wm.	40	M	Farmer	21Ma02Gf
Sarah	40	F	Farmer	21Ma02Gf
Betsey	20	F	Farmer	21Ma02Gf
Rees	16	M	Farmer	21Ma02Gf
WALKINS, Margt.	12	F	Farmer	21Ma02Gf
Wm.	12	M	Farmer	21Ma02Gf
John	7	M	Child	21Ma02Gf
Roger	.00	M	Infant	21Ma02Gf
WALSH, Wm.	2	M	Child	21Ma02Gf
Thos.	.00	M	Infant	21Ma02Gf
DALLISON, Jas.	32	M	Laborer	21Ma02Gf
Maria	34	F	Laborer	21Ma02Gf
Saml.	15	M	Laborer	21Ma02Gf
PRASSER, John	40	M	Farmer	21Ma02Gf
Ann	40	F	Farmer	21Ma02Gf
John	14	M	Farmer	21Ma02Gf
Ellis	12	M	Farmer	21Ma02Gf
Walter	9	M	Child	21Ma02Gf
WALKINS, Susan	22	F	Cooper	21Ma02Gf
Susannah	2	F	Child	21Ma02Gf
OGARA, John	16	M	Cooper	21Ma02Gf
NABAN, Jas.	28	M	Weaver	21Ma02Gf
Margt.	24	F	Weaver	21Ma02Gf
Jas.	3	M	Child	21Ma02Gf
Margt.	.00	F	Infant	21Ma02Gf
MOOREY, Joseph	28	M	Weaver	21Ma02Gf
Margt.	55	F	Weaver	21Ma02Gf
HUTTON, Wm.	32	M	Weaver	21Ma02Gf
Ann	30	F	Weaver	21Ma02Gf
Joseph	30	M	Weaver	21Ma02Gf
GREEN, Wm.	21	M	Weaver	21Ma02Gf
SIMPSON, Joseph	43	M	Weaver	21Ma02Gf
HOLDERSHAM, Edm.	30	M	Weaver	21Ma02Gf
Sarah	30	F	Weaver	21Ma02Gf
Wm.	17	M	Weaver	21Ma02Gf
Lucy	4	F	Child	21Ma02Gf
Ann	.00	F	Infant	21Ma02Gf
MOODY, John	30	M	Weaver	21Ma02Gf
Bessy	27	F	Weaver	21Ma02Gf
John	3	M	Child	21Ma02Gf
Margt.	.00	F	Infant	21Ma02Gf
RAY, John	21	M	Infant	21Ma02Gf
GALLAGHER, Margt.	20	F	Servant	21Ma02Gf
Dennis	14	M	Unknown	21Ma02Gf
JONES, Mary	60	F	Unknown	21Ma02Gf
LEWIS, Wm.	39	M	Farmer	21Ma02Gf
Mary	35	F	Unknown	21Ma02Gf
Rich.	10	M	Unknown	21Ma02Gf
JOHNSTON, Edw.	25	M	Gdnr	21Ma02Gf
DOLAN, Brid.	10	F	Gdnr	21Ma02Gf
Ann	8	F	Child	21Ma02Gf
LAVILLER, Anty	20	F	Gdnr	21Ma02Gf
CLARKE, Peggy	40	F	Unknown	21Ma02Gf
Grace	14	F	Unknown	21Ma02Gf
PACKET, Margt.	19	F	Unknown	21Ma02Gf
JONES, Mary	40	F	Unknown	21Ma02Gf
FITZPATRICK, Michl.	30	M	Unknown	21Ma02Gf
U, Elzth.	6	F	Child	21Ma02Gf
MCENTYRE, John	50	M	Child	21Ma02Gf
Peter	30	M	Unknown	21Ma02Gf
Bridget	27	F	Unknown	21Ma02Gf
Mary	.00	F	Infant	21Ma02Gf
SHARP, Wm.	28	M	Cooper	21Ma02Gf
COUGHLIN, John	18	M	Weaver	21Ma02Gf
Mary	22	F	Unknown	21Ma02Gf
Honor	20	F	Unknown	21Ma02Gf
BURN, Garrett	22	M	Tailor	21Ma02Gf
POWERS, Wm.	35	M	Tailor	21Ma02Gf
Jas.	10	M	Tailor	21Ma02Gf
BURNSIDE, Bowden	30	M	Farmer	21Ma02Gf
MCCURRY, John	25	M	Unknown	21Ma02Gf
MULLANE, Danl.	20	M	Unknown	21Ma02Gf
HUGHES, Humphrey	45	M	Unknown	21Ma02Gf
HAMMING, Edw.	30	M	Unknown	21Ma02Gf
Mary	25	F	Unknown	21Ma02Gf
TURNER, John	29	M	Unknown	21Ma02Gf
MCKENNA, Con.	37	M	Laborer	21Ma02Gf
Mary	56	F	Unknown	21Ma02Gf
Pat	30	M	Unknown	21Ma02Gf

NAMES OF PASSENGERS	AGE	SEX	OCCUPATIONS	DATE PORT SHIP
MCKENNA, Ellen	27	F	Unknown	21Ma02Gf
Owen	30	M	Unknown	21Ma02Gf
John	18	M	Unknown	21Ma02Gf
Con.	.00	M	Infant	21Ma02Gf
MCKERN, Harry	28	M	Unknown	21Ma02Gf
SHERIDAN, Arthur	26	M	Unknown	21Ma02Gf
MCEVETY, Mary	20	F	Unknown	21Ma02Gf
MCKEON, Luke	24	F	Unknown	21Ma02Gf
REILLY, Jane	20	F	Unknown	21Ma02Gf
LUNY, John	20	F	Unknown	21Ma02Gf
Brid.	21	F	Servant	21Ma02Gf
Ann	.00	F	Infant	21Ma02Gf
ALLEN, Peter	25	M	Cooper	21Ma02Gf
Dennis	27	M	Cooper	21Ma02Gf
SMITH, Mary	30	F	Servant	21Ma02Gf
SANDERSON, Wm.	37	M	Farmer	21Ma02Gf
U-Mrs.	32	F	Unknown	21Ma02Gf
Wm.	11	M	Unknown	21Ma02Gf
Albert	9	M	Child	21Ma02Gf
Sarah	6	F	Child	21Ma02Gf
Joseph	4	M	Child	21Ma02Gf
Edwin	.00	M	Infant	21Ma02Gf
Died-At-Sea				
LADOR, John	28	M	Smith	21Ma02Gf
DAGNAN, James	20	M	Weaver	21Ma02Gf
Frat	30	M	Weaver	21Ma02Gf
BOYD, George	21	M	Weaver	21Ma02Gf
WRIGHTMAN, Thos.	28	M	Laborer	21Ma02Gf
CALLAGHAN, Kate	20	F	Servant	21Ma02Gf
DENNAGHY, Pat	21	M	Unknown	21Ma02Gf
EYRE, Edw.	31	M	Unknown	21Ma02Gf
Charlotte	25	F	Unknown	21Ma02Gf
John	5	M	Child	21Ma02Gf
Geo.	3	M	Child	21Ma02Gf
Olivia	1	F	Child	21Ma02Gf
DENNAGHY, Geo.	21	M	Unknown	21Ma02Gf
Wm.	22	M	Unknown	21Ma02Gf
HALLAN, Joseph	30	M	Unknown	21Ma02Gf
Mary	25	F	Unknown	21Ma02Gf
JONES, David	35	M	Miner	21Ma02Gf
Lydia	21	F	Unknown	21Ma02Gf
Sarah	.00	F	Infant	21Ma02Gf
CHAMBERLAIN, Selin	21	M	Unknown	21Ma02Gf
PATLEY, Jacob	42	M	Unknown	21Ma02Gf
GALES, Edw.	41	M	Unknown	21Ma02Gf
KNIGHT, R.	37	M	Unknown	21Ma02Gf
DRAKE, Geo.	18	M	Laborer	21Ma02Gf
BURROWS, Wm.	43	M	Laborer	21Ma02Gf
Sarah	25	F	Unknown	21Ma02Gf
DRAKE, Wm.	15	M	Laborer	21Ma02Gf
KEATING, John	26	M	Laborer	21Ma02Gf
Maria	45	F	Servant	21Ma02Gf
BLAKEWELL, Thos.	42	M	Unknown	21Ma02Gf
Mary	42	F	Unknown	21Ma02Gf
Bridget	19	F	Unknown	21Ma02Gf
Nath.	17	M	Unknown	21Ma02Gf
Robt.	15	M	Unknown	21Ma02Gf
Mary	13	F	Unknown	21Ma02Gf
Cath.	11	F	Unknown	21Ma02Gf
Elzth.	9	F	Child	21Ma02Gf
Lawrence	8	M	Child	21Ma02Gf
Thos.	6	M	Child	21Ma02Gf
THIMDEN, Hugh	32	M	Unknown	21Ma02Gf
LESTER, John-Berry	21	M	Unknown	21Ma02Gf
Margt.	20	F	Unknown	21Ma02Gf
HAYLAND, Thos.	23	M	Unknown	21Ma02Gf
Mary	23	F	Unknown	21Ma02Gf
Jane	2	F	Child	21Ma02Gf
REYNOLDS, Wm.	20	M	Servant	21Ma02Gf
FAGAN, Pat	26	M	Servant	21Ma02Gf
John	22	M	Servant	21Ma02Gf
TURNER, Pat	25	M	Farmer	21Ma02Gf
DUFFY, Pat	20	M	Laborer	21Ma02Gf
KELLY, John	22	M	Unknown	21Ma02Gf
FARMON, John	18	M	Unknown	21Ma02Gf

NAMES OF PASSENGERS	AGE	SEX	OCCUPATIONS	DATE PORT SHIP
TIGHE, Ann	22	F	Unknown	21Ma02Gf
FELLON, Mary	20	F	Unknown	21Ma02Gf
KERNE, Wm.	45	M	Farmer	21Ma02Gf
Esther	45	F	Unknown	21Ma02Gf
Marcella	16	F	Unknown	21Ma02Gf
Esther	11	F	Unknown	21Ma02Gf
FARRELL, Thos.	25	M	Unknown	21Ma02Gf
STASSON, Margt.	24	F	Servant	21Ma02Gf
POWELL, Thos.	50	M	Farmer	21Ma02Gf
HENDREGHEN, Bridget	20	F	Unknown	21Ma02Gf
CARNEY, John	28	M	Cooper	21Ma02Gf
ROONEY, Michl.	23	M	Cooper	21Ma02Gf
Betsey	17	F	Unknown	21Ma02Gf
BURN, Owen	28	M	Unknown	21Ma02Gf
QUINN, Christy	31	M	Shoemaker	21Ma02Gf
BALLANE, John	26	M	Tailor	21Ma02Gf
Ann	28	F	Unknown	21Ma02Gf
Faith	.00	F	Infant	21Ma02Gf
ELWOOD, Bridget	40	F	Unknown	21Ma02Gf
Mary	20	F	Unknown	21Ma02Gf
Ann	16	F	Unknown	21Ma02Gf
Cath.	14	F	Unknown	21Ma02Gf
Michael	12	M	Unknown	21Ma02Gf
HACKETT, Andrew	23	M	Weaver	21Ma02Gf
WALSH, Mary	27	F	Unknown	21Ma02Gf
NICHOLSON, Wm.	44	M	Unknown	21Ma02Gf
Mary	43	F	Unknown	21Ma02Gf
Sarah	21	F	Unknown	21Ma02Gf
Mary	20	F	Unknown	21Ma02Gf
MUGGETT, Wm.	18	M	Unknown	21Ma02Gf
NICHOLSON, Betsey	16	F	Unknown	21Ma02Gf
Henry	14	M	Unknown	21Ma02Gf
Richard	12	M	Unknown	21Ma02Gf
WEAVER, John	27	M	Unknown	21Ma02Gf
HENRY, Mary	20	F	Unknown	21Ma02Gf
PATTERSON, Thos.	33	M	Unknown	21Ma02Gf
THOMAS, Jane	17	F	Unknown	21Ma02Gf
PROCTOR, John	35	M	Unknown	21Ma02Gf
Ann	30	F	Unknown	21Ma02Gf
Arthur	25	M	Unknown	21Ma02Gf
John	3	M	Child	21Ma02Gf
Wm.	.11	M	Infant	21Ma02Gf
BRADLEY, Margt.	25	F	Unknown	21Ma02Gf
KELLY, Nichl.	20	M	Unknown	21Ma02Gf
LYNCH, Michael	32	M	Unknown	21Ma02Gf
SHEA, Alice	28	F	Unknown	21Ma02Gf
JUDSON, Wm.	24	M	Unknown	21Ma02Gf
BLOOMFIELD, Wm.	20	M	Unknown	21Ma02Gf
TOOLE, Mary	50	F	Unknown	21Ma02Gf
Elizth.	30	F	Unknown	21Ma02Gf
Clement	21	M	Weaver	21Ma02Gf
Margt.	17	F	Weaver	21Ma02Gf
COSTELLO, Mary	19	F	Weaver	21Ma02Gf
Michael	25	M	Unknown	21Ma02Gf
Ann	17	F	Unknown	21Ma02Gf
KERSHAM, Henry	29	M	Farmer	21Ma02Gf
Rebecca	28	F	Unknown	21Ma02Gf
BURKE, Wm.	24	M	Unknown	21Ma02Gf
DOWNEY, Thos.	47	M	Unknown	21Ma02Gf
WHERTY, Jas.	18	M	Farmer	21Ma02Gf
ONEIL, Chris	18	M	Farmer	21Ma02Gf
HUGHES, John	17	M	Farmer	21Ma02Gf
BOOTH, Henry	28	M	Farmer	21Ma02Gf
WALTON, Henry	20	M	Farmer	21Ma02Gf
FISHER, Henry	24	M	Farmer	21Ma02Gf

WILLIAM-D.SEWALL 22 MAY 1849

From Liverpool

NAMES OF PASSENGERS		AGE	SEX	OCCUPATIONS	DATE PORT SHIP
WELSH, John		23	M	Wlmcht	22Ma02Gz
RYNES, Richard		40	M	Laborer	22Ma02Gz
LARKIN, Hiew		27	M	Blacksmith	22Ma02Gz
KAANIN, Barnard		25	M	Laborer	22Ma02Gz
Mary	(W)	27	F	Unknown	22Ma02Gz
Mary	(D)	.09	F	Infant	22Ma02Gz
LAWRANCE, Mary		17	F	Servant	22Ma02Gz
MCGURAN, Frank		15	M	Laborer	22Ma02Gz
HARTY, Locklin		17	M	Laborer	22Ma02Gz
DURGAN, Margaratt		22	F	Servant	22Ma02Gz
MCFARTY, Catherine		16	F	Servant	22Ma02Gz
CLOREY, James		27	M	Laborer	22Ma02Gz
Mary		25	F	Servant	22Ma02Gz
MORTEN, Patrick		27	M	Baker	22Ma02Gz
Mary	(W)	25	F	Unknown	22Ma02Gz
LODGE, Catherine		24	F	Dressmaker	22Ma02Gz
Susan		26	F	Dressmaker	22Ma02Gz
BANNEN, Mary		26	F	Servant	22Ma02Gz
LODGE, George		20	M	Laborer	22Ma02Gz
William		21	M	Cbtmkr	22Ma02Gz
GRIHAM, Richard		23	M	Shoemaker	22Ma02Gz
SMITH, James		25	M	Laborer	22Ma02Gz
FLRTHY, Patrick		30	M	Laborer	22Ma02Gz
RYLEY, Phillip		19	M	Laborer	22Ma02Gz
BANNON, Joseph		21	M	Laborer	22Ma02Gz
TUINAN, Biddy		00	F	Servant	22Ma02Gz
Anne		00	F	Servant	22Ma02Gz
HARNEY, William		00	M	Laborer	22Ma02Gz
Rose		40	F	Unknown	22Ma02Gz
RILEY, Edward		47	M	Laborer	22Ma02Gz
Philip		12	M	Laborer	22Ma02Gz
Barnet		13	M	Laborer	22Ma02Gz
Mary		18	F	Servant	22Ma02Gz
Abby		16	F	Servant	22Ma02Gz
Catherine		17	F	Servant	22Ma02Gz
CRANE, Anorah		27	F	Servant	22Ma02Gz
SHEERAN, Catherine		18	F	Servant	22Ma02Gz
MERRY, Eliza		32	F	Servant	22Ma02Gz
KIRWAN, Mary		50	F	Servant	22Ma02Gz
CLARK, Peter		28	M	Laborer	22Ma02Gz
Brigett	(W)	30	F	Unknown	22Ma02Gz
Hew	(S)	7	M	Child	22Ma02Gz
Thomas		23	M	Laborer	22Ma02Gz
ALLEN, Michael		29	M	Laborer	22Ma02Gz
COMESKAY, Patrick		25	M	Laborer	22Ma02Gz
GILSON, Timly		25	F	Servant	22Ma02Gz
CLOAK, Anne		19	F	Servant	22Ma02Gz
MCCAN, Patrick		26	M	Tailor	22Ma02Gz
Catherine	(M)	00	F	Unknown	22Ma02Gz
REYNOLES, John		17	M	Laborer	22Ma02Gz
LOID, Robert		15	M	Laborer	22Ma02Gz
Thomas		18	M	Laborer	22Ma02Gz
WALLICE, James		30	M	Laborer	22Ma02Gz
GERWIN, Patrick		25	M	Laborer	22Ma02Gz
HUGHES, James		18	M	Laborer	22Ma02Gz
GRANT, Anne		20	F	Servant	22Ma02Gz
HUGHES, Anne		13	F	Servant	22Ma02Gz
GRAHAM, Brigett		17	F	Servant	22Ma02Gz
DORAN, Patrick		30	M	Laborer	22Ma02Gz
MCNERREN, Donnell		22	M	Laborer	22Ma02Gz
MCTEER, Thos.		28	M	Laborer	22Ma02Gz
WALLACE, Brigett		30	F	Servant	22Ma02Gz
Patrick		12	M	Laborer	22Ma02Gz
Catherine		22	F	Servant	22Ma02Gz
SCINNIN, William		60	M	Farmer	22Ma02Gz
SCINNIN, Honori	(W)	60	F	Unknown	22Ma02Gz
Margrett		26	F	Servant	22Ma02Gz
Patrick		16	M	Farmer	22Ma02Gz
John		12	M	Farmer	22Ma02Gz
CONRUGHY, James		24	M	Laborer	22Ma02Gz
Barry		25	M	Cooper	22Ma02Gz
James		15	M	Laborer	22Ma02Gz
SHREDAN, James		20	M	Carpenter	22Ma02Gz
FOX, Ellen		35	F	Servant	22Ma02Gz
HANCKAN, Mary		25	F	Servant	22Ma02Gz
MCHANEY, Matthew		36	M	Laborer	22Ma02Gz
Jane	(D)	12	F	Unknown	22Ma02Gz
GALLIGSE, William		40	M	Weaver	22Ma02Gz
William		18	M	Laborer	22Ma02Gz
Jane		14	F	Servant	22Ma02Gz
DOLLON, Mary		50	F	Servant	22Ma02Gz
COURFEE, Mary		25	F	Servant	22Ma02Gz
LOVE, James		45	M	Laborer	22Ma02Gz
MCCORLEY, Peter		25	M	Laborer	22Ma02Gz
GARR, John		20	M	Tailor	22Ma02Gz
CARR, Anne		36	F	Weaver	22Ma02Gz
Eliza		16	F	Servant	22Ma02Gz
Marthey		19	F	Servant	22Ma02Gz
CUSHIN, Mary		30	F	Servant	22Ma02Gz
Mary		13	F	Servant	22Ma02Gz
Edmund		3	M	Child	22Ma02Gz
Ellen		1	F	Child	22Ma02Gz
HANSEY, Patrick		20	M	Draper	22Ma02Gz
Michal		19	M	Laborer	22Ma02Gz
Ellen		20	F	Servant	22Ma02Gz
Mary		18	F	Servant	22Ma02Gz
Brigett		16	F	Servant	22Ma02Gz
MCHOAN, Owen		56	M	Wheelwright	22Ma02Gz
Mary	(W)	58	F	Unknown	22Ma02Gz
Mary	(D)	16	F	Unknown	22Ma02Gz
Peter	(S)	24	M	Unknown	22Ma02Gz
Owen	(S)	2	M	Child	22Ma02Gz
LINCH, Edward		22	M	Laborer	22Ma02Gz
DIGNAN, Patrick		18	M	Laborer	22Ma02Gz
RUDDAN, Michael		25	M	Laborer	22Ma02Gz
GARRITY, James		26	M	Laborer	22Ma02Gz
Thos.		23	M	Farmer	22Ma02Gz
CASTERLY, Brigett		15	F	Servant	22Ma02Gz
Michael		11	M	Laborer	22Ma02Gz
DUYON, Patrick		38	M	Farmer	22Ma02Gz
Judith	(W)	38	F	Unknown	22Ma02Gz
Duiness	(S)	9	M	Child	22Ma02Gz
Winnifon	(D)	7	F	Child	22Ma02Gz
Judath	(D)	6	F	Child	22Ma02Gz
Mary	(D)	3	F	Child	22Ma02Gz
Brigett	(D)	1	F	Child	22Ma02Gz
BIRK, Mary		28	F	Servant	22Ma02Gz
FROTHEY, Catherine		22	F	Servant	22Ma02Gz
THRAYSAY, James		27	M	Laborer	22Ma02Gz
REIGHN, Patrick		30	M	Laborer	22Ma02Gz
Elizabeth	(W)	35	F	Unknown	22Ma02Gz
Mary	(D)	.10	F	Infant	22Ma02Gz
Margarett	(D)	14	F	Unknown	22Ma02Gz
William	(S)	12	M	Unknown	22Ma02Gz
John	(S)	10	M	Unknown	22Ma02Gz
Johanna	(D)	3	F	Child	22Ma02Gz
RYAN, Daniel		25	M	Laborer	22Ma02Gz
HASSEY, John		23	M	Laborer	22Ma02Gz
QUIRK, Patrick		38	M	Farmer	22Ma02Gz
Daniel		17	M	Laborer	22Ma02Gz
Brigett		15	F	Servant	22Ma02Gz
TURNER, John		37	M	Laborer	22Ma02Gz
Elizabeth	(W)	37	F	Unknown	22Ma02Gz
GODLEY, Andrew		25	M	Laborer	22Ma02Gz
CORNAS, Eyebell		19	F	Servant	22Ma02Gz
CASSEDY, Patrick		23	M	Mechanic	22Ma02Gz
GRIFFIN, Margarett		40	F	Servant	22Ma02Gz
James		16	M	Laborer	22Ma02Gz
Rebecca		14	F	Servant	22Ma02Gz
Jane		12	F	Servant	22Ma02Gz

NAMES OF PASSENGERS		AGE	SEX	OCCUPATIONS	DATE PORT SHIP
GRIFFIN, John		9	M	Child	22Ma02Gz
Matthew		4	M	Child	22Ma02Gz
Isaac		3	M	Child	22Ma02Gz
Thomas		3	M	Child	22Ma02Gz
PRANEFORD, Elizabeth		23	F	Servant	22Ma02Gz
GIBNEY, Owen		20	M	Laborer	22Ma02Gz
TEMPLE, Hugh		16	M	Laborer	22Ma02Gz
MCDONALD, Mick		18	M	Laborer	22Ma02Gz
MORRISON, Grace		18	F	Dressmaker	22Ma02Gz
BROGAN, Mary		20	F	Servant	22Ma02Gz
MCDONALD, Anne		22	F	Servant	22Ma02Gz
HUGHES, John		26	M	Laborer	22Ma02Gz
RORK, Patrick		27	M	Laborer	22Ma02Gz
ODONALD, John		20	M	Laborer	22Ma02Gz
FOLEY, Catherine		20	F	Servant	22Ma02Gz
HIRLY, Mary		23	F	Servant	22Ma02Gz
FITSGERALD, Patt.		26	M	Laborer	22Ma02Gz
TOWERY, Luke		25	M	Laborer	22Ma02Gz
CARREL, Patt.		18	M	Laborer	22Ma02Gz
DILLAN, Johanna		20	F	Servant	22Ma02Gz
FLYNN, Ellen		13	F	Servant	22Ma02Gz
OWNAN, Ellen		36	F	Servant	22Ma02Gz
FLARTY, Sarah		17	F	Servant	22Ma02Gz
MAHERS, John		20	M	Laborer	22Ma02Gz
KENNEDY, Thomas		23	M	Laborer	22Ma02Gz
DYER, Patrick		20	M	Laborer	22Ma02Gz
CONNELL, Dennis		35	M	Farmer	22Ma02Gz
Mary	(W)	24	F	Unknown	22Ma02Gz
Margarett	(D)	5	F	Child	22Ma02Gz
James	(S)	3	M	Child	22Ma02Gz
Charles	(S)	1	M	Child	22Ma02Gz
MCDERMOTT, Thos.		18	M	Laborer	22Ma02Gz
Patrick		15	M	Laborer	22Ma02Gz
SHEENAN, Donald		30	M	Laborer	22Ma02Gz
DONAGHONY, John		21	M	Laborer	22Ma02Gz
CAHILL, Catherine		40	F	Servant	22Ma02Gz
Margarett		14	F	Servant	22Ma02Gz
Catherine		12	F	Servant	22Ma02Gz
Honora		10	F	Servant	22Ma02Gz
Brigett		7	F	Child	22Ma02Gz
HOLORAN, Matthew		20	M	Laborer	22Ma02Gz
QUINN, Thomas		17	M	Laborer	22Ma02Gz
CASEY, Johanna		25	F	Servant	22Ma02Gz
GREENS, Fras.		60	M	Laborer	22Ma02Gz
GREEN, Thomas		27	M	Laborer	22Ma02Gz
Mary		50	F	Servant	22Ma02Gz
Alice		30	F	Servant	22Ma02Gz
MCDONALD, Thomas		34	M	Laborer	22Ma02Gz
Mary	(W)	40	F	Unknown	22Ma02Gz
MAHER, Mick		12	M	Laborer	22Ma02Gz
Ellen		13	F	Servant	22Ma02Gz
Mary		8	F	Child	22Ma02Gz
MCDONALD, Judat		25	F	Wife	22Ma02Gz
James	(S)	1	M	Child	22Ma02Gz
RYAN, Tim		30	M	Laborer	22Ma02Gz
MCDONNALD, Margarett		20	F	Servant	22Ma02Gz
LEIVY, Tim		26	M	Laborer	22Ma02Gz
MCDONNALD, John		21	M	Laborer	22Ma02Gz
WALLACE, Richard		25	M	Shoemaker	22Ma02Gz
OBRYAN, William		23	M	Coach Maker	22Ma02Gz
HARAGIN, Michael		18	M	Laborer	22Ma02Gz
SPRING, John		30	M	Schm	22Ma02Gz
MANSERGH, Elizabeth		18	F	Servant	22Ma02Gz
WALLACE, Thomas		22	M	Laborer	22Ma02Gz
Ellen	(W)	20	F	Unknown	22Ma02Gz
COUGHLAND, Malachy		52	M	Farmer	22Ma02Gz
Margarett	(W)	46	F	Unknown	22Ma02Gz
Brigett	(D)	19	F	Unknown	22Ma02Gz
Elizabeth	(D)	17	F	Unknown	22Ma02Gz
Joseph	(S)	9	M	Child	22Ma02Gz
LULLIN, Michal		40	M	Laborer	22Ma02Gz
RYAN, Mary		22	F	Wife	22Ma02Gz

FINGAL 23 MAY 1849

From Liverpool

NAMES OF PASSENGERS		AGE	SEX	OCCUPATIONS	DATE PORT SHIP
LANDY, Mil.		26	M	Laborer	23Ma02Hc
STEPLETON, Johanna		20	F	Unknown	23Ma02Hc
SYKES, Lawrence		24	M	Unknown	23Ma02Hc
MORAN, Wm.		27	M	Unknown	23Ma02Hc
DONLY, Hannah		20	F	Unknown	23Ma02Hc
ROYAN, Jenny		30	F	Unknown	23Ma02Hc
BYRNE, Matthew		50	M	Unknown	23Ma02Hc
Nelly		45	F	Unknown	23Ma02Hc
CAVANAGH, James		30	M	Unknown	23Ma02Hc
NEILL, Dolly		22	F	Unknown	23Ma02Hc
BYRNE, Mary		16	F	Unknown	23Ma02Hc
Cath.		13	F	Unknown	23Ma02Hc
Thos.		11	M	Unknown	23Ma02Hc
Ellen		9	F	Child	23Ma02Hc
Anne		7	F	Child	23Ma02Hc
LUCKER, James		21	M	Unknown	23Ma02Hc
BUNTY, Cath.		21	F	Unknown	23Ma02Hc
CAKELY, Jas.		24	M	Unknown	23Ma02Hc
Margt.		40	F	Unknown	23Ma02Hc
Died-At-Sea					
Danl.		18	M	Unknown	23Ma02Hc
Johanna		16	F	Unknown	23Ma02Hc
Cath.		13	F	Unknown	23Ma02Hc
Anne		11	F	Unknown	23Ma02Hc
CALLAHON, John		25	M	Unknown	23Ma02Hc
Mary		20	F	Unknown	23Ma02Hc
Anne		18	F	Unknown	23Ma02Hc
MAHONY, Mary		62	F	Unknown	23Ma02Hc
PUGH, Eliz.		20	F	Unknown	23Ma02Hc
MCREADY, Jas.		40	M	Unknown	23Ma02Hc
U	(W)	33	F	Unknown	23Ma02Hc
Margt.		11	F	Unknown	23Ma02Hc
Archd.		9	M	Child	23Ma02Hc
Jane		7	F	Child	23Ma02Hc
Agnes		5	F	Child	23Ma02Hc
Wm.		3	M	Child	23Ma02Hc
Patt.		.00	M	Infant	23Ma02Hc
MCCABE, Patk.		20	M	Unknown	23Ma02Hc
SANDERS, Mary-J.		28	F	Unknown	23Ma02Hc
DELANY, Patt.		30	M	Unknown	23Ma02Hc
DIVINE, Wm.		34	M	Unknown	23Ma02Hc
OLIVER, Wm.		25	M	Unknown	23Ma02Hc
Elisabeth		25	F	Unknown	23Ma02Hc
Robt.		18	M	Unknown	23Ma02Hc
Bridget		2	F	Child	23Ma02Hc
Margt.		.00	F	Infant	23Ma02H
WALSH, James		43	M	Unknown	23Ma02H
Bridgt.		30	F	Unknown	23Ma02H
MURPHY, Johanna		21	F	Unknown	23Ma02H
Bridgt.		19	F	Unknown	23Ma02H
Wm.		18	M	Unknown	23Ma02H
Ellen		16	F	Unknown	23Ma02H
KAVANAH, Margt.		21	F	Unknown	23Ma02H
DESPEN, John		25	M	Unknown	23Ma02H
MCGRATH, Mil.		16	M	Unknown	23Ma02H
Bridget		21	F	Unknown	23Ma02H
ARNOLD, Richard		16	M	Unknown	23Ma02H
CARLY, Pat		58	M	Unknown	23Ma02H
DEASEY, John		50	M	Unknown	23Ma02H
Jno.		24	M	Unknown	23Ma02H
Cath.		20	F	Unknown	23Ma02H
SWEENEY, Owen		23	M	Unknown	23Ma02H
MARSTON, Ann		30	F	Unknown	23Ma02H
Sarah		13	F	Unknown	23Ma02H
Robt.		11	M	Unknown	23Ma02H

NAMES OF PASSENGERS	AGE	SEX	OCCUPATIONS	DATE PORT SHIP
MARSTON, Mick	9	M	Child	23Ma02Hc
MCCAVIL, Jno.	22	M	Unknown	23Ma02Hc
SHEARLAND, Patt.	22	M	Unknown	23Ma02Hc
COWIN, Ann	21	F	Unknown	23Ma02Hc
BRYAN, Patt.	29	M	Unknown	23Ma02Hc
U (W)	29	F	Unknown	23Ma02Hc
MORAN, Frank	26	M	Unknown	23Ma02Hc
QUINLISH, Hugh	40	M	Unknown	23Ma02Hc
Jno.	9	M	Child	23Ma02Hc
THERIN, Cornelius	26	M	Unknown	23Ma02Hc
Cath.	26	F	Unknown	23Ma02Hc
Cath.	.00	F	Infant	23Ma02Hc
DONSEN, Edw.	26	M	Unknown	23Ma02Hc
U (W)	22	F	Unknown	23Ma02Hc
CORMICK, Adam	40	M	Unknown	23Ma02Hc
HUGHES, Mary	40	F	Unknown	23Ma02Hc
KELLY, Patt.	24	M	Unknown	23Ma02Hc
Eliza	27	F	Unknown	23Ma02Hc
Mick	5	M	Child	23Ma02Hc
Jno.	.00	F	Infant	23Ma02Hc
HANELL, Thos.	34	M	Unknown	23Ma02Hc
Mary	30	F	Unknown	23Ma02Hc
Mary	.00	F	Infant	23Ma02Hc
OWENS, Henry	55	M	Unknown	23Ma02Hc
HAND, Mary	34	F	Unknown	23Ma02Hc
Mary	15	F	Unknown	23Ma02Hc
WOOD, Jno.	30	M	Unknown	23Ma02Hc
Joseph	24	M	Unknown	23Ma02Hc
U (W)	24	F	Unknown	23Ma02Hc
MOORE, Jno.	54	M	Unknown	23Ma02Hc
Martha	47	F	Unknown	23Ma02Hc
Thos.	17	M	Unknown	23Ma02Hc
James	29	M	Unknown	23Ma02Hc
Eliz.	28	F	Unknown	23Ma02Hc
TURNER, Joseph	19	M	Unknown	23Ma02Hc
MEAD, Timothy	28	M	Unknown	23Ma02Hc
SMITH, Samuel	27	M	Unknown	23Ma02Hc
GANETT, Thos.	19	M	Unknown	23Ma02Hc
JONES, Sarah-Ann	24	F	Unknown	23Ma02Hc
LOWCOCK, U-Mrs.	25	F	Unknown	23Ma02Hc
SLATER, Jeremiah	37	M	Unknown	23Ma02Hc
Mary-Ann	35	F	Unknown	23Ma02Hc
DEEM, Alice	36	F	Unknown	23Ma02Hc
BARRACLOUGH, Geo.	24	M	Unknown	23Ma02Hc
CLAPHAM, Jno.	33	M	Unknown	23Ma02Hc
Wm.	24	M	Unknown	23Ma02Hc
EMMOTT, Francis	37	M	Unknown	23Ma02Hc
Sarah	33	F	Unknown	23Ma02Hc
HODGSON, Solomon	35	M	Unknown	23Ma02Hc
BERWISTLE, John	25	M	Unknown	23Ma02Hc
CLAPHAM, Maria	30	F	Unknown	23Ma02Hc
Mary	22	F	Unknown	23Ma02Hc
Newton	18	M	Unknown	23Ma02Hc
MILNER, Jas.	18	M	Unknown	23Ma02Hc
SMITH, Josh.	18	M	Unknown	23Ma02Hc
DEAN, Martha	22	F	Unknown	23Ma02Hc
Wm.	6	M	Child	23Ma02Hc
Hannah	8	F	Child	23Ma02Hc
MOORE, Mariah	7	F	Child	23Ma02Hc
Jno.	5	M	Child	23Ma02Hc
Hannah	2	F	Child	23Ma02Hc
SLATER, Ann	12	F	Unknown	23Ma02Hc
Zachariah	2	M	Child	23Ma02Hc
CLAPHAM, Jas.	3	M	Child	23Ma02Hc
MOORE, Mary-Ann	11	F	Unknown	23Ma02Hc
SLATER, Alfred	.00	M	Infant	23Ma02Hc
CLAPHAM, Thos.	.00	M	Infant	23Ma02Hc
FINNIGAN, Thos.	50	M	Unknown	23Ma02Hc
Margt.	47	F	Unknown	23Ma02Hc
James	22	M	Unknown	23Ma02Hc
Thos.	18	M	Unknown	23Ma02Hc
Bryan	16	M	Unknown	23Ma02Hc
Ellen	20	F	Unknown	23Ma02Hc
Cath.	14	F	Unknown	23Ma02Hc
Patt.	12	M	Unknown	23Ma02Hc
FINNIGAN, Chris	10	M	Unknown	23Ma02Hc
Bryan	45	M	Unknown	23Ma02Hc
Mary	40	F	Unknown	23Ma02Hc
Margt.	20	F	Unknown	23Ma02Hc
Margt.	18	F	Unknown	23Ma02Hc
FANIGAN, Hugh	12	M	Unknown	23Ma02Hc
Cath.	9	F	Child	23Ma02Hc
Thos.	7	M	Child	23Ma02Hc
Patt.	.00	M	Infant	23Ma02Hc
Ann	.00	F	Infant	23Ma02Hc
CARR, Ann	20	F	Unknown	23Ma02Hc
JACKSON, Henry	36	M	Unknown	23Ma02Hc
Mary	26	F	Unknown	23Ma02Hc
Thos.	4	M	Child	23Ma02Hc
Harriet	.00	F	Infant	23Ma02Hc
Da.	26	M	Unknown	23Ma02Hc
MOORE, Robert	26	M	Unknown	23Ma02Hc
Harriet	3	F	Child	23Ma02Hc
Geo.	.00	M	Infant	23Ma02Hc
Francis	30	M	Unknown	23Ma02Hc
MURRY, U-Mrs.	30	F	Unknown	23Ma02Hc
Francis	.00	M	Infant	23Ma02Hc
FANNON, Mick	40	M	Unknown	23Ma02Hc
Ann	40	F	Unknown	23Ma02Hc
Danl.	20	M	Unknown	23Ma02Hc
Mary	15	F	Unknown	23Ma02Hc
Thos.	13	M	Unknown	23Ma02Hc
Peter	11	M	Unknown	23Ma02Hc
Jno.	9	M	Child	23Ma02Hc
MCCORMICK, Margt.	20	F	Unknown	23Ma02Hc
Margt.	20	F	Unknown	23Ma02Hc
EGAN, Frank	20	M	Unknown	23Ma02Hc
JONES, Pat.	24	M	Unknown	23Ma02Hc
BORLEY, Sarah	20	F	Unknown	23Ma02Hc
DONLEY, Jas.	20	M	Unknown	23Ma02Hc
CASSIDY, Jas.	28	M	Unknown	23Ma02Hc
BAUGH, Edw.	40	M	Unknown	23Ma02Hc
Ellen	40	F	Unknown	23Ma02Hc
Margt.	20	F	Unknown	23Ma02Hc
Mary	3	F	Child	23Ma02Hc
Margt.	.00	F	Infant	23Ma02Hc
Ellen	.00	F	Infant	23Ma02Hc
Cath.	30	F	Unknown	23Ma02Hc
FAY, Lew.	30	M	Unknown	23Ma02Hc
Mary	3	F	Child	23Ma02Hc
Cath.	34	F	Unknown	23Ma02Hc
Bryan	30	M	Unknown	23Ma02Hc
BARRY, Jno.	21	M	Unknown	23Ma02Hc
DALTON, Jno.	11	M	Unknown	23Ma02Hc
WHEATON, Michl.	14	M	Unknown	23Ma02Hc
Martha	21	F	Unknown	23Ma02Hc
GAFNEY, Cath.	26	F	Unknown	23Ma02Hc
DAVIES, G.	55	M	Unknown	23Ma02Hc
Mary	18	F	Unknown	23Ma02Hc
David	20	M	Unknown	23Ma02Hc
Thos.	29	M	Unknown	23Ma02Hc
SOCHER, George	20	M	Unknown	23Ma02Hc
Charlotte	19	F	Unknown	23Ma02Hc
Isabella	21	F	Unknown	23Ma02Hc
JENNINGS, Mary	11	F	Unknown	23Ma02Hc
Smith	15	M	Unknown	23Ma02Hc
Ann	18	F	Unknown	23Ma02Hc
FLAVIN, Jno.	25	M	Unknown	23Ma02Hc
FORD, Cath.	23	F	Unknown	23Ma02Hc
JOHNSTON, Alice	55	F	Unknown	23Ma02Hc
HEALTHSTOCK, Saml.	30	M	Unknown	23Ma02Hc
Grace	25	F	Unknown	23Ma02Hc
James	19	M	Unknown	23Ma02Hc
Mary-Ann	13	F	Unknown	23Ma02Hc
Saml.	30	M	Unknown	23Ma02Hc
Maria	9	F	Child	23Ma02Hc
Ann	7	F	Child	23Ma02Hc
George	5	M	Child	23Ma02Hc
Hannah	20	F	Unknown	23Ma02Hc
METHER, John	24	M	Unknown	23Ma02Hc

NAMES OF PASSENGERS	AGE	SEX	OCCUPATIONS	DATE PORT SHIP
STOCK, Jas.	20	M	Unknown	23Ma02Hc
MIGHT, Edw.	50	M	Unknown	23Ma02Hc
COOPER, Wm.	27	M	Unknown	23Ma02Hc
KEARMAN, Pat.	26	M	Unknown	23Ma02Hc
Ann	20	F	Unknown	23Ma02Hc
BELL, Mary-Ann	20	F	Unknown	23Ma02Hc
PIT, Wm.	21	M	Unknown	23Ma02Hc
WILLIAMS, Thos.	20	M	Unknown	23Ma02Hc
MARGON, John	26	M	Unknown	23Ma02Hc
MARVISS, Walter	20	M	Unknown	23Ma02Hc
SMITH, Jas.	13	M	Unknown	23Ma02Hc
DEWIR, Pat.	26	M	Unknown	23Ma02Hc
HARPER, Robt.	33	M	Unknown	23Ma02Hc
GRALSWAG, Pat.	33	M	Unknown	23Ma02Hc
Ellen	14	F	Unknown	23Ma02Hc
Mich.	10	M	Unknown	23Ma02Hc
Mary	8	F	Child	23Ma02Hc
Jno.	6	M	Child	23Ma02Hc
Peter	4	M	Child	23Ma02Hc
Ellen	.00	F	Infant	23Ma02Hc
Danl.	17	M	Unknown	23Ma02Hc
MONAGHAN, Biddy	30	F	Unknown	23Ma02Hc
SWORD, Phil.	40	M	Unknown	23Ma02Hc
Biddy	.00	F	Infant	23Ma02Hc
Anne	50	F	Unknown	23Ma02Hc
Mary	8	F	Child	23Ma02Hc
Corns.	5	M	Child	23Ma02Hc
Jane	4	F	Child	23Ma02Hc
Joseph	2	M	Child	23Ma02Hc
Ellen	28	F	Unknown	23Ma02Hc
MURPHY, Jas.	24	M	Unknown	23Ma02Hc
Bridget	.00	F	Infant	23Ma02Hc
Mary	24	F	Unknown	23Ma02Hc
Mick	30	M	Unknown	23Ma02Hc
Patt.	28	M	Unknown	23Ma02Hc
Mary	25	F	Unknown	23Ma02Hc
REILLY, Edw.	30	M	Unknown	23Ma02Hc
Biddy	12	F	Unknown	23Ma02Hc
Rose	20	F	Unknown	23Ma02Hc
PARCEL, James	18	M	Unknown	23Ma02Hc
Will	16	M	Unknown	23Ma02Hc
DELANO, Joseph	16	M	Unknown	23Ma02Hc
BAILY, Jas.	26	M	Unknown	23Ma02Hc
HARRISON, Thos.	20	M	Unknown	23Ma02Hc
DARLING, Mick.	16	M	Unknown	23Ma02Hc
SMITH, Anne	22	F	Unknown	23Ma02Hc
LITRICK, John	20	M	Unknown	23Ma02Hc
MORLAND, Saml.	28	M	Unknown	23Ma02Hc
WILLIAMS, Jas.	27	M	Unknown	23Ma02Hc
Mary	27	F	Unknown	23Ma02Hc
BOND, Wm.	10	M	Unknown	23Ma02Hc
Jane	36	F	Unknown	23Ma02Hc
MCGRATH, Ketty	16	F	Unknown	23Ma02Hc
Johanna	12	F	Unknown	23Ma02Hc
Jeny	9	F	Child	23Ma02Hc
Mary-Ann	7	F	Child	23Ma02Hc
Honor	4	M	Child	23Ma02Hc
Cahalan	2	M	Child	23Ma02Hc
MURPHY, Law.	60	M	Unknown	23Ma02Hc
Danl.	35	M	Unknown	23Ma02Hc
Johanna	30	F	Unknown	23Ma02Hc
Patt.	.00	M	Infant	23Ma02Hc
SEROY, Mast.	25	M	Unknown	23Ma02Hc
HOLLAND, Mary	21	F	Unknown	23Ma02Hc
DEMPSEY, Wm.	36	M	Unknown	23Ma02Hc
Mary	28	F	Unknown	23Ma02Hc
Wm.	11	M	Unknown	23Ma02Hc
Danl.	9	M	Child	23Ma02Hc
Mary	7	F	Child	23Ma02Hc
DAMERY, Mary	25	F	Unknown	23Ma02Hc
DEMPSEY, John	27	M	Unknown	23Ma02Hc
Nancy	27	F	Unknown	23Ma02Hc
Mary	60	F	Unknown	23Ma02Hc
Jas.	33	M	Unknown	23Ma02Hc
Cathe.	23	F	Unknown	23Ma02Hc
DEMPSEY, Mary	.00	F	Infant	23Ma02Hc
GOOD, Richd.	52	M	Unknown	23Ma02Hc
Mary	47	F	Unknown	23Ma02Hc
Jno.	16	M	Unknown	23Ma02Hc
Sarah	14	F	Unknown	23Ma02Hc
Eliza	11	F	Unknown	23Ma02Hc
Martha	9	F	Child	23Ma02Hc
Richd.	6	M	Child	23Ma02Hc
Mary	4	F	Child	23Ma02Hc
James	.00	M	Infant	23Ma02Hc
LATRANE, Jas.	22	M	Unknown	23Ma02Hc
Cornelius	20	M	Unknown	23Ma02Hc
Cath.	19	F	Unknown	23Ma02Hc
CARCARAN, Danl.	20	M	Unknown	23Ma02Hc
Cath.	20	F	Unknown	23Ma02Hc
Jno.	.00	M	Infant	23Ma02Hc
CORNELL, Edw.	26	M	Unknown	23Ma02Hc
Cath.	26	F	Unknown	23Ma02Hc
LONG, Thos.	30	M	Unknown	23Ma02Hc
HORGAN, Cor.	30	M	Unknown	23Ma02Hc
HENRY, Lawrence	23	M	Unknown	23Ma02Hc
FORD, Edw.	40	M	Unknown	23Ma02Hc
KENNY, Mill	24	M	Unknown	23Ma02Hc
DUNN, Martin	26	M	Unknown	23Ma02Hc
Eliz.	16	F	Unknown	23Ma02Hc
FEARLY, Mary	18	F	Unknown	23Ma02Hc
FITZGERALD, Patt.	25	M	Unknown	23Ma02Hc
GRADY, Agnes	20	F	Unknown	23Ma02Hc
MCKEON, Patt.	40	M	Unknown	23Ma02Hc
Judy	39	F	Unknown	23Ma02Hc
Jno.	6	M	Child	23Ma02Hc
Margt.	3	F	Child	23Ma02Hc
Rose	13	F	Unknown	23Ma02Hc
LYNCH, Pat.	10	M	Unknown	23Ma02Hc
Bessy	13	F	Unknown	23Ma02Hc
Jno.	35	M	Unknown	23Ma02Hc
Ann	30	F	Unknown	23Ma02Hc
Mary	11	F	Unknown	23Ma02Hc
Bridget	32	F	Unknown	23Ma02Hc
Robt.	3	M	Child	23Ma02Hc
Peter	9	M	Child	23Ma02Hc
SWEENY, Ellen	20	F	Unknown	23Ma02Hc
MURRAY, Danl.	50	M	Unknown	23Ma02Hc
MURPHY, Johanna	50	F	Unknown	23Ma02Hc
Ellen	17	F	Unknown	23Ma02Hc
Johanna	18	F	Unknown	23Ma02Hc
Jno.	15	M	Unknown	23Ma02Hc
Dan.	12	M	Unknown	23Ma02Hc
Pat.	11	M	Unknown	23Ma02Hc
Mick	9	M	Child	23Ma02Hc
Mary	7	F	Child	23Ma02Hc
Wm.	.00	M	Infant	23Ma02Hc
BUCKLEY, Dennis	84	M	Unknown	23Ma02Hc
Cath.	50	F	Unknown	23Ma02Hc
Wm.	19	M	Unknown	23Ma02Hc
Jno.	18	M	Unknown	23Ma02Hc
Julia	13	F	Unknown	23Ma02Hc
Patt.	12	M	Unknown	23Ma02Hc
DUNCAN, Wm.	29	M	Unknown	23Ma02Hc
U (W)	29	F	Unknown	23Ma02Hc
FOSTER, Ann	30	F	Unknown	23Ma02Hc
Wm.	40	M	Unknown	23Ma02Hc

AMBASSADRESS 23 MAY 1849

From Liverpool

NAMES OF PASSENGERS	AGE	SEX	OCCUPATIONS	DATE PORT SHIP
MAHON, Francis	27	M	Laborer	23Ma02G
MCTAGEN, Mary	35	F	Unknown	23Ma02G

NAMES OF PASSENGERS		AGE	SEX	OCCUPATIONS	DATE PORT SHIP
LONG, Joseph		30	M	Laborer	23Ma02Gj
Ann	(W)	30	F	Unknown	23Ma02Gj
DOYLE, Bridget		16	F	Spinster	23Ma02Gj
DAVIES, Pat		30	M	Miner	23Ma02Gj
DEVINE, Mary-A.		22	F	Spinster	23Ma02Gj
NOWLAND, Jas.		21	M	Laborer	23Ma02Gj
SULLY, Susan		18	F	Spinster	23Ma02Gj
BARRATT, Eliza		20	F	Spinster	23Ma02Gj
MURRAY, Thomas		20	M	Laborer	23Ma02Gj
NEIL, Danl.		20	M	Laborer	23Ma02Gj
MORAN, Hugh		20	M	Laborer	23Ma02Gj
MONAGHAN, Eliza	(W)	20	F	Unknown	23Ma02Gj
OHARA, Brigt.		27	F	Spinster	23Ma02Gj
LYNOR, John		25	M	Laborer	23Ma02Gj
Died-At-Sea					
BURNE, Mary		18	F	Spinster	23Ma02Gj
READY, John		45	M	Laborer	23Ma02Gj
HEARY, Ellen		23	F	Spinster	23Ma02Gj
KELLY, Pat		29	M	Shoemaker	23Ma02Gj
FLYNN, Betsy		20	F	Spinster	23Ma02Gj
CAREY, Wm.		40	M	Farmer	23Ma02Gj
Judy	(W)	40	F	Unknown	23Ma02Gj
Bridget		19	F	Spinster	23Ma02Gj
Michl.		15	M	Laborer	23Ma02Gj
Mary		35	F	Unknown	23Ma02Gj
Wm.		10	M	Unknown	23Ma02Gj
Eliza		6	F	Child	23Ma02Gj
Margt.		4	F	Child	23Ma02Gj
Wm.		12	M	Unknown	23Ma02Gj
DOMSOVAN, John		35	F	Tailor	23Ma02Gj
GOODWIN, Philip		.06	M	Infant	23Ma02Gj
Jane	(W)	29	F	Unknown	23Ma02Gj
Ann		14	F	Spinster	23Ma02Gj
Arthur		8	M	Child	23Ma02Gj
Martha		5	F	Child	23Ma02Gj
JOHNSTON, Jas.		25	M	Laborer	23Ma02Gj
CARROLL, Anthy.		26	M	Farmer	23Ma02Gj
Michl.		20	M	Farmer	23Ma02Gj
FERBAY, James		20	M	Laborer	23Ma02Gj
MCGEE, Biddy		25	F	Spinster	23Ma02Gj
ROBINSON, Wm.		32	M	Farmer	23Ma02Gj
Mary		14	F	Spinster	23Ma02Gj
KENNEDY, James		16	M	Laborer	23Ma02Gj
SHEA, Jas.		25	M	Laborer	23Ma02Gj
Mary		15	F	Spinster	23Ma02Gj
WALSH, Judy		17	F	Spinster	23Ma02Gj
POWERS, Thos.		44	M	Farmer	23Ma02Gj
Judy	(W)	40	F	Unknown	23Ma02Gj
T.		.09	M	Infant	23Ma02Gj
Michl.		18	M	Farmer	23Ma02Gj
Johana		15	F	Spinster	23Ma02Gj
Margt.		12	F	Spinster	23Ma02Gj
John		8	M	Child	23Ma02Gj
Kate		5	F	Child	23Ma02Gj
EGAN, U		27	M	Wi	23Ma02Gj
FURNING, Judy		25	F	Spinster	23Ma02Gj
CAIN, Pat		41	M	Grocer	23Ma02Gj
BRITTAN, John		29	M	Blacksmith	23Ma02Gj
DANIEL, Wm.		27	M	Farmer	23Ma02Gj
THOMPSON, Mary		22	F	Spinster	23Ma02Gj
CHAMBERLAIN, Wm.		40	M	Smith	23Ma02Gj
FORD, Mary		19	M	Smith	23Ma02Gj
EAGAN, Thos.		30	M	Laborer	23Ma02Gj
KIEEFE, Mary		26	F	Spinster	23Ma02Gj
LANAGAN, Ellen		40	F	Weaver	23Ma02Gj
Mary		20	F	Spinster	23Ma02Gj
Thos.		17	M	Laborer	23Ma02Gj
Ann		9	F	Spinster	23Ma02Gj
Martin		7	M	Child	23Ma02Gj
HELANE, Andw.		25	M	Farmer	23Ma02Gj
HILARD, Thos.		20	M	Farmer	23Ma02Gj
Betsy		23	F	Wife	23Ma02Gj
Winifred		21	F	Spinster	23Ma02Gj
WHELAN, Pat		30	M	Farmer	23Ma02Gj
Cath.		28	F	Wife	23Ma02Gj

NAMES OF PASSENGERS		AGE	SEX	OCCUPATIONS	DATE PORT SHIP
WHELAN, Ann		.08	F	Infant	23Ma02Gj
DIRBY, Larry		31	M	Laborer	23Ma02Gj
BUTLER, Thos.		28	M	Laborer	23Ma02Gj
DICKINSON, Jas.F.		38	M	Miner	23Ma02Gj
Len.		9	M	Child	23Ma02Gj
Geo.		44	M	Miner	23Ma02Gj
LAMB, Geo.		48	M	Miner	23Ma02Gj
HOWDEN, Jos.		38	M	Miner	23Ma02Gj
KATON, Edwd.		20	M	Laborer	23Ma02Gj
MCNAMARA, Andw.		29	M	Farmer	23Ma02Gj
U	(W)	20	F	Unknown	23Ma02Gj
Thos.		.06	M	Infant	23Ma02Gj
MCCLUIN, Jas.		22	M	Laborer	23Ma02Gj
BYRNE, Margt.		20	F	Spinster	23Ma02Gj
GANNON, Mary		30	F	Spinster	23Ma02Gj
KELLY, Mat		26	M	Farmer	23Ma02Gj
BROWN, Jas.		24	M	Farmer	23Ma02Gj
Eliza		20	F	Wife	23Ma02Gj
KENNEDY, Amelia		22	F	Spinster	23Ma02Gj
RYAN, Michl.		20	M	Farmer	23Ma02Gj
CLARE, Jas.		.09	M	Infant	23Ma02Gj
FITZGERALD, Jas.		28	M	Mason	23Ma02Gj
PULLIER, Wm.		19	M	Grocer	23Ma02Gj
STYAN, John		23	M	Mechanic	23Ma02Gj
CLARKE, Timothy		46	M	Laborer	23Ma02Gj
Mary		40	F	Wife	23Ma02Gj
Edw.		12	M	Laborer	23Ma02Gj
Margt.		10	F	Unknown	23Ma02Gj
John		8	M	Child	23Ma02Gj
Jane		6	F	Child	23Ma02Gj
Eliza		4	F	Child	23Ma02Gj
FAGAN, Pat		19	M	Laborer	23Ma02Gj
Ruth		17	F	Spinster	23Ma02Gj
HONAHAN, Pat		34	M	Laborer	23Ma02Gj
HALL, Edw.		27	M	Laborer	23Ma02Gj
WOODS, Pat		23	M	Laborer	23Ma02Gj
Ann		21	F	Wife	23Ma02Gj
Wm.		.08	M	Infant	23Ma02Gj
MURPHY, Jas.		23	M	Laborer	23Ma02Gj
KEEGAN, Bridgt.		26	F	Spinster	23Ma02Gj
LANG, John		19	M	Laborer	23Ma02Gj
GANNON, John		50	M	Farmer	23Ma02Gj
Mary		50	F	Wife	23Ma02Gj
Wm.		20	M	Farmer	23Ma02Gj
Richd.		18	M	Farmer	23Ma02Gj
HORE, Jas.		22	M	Laborer	23Ma02Gj
COSTELLO, Thos.		20	M	Painter	23Ma02Gj
CONNELL, Jas.		21	M	Laborer	23Ma02Gj
FOGARTY, Lyl.		70	M	Farmer	23Ma02Gj
U	(W)	70	F	Wife	23Ma02Gj
Jas.		24	M	Farmer	23Ma02Gj
Thos.		20	M	Farmer	23Ma02Gj
Bridgt.		15	F	Spinster	23Ma02Gj
John		24	M	Farmer	23Ma02Gj
John		10	M	Farmer	23Ma02Gj
Cath.		20	F	Spinster	23Ma02Gj
RYAN, Pat		45	M	Farmer	23Ma02Gj
Johana		15	F	Spinster	23Ma02Gj
CARTY, J.		20	M	Laborer	23Ma02Gj
Margt.	(W)	21	F	Unknown	23Ma02Gj
FOY, Cath.		18	F	Spinster	23Ma02Gj
RYAN, Thos.		14	M	Laborer	23Ma02Gj
HEARN, Thos.		19	M	Laborer	23Ma02Gj
DEMPSEY, James		31	M	Shoemaker	23Ma02Gj
BUTLER, Jas.		21	M	Laborer	23Ma02Gj
KEEREN, Michl.		30	M	Laborer	23Ma02Gj
MCQUERY, Mary		30	F	Spinster	23Ma02Gj
LAHAN, Margt.		6	F	Child	23Ma02Gj
Winifred		4	F	Child	23Ma02Gj
Died-At-Sea					
KEEFE, David		28	M	Farmer	23Ma02Gj
FALLEN, Jas.		24	M	Laborer	23Ma02Gj
WHITE, Maurice		20	M	Carpenter	23Ma02Gj
RECENSY, Ann		50	F	Wi	23Ma02Gj
JENESEY, Jas.		16	M	Laborer	23Ma02Gj

NAMES OF PASSENGERS	AGE	SEX	OCCUPATIONS	DATE PORT SHIP
SAREY, Michl.	14	M	Laborer	23Ma02Gj
QUEENEY, Ann	11	F	Spinster	23Ma02Gj
GILLHOOLY, Hubert	20	M	Laborer	23Ma02Gj
Martin	16	M	Laborer	23Ma02Gj
Jas.	15	M	Laborer	23Ma02Gj
Ellen	11	F	Unknown	23Ma02Gj
Cath.	9	F	Child	23Ma02Gj
FEEHAN, Thos.	17	M	Bookbinder	23Ma02Gj
Hugh	25	M	Laborer	23Ma02Gj
Mary	20	F	Spinster	23Ma02Gj
SULLIVAN, Michl.	40	M	Laborer	23Ma02Gj
Johana	30	F	Wife	23Ma02Gj
John	.06	M	Infant	23Ma02Gj
MCGEE, Pat	20	M	Laborer	23Ma02Gj
DUFFEE, Michl.	11	M	Unknown	23Ma02Gj
Bridgt.	6	F	Child	23Ma02Gj
Frs.	7	M	Child	23Ma02Gj
Susan	.08	F	Infant	23Ma02Gj
QUINN, Jas.	40	M	Laborer	23Ma02Gj
Rose	18	F	Spinster	23Ma02Gj
Hugh	23	M	Laborer	23Ma02Gj
Eliza	28	F	Wife	23Ma02Gj
MCGEE, Mary	25	F	Spinster	23Ma02Gj
TALBOT, W.K.	40	M	Shoemaker	23Ma02Gj
Mary	12	F	Spinster	23Ma02Gj
BARRETTE, Edwd.	22	M	Laborer	23Ma02Gj
EARLY, John	23	M	Laborer	23Ma02Gj
Cath.	20	F	Wife	23Ma02Gj
RODGERS, Judy	20	F	Spinster	23Ma02Gj
Pete	25	M	Laborer	23Ma02Gj
Cath.	25	F	Wife	23Ma02Gj
Thos.	6	M	Child	23Ma02Gj
Margt.	3	F	Child	23Ma02Gj
LOGGAN, Mary	17	F	Spinster	23Ma02Gj
REILY, Charles	40	M	Mason	23Ma02Gj
Bridgt.	30	F	Wife	23Ma02Gj
Died-At-Sea				
John	15	M	Laborer	23Ma02Gj
Peter	14	M	Laborer	23Ma02Gj
Thos.	8	F	Child	23Ma02Gj
OBRIEN, Wm.	30	M	Laborer	23Ma02Gj
Bridgt.	26	F	Wife	23Ma02Gj
Margt.	.09	F	Infant	23Ma02Gj
CUGHLAN, Andw.	25	M	Laborer	23Ma02Gj
GILROY, Jas.	18	M	Laborer	23Ma02Gj
MCGUINESS, Peter	40	M	Laborer	23Ma02Gj
Hugh	12	M	Unknown	23Ma02Gj
Ann	5	F	Child	23Ma02Gj
DOONAN, Rose	10	F	Unknown	23Ma02Gj
LAVAN, Margt.	16	F	Spinster	23Ma02Gj
Cath.	14	F	Spinster	23Ma02Gj
DEVINE, Margt.	18	F	Spinster	23Ma02Gj
Mary	16	F	Spinster	23Ma02Gj
GILBERT, Sarah	14	F	Spinster	23Ma02Gj
CASEY, Edwd.	38	M	Tailor	23Ma02Gj
MAHON, James	40	M	Laborer	23Ma02Gj
DEELY, Ste.	21	M	Gdnr	23Ma02Gj
DAWSON, Sarah	30	F	Wife	23Ma02Gj
Pat	.08	M	Infant	23Ma02Gj
REED, Pat	28	M	Laborer	23Ma02Gj
HANNON, Jas.	20	M	Carpenter	23Ma02Gj
CONLAN, Ann	20	F	Wife	23Ma02Gj
GILLOVAN, Thos.	30	M	Laborer	23Ma02Gj
Cath.	3	F	Child	23Ma02Gj
Jos.	.09	M	Infant	23Ma02Gj
CULLIN, Robt.	21	M	Laborer	23Ma02Gj
NUGENT, Cath.	13	F	Unknown	23Ma02Gj
HORAN, John	20	M	Lawyer	23Ma02Gj
KERSY, Wm.	35	M	Tailor	23Ma02Gj
GILLAM, Mary	28	F	Wife	23Ma02Gj
CACOLEY, Pat	14	M	Laborer	23Ma02Gj
GRIMES, Ann	17	F	Spinster	23Ma02Gj
John	16	M	Laborer	23Ma02Gj
MCCORY, Ellen	16	F	Spinster	23Ma02Gj
TARIFF, Cath.	20	F	Spinster	23Ma02Gj

NAMES OF PASSENGERS	AGE	SEX	OCCUPATIONS	DATE PORT SHIP
GREGORY, Jas.	21	M	Laborer	23Ma02Gj
GILLORAN, Thos.	21	M	Laborer	23Ma02Gj
SMITH, John	29	M	Laborer	23Ma02Gj
KELLY, John	24	M	Unknown	23Ma02Gj
U-Mrs.	22	F	Farmer	23Ma02Gj
Pat	.08	M	Infant	23Ma02Gj
KILLION, Pat	20	M	Laborer	23Ma02Gj
HOGAN, Sarah	20	F	Spinster	23Ma02Gj
SCULLY, Bridgt.	20	F	Spinster	23Ma02Gj
Cath.	14	F	Spinster	23Ma02Gj
DOLAN, Jas.	30	M	Laborer	23Ma02Gj
MORAN, Edwd.	28	M	Laborer	23Ma02Gj
DONOHUE, Law.	21	M	Laborer	23Ma02Gj
GRANT, Andw.	26	M	Farmer	23Ma02Gj
James	28	M	Farmer	23Ma02Gj
James	.08	F	Infant	23Ma02Gj
DAVIS, W.	45	M	Farmer	23Ma02Gj
Dora	40	F	Wife	23Ma02Gj
Mary	21	F	Spinster	23Ma02Gj
MCCABE, Peter	27	M	Laborer	23Ma02Gj
U-Mrs.	27	F	Wife	23Ma02Gj
MCCAREY, Ellen	30	F	Spinster	23Ma02Gj
COONEY, Biddy	16	F	Spinster	23Ma02Gj
HANLON, Robt.	32	M	Printer	23Ma02Gj
CUMMINGS, Pat	25	M	Farmer	23Ma02Gj
MCGILL, Nancy	21	F	Spinster	23Ma02Gj
James	25	M	Laborer	23Ma02Gj
Owen	.09	M	Infant	23Ma02Gj
CREGAN, Mary	37	F	Unknown	23Ma02Gj
KELLY, John	24	M	Laborer	23Ma02Gj
Thos.	22	M	Laborer	23Ma02Gj
TIERNEY, Ann	18	F	Spinster	23Ma02Gj
MCDONALD, Mary	17	F	Spinster	23Ma02Gj
ROBERTS, Wm.	18	M	Laborer	23Ma02Gj
FITZPATRICK, John	28	M	Laborer	23Ma02Gj
Mary	28	F	Wife	23Ma02Gj
Mary	.06	F	Infant	23Ma02Gj
GRACE, John	16	M	Laborer	23Ma02Gj
BRYAN, Michl.	20	M	Laborer	23Ma02Gj
LYNCH, Bryant	20	M	Laborer	23Ma02Gj
BRYAN, Mary	20	F	Wife	23Ma02Gj
Cath.	18	F	Spinster	23Ma02Gj
CAREY, Pat	32	M	Farmer	23Ma02Gj
COLLINS, Lawr.	18	M	Laborer	23Ma02Gj
MCCARTLEY, Dennis	18	M	Laborer	23Ma02Gj
CONOLLY, Tiy.	24	M	Laborer	23Ma02Gj
CONNOLLY, John	23	M	Laborer	23Ma02Gj
Mary	61	F	Unknown	23Ma02Gj
MCCARTY, Peggy	6	F	Child	23Ma02Gj
DOONAN, Jas.	8	M	Child	23Ma02Gj
HILARD, Pat	27	M	Farmer	23Ma02Gj

SIBSON 23 MAY 1849

From Newcastle

NAMES OF PASSENGERS	AGE	SEX	OCCUPATIONS	DATE PORT SHIP
FLATOUN, Henry	28	M	Miner	23Ma18Gh
CLARK, John	36	M	Miner	23Ma18Gh
PROUDLOCH, Thos.	40	M	Miner	23Ma18Gh
CRACHNELL, Chas.	26	M	Miner	23Ma18Gh

NAMES OF PASSENGERS		AGE	SEX	OCCUPATIONS	DATE PORT SHIP

ABERDEEN 23 MAY 1849

From Liverpool

NAMES OF PASSENGERS		AGE	SEX	OCCUPATIONS	DATE PORT SHIP
RODGERS, U-Mrs.		27	F	Servant	23Ma02Gu
U-Mrs.		26	F	Servant	23Ma02Gu
SLINGER, Andrew		26	M	Mechanic	23Ma02Gu
U	(W)	26	F	Unknown	23Ma02Gu
Reily		10	M	Unknown	23Ma02Gu
Henry		9	M	Child	23Ma02Gu
Margaret		7	F	Child	23Ma02Gu
Jane		6	F	Child	23Ma02Gu
Ellen		4	F	Child	23Ma02Gu
John		2	M	Child	23Ma02Gu
Andrew		.00	M	Infant	23Ma02Gu
Christopher		29	M	Mechanic	23Ma02Gu
Robert		24	M	Farmer	23Ma02Gu
Anne		26	F	Wife	23Ma02Gu
U		.00	U	Infant	23Ma02Gu
ORR, John		35	M	Farmer	23Ma02Gu
Agnes	(M)	60	F	Unknown	23Ma02Gu
Margaret	(T)	27	F	Unknown	23Ma02Gu
Margaret	(W)	23	F	Unknown	23Ma02Gu
Anna	(T)	25	F	Unknown	23Ma02Gu
William		23	M	Farmer	23Ma02Gu
CAMPBELL, Alexander		22	M	Farmer	23Ma02Gu
PETTICREW, Robert		30	M	Mechanic	23Ma02Gu
MCKITTRICK, Margare	(N)	15	F	Unknown	23Ma02Gu
Jane	(N)	13	F	Unknown	23Ma02Gu
Adam	(N)	12	M	Unknown	23Ma02Gu
John	(N)	10	M	Unknown	23Ma02Gu
AGNEW, Joseph		12	M	Unknown	23Ma02Gu
MINOWEN, Andrew		22	M	Htlkpr	23Ma02Gu
U	(W)	19	F	Unknown	23Ma02Gu
HENRY, Frances		55	M	Farmer	23Ma02Gu
Mary	(W)	45	F	Unknown	23Ma02Gu
Sarah	(D)	17	F	Unknown	23Ma02Gu
Robert	(S)	15	M	Unknown	23Ma02Gu
Alexander	(S)	14	M	Unknown	23Ma02Gu
MCGOWAN, Alexander		34	M	Teacher	23Ma02Gu
Margaret	(W)	30	F	Unknown	23Ma02Gu
Robt.	(S)	9	M	Child	23Ma02Gu
Adam	(S)	4	M	Child	23Ma02Gu
Mary-Ellen	(S)	2	F	Child	23Ma02Gu
ROBERTS, Rebecca		20	F	Servant	23Ma02Gu
MCGRAN, John		35	M	Teacher	23Ma02Gu
Elizabeth	(W)	30	F	Unknown	23Ma02Gu
Jane	(D)	8	F	Child	23Ma02Gu
John	(S)	6	M	Child	23Ma02Gu
Letitia	(D)	4	F	Child	23Ma02Gu
Sarah	(D)	.00	F	Infant	23Ma02Gu
HUESTON, Hugh		25	M	Mechanic	23Ma02Gu
CAMPBELL, John		15	M	Unknown	23Ma02Gu
PARKHILL, Robt.		19	M	Mechanic	23Ma02Gu
ORR, John		25	M	Farmer	23Ma02Gu
SHASWELL, James		21	M	Mechanic	23Ma02Gu
SIGGERS, George		32	M	Mechanic	23Ma02Gu
MORGAN, William		18	M	Mechanic	23Ma02Gu
PRICE, Wm.		20	M	Mechanic	23Ma02Gu
GALLOOLY, Sally		52	F	Servant	23Ma02Gu
MARSLALY, Honora		40	F	Unknown	23Ma02Gu
Mary-Ann	(D)	20	F	Unknown	23Ma02Gu
William	(S)	17	M	Unknown	23Ma02Gu
Patrick	(S)	15	M	Unknown	23Ma02Gu
Honora	(D)	12	F	Unknown	23Ma02Gu
DUNNE, William		22	M	Farmer	23Ma02Gu
LOUGHNANE, Michael		35	M	Laborer	23Ma02Gu
James		20	M	Laborer	23Ma02Gu
Mary	(S)	21	F	Unknown	23Ma02Gu
ROWE, Michael		40	M	Farmer	23Ma02Gu
MEHAN, Martin		33	M	Mechanic	23Ma02Gu
Jane	(W)	33	F	Unknown	23Ma02Gu
John	(S)	8	M	Child	23Ma02Gu
Maria	(D)	6	F	Child	23Ma02Gu
Michael	(S)	3	M	Child	23Ma02Gu
Stephen	(S)	.00	M	Infant	23Ma02Gu
CULLEN, Jane	(C)	17	F	Unknown	23Ma02Gu
MACK, Ellen		24	F	Unknown	23Ma02Gu
Thos.	(S)	2	M	Child	23Ma02Gu
TALBOT, Thos.		33	M	Mechanic	23Ma02Gu
Anne	(W)	30	F	Unknown	23Ma02Gu
Richard	(S)	8	M	Child	23Ma02Gu
Bridget	(D)	5	F	Child	23Ma02Gu
Jane	(D)	.00	F	Infant	23Ma02Gu
MONKS, Thos.		30	M	Laborer	23Ma02Gu
Anne	(A)	30	F	Unknown	23Ma02Gu
Bridget	(W)	26	F	Unknown	23Ma02Gu
Patrick	(S)	.00	M	Infant	23Ma02Gu
Joseph		25	M	Laborer	23Ma02Gu
KELLY, Rose		27	F	Servant	23Ma02Gu
TOOLE, Nicholas		40	M	Laborer	23Ma02Gu
SERRY, Rose		22	F	Servant	23Ma02Gu
LYNCH, Philip		35	M	Laborer	23Ma02Gu
Rose	(W)	33	F	Unknown	23Ma02Gu
Pat	(S)	.00	M	Infant	23Ma02Gu
MORAN, Joseph		40	M	Laborer	23Ma02Gu
Catherine	(W)	40	F	Unknown	23Ma02Gu
Pat	(S)	6	M	Child	23Ma02Gu
William	(S)	5	M	Child	23Ma02Gu
Joseph	(S)	3	M	Child	23Ma02Gu
James	(S)	.00	M	Infant	23Ma02Gu
FOTTREL, James		26	M	Laborer	23Ma02Gu
FINN, Michael		28	M	Servant	23Ma02Gu
FITZHARRIS, James		24	M	Laborer	23Ma02Gu
SPENCER, James		26	M	Laborer	23Ma02Gu
MENTURN, James		35	M	Laborer	23Ma02Gu
Ellen	(W)	30	F	Unknown	23Ma02Gu
RYAN, John		24	M	Laborer	23Ma02Gu
CONNAL, James		21	M	Farmer	23Ma02Gu
DEGNAN, Frances		26	M	Laborer	23Ma02Gu
Mary	(D)	7	F	Child	23Ma02Gu
John	(S)	6	M	Child	23Ma02Gu
HOULDING, James		22	M	Laborer	23Ma02Gu
BOWDEN, Danl.		28	M	Laborer	23Ma02Gu
DAUGHTON, Martin		22	M	Laborer	23Ma02Gu
LYONS, Patrick		30	M	Laborer	23Ma02Gu
WHELAN, Thos.		24	M	Laborer	23Ma02Gu
MCMURDOCK, John		35	M	Laborer	23Ma02Gu
William		30	M	Engineer	23Ma02Gu
MOFFAT, James		26	M	Mechanic	23Ma02Gu
GREEN, U		30	F	Unknown	23Ma02Gu
Mary	(D)	3	F	Child	23Ma02Gu
DOUGHIN, Danl.		32	M	Mechanic	23Ma02Gu
Mary	(W)	30	F	Unknown	23Ma02Gu
CARMODY, James		32	M	Mechanic	23Ma02Gu
GARRET, William		32	M	Farmer	23Ma02Gu
QUICK, Margaret		30	F	Servant	23Ma02Gu
WADE, Robert		25	M	Seaman	23Ma02Gu
WILLIAMS, John		39	M	Farmer	23Ma02Gu
Thomas		19	M	Farmer	23Ma02Gu
RUSSELL, Lawrence		30	M	Laborer	23Ma02Gu
Catherine	(W)	30	F	Unknown	23Ma02Gu
REYNOLDS, Pat		50	M	Farmer	23Ma02Gu
Sarah	(W)	48	F	Unknown	23Ma02Gu
Ellen	(D)	16	F	Unknown	23Ma02Gu
Sarah	(D)	14	F	Unknown	23Ma02Gu
Patrick	(S)	12	M	Unknown	23Ma02Gu
Michael	(S)	8	M	Child	23Ma02Gu
REID, Stephen		35	M	Farmer	23Ma02Gu
Mary	(W)	34	F	Unknown	23Ma02Gu
Stephen	(S)	7	M	Child	23Ma02Gu
Elizabeth	(D)	6	F	Child	23Ma02Gu
Eleanor	(D)	4	F	Child	23Ma02Gu
Jeffries	(S)	2	M	Child	23Ma02Gu

NAMES OF PASSENGERS		AGE	SEX	OCCUPATIONS	DATE PORT SHIP
REID, Sarah-Anne	(D)	.00	F	Infant	23Ma02Gu
BOWERS, Rodger		52	M	Farmer	23Ma02Gu
Elizabeth	(W)	50	F	Unknown	23Ma02Gu
William	(S)	15	M	Unknown	23Ma02Gu
Jane	(D)	6	F	Child	23Ma02Gu
Elizabeth	(D)	4	F	Child	23Ma02Gu
COOGHAN, Michael		35	M	Farmer	23Ma02Gu
Catherine	(W)	33	F	Unknown	23Ma02Gu
EAGAN, William		21	M	Farmer	23Ma02Gu
RYAN, Thos.		23	M	Farmer	23Ma02Gu
Johanna	(S)	20	F	Unknown	23Ma02Gu
BARRY, John		26	M	Laborer	23Ma02Gu
SULLIVAN, Mary		20	F	Mechanic	23Ma02Gu
RADCLIFFE, John-H.		23	M	Mechanic	23Ma02Gu
CORKHILL, Thos.		23	M	Mechanic	23Ma02Gu
RADCLIFF, John		20	M	Farmer	23Ma02Gu
COLGAN, Cornls.		21	M	Mechanic	23Ma02Gu
CONNERY, Patt		26	M	Laborer	23Ma02Gu
Timothy		22	M	Laborer	23Ma02Gu
Cathrine	(S)	20	F	Unknown	23Ma02Gu
HUGHES, Patrick		40	M	Laborer	23Ma02Gu
Bridget	(W)	30	F	Unknown	23Ma02Gu
John	(S)	.00	M	Infant	23Ma02Gu
GARROW, Catherine	(C)	20	F	Unknown	23Ma02Gu
MULCALLY, William		40	M	Laborer	23Ma02Gu
DOWNEY, William		24	M	Laborer	23Ma02Gu
Tedy		23	M	Laborer	23Ma02Gu
HUGHES, Owen		27	M	Mechanic	23Ma02Gu
Elizabeth		27	F	Servant	23Ma02Gu
EVANS, Betsey		21	F	Servant	23Ma02Gu
EDWARD, William		20	M	Laborer	23Ma02Gu
Humphrey		19	M	Laborer	23Ma02Gu
CLARK, Harriet		21	F	Unknown	23Ma02Gu
DAVIES, David		28	M	Miner	23Ma02Gu
BISBY, Cornls.		30	M	Mechanic	23Ma02Gu
LEWIS, Edward		30	M	Mechanic	23Ma02Gu
RITCHIE, John		32	M	Farmer	23Ma02Gu
William		24	M	Farmer	23Ma02Gu
HICKS, James		39	M	Mechanic	23Ma02Gu
REYNOLDS, John		27	M	Mechanic	23Ma02Gu
EVANS, James		31	M	Mechanic	23Ma02Gu
JENKINS, William		31	M	Mechanic	23Ma02Gu
David		24	M	Engineer	23Ma02Gu
WILLIAMS, Richard		30	M	Collier	23Ma02Gu
EVANS, Anne		22	F	Servant	23Ma02Gu
Alice		24	F	Unknown	23Ma02Gu
Anne		2	F	Child	23Ma02Gu
PARKER, Thos.		40	M	Mechanic	23Ma02Gu
Thos.	(S)	7	M	Child	23Ma02Gu
DOUTHIVAITE, William		46	M	Mechanic	23Ma02Gu
GER, Mary		28	F	Unknown	23Ma02Gu
James	(S)	.00	M	Infant	23Ma02Gu
CASKILL, Edward		40	M	Farmer	23Ma02Gu
Jane	(W)	38	F	Unknown	23Ma02Gu
William	(S)	13	M	Unknown	23Ma02Gu
Jane	(D)	11	F	Unknown	23Ma02Gu
Margaret	(D)	10	F	Unknown	23Ma02Gu
Edward	(S)	6	M	Child	23Ma02Gu
Anne	(D)	5	F	Child	23Ma02Gu
Catherine	(D)	.00	F	Infant	23Ma02Gu
COWALL, Thos.		40	M	Laborer	23Ma02Gu
Margaret	(W)	40	F	Unknown	23Ma02Gu
Margaret	(D)	14	F	Unknown	23Ma02Gu
Anne	(D)	11	F	Unknown	23Ma02Gu
Sophia	(D)	9	F	Child	23Ma02Gu
John	(S)	7	M	Child	23Ma02Gu
William		5	M	Child	23Ma02Gu
Edward		3	M	Child	23Ma02Gu
Thomas	(S)	.00	M	Infant	23Ma02Gu
CALLOW, James		24	M	Laborer	23Ma02Gu
Mary	(T)	22	F	Unknown	23Ma02Gu
KELLY, Thomas		20	M	Laborer	23Ma02Gu
Jane	(T)	24	F	Unknown	23Ma02Gu
SHRUMININ, William		24	M	Mechanic	23Ma02Gu
CANNEL, James		24	M	Mechanic	23Ma02Gu

NAMES OF PASSENGERS		AGE	SEX	OCCUPATIONS	DATE PORT SHIP
CANNEL, John		22	M	Mechanic	23Ma02Gu
SEWELLEN, Thomas		42	M	Mechanic	23Ma02Gu
Thos.	(S)	18	M	Unknown	23Ma02Gu
Lydia	(D)	14	F	Unknown	23Ma02Gu
Mary	(D)	11	F	Unknown	23Ma02Gu
David	(S)	8	M	Child	23Ma02Gu
Louisa	(D)	3	F	Child	23Ma02Gu
Elizabeth	(D)	.00	F	Infant	23Ma02Gu
SHUTE, Joshua		24	M	Laborer	23Ma02Gu
Elizabeth	(W)	23	F	Unknown	23Ma02Gu
MACK, John		30	M	Farmer	23Ma02Gu
CLARKSON, James		21	M	Mechanic	23Ma02Gu
SYKES, Thos.		18	M	Farmer	23Ma02Gu
MCGUIRK, Pat		29	M	Laborer	23Ma02Gu
DUNLOP, Henry		24	M	Mechanic	23Ma02Gu
Isabella	(W)	20	F	Unknown	23Ma02Gu
ANDREWS, William		21	M	Farmer	23Ma02Gu
HUNTER, Thos.		22	M	Farmer	23Ma02Gu
LEWIS, Edward		20	M	Bookkeeper	23Ma02Gu
CLEARY, Michael		30	M	Mechanic	23Ma02Gu
Jeremiah		18	M	Mechanic	23Ma02Gu
CONNOLTY, John		26	M	Mechanic	23Ma02Gu
Mary-Anne	(W)	24	F	Unknown	23Ma02Gu
KELSO, Frances		32	F	Unknown	23Ma02Gu
Jane	(D)	15	F	Unknown	23Ma02Gu
Eliza	(D)	12	F	Unknown	23Ma02Gu
ROGE, Thos.		24	M	Farmer	23Ma02Gu
Frances		23	M	Farmer	23Ma02Gu
BLACKBURN, Samuel		35	M	Mechanic	23Ma02Gu
JACKSON, George		27	M	Mechanic	23Ma02Gu
DEMPSEY, Peter		28	M	Laborer	23Ma02Gu
WINPENNY, Jos.		35	M	Mechanic	23Ma02Gu
TEDIGAN, Christopher		27	M	Laborer	23Ma02Gu
Alice	(W)	24	F	Unknown	23Ma02Gu
Catherine	(D)	.00	F	Infant	23Ma02Gu
DOWLIN, Catherine	(M)	60	F	Unknown	23Ma02Gu
FINNEGAN, Patrick	(N)	10	M	Unknown	23Ma02Gu
DUMPHY, Francis		21	M	Laborer	23Ma02Gu
Jane	(T)	18	F	Unknown	23Ma02Gu
Catherine	(T)	17	F	Unknown	23Ma02Gu
SWORD, Cchristopher		26	M	Laborer	23Ma02Gu
GRACE, Patrick		55	M	Farmer	23Ma02Gu
Philip	(S)	23	M	Unknown	23Ma02Gu
Mary	(D)	22	F	Unknown	23Ma02Gu
Honora	(D)	20	F	Unknown	23Ma02Gu
Thomas	(S)	13	M	Unknown	23Ma02Gu
BOWDEN, Mary		24	F	Servant	23Ma02Gu
WHITE, Patt		30	M	Laborer	23Ma02Gu
Margaret	(T)	28	F	Unknown	23Ma02Gu
Catherine	(T)	20	F	Unknown	23Ma02Gu
CONNERFORD, Pat		30	M	Farmer	23Ma02Gu
U	(W)	26	F	Unknown	23Ma02Gu
CORCORAN, James		20	M	Farmer	23Ma02Gu
John		18	M	Clerk	23Ma02Gu
SEALY, Catherine	(S)	30	F	Unknown	23Ma02Gu
DUNNE, William		20	M	Shopkeeper	23Ma02G
NOLAN, Garret		19	M	Clerk	23Ma02G
TUSKINGTON, William		16	M	Unknown	23Ma02G
DOOLY, Catherine		16	F	Servant	23Ma02G
ONEILL, Arthur		20	M	Laborer	23Ma02G
Eleanor		22	F	Servant	23Ma02G
Savinia		18	F	Servant	23Ma02G
MCGUIGAN, Bernard		20	M	Laborer	23Ma02G
MULLEN, Bernard		20	M	Laborer	23Ma02G
Bridget		23	F	Servant	23Ma02G
MCKERVER, Henry		21	M	Laborer	23Ma02G
KERGAN, Mary		30	F	Servant	23Ma02G
Pat	(S)	4	M	Child	23Ma02G
Bridget	(D)	.00	F	Infant	23Ma02G
MULLY, Ellen		22	F	Servant	23Ma02G
PATTEN, William		21	M	Laborer	23Ma02G
MCGRAN, Mary-Jane		30	F	Unknown	23Ma02G
MURPHY, Margaret		22	F	Unknown	23Ma02G
Thomas	(S)	.00	M	Infant	23Ma02G
MCDEWIT, John		24	M	Laborer	23Ma02G

UNICORN 23 MAY 1849

From Liverpool

NAMES OF PASSENGERS		AGE	SEX	OCCUPATIONS	DATE PORT SHIP
RONEY, Nicholas		21	M	Laborer	23Ma02He
KERR, Valentine		50	M	Laborer	23Ma02He
Jane		50	F	Unknown	23Ma02He
John		10	M	Unknown	23Ma02He
DAVIS, Mick		23	M	Laborer	23Ma02He
BYRNE, Pat.		21	M	Laborer	23Ma02He
Charles		20	M	Laborer	23Ma02He
HANLON, Pat.		22	M	Laborer	23Ma02He
Mary		22	F	Unknown	23Ma02He
Betty		19	F	Unknown	23Ma02He
Dolly		16	F	Unknown	23Ma02He
Elly		16	F	Unknown	23Ma02He
Jeremiah		15	M	Unknown	23Ma02He
Morgan		50	M	Unknown	23Ma02He
Mary	(W)	50	F	Unknown	23Ma02He
REILLY, James		30	M	Unknown	23Ma02He
RYAN, Mick		25	M	Unknown	23Ma02He
ALLEN, Richard		20	M	Unknown	23Ma02He
BYRNE, John		40	M	Unknown	23Ma02He
Cathrine		40	F	Unknown	23Ma02He
Jane		18	F	Unknown	23Ma02He
Mary		16	F	Unknown	23Ma02He
Charles		11	M	Unknown	23Ma02He
Eliza		9	F	Child	23Ma02He
James		7	M	Child	23Ma02He
PRICE, Bridget		20	F	Spinster	23Ma02He
CAREY, Mick		23	M	Laborer	23Ma02He
John		20	M	Laborer	23Ma02He
Hugh		17	M	Laborer	23Ma02He
Nicholas		11	M	Laborer	23Ma02He
Sarah		24	F	Unknown	23Ma02He
Dolley		9	F	Child	23Ma02He
Mary		8	F	Child	23Ma02He
FOLEY, Pat.		23	M	Unknown	23Ma02He
LAWLER, William		24	M	Unknown	23Ma02He
ONEILL, Theresa		16	F	Spinster	23Ma02He
ADAMS, William		46	M	Farmer	23Ma02He
Samuel		14	M	Farmer	23Ma02He
Robert		20	M	Farmer	23Ma02He
Hannah		20	F	Farmer	23Ma02He
Bridget		11	F	Farmer	23Ma02He
3IGGER, David		30	M	Schm	23Ma02He
OHANLON, James		50	M	Laborer	23Ma02He
Ellen		45	F	Unknown	23Ma02He
Eliza		50	F	Unknown	23Ma02He
Catherine		17	F	Unknown	23Ma02He
Pat.		14	M	Unknown	23Ma02He
Charles		12	M	Unknown	23Ma02He
James		9	M	Child	23Ma02He
UDDY, Owen		32	M	Unknown	23Ma02He
WYER, Pat.		20	M	Tinker	23Ma02He
Catherine	(W)	27	F	Unknown	23Ma02He
Mary-Ann		9	F	Child	23Ma02He
Margarate		7	F	Child	23Ma02He
Catherine		5	F	Child	23Ma02He
Amelia		.00	F	Infant	23Ma02He
YAN, Owen		16	M	Laborer	23Ma02He
SHE, Pat.		35	F	Wife	23Ma02He
Jane		30	F	Unknown	23Ma02He
James		5	M	Child	23Ma02He
Mary		.00	F	Infant	23Ma02He
JRPHY, James		20	M	Unknown	23Ma02He
James		34	M	Unknown	23Ma02He
JFFEY, John		30	M	Unknown	23Ma02He
HITING, John		40	M	Unknown	23Ma02He

NAMES OF PASSENGERS		AGE	SEX	OCCUPATIONS	DATE PORT SHIP
SHARKEY, Pat.		30	M	Laborer	23Ma02He
HALLINON, Pat.		30	M	Laborer	23Ma02He
CUSSEN, Mick		22	M	Laborer	23Ma02He
FARRELL, Pat.		26	M	Laborer	23Ma02He
ODONNELL, John		21	M	Laborer	23Ma02He
MULLIGAN, Edmund		22	M	Laborer	23Ma02He
Martin		21	M	Laborer	23Ma02He
HIGGINS, Edmund		23	M	Laborer	23Ma02He
POWER, Mick		28	M	Laborer	23Ma02He
John		26	M	Laborer	23Ma02He
HAYNES, John		30	M	Laborer	23Ma02He
Bridget		20	F	Unknown	23Ma02He
CUNNINGHAM, Fanny		24	F	Unknown	23Ma02He
HYNES, John		.00	M	Infant	23Ma02He
NUGENT, Mick		18	M	Laborer	23Ma02He
Michael		22	M	Laborer	23Ma02He
WALSH, William		27	M	Laborer	23Ma02He
MULLAN, James		27	M	Laborer	23Ma02He
LYNCH, Pat.		27	M	Laborer	23Ma02He
PEACOCK, George		38	M	Laborer	23Ma02He
FERMOYLE, Pat.		27	M	Laborer	23Ma02He
Judith		24	F	Unknown	23Ma02He
Honora		20	F	Unknown	23Ma02He
ROE, Hugh		40	M	Laborer	23Ma02He
SMITH, Richard		30	M	Laborer	23Ma02He
ROE, Thomas		27	M	Laborer	23Ma02He
Mary		26	F	Unknown	23Ma02He
SHORT, James		26	M	Unknown	23Ma02He
MAHON, Emsty		23	U	Unknown	23Ma02He
Alice		19	F	Unknown	23Ma02He
WILLIAMS, Pat.		26	M	Unknown	23Ma02He
CHAMBERS, John		18	M	Unknown	23Ma02He
ARNOLD, Pat.		19	M	Unknown	23Ma02He
Rose		46	F	Unknown	23Ma02He
Mary		16	F	Unknown	23Ma02He
FLOY, Thomas		30	M	Unknown	23Ma02He
Nicholas		6	M	Child	23Ma02He
OBRIEN, John		16	M	Laborer	23Ma02He
MULLIGANES, James		20	M	Laborer	23Ma02He
MALONEY, Dennis		21	M	Laborer	23Ma02He
Catharine	(W)	28	F	Unknown	23Ma02He
OBOYLE, U-Revd.		27	M	Clergyman	23Ma02He
OSULLIVAN, U-Revd.		27	M	Clergyman	23Ma02He
BURKE, Pat		20	M	Laborer	23Ma02He
BYRON, Mary		30	F	Spinster	23Ma02He
NOLAN, Richard		30	M	Laborer	23Ma02He
GILMARTIN, Hugh		36	M	Laborer	23Ma02He
DUFFY, William		20	M	Laborer	23Ma02He
BEGGAN, Felix		18	M	Laborer	23Ma02He
GALLAHER, Jos.		20	M	Laborer	23Ma02He
Mary		50	F	Spinster	23Ma02He
SHERAN, Mick		25	M	Laborer	23Ma02He
SULLIVAN, James		26	M	Laborer	23Ma02He
BEATTY, David		20	M	Laborer	23Ma02He
William		20	M	Laborer	23Ma02He
FALLEY, Pat.		28	M	Laborer	23Ma02He
REILLY, Bryan		30	M	Laborer	23Ma02He
CAROLLE, Tom		25	M	Laborer	23Ma02He
BRYAN, Martin		30	M	Laborer	23Ma02He
Fanney	(W)	30	F	Unknown	23Ma02He
William		.00	M	Infant	23Ma02He
LAHEY, Richard		32	M	Laborer	23Ma02He
QUIRK, Martin		23	M	Laborer	23Ma02He
DALEY, William		25	M	Laborer	23Ma02He
COHILL, Thomas		30	M	Laborer	23Ma02He
HEALY, Thomas		27	M	Laborer	23Ma02He
MCDONNELL, Mary		20	F	Unknown	23Ma02He
CWINNAN, Bryan		20	M	Unknown	23Ma02He
MCLOUGHLIN, Margt.		18	F	Unknown	23Ma02He
MALOWNEY, Peter		20	M	Laborer	23Ma02He
DOVENY, Mick		22	M	Laborer	23Ma02He
John		14	M	Laborer	23Ma02He
BLAKE, Catharine		.00	F	Infant	23Ma02He
MURPHY, Pat.		20	M	Laborer	23Ma02He
Ellen	(W)	20	F	Unknown	23Ma02He

NAMES OF PASSENGERS		AGE	SEX	OCCUPATIONS	DATE PORT SHIP
HERAGHTY, Roger		50	M	Laborer	23Ma02He
Catharine	(W)	50	F	Unknown	23Ma02He
Mary		22	F	Spinster	23Ma02He
DICKSON, Bridget		20	F	Spinster	23Ma02He
EARLEY, Mary		16	F	Spinster	23Ma02He
CRONAN, John		28	M	Laborer	23Ma02He
GOLLAGHER, James		22	M	Laborer	23Ma02He
CARREN, Cath.		22	F	Spinster	23Ma02He
LANNING, Pat.		18	M	Laborer	23Ma02He
Peggey	(W)	20	F	Unknown	23Ma02He
DWYER, Tom		50	M	Farmer	23Ma02He
Lucy	(W)	50	F	Unknown	23Ma02He
Margaret		16	F	Unknown	23Ma02He
Jul--		16	U	Unknown	23Ma02He
Norry		21	F	Unknown	23Ma02He
Phill.		17	M	Unknown	23Ma02He
John		.00	M	Infant	23Ma02He
Patt.		9	M	Child	23Ma02He
HOWLEY, Edward		18	M	Laborer	23Ma02He
MCDONALD, Mick		36	M	Laborer	23Ma02He
Matilda	(W)	36	F	Unknown	23Ma02He
John		.00	M	Infant	23Ma02He
Robert		3	M	Child	23Ma02He
BRYAN, Hugh		16	M	Laborer	23Ma02He
HANLEY, William		36	M	Laborer	23Ma02He
Francis		36	M	Laborer	23Ma02He
Margerat		.00	F	Infant	23Ma02He
GILLAN, Peter		26	M	Laborer	23Ma02He
PARELLY, Phillip Died-At-Sea		50	M	Laborer	23Ma02He
Anne	(W)	55	F	Unknown	23Ma02He
REILLEY, Anne		30	F	Spinster	23Ma02He
QUEGLEY, Anny		25	F	Spinster	23Ma02He
MAHON, Joseph		23	M	Laborer	23Ma02He
HOGAN, Pat.		20	M	Laborer	23Ma02He
SHEAN, Jeremia		22	M	Laborer	23Ma02He
Con		24	M	Laborer	23Ma02He
CREAY, Pat.		29	M	Laborer	23Ma02He
Ellen	(W)	23	F	Unknown	23Ma02He
MALEY, Patt.		26	M	Laborer	23Ma02He
Margt.	(W)	26	F	Unknown	23Ma02He
MONAGHAN, Mary		20	F	Spinster	23Ma02He
GULLIVAN, Peter		20	M	Laborer	23Ma02He
Eliza		20	F	Unknown	23Ma02He
Anne		.00	F	Infant	23Ma02He
CALLAGHAN, Mary		20	F	Spinster	23Ma02He
DILLON, John		20	M	Laborer	23Ma02He
GEARY, William		20	M	Laborer	23Ma02He
PEARCE, Michel		35	M	Laborer	23Ma02He

CAMBRIDGE 24 MAY 1849

From Liverpool

NAMES OF PASSENGERS		AGE	SEX	OCCUPATIONS	DATE PORT SHIP
MCGUIRE, Marcella		50	F	Housekeeper	24Ma02Gk
Peter		18	M	Housekeeper	24Ma02Gk
Mathew		12	M	Housekeeper	24Ma02Gk
Marcella		10	U	Housekeeper	24Ma02Gk
REDFORTH, Alice		48	F	Dressmaker	24Ma02Gk
Eliza		9	F	Child	24Ma02Gk
MCGOWAN, John		30	M	Laborer	24Ma02Gk
Thomas		20	M	Laborer	24Ma02Gk
GREEN, Patrick		20	M	Painter	24Ma02Gk
MCANEMEY, Jane		40	F	Servant	24Ma02Gk
KEARNEY, Patk.		20	M	Laborer	24Ma02Gk
WOOD, Bridget		18	F	Servant	24Ma02Gk
FITZGERALD, U-Mrs.		30	F	Housekeeper	24Ma02Gk
Maria		6	F	Child	24Ma02Gk
Ann		4	F	Child	24Ma02Gk
BYRNES, Catharine		30	F	Tailor	24Ma02Gk
Thomas		10	M	Tailor	24Ma02Gk
Wm.		8	M	Child	24Ma02Gk
HUMPHREY, James		23	M	Plasterer	24Ma02Gk
KEALIAGHER, Julia		19	F	Milliner	24Ma02Gk
MACKAY, Catharine		35	F	Seamstress	24Ma02Gk
James		13	M	Tailor	24Ma02Gk
Ann		9	F	Child	24Ma02Gk
John		7	M	Child	24Ma02Gk
Thomas		4	M	Child	24Ma02Gk
Michael		2	M	Child	24Ma02Gk
MCCARTHY, Cathann		21	F	Servant	24Ma02Gk
SCULLY, Mary		11	F	Servant	24Ma02Gk
CARROLL, Thomas		27	M	Tinker	24Ma02Gk
BRIAN, John		25	M	Wwsh	24Ma02Gk
MCCARDLE, John		70	M	Bartender	24Ma02Gk
Catharine		66	F	Servant	24Ma02Gk
Margaret		34	F	Servant	24Ma02Gk
REARDON, Owen		30	M	Shoemaker	24Ma02Gk
Johanna		23	F	Servant	24Ma02Gk
KEEFFE, Jeny		9	F	Child	24Ma02Gk
John		6	M	Child	24Ma02Gk
MURPHY, Nancy		23	F	Cook	24Ma02Gk
DOYLE, Catharine		11	F	Cook	24Ma02Gk
SHANLY, Wm.		18	M	Bookbinder	24Ma02Gk
CARROLL, John		41	M	Printer	24Ma02Gk
MORRISON, Wm.J.		20	M	Carpenter	24Ma02Gk
Nancy		19	F	Milliner	24Ma02Gk
SMITH, Mary		5	F	Seamstress	24Ma02Gk
MCCARNEY, Patrick		20	M	Peddler	24Ma02Gk
MCASPERET, Ellen		20	F	Servant	24Ma02Gk
GARRY, Wm.		21	M	Engineer	24Ma02Gk
COLSTON, Hannah		19	F	Servant	24Ma02Gk
BRYAN, Mary		18	F	Servant	24Ma02Gk
HARRICAN, Nancy		50	F	Nurse	24Ma02Gk
Dennis		18	M	Houseboy	24Ma02Gk
Catharine		6	F	Child	24Ma02Gk
MCKNIGHT, Thomas		21	M	Printer	24Ma02Gk
Michael		22	M	Painter	24Ma02Gk
HALPENNY, Catharine		16	F	Servant	24Ma02Gk
CLARK, Alice		17	F	Cooper	24Ma02Gk
HART, Mrgaret		20	F	Cook	24Ma02Gk
BRENEN, Ellen		20	F	Cook	24Ma02Gk
CLARK, James		25	M	Brewer	24Ma02Gk
REILLY, Philip		19	M	Waiter	24Ma02Gk
Thomas		24	M	Glsbr	24Ma02Gk
HART, Mary		21	F	Servant	24Ma02Gk
James		28	M	Waiter	24Ma02Gk
HARLEY, James		18	M	Waiter	24Ma02Gk
Margaret		19	F	Servant	24Ma02Gk
GALLAGHER, James		45	M	Butcher	24Ma02Gk
Susan		36	F	Servant	24Ma02Gk
Michael		14	M	Waiter	24Ma02Gk
Saml.		7	M	Child	24Ma02Gk
Joseph		2	M	Child	24Ma02Gk
James		5	M	Child	24Ma02Gk
BENNETT, Wm.		16	M	Musician	24Ma02G
MCGUIRE, Roger		20	M	Baker	24Ma02G
MCADAM, James		45	M	Cooper	24Ma02G
Betty		10	F	Cooper	24Ma02G
MURPHY, Patrick		11	M	Cooper	24Ma02G
DUNCAN, James		20	M	Chandler	24Ma02G
TULLY, Ann		10	F	Chandler	24Ma02G
Ellen		20	F	Servant	24Ma02G
KELLY, Ann		27	F	Servant	24Ma02G
MURRAY, Patrick		21	M	Waiter	24Ma02G
James		19	M	Waiter	24Ma02G
CUNEY, Patrick		35	M	Soap Boiler	24Ma02G
DERMOTT, Lawrence		35	M	Farmer	24Ma02G
DUFFY, Rosanna		26	F	Servant	24Ma02G
MCCANNA, Mary		20	F	Cook	24Ma02G
Barney		.00	M	Infant	24Ma02G
MCNAMEE, Henry		23	M	Hod Carrier	24Ma02G
Bridget		18	F	Servant	24Ma02G
DUFFY, Patrick		24	M	Mason	24Ma02G

NAMES OF PASSENGERS	AGE	SEX	OCCUPATIONS	DATE PORT SHIP
DEMPSEY, Bridget	20	F	Cook	24Ma02Gk
GILLON, Margaret	18	F	Cook	24Ma02Gk
MURRAY, Honora	16	F	Servant	24Ma02Gk
Andrew	20	M	Gdnr	24Ma02Gk
MCDERMOTT, Charles	20	M	Carpenter	24Ma02Gk
MORGAN, Timothy	35	M	Joiner	24Ma02Gk
MCCANNA, Ellen	19	F	Servant	24Ma02Gk
DUNN, John	25	M	Engraver	24Ma02Gk
MALLON, Peter	18	M	Bell Hanger	24Ma02Gk
MCGINNIGIN, Ellen	14	M	Bell Hanger	24Ma02Gk
GALLAGHER, Ann	28	F	Servant	24Ma02Gk
HANNAHAN, Patrick	34	M	Basketmaker	24Ma02Gk
Michael	30	M	Basketmaker	24Ma02Gk
MONGHAN, Michael	14	M	Baker	24Ma02Gk
GILMINGHAN, Catharine	40	F	Servant	24Ma02Gk
MONGHAN, John	17	M	Servant	24Ma02Gk
Bridget	15	F	Servant	24Ma02Gk
MURPHY, Sally	24	F	Servant	24Ma02Gk
CLIFFORD, Catharine	20	F	Servant	24Ma02Gk
SHANNEN, Margaret	19	F	Servant	24Ma02Gk
MECHAN, Bridget	18	F	Servant	24Ma02Gk
MCBENNETT, Edward	7	M	Child	24Ma02Gk
CURIA, Patrick	11	M	Servant	24Ma02Gk
Richard	9	M	Child	24Ma02Gk
KELLY, James	21	M	Miner	24Ma02Gk
SMITH, Pegan	12	F	Miner	24Ma02Gk
Walter	10	M	Miner	24Ma02Gk
Alexr.	8	M	Child	24Ma02Gk
MULDRON, Thomas	30	M	Laborer	24Ma02Gk
Judy	30	F	Servant	24Ma02Gk
Patrick	5	M	Child	24Ma02Gk
KULDRON, Philip	2	M	Child	24Ma02Gk
MULLAN, Alice	18	F	Servant	24Ma02Gk
NOLAN, Michael	20	M	Laborer	24Ma02Gk
SCOLLON, Betsey	12	F	Laborer	24Ma02Gk
MURPHY, Eliza	20	F	Servant	24Ma02Gk
Eliza	.00	F	Infant	24Ma02Gk
ELLIOTT, Jane	19	F	Servant	24Ma02Gk
Fanny	17	F	Servant	24Ma02Gk
WYNN, Tenana	19	F	Servant	24Ma02Gk
FITZSIMMONS, Margaret	20	F	Servant	24Ma02Gk
GERATY, Kary	20	F	Servant	24Ma02Gk
MCCABE, Kary	23	F	Servant	24Ma02Gk
DONNELLY, Philip	25	M	Servant	24Ma02Gk
OWENS, Betsey	20	F	Servant	24Ma02Gk
LANCY, Bridget	11	F	Servant	24Ma02Gk
HART, Mary	10	F	Servant	24Ma02Gk
AVENNAH, Mathw.	24	M	Bricklayer	24Ma02Gk
SMITH, Betsey	22	F	Servant	24Ma02Gk
Mary	3	F	Child	24Ma02Gk
SULLIVAN, Peter	20	F	Chain Maker	24Ma02Gk
Rose	16	F	Chain Maker	24Ma02Gk
LAKELEY, Ellen	18	F	Chain Maker	24Ma02Gk
AGANLAND, Edwd.	28	M	Glazier	24Ma02Gk
CGANGHRAN, Ann	21	F	Servant	24Ma02Gk
EILEY, Sally	18	F	Servant	24Ma02Gk
ILLIAMS, Jane	20	F	Servant	24Ma02Gk
OX, Jane	23	F	Servant	24Ma02Gk
ONES, John	25	M	Miller	24Ma02Gk
Biddy	20	F	Servant	24Ma02Gk
JNN, Bernard	29	M	Pipe Layer	24Ma02Gk
YNCH, Ann	18	F	Pipe Layer	24Ma02Gk
CGWINN, John	30	M	Laborer	24Ma02Gk
Betty	3	F	Child	24Ma02Gk
CBRIDE, John	20	M	Laborer	24Ma02Gk
GES, James	62	M	Farmer	24Ma02Gk
Mary	52	F	Farmer	24Ma02Gk
Margaret	23	F	Farmer	24Ma02Gk
Maria	5	F	Child	24Ma02Gk
ADDIN, Ann	20	F	Seamstress	24Ma02Gk
RRIGAN, Mary	16	F	Seamstress	24Ma02Gk
RROLL, Mary	15	F	Seamstress	24Ma02Gk
LLOTIN, James	19	M	Hairdresser	24Ma02Gk
MPBELL, Michael	22	M	Cbtmkr	24Ma02Gk
Mary	12	F	Cbtmkr	24Ma02Gk

NAMES OF PASSENGERS	AGE	SEX	OCCUPATIONS	DATE PORT SHIP
KROUGH, Edwd.	20	M	Tailor	24Ma02Gk
Michael	9	M	Child	24Ma02Gk
MCCANN, Ann	27	F	Child	24Ma02Gk
BEHAN, John	34	M	Mechanic	24Ma02Gk
MAHAN, Mary	22	F	Servant	24Ma02Gk
COATES, Ann	21	F	Servant	24Ma02Gk
DOWNES, Alice	19	F	Servant	24Ma02Gk
Mathew	.00	M	Infant	24Ma02Gk
HESLIN, Ann	60	F	Servant	24Ma02Gk
Edwd.	18	M	Servant	24Ma02Gk
Wm.	20	M	Servant	24Ma02Gk
FORAM, Wm.	25	M	Iron Monger	24Ma02Gk
ROE, Ann	25	F	Servant	24Ma02Gk
DUNNAN, Margaret	20	F	Servant	24Ma02Gk
BYRNES, Catharine	21	F	Servant	24Ma02Gk
Denis	.00	M	Infant	24Ma02Gk
Patrick	7	M	Child	24Ma02Gk
Margaret	4	F	Child	24Ma02Gk
Thomas	3	M	Child	24Ma02Gk
DONNES, Eliza	22	F	Servant	24Ma02Gk
Ellen	.00	F	Infant	24Ma02Gk
MCGINN, Mary	18	F	Servant	24Ma02Gk
GILSEY, Hugh	27	M	Laborer	24Ma02Gk
KRAUGH, Francis	20	M	Dyer	24Ma02Gk
MCFADDEN, Sarah	27	F	Servant	24Ma02Gk
FOSTER, Elizabeth	17	F	Servant	24Ma02Gk
U	.00	U	Infant	24Ma02Gk
Wm.C.	3	M	Child	24Ma02Gk
SENTON, John	26	M	Soap Maker	24Ma02Gk
HERSEY, Henry	20	M	Laborer	24Ma02Gk
BAINBRIDGE, Robert	20	M	Builder	24Ma02Gk
Eliza	20	F	Dressmaker	24Ma02Gk
MCKIBBLIN, Anty	37	M	Hod Carrier	24Ma02Gk
MCCANLEY, Ann	19	M	Milliner	24Ma02Gk
MCCRANDALL, Saml.	23	M	Laborer	24Ma02Gk
HALL, Andrew	29	M	Laborer	24Ma02Gk
MULLIN, Susan	18	F	Servant	24Ma02Gk
STRAIN, Ann	30	F	Cook	24Ma02Gk
Handy	.00	M	Infant	24Ma02Gk
Wm.	7	M	Child	24Ma02Gk
Ann	4	F	Child	24Ma02Gk
ANDREWS, John	20	M	Mason	24Ma02Gk
DYSART, Mary	25	F	Servant	24Ma02Gk
KYLE, Ann	24	F	Servant	24Ma02Gk
DONNOGHAN, Ellen	21	F	Servant	24Ma02Gk
HENNY, Catharine	23	F	Servant	24Ma02Gk
Catharine	50	F	Servant	24Ma02Gk
Charles	20	M	Currier	24Ma02Gk
Michael	18	M	Currier	24Ma02Gk
SMITH, Lawrence	50	M	Farmer	24Ma02Gk
DEWLING, Ron	18	M	Dressmaker	24Ma02Gk
CORR, Mary-Sr.	20	F	Servant	24Ma02Gk
Mary-Jr.	18	F	Servant	24Ma02Gk
DRANEY, Mary	20	F	Servant	24Ma02Gk
MCCORMICK, Sam.	20	M	Servant	24Ma02Gk
Biddy	11	F	Servant	24Ma02Gk
PADIN, Margaret	18	F	Servant	24Ma02Gk
Ellen	11	F	Servant	24Ma02Gk
CHRISTY, John	25	M	Laborer	24Ma02Gk
FITZPATRICK, Ann	19	F	Servant	24Ma02Gk
HASTSON, Michael	21	M	Laborer	24Ma02Gk
CUNAN, Ellen	18	F	Servant	24Ma02Gk
DALEY, Jane	22	F	Servant	24Ma02Gk
COYLE, Rose	60	F	Servant	24Ma02Gk
Mathew	19	M	Servant	24Ma02Gk
Bridget	11	F	Servant	24Ma02Gk
CAMPBELL, Edwd.	19	M	Waiter	24Ma02Gk
Mary	50	F	Waiter	24Ma02Gk
ARMSTRONG, Ellen	19	F	Servant	24Ma02Gk
GRAY, Patrick	55	M	Laborer	24Ma02Gk
ROURKE, Bridget	45	F	Cook	24Ma02Gk
NALLY, Michael	18	M	Dye Sinker	24Ma02Gk
Ellen	20	F	Dye Sinker	24Ma02Gk
Sarah	59	F	Dye Sinker	24Ma02Gk
Richard	47	M	Engraver	24Ma02Gk

NAMES OF PASSENGERS	AGE	SEX	OCCUPATIONS	DATE PORT SHIP
CARREY, Dennis	24	M	Waiter	24Ma02Gk
MAHON, John	22	M	Waiter	24Ma02Gk
Ann	17	F	Servant	24Ma02Gk
MURPHY, Ellen	18	F	Servant	24Ma02Gk
FOX, Eliza	16	F	Servant	24Ma02Gk
DALEY, Catharine	30	F	Milliner	24Ma02Gk
DONNAGHAN, Bridget	60	F	Housekeeper	24Ma02Gk
Peter	18	M	Waiter	24Ma02Gk
Patrick	20	M	Waiter	24Ma02Gk
BRAY, Mary	13	F	Waiter	24Ma02Gk
Ann	10	F	Waiter	24Ma02Gk
Peter	8	M	Child	24Ma02Gk
Michl.	4	M	Child	24Ma02Gk
Christy	4	F	Child	24Ma02Gk
DUNN, Honora	16	F	Waiter	24Ma02Gk
John	27	M	Slater	24Ma02Gk
WATERS, Patrick	26	M	Stevedore	24Ma02Gk
Mary	6	F	Child	24Ma02Gk
BRENNEN, John	17	M	Stevedore	24Ma02Gk
REILEY, James	14	M	Stevedore	24Ma02Gk
DRISCALL, Ellen	20	F	Servant	24Ma02Gk
DARCEY, Teddy	6	M	Child	24Ma02Gk
Kitty	8	F	Child	24Ma02Gk
Norey	5	M	Child	24Ma02Gk
KEENAN, Mary	25	F	Seamstress	24Ma02Gk
Jeny	.00	F	Infant	24Ma02Gk
HUGES, Wm.	36	M	Weaver	24Ma02Gk
INGRAM, Margaret	22	F	Cook	24Ma02Gk
LEWIS, Bridget	20	F	Cook	24Ma02Gk
Ann	18	F	Cook	24Ma02Gk
CONTELY, Julia	21	F	Cook	24Ma02Gk
GILLION, Mary	40	F	Cook	24Ma02Gk
BYRNES, Martin	27	M	Wheelwright	24Ma02Gk
CANNANNEY, Michael	24	M	Blacksmith	24Ma02Gk
MONAGHAN, Lawrence	24	M	Locksmith	24Ma02Gk
KELLY, Bridget	20	F	Locksmith	24Ma02Gk
MCGOVERN, Ann	20	F	Locksmith	24Ma02Gk
GIBBONS, Ann	20	F	Locksmith	24Ma02Gk
IRWIN, John	20	M	Turner	24Ma02Gk
MALLON, James	17	M	Trunk Maker	24Ma02Gk
Catharine	19	F	Nurse	24Ma02Gk
HUNAY, Nicholas	35	M	Rope Maker	24Ma02Gk
Eliza	16	F	Rope Maker	24Ma02Gk
BALL, Patrick	19	M	Waiter	24Ma02Gk
DEWENEY, Patrick	30	M	Tailor	24Ma02Gk
MCCANN, Mary	20	F	Servant	24Ma02Gk
CARROLL, Catharine	20	F	Servant	24Ma02Gk
DEWANY, John	30	M	Joiner	24Ma02Gk
MCBRINE, James	20	M	Tinman	24Ma02Gk
MCCARDLE, John	22	M	Sugf	24Ma02Gk
Isaac	5	M	Child	24Ma02Gk
MURPHY, Mary	20	F	Servant	24Ma02Gk
FLYNN, Michael	25	M	Spoon Maker	24Ma02Gk
HENNY, Bartholamew	26	M	Boatmaker	24Ma02Gk
NEWMAN, Catharine	20	F	Nurse	24Ma02Gk
MATHEWS, James	22	M	Spike Maker	24Ma02Gk
HANDLIN, Ellen	21	F	Servant	24Ma02Gk
HUGES, Mary	20	F	Servant	24Ma02Gk
MAXWELL, James	22	M	Furnm	24Ma02Gk
SINEY, Nicholas	22	M	Shipwright	24Ma02Gk
HILLY, John	22	M	Nail Maker	24Ma02Gk
MCCABE, Ellen	20	F	Nurse	24Ma02Gk
FITZGERALD, Mary	23	F	Servant	24Ma02Gk
CONLAN, Mary	13	F	Servant	24Ma02Gk
MCARDLE, James	30	M	Porter	24Ma02Gk
Eliza	30	F	Porter	24Ma02Gk

ST.PATRICK 24 MAY 1849

From Liverpool

NAMES OF PASSENGERS	AGE	SEX	OCCUPATIONS	DATE PORT SHIP
CARNEY, Etty	20	F	Spinster	24Ma02Ha
FARLIN, James	44	M	None	24Ma02Ha
Judith	48	F	Wife	24Ma02Ha
Eliza	17	F	Spinster	24Ma02Ha
JAMES, Peter	10	M	Unknown	24Ma02Ha
MASTERMAN, Jane	21	F	Spinster	24Ma02Ha
KILLION, Patt	25	M	Laborer	24Ma02Ha
Michael	22	M	Blacksmith	24Ma02Ha
William	25	M	Blacksmith	24Ma02Ha
KINNION, Jane	53	F	Wife	24Ma02Ha
Mary	17	F	Spinster	24Ma02Ha
MYLLACHINE, Thomas	50	M	Weaver	24Ma02Ha
Jane	43	F	Wife	24Ma02Ha
Catherine	18	F	Spinster	24Ma02Ha
Thomas	16	M	Laborer	24Ma02Ha
Ellenor	13	F	Spinster	24Ma02Ha
Ann	11	F	Spinster	24Ma02Ha
Ann	8	F	Child	24Ma02Ha
Eliza	6	F	Child	24Ma02Ha
Jane	4	F	Child	24Ma02Ha
Robert	3	M	Child	24Ma02Ha
William	.00	M	Infant	24Ma02Ha
CAROLL, Wm.	24	M	Laborer	24Ma02Ha
CALLIN, Robt.	17	M	Joiner	24Ma02Ha
John	19	M	Laborer	24Ma02Ha
John	24	M	Laborer	24Ma02Ha
QUAYLE, Wm.	24	M	Laborer	24Ma02Ha
ROBINSON, James	18	M	Laborer	24Ma02Ha
TEERS, Dan	48	M	Weaver	24Ma02Ha
Ann	60	F	Wife	24Ma02Ha
GOMAN, Eliza	20	F	Spinster	24Ma02Ha
TEERS, James	56	M	Blacksmith	24Ma02Ha
Jane	54	F	Wife	24Ma02Ha
CROWLEY, Catherin	24	F	Wife	24Ma02Ha
John	24	M	Laborer	24Ma02Ha
John	2	M	Child	24Ma02Ha
CANE, John	22	M	Weaver	24Ma02Ha
Ann	24	F	Wife	24Ma02Ha
Ann	.00	F	Infant	24Ma02Ha
KEANS, Phillip	24	M	Blacksmith	24Ma02Ha
John	24	M	Laborer	24Ma02Ha
CHRISTIAN, James	18	M	Laborer	24Ma02Ha
CARNEY, James	25	M	Butcher	24Ma02Ha
MASDEN, David	32	M	Mechanic	24Ma02H
GARRICK, Ben	19	M	Sawer	24Ma02H
STOCKS, James-E.	32	M	Clerk	24Ma02H
Jane	32	F	Wife	24Ma02H
Henry	7	M	Child	24Ma02H
Martha	5	F	Child	24Ma02H
Mary	3	F	Child	24Ma02H
Eliza	.00	F	Infant	24Ma02H
ANDERSON, Martha	60	F	Wi	24Ma02H
Robt.	30	M	Laborer	24Ma02H
Jane	30	F	Wife	24Ma02H
CRILLEY, John	5	M	Child	24Ma02H
ANDERSON, Wm.	.00	M	Infant	24Ma02H
JACKSON, Margret	24	F	Spinster	24Ma02H
FLYNN, James	30	M	Laborer	24Ma02H
Cam----, Pat	50	M	Carpenter	24Ma02H
Honnora	24	F	Wife	24Ma02H
Julia	.00	F	Infant	24Ma02H
DAGIN, John	23	M	Laborer	24Ma02H
HARRIS, Agnis	18	F	Spinster	24Ma02H
MEAK, Fylton	21	M	Laborer	24Ma02H
Mary	18	F	Spinster	24Ma02

NAMES OF PASSENGERS	AGE	SEX	OCCUPATIONS	DATE PORT SHIP
DUNN, Pat	19	M	Laborer	24Ma02Ha
DWYER, John	20	M	Laborer	24Ma02Ha
BROWN, James	34	M	Shopkeeper	24Ma02Ha
RILEY, John	34	M	Shopkeeper	24Ma02Ha
OBRIEN, Denis	18	M	Laborer	24Ma02Ha
COABET, Margret	18	F	Spinster	24Ma02Ha
GLENN, John	28	M	Laborer	24Ma02Ha
Bridget	28	F	Spinster	24Ma02Ha
WHELEBEN, Edw.	30	M	Laborer	24Ma02Ha
KEHOE, Andrew	35	M	Laborer	24Ma02Ha
FLANINGAN, Thomas	23	M	Laborer	24Ma02Ha
CARAY, Ann	22	F	Spinster	24Ma02Ha
HEYDEN, John	30	M	Farmer	24Ma02Ha
DOOLIN, Mic	28	M	Carpenter	24Ma02Ha
DALENEY, Pat	30	M	Laborer	24Ma02Ha
Ellen	25	F	Wife	24Ma02Ha
Bridget	5	F	Child	24Ma02Ha
John	2	M	Child	24Ma02Ha
Pat	.00	M	Infant	24Ma02Ha
WILDEN, James	40	M	Laborer	24Ma02Ha
BRIEN, Thomas	40	M	Laborer	24Ma02Ha
MUNNIGIN, Mary	27	F	Spinster	24Ma02Ha
BROWN, Mary	13	F	Spinster	24Ma02Ha
Mary	10	F	Spinster	24Ma02Ha
Pat	9	M	Child	24Ma02Ha
SMITH, Bridget	18	F	Spinster	24Ma02Ha
NAUGHTON, James	24	M	Carpenter	24Ma02Ha
EAGAN, Martin	21	M	Laborer	24Ma02Ha
Rose	28	F	Wife	24Ma02Ha
HEGAN, Catherin	20	F	Spinster	24Ma02Ha
Bridget	25	F	Spinster	24Ma02Ha
Margret	29	F	Spinster	24Ma02Ha
Thomas	26	M	Laborer	24Ma02Ha
NOLAN, James	30	M	Laborer	24Ma02Ha
GRAHAM, James	37	M	Laborer	24Ma02Ha
DEMPSEY, Ann	20	F	Spinster	24Ma02Ha
RYEN, Ann	19	F	Spinster	24Ma02Ha
JOHNSON, Neil	27	M	Mechanic	24Ma02Ha
MCCRETT, Ed.	30	M	Laborer	24Ma02Ha
RYAN, Mallachy	26	M	Laborer	24Ma02Ha
LYNCH, Henry	22	M	Laborer	24Ma02Ha
COLLEY, John	20	M	Laborer	24Ma02Ha
MULLOY, Rose	23	M	Laborer	24Ma02Ha
MOLAGHNEY, Dan.	26	M	Laborer	24Ma02Ha
CURNEN, Mary	25	F	Spinster	24Ma02Ha
WELCH, Pat	25	M	Farmer	24Ma02Ha
LYNCH, Dan.	28	M	Farmer	24Ma02Ha
Thomas	30	M	Farmer	24Ma02Ha
ALEY, John	21	M	Laborer	24Ma02Ha
YAN, Mick	30	M	Laborer	24Ma02Ha
Rich.	35	M	Laborer	24Ma02Ha
Mic.	.00	M	Infant	24Ma02Ha
ENNEDY, Mgt.	18	F	Spinster	24Ma02Ha
URRAY, Denis	45	M	Laborer	24Ma02Ha
Jas.	14	M	Laborer	24Ma02Ha
Mgt.	40	F	Wife	24Ma02Ha
Mary	10	F	Spinster	24Ma02Ha
AMILTON, U-Mrs.	50	F	Wi	24Ma02Ha
ARBIN, Jane	17	F	Spinster	24Ma02Ha
LLIAMS, John	20	M	Laborer	24Ma02Ha
Henry	18	M	Laborer	24Ma02Ha
ORE, Jas.	24	M	Gdnr	24Ma02Ha
Wm.	22	M	Gdnr	24Ma02Ha
Chas.	16	M	Gdnr	24Ma02Ha
WARDS, Peter	21	M	Gdnr	24Ma02Ha
LEY, Thos.	35	M	Laborer	24Ma02Ha
LANE, Ed.	49	M	Laborer	24Ma02Ha
GGINS, Mary	42	F	Wi	24Ma02Ha
Jerry	15	M	Laborer	24Ma02Ha
Thos.	13	M	Laborer	24Ma02Ha
Mic.	16	M	Laborer	24Ma02Ha
Bridget	6	F	Child	24Ma02Ha
Jas.	9	M	Child	24Ma02Ha
DERSON, Thomas	24	M	Clerk	24Ma02Ha
JPA, Stuart	24	M	Engineer	24Ma02Ha
SHERLOCK, Pat	26	M	Engineer	24Ma02Ha
HOOLAN, Pat	22	M	Surveyor	24Ma02Ha
BRYAN, Darby	30	M	Painter	24Ma02Ha
BURKE, Thos.	22	M	Farmer	24Ma02Ha
Jos.	24	M	Farmer	24Ma02Ha
Catti	30	F	Wife	24Ma02Ha
LONDERGAN, David	24	M	Laborer	24Ma02Ha
CLAREY, Judy	28	F	Spinster	24Ma02Ha
HONESSY, Mic	25	M	Laborer	24Ma02Ha
HERMAN, Pat	23	M	Cooper	24Ma02Ha
Berd.	30	M	Laborer	24Ma02Ha
LAHAN, And.	25	M	Carpenter	24Ma02Ha
COLLINS, Pat	24	M	Stctr	24Ma02Ha
Eliza	21	F	Wife	24Ma02Ha
COFFEY, Wm.	30	F	Stctr	24Ma02Ha
FITZGERALD, Jas.	40	M	Laborer	24Ma02Ha
RILEY, Mat.	56	M	Farmer	24Ma02Ha
Ann	47	F	Wife	24Ma02Ha
Hannah	24	F	Spinster	24Ma02Ha
Eliza	28	F	Wife	24Ma02Ha
Ellen	20	F	Spinster	24Ma02Ha
Margt.	19	F	Spinster	24Ma02Ha
Mary-Ann	18	F	Spinster	24Ma02Ha
Cath.	17	F	Spinster	24Ma02Ha
KELLY, Pat	14	M	Laborer	24Ma02Ha
Julia	13	F	Spinster	24Ma02Ha
Anna	11	F	Spinster	24Ma02Ha
Jas.	12	M	Unknown	24Ma02Ha
Mat.	9	M	Child	24Ma02Ha
Thos.	30	M	Laborer	24Ma02Ha
BUMMER, Pat	20	M	Laborer	24Ma02Ha
ORR, Wm.	47	M	Laborer	24Ma02Ha
Francis	42	F	Wife	24Ma02Ha
TAVLIN, Mgt.	40	F	Wife	24Ma02Ha
FLARMAN, John	26	M	Laborer	24Ma02Ha
MIGENT, Bernard	20	M	Laborer	24Ma02Ha
EVANS, John	23	M	Baker	24Ma02Ha
WALLACE, John	28	M	Baker	24Ma02Ha
GARDINER, Jas.Robt.	20	M	Carpenter	24Ma02Ha
FITZPATRICK, James	26	M	Carpenter	24Ma02Ha
Wm.	23	M	Carpenter	24Ma02Ha
READ, John	30	M	Farmer	24Ma02Ha
PROUDFORTH, Wm.	21	M	Farmer	24Ma02Ha
Jas.	19	M	Farmer	24Ma02Ha
READ, Wm.	23	M	Farmer	24Ma02Ha
KIRKPATRICK, Robt.	26	M	Farmer	24Ma02Ha
ROGERSON, John	20	M	Farmer	24Ma02Ha
EGAN, John	26	M	Laborer	24Ma02Ha
BURNETT, Ellen	19	F	Spinster	24Ma02Ha
SWORDS, Chris	19	M	Laborer	24Ma02Ha
MURKS, Ed	19	M	Laborer	24Ma02Ha
DUGGAN, Wm.	20	M	Laborer	24Ma02Ha
Margt.	26	M	Farmer	24Ma02Ha
VAUGHAN, Mary	16	F	Spinster	24Ma02Ha
ALLAN, Peter	28	M	Wagoner	24Ma02Ha
GRIMES, Pat	18	M	Laborer	24Ma02Ha
LYNCH, Jas.	58	M	Laborer	24Ma02Ha
Jas.	15	M	Laborer	24Ma02Ha
John	28	M	Miller	24Ma02Ha
Peter	20	M	Laborer	24Ma02Ha
Cath.	18	F	Spinster	24Ma02Ha
Cath.	60	F	Wife	24Ma02Ha
ROSS, Pat	27	M	Laborer	24Ma02Ha
Mary	18	F	Spinster	24Ma02Ha
TOBIN, Chris	27	M	Laborer	24Ma02Ha
Bird	18	F	Spinster	24Ma02Ha
ANDY, John	25	M	Laborer	24Ma02Ha
MARTIN, Cath.	36	F	Wife	24Ma02Ha
MCDONALD, Pat	23	M	Laborer	24Ma02Ha
Philip	23	M	Laborer	24Ma02Ha
MCBRIDE, John	22	M	Sugar Baker	24Ma02Ha
STRINGER, Jas.	23	M	Gvn-Tut	24Ma02Ha
DENTY, Jas.	25	M	Painter	24Ma02Ha
VAUGHAN, Austin	30	M	Laborer	24Ma02Ha
DOOLEY, Pat	28	M	Laborer	24Ma02Ha

NAMES OF PASSENGERS	AGE	SEX	OCCUPATIONS	DATE PORT SHIP
LEAREY, Thos.	45	M	Sailor	24Ma02Ha
John	28	M	Laborer	24Ma02Ha
ONEILL, Fred.	23	M	Clerk	24Ma02Ha
RYAN, Tim	25	M	Laborer	24Ma02Ha
Mary	28	F	Wife	24Ma02Ha
WALL, Cath.	27	F	Spinster	24Ma02Ha
MATHEWS, Bridg.	30	F	Spinster	24Ma02Ha
Jane	25	F	Spinster	24Ma02Ha
DELANEY, Pat	22	M	Miller	24Ma02Ha
Ann	20	F	Wife	24Ma02Ha
KEENEY, Chas.	20	M	Laborer	24Ma02Ha
DELANEY, Marcella	.00	F	Infant	24Ma02Ha
KERR, Jas.	21	M	Clerk	24Ma02Ha
MCCUTCHINSON, Cath.	22	F	Wife	24Ma02Ha
Eliza-Jane	.00	F	Infant	24Ma02Ha
MONTGOMERY, Eliza	23	F	Spinster	24Ma02Ha
KEENAN, Mary	20	F	Spinster	24Ma02Ha
MEENAN, John	53	M	Wi	24Ma02Ha
CONNOR, Thos.	20	M	Laborer	24Ma02Ha
FARTY, John	30	M	Farmer	24Ma02Ha
SHEAWOOD, John	40	M	Servant	24Ma02Ha
DOOLIN, Ann	40	F	Servant	24Ma02Ha
Mary	30	F	Spinster	24Ma02Ha
SALIMON, Mic	28	M	Laborer	24Ma02Ha
KELLY, Mary	28	F	Spinster	24Ma02Ha
MCDONALD, U	50	F	Unknown	24Ma02Ha
FAYTON, Thoop	21	M	Farmer	24Ma02Ha
U-Mrs.	20	F	Wife	24Ma02Ha
MARRIAN, Edward	45	M	Farmer	24Ma02Ha
Ann	37	F	Wife	24Ma02Ha
Peter	11	M	Unknown	24Ma02Ha
Thos.	9	M	Child	24Ma02Ha
KEELAN, Mich	22	M	Laborer	24Ma02Ha
John	19	M	Laborer	24Ma02Ha
FINNIGAN, Bridgt.	27	F	Spinster	24Ma02Ha
MCCAFFY, Mich.	30	M	Mason	24Ma02Ha
KEENAN, Thomas	23	M	Farmer	24Ma02Ha
SULLIVAN, James	29	M	Farmer	24Ma02Ha
MCNANN, Hugh	26	M	Farmer	24Ma02Ha
HENDERSON, John	26	M	Farmer	24Ma02Ha
BRODRICK, Jas.	18	M	Laborer	24Ma02Ha
LYNCH, John	20	M	Miller	24Ma02Ha

MONTEZUMA 24 MAY 1849

From Demerara And St.Thomas

NAMES OF PASSENGERS	AGE	SEX	OCCUPATIONS	DATE PORT SHIP
CADELL, Alex	32	M	Engineer	24Ma53Ca
U-Mrs.	24	F	Unknown	24Ma53Ca
Elizabeth	1	F	Child	24Ma53Ca
BERRISFORD, A.	50	M	Merchant	24Ma53Ca
PAYTON, Robt.	28	M	Planter	24Ma53Ca
ROBINSON, U	42	M	Merchant	24Ma53Ca
ANDERSON, U	36	M	Mechanic	24Ma53Ca
KEENS, Fredk.	26	M	Merchant	24Ma53Ca

GARRICK 25 MAY 1849

From Liverpool

NAMES OF PASSENGERS	AGE	SEX	OCCUPATIONS	DATE PORT SHIP
ROGERS, Geo.	19	M	Painter	25Ma02Hh
REECE, Frs.	19	M	Tailor	25Ma02Hh
SCANLOW, Dennis	22	M	Laborer	25Ma02Hh
OCONNOR, Roger	28	M	Wheelwright	25Ma02Hh
LEWIS, Thos.	27	M	Laborer	25Ma02Hh
Rich.	32	M	Laborer	25Ma02Hh
BANNON, Wm.	58	M	Farmer	25Ma02Hh
Rich.	24	M	Sappr	25Ma02Hh
Thos.	18	M	Unknown	25Ma02Hh
Pat	20	M	Unknown	25Ma02Hh
Jas.	16	M	Unknown	25Ma02Hh
Judy	14	F	None	25Ma02Hh
Ann	10	F	Child	25Ma02Hh
Cath.	6	F	Child	25Ma02Hh
Mich.	4	M	Child	25Ma02Hh
BELLOW, Robt.	44	M	Farmer	25Ma02Hh
U-Mrs.	44	F	Farmer	25Ma02Hh
Pat	14	M	Unknown	25Ma02Hh
BANNON, Margt.	18	F	Housekeeper	25Ma02H
MAYBLY, Margt.	18	F	Servant	25Ma02H
SUDLERS, U	30	M	Servant	25Ma02H
Jas.	30	M	Servant	25Ma02H
ROONEY, Rich.	50	M	Laborer	25Ma02H
Margt.	28	F	Servant	25Ma02H
MCGROUL, Margt.	20	F	Servant	25Ma02H
WALSH, Jane	16	F	Servant	25Ma02H
MCCORMICK, Margt.	20	F	Dressmaker	25Ma02H
WHITE, Mary	00	F	Servant	25Ma02H
BROWN, Jcb.	50	M	Unknown	25Ma02H
U	50	M	Laborer	25Ma02H
CONNALL, Mary	18	F	Domestic	25Ma02H
FRAZER, Pat	16	M	Laborer	25Ma02H
MCCOOL, Luke	30	M	Laborer	25Ma02H
SWAIN, Jno.	25	M	Laborer	25Ma02H
DEAN, Jas.	26	M	Bricklayer	25Ma02H
RILEY, Mat.	23	M	Shepherd	25Ma02H
BUNN, Jas.	22	M	Ploughman	25Ma02H
DUNCAN, Jno.	20	M	Ploughman	25Ma02H
COUNEY, Pat	25	M	Laborer	25Ma02H
SHERIDAN, Thos.	28	M	Farmer	25Ma02H
FAGAN, Thos.	30	M	Farmer	25Ma02H
Margt.	26	F	None	25Ma02H
MCGEVIN, Mich.	17	M	Laborer	25Ma02H
MONAGHAN, Cath.	20	F	Servant	25Ma02H
Rose	18	F	Servant	25Ma02H
ALLEN, Thos.	50	M	Laborer	25Ma02H
Noah	35	M	Laborer	25Ma02H
Eliza	34	F	None	25Ma02H
CULLEN, Rose	20	F	Servant	25Ma02H
Julia	22	F	Dressmaker	25Ma02H
Anastatia	19	F	Dressmaker	25Ma02H
CONNISFIELD, B.	20	M	Laborer	25Ma02H
REILY, W.	18	M	Laborer	25Ma02H
CHEEVERS, Pat	18	M	Wagoner	25Ma02H
Cath.	20	F	Servant	25Ma02H
TUITE, Alma	20	F	Dressmaker	25Ma02
DELANY, Pat	30	M	Laborer	25Ma02
HILL, Frs.	40	M	Gdnr	25Ma02
U	40	F	None	25Ma02
Pat	15	M	Unknown	25Ma02
Fred.	8	M	Child	25Ma02
Mary	.03	F	Infant	25Ma02
CUNNINGHAM, Jas.	50	M	Waiter	25Ma02
BURNS, Mich.	26	M	Weaver	25Ma02
U-Mrs.	25	F	None	25Ma02
Mary	5	F	Child	25Ma02
KEARNS, Thos.	19	M	Servant	25Ma02
KEHOE, Jas.	18	M	Shop Boy	25Ma02
WALL, Wm.	16	M	Shop Boy	25Ma02
NOLAN, Ann	30	F	Servant	25Ma0
NOLLAN, Ewd.	60	M	Farmer	25Ma0
U-Mrs.	60	F	Farmer	25Ma0
Thos.	20	M	Unknown	25Ma0
Cath.	22	F	Unknown	25Ma0
Jno.	18	M	Unknown	25Ma0
Eliza	16	F	Unknown	25Ma0
Nina	4	F	Child	25Ma0
Phil.	15	M	Unknown	25Ma0

NAMES OF PASSENGERS	AGE	SEX	OCCUPATIONS	DATE PORT SHIP
FOX, Mary	20	F	Servant	25Ma02Hh
MARTIN, Jno.	20	M	Laborer	25Ma02Hh
GILLESPIE, Wm.	60	M	Laborer	25Ma02Hh
DOUGHERTY, Jno.	28	M	Laborer	25Ma02Hh
Mich.	16	M	Laborer	25Ma02Hh
Samuel	10	M	Child	25Ma02Hh
Henry	1	M	Child	25Ma02Hh
Eliza	14	F	None	25Ma02Hh
Mary-Ann	8	F	Child	25Ma02Hh
RICHARDS, U-Mrs.	40	F	Unknown	25Ma02Hh
Jno.	22	M	Unknown	25Ma02Hh
Thos.	11	M	Unknown	25Ma02Hh
P.	15	M	Unknown	25Ma02Hh
Jas.	71	F	Unknown	25Ma02Hh
Jane	5	F	Child	25Ma02Hh
Sarah	3	F	Child	25Ma02Hh
WILSON, Ewd.	26	M	Painter	25Ma02Hh
U-Mrs.	24	F	None	25Ma02Hh
COLLINS, Peter	30	M	Mason	25Ma02Hh
DOUNEY, John	50	M	Mason	25Ma02Hh
U-Mrs.	48	F	None	25Ma02Hh
Hugh	24	M	Mason	25Ma02Hh
Henry	18	M	Painter	25Ma02Hh
Ellen	16	F	Dressmaker	25Ma02Hh
CONLEY, Mary	18	F	Servant	25Ma02Hh
DOUNEY, Cath.	10	F	Child	25Ma02Hh
Jas.	7	M	Child	25Ma02Hh
MUSTER, Jno.	22	M	Farmer	25Ma02Hh
Thos.	18	M	Clerk	25Ma02Hh
MCCALLY, Mich.	34	M	Laborer	25Ma02Hh
MCCARTNEY, Pat	30	M	Laborer	25Ma02Hh
HOSE, Bart	30	M	Laborer	25Ma02Hh
ONEAL, U	30	M	Merchant	25Ma02Hh
U-Mrs.	26	F	None	25Ma02Hh
HILL, Danl.	20	M	Laborer	25Ma02Hh
WALSH, Pat	27	M	Laborer	25Ma02Hh
BOYLAN, Thos.	20	M	Nailer	25Ma02Hh
NEWTON, Ann	30	F	Servant	25Ma02Hh
DUFFY, Ann	20	F	Servant	25Ma02Hh
MCGUINESS, Mary	20	F	Servant	25Ma02Hh
Bridg.	25	F	Servant	25Ma02Hh
CONLAN, Judy	22	F	Servant	25Ma02Hh
MALONEY, Judy	18	F	Servant	25Ma02Hh
MCGALLAGHER, Cat.	20	F	Servant	25Ma02Hh
RYAN, Chs.	20	M	Servant	25Ma02Hh
PEARSON, Margt.	18	F	Dressmaker	25Ma02Hh
PETERS, Margt.	19	F	Dressmaker	25Ma02Hh
ANE, Jno.	19	M	Unknown	25Ma02Hh
IBSON, Jno.	20	M	Laborer	25Ma02Hh
Margt.	18	F	Servant	25Ma02Hh
PEMBERTON, Julia	20	F	Servant	25Ma02Hh
CARROLL, Phoebe	20	F	Servant	25Ma02Hh
Ellen	18	M	Servant	25Ma02Hh
ARLEY, Ewd.	26	M	Surveyor	25Ma02Hh
ARTEY, Mich.	20	M	Farmer	25Ma02Hh
DONNELL, Margt.	20	F	Unknown	25Ma02Hh
OUDRY, Honeva	20	F	Servant	25Ma02Hh
ORD, Jno.	50	M	Laborer	25Ma02Hh
Mary	50	F	None	25Ma02Hh
Jno.	20	M	Unknown	25Ma02Hh
Sarah	16	F	Unknown	25Ma02Hh
Maria	4	F	Child	25Ma02Hh
ARRISON, Pat	30	M	Farmer	25Ma02Hh
Margt.	25	F	None	25Ma02Hh
Peggy	15	F	Unknown	25Ma02Hh
Rich.	.11	M	Infant	25Ma02Hh
Brid.	.07	F	Infant	25Ma02Hh
ARKE, Mich.	30	M	Laborer	25Ma02Hh
LAN, Anth.	24	M	Laborer	25Ma02Hh
Brid.	24	F	None	25Ma02Hh
Brid.	.10	F	Infant	25Ma02Hh
UGHLEY, Wm.	30	M	Laborer	25Ma02Hh
ANAN, Owen	25	M	Laborer	25Ma02Hh
LLINS, Pat	24	M	Unknown	25Ma02Hh
Jno.	21	M	Unknown	25Ma02Hh
FOSTER, Jno.	20	M	Unknown	25Ma02Hh
JACKSON, Ellen	20	F	Dressmaker	25Ma02Hh
U-Miss	21	F	Dressmaker	25Ma02Hh
SHARKEY, Mary	20	F	Servant	25Ma02Hh
CONNOR, Andrew	18	M	Laborer	25Ma02Hh
Cat.	21	F	Servant	25Ma02Hh
ROGERS, Pat	25	M	Laborer	25Ma02Hh
CLINTON, Cat.	13	F	Servant	25Ma02Hh
DOWDELL, Ann	40	F	Servant	25Ma02Hh
Margt.	11	F	None	25Ma02Hh
Bart	7	M	Child	25Ma02Hh
Pat	6	M	Child	25Ma02Hh
BELLEN, Ann	21	F	Servant	25Ma02Hh
GRAY, Jno.	45	M	Laborer	25Ma02Hh
ANDERSON, Cath.	15	F	Servant	25Ma02Hh
Thos.	12	M	Unknown	25Ma02Hh
KEATING, Dennis	24	M	Laborer	25Ma02Hh
WADE, Nic.	22	M	Laborer	25Ma02Hh
MCNAMARA, Mary	16	F	Nurse	25Ma02Hh
DRINKLER, Jane	45	F	Unknown	25Ma02Hh
DENANEY, Sapah	20	F	Unknown	25Ma02Hh
PEURICE, Thos.	26	M	Miller	25Ma02Hh
SLACK, Jno.	21	M	Miller	25Ma02Hh
ROBERTS, Pat	20	M	Vsgn	25Ma02Hh
CULLEN, Margt.	50	F	Unknown	25Ma02Hh
GREY, Thos.	40	M	Shoemaker	25Ma02Hh
Cath.	20	F	Domestic	25Ma02Hh
HUGHES, Cath.	30	F	Cook	25Ma02Hh
Margt.	20	F	Unknown	25Ma02Hh
Pat	9	M	Child	25Ma02Hh
Jno.	6	M	Child	25Ma02Hh
Margt.	4	F	Child	25Ma02Hh
SUTTON, Ann	13	F	Servant	25Ma02Hh
RING, Brid.	50	F	Unknown	25Ma02Hh
Jas.	21	M	Unknown	25Ma02Hh
Edwd.	8	M	Child	25Ma02Hh
RILEY, Brid.	20	F	Unknown	25Ma02Hh
GALLEGAN, Ann	12	F	Servant	25Ma02Hh
GREEN, Cath.	24	F	Servant	25Ma02Hh
HOISTON, Margt.	30	F	Unknown	25Ma02Hh
Jno.	3	M	Child	25Ma02Hh
LUNNY, Marty	60	M	Farmer	25Ma02Hh
Ann	60	F	Farmer	25Ma02Hh
Mary	28	F	Farmer	25Ma02Hh
Pat	25	M	Unknown	25Ma02Hh
Ann	22	F	Unknown	25Ma02Hh
Rose	20	F	Unknown	25Ma02Hh
Abby	15	F	Unknown	25Ma02Hh
Brid.	13	F	Unknown	25Ma02Hh
Margt.	11	F	Unknown	25Ma02Hh
CAREY, Rich.	18	M	Shoemaker	25Ma02Hh
Pierce	20	M	Shoemaker	25Ma02Hh
DOUGHERTY, Wm.	22	M	Barber	25Ma02Hh
Mary	19	F	Servant	25Ma02Hh
MCCORMICK, Pat	20	M	Laborer	25Ma02Hh
DUFFY, Roger	18	M	Laborer	25Ma02Hh
FAGAN, Owen	22	M	Laborer	25Ma02Hh
MCHUGH, H.	22	M	Laborer	25Ma02Hh
GALLAGHER, Nancy	26	F	Servant	25Ma02Hh
WALL, Thos.	22	M	Laborer	25Ma02Hh
HICKEY, Mich.	21	M	Laborer	25Ma02Hh
QUINAN, Mary	22	F	Unknown	25Ma02Hh
HANY, Norah	30	F	Servant	25Ma02Hh
DOUGAN, Margt.	20	F	Boot Closer	25Ma02Hh
BIGNEY, Margt.	17	F	Servant	25Ma02Hh
BRADY, Mich.	20	M	Laborer	25Ma02Hh
SHEETING, Pat	21	M	Laborer	25Ma02Hh
FARRELL, Jno.	14	M	Laborer	25Ma02Hh
FUREY, Mich.	20	M	Laborer	25Ma02Hh
KILROY, Cath.	17	F	Unknown	25Ma02Hh
NOLAN, Mich.	11	M	Unknown	25Ma02Hh
CHEEVERS, Cath.	19	F	Dressmaker	25Ma02Hh
SHERIDAN, Jno.	24	M	Laborer	25Ma02Hh
FITZGERALD, Brid.	20	F	Unknown	25Ma02Hh
Edw.	30	M	Laborer	25Ma02Hh

NAMES OF PASSENGERS	AGE	SEX	OCCUPATIONS	DATE PORT SHIP
GERMAN, Thos.	60	M	Unknown	25Ma02Hh
Mary	27	F	Unknown	25Ma02Hh
WINKLE, Cath.	18	F	Servant	25Ma02Hh
MAHAN, Ann	27	F	Unknown	25Ma02Hh
SHERIDAN, Pat	7	M	Child	25Ma02Hh
KEEGAN, Pat	12	M	Unknown	25Ma02Hh
Thos.	9	M	Child	25Ma02Hh
Brid.	7	F	Child	25Ma02Hh
GAUGHNAN, Phil.	18	M	Laborer	25Ma02Hh
Owen	14	M	Laborer	25Ma02Hh
SMITH, Pat	21	M	Laborer	25Ma02Hh
MCMENAN, Jas.	18	M	Laborer	25Ma02Hh
MCNULTY, Martin	16	M	Laborer	25Ma02Hh
MCCOMB, Thos.	18	M	Laborer	25Ma02Hh
Sarah	18	F	Servant	25Ma02Hh
SMITH, Robt.	25	M	Laborer	25Ma02Hh
FITZIMMONS, Pat	25	M	Laborer	25Ma02Hh
MAHON, Pat	5	M	Child	25Ma02Hh
FAGAN, Pat	4	M	Child	25Ma02Hh
MCGUIRE, J.	29	M	Laborer	25Ma02Hh
DEMPSEY, Sarah	00	F	Servant	25Ma02Hh
Ann	9	F	Child	25Ma02Hh
FOGARTY, Mich.	18	M	Unknown	25Ma02Hh
FLYN, Julia	25	F	Servant	25Ma02Hh
SCALLAN, Dan.	33	M	Laborer	25Ma02Hh
BRANAGHAN, Pat	58	M	Flaxdr	25Ma02Hh
Hanah	58	F	None	25Ma02Hh
Cath.	24	F	None	25Ma02Hh
CONWAY, Rose	24	F	Servant	25Ma02Hh
GRITTEN, Cat.	21	F	Servant	25Ma02Hh
MCAVERY, Ann	28	F	Servant	25Ma02Hh
BRASELLE, Mary	18	F	Servant	25Ma02Hh
MONAGHAN, Pat	37	M	Laborer	25Ma02Hh
LYNCH, Walter	7	M	Child	25Ma02Hh
Luke	5	M	Child	25Ma02Hh
KEEFE, Margt.	20	F	Unknown	25Ma02Hh
BRIEN, Ann	7	F	Child	25Ma02Hh
SHEPPERD, Wm.	16	M	Laborer	25Ma02Hh
Margt.	14	F	Servant	25Ma02Hh
MURRY, Rose	18	F	Servant	25Ma02Hh
QUINAN, Brid.	20	F	Servant	25Ma02Hh
BANNON, Ann	25	F	Servant	25Ma02Hh
NUGENT, Brid.	60	F	Unknown	25Ma02Hh
Jas.	22	M	Gdnr	25Ma02Hh
Thos.	24	M	Unknown	25Ma02Hh
Ann	22	F	None	25Ma02Hh
FINNEGAN, Eliz.	20	F	Servant	25Ma02Hh

NEW-WORLD 26 MAY 1849

From Liverpool

NAMES OF PASSENGERS	AGE	SEX	OCCUPATIONS	DATE PORT SHIP
KEEGAN, Michael	50	M	Blacksmith	26Ma02Hg
Catherine	23	F	Unknown	26Ma02Hg
BELLEW, Michael	20	M	Laborer	26Ma02Hg
ROBINSON, John	21	M	Laborer	26Ma02Hg
Mary	20	F	Unknown	26Ma02Hg
CAREY, William	40	M	Shoemaker	26Ma02Hg
Mary	35	F	Unknown	26Ma02Hg
TIERNEY, Eliza	25	F	Unknown	26Ma02Hg
WATERSON, Arthur	37	M	Laborer	26Ma02Hg
ARMSTRONG, Denis	23	M	Laborer	26Ma02Hg
Margaret	21	F	Unknown	26Ma02Hg
KEHOE, Michael	20	M	Laborer	26Ma02Hg
ADAMS, Robert	20	M	Clerk	26Ma02Hg
BLEAKELY, Guy	20	M	Clerk	26Ma02Hg
Sarah	19	F	Unknown	26Ma02Hg
ROOKE, Rose	18	F	Unknown	26Ma02Hg
GALLAGHER, Barney	38	M	Paper Maker	26Ma02Hg

NAMES OF PASSENGERS	AGE	SEX	OCCUPATIONS	DATE PORT SHIP
RORKE, James	25	M	Laborer	26Ma02H
HOGAN, Rody	25	M	Laborer	26Ma02H
CLEAR, Eliza	20	F	Unknown	26Ma02H
SMITH, Michael	20	M	Laborer	26Ma02H
COLANTINE, Thomas	16	M	Laborer	26Ma02H
Mary	14	F	Unknown	26Ma02H
LEONARD, Eliza	24	F	Unknown	26Ma02H
CLANCY, William	18	M	Laborer	26Ma02H
HIGGINS, Peter	50	M	Laborer	26Ma02H
Nancy	35	F	Unknown	26Ma02H
Anne	2	F	Child	26Ma02H
Biddy	.10	F	Infant	26Ma02H
HALLINGER, Joseph	36	M	Laborer	26Ma02H
Nancy	11	F	Unknown	26Ma02H
Margaret	9	F	Child	26Ma02H
MCCRORY, Elenor	20	F	Unknown	26Ma02H
ODONNELL, Richard	35	M	Shoemaker	26Ma02H
Hannah	32	F	Unknown	26Ma02H
BYRNE, Michael	38	M	Laborer	26Ma02H
Catherine	24	F	Unknown	26Ma02H
Margaret	10	F	Unknown	26Ma02H
Bridget	6	F	Child	26Ma02H
Patrick	4	M	Child	26Ma02H
Michael	.09	M	Infant	26Ma02H
PARKES, Samuel	50	M	Farmer	26Ma02H
Rose	50	F	Unknown	26Ma02H
Mary-Anne	18	F	Unknown	26Ma02H
MACKAY, Samuel	2	M	Child	26Ma02H
BODIN, Biddy	11	F	Unknown	26Ma02H
COLLIN, Philip	23	M	Laborer	26Ma02H
CASEY, Bernard	20	M	Laborer	26Ma02H
WARD, Catherine	50	F	Unknown	26Ma02H
Patrick	16	M	Laborer	26Ma02H
FOX, John	27	M	Farmer	26Ma02H
Rose	26	F	Unknown	26Ma02H
James	6	M	Child	26Ma02H
Marcella	5	F	Child	26Ma02H
Thomas	2	M	Child	26Ma02H
Eliza	.11	F	Infant	26Ma02H
RENEHAN, John	26	M	Laborer	26Ma02H
REILLY, Michael	30	M	Laborer	26Ma02H
FITZSIMONS, Mary	21	F	Unknown	26Ma02H
TULLY, Mary	20	F	Unknown	26Ma02H
FLOYD, Eliza	16	F	Unknown	26Ma02H
CONNOLLY, John	23	M	Laborer	26Ma02H
WALL, Thomas	22	M	Laborer	26Ma02
Lawrence	10	M	Laborer	26Ma02
FAY, Margaret	17	F	Unknown	26Ma02
Catherine	3	F	Child	26Ma02
FITZPATRICK, Catherine	20	F	Unknown	26Ma02
Margaret	19	F	Unknown	26Ma02
SULLIVAN, Biddy	21	F	Unknown	26Ma02
OREGAN, James	42	M	Laborer	26Ma02
Honora	16	F	Unknown	26Ma02
Eliza	12	F	Unknown	26Ma02
Maurice	9	M	Child	26Ma02
MURPHY, Edward	35	M	Draper	26Ma02
Edward	9	M	Child	26Ma02
RYAN, Michael	20	M	Laborer	26Ma02
Mary	22	F	Unknown	26Ma0
BYRNE, Michael	25	M	Laborer	26Ma0
KELLY, William	26	M	Sawer	26Ma0
STACPOOLE, Peter	25	M	Laborer	26Ma0
GAFNEY, Hugh	28	M	Butcher	26Ma0
JOYCE, Austin	32	M	Shoemaker	26Ma0
Bridget	20	F	Unknown	26Ma0
CRIBBIN, Tobias	30	M	Tailor	26Ma0
MCDONALD, Catherine	14	F	Unknown	26Ma0
DOWDLE, Patrick	12	M	Unknown	26Ma0
Thomas	10	M	Unknown	26Ma0
Patrick	35	M	Laborer	26Ma0
Anne	28	F	Unknown	26Ma0
Mary	6	F	Child	26Ma0
MCIVER, Thomas	35	M	Carpenter	26Ma0
DOWDLE, Pat	25	M	Laborer	26Ma0

NAMES OF PASSENGERS	AGE	SEX	OCCUPATIONS	DATE PORT SHIP
MCMULLEN, Jas.	60	M	Horn Shiner	26Ma02Hg
Katherine	60	F	Unknown	26Ma02Hg
Jericho	27	M	Laborer	26Ma02Hg
Margaret	18	F	Unknown	26Ma02Hg
Julia	17	F	Unknown	26Ma02Hg
HOWARD, John	20	M	Laborer	26Ma02Hg
Peter	18	M	Laborer	26Ma02Hg
Mary	20	F	Unknown	26Ma02Hg
DOLAN, John	22	M	Laborer	26Ma02Hg
TRAYNOR, Owen	22	M	Laborer	26Ma02Hg
CARROL, Rose	23	F	Unknown	26Ma02Hg
WHITE, James	29	M	Servant	26Ma02Hg
Susan	29	F	Unknown	26Ma02Hg
MCGIVAN, Thomas	70	M	Laborer	26Ma02Hg
Jane	60	F	Unknown	26Ma02Hg
MEEHAN, James	26	M	Laborer	26Ma02Hg
SCANLAN, Bridget	19	F	Unknown	26Ma02Hg
KATING, Ann	26	F	Unknown	26Ma02Hg
DURKEN, Thomas	26	M	Tailor	26Ma02Hg
FAY, Wm.	23	M	Laborer	26Ma02Hg
BALEY, Wm.	21	M	Laborer	26Ma02Hg
ROOKE, Chas.	23	M	Laborer	26Ma02Hg
RABIT, Wm.	28	M	Shoemaker	26Ma02Hg
CARTY, Thos.	30	M	Laborer	26Ma02Hg
MCCOY, Fras.	22	M	Laborer	26Ma02Hg
OHARE, Patk.	31	M	Laborer	26Ma02Hg
KEENAN, Jas.	30	M	Laborer	26Ma02Hg
BYRNE, Wm.	25	M	Cbtmkr	26Ma02Hg
Eliza	20	F	Unknown	26Ma02Hg
BRENNAN, Michael	19	M	Laborer	26Ma02Hg
MATHEWS, Michael	22	M	Tailor	26Ma02Hg
PURCELL, Patk.	24	M	Farmer	26Ma02Hg
CUMMINGS, John	27	M	Farmer	26Ma02Hg
Ann	23	F	Unknown	26Ma02Hg
Jas.	2	M	Child	26Ma02Hg
Patk.	.10	M	Infant	26Ma02Hg
HOGAN, John	36	M	Mason	26Ma02Hg
Danl.	25	M	Mason	26Ma02Hg
MADDEN, John	24	M	Farmer	26Ma02Hg
HOGAN, Michl.	34	M	Mason	26Ma02Hg
FOX, Edwd.	21	M	Laborer	26Ma02Hg
Mary	52	F	Unknown	26Ma02Hg
HOGAN, Wm.	43	M	Farmer	26Ma02Hg
MAILEY, Mary	36	F	Unknown	26Ma02Hg
HOGAN, Patk.	16	M	Laborer	26Ma02Hg
OCKTER, Mary	22	F	Unknown	26Ma02Hg
IACKETT, Patk.	48	M	Farmer	26Ma02Hg
MAILEY, Judy	22	F	Unknown	26Ma02Hg
Mary-Ann	7	F	Child	26Ma02Hg
Margaret	5	F	Child	26Ma02Hg
Dennis	3	M	Child	26Ma02Hg
James	.10	M	Infant	26Ma02Hg
ORRIGAN, Patk.	20	M	Laborer	26Ma02Hg
Margaret	18	F	Unknown	26Ma02Hg
Maria	16	F	Unknown	26Ma02Hg
JMMINS, James	38	M	Laborer	26Ma02Hg
ULLIVAN, Dennis	29	M	Laborer	26Ma02Hg
Mary	26	F	Unknown	26Ma02Hg
Silvy	40	M	Laborer	26Ma02Hg
Dennis	14	M	Laborer	26Ma02Hg
RPENTER, Mary	18	F	Unknown	26Ma02Hg
Ann	15	F	Unknown	26Ma02Hg
NOLLY, Hugh	20	M	Laborer	26Ma02Hg
GAN, Peter	25	M	Laborer	26Ma02Hg
ODS, Patrick	21	M	Laborer	26Ma02Hg
CKEY, Peter	25	M	Laborer	26Ma02Hg
LAN, Lawrence	24	M	Laborer	26Ma02Hg
Bridget	24	F	Unknown	26Ma02Hg
LINGER, Lawr.	50	M	Laborer	26Ma02Hg
Margaret	35	F	Unknown	26Ma02Hg
ACK, Edmund	30	M	Laborer	26Ma02Hg
ERNEY, Matt	22	M	Laborer	26Ma02Hg
HAN, Patk.	26	M	Laborer	26Ma02Hg
YLE, Patk.	36	M	Laborer	26Ma02Hg
CHER, Thomas	20	M	Laborer	26Ma02Hg
RICKENS, John	20	M	Laborer	26Ma02Hg
MCCLARNEN, John	21	M	Carpenter	26Ma02Hg
LENEHAN, Wm.	21	M	Founder	26Ma02Hg
WILSON, Hy.	24	M	Laborer	26Ma02Hg
MCMULLEN, Margaret	19	F	Unknown	26Ma02Hg
MCFITRIDGE, Eliza	19	F	Unknown	26Ma02Hg
TIDLEY, Margaret	19	F	Unknown	26Ma02Hg
GILLAND, Maria	28	F	Unknown	26Ma02Hg
LYONS, Wm.	30	M	Laborer	26Ma02Hg
Mary	20	F	Unknown	26Ma02Hg
CARROLL, Patrick	30	M	Laborer	26Ma02Hg
CUNNINGHAM, Wm.	23	M	Laborer	26Ma02Hg
FLANAGAN, Margaret	21	F	Milliner	26Ma02Hg
MCKEOWN, Jane	19	F	Milliner	26Ma02Hg
MCCELLELLAND, Wm.	23	M	Hpntr	26Ma02Hg
DIXON, James	22	M	Shopman	26Ma02Hg
BYRNE, John	33	M	Laborer	26Ma02Hg
Ann	25	F	Unknown	26Ma02Hg
BALLAGH, Wm.	26	M	Farmer	26Ma02Hg
DALY, Ellen	60	F	Unknown	26Ma02Hg
Patk.	25	M	Laborer	26Ma02Hg
John	22	M	Laborer	26Ma02Hg
Bridget	20	F	Unknown	26Ma02Hg
Thomas	12	M	Unknown	26Ma02Hg
ODONNELL, James	45	M	Laborer	26Ma02Hg
MOLONEY, Patk.	18	M	Laborer	26Ma02Hg
CRANAGE, Jerh.	40	M	Tailor	26Ma02Hg
MAHER, Michl.	26	M	Mason	26Ma02Hg
SHERIDAN, Terence	27	M	Laborer	26Ma02Hg
Kathe.	24	F	Unknown	26Ma02Hg
JOWIN, John	20	M	Shoemaker	26Ma02Hg
CONDON, Thos.	22	M	Laborer	26Ma02Hg
WALLACE, Thos.	40	M	Shoemaker	26Ma02Hg
Mary	40	F	Unknown	26Ma02Hg
Kathe.	14	F	Unknown	26Ma02Hg
John	13	M	Unknown	26Ma02Hg
Margt.	12	F	Unknown	26Ma02Hg
Hanora	9	F	Child	26Ma02Hg
Ellen	7	F	Child	26Ma02Hg
Mary	3	F	Child	26Ma02Hg
Eliza	.10	F	Infant	26Ma02Hg
Wm.	50	M	Laborer	26Ma02Hg
SHEA, John	22	M	Shoemaker	26Ma02Hg
ODONNELL, James	22	M	Shoemaker	26Ma02Hg
HOGAN, Patk.	28	M	Laborer	26Ma02Hg
Andy	24	F	Unknown	26Ma02Hg
Edwd.	23	M	Laborer	26Ma02Hg
BOYLAN, Andw.	17	M	Laborer	26Ma02Hg
Margt.	23	F	Unknown	26Ma02Hg
Bridget	14	F	Unknown	26Ma02Hg
TUCKER, Robt.	21	M	Laborer	26Ma02Hg
James	20	M	Laborer	26Ma02Hg
LENNAN, James	24	M	Laborer	26Ma02Hg
SMITH, Edwd.	28	M	Carpenter	26Ma02Hg
FARRELL, Thos.	63	M	Laborer	26Ma02Hg
Chrisr.	26	M	Laborer	26Ma02Hg
Kathe.	18	F	Unknown	26Ma02Hg
Mary	16	F	Unknown	26Ma02Hg
MCGUIRE, Patk.	26	M	Teacher	26Ma02Hg
BANNIN, Mathw.	35	M	Carpenter	26Ma02Hg
DEVINE, Robt.	26	M	Laborer	26Ma02Hg
WILSON, Andy	30	M	Weaver	26Ma02Hg
GLENDINNIRY, Wm.	29	M	Laborer	26Ma02Hg
CORRIGAN, Terence	20	M	Laborer	26Ma02Hg
Ann	25	F	Unknown	26Ma02Hg
MCCANNON, Eliza	24	F	Unknown	26Ma02Hg
MUNCITERICK, Wm.	19	M	Laborer	26Ma02Hg
Thos.	17	M	Laborer	26Ma02Hg
CAFFREY, Thos.	30	M	Laborer	26Ma02Hg
SMITH, James	27	M	Laborer	26Ma02Hg
DEVLIN, Thos.	25	M	Laborer	26Ma02Hg
Lawr.	19	M	Laborer	26Ma02Hg
KERSEY, John	25	M	Laborer	26Ma02Hg
Eliza	22	F	Unknown	26Ma02Hg
HYLAND, Geo.	20	M	Laborer	26Ma02Hg

NAMES OF PASSENGERS	AGE	SEX	OCCUPATIONS	DATE PORT SHIP
MCCONNELL, John	50	M	Tanner	26Ma02Hg
Patk.	54	M	Laborer	26Ma02Hg
Rosa	54	F	Unknown	26Ma02Hg
Rose	11	F	Unknown	26Ma02Hg
Alice	13	F	Unknown	26Ma02Hg
CAFFREY, Michl.	24	M	Laborer	26Ma02Hg
CARROLL, Bridget	18	F	Unknown	26Ma02Hg
FITZGIBBONS, Patk.	21	M	Smith	26Ma02Hg
HOGG, Saml.	41	M	Farmer	26Ma02Hg
Thos.	62	M	Farmer	26Ma02Hg
Jane	34	F	Unknown	26Ma02Hg
Peggy	18	F	Unknown	26Ma02Hg
MCKIVETT, Mary-Ann	25	F	Unknown	26Ma02Hg
CUMMINS, Mary-Ann	22	F	Unknown	26Ma02Hg
AGNEW, James	25	M	Laborer	26Ma02Hg
MCGILL, Patk.	27	M	Draper	26Ma02Hg
HICKEY, Geo.	25	M	Tinker	26Ma02Hg
MATHEWS, Alice	19	F	Unknown	26Ma02Hg
HICKEY, Jane	15	F	Unknown	26Ma02Hg
WALLACE, Hugh	22	M	Laborer	26Ma02Hg
Mary	17	F	Unknown	26Ma02Hg
Jane	15	F	Unknown	26Ma02Hg
Sarah	11	F	Unknown	26Ma02Hg
Thomas	18	M	Laborer	26Ma02Hg
KENNEDY, Sally	22	F	Unknown	26Ma02Hg
MATHEWS, Pat	30	M	Laborer	26Ma02Hg
Katherine	16	F	Unknown	26Ma02Hg
John	14	M	Unknown	26Ma02Hg
Jane	10	F	Unknown	26Ma02Hg
Hannah	8	F	Child	26Ma02Hg
Owen	6	M	Child	26Ma02Hg
HUGHES, James	19	M	Laborer	26Ma02Hg
Mary	18	F	Unknown	26Ma02Hg
GLASS, Alexr.	36	M	Farmer	26Ma02Hg
Margt.	35	F	Unknown	26Ma02Hg
FAY, John	19	M	Laborer	26Ma02Hg
ARMSTRONG, Saml.	50	M	Joiner	26Ma02Hg
WHERRY, James	46	M	Shoemaker	26Ma02Hg
WILKEN, Geo.	40	M	Farmer	26Ma02Hg
Mary	18	F	Unknown	26Ma02Hg
MEHAN, Henry	36	M	Shoemaker	26Ma02Hg
DOYLE, Edwd.	42	M	Laborer	26Ma02Hg
Kathl.	22	F	Unknown	26Ma02Hg
KATING, John	10	M	Unknown	26Ma02Hg
MAWHAITER, Sarah	20	F	Unknown	26Ma02Hg
MCGOWAN, Thos.	28	M	Laborer	26Ma02Hg
CUNNINGHAM, Nicholas	18	M	Laborer	26Ma02Hg
MCCONNOR, Michl.	20	M	Laborer	26Ma02Hg
WARD, Julia	36	F	Unknown	26Ma02Hg
Eugene	7	M	Child	26Ma02Hg
Mary	5	F	Child	26Ma02Hg
Ellen-Esther	3	F	Child	26Ma02Hg
Dennis	2	F	Child	26Ma02Hg
William	.10	F	Infant	26Ma02Hg
FLANERY, Kathe.	30	F	Unknown	26Ma02Hg
RITCHY, Robt.	35	M	Weaver	26Ma02Hg
Sarah	23	F	Unknown	26Ma02Hg
HANNA, Josh.	20	M	Laborer	26Ma02Hg
LYNCH, Pat	45	M	Laborer	26Ma02Hg
MCCARTHY, Caroll	50	M	Unknown	26Ma02Hg
BARRING, Wm.	19	M	Bookbinder	26Ma02Hg
CLIFFORD, Hugh	20	M	Laborer	26Ma02Hg
TANDY, Mary	18	F	Unknown	26Ma02Hg
BYRNE, Ellen	23	F	Unknown	26Ma02Hg
CRADOCK, Patk.	24	M	Shopman	26Ma02Hg
RYAN, James	33	M	Shopman	26Ma02Hg
BRADY, Thomas	40	M	Laborer	26Ma02Hg
Edwd.	5	M	Child	26Ma02Hg
HARRIS, John	22	M	Varnisher	26Ma02Hg
GORMAN, Jane	25	F	Unknown	26Ma02Hg
Sarah	22	F	Unknown	26Ma02Hg
BELL, Mary	20	F	Unknown	26Ma02Hg
HARRIS, Jane	45	F	Unknown	26Ma02Hg
MCCORD, Ellen	19	F	Unknown	26Ma02Hg
WILSON, M.J.	23	F	Unknown	26Ma02Hg
GODSELL, Eliza	22	F	Unknown	26Ma02Hg
BRANAGAN, Thos.	22	M	Hrsdlr	26Ma02Hg
CROSBY, Hugh	24	M	Saddler	26Ma02Hg
BRANAGAN, James	11	M	Unknown	26Ma02Hg
CROTTY, Michl.	21	M	Carpenter	26Ma02Hg
SULLIVAN, Patk.	21	M	Tailor	26Ma02Hg
BARKER, Jas.	28	M	Mason	26Ma02Hg
BAILEY, Michl.	33	M	Mason	26Ma02Hg
MCGUIRK, Michl.	24	M	Herd	26Ma02Hg
LEONARD, John	30	M	Laborer	26Ma02Hg
BARRY, Wm.	55	M	Laborer	26Ma02Hg
Maryann	17	F	Unknown	26Ma02Hg
Cathn.	36	F	Unknown	26Ma02Hg
Thos.	40	M	Laborer	26Ma02Hg
Ellen	24	F	Unknown	26Ma02Hg
FINTON, John	23	M	Laborer	26Ma02Hg
BARRY, Richd.	28	M	Laborer	26Ma02Hg
Mary	30	F	Unknown	26Ma02Hg
Jerry	22	M	Laborer	26Ma02Hg
Wm.	21	M	Laborer	26Ma02Hg
John	13	M	Laborer	26Ma02Hg
Robt.	19	M	Laborer	26Ma02Hg
Ann	27	F	Unknown	26Ma02Hg
FOLEY, Frances	21	M	Laborer	26Ma02Hg
DONGAL, Mary	21	F	Unknown	26Ma02Hg
CUNNINGHAM, Alice	15	F	Unknown	26Ma02Hg
Kathe.	60	F	Unknown	26Ma02Hg
BENSON, Charles	31	M	Weaver	26Ma02Hg
CROSBY, Ann	18	F	Unknown	26Ma02Hg
RORKE, Ann	17	F	Unknown	26Ma02Hg
CAREY, Kathe.	18	F	Unknown	26Ma02Hg
BLIGH, M.A.	20	F	Unknown	26Ma02Hg
PHILLIPS, Christr.	20	M	Tailor	26Ma02Hg
Anna	25	F	Unknown	26Ma02Hg
CORNEY, John-H.	21	M	Baker	26Ma02Hg
MCCARTHY, Michl.	20	M	Baker	26Ma02Hg
KELLY, Kathe.	18	F	Unknown	26Ma02Hg
SPEED, George	22	M	Clerk	26Ma02Hg
MOHAN, Timothy	24	M	Clerk	26Ma02Hg
MAHONEY, Thos.	28	M	Weaver	26Ma02Hg
BOHAN, Thos.	35	M	Shopman	26Ma02Hg
EYRES, Philp.	35	M	Plasterer	26Ma02Hg
MCGUIRE, John	26	M	Mason	26Ma02Hg
MCCANN, Ann	30	F	Unknown	26Ma02Hg
Rose	.10	F	Infant	26Ma02Hg
CURRAN, Margt.	18	F	Unknown	26Ma02Hg
Kathe.	16	F	Unknown	26Ma02H
CAFFRAY, John	35	M	Gdnr	26Ma02Hg
Martha	30	F	Unknown	26Ma02H
John	10	M	Unknown	26Ma02H
Charles	7	M	Child	26Ma02H
Micheal	3	M	Child	26Ma02H
Thomas	.11	M	Infant	26Ma02H
BOYLAN, Mick	54	M	Laborer	26Ma02H
ARMSTRONG, Adam	24	M	Farmer	26Ma02H
ALLEN, John	20	M	Farmer	26Ma02H
MILLER, James	48	M	Weaver	26Ma02H
Alexr.	73	M	Bleacher	26Ma02H
Margaret	67	F	Unknown	26Ma02H
SEXTON, Peter	22	M	Laborer	26Ma02H
GILLESPIE, Saml.	23	M	Upholsterer	26Ma02H
WATSON, Thomas	25	M	Upholsterer	26Ma02H
GILLESPIE, Mary	60	F	Unknown	26Ma02H
HERRON, M.Jane	20	F	Unknown	26Ma02H
HUMPHREYS, Michl.	24	M	Laborer	26Ma02H
FOLEY, Connor	22	M	Laborer	26Ma02H
James	24	M	Laborer	26Ma02
Kathe.	20	F	Unknown	26Ma02
Ellen	19	F	Unknown	26Ma02
Jane	18	F	Unknown	26Ma02
Joanna	27	F	Unknown	26Ma02
COLLIGAN, Patk.	24	M	Laborer	26Ma02
FORAN, M.A.	20	F	Unknown	26Ma02
CAMPBELL, Ann	21	F	Unknown	26Ma02
WILSON, Mary	10	F	Unknown	26Ma02

NAMES OF PASSENGERS	AGE	SEX	OCCUPATIONS	DATE PORT SHIP
WILSON, Nancy	12	F	Unknown	26Ma02Hg
Martha	.06	F	Infant	26Ma02Hg
MCQUILLAN, Mary	60	F	Unknown	26Ma02Hg
Thomas	30	M	Laborer	26Ma02Hg
Margaret	32	F	Unknown	26Ma02Hg
Anne	28	F	Unknown	26Ma02Hg
CALLAN, Patk.	21	M	Laborer	26Ma02Hg
STEWART, Frank	20	M	Laborer	26Ma02Hg
MCCONNAN, John	22	M	Laborer	26Ma02Hg
MCDONNELL, Mary	25	F	Unknown	26Ma02Hg
MCFARLIN, John	30	M	Farmer	26Ma02Hg
Sarah	27	F	Unknown	26Ma02Hg
Kathe.	2	F	Child	26Ma02Hg
Henry	.07	M	Infant	26Ma02Hg
MULLIN, Michl.	23	M	Laborer	26Ma02Hg
ROACH, John	47	M	Laborer	26Ma02Hg
TAAFFE, Thomas	25	M	Milkman	26Ma02Hg
TOOLE, Jas.	21	M	Groom	26Ma02Hg
LYNAM, Peter	27	M	Laborer	26Ma02Hg
CARROLL, Thomas	35	M	Laborer	26Ma02Hg
Thomas	13	M	Laborer	26Ma02Hg
MCMAHON, Margt.	45	F	Unknown	26Ma02Hg
John	50	M	Laborer	26Ma02Hg
Mary	20	F	Unknown	26Ma02Hg
Margt.	20	F	Unknown	26Ma02Hg
Kitty	9	F	Child	26Ma02Hg
LENEHAN, Margt.	20	F	Unknown	26Ma02Hg
KELLY, Bridget	17	F	Unknown	26Ma02Hg
CLANCY, Mary	18	F	Unknown	26Ma02Hg
RYAN, Murtagh	30	M	Laborer	26Ma02Hg
DWYER, John	27	M	Shoemaker	26Ma02Hg
LAVERY, Richd.	19	M	Draper	26Ma02Hg
James	23	M	Draper	26Ma02Hg
HEALEY, Denis	34	M	Tanner	26Ma02Hg
BROWN, Ward	33	M	Coach Maker	26Ma02Hg
George	36	M	Coach Maker	26Ma02Hg
PEPPER, Thomas	26	M	Clerk	26Ma02Hg
Maryann	18	F	Unknown	26Ma02Hg
CROHAN, Patk.	24	M	Clerk	26Ma02Hg
MCADAM, John	26	M	Cooper	26Ma02Hg
BRADY, John	22	M	Smith	26Ma02Hg
MCMANERS, Ann	19	F	Unknown	26Ma02Hg
COLLINS, Jane	17	F	Unknown	26Ma02Hg
SMITH, Chas.	23	M	Clerk	26Ma02Hg
Thos.	19	M	Clerk	26Ma02Hg
ODONALD, Michl.	26	M	Clerk	26Ma02Hg
Eliza	25	F	Unknown	26Ma02Hg
OWRY, Isabel	21	F	Unknown	26Ma02Hg
ICROBERTS, Hugh	17	M	Grocer	26Ma02Hg
ICNAUGHTON, Agnes	25	F	Unknown	26Ma02Hg
IBSON, Charles	18	M	Spinner	26Ma02Hg
IAMILTON, Mary	22	F	Unknown	26Ma02Hg
ATTERSON, John	50	M	Farmer	26Ma02Hg
ICCATCHEN, Sarah	18	F	Unknown	26Ma02Hg
ORROW, Bess	19	F	Unknown	26Ma02Hg
Jane	17	F	Unknown	26Ma02Hg
OWNES, Patk.	26	M	Laborer	26Ma02Hg
YNAN, Michl.	20	M	Laborer	26Ma02Hg
ALONEY, Biddy	21	F	Unknown	26Ma02Hg
Ann	17	F	Unknown	26Ma02Hg
UNNE, Michl.	25	M	Laborer	26Ma02Hg
Bridget	19	F	Unknown	26Ma02Hg
MITH, Michl.	22	M	Laborer	26Ma02Hg
HITE, John	30	M	Laborer	26Ma02Hg
Margaret	30	F	Unknown	26Ma02Hg
ROWNE, Margaret	40	F	Unknown	26Ma02Hg
Henry	20	M	Clerk	26Ma02Hg
John	17	M	Clerk	26Ma02Hg
Mary	15	F	Unknown	26Ma02Hg
Arthur	14	M	Clerk	26Ma02Hg
Flora	12	F	Unknown	26Ma02Hg
Percy	10	M	Unknown	26Ma02Hg
Benn.	8	M	Child	26Ma02Hg
RRAY, Honor	17	F	Servant	26Ma02Hg
GGINS, John	53	M	Farmer	26Ma02Hg

NAMES OF PASSENGERS	AGE	SEX	OCCUPATIONS	DATE PORT SHIP
MARSHALL, Eliza	45	F	Unknown	26Ma02Hg
Sarah	40	F	Unknown	26Ma02Hg
MCCULLAGH, Jas.	22	M	Ckasst	26Ma02Hg
GRAHAM, Pat	25	M	Ckasst	26Ma02Hg
FOLEY, Moses	45	M	Shoemaker	26Ma02Hg
Joanna	40	F	Unknown	26Ma02Hg
Moses	2	M	Child	26Ma02Hg
Mary	4	F	Child	26Ma02Hg
HENDERSON, Harriett	18	F	Servant	26Ma02Hg
LEONARD, Richd.	50	M	Laborer	26Ma02Hg
Judith	50	F	Unknown	26Ma02Hg
John	20	M	Laborer	26Ma02Hg
BUTLER, Alice	23	F	Servant	26Ma02Hg
HARVEY, Jane	35	F	Unknown	26Ma02Hg
NOUD, Ann	19	F	Servant	26Ma02Hg
PAYN, Eliza-T.	19	F	Lady	26Ma02Hg
HASLET, Mary	19	F	Lady	26Ma02Hg
CARPENTER, Richd.	30	M	Merchant	26Ma02Hg
DICKSON, Robt.	30	M	Clergyman	26Ma02Hg
BROPHY, Saml.R.	25	M	Merchant	26Ma02Hg

WEST-POINT 26 MAY 1849

From Liverpool

NAMES OF PASSENGERS	AGE	SEX	OCCUPATIONS	DATE PORT SHIP
TENCH, Geo.	28	M	Unknown	26Ma02Hl
NORCOTT, N.	24	U	Unknown	26Ma02Hl
R.	22	U	Unknown	26Ma02Hl
THORPE, U	56	M	Painter	26Ma02Hl
U (W)	56	F	Unknown	26Ma02Hl
BROWN, U-Mrs.	35	F	Unknown	26Ma02Hl
Geo.	.10	M	Infant	26Ma02Hl
RICE, U	28	M	Unknown	26Ma02Hl
U (W)	22	F	Unknown	26Ma02Hl
KELLY, U	25	M	Unknown	26Ma02Hl
U (W)	23	F	Unknown	26Ma02Hl
BALL, Geo.	29	M	Unknown	26Ma02Hl
MALONEY, Michael	22	M	Laborer	26Ma02Hl
BLAKE, Michael	19	M	Laborer	26Ma02Hl
MCKENNA, James	45	M	Unknown	26Ma02Hl
MANIX, John	24	M	Laborer	26Ma02Hl
HEATHCOTE, James	34	M	Unknown	26Ma02Hl
THORPE, Elizabeth	27	F	Unknown	26Ma02Hl
James	23	M	Painter	26Ma02Hl
Frederick	25	M	Painter	26Ma02Hl
Dominick	21	M	Painter	26Ma02Hl
Essy	20	F	Unknown	26Ma02Hl
CONDHILL, Jane	25	F	Unknown	26Ma02Hl
BYRNE, Simon	30	M	Unknown	26Ma02Hl
Elizabeth	25	F	Unknown	26Ma02Hl
OBRIEN, Johan	19	M	Unknown	26Ma02Hl
Winnifred	27	F	Unknown	26Ma02Hl
JOHNSON, John	23	M	Laborer	26Ma02Hl
MALONEY, Henry	17	M	Laborer	26Ma02Hl
Hannah	14	F	Unknown	26Ma02Hl
BRADY, Thomas	25	M	Laborer	26Ma02Hl
WALSH, Mat.	25	M	Blacksmith	26Ma02Hl
RILEY, Miles	25	M	Laborer	26Ma02Hl
LINN, Mary	15	F	Tailor	26Ma02Hl
MCDONALD, Michael	26	M	Laborer	26Ma02Hl
MCMAHON, Ann	17	F	Unknown	26Ma02Hl
FINLEY, Mary	20	F	Unknown	26Ma02Hl
MCCALL, Ann	27	F	Unknown	26Ma02Hl
CRONAN, Dennis	45	M	Unknown	26Ma02Hl
John	11	M	Unknown	26Ma02Hl
MADDEN, Bridget	26	F	Unknown	26Ma02Hl
MCAULIFF, Con.	26	M	Laborer	26Ma02Hl
DELANEY, Thomas	25	M	Unknown	26Ma02Hl
CARPENTER, John	30	M	Laborer	26Ma02Hl

NAMES OF PASSENGERS	AGE	SEX	OCCUPATIONS	DATE PORT SHIP
CLIFFORD, Michael	26	M	Unknown	26Ma02HI
GIRON, Bridget	45	F	Unknown	26Ma02HI
KELLY, Bridget	13	F	Unknown	26Ma02HI
MULDOWN, John	23	M	Tailor	26Ma02HI
BYRNE, Pat.	30	M	Laborer	26Ma02HI
DAVIES, Thomas	32	M	Laborer	26Ma02HI
BYRNE, Ann	25	F	Unknown	26Ma02HI
MCKEOWN, Mary	25	F	Unknown	26Ma02HI
FLAHERTY, Ellen	25	F	Unknown	26Ma02HI
Margaret	4	F	Child	26Ma02HI
Thomas	3	M	Child	26Ma02HI
Ellen	20	F	Unknown	26Ma02HI
HEANY, Ann	21	F	Unknown	26Ma02HI
MELVILLE, John	40	M	Laborer	26Ma02HI
Mary	35	F	Unknown	26Ma02HI
Catharine	14	F	Unknown	26Ma02HI
PRENDERGAST, John	40	M	Laborer	26Ma02HI
John	40	M	Laborer	26Ma02HI
Patrick	20	M	Laborer	26Ma02HI
Bridget	14	F	Unknown	26Ma02HI
Margaret	18	F	Unknown	26Ma02HI
John	25	M	Laborer	26Ma02HI
KELLY, Hugh	28	M	Laborer	26Ma02HI
NALLY, Margaret	18	F	Unknown	26Ma02HI
CAIN, Thomas	20	M	Laborer	26Ma02HI
DELANEY, Anty	20	M	Laborer	26Ma02HI
Peter	18	M	Laborer	26Ma02HI
Thomas	21	M	Laborer	26Ma02HI
COUGHLIN, Pat.	20	M	Laborer	26Ma02HI
Ellen	20	F	Unknown	26Ma02HI
WALSH, David	21	M	Laborer	26Ma02HI
Pat.	18	M	Laborer	26Ma02HI
Margaret	14	F	Unknown	26Ma02HI
HYLAND, Michael	20	M	Laborer	26Ma02HI
FINN, James	20	M	Baker	26Ma02HI
Mary	18	F	Unknown	26Ma02HI
DOWRY, Nancy	20	F	Unknown	26Ma02HI
FALLON, John	20	M	Laborer	26Ma02HI
CUNNAN, Pat.	20	M	Carter	26Ma02HI
SLATREY, David	30	M	Laborer	26Ma02HI
DALEY, Michael	18	M	Laborer	26Ma02HI
Catharine	20	F	Unknown	26Ma02HI
BRADY, James	20	M	Laborer	26Ma02HI
FORMEY, Thomas	20	M	Laborer	26Ma02HI
PRENDERGAST, Thomas	20	M	Laborer	26Ma02HI
LEONARD, Bridget	12	F	Unknown	26Ma02HI
MATTHEWS, Bridget	30	F	Unknown	26Ma02HI
MCNAMARA, Mary	17	F	Unknown	26Ma02HI
Thomas	5	M	Child	26Ma02HI
HEERY, John	18	M	Laborer	26Ma02HI
NUGENT, Pat.	21	M	Unknown	26Ma02HI
MORLEY, Matty	19	M	Laborer	26Ma02HI
MAHON, Julia	16	F	Unknown	26Ma02HI
ROWNE, W.	30	M	Laborer	26Ma02HI
U (W)	20	F	Unknown	26Ma02HI
U	.00	U	Infant	26Ma02HI
Michael	20	M	Laborer	26Ma02HI
BARRETT, Bridget	20	F	Unknown	26Ma02HI
SCOTT, John	24	M	Gdnr	26Ma02HI
GAGAN, Edward	34	M	Laborer	26Ma02HI
U (W)	25	F	Unknown	26Ma02HI
U	.00	U	Infant	26Ma02HI
CARNADINE, John	24	M	Unknown	26Ma02HI
Mary	23	F	Unknown	26Ma02HI
Ann	18	F	Unknown	26Ma02HI
Elizabeth	16	F	Unknown	26Ma02HI
Jane	11	F	Unknown	26Ma02HI
Geo.	8	M	Child	26Ma02HI
Elizabeth	6	F	Child	26Ma02HI
Thomas	4	M	Child	26Ma02HI
Martha	2	F	Child	26Ma02HI
MORLEY, Pat	17	M	Laborer	26Ma02HI
FURLONG, Phil.	28	M	Farmer	26Ma02HI
U (W)	23	F	Unknown	26Ma02HI
U	.00	U	Infant	26Ma02HI

NAMES OF PASSENGERS	AGE	SEX	OCCUPATIONS	DATE PORT SHIP
FURLONG, Pat	25	M	Laborer	26Ma02HI
MAGUIRE, James	38	M	Laborer	26Ma02HI
U (W)	32	F	Unknown	26Ma02HI
U	.00	U	Infant	26Ma02HI
James	22	M	Laborer	26Ma02HI
MATTHEWS, Henry	35	M	Farmer	26Ma02HI
U (W)	38	F	Unknown	26Ma02HI
HYLAND, Michael	50	M	Laborer	26Ma02HI
Catharine	48	F	Unknown	26Ma02HI
Mary	20	F	Unknown	26Ma02HI
Margaret	18	F	Unknown	26Ma02HI
Elizabeth	16	F	Unknown	26Ma02HI
Catharine	14	F	Unknown	26Ma02HI
Judith	12	F	Unknown	26Ma02HI
Bridget	11	F	Unknown	26Ma02HI
BRANNAN, Mark	25	M	Unknown	26Ma02HI
KENNA, James	30	M	Laborer	26Ma02HI
Mary	26	F	Unknown	26Ma02HI
DUNN, Geo.	30	M	Laborer	26Ma02HI
Mary	18	F	Unknown	26Ma02HI
FINLEY, Pat	21	M	Laborer	26Ma02HI
MURRAY, Pat	25	M	Shoemaker	26Ma02HI
MOORE, Pat	24	M	Paper Maker	26Ma02HI
MCKENNA, Simon	25	M	Mason	26Ma02HI
Mary	22	F	Unknown	26Ma02HI
KING, Mat	25	M	Laborer	26Ma02HI
GOUGH, Michael	20	M	Laborer	26Ma02HI
SHEEN, Christopher	18	M	Unknown	26Ma02HI
GREER, Essy	15	F	Unknown	26Ma02HI
DREW, John	18	M	Unknown	26Ma02HI
CHAMBERS, Wm.	13	M	Laborer	26Ma02HI
Robert	12	M	Laborer	26Ma02HI
DYSON, Michael	18	M	Laborer	26Ma02HI
Mary	21	F	Unknown	26Ma02HI
DOOLAN, Arthur	45	M	Laborer	26Ma02HI
William	11	M	Laborer	26Ma02HI
SLATREY, John	20	M	Laborer	26Ma02HI
HYLAND, Arthur	27	M	Laborer	26Ma02HI
DALEY, Honor	20	F	Unknown	26Ma02HI
SHERIDAN, Catharine	21	F	Unknown	26Ma02HI
CLONAN, Stephen	40	M	Laborer	26Ma02HI
Pat	23	M	Laborer	26Ma02HI
Eliza	20	F	Unknown	26Ma02HI
Rose	17	F	Unknown	26Ma02HI
Catharine	15	F	Unknown	26Ma02HI
Daniel	14	M	Unknown	26Ma02HI
Maria	20	F	Unknown	26Ma02HI
ROONEY, Ann	18	F	Unknown	26Ma02HI
GORMAN, Edward	23	M	Laborer	26Ma02HI
ROURKE, Owen	21	M	Laborer	26Ma02HI
Catharine	18	F	Unknown	26Ma02HI
MULLANY, Wm.	48	M	Printer	26Ma02HI
Mary-A.	30	F	Unknown	26Ma02HI
U	.00	U	Infant	26Ma02HI
Wm.	2	M	Child	26Ma02HI
FITZGERALD, Francis	22	M	Printer	26Ma02HI
BUTLER, Margaret	14	U	Unknown	26Ma02HI
QUIGLEY, Catharine	30	F	Unknown	26Ma02HI
CAHILL, Bridget	33	F	Unknown	26Ma02HI
DONOHUE, Jno.	17	M	Laborer	26Ma02HI
OBRIEN, Thomas	26	M	Unknown	26Ma02HI
ROOSE, Pat	20	M	Laborer	26Ma02HI
MCKEOWN, Michael	22	M	Laborer	26Ma02HI
BERRIGAN, John	27	M	Unknown	26Ma02HI
Ann	20	F	Unknown	26Ma02HI
James	24	M	Unknown	26Ma02HI
U (W)	20	F	Unknown	26Ma02HI
KIRNAN, Christopher	20	M	Laborer	26Ma02HI
KINSELLA, Ann	20	F	Unknown	26Ma02HI
ORNIAN, Michael	21	M	Laborer	26Ma02HI
WINN, James	30	M	Laborer	26Ma02HI
CROTHY, James	25	M	Laborer	26Ma02HI
HENNESY, Michael	18	M	Carpenter	26Ma02HI
Margaret	16	F	Unknown	26Ma02HI
TEARNEY, Pat	26	M	Carpenter	26Ma02HI

NAMES OF PASSENGERS	AGE	SEX	OCCUPATIONS	DATE PORT SHIP
HAYES, John	21	M	Laborer	26Ma02HI
QUALEY, Stephen	23	M	Laborer	26Ma02HI
BRIEN, Mary	24	F	Unknown	26Ma02HI
PLUMMER, Thomas	28	M	Saddler	26Ma02HI
Marg.A.	24	F	Unknown	26Ma02HI
OHARE, Mary-A.	21	F	Unknown	26Ma02HI
CLARKIN, Michael	22	M	Laborer	26Ma02HI
LACEY, Mary	20	F	Unknown	26Ma02HI
MONTGOMERY, John	24	M	Surveyor	26Ma02HI
CAVANAGH, John	20	M	Shopman	26Ma02HI
DALAHANTY, John	40	M	Laborer	26Ma02HI
U (W)	40	F	Unknown	26Ma02HI
John	24	M	Laborer	26Ma02HI
William	19	M	Laborer	26Ma02HI
Mary	18	F	Unknown	26Ma02HI
Sarah	16	F	Unknown	26Ma02HI
Pat	13	M	Unknown	26Ma02HI
Tom	11	M	Unknown	26Ma02HI
Pat.	10	M	Unknown	26Ma02HI
Grace	8	F	Child	26Ma02HI
Sarah	20	F	Unknown	26Ma02HI
FLYNN, Wm.	27	M	Unknown	26Ma02HI
SMITH, Thomas	27	M	Laborer	26Ma02HI
WALLACE, Geo.	30	M	Laborer	26Ma02HI
CORMICK, Thomas	22	M	Laborer	26Ma02HI
PURCELL, Wm.	21	M	Laborer	26Ma02HI
BURKE, Thomas	25	M	Laborer	26Ma02HI
FANIN, Pat.	21	M	Laborer	26Ma02HI
KENNEDY, Bridget	21	F	Unknown	26Ma02HI
OHARAN, Dan	30	M	Laborer	26Ma02HI
Margaret	25	F	Unknown	26Ma02HI
MCGIVEN, Pat.	30	M	Laborer	26Ma02HI
U (W)	20	F	Unknown	26Ma02HI
BERRIGAN, John	27	M	Laborer	26Ma02HI
MATTHEWS, James	28	M	Laborer	26Ma02HI
John	32	M	Tailor	26Ma02HI
MCENIRY, Bernd.	27	M	Hatter	26Ma02HI
DALEY, Denis	27	M	Laborer	26Ma02HI
Margaret	25	F	Unknown	26Ma02HI
Ann	.00	F	Infant	26Ma02HI
HENDY, Michael	27	M	Grocer	26Ma02HI
KEENAN, Edward	20	M	Grocer	26Ma02HI
Fanny	18	F	Unknown	26Ma02HI
Honey	20	F	Unknown	26Ma02HI
OBRIEN, Michael	30	M	Farmer	26Ma02HI
KERNIN, Malachi	26	M	Laborer	26Ma02HI
HAND, Bernard	22	M	Laborer	26Ma02HI
WOOD, Francis	27	M	Maurer	26Ma02HI
U (W)	25	F	Unknown	26Ma02HI
U	.00	U	Infant	26Ma02HI
Andrew	18	M	Maurer	26Ma02HI
EGANS, James	23	M	Grocer	26Ma02HI
Mary-A.	21	F	Unknown	26Ma02HI
HEAD, Ann	25	F	Unknown	26Ma02HI
RILEY, Pat	20	M	Laborer	26Ma02HI
MCGIVRAN, Mary	20	F	Dressmaker	26Ma02HI
CONNELL, Thomas	20	M	Mason	26Ma02HI
Peter	27	M	Mason	26Ma02HI
BRANDLEY, Danl.	18	M	Nail Maker	26Ma02HI
MCCORMICK, Mary	18	F	Unknown	26Ma02HI
MCROBERTS, John	00	M	Unknown	26Ma02HI
MULLEN, U	00	U	Unknown	26Ma02HI

SILAS-RICHARDS 26 MAY 1849

From London

NAMES OF PASSENGERS	AGE	SEX	OCCUPATIONS	DATE PORT SHIP
SHARP, Jas.	30	M	Laborer	26Ma13Hk
Sophia	26	F	Unknown	26Ma13Hk
BAKER, Ebenezer	20	M	Unknown	26Ma13Hk
MORRIS, Geo.	2	M	Unknown	26Ma13Hk
Danl.	20	M	Unknown	26Ma13Hk
DENCE, Thos.	26	M	Unknown	26Ma13Hk
Jas.	23	M	Unknown	26Ma13Hk
COX, Wm.	25	M	Unknown	26Ma13Hk
R.	25	U	Unknown	26Ma13Hk
Chas.	.00	M	Infant	26Ma13Hk
SELLS, Jno.	31	M	Unknown	26Ma13Hk
Thomas	39	M	Unknown	26Ma13Hk
SMITH, William	27	M	Unknown	26Ma13Hk
WELLS, Robt.H.	32	M	Unknown	26Ma13Hk
BENSON, Richard	37	M	Unknown	26Ma13Hk
Lucy	33	F	Unknown	26Ma13Hk
Daniel	10	M	Unknown	26Ma13Hk
Joseph	7	M	Child	26Ma13Hk
Elizabeth	5	F	Child	26Ma13Hk
Eliza	2	F	Child	26Ma13Hk
Chas.	18	M	Unknown	26Ma13Hk
POPE, Jeremiah	23	M	Unknown	26Ma13Hk
KING, George	28	M	Unknown	26Ma13Hk
Sarah	25	F	Unknown	26Ma13Hk
GAISED, Edward	18	M	Unknown	26Ma13Hk
COOK, Joseph	34	M	Unknown	26Ma13Hk
SIMMONS, Thomas	18	M	Unknown	26Ma13Hk
LOVELOCK, Jno.	26	M	Unknown	26Ma13Hk
Lewis	9	M	Child	26Ma13Hk
PITTEPHER, Jno.	33	M	Unknown	26Ma13Hk
Mary	33	F	Unknown	26Ma13Hk
Richard	12	M	Unknown	26Ma13Hk
TILLEY, Henry	30	M	Unknown	26Ma13Hk
Elizabeth	30	F	Unknown	26Ma13Hk
Wm.	5	M	Child	26Ma13Hk
Elizabeth	2	F	Child	26Ma13Hk
HALL, Jas.	43	M	Unknown	26Ma13Hk
Jas.	14	M	Unknown	26Ma13Hk
SHORLAND, Robt.	30	M	Unknown	26Ma13Hk
DOWDAN, Chas.	30	M	Unknown	26Ma13Hk
STONEHAM, Jno.	27	M	Unknown	26Ma13Hk
Eliza	23	F	Unknown	26Ma13Hk
Thomas	5	M	Child	26Ma13Hk
STACE, Ann	67	F	Unknown	26Ma13Hk
NORTHOVER, Henry	30	M	Unknown	26Ma13Hk
WHISTLER, Wm.	24	M	Unknown	26Ma13Hk
WATKINS, Seth	20	M	Unknown	26Ma13Hk
STACEY, Chas.	22	M	Unknown	26Ma13Hk
Elizabeth	23	F	Unknown	26Ma13Hk
PICK, Charles	30	M	Unknown	26Ma13Hk
BAILEY, Elizabeth	18	F	Unknown	26Ma13Hk
POWELL, Thos.	39	M	Unknown	26Ma13Hk
F.M.	33	U	Unknown	26Ma13Hk
F.Wm.	11	M	Unknown	26Ma13Hk
M.Fanny	8	F	Child	26Ma13Hk
Edith	4	F	Child	26Ma13Hk
George-E.	.00	M	Infant	26Ma13Hk
BARNETT, Jno.	38	M	Unknown	26Ma13Hk
Eliza	33	F	Unknown	26Ma13Hk
Eliza	11	F	Unknown	26Ma13Hk
Mary	9	F	Child	26Ma13Hk
Thomas	4	M	Child	26Ma13Hk
Harriet	5	F	Child	26Ma13Hk
Jane	3	F	Child	26Ma13Hk
Edward	.00	M	Infant	26Ma13Hk
RUSSELL, Edward	29	M	Unknown	26Ma13Hk
DAY, George	31	M	Unknown	26Ma13Hk
Anna	31	F	Unknown	26Ma13Hk
George	11	M	Unknown	26Ma13Hk
Emily	7	F	Child	26Ma13Hk
Priscilla	4	F	Child	26Ma13Hk
Henry	.00	M	Infant	26Ma13Hk
MEYER, Henry	22	M	Unknown	26Ma13Hk
BANKS, Wm.	36	M	Unknown	26Ma13Hk
Eliza	34	F	Unknown	26Ma13Hk
Eliza	10	F	Unknown	26Ma13Hk
William	8	M	Child	26Ma13Hk

NAMES OF PASSENGERS	AGE	SEX	OCCUPATIONS	DATE PORT SHIP
BANKS, Ursala	5	F	Child	26Ma13Hk
Esther	3	F	Child	26Ma13Hk
Martha	.00	F	Infant	26Ma13Hk
JEFFERSON, Danl.	28	M	Unknown	26Ma13Hk
Mary	20	F	Unknown	26Ma13Hk
Danl.	.00	M	Infant	26Ma13Hk
DIXON, Zacharrah	36	F	Unknown	26Ma13Hk
Deborah	34	F	Unknown	26Ma13Hk
Alfred	13	M	Unknown	26Ma13Hk
Walter	11	M	Unknown	26Ma13Hk
Albert	9	M	Child	26Ma13Hk
Zahrab	7	M	Child	26Ma13Hk
Deborah	5	F	Child	26Ma13Hk
Ellen	3	F	Child	26Ma13Hk
William	.00	M	Infant	26Ma13Hk
HARPER, William	42	M	Unknown	26Ma13Hk
Elenor	42	F	Unknown	26Ma13Hk
SHEETER, Henry	21	M	Unknown	26Ma13Hk
CATT, Rosoland	18	U	Unknown	26Ma13Hk
DALE, George	18	M	Unknown	26Ma13Hk
MCLEOD, Jno.	28	M	Unknown	26Ma13Hk
Deborah	23	F	Unknown	26Ma13Hk
LOUGH, Jno.	41	M	Unknown	26Ma13Hk
Emma	19	F	Unknown	26Ma13Hk
FERRIS, G.E.	26	U	Unknown	26Ma13Hk
Sarah-C.	26	F	Unknown	26Ma13Hk
CHAMP, Edwin	22	M	Unknown	26Ma13Hk
Elizabeth	22	F	Unknown	26Ma13Hk
BULL, Edward	56	M	Unknown	26Ma13Hk
Mary	50	F	Unknown	26Ma13Hk
Jno.	23	M	Unknown	26Ma13Hk
BASSETT, Henry	38	M	Unknown	26Ma13Hk
Sarah	30	F	Unknown	26Ma13Hk
CASTLE, Jno.	30	M	Unknown	26Ma13Hk
Elizabeth	32	F	Unknown	26Ma13Hk
Emma	.00	F	Infant	26Ma13Hk
HOUSEMAN, George	37	M	Unknown	26Ma13Hk
Marion	33	F	Unknown	26Ma13Hk
Marion	8	F	Child	26Ma13Hk
Elizabeth	5	F	Child	26Ma13Hk
Mary-Ann	.00	F	Infant	26Ma13Hk
BOLTON, Henry	20	M	Unknown	26Ma13Hk
VENNER, Jno.	26	M	Unknown	26Ma13Hk
Sarah	22	F	Unknown	26Ma13Hk
SMITH, Jeremiah	19	M	Unknown	26Ma13Hk
FUGGLE, Stephen	29	M	Unknown	26Ma13Hk
Mary	31	F	Unknown	26Ma13Hk
R.	7	U	Child	26Ma13Hk
Stephen	5	M	Child	26Ma13Hk
SLAYTER, William	23	M	Unknown	26Ma13Hk
SUTHERDEN, Wm.	23	M	Unknown	26Ma13Hk
SHOWBRIDGE, Jas.	19	M	Unknown	26Ma13Hk
CHARLTON, Charley	27	M	Unknown	26Ma13Hk
Mary	39	F	Unknown	26Ma13Hk
Sussana	.00	F	Infant	26Ma13Hk
STAPLER, William	27	M	Unknown	26Ma13Hk
CLARK, Chas.	21	M	Unknown	26Ma13Hk
DENBY, George	25	M	Unknown	26Ma13Hk
Mary	27	F	Unknown	26Ma13Hk
HUGGINS, William	22	M	Unknown	26Ma13Hk

MIDWAY 26 MAY 1849

From Halifax

NAMES OF PASSENGERS	AGE	SEX	OCCUPATIONS	DATE PORT SHIP
GLENN, A.	31	M	Laborer	26Ma43Gg
DOYLE, Francis	7	M	Child	26Ma43Gg
Cath.	13	F	Unknown	26Ma43Gg
Peter	11	M	Unknown	26Ma43Gg
DOYLE, George	9	M	Child	26Ma43Gg
M.	15	M	Unknown	26Ma43Gg
NOVIL, Agnes	17	F	Unknown	26Ma43Gg
WELCH, Mary	29	F	Servant	26Ma43Gg
U	1	F	Child	26Ma43Gg

BOLTON-ABBEY 26 MAY 1849

From Londonderry

NAMES OF PASSENGERS	AGE	SEX	OCCUPATIONS	DATE PORT SHIP
LOGAN, John	30	M	None	26Ma01Gi
SHIELS, Biddy	19	F	None	26Ma01Gi
LOGAN, Grace	26	F	None	26Ma01Gi
MCLAUGHLIN, Paddy	9	M	Child	26Ma01Gi
James	7	M	Child	26Ma01Gi
John	5	M	Child	26Ma01Gi
Michael	30	M	Farmer	26Ma01Gi
Nancy	30	F	Farmer	26Ma01Gi
Unity	18	F	None	26Ma01Gi
MCCAULEY, John	20	M	None	26Ma01Gi
MCSHANE, Jeremiah	18	M	Saddler	26Ma01Gi
DOHERTY, Neil	10	M	None	26Ma01Gi
WILKIE, William	24	M	None	26Ma01Gi
John	20	M	None	26Ma01Gi
Henry	15	M	None	26Ma01Gi
Mary	64	F	None	26Ma01Gi
DOHERTY, Unity	28	F	None	26Ma01Gi
Mary	10	F	None	26Ma01Gi
CAMPBELL, David	20	M	Farmer	26Ma01Gi
James	26	M	Farmer	26Ma01Gi
HARKEN, Michael	24	M	Farmer	26Ma01Gi
HARRIOT, James	23	M	Farmer	26Ma01Gi
ELLIOT, Mary	19	F	None	26Ma01Gi
CALDWELL, Robert	12	M	None	26Ma01Gi
John	10	M	None	26Ma01Gi
FORBUSH, Isabella	16	F	None	26Ma01Gi
James	20	M	None	26Ma01Gi
Andrew	6	M	Child	26Ma01Gi
SPROULE, Andrew	27	M	None	26Ma01Gi
FORBUSH, Kitty	40	F	None	26Ma01Gi
Eliza	8	F	Child	26Ma01Gi
ALLISON, Ann-E.	24	F	None	26Ma01Gi
LITTLE, Jane	40	F	None	26Ma01Gi
John	17	M	None	26Ma01Gi
DOHERTY, Michael	8	M	Child	26Ma01Gi
LITTLE, Betty	15	F	None	26Ma01Gi
Sally	13	F	None	26Ma01Gi
WATERS, William	25	M	Wwsh	26Ma01Gi
Catherine	26	F	None	26Ma01Gi
Mary	6	F	Child	26Ma01Gi
MCCAE, Mary	11	F	None	26Ma01Gi
MARTIN, James	31	M	None	26Ma01Gi
Mary	31	F	None	26Ma01Gi
WATERS, Mary	18	F	None	26Ma01Gi
MCCAUFIELD, Barry	26	M	Tailor	25Ma01Gi
Mary	26	F	None	26Ma01Gi
Margaret	40	F	None	26Ma01Gi
SWEENEY, Ann	20	F	None	26Ma01Gi
GALLAGHER, Edward	18	M	None	26Ma01Gi
Catherine	15	F	None	26Ma01Gi
CALLION, Catherine	20	F	None	26Ma01Gi
MCLAUGHLIN, Jane	57	F	None	26Ma01Gi
Eliza	20	F	None	26Ma01Gi
Jane	18	F	None	26Ma01Gi
Martha	12	F	None	26Ma01Gi
JOHNSON, John	22	M	None	26Ma01Gi
Ann	24	F	None	26Ma01G
Mary	20	F	None	26Ma01G
REID, William	21	M	None	26Ma01G

NAMES OF PASSENGERS	AGE	SEX	OCCUPATIONS	DATE PORT SHIP
VERRIL, Betsy	19	F	None	26Ma01Gi
MCMULLIN, Catharine	20	F	None	26Ma01Gi
Susan	20	F	None	26Ma01Gi
LYNCH, Mary	37	F	None	26Ma01Gi
LEONARD, Betsy	20	F	None	26Ma01Gi
Margaret	16	F	None	26Ma01Gi
SULVER, Susan	17	F	None	26Ma01Gi
POTTER, William	21	M	None	26Ma01Gi
Rose	19	F	None	26Ma01Gi
John	17	M	None	26Ma01Gi
Joseph	13	M	None	26Ma01Gi
Samuel	13	M	None	26Ma01Gi
Samuel	14	M	None	26Ma01Gi
MCLAUGH, James	27	M	Miller	26Ma01Gi
HUNTER, William	22	M	None	26Ma01Gi
RODGERS, Mary	45	F	None	26Ma01Gi
FLEMING, Mary	18	F	None	26Ma01Gi
MCDOCK, Mary	18	F	None	26Ma01Gi
MCGILLEN, Ann	19	F	None	26Ma01Gi
PHILLIPS, Eliza	19	F	None	26Ma01Gi
GRIFFIN, James	23	M	Farmer	26Ma01Gi
MCLAUGHLIN, William	21	M	Gdnr	26Ma01Gi
GRAY, John	24	M	Farmer	26Ma01Gi
MCGINTY, James	20	M	Farmer	26Ma01Gi
MCLAUGHLIN, Margaret	18	F	None	26Ma01Gi
JONES, Catharine	20	F	None	26Ma01Gi
MCLAUGHLIN, Mary	16	F	None	26Ma01Gi
MCGAGHRAN, Betty	20	F	None	26Ma01Gi
WATERS, Neil	30	M	None	26Ma01Gi
Nancy	9	F	Child	26Ma01Gi
John	.06	M	Infant	26Ma01Gi
MCMULLIN, Darby	30	M	Farmer	26Ma01Gi
GOULD, Robert	19	M	Farmer	26Ma01Gi
LAFFERTY, Robert	23	M	Farmer	26Ma01Gi
CONNELL, Mary-Ann	17	F	Dressmaker	26Ma01Gi
Catty	14	F	Dressmaker	26Ma01Gi
GILLEN, Hannah	18	F	Dressmaker	26Ma01Gi
COLLINS, Biddy	20	F	Dressmaker	26Ma01Gi
THOMPSON, Alexander	37	M	Boatman	26Ma01Gi
REID, James	27	M	Slater	26Ma01Gi
DIFFY, John	28	M	Tailor	26Ma01Gi
Catherine	25	F	None	26Ma01Gi
John	.06	M	Infant	26Ma01Gi
Edward	4	M	Child	26Ma01Gi
OCONNOR, Terence	18	M	None	26Ma01Gi
MCGOWAN, James	17	M	None	26Ma01Gi
CLANCEY, James	22	M	None	26Ma01Gi
MCGOWAN, John	10	M	None	26Ma01Gi
CONNOLLY, Libby	16	F	None	26Ma01Gi
HARKIN, Daniel	36	M	None	26Ma01Gi
Eliza	34	F	None	26Ma01Gi
James	13	M	None	26Ma01Gi
Patrick	10	M	None	26Ma01Gi
Isabella	12	F	None	26Ma01Gi
John	7	M	Child	26Ma01Gi
Daniel	3	M	Child	26Ma01Gi
Ann-Maria	.06	F	Infant	26Ma01Gi
CARLAND, Sarah	22	F	None	26Ma01Gi
CONNOR, John	22	M	None	26Ma01Gi
SWEENEY, John	24	M	None	26Ma01Gi
LELAND, Patrick	18	M	None	26Ma01Gi
DAIVIR, John	21	M	None	26Ma01Gi
OCONNOR, Sally	20	F	None	26Ma01Gi
DOCKADY, Rose-Ann	22	F	None	26Ma01Gi
DEMPSEY, Mary	25	F	None	26Ma01Gi
CONNOR, William	.06	M	Infant	26Ma01Gi
MCCARD, Elizabeth	26	F	None	26Ma01Gi
MULLIGAN, Jane	19	F	None	26Ma01Gi
David	18	M	Farmer	26Ma01Gi
Ann	16	F	None	26Ma01Gi
Samuel	14	M	Farmer	26Ma01Gi
Eliza	12	F	None	26Ma01Gi
Ann	38	F	None	26Ma01Gi
MODDY, Robert	26	M	Farmer	26Ma01Gi
ENNON, Thomas	24	M	Joiner	26Ma01Gi
KNOX, John	23	M	None	26Ma01Gi
DOHIRT, George	19	M	None	26Ma01Gi
GILMORE, John	21	M	Fisherman	26Ma01Gi
MCNUTT, John	24	M	None	26Ma01Gi
Ester	28	F	None	26Ma01Gi
Ester	74	F	None	26Ma01Gi
BRADLEY, Mary	40	F	None	26Ma01Gi
GILLON, Mary	35	F	None	26Ma01Gi
Ann	11	F	None	26Ma01Gi
Henry	14	M	None	26Ma01Gi
MODDY, Mary	26	F	None	26Ma01Gi
Mary-Ann	4	F	Child	26Ma01Gi
Margaret	72	F	None	26Ma01Gi
John	70	M	None	26Ma01Gi
WALSH, Henry	20	M	None	26Ma01Gi
GOODY, John	17	M	Cooper	26Ma01Gi
OBRIEN, Sally	30	F	None	26Ma01Gi
Daniel	11	M	None	26Ma01Gi
Bennet	9	M	Child	26Ma01Gi
Michael	.06	M	Infant	26Ma01Gi
HUTCHINSON, Catharine	34	F	None	26Ma01Gi
Thomas	1	M	Child	26Ma01Gi
Martha	6	F	Child	26Ma01Gi
Mary	.09	F	Infant	26Ma01Gi
MCCONNELL, Mary	27	F	Dressmaker	26Ma01Gi
Joseph	20	M	None	26Ma01Gi
MCMULLEN, James	22	M	None	26Ma01Gi
CARLIN, James	21	M	None	26Ma01Gi
KERR, James	21	M	None	26Ma01Gi
BARR, Mary	23	F	None	26Ma01Gi
SWEENEY, Betty	21	F	None	26Ma01Gi
LAUGRIN, Caroline	19	F	None	26Ma01Gi
CLARREN, Betty	20	F	None	26Ma01Gi
RODGER, Francis	20	M	Baker	26Ma01Gi
TAYLOR, Francis	20	M	None	26Ma01Gi
TATE, Jane	18	F	None	26Ma01Gi
MCCLELLAND, Jane	12	F	None	26Ma01Gi
John	10	M	None	26Ma01Gi
Mary-Ann	8	F	Child	26Ma01Gi
Thomas	6	M	Child	26Ma01Gi
CAMPBELL, John	24	M	None	26Ma01Gi
MCDEVIR, Robert	20	M	None	26Ma01Gi
DIFFIN, Edward	20	M	None	26Ma01Gi
BURK, Edward	24	M	None	26Ma01Gi
SHEILDS, Charles	28	M	Farmer	26Ma01Gi
Mary	30	F	None	26Ma01Gi
HAMILTON, James	32	M	Blacksmith	26Ma01Gi
Eliza	26	F	None	26Ma01Gi
RAMSAY, Eliza	27	F	None	26Ma01Gi
CHURCH, Mary	18	F	Milliner	26Ma01Gi
DOWNS, Eliza	20	F	None	26Ma01Gi
LYNCH, John	22	M	None	26Ma01Gi
DOWNS, Samuel	19	M	None	26Ma01Gi
HUTCHINSON, James	18	M	None	26Ma01Gi
KILLGREW, William	20	M	None	26Ma01Gi
HISLET, William	21	M	None	26Ma01Gi
Eleanor	16	F	None	26Ma01Gi
MCLENNAN, Sally	16	F	None	26Ma01Gi
YOUNG, Thomas	47	M	Farmer	26Ma01Gi
Margaret	35	F	None	26Ma01Gi
John	19	M	None	26Ma01Gi
Ann	14	F	None	26Ma01Gi
William	7	M	Child	26Ma01Gi
Robert	5	M	Child	26Ma01Gi
Margaret	2	F	Child	26Ma01Gi
Thomas	.06	M	Infant	26Ma01Gi
MCFARLANE, Thomas	20	M	None	26Ma01Gi
MCLAUGHLIN, Hugh	18	M	Blacksmith	26Ma01Gi
MCCAULEY, William	20	M	None	26Ma01Gi
CAMPBELL, Alexander	35	M	Farmer	26Ma01Gi
MORRISON, Robert	21	M	Clerk	26Ma01Gi
LOUGHHEAD, Archy	18	M	None	26Ma01Gi

BRITANNIA 28 MAY 1849

From Liverpool

NAMES OF PASSENGERS	AGE	SEX	OCCUPATIONS	DATE PORT SHIP
LAWSON, Mary	30	F	Spinster	28Ma02Hm
OCONNELL, James	40	M	Farmer	28Ma02Hm
Danl.	25	M	Farmer	28Ma02Hm
NEILAN, Thomas	38	M	Farmer	28Ma02Hm
James	38	M	Farmer	28Ma02Hm
DRIVER, Thomas	35	M	Farmer	28Ma02Hm
HANNAY, George	24	M	Carpenter	28Ma02Hm
FORD, Catharine	34	F	Nurse	28Ma02Hm
FIELDING, William	24	M	Blacksmith	28Ma02Hm
Ann	24	F	Unknown	28Ma02Hm
Henry	.00	M	Infant	28Ma02Hm
KENRICK, Agnes	24	F	Unknown	28Ma02Hm
BOWMAN, Jane	24	F	Unknown	28Ma02Hm
FARNEY, Solomon	56	M	Farmer	28Ma02Hm
U (W)	63	F	Unknown	28Ma02Hm
George	20	M	Fsvnt	28Ma02Hm
BRADLEY, Anne	16	F	Servant	28Ma02Hm
NAILOR, Saml.	40	M	Shoemaker	28Ma02Hm
KAITHBY, George	28	M	Shoemaker	28Ma02Hm
STEPHENSON, Joseph	42	M	Goldsmith	28Ma02Hm
U (W)	42	F	Unknown	28Ma02Hm
William	11	M	Unknown	28Ma02Hm
HOTWILL, U	25	F	Unknown	28Ma02Hm
Mary	.00	F	Infant	28Ma02Hm
HOWELL, William	30	M	Plumber	28Ma02Hm
Mary-Ann	35	F	Unknown	28Ma02Hm
William	2	M	Child	28Ma02Hm
Hannah	.00	F	Infant	28Ma02Hm
LOBEY, William	25	M	Laborer	28Ma02Hm
Caroline	37	F	Unknown	28Ma02Hm
KELLY, Catharine	23	F	Unknown	28Ma02Hm
Rose	3	F	Child	28Ma02Hm
LLOYD, Edward	44	M	Farmer	28Ma02Hm
NICHOLS, George	22	M	Farmer	28Ma02Hm
BUSHBY, George	17	M	Servant	28Ma02Hm
NICHOLS, Fred	12	M	Servant	28Ma02Hm
Mary	21	F	Servant	28Ma02Hm
KERR, Mary	22	F	Servant	28Ma02Hm
Henry	.00	M	Infant	28Ma02Hm
NICHOLS, Jerry	.00	M	Infant	28Ma02Hm
KENNEDY, Michael	30	M	Tinsmith	28Ma02Hm
Matt.	19	M	Tinsmith	28Ma02Hm
Edward	18	M	Tinsmith	28Ma02Hm
Ellen	50	F	Unknown	28Ma02Hm
Anne	23	F	Seamstress	28Ma02Hm
HENDERSON, Thomas	40	M	Farmer	28Ma02Hm
MCCREANER, Cath.	20	F	Servant	28Ma02Hm
WATTS, James	26	M	Barber	28Ma02Hm
COSBEY, Matthew	26	M	Hatter	28Ma02Hm
STOREY, Miles	27	M	Joiner	28Ma02Hm
Mary	27	F	Unknown	28Ma02Hm
William	1	M	Child	28Ma02Hm
FINEGAN, Betty	20	F	Servant	28Ma02Hm
COYLE, Catherine	20	F	Seamstress	28Ma02Hm
Thomas	18	M	Farmer	28Ma02Hm
ROONEY, Francis	22	M	Farmer	28Ma02Hm
MCGIVERN, Michl.	20	M	Farmer	28Ma02Hm
MARTIN, John	47	M	Farmer	28Ma02Hm
Mary	46	F	Unknown	28Ma02Hm
Edward	22	M	Servant	28Ma02Hm
John	20	M	Servant	28Ma02Hm
Stephen	18	M	Servant	28Ma02Hm
Mary	5	F	Child	28Ma02Hm
James	.00	M	Infant	28Ma02Hm
BRIEN, Wm.	20	M	Laborer	28Ma02Hm

NAMES OF PASSENGERS	AGE	SEX	OCCUPATIONS	DATE PORT SHIP
BRIEN, Thomas	20	M	Laborer	28Ma02Hm
BRYNE, Thomas	35	M	Laborer	28Ma02Hm
Edward	17	M	Laborer	28Ma02Hm
KEOGH, James	17	M	Laborer	28Ma02Hm
BRIEN, David	26	M	Laborer	28Ma02Hm
Mary	25	F	Unknown	28Ma02Hm
Mary	26	F	Unknown	28Ma02Hm
BEHAN, Michael	25	M	Farmer	28Ma02Hm
HORE, Edward	26	M	Farmer	28Ma02Hm
FARRELL, Eliza	50	F	Unknown	28Ma02Hm
MCCOYNE, William	20	M	Laborer	28Ma02Hm
KELLY, Johanna	56	F	Unknown	28Ma02Hm
LACEY, James	19	M	Servant	28Ma02Hm
HANNAY, Sarah	29	F	Nurse	28Ma02Hm
TOBIN, Catharine	18	F	Servant	28Ma02Hm
WALSH, Catharine	20	F	Seamstress	28Ma02Hm
BLANE, John	50	M	Farmer	28Ma02Hm
ROBINSON, William	23	M	Farmer	28Ma02Hm
ADSON, Richard	30	M	Farmer	28Ma02Hm
Betsey	26	F	Unknown	28Ma02Hm
LEAREY, John	26	M	Laborer	28Ma02Hm
Julia	22	F	Unknown	28Ma02Hm
HORAN, William	27	M	Cooper	28Ma02Hm
LEAREY, David	.00	M	Infant	28Ma02Hm
CURRAN, Hugh	20	M	Fsvnt	28Ma02Hm
SHERIDAN, Catharine	19	F	Fsvnt	28Ma02Hm
RICHES, John	22	M	Fsvnt	28Ma02Hm
James	20	M	Fsvnt	28Ma02Hm
FOUNTAIN, William	25	M	Fsvnt	28Ma02Hm
MURRAY, Charles	40	M	Carpenter	28Ma02Hm
Mary	36	F	Unknown	28Ma02Hm
Wm.	26	M	Carpenter	28Ma02Hm
John	23	M	Carpenter	28Ma02Hm
John	3	M	Child	28Ma02Hm
John	.00	M	Infant	28Ma02Hm
Charles	.00	M	Infant	28Ma02Hm
WALSH, Mary	20	F	Seamstress	28Ma02Hm
KERWIN, John	23	M	Servant	28Ma02Hm
TIERNAN, Michl.	19	M	Servant	28Ma02Hm
KELLY, William	19	M	Servant	28Ma02Hm
MCSORLAND, Susan	19	F	Seamstress	28Ma02Hm
FETHERSTONE, Thomas	53	M	Farmer	28Ma02Hm
Bridget	36	F	Unknown	28Ma02Hm
Thomas	18	M	Unknown	28Ma02Hm
Mary	16	F	Unknown	28Ma02Hm
Patrick	13	M	Unknown	28Ma02Hm
HOGAN, Chris	24	M	Blacksmith	28Ma02Hm
KING, Ellen	24	F	Servant	28Ma02Hm
DOOLAN, Michael	22	M	Tailor	28Ma02Hm
CARTWRIGHT, Benjamin	30	M	Stctr	28Ma02Hm
Jane	20	F	Unknown	28Ma02Hm
AIGAN, Owen	22	M	Mason	28Ma02Hm
HERCHENLEIGH, Pat	20	M	Fsvnt	28Ma02Hm
DILLON, Thomas	16	M	Fsvnt	28Ma02Hm
RAFFERTY, Michl.	12	M	Unknown	28Ma02Hm
AIGAN, Pat	10	M	Unknown	28Ma02Hm
BURKE, John	30	M	Laborer	28Ma02Hm
Thomas	25	M	Laborer	28Ma02Hm
COSTELLO, Danl.	35	M	Laborer	28Ma02Hm
GLENNON, Margt.	21	F	Seamstress	28Ma02Hm
POMON, Michl.	18	M	Laborer	28Ma02Hm
JENNINGS, Mary	21	F	Servant	28Ma02Hm
SHEIN, Cathr.	40	F	Servant	28Ma02Hm
Cathr.	10	F	Servant	28Ma02Hm
BURNS, Michl.	35	M	Farmer	28Ma02Hm
IRELAND, Joseph	50	M	Farmer	28Ma02Hm
U (W)	50	F	Unknown	28Ma02Hm
George	18	M	Fsvnt	28Ma02Hm
John	16	M	Fsvnt	28Ma02Hm
Emily	10	F	Fsvnt	28Ma02Hm
Richd.	8	M	Child	28Ma02Hm
SPINSON, Richd.	41	M	Bookmaker	28Ma02Hm
RICHARDSON, Walter	31	M	Shoemaker	28Ma02Hm
HOPKINS, John	41	M	Glsbr	28Ma02Hm
MCCABE, Margt.	29	F	Servant	28Ma02Hm

NAMES OF PASSENGERS	AGE	SEX	OCCUPATIONS	DATE PORT SHIP
MCCABE, James	19	M	Farmer	28Ma02Hm
ONEIL, Mary-Ann	19	F	Seamstress	28Ma02Hm
MANAHAN, Thos.	22	M	Laborer	28Ma02Hm
MULLIGAN, Ellen	20	F	Servant	28Ma02Hm
CONNOLLY, Phillip	00	M	Laborer	28Ma02Hm
SMITH, William	18	M	Tailor	28Ma02Hm
MASON, Joseph	60	M	Carver	28Ma02Hm
Jane	60	F	Unknown	28Ma02Hm
Eliza	22	F	Unknown	28Ma02Hm
WATERS, Bridget	40	F	Nurse	28Ma02Hm
SMITH, George	30	M	Turner	28Ma02Hm
DOUGHERTY, James	22	M	Laborer	28Ma02Hm
MARTIN, Jacob	28	M	Laborer	28Ma02Hm
Sarah	16	F	Unknown	28Ma02Hm
STACEY, John	35	M	Blacksmith	28Ma02Hm
Wm.	11	M	Unknown	28Ma02Hm
Francis	16	M	Unknown	28Ma02Hm
MEANEY, Ann	22	F	Servant	28Ma02Hm
SEATON, Thos.	18	M	Fsvnt	28Ma02Hm
Adam	20	M	Servant	28Ma02Hm
HENRY, James	18	M	Servant	28Ma02Hm
IRVEN, Chas.	18	M	Servant	28Ma02Hm
ELVERY, Stewart	18	M	Servant	28Ma02Hm
Sarah-Ann	20	F	Seamstress	28Ma02Hm
MCKINSIE, Wm.	30	M	Barber	28Ma02Hm
FLEMING, Thomas	20	M	Mason	28Ma02Hm
BURKE, James	20	M	Carpenter	28Ma02Hm
MADDEN, John	20	M	Rope Maker	28Ma02Hm
HEFFORIN, Martin	35	M	Joiner	28Ma02Hm
BARRETT, Maria	25	F	Seamstress	28Ma02Hm
Mathew	45	M	Farmer	28Ma02Hm
Mary	2	F	Child	28Ma02Hm
John	.00	M	Infant	28Ma02Hm
HAYS, Mary	25	F	Servant	28Ma02Hm
WALSH, Cre.	28	F	Servant	28Ma02Hm
WINNER, Joseph	25	M	Turner	28Ma02Hm
Wm.	12	M	Unknown	28Ma02Hm
MORISON, John	26	M	Cooper	28Ma02Hm
MCGINNESS, Alley	20	F	Servant	28Ma02Hm
CARROLL, Wm.	25	M	Carpenter	28Ma02Hm
FIMESSY, Mary	25	F	House Maid	28Ma02Hm
BURNS, Mary	16	F	House Maid	28Ma02Hm
Nancy	14	F	House Maid	28Ma02Hm
Bridget	14	F	House Maid	28Ma02Hm
SHEERLY, Mary	20	F	House Maid	28Ma02Hm
PARNELL, Saml.	20	M	Spinner	28Ma02Hm
CORRIGAN, Patk.	25	M	Laborer	28Ma02Hm
U (W)	25	F	Unknown	28Ma02Hm
Mary	.00	F	Infant	28Ma02Hm
COOPER, Ellen	20	F	House Maid	28Ma02Hm
Mary-Jane	20	F	House Maid	28Ma02Hm
LOWFORK, U-Mrs.	50	F	House Maid	28Ma02Hm
Ellen	20	F	House Maid	28Ma02Hm
Susanah	19	F	House Maid	28Ma02Hm
LAWCOCK, Mary	17	F	House Maid	28Ma02Hm
Ann	15	F	Unknown	28Ma02Hm
Jane	7	F	Child	28Ma02Hm
KINNEY, Martin	48	M	Farmer	28Ma02Hm
Ann	46	F	Unknown	28Ma02Hm
Maurice	22	M	Farmer	28Ma02Hm
.ARKIN, Cathr.	22	F	Unknown	28Ma02Hm
:ELLY, Isabella	22	F	Seamstress	28Ma02Hm
OBBIN, James	25	M	Farmer	28Ma02Hm
RADY, Michl.	25	M	Farmer	28Ma02Hm
MCGAVIN, Robt.	20	M	Fsvnt	28Ma02Hm
ORISTER, Eliza	18	F	House Maid	28Ma02Hm
OODARD, Wm.	24	M	Farmer	28Ma02Hm
LEESON, Thos.	21	M	Farmer	28Ma02Hm
LACKEY, Thos.	21	M	Blacksmith	28Ma02Hm
ATTON, Thos.	20	M	Tailor	28Ma02Hm
YAN, Mathew	20	M	Brick Maker	28Ma02Hm
WYRE, Judy	18	F	Seamstress	28Ma02Hm
ENNEDY, John	19	M	Laborer	28Ma02Hm
CANALLY, Robert	19	M	Laborer	28Ma02Hm
ARTIN, Thos.	20	M	Laborer	28Ma02Hm
SMITH, Thos.	20	M	Laborer	28Ma02Hm
MCERIFF, Eliza	19	F	House Maid	28Ma02Hm
MAHER, John	30	M	Farmer	28Ma02Hm
Patk.	27	M	Farmer	28Ma02Hm
Timothy	25	M	Farmer	28Ma02Hm
BOHIN, Wm.	28	M	Farmer	28Ma02Hm
James	22	M	Farmer	28Ma02Hm
Tha.	26	M	Farmer	28Ma02Hm
U-Mrs.	25	F	Unknown	28Ma02Hm
James	2	M	Child	28Ma02Hm
James	23	M	Laborer	28Ma02Hm
DWYRE, Thos.	24	M	Cooper	28Ma02Hm
BOHIN, Danl.	.00	M	Infant	28Ma02Hm
RYAN, Thos.	25	M	Molder	28Ma02Hm
TRACEY, Daniel	25	M	Molder	28Ma02Hm
CASEY, Thos.	24	M	Builder	28Ma02Hm
LAHEY, Bridget	18	F	House Maid	28Ma02Hm
RYAN, Margt.	18	F	House Maid	28Ma02Hm
CARROLL, Mary	17	F	House Maid	28Ma02Hm
WALKER, Mary	18	F	House Maid	28Ma02Hm
BOHIN, Margt.	22	F	House Maid	28Ma02Hm
MOONEY, Michl.	24	M	Laborer	28Ma02Hm
CONNER, James	28	M	Laborer	28Ma02Hm
KIGAN, Michl.	30	M	Laborer	28Ma02Hm
Ann	20	F	Seamstress	28Ma02Hm
FISHWICK, Richd.	25	M	Farmer	28Ma02Hm
U (W)	25	F	Unknown	28Ma02Hm
MCCLAIN, Robt.	20	M	Servant	28Ma02Hm
MCDONALD, Patk.	29	M	Laborer	28Ma02Hm
RYANS, Thos.	35	M	Laborer	28Ma02Hm
GIFFONS, Patk.	23	M	Laborer	28Ma02Hm
Ann	19	F	Unknown	28Ma02Hm
William	2	M	Child	28Ma02Hm
Mary-Ann	.00	F	Infant	28Ma02Hm
SHEATY, Dennis	27	M	Farmer	28Ma02Hm
Mary	27	F	Unknown	28Ma02Hm
John	2	M	Child	28Ma02Hm
Thomas	.00	M	Infant	28Ma02Hm
HOOPER, James	23	M	Laborer	28Ma02Hm
EARLEY, Owen	21	M	Laborer	28Ma02Hm
Cathr.	20	F	Unknown	28Ma02Hm
MCGUIRE, John	20	M	Tailor	28Ma02Hm
LYONS, Peter	30	M	Barber	28Ma02Hm
Ann	28	F	Seamstress	28Ma02Hm
Patk.	5	M	Child	28Ma02Hm
James	3	M	Child	28Ma02Hm
FARRELL, Margt.	19	F	Servant	28Ma02Hm
Cathr.	20	F	Servant	28Ma02Hm
HEFFERNAN, Michl.	24	M	Brick Maker	28Ma02Hm
BENSON, James	40	M	Brick Maker	28Ma02Hm
DOYLE, James	56	M	Stctr	28Ma02Hm
Michl.	12	M	None	28Ma02Hm
Alexr.	18	M	None	28Ma02Hm
DUGGAN, James	28	M	Fsvnt	28Ma02Hm
DOYLE, Ann	26	F	Seamstress	28Ma02Hm
CLOYNE, Ann	21	F	Seamstress	28Ma02Hm
DUGHAM, Anne	.00	F	Infant	28Ma02Hm
DALTON, Richd.	18	M	Tailor	28Ma02Hm
FLANNAGAN, John	30	M	Barber	28Ma02Hm
DOUGHERTY, John	30	M	Carpenter	28Ma02Hm
DUFFY, Francis	30	M	Unknown	28Ma02Hm
CALDWELL, Dominick	20	M	Cooper	28Ma02Hm
CASKER, Thos.	27	M	Farmer	28Ma02Hm
SHIRE, Henry	25	M	Farmer	28Ma02Hm
Danl.	23	M	Farmer	28Ma02Hm
Bridget	20	F	None	28Ma02Hm
SULLIVAN, John	22	M	Laborer	28Ma02Hm
Margt.	18	F	Unknown	28Ma02Hm
CONNELL, Ellen	24	F	Seamstress	28Ma02Hm
KELLY, John	33	M	Farmer	28Ma02Hm

CATHERINE 28 MAY 1849

From Liverpool

NAMES OF PASSENGERS	AGE	SEX	OCCUPATIONS	DATE PORT SHIP
HESTER, Martin	40	M	Laborer	28Ma02Hn
Th--	5	M	Child	28Ma02Hn
Bridget	60	F	Unknown	28Ma02Hn
BANNING, Thomas	30	M	Laborer	28Ma02Hn
MULLEN, Mary	25	F	Unknown	28Ma02Hn
CLARKE, Jane	40	F	Unknown	28Ma02Hn
READ, Mathies	22	M	Servant	28Ma02Hn
WATERS, Margaret	24	F	Servant	28Ma02Hn
COSGROVE, Joseph	22	M	Laborer	28Ma02Hn
COWLEY, Barnard	20	M	Laborer	28Ma02Hn
MARIN, Judy	20	F	Servant	28Ma02Hn
Margaret	18	F	Servant	28Ma02Hn
GARTLING, Sarah	18	F	Servant	28Ma02Hn
QUIGLEY, Mary	23	F	Servant	28Ma02Hn
RYAN, Hannah	20	F	Servant	28Ma02Hn
Ann	23	F	Servant	28Ma02Hn
Mary	22	F	Servant	28Ma02Hn
Dennis	20	M	Laborer	28Ma02Hn
CLIFFORD, Partrick	26	M	Tailor	28Ma02Hn
Daniel	24	M	Laborer	28Ma02Hn
WOOD, Mary	18	F	Servant	28Ma02Hn
OCONNOR, James	18	M	Shoemaker	28Ma02Hn
John	26	M	Shoemaker	28Ma02Hn
MONAGHAN, John	24	M	Laborer	28Ma02Hn
Nancy	30	F	Unknown	28Ma02Hn
REISTON, John	21	M	Laborer	28Ma02Hn
Bridget	28	F	Laborer	28Ma02Hn
STANKARD, William	32	M	Laborer	28Ma02Hn
Ellen	26	F	None	28Ma02Hn
NAVIN, Bridget	20	F	Servant	28Ma02Hn
MCMAN, Michael	20	M	Laborer	28Ma02Hn
FITZGERALD, Michael	21	M	Laborer	28Ma02Hn
DONOHUE, Henry	30	M	Laborer	28Ma02Hn
MEINON, Malachi	18	M	Laborer	28Ma02Hn
HORRAN, Martin	20	M	Laborer	28Ma02Hn
MCGOVERAN, Biddy	18	F	Servant	28Ma02Hn
Mary	16	F	Servant	28Ma02Hn
ROOKE, Ann	30	F	Servant	28Ma02Hn
DEGNIN, Domnick	22	M	Laborer	28Ma02Hn
Catherine	20	F	None	28Ma02Hn
FOX, Patrick	40	M	Laborer	28Ma02Hn
Eliza	40	F	None	28Ma02Hn
Catherine	13	F	Servant	28Ma02Hn
Arthur	10	M	Child	28Ma02Hn
Robert	8	M	Child	28Ma02Hn
Margaret	00	F	Child	28Ma02Hn
Emily	.00	F	Infant	28Ma02Hn
Catharine	12	F	None	28Ma02Hn
Sarah	10	F	Child	28Ma02Hn
SENNOT, John	40	M	Laborer	28Ma02Hn
DOYLE, Laurence	30	M	Miner	28Ma02Hn
BYRNE, James	42	M	Laborer	28Ma02Hn
Elizabeth	33	F	None	28Ma02Hn
James	3	M	Child	28Ma02Hn
Grace	.00	F	Infant	28Ma02Hn
MOONEY, Catherine	23	F	Servant	28Ma02Hn
Mary	20	F	Servant	28Ma02Hn
CLARKE, Miles	24	M	Clerk	28Ma02Hn
AILEY, John	24	M	Laborer	28Ma02Hn
MCREDMOND, Michael	19	M	Laborer	28Ma02Hn
LENNON, Simon	25	M	Farmer	28Ma02Hn
Edward	20	M	Farmer	28Ma02Hn
CARR, Catherine	16	F	Servant	28Ma02Hn
GREEN, Mary	17	F	Servant	28Ma02Hn
CARR, James	30	M	Laborer	28Ma02Hn
TROUS, Rebecca	22	F	Dressmaker	28Ma02Hn
LEONARD, Michael	24	M	Laborer	28Ma02Hn
RILEY, Thomas	25	M	Laborer	28Ma02Hn
CHESHIRE, John	25	M	Laborer	28Ma02Hn
KEARY, Timothy	18	M	Laborer	28Ma02Hn
Mary	23	F	None	28Ma02Hn
MEARA, Catherine	17	F	Servant	28Ma02Hn
REARDON, Rody	27	M	Laborer	28Ma02Hn
Dennis	17	M	Laborer	28Ma02Hn
RIELY, Mary	20	F	Servant	28Ma02Hn
Edward	22	M	Laborer	28Ma02Hn
PATTISON, Ellen	13	F	Servant	28Ma02Hn
Patrick	21	M	Laborer	28Ma02Hn
HIGGENS, Stephen	23	M	Laborer	28Ma02Hn
CONDRY, Merty	22	M	Laborer	28Ma02Hn
GILMOUR, Ann	22	F	Servant	28Ma02Hn
THOMAS, William	49	M	Miner	28Ma02Hn
BRENNAN, Michael	32	M	Miner	28Ma02Hn
JOHNSTON, Margret	20	F	Servant	28Ma02Hn
MCGUIRE, Mary	18	F	Servant	28Ma02Hn
MEHAN, Margaret	18	F	Servant	28Ma02Hn
Mary	20	F	Servant	28Ma02Hn
DULAN, Fanny	14	F	Servant	28Ma02Hn
MCCORMICK, Bryan	48	M	Farmer	28Ma02Hn
Rose	26	F	Nurse	28Ma02Hn
KENNEDY, James	16	M	Laborer	28Ma02Hn
MOORE, Michael	19	M	Laborer	28Ma02Hn
CASEY, Michael	26	M	Laborer	28Ma02Hn
MARY, Barnard	21	M	Laborer	28Ma02Hn
FEHY, Archibald	29	M	Blacksmith	28Ma02Hn
Rosaly	27	F	None	28Ma02Hn
DIFLEY, Mary	35	F	Servant	28Ma02Hn
DILLON, Mary	30	F	Servant	28Ma02Hn
HOLOHAN, John	30	M	Laborer	28Ma02Hn
MURPHY, Timothy	25	M	Laborer	28Ma02Hn
RYAN, Mary	27	F	Servant	28Ma02Hn
SHORTLE, Mary	20	F	Servant	28Ma02Hn
PHILLIPS, Mary	30	F	Dressmaker	28Ma02Hn
TRYNAN, Margaret	26	F	Servant	28Ma02Hn
LYNCH, Mary	14	F	Servant	28Ma02Hn
Ann	10	F	Servant	28Ma02Hn
Peter	5	M	Child	28Ma02Hn
Timothy	43	M	Laborer	28Ma02Hn
Bridget	36	F	None	28Ma02Hn
Michael	13	M	Laborer	28Ma02Hn
Thomas	17	M	Laborer	28Ma02Hn
John	21	M	Laborer	28Ma02Hn
Timothy	7	M	Child	28Ma02Hn
Robert	2	M	Child	28Ma02Hn
MOORE, Robert	56	M	Farmer	28Ma02Hn
HAYS, Michael	29	M	Farmer	28Ma02Hn
MYLES, Patrick	27	M	Farmer	28Ma02Hn
WELCH, Thomas	30	M	Farmer	28Ma02Hn
WALIN, Batt	26	M	Laborer	28Ma02Hn
DURALL, Patrick	30	M	Clerk	28Ma02Hn
DWYER, John	30	M	Laborer	28Ma02Hn
Pat	25	M	Laborer	28Ma02Hn
GLEASON, Timothy	40	M	Laborer	28Ma02Hn
MILLER, Alexander	28	M	Laborer	28Ma02Hn
WOOD, Ann	19	F	Servant	28Ma02Hn
Margaret	24	F	Servant	28Ma02Hn
Jane	16	F	Servant	28Ma02Hn
Ann	19	F	Servant	28Ma02Hn
Mary	15	F	Servant	28Ma02Hn
WILSON, John	22	M	Farmer	28Ma02Hn
Eliza	18	F	None	28Ma02Hn
GILLON, Thomas	21	M	Bookkeeper	28Ma02Hn
Bernard	19	M	Farmer	28Ma02Hn
Mary	16	F	Servant	28Ma02Hn
Ann	11	F	Servant	28Ma02Hn
CARROLL, Pat.	30	M	Farmer	28Ma02Hn
Mary	7	F	Child	28Ma02Hn
Anthony	4	M	Child	28Ma02Hn
REYNOLDS, Ann	11	F	None	28Ma02Hn
DONOHUE, Pat.	22	M	Farmer	28Ma02Hn

NAMES OF PASSENGERS	AGE	SEX	OCCUPATIONS	DATE PORT SHIP
HECTOR, Pat.	21	M	Farmer	28Ma02Hn
GUNNAN, John	26	M	Farmer	28Ma02Hn
KENNOR, Pat.	26	M	Farmer	28Ma02Hn
Mary	18	F	None	28Ma02Hn
WILLIAMS, Ann	19	F	Servant	28Ma02Hn
JUSTINGS, Eliza	36	F	Servant	28Ma02Hn
MCGULLEN, Catherine	19	F	Servant	28Ma02Hn
BRADY, Rose	20	F	Servant	28Ma02Hn
HINDS, Auty	21	F	Servant	28Ma02Hn
PRICE, Mary	18	F	Servant	28Ma02Hn
KEHOE, Ellen	20	F	Servant	28Ma02Hn
FARRELL, Thomas	20	M	Blacksmith	28Ma02Hn
MARDELL, Nicholas	23	M	Laborer	28Ma02Hn
CLEAHY, Pat.	22	M	Laborer	28Ma02Hn
GALVIN, Catherine	35	F	None	28Ma02Hn
James	13	M	Unknown	28Ma02Hn
Elizabeth	11	F	Unknown	28Ma02Hn
Peter	9	M	Child	28Ma02Hn
Mary	7	F	Child	28Ma02Hn
Biddy	5	F	Child	28Ma02Hn
Ann	2	F	Child	28Ma02Hn
FLEMING, John	23	M	Laborer	28Ma02Hn
MCFADDEN, James	18	M	Laborer	28Ma02Hn
FAHEY, Michael	50	M	Farmer	28Ma02Hn
Julia	40	F	None	28Ma02Hn
William	12	M	Farmer	28Ma02Hn
LEESON, Margaret	25	F	Dressmaker	28Ma02Hn
Michael	5	M	Child	28Ma02Hn
James	3	M	Child	28Ma02Hn
Eliza	2	F	Child	28Ma02Hn
Margaret	.00	F	Infant	28Ma02Hn
NORTON, Pat.	18	M	Laborer	28Ma02Hn
Michael	12	M	Laborer	28Ma02Hn
MURRAY, Julia	40	F	Grocer	28Ma02Hn
Ann	23	F	Grocer	28Ma02Hn
Mary	19	F	Servant	28Ma02Hn
Pat.	7	M	Child	28Ma02Hn
GARRAHER, Mary	19	F	Servant	28Ma02Hn
MCSHANE, Henry	20	M	Valet	28Ma02Hn
WILSON, Mary	25	F	None	28Ma02Hn
William	21	M	Groom	28Ma02Hn
MURRAY, Rose	20	F	Servant	28Ma02Hn
REYNOLDS, Rose	16	F	Servant	28Ma02Hn
GRADY, Mary	20	F	Servant	28Ma02Hn
QUINN, Biddy	18	F	Servant	28Ma02Hn
CONCANNON, Michael	28	M	Waiter	28Ma02Hn
SMYTH, Laurence	20	M	Servant	28Ma02Hn
SINGLETON, Peter	19	M	Laborer	28Ma02Hn
HEGAN, Margaret	20	F	Servant	28Ma02Hn

YORKTOWN 28 MAY 1849

From London

NAMES OF PASSENGERS	AGE	SEX	OCCUPATIONS	DATE PORT SHIP
GERSON, Julius	24	M	Merchant	28Ma13Hs
CHATFIELD, Hugh	24	M	Surveyor	28Ma13Hs
RANKIN, Francis	43	M	Surgeon	28Ma13Hs
Ann	40	F	None	28Ma13Hs
CHILD, Henry	51	M	Goldsmith	28Ma13Hs
Allice	28	F	None	28Ma13Hs
FORESYTH, Jane	32	F	None	28Ma13Hs
BYRNE, Edmund	55	M	Surgeon	28Ma13Hs
Mary	54	F	None	28Ma13Hs
WOODHAM, James	47	M	Farmer	28Ma13Hs
Sarah	46	F	None	28Ma13Hs
Sarah	18	F	None	28Ma13Hs
Mary	15	F	None	28Ma13Hs
David	4	M	Child	28Ma13Hs
KATTE, Isabella	41	F	None	28Ma13Hs
KATTE, Walter	18	M	Engineer	28Ma13Hs
STROUD, Robert	35	M	Grocer	28Ma13Hs
Sarah	30	F	None	28Ma13Hs
Sarah	4	F	Child	28Ma13Hs
Kate	2	F	Child	28Ma13Hs
Robert	.00	M	Infant	28Ma13Hs
CASE, William	28	M	Chtmr	28Ma13Hs
Emma	27	F	None	28Ma13Hs
LORD, Thomas	22	M	Mariner	28Ma13Hs
Mary	22	F	None	28Ma13Hs
BROOKS, George	29	M	Carpenter	28Ma13Hs
Ann	27	F	None	28Ma13Hs
George	.00	M	Infant	28Ma13Hs
RANDALL, Henry	27	M	Tinman	28Ma13Hs
Harriet	36	F	None	28Ma13Hs
FARMER, Henry	22	M	Porter	28Ma13Hs
BOYLE, Robert	34	M	Unknown	28Ma13Hs
FREENA, John	47	M	Tinman	28Ma13Hs
Jane	48	F	None	28Ma13Hs
HORE, Henry	35	M	Porter	28Ma13Hs
Joseph	24	M	Porter	28Ma13Hs
Elisabeth	48	F	Dressmaker	28Ma13Hs
GILLIARD, Pullen	33	M	Builder	28Ma13Hs
Susan	32	F	None	28Ma13Hs
Nathaniel	3	M	Child	28Ma13Hs
Sylvanus	35	M	Unknown	28Ma13Hs
Elisabeth	28	F	None	28Ma13Hs
Peggy	50	F	Servant	28Ma13Hs
PEPPER, James	33	M	Goldbeater	28Ma13Hs
ELLISON, Thomas	22	M	Mason	28Ma13Hs
CARPENTER, Nicholas	54	M	Bookseller	28Ma13Hs
Sarah	58	F	None	28Ma13Hs
BAILEY, William	35	M	Laborer	28Ma13Hs
GREATBACK, Joseph	22	M	Laborer	28Ma13Hs
GREEN, Mary	22	M	Laborer	28Ma13Hs
MONK, John	20	M	Laborer	28Ma13Hs
WELCH, Phillip	21	M	Laborer	28Ma13Hs
JAMES, Harriet	36	F	Artist	28Ma13Hs
Emily	15	F	None	28Ma13Hs
Lucy	10	F	Child	28Ma13Hs
Julia	9	F	Child	28Ma13Hs
Allice	8	F	Child	28Ma13Hs
Francis	11	M	None	28Ma13Hs
CHATFIELD, Thomas	33	M	Brazier	28Ma13Hs
Jane	33	F	None	28Ma13Hs
Jane	10	F	Child	28Ma13Hs
Henry	3	M	Child	28Ma13Hs
William	.00	M	Infant	28Ma13Hs
PEARD, William	27	M	Carpenter	28Ma13Hs
Harriet	30	F	None	28Ma13Hs
Grace	19	F	None	28Ma13Hs
MILES, Thomas	42	M	Unknown	28Ma13Hs
Eliza	36	F	None	28Ma13Hs
Thomas	7	M	Child	28Ma13Hs
Peter	6	M	Child	28Ma13Hs
Richard	3	M	Child	28Ma13Hs
George	1	M	Child	28Ma13Hs
BOYLE, William	64	M	Unknown	28Ma13Hs
Eliza	63	F	None	28Ma13Hs
MACAVOY, John	34	M	Farmer	28Ma13Hs
Margaret	31	F	None	28Ma13Hs
Henry	1	M	Child	28Ma13Hs
LUCKER, Thomas	39	M	Carpenter	28Ma13Hs
WILLIAMS, Joseph	45	M	Weaver	28Ma13Hs
Charles	12	M	Weaver	28Ma13Hs
LEGGETT, Charlotte	26	F	None	28Ma13Hs
George	00	M	Infant	28Ma13Hs
HITCHCOCK, James	36	M	Farmer	28Ma13Hs
Eliza	35	F	None	28Ma13Hs
Daniel	16	M	Unknown	28Ma13Hs
John	8	M	Child	28Ma13Hs
Thomas	6	M	Child	28Ma13Hs
James	2	M	Child	28Ma13Hs
Martha	.00	F	Infant	28Ma13Hs
BLIZARD, Thomas	17	M	Laborer	28Ma13Hs

NAMES OF PASSENGERS	AGE	SEX	OCCUPATIONS	DATE PORT SHIP
MAY, Mary	46	F	Dressmaker	28Ma13Hs
REED, Sarah	45	F	Dressmaker	28Ma13Hs
SIMPKINS, Henry	45	M	Laborer	28Ma13Hs
Jane	44	F	None	28Ma13Hs
George	6	M	Child	28Ma13Hs
Mark	5	M	Child	28Ma13Hs
Emma	3	F	Child	28Ma13Hs
Thomas	.00	M	Infant	28Ma13Hs
ANGLE, Isaac	27	M	Laborer	28Ma13Hs
CARTER, Henry	27	M	Laborer	28Ma13Hs
Hannah	28	F	None	28Ma13Hs
Alfred	2	M	Child	28Ma13Hs
Sarah	.00	F	Infant	28Ma13Hs
HOPKINS, Eliza	29	F	Lad	28Ma13Hs
Ann	2	F	Child	28Ma13Hs
LOCK, John	38	M	Grocer	28Ma13Hs
Ann	38	F	None	28Ma13Hs
Mary	16	F	None	28Ma13Hs
Ann	12	F	None	28Ma13Hs
Daniel	10	M	Child	28Ma13Hs
Sarah	8	F	Child	28Ma13Hs
John	6	M	Child	28Ma13Hs
Eliza	4	F	Child	28Ma13Hs
Francis	1	M	Child	28Ma13Hs
MALTWOOD, Francis	52	M	Sailor	28Ma13Hs
WEEKS, Francis	18	M	Porter	28Ma13Hs
CHAPMAN, Harriet	27	F	None	28Ma13Hs
Richard	29	M	Farmer	28Ma13Hs
TREY, William	27	M	Laborer	28Ma13Hs
CASEY, Johana	27	F	Servant	28Ma13Hs
Ellen	25	F	Servant	28Ma13Hs
TORRINGTON, Thomas	23	M	Laborer	28Ma13Hs
AFFORD, Nathaniel	30	M	Laborer	28Ma13Hs
MINDENHALL, William	23	M	Engineer	28Ma13Hs
WADE, John	25	M	Engineer	28Ma13Hs
RAINFORD, George	37	M	Brewer	28Ma13Hs
Harriet	33	F	None	28Ma13Hs
George	11	M	None	28Ma13Hs
Mary	8	F	Child	28Ma13Hs
Harriet	4	F	Child	28Ma13Hs
CHURCHER, Hellen	29	F	None	28Ma13Hs
Mary	2	F	Child	28Ma13Hs
WILFORD, Sarah	2	F	Child	28Ma13Hs
Mary	30	F	None	28Ma13Hs
MAYNARD, John	25	M	Laborer	28Ma13Hs
BURDEN, John	33	M	Laborer	28Ma13Hs
Damaris	34	F	None	28Ma13Hs
Peter	9	M	Child	28Ma13Hs
Sarah	.00	F	Infant	28Ma13Hs
MARCH, Charles	34	M	Laborer	28Ma13Hs
WATSON, David	29	M	Gdnr	28Ma13Hs
SAMPSON, Sarah	22	F	None	28Ma13Hs
Eben.	3	M	Child	28Ma13Hs
LEE, John	31	M	Laborer	28Ma13Hs
Rebecca	31	F	None	28Ma13Hs
Matilda	5	F	Child	28Ma13Hs
John	.00	M	Infant	28Ma13Hs
TODMAN, John	15	M	Laborer	28Ma13Hs
SAVAGE, John	39	M	Laborer	28Ma13Hs
Lucy	46	F	None	28Ma13Hs
Maria	8	F	Child	28Ma13Hs
STONE, John	17	M	Shoemaker	28Ma13Hs
BROWN, Elias	28	M	Mason	28Ma13Hs
MORRING, Ruben	30	M	Laborer	28Ma13Hs
BROWN, Lydia	26	F	None	28Ma13Hs
Sarah	.00	F	Infant	28Ma13Hs
Mary	.00	F	Infant	28Ma13Hs
Born-At-Sea				
WOOD, Emma	25	F	None	28Ma13Hs
James	4	M	Child	28Ma13Hs
Emma	1	F	Child	28Ma13Hs
BENNETT, Henry	22	M	Laborer	28Ma13Hs
Daniel	10	M	Child	28Ma13Hs
KNIGHT, Stephen	40	M	Shoemaker	28Ma13Hs
Stephen	12	M	Shoemaker	28Ma13Hs

NAMES OF PASSENGERS	AGE	SEX	OCCUPATIONS	DATE PORT SHIP
MORELAND, John	42	M	Carpenter	28Ma13Hs
ABSELL, William	21	M	Cooper	28Ma13Hs
BENNETT, Robert	29	M	Laborer	28Ma13Hs
STOWALD, Frederick	26	M	Laborer	28Ma13Hs
COOPER, Christopher	20	M	Pmbr-Gzr	28Ma13Hs
Mathew	24	M	Painter	28Ma13Hs
MILES, Joseph	45	M	Carpenter	28Ma13Hs
LACY, William	25	M	Laborer	28Ma13Hs
KIRKPATRICK, George	35	M	Gdnr	28Ma13Hs
Ann	40	F	None	28Ma13Hs
Walter	3	M	Child	28Ma13Hs
Guy	.00	M	Infant	28Ma13Hs
LOURY, John	30	M	Joiner	28Ma13Hs
ROGERS, Jane	47	F	Dressmaker	28Ma13Hs
WALFORD, Sarah	50	F	Dressmaker	28Ma13Hs
Emma	20	F	Dressmaker	28Ma13Hs
Jane	19	F	Dressmaker	28Ma13Hs
COATES, William	21	M	Mason	28Ma13Hs
BIRCH, John	25	M	Shoemaker	28Ma13Hs
DUNSCOMBE, John	29	M	Shoemaker	28Ma13Hs
Lydia	30	F	None	28Ma13Hs
Edward	1	M	Child	28Ma13Hs
TRESLER, John	60	M	Smith	28Ma13Hs
TRUSLER, Jemima	53	F	None	28Ma13Hs
Thomas	22	M	Unknown	28Ma13Hs
Maria	17	F	Unknown	28Ma13Hs
William	25	M	Smith	28Ma13Hs
Mary	20	F	None	28Ma13Hs
William	1	M	Child	28Ma13Hs
James	25	M	Smith	28Ma13Hs
Charlotte	25	F	None	28Ma13Hs
Ellen	1	F	Child	28Ma13Hs
WOODYER, Thomas	62	M	Laborer	28Ma13Hs
John	26	M	Laborer	28Ma13Hs
WALKER, Eliza	31	F	None	28Ma13Hs
Eliza	7	F	Child	28Ma13Hs
Edith	5	F	Child	28Ma13Hs
DAY, Henry	17	M	Laborer	28Ma13Hs
KING, James	25	M	Farmer	28Ma13Hs
WILLIAMS, Obadiah	52	M	Hatter	28Ma13Hs
BAILEY, Benjamin	57	M	Ptdsgr	28Ma13Hs
Eliza	59	F	None	28Ma13Hs
DIBLEY, Henry	46	M	Farmer	28Ma13Hs
Eliza	38	F	None	28Ma13Hs
PARK, Edward	41	M	Servant	28Ma13Hs
FREEMAN, William	43	M	Carpenter	28Ma13Hs
JACKSON, Isaac	30	M	Merchant	28Ma13Hs
BRADSHAW, Henry	45	M	Cbtmkr	28Ma13Hs
HOOPER, James	18	M	Porter	28Ma13Hs
William	20	M	Porter	28Ma13Hs
RAYNOR, George	30	M	Carpenter	28Ma13Hs
Frances	31	F	None	28Ma13Hs
John	3	M	Child	28Ma13Hs
George	.00	M	Infant	28Ma13Hs
HUGHES, John	30	M	Carpenter	28Ma13Hs
GLAZEBROOK, George	23	M	Smith	28Ma13Hs
Mary	19	F	None	28Ma13Hs
Margaret	.00	F	Infant	28Ma13Hs
BENNETT, Martha	35	F	Servant	28Ma13Hs
DEUYER, Sarah	24	F	Servant	28Ma13Hs
MILES, John	34	M	Mason	28Ma13Hs
Ann	33	F	None	28Ma13Hs
MACHRELL, Albert	32	M	Upholsterer	28Ma13Hs
WALFORD, Charles	52	M	Watchmaker	28Ma13Hs
Ann	48	F	None	28Ma13Hs
Charles	23	M	Clerk	28Ma13Hs
George	21	M	Baker	28Ma13Hs
Sarah	20	F	None	28Ma13Hs
Rebecca	18	F	None	28Ma13Hs
Fanny	14	F	None	28Ma13Hs
Thomas	12	M	None	28Ma13Hs
RICHARDS, Richard	16	M	Farmer	28Ma13Hs
LAMBERN, George	29	M	Brush Maker	28Ma13Hs
Sarah	29	F	None	28Ma13Hs
BOUFFLER, James	33	M	Bootmaker	28Ma13Hs

NAMES OF PASSENGERS	AGE	SEX	OCCUPATIONS	DATE PORT SHIP
BOUFFLER, Jane	34	F	None	28Ma13Hs
James	7	M	Child	28Ma13Hs
Edward	5	M	Child	28Ma13Hs
BISHOP, Ann	30	F	Seamstress	28Ma13Hs
EVERNDEN, Thomas	23	M	Shoemaker	28Ma13Hs
James	22	M	Shoemaker	28Ma13Hs
Emma	3	F	Child	28Ma13Hs
George	1	M	Child	28Ma13Hs
Henry	.00	M	Infant	28Ma13Hs
PEARCE, Henry	25	M	Gdnr	28Ma13Hs
Sarah	20	F	None	28Ma13Hs
HAMMOND, William	23	M	Gdnr	28Ma13Hs
Matilda	23	F	None	28Ma13Hs
TRESLER, Charles	31	M	Smith	28Ma13Hs
Hannah	31	F	None	28Ma13Hs
Amelia	7	F	Child	28Ma13Hs
Mary	5	F	Child	28Ma13Hs
Emma	4	F	Child	28Ma13Hs
Joseph	.00	M	Infant	28Ma13Hs
CHALLIS, James	32	M	Grocer	28Ma13Hs
Susan	30	F	None	28Ma13Hs
Susan	9	F	Child	28Ma13Hs
Jane	7	F	Child	28Ma13Hs
Josiah	5	M	Child	28Ma13Hs
Ruth	3	F	Child	28Ma13Hs
Ann	1	F	Child	28Ma13Hs
WATKINS, Mary	28	F	Dressmaker	28Ma13Hs
JONES, Martin	24	M	Laborer	28Ma13Hs
COLES, Henry	18	M	Weaver	28Ma13Hs
WOLF, Joseph	24	M	Weaver	28Ma13Hs
SHELLY, Michael	32	M	Tinman	28Ma13Hs
CALLICUN, Mary	35	F	Servant	28Ma13Hs
TURNER, Sophia	34	F	Servant	28Ma13Hs
HELY, Alice	39	F	Servant	28Ma13Hs
BRADFORD, George	39	M	Shoemaker	28Ma13Hs
ALLEN, Jesse	39	M	Tailor	28Ma13Hs
CUMMINGS, Henry	34	M	Butcher	28Ma13Hs
Mary	42	F	None	28Ma13Hs
Thomas	7	M	Child	28Ma13Hs
NASH, James	18	M	Porter	28Ma13Hs
TAYLOR, William	36	M	Goldsmith	28Ma13Hs
Mary	37	F	None	28Ma13Hs
Mary	10	F	Child	28Ma13Hs
Rebecca	8	F	Child	28Ma13Hs
Mary	6	F	Child	28Ma13Hs
William	4	M	Child	28Ma13Hs
Sarah	2	F	Child	28Ma13Hs
James	.00	M	Infant	28Ma13Hs
LILLIBOURNE, Thomas	29	M	Grocer	28Ma13Hs
Esther	30	F	Grocer	28Ma13Hs
WEST, Henry	43	M	Shoemaker	28Ma13Hs
Fanny	42	F	None	28Ma13Hs
Caroline	19	F	None	28Ma13Hs
Louisa	17	F	None	28Ma13Hs
Matilda	14	F	None	28Ma13Hs
Julia	11	F	None	28Ma13Hs
Emily	9	F	None	28Ma13Hs
Henry	7	M	Child	28Ma13Hs
JOURDAN, Daniel	18	M	Mariner	28Ma13Hs

JAVA 28 MAY 1849

From Londonderry

NAMES OF PASSENGERS	AGE	SEX	OCCUPATIONS	DATE PORT SHIP
TOLAN, Nancy	20	F	Unknown	28Ma01Al
MCDEVITT, Peggy	19	F	Unknown	28Ma01Al
BANNON, Felix	35	M	Unknown	28Ma01Al
MULLEN, James	36	M	Unknown	28Ma01Al
LONG, John	20	M	Unknown	28Ma01Al
BOYLE, Daniel	21	M	Unknown	28Ma01Al
MCLOUGHLIN, Patrick	19	M	Unknown	28Ma01Al
FLEMING, Arthur	45	M	Unknown	28Ma01Al
Jane	25	F	Unknown	28Ma01Al
MCLARKY, Francis	28	M	Unknown	28Ma01Al
Ellen	25	F	Unknown	28Ma01Al
MCLOUGHLIN, James	25	M	Unknown	28Ma01Al
Biddy	19	F	Unknown	28Ma01Al
KEARNEY, Dennis	19	M	Unknown	28Ma01Al
MCDEVITT, Robert	18	M	Unknown	28Ma01Al
MCLOUGHLIN, Sally	17	F	Unknown	28Ma01Al
Biddy	18	F	Unknown	28Ma01Al
Patrick	19	M	Unknown	28Ma01Al
COLGIN, John	20	M	Unknown	28Ma01Al
COSTELLO, James	21	M	Unknown	28Ma01Al
MULLEN, Patrick	45	M	Unknown	28Ma01Al
Belinda	40	F	Unknown	28Ma01Al
Mary	15	F	Unknown	28Ma01Al
Henry	18	M	Unknown	28Ma01Al
Easey	12	F	Unknown	28Ma01Al
Patk.	10	M	Unknown	28Ma01Al
BELL, Jane	20	F	Unknown	28Ma01Al
MCKIERNAN, Margaret	20	F	Unknown	28Ma01Al
Mary-Ann	18	F	Unknown	28Ma01Al
MCNEELY, Lawrence	20	M	Unknown	28Ma01Al
KERNAN, Bridget	25	F	Unknown	28Ma01Al
BOYLE, John	26	M	Unknown	28Ma01Al
MCCALLEN, Daniel	28	M	Unknown	28Ma01Al
MCLELLAND, Mary-Jane	18	F	Unknown	28Ma01Al
Ellen	20	F	Unknown	28Ma01Al
KEARNEY, Neal	21	M	Unknown	28Ma01Al
MCGRANNAGH, Hugh	20	M	Unknown	28Ma01Al
Margaret	23	F	Unknown	28Ma01Al
MCNULTY, Ellen	.00	F	Infant	28Ma01Al
MCLOUGHLIN, William	40	M	Unknown	28Ma01Al
MCGEOGHGAN, Dennis	20	M	Unknown	28Ma01Al
Catherine	18	F	Unknown	28Ma01Al
DOHERTY, Edward	20	M	Unknown	28Ma01Al
TRACY, Betty	18	F	Unknown	28Ma01Al
KEAN, Ann	20	F	Unknown	28Ma01Al
FLANNAGHAN, Bernd.	21	M	Unknown	28Ma01Al
STEVENSON, Andrew	20	M	Unknown	28Ma01Al
Jane	18	F	Unknown	28Ma01Al
CONNELL, Catherine	20	F	Unknown	28Ma01Al
MCNEILL, Hugh	21	M	Unknown	28Ma01Al
MCDADE, Madge	20	F	Unknown	28Ma01Al
MCLOUGHLIN, William	21	M	Unknown	28Ma01Al
NUGENT, Ann	46	F	Unknown	28Ma01Al
KEARNEY, Ellen	22	F	Unknown	28Ma01Al
THORPE, Jane	24	F	Unknown	28Ma01Al
Elizabeth	.00	F	Infant	28Ma01Al
MENSON, Ann	10	F	Unknown	28Ma01Al
Charles	8	M	Child	28Ma01Al
GEARNEY, Wm.	20	M	Unknown	28Ma01Al
CUNNINGHAM, Elizabeth	22	F	Unknown	28Ma01Al
John	18	M	Unknown	28Ma01Al
MOOR, Robert	20	M	Unknown	28Ma01Al
HUNTER, Jane	25	F	Unknown	28Ma01Al
BENSON, John	50	M	Unknown	28Ma01Al
Jane	50	F	Unknown	28Ma01Al
Rich.	28	M	Unknown	28Ma01Al
Cath.	25	F	Unknown	28Ma01Al
Frances	25	F	Unknown	28Ma01Al
John	9	M	Child	28Ma01Al
Margaret	9	F	Child	28Ma01Al
Jane	7	F	Child	28Ma01Al
Martha	4	F	Child	28Ma01Al
William	25	M	Unknown	28Ma01Al
HAGARTY, Patk.	20	M	Unknown	28Ma01Al
MCLOUGHLIN, John	22	M	Unknown	28Ma01Al
DOHERTY, Charles	35	M	Unknown	28Ma01Al
MCLEAN, Catherine	20	F	Unknown	28Ma01Al
MAGUINNESS, Henry	38	M	Unknown	28Ma01Al
Sarah	13	F	Unknown	28Ma01Al
KEAN, Daniel	20	M	Unknown	28Ma01Al

NAMES OF PASSENGERS	AGE	SEX	OCCUPATIONS	DATE PORT SHIP
ANDERSON, John	20	M	Unknown	28Ma01Al
MCLOUGHLIN, James	21	M	Unknown	28Ma01Al
MILLER, George	30	M	Unknown	28Ma01Al
Ellen	28	F	Unknown	28Ma01Al
Isaac	3	M	Child	28Ma01Al
MCGANNEGALL, Rebecca	21	F	Unknown	28Ma01Al
BLANCEY, Catherine	25	F	Unknown	28Ma01Al
FREEL, Patrick	35	M	Unknown	28Ma01Al
CUNNINGHAM, John	24	M	Unknown	28Ma01Al
MURRAY, David	20	M	Unknown	28Ma01Al
OBRIEN, James	21	M	Unknown	28Ma01Al
GALLAGHER, Patk.	18	M	Unknown	28Ma01Al
BRADLEY, Dennis	22	M	Unknown	28Ma01Al
MCLOUGHLIN, Patk.	18	M	Unknown	28Ma01Al
Patk.	40	M	Unknown	28Ma01Al
MCLARNY, Dennis	18	M	Unknown	28Ma01Al
George	17	M	Unknown	28Ma01Al
MCCAULLAN, Phillip	22	M	Unknown	28Ma01Al
CULMERY, Daniel	18	M	Unknown	28Ma01Al
MOORHEAD, Robert	55	M	Unknown	28Ma01Al
Mary	55	F	Unknown	28Ma01Al
David	17	M	Unknown	28Ma01Al
William	13	M	Unknown	28Ma01Al
John	9	M	Child	28Ma01Al
Cath.	5	F	Child	28Ma01Al
MCGROSSIN, Hannah	25	F	Unknown	28Ma01Al
Mary	21	F	Unknown	28Ma01Al
ERWIN, George	25	M	Unknown	28Ma01Al
Catherine	25	F	Unknown	28Ma01Al
Margaret	10	F	Unknown	28Ma01Al
Catherine	.00	F	Infant	28Ma01Al
WATSON, Robert	21	M	Unknown	28Ma01Al
DOHERTY, Nancy	18	F	Unknown	28Ma01Al
HELFERTY, Biddy	17	F	Unknown	28Ma01Al
ODONNELL, Roger	23	M	Unknown	28Ma01Al
Jane	23	F	Unknown	28Ma01Al
Mary	.00	F	Infant	28Ma01Al
GELLESPIE, James	21	M	Unknown	28Ma01Al
VEITCH, George	20	M	Unknown	28Ma01Al
Jane	19	F	Unknown	28Ma01Al
BRIEN, James	20	M	Unknown	28Ma01Al
SWANSON, Irwin	20	M	Unknown	28Ma01Al
OBRIEN, Andrew	30	M	Unknown	28Ma01Al
Sarah	28	F	Unknown	28Ma01Al
James	7	M	Child	28Ma01Al
Mary	6	F	Child	28Ma01Al
Peter	2	M	Child	28Ma01Al
Sarah	.00	F	Infant	28Ma01Al
Margaret	20	F	Unknown	28Ma01Al
SWEENEY, Charles	24	M	Unknown	28Ma01Al
GORMLEY, Catherine	23	F	Unknown	28Ma01Al
OBRIEN, Ann	14	F	Unknown	28Ma01Al
DARCUS, Henry	20	M	Unknown	28Ma01Al
MCLOUGHLIN, Margery	50	F	Unknown	28Ma01Al
Bernard	8	M	Child	28Ma01Al
GILLEN, William	45	M	Unknown	28Ma01Al
Mary	52	F	Unknown	28Ma01Al
Margaret	27	F	Unknown	28Ma01Al
GORDEN, Samuel	23	M	Unknown	28Ma01Al
WILSON, James	17	M	Unknown	28Ma01Al
MCGRANN, James	18	M	Unknown	28Ma01Al
MCNEILL, Robert	43	M	Unknown	28Ma01Al
Easey	16	F	Unknown	28Ma01Al
Mary-I.	13	F	Unknown	28Ma01Al
Robert	11	M	Unknown	28Ma01Al
John	9	M	Child	28Ma01Al
David	7	M	Child	28Ma01Al
Letitia	4	F	Child	28Ma01Al
CANNING, James	25	M	Unknown	28Ma01Al
NUGENT, Patrick	45	M	Unknown	28Ma01Al
Ann	15	F	Unknown	28Ma01Al
COYLE, Ann	18	F	Unknown	28Ma01Al
BROWNE, Rhoda	35	F	Unknown	28Ma01Al
MCNULTY, David	25	M	Unknown	28Ma01Al
MILLER, Isaac	15	M	Unknown	28Ma01Al
COX, Abraham	28	M	Unknown	28Ma01Al
BLAKELY, Robert	23	M	Unknown	28Ma01Al
Jane	19	F	Unknown	28Ma01Al
Ellen	19	F	Unknown	28Ma01Al
HART, Mary	38	F	Unknown	28Ma01Al
STEVENSON, Mary-J.	18	F	Unknown	28Ma01Al
Margaret	15	F	Unknown	28Ma01Al
DIAMOND, Margaret	19	F	Unknown	28Ma01Al
AIKEN, Robert	20	M	Unknown	28Ma01Al
John	19	M	Unknown	28Ma01Al
DOHERTY, Hugh	30	M	Unknown	28Ma01Al
Margaret	27	F	Unknown	28Ma01Al
ARBUCKLE, Margaret	23	F	Unknown	28Ma01Al
Thos.	21	M	Unknown	28Ma01Al
William	7	M	Child	28Ma01Al
GALLAGHER, William	40	M	Unknown	28Ma01Al
LOCKHART, Samuel	18	M	Unknown	28Ma01Al
LYNCH, John	23	M	Unknown	28Ma01Al
Sally	22	F	Unknown	28Ma01Al
HUNTER, David	18	M	Unknown	28Ma01Al
CORGILL, Mary	26	F	Unknown	28Ma01Al

JAMES-REDDIN 28 MAY 1849

From Limerick

NAMES OF PASSENGERS	AGE	SEX	OCCUPATIONS	DATE PORT SHIP
MCDONNELL, James	30	M	Farmer	28Ma35Gt
MCDONALD, Michael	27	M	Farmer	28Ma35Gt
OBRIEN, John	22	M	Farmer	28Ma35Gt
MCINERNY, John	50	M	Farmer	28Ma35Gt
Mary (W)	50	F	Wife	28Ma35Gt
Patt	26	M	Farmer	28Ma35Gt
James	24	M	Farmer	28Ma35Gt
John	25	M	Farmer	28Ma35Gt
Mary	17	F	Spinster	28Ma35Gt
Margt.	14	F	Spinster	28Ma35Gt
Thomas	12	M	Child	28Ma35Gt
Ann	10	F	Child	28Ma35Gt
Biddy	8	F	Child	28Ma35Gt
WALSH, Patt	32	M	Farmer	28Ma35Gt
Michl.	22	M	Farmer	28Ma35Gt
Bridget	19	F	Spinster	28Ma35Gt
HICKEY, Fanny	20	F	Spinster	28Ma35Gt
BURKE, Edmund	30	M	Laborer	28Ma35Gt
Patt	28	M	Laborer	28Ma35Gt
HAYTON, Ellen	19	F	Spinster	28Ma35Gt
CUMMINS, Ellen	19	F	Spinster	28Ma35Gt
FITZGERALD, Maurice	20	M	Laborer	28Ma35Gt
James	25	M	Laborer	28Ma35Gt
FORD, Wm. Died-At-Sea	22	M	Laborer	28Ma35Gt
DOYLE, Patt	22	M	Laborer	28Ma35Gt
FITZGERALD, Wm.	30	M	Laborer	28Ma35Gt
SCANLON, Michl.	20	M	Laborer	28Ma35Gt
John	18	M	Laborer	28Ma35Gt
BLAKE, Michl. Died-At-Sea	30	M	Laborer	28Ma35Gt
HOWARD, Mary	22	F	Spinster	28Ma35Gt
MORGAN, Patt	26	M	Laborer	28Ma35Gt
CULLINEY, John	35	M	Laborer	28Ma35Gt
Margt. (W)	30	F	Wife	28Ma35Gt
Ellen	6	F	Child	28Ma35Gt
Patt	4	M	Child	28Ma35Gt
NEALON, Pat	55	M	Farmer	28Ma35Gt
Mary (W)	50	F	Wife	28Ma35Gt
Darby	25	M	Farmer	28Ma35Gt
Thomas	19	M	Farmer	28Ma35Gt
David	17	M	Farmer	28Ma35Gt
Patrick	13	M	None	28Ma35Gt

NAMES OF PASSENGERS		AGE	SEX	OCCUPATIONS	DATE PORT SHIP
NEALON, Ellen		20	F	Spinster	28Ma35Gt
Margt.		11	F	Child	28Ma35Gt
OBRIEN, Thomas		55	M	Farmer	28Ma35Gt
Elizabeth	(W)	50	F	Wife	28Ma35Gt
John		30	M	Farmer	28Ma35Gt
Pat		27	M	Farmer	28Ma35Gt
Thomas		24	M	Farmer	28Ma35Gt
Morris		21	M	Farmer	28Ma35Gt
James		18	M	Farmer	28Ma35Gt
Michl.		15	M	Farmer	28Ma35Gt
William		12	M	Child	28Ma35Gt
DWYER, Mary		24	F	Spinster	28Ma35Gt
COFFEY, James		37	M	Farmer	28Ma35Gt
BRYAN, Pat		22	M	Farmer	28Ma35Gt
Ellen		20	F	Spinster	28Ma35Gt
SHEEDY, John		30	M	Farmer	28Ma35Gt
Michl.		26	M	Farmer	28Ma35Gt
DAWSON, Julia		21	F	Spinster	28Ma35Gt
EDWARDS, Mary		20	F	Spinster	28Ma35Gt
EGAN, Bryan		20	M	Farmer	28Ma35Gt
SHERRY, John		32	M	Farmer	28Ma35Gt
John		15	M	Farmer	28Ma35Gt
MCDONNELL, Ann		15	F	Spinster	28Ma35Gt
HALLORAN, John		30	M	Farmer	28Ma35Gt
Anne		16	F	Spinster	28Ma35Gt
Peggy		14	F	Spinster	28Ma35Gt
GLEESON, Daniel		26	M	Laborer	28Ma35Gt
Mary		21	F	Spinster	28Ma35Gt
POWER, Mary		21	F	Wi	28Ma35Gt
Bridget Died-At-Sea		.00	F	Infant	28Ma35Gt
ALLEN, Patt		28	M	Farmer	28Ma35Gt
RYAN, Michl.		27	M	Farmer	28Ma35Gt
Martin		24	M	Farmer	28Ma35Gt
Margt.		14	F	Spinster	28Ma35Gt
MCNAMARA, Dan.		25	M	Farmer	28Ma35Gt
Catherine		26	F	Spinster	28Ma35Gt
OBRIEN, Johanna		45	F	Matron	28Ma35Gt
Bridget		20	F	Matron	28Ma35Gt
MCNAMEE, Mathew		30	M	Farmer	28Ma35Gt
WHITE, Margt.		22	F	Spinster	28Ma35Gt
Catherine		18	F	Spinster	28Ma35Gt
AHERN, Francis		21	M	Saddler	28Ma35Gt
OBRIEN, Daniel		14	M	Farmer	28Ma35Gt
DONOHUE, Wm.		36	M	Farmer	28Ma35Gt
Mary	(W)	27	F	Wife	28Ma35Gt
OSHEA, Michl.		33	M	Farmer	28Ma35Gt
Debora	(W)	40	F	Wife	28Ma35Gt
John		.11	M	Infant	28Ma35Gt

ELIJAH-SWIFT 28 MAY 1849

From Glasgow

NAMES OF PASSENGERS	AGE	SEX	OCCUPATIONS	DATE PORT SHIP
GALLAGHER, Mary	21	F	Unknown	28Ma04Gs
CONWAY, Michael	26	M	Boatmaker	28Ma04Gs
MCLACHLAN, Patrick	35	M	Laborer	28Ma04Gs
BROGAN, Felix	38	M	Spinner	28Ma04Gs
PETERSON, Wm.	37	M	Laborer	28Ma04Gs
KENNEDY, John	31	M	Unknown	28Ma04Gs
Marion Died-At-Sea	30	F	Unknown	28Ma04Gs
Marion	7	F	Child	28Ma04Gs
Alex	.11	M	Infant	28Ma04Gs
SUTHERLAND, Dennis	37	M	Laborer	28Ma04Gs
Betsey	37	F	Unknown	28Ma04Gs
COOPER, Wm.	19	M	Wright	28Ma04Gs
MURPHY, Alice	18	F	Servant	28Ma04Gs
MCNICOL, Susan	17	F	Servant	28Ma04Gs
STEVENSON, Michael	40	M	Unknown	28Ma04Gs
CASEY, Patrick	30	M	Laborer	28Ma04Gs
SWEENIE, Daniel	40	M	Weaver	28Ma04Gs
Catherine	35	F	Unknown	28Ma04Gs
Susan	7	F	Child	28Ma04Gs
Mary	70	F	Unknown	28Ma04Gs
Henry	5	M	Child	28Ma04Gs
James	16	M	Unknown	28Ma04Gs
Catherine	3	F	Child	28Ma04Gs
FOY, Patrick	24	M	Laborer	28Ma04Gs
Henry	29	M	Laborer	28Ma04Gs
HARKER, Wm.	12	M	None	28Ma04Gs
MCKENNEY, Hugh	28	M	Tailor	28Ma04Gs

MARY-AND-MARTHA 28 MAY 1849

From Buenos Aires

NAMES OF PASSENGERS	AGE	SEX	OCCUPATIONS	DATE PORT SHIP
GRAY, John	25	M	Digger	28Ma64Gq

HELEN-THOMPSON 29 MAY 1849

From Belfast

NAMES OF PASSENGERS	AGE	SEX	OCCUPATIONS	DATE PORT SHIP
ANDERSEN, Jane	23	F	Unknown	29Ma05Hu
Sarah	19	F	Unknown	29Ma05Hu
BLAIR, James	17	M	Unknown	29Ma05Hu
LOWRY, William	28	M	Unknown	29Ma05Hu
Eliza	24	F	Unknown	29Ma05Hu
George	28	M	Unknown	29Ma05Hu
Ann	21	F	Unknown	29Ma05Hu
MCBRIDE, Robert	31	M	Unknown	29Ma05Hu
Jane	24	F	Unknown	29Ma05Hu
Robert	.00	M	Infant	29Ma05Hu
STEVENSON, James	21	M	Unknown	29Ma05Hu
BLAIR, Robert	16	M	Unknown	29Ma05Hu
John	12	M	Unknown	29Ma05Hu
Mary	18	F	Unknown	29Ma05Hu
JEFFREY, Mary	40	F	Unknown	29Ma05Hu
Margaret	18	F	Unknown	29Ma05Hu
Lydia	16	F	Unknown	29Ma05Hu
William	12	M	Unknown	29Ma05Hu
SHARK, David	19	M	Unknown	29Ma05Hu
FLINN, Hugh	20	M	Unknown	29Ma05Hu
MCBRIDE, Bernard	21	M	Unknown	29Ma05Hu
John	21	M	Unknown	29Ma05Hu
Mary	20	F	Unknown	29Ma05Hu
Mary	.00	F	Infant	29Ma05Hu
MCCONNELL, Joseph	20	M	Unknown	29Ma05Hu
Ellen	20	F	Unknown	29Ma05Hu
MCCUTCHEN, Margt.	40	F	Unknown	29Ma05Hu
John	15	M	Unknown	29Ma05Hu
David	12	M	Unknown	29Ma05Hu
Alexander	9	M	Child	29Ma05Hu
Mary	7	F	Child	29Ma05Hu
Margaret	5	F	Child	29Ma05Hu
James	3	M	Child	29Ma05Hu
Andrew	.00	M	Infant	29Ma05Hu
NIXON, John	24	M	Unknown	29Ma05Hu
Mary	20	F	Unknown	29Ma05Hu
Ann	.00	F	Infant	29Ma05Hu
MCMICHAN, James	40	M	Unknown	29Ma05Hu
KELLY, Hugh	12	M	Unknown	29Ma05Hu

NAMES OF PASSENGERS	AGE	SEX	OCCUPATIONS	DATE PORT SHIP
HANVEY, John	18	M	Unknown	29Ma05Hu
KANE, John	20	M	Unknown	29Ma05Hu
WARNOCK, Wm.	20	M	Unknown	29Ma05Hu
GAMBLE, James	17	M	Unknown	29Ma05Hu
MCCLARTY, Mary	28	F	Unknown	29Ma05Hu
Mary	5	F	Child	29Ma05Hu
John	3	M	Child	29Ma05Hu
David	.00	M	Infant	29Ma05Hu
MCCORVILLE, James	30	M	Unknown	29Ma05Hu
Biddy	18	F	Unknown	29Ma05Hu
Mary	22	F	Unknown	29Ma05Hu
WARD, William	27	M	Unknown	29Ma05Hu
George	28	M	Unknown	29Ma05Hu
Elisie	20	F	Unknown	29Ma05Hu
KIRKPATRICK, Jas.	22	M	Unknown	29Ma05Hu
Jane	18	F	Unknown	29Ma05Hu
MCBRIDE, Sally	20	F	Unknown	29Ma05Hu
MAHAFFREY, James	20	M	Unknown	29Ma05Hu
PATTERSON, Eliza	20	F	Unknown	29Ma05Hu
MCMULLEN, Richard	30	M	Unknown	29Ma05Hu
Rose	20	F	Unknown	29Ma05Hu
BERTLEY, James	48	M	Unknown	29Ma05Hu
Pat.	18	M	Unknown	29Ma05Hu
Mary	21	F	Unknown	29Ma05Hu
CAUGHEY, Eliza	48	F	Unknown	29Ma05Hu
DOWNEY, Nicholas	27	M	Unknown	29Ma05Hu
SAVAGE, John	21	M	Unknown	29Ma05Hu
Ann	21	F	Unknown	29Ma05Hu
BLACK, John	20	M	Unknown	29Ma05Hu
BAILEY, James	21	M	Unknown	29Ma05Hu
MILLAR, Thomas	46	M	Unknown	29Ma05Hu
Eliza	40	F	Unknown	29Ma05Hu
Jane	20	F	Unknown	29Ma05Hu
Robert	17	M	Unknown	29Ma05Hu
Ruth	12	F	Unknown	29Ma05Hu
Eliza	10	F	Unknown	29Ma05Hu
Mary	8	F	Child	29Ma05Hu
Thomas	7	M	Child	29Ma05Hu
Margaret	3	F	Child	29Ma05Hu
Ann	.00	F	Infant	29Ma05Hu
DELWIRTH, Sarah	10	F	Unknown	29Ma05Hu
Andrew	8	M	Child	29Ma05Hu
Mary	6	F	Child	29Ma05Hu
Margaret	3	F	Child	29Ma05Hu
Maria	.00	F	Infant	29Ma05Hu
MALLEN, James	40	M	Unknown	29Ma05Hu
Mary	37	F	Unknown	29Ma05Hu
John	16	M	Unknown	29Ma05Hu
James	14	M	Unknown	29Ma05Hu
Patt	11	M	Unknown	29Ma05Hu
Sarah	9	F	Child	29Ma05Hu
Peter	7	M	Child	29Ma05Hu
Mary	5	F	Child	29Ma05Hu
DONNOLLY, Hugh	53	M	Unknown	29Ma05Hu
Thelim	52	M	Unknown	29Ma05Hu
Margaret	50	F	Unknown	29Ma05Hu
NUGENT, Pat	9	M	Child	29Ma05Hu
DONNOLLY, Biddy	20	F	Unknown	29Ma05Hu
MCLOUGHLIN, Henry	60	M	Unknown	29Ma05Hu
Sarah	62	F	Unknown	29Ma05Hu
Jane	16	F	Unknown	29Ma05Hu
Robert	14	M	Unknown	29Ma05Hu
Sarah	12	F	Unknown	29Ma05Hu
MALLEN, Cath.	50	F	Unknown	29Ma05Hu
James	10	M	Unknown	29Ma05Hu
Alice	12	F	Unknown	29Ma05Hu
DONNOLLY, Owen	27	M	Unknown	29Ma05Hu
Arthur	21	M	Unknown	29Ma05Hu
Thomas	19	M	Unknown	29Ma05Hu
Mary	23	F	Unknown	29Ma05Hu
Veronica	25	F	Unknown	29Ma05Hu
NELSEN, William	46	M	Unknown	29Ma05Hu
Isabella	40	F	Unknown	29Ma05Hu
Eliza	16	F	Unknown	29Ma05Hu
Sarah	9	F	Child	29Ma05Hu

NAMES OF PASSENGERS	AGE	SEX	OCCUPATIONS	DATE PORT SHIP
MCKINLEY, U-Mrs.	30	F	Unknown	29Ma05Hu
Ellen	21	F	Unknown	29Ma05Hu
Hugh	16	M	Unknown	29Ma05Hu
COWAN, James	22	M	Unknown	29Ma05Hu
Margt.	40	F	Unknown	29Ma05Hu
Margaret	24	F	Unknown	29Ma05Hu
Mary	18	F	Unknown	29Ma05Hu
QUINN, John	30	M	Unknown	29Ma05Hu
Margaret	26	F	Unknown	29Ma05Hu
Mary	3	F	Child	29Ma05Hu
Isabella	.00	F	Infant	29Ma05Hu
NEILSEN, James	40	M	Unknown	29Ma05Hu
Mary	36	F	Unknown	29Ma05Hu
James	16	M	Unknown	29Ma05Hu
Ann	9	F	Child	29Ma05Hu
John	6	M	Child	29Ma05Hu
Margaret	4	F	Child	29Ma05Hu
CROSS, Margaret	55	F	Unknown	29Ma05Hu
John	30	M	Unknown	29Ma05Hu
Eliza	22	F	Unknown	29Ma05Hu
Jane	19	F	Unknown	29Ma05Hu
BUTLER, Felix	33	M	Unknown	29Ma05Hu
Rose	26	F	Unknown	29Ma05Hu
Isabella	30	F	Unknown	29Ma05Hu
James	6	M	Child	29Ma05Hu
Margaret	3	F	Child	29Ma05Hu
CASEY, Cath	29	F	Unknown	29Ma05Hu
WATSON, Jane	50	F	Unknown	29Ma05Hu
Robert	23	M	Unknown	29Ma05Hu
Ann	20	F	Unknown	29Ma05Hu
Eliza	18	F	Unknown	29Ma05Hu
Joseph	15	M	Unknown	29Ma05Hu
Sarah	12	F	Unknown	29Ma05Hu
HELHINGTON, George	20	M	Unknown	29Ma05Hu
John	18	M	Unknown	29Ma05Hu
William	12	M	Unknown	29Ma05Hu
DALEY, Arthur	40	M	Unknown	29Ma05Hu
Sarah	38	F	Unknown	29Ma05Hu
Mary	17	F	Unknown	29Ma05Hu
James	13	M	Unknown	29Ma05Hu
Ann	11	F	Unknown	29Ma05Hu
Thomas	4	M	Child	29Ma05Hu
Jane	.00	F	Infant	29Ma05Hu
MAGEE, John	64	M	Unknown	29Ma05Hu
Ann	57	F	Unknown	29Ma05Hu
Alexander	18	M	Unknown	29Ma05Hu
Robert	12	M	Unknown	29Ma05Hu
DELWIRTH, Thomas	36	M	Unknown	29Ma05Hu
Maria	35	F	Unknown	29Ma05Hu
Jane	14	F	Unknown	29Ma05Hu
John	12	M	Unknown	29Ma05Hu
COWAN, Isabella	14	F	Unknown	29Ma05Hu
Thomas	40	F	Unknown	29Ma05Hu
STEWART, Eliza	.00	F	Infant	29Ma05Hu
HALL, William	40	M	Unknown	29Ma05Hu
DEVLIN, Ber.	21	M	Unknown	29Ma05Hu
WELSH, Ellen	18	F	Unknown	29Ma05Hu
Catharine	16	F	Unknown	29Ma05Hu
MCCLORY, Margaret	15	F	Unknown	29Ma05Hu
Ellen	16	F	Unknown	29Ma05Hu
FRASER, Lesselie	40	M	Unknown	29Ma05Hu
Ellen	40	F	Unknown	29Ma05Hu
John	17	M	Unknown	29Ma05Hu
Ann	18	M	Unknown	29Ma05Hu
Caldwell	14	M	Unknown	29Ma05Hu
Rachael	12	F	Unknown	29Ma05Hu
William	9	M	Child	29Ma05Hu
Robert	6	M	Child	29Ma05Hu
MAGEE, Ann	24	F	Unknown	29Ma05Hu
THORNTON, Ann	21	F	Unknown	29Ma05Hu
SCOTT, Robert	21	M	Unknown	29Ma05Hu
ADAMS, Robert	24	M	Unknown	29Ma05Hu
FLANIGAN, Ber.	25	M	Unknown	29Ma05Hu
LYTLE, Robert	20	M	Unknown	29Ma05Hu
FLANIGAN, Edward	14	M	Unknown	29Ma05Hu

NAMES OF PASSENGERS	AGE	SEX	OCCUPATIONS	DATE PORT SHIP
FAVEY, James	18	M	Unknown	29Ma05Hu
FLANIGAN, Rose	14	F	Unknown	29Ma05Hu
MARTIN, James	20	M	Unknown	29Ma05Hu
MCDOWELL, Eliza	25	F	Unknown	29Ma05Hu
MILLAR, James	19	M	Unknown	29Ma05Hu

SERAPHINE 29 MAY 1849

From Newry

NAMES OF PASSENGERS	AGE	SEX	OCCUPATIONS	DATE PORT SHIP
DONNELLY, Patrick	24	M	Farmer	29Ma11Hf
ROCHS, Sarah	30	F	Unknown	29Ma11Hf
SHORT, Cathern	27	F	Laborer	29Ma11Hf
Ann	20	F	Unknown	29Ma11Hf
ROCHS, Cathern	32	F	Unknown	29Ma11Hf
Owen	30	M	Unknown	29Ma11Hf
Ann	19	F	Unknown	29Ma11Hf
Margret	17	F	Unknown	29Ma11Hf
Sarah-Jane	15	F	Unknown	29Ma11Hf
HANNES, George	21	M	Unknown	29Ma11Hf
Mary	20	F	Unknown	29Ma11Hf
Margret	.00	F	Infant	29Ma11Hf
MCKEOWN, John	25	M	Unknown	29Ma11Hf
RAFFERTY, Bridget	20	F	Unknown	29Ma11Hf
DORAN, Jane	31	F	Unknown	29Ma11Hf
Samuel	30	M	Unknown	29Ma11Hf
Isabella	9	F	Child	29Ma11Hf
Andrew	.00	M	Infant	29Ma11Hf
DALY, John	24	M	Unknown	29Ma11Hf
Cath.	20	F	Unknown	29Ma11Hf
BOYLE, Ann	34	F	Unknown	29Ma11Hf
Denice	32	F	Unknown	29Ma11Hf
Rose	19	M	Unknown	29Ma11Hf
Mary	18	F	Unknown	29Ma11Hf
Thomas	17	M	Unknown	29Ma11Hf
Ann	16	F	Unknown	29Ma11Hf
Margret	15	F	Unknown	29Ma11Hf
Michal	14	M	Unknown	29Ma11Hf
Ellen	12	F	Unknown	29Ma11Hf
Cathrin.	10	F	Unknown	29Ma11Hf
Jane	7	F	Child	29Ma11Hf
Rose	.00	F	Infant	29Ma11Hf
MCDONNELL, Cathn.	27	F	Unknown	29Ma11Hf
Ann	24	F	Unknown	29Ma11Hf
SHANE, Robert	20	M	Unknown	29Ma11Hf
Sarah-Jane	21	F	Unknown	29Ma11Hf
CLARK, John	42	M	Unknown	29Ma11Hf
SHANE, Christian	20	M	Unknown	29Ma11Hf
Eliza	19	F	Unknown	29Ma11Hf
RIDLY, Sally	40	F	Unknown	29Ma11Hf
Hannah	42	F	Unknown	29Ma11Hf
MULHOLLAND, Charles	29	M	Unknown	29Ma11Hf
MAGEE, Bernard	42	M	Unknown	29Ma11Hf
Felix	40	M	Unknown	29Ma11Hf
Charles	20	M	Unknown	29Ma11Hf
Patrick	19	M	Unknown	29Ma11Hf
Nancy	17	F	Unknown	29Ma11Hf
Sally	16	F	Unknown	29Ma11Hf
Rose	15	F	Unknown	29Ma11Hf
Mary	14	F	Unknown	29Ma11Hf
Mragret	13	F	Unknown	29Ma11Hf
Ellen	7	F	Child	29Ma11Hf
MCKERNAN, Patrick	29	M	Unknown	29Ma11Hf
Charles	27	M	Unknown	29Ma11Hf
DOLAN, Danial	40	M	Unknown	29Ma11Hf
Elizabeth	43	F	Unknown	29Ma11Hf
Bridget	19	F	Unknown	29Ma11Hf
Mary	17	F	Unknown	29Ma11Hf
Margret	16	F	Unknown	29Ma11Hf
DOLAN, Ann	15	F	Unknown	29Ma11Hf
MCCOLLOUGH, Thomas	29	M	Unknown	29Ma11Hf
CALWELL, Thomas	22	M	Unknown	29Ma11Hf
HALLINGSOUTH, Ann	27	F	Unknown	29Ma11Hf
Sally	25	F	Unknown	29Ma11Hf
TUFT, James	21	M	Unknown	29Ma11Hf
Ann	20	F	Unknown	29Ma11Hf
Nancy	10	F	Unknown	29Ma11Hf
MALLONY, Michal	42	M	Unknown	29Ma11Hf
Sarah	22	F	Unknown	29Ma11Hf
Ann	10	F	Unknown	29Ma11Hf
Ellen	9	F	Child	29Ma11Hf
Michael	7	M	Child	29Ma11Hf
FAY, Francis	29	M	Unknown	29Ma11Hf
KERNING, James	40	M	Unknown	29Ma11Hf
WRIGHT, David	40	M	Unknown	29Ma11Hf
Mancy	40	F	Unknown	29Ma11Hf
Thomas	20	M	Unknown	29Ma11Hf
Sally-Ann	17	F	Unknown	29Ma11Hf
Margret-Jane	.00	F	Infant	29Ma11Hf
Thomas	40	M	Unknown	29Ma11Hf
Jane	34	F	Unknown	29Ma11Hf
Sally	19	F	Unknown	29Ma11Hf
Martha	17	F	Unknown	29Ma11Hf
Sarah-Jane	.00	F	Infant	29Ma11Hf
MAGNUM, Michal	21	M	Unknown	29Ma11Hf
MCCONNSKY, Margret	27	F	Unknown	29Ma11Hf
Biddy	25	F	Unknown	29Ma11Hf
Patrick	12	M	Unknown	29Ma11Hf
Michal	10	M	Unknown	29Ma11Hf
John	9	M	Child	29Ma11Hf
CULL, Hew	42	M	Unknown	29Ma11Hf
Michal	20	M	Unknown	29Ma11Hf
Susan	9	F	Child	29Ma11Hf
Anne	7	F	Child	29Ma11Hf
PUTERFIELD, Sarah	32	F	Unknown	29Ma11Hf
Patrick	30	M	Unknown	29Ma11Hf
Biddy	10	F	Unknown	29Ma11Hf
Ann	9	F	Child	29Ma11Hf
POWELL, Agnas	29	F	Unknown	29Ma11Hf
MCDONNELL, Patrick	43	M	Unknown	29Ma11Hf
BRADY, Bernard	19	M	Unknown	29Ma11Hf
WRICH, Agnus	.00	F	Infant	29Ma11Hf
QUINN, Denice	42	M	Unknown	29Ma11Hf
ACHISON, James	42	M	Unknown	29Ma11Hf
Agnes	40	F	Unknown	29Ma11Hf
Thomas	19	M	Unknown	29Ma11Hf
Agnes	17	F	Unknown	29Ma11Hf
Priscilla	15	F	Unknown	29Ma11Hf
Elizibeth	13	F	Unknown	29Ma11Hf
Sarah	11	F	Unknown	29Ma11Hf
John	9	M	Child	29Ma11Hf
Emily	.00	F	Infant	29Ma11Hf
HUNTIN, Margret-J.	47	F	Unknown	29Ma11Hf
MCCOWELLE, Biddy	33	F	Unknown	29Ma11Hf
LOW, Ellen	14	F	Unknown	29Ma11Hf
OHIAR, Thomas	17	M	Unknown	29Ma11Hf
Kitty	16	F	Unknown	29Ma11Hf
CAMPBELL, Mary	42	F	Unknown	29Ma11Hf
OHEAR, Kitty	14	F	Unknown	29Ma11Hf
PRISTON, John	27	M	Unknown	29Ma11Hf
Eliza	25	F	Unknown	29Ma11Hf
Thomas	.00	M	Infant	29Ma11Hf
KEENAN, Mary	42	F	Unknown	29Ma11Hf
HEURLY, Peggy	27	F	Unknown	29Ma11Hf
Sarah	21	F	Unknown	29Ma11Hf
MCSHANE, James	25	M	Unknown	29Ma11Hf
PILAN, Rose	42	F	Unknown	29Ma11Hf
Mary	41	F	Unknown	29Ma11Hf
MCKEE, Hew.	49	M	Unknown	29Ma11Hf
Joseph	40	M	Unknown	29Ma11Hf
ALLEN, Alexander	27	M	Unknown	29Ma11Hf
WHITE, Denice	24	M	Unknown	29Ma11Hf
SMYTH, Robert	20	M	Unknown	29Ma11Hf
PATTON, Isabella	27	F	Unknown	29Ma11Hf

NAMES OF PASSENGERS	AGE	SEX	OCCUPATIONS	DATE PORT SHIP
PATTON, Joseph	25	M	Unknown	29Ma11Hf
Margret	19	F	Unknown	29Ma11Hf
John	17	M	Unknown	29Ma11Hf
Isabella	10	F	Unknown	29Ma11Hf
GONLAY, Samuel	42	M	Unknown	29Ma11Hf
Sarah-Ann	27	F	Unknown	29Ma11Hf
BOYD, Samuel	21	M	Unknown	29Ma11Hf
CLARK, Martha	27	F	Unknown	29Ma11Hf
SWAN, William	28	M	Unknown	29Ma11Hf
Eliza	24	F	Unknown	29Ma11Hf
John	.00	M	Infant	29Ma11Hf
MCCLEARHAN, Sarah	42	F	Unknown	29Ma11Hf
CARR, Peter	14	M	Unknown	29Ma11Hf
Mary	9	F	Child	29Ma11Hf
PRISTON, Jane	27	F	Unknown	29Ma11Hf
COOK, Mary	24	F	Unknown	29Ma11Hf
SIMPSON, James	22	M	Unknown	29Ma11Hf
Ann	21	F	Unknown	29Ma11Hf
GRANT, Bridget	42	F	Unknown	29Ma11Hf
MORROW, Hector	27	M	Unknown	29Ma11Hf
CULGGESH, Eliza	24	F	Unknown	29Ma11Hf
COWAN, Mary	27	F	Unknown	29Ma11Hf
Agnas	25	F	Unknown	29Ma11Hf
Cathe.	12	F	Unknown	29Ma11Hf
William	10	M	Unknown	29Ma11Hf
John	9	M	Child	29Ma11Hf
FULTS, John	42	M	Unknown	29Ma11Hf
CAMPILES, James	30	M	Unknown	29Ma11Hf
MCARDLE, Mary	29	F	Unknown	29Ma11Hf
Bernard	21	M	Unknown	29Ma11Hf
CAMPBELL, Catherin	43	F	Unknown	29Ma11Hf
OHANLAN, Bridget	42	F	Unknown	29Ma11Hf
MEIGHAN, Thomas	14	M	Unknown	29Ma11Hf
Mary	21	F	Unknown	29Ma11Hf
IRWIN, Andrew	27	M	Unknown	29Ma11Hf
HENING, John	20	M	Unknown	29Ma11Hf
MCCANN, Elizabeth	42	F	Unknown	29Ma11Hf
OHEAR, Margret	21	F	Unknown	29Ma11Hf
Mary	19	F	Unknown	29Ma11Hf
MCGOWAN, Biddy	42	F	Unknown	29Ma11Hf
BARLY, William	22	M	Unknown	29Ma11Hf
OHEAR, Domonich	20	M	Unknown	29Ma11Hf
MCPARLAN, Biddy	27	F	Unknown	29Ma11Hf
JOLE, Cathern	33	M	Unknown	29Ma11Hf
COUPTES, John	42	M	Unknown	29Ma11Hf
ROCHS, Biddy	14	F	Unknown	29Ma11Hf
MCGENUS, Thomas	32	M	Unknown	29Ma11Hf
CONLON, Michal	27	M	Unknown	29Ma11Hf
MCEVOY, Eliza	21	F	Unknown	29Ma11Hf
RUSSELL, Robert	42	M	Unknown	29Ma11Hf
Margret	27	F	Unknown	29Ma11Hf
MCCARTHY, Rose-Ann	20	F	Unknown	29Ma11Hf
BOYLE, Mary	20	F	Unknown	29Ma11Hf
PRISTON, Eliza	14	F	Unknown	29Ma11Hf
PARR, William	41	M	Unknown	29Ma11Hf
Eliza	40	F	Unknown	29Ma11Hf
Susan	19	F	Unknown	29Ma11Hf
HANNLON, George	22	M	Unknown	29Ma11Hf
MAGUIRE, Margret	20	F	Unknown	29Ma11Hf
Margret	.00	F	Infant	29Ma11Hf
MCMITTEN, James	40	M	Unknown	29Ma11Hf
WARREN, William-J.	27	M	Unknown	29Ma11Hf
MCKEOWN, Edward	27	M	Unknown	29Ma11Hf
MOONEY, Biddy	14	F	Unknown	29Ma11Hf
MCMULLEN, Michal	27	M	Unknown	29Ma11Hf
JOHNSTON, James	20	M	Unknown	29Ma11Hf
MCCANN, James	17	M	Unknown	29Ma11Hf
JOHNSTON, Robert	42	M	Unknown	29Ma11Hf
Thomas	40	M	Unknown	29Ma11Hf
MURPHY, Terence	45	M	Unknown	29Ma11Hf
John	42	M	Unknown	29Ma11Hf
Elizabeth	17	M	Unknown	29Ma11Hf
Bridget	10	F	Unknown	29Ma11Hf
BELL, Robert	14	M	Unknown	29Ma11Hf
MARTON, John	38	M	Unknown	29Ma11Hf

NAMES OF PASSENGERS	AGE	SEX	OCCUPATIONS	DATE PORT SHIP
MCCUDDEN, Ann	21	F	Unknown	29Ma11Hf
DOYLE, James	27	M	Unknown	29Ma11Hf
QUINN, Elizabeth	22	F	Unknown	29Ma11Hf
MATHEW, Alice	41	F	Unknown	29Ma11Hf
LANDY, Ann	22	F	Unknown	29Ma11Hf
MCMARTORY, Ann	41	F	Unknown	29Ma11Hf
CAMPBELL, Christy	38	M	Unknown	29Ma11Hf
Rose	27	F	Unknown	29Ma11Hf
GALICA, Rose	22	F	Unknown	29Ma11Hf
Mary	12	F	Unknown	29Ma11Hf
Henry	9	M	Child	29Ma11Hf
MAGEE, James	42	M	Unknown	29Ma11Hf
WOODS, Patrick	27	M	Unknown	29Ma11Hf
BARDON, Henry	49	M	Unknown	29Ma11Hf
Mary	42	F	Unknown	29Ma11Hf
Charlott	.00	F	Infant	29Ma11Hf
CURIGEL, Patrick	22	M	Unknown	29Ma11Hf
James	20	M	Unknown	29Ma11Hf
FOX, William	41	M	Unknown	29Ma11Hf
WHITE, Sarah	40	F	Unknown	29Ma11Hf
MURPHY, Richard	42	M	Unknown	29Ma11Hf
Cathn.	27	F	Unknown	29Ma11Hf
Margret	22	F	Unknown	29Ma11Hf
Anne	21	F	Unknown	29Ma11Hf

CONRAD 29 MAY 1849

From Greenock

NAMES OF PASSENGERS	AGE	SEX	OCCUPATIONS	DATE PORT SHIP
MCRITCHIE, Wm.	40	M	Blacksmith	29Ma33Hi
James	38	M	Blacksmith	29Ma33Hi
GEMMILL, Andrew	39	M	Farmer	29Ma33Hi
Elizth.	39	F	Relative	29Ma33Hi
Elizth.	11	F	Relative	29Ma33Hi
Robert	4	M	Child	29Ma33Hi
James	2	M	Child	29Ma33Hi
HAMILTON, Alexr.	24	M	Laborer	29Ma33Hi
OHAIR, John	41	M	Farmer	29Ma33Hi
Roseann	39	F	Relative	29Ma33Hi
James	11	M	Relative	29Ma33H
William	8	M	Child	29Ma33H
Philip	5	M	Child	29Ma33H
Michael	3	M	Child	29Ma33H
Henry	.11	M	Infant	29Ma33H
DONNELLY, Jane	18	F	Spinster	29Ma33H
WILSON, George	39	M	Baker	29Ma33H
GAVIN, John	33	M	Cnf	29Ma33H
Mary	33	F	Relative	29Ma33H
Robert	11	M	Relative	29Ma33H
DAVIS, Wm.	24	M	Dyer	29Ma33H
Jane	22	F	Wife	29Ma33H
Michael	18	M	Unknown	29Ma33H
SMITH, Alexr.	19	M	Shoemaker	29Ma33H
Jane	48	F	Spinster	29Ma33H
Sarah	18	F	Spinster	29Ma33H
Elizth.	7	F	Child	29Ma33H
GEMNELL, Robt.	14	M	Tailor	29Ma33H
MCRITCHIE, Jane	6	F	Child	29Ma33H
James	3	M	Child	29Ma33H
JAMIESON, Robert	24	M	Laborer	29Ma33H
NISBETT, Robt.	63	M	Farmer	29Ma33H
Marion	56	F	Relative	29Ma33H
Elzth.	24	F	Relative	29Ma33H
Janet	22	F	Relative	29Ma33H
John	20	M	Relative	29Ma33H
Robert	17	M	Relative	29Ma33H
MAN, Thomas	27	M	Farmer	29Ma33H
Agnes	22	F	Relative	29Ma33H
Charles	4	M	Child	29Ma33H

NAMES OF PASSENGERS	AGE	SEX	OCCUPATIONS	DATE PORT SHIP	NAMES OF PASSENGERS	AGE	SEX	OCCUPATIONS	DATE PORT SHIP
MAN, Janet	.11	F	Infant	29Ma33Hi	BOYLE, Andrew	20	M	Laborer	29Ma33Hi
NESBET, James	20	M	Farmer	29Ma33Hi	WILKILL, Robert	34	M	Laborer	29Ma33Hi
FINDLAY, Janet	50	F	Spinster	29Ma33Hi	U-Mrs.	28	F	Wife	29Ma33Hi
WILSON, Robert	30	M	Farmer	29Ma33Hi	WOOD, Thos.	50	M	Laborer	29Ma33Hi
Janet	30	F	Relative	29Ma33Hi	Mary	46	F	Wife	29Ma33Hi
James	9	M	Child	29Ma33Hi	George	16	M	Unknown	29Ma33Hi
Hugh	7	M	Child	29Ma33Hi	Jane	12	F	Unknown	29Ma33Hi
John	3	M	Child	29Ma33Hi	Isabella	10	F	Unknown	29Ma33Hi
Robert	.08	M	Infant	29Ma33Hi	Thos.	8	F	Child	29Ma33Hi
ALLAN, Gavin	22	M	Laborer	29Ma33Hi	MURRAY, U-Mrs.	46	F	Wife	29Ma33Hi
SHAW, Wm.	18	M	Laborer	29Ma33Hi	Margt.	19	F	Unknown	29Ma33Hi
HARPER, Wm.	38	M	Laborer	29Ma33Hi	CRAIG, Anna	27	F	Spinster	29Ma33Hi
COCHRAN, Wm.	40	M	Laborer	29Ma33Hi	DONALDSON, Andw.	21	M	Laborer	29Ma33Hi
WILSON, John	27	M	Farmer	29Ma33Hi	Elizth.	20	F	Wife	29Ma33Hi
Isabella	26	F	Relative	29Ma33Hi	John	.10	M	Infant	29Ma33Hi
Catharine	5	F	Child	29Ma33Hi	CASWELL, Robert	40	M	Laborer	29Ma33Hi
Wm.	3	M	Child	29Ma33Hi	MCCARTON, James	25	M	Laborer	29Ma33Hi
Isabella	.07	F	Infant	29Ma33Hi	Sarah	22	F	Wife	29Ma33Hi
MCLEAN, John	35	M	Carver	29Ma33Hi	Patrick	.09	M	Infant	29Ma33Hi
Margt.	50	F	Spinster	29Ma33Hi	BOYLAN, Hugh	26	M	Laborer	29Ma33Hi
SMALL, James	20	M	Tailor	29Ma33Hi	MURRAY, Bridget	25	F	Spinster	29Ma33Hi
Margt.	5	F	Child	29Ma33Hi	CORK, John	20	M	Laborer	29Ma33Hi
HENDERSON, Thos.	25	M	Wright	29Ma33Hi	HUGHES, Hannah	18	F	Spinster	29Ma33Hi
SMITH, Mary	22	F	Spinster	29Ma33Hi	COLLINS, Mary	18	F	Spinster	29Ma33Hi
Sarah	20	F	Spinster	29Ma33Hi	EVANS, Pat	24	M	Laborer	29Ma33Hi
Christina	7	F	Child	29Ma33Hi	MCARDLE, James	21	M	Laborer	29Ma33Hi
CLARK, John	48	M	Joiner	29Ma33Hi	DONNELLY, Peter	23	M	Laborer	29Ma33Hi
Margt.	50	F	Wife	29Ma33Hi	DORLEY, Elizth.	17	F	Spinster	29Ma33Hi
Robert	21	M	Unknown	29Ma33Hi	KEAN, James	26	M	Laborer	29Ma33Hi
RALSTON, Duncan	20	M	Laborer	29Ma33Hi	HAUGHNEY, John	25	M	Laborer	29Ma33Hi
MCRITCHIE, James	44	M	Farmer	29Ma33Hi	NEILSON, John	26	M	Laborer	29Ma33Hi
U-Mrs.	45	F	Relative	29Ma33Hi	MCCARR, Pat	16	M	Laborer	29Ma33Hi
Margt.	22	F	Relative	29Ma33Hi	Ann	13	F	Unknown	29Ma33Hi
Daniel	11	M	Relative	29Ma33Hi	MCGUINNESS, Ellen	30	F	Spinster	29Ma33Hi
THOMPSON, E.	9	F	Child	29Ma33Hi	LOURINSON, Sarah	16	F	Spinster	29Ma33Hi
Ann	7	F	Child	29Ma33Hi	PATTERSON, John	18	M	Laborer	29Ma33Hi
Margt.	37	F	Spinster	29Ma33Hi	CROULL, James	30	M	Laborer	29Ma33Hi
Janet	39	F	Spinster	29Ma33Hi	DEARIE, John	23	M	Laborer	29Ma33Hi
Catharine	15	F	Spinster	29Ma33Hi	FULLA, Robert	21	M	Laborer	29Ma33Hi
MCDERMID, James	27	M	Laborer	29Ma33Hi	WRIGHT, John	26	M	Laborer	29Ma33Hi
FORRESTER, Mary	21	F	Laborer	29Ma33Hi	Andrew	24	M	Laborer	29Ma33Hi
POLLOCK, Cathe.	19	F	Spinster	29Ma33Hi	DEARIE, Bernard	26	M	Laborer	29Ma33Hi
MARSHALL, Matthew	25	M	Smith	29Ma33Hi	HARKINS, Mary	18	F	Spinster	29Ma33Hi
BROWN, John	33	M	Smith	29Ma33Hi	PAXTON, John	35	M	Farmer	29Ma33Hi
HUNTER, Alexr.	30	M	Farmer	29Ma33Hi	Margt.	33	F	Wife	29Ma33Hi
U-Mrs.	26	F	Relative	29Ma33Hi	Martha	16	F	Unknown	29Ma33Hi
Margt.	7	F	Child	29Ma33Hi	ROBSON, Wm.	27	M	Laborer	29Ma33Hi
Mary	5	F	Child	29Ma33Hi	MCKENNY, Wm.	19	M	Laborer	29Ma33Hi
Janet	2	F	Child	29Ma33Hi	SIMON, Julius	23	M	Laborer	29Ma33Hi
Ann	.04	F	Infant	29Ma33Hi	GILLESPIE, Ann	18	F	Spinster	29Ma33Hi
HAMILTON, Daniel	22	M	Farmer	29Ma33Hi	Jane	16	F	Spinster	29Ma33Hi
Mary	18	F	Relative	29Ma33Hi	AGNEW, Alexr.	43	M	Laborer	29Ma33Hi
Eliza	20	F	Relative	29Ma33Hi	MCGUIRE, Alexr.	26	M	Smith	29Ma33Hi
Rebecca	19	F	Relative	29Ma33Hi	Frances	14	M	Unknown	29Ma33Hi
Jane	40	F	Relative	29Ma33Hi	BLACK, Jane	19	F	Spinster	29Ma33Hi
Isabella	13	F	Relative	29Ma33Hi	MCMANUS, Felix	60	M	Farmer	29Ma33Hi
DOHERTY, Patrick	28	M	Laborer	29Ma33Hi	Cathe.	22	F	Wife	29Ma33Hi
EWING, Robert	40	M	Laborer	29Ma33Hi	John	25	M	Unknown	29Ma33Hi
Andw.	39	M	Laborer	29Ma33Hi	MCPHARE, Jas.	15	M	Unknown	29Ma33Hi
Eliza	29	F	Wife	29Ma33Hi	LUDLEY, Charles	35	M	Laborer	29Ma33Hi
CAMERON, Wm.	30	M	Laborer	29Ma33Hi	SWIFT, Abm.	55	M	Merchant	29Ma33Hi
Ellen	28	F	Wife	29Ma33Hi	Rosalie	26	F	Relative	29Ma33Hi
REILEY, Margt.	25	F	Unknown	29Ma33Hi	Lisaletta	24	F	Relative	29Ma33Hi
Mary	10	F	Unknown	29Ma33Hi	Franz	22	M	Relative	29Ma33Hi
Margt.	8	F	Child	29Ma33Hi	ENGLANDER, Marquiz	25	M	Goldsmith	29Ma33Hi
Sally	3	F	Child	29Ma33Hi	HAACK, Constantine	24	M	Engineer	29Ma33Hi
Ann	.06	F	Infant	29Ma33Hi	DAVID, Abm.	30	M	Merchant	29Ma33Hi
BROWN, Joseph	30	M	Farmer	29Ma33Hi	Hannah	24	F	Wife	29Ma33Hi
Ann	26	F	Wife	29Ma33Hi	SHRADER, Casper	34	M	Farmer	29Ma33Hi
Mary	.03	F	Infant	29Ma33Hi	Marie	33	F	Relative	29Ma33Hi
DUFFY, Patk.	18	M	Laborer	29Ma33Hi	Alvelin	7	F	Child	29Ma33Hi
Mary	26	F	Relative	29Ma33Hi	Marie	5	F	Child	29Ma33Hi
Martha	22	F	Relative	29Ma33Hi	Wilhelmina	2	F	Child	29Ma33Hi
Helen	20	F	Relative	29Ma33Hi	MEALKA, Fredk.	23	M	Mason	29Ma33Hi
FLANNIGAN, Daniel	25	M	Laborer	29Ma33Hi	PAPST, Oscar	23	M	Shoemaker	29Ma33Hi

NAMES OF PASSENGERS	AGE	SEX	OCCUPATIONS	DATE PORT SHIP
VENSCH, Fredk.	22	M	Cbtmkr	29Ma33Hi
ADAM, Elias	25	M	Tailor	29Ma33Hi
LEISTHER, Wilhelm	26	M	Cbtmkr	29Ma33Hi
KOCH, Fredk.	26	M	Cbtmkr	29Ma33Hi
FINN, Carl	27	M	Wheelwright	29Ma33Hi
Augusta	20	F	Wife	29Ma33Hi
GIMSCHE, Edward	24	M	Carpenter	29Ma33Hi
LEACHART, Wm.	28	M	Painter	29Ma33Hi
NAMMANN, Alexr.	30	M	Painter	29Ma33Hi
Maria	30	F	Wife	29Ma33Hi
FRITZ, August	19	M	Cbtmkr	29Ma33Hi
WILLIAMS, Mary-Ann	19	F	Spinster	29Ma33Hi
WELSH, Mary	40	F	Wife	29Ma33Hi
Robert	17	M	Relative	29Ma33Hi
Eliza	15	F	Relative	29Ma33Hi
Samuel	13	M	Relative	29Ma33Hi
George	11	M	Relative	29Ma33Hi
DARBY, James	20	M	Laborer	29Ma33Hi
Patrick	18	M	Laborer	29Ma33Hi
John	14	M	Laborer	29Ma33Hi
Catharine	40	F	Spinster	29Ma33Hi
CURLY, Mary	50	F	Unknown	29Ma33Hi
Owen	18	M	Relative	29Ma33Hi
Cathe.	16	F	Relative	29Ma33Hi
Michael	13	M	Relative	29Ma33Hi
Susan	11	F	Relative	29Ma33Hi
Ann	9	F	Child	29Ma33Hi
Margt.	7	F	Child	29Ma33Hi
MCCAGLEY, Arnold	28	M	Laborer	29Ma33Hi
RYAN, Patk.	24	M	Farmer	29Ma33Hi
Rosey	18	F	Wife	29Ma33Hi
Catharine	16	F	Unknown	29Ma33Hi
John	2	M	Child	29Ma33Hi
BYRNES, Francis	30	M	Laborer	29Ma33Hi
MCGURK, Michael	20	M	Laborer	29Ma33Hi
MCGILDUFF, Patk.	20	M	Laborer	29Ma33Hi
TIERNAY, Ann	18	F	Spinster	29Ma33Hi
DUFF, Ann	25	F	Spinster	29Ma33Hi
DONNELLY, Rose	30	F	Spinster	29Ma33Hi
MCCHRYSTAL, Danl.	24	M	Laborer	29Ma33Hi
MCGAVIN, Peter	35	M	Laborer	29Ma33Hi
Rosanna	25	F	Wife	29Ma33Hi
BRADLEY, Ann	18	F	Spinster	29Ma33Hi
BURKETT, Ann	18	F	Spinster	29Ma33Hi
MORAN, Bernard	30	M	Laborer	29Ma33Hi
Bridget	30	F	Wife	29Ma33Hi
James	.09	M	Infant	29Ma33Hi
HALL, Francis	20	M	Laborer	29Ma33Hi
LOGAN, Wm.	18	M	Laborer	29Ma33Hi
DALLY, Ann	24	F	Spinster	29Ma33Hi
James	12	M	Unknown	29Ma33Hi
Fredk.	18	M	Laborer	29Ma33Hi
Matilda	4	F	Child	29Ma33Hi
Theresa	2	F	Child	29Ma33Hi
LAFAN, John	24	M	Laborer	29Ma33Hi
BOND, John	24	M	Laborer	29Ma33Hi
MCWHER, Cathe.	50	F	Unknown	29Ma33Hi
Wm.	24	M	Relative	29Ma33Hi
Eliza	22	F	Relative	29Ma33Hi
Margt.	20	F	Relative	29Ma33Hi
Grace	18	F	Relative	29Ma33Hi
Mary	11	F	Relative	29Ma33Hi
HENDRY, Michael	40	M	Laborer	29Ma33Hi
DONAGHEY, James	24	M	Laborer	29Ma33Hi
Ann	22	F	Wife	29Ma33Hi
Andrew	23	M	Unknown	29Ma33Hi
WARD, Margt.	22	F	Laborer	29Ma33Hi
ONEIL, Bernard	20	M	Laborer	29Ma33Hi
Patk.	25	M	Laborer	29Ma33Hi
Wm.	30	M	Laborer	29Ma33Hi
WILLIAMSON, Robt.	21	M	Laborer	29Ma33Hi
POWELL, Mary	48	F	Spinster	29Ma33Hi
GORMLAY, Mary	40	F	Spinster	29Ma33Hi
POWELL, Eliza	12	F	Unknown	29Ma33Hi
John	10	M	Unknown	29Ma33Hi
GORMLAY, Patk.	10	M	Unknown	29Ma33Hi
POWELL, Mary	8	F	Child	29Ma33Hi
Cathe.	6	F	Child	29Ma33Hi
GILLIES, Alexr.	44	M	Laborer	29Ma33Hi
SYMMINGTON, Danl.	26	M	Laborer	29Ma33Hi
Fanny	28	F	Wife	29Ma33Hi
RODGER, James	25	M	Farmer	29Ma33Hi
DOLLY, Mary	50	F	Spinster	29Ma33Hi
BOYLE, Andrew	20	M	Laborer	29Ma33Hi
FROGGART, George	25	M	Laborer	29Ma33Hi
GORMLEY, Barney	20	M	Laborer	29Ma33Hi
RUTZER, S.D.	40	M	Laborer	29Ma33Hi
HAHUS, A.	50	F	Laborer	29Ma33Hi
BOSCHER, E.A.	22	M	Laborer	29Ma33Hi
T.G.	24	M	Laborer	29Ma33Hi
MCRICHIE, Cathe.	.03	F	Infant	29Ma33Hi
MCKENZIE, Murdoch	23	M	Laborer	29Ma33Hi

CHIEFTAIN 29 MAY 1849

From Belfast

NAMES OF PASSENGERS	AGE	SEX	OCCUPATIONS	DATE PORT SHIP
BUTLER, Simon	40	M	Unknown	29Ma05Ht
Jane	30	F	Unknown	29Ma05Ht
John	13	M	Unknown	29Ma05Ht
James	11	M	Unknown	29Ma05Ht
Dorcas	3	M	Child	29Ma05Ht
Mary-Jane	.00	F	Infant	29Ma05Ht
MADDEN, Susan	20	F	Unknown	29Ma05Ht
GAYNOR, John	16	M	Unknown	29Ma05Ht
KEATING, John	22	M	Unknown	29Ma05Ht
Catherine	19	F	Unknown	29Ma05Ht
Catherine	40	F	Unknown	29Ma05Ht
Mary-Jane	14	F	Unknown	29Ma05Ht
Daniel	13	M	Unknown	29Ma05Ht
MCLARIM, John	25	M	Unknown	29Ma05Ht
MCLEAN, Arch	20	M	Unknown	29Ma05Ht
MCKEAG, James	70	M	Unknown	29Ma05Ht
John	40	M	Unknown	29Ma05Ht
Mary	20	F	Unknown	29Ma05Ht
Mary	70	F	Unknown	29Ma05Ht
Rose	17	F	Unknown	29Ma05Ht
WOODSIDE, Samuel	17	M	Unknown	29Ma05Ht
Jane	20	F	Unknown	29Ma05Ht
DONNOLLY, Margaret	35	F	Unknown	29Ma05Ht
Mary	3	F	Child	29Ma05Ht
Susan	.00	F	Infant	29Ma05Ht
MCCLURE, John	28	M	Unknown	29Ma05Ht
Isabella	35	F	Unknown	29Ma05Ht
Wm.John	6	M	Child	29Ma05Ht
William	2	M	Child	29Ma05Ht
Agnes	.00	F	Infant	29Ma05Ht
David	.00	M	Infant	29Ma05Ht
Sarah	28	F	Unknown	29Ma05Ht
DARRAGH, John	24	M	Unknown	29Ma05Ht
Margaret	24	F	Unknown	29Ma05Ht
THOMPSON, Francis	32	M	Unknown	29Ma05Ht
David	13	M	Unknown	29Ma05Ht
HARE, John	30	M	Unknown	29Ma05Ht
Margaret	30	F	Unknown	29Ma05Ht
Fanny	4	F	Child	29Ma05Ht
William	.00	M	Infant	29Ma05Ht
MAHOOD, James	35	M	Unknown	29Ma05Ht
Nancy	30	F	Unknown	29Ma05Ht
David	13	M	Unknown	29Ma05Ht
James	12	M	Unknown	29Ma05Ht
Eliza	9	F	Child	29Ma05Ht
Richard	8	M	Child	29Ma05Ht
William	5	M	Child	29Ma05Ht

NAMES OF PASSENGERS	AGE	SEX	OCCUPATIONS	DATE PORT SHIP
MCKEE, Thomas	20	M	Unknown	29Ma05Ht
HANNA, Robert	20	M	Unknown	29Ma05Ht
MARSHALL, Robert	20	M	Unknown	29Ma05Ht
SIMPSON, Samuel	48	M	Unknown	29Ma05Ht
Ann	30	F	Unknown	29Ma05Ht
Jane	15	F	Unknown	29Ma05Ht
Lowry	13	M	Unknown	29Ma05Ht
Sarah	12	F	Unknown	29Ma05Ht
Rebecca-Ann	10	F	Unknown	29Ma05Ht
Samuel	8	M	Child	29Ma05Ht
David	5	M	Child	29Ma05Ht
KERR, Mary	20	F	Unknown	29Ma05Ht
BLAKELY, Elizabeth	20	F	Unknown	29Ma05Ht
MATEER, Jane	60	F	Unknown	29Ma05Ht
Susanna	30	F	Unknown	29Ma05Ht
David	22	M	Unknown	29Ma05Ht
John	20	M	Unknown	29Ma05Ht
Mary	18	F	Unknown	29Ma05Ht
LOWRY, Alexander	15	M	Unknown	29Ma05Ht
MCILVENE, Sarah	20	F	Unknown	29Ma05Ht
FLANIGAN, John	21	M	Unknown	29Ma05Ht
Margaret	17	F	Unknown	29Ma05Ht
Ann	.00	F	Infant	29Ma05Ht
SIMPSON, Alexander	25	M	Unknown	29Ma05Ht
Mary	23	F	Unknown	29Ma05Ht
WILSON, George	22	M	Unknown	29Ma05Ht
BLAKELY, Hans	48	M	Unknown	29Ma05Ht
Elizabeth	36	F	Unknown	29Ma05Ht
Hans	12	M	Unknown	29Ma05Ht
Mary	10	F	Unknown	29Ma05Ht
Wm.John	8	M	Child	29Ma05Ht
Eliza-Jane	6	F	Child	29Ma05Ht
Nancy-Ann	3	F	Child	29Ma05Ht
David	.00	M	Infant	29Ma05Ht
STEWART, John	32	M	Unknown	29Ma05Ht
John	25	M	Unknown	29Ma05Ht
ROSS, Hugh	18	M	Unknown	29Ma05Ht
MARSHALL, Robert	19	M	Unknown	29Ma05Ht
KEELER, Robert	16	M	Unknown	29Ma05Ht
WARD, Houston	35	M	Unknown	29Ma05Ht
Eliza	9	F	Child	29Ma05Ht
Thomas	7	M	Child	29Ma05Ht
John	5	M	Child	29Ma05Ht
Thomas	50	M	Unknown	29Ma05Ht
Sarah	25	F	Unknown	29Ma05Ht
Jane	21	F	Unknown	29Ma05Ht
DRAKE, Thomas	26	M	Unknown	29Ma05Ht
Martha	20	F	Unknown	29Ma05Ht
MCBRIDE, Wm.	60	M	Unknown	29Ma05Ht
Elizabeth	55	F	Unknown	29Ma05Ht
Jane	40	F	Unknown	29Ma05Ht
James	24	M	Unknown	29Ma05Ht
John	18	M	Unknown	29Ma05Ht
Eliza	16	F	Unknown	29Ma05Ht
William	13	M	Unknown	29Ma05Ht
Moses	10	M	Unknown	29Ma05Ht
Robert	7	M	Child	29Ma05Ht
Thomas	4	M	Child	29Ma05Ht
NORWOOD, Graham	22	M	Unknown	29Ma05Ht
STRANEY, William	50	M	Unknown	29Ma05Ht
Catharine	16	F	Unknown	29Ma05Ht
Mary	13	F	Unknown	29Ma05Ht
MACLURCAN, Thomas	35	M	Unknown	29Ma05Ht
RAMSAY, John	22	M	Unknown	29Ma05Ht
MURRAY, Edward	40	M	Unknown	29Ma05Ht
Jane	40	F	Unknown	29Ma05Ht
Henry	15	M	Unknown	29Ma05Ht
Daniel	13	M	Unknown	29Ma05Ht
Agnes	11	F	Unknown	29Ma05Ht
William	9	M	Child	29Ma05Ht
James	7	M	Child	29Ma05Ht
Jane	5	F	Child	29Ma05Ht
Hugh	3	M	Child	29Ma05Ht
Edward	2	M	Child	29Ma05Ht
Margaret	.00	F	Infant	29Ma05Ht
KANE, John	24	M	Unknown	29Ma05Ht
CARLISLE, Robert	34	M	Unknown	29Ma05Ht
MEGANY, Mary	30	F	Unknown	29Ma05Ht
GEDDES, Samuel	18	M	Unknown	29Ma05Ht
SCULLIEN, Thomas	42	M	Unknown	29Ma05Ht
Kill	18	M	Unknown	29Ma05Ht
TAYLOR, Isabella	27	F	Unknown	29Ma05Ht
WALKER, John	25	M	Unknown	29Ma05Ht
KERR, Eliza	20	F	Unknown	29Ma05Ht
LOWRY, Robert	23	M	Unknown	29Ma05Ht
Ann	20	F	Unknown	29Ma05Ht
CAMBRIDGE, John-M.	40	M	Unknown	29Ma05Ht
Mary	40	F	Unknown	29Ma05Ht
Ellen	13	F	Unknown	29Ma05Ht
EARL, Mary	20	F	Unknown	29Ma05Ht
MCCULLOGH, Arch.	20	M	Unknown	29Ma05Ht
WILSON, Maria	20	F	Unknown	29Ma05Ht
MCNEILL, Michael	25	M	Unknown	29Ma05Ht
Biddy	25	F	Unknown	29Ma05Ht
SMITH, Lawrence	30	M	Unknown	29Ma05Ht
Nancy	24	F	Unknown	29Ma05Ht
MCKENNA, Mary	20	F	Unknown	29Ma05Ht
BOYDE, Thomas	20	M	Unknown	29Ma05Ht
MCAREE, Betty	35	F	Unknown	29Ma05Ht
Michael	13	M	Unknown	29Ma05Ht
Owen	3	M	Child	29Ma05Ht
HENRY, Patrick	18	M	Unknown	29Ma05Ht
Catharine	17	F	Unknown	29Ma05Ht
NEILL, William	22	M	Unknown	29Ma05Ht
Mary	23	F	Unknown	29Ma05Ht
JOHNSON, William	21	M	Unknown	29Ma05Ht
MOFFATT, John	24	M	Unknown	29Ma05Ht
MCCAMBRIDGE, Betsey	2	F	Child	29Ma05Ht

ANN-HARLEY 29 MAY 1849

From Glasgow

NAMES OF PASSENGERS		AGE	SEX	OCCUPATIONS	DATE PORT SHIP
MCVEAN, Duncan		22	M	Laborer	29Ma04Hj
HERCANS, Ann		26	F	Spinster	29Ma04Hj
MCMURRAY, George		30	M	Farmer	29Ma04Hj
Ann	(W)	26	F	Wife	29Ma04Hj
Martha	(D)	5	F	Child	29Ma04Hj
Sarah	(D)	2	F	Child	29Ma04Hj
George	(S)	.02	M	Infant	29Ma04Hj
BIRD, Peter		20	M	Laborer	29Ma04Hj
KELLS, John		23	M	Laborer	29Ma04Hj
GEATINGS, Margt.		3	F	Child	29Ma04Hj
Hugh		24	M	Laborer	29Ma04Hj
CONROY, Bridget		24	F	Spinster	29Ma04Hj
QUINN, Bernard		25	M	Laborer	29Ma04Hj
RORRAN, James		40	M	Farmer	29Ma04Hj
Margt.	(W)	35	F	Wife	29Ma04Hj
CALLIHAN, Thomas		23	M	Laborer	29Ma04Hj
MCTAGGART, John		18	M	Laborer	29Ma04Hj
HAGGARTY, Andrew		23	M	Laborer	29Ma04Hj
Mary	(W)	20	F	Wife	29Ma04Hj
CREELY, Betty		22	F	Spinster	29Ma04Hj
Patrick		14	M	Unknown	29Ma04Hj
FANNAGAN, Catherine		30	F	Wife	29Ma04Hj
Catherine	(D)	3	F	Child	29Ma04Hj
FLOYD, Hugh		21	M	Laborer	29Ma04Hj
MOSS, Samuel		22	M	Laborer	29Ma04Hj
KELLY, Peter		20	M	Laborer	29Ma04Hj
BADLEY, David		19	M	Laborer	29Ma04Hj
DIAMOND, Catherine		20	F	Spinster	29Ma04Hj
BOYD, James-Baxter		20	M	Laborer	29Ma04Hj
MOONEY, James		20	M	Laborer	29Ma04Hj
JONES, Samuel		22	M	Laborer	29Ma04Hj

NAMES OF PASSENGERS		AGE	SEX	OCCUPATIONS	DATE PORT SHIP
CLIFFORD, James		22	M	Laborer	29Ma04Hj
William		24	M	Laborer	29Ma04Hj
Margaret		22	F	Spinster	29Ma04Hj
RINTOUL, Robt.		22	M	Laborer	29Ma04Hj
MOONEY, James		20	M	Laborer	29Ma04Hj

MILICETE 30 MAY 1849

From Liverpool

NAMES OF PASSENGERS		AGE	SEX	OCCUPATIONS	DATE PORT SHIP
HACKETT, William		45	M	Carpenter	30Ma13Hx
U-Mrs.	(W)	45	F	None	30Ma13Hx
William		7	M	Child	30Ma13Hx
Michael		.00	M	Infant	30Ma13Hx
REGAN, William		40	M	Laborer	30Ma13Hx
KEGAN, James		30	M	Laborer	30Ma13Hx
MORGAN, William		40	M	Laborer	30Ma13Hx
DONALY, Francis		37	M	Laborer	30Ma13Hx
U-Mrs.	(W)	26	F	None	30Ma13Hx
Mary		4	F	Child	30Ma13Hx
BAGNALL, William		21	M	Carpenter	30Ma13Hx
EAVERSY, Thomas		20	M	Laborer	30Ma13Hx
BURKE, William		20	M	Laborer	30Ma13Hx
TOOLY, Martin		25	M	Laborer	30Ma13Hx
HOGAN, Thos.		20	M	Mason	30Ma13Hx
WEST, James		20	M	Laborer	30Ma13Hx
LANGAN, Pat.		20	M	Laborer	30Ma13Hx
BROPHY, Mich.		33	M	Laborer	30Ma13Hx
U-Mrs.	(W)	33	F	None	30Ma13Hx
Ellen		.00	F	Infant	30Ma13Hx
Dennis		26	M	Laborer	30Ma13Hx
WHEELER, Mary		40	F	None	30Ma13Hx
Catherine		.00	F	Infant	30Ma13Hx
DEFFY, Pat.		30	M	Laborer	30Ma13Hx
FARRELL, Dan		14	M	Laborer	30Ma13Hx
MCEVERY, Pat		30	M	Laborer	30Ma13Hx
MURRAY, James		18	M	Laborer	30Ma13Hx
HILISPY, James		40	M	Farmer	30Ma13Hx
U-Mrs.	(W)	40	F	Farmer	30Ma13Hx
George		25	M	Farmer	30Ma13Hx
James		19	M	Farmer	30Ma13Hx
Eliza		20	F	Farmer	30Ma13Hx
Thomas		14	F	Farmer	30Ma13Hx
Mary		11	F	Farmer	30Ma13Hx
John		21	M	Farmer	30Ma13Hx
BROPHY, Ellen		25	F	Servant	30Ma13Hx
HESLOPP, George		40	M	Laborer	30Ma13Hx
CUNNINGHAM, John		21	M	Laborer	30Ma13Hx
DIJON, Charles		20	M	Laborer	30Ma13Hx
DONALY, Richard		27	M	Carpenter	30Ma13Hx
GREGORY, Pat.		25	M	Laborer	30Ma13Hx
MATTHEWS, Mich.		15	M	Laborer	30Ma13Hx
DEAN, James		17	M	Laborer	30Ma13Hx
SHEFFY, Mary		25	F	Servant	30Ma13Hx
MYERS, Pat.		40	M	Laborer	30Ma13Hx
U-Mrs.	(W)	36	F	None	30Ma13Hx
Cath.		11	F	None	30Ma13Hx
John		9	M	Child	30Ma13Hx
Julia		7	F	Child	30Ma13Hx
Mary		5	F	Child	30Ma13Hx
Pat.		3	M	Child	30Ma13Hx
Thomas		.00	M	Infant	30Ma13Hx
BRYAN, Patrick		36	M	Farmer	30Ma13Hx
U-Mrs.	(W)	25	F	Farmer	30Ma13Hx
Daniel		40	M	Farmer	30Ma13Hx
Patrick		25	M	Farmer	30Ma13Hx
Mary		15	F	Farmer	30Ma13Hx
John		14	M	Farmer	30Ma13Hx
Margaret		2	F	Child	30Ma13Hx

NAMES OF PASSENGERS		AGE	SEX	OCCUPATIONS	DATE PORT SHIP
BRYAN, Ellen		.00	F	Infant	30Ma13Hx
Died-At-Sea					
CONNELL, John		21	M	Laborer	30Ma13Hx
LARKIN, Mich.		24	M	Laborer	30Ma13Hx
MORISY, Thomas		24	M	Laborer	30Ma13Hx
DELANY, John		24	M	Laborer	30Ma13Hx
RYAN, James		16	M	Laborer	30Ma13Hx
STICSEY, Mary		20	F	Laborer	30Ma13Hx
CUMMINGS, John		21	M	Laborer	30Ma13Hx
CUE, Edward		21	M	Laborer	30Ma13Hx
Pat.		17	M	Laborer	30Ma13Hx
CARNEY, Sam		25	M	Laborer	30Ma13Hx
BURKE, Thos.		30	M	Laborer	30Ma13Hx
Ellen		28	F	Laborer	30Ma13Hx
MCQUADE, Mary		21	F	Dressmaker	30Ma13Hx
RYLEY, Owen		21	M	Laborer	30Ma13Hx
HENDERSON, Thos.		20	M	Laborer	30Ma13Hx
NEVESY, James		25	M	Laborer	30Ma13Hx
Charles		23	M	Laborer	30Ma13Hx
Pat.		23	M	Laborer	30Ma13Hx
Ellen		20	F	Laborer	30Ma13Hx
Thomas		18	M	Laborer	30Ma13Hx
Bernd.		16	M	Laborer	30Ma13Hx
KILKENNY, Edward		28	M	Laborer	30Ma13Hx
U-Mrs.	(W)	28	F	None	30Ma13Hx
Mary-Ann		.00	F	Infant	30Ma13Hx
DENNY, Mary		25	F	Laborer	30Ma13Hx
Margaret		.00	F	Infant	30Ma13Hx
OBRIEN, Thomas		25	M	Farmer	30Ma13Hx
U-Mrs.	(W)	25	F	Farmer	30Ma13Hx
Mary		.00	F	Infant	30Ma13Hx
BRANNAN, James		20	M	Farmer	30Ma13Hx
Cath.		20	F	Farmer	30Ma13Hx
KELLY, Edw.		18	M	Farmer	30Ma13Hx
OBRIEN, James		20	M	Farmer	30Ma13Hx
DUFFY, John		40	M	Farmer	30Ma13Hx
U-Mrs.	(W)	40	F	None	30Ma13Hx
Thomas		23	M	Farmer	30Ma13Hx
Michael		19	M	Farmer	30Ma13Hx
Margaret		18	F	Farmer	30Ma13Hx
Cath.		15	F	Farmer	30Ma13Hx
Edward		11	M	Farmer	30Ma13Hx
Phil.		9	M	Child	30Ma13Hx
CORAGAN, Mich.		12	M	Laborer	30Ma13Hx
CAVANNAH, Peter		45	M	Laborer	30Ma13Hx
U-Miss		20	F	Laborer	30Ma13Hx
U-Mrs.		20	F	Laborer	30Ma13Hx
MEE, James		25	M	Laborer	30Ma13Hx
HERBERT, Michl.		20	M	Laborer	30Ma13Hx
MCGUIRE, John		20	M	Unknown	30Ma13Hx
MCDERMOT, Danl.		40	M	Farmer	30Ma13Hx
U-Mrs.	(W)	40	F	Farmer	30Ma13Hx
Ellen		8	F	Child	30Ma13Hx
Lawrence		5	M	Child	30Ma13Hx
James		17	M	Farmer	30Ma13Hx
MANNY, Judy		20	F	Farmer	30Ma13Hx
MALONEY, Mary		20	F	Farmer	30Ma13Hx
COSGROVE, Edw.		24	M	Laborer	30Ma13Hx
BUCKET, Bridget		20	F	Servant	30Ma13Hx
EVERS, James		25	M	Laborer	30Ma13Hx
Margaret		20	F	Laborer	30Ma13Hx
Margaret		40	F	Laborer	30Ma13Hx
BOYLES, Mary		16	F	Laborer	30Ma13Hx
CARVEL, John		37	M	Laborer	30Ma13Hx
MORICY, Michl.		24	M	Laborer	30Ma13Hx
FITZPATRICK, Michl.		55	M	Laborer	30Ma13Hx
Bridt.	(W)	50	F	None	30Ma13Hx
Pat.		26	M	Laborer	30Ma13Hx
Nicholas		20	M	Laborer	30Ma13Hx
Bridt.		22	F	None	30Ma13Hx
Margaret		18	F	None	30Ma13Hx
JARGON, Dennis		29	M	Laborer	30Ma13Hx
RUDDY, Thomas		20	M	Laborer	30Ma13Hx
SHELLEY, Edward		30	M	Laborer	30Ma13Hx
MALONEY, Catherine		12	F	Laborer	30Ma13Hx

NAMES OF PASSENGERS	AGE	SEX	OCCUPATIONS	DATE PORT SHIP
BURNE, William	23	M	Laborer	30Ma13Hx
Mary	21	F	Laborer	30Ma13Hx
EDGEWORTH, Eliza	18	F	Servant	30Ma13Hx
LORAN, James	37	M	Shoemaker	30Ma13Hx
Eliza	33	F	None	30Ma13Hx
Martha	13	F	None	30Ma13Hx
John	3	M	Child	30Ma13Hx
Chris	.00	M	Infant	30Ma13Hx
FLEMING, Thomas	25	M	Laborer	30Ma13Hx
MURPHY, Ann	26	F	Laborer	30Ma13Hx
BURNEY, Thomas	28	M	Laborer	30Ma13Hx
Susan	20	F	Laborer	30Ma13Hx
GOLDING, James	30	M	Laborer	30Ma13Hx
HAYES, John	25	M	Laborer	30Ma13Hx
RILEY, Julia	28	F	Laborer	30Ma13Hx
Charles	24	M	Laborer	30Ma13Hx
TOOLE, William	22	M	Laborer	30Ma13Hx
Michl.	25	M	Laborer	30Ma13Hx
GRANISAN, Marg.	25	F	Laborer	30Ma13Hx
CULLEN, John	20	M	Laborer	30Ma13Hx
John	21	M	Laborer	30Ma13Hx
Pat.	20	M	Laborer	30Ma13Hx
CARROLL, Thomas	22	M	Laborer	30Ma13Hx
RIDING, John	21	M	Laborer	30Ma13Hx
James	26	M	Laborer	30Ma13Hx
MCGUIRE, Richrd	25	M	Laborer	30Ma13Hx
HARTLEY, Morris	32	M	Laborer	30Ma13Hx
Edward	34	M	Laborer	30Ma13Hx
QUIRK, Morris	30	M	Laborer	30Ma13Hx
EDWARDS, William	30	M	Clerk	30Ma13Hx
CUMMINGS, Jeffrey	55	M	Farmer	30Ma13Hx
Jeffrey	18	M	Farmer	30Ma13Hx
Johannah	16	F	Farmer	30Ma13Hx
Alice	24	F	Farmer	30Ma13Hx
Mary	22	F	Farmer	30Ma13Hx
Hannah	50	F	Farmer	30Ma13Hx
Ellen	20	F	Farmer	30Ma13Hx
HARTLEY, Mary	20	F	Farmer	30Ma13Hx
CUMMINGS, Matthew	20	M	Farmer	30Ma13Hx
Johannah	18	F	Farmer	30Ma13Hx
WELSH, Mary	20	F	Farmer	30Ma13Hx
Bridget	18	F	Farmer	30Ma13Hx
POWER, Pat.	23	M	Mason	30Ma13Hx
DWYER, John	20	M	Laborer	30Ma13Hx
Mary	18	M	Laborer	30Ma13Hx
RYAN, Pat.	26	M	Laborer	30Ma13Hx
Ellen	27	F	Laborer	30Ma13Hx
LYNCH, Pat.	25	M	Laborer	30Ma13Hx
Jane	18	F	Laborer	30Ma13Hx
Eliza	.00	F	Infant	30Ma13Hx
HICKEY, Mary	22	F	Dressmaker	30Ma13Hx
MOORE, James	28	M	Laborer	30Ma13Hx
MAHON, Pat.	30	M	Farmer	30Ma13Hx
CAHILL, Pat.	30	M	Laborer	30Ma13Hx
MCGARTH, Pat.	29	M	Laborer	30Ma13Hx
MCALLEN, J.	29	M	Laborer	30Ma13Hx
MCGUIRE, Phil	40	M	Blacksmith	30Ma13Hx
RUDDY, John	20	M	Laborer	30Ma13Hx
MURPHY, Cath.	30	F	Servant	30Ma13Hx
CONAUGHTY, Pat.	20	M	Laborer	30Ma13Hx
Thos.	20	M	Laborer	30Ma13Hx
John	25	M	Laborer	30Ma13Hx
CUNNINGHAM, Bernard	24	M	Laborer	30Ma13Hx
MCGREARY, John	21	M	Carpenter	30Ma13Hx
KILLY, Ann	26	F	Servant	30Ma13Hx
FITZGIBBON, Edward	20	M	Laborer	30Ma13Hx
Julia	45	F	Laborer	30Ma13Hx
Cornelius	2	M	Child	30Ma13Hx
MCNAMARAH, James	45	M	Laborer	30Ma13Hx
Bridget	48	F	Laborer	30Ma13Hx
Mary	12	F	Laborer	30Ma13Hx
Jane	8	F	Child	30Ma13Hx
Maria	4	F	Child	30Ma13Hx
Charles	2	M	Child	30Ma13Hx
ANEY, John	35	M	Laborer	30Ma13Hx
CANEY, Thomas	25	M	Laborer	30Ma13Hx
MCCARLIFF, Richard	28	M	Laborer	30Ma13Hx
MCCALL, John	20	M	Laborer	30Ma13Hx
GEARN, Danl.	20	M	Laborer	30Ma13Hx
MURTIN, Michl.	20	M	Laborer	30Ma13Hx
SULLIVAN, Rowd.	30	M	Tailor	30Ma13Hx
Margaret	28	F	None	30Ma13Hx
Jeremiah	2	M	Child	30Ma13Hx
Edward	.00	M	Infant	30Ma13Hx
Tim.	25	M	Laborer	30Ma13Hx
BURKE, Walter	50	M	Laborer	30Ma13Hx
Pat.	21	M	Laborer	30Ma13Hx
Mary	25	F	Laborer	30Ma13Hx
Nelly	24	F	Laborer	30Ma13Hx
Bridget	21	F	Laborer	30Ma13Hx
Julia	20	F	Laborer	30Ma13Hx
Eliza	13	F	Laborer	30Ma13Hx
SMITH, Michl.	35	M	Laborer	30Ma13Hx
Pat.	21	M	Laborer	30Ma13Hx
Pat.	13	M	Laborer	30Ma13Hx
James	35	M	Laborer	30Ma13Hx
Cath.	22	F	Laborer	30Ma13Hx
Judy	22	F	Laborer	30Ma13Hx
Ann	00	F	Infant	30Ma13Hx
RIGGS, Eliza	25	F	Laborer	30Ma13Hx
William	.00	M	Infant	30Ma13Hx
GITTCHINA, Fanny	23	F	Laborer	30Ma13Hx
DOYLE, Mary	19	F	Laborer	30Ma13Hx
KESHEYN, John	25	M	Laborer	30Ma13Hx
Pat.	21	M	Laborer	30Ma13Hx
MORRIS, Thomas	21	M	Laborer	30Ma13Hx
Ann	45	F	Laborer	30Ma13Hx
Sally	22	F	Laborer	30Ma13Hx
Eliza	5	F	Child	30Ma13Hx
MCWILLIAM, Pat.	30	M	Mariner	30Ma13Hx
YAWL, Edward	25	M	Laborer	30Ma13Hx
Jane	22	F	Laborer	30Ma13Hx
RILEY, Bridgt.	50	F	Wi	30Ma13Hx
Bridgt.	20	F	Wi	30Ma13Hx
Maria	14	F	None	30Ma13Hx
Dennis	13	M	None	30Ma13Hx
GREGSON, George	00	M	Unknown	30Ma13Hx
LONGBOTTOM, U-Mrs.	00	F	Unknown	30Ma13Hx
U	00	U	Child	30Ma13Hx
U	00	U	Child	30Ma13Hx
U, U	00	U	Servant	30Ma13Hx

EFFINGHAM 30 MAY 1849

From Cork

NAMES OF PASSENGERS	AGE	SEX	OCCUPATIONS	DATE PORT SHIP
DONOGHUE, Peggy	20	F	Spinster	30Ma08Hb
BRESNAN, Tim	20	M	Laborer	30Ma08Hb
MORAN, Pady	20	F	Unknown	30Ma08Hb
OCONNOR, Thos.	20	M	Unknown	30Ma08Hb
HENNESEY, Patt	20	M	Unknown	30Ma08Hb
COLLIER, John	20	M	Unknown	30Ma08Hb
BOLDERS, Rich.	20	M	Unknown	30Ma08Hb
John	20	M	Unknown	30Ma08Hb
Bridget	20	F	Unknown	30Ma08Hb
Ally	20	M	Unknown	30Ma08Hb
CRONIN, Mary	20	F	Unknown	30Ma08Hb
MURRAY, Tim	20	M	Unknown	30Ma08Hb
Johanna	20	F	Unknown	30Ma08Hb
DWYER, Batt	20	M	Unknown	30Ma08Hb
COLLINS, Curley	20	M	Unknown	30Ma08Hb
Patk.	20	M	Unknown	30Ma08Hb
GOULDING, James	20	M	Unknown	30Ma08Hb
Johanna	20	F	Unknown	30Ma08Hb

NAMES OF PASSENGERS	AGE	SEX	OCCUPATIONS	DATE PORT SHIP
SHEEHAN, Cath.	20	F	Unknown	30Ma08Hb
CURTIN, Peggy	20	F	Unknown	30Ma08Hb
MULCHAHY, Hannah	20	F	Unknown	30Ma08Hb
DOOLEY, Mary	20	F	Unknown	30Ma08Hb
WING, James	20	M	Unknown	30Ma08Hb
CASEY, Batt	20	M	Unknown	30Ma08Hb
DOWNING, John	20	M	Unknown	30Ma08Hb
Judith	20	F	Unknown	30Ma08Hb
WALSH, John	20	M	Unknown	30Ma08Hb
LEAHY, Mary-Ann	20	F	Unknown	30Ma08Hb
Died-At-Sea				
AHERN, John	20	M	Unknown	30Ma08Hb
FOLEY, James	20	M	Unknown	30Ma08Hb
Died-At-Sea				
LOMBARD, Rich.	20	M	Unknown	30Ma08Hb
John	20	M	Unknown	30Ma08Hb
Jane	20	F	Unknown	30Ma08Hb
Mary	20	F	Unknown	30Ma08Hb
FRAZER, John	25	M	Unknown	30Ma08Hb
NOONAN, Margt.	22	F	Unknown	30Ma08Hb
HEAFFY, Ann	22	F	Unknown	30Ma08Hb
COX, Wm.	22	M	Unknown	30Ma08Hb
WALLACE, Patt	22	M	Unknown	30Ma08Hb
John	20	M	Unknown	30Ma08Hb
NEAL, Dennis	20	M	Unknown	30Ma08Hb
GOULDING, Hannah	5	F	Child	30Ma08Hb
DUNCAN, Patk.	20	M	Unknown	30Ma08Hb
DRISCOLL, Con.	20	M	Unknown	30Ma08Hb
WALLACE, Wm.	26	M	Unknown	30Ma08Hb
CURTIS, Jerry	26	M	Unknown	30Ma08Hb
MULLIN, Michl.	26	M	Unknown	30Ma08Hb
TWONEY, Joseph	20	M	Unknown	30Ma08Hb
GRIFFIN, Wm.	30	M	Unknown	30Ma08Hb
Kate	26	F	Unknown	30Ma08Hb
John	.00	M	Infant	30Ma08Hb
Mary	.00	F	Infant	30Ma08Hb
BARRY, Mihl.	22	M	Unknown	30Ma08Hb
MULLANE, Margt.	20	F	Unknown	30Ma08Hb
Ellen	12	F	Unknown	30Ma08Hb
HENNESEY, John	26	M	Unknown	30Ma08Hb
BRIEN, Mary	30	F	Unknown	30Ma08Hb
Denis	.00	M	Infant	30Ma08Hb
COTTER, Batt	30	M	Unknown	30Ma08Hb
Patt	.00	M	Infant	30Ma08Hb
Elizabeth	.00	F	Infant	30Ma08Hb
Died-At-Sea				
CASEY, Wm.	30	M	Unknown	30Ma08Hb
JACKSON, Ellen	25	F	Unknown	30Ma08Hb
DONOVAN, Jackson	8	M	Child	30Ma08Hb
DRISCOLL, Michl.	20	M	Unknown	30Ma08Hb
Timothy	25	M	Unknown	30Ma08Hb
Margaret	25	F	Unknown	30Ma08Hb
DONOVAN, Denis	30	M	Unknown	30Ma08Hb
COUGHLAN, Danl.	25	M	Unknown	30Ma08Hb
Con.	20	M	Unknown	30Ma08Hb
PIGOTT, Ann	22	F	Unknown	30Ma08Hb
LYNCH, Danl.	20	M	Unknown	30Ma08Hb
Mary	17	F	Unknown	30Ma08Hb
GLEESON, James	20	M	Unknown	30Ma08Hb
Mary	21	F	Unknown	30Ma08Hb
TWOMEY, Mary	22	F	Unknown	30Ma08Hb
SKEHIN, John	30	M	Unknown	30Ma08Hb
Margaret	30	F	Unknown	30Ma08Hb
James	7	M	Child	30Ma08Hb
James	.00	M	Infant	30Ma08Hb
Denis	9	M	Child	30Ma08Hb
Anne	9	F	Child	30Ma08Hb
Cath.	30	F	Unknown	30Ma08Hb
RIORDAN, John	20	M	Unknown	30Ma08Hb
Johanna	20	F	Unknown	30Ma08Hb
HIGGINS, John	20	M	Unknown	30Ma08Hb
MOHER, John	20	M	Unknown	30Ma08Hb
Hannah	20	F	Unknown	30Ma08Hb
BAREN, Hannah	20	F	Unknown	30Ma08Hb
FOLEY, John	30	M	Unknown	30Ma08Hb
FOLEY, Margaret	30	F	Unknown	30Ma08Hb
Wm.	.00	M	Infant	30Ma08Hb
James	.00	M	Infant	30Ma08Hb
CASHEN, James	30	M	Unknown	30Ma08Hb
Wm.	30	M	Unknown	30Ma08Hb
James	20	M	Unknown	30Ma08Hb
Patk.	40	M	Unknown	30Ma08Hb
James	20	M	Unknown	30Ma08Hb
Hanora	30	F	Unknown	30Ma08Hb
Hanora	40	F	Unknown	30Ma08Hb
Francis	.00	M	Infant	30Ma08Hb
Joyce	.00	M	Infant	30Ma08Hb
Joyce	30	M	Unknown	30Ma08Hb
Anna	11	F	Unknown	30Ma08Hb
Wm.	17	M	Unknown	30Ma08Hb
Eliza	20	F	Unknown	30Ma08Hb
Henry	22	M	Unknown	30Ma08Hb
CURT, Joyce	30	M	Unknown	30Ma08Hb
CONNELL, Richd.	24	M	Unknown	30Ma08Hb
Hanora	22	F	Unknown	30Ma08Hb
Died-At-Sea				
Charles	6	M	Child	30Ma08Hb
Mary	23	F	Unknown	30Ma08Hb
Mary	.00	F	Infant	30Ma08Hb
Michl.	30	M	Unknown	30Ma08Hb
Hannah	.00	F	Infant	30Ma08Hb
FITZGERALD, George	20	M	Unknown	30Ma08Hb
HENNESEY, Wm.	20	M	Unknown	30Ma08Hb
Mary	21	F	Unknown	30Ma08Hb
Michl.	22	M	Unknown	30Ma08Hb
MCLEUR, John	24	M	Unknown	30Ma08Hb
MAHONY, Ellen	25	F	Unknown	30Ma08Hb
BRIEN, James	26	M	Unknown	30Ma08Hb
STACK, John	22	M	Unknown	30Ma08Hb
Ellen	24	F	Unknown	30Ma08Hb
Richd.	.00	M	Infant	30Ma08Hb
MANSFIELD, James	19	M	Unknown	30Ma08Hb
RIORDAN, Wm.	35	M	Unknown	30Ma08Hb
Mary	30	F	Unknown	30Ma08Hb
Cath.	20	F	Unknown	30Ma08Hb
Cath.	.00	F	Infant	30Ma08Hb
CONNELL, Wm.	20	M	Unknown	30Ma08Hb
Thomas	21	M	Unknown	30Ma08Hb
Ellen	26	F	Unknown	30Ma08Hb
Cath.	13	F	Unknown	30Ma08Hb
FITZGERALD, Maurice	29	M	Unknown	30Ma08H
KELLY, Danl.	26	M	Unknown	30Ma08H
MURPHY, James	20	M	Unknown	30Ma08H
James	21	M	Unknown	30Ma08H
Michl.	21	M	Unknown	30Ma08H
CONNOR, Julia	20	F	Unknown	30Ma08H
Cath.	21	F	Unknown	30Ma08H
BRYAN, Michl.	30	M	Unknown	30Ma08H
LUDDY, Wm.	20	M	Unknown	30Ma08H
MAHONY, John	20	M	Unknown	30Ma08H
MURPHY, Wm.	20	M	Unknown	30Ma08H
SHEAHAN, Patt	25	M	Unknown	30Ma08H
CURTIN, John	26	M	Unknown	30Ma08H
BAWLEY, Wm.	23	M	Unknown	30Ma08H
CLANCY, Patt	22	M	Unknown	30Ma08H
FITZGIBBON, Wm.	18	M	Unknown	30Ma08H
Mary	20	F	Unknown	30Ma08H
LEARY, Flora	20	F	Unknown	30Ma08H
COLLINS, Patt	18	M	Unknown	30Ma08H
HAYES, Julia	21	F	Unknown	30Ma08H
CRAWLEY, Mary	20	F	Unknown	30Ma08H
Mary	25	F	Unknown	30Ma08H
DONOVAN, Michl.	28	M	Unknown	30Ma08H
BANANE, Chs.	30	M	Unknown	30Ma08H
Died-At-Sea				
SULLIVAN, Dennis	30	M	Unknown	30Ma08
MAHONY, Dick	20	M	Unknown	30Ma08
POWER, Edmund	20	M	Unknown	30Ma08
CRAWLEY, Julia	20	F	Unknown	30Ma08
CONNELL, Jinny	25	F	Unknown	30Ma08

NAMES OF PASSENGERS	AGE	SEX	OCCUPATIONS	DATE PORT SHIP
HEALY, Con.	30	M	Unknown	30Ma08Hb
Mary	30	F	Unknown	30Ma08Hb
REILY, John	20	M	Unknown	30Ma08Hb
Maria	18	F	Unknown	30Ma08Hb
CRAWLEY, Timothy	40	M	Unknown	30Ma08Hb
Ellen	38	F	Unknown	30Ma08Hb
Died-At-Sea				
Dan	30	M	Unknown	30Ma08Hb
HEGGARTY, Dan	22	M	Unknown	30Ma08Hb
CRAWLEY, Tim	12	M	Unknown	30Ma08Hb
Con.	10	M	Unknown	30Ma08Hb
Denis	8	M	Child	30Ma08Hb
John	6	M	Child	30Ma08Hb
Ellen	.00	F	Infant	30Ma08Hb
SULLIVAN, Dennis	40	M	Unknown	30Ma08Hb
Died-At-Sea				
HENNESEY, Thos.	28	M	Unknown	30Ma08Hb
Died-At-Sea				
MURRAY, Edmund	28	M	Unknown	30Ma08Hb
KEEFE, Owen	12	M	Unknown	30Ma08Hb
Julia	10	F	Unknown	30Ma08Hb
FLANAGAN, John	20	M	Unknown	30Ma08Hb
BRO, Michl.	20	M	Unknown	30Ma08Hb
BRIEN, Julia	25	F	Unknown	30Ma08Hb
MCGRATH, Roger	25	M	Unknown	30Ma08Hb
Ellen	20	F	Unknown	30Ma08Hb
KELLY, Hannah	15	F	Unknown	30Ma08Hb
CAHILL, Wm.	25	M	Unknown	30Ma08Hb
Mary	26	F	Unknown	30Ma08Hb
CORCORAN, Mary	24	F	Unknown	30Ma08Hb
Mary	8	F	Child	30Ma08Hb
Alice	6	F	Child	30Ma08Hb
DELANY, Bridget	20	F	Unknown	30Ma08Hb
MCDONNELL, Thos.	20	M	Unknown	30Ma08Hb
Bridget	25	F	Unknown	30Ma08Hb
MAHONY, James	20	M	Unknown	30Ma08Hb
CONWELL, Nelly	20	F	Unknown	30Ma08Hb
DONOVAN, Timothy	20	M	Unknown	30Ma08Hb
SEAN, Jerry	20	M	Unknown	30Ma08Hb
NASH, Mary	20	F	Unknown	30Ma08Hb
REGAN, Ellen	28	F	Unknown	30Ma08Hb
Mary	20	F	Unknown	30Ma08Hb
KIDNEY, Hannah	24	F	Unknown	30Ma08Hb
VAUGHAN, John	22	M	Unknown	30Ma08Hb
MCDONNELL, Johanna	40	F	Unknown	30Ma08Hb
Hannah	10	F	Unknown	30Ma08Hb
Joseph	7	M	Child	30Ma08Hb
Robert	12	M	Unknown	30Ma08Hb
REILY, Philipp	20	M	Unknown	30Ma08Hb
HIGGINS, John	28	M	Unknown	30Ma08Hb
Mary-Ann	25	F	Unknown	30Ma08Hb
LOONY, Michl.	28	M	Unknown	30Ma08Hb
MCCARTHY, Ellen	20	F	Unknown	30Ma08Hb
BURCHELL, John	26	M	Unknown	30Ma08Hb
OLIFFE, Sheans	22	M	Unknown	30Ma08Hb
FITZGERALD, John	22	M	Unknown	30Ma08Hb
MURPHY, Ellen	18	F	Unknown	30Ma08Hb
Bess	13	F	Unknown	30Ma08Hb
GRIFFEN, Bridget	20	F	Unknown	30Ma08Hb
LYNCH, Cath.	20	F	Unknown	30Ma08Hb
MALONY, James	20	M	Unknown	30Ma08Hb
FOLEY, Wm.	30	M	Unknown	30Ma08Hb
HAWKES, Michl.	26	M	Unknown	30Ma08Hb
SCOLLARD, Maurice	26	M	Unknown	30Ma08Hb
Cath.	24	F	Unknown	30Ma08Hb
MAHONY, Eliza	24	F	Unknown	30Ma08Hb
HERRICK, Jane	26	F	Unknown	30Ma08Hb
WALSH, Michl.	20	M	Unknown	30Ma08Hb
DAWSON, Wm.	33	M	Unknown	30Ma08Hb
Sarah	20	F	Unknown	30Ma08Hb
James	30	M	Unknown	30Ma08Hb
Richd.	9	M	Child	30Ma08Hb
Cath.	.00	F	Infant	30Ma08Hb
Wm.	5	F	Child	30Ma08Hb
Mary	.00	F	Infant	30Ma08Hb

NAMES OF PASSENGERS	AGE	SEX	OCCUPATIONS	DATE PORT SHIP
CURTIN, Danl.	26	M	Unknown	30Ma08Hb
MURPHY, Danl.	24	M	Unknown	30Ma08Hb
Died-At-Sea				
HERLEHY, Wm.	28	M	Unknown	30Ma08Hb
DONOVAN, Jerry	26	M	Unknown	30Ma08Hb
KENNY, Thos.	25	M	Unknown	30Ma08Hb
John	22	M	Unknown	30Ma08Hb
Batt	21	M	Unknown	30Ma08Hb
John	18	M	Unknown	30Ma08Hb
John	13	M	Unknown	30Ma08Hb
Ellen	10	F	Unknown	30Ma08Hb
COUGHLAN, Michl.	40	M	Unknown	30Ma08Hb
Margt.	40	F	Unknown	30Ma08Hb
Peter	24	M	Unknown	30Ma08Hb
Michl.	16	M	Unknown	30Ma08Hb
HOPKINS, J.	00	M	Unknown	30Ma08Hb
HOSKIN, Thos.	00	M	Unknown	30Ma08Hb
WRIGHT, Cath.	00	F	Unknown	30Ma08Hb
HEARD, Ellen	00	F	Unknown	30Ma08Hb
ATKINS, Ben	00	F	Unknown	30Ma08Hb
BURKE, Rebecca	00	F	Unknown	30Ma08Hb
STANLY, Joseph	00	M	Unknown	30Ma08Hb
GREAVES, W.M.	40	M	Unknown	30Ma08Hb
U-Mrs.	20	F	Unknown	30Ma08Hb
U-Miss	20	F	Unknown	30Ma08Hb
G.	19	F	Unknown	30Ma08Hb
H.	17	F	Unknown	30Ma08Hb
Chs.	19	M	Unknown	30Ma08Hb
TOTTENHAM, G.	21	M	Unknown	30Ma08Hb
GREAVES, F.	11	M	Unknown	30Ma08Hb
Maria	8	F	Child	30Ma08Hb
EDWARDS, John	48	M	Unknown	30Ma08Hb
Eliza-Ann	20	F	Unknown	30Ma08Hb
Sarah	19	F	Unknown	30Ma08Hb
Jane	17	F	Unknown	30Ma08Hb
HARRIS, U-Mr.	30	M	Unknown	30Ma08Hb
TELLINGHINT, Cap.	28	M	Unknown	30Ma08Hb
OKEEFE, H.	18	M	Unknown	30Ma08Hb
EDWARDS, B.	17	M	Unknown	30Ma08Hb
Mary-A.	14	F	Unknown	30Ma08Hb
Cath.	13	F	Unknown	30Ma08Hb
Emily	7	M	Child	30Ma08Hb
Robert	10	M	Unknown	30Ma08Hb
James	8	M	Child	30Ma08Hb
NEVILLE, U	20	M	Unknown	30Ma08Hb
BAKER, Richd.	20	M	Unknown	30Ma08Hb
TWOMEY, John	24	M	Unknown	30Ma08Hb
HAYES, Danl.	20	M	Unknown	30Ma08Hb
GLEESON, Pat	17	M	Unknown	30Ma08Hb
AHERN, David	23	M	Unknown	30Ma08Hb
POWER, John	19	M	Unknown	30Ma08Hb
HADIGAN, Patt	19	M	Unknown	30Ma08Hb
AHERN, Mary	20	F	Unknown	30Ma08Hb

RICHARD-N.PARKER 30 MAY 1849

From Cork

NAMES OF PASSENGERS	AGE	SEX	OCCUPATIONS	DATE PORT SHIP
DEBAHAUT, Diana	22	F	Servant	30Ma08Gr
OCONNOR, Michl.	23	M	Farmer	30Ma08Gr
HARRINGTON, Fras.	20	M	Farmer	30Ma08Gr
GALAVIN, Ellen	20	F	Servant	30Ma08Gr
DELANY, Michl.	20	M	Laborer	30Ma08Gr
Maty	11	F	Servant	30Ma08Gr
AHERN, John	20	M	Farmer	30Ma08Gr
WELAND, Thos.	24	M	Farmer	30Ma08Gr
BURCHELL, Henry	13	M	None	30Ma08Gr
Susan	13	F	Servant	30Ma08Gr
WHOLLEY, Michl.	25	M	Farmer	30Ma08Gr

NAMES OF PASSENGERS	AGE	SEX	OCCUPATIONS	DATE PORT SHIP
WHOLLEY, Andrew	23	M	Farmer	30Ma08Gr
Margt.	21	F	Servant	30Ma08Gr
Catherine	60	F	Servant	30Ma08Gr
NEWMAN, Catherine	25	F	Servant	30Ma08Gr
WHOLLEY, Thos.	5	M	Child	30Ma08Gr
Jas.	.00	M	Infant	30Ma08Gr
SULLIVAN, Danl.	30	M	Farmer	30Ma08Gr
Mary	26	F	None	30Ma08Gr
Mary	.00	F	Infant	30Ma08Gr
LEWIS, Ellen	16	F	None	30Ma08Gr
FLANIGAN, Ellen	.00	F	Infant	30Ma08Gr
SWEENEY, Jas.	25	M	Farmer	30Ma08Gr
Mary	20	F	None	30Ma08Gr
DONOVAN, Danl.	22	M	Laborer	30Ma08Gr
DEACY, Jas.	40	M	Farmer	30Ma08Gr
Johanna	35	F	None	30Ma08Gr
William	10	M	None	30Ma08Gr
Margt.	8	F	Child	30Ma08Gr
Patrick	6	M	Child	30Ma08Gr
Mary	.00	F	Infant	30Ma08Gr
ROCHE, Mary	30	F	Servant	30Ma08Gr
REARDON, Danl.	25	M	Shoemaker	30Ma08Gr
GLEESON, Ellen	20	F	Servant	30Ma08Gr
SLATTERY, Mary	24	F	Servant	30Ma08Gr
COLLINS, Corns.	25	M	Farmer	30Ma08Gr
Margt.	20	F	Servant	30Ma08Gr
CALLANAN, Ann	23	F	Servant	30Ma08Gr
MULCAHY, Ann	23	F	Servant	30Ma08Gr
BOYD, Jas.	25	M	Farmer	30Ma08Gr
Joseph	20	M	Farmer	30Ma08Gr
William	18	M	Farmer	30Ma08Gr
CROWLEY, Dennis	23	M	Farmer	30Ma08Gr
COFFEE, Timothy	25	M	Farmer	30Ma08Gr
CARTIN, Ellen	21	F	Servant	30Ma08Gr
REILLY, Ellen	23	F	Servant	30Ma08Gr
SULLIVAN, Marty	24	M	Laborer	30Ma08Gr
HICKEY, James	25	M	Laborer	30Ma08Gr
John	18	M	Laborer	30Ma08Gr
Bridget	16	F	None	30Ma08Gr
Cath.	10	F	None	30Ma08Gr
Ellen	.00	F	Infant	30Ma08Gr
CONNOLLY, Julia	7	F	Child	30Ma08Gr
MURRAY, Patrick	23	M	Laborer	30Ma08Gr
Johanna	17	F	None	30Ma08Gr
Danl.	.00	M	Infant	30Ma08Gr
DONOVAN, Chas.	30	M	Farmer	30Ma08Gr
Michl.	24	M	Farmer	30Ma08Gr
Ellen	27	F	Servant	30Ma08Gr
CROWLEY, John	27	M	Laborer	30Ma08Gr
Mary	20	F	Servant	30Ma08Gr
MAHONY, Jerry	27	M	Farmer	30Ma08Gr
Cath.	20	F	Servant	30Ma08Gr
SHEEHAN, Mary	20	F	Servant	30Ma08Gr
DONOVAN, Julia	.00	F	Infant	30Ma08Gr
CONNELL, Joseph	30	M	Laborer	30Ma08Gr
REGAN, John	26	M	Laborer	30Ma08Gr
BROWN, Edwd.	26	M	Laborer	30Ma08Gr
WEYMOUTH, Ann	24	F	Servant	30Ma08Gr
MCCARTHY, Patrick	25	M	Farmer	30Ma08Gr
Died-At-Sea				
SWEENEY, Owen	50	M	Farmer	30Ma08Gr
SULLIVAN, Michl.	30	M	Farmer	30Ma08Gr
Cath.	26	F	Servant	30Ma08Gr
Michl.	.00	M	Infant	30Ma08Gr
COLLINS, Jim	50	M	Laborer	30Ma08Gr
Dennis	17	M	Laborer	30Ma08Gr
Timothy	18	M	Laborer	30Ma08Gr
James	.00	M	Infant	30Ma08Gr
John	20	M	Laborer	30Ma08Gr
FITZGERALD, John	46	M	Farmer	30Ma08Gr
Mary	21	F	None	30Ma08Gr
Kate	15	F	None	30Ma08Gr
Betty	13	F	None	30Ma08Gr
Jas.	10	M	None	30Ma08Gr
Edmund	8	M	Child	30Ma08Gr

NAMES OF PASSENGERS		AGE	SEX	OCCUPATIONS	DATE PORT SHIP
FITZGERALD, John		7	M	Child	30Ma08Gr
David		.00	M	Infant	30Ma08Gr

LADY-HARVEY 30 MAY 1849

From Limerick

NAMES OF PASSENGERS		AGE	SEX	OCCUPATIONS	DATE PORT SHIP
HICKIN, John		24	M	Farmer	30Ma35Gp
Johanna	(W)	22	F	Wife	30Ma35Gp
Margaret	(D)	13	F	Daughter	30Ma35Gp
BYRNES, Wm.		58	M	Farmer	30Ma35Gp
Thomas	(S)	25	M	Farmer	30Ma35Gp
John	(S)	18	M	Farmer	30Ma35Gp
Johanna	(W)	22	F	Wife	30Ma35Gp
Hannorah	(D)	19	F	Daughter	30Ma35Gp
CLOHECY, Mary		40	F	Farmer	30Ma35Gp
QUINN, John		22	M	Farmer	30Ma35Gp
Michael		22	M	Unknown	30Ma35Gp
Pat		20	M	Unknown	30Ma35Gp
Hannora		21	F	Wife	30Ma35Gp
Bridget		18	F	Unknown	30Ma35Gp
Ellen		16	F	Unknown	30Ma35Gp
CALLAGHAN, Thomas		25	M	Laborer	30Ma35Gp
Sarah	(W)	21	F	Wife	30Ma35Gp
WALSH, T.		25	M	Farmer	30Ma35Gp
HANNA, Johanna		27	F	Wife	30Ma35Gp
COSTOLOE, Bridget		19	F	Unknown	30Ma35Gp
LAW, Michael		30	M	Trade Man	30Ma35Gp
CONNORS, John		35	M	Farmer	30Ma35Gp
ADAMS, Mary-Ann		19	F	Wife	30Ma35Gp
CUNNINGHAM, Terrence		23	M	Farmer	30Ma35Gp
BOLAND, John		30	M	Farmer	30Ma35Gp
Margt.	(W)	25	F	Wife	30Ma35Gp
MONEY, Johanna		25	F	Unknown	30Ma35Gp
HANNEN, Wm.		20	M	Farmer	30Ma35Gp
MCMAHON, Bridget		22	F	Unknown	30Ma35Gp
FITZGERALD, Michl.		40	M	Laborer	30Ma35Gp
GORMAN, John		10	M	Child	30Ma35Gp
Jerry		6	M	Child	30Ma35Gp
MCMAHON, James		24	M	Laborer	30Ma35Gp
MALONEY, James		48	M	Farmer	30Ma35Gp
Cath.	(W)	52	F	Wife	30Ma35Gp
Mary	(D)	13	F	Daughter	30Ma35Gp
John	(S)	21	M	Son	30Ma35Gp
Thomas	(S)	18	M	Son	30Ma35Gp
Michael	(S)	20	M	Son	30Ma35Gp
MARRIBY, Thomas		30	M	Farmer	30Ma35Gp
Ellen	(W)	23	F	Wife	30Ma35Gp
John		.06	M	Infant	30Ma35Gp
HOGAN, Michael		30	M	Laborer	30Ma35Gp
LYNCH, John		32	M	Laborer	30Ma35Gp
Nerry	(T)	13	F	Sister	30Ma35Gp
CONNELLY, Pat		30	M	Laborer	30Ma35Gp
MCINERNY, Thomas		30	M	Laborer	30Ma35Gp
Mary	(T)	20	F	Sister	30Ma35Gp
Cathl.	(T)	4	F	Child	30Ma35Gp
DONNALLAN, Sarah		19	F	Unknown	30Ma35Gp
DOYLE, Michael		19	M	Laborer	30Ma35Gp
MCINERNY, Pat		24	M	Farmer	30Ma35Gp
Cathl.	(T)	25	F	Sister	30Ma35Gp
KELLY, Darby		45	M	Farmer	30Ma35Gp
Bridget	(D)	19	F	Unknown	30Ma35Gp
Pat	(S)	18	F	Unknown	30Ma35Gp
Mary	(D)	16	F	Unknown	30Ma35Gp
Ellen	(D)	14	F	Unknown	30Ma35Gp
Honora	(D)	12	F	Unknown	30Ma35Gp
BROWN, Francis		29	M	Laborer	30Ma35Gp
LEARY, Andrew		30	M	Laborer	30Ma35Gp
MCGRUEN, Hugh		30	M	Laborer	30Ma35Gp

NAMES OF PASSENGERS		AGE	SEX	OCCUPATIONS	DATE PORT SHIP
MCGRUEN, Bridget	(W)	24	F	Wife	30Ma35Gp
Mary	(D)	3	F	Child	30Ma35Gp
Honora	(D)	.03	F	Infant	30Ma35Gp
WOLFE, Raffe		30	M	Farmer	30Ma35Gp
Mary	(W)	50	F	Wife	30Ma35Gp
BOYLE, Eliza		26	F	Unknown	30Ma35Gp
KEOGAN, Michl.		32	M	Farmer	30Ma35Gp
Mary	(W)	40	F	Wife	30Ma35Gp
Michl.	(S)	17	M	Son	30Ma35Gp
Mary	(D)	15	F	Daughter	30Ma35Gp
Dennis		28	M	Unknown	30Ma35Gp
MCINERNY, Pat		25	M	Laborer	30Ma35Gp
SLATERTY, Mary		20	F	Unknown	30Ma35Gp
Margt.	(T)	15	F	Sister	30Ma35Gp
GLEASON, John		17	M	Laborer	30Ma35Gp
KENNY, Thos.		20	M	Laborer	30Ma35Gp
CONSIDINE, Wm.		37	M	Farmer	30Ma35Gp
OBRIEN, Timothy		35	M	Farmer	30Ma35Gp
MUNBY, Martin		25	M	Laborer	30Ma35Gp
KIRKPATRICK, John		34	M	Laborer	30Ma35Gp
Anne	(W)	20	F	Wife	30Ma35Gp
COGHAM, Simon		20	M	Laborer	30Ma35Gp
DOHERTY, James		24	M	Laborer	30Ma35Gp
Mary		20	F	Wife	30Ma35Gp
Judy	(T)	26	F	Sister	30Ma35Gp
Mary-Ann		2	F	Child	30Ma35Gp
CALLINAN, Mary		20	F	Wife	30Ma35Gp
Mgt.		26	F	Wife	30Ma35Gp
KINNCAN, Pat		.02	M	Infant	30Ma35Gp
DALY, Martin		40	M	Farmer	30Ma35Gp
KINNCAN, John		50	M	Farmer	30Ma35Gp

JAMES-HALL 30 MAY 1849

From St.Croix

NAMES OF PASSENGERS		AGE	SEX	OCCUPATIONS	DATE PORT SHIP
JOHNSON, Wm.John		43	M	Planter	30Ma39Gn

ROSETTA 30 MAY 1849

From Liverpool

NAMES OF PASSENGERS		AGE	SEX	OCCUPATIONS	DATE PORT SHIP
JENNINGS, Edw.		40	M	Farmer	30Ma02Gy
Anne	(W)	30	F	Wife	30Ma02Gy
Edw.		6	M	Child	30Ma02Gy
Robert		4	M	Child	30Ma02Gy
Jane		.09	F	Infant	30Ma02Gy
BRIEN, Bridget		14	F	Spinster	30Ma02Gy
JENNINGS, Mary-Ann		2	F	Child	30Ma02Gy
SUMINS, Mary		36	F	Wi	30Ma02Gy
HOGAN, Jas.		27	M	Farmer	30Ma02Gy
GERR, Patrick		30	M	Weaver	30Ma02Gy
KELLY, Malachi		29	M	Farmer	30Ma02Gy
MONAHAN, Anthy		30	M	Farmer	30Ma02Gy
Philip		22	M	Farmer	30Ma02Gy
CREGG, Wm.		22	M	Gasfitter	30Ma02Gy
CONNELL, Patrick		29	M	Farmer	30Ma02Gy
RYAN, Mary		30	F	Wife	30Ma02Gy
Norah		20	F	Servant	30Ma02Gy
CONNELL, Ellen		.09	F	Infant	30Ma02Gy
Mary		7	F	Child	30Ma02Gy
John		4	M	Child	30Ma02Gy
MCGRATH, John		30	M	Farmer	30Ma02Gy
MCGRATH, Peggy	(W)	20	F	Wife	30Ma02Gy
John		.06	M	Infant	30Ma02Gy
ENGLISH, Nancy		19	F	Servant	30Ma02Gy
KAY, Mary		16	F	Servant	30Ma02Gy
MCGRATH, Mary		2	F	Child	30Ma02Gy
Ellen		3	F	Child	30Ma02Gy
FAY, Pat		27	M	Laborer	30Ma02Gy
Margt.		17	F	Servant	30Ma02Gy
COLE, Cath.		22	F	Servant	30Ma02Gy
CLARK, Christy		27	M	Laborer	30Ma02Gy
MORGAN, Pat		21	M	Laborer	30Ma02Gy
ASHLEY, Lawrence		26	M	Laborer	30Ma02Gy
RICHARDSON, Arthur		22	M	Shoemaker	30Ma02Gy
NELTY, Stephen		30	M	Laborer	30Ma02Gy
MASTERSON, Kate		16	F	Servant	30Ma02Gy
MADE, Pat		24	M	Laborer	30Ma02Gy
DUFFY, Pat		40	M	Shopkeeper	30Ma02Gy
FALLEN, James		20	M	Laborer	30Ma02Gy
GALOBY, John		25	M	Laborer	30Ma02Gy
CUNNINGHAM, Bridget		40	F	Wife	30Ma02Gy
Sarah		13	F	Spinster	30Ma02Gy
Bridget		20	F	Servant	30Ma02Gy
SHERDEN, Jas.		49	M	Laborer	30Ma02Gy
Pat		18	M	Laborer	30Ma02Gy
SMITH, Philip		64	M	Farmer	30Ma02Gy
Rose	(W)	60	F	Wife	30Ma02Gy
Philip		20	M	Farmer	30Ma02Gy
Margt.		18	F	Servant	30Ma02Gy
FINGAN, Margt.		20	F	Dressmaker	30Ma02Gy
SHERDAN, Ellen		25	F	Servant	30Ma02Gy
GAFFREY, Chas.		30	M	Laborer	30Ma02Gy
FITZPATRICK, Mary		20	F	Servant	30Ma02Gy
RILEY, Rose		19	F	Servant	30Ma02Gy
John		16	M	Laborer	30Ma02Gy
DUFFY, Alice		30	F	Servant	30Ma02Gy
CALLAGHAN, Mary		6	F	Child	30Ma02Gy
HERST, Joseph		40	M	Miner	30Ma02Gy
JOHNSTON, Henry		30	M	Farmer	30Ma02Gy
HERMAN, Rich.		36	M	Mechanic	30Ma02Gy
KINNY, John		30	M	Laborer	30Ma02Gy
WELSH, Michl.		27	M	Farmer	30Ma02Gy
JENKINS, Wm.		50	M	Farmer	30Ma02Gy
Elizabeth	(W)	45	F	Wife	30Ma02Gy
Sarah		17	F	Spinster	30Ma02Gy
Elizabeth		13	F	Spinster	30Ma02Gy
Ann		12	F	Spinster	30Ma02Gy
Thos.		13	M	Unknown	30Ma02Gy
William		27	M	Farmer	30Ma02Gy
LONG, Danl.		30	M	Farmer	30Ma02Gy
Mary		32	F	Servant	30Ma02Gy
Bridget		28	F	Servant	30Ma02Gy
SMITH, Michl.		28	M	Mason	30Ma02Gy
Sarah	(W)	20	F	Wife	30Ma02Gy
ANDERSON, Pat		20	M	Bootmaker	30Ma02Gy
NACH, Nathan		21	M	Shoemaker	30Ma02Gy
HUTCHINSON, Thos.		20	M	Farmer	30Ma02Gy
SMITH, Thos.		20	M	Laborer	30Ma02Gy
KAGAN, Thos.		31	M	Laborer	30Ma02Gy
GALLAGH, John		18	M	Farmer	30Ma02Gy
KING, James		60	M	Laborer	30Ma02Gy
DRUMM, John		40	M	Farmer	30Ma02Gy
Bridget	(W)	40	M	Farmer	30Ma02Gy
Margt.		.09	F	Infant	30Ma02Gy
Eliza		2	F	Child	30Ma02Gy
Catherine		12	F	Spinster	30Ma02Gy
Bridget		14	F	Spinster	30Ma02Gy
MURRAY, Judy		20	F	Servant	30Ma02Gy
GALLAGHER, Ann		24	F	Servant	30Ma02Gy
DRUMM, Mary		20	F	Dressmaker	30Ma02Gy
FAY, Michl.		50	M	Farmer	30Ma02Gy
Ellen	(W)	47	F	Wife	30Ma02Gy
Ann		11	F	Spinster	30Ma02Gy
Michl.		13	M	Unknown	30Ma02Gy
DUGAN, Michl.		22	M	Farmer	30Ma02Gy
SHAY, Thos.		26	M	Laborer	30Ma02Gy

NAMES OF PASSENGERS		AGE	SEX	OCCUPATIONS	DATE PORT SHIP
TURNY, Bridget		20	F	Servant	30Ma02Gy
MCPHILLIPS, Pat		40	M	Farmer	30Ma02Gy
John		18	M	None	30Ma02Gy
Ellen		16	F	Spinster	30Ma02Gy
Pat		12	M	Laborer	30Ma02Gy
SMITH, Biddy		22	F	Servant	30Ma02Gy
MCGINILE, John		40	M	Laborer	30Ma02Gy
Bridget	(W)	35	F	Wife	30Ma02Gy
LAYLOR, John		36	M	Carpenter	30Ma02Gy
Mary	(W)	22	F	Wife	30Ma02Gy
Cath.		3	F	Child	30Ma02Gy
Ellen		.09	F	Infant	30Ma02Gy
KIRKIN, Ann		16	F	Servant	30Ma02Gy
BRADY, Coner		14	M	Laborer	30Ma02Gy
LARLEY, James		12	M	Laborer	30Ma02Gy
SULLIVAN, John		60	M	Farmer	30Ma02Gy
FAGAN, Mary		20	F	Servant	30Ma02Gy
FAHY, Hugh		25	M	Gasfitter	30Ma02Gy
Jane	(W)	20	F	Wife	30Ma02Gy
SLATTERY, Jas.		20	M	Laborer	30Ma02Gy
MULDOON, Owen		30	M	Gdnr	30Ma02Gy
Julia	(W)	29	F	Wife	30Ma02Gy
Jas.		.06	M	Infant	30Ma02Gy
CUNNINGHAM, Ann		9	F	Child	30Ma02Gy
Margt.		7	F	Child	30Ma02Gy
CONER, John		40	M	Farmer	30Ma02Gy
BIRGIN, Danl.		22	M	Servant	30Ma02Gy
Biddy		15	F	Servant	30Ma02Gy
WHALEN, Cath.		25	F	Servant	30Ma02Gy
Mary		18	F	Servant	30Ma02Gy
Jane		21	F	Servant	30Ma02Gy
Honora		15	F	Servant	30Ma02Gy
KAVANAGH, Rebecca		18	F	Servant	30Ma02Gy
DORAN, Pat		25	M	Laborer	30Ma02Gy
DWIER, Martin		49	M	Mason	30Ma02Gy
MCKENNA, Jane		30	F	Servant	30Ma02Gy
PATTERSON, John		30	M	Laborer	30Ma02Gy
Cath.	(W)	22	F	Wife	30Ma02Gy
Wm.		19	M	Servant	30Ma02Gy
RILEY, Pat		20	M	Laborer	30Ma02Gy
DONNOLLY, Peter		18	M	Laborer	30Ma02Gy
Cath.		18	F	Spinster	30Ma02Gy
MCGUIRK, Pat		20	M	Tailor	30Ma02Gy
BOWER, Wm.		25	M	Tailor	30Ma02Gy
HAGARTY, Robt.		21	M	Tailor	30Ma02Gy
FALEY, Ellen		16	F	Spinster	30Ma02Gy

VELOCITY 31 MAY 1849

From Waterford

NAMES OF PASSENGERS	AGE	SEX	OCCUPATIONS	DATE PORT SHIP
MARCHELLA, Michael	30	M	Laborer	31Ma15Gx
COLLINS, Mary	25	F	Spinster	31Ma15Gx
Ellen	19	F	Spinster	31Ma15Gx
Anne	13	F	Spinster	31Ma15Gx
FOLEY, John	29	M	Laborer	31Ma15Gx
Bridget	21	F	Spinster	31Ma15Gx
CARROLL, Thomas	30	M	Laborer	31Ma15Gx
CONNOR, Patk.	25	M	Laborer	31Ma15Gx
POWER, Jno.	27	M	Laborer	31Ma15Gx
QUINLAN, Mary	20	F	Spinster	31Ma15Gx
MULLOUNEY, Ryan	31	M	Laborer	31Ma15Gx
Judith	28	F	Spinster	31Ma15Gx
Edward	18	M	Laborer	31Ma15Gx
CONNELLY, Bridget	24	F	Spinster	31Ma15Gx
BRYAN, James	25	M	Laborer	31Ma15Gx
SHARKEY, Geo.	23	M	Laborer	31Ma15Gx
POWER, Maurice	21	M	Laborer	31Ma15Gx
HAINEY, Margt.	25	F	Spinster	31Ma15Gx
HARRIGAN, John	30	M	Laborer	31Ma15Gx
Patk.	13	M	Laborer	31Ma15Gx
Ellen	12	F	Spinster	31Ma15Gx
CROTTY, Thomas	23	M	Laborer	31Ma15Gx
Lawrence	13	M	Laborer	31Ma15Gx
MOORE, Edw.	27	M	Unknown	31Ma15Gx
Mary	24	F	Spinster	31Ma15Gx
FENNILL, John	29	M	Laborer	31Ma15Gx
Mat	24	M	Laborer	31Ma15Gx
Lucy	19	F	Spinster	31Ma15Gx
Anne	.00	F	Infant	31Ma15Gx
DELANEY, Matt.	33	M	Laborer	31Ma15Gx
Ellen	29	F	Spinster	31Ma15Gx
Bridget	24	F	Spinster	31Ma15Gx
POWER, Robt.	29	M	Laborer	31Ma15Gx
Anne	12	F	Spinster	31Ma15Gx
Bridget	.00	F	Infant	31Ma15Gx
KEANE, John	27	M	Laborer	31Ma15Gx
HOLLY, Mary	24	F	Spinster	31Ma15Gx
MALONEY, Thomas	25	M	Laborer	31Ma15Gx
Alice	20	F	Spinster	31Ma15Gx
STEWARD, Jno.	35	M	Laborer	31Ma15Gx
Cath.	29	F	Spinster	31Ma15Gx
Anne	20	F	Spinster	31Ma15Gx
Robt.	13	M	Laborer	31Ma15Gx
Mary	18	F	Spinster	31Ma15Gx
John	12	M	Laborer	31Ma15Gx
Jane	19	F	Spinster	31Ma15Gx
Alex	14	M	Laborer	31Ma15Gx
ODONNELL, Bart	39	M	Laborer	31Ma15Gx
Ellen	36	F	Spinster	31Ma15Gx
Stephen	13	M	Spinster	31Ma15Gx
Bridget	30	F	Spinster	31Ma15Gx
John	13	M	Laborer	31Ma15Gx
Died-At-Sea				
Johanna	12	F	Spinster	31Ma15Gx
Mary	.00	F	Infant	31Ma15Gx
FLYNN, Edw.	40	M	Piper	31Ma15Gx
POWER, Jiffy	37	F	Spinster	31Ma15Gx
WHITTLE, Thomas	29	M	Laborer	31Ma15Gx
BERSEN, Cath.	25	F	Spinster	31Ma15Gx
LONIGAN, Patk.	20	M	Laborer	31Ma15Gx
WHITE, Geo.	19	M	Laborer	31Ma15Gx
ROCHE, Thomas	31	M	Laborer	31Ma15Gx
HAYES, John	29	M	Laborer	31Ma15Gx
Alice	24	F	Spinster	31Ma15Gx
FLYNN, Jno.	29	M	Laborer	31Ma15Gx
CORCORAN, Darby	31	M	Laborer	31Ma15Gx
MOORE, Mary	.00	F	Infant	31Ma15Gx

WOLFVILLE 31 MAY 1849

From Belfast

NAMES OF PASSENGERS	AGE	SEX	OCCUPATIONS	DATE PORT SHIP
FORBES, Margaret	23	F	Unknown	31Ma05Hc
Nancy	18	F	Unknown	31Ma05Hc
Mathew	.00	M	Infant	31Ma05H
HANNA, Ellen	20	F	Unknown	31Ma05H
MAGEE, Sarah	56	F	Unknown	31Ma05H
Eliza	21	F	Unknown	31Ma05H
James	20	M	Unknown	31Ma05H
SPRATE, James	29	M	Unknown	31Ma05H
Mary	27	F	Unknown	31Ma05H
WILSON, Robert	21	M	Unknown	31Ma05H
BLAIR, Jane	20	F	Unknown	31Ma05H
PATTERSON, James	35	M	Unknown	31Ma05H
Jane	25	F	Unknown	31Ma05H
MARTON, Joseph	60	M	Unknown	31Ma05H
Agnes	55	F	Unknown	31Ma05H

NAMES OF PASSENGERS	AGE	SEX	OCCUPATIONS	DATE PORT SHIP
MARTON, Alexander	21	M	Unknown	31Ma05Ho
Eliza	.00	F	Infant	31Ma05Ho
JELLY, Bessy	18	F	Unknown	31Ma05Ho
GLOVE, Mary	18	F	Unknown	31Ma05Ho
MASON, Susan	30	F	Unknown	31Ma05Ho
William	23	M	Unknown	31Ma05Ho
David	2	M	Child	31Ma05Ho
Robert	.00	M	Infant	31Ma05Ho
MAVINCHEY, Bridget	50	F	Unknown	31Ma05Ho
Patrick	42	M	Unknown	31Ma05Ho
Ann	16	M	Unknown	31Ma05Ho
John	7	M	Child	31Ma05Ho
Peter	.00	M	Infant	31Ma05Ho
RAFFERTY, Catherine	18	F	Unknown	31Ma05Ho
PORTER, John	24	M	Unknown	31Ma05Ho
MCCUNE, James	24	M	Unknown	31Ma05Ho
GARRIGAN, James	26	M	Unknown	31Ma05Ho
Margaret	24	F	Unknown	31Ma05Ho
ALEXANDER, James	63	M	Unknown	31Ma05Ho
Eliza	34	F	Unknown	31Ma05Ho
Fanny	32	F	Unknown	31Ma05Ho
SHEPHEN, William	10	M	Unknown	31Ma05Ho
ONEILL, Rose	21	F	Unknown	31Ma05Ho
Mary	20	F	Unknown	31Ma05Ho
JACKSON, Sarah	17	F	Unknown	31Ma05Ho
GORMLY, Frances	21	F	Unknown	31Ma05Ho
HICKS, Henry	18	M	Unknown	31Ma05Ho
TAYLOR, John	20	M	Unknown	31Ma05Ho
THOMPSON, Mary	22	F	Unknown	31Ma05Ho
MCQUADE, Margaret	18	F	Unknown	31Ma05Ho
LYNCH, Thomas	29	M	Unknown	31Ma05Ho
FERGASON, William	20	M	Unknown	31Ma05Ho
NAPIER, Mary	26	F	Unknown	31Ma05Ho
HOOLY, James	19	M	Unknown	31Ma05Ho
Margaret	21	F	Unknown	31Ma05Ho
SURPLUS, Charles	18	M	Unknown	31Ma05Ho
ROBINSON, William	18	M	Unknown	31Ma05Ho
TULFORD, Alexander	20	M	Unknown	31Ma05Ho
NELSON, Hugh	21	M	Unknown	31Ma05Ho
SMITH, Jonathan	30	M	Unknown	31Ma05Ho
BLACK, Andrew	35	M	Unknown	31Ma05Ho
GRAY, William	20	M	Unknown	31Ma05Ho
Mary	20	F	Unknown	31Ma05Ho
Thomas	.00	M	Infant	31Ma05Ho
BURNSIDE, James	25	M	Unknown	31Ma05Ho
SCOTT, Hugh	20	M	Unknown	31Ma05Ho
BOYD, William	20	M	Unknown	31Ma05Ho
THOMPSON, Alexer	20	M	Unknown	31Ma05Ho
HARRINGTON, William	20	M	Unknown	31Ma05Ho
BURNS, Matilda	20	F	Unknown	31Ma05Ho
MCCLANGYHAM, Thomas	20	M	Unknown	31Ma05Ho
MOONEY, Catherine	17	F	Unknown	31Ma05Ho
Mary	12	F	Unknown	31Ma05Ho
JOHNSTON, William	20	M	Unknown	31Ma05Ho
MCBRIAN, Jhon	24	M	Unknown	31Ma05Ho
MOONEY, John	20	M	Unknown	31Ma05Ho
ADAMS, Hugh	30	M	Unknown	31Ma05Ho
BELL, James	30	M	Unknown	31Ma05Ho
Jane	21	F	Unknown	31Ma05Ho
William	12	M	Unknown	31Ma05Ho
MOORE, Mary	20	F	Unknown	31Ma05Ho
KEENAN, Mary	30	F	Unknown	31Ma05Ho
RICE, William	50	M	Unknown	31Ma05Ho
James	22	M	Unknown	31Ma05Ho
NOX, William	21	M	Unknown	31Ma05Ho
MCKEY, Ann	30	F	Unknown	31Ma05Ho
GAHAN, James	30	M	Unknown	31Ma05Ho
Mary	28	F	Unknown	31Ma05Ho
Diana	15	F	Unknown	31Ma05Ho
Margaret	13	F	Unknown	31Ma05Ho
Florenda	.00	F	Infant	31Ma05Ho
MOORE, William	19	M	Unknown	31Ma05Ho
COGHERTY, Joseph	25	M	Unknown	31Ma05Ho
MULLAN, James	20	M	Unknown	31Ma05Ho
TAYLOR, Thomas	50	M	Unknown	31Ma05Ho
TAYLOR, James	23	M	Unknown	31Ma05Ho
MCGRATH, Peter	40	M	Unknown	31Ma05Ho
Sarah	30	F	Unknown	31Ma05Ho
Margaret	6	F	Child	31Ma05Ho
James	.00	M	Infant	31Ma05Ho
MCGRAN, Jno.	30	M	Unknown	31Ma05Ho
DICKEY, Mase	50	U	Unknown	31Ma05Ho
Rose	50	F	Unknown	31Ma05Ho
Robert	20	M	Unknown	31Ma05Ho
Peggy	19	F	Unknown	31Ma05Ho
David	12	M	Unknown	31Ma05Ho
Matilda	.00	F	Infant	31Ma05Ho
RIDE, Mary	21	F	Unknown	31Ma05Ho
MCDONNELL, Jane	24	F	Unknown	31Ma05Ho
MARSHALL, Mathew	22	M	Unknown	31Ma05Ho
ANDERSON, David	20	M	Unknown	31Ma05Ho
DORAN, Catherine	20	F	Unknown	31Ma05Ho
DUNCAN, James	21	M	Unknown	31Ma05Ho
MCCULLOUGH, Peter	22	M	Unknown	31Ma05Ho
KILCHRIST, Hugh	22	M	Unknown	31Ma05Ho
MCBRIDE, Neal	21	M	Unknown	31Ma05Ho
BROWN, Matthew	17	M	Unknown	31Ma05Ho
MCSHANNOCK, Hugh	22	M	Unknown	31Ma05Ho
RANSON, Jane	23	F	Unknown	31Ma05Ho
Sarah	.00	F	Infant	31Ma05Ho
MCLAUGHLIN, Catherine	22	F	Unknown	31Ma05Ho
Mary	20	F	Unknown	31Ma05Ho
Rose	16	F	Unknown	31Ma05Ho
Hanna	.00	F	Infant	31Ma05Ho
CHAMBAS, Esther	24	F	Unknown	31Ma05Ho
MCMILLAN, Denis	22	M	Unknown	31Ma05Ho
CUNNINGHAM, Leticid	22	U	Unknown	31Ma05Ho
SMITH, Thomas	28	M	Unknown	31Ma05Ho
Jane	26	F	Unknown	31Ma05Ho
William	.00	M	Infant	31Ma05Ho
PATTERSON, John	16	M	Unknown	31Ma05Ho
FERGASON, David	30	M	Unknown	31Ma05Ho
KERNEY, Mary	20	F	Unknown	31Ma05Ho
SCOTT, Eliza	23	F	Unknown	31Ma05Ho
Ellen	21	F	Unknown	31Ma05Ho
COCHRAN, Irwin	21	M	Unknown	31Ma05Ho
ARNOTT, Grase	25	F	Unknown	31Ma05Ho
WILERT, William	25	M	Unknown	31Ma05Ho
MILLS, James	24	M	Unknown	31Ma05Ho
Margaret	18	F	Unknown	31Ma05Ho
LOWREY, Samuel	60	M	Unknown	31Ma05Ho
Christiana	50	F	Unknown	31Ma05Ho
Margaret	22	F	Unknown	31Ma05Ho
Mary	20	F	Unknown	31Ma05Ho
Jane	18	F	Unknown	31Ma05Ho
Eliza	16	F	Unknown	31Ma05Ho
John	13	M	Unknown	31Ma05Ho
Christiana	9	F	Child	31Ma05Ho
Susan	.00	F	Infant	31Ma05Ho
CAMPBELL, Fad	24	U	Unknown	31Ma05Ho
HAMMELL, Thomas	16	M	Unknown	31Ma05Ho
Sarah	22	F	Unknown	31Ma05Ho
COCHRAN, Thomas	24	M	Unknown	31Ma05Ho
CAMPBELL, Gowan	24	M	Unknown	31Ma05Ho
CLEELAND, William	22	M	Unknown	31Ma05Ho
HAMMELL, Eliza	21	F	Unknown	31Ma05Ho
Sarah	21	F	Unknown	31Ma05Ho
KANE, Margaret	21	F	Unknown	31Ma05Ho
MCCLANAGHAN, Robert	25	M	Unknown	31Ma05Ho
WILSON, James	21	M	Unknown	31Ma05Ho
Margaret	23	F	Unknown	31Ma05Ho
Elizabeth	18	F	Unknown	31Ma05Ho
CAMPBELL, Margaret	26	F	Unknown	31Ma05Ho
MCMULLEN, Bernard	40	M	Unknown	31Ma05Ho
Nancy	40	F	Unknown	31Ma05Ho
Patrick	2	M	Child	31Ma05Ho
Elizabeth	.00	F	Infant	31Ma05Ho
GILLESPIE, Ann	45	F	Unknown	31Ma05Ho
William	12	M	Unknown	31Ma05Ho
ANUDO, Mary	16	F	Unknown	31Ma05Ho

NAMES OF PASSENGERS	AGE	SEX	OCCUPATIONS	DATE PORT SHIP
ANUDO, Elizabeth	11	F	Unknown	31Ma05Ho
GILLESPIE, Brownlon	7	U	Child	31Ma05Ho
Sarah	.00	F	Infant	31Ma05Ho
MCALLEN, James	40	M	Unknown	31Ma05Ho
Jno.	42	M	Unknown	31Ma05Ho
Margaret	25	F	Unknown	31Ma05Ho
COCHRAN, John	20	M	Unknown	31Ma05Ho
KERNS, William	22	M	Unknown	31Ma05Ho
Biddy	22	F	Unknown	31Ma05Ho

MALABER 31 MAY 1849

From Greenock

NAMES OF PASSENGERS	AGE	SEX	OCCUPATIONS	DATE PORT SHIP
DAVIDSON, William	28	M	Shoemaker	31Ma33le
MCGILL, Jane	28	F	Matron	31Ma33le
KENT, James	16	M	Fsvnt	31Ma33le
DAVIDSON, Mary	5	F	Child	31Ma33le
Thomas	3	M	Child	31Ma33le
AUBRY, John	22	M	Laborer	31Ma33le
MCKINLAY, William	25	M	Tinsmith	31Ma33le
CLARK, Janet	62	F	Matron	31Ma33le
William	25	M	Weaver	31Ma33le
Catherine	23	F	Servant	31Ma33le
Janet	20	F	Servant	31Ma33le
Nathaniel	11	M	None	31Ma33le
John	7	M	Child	31Ma33le
Wm.	5	M	Child	31Ma33le
John-Davidson	3	M	Child	31Ma33le
STODDART, John	43	M	Mnftr	31Ma33le
Ann	30	F	Matron	31Ma33le
Ann	16	F	Spinster	31Ma33le
Thomas	13	M	None	31Ma33le
William	12	M	None	31Ma33le
John	7	M	Child	31Ma33le
Andrew	5	M	Child	31Ma33le
Agnes	.11	F	Infant	31Ma33le
David	3	M	Child	31Ma33le
Thomas	33	M	Bookseller	31Ma33le
Sophia	33	F	Matron	31Ma33le
RICHARDSON, George	60	M	Laborer	31Ma33le
Sophia	60	F	Matron	31Ma33le
Thomas	27	M	Blacksmith	31Ma33le
George	12	M	None	31Ma33le
Eliza	8	F	Child	31Ma33le
DORY, Thomas	45	M	Laborer	31Ma33le
Died-At-Sea				
RODGER, John	30	M	Laborer	31Ma33le
OLLIPHANT, Ann	37	F	Matron	31Ma33le
COOK, Jessie	21	F	Spinster	31Ma33le
SRIMGLAN, Robt.	37	M	Prntctr	31Ma33le
Janet	42	F	Matron	31Ma33le
Robert	19	M	Prntctr	31Ma33le
Archibald	17	M	Plumber	31Ma33le
Janet	15	F	Spinster	31Ma33le
Helen	13	F	None	31Ma33le
Ann	10	F	None	31Ma33le
John	8	M	Child	31Ma33le
James	6	M	Child	31Ma33le
Francis	3	M	Child	31Ma33le
Betsy	.02	F	Infant	31Ma33le
JOHNSTON, David	36	M	Mill Owner	31Ma33le
Eliza	32	F	Matron	31Ma33le
Duncan	4	M	Child	31Ma33le
Eliza	6	F	Child	31Ma33le
HANE, Moses	27	M	Joiner	31Ma33le
Jessie	22	F	Matron	31Ma33le
ERSKINE, M.	22	M	Laborer	31Ma33le
MCCONNELL, Alexander-G	30	M	Engd	31Ma33le
MCCONNELL, Janet	30	F	Matron	31Ma33le
Margaret	5	F	Child	31Ma33le
John	.11	M	Infant	31Ma33le
Mary	3	F	Child	31Ma33le
STRATHRAM, Thomas	33	M	Shoemaker	31Ma33le
STRATHRAN, Helen	34	F	Matron	31Ma33le
John	10	M	None	31Ma33le
Margaret	8	F	Child	31Ma33le
James	5	M	Child	31Ma33le
Alexander	2	M	Child	31Ma33le
BROWN, John	38	M	Bootmaker	31Ma33le
Agnes	30	F	Matron	31Ma33le
MALCOLM, Jean	30	F	Matron	31Ma33le
Martha	12	F	None	31Ma33le
Mary	9	F	Child	31Ma33le
MILLER, Peter	40	M	Shoemaker	31Ma33le
Margaret	33	F	Matron	31Ma33le
Isabella	11	F	None	31Ma33le
Margaret	5	F	Child	31Ma33le
Ann	3	F	Child	31Ma33le
Mary	.11	F	Infant	31Ma33le
TODD, Wm.	17	M	Shoemaker	31Ma33le
MCLACHLAN, Wm.	36	M	Tailor	31Ma33le
Catherine	40	F	Matron	31Ma33le
WISHART, Margaret	14	F	Spinster	31Ma33le
MCLACHLAN, James	7	M	Child	31Ma33le
Wm.	5	M	Child	31Ma33le
John-Gray	3	M	Child	31Ma33le
Catherine	.10	F	Infant	31Ma33le
Died-At-Sea				
MURRAN, Patrick	20	M	Laborer	31Ma33le
John	47	M	Laborer	31Ma33le
WARD, Peter	32	M	Laborer	31Ma33le
MCKINZIE, Donald	35	M	Laborer	31Ma33le
Ann	30	F	Matron	31Ma33le
Wm.	4	M	Child	31Ma33le
Ann	2	F	Child	31Ma33le
Margaret	50	F	Matron	31Ma33le
TAIT, Robert	28	M	Shoemaker	31Ma33le
MCKAY, Jane	26	F	Matron	31Ma33le
Mary-Ann	7	F	Child	31Ma33le
Margaret	5	F	Child	31Ma33le
Jane	.05	F	Infant	31Ma33le
CLELLAND, Joseph	40	M	Laborer	31Ma33le
Jane	40	M	Matron	31Ma33le
John	20	M	Farmer	31Ma33le
Eliza	17	F	Spinster	31Ma33le
Hugh	17	M	Farmer	31Ma33le
Mary-Ann	15	F	Spinster	31Ma33le
Wm.	13	M	None	31Ma33le
Ann	11	F	None	31Ma33le
Eliza	8	F	Child	31Ma33le
James	3	M	Child	31Ma33le
Robert	.10	M	Infant	31Ma33le
MCCASHAN, Dennis	30	M	Laborer	31Ma33le
Jane	25	F	Matron	31Ma33le
Patrick	5	M	Child	31Ma33le
Catherine	3	F	Child	31Ma33le
John	.01	M	Infant	31Ma33le
FINNEGAN, James	25	M	Laborer	31Ma33le
John	20	M	Laborer	31Ma33le
MCDONNELL, Henry	20	M	Shoemaker	31Ma33le
BROWN, Farrell	18	M	Shoemaker	31Ma33le
SHAW, John	47	M	Farmer	31Ma33le
Isabella	36	F	Matron	31Ma33le
Wm.	20	M	Farmer	31Ma33le
John	18	M	Farmer	31Ma33le
Thomas	16	M	Farmer	31Ma33le
Janet	13	F	None	31Ma33le
David	10	M	None	31Ma33le
James	8	M	Child	31Ma33le
Hugh	4	M	Child	31Ma33le
CLARKSON, John	38	M	Farmer	31Ma33le
Mary	32	F	Matron	31Ma33le
James	6	M	Child	31Ma33le

NAMES OF PASSENGERS	AGE	SEX	OCCUPATIONS	DATE PORT SHIP
CLARKSON, Janet	5	F	Child	31Ma33le
John	3	M	Child	31Ma33le
Thomas	.07	M	Infant	31Ma33le
MAGUIRE, Phillip	40	M	Farmer	31Ma33le
GUEN, Matthew	19	M	Farmer	31Ma33le
MAHAR, Catherine	22	F	Spinster	31Ma33le
FARMER, Catherine	22	F	Spinster	31Ma33le
SPANKS, John	21	M	Flaxworker	31Ma33le
COWLY, John	25	M	Mason	31Ma33le
Ann	23	F	Matron	31Ma33le
Ann	.06	F	Infant	31Ma33le
MCANDREW, John	56	M	Painter	31Ma33le
Mary	58	F	Matron	31Ma33le
OLLIPHANT, Jane	37	F	Spinster	31Ma33le
MCANDREW, Ann	34	F	Matron	31Ma33le
OLLIPHANT, John	25	M	Painter	31Ma33le
EOIR, George	24	M	Hat Dresser	31Ma33le
SNULLER, William	25	M	Enkr	31Ma33le
THOMSON, Andrew	21	M	Machmkr	31Ma33le
GARRARDS, Henry	50	M	Printer	31Ma33le
Mary	48	F	Matron	31Ma33le
MCGOWAN, Catherine	22	F	Spinster	31Ma33le
EDWARDS, Helen	17	F	Spinster	31Ma33le
Margaret	13	F	None	31Ma33le
Peter	8	M	Child	31Ma33le
James	7	M	Child	31Ma33le
FORBES, John	6	M	Child	31Ma33le
CURRIS, John	24	M	Block Maker	31Ma33le
SMEE, Hugh	32	M	Mill Worker	31Ma33le
Jane	32	F	Matron	31Ma33le
BACON, Mary	7	F	Child	31Ma33le
Samuel	5	M	Child	31Ma33le
DUNCAN, Thomas	23	M	Victualler	31Ma33le
BELL, Martha	24	F	Unknown	31Ma33le
DUNCAN, Elizabeth	33	F	Matron	31Ma33le
MACHOOKE, John	20	M	Ctnsp	31Ma33le
MCINTYRE, Margaret	56	F	Matron	31Ma33le
Rebecca	32	F	Matron	31Ma33le
Sarah	20	F	Matron	31Ma33le
James	12	M	None	31Ma33le
GILDERSLEEVES, Ann	22	F	Servant	31Ma33le
MCGREGOR, Hannah	16	F	Servant	31Ma33le
SEGGAN, James	25	M	Laborer	31Ma33le
Mathew	20	M	Laborer	31Ma33le
GLASGOW, Robert	40	M	Unknown	31Ma33le
Elizabeth	40	F	Unknown	31Ma33le
Margaret	8	F	Child	31Ma33le
James	16	M	Unknown	31Ma33le
Jane	13	F	None	31Ma33le
Elizabeth	11	F	None	31Ma33le
Samuel	6	M	Child	31Ma33le
Robert	4	M	Child	31Ma33le
ERBINE, James	40	M	Unknown	31Ma33le
Ann	39	F	Unknown	31Ma33le
Jane	18	F	Spinster	31Ma33le
Margt.	13	F	None	31Ma33le
Maly	12	F	None	31Ma33le
Wm.	10	M	None	31Ma33le
John	7	M	Child	31Ma33le
Sarah	5	M	Child	31Ma33le
Robert	2	M	Child	31Ma33le
ALAGHER, Patrick	25	M	Laborer	31Ma33le
LEXANDER, Cochrane	27	M	Farmer	31Ma33le
AWRENCE, Samuel	26	M	Farmer	31Ma33le
EAN, Thomas	45	M	Laborer	31Ma33le
Patrick	19	M	Laborer	31Ma33le
Mary	17	F	Spinster	31Ma33le
ACMANUS, Mary	27	F	Spinster	31Ma33le
EAN, Dennis	50	M	Laborer	31Ma33le
John	17	M	Laborer	31Ma33le
ANAGHAN, Biddy	23	F	Spinster	31Ma33le
ENANCY, John	20	M	Laborer	31Ma33le
Catherine	22	F	Spinster	31Ma33le
GEE, Barnard	36	M	Laborer	31Ma33le
ENANCY, Ann	13	F	None	31Ma33le
TENANCY, Margaret	8	F	Child	31Ma33le
Eliza	6	F	Child	31Ma33le
MCGUINN, Thomas	20	M	Laborer	31Ma33le
HAGHARTY, Bridget	20	F	Spinster	31Ma33le
KERRIGAN, Honor	22	F	Spinster	31Ma33le
Mary	11	F	None	31Ma33le
GIBSON, John	27	M	Painter	31Ma33le
Eliza-Jane	24	F	Matron	31Ma33le
Eliza-Jane	.10	F	Infant	31Ma33le
HUNTER, George	21	M	Brf	31Ma33le
FRASER, James	25	M	Brf	31Ma33le
GOLD, James	19	M	Druggist	31Ma33le
WYLIE, Andrew	22	M	Blacksmith	31Ma33le
KEECOLM, Elizabeth	26	F	Matron	31Ma33le
John	3	M	Child	31Ma33le
MCINTYRE, May	40	F	Matron	31Ma33le
HANEGHAN, John	22	M	Laborer	31Ma33le
Mary	21	F	Spinster	31Ma33le
GLASGOW, John	76	M	Unknown	31Ma33le
Jane	60	F	Unknown	31Ma33le
James	26	M	Unknown	31Ma33le
John	12	M	None	31Ma33le
HANY, Wm.	27	M	Unknown	31Ma33le
Eliza	26	F	Unknown	31Ma33le
Eliza-Jane	.07	F	Infant	31Ma33le
Abraham	25	M	Laborer	31Ma33le
Nancy	26	F	Matron	31Ma33le
Nancy-Ann	22	F	Spinster	31Ma33le
John	26	M	Laborer	31Ma33le
QUINN, John	35	M	Laborer	31Ma33le
Nancy	33	F	Unknown	31Ma33le
HUGHES, Eliza	18	F	Spinster	31Ma33le
BICKMER, Henry	21	M	Bookbinder	31Ma33le
DOULLS, David	23	M	Hrsm	31Ma33le
BROADFOOT, Adam	23	M	Laborer	31Ma33le
RALSTON, Hugh	24	M	Laborer	31Ma33le
BLYTHE, Thomas	21	M	Gdnr	31Ma33le
FLUIT, George	25	M	Gdnr	31Ma33le
FERGUSON, Richard	28	M	Joiner	31Ma33le
BELL, David	40	M	Sawer	31Ma33le
QUINN, Hugh	9	M	Child	31Ma33le
Mary	2	F	Child	31Ma33le
MACCARD, James	27	M	None	31Ma33le
Nancy	27	F	None	31Ma33le
John	5	M	Child	31Ma33le
Eliza	3	F	Child	31Ma33le
Mary-Ann	.11	F	Infant	31Ma33le
HONEY, Edward	21	M	Shpc	31Ma33le
MCMANEY, James	21	M	Flesher	31Ma33le
HENRY, James	46	M	Laborer	31Ma33le
Bridget	16	F	Spinster	31Ma33le
BOCHNANE, John	39	M	Carpenter	31Ma33le
Mary	6	F	Child	31Ma33le
DONAS, John	40	M	Laborer	31Ma33le
Sarah	16	F	Spinster	31Ma33le
John	13	M	None	31Ma33le
Edward	13	M	None	31Ma33le
MCCADDEN, George	16	M	Laborer	31Ma33le
COCHRANE, Isabella	6	F	Child	31Ma33le
MCENENNY, James	30	M	Laborer	31Ma33le
ANDERSON, James	39	M	Millwright	31Ma33le
Peter	35	M	Mason	31Ma33le
DONAS, Bridget	40	F	Matron	31Ma33le
MCDAUGALL, John	28	M	Shoemaker	31Ma33le
LITTLE, Matthew	20	M	Shoemaker	31Ma33le
SCOTT, William	28	M	Farmer	31Ma33le
STEVENS, Allan	23	M	Miller	31Ma33le
LINDSAY, Matthew	24	M	Farmer	31Ma33le
PATRICK, Alex.	28	M	Engineer	31Ma33le
Elizabeth	.08	F	Infant	31Ma33le
Elizabeth	26	F	Matron	31Ma33le
ALLAN, Mary	36	F	Matron	31Ma33le
Margaret	18	F	Spinster	31Ma33le
Mary	16	F	None	31Ma33le
Jane	12	F	None	31Ma33le

-5-

NAMES OF PASSENGERS	AGE	SEX	OCCUPATIONS	DATE PORT SHIP
ALLAN, William	10	M	None	31Ma33le
Elizabeth	8	F	Child	31Ma33le
KEENAN, Neil	50	M	Wheelwright	31Ma33le
Elizabeth	40	F	Matron	31Ma33le
Catherine	12	F	None	31Ma33le
Michael	10	M	None	31Ma33le
Hugh	8	M	Child	31Ma33le
Hannah	6	F	Child	31Ma33le
Bryan	.02	M	Infant	31Ma33le
HARDMAN, Henry	21	M	Tipwkr	31Ma33le
COOK, Rosanna	35	F	Matron	31Ma33le
Mary-Ann	18	F	Spinster	31Ma33le
Helen	9	F	Child	31Ma33le
Francis	4	M	Child	31Ma33le
Joseph	4	M	Child	31Ma33le
Rosanna	.10	F	Infant	31Ma33le
WARDROP, Walter	49	M	Weaver	31Ma33le
STRUTHERS, Jean	28	F	Matron	31Ma33le
Jean	4	F	Child	31Ma33le
EWING, Robert	30	M	Farmer	31Ma33le
Mary	24	F	Matron	31Ma33le
FOYNSON, Helen	50	F	Matron	31Ma33le
MCLAREN, Robert	22	M	Laborer	31Ma33le
REDWICK, Alex.	32	M	Mechanic	31Ma33le
Catherine	24	F	Matron	31Ma33le
Janet	5	F	Child	31Ma33le
Elizabeth	2	F	Child	31Ma33le
Alexander	.06	M	Infant	31Ma33le
William	24	M	Clerk	31Ma33le
JOHNSON, Thomas	34	M	Mechanic	31Ma33le
CONNELY, Wm.	22	M	Laborer	31Ma33le
Patrick	12	M	None	31Ma33le
Margaret	17	F	Spinster	31Ma33le
SCOTT, Peter	24	M	Laborer	31Ma33le
Ann	23	F	Matron	31Ma33le
NEILSON, James	20	M	Laborer	31Ma33le
SAUL, Wm.	25	M	Carpenter	31Ma33le
Mary	21	F	Matron	31Ma33le
Hugh	2	M	Child	31Ma33le
Thomas	.02	M	Infant	31Ma33le
CUNNINGHAM, Ann	25	F	Servant	31Ma33le
GOWANS, Thomas	27	M	Printer	31Ma33le
HARRY, Barney	45	M	Laborer	31Ma33le
Sally	20	F	Spinster	31Ma33le
TALCHER, Hannah-J.	17	F	Spinster	31Ma33le
Mcka--, Hugh	27	M	Laborer	31Ma33le
Ma--, Dennis	40	M	Carter	31Ma33le
Sarah	35	F	Matron	31Ma33le
Daniel	.11	M	Infant	31Ma33le
COLVILLE, John	21	M	Carpenter	31Ma33le
MCGEE, Mary-Ann	20	F	Spinster	31Ma33le
MCCORMICK, Peter	20	M	Laborer	31Ma33le
BARRY, Hannah	17	F	Spinster	31Ma33le
MCALACE, Mary	17	F	Spinster	31Ma33le
KANTER, Alexander	34	M	Farmer	31Ma33le
Mary	20	F	Matron	31Ma33le
LEGGAT, George	20	M	Unknown	31Ma33le
MCGEE, Mary	22	F	Servant	31Ma33le
SHIELS, David	24	M	Carpenter	31Ma33le
SCALLAN, James	30	M	Laborer	31Ma33le
Catherine	30	F	Matron	31Ma33le
Ann	60	F	Matron	31Ma33le
Ann	7	F	Child	31Ma33le
SHIELS, Margery	23	F	Servant	31Ma33le
CUNNINGHAM, Peggy-Jean	16	F	Spinster	31Ma33le
SCOLLAN, Ann	.10	F	Infant	31Ma33le
HANKER, John	22	M	Laborer	31Ma33le
PORKES, Alexander	26	M	Laborer	31Ma33le
HOWE, John	27	M	Joiner	31Ma33le
WILSON, Alexander	20	M	Joiner	31Ma33le
SOMMERVILLE, Adam	19	M	Laborer	31Ma33le
STRATHERS, Wm.	30	M	Farmer	31Ma33le
Archd.	3	M	Child	31Ma33le
Mary	8	F	Child	31Ma33le
Mary	27	F	Matron	31Ma33le

NAMES OF PASSENGERS	AGE	SEX	OCCUPATIONS	DATE PORT SHIP
STRATHERS, William	.07	M	Infant	31Ma33l
Andrew	23	M	Joiner	31Ma33l
Jane	20	F	Matron	31Ma33l
ANDERSON, Wm.	20	M	Laborer	31Ma33l
FORBES, James	36	M	Laborer	31Ma33l
BURGESS, Thomas	20	M	Laborer	31Ma33l
GALBREATH, George	21	M	Laborer	31Ma33l
BLACK, Wm.	41	M	Cartwright	31Ma33l
MCKINLEY, John	25	M	Smith	31Ma33l
INGLIS, Mary	36	F	Matron	31Ma33l
MCKINLEY, Elizabeth	.08	F	Infant	31Ma33l
MCLAREN, Robert	50	M	Laborer	31Ma33l
Elizabeth	46	F	Matron	31Ma33l
Robt.Jr.	24	M	Carver	31Ma33l
MCKINLEY, Elizabeth	26	F	Matron	31Ma33l
MCLAREN, Rosina	20	F	Matron	31Ma33l
FINNIE, Hugh	20	M	Printer	31Ma33l
CRAY, James	22	M	Wheelwright	31Ma33l
SHEDDON, Robert	19	M	Farmer	31Ma33l
BAHRMAN, John-F.	28	M	Broker	31Ma33l
Ann	26	F	Matron	31Ma33l
Andrew	4	M	Child	31Ma33l
Barnnet	2	M	Child	31Ma33l
Mary-Ann	.08	F	Infant	31Ma33l
CUFF, John	28	M	Clerk	31Ma33l
GRANT, James	33	M	Merchant	31Ma33l
QUINLAND, John	14	M	None	31Ma33l

BROTHERS 31 MAY 1849

From Newry

NAMES OF PASSENGERS		AGE	SEX	OCCUPATIONS	DATE PORT SHIP
FREEBURN, Archibald		19	M	Saddler	31Ma11H
HARRISON, William		18	M	Blacksmith	31Ma11H
Mary-Anne		16	F	Spinster	31Ma11H
RICE, Patrick		34	M	Carpenter	31Ma11H
RAY, Michael		40	M	Farmer	31Ma11H
Rose	(W)	40	F	Wife	31Ma11H
Oliver		10	M	Child	31Ma11H
Margaret		8	F	Child	31Ma11H
Michael		5	M	Child	31Ma11H
Susanna		3	F	Child	31Ma11H
Alice		.00	F	Infant	31Ma11H
Rose		.00	F	Infant	31Ma11H
WALSH, Alice		24	F	Spinster	31Ma11H
GRIBBEN, Hugh		21	M	Currier	31Ma11H
FREEBURN, George		45	M	Smith	31Ma11H
Jane	(W)	47	F	Wife	31Ma11H
Abigan		21	F	Relative	31Ma11H
Margaret		17	F	Relative	31Ma11H
Sarah		15	F	Relative	31Ma11H
Mary-Ann		13	F	Relative	31Ma11H
George		11	M	Relative	31Ma11H
Robert		9	M	Child	31Ma11
Jane		7	F	Child	31Ma11
William		5	M	Child	31Ma11
Eliza		.00	F	Infant	31Ma11
MCCASTER, Michael		22	M	Shoemaker	31Ma11
ROWAN, Esther		16	F	Spinster	31Ma11
ROONEY, Mary		24	F	Spinster	31Ma11
Alice		20	F	Spinster	31Ma11
MOONEY, Hugh		22	M	Wood Cutter	31Ma11
MCCLEAN, Ellen		20	F	Spinster	31Ma11
CARROLL, Ann		25	F	Spinster	31Ma11
TREANOR, Daniel		24	M	Bootmaker	31Ma11
BARON, Charles		25	M	Carpenter	31Ma11
DENSIMORE, William		24	M	Compositor	31Ma11
KINNEAR, John		40	M	Farmer	31Ma11
Eliza	(W)	35	F	Wife	31Ma11

NAMES OF PASSENGERS	AGE	SEX	OCCUPATIONS	DATE PORT SHIP
KINNEAR, Jane	60	F	Relative	31Ma11Hd
Mary	15	F	Relative	31Ma11Hd
FLANIGAN, Mary	17	F	Unknown	31Ma11Hd
KINNEAR, Jane	13	F	Relative	31Ma11Hd
George	10	M	Relative	31Ma11Hd
Joseph	8	M	Child	31Ma11Hd
Eliza	5	F	Child	31Ma11Hd
Margaret	.00	F	Infant	31Ma11Hd
MCATTEE, Mary	18	F	Spinster	31Ma11Hd
Rose	14	F	Spinster	31Ma11Hd
MCINTEGART, Stephen	25	M	Watchmaker	31Ma11Hd
FITZPATRICK, Judith	25	F	Spinster	31Ma11Hd
BRANIGAN, Patrick	20	M	Baker	31Ma11Hd
DRUMMOND, William	63	M	Farmer	31Ma11Hd
Ann	19	F	Relative	31Ma11Hd
Mary	17	F	Relative	31Ma11Hd
William	14	M	Relative	31Ma11Hd
LEMON, John	21	M	Millwright	31Ma11Hd
Eliza (W)	18	F	Wife	31Ma11Hd
THOMPSON, Ann	18	F	Spinster	31Ma11Hd
Robert	23	M	Stone Mason	31Ma11Hd
Margaret (T)	20	F	Sister	31Ma11Hd
SHANES, Thomas	32	M	Farmer	31Ma11Hd
Alexander	30	M	Brother	31Ma11Hd
Joseph	25	M	Brother	31Ma11Hd
Nancy	21	F	Sister	31Ma11Hd
Jane	21	F	Sister	31Ma11Hd
KINNELL, Joseph	23	M	Coppersmith	31Ma11Hd
MCNEALY, James	32	M	Baker	31Ma11Hd
BROWN, John	50	M	Farmer	31Ma11Hd
Eleanor (W)	45	F	Wife	31Ma11Hd
Jane (D)	16	F	Daughter	31Ma11Hd
Elizabeth (D)	14	F	Daughter	31Ma11Hd
WALLACE, Samuel	19	M	Whitesmith	31Ma11Hd
BYRNE, Michael	28	M	Brf	31Ma11Hd
MCGUINESS, Eliza	29	F	Spinster	31Ma11Hd
CRAWLEY, James	24	M	Carpenter	31Ma11Hd
Sarah (W)	24	F	Wife	31Ma11Hd
Catherine	24	F	Spinster	31Ma11Hd
HANLON, Michael	24	M	Laborer	31Ma11Hd
BOYLE, Bernard	20	M	Slater	31Ma11Hd
Mary (W)	20	F	Wife	31Ma11Hd
CONNOLLY, Biddy	40	F	Wi	31Ma11Hd
PALMER, Adam	14	M	Unknown	31Ma11Hd
Eleanor (T)	12	F	Sister	31Ma11Hd
MURPHY, James	35	M	Farmer	31Ma11Hd
Ann (W)	35	F	Wife	31Ma11Hd
Mary	7	F	Child	31Ma11Hd
Hannah	4	F	Child	31Ma11Hd
Biddy	.00	F	Infant	31Ma11Hd
Died-At-Sea				
Alice	22	F	Spinster	31Ma11Hd
GRIMES, Patrick	22	M	Shipwright	31Ma11Hd
Ellen	60	F	Unknown	31Ma11Hd
MCKINLEY, William	60	M	Currier	31Ma11Hd
MCKEWN, Ann	22	F	Spinster	31Ma11Hd
James	23	M	Brother	31Ma11Hd
OMERVILLE, Anne	20	F	Spinster	31Ma11Hd
ERR, John	48	M	Farmer	31Ma11Hd
Betty (W)	50	F	Wife	31Ma11Hd
CKNIGHT, Mary	54	F	Relative	31Ma11Hd
ERR, George	16	M	Relative	31Ma11Hd
Robert	11	M	Relative	31Ma11Hd
Eliza	7	F	Child	31Ma11Hd
LEAKLY, James	26	M	Shoemaker	31Ma11Hd
Margaret (W)	30	F	Wife	31Ma11Hd
Eliza	3	F	Child	31Ma11Hd
John	.00	M	Infant	31Ma11Hd
URRAY, Henry	35	M	Couch Maker	31Ma11Hd
Ann (T)	38	F	Sister	31Ma11Hd
EARIGHT, Marcus	9	M	Child	31Ma11Hd
CKEWN, Patt	20	M	Farmer	31Ma11Hd
John	18	M	Relative	31Ma11Hd
Bridget	15	F	Relative	31Ma11Hd
Peter	13	M	Relative	31Ma11Hd

NAMES OF PASSENGERS	AGE	SEX	OCCUPATIONS	DATE PORT SHIP
MCKEWN, Felix	10	M	Relative	31Ma11Hd
Ann	8	F	Child	31Ma11Hd
Thomas	6	M	Child	31Ma11Hd
Catherine	2	F	Child	31Ma11Hd
Michael	.00	M	Infant	31Ma11Hd
James	40	M	Farmer	31Ma11Hd
Mary (W)	35	F	Wife	31Ma11Hd
HARRISON, Mary	20	F	Spinster	31Ma11Hd
MCSHANE, Elizabeth	25	F	Spinster	31Ma11Hd
WHITE, Mary	20	F	Spinster	31Ma11Hd
Margaret	22	F	Spinster	31Ma11Hd
BOYLE, Bernard	36	M	Joiner	31Ma11Hd
Julia (W)	38	F	Wife	31Ma11Hd
Julia	.00	F	Infant	31Ma11Hd
BOYD, Samuel	32	M	Sail Maker	31Ma11Hd
CUMMING, Margaret	25	F	Spinster	31Ma11Hd
BLACK, David	22	M	Weaver	31Ma11Hd
Mary	20	F	Spinster	31Ma11Hd
MCNEILY, David	30	M	Laborer	31Ma11Hd
DONALDSON, Elizabeth	26	F	Spinster	31Ma11Hd
Anne	25	F	Spinster	31Ma11Hd
MCGIVERN, Catherine	26	F	Spinster	31Ma11Hd
JOHNSON, Thomas	24	M	Wdpr	31Ma11Hd
MORGAN, Peter	22	M	Locksmith	31Ma11Hd
TAIT, Robert	18	M	Carpenter	31Ma11Hd
MCATEER, Alice	26	F	Spinster	31Ma11Hd
CASSIDY, William	23	M	Joiner	31Ma11Hd
MCGUINESS, Patrick	22	M	Blwmkr	31Ma11Hd
DOOGAN, Mary	20	F	Spinster	31Ma11Hd
KING, Stephen	26	M	Farmer	31Ma11Hd
Mary (T)	18	F	Sister	31Ma11Hd
MONAGHAN, Patt	24	M	Slater	31Ma11Hd
GORMAN, Mary-Ann	12	F	Spinster	31Ma11Hd
FEARON, Daniel	35	M	Chandler	31Ma11Hd
Thomas (S)	10	M	Son	31Ma11Hd
MURPHY, James	19	M	Cutler	31Ma11Hd
Michael	20	M	Tanner	31Ma11Hd
HERRING, Ralph	30	M	Butcher	31Ma11Hd
Jane (W)	30	F	Wife	31Ma11Hd
PORTER, Susan	55	F	Spinster	31Ma11Hd
CONE, Charles	24	M	Barber	31Ma11Hd
FINNIGAN, Owen	24	M	Locksmith	31Ma11Hd
MCKENNA, Patt	18	M	Bootmaker	31Ma11Hd
TEMPLETON, Ann	28	F	Spinster	31Ma11Hd
MCGUIRE, Ann	20	F	Spinster	31Ma11Hd
CALL, Bernard	20	M	Mechanic	31Ma11Hd
MORGAN, Bessy	18	F	Spinster	31Ma11Hd
BARRETT, Jane	41	F	Spinster	31Ma11Hd
SINCLAIR, Archibald	21	M	Painter	31Ma11Hd
Nathaniel	24	M	Painter	31Ma11Hd
Ann	50	F	Unknown	31Ma11Hd
Jane	25	F	Relative	31Ma11Hd
Ann-Eliza	23	F	Relative	31Ma11Hd
Susan	22	F	Relative	31Ma11Hd
Margaret	20	F	Relative	31Ma11Hd
BARRETT, Bessy	8	F	Child	31Ma11Hd
MCHENRY, Charles	50	M	Farmer	31Ma11Hd
MCGREEHAN, Owen	21	M	Glazier	31Ma11Hd
MCPORTER, James	24	M	Farmer	31Ma11Hd
CARROLL, Alice	20	F	Spinster	31Ma11Hd
Betty	27	F	Spinster	31Ma11Hd
MCCLURE, Ann	45	F	Wi	31Ma11Hd
Susan	26	F	Relative	31Ma11Hd
William	11	M	Child	31Ma11Hd
James	9	M	Child	31Ma11Hd
Henry	4	M	Child	31Ma11Hd
MOONEY, Peter	26	M	Baker	31Ma11Hd
HANLON, Elizabeth	20	F	Spinster	31Ma11Hd
DORAN, Paul	30	M	Carpenter	31Ma11Hd
WALLACE, John	24	M	Laborer	31Ma11Hd
HUGHES, Edward	38	M	Farmer	31Ma11Hd
Biddy	16	F	Spinster	31Ma11Hd
MORGAN, Margaret	20	F	Spinster	31Ma11Hd
John	.00	M	Infant	31Ma11Hd
BURNS, Ann	26	F	Seamstress	31Ma11Hd

NAMES OF PASSENGERS		AGE	SEX	OCCUPATIONS	DATE PORT SHIP
MURPHY, Alex		18	M	Farmer	31Ma11Hd
MORGAN, Judy		17	F	Servant	31Ma11Hd
WALKER, George		46	M	Land Owner	31Ma11Hd
Elizabeth	(W)	35	F	Wife	31Ma11Hd
Mary-Ann		18	F	Relative	31Ma11Hd
Thomas		15	M	Relative	31Ma11Hd
Elizabeth		13	F	Relative	31Ma11Hd
George		12	M	Relative	31Ma11Hd
Letitia		10	F	Relative	31Ma11Hd
LINDSAY, Richard		22	M	Gentleman	31Ma11Hd
MALONE, Ann		30	F	Lady	31Ma11Hd
WALKER, Sarah		17	F	Unknown	31Ma11Hd
RESSICK, Mary		22	F	Servant	31Ma11Hd
OHAGAN, Maria		20	F	Servant	31Ma11Hd

OSCEOLA 31 MAY 1849

From Liverpool

NAMES OF PASSENGERS		AGE	SEX	OCCUPATIONS	DATE PORT SHIP
SMITH, Anne		35	F	Unknown	31Ma02Hq
Ellen		16	F	Unknown	31Ma02Hq
QUIRK, Pat		13	M	Unknown	31Ma02Hq
REYNOLDS, Mary		56	F	Unknown	31Ma02Hq
Peter		11	M	Unknown	31Ma02Hq
FLEMING, John		26	M	Laborer	31Ma02Hq
Michael		27	M	Unknown	31Ma02Hq
Jane		30	F	Unknown	31Ma02Hq
GOLDING, Matthew		22	M	Laborer	31Ma02Hq
KENNAN, John		20	M	Shoemaker	31Ma02Hq
Jane		28	F	Unknown	31Ma02Hq
EAGAN, Pat		40	M	Laborer	31Ma02Hq
MULLEN, Mary		30	F	Unknown	31Ma02Hq
HUNT, John		20	M	Laborer	31Ma02Hq
KEENE, Michl.		20	M	Laborer	31Ma02Hq
HEYDON, James		21	M	Watchmaker	31Ma02Hq
MITCHELL, Thos.		44	M	Farmer	31Ma02Hq
Rachel		40	F	Unknown	31Ma02Hq
Sarah		11	F	Unknown	31Ma02Hq
Emma		6	F	Child	31Ma02Hq
Mary		4	F	Child	31Ma02Hq
DAVIS, Esau		26	M	Laborer	31Ma02Hq
Eliza		24	F	Unknown	31Ma02Hq
Mary		.00	F	Infant	31Ma02Hq
KEASE, John		46	M	Farmer	31Ma02Hq
DAVIS, David		18	M	Farmer	31Ma02Hq
THOMAS, Diana		23	M	Unknown	31Ma02Hq
JONES, James		22	M	Laborer	31Ma02Hq
DAVIS, Ellen		23	F	Unknown	31Ma02Hq
WILLIAMS, Mary		22	F	Unknown	31Ma02Hq
GOODALL, Wm.		40	M	Gdnr	31Ma02Hq
Charlotte		41	F	Unknown	31Ma02Hq
Eliza		16	F	Unknown	31Ma02Hq
Rebecca		7	F	Child	31Ma02Hq
TUCKWAY, Wm.		28	M	Engineer	31Ma02Hq
U	(W)	25	F	Unknown	31Ma02Hq
Agnes		4	F	Child	31Ma02Hq
HENRY, Wm.		1	M	Child	31Ma02Hq
Saml.		23	M	Engineer	31Ma02Hq
DUFFEY, James		26	M	Miller	31Ma02Hq
MULVANY, John		18	M	Accountant	31Ma02Hq
ROACH, Robert		58	M	Farmer	31Ma02Hq
U	(W)	50	F	Unknown	31Ma02Hq
Anne		28	F	Unknown	31Ma02Hq
Pat		27	M	Laborer	31Ma02Hq
John		25	M	Unknown	31Ma02Hq
Mary		22	F	Unknown	31Ma02Hq
Cathe.		20	F	Unknown	31Ma02Hq
Jane		18	F	Unknown	31Ma02Hq
Bernard		15	M	Servant	31Ma02Hq
ROACH, Henry		15	M	Unknown	31Ma02Hq
Ellen		12	F	Unknown	31Ma02Hq
MCGOVERN, Dan		28	M	Unknown	31Ma02Hq
U	(W)	23	F	Unknown	31Ma02Hq
John		5	M	Child	31Ma02Hq
PETERS, Margt.		4	F	Child	31Ma02Hq
MCCABE, John		20	M	Surveyor	31Ma02Hq
DUFFEY, Pat		20	M	Coppersmith	31Ma02Hq
HUGHES, John		19	M	Tinsmith	31Ma02Hq
FARLEY, Dennis		36	M	Laborer	31Ma02Hq
John		28	M	Laborer	31Ma02Hq
MURPHEY, Pat		28	M	Laborer	31Ma02Hq
MCCARTHY, John		30	M	Farmer	31Ma02Hq
Cathn.		27	F	Unknown	31Ma02Hq
Dan		19	M	Clerk	31Ma02Hq
Ellen		26	F	Unknown	31Ma02Hq
Mary		28	F	Unknown	31Ma02Hq
BRATUSKY, Maurice		40	M	Clerk	31Ma02Hq
U	(W)	38	F	Unknown	31Ma02Hq
Esther		10	F	Unknown	31Ma02Hq
Hannah		12	F	Unknown	31Ma02Hq
Andrew		.00	M	Infant	31Ma02Hq
Rachel		.00	F	Infant	31Ma02Hq
Samuel		7	M	Child	31Ma02Hq
Dorothy		60	F	Unknown	31Ma02Hq
Leah		18	F	Unknown	31Ma02Hq
BREENE, Pat		21	M	Gdnr	31Ma02Hq
Walter		18	M	Clerk	31Ma02Hq
Cath.		18	F	Unknown	31Ma02Hq
PENNESEY, John		28	M	Laborer	31Ma02Hq
SHERWICK, Wm.		31	M	Blacksmith	31Ma02Hq
John		27	M	Blacksmith	31Ma02Hq
BURKE, Michael		26	M	Laborer	31Ma02H
Johannah		21	F	Unknown	31Ma02H
MULCAHY, Wm.		24	M	Laborer	31Ma02H
BRIEN, Ellen		40	F	Unknown	31Ma02H
MARTIN, John		40	M	Blacksmith	31Ma02H
U	(W)	45	F	Unknown	31Ma02H
Wm.		18	M	Blacksmith	31Ma02H
John		14	M	Blacksmith	31Ma02H
James		16	M	Blacksmith	31Ma02H
Thomas		12	M	Unknown	31Ma02H
Joseph		10	M	Unknown	31Ma02H
Gilbert		4	M	Child	31Ma02H
Bessy		6	F	Child	31Ma02H
EVANS, Margt.		21	F	Unknown	31Ma02H
Matt.		19	M	Unknown	31Ma02H
MCGRATH, Peter		50	M	Blacksmith	31Ma02H
MAHAN, Andrew		28	M	Laborer	31Ma02H
Bridget		26	F	Unknown	31Ma02H
KIRLAN, John		22	M	Laborer	31Ma02H
Fanny		16	F	Unknown	31Ma02H
Michael		30	M	Laborer	31Ma02H
HANNAHAN, Ellen		45	F	Unknown	31Ma02H
Bridget		18	F	Unknown	31Ma02H
Pat		15	M	Laborer	31Ma02H
Catherine		10	F	Unknown	31Ma02H
COOKIN, Edwd.		27	M	Carpenter	31Ma02H
KEATING, James		25	M	Gdnr	31Ma02H
GORMAN, John		25	M	Laborer	31Ma02H
U	(W)	22	F	Unknown	31Ma02H
Michael		4	M	Child	31Ma02H
Winny		2	M	Child	31Ma02H
William		1	M	Child	31Ma02H
BROPHY, Cathn.		18	F	Unknown	31Ma02H
MORRISSY, Jane		46	F	Unknown	31Ma02H
MURPHY, Mark		45	M	Farmer	31Ma02H
Edwd.		11	M	Unknown	31Ma02H
HEALY, James		26	M	Farmer	31Ma02H
U	(W)	23	F	Unknown	31Ma02H
HANNAHAN, Michael		22	M	Farmer	31Ma02H
HEALY, U		.00	U	Infant	31Ma02H
DONOVAN, John		16	M	Saddler	31Ma02H
Pat		20	M	Saddler	31Ma02H
KELLY, U-Mrs.		29	F	Unknown	31Ma02H

NAMES OF PASSENGERS		AGE	SEX	OCCUPATIONS	DATE PORT SHIP
CONNOR, Michael		33	M	Laborer	31Ma02Hq
SHEA, Pat		28	M	Laborer	31Ma02Hq
WALSH, Jane		12	F	Unknown	31Ma02Hq
FENNETY, Wm.		19	M	Farrier	31Ma02Hq
GROGAN, Cath.		20	F	Unknown	31Ma02Hq
PRENDERGAST, Mary		17	F	Unknown	31Ma02Hq
MADDEN, Helen		19	F	Unknown	31Ma02Hq
Rose		22	F	Unknown	31Ma02Hq
CONRAY, Mary		55	F	Unknown	31Ma02Hq
James		.00	M	Infant	31Ma02Hq
KELLY, John		30	M	Farmer	31Ma02Hq
U	(W)	20	F	Unknown	31Ma02Hq
Cath.		60	F	Farmer	31Ma02Hq
U-Mrs.		60	F	Unknown	31Ma02Hq
Pat		22	M	Farmer	31Ma02Hq
John		20	M	Unknown	31Ma02Hq
Michael		13	M	Unknown	31Ma02Hq
Anne		15	F	Unknown	31Ma02Hq
MULDOON, James		20	M	Farmer	31Ma02Hq
MULLIN, Martin		30	M	Farmer	31Ma02Hq
U	(W)	28	M	Unknown	31Ma02Hq
QUINN, Michael		25	M	Unknown	31Ma02Hq
HARD, Maria		20	F	Unknown	31Ma02Hq
Rose		2	F	Unknown	31Ma02Hq
CONWAY, Pat		.00	M	Infant	31Ma02Hq
MCCHOLE, Mary		26	F	Unknown	31Ma02Hq
Margaret		5	F	Child	31Ma02Hq
Nicolas		3	M	Child	31Ma02Hq
CARROLL, Richd.		35	M	Blacksmith	31Ma02Hq
CONNOLLY, Helen		18	F	Unknown	31Ma02Hq
FARRELLY, Cath.		18	F	Unknown	31Ma02Hq
HOMEDY, Margt.		22	F	Unknown	31Ma02Hq
FITZGERALD, John		28	M	Mason	31Ma02Hq
Mary		18	F	Unknown	31Ma02Hq
U		.00	U	Infant	31Ma02Hq
FARRELL, Pat		28	M	Laborer	31Ma02Hq
John		21	M	Clerk	31Ma02Hq
Anne		22	F	Unknown	31Ma02Hq
NOLAN, James		30	M	Farmer	31Ma02Hq
GILLAN, Eliz.		48	F	Unknown	31Ma02Hq
Edwd.		13	M	Unknown	31Ma02Hq
Frances		9	F	Child	31Ma02Hq
CONNOLLY, Michael		24	M	Laborer	31Ma02Hq
WHITE, John		20	M	Laborer	31Ma02Hq
MCCABE, Bridget		20	F	Unknown	31Ma02Hq
BRADY, John		20	M	Farmer	31Ma02Hq
MCGUIRE, Richd.		13	M	Unknown	31Ma02Hq
MURRAY, Mary		14	F	Unknown	31Ma02Hq
GILLAN, Wm.		46	M	Tailor	31Ma02Hq
REILLY, Pat		21	M	Laborer	31Ma02Hq
LAWLER, Cath.		18	F	Laborer	31Ma02Hq
MCCALL, Edwd.		21	M	Laborer	31Ma02Hq
REEFE, John		28	M	Laborer	31Ma02Hq
Timothy		24	M	Laborer	31Ma02Hq
Margaret		20	F	Laborer	31Ma02Hq
HAYES, Pat		30	M	Laborer	31Ma02Hq
U	(W)	27	F	Unknown	31Ma02Hq
Maria		3	F	Child	31Ma02Hq
Anne		1	F	Child	31Ma02Hq
HOGAN, Michael		20	M	Blacksmith	31Ma02Hq
Mary		17	F	Unknown	31Ma02Hq
KEATING, James		14	M	Unknown	31Ma02Hq
DEVINE, Martin		26	M	Laborer	31Ma02Hq
HARKIN, John		24	M	Laborer	31Ma02Hq
NEPON, Biddy		16	F	Unknown	31Ma02Hq
DUNNE, Michael		30	M	Laborer	31Ma02Hq
U	(W)	28	F	Unknown	31Ma02Hq
Ellen		50	F	Unknown	31Ma02Hq
Eliza		13	F	Unknown	31Ma02Hq
Biddy		11	F	Unknown	31Ma02Hq
Pat		9	M	Child	31Ma02Hq
Peter		6	M	Child	31Ma02Hq
Mary		3	F	Child	31Ma02Hq
Julia		.00	F	Infant	31Ma02Hq
DWYER, James		32	M	Laborer	31Ma02Hq
DWYER, James		16	M	Laborer	31Ma02Hq
Mary		13	F	Laborer	31Ma02Hq
Edmund		34	M	Laborer	31Ma02Hq
KEEFE, John		22	M	Laborer	31Ma02Hq
Timothy		21	M	Laborer	31Ma02Hq
FITZGERALD, Garret		24	M	Laborer	31Ma02Hq
U	(W)	22	F	Unknown	31Ma02Hq
Cathn.		1	F	Child	31Ma02Hq
CONWAY, Thos.		28	M	Laborer	31Ma02Hq
MURPHY, Edwd.		45	M	Laborer	31Ma02Hq
MAYLER, Edwd.		34	M	Laborer	31Ma02Hq
Denis		32	M	Laborer	31Ma02Hq
Lawrence		22	M	Laborer	31Ma02Hq
RYAN, Jerry		25	M	Laborer	31Ma02Hq
John		26	M	Laborer	31Ma02Hq
NOLAN, James		24	M	Laborer	31Ma02Hq
MOONEY, Eliza		12	F	Unknown	31Ma02Hq
FINN, Lawrence		40	M	Laborer	31Ma02Hq
Mary		18	F	Unknown	31Ma02Hq
REEFE, Thomas		18	M	Laborer	31Ma02Hq
CUSTIN, James		20	M	Laborer	31Ma02Hq
Anne		16	F	Unknown	31Ma02Hq
CONNOR, John		23	M	Laborer	31Ma02Hq
MAHAN, Pat		23	M	Laborer	31Ma02Hq
MARRINAN, James		24	M	Laborer	31Ma02Hq
Samuel		25	M	Laborer	31Ma02Hq
AGNEW, Thomas		25	M	Laborer	31Ma02Hq
DUFFEY, Thomas		25	M	Laborer	31Ma02Hq
Bridget		20	F	Unknown	31Ma02Hq
Judith		22	F	Unknown	31Ma02Hq
COOLIDGE, Bridget		23	F	Unknown	31Ma02Hq
CARTNEY, Mary		17	F	Unknown	31Ma02Hq
CEARNS, Anne		19	F	Unknown	31Ma02Hq
MCNARRY, Cath.		19	F	Unknown	31Ma02Hq
ENGLISH, Rose		20	F	Unknown	31Ma02Hq
BOLAND, John		15	M	Laborer	31Ma02Hq
James		28	M	Laborer	31Ma02Hq
Boni		30	M	Unknown	31Ma02Hq
VARASA, Sande		32	M	Tailor	31Ma02Hq
U	(W)	30	F	Unknown	31Ma02Hq
James		4	F	Child	31Ma02Hq
Mary		.00	F	Infant	31Ma02Hq
HEATON, Wm.		30	M	Clothier	31Ma02Hq
EAGAN, Cath.		26	F	Unknown	31Ma02Hq
John		36	M	Cbtmkr	31Ma02Hq
DOYLE, Risto		23	M	Gdnr	31Ma02Hq
Jerry		20	M	Gdnr	31Ma02Hq
Christopher		18	M	Gdnr	31Ma02Hq
KITCHIN, Wm.		32	M	Laborer	31Ma02Hq
WHYBURN, Richd.		39	M	Laborer	31Ma02Hq
KITCHIN, U-Mrs.		30	F	Mason	31Ma02Hq
WHYBURN, George		21	M	Laborer	31Ma02Hq
Charlotte		20	F	Laborer	31Ma02Hq
Emma		17	F	Unknown	31Ma02Hq
Edward		15	M	Laborer	31Ma02Hq
Margaret		9	F	Child	31Ma02Hq
Ellen		4	F	Child	31Ma02Hq
Oppercue		1	F	Child	31Ma02Hq
GABBET, Frances		40	F	Laborer	31Ma02Hq
MCGUIRE, John		25	M	Unknown	31Ma02Hq
DOWELL, Margt.		18	F	Unknown	31Ma02Hq
FLOOD, Pat		22	M	Baker	31Ma02Hq
ANGEL, Pat		24	M	Laborer	31Ma02Hq
CASTER, Francis		24	M	Laborer	31Ma02Hq
U	(W)	27	F	Unknown	31Ma02Hq
U		.00	F	Infant	31Ma02Hq
THOMAS, Wm.		24	M	Laborer	31Ma02Hq
BEGLIN, Alley		26	M	Unknown	31Ma02Hq
Mary		18	F	Unknown	31Ma02Hq
CASSIDY, John		30	M	Laborer	31Ma02Hq
BROPHY, Bridgt.		20	F	Laborer	31Ma02Hq
STAR, Thomas		30	M	Laborer	31Ma02Hq
COOPER, Wm.		40	M	Laborer	31Ma02Hq
Edwin		18	M	Laborer	31Ma02Hq
HEELY, Andrew		25	M	Laborer	31Ma02Hq

NAMES OF PASSENGERS		AGE	SEX	OCCUPATIONS	DATE PORT SHIP
LAWLER, Pat		25	M	Unknown	31Ma02Hq
COLLINS, Edwd.		30	M	Laborer	31Ma02Hq
MURPHY, Edwd.		19	M	Laborer	31Ma02Hq
NEWTON, Isaac		26	M	Wheelwright	31Ma02Hq
U	(W)	26	F	Unknown	31Ma02Hq
Elizabeth		7	F	Child	31Ma02Hq
Mary		5	F	Child	31Ma02Hq
Isaac		3	M	Child	31Ma02Hq
Alfred		1	M	Child	31Ma02Hq
TAFFORD, Edwd.		59	M	Farmer	31Ma02Hq
U	(W)	55	F	Unknown	31Ma02Hq
Edwd.		30	M	Miller	31Ma02Hq
CROWS, Wm.		30	M	Laborer	31Ma02Hq
U	(W)	26	F	Unknown	31Ma02Hq
Edwd.		10	M	Unknown	31Ma02Hq
Mark		8	M	Child	31Ma02Hq
John		6	M	Child	31Ma02Hq
Charles		3	M	Child	31Ma02Hq
Mary		1	F	Child	31Ma02Hq
WHYBURN, U-Mrs.		40	F	Unknown	31Ma02Hq
DAVIS, Mary		18	F	Unknown	31Ma02Hq
Rachel		21	F	Unknown	31Ma02Hq
EVANS, Eliza		19	F	Unknown	31Ma02Hq

FIDELIA 31 MAY 1849

From Liverpool

NAMES OF PASSENGERS		AGE	SEX	OCCUPATIONS	DATE PORT SHIP
DAVIS, Mary		21	F	Unknown	31Ma02Ic
HUNT, Thomas		30	M	Farmer	31Ma02Ic
Susan	(W)	30	F	Wife	31Ma02Ic
STEPHENSON, John		45	M	Pmfr	31Ma02Ic
Eliza		40	F	None	31Ma02Ic
JEFFERIES, Jane		40	F	None	31Ma02Ic
Catherine		25	F	None	31Ma02Ic
HIGGINS, Charles		25	M	Draper	31Ma02Ic
CROTTY, James		22	M	Stone Mason	31Ma02Ic
Eliza	(W)	21	F	Wife	31Ma02Ic
FALON, Michal		27	M	Stone Mason	31Ma02Ic
MARRALL, Patrick		27	M	Stone Mason	31Ma02Ic
KINSLAR, Jeremiah		18	M	Shopman	31Ma02Ic
Garrat		75	M	Farmer	31Ma02Ic
Margaret	(W)	60	F	Wife	31Ma02Ic
Terresa		18	F	None	31Ma02Ic
CONNERFORD, Eliza		20	F	None	31Ma02Ic
CLOWERY, William		25	M	Student	31Ma02Ic
KAHOA, Arthur		50	M	Farmer	31Ma02Ic
DALTON, Lawrence		17	M	Farmer	31Ma02Ic
Margaret		30	F	Servant	31Ma02Ic
MCCULLY, Jane		20	F	None	31Ma02Ic
ARCHDEACON, Ellen		25	F	Unknown	31Ma02Ic
MCGERVEY, Bridget		25	F	Unknown	31Ma02Ic
CONNOR, Rose		16	F	None	31Ma02Ic
MCCULLY, Mary-Jane		17	F	None	31Ma02Ic
RYAN, Bridget		20	F	None	31Ma02Ic
BERLY, Ann		20	F	Unknown	31Ma02Ic
Fill		25	M	Laborer	31Ma02Ic
RYAN, Catherine		25	F	Servant	31Ma02Ic
LOUDER, Ann		26	F	Unknown	31Ma02Ic
Thomas		.00	M	Infant	31Ma02Ic
MCCONNOR, Mick		21	M	Unknown	31Ma02Ic
Mary		40	F	Unknown	31Ma02Ic
Catherine		25	F	Unknown	31Ma02Ic
Mary		20	F	Unknown	31Ma02Ic
John		18	M	Unknown	31Ma02Ic
Hesser		17	U	Unknown	31Ma02Ic
Margaret		14	F	Unknown	31Ma02Ic
Ellen		15	F	Unknown	31Ma02Ic
Felix		12	M	None	31Ma02Ic
MCCONNOR, Jane		10	F	None	31Ma02Ic
MCLANE, Martha		25	F	Unknown	31Ma02Ic
MCCOURTNEY, Nancy		24	F	Unknown	31Ma02Ic
MITCHELL, Mary		17	F	Unknown	31Ma02Ic
GRAY, Jane		18	F	Unknown	31Ma02Ic
JAMISON, Samuel		40	M	Shoemaker	31Ma02Ic
Sarah	(W)	29	F	Wife	31Ma02Ic
John		7	M	Child	31Ma02Ic
Margaret		5	F	Child	31Ma02Ic
Robert		3	M	Child	31Ma02Ic
Matilda		.00	F	Infant	31Ma02Ic
WALLACE, Sarah		50	F	Unknown	31Ma02Ic
Archibald		22	M	Laborer	31Ma02Ic
Jane		20	F	Servant	31Ma02Ic
Charles		18	M	Laborer	31Ma02Ic
Thomas		16	M	Laborer	31Ma02Ic
John		14	M	Laborer	31Ma02Ic
James		12	M	Laborer	31Ma02Ic
JOHNSTON, Barbery		17	U	Unknown	31Ma02Ic
DUFFY, Charles		26	M	Unknown	31Ma02Ic
GALDON, John		26	M	Laborer	31Ma02Ic
TRAVIS, Patrick		30	M	Laborer	31Ma02Ic
REILLY, Mathew		25	M	Laborer	31Ma02Ic
CURRY, Margaret		19	F	Unknown	31Ma02Ic
PERCIL, Ann		22	F	Servant	31Ma02Ic
LEDWARDS, Ellen		18	F	Servant	31Ma02Ic
BOWAN, Ellen		15	F	Servant	31Ma02Ic
HERAN, Catherine		22	F	Servant	31Ma02Ic
MOORE, Andrew		36	M	Laborer	31Ma02Ic
Mary	(W)	35	F	Wife	31Ma02Ic
John		12	M	Unknown	31Ma02Ic
Mary-Jane		10	F	Unknown	31Ma02Ic
Margaret		8	F	Child	31Ma02Ic
James		6	M	Child	31Ma02Ic
Nancy		4	F	Child	31Ma02Ic
Martha		.00	F	Infant	31Ma02Ic
FITZPATRICK, Margaret		25	F	Unknown	31Ma02Ic
DELANY, Margaret		22	F	Unknown	31Ma02Ic
MAHONY, Catherine		16	F	Unknown	31Ma02Ic
TOWELL, Mary		15	F	Servant	31Ma02Ic
MURRY, Margret		26	F	Servant	31Ma02Ic
LYND, Mary		26	F	Dressmaker	31Ma02Ic
Robert		8	M	Child	31Ma02Ic
Samuel		5	M	Child	31Ma02Ic
Eliza		3	F	Child	31Ma02Ic
HAMMON, James		29	M	Shoemaker	31Ma02Ic
GERRY, James		13	M	Unknown	31Ma02Ic
NERAN, Daniel		20	M	Laborer	31Ma02Ic
COLLINS, Timothy		25	M	Unknown	31Ma02Ic
PERRY, Mathew		35	M	Weaver	31Ma02Ic
John		69	M	Unknown	31Ma02Ic
Elizabeth		32	F	None	31Ma02Ic
John		.00	M	Infant	31Ma02Ic
Died-At-Sea					
CORRAGAN, Bessey		19	F	Servant	31Ma02Ic
NICHOLSON, Jane		18	F	Servant	31Ma02Ic
Mary		45	F	Servant	31Ma02Ic
BAKER, Ellen		15	F	Servant	31Ma02Ic
BLACK, John		36	M	Farmer	31Ma02Ic
Sarah	(W)	30	F	Wife	31Ma02Ic
Nancy		14	F	Unknown	31Ma02Ic
John		11	M	Unknown	31Ma02Ic
William		9	M	Child	31Ma02Ic
PERRY, Andrew		40	M	Laborer	31Ma02Ic
Sarah		35	F	None	31Ma02Ic
Jane		12	F	None	31Ma02Ic
Samuel		10	M	None	31Ma02Ic
Andrew		5	M	Child	31Ma02Ic
PATTERSON, Robert		21	M	Laborer	31Ma02Ic
Hamilton		18	U	Unknown	31Ma02Ic
CROSBY, Patrick		25	M	Unknown	31Ma02Ic
MAGUIRE, Patrick		18	M	Unknown	31Ma02Ic
HAILY, Patrick		25	M	Unknown	31Ma02Ic
REILLY, Daniel		21	M	Unknown	31Ma02Ic
MCGEFF, Thomas		50	M	Unknown	31Ma02Ic

NAMES OF PASSENGERS	AGE	SEX	OCCUPATIONS	DATE PORT SHIP
CLERK, Margaret	30	F	Servant	31Ma02lc
GANDRY, Sarah	50	F	Servant	31Ma02lc
HICKEY, Mary	50	F	Servant	31Ma02lc
CONAGAN, Edward	26	M	Laborer	31Ma02lc
MCINTIRE, Moses	24	M	Laborer	31Ma02lc
BAGAN, Mark	23	M	Laborer	31Ma02lc
MCGLYN, Andrew	20	M	Laborer	31Ma02lc
FARLEY, John	21	M	Laborer	31Ma02lc
CLARK, Mick	18	M	Laborer	31Ma02lc
Connor	15	M	Laborer	31Ma02lc
FARLAN, Pat	17	M	Laborer	31Ma02lc
CARLAN, Mick	18	M	Laborer	31Ma02lc
CAIN, John	16	M	Laborer	31Ma02lc
DENEGAN, Pat	21	M	Laborer	31Ma02lc
DUNLAVY, James	20	M	Laborer	31Ma02lc
CRAIN, Jack	70	M	Laborer	31Ma02lc
John	7	M	Child	31Ma02lc
Ann	5	F	Child	31Ma02lc
LYANN, Pat	12	M	Unknown	31Ma02lc
MCGIRL, Ann	16	F	Servant	31Ma02lc
Daniel	12	M	Unknown	31Ma02lc
GERVY, Catherine	16	F	Unknown	31Ma02lc
NASH, William	32	M	Laborer	31Ma02lc
Bessy	8	F	Child	31Ma02lc
Ellen	10	F	Unknown	31Ma02lc
PERCIL, Johanna	20	F	Servant	31Ma02lc
MCMARROW, Mary	30	F	Servant	31Ma02lc
FOGARTY, John	46	M	Laborer	31Ma02lc
Judy (W)	34	F	Wife	31Ma02lc
Edward	.00	M	Infant	31Ma02lc
Mick	.00	M	Infant	31Ma02lc
Ann	13	F	Unknown	31Ma02lc
MILAN, Mary	30	F	Unknown	31Ma02lc
Mick	7	M	Child	31Ma02lc
Catherine	5	F	Child	31Ma02lc
MAHAR, Margaret	20	F	Unknown	31Ma02lc
OGAN, Antony	47	M	Laborer	31Ma02lc
FOGARTY, John	18	M	Laborer	31Ma02lc
Pat	6	M	Child	31Ma02lc
WIGHT, Amy	4	F	Child	31Ma02lc
New	22	M	Unknown	31Ma02lc
Ellen	16	F	Unknown	31Ma02lc
Judy	19	F	Unknown	31Ma02lc
MCCARL, Catherine	19	F	Unknown	31Ma02lc
HINAIS, James	6	M	Child	31Ma02lc
CONWAY, Edward	23	M	Laborer	31Ma02lc
LONGRIN, William	20	M	Laborer	31Ma02lc
WILSON, James	18	M	Laborer	31Ma02lc
CURRY, Nicholas	18	M	Laborer	31Ma02lc
FITZGERALD, Wm.	17	M	Laborer	31Ma02lc
NICKOLSON, George	20	M	Laborer	31Ma02lc
GASKELL, Patrick	27	M	Laborer	31Ma02lc
MCGRATH, Daniel	25	M	Laborer	31Ma02lc
Thomas	20	M	Laborer	31Ma02lc
DOLAN, Thomas	50	M	Laborer	31Ma02lc
ECCLES, John	18	M	Laborer	31Ma02lc
CARRY, Andrew	16	M	Laborer	31Ma02lc
RYO, Anty	18	F	Unknown	31Ma02lc
CAHAN, Bridget	23	F	Unknown	31Ma02lc
KNOWLES, Judy	25	F	Servant	31Ma02lc
GLANCY, Mary	16	F	Servant	31Ma02lc
TRAVIS, Catherine	21	F	Servant	31Ma02lc
DARKES, Catherine	20	F	Servant	31Ma02lc
MAXWELL, Mary-Ann	19	F	Servant	31Ma02lc
KILMARTIN, John	25	M	Unknown	31Ma02lc
Johanna	28	F	Servant	31Ma02lc
SHARKEY, John	22	M	Unknown	31Ma02lc
Mary	18	F	Servant	31Ma02lc
MORAN, Pat	30	M	Laborer	31Ma02lc
FOGARTY, Winnie	42	U	Unknown	31Ma02lc
Rose	16	F	Unknown	31Ma02lc
Albert	18	M	Unknown	31Ma02lc
MURPHY, Ellen	12	F	Unknown	31Ma02lc
MCDUNN, Catherine	13	F	Unknown	31Ma02lc
MURPHY, Margaret	12	F	Unknown	31Ma02lc
LINARD, Seisley	44	U	Unknown	31Ma02lc
ORAH, Thomas	15	M	Unknown	31Ma02lc
Mick	17	M	Unknown	31Ma02lc
Peter	5	M	Child	31Ma02lc
Peggy	14	F	Unknown	31Ma02lc
WELSH, Mary	18	F	Unknown	31Ma02lc
Ellen	9	F	Child	31Ma02lc
John	6	M	Child	31Ma02lc
SHERWOOD, Sarah	16	F	Unknown	31Ma02lc
MURPHY, Wm.	24	M	Unknown	31Ma02lc
Hessa	22	U	Unknown	31Ma02lc
Ellen	.00	F	Infant	31Ma02lc
CALAGAN, Patrick	30	M	Unknown	31Ma02lc
Bridget	30	F	Unknown	31Ma02lc
Margaret	10	F	Unknown	31Ma02lc
Mary-Ann	7	F	Child	31Ma02lc
John	5	M	Child	31Ma02lc
Sabina	.00	F	Infant	31Ma02lc
MAGAN, Homa	20	U	Unknown	31Ma02lc
COX, Rosa	20	F	Unknown	31Ma02lc
MCGOVERN, Phill	23	M	Unknown	31Ma02lc
MCGIRL, Pat	20	M	Unknown	31Ma02lc
REILY, James	27	M	Unknown	31Ma02lc
HAYGINS, Mary	20	F	Unknown	31Ma02lc
JORDAN, Ann	17	F	Servant	31Ma02lc
HIGGINS, Mary	16	F	Unknown	31Ma02lc
COMLOW, Bridget	.11	F	Infant	31Ma02lc
MAGAN, Bridget	20	F	Unknown	31Ma02lc
MURPHY, Edward	60	M	Unknown	31Ma02lc
Rosa	60	F	Unknown	31Ma02lc
Thomas	19	M	Laborer	31Ma02lc
Francis	16	M	Laborer	31Ma02lc
JORDAN, Andrew	20	M	Cooper	31Ma02lc
LOCKEAD, Joseph	25	M	Smith	31Ma02lc
DESMOND, Wm.	20	M	Cbtmkr	31Ma02lc
LOCKEAD, Maria	.00	F	Infant	31Ma02lc
MCGOVERN, Rose	16	F	Servant	31Ma02lc
SMITH, Rosa	30	F	Servant	31Ma02lc
ROCCH, Ellen	23	F	Servant	31Ma02lc
BEYS, Bessy	8	F	Child	31Ma02lc
MCGUIRE, Pat	40	M	Laborer	31Ma02lc
Margaret	35	F	Unknown	31Ma02lc
Pat	12	M	Unknown	31Ma02lc
Mary	5	F	Child	31Ma02lc
SULLIVAN, Catherine	18	F	Unknown	31Ma02lc
CALAGAN, Catherine	20	F	Unknown	31Ma02lc
Johanna	11	F	Unknown	31Ma02lc
BARRY, Margaret	20	F	Servant	31Ma02lc
MCNALTY, John	20	M	Unknown	31Ma02lc
OWENS, Daniel	20	M	Unknown	31Ma02lc
HARVEY, Owen	20	M	Laborer	31Ma02lc
HARRALS, Edmond	60	M	Laborer	31Ma02lc
Ellen	14	F	Unknown	31Ma02lc
Anna	13	F	Unknown	31Ma02lc
RONEY, Mary	40	F	Unknown	31Ma02lc
John	18	M	Unknown	31Ma02lc
MITCHEL, John	18	M	Unknown	31Ma02lc
Rose	16	F	Unknown	31Ma02lc
OWEN, Margaret	12	F	Unknown	31Ma02lc
OKIEFF, John	26	M	Laborer	31Ma02lc
RERIANS, James	16	M	Laborer	31Ma02lc
DAVISON, James	15	M	Laborer	31Ma02lc
MURPHY, James	36	M	Laborer	31Ma02lc
GAFNEY, Mary	30	F	Servant	31Ma02lc
LARVAN, Dora	48	F	Servant	31Ma02lc
GAFNEY, Ode	10	M	Unknown	31Ma02lc
James	8	M	Child	31Ma02lc
Catherine	4	F	Child	31Ma02lc
Ann	.00	F	Infant	31Ma02lc
RERRIN, Jane	15	F	Servant	31Ma02lc
LYON, Margaret	30	F	Servant	31Ma02lc
CAHAN, Mary	21	F	Unknown	31Ma02lc
LYON, Martin	31	M	Unknown	31Ma02lc
CORD, Catherine	30	F	Unknown	31Ma02lc
GERVY, James	14	M	Unknown	31Ma02lc

NAMES OF PASSENGERS	AGE	SEX	OCCUPATIONS	DATE PORT SHIP
HERBY, James	11	M	Unknown	31Ma02lc
HARVEY, Mary	60	F	Unknown	31Ma02lc
CORD, Margaret	26	F	Unknown	31Ma02lc
Michl.	5	M	Child	31Ma02lc
James	.00	M	Infant	31Ma02lc
MCANTY, Pat	65	M	Laborer	31Ma02lc
Susan (W)	60	F	Wife	31Ma02lc
Francis	18	M	Laborer	31Ma02lc
LEE, Pat	16	M	Laborer	31Ma02lc
CUSHMAN, Johanna	30	F	Servant	31Ma02lc
William	9	M	Child	31Ma02lc
Thomas	10	M	Unknown	31Ma02lc
Mary	33	F	Unknown	31Ma02lc
CROKE, James	18	M	Laborer	31Ma02lc
KIEFE, Thomas	21	M	Laborer	31Ma02lc
CROWLY, John	23	M	Laborer	31Ma02lc
WALGLOW, Thomas	20	M	Laborer	31Ma02lc
GAFNEY, Farrel	20	M	Laborer	31Ma02lc
MORTON, Margaret	8	F	Child	31Ma02lc
MCSARAH, Thomas	.00	F	Infant	31Ma02lc
COULON, Michl.	12	M	Unknown	31Ma02lc
OCONNOR, John	19	M	Laborer	31Ma02lc
MCMANNUS, Margaret	24	F	Servant	31Ma02lc
Mary	22	F	Servant	31Ma02lc
MCDERMOT, Sarah	21	F	Servant	31Ma02lc
GALLARD, Ann	22	F	Servant	31Ma02lc
MULLVANY, Mary	35	F	Servant	31Ma02lc
Catherine	4	F	Child	31Ma02lc
SCOLLAN, Charles	22	M	Servant	31Ma02lc
Catherine	9	F	Child	31Ma02lc
MULLVANY, Mary	.00	F	Infant	31Ma02lc
FALL, Pat	14	M	Unknown	31Ma02lc
Catherine	8	F	Child	31Ma02lc
ACHSON, John	18	M	Unknown	31Ma02lc
Eliza	11	F	Unknown	31Ma02lc
BOND, Mary-Ann	28	F	Bookbinder	31Ma02lc
Edward	.00	M	Infant	31Ma02lc
William	4	M	Child	31Ma02lc
BRENNAN, Jane	22	F	Servant	31Ma02lc
SHY, Elizabeth	17	F	Servant	31Ma02lc
Ellen	19	F	Servant	31Ma02lc
SHANNAH, Alice	19	F	Servant	31Ma02lc
BERK, Judy	20	F	Servant	31Ma02lc
CONLEY, Mary	20	F	Servant	31Ma02lc
Margaret	27	F	Servant	31Ma02lc
WELSH, Margaret	17	F	Servant	31Ma02lc
MALONEY, Ann	16	F	Servant	31Ma02lc
MAGUIRE, Catherine	20	F	Servant	31Ma02lc
MCDONALD, John	18	M	Shop Boy	31Ma02lc
LAMB, Michel	22	M	Servant	31Ma02lc
CASLO, Eliza	17	F	Servant	31Ma02lc
STRICKLAN, Catherine	19	F	Servant	31Ma02lc
FLYN, Agnes	29	F	Servant	31Ma02lc
STRICKLAN, Martha	15	F	Servant	31Ma02lc
MCMANNAS, Pat	30	M	Servant	31Ma02lc
CONNOR, James	13	M	Servant	31Ma02lc
MCCURRY, John	13	M	Servant	31Ma02lc
PERSONS, Jane	20	F	Servant	31Ma02lc
MURPHY, Winafred	18	F	Servant	31Ma02lc
BOYLE, Sarah	18	F	Servant	31Ma02lc
CLERRY, Rose	14	F	Servant	31Ma02lc
GRAY, Pat	20	M	Batter	31Ma02lc
HUMPHRY, George	19	M	Servant	31Ma02lc
DALTON, George	18	M	Servant	31Ma02lc
ELLIOT, Robert	18	M	Servant	31Ma02lc
DALTON, Margaret	17	F	Servant	31Ma02lc
HUMPHRY, Mary-Ann	17	F	Servant	31Ma02lc
GRAHAM, Aryial	15	U	Servant	31Ma02lc
Ann-Jane	9	F	Child	31Ma02lc
CARROL, Julia	15	F	Servant	31Ma02lc
DOGARTY, Thomas	25	M	Carpenter	31Ma02lc
HESSLIN, James	18	M	Baker	31Ma02lc
DELANY, John	26	M	Shoemaker	31Ma02lc
LEE, Charles	17	M	Tailor	31Ma02lc
LYNCH, Owen	17	M	Laborer	31Ma02lc
DAVAN, Maria	18	F	Servant	31Ma02lc
GRIFFIN, Mary-Ann	9	F	Child	31Ma02lc
Bridget	15	F	Servant	31Ma02lc
ARMSTRONG, Ann	18	F	Servant	31Ma02lc
REILLY, Catherine	8	F	Child	31Ma02lc
LYONS, Biddy	17	F	Servant	31Ma02lc
CARRIGAN, Owen	18	M	None	31Ma02lc
KNOWLAN, Stertan	50	U	None	31Ma02lc
John	35	M	None	31Ma02lc
MCGUINIS, Margaret	40	F	Unknown	31Ma02lc
BRIGNEY, Pat	24	M	Unknown	31Ma02lc
MCGUINES, Arthur	3	M	Child	31Ma02lc
CALAGAN, Margaret	30	F	Unknown	31Ma02lc
MULLAN, Mary	14	F	Servant	31Ma02lc
Biddy	16	F	Servant	31Ma02lc
CALLERY, Ann	16	F	Servant	31Ma02lc
Bridget	18	F	Servant	31Ma02lc
OWENS, Alice	30	F	Servant	31Ma02lc
MALICK, Mary	11	F	Servant	31Ma02lc
John	12	M	Servant	31Ma02lc
REILY, Mary	17	F	Servant	31Ma02lc
FLANAGAN, Terry	20	M	Servant	31Ma02lc
MULICK, Catherine	20	F	Servant	31Ma02lc
CASSADY, Mary	30	F	Servant	31Ma02lc
Francis	8	M	Child	31Ma02lc
Thomas	4	M	Child	31Ma02lc
James	.00	M	Infant	31Ma02lc
MURRY, Ann	16	F	None	31Ma02lc
LYNCH, James	28	M	Carpenter	31Ma02lc
TIERNY, Anna	20	F	Dressmaker	31Ma02lc
MCGUINNAS, Edward	7	M	Child	31Ma02lc
George-Henry	5	M	Child	31Ma02lc
Josep	.00	M	Infant	31Ma02lc
Thomas	11	M	Unknown	31Ma02lc
John	13	M	Unknown	31Ma02lc
PLATT, James	25	M	Unknown	31Ma02lc
GREEN, Ellen	21	F	Unknown	31Ma02lc

JAMES-PENNELL 31 MAY 1849

From Liverpool

NAMES OF PASSENGERS	AGE	SEX	OCCUPATIONS	DATE PORT SHIP
STEEL, Pat	00	M	Laborer	31Ma02lh
ELTON, John	45	M	Laborer	31Ma02lh
DEVINE, Margt.	30	F	Laborer	31Ma02lh
COTTON, M.	22	F	Laborer	31Ma02lh
U	.00	U	Infant	31Ma02lh
Daniel	4	M	Child	31Ma02lh
Ebensgen	2	M	Child	31Ma02lh
CAREY, Andrew	21	M	Unknown	31Ma02lh
CUSHMAN, Darbery	42	M	Unknown	31Ma02lh
MACKEY, John	50	M	Unknown	31Ma02lh
AHERN, Ellen	22	F	Unknown	31Ma02lh
CORBIT, John	40	M	Unknown	31Ma02lh
CRONIN, Thos.	32	M	Unknown	31Ma02lh
SULLIVAN, Tim	16	M	Unknown	31Ma02lh
KINENY, James	34	M	Unknown	31Ma02lh
Joshua	39	M	Unknown	31Ma02lh
OCONNOR, Denis	19	M	Unknown	31Ma02lh
Jane	26	F	Unknown	31Ma02lh
OMALLY, Eliza	28	F	Unknown	31Ma02lh
Susan	33	F	Unknown	31Ma02lh
MOON, Mary	42	F	Unknown	31Ma02lh
John	61	M	Unknown	31Ma02lh
BRYAN, Ellen	54	F	Unknown	31Ma02lh
HALLERSEY, Jenny	32	F	Unknown	31Ma02lh
DUGGAN, Ellen	46	F	Unknown	31Ma02lh
DISEBY, Ellen	32	F	Unknown	31Ma02l
BROWN, James	21	M	Unknown	31Ma02l

NAMES OF PASSENGERS	AGE	SEX	OCCUPATIONS	DATE PORT SHIP
BROWN, Ann	30	F	Unknown	31Ma02lh
DONOHUE, Mich.	21	M	Unknown	31Ma02lh
Mary	31	F	Unknown	31Ma02lh
SIMSON, Tim	42	M	Unknown	31Ma02lh
Cathn.	54	F	Unknown	31Ma02lh
Dan	43	M	Unknown	31Ma02lh
Mary	44	F	Unknown	31Ma02lh
CONNOR, Pat	56	M	Unknown	31Ma02lh
Margt.	19	F	Unknown	31Ma02lh
U	.00	U	Infant	31Ma02lh
Ellen	23	F	Unknown	31Ma02lh
Anne	25	F	Unknown	31Ma02lh
WHISTOR, Denis	31	M	Unknown	31Ma02lh
Margt.	36	F	Unknown	31Ma02lh
KONNELY, Mich.	34	M	Unknown	31Ma02lh
Anne	61	F	Unknown	31Ma02lh
Mary	71	F	Unknown	31Ma02lh
DOOLEY, Bridget	00	F	Unknown	31Ma02lh
U	.00	U	Infant	31Ma02lh
Mary	14	F	Unknown	31Ma02lh
Tim	29	M	Unknown	31Ma02lh
John	17	M	Unknown	31Ma02lh
Bridget	42	F	Unknown	31Ma02lh
KENALLY, Pat	36	M	Unknown	31Ma02lh
Denis	18	M	Unknown	31Ma02lh
Mary	45	F	Unknown	31Ma02lh
Margt.	49	F	Unknown	31Ma02lh
REDDY, Mrgt.	00	U	Unknown	31Ma02lh
U	.00	U	Infant	31Ma02lh
Bridget	48	F	Unknown	31Ma02lh
BARKER, Bess	47	F	Unknown	31Ma02lh
WALLACE, Ann	39	F	Unknown	31Ma02lh
MAHON, Pat	46	M	Unknown	31Ma02lh
WHELAN, James	45	M	Unknown	31Ma02lh
BATT, James	25	M	Unknown	31Ma02lh
CAMPION, Pat	26	M	Unknown	31Ma02lh
REDDY, Ellen	27	F	Unknown	31Ma02lh
KEVIN, Bridget	24	F	Unknown	31Ma02lh
MAHONE, Francis	32	M	Unknown	31Ma02lh
KENNY, Bridget	34	F	Unknown	31Ma02lh
Mary	39	F	Unknown	31Ma02lh
Bess	38	F	Unknown	31Ma02lh
Maria	60	F	Unknown	31Ma02lh
KINEY, Anna	61	F	Unknown	31Ma02lh
Bridget	45	F	Unknown	31Ma02lh
BURKE, Bess	44	F	Unknown	31Ma02lh
NEWMAN, John	43	M	Unknown	31Ma02lh
Anne	41	F	Unknown	31Ma02lh
CAHILL, Joseph	49	M	Unknown	31Ma02lh
John	50	M	Unknown	31Ma02lh
Bridget	29	F	Unknown	31Ma02lh
CORMACK, U-Mrs.	19	F	Unknown	31Ma02lh
Richard	32	M	Unknown	31Ma02lh
Mary	45	F	Unknown	31Ma02lh
Peter	36	M	Unknown	31Ma02lh
Mary	12	F	Unknown	31Ma02lh
Eliza	10	F	Unknown	31Ma02lh
Peter	12	M	Unknown	31Ma02lh
BRYAN, Cath.	00	F	Unknown	31Ma02lh
BOADEN, Pat	19	M	Unknown	31Ma02lh
John	41	M	Unknown	31Ma02lh
Norry	25	F	Unknown	31Ma02lh
Margt.	32	F	Unknown	31Ma02lh
SCOTT, Wm.	35	M	Unknown	31Ma02lh
MILLAR, Eliza	39	F	Unknown	31Ma02lh
MAHON, Nicholas	40	M	Unknown	31Ma02lh
MORAN, Mich.	32	M	Unknown	31Ma02lh
MALLARY, John	23	M	Unknown	31Ma02lh
MORAN, Margt.	19	F	Unknown	31Ma02lh
MANLEY, James	21	M	Unknown	31Ma02lh
FINNA, Pat	23	M	Unknown	31Ma02lh
CASEY, Anne	25	F	Unknown	31Ma02lh
KENNING, Mary	29	F	Unknown	31Ma02lh
HASLEY, Joseph	36	M	Unknown	31Ma02lh
PUGH, Thos.	37	M	Unknown	31Ma02lh
KENNEDY, Edwd.	44	M	Unknown	31Ma02lh
DONNELL, Margt.	00	F	Unknown	31Ma02lh
BURLINGTON, Margt.	24	F	Unknown	31Ma02lh
MANIGDON, Cathe.	29	F	Unknown	31Ma02lh
RICE, Richd.	31	M	Unknown	31Ma02lh
Cath.	14	F	Unknown	31Ma02lh
Ellen	45	F	Unknown	31Ma02lh
MCDONNELL, Dan	54	M	Unknown	31Ma02lh
HONNOR, Thos.	19	M	Unknown	31Ma02lh
CREAN, John	27	M	Unknown	31Ma02lh
Mary	37	F	Unknown	31Ma02lh
CARTHY, Denis	45	M	Unknown	31Ma02lh
BASSET, Wm.	61	M	Unknown	31Ma02lh
CORCORAN, Cath.	33	F	Unknown	31Ma02lh
HIGGINS, Sally	44	F	Unknown	31Ma02lh
BARKER, Kelly	45	U	Unknown	31Ma02lh
TULLY, Bridget	43	F	Unknown	31Ma02lh
KEARNEY, John	41	M	Unknown	31Ma02lh
CLINTON, Joseph	36	M	Unknown	31Ma02lh
CORCORAN, Pat	22	M	Unknown	31Ma02lh
MANNING, Dennis	33	M	Unknown	31Ma02lh
CARTHY, Mick	29	M	Unknown	31Ma02lh
CORCORAN, John	14	M	Unknown	31Ma02lh
MURPHY, Pat	19	M	Unknown	31Ma02lh
MCMAMIRE, Thos.	23	M	Unknown	31Ma02lh
MARTIN, Rose	32	F	Unknown	31Ma02lh
MCLOUGHLIN, John	44	M	Unknown	31Ma02lh
MCCAN, Lib.	45	F	Unknown	31Ma02lh
HENSON, Mich.	48	M	Unknown	31Ma02lh
Pat	47	M	Unknown	31Ma02lh
Cath.	39	F	Unknown	31Ma02lh
FAMISON, John	22	M	Unknown	31Ma02lh
HAWSON, Joseph	52	M	Unknown	31Ma02lh
Martin	36	M	Unknown	31Ma02lh
James	25	M	Unknown	31Ma02lh
Mary	43	F	Unknown	31Ma02lh
Joseph	29	M	Unknown	31Ma02lh
Ann	28	F	Unknown	31Ma02lh
COLLIN, Anne	26	F	Unknown	31Ma02lh
SCULLY, John	17	M	Unknown	31Ma02lh
HATTON, Phi	23	U	Unknown	31Ma02lh
SHARKEY, Thos.	43	M	Unknown	31Ma02lh
MCDERMOT, Ellen	24	F	Unknown	31Ma02lh
MANING, Mary	49	F	Unknown	31Ma02lh
JONES, Mary-Anne	63	F	Unknown	31Ma02lh
JOHNE, John	42	M	Unknown	31Ma02lh
Sarah	40	F	Unknown	31Ma02lh
Sam	34	M	Unknown	31Ma02lh
Thomas	24	M	Unknown	31Ma02lh
HASLEY, John	22	M	Unknown	31Ma02lh
Mary-Anne	50	F	Unknown	31Ma02lh
JONES, Wm.	52	M	Unknown	31Ma02lh
Mary	53	F	Unknown	31Ma02lh
CROWLEY, Mich.	54	M	Unknown	31Ma02lh
Mich.	21	M	Unknown	31Ma02lh
Owen	31	M	Unknown	31Ma02lh
Julin	29	M	Unknown	31Ma02lh
MARKEY, Cath.	31	F	Unknown	31Ma02lh
SMITH, Ellen	44	F	Unknown	31Ma02lh
CARNE, Julian	45	M	Unknown	31Ma02lh
Margt.	16	F	Unknown	31Ma02lh
MCCREATIN, Owen	18	M	Unknown	31Ma02lh
Mich.	24	M	Unknown	31Ma02lh
Bridget	54	F	Unknown	31Ma02lh
RICH, Dick	19	M	Unknown	31Ma02lh
John	42	M	Unknown	31Ma02lh
Thomas	14	M	Unknown	31Ma02lh
Eliza	18	F	Unknown	31Ma02lh
FINEGAN, Mich.	32	M	Unknown	31Ma02lh
Rose	43	F	Unknown	31Ma02lh
GLEASON, Bridget	61	F	Unknown	31Ma02lh
Thomas	18	M	Unknown	31Ma02lh
Margt.	27	F	Unknown	31Ma02lh
Bridget	32	F	Unknown	31Ma02lh
John	36	M	Unknown	31Ma02lh

NAMES OF PASSENGERS	AGE	SEX	OCCUPATIONS	DATE PORT SHIP
GLEASON, Pat	39	M	Unknown	31Ma02Ih
NEARY, Mary	44	F	Unknown	31Ma02Ih
SEOBEY, Mich.	49	M	Unknown	31Ma02Ih
OBRIAN, Cath.	50	F	Unknown	31Ma02Ih
Thos.	27	M	Unknown	31Ma02Ih
Julia	32	F	Unknown	31Ma02Ih
MORGAN, Pat	49	M	Unknown	31Ma02Ih
MCDONNELL, Ann	45	F	Unknown	31Ma02Ih
RICE, John	46	M	Unknown	31Ma02Ih
MCCARTHY, John	47	M	Unknown	31Ma02Ih
HALEY, Tim	18	M	Unknown	31Ma02Ih
MORRISY, Ellen	24	F	Unknown	31Ma02Ih
Rose	29	F	Unknown	31Ma02Ih
FLEMMING, Julia	19	F	Unknown	31Ma02Ih
FLANAGAN, Red	36	M	Unknown	31Ma02Ih
GODSAL, Mary	37	F	Unknown	31Ma02Ih
MAHON, Thos.	22	M	Unknown	31Ma02Ih
QUIN, Mary	41	F	Unknown	31Ma02Ih
SULIVAN, Patt	19	M	Unknown	31Ma02Ih
JOYCE, Elias	23	M	Unknown	31Ma02Ih
FERRIS, Cath.	29	F	Unknown	31Ma02Ih
FLOYD, James	41	M	Unknown	31Ma02Ih
Thos.	39	M	Unknown	31Ma02Ih
TOOLERY, Ann	27	F	Unknown	31Ma02Ih
Denis	54	M	Unknown	31Ma02Ih
WALLACE, Ed.	39	M	Unknown	31Ma02Ih
MORRISAY, Mary	45	F	Unknown	31Ma02Ih
DESHAN, Chas.	18	M	Unknown	31Ma02Ih
Margt.	31	F	Unknown	31Ma02Ih
U	.00	U	Infant	31Ma02Ih
REARDON, John	14	M	Unknown	31Ma02Ih
DUFFY, Cath.	27	F	Unknown	31Ma02Ih
CARREY, Mary	34	F	Unknown	31Ma02Ih
QUIN, Pat	51	M	Unknown	31Ma02Ih
DUNNON, Mary	36	F	Unknown	31Ma02Ih
COTTON, Emma	45	F	Unknown	31Ma02Ih
BRYAN, John	34	M	Unknown	31Ma02Ih
BRIDDEN, Ellen	27	F	Unknown	31Ma02Ih
CONWAY, James	39	M	Unknown	31Ma02Ih
BARKER, Ketty	00	U	Unknown	31Ma02Ih
POWERS, U	00	M	Unknown	31Ma02Ih
MCGREGORY, U	00	M	Unknown	31Ma02Ih

ELIZABETH 31 MAY 1849

From Dublin

NAMES OF PASSENGERS	AGE	SEX	OCCUPATIONS	DATE PORT SHIP
CLARAN, John	17	M	Farmer	31Ma12Bk
FLETCHER, Ann	20	F	Unknown	31Ma12Bk
DALEY, Patt	35	M	Laborer	31Ma12Bk
Mary	9	F	Child	31Ma12Bk
DONNOLLY, Bryan	25	M	Unknown	31Ma12Bk
REILLY, Patt	25	M	Unknown	31Ma12Bk
CASEY, Farrell	40	M	Unknown	31Ma12Bk
Margaret	35	F	Unknown	31Ma12Bk
John	16	M	Unknown	31Ma12Bk
William	12	M	Unknown	31Ma12Bk
Mary	13	F	Unknown	31Ma12Bk
James	10	M	Unknown	31Ma12Bk
Eliza	5	F	Child	31Ma12Bk
Thomas	.00	M	Infant	31Ma12Bk
MULLIGAN, Michael	30	M	Unknown	31Ma12Bk
Peter	19	M	Unknown	31Ma12Bk
Margaret	18	F	Unknown	31Ma12Bk
Margaret	16	F	Unknown	31Ma12Bk
Michael	13	M	Unknown	31Ma12Bk
Bess	10	F	Unknown	31Ma12Bk
Patt	.00	M	Infant	31Ma12Bk
LEWIS, Bernard	25	M	Unknown	31Ma12Bk
CHIVERS, Joseph	45	M	Unknown	31Ma12Bk
CUSLEY, Michael	20	M	Unknown	31Ma12Bk
Jane	18	F	Unknown	31Ma12Bk
HEALLY, Matt	20	M	Unknown	31Ma12Bk
EGAN, Eliza	20	F	Unknown	31Ma12Bk
DOOLEY, Mary	13	F	Unknown	31Ma12Bk
Ann	11	F	Unknown	31Ma12Bk
John	9	M	Child	31Ma12Bk
DEMPSEY, Andy	40	M	Unknown	31Ma12Bk
Ann	40	F	Unknown	31Ma12Bk
John	34	M	Unknown	31Ma12Bk
Mary	13	F	Unknown	31Ma12Bk
Catherine	11	F	Unknown	31Ma12Bk
John	9	M	Child	31Ma12Bk
Andy	.00	M	Infant	31Ma12Bk
GRAHAM, U-Miss	22	F	Unknown	31Ma12Bk
Mary	20	F	Unknown	31Ma12Bk
LYNCH, John	30	M	Unknown	31Ma12Bk
RYAN, Michael	20	M	Unknown	31Ma12Bk
OMARA, Denis	20	M	Unknown	31Ma12Bk
RYAN, Susan	13	F	Unknown	31Ma12Bk
MAHON, Mary	35	F	Unknown	31Ma12Bk
GLYNN, Ann	20	F	Unknown	31Ma12Bk
Mary	20	F	Unknown	31Ma12Bk
Peter	25	M	Unknown	31Ma12Bk
BATES, Robert	45	M	Unknown	31Ma12Bk
Mary	60	F	Unknown	31Ma12Bk
MULLAN, Michl.	50	M	Unknown	31Ma12Bk
READY, Julia	25	F	Unknown	31Ma12Bk
Rosey	20	F	Unknown	31Ma12Bk
DOYLE, U-Mrs.	45	F	Unknown	31Ma12Bk
John	18	M	Unknown	31Ma12Bk
EGAN, James	20	M	Unknown	31Ma12Bk
William	20	M	Unknown	31Ma12Bk
Michael	20	M	Unknown	31Ma12Bk
FEE, Isabella	18	F	Unknown	31Ma12Bk
MEELY, Bridget	20	F	Unknown	31Ma12Bk
U-Mrs.	30	F	Unknown	31Ma12Bk
GAWLEY, Michael	60	M	Unknown	31Ma12Bk
John	28	M	Unknown	31Ma12Bk
Michael	26	M	Unknown	31Ma12Bk
Mary	20	F	Unknown	31Ma12Bk
Judy	19	F	Unknown	31Ma12Bk
Patt	16	M	Unknown	31Ma12Bk
MEEHAN, Michl.	44	M	Unknown	31Ma12Bk
Mary-Ann	30	F	Unknown	31Ma12Bk
Bridget	24	F	Unknown	31Ma12Bk
John	8	M	Child	31Ma12Bk
Margaret	.00	F	Infant	31Ma12Bk
BYRNE, Patt	40	M	Unknown	31Ma12Bk
Lawrence	26	M	Unknown	31Ma12Bk
Mary	23	F	Unknown	31Ma12Bk
CAREY, Mary	50	F	Unknown	31Ma12Bk
William	24	M	Unknown	31Ma12Bk
Mary	22	F	Unknown	31Ma12Bk
Catherine	17	F	Unknown	31Ma12Bk
Elizabeth	16	F	Unknown	31Ma12Bk
John	10	M	Unknown	31Ma12Bk
Bridget	.00	F	Infant	31Ma12Bk
MCMANUS, Phillip	28	M	Unknown	31Ma12Bk
Catherine	30	F	Unknown	31Ma12Bk
Bridget	2	F	Child	31Ma12Bk
CROWLEY, Mary	28	F	Unknown	31Ma12Bk
Bridget	20	F	Unknown	31Ma12Bk
BROOKS, James	20	M	Unknown	31Ma12B
MCGAWLEY, Ann	35	F	Unknown	31Ma12B
MELLS, Thomas	34	M	Unknown	31Ma12Bk
U-Mrs.	34	F	Unknown	31Ma12Bk
Margaret	4	F	Child	31Ma12Bk
Mary	.00	F	Infant	31Ma12Bk
CARTER, John	24	M	Unknown	31Ma12Bk
BEHAN, Patt	28	M	Unknown	31Ma12Bk
MEEHAN, James	25	M	Unknown	31Ma12B
MCCLARE, Thos.	18	M	Unknown	31Ma12B
CUMMINS, Patt	24	M	Unknown	31Ma12B

NAMES OF PASSENGERS	AGE	SEX	OCCUPATIONS	DATE PORT SHIP
CUMMINS, John	20	M	Unknown	31Ma12Bk
Thomas	12	M	Unknown	31Ma12Bk
MESKELL, Wm.	24	M	Unknown	31Ma12Bk
U-Mrs.	26	F	Unknown	31Ma12Bk
SMITH, Elizabeth	21	F	Unknown	31Ma12Bk
CARROLL, John	20	M	Unknown	31Ma12Bk
MITCHELL, Mary	21	F	Unknown	31Ma12Bk
HIGGINS, Jane	26	F	Unknown	31Ma12Bk
MOONEY, Biddy	30	F	Unknown	31Ma12Bk
Ellen	5	F	Child	31Ma12Bk
John	.00	M	Infant	31Ma12Bk
REPTON, John	21	M	Unknown	31Ma12Bk

CHARLOTTE-HARRISON 31 MAY 1849

From Greenock

NAMES OF PASSENGERS	AGE	SEX	OCCUPATIONS	DATE PORT SHIP
MCCANN, William	19	M	Laborer	31Ma33Hz
SMITH, James	19	M	Laborer	31Ma33Hz
Margaret	17	F	Servant	31Ma33Hz
John	10	M	Child	31Ma33Hz
Samuel	6	M	Child	31Ma33Hz
MURDOCK, Thomas	20	M	Miner	31Ma33Hz
HAMILL, Samuel	19	M	Unknown	31Ma33Hz
Catherine	50	F	Unknown	31Ma33Hz
George	11	M	Unknown	31Ma33Hz
FINNIE, Thomas	25	M	Laborer	31Ma33Hz
HILL, James	70	M	Mason	31Ma33Hz
Jane	55	F	Unknown	31Ma33Hz
William	20	M	Laborer	31Ma33Hz
Robert	17	M	Laborer	31Ma33Hz
Mary-Jane	13	F	Unknown	31Ma33Hz
George	10	M	Child	31Ma33Hz
James	8	M	Child	31Ma33Hz
LOUTTER, William	34	M	Mason	31Ma33Hz
Abigail	30	F	Unknown	31Ma33Hz
Thomas	5	M	Child	31Ma33Hz
John	3	M	Child	31Ma33Hz
Elizabeth	2	F	Child	31Ma33Hz
COBURN, Susanna	22	F	Servant	31Ma33Hz
WINTERS, Mary	40	F	Unknown	31Ma33Hz
Margaret	6	F	Child	31Ma33Hz
WILSON, William	56	M	Sawer	31Ma33Hz
Jane	51	F	Unknown	31Ma33Hz
Robert	29	M	Sawer	31Ma33Hz
Thomas	27	M	Sawer	31Ma33Hz
William	20	M	Sawer	31Ma33Hz
Rebecca	27	F	Servant	31Ma33Hz
Richard	13	M	Unknown	31Ma33Hz
Grace	18	F	Servant	31Ma33Hz
Catherine	11	F	Unknown	31Ma33Hz
STEWART, Robert	13	M	Unknown	31Ma33Hz
HUNTER, William	40	M	Wright	31Ma33Hz
Sarah	35	F	Unknown	31Ma33Hz
Ellen	10	F	Unknown	31Ma33Hz
William	8	M	Child	31Ma33Hz
Mary	6	F	Child	31Ma33Hz
Ann	4	F	Child	31Ma33Hz
Isabella	1	F	Child	31Ma33Hz
BRYCE, James	30	M	Laborer	31Ma33Hz
Isabella	26	F	Unknown	31Ma33Hz
Peter	6	M	Child	31Ma33Hz
Elizabeth	4	F	Child	31Ma33Hz
Thomas	1	M	Child	31Ma33Hz
SLATER, Alexander	24	M	Slater	31Ma33Hz
CAMPBELL, William	30	M	Merchant	31Ma33Hz
Margaret	28	F	Unknown	31Ma33Hz
James	22	M	Laborer	31Ma33Hz
Thomas	3	M	Child	31Ma33Hz
CAMPBELL, James	1	M	Child	31Ma33Hz
WILLIAMSON, James	55	M	Laborer	31Ma33Hz
Ellen	57	F	Unknown	31Ma33Hz
William	31	M	Laborer	31Ma33Hz
Peter	29	M	Laborer	31Ma33Hz
Margaret	29	F	Servant	31Ma33Hz
Elizabeth	34	F	Servant	31Ma33Hz
Margaret	.08	F	Infant	31Ma33Hz
MILLER, Alexander	28	M	Unknown	31Ma33Hz
Jane	23	F	Unknown	31Ma33Hz
Elizabeth	2	F	Child	31Ma33Hz
Jannet	.08	F	Infant	31Ma33Hz
PATTERSON, Robert	33	M	Laborer	31Ma33Hz
Sarah	24	F	Unknown	31Ma33Hz
Sophia	1	F	Child	31Ma33Hz
SWAN, David	47	M	Miner	31Ma33Hz
James	23	M	Miner	31Ma33Hz
William	27	M	Wright	31Ma33Hz
Agnes	19	F	Servant	31Ma33Hz
Thomas	.08	M	Infant	31Ma33Hz
FREELAND, John	21	M	Laborer	31Ma33Hz
HILL, John	46	M	Laborer	31Ma33Hz
MICKLE, John	39	M	Mason	31Ma33Hz
John	12	M	Unknown	31Ma33Hz
James	10	M	Unknown	31Ma33Hz
GREEN, Michael	28	M	Laborer	31Ma33Hz
MCKENZIE, James	22	M	Molder	31Ma33Hz
Robert	20	M	Molder	31Ma33Hz
BOA, Andrew	42	M	Mason	31Ma33Hz
SHENNER, Alexander	45	M	Mechanic	31Ma33Hz
Agnes	40	F	Unknown	31Ma33Hz
Alexander	20	M	Laborer	31Ma33Hz
LAMB, James	20	M	Laborer	31Ma33Hz
NEIL, Robert	29	M	Laborer	31Ma33Hz
Ellen	27	F	Servant	31Ma33Hz
CONTRAIL, Sarah	21	F	Servant	31Ma33Hz
FORSYTH, Peter	22	M	Wright	31Ma33Hz
STRONG, George	49	M	Laborer	31Ma33Hz
Mary	38	F	Unknown	31Ma33Hz
AITCHISON, Alex	34	M	Potter	31Ma33Hz
INGLIS, William	26	M	Potter	31Ma33Hz
OSWALD, George	20	M	Fefndr	31Ma33Hz
HALL, Alex	20	M	Fefndr	31Ma33Hz
FINNEY, Margaret	30	F	Servant	31Ma33Hz
BURDON, Alex	28	M	Laborer	31Ma33Hz
JOHNTSON, Ephraim	38	M	Laborer	31Ma33Hz
HARPER, Maria-O.	28	F	Servant	31Ma33Hz
STEWART, Thomas	40	M	Miner	31Ma33Hz
Jane	35	F	Unknown	31Ma33Hz
David	12	M	Unknown	31Ma33Hz
Margaret	10	F	Child	31Ma33Hz
William	8	M	Child	31Ma33Hz
Mary-Jane	6	F	Child	31Ma33Hz
Sarah-Anne	2	F	Child	31Ma33Hz
GILL, Ann	40	F	Servant	31Ma33Hz
Andrew	9	M	Child	31Ma33Hz
Mary	7	F	Child	31Ma33Hz
Susan	5	F	Child	31Ma33Hz
Alicin	4	F	Child	31Ma33Hz
Elizabeth	1	F	Child	31Ma33Hz
GOGGIN, Elizabeth	68	F	Unknown	31Ma33Hz
JOHNSTON, William	28	M	Laborer	31Ma33Hz
WARD, Sarah	30	F	Servant	31Ma33Hz
MCGECHAN, Nancy	25	F	Servant	31Ma33Hz
Bridget	20	F	Servant	31Ma33Hz
MCDREE, Mary	20	F	Servant	31Ma33Hz
MORRISON, William	18	M	Laborer	31Ma33Hz
MILLER, William	17	M	Laborer	31Ma33Hz
MCSERNON, Jane	24	F	Unknown	31Ma33Hz
Sarah	2	F	Child	31Ma33Hz
Hugh	1	M	Child	31Ma33Hz
SPENCER, Thomas	8	M	Child	31Ma33Hz
MCCUSHIAN, Catherine	13	F	Unknown	31Ma33Hz
BLAIR, Samuel	32	M	Laborer	31Ma33Hz
MCBRIDE, Agnes	32	F	Unknown	31Ma33Hz

NAMES OF PASSENGERS	AGE	SEX	OCCUPATIONS	DATE PORT SHIP
MCBRIDE, David	20	M	Laborer	31Ma33Hz
Martha	18	F	Servant	31Ma33Hz
Margaret	17	F	Servant	31Ma33Hz
Mary	13	F	Unknown	31Ma33Hz
Sarah	11	F	Unknown	31Ma33Hz
GREEN, Joseph	20	M	Farmer	31Ma33Hz
RUTHERFORD, John	25	M	Farmer	31Ma33Hz
Robert	22	M	Farmer	31Ma33Hz
Adam	20	M	Farmer	31Ma33Hz
MCADAM, Thomas	22	M	Farmer	31Ma33Hz
BARRY, James	25	M	Farmer	31Ma33Hz
CAULFIELD, Mary	50	F	Unknown	31Ma33Hz
James	20	M	Laborer	31Ma33Hz
Eliza-Jane	16	F	Servant	31Ma33Hz
William-John	10	M	Unknown	31Ma33Hz
SHARP, Joseph	26	M	Laborer	31Ma33Hz
Mary-Ann	23	F	Unknown	31Ma33Hz
James	5	M	Child	31Ma33Hz
Mary	2	F	Child	31Ma33Hz
Robert	1	M	Child	31Ma33Hz
LARKIN, Edward	25	M	Laborer	31Ma33Hz
James	23	M	Laborer	31Ma33Hz
Patrick	21	M	Laborer	31Ma33Hz
BLAIR, William	27	M	Laborer	31Ma33Hz
Agnes	30	F	Laborer	31Ma33Hz
MEREDITH, Joseph	30	M	Unknown	31Ma33Hz
Mary	35	F	Unknown	31Ma33Hz
TULLY, Ann-Maria	32	F	Unknown	31Ma33Hz
Susannah	10	F	Child	31Ma33Hz
Achison	6	M	Child	31Ma33Hz
EVANS, Maria	25	F	Servant	31Ma33Hz
FLEMING, John	24	M	Laborer	31Ma33Hz
ONEIL, Ann	29	F	Unknown	31Ma33Hz
Matthew	7	M	Child	31Ma33Hz
MORISON, Wm.Jno.	22	M	Laborer	31Ma33Hz
LEE, William-A.	33	M	Farmer	31Ma33Hz
Francis	13	M	Unknown	31Ma33Hz
MCSWAGGAN, John	40	M	Laborer	31Ma33Hz
DARLIN, Edward	45	M	Laborer	31Ma33Hz
Ellen	13	F	Unknown	31Ma33Hz
AGERBY, John-H.	45	M	Laborer	31Ma33Hz
Jane	50	F	Unknown	31Ma33Hz
WEIR, Jane	24	F	Servant	31Ma33Hz
MCGAVIN, John	25	M	Laborer	31Ma33Hz
Charles	22	M	Laborer	31Ma33Hz
Elizabeth	23	F	Unknown	31Ma33Hz
CAGLE, John	45	M	Laborer	31Ma33Hz
MCCLOSKY, Mary-A.	16	F	Servant	31Ma33Hz
BEAL, Robert	30	M	Laborer	31Ma33Hz
HORM, Alex	30	M	Unknown	31Ma33Hz
Ann	30	F	Unknown	31Ma33Hz
James	3	M	Unknown	31Ma33Hz
Mary	13	F	Unknown	31Ma33Hz
Rebecca	11	F	Unknown	31Ma33Hz
Jane	9	F	Child	31Ma33Hz
Isabella	7	F	Child	31Ma33Hz
William	4	M	Child	31Ma33Hz
Thomas	1	M	Child	31Ma33Hz
MCGALRICK, Mary	20	F	Servant	31Ma33Hz
MCNATTY, Michael	50	M	Laborer	31Ma33Hz
John	18	M	Laborer	31Ma33Hz
Patrick	20	M	Laborer	31Ma33Hz
Terence	14	M	Unknown	31Ma33Hz
Mary	12	F	Unknown	31Ma33Hz
Agnes	4	F	Child	31Ma33Hz
MULHEARN, Charles	18	M	Laborer	31Ma33Hz
CAN, David	20	M	Laborer	31Ma33Hz
Jane	18	F	Servant	31Ma33Hz
HARN, John	22	M	Laborer	31Ma33Hz
CROMBY, Edward	45	M	Laborer	31Ma33Hz
Rose	45	F	Unknown	31Ma33Hz
Catherine	19	F	Servant	31Ma33Hz
Aron	11	M	Unknown	31Ma33Hz
Biddy	4	F	Child	31Ma33Hz
Mary	7	F	Child	31Ma33Hz

NAMES OF PASSENGERS	AGE	SEX	OCCUPATIONS	DATE PORT SHIP
CROMBY, Edward	5	M	Child	31Ma33Hz
Peter	2	M	Child	31Ma33Hz
James	13	M	Unknown	31Ma33Hz
SMITH, William	25	M	Laborer	31Ma33Hz
LLOYD, Patrick	24	M	Laborer	31Ma33Hz
CUNEAN, Bridget	20	F	Servant	31Ma33Hz
MULHEARN, Mary	12	F	Unknown	31Ma33Hz
MCCLOSKY, Patrick	20	M	Laborer	31Ma33Hz
ARBUCKLE, Margaret	25	F	Servant	31Ma33Hz
NUGENT, Michael	14	M	Laborer	31Ma33Hz
BROADLEY, David	29	M	Laborer	31Ma33Hz
DAVIDSON, Henry	20	M	Laborer	31Ma33Hz
ANDERSON, Isabella	20	F	Servant	31Ma33Hz
BOYCE, Ellen	25	F	Servant	31Ma33Hz
JOHNSTON, Mary	38	F	Unknown	31Ma33Hz
MORTON, David	23	M	Merchant	31Ma33Hz

ANN-MCLESTER 01 JUNE 1849

From Dublin

NAMES OF PASSENGERS	AGE	SEX	OCCUPATIONS	DATE PORT SHIP
MCEVOY, Ellen	17	F	Unknown	01Ju12Hy
MCKEE, James	8	M	Child	01Ju12Hy
GILES, Catherine	20	F	Unknown	01Ju12Hy
DUFFEY, Bridget	26	F	Unknown	01Ju12Hy
HAYDEN, Julia	26	F	Unknown	01Ju12Hy
DANIEL, James	23	M	Unknown	01Ju12Hy
U-Mrs.	20	F	Unknown	01Ju12Hy
CHARLES, Robert	20	M	Unknown	01Ju12Hy
Richard	24	M	Unknown	01Ju12Hy
WHELEN, George	54	M	Unknown	01Ju12Hy
U-Mrs.	40	F	Unknown	01Ju12Hy
George	24	M	Unknown	01Ju12Hy
William	21	M	Unknown	01Ju12Hy
Patt	19	M	Unknown	01Ju12Hy
Betsey	23	F	Unknown	01Ju12Hy
Maria	16	F	Unknown	01Ju12Hy
Bridget	.00	F	Infant	01Ju12Hy
BERGAN, Denis	35	M	Unknown	01Ju12Hy
HOLLANDS, Alexander	15	M	Unknown	01Ju12Hy
U-Mrs.	30	F	Unknown	01Ju12Hy
William	35	M	Unknown	01Ju12Hy
MARTIN, Patt	45	M	Unknown	01Ju12Hy
U-Mrs.	40	F	Unknown	01Ju12Hy
Daniel	16	M	Unknown	01Ju12Hy
Catherine	13	F	Unknown	01Ju12Hy
MURPHY, John	16	M	Unknown	01Ju12Hy
Stephen	14	M	Unknown	01Ju12Hy
CALSEN, Robert	54	M	Unknown	01Ju12Hy
DYAS, George	35	M	Unknown	01Ju12Hy
U-Mrs.	30	F	Unknown	01Ju12Hy
Edward	9	M	Child	01Ju12Hy
Mary-Jane	7	F	Child	01Ju12Hy
George	8	M	Child	01Ju12Hy
William	.00	M	Infant	01Ju12Hy
CRAWFORD, Mary	50	F	Unknown	01Ju12Hy
RYAN, Sophia	27	F	Unknown	01Ju12Hy
GREEN, Mary	24	F	Unknown	01Ju12Hy
MCCARTHY, John	27	M	Unknown	01Ju12Hy
JULIEN, John	19	M	Unknown	01Ju12Hy
Margaret	18	F	Unknown	01Ju12Hy
MELHAM, John	26	M	Unknown	01Ju12Hy
MCMACLIN, John	46	M	Unknown	01Ju12Hy
KELLY, Francis	25	M	Unknown	01Ju12Hy
SEALLY, Bryan	35	M	Unknown	01Ju12Hy
Bridget	15	F	Unknown	01Ju12Hy
SMITH, Elizabeth	25	F	Unknown	01Ju12Hy
Julia	23	F	Unknown	01Ju12Hy
LEAREY, Patt	25	M	Unknown	01Ju12Hy

NAMES OF PASSENGERS	AGE	SEX	OCCUPATIONS	DATE PORT SHIP
SWEENEY, Patt	24	M	Unknown	01Ju12Hy
Letitia	26	F	Unknown	01Ju12Hy
REILLY, Mary	21	F	Unknown	01Ju12Hy
CUNEN, Richard	25	M	Unknown	01Ju12Hy
MAGGIN, John	22	M	Unknown	01Ju12Hy
CAIN, Man	21	M	Unknown	01Ju12Hy
DURHAM, Mary	40	F	Unknown	01Ju12Hy
Henry	16	M	Unknown	01Ju12Hy
Catherine	10	F	Unknown	01Ju12Hy
Maria	.00	F	Infant	01Ju12Hy
MULHAM, Biddy	23	F	Unknown	01Ju12Hy
SWEENY, John	45	M	Unknown	01Ju12Hy
U-Mrs.	33	F	Unknown	01Ju12Hy
Patt	5	M	Child	01Ju12Hy
To--	.00	F	Infant	01Ju12Hy
CAFFREY, Mary	12	F	Unknown	01Ju12Hy
LEAG, Rosa	.00	F	Infant	01Ju12Hy
DUNN, Corn	24	M	Unknown	01Ju12Hy
LORD, Jno.	20	M	Unknown	01Ju12Hy
MONTGOMERY, Chris	50	F	Unknown	01Ju12Hy
GILES, Edward	28	M	Unknown	01Ju12Hy
MONTGOMERY, Matt	40	M	Unknown	01Ju12Hy
U-Mrs.	35	F	Unknown	01Ju12Hy
Matt	16	M	Unknown	01Ju12Hy
Bridget	14	F	Unknown	01Ju12Hy
Mary	12	F	Unknown	01Ju12Hy
Helen	10	F	Unknown	01Ju12Hy
Rose	8	F	Child	01Ju12Hy
James	6	M	Child	01Ju12Hy
John	.00	M	Infant	01Ju12Hy
CORNELL, Matt	21	M	Unknown	01Ju12Hy
CORNES, Tom	20	M	Unknown	01Ju12Hy
LUITE, John	19	M	Unknown	01Ju12Hy
LARKER, Mich	23	M	Unknown	01Ju12Hy
GIBBONS, Rose	56	F	Unknown	01Ju12Hy
James	26	M	Unknown	01Ju12Hy
Christopher	20	M	Unknown	01Ju12Hy
Tim	24	M	Unknown	01Ju12Hy
Rose	22	F	Unknown	01Ju12Hy
MARTIN, James	23	M	Unknown	01Ju12Hy
CAFFREY, Patt	20	M	Unknown	01Ju12Hy
Tom	20	M	Unknown	01Ju12Hy
Judy	24	F	Unknown	01Ju12Hy
NUGENT, Peter	19	M	Unknown	01Ju12Hy
Bridget	26	F	Unknown	01Ju12Hy
Elizabeth	20	F	Unknown	01Ju12Hy
Margaret	.00	F	Infant	01Ju12Hy
LACEY, Terry	35	F	Unknown	01Ju12Hy
MULROONEY, Tom	21	M	Unknown	01Ju12Hy
GIBBON, Martha	21	F	Unknown	01Ju12Hy
NELDON, Patt	20	M	Unknown	01Ju12Hy
Mary	12	F	Unknown	01Ju12Hy
WYER, Martin	33	M	Unknown	01Ju12Hy
Patt	12	M	Unknown	01Ju12Hy
MCDERMOTT, Sarry	22	F	Unknown	01Ju12Hy
Alicia	18	F	Unknown	01Ju12Hy
JULIEN, Margaret	18	F	Unknown	01Ju12Hy
CALLAGAN, Peter	35	M	Unknown	01Ju12Hy
Teely	35	F	Unknown	01Ju12Hy
Bryan	16	M	Unknown	01Ju12Hy
Michael	12	M	Unknown	01Ju12Hy
John	10	M	Unknown	01Ju12Hy
ACEY, Patt	37	M	Unknown	01Ju12Hy
U-Mrs.	37	F	Unknown	01Ju12Hy
Mary	8	F	Child	01Ju12Hy
Daniel	7	M	Child	01Ju12Hy
Michael	5	M	Child	01Ju12Hy
Judy	3	F	Child	01Ju12Hy
Margaret	.00	F	Infant	01Ju12Hy
EAREY, Thos.	23	M	Unknown	01Ju12Hy
Maria	20	F	Unknown	01Ju12Hy
Catherine	18	M	Unknown	01Ju12Hy
ENNY, Red	22	F	Unknown	01Ju12Hy
U-Mrs.	21	F	Unknown	01Ju12Hy
OSTELLO, Edward	28	M	Unknown	01Ju12Hy
COSTELLO, Thomas	7	M	Child	01Ju12Hy
Bridget	40	F	Unknown	01Ju12Hy
REILLY, Ann	16	F	Unknown	01Ju12Hy
ALLWELL, Phill	23	M	Unknown	01Ju12Hy
Mary	20	F	Unknown	01Ju12Hy
DOWNES, Patt	20	M	Unknown	01Ju12Hy
Michael	16	M	Unknown	01Ju12Hy
CONNELLY, Patt	16	M	Unknown	01Ju12Hy
TRAVERS, Edw.	30	M	Unknown	01Ju12Hy
MANNOX, Patt	22	M	Unknown	01Ju12Hy
KELLY, Francis	25	M	Unknown	01Ju12Hy
TULLY, Owen	25	M	Unknown	01Ju12Hy
MOLONY, Patt	24	M	Unknown	01Ju12Hy
Wm.	23	M	Unknown	01Ju12Hy
LANDS, Michael	.00	M	Infant	01Ju12Hy
LITTLE, Mary	23	F	Unknown	01Ju12Hy
DOOLEY, Edward	30	M	Unknown	01Ju12Hy
KERRIGAN, U-Mr.	18	M	Unknown	01Ju12Hy
HAGERTY, U-Mrs.	17	F	Unknown	01Ju12Hy
MULAIDY, U-Mr.	18	M	Unknown	01Ju12Hy
DAVIS, U-Mr.	17	M	Unknown	01Ju12Hy
Alicia	16	F	Unknown	01Ju12Hy
KEENAN, U	7	M	Child	01Ju12Hy
FLLOYD, U-Mr.	18	M	Unknown	01Ju12Hy
PARSEN, U-Mr.	17	M	Unknown	01Ju12Hy
IRVINE, U-Mr.	20	M	Unknown	01Ju12Hy
Amelia	19	F	Unknown	01Ju12Hy
KEENAN, U-Mrs.	30	F	Unknown	01Ju12Hy
CURTIS, Wm.	21	M	Unknown	01Ju12Hy
KENNEDY, Mary	20	F	Unknown	01Ju12Hy
Ann	19	F	Unknown	01Ju12Hy
William	18	M	Unknown	01Ju12Hy
Daniel	17	M	Unknown	01Ju12Hy
LAWLER, Catherine	20	F	Unknown	01Ju12Hy
DOOLEY, Catherine	18	F	Unknown	01Ju12Hy
DELANEY, Sarah	15	F	Unknown	01Ju12Hy
Margaret	10	F	Unknown	01Ju12Hy
John	11	M	Unknown	01Ju12Hy
Maria	15	F	Unknown	01Ju12Hy
DOYLE, John	24	M	Unknown	01Ju12Hy
MARTIN, Patt	24	M	Unknown	01Ju12Hy
MCKEE, Nora	35	F	Unknown	01Ju12Hy

COLUMBIA 01 JUNE 1849

From Belfast

NAMES OF PASSENGERS		AGE	SEX	OCCUPATIONS	DATE PORT SHIP
DAVIS, Bernard		26	M	Laborer	01Ju05Il
Mary	(W)	24	F	Wife	01Ju05Il
KELLY, Wm.John		19	M	Laborer	01Ju05Il
Elizabeth		45	F	Wi	01Ju05Il
Sally-Ann		21	F	Spinster	01Ju05Il
Mary-Jane		24	F	Spinster	01Ju05Il
Margaret		28	F	Spinster	01Ju05Il
KNOX, James		27	M	Laborer	01Ju05Il
Peggy	(W)	27	F	Wife	01Ju05Il
John		2	M	Child	01Ju05Il
WALLACE, Frances		26	M	Laborer	01Ju05Il
MCREARDON, Susan		26	F	Spinster	01Ju05Il
Elizabeth		13	F	Unknown	01Ju05Il
Sophia		6	F	Child	01Ju05Il
BRYAN, Wm.		24	M	Laborer	01Ju05Il
BAXTER, Henry		21	M	Laborer	01Ju05Il
WHEATON, John		40	M	Farmer	01Ju05Il
Mary-Ann	(W)	40	F	Wife	01Ju05Il
John		8	M	Child	01Ju05Il
Mary-Ann		6	F	Child	01Ju05Il
Elizabeth		3	F	Child	01Ju05Il
Wm.		.10	M	Infant	01Ju05Il

NAMES OF PASSENGERS		AGE	SEX	OCCUPATIONS	DATE PORT SHIP
OHAIRE, John		24	M	Laborer	01Ju05II
Margaret	(W)	20	F	Wife	01Ju05II
MATTERS, Hugh		33	M	Laborer	01Ju05II
GREEN, Michael		26	M	Laborer	01Ju05II
HYNES, Patrick		24	M	Laborer	01Ju05II
MCGEENOY, Danl.		16	M	Laborer	01Ju05II
CAMPBELL, Mary		20	F	Spinster	01Ju05II
KEATON, Mary		23	F	Spinster	01Ju05II
James		.11	M	Infant	01Ju05II
CARR, Elizabeth		32	F	Spinster	01Ju05II
FRAZER, James		20	M	Laborer	01Ju05II
HUGHES, Edward		21	M	Laborer	01Ju05II
Robert		17	M	Laborer	01Ju05II
GRACEY, Jane		30	F	Spinster	01Ju05II
MCCADE, Joseph		30	M	Laborer	01Ju05II
Mary		60	F	Wi	01Ju05II
CARAGHAN, Michael		22	M	Laborer	01Ju05II
BOURKE, Robert		20	M	Laborer	01Ju05II
Alexander		17	M	Laborer	01Ju05II
CUMMINS, John		25	M	Laborer	01Ju05II
CAMPBELL, Mary		20	F	Spinster	01Ju05II
TARKINGTON, Eliz.		20	F	Spinster	01Ju05II
BANAGHAN, Chas.		18	M	Laborer	01Ju05II
TAGGAN, Wm.		31	M	Laborer	01Ju05II
MOORE, James		25	M	Laborer	01Ju05II
BOYCE, John		35	M	Laborer	01Ju05II
STREANY, Ann		17	F	Spinster	01Ju05II
HUGHES, Mary		22	F	Spinster	01Ju05II
DECKER, Mary		22	F	Spinster	01Ju05II
DORCAN, Margt.		19	F	Spinster	01Ju05II
ANDERSON, Mary		35	F	Spinster	01Ju05II
Jane		16	F	Spinster	01Ju05II
Letitia		13	F	Unknown	01Ju05II
Robert		12	M	Unknown	01Ju05II
DANER, John		25	M	Laborer	01Ju05II
LONGHRAN, Bridget		15	F	Spinster	01Ju05II
Ann		12	F	Unknown	01Ju05II
DOUGGHY, Cath.		20	F	Spinster	01Ju05II
Patk.		17	M	Laborer	01Ju05II
KELLY, Wm.		14	M	Laborer	01Ju05II
JOHNSTON, Jane		28	F	Spinster	01Ju05II
GRAHAM, Joseph		17	M	Laborer	01Ju05II
John		20	M	Laborer	01Ju05II
Matilda		20	F	Spinster	01Ju05II
KELLY, Samuel		30	M	Laborer	01Ju05II
Mary	(W)	30	F	Wife	01Ju05II
WILSON, Mary		70	F	Wi	01Ju05II
3)QLLY, Jane		9	F	Child	01Ju05II
John		11	M	Unknown	01Ju05II
HAWTHORNE, Joseph		20	M	Laborer	01Ju05II
HAWORTH, Joseph		21	M	Laborer	01Ju05II
HIGGIN, Andrew		21	M	Laborer	01Ju05II
HARRISON, Edwd.		40	M	Laborer	01Ju05II
MCWRIGHT, Jas.		22	M	Laborer	01Ju05II
LEDGET, Eliz.		23	F	Spinster	01Ju05II
Hannah		25	F	Spinster	01Ju05II
TAGGART, Jas.		30	M	Farmer	01Ju05II
Mary	(W)	30	F	Wife	01Ju05II
SMITH, Isabella		5	F	Child	01Ju05II
Dennis		2	M	Child	01Ju05II
Catharine		44	F	Spinster	01Ju05II
HAMILTON, Thos.		35	M	Laborer	01Ju05II
MCCLENAHAN, Job.		25	M	Laborer	01Ju05II
Margaret	(W)	25	F	Wife	01Ju05II
Elizabeth		3	F	Child	01Ju05II
Mary-Ellen		.00	F	Infant	01Ju05II
BECK, Joshua		23	M	Laborer	01Ju05II
Jane		22	F	Spinster	01Ju05II
FLETCHER, Frances		18	M	Laborer	01Ju05II
HYNDS, Bernard		24	M	Laborer	01Ju05II
MCCULLEN, Bernard		30	M	Farmer	01Ju05II
Eliza		24	F	Wife	01Ju05II
Sarah		.00	F	Infant	01Ju05II
Mary-Ann		2	F	Child	01Ju05II
William		22	M	Farmer	01Ju05II

NAMES OF PASSENGERS		AGE	SEX	OCCUPATIONS	DATE PORT SHIP
MCCULLEN, John		20	M	Farmer	01Ju05II
MCKERWIN, Biddy		20	F	Spinster	01Ju05II
GRAY, Wm.		45	M	Farmer	01Ju05II
Ellen	(W)	45	F	Wife	01Ju05II
Rebecca		23	F	Spinster	01Ju05II
Alexander		22	M	Farmer	01Ju05II
Ellen		19	F	Spinster	01Ju05II
Margaret		16	F	Spinster	01Ju05II
GARDNER, Samuel		40	M	Farmer	01Ju05II
Jane	(W)	39	F	Wife	01Ju05II
Margt.		15	F	Spinster	01Ju05II
James		13	M	Unknown	01Ju05II
Agnes		11	F	Unknown	01Ju05II
Eliza		9	F	Child	01Ju05II
Susanna		5	F	Child	01Ju05II
Robert		.00	M	Infant	01Ju05II
MOORE, Hugh		21	M	Farmer	01Ju05II
Mary		18	F	Spinster	01Ju05II
Robt.Jas.		14	M	Laborer	01Ju05II
DUNDEE, Thomas		22	M	Laborer	01Ju05II
DOUGHERTY, Michael		20	M	Laborer	01Ju05II
CAMPBELL, Susan		22	F	Spinster	01Ju05II
RANKIN, Wm.		23	M	Laborer	01Ju05II
CARR, John		30	M	Laborer	01Ju05II
NEWWORTHY, Jane		25	F	Spinster	01Ju05II
NEWORTHY, Lucinda		22	F	Spinster	01Ju05II
Elizabeth		24	F	Spinster	01Ju05II
DICKSON, Mary	(W)	25	F	Wife	01Ju05II
Robt.		1	M	Child	01Ju05II
MCCARRY, Wm.		25	M	Laborer	01Ju05II
GILLESPIE, Fanihan		24	M	Laborer	01Ju05II
Margaret	(W)	23	F	Wife	01Ju05II
Leonard		.00	M	Infant	01Ju05II
MCGEE, Peter		18	M	Laborer	01Ju05II
MCGROIN, Margt.		18	F	Spinster	01Ju05II
HALL, Mary-Ann		20	F	Spinster	01Ju05II
DAVIDSON, Sarah		50	F	Farmer	01Ju05II
Wm.John		24	M	Farmer	01Ju05I
Rachel		22	F	Spinster	01Ju05I
Sarah		18	F	Spinster	01Ju05I
Francis		14	F	Spinster	01Ju05I
Isabella		12	F	Unknown	01Ju05I
MARREN, Andrew		40	M	Gentleman	01Ju05I

SENATOR 01 JUNE 1849

From Liverpool

NAMES OF PASSENGERS	AGE	SEX	OCCUPATIONS	DATE PORT SHIP
DAWSON, John	36	M	Farmer	01Ju02
Mary	37	F	None	01Ju02
William	14	M	None	01Ju02
Bernard	12	M	None	01Ju02
Mary-Anne	10	F	Child	01Ju02
Thomas	8	M	Child	01Ju02
Eliza.	6	F	Child	01Ju02
Bridget	3	F	Child	01Ju02
Rose	.09	F	Infant	01Ju02
SWEENEY, Bryan	25	M	Sailor	01Ju02
Margaret	23	F	Spinster	01Ju02
WARDE, Daniel	25	M	Laborer	01Ju02
Patrick	34	M	Laborer	01Ju02
Mary	27	F	None	01Ju02
Martin	6	M	Child	01Ju02
John	24	M	Laborer	01Ju02
Bridget	20	F	None	01Ju02
DWIER, Michael	18	M	Laborer	01Ju02
RYAN, Thomas	35	M	Shoemaker	01Ju02
JOHNSON, Eliza	23	F	Spinster	01Ju02
REED, Patrick	28	M	Spinner	01Ju02

NAMES OF PASSENGERS	AGE	SEX	OCCUPATIONS	DATE PORT SHIP	NAMES OF PASSENGERS	AGE	SEX	OCCUPATIONS	DATE PORT SHIP
CANTWELL, John	28	M	Shoemaker	01Ju02Ir	WALSH, John	45	M	Farmer	01Ju02Ir
QUIRK, William	24	M	Shoemaker	01Ju02Ir	Alice	40	F	None	01Ju02Ir
SHERIDAN, Thomas	32	M	Laborer	01Ju02Ir	Bridget	9	F	Child	01Ju02Ir
KEAUGH, Rose	14	F	Spinster	01Ju02Ir	LAWLO, James	45	M	Farmer	01Ju02Ir
HUTCHINSON, William	42	M	Grocer	01Ju02Ir	ANDERSON, John	28	M	Farmer	01Ju02Ir
Elizabeth	11	F	None	01Ju02Ir	MALADY, Thomas	28	M	Farmer	01Ju02Ir
John	15	M	None	01Ju02Ir	Mary	21	F	None	01Ju02Ir
WELSH, Edmund	21	M	Laborer	01Ju02Ir	WALKMAN, James	18	M	None	01Ju02Ir
STORAN, Michael	27	M	Laborer	01Ju02Ir	KENNY, James	23	M	None	01Ju02Ir
FITZPATRICK, John	25	M	Laborer	01Ju02Ir	KIRK, James	30	M	Currier	01Ju02Ir
Margaret	18	F	Spinster	01Ju02Ir	Patrick	25	M	Laborer	01Ju02Ir
GAOGHGIN, Christopher	34	M	Plasterer	01Ju02Ir	MAGHER, Thomas	23	M	Carpenter	01Ju02Ir
HAMPSON, James	22	M	Painter	01Ju02Ir	SHEA, Phillipp	31	M	Laborer	01Ju02Ir
READY, Richard	22	M	Blacksmith	01Ju02Ir	BUIRNE, Anastatia	16	F	Spinster	01Ju02Ir
MURRAY, John	23	M	Shoemaker	01Ju02Ir	BAGNALL, James	25	M	Laborer	01Ju02Ir
Thomas	24	M	Shoemaker	01Ju02Ir	MAGOUGH, Joseph	65	M	Farmer	01Ju02Ir
RILEY, Kevin	24	M	Laborer	01Ju02Ir	Nicholas	17	M	Farmer	01Ju02Ir
TIERNEY, Daniel	24	M	Laborer	01Ju02Ir	Michael	13	M	Farmer	01Ju02Ir
Anne	18	F	Spinster	01Ju02Ir	Mary	15	F	None	01Ju02Ir
WELSH, Eliza	20	F	Spinster	01Ju02Ir	CURTIS, John	21	M	Laborer	01Ju02Ir
MURPHY, Thomas	32	M	Laborer	01Ju02Ir	MAHONEY, John	50	M	Laborer	01Ju02Ir
DONOGHUE, Martin	25	M	Laborer	01Ju02Ir	KNOX, Richard	26	M	Clerk	01Ju02Ir
MURRAY, William	28	M	Laborer	01Ju02Ir	Mary	35	F	None	01Ju02Ir
JENNINGS, Patrick	31	M	Laborer	01Ju02Ir	MCIVER, Nicholas	12	M	None	01Ju02Ir
KEGAN, John	35	M	Laborer	01Ju02Ir	MCMANUS, Barnard	40	M	Farmer	01Ju02Ir
MAYER, John	25	M	Laborer	01Ju02Ir	Bridget	40	F	None	01Ju02Ir
Jeremiah	25	M	Laborer	01Ju02Ir	Bridget	14	F	None	01Ju02Ir
Margaret	60	F	Wi	01Ju02Ir	NANGLE, Francis	25	M	Laborer	01Ju02Ir
MORRISS, Judy	50	F	Wi	01Ju02Ir	Elizabeth	21	F	None	01Ju02Ir
MONIGHAN, Mathew	23	M	Servant	01Ju02Ir	CURRAN, William	35	M	Farmer	01Ju02Ir
KARNEY, Andrew	24	M	Hawker	01Ju02Ir	Mary	26	F	None	01Ju02Ir
MASTERSON, John	24	M	Farmer	01Ju02Ir	Marianne	.06	F	Infant	01Ju02Ir
WELSH, James	20	M	Farmer	01Ju02Ir	KANE, Ann	23	F	Spinster	01Ju02Ir
CALLAGHAN, John	24	M	Miner	01Ju02Ir	KELLY, John	26	M	Farmer	01Ju02Ir
KNELINS, Daniel	41	M	Farmer	01Ju02Ir	MURPHY, Bartholomew	26	M	Farmer	01Ju02Ir
Sarah	41	F	None	01Ju02Ir	SMITH, John	24	M	Farmer	01Ju02Ir
Robert	15	M	None	01Ju02Ir	KILLAN, Bridget	26	F	Cook	01Ju02Ir
William	13	M	None	01Ju02Ir	BRENNEN, James	24	M	Farmer	01Ju02Ir
James	11	M	None	01Ju02Ir	HENRY, Bridget	26	F	Spinster	01Ju02Ir
Rebekhah	6	F	Child	01Ju02Ir	MCGRATH, Margaret	26	F	Spinster	01Ju02Ir
George	4	M	Child	01Ju02Ir	PHELAN, John	30	M	Laborer	01Ju02Ir
Abraham	3	M	Child	01Ju02Ir	Judy	20	F	Servant	01Ju02Ir
Richard	.08	M	Infant	01Ju02Ir	GRADY, John	21	M	Laborer	01Ju02Ir
MONGIN, Richard	13	M	None	01Ju02Ir	DELANEY, Martin	30	M	Laborer	01Ju02Ir
MONAHAN, Bridget	50	F	None	01Ju02Ir	MAGHER, Thomas	23	M	Laborer	01Ju02Ir
Michael	50	M	Tailor	01Ju02Ir	GRADEY, John	25	M	Laborer	01Ju02Ir
Malloch	21	M	Laborer	01Ju02Ir	DEGAN, Malachy	35	M	Laborer	01Ju02Ir
ANDREW, Salmon	20	M	Laborer	01Ju02Ir	DELANEY, William	25	M	Laborer	01Ju02Ir
KELDUFF, Michael	26	M	Laborer	01Ju02Ir	MARAH, Patrick	30	M	Laborer	01Ju02Ir
Bridget	14	F	Spinster	01Ju02Ir	Marah	25	F	None	01Ju02Ir
BRYAN, James	30	M	Laborer	01Ju02Ir	REILLY, Nichols	30	M	Laborer	01Ju02Ir
CARLETON, Charles	28	M	Farmer	01Ju02Ir	GRADY, Margaret	24	F	Servant	01Ju02Ir
HARVEY, James	19	M	Grocer	01Ju02Ir	MARTIN, Catharine	22	F	Servant	01Ju02Ir
MOONAN, Catharine	17	F	Spinster	01Ju02Ir	GRADEY, Mary	27	F	Servant	01Ju02Ir
HOGAN, James	36	M	Draper	01Ju02Ir	BURGIN, Dennis	30	M	Servant	01Ju02Ir
Denniss	26	M	Blacksmith	01Ju02Ir	GRADEY, Judy	50	F	Servant	01Ju02Ir
Mary	21	F	Spinster	01Ju02Ir	HOOLY, Patrick	25	F	Laborer	01Ju02Ir
LEESON, Patrick	31	M	Clerk	01Ju02Ir	DELANEY, Martin	25	F	Laborer	01Ju02Ir
ASSON, William	22	M	Cver	01Ju02Ir	BRENNEN, Andrew	28	M	Ostler	01Ju02Ir
CANLIN, John	20	M	Laborer	01Ju02Ir	MURPHY, Thomas	34	M	Farmer	01Ju02Ir
IGOTT, Richard	30	M	Fellmonger	01Ju02Ir	FRANCIS, Thomas	40	M	Farmer	01Ju02Ir
UGHES, Edward	35	M	Servant	01Ju02Ir	DOGHERTY, Daniel	38	M	Shoemaker	01Ju02Ir
IBSON, Archibald	25	M	Clerk	01Ju02Ir	HOGAN, William	45	M	Carpenter	01Ju02Ir
ENRY, Margaret	20	F	Spinster	01Ju02Ir	Judith	36	F	None	01Ju02Ir
YONS, Timothy	29	M	Mason	01Ju02Ir	Marianne	10	F	None	01Ju02Ir
RIEN, Patrick	26	M	Laborer	01Ju02Ir	COSTELLO, Sally	45	F	Wi	01Ju02Ir
ENNEN, Michael	28	M	Laborer	01Ju02Ir	William	20	M	Laborer	01Ju02Ir
Margaret	28	F	None	01Ju02Ir	Edward	18	M	Laborer	01Ju02Ir
Charles	.02	M	Infant	01Ju02Ir	Patrick	16	M	Laborer	01Ju02Ir
ENNELLEY, Johannah	35	F	None	01Ju02Ir	Mary	14	F	None	01Ju02Ir
Richard	7	M	Child	01Ju02Ir	Anne	12	F	None	01Ju02Ir
James	5	M	Child	01Ju02Ir	Catharine	10	F	None	01Ju02Ir
Elizabeth	2	F	Child	01Ju02Ir	James	8	M	Child	01Ju02Ir
YAN, Patrick	45	M	Carpenter	01Ju02Ir	GRAINGER, Peter	27	M	Laborer	01Ju02Ir
NOLLY, John	30	M	Laborer	01Ju02Ir	Mary	25	F	None	01Ju02Ir

NAMES OF PASSENGERS	AGE	SEX	OCCUPATIONS	DATE PORT SHIP
GRAINGER, Judy	6	F	Child	01Ju02Ir
Mary	22	F	Spinster	01Ju02Ir
FOLEY, Mary	40	F	Spinster	01Ju02Ir
John	17	M	Laborer	01Ju02Ir
Mary	12	F	None	01Ju02Ir
Jeremiah	6	M	Child	01Ju02Ir
BRIEN, Timothy	15	M	Laborer	01Ju02Ir
HANNAY, William-John	21	M	Clerk	01Ju02Ir
CARROLL, John	20	M	Laborer	01Ju02Ir
WOGAN, Mary	22	F	Servant	01Ju02Ir
CULLAN, Patrick	27	M	Shoemaker	01Ju02Ir
MORAN, James	50	M	Laborer	01Ju02Ir
James	17	M	Laborer	01Ju02Ir
SMITH, Mary	20	F	Spinster	01Ju02Ir
FURLEY, Patrick	23	M	Clerk	01Ju02Ir
Marianne	16	F	None	01Ju02Ir
SUTCLIFFE, Isabella	30	F	Wi	01Ju02Ir
William-Henry-F.	.11	M	Infant	01Ju02Ir
FITZGERALD, Helenda	16	F	Spinster	01Ju02Ir
GREGG, Edmund	25	M	Laborer	01Ju02Ir
LEARY, Denniss	20	M	Laborer	01Ju02Ir
HORAN, Ellen	27	F	Servant	01Ju02Ir
OSHEAY, Mark	30	M	Servant	01Ju02Ir
COSTELLO, Denniss	30	M	Servant	01Ju02Ir
FARRELL, Bridget	15	F	Spinster	01Ju02Ir
STEWART, Anne	23	F	Servant	01Ju02Ir
MORAN, Michael	22	M	Laborer	01Ju02Ir
STRINGER, Mary-Jane	27	F	Servant	01Ju02Ir
GRAHAM, Isabella	15	F	Servant	01Ju02Ir
STRINGER, Jane	8	F	Child	01Ju02Ir
Robert	5	M	Child	01Ju02Ir
John	3	M	Child	01Ju02Ir
William	.04	M	Infant	01Ju02Ir
JOHNSON, Ellen	26	F	Servant	01Ju02Ir
CAREY, Barnard	41	M	Laborer	01Ju02Ir
Thomas	30	M	Carpenter	01Ju02Ir
Anne	18	F	Spinster	01Ju02Ir
FENNEGAN, Mary	40	F	Servant	01Ju02Ir
MCLOCKLIN, Thos	32	M	Servant	01Ju02Ir
DONLAN, James	22	M	Servant	01Ju02Ir
Maria	22	F	None	01Ju02Ir
John	.11	M	Infant	01Ju02Ir
GIBSON, William	21	M	Farmer	01Ju02Ir
MCVAE, Catharine	12	F	None	01Ju02Ir
SMITH, Patrick	24	M	Laborer	01Ju02Ir
Mary	20	F	Servant	01Ju02Ir
MAYER, Ann	21	F	Spinster	01Ju02Ir

SHANNON 02 JUNE 1849

From Liverpool

NAMES OF PASSENGERS	AGE	SEX	OCCUPATIONS	DATE PORT SHIP
MURRY, John	25	M	Laborer	02Ju02Id
Mary	22	F	Servant	02Ju02Id
Kate	20	F	Servant	02Ju02Id
Nelly	18	F	Servant	02Ju02Id
WALSH, Dorah	20	F	Servant	02Ju02Id
Maria	24	F	Servant	02Ju02Id
Peter	23	M	Servant	02Ju02Id
BUTLER, James	30	M	Laborer	02Ju02Id
Bridget	26	F	Servant	02Ju02Id
Laurence	14	M	Servant	02Ju02Id
CARROLE, Anne	24	F	Servant	02Ju02Id
HOPKINS, Michael	20	M	Farmer	02Ju02Id
SEERY, Margt.	23	F	Servant	02Ju02Id
Mary-Anne	21	F	Servant	02Ju02Id
DUNNE, James	27	M	Farmer	02Ju02Id
Daniel	18	M	Farmer	02Ju02Id
Catherine	16	F	Servant	02Ju02Id
HARRINGTON, John	60	M	Farmer	02Ju02Id
Samuel	19	M	Farmer	02Ju02Id
SCULLY, John	60	M	Farmer	02Ju02Id
Patrick	40	M	Farmer	02Ju02Id
Catherine	24	F	Servant	02Ju02Id
Julia	20	F	Servant	02Ju02Id
HICKEY, Thomas	20	M	Farmer	02Ju02Id
LANE, Peter	27	M	Farmer	02Ju02Id
WALSH, Mary	24	F	Servant	02Ju02Id
Kate	22	F	Servant	02Ju02Id
Essy	20	F	Servant	02Ju02Id
Bridget	18	F	Servant	02Ju02Id
Sarah	16	F	Servant	02Ju02Id
BRYNE, William	23	M	Farmer	02Ju02Id
PARROTT, Mary-Anne	28	F	Servant	02Ju02Id
John	17	M	Servant	02Ju02Id
David	14	M	Servant	02Ju02Id
BINKS, Thomas	20	M	Servant	02Ju02Id
BURTON, Henry	26	M	Servant	02Ju02Id
CAMART, Hannah	21	F	Servant	02Ju02Id
BRINDLE, Daniel	38	M	Farmer	02Ju02Id
Rose	26	F	Servant	02Ju02Id
Michael	21	M	Servant	02Ju02Id
SHANNON, Thady	38	M	Laborer	02Ju02Id
Timothy	26	M	Laborer	02Ju02Id
Mary	21	F	Laborer	02Ju02Id
FLANAGAN, Owen	17	M	Laborer	02Ju02Id
FOX, William	20	M	Laborer	02Ju02Id
Patrick	18	M	Laborer	02Ju02Id
SHANNON, Patrick	15	M	Laborer	02Ju02Id
Catherine	18	F	Servant	02Ju02Id
John	16	M	Laborer	02Ju02Id
MULANY, Pat	18	M	Laborer	02Ju02Id
LEVEER, James	40	M	Laborer	02Ju02Id
Betsy	26	F	Wife	02Ju02Id
REGAN, Patt	56	M	Farmer	02Ju02Id
U (W)	48	F	Wife	02Ju02Id
Martin	25	M	Farmer	02Ju02Id
James	20	M	Farmer	02Ju02Id
Winner	18	M	Farmer	02Ju02Id
Honora	32	F	Servant	02Ju02Id
Ellen	16	F	Servant	02Ju02Id
DALAGAN, John	40	M	Farmer	02Ju02Id
DARGAN, James	14	M	Servant	02Ju02Id
OSHAUNESSY, Michael	22	M	Farmer	02Ju02Id
BURKE, William	25	M	Farmer	02Ju02Id
MEALY, William	30	M	Farmer	02Ju02Id
Mary-Anne	30	F	Servant	02Ju02Id
Turner	20	M	Laborer	02Ju02Id
Frances	18	F	Laborer	02Ju02Id
HAYE, Robert	28	M	Laborer	02Ju02Id
Anne	26	F	Servant	02Ju02Id
Thomas	18	M	Laborer	02Ju02Id
John	22	M	Farmer	02Ju02Id
Elizabeth	21	F	Wife	02Ju02Id
John	18	M	Farmer	02Ju02Id
ASHURST, John	25	M	Gentleman	02Ju02Id
JOHNSON, Robert	21	M	Farmer	02Ju02Id
BEVAN, Bridget	24	F	Servant	02Ju02Id
TIMMINS, Mary	26	F	Servant	02Ju02Id
TRAVERS, Anne	28	F	Servant	02Ju02Id
BANNISTER, George	29	M	Laborer	02Ju02Id
HOLLAND, George	60	M	Laborer	02Ju02Id
Rhoda (W)	44	F	Wife	02Ju02Id
William	14	M	Servant	02Ju02Id
BLEWITT, John	22	M	Servant	02Ju02Id
U-Mrs. (W)	21	F	Wife	02Ju02Id
TAILOR, William	32	M	Laborer	02Ju02Id
BOWYER, Samuel	27	M	Farmer	02Ju02Id
U-Mrs. (W)	22	F	Wife	02Ju02Id
DUGGAN, Margt.	21	F	Servant	02Ju02Id
LONERGAN, Ellen	21	F	Servant	02Ju02Id
ENGLISH, William	26	M	Farmer	02Ju02Id
CAIN, Patrick	30	M	Farmer	02Ju02Id
Anne	14	F	Servant	02Ju02Id

NAMES OF PASSENGERS		AGE	SEX	OCCUPATIONS	DATE PORT SHIP
CAIN, Catherine		18	F	Servant	02Ju02Id
Laurence		20	M	Farmer	02Ju02Id
BROWN, Charles		24	M	Farmer	02Ju02Id
WALLS, Patrick		17	M	Farmer	02Ju02Id
Ellen		19	F	Wife	02Ju02Id
DOWNEY, Allice		18	F	Servant	02Ju02Id
KELLEY, Catherine		30	F	Servant	02Ju02Id
HAMILTON, Mary		30	F	Servant	02Ju02Id
Fanny		18	F	Servant	02Ju02Id
FITZSIMMONS, Hugh		20	M	Farmer	02Ju02Id
QUINN, Patrick		30	M	Farmer	02Ju02Id
Catherine		29	F	Wife	02Ju02Id
Patrick		17	M	Servant	02Ju02Id
Margaret		16	F	Servant	02Ju02Id
Anne		20	F	Servant	02Ju02Id
Frances		18	F	Servant	02Ju02Id
MELONE, Patrick		24	M	Servant	02Ju02Id
Mary-Anne		18	F	Servant	02Ju02Id
MCGLINCHY, Sophia		17	F	Servant	02Ju02Id
John-Paul		25	M	Farmer	02Ju02Id
CARROLTON, John		30	M	Mechanic	02Ju02Id
WHITE, Joseph		28	M	Farmer	02Ju02Id
BRADY, Bernard		23	M	Farmer	02Ju02Id
Edward		22	M	Farmer	02Ju02Id
DAVIES, U-Mrs.		30	F	Servant	02Ju02Id
SATRO, Sall		22	M	Carpenter	02Ju02Id
MANGAN, John		30	M	Laborer	02Ju02Id
U	(W)	30	F	Wife	02Ju02Id
U		.00	U	Infant	02Ju02Id
SHARKEY, James		30	M	Mason	02Ju02Id
SWINTON, Robert		34	M	Farmer	02Ju02Id
Eliza	(W)	30	F	Wife	02Ju02Id
Elizabeth		9	F	Child	02Ju02Id
Anne-Maria		8	F	Child	02Ju02Id
Walter		5	M	Child	02Ju02Id
Wilfred		.00	M	Infant	02Ju02Id
GANTLEY, Anne		23	F	Servant	02Ju02Id
SPRAY, John		26	M	Farmer	02Ju02Id
U	(W)	24	F	Wife	02Ju02Id
MURPHY, Patrick		26	M	Laborer	02Ju02Id
WALSH, Philip		26	M	Laborer	02Ju02Id
MURPHY, Moses		30	M	Laborer	02Ju02Id
Anne		26	F	Wife	02Ju02Id
Besse		20	F	Servant	02Ju02Id
Michael		5	M	Child	02Ju02Id
Martin		2	M	Child	02Ju02Id
Eliza		.00	F	Infant	02Ju02Id
HERRIMAN, William		25	M	Farmer	02Ju02Id
BRADY, Susanna		16	F	Servant	02Ju02Id
GAFFNEY, Mary		17	F	Servant	02Ju02Id
FURY, John		24	M	Shoemaker	02Ju02Id
BRYNE, Laurence		22	M	Farmer	02Ju02Id
Eliza		24	F	Servant	02Ju02Id
MCNALLY, Anna		18	F	Laborer	02Ju02Id
ASPELL, Ellen		23	F	Servant	02Ju02Id
COTES, William		28	M	Servant	02Ju02Id
MALONE, James		24	M	Servant	02Ju02Id
Mary		22	F	Wife	02Ju02Id
KENNY, John		28	M	Mechanic	02Ju02Id
RUDD, Samuel		24	M	Farmer	02Ju02Id
Jane		22	F	Servant	02Ju02Id
BENNETT, William		22	M	Tailor	02Ju02Id
MCSHANE, James		28	M	Tailor	02Ju02Id
Ellen		22	F	Wife	02Ju02Id
Mary		2	F	Child	02Ju02Id
HEARTY, Owen		30	M	Laborer	02Ju02Id
Catherine		19	F	Servant	02Ju02Id
Ellen		18	F	Servant	02Ju02Id
Patrick		13	M	None	02Ju02Id
LEMMON, Mary		18	F	Servant	02Ju02Id
MCGENNESS, William		24	M	Laborer	02Ju02Id
Hugh		23	M	Laborer	02Ju02Id
KELAHER, Daniel		22	M	Laborer	02Ju02Id
BYRNE, John		22	M	Farmer	02Ju02Id
Jane	(W)	30	F	Wife	02Ju02Id

NAMES OF PASSENGERS		AGE	SEX	OCCUPATIONS	DATE PORT SHIP
MOORE, U-Mrs.		24	F	Servant	02Ju02Id
MCDONNELL, Owen		24	M	Laborer	02Ju02Id
POWELL, David		60	M	Laborer	02Ju02Id
Morgan		37	M	Laborer	02Ju02Id
Margt.		30	F	Servant	02Ju02Id
Rachel		19	F	Servant	02Ju02Id
DAVIES, Daniel		12	M	None	02Ju02Id
JOHN, John		18	M	Mason	02Ju02Id
HANSLOW, Edward		24	M	Farmer	02Ju02Id
GALVIN, Mark		40	M	Farmer	02Ju02Id
DODSON, George		29	M	Laborer	02Ju02Id
GREENBATCH, Lambert		39	M	Laborer	02Ju02Id
DOLLARD, Phillard		30	M	Laborer	02Ju02Id
MAKER, Edmund		19	M	Tailor	02Ju02Id
LANEGAN, Edward		30	M	Farmer	02Ju02Id
Bridget		20	F	Wife	02Ju02Id
KENEDY, Bridget		21	F	Servant	02Ju02Id
CAHILL, William		30	M	Laborer	02Ju02Id
MAKER, Anthony		33	M	Laborer	02Ju02Id
Eliza		30	F	Servant	02Ju02Id
Anne		4	F	Child	02Ju02Id
William		3	M	Child	02Ju02Id
Philip		.00	M	Infant	02Ju02Id
Julia		20	F	Servant	02Ju02Id
FROGGATT, Edward		24	M	Farmer	02Ju02Id
STEPHENSON, James		50	M	Farmer	02Ju02Id
SHIEL, John		26	M	Farmer	02Ju02Id
Catherine		20	F	Wife	02Ju02Id
Patrick		.00	M	Infant	02Ju02Id
MCCANN, Peter		28	M	Laborer	02Ju02Id
FARRELL, Thomas		30	M	Laborer	02Ju02Id
CONNOR, Michael		26	M	Laborer	02Ju02Id
U	(W)	18	F	Wife	02Ju02Id
SMITH, Catherine		50	F	Servant	02Ju02Id
Jane		18	F	Servant	02Ju02Id
Joseph		17	M	Laborer	02Ju02Id
THOMPSON, Eliza		17	F	Servant	02Ju02Id
STORLY, Mary-Anna		18	F	Servant	02Ju02Id
Robert		17	M	Servant	02Ju02Id
Frances		18	F	Servant	02Ju02Id
VENEBLES, Peter		29	M	Farmer	02Ju02Id
Catherine		24	F	Wife	02Ju02Id
GOODWIN, Jane		20	F	Servant	02Ju02Id
MITCHELL, Joseph		21	M	Servant	02Ju02Id
HAYES, John		25	M	Farmer	02Ju02Id
BARRETT, Richard		22	M	Farmer	02Ju02Id
Jeremiah		30	M	Farmer	02Ju02Id
HENNESSY, Patrick		21	M	Laborer	02Ju02Id
RYAN, David		22	M	Laborer	02Ju02Id
CUSHIN, Andrew		36	M	Laborer	02Ju02Id
TRAVERSE, Charles		21	M	Farmer	02Ju02Id
EAGAN, Bridget		18	F	Farmer	02Ju02Id
KENNEY, Stephen		19	M	Farmer	02Ju02Id
LEO, Richard		19	M	Farmer	02Ju02Id
KIRKPATRICK, Elizabt.		22	F	Servant	02Ju02Id
SHILOCK, Mary		22	F	Servant	02Ju02Id
GALAHER, Patrick		22	M	Laborer	02Ju02Id
Mary		20	F	Servant	02Ju02Id
Rose		25	F	Servant	02Ju02Id
John		8	M	Child	02Ju02Id
HIGGINS, Luke		25	M	Farmer	02Ju02Id
Margaret		22	F	Laborer	02Ju02Id
Thomas		5	M	Child	02Ju02Id
Mary		3	F	Child	02Ju02Id
LEONARD, Anne		19	F	Servant	02Ju02Id
MCMAUGH, Charles		50	M	Laborer	02Ju02Id
Mary		50	F	Wife	02Ju02Id
John-C.		15	M	Laborer	02Ju02Id
Peter		11	M	Unknown	02Ju02Id
MULLIGAN, Ellen		21	F	Laborer	02Ju02Id
John		21	M	Laborer	02Ju02Id
Rosanna		11	F	Laborer	02Ju02Id
MCCABE, Michl.		30	M	Laborer	02Ju02Id
KIERNAN, Christy		20	M	Laborer	02Ju02Id
BRENNAN, Thos.		26	M	Laborer	02Ju02Id

NAMES OF PASSENGERS		AGE	SEX	OCCUPATIONS	DATE PORT SHIP
BRENNAN, Roger		24	M	Laborer	02Ju02Id
MCMURRAY, Peter		18	M	Laborer	02Ju02Id
Mary		20	F	Laborer	02Ju02Id
COFFNEY, Julia		40	F	Laborer	02Ju02Id
Edward		16	M	Laborer	02Ju02Id
Ann		14	F	Laborer	02Ju02Id
Cathe.		16	F	Laborer	02Ju02Id
Pat.		6	M	Child	02Ju02Id
Henry		4	M	Child	02Ju02Id
FLYNNE, Jane		45	F	Laborer	02Ju02Id
James		28	M	Laborer	02Ju02Id
SHAUGNESSY, Wm.		20	M	Laborer	02Ju02Id
WHELAN, P.		30	M	Unknown	02Ju02Id
U	(W)	25	F	Wife	02Ju02Id
U		00	U	Child	02Ju02Id
U		00	U	Child	02Ju02Id
U		00	U	Child	02Ju02Id
U		00	U	Child	02Ju02Id
U, U		30	M	Unknown	02Ju02Id
U-Mrs.	(W)	25	F	Unknown	02Ju02Id
MOSER, U		30	M	Unknown	02Ju02Id
BOLTON, U		50	M	Unknown	02Ju02Id
WHELAN, U-Miss		21	F	Unknown	02Ju02Id

BRITISH-QUEEN 02 JUNE 1849

From Dublin

NAMES OF PASSENGERS	AGE	SEX	OCCUPATIONS	DATE PORT SHIP
GRAVES, James	38	M	Laborer	02Ju12Hw
Elizabeth	25	F	Laborer	02Ju12Hw
GREGAN, William	40	M	Laborer	02Ju12Hw
Margt.	36	F	Laborer	02Ju12Hw
Thomas	15	M	Laborer	02Ju12Hw
MCQUE, James	19	M	Laborer	02Ju12Hw
MORGAN, James	23	M	Laborer	02Ju12Hw
Mary	22	F	Laborer	02Ju12Hw
FLANAGAN, John	23	M	Laborer	02Ju12Hw
Maria	24	F	Laborer	02Ju12Hw
HALPRIN, John	30	M	Laborer	02Ju12Hw
CALLAGAN, Pat	25	M	Laborer	02Ju12Hw
Eliza	20	F	Laborer	02Ju12Hw
MCKEEVER, Pat	21	M	Laborer	02Ju12Hw
MURPHY, John	26	M	Laborer	02Ju12Hw
COMESKEAL, Edward	27	M	Laborer	02Ju12Hw
Anne	20	F	Laborer	02Ju12Hw
Rosanna	.07	F	Infant	02Ju12Hw
COYLE, Pat	25	M	Laborer	02Ju12Hw
MCGINESS, James	40	M	Laborer	02Ju12Hw
DOYLE, Robert	50	M	Laborer	02Ju12Hw
Mary	48	F	Laborer	02Ju12Hw
James	21	M	Laborer	02Ju12Hw
John	18	M	Laborer	02Ju12Hw
Pat	17	M	Laborer	02Ju12Hw
Mary	15	F	Laborer	02Ju12Hw
Michael	13	M	Laborer	02Ju12Hw
Robert	11	M	Laborer	02Ju12Hw
Sarah	8	F	Child	02Ju12Hw
Peter	6	M	Child	02Ju12Hw
William	3	M	Child	02Ju12Hw
Joseph	.05	M	Infant	02Ju12Hw
GAVIN, James	31	M	Laborer	02Ju12Hw
BOOTH, Ellen	21	F	Laborer	02Ju12Hw
CAHAN, James	25	M	Laborer	02Ju12Hw
WARD, Winifred	45	F	Laborer	02Ju12Hw
Mary	25	F	Laborer	02Ju12Hw
MCCORMICK, John	18	M	Laborer	02Ju12Hw
COCHLIN, Andrew	27	M	Laborer	02Ju12Hw
BUTLER, Timothy	45	M	Laborer	02Ju12Hw
H---	32	U	Laborer	02Ju12Hw
BUTLER, Peter	11	M	Laborer	02Ju12Hw
John	9	M	Child	02Ju12Hw
QUANN, David	29	M	Laborer	02Ju12Hw
HOPKINS, Frances	26	F	Laborer	02Ju12Hw
LYNCH, Christopher	54	M	Laborer	02Ju12Hw
Eliza	45	F	Laborer	02Ju12Hw
Lawrence	20	M	Laborer	02Ju12Hw
Cathe.	18	F	Laborer	02Ju12Hw
James	16	M	Laborer	02Ju12Hw
Margaret	13	F	Laborer	02Ju12Hw
Julia	14	F	Laborer	02Ju12Hw
John	12	M	Laborer	02Ju12Hw
Thomas	4	M	Child	02Ju12Hw
Chris.	2	M	Child	02Ju12Hw
Elizabeth	13	F	Laborer	02Ju12Hw
DEMPSEY, Peter	53	M	Laborer	02Ju12Hw
Cath.	48	F	Laborer	02Ju12Hw
John	24	M	Laborer	02Ju12Hw
Dennis	22	M	Laborer	02Ju12Hw
Mary-Ann	20	F	Laborer	02Ju12Hw
James	18	M	Laborer	02Ju12Hw
Catherine	16	F	Laborer	02Ju12Hw
Teresa	14	F	Laborer	02Ju12Hw
Julia	8	F	Child	02Ju12Hw
Henry	6	M	Child	02Ju12Hw
Martha	3	F	Child	02Ju12Hw
WILEY, John	28	M	Laborer	02Ju12Hw
Mary-Ann	36	F	Laborer	02Ju12Hw
Bridget	3	F	Child	02Ju12Hw
Thomas	6	M	Child	02Ju12Hw
WAUGH, William	27	M	Laborer	02Ju12Hw
BURKE, Thomas	25	M	Laborer	02Ju12Hw
H---	4	U	Child	02Ju12Hw
John	.08	M	Infant	02Ju12Hw
Mary-Ann	26	F	Laborer	02Ju12Hw
SHORTHALL, Elizabeth	17	F	Laborer	02Ju12Hw
HUMBERT, Frances	50	F	Laborer	02Ju12Hw
RAFTER, Darby	40	M	Laborer	02Ju12Hw
Thomas	17	M	Laborer	02Ju12Hw
William	5	M	Child	02Ju12Hw
Darby	4	M	Child	02Ju12Hw
James	3	M	Child	02Ju12Hw
Pat	.10	M	Infant	02Ju12Hw
Mary	.00	F	Infant	02Ju12Hw
KEARNEY, Peter	26	M	Laborer	02Ju12Hw
Margt.	18	F	Laborer	02Ju12Hw
MURRAY, Alex	21	M	Laborer	02Ju12Hw
Mary	20	F	Laborer	02Ju12Hw
Rose	22	F	Laborer	02Ju12Hw
HANLON, Pat	27	M	Laborer	02Ju12Hw
FRASER, John	19	M	Laborer	02Ju12Hw
FITZPATRICK, John	26	M	Laborer	02Ju12Hw
DOYLE, Mich.	22	M	Laborer	02Ju12Hw
STAFFORD, Henry	40	M	Laborer	02Ju12Hw
Sarah	36	F	Laborer	02Ju12Hw
James	14	M	Laborer	02Ju12Hw
CASSIDY, Cath.	21	F	Laborer	02Ju12Hw
LEE, Francis	27	M	Laborer	02Ju12Hw
HEYFRON, Pat	20	M	Laborer	02Ju12Hw
DILLON, James	23	M	Laborer	02Ju12Hw
SANOTT, John	35	M	Laborer	02Ju12Hw
FLINN, Lawrence	50	M	Laborer	02Ju12Hw
John	25	M	Laborer	02Ju12Hw
Thomas	16	M	Laborer	02Ju12Hw
Heessy	20	F	Laborer	02Ju12Hw
TOOLE, Pat	50	M	Laborer	02Ju12Hw
DAVIS, Peter	27	M	Laborer	02Ju12Hw
Hana	26	F	Laborer	02Ju12Hw
DOYLE, Eleanor	30	F	Laborer	02Ju12Hw
WARWICK, Jane	27	F	Laborer	02Ju12Hw
DOYLE, John	27	M	Laborer	02Ju12Hw
BOYLE, Edward	18	M	Laborer	02Ju12Hw
DAVIS, Robert	.09	M	Infant	02Ju12Hw
BURKE, John	24	M	Laborer	02Ju12Hw
HENRY, Jeremiah	23	M	Laborer	02Ju12Hw

NAMES OF PASSENGERS	AGE	SEX	OCCUPATIONS	DATE PORT SHIP
HENRY, Eliza	20	F	Laborer	02Ju12Hw
SAVAGH, John	61	M	Laborer	02Ju12Hw
Eliza	44	F	Laborer	02Ju12Hw
Mary	19	F	Laborer	02Ju12Hw
Pat	15	M	Laborer	02Ju12Hw
Rosana	10	F	Laborer	02Ju12Hw
COX, Mary	24	F	Laborer	02Ju12Hw
ORINEY, Sarah	20	F	Laborer	02Ju12Hw
CURTIS, James	21	M	Laborer	02Ju12Hw
COLLIER, Michl.	23	M	Laborer	02Ju12Hw
KELLY, Mich.	21	M	Laborer	02Ju12Hw
WAUGH, Joseph	24	M	Laborer	02Ju12Hw
Emily	21	F	Laborer	02Ju12Hw
CAVANAUGH, Mary	35	F	Laborer	02Ju12Hw
Eleanor	29	F	Laborer	02Ju12Hw
Jane	19	F	Laborer	02Ju12Hw
MCCOURT, Terrence	29	M	Laborer	02Ju12Hw
WALSH, Chris.	25	M	Laborer	02Ju12Hw
BARBER, James	28	M	Laborer	02Ju12Hw
FAGAN, Pat	24	M	Laborer	02Ju12Hw
KAVANAUGH, Pat	22	M	Laborer	02Ju12Hw
MCCLOON, William	22	M	Laborer	02Ju12Hw
SAVAGH, John	30	M	Laborer	02Ju12Hw
CANFIELD, Edward	20	M	Laborer	02Ju12Hw
KIERNAN, Thomas	25	M	Laborer	02Ju12Hw
Ann	27	F	Laborer	02Ju12Hw
CARR, John	28	M	Laborer	02Ju12Hw
H---	19	U	Laborer	02Ju12Hw
FOX, Bridget	20	F	Laborer	02Ju12Hw
COOGAN, John	19	M	Laborer	02Ju12Hw
CLARK, Walter	24	M	Laborer	02Ju12Hw
KELLY, Agnes	19	F	Laborer	02Ju12Hw
BRENNAN, John	30	M	Laborer	02Ju12Hw
HALLORAN, Elizth.	42	F	Laborer	02Ju12Hw
Mary	17	F	Laborer	02Ju12Hw
Judith	15	F	Laborer	02Ju12Hw
BYRNE, Pat	7	M	Child	02Ju12Hw
Anastasia	52	F	Laborer	02Ju12Hw
John	50	M	Laborer	02Ju12Hw
Darby	23	M	Laborer	02Ju12Hw
Bryan	20	M	Laborer	02Ju12Hw
Mary-Ann	18	F	Laborer	02Ju12Hw
Martha	19	F	Laborer	02Ju12Hw
Daniel	14	M	Laborer	02Ju12Hw
Joseph	10	M	Laborer	02Ju12Hw
Thomas	9	M	Child	02Ju12Hw
MCCABE, Charles	7	M	Child	02Ju12Hw
BYRNE, John	25	M	Laborer	02Ju12Hw
Bridget	30	F	Laborer	02Ju12Hw
H---	25	U	Laborer	02Ju12Hw
Mary	.07	F	Infant	02Ju12Hw
HARVEY, Edw.	32	M	Laborer	02Ju12Hw
Cath.	24	F	Laborer	02Ju12Hw
ARTHUR, Peter	28	M	Laborer	02Ju12Hw
ROSSITER, Mary	16	F	Laborer	02Ju12Hw
DOWD, Thomas	21	M	Laborer	02Ju12Hw
KELLY, James	28	M	Laborer	02Ju12Hw
BUT, Frances	17	F	Laborer	02Ju12Hw
KINLEY, Thomas	24	M	Laborer	02Ju12Hw
POWELL, Eliza	19	F	Laborer	02Ju12Hw
Margt.	45	F	Laborer	02Ju12Hw
COWLEY, Elizt.	30	F	Laborer	02Ju12Hw
SMITH, Charles	43	M	Laborer	02Ju12Hw
Sarah	43	F	Laborer	02Ju12Hw
Hanah	20	F	Laborer	02Ju12Hw
Frances	17	F	Laborer	02Ju12Hw
Sarah	16	F	Laborer	02Ju12Hw
Jane	12	F	Laborer	02Ju12Hw
Mary	10	F	Laborer	02Ju12Hw
Charles	5	M	Child	02Ju12Hw
CARNEY, Bridget	19	F	Laborer	02Ju12Hw
DENNIS, Miles	24	M	Laborer	02Ju12Hw
Mary	22	F	Laborer	02Ju12Hw
RYAN, Thomas	30	M	Laborer	02Ju12Hw
Pat	24	M	Laborer	02Ju12Hw

NAMES OF PASSENGERS	AGE	SEX	OCCUPATIONS	DATE PORT SHIP
RYAN, Eleanor	24	F	Laborer	02Ju12Hw
Magrt.	28	F	Laborer	02Ju12Hw
DOYLE, John	25	M	Laborer	02Ju12Hw
SHERWOOD, James	33	M	Laborer	02Ju12Hw
BOYLE, Owen	20	M	Laborer	02Ju12Hw
BALL, Edward	20	M	Laborer	02Ju12Hw
NOWLAN, Thomas	19	M	Laborer	02Ju12Hw
EARL, H---	24	U	Laborer	02Ju12Hw
Margt.	23	F	Laborer	02Ju12Hw
BYRNE, William	30	M	Laborer	02Ju12Hw
Dorothy	30	F	Laborer	02Ju12Hw
WILLIS, William	23	M	Laborer	02Ju12Hw
FINAGAN, William	23	M	Laborer	02Ju12Hw
GUNN, Mich.	20	M	Laborer	02Ju12Hw
RICHARDS, Celia	40	F	Laborer	02Ju12Hw
COLLIER, Margt.	19	F	Laborer	02Ju12Hw
BURKE, Valenine	28	M	Laborer	02Ju12Hw
RYAN, John	25	M	Laborer	02Ju12Hw
DOYLE, James	31	M	Laborer	02Ju12Hw
BARRETT, Jane	30	F	Laborer	02Ju12Hw
Margt.	22	F	Laborer	02Ju12Hw
BRADY, Owen	30	M	Laborer	02Ju12Hw
Mary	25	F	Laborer	02Ju12Hw
HUNTER, Cath.	18	F	Laborer	02Ju12Hw
DROONOGOHAM, Christoph	50	M	Gentleman	02Ju12Hw
OGORMAN, Robert	35	M	Gentleman	02Ju12Hw
Julia	40	F	Lady	02Ju12Hw
FRIZETT, Charles-F.	25	M	Gentleman	02Ju12Hw
GRAHAM, Edward-F.	28	M	Gentleman	02Ju12Hw
TOBIN, Mary	25	F	Lady	02Ju12Hw
LOONEY, Laurence	36	M	Laborer	02Ju12Hw
DILLON, Phillip	22	M	Laborer	02Ju12Hw
Margt.	23	F	Laborer	02Ju12Hw

DEFENSE 02 JUNE 1849

From Dublin

NAMES OF PASSENGERS	AGE	SEX	OCCUPATIONS	DATE PORT SHIP
ATKINSON, Edward	50	M	Farmer	02Ju12Hp
Margaret	48	F	Unknown	02Ju12Hp
REYNOLDS, Charles	45	M	Laborer	02Ju12Hp
Patt	23	M	Unknown	02Ju12Hp
Bridget	19	F	Unknown	02Ju12Hp
Christian	13	M	Unknown	02Ju12Hp
REILLY, Cath.	24	F	Unknown	02Ju12Hp
HANLEY, John	20	M	Unknown	02Ju12Hp
BYRNE, Mary	20	F	Unknown	02Ju12Hp
LANDELS, Jane	25	F	Unknown	02Ju12Hp
WALSH, Nick	14	M	Unknown	02Ju12Hp
Catharne	19	F	Unknown	02Ju12Hp
SMITH, Sarah	21	F	Unknown	02Ju12Hp
FLYNN, Peter	35	M	Unknown	02Ju12Hp
DEVINE, Cath.	8	F	Child	02Ju12Hp
KIRWANE, Jas.	27	M	Unknown	02Ju12Hp
ROGERSON, U-Mr.	28	M	Unknown	02Ju12Hp
RICHARDSON, U-Mr.	19	M	Unknown	02Ju12Hp
MORGAN, U-Mr.	19	M	Unknown	02Ju12Hp
CONNOR, Michl.	22	M	Unknown	02Ju12Hp
READY, Julia	25	F	Unknown	02Ju12Hp
Rosey	25	F	Unknown	02Ju12Hp
DOYLE, U.Mrs.	23	F	Unknown	02Ju12Hp
OREILLY, Thos.	32	M	Unknown	02Ju12Hp
U-Mrs.	28	F	Unknown	02Ju12Hp
Charlotte	7	F	Child	02Ju12Hp
Robert	5	M	Child	02Ju12Hp
Bernard	.00	M	Infant	02Ju12Hp
MCINTYRE, Peter	35	M	Unknown	02Ju12Hp
U-Mrs.	24	F	Unknown	02Ju12Hp
John	.00	M	Infant	02Ju12Hp

NAMES OF PASSENGERS	AGE	SEX	OCCUPATIONS	DATE PORT SHIP
COTTER, Wm.	27	M	Unknown	02Ju12Hp
Ellen	54	F	Unknown	02Ju12Hp
Eliza	22	F	Unknown	02Ju12Hp
Ellen	17	F	Unknown	02Ju12Hp
HOGAN, Phil.	25	M	Unknown	02Ju12Hp
KIERNAN, Ellen	23	F	Unknown	02Ju12Hp
Ellen	18	F	Unknown	02Ju12Hp
MCCORMACK, Hugh	28	M	Unknown	02Ju12Hp
Ann	26	F	Unknown	02Ju12Hp
HORAN, Matt	20	M	Unknown	02Ju12Hp
CONVEY, Michl.	21	M	Unknown	02Ju12Hp
LOWERY, Cath.	20	F	Unknown	02Ju12Hp
CREVIN, Peter	24	M	Unknown	02Ju12Hp
Mary	20	F	Unknown	02Ju12Hp
NEILL, Margt.	25	F	Unknown	02Ju12Hp
KENETT, Rich.S.	20	M	Unknown	02Ju12Hp
U-Mrs.	20	F	Unknown	02Ju12Hp
KELLY, Simon	60	M	Unknown	02Ju12Hp
Bridget	40	F	Unknown	02Ju12Hp
Mary-Ann	16	F	Unknown	02Ju12Hp
Joe	13	M	Unknown	02Ju12Hp
Eliza	11	F	Unknown	02Ju12Hp
Judith	10	F	Unknown	02Ju12Hp
John	9	M	Child	02Ju12Hp
Teresa	.00	F	Infant	02Ju12Hp
MOFFATT, U-Mrs.	58	F	Unknown	02Ju12Hp
John	19	M	Unknown	02Ju12Hp
Eliza	18	F	Unknown	02Ju12Hp
Ann	17	F	Unknown	02Ju12Hp
Owen	14	M	Unknown	02Ju12Hp
GWYMER, Maria	25	F	Unknown	02Ju12Hp
Sarah	23	F	Unknown	02Ju12Hp
Susan	20	F	Unknown	02Ju12Hp
ARMSTRONG, U-Mr.	20	M	Unknown	02Ju12Hp
DOOLEY, Jas.	30	M	Unknown	02Ju12Hp
Margaret	20	F	Unknown	02Ju12Hp
Patt	20	M	Unknown	02Ju12Hp
Ann	18	F	Unknown	02Ju12Hp
MCGUN, John	22	M	Unknown	02Ju12Hp
DOOLEY, Eliza	15	F	Unknown	02Ju12Hp
CAULFIELDS, Patt	21	M	Unknown	02Ju12Hp
FINN, Bridget	22	F	Unknown	02Ju12Hp
Catharine	.00	F	Infant	02Ju12Hp
MCLAUGHLIN, Jas.	25	M	Unknown	02Ju12Hp
Catharine	20	F	Unknown	02Ju12Hp
MOLLOWNEY, John	19	M	Unknown	02Ju12Hp
KINCH, Wm.	40	M	Unknown	02Ju12Hp
James	23	M	Unknown	02Ju12Hp
Catharine	18	F	Unknown	02Ju12Hp
MCGOVERN, U-Miss	28	F	Unknown	02Ju12Hp
U-Miss	25	F	Unknown	02Ju12Hp
Stephen	.00	M	Infant	02Ju12Hp
REED, John	25	M	Unknown	02Ju12Hp
MONK, Andrew	23	M	Unknown	02Ju12Hp
FLANIGAN, Patt	30	M	Unknown	02Ju12Hp
U-Mrs.	25	F	Unknown	02Ju12Hp
Patt	.00	M	Infant	02Ju12Hp
CARROLL, Con	45	M	Unknown	02Ju12Hp
U-Mrs.	40	F	Unknown	02Ju12Hp
Matt	28	M	Unknown	02Ju12Hp
Biddy	20	F	Unknown	02Ju12Hp
Thomas	18	M	Unknown	02Ju12Hp
Con	13	M	Unknown	02Ju12Hp
Teresa	12	F	Unknown	02Ju12Hp
Edward	.00	M	Infant	02Ju12Hp
FRENCH, Lucy	20	F	Unknown	02Ju12Hp
ENEIS, Tom	22	M	Unknown	02Ju12Hp
Mary	21	F	Unknown	02Ju12Hp
DILLON, Margaret	23	F	Unknown	02Ju12Hp
GALVIN, Ann	24	F	Unknown	02Ju12Hp
BRAALY, John	27	M	Unknown	02Ju12Hp
FLxDANIGAN, Patt	21	M	Unknown	02Ju12Hp
Catharine	24	F	Unknown	02Ju12Hp
KINSELLA, John	22	M	Unknown	02Ju12Hp
LOGAN, James	30	M	Unknown	02Ju12Hp
LOGAN, U-Mrs.	30	F	Unknown	02Ju12Hp
Patt	10	M	Unknown	02Ju12Hp
Ann	8	F	Child	02Ju12Hp
Maria	.00	F	Infant	02Ju12Hp
COOLIN, U-Mr.	40	M	Unknown	02Ju12Hp
U-Mrs.	30	F	Unknown	02Ju12Hp
James	12	M	Unknown	02Ju12Hp
Ann	10	F	Unknown	02Ju12Hp
Maria	8	F	Child	02Ju12Hp
John	6	M	Child	02Ju12Hp
Peter	4	M	Child	02Ju12Hp
Susan	2	F	Child	02Ju12Hp
MASON, Samuel	40	M	Unknown	02Ju12Hp
ALLPREN, James	20	M	Unknown	02Ju12Hp
BELL, Alexander	19	M	Unknown	02Ju12Hp
MALON, Edward	24	M	Unknown	02Ju12Hp
KINSELLA, Sarah	18	F	Unknown	02Ju12Hp
DAVIS, James	22	M	Unknown	02Ju12Hp
CLINTON, John	20	M	Unknown	02Ju12Hp
HEALEY, Francis	20	M	Unknown	02Ju12Hp
CLINTON, Mary	20	F	Unknown	02Ju12Hp
WARD, Joe	21	M	Unknown	02Ju12Hp
WALSH, John	40	M	Unknown	02Ju12Hp
CULLEN, John	29	M	Unknown	02Ju12Hp
Margaret	20	F	Unknown	02Ju12Hp
BRYAN, James	22	M	Unknown	02Ju12Hp
Mary	20	F	Unknown	02Ju12Hp
MAHAN, Peter	21	M	Unknown	02Ju12Hp
BRYAN, Thomas	.00	M	Infant	02Ju12Hp
DUNN, John	23	M	Unknown	02Ju12Hp
GERAGHTY, Ann	25	F	Unknown	02Ju12Hp
QUINN, Biddy	27	F	Unknown	02Ju12Hp
MURPHY, James	22	M	Unknown	02Ju12Hp
TOOHILL, Mary	20	F	Unknown	02Ju12Hp
MEDCALF, Christy	25	F	Unknown	02Ju12Hp
Christy	.00	F	Infant	02Ju12Hp
CAVANAGH, U-Mrs.	27	F	Unknown	02Ju12Hp
DALEY, John	21	M	Unknown	02Ju12Hp
MAHER, Thos.	50	M	Unknown	02Ju12Hp
MURPHY, Patt	20	M	Unknown	02Ju12Hp
BRIESTAGE, George	26	M	Unknown	02Ju12Hp
BRYAN, Lawrence	40	M	Unknown	02Ju12Hp
PURCELL, Tobias	22	M	Unknown	02Ju12Hp
Michael	17	M	Unknown	02Ju12Hp
John	13	M	Unknown	02Ju12Hp
WALSH, Margaret	20	F	Unknown	02Ju12Hp
CALLAGHER, Mary	36	F	Unknown	02Ju12Hp
Mary	19	F	Unknown	02Ju12Hp
HAYES, John	21	M	Unknown	02Ju12Hp
Patt	19	M	Unknown	02Ju12Hp
Honor	26	F	Unknown	02Ju12Hp
Michael	17	M	Unknown	02Ju12Hp
Michael	4	M	Child	02Ju12Hp
William	.00	M	Infant	02Ju12Hp
SCULLY, Eliza	17	F	Unknown	02Ju12Hp
CREEVEY, John	22	M	Unknown	02Ju12Hp
MORAN, Thos.	40	M	Unknown	02Ju12Hp
RESHAM, Margt.	20	F	Unknown	02Ju12Hp
CONNOR, Thos.	27	M	Unknown	02Ju12Hp
BROWN, Ann	24	F	Unknown	02Ju12Hp
John	.00	M	Infant	02Ju12Hp
MARKS, Joe	20	M	Unknown	02Ju12Hp
BRADY, U-Miss	20	F	Unknown	02Ju12Hp
SHERIDAN, U-Miss	20	F	Unknown	02Ju12Hp
MCMANUS, Jas	27	M	Unknown	02Ju12Hp
SMITH, John	21	M	Unknown	02Ju12Hp
GILL, Edward	40	M	Unknown	02Ju12Hp
DOWLING, Eliza	30	F	Unknown	02Ju12Hp
John	11	M	Unknown	02Ju12Hp
REILLY, Mary	20	F	Unknown	02Ju12Hp
CONNOR, Jas	20	M	Unknown	02Ju12Hp
MOORE, Mary	23	F	Unknown	02Ju12
Peggy	20	F	Unknown	02Ju12Hp
KENNY, John	48	M	Unknown	02Ju12Hp
U-Mrs.	45	F	Unknown	02Ju12Hp

NAMES OF PASSENGERS	AGE	SEX	OCCUPATIONS	DATE PORT SHIP
KENNY, John	27	M	Unknown	02Ju12Hp
Thomas	23	M	Unknown	02Ju12Hp
Bryan	18	M	Unknown	02Ju12Hp
Patt	13	M	Unknown	02Ju12Hp
James	11	M	Unknown	02Ju12Hp
FAHEY, Eliza	36	F	Unknown	02Ju12Hp
John	19	M	Unknown	02Ju12Hp
Bridget	12	F	Unknown	02Ju12Hp
Eliza	10	F	Unknown	02Ju12Hp
Tim	11	M	Unknown	02Ju12Hp
Patt	9	M	Child	02Ju12Hp
CONWAY, Peter	28	M	Unknown	02Ju12Hp
Bridget	20	F	Unknown	02Ju12Hp
William	.00	M	Infant	02Ju12Hp
CLAVIN, Bridget	18	F	Unknown	02Ju12Hp
KEARNEY, Bridget	18	F	Unknown	02Ju12Hp
HORAN, Thos.	19	M	Unknown	02Ju12Hp
EGAN, Bridget	18	F	Unknown	02Ju12Hp
CUMMINS, Rich	18	M	Unknown	02Ju12Hp
GERAGHTY, Patt	20	M	Unknown	02Ju12Hp
Bridget	10	F	Unknown	02Ju12Hp
MORAN, Thos.	21	M	Unknown	02Ju12Hp
DONNOLLY, David	25	M	Unknown	02Ju12Hp
GERAGHTY, Tim	13	M	Unknown	02Ju12Hp
Mary	10	F	Unknown	02Ju12Hp
Bridget	6	F	Child	02Ju12Hp
Fanny	.00	F	Infant	02Ju12Hp
DONNOLLY, U-Mrs.	36	F	Unknown	02Ju12Hp
CAVANAGH, Bridget	21	F	Unknown	02Ju12Hp
Margaret	.00	F	Infant	02Ju12Hp

SEA 04 JUNE 1849

From London

NAMES OF PASSENGERS	AGE	SEX	OCCUPATIONS	DATE PORT SHIP
DOODY, Crist.	54	M	Farmer	04Ju13Ia
Rose	50	F	None	04Ju13Ia
Anne	29	F	None	04Ju13Ia
Ctty.	23	U	None	04Ju13Ia
Patrick	21	M	Unknown	04Ju13Ia
Thomas	16	M	Unknown	04Ju13Ia
Mary	11	F	None	04Ju13Ia
MILEY, Catharine	24	F	Servant	04Ju13Ia
Anne	20	F	Servant	04Ju13Ia
James	18	M	Servant	04Ju13Ia
KERR, William	26	M	Carpenter	04Ju13Ia
GRANT, Joseph	22	M	Schm	04Ju13Ia
IRELAND, James-W.	21	M	Farmer	04Ju13Ia
REDMOND, John	21	M	Laborer	04Ju13Ia
TAYLOR, Edward	35	M	Blacksmith	04Ju13Ia
Martha	25	F	None	04Ju13Ia
William	30	M	Blacksmith	04Ju13Ia
Jane	25	F	None	04Ju13Ia
Thomas	7	M	Child	04Ju13Ia
James	6	M	Child	04Ju13Ia
Edward	4	M	Child	04Ju13Ia
William	2	M	Child	04Ju13Ia
Edward	3	M	Child	04Ju13Ia
Eliza	.00	F	Infant	04Ju13Ia
Died-At-Sea				
FERRIS, John	28	M	Farmer	04Ju13Ia
SHIPLEY, Cad	25	U	Farmer	04Ju13Ia
HORN, James	25	M	Farmer	04Ju13Ia
NOBLE, Sarah	16	F	Servant	04Ju13Ia
HARRISON, John	34	M	Weaver	04Ju13Ia
EVANS, James	30	M	Farmer	04Ju13Ia
Walter	15	M	Farmer	04Ju13Ia
MAHER, Nissy	40	F	None	04Ju13Ia
Esther	24	F	None	04Ju13Ia
MAHER, Mary	21	F	None	04Ju13Ia
Michael	18	M	Unknown	04Ju13Ia
James	17	M	Unknown	04Ju13Ia
Thomas	14	M	Unknown	04Ju13Ia
Alicia	9	F	Child	04Ju13Ia
Catharine	7	F	Child	04Ju13Ia
MURPHY, James	25	M	Farmer	04Ju13Ia
MATTHEWS, Rose	30	F	None	04Ju13Ia
Died-At-Sea				
Anne	10	F	Child	04Ju13Ia
Patrick	9	M	Child	04Ju13Ia
Michael	2	M	Child	04Ju13Ia
Thomas	.00	M	Infant	04Ju13Ia
Died-At-Sea				
DOLAN, Mary	30	F	Servant	04Ju13Ia
John	9	M	Child	04Ju13Ia
Mary	12	M	Unknown	04Ju13Ia
HARFORD, Simeon	32	M	Farmer	04Ju13Ia
Anne	25	F	None	04Ju13Ia
James	5	M	Child	04Ju13Ia
Patrick	4	M	Child	04Ju13Ia
Margaret	.00	F	Infant	04Ju13Ia
CONNELL, Edward	25	M	Laborer	04Ju13Ia
Catharine	30	F	None	04Ju13Ia
DEVINE, John	26	F	Unknown	04Ju13Ia
WHITE, William	25	M	Unknown	04Ju13Ia
GILMORE, James	35	M	Farmer	04Ju13Ia
Eleanor	30	F	None	04Ju13Ia
John	10	F	None	04Ju13Ia
Letitia	8	F	Child	04Ju13Ia
James	5	M	Child	04Ju13Ia
Elizabeth	12	F	None	04Ju13Ia
GRIER, Samuel	35	M	Unknown	04Ju13Ia
Margaret	35	F	None	04Ju13Ia
Jane	18	F	None	04Ju13Ia
Nancy	16	F	None	04Ju13Ia
Bess	15	F	None	04Ju13Ia
Margaret	14	F	None	04Ju13Ia
Isabella	14	F	None	04Ju13Ia
Martha	10	F	Child	04Ju13Ia
Samuel	7	M	Child	04Ju13Ia
FREEMAN, Thomas	24	M	Laborer	04Ju13Ia
BRYAN, John	22	M	Laborer	04Ju13Ia
James	20	M	Laborer	04Ju13Ia
Mary	18	F	None	04Ju13Ia
Johanna	11	F	None	04Ju13Ia
Lawrence	22	M	Unknown	04Ju13Ia
Mary	26	F	None	04Ju13Ia
John	.00	M	Infant	04Ju13Ia
SEHAIN, James	24	M	Unknown	04Ju13Ia
Margaret	28	F	None	04Ju13Ia
Mary	12	F	None	04Ju13Ia
John	9	M	Child	04Ju13Ia
Ellen	7	F	Child	04Ju13Ia
Thomas	3	M	Child	04Ju13Ia
Mary	24	F	Unknown	04Ju13Ia
CARROLL, Patrick	20	M	Laborer	04Ju13Ia
SMITH, James	28	M	Teacher	04Ju13Ia
KEATING, Ambrose	21	M	Laborer	04Ju13Ia
Mary	19	F	None	04Ju13Ia
Ann	18	F	None	04Ju13Ia
FARRELL, Thos.	27	M	Laborer	04Ju13Ia
MCCABE, James	24	M	Laborer	04Ju13Ia
DONLADY, Margaret	22	F	Servant	04Ju13Ia
MCNALLY, Margaret	21	F	Servant	04Ju13Ia
DUGDALE, Bridget	22	F	Servant	04Ju13Ia
Mary	14	F	Servant	04Ju13Ia
GORMAN, Daniel	22	M	Laborer	04Ju13Ia
David	24	M	Laborer	04Ju13Ia
MURPHY, Edward	20	M	Laborer	04Ju13Ia
SHEA, James	22	M	Laborer	04Ju13Ia
Mary	14	F	None	04Ju13Ia
BERRY, Jeonagh	24	M	Laborer	04Ju13Ia
MULLIN, Michael	20	M	Laborer	04Ju13Ia
LYNCH, Alice	17	F	Servant	04Ju13Ia

NAMES OF PASSENGERS	AGE	SEX	OCCUPATIONS	DATE PORT SHIP
SHERRY, John	16	M	Laborer	04Ju13la
Owen	15	M	Laborer	04Ju13la
Ellen	4	F	Child	04Ju13la
Died-At-Sea				
Anne	3	F	Child	04Ju13la
GREENAN, John	50	M	Unknown	04Ju13la
Betty	40	F	None	04Ju13la
Peter	22	M	Unknown	04Ju13la
Isabella	24	F	Unknown	04Ju13la
Died-At-Sea				
Alice	19	F	None	04Ju13la
Rose	17	F	None	04Ju13la
Died-At-Sea				
Edward	12	M	Unknown	04Ju13la
Died-At-Sea				
Patrick	9	M	Child	04Ju13la
John	4	M	Child	04Ju13la
James	4	M	Child	04Ju13la
Peter	1	M	Child	04Ju13la
DORAN, James	24	M	Unknown	04Ju13la
Mary	22	F	None	04Ju13la
MOODY, Thomas	24	M	Farmer	04Ju13la
OBRIEN, Lawrence	24	M	Carpenter	04Ju13la
WHITTLE, Joseph	26	M	Farmer	04Ju13la
REILY, Sarah	20	F	Servant	04Ju13la
REILLY, Winifred	17	F	Servant	04Ju13la
HAYES, Daniel	25	M	Farmer	04Ju13la
Mary	32	F	None	04Ju13la
Mary	11	F	None	04Ju13la
Alice	9	F	Child	04Ju13la
Catherine	7	F	Child	04Ju13la
Honora	4	F	Child	04Ju13la
Michael	3	M	Child	04Ju13la
CODY, Henry	35	M	Laborer	04Ju13la
DUNAGAN, Mary	20	F	None	04Ju13la
Died-At-Sea				
HAYES, Martin	23	M	Unknown	04Ju13la
NEWMAN, Michael	45	M	Unknown	04Ju13la
Anne	42	F	None	04Ju13la
James	18	M	None	04Ju13la
Christopher	14	M	None	04Ju13la
Thomas	13	M	None	04Ju13la
Michael	10	M	Child	04Ju13la
Mary	8	F	Child	04Ju13la
Simon	5	M	Child	04Ju13la
Anne	3	F	Child	04Ju13la
Patrick	.00	M	Infant	04Ju13la
CONLON, Edward	22	M	Laborer	04Ju13la
WHITE, Briget	29	F	Unknown	04Ju13la
HARTNELL, Daniel	24	M	Unknown	04Ju13la
WALSH, James	22	M	Unknown	04Ju13la
John	27	M	Unknown	04Ju13ia
GRIFFIN, Thomas	30	M	Unknown	04Ju13la
Catharine	22	F	Unknown	04Ju13la
WALSH, Bridget	17	F	Unknown	04Ju13la
HAYES, Patrick	40	M	Farmer	04Ju13la
RASPIN, Eliza	22	F	Servant	04Ju13la
HUGHS, U-Miss	22	F	Unknown	04Ju13la
PRICE, Alice	23	F	Cook	04Ju13la
BOYLE, Michael	24	M	Unknown	04Ju13la
MCDONNELL, Ruth	26	F	Unknown	04Ju13la
RUTTER, Thomas	24	M	Unknown	04Ju13la
WINKEL, John	26	M	Weaver	04Ju13la
KEENAN, Thomas	50	M	Laborer	04Ju13la
Peter	27	M	Laborer	04Ju13la
Mary	50	F	None	04Ju13la
CONNELL, Patrick	24	M	Carpenter	04Ju13la
Catharine	24	F	None	04Ju13la
MELONEY, Robert	24	M	Unknown	04Ju13la
SKANE, Thomas	28	M	Nailer	04Ju13la
NOLAN, Honora	22	F	Servant	04Ju13la
FOLEY, Margaret	21	F	Unknown	04Ju13la
Eliza	22	F	Unknown	04Ju13la
HAYES, Michael	21	M	Unknown	04Ju13la
LELLAS, Michael	50	M	Baker	04Ju13la

NAMES OF PASSENGERS	AGE	SEX	OCCUPATIONS	DATE PORT SHIP
LELLAS, Briget	16	F	None	04Ju13la
Mary	18	F	None	04Ju13la
Margaret	13	F	None	04Ju13la
Michael	7	M	Child	04Ju13la
HAYES, Julia	40	F	None	04Ju13la
CUDDY, Mary	29	F	Unknown	04Ju13la
LUIRA, Mary	18	F	Unknown	04Ju13la
MEAD, Patrick	50	M	Unknown	04Ju13la
Betty	50	F	None	04Ju13la
Phillip	15	M	Unknown	04Ju13la
Patrick	14	M	Unknown	04Ju13la
Margaret	16	F	Unknown	04Ju13la
Betty	10	F	Child	04Ju13la
James	8	M	Child	04Ju13la
TUNNEY, Phillip	30	M	Unknown	04Ju13la
BRITCH, John	30	M	Unknown	04Ju13la
Eliza	29	F	None	04Ju13la
Sarah	5	F	Child	04Ju13la
George	2	M	Child	04Ju13la
BATTY, John	24	M	Unknown	04Ju13la
Jane	25	F	None	04Ju13la
Thomas	.00	M	Infant	04Ju13la
MORROW, John	.00	M	Infant	04Ju13la
CONNOR, James	24	M	Farmer	04Ju13la
Margaret	21	F	None	04Ju13la
Patrick	24	M	Unknown	04Ju13la
RYAN, Edward	30	M	Unknown	04Ju13la
Died-At-Sea				
Mary	25	F	None	04Ju13la
KANE, Maurice	28	M	Unknown	04Ju13la
READY, David	26	M	Unknown	04Ju13la
DOWNES, William	30	M	Unknown	04Ju13la
Mary	30	F	None	04Ju13la
Rebecca	3	F	Child	04Ju13la
PLUNCKET, Richard	22	M	Smith	04Ju13la
CARTER, Robert	23	M	Unknown	04Ju13la
HUGHES, James	25	M	Unknown	04Ju13la
CRONAN, Mary	26	F	None	04Ju13la
Dennis	8	M	Child	04Ju13la
BARRON, Margaret	20	M	Unknown	04Ju13la
DOWNEY, Peter	00	M	Unknown	04Ju13la
TAYLOR, Eliza	24	F	None	04Ju13la
GORMAN, William	22	M	Farmer	04Ju13la
STARK, Richard	24	M	Unknown	04Ju13la

OSCEOLA 04 MAY 1849

From Lanzarata

NAMES OF PASSENGERS	AGE	SEX	OCCUPATIONS	DATE PORT SHIP
TOLE, M.L.	28	M	Apothecary	04Ma65Hq

ADELINE 04 JUNE 1849

From Liverpool

NAMES OF PASSENGERS	AGE	SEX	OCCUPATIONS	DATE PORT SHIP
DONNOLY, Michl.	25	M	Laborer	04Ju02lu
DOLAN, Lucy	20	F	Laborer	04Ju02lu
Thos.	25	M	Servant	04Ju02lu
FOGGIN, John	51	M	Artist	04Ju02lu
U-Mrs.	50	F	Artist	04Ju02lu
Mary	24	F	Artist	04Ju02lu
Rebecca	16	F	Artist	04Ju02lu
Rachael	12	F	Artist	04Ju02lu

NAMES OF PASSENGERS	AGE	SEX	OCCUPATIONS	DATE PORT SHIP
FOGGIN, John	9	M	Child	04Ju02lu
Eliza	6	F	Child	04Ju02lu
FARRELL, Darby	50	M	Farmer	04Ju02lu
Mary	50	F	Farmer	04Ju02lu
Kate	18	F	Farmer	04Ju02lu
James	17	M	Farmer	04Ju02lu
MCGUIRE, Mary	20	F	Servant	04Ju02lu
GARTY, Bridgt.	36	F	Farmer	04Ju02lu
John	17	M	Farmer	04Ju02lu
Henry	16	M	Farmer	04Ju02lu
Michael	14	M	Farmer	04Ju02lu
Josh.	8	M	Child	04Ju02lu
Owen	6	M	Child	04Ju02lu
Ellen	4	F	Child	04Ju02lu
NAUGHTEN, Mary	18	F	Child	04Ju02lu
Jane	3	F	Child	04Ju02lu
Barnd.	2	M	Child	04Ju02lu
Maria	.00	F	Infant	04Ju02lu
MCGUIRE, Ellen	18	F	Servant	04Ju02lu
RILEY, Pat	24	M	Laborer	04Ju02lu
CONGLIN, Frank	24	M	Laborer	04Ju02lu
Peggy	50	F	Servant	04Ju02lu
Ally	18	F	Servant	04Ju02lu
Kitty	20	F	Servant	04Ju02lu
CULRALIN, Martin	7	M	Child	04Ju02lu
Pat	4	M	Child	04Ju02lu
DOOGAN, Lou	30	M	Laborer	04Ju02lu
CORMICK, Bridt.	39	F	Servant	04Ju02lu
MURPHY, Jas.	60	M	Farmer	04Ju02lu
Edwd.	16	M	Farmer	04Ju02lu
Cathe.	22	F	Servant	04Ju02lu
BYRNE, Wills	25	F	Servant	04Ju02lu
RILEY, Danl.	22	M	Laborer	04Ju02lu
FLYNN, Thos.	30	M	Laborer	04Ju02lu
Margt.	28	F	Laborer	04Ju02lu
Jno.	.00	M	Infant	04Ju02lu
ONEIL, John	25	M	Laborer	04Ju02lu
KELLY, Michl.	20	M	Laborer	04Ju02lu
HEALEY, Margt.	30	F	Servant	04Ju02lu
ODONNELL, John	21	M	Farmer	04Ju02lu
MAHONEY, James	20	M	Farmer	04Ju02lu
COUGLIN, Bridt.	20	F	Servant	04Ju02lu
CATALAN, Mary	20	F	Servant	04Ju02lu
MAHONEY, Mary	20	F	Servant	04Ju02lu
HONGAN, Mary	20	F	Servant	04Ju02lu
COUGHLAN, Con.	22	M	Farmer	04Ju02lu
Morris	17	M	Farmer	04Ju02lu
Mary	26	F	Farmer	04Ju02lu
Mary	56	F	Farmer	04Ju02lu
FITZPATRICK, Pat	24	M	Carpenter	04Ju02lu
Ellen	24	F	Carpenter	04Ju02lu
Ellen	.00	F	Infant	04Ju02lu
BUNNEN, Pat	20	M	Laborer	04Ju02lu
BYRNE, Patk.	40	M	Laborer	04Ju02lu
FLYNN, M.	32	M	Fisherman	04Ju02lu
EGANS, Mary	25	F	Servant	04Ju02lu
DONOVAN, Danl.	40	M	Laborer	04Ju02lu
John	20	M	Laborer	04Ju02lu
MCAUGHTY, John	25	M	Blacksmith	04Ju02lu
TRAYNER, Frank	18	M	Farmer	04Ju02lu
EGAN, Edward	24	M	Laborer	04Ju02lu
LENARD, Joseph	21	M	Laborer	04Ju02lu
GAINTZ, Bridgt.	17	F	Laborer	04Ju02lu

WARD-CHIPMAN 05 JUNE 1849

From Liverpool

NAMES OF PASSENGERS	AGE	SEX	OCCUPATIONS	DATE PORT SHIP
MCCART, Thos.	30	M	Unknown	05Ju02lf
Cath.	28	F	Unknown	05Ju02lf
Alice	24	F	Unknown	05Ju02lf
Jane	22	F	Unknown	05Ju02lf
James	20	M	Unknown	05Ju02lf
Richard	19	M	Unknown	05Ju02lf
Ann	13	F	Unknown	05Ju02lf
Margaret	11	F	Unknown	05Ju02lf
EAGAN, Ann	25	F	Unknown	05Ju02lf
Alice	20	F	Unknown	05Ju02lf
JONES, Mary	21	F	Unknown	05Ju02lf
DOUGHAN, Thos.	55	M	Unknown	05Ju02lf
Cath.	50	F	Unknown	05Ju02lf
Farrell	24	M	Unknown	05Ju02lf
Bridget	22	F	Unknown	05Ju02lf
Judy	20	F	Unknown	05Ju02lf
Pat	18	M	Unknown	05Ju02lf
Ellen	16	F	Unknown	05Ju02lf
Margaret	14	F	Unknown	05Ju02lf
LYNCH, Danl.	50	M	Unknown	05Ju02lf
U-Mrs.	48	F	Unknown	05Ju02lf
Lawrence	23	M	Unknown	05Ju02lf
Pat	26	M	Unknown	05Ju02lf
Pat	11	M	Unknown	05Ju02lf
MOLLY, Wm.	24	M	Unknown	05Ju02lf
Bridget	20	F	Unknown	05Ju02lf
BYRNE, James	24	M	Unknown	05Ju02lf
MCCABE, Francis	30	M	Unknown	05Ju02lf
Ann	27	F	Unknown	05Ju02lf
Mary	4	F	Child	05Ju02lf
Patrick	2	M	Child	05Ju02lf
Fanny	.00	F	Infant	05Ju02lf
LUNT, Jno.	27	M	Unknown	05Ju02lf
MCGURR, Francis	29	M	Unknown	05Ju02lf
MCBRIEN, Owen	20	M	Unknown	05Ju02lf
MULLALY, James	20	M	Unknown	05Ju02lf
CARNEY, Fanny	48	F	Unknown	05Ju02lf
MCCARTRY, Bridget	20	F	Unknown	05Ju02lf
Fanny	18	F	Unknown	05Ju02lf
JONES, Mich	22	M	Unknown	05Ju02lf
Mary	22	F	Unknown	05Ju02lf
LEWIS, Faulks	25	M	Unknown	05Ju02lf
LOUGHLIN, James	30	M	Unknown	05Ju02lf
Mary	30	F	Unknown	05Ju02lf
James	3	M	Child	05Ju02lf
Maria	.00	F	Infant	05Ju02lf
ANDERSON, Geo.	18	M	Unknown	05Ju02lf
LYNCH, Rose	16	F	Unknown	05Ju02lf
COX, Cath.	18	F	Unknown	05Ju02lf
KELLY, Dan	24	M	Unknown	05Ju02lf
Keron	18	M	Unknown	05Ju02lf
WRIGHT, W.H. Died-At-Sea	21	M	Unknown	05Ju02lf
SMITH, Alex.	29	M	Unknown	05Ju02lf
HARRIS, Wm.	30	M	Unknown	05Ju02lf
Ann	22	F	Unknown	05Ju02lf
Ellen	2	F	Child	05Ju02lf
Joanna	.00	F	Infant	05Ju02lf
OROURKE, Ann	21	F	Unknown	05Ju02lf
MARSHALL, Geo.	24	M	Unknown	05Ju02lf
REDFORN, Jno.	26	M	Unknown	05Ju02lf
HADE, Edwd.	37	M	Unknown	05Ju02lf
DUNN, Margt.	40	F	Unknown	05Ju02lf
RILEY, Pat	4	M	Child	05Ju02lf
Thos.	5	M	Child	05Ju02lf

NAMES OF PASSENGERS	AGE	SEX	OCCUPATIONS	DATE PORT SHIP
KENDALL, Jacob	37	M	Unknown	05Ju02lf
ROBINSON, Thos.	29	M	Unknown	05Ju02lf
Harriet	27	F	Unknown	05Ju02lf
Elizabeth	4	F	Child	05Ju02lf
Jno.	2	M	Child	05Ju02lf
Jno.	.00	M	Infant	05Ju02lf
COLLING, Jno.	21	M	Unknown	05Ju02lf
Johanna	22	F	Unknown	05Ju02lf
POWER, Thos.	40	M	Unknown	05Ju02lf
Ellen	40	F	Unknown	05Ju02lf
Mic.	16	M	Unknown	05Ju02lf
Pat.	12	M	Unknown	05Ju02lf
Pierce	10	M	Unknown	05Ju02lf
Thos.	8	M	Child	05Ju02lf
Bridget	7	F	Child	05Ju02lf
Cath.	5	F	Child	05Ju02lf
Mitchell	3	M	Child	05Ju02lf
Ellen	.00	F	Infant	05Ju02lf
MCGRATH, Thos.	45	M	Unknown	05Ju02lf
Jno.	30	M	Unknown	05Ju02lf
Biddy	25	F	Unknown	05Ju02lf
DERMOTT, Dan	40	M	Unknown	05Ju02lf
Thos.	9	M	Child	05Ju02lf
Edwd.	7	M	Child	05Ju02lf
BULGER, Pat	25	M	Unknown	05Ju02lf
MULLIGAN, Bridget	21	F	Unknown	05Ju02lf
Mich	28	M	Unknown	05Ju02lf
Jno.	28	M	Unknown	05Ju02lf
CORCORAN, Jno.	30	M	Unknown	05Ju02lf
SCALLY, Mich	18	M	Unknown	05Ju02lf
HANLEY, Honora	20	F	Unknown	05Ju02lf
CONLAY, Biddy	40	F	Unknown	05Ju02lf
LACE, Cath.	16	F	Unknown	05Ju02lf
BURKE, Jno.	30	M	Unknown	05Ju02lf
RAWKIES, Robt.	40	M	Unknown	05Ju02lf
Mary	12	F	Unknown	05Ju02lf
BURKE, Thos.	28	M	Unknown	05Ju02lf
Ellen	14	F	Unknown	05Ju02lf
WILSON, Alex	35	M	Unknown	05Ju02lf
BRIAND, Wm.	30	M	Unknown	05Ju02lf
KERNS, Jno.	35	M	Unknown	05Ju02lf
HAMELTON, Dan	40	M	Unknown	05Ju02lf
Wm.	25	M	Unknown	05Ju02lf
BROWN, Ed	22	M	Unknown	05Ju02lf
HEFFRON, Pat	22	F	Unknown	05Ju02lf
BLUATT, Thos.	16	M	Unknown	05Ju02lf
NOON, Mic.	26	M	Unknown	05Ju02lf
SHINA, Thos.	3	M	Child	05Ju02lf
GUNDON, Jno.	23	M	Unknown	05Ju02lf
GREEN, Ric.	50	M	Unknown	05Ju02lf
BELFORTH, Wm.	20	M	Unknown	05Ju02lf
WALKER, Jno.	22	M	Unknown	05Ju02lf
WHITLOCK, Jas.	20	M	Unknown	05Ju02lf
SMITH, Thos.	19	M	Unknown	05Ju02lf
Cath.	21	F	Unknown	05Ju02lf
FARRELL, Wm.	18	M	Unknown	05Ju02lf
CREGAN, Mary	22	F	Unknown	05Ju02lf
JOHNSTON, Jno.	29	M	Unknown	05Ju02lf
CORCORAN, Pat	21	M	Unknown	05Ju02lf
DAWKINS, Henry	29	M	Unknown	05Ju02lf
MAHONEY, Mic.	28	M	Unknown	05Ju02lf
Mary	28	F	Unknown	05Ju02lf
GRIFFIN, Mary	10	F	Unknown	05Ju02lf
Johanna	5	F	Child	05Ju02lf
MAHONEY, Eliz.	2	F	Child	05Ju02lf
Bridget	.00	F	Infant	05Ju02lf
Pat	20	M	Unknown	05Ju02lf
FLINN, Mary	20	F	Unknown	05Ju02lf
CUNNINGHAM, Cath.	35	F	Unknown	05Ju02lf
Ann	14	F	Unknown	05Ju02lf
Cath.	11	F	Unknown	05Ju02lf
Bridget	9	F	Child	05Ju02lf
Mic.	4	M	Child	05Ju02lf
KELLY, Cath.	18	F	Unknown	05Ju02lf
GILL, Bridget	20	F	Unknown	05Ju02lf
CLINE, Jas.	20	M	Unknown	05Ju02lf
Barney	18	M	Unknown	05Ju02lf
CASSON, Wm.	20	M	Unknown	05Ju02lf
HAWKINS, Frank	30	M	Unknown	05Ju02lf
Mgt.	10	F	Unknown	05Ju02lf
PENDER, Mgt.	35	F	Unknown	05Ju02lf
BOYNE, Cath.	20	F	Unknown	05Ju02lf
DEVLIN, Dan	28	M	Unknown	05Ju02lf
Mary-A.	25	F	Unknown	05Ju02lf
Martha	.00	F	Infant	05Ju02lf
BURINER, Jno.	20	M	Unknown	05Ju02lf
ANDREWS, Thos.	23	M	Unknown	05Ju02lf
LIGHTFOOT, Thos.	25	M	Unknown	05Ju02lf
Sarah	25	F	Unknown	05Ju02lf
Geo.	10	M	Unknown	05Ju02lf
Eliza	2	F	Child	05Ju02lf
EAGAN, Jas.	30	M	Unknown	05Ju02lf
FLYNN, Edward	30	M	Unknown	05Ju02lf
MASKAY, Mgt.	21	F	Unknown	05Ju02lf
RILEY, Jno.	25	M	Unknown	05Ju02lf
Mary	30	F	Unknown	05Ju02lf
THORNTON, Jno.	23	M	Unknown	05Ju02lf
RILEY, Mic.	27	M	Unknown	05Ju02lf
BALE, Sam	20	M	Unknown	05Ju02lf
COULTER, Jno.	20	M	Unknown	05Ju02lf
MCSWIGGER, Mgt.	20	F	Unknown	05Ju02lf
LOVETE, Jane	20	F	Unknown	05Ju02lf
KELLY, Jas.	26	M	Unknown	05Ju02lf
Edward	24	M	Unknown	05Ju02lf
Mic.	13	M	Unknown	05Ju02lf
RILEY, Ellen	21	F	Unknown	05Ju02lf
Luke	12	M	Unknown	05Ju02lf
BOOR, Jno.	30	M	Unknown	05Ju02lf
Ann	31	F	Unknown	05Ju02lf
Geo.	4	M	Child	05Ju02lf
Jno.	1	M	Child	05Ju02lf
ALLEN, Jas.	33	M	Unknown	05Ju02lf
FEHAN, Jno.	28	M	Unknown	05Ju02lf
BREEGAN, Honora	20	F	Unknown	05Ju02lf
COMERFORD, Cath.	24	F	Unknown	05Ju02lf
Julia	21	F	Unknown	05Ju02lf
Bridget	18	F	Unknown	05Ju02lf
Wm.	20	M	Unknown	05Ju02lf
Jas.	25	M	Unknown	05Ju02lf
Ellen	25	F	Unknown	05Ju02lf
Mary	20	F	Unknown	05Ju02lf
Jno.	2	M	Child	05Ju02lf
Mich.	.00	M	Infant	05Ju02lf
Ned	12	M	Unknown	05Ju02lf
STAPLETON, Jno.	20	M	Unknown	05Ju02lf
Cath.	18	F	Unknown	05Ju02lf
FOGARTY, Mic.	25	M	Unknown	05Ju02lf
Cath.	18	F	Unknown	05Ju02lf
FRAZER, Mich.	28	M	Unknown	05Ju02lf
BRYAN, Jno.	26	M	Unknown	05Ju02lf
KEVAN, Jno.	27	M	Unknown	05Ju02lf
BRYAN, Mary	22	F	Unknown	05Ju02lf
MCDONNELL, Jno.	15	M	Unknown	05Ju02lf
KELLY, Mich.	21	M	Unknown	05Ju02lf
MCGARN, Ann	24	F	Unknown	05Ju02lf
STEWART, Hugh	30	M	Unknown	05Ju02lf
Sarah	24	F	Unknown	05Ju02lf
FLEYES, Jno.	25	M	Unknown	05Ju02lf
DEVARY, Dan	26	M	Unknown	05Ju02l
Ann	24	F	Unknown	05Ju02lf
RILEY, Mary	18	F	Unknown	05Ju02l
BURETON, Wm.	24	M	Unknown	05Ju02l
FOSTER, Andrew	24	M	Unknown	05Ju02l
PERSALE, Alice	24	F	Unknown	05Ju02l
LEWIN, Mary	24	F	Unknown	05Ju02l
GRAY, Robt.	48	M	Unknown	05Ju02l
MCCARTNEY, Thos.	24	M	Unknown	05Ju02l
Elizabeth	20	F	Unknown	05Ju02l
Margt.	7	F	Child	05Ju02l
Thos.	21	M	Unknown	05Ju02l

NAMES OF PASSENGERS		AGE	SEX	OCCUPATIONS	DATE PORT SHIP
FLONEY, Martin		31	M	Unknown	05Ju02If
Jane		31	F	Unknown	05Ju02If
Mary		2	F	Child	05Ju02If
FLAGAN, Thos.		26	M	Unknown	05Ju02If
BLOWN, Robt.		26	M	Unknown	05Ju02If
FITZPATRICK, Chs.		57	M	Unknown	05Ju02If
Wm.		22	M	Unknown	05Ju02If
KELLY, Jno.		26	M	Unknown	05Ju02If
CULISS, Wm.		45	M	Unknown	05Ju02If
Henry		19	M	Unknown	05Ju02If
BUCHER, Wm.		27	M	Unknown	05Ju02If
FLANNIGAN, Brio.		25	M	Unknown	05Ju02If
SHEELS, Edwd.		24	M	Unknown	05Ju02If
Sam		17	M	Unknown	05Ju02If
Jno.		15	M	Unknown	05Ju02If
FLANNIGAN, Brio.		44	M	Unknown	05Ju02If
MUIS, Elizh.		19	F	Unknown	05Ju02If
STOREY, Jno.		38	M	Unknown	05Ju02If
RYAN, Mary		41	F	Unknown	05Ju02If
Jno.		18	M	Unknown	05Ju02If
Mary		16	F	Unknown	05Ju02If
Honora		13	F	Unknown	05Ju02If
Judy		11	F	Unknown	05Ju02If
Cath.		8	F	Child	05Ju02If
Margt.		4	F	Child	05Ju02If
GAVIN, Pat		21	M	Unknown	05Ju02If
DUGGAN, Wm.		21	M	Unknown	05Ju02If
Mgt.		25	F	Unknown	05Ju02If
SMITH, Bridget		18	F	Unknown	05Ju02If
HAMILTON, Jno.		23	M	Unknown	05Ju02If
GOWAN, Pat		21	M	Unknown	05Ju02If
MOONEY, Ann		19	F	Unknown	05Ju02If
MAYORSON, Geo.		49	M	Unknown	05Ju02If
Isabella		47	F	Unknown	05Ju02If
Jno.		18	M	Unknown	05Ju02If
Jas.		16	M	Unknown	05Ju02If
Mgt.		18	F	Unknown	05Ju02If
Janet		14	F	Unknown	05Ju02If
Isabella		12	F	Unknown	05Ju02If
COONES, Jno.		25	M	Unknown	05Ju02If
ROURKE, Jas.		27	M	Unknown	05Ju02If
Biddy		25	F	Unknown	05Ju02If
DEVINE, Pat		30	M	Unknown	05Ju02If
Bartle		22	M	Unknown	05Ju02If
WHITE, Jno.		24	M	Unknown	05Ju02If
Anastalea		23	F	Unknown	05Ju02If

JAVA 05 JUNE 1849

From Bristol

NAMES OF PASSENGERS		AGE	SEX	OCCUPATIONS	DATE PORT SHIP
HAWKINS, William		28	M	Farmer	05Ju10AI
Sarah	(W)	25	F	None	05Ju10AI
Joseph	(S)	1	M	Child	05Ju10AI
Benjamin	(S)	1	M	Child	05Ju10AI
JEFFRIES, Robert		18	M	Laborer	05Ju10AI
BATTER, Hugh		20	M	Laborer	05Ju10AI
CARNLY, George		26	M	Painter	05Ju10AI
DAINSEN, Charles		29	M	Innkeeper	05Ju10AI
Eliza	(W)	27	F	None	05Ju10AI
Maria	(D)	.10	F	Infant	05Ju10AI
Sophie	(D)	3	F	Child	05Ju10AI
George	(S)	4	M	Child	05Ju10AI
HART, John		28	M	Laborer	05Ju10AI
PARSENS, Joseph		26	M	Laborer	05Ju10AI
Harriett	(W)	19	F	None	05Ju10AI
PEARSE, William		22	M	Plasterer	05Ju10AI
Augustin		23	M	Yeoman	05Ju10AI
ESTCOTT, Mary-Anne		29	F	Unknown	05Ju10AI
WESTCOTT, Bessey	(D)	10	F	None	05Ju10AI
Marianna	(D)	8	F	Child	05Ju10AI
GAY, Tir	(M)	8	F	Child	05Ju10AI
SPENCER, Henry		16	M	Shoemaker	05Ju10AI
FRY, Joseph		20	M	Farmer	05Ju10AI
LOTT, F.		19	M	Laborer	05Ju10AI
MOULTEN, Wm.		23	M	Laborer	05Ju10AI
WILLIAMS, John		42	M	Laborer	05Ju10AI
MILTEN, Wm.		32	M	Yeoman	05Ju10AI
Mary	(W)	28	F	None	05Ju10AI
Elizabeth	(D)	1	F	Child	05Ju10AI
STRINGE, Chas.		18	M	Laborer	05Ju10AI
HADE, Michl.		16	M	Laborer	05Ju10AI
HARKINS, Robt.		27	M	Laborer	05Ju10AI
Samuel		27	M	Laborer	05Ju10AI
SMITH, John		15	M	Laborer	05Ju10AI
PARKER, Robert		25	M	Mason	05Ju10AI
PITCHER, Edmund		48	M	Farmer	05Ju10AI
Mary	(D)	4	F	Child	05Ju10AI
Thomas	(S)	10	M	None	05Ju10AI
Prudence	(D)	8	F	Child	05Ju10AI
Edward	(S)	7	M	Child	05Ju10AI
Heleen	(S)	5	F	Child	05Ju10AI
WEEKS, James		29	M	Mason	05Ju10AI
Mary	(W)	28	F	None	05Ju10AI
Charles	(S)	3	M	Child	05Ju10AI
Mary	(D)	1	F	Child	05Ju10AI
HILL, Martha		22	F	Unknown	05Ju10AI
EVANS, Richard		21	M	Farmer	05Ju10AI
HAM, Henry		27	M	Farmer	05Ju10AI
Betsey	(W)	23	F	Farmer	05Ju10AI
Sarah	(D)	3	F	Child	05Ju10AI
Emily	(D)	1	F	Child	05Ju10AI
TAYLOR, George		19	M	Painter	05Ju10AI
Luke		22	M	Painter	05Ju10AI
WILCOX, Abbott		25	M	Farmer	05Ju10AI
BLACKMERE, Richd.		19	M	Laborer	05Ju10AI
STONE, Thomas		23	M	Engineer	05Ju10AI
Mary-Anne	(W)	19	F	None	05Ju10AI
BURGE, William		32	M	Plasterer	05Ju10AI
William-Jr.	(S)	10	M	None	05Ju10AI
HILL, John		24	M	Laborer	05Ju10AI
SULLIVAN, John		18	M	Laborer	05Ju10AI
James		23	M	Laborer	05Ju10AI
COOKE, Henry		26	M	Unknown	05Ju10AI
LYNE, Saml.		38	M	Carpenter	05Ju10AI
Anne	(W)	35	F	None	05Ju10AI
Anne	(D)	11	F	None	05Ju10AI
Saul	(S)	10	M	None	05Ju10AI
George	(S)	8	M	Child	05Ju10AI
Thomas	(S)	7	M	Child	05Ju10AI
Louisa	(D)	6	F	Child	05Ju10AI
Charles	(S)	4	M	Child	05Ju10AI
William	(S)	3	M	Child	05Ju10AI
Henry		1	M	Child	05Ju10AI
STACEY, William		45	M	Laborer	05Ju10AI
Anne	(W)	43	F	None	05Ju10AI
Mary	(D)	10	F	None	05Ju10AI
Honora	(D)	9	F	Child	05Ju10AI
Elizabeth	(D)	7	F	Child	05Ju10AI
Henry	(S)	5	M	Child	05Ju10AI
BRADFIELD, Saml.		40	M	Cordwainer	05Ju10AI
Patience	(W)	38	F	None	05Ju10AI
William	(S)	11	M	None	05Ju10AI
Thomas	(S)	8	M	Child	05Ju10AI
NOTT, William		24	M	Turner	05Ju10AI
Mary	(W)	25	F	None	05Ju10AI
HONEYWELL, Chas.		31	M	Carpenter	05Ju10AI
Susan	(W)	25	F	None	05Ju10AI
WEEKS, James		28	M	Laborer	05Ju10AI
FIELD, William		19	M	Laborer	05Ju10AI
SKINNER, Chas.		34	M	Laborer	05Ju10AI
Eliza	(W)	30	F	None	05Ju10AI
Thomas	(S)	6	M	Child	05Ju10AI
Stephen	(S)	4	M	Child	05Ju10AI

NAMES OF PASSENGERS		AGE	SEX	OCCUPATIONS	DATE PORT SHIP
HUNT, Elizabeth		19	F	Spinster	05Ju10Al
FRANKLING, Thomas		50	M	Farmer	05Ju10Al
Sarah	(W)	52	F	None	05Ju10Al
Thomas-Jr.	(S)	29	M	Farmer	05Ju10Al
William		17	M	Farmer	05Ju10Al
Phebe		22	F	Spinster	05Ju10Al
CATTLE, Henry-John		26	M	Unknown	05Ju10Al
DICKS, James		32	M	Laborer	05Ju10Al
Dinah	(W)	29	F	None	05Ju10Al
PRICE, William		29	M	Innkeeper	05Ju10Al
Anne	(W)	22	F	None	05Ju10Al
LANDER, Saml.		25	F	None	05Ju10Al
H-----, Robt.		23	M	Farmer	05Ju10Al
FREITHY, H.		24	M	Butcher	05Ju10Al
ARTHUR, Richd.Clean		30	M	Farmer	05Ju10Al
Mary	(W)	33	F	None	05Ju10Al
TAYLER, Thos.Tucker		42	M	Coppersmith	05Ju10Al
Elizabeth	(W)	38	F	None	05Ju10Al
James	(S)	9	M	Child	05Ju10Al
FAWKES, Hope		22	F	Spinster	05Ju10Al
HUDSON, Jesse		30	M	Cooper	05Ju10Al
STARR, William		26	M	Laborer	05Ju10Al
Sarah	(W)	23	F	None	05Ju10Al
KENNEDY, John		22	M	Laborer	05Ju10Al
HENNESSY, James		19	M	Unknown	05Ju10Al
BUTT, George		42	M	Unknown	05Ju10Al
Mary	(M)	40	F	None	05Ju10Al
Elisiah		35	M	Laborer	05Ju10Al
Ellen	(W)	29	F	None	05Ju10Al
Laura	(D)	6	F	Child	05Ju10Al
Frank	(S)	.10	M	Infant	05Ju10Al
Charles	(S)	2	M	Child	05Ju10Al
DUNCAN, James		29	M	Engineer	05Ju10Al
FRANCIS, Mary		23	F	Spinster	05Ju10Al
FRANKLING, Robt.		22	M	Engineer	05Ju10Al
Susan		11	F	None	05Ju10Al
BENSEN, John-James		23	M	Engineer	05Ju10Al
BUTLER, Isaac		22	M	Carpenter	05Ju10Al
Anne	(W)	19	F	None	05Ju10Al
GIBBONS, Robt.		39	M	Farmer	05Ju10Al
Anne	(W)	41	F	None	05Ju10Al
Adelaide	(D)	6	F	Child	05Ju10Al
Evan	(S)	3	M	Child	05Ju10Al
Agnes	(D)	2	F	Child	05Ju10Al
OATRIDGE, Robt.		19	M	Farmer	05Ju10Al
Elizabeth		27	F	Spinster	05Ju10Al
WEST, Luke		24	M	Farmer	05Ju10Al
WEBB, John		36	M	Laborer	05Ju10Al
Elizabeth	(W)	39	F	None	05Ju10Al
Charles	(S)	9	M	Child	05Ju10Al
Anna	(D)	8	F	Child	05Ju10Al
William	(S)	6	M	Child	05Ju10Al
George	(S)	2	M	Child	05Ju10Al
MILES, Mark		29	M	Miner	05Ju10Al
Mary	(W)	25	F	None	05Ju10Al
HERIN, William		34	M	Laborer	05Ju10Al
Anna	(W)	30	F	None	05Ju10Al
John	(S)	6	M	Child	05Ju10Al
Anna	(D)	4	F	Child	05Ju10Al
WELLS, Robt.		27	M	Laborer	05Ju10Al
Elizabeth		27	F	Laborer	05Ju10Al
BAKER, John		22	M	Accountant	05Ju10Al
TILLING, George		23	M	Laborer	05Ju10Al
SEYMOUR, Harry		19	M	Laborer	05Ju10Al
ORCHARD, John		38	M	Laborer	05Ju10Al
Jane-Anne	(W)	34	F	None	05Ju10Al
Guye	(S)	8	M	Child	05Ju10Al
Richard	(S)	7	M	Child	05Ju10Al
THOMAS, John		00	M	Accountant	05Ju10Al
Ann	(W)	00	F	None	05Ju10Al
PRIDAY, William		16	M	Seaman	05Ju10Al
ANDREWS, John		23	M	Laborer	05Ju10Al
Louisa	(W)	18	F	None	05Ju10Al
LEWIS, William		20	M	Miner	05Ju10Al
WILLIAMS, Hannah		27	F	W-Mnr	05Ju10Al
COOKE, Eliza		32	F	W-Mnr	05Ju10Al
Anne	(D)	1	F	Child	05Ju10Al
BOND, Harvey		32	M	Carpenter	05Ju10Al
William		23	M	Builder	05Ju10Al
HARPER, John		24	M	Farmer	05Ju10Al
MANNING, Nich.		25	M	Farmer	05Ju10Al
Ellen	(W)	19	F	None	05Ju10Al
HOUGH, Frederick		24	M	Tailor	05Ju10Al
Susan	(W)	25	F	None	05Ju10Al
ANSTIC, Jane		19	F	Spinster	05Ju10Al
LANDEN, Edw.		32	M	Engineer	05Ju10Al
Mary	(W)	35	F	None	05Ju10Al
William	(S)	10	M	None	05Ju10Al
Edw.	(S)	9	M	Child	05Ju10Al
Mary	(D)	6	F	Child	05Ju10Al
Eliza	(D)	2	F	Child	05Ju10Al
ALYCE, Chs.		28	M	Farmer	05Ju10Al
Caroline	(W)	23	F	None	05Ju10Al
FAY, Athaliah		33	F	W-Fmr	05Ju10Al
Mary-Anne	(D)	11	F	None	05Ju10Al
Elizabeth		10	F	None	05Ju10Al
Emma	(D)	8	F	Child	05Ju10Al
John	(S)	4	M	Child	05Ju10Al

EARL-OF-DURHAM 05 JUNE 1849

From London

NAMES OF PASSENGERS		AGE	SEX	OCCUPATIONS	DATE PORT SHIP
STEVENS, John		32	M	None	05Ju13Is
Jane		23	F	None	05Ju13Is
TAYLOR, Wm.		17	M	Unknown	05Ju13Is
STRELLY, Henry		20	M	Unknown	05Ju13Is
Emily		27	F	Unknown	05Ju13Is
CONSTABLE, John		32	M	Unknown	05Ju13Is
WALKER, Wm.		25	M	Unknown	05Ju13Is
Sarah		18	F	Unknown	05Ju13Is
HEFFERMAN, Timothy		30	M	Unknown	05Ju13Is
JENKINS, Lydia		30	F	Unknown	05Ju13Is
Wm.		5	M	Child	05Ju13Is
John		3	M	Child	05Ju13Is
Emma		1	F	Child	05Ju13Is
HUDSON, Wm.		30	M	Unknown	05Ju13Is
COLENE, Caroline		25	F	Unknown	05Ju13Is
CRAMER, Daniel		42	M	Unknown	05Ju13Is
LEE, John		27	M	Unknown	05Ju13Is
HOWARD, Henry		35	M	Mechanic	05Ju13Is
Fredk.		15	M	Mechanic	05Ju13Is
Walter		7	M	Child	05Ju13Is
JONES, Wm.		40	M	Mechanic	05Ju13Is
Edith		39	F	Mechanic	05Ju13Is
Francis		14	M	Mechanic	05Ju13Is
Edith		12	F	Mechanic	05Ju13Is
Emma		10	F	Mechanic	05Ju13Is
William		11	M	Mechanic	05Ju13Is
John		6	M	Child	05Ju13Is
Jane		6	F	Child	05Ju13Is
ALEXANDER, Wm.		1	M	Child	05Ju13Is
MATTHEWS, Wm.		17	M	Mechanic	05Ju13Is
Wm.		45	M	Mechanic	05Ju13I
Wm.		46	M	Mechanic	05Ju13I
Elizabeth		20	F	Mechanic	05Ju13I
Elizabeth		11	F	Mechanic	05Ju13I
ADDISON, Wm.		26	M	Mechanic	05Ju13I
Mary		21	F	None	05Ju13I
Robert		29	M	None	05Ju13I
OCONNELL, Richard		45	M	None	05Ju13I
AHERN, John		20	M	Laborer	05Ju13I
NICHOLAS, Mary		21	F	Laborer	05Ju13
WILLIAMSON, Wm.		35	M	Laborer	05Ju13

NAMES OF PASSENGERS	AGE	SEX	OCCUPATIONS	DATE PORT SHIP
ARNOLD, Geo.	23	M	Laborer	05Ju13ls
Eliza	21	F	Laborer	05Ju13ls
WALKER, Saml.	30	M	Laborer	05Ju13ls
Eliza	27	F	Laborer	05Ju13ls
NEHOME, Eliza	24	F	Laborer	05Ju13ls
Ada	1	F	Child	05Ju13ls
WHITEHOUSE, Mary-Ann	21	F	Laborer	05Ju13ls
Alfred	13	M	Laborer	05Ju13ls
Edward	26	M	Laborer	05Ju13ls
ROGERS, Wm.	00	M	Laborer	05Ju13ls
Martha	48	F	Laborer	05Ju13ls
Edwin	19	M	Unknown	05Ju13ls
Louisa	17	F	Unknown	05Ju13ls
Julia	15	F	Unknown	05Ju13ls
Emma	13	F	Unknown	05Ju13ls
George	21	M	Unknown	05Ju13ls
LEWIS, Anna	00	F	Unknown	05Ju13ls
MAGNESS, Phebe	17	F	Unknown	05Ju13ls
HAMILTON, John	54	M	Unknown	05Ju13ls
John	18	M	Unknown	05Ju13ls
WALKER, Henry	30	M	Unknown	05Ju13ls
BROWN, Geo.	23	M	Unknown	05Ju13ls
Sophia	20	F	Unknown	05Ju13ls
CORNWALL, Thos.	33	M	Unknown	05Ju13ls
David	32	M	Unknown	05Ju13ls
WALKER, John	28	M	Unknown	05Ju13ls
SCULLY, Margt.	24	F	Unknown	05Ju13ls
TAYLOR, Geo.	24	F	Unknown	05Ju13ls
Henry	21	M	Unknown	05Ju13ls
HEFFERMAN, John	28	M	Unknown	05Ju13ls
COLEMAN, John	42	M	Unknown	05Ju13ls
DOWMAN, Edwd.	25	M	Unknown	05Ju13ls
IMPETT, John	22	M	Unknown	05Ju13ls
MEDHERST, Wm.	44	M	Unknown	05Ju13ls
Ann	44	F	Unknown	05Ju13ls
Thos.	12	M	Unknown	05Ju13ls
Fredk.	7	M	Child	05Ju13ls
FAIRLESS, Ann	28	F	Unknown	05Ju13ls
HESLOP, Robt.	28	M	Unknown	05Ju13ls
Sarah	30	F	Unknown	05Ju13ls
HARRINGTON, Timothy	21	M	Unknown	05Ju13ls
RATCLIFFE, Wm.	40	M	Unknown	05Ju13ls
MOSER, Margt.	22	F	Unknown	05Ju13ls
Barbara	23	F	Unknown	05Ju13ls
SHEFFER, Catherine	30	F	Unknown	05Ju13ls
KNIGHT, Robt.	25	M	Unknown	05Ju13ls
RUTLEY, Robt.	25	M	Unknown	05Ju13ls
LAYCOCK, Jas.	24	M	Unknown	05Ju13ls
HENNESEY, Catherine	27	F	Unknown	05Ju13ls
SMITH, Marcus	30	M	Unknown	05Ju13ls
Henry	00	M	Unknown	05Ju13ls
ROBINSON, Edwd.	27	M	Unknown	05Ju13ls
U-Mrs.	24	F	Unknown	05Ju13ls
FELL, Thos.B.	41	M	Unknown	05Ju13ls
Mary-Ann	36	F	Unknown	05Ju13ls
Mary-Ann	18	F	Unknown	05Ju13ls
Jane	12	F	Unknown	05Ju13ls
Caroline	10	F	Unknown	05Ju13ls
Chas.	7	M	Child	05Ju13ls
Emma	8	F	Child	05Ju13ls
Margaret	6	F	Child	05Ju13ls
Eliza	5	F	Child	05Ju13ls
Harriet	10	F	Unknown	05Ju13ls
SUSAN, Chas.	40	M	Unknown	05Ju13ls
Esther-K.	13	F	Unknown	05Ju13ls
Kezia	37	U	Unknown	05Ju13ls
Chas.J.	9	M	Child	05Ju13ls
Joseph	7	M	Child	05Ju13ls
Geo.J.	6	M	Child	05Ju13ls
Alfred-H.	4	M	Child	05Ju13ls
Susan	2	F	Child	05Ju13ls
ASON, Thos.	24	M	Unknown	05Ju13ls
ULIER, Thos.	30	M	Unknown	05Ju13ls
EAD, Chas.	29	M	Unknown	05Ju13ls
JSAN, Mary-F.	62	F	Unknown	05Ju13ls
VETTE, Magdaline	25	F	Unknown	05Ju13ls
ECKERT, Thos.	26	F	Unknown	05Ju13ls
KELLY, Peter	22	M	Unknown	05Ju13ls
BANKS, Jane	76	F	Unknown	05Ju13ls
JOHNSTON, Mary-Ann	31	F	Unknown	05Ju13ls
Mary-Ann	14	F	Unknown	05Ju13ls
Margt.	13	F	Unknown	05Ju13ls
Jane	12	F	Unknown	05Ju13ls
John	7	M	Child	05Ju13ls
Anne	8	F	Child	05Ju13ls
Helen	4	F	Child	05Ju13ls
HUGHES, John	48	M	Unknown	05Ju13ls
Mary	42	F	Unknown	05Ju13ls
ROTH, Lewis	42	M	Unknown	05Ju13ls
Emma	24	F	Unknown	05Ju13ls
HOFFMAN, Edwd.	50	M	Unknown	05Ju13ls
SPOLER, Fred	40	M	Unknown	05Ju13ls
HOBSON, John	21	M	Unknown	05Ju13ls
Margt.	20	M	Unknown	05Ju13ls
STEEN, Geo.	44	M	Unknown	05Ju13ls
Hannah	42	F	Unknown	05Ju13ls
Edward	21	M	Unknown	05Ju13ls
Emma	17	F	Unknown	05Ju13ls
Ann	10	F	Unknown	05Ju13ls
SMITH, Alex.	18	M	Unknown	05Ju13ls
SUSAN, Mary-Ann	11	F	Unknown	05Ju13ls

JANE 05 JUNE 1849

From Cork

NAMES OF PASSENGERS	AGE	SEX	OCCUPATIONS	DATE PORT SHIP
COLLINS, Catharine	32	F	Servant	05Ju08lb
MANSFIELD, P.	29	M	Laborer	05Ju08lb
RIELY, J.	40	M	Laborer	05Ju08lb
SULLIVAN, J.	36	M	Laborer	05Ju08lb
TERRY, J.	29	M	Laborer	05Ju08lb
HOXSON, T.	26	M	Farmer	05Ju08lb
J.	31	M	Farmer	05Ju08lb
Mary	19	F	Farmer	05Ju08lb
FLEMING, Thos.	20	M	Farmer	05Ju08lb
A.	23	M	Farmer	05Ju08lb
B.	18	M	Farmer	05Ju08lb
GEARY, Thomas	41	M	Farmer	05Ju08lb
Mary	38	F	Servant	05Ju08lb
OBRIEN, Mary	26	F	Servant	05Ju08lb
CUNNINGHAM, T.	19	M	Farmer	05Ju08lb
Pat	32	M	Farmer	05Ju08lb
HEERY, Mary	43	F	Farmer	05Ju08lb
CONWAY, William	19	M	Laborer	05Ju08lb
BERRY, Mary	11	F	Servant	05Ju08lb
MURPHY, C.	26	M	Unknown	05Ju08lb
BAGE, T.	34	M	Unknown	05Ju08lb
NAVON, T.	32	M	Unknown	05Ju08lb
MAGNER, M.	30	M	Unknown	05Ju08lb
COSHMAN, M.	28	M	Unknown	05Ju08lb
DUGGAN, W.	31	M	Unknown	05Ju08lb
Ally	00	F	Unknown	05Ju08lb
HERRAN, Mary	26	F	Unknown	05Ju08lb
DUGGAN, Jane	24	F	Unknown	05Ju08lb
Ally	23	F	Unknown	05Ju08lb
M.	00	M	Unknown	05Ju08lb
E.	41	M	Unknown	05Ju08lb
D.	10	M	Unknown	05Ju08lb
RYAN, E.	30	M	Unknown	05Ju08lb
P.	28	M	Unknown	05Ju08lb
E.	18	M	Unknown	05Ju08lb
E.	17	M	Unknown	05Ju08lb
P.	14	M	Unknown	05Ju08lb
Jh.	12	M	Unknown	05Ju08lb

NAMES OF PASSENGERS	AGE	SEX	OCCUPATIONS	DATE PORT SHIP
BARRY, Peggy	10	F	Unknown	05Ju08lb
MILLINEK, T.	27	M	Unknown	05Ju08lb
CONWAY, T.	20	M	Unknown	05Ju08lb
NAVON, E.	22	M	Unknown	05Ju08lb
KELLY, Daylen	30	M	Unknown	05Ju08lb
ONEILL, Mary	20	F	Unknown	05Ju08lb
POWER, John	34	M	Unknown	05Ju08lb
MONOFARY, John	14	M	Unknown	05Ju08lb
CONDON, Pat.	30	M	Unknown	05Ju08lb
FLEMING, R.	30	M	Farmer	05Ju08lb
R.	30	M	Farmer	05Ju08lb

MANILA 05 JUNE 1849

From Liverpool

NAMES OF PASSENGERS	AGE	SEX	OCCUPATIONS	DATE PORT SHIP
MATTISON, Wm.	23	M	Unknown	05Ju02lv
NEILL, John	17	M	Unknown	05Ju02lv
COMMON, Mich.	40	M	Unknown	05Ju02lv
Mary	14	F	Unknown	05Ju02lv
SULLIVAN, Roger	27	M	Unknown	05Ju02lv
CURRAN, John	38	M	Unknown	05Ju02lv
Mary	30	F	Unknown	05Ju02lv
CARTY, Dennis	20	M	Unknown	05Ju02lv
MAHONEY, Mary	35	F	Unknown	05Ju02lv
Cornelius	11	M	Unknown	05Ju02lv
John	9	M	Child	05Ju02lv
HOWARD, Mick	22	M	Unknown	05Ju02lv
Ellen	4	F	Child	05Ju02lv
Mary	3	F	Child	05Ju02lv
SHEEHAN, Mary	13	F	Unknown	05Ju02lv
MCAULIFFE, Denis	20	M	Unknown	05Ju02lv
FLAHERTY, U	21	M	Doctor	05Ju02lv
RIVELLER, Ellen	7	F	Child	05Ju02lv
Edward	26	M	Unknown	05Ju02lv
BYRNE, John	21	M	Unknown	05Ju02lv
CORVEY, James	15	M	Unknown	05Ju02lv
CAFFREY, Rose	19	M	Unknown	05Ju02lv
Ellen	11	F	Unknown	05Ju02lv
Margt.	13	F	Unknown	05Ju02lv
LAWLER, Mich.	9	M	Child	05Ju02lv
SMITH, Thos.	11	M	Unknown	05Ju02lv
Emma	24	F	Unknown	05Ju02lv
Isabelle	46	F	Unknown	05Ju02lv
LANE, Sarah	30	F	Unknown	05Ju02lv
HOLDEN, John	2	M	Child	05Ju02lv
MCELAINE, Thos.	13	M	Unknown	05Ju02lv
CARSEY, Thos.	29	M	Unknown	05Ju02lv
MCDONALD, U-Mrs.	24	F	Unknown	05Ju02lv
GREELY, Maria	20	F	Unknown	05Ju02lv
NOOLAN, Ann	25	F	Unknown	05Ju02lv
MCGERSEY, Margt.	6	F	Child	05Ju02lv
CONNOR, Margt.	4	F	Child	05Ju02lv
Mary	2	F	Child	05Ju02lv
STIRCH, Jas.	30	M	Unknown	05Ju02lv
WASON, Pat.	28	M	Unknown	05Ju02lv
CASILL, A.	40	U	Unknown	05Ju02lv
MCDONNELL, Cath.	35	F	Unknown	05Ju02lv
CARROLL, Mary	37	F	Unknown	05Ju02lv
AKINSON, Wm.	40	M	Unknown	05Ju02lv
Thos.	18	M	Unknown	05Ju02lv
ATKINS, Isabella	11	F	Unknown	05Ju02lv
William	56	M	Unknown	05Ju02lv
FLANAGAN, John	30	M	Unknown	05Ju02lv
RYAN, A.	24	U	Unknown	05Ju02lv
BRACH, Mark	23	M	Unknown	05Ju02lv
CLARK, Francis	27	M	Unknown	05Ju02lv
U-Mrs. (W)	27	F	Unknown	05Ju02lv
Harriet	8	F	Child	05Ju02lv

NAMES OF PASSENGERS	AGE	SEX	OCCUPATIONS	DATE PORT SHIP
CLARK, John	6	M	Child	05Ju02lv
Susanna	3	F	Child	05Ju02lv
BURKE, Rose	30	U	Unknown	05Ju02lv
Wm.	22	M	Unknown	05Ju02lv
Ann	13	F	Unknown	05Ju02lv
HAY, Robert	27	M	Unknown	05Ju02lv
U-Mrs. (W)	27	F	Unknown	05Ju02lv
U	.00	U	Infant	05Ju02lv
Jas.	5	M	Child	05Ju02lv
Richard	3	M	Child	05Ju02lv
CONNOR, Denis	22	M	Unknown	05Ju02lv
L--	20	U	Unknown	05Ju02lv
NULLY, Eliza	18	F	Unknown	05Ju02lv
Susan	16	F	Unknown	05Ju02lv
HICKEY, U	30	M	Unknown	05Ju02lv
John	20	M	Unknown	05Ju02lv
Mich.	7	M	Child	05Ju02lv
DUFFY, Mich.	30	M	Unknown	05Ju02lv
MCAVERY, H.	30	U	Unknown	05Ju02lv
Thos.	26	M	Unknown	05Ju02lv
Ellen	89	F	Unknown	05Ju02lv
Elisa.	24	F	Unknown	05Ju02lv
RUSSELL, M.	34	U	Unknown	05Ju02lv
HARRISON, John	34	M	Unknown	05Ju02lv
KELLY, Margt.	26	F	Unknown	05Ju02lv
CLEAR, Mary	28	F	Unknown	05Ju02lv
WILLIAMS, Ben	44	F	Unknown	05Ju02lv
U-Mrs.	40	F	Unknown	05Ju02lv
Ben	13	M	Unknown	05Ju02lv
Ann	8	F	Child	05Ju02lv
John	10	M	Child	05Ju02lv
CARTY, Mich.	29	M	Unknown	05Ju02lv
Wm.	10	M	Child	05Ju02lv
GLEASSON, Wm.	24	M	Unknown	05Ju02lv
MEYHER, Denis	21	M	Unknown	05Ju02lv
FLANAGAN, Jas.	19	M	Unknown	05Ju02lv
Judy	24	F	Unknown	05Ju02lv
Bridget	15	F	Unknown	05Ju02lv
KENEDY, Margt.	15	F	Unknown	05Ju02lv
NAUGHTON, John	24	M	Unknown	05Ju02lv
KELLY, John	26	M	Unknown	05Ju02lv
Ellen	26	F	Unknown	05Ju02lv
U	.00	U	Infant	05Ju02lv
Pat	26	M	Unknown	05Ju02lv
SHANAHAN, Pat	2	M	Child	05Ju02lv
HACKEY, Ca--	20	U	Unknown	05Ju02lv
RYDER, Dan	22	M	Unknown	05Ju02lv
Mary	30	F	Unknown	05Ju02lv
Quinn	18	M	Unknown	05Ju02lv
MCCAFFREY, Dennis	25	M	Unknown	05Ju02lv
MALLEN, Jas.	21	M	Unknown	05Ju02lv
BRADY, Ed.	26	M	Unknown	05Ju02lv
CAHILL, John	26	M	Unknown	05Ju02lv
Ann	2	F	Child	05Ju02lv
Margt.	32	F	Child	05Ju02lv
CORCOREN, Pat.	31	M	Unknown	05Ju02lv
Margt.	29	F	Unknown	05Ju02lv
U	.00	U	Infant	05Ju02lv
Ellen	25	F	Unknown	05Ju02lv
Ann	35	F	Unknown	05Ju02lv
BLACKLIN, John	35	M	Unknown	05Ju02lv
ALEXANDER, John	22	M	Unknown	05Ju02lv
CONWAY, John	20	M	Unknown	05Ju02lv
Judy	19	F	Unknown	05Ju02lv
MURPHY, Jas.	17	M	Unknown	05Ju02lv
John	15	M	Unknown	05Ju02lv
Cath.	9	F	Child	05Ju02lv
Bridget	20	F	Unknown	05Ju02lv
Ellen	16	F	Unknown	05Ju02lv
Cath.	40	F	Unknown	05Ju02lv
JONES, Wm.	30	M	Unknown	05Ju02lv
ROBSON, John	21	M	Unknown	05Ju02lv
WHITSON, Denis	23	M	Unknown	05Ju02lv
Margt.	21	F	Unknown	05Ju02lv
COSGREN, John	20	M	Unknown	05Ju02lv

NAMES OF PASSENGERS	AGE	SEX	OCCUPATIONS	DATE PORT SHIP
COONEY, Pat.	25	M	Unknown	05Ju02lv
Margt.	12	F	Unknown	05Ju02lv
Pat.	10	M	Unknown	05Ju02lv
Mary	6	F	Unknown	05Ju02lv
CARROLL, Pat	40	M	Unknown	05Ju02lv
Cath.	35	F	Unknown	05Ju02lv
U	.00	U	Infant	05Ju02lv
Phil.	12	M	Unknown	05Ju02lv
Tim.	10	M	Unknown	05Ju02lv
John	8	M	Child	05Ju02lv
Wm.	6	M	Child	05Ju02lv
Cent.	4	U	Child	05Ju02lv
RYAN, John	00	M	Unknown	05Ju02lv
Henry	00	M	Unknown	05Ju02lv
POWERS, Mich.	00	M	Unknown	05Ju02lv
MUCH, Elisa	00	M	Unknown	05Ju02lv
CARROLL, Wm.	00	M	Unknown	05Ju02lv
NEWLEN, Thos.	50	M	Unknown	05Ju02lv
REDMON, Mich.	00	M	Unknown	05Ju02lv
WHEELAN, Pat.	60	M	Unknown	05Ju02lv
MOORE, Mary	00	F	Unknown	05Ju02lv
John	00	F	Unknown	05Ju02lv
MAHER, Pat.	17	F	Unknown	05Ju02lv
KELLY, U	00	F	Unknown	05Ju02lv
LYNCH, Dan.	00	F	Unknown	05Ju02lv
WILSON, Sarah	18	F	Unknown	05Ju02lv
A.	00	U	Unknown	05Ju02lv
John	00	M	Unknown	05Ju02lv
Robert	00	M	Unknown	05Ju02lv
Racine	00	U	Unknown	05Ju02lv
CLARKE, Wm.	00	M	Unknown	05Ju02lv
DOLLAN, John	00	M	Unknown	05Ju02lv
DOLAN, Cath.	40	F	Unknown	05Ju02lv
Mich.	28	M	Unknown	05Ju02lv
CRATTY, Mich.	30	M	Unknown	05Ju02lv
FITRINGERALD, Ellen	00	F	Unknown	05Ju02lv
ONEIL, Cat.	00	F	Unknown	05Ju02lv
MAHER, Mich.	16	M	Unknown	05Ju02lv
WHEELAN, Pat.	00	M	Unknown	05Ju02lv
PURCELL, Rose	70	M	Unknown	05Ju02lv
GUINN, C.	00	M	Unknown	05Ju02lv
CONWELL, Dick	4	M	Child	05Ju02lv
Bren---, Pat.	5	M	Child	05Ju02lv
SHEA, Celia	00	F	Unknown	05Ju02lv
BARRIGAN, Wm.	10	M	Child	05Ju02lv
Jas.	6	M	Child	05Ju02lv
DERRY, John	8	M	Child	05Ju02lv
Jas.	12	M	Unknown	05Ju02lv
FLYN, Thos.	40	M	Unknown	05Ju02lv
MORING, Th.	42	M	Unknown	05Ju02lv
MURPHY, Pat.	23	M	Unknown	05Ju02lv
WALLNUTT, Chris.	25	M	Unknown	05Ju02lv
ROBESON, John	60	M	Unknown	05Ju02lv
BURNS, Pat.	41	M	Unknown	05Ju02lv
John	20	M	Unknown	05Ju02lv
Ann	18	F	Unknown	05Ju02lv
Magt.	12	F	Unknown	05Ju02lv
COTT, Wm.	40	M	Unknown	05Ju02lv
OOLEY, Ed.	30	M	Unknown	05Ju02lv
URLEY, U-Mr.	28	U	Unknown	05Ju02lv
EWMAN, Thos.	25	M	Unknown	05Ju02lv
UNLOP, Hugh	41	M	Unknown	05Ju02lv
TEWART, Wm.	60	M	Unknown	05Ju02lv
OOLEY, Ed.	38	M	Unknown	05Ju02lv
URLEY, U-Mr.	27	M	Unknown	05Ju02lv
EWMAN, Thos.	29	M	Unknown	05Ju02lv
NLOP, Hugh	31	M	Unknown	05Ju02lv
TEWART, Wm.	27	M	Unknown	05Ju02lv
RPHY, D.	25	M	Unknown	05Ju02lv
GUIRE, John	26	M	Unknown	05Ju02lv
DOUGH, U-Mr.	30	M	Unknown	05Ju02lv
Mary	28	F	Unknown	05Ju02lv
EIL, J.	18	M	Unknown	05Ju02lv
NE, Jos.	19	M	Unknown	05Ju02lv
Sarah	10	F	Child	05Ju02lv
KANE, Pat.	12	M	Unknown	05Ju02lv
STELE, Lucy	40	F	Unknown	05Ju02lv
CARRAGH, F.	30	F	Unknown	05Ju02lv
Wm.	12	M	Unknown	05Ju02lv
John	10	M	Child	05Ju02lv
Hannah	8	F	Child	05Ju02lv
Joseph	6	M	Child	05Ju02lv
DIXON, Thos.	38	M	Unknown	05Ju02lv
Judy	36	F	Unknown	05Ju02lv
Joseph	6	M	Child	05Ju02lv
PICKENS, Thos.	6	M	Child	05Ju02lv
U-Mrs.	21	F	Unknown	05Ju02lv
Sarah	20	F	Unknown	05Ju02lv
Mary	18	F	Unknown	05Ju02lv
Harold	12	M	Unknown	05Ju02lv
Ian	6	M	Child	05Ju02lv
Hugh	4	M	Child	05Ju02lv
WALLACE, B.	40	M	Unknown	05Ju02lv
Mary	38	F	Unknown	05Ju02lv
Ann	12	F	Unknown	05Ju02lv
John	10	M	Child	05Ju02lv
Watson	6	M	Child	05Ju02lv
Hannah	8	F	Child	05Ju02lv
Thos.	4	M	Child	05Ju02lv
Jas.	3	M	Child	05Ju02lv
HETHINGTON, Mary	28	F	Unknown	05Ju02lv
Joseph	30	M	Unknown	05Ju02lv
SIMPSON, Joseph	22	M	Unknown	05Ju02lv
CARROLL, Bridget	6	F	Child	05Ju02lv

ASHLAND 05 JUNE 1849

From Liverpool

NAMES OF PASSENGERS	AGE	SEX	OCCUPATIONS	DATE PORT SHIP
KEARNY, Michael	22	M	Laborer	05Ju02lk
MURRAY, Michael	24	M	Tailor	05Ju02lk
HARRISON, Catherine	45	F	Unknown	05Ju02lk
Martin	4	M	Child	05Ju02lk
Catherine	2	F	Child	05Ju02lk
MCDERMOTT, Thos.	30	M	Mason	05Ju02lk
MORRISON, John	28	M	Mason	05Ju02lk
DOHERTY, Michael	35	M	Rope Maker	05Ju02lk
Mary	24	F	Unknown	05Ju02lk
U	.00	U	Infant	05Ju02lk
NEARY, Maria	30	F	Unknown	05Ju02lk
HAMILTON, Wm.	25	M	Laborer	05Ju02lk
COLLINS, Ed.	18	M	Laborer	05Ju02lk
LYNCH, Michael	50	M	Farmer	05Ju02lk
Michael-Jr.	26	M	Farmer	05Ju02lk
Betty	24	F	Unknown	05Ju02lk
Ann	21	F	Unknown	05Ju02lk
CORCORAN, John	26	M	Farmer	05Ju02lk
MURRAY, John	35	M	Laborer	05Ju02lk
Alice	25	F	Unknown	05Ju02lk
BERRIGAN, John	29	M	Baker	05Ju02lk
REILLY, Owen	25	M	Laborer	05Ju02lk
BYRNE, Jas.	21	M	Laborer	05Ju02lk
WALCH, John	24	M	Laborer	05Ju02lk
KING, Jas.	24	M	Laborer	05Ju02lk
MURPHY, Thos.	30	M	Laborer	05Ju02lk
SHORTELL, P.	29	M	Laborer	05Ju02lk
WHELAN, Jsa.	31	M	Laborer	05Ju02lk
CAMPION, Patt	20	M	Laborer	05Ju02lk
BATES, Jas.	20	M	Laborer	05Ju02lk
KEVAN, Bridget	25	F	Unknown	05Ju02lk
RIDDY, Ellen	24	F	Unknown	05Ju02lk
MULLY, Judy	25	F	Unknown	05Ju02lk
KEEFEE, Judy	30	F	Unknown	05Ju02lk
POWELL, Mary	45	F	Unknown	05Ju02lk

NAMES OF PASSENGERS	AGE	SEX	OCCUPATIONS	DATE PORT SHIP
HARDEN, Jas.	42	M	Laborer	05Ju02lk
OBRIEN, Margaret	19	F	Unknown	05Ju02lk
HOGAN, Edward	48	M	Clerk	05Ju02lk
CLARK, Thos.	50	M	Laborer	05Ju02lk
Ann	48	F	Unknown	05Ju02lk
Jas.	19	M	Unknown	05Ju02lk
Mary-Ann	17	F	Unknown	05Ju02lk
Joseph	3	M	Child	05Ju02lk
GRAHAM, John	18	M	Laborer	05Ju02lk
THOMPSON, Sarah	23	F	Laborer	05Ju02lk
RYAN, John	40	M	Mason	05Ju02lk
LALLY, John	24	M	Blacksmith	05Ju02lk
STRAHAN, Andrew	20	M	Laborer	05Ju02lk
OWENS, Edward	21	M	Laborer	05Ju02lk
TOOLE, John	24	M	Laborer	05Ju02lk
MURRAY, Patt	35	M	Laborer	05Ju02lk
GARGAN, John	25	M	Blacksmith	05Ju02lk
RELLIGAN, Michael	28	M	Laborer	05Ju02lk
OCONNER, Morris	18	M	Laborer	05Ju02lk
KANE, Wm.	35	M	Laborer	05Ju02lk
Michael	32	M	Laborer	05Ju02lk
Biddy	30	F	Laborer	05Ju02lk
BELSON, Ann	40	F	Unknown	05Ju02lk
Edward	14	M	Unknown	05Ju02lk
BARRETT, Thos.	21	M	Unknown	05Ju02lk
DARCY, John	25	M	Laborer	05Ju02lk
FAUSEY, Margaret	24	F	Unknown	05Ju02lk
FAHY, Bridget	19	F	Unknown	05Ju02lk
Mary	7	F	Child	05Ju02lk
REILLY, Jas.	24	M	Farmer	05Ju02lk
Mary	20	F	Unknown	05Ju02lk
Julia	18	F	Unknown	05Ju02lk
FITZPATRICK, Patt	38	M	Unknown	05Ju02lk
Mary	33	F	Unknown	05Ju02lk
U	.00	U	Infant	05Ju02lk
Cath.	7	F	Child	05Ju02lk
Mary	4	F	Child	05Ju02lk
ROCHE, Danl.	35	M	Blacksmith	05Ju02lk
Ann	30	F	Unknown	05Ju02lk
DONOVAN, Danl.	45	M	Laborer	05Ju02lk
Ellen	35	F	Laborer	05Ju02lk
U	.00	U	Infant	05Ju02lk
Michael	2	M	Child	05Ju02lk
BRENNAN, Margaret	45	F	Unknown	05Ju02lk
GALLIGHAR, Edward	24	M	Laborer	05Ju02lk
CONNELL, Richard	45	M	Laborer	05Ju02lk
Mary	40	F	Unknown	05Ju02lk
U	.00	U	Infant	05Ju02lk
Catherine	11	F	Unknown	05Ju02lk
Ellen	9	F	Child	05Ju02lk
Philip	7	M	Child	05Ju02lk
John	5	M	Child	05Ju02lk
Mary	2	F	Child	05Ju02lk
CANTWELL, Mathew	30	M	Laborer	05Ju02lk
Rose	28	F	Unknown	05Ju02lk
Henry	18	M	Unknown	05Ju02lk
Biff	15	M	Unknown	05Ju02lk
CONDOR, Jas.	30	M	Laborer	05Ju02lk
KERWAN, Jas.	30	M	Laborer	05Ju02lk
SPELMAN, Martin	29	M	Laborer	05Ju02lk
CONNELL, Jas.	25	M	Laborer	05Ju02lk
FOLEY, Wm.	20	M	Laborer	05Ju02lk
Michael	18	M	Laborer	05Ju02lk
CONNELL, Norry	24	F	Unknown	05Ju02lk
GRAY, Catherine	20	F	Unknown	05Ju02lk
KELLY, John	30	M	Laborer	05Ju02lk
COLLUM, Thos.	50	M	Laborer	05Ju02lk
Betsey	35	F	Unknown	05Ju02lk
U	.00	U	Infant	05Ju02lk
DOYLE, Mary	18	F	Unknown	05Ju02lk
Margaret	17	F	Unknown	05Ju02lk
FARELL, Ann	19	F	Unknown	05Ju02lk
DONOHOE, Catherine	20	F	Unknown	05Ju02lk
DUGGAN, Rose	20	F	Unknown	05Ju02lk
MADDEN, Morris	30	M	Laborer	05Ju02lk
MADDEN, Jas.	28	M	Laborer	05Ju02lk
Martin	22	M	Laborer	05Ju02lk
Pat	19	M	Unknown	05Ju02lk
KENNEDY, John	14	M	Unknown	05Ju02lk
Ellen	17	F	Unknown	05Ju02lk
QUINLAN, Biddy	16	F	Unknown	05Ju02lk
KEEFEE, Catherine	45	F	Unknown	05Ju02lk
Patrick	12	M	Unknown	05Ju02lk
Catherine	9	F	Child	05Ju02lk
COLLINS, John	55	M	Laborer	05Ju02lk
Mary	50	F	Unknown	05Ju02lk
Margaret	14	F	Unknown	05Ju02lk
RIELLY, Bridget	25	F	Unknown	05Ju02lk
MALIN, Bitsy	22	F	Unknown	05Ju02lk
WALSH, John	50	M	Laborer	05Ju02lk
Ellen	15	F	Unknown	05Ju02lk
Catherine	8	F	Child	05Ju02lk
William	6	M	Child	05Ju02lk
BRADLY, Jas.	35	M	Laborer	05Ju02lk
Betty	25	F	Unknown	05Ju02lk
FITZGERALD, Johanna	17	F	Unknown	05Ju02lk
MCCABE, Ann	21	F	Unknown	05Ju02lk
LEARY, Thos.	55	M	Carpenter	05Ju02lk
Margaret	50	F	Unknown	05Ju02lk
Patrick	13	M	Unknown	05Ju02lk
John	10	M	Unknown	05Ju02lk
Margaret	7	F	Child	05Ju02lk
William	4	F	Child	05Ju02lk
Ann	2	F	Child	05Ju02lk
MCAVOY, Jane	26	F	Unknown	05Ju02lk
Catherine	23	F	Unknown	05Ju02lk
CONNOR, John	30	M	Farmer	05Ju02lk
BRIEN, Danl.	26	M	Carpenter	05Ju02lk
FEARAN, Michael	32	M	Laborer	05Ju02lk
SPELMAN, Jas.	28	M	Laborer	05Ju02lk
DOYLE, Lawrence	24	M	Laborer	05Ju02lk
TOOLE, Peter	25	M	Laborer	05Ju02lk
CONNERY, Joseph	24	M	Laborer	05Ju02lk
DOOLEY, John	27	M	Laborer	05Ju02lk
MCDONOUGH, Michael	23	M	Laborer	05Ju02lk
DUNN, Thomas	18	M	Laborer	05Ju02lk
MURPHY, Patt	25	M	Laborer	05Ju02lk
PUSDEN, Tesina	24	M	Saddler	05Ju02lk
BRIEN, Patt	20	M	Laborer	05Ju02lk
MURRAY, Mary	18	F	Laborer	05Ju02lk
DAWNE, John	40	M	Laborer	05Ju02lk
MCGUIRE, Thos.	40	M	Laborer	05Ju02lk
KEEFER, Patt	22	M	Laborer	05Ju02lk
RIELLY, Jas.	30	M	Laborer	05Ju02lk
MCNALLY, Patt	25	M	Laborer	05Ju02lk
KELLY, Jas.	30	M	Laborer	05Ju02lk
GALLAHER, Betsey	24	F	Unknown	05Ju02lk
FOSSICH, Thos.	30	M	Mason	05Ju02lk
CASEY, Patrick	25	M	Mason	05Ju02lk
GILMOUR, Patrick	23	M	Farmer	05Ju02lk
Margaret	22	F	Unknown	05Ju02lk
U	.00	U	Infant	05Ju02lk
CLUNN, Robt.	30	M	Laborer	05Ju02lk
BROWN, Patrick	40	M	Laborer	05Ju02lk
John	38	M	Laborer	05Ju02lk
Catherine	40	F	Unknown	05Ju02lk
MCCABE, Mary	35	F	Unknown	05Ju02lk
REDDYT, John	24	M	Laborer	05Ju02lk
DIVINE, Ann	50	F	Unknown	05Ju02lk
Patk.	12	M	Unknown	05Ju02lk
BROWN, Michael	40	M	Laborer	05Ju02lk
Ellen	30	F	Unknown	05Ju02l
COUGHLAN, Patrick	20	M	Laborer	05Ju02l
Johanna	18	F	Unknown	05Ju02l
Mary	15	F	Unknown	05Ju02l
FITZGERALD, Bridget	30	F	Unknown	05Ju02l
BARRY, John	45	M	Laborer	05Ju02l
LAVERTY, John	22	M	Baker	05Ju02l
MAHON, John	28	M	Laborer	05Ju02
GREENWOOD, Robt.	20	M	Laborer	05Ju02

NAMES OF PASSENGERS	AGE	SEX	OCCUPATIONS	DATE PORT SHIP
BUCKLEY, John	21	M	Tailor	05Ju02lk

NIAGARA 05 JUNE 1849

From Liverpool

NAMES OF PASSENGERS	AGE	SEX	OCCUPATIONS	DATE PORT SHIP
WILSON, U	36	M	Merchant	05Ju02lg
BAUER, G.B.	25	M	Merchant	05Ju02lg
REDDY, U-Mrs.	39	F	Lady	05Ju02lg
Wm.	20	M	Mechanic	05Ju02lg
James	18	M	Mechanic	05Ju02lg
ARROWSMITH, Wm.	33	M	Mechanic	05Ju02lg

A.Z. 05 JUNE 1849

From Liverpool

NAMES OF PASSENGERS	AGE	SEX	OCCUPATIONS	DATE PORT SHIP
DARES, U	20	F	Unknown	05Ju02lp
Jane	25	F	Unknown	05Ju02lp
BURNS, Tim	30	M	Laborer	05Ju02lp
CAFFREY, Judy	16	F	Servant	05Ju02lp
HOEY, Ann	16	F	Servant	05Ju02lp
Rose	9	F	Child	05Ju02lp
GLAGHY, Wm.	48	M	Clerk	05Ju02lp
Sarah	10	F	Servant	05Ju02lp
Margret	8	F	Child	05Ju02lp
Ellen	6	F	Child	05Ju02lp
MCALEER, Mary	48	F	Servant	05Ju02lp
Ellen	20	F	Servant	05Ju02lp
Hugh	12	M	Servant	05Ju02lp
ROURKE, Ed.	18	M	Servant	05Ju02lp
MCKERNAN, Pat	22	M	Laborer	05Ju02lp
BEARD, James	16	M	Laborer	05Ju02lp
Margret	30	F	Laborer	05Ju02lp
Michall	9	M	Child	05Ju02lp
Margret	10	F	Unknown	05Ju02lp
GINN, Thos.	29	M	Laborer	05Ju02lp
HIGGINS, Pat	30	M	Laborer	05Ju02lp
MCSHERRY, Margt.	25	F	Laborer	05Ju02lp
MILINNON, Cath.	31	F	Laborer	05Ju02lp
Bigt.	21	F	Servant	05Ju02lp
ACKESON, Alex.	10	M	Servant	05Ju02lp
Thos.	8	M	Child	05Ju02lp
MARTIN, Morris	24	M	Laborer	05Ju02lp
BLYAND, Ellen	26	F	Laborer	05Ju02lp
HAMILTON, Henry	23	M	Gdnr	05Ju02lp
KALAKER, Pat	20	M	Laborer	05Ju02lp
CLEAR, Thos.	22	M	Laborer	05Ju02lp
RYAN, Sam	25	M	Laborer	05Ju02lp
HAMILTON, Rachel	20	F	Unknown	05Ju02lp
MCQUESTIN, Esther	18	F	Unknown	05Ju02lp
SULLIVAN, Mary	24	F	Unknown	05Ju02lp
SIMMINS, Cath.	24	F	Unknown	05Ju02lp
HUGH, Pat	20	M	Laborer	05Ju02lp
TERELL, Judy	20	F	Servant	05Ju02lp
OCALLAGHAN, Mary	40	F	Unknown	05Ju02lp
Robt.	13	M	Unknown	05Ju02lp
Pat	11	M	Unknown	05Ju02lp
Danl.	9	M	Child	05Ju02lp
Maria	7	F	Child	05Ju02lp
Thos.	5	M	Child	05Ju02lp
AVANAGH, John	36	M	Laborer	05Ju02lp
CHUGH, Danl.	20	M	Laborer	05Ju02lp
MCHUGH, Peter	18	M	Laborer	05Ju02lp
MCGUIRE, Margret	20	F	Unknown	05Ju02lp
BREEN, Sarah	11	F	Unknown	05Ju02lp
KEATING, John	40	M	Laborer	05Ju02lp
ANGTEY, Ellen	20	F	Laborer	05Ju02lp
MEHAN, Anna	18	F	Laborer	05Ju02lp
SMITH, Brigt.	50	F	Laborer	05Ju02lp
MCENROE, Rose	16	F	Laborer	05Ju02lp
TALLY, Michal	23	M	Laborer	05Ju02lp
MCENROE, Pat	33	M	Laborer	05Ju02lp
Margret	50	F	Laborer	05Ju02lp
Margret	11	F	Laborer	05Ju02lp
Mary	8	F	Child	05Ju02lp
Peter	4	M	Child	05Ju02lp
Margret	7	F	Child	05Ju02lp
RYAND, Ellen	23	F	Unknown	05Ju02lp
LODAN, Mary	40	F	Unknown	05Ju02lp
CLARKIN, Susan	10	F	Unknown	05Ju02lp
RYAN, John	25	M	Shoemaker	05Ju02lp
COONEY, Saml.	32	M	Laborer	05Ju02lp
CONNEY, Maria	30	F	Wife	05Ju02lp
SHENYNESSEY, Cathn.	32	F	Servant	05Ju02lp
MCMAHON, Owen	19	M	Laborer	05Ju02lp
Bridgt.	21	F	Unknown	05Ju02lp
LOOBY, Wm.	26	M	Laborer	05Ju02lp
MCWEENY, John	19	M	Laborer	05Ju02lp
GRATH, Ann	30	F	Laborer	05Ju02lp
FLYNN, Luke	19	M	Laborer	05Ju02lp
GILLERN, James	21	M	Laborer	05Ju02lp
BURKE, James	22	M	Laborer	05Ju02lp
WALSH, Cath.	29	F	Unknown	05Ju02lp
CALLAGHEM, Margaret	17	F	Unknown	05Ju02lp
DALEY, Thos.	36	M	Laborer	05Ju02lp
KELLY, Michal	25	M	Laborer	05Ju02lp
SCULLY, Pat	50	M	Carpenter	05Ju02lp
Mary (D)	10	F	Unknown	05Ju02lp
Birgt. (D)	6	F	Child	05Ju02lp
Cath. (D)	5	F	Child	05Ju02lp
FLYNN, Michal	38	M	Laborer	05Ju02lp
ARDLE, John	22	M	Carpenter	05Ju02lp
ELLIS, Eliza	21	F	Unknown	05Ju02lp
MOORE, Robt.	26	M	Laborer	05Ju02lp
CORIGAN, Andrew	37	M	Laborer	05Ju02lp
Sarah	30	F	Unknown	05Ju02lp
Brigt. (D)	12	F	Unknown	05Ju02lp
Sally (D)	10	F	Unknown	05Ju02lp
Mary (D)	5	F	Child	05Ju02lp
John (S)	4	M	Child	05Ju02lp
Essy (D)	3	F	Child	05Ju02lp
Thos. (S)	.00	M	Infant	05Ju02lp
GRIFFIN, John	20	M	Laborer	05Ju02lp
BRENNAN, Wm.	28	M	Laborer	05Ju02lp
Cath.	28	F	Wife	05Ju02lp
KENNEDY, John	35	M	Weaver	05Ju02lp
Michal	30	M	Weaver	05Ju02lp
Brigt.	37	F	Wife	05Ju02lp
BYRONE, John	28	M	Laborer	05Ju02lp
Ally	47	F	Laborer	05Ju02lp
Phil.	27	M	Laborer	05Ju02lp
Winni	22	M	Laborer	05Ju02lp
Ellen	15	F	Laborer	05Ju02lp
Cath.	11	F	Laborer	05Ju02lp
MAINS, Winni	28	M	Laborer	05Ju02lp
Ihr	3	U	Child	05Ju02lp
James	.00	M	Infant	05Ju02lp
WALSH, John	22	M	Laborer	05Ju02lp
Brigt.	24	F	Laborer	05Ju02lp
HINIEGAN, Mary	28	F	Unknown	05Ju02lp
Ellen	24	F	Unknown	05Ju02lp
NOLAN, Mary	21	F	Servant	05Ju02lp
BEROKE, James	21	M	Tailor	05Ju02lp
MURPHY, Martin	28	M	Laborer	05Ju02lp
Thos.	24	M	Laborer	05Ju02lp
DENNON, Edwd.	21	M	Tailor	05Ju02lp
COFFEY, Mary-Ann	21	F	Unknown	05Ju02lp

NAMES OF PASSENGERS		AGE	SEX	OCCUPATIONS	DATE PORT SHIP
COFFEY, Peter		16	M	Unknown	05Ju02Ip
SAYERS, Jane		20	F	Unknown	05Ju02Ip
FARMONS, Wm.		24	M	Laborer	05Ju02Ip
FOX, Thos.		21	M	Laborer	05Ju02Ip
Cathn.		20	F	Wife	05Ju02Ip
MAGRAW, Thos.		23	M	Farmer	05Ju02Ip
REARDON, Mary		23	F	Servant	05Ju02Ip
KEEFFE, Pat		21	M	Laborer	05Ju02Ip
MCCARTY, Michal		30	M	Laborer	05Ju02Ip
Julia		26	F	Laborer	05Ju02Ip
SHERIDAN, Mary		18	F	Servant	05Ju02Ip
HIGGINS, Mary		18	F	Servant	05Ju02Ip
HALEY, Mary		20	F	Servant	05Ju02Ip
DANDAN, John		23	M	Plasterer	05Ju02Ip
U		23	M	Plasterer	05Ju02Ip
CRONAN, David		25	M	Laborer	05Ju02Ip
John		23	M	Laborer	05Ju02Ip
Danl.		14	M	Laborer	05Ju02Ip
MCCOONEY, Wm.		25	M	Laborer	05Ju02Ip
U	(W)	22	F	Unknown	05Ju02Ip
Ann	(D)	.00	F	Infant	05Ju02Ip
CAVANAGH, Brigt.		22	F	Servant	05Ju02Ip
Mary		20	F	Servant	05Ju02Ip
Bryan		18	M	Servant	05Ju02Ip
Judy		16	F	Servant	05Ju02Ip
SHERRY, James		33	M	Laborer	05Ju02Ip
Ann		20	F	Wife	05Ju02Ip
HORNER, John		42	M	Grocer	05Ju02Ip
U	(W)	31	F	Unknown	05Ju02Ip
Mary	(D)	.00	F	Infant	05Ju02Ip
RILEY, Margret		18	F	Servant	05Ju02Ip
COSTLOW, Edw.		25	M	Laborer	05Ju02Ip
Nancy		23	F	Wife	05Ju02Ip
HOYLE, Margret		25	F	Servant	05Ju02Ip
ALLEN, Pat		21	M	Laborer	05Ju02Ip
CAVANAGH, Pater		19	M	Laborer	05Ju02Ip
MCANALLEY, John		17	M	Laborer	05Ju02Ip
LAWN, Mary		24	F	Servant	05Ju02Ip
DIXON, Elisa		18	F	Servant	05Ju02Ip
MCGARONEY, Ellen		20	F	Servant	05Ju02Ip
BYRES, Simon		35	M	Farmer	05Ju02Ip
U	(W)	30	F	Unknown	05Ju02Ip
FINNIUS, Michal		50	M	Unknown	05Ju02Ip
FITZGERALD, M.		45	M	Unknown	05Ju02Ip
M.		37	M	Unknown	05Ju02Ip
CLANCEY, James		50	M	Farmer	05Ju02Ip
Mary	(W)	50	F	Unknown	05Ju02Ip
Wm.		24	M	Laborer	05Ju02Ip
Con.		22	M	Laborer	05Ju02Ip
Cath.	(D)	18	F	Unknown	05Ju02Ip
Lolana	(D)	12	F	Unknown	05Ju02Ip
Mary	(D)	28	F	Unknown	05Ju02Ip
QUIRK, Mat		52	M	Farmer	05Ju02Ip
Cath.	(W)	52	F	Unknown	05Ju02Ip
Matilda		10	F	Unknown	05Ju02Ip
CORMICK, Mary		18	F	Unknown	05Ju02Ip
GLAVIN, Edw.		28	M	Bone-Letter	05Ju02Ip
Pat		10	M	Bone-Letter	05Ju02Ip
KELLY, James		20	M	Brick Maker	05Ju02Ip
CLAREY, James		30	M	Laborer	05Ju02Ip
BOWLING, Honor		25	M	Laborer	05Ju02Ip
MOMACY, Mary		15	F	Servant	05Ju02Ip
BYRNE, Pat		5	M	Child	05Ju02Ip
DELANY, Pat		22	M	Sawer	05Ju02Ip
MITCHELL, Pat		41	M	Carpenter	05Ju02Ip
Pat		13	M	Carpenter	05Ju02Ip
Brigt.		40	F	Wife	05Ju02Ip
Ellen	(D)	11	F	Unknown	05Ju02Ip
HUGHES, Ellen		25	F	Servant	05Ju02Ip

CLARE 06 JUNE 1849

From Donegal

NAMES OF PASSENGERS	AGE	SEX	OCCUPATIONS	DATE PORT SHIP
SPROUL, Catharine	30	F	None	06Ju34Jd
Jane	5	F	Child	06Ju34Jd
HAMMOND, Fanny-Maria	32	F	None	06Ju34Jd
MONAGHAN, Jane	22	F	None	06Ju34Jd
MCGANIGLE, Winny	20	F	Dressmaker	06Ju34Jd
DONLEVY, John	30	M	Tanner	06Ju34Jd
CASSIDY, Francis	32	M	Carpenter	06Ju34Jd
MCNEELY, Isabella	20	F	Spinster	06Ju34Jd
Elizabeth	19	F	Spinster	06Ju34Jd
MCCREADY, William	25	M	Farmer	06Ju34Jd
Margaret	23	F	Spinster	06Ju34Jd
GILLESPIE, Andrew	28	M	Farmer	06Ju34Jd
MARTIN, John	22	M	Laborer	06Ju34Jd
MEEGHAN, James	25	M	Laborer	06Ju34Jd
Mary	23	F	Spinster	06Ju34Jd
Thomas	.09	M	Infant	06Ju34Jd
Dennis	40	M	Laborer	06Ju34Jd
Hannah	20	F	Spinster	06Ju34Jd
KIRK, Margaret	22	F	Spinster	06Ju34Jd
Tessy	21	F	Spinster	06Ju34Jd
MCCALLIAN, Fanny	19	F	Spinster	06Ju34Jd
CUNNINGHAM, Hugh	19	M	Laborer	06Ju34Jd
MEEGHAN, Betty	23	F	Spinster	06Ju34Jd
HANAUGHEY, Patrick	18	M	Laborer	06Ju34Jd
Mary	17	F	Spinster	06Ju34Jd
MEEGHAN, Mary	19	F	Spinster	06Ju34Jd
CASSIDY, Andrew	28	M	Farmer	06Ju34Jd
Mary-Jane	26	F	Spinster	06Ju34Jd
DIVER, John	20	M	Laborer	06Ju34Jd
GALLAGHER, Elizabeth	18	F	Spinster	06Ju34Jd
JOHNSTON, Mary	30	F	Matron	06Ju34Jd
Robert	13	M	Student	06Ju34Jd
John	10	M	Student	06Ju34Jd
William	9	M	Student	06Ju34Jd
James	7	M	Student	06Ju34Jd
Ann-Jane	6	F	Student	06Ju34Jd
Mary	.02	F	Infant	06Ju34Jd
George	34	M	Laborer	06Ju34Jd
SCOTT, David	58	M	Farmer	06Ju34Jd
Rebecca	55	F	Matron	06Ju34Jd
Jane	28	F	Spinster	06Ju34Jd
Robert	21	M	Laborer	06Ju34Jd
HAMOND, Mary	12	F	Student	06Ju34Jd
Benjamin	10	M	Student	06Ju34Jd
Rebecca	8	F	Student	06Ju34Jd
Susan	5	F	Child	06Ju34Jd
DAVIS, Jane	19	F	Spinster	06Ju34J
MCBREARTY, Mary	21	F	Spinster	06Ju34J
Jane	14	F	Student	06Ju34J
OCONNELL, Valentine	19	M	Laborer	06Ju34J
BROGAN, Isabella	22	F	Spinster	06Ju34J
GALLAGHER, Margaret	20	F	Spinster	06Ju34J
Bridget	15	F	Spinster	06Ju34J
MONTGOMERY, Bessy	16	F	Spinster	06Ju34J
MCJUNKEN, Margaret	35	F	Matron	06Ju34J
RHODDY, Margaret	20	F	Spinster	06Ju34J
MCJUNKEN, Robert	12	M	Student	06Ju34J
Mary-Jane	10	F	Student	06Ju34J
John	7	M	Student	06Ju34J
CARR, Elizabeth	35	F	Matron	06Ju34J
Mary	25	F	Spinster	06Ju34J
MCJUNKEN, William-Jame	2	M	Child	06Ju34J
KILDEA, John	22	M	Laborer	06Ju34J
STEPHENSON, Charles	23	M	Laborer	06Ju34
MCFADDEN, Connell	20	M	Laborer	06Ju34

NAMES OF PASSENGERS	AGE	SEX	OCCUPATIONS	DATE PORT SHIP
MELLY, Margaret	23	F	Matron	06Ju34Jd
GALLAGHER, Maria	25	F	Spinster	06Ju34Jd
WREN, Joseph	28	M	Farmer	06Ju34Jd
Jane	26	F	Spinster	06Ju34Jd
Isabella	13	M	Student	06Ju34Jd
Joseph	.06	M	Infant	06Ju34Jd
BARTON, John	23	M	Laborer	06Ju34Jd
WREN, James	24	M	Laborer	06Ju34Jd
MEEGHAN, Mary	32	F	Spinster	06Ju34Jd
Mary	15	F	Spinster	06Ju34Jd
LITTLE, Robert	20	M	Laborer	06Ju34Jd
GALLAGHER, Patrick	14	M	Laborer	06Ju34Jd
SHEEVUNN, Hannah	17	F	Spinster	06Ju34Jd
KENNEDY, Patrick	22	M	Laborer	06Ju34Jd
MEEGHAN, Ann	20	F	Spinster	06Ju34Jd
GRIFFITH, Patrick	15	M	Laborer	06Ju34Jd
NEWMAN, Catherine	18	F	Spinster	06Ju34Jd
MCINTIRE, Winfred	20	F	Spinster	06Ju34Jd
SCARLET, Elizabeth	18	F	Spinster	06Ju34Jd
GALLAGHER, John	25	M	Laborer	06Ju34Jd
Catherine	23	F	Spinster	06Ju34Jd
DOHERTY, Patrick	23	M	Laborer	06Ju34Jd
CANON, Rose	24	F	Spinster	06Ju34Jd
MEEGHAN, John	25	M	Laborer	06Ju34Jd
Kitty	23	F	Spinster	06Ju34Jd
SCARLET, Ann	18	F	Spinster	06Ju34Jd
LALLY, Bridget	20	F	Spinster	06Ju34Jd
LAVANDER, Patrick	40	M	Coachman	06Ju34Jd
Bridget	38	F	Matron	06Ju34Jd
Thomas	12	M	Student	06Ju34Jd
Bridget	10	F	Child	06Ju34Jd
Eleanor	.10	F	Infant	06Ju34Jd
BRADLY, Catherine	18	F	Spinster	06Ju34Jd
CAMPBELL, Rose	20	F	Spinster	06Ju34Jd
GWYNN, William	23	M	Saddler	06Ju34Jd
MCBREARTY, Isabella	15	F	Spinster	06Ju34Jd
CUNNINGHAM, Ellen	18	F	Spinster	06Ju34Jd
MCJUNKIN, Catherine	24	F	Spinster	06Ju34Jd
SPROUL, Charles	50	M	Farmer	06Ju34Jd
MCCREADY, Ann	20	F	Spinster	06Ju34Jd
BYRNES, Rose	22	F	Spinster	06Ju34Jd
HUGHES, Thomas	18	M	Clerk	06Ju34Jd
COULTER, Mary	28	F	Matron	06Ju34Jd
John	30	M	Laborer	06Ju34Jd
Isabella	5	F	Student	06Ju34Jd
Mary	2	F	Child	06Ju34Jd
MCBREARTY, John	23	M	Laborer	06Ju34Jd
GRAHAM, Ann	20	F	Spinster	06Ju34Jd
WARD, Margaret	22	F	Spinster	06Ju34Jd
GORMAN, Anthony	24	M	Laborer	06Ju34Jd
GALLAGHER, James	26	M	Laborer	06Ju34Jd
NESBITT, Thomas	23	M	Laborer	06Ju34Jd
MCSHANNY, Marcus	20	M	Laborer	06Ju34Jd
MONAGHAN, Hugh	19	M	Laborer	06Ju34Jd
MCQUADE, Mary	18	F	Spinster	06Ju34Jd
CRUMLY, Thomas	40	M	Smith	06Ju34Jd
PETERSON, Mary	25	F	Spinster	06Ju34Jd
MONAGHAN, Patrick	12	M	Student	06Ju34Jd

BERLIN 06 JUNE 1849

From Liverpool

NAMES OF PASSENGERS	AGE	SEX	OCCUPATIONS	DATE PORT SHIP
UINN, Biddy	36	F	None	06Ju02It
Alice	14	F	None	06Ju02It
Mary	12	F	None	06Ju02It
Biddy	8	F	Child	06Ju02It
Charles	6	M	Child	06Ju02It
Peggy	4	F	Child	06Ju02It
CAMPBELL, James	26	M	Laborer	06Ju02It
Sarah	50	F	None	06Ju02It
Siddy	20	F	None	06Ju02It
Charles	16	M	None	06Ju02It
Sarah	14	F	None	06Ju02It
Pat	11	M	None	06Ju02It
Biddy	9	F	Child	06Ju02It
DONAHY, Mary	20	F	None	06Ju02It
WALSH, Judith	20	F	Servant	06Ju02It
Catherine	18	F	Servant	06Ju02It
DOYER, Andrew	30	M	Laborer	06Ju02It
John	27	M	Laborer	06Ju02It
BARRY, James-M.	35	M	Laborer	06Ju02It
SMITH, John	45	M	Laborer	06Ju02It
Stephen	27	M	Laborer	06Ju02It
LITTLE, Peter	18	M	Laborer	06Ju02It
OBARA, John	24	M	Laborer	06Ju02It
Wm.	23	M	Laborer	06Ju02It
Mary	18	F	None	06Ju02It
Ann	45	F	None	06Ju02It
MILLS, Mary	14	F	None	06Ju02It
Catherine	12	F	None	06Ju02It
DONAGHAN, Wm.	20	M	None	06Ju02It
Peter	16	M	None	06Ju02It
Nancy	30	F	None	06Ju02It
MITCHELL, Ben	33	M	Mechanic	06Ju02It
Maria	29	F	None	06Ju02It
Ann	9	F	Child	06Ju02It
Alfred	.00	M	Infant	06Ju02It
DARCY, Mick	24	M	None	06Ju02It
DOYLE, Pat	26	M	Laborer	06Ju02It
Margt.	26	F	None	06Ju02It
SHIELDS, John	20	M	Laborer	06Ju02It
Margt.	19	F	Laborer	06Ju02It
WILKS, John	24	M	Laborer	06Ju02It
WITHAM, Richd.	25	M	Laborer	06Ju02It
SMITH, Martin	30	M	Laborer	06Ju02It
Andrew	15	M	Laborer	06Ju02It
Pat	22	M	Laborer	06Ju02It
Bridget	20	F	Laborer	06Ju02It
Catherine	24	F	Laborer	06Ju02It
SHERIDAN, James	26	M	Laborer	06Ju02It
Peter	20	M	Laborer	06Ju02It
DOOGAN, Mary	32	F	Laborer	06Ju02It
Mick	3	M	Laborer	06Ju02It
Andrew	.00	M	Infant	06Ju02It
PALMER, Pierce	27	F	Laborer	06Ju02It
COOLAN, Pat	30	M	Laborer	06Ju02It
BRENAN, Catherine	47	F	Laborer	06Ju02It
MAHER, Wm.	47	M	Laborer	06Ju02It
Mick	2	M	Laborer	06Ju02It
Bridget	20	F	Laborer	06Ju02It
Eliza	18	F	Laborer	06Ju02It
Catherine	16	F	Laborer	06Ju02It
Dennis	9	M	Child	06Ju02It
MCGARRY, Thos.	36	M	Laborer	06Ju02It
Ellen	30	F	Laborer	06Ju02It
James	4	M	Child	06Ju02It
Richd.	3	M	Child	06Ju02It
Eliza	.00	F	Infant	06Ju02It
SIMEON, Pat	20	M	Laborer	06Ju02It
Thos.	3	M	Child	06Ju02It
WALDRON, John	23	M	Laborer	06Ju02It
GLASSWOOD, Ellen	25	F	Laborer	06Ju02It
Jane	16	F	Laborer	06Ju02It
Mary	14	F	Laborer	06Ju02It
George	9	M	Child	06Ju02It
Ann	5	F	Child	06Ju02It
GREEN, John	18	M	Laborer	06Ju02It
MURPHY, James	25	M	Laborer	06Ju02It
Margt.	20	F	Laborer	06Ju02It
Michl.	4	M	Child	06Ju02It
SCOTT, Thos.	25	M	Laborer	06Ju02It
MCLEARY, Jas.	20	M	Laborer	06Ju02It
Margt.	20	F	Laborer	06Ju02It

NAMES OF PASSENGERS	AGE	SEX	OCCUPATIONS	DATE PORT SHIP	NAMES OF PASSENGERS	AGE	SEX	OCCUPATIONS	DATE PORT SHIP
DONOGAN, Martha	28	F	Laborer	06Ju02It	REYNOLDS, Sylvester	20	M	Laborer	06Ju02It
Margt.	28	F	Laborer	06Ju02It	U-Mrs.	26	F	Laborer	06Ju02It
BROHAN, Margt.	18	F	Laborer	06Ju02It	Biddy	35	F	Laborer	06Ju02It
LYONS, Joseph	29	M	Laborer	06Ju02It	MORAN, Cormick	25	M	Laborer	06Ju02It
Wm.	28	M	Laborer	06Ju02It	MOORRISEY, Wm.	25	M	Laborer	06Ju02It
WOODS, James	23	M	Laborer	06Ju02It	WARD, Wm.	36	M	Laborer	06Ju02It
GORMAN, John	24	M	Laborer	06Ju02It	U-Mrs.	26	F	Laborer	06Ju02It
Judith	50	F	Laborer	06Ju02It	Bess	.00	F	Infant	06Ju02It
Bridget	22	F	Laborer	06Ju02It	John	23	M	Laborer	06Ju02It
Johannah	20	F	Laborer	06Ju02It	Bridget	22	F	Laborer	06Ju02It
Harriet	4	F	Laborer	06Ju02It	Jane	24	F	Laborer	06Ju02It
Patt	25	M	Laborer	06Ju02It	Alice	3	F	Child	06Ju02It
Catherine	25	F	Laborer	06Ju02It	John	.00	M	Infant	06Ju02It
Wm.	.00	M	Infant	06Ju02It	COSTILLS, Cathe.	22	F	Laborer	06Ju02It
TUMNEY, Wm.	25	M	Laborer	06Ju02It	WARD, Bess	19	F	Laborer	06Ju02It
OBRIEN, Thos.	25	M	Laborer	06Ju02It	Cathe.	17	F	Laborer	06Ju02It
Eliza	18	F	Laborer	06Ju02It	SHERNEY, James	20	M	Laborer	06Ju02It
BYRNES, Thos.	22	M	Laborer	06Ju02It	RAFFERTY, Rose	22	F	Laborer	06Ju02It
Fanny	20	F	Laborer	06Ju02It	GALVIN, Mary	22	F	Laborer	06Ju02It
Mary-Ann	20	F	Laborer	06Ju02It	LAWRENCE, John	22	M	Laborer	06Ju02It
Ellen	20	F	Laborer	06Ju02It	DEGAN, Jack	50	M	Laborer	06Ju02It
MCGORY, Anne	21	F	Laborer	06Ju02It	U-Mrs.	48	F	Laborer	06Ju02It
CLARK, May	20	F	Laborer	06Ju02It	John	19	M	Laborer	06Ju02It
WHOLAHAN, Cathe.	20	F	Laborer	06Ju02It	Mary-Anne	13	F	Laborer	06Ju02It
Anne	20	F	Laborer	06Ju02It	Bridget	13	F	Laborer	06Ju02It
Jessie	20	M	Laborer	06Ju02It	Joseph	9	M	Child	06Ju02It
BYRES, Barnan	25	M	Laborer	06Ju02It	Margt.	7	F	Child	06Ju02It
U-Mrs.	25	F	Laborer	06Ju02It	Jeremiah	5	M	Child	06Ju02It
BERRY, James	24	M	Laborer	06Ju02It	Jack	3	M	Child	06Ju02It
LUCEY, William	55	M	Laborer	06Ju02It	James	39	M	Laborer	06Ju02It
U-Mrs.	55	F	Laborer	06Ju02It	U-Mrs.	33	F	Laborer	06Ju02It
IRONS, May	70	F	Laborer	06Ju02It	Maria	15	F	Laborer	06Ju02It
ANDERSON, Thos.	26	M	Laborer	06Ju02It	Michl.	13	M	Laborer	06Ju02It
U-Mrs. (W)	24	F	Laborer	06Ju02It	Jeremiah	.00	M	Infant	06Ju02It
BROYDON, Saml.	20	M	Laborer	06Ju02It	MARRIAN, Pat	19	M	Laborer	06Ju02It
BRIOLS, Saml.F.	20	M	Laborer	06Ju02It	MAGEE, Matt	23	M	Laborer	06Ju02It
BOWLS, Isabella	20	F	Laborer	06Ju02It	INGARTY, Mick	23	M	Laborer	06Ju02It
GRAHAM, William	20	M	Laborer	06Ju02It	PATCHILL, Alice	23	F	Laborer	06Ju02It
MCMANUS, Ellen	19	F	Laborer	06Ju02It	HALPHIN, Michl.	25	M	Laborer	06Ju02It
FLEMING, Eliza	20	F	Laborer	06Ju02It	Judith	20	F	Laborer	06Ju02It
ELLIOTT, William	30	M	Laborer	06Ju02It	BIRD, Peter	30	M	Laborer	06Ju02It
MCGUIRE, William	20	M	Laborer	06Ju02It	FITTHAM, James	19	M	Laborer	06Ju02It
GILLES, John	28	M	Laborer	06Ju02It	CONNELLY, Rosy	46	F	Laborer	06Ju02It
MONOGHAN, Barnard	25	M	Laborer	06Ju02It	MCMAHON, Francis	20	M	Laborer	06Ju02I
LEONARD, William	29	M	Laborer	06Ju02It	Mary	18	F	Laborer	06Ju02I
James	25	M	Laborer	06Ju02It	WRAY, John	20	M	Laborer	06Ju02I
HENNESSY, Sam	25	M	Laborer	06Ju02It	DINNARD, Michl.	25	M	Laborer	06Ju02I
BERBRIDGE, Edwd.	45	M	Laborer	06Ju02It	GLASSWOOD, Jane	3	F	Child	06Ju02I
Michl.	15	M	Laborer	06Ju02It	John	.00	M	Infant	06Ju02I
James	13	M	Laborer	06Ju02It	DEANE, Pat	25	M	Laborer	06Ju02I
William	10	M	Laborer	06Ju02It	LOME, U-Mrs.	35	F	Laborer	06Ju02I
COWAN, George	30	M	Laborer	06Ju02It	FLETCHER, U-Miss	16	F	Laborer	06Ju02I
U-Mrs.	30	F	Laborer	06Ju02It	LOME, Edwin	6	M	Child	06Ju02I
Mary	4	F	Child	06Ju02It	Thomas	4	M	Child	06Ju02I
John	17	M	Laborer	06Ju02It	HEANEY, Catherine	27	F	Laborer	06Ju02I
MCCORVILL, Dan	25	M	Laborer	06Ju02It	Rosy	22	F	Laborer	06Ju02I
U-Mrs.	25	F	Laborer	06Ju02It	NETLERY, Alexander	25	M	Laborer	06Ju02I
Dan	2	M	Child	06Ju02It	Ann	25	F	Laborer	06Ju02I
Patt	.00	M	Infant	06Ju02It	KANE, Mary	2	F	Child	06Ju02I
BREEN, Michl.	25	M	Laborer	06Ju02It	COULTER, Ann	22	F	Laborer	06Ju02I
AHERN, Jeffry	20	M	Laborer	06Ju02It	RUSSELL, Julia	20	F	Laborer	06Ju02I
SHEEHAN, Michl.	20	M	Laborer	06Ju02It	HOWRIGAN, Honora	30	F	Laborer	06Ju02I
U-Mrs.	20	F	Laborer	06Ju02It	BRADSHAW, Catherine	40	F	Laborer	06Ju02I
BUCKLEY, William	20	M	Laborer	06Ju02It	John	7	M	Child	06Ju02I
U-Mrs.	20	F	Laborer	06Ju02It	MCKEOWN, James	45	M	Laborer	06Ju02I
Edwd.	20	M	Laborer	06Ju02It	NICHOLAS, Wm.	32	M	Laborer	06Ju02I
Edwd.	.00	M	Infant	06Ju02It	QUICK, Joshua	26	M	Laborer	06Ju02I
BRADLEY, John	25	M	Laborer	06Ju02It	MCGANNON, Benty	20	M	Laborer	06Ju02
MEALEY, Bridget	20	F	Laborer	06Ju02It	FITZPATRICK, Mat	30	M	Laborer	06Ju02
COFFY, Ellen	20	F	Laborer	06Ju02It	MOORE, James	32	M	Laborer	06Ju02
HANAHAN, Catherine	25	F	Laborer	06Ju02It	Pat	23	M	Laborer	06Ju02
LONDERGEN, James	40	M	Laborer	06Ju02It	FARRELL, Mat	23	M	Laborer	06Ju02
Cathe.	20	F	Laborer	06Ju02It	MCQUEENY, Catherine	16	F	Laborer	06Ju02
Ellen	25	F	Laborer	06Ju02It	ORPHEUS, James	27	M	Laborer	06Ju02
John	25	M	Laborer	06Ju02It	Margt.	28	F	Laborer	06Ju02

NAMES OF PASSENGERS	AGE	SEX	OCCUPATIONS	DATE PORT SHIP
ORPHEUS, Eliza	3	F	Child	06Ju021t
Anna	2	F	Child	06Ju021t
James	.00	M	Infant	06Ju021t
HICKEN, Robert	32	M	Laborer	06Ju021t
Ann-Jane	30	F	Laborer	06Ju021t
Robert	4	M	Child	06Ju021t
John	3	M	Child	06Ju021t
Mary	.00	F	Infant	06Ju021t
STEENSON, Mary-Ann	12	F	Laborer	06Ju021t
FLETCHER, Ellen	21	F	Laborer	06Ju021t
CONNOR, Rosanna	24	F	Laborer	06Ju021t
TELFORD, James	29	M	Laborer	Ju021t
Mary	27	F	Laborer	Ju021t
David	5	M	Child	Ju021t
Wm.	4	M	Child	Ju021t
Mary-Ann	.00	F	Infant	06Ju021t
FULTON, James	19	M	Laborer	06Ju021t
MAHER, Cath.	20	F	Laborer	06Ju021t
LEWIS, Margt.	37	F	Laborer	06Ju021t
ONIEL, Hugh	40	M	Laborer	06Ju021t
Thos.	13	M	Laborer	06Ju021t
NOLAN, Wm.	20	M	Laborer	06Ju021t
Mary-Ann	22	F	Laborer	06Ju021t
JAMIESON, Edward	28	M	Laborer	06Ju021t
COX, Harry	18	M	Laborer	06Ju021t
GAFFNEY, Daniel	24	M	Laborer	06Ju021t
BROOK, John	35	M	Merchant	06Ju021t
DEFENTON, U-Mr.	30	M	Merchant	06Ju021t
U, U Born-At-Sea	.00	U	Infant	06Ju021t
U Born-At-Sea	.00	U	Infant	06Ju021t
SMITH, Luke	25	M	Laborer	06Ju021t
Michl.	20	M	Laborer	06Ju021t
COONEY, James	25	M	Laborer	06Ju021t

HEBE 06 JUNE 1849

From London

NAMES OF PASSENGERS	AGE	SEX	OCCUPATIONS	DATE PORT SHIP
OBRIEN, Terence	28	M	Laborer	06Ju1311
Ellen	28	F	Unknown	06Ju1311
REGAN, Jno.	20	M	Unknown	06Ju1311
Patrick	11	M	Unknown	06Ju1311
LOVELL, Thomas	37	M	Unknown	06Ju1311
Elizabeth	27	F	Unknown	06Ju1311
WELSTEAD, William	24	M	Unknown	06Ju1311
SHARP, Edward	24	M	Unknown	06Ju1311
LEE, Timothy	30	M	Unknown	06Ju1311
CORTENARY, Jno.	26	M	Unknown	06Ju1311
DECKER, Fredk.	23	M	Unknown	06Ju1311
WEBER, John	23	M	Unknown	06Ju1311
WARDMENT, Geo.	33	M	Unknown	06Ju1311
GRAPE, Geo.	40	M	Unknown	06Ju1311
GODERHAM, Jno.	45	M	Unknown	06Ju1311
WINTER, Wm.	48	M	Unknown	06Ju1311
Geo.	20	M	Unknown	06Ju1311
MARCH, Jno.	30	M	Unknown	06Ju1311
WALTERS, Geo.	23	M	Unknown	06Ju1311
QUESTEAD, James	22	M	Unknown	06Ju1311
JAMES, Andrew	22	M	Unknown	06Ju1311
ARNOLD, John-W.	26	M	Unknown	06Ju1311
ARGENT, Thos.	23	M	Unknown	06Ju1311
INES, Jas.	31	M	Unknown	06Ju1311
CKINSACK, Wm.	28	M	Unknown	06Ju1311
Ann	27	F	Unknown	06Ju1311
ARON, Mary	60	F	Unknown	06Ju1311
Jane	27	F	Unknown	06Ju1311
Louisa	24	F	Unknown	06Ju1311
LYNN, Jno.	22	M	Unknown	06Ju1311
LAWSON, Wm.	32	M	Unknown	06Ju1311
KIRBY, Thomas	38	M	Unknown	06Ju1311
WATT, Daniel	47	M	Unknown	06Ju1311
MILLEDGE, James	42	M	Unknown	06Ju1311
Francis	41	M	Unknown	06Ju1311
MCLOUGHTON, Daniel	35	M	Unknown	06Ju1311
Edwd.	13	M	Unknown	06Ju1311
GENTLE, James	32	M	Unknown	06Ju1311
Lucy	36	F	Unknown	06Ju1311
STOCKER, John	26	M	Unknown	06Ju1311
Mary	30	F	Unknown	06Ju1311
DEAN, Thos.	38	M	Unknown	06Ju1311
Catherine	30	M	Unknown	06Ju1311
Catherine	3	F	Child	06Ju1311
CHADWELL, James	23	M	Unknown	06Ju1311
GREEN, Lot	20	M	Unknown	06Ju1311
BENNETT, John	54	M	Unknown	06Ju1311
Elizabeth	44	F	Unknown	06Ju1311
Wm.	15	M	Unknown	06Ju1311
Elizabeth	13	F	Unknown	06Ju1311
Isabella	11	F	Unknown	06Ju1311
Henry	9	M	Child	06Ju1311
John	6	M	Child	06Ju1311
SOLOMON, Moss	12	M	Unknown	06Ju1311
Joseph	13	M	Unknown	06Ju1311
BRENNAN, Edw.	36	M	Unknown	06Ju1311
Jane	30	F	Unknown	06Ju1311
BARLETTS, Henry	21	M	Unknown	06Ju1311
REGAN, John	22	M	Unknown	06Ju1311
Wm.	18	M	Unknown	06Ju1311
Ellen	24	F	Unknown	06Ju1311
BATEMAN, Chas.	27	M	Unknown	06Ju1311
Caroline	20	F	Unknown	06Ju1311
Geo.	2	M	Child	06Ju1311
Edwd.	.00	M	Infant	06Ju1311
WINSTON, Eliza	22	F	Unknown	06Ju1311
Louisa	27	F	Unknown	06Ju1311
MITCHAEL, Edwd.	26	M	Unknown	06Ju1311
MURPHY, Cornelius	26	M	Unknown	06Ju1311
Mary	26	F	Unknown	06Ju1311
LEWIS, Timothy	28	M	Unknown	06Ju1311
FLEMING, Ellen	28	F	Unknown	06Ju1311
Ellen	.00	F	Infant	06Ju1311
BLEACHER, Joseph	37	M	Unknown	06Ju1311
Eliza	30	F	Unknown	06Ju1311
THACHER, Thos.	59	M	Unknown	06Ju1311
Mary	59	F	Unknown	06Ju1311
Henry	30	M	Unknown	06Ju1311
James	19	M	Unknown	06Ju1311
Jos.	13	M	Unknown	06Ju1311
CAGNEY, Michael	23	M	Unknown	06Ju1311
DUNN, Bridget	27	F	Unknown	06Ju1311
NEWBURY, Jno.	23	M	Unknown	06Ju1311
Ann	20	F	Unknown	06Ju1311
RAMSDALE, James	21	M	Unknown	06Ju1311
WATSON, Edwd.	22	M	Unknown	06Ju1311
FINCH, Geo.	21	M	Unknown	06Ju1311
COCUSS, John	23	M	Unknown	06Ju1311
FLYNN, John	23	M	Unknown	06Ju1311
PURCHASE, John	40	M	Unknown	06Ju1311
Louisa	36	F	Unknown	06Ju1311
SYMONS, Henry	32	M	Unknown	06Ju1311
PURCHASE, John	13	M	Unknown	06Ju1311
Stephan	12	M	Unknown	06Ju1311
Louisa	10	F	Unknown	06Ju1311
Mary	7	F	Child	06Ju1311
Wm.	6	M	Child	06Ju1311
LEE, Jas.	22	M	Unknown	06Ju1311
GORDEN, Edward	42	M	Unknown	06Ju1311
NORDEN, Mark	28	M	Unknown	06Ju1311
SHORTER, Jno.	30	M	Unknown	06Ju1311
Sarah	66	F	Unknown	06Ju1311
Harriet	24	F	Unknown	06Ju1311
HOOD, Benjamin	19	M	Unknown	06Ju1311

NAMES OF PASSENGERS	AGE	SEX	OCCUPATIONS	DATE PORT SHIP
MICHELON, Henry	18	M	Unknown	06Ju13Il
DONIVAN, Jas.	92	M	Unknown	06Ju13Il
NICHOLAS, Esther	13	F	Unknown	06Ju13Il
AGENT, Ann	28	F	Unknown	06Ju13Il
HINES, Mary	22	F	Unknown	06Ju13Il
KELLY, Jno.	40	M	Unknown	06Ju13Il
HOUGHTON, Martha	29	F	Unknown	06Ju13Il
Eliza	3	F	Child	06Ju13Il
Geo.	.00	M	Infant	06Ju13Il
SEATON, Eliza	25	F	Unknown	06Ju13Il
Abraham	.00	M	Infant	06Ju13Il
SCOTT, Thos.	24	M	Unknown	06Ju13Il
Jno.	34	M	Unknown	06Ju13Il
Ann	30	F	Unknown	06Ju13Il
Mary-Ann	.00	F	Infant	06Ju13Il
EVANS, Eliza	20	F	Unknown	06Ju13Il
KELLAID, Jno.	48	M	Unknown	06Ju13Il
HOLMAN, James	27	M	Unknown	06Ju13Il
JEFFREYS, Frederick	19	M	Unknown	06Ju13Il
ROACH, John	25	M	Unknown	06Ju13Il
SCOTT, Wm.	25	M	Unknown	06Ju13Il
Bridget	24	F	Unknown	06Ju13Il
Ellen	23	F	Unknown	06Ju13Il
Mary	2	F	Child	06Ju13Il
Ellen	.00	F	Infant	06Ju13Il
FLEMMING, Michael	43	M	Unknown	06Ju13Il
Edwd.	37	M	Unknown	06Ju13Il
WOLF, Ann	16	F	Unknown	06Ju13Il
REEFE, Patrick	34	M	Unknown	06Ju13Il
HARRIS, Jno.	25	M	Unknown	06Ju13Il
TOPSETT, Jese	34	U	Unknown	06Ju13Il
John	30	M	Unknown	06Ju13Il
TOMSETT, Mary	25	F	Unknown	06Ju13Il
James	23	M	Unknown	06Ju13Il
MANN, Edward	18	M	Unknown	06Ju13Il
LITTLE, Jesse	2	U	Unknown	06Ju13Il
MURPHY, Michael	27	M	Unknown	06Ju13Il
HEYLIN, Joseph	55	M	Unknown	06Ju13Il
MORRIS, Jane	22	F	Unknown	06Ju13Il
PURCELL, John	43	M	Unknown	06Ju13Il
COPEMAN, Edwd.	28	M	Unknown	06Ju13Il
EYRE, Benjamin	25	M	Unknown	06Ju13Il
Henrietta	24	F	Unknown	06Ju13Il
COCKLAND, Jno.	31	M	Unknown	06Ju13Il
Bridget	23	F	Unknown	06Ju13Il
NEEDHAM, Geo.	38	M	Unknown	06Ju13Il
Sarah	35	F	Unknown	06Ju13Il
Mary-Ann	12	F	Unknown	06Ju13Il
Wm.	11	M	Unknown	06Ju13Il
Robert	9	M	Child	06Ju13Il
COLLINGS, Thos.	35	M	Unknown	06Ju13Il
BANDERS, Louisa	24	F	Unknown	06Ju13Il
DEVINE, Patrick	26	M	Unknown	06Ju13Il
Johanna	29	F	Unknown	06Ju13Il
Cath.	.00	F	Infant	06Ju13Il
PENTON, Geo.	38	M	Unknown	06Ju13Il
Mary-Ann	30	F	Unknown	06Ju13Il
NORDEN, Henry	19	M	Unknown	06Ju13Il
VILES, Benjamin	22	M	Unknown	06Ju13Il
MURPHY, Patrick	26	M	Unknown	06Ju13Il
Margaret	20	F	Unknown	06Ju13Il
MCCARLY, Michael	24	M	Unknown	06Ju13Il
Mary	25	F	Unknown	06Ju13Il
John	.00	M	Infant	Q6Ju13Il
DOYER, David	30	M	Unknown	06Ju13Il
Julia	24	F	Unknown	06Ju13Il
MADEN, Cath.	28	F	Unknown	06Ju13Il
BROWNE, Jno.	24	M	Unknown	06Ju13Il
MCDERMOT, Jane	32	F	Unknown	06Ju13Il
Jemima	34	F	Unknown	06Ju13Il
MULBURY, Patrick	20	M	Unknown	06Ju13Il
ADAMS, Mary	24	F	Unknown	06Ju13Il
Ellen	16	F	Unknown	06Ju13Il
Edward	9	M	Child	06Ju13Il
HOGAN, James	45	M	Unknown	06Ju13Il
BROWN, Edward	45	M	Unknown	06Ju13Il
WINSTON, Mary	50	F	Unknown	06Ju13Il
MIDDLETON, James	23	M	Unknown	06Ju13Il

MARY 07 JUNE 1849

From Sligo

NAMES OF PASSENGERS	AGE	SEX	OCCUPATIONS	DATE PORT SHIP
SHAW, Wm.	22	M	Painter	07Ju21Im
OCONNOR, Terrence	24	M	Servant	07Ju21Im
MAQUIRE, Pat	26	M	Laborer	07Ju21Im
CONLAN, Mathew	50	M	Farmer	07Ju21Im
Catherine	52	F	Wife	07Ju21Im
Jas.	16	M	Farmer	07Ju21Im
WARD, Mary	15	F	Servant	07Ju21Im
CARLEY, Mary	23	F	Servant	07Ju21Im
MORTIMER, Lizza	22	F	Servant	07Ju21Im
GOFFENEY, Jane	20	F	Servant	07Ju21Im
TOURY, Pat	18	M	Laborer	07Ju21Im
KEEGAN, Catherine	14	F	Spinster	07Ju21Im
ATKINSON, Thos.	30	M	Laborer	07Ju21Im
MCGOWAN, Patt	23	M	Laborer	07Ju21Im
Lawrence	22	M	Laborer	07Ju21Im
SMITH, Ann	21	F	Servant	07Ju21Im
VERDON, Biddy	35	F	Servant	07Ju21Im
MULLIGAN, Mary	35	F	Servant	07Ju21Im
M.Ann	7	F	Child	07Ju21Im
HEALLY, Mary	36	F	Servant	07Ju21Im
ALLEN, Eliza	20	F	Lady	07Ju21Im
MOLLOY, Pat	35	M	Farmer	07Ju21Im
Honor	20	F	Servant	07Ju21Im
KENNEDY, Bridget	20	F	Spinster	07Ju21Im
REED, Hester	18	F	Spinster	07Ju21Im
Jane	24	F	Spinster	07Ju21Im
BRADY, Hugh	22	M	Clerk	07Ju21Im
BRENAN, John	30	M	Laborer	07Ju21Im
Bridget	28	F	Servant	07Ju21Im
RYAN, Catherine	35	F	Servant	07Ju21Im
Bridget	27	F	Servant	07Ju21Im
MCNALAME, Honor	30	F	Servant	07Ju21Im
GOWMAN, Mary	29	F	Servant	07Ju21Im
KEARENS, Bridget	25	F	Servant	07Ju21Im
Honor	19	F	Servant	07Ju21Im
Michael	18	M	Laborer	07Ju21In
MEEHAN, Pat	22	M	Laborer	07Ju21In
Frances	20	F	Servant	07Ju21In
Jane	23	F	Servant	07Ju21In
KEENY, Rose	28	F	Servant	07Ju21Ir
Margaret	21	F	Servant	07Ju21Ir
MCDERMOTT, Edward	40	M	Laborer	07Ju21Ir
SHANNAN, Jane	26	F	Servant	07Ju21Ir
SCANLANE, Ellen	30	F	Servant	07Ju21Ir
MULRONY, Biddy	30	F	Servant	07Ju21Ir
DARCY, Betty	25	F	Servant	07Ju21I
Mary	27	F	Servant	07Ju21I
JUDGE, Thos.	38	M	Laborer	07Ju21I
IRWIN, Ellen	40	F	Lady	07Ju21I
Henry	20	M	Farmer	07Ju21I
William	10	M	Farmer	07Ju21I
Hannah	24	F	Lady	07Ju21I
James	23	M	Farmer	07Ju21I
Ann	19	F	Lady	07Ju21I
Catherine	14	F	Lady	07Ju21
JUDGE, Michael	35	M	Laborer	07Ju21
FALLEN, Margt.	30	F	Servant	07Ju21
MCHUGH, Neal	35	M	Servant	07Ju21
CARSON, Jason	32	M	Servant	07Ju21
Catharine	28	F	Servant	07Ju21
Mary-Jane	7	F	Child	07Ju21

NAMES OF PASSENGERS		AGE	SEX	OCCUPATIONS	DATE PORT SHIP
CARSON, John		6	M	Child	07Ju21Im
FARLEY, John		18	M	Servant	07Ju21Im

THOS.TROWBRIDGE 07 JUNE 1849

From Santiago

NAMES OF PASSENGERS		AGE	SEX	OCCUPATIONS	DATE PORT SHIP
MURTON, J.		30	M	Merchant	07Ju37Hv
NICHOLS, W.		35	M	Merchant	07Ju37Hv
TRAVILYN, J.		28	M	Merchant	07Ju37Hv

TYRINGHAM 07 JUNE 1849

From Liverpool

NAMES OF PASSENGERS		AGE	SEX	OCCUPATIONS	DATE PORT SHIP
WILKES, Zachariah		63	M	Farmer	07Ju02Ij
Hannah	(W)	38	F	Wife	07Ju02Ij
William	(S)	16	M	Son	07Ju02Ij
Hannah	(D)	11	F	Daughter	07Ju02Ij
Thomas	(S)	9	M	Child	07Ju02Ij
Amelia	(D)	3	F	Child	07Ju02Ij
Harnett	(D)	.00	F	Infant	07Ju02Ij
STARTIN, Samuel		23	M	Laborer	07Ju02Ij
SHARP, Thomas		24	M	Farmer	07Ju02Ij
GRANGER, Elizabeth		20	F	Servant	07Ju02Ij
MOORE, George		30	M	Laborer	07Ju02Ij
Anne	(W)	33	F	Wife	07Ju02Ij
OLDACRE, Thomas		35	M	Farmer	07Ju02Ij
Sarah	(W)	33	F	Wife	07Ju02Ij
James	(S)	9	M	Child	07Ju02Ij
Andrew	(S)	7	M	Child	07Ju02Ij
Mary	(D)	5	F	Child	07Ju02Ij
Jane	(D)	3	F	Child	07Ju02Ij
POTTER, Henry		33	M	Farmer	07Ju02Ij
Mary	(W)	31	F	Wife	07Ju02Ij
James	(S)	11	M	Son	07Ju02Ij
Elizabeth	(D)	9	F	Child	07Ju02Ij
Ann	(D)	8	F	Child	07Ju02Ij
John	(S)	5	M	Child	07Ju02Ij
Henry	(S)	4	M	Child	07Ju02Ij
Martha	(D)	3	F	Child	07Ju02Ij
William	(S)	.00	M	Infant	07Ju02Ij
ODDY, Michael		30	M	Draper	07Ju02Ij
Jane	(W)	30	F	Wife	07Ju02Ij
U		.00	U	Infant	07Ju02Ij
Ann	(D)	4	F	Child	07Ju02Ij
William	(S)	2	M	Child	07Ju02Ij
ARD, Ann		64	F	Wi	07Ju02Ij
ODDY, Robert		35	M	Farmer	07Ju02Ij
Mary	(W)	34	F	Wife	07Ju02Ij
Edward	(S)	9	M	Child	07Ju02Ij
OSTELLO, Michael		20	M	Laborer	07Ju02Ij
UIN, Ann		20	F	Servant	07Ju02Ij
ORSON, James		23	M	Litgr	07Ju02Ij
CCORMICK, Peter		25	M	Farmer	07Ju02Ij
U-Mrs.	(W)	25	F	Wife	07Ju02Ij
U		.00	U	Infant	07Ju02Ij
OGAN, Richard		25	M	Fitter	07Ju02Ij
NDERSON, U-Mrs.		30	F	Servant	07Ju02Ij
ATHER, John		30	M	Sawer	07Ju02Ij
OLMES, James		30	M	Laborer	07Ju02Ij
Catherine		22	F	Servant	07Ju02Ij
YNN, Mary		30	F	Servant	07Ju02Ij
FLYNN, Michael		13	M	Servant	07Ju02Ij
COFFY, Michael		23	M	Laborer	07Ju02Ij
MCCORMICK, Mary-Ann		.00	F	Infant	07Ju02Ij
LENNON, Patrick		40	M	Servant	07Ju02Ij
WALSH, Luke		22	M	Servant	07Ju02Ij
MAGOUIN, John		24	M	Servant	07Ju02Ij
DILLON, John		22	M	Laborer	07Ju02Ij
CONNELL, James		22	M	Laborer	07Ju02Ij
Catherine		24	F	Servant	07Ju02Ij
TOOLEY, Bridget		22	F	Servant	07Ju02Ij
DEMPSEY, Patrick		28	M	Laborer	07Ju02Ij
WILLIAMS, William		25	M	Laborer	07Ju02Ij
Thomas		18	M	Laborer	07Ju02Ij
Jane		28	F	Servant	07Ju02Ij
Martha		22	F	Servant	07Ju02Ij
SMYTH, Ann		20	F	Servant	07Ju02Ij
KENNARNAN, James		26	M	Laborer	07Ju02Ij
Mary		20	F	Unknown	07Ju02Ij
OKEEFE, Daniel		34	M	Laborer	07Ju02Ij
Mary		26	F	Unknown	07Ju02Ij
MALONY, John		22	M	Laborer	07Ju02Ij
William		20	M	Mason	07Ju02Ij
KELLY, William		22	M	Tailor	07Ju02Ij
LAWLER, James		20	M	Laborer	07Ju02Ij
Maria		20	F	Servant	07Ju02Ij
Ann		20	F	Servant	07Ju02Ij
MOORE, Catherine		21	F	Servant	07Ju02Ij
BEGGS, James		27	M	Fitter	07Ju02Ij
WOODS, William-Wilson		48	M	Tailor	07Ju02Ij
HARRINGTON, Arthur		21	M	Spinner	07Ju02Ij
GLEESON, Patrick		24	M	Carpenter	07Ju02Ij
FARRELL, Patrick		24	M	Laborer	07Ju02Ij
KEVENEY, Thomas		30	M	Laborer	07Ju02Ij
Bridget	(W)	20	F	Wife	07Ju02Ij
MARLOW, Richard		20	M	Laborer	07Ju02Ij
BRANNAN, Margaret		50	F	Servant	07Ju02Ij
FITZPATRICK, Edmund		20	M	Laborer	07Ju02Ij
RAFFERTY, Patrick		23	M	Laborer	07Ju02Ij
MCSORLEY, James		23	M	Clerk	07Ju02Ij
GRAHAM, Charles		21	M	Clerk	07Ju02Ij
KILLMAN, Hugh		18	M	Clerk	07Ju02Ij
JARNEY, Patrick		20	M	Laborer	07Ju02Ij
MCLAUGHLIN, Biddy		20	F	Servant	07Ju02Ij
PALLEN, Thomas		23	M	Laborer	07Ju02Ij
CONLIN, Catherine		22	F	Servant	07Ju02Ij
COYLE, Catherine		12	F	Servant	07Ju02Ij
MORTON, Robert		30	M	Paper Maker	07Ju02Ij
MCDONALD, George		40	M	Paper Maker	07Ju02Ij
STICKS, James		37	M	Paper Maker	07Ju02Ij
LEE, Samuel		30	M	Carpenter	07Ju02Ij
COLLINS, Bernard		15	M	Servant	07Ju02Ij
SULLIVAN, William		30	M	Laborer	07Ju02Ij
U-Mrs.	(W)	30	F	Wife	07Ju02Ij
Eliza		15	F	Unknown	07Ju02Ij
Winifred		11	F	Unknown	07Ju02Ij
Patt		9	M	Child	07Ju02Ij
James		16	M	Unknown	07Ju02Ij
CROWLY, John		25	M	Laborer	07Ju02Ij
Mary		.11	F	Infant	07Ju02Ij
MCDOWELL, John		25	M	Laborer	07Ju02Ij
MCKELVY, Robert		25	M	Laborer	07Ju02Ij
Ellen	(W)	24	F	Wife	07Ju02Ij
Isabella		.00	F	Infant	07Ju02Ij
BRADY, John		30	M	Laborer	07Ju02Ij
COFFEE, James		29	M	Carpenter	07Ju02Ij
GARRAHAN, Rose		49	F	Servant	07Ju02Ij
MCKELVY, Agnes		10	F	Servant	07Ju02Ij
RYAN, Martin		20	M	Laborer	07Ju02Ij
Mary	(W)	21	F	Wife	07Ju02Ij
Thomas		7	M	Child	07Ju02Ij
William		6	M	Child	07Ju02Ij
Robert		4	M	Child	07Ju02Ij
John		2	M	Child	07Ju02Ij
Hassell		.00	M	Infant	07Ju02Ij
PERKINS, Caroline		20	F	Unknown	07Ju02Ij

NAMES OF PASSENGERS		AGE	SEX	OCCUPATIONS	DATE PORT SHIP
FOSTER, George		30	M	Farmer	07Ju02Ij
U-Mrs.	(W)	32	F	Wife	07Ju02Ij
John		3	M	Child	07Ju02Ij
Mary		.00	F	Infant	07Ju02Ij
WOODS, Margaret		50	F	Wi	07Ju02Ij
Ann		16	F	Unknown	07Ju02Ij
Bridget		12	F	Unknown	07Ju02Ij
Betty		10	F	Unknown	07Ju02Ij
Patrick		8	M	Child	07Ju02Ij
WINSPEARE, Robert		24	M	Farmer	07Ju02Ij
Charlotte	(W)	21	F	Wife	07Ju02Ij
Eliza		2	F	Child	07Ju02Ij
Sarah		.00	F	Infant	07Ju02Ij
GOODFELLOW, Robert		35	M	Farmer	07Ju02Ij
QUEST, George		30	M	Laborer	07Ju02Ij
LAWLERS, Michael		24	M	Sawer	07Ju02Ij
BYRNE, Peter		22	M	Laborer	07Ju02Ij
KINSELA, Michael		19	M	Laborer	07Ju02Ij
LAWLESS, Catherine		24	F	Servant	07Ju02Ij
DICKINSON, Thomas		51	M	Laborer	07Ju02Ij
Mary	(W)	52	F	Wife	07Ju02Ij
George		19	M	Unknown	07Ju02Ij
Joseph		18	M	Unknown	07Ju02Ij
Francis		13	M	Unknown	07Ju02Ij
Ann		11	F	Unknown	07Ju02Ij
Hartas		9	M	Child	07Ju02Ij
Samuel		7	M	Child	07Ju02Ij
Piercy		5	M	Child	07Ju02Ij
FLETCHER, Abel		30	M	Laborer	07Ju02Ij
LANGLRY, John		18	M	Laborer	07Ju02Ij
Honora		16	F	Servant	07Ju02Ij
HAYES, Patrick		25	M	Maurer	07Ju02Ij
BRANNAN, John		20	M	Carpenter	07Ju02Ij
NEAVY, Ellen		20	F	Servant	07Ju02Ij
Ann		20	F	Servant	07Ju02Ij
DISKIN, Thomas		24	M	Laborer	07Ju02Ij
Patrick		20	M	Laborer	07Ju02Ij
FEEHY, Robert		30	M	Laborer	07Ju02Ij
FREEMAN, Mary		30	F	Servant	07Ju02Ij
TYNE, Margaret		14	F	Servant	07Ju02Ij
HOGAN, Michael		25	M	Laborer	07Ju02Ij
U-Mrs.	(W)	25	F	Wife	07Ju02Ij
CAHILL, Patt		25	M	Laborer	07Ju02Ij
HOGAN, Julia		20	F	Servant	07Ju02Ij
DUFFY, James		50	M	Laborer	07Ju02Ij
Owen		17	M	Unknown	07Ju02Ij
Bridget		15	F	Unknown	07Ju02Ij
Margaret		11	F	Unknown	07Ju02Ij
Anne		8	F	Child	07Ju02Ij
MCGAVIL, James		50	M	Laborer	07Ju02Ij
U-Mrs.	(W)	48	F	Wife	07Ju02Ij
Mary		16	F	Unknown	07Ju02Ij
Pat		14	M	Unknown	07Ju02Ij
Owen		11	M	Unknown	07Ju02Ij
Francis		9	M	Child	07Ju02Ij
Dennis		9	M	Child	07Ju02Ij
DUFFY, Michael		14	M	Laborer	07Ju02Ij
Mary		11	F	Servant	07Ju02Ij
WELLS, James		31	M	Unknown	07Ju02Ij
WEEDON, George		37	M	Miner	07Ju02Ij
WELLS, Jane		27	F	Servant	07Ju02Ij
CARLING, William		23	M	Miner	07Ju02Ij
BALL, John		36	M	Miner	07Ju02Ij
MIDDLETON, Thomas		23	M	Miner	07Ju02Ij
BROWN, David		21	M	Miner	07Ju02Ij
BENBAUGH, Henry		23	M	Miner	07Ju02Ij
LOUDEN, William		18	M	Laborer	07Ju02Ij
DUFFY, Gilley		19	F	Servant	07Ju02Ij
Ann		20	F	Servant	07Ju02Ij
MCGOUGH, James		19	M	Laborer	07Ju02Ij
MCENTERE, William		19	M	Laborer	07Ju02Ij
SWEENY, Jane		10	F	Servant	07Ju02Ij
MULLEN, Thomas		30	M	Laborer	07Ju02Ij
Jane	(W)	30	F	Wife	07Ju02Ij
Christopher		14	M	Unknown	07Ju02Ij

NAMES OF PASSENGERS		AGE	SEX	OCCUPATIONS	DATE PORT SHIP
MULLEN, Alice		12	F	Unknown	07Ju02Ij
SWEENY, Peter		19	M	Laborer	07Ju02Ij
DOYLE, Thomas		20	M	Laborer	07Ju02Ij
CAHILL, Thomas		30	M	Tailor	07Ju02Ij
BODDY, Robert		22	M	Shepherd	07Ju02Ij
ELLIOT, George		21	M	Saddler	07Ju02Ij
THOMPSON, James		22	M	Farmer	07Ju02Ij
HARRISON, James		20	M	Shoemaker	07Ju02Ij
CROULY, Mary		25	F	Servant	07Ju02Ij
MCDOWELL, Isaac		17	M	Laborer	07Ju02Ij
GLEEVAN, John		20	M	Laborer	07Ju02Ij
BROOKS, Dora		60	F	Wi	07Ju02Ij
Thomas		00	M	Laborer	07Ju02Ij
Mary		00	F	Servant	07Ju02Ij
REDMOND, Edward		21	M	Laborer	07Ju02Ij
Sarah		19	F	Servant	07Ju02Ij
Margaret		00	F	Servant	07Ju02Ij
PURCELL, Bridget		20	F	Servant	07Ju02Ij
KEY, Thomas		12	M	Servant	07Ju02Ij
HEALY, James		50	M	Laborer	07Ju02Ij
QUEENAN, James		50	M	Laborer	07Ju02Ij
John		26	M	Laborer	07Ju02Ij
HANNAN, Bridget		60	F	Servant	07Ju02Ij
SWEENY, Ann		17	F	Servant	07Ju02Ij
HUGHES, Catherine		18	F	Servant	07Ju02Ij
DOLTON, Thomas		12	M	Servant	07Ju02Ij
DOWLING, Mary-Ann		24	F	Dressmaker	07Ju02Ij
FRONEY, Joseph		27	M	Painter	07Ju02Ij
Deborah	(W)	31	F	Wife	07Ju02Ij
John	(S)	4	M	Child	07Ju02Ij
Joseph	(S)	.00	M	Infant	07Ju02Ij
CAMPBELL, Hugh		35	M	Shoemaker	07Ju02Ij
SKUFFLETON, Ann		25	F	Servant	07Ju02Ij
RIERDON, Thomas		22	M	Brick Maker	07Ju02Ij
SKUFFLETON, Catherine		25	F	Servant	07Ju02Ij
FARRELL, Ann		17	F	Servant	07Ju02Ij
SADLER, James		22	M	Laborer	07Ju02Ij
DOYLE, John		25	M	Laborer	07Ju02Ij
U-Mrs.	(W)	25	F	Wife	07Ju02Ij
Patt	(S)	2	M	Child	07Ju02Ij
Thos.	(S)	.00	M	Infant	07Ju02Ij

LAWRENCE-FORESTAL 08 JUNE 1849

From Waterford

NAMES OF PASSENGERS	AGE	SEX	OCCUPATIONS	DATE PORT SHIP
CAIN, Patt	50	M	Laborer	08Ju15I
Bridget	50	F	Unknown	08Ju15I
Margaret	16	F	Unknown	08Ju15I
CASEY, Johannah	16	F	Unknown	08Ju15I
GRIFFIN, William	40	M	Unknown	08Ju15I
Ellen	44	F	Unknown	08Ju15I
Catherine	38	F	Unknown	08Ju15I
TURNEY, Catherine	17	F	Unknown	08Ju15I
POWER, Johanna	24	F	Unknown	08Ju15I
MURRAY, Thomas	50	M	Unknown	08Ju15I
Michael	40	M	Unknown	08Ju15I
Bridget	17	F	Unknown	08Ju15I
Patt	10	M	Unknown	08Ju15I
Mary	17	F	Unknown	08Ju15I
Patt	13	M	Unknown	08Ju15
John	11	M	Unknown	08Ju15
William	.00	M	Infant	08Ju15
QUINN, Patt	22	M	Unknown	08Ju15
WALSH, Edward	24	M	Unknown	08Ju15
LYONS, Denis	30	M	Unknown	08Ju15
POWER, Thomas	30	M	Unknown	08Ju15
Patt	26	M	Unknown	08Ju15
FLYNN, Edmond	24	M	Unknown	08Ju15

NAMES OF PASSENGERS	AGE	SEX	OCCUPATIONS	DATE PORT SHIP
GOUGH, Nicholas	21	M	Unknown	08Ju15In
DUNPHY, Patrick	35	M	Unknown	08Ju15In
CAIN, Thomas	30	M	Unknown	08Ju15In
Ellen	30	F	Unknown	08Ju15In
Bridget	3	F	Child	08Ju15In
Patt	.00	M	Infant	08Ju15In
BOATES, Edward	22	M	Unknown	08Ju15In
HILAND, Ellen	19	F	Unknown	08Ju15In
MURPHY, Walter	50	M	Unknown	08Ju15In
Edward	21	M	Unknown	08Ju15In
Michal	17	M	Unknown	08Ju15In
Bridget	22	F	Unknown	08Ju15In
Catherine	19	F	Unknown	08Ju15In
Ann	15	F	Unknown	08Ju15In
GONNAN, Thomas	22	M	Unknown	08Ju15In
FAHEY, John	22	M	Unknown	08Ju15In
Bridget	20	F	Unknown	08Ju15In
MCCARTHY, Denis	32	M	Unknown	08Ju15In
BROWNE, Thomas	25	M	Unknown	08Ju15In
SUTTON, Mary	27	F	Unknown	08Ju15In
DUNFORD, Michal	21	M	Unknown	08Ju15In
Thomas	20	M	Unknown	08Ju15In
John	18	M	Unknown	08Ju15In
RENNEY, Margaret	23	F	Unknown	08Ju15In
TOBIN, Edward	23	M	Unknown	08Ju15In
COLFORD, Anne	23	F	Unknown	08Ju15In
Mary	20	F	Unknown	08Ju15In
Barney	19	M	Unknown	08Ju15In
Margaret	16	F	Unknown	08Ju15In
Patt	7	M	Child	08Ju15In
Mary	.00	F	Infant	08Ju15In
EGAN, Michal	22	M	Unknown	08Ju15In
WALSH, Henry	28	M	Unknown	08Ju15In
EUNES, Edward	29	M	Unknown	08Ju15In
MORGAN, John	32	M	Unknown	08Ju15In
ROCHE, Richard	29	M	Unknown	08Ju15In
NASH, Catherine	18	F	Unknown	08Ju15In
Mary	17	F	Unknown	08Ju15In
GORMAN, John	19	M	Unknown	08Ju15In
FLYNN, Anastatia	22	F	Unknown	08Ju15In
HEMBURY, Thomas	48	M	Unknown	08Ju15In
Anastatia	41	F	Unknown	08Ju15In
Mary	14	F	Unknown	08Ju15In
Joseph	12	M	Unknown	08Ju15In
Catherine	7	F	Child	08Ju15In
Thomas	.00	M	Infant	08Ju15In
BARRON, Martin	26	M	Unknown	08Ju15In
CORCORAN, Johanna	21	F	Unknown	08Ju15In
DOHENEY, John	20	M	Unknown	08Ju15In
AYLWARD, Mary	17	F	Unknown	08Ju15In
BRENNAN, Denis	24	M	Unknown	08Ju15In
MCNAMARA, James	33	M	Unknown	08Ju15In
WALSH, Margaret	22	F	Unknown	08Ju15In
BURKE, Patrick	30	M	Unknown	08Ju15In
QUIRKE, William	22	M	Unknown	08Ju15In
BRIEN, James	25	M	Unknown	08Ju15In
DONNELL, Margaret	30	F	Unknown	08Ju15In
BOWERS, Margaret	23	F	Unknown	08Ju15In
MACKAY, John	20	M	Unknown	08Ju15In
CURRENT, John	23	M	Unknown	08Ju15In
CURRAN, Michal	27	M	Unknown	08Ju15In
James	20	M	Unknown	08Ju15In
HEARNE, William	20	M	Unknown	08Ju15In
MCNAMARA, William	38	M	Unknown	08Ju15In
Catherine	28	F	Unknown	08Ju15In
Edward	14	M	Unknown	08Ju15In
William	9	M	Child	08Ju15In
Joseph	6	M	Child	08Ju15In
John	4	M	Child	08Ju15In
Mary	.00	F	Infant	08Ju15In
WELSH, Mary	21	F	Unknown	08Ju15In

GOLDEN-SPRING 09 JUNE 1849

From London

NAMES OF PASSENGERS	AGE	SEX	OCCUPATIONS	DATE PORT SHIP
LIPPY, John	18	M	Child	09Ju13lo
ANDREWS, Fredr.	41	M	Child	09Ju13lo
SATTLER, Eliza	21	F	Unknown	09Ju13lo
ANGEL, Elizabeth	23	F	Unknown	09Ju13lo
CHRIST, Geo.A.	44	M	Unknown	09Ju13lo
WINDROB, Joseph	35	M	Unknown	09Ju13lo
DAPPER, John	44	M	Unknown	09Ju13lo
Catharina-Eliz.	35	F	Unknown	09Ju13lo
HERRICK, John	18	M	Unknown	09Ju13lo
Ann-Elizabeth	14	F	Unknown	09Ju13lo
HULPPERT, Benedict	28	M	Unknown	09Ju13lo
MELINET, Catherine	32	F	Unknown	09Ju13lo
OTT, John-Francis	42	M	Unknown	09Ju13lo
REED, Joseph	23	M	Unknown	09Ju13lo
RALLAS, Andrew	22	M	Unknown	09Ju13lo
LENOX, Geo.	35	M	Unknown	09Ju13lo
Fanny	40	F	Unknown	09Ju13lo
Emily	6	F	Child	09Ju13lo
APPLEGATE, Thomas	21	M	Unknown	09Ju13lo
RIED, Jas.	42	M	Child	09Ju13lo
RAGAN, Wm.	15	M	Unknown	09Ju13lo
Mary	30	F	Unknown	09Ju13lo
DONAHUE, Ellen	21	F	Unknown	09Ju13lo
Margaret	22	F	Unknown	09Ju13lo
Bridget	23	F	Unknown	09Ju13lo
REGAN, Mary	35	F	Unknown	09Ju13lo
CREAM, Austin	3	M	Child	09Ju13lo
CALLARD, Nathaniel	29	M	Unknown	09Ju13lo
PAGE, Wm.	29	M	Unknown	09Ju13lo
Maria	32	F	Unknown	09Ju13lo
Alfred	17	M	Unknown	09Ju13lo
Thos.	5	M	Child	09Ju13lo
Wm.	3	M	Child	09Ju13lo
Joe	.00	M	Infant	09Ju13lo
Richard	32	M	Unknown	09Ju13lo
Mary-Ann	28	F	Unknown	09Ju13lo
Ann	7	F	Unknown	09Ju13lo
Wm.	3	M	Child	09Ju13lo
Emma	5	M	Child	09Ju13lo
Thos.Richard	.00	M	Infant	09Ju13lo
DEVON, Wm.	28	M	Unknown	09Ju13lo
BARKER, Joseph	22	M	Unknown	09Ju13lo
Rachael	22	F	Unknown	09Ju13lo
Martin	3	M	Child	09Ju13lo
COIN, Jno.	36	M	Unknown	09Ju13lo
Ann	30	F	Unknown	09Ju13lo
Mary	3	F	Child	09Ju13lo
CLEANES, James	24	M	Unknown	09Ju13lo
KRAVEN, Wm.	27	M	Unknown	09Ju13lo
DORSANN, Joe	24	M	Unknown	09Ju13lo
HERING, Peter	26	M	Unknown	09Ju13lo
MITCHELL, James	21	M	Unknown	09Ju13lo
Ellen	21	F	Unknown	09Ju13lo
BLAKE, Wm.	40	M	Unknown	09Ju13lo
Mary	42	F	Unknown	09Ju13lo
Thomas	21	M	Unknown	09Ju13lo
POWELL, May	40	F	Unknown	09Ju13lo
CHAPPLE, Robt.	18	M	Unknown	09Ju13lo
James	13	M	Unknown	09Ju13lo
SMITH, Ann	30	F	Unknown	09Ju13lo
QUICK, Thos.	26	M	Unknown	09Ju13lo
PAINE, Wm.	30	M	Unknown	09Ju13lo
SHURS, Jno.	21	M	Unknown	09Ju13lo
GARDNER, Thos.	20	M	Unknown	09Ju13lo
BREDELL, Dennis	28	M	Unknown	09Ju13lo

NAMES OF PASSENGERS	AGE	SEX	OCCUPATIONS	DATE PORT SHIP
CASEY, Mary	28	F	Unknown	09Ju13lo
FISHER, Jno.	23	M	Unknown	09Ju13lo
Margaret	19	F	Unknown	09Ju13lo

JAMES-H.SHEPHERD 11 JUNE 1849

From Liverpool

NAMES OF PASSENGERS	AGE	SEX	OCCUPATIONS	DATE PORT SHIP
COUGHLAN, Patric	20	M	Laborer	11Ju02Jo
John	18	M	Laborer	11Ju02Jo
KILLRIDGE, Benj.	25	M	Laborer	11Ju02Jo
BYRNE, Walter	45	M	Carpenter	11Ju02Jo
Margt.	40	F	Carpenter	11Ju02Jo
Betsey	13	F	Carpenter	11Ju02Jo
Wm.	10	M	Carpenter	11Ju02Jo
Henry	8	M	Child	11Ju02Jo
Walter	3	M	Child	11Ju02Jo
Pat.	.00	M	Infant	11Ju02Jo
NAIL, Michl.	25	M	Laborer	11Ju02Jo
CARPENTER, Bdgt.	22	F	Laborer	11Ju02Jo
CONLAN, James	23	M	Servant	11Ju02Jo
NAIL, Simon	25	M	Servant	11Ju02Jo
RIELLY, Pat.	30	M	Servant	11Ju02Jo
DOGHERTY, Rose	18	F	Servant	11Ju02Jo
Margaret	2	F	Child	11Ju02Jo
James	.00	M	Infant	11Ju02Jo
BOYLE, Wm.	17	M	Servant	11Ju02Jo
KENNON, Wm.	20	M	Laborer	11Ju02Jo
NELSON, Brdgt.	25	F	Servant	11Ju02Jo
MCGUINN, Thos.	25	M	Laborer	11Ju02Jo
KELLEY, Michl.	24	M	Laborer	11Ju02Jo
HENLY, Cons.	50	M	Laborer	11Ju02Jo
Michl.	24	M	Laborer	11Ju02Jo
Jack	40	M	Tailor	11Ju02Jo
Bdgt.	9	F	Child	11Ju02Jo
HARNET, James	25	M	Tailor	11Ju02Jo
FOLEY, Jno.	23	M	Tailor	11Ju02Jo
GOLSON, Beth	35	F	Tailor	11Ju02Jo
HARE, Martin	40	M	Surveyor	11Ju02Jo
GILLEY, Michael	26	M	Servant	11Ju02Jo
MALLOY, Bdgt.	43	F	Servant	11Ju02Jo
Mary	21	F	Servant	11Ju02Jo
Magt.	18	F	Servant	11Ju02Jo
Ann	15	F	Laborer	11Ju02Jo
Martin	12	M	Laborer	11Ju02Jo
Ellen	10	F	Laborer	11Ju02Jo
DUNKER, Magt.	12	F	Laborer	11Ju02Jo
HYLAND, Jane	21	F	Laborer	11Ju02Jo
WALSH, Cath.	20	F	Laborer	11Ju02Jo
COWLEY, Cath.	20	F	Laborer	11Ju02Jo
WALSH, Honor	4	F	Child	11Ju02Jo
TUNNEY, Ann	20	F	Laborer	11Ju02Jo
MCGOUGHLIN, Cath.	20	F	Laborer	11Ju02Jo
CARNEY, Mary	50	F	Laborer	11Ju02Jo
Andy	18	M	Laborer	11Ju02Jo
David	16	M	Laborer	11Ju02Jo
Cath.	12	F	Laborer	11Ju02Jo
Margt.	10	F	Laborer	11Ju02Jo
Tim.	8	M	Child	11Ju02Jo
Jackey	6	M	Child	11Ju02Jo
James	20	M	Laborer	11Ju02Jo
MCNELLY, Pat.	30	M	Laborer	11Ju02Jo
Ellen	28	F	Laborer	11Ju02Jo
Andy	7	M	Child	11Ju02Jo
Pat.	5	M	Child	11Ju02Jo
WHITE, Pat.	24	M	Laborer	11Ju02Jo
NEILLY, Michl.	3	M	Child	11Ju02Jo
Mary	.00	F	Infant	11Ju02Jo
BURKE, Brady	18	M	Laborer	11Ju02Jo

NAMES OF PASSENGERS	AGE	SEX	OCCUPATIONS	DATE PORT SHIP
CAREY, John	40	M	Laborer	11Ju02Jo
Cath.	35	F	Laborer	11Ju02Jo
Ellen	7	F	Child	11Ju02Jo
Bdgt.	4	F	Child	11Ju02Jo
Michael	2	M	Child	11Ju02Jo
MCDONNEL, John	30	M	Laborer	11Ju02Jo
Betty	50	F	Laborer	11Ju02Jo
BOURKE, Mary	36	F	Laborer	11Ju02Jo
HUGHES, Mgt.	30	F	Carpenter	11Ju02Jo
MCDONNOL, Ellen	18	F	Carpenter	11Ju02Jo
HOLHAM, Michl.	28	M	Carpenter	11Ju02Jo
MURRY, Pat.	30	M	Carpenter	11Ju02Jo
HOLHAM, Ellen	18	F	Carpenter	11Ju02Jo
MCMAHOD, Thos.	25	M	Miner	11Ju02Jo
GALLEGHER, Mary	19	F	Servant	11Ju02Jo
BRIEN, Danl.	25	M	Farmer	11Ju02Jo
CROKE, John	24	M	Farmer	11Ju02Jo
BLAKE, Wm.	30	M	Farmer	11Ju02Jo
Peggy	22	F	Farmer	11Ju02Jo
WALSH, John	22	M	Farmer	11Ju02Jo
PURDEN, Cath.	18	F	Farmer	11Ju02Jo
CANNING, John	40	M	Farmer	11Ju02Jo
Wm.	20	M	Farmer	11Ju02Jo
Jno.	18	M	Farmer	11Ju02Jo
KELLEY, John	25	M	Grocer	11Ju02Jo
PETERS, Pat.	20	M	Grocer	11Ju02Jo
HUGHES, John	25	M	Grocer	11Ju02Jo
MUNROE, Margt.	30	F	Servant	11Ju02Jo
GRANEY, Brdgt.	12	F	Servant	11Ju02Jo
MCGRATH, Thos.	50	M	Laborer	11Ju02Jo
Honor	40	F	Laborer	11Ju02Jo
Brdgt.	19	F	Laborer	11Ju02Jo
Michl.	16	M	Laborer	11Ju02Jo
John	12	M	Laborer	11Ju02Jo
Michl.	10	M	Laborer	11Ju02Jo
Ellen	8	F	Child	11Ju02Jo
KENDRICK, Ellen	45	F	Laborer	11Ju02Jo
James	23	M	Laborer	11Ju02Jo
Thos.	20	M	Laborer	11Ju02Jo
Edwd.	7	M	Child	11Ju02Jo
BOURKE, Pat.	21	M	Laborer	11Ju02Jo
KENDRICK, Brdgt.	9	F	Child	11Ju02Jo
RYAN, Mary	24	F	Laborer	11Ju02Jo
CAVENAGH, Bernard	40	M	Farmer	11Ju02Jo
Pat.	23	M	Farmer	11Ju02Jo
John	16	M	Farmer	11Ju02Jo
Cath.	15	F	Farmer	11Ju02Jo
Ann	12	F	Farmer	11Ju02Jo
Tim.	10	F	Farmer	11Ju02Jo
WARD, Judy	25	F	Servant	11Ju02Jo
HIGGINS, John	29	M	Publican	11Ju02Jo
U (W)	26	F	Publican	11Ju02Jo
CULLEN, Michl.	18	M	Laborer	11Ju02Jo
LOUGHLEN, Pat.	25	M	Pitman	11Ju02Jo
WALLACE, John	21	M	Servant	11Ju02Jo
SPRING, Cath.	20	F	Servant	11Ju02Jo
Elisa	22	F	Servant	11Ju02Jo
CLUSKEY, Michael	21	M	Laborer	11Ju02Jo
GORMAN, James	25	M	Laborer	11Ju02Jo
LENNON, Pat.	20	M	Laborer	11Ju02Jo
OHARE, Edwd.	22	F	Laborer	11Ju02Jo
MURRY, Mary	20	F	Laborer	11Ju02Jo
INGOLDSBY, John	24	M	Farmer	11Ju02Jo
MCGUIRE, John	24	M	Laborer	11Ju02Jo
Mary	60	F	Unknown	11Ju02Jo
Rose	21	F	Unknown	11Ju02Jo
MCDONNEL, John	16	M	Carver	11Ju02Jo
Mary	18	F	Carver	11Ju02Jo
SHIELDS, Martha	49	F	Farmer	11Ju02Jo
Elisa	21	F	Farmer	11Ju02Jo
John	17	M	Farmer	11Ju02Jo
Edwd.	19	M	Farmer	11Ju02Jo
MALONY, Cath.	28	F	Laborer	11Ju02Jo
Dennis	25	M	Laborer	11Ju02Jo
SCULLY, Luke	12	M	Laborer	11Ju02Jo

NAMES OF PASSENGERS	AGE	SEX	OCCUPATIONS	DATE PORT SHIP
MULLANY, James	11	M	Laborer	11Ju02Jo
SHIELDS, Michael	20	M	Laborer	11Ju02Jo
MCMANUS, Wm.	11	M	Laborer	11Ju02Jo
BRAELY, Sarah	20	F	Servant	11Ju02Jo
PHILLIPS, Mary	40	F	Laborer	11Ju02Jo
MACKALANY, James	50	M	Laborer	11Ju02Jo
Sarah	50	F	Laborer	11Ju02Jo
Sarah	12	F	Laborer	11Ju02Jo
LAHEY, John	20	M	Laborer	11Ju02Jo
Maria	11	F	Laborer	11Ju02Jo
DOWNY, Barbara	41	F	Servant	11Ju02Jo
GERAGHTY, John	18	M	Cobbler	11Ju02Jo
GIBBINS, Michael	32	M	Gdnr	11Ju02Jo
NEEDHAM, Wm.	30	M	Laborer	11Ju02Jo
HANLEY, Thos.	18	M	Laborer	11Ju02Jo
Ellen	11	F	Laborer	11Ju02Jo
ONEILL, John	25	M	Laborer	11Ju02Jo
HART, Magt.	18	F	Laborer	11Ju02Jo
FLATTRY, Bryan	20	M	Laborer	11Ju02Jo
SPEERMAN, Mark	20	M	Laborer	11Ju02Jo
GLEASON, Wm.	20	M	Laborer	11Ju02Jo
MCGUR, Mary	18	F	Laborer	11Ju02Jo
MCCAN, Mary-A.	18	F	Servant	11Ju02Jo
BUTLER, Fanny	21	F	Servant	11Ju02Jo
LODRICK, Mary	6	F	Child	11Ju02Jo
KEARNY, Daniel	40	M	Laborer	11Ju02Jo
Mary	35	F	Laborer	11Ju02Jo
CONNERS, Pat.	30	M	Laborer	11Ju02Jo
KEARNY, John Died-At-Sea	.00	M	Infant	11Ju02Jo
Brdgt.	9	F	Child	11Ju02Jo
Cecilia	7	F	Child	11Ju02Jo
GARROHAM, Ann	18	F	Servant	11Ju02Jo
FINN, John	30	M	Laborer	11Ju02Jo
KIRK, Martin	40	M	Cobbler	11Ju02Jo
GORMAN, Tim.	19	M	Tailor	11Ju02Jo
CUNNINGHAM, Pat.	18	M	Laborer	11Ju02Jo
DOWNES, Thos.	40	M	Laborer	11Ju02Jo
Pat.	18	M	Laborer	11Ju02Jo
LOUGHLAN, Pat.	25	M	Laborer	11Ju02Jo
OROKE, Farrel	25	M	Laborer	11Ju02Jo
CAMPBELL, Ann	45	F	Laborer	11Ju02Jo
DUFFY, Barney	45	F	Laborer	11Ju02Jo
Mary	24	F	Laborer	11Ju02Jo
Rose	11	F	Laborer	11Ju02Jo
Pat.	10	M	Laborer	11Ju02Jo
ADDY, Mary	60	F	Laborer	11Ju02Jo
BARTRAM, James	21	M	Laborer	11Ju02Jo
GANT, Anty.	40	F	Servant	11Ju02Jo
Ann	13	F	Servant	11Ju02Jo
Johanna	11	F	Servant	11Ju02Jo
Agnes	9	F	Child	11Ju02Jo
Julie	7	F	Child	11Ju02Jo
John	5	M	Child	11Ju02Jo
Barney	3	M	Child	11Ju02Jo
Mgt.	.00	F	Infant	11Ju02Jo
CAVENNAGH, James	21	M	Carpenter	11Ju02Jo
ONANN, Andrew	50	M	Farmer	11Ju02Jo
U (W)	50	F	Farmer	11Ju02Jo
Mary	25	F	Farmer	11Ju02Jo
John	30	M	Farmer	11Ju02Jo
DOGHAM, Pierce	21	M	Farmer	11Ju02Jo
HARVEY, Michl.	26	M	Farmer	11Ju02Jo
MCGRATH, John	28	M	Stctr	11Ju02Jo
U (W)	28	F	Stctr	11Ju02Jo
U	.00	U	Infant	11Ju02Jo
MANRON, Jos.	30	M	Laborer	11Ju02Jo
MEARDON, Jno.	28	M	Coachman	11Ju02Jo
MITCHEL, Eliza	30	F	Unknown	11Ju02Jo
George	2	M	Child	11Ju02Jo
CLEMENTS, Thos.	37	M	Carpenter	11Ju02Jo
U (W)	30	F	Carpenter	11Ju02Jo
Michael	24	M	Carpenter	11Ju02Jo
Mary	20	F	Carpenter	11Ju02Jo
Peter	18	M	Carpenter	11Ju02Jo
CLEMENTS, James	19	M	Carpenter	11Ju02Jo
Jane	17	F	Carpenter	11Ju02Jo
Maria	15	F	Carpenter	11Ju02Jo
Ann	13	F	Carpenter	11Ju02Jo
Bessey	10	F	Carpenter	11Ju02Jo
Rosey	11	F	Carpenter	11Ju02Jo
Pat.	9	M	Child	11Ju02Jo
Ellen	5	F	Child	11Ju02Jo
Thos.	2	M	Child	11Ju02Jo
LUTH, Mgt.	13	F	Carpenter	11Ju02Jo
CUMMISKY, Pat.	40	M	Farmer	11Ju02Jo
U (W)	40	F	Farmer	11Ju02Jo
James	24	M	Farmer	11Ju02Jo
Jane	11	F	Farmer	11Ju02Jo
Teresa	9	F	Child	11Ju02Jo
BYRNE, Barney	26	M	Laborer	11Ju02Jo
MULLEN, James	19	M	Laborer	11Ju02Jo
BATTERSLEY, Ellen	30	F	Servant	11Ju02Jo
Ann	26	F	Servant	11Ju02Jo
Hugh	3	M	Child	11Ju02Jo
BAKER, James	28	M	Potter	11Ju02Jo
LAUGHEN, Michael	37	M	Blacksmith	11Ju02Jo

CORNELIA 11 JUNE 1849

From Liverpool

NAMES OF PASSENGERS	AGE	SEX	OCCUPATIONS	DATE PORT SHIP
NEVITT, Robert	35	M	Gentleman	11Ju02Jn
Jemima	40	F	Unknown	11Ju02Jn
Matilda	5	F	Child	11Ju02Jn
Charles-Henry	4	M	Child	11Ju02Jn
BYRNE, Anne-Maria	22	F	Unknown	11Ju02Jn
Jane	21	F	Unknown	11Ju02Jn
Cecilia	16	F	Unknown	11Ju02Jn
MURRAY, Cath.	20	F	Unknown	11Ju02Jn
Fanny	19	F	Unknown	11Ju02Jn
Edward	17	M	Unknown	11Ju02Jn
Emma	14	F	Unknown	11Ju02Jn
James	35	M	Gentleman	11Ju02Jn
CLYNES, Joseph	25	M	Farmer	11Ju02Jn
Mary	25	F	Unknown	11Ju02Jn
Patrick	5	M	Child	11Ju02Jn
Joseph	.00	M	Infant	11Ju02Jn
MADDEN, Mary	19	F	Unknown	11Ju02Jn
TULLY, Bridget	17	F	Unknown	11Ju02Jn
HARNEY, John	.00	M	Infant	11Ju02Jn
COX, Joseph	32	M	Servant	11Ju02Jn
Jessie	48	F	Unknown	11Ju02Jn
ARMSTRONG, John	22	M	Wool Draper	11Ju02Jn
Robert	20	M	Wool Draper	11Ju02Jn
BUCKLEY, Timothy	22	M	Laborer	11Ju02Jn
Margt.	23	F	Unknown	11Ju02Jn
James	15	M	Unknown	11Ju02Jn
DUNPHY, Thomas	30	M	Joiner	11Ju02Jn
POWERS, Margt.	43	F	Unknown	11Ju02Jn
Sarah	20	F	Unknown	11Ju02Jn
Ellen	18	F	Unknown	11Ju02Jn
Micheal	8	M	Child	11Ju02Jn
DANN, Betsey	22	F	Unknown	11Ju02Jn
WESTMAN, Alexander	23	M	Whitesmith	11Ju02Jn
Hannah	25	F	Unknown	11Ju02Jn
DUMFRIES, John	30	M	Laborer	11Ju02Jn
SWAIN, Mary	50	F	Unknown	11Ju02Jn
STRINGER, Richd.	6	M	Child	11Ju02Jn
WHITE, Thomas	40	M	Shoemaker	11Ju02Jn
NEILL, George	26	M	Farmer	11Ju02Jn
Feby	26	F	Unknown	11Ju02Jn
Nixon	2	M	Child	11Ju02Jn

NAMES OF PASSENGERS	AGE	SEX	OCCUPATIONS	DATE PORT SHIP
Eliza-Jane Died-At-Sea	.00	F	Infant	11Ju02Jn
LAWRENCE, Anne	20	F	Unknown	11Ju02Jn
Robert	.00	M	Infant	11Ju02Jn
Anne	17	F	Unknown	11Ju02Jn
GALLIGAN, Andrew	40	M	Farmer	11Ju02Jn
Anne	35	F	Unknown	11Ju02Jn
Rose	13	F	Unknown	11Ju02Jn
Bridget	11	F	Unknown	11Ju02Jn
Martha	7	F	Child	11Ju02Jn
Peter	5	M	Child	11Ju02Jn
Phillip	3	M	Child	11Ju02Jn
Anne	.00	F	Infant	11Ju02Jn
CALLAGHAN, Thomas	45	M	Laborer	11Ju02Jn
OBRIEN, Edward	20	M	Laborer	11Ju02Jn
CONNELL, Patk.	14	M	Laborer	11Ju02Jn
John	19	M	Laborer	11Ju02Jn
REAR, Bernard	42	M	Bookkeeper	11Ju02Jn
BURKE, Sarah	21	F	Unknown	11Ju02Jn
HIGGINS, Anne	28	F	Unknown	11Ju02Jn
DWYER, Jeremiah	30	M	Painter	11Ju02Jn
Mary	25	F	Unknown	11Ju02Jn
William	.00	M	Infant	11Ju02Jn
WHELAN, Andrew	14	M	Laborer	11Ju02Jn
DUNN, Michael	27	M	Laborer	11Ju02Jn
CRAWFORD, Rebecca	17	F	Unknown	11Ju02Jn
MCKENNA, Mary	21	F	Unknown	11Ju02Jn
MCCAHA, Cath.	44	F	Unknown	11Ju02Jn
HAYDEN, Margt.	35	F	Unknown	11Ju02Jn
Michl.John	11	M	Unknown	11Ju02Jn
Thomas	9	M	Child	11Ju02Jn
ELLIOTT, Thomas	31	M	Cutter	11Ju02Jn
Elisha	22	F	Unknown	11Ju02Jn
MCAVOY, Mary	21	F	Unknown	11Ju02Jn
DAY, Eliza	60	F	Unknown	11Ju02Jn
Patk.	15	M	Unknown	11Ju02Jn
CRUTHERS, John	32	M	Sawer	11Ju02Jn
LANIGAN, George	23	M	Sawer	11Ju02Jn
BUCKLEY, John	27	M	Butler	11Ju02Jn
MORRIES, John	27	M	Yeoman	11Ju02Jn
MURPHY, Jeremiah	33	M	Yeoman	11Ju02Jn
CONNOR, Thomas	20	M	Farmer	11Ju02Jn
MURPHY, Cath.	22	F	Unknown	11Ju02Jn
FOLEY, Margt.	25	F	Unknown	11Ju02Jn
Marty	25	M	Laborer	11Ju02Jn
FURLONG, Mary	20	F	Unknown	11Ju02Jn
BRADY, John	35	M	Laborer	11Ju02Jn
ODONNELL, John	26	M	Pntr-Gzr	11Ju02Jn
Wm.	14	M	Pntr-Gzr	11Ju02Jn
James	10	M	Unknown	11Ju02Jn
Honora	22	F	Unknown	11Ju02Jn
Mary	18	F	Unknown	11Ju02Jn
BURKE, Patrick	60	M	Bookseller	11Ju02Jn
Peter	25	M	Bookseller	11Ju02Jn
LYNCH, James	18	M	Bookseller	11Ju02Jn
ROONEY, Roger	26	M	Laborer	11Ju02Jn
FOLEY, Andrew	26	M	Laborer	11Ju02Jn
MCGLONE, John	26	M	Laborer	11Ju02Jn
RIORDEN, Mary	18	F	Unknown	11Ju02Jn
DUNN, Jerimiah	28	M	Laborer	11Ju02Jn
GINTY, John	23	M	Laborer	11Ju02Jn
Eliza	30	F	Unknown	11Ju02Jn
MORRIS, Margaret	25	F	Unknown	11Ju02Jn
GINTY, Eliza-Ann	6	F	Child	11Ju02Jn
William-John	.00	M	Infant	11Ju02Jn
RADDICK, Mary	25	F	Unknown	11Ju02Jn
HASLAM, Richd.	19	M	Bookkeeper	11Ju02Jn
RALBIT, Wm.	22	M	Bookkeeper	11Ju02Jn
THOMPSON, Arabella	20	F	Unknown	11Ju02Jn
RABBIT, Mary	20	F	Unknown	11Ju02Jn
DALEY, Wm.	28	M	Farmer	11Ju02Jn
Ellen	20	F	Unknown	11Ju02Jn
COOK, Patrick	24	M	Laborer	11Ju02Jn
MARLAND, Phillip	27	M	Laborer	11Ju02Jn
KENNEDY, Bridget	24	F	Unknown	11Ju02Jn
JOYCE, Richd.	21	M	Bookkeeper	11Ju02Jn
MURPHY, Mary	25	F	Unknown	11Ju02Jn
RYAN, Judy	27	F	Unknown	11Ju02Jn
CAVANNAH, Bridget	26	F	Unknown	11Ju02Jn
John	2	M	Child	11Ju02Jn
Mary-Sarah	.00	F	Infant	11Ju02Jn
DWYER, Michael	24	M	Bookkeeper	11Ju02Jn
HOOLAHAN, Cath.	19	F	Unknown	11Ju02Jn
RYAN, Anne	19	F	Unknown	11Ju02Jn
CONDON, Morris	25	M	Laborer	11Ju02Jn
LUNDIGAN, John	27	M	Enginesmith	11Ju02Jn
CASEY, Timothy	18	M	Laborer	11Ju02Jn
Mary	19	F	Unknown	11Ju02Jn
HOURIGAN, Owen	25	M	Laborer	11Ju02Jn
SULLIVAN, Cath.	20	F	Unknown	11Ju02Jn
Mary	23	F	Unknown	11Ju02Jn
Timothy	.00	M	Infant	11Ju02Jn
CONNELLY, Bridget	23	F	Unknown	11Ju02Jn
GRADY, Sarah	46	F	Unknown	11Ju02Jn
James	7	M	Child	11Ju02Jn
CALLAGHAN, John	23	M	Farmer	11Ju02Jn
PRIEST, James	46	M	Laborer	11Ju02Jn
HARVEY, Thomas	30	M	Farmer	11Ju02Jn
MCOLIVE, John	30	M	Farmer	11Ju02Jn
Bridget	32	F	Unknown	11Ju02Jn
DOOSEY, Thomas	29	M	Laborer	11Ju02Jn
Cath.	20	F	Laborer	11Ju02Jn
HOWARD, Michael	30	M	Laborer	11Ju02Jn
John	35	M	Laborer	11Ju02Jn
Margt.	17	F	Unknown	11Ju02Jn
BURKE, Sarah	19	F	Unknown	11Ju02Jn
WHELAN, Mary	34	F	Unknown	11Ju02Jn
Judith	13	F	Unknown	11Ju02Jn
Patrick	11	M	Unknown	11Ju02Jn
GALVIN, Bernard	34	M	Laborer	11Ju02Jn
FLANNIGAN, Anne	9	F	Child	11Ju02Jn
Thomas	10	M	Unknown	11Ju02Jn
John	7	M	Child	11Ju02Jn
HARDY, Sarah	45	F	Unknown	11Ju02Jn
MCALISTER, Mary	20	F	Unknown	11Ju02Jn
Wm.	22	M	Laborer	11Ju02Jn
THOMPSON, Eliza	26	F	Unknown	11Ju02Jn
HENRY, Robert	30	M	Servant	11Ju02Jn
MILLER, George	18	M	Watchmaker	11Ju02Jn
MAGINN, Ann	19	F	Unknown	11Ju02Jn
MCCARNEY, Bridget	58	F	Unknown	11Ju02Jn
TRACEY, Bridget	49	F	Unknown	11Ju02Jn
TAGUE, Patrick	29	M	Laborer	11Ju02Jn
MULKIN, Dennis	21	M	Blacksmith	11Ju02Jn
DAVIS, James	24	M	Laborer	11Ju02Jn
MCCAULEY, Charles	21	M	Weaver	11Ju02Jn
FALLON, Cath.	48	F	Unknown	11Ju02Jn
Ann	20	F	Unknown	11Ju02Jn
CASEY, Mary	8	F	Child	11Ju02Jn
DARDIS, Peter	25	M	Laborer	11Ju02Jn
REYNOLDS, Wm.	30	M	Farmer	11Ju02Jn
Mary	22	F	Unknown	11Ju02Jn
Frances	50	F	Unknown	11Ju02Jn
Esther	20	F	Unknown	11Ju02Jn
John	20	M	Unknown	11Ju02Jn
Jacob	13	M	Unknown	11Ju02Jn
KIERMAN, Thomas	28	M	Farmer	11Ju02Jn
Elizabeth	60	F	Unknown	11Ju02Jn
Anne	25	F	Unknown	11Ju02Jn
Fanny	25	F	Unknown	11Ju02Jn
John	4	M	Child	11Ju02Jn
Eliza	3	F	Child	11Ju02Jn
Margaret	.00	F	Infant	11Ju02Jn
TAYLOR, Thomas	35	M	Farmer	11Ju02Jn
NEILL, Harriet	6	F	Child	11Ju02Jn
GRIFFIN, William	48	M	Weaver	11Ju02Jn
RYAN, Michael	36	M	Laborer	11Ju02Jn
GRIFFIN, William	9	M	Child	11Ju02Jn
Patrick	34	M	Laborer	11Ju02Jn
Ellen	10	F	Unknown	11Ju02Jn

NAMES OF PASSENGERS	AGE	SEX	OCCUPATIONS	DATE PORT SHIP
GRIFFIN, Mary	4	F	Child	11Ju02Jn
John	.00	M	Infant	11Ju02Jn
HARRINGTON, Margaret	22	F	Unknown	11Ju02Jn
MADDEN, Mary	20	F	Unknown	11Ju02Jn
LARKIN, Margaret	20	F	Unknown	11Ju02Jn
LOGHLIN, Jane	19	F	Unknown	11Ju02Jn
CURRAN, Anne	20	F	Unknown	11Ju02Jn
BRENNAN, Mary	18	F	Unknown	11Ju02Jn
CONLAN, Bridget	22	F	Unknown	11Ju02Jn
TIERNEY, Bridget	20	F	Unknown	11Ju02Jn
IVORY, Peter	10	M	Unknown	11Ju02Jn
RYAN, Michael	40	M	Servant	11Ju02Jn
ONEILL, John	20	M	Laborer	11Ju02Jn
MORLEY, George	24	M	Weaver	11Ju02Jn
PARKER, Mary	40	F	Unknown	11Ju02Jn
Anne	16	F	Unknown	11Ju02Jn
Nicholas	13	M	Unknown	11Ju02Jn
Robert	11	M	Unknown	11Ju02Jn
FITZGERALD, Edward	23	M	Apothecary	11Ju02Jn
JONES, Robert	23	M	Draper	11Ju02Jn
CONNELL, John	40	M	Laborer	11Ju02Jn
Ellen	30	F	Unknown	11Ju02Jn
Margaret	28	F	Unknown	11Ju02Jn
Mary	.00	F	Infant	11Ju02Jn
PRYER, James	22	M	Laborer	11Ju02Jn
CARROLL, Patrick	21	M	Laborer	11Ju02Jn
HURST, Ewd.	29	M	Laborer	11Ju02Jn
GANNON, James	27	M	Laborer	11Ju02Jn
Peter	24	M	Laborer	11Ju02Jn
Margt.	60	F	Unknown	11Ju02Jn
DOOLAN, Mary	26	F	Unknown	11Ju02Jn
CONNELAY, Mary	20	F	Unknown	11Ju02Jn
MALINN, Patrick	25	M	Laborer	11Ju02Jn
James	10	M	Unknown	11Ju02Jn
Mary	34	F	Unknown	11Ju02Jn
MCGEE, Samuel	30	M	Laborer	11Ju02Jn
MURRAY, James	24	M	Laborer	11Ju02Jn
BRADY, Anne	16	F	Unknown	11Ju02Jn
MAGINN, Patrick	20	M	Laborer	11Ju02Jn
MATTHEWS, John	18	M	Laborer	11Ju02Jn
CONNELY, Thomas	20	M	Laborer	11Ju02Jn
GRIFFITHS, John	32	M	Laborer	11Ju02Jn
MONAHAN, Thomas	38	M	Nailer	11Ju02Jn
BARNWELL, William	24	M	Laborer	11Ju02Jn
DUNBAR, Thomas	24	M	Blacksmith	11Ju02Jn
Mary	24	F	Unknown	11Ju02Jn
Mary	.00	F	Infant	11Ju02Jn
FARROLL, David	40	M	Laborer	11Ju02Jn
DELONGERY, Cornelius	18	M	Laborer	11Ju02Jn
SAVAGE, Patrick	24	M	Laborer	11Ju02Jn
Michael	21	M	Laborer	11Ju02Jn
CONNELL, Michl.	24	M	Laborer	11Ju02Jn
CURTAIN, Michl.	25	M	Laborer	11Ju02Jn
FLING, John	21	M	Laborer	11Ju02Jn
KIRVAN, Patrick	21	M	Laborer	11Ju02Jn
Thomas	29	M	Laborer	11Ju02Jn
ONEILL, Mary	21	F	Unknown	11Ju02Jn
MCDUNAGH, John	30	M	Bookkeeper	11Ju02Jn
Bridget	30	F	Unknown	11Ju02Jn
SHERIDAN, John	16	M	Unknown	11Ju02Jn
BARRETT, Willm.	20	M	Laborer	11Ju02Jn
MAHER, Judy	19	F	Unknown	11Ju02Jn
Willm.	26	M	Laborer	11Ju02Jn
Andrew	21	M	Laborer	11Ju02Jn
SLEVIN, Margaret	21	F	Unknown	11Ju02Jn
DUGGAN, Rose	20	F	Unknown	11Ju02Jn
LYONS, James	52	M	Tailor	11Ju02Jn
James	30	M	Tailor	11Ju02Jn
James	20	M	Tailor	11Ju02Jn
NUGENT, William	27	M	Laborer	11Ju02Jn
CONWAY, James	28	M	Laborer	11Ju02Jn
RYAN, Thomas	35	M	Laborer	11Ju02Jn
CONNOR, Edward	35	M	Laborer	11Ju02Jn
Mary	35	F	Unknown	11Ju02Jn
John	17	M	Unknown	11Ju02Jn
CONNOR, Bridget	14	F	Unknown	11Ju02Jn
DOOLAN, Margaret	24	F	Unknown	11Ju02Jn
Bridget	27	F	Unknown	11Ju02Jn
SCALLY, Lawrence	25	M	Tailor	11Ju02Jn
DELAHUNTY, Patrick	28	M	Laborer	11Ju02Jn
Margaret	26	F	Unknown	11Ju02Jn
HARRISON, Patrick	21	M	Laborer	11Ju02Jn
WELCH, Micheal	27	M	Laborer	11Ju02Jn
HARRINGTON, John	.00	M	Infant	11Ju02Jn
Born-At-Sea				
HANSON, U	.00	U	Infant	11Ju02Jn
Born-At-Sea Died-At-Sea				

JAMESTOWN 11 JUNE 1849

From Liverpool

NAMES OF PASSENGERS	AGE	SEX	OCCUPATIONS	DATE PORT SHIP
DONOHUE, James	28	M	Farmer	11Ju02Jf
Patrick	26	M	Farmer	11Ju02Jf
ROURKE, Denis	26	M	Farmer	11Ju02Jf
DONOHUE, Eliza	30	F	Servant	11Ju02Jf
James	24	M	Laborer	11Ju02Jf
DEMPSEY, John	26	M	Carpenter	11Ju02Jf
Maria	19	F	Servant	11Ju02Jf
MOONEY, Anne	24	F	Servant	11Ju02Jf
TOURNEY, John	24	F	Laborer	11Ju02Jf
NOLAN, Hugh	24	F	Laborer	11Ju02Jf
BYRNE, Mary	24	F	Servant	11Ju02Jf
Sarah	18	F	Servant	11Ju02Jf
REDMAN, Mary	19	F	Dressmaker	11Ju02Jf
Margt.	17	F	Dressmaker	11Ju02Jf
KENAHAN, Margt.	34	F	Dressmaker	11Ju02Jf
Margt.	10	F	Dressmaker	11Ju02Jf
James	14	M	Shoemaker	11Ju02Jf
Henry	4	M	Child	11Ju02Jf
COMYNS, Thomas	25	M	Carpenter	11Ju02Jf
Peter	22	M	Laborer	11Ju02Jf
EUSTACE, John	20	M	Laborer	11Ju02Jf
MALALLY, Mary	22	F	Servant	11Ju02Jf
ADAMS, Mary	40	F	Farmer	11Ju02Jf
Thos.	20	M	Farmer	11Ju02Jf
MULLOY, Cooke-C.	21	M	Laborer	11Ju02Jf
Robt.C.	20	M	Laborer	11Ju02Jf
SWEETMAN, Catharine	18	F	Servant	11Ju02Jf
CROWLEY, Timothy	30	M	Laborer	11Ju02Jf
KENNEDY, John	28	M	Farmer	11Ju02Jf
JOHNSON, Wm.	20	M	Farmer	11Ju02Jf
BLANG, Alex.	24	M	Butcher	11Ju02Jf
COX, Chas.P.	26	M	Saddler	11Ju02Jf
Mary-Anne	21	F	Saddler	11Ju02Jf
WHELAN, Anne	21	F	Servant	11Ju02Jf
JONES, Mary	20	F	Servant	11Ju02Jf
BERRY, Joseph	25	M	Farmer	11Ju02Jf
Patk.	17	M	Farmer	11Ju02Jf
CONROY, Edward	23	M	Farmer	11Ju02Jf
MCGEE, Wm.	28	M	Servant	11Ju02Jf
LANE, Denis	21	M	Dealer	11Ju02Jf
Mary	50	F	Dealer	11Ju02Jf
MARY, Jane	18	F	Dealer	11Ju02Jf
CONNELL, John	24	M	Weaver	11Ju02Jf
FALLANE, John	24	M	Maurer	11Ju02Jf
Eliza	22	F	Maurer	11Ju02Jf
OGRADY, Ctharine	20	F	Dressmaker	11Ju02Jf
FARRELL, John	24	M	Engineer	11Ju02Jf
CLARK, Daniel-C.	28	M	Surgeon	11Ju02Jf

BREWER 12 JUNE 1849

From Liverpool

NAMES OF PASSENGERS	AGE	SEX	OCCUPATIONS	DATE PORT SHIP
GREVES, Jno.	54	M	Unknown	12Ju02lw
Robt.	20	M	Unknown	12Ju02lw
FOSTER, Wm.	28	M	Unknown	12Ju02lw
HUGGAN, Jno.	26	M	Unknown	12Ju02lw
Mgt.	26	F	Unknown	12Ju02lw
Matilda	28	F	Unknown	12Ju02lw
Hannah-Jane	3	F	Child	12Ju02lw
Wm.	.00	M	Infant	12Ju02lw
Elizh.	3	F	Child	12Ju02lw
DONNAGAN, Edwd.	24	M	Unknown	12Ju02lw
TODD, Jno.	44	M	Unknown	12Ju02lw
Wm.	17	M	Unknown	12Ju02lw
BECKTON, Jos.	22	M	Unknown	12Ju02lw
ATTERTON, Thos.	38	M	Unknown	12Ju02lw
HALLIDAY, Jas.	30	M	Unknown	12Ju02lw
LISTERSTON, Hannah	23	F	Unknown	12Ju02lw
Joseph	.00	M	Infant	12Ju02lw
FERGUSON, Humphrey	50	M	Unknown	12Ju02lw
Wm.	50	M	Unknown	12Ju02lw
Robt.	18	M	Unknown	12Ju02lw
LONG, Ann	15	F	Unknown	12Ju02lw
QUINN, Malachi	30	M	Unknown	12Ju02lw
NEILD, Thos.	34	M	Unknown	12Ju02lw
HUMPHREY, Robert	19	M	Unknown	12Ju02lw
ALLEN, Jno.	56	M	Unknown	12Ju02lw
Peggy	56	F	Unknown	12Ju02lw
Pat	21	M	Unknown	12Ju02lw
Jno.	19	M	Unknown	12Ju02lw
Martin	18	M	Unknown	12Ju02lw
QUINN, James	24	M	Unknown	12Ju02lw
LAWKLAND, Wm.	30	M	Unknown	12Ju02lw
ALLEN, Dennis	9	M	Child	12Ju02lw
Mary	22	F	Unknown	12Ju02lw
Edwd.	30	M	Unknown	12Ju02lw
ALGOO, Alex.	25	M	Unknown	12Ju02lw
KILPATRICK, Jas.	18	M	Unknown	12Ju02lw
AGOO, Mary	24	F	Unknown	12Ju02lw
MCDONILL, Pat	30	M	Unknown	12Ju02lw
HOGAN, James	30	M	Unknown	12Ju02lw
FOX, George	25	M	Unknown	12Ju02lw
MARTIN, Stephen	33	M	Unknown	12Ju02lw
Jno.	11	M	Unknown	12Ju02lw
GRINDLE, Jno.	22	M	Unknown	12Ju02lw
ROBSON, Jas.	20	M	Unknown	12Ju02lw
CLAYTON, Eliz.	25	F	Unknown	12Ju02lw
Fredk.	.00	M	Infant	12Ju02lw
HURCHLEFF, Martin	40	M	Unknown	12Ju02lw
Jno.	13	M	Unknown	12Ju02lw
Fergus	32	M	Unknown	12Ju02lw
Joseph	6	M	Child	12Ju02lw
Mary-Ann	.00	F	Infant	12Ju02lw
ANDERSON, James	20	M	Unknown	12Ju02lw
PARKES, Wm.	47	M	Unknown	12Ju02lw
Sarah	47	F	Unknown	12Ju02lw
Thomas	23	M	Unknown	12Ju02lw
Alfred	20	M	Unknown	12Ju02lw
Sarah	19	F	Unknown	12Ju02lw
Sarah	17	F	Unknown	12Ju02lw
William	10	M	Unknown	12Ju02lw
STRAHAM, Deborah	36	M	Unknown	12Ju02lw
Wm.	14	M	Unknown	12Ju02lw
QUINN, Judith	25	F	Unknown	12Ju02lw
GASKILL, Jonathan	31	M	Unknown	12Ju02lw
KING, Wm.	31	M	Unknown	12Ju02lw
MCKEOWN, Pat	17	M	Unknown	12Ju02lw
DALEY, Owen	35	M	Unknown	12Ju02lw
Mary	25	F	Unknown	12Ju02lw
CLOUR, Pat	24	M	Unknown	12Ju02lw
SULLIVAN, Danl.	25	M	Unknown	12Ju02lw
Ann	23	F	Unknown	12Ju02lw
MAHONE, Mick	21	M	Unknown	12Ju02lw
SULLIVAN, Danl.	22	M	Unknown	12Ju02lw
DODGSON, Jno.	20	M	Unknown	12Ju02lw
WARBRECK, Wm.	40	M	Unknown	12Ju02lw
James	40	M	Unknown	12Ju02lw
William	11	M	Unknown	12Ju02lw
ECCLESTON, Wm.	30	M	Unknown	12Ju02lw
Margt.	28	F	Unknown	12Ju02lw
James	7	M	Child	12Ju02lw
Margt.	2	F	Child	12Ju02lw
ABBOTSON, Wm.	35	M	Unknown	12Ju02lw
WRANGHAN, George	38	M	Unknown	12Ju02lw
GEE, Jno.	30	M	Unknown	12Ju02lw
COFFEE, Jno.	32	M	Unknown	12Ju02lw
LEE, Mary	30	F	Unknown	12Ju02lw
Michl.	9	M	Child	12Ju02lw
Ellen	5	F	Child	12Ju02lw
Alice	2	F	Child	12Ju02lw
WELSH, Wm.	28	M	Unknown	12Ju02lw
MCMULLEN, Hector	22	M	Unknown	12Ju02lw
MURRAY, Mwm.	24	M	Unknown	12Ju02lw
GILDING, Jno.	45	M	Unknown	12Ju02lw
Sarah	48	F	Unknown	12Ju02lw
Sarah-Ann	21	F	Unknown	12Ju02lw
Richard	19	M	Unknown	12Ju02lw
George	10	M	Unknown	12Ju02lw
Elizabeth	8	F	Child	12Ju02lw
Michl.	6	M	Child	12Ju02lw
Margt.	3	F	Child	12Ju02lw
STINSON, Timothy	23	M	Unknown	12Ju02lw
BLASKE, Robt.	18	M	Unknown	12Ju02lw
SHERDOCK, Michl.	34	M	Unknown	12Ju02lw
WALSH, Anne	17	F	Unknown	12Ju02lw
DUNN, James	28	M	Unknown	12Ju02lw
CARROLL, Christ	28	M	Unknown	12Ju02lw
GRAHAM, Edwd.	20	M	Unknown	12Ju02lw
MEEHAM, Thomas	35	M	Unknown	12Ju02lw
Edwd.	30	M	Unknown	12Ju02lw
Mary	25	F	Unknown	12Ju02lw
Kitt	2	M	Child	12Ju02lw
Cath.	.00	F	Infant	12Ju02lw
SMITH, Phelix	26	M	Unknown	12Ju02lw
MURPHY, Patt	30	M	Unknown	12Ju02lw
Mary	30	F	Unknown	12Ju02lw
Anthony	20	M	Unknown	12Ju02lw
Johanna	16	F	Unknown	12Ju02lw
Maria	10	F	Unknown	12Ju02lw
Johny	7	M	Child	12Ju02lw
Anne	3	F	Child	12Ju02lw
REDMOND, Nancy	20	F	Unknown	12Ju02lw
MOORE, Robert	20	M	Unknown	12Ju02lw
BAGLEY, Thos.	25	M	Unknown	12Ju02lw
Henry	20	M	Unknown	12Ju02lw
Joseph	20	M	Unknown	12Ju02lw
MOORE, John	20	M	Unknown	12Ju02lw
BYRNE, Patt	25	M	Unknown	12Ju02lw
OSBURNE, John	26	M	Unknown	12Ju02lw
KAVANAGH, Meg	20	F	Unknown	12Ju02lw
CONRANG, Martin	35	M	Unknown	12Ju02lw
Mary	30	F	Unknown	12Ju02lw
Bridget	4	F	Child	12Ju02lw
Margt.	2	F	Child	12Ju02lw
Michl.	.00	M	Infant	12Ju02lw
WALSH, William	50	M	Unknown	12Ju02lw
Nancy	50	F	Unknown	12Ju02lw
Rosey	20	F	Unknown	12Ju02lw
Thos.	21	M	Unknown	12Ju02lw
HIGGANS, Margt.	25	F	Unknown	12Ju02lw
KING, James	20	M	Unknown	12Ju02lw
Mary	25	F	Unknown	12Ju02lw

NAMES OF PASSENGERS	AGE	SEX	OCCUPATIONS	DATE PORT SHIP
LITTLEMAN, Jacob	20	M	Unknown	12Ju02Iw
MAHON, M.	20	M	Unknown	12Ju02Iw
CARR, Margt.	20	F	Unknown	12Ju02Iw
GROZIER, Joseph	20	M	Unknown	12Ju02Iw
ABERDEENER, Abraham	35	M	Unknown	12Ju02Iw
Moses	25	M	Unknown	12Ju02Iw
MAJOR, Leopold	25	M	Unknown	12Ju02Iw
J.B.	28	M	Unknown	12Ju02Iw
WILD, John	26	M	Unknown	12Ju02Iw
DOYLE, Michl.	25	M	Unknown	12Ju02Iw
Mary	25	F	Unknown	12Ju02Iw
RIDDLE, Wm.	28	M	Unknown	12Ju02Iw
HELPS, Saml.	25	M	Unknown	12Ju02Iw
ELLCOTT, Robert	20	M	Unknown	12Ju02Iw
JORDAN, Alice	40	F	Unknown	12Ju02Iw
KNISELLAR, James	28	M	Unknown	12Ju02Iw
Mary	25	F	Unknown	12Ju02Iw
Martin	15	M	Unknown	12Ju02Iw
Michl.	2	M	Child	12Ju02Iw
Biddy	.00	F	Infant	12Ju02Iw
KELLY, Patk.	25	M	Unknown	12Ju02Iw
SOLAN, James	28	M	Unknown	12Ju02Iw
Sarah	25	F	Unknown	12Ju02Iw
DONOHUE, Pat	25	M	Unknown	12Ju02Iw
Sarah	25	F	Unknown	12Ju02Iw
KAVANAGH, Patk.	9	M	Child	12Ju02Iw
Cath.	10	F	Unknown	12Ju02Iw
HUTCHINSON, Eliza	25	F	Unknown	12Ju02Iw
BROWN, Wm.	25	M	Unknown	12Ju02Iw
COLLINS, Wm.	30	M	Unknown	12Ju02Iw
MCNULTY, Mag	24	F	Unknown	12Ju02Iw
BOYERS, John	35	M	Unknown	12Ju02Iw
Janet	30	F	Unknown	12Ju02Iw
David	15	M	Unknown	12Ju02Iw
James	11	M	Unknown	12Ju02Iw
Mary-Jane	7	F	Child	12Ju02Iw
Wm.	3	M	Child	12Ju02Iw
CAMPBELL, Wm.	40	M	Unknown	12Ju02Iw
Sophia	30	F	Unknown	12Ju02Iw
Walter	9	M	Child	12Ju02Iw
Robert	7	M	Child	12Ju02Iw
Mary	4	F	Child	12Ju02Iw
David	.00	M	Infant	12Ju02Iw
MANSIN, Jane	30	F	Unknown	12Ju02Iw
U	16	M	Unknown	12Ju02Iw
U	18	F	Unknown	12Ju02Iw
ROBERTS, Edward	40	M	Unknown	12Ju02Iw
Mag.	38	F	Unknown	12Ju02Iw
Sewal	21	M	Unknown	12Ju02Iw
Elizh.	20	F	Unknown	12Ju02Iw
Cath	18	F	Unknown	12Ju02Iw
Anne	16	F	Unknown	12Ju02Iw
Sarah	13	F	Unknown	12Ju02Iw
Zachariah	10	M	Unknown	12Ju02Iw
Mariah	8	F	Child	12Ju02Iw
Mary	6	F	Child	12Ju02Iw
Lazarus	4	M	Child	12Ju02Iw
David-D.	24	M	Unknown	12Ju02Iw
WILLIAMS, Wm.	26	M	Unknown	12Ju02Iw
Sarah	24	F	Unknown	12Ju02Iw
HUGHES, Sarah	30	F	Unknown	12Ju02Iw
SULLIVAN, John	38	M	Unknown	12Ju02Iw
THOMAS, Gorman	50	M	Unknown	12Ju02Iw
CASH, Thomas	23	M	Unknown	12Ju02Iw
Susan	20	F	Unknown	12Ju02Iw
FARRELLY, Bryan	28	M	Unknown	12Ju02Iw
U-Mrs.	25	F	Unknown	12Ju02Iw
HOLBORN, Eliza	28	F	Unknown	12Ju02Iw
Martha	22	F	Unknown	12Ju02Iw
Anne	.00	F	Infant	12Ju02Iw
Harriott	29	F	Unknown	12Ju02Iw
Wm.	8	M	Child	12Ju02Iw
Harriott	6	F	Child	12Ju02Iw
Robert	.00	M	Infant	12Ju02Iw
KELLY, James	27	M	Unknown	12Ju02Iw
KELLY, James-Jr.	17	M	Unknown	12Ju02Iw
CONLAN, John	13	M	Unknown	12Ju02Iw
WHITTAKER, Henry	25	M	Unknown	12Ju02Iw
Jane	25	F	Unknown	12Ju02Iw
Mary-Jane	3	F	Child	12Ju02Iw
Eleanor	.00	F	Infant	12Ju02Iw
GELSHINAN, Michl.	27	M	Unknown	12Ju02Iw
COLLINSON, Jeffry	35	M	Unknown	12Ju02Iw
Joseph	34	M	Unknown	12Ju02Iw
Mary-Ann	12	F	Unknown	12Ju02Iw
Mary	14	F	Unknown	12Ju02Iw
WATTERS, Jno.W.	27	M	Unknown	12Ju02Iw
Ellen	25	F	Unknown	12Ju02Iw
CARNELL, Jane	21	F	Unknown	12Ju02Iw
MCGOUGH, A.	40	M	Clergyman	12Ju02Iw
KNOWLAND, P.	32	M	Unknown	12Ju02Iw
U-Mrs.	29	F	Unknown	12Ju02Iw
FARRIDAY, Jane	23	F	Unknown	12Ju02Iw

GOV.HINCKLEY 12 JUNE 1849

From London

NAMES OF PASSENGERS	AGE	SEX	OCCUPATIONS	DATE PORT SHIP
PROBERT, Wm.	18	M	Blacksmith	12Ju13Jp
FARMER, Chas.	22	M	Laborer	12Ju13Jp
Died-At-Sea				
DOWLEY, James	35	M	Laborer	12Ju13Jp
GIBBS, Samuel	42	M	Laborer	12Ju13Jp
Rosetta	44	F	Unknown	12Ju13Jp
Died-At-Sea				
Samuel	18	M	Laborer	12Ju13Jp
William	16	M	Laborer	12Ju13Jp
Isaac	14	M	Laborer	12Ju13Jp
Elizabeth	11	F	Unknown	12Ju13Jp
Edmund	9	M	Child	12Ju13Jp
Died-At-Sea				
Mary-Ann	7	F	Child	12Ju13Jp
Alfred	6	M	Child	12Ju13Jp
James	4	M	Child	12Ju13Jp
BURTON, Thomas	44	M	Unknown	12Ju13Jp
ALDERSON, James	49	M	Agrc	12Ju13Jp
BAYNES, Nes.	33	M	Agrc	12Ju13Jp
FANWICK, Chas.	30	M	Agrc	12Ju13Jp
JOHNSON, Geo.	28	M	Agrc	12Ju13Jp
WRIGHT, Andrew	44	M	Agrc	12Ju13Jp
HALL, Bancroft	32	M	Agrc	12Ju13Jp
QYLEDEN, Harriet	35	F	Unknown	12Ju13Jp
Caroline	4	F	Child	12Ju13Jp
WRIGHT, Geo.	33	M	Unknown	12Ju13Jp
ABRAHAM, Michael	33	M	Unknown	12Ju13Jp
HARRIGAN, Julia	33	F	Unknown	12Ju13Jp
RAYNES, Henry	33	M	Unknown	12Ju13Jp
INTCH, Henning	31	M	Laborer	12Ju13Jp
MOLTZ, Johan	31	M	Laborer	12Ju13Jp
KELLER, Johan	40	M	Laborer	12Ju13Jp
LEISER, Johan	24	M	Laborer	12Ju13Jp
BRUCKER, Jos.	20	M	Laborer	12Ju13Jp
LOTTEREN, Jos.	27	M	Laborer	12Ju13Jp
STUMMEL, Jac.	27	M	Laborer	12Ju13Jp
KOCH, Joh.	18	M	Laborer	12Ju13Jp
EISEL, Joh.	22	M	Laborer	12Ju13Jp
SPIEDER, Christian	20	F	Laborer	12Ju13Jp
PALLANT, Pleasant	1	M	Child	12Ju13Jp
George	2	M	Child	12Ju13Jp
CROWLEY, James	36	M	Farmer	12Ju13Jp
Mary	25	F	Farmer	12Ju13Jp
HYETT, John	24	M	Clock Maker	12Ju13Jp
LINCOLN, John	26	M	Clock Maker	12Ju13Jp
Caroline	24	F	Unknown	12Ju13Jp

NAMES OF PASSENGERS	AGE	SEX	OCCUPATIONS	DATE PORT SHIP
GIBBS, Matthew	1	M	Child	12Ju13Jp
Died-At-Sea				
PALMER, William	38	M	Cbtmkr	12Ju13Jp
Elizabeth	38	F	Unknown	12Ju13Jp
Richard	3	M	Child	12Ju13Jp
MILLER, Wm.	42	M	Pipe Maker	12Ju13Jp
Hannah	42	F	Pipe Maker	12Ju13Jp
SALMONS, John	26	M	Laborer	12Ju13Jp
George	27	M	Laborer	12Ju13Jp
James	19	M	Laborer	12Ju13Jp
BROWN, John	32	M	Laborer	12Ju13Jp
Died-At-Sea				
CURTIS, John	40	M	Laborer	12Ju13Jp
BROWN, Ann	20	F	Unknown	12Ju13Jp
Died-At-Sea				
Mary-Ann	2	F	Child	12Ju13Jp
Died-At-Sea				
HANIGAN, Geo.	30	M	Laborer	12Ju13Jp
Elizabeth	34	F	Unknown	12Ju13Jp
Ann	8	F	Child	12Ju13Jp
George	6	M	Child	12Ju13Jp
James	4	M	Child	12Ju13Jp
Died-At-Sea				
THOMAS, Wm.	.00	M	Infant	12Ju13Jp

SHANNON 12 JUNE 1849

From Bristol

NAMES OF PASSENGERS	AGE	SEX	OCCUPATIONS	DATE PORT SHIP
WEEKS, Eliza	20	F	Dairymaid	12Ju10ld
PENTICOST, Jesse	31	M	Farmer	12Ju10ld
Elizabeth	29	F	Unknown	12Ju10ld
Mary-Ann	7	F	Child	12Ju10ld
William	6	M	Child	12Ju10ld
Joseph	4	M	Child	12Ju10ld
CANNING, Henry	32	M	Butcher	12Ju10ld
Louisa	31	F	Unknown	12Ju10ld
Joseph	11	M	Unknown	12Ju10ld
John	7	M	Child	12Ju10ld
Caroline	4	F	Child	12Ju10ld
Ellen	3	F	Child	12Ju10ld
Alfred	19	M	Butcher	12Ju10ld
ROBERTS, Anna	25	F	Unknown	12Ju10ld
SMITH, Joseph	53	M	Laborer	12Ju10ld
Elizabeth	50	F	Unknown	12Ju10ld
Benjamin	17	M	Unknown	12Ju10ld
Joseph	14	M	Laborer	12Ju10ld
Elizabeth	11	F	Unknown	12Ju10ld
Eliza	7	F	Child	12Ju10ld
STRONG, Elizabeth	45	F	Unknown	12Ju10ld
Sarah-Caroline	19	F	Unknown	12Ju10ld
Emma	16	F	Unknown	12Ju10ld
Fanny	14	F	Unknown	12Ju10ld
FERRANT, Thomas	36	M	Merchant	12Ju10ld
Mary	26	F	Unknown	12Ju10ld
Mary	2	F	Child	12Ju10ld
COUSINS, Jno.K.	29	M	Surgeon	12Ju10ld
Mary-Ann	31	F	Unknown	12Ju10ld
WESTLAKE, William	29	M	Laborer	12Ju10ld
Harriet	40	F	Unknown	12Ju10ld
Louisa	15	F	Unknown	12Ju10ld
Albert	13	M	Unknown	12Ju10ld
HAYNS, James	54	M	Laborer	12Ju10ld
Henry	9	M	Child	12Ju10ld
BAWDEN, John	26	M	Laborer	12Ju10ld
MONK, John	38	M	Laborer	12Ju10ld
Caroline	39	F	Unknown	12Ju10ld
Edward	3	M	Child	12Ju10ld
DYKE, Joseph	34	M	Innkeeper	12Ju10ld
DYKE, Eliza	31	F	Unknown	12Ju10ld
Eliza	1	F	Child	12Ju10ld
MILTON, Benjamin	28	M	Laborer	12Ju10ld
WOOBOURN, John	21	M	Laborer	12Ju10ld
FROST, Thomas	48	M	Farmer	12Ju10ld
Fanny	47	F	Unknown	12Ju10ld
ROW, Amelia	20	F	Dairymaid	12Ju10ld
BARNETT, Jeffrey	26	M	Flabr	12Ju10ld
Eliza	22	F	Unknown	12Ju10ld
WILKINS, Matthew	31	M	Engineer	12Ju10ld
Elizabeth	31	F	Unknown	12Ju10ld
Mary-Ann	10	F	Unknown	12Ju10ld
Martha	8	F	Child	12Ju10ld
Eliza	4	F	Child	12Ju10ld
Henry	2	M	Child	12Ju10ld
HOWELL, Mary	52	F	Unknown	12Ju10ld
THOMSON, George	41	M	Engineer	12Ju10ld
Ann	41	F	Unknown	12Ju10ld
Jeffery	11	M	Unknown	12Ju10ld
Jane	8	F	Child	12Ju10ld
William	18	M	Mechanic	12Ju10ld
William	30	M	Mechanic	12Ju10ld
DUGLAS, Schoth	28	M	Mechanic	12Ju10ld
SLADE, John	25	M	Mechanic	12Ju10ld
Mary	25	F	Unknown	12Ju10ld
SPRUCE, James	24	M	Flabr	12Ju10ld
GOODENOUGH, Robert	28	M	Flabr	12Ju10ld
BRYANT, George	20	M	Flabr	12Ju10ld
MILDRUM, William	24	M	Engineer	12Ju10ld
SPARKMAN, Jacob	30	M	Engineer	12Ju10ld
Maria	30	F	Unknown	12Ju10ld
Louisa-Ann	5	F	Child	12Ju10ld
John	3	M	Child	12Ju10ld
WISHART, Andrew	27	M	Mechanic	12Ju10ld
HEDGES, Charles	31	M	Baker	12Ju10ld
Jane	30	F	Unknown	12Ju10ld
Alfred	18	M	Baker	12Ju10ld
WRIGHT, Robert	28	M	Engineer	12Ju10ld
Charles	8	M	Child	12Ju10ld
Elizabeth	4	F	Child	12Ju10ld
Charles	30	M	Engineer	12Ju10ld
Elizabeth	28	F	Unknown	12Ju10ld
AYRS, William	28	M	Mechanic	12Ju10ld
Frances	33	F	Unknown	12Ju10ld
ROBERTS, James	44	M	Shoemaker	12Ju10ld
BISHOP, Robert	28	M	Mechanic	12Ju10ld
John	20	M	Mechanic	12Ju10ld
NOAKS, George	28	M	Miner	12Ju10ld
Arrabella	28	F	Unknown	12Ju10ld
Trepharnia	3	F	Child	12Ju10ld
ROLING, Moses	21	M	Flabr	12Ju10ld
Caphaia	22	F	Unknown	12Ju10ld
CARY, Thomas	21	M	Farmer	12Ju10ld
BLACKMORE, Joseph	41	M	Vsgn	12Ju10ld
COLLINS, Charles	32	M	Mechanic	12Ju10ld
ASHTON, John	33	M	Mechanic	12Ju10ld
Anne	37	F	Unknown	12Ju10ld
WINTER, Samuel	30	M	Butcher	12Ju10ld
SOLOMON, Samuel	30	M	Carpenter	12Ju10ld
Ann	30	F	Unknown	12Ju10ld
Hugh	6	M	Child	12Ju10ld
LANE, Moses	19	M	Laborer	12Ju10ld
BAKER, Alfred	27	M	Mason	12Ju10ld
Elizabeth	27	F	Unknown	12Ju10ld
Mary	4	F	Child	12Ju10ld
Alfred	2	M	Child	12Ju10ld
WILLIAMS, James	50	M	Farmer	12Ju10ld
WILLINGTON, Louisa	38	F	Unknown	12Ju10ld
Hester	6	F	Child	12Ju10ld
WILLIAMS, John	60	M	Farmer	12Ju10l
MORRISON, W.	24	M	Grocer	12Ju10l
PAUL, Sarah	76	F	Unknown	12Ju10l
Died-At-Sea				
JOB, William-H.	28	M	Draper	12Ju10l
Elizabeth	30	F	Unknown	12Ju10l

NAMES OF PASSENGERS		AGE	SEX	OCCUPATIONS	DATE PORT SHIP
JOB, Annet		5	F	Child	12Ju10Id
Conliss		3	M	Child	12Ju10Id
ELLENY, Edward		18	M	Draper	12Ju10Id
U, U		.00	U	Infant	12Ju10Id
U		.00	U	Infant	12Ju10Id
U		.00	U	Infant	12Ju10Id
U		.00	U	Infant	12Ju10Id
U		.00	U	Infant	12Ju10Id
U		.00	U	Infant	12Ju10Id
U		.00	U	Infant	12Ju10Id
U		.00	U	Infant	12Ju10Id
U		.00	U	Infant	12Ju10Id
U		.00	U	Infant	12Ju10Id
U		.00	U	Infant	12Ju10Id

PURSUIT 12 JUNE 1849

From Glasgow

NAMES OF PASSENGERS		AGE	SEX	OCCUPATIONS	DATE PORT SHIP
MCGOWN, John		40	M	Rdcntr	12Ju04Jm
U	(W)	40	F	Unknown	12Ju04Jm
Elizabeth		21	F	Relative	12Ju04Jm
Jean		19	F	Relative	12Ju04Jm
Rebecca		6	F	Child	12Ju04Jm
Janet		.00	F	Infant	12Ju04Jm
MCCLURKEY, Henry		26	M	Unknown	12Ju04Jm
BURNS, John		36	M	Joiner	12Ju04Jm
U	(W)	28	F	Unknown	12Ju04Jm
James		.00	M	Infant	12Ju04Jm
BROWN, Patrick		32	M	Dealer	12Ju04Jm
U	(W)	35	F	Wife	12Ju04Jm
Matthew		7	M	Child	12Ju04Jm
Mary-Ann		3	F	Child	12Ju04Jm
Levinia		.00	F	Infant	12Ju04Jm
FORSYTH, James		30	M	Wright	12Ju04Jm
U	(W)	30	F	Wife	12Ju04Jm
John		8	M	Child	12Ju04Jm
Agnes		5	F	Child	12Ju04Jm
Thomas		2	M	Child	12Ju04Jm
Peter		.00	M	Infant	12Ju04Jm
MCARTHUR, U-Mrs.		26	F	Unknown	12Ju04Jm
James	(S)	4	M	Child	12Ju04Jm
Elizabeth	(D)	.00	F	Infant	12Ju04Jm
WINTER, Hugh		36	M	Fireman	12Ju04Jm
John		17	M	Lpspt	12Ju04Jm
James		12	M	Relative	12Ju04Jm
Peter		10	M	Relative	12Ju04Jm
Mary		8	F	Child	12Ju04Jm
Catharine		6	F	Child	12Ju04Jm
Hugh		4	M	Child	12Ju04Jm
Thomas		21	M	Smith	12Ju04Jm
BIGGIN, Patrick		16	M	Goldbeater	12Ju04Jm
LYLE, William		45	M	Weaver	12Ju04Jm
U	(W)	40	F	Wife	12Ju04Jm
TELFORD, Charles		20	M	Weaver	12Ju04Jm
LYLE, James		28	M	Weaver	12Ju04Jm
U	(W)	26	F	Wife	12Ju04Jm
Margaret		11	F	Relative	12Ju04Jm
Jane		7	F	Child	12Ju04Jm
Alexander		4	M	Child	12Ju04Jm
James		.00	M	Infant	12Ju04Jm
HART, William		26	M	Mason	12Ju04Jm
U	(W)	26	F	Wife	12Ju04Jm
WHITE, George		40	M	Artist	12Ju04Jm
INNIE, James		50	M	Laborer	12Ju04Jm
MCRAY, Robert		29	M	Schm	12Ju04Jm
U	(W)	23	F	Wife	12Ju04Jm
ASTON, John		55	M	Wright	12Ju04Jm
EITCH, Robert		26	M	Laborer	12Ju04Jm
LEITCH, U	(W)	24	F	Wife	12Ju04Jm
Margaret		.00	F	Infant	12Ju04Jm
CUICKSHANKS, Andrew		26	M	Laborer	12Ju04Jm
SINCLAIR, Alexander		28	M	Baker	12Ju04Jm
U	(W)	20	F	Wife	12Ju04Jm
MCGOWN, U-Mrs.		55	F	Wife	12Ju04Jm
ONEIL, Michael		35	M	Shoemaker	12Ju04Jm
MACHWEE, James		7	M	Child	12Ju04Jm
HARRIS, Alexander		40	M	Tailor	12Ju04Jm
U	(W)	30	F	Wife	12Ju04Jm
James		10	M	Relative	12Ju04Jm
Alexander		8	M	Child	12Ju04Jm
Mary		6	F	Child	12Ju04Jm
David		4	M	Child	12Ju04Jm
Thomas		2	M	Child	12Ju04Jm
BLACK, U-Mrs.		40	F	Wi	12Ju04Jm
Betsey		17	F	Relative	12Ju04Jm
Agnes		12	F	Relative	12Ju04Jm
George		10	M	Relative	12Ju04Jm
Hugh		8	M	Child	12Ju04Jm
Mary		5	F	Child	12Ju04Jm
John		3	M	Child	12Ju04Jm
James		.00	M	Infant	12Ju04Jm
SCOTT, George		20	M	Blacksmith	12Ju04Jm
James		18	M	Laborer	12Ju04Jm
CAVERS, Adam		19	M	Laborer	12Ju04Jm
MURRAY, William		35	M	Tailor	12Ju04Jm
Mary		28	F	House Maid	12Ju04Jm
FAIRBAIRN, James		19	M	Laborer	12Ju04Jm
Walter		14	M	Laborer	12Ju04Jm
HENDERSON, George		22	M	Tailor	12Ju04Jm
EASTON, Agnes		28	F	Spinster	12Ju04Jm
NISH, Alexander		30	M	Tailor	12Ju04Jm
Nathaniel		26	M	Laborer	12Ju04Jm
MCKAY, Alexander		24	M	Millwright	12Ju04Jm
THOMSON, David		34	M	Draftsman	12Ju04Jm
U-Mrs.		34	F	Tailor	12Ju04Jm
PATERSON, John		13	M	Unknown	12Ju04Jm
James		10	M	Relative	12Ju04Jm
Hellen		6	F	Child	12Ju04Jm
LEISHMAN, John		26	M	Clcp	12Ju04Jm
BLAIR, Robert		28	M	Clcp	12Ju04Jm
RAMSEY, George		22	M	Cartwright	12Ju04Jm
BOYLE, Peter		28	M	Laborer	12Ju04Jm
HOWDEN, George		28	M	Shoemaker	12Ju04Jm
LINDSAY, John		30	M	Coach Maker	12Ju04Jm
Jannes	(W)	30	F	Wife	12Ju04Jm
Hugh	(S)	4	M	Child	12Ju04Jm
John	(S)	.00	M	Infant	12Ju04Jm
Hugh		30	M	Engineer	12Ju04Jm
BOYLE, James		20	M	Laborer	12Ju04Jm
WHITELAW, James		21	M	Laborer	12Ju04Jm
HANA, William		20	M	Laborer	12Ju04Jm
DAILY, John		22	M	Laborer	12Ju04Jm
CLARK, Mary		45	F	Wi	12Ju04Jm
James		22	M	Laborer	12Ju04Jm
MCLESH, George		30	M	Carter	12Ju04Jm
BROWN, Thomas		21	M	Weaver	12Ju04Jm
GRAY, John		63	M	Weaver	12Ju04Jm
John		24	M	Weaver	12Ju04Jm
Robert		22	M	Laborer	12Ju04Jm
Thomas		20	M	Weaver	12Ju04Jm
BOYD, John		22	M	Laborer	12Ju04Jm
LOGG, Francis		23	M	Carter	12Ju04Jm
DRUMMOND, U-Mrs.		57	F	Wife	12Ju04Jm
Hellen		36	F	Wife	12Ju04Jm
John		29	M	Weaver	12Ju04Jm
Jannet	(W)	24	F	Wife	12Ju04Jm
Ann		20	F	Servant	12Ju04Jm
FERNIE, James		.00	M	Infant	12Ju04Jm
PRATT, William		22	M	Weaver	12Ju04Jm
CHRISTIE, Elizabeth		31	F	Servant	12Ju04Jm
SIMPSON, John		20	M	Tailor	12Ju04Jm
GUTHRIE, Robert		20	M	Tailor	12Ju04Jm
STRACHAN, David		26	M	Weaver	12Ju04Jm

NAMES OF PASSENGERS		AGE	SEX	OCCUPATIONS	DATE PORT SHIP
MILNE, Henry		27	M	Weaver	12Ju04Jm
U-Mrs.		30	F	Wife	12Ju04Jm
James	(S)	6	M	Child	12Ju04Jm
Jannet	(D)	4	F	Child	12Ju04Jm
CONNIE, John		23	M	Smith	12Ju04Jm
Isabella	(W)	24	F	Wife	12Ju04Jm
LAW, James		30	M	Weaver	12Ju04Jm
U-Mrs.		25	F	Wife	12Ju04Jm
Jean	(D)	2	F	Child	12Ju04Jm
John	(S)	.00	M	Infant	12Ju04Jm
LEERY, Hellen		21	F	Servant	12Ju04Jm
MCDONALD, Charlotte		50	F	Wife	12Ju04Jm
GREGG, James		26	M	Engineer	12Ju04Jm
GALLOCHER, John		26	M	Laborer	12Ju04Jm
Daniel		20	M	Laborer	12Ju04Jm
CARRON, Ann		20	F	Servant	12Ju04Jm
BRIAN, Mary		50	F	Spinster	12Ju04Jm
Ann	(D)	13	F	Relative	12Ju04Jm
John	(S)	12	M	Relative	12Ju04Jm
MCGEE, William		27	M	Laborer	12Ju04Jm
BOYLE, Edward		27	M	Tailor	12Ju04Jm
SHEVELIN, John		26	M	Laborer	12Ju04Jm
MCCALLUM, Edward		24	M	Tailor	12Ju04Jm
CAMPBELL, Nancy		30	F	Spinster	12Ju04Jm
SHERIDAN, Margaret		30	F	Servant	12Ju04Jm
Susan		26	F	Servant	12Ju04Jm
James		26	M	Laborer	12Ju04Jm
William		24	M	Shoemaker	12Ju04Jm
James		24	M	Laborer	12Ju04Jm
BOYLE, Barnabas		35	M	Laborer	12Ju04Jm
Charles		17	M	Laborer	12Ju04Jm
Brian		15	M	Laborer	12Ju04Jm
LOUGH, Dominicke		21	M	Carpenter	12Ju04Jm
COYLE, John		40	M	Laborer	12Ju04Jm
Mary		16	F	Servant	12Ju04Jm
Catharine		11	F	Servant	12Ju04Jm
BROWN, Brian		29	M	Laborer	12Ju04Jm
GALLOCHER, Mary		24	F	Wife	12Ju04Jm
BROWN, Patrick		28	M	Laborer	12Ju04Jm
Nancy	(W)	28	F	Wife	12Ju04Jm
Mary		.00	F	Infant	12Ju04Jm
ONEIL, Henry		30	M	Laborer	12Ju04Jm
Ann	(W)	25	F	Wife	12Ju04Jm
MCCALE, Ann		18	F	Spinster	12Ju04Jm
WOODS, Bridget		25	F	Spinster	12Ju04Jm
GOUGHAN, Bridget		20	F	Spinster	12Ju04Jm
FLINN, Bridget		15	F	Spinster	12Ju04Jm
LAVIN, Honor		30	F	Spinster	12Ju04Jm
BURNET, Ann		18	F	Spinster	12Ju04Jm
DAILY, Dorothy		18	F	Spinster	12Ju04Jm
GALORTY, Patrick		22	M	Laborer	12Ju04Jm
LYNCH, John		30	M	Laborer	12Ju04Jm
SKEFFINGTON, Patrick		28	M	Laborer	12Ju04Jm
U	(W)	26	F	Wife	12Ju04Jm
Patrick	(S)	2	M	Child	12Ju04Jm
MULHARN, Ann		21	F	Spinster	12Ju04Jm
GLYN, Bridget		15	F	Spinster	12Ju04Jm
DEIGNON, Patrick		22	M	Laborer	12Ju04Jm
CAVANAUGH, John		24	M	Laborer	12Ju04Jm
GERAN, Bridget		18	F	Spinster	12Ju04Jm
FAUZY, Ann		22	F	Spinster	12Ju04Jm
DOUGHERTY, Owen		40	M	Laborer	12Ju04Jm
Nancy	(W)	30	F	Wife	12Ju04Jm
Bridget		13	F	Unknown	12Ju04Jm
Mary		11	F	Unknown	12Ju04Jm
MCGEINDER, Thomas		24	M	Laborer	12Ju04Jm
Margaret	(W)	24	F	Wife	12Ju04Jm
Jane		4	F	Child	12Ju04Jm
James		2	M	Child	12Ju04Jm
SCOLEY, Nancy		19	F	Spinster	12Ju04Jm
LYON, Mary		24	F	Wife	12Ju04Jm
Samuel		.00	M	Infant	12Ju04Jm
WOODBURN, Robert		22	M	Laborer	12Ju04Jm
Jane	(W)	19	F	Wife	12Ju04Jm
MISKELLY, Jane		34	F	Spinster	12Ju04Jm
MISKELLY, Samuel		13	M	Unknown	12Ju04Jm
John	(S)	11	M	Unknown	12Ju04Jm
William	(S)	9	M	Child	12Ju04Jm
Mary-Jane	(D)	7	F	Child	12Ju04Jm
Sarah	(D)	5	F	Child	12Ju04Jm
Margaret	(D)	3	F	Child	12Ju04Jm
Eliza	(D)	2	F	Child	12Ju04Jm
James	(S)	.00	M	Infant	12Ju04Jm
MCHENDRY, Nancy		40	F	Wife	12Ju04Jm
Rose		19	F	Spinster	12Ju04Jm
Agnes		17	F	Laborer	12Ju04Jm
Martha		14	F	Spinster	12Ju04Jm
Susanna		10	F	Unknown	12Ju04Jm
DOURACH, Sally		30	F	Wife	12Ju04Jm
John		30	M	Laborer	12Ju04Jm
William	(S)	4	M	Child	12Ju04Jm
Hellen	(D)	.00	F	Infant	12Ju04Jm
KANE, John		15	M	Laborer	12Ju04Jm
KERRY, John		37	M	Laborer	12Ju04Jm
John		13	M	Unknown	12Ju04Jm
BOYLE, James		20	M	Laborer	12Ju04Jm
Patrick		40	M	Laborer	12Ju04Jm
QUIN, Mark		54	M	Laborer	12Ju04Jm
HICKEY, James		26	M	Smith	12Ju04Jm
U	(W)	26	F	Wife	12Ju04Jm
John	(S)	4	M	Child	12Ju04Jm
Mary	(D)	3	F	Child	12Ju04Jm
James	(S)	.00	M	Infant	12Ju04Jm
CRAWFORD, John		23	M	Laborer	12Ju04Jm
ROBSON, John		30	M	Laborer	12Ju04Jm
SWEENEY, Thomas		40	M	Laborer	12Ju04Jm
GRIFFEN, John		20	M	Bootmaker	12Ju04Jm
MCCULLUM, James		34	M	Shoemaker	12Ju04Jm
MCKENA, Charles		30	M	Shoemaker	12Ju04Jm
COYLE, Andrew		40	M	Shoemaker	12Ju04Jm
MCCALL, Ann		28	F	Spinster	12Ju04Jm
COYLE, James		14	M	Unknown	12Ju04Jm
SINCLAIR, Alexander		26	M	Tailor	12Ju04Jm
MCCALLUM, U-Mrs.		40	F	Wife	12Ju04Jm
William	(S)	12	M	Unknown	12Ju04Jm
John	(S)	4	M	Child	12Ju04Jm
MCMARTEN, David		32	M	Laborer	12Ju04Jm
KINGHORN, Alexander		21	M	Joiner	12Ju04Jm
CARR, Patrick		20	M	Laborer	12Ju04Jm
NAIRN, Peter		31	M	Laborer	12Ju04Jm
TEOUP, Alexander		30	M	Plant Layer	12Ju04Jm
U	(W)	28	F	Wife	12Ju04Jm
Elizabeth	(D)	.00	F	Infant	12Ju04Jm
MCCALLUM, Roden		54	M	Laborer	12Ju04Jm
CLYDESDALE, John		27	M	Laborer	12Ju04Jm
BURNS, Mary		20	F	Spinster	12Ju04Jm
MCGILL, Mary		19	F	Spinster	12Ju04Jm
BANKS, Alexander		26	M	Miller	12Ju04Jm
NICOL, James		29	M	Clerk	12Ju04Jm
MOOR, Joseph		28	M	Starcher	12Ju04Jm
LOUDON, John		36	M	Laborer	12Ju04Jm
LUNDIE, William		24	M	Laborer	12Ju04Jm
PATERSON, Andrew		31	M	Draper	12Ju04Jm
U	(W)	28	F	Wife	12Ju04Jm
Hellen	(D)	5	F	Child	12Ju04Jm
Christina	(D)	.00	F	Infant	12Ju04Jm
INNES, James		24	M	Millwright	12Ju04Jm
MILNE, John		22	M	Millwright	12Ju04Jm
COWAN, David		20	M	Draper	12Ju04Jm
ONEIL, U-Mrs.		35	F	Wife	12Ju04Jm

NAMES OF PASSENGERS	AGE	SEX	OCCUPATIONS	DATE PORT SHIP

METEOR 12 JUNE 1849

From Liverpool

NAMES OF PASSENGERS	AGE	SEX	OCCUPATIONS	DATE PORT SHIP
WILSON, Sarah	30	F	Servant	12Ju02Jz
Eliza	16	F	Servant	12Ju02Jz
James	15	M	Servant	12Ju02Jz
William	12	M	Servant	12Ju02Jz
Louisa	7	F	Child	12Ju02Jz
TAYLOR, Amelia	16	F	Servant	12Ju02Jz
ATTAWAY, K.	32	M	Mechanic	12Ju02Jz
ASH, F.	38	M	Servant	12Ju02Jz
WARDROBE, C.	31	M	Silversmith	12Ju02Jz
Ann	30	F	Silversmith	12Ju02Jz
Fredrick	7	M	Child	12Ju02Jz
Lucy	4	F	Child	12Ju02Jz
Ann	2	F	Child	12Ju02Jz
Thomas	.00	M	Infant	12Ju02Jz
JOHNSON, C.R.	19	M	Tailor	12Ju02Jz
MILLIGAN, James	36	M	Laborer	12Ju02Jz
Johanna	44	F	Laborer	12Ju02Jz
Mic.	24	M	Laborer	12Ju02Jz
Anne	22	F	Servant	12Ju02Jz
Ellen	20	F	Servant	12Ju02Jz
John	18	M	Laborer	12Ju02Jz
Laurence	17	M	Laborer	12Ju02Jz
Margaret	10	F	Servant	12Ju02Jz
James	8	M	Child	12Ju02Jz
Johanna	7	F	Child	12Ju02Jz
Simon	4	M	Child	12Ju02Jz
COLLINS, Thomas	35	M	Farmer	12Ju02Jz
Ellen	34	F	Farmer	12Ju02Jz
John	10	M	Farmer	12Ju02Jz
James	9	M	Child	12Ju02Jz
Mic.	7	M	Child	12Ju02Jz
Mary	6	F	Child	12Ju02Jz
Thomas	5	M	Child	12Ju02Jz
Pat	3	M	Child	12Ju02Jz
PRESTON, Catherine	26	F	Servant	12Ju02Jz
MCGUINNIS, Mary	25	F	Servant	12Ju02Jz
HALLIGAN, Bridget	20	F	Servant	12Ju02Jz
TIMORAN, John	26	M	Farmer	12Ju02Jz
Betty	24	F	Farmer	12Ju02Jz
Nic.	.00	M	Infant	12Ju02Jz
QUIN, Mary	28	F	Servant	12Ju02Jz
Bridget	26	F	Servant	12Ju02Jz
KANE, Eliza	20	F	Servant	12Ju02Jz
BURNS, Eliza	20	F	Servant	12Ju02Jz
FITZGERALD, John	48	M	Laborer	12Ju02Jz
KENNEDY, Nic.	28	M	Laborer	12Ju02Jz
Andrew	27	M	Laborer	12Ju02Jz
Ellen	26	F	Laborer	12Ju02Jz
Mary	25	F	Servant	12Ju02Jz
Hannah	24	F	Servant	12Ju02Jz
Daniel	6	M	Child	12Ju02Jz
FINLAY, Luke	24	M	Laborer	12Ju02Jz
DELAHUNTY, Michael	36	M	Laborer	12Ju02Jz
U (W)	25	F	Unknown	12Ju02Jz
BURNES, Eliza	18	F	Laborer	12Ju02Jz
DELAHUNTY, Mic.	6	M	Child	12Ju02Jz
Bridget	4	F	Child	12Ju02Jz
Mary	3	F	Child	12Ju02Jz
John	00	M	Unknown	12Ju02Jz
Died-At-Sea				
Catherine	.00	F	Infant	12Ju02Jz
John	50	M	Laborer	12Ju02Jz
Mary	25	F	Laborer	12Ju02Jz
Lawrence	3	M	Child	12Ju02Jz

NAMES OF PASSENGERS	AGE	SEX	OCCUPATIONS	DATE PORT SHIP
U	.00	U	Infant	12Ju02Jz
Born-At-Sea				
Nic.	7	M	Child	12Ju02Jz
Mary	5	F	Child	12Ju02Jz
WALON, Joseph	19	M	Laborer	12Ju02Jz
Margaret	14	F	Laborer	12Ju02Jz
QUINN, John	20	M	Laborer	12Ju02Jz
Catherine	18	F	Laborer	12Ju02Jz
COFFREY, James	25	M	Laborer	12Ju02Jz
KELLER, Peter	25	M	Laborer	12Ju02Jz
REILLY, Rid.	30	M	Servant	12Ju02Jz
GOLDSMITH, Sally	25	F	Servant	12Ju02Jz
MONIES, Cecilia	25	F	Servant	12Ju02Jz
REILLY, Catherine	9	F	Child	12Ju02Jz
DOOGAN, Michael	40	M	Laborer	12Ju02Jz
WILLIAMSON, John	25	M	Laborer	12Ju02Jz
Maboth	24	F	Laborer	12Ju02Jz
WATSON, Laurence	22	M	Laborer	12Ju02Jz
Pat	21	M	Laborer	12Ju02Jz
Honora	24	F	Laborer	12Ju02Jz
CONROY, Joseph	24	M	Laborer	12Ju02Jz
FENNON, Thomas	59	M	Laborer	12Ju02Jz
PATTISON, James	46	M	Farmer	12Ju02Jz
Diadem	35	F	Farmer	12Ju02Jz
Bessy	9	F	Child	12Ju02Jz
William	7	M	Child	12Ju02Jz
Eliza	40	F	Farmer	12Ju02Jz
James	16	F	Farmer	12Ju02Jz
John	14	F	Farmer	12Ju02Jz
Mary	19	F	Farmer	12Ju02Jz
Diana	5	F	Child	12Ju02Jz
MCKENNIE, Dennis	26	M	Laborer	12Ju02Jz
CROWLEY, John	30	M	Laborer	12Ju02Jz
MCCARTY, Tim.	23	M	Laborer	12Ju02Jz
HANLEY, Ellen	28	F	Laborer	12Ju02Jz
GILSHAM, Peter	55	M	Farmer	12Ju02Jz
Nancy	50	F	Farmer	12Ju02Jz
Ann	19	F	Farmer	12Ju02Jz
John	17	M	Farmer	12Ju02Jz
Betty	14	F	Farmer	12Ju02Jz
ODONNELL, John	50	F	Farmer	12Ju02Jz
U (W)	40	F	Farmer	12Ju02Jz
Harriet	12	F	Farmer	12Ju02Jz
MCKILOBODY, Ann	30	F	Farmer	12Ju02Jz
James	10	M	Child	12Ju02Jz
Elizabeth	7	F	Child	12Ju02Jz
Thomas	.00	M	Infant	12Ju02Jz
BURNES, James	30	M	Laborer	12Ju02Jz
Margaret	29	F	Unknown	12Ju02Jz
William	.00	M	Infant	12Ju02Jz
KERNAN, John	35	M	Unknown	12Ju02Jz
Mary	12	F	Unknown	12Ju02Jz
Martha	30	F	Unknown	12Ju02Jz
DUFFY, Bridget	20	F	Servant	12Ju02Jz
MAHONY, Maurice	20	M	Laborer	12Ju02Jz
GARNET, Mary	40	F	Servant	12Ju02Jz
HEATH, James	25	M	Farmer	12Ju02Jz
Humphrey	20	M	Farmer	12Ju02Jz
BROWN, Daniel	30	M	Farmer	12Ju02Jz
U (W)	32	F	Farmer	12Ju02Jz
Honora	5	F	Child	12Ju02Jz
Margaret	3	F	Child	12Ju02Jz
Ellen	.00	F	Infant	12Ju02Jz
Bridget	24	F	Farmer	12Ju02Jz
SULLIVAN, Jane	24	F	Farmer	12Ju02Jz
BISHOP, Pat.	25	M	Farmer	12Ju02Jz
Bridget	22	F	Farmer	12Ju02Jz
Catherine	.00	F	Infant	12Ju02Jz
ROONEY, Pat.	50	M	Servant	12Ju02Jz
Jane	57	F	Servant	12Ju02Jz
Pat.	22	M	Servant	12Ju02Jz
Frank	20	M	Servant	12Ju02Jz
Richd.	17	M	Servant	12Ju02Jz
John	15	M	Servant	12Ju02Jz
Kit	13	F	Servant	12Ju02Jz

NAMES OF PASSENGERS	AGE	SEX	OCCUPATIONS	DATE PORT SHIP
ROONEY, William	11	M	Servant	12Ju02Jz
Bridget	9	F	Servant	12Ju02Jz
MURREY, Pat	25	M	Servant	12Ju02Jz
Mary	25	F	Servant	12Ju02Jz
BRANNON, Dennis	26	M	Laborer	12Ju02Jz
Anne	18	F	Laborer	12Ju02Jz
CARELESS, Bridget	20	F	Laborer	12Ju02Jz
MAHONY, James	22	M	Servant	12Ju02Jz
Margaret	60	F	Servant	12Ju02Jz
CURWIN, Michael	25	M	Servant	12Ju02Jz
HEAVY, James	25	M	Servant	12Ju02Jz
KELLY, John	28	M	Servant	12Ju02Jz
WOOLAN, James	20	M	Servant	12Ju02Jz
BRYAN, James	25	M	Servant	12Ju02Jz
WOOLAN, Nic.	12	M	Servant	12Ju02Jz
Mary-Ann	20	F	Servant	12Ju02Jz
NIELD, Ann	22	F	Servant	12Ju02Jz
DOOLAN, Francis	40	M	Servant	12Ju02Jz
MCCABE, Elizabeth	25	F	Seamstress	12Ju02Jz
Catherine	22	F	Seamstress	12Ju02Jz
MILES, James	24	M	Laborer	12Ju02Jz
DANIELS, John	30	M	Laborer	12Ju02Jz
FYES, Wm.	30	M	Laborer	12Ju02Jz
HEYES, Wm.	50	M	Laborer	12Ju02Jz
Anty.	30	M	Laborer	12Ju02Jz
BURNES, Mary	30	F	Servant	12Ju02Jz
MURPHY, Ellen	22	F	Servant	12Ju02Jz
MCMANN, Ann	22	F	Servant	12Ju02Jz
Maragret	24	F	Servant	12Ju02Jz
BURNES, Biddy	30	F	Servant	12Ju02Jz
John	.00	M	Infant	12Ju02Jz
CALIS, Margaret	30	F	Servant	12Ju02Jz
MURPHY, James	4	M	Child	12Ju02Jz
BREENS, Miles	30	M	Farmer	12Ju02Jz
FORTUNE, John	30	M	Farmer	12Ju02Jz
MALONE, Bridget	24	F	Servant	12Ju02Jz
HANSON, Patrick	30	M	Servant	12Ju02Jz
COLLINS, Ellen	.00	F	Infant	12Ju02Jz

EARL-OF-DURHAM 12 JUNE 1849

From London

NAMES OF PASSENGERS	AGE	SEX	OCCUPATIONS	DATE PORT SHIP
STEEL, Timothy	24	M	Laborer	12Ju13Is
WALDRON, Maria	26	F	Servant	12Ju13Is
Elizabeth	16	F	Servant	12Ju13Is
ELLIOTT, Thomas	50	M	Unknown	12Ju13Is
Eliza	45	F	Unknown	12Ju13Is
William	24	M	Unknown	12Ju13Is
VANSTON, Robt.	28	M	Unknown	12Ju13Is
Ann	27	F	Unknown	12Ju13Is
POST, John	38	M	Unknown	12Ju13Is
STANLEY, William	32	M	Unknown	12Ju13Is
Rebecca	32	F	Unknown	12Ju13Is
Thos.W.	2	M	Child	12Ju13Is
HILL, George	25	M	Unknown	12Ju13Is
HUZZY, Mary	30	F	Unknown	12Ju13Is
FINNAMORE, Margaret	35	F	Unknown	12Ju13Is
Frederic	16	M	Unknown	12Ju13Is
John	14	M	Unknown	12Ju13Is
William	12	M	Unknown	12Ju13Is
Alfred	8	M	Child	12Ju13Is
Emily	6	F	Child	12Ju13Is
Mary-Ann	2	F	Child	12Ju13Is
Sarah	60	F	Unknown	12Ju13Is
WOOD, Wm.	24	M	Unknown	12Ju13Is
HORSBY, Wm.	28	M	Unknown	12Ju13Is
SKINNER, Edw.	23	M	Unknown	12Ju13Is
KAY, John	26	M	Unknown	12Ju13Is
KAY, Mary	26	F	Unknown	12Ju13Is
DEE, Mary	45	F	Unknown	12Ju13Is
HENRY, Margaret	22	F	Unknown	12Ju13Is
LEE, Alfred	25	M	Unknown	12Ju13Is
Hannah	22	F	Unknown	12Ju13Is
Maria	.00	F	Infant	12Ju13Is
WOOD, Saml.	25	M	Unknown	12Ju13Is
Edw.	26	M	Unknown	12Ju13Is
Eldred	20	M	Unknown	12Ju13Is
Elizabeth	22	F	Unknown	12Ju13Is
PALMER, Edward	21	M	Unknown	12Ju13Is
GEER, Charles	25	M	Unknown	12Ju13Is
SMITH, Edw.	24	M	Unknown	12Ju13Is
DAVIS, Ann	28	F	Unknown	12Ju13Is
HARRISON, Wm.	30	M	Unknown	12Ju13Is
Fanny	20	F	Unknown	12Ju13Is
LANE, Danl.	24	M	Unknown	12Ju13Is
BAILEY, James	29	M	Unknown	12Ju13Is
Jane	28	F	Unknown	12Ju13Is
Maria	52	F	Unknown	12Ju13Is
Jemima	21	F	Unknown	12Ju13Is
Jane	4	F	Child	12Ju13Is

HEROINE 12 JUNE 1849

From Newcastle

NAMES OF PASSENGERS	AGE	SEX	OCCUPATIONS	DATE PORT SHIP
FARLEY, John	42	M	Miner	12Ju18Ix
WRIGHT, Wm.	26	M	Painter	12Ju18Ix
Ann	20	F	Unknown	12Ju18Ix
Mary-Ann	.09	F	Infant	12Ju18Ix
MOORE, Deborah	60	F	Unknown	12Ju18Ix
GORDON, Saml.	28	M	Unknown	12Ju18Ix
FARLEY, James	16	M	Miner	12Ju18Ix
DREW, Edward	45	M	Laborer	12Ju18Ix
SCOTT, John-Andw.	28	M	Miner	12Ju18Ix
Ann	28	F	Unknown	12Ju18Ix
J.G.	20	M	Unknown	12Ju18Ix
CRAWFORD, Thos.	32	M	Unknown	12Ju18Ix
Mary	29	F	Unknown	12Ju18Ix
Elizabeth	.11	F	Infant	12Ju18Ix
ALDER, John	31	M	Unknown	12Ju18Ix
Ann	34	F	Unknown	12Ju18Ix
CLARK, David	23	M	Mason	12Ju18Ix
TURNER, John	38	M	Mason	12Ju18Ix
Elizth.	28	F	Unknown	12Ju18Ix
John	.09	M	Infant	12Ju18Ix
FAIRLY, Thos.	13	M	Miner	12Ju18Ix
Isabella	10	F	Unknown	12Ju18Ix
CRAWFORD, Thos.	5	M	Child	12Ju18Ix
Ralph	3	M	Child	12Ju18Ix
ALDER, Cath.	7	F	Child	12Ju18Ix
George	5	M	Child	12Ju18Ix
TURNER, Elizth.	3	F	Child	12Ju18Ix

KENT 12 JUNE 1849

From Bermuda And St.Thomas

NAMES OF PASSENGERS	AGE	SEX	OCCUPATIONS	DATE PORT SHIP
BLAIR, Robert	24	M	Farmer	12Ju47Iy
WALKER, Thomas	26	M	Farmer	12Ju47Iy
HANNIGAN, Mary	18	F	Servant	12Ju47Iy
DANE, Ellen	20	F	Servant	12Ju47Iy

NAMES OF PASSENGERS		AGE	SEX	OCCUPATIONS	DATE PORT SHIP
BURN, John		41	M	Farmer	12Ju47ly
Ellen	(W)	40	F	Wife	12Ju47ly
Biddy		18	F	Servant	12Ju47ly
GETTINS, James		22	M	Servant	12Ju47ly
BEATTY, Mary		30	F	Spinster	12Ju47ly
Mag---, Rich.		22	M	Servant	12Ju47ly
CANNON, James		24	M	Servant	12Ju47ly
Mary		20	F	Servant	12Ju47ly
MCFADDEN, Mary		20	F	Servant	12Ju47ly
KENNY, Jane		20	F	Servant	12Ju47ly
GOML, Jane		21	F	Servant	12Ju47ly
WATSON, Thomas		50	M	Farmer	12Ju47ly
HAUGHEY, Ann		20	F	Spinster	12Ju47ly
MULHANE, Henry		21	M	Farmer	12Ju47ly
MCREADY, Margt.		19	F	Spinster	12Ju47ly
MCBREATTY, Sally		30	F	Wife	12Ju47ly
John		.09	M	Infant	12Ju47ly
ERSKINE, Kitty		30	F	Spinster	12Ju47ly
LANGAM, Wm.		35	M	Laborer	12Ju47ly
SWEENY, Ann		17	F	Spinster	12Ju47ly
BOYLE, Biddy		24	F	Spinster	12Ju47ly
Cath.		19	F	Spinster	12Ju47ly
MCHUGH, Susan		24	F	Spinster	12Ju47ly
SWEENY, Mary		20	F	Spinster	12Ju47ly
DOUGHERTY, Jane		20	F	Spinster	12Ju47ly
DANE, Rebecca		18	F	Spinster	12Ju47ly
HERN, Michl.		20	M	Laborer	12Ju47ly
BRESLIN, Andrw.		21	M	Laborer	12Ju47ly
LYONS, Ann		23	F	Wife	12Ju47ly
DOUD, Rodger		50	M	Farmer	12Ju47ly
Sally	(W)	40	F	Wife	12Ju47ly
Ellen		14	F	Spinster	12Ju47ly
MEEHAN, James		60	M	Farmer	12Ju47ly
BARRY, Mary		36	F	Wife	12Ju47ly
Joseph		18	M	Laborer	12Ju47ly
Robert		14	M	Laborer	12Ju47ly
MCCONAGHER, Anne		22	F	Spinster	12Ju47ly
CALLAGHAN, Hugh		3	M	Farmer	12Ju47ly
Mary	(W)	25	F	Wife	12Ju47ly
MCCABE, Neal		26	M	Laborer	12Ju47ly
Mary	(W)	25	F	Wife	12Ju47ly
BRODDY, Pat		26	M	Laborer	12Ju47ly
SWEENY, Michl.		25	M	Laborer	12Ju47ly
Mary	(W)	21	F	Wife	12Ju47ly
MCCALEY, Anne		30	F	Spinster	12Ju47ly
SWEENY, John		.08	M	Infant	12Ju47ly
BOYLE, Bridget		28	F	Spinster	12Ju47ly
COCHRANE, James		20	M	Laborer	12Ju47ly
CASSIDY, Edw.		14	M	Laborer	12Ju47ly
RODGERS, Mary		30	F	Spinster	12Ju47ly
LOGAN, John		.09	M	Infant	12Ju47ly
SWEENY, Mary		20	F	Spinster	12Ju47ly
MCSHANE, Mary		20	F	Spinster	12Ju47ly
CARR, Margt.		35	F	Spinster	12Ju47ly
QUINN, Moses		21	M	Laborer	12Ju47ly
BURNS, John		30	M	Laborer	12Ju47ly
Biddy	(W)	22	F	Wife	12Ju47ly
Biddy		.09	F	Infant	12Ju47ly
BOYLE, Hugh		21	M	Laborer	12Ju47ly
MCQUADE, John		20	M	Laborer	12Ju47ly
LORE, Margt.		19	F	Spinster	12Ju47ly
DOUGHERTY, Andrw.		24	M	Laborer	12Ju47ly
Jane	(W)	23	F	Wife	12Ju47ly
James		.08	M	Infant	12Ju47ly
WARD, Michl.		24	M	Laborer	12Ju47ly
OBRIAN, Thos.		22	M	Laborer	12Ju47ly
BRESLAN, Pat		26	M	Laborer	12Ju47ly
MCNELAS, Frs.		24	M	Laborer	12Ju47ly
HARGHERY, Pat		24	M	Laborer	12Ju47ly
CUNNINGHAM, John		30	M	Laborer	12Ju47ly
BRODDY, Ellen		26	F	Spinster	12Ju47ly
BRADDEN, James		27	M	Laborer	12Ju47ly
Biddy	(W)	30	F	Wife	12Ju47ly
MCLOON, Ma---		26	F	Spinster	12Ju47ly
MCGILL, Ann		18	F	Spinster	12Ju47ly
FISHER, Edw.		23	M	Laborer	12Ju47ly
Candy		18	M	Laborer	12Ju47ly
Ann		23	F	Wife	12Ju47ly
Harrt.		.09	F	Infant	12Ju47ly
SHANNEN, Margt.		22	F	Spinster	12Ju47ly
CRAWFORD, Hugh		20	M	Laborer	12Ju47ly
CONNELL, John		45	M	Farmer	12Ju47ly
OBRIEN, Ann		22	F	Spinster	12Ju47ly
DAWSON, Jas.		.06	M	Infant	12Ju47ly
HOGAN, Rose		20	F	Spinster	12Ju47ly
LONG, James		20	M	Laborer	12Ju47ly
MCNULTY, Ellen		20	F	Spinster	12Ju47ly
MCGIMLEY, Wm.		16	M	Laborer	12Ju47ly
CAMPBELL, Frs.		40	M	Farmer	12Ju47ly
MCINTYRE, Sally		20	F	Spinster	12Ju47ly
KERR, James		24	M	Laborer	12Ju47ly
MCNOLAS, E.		24	F	Spinster	12Ju47ly
ODONNELL, Biddy		22	F	Spinster	12Ju47ly
MCGHEE, Mary-Ann		20	F	Spinster	12Ju47ly
BRIDE, Biddy		21	F	Spinster	12Ju47ly
DIRAN, Bernard		30	M	Laborer	12Ju47ly
BURNS, Peter		30	M	Laborer	12Ju47ly
MCCLOSKEY, Ann		20	F	Spinster	12Ju47ly
CANNON, Brian		50	M	Farmer	12Ju47ly
Marty	(W)	50	F	Wife	12Ju47ly
Bryan		.10	M	Infant	12Ju47ly
BRILENS, John		30	M	Laborer	12Ju47ly
Sally	(W)	40	F	Wife	12Ju47ly
GALLAGHER, Kitty		16	F	Spinster	12Ju47ly
Sarah		.06	F	Infant	12Ju47ly
Nelly		.06	F	Infant	12Ju47ly
MCBREARTY, James		20	M	Laborer	12Ju47ly
GALLAGHER, Danl.		25	M	Laborer	12Ju47ly
Sarah		.09	F	Infant	12Ju47ly
FRIEL, James		25	M	Farmer	12Ju47ly
FINN, John		25	M	Laborer	12Ju47ly
MCNEILS, John		21	M	Laborer	12Ju47ly
BRICE, Arthur		18	M	Laborer	12Ju47ly
MCSHANE, Hannah		18	F	Spinster	12Ju47ly
MCGRULONG, Hugh		20	M	Laborer	12Ju47ly
DEVERY, John		17	M	Laborer	12Ju47ly
SHERMAN, Chas.		24	M	Laborer	12Ju47ly
WALKER, Cath.		24	F	Spinster	12Ju47ly
DANE, Wm.		20	M	Laborer	12Ju47ly
WILKINS, Mary		20	F	Spinster	12Ju47ly
MCLAUGHLIN, Mary		24	F	Spinster	12Ju47ly
LONG, George		18	M	Laborer	12Ju47ly
MCCOY, Mary		17	F	Spinster	12Ju47ly

MORTIMER-LIVINGSTON 12 JUNE 1849

From Liverpool

NAMES OF PASSENGERS		AGE	SEX	OCCUPATIONS	DATE PORT SHIP
KEATING, Joanna		23	F	Servant	12Ju02Jr
SLATER, Mary		30	F	Servant	12Ju02Jr
BRUNNAN, Henry-F.		16	M	Surgeon	12Ju02Jr
WATKINS, John		27	M	Mechanic	12Ju02Jr
Jane		59	F	Unknown	12Ju02Jr
Prudentia		20	F	Unknown	12Ju02Jr
MULLEN, James		40	M	Servant	12Ju02Jr
SHENY, James		25	M	Farmer	12Ju02Jr
CONOVAN, James		25	M	Laborer	12Ju02Jr
MURNEY, Patrick		32	M	Laborer	12Ju02Jr
QUINN, Sarah		26	F	Servant	12Ju02Jr
PARTEN, Nicholas		50	M	Farmer	12Ju02Jr
Bridget		41	F	Farmer	12Ju02Jr
Christopher		19	M	Farmer	12Ju02Jr
Mary		17	F	Farmer	12Ju02Jr
Catherine		15	F	Farmer	12Ju02Jr

NAMES OF PASSENGERS	AGE	SEX	OCCUPATIONS	DATE PORT SHIP	NAMES OF PASSENGERS	AGE	SEX	OCCUPATIONS	DATE PORT SHIP
PARTEN, John	13	M	Farmer	12Ju02Jr	CODY, Michael	35	M	Laborer	12Ju02Jr
Michael	11	M	Farmer	12Ju02Jr	Mary	35	F	Unknown	12Ju02Jr
Banen	9	M	Child	12Ju02Jr	James	14	M	Laborer	12Ju02Jr
Peter	6	M	Child	12Ju02Jr	Mary	17	F	Unknown	12Ju02Jr
Nicholas	2	M	Child	12Ju02Jr	Catherine	5	F	Child	12Ju02Jr
GILL, Alice	19	F	Servant	12Ju02Jr	Jillan	3	F	Child	12Ju02Jr
Alice	19	F	Servant	12Ju02Jr	Bridget	.04	F	Infant	12Ju02Jr
FAGAN, John	23	M	Laborer	12Ju02Jr	GERRY, Edward	38	M	Laborer	12Ju02Jr
SPEIN, James	23	M	Mechanic	12Ju02Jr	Margaret	38	F	Unknown	12Ju02Jr
BUCKLEY, Edmund	19	M	Mechanic	12Ju02Jr	Margaret	11	F	Unknown	12Ju02Jr
William	22	M	Mechanic	12Ju02Jr	Michael	9	M	Child	12Ju02Jr
Catherine	19	F	Unknown	12Ju02Jr	Patrick	7	M	Child	12Ju02Jr
Edmund	.06	M	Infant	12Ju02Jr	John	5	M	Child	12Ju02Jr
DALY, Jane	30	F	Wi	12Ju02Jr	Ellen	4	F	Child	12Ju02Jr
Willenmena	.02	F	Infant	12Ju02Jr	John	5	M	Child	12Ju02Jr
HENRY, Henry	20	M	Farmer	12Ju02Jr	Michael	4	M	Child	12Ju02Jr
PINKERTON, Robert	20	M	Weaver	12Ju02Jr	CALLAGHAN, James	20	M	Laborer	12Ju02Jr
RYAN, John	46	M	Farmer	12Ju02Jr	Cornelius	22	M	Laborer	12Ju02Jr
Mary	44	F	Farmer	12Ju02Jr	KEGAN, Thomas	23	M	Laborer	12Ju02Jr
Bridget	23	F	Farmer	12Ju02Jr	SHOE, Bryan	44	M	Mechanic	12Ju02Jr
Catherine	20	F	Farmer	12Ju02Jr	Catherine	11	F	Unknown	12Ju02Jr
Michael	18	M	Farmer	12Ju02Jr	LISBONE, Michael	24	M	Laborer	12Ju02Jr
John	16	M	Farmer	12Ju02Jr	NEVILLE, John	24	M	Mechanic	12Ju02Jr
Julia	13	F	Unknown	12Ju02Jr	DOGHERTY, James	23	M	Laborer	12Ju02Jr
Margaret	5	F	Child	12Ju02Jr	BOYLE, Ann	25	F	Unknown	12Ju02Jr
Jeremiah	3	M	Child	12Ju02Jr	Mary	.06	M	Infant	12Ju02Jr
Edmund	.10	M	Infant	12Ju02Jr	BARBERRY, Richard	38	M	Farmer	12Ju02Jr
DEGAIN, Luke	50	M	Farmer	12Ju02Jr	Margerette	38	F	Farmer	12Ju02Jr
Mary	46	F	Unknown	12Ju02Jr	Daniel	11	M	Unknown	12Ju02Jr
John	19	M	Farmer	12Ju02Jr	Joanna	9	F	Child	12Ju02Jr
Bridget	13	F	Farmer	12Ju02Jr	Richard	9	M	Child	12Ju02Jr
Mary-Ann	12	F	Farmer	12Ju02Jr	Eliza	2	F	Child	12Ju02Jr
Joseph	10	M	Farmer	12Ju02Jr	Margerette	.10	F	Infant	12Ju02Jr
Margaret	9	F	Child	12Ju02Jr	HEINE, Geoffrey	24	M	Mechanic	12Ju02Jr
Jeremiah	7	M	Child	12Ju02Jr	SKEHEN, Michael	30	M	Laborer	12Ju02Jr
Lack	5	M	Child	12Ju02Jr	Mary	32	F	Unknown	12Ju02Jr
James	38	M	Unknown	12Ju02Jr	NOLAN, Michael	42	M	Cooper	12Ju02Jr
Mary	28	F	Unknown	12Ju02Jr	RYAN, Mary	20	F	Servant	12Ju02Jr
Maria	17	F	Unknown	12Ju02Jr	HICKIE, Rose	25	F	Servant	12Ju02Jr
Michael	15	M	Unknown	12Ju02Jr	LANNAGANY, James	50	M	Farmer	12Ju02Jr
Jeremiah	.05	M	Infant	12Ju02Jr	Catherine	16	F	Unknown	12Ju02Jr
RYAN, Judith	26	F	Servant	12Ju02Jr	CASSIN, John	26	M	Mechanic	12Ju02Jr
Michael	27	M	Mechanic	12Ju02Jr	MACFRAN, Ellen	24	F	Servant	12Ju02Jr
CAULKIN, William	27	M	Mechanic	12Ju02Jr	FLINN, Michael	24	M	Farmer	12Ju02Jr
COFFEE, John	27	M	Mechanic	12Ju02Jr	Ellen	24	F	Unknown	12Ju02Jr
Edmund	25	M	Mechanic	12Ju02Jr	Ellen	3	F	Child	12Ju02Jr
BURKE, Ellen	24	F	Servant	12Ju02Jr	Johanna	.10	F	Infant	12Ju02Jr
IVY, Timothy	26	M	Laborer	12Ju02Jr	MANNING, Mary	16	F	Servant	12Ju02Jr
DONALDSON, Letitia	48	F	Wi	12Ju02Jr	TELLANY, Thomas	23	M	Gdnr	12Ju02Jr
Jane	20	F	Servant	12Ju02Jr	CUDDALL, Samuel	20	M	Laborer	12Ju02Jr
KALUHEN, John	21	M	Laborer	12Ju02Jr	NEIL, Thomas	25	M	Mechanic	12Ju02Jr
OCONNELL, Daniel	20	M	Laborer	12Ju02Jr	Mary-Jane	23	F	Unknown	12Ju02Jr
BURKE, James	25	M	Laborer	12Ju02Jr	COHEN, James	15	M	Farmer	12Ju02Jr
Thomas	50	M	Laborer	12Ju02Jr	Andrew	17	M	Farmer	12Ju02Jr
Luke	20	M	Laborer	12Ju02Jr	FONELY, Michael	22	M	Laborer	12Ju02Jr
Mary	15	F	Unknown	12Ju02Jr	MULLENS, Mary	18	F	Servant	12Ju02Jr
RYLAIN, Michael	50	M	Laborer	12Ju02Jr	DONNOLD, John	55	M	Laborer	12Ju02Jr
Bridget	40	F	Laborer	12Ju02Jr	Judith	40	F	Unknown	12Ju02Jr
Mary	15	F	Laborer	12Ju02Jr	Nelly	12	F	Unknown	12Ju02Jr
Daniel	6	M	Child	12Ju02Jr	Margaret	10	F	Unknown	12Ju02Jr
Michael	4	M	Child	12Ju02Jr	Philip	7	M	Child	12Ju02Jr
Catherine	.04	F	Infant	12Ju02Jr	Mary	5	F	Child	12Ju02Jr
OBRIEN, Dennis	24	M	Laborer	12Ju02Jr	RYAN, Edmond	25	M	Laborer	12Ju02Jr
Mary	25	F	Unknown	12Ju02Jr	COSTELLO, Samuel	25	F	Laborer	12Ju02Jr
Honora	.04	F	Infant	12Ju02Jr	Margaret	21	F	Laborer	12Ju02Jr
Honora	21	F	Unknown	12Ju02Jr	WALLACE, Thomas	21	M	Laborer	12Ju02Jr
KENEDY, James	20	M	Laborer	12Ju02Jr	MABING, William	20	M	Laborer	12Ju02Jr
ONEIL, Redmond	22	M	Laborer	12Ju02Jr	BARKE, Robert	20	M	Servant	12Ju02Jr
MOLLAN, Morris	40	M	Laborer	12Ju02Jr	Mary-Jane	18	F	Servant	12Ju02Jr
CARY, James	28	M	Laborer	12Ju02Jr	CALLEGHAN, Thomas	28	M	Laborer	12Ju02Jr
GOLDSBY, Joseph	40	M	Laborer	12Ju02Jr	FARRELL, John	29	M	Laborer	12Ju02Jr
MATTUMKEY, Edmund	26	M	Laborer	12Ju02Jr	OWENS, John	30	M	Laborer	12Ju02Jr
MACCLISKEY, Peter	19	M	Laborer	12Ju02Jr	Ellen	28	F	Servant	12Ju02Jr
BURKE, Lawrence	42	M	Laborer	12Ju02Jr	Ann	29	F	Servant	12Ju02Jr
Bridget	11	F	Unknown	12Ju02Jr	HENDERLY, Bryan	23	M	Laborer	12Ju02Jr

NAMES OF PASSENGERS	AGE	SEX	OCCUPATIONS	DATE PORT SHIP
HENDERLY, Alice	24	F	Servant	12Ju02Jr
Anne	17	F	Servant	12Ju02Jr
WEKELY, Mary	19	F	Servant	12Ju02Jr
KIRBY, Bridget	10	F	Servant	12Ju02Jr
SMITH, Philip	23	M	Laborer	12Ju02Jr
MCCORMACK, John	17	M	Laborer	12Ju02Jr
Anne	20	F	Laborer	12Ju02Jr
MCGUIRE, Thomas	22	M	Mechanic	12Ju02Jr
Mary	24	F	Unknown	12Ju02Jr
COCKLAN, Mary	40	F	Servant	12Ju02Jr
James	18	M	Laborer	12Ju02Jr
John	18	M	Laborer	12Ju02Jr
Mary	20	F	Laborer	12Ju02Jr
BARKER, Shanne	26	F	Servant	12Ju02Jr
FAGAN, Ellen	20	F	Servant	12Ju02Jr
DOHERTY, William	45	M	Laborer	12Ju02Jr
HUNTER, Thomas	20	M	Farmer	12Ju02Jr
Eliza-Jane	22	M	Dressmaker	12Ju02Jr
MCLUCKEN, Eliza-Jane	17	F	Servant	12Ju02Jr
KILING, Robert	20	M	Mechanic	12Ju02Jr
MARTIN, Daniel	21	M	Laborer	12Ju02Jr
KILROY, Miley	00	F	Servant	12Ju02Jr
OKERLY, Micahel	00	M	Laborer	12Ju02Jr
Margaret	20	F	Servant	12Ju02Jr
GUIHERTY, Alice	20	F	Servant	12Ju02Jr
KAHY, Michael	22	M	Mechanic	12Ju02Jr
Mary	6	F	Child	12Ju02Jr
MCCABE, Peter	10	M	Laborer	12Ju02Jr
NOBLE, James	22	M	Mechanic	12Ju02Jr
Margaret	23	F	Unknown	12Ju02Jr
AIMS, Eliza	.09	F	Infant	12Ju02Jr
GUNTER, Elizabeth	18	F	Dressmaker	12Ju02Jr
BUNSLY, Margaret	24	F	Dressmaker	12Ju02Jr
MARTIN, Thomas	40	M	Gdnr	12Ju02Jr
Jane	40	F	Gdnr	12Ju02Jr
KEATON, John-S.	21	M	Laborer	12Ju02Jr
Maria	20	F	Laborer	12Ju02Jr
ANDREWS, Thomas	24	M	Mechanic	12Ju02Jr
CHEEAN, Peter	35	M	Mechanic	12Ju02Jr
DERMODY, Thomas	22	M	Mechanic	12Ju02Jr
KARMIN, Michael	22	M	Laborer	12Ju02Jr
GOLDING, Bridget	22	F	Dressmaker	12Ju02Jr
MORLAND, Grea	20	F	Servant	12Ju02Jr
Mary	18	F	Servant	12Ju02Jr
CAREW, Mary	18	F	Servant	12Ju02Jr
COLLINS, Patrick	19	M	None	12Ju02Jr
CABINE, James	18	M	Laborer	12Ju02Jr
MULLAND, Patrick	24	M	Laborer	12Ju02Jr
MULLOUGH, Mary-E.	19	F	Servant	12Ju02Jr
QUINN, Ann	40	F	Servant	12Ju02Jr
CLOWAN, Ann	14	F	Servant	12Ju02Jr
MURREY, Ann	29	F	Servant	12Ju02Jr
HADINS, James	15	M	Servant	12Ju02Jr
MILDA, Hannah	55	F	Servant	12Ju02Jr
MCKEOWN, James	18	M	Laborer	12Ju02Jr
WARD, Michael	20	M	Laborer	12Ju02Jr
TREVORE, Hugh	42	M	Laborer	12Ju02Jr
ICKENNEN, Mary	25	F	Servant	12Ju02Jr
.ARKIN, Jean	24	F	Dressmaker	12Ju02Jr

BARBARA 13 JUNE 1849

From Londonderry

NAMES OF PASSENGERS	AGE	SEX	OCCUPATIONS	DATE PORT SHIP
UGGAN, James	25	M	Unknown	13Ju01Jb
OHERTY, Owen	19	M	Unknown	13Ju01Jb
ARD, John	18	M	Unknown	13Ju01Jb
OHERTY, Charles	18	M	Unknown	13Ju01Jb
CLAUGHLIN, Bryan	35	M	Blacksmith	13Ju01Jb
RODDEN, Michael	30	M	Unknown	13Ju01Jb
DEENY, James	20	M	Tailor	13Ju01Jb
LONER, James	23	M	Unknown	13Ju01Jb
CANE, Bernard	22	M	Shoemaker	13Ju01Jb
GALLAGHER, Biddy	22	F	Unknown	13Ju01Jb
STEWART, Hamilton	26	M	Unknown	13Ju01Jb
MULLIN, Matilda	20	F	Unknown	13Ju01Jb
HENDERSON, William	24	M	Unknown	13Ju01Jb
RILEY, Thomas	30	M	Unknown	13Ju01Jb
Ellen	25	F	Unknown	13Ju01Jb
Catherine	.01	F	Infant	13Ju01Jb
FERGUSON, Eliza	24	F	Unknown	13Ju01Jb
MCCOURT, Teresa	24	F	Unknown	13Ju01Jb
DERMOTT, Magie	24	F	Unknown	13Ju01Jb
DOHERTY, Catherine	23	F	Unknown	13Ju01Jb
MCSHANE, Daniel	23	M	Unknown	13Ju01Jb
GALLAHER, Jane	31	F	Unknown	13Ju01Jb
CAREY, Martha	12	F	Unknown	13Ju01Jb
Ann	4	F	Child	13Ju01Jb
GALLAHER, Miley	18	M	Unknown	13Ju01Jb
KANE, Patrick	20	M	Unknown	13Ju01Jb
MICHALS, Thomas	22	M	Unknown	13Ju01Jb
U-Mrs.	22	F	Unknown	13Ju01Jb
ODONNELL, Jane	17	F	Unknown	13Ju01Jb
STEWART, Eliza	22	F	Unknown	13Ju01Jb
Thomas	20	M	Unknown	13Ju01Jb
SPEAR, Joseph	21	M	Unknown	13Ju01Jb
LOGNE, Eliza	19	F	Unknown	13Ju01Jb
MCGETTIGAN, James	25	M	Unknown	13Ju01Jb
BLAY, William	25	M	Unknown	13Ju01Jb
GILLEN, John	30	M	Unknown	13Ju01Jb
Bridget	30	F	Unknown	13Ju01Jb
William	24	M	Unknown	13Ju01Jb
MCCANON, Thomas	24	M	Unknown	13Ju01Jb
GILLEN, Mary Died-At-Sea	3	F	Unknown	13Ju01Jb
Ellen	00	F	Unknown	13Ju01Jb
LYNCH, Michl.	60	M	Unknown	13Ju01Jb
Catherine	40	F	Unknown	13Ju01Jb
Unity	13	F	Unknown	13Ju01Jb
Michael	10	M	Unknown	13Ju01Jb
SCOTT, Murphy	24	M	Unknown	13Ju01Jb
COOK, Robert	25	M	Unknown	13Ju01Jb
BURNS, Ellen	20	F	Unknown	13Ju01Jb
ODONNELL, Daniel	19	M	Unknown	13Ju01Jb
BONNER, Eleanor	16	F	Unknown	13Ju01Jb
MCLAUGHLIN, Sarah-Jane	20	F	Unknown	13Ju01Jb
Michael	22	M	Unknown	13Ju01Jb
Mary	25	F	Unknown	13Ju01Jb
William	26	M	Unknown	13Ju01Jb
Ann	20	F	Unknown	13Ju01Jb
Susan	19	F	Unknown	13Ju01Jb
Catherine	17	F	Unknown	13Ju01Jb
Eliza-Jane	14	F	Unknown	13Ju01Jb
Margaret	12	F	Unknown	13Ju01Jb
Rose	55	F	Unknown	13Ju01Jb
HARTIN, Ann	26	F	Unknown	13Ju01Jb
BURK, Eliza	26	F	Unknown	13Ju01Jb
MCCONNELL, Mary	24	F	Unknown	13Ju01Jb
MCCREA, Michael	25	M	Unknown	13Ju01Jb
MCGUIRE, Michael	25	M	Unknown	13Ju01Jb
RODGER, Isabella	16	F	Unknown	13Ju01Jb
MORROW, Eliza	24	F	Unknown	13Ju01Jb
MCGAHY, Mary-Jane	24	F	Unknown	13Ju01Jb
DEVER, U-Miss	24	F	Unknown	13Ju01Jb
LOCHRAY, Nancy	24	F	Unknown	13Ju01Jb
Owen	24	M	Unknown	13Ju01Jb
MCGEEHAN, Danl.	26	M	Unknown	13Ju01Jb
MCLAUGHLIN, Edward	18	M	Unknown	13Ju01Jb
Margaret	20	F	Unknown	13Ju01Jb
REID, Thomas	19	M	Unknown	13Ju01Jb
DOHERTY, Michael	30	M	Unknown	13Ju01Jb
U-Mrs.	30	F	Unknown	13Ju01Jb
Hugh	.09	M	Infant	13Ju01Jb
Edward	19	M	Unknown	13Ju01Jb

NAMES OF PASSENGERS	AGE	SEX	OCCUPATIONS	DATE PORT SHIP
PORTER, John	19	M	Unknown	13Ju01Jb
MCGOWAN, James	40	M	Unknown	13Ju01Jb
MCDEVITT, John	6	M	Unknown	13Ju01Jb
CRUMLISH, Susan	20	F	Unknown	13Ju01Jb
DEVENNY, Mary	50	F	Unknown	13Ju01Jb
Catherine	10	F	Unknown	13Ju01Jb
Sarah	13	F	Unknown	13Ju01Jb
MEARNS, Thomas	55	M	Unknown	13Ju01Jb
Anne	50	F	Unknown	13Ju01Jb
Chas.	30	M	Unknown	13Ju01Jb
Rosy	20	F	Unknown	13Ju01Jb
Patrick	22	M	Unknown	13Ju01Jb
DONAHY, Margaret	20	F	Unknown	13Ju01Jb
MCDERMOTT, John	36	M	Unknown	13Ju01Jb
Martha	35	F	Unknown	13Ju01Jb
Michael	00	M	Unknown	13Ju01Jb
CONNELL, Eliza	24	F	Unknown	13Ju01Jb
BLAKELY, Isabella	24	F	Unknown	13Ju01Jb
Rich	26	M	Unknown	13Ju01Jb
PORTER, James	24	M	Unknown	13Ju01Jb
Catherine	20	F	Unknown	13Ju01Jb
DEVLIN, John	20	M	Unknown	13Ju01Jb
Michael	22	M	Unknown	13Ju01Jb
CULBERT, William	19	M	Unknown	13Ju01Jb
FINLAY, Elisha	20	F	Unknown	13Ju01Jb
MCCLINTOCK, Eliza	21	F	Unknown	13Ju01Jb
CHAMBERS, James	25	M	Unknown	13Ju01Jb
GALLAHER, John	24	M	Unknown	13Ju01Jb
MCGOWAN, Mary	20	F	Unknown	13Ju01Jb
FRAME, Madgie	28	F	Unknown	13Ju01Jb
MCGOWAN, Henry	20	M	Unknown	13Ju01Jb
John	18	M	Unknown	13Ju01Jb
BRADLEY, Eliza	55	F	Unknown	13Ju01Jb
Jane	19	F	Unknown	13Ju01Jb
Enry	18	M	Unknown	13Ju01Jb
Ann-I.	9	F	Child	13Ju01Jb
DEVLIN, James	13	M	Unknown	13Ju01Jb
Nancy	9	F	Child	13Ju01Jb
MCGOWAN, Teresa	21	F	Unknown	13Ju01Jb
KANE, James	24	M	Unknown	13Ju01Jb
PIGOT, Fredrick	24	M	Unknown	13Ju01Jb
CARR, James	24	M	Unknown	13Ju01Jb
MOSS, Jane	25	F	Unknown	13Ju01Jb
MCGEE, Wm.	17	M	Unknown	13Ju01Jb
MONOHAN, Ann	21	F	Unknown	13Ju01Jb
CAMPBELL, Rich	18	M	Unknown	13Ju01Jb
JOHNSON, Andrew	30	M	Unknown	13Ju01Jb
MCMENNENY, Henry	28	M	Unknown	13Ju01Jb
MEEHAN, David	25	M	Unknown	13Ju01Jb
Nancy	50	F	Unknown	13Ju01Jb
MCDERMOTT, Magie	30	F	Unknown	13Ju01Jb
GALLAHER, Sarah	28	F	Unknown	13Ju01Jb
LYNCH, John	20	M	Unknown	13Ju01Jb

TWO-SISTERS 13 JUNE 1849

From Cork

NAMES OF PASSENGERS	AGE	SEX	OCCUPATIONS	DATE PORT SHIP
NOONAN, Daniel	28	M	Farmer	13Ju08Ja
Ellen	26	F	Unknown	13Ju08Ja
SCANLON, Elizabeth	20	F	Unknown	13Ju08Ja
BERRY, John	30	M	Unknown	13Ju08Ja
MCARRINGTON, John	30	M	Unknown	13Ju08Ja
DOURAN, Catherine	20	F	Unknown	13Ju08Ja
DEASEY, Catherine	18	F	Unknown	13Ju08Ja
COLLINS, Catherine	13	F	Unknown	13Ju08Ja
Hannah	10	F	Unknown	13Ju08Ja
TUM, John	24	M	Unknown	13Ju08Ja
MAHONEY, Ellen	20	F	Unknown	13Ju08Ja
LEAN, Maurice	47	F	Unknown	13Ju08Ja
Catherine	40	F	Unknown	13Ju08Ja
U, Edward	.00	M	Infant	13Ju08Ja
DONOVAN, Timothy	20	M	Unknown	13Ju08Ja
DEASEY, Michal	30	M	Unknown	13Ju08Ja
MAYER, Honora	20	F	Unknown	13Ju08Ja
Abby	20	F	Unknown	13Ju08Ja
LYNCH, Michal	19	M	Unknown	13Ju08Ja
MORGAN, William	40	M	Unknown	13Ju08Ja
Margaret	30	F	Unknown	13Ju08Ja
Mary	15	F	Unknown	13Ju08Ja
Patk.	8	M	Child	13Ju08Ja
Nancy	.00	F	Infant	13Ju08Ja
William	5	M	Child	13Ju08Ja
HONAN, William	20	M	Unknown	13Ju08Ja
BRIEN, Julia	30	F	Unknown	13Ju08Ja
FOLEY, Timothy	30	M	Unknown	13Ju08Ja
John	20	M	Unknown	13Ju08Ja
SCOTT, John	21	M	Unknown	13Ju08Ja
BOYLE, Patt	24	M	Unknown	13Ju08Ja
PRIOR, Ellen	25	F	Unknown	13Ju08Ja
CRAINE, Mark	21	M	Unknown	13Ju08Ja
NEVELLE, Michal	25	M	Unknown	13Ju08Ja
CONNOLLY, Jerry	20	M	Unknown	13Ju08Ja
Kate	25	F	Unknown	13Ju08Ja
John	13	M	Unknown	13Ju08Ja
BRITTON, Nancy	20	F	Unknown	13Ju08Ja
COLD, John	40	M	Unknown	13Ju08Ja
Richard	19	M	Unknown	13Ju08Ja
Gregary	18	M	Unknown	13Ju08Ja
Eliza	20	F	Unknown	13Ju08Ja
Ester	9	F	Child	13Ju08Ja
John	.00	M	Infant	13Ju08Ja
HENESSEY, Mary	20	F	Unknown	13Ju08Ja
CONNELLY, Kate	20	F	Unknown	13Ju08Ja
LINCHAN, Catherine	20	F	Unknown	13Ju08Ja
BAKER, Michal	14	M	Unknown	13Ju08Ja
Luke	12	M	Unknown	13Ju08Ja
WEBB, Mary	50	F	Unknown	13Ju08Ja
Henry	32	M	Unknown	13Ju08Ja
Christopher	19	M	Unknown	13Ju08Ja
Margaret	18	F	Unknown	13Ju08Ja
Margaret	20	F	Unknown	13Ju08Ja
Susan	13	F	Unknown	13Ju08Ja
George	2	M	Child	13Ju08Ja
Jane	.00	F	Infant	13Ju08Ja
MILUGAR, Con.	30	M	Unknown	13Ju08Ja
HENNAN, Michal	30	M	Unknown	13Ju08Ja
BRUCE, Joney	20	U	Unknown	13Ju08Ja
MCAULIFF, Mary	20	F	Unknown	13Ju08Ja
KILMARTON, John	20	M	Unknown	13Ju08Ja
KEFFY, Dan	30	M	Unknown	13Ju08Ja
HARTUCH, Catherine	35	F	Unknown	13Ju08Ja
WEIL, Jerry	20	M	Unknown	13Ju08Ja
HARRINGTON, Denis	20	M	Unknown	13Ju08Ja
DALY, Bridget	20	F	Unknown	13Ju08Ja
CALLAGHAN, Stephan	20	M	Unknown	13Ju08Ja
CONNORS, Michal	30	M	Unknown	13Ju08Ja
Timothy	6	M	Child	13Ju08Ja
Corn.	15	M	Unknown	13Ju08Ja
Jerry	20	M	Unknown	13Ju08Ja
Ellen	17	F	Unknown	13Ju08Ja
DOYLE, John	30	M	Unknown	13Ju08Ja
Johana	30	F	Unknown	13Ju08Ja
Patt	30	F	Unknown	13Ju08Ja
Michal	.00	M	Infant	13Ju08Ja
MCARTHY, Johanna	20	F	Unknown	13Ju08Ja
COVERY, Richard	20	M	Unknown	13Ju08Ja
BARRY, Thomas	25	M	Unknown	13Ju08Ja
Cath.	20	F	Unknown	13Ju08Ja
Edward	.00	M	Infant	13Ju08Ja
COTTER, James	16	M	Unknown	13Ju08Ja
John	12	M	Unknown	13Ju08Ja
SPITTAIN, John	20	M	Unknown	13Ju08
Mary	21	F	Unknown	13Ju08

NAMES OF PASSENGERS	AGE	SEX	OCCUPATIONS	DATE PORT SHIP
MAHONEY, John	24	M	Unknown	13Ju08Ja
FOLEY, Michal	12	M	Unknown	13Ju08Ja
WILLIAMS, Jane	28	F	Unknown	13Ju08Ja
FOLEY, Michal	40	M	Unknown	13Ju08Ja
WILLIAMS, Kate	16	F	Unknown	13Ju08Ja
Caroline	12	F	Unknown	13Ju08Ja
Stephan	4	M	Child	13Ju08Ja
Michal	.00	M	Infant	13Ju08Ja
WARNER, Agnes	20	F	Unknown	13Ju08Ja
CROLLY, Owen	20	M	Unknown	13Ju08Ja
HYDE, David	20	M	Unknown	13Ju08Ja
DESMOND, Ellen	20	F	Unknown	13Ju08Ja
THOMPSON, William	30	M	Unknown	13Ju08Ja
Jane	28	F	Unknown	13Ju08Ja
Kate	24	F	Unknown	13Ju08Ja
Mary-Jane	.00	F	Infant	13Ju08Ja
TEAT, Eliza	20	F	Unknown	13Ju08Ja
PURCELL, Stephan	22	M	Unknown	13Ju08Ja
Lucy	20	F	Unknown	13Ju08Ja
RYALL, Samuel	20	M	Unknown	13Ju08Ja
U-Mrs.	18	F	Unknown	13Ju08Ja
DOODY, Mary	20	F	Unknown	13Ju08Ja
WILSON, Jm.J.	28	U	Unknown	13Ju08Ja
William	26	M	Unknown	13Ju08Ja
U, U	.00	U	Infant	13Ju08Ja
HALLEN, John	24	M	Unknown	13Ju08Ja
GAGGIN, James	22	M	Unknown	13Ju08Ja
SHEAN, Patrick	24	M	Unknown	13Ju08Ja
MURPHY, Jeremiah	24	M	Unknown	13Ju08Ja
CULLAGHAN, Honora	20	F	Unknown	13Ju08Ja
Catherine	20	F	Unknown	13Ju08Ja
HOGAN, Johana	20	F	Unknown	13Ju08Ja
MORGAN, John	40	M	Unknown	13Ju08Ja
Johannah	35	F	Unknown	13Ju08Ja
Mary	5	F	Child	13Ju08Ja

QUEBEC-PACKET 14 JUNE 1849

From Limerick

NAMES OF PASSENGERS	AGE	SEX	OCCUPATIONS	DATE PORT SHIP
MALOWNEY, James	40	M	Farmer	14Ju35Jc
GORMAN, Mary	55	F	Matron	14Ju35Jc
BOURKE, Rich.	20	M	Laborer	14Ju35Jc
DOWLING, Johanna	25	F	Spinster	14Ju35Jc
FITZGERALD, Pat	20	M	Farmer	14Ju35Jc
Mary	17	F	Spinster	14Ju35Jc
CARNINS, Michl.	32	M	Unknown	14Ju35Jc
Bridget	28	F	Spinster	14Ju35Jc
Mary	26	F	Unknown	14Ju35Jc
Owen	4	M	Child	14Ju35Jc
John	3	M	Child	14Ju35Jc
CARMODY, Danl.	2	M	Child	14Ju35Jc
CARNINS, James	.02	M	Infant	14Ju35Jc
RAFFERTY, John	25	M	Laborer	14Ju35Jc
Catherine	23	F	Spinster	14Ju35Jc
Patt	21	M	Laborer	14Ju35Jc
Mary	17	F	Spinster	14Ju35Jc
RIORDAN, Mary	24	F	Spinster	14Ju35Jc
Bridget	20	F	Spinster	14Ju35Jc
Ellen	26	F	Spinster	14Ju35Jc
IUGENT, Mary	24	F	Spinster	14Ju35Jc
HELAN, Danl.	25	M	Laborer	14Ju35Jc
John	20	M	Laborer	14Ju35Jc
Oliver	15	M	Laborer	14Ju35Jc
YAN, John	30	M	Laborer	14Ju35Jc
EAGAN, Maurice	28	M	Laborer	14Ju35Jc
ITZGERALD, David	22	M	Laborer	14Ju35Jc
AUGHTON, Timothy	30	M	Laborer	14Ju35Jc
Mary	46	F	Milliner	14Ju35Jc
NEINAN, Denis	28	M	Laborer	14Ju35Jc
LOYONS, Edmund	20	M	Laborer	14Ju35Jc
CASEY, Honnor	18	F	Dressmaker	14Ju35Jc
CUMMINS, Owen	25	M	Laborer	14Ju35Jc
BUTLER, John	24	M	Laborer	14Ju35Jc
KEOUGH, Math.	26	M	Laborer	14Ju35Jc
GRACE, Bridget	22	F	Spinster	14Ju35Jc
FITZGERALD, David	22	M	Laborer	14Ju35Jc
CARTY, John	25	M	Laborer	14Ju35Jc
Cornelius	23	M	Laborer	14Ju35Jc
Pat	21	M	Laborer	14Ju35Jc
Danl.	19	M	Laborer	14Ju35Jc
Ellen	14	F	Spinster	14Ju35Jc
Johanna	9	F	Child	14Ju35Jc
MURPHY, Mat.	30	M	Farmer	14Ju35Jc
Cath.	25	F	Wife	14Ju35Jc
Mary	.00	F	Infant	14Ju35Jc
RYAN, Pat	24	M	Farmer	14Ju35Jc
Thos.	54	M	Farmer	14Ju35Jc
Mary	50	F	Spinster	14Ju35Jc
Johanna	20	F	Spinster	14Ju35Jc
Michl.	18	M	Farmer	14Ju35Jc
Thos.	14	M	Laborer	14Ju35Jc
Jas.	11	M	Unknown	14Ju35Jc
KELLY, Tim	27	M	Farmer	14Ju35Jc
Bridget	27	F	Wife	14Ju35Jc
Johanna	3	F	Child	14Ju35Jc
Thos.	.00	M	Infant	14Ju35Jc
MEARA, Michl.	26	M	Laborer	14Ju35Jc
Johanna	25	F	Wife	14Ju35Jc
KELLY, Ally	24	F	Spinster	14Ju35Jc
MARA, Philip	.00	M	Infant	14Ju35Jc
WHELAN, Pat	33	M	Laborer	14Ju35Jc
John	31	M	Laborer	14Ju35Jc
Mary	10	F	None	14Ju35Jc
KELLY, Thos.	22	M	Farmer	14Ju35Jc
Sarah	20	F	Spinster	14Ju35Jc
WHELAN, William	8	M	Child	14Ju35Jc
RYAN, Catherine	25	F	Spinster	14Ju35Jc
SAVAGE, Pat	30	M	Farmer	14Ju35Jc
ANGLIM, Thos.	18	M	Unknown	14Ju35Jc
KEOGH, Pat	26	M	Laborer	14Ju35Jc
BRYAN, John	30	M	Laborer	14Ju35Jc
Bridget	30	F	Wife	14Ju35Jc
Mary	25	F	Weaver	14Ju35Jc
Pat	4	M	Child	14Ju35Jc
Ellen	.00	F	Infant	14Ju35Jc
CONNOLLY, Thos.	22	M	Farmer	14Ju35Jc
NOLAN, John	35	M	Farmer	14Ju35Jc
Norry	30	F	Wife	14Ju35Jc
KELLY, Mary	26	F	Wife	14Ju35Jc
RYAN, Pat	22	M	Farmer	14Ju35Jc
DWYER, Ann	20	F	Spinster	14Ju35Jc
FAHY, Timothy	20	M	Farmer	14Ju35Jc
MURPHY, Jimmy	26	M	Farmer	14Ju35Jc
NEARIN, Sally	27	F	Spinster	14Ju35Jc
ANGLIM, John	12	M	None	14Ju35Jc
HAUGH, Mary	15	F	Spinster	14Ju35Jc

AGNES 14 JUNE 1849

From Dublin

NAMES OF PASSENGERS	AGE	SEX	OCCUPATIONS	DATE PORT SHIP
KEOUGH, James	13	M	Farmer	14Ju12Js
NEAL, Patt	24	M	Unknown	14Ju12Js
FLOYD, Wm.	25	M	Unknown	14Ju12Js
CLINCH, Michl.	24	M	Unknown	14Ju12Js
Lawrence	13	M	Unknown	14Ju12Js
MCMAHON, U-Miss.	30	F	Unknown	14Ju12Js

NAMES OF PASSENGERS	AGE	SEX	OCCUPATIONS	DATE PORT SHIP
MCMAHON, Ann	26	F	Unknown	14Ju12Js
Jane	15	F	Unknown	14Ju12Js
John	11	M	Unknown	14Ju12Js
William	8	M	Child	14Ju12Js
M-----, Thomas	00	M	Unknown	14Ju12Js
GAVIN, Francis	21	M	Unknown	14Ju12Js
RIVELL, Hanah	20	F	Unknown	14Ju12Js
MONEY, Matt	21	M	Unknown	14Ju12Js
KELLY, Charles	24	M	Unknown	14Ju12Js
MOONEY, Margaret	18	F	Unknown	14Ju12Js
GINNIS, Mary	8	F	Child	14Ju12Js
Catharine	.00	F	Infant	14Ju12Js
JACKSON, Cath.	14	F	Unknown	14Ju12Js
KELLY, Edward	30	M	Unknown	14Ju12Js
John	22	M	Unknown	14Ju12Js
OHALLARN, Michl.	24	M	Unknown	14Ju12Js
Julia	20	F	Unknown	14Ju12Js
BYNE, James	35	M	Unknown	14Ju12Js
U-Mrs.	30	F	Unknown	14Ju12Js
James	3	M	Child	14Ju12Js
Grace	.00	F	Infant	14Ju12Js
LAYLESS, Mary	25	F	Unknown	14Ju12Js
TURPIN, Joseph	19	M	Unknown	14Ju12Js
LACEY, Patt	30	M	Unknown	14Ju12Js
Margaret	24	F	Unknown	14Ju12Js
Bettey	4	F	Child	14Ju12Js
Catharine	.00	F	Infant	14Ju12Js
William	.00	M	Infant	14Ju12Js
Mick	28	M	Unknown	14Ju12Js
Jane	22	F	Unknown	14Ju12Js
Miles	4	M	Child	14Ju12Js
Betty	2	F	Child	14Ju12Js
Mick	.00	M	Infant	14Ju12Js
KINSELLA, Edward	30	M	Unknown	14Ju12Js
Catharine	24	F	Unknown	14Ju12Js
Miles	5	M	Child	14Ju12Js
John	2	M	Child	14Ju12Js
Biddy	.00	F	Infant	14Ju12Js
BUTLER, Cath.	13	F	Unknown	14Ju12Js
MOONEY, Denis	25	M	Unknown	14Ju12Js
OBRIEN, John	40	M	Unknown	14Ju12Js
Elizth.	40	F	Unknown	14Ju12Js
Ann	17	F	Unknown	14Ju12Js
Edward	10	M	Unknown	14Ju12Js
Maria	8	F	Child	14Ju12Js
HANKS, George	17	M	Unknown	14Ju12Js
Samuel	16	M	Unknown	14Ju12Js
Ann	10	F	Unknown	14Ju12Js
DWYER, Bernard	40	M	Unknown	14Ju12Js
U-Mrs.	38	F	Unknown	14Ju12Js
Hugh	10	M	Unknown	14Ju12Js
Thomas	.00	M	Infant	14Ju12Js
RUSELLA, Wm.	50	M	Unknown	14Ju12Js
John	22	M	Unknown	14Ju12Js
Michael	18	M	Unknown	14Ju12Js
John	28	M	Unknown	14Ju12Js
Mary	10	F	Unknown	14Ju12Js
James	28	M	Unknown	14Ju12Js
BOYLE, Wm.	35	M	Unknown	14Ju12Js
Mary	35	F	Unknown	14Ju12Js
DALEY, Julia	17	F	Unknown	14Ju12Js
CULAHAN, Owen	20	M	Unknown	14Ju12Js
MCGOVERN, John	26	M	Unknown	14Ju12Js
Eliza	24	F	Unknown	14Ju12Js
Ann	18	F	Unknown	14Ju12Js
Peter	.00	M	Infant	14Ju12Js
KENNEDY, Luke	18	M	Unknown	14Ju12Js
SOMMERVILLE, James	20	M	Unknown	14Ju12Js
HARPER, John	35	M	Unknown	14Ju12Js
BOURKE, Bridget	40	F	Unknown	14Ju12Js
KINSELLA, Wm.	50	M	Unknown	14Ju12Js
U-Mrs.	45	F	Unknown	14Ju12Js
William	13	M	Unknown	14Ju12Js
Benjamin	12	M	Unknown	14Ju12Js
PARKENSON, Saml.	50	M	Unknown	14Ju12Js
PARKENSON, Alicia	50	F	Unknown	14Ju12Js
HOLLAND, John	20	M	Unknown	14Ju12Js
Eliza	19	F	Unknown	14Ju12Js
COMMERFRIED, Ann	20	F	Unknown	14Ju12Js
CRISTIN, Wm.	30	M	Unknown	14Ju12Js
Wm.	24	M	Unknown	14Ju12Js
John	4	M	Child	14Ju12Js
Jane	2	F	Child	14Ju12Js
Ellen	.00	F	Infant	14Ju12Js
HUGHES, U	18	F	Unknown	14Ju12Js
MOOREHEAD, Jas.	25	M	Unknown	14Ju12Js
DOYLE, Essy	20	F	Unknown	14Ju12Js
GILL, Joseph	20	M	Unknown	14Ju12Js
COSGRIFF, Lewis	17	M	Unknown	14Ju12Js
John	12	F	Unknown	14Ju12Js
CRELLEN, Jas.	40	M	Unknown	14Ju12Js
HIGGINS, Thos.	20	M	Unknown	14Ju12Js
Bridget	22	F	Unknown	14Ju12Js
BRENNAN, Wm.	.00	M	Infant	14Ju12Js
Ann	7	F	Child	14Ju12Js
Tom	20	M	Unknown	14Ju12Js
WALSH, Joseph	20	M	Unknown	14Ju12Js
COLLONY, James	20	M	Unknown	14Ju12Js
Jane	29	F	Unknown	14Ju12Js
MOONEY, Rich	50	M	Unknown	14Ju12Js
U-Mrs.	50	F	Unknown	14Ju12Js
U-Miss.	21	F	Unknown	14Ju12Js
U-Miss.	20	F	Unknown	14Ju12Js
Arthur	19	M	Unknown	14Ju12Js
Denis	18	M	Unknown	14Ju12Js
Patt	16	M	Unknown	14Ju12Js
Richard	13	M	Unknown	14Ju12Js
Thomas	11	M	Unknown	14Ju12Js
James	9	M	Child	14Ju12Js
MULLADY, Sally	23	F	Unknown	14Ju12Js
COSTELLO, Ann	10	F	Unknown	14Ju12Js
MUNAY, Michl.	40	M	Unknown	14Ju12Js
U	40	F	Unknown	14Ju12Js
Maria	12	F	Unknown	14Ju12Js
John	10	M	Unknown	14Ju12Js
Ann	.00	F	Infant	14Ju12Js
NOLAN, U	20	F	Unknown	14Ju12Js
GORMAN, John	22	M	Unknown	14Ju12Js
Catharine	20	F	Unknown	14Ju12Js
SIMEN, Wm.	25	M	Unknown	14Ju12Js
MCCORMACK, Wm.	10	M	Unknown	14Ju12Js
COLLINS, Jas.	25	M	Unknown	14Ju12Js
FAWCETT, U	25	F	Unknown	14Ju12Js
Susan	21	F	Unknown	14Ju12Js
Ward	20	M	Unknown	14Ju12Js
R.	22	M	Unknown	14Ju12Js
Wm.	18	M	Unknown	14Ju12Js
BYRNE, Hugh	30	M	Unknown	14Ju12Js
James	28	M	Unknown	14Ju12Js
Patt	26	M	Unknown	14Ju12Js
MERGAN, Patt	30	M	Unknown	14Ju12Js
Mary	20	F	Unknown	14Ju12Js
DOYLE, Hanah	20	F	Unknown	14Ju12Js
FLETCHER, Ann	20	F	Unknown	14Ju12Js
BRYAN, John	20	M	Unknown	14Ju12Js
BRYNE, John	20	M	Unknown	14Ju12Js
KRISELLA, Michl.	20	M	Unknown	14Ju12Js
HOWARD, Tim	40	M	Unknown	14Ju12J
U	40	F	Unknown	14Ju12J
Patt	16	M	Unknown	14Ju12J
William	13	M	Unknown	14Ju12J
Mary	11	F	Unknown	14Ju12J
Tim	9	M	Child	14Ju12J
CAMPBELL, Ham	24	M	Unknown	14Ju12J
U	20	F	Unknown	14Ju12J
NOLAN, Peter	24	M	Unknown	14Ju12J
Ann	20	F	Unknown	14Ju12J
MATRON, W.	21	M	Unknown	14Ju12J
MCDONNELL, John	21	M	Unknown	14Ju12J
Ann	20	F	Unknown	14Ju12J

NAMES OF PASSENGERS	AGE	SEX	OCCUPATIONS	DATE PORT SHIP
DERAN, Bridget	40	F	Unknown	14Ju12Js
Michael	21	M	Unknown	14Ju12Js
Mary	20	F	Unknown	14Ju12Js
Brady	16	M	Unknown	14Ju12Js
Darby	12	M	Unknown	14Ju12Js
CAREY, Joseph	20	M	Unknown	14Ju12Js
WYNNE, John	21	M	Unknown	14Ju12Js
MAHEN, John	21	M	Unknown	14Ju12Js
NOWLAN, Denis	21	M	Unknown	14Ju12Js
Margaret	33	F	Unknown	14Ju12Js
KELLY, Julia	20	F	Unknown	14Ju12Js
MCDONNELL, Mich.	20	M	Unknown	14Ju12Js
U	24	F	Unknown	14Ju12Js
William	4	M	Child	14Ju12Js
Mary-A.	2	F	Child	14Ju12Js
Michael	.00	M	Infant	14Ju12Js
DEMPSY, Margt.	20	F	Unknown	14Ju12Js
BYRNE, John	26	M	Unknown	14Ju12Js
BRYAN, Mary	20	F	Unknown	14Ju12Js
CONTRY, Rich	30	M	Unknown	14Ju12Js
MURRAY, Mich	30	M	Unknown	14Ju12Js
Wm.	26	M	Unknown	14Ju12Js
MACK, Ann	50	F	Unknown	14Ju12Js
Essy	30	F	Unknown	14Ju12Js
Margaret	26	F	Unknown	14Ju12Js
Marcia	9	F	Child	14Ju12Js
KENNY, John	21	M	Unknown	14Ju12Js
EVANS, John	22	M	Unknown	14Ju12Js
CALLIN, Jas.	24	M	Unknown	14Ju12Js
BYRNE, Bridget	30	F	Unknown	14Ju12Js
Maria	9	F	Child	14Ju12Js
MULLIGAN, Wm.	27	M	Unknown	14Ju12Js
U	21	F	Unknown	14Ju12Js
Margaret	.00	F	Infant	14Ju12Js
HICKEY, John	25	M	Unknown	14Ju12Js
HERD, John	25	M	Unknown	14Ju12Js
HICKEY, Mary	25	F	Unknown	14Ju12Js
Ann	25	F	Unknown	14Ju12Js
CAREY, John	25	M	Unknown	14Ju12Js
KENNEDY, Patt	22	M	Unknown	14Ju12Js
HICKEY, Michael	22	M	Unknown	14Ju12Js
FAGAN, Jas.	24	M	Unknown	14Ju12Js
U	20	F	Unknown	14Ju12Js
SKETTEN, John	24	M	Unknown	14Ju12Js
OBRIEN, Edw.	20	M	Unknown	14Ju12Js
James	20	M	Unknown	14Ju12Js
COONAN, U	40	F	Wi	14Ju12Js
Mary	29	F	Unknown	14Ju12Js
James	26	M	Unknown	14Ju12Js
John	24	M	Unknown	14Ju12Js
Patt	16	M	Unknown	14Ju12Js
Eliza	30	F	Unknown	14Ju12Js
MOORE, Edward	30	M	Unknown	14Ju12Js
BRADLEY, Rose	35	F	Unknown	14Ju12Js
PLUNKET, Matt	25	M	Unknown	14Ju12Js
Mary	26	F	Unknown	14Ju12Js
Bessy	19	F	Unknown	14Ju12Js
John	18	M	Unknown	14Ju12Js
FITZGERALD, John	27	M	Unknown	14Ju12Js
CARROLL, Mary	20	F	Unknown	14Ju12Js
CONWAY, Bridget	20	F	Unknown	14Ju12Js
MCCULLAGH, Michl.	20	M	Unknown	14Ju12Js
LYONS, Michl.	20	M	Unknown	14Ju12Js
CANE, Michl.	20	M	Unknown	14Ju12Js
KELLY, Sally	20	F	Unknown	14Ju12Js
ICKEY, James	26	M	Unknown	14Ju12Js
FRENCH, Rich	26	M	Unknown	14Ju12Js
IGAN, Wm.	28	M	Unknown	14Ju12Js
RUTEN, Wm.	40	M	Unknown	14Ju12Js
U	36	F	Unknown	14Ju12Js
John	13	M	Unknown	14Ju12Js
James	12	M	Unknown	14Ju12Js
Ann	10	F	Unknown	14Ju12Js
Bess	8	F	Child	14Ju12Js
Sally	7	F	Child	14Ju12Js
BRUTEN, Thomas	5	M	Child	14Ju12Js
Jane	3	F	Child	14Ju12Js
Alice	2	F	Child	14Ju12Js
KELLY, Mary	20	F	Unknown	14Ju12Js
ADAMS, Wm.	40	M	Unknown	14Ju12Js
U	40	F	Unknown	14Ju12Js
John	20	M	Unknown	14Ju12Js
Joseph	18	M	Unknown	14Ju12Js
MURPHY, Thos.	32	M	Unknown	14Ju12Js
KELLY, John	30	M	Unknown	14Ju12Js
KING, Wm.	18	M	Unknown	14Ju12Js
HACKETT, John	21	M	Unknown	14Ju12Js
KENNY, Danl.	50	M	Unknown	14Ju12Js
SAMUELS, Wm.	36	M	Unknown	14Ju12Js
U	14	F	Unknown	14Ju12Js

MARIA 14 JUNE 1849

From Cork

NAMES OF PASSENGERS	AGE	SEX	OCCUPATIONS	DATE PORT SHIP
COOK, John	25	M	Unknown	14Ju08Jq
RILEY, Philipp	40	M	Unknown	14Ju08Jq
Mary	30	F	Unknown	14Ju08Jq
Tho.	5	M	Child	14Ju08Jq
Michl.	3	M	Child	14Ju08Jq
STIKY, John	21	M	Unknown	14Ju08Jq
James	12	M	Unknown	14Ju08Jq
Mary	13	F	Unknown	14Ju08Jq
MCCARTHY, Cathr.	15	F	Unknown	14Ju08Jq
COLLINS, Tho.	22	M	Unknown	14Ju08Jq
DONOVAN, Peter	40	M	Unknown	14Ju08Jq
MRAN, Martin	30	M	Unknown	14Ju08Jq
COCKERY, Jerry	30	M	Unknown	14Ju08Jq
Ellen	20	F	Unknown	14Ju08Jq
KEEFE, Betty	18	F	Unknown	14Ju08Jq
MOORE, Bat.	30	M	Unknown	14Ju08Jq
ROONEY, Danl.	22	M	Unknown	14Ju08Jq
Timothy	20	M	Unknown	14Ju08Jq
COLLINS, Ellen	22	F	Unknown	14Ju08Jq
LULEY, Tho.	33	M	Unknown	14Ju08Jq
RYAN, Jas.	27	M	Unknown	14Ju08Jq
STICKEY, Tho.	40	M	Unknown	14Ju08Jq
RYAN, Edmond	34	M	Unknown	14Ju08Jq
CRADON, Mary	40	F	Unknown	14Ju08Jq
SINGLETON, Danl.	22	M	Unknown	14Ju08Jq
WOLFE, Ann	19	F	Unknown	14Ju08Jq
REGAN, Jerry	26	M	Unknown	14Ju08Jq
DALY, John	30	M	Unknown	14Ju08Jq
CREEDON, Joseph	36	M	Unknown	14Ju08Jq
Jane	36	F	Unknown	14Ju08Jq
Jane	20	F	Unknown	14Ju08Jq
Mony	10	F	Unknown	14Ju08Jq
Timothy	7	M	Child	14Ju08Jq
Michl.	5	M	Child	14Ju08Jq
Ellen	3	F	Child	14Ju08Jq
MANAHY, Corns.	22	M	Unknown	14Ju08Jq
Julia	18	F	Unknown	14Ju08Jq
RYAN, Michl.	22	M	Unknown	14Ju08Jq
CALLAGHAN, Mary	46	F	Unknown	14Ju08Jq
John	20	M	Unknown	14Ju08Jq
Tim.	19	M	Unknown	14Ju08Jq
Jerry	13	M	Unknown	14Ju08Jq
Cons.	10	M	Unknown	14Ju08Jq
Bridget	7	F	Child	14Ju08Jq
Cathrin.	4	F	Child	14Ju08Jq
BARTON, Michl.	6	M	Child	14Ju08Jq
Danl.	5	M	Child	14Ju08Jq
WALSH, Davd.	18	M	Unknown	14Ju08Jq
MURPHY, Ellen	18	F	Unknown	14Ju08Jq

NAMES OF PASSENGERS	AGE	SEX	OCCUPATIONS	DATE PORT SHIP
REGAN, Jas.	50	M	Unknown	14Ju08Jq
Ellen	22	F	Unknown	14Ju08Jq
COLLINS, W.	16	M	Unknown	14Ju08Jq
John	11	M	Unknown	14Ju08Jq
Jas.	4	M	Child	14Ju08Jq
Kate	6	F	Child	14Ju08Jq
Mary	50	F	Unknown	14Ju08Jq
SULLIVAN, Johanna	20	F	Unknown	14Ju08Jq
VAUGHAN, John	25	M	Unknown	14Ju08Jq
KEEFE, John	21	M	Unknown	14Ju08Jq
Ellen	18	F	Unknown	14Ju08Jq
SULLIVAN, Eugene	22	M	Unknown	14Ju08Jq
Honr.	22	F	Unknown	14Ju08Jq
BOWLES, W.	26	M	Unknown	14Ju08Jq
Johanna	20	F	Unknown	14Ju08Jq
FAHY, Jas.	20	M	Unknown	14Ju08Jq
CANTY, Tho.	35	M	Unknown	14Ju08Jq
Ellen	30	F	Unknown	14Ju08Jq
Jerry	13	M	Unknown	14Ju08Jq
Johanna	11	F	Unknown	14Ju08Jq
Corns.	9	M	Child	14Ju08Jq
Tho.	5	M	Child	14Ju08Jq
Mary	.00	F	Infant	14Ju08Jq
NEALON, Tho.	32	M	Unknown	14Ju08Jq
DIVANE, J.	30	M	Unknown	14Ju08Jq
OCONNEL, Maurice	29	M	Unknown	14Ju08Jq
HAYES, U-Mr.	29	M	Unknown	14Ju08Jq
Mary	25	F	Unknown	14Ju08Jq
ROCHE, Ellen	22	F	Unknown	14Ju08Jq
Ann	4	F	Child	14Ju08Jq
SULLIVAN, John	20	M	Unknown	14Ju08Jq
KELERHER, Mary	26	F	Unknown	14Ju08Jq
DONOVAN, Pat.	40	M	Unknown	14Ju08Jq
DEARY, Ellen	24	F	Unknown	14Ju08Jq
Bridget	20	F	Unknown	14Ju08Jq
BURNETT, Josiah	17	M	Unknown	14Ju08Jq
MARSHALL, Tho.	22	M	Unknown	14Ju08Jq
BROWNE, Eliza	17	F	Unknown	14Ju08Jq
NAGLE, H.	11	F	Unknown	14Ju08Jq
TOONEY, Corns.	40	M	Unknown	14Ju08Jq
Maurice	11	M	Unknown	14Ju08Jq
CLIFFORD, W.	45	M	Unknown	14Ju08Jq
Margt.	40	F	Unknown	14Ju08Jq
Danl.	16	M	Unknown	14Ju08Jq
Ann	10	F	Unknown	14Ju08Jq
Margt.	5	F	Child	14Ju08Jq
Hanh.	3	F	Child	14Ju08Jq
DUNN, Mary	30	F	Unknown	14Ju08Jq
VIKERY, Saml.	25	M	Unknown	14Ju08Jq
Jas.	27	M	Unknown	14Ju08Jq
OMALEY, Pat.	27	M	Unknown	14Ju08Jq
REGAN, Michl.	40	M	Unknown	14Ju08Jq
HOWOGHAN, Johanna	30	F	Unknown	14Ju08Jq
Mary	23	F	Unknown	14Ju08Jq
GOSNELL, John	40	M	Unknown	14Ju08Jq
COGHLAN, John	20	M	Unknown	14Ju08Jq
COFFER, Mary	19	F	Unknown	14Ju08Jq
BRENAN, Judy	18	F	Unknown	14Ju08Jq
FITZGERALD, Edwd.	40	M	Unknown	14Ju08Jq
KENELY, Cath.	30	F	Unknown	14Ju08Jq
HASLEY, Bat.	21	M	Unknown	14Ju08Jq
DONOHUE, Honr.	24	F	Unknown	14Ju08Jq
Cath.	21	F	Unknown	14Ju08Jq
LEARY, Margt.	18	F	Unknown	14Ju08Jq
MAGROTH, Roger	24	M	Unknown	14Ju08Jq
Cath.	23	F	Unknown	14Ju08Jq
MCCARTY, Danl.	18	M	Unknown	14Ju08Jq
DONAHOE, Jerry	32	M	Unknown	14Ju08Jq
Michl.	40	M	Unknown	14Ju08Jq
GARVEY, Timothy	30	M	Unknown	14Ju08Jq
Jas.	35	M	Unknown	14Ju08Jq
HORAN, John	25	M	Unknown	14Ju08Jq
Cath.	19	F	Unknown	14Ju08Jq
MCCARTHY, G.	20	M	Unknown	14Ju08Jq
LEAHY, John	22	M	Unknown	14Ju08Jq
RISDAN, Denis	20	M	Unknown	14Ju08Jq
HEALY, Patrick	20	M	Unknown	14Ju08Jq
MURPHY, Jeremiah	30	M	Unknown	14Ju08Jq
Margaret	20	F	Unknown	14Ju08Jq
U	.00	U	Infant	14Ju08Jq
TAYLOR, M.	50	M	Unknown	14Ju08Jq
Honr.	24	F	Unknown	14Ju08Jq
Cath.	20	F	Unknown	14Ju08Jq
Ann	21	F	Unknown	14Ju08Jq
BARRY, Ellen	24	F	Unknown	14Ju08Jq
John	6	M	Child	14Ju08Jq
Bridget	3	F	Child	14Ju08Jq
MURPHY, M.	24	M	Unknown	14Ju08Jq

THETIS 14 JUNE 1849

From Limerick

NAMES OF PASSENGERS	AGE	SEX	OCCUPATIONS	DATE PORT SHIP
KINCANE, John	19	M	Laborer	14Ju35Ka
SKANLAN, John	24	M	Laborer	14Ju35Ka
Bridget	22	F	Servant	14Ju35Ka
KANE, Simon	39	M	Farmer	14Ju35Ka
Mgt.	29	F	Matron	14Ju35Ka
Michl.	.00	M	Infant	14Ju35Ka
Bridget	34	F	Spinster	14Ju35Ka
John	9	M	Child	14Ju35Ka
Park	8	M	Child	14Ju35Ka
SEXTON, Francis	29	M	Laborer	14Ju35Ka
KEARNEY, Michael	23	M	Farmer	14Ju35Ka
SULLIVAN, Matt	38	M	Farmer	14Ju35Ka
MAHONY, Jane	19	F	Servant	14Ju35Ka
HICKEY, Ellen	30	F	Servant	14Ju35Ka
HOWARD, James	23	M	Laborer	14Ju35Ka
CROWE, Bridget	19	F	Servant	14Ju35Ka
HEANEY, Ellen	19	F	Servant	14Ju35Ka
Mary	21	F	Servant	14Ju35Ka
CROTTY, Michael	20	M	Laborer	14Ju35Ka
CULLIGAN, Thos.	18	M	Laborer	14Ju35Ka
HANRANHAN, Pat	00	M	Laborer	14Ju35Ka
NORMOYLE, Thos.	00	M	Laborer	14Ju35Ka
BARRY, Mgt.	19	F	Spinster	14Ju35Ka
Cath.	9	F	Child	14Ju35Ka
MCCARTHY, Bridget	20	F	Spinster	14Ju35Ka
TIERNEY, Pierce	22	M	Laborer	14Ju35Ka
DONOVAN, Pat	40	M	Laborer	14Ju35Ka
HALLAHAN, Thos.	30	M	Laborer	14Ju35Ka
MCKEW, Mary	18	F	Servant	14Ju35Ka
MCNAMARA, Mary	34	F	Servant	14Ju35Ka
HANRAHAN, Johanna	21	F	Servant	14Ju35Ka
OBRIEN, Anne	33	F	Servant	14Ju35Ka
Joseph	13	M	Laborer	14Ju35Ka
BOURKE, Lucy	24	F	Servant	14Ju35Ka
Kate	4	F	Child	14Ju35Ka
CASTOLOE, James	30	M	Laborer	14Ju35Ka
MEAGHER, John	35	M	Laborer	14Ju35Ka
MARTIN, Mary	18	F	Servant	14Ju35K
FRAWLEY, Michael	26	M	Laborer	14Ju35K
Mary	26	F	Matron	14Ju35K
Mary	.06	F	Infant	14Ju35K
BLAKE, John	20	M	Laborer	14Ju35K
Patt.	18	M	Laborer	14Ju35K
BUTLER, Thos.	22	M	Laborer	14Ju35K
OBRIEN, James	30	M	Laborer	14Ju35K
RYAN, Michl.	18	M	Laborer	14Ju35K
KENNEDY, Michl.	25	M	Laborer	14Ju35K
DOYLE, John	25	M	Laborer	14Ju35K
ARTHUR, Wm.	30	M	Farmer	14Ju35K
Anne	30	F	Matron	14Ju35K
CAMPBELL, John	27	M	Laborer	14Ju35K

NAMES OF PASSENGERS		AGE	SEX	OCCUPATIONS	DATE PORT SHIP
HEALY, Michael		40	M	Laborer	14Ju35Ka
Bdgt.		28	F	Matron	14Ju35Ka
GRAYNOR, Ellen		26	F	Servant	14Ju35Ka
John		20	M	Laborer	14Ju35Ka
Ellen		20	F	Servant	14Ju35Ka
MCNAMEE, Mary		16	F	Servant	14Ju35Ka
Mary		25	F	Servant	14Ju35Ka
LEARY, Patt.		22	M	Farmer	14Ju35Ka
MCGORMAN, U-Mrs.		22	F	Matron	14Ju35Ka
ROURKE, Thos.		21	M	Laborer	14Ju35Ka
KEELY, Lewis		50	M	Laborer	14Ju35Ka
LOOMEY, Patt.		35	M	Laborer	14Ju35Ka
KELT, James		20	M	Laborer	14Ju35Ka
HOUGH, Patt.		35	M	Laborer	14Ju35Ka
Mary	(W)	30	F	None	14Ju35Ka
Maria		9	F	Child	14Ju35Ka
Bdgt.		5	F	Child	14Ju35Ka
Michl.		.00	M	Infant	14Ju35Ka
BOURKE, Cath.		18	F	Servant	14Ju35Ka
May		15	F	Servant	14Ju35Ka
KENNEDY, Pat		40	M	Farmer	14Ju35Ka
Bdgt.		30	F	Matron	14Ju35Ka
GLEESON, Philip		30	M	Laborer	14Ju35Ka
POWERS, Patt.		24	M	Laborer	14Ju35Ka
HOPKINS, Patt.		38	M	Laborer	14Ju35Ka
HARRIMAN, Charles		35	M	Laborer	14Ju35Ka
Julia	(W)	30	F	None	14Ju35Ka
John		7	M	Child	14Ju35Ka
Patt.		5	M	Child	14Ju35Ka
William		.00	M	Infant	14Ju35Ka
DILLON, John		35	M	Laborer	14Ju35Ka
Mary	(W)	30	F	None	14Ju35Ka
Mary		13	F	None	14Ju35Ka
Mgt.		11	F	None	14Ju35Ka
John		9	M	Child	14Ju35Ka
Francis		7	M	Child	14Ju35Ka
Johanna		5	F	Child	14Ju35Ka
Michl.		3	M	Child	14Ju35Ka
Edward		2	M	Child	14Ju35Ka
MCMAHON, Mgt.		40	F	Servant	14Ju35Ka
MORAN, John		35	M	Laborer	14Ju35Ka
LEARY, Johanna		23	F	Servant	14Ju35Ka
COUNELLA, David		35	M	Laborer	14Ju35Ka
CANADY, Mary		56	F	Servant	14Ju35Ka
GLEESON, Martin		20	M	Laborer	14Ju35Ka
Mary	(W)	17	F	None	14Ju35Ka
CAMPHION, Michl.		18	M	Laborer	14Ju35Ka
Bdgt.	(W)	20	F	None	14Ju35Ka
MARA, Mary		30	F	Servant	14Ju35Ka
Michl.	(S)	7	M	Child	14Ju35Ka
NEUSTADT, Cath.		20	F	Servant	14Ju35Ka
GWARE, Richd.		25	M	Laborer	14Ju35Ka
Cath.	(W)	20	F	None	14Ju35Ka
NEUSTADT, Cath.		00	F	Wife	14Ju35Ka
CUNNINGHAM, Patt.		24	M	Laborer	14Ju35Ka
Mary	(W)	24	F	None	14Ju35Ka
Joseph	(S)	5	M	Child	14Ju35Ka
DAGHERTY, Cath.		20	F	Servant	14Ju35Ka
DILLON, Mgt.		20	F	Servant	14Ju35Ka
VOHAN, Bridget		20	F	Servant	14Ju35Ka
KEEFEY, James		22	M	Laborer	14Ju35Ka
Cath.	(W)	20	F	None	14Ju35Ka
Martin	(S)	14	M	None	14Ju35Ka
BROMS, James		28	M	Laborer	14Ju35Ka
Bdgt.	(W)	30	F	None	14Ju35Ka
HEALY, Mgt.		24	F	Servant	14Ju35Ka
Jos.		20	M	Laborer	14Ju35Ka
CANLAN, John		30	M	Laborer	14Ju35Ka
Ellen	(W)	24	F	None	14Ju35Ka
Lynaugh	(S)	4	M	Child	14Ju35Ka
Mary	(D)	2	F	Child	14Ju35Ka
Mgt.		20	F	Servant	14Ju35Ka
James		22	M	Laborer	14Ju35Ka
Michl.		4	M	Child	14Ju35Ka
OLEY, Thaddeus		24	M	Laborer	14Ju35Ka

NAMES OF PASSENGERS	AGE	SEX	OCCUPATIONS	DATE PORT SHIP
GRADY, Eliza	26	F	Servant	14Ju35Ka
QUINLAN, Thaddeus	20	M	Laborer	14Ju35Ka
CONNOLLY, Patt	24	M	Laborer	14Ju35Ka
MADDEN, Michl.	25	M	Laborer	14Ju35Ka
BEVERIDGE, Maria-E.	38	F	Lady	14Ju35Ka
ENWRIGHT, Margt.	18	F	Lady	14Ju35Ka
READING, Honora	18	F	Lady	14Ju35Ka

HOTTINGER 14 JUNE 1849

From Liverpool

NAMES OF PASSENGERS	AGE	SEX	OCCUPATIONS	DATE PORT SHIP
CAHILL, Chas.	49	M	Surveyor	14Ju02Je
Ellen	22	F	Unknown	14Ju02Je
HENRY, Thos.	30	M	Farmer	14Ju02Je
Edwd.	25	M	Farmer	14Ju02Je
LEONARD, Michl.	18	M	Farmer	14Ju02Je
OCONNELL, Bridt.	12	F	Unknown	14Ju02Je
Margt.	17	F	Unknown	14Ju02Je
QUINLAN, Margt.	50	F	Unknown	14Ju02Je
Ellen	15	F	Unknown	14Ju02Je
COSTIGAN, Willaim	17	M	Shoemaker	14Ju02Je
BROPHY, Margt.	22	F	Unknown	14Ju02Je
NAUGHTON, Michl.	16	M	Unknown	14Ju02Je
Peter	14	M	Unknown	14Ju02Je
SWIFT, Joseph	50	M	Farmer	14Ju02Je
John	16	M	Farmer	14Ju02Je
Mary	62	F	Unknown	14Ju02Je
MCGARTY, Bridt.	17	F	Unknown	14Ju02Je
MCMULLEN, Owen	19	M	Shoemaker	14Ju02Je
LITTLE, John	52	M	Farmer	14Ju02Je
HURST, Hannah	20	F	Unknown	14Ju02Je
GEOHEGERN, Thos.	32	M	Farmer	14Ju02Je
Denis	38	M	Farmer	14Ju02Je
MCCAULEY, James	22	M	Shoemaker	14Ju02Je
MCCONNELL, Frans.	36	M	Hrsm	14Ju02Je
BENNETT, James	45	M	Farmer	14Ju02Je
ONEILL, Mary	19	F	Unknown	14Ju02Je
POWER, Brid.	23	F	Unknown	14Ju02Je
MCGRATH, Margt.	20	F	Unknown	14Ju02Je
HOLAHAN, Thos.	30	M	Farmer	14Ju02Je
Michl.	28	M	Farmer	14Ju02Je
MCKEARY, Mary	40	F	Unknown	14Ju02Je
James	11	M	Unknown	14Ju02Je
Catharine	9	F	Child	14Ju02Je
MCGEE, Henry	26	M	Farmer	14Ju02Je
Bridget	62	F	Unknown	14Ju02Je
MCQUILLAN, Eliza	20	F	Unknown	14Ju02Je
MURPHY, John	23	M	Butler	14Ju02Je
Mary	20	F	Unknown	14Ju02Je
MCCLUSKY, Michl.	25	M	Farmer	14Ju02Je
Chas.	18	M	Farmer	14Ju02Je
BOYLE, Willm.	20	M	Farmer	14Ju02Je
Ellen	19	F	Farmer	14Ju02Je
HURST, Jos.	26	M	Farmer	14Ju02Je
Eliza	20	F	Unknown	14Ju02Je
U	.00	U	Infant	14Ju02Je
Born-At-Sea				
MCCONNELL, Pat	27	M	Laborer	14Ju02Je
GALLAGHER, Rose	20	F	Unknown	14Ju02Je
KELLEN, Ann	45	F	Unknown	14Ju02Je
NORTON, James	23	M	Farmer	14Ju02Je
CAVANAGH, Pat	40	M	Farmer	14Ju02Je
James	39	M	Farmer	14Ju02Je
Ann	29	F	Farmer	14Ju02Je
Eliza	9	F	Child	14Ju02Je
Bridget	6	F	Child	14Ju02Je
Patrick	.00	M	Infant	14Ju02Je
Eliza	56	F	Unknown	14Ju02Je

NAMES OF PASSENGERS	AGE	SEX	OCCUPATIONS	DATE PORT SHIP
HANLON, Eliza	30	F	Unknown	14Ju02Je
KERRY, Michl.	28	M	Farmer	14Ju02Je
OBRIEN, John	55	M	Farmer	14Ju02Je
Lawrence	61	M	Farmer	14Ju02Je
Elizbeth	55	F	Unknown	14Ju02Je
GARNIER, Eliza	23	F	Unknown	14Ju02Je
DUKE, James	27	M	Shoemaker	14Ju02Je
Barbara	25	F	Unknown	14Ju02Je
CORDORAN, Tim	23	M	Farmer	14Ju02Je
HEARD, John	30	M	Hrsm	14Ju02Je
FINN, William	32	M	Farmer	14Ju02Je
MCCONNELL, David	27	M	Farmer	14Ju02Je
FRAWER, U-Mrs.	25	F	Unknown	14Ju02Je
HUNTER, John	25	M	Farmer	14Ju02Je
MAIN, Robt.	24	M	Farmer	14Ju02Je
COLGAN, W.	26	M	Blacksmith	14Ju02Je
Rose	30	F	Unknown	14Ju02Je
Catharine	30	F	Unknown	14Ju02Je
Margt.	22	F	Unknown	14Ju02Je
MCATEER, Rose	18	F	Unknown	14Ju02Je
LYNCH, Mary	30	F	Unknown	14Ju02Je
WILSON, Jane	20	F	Unknown	14Ju02Je
MILLER, Mary	44	F	Unknown	14Ju02Je
SCHOFIELD, Mary	47	F	Unknown	14Ju02Je
William	21	M	Weaver	14Ju02Je
Betsy	19	F	Weaver	14Ju02Je
Silas	16	M	Weaver	14Ju02Je
Hannah	13	F	Weaver	14Ju02Je
Alfred	6	M	Child	14Ju02Je
Thomas	10	M	Unknown	14Ju02Je
HOLT, Thos.	21	M	Unknown	14Ju02Je
Thos.	21	M	Unknown	14Ju02Je
BROWN, John	49	M	Miner	14Ju02Je
ROBERTS, Thos.	29	M	Cbtmkr	14Ju02Je
LORD, William	24	M	Cbtmkr	14Ju02Je
Margt.	25	F	Fwkr	14Ju02Je
CROOKS, Jos.	30	M	Mechanic	14Ju02Je
KERSHAW, Jos.	26	M	Unknown	14Ju02Je
MCKANN, Mart.	20	F	Unknown	14Ju02Je
WARD, Sarah	18	F	Unknown	14Ju02Je
LANCASTER, John	7	M	Child	14Ju02Je
CARSON, James	25	M	Shoemaker	14Ju02Je
Robt.	15	M	Farmer	14Ju02Je
Martha	18	F	Unknown	14Ju02Je
Jane	18	F	Farmer	14Ju02Je
MCALOONE, Mary	20	F	Unknown	14Ju02Je
MCKEERA, Pat	18	M	Farmer	14Ju02Je
MURPHY, Tim	41	M	Farmer	14Ju02Je
DILLON, Julia	26	F	Farmer	14Ju02Je
Eliza	5	F	Child	14Ju02Je
COLLON, Tim	40	M	Farmer	14Ju02Je
Hannah	38	F	Unknown	14Ju02Je
Catharine	8	F	Child	14Ju02Je
Timothy	6	M	Child	14Ju02Je
Eliza	5	F	Child	14Ju02Je
Con.	4	M	Child	14Ju02Je
CRANNAGE, Edwd.	40	M	Iron Worker	14Ju02Je
Anna	40	F	Wife	14Ju02Je
Benjm.	18	M	Unknown	14Ju02Je
Susan	16	F	Unknown	14Ju02Je
George	13	M	Unknown	14Ju02Je
Jane	10	F	Unknown	14Ju02Je
Thomas	8	M	Child	14Ju02Je
James	6	M	Child	14Ju02Je
William	.00	M	Infant	14Ju02Je
WILLIAMS, John	34	M	Iron Worker	14Ju02Je
Lucy	38	F	Unknown	14Ju02Je
COTTERELL, Jonah	50	M	Mason	14Ju02Je
Sarah	56	F	Unknown	14Ju02Je
Sarah	19	M	Unknown	14Ju02Je
Peter	20	M	Mason	14Ju02Je
SHUFFLEBOTTOM, Mary-An	20	F	Unknown	14Ju02Je
Hannah	3	F	Child	14Ju02Je
Emma	.00	F	Infant	14Ju02Je
WHITEHEAD, Geo.	24	M	Farmer	14Ju02Je
POULTON, Richd.	25	M	Farmer	14Ju02Je
M.	20	F	Unknown	14Ju02Je
CARSON, James	55	M	Shoemaker	14Ju02Je
MCMANNING, Con.	40	M	Laborer	14Ju02Je
MCNAMARA, Mary	22	F	Unknown	14Ju02Je
GILLEGAN, Peter	28	M	Laborer	14Ju02Je
Peter	28	M	Laborer	14Ju02Je
POLLET, Abel	40	M	Laborer	14Ju02Je
ARTHURS, Thos.	22	M	Unknown	14Ju02Je
WOOLLEY, Alfred	23	M	Laborer	14Ju02Je
RICHEY, Frank	30	M	Coach Maker	14Ju02Je
TAYLOR, Geo.	20	M	Unknown	14Ju02Je
CLOSE, Jos.	55	M	Miner	14Ju02Je
HAINER, Thos.	24	M	Laborer	14Ju02Je
BALL, Geo.	18	M	Laborer	14Ju02Je
Cath.	16	F	Unknown	14Ju02Je
NEWLANDS, John	30	M	Unknown	14Ju02Je
Agnes	25	F	Unknown	14Ju02Je
COUGHLAN, John	24	M	Farmer	14Ju02Je
MCCLERNAN, John	21	M	Shoemaker	14Ju02Je
BOYD, Ed	20	M	Farmer	14Ju02Je
BORLAND, Archie	17	M	Farmer	14Ju02Je
MCLEAN, Jane	16	F	Unknown	14Ju02Je
HOGG, Martha	24	F	Unknown	14Ju02Je
Mary-Anne	4	F	Child	14Ju02Je
RIGBY, Danl.	20	M	Farmer	14Ju02Je
DERRICK, Austin	27	M	Farmer	14Ju02Je
Ann	20	F	Unknown	14Ju02Je
Ann	2	F	Child	14Ju02Je
DEVER, Chas.	20	M	Farmer	14Ju02Je
Mary	18	F	Unknown	14Ju02Je
WALSH, C.	38	M	Sawer	14Ju02Je
L.	36	F	Unknown	14Ju02Je
Adelaide	16	F	Unknown	14Ju02Je
Emma	10	F	Unknown	14Ju02Je
Mary-Anne	9	F	Child	14Ju02Je
Charles	6	M	Child	14Ju02Je
Fanny	3	F	Child	14Ju02Je
BOWERIN, Thos.	23	M	Miner	14Ju02Je
MCLAUGHLAN, Hugh	25	M	Miner	14Ju02Je
WHITE, Thos.	22	M	Farmer	14Ju02Je
ARKWRIGHT, Abm.	24	M	Engineer	14Ju02Je
REDDISH, M.	24	M	Weaver	14Ju02Je
HOLLELY, Saml.	29	M	Weaver	14Ju02Je
Thomas	30	M	Weaver	14Ju02Je
GATCHER, Margt.	32	F	Unknown	14Ju02Je
LOUGHAN, Pat	30	M	Laborer	14Ju02Je
HOLMES, T.	32	M	Clergyman	14Ju02Je
Sarah	30	F	Unknown	14Ju02Je
Eliza	.00	M	Infant	14Ju02Je
LEITH, M.	18	F	Unknown	14Ju02Je
HARRAN, Jane	18	F	Servant	14Ju02Je
HASHER, Jane	18	F	Unknown	14Ju02Je
Thos.	17	M	Farmer	14Ju02Je
FOSTER, Thos.	23	M	Farmer	14Ju02Je
BRAMWELL, G.	33	M	Laborer	14Ju02Je
Thos.	26	M	Laborer	14Ju02Je
Ann	40	F	Unknown	14Ju02Je
Thos.	11	M	Unknown	14Ju02Je
Stephen	9	M	Child	14Ju02Je
James	6	M	Child	14Ju02Je
SHEEN, John	20	M	Laborer	14Ju02Je
BROOKS, Jane	26	F	Unknown	14Ju02Je
MONAGHAN, Mary	21	F	Unknown	14Ju02Je
PARKER, John	21	M	Laborer	14Ju02Je
KENNEDY, John	26	M	Whitesmith	14Ju02Je
Robt.	23	M	Tinner	14Ju02Je
Jane	22	F	Unknown	14Ju02Je
U	.00	U	Infant	14Ju02Je
Born-At-Sea				
EDWARDS, Nancy	16	F	Unknown	14Ju02Je
KELLY, Owen	21	M	Laborer	14Ju02Je
William	23	M	Laborer	14Ju02Je
PINKERTON, John	40	M	Farmer	14Ju02J
Sarah	40	F	Unknown	14Ju02J

NAMES OF PASSENGERS	AGE	SEX	OCCUPATIONS	DATE PORT SHIP
PINKERTON, John	16	M	Farmer	14Ju02Je
Margt.Jane	20	F	Unknown	14Ju02Je
Simeon	11	M	Unknown	14Ju02Je
Sarah	8	F	Child	14Ju02Je
Eliza	6	F	Child	14Ju02Je
Saml.	18	M	Unknown	14Ju02Je
Jos.	.00	M	Infant	14Ju02Je
SMITH, Sam	28	M	Farmer	14Ju02Je
WILLENBY, Ellen	20	F	Unknown	14Ju02Je
HAND, John	32	M	Farmer	14Ju02Je
KELLY, Thos.	20	M	Laborer	14Ju02Je
GARDINER, Jos.	22	M	Laborer	14Ju02Je
TAYLOR, J.	30	M	Unknown	14Ju02Je
GORMLEY, Bridget	40	F	Unknown	14Ju02Je
Thos.	8	M	Child	14Ju02Je
Ann	7	F	Child	14Ju02Je
Michl.	6	M	Child	14Ju02Je
Pat	4	M	Child	14Ju02Je
Luke	.00	M	Infant	14Ju02Je
MOFFAT, Michl.	18	M	Laborer	14Ju02Je
MAHAN, Thos.	21	M	Laborer	14Ju02Je
BYRD, Eliz.	20	F	Unknown	14Ju02Je
CARTWRIGHT, Mary	24	F	Unknown	14Ju02Je
Susan	60	F	Unknown	14Ju02Je
Edwd.	60	M	Unknown	14Ju02Je
Edwd.	24	M	Puddler	14Ju02Je
James	23	M	Puddler	14Ju02Je
Thomas	21	M	Roller	14Ju02Je
Chas.	19	M	Puddler	14Ju02Je
PEAKE, Geo.	26	M	Shoemaker	14Ju02Je
WASS, Artin	50	M	Farmer	14Ju02Je
Ann	45	F	Unknown	14Ju02Je
Elizabeth	20	F	Unknown	14Ju02Je
Sarah	17	F	Unknown	14Ju02Je
Rebecca	15	F	Unknown	14Ju02Je
Hannah	12	F	Unknown	14Ju02Je
Jesse	11	M	Unknown	14Ju02Je
George	7	M	Child	14Ju02Je
Thomas	7	M	Child	14Ju02Je
Eliza	2	F	Child	14Ju02Je
LODGE, Jas.	29	M	Farmer	14Ju02Je
Wm.S.	26	M	Farmer	14Ju02Je
Eliza	8	F	Child	14Ju02Je
George	6	M	Child	14Ju02Je
Edwin	4	M	Child	14Ju02Je
Amprose	2	M	Child	14Ju02Je
Hannah	.00	F	Infant	14Ju02Je
Richard	22	M	Farmer	14Ju02Je
UTHERN, Josh	35	M	Farmer	14Ju02Je
RIFFEN, Henry	37	M	Unknown	14Ju02Je
ACHELL, Ann	27	F	Unknown	14Ju02Je
OSTAN, Martin	12	M	Unknown	14Ju02Je
CGRATH, Jos.	35	M	Unknown	14Ju02Je
Ann	30	F	Unknown	14Ju02Je
YRNE, Jno.	20	M	Unknown	14Ju02Je
REAMER, Edwd.	39	M	Unknown	14Ju02Je
S.	29	F	Unknown	14Ju02Je
John	29	M	Unknown	14Ju02Je
M.	25	F	Unknown	14Ju02Je
John	.00	M	Infant	14Ju02Je
Margaret	20	F	Unknown	14Ju02Je
John	30	M	Unknown	14Ju02Je
Josh.	11	M	Unknown	14Ju02Je
Edwd.	10	M	Unknown	14Ju02Je
Molly	7	F	Child	14Ju02Je
YNE, Owen	25	M	Laborer	14Ju02Je
ITH, Owen	23	M	Laborer	14Ju02Je
Margt.	24	F	Unknown	14Ju02Je
OLEY, Thos.	22	M	Laborer	14Ju02Je
CFYFE, Judy	18	F	Unknown	14Ju02Je
FFNEY, Pat	20	M	Laborer	14Ju02Je
NG, Owen	2	M	Child	14Ju02Je
WNSON, John	29	M	Unknown	14Ju02Je
U-Mrs.	23	F	Unknown	14Ju02Je
BINSON, Edwd.	23	M	Laborer	14Ju02Je

NAMES OF PASSENGERS	AGE	SEX	OCCUPATIONS	DATE PORT SHIP
FITZPATRICK, Ann	29	F	Unknown	14Ju02Je
MORRIS, Thomas	25	M	Farmer	14Ju02Je
DUMFIL, Sarah	40	F	Unknown	14Ju02Je
MACKEY, James	20	M	Chandler	14Ju02Je
Bridget	20	F	Unknown	14Ju02Je
BURFORD, John	44	M	Laborer	14Ju02Je
GORMAN, Cath.	20	F	Unknown	14Ju02Je
SMITH, Jane	24	F	Unknown	14Ju02Je
Alice	25	F	Unknown	14Ju02Je
ROBINSON, John	35	M	Laborer	14Ju02Je
HAMPSHIRE, Chas.	24	M	Farmer	14Ju02Je
ONEILL, Michl.	28	M	Laborer	14Ju02Je
ROURK, John	27	M	Laborer	14Ju02Je
CARROLL, Dennis	29	M	Laborer	14Ju02Je
Mary	20	F	Unknown	14Ju02Je
BATESON, John	27	M	Bookkeeper	14Ju02Je
Thos.	23	M	Bookkeeper	14Ju02Je
BYRNE, Jane	20	F	Unknown	14Ju02Je
KENNEDY, Dan	24	M	Laborer	14Ju02Je
WHITTAKER, Jas.	29	M	Millwright	14Ju02Je
CATHCART, John	35	M	Farmer	14Ju02Je
Ann	35	F	Unknown	14Ju02Je
MALCAHY, Chas.R.	30	M	Farmer	14Ju02Je
Ann-Kate	25	F	Unknown	14Ju02Je
BURKE, James	25	M	Laborer	14Ju02Je
MULCAHY, Dick	30	M	Laborer	14Ju02Je
Jas.Art.	40	M	Gdnr	14Ju02Je
Eliza	30	F	Unknown	14Ju02Je
STOTT, Isaac	30	M	Laborer	14Ju02Je
CASEY, Michl.	35	M	Laborer	14Ju02Je
STETTON, Stephen	23	M	Farmer	14Ju02Je
M.	23	F	Farmer	14Ju02Je
Isaac	7	M	Child	14Ju02Je
Joseph	2	M	Child	14Ju02Je
FOX, John	23	M	Butcher	14Ju02Je
Mary-K.	44	F	Unknown	14Ju02Je
Fredk.	12	M	Unknown	14Ju02Je
PHILIPS, Wm.	23	M	Unknown	14Ju02Je
ROULSTONE, Jos.	23	M	Unknown	14Ju02Je
Thos.	30	M	Unknown	14Ju02Je
SMITH, Pat	20	M	Laborer	14Ju02Je
Farrell	24	U	Unknown	14Ju02Je
MCDERMOTT, Ml.	21	M	Farmer	14Ju02Je
ABBOTT, J.	21	M	Carpenter	14Ju02Je
Wm.S.	50	M	Unknown	14Ju02Je
A.	23	F	Unknown	14Ju02Je
RATCHFORD, Cath.	40	F	Unknown	14Ju02Je
HERRON, Albert	20	M	Laborer	14Ju02Je
HUNTER, Wm.	20	M	Shepherd	14Ju02Je
Jane	21	F	Unknown	14Ju02Je
BOWAN, Chas.	22	M	Farmer	14Ju02Je
BELL, Jno.	19	M	Farmer	14Ju02Je
PATTERSON, Danl.	18	M	Farmer	14Ju02Je
ARMSTRONG, Robt.	26	M	Farmer	14Ju02Je
ROBINSON, W.	21	M	Farmer	14Ju02Je
MCCUNE, J.	20	M	Blacksmith	14Ju02Je
HIGGINS, W.	23	M	Mason	14Ju02Je
EVANS, Thos.	26	M	Mason	14Ju02Je
BURNETT, W.	21	M	Mason	14Ju02Je
HOLLINGWORTH, Jas.	25	M	Unknown	14Ju02Je
Ann-Cath.	25	F	Unknown	14Ju02Je
Eliz.	40	F	Unknown	14Ju02Je
Henry	21	M	Unknown	14Ju02Je
Eliza	15	F	Unknown	14Ju02Je
Jac.	12	M	Unknown	14Ju02Je
DRAPER, Robt.	12	M	Unknown	14Ju02Je
Ann	10	F	Unknown	14Ju02Je
SHARPER, Richd.	30	M	Unknown	14Ju02Je
DUNN, Michl.	25	M	Farmer	14Ju02Je
KERWAN, Pat	23	M	Farmer	14Ju02Je
RUSTER, Samson	18	M	Farmer	14Ju02Je
DAVIS, Geo.	26	M	Farmer	14Ju02Je
Caroline	25	F	Unknown	14Ju02Je
Gaines	5	M	Child	14Ju02Je
Arthur	.00	M	Infant	14Ju02Je

NAMES OF PASSENGERS	AGE	SEX	OCCUPATIONS	DATE PORT SHIP
BROWN, Mary	17	F	Unknown	14Ju02Je
WALSH, Sarah	22	F	Unknown	14Ju02Je
Cath.	20	F	Unknown	14Ju02Je
BROGAN, Brid.	20	F	Unknown	14Ju02Je
CORBREAN, J.	20	M	Laborer	14Ju02Je
STEWART, Cath.	25	F	Unknown	14Ju02Je
SIMPSON, Margt.	3	F	Child	14Ju02Je
MAHER, John	20	M	Laborer	14Ju02Je
Martin	21	M	Laborer	14Ju02Je
MCGRATH, Anty	17	M	Unknown	14Ju02Je
Jas.Joy.	24	M	Farmer	14Ju02Je
MONAGHAN, Cath.	20	F	Unknown	14Ju02Je
BRADY, Phil.	20	M	Laborer	14Ju02Je
MATTHEWS, Mary	25	F	Unknown	14Ju02Je
WALLACE, Eliza	19	F	Unknown	14Ju02Je
Jane	17	F	Unknown	14Ju02Je
U	.00	U	Infant	14Ju02Je
Born-At-Sea	Died-At-Sea			
BUCKLEY, John	25	M	Laborer	14Ju02Je
FEAGAN, Pat	25	M	Laborer	14Ju02Je
MULLIGAN, Thos.	30	M	Farmer	14Ju02Je
OBRIEN, Cath.	40	F	Unknown	14Ju02Je
Eliza	17	F	Unknown	14Ju02Je
Edwd.	10	M	Unknown	14Ju02Je
Winifred	7	F	Child	14Ju02Je
CAVAGH, Mary	25	F	Unknown	14Ju02Je
MAHER, Corn.	25	M	Laborer	14Ju02Je
PILES, Margt.	20	F	Unknown	14Ju02Je
LYONS, Jas.	25	M	Laborer	14Ju02Je
Ctah.	18	F	Unknown	14Ju02Je
HENNESSY, Ann	18	F	Unknown	14Ju02Je
EGAN, Cath.	19	F	Unknown	14Ju02Je
KELLY, Michl.	18	M	Laborer	14Ju02Je
ANDERSON, Jane	17	F	Unknown	14Ju02Je
GLYNNE, Martin	21	M	Farmer	14Ju02Je
DUNNE, Chas.	24	M	Farmer	14Ju02Je
Ann	22	F	Unknown	14Ju02Je
Pat	22	M	Laborer	14Ju02Je
LODGE, Jane	11	F	Unknown	14Ju02Je
NEIL, Brid.	28	F	Unknown	14Ju02Je
Ann	7	F	Child	14Ju02Je
Maria	5	F	Child	14Ju02Je
Elizabeth	3	F	Child	14Ju02Je
NOLAN, Pat	20	M	Laborer	14Ju02Je
KELLY, Dan	24	M	Laborer	14Ju02Je
Susan	22	F	Unknown	14Ju02Je
BROWN, Wm.	30	M	Farmer	14Ju02Je
DOGHERTY, John	28	M	Farmer	14Ju02Je
Mary	18	F	Unknown	14Ju02Je
GALLAGHER, Jas.	40	M	Laborer	14Ju02Je
DILLON, Ann	20	F	Unknown	14Ju02Je
BATTLEWORTH, Jas.	20	M	Farmer	14Ju02Je
DRISCOLL, Mary	21	F	Unknown	14Ju02Je
Ellen	20	F	Unknown	14Ju02Je
SMITH, Pat	20	M	Laborer	14Ju02Je
Cath.	20	F	Unknown	14Ju02Je
LYNCH, Brid.	24	F	Unknown	14Ju02Je
Oliver	2	M	Child	14Ju02Je
Ann	.00	F	Infant	14Ju02Je

ROSCIUS 15 JUNE 1849

From Liverpool

NAMES OF PASSENGERS	AGE	SEX	OCCUPATIONS	DATE PORT SHIP
DWAR, John	30	M	Merchant	15Ju02JI
LOWRY, John	25	M	Attorney	15Ju02JI
SWANN, Abraham	28	M	Cbtmkr	15Ju02JI
Deborah	32	F	Cbtmkr	15Ju02JI
MAY, Joseph-M.	9	M	Child	15Ju02JI
FRANCK, Charles	50	M	Farmer	15Ju02JI
Charles	18	M	Farmer	15Ju02JI
John	25	M	Farmer	15Ju02JI
Jane	50	F	Farmer	15Ju02JI
Fanny	21	F	Farmer	15Ju02JI
Jane	20	F	Farmer	15Ju02JI
Elizth.	10	F	Farmer	15Ju02JI
BENJAMIN, Lawlan	22	F	Farmer	15Ju02JI
LISLER, Robt.	60	M	Farmer	15Ju02JI
MCKEAN, U	23	F	Spinster	15Ju02JI
DEVIT, Mary-Anne	45	F	Spinster	15Ju02JI
MCGRATH, Hugh	26	M	Spinster	15Ju02JI
Anne	26	F	Milliner	15Ju02JI
Hugh	2	M	Child	15Ju02JI
Charles	.00	M	Infant	15Ju02JI
Cath.	12	F	Farmer	15Ju02JI
Martha-Jane	25	F	Farmer	15Ju02JI
SMITH, Mary	26	F	Farmer	15Ju02JI
MARSHALL, Anne	40	F	Farmer	15Ju02JI
CHUMLY, Thomas	40	M	Farmer	15Ju02JI
Anne	38	F	Farmer	15Ju02JI
Eliza-Anne	.00	F	Infant	15Ju02JI
RYAN, Marlin	38	M	Farmer	15Ju02JI
OBRIEN, Matthew	2	M	Child	15Ju02JI
BARK, William	19	M	Farmer	15Ju02JI
OMEARER, Michael	28	M	Farmer	15Ju02JI
HUCKNER, James-H.	20	M	Farmer	15Ju02JI
WILLIAMSON, John	29	M	Farmer	15Ju02JI
SUDDLER, Charles	21	M	Farmer	15Ju02JI
WILLIAMSON, Sarah	21	F	Farmer	15Ju02JI
James	19	M	Farmer	15Ju02JI
CHAPMAN, William	25	M	Farmer	15Ju02JI
Mary-Anne	22	F	Farmer	15Ju02JI
LUKE, Mary	21	F	Milliner	15Ju02JI
RICH, Mary	23	F	Milliner	15Ju02JI
DUNNE, Margt.	16	F	Milliner	15Ju02JI
Anne	30	F	Pasm	15Ju02JI
GARDENER, Elizth.	30	F	Pasm	15Ju02JI
ATCHINSON, Mary	30	F	Pasm	15Ju02JI
PARISH, John	34	M	Farmer	15Ju02JI
Peter	32	M	Farmer	15Ju02JI
Emma	9	F	Child	15Ju02JI
Charles	7	M	Child	15Ju02JI
William	4	M	Child	15Ju02JI
SHAW, John-M.	4	M	Child	15Ju02JI
BEETON, John	38	M	Farmer	15Ju02JI
REYNARD, Geo.	26	M	Farmer	15Ju02JI
Mary	2	F	Child	15Ju02JI
James	.00	M	Infant	15Ju02JI
KEYNARD, Henry	40	M	Farmer	15Ju02JI
Died-At-Sea				
PROUD, James	50	M	Shoemaker	15Ju02J
Cath.	45	F	Shoemaker	15Ju02J
Thomas	22	M	Shoemaker	15Ju02J
James	28	M	Shoemaker	15Ju02J
David	18	M	Shoemaker	15Ju02J
Richard	17	M	Shoemaker	15Ju02J
Eliza	12	F	Shoemaker	15Ju02J
MAGUIRE, Susanna	10	F	Milliner	15Ju02J
PRERED, Samuel	6	M	Child	15Ju02J
Isabella	4	F	Child	15Ju02J
CONDON, John	22	M	Laborer	15Ju02J
SMITH, Margaret	7	F	Child	15Ju02J
Anthony	4	M	Child	15Ju02J
Joseph	4	M	Child	15Ju02J
SHEL, Thomas	22	M	Servant	15Ju02J
Daniel	20	M	Servant	15Ju02
NICHELSON, Mary	60	F	Servant	15Ju02
GREENWOOD, Miles	53	M	Laborer	15Ju02
EGRITH, Edward	23	M	Laborer	15Ju02
Mary	20	F	Laborer	15Ju02
Thomas	2	M	Child	15Ju02
GREENWOOD, Josep	18	M	Laborer	15Ju02
Thomas	14	M	Laborer	15Ju02
Anne	8	F	Child	15Ju02

NAMES OF PASSENGERS	AGE	SEX	OCCUPATIONS	DATE PORT SHIP
GREENWOOD, Margaret	7	F	Child	15Ju02JI
CAPSTICK, Geo.	42	M	Carpenter	15Ju02JI
Margt.	40	F	Carpenter	15Ju02JI
Jane	15	F	Carpenter	15Ju02JI
Mary	9	F	Child	15Ju02JI
Margt.	6	F	Child	15Ju02JI
Dorthea	3	F	Child	15Ju02JI
Agnis	.00	F	Infant	15Ju02JI
HAGHART, Timothy	28	M	Laborer	15Ju02JI
FAGAN, Henry	30	M	Farmer	15Ju02JI
Mary	60	F	Farmer	15Ju02JI
Patrick	60	M	Farmer	15Ju02JI
Rose	18	F	Farmer	15Ju02JI
DENHAM, Hugh	20	M	Farmer	15Ju02JI
FINNEGAN, Anne	40	F	Farmer	15Ju02JI
Patrick	26	M	Farmer	15Ju02JI
Thomas	24	M	Farmer	15Ju02JI
Mary	20	F	Farmer	15Ju02JI
Catherine	16	F	Farmer	15Ju02JI
Brien	14	M	Farmer	15Ju02JI
SCOTT, Mary	10	F	Farmer	15Ju02JI
Harriet	43	F	Farmer	15Ju02JI
Mary	44	F	Farmer	15Ju02JI
Harriet	22	F	Farmer	15Ju02JI
Elizabeth	17	F	Servant	15Ju02JI
William	15	M	Laborer	15Ju02JI
HIGHMAN, Henry	10	M	Laborer	15Ju02JI
RYAN, Martin	28	M	Laborer	15Ju02JI
Ellen	26	F	Laborer	15Ju02JI
WHITE, Martin	23	M	Laborer	15Ju02JI
GREENWOOD, James	28	M	Laborer	15Ju02JI
GRACE, Mathew	23	M	Blacksmith	15Ju02JI
Anne	18	F	Blacksmith	15Ju02JI
PARSON, Anne	20	F	Blacksmith	15Ju02JI
FORSYTH, Mary	19	F	Dressmaker	15Ju02JI
Sally	19	F	Dressmaker	15Ju02JI
CONNELL, Stephen	19	M	Laborer	15Ju02JI
Mich	15	M	Laborer	15Ju02JI
SULLIVAN, John	42	M	Laborer	15Ju02JI
PARKER, Mary	64	F	Laborer	15Ju02JI
Bridget	25	F	Laborer	15Ju02JI
William	2	M	Child	15Ju02JI
Eliza	.00	F	Infant	15Ju02JI
Mathew	23	M	Laborer	15Ju02JI
FULTON, Sarah	18	F	Laborer	15Ju02JI
MCILLHENEY, Mich.	44	M	Laborer	15Ju02JI
James	23	M	Laborer	15Ju02JI
COCKLIN, John	21	M	Laborer	15Ju02JI
Mary	25	F	Laborer	15Ju02JI
Denis	20	M	Laborer	15Ju02JI
WILLIAMS, Joseph	18	M	Laborer	15Ju02J!
RYAN, Mary	20	F	Laborer	15Ju02JI
Bridget	32	F	Laborer	15Ju02JI
JACKSON, Robert	5	M	Child	15Ju02JI
Isabella	5	F	Child	15Ju02JI
Edward	40	M	Laborer	15Ju02JI
Emily	.00	F	Infant	15Ju02JI
PORTEN, Thomas	18	M	Carpenter	15Ju02JI
Sarah	9	F	Child	15Ju02JI
WEBSTER, Charles	7	M	Child	15Ju02JI
PORTER, W.H.	5	U	Child	15Ju02JI
BERRY, Robt.	27	M	Laborer	15Ju02JI
HARTLY, Thomas	60	M	Laborer	15Ju02JI
Samuel	46	M	Laborer	15Ju02JI
Thomas	11	M	Laborer	15Ju02JI
TOFT, John	43	M	Laborer	15Ju02JI
BROWN, Henry	59	M	Laborer	15Ju02JI
LEVISLY, William	20	M	Laborer	15Ju02JI
MADDY, John	13	M	Laborer	15Ju02JI
FRANKLIN, Robert	25	M	Laborer	15Ju02JI
Mary	26	F	Laborer	15Ju02JI
James	3	M	Child	15Ju02JI
John-W.	1	M	Child	15Ju02JI
Mathew	23	M	Laborer	15Ju02JI
MCDOWELL, Robert	31	M	Laborer	15Ju02JI
MELEY, Susana	52	F	Farmer	15Ju02JI
Anne	20	F	Farmer	15Ju02JI
Sarah	17	F	Farmer	15Ju02JI
Susanna	14	F	Farmer	15Ju02JI
Barry	11	M	Farmer	15Ju02JI
MOFFAT, Joseph	18	M	Tailor	15Ju02JI
STANTON, Thomas	33	M	Laborer	15Ju02JI
GIBBONS, Joseph	13	M	Laborer	15Ju02JI
BATTY, Edward	20	M	Laborer	15Ju02JI
CARSON, Henry	19	M	Laborer	15Ju02JI
BECKETT, Mary-Anne	32	F	Laborer	15Ju02JI
WALLACE, Mary-Jane	34	F	Laborer	15Ju02JI
HUDSON, James	31	M	Laborer	15Ju02JI
MCCASTER, Elizabeth	24	F	Laborer	15Ju02JI
JOHNSTONE, Eliza	28	F	Laborer	15Ju02JI
MCKATH, Bridget	30	F	Farmer	15Ju02JI
KILPATRICK, Margt.	35	F	Farmer	15Ju02JI
KELLY, John	20	M	Farmer	15Ju02JI
CONNELL, David	40	M	Farmer	15Ju02JI
MCKINGLY, Alice	41	F	Farmer	15Ju02JI
STEWART, Emeliane	40	F	Farmer	15Ju02JI
DUNNOLY, Patrick	30	M	Farmer	15Ju02JI
KILPATRICK, Robert	60	M	Farmer	15Ju02JI
OLIVE, Anne	27	F	Hatter	15Ju02JI
MEAGHER, James	30	M	Hatter	15Ju02JI
BASTARD, William	39	M	Hatter	15Ju02JI
LAKE, Thomas	18	M	Hatter	15Ju02JI
LARENCE, Anne	22	F	Hatter	15Ju02JI
Sarah	18	F	Hatter	15Ju02JI
OBRIEN, Timothy	45	M	Farmer	15Ju02JI
Cath.	45	F	Farmer	15Ju02JI
Ellen	20	F	Farmer	15Ju02JI
Denis	18	M	Farmer	15Ju02JI
Bridget	17	F	Farmer	15Ju02JI
Philip	8	M	Child	15Ju02JI
HARTLEY, Eliza	3	F	Child	15Ju02JI
MURPHY, James	18	M	Laborer	15Ju02JI
GORDON, Robert	23	M	Laborer	15Ju02JI
MCSEEKRY, Eliza	20	F	Laborer	15Ju02JI
GORDON, Sarah	21	F	Laborer	15Ju02JI
OLDHER, William	18	M	Laborer	15Ju02JI
OLIVE, Robt.	35	M	Laborer	15Ju02JI
NASH, Robt.	24	M	Laborer	15Ju02JI
MANGHAN, John	27	M	Laborer	15Ju02JI
Anne	20	F	Laborer	15Ju02JI
Rose	18	F	Laborer	15Ju02JI
Patrick	16	M	Laborer	15Ju02JI
Anne	14	F	Laborer	15Ju02JI
DULY, John	50	M	Farmer	15Ju02JI
SMITH, James	40	M	Farmer	15Ju02JI
BRADY, Bessy	30	F	Farmer	15Ju02JI
SMITH, Bridgett	20	F	Farmer	15Ju02JI
MCCEERY, Mary	60	F	Farmer	15Ju02JI
MCCARTY, Mathew	35	M	Farmer	15Ju02JI
CARTY, Bridget	22	F	Farmer	15Ju02JI
KELLY, James	20	M	Farmer	15Ju02JI
RUSSELL, John	10	M	Farmer	15Ju02JI
MORROW, James	6	M	Child	15Ju02JI
U	4	M	Child	15Ju02JI
GRANT, Patrick	11	M	Farmer	15Ju02JI
MCCLEAN, Michael	15	M	Farmer	15Ju02JI
OCONNOR, John	60	M	Farmer	15Ju02JI
MILLIKIN, James	40	M	Farmer	15Ju02JI
Mary	30	F	Farmer	15Ju02JI
Sarah	27	F	Farmer	15Ju02JI
Elizth.	25	F	Farmer	15Ju02JI
Cath.	22	F	Farmer	15Ju02JI
DARDITH, Elizth.	40	F	Farmer	15Ju02JI
Thomas	42	M	Farmer	15Ju02JI
DUDLEY, William	49	M	Farmer	15Ju02JI
CORTLY, Louisa	50	F	Farmer	15Ju02JI
MEDCLIFF, James	35	M	Farmer	15Ju02JI
KENNEDY, Thomas	25	M	Farmer	15Ju02JI
MEAGHER, Michael	25	M	Farmer	15Ju02JI
Margaret	23	F	Farmer	15Ju02JI

NAMES OF PASSENGERS	AGE	SEX	OCCUPATIONS	DATE PORT SHIP
MCKIRKIN, Henry	17	M	Farmer	15Ju02JI
LAVERTY, Ellen	15	F	Farmer	15Ju02JI
COLLINGTON, James	30	F	Carpenter	15Ju02JI
Mary	36	F	Carpenter	15Ju02JI
RICKARD, Michael	18	M	Carpenter	15Ju02JI
John	15	M	Carpenter	15Ju02JI
Edward	10	M	Carpenter	15Ju02JI
Joseph	8	M	Child	15Ju02JI
FITZGERALD, James	33	M	Shoemaker	15Ju02JI
Hannah	25	F	Shoemaker	15Ju02JI
NOWLAN, Andrew	33	M	Shoemaker	15Ju02JI
GALLAGHER, Lewis	21	M	Laborer	15Ju02JI
Francis	13	M	Laborer	15Ju02JI
Patrick	8	M	Child	15Ju02JI
Hugh	10	M	Laborer	15Ju02JI
CARLEY, Anne	38	F	Laborer	15Ju02JI
Patrick	10	M	Laborer	15Ju02JI
Anne	6	F	Child	15Ju02JI
CUSKY, Mary	28	F	Laborer	15Ju02JI
ROWE, Thomas	4	M	Child	15Ju02JI
CROWDON, Patrick	28	M	Cooper	15Ju02JI
MULLIGAN, Edward	19	M	Cooper	15Ju02JI
MULLIN, Peter	14	M	Cooper	15Ju02JI
DAISOF, Judy	19	F	Cooper	15Ju02JI
WELCH, James	21	M	Farmer	15Ju02JI
Thomas	23	M	Farmer	15Ju02JI
SWEENEY, Ellen	35	M	Laborer	15Ju02JI
SIMPSON, David	36	M	Laborer	15Ju02JI
FIELDS, John	20	M	Laborer	15Ju02JI
BLAKE, Anne	40	F	Laborer	15Ju02JI
SCUDDY, Jane	42	F	Laborer	15Ju02JI
Catherine	16	F	Laborer	15Ju02JI
HARTY, James	29	M	Laborer	15Ju02JI
WHITE, John	19	M	Laborer	15Ju02JI
JOHNSTONE, Henry	18	M	Laborer	15Ju02JI
SINCLAIR, John	10	M	Laborer	15Ju02JI
JOHNSTONE, Agnis	11	M	Laborer	15Ju02JI
HULTON, Edwards	18	M	Laborer	15Ju02JI
JORDAN, Thomas	30	M	Laborer	15Ju02JI
BANE, Patrick	20	M	Laborer	15Ju02JI
Mary	16	F	Laborer	15Ju02JI
JORDAN, Mary	18	F	Laborer	15Ju02JI
BUTLER, Mary	18	F	Laborer	15Ju02JI
CEW, Cath.	13	F	Laborer	15Ju02JI
ROWAN, James	20	M	Laborer	15Ju02JI
WADSON, John	30	M	Laborer	15Ju02JI
MULERON, Anne	25	F	Laborer	15Ju02JI
QUINLIN, Thomas	21	M	Laborer	15Ju02JI
MCCANN, John	21	M	Laborer	15Ju02JI
HARTY, James	25	M	Laborer	15Ju02JI
WHILE, John	20	M	Laborer	15Ju02JI
JOHNSTONE, Henry	40	M	Laborer	15Ju02JI
SINCLAIR, John	19	M	Farmer	15Ju02JI
JOHNSTONE, Agnis	30	F	Farmer	15Ju02JI
MCCREA, Edward	26	M	Farmer	15Ju02JI
HANSHAW, Thomas	26	M	Farmer	15Ju02JI
Elizth.	69	F	Farmer	15Ju02JI
BINSTONE, William	44	M	Farmer	15Ju02JI
Eliza	32	F	Farmer	15Ju02JI
KELLY, Mary	30	F	Farmer	15Ju02JI
SWEENY, Patrick	34	M	Farmer	15Ju02JI
BALL, Margt.	70	F	Farmer	15Ju02JI
Bessy	16	F	Farmer	15Ju02JI
Luke	18	M	Farmer	15Ju02JI
STETSON, Bernard	19	M	Laborer	15Ju02JI
MCNANNY, Peter	20	M	Laborer	15Ju02JI
FARLEY, Michael	20	M	Laborer	15Ju02JI
MCKEEREN, Thomas	22	M	Laborer	15Ju02JI
BREEN, Mary	17	F	Laborer	15Ju02JI
BALL, Mathew	8	M	Child	15Ju02JI
Margt.	4	F	Child	15Ju02JI
Sally	18	F	Milliner	15Ju02JI
MARTEN, Catherine	19	F	Milliner	15Ju02JI
KARL, Edward	40	M	Farmer	15Ju02JI
Patrick	18	M	Farmer	15Ju02JI

NAMES OF PASSENGERS	AGE	SEX	OCCUPATIONS	DATE PORT SHIP
MOULDEN, John	30	M	Farmer	15Ju02JI
BREEN, John	26	M	Farmer	15Ju02JI
BALL, James	25	M	Laborer	15Ju02JI
Catherine	30	F	Laborer	15Ju02JI
Thomas	6	M	Child	15Ju02JI
John	4	M	Child	15Ju02JI
Bridget	5	F	Child	15Ju02JI
GRADY, Edward	45	M	Farmer	15Ju02JI
Patrick	25	M	Farmer	15Ju02JI
MURPHY, Thomas	21	M	Farmer	15Ju02JI
NORTH, John	16	M	Farmer	15Ju02JI
GRADY, Mary-A.	16	M	Farmer	15Ju02JI
HENRY, Anne	13	F	Farmer	15Ju02JI
Cath.	18	F	Farmer	15Ju02JI
ROBINSON, Joseph	8	M	Child	15Ju02JI
MCCANN, John	16	M	Child	15Ju02JI
KENNEDY, Hugh	22	M	Child	15Ju02JI
GALLAHER, Rose	40	F	Farmer	15Ju02JI
Bridget	50	F	Farmer	15Ju02JI
QUIN, Ellen	25	F	Farmer	15Ju02JI
GALLAGHER, Margt.	8	F	Child	15Ju02JI
THOMAS, Robert	24	M	Farmer	15Ju02JI
HUSTHEAD, James	28	M	Farmer	15Ju02JI
CAIN, Joseph	15	M	Farmer	15Ju02JI
GREEN, Joseph	2	M	Child	15Ju02JI
NEILL, Phelep	30	M	Shoemaker	15Ju02JI
KENN, James	18	M	Shoemaker	15Ju02JI
WINTER, Martha	22	F	Shoemaker	15Ju02JI
GAVIN, Joseph	1	M	Child	15Ju02JI
HUGHES, Denis	26	M	Shoemaker	15Ju02JI
SOUTH, Denis	11	M	Shoemaker	15Ju02JI
HANDER, Pat	23	M	Laborer	15Ju02JI
GAVIN, Denis	21	M	Laborer	15Ju02JI
CONNELL, Cath.	35	F	Laborer	15Ju02JI
WOODS, Denis	25	M	Laborer	15Ju02JI
HEDERLY, Bridget	20	F	Laborer	15Ju02JI
SCOTT, Mary	22	F	Laborer	15Ju02JI
PORTER, Sarah-A.	5	F	Child	15Ju02JI
OBRIEN, Mary	45	F	Laborer	15Ju02JI
BIRNEY, James	60	M	Laborer	15Ju02JI
MCCREED, Mathew	30	M	Laborer	15Ju02JI
DEELY, Francis	20	M	Laborer	15Ju02JI
BALL, Anne	5	F	Child	15Ju02JI

JULIET 15 JUNE 1849

From Waterford

NAMES OF PASSENGERS	AGE	SEX	OCCUPATIONS	DATE PORT SHIP
CAHILL, John	13	M	None	15Ju15J
Mich.	11	M	None	15Ju15J
Ellen	14	F	None	15Ju15J
John	35	M	Laborer	15Ju15J
FAGAN, Patrick	20	M	Spinster	15Ju15J
Mary	22	F	Spinster	15Ju15J
HICKEY, Patrick	28	M	Laborer	15Ju15J
COFFIE, Betsy	23	F	Spinster	15Ju15J
GOFF, Ellen	20	F	Spinster	15Ju15J
KEARNEY, Mary	24	F	Spinster	15Ju15J
WALSH, Mary	21	F	Spinster	15Ju15J
CLOODY, John	18	M	Laborer	15Ju15J
BYRNE, Ellen	22	F	Spinster	15Ju15J
KAVENAGH, Ellen	40	F	Spinster	15Ju15J
Ellen	14	F	Spinster	15Ju15J
WALSH, Cat.	31	F	Spinster	15Ju15
Ellen	12	F	None	15Ju15
Mat.	10	M	None	15Ju15
Pat	5	M	Child	15Ju15
Kath.	2	F	Child	15Ju15
POUDER, M.	20	M	Laborer	15Ju15

NAMES OF PASSENGERS	AGE	SEX	OCCUPATIONS	DATE PORT SHIP
KEARSEY, Wm.	19	M	Laborer	15Ju15Jh
FLAHERTY, Margt.	26	F	Spinster	15Ju15Jh
KAVENAGH, Cath.	16	F	Spinster	15Ju15Jh
HANLON, Patrick	27	M	Laborer	15Ju15Jh
NEVILLE, Miles	28	M	Laborer	15Ju15Jh
BYRNE, Martin	27	M	Laborer	15Ju15Jh
BROWN, Patr.	21	M	Laborer	15Ju15Jh
SWEETMAN, Jane	34	F	Spinster	15Ju15Jh
Mich.	17	M	Laborer	15Ju15Jh
Robr.	9	M	Child	15Ju15Jh
KENNEDY, Mary	18	F	Spinster	15Ju15Jh
QUINLAN, John	24	M	Laborer	15Ju15Jh
FURLONG, Cath.	34	F	Spinster	15Ju15Jh
CHRISTOPHER, Mich.	33	M	Laborer	15Ju15Jh
Maria	30	F	Spinster	15Ju15Jh
Ths.	6	M	Child	15Ju15Jh
Valentine	4	F	Child	15Ju15Jh
Mary	2	F	Child	15Ju15Jh
RYAN, Ellen	25	F	Spinster	15Ju15Jh
WALSH, Mary	20	F	Spinster	15Ju15Jh
LOUGHLIN, Cath.	23	F	Spinster	15Ju15Jh
Philip	21	M	Laborer	15Ju15Jh
CASTIN, Bridget	24	F	Spinster	15Ju15Jh
DONOVAN, Wm.	40	M	Laborer	15Ju15Jh
DUCEY, John	24	M	Laborer	15Ju15Jh
DROHAM, John	24	M	Laborer	15Ju15Jh
DEVINE, Pat	25	M	Laborer	15Ju15Jh
Mary	20	F	Spinster	15Ju15Jh
CORNEAGE, Mich.	20	M	Laborer	15Ju15Jh
KEHOE, Abby	28	F	Spinster	15Ju15Jh
John	8	M	Child	15Ju15Jh
Jane	10	F	Unknown	15Ju15Jh
HURLEY, John	21	M	Laborer	15Ju15Jh
FITZGERALD, Mary	24	F	Spinster	15Ju15Jh
POWER, Cath.	16	F	Spinster	15Ju15Jh
TRACY, Ellen	22	F	Spinster	15Ju15Jh
HALISEY, Patrick	22	M	Laborer	15Ju15Jh
MORRIS, John	23	M	Laborer	15Ju15Jh
MURPHY, Patrick	28	M	Laborer	15Ju15Jh
FITZGERALD, Ths.	40	M	Laborer	15Ju15Jh
John	13	M	Laborer	15Ju15Jh
Patrick	12	M	Laborer	15Ju15Jh
Bridget	9	F	Child	15Ju15Jh
Mary	17	F	Spinster	15Ju15Jh
TYRER, Mary	20	F	Spinster	15Ju15Jh
CHRISTOPHER, Mary	.08	F	Infant	15Ju15Jh
KEHOE, James	.09	M	Infant	15Ju15Jh

MARY-HARRINGTON 16 JUNE 1849

From Glasgow

NAMES OF PASSENGERS	AGE	SEX	OCCUPATIONS	DATE PORT SHIP
WALKER, William	60	M	Farmer	16Ju04Jl
William	28	M	Farmer	16Ju04Jl
Isabella	18	F	Relative	16Ju04Jl
KERR, Daniel	28	M	Farmer	16Ju04Jl
Mary	25	F	Relative	16Ju04Jl
Jesse	2	F	Child	16Ju04Jl
William	.06	M	Infant	16Ju04Jl
LAURIE, Agnes	23	F	Spinster	16Ju04Jl
RANKINE, James	19	M	Laborer	16Ju04Jl
Christina	66	F	None	16Ju04Jl
GRAHAM, Jane	40	F	Wife	16Ju04Jl
William	19	M	Relative	16Ju04Jl
Margaret	17	F	Relative	16Ju04Jl
Jane	12	F	Relative	16Ju04Jl
Elizth.	10	F	Relative	16Ju04Jl
Robert	8	M	Child	16Ju04Jl
Ann	3	F	Child	16Ju04Jl
MCGUIRE, John	40	M	Laborer	16Ju04Jl
Cath.	48	F	Spinster	16Ju04Jl
Mary	34	F	Spinster	16Ju04Jl
MORRIS, John	21	M	Laborer	16Ju04Jl
RAMSAY, Richard	24	M	Laborer	16Ju04Jl
DOWNIE, Susan	20	F	Wife	16Ju04Jl
Robert	.11	M	Infant	16Ju04Jl
KAIN, Agnes	21	F	Wife	16Ju04Jl
Hugh	.05	M	Infant	16Ju04Jl
HUME, Francis	35	M	Laborer	16Ju04Jl
Mary	15	F	Relative	16Ju04Jl
William	9	M	Child	16Ju04Jl
George	5	M	Child	16Ju04Jl
RALSTON, Duncan	20	M	Laborer	16Ju04Jl
RAMSAY, Robert	21	M	Laborer	16Ju04Jl
Jane	64	F	Wife	16Ju04Jl
WORKMAN, John	25	M	Laborer	16Ju04Jl
GALY, William	28	M	Laborer	16Ju04Jl
Elizabeth	26	F	Relative	16Ju04Jl
James	4	M	Child	16Ju04Jl
Elizabeth	.10	F	Infant	16Ju04Jl
JOHNSTONE, David	30	M	Smith	16Ju04Jl
MARTIN, John	23	M	Laborer	16Ju04Jl
Margaret	24	F	Spinster	16Ju04Jl
Mary	20	F	Spinster	16Ju04Jl
BOWMAN, Robert	13	M	None	16Ju04Jl
WHISTON, John	28	M	Laborer	16Ju04Jl
DENIGAN, Isaac	30	M	Laborer	16Ju04Jl
DEMPSTER, Isabella	21	F	Wife	16Ju04Jl
Thomas	3	M	Child	16Ju04Jl
GIBSON, James	8	M	Child	16Ju04Jl
Janet	54	F	Wife	16Ju04Jl
Thomas	17	M	Relative	16Ju04Jl
LAURIE, Charlotte	19	F	Spinster	16Ju04Jl
MCDIRRITT, Francis	20	M	Laborer	16Ju04Jl
DOLAN, Michael	28	M	Laborer	16Ju04Jl
FARRAL, Catherine	54	F	Wife	16Ju04Jl
Elizabeth	18	F	Relative	16Ju04Jl
BARNIE, Andrew	39	M	Farmer	16Ju04Jl
Elizabeth	25	F	Relative	16Ju04Jl
Elizabeth	4	F	Child	16Ju04Jl
Jessie	2	F	Child	16Ju04Jl
John	.06	M	Infant	16Ju04Jl
SMITH, Ann	27	F	Spinster	16Ju04Jl
MCLAUGHLIN, Hugh	21	M	Laborer	16Ju04Jl
MCARTHUR, James	36	M	Laborer	16Ju04Jl
CAMPBELL, Mary	25	F	Spinster	16Ju04Jl
COACH, Nathaniel	37	M	Laborer	16Ju04Jl
BOWER, Margaret	35	F	Spinster	16Ju04Jl
SHEPPARD, Janet	50	F	Spinster	16Ju04Jl
DOLAN, William	26	M	Laborer	16Ju04Jl
Catherine	21	F	Spinster	16Ju04Jl
James	13	M	None	16Ju04Jl
MCDONALD, Alex.	28	M	Laborer	16Ju04Jl
BROWNLIE, Alex.	21	M	Laborer	16Ju04Jl
MCANLAY, Patrick	40	M	Laborer	16Ju04Jl
MCGUINNESS, Chas.	39	M	Laborer	16Ju04Jl
REID, James	39	M	Laborer	16Ju04Jl
WHITE, Peter	39	M	Laborer	16Ju04Jl
SCOTT, Alexander	22	M	Laborer	16Ju04Jl
Mary	21	F	Spinster	16Ju04Jl
MCFARLAND, James	71	M	Laborer	16Ju04Jl
William	39	M	Laborer	16Ju04Jl
James	11	M	None	16Ju04Jl
BRODIE, Matthew	24	M	Laborer	16Ju04Jl
Hugh	25	M	Laborer	16Ju04Jl
John	13	M	None	16Ju04Jl
SCOTT, John	38	M	Laborer	16Ju04Jl
Isabella	33	F	Spinster	16Ju04Jl
SHERRIFF, John	28	M	Joiner	16Ju04Jl
Jean	28	M	Joiner	16Ju04Jl
PRUESY, Alexander	20	M	Smith	16Ju04Jl
Isabella	22	F	Wife	16Ju04Jl
CHRYSTAL, James	27	M	Laborer	16Ju04Jl
Esther	23	F	Wife	16Ju04Jl

NAMES OF PASSENGERS		AGE	SEX	OCCUPATIONS	DATE PORT SHIP
HAMILTON, Joseph		28	M	Laborer	16Ju04Jl
COLE, Daniel		23	M	Laborer	16Ju04Jl
HAMILTON, John		23	M	Laborer	16Ju04Jl
SHILL, Cormick		23	M	Laborer	16Ju04Jl
ALLAN, Matilda		18	F	Spinster	16Ju04Jl
GRAHAM, Thomas		25	M	Laborer	16Ju04Jl
STEEN, George		22	M	Laborer	16Ju04Jl
MCGILL, William		16	M	Laborer	16Ju04Jl
CAMPBELL, James		19	M	Laborer	16Ju04Jl
COOK, William		25	M	Laborer	16Ju04Jl
KNOX, William		23	M	Laborer	16Ju04Jl
ESLIRTH, Alexander		25	M	Laborer	16Ju04Jl
RITCHIE, James		21	M	Laborer	16Ju04Jl
MCCULLOCK, Mary		18	F	Spinster	16Ju04Jl
MCKINNON, Archd.		23	M	Laborer	16Ju04Jl
MOORE, Alex.		22	M	Laborer	16Ju04Jl
Grisilda		19	F	Spinster	16Ju04Jl
BRANDMAN, Augusta		22	M	Unknown	16Ju04Jl
TETMAN, Heinrich		30	M	Joiner	16Ju04Jl
Christina		32	F	Spinster	16Ju04Jl
Johanna		29	F	Spinster	16Ju04Jl
STRAFFNER, Heinrich		20	M	Tailor	16Ju04Jl
BERN, Herman-H.		27	M	Bookbinder	16Ju04Jl
MERTINES, Ludwig		32	M	Turner	16Ju04Jl
Englich		32	F	Relative	16Ju04Jl
Carl		5	M	Child	16Ju04Jl
Fred.		3	M	Child	16Ju04Jl
Ludwig		.11	M	Infant	16Ju04Jl
MCCANALASS, Daniel		30	M	Laborer	16Ju04Jl
Thomas		7	M	Child	16Ju04Jl
BRYSON, Sarah		26	F	Spinster	16Ju04Jl
REID, John		23	M	Laborer	16Ju04Jl
Alex.		21	M	Laborer	16Ju04Jl
BERNON, Daniel		25	M	Laborer	16Ju04Jl
BRUCE, James		24	M	Laborer	16Ju04Jl
Margaret		24	F	Relative	16Ju04Jl
Cath.		2	F	Child	16Ju04Jl
LINN, James		35	M	Laborer	16Ju04Jl
Mary	(W)	25	F	Wife	16Ju04Jl
MCILLHATTON, Michael		20	M	Laborer	16Ju04Jl
COBURNE, Thomas		20	M	Laborer	16Ju04Jl
HUGHES, Susan		19	F	Spinster	16Ju04Jl
LEGGETT, John		60	M	Laborer	16Ju04Jl
Mary		59	F	Relative	16Ju04Jl
Robt.		20	M	Relative	16Ju04Jl
Agnes		13	F	Relative	16Ju04Jl
LYNCH, Philip		71	M	Laborer	16Ju04Jl
Biddy		30	F	Relative	16Ju04Jl
James		19	M	Relative	16Ju04Jl
Joseph		16	M	Relative	16Ju04Jl
MCDONALD, Henry		28	M	Laborer	16Ju04Jl
QUINN, Wm.		27	M	Laborer	16Ju04Jl
WALSH, Jas.H.		30	M	Laborer	16Ju04Jl
DEERY, Jane		22	F	Spinster	16Ju04Jl
WALSH, Tim.		00	M	Unknown	16Ju04Jl

CAMBRIA 16 JUNE 1849

From Liverpool

NAMES OF PASSENGERS		AGE	SEX	OCCUPATIONS	DATE PORT SHIP
GRAYDON, Joseph		34	M	Merchant	16Ju02Jj
SWIFT, Pratt		28	M	Independent	16Ju02Jj
MACEDO, U		00	F	Unknown	16Ju02Jj
HAMILTON, U		36	M	Merchant	16Ju02Jj
KERRY, U		33	M	Merchant	16Ju02Jj
HEYFRON, A.		36	M	Merchant	16Ju02Jj

HARMONIA 16 JUNE 1849

From Glasgow

NAMES OF PASSENGERS		AGE	SEX	OCCUPATIONS	DATE PORT SHIP
MCDONOLD, Peter		67	M	Laborer	16Ju04Jk
Mary		67	F	Unknown	16Ju04Jk
Sarah		3	F	Child	16Ju04Jk
MCNICHOLL, Hugh		24	M	Locksmith	16Ju04Jk
HILLARY, Martin		27	M	Tailor	16Ju04Jk
HOUSTON, Robert		26	M	Unknown	16Ju04Jk
KELLY, Mary		24	F	Unknown	16Ju04Jk
Anne		.11	F	Infant	16Ju04Jk
MUREHEAD, John		22	M	Unknown	16Ju04Jk
Mary		19	F	Unknown	16Ju04Jk
HART, Wm.		25	M	Gdnr	16Ju04Jk
URE, Mathew		25	M	Unknown	16Ju04Jk
GRIVES, James		44	M	Broker	16Ju04Jk
Susan		38	F	Unknown	16Ju04Jk
John		9	M	Child	16Ju04Jk
Thomas		7	M	Child	16Ju04Jk
Susan		5	F	Child	16Ju04Jk
Rosannah		2	F	Child	16Ju04Jk
Patrick		.00	M	Infant	16Ju04Jk
MCKINLY, Hannah		40	F	Shoemaker	16Ju04Jk
Anne		30	F	Unknown	16Ju04Jk
Charles		9	M	Child	16Ju04Jk
George		7	M	Child	16Ju04Jk
Osmund		5	M	Child	16Ju04Jk
David		2	M	Child	16Ju04Jk
Samuel		.11	M	Infant	16Ju04Jk
MCNEE, Peter		45	M	Laborer	16Ju04Jk
Patrick		18	M	Unknown	16Ju04Jk
Thomes		13	M	Unknown	16Ju04Jk
PATTERSON, Robert		37	M	Farmer	16Ju04Jk
Ann		20	F	Unknown	16Ju04Jk
Sarah		3	F	Child	16Ju04Jk
Mary		2	F	Child	16Ju04Jk
Catherine		.06	F	Infant	16Ju04Jk
WILKERSON, Sarah		18	F	Unknown	16Ju04Jk
Elijah		20	M	Unknown	16Ju04Jk
THOMSON, Elizabeth		25	F	Unknown	16Ju04Jk
MCKAGE, Hugh		22	M	Unknown	16Ju04Jk
FERGURSON, Samuel		24	M	Unknown	16Ju04Jk

OREGON 16 JUNE 1849

From Liverpool

NAMES OF PASSENGERS		AGE	SEX	OCCUPATIONS	DATE PORT SHIP
BRATINAGH, L.		35	M	Merchant	16Ju02K
BENNETT, Wm.		26	M	Merchant	16Ju02K
HOLLAND, Thos.		40	M	Merchant	16Ju02K
WEIR, Chas.		30	M	Merchant	16Ju02K
WHELAN, Dennis		20	M	Laborer	16Ju02K
Peggy		20	F	Wife	16Ju02K
Bridg.		13	F	Spinster	16Ju02K
Cath.		11	F	None	16Ju02K
James		28	M	Laborer	16Ju02K
Cath.		28	F	Wife	16Ju02K
Dennis	(S)	4	M	Child	16Ju02K
Mary	(D)	3	F	Child	16Ju02K
James	(S)	.09	M	Infant	16Ju02K
MALEHY, Bridgt.		20	F	Spinster	16Ju02K
MCWEENY, John		26	M	Laborer	16Ju02K

NAMES OF PASSENGERS	AGE	SEX	OCCUPATIONS	DATE PORT SHIP
REYNOLDS, Mich.	12	M	Laborer	16Ju02Kb
Pat	11	M	Laborer	16Ju02Kb
LEACHMAN, Wm.	40	M	Farmer	16Ju02Kb
Died-At-Sea				
Charlotte	40	F	Wife	16Ju02Kb
Died-At-Sea				
Elizabeth	12	F	Spinster	16Ju02Kb
Died-At-Sea				
Harriet	10	F	Spinster	16Ju02Kb
Mary	8	F	Child	16Ju02Kb
Richd.	6	M	Child	16Ju02Kb
Fredk.	4	M	Child	16Ju02Kb
Died-At-Sea				
Wm.	.08	M	Infant	16Ju02Kb
Charlotte	.08	F	Infant	16Ju02Kb
MELEGAN, Thos.	20	M	Laborer	16Ju02Kb
Sarah	20	F	Wife	16Ju02Kb
DUFFY, John	26	M	Laborer	16Ju02Kb
U	26	F	Wife	16Ju02Kb
MCNAMARA, Mich.	25	M	Laborer	16Ju02Kb
Wm.	20	M	Laborer	16Ju02Kb
KEERNAN, Thos.	21	M	Laborer	16Ju02Kb
Died-At-Sea				
Marsia	19	F	Spinster	16Ju02Kb
K--, Mary	17	F	Spinster	16Ju02Kb
SUTTON, James	46	M	Farmer	16Ju02Kb
Died-At-Sea				
MAHY, Mich.	40	M	Farmer	16Ju02Kb
Died-At-Sea				
Sutt--, Eliza	26	F	Spinster	16Ju02Kb
FLYNN, John	20	M	Laborer	16Ju02Kb
BRADY, Pat	17	M	Laborer	16Ju02Kb
COONY, Wm.	25	M	Laborer	16Ju02Kb
BRADY, Owen	20	M	Laborer	16Ju02Kb
Pat	20	M	Laborer	16Ju02Kb
MARSELLY, Danl.	20	M	Laborer	16Ju02Kb
ODONNELL, James	30	M	Laborer	16Ju02Kb
CHARLES, H.	20	M	Laborer	16Ju02Kb
-Mott--	20	F	Wife	16Ju02Kb
Died-At-Sea				
Jane	.06	F	Infant	16Ju02Kb
HUGHES, Robert	20	M	Laborer	16Ju02Kb
EVANS, Margt.	20	F	Spinster	16Ju02Kb
VALLERY, Ellis	20	M	Laborer	16Ju02Kb
DAY, James	30	M	Farmer	16Ju02Kb
HANNAGHAN, Jas.	23	M	Farmer	16Ju02Kb
HADON, Sarah	35	F	Wi	16Ju02Kb
GANNON, John	26	M	Laborer	16Ju02Kb
GRENEHALAT, Jas.	19	M	Laborer	16Ju02Kb
RYAN, John	20	M	Laborer	16Ju02Kb
FITZGERALD, Frank	30	M	Laborer	16Ju02Kb
GARY, John	20	M	Laborer	16Ju02Kb
MEECHAM, Wm.	20	M	Laborer	16Ju02Kb
LANNON, Pat	30	M	Laborer	16Ju02Kb
James	18	M	Laborer	16Ju02Kb
KENNEDY, Michl.	30	M	Laborer	16Ju02Kb
PENDEGRAST, John	30	M	Laborer	16Ju02Kb
Died-At-Sea				
Philip	12	M	Laborer	16Ju02Kb
HANDING, Jas.	30	M	Farmer	16Ju02Kb
Ann	30	F	Wife	16Ju02Kb
Died-At-Sea				
EATON, L.	20	M	Laborer	16Ju02Kb
Hannah	11	F	Spinster	16Ju02Kb
Jane	9	F	Child	16Ju02Kb
Edw.	7	M	Child	16Ju02Kb
Eleanor	4	F	Child	16Ju02Kb
HANDAY, U-Mrs.	20	F	Wife	16Ju02Kb
Jane	8	F	Child	16Ju02Kb
Rebecca	4	F	Child	16Ju02Kb
Eliza	.10	F	Infant	16Ju02Kb
SPILMAN, John	26	M	Laborer	16Ju02Kb
MELIN, Alex	20	M	Laborer	16Ju02Kb
Martha	20	F	Laborer	16Ju02Kb
Sarah	17	F	Laborer	16Ju02Kb
MELIN, Wm.	11	M	None	16Ju02Kb
COLLINS, James	20	M	Laborer	16Ju02Kb
DONLEVY, John	21	M	Laborer	16Ju02Kb
OSEGIBY, John	30	M	Laborer	16Ju02Kb
James	30	M	Laborer	16Ju02Kb
WALSH, John	40	M	Farmer	16Ju02Kb
Died-At-Sea				
Cath.	20	F	Wife	16Ju02Kb
MCDONALD, Thos.	20	M	Laborer	16Ju02Kb
BELL, Peter	20	M	Laborer	16Ju02Kb
WHEATLEY, Edw.	30	M	Laborer	16Ju02Kb
U	30	F	Wife	16Ju02Kb
LAMES, Jas.	20	M	Laborer	16Ju02Kb
BRICE, George	30	M	Laborer	16Ju02Kb
HEASKIN, U-Mrs.	29	F	Wife	16Ju02Kb
Hannah	5	F	Child	16Ju02Kb
Robt.	.10	M	Infant	16Ju02Kb
CURRAN, Pat	29	M	Laborer	16Ju02Kb
MASH, Margt.	20	F	Spinster	16Ju02Kb
Died-At-Sea				
JOYCE, John	29	M	Laborer	16Ju02Kb
U	29	F	Wife	16Ju02Kb
Mary	.08	F	Infant	16Ju02Kb
POLK, Wm.	56	M	Farmer	16Ju02Kb
HARMELL, John	19	M	Laborer	16Ju02Kb
Christy	20	F	Wife	16Ju02Kb
BOYLE, Mary	24	F	Spinster	16Ju02Kb
JOHNSTON, Geo.	24	M	Farmer	16Ju02Kb
MIDINGTON, Chas.	22	M	Farmer	16Ju02Kb
BISHOP, Rich.	25	M	Laborer	16Ju02Kb
NUGENT, Mary	20	F	Spinster	16Ju02Kb
MIDINGTON, Henry	27	M	Farmer	16Ju02Kb
Mary	27	F	Wife	16Ju02Kb
Mary-Ann	27	F	Spinster	16Ju02Kb
Chas.	3	M	Child	16Ju02Kb
Jas.	.08	M	Infant	16Ju02Kb
MCGRATH, Mary	20	F	Spinster	16Ju02Kb
CONNER, Cath.	20	F	Spinster	16Ju02Kb
GARRY, John	21	M	Farmer	16Ju02Kb
Dennis	21	M	Farmer	16Ju02Kb
Cath.	21	F	Wife	16Ju02Kb
PENDSON, John	20	M	Laborer	16Ju02Kb
Died-At-Sea				
U	20	F	Wife	16Ju02Kb
Mary	.09	F	Infant	16Ju02Kb
MAHAN, Edw.	21	M	Laborer	16Ju02Kb
Cath.	17	F	Spinster	16Ju02Kb
NORRIS, Thos.	36	M	Farmer	16Ju02Kb
Died-At-Sea				
Margt.	22	F	Spinster	16Ju02Kb
Died-At-Sea				
MYERS, Margt.	21	F	Spinster	16Ju02Kb
CLIFFORD, Thos.	63	M	Farmer	16Ju02Kb
Died-At-Sea				
John	26	M	Farmer	16Ju02Kb
Lin--, Thos.	17	M	Farmer	16Ju02Kb
HOLLAND, Anne	10	F	None	16Ju02Kb
Died-At-Sea				
BROPHY, Michl.	27	M	Farmer	16Ju02Kb
COMPTON, John	27	M	Farmer	16Ju02Kb
FARMER, Brian	30	M	Farmer	16Ju02Kb
Biddy	27	F	Wife	16Ju02Kb
GARRIGAN, Ch.	33	F	Wi	16Ju02Kb
PATTON, Margt.	33	F	Wi	16Ju02Kb
SHAGNESHY, Jas.	25	M	Laborer	16Ju02Kb
SMITH, J.	21	M	Laborer	16Ju02Kb
MCCORSTAND, Ths.	24	M	Mechanic	16Ju02Kb
DONANE, Thos.	20	M	Mechanic	16Ju02Kb
COLLINS, Tim	35	M	Laborer	16Ju02Kb
Pat	37	M	Laborer	16Ju02Kb
Ellen	25	F	Unknown	16Ju02Kb
WALSH, Ellen	27	F	Spinster	16Ju02Kb
Died-At-Sea				
DALEY, James	25	M	Laborer	16Ju02Kb
Cath.	25	F	Wife	16Ju02Kb

NAMES OF PASSENGERS	AGE	SEX	OCCUPATIONS	DATE PORT SHIP
FITZGERALD, Pat	21	M	Laborer	16Ju02Kb
COMYTON, Martin	26	M	Laborer	16Ju02Kb
WHELAN, John	30	M	Laborer	16Ju02Kb
HUNT, Ellen	27	F	Spinster	16Ju02Kb
HUGROVE, Robt.	30	M	Farmer	16Ju02Kb
U	20	F	Wife	16Ju02Kb
John	5	M	Child	16Ju02Kb
Jos.	3	M	Child	16Ju02Kb
Agnes	.06	F	Infant	16Ju02Kb
Died-At-Sea				
NESBIT, Joseph	30	M	Mechanic	16Ju02Kb
U	30	F	Wife	16Ju02Kb
Arthur	5	M	Child	16Ju02Kb
WILLIAMS, Jas.	30	M	Farmer	16Ju02Kb
U	30	F	Wife	16Ju02Kb
ROBINSON, Edith	30	F	Spinster	16Ju02Kb
KEERNAN, John	60	M	Farmer	16Ju02Kb
Ken	30	M	Farmer	16Ju02Kb
CROWLEY, Dennis	24	M	Laborer	16Ju02Kb
FLEMING, Edw.	24	M	Laborer	16Ju02Kb
DORDERY, John	21	M	Laborer	16Ju02Kb
MCGHEE, Ann	21	F	Spinster	16Ju02Kb
BOYLAN, Cath.	30	F	Spinster	16Ju02Kb
FARRELL, Ellen	20	F	Spinster	16Ju02Kb
HARMAY, Rich.	21	M	Farmer	16Ju02Kb
HUGHES, John	50	M	Farmer	16Ju02Kb
CARNEY, Wm.	27	M	Farmer	16Ju02Kb
LEONARD, Mary	21	F	Spinster	16Ju02Kb
PLUNKET, Margt.	24	F	Spinster	16Ju02Kb
FLEANY, James	21	M	Laborer	16Ju02Kb
Ann	18	F	Wife	16Ju02Kb
MURRAY, Mary	19	F	Spinster	16Ju02Kb
MCCABE, Thos.	49	M	Farmer	16Ju02Kb
Rose	47	F	Wife	16Ju02Kb
Bridgt.	21	F	Spinster	16Ju02Kb
Philip	22	M	Farmer	16Ju02Kb
Thos.	19	M	Farmer	16Ju02Kb
NEARY, John	27	M	Laborer	16Ju02Kb
SHANOCK, U-Mrs.	50	F	Wi	16Ju02Kb
MYERS, U-Mrs.	30	F	Wi	16Ju02Kb
GRINTRY, Geo.	20	M	Laborer	16Ju02Kb
MASER, L.	20	M	Laborer	16Ju02Kb
BROGAN, Pat	20	M	Laborer	16Ju02Kb
NEILL, Mich.	20	M	Laborer	16Ju02Kb
MCCABE, Michl.	21	M	Laborer	16Ju02Kb
MCANDY, Nancy	50	F	Wi	16Ju02Kb
BRYAN, Honora	32	F	Spinster	16Ju02Kb
NORRAN, Martin	22	M	Laborer	16Ju02Kb
COMAN, Bridt.	20	F	Spinster	16Ju02Kb
MCANDY, Barty	20	M	Laborer	16Ju02Kb
MCCONN, Judy	24	F	Spinster	16Ju02Kb
HUGHES, Mary	26	F	Spinster	16Ju02Kb
HANLEY, Winifred	23	F	Spinster	16Ju02Kb
FLYNN, Bridget	40	F	Wi	16Ju02Kb
KELLY, Mary	30	F	Wife	16Ju02Kb
Bridgt.	.08	F	Infant	16Ju02Kb
MCELROY, Mich.	22	M	Laborer	16Ju02Kb
MURRY, Pat	13	M	None	16Ju02Kb
ARMSTRONG, Jno.	25	M	Farmer	16Ju02Kb
LONGUNY, Martin	20	M	Farmer	16Ju02Kb
CAMPBELL, Ths.	19	M	Farmer	16Ju02Kb
Jas.	22	M	Mechanic	16Ju02Kb
RUDDY, Edw.	30	M	Mechanic	16Ju02Kb
Rose	10	F	None	16Ju02Kb
JONES, Esth.	40	M	Farmer	16Ju02Kb
BRANAGAN, Jas.	20	M	Laborer	16Ju02Kb
Thos.	20	M	Laborer	16Ju02Kb
MORGAN, Hump.	32	M	Laborer	16Ju02Kb
SHAUGHNESSY, Anne	15	F	Spinster	16Ju02Kb
MCNALLY, Biddy	15	F	Spinster	16Ju02Kb
John	7	M	Child	16Ju02Kb
MOONEY, Mich.	5	M	Child	16Ju02Kb
STANTON, Martin	20	M	Mechanic	16Ju02Kb
MEEHAN, Thos.	15	M	None	16Ju02Kb
MCGUIRE, James	18	M	Laborer	16Ju02Kb
MANGAN, Pat	23	M	Laborer	16Ju02Kb
WHEALLY, Wm.	26	M	Laborer	16Ju02Kb
SULLY, Cath.	37	F	Wife	16Ju02Kb
Thos.	10	M	None	16Ju02Kb
Michl.	6	M	Child	16Ju02Kb
Died-At-Sea				
MARNELL, John	40	M	Farmer	16Ju02Kb
Mary	24	F	Spinster	16Ju02Kb
ONALLY, Martin	20	M	Laborer	16Ju02Kb
WALSH, Martin	12	M	Laborer	16Ju02Kb
MCMANEY, Mary	45	F	Wi	16Ju02Kb
Arthur	20	M	Laborer	16Ju02Kb
Biddy	25	F	Spinster	16Ju02Kb
KERRY, Michl.	19	M	Laborer	16Ju02Kb
HASGHER, Tim	20	M	Laborer	16Ju02Kb
Jno.	18	M	Laborer	16Ju02Kb
Martin	16	M	Laborer	16Ju02Kb
SHAGHNESSY, Jno.	25	M	Laborer	16Ju02Kb
PAYNE, Jno.	20	M	Laborer	16Ju02Kb
JOHNSTON, Jno.	26	M	Laborer	16Ju02Kb
PAYNE, Cath.	22	F	Wife	16Ju02Kb
INGHAN, Louisa	19	F	Spinster	16Ju02Kb
BIRD, Owen	25	M	Laborer	16Ju02Kb
Honora	22	F	Spinster	16Ju02Kb
PARK, Anne	25	F	Spinster	16Ju02Kb
PARKE, Mary	4	F	Child	16Ju02Kb
MCCORMICK, Saml.	26	M	Laborer	16Ju02Kb
May	27	F	Wife	16Ju02Kb
MCCALL, Jno.	17	M	Laborer	16Ju02Kb
Alex	8	M	Child	16Ju02Kb
MEEHAN, Martin	38	M	Laborer	16Ju02Kb
Mary	20	F	Spinster	16Ju02Kb
MCGEE, Cath.	19	F	Spinster	16Ju02Kb
MASON, John	36	M	Mechanic	16Ju02Kb
Eliza	20	F	Spinster	16Ju02Kb
ADAMSON, Wm.	22	M	Farmer	16Ju02Kb
Died-At-Sea				
Moses	36	M	Farmer	16Ju02Kb
John	8	M	Child	16Ju02Kb
Ellen	8	F	Child	16Ju02Kb
Edwd.	4	M	Child	16Ju02Kb
Jane	.09	F	Infant	16Ju02Kb
Died-At-Sea				
ASLAND, Wm.	20	M	Laborer	16Ju02Kb
HERNESON, R.	25	M	Farmer	16Ju02Kb
JAMESON, Thos.	20	M	Farmer	16Ju02Kb
PARKSON, Anne	29	F	Wife	16Ju02Kb
Robinson	5	M	Child	16Ju02Kb
HEADNER, Wm.	22	M	Farmer	16Ju02Kb
Eliz.	24	F	Wife	16Ju02Kb
Died-At-Sea				
MCGUIRE, Ann	28	F	Spinster	16Ju02Kb
Mary	24	F	Spinster	16Ju02Kb
MURRAY, John	21	M	Laborer	16Ju02Kb
RUDDIGAN, Hugh	20	M	Laborer	16Ju02Kb
MULLEN, Arthur	50	M	Farmer	16Ju02Kb
Arthur	30	M	Farmer	16Ju02Kb
Died-At-Sea				
Michl.	19	M	Farmer	16Ju02Kb
GRACE, John	21	M	Laborer	16Ju02Kb
SCALLY, Ann	20	F	Spinster	16Ju02Kb
TIERNAN, Mary	30	F	Spinster	16Ju02Kb
SMITH, Mary	20	F	Spinster	16Ju02Kb
HUGHES, Brian	40	M	Farmer	16Ju02Kb
DORDEY, Mich.	21	M	Farmer	16Ju02Kb
YORKE, Thos.	21	M	Farmer	16Ju02Kb
MURTAGH, Biddy	21	F	Spinster	16Ju02Kb
DUGGAN, Danl.	20	M	Laborer	16Ju02Kb
CARNY, Jno.	24	M	Laborer	16Ju02Kb
Died-At-Sea				
RYAN, Dennis	21	M	Laborer	16Ju02Kb
CORMICK, Mich.	24	M	Laborer	16Ju02Kb
DOYLE, Jas.	20	M	Laborer	16Ju02Kb
Hugh	21	M	Laborer	16Ju02Kb
SHERIDAN, Philip	49	M	Farmer	16Ju02Kb

NAMES OF PASSENGERS	AGE	SEX	OCCUPATIONS	DATE PORT SHIP
NOLAN, Edm.	29	M	Farmer	16Ju02Kb
U	29	F	Wife	16Ju02Kb
Edw.	.08	M	Infant	16Ju02Kb
VESSELL, Geo.	37	M	Laborer	16Ju02Kb
Died-At-Sea				
Jane	29	F	Wife	16Ju02Kb
Jane	3	F	Child	16Ju02Kb
Frs.	.06	M	Infant	16Ju02Kb
CLARKE, Michl.	30	M	Laborer	16Ju02Kb
MCMAHON, James	65	M	Farmer	16Ju02Kb
U	60	F	Wife	16Ju02Kb
Jas.	25	M	Farmer	16Ju02Kb
Margt.	23	F	Wife	16Ju02Kb
Peter	25	M	Farmer	16Ju02Kb
Owen	14	M	Farmer	16Ju02Kb
Eliz.	16	F	Spinster	16Ju02Kb
FOYLE, Chs.	16	M	Laborer	16Ju02Kb
BRADY, Phil	19	M	Laborer	16Ju02Kb
May	25	F	Spinster	16Ju02Kb
DONNOVAN, May	27	F	Wife	16Ju02Kb
Danl.	.09	M	Infant	16Ju02Kb
Died-At-Sea				
COLEMAN, Walter	22	M	Farmer	16Ju02Kb
Mary	21	F	Wife	16Ju02Kb
John	15	M	None	16Ju02Kb
WALSH, John	20	M	Laborer	16Ju02Kb
MORAN, Handy	26	M	Laborer	16Ju02Kb
Mary	24	F	Wife	16Ju02Kb
MURPHY, Mary	24	F	Spinster	16Ju02Kb
Cri--, Con	22	M	Laborer	16Ju02Kb
BURNETT, Andw.	24	M	Laborer	16Ju02Kb
Died-At-Sea				
ORAN, Ellen	.06	F	Infant	16Ju02Kb
SULLIVAN, Mich.	27	M	Laborer	16Ju02Kb
Margt.	25	F	Wife	16Ju02Kb
Pat	20	M	Laborer	16Ju02Kb
Margt.	25	F	Wife	16Ju02Kb
BURKE, Hny.	30	M	Laborer	16Ju02Kb
Johanna	24	F	Wife	16Ju02Kb
Sarah	.09	F	Infant	16Ju02Kb
MCCARTHY, Mary	18	F	Spinster	16Ju02Kb
LYNN, Cath.	20	F	Spinster	16Ju02Kb
OUGHEY, Pat	19	M	Laborer	16Ju02Kb
ARRELL, Andw.	50	M	Laborer	16Ju02Kb
Andw.	16	M	Laborer	16Ju02Kb
EGAN, Michl.	24	M	Laborer	16Ju02Kb
REGG, Hugh	18	M	Laborer	16Ju02Kb
ENNEDY, Thos.	27	M	Laborer	16Ju02Kb
ORMEY, Thos.	26	M	Laborer	16Ju02Kb
U	26	F	Wife	16Ju02Kb
RDY, Judith	40	F	Wi	16Ju02Kb
LEY, Mary	20	F	Spinster	16Ju02Kb
LAILY, Biddy	25	F	Spinster	16Ju02Kb
RNING, Cath.	25	F	Spinster	16Ju02Kb
EN, Cath.	24	F	Spinster	16Ju02Kb
ITH, Jno.	20	M	Laborer	16Ju02Kb
ans-Dr-SMITH, Peter	21	M	Laborer	16Ju02Kb
Died-At-Sea				
ANS, Ann	20	F	Spinster	16Ju02Kb
NNOR, Cath.	30	F	Spinster	16Ju02Kb
rey-Dr-SMITH, Wm.	37	M	Laborer	16Ju02Kb
Died-At-Sea				
REY, Ann	25	F	Spinster	16Ju02Kb
NTY, Wm.	40	M	Farmer	16Ju02Kb
TLEY, Wm.	20	M	Farmer	16Ju02Kb
John	20	M	Farmer	16Ju02Kb
Frs.	18	M	Farmer	16Ju02Kb
YES, Frs.	50	M	Farmer	16Ju02Kb
U	31	F	Wife	16Ju02Kb
Died-At-Sea				
Rich.	10	M	None	16Ju02Kb
Mary	7	F	Child	16Ju02Kb
Thos.	5	M	Child	16Ju02Kb
Frs.	4	M	Child	16Ju02Kb
Jane	.09	F	Infant	16Ju02Kb
Died-At-Sea				
MITCHELL, Rose	21	F	Spinster	16Ju02Kb

TADMOR 16 JUNE 1849

From Greenock

NAMES OF PASSENGERS		AGE	SEX	OCCUPATIONS	DATE PORT SHIP
DRUMMOND, George		60	M	Farmer	16Ju33Kj
U	(W)	60	F	None	16Ju33Kj
B.		26	U	None	16Ju33Kj
Margaret		23	F	None	16Ju33Kj
Jean		18	F	None	16Ju33Kj
Eliza		14	F	None	16Ju33Kj
MILLAR, John		28	M	Fsvnt	16Ju33Kj
U	(W)	28	F	None	16Ju33Kj
Margaret		5	F	Child	16Ju33Kj
John		3	M	Child	16Ju33Kj
GALLACHER, George		18	M	Laborer	16Ju33Kj
MOWBRAY, Thomas		49	M	Forester	16Ju33Kj
U	(W)	45	F	None	16Ju33Kj
Alice		22	F	None	16Ju33Kj
Thomas		20	M	None	16Ju33Kj
John		17	M	None	16Ju33Kj
Robert		15	M	None	16Ju33Kj
Margaret		12	F	None	16Ju33Kj
Mary		7	F	Child	16Ju33Kj
James		4	M	Child	16Ju33Kj
WATSON, Bertram		25	M	Mason	16Ju33Kj
U	(W)	25	F	None	16Ju33Kj
BISHOP, Archibald		20	M	Farmer	16Ju33Kj
WILSON, William		35	M	Farmer	16Ju33Kj
U	(W)	40	F	None	16Ju33Kj
James		3	M	Child	16Ju33Kj
Thomas		13	M	None	16Ju33Kj
David		21	M	Printer	16Ju33Kj
WALLACE, Robert		22	M	Printer	16Ju33Kj
THORN, John		27	M	Weaver	16Ju33Kj
U	(W)	26	F	None	16Ju33Kj
Sarah		4	F	Child	16Ju33Kj
William		2	M	Child	16Ju33Kj
GARDNER, John		26	M	Lthsp	16Ju33Kj
U	(W)	22	F	None	16Ju33Kj
Elizabeth		3	F	Child	16Ju33Kj
HILLIEND, Robt.		26	M	Unknown	16Ju33Kj
MCGILL, Margt.		34	F	None	16Ju33Kj
James		9	M	Child	16Ju33Kj
Agnes		3	F	Child	16Ju33Kj
William		.06	M	Infant	16Ju33Kj
FAULDS, Barbara		50	F	None	16Ju33Kj
RULE, Henry		20	M	None	16Ju33Kj
BLAIN, George		39	M	Merchant	16Ju33Kj
Helen		27	F	Weaver	16Ju33Kj
Christian		9	M	Child	16Ju33Kj
James		7	M	Child	16Ju33Kj
Margaret		4	F	Child	16Ju33Kj
PETIN, Robt.		35	M	Bookseller	16Ju33Kj
U	(W)	30	F	None	16Ju33Kj
Margaret		9	F	Child	16Ju33Kj
Elizabeth		5	F	Child	16Ju33Kj
HENDERSON, Duncan		28	M	Miller	16Ju33Kj
U	(W)	28	F	None	16Ju33Kj
Catharine		45	F	None	16Ju33Kj
BECHIM, Robt.		27	M	None	16Ju33Kj
U	(W)	27	F	None	16Ju33Kj
Mary		.07	F	Infant	16Ju33Kj
OLIVER, William		24	M	None	16Ju33Kj
U	(W)	26	F	None	16Ju33Kj
FORMAN, James		27	M	None	16Ju33Kj

NAMES OF PASSENGERS		AGE	SEX	OCCUPATIONS	DATE PORT SHIP
FORMAN, U	(W)	21	F	None	16Ju33Kj
BOUNDING, James		31	M	Coachman	16Ju33Kj
U	(W)	38	F	None	16Ju33Kj
Mary		10	F	None	16Ju33Kj
Helen		1	F	Child	16Ju33Kj
FERGUSON, U-Mrs.		28	F	None	16Ju33Kj
RENWICK, Francis		27	M	Saddler	16Ju33Kj
JAMISON, Isabella		24	F	None	16Ju33Kj
COOPER, John		23	M	Baker	16Ju33Kj
HUNTER, Mason		27	M	None	16Ju33Kj
COGHILL, Francis		24	M	None	16Ju33Kj
FARMER, Alex.		46	M	None	16Ju33Kj
U	(W)	29	F	None	16Ju33Kj
Mary		11	F	None	16Ju33Kj
Marion		9	F	Child	16Ju33Kj
Agnes		7	F	Child	16Ju33Kj
Grace		5	F	Child	16Ju33Kj
James		3	M	Child	16Ju33Kj
Gr--, Charles		28	M	Farmer	16Ju33Kj
SMITH, John		23	M	Mechanic	16Ju33Kj
MURPHY, James		25	M	Mechanic	16Ju33Kj
SMITH, John		20	M	Mechanic	16Ju33Kj
HINT, Peter		22	M	None	16Ju33Kj
TURNER, Alen		.11	M	Infant	16Ju33Kj
GLENDINNOR, David		22	M	Laborer	16Ju33Kj
DAVIDSON, Agnes		22	F	None	16Ju33Kj
WILLIAMSON, Henry		38	M	Laborer	16Ju33Kj
BEN, Walter		24	M	Laborer	16Ju33Kj
MCKAY, Arthur		26	M	Laborer	16Ju33Kj
DUNLOP, Andrew		21	M	Laborer	16Ju33Kj
SMITH, Bernard		30	M	Laborer	16Ju33Kj
SCOTT, James		32	M	Laborer	16Ju33Kj
U	(W)	31	F	None	16Ju33Kj
James		13	M	None	16Ju33Kj
George		10	M	None	16Ju33Kj
Mary		2	F	Child	16Ju33Kj
JOHNSTON, Henry		20	M	None	16Ju33Kj
HIGGINS, Cameron		30	M	None	16Ju33Kj
BROWN, Hinton		40	M	None	16Ju33Kj
THOMSON, Arch		29	M	None	16Ju33Kj
Ann		27	F	None	16Ju33Kj
Helen		.10	F	Infant	16Ju33Kj
LYNCH, James		35	M	None	16Ju33Kj
Margaret		27	F	None	16Ju33Kj
DEMPSEY, Bridget		20	F	None	16Ju33Kj
CARLON, Betsey		23	F	None	16Ju33Kj
BUNTON, John		23	F	None	16Ju33Kj
WILLIS, Robt.		26	M	None	16Ju33Kj
MCLACHLAN, Hugh		45	M	None	16Ju33Kj
U	(W)	35	F	None	16Ju33Kj
Hugh		9	M	Child	16Ju33Kj
Frances		7	F	Child	16Ju33Kj
Ann-Jane		6	F	Child	16Ju33Kj
Thomas		5	M	Child	16Ju33Kj
Margaret		2	F	Child	16Ju33Kj
WELSH, Ann		22	F	None	16Ju33Kj
NEELY, Martha		24	F	None	16Ju33Kj
HOWARD, George		30	M	None	16Ju33Kj
GREG, Andrew		27	M	None	16Ju33Kj
Mary		26	F	None	16Ju33Kj
Alexander		.08	M	Infant	16Ju33Kj
MCGOUGH, Thomas		22	M	Laborer	16Ju33Kj
BROCK, Thomas		31	M	Mason	16Ju33Kj
CRAIG, John		50	M	Farmer	16Ju33Kj
U	(W)	45	F	None	16Ju33Kj
DALRIET, John		25	M	None	16Ju33Kj
Agnes		14	F	None	16Ju33Kj
James		21	M	None	16Ju33Kj
William		19	M	None	16Ju33Kj
Janet		10	F	None	16Ju33Kj
DIVINER, Francis		40	M	Mechanic	16Ju33Kj
HAMILTON, George		31	M	Hawker	16Ju33Kj
MCEWEN, James		33	M	Unknown	16Ju33Kj
MCGUIGEN, Bridget		16	F	None	16Ju33Kj
DOOLL, Dennis		35	M	Laborer	16Ju33Kj

NAMES OF PASSENGERS		AGE	SEX	OCCUPATIONS	DATE PORT SHIP
MCGUIRE, Chas.		30	M	Laborer	16Ju33K
LYNCH, Francis		29	M	Laborer	16Ju33K
U	(W)	22	F	None	16Ju33K
James		.10	M	Infant	16Ju33K
DOHERTY, John		26	M	Laborer	16Ju33K
LAVALL, Peter		21	M	Laborer	16Ju33K
LAWSON, Wm.		30	M	Laborer	16Ju33K
BROWN, John		29	M	Laborer	16Ju33K
MARAT, John		28	M	Laborer	16Ju33K
CAMERON, Alex.		24	M	Laborer	16Ju33K
U	(W)	21	F	None	16Ju33K
MARTIN, John		18	M	Laborer	16Ju33K
FARQUHARER, Francis-L.		23	M	Saddler	16Ju33K
HIFF, John		19	M	Merchant	16Ju33K
CORRIGAN, Hugh		25	M	Laborer	16Ju33K
LESLIES, James		28	M	Mechanic	16Ju33K
Ann		23	F	None	16Ju33K
DONALD, James		33	M	Weaver	16Ju33K
DATHINE, Elizabeth		23	F	None	16Ju33K
DOW, Elspet		30	F	None	16Ju33K
DONALD, Catharine		5	F	Child	16Ju33K
KRESSION, Wm.		42	M	Cowfeeder	16Ju33K
U	(W)	43	F	None	16Ju33K
David		17	M	None	16Ju33K
Robert		13	M	Mechanic	16Ju33K
Janet		12	F	None	16Ju33K
MAIN, Robert		50	M	None	16Ju33K
Helen		12	F	None	16Ju33K
David		10	M	None	16Ju33K
Janet		8	F	Child	16Ju33K
John		20	M	None	16Ju33K
Ann		19	F	None	16Ju33K
TAYLOR, George		45	M	Farmer	16Ju33K
Andrew		18	M	Farmer	16Ju33K
POWER, Robt.		23	M	Mechanic	16Ju33K
WALKINSHAW, Andrew		25	M	Mechanic	16Ju33K
KING, James		25	M	Mechanic	16Ju33K
WILSON, John		25	M	Mechanic	16Ju33K
CORNIE, John		33	M	Unknown	16Ju33K
U	(W)	35	F	None	16Ju33K
Catharine		13	F	None	16Ju33K
Margaret		9	F	Child	16Ju33K
ADAMS, Janet		30	F	None	16Ju33K
PEIRA, Alexr.		30	M	Fefndr	16Ju33K
ROBERTSON, James		29	M	Fefndr	16Ju33K
ROMANZI, Wm.		25	M	Millwright	16Ju33K
SMITH, John		50	M	Farmer	16Ju33K
SHAALE, Colin		49	M	Farmer	16Ju33K
John		18	M	Farmer	16Ju33K
TULLOCK, James		28	M	Weaver	16Ju33K
Robert		23	M	None	16Ju33K
Agnes		24	F	None	16Ju33K
Janet		29	F	None	16Ju33K
William		.09	M	Infant	16Ju33K
William		.09	M	Infant	16Ju33K
DICKIE, Wm.		45	M	Fsvnt	16Ju33K
HOLLAND, Wm.		30	M	Tailor	16Ju33K
U	(W)	30	F	None	16Ju33K
Maria		9	F	Child	16Ju33K
Anna		5	F	Child	16Ju33K
Margaret		.06	F	Infant	16Ju33
YOUNG, James		22	M	Tailor	16Ju33
BANEL, Ann		23	F	None	16Ju33
Wm.		3	M	Child	16Ju33
Fanny		.10	F	Infant	16Ju33
MCMILLAN, Alex.		22	M	Flaxdr	16Ju33
U	(W)	18	F	None	16Ju33
HUTTON, Wm.		32	M	None	16Ju33
U	(W)	28	F	None	16Ju33
Wm.		3	M	Child	16Ju33
Mary-Ann		1	F	Child	16Ju33
James		2	M	Child	16Ju33
THOMPSON, John		27	M	Flaxdr	16Ju33
GRAY, James		20	M	Mechanic	16Ju33
STEWART, John		24	M	Mechanic	16Ju33

NAMES OF PASSENGERS	AGE	SEX	OCCUPATIONS	DATE PORT SHIP
STEWART, U (W)	26	F	None	16Ju33Kj
SMITH, Wm.	31	M	Dyer	16Ju33Kj
CAMPBELL, James	20	M	Weaver	16Ju33Kj
HAIDER, Thomas	22	M	Weaver	16Ju33Kj
U (W)	22	F	None	16Ju33Kj
GIBB, James	30	M	Farmer	16Ju33Kj
U (W)	29	F	None	16Ju33Kj
Wm.	9	M	Child	16Ju33Kj
DOVAN, Rose	20	F	None	16Ju33Kj
MACHE, John	20	M	Clerk	16Ju33Kj
MURPHY, Hugh	32	M	Laborer	16Ju33Kj
Francis	35	M	Laborer	16Ju33Kj
CAMPBELL, James	29	M	Laborer	16Ju33Kj
MCFARLANE, Hugh	40	M	Laborer	16Ju33Kj
LUNDIE, Alex.	23	M	Laborer	16Ju33Kj
BROWN, Danl.	19	M	Laborer	16Ju33Kj
HAGAN, Ann	25	F	None	16Ju33Kj
DONNELLY, Catharine	25	F	None	16Ju33Kj
QUINN, Joseph	29	M	Laborer	16Ju33Kj
Isabella	20	F	None	16Ju33Kj
KELLY, Ann	16	F	None	16Ju33Kj
RORY, Laughlin	16	M	None	16Ju33Kj
DOBSON, Wm.	35	M	Laborer	16Ju33Kj
Robert	24	M	Laborer	16Ju33Kj
SHELLINGTON, Ann	26	F	None	16Ju33Kj
MCSIRENS, Elizabeth	21	F	None	16Ju33Kj
GIBBONS, George	50	M	Merchant	16Ju33Kj
CARRICAN, Ann	20	F	Unknown	16Ju33Kj

CHATHAM 18 JUNE 1849

From St. JOHNS, N.F.

NAMES OF PASSENGERS	AGE	SEX	OCCUPATIONS	DATE PORT SHIP
MCTURK, Jas.	28	M	Farmer	18Ju56Kn
TRACEY, Thos.	20	M	Clerk	18Ju56Kn
MULLONEY, Richd.	29	M	Cooper	18Ju56Kn
TUOHY, Jas.D.	21	M	Clerk	18Ju56Kn
LARK, Henry	45	M	Farmer	18Ju56Kn
FINLAY, Robt.	26	M	Accountant	18Ju56Kn
Grace	28	F	None	18Ju56Kn
Jas.R.	3	M	Child	18Ju56Kn
Sarah-G.	1	F	Child	18Ju56Kn
CORMACK, Michl.	28	M	Laborer	18Ju56Kn
Mary	26	F	None	18Ju56Kn
Betsey	4	F	Child	18Ju56Kn
Mary	2	F	Child	18Ju56Kn
Richd.	1	M	Child	18Ju56Kn
KELLEY, Jas.	21	M	Maurer	18Ju56Kn
John	30	M	Mason	18Ju56Kn
Mary-A.	24	F	None	18Ju56Kn
Cath.	1	F	Child	18Ju56Kn
Alice	.06	F	Infant	18Ju56Kn
CARRIGAN, John	28	M	Laborer	18Ju56Kn
Mary	25	F	None	18Ju56Kn
OONEY, Jas.	45	M	Laborer	18Ju56Kn
Ellen	13	F	None	18Ju56Kn
KEEFE, Wm.	29	M	Mason	18Ju56Kn
Andrew	26	M	Mason	18Ju56Kn
EARDON, Michl.	35	M	Blacksmith	18Ju56Kn
ANT, James	27	M	Blacksmith	18Ju56Kn
Mary	30	F	None	18Ju56Kn
HEARN, Wm.	26	M	Blacksmith	18Ju56Kn
WYER, Johannah	30	F	Servant	18Ju56Kn
ROKE, George	30	M	Laborer	18Ju56Kn
ARNEY, Philipp	30	M	Laborer	18Ju56Kn
AWLER, John	26	M	Laborer	18Ju56Kn
ULLEN, John	29	M	Laborer	18Ju56Kn
HEEHY, John	35	M	Mason	18Ju56Kn
ILSON, Mary-A.	23	F	None	18Ju56Kn

NAMES OF PASSENGERS	AGE	SEX	OCCUPATIONS	DATE PORT SHIP
WILSON, Andrew	00	M	None	18Ju56Kn
FULLERTON, Wm.	28	M	Laborer	18Ju56Kn
Bridget	30	F	None	18Ju56Kn
GRADY, Michl.	26	M	Laborer	18Ju56Kn
Richd.	36	M	Laborer	18Ju56Kn
DUGGAN, Thos.	30	M	Laborer	18Ju56Kn
GEDDINS, Joseph	20	M	Laborer	18Ju56Kn
Peter	9	M	Child	18Ju56Kn
Mary	40	F	None	18Ju56Kn
ONEIL, John	43	M	Cooper	18Ju56Kn
Ann	43	F	None	18Ju56Kn
Patk.	18	M	Cooper	18Ju56Kn
Denis	17	M	Cooper	18Ju56Kn
John	9	M	Child	18Ju56Kn
BREND, Thos.	17	M	Laborer	18Ju56Kn
RYAN, Thos.	33	M	Mason	18Ju56Kn
WALSH, Jas.	25	M	Farmer	18Ju56Kn

KATE 18 JUNE 1849

From Windsor

NAMES OF PASSENGERS	AGE	SEX	OCCUPATIONS	DATE PORT SHIP
COX, Alexander	38	M	Overseer	18Ju55Kl

LAING 18 JUNE 1849

From Galway

NAMES OF PASSENGERS	AGE	SEX	OCCUPATIONS	DATE PORT SHIP
FEENEY, Margaret	16	F	Laborer	18Ju06Ko
ODEA, Ellen	18	F	Unknown	18Ju06Ko
CORCORAN, Winny	21	F	Unknown	18Ju06Ko
COONEY, James	18	M	Unknown	18Ju06Ko
GRIMES, Ellen	18	F	Unknown	18Ju06Ko
LYONS, Briget	14	F	Unknown	18Ju06Ko
KERIN, Corny	20	M	Unknown	18Ju06Ko
MALONE, Thomas	21	M	Unknown	18Ju06Ko
LOUGHRY, William	26	M	Unknown	18Ju06Ko
Edmond	14	M	Unknown	18Ju06Ko
CARROLL, James	18	M	Unknown	18Ju06Ko
FYNN, Margt.	18	F	Unknown	18Ju06Ko
REILLY, Kate	22	F	Unknown	18Ju06Ko
FOLAN, Martin	30	M	Unknown	18Ju06Ko
LORD, Martin	29	M	Unknown	18Ju06Ko
CORMICAN, Biddy	20	F	Unknown	18Ju06Ko
Peggy	17	F	Unknown	18Ju06Ko
John	8	M	Child	18Ju06Ko
BURKE, John	26	M	Unknown	18Ju06Ko
NAUGHTON, James	30	M	Unknown	18Ju06Ko
HEANY, Daniel	30	M	Unknown	18Ju06Ko
Mary	30	F	Unknown	18Ju06Ko
GERATHY, Margaret	33	F	Unknown	18Ju06Ko
BROWN, John	13	M	Unknown	18Ju06Ko
LINSKY, Martin	29	M	Unknown	18Ju06Ko
GRIFFIN, Martin	26	M	Unknown	18Ju06Ko
COOKE, Patt	24	M	Unknown	18Ju06Ko
HERBERT, Margaret	21	F	Unknown	18Ju06Ko
WALSH, Edward	23	M	Unknown	18Ju06Ko
Patt	24	M	Unknown	18Ju06Ko
John	22	M	Unknown	18Ju06Ko
FAHERTY, Judy	17	F	Unknown	18Ju06Ko
KANE, Honor	17	F	Unknown	18Ju06Ko
DUANE, Patt	20	M	Unknown	18Ju06Ko
Mary	25	F	Unknown	18Ju06Ko

NAMES OF PASSENGERS	AGE	SEX	OCCUPATIONS	DATE PORT SHIP
DUANE, Biddy	8	F	Child	18Ju06Ko
Judy	7	F	Child	18Ju06Ko
CORMICAN, Mary	18	F	Unknown	18Ju06Ko
MORAN, Timothy	22	M	Unknown	18Ju06Ko
HALL, Michael	28	M	Unknown	18Ju06Ko
RIELLY, Patt	20	M	Unknown	18Ju06Ko
DEELY, Teady	22	M	Unknown	18Ju06Ko
Briget	20	F	Unknown	18Ju06Ko
BOYLE, Judy	28	F	Unknown	18Ju06Ko
Judy	.11	F	Infant	18Ju06Ko
WALSH, Walter	21	M	Unknown	18Ju06Ko
COY, Patt.	30	M	Unknown	18Ju06Ko
MCTIGHE, Terence	24	M	Unknown	18Ju06Ko
John	22	M	Unknown	18Ju06Ko
SKARRY, Patt	26	M	Unknown	18Ju06Ko
MARTIN, James	21	M	Unknown	18Ju06Ko
WALSH, Judy	16	F	Unknown	18Ju06Ko
CONRY, Michael	30	M	Unknown	18Ju06Ko
CAHILL, Biddy	5	F	Child	18Ju06Ko
KELLY, Winny	18	F	Unknown	18Ju06Ko
GILLIGAN, Michael	25	M	Unknown	18Ju06Ko
STEELY, Thomas	27	M	Unknown	18Ju06Ko
Eliza	24	F	Unknown	18Ju06Ko
KEARNEY, Denis	19	M	Unknown	18Ju06Ko
James	16	M	Unknown	18Ju06Ko
KELLY, Margaret	36	F	Unknown	18Ju06Ko
DONOHUE, Ellen	18	F	Unknown	18Ju06Ko
CURRAN, Bartly	22	M	Unknown	18Ju06Ko
MAHON, Bryan	26	M	Unknown	18Ju06Ko
MCGRATH, Michael	21	M	Unknown	18Ju06Ko
MCDONOGH, Edward	30	M	Unknown	18Ju06Ko
KING, Martin	33	M	Unknown	18Ju06Ko
DONOHUE, John	28	M	Unknown	18Ju06Ko
RUANE, John	28	M	Unknown	18Ju06Ko
DOALARTY, Mary	18	F	Unknown	18Ju06Ko
HARDY, Briget	20	F	Unknown	18Ju06Ko
SHEANON, Patt	25	M	Unknown	18Ju06Ko
ODONNELL, James-Mrs.	36	F	Unknown	18Ju06Ko
Patt	12	M	Unknown	18Ju06Ko
Charles	10	M	Unknown	18Ju06Ko
Myles	4	M	Child	18Ju06Ko
Maria	7	F	Child	18Ju06Ko
Maryan	7	F	Child	18Ju06Ko
Teresa	5	F	Child	18Ju06Ko
Kate	5	F	Child	18Ju06Ko
IVERS, Patt	56	M	Unknown	18Ju06Ko
MCNABLE, Sally	20	F	Unknown	18Ju06Ko
DOUD, Martin	28	M	Unknown	18Ju06Ko
KELLY, Anthony	34	M	Unknown	18Ju06Ko
MURRAY, Catherine	19	F	Unknown	18Ju06Ko
CARNOR, Daniel	21	M	Unknown	18Ju06Ko
NOONE, James	21	M	Unknown	18Ju06Ko
BYRNELL, George	.09	M	Infant	18Ju06Ko
Mary	30	F	Unknown	18Ju06Ko
MCCORMICK, Thomas	26	M	Unknown	18Ju06Ko
CUNNANE, Mark	45	M	Unknown	18Ju06Ko
CONNOLLY, William	27	M	Unknown	18Ju06Ko
FOLAN, Mark	40	M	Unknown	18Ju06Ko
Sally	26	F	Unknown	18Ju06Ko
KELLY, Mark	30	M	Unknown	18Ju06Ko
FOLAN, Mary	.06	F	Infant	18Ju06Ko
SHEAN, Mary	30	F	Unknown	18Ju06Ko
ODAY, Gilbert	26	M	Unknown	18Ju06Ko

JNO.COLBY 18 JUNE 1849

From Ponce

NAMES OF PASSENGERS	AGE	SEX	OCCUPATIONS	DATE PORT SHIP
ROBINSON, John	32	M	Planter	18Ju66Kp

PROGRESS 18 JUNE 1849

From Londonderry

NAMES OF PASSENGERS	AGE	SEX	OCCUPATIONS	DATE PORT SHIP
ROBB, James	20	M	Laborer	18Ju01Ks
LYNCH, Michael	18	M	Laborer	18Ju01Ks
DALY, James	18	M	Tailor	18Ju01Ks
KELLY, Sarah	24	F	Spinster	18Ju01Ks
MELARKEY, Thomas	17	M	Laborer	18Ju01Ks
COLHUNE, Samuel	12	M	Unknown	18Ju01Ks
Letitia	13	F	Unknown	18Ju01Ks
MCLOUGHLIN, Hannah	18	F	Spinster	18Ju01Ks
BALL, Robert	60	M	Carpenter	18Ju01Ks
U (W)	58	F	Spinster	18Ju01Ks
Francis	13	M	Unknown	18Ju01Ks
HOPKINS, Abraham	18	M	Laborer	18Ju01Ks
ROGERS, John	20	M	Laborer	18Ju01Ks
GAFFENERY, Jane	35	F	Spinster	18Ju01Ks
MCGOWEN, Nancy	17	F	Spinster	18Ju01Ks
CHISUM, Sophia	35	F	Spinster	18Ju01Ks
LAFFERTY, Neil	50	M	Laborer	18Ju01Ks
Catherine	17	F	Spinster	18Ju01Ks
Mary	13	F	Unknown	18Ju01Ks
MCCOB, William	15	M	Laborer	18Ju01Ks
REDGATE, Nancy	15	F	Unknown	18Ju01Ks
Bessy	10	F	Unknown	18Ju01Ks
WALLS, John	22	M	Laborer	18Ju01Ks
Jane	15	F	Spinster	18Ju01Ks
POLSTAN, Jane	20	F	Spinster	18Ju01Ks
REID, William	50	M	Laborer	18Ju01Ks
William	12	M	Unknown	18Ju01Ks
Mary	9	F	Child	18Ju01Ks
Ann	7	F	Child	18Ju01Ks
John	4	M	Child	18Ju01Ks
MCCARSTEN, Mary-Ann	27	F	Spinster	18Ju01Ks
MCGUINESS, John	29	M	Laborer	18Ju01Ks
MORAN, Samuel	20	M	Stctr	18Ju01Ks
HAMILTON, John	18	M	Clerk	18Ju01Ks
DORAN, Hugh	20	M	Laborer	18Ju01Ks
CLUFF, John	24	M	Clerk	18Ju01Ks
MCLOUGHLIN, Hannah	20	F	Spinster	18Ju01Ks
MURRAY, John	18	M	Laborer	18Ju01Ks
MCCORKELL, William-Tho	20	M	Laborer	18Ju01Ks
MCINTYRE, Andrew	34	M	Laborer	18Ju01Ks
Mary	24	F	Spinster	18Ju01Ks
Mary-Ann	6	F	Child	18Ju01K
George	4	M	Child	18Ju01K
Elizabeth	.00	F	Infant	18Ju01K
MURRAY, Alice	16	F	Spinster	18Ju01K
BRADLEY, Catherine	18	F	Spinster	18Ju01K
DOHERTY, John	20	M	Laborer	18Ju01K
Grace	24	F	Spinster	18Ju01K
MULLEN, John	20	M	Laborer	18Ju01K
HARKEN, William	28	M	Laborer	18Ju01K
John	21	M	Laborer	18Ju01K
Peggy-Jane	23	F	Spinster	18Ju01K
LAFFERTY, Matilda	18	F	Dressmaker	18Ju01K

NAMES OF PASSENGERS	AGE	SEX	OCCUPATIONS	DATE PORT SHIP
HEGARTY, James	24	M	Land Agent	18Ju01Ks
GILLAN, James	24	M	Laborer	18Ju01Ks
MCANULTY, Mary	48	F	Wi	18Ju01Ks
John	22	M	Laborer	18Ju01Ks
James	19	M	Laborer	18Ju01Ks
George	13	M	Unknown	18Ju01Ks
QUIN, Biddy	16	F	Dressmaker	18Ju01Ks
KERIGAN, James	24	M	Laborer	18Ju01Ks
Francis	29	M	Baker	18Ju01Ks
Nancy	19	F	Spinster	18Ju01Ks
Margaret	21	F	Spinster	18Ju01Ks
MCCOURT, Owen	13	M	Unknown	18Ju01Ks
Mary	11	F	Unknown	18Ju01Ks
LYNCH, James	24	M	Laborer	18Ju01Ks
COLHORNE, Michael	23	M	Tailor	18Ju01Ks
MCGROREY, John	32	M	Laborer	18Ju01Ks
GILCHRIST, Henry	30	M	Clerk	18Ju01Ks
U (W)	24	F	Spinster	18Ju01Ks
Maria	12	F	Unknown	18Ju01Ks
Roseanna	1	F	Child	18Ju01Ks
DEVLIN, Bernard	24	M	Laborer	18Ju01Ks
LAFFERTY, Mary	35	F	Wi	18Ju01Ks
KEARNEY, Eliza	12	F	Unknown	18Ju01Ks
Patrick	5	M	Child	18Ju01Ks
James	10	M	Unknown	18Ju01Ks
MCAVERY, Francis	22	M	Laborer	18Ju01Ks
MCPHILAMEY, James	33	M	Stctr	18Ju01Ks
Thomas	60	M	Weaver	18Ju01Ks
MCGARIGLE, Patrick	24	M	Laborer	18Ju01Ks
GALLACHER, Ann	20	F	Spinster	18Ju01Ks
WELCH, Eliza	20	F	Spinster	18Ju01Ks
MCLAUGHLIN, Hugh	18	M	Laborer	18Ju01Ks

CLUTHA 19 JUNE 1849

From Liverpool

NAMES OF PASSENGERS	AGE	SEX	OCCUPATIONS	DATE PORT SHIP
GILLESPIE, Isabella	60	F	None	19Ju02Kg
SMITH, James	24	M	Laborer	19Ju02Kg
SIMPSON, Margt.	60	F	None	19Ju02Kg
CULLEN, Elizth.	17	F	None	19Ju02Kg
Ann-Jane	12	F	None	19Ju02Kg
MARTIN, Hugh	26	M	Laborer	19Ju02Kg
GIBSON, Wm.	21	M	Laborer	19Ju02Kg
WARD, Joseph	19	M	Laborer	19Ju02Kg
BEATY, Mary	40	F	Laborer	19Ju02Kg
MATTHEWS, Mary	28	F	Wife	19Ju02Kg
Elizth.	2	F	Child	19Ju02Kg
Wm.J.	.11	M	Infant	19Ju02Kg
CALLAGHAN, Sarah	21	F	Spinster	19Ju02Kg
James	35	M	Laborer	19Ju02Kg
RODGER, Andrew	23	M	Laborer	19Ju02Kg
PROUDFOOT, George	32	M	Laborer	19Ju02Kg
George	63	M	Laborer	19Ju02Kg
Christian	22	F	None	19Ju02Kg
MCGAMILL, Francis	35	M	Laborer	19Ju02Kg
ULLAN, Alex.	23	M	Laborer	19Ju02Kg
ICHAEL, Jane	22	F	Spinster	19Ju02Kg
OY, Rose	25	F	Spinster	19Ju02Kg
CDOUGALL, Mag.	22	F	Spinster	19Ju02Kg
UMMINGS, Alex.	32	M	Farmer	19Ju02Kg
Mary (W)	21	F	Wife	19Ju02Kg
OLMES, James	39	M	Laborer	19Ju02Kg
HOMPSON, Saml.	17	M	Laborer	19Ju02Kg
TEEL, Mary-Ann	22	F	Servant	19Ju02Kg
EMPLE, Mary-Ann	21	F	Servant	19Ju02Kg
CCOOL, John	35	M	Laborer	19Ju02Kg
Wm.	11	M	Laborer	19Ju02Kg
RAWFORD, Thomas	50	M	Laborer	19Ju02Kg
CRAMSIE, John	19	M	Laborer	19Ju02Kg
WALT, Sarah	84	F	None	19Ju02Kg
GRAY, Gavin	36	M	Farmer	19Ju02Kg
Mary	36	F	Wife	19Ju02Kg
John	14	M	Son	19Ju02Kg
Wm.	12	M	Son	19Ju02Kg
STODDART, John	56	M	Farmer	19Ju02Kg
John	24	M	Unknown	19Ju02Kg
Elizth.	50	F	Unknown	19Ju02Kg
Margt.	20	F	Unknown	19Ju02Kg
MCCLUSKY, James	35	M	Farmer	19Ju02Kg
U-Mrs.	30	F	Relative	19Ju02Kg
Mary	12	F	Relative	19Ju02Kg
Thomas	10	M	Relative	19Ju02Kg
James	3	M	Child	19Ju02Kg
CARROLL, Thomas	22	M	Laborer	19Ju02Kg
ADAMS, Thomas	25	M	Laborer	19Ju02Kg
ROBINSON, James	36	M	Laborer	19Ju02Kg
SMITH, John	38	M	Laborer	19Ju02Kg
WHITESWELL, Robert	36	M	Laborer	19Ju02Kg
MCMENANN, John	50	M	Laborer	19Ju02Kg
Biddy	14	F	None	19Ju02Kg
WALLS, Eleanor	20	F	None	19Ju02Kg
OKEAN, Patk.	36	M	Laborer	19Ju02Kg
Mary	26	F	Relative	19Ju02Kg
John	1	M	Child	19Ju02Kg
ADAMS, Thomas	31	M	Laborer	19Ju02Kg
MORGAN, John	37	M	Laborer	19Ju02Kg
NEWMAN, Jacob	22	M	Laborer	19Ju02Kg
KRAFT, Julius	23	M	Laborer	19Ju02Kg
NEWMAN, Casider	22	M	Laborer	19Ju02Kg
KUPPER, Hermann	24	M	Laborer	19Ju02Kg
ARCHBEIN, Meyer	20	M	Laborer	19Ju02Kg
LEVI, Ludwig	28	M	Laborer	19Ju02Kg
WENNER, Casper-G.	49	M	Farmer	19Ju02Kg
Christina	49	F	Relative	19Ju02Kg
Johanna	24	F	Relative	19Ju02Kg
Elizth.	22	F	Relative	19Ju02Kg
Sophia	20	F	Relative	19Ju02Kg
Wilhelmina	18	F	Relative	19Ju02Kg
Maria	16	F	Relative	19Ju02Kg
Theresa	9	F	Child	19Ju02Kg
Fredk.Wm.	4	M	Child	19Ju02Kg
REINSHARD, Adam	.11	M	Infant	19Ju02Kg
LULLFLEICH, Valentine	26	M	Smith	19Ju02Kg
DIAMOND, Ann	18	F	Cap Maker	19Ju02Kg
SCHWARZINGKIE, Solomon	34	M	Cap Maker	19Ju02Kg
Jutchend	30	F	Relative	19Ju02Kg
Oscar	4	M	Child	19Ju02Kg
Louisa	2	F	Child	19Ju02Kg
MULLEN, Theresa	27	F	Spinster	19Ju02Kg
JAHRIG, Johana-G.	31	F	Laborer	19Ju02Kg
CAROLINE, Augusta	17	F	Spinster	19Ju02Kg
JACOB, Johanna	21	F	Flesher	19Ju02Kg
LAUDER, Jacob	20	M	Currier	19Ju02Kg
SICHTFERS, F.A.	28	M	Bookseller	19Ju02Kg
Dorothea	20	F	Spinster	19Ju02Kg
PEYSER, Herman	31	M	Glazier	19Ju02Kg
AARON, Levy	20	M	Glazier	19Ju02Kg
WRONSKY, Abraham	13	M	None	19Ju02Kg
MILLER, Julius	30	M	Merchant	19Ju02Kg
SCHULTS, Hendrich	22	M	Architect	19Ju02Kg
ISRAEL, Louis	23	M	Hawker	19Ju02Kg
SCHEMACK, Isarael	23	M	Tailor	19Ju02Kg
MANNIBEY, Abm.	22	M	Clerk	19Ju02Kg
SIHONE, R.	43	M	Printer	19Ju02Kg
Emma	37	F	Relative	19Ju02Kg
Mary	5	F	Child	19Ju02Kg
HEINZE, Joseph	18	M	Joiner	19Ju02Kg
TWANSY, A.	20	M	Miller	19Ju02Kg
RUTHARNY, C.	37	M	Rope Maker	19Ju02Kg
Dorotha	24	F	Relative	19Ju02Kg
Augusta	.09	F	Infant	19Ju02Kg
CALMACK, Louis	20	M	Cooper	19Ju02Kg
LANGE, Julius	24	M	Baker	19Ju02Kg

NAMES OF PASSENGERS	AGE	SEX	OCCUPATIONS	DATE PORT SHIP
KRISTEN, Franze	28	M	Joiner	19Ju02Kg
KRIG, Julius	25	M	Brewer	19Ju02Kg
MAYNER, W.L.	27	M	Smith	19Ju02Kg
LERSBECK, W.	23	M	Locksmith	19Ju02Kg
SIEPLE, A.	22	M	Goldsmith	19Ju02Kg
GUFFES, A.	45	M	Miller	19Ju02Kg
TYRAMTER, F.G.	25	M	Smith	19Ju02Kg
MOIR, Albert	20	M	Merchant	19Ju02Kg
LOSCHEN, Louis	22	M	Merchant	19Ju02Kg
WAYMER, Wilhelm	30	M	Merchant	19Ju02Kg
COLMACK, Caroline	28	F	Spinster	19Ju02Kg
PESTHER, Franz	42	M	Clerk	19Ju02Kg
RAINKE, Michael-S.	24	M	Clerk	19Ju02Kg
TURK, Sande	30	M	Farmer	19Ju02Kg
Caroline	30	F	Relative	19Ju02Kg
Leopold	8	M	Child	19Ju02Kg
Tim.	7	M	Child	19Ju02Kg
Nina	5	F	Child	19Ju02Kg
Agnes	4	F	Child	19Ju02Kg
Magnes	.11	M	Infant	19Ju02Kg
VICTOR, M.	20	M	Joiner	19Ju02Kg
WADLEMAN, M.	20	M	Joiner	19Ju02Kg
SOLOMAN, Hauchon	14	M	None	19Ju02Kg
POSMAUKY, N.	20	M	Laborer	19Ju02Kg
MCGART, B.	19	M	Laborer	19Ju02Kg
RIEBER, Victor	27	M	Laborer	19Ju02Kg
COHN, Johan	23	M	Laborer	19Ju02Kg
ISAAC, Mortz	35	M	Laborer	19Ju02Kg
BEYER, Lette-	48	F	Spinster	19Ju02Kg
KNOHIS, J.	21	M	Tailor	19Ju02Kg
RISSE, Wilhelm	37	M	Shoemaker	19Ju02Kg
LEVENE, Heyman	39	M	Farmer	19Ju02Kg
Johanna	38	F	Relative	19Ju02Kg
Samuel	9	M	Child	19Ju02Kg
Dorian	6	M	Child	19Ju02Kg
Janet	4	F	Child	19Ju02Kg
Betty	.10	F	Infant	19Ju02Kg
ADAM, Wolf	27	M	Laborer	19Ju02Kg
Julian	25	M	Relative	19Ju02Kg
David	2	M	Child	19Ju02Kg
Simon	.06	M	Infant	19Ju02Kg
ISCHOOKE, K.	24	M	Laborer	19Ju02Kg
SCHMIDT, F.W.	26	M	Laborer	19Ju02Kg
WEINOCK, U	25	M	Laborer	19Ju02Kg
STEWART, Agnes	24	F	Spinster	19Ju02Kg
MCILHIND, Thos.	50	M	Farmer	19Ju02Kg
Ellen	19	F	Relative	19Ju02Kg
David	17	M	Relative	19Ju02Kg
Mary	12	F	Relative	19Ju02Kg
Margery	10	F	Relative	19Ju02Kg
Thomas	8	M	Child	19Ju02Kg
ODONNELL, Mary	21	F	Spinster	19Ju02Kg
MCILHANE, Andy	30	M	Laborer	19Ju02Kg
GOLDING, David	35	M	Laborer	19Ju02Kg
Eliza	14	F	Unknown	19Ju02Kg
DONAGHY, Ann	35	F	Spinster	19Ju02Kg
MCMENOMIE, John	30	M	Farmer	19Ju02Kg
Mary	28	F	Relative	19Ju02Kg
Michael	8	M	Child	19Ju02Kg
James	6	M	Child	19Ju02Kg
Hugh	3	M	Child	19Ju02Kg
Mary	.10	F	Infant	19Ju02Kg
BREADEN, Ellen	19	F	Spinster	19Ju02Kg
WALLACE, Elsie	76	F	Spinster	19Ju02Kg
FLEMING, Essey	26	F	Spinster	19Ju02Kg
WOODS, Hannah	18	F	Spinster	19Ju02Kg
ALEXANDER, Margaret	16	F	Spinster	19Ju02Kg
NANN, Ann	22	F	Spinster	19Ju02Kg
Mary	20	F	Spinster	19Ju02Kg
STEWART, Catharine	18	F	Spinster	19Ju02Kg
BOOMFIELD, Jane	18	F	Spinster	19Ju02Kg
BUCHANAN, James	32	M	Unknown	19Ju02Kg
STEWART, Agnes	25	F	Unknown	19Ju02Kg
CISNER, Joseph	31	M	Unknown	19Ju02Kg
POLLITZ, Morris	29	M	Unknown	19Ju02Kg

JOSEPHINE 19 JUNE 1849

From Liverpool

NAMES OF PASSENGERS	AGE	SEX	OCCUPATIONS	DATE PORT SHIP
BROWN, Rose	19	F	Unknown	19Ju02Kh
MCARENA, Chas.	33	M	Unknown	19Ju02Kh
Ann	22	F	Unknown	19Ju02Kh
CALHANES, John	26	M	Unknown	19Ju02Kh
TRACY, Michael	34	M	Unknown	19Ju02Kh
WIERS, Robert	50	M	Unknown	19Ju02Kh
WREN, Robert	10	M	Unknown	19Ju02Kh
WALTHAM, Thas.	3	M	Child	19Ju02Kh
MULRADY, Jas.	35	M	Unknown	19Ju02Kh
DUNAGAN, Peter	53	M	Unknown	19Ju02Kh
HOGAN, Dennis	18	M	Unknown	19Ju02Kh
Bidy	46	F	Unknown	19Ju02Kh
FARRELL, Danl.	24	M	Unknown	19Ju02Kh
Ellen	24	F	Unknown	19Ju02Kh
ARMSTRONG, Wm.	32	M	Unknown	19Ju02Kh
Hannah	28	F	Unknown	19Ju02Kh
Jane	5	F	Child	19Ju02Kh
Mary	3	F	Child	19Ju02Kh
Phebe	.09	F	Infant	19Ju02Kh
Died-At-Sea				
HEATHINGTON, Jas.	30	M	Unknown	19Ju02Kh
Hannah	36	F	Unknown	19Ju02Kh
SHUBBS, Thos.	28	M	Unknown	19Ju02Kh
SWINDLE, Mary	20	F	Unknown	19Ju02Kh
JONES, Wm.	25	M	Unknown	19Ju02Kh
LOYD, Ellen	25	F	Unknown	19Ju02Kh
LONG, Ann	26	F	Unknown	19Ju02Kh
JONES, Martin	58	M	Unknown	19Ju02Kh
Margaret	58	F	Unknown	19Ju02Kh
EARL, Wm.	45	M	Unknown	19Ju02Kh
HILL, Susan	28	F	Unknown	19Ju02Kh
Wm.H.	11	M	Unknown	19Ju02Kh
DALE, Thos.	32	M	Unknown	19Ju02Kh
Hariet	36	F	Unknown	19Ju02Kh
Christopher	10	M	Unknown	19Ju02Kh
Catherine	.09	M	Infant	19Ju02Kh
Margret	7	F	Child	19Ju02Kh
Mary-Ann	5	F	Child	19Ju02Kh
John-Francis	3	M	Child	19Ju02Kh
Wm.Jas.	.09	M	Infant	19Ju02Kh
MASTERSON, Christopher	30	M	Unknown	19Ju02K
HAINES, Peter	25	M	Unknown	19Ju02K
SMITH, Nathen	35	M	Unknown	19Ju02K
Mary	4	F	Child	19Ju02K
MURRAY, Ann	18	F	Unknown	19Ju02K
GARLAND, Betty	26	F	Unknown	19Ju02K
Died-At-Sea				
KEEFE, Dennis	26	M	Unknown	19Ju02K
Timothy	16	M	Unknown	19Ju02K
ROACH, Margret	40	F	Unknown	19Ju02K
John	12	M	Unknown	19Ju02K
Thos.	10	M	Unknown	19Ju02K
Susan	8	F	Child	19Ju02K
Edward	6	M	Child	19Ju02K
Wm.	3	M	Child	19Ju02K
BOYLAN, Nathan	30	M	Unknown	19Ju02K
MCGUYOR, Bridget	34	F	Unknown	19Ju02K
Mary	5	F	Child	19Ju02K
RYLEY, Thos.	22	M	Unknown	19Ju02K
MCCOFFEY, Cath.	19	F	Unknown	19Ju02K
DUFFY, Pat	19	M	Unknown	19Ju02K
KINNEY, Michael	18	M	Unknown	19Ju02K
CAVAN, Cath.	18	F	Unknown	19Ju02K
DRISCOL, John	34	M	Unknown	19Ju02K
Mary	36	F	Unknown	19Ju02K

NAMES OF PASSENGERS	AGE	SEX	OCCUPATIONS	DATE PORT SHIP
DRISCOL, Thos.	8	M	Child	19Ju02Kh
Wm.	6	M	Child	19Ju02Kh
Jas.	4	M	Child	19Ju02Kh
John	2	M	Child	19Ju02Kh
KEELAN, Jas.	26	M	Unknown	19Ju02Kh
Bridget	50	F	Unknown	19Ju02Kh
Rose	19	F	Unknown	19Ju02Kh
DAVDIS, John	30	M	Unknown	19Ju02Kh
Mary	35	F	Unknown	19Ju02Kh
Mary	50	F	Unknown	19Ju02Kh
John	50	M	Unknown	19Ju02Kh
Andrew	26	M	Unknown	19Ju02Kh
Mary	26	F	Unknown	19Ju02Kh
John	11	M	Unknown	19Ju02Kh
Ann	13	F	Unknown	19Ju02Kh
DILLSON, Jas.	33	M	Unknown	19Ju02Kh
BRAY, Jas.	50	M	Unknown	19Ju02Kh
Cath.	45	F	Unknown	19Ju02Kh
Patrick	22	M	Unknown	19Ju02Kh
Mary	20	F	Unknown	19Ju02Kh
John	18	M	Unknown	19Ju02Kh
Ann	10	F	Unknown	19Ju02Kh
Cath.	8	F	Child	19Ju02Kh
Jas.	4	M	Child	19Ju02Kh
Joseph	.11	M	Infant	19Ju02Kh
MURTHER, Jas.	21	M	Unknown	19Ju02Kh
WARD, Thos.	25	M	Unknown	19Ju02Kh
Cath.	20	F	Unknown	19Ju02Kh
Philip	27	M	Unknown	19Ju02Kh
RYAN, John	28	M	Unknown	19Ju02Kh
MARLIN, Jas.	21	M	Unknown	19Ju02Kh
MALONE, John	30	M	Unknown	19Ju02Kh
HARFORD, Nicholas	31	M	Unknown	19Ju02Kh
HINCKLEY, Chas.	25	M	Unknown	19Ju02Kh
REDDING, Jas.	26	M	Unknown	19Ju02Kh
MOON, Michael	20	M	Unknown	19Ju02Kh
OBRYEN, Daniel	30	M	Unknown	19Ju02Kh
PARKER, Benjamin	22	M	Unknown	19Ju02Kh
TEAL, Mariah	32	F	Unknown	19Ju02Kh
WAKEFIELD, Thomas	36	M	Unknown	19Ju02Kh
Cath.	4	F	Child	19Ju02Kh
Ann	14	F	Unknown	19Ju02Kh
Elizabeth	12	F	Unknown	19Ju02Kh
Mary	10	F	Unknown	19Ju02Kh
Wm.	8	M	Child	19Ju02Kh
Cath.	6	F	Child	19Ju02Kh
Emma	4	F	Child	19Ju02Kh
Hannah	2	F	Child	19Ju02Kh
BILSON, Benjamin	42	M	Unknown	19Ju02Kh
Sarah	42	F	Unknown	19Ju02Kh
Betsey	20	F	Unknown	19Ju02Kh
John	15	M	Unknown	19Ju02Kh
Thos.	11	M	Unknown	19Ju02Kh
Ann	10	F	Unknown	19Ju02Kh
Fanney	4	F	Child	19Ju02Kh
Mary	2	F	Child	19Ju02Kh
OWSON, John	26	M	Unknown	19Ju02Kh
ARAN, Wm.	21	M	Unknown	19Ju02Kh
BRYEN, Jas.	22	M	Unknown	19Ju02Kh
Mary	20	F	Unknown	19Ju02Kh
ISHERWOOD, John	32	M	Unknown	19Ju02Kh
ILSON, John	28	M	Unknown	19Ju02Kh
CDONNALD, Jas.	39	M	Unknown	19Ju02Kh
CGINNIS, Ann	20	F	Unknown	19Ju02Kh
CMARA, Robt.	20	M	Unknown	19Ju02Kh
EWELL, Wm.	25	M	Unknown	19Ju02Kh
NDREWS, Christopher	19	M	Unknown	19Ju02Kh
LLEN, John	21	M	Unknown	19Ju02Kh
MITH, Alex.	35	M	Unknown	19Ju02Kh
Margt.	35	F	Unknown	19Ju02Kh
CCHAIN, Ellen	19	F	Unknown	19Ju02Kh
ANIGAN, Peter	20	M	Unknown	19Ju02Kh
ONNOR, Mathew	29	M	Unknown	19Ju02Kh
RNEL, Geo.	21	M	Unknown	19Ju02Kh
UGH, Martin	30	M	Unknown	19Ju02Kh

NAMES OF PASSENGERS	AGE	SEX	OCCUPATIONS	DATE PORT SHIP
KOUGH, Catherine	30	F	Unknown	19Ju02Kh
Pat	9	M	Child	19Ju02Kh
Bettsey	7	F	Child	19Ju02Kh
Mary	5	F	Child	19Ju02Kh
Christopher	.11	M	Infant	19Ju02Kh
LONEY, Christopher	56	M	Unknown	19Ju02Kh
Mary	52	F	Unknown	19Ju02Kh
Mary	20	F	Unknown	19Ju02Kh
Nicholas	17	M	Unknown	19Ju02Kh
John	16	M	Unknown	19Ju02Kh
HILAND, Ann	20	F	Unknown	19Ju02Kh
WATSEN, P.	29	M	Unknown	19Ju02Kh
JACKSON, Danl.	22	M	Unknown	19Ju02Kh
DOLMAGE, Andrew	19	M	Unknown	19Ju02Kh
DALE, Thos.	25	M	Unknown	19Ju02Kh
CONLAN, Joh.	26	M	Unknown	19Ju02Kh
Mary	50	F	Unknown	19Ju02Kh
KELLY, Jerry	24	M	Unknown	19Ju02Kh
Nody	20	F	Unknown	19Ju02Kh
OLIVER, Jas.	34	M	Unknown	19Ju02Kh
Elizabeth	20	F	Unknown	19Ju02Kh
LATCHMAN, John	20	M	Unknown	19Ju02Kh
Gutler	19	M	Unknown	19Ju02Kh
CALAS, John	41	M	Unknown	19Ju02Kh
Mary-Ann	41	F	Unknown	19Ju02Kh
DAY, John	20	M	Unknown	19Ju02Kh
CURGAN, Michael	20	M	Unknown	19Ju02Kh
Bridget	18	F	Unknown	19Ju02Kh
KELLEY, John	19	M	Unknown	19Ju02Kh
DUFFEY, Owen	23	M	Unknown	19Ju02Kh
SHIPPEN, Frances	23	M	Unknown	19Ju02Kh
CONLEY, Michael	33	M	Unknown	19Ju02Kh
GAFNEY, John	25	M	Unknown	19Ju02Kh
Bridget	20	F	Unknown	19Ju02Kh
CORVISON, Cath.	34	F	Unknown	19Ju02Kh
ERVING, Wm.	24	M	Unknown	19Ju02Kh
MCNAMARA, Michael	34	M	Unknown	19Ju02Kh
Cath.	33	F	Unknown	19Ju02Kh
Daniel	8	M	Child	19Ju02Kh
John	6	M	Child	19Ju02Kh
Edmond	4	M	Child	19Ju02Kh
Cath.	3	F	Child	19Ju02Kh
Timothy	.09	M	Infant	19Ju02Kh
WELSH, Elizabeth	25	F	Unknown	19Ju02Kh
HACKETT, Geramiah	30	M	Unknown	19Ju02Kh
ATKINS, John	30	M	Unknown	19Ju02Kh
Jane	30	F	Unknown	19Ju02Kh
Cath.	7	F	Child	19Ju02Kh
FLEMINGS, John	25	M	Unknown	19Ju02Kh
HAMILTON, John	25	M	Unknown	19Ju02Kh
MCNEAL, John	23	M	Unknown	19Ju02Kh
MCKINLEY, Pat.	21	M	Unknown	19Ju02Kh
DOYLE, Jas.	23	M	Unknown	19Ju02Kh
RYAN, Jas.	23	M	Unknown	19Ju02Kh
SULIVAN, Jas.	18	M	Unknown	19Ju02Kh
EARL, Elizabeth	00	F	Unknown	19Ju02Kh

LONDON 19 JUNE 1849

From Liverpool

NAMES OF PASSENGERS	AGE	SEX	OCCUPATIONS	DATE PORT SHIP
MCDONALD, Henrietta	32	F	None	19Ju02Ju
FORAN, Patrick	29	M	None	19Ju02Ju
MCCORMICK, Wm.	43	M	None	19Ju02Ju
Mary	35	F	None	19Ju02Ju
MCCOMB, Sarah	30	F	None	19Ju02Ju
MILES, Fred.	44	M	None	19Ju02Ju
Maria	38	F	None	19Ju02Ju
Lilla-M.	12	F	None	19Ju02Ju

NAMES OF PASSENGERS	AGE	SEX	OCCUPATIONS	DATE PORT SHIP
FITZHENRY, Richd.	44	M	None	19Ju02Ju
Mary	41	F	None	19Ju02Ju
Lawrence	21	M	None	19Ju02Ju
Michael	19	M	None	19Ju02Ju
Catharine	16	F	None	19Ju02Ju
Margaret	13	F	None	19Ju02Ju
Jane	10	F	None	19Ju02Ju
Ann	6	F	Child	19Ju02Ju
Nestacia	4	F	Child	19Ju02Ju
Richard	3	M	Child	19Ju02Ju
William	30	M	Unknown	19Ju02Ju
Catharine	70	F	Unknown	19Ju02Ju
WELSH, John-Thos.	25	F	Unknown	19Ju02Ju
MCKENDRY, Andrew	25	M	Unknown	19Ju02Ju
SHIELDS, Alexr.	20	M	Unknown	19Ju02Ju
BACON, John	22	M	Unknown	19Ju02Ju
Jane	24	F	Unknown	19Ju02Ju
LEBQDY, John	26	M	Unknown	19Ju02Ju
Elesia	24	F	Unknown	19Ju02Ju
CURRAN, James	57	M	Unknown	19Ju02Ju
SMITH, Nicholas	25	M	Unknown	19Ju02Ju
FARREL, Mary	18	F	Unknown	19Ju02Ju
CARNES, Ann	23	F	Unknown	19Ju02Ju
JORDAN, Archibald	34	M	Unknown	19Ju02Ju
HOWARD, John	26	M	Unknown	19Ju02Ju
KELLY, Jerry	28	M	Unknown	19Ju02Ju
WHITE, Thos.	30	M	Unknown	19Ju02Ju
Ann	32	F	Unknown	19Ju02Ju
Edward	.04	M	Infant	19Ju02Ju
REARDON, Mary	27	F	Unknown	19Ju02Ju
SULLIVAN, Mary	19	F	Unknown	19Ju02Ju
FISHER, Robert	22	M	Unknown	19Ju02Ju
VERNON, John	19	M	Unknown	19Ju02Ju
COGLAN, James	29	M	Unknown	19Ju02Ju
CONROY, Michl.	22	M	Unknown	19Ju02Ju
FITZGERALD, James	19	M	Unknown	19Ju02Ju
KELLY, Francis	20	M	Unknown	19Ju02Ju
MCCARTY, John	30	M	Unknown	19Ju02Ju
Ann	32	F	Unknown	19Ju02Ju
Jane	5	F	Child	19Ju02Ju
Michael	3	M	Child	19Ju02Ju
Elisha	.06	F	Infant	19Ju02Ju
DONAGHUE, Patrick	34	M	Unknown	19Ju02Ju
MANNING, Frank	30	M	Unknown	19Ju02Ju
MATHEWS, John	30	M	Unknown	19Ju02Ju
Catharine	34	F	Unknown	19Ju02Ju
FADAGAN, Mary	30	F	Unknown	19Ju02Ju
POMEROY, Richd.	36	F	Unknown	19Ju02Ju
John	24	M	Unknown	19Ju02Ju
Margaret	30	F	Unknown	19Ju02Ju
Richard	11	M	Unknown	19Ju02Ju
Timothy	9	M	Child	19Ju02Ju
Henry	6	M	Child	19Ju02Ju
Mary-Ann	4	F	Child	19Ju02Ju
Ellen-Jane	1	F	Child	19Ju02Ju
OBRIEN, Ellen	20	F	Unknown	19Ju02Ju
LUCY, Mary	20	F	Unknown	19Ju02Ju
TRAINEE, Catharine	22	F	Unknown	19Ju02Ju
LOYD, Geo.	21	M	Unknown	19Ju02Ju
HICKEY, Pat	24	M	Unknown	19Ju02Ju
HANNAH, John	33	M	Unknown	19Ju02Ju
Biddy	33	F	Unknown	19Ju02Ju
COLEMAN, Pat	24	M	Unknown	19Ju02Ju
Michael	22	M	Unknown	19Ju02Ju
Kitty	27	F	Unknown	19Ju02Ju
Pat	12	M	Unknown	19Ju02Ju
Margaret	50	F	Unknown	19Ju02Ju
MULREADY, Pat	30	M	Unknown	19Ju02Ju
BRANNON, James	27	M	Unknown	19Ju02Ju
GAFF, Thos.	25	M	Unknown	19Ju02Ju
DALY, Pat	25	M	Unknown	19Ju02Ju
HUGHES, Rose	26	F	Unknown	19Ju02Ju
MILROY, Mary	23	F	Unknown	19Ju02Ju
CONACHIE, James	27	M	Unknown	19Ju02Ju
MCGUIRE, Christopher	28	M	Unknown	19Ju02Ju

NAMES OF PASSENGERS	AGE	SEX	OCCUPATIONS	DATE PORT SHIP
MCGUIRE, Eliza	23	F	Unknown	19Ju02Ju
MORGAN, Catharine	40	F	Unknown	19Ju02Ju
MCCERREN, Mary	16	F	Unknown	19Ju02Ju
WILSON, James	43	M	Unknown	19Ju02Ju
Caroline	39	F	Unknown	19Ju02Ju
FORLEY, Stephen	50	M	Unknown	19Ju02Ju
Ellen	45	F	Unknown	19Ju02Ju
Thos.	21	M	Unknown	19Ju02Ju
Mary	17	F	Unknown	19Ju02Ju
Peter	13	M	Unknown	19Ju02Ju
Bridget	11	F	Unknown	19Ju02Ju
John	9	M	Child	19Ju02Ju
SMITH, Thos.	24	M	Unknown	19Ju02Ju
WILSON, Stephen	24	M	Unknown	19Ju02Ju
COCHRAN, John	25	M	Unknown	19Ju02Ju
BRENNAN, Patrick	25	M	Unknown	19Ju02Ju
FALEN, Timothy	33	M	Unknown	19Ju02Ju
BOYLE, Mathew	30	M	Unknown	19Ju02Ju
COMMONS, Dennis	19	M	Unknown	19Ju02Ju
Thos.	21	M	Unknown	19Ju02Ju
EGGLESTON, Wm.	20	M	Unknown	19Ju02Ju
GARTER, Stephen	43	M	Unknown	19Ju02Ju
Ann	19	F	Unknown	19Ju02Ju
JONES, Edw.	40	M	Unknown	19Ju02Ju
Sarah	25	F	Unknown	19Ju02Ju
Edward	1	M	Child	19Ju02Ju
LOYD, John	21	M	Unknown	19Ju02Ju
SUMMER, Thomas	26	M	Unknown	19Ju02Ju
MORRIS, James	37	M	Unknown	19Ju02Ju
Mary	45	F	Unknown	19Ju02Ju
Mary	10	F	Unknown	19Ju02Ju
RICHARDSON, John	40	M	Unknown	19Ju02Ju
MARTIN, Peter	44	M	Unknown	19Ju02Ju
Nancy	40	F	Unknown	19Ju02Ju
MATHEWS, John	29	M	Unknown	19Ju02Ju
DOYLE, Pat	30	M	Unknown	19Ju02Ju
GRAY, Stephen	24	M	Unknown	19Ju02Ju
Mary	.06	F	Infant	19Ju02Ju
Ann	24	F	Unknown	19Ju02Ju
GLENNEN, John	25	M	Unknown	19Ju02Ju
MCGUIRE, Francis	23	M	Unknown	19Ju02Ju
LONG, Walter	24	M	Unknown	19Ju02Ju
Margaret	22	F	Unknown	19Ju02Ju
RILEY, Pat	24	M	Unknown	19Ju02Ju
CASSIDY, James	25	M	Unknown	19Ju02Ju
PLUNKET, Edward	18	M	Unknown	19Ju02Ju
CASSIDY, Jane	20	F	Unknown	19Ju02Ju
PLUNKET, Margaret	18	F	Unknown	19Ju02Ju
JOHNSON, Rose	20	F	Unknown	19Ju02Ju
BROOKS, John	45	M	Unknown	19Ju02Ju
John	21	M	Unknown	19Ju02Ju
DARROCH, John	31	M	Unknown	19Ju02Ju
SHULTZ, Ed	27	M	Unknown	19Ju02Ju
KELLY, Michl.	22	M	Unknown	19Ju02Ju
NOONAN, William	18	M	Unknown	19Ju02Ju
CALAHAN, Dennis	19	M	Unknown	19Ju02Ju
DALY, Bridget	25	F	Unknown	19Ju02Ju
Lawrence	60	M	Unknown	19Ju02Ju
REGAN, Thos.	30	M	Unknown	19Ju02Ju
CLECKIN, John	14	M	Unknown	19Ju02Ju
Mary	25	F	Unknown	19Ju02Ju
BARRY, Ellen	20	F	Unknown	19Ju02Ju
MORRIS, John	46	M	Unknown	19Ju02Ju
Barbara	46	F	Unknown	19Ju02Ju
William	20	M	Unknown	19Ju02Ju
Thos.	18	M	Unknown	19Ju02Ju
Richard	16	M	Unknown	19Ju02Ju
Mary	14	F	Unknown	19Ju02Ju
Elizabeth	12	F	Unknown	19Ju02Ju
Ann	10	F	Unknown	19Ju02Ju
Emily	7	F	Child	19Ju02Ju
Margaret	4	F	Child	19Ju02Ju
HAY, John	19	M	Unknown	19Ju02Ju
PEARSON, Robt.	40	M	Unknown	19Ju02Ju
RYAN, Patrick	18	M	Unknown	19Ju02Ju

NAMES OF PASSENGERS	AGE	SEX	OCCUPATIONS	DATE PORT SHIP
BARRY, John	21	M	Unknown	19Ju02Ju
KELLY, Michael	25	M	Unknown	19Ju02Ju
WELCH, Michael	25	M	Unknown	19Ju02Ju
GARBUT, Thos.	21	M	Unknown	19Ju02Ju
Elizabeth	22	F	Unknown	19Ju02Ju
MORTON, Elizabeth	50	F	Unknown	19Ju02Ju
Dolly	27	F	Unknown	19Ju02Ju
KIRLINGER, Pat	18	M	Unknown	19Ju02Ju
STONE, William	18	M	Unknown	19Ju02Ju
LAKIN, Peter	32	M	Unknown	19Ju02Ju
John	26	M	Unknown	19Ju02Ju
Mary	27	F	Unknown	19Ju02Ju
IRWIN, Jane	38	F	Unknown	19Ju02Ju
SMITH, Peter	22	M	Unknown	19Ju02Ju
MARTIN, Ann	22	F	Unknown	19Ju02Ju
COFFEE, Ann	26	F	Unknown	19Ju02Ju
MAHON, Pat	23	M	Unknown	19Ju02Ju
KELLY, Patrick	26	M	Unknown	19Ju02Ju
COYLE, Patrick	8	M	Child	19Ju02Ju
Edward	13	M	Unknown	19Ju02Ju
CONLAHIN, Mary	25	F	Unknown	19Ju02Ju
COCHRAN, Mary	25	F	Unknown	19Ju02Ju
HIND, Mary	25	F	Unknown	19Ju02Ju
LARKEN, Pat	18	M	Unknown	19Ju02Ju
COCHRAN, Michael	25	M	Unknown	19Ju02Ju
MOORE, Lewis	24	M	Unknown	19Ju02Ju
MAHAN, John	30	M	Unknown	19Ju02Ju
Ann	26	F	Unknown	19Ju02Ju
BURNS, Michl.	28	M	Unknown	19Ju02Ju
Shul.	30	U	Unknown	19Ju02Ju
FLANAGAN, Mary	22	F	Unknown	19Ju02Ju
CARLE, Mary	22	F	Unknown	19Ju02Ju
MCCAFFERTY, Owen	20	M	Unknown	19Ju02Ju
Mary	25	F	Unknown	19Ju02Ju
REARDON, James	40	M	Unknown	19Ju02Ju
CARSON, Bridget	25	F	Unknown	19Ju02Ju
CRUDON, Martin	26	M	Unknown	19Ju02Ju
Ellen	26	F	Unknown	19Ju02Ju
Ellen	6	F	Child	19Ju02Ju
John	4	M	Child	19Ju02Ju
Catharine	2	F	Child	19Ju02Ju
KELLY, Michl.	20	M	Unknown	19Ju02Ju
CONLIN, Pat	21	M	Unknown	19Ju02Ju
LEWIS, James	20	M	Unknown	19Ju02Ju
CONDON, Thos.	10	M	Unknown	19Ju02Ju
Mary	18	F	Unknown	19Ju02Ju
Catharine	16	F	Unknown	19Ju02Ju
HANDY, Pat	20	M	Unknown	19Ju02Ju
Margaret	18	F	Unknown	19Ju02Ju
BURNS, Patrick	30	M	Unknown	19Ju02Ju
COURMET, James	21	M	Unknown	19Ju02Ju
MALONEY, James	21	M	Unknown	19Ju02Ju
ADAMS, Christopher	26	M	Unknown	19Ju02Ju
MCGUIRE, Thos.	20	M	Unknown	19Ju02Ju
GOUNANT, Peter	27	M	Unknown	19Ju02Ju
MORTON, James	26	M	Unknown	19Ju02Ju
Rebecca	20	F	Unknown	19Ju02Ju
HENRY, Mary	30	F	Unknown	19Ju02Ju
WILLIAMSON, Eliza	28	F	Unknown	19Ju02Ju
PRIOR, John	35	M	Unknown	19Ju02Ju
Ann	25	F	Unknown	19Ju02Ju
Mary	12	F	Unknown	19Ju02Ju
John	7	M	Child	19Ju02Ju
Mathew	5	M	Child	19Ju02Ju
Rose	2	F	Child	19Ju02Ju
SMITHE, John	38	M	Unknown	19Ju02Ju
Betty	34	F	Unknown	19Ju02Ju
Peter	14	M	Unknown	19Ju02Ju
Margaret	11	F	Unknown	19Ju02Ju
Mary	9	F	Child	19Ju02Ju
BOWEN, John	34	M	Unknown	19Ju02Ju
HENNESY, John	60	M	Unknown	19Ju02Ju
Alice	17	F	Unknown	19Ju02Ju
KEEFE, Joanna	16	F	Unknown	19Ju02Ju
DONAHEN, John	13	M	Unknown	19Ju02Ju
DONAHEN, Catharine	10	F	Unknown	19Ju02Ju
RADY, Edward	30	M	Unknown	19Ju02Ju
Michael	27	M	Unknown	19Ju02Ju
SHELLA, Michael	32	M	Unknown	19Ju02Ju
DUNN, John	22	M	Unknown	19Ju02Ju
RYAN, Philip	28	M	Unknown	19Ju02Ju
COX, Thos.	20	M	Unknown	19Ju02Ju
HARRINGTON, Christie	20	M	Unknown	19Ju02Ju
MCGINNIS, Pat	24	M	Unknown	19Ju02Ju
LOUNEN, Archibald	26	M	Unknown	19Ju02Ju
CONLY, Patrick	24	M	Unknown	19Ju02Ju
Barry	14	M	Unknown	19Ju02Ju
Ann	50	F	Unknown	19Ju02Ju
Ann	11	F	Unknown	19Ju02Ju
MCCADE, Mary	25	F	Unknown	19Ju02Ju
DOWD, Michl.	20	M	Unknown	19Ju02Ju
MCGOUGH, Thos.	21	M	Unknown	19Ju02Ju
BUGGREY, John	28	M	Unknown	19Ju02Ju
BRUNNEN, Edward	28	M	Unknown	19Ju02Ju
MCCUTTER, Orvan	40	M	Unknown	19Ju02Ju
MCKEON, John	47	M	Unknown	19Ju02Ju
JOHNSON, Edward	19	M	Unknown	19Ju02Ju
QUIRK, Joseph	40	M	Unknown	19Ju02Ju
Joseph	22	M	Unknown	19Ju02Ju
Jane	40	F	Unknown	19Ju02Ju
Thomas	10	M	Unknown	19Ju02Ju
Ann	8	F	Child	19Ju02Ju
James	3	M	Child	19Ju02Ju
CARSLEY, Thomas	23	M	Unknown	19Ju02Ju
CALVIN, John	25	M	Unknown	19Ju02Ju
MCCURDY, Moore	19	M	Unknown	19Ju02Ju
BRUON, George	20	M	Unknown	19Ju02Ju
CLARK, Michael	30	M	Unknown	19Ju02Ju
John	28	M	Unknown	19Ju02Ju
WELSH, Edward	20	M	Unknown	19Ju02Ju
CLARK, Maria	22	F	Unknown	19Ju02Ju
James	2	M	Child	19Ju02Ju
Maria	.06	F	Infant	19Ju02Ju
MOORE, Michael	26	M	Unknown	19Ju02Ju
William	24	M	Unknown	19Ju02Ju
TURNEY, Ellen	40	F	Unknown	19Ju02Ju
Mary	10	F	Unknown	19Ju02Ju
Jane	8	F	Child	19Ju02Ju
CRAWLEY, Simon	45	M	Unknown	19Ju02Ju
WHITE, Ambrose	50	M	Unknown	19Ju02Ju
Elizabeth	9	F	Child	19Ju02Ju
Jane	7	F	Child	19Ju02Ju
Charles	5	M	Child	19Ju02Ju
MULLENS, Robert	25	M	Unknown	19Ju02Ju
BURNS, Thomas	14	M	Unknown	19Ju02Ju
HEINNATTE, John	26	M	Unknown	19Ju02Ju
CHAPPELL, Ann	35	F	Unknown	19Ju02Ju
Mary	14	F	Unknown	19Ju02Ju
Elizabeth	13	F	Unknown	19Ju02Ju
Sarah	9	F	Child	19Ju02Ju
Nora	2	F	Child	19Ju02Ju
LOCKWOOD, Thos.	23	M	Unknown	19Ju02Ju
Ann	24	F	Unknown	19Ju02Ju
WHITE, Herbert	3	M	Child	19Ju02Ju
Arthur	1	M	Child	19Ju02Ju
Wm.	34	M	Unknown	19Ju02Ju
LOCKWOOD, Sarah	1	F	Child	19Ju02Ju
WHITE, Ann	34	F	Unknown	19Ju02Ju
POTTER, William	32	M	Unknown	19Ju02Ju
Jane	30	F	Unknown	19Ju02Ju
Luke	.04	M	Infant	19Ju02Ju
James	8	M	Child	19Ju02Ju
Catharine	6	F	Child	19Ju02Ju
John	4	M	Child	19Ju02Ju
Ann	2	F	Child	19Ju02Ju
SMITH, Geo.	35	M	Unknown	19Ju02Ju
Mary-Ann	32	F	Unknown	19Ju02Ju
MARSDEN, Thos.	33	M	Unknown	19Ju02Ju
Ann	33	F	Unknown	19Ju02Ju
John	5	M	Child	19Ju02Ju

NAMES OF PASSENGERS	AGE	SEX	OCCUPATIONS	DATE PORT SHIP
MARSDEN, Christopher	1	M	Child	19Ju02Ju
COOLEY, Ed	34	M	Unknown	19Ju02Ju
CABLEY, Henry	31	M	Unknown	19Ju02Ju
CAMPION, Benjamin	26	M	Unknown	19Ju02Ju
Elizabeth	20	F	Unknown	19Ju02Ju
YOUNG, Jane	31	F	Unknown	19Ju02Ju
SHANNON, Catharine	19	F	Unknown	19Ju02Ju
WENHAN, James	40	M	Unknown	19Ju02Ju
Mary-Ann	19	F	Unknown	19Ju02Ju
THOMPSON, Robt.	34	M	Unknown	19Ju02Ju
Eliza	28	F	Unknown	19Ju02Ju
George	.08	M	Infant	19Ju02Ju
ALLEN, Sarah	32	F	Unknown	19Ju02Ju
Geo.	5	M	Child	19Ju02Ju
Mary	2	F	Child	19Ju02Ju
Charles	.04	M	Infant	19Ju02Ju
SILL, Daniel	30	M	Unknown	19Ju02Ju
Mary	22	F	Unknown	19Ju02Ju
MCDONOUGH, Thomas	19	M	Unknown	19Ju02Ju
SOUTHERN, Ralph-M.	37	M	Unknown	19Ju02Ju
CROMIE, David	28	M	Unknown	19Ju02Ju
LEACH, John	31	M	Unknown	19Ju02Ju
WOOD, John	30	M	Unknown	19Ju02Ju
Kesiah	30	U	Unknown	19Ju02Ju
Anna	6	F	Child	19Ju02Ju
Elizabeth	4	F	Child	19Ju02Ju
Mary	1	F	Child	19Ju02Ju
MCGINN, Mary	26	F	Unknown	19Ju02Ju
CLARK, Elizabeth	27	F	Unknown	19Ju02Ju
EMERY, John	26	M	Unknown	19Ju02Ju
KELLY, Mary	24	F	Unknown	19Ju02Ju
REARDON, Alice	40	F	Unknown	19Ju02Ju
CASTELLER, Peter	20	M	Unknown	19Ju02Ju

ANN-CARR 19 JUNE 1849

From Waterford

NAMES OF PASSENGERS	AGE	SEX	OCCUPATIONS	DATE PORT SHIP
COSTIN, Michael	27	M	Farmer	19Ju15Ki
Patt.	24	M	Farmer	19Ju15Ki
Richard	22	M	Farmer	19Ju15Ki
LERRIHAN, David	25	M	Farmer	19Ju15Ki
Patt.	28	M	Farmer	19Ju15Ki
KING, Phillip	30	M	Farmer	19Ju15Ki
Catherine	26	F	Farmer	19Ju15Ki
Judith	24	F	Spinster	19Ju15Ki
RYAN, Mary	20	F	Spinster	19Ju15Ki
DUGGAN, Margt.	18	F	Spinster	19Ju15Ki
SANSHAW, Phillip	16	M	Spinner	19Ju15Ki
DALTON, Mary	12	F	Spinster	19Ju15Ki
GRIFFIN, Jno.	40	M	Farmer	19Ju15Ki
MARWELL, Anastasia	30	F	Spinster	19Ju15Ki
GRIFFIN, Michael	28	M	Laborer	19Ju15Ki
Mary	21	F	Spinster	19Ju15Ki
Johanna	19	F	Spinster	19Ju15Ki
Patt.	10	M	Farmer	19Ju15Ki
FITZGERALD, Ellen	20	F	Spinster	19Ju15Ki
SWEETMAN, Mary	21	F	Spinster	19Ju15Ki
MOHONY, Margt.	24	F	Spinster	19Ju15Ki
COLTER, Patty	35	M	Spinner	19Ju15Ki
BOHAN, Jno.	30	M	Farmer	19Ju15Ki
HENRY, Catherine	28	F	Spinster	19Ju15Ki
MURPHY, Michael	25	M	Farmer	19Ju15Ki
WALSH, Jno.	25	M	Farmer	19Ju15Ki
HUNT, Jno.	37	M	Farmer	19Ju15Ki
COCORAN, Pat.	27	M	Farmer	19Ju15Ki
WELSH, Michael	36	M	Farmer	19Ju15Ki
KENNEDY, Peter	26	M	Farmer	19Ju15Ki
DUNNE, Thomas	27	M	Spinner	19Ju15Ki
DUNNE, Catherine	25	F	Laborer	19Ju15Ki
POWER, Michael	20	M	Laborer	19Ju15Ki
KEANE, Thomas	30	M	Laborer	19Ju15Ki
Wm.	20	M	Spinner	19Ju15Ki
Margt.	40	F	Spinster	19Ju15Ki
HICKEY, Margt.	21	F	Spinster	19Ju15Ki
HALLAHAN, Jno.	30	M	Farmer	19Ju15Ki
SLATTERY, Jno.	28	M	Farmer	19Ju15Ki
Catherine	26	F	Spinster	19Ju15Ki
Catherine	19	F	Spinster	19Ju15Ki
Margt.	16	F	Spinster	19Ju15Ki
Wm.	12	M	Laborer	19Ju15Ki
Jno.	7	M	Child	19Ju15Ki
OHEARY, David	26	M	Child	19Ju15Ki
BURKE, Wm.	24	M	Child	19Ju15Ki
CARROLL, Geo.	24	M	Child	19Ju15Ki
Anne	19	F	Spinster	19Ju15Ki
POWER, Jno.	28	M	Farmer	19Ju15Ki
MERRIMAN, David	24	M	Farmer	19Ju15Ki
MAYLAN, Jno.	30	M	Farmer	19Ju15Ki
GRACE, Pat.	22	M	Farmer	19Ju15Ki
MAYLAN, Mary	28	F	Spinster	19Ju15Ki
MCGRATH, Johanna	24	F	Spinster	19Ju15Ki
HICKEY, Martin	22	M	Farmer	19Ju15Ki
Patt.	12	M	Farmer	19Ju15Ki
HOGAN, Michael	30	M	Farmer	19Ju15Ki
HANLAN, Ellen	28	F	Spinster	19Ju15Ki
CAMPBELL, Hugh	22	M	Farmer	19Ju15Ki
SULLIVAN, Jas.	26	M	Farmer	19Ju15Ki
RAWLEY, Jno.	40	M	Farmer	19Ju15Ki
Catherine	36	F	Spinster	19Ju15Ki
Walter	7	M	Child	19Ju15Ki
Jas.	5	M	Child	19Ju15Ki
Ellen	2	F	Child	19Ju15Ki
Mary	.00	F	Infant	19Ju15Ki
POWER, Edward	24	M	Shoemaker	19Ju15Ki
GREENE, Dennis	25	M	Farmer	19Ju15Ki
MCLALEY, Catherine	22	F	Spinster	19Ju15Ki
CLEARY, Thomas	37	M	Spinner	19Ju15Ki
Honora	35	F	Spinster	19Ju15Ki
Bridget	7	F	Child	19Ju15Ki
Jno.	4	M	Child	19Ju15Ki
Cathr.	2	F	Child	19Ju15Ki
Cathr.	.00	F	Infant	19Ju15Ki
LAMBERT, Anastie	26	F	Farmer	19Ju15Ki
MAYLAN, Catherine	18	F	Spinster	19Ju15Ki
RAWLEY, Bridget	00	F	Child	19Ju15Ki
CLEARY, Mary-Ann	.00	F	Infant	19Ju15Ki
WING, Anastasia	19	F	Spinster	19Ju15Ki

TRANSIT 19 JUNE 1849

From Turks Island

NAMES OF PASSENGERS	AGE	SEX	OCCUPATIONS	DATE PORT SHIP
HOOD, Alex.	23	M	Planter	19Ju67Kq

E.FORESTAL 19 JUNE 1849

From Limerick

NAMES OF PASSENGERS	AGE	SEX	OCCUPATIONS	DATE PORT SHIP
BROWNE, Margaret	22	F	Spinster	19Ju35Kf
Mary	25	F	Spinster	19Ju35Kf
Johanna	30	F	Spinster	19Ju35Kf

NAMES OF PASSENGERS		AGE	SEX	OCCUPATIONS	DATE PORT SHIP
BARRETT, Johanna		20	F	Spinster	19Ju35Kf
Catherine		22	F	Spinster	19Ju35Kf
LEARY, Ellen		24	F	Spinster	19Ju35Kf
OBRIEN, Pat		15	M	None	19Ju35Kf
CONLON, Mary		44	F	Matron	19Ju35Kf
Patk.		26	M	Unknown	19Ju35Kf
Chas.		19	M	Unknown	19Ju35Kf
Mary		17	F	Unknown	19Ju35Kf
Terry		16	U	Unknown	19Ju35Kf
Martin		12	M	Unknown	19Ju35Kf
James		9	M	Child	19Ju35Kf
Peter		7	M	Child	19Ju35Kf
Thomas		5	M	Child	19Ju35Kf
ODED, Mary		24	F	Spinster	19Ju35Kf
COLMAN, Bridget		26	F	Spinster	19Ju35Kf
LADEN, Thos.		26	M	Farmer	19Ju35Kf
FAUL, Winny		21	F	Spinster	19Ju35Kf
LYNCH, Henry		18	M	Farmer	19Ju35Kf
HARE, Catherine		21	F	Spinster	19Ju35Kf
BROWN, Thomas		28	M	Laborer	19Ju35Kf
HANNON, Johanna		25	F	Spinster	19Ju35Kf
LYNCH, Mary		25	F	Spinster	19Ju35Kf
GLEESON, Bridget		25	F	Spinster	19Ju35Kf
RYAN, Tim.		55	M	Farmer	19Ju35Kf
U-Mrs.	(W)	40	F	Wife	19Ju35Kf
James		.06	M	Infant	19Ju35Kf
Anne		18	F	Spinster	19Ju35Kf
Ellen		16	F	Spinster	19Ju35Kf
Margaret		14	F	Spinster	19Ju35Kf
LYNCH, Edmond		20	M	Farmer	19Ju35Kf
John		.10	M	Infant	19Ju35Kf
RYAN, Mary		30	F	Spinster	19Ju35Kf
Catherine		.02	F	Infant	19Ju35Kf
Tym		4	U	Child	19Ju35Kf
CONLON, John		.05	M	Infant	19Ju35Kf
James		25	M	Unknown	19Ju35Kf
Jane	(W)	40	F	Wife	19Ju35Kf
Catherine		17	F	Spinster	19Ju35Kf
Honora		8	F	Child	19Ju35Kf
GINANE, Thomas		18	M	Laborer	19Ju35Kf
MEANY, Margt.		18	F	Spinster	19Ju35Kf
CARY, Patt-C.		50	M	Farmer	19Ju35Kf
Nancy	(W)	45	F	Wife	19Ju35Kf
Mary		17	F	Spinster	19Ju35Kf
Peggy		14	F	Spinster	19Ju35Kf
GILDEA, Thos.		25	M	Laborer	19Ju35Kf
Mary		17	F	Spinster	19Ju35Kf
MALONEY, Dannl.		21	M	Laborer	19Ju35Kf
RUSSEL, James		40	M	Laborer	19Ju35Kf
DWYER, Richard		13	M	None	19Ju35Kf
MAHER, Danl.		25	M	Laborer	19Ju35Kf
Anne	(W)	21	F	Wife	19Ju35Kf
Mary		20	F	Spinster	19Ju35Kf
John		.06	M	Infant	19Ju35Kf
MCMAHON, Mary		30	F	Spinster	19Ju35Kf
HANLON, Bridget		40	F	Spinster	19Ju35Kf
CONNORS, Martin		26	M	Laborer	19Ju35Kf
WALSH, John		36	M	Laborer	19Ju35Kf
Ellen	(W)	30	F	Wife	19Ju35Kf
RELIHAN, Maurice		50	M	Farmer	19Ju35Kf
Mary		20	F	Spinster	19Ju35Kf
Michl.		17	M	Laborer	19Ju35Kf
FOLEY, Michl.		22	M	Laborer	19Ju35Kf
Mary	(W)	20	F	Wife	19Ju35Kf
Danl.		25	M	Farmer	19Ju35Kf
Mary	(W)	20	F	Wife	19Ju35Kf
Bridget		2	F	Child	19Ju35Kf
MCMAHON, Peggy		26	F	Wife	19Ju35Kf
John		.04	M	Infant	19Ju35Kf
OSHEA, Ellen		21	F	Spinster	19Ju35Kf
WHELAN, Conn		50	U	Farmer	19Ju35Kf
Mary		10	F	None	19Ju35Kf
RYAN, Patt		22	M	Farmer	19Ju35Kf
OHERN, John		18	M	Farmer	19Ju35Kf
CUSACK, Susan		30	F	Matron	19Ju35Kf
CUSACK, Margt.		4	F	Child	19Ju35Kf
FINNUCANE, Dannl.		33	M	Farmer	19Ju35Kf
U-Mrs.	(W)	23	F	Wife	19Ju35Kf
HARRIS, Thos.		20	M	Shopkeeper	19Ju35Kf
Robt.		19	M	Shopkeeper	19Ju35Kf
DOWNEY, Thos.		17	M	Laborer	19Ju35Kf
MARK, Ellen		23	F	Spinster	19Ju35Kf
FONHIL, Michl.		00	M	Laborer	19Ju35Kf
MARKHIN, Hanna		26	F	Spinster	19Ju35Kf
CONVERS, Mary		26	F	Spinster	19Ju35Kf
FLYNN, Patt		25	M	Laborer	19Ju35Kf
GRADY, Dennis		33	M	Laborer	19Ju35Kf
LEAHY, Michl.		34	M	Laborer	19Ju35Kf
MALONEY, Margt.		20	F	Unknown	19Ju35Kf

AEOLUS 19 JUNE 1849

From Dublin

NAMES OF PASSENGERS		AGE	SEX	OCCUPATIONS	DATE PORT SHIP
AHERN, John		30	M	Farmer	19Ju12Kw
Catherine		12	F	Farmer	19Ju12Kw
MCNAMARA, James		32	M	Farmer	19Ju12Kw
Andy		20	M	Farmer	19Ju12Kw
Magt.		30	F	Farmer	19Ju12Kw
Ellen		17	F	Farmer	19Ju12Kw
AHERN, John		40	M	Farmer	19Ju12Kw
Catherine		42	F	Farmer	19Ju12Kw
Thomas		.00	M	Infant	19Ju12Kw
BRANNAN, Edward		40	M	Farmer	19Ju12Kw
Catherine		30	F	Farmer	19Ju12Kw
Patrick		11	M	Farmer	19Ju12Kw
William		7	M	Child	19Ju12Kw
Denis		32	M	Farmer	19Ju12Kw
John		8	M	Child	19Ju12Kw
Catherine		.00	F	Infant	19Ju12Kw
Pat		40	M	Farmer	19Ju12Kw
Denis		9	M	Child	19Ju12Kw
Mary		7	F	Child	19Ju12Kw
LAWLOR, Mary		20	F	Farmer	19Ju12Kw
BRENNAN, Martin		30	M	Farmer	19Ju12Kw
Mary		30	F	Farmer	19Ju12Kw
John		6	M	Child	19Ju12Kw
Biddy		.00	F	Infant	19Ju12Kw
CARROLL, Margt.		40	F	Farmer	19Ju12Kw
Francis		24	M	Farmer	19Ju12Kw
James		21	M	Farmer	19Ju12Kw
John		19	M	Farmer	19Ju12Kw
Pat		17	M	Farmer	19Ju12Kw
Mary		13	F	Farmer	19Ju12Kw
Margt.		11	F	Farmer	19Ju12Kw
Martin		9	M	Child	19Ju12Kw
Michael		9	M	Child	19Ju12Kw
Ann		.00	F	Infant	19Ju12Kw
GEOGHEGAN, Matthew		35	M	Farmer	19Ju12Kw
Judy		31	F	Farmer	19Ju12Kw
Maria		13	F	Farmer	19Ju12Kw
Thos.		12	M	Farmer	19Ju12Kw
Margt.		.00	F	Infant	19Ju12Kw
FREEMAN, Nicholas		16	M	Farmer	19Ju12Kw
Rose		21	F	Farmer	19Ju12Kw
BARRETT, U-Mrs.		35	F	Farmer	19Ju12Kw
Elizth.		17	F	Farmer	19Ju12Kw
James		12	M	Farmer	19Ju12Kw
OBYRENE, John		20	M	Farmer	19Ju12Kw
MCMAHON, Dan.		50	M	Farmer	19Ju12Kw
DORAN, Richard		26	M	Farmer	19Ju12Kw
WADE, John		20	M	Farmer	19Ju12Kw
Catherine		22	F	Farmer	19Ju12Kw
CANE, John		20	M	Farmer	19Ju12Kw

NAMES OF PASSENGERS	AGE	SEX	OCCUPATIONS	DATE PORT SHIP
FLYNN, Pat	19	M	Farmer	19Ju12Kw
BROPHY, William	27	M	Farmer	19Ju12Kw
ROBINSON, James	23	M	Farmer	19Ju12Kw
WILLIAMS, Michael	17	M	Farmer	19Ju12Kw
Mary	13	F	Farmer	19Ju12Kw
CURTIS, Michael	27	M	Farmer	19Ju12Kw
NUGENT, Thos.	21	M	Farmer	19Ju12Kw
MOORE, Peter	20	M	Farmer	19Ju12Kw
DEMPSEY, Peter	25	M	Farmer	19Ju12Kw
MCDONA, Margt.	20	F	Farmer	19Ju12Kw
CAREY, Catherine	.00	F	Infant	19Ju12Kw
MOLLOY, James	4	M	Child	19Ju12Kw
MCDONALD, Biddy	19	F	Farmer	19Ju12Kw
KELLY, Maria	10	F	Farmer	19Ju12Kw
BROWNE, Biddy	21	F	Farmer	19Ju12Kw
STANLEY, Honor	40	F	Farmer	19Ju12Kw
Teresa	20	F	Farmer	19Ju12Kw
CULLEN, Eliza	20	F	Farmer	19Ju12Kw
NORRIS, Albert	00	M	Farmer	19Ju12Kw
NOLAN, William	21	M	Farmer	19Ju12Kw
CONNELL, Thomas	30	M	Farmer	19Ju12Kw
U (W)	28	F	Farmer	19Ju12Kw
Mary	4	F	Child	19Ju12Kw
James	2	M	Child	19Ju12Kw
Anne	.00	F	Infant	19Ju12Kw
NOLAN, U-Mrs.	40	F	Farmer	19Ju12Kw
Maria	19	F	Farmer	19Ju12Kw
Simon	21	M	Farmer	19Ju12Kw
Edward	17	M	Farmer	19Ju12Kw
KEELY, Fanny	22	F	Farmer	19Ju12Kw
GATELY, U-Miss	20	F	Farmer	19Ju12Kw
MACKEN, U-Mrs.	20	F	Farmer	19Ju12Kw
SMITH, James	30	M	Farmer	19Ju12Kw
U (W)	25	F	Farmer	19Ju12Kw
Kate	24	F	Farmer	19Ju12Kw
Francis	.00	M	Infant	19Ju12Kw
DALTON, Ellen	20	F	Farmer	19Ju12Kw
Agnes	21	F	Farmer	19Ju12Kw
PHELAN, Michl.	23	M	Farmer	19Ju12Kw
U (W)	22	F	Farmer	19Ju12Kw
BURTON, U-Mrs.	20	F	Farmer	19Ju12Kw
BUTLER, John	27	M	Unknown	19Ju12Kw
Walter	26	M	Unknown	19Ju12Kw
FITZHENRY, John	25	M	Unknown	19Ju12Kw
JACKSON, U-Capt.	23	M	Unknown	19Ju12Kw
HOOLAHAN, Ann	20	F	Unknown	19Ju12Kw
MCDONALD, U-Mrs.	22	F	Unknown	19Ju12Kw
U	.00	U	Infant	19Ju12Kw
MOORE, U-Mrs.	21	F	Unknown	19Ju12Kw
HUEY, Eliza	20	F	Unknown	19Ju12Kw
LONG, James	27	M	Unknown	19Ju12Kw
BOLLAM, George	29	M	Unknown	19Ju12Kw
CLARKE, Barrington	30	M	Unknown	19Ju12Kw
U (W)	26	F	Unknown	19Ju12Kw
BRANNAN, Thos.	8	M	Child	19Ju12Kw
DUNNE, Patk.	6	M	Child	19Ju12Kw
MAHON, Pal	4	M	Child	19Ju12Kw
BYRNE, John	27	M	Unknown	19Ju12Kw
RAFFERTY, John	25	M	Unknown	19Ju12Kw
BYRNE, Patk.	22	M	Unknown	19Ju12Kw
MOORE, Joseph	22	M	Unknown	19Ju12Kw
ELLIOTT, Andrew	26	M	Unknown	19Ju12Kw
KEELEY, Sylvester	26	M	Unknown	19Ju12Kw
HALPIN, Thomas	13	M	Unknown	19Ju12Kw
WOODS, Hugh	20	M	Unknown	19Ju12Kw
CLARKE, John	21	M	Unknown	19Ju12Kw
BYRNE, James	22	M	Unknown	19Ju12Kw
THORNTON, Fanny	17	F	Unknown	19Ju12Kw
GRIFFIN, Fanny	18	F	Unknown	19Ju12Kw
THORNTON, Isabella	22	F	Unknown	19Ju12Kw
CASEY, Mary	.00	F	Infant	19Ju12Kw
MCGUINESS, Ann	22	F	Unknown	19Ju12Kw
Eliza	.00	F	Infant	19Ju12Kw
DUNNE, Catherine	25	F	Unknown	19Ju12Kw
MCCABE, James	32	M	Unknown	19Ju12Kw
MCCABE, U (W)	30	F	Unknown	19Ju12Kw
Margt.	20	F	Unknown	19Ju12Kw
Mary	6	F	Child	19Ju12Kw
Brian	3	M	Child	19Ju12Kw
Rose	.00	F	Infant	19Ju12Kw
TOOLE, Thomas	25	M	Unknown	19Ju12Kw
FULTON, Anne	23	F	Unknown	19Ju12Kw
DOWEY, Jane	20	F	Unknown	19Ju12Kw
MEHAN, Ellen	20	F	Unknown	19Ju12Kw
MCMAHON, Cathre.	20	F	Unknown	19Ju12Kw
CARHEY, Margt.	40	F	Unknown	19Ju12Kw
ELLISS, Mary	25	F	Unknown	19Ju12Kw
BUTLER, U-Miss	18	F	Unknown	19Ju12Kw
Mary	17	F	Unknown	19Ju12Kw
SHERIDAN, U-Miss	17	F	Unknown	19Ju12Kw
CHURCHILL, U-Miss	26	F	Unknown	19Ju12Kw
RICKARD, Mary	13	F	Unknown	19Ju12Kw
Sarah	11	F	Unknown	19Ju12Kw
Henry	10	M	Unknown	19Ju12Kw
Anna	8	F	Child	19Ju12Kw
Francis	5	M	Child	19Ju12Kw
Lizzy	3	F	Child	19Ju12Kw
BYRNE, Biddy	20	F	Unknown	19Ju12Kw
SCOLL, James	20	M	Unknown	19Ju12Kw
John	20	M	Unknown	19Ju12Kw
DEERING, Thos.	30	M	Unknown	19Ju12Kw
KENNEDY, Edward	17	M	Unknown	19Ju12Kw
KENNEY, Thos.	35	M	Unknown	19Ju12Kw
MAIRIN, Michl.	28	M	Unknown	19Ju12Kw
KERNAN, Patk.	24	M	Unknown	19Ju12Kw
MORAN, Bridget	35	F	Unknown	19Ju12Kw
Ann	5	F	Child	19Ju12Kw
Joseph	5	M	Child	19Ju12Kw
SULLIVAN, Teresa	50	F	Unknown	19Ju12Kw
MORAN, Michl.	30	M	Unknown	19Ju12Kw
John	20	M	Unknown	19Ju12Kw
HOGG, Robt.	22	M	Unknown	19Ju12Kw
MCMAHON, Thos.	24	M	Unknown	19Ju12Kw
OSULLIVAN, Joseph	24	M	Unknown	19Ju12Kw
DOYLE, Jane	24	F	Unknown	19Ju12Kw
James	45	M	Unknown	19Ju12Kw
Michl.	26	M	Unknown	19Ju12Kw
BUTLER, James	16	M	Unknown	19Ju12Kw
MEAD, James	16	M	Unknown	19Ju12Kw
GAGRAN, Patrick	20	M	Unknown	19Ju12Kw
Thos.	22	M	Unknown	19Ju12Kw
MADDEN, Michl.	22	M	Unknown	19Ju12Kw
SULLIVAN, Peter	23	M	Unknown	19Ju12Kw
FEGAN, John	21	M	Unknown	19Ju12Kw
KELLY, Peter	40	M	Unknown	19Ju12Kw
Mary	30	F	Unknown	19Ju12Kw
Maria	10	F	Unknown	19Ju12Kw
Margt.	4	F	Child	19Ju12Kw
Bridget	6	F	Child	19Ju12Kw
Teresa	.00	F	Infant	19Ju12Kw
GATELY, James	35	M	Unknown	19Ju12Kw
BOLTON, Owen	27	M	Unknown	19Ju12Kw
LENNAN, Thos.	50	M	Unknown	19Ju12Kw
HOGAN, Edward	20	M	Unknown	19Ju12Kw
BARRY, Frank	24	M	Unknown	19Ju12Kw
PARKER, James	24	M	Unknown	19Ju12Kw
FITZGERALD, Michl.	45	M	Unknown	19Ju12Kw
Thos.	15	M	Unknown	19Ju12Kw
Bridget	12	F	Unknown	19Ju12Kw
Rose	.00	F	Infant	19Ju12Kw
HARLEY, Mary	30	F	Unknown	19Ju12Kw
DOYLE, James	26	M	Unknown	19Ju12Kw
ROAN, James	26	M	Unknown	19Ju12Kw
BATTERSBY, Wm.	37	M	Unknown	19Ju12Kw
Catherine	33	F	Unknown	19Ju12Kw
Honor	11	F	Unknown	19Ju12Kw
Mary	9	F	Child	19Ju12Kw
James	4	M	Child	19Ju12Kw
William	6	M	Child	19Ju12Kw
STAFFORD, Edward	56	M	Unknown	19Ju12Kw

NAMES OF PASSENGERS	AGE	SEX	OCCUPATIONS	DATE PORT SHIP
STAFFORD, Ann	48	F	Unknown	19Ju12Kw
Ann	20	F	Unknown	19Ju12Kw
Biddy	15	F	Unknown	19Ju12Kw
Frank	13	M	Unknown	19Ju12Kw
Catherine	11	F	Unknown	19Ju12Kw
Margt.	9	F	Child	19Ju12Kw
NOLAN, Anne	22	F	Unknown	19Ju12Kw
Sarah	18	F	Unknown	19Ju12Kw
Mary	13	F	Unknown	19Ju12Kw
Michl.	11	M	Unknown	19Ju12Kw
WHELAN, U-Mrs.	45	F	Unknown	19Ju12Kw
Patrick	24	M	Unknown	19Ju12Kw
Ellen	20	F	Unknown	19Ju12Kw
FENAN, William	50	M	Unknown	19Ju12Kw
John	26	M	Unknown	19Ju12Kw
Timothy	24	M	Unknown	19Ju12Kw
Thos.	20	M	Unknown	19Ju12Kw
GAMLAN, Kitty	35	F	Unknown	19Ju12Kw
John	7	M	Child	19Ju12Kw
Frank	5	M	Child	19Ju12Kw
Margt.	2	F	Child	19Ju12Kw
BYRNE, Nancy	20	F	Unknown	19Ju12Kw
DUNNE, Anne	30	F	Unknown	19Ju12Kw
Catherine	20	F	Unknown	19Ju12Kw
Edward	17	M	Unknown	19Ju12Kw
Timothy	16	M	Unknown	19Ju12Kw
Sarah	11	F	Unknown	19Ju12Kw
John	6	M	Child	19Ju12Kw
James	8	M	Child	19Ju12Kw
GARMAN, Ellen	22	F	Unknown	19Ju12Kw
KILTON, L.	40	M	Unknown	19Ju12Kw
U (W)	38	F	Unknown	19Ju12Kw
U	15	F	Unknown	19Ju12Kw
U	13	F	Unknown	19Ju12Kw
Jane-T.	6	F	Child	19Ju12Kw
John-F.	16	M	Unknown	19Ju12Kw
HANDLEY, U	28	M	Unknown	19Ju12Kw
LOYDE, U	22	M	Unknown	19Ju12Kw
HEATH, U-Mrs.	28	F	Unknown	19Ju12Kw
Mary	22	F	Unknown	19Ju12Kw
CORBERRY, Ned	17	M	Unknown	19Ju12Kw
Hugh	11	M	Unknown	19Ju12Kw
Ann	13	F	Unknown	19Ju12Kw
STANLEY, Margt.	22	F	Farmer	19Ju12Kw

ENTERPRISE 19 JUNE 1849

From Liverpool

NAMES OF PASSENGERS	AGE	SEX	OCCUPATIONS	DATE PORT SHIP
FLANNELLY, Manas	30	M	Laborer	19Ju02Ga
TRIESTE, Patrick	30	F	Laborer	19Ju02Ga
Bridget	50	F	Unknown	19Ju02Ga
WALSH, William	24	M	Laborer	19Ju02Ga
EALY, Patt	20	M	Laborer	19Ju02Ga
EALY, Timth.	20	M	Laborer	19Ju02Ga
EIGH, Harvey	52	M	Laborer	19Ju02Ga
Peter	20	M	Laborer	19Ju02Ga
URPHY, James	20	M	Laborer	19Ju02Ga
ENNEL, Patrick	27	M	Laborer	19Ju02Ga
ACEY, Michl.	21	M	Maurer	19Ju02Ga
RYER, Thomas	50	M	Maurer	19Ju02Ga
Jane	45	F	Servant	19Ju02Ga
IVVER, James	25	M	Laborer	19Ju02Ga
AUGHEY, John	24	M	Laborer	19Ju02Ga
Sarah	22	F	Servant	19Ju02Ga
NEILL, John	19	M	Laborer	19Ju02Ga
CALLY, Pat	55	M	Laborer	19Ju02Ga
Mary	50	F	Servant	19Ju02Ga
RADY, John	26	M	Laborer	19Ju02Ga
GRADY, Michl.	30	M	Laborer	19Ju02Ga
Ellen	30	F	Unknown	19Ju02Ga
Edward	8	M	Child	19Ju02Ga
Patrick	7	M	Child	19Ju02Ga
Bessy	5	F	Child	19Ju02Ga
John	.00	M	Infant	19Ju02Ga
HOGAN, Lawrence	30	M	Laborer	19Ju02Ga
Cathn.	26	F	Servant	19Ju02Ga
Patrick	.02	M	Infant	19Ju02Ga
CONLAN, Thomas	40	M	Laborer	19Ju02Ga
Mary	40	F	Servant	19Ju02Ga
Thomas	9	M	Child	19Ju02Ga
Patrick	7	M	Child	19Ju02Ga
Margt.	5	F	Child	19Ju02Ga
LYNCH, Ellen	22	F	Dressmaker	19Ju02Ga
HUGHES, Cathn.	26	F	Dressmaker	19Ju02Ga
BOLLESTY, Rose	24	F	Dressmaker	19Ju02Ga
HALLENAN, Kate	21	F	Servant	19Ju02Ga
DOOLAN, Cathn.	21	F	Servant	19Ju02Ga
Hannah	19	F	Servant	19Ju02Ga
CONLAN, James	24	M	Laborer	19Ju02Ga
Mary	23	F	Unknown	19Ju02Ga
FARELLY, Pat	40	M	Laborer	19Ju02Ga
Anne	16	F	Unknown	19Ju02Ga
DERWIN, Peter	20	M	Laborer	19Ju02Ga
Bridget	16	F	Unknown	19Ju02Ga
LYNCH, Michl.	20	M	Laborer	19Ju02Ga
CASEY, Patt	30	M	Laborer	19Ju02Ga
SMITH, Ellen	25	F	Unknown	19Ju02Ga
FARRELL, Thomas	22	M	Laborer	19Ju02Ga
Mary	18	F	Servant	19Ju02Ga
JENKINS, Mary	20	F	Servant	19Ju02Ga
Frances	16	F	Servant	19Ju02Ga
BRIEN, Judith	20	F	Servant	19Ju02Ga
FAY, Ellen	30	F	Servant	19Ju02Ga
FLANNEGAN, Michl.	26	M	Laborer	19Ju02Ga
Ellen	24	F	Servant	19Ju02Ga
James	26	M	Laborer	19Ju02Ga
Mary	23	F	Servant	19Ju02Ga
MCCOY, William	21	M	Stone Mason	19Ju02Ga
MCCAFFREY, Michl.	25	M	Laborer	19Ju02Ga
AHEIRN, Rob.	45	M	Trade Man	19Ju02Ga
Rob.	19	M	Student	19Ju02Ga
FLYNE, John	38	M	Laborer	19Ju02Ga
Ellen	33	F	Unknown	19Ju02Ga
Patrick	9	M	Child	19Ju02Ga
Morris	7	M	Child	19Ju02Ga
Ellen	5	F	Child	19Ju02Ga
Thomas	.07	M	Infant	19Ju02Ga
OKEEFE, Michl.	40	M	Laborer	19Ju02Ga
LOFTUS, Bridget	20	F	Dressmaker	19Ju02Ga
BRYAN, Michael	21	M	Laborer	19Ju02Ga
Anne	20	F	Servant	19Ju02Ga
HOGAN, Michl.	50	M	Laborer	19Ju02Ga
Jane	36	F	Unknown	19Ju02Ga
Thomas	21	M	Laborer	19Ju02Ga
Cathn.	14	F	Unknown	19Ju02Ga
John	13	M	Unknown	19Ju02Ga
Cathn.	5	F	Child	19Ju02Ga
Thomas	30	M	Laborer	19Ju02Ga
CONWAY, Andrew	33	M	Laborer	19Ju02Ga
FLYNNIE, Thomas	40	M	Laborer	19Ju02Ga
KILLFOYLE, Patt	30	M	Laborer	19Ju02Ga
Anne	18	F	Servant	19Ju02Ga
TRELLY, Hugh	22	M	Laborer	19Ju02Ga
WHITE, Margt.	50	F	Unknown	19Ju02Ga
MURPHY, Margt.	25	F	Servant	19Ju02Ga
James	23	M	Laborer	19Ju02Ga
Ellen	20	F	Servant	19Ju02Ga
Barthn.	18	M	Laborer	19Ju02Ga
Honora	16	F	Unknown	19Ju02Ga
Morgan	25	M	Laborer	19Ju02Ga
Sarah	22	F	Servant	19Ju02Ga
HENNESSEY, Thomas	18	M	Laborer	19Ju02Ga
DOODY, James	22	M	Laborer	19Ju02Ga

NAMES OF PASSENGERS	AGE	SEX	OCCUPATIONS	DATE PORT SHIP
DOODY, Bridget	22	F	Servant	19Ju02Ga
Cathn.	17	F	Unknown	19Ju02Ga
Margt.	16	F	Unknown	19Ju02Ga
CAMPION, Ellen	20	F	Servant	19Ju02Ga
MURPHY, Edmund	21	M	Laborer	19Ju02Ga
FITZGERALD, Thomas	22	M	Laborer	19Ju02Ga
DUMFORD, John	40	M	Laborer	19Ju02Ga
COOTE, Thomas	21	M	Laborer	19Ju02Ga
MURPHY, Pat	22	M	Laborer	19Ju02Ga
CONWENY, Pat	19	M	Laborer	19Ju02Ga
Mary	30	F	Servant	19Ju02Ga
HICKEY, Lawrence	36	M	Laborer	19Ju02Ga
HEDEGAN, Michl.	40	M	Laborer	19Ju02Ga
Ellen	30	F	Servant	19Ju02Ga
Mary	9	F	Child	19Ju02Ga
William	7	M	Child	19Ju02Ga
Margt.	5	F	Child	19Ju02Ga
Isabel	.07	F	Infant	19Ju02Ga
MEALY, Honora	30	M	Unknown	19Ju02Ga
FLEMING, Mary	50	F	Servant	19Ju02Ga
CRONAN, David	13	M	Laborer	19Ju02Ga
COGHLAN, Margt.	21	F	Dressmaker	19Ju02Ga
SULLIVAN, Florence	15	F	Unknown	19Ju02Ga
MAHONY, Patrick	38	M	Laborer	19Ju02Ga
Mary	18	F	Unknown	19Ju02Ga
Patt	11	M	Unknown	19Ju02Ga
Cathn.	13	F	Unknown	19Ju02Ga
BUCKLEY, James	40	M	Laborer	19Ju02Ga
MCCARTHY, Pat	34	M	Laborer	19Ju02Ga
Margt.	30	F	Unknown	19Ju02Ga
GORMAN, Michl.	45	M	Laborer	19Ju02Ga
TUOMY, Timy.	38	M	Laborer	19Ju02Ga
Ellen	38	F	Unknown	19Ju02Ga
John	38	M	Laborer	19Ju02Ga
TOBIN, William	24	M	Laborer	19Ju02Ga
Richd.	00	M	Laborer	19Ju02Ga
MURPHY, Denis	00	M	Laborer	19Ju02Ga
Ellen	34	F	Servant	19Ju02Ga
Margt.	5	F	Child	19Ju02Ga
John	4	M	Child	19Ju02Ga
Julia	.11	F	Infant	19Ju02Ga
CONNORS, Margt.	50	F	Unknown	19Ju02Ga
John	2	M	Child	19Ju02Ga
MAHONY, Martin	30	M	Laborer	19Ju02Ga
Maurice	1	M	Child	19Ju02Ga
CALLEHAN, John	20	M	Laborer	19Ju02Ga
WALSH, Michl.	22	M	Laborer	19Ju02Ga
MCDONALD, Mary	25	F	Servant	19Ju02Ga
MOSS, Alice	25	F	Servant	19Ju02Ga
Mary	21	F	Servant	19Ju02Ga
LYNCH, John	19	M	Laborer	19Ju02Ga
HACKETT, Michl.	27	M	Laborer	19Ju02Ga
DALY, Denis	24	M	Laborer	19Ju02Ga
HENESSY, Patt	15	M	Laborer	19Ju02Ga
John	24	M	Laborer	19Ju02Ga
Margt.	13	F	Servant	19Ju02Ga
ONEILL, Denis	11	M	Laborer	19Ju02Ga
DONOHUE, Rose	15	F	Servant	19Ju02Ga
Anne	13	F	Servant	19Ju02Ga
MCCARTHY, Cornelia	34	F	Servant	19Ju02Ga
BRETT, Patrick	26	M	Clerk	19Ju02Ga
DONNOVAN, Bessy	18	F	Servant	19Ju02Ga
CONNORS, Mary	7	F	Child	19Ju02Ga

MARIA 20 JUNE 1849

From Limerick

NAMES OF PASSENGERS	AGE	SEX	OCCUPATIONS	DATE PORT SHIP
CUSACK, Thomas	35	M	Farmer	20Ju35Jq
Michael	30	M	Farmer	20Ju35Jq
GALVIN, Patrick	20	M	Farmer	20Ju35Jq
Michael	18	M	Farmer	20Ju35Jq
Cornelius	17	M	Farmer	20Ju35Jq
Bridget	14	F	Spinster	20Ju35Jq
LYNCH, John	25	M	Farmer	20Ju35Jq
Patrick	20	M	Farmer	20Ju35Jq
Jas.	30	M	Farmer	20Ju35Jq
CAREY, Andrew	29	M	Farmer	20Ju35Jq
Matilda	30	F	Wife	20Ju35Jq
Mary	6	F	Child	20Ju35Jq
OCONNOR, Pat.	26	M	Farmer	20Ju35Jq
LYNCH, Maurice	24	M	Farmer	20Ju35Jq
Thomas	19	M	Farmer	20Ju35Jq
Magt.	23	F	Spinster	20Ju35Jq
Cathn.	21	F	Spinster	20Ju35Jq
Mary	20	F	Spinster	20Ju35Jq
RYAN, Philip	26	M	Farmer	20Ju35Jq
Biddy	20	F	Wife	20Ju35Jq
KILVINTON, Chas.	30	M	Farmer	20Ju35Jq
Mary	30	F	Matron	20Ju35Jq
HORN, Mary	20	F	Spinster	20Ju35Jq
KILVINTON, Pat.	2	M	Child	20Ju35Jq
George	.00	M	Infant	20Ju35Jq
MULGREW, John	20	M	Farmer	20Ju35Jq
Michael	18	M	Farmer	20Ju35Jq
Harriet	22	F	Spinster	20Ju35Jq
Mary	19	F	Spinster	20Ju35Jq
MOLONEY, John	25	M	Farmer	20Ju35Jq
HOULIHAN, Edwd.	23	M	Farmer	20Ju35Jq
John	21	M	Farmer	20Ju35Jq
HICKEY, Mary	40	F	Spinster	20Ju35Jq
MOLONEY, Bridget	22	F	Unknown	20Ju35Jq
LISTON, John	25	M	Farmer	20Ju35Jq
HOGAN, Thos.	20	M	Farmer	20Ju35Jq
John	16	M	Farmer	20Ju35Jq
Cathn.	14	F	Spinster	20Ju35Jq
MCMAHON, Michl.	22	M	Farmer	20Ju35Jq
John	7	M	Child	20Ju35Jq
Michael	5	M	Child	20Ju35Jq
LISTER, Maurice	30	M	Laborer	20Ju35Jq
MCMAHON, James	12	M	Farmer	20Ju35Jq
OBRIEN, Pat.	26	M	Farmer	20Ju35Jq
DOOLADHY, Pat.	35	M	Farmer	20Ju35Jq
ROCHE, Johanna	25	F	Spinster	20Ju35Jq
FULHILL, Biddy	20	F	Spinster	20Ju35Jq
Mary	8	F	Child	20Ju35Jq
Jas.	4	M	Child	20Ju35Jq
Laurie	.00	F	Infant	20Ju35Jq
HAGAN, Michael	40	M	Farmer	20Ju35Jq
Mary	35	F	Wife	20Ju35Jq
Biddy	10	F	Spinster	20Ju35Jq
CASEY, Cathn.	40	F	Spinster	20Ju35Jq
MCGRANE, Pat.	21	M	Farmer	20Ju35J
John	19	M	Farmer	20Ju35J
CONNOR, Michael	30	M	Farmer	20Ju35J
Ann	30	F	Wife	20Ju35J
John	17	M	Laborer	20Ju35J
Marianna	9	F	Child	20Ju35J
Richd.	7	M	Child	20Ju35J
Edwd.	5	M	Child	20Ju35J
Magt.	5	F	Child	20Ju35J
HALWALL, Thos.	21	M	Farmer	20Ju35J
ODAY, Cathn.	20	F	Spinster	20Ju35J

NAMES OF PASSENGERS	AGE	SEX	OCCUPATIONS	DATE PORT SHIP
EGAN, Johanna	17	F	Spinster	20Ju35Jq
DONOHUE, Jas.	30	M	Farmer	20Ju35Jq
OCONNOR, Bryan	20	M	Farmer	20Ju35Jq
LEXTON, Pat.	27	M	Farmer	20Ju35Jq
CROLLY, Tim.	25	M	Farmer	20Ju35Jq
ROCHE, Michl.	20	M	Farmer	20Ju35Jq
OSHAUGHNESSY, Pat.	26	M	Farmer	20Ju35Jq
Cathn.	14	F	Spinster	20Ju35Jq
Bridget	13	F	Unknown	20Ju35Jq
Pat.	11	M	Unknown	20Ju35Jq
Jas.	8	M	Child	20Ju35Jq
Hannah	.00	F	Infant	20Ju35Jq
DEMPSEY, Edwin	35	M	Farmer	20Ju35Jq
Mary	32	F	Wife	20Ju35Jq
Cathn.	6	F	Child	20Ju35Jq
Maria	4	F	Child	20Ju35Jq
Margaret	2	F	Child	20Ju35Jq
FLAHAVAN, Catherine	20	F	Spinster	20Ju35Jq
MEALY, Michael	25	M	Farmer	20Ju35Jq
POMERY, Richd.	30	M	Farmer	20Ju35Jq
FRAWLEY, John	31	M	Farmer	20Ju35Jq
Mary	31	F	Wife	20Ju35Jq
Biddy	2	F	Child	20Ju35Jq
Thomas	.00	M	Infant	20Ju35Jq
HAYES, Mary	28	F	Spinster	20Ju35Jq
DONALDSON, John	20	M	Farmer	20Ju35Jq
MANNON, Biddy	20	F	Spinster	20Ju35Jq
TOHEY, Pat.	56	M	Farmer	20Ju35Jq
Pat.	30	M	Farmer	20Ju35Jq
Jas.	26	M	Farmer	20Ju35Jq
Michl.	22	M	Farmer	20Ju35Jq
Daniel	20	M	Farmer	20Ju35Jq
DONOVAN, Peggy	18	F	Spinster	20Ju35Jq
SHEEHEY, Roger	26	M	Farmer	20Ju35Jq
DONNELLY, Mary	20	F	Spinster	20Ju35Jq
PURCEL, Pat.	12	M	Unknown	20Ju35Jq
FRAWLEY, Thomas	26	M	Farmer	20Ju35Jq
Honora	19	F	Wife	20Ju35Jq
Michael	3	M	Child	20Ju35Jq
Pat.	.00	M	Infant	20Ju35Jq
DEMPSEY, --Uno	1	U	Child	20Ju35Jq
REDDINGTON, Pat.	2	M	Child	20Ju35Jq

DE-WITT-CLINTON 20 JUNE 1849

From Liverpool

NAMES OF PASSENGERS	AGE	SEX	OCCUPATIONS	DATE PORT SHIP
MURPHY, John	28	M	Shoemaker	20Ju02Jv
Catherine	2	F	Child	20Ju02Jv
Margaret	28	F	Unknown	20Ju02Jv
DRYSDALE, John	33	M	Gdnr	20Ju02Jv
Jane	26	F	Unknown	20Ju02Jv
KENNEDY, Willm.	25	M	Farmer	20Ju02Jv
Catherine	20	F	Unknown	20Ju02Jv
James	24	M	Unknown	20Ju02Jv
Jane	22	F	Unknown	20Ju02Jv
Stephen	23	M	Unknown	20Ju02Jv
OONAN, John	18	M	Laborer	20Ju02Jv
Ellen	20	F	Unknown	20Ju02Jv
SALMON, James	21	M	Unknown	20Ju02Jv
ANNELEY, Willm.	26	M	Unknown	20Ju02Jv
OGARTY, Margt.	22	F	Servant	20Ju02Jv
Honora	20	F	Unknown	20Ju02Jv
AMMOND, Patk.	33	M	Laborer	20Ju02Jv
ILLELAND, Jas.	21	M	Laborer	20Ju02Jv
ERGAN, John	35	M	Laborer	20Ju02Jv
ARR, Cathrn.	35	F	Seamstress	20Ju02Jv
Mary	30	F	Unknown	20Ju02Jv
GAN, Willm.	34	M	Farmer	20Ju02Jv
EGAN, Bridget	30	F	Unknown	20Ju02Jv
Margt.	.08	F	Infant	20Ju02Jv
SHEA, Robt.	26	M	Laborer	20Ju02Jv
HAMILTON, Wm.	30	M	Laborer	20Ju02Jv
Cathn.	29	F	Unknown	20Ju02Jv
DONOVAN, Richd.	22	M	Unknown	20Ju02Jv
HAGGARTY, Denis	22	M	Laborer	20Ju02Jv
BUCHANIN, Willm.	22	M	Tailor	20Ju02Jv
Helena	19	F	Seamstress	20Ju02Jv
DONOVAN, Ellen	35	F	Unknown	20Ju02Jv
CULLENANE, Andrew	20	M	Farmer	20Ju02Jv
GILMARTIN, Cathrn.	20	F	Servant	20Ju02Jv
KELLY, Patk.	24	M	Farmer	20Ju02Jv
Anne	22	F	Unknown	20Ju02Jv
Cathne.	19	F	Unknown	20Ju02Jv
MCENTIGART, Josh.	17	M	Laborer	20Ju02Jv
MCCANN, Cathrn.	16	F	Servant	20Ju02Jv
DORAN, Michl.	45	M	Farmer	20Ju02Jv
James	25	M	Unknown	20Ju02Jv
MAHER, Michl.	40	M	Unknown	20Ju02Jv
CAMPION, Margt.	25	F	Servant	20Ju02Jv
FREEMAN, John	24	M	Farmer	20Ju02Jv
Mary	22	F	Unknown	20Ju02Jv
BYRNE, Pat	44	M	Ffmr	20Ju02Jv
Mary-Anne	49	F	Unknown	20Ju02Jv
Patk.	3	M	Child	20Ju02Jv
MAHER, Rody	33	M	Laborer	20Ju02Jv
Mary	21	F	Unknown	20Ju02Jv
DORAN, John	3	M	Child	20Ju02Jv
Marcella	7	F	Child	20Ju02Jv
REYNOLDS, Margt.	20	F	Servant	20Ju02Jv
KERIGAN, Jas.	24	M	Laborer	20Ju02Jv
PRICE, David	28	M	Spinner	20Ju02Jv
Bridget	28	F	Unknown	20Ju02Jv
Richd.	7	M	Child	20Ju02Jv
Willm.	5	M	Child	20Ju02Jv
BIRCH, Cathne.	40	F	Servant	20Ju02Jv
HEERY, Cathne.	20	F	Seamstress	20Ju02Jv
DUFFY, Cathne.	17	F	Seamstress	20Ju02Jv
GAYNOR, Patk.	24	M	Farmer	20Ju02Jv
PAGARTY, Willm.	32	M	Unknown	20Ju02Jv
Cathn.	30	F	Unknown	20Ju02Jv
Mary	1	F	Child	20Ju02Jv
FOGARTY, Patk.	28	M	Ostler	20Ju02Jv
KEEGAN, Richd.	24	M	Shoemaker	20Ju02Jv
Bridget	22	F	Unknown	20Ju02Jv
FITZSIMONS, Willm.	24	M	Farmer	20Ju02Jv
BRADY, Danl.	30	M	Farmer	20Ju02Jv
Anne	30	F	Unknown	20Ju02Jv
Anastasia	19	F	Unknown	20Ju02Jv
Mary	8	F	Child	20Ju02Jv
Thomas	6	M	Child	20Ju02Jv
Daniel	4	M	Child	20Ju02Jv
Ellen	1	F	Child	20Ju02Jv
KENNY, John	30	M	Laborer	20Ju02Jv
Julia	30	F	Unknown	20Ju02Jv
Mary	.08	F	Infant	20Ju02Jv
CARTY, Anne	30	F	Servant	20Ju02Jv
LAVERY, Sarah	28	F	Unknown	20Ju02Jv
MCVEY, Ellen	20	F	Unknown	20Ju02Jv
MCFILLAN, John	28	M	Laborer	20Ju02Jv
MCCARTNEY, Peter	23	M	Unknown	20Ju02Jv
John	21	M	Laborer	20Ju02Jv
MCKEEVOR, John	30	M	Farmer	20Ju02Jv
Cathn.	28	F	Unknown	20Ju02Jv
OBRIEN, Cathn.	17	F	Seamstress	20Ju02Jv
Margaret	16	F	Unknown	20Ju02Jv
DALLARD, Patk.	40	M	Farmer	20Ju02Jv
Mary	33	F	Unknown	20Ju02Jv
Michl.	13	M	Unknown	20Ju02Jv
Willm.	11	M	Unknown	20Ju02Jv
Mary	9	F	Child	20Ju02Jv
Bridget	7	F	Child	20Ju02Jv
Catherine	4	F	Child	20Ju02Jv
CANLE, George	19	M	Laborer	20Ju02Jv

NAMES OF PASSENGERS	AGE	SEX	OCCUPATIONS	DATE PORT SHIP
COYLE, Patk.	25	M	Unknown	20Ju02Jv
THOMPSON, Eliza	19	F	Seamstress	20Ju02Jv
STEWART, Wm.	21	M	Laborer	20Ju02Jv
MCGINN, Jas.	17	M	Farmer	20Ju02Jv
Jane	18	F	Unknown	20Ju02Jv
BOYLE, Bernard	22	M	Farmer	20Ju02Jv
DALY, James	22	M	Farmer	20Ju02Jv
MULDOON, James	20	M	Laborer	20Ju02Jv
Cathern.	15	F	Unknown	20Ju02Jv
CULLENANE, Jas.	19	M	Laborer	20Ju02Jv
MCKENNA, Patk.	1	M	Farmer	20Ju02Jv
Rosa	20	F	Unknown	20Ju02Jv
CONNORS, Willm.	21	M	Unknown	20Ju02Jv
HILL, Patk.	21	M	Unknown	20Ju02Jv
DOHENY, Bridget	22	F	Servant	20Ju02Jv
MARTIN, Willm.	24	M	Laborer	20Ju02Jv
MCEVOY, Michl.	24	M	Farmer	20Ju02Jv
Owen	23	M	Laborer	20Ju02Jv
BRAY, Mary	20	F	Servant	20Ju02Jv
MCEVOY, Anne	20	M	Laborer	20Ju02Jv
BRIEN, Richd.	28	M	Farmer	20Ju02Jv
CROAKE, Edwd.	30	M	Unknown	20Ju02Jv
FORD, John	24	M	Unknown	20Ju02Jv
MCGRAW, John	27	M	Unknown	20Ju02Jv
SHEA, Jas.	26	M	Laborer	20Ju02Jv
DOHENY, Thos.	21	M	Unknown	20Ju02Jv
Margt.	26	F	Unknown	20Ju02Jv
WALSH, Mary	30	F	Seamstress	20Ju02Jv
MORRIS, Honora	24	F	Unknown	20Ju02Jv
MCGRAW, Cathn.	22	F	Servant	20Ju02Jv
PHELAN, Bridget	20	F	Unknown	20Ju02Jv
CAMPION, Philip	21	M	Laborer	20Ju02Jv
CRAWFORD, John	21	M	Farmer	20Ju02Jv
MCDONALD, Jas.	22	M	Mechanic	20Ju02Jv
Cathne.	25	F	Unknown	20Ju02Jv
MCDONNELL, Anne	30	F	Servant	20Ju02Jv
MARTIN, Mary	30	F	Servant	20Ju02Jv
GUILFOYLE, Ellen	37	F	Farmer	20Ju02Jv
John	21	M	Unknown	20Ju02Jv
Mary	19	F	Unknown	20Ju02Jv
Stephen	17	M	Unknown	20Ju02Jv
Cathre.	12	F	Unknown	20Ju02Jv
Ellen	11	F	Unknown	20Ju02Jv
Cornelius	9	M	Child	20Ju02Jv
KEEGAN, Mattw.	24	M	Laborer	20Ju02Jv
RIORDAN, Mary	21	F	Servant	20Ju02Jv
MALONEY, Johanna	21	F	Unknown	20Ju02Jv
RYAN, Thos.	34	M	Farmer	20Ju02Jv
KENNEDY, Martin	30	M	Unknown	20Ju02Jv
CASS, Thos.	26	M	Unknown	20Ju02Jv
James	24	M	Unknown	20Ju02Jv
Margt.	22	F	Unknown	20Ju02Jv
CULLENANE, Anty.	30	M	Laborer	20Ju02Jv
RYAN, Bridget	27	F	Servant	20Ju02Jv
GUIRY, Michl.	24	M	Tailor	20Ju02Jv
HAYES, Michl.	23	M	Laborer	20Ju02Jv
KEITH, Mattw.	24	M	Soldier	20Ju02Jv
MCCABE, Edwd.	25	M	Farmer	20Ju02Jv
REILLY, Thos.	40	M	Farmer	20Ju02Jv
CLIFFORD, Jane	20	F	Seamstress	20Ju02Jv
STEWART, Betsy	17	F	Seamstress	20Ju02Jv
LARKIN, Sally	18	F	Servant	20Ju02Jv
Jas.	50	M	Schm	20Ju02Jv
MCPHILLIPS, Edwd.	40	M	Laborer	20Ju02Jv
DUFFY, Jas.	25	M	Unknown	20Ju02Jv
Mary	20	F	Servant	20Ju02Jv
MCSTRAVICK, Mary	18	F	Servant	20Ju02Jv
CAMPBELL, Jas.	30	M	Mechanic	20Ju02Jv
POWER, John	21	M	Tailor	20Ju02Jv
Mary	19	F	Unknown	20Ju02Jv
MCMINN, Jas.	33	M	Farmer	20Ju02Jv
Mary	22	F	Unknown	20Ju02Jv
Cathn.	1	F	Child	20Ju02Jv
RUDDY, John	20	M	Laborer	20Ju02Jv
Mitchell	20	M	Unknown	20Ju02Jv
WORTH, Eliza	25	F	Seamstress	20Ju02Jv
Anne	.10	F	Infant	20Ju02Jv
ROGERS, Rosana	35	F	Unknown	20Ju02Jv
Mary	3	F	Child	20Ju02Jv
DALY, Peter	50	M	Laborer	20Ju02Jv
SHERIDAN, Pat	18	M	Unknown	20Ju02Jv
PHILLIPS, Patk.	21	M	Farmer	20Ju02Jv
Anne	19	F	Unknown	20Ju02Jv
Margt.	18	F	Unknown	20Ju02Jv
James	16	M	Unknown	20Ju02Jv
John	13	M	Unknown	20Ju02Jv
Mary	11	F	Unknown	20Ju02Jv
Thos.	7	M	Child	20Ju02Jv
Lawrence	3	M	Child	20Ju02Jv
KAIN, Francis	50	F	Unknown	20Ju02Jv
Bridget	40	F	Unknown	20Ju02Jv
Bridget	21	F	Unknown	20Ju02Jv
Ambrose	19	M	Unknown	20Ju02Jv
Margt.	16	F	Unknown	20Ju02Jv
Ellen	13	F	Unknown	20Ju02Jv
KNOX, John	46	M	Unknown	20Ju02Jv
Phillip	24	M	Unknown	20Ju02Jv
Edwd.	21	M	Unknown	20Ju02Jv
Jane	45	F	Unknown	20Ju02Jv
SHUFFREY, Bridget	24	F	Servant	20Ju02Jv
KIERNAN, Richd.	30	M	Laborer	20Ju02Jv
BAKER, Willm.	25	M	Farmer	20Ju02Jv
Cathn.	23	F	Farmer	20Ju02Jv
Mary-Clinton	.01	F	Infant	20Ju02Jv
BOWES, Jas.	42	M	Laborer	20Ju02Jv
REILLY, Thos.	20	M	Baker	20Ju02Jv
Maria	23	F	Baker	20Ju02Jv
HAYES, Jerh.	30	M	Laborer	20Ju02Jv
CONNOLLY, John	18	M	Laborer	20Ju02Jv
HAYES, Stephen	20	M	Shoemaker	20Ju02Jv
WILLIAMS, Richd.	22	M	Laborer	20Ju02Jv
DONEGAN, David	34	M	Unknown	20Ju02Jv
Patk.	16	M	Unknown	20Ju02Jv
Ellen	25	F	Unknown	20Ju02Jv
Johanna	18	F	Unknown	20Ju02Jv
Bridget	11	F	Unknown	20Ju02Jv
Mary	9	F	Child	20Ju02Jv
Eliza	7	F	Child	20Ju02Jv
GEARY, Honora	18	F	Servant	20Ju02Jv
LINEHARN, Danl.	22	M	Laborer	20Ju02Jv
OCONNELL, Michl.	30	M	Laborer	20Ju02Jv
KEELEY, Johanna	30	F	Servant	20Ju02Jv
DALY, Jane	22	F	Seamstress	20Ju02Jv
LINARD, Bella	20	F	Seamstress	20Ju02Jv
WARD, Evans	20	M	Laborer	20Ju02Jv
BOYLE, Mary	30	F	Servant	20Ju02Jv
Biddy	7	F	Child	20Ju02Jv
Patk.	3	M	Child	20Ju02Jv
Anne	1	F	Child	20Ju02Jv
KINNEALEY, Patk.	18	M	Laborer	20Ju02Jv
Thos.	13	M	Laborer	20Ju02Jv
MERIGAN, Margt.	12	F	Servant	20Ju02Jv
GUNNY, Margt.	20	F	Unknown	20Ju02Jv
BROGAN, Cathne.	30	F	Unknown	20Ju02Jv
Bridget	12	F	Unknown	20Ju02Jv
SHEPPARD, Eliza	18	F	Unknown	20Ju02Jv
KAIN, Abby	30	M	Farmer	20Ju02Jv
John	10	M	Farmer	20Ju02Jv
Timothy	4	M	Child	20Ju02Jv
MCGOWAN, Anne	30	F	Farmer	20Ju02Jv
Cathne.	4	F	Child	20Ju02Jv
Anne	.06	F	Infant	20Ju02Jv
KAVANAGH, Jane	18	F	Servant	20Ju02Jv
LANG, Thos.	24	M	Laborer	20Ju02Jv
Alice	20	F	Seamstress	20Ju02Jv
CAMPBELL, Mary	20	F	Servant	20Ju02Jv
DORAN, Thos.	35	M	Porter	20Ju02Jv
CUNIFF, Bernard	28	M	Shoemaker	20Ju02Jv
CAHILL, Judy	30	F	Unknown	20Ju02J
Margaret	14	F	Unknown	20Ju02J

NAMES OF PASSENGERS	AGE	SEX	OCCUPATIONS	DATE PORT SHIP
CAHILL, Cathne.	32	F	Unknown	20Ju02Jv
Judy	10	F	Unknown	20Ju02Jv
Betty	8	F	Child	20Ju02Jv
Bridget	4	F	Child	20Ju02Jv
BURKE, Ellen	32	F	Servant	20Ju02Jv
SMITH, David	23	M	Gentleman	20Ju02Jv
John-W.	36	M	Gentleman	20Ju02Jv

ISAAC-WRIGHT 21 JUNE 1849

From Liverpool

NAMES OF PASSENGERS	AGE	SEX	OCCUPATIONS	DATE PORT SHIP
STANTON, James	24	M	Carpenter	21Ju02Km
FARRELL, Bridget	20	F	Unknown	21Ju02Km
Bridget	3	F	Child	21Ju02Km
STANTON, Mary	22	F	Unknown	21Ju02Km
DIVINE, James	40	M	Laborer	21Ju02Km
Catherine	40	F	Unknown	21Ju02Km
Mary	13	F	Unknown	21Ju02Km
James	10	M	Unknown	21Ju02Km
Catherine	6	F	Child	21Ju02Km
Margt.	8	F	Child	21Ju02Km
Rosana	3	F	Child	21Ju02Km
ELLIOT, Robert	48	M	Laborer	21Ju02Km
DOOLEN, James	35	M	Laborer	21Ju02Km
WOLOHAN, John	50	M	Laborer	21Ju02Km
USHER, Geo.	33	M	Laborer	21Ju02Km
MONAGHAN, Ann	26	F	Spinster	21Ju02Km
LYNCH, Bridget	14	F	Spinster	21Ju02Km
Ann	12	F	Spinster	21Ju02Km
MALONE, James	20	M	Stctr	21Ju02Km
HAYDEN, Mary	40	F	Wi	21Ju02Km
MCCLUSKEY, Cathe.	50	F	Wi	21Ju02Km
GALONE, Margt.	18	F	Wi	21Ju02Km
Ann	9	F	Child	21Ju02Km
GARRAHAN, Danl.	20	M	Laborer	21Ju02Km
Bernard	18	M	Laborer	21Ju02Km
HARVEY, Dennis	50	M	Weaver	21Ju02Km
Elizth.	19	F	Spinster	21Ju02Km
James	20	M	Unknown	21Ju02Km
BRADY, Mary	12	F	Spinster	21Ju02Km
MCNAMEE, Pat	20	M	Laborer	21Ju02Km
MCGERAPHY, John	24	M	Laborer	21Ju02Km
CAREY, Margt.	40	F	Wi	21Ju02Km
Anne	19	F	Spinster	21Ju02Km
SMITH, Bridget	13	F	Spinster	21Ju02Km
Ann	20	F	Spinster	21Ju02Km
HALE, Michl.	18	M	Laborer	21Ju02Km
Winny	16	F	Spinster	21Ju02Km
HARVEY, Pat	22	M	Coach Maker	21Ju02Km
SMITH, Phillip	21	M	Laborer	21Ju02Km
CARTNEY, Lawrence	20	M	Laborer	21Ju02Km
TULLY, Owen	18	M	Tailor	21Ju02Km
GORNEY, Cathe.	50	F	Spinster	21Ju02Km
FARLEY, Margt.	21	F	Spinster	21Ju02Km
MCCABE, Ellen	20	F	Spinster	21Ju02Km
CARTNEY, Jane	15	F	Spinster	21Ju02Km
KIDGEN, John	24	M	Laborer	21Ju02Km
DANIHAN, Michl.	24	M	Laborer	21Ju02Km
ONEILL, Michl.	18	M	Laborer	21Ju02Km
HAGAN, Phillip	25	M	Laborer	21Ju02Km
Mary	30	F	Spinster	21Ju02Km
Bridget	16	F	Spinster	21Ju02Km
BRADY, Bridget	16	F	Spinster	21Ju02Km
IGO, Ellen	18	F	Spinster	21Ju02Km
CAMPBELL, John	35	M	Laborer	21Ju02Km
Mary	40	F	Unknown	21Ju02Km
Bridget	38	F	Spinster	21Ju02Km
GARNEY, Hannah	15	F	Spinster	21Ju02Km
CAMPBELL, James	23	M	Laborer	21Ju02Km
MURPHY, Hugh	15	M	Unknown	21Ju02Km
John	11	M	Unknown	21Ju02Km
Nancy	13	F	Unknown	21Ju02Km
MCCORMICK, Jno.	26	M	Carpenter	21Ju02Km
RODGERS, John	25	M	Laborer	21Ju02Km
Edward	20	M	Laborer	21Ju02Km
Mary	15	F	Unknown	21Ju02Km
David	12	M	Laborer	21Ju02Km
MURPHY, John	24	M	Laborer	21Ju02Km
Margt.	21	F	Unknown	21Ju02Km
MCKEAN, Margt.	60	F	Wi	21Ju02Km
Mary	35	F	Spinster	21Ju02Km
Eliza	25	F	Spinster	21Ju02Km
Jane	30	F	Spinster	21Ju02Km
MCCARTNEY, James	28	M	Laborer	21Ju02Km
GUNN, James	22	M	Laborer	21Ju02Km
REILLY, Michl.	23	M	Laborer	21Ju02Km
WATSON, Margt.	25	F	Unknown	21Ju02Km
Susan	21	F	Spinster	21Ju02Km
Mary	23	F	Spinster	21Ju02Km
KEEGAN, James	25	M	Laborer	21Ju02Km
MCGINN, James	20	M	Laborer	21Ju02Km
HANDYBO, Richard	20	M	Laborer	21Ju02Km
John	20	M	Laborer	21Ju02Km
Ellen	50	F	Wi	21Ju02Km
RADDLE, Edward	25	M	Laborer	21Ju02Km
MONAGHAN, James	17	M	Cooper	21Ju02Km
WHEELTON, Michl.	25	M	Cooper	21Ju02Km
MCCORMICK, Lawrence	28	M	Laborer	21Ju02Km
MURPHY, Ann	20	F	Spinster	21Ju02Km
JOHNSTON, Eliza	17	F	Spinster	21Ju02Km
FORAN, Mary	15	F	Spinster	21Ju02Km
MCGAEHAN, Mary	16	F	Spinster	21Ju02Km
MEECAN, Bridget	16	F	Spinster	21Ju02Km
James	16	M	Laborer	21Ju02Km
KOGAN, Peter	23	M	Laborer	21Ju02Km
James	20	M	Laborer	21Ju02Km
DUNN, Mary	13	F	Spinster	21Ju02Km
Bridget	20	F	Spinster	21Ju02Km
SCULLY, Pat	12	M	Unknown	21Ju02Km
Mary	13	F	Unknown	21Ju02Km
Catherine	10	F	Unknown	21Ju02Km
DONALD, Alice	18	F	Spinster	21Ju02Km
LAHEY, Anora	18	F	Spinster	21Ju02Km
DOWLEY, John	18	M	Laborer	21Ju02Km
BULKELEY, Catherine	22	F	Wi	21Ju02Km
NEILL, Bridget	55	F	Spinster	21Ju02Km
THOMPSON, Mary	60	F	Wi	21Ju02Km
John	20	M	Laborer	21Ju02Km
MOLLOY, Ellen	30	F	Wi	21Ju02Km
Ellen	7	F	Child	21Ju02Km
Bridget	9	F	Child	21Ju02Km
Edward	5	M	Child	21Ju02Km
CALLAGHAN, Henry	40	M	Laborer	21Ju02Km
HART, Pat	21	M	Laborer	21Ju02Km
CALLIGAN, James	18	M	Laborer	21Ju02Km
John	10	M	Laborer	21Ju02Km
DIXON, Mary	34	F	Wi	21Ju02Km
James	7	M	Child	21Ju02Km
Rosa	2	F	Child	21Ju02Km
SMITH, Catherine	18	F	Spinster	21Ju02Km
SHIELDS, Cathe.	18	F	Spinster	21Ju02Km
KIRKE, Bridget	17	F	Spinster	21Ju02Km
HANNINGAN, Joseph	20	F	Spinster	21Ju02Km
FITZSIMMONS, James	21	M	Laborer	21Ju02Km
REID, James	30	M	Rope Maker	21Ju02Km
COCHRAN, John	11	M	Laborer	21Ju02Km
MCGILLICK, Pat	17	M	Laborer	21Ju02Km
MCCANN, Chas.	20	M	Laborer	21Ju02Km
ATFIELD, Pat	27	M	Laborer	21Ju02Km
James	20	M	Laborer	21Ju02Km
Michael	18	M	Laborer	21Ju02Km
Catherine	24	F	Spinster	21Ju02Km
Alice	30	F	Wi	21Ju02Km

NAMES OF PASSENGERS	AGE	SEX	OCCUPATIONS	DATE PORT SHIP
ATFIELD, Catherine	24	F	Spinster	21Ju02Km
Alice	30	F	Wi	21Ju02Km
BALL, Thomas	30	M	Laborer	21Ju02Km
Betsy	30	F	Unknown	21Ju02Km
Ellen	7	F	Child	21Ju02Km
LANGAN, Wm.	23	M	Laborer	21Ju02Km
MCDERMOTT, Mary	60	F	Wi	21Ju02Km
MCCANN, Ellen	20	F	Spinster	21Ju02Km
DOHERTY, Danl.	16	M	Carpenter	21Ju02Km
DOYLE, Pat	48	M	Carpenter	21Ju02Km
Catherine	44	F	Spinster	21Ju02Km
Wm.	.00	M	Infant	21Ju02Km
Jane	13	F	Unknown	21Ju02Km
John	11	M	Unknown	21Ju02Km
Margt.	9	F	Child	21Ju02Km
Phillip	7	M	Child	21Ju02Km
Michael	3	M	Child	21Ju02Km
CUNNINGHAM, Ann	19	F	Spinster	21Ju02Km
MURRAY, John	22	M	Laborer	21Ju02Km
CUNNINGHAM, Michl.	25	M	Laborer	21Ju02Km
Pat	20	M	Laborer	21Ju02Km
TULLY, Ann	23	F	Spinster	21Ju02Km
WHITE, Essy	25	F	Spinster	21Ju02Km
MAHON, Mary	23	F	Spinster	21Ju02Km
FLAHARTY, Bridget	30	F	Spinster	21Ju02Km
Michael	3	M	Child	21Ju02Km
REILLY, Ann	24	F	Spinster	21Ju02Km
Mary-Ann	.00	F	Infant	21Ju02Km
BRADY, Liddy	24	M	Laborer	21Ju02Km
HOSEY, Pat	22	M	Laborer	21Ju02Km
FISHER, William	16	M	Laborer	21Ju02Km
CALLAN, Anne	14	F	Spinster	21Ju02Km
LYNCH, Margt.	16	F	Spinster	21Ju02Km
FALKNER, Bridget	18	F	Spinster	21Ju02Km
MCCANN, Margt.	16	F	Spinster	21Ju02Km
DAVIES, Edward	34	M	Tailor	21Ju02Km
Jane	33	F	Unknown	21Ju02Km
Frederick	9	M	Child	21Ju02Km
Emma	7	F	Child	21Ju02Km
Eliza	4	F	Child	21Ju02Km
Edward	.00	M	Infant	21Ju02Km
HANNAH, Robert	44	M	Shoemaker	21Ju02Km
Mary	45	F	Unknown	21Ju02Km
James	16	M	Unknown	21Ju02Km
William	13	M	Unknown	21Ju02Km
Jennett	10	F	Unknown	21Ju02Km
Robert	19	M	Unknown	21Ju02Km
Nancy	5	F	Child	21Ju02Km
HORNBY, Martha	42	F	Child	21Ju02Km
William	19	M	Shoemaker	21Ju02Km
James	16	M	Shoemaker	21Ju02Km
Thomas	12	M	Shoemaker	21Ju02Km
Sarah-Ann	8	F	Child	21Ju02Km
DONALDSON, John	25	M	Engineer	21Ju02Km
TALLENTIER, Thos.	23	M	Engineer	21Ju02Km
JOHNSON, John	25	M	Blacksmith	21Ju02Km
Mary	24	F	Unknown	21Ju02Km
KIRBY, Danl.	27	M	Laborer	21Ju02Km
GORMALLY, James	22	M	Laborer	21Ju02Km
DIGNAN, James	18	M	Laborer	21Ju02Km
EASTWOOD, Wm.	18	M	Weaver	21Ju02Km
DEMPSY, Richd.	20	M	Laborer	21Ju02Km
YOUNG, Simon	18	M	Laborer	21Ju02Km
GACHIN, James	20	M	Laborer	21Ju02Km
MCGOWAN, Thos.	21	M	Laborer	21Ju02Km
GONOLLEY, Betsy	20	F	Spinster	21Ju02Km
LAVIN, Betsy	18	F	Spinster	21Ju02Km
Mary	18	F	Spinster	21Ju02Km
SHERMAN, Mary-Agnes	18	F	Spinster	21Ju02Km
REILLY, Bridget	24	F	Spinster	21Ju02Km
MCBRIDE, Bridget	19	F	Spinster	21Ju02Km
MCKERN, Ann	25	F	Spinster	21Ju02Km
POCOLIS, Geo.	47	M	Blacksmith	21Ju02Km
STONES, Vincent	24	M	Blacksmith	21Ju02Km
BROWN, Margt.	30	F	Unknown	21Ju02Km
BULKELEY, Ann	32	F	Spinster	21Ju02Km
FARER, Marry	20	F	Spinster	21Ju02Km
KENNEY, Peter	21	M	Laborer	21Ju02Km
KELLY, James	16	M	Laborer	21Ju02Km
Timothy	14	M	Laborer	21Ju02Km
MURRAY, John	11	M	Unknown	21Ju02Km
HORAN, John	12	M	Unknown	21Ju02Km
MURRAY, Mary	17	F	Spinster	21Ju02Km
HARISS, Eliza	18	F	Spinster	21Ju02Km
MURRAY, Catherine	17	F	Spinster	21Ju02Km
Wm.	9	M	Child	21Ju02Km
MCLOUGHLIN, Michl.	19	M	Laborer	21Ju02Km
BLESSING, Pat	21	M	Laborer	21Ju02Km
MORON, Jno.	30	M	Laborer	21Ju02Km
KEEFE, Julia	60	F	Wi	21Ju02Km
Mary	20	F	Unknown	21Ju02Km
Michael	.00	M	Infant	21Ju02Km
Alice	19	F	Spinster	21Ju02Km
Catherine	20	F	Spinster	21Ju02Km
Mary	2	F	Child	21Ju02Km
MCCARTNEY, Danl.	33	M	Laborer	21Ju02Km
MCCAFFRY, James	21	M	Laborer	21Ju02Km
LAWLOR, Wm.	21	M	Laborer	21Ju02Km
MORAN, John	25	M	Laborer	21Ju02Km
MCKENNA, James	18	M	Laborer	21Ju02Km
GANAHAN, Cathe.	16	F	Spinster	21Ju02Km
Margt.	20	F	Spinster	21Ju02Km
FREEL, Ann	18	F	Spinster	21Ju02Km
MCGOWEN, Mary	13	F	Spinster	21Ju02Km
DOHERTY, Rodger	35	M	Laborer	21Ju02Km
Mary	30	F	Unknown	21Ju02Km
Terence	30	M	Laborer	21Ju02Km
CRONAN, John	28	M	Laborer	21Ju02Km
DARSY, Mary	25	F	Spinster	21Ju02Km
PLUNKETT, Thos.	21	M	Laborer	21Ju02Km
MCDONALD, Lawrence	28	M	Laborer	21Ju02Km
HOGAN, Michl.	20	M	Laborer	21Ju02Km
BURKE, James	21	M	Laborer	21Ju02Km
HOY, Judy	25	F	Spinster	21Ju02Km
CALLAPY, Mary	25	F	Spinster	21Ju02Km
REILLY, Johanna	25	F	Spinster	21Ju02Km
HANKARD, Mary	16	F	Spinster	21Ju02Km
BURK, Bridget	19	F	Spinster	21Ju02Km
HARDMAN, Margt.	35	F	Spinster	21Ju02Km
HOGAN, Pat	16	M	Laborer	21Ju02Km
Mary	23	F	Laborer	21Ju02Km
Pierce	.00	M	Infant	21Ju02Km
ROYAN, Mary	16	F	Laborer	21Ju02Km
HOGAN, Mary	19	F	Spinster	21Ju02Km
HAND, Mary	19	F	Spinster	21Ju02Km
DOONE, Ann	20	F	Spinster	21Ju02Km
HOGAN, Bridget	22	F	Spinster	21Ju02Km
LORING, Margt.	30	F	Unknown	21Ju02Km
James	2	M	Child	21Ju02Km
BRODERICK, Thos.	25	M	Laborer	21Ju02Km
Pat	20	M	Laborer	21Ju02Km
COLLINGS, John	28	M	Laborer	21Ju02Km
HAMILTON, Sarah	35	F	Wi	21Ju02Km
Jane	15	F	Spinster	21Ju02Km
Sarah	12	F	Unknown	21Ju02Km
TIERNAN, Thos.	27	M	Laborer	21Ju02Km
Bridget	25	F	Unknown	21Ju02Km
HEWITT, Bessy	20	F	Spinster	21Ju02Km
KELLY, Anne	23	F	Spinster	21Ju02Km
MURPHY, Edward	73	M	Tailor	21Ju02Km
MCCALLON, Pat	17	M	Shoemaker	21Ju02Km
POTTS, Mary-Ann	30	F	Spinster	21Ju02Km
MCANALLY, Alice	18	F	Spinster	21Ju02Km
HARDIGAN, Andrew	25	M	Laborer	21Ju02Km
SULLIVAN, John	16	M	Laborer	21Ju02Km
MURPHY, John	20	M	Laborer	21Ju02Km
NUGENT, Jane	18	F	Spinster	21Ju02Km
NOLAN, Wm.	28	M	Carpenter	21Ju02Km
Margt.	26	F	Unknown	21Ju02Km
Mary	.00	F	Infant	21Ju02Km

NAMES OF PASSENGERS	AGE	SEX	OCCUPATIONS	DATE PORT SHIP
NOLAN, Thos.	27	M	Laborer	21Ju02Km
SHANLEY, Wm.	60	M	Cartwright	21Ju02Km
Susanna	50	F	Unknown	21Ju02Km
Michl.	20	M	Laborer	21Ju02Km
Susanna	9	F	Child	21Ju02Km
ODWYER, Ellen	38	F	Unknown	21Ju02Km
FLAHARTY, Michl.	45	M	Laborer	21Ju02Km
COOK, John	18	M	Laborer	21Ju02Km
ROYAL, Bernard	23	M	Laborer	21Ju02Km
MOOR, James	20	M	Laborer	21Ju02Km
PORTER, Wm.	23	M	Laborer	21Ju02Km
Mary	22	F	Unknown	21Ju02Km
Joseph	8	M	Child	21Ju02Km
Jane	11	F	Unknown	21Ju02Km
MCCABE, Rose	50	F	Wi	21Ju02Km
Rose	25	F	Spinster	21Ju02Km
KELLY, Alice	20	F	Spinster	21Ju02Km
CARROLL, Bernard	29	M	Laborer	21Ju02Km
Eliza	20	F	Unknown	21Ju02Km
FITZPATRICK, Mary	18	F	Spinster	21Ju02Km
MARRON, Bridget	4	F	Child	21Ju02Km
FANELL, Terry	18	M	Unknown	21Ju02Km
Mary	16	F	Unknown	21Ju02Km
DONOVAN, Mary	18	F	Spinster	21Ju02Km
KELLY, Cathe.	14	F	Spinster	21Ju02Km
FITZSIMMONS, Cathe.	57	F	Wi	21Ju02Km
John	18	M	Unknown	21Ju02Km
GAEHAN, Bryan	15	M	Unknown	21Ju02Km
FARRELL, Joseph	16	M	Laborer	21Ju02Km
SIMES, James	33	M	Laborer	21Ju02Km
DOYLE, Dennis	22	M	Laborer	21Ju02Km
Garrick	20	M	Laborer	21Ju02Km
VERNARD, Jno.	26	M	Laborer	21Ju02Km
MCDERMOTT, Edwd.	25	M	Laborer	21Ju02Km
SMITH, Michl.	20	M	Gdnr	21Ju02Km
FITZPATRICK, Thos.	20	M	Laborer	21Ju02Km
CALLAGHAN, Cathe.	20	F	Spinster	21Ju02Km
Pat	24	M	Laborer	21Ju02Km
CUDDYHA, Ann	20	F	Spinster	21Ju02Km
CONNOR, Ellen	20	F	Spinster	21Ju02Km
MCDONONGH, Pat	3	M	Child	21Ju02Km
HANLAN, Bridget	60	F	Wi	21Ju02Km
Ellen	15	F	Spinster	21Ju02Km
Bridget	23	F	Spinster	21Ju02Km
Pat	3	M	Child	21Ju02Km
MCKEN, Ann	28	F	Spinster	21Ju02Km
OWEN, Charles	21	M	Joiner	21Ju02Km
Jane	20	F	Joiner	21Ju02Km
Mary	.00	F	Infant	21Ju02Km
CAWLEY, Thomas	24	M	Blacksmith	21Ju02Km
Mary	27	F	Unknown	21Ju02Km
Sarah	2	F	Child	21Ju02Km
FOSTER, Wm.Whittaker	44	M	Yeoman	21Ju02Km
Jane	50	F	Unknown	21Ju02Km
TAYLOR, Robert	29	M	Laborer	21Ju02Km
NOONS, Janson	21	M	Farmer	21Ju02Km
BATHERS, Agnes	48	F	Unknown	21Ju02Km
Mary	20	F	Unknown	21Ju02Km
Andrew	8	M	Child	21Ju02Km
MELLOR, Matthew	50	M	Laborer	21Ju02Km
Sarah	36	F	Unknown	21Ju02Km
COUGHLAN, Wm.	39	M	Miller	21Ju02Km
Ellen	34	F	Unknown	21Ju02Km
Catherine	3	F	Child	21Ju02Km
Mary	13	F	Unknown	21Ju02Km
Frances	8	M	Child	21Ju02Km
Ellen	5	F	Child	21Ju02Km
Eliza	35	F	Unknown	21Ju02Km
ROWLEY, Mary	18	F	Spinster	21Ju02Km
HUNTINGTON, John	45	M	Blacksmith	21Ju02Km
Margt.	39	F	Unknown	21Ju02Km
Thomas	15	M	Unknown	21Ju02Km
George	8	M	Child	21Ju02Km
Louisa	6	F	Child	21Ju02Km
William	4	M	Child	21Ju02Km
HUNTINGTON, John	2	M	Child	21Ju02Km
Charles	.00	M	Infant	21Ju02Km
SHAW, George	28	M	Baker	21Ju02Km
CROSSLEY, Edward	45	M	Farmer	21Ju02Km
Jane	39	F	Unknown	21Ju02Km
Mary	13	F	Unknown	21Ju02Km
John	6	M	Child	21Ju02Km
Thomas	2	M	Child	21Ju02Km
IRVING, Elizth.	32	F	Spinster	21Ju02Km
BERK, Elizth.	21	F	Spinster	21Ju02Km
GEARY, James	22	M	Laborer	21Ju02Km
WASON, Samuel	40	M	Laborer	21Ju02Km
Mary	35	F	Unknown	21Ju02Km
Margt.	19	F	Unknown	21Ju02Km
Ann	5	F	Child	21Ju02Km
WYNNE, Thomas	40	M	Farmer	21Ju02Km
Catharine	40	F	Unknown	21Ju02Km
Mary	15	F	Unknown	21Ju02Km
Mark	14	M	Unknown	21Ju02Km
Daniel	12	M	Unknown	21Ju02Km
HURLEY, Ann	20	F	Spinster	21Ju02Km
WYNNE, Michl.	18	M	Laborer	21Ju02Km
HOWARD, Abraham	40	M	Laborer	21Ju02Km
Anne	45	F	Unknown	21Ju02Km
HIBBERT, Martha	13	F	Unknown	21Ju02Km
DAIL, Ann	21	F	Spinster	21Ju02Km
WHITEHEAD, Anne	60	F	Wi	21Ju02Km
STIZAKER, Anne	21	F	Spinster	21Ju02Km
WHITEHEAD, Danl.	47	M	Laborer	21Ju02Km
BECK, George	27	M	Cord Winder	21Ju02Km
MURPHY, Thomas	25	M	Cord Winder	21Ju02Km
Frances	23	F	Spinster	21Ju02Km
Elizabeth	29	F	Spinster	21Ju02Km
ASHBURY, Thomas	29	M	Cutler	21Ju02Km
Emma	6	F	Child	21Ju02Km
Lucy	.00	F	Infant	21Ju02Km
Sarah	30	F	Unknown	21Ju02Km
BELL, John	26	M	Cutler	21Ju02Km
HUNTINGDON, George	40	M	Unknown	21Ju02Km
Sarah	43	F	Unknown	21Ju02Km
Henry	11	M	Unknown	21Ju02Km
Thomas	9	M	Child	21Ju02Km
Caroline	7	F	Child	21Ju02Km
Mary	5	F	Child	21Ju02Km
George	.00	M	Infant	21Ju02Km
Martha	13	F	Unknown	21Ju02Km
MAY, Margt.	40	F	Unknown	21Ju02Km
GILPATRICK, John	29	M	Unknown	21Ju02Km
TOWNSEND, Lewis	30	M	Unknown	21Ju02Km
Sarah	30	F	Unknown	21Ju02Km
Eliza-May	30	F	Unknown	21Ju02Km
Margt.	12	F	Unknown	21Ju02Km
George	10	M	Unknown	21Ju02Km
NICKLIN, James	46	M	Joiner	21Ju02Km
Harriet	38	F	Unknown	21Ju02Km
Frederick	24	M	Unknown	21Ju02Km
John	10	M	Unknown	21Ju02Km
William	9	M	Child	21Ju02Km
Thomas	3	M	Child	21Ju02Km
Edwin	5	M	Child	21Ju02Km
CHILD, Wm.	26	M	Gentleman	21Ju02Km
HAINES, Joseph	21	M	Saddler	21Ju02Km
MCCLUSKEY, Pat	20	M	Laborer	21Ju02Km
Phillip	18	M	Laborer	21Ju02Km
Bernard	16	M	Laborer	21Ju02Km
BIGLEY, Owen	20	M	Grocer	21Ju02Km
DOWD, James	29	M	Laborer	21Ju02Km
HARRIS, Henry	26	M	Printer	21Ju02Km
NUONES, Edwd.	27	M	Brewer	21Ju02Km
GREAVES, Jane	43	M	Unknown	21Ju02Km
James	18	M	Unknown	21Ju02Km
Sarah	16	F	Unknown	21Ju02Km
Joseph	14	M	Unknown	21Ju02Km
Margt.	12	F	Unknown	21Ju02Km
Elizabeth	8	F	Child	21Ju02Km

NAMES OF PASSENGERS	AGE	SEX	OCCUPATIONS	DATE PORT SHIP
GREAVES, John	6	M	Child	21Ju02Km
Jane	2	M	Child	21Ju02Km
Thomas	.00	M	Infant	21Ju02Km
WHITEHEAD, Ann	31	F	Weaver	21Ju02Km
COOPER, Thos.	30	M	Plasterer	21Ju02Km
Sarah	36	F	Unknown	21Ju02Km
Alva	.00	F	Infant	21Ju02Km
READ, John	44	M	Farmer	21Ju02Km
John	19	M	Farmer	21Ju02Km
HARRIS, Thos.	46	M	Painter	21Ju02Km
GUY, Joseph	19	M	Brf	21Ju02Km
PALPEYMAN, John	40	M	Farmer	21Ju02Km
George	12	M	Unknown	21Ju02Km
Susan	40	F	Unknown	21Ju02Km
John	15	M	Unknown	21Ju02Km
Mary	11	F	Unknown	21Ju02Km
Esther	9	F	Child	21Ju02Km
Charles	7	M	Child	21Ju02Km
Frederick	5	M	Child	21Ju02Km
Thomasine	3	F	Child	21Ju02Km
COUGHLIN, Bartholomew	35	M	Unknown	21Ju02Km
DOHENY, Mary-Jane	30	F	Unknown	21Ju02Km
Michael	8	M	Child	21Ju02Km
Morgan-Odwyer	5	M	Child	21Ju02Km
Ellen	3	F	Child	21Ju02Km
Catherine	.00	F	Infant	21Ju02Km
ODWYER, Ellen	26	F	Unknown	21Ju02Km
OWEN, Sophia-Ann	30	F	Unknown	21Ju02Km
ANDERSON, Peter	11	M	Unknown	21Ju02Km
JONES, Mary	21	F	Unknown	21Ju02Km
REILLY, Margt.	30	F	Unknown	21Ju02Km
ALANSON, Jno.	23	M	Unknown	21Ju02Km

COLUMBUS 23 JUNE 1849

From Liverpool

NAMES OF PASSENGERS	AGE	SEX	OCCUPATIONS	DATE PORT SHIP
FIFE, Elizabeth	28	F	Unknown	23Ju02Jy
Wm.Del.	4	M	Child	23Ju02Jy
Matilda-L.	2	F	Child	23Ju02Jy
TYRRELL, Adam	28	M	Unknown	23Ju02Jy
GLENDEINIE, Alexr.	22	M	Unknown	23Ju02Jy
GRANT, Jane	25	F	Unknown	23Ju02Jy
KENNEDY, Catherine	20	F	Unknown	23Ju02Jy
MCDONNELL, James	26	M	Unknown	23Ju02Jy
Eliza	18	F	Unknown	23Ju02Jy
Joseph	16	F	Unknown	23Ju02Jy
DORAN, Thomas	28	M	Unknown	23Ju02Jy
QUINN, William	25	M	Unknown	23Ju02Jy
COONEY, Jno.	23	F	Unknown	23Ju02Jy
Jno.	28	F	Unknown	23Ju02Jy
SHEA, Daniel	26	M	Unknown	23Ju02Jy
Peter	28	M	Unknown	23Ju02Jy
John	30	M	Unknown	23Ju02Jy
CONNELL, Dennis	23	M	Unknown	23Ju02Jy
LEARY, Isovey	30	M	Unknown	23Ju02Jy
HOLOHANN, Ellen	28	F	Unknown	23Ju02Jy
CALLAHAN, Mary	21	F	Unknown	23Ju02Jy
CONNELL, Mick	20	M	Unknown	23Ju02Jy
HOGAN, Sylvester	57	M	Unknown	23Ju02Jy
Daniel	22	M	Unknown	23Ju02Jy
John	24	M	Unknown	23Ju02Jy
HUSEY, Michael	30	M	Unknown	23Ju02Jy
HEMPSEY, Bridget	40	F	Unknown	23Ju02Jy
HENNESSY, Michael	17	M	Unknown	23Ju02Jy
Owen	16	M	Unknown	23Ju02Jy
Richd.	12	M	Unknown	23Ju02Jy
Wm.	10	M	Unknown	23Ju02Jy
KEEFE, Wm.	20	M	Unknown	23Ju02Jy
BURKE, Michael	21	M	Unknown	23Ju02Jy
TERRALL, Patrick	28	M	Unknown	23Ju02Jy
REILLY, Peter	24	M	Unknown	23Ju02Jy
DUNN, Peter	26	M	Unknown	23Ju02Jy
MALONEY, Johanna	24	F	Unknown	23Ju02Jy
MORRAN, Eliza	21	F	Unknown	23Ju02Jy
MALOONEY, Thomas	14	M	Unknown	23Ju02Jy
GLARGAN, Charles	26	M	Unknown	23Ju02Jy
KEEFE, Wm.	24	M	Unknown	23Ju02Jy
HASTEN, Michael	22	M	Unknown	23Ju02Jy
COLES, Patrick	18	M	Unknown	23Ju02Jy
BRIAN, Richd.	28	M	Unknown	23Ju02Jy
Michael	16	M	Unknown	23Ju02Jy
LYWECKE, Michael	26	M	Unknown	23Ju02Jy
Catherine	22	F	Unknown	23Ju02Jy
MCINERNY, Brian	24	M	Unknown	23Ju02Jy
Catherine	21	F	Unknown	23Ju02Jy
CUSACK, Mose	53	F	Unknown	23Ju02Jy
Anne	23	F	Unknown	23Ju02Jy
EUSECT, Michael	25	M	Unknown	23Ju02Jy
EAGAN, Maurice	27	M	Unknown	23Ju02Jy
CONOLLY, John	50	M	Unknown	23Ju02Jy
Mary	50	F	Unknown	23Ju02Jy
John	15	M	Unknown	23Ju02Jy
Mary	12	F	Unknown	23Ju02Jy
Thos.	11	M	Unknown	23Ju02Jy
CONNOLLY, Margt.	9	F	Child	23Ju02Jy
Michael	7	M	Child	23Ju02Jy
James	5	M	Child	23Ju02Jy
Patrick	3	M	Child	23Ju02Jy
WASON, Patrick	50	M	Unknown	23Ju02Jy
GLEASON, Mary	27	F	Unknown	23Ju02Jy
James	16	M	Unknown	23Ju02Jy
Patrick	15	M	Unknown	23Ju02Jy
BRIAN, Thos.	24	M	Unknown	23Ju02Jy
John	25	M	Unknown	23Ju02Jy
FLANNEGAN, Margt.	20	F	Unknown	23Ju02Jy
MUSTOGH, Bridget	22	F	Unknown	23Ju02Jy
Betty	20	F	Unknown	23Ju02Jy
MCMANUS, Patrick	27	M	Unknown	23Ju02Jy
Terrence	16	M	Unknown	23Ju02Jy
Mary	16	F	Unknown	23Ju02Jy
Campbell	27	M	Unknown	23Ju02Jy
CREA, Maria	25	F	Unknown	23Ju02Jy
JUDGE, Patrick	28	M	Unknown	23Ju02Jy
CONNOLLY, Thos.	26	M	Unknown	23Ju02Jy
FARRELL, Edward	28	M	Unknown	23Ju02Jy
KELLY, James	18	M	Unknown	23Ju02Jy
MCEARLY, Mary	29	F	Unknown	23Ju02Jy
SULLIVAN, Bridget	30	F	Unknown	23Ju02Jy
MCNAMARER, Eliza	30	F	Unknown	23Ju02Jy
MCMURTY, Hugh	19	M	Unknown	23Ju02Jy
FARRELLY, Patrick	45	M	Unknown	23Ju02Jy
CANIMANER, Ellen	20	F	Unknown	23Ju02Jy
BURKE, John	15	M	Unknown	23Ju02Jy
HENNING, John	40	M	Unknown	23Ju02Jy
MALONY, Anne	17	F	Unknown	23Ju02Jy
HOGAN, Michael	19	M	Unknown	23Ju02Jy
Daniel	10	M	Unknown	23Ju02Jy
MCGILL, Thos.	18	M	Unknown	23Ju02Jy
WHEALAN, John	30	M	Unknown	23Ju02Jy
CAHALANN, Thos.	35	M	Unknown	23Ju02Jy
Ann	40	F	Unknown	23Ju02Jy
Bridget	14	F	Unknown	23Ju02Jy
John	11	M	Unknown	23Ju02Jy
Thos.	8	M	Child	23Ju02Jy
MCKEE, Susan	20	F	Unknown	23Ju02Jy
Neal	18	M	Unknown	23Ju02Jy
MCKENNA, Terrence	20	M	Unknown	23Ju02Jy
RAFFERTY, Sarah-Ann	20	F	Unknown	23Ju02Jy
MOLLIN, Dennis	12	M	Unknown	23Ju02Jy
HEALIN, Bridget	14	F	Unknown	23Ju02Jy
MCCAB, Rearden	14	F	Unknown	23Ju02Jy
CARROLL, Patrick	19	M	Unknown	23Ju02Jy
NEILLY, Patrick	14	M	Unknown	23Ju02Jy

NAMES OF PASSENGERS	AGE	SEX	OCCUPATIONS	DATE PORT SHIP
COOLLY, Francis	13	M	Unknown	23Ju02Jy
Patrick	10	M	Unknown	23Ju02Jy
MCGRATH, Catherine	24	F	Unknown	23Ju02Jy
FIELY, Catherine	17	F	Unknown	23Ju02Jy
Anne	11	F	Unknown	23Ju02Jy
SULLIVAN, John	24	M	Unknown	23Ju02Jy
MCGUIRE, Abbey	17	F	Unknown	23Ju02Jy
Frances	19	F	Unknown	23Ju02Jy
MCQUINN, Patrick	23	M	Unknown	23Ju02Jy
CONNOLLY, Mary	20	F	Unknown	23Ju02Jy
FARLEY, Mary	28	F	Unknown	23Ju02Jy
James	4	M	Child	23Ju02Jy
Lawrence	8	M	Child	23Ju02Jy
REILLY, John	20	M	Unknown	23Ju02Jy
Phillip	22	M	Unknown	23Ju02Jy
Cathe.	15	F	Unknown	23Ju02Jy
Johanna	11	F	Unknown	23Ju02Jy
HEGAN, James	18	M	Unknown	23Ju02Jy
Sarah	18	F	Unknown	23Ju02Jy
MULLEN, Michael	14	M	Unknown	23Ju02Jy
CONNOR, Mary	25	F	Unknown	23Ju02Jy
Louisa	17	F	Unknown	23Ju02Jy
EGDELL, U	.10	M	Infant	23Ju02Jy
MCCABE, Owen	22	M	Unknown	23Ju02Jy
Terrance	16	M	Unknown	23Ju02Jy
Bridget	20	F	Unknown	23Ju02Jy
MONAGHAN, Patk.	21	M	Unknown	23Ju02Jy
Anne	18	F	Unknown	23Ju02Jy
MCKERWAN, John	20	M	Unknown	23Ju02Jy
CABELL, Pat	26	M	Unknown	23Ju02Jy
MCCANN, Betsey	18	F	Unknown	23Ju02Jy
CARR, Biddy	18	F	Unknown	23Ju02Jy
WATTERSON, Pat	36	M	Unknown	23Ju02Jy
Rose	28	F	Unknown	23Ju02Jy
Margt.	26	F	Unknown	23Ju02Jy
John	8	M	Child	23Ju02Jy
DOOGAN, Thos.	15	M	Unknown	23Ju02Jy
MALLIGAN, Wm.	21	M	Unknown	23Ju02Jy
BURKE, Thos.	21	M	Unknown	23Ju02Jy
Mary	19	F	Unknown	23Ju02Jy
MEWLAN, John	26	F	Unknown	23Ju02Jy
Thos.	23	M	Unknown	23Ju02Jy
Richd.	18	M	Unknown	23Ju02Jy
Henry	19	M	Unknown	23Ju02Jy
Peter	16	M	Unknown	23Ju02Jy
MAGOWAN, John	35	M	Unknown	23Ju02Jy
Isabella	34	F	Unknown	23Ju02Jy
QUITY, James	22	M	Unknown	23Ju02Jy
KENNAN, Catherine	25	F	Unknown	23Ju02Jy

E.Z. 23 JUNE 1849

From Liverpool

NAMES OF PASSENGERS	AGE	SEX	OCCUPATIONS	DATE PORT SHIP
DONAHY, Thos.	29	M	Carpenter	23Ju02Ky
BURKE, John	28	M	Carpenter	23Ju02Ky
MCCARTHY, Therence	40	M	Laborer	23Ju02Ky
CROWLEY, James	28	M	Laborer	23Ju02Ky
Ellen	21	F	Laborer	23Ju02Ky
Michl.	19	M	Laborer	23Ju02Ky
TIRNEY, Chrisotpher	18	M	Laborer	23Ju02Ky
Cathn.	16	F	Laborer	23Ju02Ky
FLOOD, Rose	18	F	Laborer	23Ju02Ky
MCCABE, Mary	18	F	Laborer	23Ju02Ky
EARLY, Bridget	18	F	Laborer	23Ju02Ky
Thos.	20	M	Laborer	23Ju02Ky
REILLY, Patt	22	M	Laborer	23Ju02Ky
Margt.	20	F	Laborer	23Ju02Ky
IGO, Thos.	29	M	Laborer	23Ju02Ky
IGO, Ellen	16	F	Laborer	23Ju02Ky
BRINNANT, Geo.	20	M	Laborer	23Ju02Ky
Cath.	30	F	Farmer	23Ju02Ky
Nicholas	29	M	Farmer	23Ju02Ky
BRENNANT, James	19	M	Farmer	23Ju02Ky
Eliza	44	F	Farmer	23Ju02Ky
CUSACK, Eliza	29	F	Farmer	23Ju02Ky
Thomas	21	M	Farmer	23Ju02Ky
RYAN, Jno.	30	M	Farmer	23Ju02Ky
MCDERMOTT, Mary-A.	30	F	Farmer	23Ju02Ky
MULKMAN, Mary	21	F	Farmer	23Ju02Ky
MULKENNAN, Ann	18	F	Farmer	23Ju02Ky
Honora	16	F	Farmer	23Ju02Ky
CORMICK, Marella	22	F	Farmer	23Ju02Ky
Julia	20	F	Farmer	23Ju02Ky
Margaret	40	M	Carpenter	23Ju02Ky
Michl.	20	M	Carpenter	23Ju02Ky
Edward	40	M	Carpenter	23Ju02Ky
MEHANT, James	25	M	Laborer	23Ju02Ky
CREIDEN, James	25	M	Laborer	23Ju02Ky
HIGGINS, Patt	30	M	Laborer	23Ju02Ky
TOOHEY, Darby	28	M	Laborer	23Ju02Ky
Martin	26	M	Laborer	23Ju02Ky
John	25	M	Laborer	23Ju02Ky
MAHEN, James	40	M	Farmer	23Ju02Ky
Lawrence	17	M	Farmer	23Ju02Ky
Julia	20	F	Unknown	23Ju02Ky
Ann	6	F	Child	23Ju02Ky
MAHER, Cathn.	11	F	Unknown	23Ju02Ky
MAHEN, Thos.	13	M	Farmer	23Ju02Ky
CONEY, James	45	M	Farmer	23Ju02Ky
Michael	18	M	Farmer	23Ju02Ky
Mary	22	F	Farmer	23Ju02Ky
Jane	13	F	Farmer	23Ju02Ky
HARTNEY, Michael	25	M	Farmer	23Ju02Ky
MCDUNNELL, James	25	M	Farmer	23Ju02Ky
FEELEY, Michael	18	M	Farmer	23Ju02Ky
John	13	M	Farmer	23Ju02Ky
GALIN, Patt	27	M	Farmer	23Ju02Ky
Michael	20	M	Farmer	23Ju02Ky
Michael	22	M	Farmer	23Ju02Ky
Bridget	23	F	Farmer	23Ju02Ky
SULLIVAN, Thos.	29	M	Laborer	23Ju02Ky
KELLY, Patt	45	M	Laborer	23Ju02Ky
Patt	7	M	Child	23Ju02Ky
Sarah	30	F	Laborer	23Ju02Ky
Cathiern.	10	F	Laborer	23Ju02Ky
Margaret	20	F	Unknown	23Ju02Ky
GATTLY, John	40	M	Laborer	23Ju02Ky
TRUMBLE, Michl.	25	M	Laborer	23Ju02Ky
HUNT, Cathrine	20	F	Laborer	23Ju02Ky
WILNE, Sarah	50	F	Laborer	23Ju02Ky
MCGARRY, Patt	45	M	Laborer	23Ju02Ky
KENNEDY, Ellen	20	F	Laborer	23Ju02Ky
BRYAN, David	50	M	Farmer	23Ju02Ky
John	24	M	Farmer	23Ju02Ky
Wm.	26	M	Farmer	23Ju02Ky
Honora	30	F	Farmer	23Ju02Ky
Ellen	17	F	Farmer	23Ju02Ky
MURPHY, David	30	M	Farmer	23Ju02Ky
Dennis	3	M	Child	23Ju02Ky
U	30	F	Unknown	23Ju02Ky
Ann	.06	F	Infant	23Ju02Ky
Ellen	2	F	Child	23Ju02Ky
Nancy	.06	F	Infant	23Ju02Ky
RAY, Ellen	18	F	Unknown	23Ju02Ky
Dennis	20	M	Unknown	23Ju02Ky
SWEENY, Wm.	20	M	Unknown	23Ju02Ky
Mary	18	F	Unknown	23Ju02Ky
KEARY, Mary	22	F	Laborer	23Ju02Ky
David	20	M	Laborer	23Ju02Ky
Ellen	10	F	Laborer	23Ju02Ky
CLARK, James	25	M	Laborer	23Ju02Ky
MURPHY, John	27	M	Laborer	23Ju02Ky
MORITY, John	20	M	Laborer	23Ju02Ky

NAMES OF PASSENGERS	AGE	SEX	OCCUPATIONS	DATE PORT SHIP
CHRISTY, John	20	M	Laborer	23Ju02Ky
LAPLER, Michl.	24	M	Laborer	23Ju02Ky
BRADY, Patt	24	M	Laborer	23Ju02Ky
Mary	20	F	Laborer	23Ju02Ky
COOK, Owen	24	M	Laborer	23Ju02Ky
MARTIN, John	18	M	Laborer	23Ju02Ky
FLOOD, Michael	29	M	Laborer	23Ju02Ky
John	17	M	Laborer	23Ju02Ky
SMITH, Robt.	15	M	Laborer	23Ju02Ky
Ann	15	F	Laborer	23Ju02Ky
LYNCH, Biddy	18	F	Laborer	23Ju02Ky
KELLY, Margt.	12	F	Laborer	23Ju02Ky
FITZPATRICK, Hugh	24	M	Laborer	23Ju02Ky
MARTIN, John	27	M	Laborer	23Ju02Ky
Mary	21	F	Laborer	23Ju02Ky
HANAGAN, Patt	24	M	Laborer	23Ju02Ky
James	26	M	Laborer	23Ju02Ky
HANEGAN, Mary	21	F	Laborer	23Ju02Ky
ROURKE, Terence	40	M	Laborer	23Ju02Ky
CRONAN, Pat	20	M	Laborer	23Ju02Ky
KELCHER, Thos.	20	M	Laborer	23Ju02Ky
CLARKE, Tim	39	M	Laborer	23Ju02Ky
BUCKLEY, John	20	M	Laborer	23Ju02Ky
CRINELL, Robt.	27	M	Laborer	23Ju02Ky
U	27	F	Laborer	23Ju02Ky
Ann	.04	F	Infant	23Ju02Ky
WRIGHT, Geo.	20	M	Laborer	23Ju02Ky
BIRMINGHAM, Thos.	30	M	Laborer	23Ju02Ky
U	30	F	Laborer	23Ju02Ky
Ann	.06	F	Infant	23Ju02Ky
WALSH, Mary	30	F	Unknown	23Ju02Ky
SHANNEN, Patt	18	M	Unknown	23Ju02Ky
SHIRT, Patt	27	M	Unknown	23Ju02Ky
MALY, Patt	20	M	Unknown	23Ju02Ky
BLAKELY, Jane	17	F	Unknown	23Ju02Ky
Maria	28	F	Unknown	23Ju02Ky
John	24	M	Unknown	23Ju02Ky
MARSDEN, John	48	M	Joiner	23Ju02Ky
U	29	F	Unknown	23Ju02Ky
Mari	19	F	Unknown	23Ju02Ky
STEAD, David	24	M	Unknown	23Ju02Ky
John-E.	.11	M	Infant	23Ju02Ky
Ann	22	F	Unknown	23Ju02Ky
ASHTEN, Thomas	12	M	Miller	23Ju02Ky
Thomas	13	M	Miller	23Ju02Ky
John	11	M	Miller	23Ju02Ky
William	7	M	Child	23Ju02Ky
Jane	39	F	Unknown	23Ju02Ky
Mary	18	F	Unknown	23Ju02Ky
Eliza	16	F	Unknown	23Ju02Ky
KAY, Matt	29	M	Unknown	23Ju02Ky
GIDDISEN, Benjm.	28	M	Unknown	23Ju02Ky
FITZSIMMONS, John	20	M	Unknown	23Ju02Ky
Cathn.	20	F	Unknown	23Ju02Ky
WALKER, C.	20	F	Unknown	23Ju02Ky
Margaret	18	F	Unknown	23Ju02Ky
Mary	16	F	Unknown	23Ju02Ky
Robt.	18	M	Unknown	23Ju02Ky
DUNN, Matt.	40	M	Unknown	23Ju02Ky
LYNCH, Biddy	21	F	Unknown	23Ju02Ky
HEALY, Mary	20	F	Unknown	23Ju02Ky
LARKIN, Julia	22	F	Unknown	23Ju02Ky
BARCLAY, James	27	M	Unknown	23Ju02Ky
MASTERS, John	23	M	Unknown	23Ju02Ky
SMITH, James	20	M	Laborer	23Ju02Ky
Margaret	20	F	Laborer	23Ju02Ky
MASTERSON, Cath.	20	F	Laborer	23Ju02Ky
Michl.	20	M	Laborer	23Ju02Ky
WARD, John	20	M	Laborer	23Ju02Ky
HARTNER, Mary	20	F	Laborer	23Ju02Ky
PHALEN, Ann	30	F	Laborer	23Ju02Ky
Jane	.08	F	Infant	23Ju02Ky
Patt	9	M	Child	23Ju02Ky
CASHIER, John	20	M	Unknown	23Ju02Ky
CASSIDY, Patt	30	M	Unknown	23Ju02Ky

NAMES OF PASSENGERS	AGE	SEX	OCCUPATIONS	DATE PORT SHIP
MCCORMACK, Patt	30	M	Unknown	23Ju02Ky
KNIGHT, Eliza	26	F	Unknown	23Ju02Ky
QUIGLEY, Edwd.	26	M	Unknown	23Ju02Ky
SMITH, John	20	M	Unknown	23Ju02Ky
BERTH, Geo.	20	M	Unknown	23Ju02Ky
PEARSON, John	25	M	Unknown	23Ju02Ky
FARRELL, Ann	18	F	Laborer	23Ju02Ky
ANDERSON, H.	20	F	Laborer	23Ju02Ky
BRACKEN, Sarah	20	F	Laborer	23Ju02Ky
James	18	M	Laborer	23Ju02Ky
CHOIR, Patt	25	M	Laborer	23Ju02Ky
ROHE, Christ.	30	M	Laborer	23Ju02Ky
BOUGHEN, James	16	M	Laborer	23Ju02Ky
GAHARTY, David	30	M	Laborer	23Ju02Ky
Mary	25	F	Laborer	23Ju02Ky
Ann	4	F	Child	23Ju02Ky
MCCABE, Miles	25	M	Child	23Ju02Ky
RUSSELL, John	28	M	Child	23Ju02Ky
BOOLIN, John	28	M	Child	23Ju02Ky
BRADLY, John	25	M	Child	23Ju02Ky
Patt	23	M	Unknown	23Ju02Ky
FLORING, John	27	M	Clerk	23Ju02Ky
BURNES, John	33	M	Unknown	23Ju02Ky
COLEMAN, Michl.	29	M	Unknown	23Ju02Ky
BRAUGHEL, James	23	M	Unknown	23Ju02Ky
Eliza	22	F	Unknown	23Ju02Ky
BRADLY, James	33	M	Unknown	23Ju02Ky
James	33	M	Laborer	23Ju02Ky
Ann	7	F	Child	23Ju02Ky
BURKE, Patt	20	M	Unknown	23Ju02Ky
KEGAN, Bridget	20	F	Unknown	23Ju02Ky
CARROLL, Mary	40	F	Unknown	23Ju02Ky
Maria	16	F	Unknown	23Ju02Ky
James	6	M	Child	23Ju02Ky
DINEGAN, Wm.	11	M	Unknown	23Ju02Ky
KEANY, Barny	15	M	Unknown	23Ju02Ky
KENAN, Phil.	21	M	Unknown	23Ju02Ky
RYAN, Thos.	19	M	Unknown	23Ju02Ky
KENEDY, Jane	34	F	Unknown	23Ju02Ky
CLARKE, Matt	20	M	Unknown	23Ju02Ky
CINLIN, Luke	27	M	Unknown	23Ju02Ky
CLARKE, Michl.	4	M	Child	23Ju02Ky
KELLY, Cathr.	22	F	Unknown	23Ju02Ky
CHANCE, Margt.	14	F	Unknown	23Ju02Ky
KELLY, Brid.	20	F	Unknown	23Ju02Ky
MARTIN, James	29	F	Unknown	23Ju02Ky
Cathrine	40	F	Unknown	23Ju02Ky
Mary	15	F	Unknown	23Ju02Ky
TIGH, Biddy	24	F	Unknown	23Ju02Ky
DRISCOLL, Ellen	40	F	Unknown	23Ju02Ky
WALSH, Wm.	42	M	Unknown	23Ju02Ky
DENELLY, Patt	25	M	Unknown	23Ju02Ky
Owen	26	M	Unknown	23Ju02Ky
MEKEEN, John	20	M	Unknown	23Ju02Ky
GILSHINAN, Pat	29	M	Unknown	23Ju02Ky
MARTIN, Lawr.	17	M	Unknown	23Ju02Ky
REYNOLDS, Jno.M.	36	M	Unknown	23Ju02Ky
GREYING, Cathn.	13	F	Unknown	23Ju02Ky
DALY, Frank	25	M	Unknown	23Ju02Ky
Eliza	20	F	Unknown	23Ju02Ky
EGAR, U-Mrs.	70	F	Unknown	23Ju02Ky
Thos.	40	M	Unknown	23Ju02Ky
John	36	M	Unknown	23Ju02Ky
ROCHE, Alice	30	F	Laborer	23Ju02Ky
GRAY, Michl.	22	M	Laborer	23Ju02Ky
FERRIS, Arthur	25	M	Laborer	23Ju02Ky
QUIGLY, Eliza	29	F	Laborer	23Ju02Ky
FINNAR, Mary	29	F	Laborer	23Ju02Ky
BORDEN, Bridget	30	F	Laborer	23Ju02Ky
MCCORMICK, John	24	M	Laborer	23Ju02Ky
FITZPATRICK, Danl.	20	M	Laborer	23Ju02Ky
HANAGHAN, Jane	17	F	Laborer	23Ju02Ky

ARGYLE 26 JUNE 1849

From Liverpool

NAMES OF PASSENGERS	AGE	SEX	OCCUPATIONS	DATE PORT SHIP
HEALY, Thos.	33	M	Laborer	26Ju02Lf
Bridget	24	F	Laborer	26Ju02Lf
Thos.	.06	M	Infant	26Ju02Lf
Donald	28	M	Laborer	26Ju02Lf
Mgt.	28	F	Laborer	26Ju02Lf
Ellen	18	F	Laborer	26Ju02Lf
REARDON, Michl.	16	M	Laborer	26Ju02Lf
Mary	18	F	Laborer	26Ju02Lf
MONGORY, Daniel	25	M	Laborer	26Ju02Lf
Nancy	25	F	Laborer	26Ju02Lf
MCKELFY, Hen.	18	M	Laborer	26Ju02Lf
HEARTHY, Timothy	40	M	Laborer	26Ju02Lf
Mary	36	F	Laborer	26Ju02Lf
Mary	8	F	Child	26Ju02Lf
James	6	M	Child	26Ju02Lf
William	4	M	Child	26Ju02Lf
Thos.	.06	M	Infant	26Ju02Lf
REES, Wm.	24	M	Laborer	26Ju02Lf
Magdalene	20	F	Laborer	26Ju02Lf
Wm.	5	M	Child	26Ju02Lf
Jane	1	F	Child	26Ju02Lf
Maria	.04	F	Infant	26Ju02Lf
WILLIAMS, Philip	28	M	Laborer	26Ju02Lf
Mary	32	F	Laborer	26Ju02Lf
Sarah	10	F	Laborer	26Ju02Lf
STEWART, John	30	M	Laborer	26Ju02Lf
Chars.	25	M	Laborer	26Ju02Lf
MOONEY, Ann	13	F	Laborer	26Ju02Lf
MCNAMARA, Thos.	30	M	Laborer	26Ju02Lf
Margt.	40	F	Laborer	26Ju02Lf
James	10	M	Laborer	26Ju02Lf
Bridget	20	F	Laborer	26Ju02Lf
ROSS, Mark	29	M	Laborer	26Ju02Lf
SHANE, Henry	34	M	Laborer	26Ju02Lf
MONAGHAN, Judy	25	F	Laborer	26Ju02Lf
WREN, John	28	M	Laborer	26Ju02Lf
Margt.	24	F	Laborer	26Ju02Lf
Sarah-Jane	5	F	Child	26Ju02Lf
Mary-E.	1	F	Child	26Ju02Lf
ANGMER, John	32	M	Laborer	26Ju02Lf
CONOLLY, Pat	30	M	Laborer	26Ju02Lf
Margt.	20	F	Laborer	26Ju02Lf
Ellen	2	F	Child	26Ju02Lf
John	.11	M	Infant	26Ju02Lf
Mary	.01	F	Infant	26Ju02Lf
LUNGAN, Daniel	56	M	Laborer	26Ju02Lf
Mary	40	F	Laborer	26Ju02Lf
Edward	13	M	Laborer	26Ju02Lf
Mary	11	F	Laborer	26Ju02Lf
ATHELD, Wm.	18	M	Laborer	26Ju02Lf
QUINLAN, Lawrence	26	M	Laborer	26Ju02Lf
KINGSTON, John	29	M	Laborer	26Ju02Lf
BRYAN, Pat	18	M	Laborer	26Ju02Lf
Ann	16	F	Laborer	26Ju02Lf
DORGAN, Terrence	22	M	Laborer	26Ju02Lf
HESSBERG, Jeremiah	21	M	Laborer	26Ju02Lf
RORKE, Edward	21	M	Laborer	26Ju02Lf
LEARY, Edward	17	M	Laborer	26Ju02Lf
CONAHAN, Mary	21	F	Laborer	26Ju02Lf
WALSH, Ellen	18	F	Laborer	26Ju02Lf
WHITE, John	40	M	Laborer	26Ju02Lf
George	16	M	Laborer	26Ju02Lf
Mary	12	F	Laborer	26Ju02Lf
Wm.	9	M	Child	26Ju02Lf
RORKE, Pat	20	M	Laborer	26Ju02Lf
LEAMY, Thos.	12	M	Laborer	26Ju02Lf
MORRISON, Thos.	25	M	Laborer	26Ju02Lf
ODONNELL, Barbara	50	F	Laborer	26Ju02Lf
James	30	M	Laborer	26Ju02Lf
John	20	M	Laborer	26Ju02Lf
Pat	24	M	Laborer	26Ju02Lf
Bridget	20	F	Laborer	26Ju02Lf
Cath.	18	F	Laborer	26Ju02Lf
Barbara	7	F	Child	26Ju02Lf
WALSH, Martin	24	M	Laborer	26Ju02Lf
FORT, John	28	M	Laborer	26Ju02Lf
Margt.	28	F	Laborer	26Ju02Lf
FOY, John	30	M	Laborer	26Ju02Lf
BYRNE, Wm.	25	M	Laborer	26Ju02Lf
WHITE, Pat	18	M	Laborer	26Ju02Lf
HALE, Henry	50	M	Laborer	26Ju02Lf
Mary	61	F	Laborer	26Ju02Lf
Robt.	22	M	Laborer	26Ju02Lf
Geo.	13	M	Laborer	26Ju02Lf
BULLEN, Susan	11	F	Laborer	26Ju02Lf
HALL, John	22	M	Laborer	26Ju02Lf
MCCULLERS, Pat	22	M	Laborer	26Ju02Lf
MCNANE, Cath.	25	F	Laborer	26Ju02Lf
ONEIL, Henry	20	M	Laborer	26Ju02Lf
Mary	21	F	Laborer	26Ju02Lf
JOHNSTON, John	25	M	Laborer	26Ju02Lf
James	20	M	Laborer	26Ju02Lf
Thomas	32	M	Laborer	26Ju02Lf
LALLY, John	25	M	Laborer	26Ju02Lf
Wm.	20	M	Laborer	26Ju02Lf
Mary	21	F	Laborer	26Ju02Lf
JOHNSTON, Francis	25	M	Laborer	26Ju02Lf
STEWART, Samuel	20	M	Laborer	26Ju02Lf
MCMENOMY, Ann	20	F	Laborer	26Ju02Lf
Margt.	16	F	Laborer	26Ju02Lf
MCGRATH, Edward	20	M	Laborer	26Ju02Lf
Johanna	20	F	Laborer	26Ju02Lf
WALKER, Francis	36	M	Laborer	26Ju02Lf
Frances	32	F	Laborer	26Ju02Lf
Joseph	10	M	Laborer	26Ju02Lf
METLIZE, Sebastn.	52	M	Laborer	26Ju02Lf
Ann	28	F	Laborer	26Ju02Lf
Ann	6	F	Child	26Ju02Lf
Martha	4	F	Child	26Ju02Lf
MCRUAN, Pat	22	M	Laborer	26Ju02Lf
John	28	M	Laborer	26Ju02Lf
FAY, Pat	60	M	Laborer	26Ju02Lf
Mary	19	F	Laborer	26Ju02Lf
Anne	17	F	Laborer	26Ju02Lf
Michl.	13	M	Laborer	26Ju02Lf
John	13	M	Laborer	26Ju02Lf
Pat	10	M	Laborer	26Ju02Lf
Ellen	7	F	Child	26Ju02Lf
James	6	M	Child	26Ju02Lf
FLINN, Biddy	30	F	Laborer	26Ju02Lf
FARRELL, Thos.	25	M	Laborer	26Ju02Lf
FLYNN, Michl.	9	M	Child	26Ju02Lf
Mary	7	F	Child	26Ju02Lf
James	4	M	Child	26Ju02Lf
M---	2	U	Child	26Ju02Lf
Thos.	.00	M	Infant	26Ju02Lf
DAVEN, John	25	M	Laborer	26Ju02Lf
WALLACE, Thos.	28	M	Laborer	26Ju02Lf
HEFFERAN, James	35	M	Laborer	26Ju02Lf
MCGRATH, John	28	M	Laborer	26Ju02Lf
ENNIS, Edw.	20	M	Laborer	26Ju02Lf
BOUCHER, Richd.	25	M	Laborer	26Ju02Lf
Mary	23	F	Laborer	26Ju02Lf
Michl.	22	M	Laborer	26Ju02Lf
Cath.	30	F	Laborer	26Ju02Lf
NOONAN, Pat	15	M	Laborer	26Ju02Lf
Thos.	20	M	Laborer	26Ju02Lf
WALLACE, John	18	M	Laborer	26Ju02Lf
BOUCHER, Mary	11	F	Laborer	26Ju02Lf
Mary	7	F	Child	26Ju02Lf

NAMES OF PASSENGERS	AGE	SEX	OCCUPATIONS	DATE PORT SHIP
BOUCHER, Michl.	6	M	Child	26Ju02Lf
James	3	M	Child	26Ju02Lf
HANLEY, Ann	18	F	Laborer	26Ju02Lf
Peter	16	M	Laborer	26Ju02Lf
DOHERTY, James	30	M	Laborer	26Ju02Lf
Mary	45	F	Laborer	26Ju02Lf
John	25	M	Laborer	26Ju02Lf
MCALLISTER, Saml.	3	M	Child	26Ju02Lf
HEALY, Cath.	2	F	Child	26Ju02Lf
HALL, Henry	27	M	Merchant	26Ju02Lf
Maria	25	F	Merchant	26Ju02Lf
Sarah	9	F	Child	26Ju02Lf
Edward-Thos.	7	M	Child	26Ju02Lf
Ann-Jane	7	F	Child	26Ju02Lf
Henry	6	M	Child	26Ju02Lf
James	3	M	Child	26Ju02Lf

SHELTON 26 JUNE 1849

From Belfast

NAMES OF PASSENGERS	AGE	SEX	OCCUPATIONS	DATE PORT SHIP
PARK, William	60	M	Laborer	26Ju05Kr
Eliza	54	F	Unknown	26Ju05Kr
Eliza	25	F	Unknown	26Ju05Kr
Nancy	23	F	Unknown	26Ju05Kr
William	19	M	Unknown	26Ju05Kr
James	16	M	Unknown	26Ju05Kr
John	14	M	Unknown	26Ju05Kr
Alexander	12	M	Unknown	26Ju05Kr
ADAMS, William	55	M	Unknown	26Ju05Kr
Elizabeth	40	F	Unknown	26Ju05Kr
Alexander	18	M	Unknown	26Ju05Kr
William	16	M	Unknown	26Ju05Kr
Martha	13	F	Unknown	26Ju05Kr
BECK, Thomas	20	M	Unknown	26Ju05Kr
BAILEY, James	19	M	Unknown	26Ju05Kr
QUINN, Jane-E.	31	F	Unknown	26Ju05Kr
Ann	.00	F	Infant	26Ju05Kr
WRITE, William	18	M	Unknown	26Ju05Kr
LONG, William	23	M	Unknown	26Ju05Kr
MOORE, William	17	M	Unknown	26Ju05Kr
Margaret	31	F	Unknown	26Ju05Kr
MARTIN, Eliza	21	F	Unknown	26Ju05Kr
MORRISON, Eliza	19	F	Unknown	26Ju05Kr
COPELAND, Sarah	20	F	Unknown	26Ju05Kr
MCQUITTY, Wm.J.	19	M	Unknown	26Ju05Kr
DAVEY, Henry	27	M	Unknown	26Ju05Kr
MCGORIE, Pat	23	M	Unknown	26Ju05Kr
TROOPE, Mary	25	F	Unknown	26Ju05Kr
MCILVOGUE, Ellen	21	F	Unknown	26Ju05Kr
DONOHUE, Rose	25	F	Unknown	26Ju05Kr
PRESLEY, Wm.	30	M	Unknown	26Ju05Kr
Latitia	28	F	Unknown	26Ju05Kr
Sophia	11	F	Unknown	26Ju05Kr
Jane-E.	7	F	Child	26Ju05Kr
William	5	M	Child	26Ju05Kr
Isabella	.00	F	Infant	26Ju05Kr
WATSON, Joseph	24	M	Unknown	26Ju05Kr
Isabella	20	F	Unknown	26Ju05Kr
John	20	M	Unknown	26Ju05Kr
PATTERSON, Wm.	44	M	Unknown	26Ju05Kr
Samuel	17	M	Unknown	26Ju05Kr
James	15	M	Unknown	26Ju05Kr
AGNEW, Daniel	38	M	Unknown	26Ju05Kr
HUGHES, Bridget	24	F	Unknown	26Ju05Kr
HUNTER, John	62	M	Unknown	26Ju05Kr
Elizth.	52	F	Unknown	26Ju05Kr
James	18	M	Unknown	26Ju05Kr
Jannett	26	F	Unknown	26Ju05Kr
HUNTER, Robt.J.	13	M	Unknown	26Ju05Kr
Rosannah	.00	F	Infant	26Ju05Kr
EVANS, Thos.	60	M	Unknown	26Ju05Kr
Thos.	32	M	Unknown	26Ju05Kr
Kate	20	F	Unknown	26Ju05Kr
Mary	.00	F	Infant	26Ju05Kr
Chris	.00	M	Infant	26Ju05Kr
MORAN, Ann	30	F	Unknown	26Ju05Kr
WHITEMAN, Adam	24	M	Unknown	26Ju05Kr
KEATING, John	28	M	Unknown	26Ju05Kr
PARKINSON, William	28	M	Unknown	26Ju05Kr
DUNN, Robert	25	M	Unknown	26Ju05Kr
HENDERSON, David	15	M	Unknown	26Ju05Kr
DICKSON, Nancy	21	F	Unknown	26Ju05Kr
RANSOM, Ann-J.	20	F	Unknown	26Ju05Kr
MCCAFFREY, James	26	M	Unknown	26Ju05Kr
PENY, James	24	M	Unknown	26Ju05Kr
CRAIG, Thos.	24	M	Unknown	26Ju05Kr
Mary	25	F	Unknown	26Ju05Kr
LITTLE, Margt.	24	F	Unknown	26Ju05Kr
HONEYFORD, Elizth.	28	F	Unknown	26Ju05Kr
Ann	14	F	Unknown	26Ju05Kr
NICKELSON, Elizth.	23	F	Unknown	26Ju05Kr
PORTER, Wm.	50	M	Unknown	26Ju05Kr
Agnes	45	F	Unknown	26Ju05Kr
VALLELY, Mathew	24	M	Unknown	26Ju05Kr
Mary	22	F	Unknown	26Ju05Kr
John	.00	M	Infant	26Ju05Kr
STEWART, David	23	M	Unknown	26Ju05Kr
ELLIS, William	15	M	Unknown	26Ju05Kr
BELL, Wm.	50	M	Unknown	26Ju05Kr
Elizt.	50	F	Unknown	26Ju05Kr
Ann	20	F	Unknown	26Ju05Kr
James	18	M	Unknown	26Ju05Kr
Jane	16	F	Unknown	26Ju05Kr
Eliza	14	F	Unknown	26Ju05Kr
John	12	M	Unknown	26Ju05Kr
Susan	10	F	Unknown	26Ju05Kr
HANA, Margt.	24	F	Unknown	26Ju05Kr
Mary-M.	.00	F	Infant	26Ju05Kr
Elizt.	.00	F	Infant	26Ju05Kr
MCCREADY, Mary	20	F	Unknown	26Ju05Kr
MCKEOWN, Sarah	19	F	Unknown	26Ju05Kr
MCROBERTS, Wm.	35	M	Unknown	26Ju05Kr
Mary-A.	30	F	Unknown	26Ju05Kr
Jane	15	F	Unknown	26Ju05Kr
Charles	14	M	Unknown	26Ju05Kr
Mary-A.	10	F	Unknown	26Ju05Kr
Sarah	8	F	Child	26Ju05Kr
Wm.	6	M	Child	26Ju05Kr
Samuel	.00	M	Infant	26Ju05Kr
KEEMAN, James	21	M	Unknown	26Ju05Kr
SMITH, Alex.	23	M	Unknown	26Ju05Kr
MITCHELL, Wm.	20	M	Unknown	26Ju05Kr
CARMICHAEL, Jas.	22	M	Unknown	26Ju05Kr
HAGG, Robt.	19	M	Unknown	26Ju05Kr
GORMAN, Margt.	00	F	Unknown	26Ju05Kr
STRAINEY, Rich.	22	M	Unknown	26Ju05Kr
KEAMES, John	28	M	Unknown	26Ju05Kr
STEWART, James	19	M	Unknown	26Ju05Kr
FEGAN, John	35	M	Unknown	26Ju05Kr
Ann	26	F	Unknown	26Ju05Kr
MCVEIGH, Wm.	20	M	Unknown	26Ju05Kr
DAVIDSON, James	28	M	Unknown	26Ju05Kr
Sarah	25	F	Unknown	26Ju05Kr
Mary	17	F	Unknown	26Ju05Kr
Martha	14	F	Unknown	26Ju05Kr
KAIG, Jane	20	F	Unknown	26Ju05Kr
CUMMINGS, Chas.	27	M	Unknown	26Ju05Kr
COSTELLO, Hugh	22	M	Unknown	26Ju05Kr
Rosa	23	F	Unknown	26Ju05Kr
HOOD, James	23	M	Unknown	26Ju05Kr
BELL, Eliza	20	F	Unknown	26Ju05Kr
MCCAULEY, Jas.	19	M	Unknown	26Ju05Kr
Jas.	20	M	Unknown	26Ju05Kr

NAMES OF PASSENGERS	AGE	SEX	OCCUPATIONS	DATE PORT SHIP
MCCABE, Betty	50	F	Unknown	26Ju05Kr
MCKILLUP, Nancy	13	F	Unknown	26Ju05Kr
WARSON, Margt.	14	F	Unknown	26Ju05Kr
ROBERTS, Hamilton	39	M	Unknown	26Ju05Kr
Hamilton	13	M	Unknown	26Ju05Kr
SAVAGE, Henry	16	M	Unknown	26Ju05Kr
CORVILLE, Kity	23	F	Unknown	26Ju05Kr
ALEXANDER, Elizt.	19	F	Unknown	26Ju05Kr
NICOLL, Mary-J.	19	F	Unknown	26Ju05Kr
MCCLUSKEY, Mary-T.	20	F	Unknown	26Ju05Kr
KILPATRICK, Alex.	20	M	Unknown	26Ju05Kr
VALENTINE, Robt.	20	M	Unknown	26Ju05Kr
KILPATRICK, Jane	25	F	Unknown	26Ju05Kr
SLOAN, Chas.	35	M	Unknown	26Ju05Kr
Mary-A.	30	F	Unknown	26Ju05Kr
Wm.	5	M	Child	26Ju05Kr
James	.00	M	Infant	26Ju05Kr
John	.00	M	Infant	26Ju05Kr
HUGHES, Henry	35	M	Unknown	26Ju05Kr
Mary	17	F	Unknown	26Ju05Kr
Francis	13	F	Unknown	26Ju05Kr
Kitty	8	F	Child	26Ju05Kr
Elizt.	.00	F	Infant	26Ju05Kr
Pat	36	M	Unknown	26Ju05Kr
FRAZIER, Jane	22	F	Unknown	26Ju05Kr
HUGHES, Margt.	22	F	Unknown	26Ju05Kr
MCCREA, Teresa	23	F	Unknown	26Ju05Kr
CARRIGAN, John	30	M	Unknown	26Ju05Kr
HEANY, Anthony	34	M	Unknown	26Ju05Kr
HUGHES, John	17	M	Unknown	26Ju05Kr
HEANY, John	22	M	Unknown	26Ju05Kr
Eliza	22	F	Unknown	26Ju05Kr
HUNTER, Mary	22	F	Unknown	26Ju05Kr
MCCLOUGH, Mary	19	F	Unknown	26Ju05Kr
KIRKPATRICK, Nancy	19	F	Unknown	26Ju05Kr
STEWART, Chas.	27	M	Unknown	26Ju05Kr
Elizt.	21	F	Unknown	26Ju05Kr
Ann	.00	F	Infant	26Ju05Kr
HUGHES, Jane	48	F	Unknown	26Ju05Kr
Danl.	16	M	Unknown	26Ju05Kr
Ann	13	F	Unknown	26Ju05Kr
Cath.	13	F	Unknown	26Ju05Kr
Sarah	12	F	Unknown	26Ju05Kr
John	7	M	Child	26Ju05Kr
KIRKPATRICK, Robt.	19	M	Unknown	26Ju05Kr
Jane	26	F	Unknown	26Ju05Kr
ELLIOT, Mary-A.	18	F	Unknown	26Ju05Kr
MOORE, Margt.	18	F	Unknown	26Ju05Kr
MALLEN, Mary	19	F	Unknown	26Ju05Kr
DONNELLY, John	23	M	Unknown	26Ju05Kr
MCGORDAN, Bridget	19	F	Unknown	26Ju05Kr
ELLER, Betty	17	F	Unknown	26Ju05Kr
Latitia	19	F	Unknown	26Ju05Kr
John	18	M	Unknown	26Ju05Kr
ORCE, Alex.	24	M	Unknown	26Ju05Kr
ESBITT, Wm.	25	M	Unknown	26Ju05Kr
UIN, U	.00	U	Infant	26Ju05Kr
ADDEN, D.H.	50	U	Unknown	26Ju05Kr
IYOM, U	30	U	Unknown	26Ju05Kr
YAN, Geo.	25	M	Unknown	26Ju05Kr
DON, M.J.Mrs.	20	F	Unknown	26Ju05Kr
ECKETTES, C.	30	U	Unknown	26Ju05Kr
OATES, A.F.	25	U	Unknown	26Ju05Kr
John	30	M	Unknown	26Ju05Kr

OREGON 26 JUNE 1849

From Limerick

NAMES OF PASSENGERS	AGE	SEX	OCCUPATIONS	DATE PORT SHIP
COUDON, Wm.	40	M	Farmer	26Ju35Kb
Anne	40	F	Unknown	26Ju35Kb
DWYER, Cath.	25	F	Unknown	26Ju35Kb
Cath.	16	F	Unknown	26Ju35Kb
CONDEN, Cath.	3	F	Child	26Ju35Kb
Mary	2	F	Child	26Ju35Kb
David	.00	M	Infant	26Ju35Kb
HARTIGAN, Maurice	23	M	Unknown	26Ju35Kb
Mary	20	F	Unknown	26Ju35Kb
HOGAN, Ellen	25	F	Unknown	26Ju35Kb
CARNEY, John	23	M	Unknown	26Ju35Kb
BRUNANE, John	50	M	Unknown	26Ju35Kb
Mary	40	F	Unknown	26Ju35Kb
Cath.	26	F	Unknown	26Ju35Kb
Thos.	8	M	Child	26Ju35Kb
Rich.	6	M	Child	26Ju35Kb
Cath.	.00	F	Infant	26Ju35Kb
LOONEY, Johannah	26	F	Unknown	26Ju35Kb
Pat	24	M	Unknown	26Ju35Kb
COLEMAN, James	26	M	Unknown	26Ju35Kb
MEEHAN, John	30	M	Unknown	26Ju35Kb
Ellen	22	F	Unknown	26Ju35Kb
Mich.	.00	M	Infant	26Ju35Kb
HARTIGAN, Biddy	26	F	Unknown	26Ju35Kb
QUAID, Cath.	25	F	Unknown	26Ju35Kb
QUADE, Tim	.00	M	Infant	26Ju35Kb
MULCAHY, Jas.	25	M	Unknown	26Ju35Kb
DWYER, Pat.	22	M	Unknown	26Ju35Kb
HILAND, Mich.	20	M	Unknown	26Ju35Kb
Edmond	20	M	Unknown	26Ju35Kb
CORMACK, Margt.	40	F	Unknown	26Ju35Kb
Ellen	25	F	Unknown	26Ju35Kb
HILAND, Cath.	20	F	Unknown	26Ju35Kb
DIRKIN, Mary	24	F	Unknown	26Ju35Kb
DOOLEY, Thady	28	M	Unknown	26Ju35Kb
DONOVAN, Jno.	28	M	Unknown	26Ju35Kb
Biddy	20	F	Unknown	26Ju35Kb
MUNNANE, Jas.	28	M	Unknown	26Ju35Kb
HILAND, Michl.	20	M	Unknown	26Ju35Kb
RYAN, John	26	M	Unknown	26Ju35Kb
Mary	30	F	Unknown	26Ju35Kb
NUNAN, Thos.	25	M	Farmer	26Ju35Kb
CONNORS, John	30	M	Unknown	26Ju35Kb
MCNAMARA, Ellen	19	F	Unknown	26Ju35Kb
Margt.	15	F	Unknown	26Ju35Kb
HALEY, Anne	28	F	Unknown	26Ju35Kb
Mary	4	F	Child	26Ju35Kb
Margt.	.00	F	Infant	26Ju35Kb
HERBERT, Stephen	24	M	Unknown	26Ju35Kb
BEHANE, Tos.	25	M	Unknown	26Ju35Kb
SLATTERY, Margt.	40	F	Unknown	26Ju35Kb
Ellen	7	F	Child	26Ju35Kb
CANNY, Ellen	20	F	Unknown	26Ju35Kb
CULLIHANE, Margt.	24	F	Unknown	26Ju35Kb
OKEEFE, Eliza	24	F	Unknown	26Ju35Kb
Cath.	22	F	Unknown	26Ju35Kb
MAID, John	28	M	Unknown	26Ju35Kb
MORAN, James	45	M	Unknown	26Ju35Kb
Margt.	25	F	Unknown	26Ju35Kb
Mary	15	F	Unknown	26Ju35Kb
Michl.	12	M	Unknown	26Ju35Kb
Patt	5	M	Child	26Ju35Kb
Ellen	.00	F	Infant	26Ju35Kb
MORRISSY, James	30	M	Unknown	26Ju35Kb
CONNELL, Jeffry	25	M	Unknown	26Ju35Kb

NAMES OF PASSENGERS	AGE	SEX	OCCUPATIONS	DATE PORT SHIP
COSGRIFF, Cath.	17	F	Unknown	26Ju35Kb
Mary	26	F	Unknown	26Ju35Kb
HARTIGAN, Bridget	22	F	Unknown	26Ju35Kb
RYAN, Michl.	30	M	Unknown	26Ju35Kb
MOONEY, Owen	30	M	Unknown	26Ju35Kb
CURTIN, Jas.	22	M	Unknown	26Ju35Kb
MCMAHON, John	20	M	Unknown	26Ju35Kb
SLATTERY, Danl.	6	M	Child	26Ju35Kb
KENNEDY, Hannah	16	F	Unknown	26Ju35Kb
HINCHY, Dennis	20	M	Unknown	26Ju35Kb
BAKER, Patt	28	M	Unknown	26Ju35Kb
SWEENEY, Danl.	28	M	Unknown	26Ju35Kb
James	19	M	Unknown	26Ju35Kb
Ellen	20	F	Unknown	26Ju35Kb
HINCHY, Bridget	23	F	Unknown	26Ju35Kb
BURNS, Elecia	20	F	Unknown	26Ju35Kb
WHEALON, Cath.	20	F	Unknown	26Ju35Kb
SHAUGHNESSY, Hannah	20	F	Unknown	26Ju35Kb
Margt.	16	F	Unknown	26Ju35Kb
HOGAN, Johannah	20	F	Unknown	26Ju35Kb
Honor	20	F	Unknown	26Ju35Kb
RYAN, Timy.	20	M	Unknown	26Ju35Kb
HOGAN, John	40	M	Unknown	26Ju35Kb
Mary	40	F	Unknown	26Ju35Kb
Ellen	12	F	Unknown	26Ju35Kb
Judy	10	F	Unknown	26Ju35Kb
Patt.	5	M	Child	26Ju35Kb
James	2	M	Child	26Ju35Kb
Margt.	.00	F	Infant	26Ju35Kb
MCDONNELL, Michl.	35	M	Unknown	26Ju35Kb
Honor	35	F	Unknown	26Ju35Kb
Maria	16	F	Unknown	26Ju35Kb
Michl.	12	M	Unknown	26Ju35Kb
John	12	M	Unknown	26Ju35Kb
William	6	M	Child	26Ju35Kb
Edmund	4	M	Child	26Ju35Kb
Biddy	.00	F	Infant	26Ju35Kb
HANALY, Darby	30	M	Unknown	26Ju35Kb
Ellen	30	F	Unknown	26Ju35Kb
Eliza	.00	F	Infant	26Ju35Kb
RYAN, Mary	20	F	Unknown	26Ju35Kb
CLANCHY, Biddy	26	F	Unknown	26Ju35Kb
Patt.	.00	M	Infant	26Ju35Kb
GLEESON, John	40	M	Unknown	26Ju35Kb
Nory	13	F	Unknown	26Ju35Kb
RYAN, John	20	M	Unknown	26Ju35Kb
FLYNN, Wm.	22	M	Unknown	26Ju35Kb
QUIRK, M.	21	M	Unknown	26Ju35Kb
HANNIEN, Margt.	36	F	Unknown	26Ju35Kb
Nancy	14	F	Unknown	26Ju35Kb
Cath.	16	F	Unknown	26Ju35Kb
NIHILL, Jno.	26	M	Unknown	26Ju35Kb
HALORAN, Cath.	18	F	Unknown	26Ju35Kb
CULLIGAN, Thos.	20	M	Unknown	26Ju35Kb
Cath.	21	F	Unknown	26Ju35Kb
OLOUGHLIN, M.	14	M	Unknown	26Ju35Kb
Lucy	6	F	Child	26Ju35Kb
RYAN, Jno.	22	M	Unknown	26Ju35Kb
DINEEN, Jno.	20	M	Unknown	26Ju35Kb
Patt.	20	M	Unknown	26Ju35Kb
OKELLY, Mary	35	F	Unknown	26Ju35Kb
John	5	M	Child	26Ju35Kb
YOUNG, Leonard	35	M	Unknown	26Ju35Kb
Anne	25	F	Unknown	26Ju35Kb
MANS, Margt.	20	F	Unknown	26Ju35Kb
CLIFFORD, Wm.	16	M	Unknown	26Ju35Kb

ELIZA-CAROLINE 26 JUNE 1849

From Liverpool

NAMES OF PASSENGERS	AGE	SEX	OCCUPATIONS	DATE PORT SHIP
LEANANON, Mary	20	F	Spinster	26Ju02Lb
LENANON, Ann	18	F	Spinster	26Ju02Lb
Francis	26	M	Laborer	26Ju02Lb
PRIOR, Peter	22	M	Laborer	26Ju02Lb
HESLEY, Thos.	40	M	Laborer	26Ju02Lb
MCCARTHY, Elizabeth	20	F	Spinster	26Ju02Lb
RICE, Edwd.	27	M	Farmer	26Ju02Lb
Jane (W)	25	F	None	26Ju02Lb
John	3	M	Child	26Ju02Lb
Jane	.09	F	Infant	26Ju02Lb
CLOKER, Edwd.	25	M	Blacksmith	26Ju02Lb
Willia--, Thos.	25	M	Unknown	26Ju02Lb
JENKINS, John	20	M	Farmer	26Ju02Lb
Mary (W)	25	F	None	26Ju02Lb
Thos.	4	M	Child	26Ju02Lb
Isaac	.08	M	Infant	26Ju02Lb
EVANS, John	50	M	Farmer	26Ju02Lb
U (W)	50	F	None	26Ju02Lb
Ann	27	F	Spinster	26Ju02Lb
Eliza	24	F	Spinster	26Ju02Lb
Charlotte	18	F	Spinster	26Ju02Lb
Margt.	14	F	Spinster	26Ju02Lb
Evan	13	M	None	26Ju02Lb
Sophia	10	F	Spinster	26Ju02Lb
Wm.	7	M	Child	26Ju02Lb
Mary	7	F	Child	26Ju02Lb
Reece	6	M	Child	26Ju02Lb
Martha	.09	F	Infant	26Ju02Lb
JONES, Edw.	39	M	Weaver	26Ju02Lb
U (W)	30	F	None	26Ju02Lb
Mary	8	F	Child	26Ju02Lb
Winifred	6	F	Child	26Ju02Lb
Jane	4	F	Child	26Ju02Lb
Margt. Died-At-Sea	.06	F	Infant	26Ju02Lb
WELCH, Edwd.	30	M	Laborer	26Ju02L
U (W)	30	F	None	26Ju02L
U Born-At-Sea	.00	U	Infant	26Ju02L
CUNNINGHAM, Wm.	30	M	Mechanic	26Ju02L
Jane (W)	24	F	None	26Ju02L
MCDONELL, Ann	30	F	Spinster	26Ju02L
RILEY, Brien	26	M	Laborer	26Ju02L
GAUGHEN, Edwd.	20	M	Laborer	26Ju02L
HERBERT, Mary	21	F	Spinster	26Ju02L
MOONEY, Mary	24	F	Spinster	26Ju02L
DALEY, Jas.	26	M	Laborer	26Ju02L
DEGNAN, Jas.	30	M	Gdnr	26Ju02L
FLANEGAN, Thos.	26	M	Laborer	26Ju02L
Michl.	22	M	Laborer	26Ju02L
Bridgt.	60	F	Wi	26Ju02L
DONLEY, Mary	3	F	Child	26Ju02L
GAMON, Christ.	50	M	Farmer	26Ju02L
GARMON, Cath. (W)	54	F	None	26Ju02L
James	60	M	Farmer	26Ju02L
Pat	20	F	Farmer	26Ju02L
Peter	18	M	Farmer	26Ju02L
Lawrence	15	M	Farmer	26Ju02L
Bridgt.	12	F	None	26Ju02
GANNON, John	10	M	None	26Ju02
Catha.	7	F	Child	26Ju02
Elizabeth	5	F	Child	26Ju02
Luke	38	M	Farmer	26Ju02
Owen	36	M	Farmer	26Ju02
Mary (W)	22	F	None	26Ju02

NAMES OF PASSENGERS		AGE	SEX	OCCUPATIONS	DATE PORT SHIP
NEARMAN, Math.		50	M	Farmer	26Ju02Lb
Julia	(W)	30	F	None	26Ju02Lb
John		9	M	Child	26Ju02Lb
Peter		7	M	Child	26Ju02Lb
Mary		5	F	Child	26Ju02Lb
Bridgt.		3	F	Child	26Ju02Lb
Julia		.09	F	Infant	26Ju02Lb
RILEY, John		40	M	Laborer	26Ju02Lb
CULLIN, Rich.		40	M	Carpenter	26Ju02Lb
BLUNTAL, Cath.		18	F	None	26Ju02Lb
LOUGHLAN, Pat		45	M	Laborer	26Ju02Lb
Pat		20	M	Laborer	26Ju02Lb
CAHILL, Michl.		35	M	Laborer	26Ju02Lb
Cath.	(W)	30	F	None	26Ju02Lb
Mary		10	F	None	26Ju02Lb
Frs.		.09	M	Infant	26Ju02Lb
CURLEY, Mary		17	F	Spinster	26Ju02Lb
DILLON, Martin		44	M	Farmer	26Ju02Lb
Peggy	(W)	40	F	None	26Ju02Lb
Ann		14	F	Spinster	26Ju02Lb
Judith		11	F	Spinster	26Ju02Lb
Lawrence		9	M	Child	26Ju02Lb
Pat		5	M	Child	26Ju02Lb
Margt.		2	F	Child	26Ju02Lb
FALNER, Elizabeth		25	F	Spinster	26Ju02Lb
MULLEN, Julia		20	F	Spinster	26Ju02Lb
Ellen		8	F	Child	26Ju02Lb
ONELLE, Honora		25	F	Spinster	26Ju02Lb
CAHILL, Jas.		10	M	None	26Ju02Lb
GABIN, Thos.		25	M	Farmer	26Ju02Lb
U	(W)	25	F	None	26Ju02Lb
GRAY, Thos.		20	M	Laborer	26Ju02Lb
BRENNEN, John		30	M	Laborer	26Ju02Lb
BRENAN, Cath.	(W)	25	F	None	26Ju02Lb
WHEALAN, Wm.		21	M	Shoemaker	26Ju02Lb
Jane	(W)	20	F	None	26Ju02Lb
THOMPSON, Sarah		20	F	Spinster	26Ju02Lb
ROSS, George		33	M	Goldsmith	26Ju02Lb
MORGAN, John		30	M	Farmer	26Ju02Lb
Evan		20	M	Carpenter	26Ju02Lb
BENNETT, Mary		20	F	Spinster	26Ju02Lb
GAVON, John		12	M	Farmer	26Ju02Lb
Maria		10	F	None	26Ju02Lb
Charles		9	M	Child	26Ju02Lb
JOHNSTON, Thos.		40	M	Cnf	26Ju02Lb
Maria		20	F	Spinster	26Ju02Lb
MCCAWEN, Can.		40	M	Laborer	26Ju02Lb
TIRENEY, John		30	M	Laborer	26Ju02Lb
KENNADY, James		25	M	Laborer	26Ju02Lb
WARD, Mich.		20	M	Laborer	26Ju02Lb
DORAN, Wm.		21	M	Laborer	26Ju02Lb
John		20	M	Laborer	26Ju02Lb
MULLVANY, Wm.		24	M	Farmer	26Ju02Lb
Chas.		24	M	Farmer	26Ju02Lb
Jane	(W)	21	F	None	26Ju02Lb
James		24	M	Farmer	26Ju02Lb
BLODSWORTH, Robt.		30	M	Laborer	26Ju02Lb
Elizabeth	(W)	26	F	None	26Ju02Lb
Thos.		2	M	Child	26Ju02Lb
Wm.		.06	M	Infant	26Ju02Lb
SMITH, Jerry		29	M	Laborer	26Ju02Lb
Eliza		16	F	Spinster	26Ju02Lb
John		11	M	None	26Ju02Lb
BLACKBURN, Wm.		31	M	Miner	26Ju02Lb
John		3	M	Child	26Ju02Lb
Sarah		.10	F	Infant	26Ju02Lb
U-Mrs.		20	F	Wife	26Ju02Lb
JOHNSTON, Rich.		30	M	Gdnr	26Ju02Lb
Jane	(W)	23	F	None	26Ju02Lb
PURSEL, Mary-Ann		19	F	Spinster	26Ju02Lb
Rose		30	F	Spinster	26Ju02Lb
STRANGE, James		30	M	Gdnr	26Ju02Lb
Margt.	(W)	25	F	None	26Ju02Lb
ENTRY, John		20	M	Laborer	26Ju02Lb
ULLAN, Michl.		20	M	Laborer	26Ju02Lb
MULLAN, Peter		21	M	Laborer	26Ju02Lb
SAUNDERS, Sarah		24	F	Spinster	26Ju02Lb
Mary		20	F	Spinster	26Ju02Lb
PATRICK, Ann-F.		20	F	Spinster	26Ju02Lb
WOOD, Mary		20	F	Spinster	26Ju02Lb
Thos.		8	M	Child	26Ju02Lb
POWELL, James		28	M	Painter	26Ju02Lb
MARTIN, James		30	M	Ppstr	26Ju02Lb
TOWER, Pat		26	M	Stone Mason	26Ju02Lb
LIONS, Pat		30	M	Laborer	26Ju02Lb
U	(W)	30	F	None	26Ju02Lb
U		.00	U	Infant	26Ju02Lb
Born-At-Sea					
BRENNAN, Ann		25	F	None	26Ju02Lb
HORAN, Terence		28	M	Laborer	26Ju02Lb
DOWNS, George		21	M	Saddler	26Ju02Lb
JAMES, John		24	M	Stone Mason	26Ju02Lb
MCGOWAN, Andw.		27	M	Laborer	26Ju02Lb
Cath.		27	F	Spinster	26Ju02Lb
Rose	(W)	25	F	None	26Ju02Lb
Pat		.06	M	Infant	26Ju02Lb
MEEHAN, James		50	M	Laborer	26Ju02Lb
KEELY, Martha		30	F	Spinster	26Ju02Lb
HAWKS, Edwd.		23	M	Mason	26Ju02Lb
COULTON, Joseph		25	M	Mason	26Ju02Lb
RILEY, Brien		30	M	Laborer	26Ju02Lb
SUEENY, Thos.		38	M	Laborer	26Ju02Lb
Mary	(W)	30	F	None	26Ju02Lb
Kate		6	F	Child	26Ju02Lb
Mary		5	F	Child	26Ju02Lb
DORAN, Mary		17	F	Spinster	26Ju02Lb
CAVANAGH, John		20	M	Laborer	26Ju02Lb
LOCKHURST, John		20	M	Laborer	26Ju02Lb
NOWLAND, Nicholas		20	M	Laborer	26Ju02Lb
KELLY, John		40	M	Laborer	26Ju02Lb
Pat		40	M	Laborer	26Ju02Lb
Eliza	(W)	25	F	None	26Ju02Lb
Chas.		23	M	Laborer	26Ju02Lb
Joseph		16	M	Laborer	26Ju02Lb
Bridget		.09	F	Infant	26Ju02Lb
James		12	M	Laborer	26Ju02Lb
LANGAN, Chas.		40	M	Laborer	26Ju02Lb
HANLON, John		27	M	Laborer	26Ju02Lb
EGLINTON, Danl.		19	M	Laborer	26Ju02Lb
RILEY, Mary		30	F	Wife	26Ju02Lb
Chas.		.06	M	Infant	26Ju02Lb
FARRELL, Jane		39	F	Wi	26Ju02Lb
Eliza		15	F	Spinster	26Ju02Lb
KERR, Thos.		24	M	Laborer	26Ju02Lb
GRAHAM, Joseph		26	M	Laborer	26Ju02Lb
HOUSMAN, Wm.		50	M	Miller	26Ju02Lb
John		20	M	Laborer	26Ju02Lb
WILSON, George		36	M	Blacksmith	26Ju02Lb
Mary	(W)	25	F	None	26Ju02Lb
L.		4	F	Child	26Ju02Lb
Isabella		2	F	Child	26Ju02Lb
Sarah		.06	F	Infant	26Ju02Lb
John		7	M	Child	26Ju02Lb
MCMANUS, Biddy		27	F	Spinster	26Ju02Lb
DUFFY, Thos.		40	M	Laborer	26Ju02Lb
CAIN, David		50	M	Laborer	26Ju02Lb
Mary	(W)	59	F	None	26Ju02Lb
David		12	M	Laborer	26Ju02Lb
Ellen		5	F	Child	26Ju02Lb
Christy		50	F	Wi	26Ju02Lb
Julia		50	F	Wi	26Ju02Lb
Paddy		12	M	None	26Ju02Lb
Timothy		2	M	Child	26Ju02Lb
HAUGHEN, Pat		18	M	Laborer	26Ju02Lb
BEAKIN, Simon		20	M	Laborer	26Ju02Lb
HARRISS, Frank		40	M	Farmer	26Ju02Lb
DAVIES, John		30	M	Farmer	26Ju02Lb
FINLAY, John		30	M	Farmer	26Ju02Lb
FAIN, Frank		16	M	Shoemaker	26Ju02Lb
DILLON, Ann		25	F	Spinster	26Ju02Lb

NAMES OF PASSENGERS	AGE	SEX	OCCUPATIONS	DATE PORT SHIP
BOSTOCK, George	50	M	Farmer	26Ju02Lb
Eliza	19	F	Spinster	26Ju02Lb
HOGG, Cath.	17	F	Spinster	26Ju02Lb
JONES, Lewis	30	M	Laborer	26Ju02Lb
David	30	M	Laborer	26Ju02Lb
Mich.	29	M	Shoemaker	26Ju02Lb
MANGAN, Wm.	19	M	Shoemaker	26Ju02Lb
CLEFIELD, John	25	M	Shoemaker	26Ju02Lb
KANE, David	26	M	Miner	26Ju02Lb
MORRIS, Robt.	21	M	Miner	26Ju02Lb
STAFFORD, Bernd.	60	M	Farmer	26Ju02Lb
Mary (W)	60	F	None	26Ju02Lb
WHITE, Elizabeth	20	F	Spinster	26Ju02Lb
FORRESTER, Mary	20	F	Spinster	26Ju02Lb
DECANON, Ann	30	F	Spinster	26Ju02Lb
ROBERTS, Robert	30	M	Farmer	26Ju02Lb
GALVIN, Joseph	28	M	Laborer	26Ju02Lb
Eliza (W)	33	F	None	26Ju02Lb
Mary	9	F	Child	26Ju02Lb
Laurence	8	M	Child	26Ju02Lb
Joseph	5	M	Child	26Ju02Lb
Eleanor	.09	F	Infant	26Ju02Lb
FARRELL, Mary	33	F	Wife	26Ju02Lb
Ellen	.08	F	Infant	26Ju02Lb
EARLEY, Martin	21	M	Surveyor	26Ju02Lb
FRANKLIN, Jno.	20	M	Laborer	26Ju02Lb
Hannah	20	F	Spinster	26Ju02Lb
GALLAGHER, Edwd.	20	M	Surveyor	26Ju02Lb
SAVAGE, Cath.	20	F	Spinster	26Ju02Lb
Fanny	20	F	Spinster	26Ju02Lb
HANGON, Nancy	30	F	Spinster	26Ju02Lb
HANEGAN, Peter	20	M	Laborer	26Ju02Lb
ENGLISH, Fredk.	27	M	Laborer	26Ju02Lb
CHAPMAN, Wm.	26	M	Laborer	26Ju02Lb
Thos.	26	M	Baker	26Ju02Lb
MONAHAN, James	21	M	Laborer	26Ju02Lb
John	21	M	Laborer	26Ju02Lb
Pat	21	M	Laborer	26Ju02Lb
CAROLL, Danl.	14	M	Laborer	26Ju02Lb
JALES, Wm.	26	M	Laborer	26Ju02Lb
TEMPLE, Henry	30	M	Miner	26Ju02Lb
Mary (W)	29	F	None	26Ju02Lb
John	4	M	Child	26Ju02Lb
James	2	M	Child	26Ju02Lb
Hannah	.09	F	Infant	26Ju02Lb
WELDON, Thos.	36	M	Laborer	26Ju02Lb
TIERNEY, Wm.	23	M	Mechanic	26Ju02Lb
John	21	M	Mechanic	26Ju02Lb
DONNOVAN, Wm.	22	M	Laborer	26Ju02Lb
HEANEY, Rose	26	F	Wife	26Ju02Lb
HUGHES, Henry	26	M	Miller	26Ju02Lb
BRENNAN, Laurence	24	M	Carpenter	26Ju02Lb
Eliza (W)	19	F	None	26Ju02Lb
Eleanor	.06	F	Infant	26Ju02Lb
FARRELL, Mary	24	F	Spinster	26Ju02Lb
KING, Rich.	28	M	Carpenter	26Ju02Lb
Mary (W)	28	F	None	26Ju02Lb
Danl.	3	M	Child	26Ju02Lb
Maria	.09	F	Infant	26Ju02Lb
LEESON, Martha	23	F	Wife	26Ju02Lb
Mary-Ann	2	F	Child	26Ju02Lb
John	.06	M	Infant	26Ju02Lb
RILEY, Brien	22	M	Laborer	26Ju02Lb
La--, Michl.	49	M	Carpenter	26Ju02Lb
LAINDRY, Jos.	16	M	Laborer	26Ju02Lb
DOOLEY, Mich.	25	M	Laborer	26Ju02Lb
GEAHAN, Cons.	42	M	Laborer	26Ju02Lb
James	11	M	Clerk	26Ju02Lb
SHERIDAN, Thos.	19	M	Laborer	26Ju02Lb
TRYELL, Ellen	.06	F	Infant	26Ju02Lb
FISHER, Mary	38	F	Wife	26Ju02Lb
Thos.	44	M	Laborer	26Ju02Lb
Maria	8	F	Child	26Ju02Lb
TRYELL, Margt.	20	F	Wife	26Ju02Lb
FISHER, Jonathan	5	M	Child	26Ju02Lb

NAMES OF PASSENGERS	AGE	SEX	OCCUPATIONS	DATE PORT SHIP
FOLEY, John	24	M	Laborer	26Ju02Lb
EVANS, Sarah	21	F	Spinster	26Ju02Lb
COULTON, Michl.	20	M	Mason	26Ju02Lb
KELLY, Danl.	19	M	Laborer	26Ju02Lb

ST.LAWRENCE 27 JUNE 1849

From Liverpool

NAMES OF PASSENGERS	AGE	SEX	OCCUPATIONS	DATE PORT SHIP
KIRBY, James	24	M	Unknown	27Ju02Bh
RYAN, Mary	50	F	Unknown	27Ju02Bh
Robert	25	M	Unknown	27Ju02Bh
DOOLAN, Bridget	10	F	Unknown	27Ju02Bh
DRUM, Ann	18	F	Unknown	27Ju02Bh
NEVILLE, Cathn.	18	F	Unknown	27Ju02Bh
SHORTALL, Margt.	22	F	Unknown	27Ju02Bh
BUCHANON, Jane	25	F	Unknown	27Ju02Bh
Died-At-Sea				
Eliza-Ann	9	F	Child	27Ju02Bh
Debora	7	F	Child	27Ju02Bh
John	3	M	Child	27Ju02Bh
Joseph	26	M	Unknown	27Ju02Bh
Died-At-Sea				
Jane	30	F	Unknown	27Ju02Bh
U	.03	U	Infant	27Ju02Bh
Died-At-Sea				
William	20	M	Unknown	27Ju02Bh
TOP, Silina	18	F	Unknown	27Ju02Bh
Died-At-Sea				
WHELAN, Thomas	25	M	Unknown	27Ju02Bh
LONG, Margt.	40	F	Unknown	27Ju02Bh
Died-At-Sea				
James	18	M	Unknown	27Ju02Bh
Bridget	17	F	Unknown	27Ju02Bh
MORRISON, Patr.	19	M	Unknown	27Ju02Bh
WAUGH, Nancy	24	F	Unknown	27Ju02Bh
Jane	22	F	Unknown	27Ju02Bh
Died-At-Sea				
Sarah	20	F	Unknown	27Ju02Bh
Died-At-Sea				
HENESSY, David	35	M	Unknown	27Ju02Bh
BYRNES, Bridget	20	F	Unknown	27Ju02Bh
MCANALLY, Bernard	19	M	Unknown	27Ju02Bh
Cathn.	12	F	Unknown	27Ju02Bh
LOU, Susan	18	F	Unknown	27Ju02Bh
KEARNY, Patk.	23	M	Unknown	27Ju02Bh
GUTY, Condy	22	M	Unknown	27Ju02Bh
MCGOVERN, James	21	M	Unknown	27Ju02Bh
TRAINER, Bridget	23	F	Unknown	27Ju02Bh
MCANALTY, Bernard	22	M	Unknown	27Ju02Bh
MCCANN, Thomas	21	M	Unknown	27Ju02Bh
MCGLINN, James	43	M	Unknown	27Ju02Bh
Died-At-Sea				
MONAGHAN, Eliza	19	F	Unknown	27Ju02Bh
MCGLINN, Patr.	12	M	Unknown	27Ju02Bh
Thomas	10	M	Unknown	27Ju02Bh
Mary	5	F	Child	27Ju02Bh
DALTON, Widow	40	F	Unknown	27Ju02Bh
Charles	18	M	Unknown	27Ju02Bh
MCANALTY, John	24	M	Unknown	27Ju02B
MCCANN, John	23	M	Unknown	27Ju02B
Died-At-Sea				
BANNON, John	22	M	Unknown	27Ju02B
LINCEY, Robert	17	M	Unknown	27Ju02B
Robert	17	M	Unknown	27Ju02B
Ann	15	F	Unknown	27Ju02B
MALONY, Rosanna	14	F	Unknown	27Ju02B
POWER, Christopher	24	M	Unknown	27Ju02B
HOTCHEN, John	30	M	Unknown	27Ju02B

NAMES OF PASSENGERS	AGE	SEX	OCCUPATIONS	DATE PORT SHIP
COMMENS, Sylvester	24	M	Unknown	27Ju02Bh
DELANCY, John	23	M	Unknown	27Ju02Bh
Mary	20	F	Unknown	27Ju02Bh
COMMINS, Thomas	22	M	Unknown	27Ju02Bh
Cathn.	26	F	Unknown	27Ju02Bh
HYNE, Andrew	20	M	Unknown	27Ju02Bh
BURNS, Michl.	20	M	Unknown	27Ju02Bh
FARRELLY, Michl.	26	M	Unknown	27Ju02Bh
Cathn.	26	F	Unknown	27Ju02Bh
MURPHY, Margaret	16	F	Unknown	27Ju02Bh
Remmi----, Michl.	20	M	Unknown	27Ju02Bh
James	20	M	Unknown	27Ju02Bh
MALONE, John	20	M	Unknown	27Ju02Bh
Died-At-Sea				
BRIAN, Jeremiah	50	M	Unknown	27Ju02Bh
Died-At-Sea				
Bridget	50	F	Unknown	27Ju02Bh
Edward	30	M	Unknown	27Ju02Bh
Michl.	25	M	Unknown	27Ju02Bh
Cathn.	20	F	Unknown	27Ju02Bh
Honora	20	F	Unknown	27Ju02Bh
Died-At-Sea				
Peter	16	M	Unknown	27Ju02Bh
TAHANY, Rody	30	M	Unknown	27Ju02Bh
Margt.	30	F	Unknown	27Ju02Bh
Thomas	10	M	Unknown	27Ju02Bh
Bridget	8	F	Child	27Ju02Bh
John	5	M	Child	27Ju02Bh
Mary	3	F	Child	27Ju02Bh
Edward	.06	M	Infant	27Ju02Bh
COLLINS, Richard	40	M	Unknown	27Ju02Bh
Mary	30	F	Unknown	27Ju02Bh
Sarah	50	F	Unknown	27Ju02Bh
William	10	M	Unknown	27Ju02Bh
John	8	M	Child	27Ju02Bh
Sarah	6	F	Child	27Ju02Bh
Robert	2	M	Child	27Ju02Bh
LEDGER, Joseph-A.	30	M	Unknown	27Ju02Bh
DAILY, Patr.	20	M	Unknown	27Ju02Bh
DELAHANTY, James	20	M	Unknown	27Ju02Bh
Biddy	25	F	Unknown	27Ju02Bh
Ann	22	F	Unknown	27Ju02Bh
Died-At-Sea				
CUDDY, Biddy	24	F	Unknown	27Ju02Bh
CURHEIN, Cathr.	23	F	Unknown	27Ju02Bh
Died-At-Sea				
LODDIX, Elizabeth	27	F	Unknown	27Ju02Bh
BERRY, Patrick	25	M	Unknown	27Ju02Bh
Died-At-Sea				
Ann	60	F	Unknown	27Ju02Bh
CONNORS, James	20	M	Unknown	27Ju02Bh
FERGUSON, Margt.	60	F	Unknown	27Ju02Bh
Ann	30	F	Unknown	27Ju02Bh
Isaac	23	M	Unknown	27Ju02Bh
William	21	M	Unknown	27Ju02Bh
RANT, Mary	5	F	Husband	27Ju02Bh
OSSERY, William	30	M	Unknown	27Ju02Bh
Bridget	31	F	Unknown	27Ju02Bh
RADY, Mary	24	F	Unknown	27Ju02Bh
Michl.	.09	M	Infant	27Ju02Bh
Matthew	30	M	Unknown	27Ju02Bh
HORNBERRY, Thoms.S.	20	M	Unknown	27Ju02Bh
OONEY, William	38	M	Unknown	27Ju02Bh
Mary	42	F	Unknown	27Ju02Bh
RYAN, John	24	M	Unknown	27Ju02Bh
U-Mrs.	24	F	Unknown	27Ju02Bh
ONOVAN, Cornelius	22	M	Unknown	27Ju02Bh
James	21	M	Unknown	27Ju02Bh
Bridget	24	F	Unknown	27Ju02Bh
ANY, Margt.	24	F	Unknown	27Ju02Bh
IGGINS, Barthw.	34	M	Unknown	27Ju02Bh
IEA, Margt.	60	F	Unknown	27Ju02Bh
Mary	20	F	Unknown	27Ju02Bh
Bridgt.	26	F	Unknown	27Ju02Bh
AN, Mary	23	F	Unknown	27Ju02Bh

NAMES OF PASSENGERS	AGE	SEX	OCCUPATIONS	DATE PORT SHIP
BURKE, Alexander	28	M	Unknown	27Ju02Bh
TRAINER, James	35	M	Unknown	27Ju02Bh
MARSDEN, Mary	16	F	Unknown	27Ju02Bh
GALLAGHER, Betsy	16	F	Unknown	27Ju02Bh
BANNON, Bridgt.	17	F	Unknown	27Ju02Bh
QUINN, James	25	M	Unknown	27Ju02Bh
GAINOR, Edward	22	M	Unknown	27Ju02Bh
REARDON, David	26	M	Unknown	27Ju02Bh
Jeremiah	20	M	Unknown	27Ju02Bh
CHAPMAN, Henry	26	M	Unknown	27Ju02Bh
BRYAN, Michl.	30	M	Unknown	27Ju02Bh
BANNON, Mary	20	F	Unknown	27Ju02Bh
MCCAFFERY, Ellen	20	F	Unknown	27Ju02Bh
DAUGHERTY, Jane	30	F	Unknown	27Ju02Bh
Ann	11	F	Unknown	27Ju02Bh
Eliza	8	F	Child	27Ju02Bh
FLYNN, Edmond	20	M	Unknown	27Ju02Bh
HICKEY, Anthony	16	M	Unknown	27Ju02Bh
CLEARY, Mary	18	F	Unknown	27Ju02Bh
Died-At-Sea				
ODONNELL, Mary	18	F	Unknown	27Ju02Bh
MCGINLEY, Dennis	24	M	Unknown	27Ju02Bh
KARR, Bridget	18	F	Unknown	27Ju02Bh
MULLEN, Patr.	20	M	Unknown	27Ju02Bh
Hugh	18	M	Unknown	27Ju02Bh
CONNELL, William	26	M	Unknown	27Ju02Bh
DORAN, James	25	M	Unknown	27Ju02Bh
DELAHAUNTY, Patkr.	28	M	Unknown	27Ju02Bh
BUTLER, James	30	M	Unknown	27Ju02Bh
DUFFY, Michl.	15	M	Unknown	27Ju02Bh
CAWLEY, Patrick	24	M	Unknown	27Ju02Bh
DUFFY, Honora	10	F	Unknown	27Ju02Bh
Thomas	8	M	Child	27Ju02Bh
SWEENEY, Bridget	40	F	Unknown	27Ju02Bh
Michael	9	M	Child	27Ju02Bh
Thomas	11	M	Unknown	27Ju02Bh
Peter	7	M	Child	27Ju02Bh
Alice	5	F	Child	27Ju02Bh
Eleanor	2	F	Child	27Ju02Bh
Died-At-Sea				
MCCAFFREY, Mary	16	F	Unknown	27Ju02Bh
CALLICY, John	20	M	Unknown	27Ju02Bh
Died-At-Sea				
MCCABE, Michl.	17	M	Unknown	27Ju02Bh
DOLAN, Patrk.	15	M	Unknown	27Ju02Bh
MCEVOY, Mary	20	F	Unknown	27Ju02Bh
MCMAHON, John	30	M	Unknown	27Ju02Bh
Margt.	26	F	Unknown	27Ju02Bh
John	7	M	Child	27Ju02Bh
Died-At-Sea				
Cathn.	.06	F	Infant	27Ju02Bh
Bridget	.06	F	Infant	27Ju02Bh
Died-At-Sea				
MCGARY, Mary	22	F	Unknown	27Ju02Bh
Died-At-Sea				
DUNLAY, Margaret	20	F	Unknown	27Ju02Bh
William	20	M	Unknown	27Ju02Bh
Died-At-Sea				
GAFFNEY, Bridget	20	F	Unknown	27Ju02Bh
Died-At-Sea				
Patrick	.04	M	Infant	27Ju02Bh
Died-At-Sea				
DUNLAS, Abby	19	M	Unknown	27Ju02Bh
CRAWLEY, Mary	18	F	Unknown	27Ju02Bh
LEAHY, Ann	17	F	Unknown	27Ju02Bh

DEVONIA 27 JUNE 1849

From Bristol

NAMES OF PASSENGERS	AGE	SEX	OCCUPATIONS	DATE PORT SHIP
BOARD, Geo.	43	M	Farmer	27Ju10Kx
Martha	36	F	Unknown	27Ju10Kx
Elizt.	12	F	Unknown	27Ju10Kx
Ferdinand	10	M	Unknown	27Ju10Kx
Sarah-Ann	8	F	Child	27Ju10Kx
Geo.	6	M	Child	27Ju10Kx
Stepn.	4	M	Child	27Ju10Kx
Martha	.00	F	Infant	27Ju10Kx
Robert	23	M	Farmer	27Ju10Kx
Ann	25	F	Unknown	27Ju10Kx
Maria	.00	F	Infant	27Ju10Kx
BRYANT, Abraham	34	M	Carpenter	27Ju10Kx
HITCHCOCK, Felix	23	M	Baker	27Ju10Kx
CHAPMAN, Wm.	29	M	Farmer	27Ju10Kx
TOOMAN, John	45	M	Farmer	27Ju10Kx
Eliza	44	F	Unknown	27Ju10Kx
Julia	12	F	Unknown	27Ju10Kx
Hester	10	F	Unknown	27Ju10Kx
Mary	7	F	Child	27Ju10Kx
Eilza	6	F	Child	27Ju10Kx
YOUNG, Wm.	28	M	Laborer	27Ju10Kx
James	17	M	Laborer	27Ju10Kx
May	24	F	Laborer	27Ju10Kx
Elizt.	3	F	Child	27Ju10Kx
HILL, Geo.	29	M	Laborer	27Ju10Kx
NEAR, Geo.	38	M	Laborer	27Ju10Kx
Maria	28	F	Laborer	27Ju10Kx
Hannah	9	F	Child	27Ju10Kx
Mary	7	F	Child	27Ju10Kx
Charlotte	5	F	Child	27Ju10Kx
Louisa	.00	F	Infant	27Ju10Kx
SCRIBBINS, Jemima	30	F	Laborer	27Ju10Kx
Julia	9	F	Child	27Ju10Kx
Mary	8	F	Child	27Ju10Kx
Geo.	5	M	Child	27Ju10Kx
Mark	4	M	Child	27Ju10Kx
Thos.	.00	M	Infant	27Ju10Kx
BARRINGTON, John	20	M	Laborer	27Ju10Kx
GATE, John	56	M	Shoemaker	27Ju10Kx
Charlotte	43	F	Unknown	27Ju10Kx
Hannah	4	F	Child	27Ju10Kx
John	3	M	Child	27Ju10Kx
PEPPARD, Geo.	41	M	Farmer	27Ju10Kx
Hannah	41	F	Unknown	27Ju10Kx
Geo.	15	M	Unknown	27Ju10Kx
Sarah	13	F	Unknown	27Ju10Kx
Charles	11	M	Unknown	27Ju10Kx
Frank	9	M	Child	27Ju10Kx
Betsey	6	F	Child	27Ju10Kx
Elizt.	4	F	Child	27Ju10Kx
FOORD, Geo.	25	M	Laborer	27Ju10Kx
Ann	30	F	Unknown	27Ju10Kx
PERKINS, John	30	M	Farmer	27Ju10Kx
ROGERS, Joseph	37	M	Engineer	27Ju10Kx
Ann	37	F	Unknown	27Ju10Kx
Jane	16	F	Unknown	27Ju10Kx
Sarah-Ann	7	F	Child	27Ju10Kx
FRENCH, Chas.	31	M	Unknown	27Ju10Kx
Elizt.	31	F	Unknown	27Ju10Kx
Ellen	10	F	Child	27Ju10Kx
Alfred	8	M	Child	27Ju10Kx
Ann	6	F	Child	27Ju10Kx
Louisa	2	F	Child	27Ju10Kx
NORTHOVER, Martha	27	F	Spinster	27Ju10Kx
YEO, Jane	28	F	Unknown	27Ju10Kx

NAMES OF PASSENGERS	AGE	SEX	OCCUPATIONS	DATE PORT SHIP
MORSE, Elizabeth	21	F	Unknown	27Ju10Kx
HILL, Thos.	30	M	Unknown	27Ju10Kx
Ann	30	F	Unknown	27Ju10Kx
Elizt.	7	F	Child	27Ju10Kx
Frederick	5	M	Child	27Ju10Kx
WYATT, Francis	40	M	Cooper	27Ju10Kx
Charlotte	33	F	Unknown	27Ju10Kx
Jemima	19	F	Unknown	27Ju10Kx
Julia	10	F	Unknown	27Ju10Kx
Mary-Jane	7	F	Child	27Ju10Kx
Wm.	4	M	Child	27Ju10Kx
Celia	2	F	Child	27Ju10Kx
PARKER, Thos.	32	M	Farmer	27Ju10Kx
Patience	32	F	Unknown	27Ju10Kx
Betsey	18	F	Unknown	27Ju10Kx
Sarah	16	F	Unknown	27Ju10Kx
Thos.	11	M	Unknown	27Ju10Kx
PITTMAN, Eliza	22	F	Engineer	27Ju10Kx
Geo.	3	M	Child	27Ju10Kx
Henry	.00	M	Infant	27Ju10Kx
PORTER, Richd.	32	M	Unknown	27Ju10Kx
MALLETH, Elizth.	31	F	Spinster	27Ju10Kx
PORTER, Mary	35	F	Unknown	27Ju10Kx
JAMES, Mary	35	F	Unknown	27Ju10Kx
Mary-Ann	4	F	Child	27Ju10Kx
Geo.	2	M	Child	27Ju10Kx
PORTER, Julia	3	F	Child	27Ju10Kx
JAMES, Josiah	27	M	Blacksmith	27Ju10Kx
SAMUEL, Elizt.	73	F	Unknown	27Ju10Kx
Mary-Ann	31	F	Unknown	27Ju10Kx
BRAY, Amelia	29	F	Spinster	27Ju10Kx
James	8	M	Child	27Ju10Kx
Geo.	5	M	Child	27Ju10Kx
Wm.	3	M	Child	27Ju10Kx
EARLE, John	44	M	Grocer	27Ju10Kx
Mary	45	F	Unknown	27Ju10Kx
Wm.	17	M	Unknown	27Ju10Kx
Mercy	11	F	Unknown	27Ju10K
Cleo	9	F	Child	27Ju10K
James	37	M	Unknown	27Ju10K
GARDENER, Wm.	00	M	Unknown	27Ju10K
ELLIS, Aldred	20	M	Carpenter	27Ju10K
John	17	M	Blacksmith	27Ju10K
COX, Henry	22	M	Laborer	27Ju10K
PITTARD, Joseph	30	M	Mason	27Ju10K
Mary-Ann	30	F	Unknown	27Ju10K
BARKER, Jno.	23	M	Laborer	27Ju10K
WINGRAVE, Jno.	37	M	Laborer	27Ju10K
Mary	34	F	Unknown	27Ju10K
Jno.	9	M	Child	27Ju10K
Wm.	7	M	Child	27Ju10K
Mary-Grace	5	F	Child	27Ju10K
Clara	3	F	Child	27Ju10K
Sarah	.00	F	Infant	27Ju10K
TOOMER, Wm.	30	M	Plumber	27Ju10K
Sophia	25	F	Unknown	27Ju10K
Geo.	8	M	Child	27Ju10K
John	6	M	Child	27Ju10K
Harriett	4	F	Child	27Ju10K
Elizt.	2	F	Child	27Ju10K
Ann	.00	F	Infant	27Ju10K
DARE, Wm.	30	M	Laborer	27Ju10K
Eliza	20	F	Unknown	27Ju10K
BROOKS, Thos.	23	M	Farmer	27Ju10K
Caroline	19	F	Unknown	27Ju10
NORRISH, Fanny	27	F	Spinster	27Ju10
Caroline	24	F	Unknown	27Ju10
IRELAND, Jno.	21	M	Cbtmkr	27Ju10
DYER, Charles	50	M	Farmer	27Ju10
RICHARDS, Eliza	27	F	Unknown	27Ju10
Elizth.	5	F	Child	27Ju10
TUCKER, Wm.	21	M	Laborer	27Ju10
TAYLOR, Edwin	24	M	Laborer	27Ju10
BARON, Wm.	27	M	Laborer	27Ju10
SWEET, John	24	M	Laborer	27Ju10

NAMES OF PASSENGERS	AGE	SEX	OCCUPATIONS	DATE PORT SHIP
ATKINS, Walter	22	M	Shoemaker	27Ju10Kx
BUNNING, Ann	14	F	Spinster	27Ju10Kx
CHAPMAN, Rob.	20	M	Laborer	27Ju10Kx
GILBERT, Louisa	30	F	Unknown	27Ju10Kx
Ann	9	F	Child	27Ju10Kx
Charlotte	7	F	Child	27Ju10Kx
Albert	5	M	Child	27Ju10Kx
Louisa	2	F	Child	27Ju10Kx
George	.00	M	Infant	27Ju10Kx
PERNITON, Thos.	25	M	Farmer	27Ju10Kx
Anna-Maria	26	F	Unknown	27Ju10Kx
Ellen	.00	F	Infant	27Ju10Kx
EVANS, Saml.	22	M	Laborer	27Ju10Kx
Jane	23	F	Laborer	27Ju10Kx
ROPER, Jane	55	F	Laborer	27Ju10Kx
GIBBS, Geo.	24	M	Farmer	27Ju10Kx
BUNNING, Wm.	32	M	Farmer	27Ju10Kx
WOOLLY, Mary-Ann	25	F	Spinster	27Ju10Kx
BUNNING, Jno.	22	M	Carpenter	27Ju10Kx
BARTLETT, Jas.	25	M	Laborer	27Ju10Kx
POPLE, Jno.	25	M	Laborer	27Ju10Kx
DURSTON, Ruth	22	F	Unknown	27Ju10Kx
James	20	M	Farmer	27Ju10Kx
Jno.	50	M	Farmer	27Ju10Kx
Sarah	49	F	Unknown	27Ju10Kx
Geo.	48	M	Farmer	27Ju10Kx
Wm.	25	M	Farmer	27Ju10Kx
Edwd.	17	M	Farmer	27Ju10Kx
Ann	22	F	Spinster	27Ju10Kx
Jno.	11	M	Unknown	27Ju10Kx
Betsey	10	F	Unknown	27Ju10Kx
Maria	7	F	Child	27Ju10Kx
HES, Henry	60	M	Mason	27Ju10Kx
Thos.	41	M	Mason	27Ju10Kx
Sarah	42	F	Unknown	27Ju10Kx
Martha	18	F	Unknown	27Ju10Kx
Elizt.	15	F	Unknown	27Ju10Kx
Rob.	11	M	Unknown	27Ju10Kx
Lucy	6	F	Child	27Ju10Kx
Emily	2	F	Child	27Ju10Kx
HOCKINS, Thos.	18	M	Laborer	27Ju10Kx
Richd.	25	M	Carpenter	27Ju10Kx
JONES, Geo.	46	M	Stone Mason	27Ju10Kx
Emma	36	F	Unknown	27Ju10Kx
Geo.	21	M	Unknown	27Ju10Kx
Thos.	19	M	Stone Mason	27Ju10Kx
Sarah	12	F	Unknown	27Ju10Kx
Mary	10	F	Unknown	27Ju10Kx
Matilda	8	F	Child	27Ju10Kx
Hubert	4	M	Child	27Ju10Kx
Arabella	.00	F	Infant	27Ju10Kx
ORGAN, Jas.	30	M	Miner	27Ju10Kx
Elizt.	22	F	Unknown	27Ju10Kx
Thos.	2	M	Child	27Ju10Kx
Elizt.	.00	F	Infant	27Ju10Kx
EAL, Enoch	25	M	Mason	27Ju10Kx
Elizt.	24	F	Unknown	27Ju10Kx
Elizt.	4	F	Child	27Ju10Kx
Agatha	.00	F	Infant	27Ju10Kx
PER, Jno.	35	M	Laborer	27Ju10Kx
CKLAND, Jno.	19	M	Carpenter	27Ju10Kx
VEY, Henry	26	M	Farmer	27Ju10Kx
OK, Fredk.	22	M	Farmer	27Ju10Kx
PE, Eliza	20	F	Unknown	27Ju10Kx
James	11	M	Unknown	27Ju10Kx
WIS, Jno.	38	M	Carpenter	27Ju10Kx
Wm.	13	M	Carpenter	27Ju10Kx
Urban	7	M	Child	27Ju10Kx
ONE, Ann	40	F	Unknown	27Ju10Kx
Ellen	4	F	Child	27Ju10Kx
TTS, Geo.	18	M	Farmer	27Ju10Kx
NTON, U-Dr.	25	M	Surgeon	27Ju10Kx
CK, James	32	M	Farmer	27Ju10Kx
PP, Caroline	45	F	Unknown	27Ju10Kx
Henry	18	M	Unknown	27Ju10Kx

NAMES OF PASSENGERS	AGE	SEX	OCCUPATIONS	DATE PORT SHIP
COPP, Edwin	9	M	Child	27Ju10Kx
LEWIS, Lucy	39	F	Carpenter	27Ju10Kx
Jno.	12	M	Unknown	27Ju10Kx
Richd.	4	M	Child	27Ju10Kx
STONE, Sarah	13	F	Unknown	27Ju10Kx
HEAL, Elizt.	21	F	Unknown	27Ju10Kx
Emma	2	F	Child	27Ju10Kx
WHITE, Wm.	32	M	Unknown	27Ju10Kx
Ann	24	F	Unknown	27Ju10Kx
Eliza	.00	F	Infant	27Ju10Kx
HOCKINS, Thos.	17	M	Laborer	27Ju10Kx

HERALD 28 JUNE 1849

From Greenock

NAMES OF PASSENGERS	AGE	SEX	OCCUPATIONS	DATE PORT SHIP
MCGILP, Duncan	30	M	Farmer	28Ju33Kz
MELLIS, John	27	M	Mason	28Ju33Kz
Mary	23	F	Unknown	28Ju33Kz
William	3	M	Child	28Ju33Kz
Jessie	.10	F	Infant	28Ju33Kz
ELLISON, Henry	20	M	Valet	28Ju33Kz
FAIRLEY, John	19	M	Laborer	28Ju33Kz
JOHNSTONE, John	35	M	Laborer	28Ju33Kz
JAMIESON, James	60	M	Laborer	28Ju33Kz
ODONNELL, Mary	17	F	Servant	28Ju33Kz
WADDELL, Alexr.	25	M	Laborer	28Ju33Kz
KENNEDY, Andrew-H.	22	M	Joiner	28Ju33Kz
FRIEDLANDER, Fanny	45	F	Unknown	28Ju33Kz
Caroline	3	F	Child	28Ju33Kz
Hannah	.10	F	Infant	28Ju33Kz
Nathaniel	5	M	Child	28Ju33Kz
Barnet	11	M	Unknown	28Ju33Kz
BOWIN, Rachel	27	F	Unknown	28Ju33Kz
Hannah	4	F	Unknown	28Ju33Kz
Abram.	2	M	Unknown	28Ju33Kz
Henry	.09	M	Infant	28Ju33Kz
MORIS, Hyam	13	M	Unknown	28Ju33Kz
BARNET, Samuel	23	M	Laborer	28Ju33Kz
ISAAC, John	23	M	Laborer	28Ju33Kz
LYLE, Charles	40	M	Ctnsp	28Ju33Kz
Mary	38	F	Unknown	28Ju33Kz
Elizabeth	20	F	Servant	28Ju33Kz
Charles	18	M	Laborer	28Ju33Kz
Helen	16	F	Unknown	28Ju33Kz
James	13	M	Unknown	28Ju33Kz
John	12	M	Unknown	28Ju33Kz
Alexander	7	M	Child	28Ju33Kz
Eliza	5	F	Child	28Ju33Kz
William	10	M	Unknown	28Ju33Kz
Robert	3	M	Child	28Ju33Kz
George	.09	M	Infant	28Ju33Kz
GOLDIE, Peter	25	M	Cooper	28Ju33Kz
Mary	24	F	Unknown	28Ju33Kz
Robert	15	M	Cooper	28Ju33Kz
THOMSON, William	27	M	Blacksmith	28Ju33Kz
ANDERSON, John	30	M	Sawer	28Ju33Kz
Mary	29	F	Unknown	28Ju33Kz
John	2	M	Child	28Ju33Kz
WALLACE, John	29	M	Sawer	28Ju33Kz
MCLEAN, Jane	30	F	Unknown	28Ju33Kz
Agnes	2	F	Child	28Ju33Kz
Janet	.11	F	Infant	28Ju33Kz
Died-At-Sea				
GILFILLAN, Mary	25	F	Unknown	28Ju33Kz
William	2	M	Child	28Ju33Kz
Joseph	.09	M	Infant	28Ju33Kz
SHANKS, William	25	M	Laborer	28Ju33Kz
Isabella	30	F	Servant	28Ju33Kz

NAMES OF PASSENGERS	AGE	SEX	OCCUPATIONS	DATE PORT SHIP
SHANKS, Janet	9	F	Child	28Ju33Kz
James	7	M	Child	28Ju33Kz
Gavin	5	M	Child	28Ju33Kz
John	3	M	Child	28Ju33Kz
PINKERTON, Alexr.	35	M	Weaver	28Ju33Kz
Meam	26	F	Unknown	28Ju33Kz
Ann	1	F	Child	28Ju33Kz
BATHGATE, John	49	M	Miner	28Ju33Kz
Mary	49	F	Unknown	28Ju33Kz
Agnes	24	F	Servant	28Ju33Kz
Jean	22	F	Servant	28Ju33Kz
Adam	20	M	Miner	28Ju33Kz
William	13	M	Miner	28Ju33Kz
John	10	M	Unknown	28Ju33Kz
Ann	12	F	Unknown	28Ju33Kz
LANG, Duncan	30	M	Shoemaker	28Ju33Kz
Mary	30	F	Unknown	28Ju33Kz
Alexr.	3	M	Child	28Ju33Kz
Ellen	2	F	Child	28Ju33Kz
NORMOND, Thomas	33	M	Blacksmith	28Ju33Kz
Elizabeth	35	F	Unknown	28Ju33Kz
Elizabeth	7	F	Child	28Ju33Kz
Ellen	5	F	Child	28Ju33Kz
John	3	M	Child	28Ju33Kz
William	1	M	Child	28Ju33Kz
Died-At-Sea				
MCNEE, William	26	M	Servant	28Ju33Kz
YOUNG, Alexander	18	M	Engineer	28Ju33Kz
PHILIP, John	48	M	Cbtmkr	28Ju33Kz
Mary	48	F	Unknown	28Ju33Kz
Rachel	18	F	Servant	28Ju33Kz
SHIELDS, Robert	24	M	Engineer	28Ju33Kz
PATERSON, James	34	M	Weaver	28Ju33Kz
Jane	34	F	Unknown	28Ju33Kz
William	6	M	Child	28Ju33Kz
Janet	3	F	Child	28Ju33Kz
MCGOWAN, Duncan	34	M	Weaver	28Ju33Kz
Mary	34	F	Unknown	28Ju33Kz
John	5	M	Child	28Ju33Kz
Robert	3	M	Child	28Ju33Kz
Mary	.06	F	Infant	28Ju33Kz
THOMSON, Robert	29	M	Farmer	28Ju33Kz
LENNOX, James	22	M	Laborer	28Ju33Kz
Mary	22	F	Unknown	28Ju33Kz
ESPIE, David	28	M	Laborer	28Ju33Kz
DONAGHY, Simon	18	M	Laborer	28Ju33Kz
MUNRO, Duncan	40	M	Writer	28Ju33Kz
Jane	36	F	Unknown	28Ju33Kz
Ann	18	F	Servant	28Ju33Kz
Duncan	10	M	Unknown	28Ju33Kz
GRIFFITH, Homer	25	M	Farmer	28Ju33Kz
PATTEN, William	43	M	Writer	28Ju33Kz
Kate	40	F	Unknown	28Ju33Kz
Catherine	19	F	Servant	28Ju33Kz
James	15	M	Writer	28Ju33Kz
George	13	M	Unknown	28Ju33Kz
Duncan	11	M	Unknown	28Ju33Kz
William	8	M	Child	28Ju33Kz
Mary	5	F	Child	28Ju33Kz
Robert	3	M	Child	28Ju33Kz
Margaret	.11	F	Infant	28Ju33Kz
MONTGOMERY, William	22	M	Joiner	28Ju33Kz
NIELSON, Philip	22	M	Writer	28Ju33Kz
POPE, Duncan	22	M	Smith	28Ju33Kz
ROBERTSON, Thomas	22	M	Smith	28Ju33Kz
LINDSAY, John	52	M	Surgeon	28Ju33Kz
Henrietta	18	F	Servant	28Ju33Kz
Margaret	16	F	Servant	28Ju33Kz
David-G.	14	M	Unknown	28Ju33Kz
John	12	M	Unknown	28Ju33Kz
MCCOMBE, Agnes	17	F	Servant	28Ju33Kz
MCGOWN, Ann	18	F	Servant	28Ju33Kz
REID, Mary	28	F	Unknown	28Ju33Kz
Alexander	8	M	Child	28Ju33Kz
Alan	6	M	Child	28Ju33Kz
REID, William	3	M	Child	28Ju33Kz
BONAR, John	40	M	Machinist	28Ju33Kz
Mary	40	F	Unknown	28Ju33Kz
John	6	M	Child	28Ju33Kz
WILSON, Mary	22	F	Unknown	28Ju33Kz
John	3	M	Child	28Ju33Kz
James	1	M	Child	28Ju33Kz
HADDON, John	22	M	Mechanic	28Ju33Kz
MELVIN, Thomas	27	M	Mechanic	28Ju33Kz
Mary	25	F	Unknown	28Ju33Kz
Thomas	.03	M	Infant	28Ju33Kz
WATSON, William	42	M	Miner	28Ju33Kz
MITCHELL, Jean	24	F	Unknown	28Ju33Kz
Mary	2	F	Child	28Ju33Kz
Agnes	.10	F	Infant	28Ju33Kz
Robert	20	M	Miner	28Ju33Kz
MURRAY, Roger	27	M	Miner	28Ju33Kz
Mary	26	F	Unknown	28Ju33Kz
Agnes	3	F	Child	28Ju33Kz
David	7	M	Child	28Ju33Kz
John	4	M	Child	28Ju33Kz
David	.11	M	Infant	28Ju33Kz
LECKIE, Janet	20	F	Servant	28Ju33Kz
RILEY, Mary	27	F	Unknown	28Ju33Kz
Mary	3	F	Child	28Ju33Kz
William	2	M	Child	28Ju33Kz
MARTIN, John	35	M	Laborer	28Ju33Kz
Mary	45	F	Unknown	28Ju33Kz
PARK, Boyd	12	M	Unknown	28Ju33Kz
STEVENSON, Mirion	35	F	Servant	28Ju33Kz
Janet	7	F	Child	28Ju33Kz
SHEARER, Alexr.	25	M	Grinder	28Ju33Kz
Jane	25	F	Unknown	28Ju33Kz
Elizabeth	3	F	Child	28Ju33Kz
ANDERSON, Joseph	25	M	Laborer	28Ju33Kz
JAMIESON, Robert	23	M	Laborer	28Ju33Kz
IRVINE, Thomas	25	M	Laborer	28Ju33Kz
Jane	25	F	Unknown	28Ju33Kz
Elizabeth	12	F	Unknown	28Ju33Kz
Thomas	.10	M	Infant	28Ju33Kz
HARVEY, Edward	24	M	Laborer	28Ju33Kz
Catherine	24	F	Unknown	28Ju33K
Thomas	4	M	Child	28Ju33K
Died-At-Sea				
Mary	2	F	Child	28Ju33K
Died-At-Sea				
Catherine	.05	F	Infant	28Ju33K
Died-At-Sea				
LAWSON, Thomas	45	M	Laborer	28Ju33K
Elizabeth	45	F	Unknown	28Ju33K
Sarah	10	F	Unknown	28Ju33K
Joseph	8	M	Child	28Ju33K
MCAULAY, Robert	26	M	Laborer	28Ju33K
Barbara	20	F	Unknown	28Ju33K
STUART, James	17	M	Laborer	28Ju33K
MCKOOPREY, Nancy	13	F	Unknown	28Ju33K
BROWN, Mary	30	F	Dressmaker	28Ju33K
Eliza	12	F	Unknown	28Ju33K
Sarah	11	F	Unknown	28Ju33K
John	9	M	Child	28Ju33K
Jane-Stett	7	F	Child	28Ju33K
Rebecca	5	F	Child	28Ju33K
Robert	3	M	Child	28Ju33K
MCGHEE, Maria	40	F	Spinster	28Ju33K
FERGUSON, Mathers	50	M	Laborer	28Ju33K
Elizabeth	45	F	Unknown	28Ju33K
Robert	18	M	Laborer	28Ju33K
William-Alexander	16	M	Laborer	28Ju33K
James	13	M	Laborer	28Ju33K
Samuel	12	M	Laborer	28Ju33K
Mary-Ann	7	F	Child	28Ju33K
George	5	M	Child	28Ju33K
WILSON, Henry	42	M	Laborer	28Ju33K
GONE, John	24	M	Laborer	28Ju33K
IRWIN, David	40	M	Laborer	28Ju33K

NAMES OF PASSENGERS	AGE	SEX	OCCUPATIONS	DATE PORT SHIP
IRWIN, Margaret	30	F	Unknown	28Ju33Kz
Charles	11	M	Unknown	28Ju33Kz
Mary	8	M	Child	28Ju33Kz
William-John	6	M	Child	28Ju33Kz
Jas.Henry	4	M	Child	28Ju33Kz
Elizabeth	.06	F	Infant	28Ju33Kz
PORTER, Elizabeth	30	F	Spinster	28Ju33Kz
Eleanor	30	F	Servant	28Ju33Kz
GAMBLE, Jane	13	F	Unknown	28Ju33Kz
BLOOMFIELD, John	40	M	Farmer	28Ju33Kz
Jane	30	F	Unknown	28Ju33Kz
John	3	M	Child	28Ju33Kz
BEATTY, John	21	M	Laborer	28Ju33Kz
MCWILLIAMS, Elizabeth	20	F	Servant	28Ju33Kz
Ann-Jane	11	F	Unknown	28Ju33Kz
ELLIOTT, Patrick	19	M	Laborer	28Ju33Kz
DOHERTY, John	17	M	Laborer	28Ju33Kz
DUER, Bernard	24	M	Laborer	28Ju33Kz
HENRY, Sarah	15	F	Servant	28Ju33Kz
MULLEN, John	13	M	Unknown	28Ju33Kz
PORTER, Robert	40	M	Laborer	28Ju33Kz
Mary-Jane	40	F	Unknown	28Ju33Kz
Samuel	59	M	Laborer	28Ju33Kz
Isabella	58	F	Unknown	28Ju33Kz
William	13	M	Unknown	28Ju33Kz
Mary-Jane	12	F	Unknown	28Ju33Kz
John	10	M	Unknown	28Ju33Kz
Martha	8	F	Child	28Ju33Kz
Ellen	5	F	Child	28Ju33Kz
Samuel	.07	M	Infant	28Ju33Kz
HANA, Jemina	40	F	Servant	28Ju33Kz
Margaret	40	F	Servant	28Ju33Kz
Jemina	8	F	Child	28Ju33Kz
Margaret	4	F	Child	28Ju33Kz
Patrick	.08	M	Infant	28Ju33Kz
MCKENNA, Ann-Jane	14	F	Unknown	28Ju33Kz
PATERSON, Thomas	22	M	Laborer	28Ju33Kz
MCCLEENY, Susan	21	F	Servant	28Ju33Kz
MCEMONY, Martha	16	F	Servant	28Ju33Kz
HARE, Patrick	14	M	Laborer	28Ju33Kz
MCRORY, John	19	M	Laborer	28Ju33Kz
MCSWEENY, Stephen	30	M	Laborer	28Ju33Kz
Hanna	10	F	Unknown	28Ju33Kz
William	8	M	Child	28Ju33Kz
MCKEAN, Mary	15	F	Servant	28Ju33Kz
COOPER, Eliza	21	F	Servant	28Ju33Kz
Matilda	50	F	Servant	28Ju33Kz
BROWN, Fanny	24	F	Servant	28Ju33Kz
DOHERTY, George	22	M	Laborer	28Ju33Kz
DUNBAR, Samuel	27	M	Laborer	28Ju33Kz
COLL, John	40	M	Laborer	28Ju33Kz
Mary	40	M	Unknown	28Ju33Kz
Bryan	6	M	Child	28Ju33Kz
Mary	2	F	Child	28Ju33Kz
Margaret	1	F	Child	28Ju33Kz
MULLEN, James	28	M	Laborer	28Ju33Kz
MCCOLLEN, James	26	M	Laborer	28Ju33Kz
Catherine	27	F	Unknown	28Ju33Kz
ADAM, Neil	21	M	Laborer	28Ju33Kz
MAINHEAD, Wallace	17	M	Laborer	28Ju33Kz
LINCH, Samuel	30	M	Laborer	28Ju33Kz
DUNNING, Giles	15	M	Laborer	28Ju33Kz
LOGG, Mathew	30	M	Laborer	28Ju33Kz
WELLER, William	15	M	Laborer	28Ju33Kz
PORTEONS, Peter	22	M	Laborer	28Ju33Kz
ORR, Joseph	29	M	Laborer	28Ju33Kz
HILL, George	18	M	Laborer	28Ju33Kz
CARMICHAEL, John	26	M	Laborer	28Ju33Kz
Mary	24	F	Unknown	28Ju33Kz
WRIGHT, John	24	M	Laborer	28Ju33Kz
CAMERON, Hugh	21	M	Laborer	28Ju33Kz
BLACK, William	70	M	Laborer	28Ju33Kz
Isabella	70	F	Unknown	28Ju33Kz
FAIRLEY, James	29	M	Laborer	28Ju33Kz
Elizabeth	27	F	Unknown	28Ju33Kz
FAIRLEY, Benjamin-C.	5	M	Child	28Ju33Kz
William	3	M	Child	28Ju33Kz
James	.09	M	Infant	28Ju33Kz
Died-At-Sea				
BLAIR, John	29	M	Laborer	28Ju33Kz
Jane	26	F	Unknown	28Ju33Kz
BLACK, William-Jr.	35	M	Laborer	28Ju33Kz
MARTIN, James	18	M	Laborer	28Ju33Kz
SHEARER, Mary	.06	F	Infant	28Ju33Kz
BROWN, Robert	60	M	Unknown	28Ju33Kz
Christina	58	F	Unknown	28Ju33Kz
Henry	26	M	Unknown	28Ju33Kz
Matilda	24	F	Unknown	28Ju33Kz
Robert	4	M	Child	28Ju33Kz
Christina	.04	F	Infant	28Ju33Kz
Janet	26	F	Unknown	28Ju33Kz
Christina	18	F	Unknown	28Ju33Kz
Robert	30	M	Unknown	28Ju33Kz
CAIRNCROFT, William	25	M	Unknown	28Ju33Kz
FALCONER, John	30	M	Unknown	28Ju33Kz
Wm.	28	M	Unknown	28Ju33Kz
JOHNSTON, John	24	M	Unknown	28Ju33Kz
Agnes	26	F	Unknown	28Ju33Kz
MCCOMOCHIE, Wm.	23	M	Unknown	28Ju33Kz
Alexr.	22	M	Unknown	28Ju33Kz
LANIG, John-E.	21	M	Unknown	28Ju33Kz
Mary	21	F	Unknown	28Ju33Kz
RALSTON, Alexander	20	M	Unknown	28Ju33Kz
BROWN, Janet	30	F	Unknown	28Ju33Kz
Died-At-Sea				
RALSTON, Margaret	29	F	Unknown	28Ju33Kz
Isabella	3	F	Child	28Ju33Kz
Jane	.09	F	Infant	28Ju33Kz
JOHNSTON, Jean	2	F	Child	28Ju33Kz
Isabella	.09	F	Infant	28Ju33Kz
CHALMERS, Robert	45	M	Unknown	28Ju33Kz
Isabella	43	F	Unknown	28Ju33Kz
MCRITCHIE, Elizabeth	27	F	Unknown	28Ju33Kz
CHALMERS, Elizabeth	2	F	Child	28Ju33Kz
John	.10	M	Infant	28Ju33Kz
MCRITCHIE, Ann	11	F	Unknown	28Ju33Kz
CUTHEL, Mary	40	F	Unknown	28Ju33Kz
Jean	9	F	Child	28Ju33Kz
Agnes	7	F	Child	28Ju33Kz
BLAIN, Ellen	25	F	Unknown	28Ju33Kz
Margaret	4	F	Child	28Ju33Kz
Ellen	.10	F	Infant	28Ju33Kz
DOUGLAS, Margaret	24	F	Unknown	28Ju33Kz
DUDDY, Ellen	17	F	Servant	28Ju33Kz

CYNTHIA 28 JUNE 1849

From Berbice

NAMES OF PASSENGERS	AGE	SEX	OCCUPATIONS	DATE PORT SHIP
MCKENZIA, Donald	25	M	Carpenter	28Ju17Mm
FAIRFIELD, Isaac	30	M	None	28Ju17Mm

FALCON 28 JUNE 1849

From HAMILTON, Bermuda

NAMES OF PASSENGERS	AGE	SEX	OCCUPATIONS	DATE PORT SHIP
OUTERBRIDGE, W.R.O.	45	M	Merchant	28Ju60Kd
U	18	F	Lady	28Ju60Kd

NAMES OF PASSENGERS	AGE	SEX	OCCUPATIONS	DATE PORT SHIP
TUCKER, James	23	M	Gentleman	28Ju60Kd
LIGHTBOURN, Alexander	20	M	Clerk	28Ju60Kd
SMITH, Daniel	22	M	Merchant	28Ju60Kd
WEST, J.	30	M	Mechanic	28Ju60Kd
LEON, Daniel	10	M	Unknown	28Ju60Kd
HARVEY, U	25	F	Unknown	28Ju60Kd
STEELE, U	18	F	Unknown	28Ju60Kd
PITT, U-Mrs.	43	F	Unknown	28Ju60Kd

GUY-MANNERING 28 JUNE 1849

From Liverpool

NAMES OF PASSENGERS	AGE	SEX	OCCUPATIONS	DATE PORT SHIP
BENSON, Willis-A.	27	M	Gentleman	28Ju02Lc
SIKES, John-S.	26	M	Merchant	28Ju02Lc
PRATT, Jacob-B.	23	M	Olmcht	28Ju02Lc
WICKHAM, Henry-T.	28	M	Gentleman	28Ju02Lc
BUTTERLEY, Nicholas	26	M	Merchant	28Ju02Lc
Ellen	21	F	None	28Ju02Lc
Ellen	21	F	None	28Ju02Lc
WILLIAMS, David	49	M	Minister	28Ju02Lc
Mary	42	F	None	28Ju02Lc
Mary	15	F	None	28Ju02Lc
Elizabeth	13	F	None	28Ju02Lc
Benjamin	11	M	None	28Ju02Lc
Margaret	9	F	Child	28Ju02Lc
Jane	7	F	Child	28Ju02Lc
Amelia	5	F	Child	28Ju02Lc
Martha	3	F	Child	28Ju02Lc
John	.11	M	Infant	28Ju02Lc
David	.11	M	Infant	28Ju02Lc
Ann	22	F	None	28Ju02Lc
LEWIS, Mary	19	F	None	28Ju02Lc
GRIFFITHS, Thomas	27	M	Farmer	28Ju02Lc
THOMAS, Richard	30	M	Farmer	28Ju02Lc
Mary	29	F	None	28Ju02Lc
Mary	10	F	Child	28Ju02Lc
Margaret	8	F	Child	28Ju02Lc
Eliza	4	F	Child	28Ju02Lc
Eleanor	2	F	Child	28Ju02Lc
KNOTT, James	45	M	Gentleman	28Ju02Lc
William	18	M	Gentleman	28Ju02Lc
Ann	20	F	None	28Ju02Lc
Elizabeth	16	F	None	28Ju02Lc
Frederick	12	M	None	28Ju02Lc
BLOWER, John	39	M	Clergyman	28Ju02Lc
WOOD, Owen	24	M	Blacksmith	28Ju02Lc
WINCHIN, William-H.	18	M	Unknown	28Ju02Lc
MAHER, James	33	M	Farmer	28Ju02Lc
Kate	30	M	Farmer	28Ju02Lc
Mary	22	F	Farmer	28Ju02Lc
Eliza	20	F	Farmer	28Ju02Lc
Honora	12	F	Child	28Ju02Lc
James	10	M	Child	28Ju02Lc
Emily	9	F	Child	28Ju02Lc
Jane	7	M	Child	28Ju02Lc
John	5	M	Child	28Ju02Lc
Laura	2	M	Child	28Ju02Lc
MCGROWTHER, Charles	21	M	Laborer	28Ju02Lc
KELLY, Mary	22	F	None	28Ju02Lc
FAGAN, Peter	26	M	Laborer	28Ju02Lc
Died-At-Sea				
KELLY, Patrick	27	M	Laborer	28Ju02Lc
MOLLOY, Charles	24	M	Merchant	28Ju02Lc
DOBBS, William	26	M	Surveyor	28Ju02Lc
GLEESON, Andrew	26	M	Laborer	28Ju02Lc
HARRINGTON, Peter	26	M	Laborer	28Ju02Lc
Mary	21	F	None	28Ju02Lc
BUCKLEY, John	40	M	Blacksmith	28Ju02Lc
NOONAN, Patrick	21	M	Laborer	28Ju02Lc
REMICK, George	21	M	Servant	28Ju02Lc
Elizabeth	19	F	Servant	28Ju02Lc
MAHER, William	45	M	Laborer	28Ju02Lc
Daniel	19	M	Laborer	28Ju02Lc
SPINKS, Elizabeth	20	F	Lad	28Ju02Lc
HUNT, Ann	40	F	Dressmaker	28Ju02Lc
Amelia	20	F	Dressmaker	28Ju02Lc
Ann	17	F	Dressmaker	28Ju02Lc
Ellen	14	F	Dressmaker	28Ju02Lc
Astasia	16	F	Dressmaker	28Ju02Lc
Catherine	10	F	Child	28Ju02Lc
LYNCH, Michael	21	M	Laborer	28Ju02Lc
Died-At-Sea				
MAHONY, John	26	M	Engineer	28Ju02Lc
John-Fitz	27	M	Engineer	28Ju02Lc
MCCARTHY, Owen	22	M	Steward	28Ju02Lc
WARD, Patrick	30	M	Upholsterer	28Ju02Lc
COURTENAY, Patrick	21	M	Pawn Broker	28Ju02Lc
Bartholemew	19	M	Pawn Broker	28Ju02Lc
DILLON, John	31	M	Farmer	28Ju02Lc
Susan	28	F	None	28Ju02Lc
Died-At-Sea				
Robert	9	M	Child	28Ju02Lc
Michael	3	M	Child	28Ju02Lc
Margaret	2	F	Child	28Ju02Lc
Died-At-Sea				
Thomas	.09	M	Infant	28Ju02Lc
Died-At-Sea				
MOLONEY, James	30	M	Laborer	28Ju02Lc
PURCELL, Michael	25	M	Laborer	28Ju02Lc
CULLEN, Jeffrey	27	M	Laborer	28Ju02Lc
Stephen	27	M	Laborer	28Ju02Lc
Died-At-Sea				
Peter	24	M	Laborer	28Ju02Lc
Mary	60	F	Laborer	28Ju02Lc
GAYNOR, Martha	24	F	Laborer	28Ju02Lc
SMITH, Philip	46	F	Laborer	28Ju02Lc
MCGWYN, Christr.	50	F	Laborer	28Ju02Lc
THANAGHAN, Catherine	24	M	Servant	28Ju02Lc
RICKERBY, John	25	M	Laborer	28Ju02Lc
Ralph	16	M	Laborer	28Ju02Lc
HILL, George	25	M	Laborer	28Ju02Lc
WALSH, John	34	M	Laborer	28Ju02Lc
Ann	34	F	Laborer	28Ju02Lc
Morris	9	M	Child	28Ju02Lc
Daniel	4	M	Child	28Ju02Lc
Mary	3	F	Child	28Ju02Lc
David	.06	M	Infant	28Ju02Lc
MULLEN, Dennis	34	M	Laborer	28Ju02Lc
CARROLL, Johanna	20	F	Laborer	28Ju02Lc
CROTTY, Thomas	24	M	Laborer	28Ju02Lc
ROSBOTTOM, Robert	16	M	Plasterer	28Ju02Lc
BENNET, William	50	M	Farmer	28Ju02Lc
Elizabeth	50	F	None	28Ju02Lc
Thomas	24	M	None	28Ju02Lc
William	22	M	None	28Ju02Lc
Hugh	19	M	None	28Ju02Lc
Elizabeth	17	F	None	28Ju02Lc
Bridget	12	F	None	28Ju02Lc
John	6	M	Child	28Ju02Lc
Bridget	50	F	None	28Ju02Lc
Jane	30	F	None	28Ju02Lc
DEVIN, Catherine	24	F	None	28Ju02Lc
MARKEY, Ann	26	F	None	28Ju02L
GEFNEY, Bartholemew	27	M	Laborer	28Ju02Lc
MCGRATH, Roger	60	M	Laborer	28Ju02L
Ellen	55	F	None	28Ju02L
Roger	21	M	None	28Ju02L
Catherine	24	F	None	28Ju02L
Eliza.	22	F	None	28Ju02L
Johanna	18	F	None	28Ju02L
DONNEGAN, Johanna	16	F	None	28Ju02L
OBRIEN, Julia	22	F	None	28Ju02L
Mary	60	F	None	28Ju02L

NAMES OF PASSENGERS	AGE	SEX	OCCUPATIONS	DATE PORT SHIP
OBRIEN, Peggy	.11	F	Infant	28Ju02Lc
KEEFF, Mary	26	F	None	28Ju02Lc
John	.10	M	Infant	28Ju02Lc
MCDONNEL, James	27	M	Blacksmith	28Ju02Lc
Catherine	24	M	None	28Ju02Lc
Theresa	2	F	Child	28Ju02Lc
HAYES, John	26	M	Laborer	28Ju02Lc
Honora	24	F	Servant	28Ju02Lc
Mary	25	F	None	28Ju02Lc
DWYER, Ellen	25	F	None	28Ju02Lc
HAYES, Bridget	15	F	None	28Ju02Lc
GALLAVAN, Murty	40	M	Laborer	28Ju02Lc
John	18	M	Laborer	28Ju02Lc
Thomas	15	M	Laborer	28Ju02Lc
Margaret	13	F	None	28Ju02Lc
MULLANE, Patrick	30	M	Farmer	28Ju02Lc
Honora	25	F	None	28Ju02Lc
Michael	2	M	Child	28Ju02Lc
Kate	1	F	Child	28Ju02Lc
James	.01	M	Infant	28Ju02Lc
GILLIVAN, Kate	21	F	Servant	28Ju02Lc
NOLAN, Bridget	21	F	Servant	28Ju02Lc
HARGATE, Margaret	18	F	Servant	28Ju02Lc
REYAN, John	13	M	Laborer	28Ju02Lc
MONTGOMERY, George	24	M	Carpenter	28Ju02Lc
MCCARTHY, Jeremiah	32	M	Butcher	28Ju02Lc
MCGIRL, Jeremiah	21	M	Laborer	28Ju02Lc
MCCAFFREY, John	16	M	Laborer	28Ju02Lc
BURKE, Walter	27	M	Farmer	28Ju02Lc
FINNESY, Thomas	27	M	Laborer	28Ju02Lc
MORRIS, Michael	30	M	Laborer	28Ju02Lc
LOMNESSY, William	25	M	Laborer	28Ju02Lc
ONEIL, Patrick	22	M	Laborer	28Ju02Lc
PHELAN, Margaret	15	M	Servant	28Ju02Lc
PHIDDERSON, Thomas	13	M	Laborer	28Ju02Lc
MANNING, James	20	M	Farmer	28Ju02Lc
Bessy	50	F	Farmer	28Ju02Lc
Bessy	18	F	Farmer	28Ju02Lc
DOYLE, James	21	M	Farmer	28Ju02Lc
MCLAUGHLIN, John	18	M	Farmer	28Ju02Lc
DOOLING, Marcella	50	F	Farmer	28Ju02Lc
Edward	22	M	Farmer	28Ju02Lc
Eliza	20	F	Farmer	28Ju02Lc
Patrick	12	M	Farmer	28Ju02Lc
Mary	10	F	Child	28Ju02Lc
DUNNE, Ellen	40	F	Farmer	28Ju02Lc
ARMSTRONG, William	56	M	Laborer	28Ju02Lc
Jane	42	F	None	28Ju02Lc
John	16	M	None	28Ju02Lc
Mary-Ann	14	F	None	28Ju02Lc
Ellen	8	F	Child	28Ju02Lc
John	16	M	None	28Ju02Lc
GREENAN, Mary	17	F	None	28Ju02Lc
MCKENNAH, Hugh	24	M	Farmer	28Ju02Lc
Bernard	22	M	Farmer	28Ju02Lc
SULLIVAN, John	40	M	Farmer	28Ju02Lc
WALSH, William	32	M	Laborer	28Ju02Lc
Died-At-Sea				
Margaret	40	F	Laborer	28Ju02Lc
Died-At-Sea				
MAUGEN, Pat.	6	M	Child	28Ju02Lc
Mary	4	F	Child	28Ju02Lc
Margaret	20	F	Laborer	28Ju02Lc
CLARKE, Catherine	26	F	Laborer	28Ju02Lc
Catherine	15	F	Laborer	28Ju02Lc
Biddy	8	F	Child	28Ju02Lc
MORLEY, James	20	M	Laborer	28Ju02Lc
CATLIN, Mary	14	F	Laborer	28Ju02Lc
WILEY, William	25	M	Laborer	28Ju02Lc
MULLEN, Patrick	40	M	Stctr	28Ju02Lc
Catherine	38	F	None	28Ju02Lc
James	9	M	Child	28Ju02Lc
Bridget	4	F	Child	28Ju02Lc
MORRAY, David	25	M	Laborer	28Ju02Lc
CURRAN, Marcella	20	F	Servant	28Ju02Lc
RYAN, Mary	22	F	Servant	28Ju02Lc
MORESSY, Catherine	22	F	Servant	28Ju02Lc
ROCHE, Catherine	16	F	Servant	28Ju02Lc
COFFEY, William	22	M	Laborer	28Ju02Lc
PIERCEY, John	24	M	Laborer	28Ju02Lc
CARTY, William	25	M	Laborer	28Ju02Lc
ODAY, Michael	26	M	Laborer	28Ju02Lc
MCNAUGHTEN, Francis	50	M	Laborer	28Ju02Lc
Margaret	20	F	None	28Ju02Lc
Henry	22	M	None	28Ju02Lc
Eliza	18	F	None	28Ju02Lc
CONNOR, Patrick	30	M	None	28Ju02Lc
Ellen	21	F	None	28Ju02Lc
CASTIGAN, Maurice	16	M	Farmer	28Ju02Lc
Catherine	11	F	Farmer	28Ju02Lc
Mary	6	F	Child	28Ju02Lc
CAFFREY, Patrick	20	M	Farmer	28Ju02Lc
MAHER, James	20	M	Farmer	28Ju02Lc
SPILLANE, John	20	M	Farmer	28Ju02Lc
Patrick	16	M	Farmer	28Ju02Lc
FARREN, John	27	M	Laborer	28Ju02Lc
MURPHY, Dennis	50	M	Laborer	28Ju02Lc
Margaret	20	F	None	28Ju02Lc
COONEY, Bridget	18	F	None	28Ju02Lc
MULDOON, Peter	20	M	Farmer	28Ju02Lc
Died-At-Sea				
Michael	23	M	Farmer	28Ju02Lc
Patrick	24	M	Farmer	28Ju02Lc
MORGAN, John	19	M	None	28Ju02Lc
CARR, Charles	36	M	None	28Ju02Lc
CARRIGAN, Ann	22	F	None	28Ju02Lc
QUIN, Margaret	22	F	None	28Ju02Lc
MULDOON, Maria	18	F	None	28Ju02Lc
Theresa	12	F	None	28Ju02Lc
Elizabeth	16	F	None	28Ju02Lc
CAVANAGH, Charles	45	M	Farmer	28Ju02Lc
LITTLE, James	26	M	Laborer	28Ju02Lc
DILLON, John	18	M	Laborer	28Ju02Lc
Joseph	15	M	Laborer	28Ju02Lc
HUDSON, John	22	M	Laborer	28Ju02Lc
BROWN, Patrick	18	M	Laborer	28Ju02Lc
MCDOOLE, Alexder.	39	M	Laborer	28Ju02Lc
DEVILLING, Maria	21	F	Laborer	28Ju02Lc
MCDOOLE, Betty	4	F	Child	28Ju02Lc
WRIGHT, Joseph	21	M	Laborer	28Ju02Lc
Sally	18	F	None	28Ju02Lc
MCGEE, Robert	25	M	Laborer	28Ju02Lc
Margaret	21	F	None	28Ju02Lc
GILES, Alexder.	19	M	Laborer	28Ju02Lc
Abraham	25	M	Laborer	28Ju02Lc
MCQUIRK, Pat.	18	M	Laborer	28Ju02Lc
Catherine	12	F	None	28Ju02Lc
Hannah	21	F	None	28Ju02Lc
MCKENNAH, Francis	20	M	Laborer	28Ju02Lc
OSULLIVAN, James	45	M	Laborer	28Ju02Lc
Nancy	40	F	None	28Ju02Lc
Nancy	15	F	None	28Ju02Lc
James	6	M	Child	28Ju02Lc
Mary	8	F	Child	28Ju02Lc
Timothy	19	M	Farmer	28Ju02Lc
RYAN, Patrick	20	M	Laborer	28Ju02Lc
Died-At-Sea				
MCQUILLAN, Ellen	22	M	Servant	28Ju02Lc
MCDONNEL, Francis	22	M	Laborer	28Ju02Lc
FRAINON, Bernard	22	M	Laborer	28Ju02Lc
GILMORE, Ann	21	F	Servant	28Ju02Lc
Died-At-Sea				
DUFFY, Margaret	30	F	Servant	28Ju02Lc
MCGIRR, Ann	20	F	Servant	28Ju02Lc
COLLINGS, Mary	20	F	Servant	28Ju02Lc
EUSTACE, Michael	45	M	Farmer	28Ju02Lc
Died-At-Sea				
Mary	45	F	None	28Ju02Lc
Michael	20	M	None	28Ju02Lc
Thomas	.11	M	Infant	28Ju02Lc

NAMES OF PASSENGERS	AGE	SEX	OCCUPATIONS	DATE PORT SHIP
FORD, Pierce	26	M	Farmer	28Ju02Lc
Died-At-Sea				
Mary	23	F	Farmer	28Ju02Lc
Mary	.03	F	Infant	28Ju02Lc
Died-At-Sea				
KEELY, Patrick	17	M	Gdnr	28Ju02Lc
James	40	M	Gdnr	28Ju02Lc
Margaret	44	F	None	28Ju02Lc
MURPHY, Michael	36	M	Laborer	28Ju02Lc
John	34	M	Laborer	28Ju02Lc
Died-At-Sea				
KILDEE, Brian	21	M	Laborer	28Ju02Lc
Nabby	50	F	None	28Ju02Lc
John	23	M	Laborer	28Ju02Lc
Hugh	16	M	Laborer	28Ju02Lc
BOYD, Thomas	24	M	Laborer	28Ju02Lc
Eliza	20	F	None	28Ju02Lc
MAINES, Francis	31	M	Laborer	28Ju02Lc
GILLESPIE, William	21	M	Laborer	28Ju02Lc
BOYD, John	20	M	Laborer	28Ju02Lc
BANKES, George	26	M	Laborer	28Ju02Lc
Honora	24	F	None	28Ju02Lc
GRIMES, Catherine	30	F	Servant	28Ju02Lc
Margaret	11	F	None	28Ju02Lc
Catherine	6	F	Child	28Ju02Lc
Francis	3	F	Child	28Ju02Lc
MCAVERY, Alice	19	F	Servant	28Ju02Lc
HOGAN, Martha	36	F	Servant	28Ju02Lc
BURN, James	26	M	Laborer	28Ju02Lc
FOLEY, Bridget	45	F	Servant	28Ju02Lc
James	22	M	None	28Ju02Lc
John	10	M	Child	28Ju02Lc
Catherine	6	F	Child	28Ju02Lc
HENNESSY, Thomas	54	M	Laborer	28Ju02Lc
OKEEFE, Mary	25	F	None	28Ju02Lc
Mary	9	F	Child	28Ju02Lc
Thomas	2	M	Child	28Ju02Lc
JACKSON, Dennis	40	M	Farmer	28Ju02Lc
Johanna	35	F	None	28Ju02Lc
Dennis	10	M	Child	28Ju02Lc
Kate	8	F	Child	28Ju02Lc
Ellen	6	F	Child	28Ju02Lc
John	4	M	Child	28Ju02Lc
Mary	1	F	Child	28Ju02Lc
MANGEN, Ellen	40	F	None	28Ju02Lc
COGHLAN, Mary	19	F	None	28Ju02Lc
FITZGERALD, Catherine	22	F	None	28Ju02Lc
STEEL, William	30	M	Farmer	28Ju02Lc
Hannah	22	F	Farmer	28Ju02Lc
Henry	18	M	Farmer	28Ju02Lc
Sarah-Ann	6	F	Child	28Ju02Lc
Mary-Jane	4	F	Child	28Ju02Lc
Elizabeth	.07	F	Infant	28Ju02Lc
REGAN, Elizabeth	18	F	Farmer	28Ju02Lc
BRENNAN, Bridget	13	F	Servant	28Ju02Lc
LINNIGHAN, Catherine	50	F	Servant	28Ju02Lc
BYRON, Mary	30	F	Servant	28Ju02Lc
RYAN, Patrick	30	M	Laborer	28Ju02Lc
Catherine	20	F	Laborer	28Ju02Lc
FITZGERALD, Garrick	30	M	Laborer	28Ju02Lc
Mary	30	F	Laborer	28Ju02Lc
Richard	3	M	Child	28Ju02Lc
John	2	M	Child	28Ju02Lc
Catherine	.03	F	Infant	28Ju02Lc
MCCULLOUGH, Daniel	30	M	Laborer	28Ju02Lc
Rachael	24	F	None	28Ju02Lc
BELL, Matty	18	F	Servant	28Ju02Lc
MORRISON, Mary	25	F	Servant	28Ju02Lc
HALL, William	25	M	Laborer	28Ju02Lc
MULLEN, John	21	M	Laborer	28Ju02Lc
GORDON, Richard	20	M	Laborer	28Ju02Lc
Sarah	19	F	None	28Ju02Lc
KENNEDY, John	24	M	Farmer	28Ju02Lc
NAGLE, Michael	20	M	Farmer	28Ju02Lc
RYAN, William-F.	20	M	Laborer	28Ju02Lc
RYAN, Bridget	20	F	None	28Ju02Lc
SULLIGAN, James	40	M	Laborer	28Ju02Lc
Died-At-Sea				
KEENAN, Bridget	60	F	Laborer	28Ju02Lc
KELLY, Patrick	11	M	Laborer	28Ju02Lc
NOONAN, Mary	26	F	Servant	28Ju02Lc
MAHER, Daniel	20	M	Laborer	28Ju02Lc
Died-At-Sea				
Patrick	21	M	Laborer	28Ju02Lc
HARA, Owen-A.	23	M	Laborer	28Ju02Lc
James	20	M	Laborer	28Ju02Lc
HANNEGAN, Thomas	18	M	Laborer	28Ju02Lc
HARA, Bridget	22	F	Laborer	28Ju02Lc
Mary	.06	F	Infant	28Ju02Lc
Died-At-Sea				
MCCANN, Margaret	44	F	Laborer	28Ju02Lc
Margaret	18	F	Laborer	28Ju02Lc
Margaret	7	F	Child	28Ju02Lc
DOLAN, Michael	30	M	Laborer	28Ju02Lc
Grace	20	F	Laborer	28Ju02Lc
Thomas	.05	M	Infant	28Ju02Lc
LANGAN, Margaret	20	F	Servant	28Ju02Lc
Mary	7	F	Child	28Ju02Lc
Mary	9	F	Child	28Ju02Lc
DONDALL, Henry	22	M	Laborer	28Ju02Lc
Michael	30	M	Laborer	28Ju02Lc
KENEFIC, Michael	21	M	Laborer	28Ju02Lc
Honora	20	F	Laborer	28Ju02Lc
John	8	M	Child	28Ju02Lc
MASON, Chris.	40	M	Laborer	28Ju02Lc
Ellen	35	M	Laborer	28Ju02Lc
John	6	M	Child	28Ju02Lc
Ellen	4	F	Child	28Ju02Lc
Nathan	2	M	Child	28Ju02Lc
Isabella	16	F	Laborer	28Ju02Lc
BARNES, Thomas	60	M	Laborer	28Ju02Lc
Henry	21	M	Laborer	28Ju02Lc
James	22	M	Laborer	28Ju02Lc
Mary	20	F	Laborer	28Ju02Lc
CALLAGHAN, Robert	22	M	Laborer	28Ju02Lc
WALSH, Mary	40	F	Laborer	28Ju02Lc
James	19	M	Laborer	28Ju02Lc
Died-At-Sea				
Edward	17	M	Laborer	28Ju02Lc
Died-At-Sea				
John	13	M	Laborer	28Ju02Lc
Thomas	11	M	Laborer	28Ju02Lc
Maria	8	F	Child	28Ju02Lc
Bridget	6	F	Child	28Ju02Lc
Margaret	20	F	Laborer	28Ju02Lc
KENNEDY, John	46	M	Laborer	28Ju02Lc
CARNEY, John	14	M	Laborer	28Ju02Lc
MINCHIN, George	22	M	Laborer	28Ju02Lc
FINTON, Dennis	25	M	Laborer	28Ju02Lc
Ann	25	F	Laborer	28Ju02Lc
JONES, Thomas	21	M	Laborer	28Ju02Lc
OBRIEN, John	24	M	Laborer	28Ju02Lc
Mary	22	F	Laborer	28Ju02Lc
Michael	.06	M	Infant	28Ju02Lc
Died-At-Sea				
COLLINGS, Bridet	11	F	Child	28Ju02Lc
KELLY, Francis	20	M	Laborer	28Ju02Lc
CARMODY, Mary	23	F	Laborer	28Ju02Lc
Catherine	22	F	Laborer	28Ju02Lc
Dennis	20	M	Laborer	28Ju02Lc
Ellen	12	F	Laborer	28Ju02Lc
Michael	10	M	Child	28Ju02Lc
Cornelius	7	M	Child	28Ju02Lc
Martin	3	M	Child	28Ju02Lc
QUIN, Edward	40	M	Laborer	28Ju02Lc
Margaret	40	F	Laborer	28Ju02Lc
Catherine	16	F	Laborer	28Ju02Lc
Charles	10	M	Child	28Ju02Lc
Edmund	8	M	Child	28Ju02Lc
John	6	M	Child	28Ju02Lc

NAMES OF PASSENGERS	A G E	S E X	OCCUPATIONS	DATE PORT SHIP
QUIN, Margaret	3	F	Child	28Ju02Lc
GRUGAN, Owen	35	M	Laborer	28Ju02Lc
HOEY, Patrick	28	M	Laborer	28Ju02Lc
CAMPBELL, Bridget	20	F	Servant	28Ju02Lc
FENNEL, John	23	M	Farmer	28Ju02Lc
DUFFIN, Michael	23	M	Farmer	28Ju02Lc
HICKEY, Patrick	22	M	Laborer	28Ju02Lc
MCGARRY, Timothy	21	M	Laborer	28Ju02Lc
James	18	M	Laborer	28Ju02Lc
WILLIAMS, John	20	M	Laborer	28Ju02Lc
CONNELL, John	18	M	Laborer	28Ju02Lc
MCCAMBRIDGE, Benjm.	20	M	Laborer	28Ju02Lc
Archibald	18	M	Laborer	28Ju02Lc
MCNALLY, Patrick	18	M	Laborer	28Ju02Lc
HEIMAN, Rose	20	F	Laborer	28Ju02Lc
EARLY, John	24	M	Laborer	28Ju02Lc
BARRY, Edward	24	M	Laborer	28Ju02Lc
Died-At-Sea				
Catherine	50	F	Laborer	28Ju02Lc
Died-At-Sea				
John	16	M	Laborer	28Ju02Lc
Charles	11	M	Laborer	28Ju02Lc
Mary	9	F	Child	28Ju02Lc
FORD, Mary	20	F	Laborer	28Ju02Lc
CARR, Owen	16	M	Laborer	28Ju02Lc
Anne	18	F	Laborer	28Ju02Lc
RYAN, Thomas	25	M	Laborer	28Ju02Lc
REEDY, Michael	18	M	Laborer	28Ju02Lc
CLANCEY, Henry	30	M	Laborer	28Ju02Lc
Betsy	28	F	Laborer	28Ju02Lc
DUGGAN, William	30	M	Farmer	28Ju02Lc
RYAN, Teddy	24	M	Laborer	28Ju02Lc
QUIRK, Johanna	24	F	Laborer	28Ju02Lc
James	11	M	Laborer	28Ju02Lc
HEATHERSTONE, Patrick	20	M	Miller	28Ju02Lc
KELLY, Timothy	50	M	Laborer	28Ju02Lc
Catherine	50	F	None	28Ju02Lc
Ellen	6	F	Child	28Ju02Lc
LEWIS, Thomas	25	M	Laborer	28Ju02Lc
Mary	20	F	None	28Ju02Lc
VAHY, Mathew	20	M	Laborer	28Ju02Lc
HUMPHREY, William	19	M	Laborer	28Ju02Lc
LONG, Frances	16	M	Laborer	28Ju02Lc
Died-At-Sea				
ROBERTS, Charles	28	M	Laborer	28Ju02Lc
Mary	26	F	Laborer	28Ju02Lc
Died-At-Sea				
U	.00	M	Infant	28Ju02Lc
Born-At-Sea				
John	6	M	Child	28Ju02Lc
George	4	M	Child	28Ju02Lc
Died-At-Sea				
MCCROSY, James	25	M	Laborer	28Ju02Lc
FIELD, Mary	40	F	None	28Ju02Lc
James	7	M	Child	28Ju02Lc
CALLEY, Eliza.	20	F	Laborer	28Ju02Lc
GEORDY, Bridget	24	F	Laborer	28Ju02Lc
HEARN, Mich.A.	21	M	Laborer	28Ju02Lc
WALPOLE, Mary-A.	22	F	Laborer	28Ju02Lc
RYAN, John	26	M	Laborer	28Ju02Lc
DUGGAN, Anne	22	F	Laborer	28Ju02Lc
OCONNELL, Margt.	20	F	Laborer	28Ju02Lc
WARD, Mary-Ann	25	F	Servant	28Ju02Lc

SARDINIA 29 JUNE 1849

From Liverpool

NAMES OF PASSENGERS	A G E	S E X	OCCUPATIONS	DATE PORT SHIP
MURPHY, Edw.	25	M	Laborer	29Ju02Jw
SULLIVAN, John	23	M	Laborer	29Ju02Jw
CORLAN, Saml.	27	M	Laborer	29Ju02Jw
MCGOWAN, Jane	17	F	Servant	29Ju02Jw
MULLOY, Wm.	16	M	Unknown	29Ju02Jw
FLOOD, Cath.	14	F	Unknown	29Ju02Jw
PARKER, John	27	M	Laborer	29Ju02Jw
Mary	24	F	Unknown	29Ju02Jw
Matthew	4	M	Child	29Ju02Jw
Saml.	.00	M	Infant	29Ju02Jw
MCCARLIN, Michl.	12	M	Smith	29Ju02Jw
Mary	11	F	Smith	29Ju02Jw
Eliza	8	F	Child	29Ju02Jw
OCONNELL, Jas.	29	M	Farmer	29Ju02Jw
WALKER, Michl.	40	M	Unknown	29Ju02Jw
CLARKE, Wm.	20	M	Farmer	29Ju02Jw
FOSTER, George	22	M	Clerk	29Ju02Jw
HIGGINS, Pat.	22	M	Laborer	29Ju02Jw
MCINTYRE, John	24	M	Unknown	29Ju02Jw
HIGGINS, Bessy	24	F	Laborer	29Ju02Jw
RILEY, Honor	22	F	Laborer	29Ju02Jw
BRADY, Mary	20	F	Laborer	29Ju02Jw
FAY, Jas.	18	M	Laborer	29Ju02Jw
SMITH, Thos.	20	M	Laborer	29Ju02Jw
MCKEOWN, Ann	22	F	Laborer	29Ju02Jw
CAVANAGH, Thos.	20	M	Laborer	29Ju02Jw
Bridget	20	F	Laborer	29Ju02Jw
LINAGH, Cath.	20	F	Laborer	29Ju02Jw
TULLY, Ann	24	F	Laborer	29Ju02Jw
FRISH, John	30	M	Unknown	29Ju02Jw
NORTON, Cath.	20	F	Unknown	29Ju02Jw
BRADY, Mary	20	F	Servant	29Ju02Jw
BROWN, Margt.	22	F	Servant	29Ju02Jw
MAHON, Michl.	23	M	Farmer	29Ju02Jw
QUILL, Mary	20	F	Servant	29Ju02Jw
Margt.	22	F	Unknown	29Ju02Jw
Thos.	22	M	Unknown	29Ju02Jw
DEWS, Geo.	35	M	Farmer	29Ju02Jw
Wm.	11	M	Unknown	29Ju02Jw
ROBINS, Henry	30	M	Farmer	29Ju02Jw
Ann	30	F	Unknown	29Ju02Jw
Joseph	7	M	Child	29Ju02Jw
Amelia	2	F	Child	29Ju02Jw
EVANS, John	23	M	Laborer	29Ju02Jw
BAILY, Geo.	21	M	Cpt	29Ju02Jw
MATTHEWS, Saml.	23	M	Weaver	29Ju02Jw
Thos.	33	M	Weaver	29Ju02Jw
MURPHY, Sarah	23	F	Servant	29Ju02Jw
MCKERNEY, Ellen	17	F	Servant	29Ju02Jw
MCCARROLL, John	21	M	Groom	29Ju02Jw
MORGAN, Mary	16	F	Servant	29Ju02Jw
WRIGHT, Richd.	22	M	Servant	29Ju02Jw
Harriet	24	F	Servant	29Ju02Jw
JOHNSTON, John-G.	25	M	Laborer	29Ju02Jw
HAYES, Jas.	35	M	Laborer	29Ju02Jw
CAMPBELL, Danl.	19	M	Laborer	29Ju02Jw
FITZGERALD, Johannah	30	F	Servant	29Ju02Jw
FOLEY, Thos.	21	M	Servant	29Ju02Jw
FLAHARAN, Jas.	21	M	Servant	29Ju02Jw
Jerh.	20	M	Servant	29Ju02Jw
HANNIGAN, Wm.	14	M	Unknown	29Ju02Jw
HAYES, Peter	29	M	Smith	29Ju02Jw
MCDONALD, Bridget	25	F	Servant	29Ju02Jw
DOUGHERTY, John	18	M	Cooper	29Ju02Jw
GREENAN, Mary	19	F	Servant	29Ju02Jw

NAMES OF PASSENGERS	AGE	SEX	OCCUPATIONS	DATE PORT SHIP
BRADY, Chas.	22	M	Laborer	29Ju02Jw
MCCANN, Mary	34	F	Servant	29Ju02Jw
Mary	8	F	Child	29Ju02Jw
Sarah	4	F	Child	29Ju02Jw
MCQUAID, Mary	35	F	Servant	29Ju02Jw
RUSSELL, Richd.	21	M	Farmer	29Ju02Jw
FAY, Jas.	22	M	Cooper	29Ju02Jw
JONES, Ann	16	F	Servant	29Ju02Jw
RICHARDS, Sarah	37	F	Servant	29Ju02Jw
Mary-Ann	10	F	Servant	29Ju02Jw
Eliza	7	F	Child	29Ju02Jw
Chas.	5	M	Child	29Ju02Jw
John	2	M	Child	29Ju02Jw
FLESH, Thos.	30	M	Farmer	29Ju02Jw
Edwd.	28	M	Farmer	29Ju02Jw
Bridget	50	F	Unknown	29Ju02Jw
MCBRIDE, Cath.	22	F	Servant	29Ju02Jw
Bridget	3	F	Child	29Ju02Jw
MURPHY, Michl.	25	M	Weaver	29Ju02Jw
U (W)	25	F	Weaver	29Ju02Jw
Ruth	20	F	Weaver	29Ju02Jw
Ruth	18	F	Weaver	29Ju02Jw
James	.00	M	Infant	29Ju02Jw
SHORT, Pat.	25	M	Cooper	29Ju02Jw
Mary	18	F	Cooper	29Ju02Jw
FURNESS, Mary	22	F	Cooper	29Ju02Jw
Ruth	.00	F	Infant	29Ju02Jw
MCCANN, U	.00	U	Infant	29Ju02Jw
MULLIGAN, Margt.	25	F	Servant	29Ju02Jw
Margt.	5	F	Child	29Ju02Jw
KIERNAN, Danl.	14	M	Unknown	29Ju02Jw
SMITH, John	40	M	Laborer	29Ju02Jw
RIELLY, John	18	M	Laborer	29Ju02Jw
DRIMSON, Joseph	40	M	Laborer	29Ju02Jw
Elizth.	45	F	Laborer	29Ju02Jw
Margt.	14	F	Laborer	29Ju02Jw
Thomas	9	M	Child	29Ju02Jw
Mary	7	F	Child	29Ju02Jw
SMITH, Peter	62	M	Farmer	29Ju02Jw
Jane	65	F	Farmer	29Ju02Jw
Nancy	39	F	Farmer	29Ju02Jw
Peter	31	M	Farmer	29Ju02Jw
Jonathan	27	M	Farmer	29Ju02Jw
BARZH, Richd.	24	M	Farmer	29Ju02Jw
WALKER, John	54	M	Farmer	29Ju02Jw
DORRAN, Sarah	60	F	Farmer	29Ju02Jw
Cath.	20	F	Farmer	29Ju02Jw
Eliza	14	F	Farmer	29Ju02Jw
TRAIN, Martin	28	M	Laborer	29Ju02Jw
RONDON, Chas.	22	M	Laborer	29Ju02Jw
HURST, Henry	30	M	Laborer	29Ju02Jw
NATHAN, Michl.	37	M	Laborer	29Ju02Jw
HENZER, Reddy	30	M	Laborer	29Ju02Jw
Biddy	28	F	Laborer	29Ju02Jw
Thos.	4	M	Child	29Ju02Jw
Wm.	2	M	Child	29Ju02Jw
Margt.	.00	F	Infant	29Ju02Jw
ALLOT, Wm.	32	M	Farmer	29Ju02Jw
Henry	26	M	Farmer	29Ju02Jw
FLOOD, John	23	M	Farmer	29Ju02Jw
MORONE, Margt.	20	F	Farmer	29Ju02Jw
RILEY, John	18	M	Farmer	29Ju02Jw
REYNOLDS, Michl.	22	M	Farmer	29Ju02Jw
Bridget	18	F	Unknown	29Ju02Jw
FARRELL, Owen	18	M	Laborer	29Ju02Jw
Michl.	15	M	Laborer	29Ju02Jw
MORAN, John	18	M	Laborer	29Ju02Jw
MAHER, Mary	15	F	Unknown	29Ju02Jw
Pat.	14	M	Unknown	29Ju02Jw
RYAN, Pat.	23	M	Laborer	29Ju02Jw
Alice	21	F	Laborer	29Ju02Jw
DOYLE, John	21	M	Laborer	29Ju02Jw
FARMER, Judy	25	F	Servant	29Ju02Jw
CAMBIC, Ann	16	F	Unknown	29Ju02Jw
Esther	15	F	Unknown	29Ju02Jw
BARNSHAW, Magt.	22	F	Laborer	29Ju02Jw
MCCORMICK, Marcella	18	F	Servant	29Ju02Jw
HODGIN, Margt.	20	F	Servant	29Ju02Jw
DRURY, Thos.	50	M	Mat	29Ju02Jw
Sarah	45	F	Mat	29Ju02Jw
George	19	M	Mat	29Ju02Jw
Emma	18	F	Mat	29Ju02Jw
Chas.	15	M	Mat	29Ju02Jw
Wm.	12	M	Mat	29Ju02Jw
Alfred	10	M	Mat	29Ju02Jw
Joseph	9	M	Child	29Ju02Jw
Joseph	21	M	Laborer	29Ju02Jw
ALFORD, Thos.	36	M	Laborer	29Ju02Jw
Maria	30	F	Laborer	29Ju02Jw
BARLOW, Geo.	26	M	Laborer	29Ju02Jw
MCGUIRE, James	21	M	Laborer	29Ju02Jw
SINNOT, John	49	M	Laborer	29Ju02Jw
Susan	52	F	Laborer	29Ju02Jw
Ellen	18	F	Laborer	29Ju02Jw
FEENY, Michl.	50	M	Farmer	29Ju02Jw
Margt.	40	F	Farmer	29Ju02Jw
Elizh.	18	F	Farmer	29Ju02Jw
Michl.	.00	M	Infant	29Ju02Jw
LINAGH, Mary	20	F	Laborer	29Ju02Jw

PELTONA 29 JUNE 1849

From Belfast

NAMES OF PASSENGERS	AGE	SEX	OCCUPATIONS	DATE PORT SHIP
ARCHER, Lewis	25	M	Farmer	29Ju05Ld
CHEPSTER, Henry	30	M	Farmer	29Ju05Ld
YOUNG, Thomas	25	M	Farmer	29Ju05Ld
Eva (W)	25	F	Wife	29Ju05Ld
Jane	3	F	Child	29Ju05Ld
Thos.	.09	M	Infant	29Ju05Ld
MCCLOUD, Wm.	20	M	Laborer	29Ju05Ld
WATT, Jno.	25	M	Laborer	29Ju05Ld
MCMILLAN, John	20	M	Laborer	29Ju05Ld
CARNS, Aaron	21	M	Laborer	29Ju05Ld
MARTIN, Wm.	20	M	Laborer	29Ju05Ld
Mary (W)	18	F	Wife	29Ju05Ld
MCKERNAN, Hugh	21	M	Weaver	29Ju05Ld
HENRY, Cath.	22	F	Spinster	29Ju05Ld
BRADLEY, Hugh	18	M	Farmer	29Ju05Ld
TODD, James	20	M	Farmer	29Ju05Ld
Sam.	27	M	Farmer	29Ju05Ld
Elizabeth (W)	26	F	Wife	29Ju05Ld
Mary	17	F	Spinster	29Ju05Ld
Wm.	12	M	Unknown	29Ju05Ld
Margt.	15	F	Spinster	29Ju05Ld
James	.06	M	Infant	29Ju05Ld
KILLAN, Mark	30	M	Farmer	29Ju05Ld
Jane (W)	18	F	Wife	29Ju05Ld
OKAY, Pat.	21	M	Farmer	29Ju05Ld
Bessy	14	F	Spinster	29Ju05Ld
COFFEE, James	28	M	Farmer	29Ju05Ld
Ann (W)	20	F	Wife	29Ju05Ld
Jas.	4	M	Child	29Ju05Ld
CAFFEN, Elizabeth	.08	F	Infant	29Ju05Ld
LYNCH, Thos.	22	M	Laborer	29Ju05Ld
SHEERAN, Wm.	49	M	Laborer	29Ju05Ld
Mary	20	F	Spinster	29Ju05Ld
Eliza	18	F	Spinster	29Ju05Ld
Nancy	16	F	Spinster	29Ju05Ld
John	12	M	None	29Ju05Ld
Margt.	11	F	Spinster	29Ju05Ld
HOOPER, David	25	M	Laborer	29Ju05Ld
Martha (W)	20	F	Wife	29Ju05Ld
MAFARLAN, Eliza	20	F	Spinster	29Ju05Ld

NAMES OF PASSENGERS		AGE	SEX	OCCUPATIONS	DATE PORT SHIP
UNIACKE, Edwd.		25	M	Farmer	29Ju05Ld
Rachel	(W)	23	F	Wife	29Ju05Ld
Mary		4	F	Child	29Ju05Ld
Cath.		2	F	Child	29Ju05Ld
KANE, James		12	M	None	29Ju05Ld
HANLON, Sarah		18	F	Spinster	29Ju05Ld
MORRISON, Wm.		19	M	Laborer	29Ju05Ld
DAVISON, Jno.		19	M	Laborer	29Ju05Ld
MANNING, Luke		33	M	Laborer	29Ju05Ld
MCDINAH, Henry		30	M	Laborer	29Ju05Ld
MARSHALL, Michl.		21	M	Laborer	29Ju05Ld
MCGATYM, Wm.		30	M	Laborer	29Ju05Ld
ROCHE, Mary		20	F	Spinster	29Ju05Ld
Mary-Ann		23	F	Spinster	29Ju05Ld
Elizath.		20	F	Spinster	29Ju05Ld
MCGRAW, Eliza		20	F	Spinster	29Ju05Ld
MCKINLAY, Eliza		21	F	Spinster	29Ju05Ld
Sarah		19	F	Spinster	29Ju05Ld
MURPHY, Cath.		22	F	Spinster	29Ju05Ld
John		18	M	Baker	29Ju05Ld
DEVLIN, James		50	M	Baker	29Ju05Ld
Edw.		12	M	Unknown	29Ju05Ld
SMITH, Richd.		30	M	Unknown	29Ju05Ld
RILEY, Pat.		25	M	Unknown	29Ju05Ld
STEWART, Eliza		24	F	Servant	29Ju05Ld
MCMITCHELL, Sarah		20	F	Servant	29Ju05Ld
Jane		18	F	Servant	29Ju05Ld
WARD, Rose		24	F	Servant	29Ju05Ld
GILLMORE, James		21	M	Laborer	29Ju05Ld
Mary		25	F	Servant	29Ju05Ld
GUBBIN, Mary		21	F	Servant	29Ju05Ld
KERNAN, Margt.		16	F	Servant	29Ju05Ld
DAVISON, Mary		50	F	Servant	29Ju05Ld
Elizth.		17	F	Servant	29Ju05Ld
LORING, Alice		20	F	Servant	29Ju05Ld
DAVISON, Rachel		16	F	Servant	29Ju05Ld
BAILLIE, Sophia		20	F	Spinster	29Ju05Ld
BRADLEY, Bernard		48	M	Farmer	29Ju05Ld
Mary	(W)	19	F	Wife	29Ju05Ld
Mary		8	F	Child	29Ju05Ld
MCTIER, Ann		40	F	Wi	29Ju05Ld
Cath.		20	F	Spinster	29Ju05Ld
Ally		18	F	Spinster	29Ju05Ld
Pat.		17	M	Laborer	29Ju05Ld
Ellen		15	F	Spinster	29Ju05Ld
Mary-Ann		11	F	Spinster	29Ju05Ld
Sarah		9	F	Child	29Ju05Ld
Margt.		7	F	Child	29Ju05Ld
Chas.		5	M	Child	29Ju05Ld
LYMOND, Jas.		21	M	Carpenter	29Ju05Ld
DAVISON, James		24	M	Carpenter	29Ju05Ld
COOPER, James		55	M	Carpenter	29Ju05Ld
Susannah	(W)	54	F	Wife	29Ju05Ld
Geo.		20	M	Laborer	29Ju05Ld
James		18	M	Laborer	29Ju05Ld
Adam		11	M	None	29Ju05Ld
Jane		21	F	Spinster	29Ju05Ld
CALWELL, John		21	M	Laborer	29Ju05Ld
BOYD, Wm.		24	M	Farmer	29Ju05Ld
MCDONELL, Eliza		29	F	Wife	29Ju05Ld
Joseph		12	M	None	29Ju05Ld
Eliza		10	F	Spinster	29Ju05Ld
HAYNES, Rose		24	F	Spinster	29Ju05Ld
MCGREELAN, Nancy		25	F	Spinster	29Ju05Ld
GILLAN, Pat.		28	M	Mason	29Ju05Ld
MCILROY, Mary		25	F	Wife	29Ju05Ld
KANE, Mary		30	F	Spinster	29Ju05Ld
John		35	M	Laborer	29Ju05Ld
WHITE, John		27	M	Laborer	29Ju05Ld
LOVE, John		48	M	Farmer	29Ju05Ld
Ann	(W)	40	F	Wife	29Ju05Ld
Mary		14	F	Spinster	29Ju05Ld
Matilda		12	F	Spinster	29Ju05Ld
Nancy		10	F	Spinster	29Ju05Ld
Wm.		8	M	Child	29Ju05Ld

NAMES OF PASSENGERS		AGE	SEX	OCCUPATIONS	DATE PORT SHIP
LOVE, Maria		5	F	Child	29Ju05Ld
Jane		2	F	Child	29Ju05Ld
Alex.		.06	M	Infant	29Ju05Ld
MCMANUS, Cath.		20	F	Spinster	29Ju05Ld
FALOM, John		19	M	Laborer	29Ju05Ld
SEATON, John		22	M	Farmer	29Ju05Ld
Sarah	(W)	20	F	Wife	29Ju05Ld
Matilda		18	F	Spinster	29Ju05Ld
Sarah-J.		20	F	Spinster	29Ju05Ld
FERRIS, Mart.		18	F	Spinster	29Ju05Ld
FERGUSON, Selena		21	F	Servant	29Ju05Ld
BELL, James		22	M	Laborer	29Ju05Ld
MCCLUSKEY, Paul		58	M	Laborer	29Ju05Ld
FERGUSON, Arch.		25	M	Laborer	29Ju05Ld
GOODFELLOW, Pat.		20	M	Carpenter	29Ju05Ld
KERR, John		28	M	Carpenter	29Ju05Ld
GORMEN, Henry		26	M	Carpenter	29Ju05Ld
Sarah	(W)	24	F	Wife	29Ju05Ld
Sarah		.06	F	Infant	29Ju05Ld
KENNY, Matt.		25	M	Laborer	29Ju05Ld
FINLAY, Martha		25	F	Spinster	29Ju05Ld
BRATTEN, Fany		20	F	Spinster	29Ju05Ld
THOMPSON, Thomas		40	M	Laborer	29Ju05Ld
Jane	(T)	40	F	Sister	29Ju05Ld
CAMPBELL, Mary		19	F	Spinster	29Ju05Ld
MCGRADY, Eliza		20	F	Spinster	29Ju05Ld
LUNDY, Matt.		40	M	Laborer	29Ju05Ld
Mary	(W)	40	F	Wife	29Ju05Ld
LANDY, Mary		25	F	Spinster	29Ju05Ld
Ellen		20	F	Spinster	29Ju05Ld
Eliza		18	F	Spinster	29Ju05Ld
Pat		15	M	Laborer	29Ju05Ld
Eliza		17	F	Spinster	29Ju05Ld
STRANG, Pat		25	M	Laborer	29Ju05Ld
STROUD, Wm.		16	M	Laborer	29Ju05Ld
COULTER, Wm.		40	M	Laborer	29Ju05Ld
Mary	(W)	40	F	Wife	29Ju05Ld
Cath.		15	F	Spinster	29Ju05Ld
MAHON, John		3	M	Child	29Ju05Ld
COULTER, Margt.		30	F	Wife	29Ju05Ld
ARMSTRONG, Frs.		25	M	Laborer	29Ju05Ld
James		30	M	Farmer	29Ju05Ld
PATTINGER, David		63	M	Farmer	29Ju05Ld
Sarah	(W)	63	M	Farmer	29Ju05Ld
Ellen		23	F	Spinster	29Ju05Ld
Robt.		21	M	Laborer	29Ju05Ld
WAIGH, Rich.		26	M	Laborer	29Ju05Ld
Ellen		6	F	Child	29Ju05Ld
Maud		.08	F	Infant	29Ju05Ld
MCKEREN, Cath.		18	F	Spinster	29Ju05Ld
PETTYGREW, Robt.		23	M	Mason	29Ju05Ld
MCCAHITY, Thos.		20	M	Mason	29Ju05Ld
MCAEREILLY, James		25	M	Mason	29Ju05Ld
MCLECAL, Hugh		26	M	Mason	29Ju05Ld
GRAHAM, Geo.		18	M	Carpenter	29Ju05Ld
PATTERSON, W.		25	M	Laborer	29Ju05Ld
MCCORMACK, John		20	M	Laborer	29Ju05Ld
Mary	(W)	18	F	Wife	29Ju05Ld
MOONEY, Hugh		18	M	Servant	29Ju05Ld
Charlotte		18	F	Servant	29Ju05Ld
MCCONLEY, Jno.		16	M	Clerk	29Ju05Ld
MCCURDY, Rose		30	F	Wi	29Ju05Ld
Mary		8	F	Child	29Ju05Ld
Margt.		6	F	Child	29Ju05Ld
M.		2	M	Child	29Ju05Ld
MCCAW, Wm.		20	M	Laborer	29Ju05Ld
FRAZER, Cath.		30	F	Laborer	29Ju05Ld
Alex.		16	M	Unknown	29Ju05Ld
John		13	M	Unknown	29Ju05Ld
Sarah		11	F	Unknown	29Ju05Ld
CHAMBERS, Chit.		30	M	Unknown	29Ju05Ld
Wm.		12	M	Unknown	29Ju05Ld
John		11	M	Unknown	29Ju05Ld
RODGERS, Margt.		16	F	Spinster	29Ju05Ld
MCCURDY, Margt.		20	F	Wife	29Ju05Ld

NAMES OF PASSENGERS	AGE	SEX	OCCUPATIONS	DATE PORT SHIP
GALIGHER, Pat.	25	M	Unknown	29Ju05Ld
MCCURDY, Nancy	20	F	Spinster	29Ju05Ld
KELLY, R.	20	M	Clerk	29Ju05Ld
BRITAN, Jas.	25	M	Clerk	29Ju05Ld
MCGLAUGHLIN, Jane	30	F	Spinster	29Ju05Ld
U, U Born-At-Sea	.00	U	Infant	29Ju05Ld

GERTRUDE 29 JUNE 1849

From Liverpool

NAMES OF PASSENGERS	AGE	SEX	OCCUPATIONS	DATE PORT SHIP
FITZGERALD, Cathn.	17	F	Servant	29Ju02Ek
LEAVY, Arthur	20	M	Unknown	29Ju02Ek
CARTELL, Jno.	26	M	Servant	29Ju02Ek
MOON, Mary	15	F	Servant	29Ju02Ek
LEAVY, Patrick	20	M	Servant	29Ju02Ek
MENTAGER, Bridget	18	F	Servant	29Ju02Ek
SHERDONE, Mary	21	F	Servant	29Ju02Ek
MARTEN, Jno.	21	M	Servant	29Ju02Ek
DONLY, Margt.	17	F	Servant	29Ju02Ek
REIL, Archy	22	M	Servant	29Ju02Ek
HARRIS, Patrick	21	M	Servant	29Ju02Ek
FARRELL, Peter	20	M	Servant	29Ju02Ek
KELLY, Jno.	23	M	Servant	29Ju02Ek
NOLAN, Michl.	24	M	Blacksmith	29Ju02Ek
COYLE, Michl.	43	M	Farmer	29Ju02Ek
BLACKBURN, Mary	18	F	Servant	29Ju02Ek
MCGARRY, Margt.	20	F	Servant	29Ju02Ek
MOFFAT, Patrick	22	M	Servant	29Ju02Ek
MORGAN, Hugh	25	M	Servant	29Ju02Ek
HURT, Cathn.	18	F	Servant	29Ju02Ek
KENNAN, Mary	30	F	Servant	29Ju02Ek
Mathew	9	M	Child	29Ju02Ek
Michl.	7	M	Child	29Ju02Ek
Ann	.00	F	Infant	29Ju02Ek
WATRIN, Percival	30	M	Mechanic	29Ju02Ek
Mgt.	33	F	Unknown	29Ju02Ek
Eliza	9	F	Child	29Ju02Ek
Anne	8	F	Child	29Ju02Ek
HENRY, Jno.	6	M	Child	29Ju02Ek
Percival	.00	M	Infant	29Ju02Ek
BRADY, Bernd.	19	M	Servant	29Ju02Ek
SHEADY, Marcella	19	M	Servant	29Ju02Ek
FLYNN, Bridgt.	17	F	Servant	29Ju02Ek
CARROLL, Michl.	26	M	Farmer	29Ju02Ek
CONNOLLY, James	16	M	Farmer	29Ju02Ek
ODONNELL, Ann	23	F	Servant	29Ju02Ek
KENNY, Thos.	25	M	Servant	29Ju02Ek
MENTAGH, Bridgt.	20	F	Servant	29Ju02Ek
DONOHUE, Mary	20	F	Servant	29Ju02Ek
SANDERSON, Michl.	18	M	Servant	29Ju02Ek
FITZPATRICK, Mary	28	F	Servant	29Ju02Ek
FARRELLY, Bridgt.	18	F	Servant	29Ju02Ek
LEWIS, Ann	14	F	Servant	29Ju02Ek
HUGHES, Ellen	20	F	Servant	29Ju02Ek
BRIAN, Stephen	30	M	Laborer	29Ju02Ek
Bridgt.	30	F	Unknown	29Ju02Ek
Timothy	4	M	Child	29Ju02Ek
Cornelius	.00	M	Infant	29Ju02Ek
MCGOVERN, Mary	50	F	Servant	29Ju02Ek
SANNTORY, Dennis	50	M	Servant	29Ju02Ek
Jane	20	F	Servant	29Ju02Ek
RYAN, Margt.	20	F	Servant	29Ju02Ek
BRYAN, Mary-D.	40	F	Servant	29Ju02Ek
Danl.	9	M	Child	29Ju02Ek
FAHEY, Johanna	30	F	Servant	29Ju02Ek
James	9	M	Child	29Ju02Ek
Daniel	7	M	Child	29Ju02Ek

NAMES OF PASSENGERS	AGE	SEX	OCCUPATIONS	DATE PORT SHIP
TROY, Michl.	23	M	Servant	29Ju02Ek
REKET, Garret	40	M	Farmer	29Ju02Ek
MCCOWLEY, Ann	20	F	Servant	29Ju02Ek
MURPHY, Ellen	28	F	Dressmaker	29Ju02Ek
Jno.	27	M	Servant	29Ju02Ek
BARRETT, Jno.	20	M	Servant	29Ju02Ek
FOLEY, Dennis	20	M	Servant	29Ju02Ek
FURY, Mary	60	F	Servant	29Ju02Ek
HARA, Patrick	21	M	Servant	29Ju02Ek
Bridgt.	18	F	Servant	29Ju02Ek
MCMANNUS, Bryan	16	M	Servant	29Ju02Ek
Bridgt.	18	F	Servant	29Ju02Ek
EARLY, Jon.	16	M	Servant	29Ju02Ek
Tedy	13	F	Servant	29Ju02Ek
LEDWIDGE, Ellen	20	F	Servant	29Ju02Ek
BRIME, Cathn.	30	F	Servant	29Ju02Ek
Ellen	20	F	Servant	29Ju02Ek
HOGAN, Ellen	23	F	Servant	29Ju02Ek
KELLY, Danl.	26	M	Farmer	29Ju02Ek
WINTER, Julius-A.	20	F	Servant	29Ju02Ek
BRICKLAND, Chas.	36	M	Shoemaker	29Ju02Ek
DEAN, Jno.	20	F	Servant	29Ju02Ek
GERY, Jane	22	F	Servant	29Ju02Ek
FLYNN, Cathn.	19	F	Servant	29Ju02Ek
KEATING, Mary	18	F	Servant	29Ju02Ek
TAFFER, Bridgt.	35	F	Servant	29Ju02Ek
TAMERY, Andy	40	M	Laborer	29Ju02Ek
Nancy	35	F	Unknown	29Ju02Ek
Betty	10	F	Unknown	29Ju02Ek
Patrick	8	M	Child	29Ju02Ek
James	6	M	Child	29Ju02Ek
Peter	4	M	Child	29Ju02Ek
SMITH, Barry	2	M	Child	29Ju02Ek
Ketty	.00	F	Infant	29Ju02Ek
CLOVER, Ketty	30	F	Servant	29Ju02Ek
KERR, U	25	F	Servant	29Ju02Ek
Jane	15	F	Servant	29Ju02Ek
Kelly	18	F	Servant	29Ju02Ek
James	9	M	Child	29Ju02Ek
MCMANAN, Michl.	45	M	Laborer	29Ju02Ek
Jno.	35	M	Laborer	29Ju02Ek
MURRY, Bridgt.	20	F	Servant	29Ju02Ek
DUGGAN, Jno.	18	M	Servant	29Ju02Ek
MCGER, Jno.	20	M	Servant	29Ju02Ek
GRIBBIN, Ann	15	F	Servant	29Ju02Ek
FARLLEY, Peter	18	M	Servant	29Ju02Ek
CANTWELL, Danl.	23	M	Servant	29Ju02Ek
MCGIVEN, Cathn.	15	F	Servant	29Ju02Ek
DERKEY, Jno.	60	M	Farmer	29Ju02Ek
U	48	F	Unknown	29Ju02Ek
Saml.	19	M	Farmer	29Ju02Ek
James	17	M	Farmer	29Ju02Ek
SULLIVAN, Michl.	34	M	Mechanic	29Ju02Ek
MCBRIDE, Margt.	22	F	Servant	29Ju02Ek
SMITH, Jno.	21	M	Servant	29Ju02Ek
MUNTEN, Alex	18	M	Servant	29Ju02Ek
CALDWELL, Mary	24	F	Servant	29Ju02Ek
Sarah	20	F	Servant	29Ju02Ek
Sarah	20	F	Servant	29Ju02Ek
DAMORCE, Mary	13	F	Servant	29Ju02Ek
LEVINTHON, Edna	18	F	Servant	29Ju02Ek
U	.00	U	Infant	29Ju02Ek
SWIGAN, James-M.	45	M	Laborer	29Ju02Ek
James	13	M	Laborer	29Ju02Ek
Margt.	13	F	Laborer	29Ju02Ek
Henry	15	M	Laborer	29Ju02Ek
Mary-Ann	12	F	Unknown	29Ju02Ek
Arthur	10	M	Unknown	29Ju02Ek
Hugh	8	M	Child	29Ju02Ek
Cathn.	6	F	Child	29Ju02Ek
Chas.	.00	M	Infant	29Ju02Ek
BROWN, Betsy	17	F	Servant	29Ju02Ek
James	15	M	Servant	29Ju02Ek
FRIEL, Michl.	24	M	Servant	29Ju02Ek
Ellen	22	F	Servant	29Ju02Ek

NAMES OF PASSENGERS	AGE	SEX	OCCUPATIONS	DATE PORT SHIP
HALPIN, Tho.	25	M	Servant	29Ju02Ek
NEVEN, Martin	22	M	Servant	29Ju02Ek
Patrick	2	M	Child	29Ju02Ek
MCGALIN, Deven	28	M	Servant	29Ju02Ek
MARTIN, Connor	26	M	Servant	29Ju02Ek
MAHON, Wm.	27	M	Servant	29Ju02Ek
MOORE, James	25	M	Servant	29Ju02Ek
COREGROVE, Pat	20	M	Servant	29Ju02Ek
CORBY, Thos	30	M	Servant	29Ju02Ek
BRIDNECK, Mather	30	M	Servant	29Ju02Ek
Jno.	28	M	Servant	29Ju02Ek
HANBURY, Cathn.	40	F	Servant	29Ju02Ek
KENNEDY, Jno.	21	M	Servant	29Ju02Ek
CONRAN, Dave	22	M	Laborer	29Ju02Ek
MCGRATTY, Martin	20	M	Laborer	29Ju02Ek
BURK, Nancy	22	F	Servant	29Ju02Ek
BRACEY, Margt.	15	F	Servant	29Ju02Ek
PATTERSON, Mother	19	F	Servant	29Ju02Ek
CORRY, Peggy	20	F	Servant	29Ju02Ek
MCMAHON, James	25	M	Servant	29Ju02Ek
NOLAN, Cathn.	22	F	Servant	29Ju02Ek
WANE, Patrick	30	M	Servant	29Ju02Ek
RIDER, Wm.	27	M	Servant	29Ju02Ek
MONAGHAN, Ann	27	F	Servant	29Ju02Ek
Ann	22	F	Servant	29Ju02Ek
BROWN, Wm.	60	M	Laborer	29Ju02Ek
U	56	F	Unknown	29Ju02Ek
MCGUINNESS, Hughey	26	M	Servant	29Ju02Ek
OLIVER, Mary-Ann	24	F	Servant	29Ju02Ek
MCRENTURE, Jno.	24	F	Servant	29Ju02Ek
MCNAMARA, Tho.	25	M	Servant	29Ju02Ek
RUSSELL, Sally	25	F	Servant	29Ju02Ek
GALLAGHER, U	21	F	Unknown	29Ju02Ek
WHALAN, Mary	20	F	Unknown	29Ju02Ek
SHERIDAN, Simon	30	M	Unknown	29Ju02Ek
CLARK, Wm.	24	M	Unknown	29Ju02Ek
BRADY, James	80	M	Unknown	29Ju02Ek
HUGHES, Joseph	25	M	Laborer	29Ju02Ek
BERY, Tho.	25	M	Laborer	29Ju02Ek
CROSBY, Ally	19	F	Servant	29Ju02Ek
COBURN, Henry	19	F	Servant	29Ju02Ek
MARKEY, Jno.	35	F	Servant	29Ju02Ek
OGANE, James	21	M	Servant	29Ju02Ek
KENNEDY, James	28	M	Servant	29Ju02Ek
BYRNE, Simon	22	M	Servant	29Ju02Ek
INGHAM, Elizbth.	30	F	Servant	29Ju02Ek
EARLY, Bridgt.	48	F	Servant	29Ju02Ek
CALDWELL, Isabella	45	F	Dressmaker	29Ju02Ek
Eliza	22	F	Dressmaker	29Ju02Ek
MCBRIDE, Elizbth.	24	F	Servant	29Ju02Ek
Phillip	18	M	Servant	29Ju02Ek
POWELL, James	33	M	Servant	29Ju02Ek
Emma	9	F	Child	29Ju02Ek
DENNIS, Chas.	30	M	Laborer	29Ju02Ek
U	30	F	Unknown	29Ju02Ek
U	.00	U	Infant	29Ju02Ek
Henry	14	M	Unknown	29Ju02Ek
Cathn.	11	F	Unknown	29Ju02Ek
Martha-Ann	2	F	Child	29Ju02Ek
MCDONOGAL, Ann	19	F	Servant	29Ju02Ek
MCDONALD, Cathn.	25	F	Servant	29Ju02Ek
MURRAY, Ann	20	F	Servant	29Ju02Ek
RUTTEGER, Margt.	20	F	Servant	29Ju02Ek
FENNEGAN, Bridgt.	20	F	Servant	29Ju02Ek
CAMEKEY, Luke	20	M	Servant	29Ju02Ek
Elizabeth	22	F	Servant	29Ju02Ek
PLANNER, Martin	24	M	Servant	29Ju02Ek
CONDUIN, Eliza	20	F	Servant	29Ju02Ek
FLYNN, Ann	23	F	Servant	29Ju02Ek
DUFFEY, Owen	17	M	Servant	29Ju02Ek
HULLAND, Margt.	20	F	Servant	29Ju02Ek
WATERS, Domnick	19	M	Servant	29Ju02Ek
BOLTON, Tho.	19	M	Servant	29Ju02Ek
Mary	20	F	Servant	29Ju02Ek
HOGG, Eliza	20	F	Servant	29Ju02Ek

NAMES OF PASSENGERS	AGE	SEX	OCCUPATIONS	DATE PORT SHIP
FALLON, Danl.	17	M	Servant	29Ju02Ek
MCALHNE, Jno.	16	M	Servant	29Ju02Ek
Janice	14	F	Servant	29Ju02Ek
BRADLY, Patrick	25	M	Laborer	29Ju02Ek
MCGONAGLE, Edwd.	23	M	Laborer	29Ju02Ek
MCCANIT, Susan	18	F	Servant	29Ju02Ek
DORNEY, Bridgt.	21	F	Servant	29Ju02Ek
Patrick	13	M	Unknown	29Ju02Ek
George	10	M	Unknown	29Ju02Ek
HUGHES, James	35	M	Unknown	29Ju02Ek
MURPHY, Eliza	16	F	Unknown	29Ju02Ek
Tho.	20	M	Unknown	29Ju02Ek
COLLINS, Alice	19	F	Unknown	29Ju02Ek
MCDONNELL, Peter	20	M	Unknown	29Ju02Ek
BRYAN, Patrick	15	M	Servant	29Ju02Ek
MCBRIDE, Elizbth.	21	F	Servant	29Ju02Ek
GARLAND, Owen	19	M	Servant	29Ju02Ek
OBRIEN, Ellen	21	F	Servant	29Ju02Ek
GIBSON, Jno.	32	M	Servant	29Ju02Ek
THOMPSON, Bridgt.	30	F	Servant	29Ju02Ek
Mather	16	M	Servant	29Ju02Ek
Richd.	3	M	Child	29Ju02Ek
POWELL, Ann	17	F	Servant	29Ju02Ek
CONNOR, Margt.	22	F	Servant	29Ju02Ek
POWELL, Jno.	22	M	Servant	29Ju02Ek
QUINN, Timothy	16	M	Servant	29Ju02Ek
BANE, Patrick	15	M	Servant	29Ju02Ek
Cathn.	22	F	Servant	29Ju02Ek
John	10	M	Servant	29Ju02Ek
Mary	8	F	Child	29Ju02Ek
Bridgt.	6	F	Child	29Ju02Ek
OHARA, James	22	M	Servant	29Ju02Ek
CONNONS, Jno.	21	M	Servant	29Ju02Ek
Margt.	22	F	Servant	29Ju02Ek
GREEN, Nathn.	56	M	Laborer	29Ju02Ek
U	50	F	Unknown	29Ju02Ek
Edwd.	16	M	Unknown	29Ju02Ek
Johanna	11	F	Unknown	29Ju02Ek
Nathn.	9	M	Child	29Ju02Ek
Hannah	6	F	Child	29Ju02Ek
FENNERAN, Mary	25	F	Servant	29Ju02Ek
Patrick	9	M	Child	29Ju02Ek
HUSON, Eliza-Jane	24	F	Servant	29Ju02Ek
Lettice	15	F	Servant	29Ju02Ek
NEWMAN, Jno.	22	M	Servant	29Ju02Ek
Honer	20	M	Servant	29Ju02Ek
MCANALLY, Francis	17	M	Servant	29Ju02Ek
MCCLEAN, Jno.	25	M	Servant	29Ju02Ek
CONROY, Jno.	23	M	Servant	29Ju02Ek
James	16	M	Servant	29Ju02Ek
MCCANN, Ellen	49	F	Servant	29Ju02Ek
HAMILTON, Wm.	22	M	Servant	29Ju02Ek
James	24	M	Servant	29Ju02Ek
Mary	27	F	Servant	29Ju02Ek
WRIGHT, Elizabeth	50	F	Servant	29Ju02Ek
MCCAFFREY, Jno.	30	M	Servant	29Ju02Ek
MCBENNETT, Bridget	50	F	None	29Ju02Ek

WILBERFORCE 30 JUNE 1849

From Limerick

NAMES OF PASSENGERS	AGE	SEX	OCCUPATIONS	DATE PORT SHIP
BARRY, Mary	44	F	Servant	30Ju35Ku
Mary	21	F	Unknown	30Ju35Ku
Cath.	15	F	Unknown	30Ju35Ku
John	13	M	Unknown	30Ju35Ku
Bridget	11	F	Unknown	30Ju35Ku
RYAN, Michael	30	M	Laborer	30Ju35Ku
Mary	20	F	Servant	30Ju35Ku

NAMES OF PASSENGERS	AGE	SEX	OCCUPATIONS	DATE PORT SHIP
MINNEY, Bridget	28	F	Unknown	30Ju35Ku
BEGLEY, Margt.	27	F	Unknown	30Ju35Ku
Cath.	20	F	Unknown	30Ju35Ku
RYAN, Jno.	.09	M	Infant	30Ju35Ku
REYNOLDS, Margt.	21	F	Unknown	30Ju35Ku
OBRIEN, James	21	M	Laborer	30Ju35Ku
Cath.	48	F	Unknown	30Ju35Ku
John	13	M	Unknown	30Ju35Ku
Wm.	11	M	Unknown	30Ju35Ku
Henry	9	M	Child	30Ju35Ku
BOLFREY, George	22	M	Unknown	30Ju35Ku
HAILEY, Anty	60	F	Unknown	30Ju35Ku
William	17	M	Unknown	30Ju35Ku
John	15	M	Unknown	30Ju35Ku
MCGUIAN, Pat.	35	M	Unknown	30Ju35Ku
Honora	30	F	Unknown	30Ju35Ku
OGRADY, Jno.	38	M	Farmer	30Ju35Ku
Margt.	36	F	Unknown	30Ju35Ku
MOLONEY, Anna	32	F	Unknown	30Ju35Ku
HEALY, Edward	30	M	Laborer	30Ju35Ku
Michael	26	M	Unknown	30Ju35Ku
CASSACK, Jno.	28	M	Unknown	30Ju35Ku
CALLAHAN, Margt.	20	F	Unknown	30Ju35Ku
CASSACK, Michael	26	M	Unknown	30Ju35Ku
WALSH, Ellen	26	F	Unknown	30Ju35Ku
MEALY, Pat.	24	M	Unknown	30Ju35Ku
Edmund	28	M	Unknown	30Ju35Ku
Margt.	55	F	Unknown	30Ju35Ku
Ellen	20	F	Unknown	30Ju35Ku
Mary	18	F	Unknown	30Ju35Ku
OBRIEN, Thos.	35	M	Unknown	30Ju35Ku
RYAN, Michael	22	M	Unknown	30Ju35Ku
LOONEY, Jno.	26	M	Unknown	30Ju35Ku
Margt.	24	F	Unknown	30Ju35Ku
BOURKE, Michl.	20	M	Unknown	30Ju35Ku
BUTLER, Thos.	30	M	Unknown	30Ju35Ku
Pat.	30	M	Unknown	30Ju35Ku
MCNAMARA, M.	20	M	Unknown	30Ju35Ku
HICKEY, Danl.	21	M	Unknown	30Ju35Ku
WALSH, Cath.	21	F	Unknown	30Ju35Ku
OBRIEN, John	22	M	Unknown	30Ju35Ku
BUTLER, Wm.	36	M	Unknown	30Ju35Ku
WALSH, Pat.	35	M	Unknown	30Ju35Ku
HANCOCK, Michl.	20	M	Unknown	30Ju35Ku
LYNCH, Bridget	21	F	Unknown	30Ju35Ku
Hannah	14	F	Unknown	30Ju35Ku
MURRANE, Michl.	18	M	Unknown	30Ju35Ku
HIGGINS, James	20	M	Unknown	30Ju35Ku
RUTTLE, Pat.	35	M	Unknown	30Ju35Ku
Andy	7	M	Child	30Ju35Ku
MURPHY, Bridget	24	F	Unknown	30Ju35Ku
MCNAMARA, Michael	50	M	Unknown	30Ju35Ku
QUINN, Michl.	30	M	Unknown	30Ju35Ku
DUHIGG, Timothy	16	M	Unknown	30Ju35Ku
TRACY, Andy	35	M	Unknown	30Ju35Ku
Hannah	30	F	Unknown	30Ju35Ku
Edmund	.02	M	Infant	30Ju35Ku
AHERN, Jno.	36	M	Unknown	30Ju35Ku
BOURKE, Richd.	30	M	Unknown	30Ju35Ku
CORCORAN, James	28	M	Unknown	30Ju35Ku
LEE, Pat.	30	M	Unknown	30Ju35Ku
FLYNN, Michael	40	M	Unknown	30Ju35Ku
RUSSEL, Martin	24	M	Unknown	30Ju35Ku
Pat	22	M	Unknown	30Ju35Ku
DONOVAN, Wm.	36	M	Unknown	30Ju35Ku
Cath.	24	F	Unknown	30Ju35Ku
HOLLARAN, James	20	M	Unknown	30Ju35Ku
Mary	00	M	Unknown	30Ju35Ku
BYRNES, Johanna	24	F	Unknown	30Ju35Ku
John	23	M	Unknown	30Ju35Ku
DILLON, Pat.	24	M	Unknown	30Ju35Ku
YOONEY, Cath.	20	F	Unknown	30Ju35Ku
Wm.	13	M	Unknown	30Ju35Ku
BUCKLEY, Ellen	18	F	Unknown	30Ju35Ku
COSTOLOES, Edwd.	24	M	Unknown	30Ju35Ku
AHERN, Martin	18	M	Unknown	30Ju35Ku
ROURKE, Wm.	30	M	Unknown	30Ju35Ku
ROBINSON, Wm.	54	M	Gentleman	30Ju35Ku
Jane	44	F	Unknown	30Ju35Ku
HUTCHINGS, Elizabeth	26	F	Lady	30Ju35Ku
Ellen	6	F	Child	30Ju35Ku
Phoebe	22	F	Unknown	30Ju35Ku
Mary	29	F	Unknown	30Ju35Ku
Jane	18	F	Unknown	30Ju35Ku
Charlotte	16	F	Unknown	30Ju35Ku
Robt.	17	M	Unknown	30Ju35Ku
Sarah	15	F	Unknown	30Ju35Ku
Henrietta	11	F	Unknown	30Ju35Ku
Anna	13	F	Unknown	30Ju35Ku
SHEEHEY, James	20	M	Unknown	30Ju35Ku
EVANS, Francis	18	M	Unknown	30Ju35Ku
SHEEHEY, Myles	58	M	Unknown	30Ju35Ku
Mary	20	F	Unknown	30Ju35Ku
SHAUNESSY, James	28	M	Unknown	30Ju35Ku
CORCORAN, Corn.	40	M	Unknown	30Ju35Ku
Mary	40	F	Unknown	30Ju35Ku
SHEEHEY, Johanna	25	F	Unknown	30Ju35Ku
Kate	23	F	Unknown	30Ju35Ku
Mary	21	F	Unknown	30Ju35Ku
MCDONALD, Eliza	20	F	Unknown	30Ju35Ku

HYPERION 30 JUNE 1849

From Liverpool

NAMES OF PASSENGERS	AGE	SEX	OCCUPATIONS	DATE PORT SHIP
WILLIAMS, Hugh	22	M	Unknown	30Ju02Kt
Richard	24	M	Unknown	30Ju02Kt
Wm.	26	M	Unknown	30Ju02Kt
Jno.	28	M	Unknown	30Ju02Kt
Elizth.	29	F	Unknown	30Ju02Kt
Jane	25	F	Unknown	30Ju02Kt
Jno.	6	M	Child	30Ju02Kt
Richard	4	M	Child	30Ju02Kt
Mary	2	F	Child	30Ju02Kt
Jno.	.00	M	Infant	30Ju02Kt
BERCSFORD, Jos.	31	M	Unknown	30Ju02Kt
LUDLOW, Stephen	18	M	Unknown	30Ju02Kt
MORAN, Michl.	40	M	Unknown	30Ju02Kt
Margt.	40	F	Unknown	30Ju02Kt
Michl.	12	M	Unknown	30Ju02Kt
Ann	10	F	Unknown	30Ju02Kt
Bridget	8	F	Child	30Ju02Kt
REYNOLDS, Tim	22	M	Unknown	30Ju02Kt
HUGHES, Martin	26	M	Unknown	30Ju02Kt
WELSH, Jno.	36	M	Unknown	30Ju02Kt
MORAN, Mary	36	F	Unknown	30Ju02Kt
KELLY, Cath.	28	F	Unknown	30Ju02Kt
CLESHAW, Andrew	40	M	Unknown	30Ju02Kt
Michl.	15	M	Unknown	30Ju02Kt
Mary	12	F	Unknown	30Ju02Kt
MCKENNA, Thomas	17	M	Unknown	30Ju02Kt
CONNOLLY, Mick	26	M	Unknown	30Ju02Kt
KELLY, Martin	45	M	Unknown	30Ju02Kt
THOMAS, Wm.	48	M	Unknown	30Ju02Kt
DAVIS, Jno.	21	M	Unknown	30Ju02Kt
WILLIAMS, Wm.	35	M	Unknown	30Ju02Kt
Sarah	42	F	Unknown	30Ju02Kt
Eleanor	13	F	Unknown	30Ju02Kt
Thomas	12	M	Unknown	30Ju02Kt
Ann	3	F	Child	30Ju02Kt
Mary-Ann	.00	F	Infant	30Ju02Kt
MURPHY, Nory	30	M	Unknown	30Ju02Kt
Mary	18	F	Unknown	30Ju02Kt
CLARAN, Michl.	25	M	Unknown	30Ju02K

NAMES OF PASSENGERS	AGE	SEX	OCCUPATIONS	DATE PORT SHIP
WILLIAMS, James	6	M	Child	30Ju02K+
KELLY, Wm.	28	M	Unknown	30Ju02K+
Julia	25	F	Unknown	30Ju02K+
July	14	F	Unknown	30Ju02K+
JAMES, Stephen	48	M	Unknown	30Ju02K+
Mary	38	F	Unknown	30Ju02K+
Mathew	13	M	Unknown	30Ju02K+
Hannah	11	F	Unknown	30Ju02K+
Jno.	9	M	Child	30Ju02K+
David	7	M	Child	30Ju02K+
Charles	5	M	Child	30Ju02K+
Wm.	4	M	Child	30Ju02K+
Joseph	2	M	Child	30Ju02K+
BROCK, George	33	M	Unknown	30Ju02K+
ROBBINS, Elisha	49	M	Unknown	30Ju02K+
MULDOWRY, And.	30	M	Unknown	30Ju02K+
QUINN, Martin	16	M	Unknown	30Ju02K+
GION, James	26	M	Unknown	30Ju02K+
MCCORMACK, Peter	40	M	Unknown	30Ju02K+
Margt.	36	F	Unknown	30Ju02K+
Cath.	13	F	Unknown	30Ju02K+
Peter	17	M	Unknown	30Ju02K+
Jno.	11	M	Unknown	30Ju02K+
James	9	M	Child	30Ju02K+
Joseph	7	M	Child	30Ju02K+
Margt.	5	F	Child	30Ju02K+
Biddy	3	F	Child	30Ju02K+
Wm.	.00	M	Infant	30Ju02K+
Owen	22	M	Unknown	30Ju02K+
WARD, James	22	M	Unknown	30Ju02K+
KING, Henry	26	M	Unknown	30Ju02K+
GONEZ, Jno.	30	M	Unknown	30Ju02K+
Biddy	10	F	Unknown	30Ju02K+
CONNOLLY, Thos.	22	M	Unknown	30Ju02K+
Mary	20	F	Unknown	30Ju02K+
MCCARTLY, Danl.	40	M	Unknown	30Ju02K+
GREEN, James	26	M	Unknown	30Ju02K+
PARRINGTON, Thos.	15	M	Unknown	30Ju02K+
HOHAG, Toby	13	M	Unknown	30Ju02K+
RYAN, Pat	18	M	Unknown	30Ju02K+
LYNCH, Pat	22	M	Unknown	30Ju02K+
SCANDLAN, Pat	20	M	Unknown	30Ju02K+
QUINN, Timothy	56	M	Unknown	30Ju02K+
OHARE, Thos.	40	M	Unknown	30Ju02K+
Margaret	15	F	Unknown	30Ju02K+
ROSENBURGH, Hyram	26	M	Unknown	30Ju02K+
MILLWOOD, E.	18	F	Unknown	30Ju02K+
CASEY, Johanna	18	F	Unknown	30Ju02K+
BARNAY, Thos.	20	M	Unknown	30Ju02K+
QUILAN, Thos.	13	M	Unknown	30Ju02K+
HACKETT, Michell	20	M	Unknown	30Ju02K+
HOLT, Dennis	16	M	Unknown	30Ju02K+
Alicca	13	F	Unknown	30Ju02K+
GRAY, James	25	M	Unknown	30Ju02K+
FLYNN, Michl.	26	M	Unknown	30Ju02K+
Bridget	26	F	Unknown	30Ju02K+
CONNOY, Biddy	20	F	Unknown	30Ju02K+
KING, Margt.	5	F	Child	30Ju02K+
MCKENNA, Pat	20	M	Unknown	30Ju02K+
MATHEWS, Mary	30	F	Unknown	30Ju02K+
Richard	10	M	Unknown	30Ju02K+
Jno.	9	M	Child	30Ju02K+
Eli	7	M	Child	30Ju02K+
Jane	5	F	Child	30Ju02K+
WOOD, Thomas	40	M	Unknown	30Ju02K+
Sarah	40	F	Unknown	30Ju02K+
ADGIN, Saml.	20	M	Unknown	30Ju02K+
HENARAW, Richard	25	M	Unknown	30Ju02K+
LARAN, John	29	M	Unknown	30Ju02K+
HAINES, Jno.	30	M	Unknown	30Ju02K+
FOX, Wm.	29	M	Unknown	30Ju02K+
GOVEN, Thos.M.	17	M	Unknown	30Ju02K+
Bridget	15	F	Unknown	30Ju02K+
DELAHARTY, Rose	20	F	Unknown	30Ju02K+
Cathn.	18	F	Unknown	30Ju02K+
HANEY, Cath.	30	F	Unknown	30Ju02K+
Kate	12	F	Unknown	30Ju02K+
Elliot	2	M	Child	30Ju02K+
Edwd.	.00	M	Infant	30Ju02K+
CLIFFORD, Mary	25	F	Unknown	30Ju02K+
CLACKIN, James	30	M	Unknown	30Ju02K+
CUNNINGHAM, Bridget	20	F	Unknown	30Ju02K+
MAGUIRE, Betty	20	F	Unknown	30Ju02K+
GARRATTY, Mary	36	F	Unknown	30Ju02K+
Cath.	12	F	Unknown	30Ju02K+
Michael	10	M	Unknown	30Ju02K+
Jno.	8	M	Child	30Ju02K+
FINEGAN, Jno.	20	M	Unknown	30Ju02K+
GOLD, Johannah	25	F	Unknown	30Ju02K+
MAGUIRE, Judy	50	F	Unknown	30Ju02K+
POYHTS, Thomas	40	M	Unknown	30Ju02K+
Elizht.	36	F	Unknown	30Ju02K+
KILLOCK, Jno.	32	M	Unknown	30Ju02K+
DOWNEY, Thomas	18	M	Unknown	30Ju02K+
JONES, Hugh	40	M	Unknown	30Ju02K+
Eliza	40	F	Unknown	30Ju02K+
Hugh	9	M	Child	30Ju02K+
Susannah	7	F	Child	30Ju02K+
Jno.	4	M	Child	30Ju02K+
Eliza	2	F	Child	30Ju02K+
HIGGANS, Richard	22	M	Unknown	30Ju02K+
EINON, Jane	22	F	Unknown	30Ju02K+
KEALY, James	20	M	Unknown	30Ju02K+
MULLIGAN, Berd.	23	M	Unknown	30Ju02K+
KELLY, Jno.	40	M	Unknown	30Ju02K+
Bridget	20	F	Unknown	30Ju02K+
Owen	16	M	Unknown	30Ju02K+
GURALTY, Thos.	24	M	Unknown	30Ju02K+
HUGHES, Thos.	48	M	Unknown	30Ju02K+
Cath.	49	F	Unknown	30Ju02K+
ELLIS, Wm.	33	M	Unknown	30Ju02K+
Jane	28	F	Unknown	30Ju02K+
James	24	M	Unknown	30Ju02K+
MORGAN, Eliza	43	F	Unknown	30Ju02K+
Evan	16	M	Unknown	30Ju02K+
Cath.	9	F	Child	30Ju02K+
Grace	6	F	Child	30Ju02K+
Mary	4	F	Child	30Ju02K+
Jno.	1	M	Child	30Ju02K+
DAVIS, David	33	M	Unknown	30Ju02K+
Ann	35	F	Unknown	30Ju02K+
Mary	3	F	Child	30Ju02K+
Isaac	.00	M	Infant	30Ju02K+
JONES, Richard	34	M	Unknown	30Ju02K+
Mary	32	F	Unknown	30Ju02K+
Jane	7	F	Child	30Ju02K+
Jno.	.00	M	Infant	30Ju02K+
EVANS, Eram	45	M	Unknown	30Ju02K+
Cath.	44	F	Unknown	30Ju02K+
Jno.	16	M	Unknown	30Ju02K+
Cath.	12	F	Unknown	30Ju02K+
Martha	10	F	Unknown	30Ju02K+
Eliza	8	F	Child	30Ju02K+
Mary	6	F	Child	30Ju02K+
Evan	1	M	Child	30Ju02K+
EDWARDS, Hugh	38	M	Unknown	30Ju02K+
Jno.	18	M	Unknown	30Ju02K+
STEPHENSON, Danl.	30	M	Unknown	30Ju02K+
Maria	25	F	Unknown	30Ju02K+
Sarah	3	F	Child	30Ju02K+
Charles	.00	M	Infant	30Ju02K+
ROSBOROGH, Thos.	24	M	Unknown	30Ju02K+
Anna	20	F	Unknown	30Ju02K+
James	.00	M	Infant	30Ju02K+
WATTS, Saml.	33	M	Unknown	30Ju02K+
Eliza	39	F	Unknown	30Ju02K+
Elizth.	11	F	Unknown	30Ju02K+
Mary-Jane	7	F	Child	30Ju02K+
Henry	2	M	Child	30Ju02K+
Alfred	6	M	Child	30Ju02K+

NAMES OF PASSENGERS	AGE	SEX	OCCUPATIONS	DATE PORT SHIP
STAR, Jno.	39	M	Unknown	30Ju02Kt
POWER, Michl.	30	M	Unknown	30Ju02Kt
Allen	30	M	Unknown	30Ju02Kt
DEWEY, Bridget	25	F	Unknown	30Ju02Kt
KING, Margt.	13	F	Unknown	30Ju02Kt
MCDONNELL, Mary	16	F	Unknown	30Ju02Kt
CAMMON, Edwd.	26	M	Unknown	30Ju02Kt
MCCULL, James	18	M	Unknown	30Ju02Kt
FLANNAGAN, Thos.	30	M	Unknown	30Ju02Kt
BYRNES, Mary	17	F	Unknown	30Ju02Kt
FEEHAN, Michl.	24	M	Unknown	30Ju02Kt
LONGHAN, Ellen	32	F	Unknown	30Ju02Kt
CUMMINS, Andrew	46	M	Unknown	30Ju02Kt
Edwd.	13	M	Unknown	30Ju02Kt
LAMBILL, Saml.	25	M	Unknown	30Ju02Kt
GIFFIN, Mary	24	F	Unknown	30Ju02Kt
DEAN, James	26	M	Unknown	30Ju02Kt
EAGAN, Ellen	35	F	Unknown	30Ju02Kt
Mary	19	F	Unknown	30Ju02Kt
Ann	12	F	Unknown	30Ju02Kt
Patrick	9	M	Child	30Ju02Kt
Jno.	8	M	Child	30Ju02Kt
PIKE, Martin	22	M	Unknown	30Ju02Kt
Pat	22	M	Unknown	30Ju02Kt
HEGAN, Dennis	22	M	Unknown	30Ju02Kt
Cath.	20	F	Unknown	30Ju02Kt
Mary	18	F	Unknown	30Ju02Kt
QUINK, Thomas	20	M	Unknown	30Ju02Kt
HILL, Ann	21	F	Unknown	30Ju02Kt
Elizth.	2	F	Child	30Ju02Kt
Robt.	.00	M	Infant	30Ju02Kt
RYAN, Bridget	25	F	Unknown	30Ju02Kt
CARROLL, Wm.	30	M	Unknown	30Ju02Kt
QUARRY, Michl.	28	M	Unknown	30Ju02Kt
WILLIS, Thomas	37	M	Unknown	30Ju02Kt
HORN, Joseph	21	M	Unknown	30Ju02Kt
MULLIVAN, Saml.	26	M	Unknown	30Ju02Kt
Betty	25	F	Unknown	30Ju02Kt
Mary	.00	F	Infant	30Ju02Kt
STANTON, Cath.	24	F	Unknown	30Ju02Kt
MAHER, Michl.	25	M	Unknown	30Ju02Kt
CONLAN, Cath.	30	F	Unknown	30Ju02Kt
BACHAS, Elizth.	17	F	Unknown	30Ju02Kt
DIREFF, Edwd.	25	M	Unknown	30Ju02Kt
HAGAR, Phillip	27	M	Unknown	30Ju02Kt
Jeremiah	18	M	Unknown	30Ju02Kt
HIGGANS, Henry	26	M	Unknown	30Ju02Kt
Ann	20	F	Unknown	30Ju02Kt
Pat	4	M	Child	30Ju02Kt
Maria	2	F	Child	30Ju02Kt
James	.00	M	Infant	30Ju02Kt
GLESHAN, John	25	M	Unknown	30Ju02Kt
Mary	20	F	Unknown	30Ju02Kt
RYAN, Mary	40	F	Unknown	30Ju02Kt
Cath.	25	F	Unknown	30Ju02Kt
FITZGERALD, James	10	M	Unknown	30Ju02Kt
BRADY, Pat	19	M	Unknown	30Ju02Kt
RYAN, Wm.	40	M	Unknown	30Ju02Kt
Margt.	26	F	Unknown	30Ju02Kt
HARLAND, James	32	M	Unknown	30Ju02Kt
Hannah	35	F	Unknown	30Ju02Kt
Henry	9	M	Child	30Ju02Kt
HUNT, Sarah	15	F	Unknown	30Ju02Kt
FINIGAN, Margt.	15	F	Unknown	30Ju02Kt
HAREY, James	40	M	Unknown	30Ju02Kt
EVANS, Garret	27	M	Unknown	30Ju02Kt
Mary	30	F	Unknown	30Ju02Kt
Mick	2	M	Child	30Ju02Kt
Mary	.00	F	Infant	30Ju02Kt
POWIE, Thomas	30	M	Unknown	30Ju02Kt
COTTER, Mary	23	F	Unknown	30Ju02Kt
DIVAN, Mary	19	F	Unknown	30Ju02Kt
CONNOR, Elizabeth	28	F	Unknown	30Ju02Kt
Margt.	21	F	Unknown	30Ju02Kt
Mary	19	F	Unknown	30Ju02Kt
MCKENNA, Mary Died-At-Sea	50	F	Unknown	30Ju02Kt
Owen Died-At-Sea	50	M	Unknown	30Ju02Kt
FAY, U	60	F	Unknown	30Ju02Kt
ROGERS, Ann	30	F	Unknown	30Ju02Kt
CLIFFORD, George	28	M	Unknown	30Ju02Kt
OWENS, Richard	25	M	Unknown	30Ju02Kt
PRICE, Thos.	24	M	Unknown	30Ju02Kt
MORROW, John	23	M	Unknown	30Ju02Kt
RADLEY, John	33	M	Unknown	30Ju02Kt

MONTREAL-OF-NY 30 JUNE 1849

From Limerick

NAMES OF PASSENGERS	AGE	SEX	OCCUPATIONS	DATE PORT SHIP
SCANLON, James	55	M	Baker	30Ju35Lh
GILMORE, John	25	M	Baker	30Ju35Lh
U (W)	22	F	Wife	30Ju35Lh
SCANLON, U-Mrs.	52	F	Unknown	30Ju35Lh
ONEILL, U-Mrs.	27	F	Unknown	30Ju35Lh
SCANLON, Anne	18	F	Unknown	30Ju35Lh
Margt.	16	F	Unknown	30Ju35Lh
GILMORE, Anne	2	F	Child	30Ju35Lh
Jane	.02	F	Infant	30Ju35Lh
ONEILL, Jane	1	F	Child	30Ju35Lh
FITZGERALD, James	36	M	Grocer	30Ju35Lh
Johannah (W)	36	F	Wife	30Ju35Lh
Edward	12	M	Unknown	30Ju35Lh
Joseph	10	M	Unknown	30Ju35Lh
Helena	5	F	Child	30Ju35Lh
Kate	.10	F	Infant	30Ju35Lh
OREGH, Michl.	36	M	Carpenter	30Ju35Lh
Mary (W)	36	F	Wife	30Ju35Lh
LYNCH, Catherine	20	F	Servant	30Ju35Lh
MORGAN, Denis	40	M	Unknown	30Ju35Lh
U, Denis	00	M	Unknown	30Ju35Lh
Eliza	00	F	Unknown	30Ju35Lh
OSHEA, Mary	28	F	Servant	30Ju35Lh
HAYSE, Patt	50	M	Laborer	30Ju35Lh
Mary (W)	50	F	Wife	30Ju35Lh
Michael	20	M	Laborer	30Ju35Lh
Patt	18	M	Laborer	30Ju35Lh
Johanna	15	F	Servant	30Ju35Lh
James	8	M	Child	30Ju35Lh
Mary	10	F	Servant	30Ju35Lh
WHITE, Michael	28	M	Farmer	30Ju35Lh
Henry	22	M	Farmer	30Ju35Lh
U-Mrs.	50	F	Wife	30Ju35Lh
Mary-Ann	17	F	Servant	30Ju35Lh
Margt.	11	F	Servant	30Ju35Lh
DALY, Patt	19	M	Clerk	30Ju35Lh
COLEMAN, John	18	M	Farmer	30Ju35Lh
RYAN, James	55	M	Laborer	30Ju35Lh
BOLAND, John	20	M	Laborer	30Ju35Lh
HANNE, John	22	M	Laborer	30Ju35Lh
Michael	20	M	Laborer	30Ju35Lh
MALONEY, Thomas	17	M	Farmer	30Ju35Lh
MCGRATH, Amelia	23	F	Dressmaker	30Ju35Lh
RYAN, Johanah	24	F	Dressmaker	30Ju35Lh
POWER, Mary	22	F	Servant	30Ju35Lh
Catherine	18	F	Servant	30Ju35Lh
Simon	16	M	Servant	30Ju35Lh
AHERN, Patt	23	M	Farmer	30Ju35Lh
CARRIG, David	26	M	Laborer	30Ju35Lh
MALONEY, Michael	25	M	Laborer	30Ju35Lh
HIGGINS, John	30	M	Farmer	30Ju35Lh
DAREY, Wm.	22	M	Tailor	30Ju35Lh
MAIDE, Maurice	21	M	Farmer	30Ju35Lh

NAMES OF PASSENGERS	AGE	SEX	OCCUPATIONS	DATE PORT SHIP
CASEY, Daniel	28	M	Farmer	30Ju35Lh
BLAKE, James	26	M	Laborer	30Ju35Lh
Johanah	50	F	Matron	30Ju35Lh
John	20	M	Laborer	30Ju35Lh
KELLEY, Morty	32	M	Laborer	30Ju35Lh
HENNESSY, John	30	M	Laborer	30Ju35Lh
MCNAMARA, Margt.	18	F	Servant	30Ju35Lh
HICKSON, Sarah	4	F	Child	30Ju35Lh
Lucy	2	F	Child	30Ju35Lh
MARSHELL, Mary	28	F	Nurse	30Ju35Lh
DAY, Margt.	12	F	Servant	30Ju35Lh
DOOLAN, Paddy	45	M	Laborer	30Ju35Lh
John	13	M	Laborer	30Ju35Lh
Mary	12	F	Servant	30Ju35Lh
LEO, Patt	18	M	Laborer	30Ju35Lh
HASTINGS, George	22	M	Laborer	30Ju35Lh
KENNELLY, John	56	M	Farmer	30Ju35Lh
NEVIL, Patt	20	M	Laborer	30Ju35Lh
Honnor	17	F	Servant	30Ju35Lh
HERBERT, Dillon	30	M	Couch Maker	30Ju35Lh
DOHERTY, Michael	40	M	Laborer	30Ju35Lh
GREEN, Daniel	23	M	Blacksmith	30Ju35Lh
DALTON, Michael	30	M	Laborer	30Ju35Lh
MCGRATH, Wm.	56	M	Farmer	30Ju35Lh
Denis	30	M	Farmer	30Ju35Lh
James	23	M	Farmer	30Ju35Lh
ONEILL, Denis	22	M	Farmer	30Ju35Lh
Michael	18	M	Farmer	30Ju35Lh
HALL, Henry	30	M	Clerk	30Ju35Lh
DALE, James	28	M	Gdnr	30Ju35Lh
VAUGHAN, Patt	17	M	Laborer	30Ju35Lh
SECTAN, John	26	M	Laborer	30Ju35Lh
HASTINGS, Thomas	20	M	Laborer	30Ju35Lh
Mary	18	F	Laborer	30Ju35Lh
HALLERON, James	30	M	Farmer	30Ju35Lh
Maurice	26	M	Farmer	30Ju35Lh
Thos.	23	M	Farmer	30Ju35Lh
FRANKEY, Bridget	24	F	Servant	30Ju35Lh
NUNAN, Ned	38	M	Laborer	30Ju35Lh
MADE, Patt	19	M	Laborer	30Ju35Lh
TRACY, Timothy	27	M	Laborer	30Ju35Lh
Bridget	21	F	Servant	30Ju35Lh
Margt.	18	F	Servant	30Ju35Lh
OBRIEN, Thomas	36	M	Carpenter	30Ju35Lh
HALLERON, Ellen	30	F	Servant	30Ju35Lh
Mary	14	F	Servant	30Ju35Lh
John	10	M	Laborer	30Ju35Lh
Michael	8	M	Child	30Ju35Lh
Patk.	6	M	Child	30Ju35Lh
Margt.	.11	F	Infant	30Ju35Lh
HALPIN, Michael	30	M	Laborer	30Ju35Lh
Bridget	26	F	Servant	30Ju35Lh
KEOGH, Patt	30	M	Farmer	30Ju35Lh
Thomas	19	M	Farmer	30Ju35Lh
Mary	24	F	Servant	30Ju35Lh
Mary	18	F	Servant	30Ju35Lh
HARTIGAN, Ellen	30	F	Servant	30Ju35Lh
BRICK, Catherine	20	F	Servant	30Ju35Lh
DAWSON, Wm.	40	M	Laborer	30Ju35Lh
FITZGERALD, James	20	M	Laborer	30Ju35Lh
MCENERNY, Mary	26	F	Servant	30Ju35Lh
Margt.	23	F	Servant	30Ju35Lh
Thomas	14	M	Servant	30Ju35Lh
QUADE, Timothy	36	M	Laborer	30Ju35Lh
HALPIN, John	28	M	Laborer	30Ju35Lh
POWER, James	58	M	Farmer	30Ju35Lh
COFFEE, David	22	M	Laborer	30Ju35Lh
MOLERY, Thomas	22	M	Laborer	30Ju35Lh
SHEHAN, Anne	18	F	Servant	30Ju35Lh
OMALEY, Owen	18	M	Clerk	30Ju35Lh
James	24	M	Farmer	30Ju35Lh
MCMAHON, Edward	30	M	Farmer	30Ju35Lh
Anne	25	F	Dressmaker	30Ju35Lh
SHEHAN, Catherine	14	F	Servant	30Ju35Lh
CARRIGAN, Edward	36	M	Laborer	30Ju35Lh
KENNEDY, Thomas	35	M	Blacksmith	30Ju35Lh
MCCORMACK, John	25	M	Farmer	30Ju35Lh
Mary (W)	19	F	Wife	30Ju35Lh
Mary-Ann	.05	F	Infant	30Ju35Lh
RABALDI, Joseph	27	M	Cvr-Gldr	30Ju35Lh
HOURIGIN, James	45	M	Farmer	30Ju35Lh
Connor	26	M	Farmer	30Ju35Lh
Ellen	24	F	Servant	30Ju35Lh
James	17	M	Farmer	30Ju35Lh
Lawrence	13	M	Farmer	30Ju35Lh
Timothy	10	M	Farmer	30Ju35Lh
BROWN, Paddy	36	M	Laborer	30Ju35Lh
MCENERNY, James	30	M	Laborer	30Ju35Lh
TOUHALL, Mary-Anne	20	F	Servant	30Ju35Lh
GRANT, Maris-Mrs.	23	F	Dressmaker	30Ju35Lh
Mary	3	F	Child	30Ju35Lh
MCENERNY, Mary	20	F	Servant	30Ju35Lh
SHEPPHARD, Mary	22	F	Servant	30Ju35Lh
CONNOR, Thos.	45	M	Laborer	30Ju35Lh
FRINEGIN, John	22	M	Laborer	30Ju35Lh
GRIFFIN, James	30	M	Tchrl	30Ju35Lh
COLBERT, Patt	29	M	Laborer	30Ju35Lh
CASEY, Mary	37	F	Servant	30Ju35Lh
GRIFFIN, Bridget	30	F	Servant	30Ju35Lh
CREGHAN, Ellen	22	F	Servant	30Ju35Lh
Norry	20	F	Servant	30Ju35Lh
BRASSELL, Wm.	30	M	Farmer	30Ju35Lh
SHEHAN, Patt	23	M	Laborer	30Ju35Lh
OBRIEN, Wm.	25	M	Farmer	30Ju35Lh
Mary	23	F	Servant	30Ju35Lh
OKEIFFER, Honor	10	F	Servant	30Ju35Lh
SULLIVAN, Bridget	30	F	Servant	30Ju35Lh
CANDON, Betty	20	F	Servant	30Ju35Lh
WALSH, James	20	M	Laborer	30Ju35Lh
OKEIFFER, Timothy	57	M	Laborer	30Ju35Lh
EGIN, Thos.	30	M	Baker	30Ju35Lh
QUERIN, James	17	M	Laborer	30Ju35Lh
MARTIN, Michael	20	M	Gdnr	30Ju35Lh
MULGUINE, Margt.	16	F	Servant	30Ju35Lh
SPELLISY, Margt.	22	F	Dressmaker	30Ju35Lh
Wm.	.10	M	Infant	30Ju35Lh
MALONEY, John	17	M	Clerk	30Ju35Lh
BOHAN, Denis	40	M	Farmer	30Ju35Lh
BROWN, Anne	18	F	Servant	30Ju35Lh
POWER, Michael	9	M	Child	30Ju35Lh
MALONEY, Michael	9	M	Child	30Ju35Lh
OBRIEN, Patt.	30	M	Farmer	30Ju35Lh
Margt. (W)	27	F	Wife	30Ju35Lh
Bridget	.11	F	Infant	30Ju35Lh
MULLINS, Ellen	20	F	Matron	30Ju35Lh
CALLINAN, Mary	40	F	Dressmaker	30Ju35Lh
Anne	18	F	Dressmaker	30Ju35Lh
BURK, Catherine	42	F	Servant	30Ju35Lh
CALLINAN, Denis	5	M	Child	30Ju35Lh
WILSON, Wm.	31	M	Merchant	30Ju35Lh
U (W)	28	F	Wife	30Ju35Lh
John	3	M	Child	30Ju35Lh
Wm.Jr.	1	M	Child	30Ju35Lh
BLACK, John	19	M	Clerk	30Ju35Lh
Allicia	20	F	Milliner	30Ju35Lh
Anne	18	F	Dressmaker	30Ju35Lh
MANAHAN, Elizabeth	20	F	Milliner	30Ju35Lh
JAMES, Mary-J.	26	F	Governess	30Ju35Lh
ENGLISH, John	30	M	Clerk	30Ju35Lh
OHALLERON, Eliza	24	F	Governess	30Ju35Lh
JAMES, John	30	M	Clerk	30Ju35Lh
Charles	27	M	Clerk	30Ju35Lh
HALLERON, Anne	00	F	Servant	30Ju35Lh

HIBERNIA 30 JUNE 1849

From Liverpool

NAMES OF PASSENGERS	AGE	SEX	OCCUPATIONS	DATE PORT SHIP
SWEETLAND, Edwd.M.	27	M	Merchant	30Ju02Go
BIRTY, Richard	37	M	Mnftr	30Ju02Go
PIERCE, George	35	M	Merchant	30Ju02Go
MURRAY, J.	24	M	Merchant	30Ju02Go
BLACK, William	38	M	Mmrnr	30Ju02Go
PAULSON, Charles	32	M	Merchant	30Ju02Go
WOODCOCK, A.B.	38	M	Cver	30Ju02Go
CUNYNGHAME, A.S.	36	M	Lt.Colonel	30Ju02Go
U-Hon. (W)	24	F	None	30Ju02Go
U	00	U	Child	30Ju02Go
DARELS, Emma-Mrs.	21	F	Servant	30Ju02Go
HORNBY, E.O.	30	M	Barrister	30Ju02Go
Martha	29	F	None	30Ju02Go
WILLIAMS, J.R.	52	M	Ship Owner	30Ju02Go
Charlotte	55	F	None	30Ju02Go
HENRY, Sarah	14	F	Servant	30Ju02Go
SIMSON, Henry	30	M	Merchant	30Ju02Go
U (W)	30	F	None	30Ju02Go
U	2	U	Child	30Ju02Go
NEILSON, Wm.	27	M	None	30Ju02Go
KELLY, John-J.	33	M	Merchant	30Ju02Go
THORNTON, William	31	M	Gentleman	30Ju02Go
TOBIN, James	29	M	Physician	30Ju02Go
MELLISS, D.	45	M	Merchant	30Ju02Go
HAMEL, Richard-B.	17	M	Merchant	30Ju02Go
HENLEY, H.R.E.	22	M	Gentleman	30Ju02Go
THORNTON, Mary	20	F	None	30Ju02Go
PERRIER, William	26	M	Merchant	30Ju02Go
GOODLAND, John	42	M	Merchant	30Ju02Go
MACNAB, Duncan	28	M	None	30Ju02Go
MONYSY, Timothy	44	M	Clerk	30Ju02Go

ASHBURTON 30 JUNE 1849

From Liverpool

NAMES OF PASSENGERS	AGE	SEX	OCCUPATIONS	DATE PORT SHIP
BYRNE, Mary	26	F	Unknown	30Ju02Le
MATHEW, Theobald-Rev.	59	M	Clergyman	30Ju02Le
DORAN, Wm.Rev.	36	M	Clergyman	30Ju02Le
WARD, David-O.	28	M	Unknown	30Ju02Le
QUINLAN, James	34	M	Unknown	30Ju02Le
MAGUIRE, Henry	25	M	Unknown	30Ju02Le
FOSTER, Wm.	62	M	Unknown	30Ju02Le
LAWLOR, Richard-Wm.	24	M	Unknown	30Ju02Le
COLLINS, Henry	29	M	File Cutter	30Ju02Le
CLANCY, Richard	18	M	Tailor	30Ju02Le
WALSH, John	40	M	Unknown	30Ju02Le
VITTEY, Eliza.	19	F	Unknown	30Ju02Le
James	18	M	Tailor	30Ju02Le
Henry	16	M	Tailor	30Ju02Le
WALSH, Letisa	8	F	Child	30Ju02Le
Anna	6	F	Child	30Ju02Le
John	4	M	Child	30Ju02Le
Sarah	2	F	Child	30Ju02Le
WINTER, David	24	M	Farmer	30Ju02Le
WILSON, William	26	M	Farmer	30Ju02Le
ARMSTRONG, James	30	M	Farmer	30Ju02Le
SULLIVAN, John	32	M	Clerk	30Ju02Le
BURNES, Thady	24	M	Laborer	30Ju02Le
KEIRENS, Cath.	18	F	Servant	30Ju02Le
FLINN, Patk.	20	M	Laborer	30Ju02Le
FITZPATRICK, Pat.	28	M	Smith	30Ju02Le
NUNEN, Danl.	30	M	Farmer	30Ju02Le
BICKERS, Luke	24	M	Maurer	30Ju02Le
CUMMINS, Michael	25	M	Laborer	30Ju02Le
Maria	18	F	Unknown	30Ju02Le
MURTHA, Patrick	30	M	Laborer	30Ju02Le
Ellen	27	F	Unknown	30Ju02Le
HUGHES, John	45	M	Farmer	30Ju02Le
Catherine	40	F	Unknown	30Ju02Le
James	17	M	Farmer	30Ju02Le
Patrick	15	M	Farmer	30Ju02Le
Thomas	13	M	Farmer	30Ju02Le
Jolin	13	M	Farmer	30Ju02Le
Mary	11	F	Unknown	30Ju02Le
ONEIL, Jane	40	F	Unknown	30Ju02Le
Jane	18	F	Unknown	30Ju02Le
Margaret	14	F	Unknown	30Ju02Le
BERGIN, Pat	35	M	Laborer	30Ju02Le
Eliza	30	F	Unknown	30Ju02Le
HIRST, George	34	M	Laborer	30Ju02Le
MINER, Maria	20	F	Unknown	30Ju02Le
RYAN, Jerimiah	20	M	Laborer	30Ju02Le
PENDERGAST, Michael	16	M	Laborer	30Ju02Le
BRANNEN, Richard	33	M	Laborer	30Ju02Le
U-Mrs.	26	F	Unknown	30Ju02Le
John	2	M	Child	30Ju02Le
CACY, Lawrence	28	M	Laborer	30Ju02Le
WALSH, Ellen	28	F	Unknown	30Ju02Le
OREORDEN, James	22	M	Laborer	30Ju02Le
MILLER, Alex	42	M	Miller	30Ju02Le
U-Mrs.	37	F	Unknown	30Ju02Le
Ellen	16	F	Unknown	30Ju02Le
William	14	M	Unknown	30Ju02Le
Margaret	12	F	Unknown	30Ju02Le
Anna	7	F	Child	30Ju02Le
Mary	5	F	Child	30Ju02Le
Catherine	2	F	Child	30Ju02Le
Allex	7	M	Child	30Ju02Le
FLEMING, Mary	6	F	Child	30Ju02Le
HANLON, Michael	30	M	Laborer	30Ju02Le
FITZPATRICK, John	30	M	Laborer	30Ju02Le
KAY, Michael	45	M	Laborer	30Ju02Le
BLACKILM, Conrad	28	M	Servant	30Ju02Le
MACKEN, Mark	21	M	Laborer	30Ju02Le
DREW, John	50	M	Farmer	30Ju02Le
OCONNER, Bridget	25	F	Unknown	30Ju02Le
CARR, Margaret	20	F	Servant	30Ju02Le
WHITE, Joseph	19	M	Laborer	30Ju02Le
DUNBAR, John	60	M	Tailor	30Ju02Le
Mary	50	F	Unknown	30Ju02Le
Ellen	30	F	Unknown	30Ju02Le
Joseph	12	M	Unknown	30Ju02Le
Mary	9	F	Child	30Ju02Le
DONAHUE, Corn.	21	M	Farmer	30Ju02Le
Johanna	50	F	Unknown	30Ju02Le
Bridget	11	F	Unknown	30Ju02Le
Patrick	9	M	Child	30Ju02Le
Mary	7	F	Child	30Ju02Le
WALSH, Ellen	20	F	Servant	30Ju02Le
HENRY, Ellen	20	F	Unknown	30Ju02Le
BONNER, Sarah	28	F	Unknown	30Ju02Le
Catherine	24	F	Unknown	30Ju02Le
CORDENEY, Elizabeth	17	F	Unknown	30Ju02Le
MCMANUS, Bridget	13	F	Unknown	30Ju02Le
QUINLAN, Daniel	49	M	Farmer	30Ju02Le
Bridget	40	F	Unknown	30Ju02Le
Pat	13	M	Unknown	30Ju02Le
Honer.	11	F	Unknown	30Ju02Le
Margaret	9	F	Child	30Ju02Le
Maria	7	F	Child	30Ju02Le
Kate	5	F	Child	30Ju02Le
Bridget	4	F	Child	30Ju02Le
Anna	2	F	Child	30Ju02Le

NAMES OF PASSENGERS	AGE	SEX	OCCUPATIONS	DATE PORT SHIP
QUINLAN, Daniel	.00	M	Infant	30Ju02Le
CAHAN, Mary	16	F	Unknown	30Ju02Le
MAHER, Margaret	17	F	Unknown	30Ju02Le
Mary	10	F	Unknown	30Ju02Le
HARLAND, Mathew	24	M	Clerk	30Ju02Le
KEORS, Michael	22	M	Laborer	30Ju02Le
FOGARTY, Edmond	20	M	Laborer	30Ju02Le
CASHILL, James	22	M	Laborer	30Ju02Le
KENNY, James	22	M	Laborer	30Ju02Le
Biddy	27	F	Unknown	30Ju02Le
DEKO, Eliza	18	F	Unknown	30Ju02Le
Susan	25	F	Unknown	30Ju02Le
HORAN, Daniel	30	M	Farmer	30Ju02Le
Catherine	25	F	Unknown	30Ju02Le
Xxxxx	3	M	Child	30Ju02Le
Daniel	1	M	Child	30Ju02Le
Charles	.00	M	Infant	30Ju02Le
DALTON, Sally	20	F	Servant	30Ju02Le
MCNULTY, Margaret	23	F	Milliner	30Ju02Le
ROE, James	39	M	Laborer	30Ju02Le
Catherine	25	F	Unknown	30Ju02Le
FLEMING, Pat	30	M	Miller	30Ju02Le
Anna	20	F	Unknown	30Ju02Le
EYLETON, Thomas	20	M	Laborer	30Ju02Le
DUNN, Mary	23	F	Unknown	30Ju02Le
WEEKS, Margaret	33	F	Unknown	30Ju02Le
John	30	M	Laborer	30Ju02Le
DUNN, Eliza	4	F	Child	30Ju02Le
CONNORS, Mary	20	F	Unknown	30Ju02Le
Johann	19	M	Unknown	30Ju02Le
MURRAY, Anna	58	F	Unknown	30Ju02Le
Catherine	19	F	Unknown	30Ju02Le
RING, James	22	M	Laborer	30Ju02Le
LARKEN, Catherine	45	F	Unknown	30Ju02Le
ARTHURS, John	13	M	Unknown	30Ju02Le
WARREN, James	18	M	Unknown	30Ju02Le
Margt.	21	F	Unknown	30Ju02Le
KELLY, Patrick	18	M	Laborer	30Ju02Le
Martha-J.	20	F	Unknown	30Ju02Le
HOPPER, James	50	M	Laborer	30Ju02Le
Jane	50	F	Unknown	30Ju02Le
Arthur	28	M	Laborer	30Ju02Le
Robert	18	M	Unknown	30Ju02Le
Samuel	10	M	Unknown	30Ju02Le
John	14	M	Unknown	30Ju02Le
Thomas	14	M	Unknown	30Ju02Le
Elizabeth	32	F	Unknown	30Ju02Le
Agnes	17	F	Unknown	30Ju02Le
James	21	M	Laborer	30Ju02Le
COLLIN, Charles	16	M	Unknown	30Ju02Le
Anna	10	F	Unknown	30Ju02Le
TRIMBLE, Robert	23	M	Farmer	30Ju02Le
OBRIEN, Mary	25	F	Unknown	30Ju02Le
CUNNINGHAM, Patrick	00	M	Laborer	30Ju02Le
MORTON, A.Jr.	00	M	Unknown	30Ju02Le
A.Sr.	00	M	Unknown	30Ju02Le
Mary-Anna	25	F	Unknown	30Ju02Le
MOONEY, Rose	22	F	Milliner	30Ju02Le
FANELL, Anna	20	F	Unknown	30Ju02Le
Karin	38	F	Unknown	30Ju02Le
NEWLAND, Anna	50	F	Unknown	30Ju02Le
John	17	M	Unknown	30Ju02Le
John	9	M	Child	30Ju02Le
LITTLE, Charles	22	M	Laborer	30Ju02Le
Matilda	20	F	Unknown	30Ju02Le
MCFEETERS, William	13	M	Unknown	30Ju02Le
MURPHY, Michael	25	M	Laborer	30Ju02Le
COYLE, Hugh	16	M	Laborer	30Ju02Le
RYAN, Honor	16	F	Unknown	30Ju02Le
GOLDON, James	22	M	Laborer	30Ju02Le
SHERIDAN, Peter	15	M	Unknown	30Ju02Le
Margaret	16	F	Unknown	30Ju02Le
CALLAHAN, Catherine	20	F	Unknown	30Ju02Le
SULLIVAN, Timothy	18	M	Laborer	30Ju02Le
MULLOY, Margaret	20	F	Unknown	30Ju02Le
WARD, Bernard	18	M	Shoemaker	30Ju02Le
HALPIN, John	4	M	Child	30Ju02Le
QUIGLEY, Michael	19	M	Tailor	30Ju02Le
HOWAN, Mary	25	F	Unknown	30Ju02Le
WEST, John	24	M	Carpenter	30Ju02Le
HUMPHRYS, David	28	M	Draper	30Ju02Le
MAGEE, Mary	48	F	Unknown	30Ju02Le
Mary-Jr.	10	F	Unknown	30Ju02Le
MAYCE, James	8	M	Unknown	30Ju02Le
KEEGAN, Patrick	45	M	Laborer	30Ju02Le
Catherine	35	F	Unknown	30Ju02Le
Lawrence	6	M	Child	30Ju02Le
James	4	M	Child	30Ju02Le
BOLAND, John	50	M	Shoemaker	30Ju02Le
Mary	48	F	Shoemaker	30Ju02Le
John	29	M	Shoemaker	30Ju02Le
Walter	22	M	Shoemaker	30Ju02Le
Mary	24	F	Unknown	30Ju02Le
Julia	21	F	Unknown	30Ju02Le
Nicholas	15	M	Unknown	30Ju02Le
Catherine	12	F	Unknown	30Ju02Le
Joseph	9	M	Child	30Ju02Le
James	7	M	Child	30Ju02Le
TOOMY, Andrew	25	M	Carpenter	30Ju02Le
James	26	M	Farmer	30Ju02Le
MAGEE, John	25	M	Butcher	30Ju02Le
Margaret	23	F	Unknown	30Ju02Le
CRINEN, Austin	25	M	Laborer	30Ju02Le
Mary	17	F	Unknown	30Ju02Le
DROMGOOLE, Christopher	36	M	Saddler	30Ju02Le
OKEEF, Michael	31	M	Laborer	30Ju02Le
WELWORTH, George	30	M	Farmer	30Ju02Le
Anna	25	F	Unknown	30Ju02Le
David	20	M	Farmer	30Ju02Le
WILSON, U-Mrs.	60	F	Unknown	30Ju02Le
IVARY, James	20	M	Saddler	30Ju02Le
KEARY, Mary	20	F	Unknown	30Ju02Le
CORIGAN, John	17	M	Tailor	30Ju02Le
SHEILL, Peter	24	M	Farmer	30Ju02Le
Catherine	20	F	Unknown	30Ju02Le
BOURKE, James	17	M	Laborer	30Ju02Le
DEVEY, Michael	36	M	Carpenter	30Ju02Le
Elizabeth	25	F	Unknown	30Ju02Le
STANTON, John	22	M	Shoemaker	30Ju02Le
OBRIEN, Timothy	22	M	Shoemaker	30Ju02Le
Cornelius	21	M	Tailor	30Ju02Le
Eliza	18	F	Dressmaker	30Ju02Le
GRIFFEN, James	24	M	Shoemaker	30Ju02Le
GHARINASSY, Morris	20	M	Laborer	30Ju02Le
ANDERSON, Francis	25	M	Laborer	30Ju02Le
FOSTER, Samuel	45	M	Laborer	30Ju02Le
CAIRNS, William	22	M	Farmer	30Ju02Le
HENNESY, David	28	M	Clerk	30Ju02Le
OCONNER, Maurice	25	M	Laborer	30Ju02Le
ROACH, Mary	21	F	Unknown	30Ju02Le
DALEY, Mary	30	F	Unknown	30Ju02Le
MCCARTHY, Dennis	26	M	Laborer	30Ju02Le
Margaret	20	F	Unknown	30Ju02Le
Julia	20	F	Unknown	30Ju02Le
MULLINS, Richard	22	M	Shoemaker	30Ju02Le
Margaret	36	F	Unknown	30Ju02Le
REEVES, Mary-Mrs.	34	F	Unknown	30Ju02Le
WHITE, Richard	7	M	Child	30Ju02Le
BANETT, John	27	M	Coach Maker	30Ju02Le
GILCHRIST, Letty	18	F	Unknown	30Ju02Le
ADDY, Margaret	18	F	Unknown	30Ju02Le
GEDDES, William	25	M	Laborer	30Ju02Le
Margaret	23	F	Unknown	30Ju02Le
Joseph	.00	M	Infant	30Ju02Le
FANNING, Hugh	25	M	Laborer	30Ju02Le
FLYNN, John	25	M	Laborer	30Ju02Le
Ellen	18	F	Unknown	30Ju02Le
HASLETT, Sarah	12	F	Unknown	30Ju02Le
JACKSON, William-J.	44	M	Draper	30Ju02Le
Margaret	40	F	Unknown	30Ju02Le

NAMES OF PASSENGERS		AGE	SEX	OCCUPATIONS	DATE PORT SHIP
JACKSON, Charles		16	M	Unknown	30Ju02Le
Margaret-F.		13	F	Unknown	30Ju02Le
Anna		12	M	Unknown	30Ju02Le
Mary-F.		9	F	Child	30Ju02Le
Jane		7	F	Child	30Ju02Le
William		1	M	Child	30Ju02Le
DELANY, Mary		30	F	Unknown	30Ju02Le
OROURKE, Francis		30	M	Draper	30Ju02Le
BLAKE, William		30	M	Farmer	30Ju02Le
OCALLAGHAN, Timothy		15	M	Saddler	30Ju02Le
MURPHY, John		40	M	Chandler	30Ju02Le
Mary		30	F	Unknown	30Ju02Le
ALLENDER, Thomas		26	M	Laborer	30Ju02Le
MCELROY, Patrick		20	M	Laborer	30Ju02Le
Mary		40	F	Unknown	30Ju02Le
QUIGLEY, John		36	M	Farmer	30Ju02Le
Charlotte		25	F	Unknown	30Ju02Le
CURRY, Peter		25	M	Farmer	30Ju02Le
William		24	M	Farmer	30Ju02Le
DELANEY, Patrick		20	M	Laborer	30Ju02Le
HUTCHISON, Ellen		22	F	Servant	30Ju02Le
GRIFFEN, Mary		23	F	Servant	30Ju02Le
BOYLE, William		40	M	Cver	30Ju02Le
WALAN, Anna		22	F	None	30Ju02Le
TERNELL, Edward		40	M	Shoemaker	30Ju02Le
James		16	M	Shoemaker	30Ju02Le
Louisa		11	F	None	30Ju02Le
MOORE, James		30	M	Clerk	30Ju02Le
CONNELLY, Patrick		25	M	Farmer	30Ju02Le
Judith		25	F	None	30Ju02Le
Catherine		20	F	None	30Ju02Le
James		9	M	Child	30Ju02Le
SCHOLES, Francis		21	M	Teacher	30Ju02Le
BURNES, Charles		50	M	Joiner	30Ju02Le
Anna		40	F	None	30Ju02Le
Jane		15	F	None	30Ju02Le
Eliza		11	F	None	30Ju02Le
Anna		10	F	None	30Ju02Le
PATTEN, John		40	M	Farmer	30Ju02Le
CULLEN, Thomas		18	M	Laborer	30Ju02Le
MCLAUGHLIN, Wm.		32	M	Gentleman	30Ju02Le
Peter		20	M	Gentleman	30Ju02Le
WALKER, William-Mrs.		22	F	None	30Ju02Le
SMITH, John		45	M	Builder	30Ju02Le
RICHARDSON, David		22	M	Laborer	30Ju02Le
Betsy		22	F	None	30Ju02Le
WILSON, John		33	M	Gentleman	30Ju02Le
WILLIAMS, U-Mrs.		21	F	None	30Ju02Le
HALPIN, Elizabeth		4	F	Child	30Ju02Le
WILSON, William		30	M	Servant	30Ju02Le
NUGENT, Mary		19	F	Servant	30Ju02Le

RICHARD-ALSOP 02 JULY 1849

From Liverpool

NAMES OF PASSENGERS		AGE	SEX	OCCUPATIONS	DATE PORT SHIP
CORKEN, Frederic-W.		36	M	None	02Jl02Lg
Sarah		30	F	None	02Jl02Lg
Henry		10	M	None	02Jl02Lg
John		3	M	Child	02Jl02Lg
RUSK, George		24	M	Dealer	02Jl02Lg
U	(W)	22	F	Dealer	02Jl02Lg
IRWIN, Robr.		23	M	Laborer	02Jl02Lg
U	(W)	21	F	Laborer	02Jl02Lg
BAXTER, Robt.		22	M	Laborer	02Jl02Lg
DOLAN, Thomas		30	M	Unknown	02Jl02Lg
TOOLE, Hm.		30	M	Unknown	02Jl02Lg
Eliza		29	F	Unknown	02Jl02Lg
U		.09	M	Infant	02Jl02Lg
BOYNE, Hugh		32	M	Unknown	02Jl02Lg
Bridget		30	F	Unknown	02Jl02Lg
Cathn.		6	F	Child	02Jl02Lg
Ellen		4	F	Child	02Jl02Lg
U		.07	F	Infant	02Jl02Lg
DEBERY, Owen		24	M	Laborer	02Jl02Lg
Margt.		22	F	Laborer	02Jl02Lg
Fanny		40	F	Laborer	02Jl02Lg
IRWIN, James		50	M	Farmer	02Jl02Lg
GRADY, Biddy		26	F	Servant	02Jl02Lg
GOLOHER, Winefred		25	F	Servant	02Jl02Lg
KELLY, Joseph		54	M	Farmer	02Jl02Lg
Cathn.		52	F	Farmer	02Jl02Lg
Cathn.		18	F	Farmer	02Jl02Lg
James		13	M	Farmer	02Jl02Lg
Bridget		10	F	Farmer	02Jl02Lg
Patrick		8	M	Child	02Jl02Lg
BURNS, Edward		56	M	Farmer	02Jl02Lg
U	(W)	50	F	Farmer	02Jl02Lg
CONNOR, Margt.		3	F	Child	02Jl02Lg
BERGEN, Cathn.		57	F	Laborer	02Jl02Lg
James		35	M	Laborer	02Jl02Lg
Thomas		30	M	Laborer	02Jl02Lg
Honora		28	F	Laborer	02Jl02Lg
HICKEY, Thomas		30	M	Laborer	02Jl02Lg
MULCAHY, Patt.		20	M	Laborer	02Jl02Lg
BERGEN, Cathn.		11	F	Laborer	02Jl02Lg
Lawrence		9	M	Child	02Jl02Lg
Bridget		8	F	Child	02Jl02Lg
Patrick		7	M	Child	02Jl02Lg
MOCKLEN, Michl.		35	M	Tanner	02Jl02Lg
Cathn.		32	F	Unknown	02Jl02Lg
Judy		19	F	Unknown	02Jl02Lg
Patrick		17	M	Unknown	02Jl02Lg
John		15	M	Unknown	02Jl02Lg
Thomas		11	M	Unknown	02Jl02Lg
Cathn.		9	F	Child	02Jl02Lg
BERGEN, Margt.		40	F	Unknown	02Jl02Lg
HEFFERIN, John		50	M	Tanner	02Jl02Lg
Judy		48	F	Tanner	02Jl02Lg
Michl.		17	M	Tanner	02Jl02Lg
Winefred		15	F	Tanner	02Jl02Lg
CLEARY, Patrick		25	M	Tanner	02Jl02Lg
HART, U-Miss		28	F	Unknown	02Jl02Lg
MARKEY, Patrick		25	M	Laborer	02Jl02Lg
Anne		12	F	Laborer	02Jl02Lg
FARRELLY, James		28	M	Laborer	02Jl02Lg
HAND, Rose		28	F	Laborer	02Jl02Lg
MCMAHON, Bernard		21	M	Laborer	02Jl02Lg
HUEY, Owen		21	M	Laborer	02Jl02Lg
MCKEEVER, Nichl.		21	M	Laborer	02Jl02Lg
HUGHES, Geo.		21	M	Laborer	02Jl02Lg
Mary		18	F	Laborer	02Jl02Lg
HEALY, Lawrence		21	M	Stone Mason	02Jl02Lg
Patrick		18	M	Stone Mason	02Jl02Lg
Anne		20	F	Stone Mason	02Jl02Lg
GERATY, James		20	M	Stone Mason	02Jl02Lg
SMITH, Felix		24	M	Laborer	02Jl02Lg
Margt.		28	F	Laborer	02Jl02Lg
Cathn.		19	F	Laborer	02Jl02Lg
MCKENNA, Honora		30	F	Laborer	02Jl02Lg
MAGEE, James		24	M	Laborer	02Jl02Lg
MILLER, Andrew		24	M	Laborer	02Jl02Lg
Anne	(W)	20	F	Laborer	02Jl02Lg
KAVANAGH, Anne		20	F	Laborer	02Jl02Lg
HOGAN, Charles		22	M	Laborer	02Jl02Lg
U	(W)	22	M	Laborer	02Jl02Lg
MANAMY, Thomas		40	M	Laborer	02Jl02Lg
BERJAN, Maria		35	F	Laborer	02Jl02Lg
CARROLL, Thomas		40	M	Laborer	02Jl02Lg
BYRNE, Mary		50	F	Laborer	02Jl02Lg
John		30	M	Laborer	02Jl02Lg
Edward		25	M	Laborer	02Jl02Lg
MAHAN, Thomas		25	M	Laborer	02Jl02Lg
MURPHY, Thomas		21	M	Laborer	02Jl02Lg

NAMES OF PASSENGERS	AGE	SEX	OCCUPATIONS	DATE PORT SHIP
TIMMONS, Temp.	22	F	Laborer	02JI02Lg
SYMONDS, George	21	M	Laborer	02JI02Lg
MCCONNELL, Anne	21	F	Laborer	02JI02Lg
KING, Thos.	11	M	Laborer	02JI02Lg
WHITE, John	50	M	Carpenter	02JI02Lg
James	20	M	Carpenter	02JI02Lg
CLARKE, Mary	18	F	Carpenter	02JI02Lg
FARRELLY, James	14	M	Laborer	02JI02Lg
Thomas	10	M	Laborer	02JI02Lg
Peter	8	M	Child	02JI02Lg
FARRELL, John	15	M	Laborer	02JI02Lg
Anne	12	F	Laborer	02JI02Lg
PHELAN, John	50	M	Farmer	02JI02Lg
Margt.	48	F	Farmer	02JI02Lg
Patrick	25	M	Farmer	02JI02Lg
Mary	26	F	Farmer	02JI02Lg
John	24	M	Farmer	02JI02Lg
James	22	M	Farmer	02JI02Lg
Michl.	20	M	Farmer	02JI02Lg
Margt.	18	F	Farmer	02JI02Lg
Bridget	15	F	Farmer	02JI02Lg
Cathn.	11	F	Farmer	02JI02Lg
WALSH, Patt.	28	M	Farmer	02JI02Lg
Mary	16	F	Farmer	02JI02Lg
Elizth.	14	F	Farmer	02JI02Lg
DUFF, Patrick	20	M	Farmer	02JI02Lg
Mary	16	F	Farmer	02JI02Lg
CORGAN, Michl.	30	M	Farmer	02JI02Lg
FLANAGAN, Edward	34	M	Farmer	02JI02Lg
Mary	30	F	Farmer	02JI02Lg
Hugh	.00	M	Infant	02JI02Lg
LEMAN, Patt.	50	M	Farmer	02JI02Lg
HUEY, Mary	21	F	Farmer	02JI02Lg
Mary	.04	F	Infant	02JI02Lg
HUGHES, Alicia	18	F	Farmer	02JI02Lg
Elizth.	11	F	Farmer	02JI02Lg
HAGAN, James	20	M	Farmer	02JI02Lg
Cathn.	20	F	Farmer	02JI02Lg
Susan	18	F	Farmer	02JI02Lg
Daniel	14	M	Farmer	02JI02Lg
MULLHOLEN, Rose	21	F	Farmer	02JI02Lg
EGAN, Martha	21	F	Gdnr	02JI02Lg
CLYNE, John	25	M	Gdnr	02JI02Lg
BRADY, Bernard	21	M	Gdnr	02JI02Lg
Philip	24	M	Gdnr	02JI02Lg
Lawrence	20	M	Gdnr	02JI02Lg
Patrick	19	M	Gdnr	02JI02Lg
Anne	18	F	Gdnr	02JI02Lg
SMITH, James	26	M	Miner	02JI02Lg
Cathn.	26	F	Miner	02JI02Lg
Maria	.07	F	Infant	02JI02Lg
QUINLAND, Patt.	30	M	Infant	02JI02Lg
FLANAGAN, Rose	30	F	None	02JI02Lg
Patrick	16	M	None	02JI02Lg
James	14	M	None	02JI02Lg
Mary	11	F	None	02JI02Lg
Wm.	6	M	Child	02JI02Lg
Michl.	.03	M	Infant	02JI02Lg
WALL, Mary	22	F	None	02JI02Lg
Julia	20	F	None	02JI02Lg
KANE, John	20	M	Laborer	02JI02Lg
PHILIPS, Michl.	50	M	Farmer	02JI02Lg
Bridget	19	F	Farmer	02JI02Lg
Margt.	15	F	Farmer	02JI02Lg
Mary	14	F	Farmer	02JI02Lg
KELLY, Anne	25	F	Farmer	02JI02Lg
ROURKE, James	27	M	Farmer	02JI02Lg
CLARK, Joseph	36	M	Miller	02JI02Lg
AMB, James	26	M	Farmer	02JI02Lg
LANAGAN, Patt.	26	M	Farmer	02JI02Lg
AMB, Mary	25	M	Farmer	02JI02Lg
ENNIS, Thomas	16	M	Farmer	02JI02Lg
MITH, Andrew	21	M	Farmer	02JI02Lg
AISLEY, James	40	M	Laborer	02JI02Lg
Michl.	11	M	Laborer	02JI02Lg

NAMES OF PASSENGERS	AGE	SEX	OCCUPATIONS	DATE PORT SHIP
LAUREY, Edward	25	M	Laborer	02JI02Lg
MULIGAN, Bryan	25	M	Laborer	02JI02Lg
CLARK, Mary	26	F	Laborer	02JI02Lg
KLERIN, Francis	18	F	Laborer	02JI02Lg
STRAHAN, James	26	M	Servant	02JI02Lg
GRAHAM, Henry	28	M	Laborer	02JI02Lg
DELANCY, James	30	M	Laborer	02JI02Lg
James	30	M	Laborer	02JI02Lg
Bridget	24	F	Laborer	02JI02Lg
Ellen	26	F	Laborer	02JI02Lg
MCGIRR, Robert	21	M	Laborer	02JI02Lg
BYRN, John	25	M	Laborer	02JI02Lg
MCNALLY, Charles	25	M	Laborer	02JI02Lg
MCLALLY, James	30	M	Farmer	02JI02Lg
Mary	30	F	Farmer	02JI02Lg
Mary	22	F	Farmer	02JI02Lg
John	14	M	Farmer	02JI02Lg
Ellen	26	F	Farmer	02JI02Lg
FITZSIMONS, George	48	M	Farmer	02JI02Lg
U (W)	48	F	Farmer	02JI02Lg
Thos.	27	M	Farmer	02JI02Lg
Cathn.	26	F	Farmer	02JI02Lg
Bridget	.10	F	Infant	02JI02Lg
Mary	23	F	Farmer	02JI02Lg
Anne	19	F	Farmer	02JI02Lg
Michl.	18	M	Farmer	02JI02Lg
Cathn.	14	F	Farmer	02JI02Lg
Rose	8	F	Child	02JI02Lg
LARKIN, James	26	M	Laborer	02JI02Lg
Mary	20	F	Laborer	02JI02Lg
BRADY, Francis	18	M	Laborer	02JI02Lg
MACKEN, Ellen	26	F	Laborer	02JI02Lg
MCGLYNN, Mary	16	F	Laborer	02JI02Lg
SMITH, Cathn.	15	F	Laborer	02JI02Lg
SHANNON, Patrick	28	M	Baker	02JI02Lg
JACKSON, John	28	M	Baker	02JI02Lg
Hannah	26	F	Baker	02JI02Lg
Maria	5	F	Child	02JI02Lg
Wm.	2	M	Child	02JI02Lg
MOORE, Edward	24	M	Baker	02JI02Lg
Rachel	21	F	Baker	02JI02Lg
DOYLE, Mary	30	F	Laborer	02JI02Lg
Patrick	17	M	Laborer	02JI02Lg
Ellen	9	F	Child	02JI02Lg
Anne	7	F	Child	02JI02Lg
Alice	6	F	Child	02JI02Lg
Lawrence	4	M	Child	02JI02Lg
Margt.	.03	F	Infant	02JI02Lg
AUGLY, Peter	25	M	Laborer	02JI02Lg
SMITH, Mary	24	F	Laborer	02JI02Lg
FARRAN, Rose	40	F	Laborer	02JI02Lg
GILLERAN, Mary	21	F	Servant	02JI02Lg
FITZPATRICK, Owen	38	M	Laborer	02JI02Lg
Bridget	35	F	Laborer	02JI02Lg
Edward	8	M	Child	02JI02Lg
Margt.	5	F	Child	02JI02Lg
SHEILDS, Wm.	40	M	Coachman	02JI02Lg
MCDERMOT, Hugh	26	M	Laborer	02JI02Lg
U (W)	22	F	Laborer	02JI02Lg
Charles	.09	M	Infant	02JI02Lg
WALSH, Mary	20	F	Laborer	02JI02Lg
BOYD, Temp.	26	F	Servant	02JI02Lg
MCGEE, Bernard	40	F	Farmer	02JI02Lg
WILLSON, Thomas	35	M	Unknown	02JI02Lg
CAMBELL, David	23	M	Farmer	02JI02Lg
Cathn.	21	F	Farmer	02JI02Lg
DOLAN, Hugh	30	M	Farmer	02JI02Lg
CAVANAGH, Patt.	30	M	Carpenter	02JI02Lg
FARRELL, Michl.	20	M	Laborer	02JI02Lg
BUCKLEY, Patt.	40	M	Laborer	02JI02Lg
LEE, Patrick	40	M	Farmer	02JI02Lg
Cath.	10	F	Farmer	02JI02Lg
LYNCH, Ellen	35	F	Servant	02JI02Lg
HAUGH, Thomas	40	M	Servant	02JI02Lg
ROYDAN, Daniel	26	M	Servant	02JI02Lg

K

NAMES OF PASSENGERS	AGE	SEX	OCCUPATIONS	DATE PORT SHIP
REAY, Archibald	46	M	Laborer	02JI02Lg
Jane	44	F	Laborer	02JI02Lg
Henry	19	M	Laborer	02JI02Lg
Mary-Anne	7	F	Child	02JI02Lg
George	5	M	Child	02JI02Lg
Martha	3	F	Child	02JI02Lg
Jane	.05	F	Infant	02JI02Lg
Died-At-Sea				
COUGLIN, Margt.	20	F	Servant	02JI02Lg
FORNEY, James	19	M	Servant	02JI02Lg
COWDEN, Mary	21	F	Servant	02JI02Lg
MCGUIRE, Mary	19	F	Servant	02JI02Lg
MCKENNA, Sarah	30	F	Laborer	02JI02Lg
Patrick	11	M	Laborer	02JI02Lg
Richard	9	M	Child	02JI02Lg
Andrew	7	M	Child	02JI02Lg
Francis	3	M	Child	02JI02Lg
KILCREEN, Michl.	18	M	Laborer	02JI02Lg
CREAMER, Rose	12	F	Laborer	02JI02Lg
Anne	11	F	Laborer	02JI02Lg
KING, Margt.	17	F	Laborer	02JI02Lg
CONWAY, Ellen	25	F	Laborer	02JI02Lg
GUNN, James	30	M	Laborer	02JI02Lg
Anne	28	F	Laborer	02JI02Lg
OHALORAN, Wm.	40	M	Unknown	02JI02Lg

AYOFF 02 JULY 1849

From Londonderry

NAMES OF PASSENGERS	AGE	SEX	OCCUPATIONS	DATE PORT SHIP
MCDADE, Jane	24	F	Spinster	02JI01Mf
DERLIN, James	50	M	Laborer	02JI01Mf
U	54	F	Spinster	02JI01Mf
Kitty	14	F	Spinster	02JI01Mf
Patrick	11	M	Laborer	02JI01Mf
BANAN, Charles	25	M	Laborer	02JI01Mf
MCDADE, John	34	M	Laborer	02JI01Mf
FAULKNER, Rosie	28	F	Spinster	02JI01Mf
MCDADE, Mary	28	F	Spinster	02JI01Mf
FLEMING, Edw.	18	M	Laborer	02JI01Mf
T.	19	M	Laborer	02JI01Mf
KINCAID, Sahra	16	F	Spinster	02JI01Mf
MELVIN, K.A.	17	F	Spinster	02JI01Mf
MULLEN, James-A.	13	M	Laborer	02JI01Mf
MAYER, Susanne	54	F	Spinster	02JI01Mf
MCGREGOR, Catherine	16	F	Spinster	02JI01Mf
RYAN, Margaret	39	F	Spinster	02JI01Mf
Neal	18	M	Laborer	02JI01Mf
Mar.	14	F	Spinster	02JI01Mf
LEMLIN, Rose	16	F	Spinster	02JI01Mf
May	20	F	Spinster	02JI01Mf
MCFADDEN, Biddy	17	F	Spinster	02JI01Mf
HURFE, James	18	M	Laborer	02JI01Mf
BAIRN, Charles	23	M	Laborer	02JI01Mf
MORROW, John	18	M	Laborer	02JI01Mf
DUNNELE, May-P.	13	F	Spinster	02JI01Mf
SHERA, James	24	M	Laborer	02JI01Mf
MCDERMOTT, Sarah	15	F	Spinster	02JI01Mf
MCGOWEN, John	19	M	Laborer	02JI01Mf
RUPPERT, Ann	23	F	Spinster	02JI01Mf
GALLAGHER, Mary-A.	16	F	Spinster	02JI01Mf
ALLISON, John	27	M	Laborer	02JI01Mf
Ann	25	F	Spinster	02JI01Mf
HOOD, Isabella	20	F	Spinster	02JI01Mf
MCGAHAN, Mary	40	F	Spinster	02JI01Mf
Susan	18	F	Spinster	02JI01Mf
Eliza.	14	F	Spinster	02JI01Mf
John	11	M	Laborer	02JI01Mf
HENRY, James	20	M	Laborer	02JI01Mf
DOHERTY, Wm.	26	M	Laborer	02JI01Mf
Fanny	23	F	Spinster	02JI01Mf
May	4	F	Child	02JI01Mf
Ellen	2	F	Child	02JI01Mf
CONNALY, Mary-A.	17	F	Spinster	02JI01Mf
MCGEEHAN, James	19	M	Laborer	02JI01Mf
MCKINNEY, John	15	M	Laborer	02JI01Mf
GARVIN, Marg.	60	F	Spinster	02JI01Mf
Mary-A.	20	F	Spinster	02JI01Mf
DENNY, Cath.	60	F	Spinster	02JI01Mf
SMITHE, Margaret	46	F	Spinster	02JI01Mf
Eliza.	38	F	Spinster	02JI01Mf
MULHENNEY, James	20	M	Laborer	02JI01Mf
DOHERTY, Mary	18	F	Spinster	02JI01Mf
GAHEN, James	24	M	Laborer	02JI01Mf
Edward	22	M	Laborer	02JI01Mf
Catherine	13	F	Spinster	02JI01Mf
Thomas	20	M	Laborer	02JI01Mf
Richard	11	M	Laborer	02JI01Mf
SWEMBY, Mary	19	F	Spinster	02JI01Mf
Nancy	15	F	Spinster	02JI01Mf
MCLAUGHTON, Charles	20	M	Laborer	02JI01Mf
MCCARNEL, Biddy	21	F	Spinster	02JI01Mf
HUTCHISON, Maryan	21	F	Spinster	02JI01Mf
OHARA, Letitia	17	F	Spinster	02JI01Mf
BURNSIDES, Wm.	41	M	Laborer	02JI01Mf
CUNNINGHAM, Alexander	22	M	Laborer	02JI01Mf
DOHERTY, Patrick	19	M	Laborer	02JI01Mf
SPROULE, Ann	23	F	Spinster	02JI01Mf
PATTERSON, John	20	M	Laborer	02JI01Mf
Bitty	18	F	Spinster	02JI01Mf
NEALS, Rebecca	16	F	Spinster	02JI01Mf
DOHERTY, James	25	M	Laborer	02JI01Mf
MCCONNELL, Cath.	30	F	Spinster	02JI01Mf
Cath.	18	F	Spinster	02JI01Mf
Rachel	14	F	Spinster	02JI01Mf
Eliza.	8	F	Child	02JI01Mf
Sarah-Ann	1	F	Child	02JI01Mf
HAGEN, Michael	20	M	Laborer	02JI01Mf
MCCLARK, John	14	M	Laborer	02JI01Mf
GALLAGHER, Wm.	17	M	Laborer	02JI01Mf
KIRROCH, Geo.	21	M	Laborer	02JI01Mf
GALLAGHER, Mary	35	F	Spinster	02JI01Mf
John	15	M	Laborer	02JI01Mf
FRIELE, Sally	24	F	Spinster	02JI01Mf
GALLAGHER, Joseph	6	M	Child	02JI01Mf
MCCONNELL, Margaret	20	F	Spinster	02JI01Mf
HENRY, John-A.	22	M	Laborer	02JI01Mf
Margaret-A.	20	F	Spinster	02JI01Mf
THORNTON, James	20	F	Spinster	02JI01Mf
MCLAUGHLIN, Dennis	20	M	Laborer	02JI01Mf
MCMENNES, James	19	M	Laborer	02JI01Mf
WILSON, Sarah	65	M	Laborer	02JI01Mf
MONTGOMERY, Thomas	20	M	Laborer	02JI01Mf
John	17	M	Laborer	02JI01Mf
ONEIL, John	22	M	Laborer	02JI01Mf
Margaret	19	F	Spinster	02JI01Mf
MOODY, Alexander	18	M	Laborer	02JI01Mf
DOUGHERTY, Wm.	17	M	Laborer	02JI01Mf
MCDADE, Isabella	20	F	Spinster	02JI01Mf
MOONY, James	20	M	Laborer	02JI01Mf
DOHERTY, Danl.	35	M	Laborer	02JI01Mf
Cornelius	60	M	Laborer	02JI01Mf
SWAN, Nancy	40	F	Spinster	02JI01Mf
DOHERTY, James	22	M	Laborer	02JI01Mf
MCGLOUGHLIN, Ann	24	F	Spinster	02JI01Mf
Mary-A.	8	F	Child	02JI01Mf
Biddy	6	F	Child	02JI01Mf
JAMES, John	14	M	Laborer	02JI01M
MCCONNELL, John	21	M	Laborer	02JI01M
GALLAGHER, Ann	18	F	Spinster	02JI01M
BRYSON, Catherine	18	F	Spinster	02JI01M
SCHER, David	55	M	Laborer	02JI01M
HARRIS, Patrick	20	M	Laborer	02JI01M
FENNY, Daniel	39	M	Laborer	02JI01M

NAMES OF PASSENGERS	AGE	SEX	OCCUPATIONS	DATE PORT SHIP
FENNY, James	16	M	Laborer	02JI01Mf
Elizabeth	18	F	Spinster	02JI01Mf
SWEENEY, Neil	33	M	Laborer	02JI01Mf
Nancy	21	F	Spinster	02JI01Mf
Susan	1	F	Child	02JI01Mf
CAINE, Rebecca	52	F	Spinster	02JI01Mf
Margt.	19	F	Spinster	02JI01Mf
SHNOUT, Ian	23	M	Laborer	02JI01Mf
Alexander	18	M	Laborer	02JI01Mf
Jane	14	F	Spinster	02JI01Mf
CANNA, John	35	M	Laborer	02JI01Mf
ODONNELL, Charles	25	M	Laborer	02JI01Mf
KELLY, John	20	M	Laborer	02JI01Mf
HUMPHREY, Elizabeth	40	F	Spinster	02JI01Mf
CONNAGHER, R.	16	F	Spinster	02JI01Mf
Graham	21	M	Laborer	02JI01Mf
MAGUIRE, Ellen	27	F	Spinster	02JI01Mf
Ellen	38	F	Spinster	02JI01Mf
Mary-Ann	8	F	Child	02JI01Mf
Thomas	14	M	Laborer	02JI01Mf
Susan	10	F	Child	02JI01Mf
Lucey	7	F	Child	02JI01Mf
BANNEN, James	7	M	Child	02JI01Mf
CANNING, Wm.T.	27	M	Dd	02JI01Mf
STEEN, Mary	25	F	Spinster	02JI01Mf
RIDER, Jemima	18	F	Spinster	02JI01Mf
CATHER, Joseph	39	M	Merchant	02JI01Mf
Isabella	38	F	Spinster	02JI01Mf
WALKER, Sarah	20	F	Spinster	02JI01Mf
CATHER, Isabella	8	F	Child	02JI01Mf
Lawrence	2	M	Child	02JI01Mf

NICOLAI-AND-JOVAN 02 JULY 1849

From London

NAMES OF PASSENGERS	AGE	SEX	OCCUPATIONS	DATE PORT SHIP
JACOBS, Levy	51	M	Unknown	02JI13Mi
HOLLINSHEAD, John	39	M	Unknown	02JI13Mi
HERNE, Isaac	28	M	Unknown	02JI13Mi
HARVEY, Wm.	24	M	Unknown	02JI13Mi
Sarah	28	F	Unknown	02JI13Mi
MILLY, Thos.	24	M	Unknown	02JI13Mi
BARTELLY, Wm.	33	M	Unknown	02JI13Mi
Hannah	35	F	Unknown	02JI13Mi
Francis	10	M	Unknown	02JI13Mi
Jane	.00	F	Infant	02JI13Mi
WYCHERLY, John	58	M	Unknown	02JI13Mi
MULLEN, Catherine	28	F	Unknown	02JI13Mi
Fanny	4	F	Child	02JI13Mi
John	.00	M	Infant	02JI13Mi
MILLER, Ann	45	F	Unknown	02JI13Mi
Thos.	23	M	Unknown	02JI13Mi
Henry	21	M	Unknown	02JI13Mi
Maria	19	F	Unknown	02JI13Mi
Sarah	9	F	Child	02JI13Mi
FLETCHER, John	59	M	Unknown	02JI13Mi
Mary	50	F	Unknown	02JI13Mi
Mary-Ann	30	F	Unknown	02JI13Mi
Kezia	13	F	Unknown	02JI13Mi
Maria	11	F	Unknown	02JI13Mi
LEE, Susan	10	F	Unknown	02JI13Mi
Thos.	9	M	Child	02JI13Mi
ARETT, Eliza	26	F	Unknown	02JI13Mi
Cathe.	21	F	Unknown	02JI13Mi
HATTEN, Jas.	23	M	Unknown	02JI13Mi
TAYLOR, Thos.	33	M	Unknown	02JI13Mi
Mary	33	F	Unknown	02JI13Mi
Henry	8	M	Child	02JI13Mi
Ellen	6	F	Child	02JI13Mi
TAYLOR, Ann	5	F	Child	02JI13Mi
Edwin	2	M	Child	02JI13Mi
Sarah	.00	F	Infant	02JI13Mi
HANESER, Ann	35	F	Unknown	02JI13Mi
MARTIN, Wm.	59	M	Unknown	02JI13Mi
CROSS, Rebecca	33	F	Unknown	02JI13Mi
Ann	.00	F	Infant	02JI13Mi
Lydia	.00	F	Infant	02JI13Mi
ROBINS, Ann	36	F	Unknown	02JI13Mi
Elizabeth	11	F	Unknown	02JI13Mi
Roland	9	M	Child	02JI13Mi
Jos.	6	M	Child	02JI13Mi
SEVENOAKS, Wm.	19	M	Unknown	02JI13Mi
COLETT, Henry	41	M	Unknown	02JI13Mi
Harriet	36	F	Unknown	02JI13Mi
Henry	16	M	Unknown	02JI13Mi
BAYLEY, Robt.	29	M	Unknown	02JI13Mi
Caroline	24	F	Unknown	02JI13Mi
Robt.	6	M	Child	02JI13Mi
Nichas.	4	M	Child	02JI13Mi
Saml.	.00	M	Infant	02JI13Mi
TILLEY, Wm.	29	M	Unknown	02JI13Mi
BOWMAN, Esther	21	F	Unknown	02JI13Mi
DRALE, Hannah	34	F	Unknown	02JI13Mi
Angeline	10	F	Unknown	02JI13Mi
Thos.	8	M	Child	02JI13Mi
Wm.	4	M	Child	02JI13Mi
BESSLEY, John	24	M	Unknown	02JI13Mi
CRICKMORE, Benj.	30	M	Unknown	02JI13Mi
DOALE, Jane	6	F	Child	02JI13Mi
E.Ann	.00	F	Infant	02JI13Mi
WILSON, John	38	M	Unknown	02JI13Mi
Thos.	11	M	Unknown	02JI13Mi
SULLIVAN, M.	33	U	Unknown	02JI13Mi
Ellen	30	F	Unknown	02JI13Mi
LYON, Mary	40	F	Unknown	02JI13Mi
Roger	23	M	Unknown	02JI13Mi
DEADY, Danl.	29	M	Unknown	02JI13Mi
Betsey	22	F	Unknown	02JI13Mi
PRATT, Chs.	35	M	Unknown	02JI13Mi
MOSES, Rosa	34	F	Unknown	02JI13Mi
ESSEX, Robt.	32	M	Unknown	02JI13Mi
ROCHE, Ellen	60	F	Unknown	02JI13Mi
MAHER, Julia	25	F	Unknown	02JI13Mi
ALLEN, Wm.	34	M	Unknown	02JI13Mi
BUTTERFIELD, Sarah	22	F	Unknown	02JI13Mi
HARLEY, John	40	M	Unknown	02JI13Mi
HORAN, Michl.	34	M	Unknown	02JI13Mi
TOWNSEND, Wm.	21	M	Unknown	02JI13Mi
Nichl.	25	M	Unknown	02JI13Mi
TIMMERN, Phillip	13	M	Unknown	02JI13Mi
KEAR, John-C.	31	M	Unknown	02JI13Mi
Elizth.	33	F	Unknown	02JI13Mi
John-D.	10	M	Unknown	02JI13Mi
Peter	5	M	Child	02JI13Mi
Wm.	3	M	Child	02JI13Mi
Gustave	.00	U	Infant	02JI13Mi
WEBER, Phillip	10	M	Unknown	02JI13Mi
TEXTON, Ellen	16	F	Unknown	02JI13Mi
BROWN, John	30	M	Unknown	02JI13Mi
SHARP, Francis	21	M	Unknown	02JI13Mi
MATTHEWS, Wm.	30	M	Unknown	02JI13Mi
Amelia	25	F	Unknown	02JI13Mi
Mary-Ann	4	F	Child	02JI13Mi
Thos.Henry	.00	M	Infant	02JI13Mi
DARE, Kilburn	40	M	Unknown	02JI13Mi
CONMORE, Thos.	26	M	Unknown	02JI13Mi
LITTLER, Chs.	32	M	Unknown	02JI13Mi
Ann	31	F	Unknown	02JI13Mi
ORBURTON, George	24	M	Unknown	02JI13Mi
HOWLIT, Robt.	24	M	Unknown	02JI13Mi
CARDY, George	25	M	Unknown	02JI13Mi
MOORE, Martha	22	F	Unknown	02JI13Mi
Thos.	31	M	Unknown	02JI13Mi
Celina	.00	F	Infant	02JI13Mi

NAMES OF PASSENGERS	AGE	SEX	OCCUPATIONS	DATE PORT SHIP
WILLIAMS, Jane	50	F	Unknown	02J113Mi
TUSTIN, Mary	36	F	Unknown	02J113Mi
Edw.	30	M	Unknown	02J113Mi
Frances	8	F	Unknown	02J113Mi
BLUNFIELD, John	25	M	Farmer	02J113Mi
SPENCE, Wm.	30	M	Farmer	02J113Mi
NICHY, Nichs.	30	M	Farmer	02J113Mi
CROW, Geo.	18	M	Farmer	02J113Mi
Saml.	19	M	Farmer	02J113Mi
SMITH, Wm.	30	M	Unknown	02J113Mi
CONCKLIN, Chs.	30	M	Unknown	02J113Mi
U (W)	25	F	Unknown	02J113Mi
John	10	M	Unknown	02J113Mi
Ellen	.00	F	Infant	02J113Mi
WHITE, Edw.	27	M	Unknown	02J113Mi
MOON, Chs.	20	M	Unknown	02J113Mi
BAILEY, Robt.	22	M	Unknown	02J113Mi
ELLIOTT, Eliza	28	F	Unknown	02J113Mi
BAYLEY, Robt.	30	M	Unknown	02J113Mi
KILBURN, Mary-C.	39	F	Unknown	02J113Mi
Francis-H.	9	M	Child	02J113Mi
Michl.	7	M	Child	02J113Mi
Elizh.	5	F	Child	02J113Mi
Alice	2	F	Child	02J113Mi
Francis	.00	M	Infant	02J113Mi
BICKNELL, David	33	M	Unknown	02J113Mi
Dorcas	30	U	Unknown	02J113Mi
Willm.	2	M	Child	02J113Mi
Adelaide	6	F	Child	02J113Mi
CHILD, Henry	32	M	Unknown	02J113Mi
SALOMAN, Leond.	23	M	Unknown	02J113Mi
Morty	22	M	Unknown	02J113Mi
ANTHY, Wm.	24	M	Unknown	02J113Mi
TURNER, Donald	58	M	Unknown	02J113Mi
Isabella	50	F	Unknown	02J113Mi
Hugh	34	M	Unknown	02J113Mi
Duncan	22	M	Unknown	02J113Mi
Ann	20	F	Unknown	02J113Mi
James	18	M	Unknown	02J113Mi
Charles	16	M	Unknown	02J113Mi
CAMPBELL, James	28	M	Unknown	02J113Mi
Ann	28	F	Unknown	02J113Mi
John	38	M	Unknown	02J113Mi

MARIANE 02 JULY 1849

From Belfast

NAMES OF PASSENGERS	AGE	SEX	OCCUPATIONS	DATE PORT SHIP
GRIBBON, Wm.	20	M	Laborer	02J105Ly
Margt.	26	F	Unknown	02J105Ly
CRAWFORD, Esther	28	F	Unknown	02J105Ly
KELLEN, Nath.	25	M	Unknown	02J105Ly
GLASGOW, Wm.	50	M	Unknown	02J105Ly
Nancy	46	F	Unknown	02J105Ly
Matilda	23	F	Unknown	02J105Ly
Jane	21	F	Unknown	02J105Ly
Henry	19	M	Unknown	02J105Ly
Adam	15	M	Unknown	02J105Ly
Isaac	12	M	Unknown	02J105Ly
Benjamin	12	M	Child	02J105Ly
Alexander	5	M	Child	02J105Ly
FARLEY, Mary	23	F	Unknown	02J105Ly
Robert	20	M	Unknown	02J105Ly
J.	00	U	Unknown	02J105Ly
LETTE, Wm.	24	M	Unknown	02J105Ly
Hessy	21	F	Unknown	02J105Ly
MCGAHAN, John	19	M	Unknown	02J105Ly
FALOON, Daniel	21	M	Unknown	02J105Ly
Hugh	18	M	Unknown	02J105Ly
CRAWFORD, James	22	M	Unknown	02J105Ly
MCCAVANA, Bernd.	28	M	Unknown	02J105Ly
GILMOR, James	28	M	Unknown	02J105Ly
SLOAN, John	31	M	Unknown	02J105Ly
Jane	25	F	Unknown	02J105Ly
CHAMBERS, James	25	M	Unknown	02J105Ly
Sarah	25	F	Unknown	02J105Ly
Jane	30	F	Unknown	02J105Ly
Jane	22	F	Unknown	02J105Ly
MCIHRAIN, Hans	26	M	Unknown	02J105Ly
Barbara	26	F	Unknown	02J105Ly
CHAMBERS, Sarah	24	F	Unknown	02J105Ly
MATAR, Alex.	23	M	Unknown	02J105Ly
Martha	29	F	Unknown	02J105Ly
Agnes	8	F	Child	02J105Ly
Alex.	.00	M	Infant	02J105Ly
HANNA, Sarah	26	F	Unknown	02J105Ly
Margt.	22	F	Unknown	02J105Ly
Susana	.00	F	Infant	02J105Ly
LIGHTBODY, Hugh	55	M	Unknown	02J105Ly
Betsey	45	F	Unknown	02J105Ly
Andrew	13	M	Unknown	02J105Ly
SMYLIE, James	32	M	Unknown	02J105Ly
Charlotte	21	F	Unknown	02J105Ly
MCKEE, Alex.	26	M	Unknown	02J105Ly
Nicholas	26	M	Unknown	02J105Ly
Eliza	22	F	Unknown	02J105Ly
ACKSON, Henry	26	M	Unknown	02J105Ly
MCCLURY, John	23	M	Unknown	02J105Ly
Isabella	23	F	Unknown	02J105Ly
Edward	1	M	Child	02J105Ly
MCKELLOP, Sarah	20	F	Unknown	02J105Ly
Jane	16	F	Unknown	02J105Ly
WILSON, Thos.	20	M	Unknown	02J105Ly
STEVINSON, Abigael	23	F	Unknown	02J105Ly
GUNNING, George	29	M	Unknown	02J105Ly
Martha	23	F	Unknown	02J105Ly
Martha	63	F	Unknown	02J105Ly
Anna	4	F	Child	02J105Ly
George	.00	M	Infant	02J105Ly
John	15	M	Unknown	02J105Ly
GILMORE, Robert	20	M	Unknown	02J105Ly
MAGUIRE, Isabella	20	F	Unknown	02J105Ly
Margt.	20	F	Unknown	02J105Ly
BOYD, Robert	68	M	Unknown	02J105Ly
MCCAPPIN, Robert	20	M	Unknown	02J105Ly
WALMSEY, Eliza	46	F	Unknown	02J105Ly
GAUDY, Wm.	50	M	Unknown	02J105Ly
Jane	40	F	Unknown	02J105Ly
James	22	M	Unknown	02J105Ly
John	21	M	Unknown	02J105Ly
Robert	18	M	Unknown	02J105L
Hugh	16	M	Unknown	02J105L
Jane	15	F	Unknown	02J105L
Wm.	11	M	Unknown	02J105L
George	10	M	Unknown	02J105L
Thomas	8	M	Child	02J105L
MCCULLY, Agnes	40	F	Unknown	02J105L
Robert	23	M	Unknown	02J105L
John	20	M	Unknown	02J105L
Eliza	18	F	Unknown	02J105L
Jane	16	F	Unknown	02J105L
James	14	M	Unknown	02J105L
Agnes	12	F	Unknown	02J105L
ALLEN, Hugh	25	M	Unknown	02J105L
SPENCER, Mariane	20	F	Unknown	02J105L
SCULLION, Mary	25	F	Unknown	02J105L
SEED, John	21	M	Unknown	02J105L
Eliza	40	F	Unknown	02J105L
Eliza	19	F	Unknown	02J105L
Ann	17	F	Unknown	02J105L
Wm.	14	M	Unknown	02J105L
LAWSON, Samuel	24	M	Unknown	02J105L
ENGLISH, Hugh	23	M	Unknown	02J105L
MCCULLY, Pearce	28	M	Unknown	02J105L

NAMES OF PASSENGERS	AGE	SEX	OCCUPATIONS	DATE PORT SHIP
WALKER, Ruth	20	F	Unknown	02JI05Ly
TAGGART, Margt.	28	F	Unknown	02JI05Ly
MARTIN, Robert	50	M	Unknown	02JI05Ly
Ann	50	F	Unknown	02JI05Ly
Amelia	24	F	Unknown	02JI05Ly
Margt.	22	F	Unknown	02JI05Ly
Robert	20	M	Unknown	02JI05Ly
Anna	11	F	Unknown	02JI05Ly
John	9	M	Child	02JI05Ly
ELLIOT, Ben.	18	M	Unknown	02JI05Ly
SMYLIE, George	33	M	Unknown	02JI05Ly
NELSON, Wm.	27	M	Unknown	02JI05Ly
CHANIBAD, Joseph	17	M	Unknown	02JI05Ly
LENNON, Sarah	26	F	Unknown	02JI05Ly
WILLIAMS, Emma	13	F	Unknown	02JI05Ly
MCCLEMENT, Mary	35	F	Unknown	02JI05Ly
PATTERSON, Eleanor	16	F	Unknown	02JI05Ly
MCCOMB, Jane	25	F	Unknown	02JI05Ly
CONLAN, Patk.	19	M	Unknown	02JI05Ly
MCNICHOLS, Hugh	26	M	Unknown	02JI05Ly
CHAMBER, James	24	M	Unknown	02JI05Ly
GRAHAM, David	21	M	Unknown	02JI05Ly
CASSEDY, John	24	M	Unknown	02JI05Ly
KENNEDY, Michl.	23	M	Unknown	02JI05Ly
DONAGHY, Margt.	23	F	Unknown	02JI05Ly
CROSKERY, Wm.	20	M	Unknown	02JI05Ly
GILLESPIE, Eliza	25	F	Unknown	02JI05Ly
HENEY, Alex.	30	M	Unknown	02JI05Ly
Nancy	30	F	Unknown	02JI05Ly
Joseph	35	M	Unknown	02JI05Ly
Ann	26	F	Unknown	02JI05Ly
KIRK, Jane	32	F	Unknown	02JI05Ly
Nancy	17	F	Unknown	02JI05Ly
David	13	M	Unknown	02JI05Ly
Alex.	11	M	Unknown	02JI05Ly
HENEY, Mary	30	F	Unknown	02JI05Ly
HARSHAW, Eliza	38	F	Unknown	02JI05Ly
Margt.	18	F	Unknown	02JI05Ly
Eleanor	17	F	Unknown	02JI05Ly
James	14	M	Unknown	02JI05Ly
Sarah	11	F	Unknown	02JI05Ly
Wm.	10	M	Unknown	02JI05Ly
Andrew	9	M	Child	02JI05Ly
Francis	8	M	Child	02JI05Ly
SIMPSON, Andrew	40	M	Unknown	02JI05Ly
JOHNSON, Robert	59	M	Unknown	02JI05Ly
Betty	47	F	Unknown	02JI05Ly
Sarah	24	F	Unknown	02JI05Ly
John	20	M	Unknown	02JI05Ly
Thomas	20	M	Unknown	02JI05Ly
James	18	M	Unknown	02JI05Ly
Eliza	15	F	Unknown	02JI05Ly
Robert	13	M	Unknown	02JI05Ly
Nancy	11	F	Unknown	02JI05Ly
Wm.	8	M	Child	02JI05Ly
David	6	M	Child	02JI05Ly
WEATHERUP, John	24	M	Unknown	02JI05Ly
HANNALLY, Ann	26	F	Unknown	02JI05Ly
John	6	M	Child	02JI05Ly
BRADFORD, Hugh	18	M	Unknown	02JI05Ly
WILSON, John	18	M	Unknown	02JI05Ly
BAXTER, Susan	40	F	Unknown	02JI05Ly
LINDSAY, Isabella	21	F	Unknown	02JI05Ly
MCGORIAN, Hugh	40	M	Unknown	02JI05Ly
Eliza	25	F	Unknown	02JI05Ly
TELFORD, Eliza	24	F	Unknown	02JI05Ly
Mary	22	F	Unknown	02JI05Ly
OKANE, John	45	M	Unknown	02JI05Ly
Bridget	40	F	Unknown	02JI05Ly
Peter	23	M	Unknown	02JI05Ly
Eliza	21	F	Unknown	02JI05Ly
John	3	M	Child	02JI05Ly
MCCAFFERTY, Patk.	.00	M	Infant	02JI05Ly
SAUNDERS, Isabella	30	F	Unknown	02JI05Ly
WADDELL, Rachael	20	F	Unknown	02JI05Ly

NAMES OF PASSENGERS	AGE	SEX	OCCUPATIONS	DATE PORT SHIP
WADDELL, William-H.	3	M	Child	02JI05Ly
Robert	2	M	Child	02JI05Ly
HUNTER, Margt.	20	F	Unknown	02JI05Ly
COWAN, William	20	M	Unknown	02JI05Ly
MCCARTNEY, Jane	26	F	Unknown	02JI05Ly
BLACK, John	22	M	Unknown	02JI05Ly
LYONS, James	20	M	Unknown	02JI05Ly
JOHNSTON, Jane	22	F	Unknown	02JI05Ly
SOANE, Henry	25	M	Unknown	02JI05Ly
SEEBODY, Elizabeth	35	F	Unknown	02JI05Ly
HAMILTON, Oliver	65	M	Unknown	02JI05Ly
Sarah	64	F	Unknown	02JI05Ly
Sarah	30	F	Unknown	02JI05Ly
Martha	23	F	Unknown	02JI05Ly
Anne	20	F	Unknown	02JI05Ly
MCNEIGHT, Edwin	4	M	Child	02JI05Ly
THOMPSON, David	20	M	Unknown	02JI05Ly
KEON, Thomas	18	M	Unknown	02JI05Ly
MCKENNA, Cath.	15	F	Unknown	02JI05Ly
MCDONALD, Mary	30	F	Unknown	02JI05Ly
Alice	12	F	Unknown	02JI05Ly
Rose-Ann	10	F	Unknown	02JI05Ly
MORROW, Jane	21	F	Unknown	02JI05Ly
MAGILL, Hugh	25	M	Unknown	02JI05Ly
Sarah	22	F	Unknown	02JI05Ly
Jane	5	F	Child	02JI05Ly
Sarah	2	F	Child	02JI05Ly
Cecilia	.00	F	Infant	02JI05Ly
FALLOON, Mary	30	F	Unknown	02JI05Ly
OWENS, David	50	M	Unknown	02JI05Ly
William-J.	12	M	Unknown	02JI05Ly
Sarah-Ellen	35	F	Unknown	02JI05Ly
Julia	11	F	Unknown	02JI05Ly
Sophia	6	F	Child	02JI05Ly
COWAN, Mary	28	F	Unknown	02JI05Ly
MACONN, Joseph	30	M	Unknown	02JI05Ly
THOMPSON, Joseph	18	M	Unknown	02JI05Ly
RAINEY, John	30	M	Unknown	02JI05Ly
Jane	20	F	Unknown	02JI05Ly
Hugh	22	M	Unknown	02JI05Ly
Wm.Robt.	21	M	Unknown	02JI05Ly
David	12	M	Unknown	02JI05Ly
Mary-A.	15	F	Unknown	02JI05Ly
Joseph	10	M	Unknown	02JI05Ly
Hugh	.00	M	Infant	02JI05Ly
MAY, James	35	M	Unknown	02JI05Ly
William	25	M	Unknown	02JI05Ly
SIMMS, Robert	50	M	Unknown	02JI05Ly
CHARLES, John	15	M	Unknown	02JI05Ly
BENSON, Robt.	28	M	Unknown	02JI05Ly
Jane	25	F	Unknown	02JI05Ly
Ellen	5	F	Child	02JI05Ly
Sarah	1	F	Child	02JI05Ly
GLASGOW, James	20	M	Unknown	02JI05Ly
RESEDE, Mary	24	F	Unknown	02JI05Ly
CAPLES, Margt.	25	F	Unknown	02JI05Ly
SPENCE, Margt.	16	F	Unknown	02JI05Ly
BRADBURY, Eliza	40	F	Unknown	02JI05Ly
WILSON, George	14	M	Unknown	02JI05Ly
MAXWELL, Wm.	13	M	Unknown	02JI05Ly
OFFIET, John	22	M	Unknown	02JI05Ly
James	22	M	Unknown	02JI05Ly
Margt.	23	F	Unknown	02JI05Ly
KIRKPATRICK, Ann	29	F	Unknown	02JI05Ly
Sarah	2	F	Child	02JI05Ly
ALLEN, Wm.	29	M	Unknown	02JI05Ly
Ann	20	F	Unknown	02JI05Ly
DICK, Elizabeth	30	F	Unknown	02JI05Ly
CHARLES, Eliza	10	F	Unknown	02JI05Ly
MCCAUGHNEY, Maria	20	F	Unknown	02JI05Ly
Margt.	18	F	Unknown	02JI05Ly
LOWERY, Hugh	25	M	Unknown	02JI05Ly
MCKAVOY, Mary	18	F	Unknown	02JI05Ly
Rosa	17	F	Unknown	02JI05Ly
MCALONAN, Mary	20	F	Unknown	02JI05Ly

NAMES OF PASSENGERS	AGE	SEX	OCCUPATIONS	DATE PORT SHIP
FORD, Ann	22	F	Unknown	02JI05Ly
MCCUTCHEN, Mary	20	F	Unknown	02JI05Ly
Jane	18	F	Unknown	02JI05Ly
REDMOND, Patk.	20	M	Unknown	02JI05Ly
AVILSON, James	20	M	Unknown	02JI05Ly
VANDAL, Eliza	20	F	Unknown	02JI05Ly
MCCLEAN, Cath.	25	F	Unknown	02JI05Ly
HOLLAND, Mary	19	F	Unknown	02JI05Ly
DOUGLAS, Ann	30	F	Unknown	02JI05Ly
GILLESPIE, Robert	22	M	Unknown	02JI05Ly
FURGESON, John	49	M	Unknown	02JI05Ly
BAXTER, Robt.	18	M	Unknown	02JI05Ly
SANDERSON, Wm.	25	M	Unknown	02JI05Ly
Nath.	22	M	Unknown	02JI05Ly
THOMAS, Wm.	18	M	Unknown	02JI05Ly
LEWIS, John	18	M	Unknown	02JI05Ly
WILLIAMS, Geo.W.	30	M	Unknown	02JI05Ly
GRAHAM, Sarah	33	F	Unknown	02JI05Ly
TELFORD, Robert	26	M	Unknown	02JI05Ly
CHAMBER, Eliza	20	F	Unknown	02JI05Ly
FRANCE, Jane	20	F	Unknown	02JI05Ly
LIGHTBODY, Chas.	55	M	Unknown	02JI05Ly
Agnes	55	F	Unknown	02JI05Ly
Rebecca	27	F	Unknown	02JI05Ly
HUNTER, Hugh	20	M	Unknown	02JI05Ly
Eliza	20	F	Unknown	02JI05Ly
BENNETT, Mary	22	F	Unknown	02JI05Ly
MCGINNIS, Sarah	55	F	Unknown	02JI05Ly
SIMPSON, Thos.	21	M	Unknown	02JI05Ly
BLAKELY, David	21	M	Unknown	02JI05Ly
Eliza	30	F	Unknown	02JI05Ly
JAMISON, Hugh	18	M	Unknown	02JI05Ly
Eliza	16	F	Unknown	02JI05Ly
MULHOLLAND, Hy.	45	M	Unknown	02JI05Ly
BROWN, Wm.	23	M	Unknown	02JI05Ly
GARTEN, Wm.	58	M	Unknown	02JI05Ly
Robt.	21	M	Unknown	02JI05Ly
Jane	20	F	Unknown	02JI05Ly
Matilda	18	F	Unknown	02JI05Ly
MCBRIDE, Ann	23	F	Unknown	02JI05Ly
Eliza	21	F	Unknown	02JI05Ly
SPINKS, Wm.	20	M	Unknown	02JI05Ly
DOUGLAS, John	20	M	Unknown	02JI05Ly
FLAVELL, Thos.	22	M	Unknown	02JI05Ly
Rosa	21	F	Unknown	02JI05Ly

CAROLINE-NESMITH 02 JULY 1849

From Liverpool

NAMES OF PASSENGERS	AGE	SEX	OCCUPATIONS	DATE PORT SHIP
SHAW, Jno.	44	M	Unknown	02JI02Ma
Mary	49	F	Unknown	02JI02Ma
Tom	25	M	Unknown	02JI02Ma
Geo.	19	M	Unknown	02JI02Ma
Mary	13	F	Unknown	02JI02Ma
Geo.	7	M	Child	02JI02Ma
Elias	1	M	Child	02JI02Ma
COWAN, Geo.	23	M	Unknown	02JI02Ma
SHIPLEY, Jno.	26	M	Unknown	02JI02Ma
Ann	25	F	Unknown	02JI02Ma
ARMSTRONG, Adam	32	M	Unknown	02JI02Ma
Isabella	32	F	Unknown	02JI02Ma
Marcella	6	F	Child	02JI02Ma
Isabella	3	F	Child	02JI02Ma
Jane	.00	F	Infant	02JI02Ma
HUNTER, Jno.	33	M	Unknown	02JI02Ma
Mgt.	26	F	Unknown	02JI02Ma
Richd.	.00	M	Infant	02JI02Ma
TATE, Andrew	30	M	Unknown	02JI02Ma
TATE, Robt.	16	M	Unknown	02JI02Ma
GRANGER, Thos.	26	M	Unknown	02JI02Ma
BENROSE, Wm.	37	M	Unknown	02JI02Ma
LAHEY, Jos.	23	M	Unknown	02JI02Ma
WATTS, Thos.	29	M	Unknown	02JI02Ma
Henry	21	M	Unknown	02JI02Ma
JONES, Richd.	41	M	Unknown	02JI02Ma
WHELAN, Peter	30	M	Unknown	02JI02Ma
Mary	23	F	Unknown	02JI02Ma
DALEY, Peter	50	M	Unknown	02JI02Ma
BRENNAN, Michl.	50	M	Unknown	02JI02Ma
Sally	50	F	Unknown	02JI02Ma
Biddy	14	F	Unknown	02JI02Ma
Pat	11	M	Unknown	02JI02Ma
KELLY, Michl.	28	M	Unknown	02JI02Ma
BUTLER, Pat	24	M	Unknown	02JI02Ma
Wm.	26	M	Unknown	02JI02Ma
REILLY, Terence	44	M	Unknown	02JI02Ma
MURRAY, Jas.	40	M	Unknown	02JI02Ma
Mgt.	36	F	Unknown	02JI02Ma
Mary	8	F	Child	02JI02Ma
REILLY, Jno.	40	M	Unknown	02JI02Ma
BYRNES, Bryan	20	M	Unknown	02JI02Ma
Mary	20	F	Unknown	02JI02Ma
LOVE, Jno.M.	35	M	Unknown	02JI02Ma
Pat	15	M	Unknown	02JI02Ma
MCCUE, Thos.	50	M	Unknown	02JI02Ma
Wm.	23	M	Unknown	02JI02Ma
KEOGH, Phil.	40	M	Unknown	02JI02Ma
JONES, Wm.	30	M	Unknown	02JI02Ma
BRIEN, Thos.	28	M	Unknown	02JI02Ma
HEWIT, Jno.	30	M	Unknown	02JI02Ma
JOBSON, Jno.	23	M	Unknown	02JI02Ma
CASE, Jane	40	F	Unknown	02JI02Ma
Abm.	11	M	Unknown	02JI02Ma
Mary	9	F	Child	02JI02Ma
Sarah	7	F	Child	02JI02Ma
Ellen	5	F	Child	02JI02Ma
Eliza	3	F	Child	02JI02Ma
QUIRK, Peirce	40	M	Unknown	02JI02Ma
Mary	40	F	Unknown	02JI02Ma
Bridget	16	F	Unknown	02JI02Ma
Alley	14	F	Unknown	02JI02Ma
Wm.	13	M	Unknown	02JI02Ma
Jas.	12	M	Unknown	02JI02Ma
Michl.	10	M	Unknown	02JI02Ma
Johanna	8	F	Child	02JI02Ma
John	6	M	Child	02JI02Ma
BUTLER, Judy	35	F	Unknown	02JI02Ma
KENNER, Jno.	30	M	Unknown	02JI02Ma
FANNING, Stephen	20	M	Unknown	02JI02Ma
STAPLETON, Jno.	25	M	Unknown	02JI02Ma
SAFFAN, Jno.	30	M	Unknown	02JI02Ma
KILLAN, Mary	23	F	Unknown	02JI02Ma
ODOWD, Peter	25	M	Unknown	02JI02Ma
SCUNLAN, Peter	20	M	Unknown	02JI02Ma
WALIS, Ann	20	F	Unknown	02JI02Ma
Bridget	5	F	Child	02JI02Ma
BREE, Jno.	20	M	Unknown	02JI02Ma
Pat	25	M	Unknown	02JI02Ma
Mary	23	F	Unknown	02JI02Ma
SCUNLAN, Mary	26	F	Unknown	02JI02Ma
SARRITY, Mary	23	F	Unknown	02JI02Ma
CONWAY, Ellen	18	F	Unknown	02JI02Ma
OBRIEN, Jas.	20	M	Unknown	02JI02M
CASEY, Eliza	34	F	Unknown	02JI02M
Mary	4	F	Child	02JI02M
U	2	U	Child	02JI02M
DALEY, Con.	20	M	Unknown	02JI02M
CONDON, Jno.	20	M	Unknown	02JI02M
RICHARDS, Thos.	35	M	Unknown	02JI02M
NEPHSEY, Martin	25	M	Unknown	02JI02M
SHEAN, Fras.	45	M	Unknown	02JI02M
Fras.	18	M	Unknown	02JI02M
Judy	15	F	Unknown	02JI02M

NAMES OF PASSENGERS	AGE	SEX	OCCUPATIONS	DATE PORT SHIP
SHEAN, Wm.	35	M	Unknown	02JI02Ma
Rose	30	F	Unknown	02JI02Ma
Jno.	.00	M	Infant	02JI02Ma
FARRELL, Mgt.	20	F	Unknown	02JI02Ma
CONNAN, Duncan	27	M	Unknown	02JI02Ma
CROWE, Mic.	28	M	Unknown	02JI02Ma
Kate	23	F	Unknown	02JI02Ma
Jno.	2	M	Child	02JI02Ma
CUCKE, Dan.	28	M	Unknown	02JI02Ma
MARRICAN, Biddy	20	F	Unknown	02JI02Ma
CROWE, Pat	25	M	Unknown	02JI02Ma
Jno.	22	M	Unknown	02JI02Ma
Biddy	22	F	Unknown	02JI02Ma
SCULLIAN, Jno.	23	M	Unknown	02JI02Ma
MULLINS, Jas.	13	M	Unknown	02JI02Ma
Maurice	11	M	Unknown	02JI02Ma
Pat	8	M	Child	02JI02Ma
Wm.	5	M	Child	02JI02Ma
Honora	2	F	Child	02JI02Ma
Pat	50	M	Unknown	02JI02Ma
Biddy	45	F	Unknown	02JI02Ma
Mary	20	F	Unknown	02JI02Ma
Jno.	18	M	Unknown	02JI02Ma
Biddy	16	F	Unknown	02JI02Ma
EGAN, Wm.	45	M	Unknown	02JI02Ma
CURDON, Mary	20	F	Unknown	02JI02Ma
Bridget	18	F	Unknown	02JI02Ma
FURY, Thos.	35	M	Unknown	02JI02Ma
Peggy	30	F	Unknown	02JI02Ma
Jno.	11	M	Unknown	02JI02Ma
Ellen	9	F	Child	02JI02Ma
WALLACE, Pat	50	M	Unknown	02JI02Ma
OHARE, Richd.	18	M	Unknown	02JI02Ma
Thos.	16	M	Unknown	02JI02Ma
KIRKBUT, Robt.	36	M	Unknown	02JI02Ma
FITZGERALD, Jno.	30	M	Unknown	02JI02Ma
Geo.	30	M	Unknown	02JI02Ma
Ann	20	F	Unknown	02JI02Ma
Sarah	5	F	Child	02JI02Ma
Jas.	.00	M	Infant	02JI02Ma
MILES, Maria	16	F	Unknown	02JI02Ma
Jas.	14	M	Unknown	02JI02Ma
Dora	12	F	Unknown	02JI02Ma
Bridget	9	F	Child	02JI02Ma
Pat	7	M	Child	02JI02Ma
Owen	5	M	Child	02JI02Ma
DUGGAN, Mary	27	F	Unknown	02JI02Ma
BURNES, Jno.	5	M	Child	02JI02Ma
DAW, Michl.	40	M	Unknown	02JI02Ma
Pat	14	M	Unknown	02JI02Ma
Ann	17	F	Unknown	02JI02Ma
HURRY, Jane	22	F	Unknown	02JI02Ma
CREEHAN, Margt.	5	F	Child	02JI02Ma
Pat	5	M	Child	02JI02Ma
NORTON, Richd.	35	M	Unknown	02JI02Ma
CLARK, Pat	20	M	Unknown	02JI02Ma
MORGAN, Mary	26	F	Unknown	02JI02Ma
RILEY, Pat	28	M	Unknown	02JI02Ma
Cathe.	22	F	Unknown	02JI02Ma
SMITH, Thos.	26	M	Unknown	02JI02Ma
RILEY, Thos.	36	M	Unknown	02JI02Ma
Ann	50	F	Unknown	02JI02Ma
HEALEY, Phil.	40	M	Unknown	02JI02Ma
Dan.	28	M	Unknown	02JI02Ma
Bessy	20	F	Unknown	02JI02Ma
Jas.	1	M	Child	02JI02Ma
Michl.	.00	M	Infant	02JI02Ma
KELLY, Frank	20	M	Unknown	02JI02Ma
Cath.	26	F	Unknown	02JI02Ma
RICHARDSON, Wm.	33	M	Unknown	02JI02Ma
EMSEY, Pat	25	M	Unknown	02JI02Ma
Dan.	30	M	Unknown	02JI02Ma
Ann	18	F	Unknown	02JI02Ma
Anthy.	12	M	Unknown	02JI02Ma
OLT, Jno.	39	M	Unknown	02JI02Ma
NIXON, Mary	44	F	Unknown	02JI02Ma
Lee	23	M	Unknown	02JI02Ma
Thos.	18	M	Unknown	02JI02Ma
Ralph	16	M	Unknown	02JI02Ma
Wm.	13	M	Unknown	02JI02Ma
Jno.	8	M	Child	02JI02Ma
MCFADDEN, Nelly	26	F	Unknown	02JI02Ma
NEWMAN, Jas.	16	M	Unknown	02JI02Ma
BURKE, Milly	19	M	Unknown	02JI02Ma
FOX, Richd.	45	M	Unknown	02JI02Ma
Thos.	20	M	Unknown	02JI02Ma
Robt.	17	M	Unknown	02JI02Ma
DEMPSEY, Michl.	20	M	Unknown	02JI02Ma
DONELLY, Jno.	35	M	Unknown	02JI02Ma
MCGUIRE, Hy.	50	M	Unknown	02JI02Ma
Anne	51	F	Unknown	02JI02Ma
Henry	20	M	Unknown	02JI02Ma
Mary	22	F	Unknown	02JI02Ma
Ann	18	F	Unknown	02JI02Ma
Eliza	14	F	Unknown	02JI02Ma
Pat	7	M	Child	02JI02Ma
WALLACE, Jno.	28	M	Unknown	02JI02Ma
Ann	28	F	Unknown	02JI02Ma
DONOVAN, Jas.	25	M	Unknown	02JI02Ma
Honora	25	F	Unknown	02JI02Ma
DWYER, Pat	21	M	Unknown	02JI02Ma
RYAN, Launce.	21	M	Unknown	02JI02Ma
Wm.	36	M	Unknown	02JI02Ma
MAYERS, Edwd.	28	M	Unknown	02JI02Ma
CREDDY, Pat	28	M	Unknown	02JI02Ma
Ann	30	F	Unknown	02JI02Ma
Sarah	18	F	Unknown	02JI02Ma
MCGOUGH, Terry	55	M	Unknown	02JI02Ma
LYGON, Francis	30	M	Unknown	02JI02Ma
TRACEY, Jno.	29	M	Unknown	02JI02Ma
ALLWELL, Mic.	20	M	Unknown	02JI02Ma
Mary	18	F	Unknown	02JI02Ma
MCPARLANE, Mgt.	25	F	Unknown	02JI02Ma
RILEY, Hugh	18	M	Unknown	02JI02Ma
CROSTON, Pat	19	M	Unknown	02JI02Ma
Judy	17	F	Unknown	02JI02Ma
KIMON, Fras.	20	M	Unknown	02JI02Ma
Cath.	16	F	Unknown	02JI02Ma
Richd.	10	M	Unknown	02JI02Ma
CARROLL, Jno.	25	M	Unknown	02JI02Ma
OCONNELL, Jas.	26	M	Unknown	02JI02Ma
MCDONNELL, Cathe.	17	F	Unknown	02JI02Ma
Thos.	9	M	Child	02JI02Ma
JORDAN, Pat	26	M	Unknown	02JI02Ma
FITZSIMONS, Honor	10	F	Unknown	02JI02Ma
FITZPATRICK, Mary	22	F	Unknown	02JI02Ma
DONOVAN, Bridget	22	F	Unknown	02JI02Ma
DELLARD, Thos.	12	M	Unknown	02JI02Ma
JONES, Stephen	42	M	Unknown	02JI02Ma
Mgt.	38	F	Unknown	02JI02Ma
Rees	15	M	Unknown	02JI02Ma
Wm.	12	M	Unknown	02JI02Ma
Ems.	9	M	Child	02JI02Ma
Evan	7	M	Child	02JI02Ma
Stephen	4	M	Child	02JI02Ma
Jno.	4	M	Child	02JI02Ma
Dan.	2	M	Child	02JI02Ma
EVANS, Mgt.	25	F	Unknown	02JI02Ma
THOMAS, Wm.	67	M	Unknown	02JI02Ma
Eliza	67	F	Unknown	02JI02Ma
Eliza	23	F	Unknown	02JI02Ma
Mgt.	21	F	Unknown	02JI02Ma
EVANS, Jno.	25	M	Unknown	02JI02Ma
Mary	66	F	Unknown	02JI02Ma
DAVIS, Mgt.	3	F	Child	02JI02Ma
WILLIAMS, David	40	M	Unknown	02JI02Ma
Jane	35	F	Unknown	02JI02Ma
Moses	3	M	Child	02JI02Ma
DAVIES, Evan	40	F	Unknown	02JI02Ma
EVAN, Doria	33	F	Unknown	02JI02Ma

NAMES OF PASSENGERS	AGE	SEX	OCCUPATIONS	DATE PORT SHIP
EVAN, Ann	28	F	Unknown	02JI02Ma
Jno.	7	M	Child	02JI02Ma
Mgt.	5	F	Child	02JI02Ma
Jane	1	F	Child	02JI02Ma
MORGAN, Margt.	23	F	Unknown	02JI02Ma
JONES, David	40	M	Unknown	02JI02Ma
Mgt.	38	F	Unknown	02JI02Ma
Heary	9	M	Child	02JI02Ma
Mary	7	F	Child	02JI02Ma
Mgt.	5	F	Child	02JI02Ma
Abnaca	.00	F	Infant	02JI02Ma
EVANS, Jno.	26	M	Unknown	02JI02Ma
Mary	44	F	Unknown	02JI02Ma
Evan	19	M	Unknown	02JI02Ma
Eliza	16	F	Unknown	02JI02Ma
Jno.	13	M	Unknown	02JI02Ma
Elenor	12	F	Unknown	02JI02Ma
Wm.	2	M	Child	02JI02Ma
HAKINS, Jno.	37	M	Unknown	02JI02Ma
Jane	40	F	Unknown	02JI02Ma
Margt.	8	F	Child	02JI02Ma
Sarah	6	F	Child	02JI02Ma
Mary	3	F	Child	02JI02Ma
Jane	.00	F	Infant	02JI02Ma
JONES, Evan	62	M	Unknown	02JI02Ma
Mgt.	29	F	Unknown	02JI02Ma
Mary	24	F	Unknown	02JI02Ma
Ann	21	F	Unknown	02JI02Ma
PEW, David	25	M	Unknown	02JI02Ma
PRICE, David	23	M	Unknown	02JI02Ma
JONES, Thos.	27	M	Unknown	02JI02Ma
Mgt.	27	F	Unknown	02JI02Ma
JENKINS, Dan.	28	M	Unknown	02JI02Ma
Elias	29	M	Unknown	02JI02Ma
RICHARD, Dan.	35	M	Unknown	02JI02Ma
HULSE, Chris.	27	M	Unknown	02JI02Ma
Ann	23	F	Unknown	02JI02Ma
Henry	3	M	Child	02JI02Ma
Mgt.	.00	F	Infant	02JI02Ma
SULLIVAN, Fras.	28	M	Unknown	02JI02Ma
CRIAN, Michl.	30	M	Unknown	02JI02Ma
LEDGETT, Jno.	27	M	Unknown	02JI02Ma
LAVERTY, Rose	24	F	Unknown	02JI02Ma
Mary	25	F	Unknown	02JI02Ma
Ann	19	F	Unknown	02JI02Ma
CAN, Jno.	46	M	Unknown	02JI02Ma
Jno.	42	M	Unknown	02JI02Ma
Jno.	18	M	Unknown	02JI02Ma
Mary	15	F	Unknown	02JI02Ma
MCNULTY, Wm.	35	M	Unknown	02JI02Ma
Jno.	14	M	Unknown	02JI02Ma
Henry	12	M	Unknown	02JI02Ma
Susan	10	F	Unknown	02JI02Ma
Jane	8	F	Child	02JI02Ma
CONNE, Mary	20	F	Unknown	02JI02Ma
DEVINE, Jas.	30	M	Unknown	02JI02Ma
Ellen	28	F	Unknown	02JI02Ma
BRINEN, Richard	25	M	Unknown	02JI02Ma
MATHEWS, Richard	41	M	Unknown	02JI02Ma
RICHARDS, Thos.	42	M	Unknown	02JI02Ma
BENROSE, Wm.	37	M	Unknown	02JI02Ma
WYATT, Thos.	29	M	Unknown	02JI02Ma
Hy.	21	M	Unknown	02JI02Ma
GABY, Joseph	23	M	Unknown	02JI02Ma
FORDE, G.T.	20	M	Unknown	02JI02Ma
COONEY, Jas.	34	M	Unknown	02JI02Ma
Amelia	50	F	Unknown	02JI02Ma
MAHER, Jno.	22	M	Unknown	02JI02Ma
COOPER, Wm.	43	M	Unknown	02JI02Ma
ADAMS, R.	26	M	Unknown	02JI02Ma
DONNELL, J.	26	M	Unknown	02JI02Ma
PURCELL, Tobias	24	M	Unknown	02JI02Ma
BRIEN, Patrick	18	M	Unknown	02JI02Ma
LANEY, Thos.	21	M	Unknown	02JI02Ma

ABEONA 03* JULY 1849

From London

NAMES OF PASSENGERS	AGE	SEX	OCCUPATIONS	DATE PORT SHIP
BAKER, U	28	M	Carpenter	03JI13Mb
U-Mrs.	22	F	None	03JI13Mb
BARROW, U-Miss	35	F	None	03JI13Mb
HAMILTON, Wm.	30	M	Shoemaker	03JI13Mb
Alice	31	F	None	03JI13Mb
FARNES, Thomas	31	M	Unknown	03JI13Mb
KELLY, Michael	30	M	Smith	03JI13Mb
CARMODY, John	40	M	Carpenter	03JI13Mb
Mary	30	F	None	03JI13Mb
Johanna	8	F	Child	03JI13Mb
Mary	.06	F	Infant	03JI13Mb
Jeremiah	6	M	Child	03JI13Mb
HACKET, Johanna	19	F	None	03JI13Mb
MORLY, Stephen	24	M	Laborer	03JI13Mb
Mary	26	F	Laborer	03JI13Mb
DAVIES, George	29	M	Unknown	03JI13Mb
SAYER, James	30	M	Appraiser	03JI13Mb
BRENNAN, John	44	M	Smith	03JI13Mb
Neil	42	M	None	03JI13Mb
Mary	43	F	None	03JI13Mb
MULDOON, Catherine	40	F	None	03JI13Mb
Patk.	9	M	Child	03JI13Mb
Edwd.	7	M	Child	03JI13Mb
BOLAN, Thomas	24	M	Laborer	03JI13Mb
MORAND, Maria	40	F	None	03JI13Mb
John	9	M	Child	03JI13Mb
TURNER, John	49	M	Hatter	03JI13Mb
Hannah	42	F	None	03JI13Mb
Elise	12	F	Child	03JI13Mb
William	10	M	Child	03JI13Mb
Henry	7	M	Child	03JI13Mb
Hannah	5	F	Child	03JI13Mb
Jesse	3	M	Child	03JI13Mb
Jane	.06	F	Infant	03JI13Mb
KEYWORTH, William	23	M	Cutler	03JI13Mb
LAMB, John	31	M	Jeweller	03JI13Mb
SULLIVAN, Anne	34	F	None	03JI13Mb
John	9	M	Child	03JI13Mb
Kate	7	F	Child	03JI13Mb
Catherine	26	F	None	03JI13Mb
DUNNALY, John	28	M	Laborer	03JI13Mb
BOYD, John	67	M	Laborer	03JI13Mb
Sarah	53	F	None	03JI13Mb
RESS, Thomas	10	M	Child	03JI13Mb
SEARLE, Jesse	30	M	Surveyor	03JI13Mb
Rosina	31	F	None	03JI13Mb
CHADWICK, Maria	54	F	None	03JI13M
KELLY, John	24	M	Tailor	03JI13M
Thomas	30	M	Grocer	03JI13M
SMITH, John	36	M	Dyer	03JI13M
STAVART, William	28	M	Butcher	03JI13M
DIDEN, Edwd.	44	M	Weaver	03JI13M
Esther	65	F	None	03JI13M
Edwd.	23	M	Unknown	03JI13M
Mary-Anne	20	F	None	03JI13M
Esther	13	F	None	03JI13M
Thomas	9	M	Child	03JI13M
Eliza	6	F	Child	03JI13M
John	3	M	Child	03JI13M
BURNS, Patk.	26	M	Smith	03JI13M
DANLON, Saml.	20	M	Bookseller	03JI13M
Katherine	20	F	None	03JI13M
QUILL, Ellen	23	F	None	03JI13M
OCONNELL, Margt.	20	F	None	03JI13M
HAYES, Dennis	37	M	Laborer	03JI13M

* should be 02 July

NAMES OF PASSENGERS	AGE	SEX	OCCUPATIONS	DATE PORT SHIP
HAYES, Katherine	36	F	None	03J113Mb
Nicholas	7	M	Child	03J113Mb
Michael	7	M	Child	03J113Mb
Ellen	9	F	Child	03J113Mb
Mary	23	F	None	03J113Mb
BARKER, Thomas	48	M	Smith	03J113Mb
CHATTERS, George	20	M	Laborer	03J113Mb
MARCARDY, Jeremiah	32	M	Tailor	03J113Mb
CASEY, Thomas	32	M	Tailor	03J113Mb
Georgiana	30	F	None	03J113Mb
HOPE, Fletcher	22	M	Tailor	03J113Mb
TREMLOTT, John	24	M	Lace Maker	03J113Mb
TRIGG, James	33	M	Shoemaker	03J113Mb
Kath.	30	F	None	03J113Mb
John	2	M	Child	03J113Mb
Henry	.10	M	Infant	03J113Mb
JACKSON, Michael	25	M	Laborer	03J113Mb
TODD, William	24	M	Laborer	03J113Mb
HARVEY, John	21	M	Butcher	03J113Mb
WILKES, John	23	M	Engineer	03J113Mb
HOPE, Thomas	29	M	Laborer	03J113Mb
Mary	29	F	None	03J113Mb
John	3	M	Child	03J113Mb
Edwin	1	M	Child	03J113Mb
Robert	5	M	Child	03J113Mb
REILLY, John	22	M	Laborer	03J113Mb
WALTER, Michl.	40	M	Laborer	03J113Mb
RUSH, Thomas	35	M	Laborer	03J113Mb
COSGRAVE, Patk.	27	M	Laborer	03J113Mb
ANDERSON, John	50	M	Laborer	03J113Mb
Mary	50	F	Laborer	03J113Mb
Lucy	22	F	None	03J113Mb
BENNES, Ellen	18	F	None	03J113Mb
Katherine	25	F	None	03J113Mb
BIBLE, Hannah	22	F	None	03J113Mb
John	6	M	Child	03J113Mb
CONNER, Katherine	25	F	None	03J113Mb
GRANT, Ann	17	F	None	03J113Mb
LANE, Catherine	21	F	None	03J113Mb
Anne	19	F	None	03J113Mb
BRENNAN, Samuel	31	M	Laborer	03J113Mb
ELMES, Wm.	30	M	Laborer	03J113Mb
MANNOX, John	42	M	None	03J113Mb
KELLY, James	31	M	Laborer	03J113Mb
Mary	30	F	None	03J113Mb
James	11	M	Laborer	03J113Mb
Thomas	6	M	Child	03J113Mb
TURLEY, Thomas	21	M	Laborer	03J113Mb
HURLY, John	33	M	Laborer	03J113Mb

IVANHOE 02 JULY 1849

From Liverpool

NAMES OF PASSENGERS	AGE	SEX	OCCUPATIONS	DATE PORT SHIP
BEALE, John	70	M	Grocer	02J102Lw
Charlotte	21	F	None	02J102Lw
Eliza	19	F	None	02J102Lw
Adelaide	17	F	None	02J102Lw
COLEMAN, James	32	M	Laborer	02J102Lw
U, Ann	00	F	Unknown	02J102Lw
Mary-Ann	9	F	Child	02J102Lw
DOUGH, James	21	M	Laborer	02J102Lw
Jane	26	F	None	02J102Lw
Harry	4	M	Child	02J102Lw
IGGOLDEN, Richard	19	M	Butcher	02J102Lw
WINSTONCLIFF, Emanuel	25	M	Spinner	02J102Lw
Mary	24	F	Warper	02J102Lw
JARVIS, William	26	M	Spinner	02J102Lw
SUNUN, Wm.	35	M	Saddler	02J102Lw
SUNUN, Jemima	35	F	None	02J102Lw
John	13	M	None	02J102Lw
Thomas	9	M	Child	02J102Lw
Sarah-Ann	5	F	Child	02J102Lw
Jemima	2	F	Child	02J102Lw
SULLIVAN, John	30	M	Farmer	02J102Lw
Mary	25	F	None	02J102Lw
Mary	1	F	Child	02J102Lw
GREENWALSH, James	24	M	Bleacher	02J102Lw
LESTER, Margt.	31	F	Weaver	02J102Lw
Lydia	11	F	None	02J102Lw
Ellen	8	F	Child	02J102Lw
Thomas	4	M	Child	02J102Lw
KITCHEN, Edward	31	M	Farmer	02J102Lw
U (W)	21	F	None	02J102Lw
HOARE, Maria	21	F	Laborer	02J102Lw
BOWMAN, Daniel	35	M	Carpenter	02J102Lw
BROWN, Jno.	30	M	Laborer	02J102Lw
Eliza	24	F	Laborer	02J102Lw
HENRY, John	8	M	Child	02J102Lw
BRADWELL, James	50	M	Engineer	02J102Lw
MCDONNELL, Randall	22	M	Carpenter	02J102Lw
MCCAUL, James	20	M	Laborer	02J102Lw
BELL, Joseph	30	M	Miner	02J102Lw
Elizabeth	30	F	Dressmaker	02J102Lw
William	6	M	Child	02J102Lw
James	4	M	Child	02J102Lw
Jane	2	F	Child	02J102Lw
Matthew	20	M	Miner	02J102Lw
MITCHELL, John	40	M	Miner	02J102Lw
WOOLLETT, Thomas	28	M	Miner	02J102Lw
Mary	25	F	Dressmaker	02J102Lw
Elizabeth	1	F	Child	02J102Lw
Sarah	.00	F	Infant	02J102Lw
ELLIOTT, John	19	M	Engineer	02J102Lw
GRAHAM, Francis	40	M	Miner	02J102Lw
RIDGEWAY, John	21	M	Pianist	02J102Lw
ANDERSON, John	21	M	Farmer	02J102Lw
SMITH, William	25	M	Miller	02J102Lw
U (W)	22	F	None	02J102Lw
BULLOUGH, Joseph	40	M	Farmer	02J102Lw
FARRELL, Thomas	18	M	Bootmaker	02J102Lw
DILLON, Thomas	26	M	Bootmaker	02J102Lw
FARLEY, Ellen	28	F	Farmer	02J102Lw
Mary	.00	F	Infant	02J102Lw
DWYER, William	40	M	Farmer	02J102Lw
U (W)	35	F	None	02J102Lw
Mary	11	F	None	02J102Lw
John	2	M	Child	02J102Lw
Catherine	.00	F	Infant	02J102Lw
WEEKS, Mary	18	F	Farmer	02J102Lw
MANNERING, John	48	M	Builder	02J102Lw
John	28	M	Builder	02J102Lw
Daniel	20	M	Builder	02J102Lw
BLAIR, John	29	M	Farmer	02J102Lw
JUNK, Daniel	25	M	Farmer	02J102Lw
DAVIDSON, James	21	M	Farmer	02J102Lw
Smith	21	M	Farmer	02J102Lw
FLEMMING, Joseph	25	M	Farmer	02J102Lw
WHITEHEAD, Benjamin	50	M	Miner	02J102Lw
Elizabeth	50	F	None	02J102Lw
James	24	M	Miner	02J102Lw
Jane	24	F	None	02J102Lw
Mary	11	F	None	02J102Lw
Sarah	.00	F	Infant	02J102Lw
HULLEN, Thomas	20	M	Laborer	02J102Lw
MCGUIRE, Ann	24	F	None	02J102Lw
Agnes	23	F	Knitter	02J102Lw
CLARENDON, George	20	M	Farmer	02J102Lw
James	17	M	None	02J102Lw
Rebecca	17	F	None	02J102Lw
Eliza	15	F	None	02J102Lw
BROWNE, John	23	M	Fimft	02J102Lw
GRAHAM, Arthur	21	M	Tailor	02J102Lw
MCGUINNESS, Mary	20	F	Servant	02J102Lw

NAMES OF PASSENGERS	AGE	SEX	OCCUPATIONS	DATE PORT SHIP	NAMES OF PASSENGERS	AGE	SEX	OCCUPATIONS	DATE PORT SHIP
LYNCH, Margt.	17	F	Servant	02JI02Lw	MURPHY, David	21	M	Laborer	02JI02Lw
Mary	15	F	Servant	02JI02Lw	CASEY, Mary	50	F	Grocer	02JI02Lw
COSTELLO, James	30	M	Farmer	02JI02Lw	FINNALLY, Patk.	28	M	Farmer	02JI02Lw
CAHILL, Thomas	20	M	Farmer	02JI02Lw	Mary	28	F	None	02JI02Lw
DENRY, Richard	23	M	Laborer	02JI02Lw	Richard	8	M	Child	02JI02Lw
CHESTER, Geo.	26	M	Farmer	02JI02Lw	Anastatia	6	F	Child	02JI02Lw
SIMPLE, Wm.	26	M	Boatman	02JI02Lw	Mary-Ann	3	F	Child	02JI02Lw
HALL, John	26	M	Unknown	02JI02Lw	John	.00	M	Infant	02JI02Lw
WILLIS, Michl.	30	M	Miner	02JI02Lw	RYAN, Margaret	20	F	Servant	02JI02Lw
Mary	28	F	None	02JI02Lw	BUTLER, Martin	24	M	Farmer	02JI02Lw
William	5	M	Child	02JI02Lw	FLAGHERTY, Edward	20	M	Laborer	02JI02Lw
INGLEBY, James	23	M	Miner	02JI02Lw	SIMPLE, John	23	M	Carpenter	02JI02Lw
Thomas	20	M	Miner	02JI02Lw	RYAN, Bridget	21	F	None	02JI02Lw
NELANEY, Michael	26	M	Farmer	02JI02Lw	CARROLL, Jno.	22	M	Farmer	02JI02Lw
Margaret	20	F	None	02JI02Lw	Mary	20	F	None	02JI02Lw
William	.00	M	Infant	02JI02Lw	MURPHY, Mary	21	F	None	02JI02Lw
Johanna	.00	F	Infant	02JI02Lw	COTTER, Mary	21	F	None	02JI02Lw
MEANEY, Catherine	21	F	Servant	02JI02Lw	BRIEN, Patrick	30	M	Laborer	02JI02Lw
KELLY, John	21	M	Laborer	02JI02Lw	MCCABE, Rosannah	27	F	None	02JI02Lw
FLYNNE, Pat	24	M	Farmer	02JI02Lw	IRWIN, Thomas	23	M	Farmer	02JI02Lw
DONAGHUE, Francis	21	M	Laborer	02JI02Lw	CORROL, Elizabeth	21	F	Dressmaker	02JI02Lw
EAGAN, Michael	18	M	Laborer	02JI02Lw	SMITH, James	26	M	Laborer	02JI02Lw
Mary	21	F	Servant	02JI02Lw	LYNCH, Jno.	21	M	Shepherd	02JI02Lw
ROONEY, Pat	21	M	Laborer	02JI02Lw	DENNAN, Pat	30	M	Laborer	02JI02Lw
WILSON, John	28	M	Farmer	02JI02Lw	GOVERN, Mary	19	F	None	02JI02Lw
Ellen	24	F	None	02JI02Lw	MARTIN, Bridget	19	F	None	02JI02Lw
Bridget	.00	F	Infant	02JI02Lw	Judith	16	F	None	02JI02Lw
CARPENTER, Bryan	45	M	Shepherd	02JI02Lw	JENKINS, David	28	M	Miner	02JI02Lw
Ann	40	F	None	02JI02Lw	Elizabeth	29	F	None	02JI02Lw
Bridget	19	F	None	02JI02Lw	Evan	23	M	None	02JI02Lw
Matthew	16	M	None	02JI02Lw	MORRIS, David	32	M	Miner	02JI02Lw
James	12	M	None	02JI02Lw	MURRAY, Thomas	28	M	Laborer	02JI02Lw
Mary	11	F	None	02JI02Lw	Pat	24	M	Laborer	02JI02Lw
Bryan	6	M	Child	02JI02Lw	DANIEL, Robert	17	M	Laborer	02JI02Lw
Catherine	3	F	Child	02JI02Lw	GILSINAN, Jas.	24	M	Laborer	02JI02Lw
John	2	M	Child	02JI02Lw	FOX, Thomas	24	M	Laborer	02JI02Lw
BANNON, Owen	30	M	Laborer	02JI02Lw	Catherine	22	F	Laborer	02JI02Lw
SMITH, Peter	40	M	Laborer	02JI02Lw	MCGARRY, Mary-A.	22	F	Laborer	02JI02Lw
DIGNAN, James	30	M	Laborer	02JI02Lw	BULGER, Anthony	25	M	Laborer	02JI02Lw
CONNELL, Peter	30	M	Servant	02JI02Lw	WILLSON, Patk.	29	M	Cap Maker	02JI02Lw
Bridget	20	F	Servant	02JI02Lw	U (W)	25	F	None	02JI02Lw
BRIEN, Catherine	20	F	Servant	02JI02Lw	Susan	.00	F	Infant	02JI02Lw
QUINN, Michael	30	M	Tailor	02JI02Lw	MCHALE, Mary-Ann	28	F	Cap Maker	02JI02Lw
MURRAY, Larry	30	M	Laborer	02JI02Lw	MYERS, Joseph	29	M	Maurer	02JI02Lw
ROBERTS, James	28	M	Laborer	02JI02Lw	DWYER, Pat	19	M	Laborer	02JI02Lw
Catherine	24	F	Laborer	02JI02Lw	ALLISON, Thomas	24	M	Engineer	02JI02Lw
STEVENS, E.B.	22	M	Saddler	02JI02Lw	BROWNE, Robert	25	M	Farmer	02JI02Lw
Samuel	23	M	Saddler	02JI02Lw	WHITTINGTON, Richard	22	M	Clerk	02JI02Lw
MORGAN, David	33	M	Shopman	02JI02Lw	Ann	20	F	None	02JI02Lw
RYAN, William	33	M	Laborer	02JI02Lw	CURRAN, Margaret	50	F	None	02JI02Lw
MCKENNA, Jas.	27	M	Blacksmith	02JI02Lw	WOODHEAD, Joseph	23	M	Farmer	02JI02Lw
Ann	22	F	Weaver	02JI02Lw	QUINLAN, Jno.	25	M	Tailor	02JI02Lw
TIERNAN, Mary	22	F	Weaver	02JI02Lw	Mary	22	F	None	02JI02Lw
RUDDY, Catherine	20	F	Weaver	02JI02Lw	POLE, W.	25	M	Joiner	02JI02Lw
BROGAN, Henry	25	M	Laborer	02JI02Lw	CAREY, Ann	35	F	Farmer	02JI02Lw
MCKEE, Mary	40	F	None	02JI02Lw	John	13	M	Farmer	02JI02Lw
COOTE, U	26	M	Farmer	02JI02Lw	Thomas	11	M	Farmer	02JI02Lw
ODONAHUE, U	22	M	Farmer	02JI02Lw	Philip	9	M	Farmer	02JI02Lw
LEARY, John	27	M	Engineer	02JI02Lw	JONES, Mary	40	F	Housekeeper	02JI02Lw
Ann	24	F	None	02JI02Lw	Jno.	13	M	Tailor	02JI02Lw
CROWTHER, Richard	27	M	Mechanic	02JI02Lw	CORCORAN, Jno.	50	M	Blacksmith	02JI02Lw
BOWLAND, Robert	24	M	Clerk	02JI02Lw	Jno.	19	M	Blacksmith	02JI02Lw
Margaret	21	F	None	02JI02Lw	Mary	15	F	None	02JI02Lw
LYSATT, Ellen	10	F	None	02JI02Lw	KEHOE, James	30	M	Stctr	02JI02Lw
CAMPBELL, Margt.	48	F	Farmer	02JI02Lw	SMITH, Jno.	25	M	Grocer	02JI02Lw
MANNERING, John	36	M	Laborer	02JI02Lw	STOCKDALE, Joseph	28	M	Farmer	02JI02Lw
RYAN, John	23	M	Smith	02JI02Lw	GIBBONS, Thomas	26	M	Locksmith	02JI02Lw
WILLIAMS, Jane	25	F	None	02JI02Lw	MURTAGH, Mary	25	F	Farmer	02JI02Lw
NORTON, John	50	M	Farmer	02JI02Lw	THOMAS, Geo.	34	M	Blacksmith	02JI02Lw
Thomas	18	M	Farmer	02JI02Lw	BOWAN, Jno.	28	M	Shoemaker	02JI02Lw
OROURKE, Martin	20	M	Farmer	02JI02Lw	SHEEDY, Roger	30	M	Laborer	02JI02Lw
TEMPLE, John	36	M	Shoemaker	02JI02Lw	MARTIN, Margt.	25	F	None	02JI02Lw
PEPPARD, Michl.	21	M	Draper	02JI02Lw	MALOWNEY, Mary	24	F	None	02JI02Lw
TYNAN, John	22	M	Laborer	02JI02Lw	Francis	22	M	None	02JI02Lw
Patrick	24	M	Laborer	02JI02Lw	REID, Alexander	21	M	Ppstr	02JI02Lw

NAMES OF PASSENGERS	AGE	SEX	OCCUPATIONS	DATE PORT SHIP	NAMES OF PASSENGERS	AGE	SEX	OCCUPATIONS	DATE PORT SHIP
PATRIDGE, John	30	M	Sawer	02Jl02Lw	LYNCH, Mary	50	F	None	02Jl02Lw
RICE, Lawrence	24	M	Servant	02Jl02Lw	MOORE, Mary	47	F	None	02Jl02Lw
Patrick	25	M	Servant	02Jl02Lw	Ann	19	F	None	02Jl02Lw
RABBITT, Dennis	26	M	Oat	02Jl02Lw	Rose	17	F	None	02Jl02Lw
BELL, Jas.	23	M	Farmer	02Jl02Lw	Mary	15	F	None	02Jl02Lw
BROWN, Wm.	31	M	Laborer	02Jl02Lw	Catherine	10	F	None	02Jl02Lw
LAWLER, Jeremiah	30	M	Laborer	02Jl02Lw	John	7	M	Child	02Jl02Lw
Mary	26	F	None	02Jl02Lw	CADDEN, Thos.	30	M	Laborer	02Jl02Lw
Martin	.00	M	Infant	02Jl02Lw	PHILIPS, Robert	30	M	Laborer	02Jl02Lw
OBRIEN, Stephen	25	M	Shipwright	02Jl02Lw	BRYAN, James	21	M	Car Man	02Jl02Lw
U (W)	23	F	None	02Jl02Lw	KAVANAGH, Wm.	40	M	Soap Boiler	02Jl02Lw
Julia	.00	F	Infant	02Jl02Lw	Maria	35	F	None	02Jl02Lw
VOSE, Frederick	26	M	Glsctr	02Jl02Lw	Arthur	9	M	Child	02Jl02Lw
CARNEY, Dennis	35	M	Farmer	02Jl02Lw	KINGSTON, Abraham	24	M	Shoemaker	02Jl02Lw
Michael	24	M	Laborer	02Jl02Lw	KAVANAGH, Thomas	5	M	Child	02Jl02Lw
Edmund	22	M	Labcrer	02Jl02Lw	LINN, James	33	M	Rp	02Jl02Lw
MCCARTHY, Johannah	20	F	Farmer	02Jl02Lw	BRIEN, Thomas	40	M	Farmer	02Jl02Lw
Dennis	22	M	Farmer	02Jl02Lw	INGLEBY, James	24	M	Miner	02Jl02Lw
CONNOR, Daniel	40	M	Farmer	02Jl02Lw	STOREY, James	26	M	Miner	02Jl02Lw
John	25	M	Farmer	02Jl02Lw	GAVIN, John	24	M	Laborer	02Jl02Lw
Darby	23	M	Farmer	02Jl02Lw	LESGRAVE, Michl.	20	M	Laborer	02Jl02Lw
Ellen	40	F	None	02Jl02Lw	RAMSEY, Andrew	24	M	Linen Maker	02Jl02Lw
Honora	20	F	None	02Jl02Lw	James	21	M	Iron Monger	02Jl02Lw
Ellen	.00	F	Infant	02Jl02Lw	QUINLAN, John	27	M	Cver	02Jl02Lw
SULLIVAN, John	30	M	Laborer	02Jl02Lw	Michael	21	M	Engineer	02Jl02Lw
ODONNELL, Philip	37	M	Farmer	02Jl02Lw	CARNING, James	21	M	Laborer	02Jl02Lw
U (W)	35	F	None	02Jl02Lw	BROWN, William	27	M	Laborer	02Jl02Lw
Patrick	6	M	Child	02Jl02Lw	FOSTER, John-Orr	25	M	Cmagt	02Jl02Lw
Catherine	4	F	Child	02Jl02Lw	HOLBY, William	23	M	Laborer	02Jl02Lw
Jeremiah	2	M	Child	02Jl02Lw	Margaret	20	F	Laborer	02Jl02Lw
MCAULIFFE, Mary	34	F	None	02Jl02Lw	COGHLAN, Bridget	19	F	Laborer	02Jl02Lw
Jeremiah	10	M	None	02Jl02Lw	Patrick	17	M	Laborer	02Jl02Lw
Eve	8	F	Child	02Jl02Lw	WALSH, Michael	11	M	Laborer	02Jl02Lw
Cathernie	6	F	Child	02Jl02Lw	John	9	M	Laborer	02Jl02Lw
Dennis	.00	M	Infant	02Jl02Lw	MURPHY, Patrick	22	M	Car Man	02Jl02Lw
CONNELL, Johannah	25	F	Servant	02Jl02Lw	BRUTHER, Michael	48	M	Farmer	02Jl02Lw
BARRY, Mary	16	F	Servant	02Jl02Lw	Patrick	25	M	Farmer	02Jl02Lw
COLLINS, Jeremiah	22	M	Farmer	02Jl02Lw	Mary	25	F	None	02Jl02Lw
Ellen	50	F	None	02Jl02Lw	CARTHY, Daniel	25	M	Farmer	02Jl02Lw
Julia	18	F	None	02Jl02Lw	KINSHAW, Bridget	20	F	None	02Jl02Lw
Julia	4	F	Child	02Jl02Lw	EVANS, Ellen	30	F	None	02Jl02Lw
LONG, Catherine	22	F	None	02Jl02Lw	William	18	M	Laborer	02Jl02Lw
GARDNER, Nathaniel	28	M	Gdnr	02Jl02Lw	Mary	6	F	Child	02Jl02Lw
Margaret	24	F	None	02Jl02Lw	William	4	M	Child	02Jl02Lw
HANAN, James	27	M	Laborer	02Jl02Lw	SPAIN, Ellen	25	F	None	02Jl02Lw
NIHILL, Patk.	20	M	Laborer	02Jl02Lw	MURPHY, Mary	25	F	None	02Jl02Lw
CARROLL, John	45	M	Laborer	02Jl02Lw	Julia	25	F	None	02Jl02Lw
Honora	13	F	None	02Jl02Lw	GLYNNE, Pat	24	M	Laborer	02Jl02Lw
Ellen	8	F	Child	02Jl02Lw	BLAIR, Elizabeth	35	F	None	02Jl02Lw
Mary	3	F	Child	02Jl02Lw	Ann	12	F	None	02Jl02Lw
Margaret	.00	F	Infant	02Jl02Lw	John	6	M	None	02Jl02Lw
HARTNELL, William	20	M	Laborer	02Jl02Lw	Charlotte	10	F	None	02Jl02Lw
BARRY, Patk.	22	M	Farmer	02Jl02Lw	Elizabeth	1	F	None	02Jl02Lw
FALVEY, Mary	16	F	None	02Jl02Lw	GLYNNE, Michael	30	M	Carpenter	02Jl02Lw
HOWLEY, Thomas	22	M	Farmer	02Jl02Lw	PIGEON, Patrick	17	M	Laborer	02Jl02Lw
BOURKE, John	35	M	Farmer	02Jl02Lw	Lawrence	15	M	Laborer	02Jl02Lw
FLANAGHAN, Maurice	35	M	Laborer	02Jl02Lw	Bridget	33	F	Laborer	02Jl02Lw
TIERNEY, John	26	M	Farmer	02Jl02Lw	QUINN, Thomas	21	M	Laborer	02Jl02Lw
KELLY, Michael	35	M	Farmer	02Jl02Lw	LARKEN, Mary	20	F	Laborer	02Jl02Lw
Margaret	19	F	None	02Jl02Lw	HENRY, Patrick	23	M	Laborer	02Jl02Lw
Bridget	.00	F	Infant	02Jl02Lw	WALSH, Catherine	24	F	None	02Jl02Lw
HOWARD, Martin	19	M	Farmer	02Jl02Lw	MCHOLENE, Patrick	20	M	Laborer	02Jl02Lw
John	17	M	Farmer	02Jl02Lw	MCCHRISTY, Elizabeth	20	F	None	02Jl02Lw
Margaret	22	F	None	02Jl02Lw	SCANLON, Michael	35	M	Laborer	02Jl02Lw
Honora	12	F	None	02Jl02Lw	Ellen	30	F	None	02Jl02Lw
HICKEY, James	46	M	Farmer	02Jl02Lw	Margaret	8	F	Child	02Jl02Lw
Margaret	30	F	None	02Jl02Lw	BRADY, Terence	22	M	Laborer	02Jl02Lw
SMITH, Mary	21	F	Servant	02Jl02Lw	Bridget	4	F	Child	02Jl02Lw
CANBEN, Ann	18	F	Servant	02Jl02Lw	James	2	M	Child	02Jl02Lw
Martha	16	F	Servant	02Jl02Lw	GILLHANY, James	16	M	Laborer	02Jl02Lw
LYNCH, Philip	36	M	Farmer	02Jl02Lw	MCLOUGHLEN, Ann	20	F	Laborer	02Jl02Lw
Catherine	8	F	Child	02Jl02Lw	HEANEY, Ann	20	F	Laborer	02Jl02Lw
Ann	6	F	Child	02Jl02Lw	MCGRATH, Julia	22	F	Laborer	02Jl02Lw
Patrick	4	M	Child	02Jl02Lw	POLLARD, Mary	45	F	None	02Jl02Lw
Mary	2	F	Child	02Jl02Lw	Charles	11	M	None	02Jl02Lw

NAMES OF PASSENGERS	AGE	SEX	OCCUPATIONS	DATE PORT SHIP
DACEY, Timothy	40	M	Laborer	02J102Lw
Ellen	40	F	Laborer	02J102Lw
FITZGERALD, Joseph	5	M	Child	02J102Lw
SULLIVAN, Thomas	22	M	Farmer	02J102Lw

Z.RING 02 JULY 1849

From Livorno

NAMES OF PASSENGERS	AGE	SEX	OCCUPATIONS	DATE PORT SHIP
CALLAGHEN, Julia	17	F	Unknown	02J169Mh

CENTURION 03 JULY 1849

From Liverpool

NAMES OF PASSENGERS	AGE	SEX	OCCUPATIONS	DATE PORT SHIP
PARK, William	21	M	Farmer	03J102Lq
Sarah	18	F	Unknown	03J102Lq
TIERNEY, Margt.	20	F	Unknown	03J102Lq
Nora	18	F	Unknown	03J102Lq
MARGIN, Margt.	24	F	Unknown	03J102Lq
SUFFERRY, Bridget	19	F	Unknown	03J102Lq
CUNNINGHAM, Cath.	25	F	Unknown	03J102Lq
NORTEN, Wm.	40	M	Unknown	03J102Lq
HAY, Ann	24	F	Unknown	03J102Lq
Michael	4	M	Child	03J102Lq
WILSON, Jane	.06	F	Infant	03J102Lq
KELLY, Michael	32	M	Unknown	03J102Lq
Wm.	25	M	Unknown	03J102Lq
Pat.	7	M	Child	03J102Lq
DORAN, Mary	20	F	Unknown	03J102Lq
CONAST, Jas.	14	M	Unknown	03J102Lq
TEMPLE, John	36	M	Unknown	03J102Lq
Died-At-Sea				
MURRAY, Thos.	20	M	Unknown	03J102Lq
Mary	14	F	Unknown	03J102Lq
BROWN, Rich.	20	M	Unknown	03J102Lq
Eliza	22	F	Unknown	03J102Lq
HADWICK, Bridget	16	F	Unknown	03J102Lq
CALLIGAN, Daniel	38	M	Unknown	03J102Lq
QUINLAN, Danl.	50	M	Unknown	03J102Lq
Cath.	22	F	Unknown	03J102Lq
CONTILLAN, Mary	24	F	Unknown	03J102Lq
MURPHY, Cath.	24	F	Unknown	03J102Lq
MAKORY, Mary	23	F	Unknown	03J102Lq
Honor	21	F	Unknown	03J102Lq
CONNER, Thomas	26	M	Unknown	03J102Lq
NORAN, Wm.	21	M	Unknown	03J102Lq
DIRIAN, Jerri	23	M	Unknown	03J102Lq
Margt.	22	F	Unknown	03J102Lq
Danl.	7	M	Child	03J102Lq
Con.	6	M	Child	03J102Lq
Pat.	3	M	Child	03J102Lq
MURPHY, Margt.	20	F	Unknown	03J102Lq
LEARY, Jim.	15	M	Unknown	03J102Lq
Humphry	13	M	Unknown	03J102Lq
FOX, Wm.	30	M	Unknown	03J102Lq
John	30	M	Unknown	03J102Lq
Ellen	33	F	Unknown	03J102Lq
Robt.	.06	M	Infant	03J102Lq
HOWARD, John	24	M	Unknown	03J102Lq
BERT, Martha	25	F	Unknown	03J102Lq
GREGORY, A.	21	M	Unknown	03J102Lq
U-Mrs.	21	F	Unknown	03J102Lq
MCNULTY, John	34	M	Unknown	03J102Lq
BRADY, Benj.	26	M	Unknown	03J102Lq
Hugh	22	M	Unknown	03J102Lq
RYAN, Wm.	24	M	Unknown	03J102Lq
Mary	21	F	Unknown	03J102Lq
TEIRNAN, Col.	28	F	Unknown	03J102Lq
CHEETHAM, John	23	M	Unknown	03J102Lq
Eliza	21	F	Unknown	03J102Lq
Died-At-Sea				
WHEATLY, Jim.	37	M	Unknown	03J102Lq
EVERRETT, Thomas	20	M	Unknown	03J102Lq
LYMAN, Rich.	60	M	Unknown	03J102Lq
WYLDE, Sarah	36	F	Unknown	03J102Lq
Henry	10	M	Unknown	03J102Lq
Sarah	7	F	Child	03J102Lq
Emily	3	F	Child	03J102Lq
BRINDLE, Ralph	23	M	Unknown	03J102Lq
QUARREL, Thos.	28	M	Unknown	03J102Lq
FLETCHER, Wm.	25	M	Unknown	03J102Lq
STOUT, Wm.	56	M	Unknown	03J102Lq
DELAY, J.	21	M	Unknown	03J102Lq
DENNEL, Benj.	22	M	Unknown	03J102Lq
FARRELL, Wm.	18	M	Unknown	03J102Lq
SMITH, Cath.	30	F	Unknown	03J102Lq
MCDERMOT, Mick.	20	M	Unknown	03J102Lq
Thos.	50	M	Unknown	03J102Lq
Cath.	50	F	Unknown	03J102Lq
Eliza	26	F	Unknown	03J102Lq
Ann	18	F	Unknown	03J102Lq
Mick.	15	M	Unknown	03J102Lq
Eliza	20	F	Unknown	03J102Lq
FEERY, Thomas	25	M	Unknown	03J102Lq
Ann	19	F	Unknown	03J102Lq
NORWICK, Wm.	16	M	Unknown	03J102Lq
MITCHEL, John	18	M	Unknown	03J102Lq
HICKEY, Ed.	23	M	Unknown	03J102Lq
DOWD, Thomas	30	M	Unknown	03J102Lq
HALTEN, Margt.	25	F	Unknown	03J102Lq
HICKEY, Bridget	18	F	Unknown	03J102Lq
HOGAN, Con.	45	M	Unknown	03J102Lq
Mary	40	F	Unknown	03J102Lq
Ellen	12	F	Unknown	03J102Lq
Con.	10	M	Unknown	03J102Lq
Mary	8	F	Child	03J102Lq
Danl.	5	M	Child	03J102Lq
John	3	M	Child	03J102Lq
Nancy	.03	F	Infant	03J102Lq
VAUGHN, John	45	M	Unknown	03J102Lq
U-Mrs.	40	F	Unknown	03J102Lq
CLEARY, Dennis	25	M	Unknown	03J102Lq
DOWNY, John	45	M	Unknown	03J102Lq
DALY, Mary	28	F	Unknown	03J102Lq
MCMAHON, John	48	M	Unknown	03J102Lq
DOYLE, U	25	M	Unknown	03J102Lq
SCALLEY, U-Mrs.	22	F	Unknown	03J102Lq
ELLIS, Rich.	33	M	Unknown	03J102Lq
Sarah	29	F	Unknown	03J102Lq
KELLAR, Wm.	35	M	Unknown	03J102Lq
Robt.	36	M	Unknown	03J102Lq
Ann	27	F	Unknown	03J102Lq
MCGRATH, Pat.	25	M	Unknown	03J102Lq
FAGAN, John	40	M	Unknown	03J102Lq
U-Mrs.	35	F	Unknown	03J102Lq
Pat.	8	M	Child	03J102Lq
Ann	6	F	Child	03J102Lq
SHERIDAN, Bridget	20	F	Unknown	03J102Lq
Cath.	20	F	Unknown	03J102Lq
HOLTEN, Mary	21	F	Unknown	03J102Lq
MORAN, Agnes	20	F	Unknown	03J102Lq
COOLEY, Pat.	20	M	Unknown	03J102Lq
Cath.	20	F	Unknown	03J102Lq
Mary	20	F	Unknown	03J102Lq
CARRIGAN, Margt.	24	F	Unknown	03J102Lq
MITCHEL, Ann	23	F	Unknown	03J102Lq
HANLIN, Jas.	50	M	Unknown	03J102Lq

NAMES OF PASSENGERS	AGE	SEX	OCCUPATIONS	DATE PORT SHIP
HANLIN, Mick.	29	M	Unknown	03J102Lq
REID, Jas.	30	M	Unknown	03J102Lq
HILL, Thos.	45	M	Unknown	03J102Lq
U-Mrs.	45	F	Unknown	03J102Lq
CLARK, Cath.	30	F	Unknown	03J102Lq
NULTY, Mary	18	F	Unknown	03J102Lq
HILL, Jas.	22	M	Unknown	03J102Lq
FINLAN, Jas.	25	M	Unknown	03J102Lq
BROWN, Ab.	45	M	Unknown	03J102Lq
HIGGINS, John	20	M	Unknown	03J102Lq
U-Mrs.	22	F	Unknown	03J102Lq
TAFT, Henry	30	M	Unknown	03J102Lq
HUGES, John	23	M	Unknown	03J102Lq
HARPER, Ed.	45	M	Unknown	03J102Lq
Mary	30	F	Unknown	03J102Lq
Mary	14	F	Unknown	03J102Lq
Pat.	12	M	Unknown	03J102Lq
John	9	M	Child	03J102Lq
DOYLE, Tom.	23	M	Unknown	03J102Lq
CONROY, Pat	25	M	Unknown	03J102Lq
SHUNSHANNON, Pat.	25	M	Unknown	03J102Lq
BELL, Mat.	50	M	Unknown	03J102Lq
Cath.	50	F	Unknown	03J102Lq
Phil.	7	M	Child	03J102Lq
CORCORAN, Thos.	30	M	Child	03J102Lq
Cath.	17	F	Child	03J102Lq
Ellen	4	F	Child	03J102Lq
Mary	18	F	Unknown	03J102Lq
MOLE, Lora	30	F	Unknown	03J102Lq
BRANSON, John	25	M	Unknown	03J102Lq
FERGUSSEN, Mat.	48	M	Unknown	03J102Lq
PORTER, Jane	18	F	Unknown	03J102Lq
Phebe	12	F	Unknown	03J102Lq
Bridget	53	F	Unknown	03J102Lq
MITCHEL, Alex.	24	M	Unknown	03J102Lq
HOLDEN, Thomas	20	M	Unknown	03J102Lq
REILY, John	30	M	Unknown	03J102Lq
MARLIN, Susan	20	F	Unknown	03J102Lq
SMITH, Richd.	35	M	Unknown	03J102Lq
Eliza	32	F	Unknown	03J102Lq
Jas.	10	M	Unknown	03J102Lq
Fanny	9	F	Child	03J102Lq
Mary	7	F	Child	03J102Lq
Pat	5	M	Child	03J102Lq
Margt.	2	F	Child	03J102Lq
Eliza	.06	F	Infant	03J102Lq
SEBRIEY, John	30	M	Unknown	03J102Lq
U	.03	F	Infant	03J102Lq
Thos.	29	M	Unknown	03J102Lq
BRADY, Pat.	29	M	Unknown	03J102Lq
MCGRATH, Wm.	18	M	Unknown	03J102Lq
MATHEWS, Ed.	17	M	Unknown	03J102Lq
REILY, Rose	18	F	Unknown	03J102Lq
DISMAN, Bryan	23	M	Unknown	03J102Lq
FITZSIMMONS, Cath.	21	F	Unknown	03J102Lq
MCGALLEN, Mick.	30	M	Unknown	03J102Lq
MATHEWS, Con.	18	M	Unknown	03J102Lq
MULLEN, David	45	M	Unknown	03J102Lq
U-Mrs.	40	F	Unknown	03J102Lq
Mary	11	F	Unknown	03J102Lq
Wm.	9	M	Child	03J102Lq
Jas.	7	M	Child	03J102Lq
Margt.	4	F	Child	03J102Lq
Brid.	2	F	Child	03J102Lq
Jane	.06	F	Infant	03J102Lq
SMITH, Jas.	20	M	Unknown	03J102Lq
REILY, Pat.	20	M	Unknown	03J102Lq
QUIRN, Thos.	27	M	Unknown	03J102Lq
WALSH, Thos.	25	M	Unknown	03J102Lq
Mary	20	F	Unknown	03J102Lq
Jos.	24	M	Unknown	03J102Lq
KINNEDY, Ed.	20	M	Unknown	03J102Lq
Mary	20	F	Unknown	03J102Lq
POWEL, James	20	M	Unknown	03J102Lq
MARGEN, Henry	20	M	Unknown	03J102Lq
MURPHY, Cath.	20	F	Unknown	03J102Lq
Thos.	22	M	Unknown	03J102Lq
Thos.	20	M	Unknown	03J102Lq
LYNCH, Cath.	25	F	Unknown	03J102Lq
CROAL, Jas.	22	M	Unknown	03J102Lq
Margt.	26	F	Unknown	03J102Lq
MORRIS, Pat.	21	M	Unknown	03J102Lq
RYAN, Wm.	18	M	Unknown	03J102Lq
Dennis	23	M	Unknown	03J102Lq
FINLEY, Thos.	20	M	Unknown	03J102Lq
Brid.	29	F	Unknown	03J102Lq
NANGLE, Thos.	29	M	Unknown	03J102Lq
BRONSON, Rich.	28	M	Unknown	03J102Lq
U-Mrs.	27	F	Unknown	03J102Lq
Robt.	6	M	Child	03J102Lq
John	3	M	Child	03J102Lq
Rich.	.03	M	Infant	03J102Lq
JONES, John	30	M	Unknown	03J102Lq
U-Mrs.	28	F	Unknown	03J102Lq
CURRY, Robt.	25	M	Unknown	03J102Lq
U-Mrs.	22	F	Unknown	03J102Lq
Robt.	.03	M	Infant	03J102Lq
SMITH, Andw.	43	M	Unknown	03J102Lq
Mary	38	F	Unknown	03J102Lq
Wm.	16	M	Unknown	03J102Lq
Wm.	13	M	Unknown	03J102Lq
Sarah	8	F	Child	03J102Lq
Ellen	6	F	Child	03J102Lq
Jannet	4	F	Child	03J102Lq
Peter	.03	M	Infant	03J102Lq
BURKE, Mick.	20	M	Unknown	03J102Lq
BROWN, John	27	M	Unknown	03J102Lq
Mary	28	F	Unknown	03J102Lq
Mary	.06	F	Infant	03J102Lq
John	.06	M	Infant	03J102Lq
ASHBRIGE, U-Mrs.	28	F	Unknown	03J102Lq
Died-At-Sea				
Mary	30	F	Unknown	03J102Lq
Nabby	4	F	Child	03J102Lq
BROWN, Jas.	19	M	Unknown	03J102Lq
Harriet	17	F	Unknown	03J102Lq
Jno.	27	M	Unknown	03J102Lq
BEST, George	29	M	Unknown	03J102Lq
HERRON, Henry	22	M	Unknown	03J102Lq
St.GEORGE, Ellen	40	F	Unknown	03J102Lq
Mary	22	F	Unknown	03J102Lq
Cath.	18	F	Unknown	03J102Lq
Mick.	13	M	Unknown	03J102Lq
Jeffry	7	M	Child	03J102Lq
MALEY, Bridget	20	F	Unknown	03J102Lq
CUNNINGHAM, D.	20	M	Unknown	03J102Lq
MCCAULY, Ann	22	F	Unknown	03J102Lq
MARTIN, Danl.	20	M	Unknown	03J102Lq
FORD, Martha	34	F	Unknown	03J102Lq
Jas.	12	M	Unknown	03J102Lq
Jas.	10	M	Unknown	03J102Lq
Priscilla	8	F	Child	03J102Lq
Oswald	6	M	Child	03J102Lq
John	3	M	Child	03J102Lq
Died-At-Sea				
GILLHOOLY, Rose	50	F	Unknown	03J102Lq
Peter	22	M	Unknown	03J102Lq
Pat	20	M	Unknown	03J102Lq
Jno.	11	M	Unknown	03J102Lq
Cath.	9	F	Child	03J102Lq
KENNEY, Jas.	20	M	Unknown	03J102Lq
WILLIAMS, Mary	30	F	Unknown	03J102Lq
Amos	9	M	Child	03J102Lq
CONNERTY, John	57	M	Unknown	03J102Lq
Mary	33	F	Unknown	03J102Lq
DENNEL, Jeffrey	45	M	Unknown	03J102Lq
MAXIL, Mary	23	F	Unknown	03J102Lq
MORRISEY, Bridget	11	F	Unknown	03J102Lq
SHEILDEN, Cath.	20	F	Unknown	03J102Lq
KILLEN, Jas.	16	M	Unknown	03J102Lq

NAMES OF PASSENGERS	AGE	SEX	OCCUPATIONS	DATE PORT SHIP
KILLEN, Brid.	15	F	Unknown	03J102Lq
Mary	11	F	Unknown	03J102Lq
MCDONNEL, Terrance	51	M	Unknown	03J102Lq
John	17	M	Unknown	03J102Lq
Mary	8	F	Child	03J102Lq
MULLARY, Morris	50	M	Unknown	03J102Lq
Mary	50	F	Unknown	03J102Lq
Mary	22	F	Unknown	03J102Lq
Cath.	24	F	Unknown	03J102Lq
HADDOCK, John	25	M	Unknown	03J102Lq
Brid.	18	F	Unknown	03J102Lq
Phelix	24	M	Unknown	03J102Lq
KIRBY, Jas.	23	M	Unknown	03J102Lq
Mary	21	F	Unknown	03J102Lq
CONWAY, Wm.	20	M	Unknown	03J102Lq
Tim.	22	M	Unknown	03J102Lq
KILNER, Wm.	43	M	Unknown	03J102Lq
U-Mrs.	33	F	Unknown	03J102Lq
Jas.	19	M	Unknown	03J102Lq
Wm.	19	M	Unknown	03J102Lq
Gor.	22	M	Unknown	03J102Lq
James	10	M	Unknown	03J102Lq
Jane	8	F	Child	03J102Lq
Edward	6	M	Child	03J102Lq
John	.03	M	Infant	03J102Lq
KELS, Thos.	20	M	Unknown	03J102Lq
CUNNINGHAM, Thos.	21	M	Unknown	03J102Lq
FLANNIGAN, Langlen	50	M	Unknown	03J102Lq
James	20	M	Unknown	03J102Lq
Mary	16	F	Unknown	03J102Lq
Peggy	13	F	Unknown	03J102Lq
U	20	F	Unknown	03J102Lq
Mary	50	F	Unknown	03J102Lq
Pat.	22	M	Unknown	03J102Lq
Mary	.06	F	Infant	03J102Lq
THERP, Jas.	22	M	Unknown	03J102Lq

VIRGINIA 03 JULY 1849

From Liverpool

NAMES OF PASSENGERS	AGE	SEX	OCCUPATIONS	DATE PORT SHIP
COOK, Pat.	30	M	Farmer	03J102Lv
Mary	35	F	Farmer	03J102Lv
Edward	17	M	Farmer	03J102Lv
Margaret	16	F	Farmer	03J102Lv
John	13	M	Farmer	03J102Lv
Pat	.00	M	Infant	03J102Lv
OSBORNE, William	45	M	Butcher	03J102Lv
George	36	M	Butcher	03J102Lv
John	43	M	Butcher	03J102Lv
Judy	45	F	None	03J102Lv
Michael	18	M	Butcher	03J102Lv
Honora	15	F	None	03J102Lv
Ellen	9	F	Child	03J102Lv
John	6	M	Child	03J102Lv
James	15	M	Unknown	03J102Lv
Margaret	12	F	None	03J102Lv
Mary-Ann	9	F	Child	03J102Lv
Thomas	40	M	Butcher	03J102Lv
Deborah	20	F	None	03J102Lv
Catherine	3	F	Child	03J102Lv
MAKEN, Stephen	25	M	Laborer	03J102Lv
John	23	M	Laborer	03J102Lv
KEINAN, Thomas	13	M	Laborer	03J102Lv
FOX, Charles	30	M	Laborer	03J102Lv
BRADY, Mathew	50	M	Laborer	03J102Lv
Pat.	25	M	Laborer	03J102Lv
Mathew	15	M	Laborer	03J102Lv
MCGREARY, Pat.	18	M	Laborer	03J102Lv

NAMES OF PASSENGERS	AGE	SEX	OCCUPATIONS	DATE PORT SHIP
SHANLEY, Owen	30	M	Laborer	03J102Lv
DOHERTY, Henry	26	M	Farmer	03J102Lv
Fanny	22	F	Farmer	03J102Lv
Jane	24	F	Farmer	03J102Lv
John	.00	M	Infant	03J102Lv
CALHOUN, Arthur	30	M	Farmer	03J102Lv
Eliza.	28	F	None	03J102Lv
William	12	M	None	03J102Lv
Margaret	9	F	Child	03J102Lv
Susan	.00	F	Infant	03J102Lv
FLEMING, Nancy	23	F	None	03J102Lv
BRACKEN, Catherine	30	F	Spinster	03J102Lv
OWENS, Ann	25	F	Spinster	03J102Lv
BRACKEN, Jane	15	F	Spinster	03J102Lv
Sarah	12	F	Spinster	03J102Lv
Ann	9	F	Child	03J102Lv
Catherine	6	F	Child	03J102Lv
Mary	.00	F	Infant	03J102Lv
DONNELLY, Catherine	22	F	Spinster	03J102Lv
FOGARTY, Charles	18	M	Laborer	03J102Lv
BUTLER, Thomas	26	M	Laborer	03J102Lv
FOGARTY, Peggy	10	F	Child	03J102Lv
Ellen	15	F	None	03J102Lv
RYAN, Denis	60	M	Laborer	03J102Lv
Denis	32	M	Laborer	03J102Lv
James	26	M	Laborer	03J102Lv
Grace	60	F	None	03J102Lv
Deborah	32	F	Laborer	03J102Lv
Dennis	3	M	Child	03J102Lv
Mary	.00	F	Infant	03J102Lv
FINNERTY, James	29	M	Laborer	03J102Lv
BRENNAN, Michael	27	M	Laborer	03J102Lv
Catherine	29	F	Laborer	03J102Lv
MCLAUGHLIN, Pat.	55	M	Laborer	03J102Lv
Mary	50	F	None	03J102Lv
John	19	M	Laborer	03J102Lv
Ellen	17	F	Laborer	03J102Lv
Betty-Ann	15	F	Laborer	03J102Lv
Daniel	13	M	Laborer	03J102Lv
Mary	11	M	Laborer	03J102Lv
Cecelia	7	F	Child	03J102Lv
James	5	M	Child	03J102Lv
REARDEN, Michael	22	M	Laborer	03J102Lv
MAHONEY, Pat.	22	M	Laborer	03J102Lv
FLYNN, William	22	M	Laborer	03J102Lv
REGAN, William	25	M	Laborer	03J102Lv
QUINNE, Lawrence	25	M	Laborer	03J102Lv
LOOBY, Edward	25	M	Laborer	03J102Lv
HALPRIN, Pat.	38	M	Laborer	03J102Lv
SLATTERY, James	30	M	Laborer	03J102Lv
OBRIEN, Tim.	30	M	Laborer	03J102Lv
EAGLE, Sarah	20	F	Laborer	03J102Lv
MCNANELY, John	13	M	Laborer	03J102Lv
MCGINLEY, Pat.	26	M	Laborer	03J102Lv
KEENAN, Mary	16	F	Laborer	03J102Lv
TODD, Jane	50	F	Laborer	03J102Lv
John	12	M	Laborer	03J102Lv
MCMURRY, Mary	20	F	Laborer	03J102Lv
Ann-Jane	.00	F	Infant	03J102Lv
KEARNEY, Richard	22	M	Laborer	03J102Lv
Lydia	21	F	Laborer	03J102Lv
FINLEY, Martin	30	M	Laborer	03J102Lv
MOONEY, Tim.	25	M	Laborer	03J102Lv
MITCHELL, Michael	60	M	Laborer	03J102Lv
John	30	M	Laborer	03J102Lv
Pat.	27	M	Laborer	03J102Lv
Daniel	24	M	Laborer	03J102Lv
Joseph	22	M	Laborer	03J102Lv
FERGUSON, James	14	M	Laborer	03J102Lv
MCKEOGH, Bernard	22	M	Laborer	03J102Lv
Mary	16	F	Laborer	03J102Lv
MCKENNERTY, John	35	M	Laborer	03J102Lv
Michael	30	M	Laborer	03J102Lv
Honora	25	F	Laborer	03J102Lv
GARDLIN, Bernard	25	M	Laborer	03J102Lv

NAMES OF PASSENGERS	AGE	SEX	OCCUPATIONS	DATE PORT SHIP
MCCARTLEY, Bernard	35	M	Laborer	03J102Lv
MCGOWAN, Pat.	28	M	Laborer	03J102Lv
Mary	26	F	Laborer	03J102Lv
MCKENNEY, Pat.	19	M	Laborer	03J102Lv
SCOTT, William	25	M	Laborer	03J102Lv
John	22	M	Laborer	03J102Lv
WRIGHT, Joshua	20	M	Laborer	03J102Lv
MILLON, Mary	22	F	Laborer	03J102Lv
Mary	.00	F	Infant	03J102Lv
PATTESON, Joseph	55	M	Laborer	03J102Lv
Jane	50	F	Laborer	03J102Lv
Nancy	13	F	Laborer	03J102Lv
John	12	M	Laborer	03J102Lv
Mary-Jane	7	F	Child	03J102Lv
JOHNSON, William	20	M	Laborer	03J102Lv
JAMIESON, Robert	20	M	Laborer	03J102Lv
WELCH, Richard	40	M	Laborer	03J102Lv
Nancy	50	F	Laborer	03J102Lv
Rose	7	F	Child	03J102Lv
OHARA, Hugh	13	M	Laborer	03J102Lv
EGAN, Catherine	27	F	Laborer	03J102Lv
DOWNEY, Pat.	36	M	Laborer	03J102Lv
Michael	34	M	Laborer	03J102Lv
Mary	20	F	Laborer	03J102Lv
Johanna	.00	F	Infant	03J102Lv
KENNEDY, Michael	30	M	Laborer	03J102Lv
Catherine	20	F	Laborer	03J102Lv
NOWLAN, Richard	40	M	Laborer	03J102Lv
CANANE, Michael	20	M	Laborer	03J102Lv
CARDIFF, John	35	M	Mechanic	03J102Lv
Eliza.	20	F	None	03J102Lv
William	4	M	Child	03J102Lv
Francis	.00	F	Infant	03J102Lv
Died-At-Sea				
MCDONNELL, Catherine	18	F	None	03J102Lv
CAMPBELL, Pat.	21	M	Laborer	03J102Lv
John	17	M	Laborer	03J102Lv
FEELAN, Mary	30	F	None	03J102Lv
John	.00	M	Infant	03J102Lv
MEEHAN, James	20	M	Laborer	03J102Lv
RYAN, Henry	25	M	Laborer	03J102Lv
Betty	20	F	None	03J102Lv
Judy	20	F	None	03J102Lv
KEARNEY, Ann	20	F	None	03J102Lv
BROPHY, Margaret	36	F	None	03J102Lv
KEARNEY, Catherine	26	F	None	03J102Lv
Julia	6	F	Child	03J102Lv
Catherine	.00	F	Infant	03J102Lv
BOYHAM, James	25	M	Laborer	03J102Lv
HOUGHTON, William	33	M	Laborer	03J102Lv
CAUGHLIN, James	25	M	Laborer	03J102Lv
CONWAY, Mary	30	F	Laborer	03J102Lv
BUTLER, John	23	M	Laborer	03J102Lv
Michael	20	M	Laborer	03J102Lv
LEARY, Daniel	16	M	Laborer	03J102Lv
WARD, William	40	M	Laborer	03J102Lv
BRADLEY, Elizabeth	22	F	Laborer	03J102Lv
DOWELL, Pat.	40	M	Laborer	03J102Lv
Mary	32	F	Laborer	03J102Lv
Edmund	.00	M	Infant	03J102Lv
Mary	.00	F	Infant	03J102Lv
MCKENNA, Margt.	60	F	None	03J102Lv
MCCALVAGH, M	2	M	Child	03J102Lv
PURCELL, William	26	M	Laborer	03J102Lv
CROMPTON, William	30	M	Laborer	03J102Lv
MCDERMOTT, Thomas	19	M	Laborer	03J102Lv
REGAN, Cornelius	20	M	Laborer	03J102Lv
HEGARTY, Daniel	10	M	Child	03J102Lv
KEENAN, Henry	20	M	Laborer	03J102Lv
SALLY, Margt.	40	F	Laborer	03J102Lv
Catherine	16	F	Laborer	03J102Lv
Eliza.	14	F	Laborer	03J102Lv
James	9	M	Laborer	03J102Lv
Mary	7	F	Child	03J102Lv
HAYES, Betsy	20	F	Laborer	03J102Lv
DONOVAN, Margaret	20	F	Spinster	03J102Lv
THOMPSON, James	30	M	Farmer	03J102Lv
U-Mrs.	30	F	Farmer	03J102Lv
REILLY, Thomas	20	M	Farmer	03J102Lv
Rose	14	F	Farmer	03J102Lv
MURPHY, James	30	M	Laborer	03J102Lv
MULLHOLLAND, William	28	M	Laborer	03J102Lv
Rose	25	F	Laborer	03J102Lv
GANNAH, Thomas	14	M	Laborer	03J102Lv
CAUGHLIN, Catherine	25	F	Laborer	03J102Lv
MCCLUSKY, Catherine	20	F	Laborer	03J102Lv
RATTIGAN, Catherine	20	F	Laborer	03J102Lv
Michael	21	M	Laborer	03J102Lv
FLYNN, James	20	M	Laborer	03J102Lv
CALLAGHER, Pat.	20	M	Laborer	03J102Lv
FEE, Jane	15	F	Laborer	03J102Lv
JOYCE, Martin	23	M	Laborer	03J102Lv
LEELEY, Mary	25	F	Laborer	03J102Lv
REGAN, Pat.	26	M	Laborer	03J102Lv
CAMPBELL, Andrew	26	M	Laborer	03J102Lv
PERRY, Fanny	28	F	Laborer	03J102Lv
PAYNE, William	23	M	Laborer	03J102Lv
MCCOY, John	19	M	Laborer	03J102Lv
Martha	17	F	Laborer	03J102Lv
THOMPSON, James	17	M	Laborer	03J102Lv
GREEN, Mary	20	F	Laborer	03J102Lv
MCCOY, Alex	13	M	Laborer	03J102Lv
Margt.	22	F	Laborer	03J102Lv
MAHONEY, Tim.	24	M	Laborer	03J102Lv
SPEAKMAN, Margt.	20	F	Laborer	03J102Lv
CASH, Pat.	29	M	Laborer	03J102Lv
U-Mrs.	29	F	Laborer	03J102Lv
Margt.	.00	F	Infant	03J102Lv
MULLONEY, James	27	M	Laborer	03J102Lv
U-Mrs.	27	F	Laborer	03J102Lv
ARMSTRONG, Thomas	30	M	Laborer	03J102Lv
FENN, John	30	M	Laborer	03J102Lv
Mary	60	F	None	03J102Lv
Mary	18	F	None	03J102Lv
HESSEN, Thomas	25	M	Laborer	03J102Lv
BOYD, John	22	M	Laborer	03J102Lv
GILLESPIE, George	25	M	Laborer	03J102Lv
U-Mrs.	25	F	Laborer	03J102Lv
Susan	.00	F	Infant	03J102Lv
Margt.	.00	F	Infant	03J102Lv
MORROW, Sally	15	F	None	03J102Lv
Catherine	12	F	None	03J102Lv
MULLONEY, James	30	M	Laborer	03J102Lv
Charles	20	M	Laborer	03J102Lv
BUTLER, John	20	M	Laborer	03J102Lv
EGAN, Catherine	40	F	Laborer	03J102Lv
MCMAHON, Pat	35	M	Laborer	03J102Lv
Marcella	36	F	Laborer	03J102Lv
Thomas	12	M	Laborer	03J102Lv
Catherine	6	F	Child	03J102Lv
Peter	.00	M	Infant	03J102Lv
QUIRK, William	17	M	Laborer	03J102Lv
MURPHY, John	28	M	Mason	03J102Lv
CAMPBELL, James	18	M	Unknown	03J102Lv
BOYCE, James	28	M	Unknown	03J102Lv
FEENEY, Mary	10	F	None	03J102Lv
TODD, Jane	00	F	None	03J102Lv
OSBORNE, Geo.	00	M	None	03J102Lv
MCLAUGHLIN, Ellen	00	F	None	03J102Lv
CARDIFF, Michael	00	M	None	03J102Lv

CHARLES-SAUNDERS 03 JULY 1849

From Liverpool

NAMES OF PASSENGERS	AGE	SEX	OCCUPATIONS	DATE PORT SHIP
RICHARDSON, Wm.	42	M	Grocer	03Jl02Lu
Thos.	18	M	Unknown	03Jl02Lu
Robert	12	M	Unknown	03Jl02Lu
William	18	M	Unknown	03Jl02Lu
Eliza	8	F	Child	03Jl02Lu
Maria	5	F	Child	03Jl02Lu
John	.00	M	Infant	03Jl02Lu
RUSSELL, Robert	30	M	Nailer	03Jl02Lu
MCIVER, Robert	28	M	Unknown	03Jl02Lu
GORMAN, Sylvester	35	M	Laborer	03Jl02Lu
DONOHOE, Pat	23	M	Laborer	03Jl02Lu
CORISTINE, Peter	24	M	Laborer	03Jl02Lu
KEARY, Bridget	26	F	Unknown	03Jl02Lu
GRIMES, Thos.	36	M	Unknown	03Jl02Lu
Bridget	23	F	Coach Maker	03Jl02Lu
Cathn.	.00	F	Infant	03Jl02Lu
Died-At-Sea				
SCANLIN, Hugh	59	M	Farmer	03Jl02Lu
Mary-Ann	16	F	Unknown	03Jl02Lu
SAVAGE, James	20	M	Gdnr	03Jl02Lu
Cathn.	21	F	Unknown	03Jl02Lu
MCCORMICK, Pat.	40	M	Clerk	03Jl02Lu
TIGHE, Pat.	27	M	Farmer	03Jl02Lu
GLENNIN, Pat.	45	M	Laborer	03Jl02Lu
Thos.	18	M	Mason	03Jl02Lu
BOURKE, Bernard	28	M	Joiner	03Jl02Lu
Bridget	24	F	Unknown	03Jl02Lu
Mary	.00	F	Infant	03Jl02Lu
MCVEY, Lawrence	36	M	Mason	03Jl02Lu
Magt.	35	F	Unknown	03Jl02Lu
Maria	10	F	Unknown	03Jl02Lu
James	8	M	Child	03Jl02Lu
John	6	M	Child	03Jl02Lu
Bridget	4	F	Child	03Jl02Lu
George	.00	M	Infant	03Jl02Lu
MOONEY, Thos.	24	M	Farmer	03Jl02Lu
MCMULLIN, Jas.	23	M	Laborer	03Jl02Lu
ASHPINE, John	34	M	Blacksmith	03Jl02Lu
HARRISON, Geo.	34	M	Blacksmith	03Jl02Lu
MARTIN, Thos.	38	M	Joiner	03Jl02Lu
Mary	24	F	Unknown	03Jl02Lu
Teresa	.00	F	Infant	03Jl02Lu
SMITH, Judy	30	F	Unknown	03Jl02Lu
Cath.	.00	F	Infant	03Jl02Lu
WILLIAMS, Anne	22	F	Unknown	03Jl02Lu
Rose	3	F	Child	03Jl02Lu
James	2	M	Child	03Jl02Lu
BUTTER, Pat.	28	M	Farmer	03Jl02Lu
Ellen	24	F	Unknown	03Jl02Lu
Betty	11	F	Unknown	03Jl02Lu
Terence	10	M	Unknown	03Jl02Lu
GIBBON, James	30	M	Laborer	03Jl02Lu
BOURKE, Patrick	40	M	Farmer	03Jl02Lu
Elizth.	30	F	Unknown	03Jl02Lu
Alice	6	F	Child	03Jl02Lu
Peter	4	M	Child	03Jl02Lu
WHITE, Ellen	21	F	Unknown	03Jl02Lu
BAGNET, Cath.	19	F	Unknown	03Jl02Lu
GIBNEY, Luke	25	M	Laborer	03Jl02Lu
MCEVOY, Michl.	33	M	Farmer	03Jl02Lu
Lucy	28	F	Unknown	03Jl02Lu
Mary	11	F	Unknown	03Jl02Lu
Winifred	8	F	Child	03Jl02Lu
Cathr.	6	F	Child	03Jl02Lu
MCGUINN, Anne	17	F	Unknown	03Jl02Lu
HIGGINS, Michl.	24	M	Laborer	03Jl02Lu
GALHOOLY, Michl.	24	M	Laborer	03Jl02Lu
John	22	M	Laborer	03Jl02Lu
EVERY, Philip	36	M	Flaxdr	03Jl02Lu
DUFFY, Bernard	24	M	Laborer	03Jl02Lu
SWEENY, John	24	M	Butler	03Jl02Lu
NEAGLE, James	24	M	Laborer	03Jl02Lu
Cath.	22	F	Unknown	03Jl02Lu
Mary	6	F	Child	03Jl02Lu
Nancy	21	F	Unknown	03Jl02Lu
STAGG, Joseph	45	M	Basketmaker	03Jl02Lu
Anne	42	F	Unknown	03Jl02Lu
Anne	23	F	Unknown	03Jl02Lu
Arthur	3	M	Child	03Jl02Lu
LINDSAY, Wm.	21	M	Coach Maker	03Jl02Lu
Martha	21	F	Unknown	03Jl02Lu
SCANLIN, Pat.	24	M	Farmer	03Jl02Lu
MOORE, Robt.	26	M	Fisherman	03Jl02Lu
WATERSON, Robert	29	M	Nailer	03Jl02Lu
Ann	25	F	Unknown	03Jl02Lu
Christopher	2	M	Child	03Jl02Lu
Eliza	5	F	Child	03Jl02Lu
Eleanor	.00	F	Infant	03Jl02Lu
QUIGLEY, Patrick	24	M	Laborer	03Jl02Lu
DALE, Patrick	23	M	Laborer	03Jl02Lu
KENNEDY, Dennis	24	M	Laborer	03Jl02Lu
DOOLEY, Andy	24	M	Laborer	03Jl02Lu
CLEARY, Pat.	21	M	Laborer	03Jl02Lu
TAYLOR, Mary	25	F	Laborer	03Jl02Lu
Sam.	6	M	Child	03Jl02Lu
Hubert	4	M	Child	03Jl02Lu
STUBBS, James	23	M	Unknown	03Jl02Lu
RUTHERFORD, Willm.	24	M	Blr	03Jl02Lu
Isabella	21	F	Unknown	03Jl02Lu
TOOLE, Edw.	40	M	Laborer	03Jl02Lu
BLACK, Duncan	28	M	Shpc	03Jl02Lu
MCNAIR, Duncan	24	M	Laborer	03Jl02Lu
LIVINGSTON, Alexr.	21	M	Farmer	03Jl02Lu
Sarah	20	F	Unknown	03Jl02Lu
BLACK, Loughlin	3	M	Child	03Jl02Lu
Mary	.00	F	Infant	03Jl02Lu
LONG, Robt.	24	M	Laborer	03Jl02Lu
PARSON, Sextus	24	M	Tailor	03Jl02Lu
ILEY, Willm.	24	M	Sawer	03Jl02Lu
TAYLOR, James	24	M	Weaver	03Jl02Lu
NEWBY, Wilson	24	M	Mariner	03Jl02Lu
CORCORAN, Jas.	38	M	Farmer	03Jl02Lu
Johannah	30	F	Unknown	03Jl02Lu
Mary	5	F	Child	03Jl02Lu
John	3	M	Child	03Jl02Lu
Thos.	.00	M	Infant	03Jl02Lu
POWER, John	20	M	Laborer	03Jl02Lu
MULLEN, Wm.	25	M	Butcher	03Jl02Lu
CONROY, Michl.	26	M	Laborer	03Jl02Lu
WALTERS, David	40	M	Joiner	03Jl02Lu
MCGUIRE, John	46	M	Farmer	03Jl02Lu
Crn.	10	F	Unknown	03Jl02Lu
TRACY, Martin	28	M	Farmer	03Jl02Lu
OLEARY, Jno.	24	M	Grocer	03Jl02Lu
MARYAN, Jno.	30	M	Laborer	03Jl02Lu
Mary	18	F	Unknown	03Jl02Lu
GANNON, Michl.	28	M	Laborer	03Jl02Lu
ADLER, David	27	M	Butcher	03Jl02Lu
Beteke	31	F	Unknown	03Jl02Lu
Hancke	29	M	Unknown	03Jl02Lu
Solomon	6	M	Child	03Jl02Lu
Adelheid	3	F	Child	03Jl02Lu
QUINNEGAN, Winefred	8	F	Child	03Jl02Lu
Mary	16	F	Unknown	03Jl02Lu
MCNALLY, Mary-Ann	16	F	Unknown	03Jl02Lu
Mary	22	F	Unknown	03Jl02Lu
GIBBIN, John	23	M	Blacksmith	03Jl02L
James	22	M	Blacksmith	03Jl02Lu
LARKIN, Anne	24	F	Unknown	03Jl02Lu
CONNAUGHTON, John	24	M	Farmer	03Jl02L

NAMES OF PASSENGERS	AGE	SEX	OCCUPATIONS	DATE PORT SHIP
CONNAUGHTON, Patrick	36	M	Farmer	03J102Lu
Wm.	24	M	Laborer	03J102Lu
PADEN, Henry	26	M	Laborer	03J102Lu
CONNAUGHTON, Benj.	18	M	Laborer	03J102Lu
Mary-Ann	12	F	Unknown	03J102Lu
DUFFY, Patrick	10	M	Unknown	03J102Lu
Maria	6	F	Child	03J102Lu
DONLIN, Thos.	20	M	Laborer	03J102Lu
ROURKE, Mary	18	F	Unknown	03J102Lu
KENNEDY, Anne	18	F	Unknown	03J102Lu
PRESTON, James	20	M	Laborer	03J102Lu
BRIEN, Daniel	24	M	Plasterer	03J102Lu
Magt.	21	F	Unknown	03J102Lu
FARRELL, John	24	M	Farmer	03J102Lu
U (W)	24	F	Unknown	03J102Lu
U	.00	F	Infant	03J102Lu
Mary	17	F	Unknown	03J102Lu
Anne	20	F	Unknown	03J102Lu
CASHIER, Wm.	20	M	Laborer	03J102Lu
MCCORMICK, Anne	19	F	Unknown	03J102Lu
MURPHY, James	21	M	Shpc	03J102Lu
John	17	M	Shpc	03J102Lu
CONNEFORD, George	40	M	Laborer	03J102Lu
Mary	40	F	Unknown	03J102Lu
John	16	M	Laborer	03J102Lu
Cathr.	12	F	Unknown	03J102Lu
Bridget	10	F	Unknown	03J102Lu
Rose	5	F	Child	03J102Lu
Lawrence	3	M	Child	03J102Lu
Jane	.00	F	Infant	03J102Lu
BYRNE, Thos.	26	M	Laborer	03J102Lu
HENNESY, Mar[illegible]n	14	M	Laborer	03J102Lu
MURPHY, Eliza	14	F	Unknown	03J102Lu
GALVIN, Mary-Ann	21	F	Unknown	03J102Lu
DUNNE, Ann	18	F	Unknown	03J102Lu
CASSIDY, Ann	20	F	Unknown	03J102Lu
BAGNET, John	58	M	Laborer	03J102Lu
MAHAN, Pat.	21	M	Unknown	03J102Lu
Anne	19	F	Unknown	03J102Lu
CASSIN, Robt.	17	M	Unknown	03J102Lu
GILMORE, Wm.	42	M	Laborer	03J102Lu
MULLIN, Margt.	23	F	Unknown	03J102Lu
Bridget	21	F	Unknown	03J102Lu
MCGUIRE, Ellen	21	F	Unknown	03J102Lu
LIVINGSTIN, Rose-Ann	15	F	Unknown	03J102Lu
NOWLEN, Mary	50	F	Unknown	03J102Lu
Bridget	19	F	Unknown	03J102Lu
Eliza	20	F	Unknown	03J102Lu
KEAN, John	7	M	Child	03J102Lu
DONNELLY, Wm.	24	M	Laborer	03J102Lu
U	.00	F	Infant	03J102Lu
HAFERTY, John	24	M	Laborer	03J102Lu
COSGRAVE, James	22	M	Bleacher	03J102Lu
James	22	M	Laborer	03J102Lu
John	20	M	Laborer	03J102Lu
Bessy	17	F	Laborer	03J102Lu
SIXTON, C.	52	F	Unknown	03J102Lu
Thos.	20	M	Laborer	03J102Lu
KELLY, John	17	M	Unknown	03J102Lu
CLUNY, James	23	M	Laborer	03J102Lu
FOX, Cath.	18	F	Unknown	03J102Lu
WILLIN, Charlotte	30	F	Unknown	03J102Lu
RICHY, Bridget	20	F	Unknown	03J102Lu
ROURKE, Michl.	26	M	Unknown	03J102Lu
CONNIFFE, Jno.	20	M	Unknown	03J102Lu
MULLEN, James	23	M	Unknown	03J102Lu
BRYSON, Anne	15	F	Unknown	03J102Lu
NOWLEN, Dennis	19	M	Laborer	03J102Lu
FORESTER, Eliza	24	F	Unknown	03J102Lu
DONNELLY, Patrick	25	M	Laborer	03J102Lu
COLERICK, Rosey	25	F	Unknown	03J102Lu
BAYLESS, Wm.	21	M	Laborer	03J102Lu
MATTHEWS, Henry	18	M	Laborer	03J102Lu
SHEARLOCK, Edwd.	13	M	Yeoman	03J102Lu
Mary	15	F	Unknown	03J102Lu
BREEKINZY, John	28	M	Laborer	03J102Lu
Jane	24	F	Unknown	03J102Lu
ARMSTRONG, John	20	M	Laborer	03J102Lu
MALONE, Richd.	24	M	Laborer	03J102Lu
Bridget	20	F	Unknown	03J102Lu
GAHAN, Mary	21	F	Unknown	03J102Lu
KINNEGAN, John	24	M	Farmer	03J102Lu
OHARA, Morris	20	M	Laborer	03J102Lu
FLEMMING, Sarah	18	F	Unknown	03J102Lu
LAUGHLIN, Pat.	24	M	Laborer	03J102Lu
MULLINS, Thos.	20	M	Unknown	03J102Lu
CARTY, Mary	20	F	Unknown	03J102Lu
DOWD, Winny	18	F	Unknown	03J102Lu
Mary	18	F	Unknown	03J102Lu
SWEENEY, Owen	60	M	Farmer	03J102Lu
Mary	18	F	Unknown	03J102Lu
Ellen	16	F	Unknown	03J102Lu
Margt.	12	F	Unknown	03J102Lu
Owen	10	M	Unknown	03J102Lu
Willm.	8	M	Child	03J102Lu
Hugh	3	M	Child	03J102Lu
Patrick	25	M	Laborer	03J102Lu
Julia	24	F	Unknown	03J102Lu
Margt.	11	F	Unknown	03J102Lu
DUNNE, John	30	M	Laborer	03J102Lu
Julia	24	F	Unknown	03J102Lu
Mary	.00	F	Infant	03J102Lu
GREENE, Joseph	24	M	Sawer	03J102Lu
John	22	M	Sawer	03J102Lu
MURRAY, Francis	20	M	Mason	03J102Lu
BYRNE, John	45	M	Chptr	03J102Lu
BRADY, Francis	24	M	Tailor	03J102Lu
MCSMALL, Peter	20	M	Unknown	03J102Lu
Honora	21	F	Unknown	03J102Lu
MCDONALD, Honora-Henry	8	F	Child	03J102Lu
MCNUNN, Maria	22	F	Unknown	03J102Lu
Sarah	20	F	Unknown	03J102Lu
CASTINE, Dennis	40	M	Laborer	03J102Lu
Patrick	10	M	Laborer	03J102Lu
Cornelius	8	M	Child	03J102Lu
TENNINE, Mary	30	F	Unknown	03J102Lu
NEWCUMMIN, Rach.	17	F	Unknown	03J102Lu
TULLY, Mich.	24	M	Laborer	03J102Lu
SULLIVAN, Mary	28	F	Unknown	03J102Lu
Bessy	18	F	Unknown	03J102Lu
OSHEA, Pierce	35	M	Draper	03J102Lu
Johanna	30	F	Unknown	03J102Lu
Jane	6	F	Child	03J102Lu
Edwd.	5	M	Child	03J102Lu
Wm.	3	M	Child	03J102Lu
Catherine	1	F	Child	03J102Lu
DELANY, Mary	28	F	Unknown	03J102Lu
GLEESON, Mary	17	F	Unknown	03J102Lu
FITZGERALD, Mary	35	F	Unknown	03J102Lu
OLEARY, Margt.	40	F	Unknown	03J102Lu
Mary	17	F	Unknown	03J102Lu
HENRY, Jas.Rev.	45	M	Clergyman	03J102Lu
HEWIT, Edwd.	38	M	Unknown	03J102Lu
Died-At-Sea				
POWER, Cath.	24	F	Unknown	03J102Lu
Died-At-Sea				
John	.00	M	Infant	03J102Lu
Died-At-Sea				
ONEIL, Magt.	30	F	Unknown	03J102Lu
Died-At-Sea				
LYONS, Anne	20	F	Unknown	03J102Lu
Died-At-Sea				
DONNELLY, Jane	26	F	Unknown	03J102Lu
NOWLEN, Anne	12	F	Unknown	03J102Lu

NAMES OF PASSENGERS	AGE	SEX	OCCUPATIONS	DATE PORT SHIP

ESCORT 03 JULY 1849

From Newport

NAMES OF PASSENGERS	AGE	SEX	OCCUPATIONS	DATE PORT SHIP
STABB, John	40	M	Mechanic	03J131Ln
Wm.	18	M	Mechanic	03J131Ln
ANSTEY, Fredk.	23	M	Mechanic	03J131Ln

W.H.HARBECK 03 JULY 1849

From Liverpool

NAMES OF PASSENGERS	AGE	SEX	OCCUPATIONS	DATE PORT SHIP
MCMAHON, Dennis	21	M	Laborer	03J102Lr
HOGAN, Mary-J.	9	F	Child	03J102Lr
COSE, Michael	28	M	Laborer	03J102Lr
REACH, Mary	20	F	Servant	03J102Lr
GANNON, Thomas	68	M	Farmer	03J102Lr
James	30	M	Farmer	03J102Lr
OAKLEY, Martin	27	M	Spinster	03J102Lr
Catharine	21	F	Joiner	03J102Lr
GANNON, Mary	32	F	Spinster	03J102Lr
MULLENARY, Ann	50	F	WI	03J102Lr
Bridget	11	F	Spinster	03J102Lr
Rachael	9	F	Child	03J102Lr
Mary	19	F	Spinster	03J102Lr
DUGGIN, Catharine	17	F	Spinster	03J102Lr
MCHEALY, Catharine	15	F	Spinster	03J102Lr
MUCKIDY, Thomas	13	M	None	03J102Lr
CRANNOW, Matt	28	M	Laborer	03J102Lr
Mary	10	F	None	03J102Lr
Peter	11	M	None	03J102Lr
Patt	9	M	Child	03J102Lr
DORAN, Edward	13	M	None	03J102Lr
COUGHTON, Richard	20	M	Laborer	03J102Lr
Eliza	19	F	Spinster	03J102Lr
KENEDY, Mary	21	F	Spinster	03J102Lr
CLANCY, Mary	50	F	WI	03J102Lr
FLYNN, Thomas	13	M	Laborer	03J102Lr
JORDAN, Mary	27	F	Servant	03J102Lr
John	10	M	None	03J102Lr
Hugh	6	M	Child	03J102Lr
WADE, James	18	M	None	03J102Lr
DIVINE, Owen	22	M	None	03J102Lr
MUSTER, John	22	M	None	03J102Lr
FITZGIBBON, Michael	29	M	Laborer	03J102Lr
John	21	M	Laborer	03J102Lr
VAUGHN, Patk.	23	M	Laborer	03J102Lr
Wm.	20	M	Laborer	03J102Lr
BENNETT, Catharine	22	F	Laborer	03J102Lr
Mary	16	F	Laborer	03J102Lr
HUGH, Thos.M.	27	M	Watchmaker	03J102Lr
Jane-M.	20	F	None	03J102Lr
ARMSTRONG, Jane	43	F	Draper	03J102Lr
Mary-Ann	22	F	Yarn Winder	03J102Lr
Daniel	15	M	Office Boy	03J102Lr
Ellen	10	F	Spinster	03J102Lr
BATTLE, Matt	20	M	Dyer	03J102Lr
FINN, Pattk.	25	M	Dyer	03J102Lr
HENRY, Auther	34	M	Tanner	03J102Lr
GRAY, Patk.	23	M	Laborer	03J102Lr
MCDONALD, Wm.	25	M	Farmer	03J102Lr
DONELLES, Micheal	23	M	Farmer	03J102Lr
CONNELLY, Thomas	23	M	Blacksmith	03J102Lr
CONNELL, Daniel	22	M	Farmer	03J102Lr
Susan	18	F	Farmer	03J102Lr
IGO, Thomas	37	M	Laborer	03J102Lr
WALLACE, Mary-Ann	25	F	Spinster	03J102Lr
REEVES, Ellen	20	F	Spinster	03J102Lr
REILEY, Catherine	24	F	Spinster	03J102Lr
OBRIEN, John	34	M	Tailor	03J102Lr
Margaret	30	F	Tailor	03J102Lr
Mary	10	F	Tailor	03J102Lr
CUMMINS, John	16	M	Servant	03J102Lr
HOGAN, Michael	17	M	Carpenter	03J102Lr
ENNIS, Wm.	13	M	None	03J102Lr
NEARY, John	20	M	Farmer	03J102Lr
SHENAN, Corns.	40	M	Farmer	03J102Lr
Ellen	30	F	Farmer	03J102Lr
Ann	8	F	Child	03J102Lr
Hannah	2	F	Child	03J102Lr
Ellen	.09	F	Infant	03J102Lr
BARBERRY, Phillip	60	M	Bleacher	03J102Lr
John	20	M	Bleacher	03J102Lr
RACK, Daniel	21	M	Laborer	03J102Lr
GOUGH, Thomas	25	M	Shepherd	03J102Lr
ROCECK, Mary	20	F	Servant	03J102Lr
MAKEY, Bridget	25	F	Servant	03J102Lr
Mary	28	F	Servant	03J102Lr
HOGAN, Timothy	22	M	Plasterer	03J102Lr
PEMBROKE, Thomas	22	M	Servant	03J102Lr
MURPHY, Joseph	23	M	Laborer	03J102Lr
MACK, Garrett	38	M	Laborer	03J102Lr
Ellen	14	F	Laborer	03J102Lr
Ann	21	F	Laborer	03J102Lr
BROWN, Ellen	15	F	Spinster	03J102Lr
MCCHURCH, Ellen	18	F	Spinster	03J102Lr
DOWNES, James	27	M	Laborer	03J102Lr
FLYNNE, William	20	M	Laborer	03J102Lr
CLANCY, Richard	25	M	Unknown	03J102Lr
Mary	50	F	Servant	03J102Lr
Magt.	22	F	Servant	03J102Lr
DUFFEE, Catharine	60	F	WI	03J102Lr
Bernard	30	M	Laborer	03J102Lr
IRELAND, Patk.	22	M	Laborer	03J102Lr
DEAN, John	17	M	Laborer	03J102Lr
MCDONOUGH, Thomas	18	M	Laborer	03J102Lr
HEALY, Micheal	23	M	Laborer	03J102Lr
CONWAY, Owen	18	M	Laborer	03J102Lr
MAHONY, Daniel	32	M	Laborer	03J102Lr
HILL, William	31	M	Shoemaker	03J102Lr
CALLAGHAN, John	38	M	Laborer	03J102Lr
Died-At-Sea				
BIGGIN, Patk.	35	M	Laborer	03J102Lr
MARG, Danl.	34	M	Laborer	03J102Lr
KEWNAN, Thomas	30	M	Laborer	03J102Lr
Mary	30	F	Laborer	03J102Lr
Mary	6	F	Child	03J102Lr
MCNAMARA, James	24	M	Child	03J102Lr
AUSHE, Richd.	51	M	Laborer	03J102Lr
Thomas	38	M	Laborer	03J102Lr
Ellen	16	F	Spinster	03J102Lr
Magt.	11	F	Spinster	03J102Lr
CALLAGHAN, Catherine	13	F	Spinster	03J102Lr
SULLIVAN, Mich.	20	M	Laborer	03J102Lr
MCCONNELL, Mary	30	F	Servant	03J102Lr
Died-At-Sea				
NELLIGAN, Michl.	25	M	Laborer	03J102Lr
Julia	18	F	Spinster	03J102Lr
OAKLEY, John	36	M	Laborer	03J102Lr
DONNOVAN, Danl.	22	M	Shoemaker	03J102Lr
OLEARY, John	23	M	Farmer	03J102Lr
Ellen	17	F	Spinster	03J102Lr
COAKLEY, Janes	60	M	Spinster	03J102Lr
MEALY, James	60	M	Spinster	03J102Lr
WALSH, Mary	20	F	Spinster	03J102Lr
KELLY, Michl.	80	M	Laborer	03J102Lr
James	24	M	Laborer	03J102Lr
James	23	M	Laborer	03J102Lr

NAMES OF PASSENGERS	AGE	SEX	OCCUPATIONS	DATE PORT SHIP
MEAGHEN, John	20	M	Laborer	03J102Lr
FLANNAGAN, Thomas	17	M	Laborer	03J102Lr
Michael	16	M	Laborer	03J102Lr
TURNEY, Dennis	20	M	Laborer	03J102Lr
GLENNAN, James	32	M	Laborer	03J102Lr
Patrick	10	M	Spinster	03J102Lr
HEFFERMAN, Michl.	30	M	Spinster	03J102Lr
SLATTERY, Wm.	18	M	Spinster	03J102Lr
GALWAN, Patrick	20	M	Laborer	03J102Lr
Mary	20	F	Laborer	03J102Lr
COLEMAN, Bernard	22	M	Sail Maker	03J102Lr
John	30	M	Sail Maker	03J102Lr
KELLY, Patk.	19	M	Sail Maker	03J102Lr
HANNAN, Jeremiah	20	M	Laborer	03J102Lr
John	21	M	Laborer	03J102Lr
Margt.	28	F	Laborer	03J102Lr
Julia	17	F	Laborer	03J102Lr
FLYNNE, Michel	24	M	Laborer	03J102Lr
COTTEN, Wm.H.	40	M	Unknown	03J102Lr
Christina	34	F	None	03J102Lr
Barney	15	M	Unknown	03J102Lr
Joseph	11	M	None	03J102Lr
Blenerhasset	9	M	Child	03J102Lr
Catharine	6	F	Child	03J102Lr
Louisa	5	F	Child	03J102Lr
Eliza	2	F	Child	03J102Lr
HAMILTON, A.B.	34	M	Clerk	03J102Lr
HEALY, Eliza	26	F	Spinster	03J102Lr
Daniel	22	M	Laborer	03J102Lr
Margaret	12	F	Laborer	03J102Lr
DEMPSEY, Wm.	12	M	None	03J102Lr
SHIELDS, Christy	23	M	Carpenter	03J102Lr
Catharine	21	F	Spinster	03J102Lr
FOX, John	18	M	Laborer	03J102Lr
MONTGOMERY, Patk.	36	M	Laborer	03J102Lr
ORR, Joseph	24	M	Laborer	03J102Lr
James	20	M	Laborer	03J102Lr
KEWMAN, James	18	M	Laborer	03J102Lr
SHAW, James	40	M	Shoemaker	03J102Lr
DUGGAN, John	17	M	Laborer	03J102Lr
MCFEETRUS, John	21	M	Laborer	03J102Lr
MCJEFFEE, John	22	M	Shoemaker	03J102Lr
BLACK, Thomas	54	M	Laborer	03J102Lr
Mary	56	F	None	03J102Lr
Patk.	18	M	Servant	03J102Lr
Thomas	16	M	Servant	03J102Lr
BANNAN, Susan	25	F	Servant	03J102Lr
LYNCH, Sarah	24	F	Servant	03J102Lr
GODFREY, Jane	15	F	Laborer	03J102Lr
ARCHEW, Amelia	26	F	Laborer	03J102Lr
GANNERY, Thomas	40	M	Laborer	03J102Lr
CHOOLEHAN, Michel.	22	M	Laborer	03J102Lr
SHELY, Michel.	26	M	Laborer	03J102Lr
MALONE, Patk.	26	M	Laborer	03J102Lr
FOSTER, Mary	39	F	Wi	03J102Lr
Francis	10	F	Spinster	03J102Lr
Richd.	8	M	Child	03J102Lr
William	4	M	Child	03J102Lr
MCEVERY, Ellen	18	F	None	03J102Lr
Margt.	17	F	Spinster	03J102Lr
Mary	17	F	Spinster	03J102Lr
MCMANUS, Mary	7	F	Child	03J102Lr
HART, Ann	18	F	Spinster	03J102Lr
GORDON, Catharine	13	F	Spinster	03J102Lr
FLYNN, John	38	M	Unknown	03J102Lr
Rose	35	F	None	03J102Lr
Edward	13	M	None	03J102Lr
Joseph	11	M	None	03J102Lr
Mary	10	F	None	03J102Lr
Arthur	8	M	Child	03J102Lr
James	6	M	Child	03J102Lr
John	3	M	Child	03J102Lr
LEACY, Thomas	37	M	None	03J102Lr
MCMANUS, Rose	17	F	Coachman	03J102Lr
MONKS, Patk.	20	M	Tanner	03J102Lr
KENNEDY, Thos.	25	M	Blacksmith	03J102Lr
HEWMAN, Patk.	19	M	Laborer	03J102Lr
MERA, Catharine	3	F	Child	03J102Lr
KELLY, Rose	37	F	Wi	03J102Lr
BARKE, Richd.	52	M	Weaver	03J102Lr
Brigt.	50	F	Weaver	03J102Lr
HEEKEE, Alice	14	F	Weaver	03J102Lr
BURKE, Thomas	10	M	Weaver	03J102Lr
HECKE, Mah.	20	F	Spinster	03J102Lr
COBALLY, John	50	M	Laborer	03J102Lr
MALONE, James	28	M	Laborer	03J102Lr
DORAN, Thomas	27	M	Laborer	03J102Lr
Magt.	26	F	Farmer	03J102Lr
Mary	25	F	Farmer	03J102Lr
MEAGHEN, Johana	23	F	Spinster	03J102Lr
BENSON, John	26	M	Spinster	03J102Lr
CARROLL, Wm.	26	M	Laborer	03J102Lr
CARTHY, Jeremiah	26	M	Laborer	03J102Lr
MCDONALD, Stephen	56	M	Laborer	03J102Lr
OBRIEN, Lawrence	36	M	Laborer	03J102Lr
Mary	14	F	Spinster	03J102Lr
Danl.	45	M	Farmer	03J102Lr
Ester	30	F	Farmer	03J102Lr
Ann	14	F	Spinster	03J102Lr
Eliza	13	F	None	03J102Lr
Patrick	11	M	None	03J102Lr
Mathew	9	M	Child	03J102Lr
James	7	M	Child	03J102Lr
Mary	2	F	Child	03J102Lr
Daniel	1	M	Child	03J102Lr
KELLY, Catharine	23	F	Spinster	03J102Lr
WHEELAN, Dennis	29	M	Blacksmith	03J102Lr
Ann	24	F	Spinster	03J102Lr
Eliza	22	F	Spinster	03J102Lr
FOSTER, Thom.	20	M	Spinster	03J102Lr
BARRETT, Andrew	22	M	Land Agent	03J102Lr
MATTHEWS, Patrick	27	M	Land Agent	03J102Lr
BARRETT, Alice	27	F	Unknown	03J102Lr
HERON, Fanny	20	F	Spinster	03J102Lr
BOISE, Rebecca	20	F	Spinster	03J102Lr
CONNOVAN, Pat	26	M	Butcher	03J102Lr
MULLIGAN, Michael	42	M	Farmer	03J102Lr
FARRELL, Margaret	38	F	Wi	03J102Lr
Eliza	20	F	Spinster	03J102Lr
WOODS, Dennis	22	M	Spinster	03J102Lr
MCELLERNY, John	51	M	Spinster	03J102Lr
STARTY, Thoms.	37	M	Unknown	03J102Lr
DUFFY, Michael	24	M	Laborer	03J102Lr
MALIEDY, Thomas	25	M	Laborer	03J102Lr
GANNON, Patrk.	20	M	Laborer	03J102Lr
LANGDON, Ann	21	F	Spinster	03J102Lr
KENNER, Mary-Ann	19	F	Spinster	03J102Lr
WARD, Eliza	35	F	Servant	03J102Lr
VAID, Wm.	36	M	Farmer	03J102Lr
Julia	35	F	Farmer	03J102Lr
Joseph	11	M	Farmer	03J102Lr
Corns.	9	M	Child	03J102Lr
John	7	M	Child	03J102Lr
Margt.	3	F	Child	03J102Lr
Joseph	79	M	Farmer	03J102Lr
Mary	17	F	Spinster	03J102Lr
BRENNAN, Sarah	27	F	Spinster	03J102Lr
CLEARY, Patk.	35	M	Laborer	03J102Lr
CROSS, John	23	M	Laborer	03J102Lr
KELLY, James	25	M	Laborer	03J102Lr
BRIEN, Patk.	21	M	Laborer	03J102Lr
KENNELLER, Wm.	27	M	Laborer	03J102Lr
WEHELAN, Pat	30	M	Laborer	03J102Lr
MCREDMOND, John	43	M	Laborer	03J102Lr
CLEARY, Jeremiah	24	M	Turner	03J102Lr
Mary	30	F	Laborer	03J102Lr
Margt.	7	F	Child	03J102Lr
MEAGHEN, Ellen	18	F	Spinster	03J102Lr
Margt.	18	F	Servant	03J102Lr
LANLON, Allen	30	M	Bttbyr	03J102Lr

NAMES OF PASSENGERS	AGE	SEX	OCCUPATIONS	DATE PORT SHIP
WALSH, W.B.	25	M	Bttbyr	03JI02Lr
Mary	26	F	Spinster	03JI02Lr
Catharine	24	F	Spinster	03JI02Lr
HANLON, Phillip	30	M	Unknown	03JI02Lr
Mary-Ann	20	F	Unknown	03JI02Lr
Michael	3	M	Child	03JI02Lr
James	24	M	Unknown	03JI02Lr
FORTUNE, James	30	M	Cord Winder	03JI02Lr
MAHONEY, Eliza	38	F	Wi	03JI02Lr
Ann	17	F	Spinster	03JI02Lr
Francis	10	F	None	03JI02Lr
DONOVAN, John	28	M	Farmer	03JI02Lr
James-D.	23	M	Farmer	03JI02Lr
Rose-D.	5	F	Child	03JI02Lr
Anne	3	F	Child	03JI02Lr
DELANON, Wm.	29	M	Stationer	03JI02Lr

CONSTELLATION 03 JULY 1849

From Liverpool

NAMES OF PASSENGERS	AGE	SEX	OCCUPATIONS	DATE PORT SHIP
KELLY, William	30	M	Draper	03JI02Li
Charlotta	21	F	Draper	03JI02Li
FLANNIGAN, Luke	40	M	Mason	03JI02Li
LAWLER, Patrick	26	M	Laborer	03JI02Li
CURTIS, Thomas	17	M	Laborer	03JI02Li
BOYLE, John	25	M	Joiner	03JI02Li
Martha	25	F	None	03JI02Li
RIED, Catherine	20	F	None	03JI02Li
LYNCH, Matthew	30	M	Carpenter	03JI02Li
RIELLY, Robert-B.	22	M	Farmer	03JI02Li
MALONEY, Michael	20	M	Accountant	03JI02Li
WALSH, Michael	20	M	Laborer	03JI02Li
MILES, William	24	M	Laborer	03JI02Li
MCGUIRE, Mary	20	F	None	03JI02Li
WALSH, Ann	21	F	None	03JI02Li
HANNIGAN, Mary	30	F	None	03JI02Li
CRANE, Honora	51	F	None	03JI02Li
Michael	15	M	None	03JI02Li
HONOHAN, Joseph	30	M	Agent	03JI02Li
Mary	30	F	None	03JI02Li
Richard	10	M	None	03JI02Li
William	2	M	Child	03JI02Li
STAPLETON, James	24	M	Laborer	03JI02Li
GOUGH, William	24	M	Laborer	03JI02Li
LAWLER, Michael	24	M	Laborer	03JI02Li
Catherine	14	F	None	03JI02Li
Ellen	18	F	None	03JI02Li
GOUGH, Bridget	18	F	None	03JI02Li
BERGEN, Martin	30	M	Laborer	03JI02Li
WILSON, Ann	50	F	None	03JI02Li
Sarah	9	F	Child	03JI02Li
MALONEY, Catherine	40	F	None	03JI02Li
Michael	11	M	None	03JI02Li
Pat	7	M	Child	03JI02Li
Ellen	3	F	Child	03JI02Li
GUINAN, John	40	M	Laborer	03JI02Li
Catherine	27	F	None	03JI02Li
U	.00	U	Infant	03JI02Li
MURPHY, Dennis	28	M	Laborer	03JI02Li
Bridget	27	F	None	03JI02Li
MCKAY, Pat	22	M	Laborer	03JI02Li
QUINN, Dennis	30	M	Laborer	03JI02Li
KANE, Thomas	40	M	Laborer	03JI02Li
Bridget	16	F	None	03JI02Li
Mary	11	F	None	03JI02Li
MACKAY, Thomas	26	M	Laborer	03JI02Li
William	21	M	Laborer	03JI02Li
Susan	27	F	None	03JI02Li

NAMES OF PASSENGERS	AGE	SEX	OCCUPATIONS	DATE PORT SHIP
RAY, Ann	27	F	None	03JI02Li
John	3	M	Child	03JI02Li
U	.00	U	Infant	03JI02Li
DONALDSON, Robert	30	M	Laborer	03JI02Li
GOODWIN, William	13	M	None	03JI02Li
SULLIVAN, Catherine	50	F	None	03JI02Li
Margaret	25	F	None	03JI02Li
Ellen	20	F	None	03JI02Li
CAMBLE, Barney	23	M	Laborer	03JI02Li
Eliza	20	F	None	03JI02Li
RIELLY, Owen	23	M	Laborer	03JI02Li
Bernard	22	M	Laborer	03JI02Li
FLANNING, Pat	26	M	Laborer	03JI02Li
Catherine	24	F	None	03JI02Li
U	.00	U	Infant	03JI02Li
BRADY, James	21	M	Plasterer	03JI02Li
Mary	25	F	None	03JI02Li
RICE, John	23	M	Shoemaker	03JI02Li
Michael	27	M	Laborer	03JI02Li
RYAN, Michael	40	M	Laborer	03JI02Li
Johanna	38	F	None	03JI02Li
U	.00	U	Infant	03JI02Li
Bridget	7	F	Child	03JI02Li
Mat	4	M	Child	03JI02Li
Maggy	2	F	Child	03JI02Li
BLACK, John	40	M	Laborer	03JI02Li
BENNET, Thomas	24	M	Gdnr	03JI02Li
RUBIE, Thos.	23	M	Iron Monger	03JI02Li
RYAN, Pierce	30	M	Carpenter	03JI02Li
Johan.	24	U	Unknown	03JI02Li
Honora	26	F	None	03JI02Li
GILLON, Sarah	17	F	None	03JI02Li
U	.00	U	Infant	03JI02Li
DUFFY, Kitty	25	F	None	03JI02Li
TOWMY, John	40	M	Farmer	03JI02Li
Mary	36	F	None	03JI02Li
Joseph	7	M	Child	03JI02Li
RYAN, William	28	M	Farmer	03JI02Li
FARREL, William	40	M	Farmer	03JI02Li
Walter	16	M	Farmer	03JI02Li
Jane	20	F	None	03JI02Li
George	17	M	Farmer	03JI02Li
Michl.	15	M	Farmer	03JI02Li
KILLIAN, Thomas	30	M	Laborer	03JI02Li
CROWLEY, Phill.	24	M	Surveyor	03JI02Li
ODONOHUE, Thos.C.	24	M	None	03JI02Li
MAHER, Con	21	M	None	03JI02Li
CROWLEY, Julia	20	F	None	03JI02Li
COSTELLO, Ellen	18	F	None	03JI02Li
Mary	19	F	None	03JI02Li
HALLEY, Ann	18	F	None	03JI02Li
MURPHY, James	18	M	Laborer	03JI02Li
Marcella	16	F	None	03JI02Li
CAREW, Catherine	30	F	None	03JI02Li
Edward	30	M	Laborer	03JI02Li
Died-At-Sea				
KELLER, Thomas	19	M	Laborer	03JI02Li
MONOHAN, James	30	M	Laborer	03JI02Li
MAHER, James	25	M	Laborer	03JI02Li
Honora	30	F	None	03JI02Li
FULTON, Elizabeth	20	F	None	03JI02Li
Bridget	14	F	None	03JI02Li
WATERS, P.Revd.	40	M	Priest	03JI02Li
MCGOVERN, Pat	22	M	Butler	03JI02Li
Mary	18	F	None	03JI02Li
Mick	20	M	Butler	03JI02Li
SHANAHAN, Mat	19	M	Laborer	03JI02Li
FINN, Pat	30	M	Laborer	03JI02Li
LEWIS, Samuel	21	M	Laborer	03JI02Li
NELSON, Margaret	20	F	None	03JI02Li
FINLAY, Ellen	17	F	None	03JI02L
COOPER, John-M.	22	M	Laborer	03JI02L
Thomas	16	M	Laborer	03JI02L
Sarah	20	F	None	03JI02L
U	.00	U	Infant	03JI02L

NAMES OF PASSENGERS	AGE	SEX	OCCUPATIONS	DATE PORT SHIP
FANNING, Thomas	50	M	Laborer	03JI02Li
Ann	16	F	None	03JI02Li
FLANAGIN, Henry	40	M	Laborer	03JI02Li
RODGERS, Ambler	12	U	None	03JI02Li
BIRMINGHAM, Bridget	30	F	None	03JI02Li
Honora	2	F	Child	03JI02Li
Brid.	.00	F	Infant	03JI02Li
Rose	13	F	None	03JI02Li
MCGRATH, Margt.	12	F	None	03JI02Li
KELLY, Mary	18	F	None	03JI02Li
MCGUFFNEY, Sarah	24	F	None	03JI02Li
RAN, James	26	M	Laborer	03JI02Li
HOWARD, James	23	M	Laborer	03JI02Li
CONLEY, Win.	30	U	Unknown	03JI02Li
Ellen	6	F	Child	03JI02Li
Ann	4	F	Child	03JI02Li
HASKILL, Jonah	46	M	Laborer	03JI02Li
James	16	M	Laborer	03JI02Li
WARD, Pat	25	M	Laborer	03JI02Li
Died-At-Sea				
LANDY, Peter	28	M	Stcwkr	03JI02Li
DIRMODY, Chas.	26	M	Laborer	03JI02Li
FLOOD, Thos.	22	M	Tailor	03JI02Li
WRIGHT, Pat	32	M	Plasterer	03JI02Li
Brid.	34	F	None	03JI02Li
Mary	1	F	Child	03JI02Li
CANTY, Mary	18	F	None	03JI02Li
HINSEY, Thomas	24	M	Laborer	03JI02Li
HEART, Peter	18	M	Laborer	03JI02Li
MALONE, Michael	48	M	Laborer	03JI02Li
Mary	45	F	None	03JI02Li
HART, Loughlin	19	M	Laborer	03JI02Li
Eliza	11	F	None	03JI02Li
Ally	6	U	Child	03JI02Li
SLEITH, James	18	M	Seaman	03JI02Li
BURKE, Richard	20	M	Laborer	03JI02Li
Edward	10	M	None	03JI02Li
KILLDUFF, Catherine	20	F	None	03JI02Li
U	.00	U	Infant	03JI02Li
Thos.	5	M	Child	03JI02Li
Brid.	3	F	Child	03JI02Li
DOWLING, Dennis	50	M	Laborer	03JI02Li
Ann	42	F	None	03JI02Li
U	.00	U	Infant	03JI02Li
Pat	20	M	Laborer	03JI02Li
Peter	18	M	Laborer	03JI02Li
John	15	M	Laborer	03JI02Li
Mary	13	F	None	03JI02Li
Alice	11	F	None	03JI02Li
Dennis	8	M	Child	03JI02Li
MCLOUGHLIN, Michael	34	M	Laborer	03JI02Li
RYAN, Phill.	30	M	Laborer	03JI02Li
QUINN, Pat	9	M	Child	03JI02Li
Biddy	7	F	Child	03JI02Li
MOLOGHREY, Catherine	21	F	None	03JI02Li
BUSH, William	20	M	Laborer	03JI02Li
MCGUIRE, Pat	20	M	Laborer	03JI02Li
MCCABE, Bernd.	19	M	Laborer	03JI02Li
COLLYER, Martin	35	M	Jailer	03JI02Li
HARRINGTON, Jerem.	20	M	Laborer	03JI02Li
DEAVIN, Brid.	20	F	None	03JI02Li
GLYNN, Margt.	18	F	None	03JI02Li
BUTLER, Ellen	18	F	None	03JI02Li
SIMPSON, James	35	M	Laborer	03JI02Li
CORBLY, J.	40	U	Unknown	03JI02Li
HOPWOOD, James	30	M	Shoemaker	03JI02Li
DAY, Margaret	27	F	None	03JI02Li
BYRNES, Edward	25	M	Laborer	03JI02Li
STEWART, Charles	25	M	Laborer	03JI02Li
Margt.	23	F	None	03JI02Li
RIGNEY, Ellen	62	F	None	03JI02Li
Died-At-Sea				
Margt.	13	F	None	03JI02Li
MADDEN, John	20	M	Laborer	03JI02Li
DOHERTY, Judy	58	F	None	03JI02Li

NAMES OF PASSENGERS	AGE	SEX	OCCUPATIONS	DATE PORT SHIP
DOHERTY, James	18	M	Laborer	03JI02Li
CODY, Peter	22	M	Laborer	03JI02Li
John	19	M	Laborer	03JI02Li
STANTON, Peter	35	M	Laborer	03JI02Li
Pat	24	M	Laborer	03JI02Li
MCCORMICK, Pat	24	M	Laborer	03JI02Li
MADDEN, John	25	M	Laborer	03JI02Li
COSTELLO, John	24	M	Laborer	03JI02Li
SLATTERY, John	30	M	Laborer	03JI02Li
CARROL, Irena	40	F	None	03JI02Li
Mary	36	F	None	03JI02Li
U	.00	U	Infant	03JI02Li
Joseph	18	M	Laborer	03JI02Li
Andrea	9	F	Child	03JI02Li
Catherine	9	F	Child	03JI02Li
James	3	M	Child	03JI02Li
Julia	2	F	Child	03JI02Li
REED, James	40	M	Shoemaker	03JI02Li
Brid.	32	F	None	03JI02Li
U	.00	U	Infant	03JI02Li
Jacob	18	M	Shoemaker	03JI02Li
Mary	14	F	None	03JI02Li
Eliza	12	F	None	03JI02Li
J.	10	U	None	03JI02Li
John	8	M	Child	03JI02Li
J.	8	U	Child	03JI02Li
Emily	6	F	Child	03JI02Li
Ann	4	F	Child	03JI02Li
KELBURN, Pat	25	M	Laborer	03JI02Li
BURN, Michael	22	M	Laborer	03JI02Li
DOYLE, Bernd.	36	M	Laborer	03JI02Li
MAX, Brid.	20	F	None	03JI02Li
LEONARD, Jane	20	F	None	03JI02Li
REYNOLDS, Mary	18	F	None	03JI02Li
Bess	20	F	None	03JI02Li
HOGAN, Thos.	30	M	Laborer	03JI02Li
Nancy	28	F	None	03JI02Li
U	.00	U	Infant	03JI02Li
Edward	9	M	Child	03JI02Li
TAGGART, Peter	24	M	Laborer	03JI02Li
Betty	32	F	None	03JI02Li
John	6	M	Child	03JI02Li
Mary	4	F	Child	03JI02Li
M--THEN, Jane	22	F	None	03JI02Li
Julia	18	F	None	03JI02Li
Pat	16	M	None	03JI02Li
MCDONALD, James	13	M	None	03JI02Li
Edward	12	M	None	03JI02Li
LEONARD, John	20	M	Laborer	03JI02Li
SHANNON, Thos.	22	M	Laborer	03JI02Li
Hugh	18	M	Laborer	03JI02Li
Margaret	18	F	None	03JI02Li
MCCABE, Catherine	20	F	None	03JI02Li
John	22	M	Shoemaker	03JI02Li
KELLY, Thos.	30	M	Laborer	03JI02Li
RYAN, Mary	8	F	Child	03JI02Li
KING, Mary	25	F	None	03JI02Li
MEAD, Catherine	25	F	None	03JI02Li
Joseph	6	M	Child	03JI02Li
Laurence	4	M	Child	03JI02Li
Thos.	2	M	Child	03JI02Li
HEALEY, Eliza	36	F	None	03JI02Li
FAHY, Wm.	40	M	Laborer	03JI02Li
MCLOUGHLIN, Martin	15	M	Mason	03JI02Li
Ann	5	F	Child	03JI02Li
HEALLY, Eliza	18	F	None	03JI02Li
DOONEY, Catherine	30	F	None	03JI02Li
Cath.	7	F	Child	03JI02Li
Ann	4	F	Child	03JI02Li
Thos.	1	M	Child	03JI02Li
DONALDSON, Mary	18	F	None	03JI02Li
LEONARD, Wm.	16	M	Laborer	03JI02Li
TRAVERS, Peter	35	M	Laborer	03JI02Li
MCNULTY, Margt.	18	F	None	03JI02Li
TANIER, Robt.	21	M	Clerk	03JI02Li

NAMES OF PASSENGERS	AGE	SEX	OCCUPATIONS	DATE PORT SHIP
CUNNINGHAM, Eliza	25	F	None	03J102Li
SULLIVAN, Corns.	27	M	Laborer	03J102Li
John	21	M	Laborer	03J102Li
Mary	45	F	None	03J102Li
Mary	18	F	None	03J102Li
Cath.	15	F	None	03J102Li
Andrew	26	M	Laborer	03J102Li
Thos.	30	M	Laborer	03J102Li
DELANEY, Wm.	25	M	Laborer	03J102Li
SCULLY, Margt.	20	F	None	03J102Li
WHALLEN, John	21	M	Laborer	03J102Li
ONIELL, Ann	50	F	None	03J102Li
Susan	20	F	None	03J102Li
HEAVEY, Margt.	22	F	None	03J102Li
ROCHE, Mary	21	F	None	03J102Li
MCDONNELL, Catherine	26	F	None	03J102Li
Joseph	5	M	Child	03J102Li
Mary	2	F	Child	03J102Li
MCLOUGHLIN, Mic.	23	M	Laborer	03J102Li
Bridget	11	F	None	03J102Li
LYNCH, Honora	40	F	None	03J102Li
Cath.	9	F	Child	03J102Li
Mary	7	F	Child	03J102Li
Edward	15	M	None	03J102Li
Peter	13	M	None	03J102Li
HAGGARTY, Mary	24	F	None	03J102Li
PHILLIPS, Mary	50	F	None	03J102Li
WATERS, Margt.	22	F	None	03J102Li
KERWIN, Mary	45	F	None	03J102Li
Margt.	2	F	Child	03J102Li
MURRAY, John	15	M	None	03J102Li
RILEY, Dennis	18	M	None	03J102Li
VAUGHAN, John	17	M	Maurer	03J102Li
James	14	M	Maurer	03J102Li
HANNTON, Mary	20	F	None	03J102Li
Ann	5	F	Child	03J102Li
MAHON, Catherine	17	F	None	03J102Li
Honora	16	F	None	03J102Li
PURCELL, William	40	M	Laborer	03J102Li
QUINN, U	14	U	None	03J102Li
BRADY, Peter	20	M	Laborer	03J102Li
GORMBY, John	20	M	Laborer	03J102Li
DOHERTY, Berd.	18	M	Painter	03J102Li
GORMBY, Winifd.	18	F	None	03J102Li
CONNER, Brid.	18	F	None	03J102Li
BEACON, Elizt.	20	F	None	03J102Li
Margt.	19	F	None	03J102Li
DALY, Pat	19	M	Laborer	03J102Li
Mary	18	F	None	03J102Li
CULLEN, Brid.	26	F	None	03J102Li
James	3	M	Child	03J102Li
FIELD, Ann	28	F	None	03J102Li
U	.00	U	Infant	03J102Li
Cathe.	8	F	Child	03J102Li
Edward	3	M	Child	03J102Li
MURRAY, Bernard	40	M	Laborer	03J102Li
KELLY, James	24	M	Laborer	03J102Li
Brid.	21	F	None	03J102Li
WHITE, Wm.	40	M	Baker	03J102Li
U (W)	36	F	None	03J102Li
Eliza	18	F	None	03J102Li
Wm.	16	M	None	03J102Li
Benj.	14	M	None	03J102Li
Ann	6	F	Child	03J102Li
Ellen	4	F	Child	03J102Li
DANIELS, Anthony	22	M	Laborer	03J102Li
CONOLLY, Mary	38	F	None	03J102Li
SHELLY, Michl.	40	M	Laborer	03J102Li
MCGRULEY, Wm.	21	M	Laborer	03J102Li
BARROW, John	28	M	Joiner	03J102Li
FORMBY, Ellen	20	F	None	03J102Li
MICHA, Brid.	30	F	None	03J102Li
MCANNENY, Judy	15	F	None	03J102Li
MILLIGAN, Pat	35	M	Laborer	03J102Li
BROPHY, Mother	30	F	None	03J102Li
BRODY, Cathy	28	F	None	03J102Li
KING, Pat	21	M	Laborer	03J102Li
Alice	22	F	None	03J102Li
JACKSON, Ann	19	F	None	03J102Li
MCANNERAY, Ellen	20	F	None	03J102Li
SHERLIN, Ann	18	F	None	03J102Li
SMITH, Cathe.	21	F	None	03J102Li
MULROONEY, Jim	34	M	Laborer	03J102Li
CALLAGHAN, Wm.	21	M	Laborer	03J102Li
CURLEY, Barney	24	M	Laborer	03J102Li
DAY, Mary	27	F	None	03J102Li
MEADE, Danl.	26	M	Laborer	03J102Li
GOODWIN, Peter	57	M	Sawer	03J102Li
JONES, Thos.	25	M	Clerk	03J102Li
SMITH, Cath.	12	F	None	03J102Li
ROUNDFIELD, Jno.	32	M	Laborer	03J102Li
MORRIS, Jas.	36	M	Laborer	03J102Li
QUINLAN, Jas.	40	M	Laborer	03J102Li
MARTIN, Mary	58	F	None	03J102Li
CONNELL, Jno.	48	M	None	03J102Li
Mary	23	F	None	03J102Li
Julia	21	F	None	03J102Li
Bridget	20	F	None	03J102Li
David	19	M	None	03J102Li
REARDON, Ellen	24	F	None	03J102Li
Julia	20	F	None	03J102Li
DALY, Mary	17	F	None	03J102Li
CALLON, Con	23	M	None	03J102Li
ODONNELL, Morris	23	M	None	03J102Li
RUSSELL, John	36	M	None	03J102Li
Eliza	24	F	None	03J102Li
Susan	7	F	Child	03J102Li
Nath.	16	M	None	03J102Li
Ferman	13	M	None	03J102Li
HOLLIS, Michl.	48	M	None	03J102Li
Mich.	18	M	None	03J102Li
BYRNE, Jno.	25	M	None	03J102Li
CORGAN, Pat	28	M	None	03J102Li
ODONNELL, Jno.	23	M	None	03J102Li
OKEEFE, Mary	24	F	None	03J102Li
Charles	4	M	Child	03J102Li
Alfred	2	M	Child	03J102Li
SAINT, Margt.	24	F	None	03J102Li
CANTY, Mary	18	F	None	03J102Li
GIVENNY, Thos.	30	M	Laborer	03J102Li
Ann	30	F	None	03J102Li
ROCHE, Thos.	35	M	Laborer	03J102Li
ELLE, Edwd.	30	M	Laborer	03J102Li
Ellen	40	F	None	03J102Li
DANEHY, James	20	M	Laborer	03J102Li
ELLICOT, Thos.	18	M	Laborer	03J102Li
SWIFT, Peter	23	M	Laborer	03J102Li
MONAGHAN, Jno.	9	M	Child	03J102Li
FLANNIGAN, Jno.	17	M	Laborer	03J102Li
FLINN, Margt.	20	F	None	03J102Li
DOYLE, Peter	40	M	Laborer	03J102Li
NOWLAN, Mich.	27	M	Laborer	03J102Li
CONNAN, Mich.	18	M	Laborer	03J102Li
Ann	19	F	None	03J102Li
Betsy	20	F	None	03J102Li
DRISCOLL, Mary	3	F	Child	03J102Li
MCCARTHY, Brian	19	M	Laborer	03J102Li
CARROL, Betsy	24	F	None	03J102Li
Rose	22	F	None	03J102Li
FARRELL, Judy	28	F	None	03J102Li
MCCARTHY, Mike	40	M	Laborer	03J102Li
Margt.	7	F	Child	03J102Li
Mary	4	F	Child	03J102Li
HARRINGTON, Margt.	23	F	None	03J102Li
SULLIVAN, Dennis	21	M	Laborer	03J102Li
MURPHY, Maria	21	F	None	03J102Li
MARSDEN, John	56	M	Laborer	03J102Li
DOOLEY, Norry	19	F	None	03J102Li
WHITEHEAD, Martha	4	F	Child	03J102Li
SPORTWOOD, Peter	24	M	Laborer	03J102Li

NAMES OF PASSENGERS		AGE	SEX	OCCUPATIONS	DATE PORT SHIP
LAYCOCK, Henry		26	M	Laborer	03JI02Li
CROSS, Mary		30	F	None	03JI02Li
John		28	M	Laborer	03JI02Li
U		.00	U	Infant	03JI02Li
Mary		20	F	None	03JI02Li
Mary		6	F	Child	03JI02Li
Eliza		4	F	Child	03JI02Li
Susan		2	F	Child	03JI02Li
Died-At-Sea					
CRAUFORD, Mike		28	M	Laborer	03JI02Li
Judith		25	F	None	03JI02Li
James		23	M	Laborer	03JI02Li
Patrick		20	M	Laborer	03JI02Li
Margt.Ann		23	F	None	03JI02Li
LAFFY, Mike		22	M	Laborer	03JI02Li
HARRINGTON, James		28	M	Laborer	03JI02Li
Daniel		24	M	Laborer	03JI02Li
ELLIS, Wm.		25	M	Farmer	03JI02Li
Asher		23	M	Farmer	03JI02Li
Samuel		18	M	Farmer	03JI02Li
ROBINSON, Ben		20	M	Laborer	03JI02Li
EVANS, Elias		38	M	Laborer	03JI02Li
LYNCH, Thomas		40	M	Laborer	03JI02Li
U	(W)	40	F	None	03JI02Li
Rose		16	F	None	03JI02Li
Mary		13	F	None	03JI02Li
Ann		8	F	Child	03JI02Li
Thomas		4	M	Child	03JI02Li
Ellen		2	F	Child	03JI02Li
TOBIN, Jane		18	F	None	03JI02Li
CUNNINGHAM, James		30	M	Laborer	03JI02Li
DOYLE, Peter		18	M	Laborer	03JI02Li
HARRINGTON, Dan		16	M	Laborer	03JI02Li
CARNEY, Thos.		23	M	Laborer	03JI02Li
DUGAN, Pat		26	M	Laborer	03JI02Li
HAFFY, Con		25	M	Laborer	03JI02Li
MCCORVY, Thos.		17	M	Laborer	03JI02Li
MCSHANE, Brid.		17	F	None	03JI02Li
WRIGHT, Jno.		60	M	Farmer	03JI02Li
HYLAND, Len.		20	M	Laborer	03JI02Li
HASKILL, Josiah		46	M	Laborer	03JI02Li
James		16	M	Laborer	03JI02Li
MCDONALD, Mike		30	M	Laborer	03JI02Li
Margt.		25	F	None	03JI02Li
U		.00	U	Infant	03JI02Li
Cath.		11	F	None	03JI02Li
Alex		8	M	Child	03JI02Li
CLARKE, Mary		27	F	None	03JI02Li
Laurence		10	M	None	03JI02Li
U		.00	U	Infant	03JI02Li
James		2	M	Child	03JI02Li
HURST, Kate		34	F	None	03JI02Li
Cath.		34	F	None	03JI02Li
Jane		1	F	Child	03JI02Li
BURKE, Mary		37	F	None	03JI02Li
LAHEY, Denis		28	M	Laborer	03JI02Li
QUINN, Jas.		22	M	Laborer	03JI02Li
MOLLOY, Jas.		27	M	Laborer	03JI02Li
HAND, Pat		24	M	Laborer	03JI02Li
GALLAGHER, Pat		30	M	Laborer	03JI02Li
MULLALY, Ann		22	F	None	03JI02Li
LAFFY, Mike		45	M	Laborer	03JI02Li
HENRY, David		36	M	Laborer	03JI02Li
DOWLING, John		30	M	Laborer	03JI02Li
FANIER, Robt.		21	M	Laborer	03JI02Li
CARTY, Thos.		21	M	Laborer	03JI02Li
COOLLY, Jas.		50	M	Laborer	03JI02Li
FINN, Thos.		45	M	Laborer	03JI02Li
HOLT, Valentine		23	M	Laborer	03JI02Li
CLASKEY, Pat		20	M	Laborer	03JI02Li
CORBLY, Laurence		40	M	Laborer	03JI02Li
RYAN, James		20	M	Laborer	03JI02Li
WHITE, James		19	M	Laborer	03JI02Li
HERON, Pat		30	M	Laborer	03JI02Li
KENT, Jno.		50	M	Laborer	03JI02Li
KENT, Jno.		20	M	Laborer	03JI02Li
Thos.		16	M	Laborer	03JI02Li
Brid.		15	F	None	03JI02Li
Brid.		20	F	None	03JI02Li
Johan		18	U	Unknown	03JI02Li
ROGERS, Mary		20	F	None	03JI02Li
FLANNIGAN, Margt.		34	F	None	03JI02Li
Edwd.		10	M	None	03JI02Li
Mary		8	F	Child	03JI02Li
Nicholas		5	M	Child	03JI02Li
Margt.		2	F	Child	03JI02Li
ALLEN, Jas.		20	M	Laborer	03JI02Li
LEMON, Mary		18	F	None	03JI02Li
RYAN, Pat		21	M	Laborer	03JI02Li
Jno.		34	M	Laborer	03JI02Li
Mary		25	F	None	03JI02Li
CLASHBY, Jno.		18	M	Laborer	03JI02Li
BOOTH, Jas.		18	M	Laborer	03JI02Li
KELLY, Hugh		50	M	Laborer	03JI02Li
Biddy		20	F	None	03JI02Li
TARBUT, Alice		20	F	None	03JI02Li
BOOTH, Josh.		17	M	Laborer	03JI02Li
FAHY, John		50	M	Laborer	03JI02Li
CONLON, Tim		38	M	Tailor	03JI02Li
BRODERICK, Mike		24	M	Laborer	03JI02Li
ODONOHUE, Mike		36	M	Laborer	03JI02Li
U	(W)	30	F	None	03JI02Li
Jane		8	F	Child	03JI02Li
Alice		5	F	Child	03JI02Li
DILLON, David		22	M	Laborer	03JI02Li
Mary		20	F	None	03JI02Li
GRAHAM, Jas.		25	M	Laborer	03JI02Li
KILNEY, Sarah		26	F	None	03JI02Li
MCADA, Pat		28	M	Laborer	03JI02Li
BURNS, John		20	M	Laborer	03JI02Li
STAPLETON, John		30	M	Laborer	03JI02Li
DANECON, Pat		28	M	Laborer	03JI02Li
GOGHLAN, John		25	M	Laborer	03JI02Li

CHENANGO 03 JULY 1849

From Belfast

NAMES OF PASSENGERS		AGE	SEX	OCCUPATIONS	DATE PORT SHIP
MCEWIN, Wm.		40	M	Clergyman	03JI05Lo
Bessie	(W)	35	F	Wife	03JI05Lo
Martha	(M)	70	F	Mother	03JI05Lo
James	(S)	17	M	None	03JI05Lo
Wm.	(S)	13	M	None	03JI05Lo
Jno.	(S)	4	M	Child	03JI05Lo
Jemima	(D)	7	F	Child	03JI05Lo
Bessie	(D)	2	F	Child	03JI05Lo
Emily	(D)	.06	F	Infant	03JI05Lo
MCDONALD, Jane		25	F	Servant	03JI05Lo
MITCHELL, Geo.		25	M	Farmer	03JI05Lo
ELLCOCK, John		18	M	Farmer	03JI05Lo
MCVEIGH, John		30	M	Farmer	03JI05Lo
John		20	M	Farmer	03JI05Lo
WELDEN, Thomas		19	M	Farmer	03JI05Lo
HUGHES, Mary		24	F	Spinster	03JI05Lo
CURRY, John		25	M	Farmer	03JI05Lo
HAMILL, William		20	M	Farmer	03JI05Lo
LOCKHART, James		25	M	Farmer	03JI05Lo
CRAIG, John		22	M	Farmer	03JI05Lo
Nancy	(M)	40	F	Mother	03JI05Lo
Matilda	(T)	18	F	Sister	03JI05Lo
Sarah	(T)	14	F	Sister	03JI05Lo
William	(B)	10	M	Brother	03JI05Lo
Nancy	(T)	7	F	Sister	03JI05Lo
MCANALLY, Alice		40	F	Wi	03JI05Lo

NAMES OF PASSENGERS		AGE	SEX	OCCUPATIONS	DATE PORT SHIP
MCANALLY, Arthur	(S)	4	M	Child	03JI05Lo
KELLY, John		25	M	Carpenter	03JI05Lo
Ellen	(W)	20	F	Wife	03JI05Lo
DONAGHY, David		20	M	Servant	03JI05Lo
HUTCHESON, James		48	M	Farmer	03JI05Lo
Mary	(W)	56	F	Wife	03JI05Lo
Saml.	(S)	26	M	None	03JI05Lo
Ellen	(D)	34	F	None	03JI05Lo
BEDLOW, Mary		20	F	Servant	03JI05Lo
Mary-Jane		.10	F	Infant	03JI05Lo
HENRY, Ann		20	F	Servant	03JI05Lo
SMITH, Mary		20	F	Servant	03JI05Lo
MCALARNEY, James		28	M	Farmer	03JI05Lo
BOYD, Joseph		20	M	Farmer	03JI05Lo
MCGLENGHAN, Jane		20	F	Spinster	03JI05Lo
HUMPHRIES, Eliza		20	F	Spinster	03JI05Lo
HIND, James		65	M	Farmer	03JI05Lo
MCGOWAN, John		48	M	Farmer	03JI05Lo
DUGAN, Peter		22	M	Farmer	03JI05Lo
HAWTHORN, Ann		21	F	Spinster	03JI05Lo
Margaret		18	F	Spinster	03JI05Lo
DUNN, Margaret		15	F	Spinster	03JI05Lo
MCCRACKEN, Malcolm		18	M	Clerk	03JI05Lo
DONNELLY, Patrick		20	M	Clerk	03JI05Lo
Mary		19	F	Wife	03JI05Lo
MCWACKIN, James		24	M	Farmer	03JI05Lo
MCSHERRY, Hannah		22	F	Spinster	03JI05Lo
KERR, Mary		23	F	Spinster	03JI05Lo
YOUNG, Wm.		30	M	Mason	03JI05Lo
MCVICKERS, Robert		25	M	Mason	03JI05Lo
DONAGHY, Mary		28	F	Spinster	03JI05Lo
HODGEN, John		26	M	Weaver	03JI05Lo
William		20	M	Weaver	03JI05Lo
Anna	(W)	19	F	Wife	03JI05Lo
JAMESON, James		15	M	Farmer	03JI05Lo
ROBINSON, David		30	M	Farmer	03JI05Lo
Eliza	(W)	28	F	Wife	03JI05Lo
MURRAY, Anne-Jane		30	F	Spinster	03JI05Lo
CONNOR, William		18	M	Weaver	03JI05Lo
SMITH, John		24	M	Weaver	03JI05Lo
ATKINSON, Jane		24	F	Spinster	03JI05Lo
KENT, Diana		20	F	Spinster	03JI05Lo
WILSON, Margaret		15	F	Spinster	03JI05Lo
MCGURK, Martha		24	F	Spinster	03JI05Lo
MARTIN, John		22	M	Carpenter	03JI05Lo
MURROW, Jane		18	F	Spinster	03JI05Lo
DAVIDSON, Catharine		43	F	Wi	03JI05Lo
Jane	(D)	15	F	None	03JI05Lo
Catharine	(D)	7	F	Child	03JI05Lo
OAKMAN, Wm.		24	M	None	03JI05Lo
BRANKEN, Patrick		20	M	Farmer	03JI05Lo
HUNTLY, Catharine		20	F	Spinster	03JI05Lo
ROGAN, Michael		30	M	Tailor	03JI05Lo
Ann	(W)	25	F	Wife	03JI05Lo
STEWART, James		15	M	Tailor	03JI05Lo
BAWN, Wm.		28	M	Carpenter	03JI05Lo
Mary	(W)	25	F	Wife	03JI05Lo
BLOOMER, Joseph		30	M	Tailor	03JI05Lo
MCALLISTER, Catharine		20	M	Tailor	03JI05Lo
CUNNINGHAM, Catharine		20	M	Tailor	03JI05Lo
KILLEN, Wm.		50	M	Farmer	03JI05Lo
Mary	(W)	50	F	Wife	03JI05Lo
Eliza	(D)	15	F	None	03JI05Lo
Susana	(D)	11	F	None	03JI05Lo
ROBINSON, Margaret		20	F	Servant	03JI05Lo
MCKENNA, Margaret		30	F	Servant	03JI05Lo
GRIBBEN, James		25	M	Baker	03JI05Lo
Frances	(W)	25	F	Wife	03JI05Lo
MOORE, Thomas		30	M	Laborer	03JI05Lo
FISHER, Wm.J.		24	M	Laborer	03JI05Lo
MCLARNON, Agnes		21	F	Servant	03JI05Lo
ROGAN, Hugh		35	M	Laborer	03JI05Lo
MOORE, Robert		25	M	Laborer	03JI05Lo
WALLACE, James		20	M	Laborer	03JI05Lo
MURRAY, Patrick		30	M	Laborer	03JI05Lo

NAMES OF PASSENGERS		AGE	SEX	OCCUPATIONS	DATE PORT SHIP
MURRAY, Margt.	(W)	30	F	Wife	03JI05Lo
Catherine	(D)	16	F	None	03JI05Lo
Eliza	(D)	9	F	Child	03JI05Lo
Margt.	(D)	6	F	Child	03JI05Lo
LARMON, James		25	M	Weaver	03JI05Lo
MCGARVEY, Henry		25	M	Weaver	03JI05Lo
LOWRY, Robert		25	M	Weaver	03JI05Lo
NEVILLE, Catharine		21	F	Spinster	03JI05Lo
DONNELLY, Mary-J.		20	F	Spinster	03JI05Lo
MCGEE, John		20	M	Tailor	03JI05Lo
HALL, Richard		25	M	Tailor	03JI05Lo
NICHOLSON, Margt.		23	F	Spinster	03JI05Lo
MCMULLAN, Wm.		20	M	Farmer	03JI05Lo
BRIGGS, Wm.		22	M	Farmer	03JI05Lo
MCARING, Alice		24	F	Wi	03JI05Lo
Alice	(T)	22	F	Sister	03JI05Lo
Eliza	(D)	2	F	Child	03JI05Lo
MCARNEY, Alice		.11	F	Infant	03JI05Lo
BARNEY, Mary		14	F	Spinster	03JI05Lo
John		13	M	None	03JI05Lo
SMALL, Henry		23	M	Carpenter	03JI05Lo
MCMULLEN, John		35	M	Carpenter	03JI05Lo
KIRKLAND, James		25	M	Carpenter	03JI05Lo
Martha	(W)	20	F	Wife	03JI05Lo
JOHNSTONE, James		25	M	Weaver	03JI05Lo
ATKINSON, Mary		20	F	Spinster	03JI05Lo
Sarah	(T)	22	F	Sister	03JI05Lo
HALLIDAY, Isabella		17	F	Servant	03JI05Lo
GLASS, Nancy		30	F	Servant	03JI05Lo
MCCORMICK, Dan		20	M	Mason	03JI05Lo
CLARK, Letty		18	F	Spinster	03JI05Lo
Ellen		16	F	Spinster	03JI05Lo
REID, Wm.		19	M	Laborer	03JI05Lo
MORELAND, James		20	M	Laborer	03JI05Lo
ARCHER, John		35	M	Farmer	03JI05Lo
Sarah	(W)	40	F	Wife	03JI05Lo
Nancy	(D)	7	F	Child	03JI05Lo
KANE, Betty		25	F	Servant	03JI05Lo
HIGGINS, Patrick		24	M	Laborer	03JI05Lo
BISHOP, Susan		18	F	Servant	03JI05Lo
Bridget		16	F	Servant	03JI05Lo
SHIELDS, Susan		25	F	Servant	03JI05Lo
FITZSIMMONS, Patrick		30	M	Laborer	03JI05Lo
MCLOUGHLAN, Wm.		35	M	Gentleman	03JI05Lo
Ellen		30	F	Lady	03JI05Lo
THOMPSON, J.W.		26	M	Gentleman	03JI05Lo

THOMAS-BAKER 03 JULY 1849

From Galway

NAMES OF PASSENGERS		AGE	SEX	OCCUPATIONS	DATE PORT SHIP
OMALLY, Elleanor		26	F	Unknown	03JI06Lm
FORD, Margret.		25	F	Unknown	03JI06Lm
OBRIEN, Mary		20	F	Unknown	03JI06Lm
Michal		15	M	Unknown	03JI06Lm
VERLIN, Patk.		20	M	Unknown	03JI06Lm
SILVER, Patrick		26	M	Unknown	03JI06Lm
HAVERTY, Thomas		28	M	Unknown	03JI06Lm
CONNOR, Bryan		17	M	Unknown	03JI06Lm
RILEY, James		50	M	Unknown	03JI06Lm
Biddy		40	F	Unknown	03JI06Lm
REILY, Nicholas		22	M	Unknown	03JI06Lm
James		18	M	Unknown	03JI06Lm
MCDONOUGH, Patt.		25	M	Unknown	03JI06Lm
Michal		3	M	Child	03JI06Lm
Mary		.00	F	Infant	03JI06Lm
Mary		23	F	Unknown	03JI06Lm
MADDIN, Patt.		30	M	Unknown	03JI06Lm
William		30	M	Unknown	03JI06Lm

NAMES OF PASSENGERS	AGE	SEX	OCCUPATIONS	DATE PORT SHIP
MCDONOUGH, John	26	M	Unknown	03J106Lm
Mary	30	F	Unknown	03J106Lm
FAHERTY, Mary	16	F	Unknown	03J106Lm
COAN, John	45	M	Unknown	03J106Lm
CAHILL, Michal	26	M	Unknown	03J106Lm
MCLOUGHLIN, Bridget	25	F	Unknown	03J106Lm
HEALY, David	40	M	Unknown	03J106Lm
GEROUGHTY, James	40	M	Unknown	03J106Lm
Catherine	35	F	Unknown	03J106Lm
Ann	7	F	Child	03J106Lm
Margret	.00	F	Infant	03J106Lm
SHAUGNESSY, Ann	25	F	Unknown	03J106Lm
NELSON, Thomas	20	M	Unknown	03J106Lm
GLYNN, Judy	20	F	Unknown	03J106Lm
CARR, John	20	M	Unknown	03J106Lm
Patrick	18	M	Unknown	03J106Lm
GRILY, John	22	M	Unknown	03J106Lm
CARTY, Bridget	25	F	Unknown	03J106Lm
RAMAHAN, Ellen	17	F	Unknown	03J106Lm
FITTEN, Mary	21	F	Unknown	03J106Lm
LAWLER, Patrick	26	M	Unknown	03J106Lm
ELLIOT, Sarah	40	F	Unknown	03J106Lm
William	16	M	Unknown	03J106Lm
Robert	14	M	Unknown	03J106Lm
Thomas	12	M	Unknown	03J106Lm
Mary-Jane	8	F	Child	03J106Lm
Fanny	4	F	Child	03J106Lm
SHEA, Mathew	30	M	Unknown	03J106Lm
MCGLYNN, Bridget	17	F	Unknown	03J106Lm
MCDONALD, Peter	12	M	Unknown	03J106Lm
HORDANAN, Honor	20	F	Unknown	03J106Lm
CAIN, Connor	22	U	Unknown	03J106Lm
EGAN, Patt.	17	M	Unknown	03J106Lm
Mary	19	F	Unknown	03J106Lm
CARR, Mary	27	F	Unknown	03J106Lm
NOLAN, Ann	24	F	Unknown	03J106Lm
GREALISH, John	35	M	Unknown	03J106Lm
Monica	25	F	Unknown	03J106Lm
Mary	2	F	Child	03J106Lm
Patt.	.00	M	Infant	03J106Lm
FALEY, Ann	30	F	Unknown	03J106Lm
DOLLY, Mary	26	F	Unknown	03J106Lm
MULKUM, Margret	21	F	Unknown	03J106Lm
BOYLE, James	12	M	Unknown	03J106Lm
Martin	8	M	Child	03J106Lm
FERRIGHARTY, John	24	M	Unknown	03J106Lm
Cath.	20	F	Unknown	03J106Lm
QUINLIN, Phillip	34	M	Unknown	03J106Lm
Ann	34	F	Unknown	03J106Lm
SHANNON, Patt.	26	M	Unknown	03J106Lm
FLEMMING, Honor	26	F	Unknown	03J106Lm
GREEN, Ellen	30	F	Unknown	03J106Lm
FALY, Mary	15	F	Unknown	03J106Lm
KILMARTIN, John	25	M	Unknown	03J106Lm
Honor	20	F	Unknown	03J106Lm
CARROLL, Maria	15	F	Unknown	03J106Lm
BARRETT, Honor	19	F	Unknown	03J106Lm
RYDER, Thomas	19	M	Unknown	03J106Lm
FANY, Peter	13	M	Unknown	03J106Lm
FLYNN, John	14	M	Unknown	03J106Lm
Mary	17	F	Unknown	03J106Lm
BERMINGHAM, John	19	M	Unknown	03J106Lm
CAUFIELD, Martin	30	M	Unknown	03J106Lm
CARROLL, Bridget	18	F	Unknown	03J106Lm
KELLY, John	36	M	Unknown	03J106Lm
GLYNN, Mary	25	F	Unknown	03J106Lm
CAVANAGH, Honor	24	F	Unknown	03J106Lm
PARKER, John	22	M	Unknown	03J106Lm
KENNEDY, William	21	M	Unknown	03J106Lm
SCULLY, Patt.	30	M	Unknown	03J106Lm
DUNNE, Larance	14	M	Unknown	03J106Lm
CANNON, John	45	M	Unknown	03J106Lm
HENERTY, Michal	26	M	Unknown	03J106Lm
OMALLY, Celia	15	F	Unknown	03J106Lm
CAREY, Catherine	18	F	Unknown	03J106Lm

CALEDONIA 05 JULY 1849

From Londonderry

NAMES OF PASSENGERS	AGE	SEX	OCCUPATIONS	DATE PORT SHIP
COLLINS, Philip	20	M	Unknown	05J101Af
GIVENS, Robert-H.	20	M	Unknown	05J101Af
GREEN, Patrick	50	M	Unknown	05J101Af
CRERON, Chas.	45	M	Unknown	05J101Af
MCFADDON, Dennis	32	M	Unknown	05J101Af
MILLS, Robert	32	M	Unknown	05J101Af
CARTER, Ninian	49	M	Unknown	05J101Af
PORTER, Geo.	41	M	Unknown	05J101Af
John	14	M	Unknown	05J101Af
IRVINE, Wm.	23	M	Unknown	05J101Af
Anne	19	F	Unknown	05J101Af
BRITTON, Geo.	16	M	Unknown	05J101Af
IRVINE, Henry	16	M	Unknown	05J101Af
Thos.	17	M	Unknown	05J101Af
Ann	18	F	Unknown	05J101Af
WILSON, Mary	18	F	Unknown	05J101Af
CALLION, Wm.W.	17	M	Unknown	05J101Af
WEIR, Jane	23	F	Unknown	05J101Af
KILLUM, Hugh	29	M	Unknown	05J101Af
Mary	16	F	Unknown	05J101Af
Ally	17	F	Unknown	05J101Af
FINLEY, Wm.	34	M	Unknown	05J101Af
CALDWELL, Moses	37	M	Unknown	05J101Af
RAULSTON, James	31	M	Unknown	05J101Af
ALYNGHOW, Mary	45	F	Unknown	05J101Af
GAULOGHER, Jas.	40	M	Unknown	05J101Af
HORKIN, Dominick	36	M	Unknown	05J101Af
BROWNLEA, Thos.	17	M	Unknown	05J101Af
Alex.	18	M	Unknown	05J101Af
BROWN, Eliz.	21	F	Unknown	05J101Af
Cath.	39	F	Unknown	05J101Af
NOLIK, Martha	34	F	Unknown	05J101Af
TOWER, Eliz.	26	F	Unknown	05J101Af
MCKENNA, Ellen	22	F	Unknown	05J101Af
MILLER, Margt.	16	F	Unknown	05J101Af
DONOGHY, Mich.	19	M	Unknown	05J101Af
Mary	14	F	Unknown	05J101Af
HANEGAN, Ann	33	F	Unknown	05J101Af
SHORKY, Margt.	18	F	Unknown	05J101Af
MCGUINESS, Biddy	16	F	Unknown	05J101Af
BEATTY, Wm.	13	M	Unknown	05J101Af
James	14	M	Unknown	05J101Af
FITZPATRICK, Joseph	38	M	Unknown	05J101Af
MCCAULEY, Wm.	31	M	Unknown	05J101Af
John	19	M	Unknown	05J101Af
Jane	18	F	Unknown	05J101Af
EARLY, Reuben	17	M	Unknown	05J101Af
Mary	16	F	Unknown	05J101Af
WOLVER, Jane	31	F	Unknown	05J101Af
MCNULTY, James	38	M	Unknown	05J101Af
Cath.	40	F	Unknown	05J101Af
MCSHANEY, Michael	26	M	Unknown	05J101Af
ROBINSON, Ecey	28	M	Unknown	05J101Af
MCDODE, Margt.	30	F	Unknown	05J101Af
DOUGHERTY, James	19	M	Unknown	05J101Af
Biddy	17	F	Unknown	05J101Af
Mary	19	F	Unknown	05J101Af
Alex.	27	M	Unknown	05J101Af
MCEHHILL, Ann	29	F	Unknown	05J101Af
MCCONDBEN, Leslin	21	F	Unknown	05J101Af
Jane	23	F	Unknown	05J101Af
Jane-A.	19	F	Unknown	05J101Af
REID, Joh.	17	M	Unknown	05J101Af
FORBES, Mary	16	F	Unknown	05J101Af
MILTON, James	18	M	Unknown	05J101Af

NAMES OF PASSENGERS	AGE	SEX	OCCUPATIONS	DATE PORT SHIP
HILL, James	37	M	Unknown	05J101Af
Stewart	48	M	Unknown	05J101Af
Margt.	43	F	Unknown	05J101Af
LITTLE, Ann	42	F	Unknown	05J101Af
MCGEA, Edwin	50	M	Unknown	05J101Af
ANDERSON, John	36	M	Unknown	05J101Af
KEENAN, John	39	M	Unknown	05J101Af
SCOTT, Ellen	17	F	Unknown	05J101Af
FARREN, James	16	M	Unknown	05J101Af
MENENIG, Peter-M.	21	M	Unknown	05J101Af
PAUL, Wm.	28	M	Unknown	05J101Af
KELLY, Anna	50	F	Unknown	05J101Af
Leonard	49	M	Unknown	05J101Af
Sarah	38	F	Unknown	05J101Af
Ellen	20	F	Unknown	05J101Af
Rebecca	19	F	Unknown	05J101Af
James	17	M	Unknown	05J101Af
Eliz.	20	F	Unknown	05J101Af
HORSHON, Mary-J.	19	F	Unknown	05J101Af
HASSIN, James	27	M	Unknown	05J101Af
PATTERSON, Joseph	19	M	Unknown	05J101Af
Mary	22	F	Unknown	05J101Af
U, James	29	M	Unknown	05J101Af
Gily	36	M	Unknown	05J101Af
Bidy	28	F	Unknown	05J101Af
Edwd.	31	M	Unknown	05J101Af
JOLAND, Robt.	27	M	Unknown	05J101Af
CAMPBELL, Mary-J.	25	F	Unknown	05J101Af
MCCOMB, Cath.	27	F	Unknown	05J101Af
MCCULLOUGH, Pat.	21	M	Unknown	05J101Af
TAGUE, Pat.	19	M	Unknown	05J101Af
WORK, Rebecca	29	F	Unknown	05J101Af
CONNOR, Dennis	16	M	Unknown	05J101Af
BROWN, James	17	M	Unknown	05J101Af
LAHERTY, Ann	14	F	Unknown	05J101Af
SHIRT, Patrick	15	M	Unknown	05J101Af
Mary	17	F	Unknown	05J101Af
Wm.	13	M	Unknown	05J101Af
BOYER, John	19	M	Unknown	05J101Af
WILSON, Robert	19	M	Unknown	05J101Af
Ann-J.	21	F	Unknown	05J101Af
Isabella	19	F	Unknown	05J101Af
Mary	23	F	Unknown	05J101Af
Robert	14	M	Unknown	05J101Af
John	17	M	Unknown	05J101Af
Thomas	18	M	Unknown	05J101Af
CILLEN, Cath.	17	F	Unknown	05J101Af
MCEHLING, Isabella	18	F	Unknown	05J101Af
WOODS, Jane	21	F	Unknown	05J101Af
MOOD, Wm.	27	M	Unknown	05J101Af
MCELROY, Wm.	29	M	Unknown	05J101Af
HACKETT, U-Mr.	41	M	Unknown	05J101Af
WATSON, Ellen	19	F	Unknown	05J101Af
FOX, Edwin	29	M	Unknown	05J101Af
ORR, Wm.	30	M	Unknown	05J101Af
PATTON, Margt.	32	F	Unknown	05J101Af
GRESHOW, David	37	M	Unknown	05J101Af
Margt.	39	F	Unknown	05J101Af
Sarah	29	F	Unknown	05J101Af
Wm.	38	M	Unknown	05J101Af
Margt.	36	F	Unknown	05J101Af
Mary-A.	38	F	Unknown	05J101Af
Bessy	27	F	Unknown	05J101Af
MCQUILKEN, David	49	M	Unknown	05J101Af
Sarah	38	F	Unknown	05J101Af
Jane	1	F	Child	05J101Af
STEWART, Chas.	17	M	Unknown	05J101Af
BREEN, Mary	18	F	Unknown	05J101Af
Bridget	25	F	Unknown	05J101Af
WOUGH, David	27	M	Unknown	05J101Af
MCCAULEY, Samuel	29	M	Unknown	05J101Af
FERRY, Cornelius	36	M	Unknown	05J101Af
LOUGHLIN, Lary	38	U	Unknown	05J101Af
Anny	47	F	Unknown	05J101Af
MCLAUGHLIN, Wm.	44	M	Unknown	05J101Af
GALWAY, Alex.	30	M	Unknown	05J101Af
MCGEE, Mary-A.	18	F	Unknown	05J101Af
KELLY, James	17	M	Unknown	05J101Af
Ellen	37	F	Unknown	05J101Af
KIRNEY, John	35	M	Unknown	05J101Af
Biddy	35	M	Unknown	05J101Af
MONAGHAN, Margt.	29	F	Unknown	05J101Af
BOLENTINE, Jane	27	F	Unknown	05J101Af
Jane	25	F	Unknown	05J101Af
ARMSTRONG, Joh.	27	M	Unknown	05J101Af
FRYSE, Sarah	19	F	Unknown	05J101Af
BOYLE, May	19	F	Unknown	05J101Af
MCCOWEN, Matilda	20	F	Unknown	05J101Af
DONOGHY, Ellen	19	F	Unknown	05J101Af
KILPATRICK, Wm.	18	M	Unknown	05J101Af
MILLER, James	31	M	Unknown	05J101Af
Margt.	32	F	Unknown	05J101Af
DIVETT, W.	29	U	Unknown	05J101Af
FEELY, James-M.	40	M	Unknown	05J101Af
MCGIRLY, James	39	M	Unknown	05J101Af
MCCLOSKY, Hugh	27	M	Unknown	05J101Af
James	25	M	Unknown	05J101Af
BONER, Pat.	24	M	Unknown	05J101Af
CORBITT, David	18	M	Unknown	05J101Af
Jane	19	F	Unknown	05J101Af
ODONNELL, Patrick	21	M	Unknown	05J101Af
WARNOCK, Jane	27	F	Unknown	05J101Af
BOYLE, Edwd.	26	M	Unknown	05J101Af
Neal	24	M	Unknown	05J101Af
COYLE, Sarah	27	F	Unknown	05J101Af
DOUGHERTY, Tomy	29	M	Unknown	05J101Af
PATTERSON, Joh.	28	M	Unknown	05J101Af
PEOPLES, Mary	21	F	Unknown	05J101Af
MCCLEON, Thomas	21	M	Unknown	05J101Af
MCCLOSKY, Ellen	22	F	Unknown	05J101Af
DUFFY, Pat.	19	M	Unknown	05J101Af
Cath.	18	F	Unknown	05J101Af
MCCON, Thomas	16	M	Unknown	05J101Af
WILLSON, Wm.	17	M	Unknown	05J101Af
CAMPBELL, Michl.	20	M	Unknown	05J101Af
Ellen	21	F	Unknown	05J101Af
U	1	F	Child	05J101Af
ANDERSON, James	17	M	Unknown	05J101Af
NOBLE, Ann	21	F	Unknown	05J101Af
Eliza	28	F	Unknown	05J101Af
John	31	M	Unknown	05J101Af
STEWART, Mary	20	F	Unknown	05J101Af
REYNOLDS, James-M.	18	M	Unknown	05J101Af
RODGERS, Eliz.	37	F	Unknown	05J101Af
MCHENRY, James	21	M	Unknown	05J101Af
DEAN, John	21	M	Unknown	05J101Af
CREAN, Margt.	30	F	Unknown	05J101Af
MCLOUGHLIN, John-W.	29	M	Unknown	05J101Af
Ann	25	F	Unknown	05J101Af
Margt.	27	F	Unknown	05J101Af
Hugh	22	M	Unknown	05J101Af
Wm.	21	M	Unknown	05J101Af
CARLON, Philip	20	M	Unknown	05J101Af
Sarah	19	F	Unknown	05J101Af
John	19	M	Unknown	05J101Af
Mary	15	F	Unknown	05J101Af
Eliz.	16	F	Unknown	05J101Af
James	17	M	Unknown	05J101A
Hugh	18	M	Unknown	05J101A
DEMPSEY, Nancy	19	F	Unknown	05J101A
LEITCH, Rebecca	19	F	Unknown	05J101A
BARD, Jas.	22	M	Unknown	05J101A
DAULY, John	19	M	Unknown	05J101A
Ellen	26	F	Unknown	05J101A
DUFFY, Danl.	24	M	Unknown	05J101A
MCQUADE, Jane	27	F	Unknown	05J101A
ORR, Margt.	21	F	Unknown	05J101A
POLLOCK, Isabella	21	F	Unknown	05J101A
RODDEY, Chas.	29	M	Unknown	05J101A
GREEN, Nancy	30	F	Unknown	05J101A

NAMES OF PASSENGERS	AGE	SEX	OCCUPATIONS	DATE PORT SHIP
COLLINS, James	31	M	Unknown	05J101Af
SNEA, Ellen	36	F	Unknown	05J101Af
John	39	M	Unknown	05J101Af
SWEENEY, Nancy	33	F	Unknown	05J101Af
CORBITT, David	37	M	Unknown	05J101Af
Jane	29	F	Unknown	05J101Af
GLENHOLME, U-Miss	21	F	Unknown	05J101Af
BLAKELEY, Robert	18	M	Unknown	05J101Af
Hugh	19	M	Unknown	05J101Af
HENDERSON, Ann	30	F	Unknown	05J101Af
James	29	M	Unknown	05J101Af
LIVINGSTON, James	35	M	Unknown	05J101Af
BURNS, Wm.	36	M	Unknown	05J101Af
BRONDON, James	39	M	Unknown	05J101Af
CARLON, U	.00	U	Infant	05J101Af
HENDERSON, U	.00	U	Infant	05J101Af

HENRY-POTTINGER 05 JULY 1849

From Liverpool

NAMES OF PASSENGERS	AGE	SEX	OCCUPATIONS	DATE PORT SHIP
PAISLEY, Richard	20	M	Laborer	05J102Ls
U-Mrs.	20	F	Laborer	05J102Ls
SMITH, Priscilla	21	F	Laborer	05J102Ls
PAISLEY, Richd.	3	M	Child	05J102Ls
Arthur	.00	M	Infant	05J102Ls
COLLIER, Jane	20	F	Laborer	05J102Ls
KELLY, Wm.	18	M	Laborer	05J102Ls
COLLINS, James	23	M	Laborer	05J102Ls
REILLY, Pat.	27	M	Laborer	05J102Ls
Ann	32	F	Laborer	05J102Ls
Edward	10	M	Child	05J102Ls
Ann	.00	F	Infant	05J102Ls
MCVEIGH, John	20	M	Laborer	05J102Ls
TAGGERT, Jane	20	F	Laborer	05J102Ls
WHITE, Thos.	20	M	Laborer	05J102Ls
GILROY, Lawr.	20	M	Laborer	05J102Ls
EWING, Edwd.	30	M	Laborer	05J102Ls
Ellen	70	F	Laborer	05J102Ls
Pat.	12	M	Laborer	05J102Ls
CONNELL, Mary	19	F	Laborer	05J102Ls
CAREY, Fran.	30	U	Laborer	05J102Ls
Rose	30	F	Laborer	05J102Ls
Biddy	10	F	Child	05J102Ls
Ann	8	F	Child	05J102Ls
Barney	7	M	Child	05J102Ls
Mary	51	F	Laborer	05J102Ls
Betty	.00	F	Infant	05J102Ls
Mary-A.	.00	F	Infant	05J102Ls
John	25	M	Laborer	05J102Ls
MADDEN, Jas.	30	M	Laborer	05J102Ls
HEATON, Sarah	40	F	Laborer	05J102Ls
CHAPMAN, Wm.	20	M	Laborer	05J102Ls
HENBRY, Simon	28	M	Laborer	05J102Ls
Maria	22	F	Laborer	05J102Ls
MORRIS, M.	17	U	Laborer	05J102Ls
MONTAGUE, Thos.	20	M	Laborer	05J102Ls
COLEBROOK, Robt.	32	M	Laborer	05J102Ls
U-Mrs.	32	F	Laborer	05J102Ls
Robt.	8	M	Child	05J102Ls
Sarah	5	F	Child	05J102Ls
Harriet	.00	F	Infant	05J102Ls
HEARN, Stephen	46	M	Laborer	05J102Ls
Alfred	.00	M	Infant	05J102Ls
Died-At-Sea				
MORDON, Mathew	70	M	Laborer	05J102Ls
HEARN, James	.00	M	Infant	05J102Ls
MCCANN, Mich.	25	M	Laborer	05J102Ls
U-Mrs.	25	F	Laborer	05J102Ls
MCCANN, Mich.	.00	M	Infant	05J102Ls
TORCH, John	25	M	Laborer	05J102Ls
CONNOLLY, Phobe	30	F	Laborer	05J102Ls
HUGHES, Mary	40	F	Laborer	05J102Ls
Mary	16	F	Laborer	05J102Ls
Edw.	13	M	Laborer	05J102Ls
Cath.	18	F	Laborer	05J102Ls
SHAW, Eliza.	16	F	Laborer	05J102Ls
LEARY, Pat.	20	M	Laborer	05J102Ls
CASEY, Michl.	25	M	Laborer	05J102Ls
Margt.	20	F	Laborer	05J102Ls
HUNT, Jas.	18	M	Laborer	05J102Ls
GALLAGHER, Pat.	19	M	Laborer	05J102Ls
HUNT, Cath.	17	F	Laborer	05J102Ls
GALLAGHER, Cath.	18	F	Laborer	05J102Ls
RYAN, Margt.	17	F	Laborer	05J102Ls
LEWIS, Dan.	25	M	Laborer	05J102Ls
MARLEY, Thos.	35	M	Laborer	05J102Ls
U-Mrs.	30	F	Laborer	05J102Ls
Richd.	.00	M	Infant	05J102Ls
Mary	27	F	Laborer	05J102Ls
KIRKWOOD, Wm.	20	M	Laborer	05J102Ls
BRIANS, Thos.	20	M	Laborer	05J102Ls
SWIFT, Chris.	20	M	Laborer	05J102Ls
FAY, Chris.	20	M	Laborer	05J102Ls
MALONE, Esther	20	F	Laborer	05J102Ls
DONOHER, Bridgt.	7	F	Child	05J102Ls
GALLAGHER, Pat.	20	M	Laborer	05J102Ls
MULLIGAN, Jas.	23	M	Laborer	05J102Ls
Eliza.	25	F	Laborer	05J102Ls
LIDON, John	20	M	Laborer	05J102Ls
MCGOUGH, Cath.	18	F	Laborer	05J102Ls
DAVIES, Wm.	36	M	Laborer	05J102Ls
MCLAUGHLIN, Michl.	50	M	Laborer	05J102Ls
Michl.	24	M	Laborer	05J102Ls
GIBSON, John	28	M	Laborer	05J102Ls
Susan (W)	25	F	None	05J102Ls
DELANEY, Cath.	24	F	Laborer	05J102Ls
BURKES, Edw.	18	M	Laborer	05J102Ls
Bridget	16	F	Laborer	05J102Ls
Hannah	13	F	Laborer	05J102Ls
Mary	.00	F	Infant	05J102Ls
DONOVAN, B.	22	U	Infant	05J102Ls
REILLY, Hugh	30	M	Laborer	05J102Ls
MURPHY, Pat.	35	M	Laborer	05J102Ls
U-Mrs.	22	F	Laborer	05J102Ls
Margt.	.00	F	Infant	05J102Ls
John	25	M	Laborer	05J102Ls
ARMSTRONG, Wm.	18	M	Laborer	05J102Ls
MURPHY, Ellen	22	F	Laborer	05J102Ls
ARMSTRONG, Honora	45	F	Laborer	05J102Ls
MELTRO, Michl.	25	M	Laborer	05J102Ls
BARLOW, Pat.	37	M	Laborer	05J102Ls
NICHOLS, John	19	M	Laborer	05J102Ls
MCNULTY, David	19	M	Laborer	05J102Ls
EDWARD, David	19	M	Laborer	05J102Ls
GUINN, Thos.	18	M	Laborer	05J102Ls
KELLY, Pat.	25	M	Laborer	05J102Ls
U-Mrs.	25	F	Laborer	05J102Ls
GORDON, Michl.	40	M	Laborer	05J102Ls
MALONEY, Bessey	40	F	Laborer	05J102Ls
MCDERMOTT, M.	23	U	Laborer	05J102Ls
OWEN, John	24	M	Laborer	05J102Ls
MCAVOY, John	45	M	Laborer	05J102Ls
Bridget	19	F	Laborer	05J102Ls
CAREHER, John	30	M	Laborer	05J102Ls
KANE, Michl.	28	M	Laborer	05J102Ls
CRAWLEY, Mary	30	F	Laborer	05J102Ls
OATES, James	20	M	Laborer	05J102Ls
CORCORAN, Pat.	26	M	Laborer	05J102Ls
MURPHY, Michl.	26	M	Laborer	05J102Ls
SMITH, Francis	30	M	Laborer	05J102Ls
Margt.	25	F	Laborer	05J102Ls
KNOTWELL, Wm.	58	M	Laborer	05J102Ls
John	18	M	Laborer	05J102Ls

NAMES OF PASSENGERS	AGE	SEX	OCCUPATIONS	DATE PORT SHIP
DERIN, Bridgt.	35	F	Laborer	05JI02Ls
Mary	30	F	Laborer	05JI02Ls
MELVIN, Jas.	30	M	Laborer	05JI02Ls
Geo.	14	M	Laborer	05JI02Ls
CLINTON, John	24	M	Laborer	05JI02Ls
GARRY, Thomas	18	M	Laborer	05JI02Ls
Jas.	16	M	Laborer	05JI02Ls
FORBES, Walter	18	M	Laborer	05JI02Ls
ROGERS, Dolly	25	F	Laborer	05JI02Ls
WALSH, Josh.	21	M	Laborer	05JI02Ls
GERETY, Wm.	30	M	Laborer	05JI02Ls
Margt.	28	F	Laborer	05JI02Ls
James	5	M	Child	05JI02Ls
Thos.	.00	M	Infant	05JI02Ls
DENNERRY, Michl.	26	M	Laborer	05JI02Ls
Mary	10	F	Child	05JI02Ls
Pat	18	M	Laborer	05JI02Ls
CROSBY, Thos.	24	M	Laborer	05JI02Ls
DOOGAN, Pat.	15	M	Laborer	05JI02Ls
Jas.	.00	M	Infant	05JI02Ls
ROBINSON, Mat.	32	M	Laborer	05JI02Ls
MCKAY, Cath.	40	F	Laborer	05JI02Ls
Mary	11	F	Laborer	05JI02Ls
Cath.	.00	F	Infant	05JI02Ls
SHAUGHNESSY, Pat.	29	M	Laborer	05JI02Ls
MORGAN, Pat.	26	M	Laborer	05JI02Ls
COSGROVE, Judith	30	F	Laborer	05JI02Ls
WILSON, Edwd.	26	M	Laborer	05JI02Ls
Jno.	23	M	Laborer	05JI02Ls
CROW, Jas.	22	M	Laborer	05JI02Ls
Jno.	18	M	Laborer	05JI02Ls
MCALISTER, Jno.	22	M	Laborer	05JI02Ls
CONNOR, Pat.	28	M	Laborer	05JI02Ls
Dennis	20	M	Laborer	05JI02Ls
HASTINGS, John	24	M	Laborer	05JI02Ls
Jane	21	F	Laborer	05JI02Ls
BOYLE, Jas.	31	M	Laborer	05JI02Ls
CUNNAHAN, Ann	30	F	Laborer	05JI02Ls
Eliza.	.00	F	Infant	05JI02Ls
YOUNG, Wm.	26	M	Laborer	05JI02Ls
HARDEN, Wm.	31	M	Laborer	05JI02Ls
MURPHY, Michl.	50	M	Laborer	05JI02Ls
Pat.	13	M	Laborer	05JI02Ls
Jas.	11	M	Laborer	05JI02Ls
WHELAN, Michl.	20	M	Laborer	05JI02Ls
Cath. (W)	23	F	Laborer	05JI02Ls
DUGAN, Betty	20	F	Laborer	05JI02Ls
SCREM, John	25	M	Laborer	05JI02Ls
JARVIS, John	20	M	Laborer	05JI02Ls
WILLIAMS, Geo.	30	M	Laborer	05JI02Ls
HYNES, Thos.	28	M	Laborer	05JI02Ls
Margt.	27	F	Laborer	05JI02Ls
FLYNN, Michl.	25	M	Laborer	05JI02Ls
Jas.	24	M	Laborer	05JI02Ls
BURN, John	26	M	Laborer	05JI02Ls
HYNES, Johana	.00	F	Infant	05JI02Ls
KIRBY, Danl.	28	M	Laborer	05JI02Ls
MCGUIRE, Dennis	20	M	Laborer	05JI02Ls
MURPHY, Tim.	30	M	Laborer	05JI02Ls
TOLEIN, Edwd.	20	M	Laborer	05JI02Ls
CLIFFORD, Judy	24	F	Laborer	05JI02Ls
CUNNINGHAM, Thos.	19	M	Laborer	05JI02Ls
Peter	20	M	Laborer	05JI02Ls
GRAY, Alexr.	24	M	Laborer	05JI02Ls
GRUBB, Mary	24	F	Laborer	05JI02Ls
GERRETY, Mary	20	F	Laborer	05JI02Ls
OHERN, Thos.	25	M	Laborer	05JI02Ls
Ellen	19	F	Laborer	05JI02Ls
Bridget	.00	F	Infant	05JI02Ls
Danl.	18	M	Laborer	05JI02Ls
HASTINGS, Hope	18	F	Laborer	05JI02Ls
SAVAGE, Geo.B.	25	M	Laborer	05JI02Ls
GRAND, Geo.	26	M	Laborer	05JI02Ls
Crane-TARNE, Sarah	30	F	Laborer	05JI02Ls
Thos.	33	M	Laborer	05JI02Ls
Crane-TARNE, Jas.	50	M	Laborer	05JI02Ls
John	8	M	Child	05JI02Ls
SMITH, Wm.M.	21	M	Laborer	05JI02Ls
COWAN, Francis	40	M	Laborer	05JI02Ls
U-Mrs.	35	F	Laborer	05JI02Ls
Cath.	30	F	Laborer	05JI02Ls
BRADBURN, John	20	M	Laborer	05JI02Ls
COWAN, Henry	5	M	Child	05JI02Ls
LIVINGSTON, Jas.	.00	M	Infant	05JI02Ls
KELLY, Henry	40	M	Laborer	05JI02Ls
BAXTER, Robt.	23	M	Laborer	05JI02Ls
SORBY, Richd.	29	M	Laborer	05JI02Ls
MCCARTHY, Dennis	34	M	Laborer	05JI02Ls
MURPHY, Margt.	15	F	Laborer	05JI02Ls
Hogey-FOLEY, Bridget	16	F	Laborer	05JI02Ls
Maguire-MORGAN, Judy	19	F	Laborer	05JI02Ls
BYRNE, Pat.	18	M	Laborer	05JI02Ls
Thos.	34	M	Laborer	05JI02Ls
NEVIN, Michl.	26	M	Laborer	05JI02Ls
Mary	14	F	Laborer	05JI02Ls
Bridget	7	F	Child	05JI02Ls
MCLAUGHLIN, Maggy	40	F	Laborer	05JI02Ls
Cath.	6	F	Child	05JI02Ls
Edw.	4	M	Child	05JI02Ls
Mary	.00	F	Infant	05JI02Ls
John	.00	M	Infant	05JI02Ls
HUGHES, John	26	M	Laborer	05JI02Ls
FARRELL, Pat.	25	M	Laborer	05JI02Ls
MCCULLOUGH, Eliza.	18	F	Laborer	05JI02Ls
MOLDON, Mary	30	F	Laborer	05JI02Ls
RIORDAN, Pat	20	M	Laborer	05JI02Ls
NEVEN, Michl.	50	M	Laborer	05JI02Ls
KELLY, Ann	20	F	Laborer	05JI02Ls
HOLMES, Thorpe	30	M	Laborer	05JI02Ls
MAHER, Pat.	20	M	Laborer	05JI02Ls
COYNE, Thos.	21	M	Laborer	05JI02Ls
BURKE, Anty.	21	M	Laborer	05JI02Ls
Bridget	18	F	Laborer	05JI02Ls
OCONNOR, U-Miss	20	F	Laborer	05JI02Ls
ROLLISTER, Wm.	21	M	Laborer	05JI02Ls

HERMES 05 JULY 1849

From Newcastle

NAMES OF PASSENGERS	AGE	SEX	OCCUPATIONS	DATE PORT SHIP
BYRON, Julia-Amelia	24	F	Spinster	05JI18La
RIDLEY, Elizabeth-Ann	18	F	Spinster	05JI18La
HUNTER, Walter	17	M	Smith	05JI18La
COULSON, James	23	M	Clerk	05JI18La
TAYLERSON, Robert	58	M	Joiner	05JI18La
Thomas	27	M	Joiner	05JI18La
Ann (W)	25	F	Wife	05JI18La
Isabella (D)	19	F	None	05JI18La
Frances (D)	17	F	None	05JI18La
Esther-Emma (D)	15	F	None	05JI18La
Mary-Ann (D)	12	F	None	05JI18La
Robert (S)	10	M	None	05JI18La
George (S)	1	M	Child	05JI18La

YORKSHIRE 05 JULY 1849

From Liverpool

NAMES OF PASSENGERS	AGE	SEX	OCCUPATIONS	DATE PORT SHIP
MCEVOY, Cornelius	29	M	Printer	05JI02Lz
Anna-Jane	29	F	Printer	05JI02Lz
James-Murray	2	M	Child	05JI02Lz
Hugh-Barned	.05	M	Infant	05JI02Lz
Bridget	22	F	Unknown	05JI02Lz
ROWAN, Patrick	35	M	Farmer	05JI02Lz
Elizabeth	22	F	Farmer	05JI02Lz
Antony	.06	M	Infant	05JI02Lz
SMITH, James	30	M	Farmer	05JI02Lz
MALONE, James	23	M	Farmer	05JI02Lz
FITZGERALD, Richard	21	M	Servant	05JI02Lz
HAND, Alice	24	F	Unknown	05JI02Lz
GILLAN, Thomas	50	M	Farmer	05JI02Lz
Frances	25	M	Brf	05JI02Lz
SPENCE, Robert	66	M	Weaver	05JI02Lz
MURRAY, Anne	60	F	Unknown	05JI02Lz
SHEEHAN, Margaret	24	F	Unknown	05JI02Lz
CROKER, Mary	70	F	Unknown	05JI02Lz
FLYNN, Catherine	30	F	Unknown	05JI02Lz
MCALISTER, Nancy	32	F	Unknown	05JI02Lz
RUTLEDGE, Mary-Jane	26	F	Unknown	05JI02Lz
CAMPBELL, Nancy	16	F	Unknown	05JI02Lz
DEWELYEN, Anne	34	F	Unknown	05JI02Lz
SMITH, Jane	35	F	Unknown	05JI02Lz
Jane	12	F	Unknown	05JI02Lz
William	9	M	Child	05JI02Lz
Thomas	7	M	Child	05JI02Lz
John	3	M	Child	05JI02Lz
Mary-Anne	1	F	Child	05JI02Lz
MCGALL, Mary	20	F	Unknown	05JI02Lz
FLYNN, John	36	M	Laborer	05JI02Lz
Mary	1	F	Child	05JI02Lz
Edward	.04	M	Infant	05JI02Lz
DALY, Michael	30	M	Laborer	05JI02Lz
Mathew	3	M	Child	05JI02Lz
Mary	10	F	Unknown	05JI02Lz
Lawrence	6	M	Child	05JI02Lz
MCKERNAN, Barney	25	M	Laborer	05JI02Lz
DARBY, William	21	M	Laborer	05JI02Lz
DONEGAN, Owen	28	M	Laborer	05JI02Lz
RUTLEDGE, Hugh	27	M	Shoemaker	05JI02Lz
William	1	M	Child	05JI02Lz
NEIL, Judith	20	F	Unknown	05JI02Lz
LYNCH, Thomas	3	M	Child	05JI02Lz
Margaret	5	F	Child	05JI02Lz
COGHLAN, Margaret	28	F	Unknown	05JI02Lz
NAGLE, Garrett	15	M	Unknown	05JI02Lz
DUNN, Christopher	15	M	Unknown	05JI02Lz
SHANAHAN, Ellen	12	F	Unknown	05JI02Lz
Margaret	10	F	Unknown	05JI02Lz
ROCK, Ellen	32	F	Unknown	05JI02Lz
MILES, Mary-Jane	16	F	Unknown	05JI02Lz
HARTY, Alice	30	F	Unknown	05JI02Lz
Andrew	2	M	Child	05JI02Lz
NICOLE, Jane	21	F	Unknown	05JI02Lz
SHAUGHNESSY, Patrick	30	M	Laborer	05JI02Lz
SHARR, Ann	40	F	Unknown	05JI02Lz
Margaret	3	F	Child	05JI02Lz
MCGUIRE, John	40	M	Laborer	05JI02Lz
Michael	7	M	Child	05JI02Lz
WARD, John	27	M	Blacksmith	05JI02Lz
HANRATTY, Thomas	19	M	Shopkeeper	05JI02Lz
John	6	M	Child	05JI02Lz
DWELYR, William	30	M	Blacksmith	05JI02Lz
MCINERNEY, Anne	32	F	Unknown	05JI02Lz
MCINNERNY, James	22	M	Shop Boy	05JI02Lz
MCGULL, Robert-John	18	M	Weaver	05JI02Lz
MCDONALD, James	18	M	Unknown	05JI02Lz
MURRAY, Sarah	12	F	Unknown	05JI02Lz
EGAN, Thomas	30	M	Groom	05JI02Lz
Ellen	2	F	Child	05JI02Lz
Mary	25	F	Unknown	05JI02Lz
Patrick	3	M	Child	05JI02Lz
BYRNE, Mary	22	F	Unknown	05JI02Lz
MCGUIRE, Mary	30	F	Unknown	05JI02Lz
Mary	.03	F	Infant	05JI02Lz
John	10	M	Unknown	05JI02Lz
Nicholas	5	M	Child	05JI02Lz
CAMPBELL, Margaret	25	F	Unknown	05JI02Lz
FARNAN, Michael	25	M	Laborer	05JI02Lz
MCGONNELL, Ellen	40	F	Unknown	05JI02Lz
KILROY, Sarah	17	F	Unknown	05JI02Lz
Ellen	19	F	Unknown	05JI02Lz
REINEY, Marylon	14	F	Unknown	05JI02Lz
DONNELLY, Ellen	26	F	Unknown	05JI02Lz
MCCONERIN, Anne	20	F	Unknown	05JI02Lz
DONNELLY, Catherine	20	F	Unknown	05JI02Lz
MCGERR, Ellen	20	F	Unknown	05JI02Lz
Nancy	18	F	Unknown	05JI02Lz
DANIEL, Judith	14	F	Unknown	05JI02Lz
BLACKBURNE, Thomas	19	M	Clerk	05JI02Lz
MORROH, Eliza	10	F	Unknown	05JI02Lz
MULLIGAN, Mary	26	F	Unknown	05JI02Lz
CARRIGAN, James	30	M	Unknown	05JI02Lz
MULLIGAN, Bridget	16	F	Unknown	05JI02Lz
KIRKLAND, Eliza	30	F	Unknown	05JI02Lz
MCINTRIE, Winiford	15	F	Unknown	05JI02Lz
MCANDREW, Mary	17	M	Unknown	05JI02Lz
LEE, Michael	20	M	Unknown	05JI02Lz
FLYNN, Susannah	28	F	Unknown	05JI02Lz
Thomas	3	M	Child	05JI02Lz
SHIELDS, Margery	60	F	Unknown	05JI02Lz
DONNELLY, Catherine	18	F	Unknown	05JI02Lz
NALLY, John	20	M	Unknown	05JI02Lz
GRAY, Catherine	30	F	Unknown	05JI02Lz
John	5	M	Child	05JI02Lz
COYNE, Bridget	20	F	Unknown	05JI02Lz
CORCORAN, Patrick	19	M	Unknown	05JI02Lz
MCCHEANS, Patrick	13	M	Unknown	05JI02Lz
MCGEE, Sarah	18	F	Unknown	05JI02Lz
KELLY, Ellen	16	F	Unknown	05JI02Lz
SHEA, Nancy	12	F	Unknown	05JI02Lz
BROWN, Anne	20	F	Unknown	05JI02Lz
SPEAR, James	24	M	Weaver	05JI02Lz
FLYNN, John	26	M	Sailor	05JI02Lz
MCCLENAHAN, James	19	M	Weaver	05JI02Lz
DONNELLY, John	20	M	Weaver	05JI02Lz
CARROLL, William	18	M	Unknown	05JI02Lz
KIRKLAND, Robinson	19	M	Farmer	05JI02Lz
MCGLOUGHLIN, Andrew	20	M	Carpenter	05JI02Lz
MOLLORY, James	35	M	Shoemaker	05JI02Lz
MCCONNELL, Mary	58	F	Unknown	05JI02Lz
SHAUGHNESSEY, Bridget	20	F	Unknown	05JI02Lz
BILLET, Harriet	53	F	Unknown	05JI02Lz
HOWARTH, Hannah	27	F	Weaver	05JI02Lz
CORCORAN, Cather.	15	F	Unknown	05JI02Lz
MCGILLAN, Rosa	17	F	Unknown	05JI02Lz
BYRNE, Judith	18	F	Unknown	05JI02Lz
KILFADEN, James	3	M	Child	05JI02Lz
MCCRUMLISH, Edmund	16	M	Carpenter	05JI02Lz
MCCUMBERT, Rosa	16	F	Unknown	05JI02Lz
FOX, Jno.	18	M	Unknown	05JI02Lz
QUIN, Johana	20	F	Unknown	05JI02Lz
CALLAHAN, Martha	22	F	Unknown	05JI02Lz
KEARNAN, Michl.	23	M	Unknown	05JI02Lz
CASEY, Mary-H.	20	F	Unknown	05JI02Lz
SMITH, Sarah	28	F	Unknown	05JI02Lz
SHEEHAN, Ellen	30	F	Unknown	05JI02Lz
ODONNELL, John	56	M	Unknown	05JI02Lz
MCCHEANE, Charles	12	M	Unknown	05JI02Lz

NAMES OF PASSENGERS	AGE	SEX	OCCUPATIONS	DATE PORT SHIP
BURKER, Ellen	19	F	Unknown	05JI02Lz
MCILROY, Bridget	30	F	Unknown	05JI02Lz
GRAHAM, Mary	16	F	Unknown	05JI02Lz
BURKE, Margt.	20	F	Unknown	05JI02Lz
GAHNOR, Bridgt.	25	F	Unknown	05JI02Lz
HAGAN, Charles	12	M	Unknown	05JI02Lz
Mary	50	F	Unknown	05JI02Lz
Patrick	9	M	Child	05JI02Lz
ORDON, Ellen	22	F	Unknown	05JI02Lz
MOLONY, Mary	18	F	Unknown	05JI02Lz
MCCHEANE, Bridget	40	F	Unknown	05JI02Lz
John	10	M	Unknown	05JI02Lz
Mary	8	F	Child	05JI02Lz
GRYMES, Margt.	20	F	Unknown	05JI02Lz
MULLIGAN, Denis	23	M	Unknown	05JI02Lz
CASSIDY, Mary	30	F	Unknown	05JI02Lz
BISHOP, Mary	33	F	Unknown	05JI02Lz
Betsey	5	F	Child	05JI02Lz
HALPIN, Mary	23	F	Unknown	05JI02Lz
DALY, Michael	8	M	Child	05JI02Lz
CASSIDY, Patrick	4	M	Child	05JI02Lz
James	2	M	Child	05JI02Lz
TWIGS, Christopher	23	M	Stctr	05JI02Lz
BOYLE, Owen	24	M	Laborer	05JI02Lz
RIELY, Patrick	35	M	Unknown	05JI02Lz
CASTEN, Anne	8	F	Child	05JI02Lz
HAZLETON, James	24	M	Farmer	05JI02Lz
MCEVETT, James	16	M	Unknown	05JI02Lz
EUSTON, George	19	M	Unknown	05JI02Lz
GRYMES, Thomas	35	M	Unknown	05JI02Lz
MURTAGH, Anne	55	F	Unknown	05JI02Lz
MASTERSON, James	27	M	Unknown	05JI02Lz
DARRAGH, John	20	M	Unknown	05JI02Lz
FARRELL, John	23	M	Engineer	05JI02Lz
DOOHAN, Michael	24	M	Unknown	05JI02Lz
HAGARTY, Daniel	20	M	Unknown	05JI02Lz
CONNERS, Mary	19	F	Unknown	05JI02Lz
BYRNE, Frances	25	F	Unknown	05JI02Lz
BANNON, Ellen	25	F	Unknown	05JI02Lz
DARCY, Kenny	14	M	Unknown	05JI02Lz
MARTIN, Joseph	20	M	Unknown	05JI02Lz
BIND, Felix	21	M	Unknown	05JI02Lz
John	7	M	Child	05JI02Lz
LYNCH, Michael	24	M	Unknown	05JI02Lz
CONNOR, Thomas	18	M	Unknown	05JI02Lz
CASEY, Patrick	12	M	Unknown	05JI02Lz
KILGOLLAN, Mary	16	F	Unknown	05JI02Lz
DONNELLY, Mary	30	F	Unknown	05JI02Lz
STEWARD, Mary	17	F	Unknown	05JI02Lz
FARNAN, Jane	14	F	Unknown	05JI02Lz
HEFFERNAN, Michael	20	M	Unknown	05JI02Lz
CULLEN, Mary-Ann	18	F	Unknown	05JI02Lz
CUNAN, Patrick	28	M	Unknown	05JI02Lz
MYLOT, Edward	40	M	Unknown	05JI02Lz
Michael	11	M	Unknown	05JI02Lz
MCCLENNE, Jane	16	F	Unknown	05JI02Lz
CAUSBY, Isabella	14	F	Unknown	05JI02Lz
MCALISTER, Michael	35	M	Stone Mason	05JI02Lz
NULTY, John	21	M	Unknown	05JI02Lz
MCCORMICK, Peter	19	M	Unknown	05JI02Lz
CARVEN, Richard	50	M	Unknown	05JI02Lz
WHITE, Margt.Jane	24	F	Seamstress	05JI02Lz
FARLEY, Mary	23	F	Unknown	05JI02Lz
GABAN, Bridgt.	21	F	Unknown	05JI02Lz
LOUTH, Thomas	24	F	Unknown	05JI02Lz
DWELYR, Sarah	23	F	Unknown	05JI02Lz
CASEY, Morris	7	M	Child	05JI02Lz
LOGAN, Mary	23	F	Weaver	05JI02Lz
BRADY, Alice	20	F	Unknown	05JI02Lz
Alice	50	F	Unknown	05JI02Lz
CULLEN, William	27	M	Maurer	05JI02Lz
GALVIN, Michael	25	M	Unknown	05JI02Lz
CLARKE, Anne	19	F	Unknown	05JI02Lz
DUNN, Catherine	10	F	Unknown	05JI02Lz
Ellen	7	F	Child	05JI02Lz
BURKE, Thomas	46	M	Blacksmith	05JI02Lz
CLARKE, Patrick	30	M	Unknown	05JI02Lz
MCCAREY, Johannah	22	F	Unknown	05JI02Lz
CURTAIN, Ellen	9	F	Child	05JI02Lz
CONNOR, Ellen	20	F	Unknown	05JI02Lz
HENRY, Robert	25	M	Unknown	05JI02Lz
ROCHE, Timothy	27	M	Unknown	05JI02Lz
BROGHAN, John	21	M	Laborer	05JI02Lz
WOOD, Martha	16	F	Unknown	05JI02Lz
CONNOR, Christopher	20	M	Unknown	05JI02Lz
MCCABE, Edward	22	M	Unknown	05JI02Lz
BYRNE, Thomas	16	M	Unknown	05JI02Lz
CONN, John	21	M	Unknown	05JI02Lz
CONWAY, Peter	18	M	Unknown	05JI02Lz
FOX, Wm.	30	M	Carpenter	05JI02Lz
MCGLOUGHLAN, George	26	M	Unknown	05JI02Lz
HALPIN, Michael	30	M	Unknown	05JI02Lz
QUIRNEY, Owen	29	M	Unknown	05JI02Lz
KEATIN, Morris	29	M	Unknown	05JI02Lz
DOLOIN, Anne	17	F	Unknown	05JI02Lz
MCCHEANE, Catherine	6	F	Child	05JI02Lz
KEE, James	22	M	Unknown	05JI02Lz
GALLAGHER, Ellen	20	F	Unknown	05JI02Lz
ROWLANDS, Rachael	10	F	Unknown	05JI02Lz
ROGERS, Hugh	23	F	Sailor	05JI02Lz
MCGONNELL, Sarah	10	F	Unknown	05JI02Lz
COYLAN, Mary	9	F	Child	05JI02Lz
CAMPBELL, Andrew	20	M	Unknown	05JI02Lz

SATELLITE 05 JULY 1849

From Dublin

NAMES OF PASSENGERS	AGE	SEX	OCCUPATIONS	DATE PORT SHIP
KEOUGH, James	40	M	Farmer	05JI12Lp
Mary	35	F	Unknown	05JI12Lp
Henry	13	M	Unknown	05JI12Lp
Jas.	11	M	Unknown	05JI12Lp
James	9	M	Child	05JI12Lp
Anne	.00	F	Infant	05JI12Lp
ROSS, Richard	24	M	Unknown	05JI12Lp
MURPHY, Thomas	22	M	Unknown	05JI12Lp
Ellen	20	F	Unknown	05JI12Lp
ONEILL, U	31	M	Unknown	05JI12Lp
U-Mrs.	30	F	Unknown	05JI12Lp
Lawrence	8	M	Child	05JI12Lp
Mary-Anne	6	F	Child	05JI12Lp
Kate	4	F	Child	05JI12Lp
Jane	.00	F	Infant	05JI12Lp
DALTAN, Margt.	16	F	Unknown	05JI12Lp
ENNISS, U-Miss	27	F	Unknown	05JI12Lp
MEDCAFF, U	22	M	Unknown	05JI12Lp
MASAIN, Edwd.	40	M	Unknown	05JI12Lp
Eilizabeth	35	F	Unknown	05JI12Lp
Eiliza	20	F	Unknown	05JI12Lp
Kate	14	F	Unknown	05JI12Lp
Julia	12	F	Unknown	05JI12Lp
Kyran	21	M	Unknown	05JI12Lp
Edward	17	M	Unknown	05JI12Lp
Fanny	18	F	Unknown	05JI12Lp
Hariett	.00	F	Infant	05JI12Lp
COMEFORD, Anty	18	F	Unknown	05JI12Lp
COSTELLO, Andy	16	M	Unknown	05JI12Lp
KEEGAN, Mary	25	F	Unknown	05JI12Lp
Mary-Anne	13	F	Unknown	05JI12Lp
Eliza	12	F	Unknown	05JI12Lp
TULLY, Peter	25	M	Unknown	05JI12Lp
CASSIDY, John	40	M	Unknown	05JI12Lp
John	16	M	Unknown	05JI12Lp
Patt.	12	M	Unknown	05JI12Lp

NAMES OF PASSENGERS	AGE	SEX	OCCUPATIONS	DATE PORT SHIP
BLAKE, Eliza	40	F	Unknown	05JI12Lp
Andrew	10	M	Unknown	05JI12Lp
John	.00	M	Infant	05JI12Lp
FARRELL, Catherine	20	F	Unknown	05JI12Lp
KENNEDY, Margt.	20	F	Unknown	05JI12Lp
RUSSELL, Wm.	30	M	Unknown	05JI12Lp
U-Mrs.	30	M	Unknown	05JI12Lp
CALLAGHAN, Margt.	23	F	Unknown	05JI12Lp
CONNOR, John	19	M	Unknown	05JI12Lp
LYONS, Robt.	20	M	Unknown	05JI12Lp
LEE, Catherine	18	F	Unknown	05JI12Lp
FITZHARRIS, Pat.	22	M	Unknown	05JI12Lp
NEAL, Pat.	36	M	Unknown	05JI12Lp
John	45	M	Unknown	05JI12Lp
Mary	28	F	Unknown	05JI12Lp
Ann	30	F	Unknown	05JI12Lp
CUFFE, Biddy	20	F	Unknown	05JI12Lp
BUCKLEY, U	28	M	Unknown	05JI12Lp
HORAN, Margt.	13	F	Unknown	05JI12Lp
Richd.	11	M	Unknown	05JI12Lp
MURTEE, Mat.	20	M	Unknown	05JI12Lp
BROWN, U	13	F	Unknown	05JI12Lp
GILBERT, U	40	M	Unknown	05JI12Lp
U-Mrs.	31	F	Unknown	05JI12Lp
Bridget	14	F	Unknown	05JI12Lp
Anne	12	F	Unknown	05JI12Lp
Mary	10	F	Unknown	05JI12Lp
Richard	8	M	Child	05JI12Lp
Thomas	6	M	Child	05JI12Lp
Hand	4	M	Child	05JI12Lp
Eliza	.00	F	Infant	05JI12Lp
CLARKE, U	25	M	Unknown	05JI12Lp
TYE, U	21	M	Unknown	05JI12Lp
MCGOWAN, U	22	M	Unknown	05JI12Lp
U-Mrs.	21	F	Unknown	05JI12Lp
MOORE, J.	32	M	Unknown	05JI12Lp
U-Mrs.	30	F	Unknown	05JI12Lp
Alexander	6	M	Child	05JI12Lp
Dorthea	3	F	Child	05JI12Lp
John	2	M	Child	05JI12Lp
Isabella	.00	F	Infant	05JI12Lp
Anne	34	F	Unknown	05JI12Lp
MANNING, John	30	M	Unknown	05JI12Lp
Elizabeth	24	F	Unknown	05JI12Lp
Hays	3	M	Child	05JI12Lp
Wm.	2	M	Child	05JI12Lp
Robt.	.00	M	Infant	05JI12Lp
MALONE, Sarah	26	F	Unknown	05JI12Lp
FITZSIMONS, Patt.	23	M	Unknown	05JI12Lp
Sarah	20	F	Unknown	05JI12Lp
HAWKINS, Wm.	28	M	Unknown	05JI12Lp
U-Mrs.	22	F	Unknown	05JI12Lp
JACKSON, Catherine	20	F	Unknown	05JI12Lp
POLLARD, Ellen	24	F	Unknown	05JI12Lp
TOTTER, Edwd.	22	M	Unknown	05JI12Lp
BYRNE, James	38	M	Unknown	05JI12Lp
U-Mrs.	30	F	Unknown	05JI12Lp
John	3	M	Child	05JI12Lp
James	.00	M	Infant	05JI12Lp
FRANINE, U	26	M	Unknown	05JI12Lp
GRELIS, Mary	25	F	Unknown	05JI12Lp
MULLINS, P.	24	M	Unknown	05JI12Lp
James	27	M	Unknown	05JI12Lp
John	60	M	Unknown	05JI12Lp
John	60	M	Unknown	05JI12Lp
Jane	28	F	Unknown	05JI12Lp
Mary	7	F	Child	05JI12Lp
RIELLY, P.	55	M	Unknown	05JI12Lp
Rose	55	F	Unknown	05JI12Lp
Mary	25	F	Unknown	05JI12Lp
Andy	30	M	Unknown	05JI12Lp
Owen	32	M	Unknown	05JI12Lp
MATHEWS, Pat.	28	M	Unknown	05JI12Lp
Elizabeth	28	F	Unknown	05JI12Lp
MCCABE, Anne	14	F	Unknown	05JI12Lp
MATHEWS, John	3	M	Child	05JI12Lp
Michl.	.00	M	Infant	05JI12Lp
RIELLY, Mary-A.	25	F	Unknown	05JI12Lp
POLLARD, Mary	18	F	Unknown	05JI12Lp
HOLLYWOOD, Andy	32	M	Unknown	05JI12Lp
U-Mrs.	28	F	Unknown	05JI12Lp
FARRELL, Ann	20	F	Unknown	05JI12Lp
Eliza	12	F	Unknown	05JI12Lp
ROACH, Ellen	63	F	Unknown	05JI12Lp
CASSAN, Harett	20	F	Unknown	05JI12Lp
CURRAN, Peter	40	M	Unknown	05JI12Lp
THOMAS, Ellen	36	F	Unknown	05JI12Lp
Edward	7	M	Child	05JI12Lp
HOLMES, U	28	M	Unknown	05JI12Lp
QUIN, James	35	M	Unknown	05JI12Lp
COGLAN, Pat.	30	M	Unknown	05JI12Lp
Mary	30	F	Unknown	05JI12Lp
Michl.	15	M	Unknown	05JI12Lp
Pat	9	M	Child	05JI12Lp
Wm.	6	M	Child	05JI12Lp
MARTIN, Pat.	36	M	Unknown	05JI12Lp
Anne	36	F	Unknown	05JI12Lp
Julia	9	F	Child	05JI12Lp
DELANY, Pat.	40	M	Unknown	05JI12Lp
Anne	40	F	Unknown	05JI12Lp
Michael	13	M	Unknown	05JI12Lp
MCDONNELL, James	23	M	Unknown	05JI12Lp
Eliza	26	F	Unknown	05JI12Lp
Eliza	25	F	Unknown	05JI12Lp
CONNOR, Mary	18	F	Unknown	05JI12Lp
Peter	13	M	Unknown	05JI12Lp
LEVY, U	40	M	Unknown	05JI12Lp
Eliza	22	F	Unknown	05JI12Lp
Mary-A.	14	F	Unknown	05JI12Lp
COOPER, L.	20	M	Unknown	05JI12Lp
Emily	20	F	Unknown	05JI12Lp
HOOLEY, Catherine	20	F	Unknown	05JI12Lp
DARREDY, Margt.	20	F	Unknown	05JI12Lp
FLANAGAN, John	30	M	Unknown	05JI12Lp
Mary	26	F	Unknown	05JI12Lp
MCCARTHY, U-Mrs.	30	F	Unknown	05JI12Lp
Kate	.00	F	Infant	05JI12Lp
FANINAN, Michael	30	M	Unknown	05JI12Lp
Ellen	31	F	Unknown	05JI12Lp
Anne	28	F	Unknown	05JI12Lp
Mary	.00	F	Infant	05JI12Lp
DEMPSEY, U	26	M	Unknown	05JI12Lp
U-Mrs.	36	F	Unknown	05JI12Lp
Thomas	22	M	Unknown	05JI12Lp
Michl.	20	M	Unknown	05JI12Lp
Edward	15	M	Unknown	05JI12Lp
WILSON, Richard	16	M	Unknown	05JI12Lp
WHELAN, Denis	30	M	Unknown	05JI12Lp
MCALASTER, John	40	M	Unknown	05JI12Lp
DOWNY, Michael	35	M	Unknown	05JI12Lp
MCCOWAN, Catherine	17	F	Unknown	05JI12Lp
GIBSON, U	18	M	Unknown	05JI12Lp
U-Mrs.	24	F	Unknown	05JI12Lp
MATES, Richard	26	M	Unknown	05JI12Lp
BUTTERLY, Matt	15	M	Unknown	05JI12Lp
DEMPSEY, Margt.	20	F	Unknown	05JI12Lp
COSTELLO, John	50	M	Unknown	05JI12Lp
MOORE, Edwd.	28	M	Unknown	05JI12Lp
Mary	17	F	Unknown	05JI12Lp
Wm.	4	M	Child	05JI12Lp
Mary	.00	F	Infant	05JI12Lp
Margt.	21	F	Unknown	05JI12Lp
GILENY, Catherine	21	F	Unknown	05JI12Lp
DOWD, Catherine	22	F	Unknown	05JI12Lp
Mary	20	F	Unknown	05JI12Lp
COFFY, Mary	20	F	Unknown	05JI12Lp
KELLEY, Thos.	24	M	Unknown	05JI12Lp
COYLE, Elizabeth	20	F	Unknown	05JI12Lp
John	21	M	Unknown	05JI12Lp
BROWN, Eliza	20	F	Unknown	05JI12Lp

NAMES OF PASSENGERS	AGE	SEX	OCCUPATIONS	DATE PORT SHIP
JACKSON, U-Miss	24	F	Unknown	05JI12Lp
HUNT, Mary-A.	20	F	Unknown	05JI12Lp
REDMOND, Martin	18	M	Unknown	05JI12Lp
CROSS, Sarah	23	F	Unknown	05JI12Lp
LUSON, Matt.	36	M	Unknown	05JI12Lp
DUNCHAN, Wm.	24	M	Unknown	05JI12Lp
RIELLY, Ann	20	F	Unknown	05JI12Lp
KELLY, John	25	M	Unknown	05JI12Lp
HYLAND, Edward	50	M	Unknown	05JI12Lp
Catherine	13	F	Unknown	05JI12Lp
Anne	8	M	Child	05JI12Lp
LEG, Eliza	20	F	Unknown	05JI12Lp
FAY, Matt	21	M	Unknown	05JI12Lp
DUFFY, Michl.	28	M	Unknown	05JI12Lp
ROARKE, James	24	M	Unknown	05JI12Lp
WALSH, Oliver	26	M	Unknown	05JI12Lp
Mary	22	F	Unknown	05JI12Lp
EVANS,. Tom.	40	M	Unknown	05JI12Lp
DUNNING, James	50	M	Unknown	05JI12Lp
Biddy	40	F	Unknown	05JI12Lp
Thos.	18	M	Unknown	05JI12Lp
Biddy	16	F	Unknown	05JI12Lp
Mary	14	F	Unknown	05JI12Lp
Ellen	12	F	Unknown	05JI12Lp
Honor	10	F	Unknown	05JI12Lp
Anne	8	F	Child	05JI12Lp
Francis	4	F	Child	05JI12Lp
Pat	.00	M	Infant	05JI12Lp
HENRY, Mick.	50	M	Unknown	05JI12Lp
Mary	40	F	Unknown	05JI12Lp
Bridget	14	F	Unknown	05JI12Lp
Martin	12	M	Unknown	05JI12Lp
Kitty	10	F	Unknown	05JI12Lp
Mick.	8	M	Child	05JI12Lp
Maria	6	F	Child	05JI12Lp
John	4	M	Child	05JI12Lp
Patt	.00	M	Infant	05JI12Lp
DOYLE, Mary	56	F	Unknown	05JI12Lp
NEILL, John	20	M	Unknown	05JI12Lp
LARKIN, Denis	30	M	Unknown	05JI12Lp
U-Mrs.	33	F	Unknown	05JI12Lp
Catherine	.00	F	Infant	05JI12Lp
TROY, Wm.	30	M	Unknown	05JI12Lp
DOWLING, Michael	30	M	Unknown	05JI12Lp
NOLAN, Michael	40	M	Unknown	05JI12Lp
Anne	30	F	Unknown	05JI12Lp
Catherine	18	F	Unknown	05JI12Lp
Margt.	5	F	Child	05JI12Lp
James	.00	M	Infant	05JI12Lp

LADY-MILTON 05 JULY 1849

From Dublin

NAMES OF PASSENGERS	AGE	SEX	OCCUPATIONS	DATE PORT SHIP
CULLIN, Mary	40	F	Spinster	05JI12MI
Margret	18	F	Spinster	05JI12MI
Catherine	22	F	Spinster	05JI12MI
Richard	20	M	Farmer	05JI12MI
DANIEL, Jane	33	F	Spinster	05JI12MI
Jane	.00	F	Infant	05JI12MI
MOLLY, U-Miss	18	F	Spinster	05JI12MI
HAYSLEX, George	20	M	Farmer	05JI12MI
GILOULY, Catherine	21	F	Farmer	05JI12MI
CALHANE, James	35	M	Farmer	05JI12MI
Bridget	28	F	Farmer	05JI12MI
Mary	5	F	Child	05JI12MI
Denis	2	M	Child	05JI12MI
Michael	.00	M	Infant	05JI12MI
OCONNOR, Catherine	23	F	Farmer	05JI12MI
FITZGERALD, John	25	M	Farmer	05JI12MI
FARLEY, Thomas	30	M	Farmer	05JI12MI
KEOGH, Miles	21	M	Farmer	05JI12MI
KENNY, U-Mrs.	30	F	Farmer	05JI12MI
Lucy	12	F	Farmer	05JI12MI
Filena	10	F	Farmer	05JI12MI
Mick	4	M	Child	05JI12MI
Ann	.00	F	Infant	05JI12MI
CHRISTEN, U-Mrs.	40	F	Farmer	05JI12MI
Robert	20	M	Farmer	05JI12MI
Fred	15	M	Farmer	05JI12MI
Mary-J.	13	F	Farmer	05JI12MI
Sophia	10	F	Farmer	05JI12MI
Marcella	4	F	Child	05JI12MI
Edwd.	.00	M	Infant	05JI12MI
HARRELL, Thomas	20	M	Farmer	05JI12MI
Denis	19	M	Farmer	05JI12MI
KILFOYLE, John	20	M	Farmer	05JI12MI
EGAN, John	45	M	Farmer	05JI12MI
U (W)	40	F	Farmer	05JI12MI
Joseph	18	M	Farmer	05JI12MI
Thomas	15	M	Farmer	05JI12MI
James	13	M	Farmer	05JI12MI
Patt	11	M	Farmer	05JI12MI
John	9	M	Child	05JI12MI
Rose	.00	F	Infant	05JI12MI
FURNY, Ann	25	F	Farmer	05JI12MI
HART, U-Miss	20	F	Farmer	05JI12MI
BROPHY, U-Miss	20	F	Farmer	05JI12MI
HARRISON, U	20	M	Farmer	05JI12MI
Susan	45	F	Farmer	05JI12MI
William	21	M	Farmer	05JI12MI
Thomas	19	M	Farmer	05JI12MI
George	13	M	Farmer	05JI12MI
HINES, Mary	13	F	Farmer	05JI12MI
OLDHAM, Henry	22	M	Farmer	05JI12MI
CREGG, Samuel	24	M	Farmer	05JI12MI
REILLY, Patt	30	M	Farmer	05JI12MI
U (W)	24	F	Farmer	05JI12MI
James	24	M	Farmer	05JI12MI
Thomas	5	M	Child	05JI12MI
Mary-A.	2	F	Child	05JI12MI
Patt	.00	M	Infant	05JI12MI
YOUNG, Isabella	25	F	Farmer	05JI12MI
CUNNINGHAM, John	30	M	Farmer	05JI12MI
U (W)	26	F	Farmer	05JI12MI
Mary-A.	.00	F	Infant	05JI12MI
Jas.	26	M	Farmer	05JI12MI
U-Mrs.	22	F	Farmer	05JI12MI
Kate	20	F	Farmer	05JI12MI
TOOLE, Michael	24	M	Farmer	05JI12MI
U (W)	21	F	Farmer	05JI12MI
KENNA, Patt	20	M	Farmer	05JI12MI
CUMISKY, Thomas	20	M	Farmer	05JI12MI
RYAN, Rich.	28	M	Farmer	05JI12MI
U (W)	26	F	Farmer	05JI12MI
LYNCH, John	21	M	Farmer	05JI12MI
U (W)	21	F	Farmer	05JI12MI
HENESSY, John	26	M	Farmer	05JI12MI
Eliza	26	F	Farmer	05JI12MI
CULLEN, Frank	28	M	Farmer	05JI12MI
William	20	M	Farmer	05JI12MI
MCGOVERN, Ann	30	F	Farmer	05JI12MI
Teresa	8	F	Child	05JI12MI
COX, Eliza	21	F	Farmer	05JI12MI
SHEA, Michael	24	M	Farmer	05JI12MI
Anne	22	F	Farmer	05JI12MI
KILLVAN, Christy	36	M	Farmer	05JI12MI
Judith	30	F	Farmer	05JI12MI
Bess	8	F	Child	05JI12MI
Margret	6	F	Child	05JI12MI
John	4	M	Child	05JI12MI
Mary	.00	F	Infant	05JI12MI
MCCORMACK, William	20	M	Farmer	05JI12MI
Margret	20	F	Farmer	05JI12MI

NAMES OF PASSENGERS	AGE	SEX	OCCUPATIONS	DATE PORT SHIP
MCCORMACK, Eliza	20	F	Farmer	05JI12MI
MURPHY, Mary	20	F	Farmer	05JI12MI
YOUNGS, Mic-J.	30	M	Farmer	05JI12MI
Jane	12	F	Farmer	05JI12MI
Mary-Jane	7	F	Child	05JI12MI
Sarah	.00	F	Infant	05JI12MI
HARPER, U	21	M	Farmer	05JI12MI
CANNON, Michal	28	M	Farmer	05JI12MI
William	24	M	Farmer	05JI12MI
Jane	24	F	Farmer	05JI12MI
CONNOR, Mary	2	F	Child	05JI12MI
William	.00	F	Infant	05JI12MI
MAHONY, Bryan	20	M	Farmer	05JI12MI
LEE, Luke	17	M	Farmer	05JI12MI
Patt	15	M	Farmer	05JI12MI
HEOY, Fanny	24	F	Farmer	05JI12MI
HALPEN, William	20	M	Farmer	05JI12MI
NOLAN, James	20	M	Farmer	05JI12MI
MURRAY, Michal	20	M	Farmer	05JI12MI
Mary	28	F	Farmer	05JI12MI
WHISTON, Ann	18	F	Farmer	05JI12MI
GAHARAN, James	24	M	Farmer	05JI12MI
MANN, Thomas	30	M	Farmer	05JI12MI
U (W)	50	F	Farmer	05JI12MI
Mary	48	F	Farmer	05JI12MI
Patt	26	M	Farmer	05JI12MI
Ann	24	F	Farmer	05JI12MI
Catherine	20	F	Farmer	05JI12MI
Ellen	16	F	Farmer	05JI12MI
Eliza	13	F	Farmer	05JI12MI
MALLON, Patt	24	M	Farmer	05JI12MI
KILLAGHER, John	28	M	Farmer	05JI12MI
QUALLEN, Ann	40	F	Farmer	05JI12MI
Ellen	15	F	Farmer	05JI12MI
CALCAMON, Catherine	30	F	Farmer	05JI12MI
Patt	7	M	Child	05JI12MI
Mary	.00	F	Infant	05JI12MI
MURPHY, William	21	M	Farmer	05JI12MI
HEOY, Judith	17	F	Farmer	05JI12MI
Mary	13	F	Farmer	05JI12MI
MULLENS, U-Miss	16	F	Farmer	05JI12MI
DALEY, William	20	M	Farmer	05JI12MI
FLANAGAN, Michal	20	M	Farmer	05JI12MI
MARA, U-Mrs.	24	M	Farmer	05JI12MI
Rosana	6	F	Child	05JI12MI
Anne	18	F	Farmer	05JI12MI
RIELLY, Mary	22	F	Farmer	05JI12MI
Ellen	18	F	Farmer	05JI12MI
Esther	13	F	Farmer	05JI12MI
MCPARLAND, George	28	M	Farmer	05JI12MI
John	32	M	Farmer	05JI12MI
Robert	8	M	Child	05JI12MI
John	.00	M	Infant	05JI12MI
MURPHY, U	30	M	Farmer	05JI12MI
LEE, Owen	20	M	Farmer	05JI12MI
FOLEY, Patt	20	M	Farmer	05JI12MI
REFFERTY, Owen	26	M	Farmer	05JI12MI
Honor	26	F	Farmer	05JI12MI
KENAN, Judith	20	F	Farmer	05JI12MI
MURTAGH, William	20	M	Farmer	05JI12MI
NAUGHTON, Anne	45	F	Farmer	05JI12MI
KINNAN, Thomas	20	M	Farmer	05JI12MI
DUFFY, John	18	M	Farmer	05JI12MI
PHALAN, Julia	20	F	Farmer	05JI12MI
LARACY, Bridget	20	F	Farmer	05JI12MI
LYNCH, Jas.	20	M	Farmer	05JI12MI
BRYNE, Arthur	29	M	Farmer	05JI12MI
BARGAN, Margret	20	F	Farmer	05JI12MI
LAWLOR, Patt	20	M	Farmer	05JI12MI
WYNN, Mary	20	F	Farmer	05JI12MI
BYRNE, Patt	30	F	Farmer	05JI12MI
Margt.	26	F	Farmer	05JI12MI
Julia	24	F	Farmer	05JI12MI
MCCANN, P.	20	U	Farmer	05JI12MI
FLYNN, Michal	20	M	Farmer	05JI12MI
FLYNN, Michal	38	M	Farmer	05JI12MI
Mary	38	F	Farmer	05JI12MI
KIERNAN, Ellen	24	F	Farmer	05JI12MI
FLYNN, Michal	30	M	Farmer	05JI12MI
William	7	M	Child	05JI12MI
Mary	6	F	Child	05JI12MI
Judy	4	F	Child	05JI12MI
Patt	.00	M	Infant	05JI12MI
HUGHS, Richard	40	M	Farmer	05JI12MI
Janns	34	F	Farmer	05JI12MI
Walter	9	M	Child	05JI12MI
CARTER, U	21	M	Farmer	05JI12MI
BARTON, U	24	M	Farmer	05JI12MI
ROGERDON, Robert	21	M	Farmer	05JI12MI
HEARN, Margret	45	F	Farmer	05JI12MI
Biddy	14	F	Farmer	05JI12MI
Mary	11	F	Farmer	05JI12MI
MURPHY, Charles	32	M	Farmer	05JI12MI
Jane	40	F	Farmer	05JI12MI
Mary	.00	F	Infant	05JI12MI
ROBERSON, John	20	M	Farmer	05JI12MI
RYAN, John	20	M	Farmer	05JI12MI
CASSIDY, Eliza	29	F	Farmer	05JI12MI
MARTIN, Patt	28	M	Farmer	05JI12MI
Anne	23	F	Farmer	05JI12MI
Michal	4	M	Child	05JI12MI
Peter	.00	M	Infant	05JI12MI
Peter	25	M	Farmer	05JI12MI
SHAUGHNESSY, Daniel	30	M	Farmer	05JI12MI
Miles	48	M	Farmer	05JI12MI
Catherine	28	M	Farmer	05JI12MI
Mary	4	F	Child	05JI12MI
Hugh	.00	M	Infant	05JI12MI
GLEENAM, Richard	25	M	Farmer	05JI12MI
DEWY, Bridget	22	F	Farmer	05JI12MI
MOORE, Mary	20	F	Farmer	05JI12MI
BOLAND, Mary	29	F	Farmer	05JI12MI
MOLLANY, Mary	36	F	Farmer	05JI12MI
CASSIDY, James	25	M	Farmer	05JI12MI
HICKEY, Mick	28	M	Farmer	05JI12MI
Ann	30	F	Farmer	05JI12MI
Mary	10	F	Farmer	05JI12MI
Sarah	7	F	Child	05JI12MI
DALEY, William	35	M	Farmer	05JI12MI
Ann	30	F	Farmer	05JI12MI
Denis	11	M	Farmer	05JI12MI
Sarah	7	F	Child	05JI12MI
Eliza	.00	F	Infant	05JI12MI
FROST, James	20	M	Farmer	05JI12MI
COLEMAN, Mary	21	F	Farmer	05JI12MI
CRUSE, U	24	M	Farmer	05JI12MI
WALSH, John	13	M	Farmer	05JI12MI
ROBISON, Edward	24	M	Farmer	05JI12MI
Eliza	22	F	Farmer	05JI12MI
Catherine	20	F	Farmer	05JI12MI
READ, Bridget	22	F	Farmer	05JI12MI
PUGH, John	20	M	Farmer	05JI12MI
GRANT, Andrew	24	M	Farmer	05JI12MI
John	22	M	Farmer	05JI12MI
Ann	20	F	Farmer	05JI12MI
DEOWN, James	16	M	Farmer	05JI12MI
Margaret	14	F	Farmer	05JI12MI
MCDERMOTT, Owen	30	M	Farmer	05JI12MI
U (W)	30	F	Farmer	05JI12MI
KEEGAN, U	10	M	Farmer	05JI12MI
MCEAVY, Andrew	16	M	Farmer	05JI12MI

NAMES OF PASSENGERS		AGE	SEX	OCCUPATIONS	DATE PORT SHIP

MARTHA-J.WARD 05 JULY 1849

From Liverpool

NAMES OF PASSENGERS		AGE	SEX	OCCUPATIONS	DATE PORT SHIP
MCNAMARA, John		28	M	Laborer	05JI02Lj
BYRNE, John		17	M	Laborer	05JI02Lj
RILEY, Bridget		18	F	Servant	05JI02Lj
LEONARD, Ellen		30	F	Servant	05JI02Lj
Michael	(S)	10	M	Son	05JI02Lj
Thomas	(S)	9	M	Child	05JI02Lj
DOHERTY, Philip		50	M	Laborer	05JI02Lj
Kitty	(W)	25	F	Wife	05JI02Lj
Daniel	(S)	.00	M	Infant	05JI02Lj
JOYCE, Margt.		22	F	Servant	05JI02Lj
CONNELL, William		23	M	Laborer	05JI02Lj
MULLICKEN, Bartw.		20	M	Laborer	05JI02Lj
LOUGHLAN, John		18	M	Laborer	05JI02Lj
LINSKEY, Rose		37	F	Servant	05JI02Lj
COLLINS, John		25	M	Laborer	05JI02Lj
HUNT, Ellen		20	F	Servant	05JI02Lj
FICHALEY, Catherine		22	F	Servant	05JI02Lj
SIMPSON, Margt.		16	F	Servant	05JI02Lj
RILEY, Elizabeth		20	F	Servant	05JI02Lj
HUNT, Mary		34	F	Wife	05JI02Lj
Thomas		11	M	None	05JI02Lj
Richard		9	M	Child	05JI02Lj
Anne		6	F	Child	05JI02Lj
Susan		2	F	Child	05JI02Lj
John		.00	M	Infant	05JI02Lj
MCGLOUGHLIN, Ann		20	F	Servant	05JI02Lj
BELLEW, Catherine		40	F	Servant	05JI02Lj
Catherine		25	F	Servant	05JI02Lj
John		23	M	Laborer	05JI02Lj
Michael		19	M	Laborer	05JI02Lj
MALEY, Anthy.		25	M	Laborer	05JI02Lj
CUMMINS, William		15	M	Laborer	05JI02Lj
GLANCY, Martin		15	M	Laborer	05JI02Lj
Bridget	(T)	8	F	Child	05JI02Lj
DELANY, Johanna		20	F	Servant	05JI02Lj
Patrick		16	M	Laborer	05JI02Lj
Margt.		18	F	Servant	05JI02Lj
MURPHY, Daniel		27	M	Laborer	05JI02Lj
COFFEE, Jeremiah		20	M	Laborer	05JI02Lj
MCILOY, Michael		21	M	Laborer	05JI02Lj
Ellen	(W)	21	F	Wife	05JI02Lj
HAGGERTY, Anne		30	F	Wife	05JI02Lj
Mary-Anne	(T)	27	F	Sister	05JI02Lj
James		3	M	Child	05JI02Lj
LATIMER, Thomas		30	M	Nailer	05JI02Lj
JEFF, James		20	M	Mechanic	05JI02Lj
LACKEY, Margt.		18	F	Servant	05JI02Lj
CUSSACK, Catherine		19	F	Servant	05JI02Lj
Duffy		17	M	Laborer	05JI02Lj
WRIGHT, Thomas		22	M	Laborer	05JI02Lj
MULRYAN, Catherine		23	F	Servant	05JI02Lj
MULHOLLAND, Bridget		20	F	Servant	05JI02Lj
WARD, Pat.		17	M	Laborer	05JI02Lj
CONNOLLY, John		35	M	Laborer	05JI02Lj
BYRNE, Hugh		50	M	Laborer	05JI02Lj
Celia	(W)	30	F	Wife	05JI02Lj
Mary	(D)	8	F	Child	05JI02Lj
John	(S)	6	M	Child	05JI02Lj
Biddy	(D)	7	F	Child	05JI02Lj
Hugh	(S)	.00	M	Infant	05JI02Lj
MCCANN, Bernd.		27	M	Laborer	05JI02Lj
WILLIAMS, Catherine		20	F	Servant	05JI02Lj
KIERNAN, Michael		22	M	Servant	05JI02Lj
COFTY, John		35	M	Laborer	05JI02Lj
KELLY, Mary		49	F	Wife	05JI02Lj

NAMES OF PASSENGERS		AGE	SEX	OCCUPATIONS	DATE PORT SHIP
KELLY, Mary	(D)	12	F	Daughter	05JI02Lj
Bridget	(D)	11	F	Daughter	05JI02Lj
BRYAN, Rose		10	F	None	05JI02Lj
DONOHOE, Mathew		47	M	Weaver	05JI02Lj
Mary	(W)	47	F	Wife	05JI02Lj
WARD, Bridget		40	F	Wife	05JI02Lj
MCDONOUGH, Margt.		10	F	None	05JI02Lj
Michael		7	M	None	05JI02Lj
Catherine		5	F	Child	05JI02Lj
John		.00	M	Infant	05JI02Lj
HUNWIN, Catherine		18	F	Servant	05JI02Lj
MCMANUS, Bridget		24	F	Servant	05JI02Lj
LEARY, Bernard		25	M	Laborer	05JI02Lj
MCNEIL, Catherine		52	F	Wife	05JI02Lj
John		20	M	Laborer	05JI02Lj
Charles		15	M	Laborer	05JI02Lj
Pat		12	M	Laborer	05JI02Lj
Henry		11	M	Laborer	05JI02Lj
Anne		9	M	Child	05JI02Lj
DICKSON, Mary		60	F	Wife	05JI02Lj
James		20	M	Unknown	05JI02Lj
Felix		18	M	Unknown	05JI02Lj
Richard		10	M	Unknown	05JI02Lj
Grace		25	F	Servant	05JI02Lj
CLEARY, Martin		40	M	Carpenter	05JI02Lj
LOUGHLIN, Norry		24	M	Laborer	05JI02Lj
Johanna		16	F	Servant	05JI02Lj
Catherine		14	F	Servant	05JI02Lj
Edmund		5	M	Child	05JI02Lj
Margt.		.00	F	Infant	05JI02Lj
BRADY, Barny		38	M	Weaver	05JI02Lj
Julia	(W)	38	F	Wife	05JI02Lj
HARRARTY, Peter		35	M	Laborer	05JI02Lj
Anne	(W)	22	F	Wife	05JI02Lj
MCPHILIPS, John		4	M	Child	05JI02Lj
MOONEY, Thomas		20	M	Laborer	05JI02Lj
Selina	(T)	12	F	Sister	05JI02Lj
Catherine		.00	F	Infant	05JI02Lj
MCELROY, Mary		20	F	Servant	05JI02Lj
BRADY, Mary		30	F	Servant	05JI02Lj
MCCABE, Michael		10	M	Laborer	05JI02Lj
Anne	(T)	8	F	Child	05JI02Lj
John	(B)	5	M	Child	05JI02Lj
Lawrence	(B)	3	M	Child	05JI02Lj
CAROLAN, Bridget		20	F	Servant	05JI02Lj
COYLE, Pat.		25	M	Laborer	05JI02Lj
John		22	M	Laborer	05JI02Lj
MURRAY, Catherine		60	F	Servant	05JI02Lj
CLARY, Martha		14	F	Laborer	05JI02Lj
FARRELL, Peter		20	M	Laborer	05JI02Lj
CARTY, Thomas		16	M	Laborer	05JI02Lj
GAVIN, Margt.		19	F	Servant	05JI02Lj
MITCHELL, David		20	M	Laborer	05JI02Lj
TAYLOR, Alexander		20	M	Millwright	05JI02Lj
QUIGLY, Mary		23	F	Servant	05JI02Lj
MONAGHAN, Pat.		35	M	Stationer	05JI02Lj
MCKAY, Edward		20	M	Baker	05JI02Lj
BURNS, John		21	M	Mechanic	05JI02Lj
WRIGHT, John		25	M	Mechanic	05JI02Lj
LYNHAM, Pat.		35	M	Mechanic	05JI02Lj
Mary	(W)	25	F	Wife	05JI02Lj
FITZSIMMONS, Michael		34	M	Laborer	05JI02Lj
SLATER, Thomas		18	M	Cver	05JI02Lj
John		16	M	Cver	05JI02Lj
FARRELL, Mary		20	F	Servant	05JI02Lj
RIELY, Phillip		00	M	Unknown	05JI02Lj
MONAGAN, Patrick		00	M	Unknown	05JI02Lj

RAPPAHANNOCK 05 JULY 1849

From Liverpool

NAMES OF PASSENGERS	AGE	SEX	OCCUPATIONS	DATE PORT SHIP
BUTLER, Edward	25	M	Laborer	05JI02Mk
John	24	M	Laborer	05JI02Mk
BYRNE, William	25	M	Laborer	05JI02Mk
LANGLEY, James	30	M	Plasterer	05JI02Mk
Mary	30	F	None	05JI02Mk
Richard	25	M	Plasterer	05JI02Mk
John	6	M	Child	05JI02Mk
Mary	1	F	Child	05JI02Mk
Julia	.00	F	Infant	05JI02Mk
KENNEDY, John	24	M	Tinker	05JI02Mk
CARROLL, Patrick	26	M	Shepherd	05JI02Mk
Eliza	26	M	Shepherd	05JI02Mk
FORD, Patrick	20	M	Laborer	05JI02Mk
HOLMES, William	21	M	Laborer	05JI02Mk
HANELY, Catherine	20	F	Servant	05JI02Mk
DECKAN, Thomas	23	M	Laborer	05JI02Mk
Ellen	20	F	Servant	05JI02Mk
MCGUINNESS, John	20	M	Laborer	05JI02Mk
DUFFY, Patrick	30	M	Laborer	05JI02Mk
MOULDEN, Thomas	20	M	Sawer	05JI02Mk
NOON, Margaret	20	F	Servant	05JI02Mk
MEBODY, Ann	55	F	Dressmaker	05JI02Mk
MELOLLY, Mary	18	F	Dressmaker	05JI02Mk
CUMMINS, Michael	30	M	Laborer	05JI02Mk
Patrick	25	M	Farmer	05JI02Mk
Bridgett	5	F	Child	05JI02Mk
Margaret	25	F	Farmer	05JI02Mk
WINCATE, John	45	M	Farmer	05JI02Mk
MAHER, Michael	45	M	Laborer	05JI02Mk
Mary	45	F	Servant	05JI02Mk
Michael	17	F	Servant	05JI02Mk
Mary	9	F	Child	05JI02Mk
Honor	7	F	Child	05JI02Mk
LAWLER, Susan	22	F	Mtmkr	05JI02Mk
MELLON, George	43	M	Sawer	05JI02Mk
FINN, Thomas	40	M	Sawer	05JI02Mk
NOLAN, Thomas	26	M	Sawer	05JI02Mk
DOYLE, Michael	27	M	Sawer	05JI02Mk
GAINOR, Thomas	29	M	Sawer	05JI02Mk
EUSTICE, Mary	22	F	Dressmaker	05JI02Mk
James	.00	M	Infant	05JI02Mk
KELLEY, Robert	30	M	Sawer	05JI02Mk
Catherine	20	F	Servant	05JI02Mk
BRUTON, Michael	25	M	Laborer	05JI02Mk
MANLY, Bridget	21	F	Servant	05JI02Mk
DOOLY, Thomas	45	M	Laborer	05JI02Mk
Nyles	17	M	Laborer	05JI02Mk
James	10	M	Child	05JI02Mk
TOBEY, Haner	21	F	Seamstress	05JI02Mk
MARTIN, Bessy	9	F	Child	05JI02Mk
MCKEOGH, John	36	M	Farmer	05JI02Mk
Catherine	36	F	Farmer	05JI02Mk
Margaret	12	F	Child	05JI02Mk
Patrick	11	M	Child	05JI02Mk
Michael	9	M	Child	05JI02Mk
Thomas	6	M	Child	05JI02Mk
James	3	M	Child	05JI02Mk
John	.00	M	Infant	05JI02Mk
William	20	M	Farmer	05JI02Mk
DUNN, Mary	18	F	Servant	05JI02Mk
DOWLING, Michael	32	M	Laborer	05JI02Mk
Mary	24	F	Laborer	05JI02Mk
MCDONNELL, Cornelius	31	M	Farmer	05JI02Mk
RYAN, Cornelius	30	M	Laborer	05JI02Mk
John	7	M	Child	05JI02Mk
HEBEHAR, James	20	M	Laborer	05JI02Mk
MCCARTHY, Catherine	26	F	Servant	05JI02Mk
COLEMAN, Catherine	18	F	Servant	05JI02Mk
Mary	2	F	Child	05JI02Mk
CONNER, Catherine	17	F	Servant	05JI02Mk
MCDONNELL, Elin	15	F	Servant	05JI02Mk
MURPHY, Margaret	36	F	Servant	05JI02Mk
Ellen	26	F	Servant	05JI02Mk
Mary	12	F	Servant	05JI02Mk
MURRAY, Thomas	23	M	Laborer	05JI02Mk
CONLAN, Bridget	30	F	Servant	05JI02Mk
Bridget	11	F	Servant	05JI02Mk
Wini.	6	M	Child	05JI02Mk
Bridget	16	F	Servant	05JI02Mk
Ann	4	F	Child	05JI02Mk
KEARNEY, Susan	22	F	Dressmaker	05JI02Mk
EVERITT, William	17	M	Laborer	05JI02Mk
MCNELTY, Catherine	19	F	Bomkr	05JI02Mk
MURPHY, Thomas	20	M	Laborer	05JI02Mk
DRUMGOOL, Michael	17	M	Laborer	05JI02Mk
BURNES, Mary	20	F	Servant	05JI02Mk
DUFFY, Catherine	35	F	Servant	05JI02Mk
JONES, John	39	M	Farmer	05JI02Mk
Died-At-Sea				
Mary	35	F	Farmer	05JI02Mk
Molly	.00	F	Infant	05JI02Mk
David	13	M	None	05JI02Mk
Ann	10	F	Child	05JI02Mk
REILLY, Dennis	70	M	Laborer	05JI02Mk
Ellen	16	F	Laborer	05JI02Mk
MCMAHAN, Mary	22	F	Servant	05JI02Mk
HAYES, Julia	17	F	Servant	05JI02Mk
MULCAHY, Margaret	30	F	Servant	05JI02Mk
HENNY, William	7	M	Child	05JI02Mk
MCDONNELL, Julia	23	F	Servant	05JI02Mk
BYRNE, John	16	M	Laborer	05JI02Mk
BRADY, Catherine	15	F	Servant	05JI02Mk
KELEHER, Bess	18	F	Servant	05JI02Mk
BURKE, Patrick	12	M	Laborer	05JI02Mk
Ann	19	F	Dressmaker	05JI02Mk
CUNNINGHAM, Molly	28	F	Dressmaker	05JI02Mk
FENTON, Patrick	24	M	Laborer	05JI02Mk
CROSSAN, Rose	40	F	Servant	05JI02Mk
RYAN, Mary	20	F	Housekeeper	05JI02Mk
BARRETT, Mary	20	F	Housekeeper	05JI02Mk
POWELL, John	25	M	Laborer	05JI02Mk
BARRETT, John	11	M	Laborer	05JI02Mk
Ann	8	F	Child	05JI02Mk
Martin	4	M	Child	05JI02Mk
MCMAHAN, James	18	M	Laborer	05JI02Mk
Owen	25	M	Laborer	05JI02Mk
MACKLIN, Patrick	65	M	Laborer	05JI02Mk
Hugh	25	M	Laborer	05JI02Mk
Mary	20	F	Laborer	05JI02Mk
Patrick	19	M	Laborer	05JI02Mk
KENAN, Rose	19	F	Servant	05JI02Mk
CORRIGAN, Rose	9	F	Child	05JI02Mk
MORGAN, Peter	21	M	Laborer	05JI02Mk
MCCOY, Sarah	16	F	Servant	05JI02Mk
ABTHOUSE, Elizabeth	22	F	Servant	05JI02Mk
MULLIGAN, Mary	40	F	Servant	05JI02Mk
BRENNAN, Catherine	19	F	Servant	05JI02Mk
DONAHUE, Margaret	30	F	Servant	05JI02Mk
CORRIGAN, Sarah	17	F	Servant	05JI02Mk
GALLAGHER, Thomas	17	M	Servant	05JI02Mk
FINNAN, Catherine	35	F	Servant	05JI02Mk
ROURKE, Patrick	25	M	Servant	05JI02Mk
SULLIVAN, Honora	30	F	Servant	05JI02Mk
MOLLEY, Margaret	25	F	Servant	05JI02Mk
MALONEY, James	22	M	Servant	05JI02Mk
SPELLOVEY, Bridget	17	F	Servant	05JI02Mk
MCMAHAN, Andrew	20	M	Servant	05JI02Mk
FAHY, Mary	17	F	Servant	05JI02Mk
MARTIN, Catherine	16	F	Servant	05JI02Mk
HARKIN, Mary	16	F	Servant	05JI02Mk

NAMES OF PASSENGERS	AGE	SEX	OCCUPATIONS	DATE PORT SHIP
CONNER, Margaret	20	F	Servant	05JI02Mk
OBRIEN, Bridget	26	F	Servant	05JI02Mk
Thomas	.00	M	Infant	05JI02Mk
LYNCH, Patrick	5	M	Child	05JI02Mk
BAINE, Bridget	10	F	Child	05JI02Mk
NERA, Thomas	75	M	Farmer	05JI02Mk
Margaret	65	F	Farmer	05JI02Mk
CONLERY, Mary	20	F	Servant	05JI02Mk
NERA, William	40	M	Farmer	05JI02Mk
CAGAN, James	8	M	Child	05JI02Mk
REILLY, Catherine	11	F	Servant	05JI02Mk
CAGAN, Hugh	45	M	Laborer	05JI02Mk
OBRIEN, Thomas	20	M	Laborer	05JI02Mk
Michael	17	M	Laborer	05JI02Mk
William	21	M	Laborer	05JI02Mk
HICKEY, James	25	M	Laborer	05JI02Mk
MERAN, Elsie	20	F	Servant	05JI02Mk
BRYAN, Catherine	18	F	Servant	05JI02Mk
CARROLES, Betsey	20	F	Servant	05JI02Mk
BEATY, Charles	60	M	Farmer	05JI02Mk
Fanny	60	F	Farmer	05JI02Mk
SMITH, Rebecca	20	F	Servant	05JI02Mk
BEATY, John	20	M	Farmer	05JI02Mk
Charles	18	M	Farmer	05JI02Mk
William	12	M	Farmer	05JI02Mk
Eliza.	35	F	Farmer	05JI02Mk
Eliza.	.00	F	Infant	05JI02Mk
Mary	14	F	Farmer	05JI02Mk
William	35	M	Farmer	05JI02Mk
Samuel	3	M	Child	05JI02Mk
BENNETT, Susan	24	F	Servant	05JI02Mk
JOHNSON, Margaret	20	F	Servant	05JI02Mk
GREENHALGH, Squire	23	M	Joiner	05JI02Mk
Mary	23	F	None	05JI02Mk
Margaret	.00	F	Infant	05JI02Mk
HEALY, Thomas	20	M	Farmer	05JI02Mk
Ann	27	F	Servant	05JI02Mk
GALL, Steven	24	M	Miller	05JI02Mk
James	16	M	Miller	05JI02Mk
OKEGAN, Thomas	17	M	Servant	05JI02Mk
Catherine	46	F	Servant	05JI02Mk
Margaret	10	F	Child	05JI02Mk
Austin	7	M	Child	05JI02Mk
Catherine	4	F	Child	05JI02Mk
William	2	M	Child	05JI02Mk
John	.00	M	Infant	05JI02Mk
DWYER, Ann	20	F	Servant	05JI02Mk
SHEEHAN, Michael	20	M	Laborer	05JI02Mk
KENNEY, James	27	M	Laborer	05JI02Mk
MCGUINNESS, John	30	M	Laborer	05JI02Mk
U-Mrs.	25	F	None	05JI02Mk
Alexander	2	M	Child	05JI02Mk
PUSEE, Margaret	20	F	Servant	05JI02Mk
MORRISY, John	40	M	Mason	05JI02Mk
Thomas	20	M	Mason	05JI02Mk
Pierce	23	M	Mason	05JI02Mk
John	8	M	Child	05JI02Mk
CANNONS, Michael	19	M	Child	05JI02Mk
RYAN, Ellen	23	F	Housekeeper	05JI02Mk
REED, John	24	M	Laborer	05JI02Mk
DUFFY, Mary	17	F	Servant	05JI02Mk
Catherine	13	F	Servant	05JI02Mk
Margaret	9	F	Child	05JI02Mk
FITZPATRICK, Mary	27	F	Servant	05JI02Mk
Margaret	2	F	Child	05JI02Mk
CALLON, William	20	M	Servant	05JI02Mk
Ann	20	F	Servant	05JI02Mk
BEAZLEY, Constance	23	F	Servant	05JI02Mk
MCGEE, Bridget	20	F	Servant	05JI02Mk
FERGUSON, James	28	M	Laborer	05JI02Mk
GEDDAS, John	17	M	Laborer	05JI02Mk
WALSH, Edward	50	M	Laborer	05JI02Mk
U-Mrs.	30	F	Laborer	05JI02Mk
Patrick	24	M	Laborer	05JI02Mk
Ellen	20	F	Laborer	05JI02Mk
WALSH, Bridget	17	F	Laborer	05JI02Mk
Mary	12	F	Laborer	05JI02Mk
Thomas	10	M	Child	05JI02Mk
Catherine	22	F	Laborer	05JI02Mk
Ann	3	F	Child	05JI02Mk
Edward	2	M	Child	05JI02Mk
GALLAGHER, Martin	30	M	Child	05JI02Mk
U-Mrs.	20	F	Servant	05JI02Mk
MCANDREW, John	24	M	Laborer	05JI02Mk
ROSE, Oliver	40	M	Laborer	05JI02Mk
U-Mrs.	30	F	Laborer	05JI02Mk
Ann-J.	3	F	Child	05JI02Mk
Oliver	.00	M	Infant	05JI02Mk
MOOREHEAD, Hannah	35	F	Servant	05JI02Mk
Isaiah	35	M	Servant	05JI02Mk
Hannah	10	F	Child	05JI02Mk
CONROY, Ellen	40	F	Child	05JI02Mk
Dennis	18	M	Child	05JI02Mk
Bridget	10	F	Child	05JI02Mk
JOHNSON, Robert	25	M	Laborer	05JI02Mk
MCANALLY, Mary	20	F	Servant	05JI02Mk
DUFFY, Mary	20	F	Servant	05JI02Mk
LEE, Thomas	23	M	Keeper	05JI02Mk
LANDAY, James	21	M	Farmer	05JI02Mk
HEGAN, Michael	23	M	Mason	05JI02Mk
MATHEWS, Ellen	18	F	Servant	05JI02Mk
SALIN, Patrick	28	M	Laborer	05JI02Mk
FINN, Cornelius	27	M	Farmer	05JI02Mk
John	29	M	Farmer	05JI02Mk
William	.00	M	Infant	05JI02Mk
CASTOR, James	30	M	Farmer	05JI02Mk
SULLIVAN, William	38	M	Farmer	05JI02Mk
KILDRIGE, Andrew	18	M	Laborer	05JI02Mk
GILLON, James	38	M	Laborer	05JI02Mk
Margaret	32	F	Laborer	05JI02Mk
Mary	.00	F	Infant	05JI02Mk
BOYLE, Patrick	26	M	Mason	05JI02Mk
U-Mrs.	25	F	Mason	05JI02Mk
Edward	2	M	Mason	05JI02Mk
Jane	.00	F	Infant	05JI02Mk
KELLEY, Ellen	22	F	Dressmaker	05JI02Mk
MURPHY, Julia	20	F	Servant	05JI02Mk
MCLOUGHLIN, Ellen	23	F	Servant	05JI02Mk
CLARK, Thomas	50	M	Laborer	05JI02Mk
MORE, Catherine	8	F	Child	05JI02Mk
OCONNER, Timothy	26	M	Laborer	05JI02Mk
OLEARY, Catherine	24	F	Servant	05JI02Mk
Ellen	29	F	Servant	05JI02Mk
Anthony	18	M	Laborer	05JI02Mk
HIGGINS, John	16	M	Laborer	05JI02Mk
GILLESPIE, Anthony	20	M	Laborer	05JI02Mk
CONWAY, Catherine	24	F	Servant	05JI02Mk
GILLESPIE, Mary	40	F	Laborer	05JI02Mk
Michael	3	M	Child	05JI02Mk
THOMPSON, John	25	M	Laborer	05JI02Mk
Eliza	45	F	Servant	05JI02Mk
Ann	20	F	Servant	05JI02Mk
Catherine	22	F	Servant	05JI02Mk
CLIFFORD, William	30	M	Farmer	05JI02Mk
U-Mrs.	30	M	Farmer	05JI02Mk
FELDEN, Mary	23	F	Servant	05JI02Mk
DOOLIN, John	22	M	Servant	05JI02Mk
RYAN, Patrick	33	M	Farmer	05JI02Mk
Catherine	25	F	Farmer	05JI02Mk
GILLIGAN, Margaret	24	F	Farmer	05JI02Mk
Maria	20	F	Farmer	05JI02Mk
John	19	M	Farmer	05JI02Mk
Elizabeth	17	F	Farmer	05JI02Mk
Julia	12	F	Farmer	05JI02Mk
Thomas	9	M	Child	05JI02Mk
William	7	M	Child	05JI02Mk
Margaret	3	F	Child	05JI02Mk
Joseph	.00	M	Infant	05JI02Mk
LITTLE, Arch.	34	M	Farmer	05JI02Mk
U-Mrs.	34	F	None	05JI02Mk

NAMES OF PASSENGERS	AGE	SEX	OCCUPATIONS	DATE PORT SHIP
LITTLE, Francis	28	M	Farmer	05JI02Mk
Ellen	32	F	Farmer	05JI02Mk
Margaret	16	F	Farmer	05JI02Mk
Andrew	20	M	Farmer	05JI02Mk
John	19	M	Farmer	05JI02Mk
FRAZIER, John	18	M	Farmer	05JI02Mk
MCCORMACK, James	27	M	Farmer	05JI02Mk
Dorothy	22	F	Servant	05JI02Mk
Mary	26	F	Servant	05JI02Mk
HAMILTON, Margaret	16	F	Servant	05JI02Mk
FERNAN, Rose	22	F	Servant	05JI02Mk
GILLIGAN, Edward	6	M	Child	05JI02Mk
CARDUE, Ann	18	F	Servant	05JI02Mk
OHARAH, William	20	M	Servant	05JI02Mk
KEARY, William	22	M	Laborer	05JI02Mk
GILLNEY, Mary	40	F	Servant	05JI02Mk
HAND, John	18	M	Laborer	05JI02Mk
Bridget	25	F	Servant	05JI02Mk
PÀRK, Margaret	20	F	Servant	05JI02Mk
DONNELLY, Magnus	18	F	Servant	05JI02Mk
DORATY, Hugh	27	M	Servant	05JI02Mk
U-Mrs.	25	F	Servant	05JI02Mk
William	.00	M	Infant	05JI02Mk
Patrick	29	M	Servant	05JI02Mk
GOFFE, Patrick	25	M	Grocer	05JI02Mk
CASTILLA, John	38	M	Laborer	05JI02Mk
MAGEE, Lawrence	18	M	Servant	05JI02Mk
FORD, Jeremiah	18	M	Shoemaker	05JI02Mk
JOLLIFF, Henry	54	M	Laborer	05JI02Mk
GILLON, James	52	M	Laborer	05JI02Mk
CORMACK, John	18	M	Farmer	05JI02Mk
RAFTER, Patrick	22	M	Wheelwright	05JI02Mk
HAYS, Martin	40	M	Carpenter	05JI02Mk
RAFTER, Thomas	19	M	Laborer	05JI02Mk
Mary	20	F	Laborer	05JI02Mk
WILKINS, Eliza.	25	F	Servant	05JI02Mk
NORA, Sarah	40	F	Servant	05JI02Mk
William	46	M	Servant	05JI02Mk
KAEY, Mary	18	F	Servant	05JI02Mk
KILLANE, Patrick	40	M	Laborer	05JI02Mk
MALARKEY, Thomas	19	M	Laborer	05JI02Mk
MELONEY, Bridget	45	F	Servant	05JI02Mk
MALONEY, Bridget	22	F	Servant	05JI02Mk
Rose	10	F	Child	05JI02Mk
RAFTER, James	30	M	Unknown	05JI02Mk
Hannah	30	F	Servant	05JI02Mk
KENNEY, U-Mr.	50	M	Farmer	05JI02Mk
U-Mrs.	46	F	Farmer	05JI02Mk
Mary	18	F	Farmer	05JI02Mk
Sarah	20	F	Farmer	05JI02Mk
Ellen	9	F	Child	05JI02Mk
Conner	8	M	Child	05JI02Mk
John	6	M	Child	05JI02Mk
OHALLORAN, John	29	M	Farmer	05JI02Mk
MANYAN, Ann	25	F	Servant	05JI02Mk
LYNCH, John	26	M	Shoemaker	05JI02Mk
SHEENY, Patrick	27	M	Laborer	05JI02Mk
U-Mrs.	26	F	Laborer	05JI02Mk
SHELAN, Nancy	21	F	Servant	05JI02Mk
Catherine	20	F	Servant	05JI02Mk
BROPHY, Michael	25	M	Laborer	05JI02Mk
Mary	21	F	Servant	05JI02Mk
Eliza.	.00	F	Infant	05JI02Mk
GARRATY, Michael	17	M	Baker	05JI02Mk
REILY, James	40	M	Saddler	05JI02Mk
Margaret	40	F	None	05JI02Mk
ODONAHUE, Joseph	8	M	Child	05JI02Mk
CUMMINGS, Ann	46	F	None	05JI02Mk
MARCEY, Melvin	30	M	Nailer	05JI02Mk
KELLY, Edward	26	M	Optician	05JI02Mk
U-Mrs.	24	F	None	05JI02Mk
DEVERHAN, Patrick	26	M	Shoemaker	05JI02Mk
U-Mrs.	24	F	None	05JI02Mk
Ellen	.00	F	Infant	05JI02Mk
CAEKEVAN, James	13	M	Farmer	05JI02Mk
CAEKAVAN, Joseph	45	M	Farmer	05JI02Mk
SHIELDS, William	20	M	Laborer	05JI02Mk
MCANARIS, Thomas	28	M	Weaver	05JI02Mk
Ann	24	F	Weaver	05JI02Mk
MULLIGAN, John	40	M	Laborer	05JI02Mk
BURKE, Michael	20	M	Laborer	05JI02Mk
LYNN, Anthony	30	M	Laborer	05JI02Mk
U-Mrs.	26	F	Laborer	05JI02Mk
SHERIDAN, John	26	M	Laborer	05JI02Mk
U-Mrs.	24	F	Laborer	05JI02Mk
Ann	.00	F	Infant	05JI02Mk
MCCARDON, Mary	30	F	Weaver	05JI02Mk
MCCARROLL, Mary	20	F	Servant	05JI02Mk
CAMPBELL, Bridget	25	F	Servant	05JI02Mk
MALONEY, Bridget	18	F	Servant	05JI02Mk
INGATE, James	21	M	Laborer	05JI02Mk
MCMALLON, Ann	27	F	Servant	05JI02Mk
MANSON, William	27	M	Servant	05JI02Mk
ROSS, Ann	30	F	Servant	05JI02Mk
MANSON, Alexander	16	M	Ploughman	05JI02Mk
U-Mrs.	40	F	None	05JI02Mk
James	20	M	Ploughman	05JI02Mk
MANYON, Patrick	35	M	Farmer	05JI02Mk
MAYON, U-Mrs.	25	F	Farmer	05JI02Mk
Patrick	.00	M	Infant	05JI02Mk
FAGARTY, Ellen	22	F	Servant	05JI02Mk
SAFFREY, John	29	M	Laborer	05JI02Mk
CAVANAGH, Patrick	29	M	Laborer	05JI02Mk
Catherine	18	F	Servant	05JI02Mk
CARR, Catherine	50	F	Servant	05JI02Mk
CRUISE, Margaret	18	F	Servant	05JI02Mk
ROAN, Hugh	40	M	Laborer	05JI02Mk
MCDONNELL, John	26	M	Blacksmith	05JI02Mk
CONELY, George	24	M	Laborer	05JI02Mk
ALLEN, Thomas	22	M	Laborer	05JI02Mk
MCCLURE, Ellen	55	F	Servant	05JI02Mk
Mary	24	F	Servant	05JI02Mk
OREILY, Catherine	30	F	Servant	05JI02Mk
WEAVER, Robert	20	M	Laborer	05JI02Mk
COX, Mary	25	F	Storekeeper	05JI02Mk
PARK, Jonathan	18	M	Farmer	05JI02Mk
FITZPATRICK, Thomas	24	M	Farmer	05JI02Mk
Margaret	34	F	Farmer	05JI02Mk
Michael	13	M	Farmer	05JI02Mk
Catherine	11	F	Farmer	05JI02Mk
John	10	M	Child	05JI02Mk
Maria	7	F	Child	05JI02Mk
Margaret	7	F	Child	05JI02Mk
DOYLE, Patrick	21	M	Laborer	05JI02Mk
ROLLINS, Ann	21	F	Servant	05JI02Mk
FITZPATRICK, Bridget	9	F	Child	05JI02Mk
MCDONALL, Michael	27	M	Farmer	05JI02Mk
Eliza.	21	F	Farmer	05JI02Mk
DEVAN, Martin	25	M	Farmer	05JI02Mk
BONDY, William	27	M	Laborer	05JI02Mk
BOYLE, Jane-R.	30	F	Servant	05JI02Mk
MCDERMIT, Bridget	21	F	Servant	05JI02Mk
GALLAGHER, Rebecca	21	F	Servant	05JI02Mk
CONWAY, Peter	18	M	Laborer	05JI02Mk
MCLAUGHLEY, Patrick	20	M	Laborer	05JI02Mk
CARNEY, Bridget	21	F	House Maid	05JI02Mk
GABOIN, John	25	M	Laborer	05JI02Mk
CONLIN, James	25	M	Unknown	05JI02Mk
WARD, James	22	M	Laborer	05JI02Mk
Mark	20	M	Laborer	05JI02Mk
Mary	25	F	Servant	05JI02Mk
DONAHUE, Martin	35	M	Carpenter	05JI02Mk
U-Mrs.	30	F	None	05JI02Mk
John	55	M	Carpenter	05JI02Mk
Mary	4	F	Child	05JI02Mk
MCANARIS, Ann	25	F	None	05JI02Mk
GOWIN, Thomas	47	M	Carpenter	05JI02Mk
PALMER, Charles	30	M	Unknown	05JI02Mk
U-Mrs.	30	F	None	05JI02Mk
Steven	15	M	Unknown	05JI02Mk

NAMES OF PASSENGERS	AGE	SEX	OCCUPATIONS	DATE PORT SHIP
BREAN, Richard	30	M	Unknown	05JI02Mk
BRADY, U-Dr.	00	M	Unknown	05JI02Mk
U-Mrs.	00	F	Unknown	05JI02Mk
John	11	M	Unknown	05JI02Mk
Eliza.	10	F	Child	05JI02Mk
Died-At-Sea				
Mary	5	F	Child	05JI02Mk
James	2	M	Child	05JI02Mk

ASIA 05 JULY 1849

From Cork

NAMES OF PASSENGERS	AGE	SEX	OCCUPATIONS	DATE PORT SHIP
FARRELL, Michael	50	U	Laborer	05JI08Mj
Mary	50	F	Servant	05JI08Mj
Maurice	24	M	Laborer	05JI08Mj
Patrick	17	M	Laborer	05JI08Mj
Johanna	18	F	Servant	05JI08Mj
AHERN, Denis	16	M	Laborer	05JI08Mj
APPLEBY, Charles	26	M	Laborer	05JI08Mj
CAHILL, Wm.	25	M	Laborer	05JI08Mj
EGAN, James	24	M	Laborer	05JI08Mj
GALAVANE, James	21	M	Laborer	05JI08Mj
HENNESSY, James	26	M	Laborer	05JI08Mj
Mary	20	F	Servant	05JI08Mj
MURPHY, Jerry	20	M	Laborer	05JI08Mj
DAILY, David	38	M	Laborer	05JI08Mj
MULCAHY, Julia	18	F	Servant	05JI08Mj
SULLIVAN, Ellen	22	F	Servant	05JI08Mj
SHEA, Johanna	22	F	Servant	05JI08Mj
BOHANE, Denis	35	M	Laborer	05JI08Mj
Mary	26	F	Servant	05JI08Mj
Joseph	6	M	Child	05JI08Mj
James	4	M	Child	05JI08Mj
Ellen	.00	F	Infant	05JI08Mj
James	25	M	Laborer	05JI08Mj
DONOVAN, Mary	20	F	Servant	05JI08Mj
DALY, Margt.	18	F	Servant	05JI08Mj
DEMPSEY, Johanna	20	F	Servant	05JI08Mj
HANRAHAN, Bridget	18	F	Servant	05JI08Mj
SCANNELL, Jerry	17	M	Laborer	05JI08Mj
BOURK, John	21	M	Unknown	05JI08Mj
BOHAN, Cor.	23	M	Laborer	05JI08Mj
AHERN, James	21	M	Laborer	05JI08Mj
Died-At-Sea				
WALSH, Michael	40	M	Laborer	05JI08Mj
JOICE, John	45	M	Laborer	05JI08Mj
Mary	40	F	Servant	05JI08Mj
Richard	21	M	Laborer	05JI08Mj
Catherine	17	F	Servant	05JI08Mj
Ellen	12	F	Child	05JI08Mj
John	10	M	Child	05JI08Mj
HALLARAN, John	26	M	Laborer	05JI08Mj
BENNETT, Richard	28	M	Laborer	05JI08Mj
Mary	25	F	Servant	05JI08Mj
Mary	.00	F	Infant	05JI08Mj
SULLIVAN, Peggy	50	F	Servant	05JI08Mj
Catherine	24	F	Servant	05JI08Mj
Mary	17	F	Servant	05JI08Mj
Julia	14	F	Servant	05JI08Mj
KEANE, Johanna	60	F	Servant	05JI08Mj
John	30	M	Laborer	05JI08Mj
Mary	27	F	Servant	05JI08Mj
Daniel	22	M	Laborer	05JI08Mj
Thomas	26	M	Laborer	05JI08Mj
PALMER, Catherine	35	F	Servant	05JI08Mj
SULLIVAN, Jerry	30	M	Laborer	05JI08Mj
Nelly	11	F	Child	05JI08Mj
HARRINGTON, Edmond	21	M	Laborer	05JI08Mj
DYER, Anthony	45	M	Laborer	05JI08Mj
POOR, John	20	M	Laborer	05JI08Mj
WHITE, Ellen	50	F	Servant	05JI08Mj
RICE, John	16	M	Laborer	05JI08Mj
John	20	M	Laborer	05JI08Mj
James	16	M	Laborer	05JI08Mj
GOOLDEN, Catherine	18	F	Servant	05JI08Mj
SULLIVAN, Jerry	22	M	Laborer	05JI08Mj
Daniel	40	M	Laborer	05JI08Mj
GRIFFIN, Wm.	20	M	Laborer	05JI08Mj
LEARY, Cornelius	12	M	Laborer	05JI08Mj
Ellen	40	F	Servant	05JI08Mj
Michael	45	M	Laborer	05JI08Mj
DALY, Eugene	19	M	Laborer	05JI08Mj
Daniel	23	M	Laborer	05JI08Mj
Died-At-Sea				
LEARY, Judy	30	F	Servant	05JI08Mj
SCULLY, Jerry	26	F	Laborer	05JI08Mj
Honora	24	F	Servant	05JI08Mj
LEANE, Denis	20	M	Laborer	05JI08Mj
SCULLY, Michael	20	M	Laborer	05JI08Mj
Ellen	25	F	Servant	05JI08Mj
Abbey	.00	F	Infant	05JI08Mj
MURPHY, Julia	22	F	Servant	05JI08Mj
DEASY, Cors.	26	M	Laborer	05JI08Mj
HURLY, Jane	25	M	Servant	05JI08Mj
HAYES, Mary	24	F	Servant	05JI08Mj
WALSH, Mary	23	F	Servant	05JI08Mj
FLYNN, John	30	M	Laborer	05JI08Mj
Phil.	22	M	Laborer	05JI08Mj
Hannah	24	F	Servant	05JI08Mj
BYRNES, James	24	M	Laborer	05JI08Mj
HOSFORD, Wm.	22	M	Laborer	05JI08Mj
Martha	20	F	Servant	05JI08Mj
SMUDDY, Pierce	22	M	Laborer	05JI08Mj
QUIRK, Mary	25	F	Servant	05JI08Mj
HANNESY, Daniel	20	M	Laborer	05JI08Mj
BURNS, Jerry	20	M	Laborer	05JI08Mj
CRONIN, Pat.	20	M	Laborer	05JI08Mj
MURPHY, John	20	M	Laborer	05JI08Mj
GUIRY, Catherine	34	F	Servant	05JI08Mj
CAPELL, Eliza	14	F	Servant	05JI08Mj
CALLAGHAN, Michael	28	M	Laborer	05JI08Mj
Mary	25	F	Servant	05JI08Mj
Simon	30	M	Laborer	05JI08Mj
Ellen	26	F	Servant	05JI08Mj
Margaret	2	F	Child	05JI08Mj
Hannah	.00	F	Infant	05JI08Mj
Daniel	4	M	Child	05JI08Mj
Michael	3	M	Child	05JI08Mj
Margaret	2	F	Child	05JI08Mj
Died-At-Sea				
Michael	30	M	Laborer	05JI08Mj
Catherine	24	F	Servant	05JI08Mj
Michael	6	M	Child	05JI08Mj
CARY, Patk.	26	M	Laborer	05JI08Mj
MURPHY, Paddy	30	F	Servant	05JI08Mj
BURNS, Mary	20	F	Servant	05JI08Mj
SULLIVAN, Jerry	30	M	Laborer	05JI08Mj
Betty	28	F	Servant	05JI08Mj
Jerry	.00	M	Infant	05JI08Mj
MURPHY, David	30	M	Laborer	05JI08Mj
KENEDY, Peggy	25	F	Servant	05JI08Mj
HAGARTY, Denis	45	M	Laborer	05JI08Mj
Died-At-Sea				
Ellen	5	F	Child	05JI08Mj
Julia	40	F	Servant	05JI08Mj
Peter	4	M	Child	05JI08Mj
Died-At-Sea				
Julia	.00	F	Infant	05JI08Mj
LINEHAM, Michael	40	M	Laborer	05JI08Mj
Honora	30	F	Servant	05JI08Mj
Michael	.00	M	Infant	05JI08Mj
MCCARTHY, Owen	40	M	Laborer	05JI08Mj
John	12	M	Laborer	05JI08Mj

NAMES OF PASSENGERS	AGE	SEX	OCCUPATIONS	DATE PORT SHIP
SURFIN, Eliza.	21	F	Servant	05J108Mj
BRACEY, Wm.	30	M	Laborer	05J108Mj
Johanna	30	F	Servant	05J108Mj
Michael	4	M	Child	05J108Mj
PRAY, Patt.	.00	M	Infant	05J108Mj
FLANNAGAN, Michael	30	M	Laborer	05J108Mj
Catherine	25	F	Servant	05J108Mj
Margt.	26	F	Servant	05J108Mj
Timothy	.00	M	Infant	05J108Mj
HIGGINS, Johanna	40	F	Servant	05J108Mj
Jerry	18	M	Laborer	05J108Mj
Lawrence	16	M	Laborer	05J108Mj
Michael	14	M	Laborer	05J108Mj
Daniel	6	M	Child	05J108Mj
John	4	M	Child	05J108Mj
BRYAN, James	22	M	Laborer	05J108Mj
RUFFE, Joseph	22	M	Laborer	05J108Mj
LYNCH, Jerry	30	M	Laborer	05J108Mj
FORREST, Patt	26	M	Laborer	05J108Mj
Mary	26	F	Servant	05J108Mj
John	2	M	Child	05J108Mj
BUCKLY, Mary	26	F	Servant	05J108Mj
Margt.	28	F	Servant	05J108Mj
FLINN, Nicholas-Jane	24	M	Laborer	05J108Mj
Eliza	24	M	Servant	05J108Mj
LOVELL, Eliza	22	M	Servant	05J108Mj
NOYLE, Wm.	40	M	Laborer	05J108Mj
Mary	25	F	Servant	05J108Mj
BARRY, Patt	20	M	Laborer	05J108Mj
Michael	21	M	Laborer	05J108Mj
Nancy	14	F	Servant	05J108Mj
CANDEN, John	48	M	Laborer	05J108Mj
Mary	40	F	Servant	05J108Mj
DUMFEY, Mary	40	F	Servant	05J108Mj
FARRALL, John	23	M	Laborer	05J108Mj
DUMFEY, Ellen	16	F	Servant	05J108Mj
Michael	14	M	Child	05J108Mj
Margt.	11	F	Child	05J108Mj
Patt.	9	M	Child	05J108Mj
James	7	M	Child	05J108Mj
Martin	3	M	Child	05J108Mj
BOURK, James	28	M	Laborer	05J108Mj
Honora	5	F	Child	05J108Mj
MCCARTHY, Catherine	20	F	Servant	05J108Mj
LYNCH, Martin	40	M	Laborer	05J108Mj
Peggy	12	F	Child	05J108Mj
John	10	M	Child	05J108Mj
HEGERTY, Daniel	22	M	Laborer	05J108Mj
ACHISON, Samuel	25	M	Laborer	05J108Mj
Robert	22	M	Laborer	05J108Mj
MURPHY, Julia	25	F	Servant	05J108Mj
Daniel	25	M	Laborer	05J108Mj
PALMER, Wm.	20	M	Laborer	05J108Mj
DWYER, Ellen	21	F	Servant	05J108Mj
CONNELL, Thomas	14	M	Laborer	05J108Mj
BIRD, Robert	28	M	Laborer	05J108Mj
COLLINS, Con.	28	M	Laborer	05J108Mj
CRONIN, Julia	24	F	Servant	05J108Mj
FITZGERALD, Daniel	26	M	Laborer	05J108Mj
CROULY, Joseph	24	M	Laborer	05J108Mj
SWING, Patt.	30	M	Laborer	05J108Mj
Daniel	25	M	Laborer	05J108Mj
JOYCE, Eliza.	20	F	Servant	05J108Mj
BRODERICK, John	18	M	Laborer	05J108Mj
DOULING, James	20	M	Laborer	05J108Mj
DELANEY, Daniel	20	M	Laborer	05J108Mj
CONTY, Patt.	30	M	Laborer	05J108Mj
HANNIFAN, John	20	M	Laborer	05J108Mj
COTTER, Johanna	21	F	Servant	05J108Mj
CONWAY, Catherine	22	F	Servant	05J108Mj
STACK, James	23	M	Laborer	05J108Mj
Died-At-Sea				
Bridget	20	F	Servant	05J108Mj
Mary	18	F	Servant	05J108Mj
PIERCE, Catherine	24	F	Servant	05J108Mj
STACK, Garrett	21	M	Laborer	05J108Mj
CURTEN, Darly	23	M	Laborer	05J108Mj
John	20	M	Laborer	05J108Mj
ROCHE, Michael	40	M	Laborer	05J108Mj
CRONIN, Catherine	20	F	Servant	05J108Mj
MURPHY, Mary	41	F	Laborer	05J108Mj
Mary	20	F	Laborer	05J108Mj
Margt.	17	F	Laborer	05J108Mj
Jane	16	F	Laborer	05J108Mj
Jerry	14	M	Laborer	05J108Mj
MCCARTHY, Honora	48	F	Laborer	05J108Mj
Ally	48	M	Laborer	05J108Mj
Daniel	22	M	Laborer	05J108Mj
Denis	19	M	Laborer	05J108Mj
Sandy	17	M	Laborer	05J108Mj
James	14	M	Laborer	05J108Mj
Anne	15	F	Servant	05J108Mj
Susan	14	F	Servant	05J108Mj
Horince	8	F	Child	05J108Mj
DOYLE, John	22	M	Laborer	05J108Mj
Margt.	14	F	Servant	05J108Mj
CORCORAN, Cornelius	24	M	Laborer	05J108Mj
Biddy	20	F	Servant	05J108Mj
MOORE, Ellen	22	F	Servant	05J108Mj
Betty	20	F	Servant	05J108Mj
JONES, Mary	16	F	Servant	05J108Mj
MALONE, Johanna	19	F	Servant	05J108Mj
TUOKY, Denis	40	M	Laborer	05J108Mj
Julia	25	F	Servant	05J108Mj
MCANLIFFE, Martha	18	F	Servant	05J108Mj
SHEEHAN, John	18	M	Laborer	05J108Mj
KEEFFE, John	26	M	Laborer	05J108Mj
Mary	30	F	Servant	05J108Mj
DALY, Mary	30	F	Servant	05J108Mj
LINEHAM, Honora	20	F	Servant	05J108Mj
COONEY, Bridget	20	F	Servant	05J108Mj
KENNY, Wm.	30	M	Laborer	05J108Mj
COUGHLAN, Mary	28	F	Servant	05J108Mj
BELLAW, Hannah	30	F	Servant	05J108Mj
MURPHY, Jerry	28	M	Laborer	05J108Mj
DONAVAN, Pattk.	21	M	Laborer	05J108Mj
Catherine	19	F	Servant	05J108Mj
FOLEY, Mary	15	F	Servant	05J108Mj
HENTY, U	.00	M	Infant	05J108Mj
Born-At-Sea				

MECCA 05 JULY 1849

From Penzance

NAMES OF PASSENGERS	AGE	SEX	OCCUPATIONS	DATE PORT SHIP
SIMMONS, Peggy	56	F	None	05J120Mq
Saml.	35	M	Miner	05J120Mq
John	21	M	Miner	05J120Mq
Susannah	18	F	None	05J120Mq
Joseph	13	M	None	05J120Mq
U, U	37	F	None	05J120Mq
Saml.	20	M	Miner	05J120Mq
Mary	13	F	None	05J120Mq
Elizth.	00	F	None	05J120Mq
Emily	9	F	Child	05J120Mq
DUNN, Richd.	00	M	Unknown	05J120Mq
THOMAS, Jane	00	F	Unknown	05J120Mq
Mary	00	F	Unknown	05J120Mq
Savina	00	F	Unknown	05J120Mq
Margt.	00	F	Unknown	05J120Mq
Emily	11	F	None	05J120Mq
Benj.	9	M	Child	05J120Mq
Anne	60	F	None	05J120Mq
WEARE, Elizth.	23	F	None	05J120Mq

NAMES OF PASSENGERS	AGE	SEX	OCCUPATIONS	DATE PORT SHIP
WEARE, Caroline	.00	F	Infant	05J120Mq
BURGESS, John	32	M	Miner	05J120Mq
WATERS, Henry	53	M	Farmer	05J120Mq
Sarah	53	F	None	05J120Mq
Peggy	24	F	None	05J120Mq
Martha	21	F	None	05J120Mq
Mary	21	F	None	05J120Mq
Priscilla	20	F	None	05J120Mq
Jacob	18	M	Farmer	05J120Mq
Sarah	15	F	None	05J120Mq
Wm.	13	F	None	05J120Mq
Abraham	12	M	None	05J120Mq
Isaac	10	M	None	05J120Mq
Jane	23	F	None	05J120Mq
John	.00	M	Infant	05J120Mq
WARNINGTON, Joseph	24	M	Farmer	05J120Mq
HOOKER, Margt.	29	F	None	05J120Mq
RADDER, Margt.	23	F	None	05J120Mq
Matthew	.00	M	Infant	05J120Mq
TAYLOR, John	21	M	Miner	05J120Mq
PHILLIPS, Thos.	30	M	Miner	05J120Mq
SKEWES, Thos.	27	M	Miner	05J120Mq
PHILLIPS, James	25	M	Miner	05J120Mq

ST.JOHN 05 JULY 1849

From Liverpool

NAMES OF PASSENGERS	AGE	SEX	OCCUPATIONS	DATE PORT SHIP
BARNES, Thomas	15	M	Laborer	05J102Mp
Bella	11	F	Laborer	05J102Mp
James	10	M	Laborer	05J102Mp
MADDEN, Dorothea	45	F	Laborer	05J102Mp
KEENAN, Thomas	15	M	Laborer	05J102Mp
WARD, Bridget	24	F	Laborer	05J102Mp
MURRAY, Timothy	31	M	Laborer	05J102Mp
Nerry	22	U	Laborer	05J102Mp
Daniel	32	M	Laborer	05J102Mp
CEONDY, Patrick	35	M	Laborer	05J102Mp
Julia	24	F	Laborer	05J102Mp
MURPHY, Andrew	23	M	Laborer	05J102Mp
MOORE, Wm.	28	M	Laborer	05J102Mp
Catherine	27	F	Laborer	05J102Mp
Bernard	00	M	Unknown	05J102Mp
Elizabeth	00	F	Unknown	05J102Mp
JONES, Robert	23	M	Laborer	05J102Mp
CORENEY, Charles	46	M	Laborer	05J102Mp
Catherine	46	F	Laborer	05J102Mp
REARDON, Timothy	35	M	Laborer	05J102Mp
Mary	35	F	Laborer	05J102Mp
CARVER, Johanna	30	F	Laborer	05J102Mp
John	5	M	Child	05J102Mp
HAYS, Peter	25	M	Laborer	05J102Mp
FENTON, Wm.	26	M	Laborer	05J102Mp
HOLLY, John	45	M	Laborer	05J102Mp
JONES, Richard	30	M	Laborer	05J102Mp
Mary	30	F	Laborer	05J102Mp
John	5	M	Child	05J102Mp
Richard	4	M	Child	05J102Mp
CUMMINGS, Mary	23	F	Laborer	05J102Mp
GALLAGHAN, Irving	27	M	Laborer	05J102Mp
Julia	20	F	Laborer	05J102Mp
BUTLER, James	30	M	Laborer	05J102Mp
Mary	25	F	Laborer	05J102Mp
FITZGERALD, David	26	M	Laborer	05J102Mp
RYAN, Daniel	34	M	Laborer	05J102Mp
Daniel	17	M	Laborer	05J102Mp
Daniel	5	M	Child	05J102Mp
SULLIVAN, Patrick	26	M	Laborer	05J102Mp
Julia	26	F	Laborer	05J102Mp

NAMES OF PASSENGERS	AGE	SEX	OCCUPATIONS	DATE PORT SHIP
DOWNING, Wm.	26	M	Laborer	05J102Mp
Johannah	26	F	Laborer	05J102Mp
MAHONY, Dennis	33	M	Laborer	05J102Mp
Honora	33	F	Laborer	05J102Mp
HALLAHAN, Levi	27	M	Laborer	05J102Mp
TOBEN, Wm.	20	M	Laborer	05J102Mp
Mary	25	F	Laborer	05J102Mp
CARY, Michael	26	M	Laborer	05J102Mp
HENESSY, Mary	31	F	Laborer	05J102Mp
SHALVERY, Edwd.	34	M	Laborer	05J102Mp
WEARS, Cath.	21	F	Laborer	05J102Mp
SHALVERY, Mary	12	F	Laborer	05J102Mp
MCGRATH, Wm.	27	M	Laborer	05J102Mp
Mary	27	F	Laborer	05J102Mp
VICKERS, Patrick	20	M	Laborer	05J102Mp
HOY, Wm.	21	M	Laborer	05J102Mp
RILLY, Bernard	40	M	Laborer	05J102Mp
James	16	M	Laborer	05J102Mp
HARDING, Hannah	40	F	Laborer	05J102Mp
Henry	20	M	Laborer	05J102Mp
Hannah	17	F	Laborer	05J102Mp
Richard	15	M	Laborer	05J102Mp
Sarah	13	F	Laborer	05J102Mp
William	11	M	Laborer	05J102Mp
Ann	8	F	Child	05J102Mp
Susan	4	F	Child	05J102Mp
GALVIN, Patrick	29	M	Laborer	05J102Mp
WHITE, Cornelius	3	M	Child	05J102Mp
BRODNICK, Maria	12	F	Laborer	05J102Mp
CORMSKEY, James	20	M	Laborer	05J102Mp
CLARKIN, May	18	F	Laborer	05J102Mp
Eliza	16	F	Laborer	05J102Mp
Philip	14	M	Laborer	05J102Mp
Ann	13	F	Laborer	05J102Mp
John	12	M	Laborer	05J102Mp
HAND, Bernard	18	M	Laborer	05J102Mp
COLLINS, May	18	F	Laborer	05J102Mp
MOORE, Daniel	21	M	Laborer	05J102Mp
John	18	M	Laborer	05J102Mp
Catherine	23	F	Laborer	05J102Mp
Margaret	16	F	Laborer	05J102Mp
COOKE, Martin	30	M	Laborer	05J102Mp
BRYAN, Michael	28	M	Laborer	05J102Mp
LYONS, Dennis	40	M	Laborer	05J102Mp
Daniel	11	M	Laborer	05J102Mp
MURPHY, Daniel	22	M	Laborer	05J102Mp
LYONS, Margt.	32	F	Laborer	05J102Mp
Mary	11	F	Laborer	05J102Mp
Patrick	8	M	Child	05J102Mp
James	4	M	Child	05J102Mp
John	4	M	Child	05J102Mp
MAHONY, Honora	20	F	Laborer	05J102Mp
LEATING, Wm.	40	M	Laborer	05J102Mp
Ellen	40	F	Laborer	05J102Mp
MURPHY, Thomas	22	M	Laborer	05J102Mp
John	20	M	Laborer	05J102Mp
BUCKLEY, Stephen	30	M	Laborer	05J102Mp
LEALEY, James	40	M	Laborer	05J102Mp
Mary	13	F	Laborer	05J102Mp
DORLAN, Johannah	30	M	Laborer	05J102Mp
FITZPATRICK, Peggy	34	F	Laborer	05J102Mp
GORMAN, John	20	M	Laborer	05J102Mp
OCONNELL, Mich.	29	M	Laborer	05J102Mp
GRIFFEN, John	20	M	Laborer	05J102Mp
OBRIEN, Daniel	00	M	Laborer	05J102Mp
Ellen	54	F	Laborer	05J102Mp
Daniel	10	M	Laborer	05J102Mp
DALY, John	17	M	Laborer	05J102Mp
Mary	9	F	Child	05J102Mp
DEMKILLHAVEN, Terrence	17	M	Laborer	05J102Mp
POINDEGRAST, Rose	14	F	Laborer	05J102Mp
QUINN, Christian	24	M	Laborer	05J102Mp
Mary	24	F	Laborer	05J102Mp
BRYAN, Thomas	18	M	Laborer	05J102Mp
Patrick	16	M	Laborer	05J102Mp

NAMES OF PASSENGERS	AGE	SEX	OCCUPATIONS	DATE PORT SHIP
SIMPKINS, Sarah	35	F	Laborer	05JI02Mp
Thomas	7	M	Child	05JI02Mp
MASON, Samuel	36	M	Laborer	05JI02Mp
Jemima	23	F	Laborer	05JI02Mp
CALINAN, James	39	M	Laborer	05JI02Mp
EVANS, Eliza	25	F	Laborer	05JI02Mp
William	4	M	Child	05JI02Mp
George	3	M	Child	05JI02Mp
MCGADE, Ann	24	F	Laborer	05JI02Mp
LORAND, George	27	M	Laborer	05JI02Mp
Charles	3	M	Child	05JI02Mp
KEMSH, Mary	25	F	Laborer	05JI02Mp
Emma	7	F	Child	05JI02Mp
LORAND, Emma	20	F	Laborer	05JI02Mp
BLACK, George	22	M	Laborer	05JI02Mp
SMITH, Henry	30	M	Laborer	05JI02Mp
GRADY, Mary	20	F	Laborer	05JI02Mp
Michael	3	M	Child	05JI02Mp
COYLE, Mary	30	F	Laborer	05JI02Mp
Catherine	9	F	Child	05JI02Mp
John	4	M	Child	05JI02Mp
Patrick	3	M	Child	05JI02Mp
ROCHE, James	27	M	Laborer	05JI02Mp
Ann	40	F	Laborer	05JI02Mp
MORRISSAY, Michl.	40	M	Laborer	05JI02Mp
Mary	40	F	Laborer	05JI02Mp
Michl.	3	M	Child	05JI02Mp
GRADY, Ally	50	F	Laborer	05JI02Mp
Henry	24	M	Laborer	05JI02Mp
Henry	60	M	Laborer	05JI02Mp
COOKE, Robert	60	M	Laborer	05JI02Mp
Sarah	60	F	Laborer	05JI02Mp
JOHNSON, Alexander	22	M	Laborer	05JI02Mp
CORTRET, Michl.	40	M	Laborer	05JI02Mp
BULLER, James	25	M	Laborer	05JI02Mp
CARROL, Wm.	25	M	Laborer	05JI02Mp
DAWSON, John	30	M	Laborer	05JI02Mp
Wm.	35	M	Laborer	05JI02Mp
Catherine	18	F	Laborer	05JI02Mp
Mary	16	F	Laborer	05JI02Mp
Bridget	14	F	Laborer	05JI02Mp
Peter	12	M	Laborer	05JI02Mp
Ann	10	F	Laborer	05JI02Mp
John	6	M	Child	05JI02Mp
Thomas	4	M	Child	05JI02Mp
FLAHERTY, Mary	23	F	Laborer	05JI02Mp
MCDONALD, Bernard	16	M	Laborer	05JI02Mp
Rose	14	F	Laborer	05JI02Mp
MCENTEE, Rose	9	F	Child	05JI02Mp
JONES, Mary	42	F	Laborer	05JI02Mp
Mary	23	F	Laborer	05JI02Mp
CLIMEH, George	26	M	Laborer	05JI02Mp
CESS, Terrence	24	M	Laborer	05JI02Mp
STAFFORD, Thomas	24	M	Laborer	05JI02Mp
Catherine	24	F	Laborer	05JI02Mp
SAVAGE, Christy	22	M	Laborer	05JI02Mp
WARD, Patrick	25	M	Laborer	05JI02Mp
TIGHE, John	25	M	Laborer	05JI02Mp
HAGAN, Patrick	30	M	Laborer	05JI02Mp
Nancy	30	F	Laborer	05JI02Mp
Bridget	2	F	Child	05JI02Mp
DONNELLY, John	24	M	Laborer	05JI02Mp
Joseph	9	M	Child	05JI02Mp
CLIFFORD, Samuel	37	M	Laborer	05JI02Mp
Eliza	30	F	Laborer	05JI02Mp
Susan	11	F	Laborer	05JI02Mp
J.	6	U	Child	05JI02Mp
Edward	3	M	Child	05JI02Mp
INSY, John	50	M	Laborer	05JI02Mp
ILTAN, Wm.	26	M	Laborer	05JI02Mp
ITTAMORE, Wm.	26	M	Laborer	05JI02Mp
ALSH, John	26	M	Laborer	05JI02Mp
Catherine	26	F	Laborer	05JI02Mp
Margaret	26	F	Laborer	05JI02Mp
TEPHENS, James	30	M	Laborer	05JI02Mp
READY, Mary	22	F	Laborer	05JI02Mp
BURKE, Patrick	27	M	Laborer	05JI02Mp
JAW, Edward	21	M	Laborer	05JI02Mp
DALTON, James	40	M	Laborer	05JI02Mp
Honor	20	F	Laborer	05JI02Mp
FIX, Michl.	26	M	Laborer	05JI02Mp
SEERY, James	20	M	Laborer	05JI02Mp
SHANLEY, Mary	20	F	Laborer	05JI02Mp
FOYLE, Mary	20	F	Laborer	05JI02Mp
CROOGAN, Andy	21	M	Laborer	05JI02Mp
Eliza	20	F	Laborer	05JI02Mp
GASKEN, Patrick	20	M	Laborer	05JI02Mp
Ann	20	F	Laborer	05JI02Mp
MONOSHAN, Frank	30	M	Laborer	05JI02Mp
LYNCH, Edward	21	M	Laborer	05JI02Mp
FEGAN, Christy	3	M	Child	05JI02Mp
DALY, Bessy	20	F	Laborer	05JI02Mp
DELAHUNTY, Matthew	50	M	Laborer	05JI02Mp
BURGER, Catherine	44	F	Laborer	05JI02Mp
MAGUIRE, Thomas	24	M	Laborer	05JI02Mp
HALPENNY, John	20	M	Laborer	05JI02Mp
MCCABE, Margt.	40	F	Laborer	05JI02Mp
Nancy	9	F	Child	05JI02Mp
KELLY, Bridget	20	F	Laborer	05JI02Mp
TOWNSEND, Charles	24	M	Laborer	05JI02Mp
DALY, Mark	27	M	Laborer	05JI02Mp
KELSHER, Richd.	27	M	Laborer	05JI02Mp
FARRELLY, Margt.	24	F	Laborer	05JI02Mp
DONNELLY, Eliza	20	F	Laborer	05JI02Mp
Eliza	20	F	Laborer	05JI02Mp
TRACY, Ann	40	F	Laborer	05JI02Mp
Margt.	6	F	Child	05JI02Mp
KALAHIN, Patrick	26	M	Laborer	05JI02Mp
DARLIN, Michl.	40	M	Laborer	05JI02Mp
Bridget	20	F	Laborer	05JI02Mp
CAHILL, Matthew	20	M	Laborer	05JI02Mp
Mary	00	F	Laborer	05JI02Mp
BRADY, Philip	20	M	Laborer	05JI02Mp
Mary	20	F	Laborer	05JI02Mp
MONOGHAN, James	40	M	Laborer	05JI02Mp
COLLINS, Richard	44	M	Laborer	05JI02Mp
Louisa	20	F	Laborer	05JI02Mp
MASTERMAN, Hugh	20	M	Laborer	05JI02Mp
Bridget	22	F	Laborer	05JI02Mp
MURPHY, Dennis	28	M	Laborer	05JI02Mp
LANGAN, Cath.	35	F	Laborer	05JI02Mp
DOWEL, John	25	M	Laborer	05JI02Mp
WEBB, Ann	40	F	Laborer	05JI02Mp
SHERMAN, Saml.	40	M	Laborer	05JI02Mp
Mary	40	F	Laborer	05JI02Mp
FITZPATRICK, Kelly	24	M	Laborer	05JI02Mp
RODDY, Michl.	24	M	Laborer	05JI02Mp
DALY, John	20	M	Laborer	05JI02Mp
RODDY, John	20	M	Laborer	05JI02Mp
Wm.	20	M	Laborer	05JI02Mp
Mary	5	F	Child	05JI02Mp
CARLY, Patrick	27	M	Laborer	05JI02Mp
Catherine	24	F	Laborer	05JI02Mp
MURPHY, Mary	40	F	Laborer	05JI02Mp
Catherine	10	F	Laborer	05JI02Mp
Margt.	8	F	Child	05JI02Mp
REMNUS, Mary	20	F	Laborer	05JI02Mp
GILLON, Francis	22	M	Laborer	05JI02Mp
CURIG, Michl.	26	M	Laborer	05JI02Mp
CONNOR, John	24	M	Laborer	05JI02Mp
CRANE, Ellen	20	F	Laborer	05JI02Mp
Margt.	23	F	Laborer	05JI02Mp
TUMMERING, Bridget	22	F	Laborer	05JI02Mp
CORBITT, Pat.	40	M	Laborer	05JI02Mp
Catherine	11	F	Laborer	05JI02Mp
James	9	M	Child	05JI02Mp
DWYER, John	25	M	Laborer	05JI02Mp
CONDER, Pet	28	M	Laborer	05JI02Mp
MCGIVEN, Peter	18	M	Laborer	05JI02Mp
ROCHE, Ellen	16	F	Laborer	05JI02Mp

NAMES OF PASSENGERS	AGE	SEX	OCCUPATIONS	DATE PORT SHIP
ROCHE, Johanna	14	F	Laborer	05J102Mp
Ellen	13	F	Laborer	05J102Mp
Margt.	21	F	Laborer	05J102Mp
Wm.	21	M	Laborer	05J102Mp
SULLIVAN, Mary	16	F	Laborer	05J102Mp
HENESSY, Pat.	18	M	Laborer	05J102Mp
FOLIG, Robert	35	M	Laborer	05J102Mp
BUCKLEY, John	35	M	Laborer	05J102Mp
Ellen	32	F	Laborer	05J102Mp
COLLINS, Mich.	24	M	Laborer	05J102Mp
Honora	21	F	Laborer	05J102Mp
CONNOR, Nancy	28	F	Laborer	05J102Mp
William	29	M	Laborer	05J102Mp
TEVOR, Sarah	8	F	Child	05J102Mp
Sarah	29	F	Laborer	05J102Mp
BAGNES, Eliz.	25	F	Laborer	05J102Mp
MORANE, Eliza	20	F	Laborer	05J102Mp
WEED, Mary	20	F	Laborer	05J102Mp
REILLY, Eliza	22	F	Laborer	05J102Mp
KEGAN, Thomas	22	M	Laborer	05J102Mp
DALEY, Tho.	24	M	Laborer	05J102Mp
RESAN, Jas.	24	M	Laborer	05J102Mp
GERITTY, Pat.	24	M	Laborer	05J102Mp
READING, Edwd.	36	M	Laborer	05J102Mp
HOWELL, Ambrose	24	M	Laborer	05J102Mp
FOLEY, Hugh	35	M	Laborer	05J102Mp
LORAND, George	3	M	Child	05J102Mp
MYNCH, Mich.	24	M	Laborer	05J102Mp

BRYAN-ABBS 05 JULY 1849

From Limerick

NAMES OF PASSENGERS	AGE	SEX	OCCUPATIONS	DATE PORT SHIP
ROONEY, Ellen	43	F	Farmer	05J135Mn
Cath.	22	F	Farmer	05J135Mn
MCMAHON, Ann	32	F	Farmer	05J135Mn
Mary	11	F	Farmer	05J135Mn
Patt	7	M	Child	05J135Mn
John	6	M	Child	05J135Mn
BRANN, Andrew	45	M	Farmer	05J135Mn
Mary	45	F	Farmer	05J135Mn
Biddy	20	F	Farmer	05J135Mn
Anne	16	F	Farmer	05J135Mn
Henry	14	M	Farmer	05J135Mn
MOLONY, Sally	36	F	Farmer	05J135Mn
FRAWLEY, Mary	20	F	Farmer	05J135Mn
FOGARTY, John	21	M	Farmer	05J135Mn
SANDS, Cath.	30	F	Farmer	05J135Mn
KIRBY, Denis	20	M	Farmer	05J135Mn
HALLORAN, Biddy	20	F	Farmer	05J135Mn
THORNTON, Bernard	25	M	Farmer	05J135Mn
RYAN, Thomas	30	M	Farmer	05J135Mn
MURPHY, Biddy	23	F	Farmer	05J135Mn
REDDIN, Julia	26	F	Farmer	05J135Mn
HEHIR, Michl.	40	M	Farmer	05J135Mn
Jane	35	F	Farmer	05J135Mn
Margt.	15	F	Farmer	05J135Mn
KEEFE, James	18	M	Farmer	05J135Mn
Michl.	16	M	Farmer	05J135Mn
Sally	14	F	Farmer	05J135Mn
MOLONY, Mary	11	F	Farmer	05J135Mn
GRIFFIN, Patt	15	M	Farmer	05J135Mn
John	30	M	Farmer	05J135Mn
GARRICK, Patt	20	M	Farmer	05J135Mn
CLUNE, Margt.	42	F	Farmer	05J135Mn
Biddy	16	F	Farmer	05J135Mn
Margt.	14	F	Farmer	05J135Mn
Michl.	6	M	Child	05J135Mn
FLYNN, Mary	12	F	Farmer	05J135Mn
KINNANE, U	23	M	Farmer	05J135Mn
Andrew	20	M	Farmer	05J135Mn
CONNORS, Danl.	20	M	Farmer	05J135Mn
CONWAY, John	25	M	Farmer	05J135Mn
CASEY, Laurence	40	M	Farmer	05J135Mn
Mary	34	F	Farmer	05J135Mn
Michl.	18	M	Farmer	05J135Mn
HORAN, John	18	M	Farmer	05J135Mn
MCMAHON, Anne	19	F	Farmer	05J135Mn
DONNELLAN, Biddy	21	F	Farmer	05J135Mn
LYNCH, Michl.	22	M	Farmer	05J135Mn
Kate	21	F	Farmer	05J135Mn
Mary	16	F	Farmer	05J135Mn
HEHIR, Mary	18	F	Farmer	05J135Mn
Susan	17	F	Farmer	05J135Mn
CURTY, Biddy	11	F	Farmer	05J135Mn
CONNORS, Mary	18	F	Farmer	05J135Mn
LEYDEN, Batt	50	M	Farmer	05J135Mn
Ellen	44	F	Farmer	05J135Mn
Cath.	22	F	Farmer	05J135Mn
Connor	20	M	Farmer	05J135Mn
Mary	18	F	Farmer	05J135Mn
Peter	16	M	Farmer	05J135Mn
Nancy	12	F	Farmer	05J135Mn
John	10	M	Farmer	05J135Mn
Batt	8	M	Child	05J135Mn
James	6	M	Child	05J135Mn
Patt	3	M	Child	05J135Mn
Mary	24	F	Farmer	05J135Mn
Cath.	22	F	Farmer	05J135Mn
Hannah	22	F	Farmer	05J135Mn
MOWNEY, Biddy	18	F	Farmer	05J135Mn
MCNAMARA, Biddy	21	F	Farmer	05J135Mn
LYNCH, Margt.	18	F	Farmer	05J135Mn
RYAN, Mary	30	F	Farmer	05J135Mn
Thady	5	M	Child	05J135Mn
John	3	M	Child	05J135Mn
OBRIEN, Denis	35	M	Farmer	05J135Mn
CONNELLY, Edmond	40	M	Farmer	05J135Mn
Ann	30	F	Farmer	05J135Mn
John	30	M	Farmer	05J135Mn
FENTON, Cath.	30	F	Farmer	05J135Mn
RALEIGH, Stephen	30	M	Farmer	05J135Mn
Patt	22	M	Farmer	05J135Mn
Alley	25	M	Farmer	05J135Mn
Mary	20	F	Farmer	05J135Mn
Biddy	16	F	Farmer	05J135Mn
Cath.	18	F	Farmer	05J135Mn
OBRIEN, Mary	19	F	Farmer	05J135Mn
HAYES, Cath.	18	F	Farmer	05J135Mn
HUNT, Mary-A.	16	F	Farmer	05J135Mn
BOURKE, John	20	M	Farmer	05J135Mn
Margt.	20	F	Farmer	05J135Mn
Mary	20	F	Farmer	05J135Mn
DUNDON, Nancy	24	F	Farmer	05J135Mn
BOURKE, Patt	24	M	Farmer	05J135Mn
Hannah	25	F	Farmer	05J135Mn
CONNELLY, Patt	25	M	Farmer	05J135Mn
BYRNS, Arthur	19	M	Farmer	05J135Mn
HUNT, Cath.	17	F	Farmer	05J135Mn
WILLIAMS, Ann	27	F	Farmer	05J135Mn
FORD, John	40	M	Farmer	05J135Mn
FITZGERALD, W.	24	M	Farmer	05J135Mn
Johanna	20	F	Farmer	05J135Mn
Ann	18	F	Farmer	05J135Mn
HANNAN, Cath.	6	F	Child	05J135Mn
MORRISEY, Rebecca	26	F	Farmer	05J135Mn
Johanna	3	F	Child	05J135M
Mary	2	F	Child	05J135M
MCMAHON, Cath.	3	F	Child	05J135M
BARTLEY, Jane	24	F	Farmer	05J135M
MORRISSY, Ann	22	F	Farmer	05J135M
NEESON, Wm.	22	M	Farmer	05J135M
QUAIN, Johanna	18	F	Farmer	05J135M
REIDY, David	27	M	Farmer	05J135M

NAMES OF PASSENGERS	AGE	SEX	OCCUPATIONS	DATE PORT SHIP
KEANE, Mary	45	F	Farmer	05J135Mn
Jane	20	F	Farmer	05J135Mn
Eliza	19	F	Farmer	05J135Mn
FETHERTON, Michl.	20	M	Farmer	05J135Mn
MOLONY, Bridget	18	F	Farmer	05J135Mn
RYAN, Ann	20	F	Farmer	05J135Mn
Bridget	18	F	Farmer	05J135Mn
HAYES, Mary	20	F	Farmer	05J135Mn
MULQUEENEY, Cath.	18	F	Farmer	05J135Mn
CLIFFORD, Barth.	20	M	Farmer	05J135Mn

NAOMI 06 JULY 1849

From Liverpool

NAMES OF PASSENGERS	AGE	SEX	OCCUPATIONS	DATE PORT SHIP
MCINTER, Michael	30	M	Farmer	06J102Lt
BROPHY, George	50	M	Farmer	06J102Lt
Judy	50	F	Farmer	06J102Lt
John	22	M	Farmer	06J102Lt
Mary	18	F	Farmer	06J102Lt
Nancy	16	F	Farmer	06J102Lt
CORLETT, William	20	M	Shoemaker	06J102Lt
COLLINS, William	21	M	Laborer	06J102Lt
FINNER, Patk.	21	M	Carpenter	06J102Lt
MURPHY, Honor	19	F	Servant	06J102Lt
KEAN, Ann	19	F	Servant	06J102Lt
REILEY, Thomas	20	M	Tanner	06J102Lt
GIBBON, Ann	30	F	Servant	06J102Lt
MURRAY, Joseph	21	M	Laborer	06J102Lt
ROE, Robt.	30	M	Farmer	06J102Lt
Jane	40	F	Unknown	06J102Lt
Mary-Ann	24	F	Unknown	06J102Lt
Margaret	16	F	Unknown	06J102Lt
Mary-Ann	14	F	Unknown	06J102Lt
ANDERSON, Pattk.	21	M	Farmer	06J102Lt
FANNON, Phillip	37	M	Carpenter	06J102Lt
Elizabeth	14	F	Servant	06J102Lt
DONNELLY, Catharine	12	F	Servant	06J102Lt
CRONNIN, Pattk.	48	M	Laborer	06J102Lt
Daniel	4	M	Child	06J102Lt
PURSELL, James	40	M	Farmer	06J102Lt
U-Mrs.	40	F	Unknown	06J102Lt
James	18	M	Farmer	06J102Lt
John	12	M	Farmer	06J102Lt
Aurora	.00	F	Infant	06J102Lt
HARNEY, Patrick	24	M	Farmer	06J102Lt
FOGARTY, James	35	M	Shoemaker	06J102Lt
PURSELL, Martin	36	M	Farmer	06J102Lt
POWERS, Bridget	23	F	Servant	06J102Lt
FOGARTY, Honor	26	F	Servant	06J102Lt
BOURKE, John	20	M	Shoemaker	06J102Lt
Julia	23	F	Shoemaker	06J102Lt
Helen	20	F	Shoemaker	06J102Lt
Denis	.00	M	Infant	06J102Lt
CARROLL, Phillip	22	M	Farmer	06J102Lt
RYAN, John	45	M	Farmer	06J102Lt
Honor	20	F	Servant	06J102Lt
MAHER, Joseph	22	M	Laborer	06J102Lt
Mary	20	F	Unknown	06J102Lt
KEELEY, Charles	24	M	Unknown	06J102Lt
REILLY, James	20	M	Laborer	06J102Lt
Mary	20	F	Laborer	06J102Lt
BOURKE, William	40	M	Farmer	06J102Lt
Winifred	40	F	Unknown	06J102Lt
BRANNON, Thos.	26	M	Laborer	06J102Lt
RACHFORD, Patt	29	M	Laborer	06J102Lt
DOYLE, Michael	40	M	Laborer	06J102Lt
ANNON, James	26	M	Laborer	06J102Lt
CANDREW, Michael	30	M	Laborer	06J102Lt
STONEY, William	30	M	Farmer	06J102Lt
U-Mrs.	40	F	Farmer	06J102Lt
Mary	19	F	Farmer	06J102Lt
William	16	M	Farmer	06J102Lt
James	14	M	Farmer	06J102Lt
LOWTHER, Ann	4	F	Child	06J102Lt
CONNELL, Patt	21	M	Laborer	06J102Lt
William	19	M	Laborer	06J102Lt
MCGAGAN, Mary	21	F	Servant	06J102Lt
KEARNEY, Mary	27	F	Servant	06J102Lt
Richard	20	M	Laborer	06J102Lt
BROGAN, Thomas	40	M	Unknown	06J102Lt
SHEERLY, Michael	22	M	Farmer	06J102Lt
Margaret	20	F	Unknown	06J102Lt
John	18	M	Farmer	06J102Lt
ALLEN, Walter	12	M	Farmer	06J102Lt
Bridget	16	F	Farmer	06J102Lt
Maria	3	F	Child	06J102Lt
HALL, Mary	20	F	Servant	06J102Lt
KINNEY, Daniel	30	M	Laborer	06J102Lt
EGAN, Michael	30	M	Cbtmkr	06J102Lt
DELANY, Catherine	20	F	Unknown	06J102Lt
Ellen	14	F	Unknown	06J102Lt
DORE, Patrick	40	M	Farmer	06J102Lt
Elizabeth	36	F	Farmer	06J102Lt
Robert	25	M	Farmer	06J102Lt
John	19	M	Farmer	06J102Lt
Patrick	14	M	Farmer	06J102Lt
Johanna	18	F	Farmer	06J102Lt
SULLIVAN, John	25	M	Farmer	06J102Lt
KENNEDY, James	23	M	Laborer	06J102Lt
CONNOR, Thos.	22	M	Laborer	06J102Lt
Richard	30	M	Laborer	06J102Lt
Mary	23	F	Laborer	06J102Lt
RENSHAW, Thomas	21	M	Laborer	06J102Lt
Catharine	18	F	Laborer	06J102Lt
Eliza	21	F	Laborer	06J102Lt
DOHERTY, Sophia	17	F	Servant	06J102Lt
SKANLAN, John	18	M	Farmer	06J102Lt
DUMPHY, John	21	M	Shopman	06J102Lt
Ann	50	F	Unknown	06J102Lt
KELLEY, John	27	M	Laborer	06J102Lt
Thomas	23	M	Laborer	06J102Lt
GANGRIN, Helen	18	F	Servant	06J102Lt
DILLON, Robert	24	M	Miller	06J102Lt
SULLIVAN, William	30	M	Shopman	06J102Lt
Mary	26	F	Unknown	06J102Lt
John	3	M	Child	06J102Lt
James	.06	M	Infant	06J102Lt
HANNAGHTY, Mary	22	F	Servant	06J102Lt
DAWSON, Patrick	21	M	Farmer	06J102Lt
WARD, Alice	20	F	Servant	06J102Lt
FARRELL, Mathew	17	M	Laborer	06J102Lt
Mary	19	F	Laborer	06J102Lt
KEARNEY, Patt	24	M	Laborer	06J102Lt
CALAGHAN, Patt	24	M	Laborer	06J102Lt
MASTERSON, Michael	22	M	Laborer	06J102Lt
KELLEY, Patt	18	M	Laborer	06J102Lt
REILLY, Charles	21	M	Laborer	06J102Lt
Mary	30	F	Laborer	06J102Lt
PLUNKETT, Patt	40	M	Laborer	06J102Lt
Bessy	19	F	Laborer	06J102Lt
Helen	15	F	Laborer	06J102Lt
Helen	7	F	Child	06J102Lt
DONOHOE, Thomas	37	M	Laborer	06J102Lt
DUGGAN, Michael	23	M	Laborer	06J102Lt
HICKEY, Michael	21	M	Laborer	06J102Lt
MCCARTHY, Owen	27	M	Farmer	06J102Lt
Charles	35	M	Farmer	06J102Lt
John	23	M	Farmer	06J102Lt
Daniel	21	M	Farmer	06J102Lt
Charles	19	M	Farmer	06J102Lt
Daniel	26	M	Farmer	06J102Lt
Peggy	24	F	Farmer	06J102Lt
Catharine	37	F	Farmer	06J102Lt

NAMES OF PASSENGERS	AGE	SEX	OCCUPATIONS	DATE PORT SHIP
MCCARTHY, Catharine	22	F	Farmer	06J102Lt
BRENNAN, Andrew	19	M	Farmer	06J102Lt
Timothy	30	M	Farmer	06J102Lt
Peggy	24	F	Farmer	06J102Lt
Michael	.05	M	Infant	06J102Lt
Helen	14	F	Unknown	06J102Lt
TRACEY, Michael	19	M	Laborer	06J102Lt
CAMPBELL, John	20	M	Laborer	06J102Lt
HICKEY, Thomas	25	M	Laborer	06J102Lt
Garret	20	M	Laborer	06J102Lt
John	23	M	Laborer	06J102Lt
CONNELL, Patt	21	M	Laborer	06J102Lt
DILLON, Catharine	14	F	Laborer	06J102Lt
James	20	M	Laborer	06J102Lt
BRADY, John	25	M	Laborer	06J102Lt
DONAGHY, Michael	25	M	Laborer	06J102Lt
INGLISBY, Owen	20	M	Laborer	06J102Lt
FARRELL, Patt	28	M	Laborer	06J102Lt
MCGOVERN, Margaret	24	F	Servant	06J102Lt
Honor	25	F	Servant	06J102Lt
CONNELLY, Mary	22	F	Servant	06J102Lt
KEALLY, James	49	M	Laborer	06J102Lt
Died-At-Sea				
Rose	39	F	Laborer	06J102Lt
CLAHEY, Ann	14	F	Servant	06J102Lt
Rose	12	F	Servant	06J102Lt
MAGLAN, Eliza	22	F	Servant	06J102Lt
WYER, Mary	22	F	Servant	06J102Lt
MULLEN, Patrick	45	M	Laborer	06J102Lt
Bridget	33	F	Laborer	06J102Lt
Mary	12	F	Laborer	06J102Lt
Catharine	10	F	Laborer	06J102Lt
John	8	M	Child	06J102Lt
Patt	6	M	Child	06J102Lt
KING, John	43	M	Farmer	06J102Lt
Margaret	41	F	Farmer	06J102Lt
Margaret	7	F	Child	06J102Lt
Mary	5	F	Child	06J102Lt
Patt	.00	M	Infant	06J102Lt
WOODS, Thomas	20	M	Laborer	06J102Lt
FOX, Patrick	20	M	Laborer	06J102Lt
COFFY, Michael	50	M	Laborer	06J102Lt
Margaret	20	F	Laborer	06J102Lt
Michael	30	M	Laborer	06J102Lt
DORSETT, Eliza	25	F	Servant	06J102Lt
PHILLIPS, George	24	M	Farmer	06J102Lt
Richard	25	M	Farmer	06J102Lt
COSGROVE, Thos.	16	M	Shopman	06J102Lt
BAKER, William	19	M	Laborer	06J102Lt
CAMPBELL, Margaret	25	F	Servant	06J102Lt
CASSIDY, John	25	M	Laborer	06J102Lt
MCGRATH, Thomas	24	M	Laborer	06J102Lt
Mary	28	F	Unknown	06J102Lt
CODY, James	22	M	Farmer	06J102Lt
KELLEY, Thomas	45	M	Farmer	06J102Lt
Biddy	35	F	Farmer	06J102Lt
Helen	19	F	Farmer	06J102Lt
Biddy	17	F	Farmer	06J102Lt
Mary	15	F	Farmer	06J102Lt
Susannah	13	F	Farmer	06J102Lt
Mary	11	F	Farmer	06J102Lt
John	11	M	Farmer	06J102Lt
Patt	9	M	Child	06J102Lt
Timothy	7	M	Child	06J102Lt
Thomas	5	M	Child	06J102Lt
Margaret	3	F	Child	06J102Lt
MCGRATH, Michael	30	M	Farmer	06J102Lt
Michael	.11	M	Infant	06J102Lt
DORLAN, James	50	M	Farmer	06J102Lt
Thomas	32	M	Laborer	06J102Lt
John	10	M	Laborer	06J102Lt
CARTWELL, James	26	M	Laborer	06J102Lt
DELANY, James	21	M	Laborer	06J102Lt
CERNES, Daniel	20	M	Laborer	06J102Lt
NAGLE, Thomas	16	M	Laborer	06J102Lt
SEONE, Edwin	33	M	Laborer	06J102Lt
TRACEY, Ann	45	F	Farmer	06J102Lt
Richd.	17	M	Farmer	06J102Lt
MONESSY, William	40	M	Shopman	06J102Lt
James	20	M	Shopman	06J102Lt
Helen	22	F	Shopman	06J102Lt
HAYES, John	22	M	Shopman	06J102Lt
LACEY, Patt	20	M	Laborer	06J102Lt
CASSIDY, Bridget	18	F	Servant	06J102Lt
MULROY, Mary	16	F	Servant	06J102Lt
CASSIDY, John	30	M	Laborer	06J102Lt
MULROY, Jane	12	F	Servant	06J102Lt
SLACK, Susan	11	F	Servant	06J102Lt
HUNT, Bridget	50	F	Farmer	06J102Lt
Thomas	13	M	Farmer	06J102Lt
Mary	11	F	Farmer	06J102Lt
BARRY, James	24	M	Farmer	06J102Lt
FANNY, Ann	40	F	Servant	06J102Lt
CAVANAGH, Mary	18	F	Servant	06J102Lt
DWYER, William	30	M	Laborer	06J102Lt
U-Mrs.	30	F	Laborer	06J102Lt
Mary	10	F	Laborer	06J102Lt
CLAFFEY, William	21	M	Laborer	06J102Lt

GLENLYON 06 JULY 1849

From Liverpool

NAMES OF PASSENGERS	AGE	SEX	OCCUPATIONS	DATE PORT SHIP
MCGALLAGHER, Rose	40	F	Unknown	06J102Mr
John	20	M	Unknown	06J102Mr
HAMILL, James	40	M	Unknown	06J102Mr
Laurence	17	M	Unknown	06J102Mr
Mary	15	F	Unknown	06J102Mr
Catherine	13	F	Unknown	06J102Mr
Bridget	12	F	Unknown	06J102Mr
DERMOT, Garret	16	M	Unknown	06J102Mr
MCCABE, Thomas	28	M	Unknown	06J102Mr
Catherine	24	F	Unknown	06J102Mr
James	3	M	Child	06J102Mr
Ann	.00	F	Infant	06J102Mr
Mcgu--, John	28	M	Unknown	06J102Mr
HART, Ann	39	F	Unknown	06J102Mr
Kate	18	F	Unknown	06J102Mr
Ellen	.00	F	Infant	06J102Mr
MULLOWNY, John	40	M	Unknown	06J102Mr
John	20	M	Unknown	06J102Mr
MIERS, Julia	30	F	Unknown	06J102M
Bridget	30	F	Unknown	06J102M
MURPHEY, Michael	22	M	Unknown	06J102M
RYAN, May	20	F	Unknown	06J102M
WHITE, Luke	20	M	Unknown	06J102M
MCANN, Michael	30	M	Unknown	06J102M
MORRIS, Ann	20	F	Unknown	06J102M
GALEN, Bridget	25	F	Unknown	06J102M
Patrick	3	M	Child	06J102M
LEARY, B.	20	M	Unknown	06J102M
U (W)	20	F	Unknown	06J102M
Enos	.00	M	Infant	06J102M
DOBSON, Furies	39	M	Unknown	06J102M
James	16	M	Unknown	06J102M
MCGUTH, James	23	M	Unknown	06J102M
U-Miss	23	F	Unknown	06J102M
WALTERS, Geo.	23	M	Unknown	06J102M
NOONAN, Timothy	25	M	Unknown	06J102M
KERAN, J.	25	M	Unknown	06J102M
Cahterine	40	F	Unknown	06J102M
CAMPBELL, John	10	M	Unknown	06J102M
Thomas	13	M	Unknown	06J102M
OBRIEN, Wm.	20	M	Unknown	06J102

NAMES OF PASSENGERS	AGE	SEX	OCCUPATIONS	DATE PORT SHIP
RYAN, John	23	M	Unknown	06JI02Mr
Edwd.	21	M	Unknown	06JI02Mr
Wm.	26	M	Unknown	06JI02Mr
MCGATH, John	24	M	Unknown	06JI02Mr
DUNN, Thomas	24	M	Unknown	06JI02Mr
KEATING, Ellen	19	F	Unknown	06JI02Mr
SUTTER, Hanna	30	F	Unknown	06JI02Mr
RYAN, Julia	25	F	Unknown	06JI02Mr
ONEILL, John	68	M	Unknown	06JI02Mr
Con	32	M	Unknown	06JI02Mr
Jem	28	M	Unknown	06JI02Mr
Ellen	60	F	Unknown	06JI02Mr
John	15	M	Unknown	06JI02Mr
DONNELLY, Francis	20	M	Unknown	06JI02Mr
U (W)	20	F	Unknown	06JI02Mr
FOX, Barnard	20	M	Unknown	06JI02Mr
DONNELLY, John	20	M	Unknown	06JI02Mr
FITZSIMMONS, Jas.	30	M	Unknown	06JI02Mr
U (W)	30	F	Unknown	06JI02Mr
Thomas	5	M	Child	06JI02Mr
Mary	3	F	Child	06JI02Mr
John	.00	M	Infant	06JI02Mr
CLARK, Cahane	20	F	Unknown	06JI02Mr
LEALY, John	25	M	Unknown	06JI02Mr
U (W)	25	F	Unknown	06JI02Mr
NAUGHTER, Da.	25	M	Unknown	06JI02Mr
NOULAN, Martin	25	M	Unknown	06JI02Mr
DANNEHER, Michael	40	M	Unknown	06JI02Mr
SULLIVAN, Patk.	30	M	Unknown	06JI02Mr
Eliza	31	F	Unknown	06JI02Mr
FEEHAN, Daniel	18	M	Unknown	06JI02Mr
DALE, Peter	20	M	Unknown	06JI02Mr
Ellen	19	F	Unknown	06JI02Mr
MARTIN, John	20	M	Unknown	06JI02Mr
Bridget	20	F	Unknown	06JI02Mr
CARRON, Mary	20	F	Unknown	06JI02Mr
REYNOLDS, Mary	30	F	Unknown	06JI02Mr
RODGERS, Rose	25	F	Unknown	06JI02Mr
MONAGHAN, Jem	28	M	Unknown	06JI02Mr
U (W)	20	F	Unknown	06JI02Mr
COLLINS, John	26	M	Unknown	06JI02Mr
RICHELL, Barnd.	20	M	Unknown	06JI02Mr
Cath.	18	F	Unknown	06JI02Mr
FLOOD, Michael	30	M	Unknown	06JI02Mr
ORR, Mathew	17	M	Unknown	06JI02Mr
WHITNEY, U-Mrs.	35	F	Unknown	06JI02Mr
FINNESSY, Bridget	40	F	Unknown	06JI02Mr
CANNELL, John	30	M	Unknown	06JI02Mr
MCCULLY, Ann	30	F	Unknown	06JI02Mr
Ann	3	F	Child	06JI02Mr
DONNAHUE, Ann	18	F	Unknown	06JI02Mr
WARNOCK, John	19	M	Unknown	06JI02Mr
Wm.	17	M	Unknown	06JI02Mr
BRADY, Mathew	19	M	Unknown	06JI02Mr
DOYLE, M.	25	F	Unknown	06JI02Mr
MORHE, Michael	26	M	Unknown	06JI02Mr
BEHAN, Patk.	26	M	Unknown	06JI02Mr
DOWD, Hannah	17	F	Unknown	06JI02Mr
MAHAN, Wm.	35	M	Unknown	06JI02Mr
Dennis	25	M	Unknown	06JI02Mr
GLEESON, Wm.	21	M	Unknown	06JI02Mr
MORRIS, Mary	20	F	Unknown	06JI02Mr
MCCOY, Mary	23	F	Unknown	06JI02Mr
CADRY, July	18	F	Unknown	06JI02Mr
CANAH, James	25	M	Unknown	06JI02Mr
DELAHUNTY, Mary	20	F	Unknown	06JI02Mr
MCCORMICK, M.	25	F	Unknown	06JI02Mr
Michael	25	M	Unknown	06JI02Mr
SHIELDS, Patk.	21	M	Unknown	06JI02Mr
Cath.	16	F	Unknown	06JI02Mr
YNCH, Hugh	40	M	Unknown	06JI02Mr
Daphne	40	F	Unknown	06JI02Mr
Patk.	6	M	Child	06JI02Mr
Bridget	40	F	Unknown	06JI02Mr
ITZSIMMONS, Thomas	40	M	Unknown	06JI02Mr
FITZSIMMONS, Ellen	40	F	Unknown	06JI02Mr
REILLY, Patk.	40	M	Unknown	06JI02Mr
RELINGTON, James	18	M	Unknown	06JI02Mr
HALL, Frank	30	M	Unknown	06JI02Mr
Mary	28	F	Unknown	06JI02Mr
RYAN, Patk.	55	M	Unknown	06JI02Mr
Michael	33	M	Unknown	06JI02Mr
MCCORMACK, Bryan	41	M	Unknown	06JI02Mr
U-Miss	40	F	Unknown	06JI02Mr
Catherine	10	F	Unknown	06JI02Mr
Mary	8	F	Child	06JI02Mr
John	6	M	Child	06JI02Mr
Laurence	3	M	Child	06JI02Mr
GALLAGHER, Susan Died-At-Sea	45	F	Unknown	06JI02Mr
James	17	M	Unknown	06JI02Mr
Ma.	15	M	Unknown	06JI02Mr
KENNEY, Honora	40	F	Unknown	06JI02Mr
Patk.	16	M	Unknown	06JI02Mr
CALLAGHER, Turney	36	M	Unknown	06JI02Mr
Mary	30	F	Unknown	06JI02Mr
SULLIVAN, John	26	M	Unknown	06JI02Mr
HANEY, James	35	M	Unknown	06JI02Mr
MAHONY, Margret	19	M	Unknown	06JI02Mr
CACHRINE, John	40	M	Unknown	06JI02Mr
KEEF, Daniel	27	M	Unknown	06JI02Mr
CAIRNS, Patk.	30	M	Unknown	06JI02Mr
ATTRY, John	50	M	Unknown	06JI02Mr
HEEBEN, Edw.	50	M	Unknown	06JI02Mr
RYAN, Ellen	3	F	Child	06JI02Mr
Michael	.00	M	Infant	06JI02Mr
MCDONALD, Cath.	12	F	Unknown	06JI02Mr
Br.	11	F	Unknown	06JI02Mr
Mary	9	F	Child	06JI02Mr
Ann	7	F	Child	06JI02Mr
Ellen	5	F	Child	06JI02Mr
Michael	.00	M	Infant	06JI02Mr
MOORE, Michael	30	M	Unknown	06JI02Mr
CHURLY, Wm.	24	M	Unknown	06JI02Mr
COLLINS, Catharine	20	F	Unknown	06JI02Mr
WALSH, Thomas	22	M	Unknown	06JI02Mr
ROURKE, Moses	20	M	Unknown	06JI02Mr
OHARE, Owen	22	M	Unknown	06JI02Mr
DALON, Patk.	30	M	Unknown	06JI02Mr
SHANLY, Michael	23	M	Unknown	06JI02Mr
DELANY, Bridget	18	F	Unknown	06JI02Mr
MCGLINY, Bridy	18	F	Unknown	06JI02Mr
HICKEY, Wm.	25	M	Unknown	06JI02Mr
DESPARD, Richd.	20	M	Unknown	06JI02Mr
OBRIEN, Wm.	20	M	Unknown	06JI02Mr
MCGRAH, Cathne.	20	F	Unknown	06JI02Mr
Bridy	20	F	Unknown	06JI02Mr
STENEY, Wm.	25	M	Unknown	06JI02Mr
MARA, Bridget	25	F	Unknown	06JI02Mr
BEADY, James	20	M	Unknown	06JI02Mr
HIGGINS, Wm.	28	M	Unknown	06JI02Mr
Richard	21	M	Unknown	06JI02Mr
Ann	27	F	Unknown	06JI02Mr
Elizabeth	49	F	Unknown	06JI02Mr
Martin	16	M	Unknown	06JI02Mr
METCALF, Wm.	21	M	Unknown	06JI02Mr
John	21	M	Unknown	06JI02Mr
JACKSON, Thomas	25	M	Unknown	06JI02Mr
MCNAMARA, John	22	M	Unknown	06JI02Mr
MCELENEY, Patk.	30	M	Unknown	06JI02Mr
U-Miss	20	F	Unknown	06JI02Mr
RICH, Thomas	54	M	Unknown	06JI02Mr
Mary	28	F	Unknown	06JI02Mr
Bridget	18	F	Unknown	06JI02Mr
John	15	M	Unknown	06JI02Mr
Thomas	13	M	Unknown	06JI02Mr
BAGGS, Ellen	18	F	Unknown	06JI02Mr
FINN, Timothy	25	M	Unknown	06JI02Mr
Edward	25	M	Unknown	06JI02Mr
KEANEY, Margaret	24	F	Unknown	06JI02Mr

NAMES OF PASSENGERS	AGE	SEX	OCCUPATIONS	DATE PORT SHIP
BROPHY, Michael	30	M	Unknown	06J102Mr
CARNER, John	30	M	Unknown	06J102Mr
EGAN, An.	26	M	Unknown	06J102Mr
FERRICK, Thomas	20	M	Unknown	06J102Mr
MONAGHAN, Patk.	30	M	Unknown	06J102Mr
GAFFNEY, Patk.	26	M	Unknown	06J102Mr
CLENKIN, John	33	M	Unknown	06J102Mr
BRADY, Peter	30	M	Unknown	06J102Mr
SCANNELL, John	13	M	Unknown	06J102Mr
James	20	M	Unknown	06J102Mr
BENNETT, Samuel	41	M	Unknown	06J102Mr
Ann	49	F	Unknown	06J102Mr
OLDHAM, Thomas	30	M	Unknown	06J102Mr
BATEMAN, Jonathan	34	M	Unknown	06J102Mr
Elizabeth	24	F	Unknown	06J102Mr
Geo.	22	M	Unknown	06J102Mr
H.	18	M	Unknown	06J102Mr
Josiah	16	M	Unknown	06J102Mr
Lucy	13	F	Unknown	06J102Mr
Ann	10	F	Unknown	06J102Mr
David	8	M	Child	06J102Mr
Thomas	6	M	Child	06J102Mr
Jane	2	F	Child	06J102Mr
Susan	.00	F	Infant	06J102Mr
LEVENTH, Geo.	24	M	Unknown	06J102Mr
DINTON, Wm.	16	M	Unknown	06J102Mr
MAYEN, Geo.	31	M	Unknown	06J102Mr
RYAN, Thomas	17	M	Unknown	06J102Mr
Margaret	17	F	Unknown	06J102Mr
GODFREY, Mich.	21	M	Unknown	06J102Mr
BOALE, Margaret	34	F	Unknown	06J102Mr
Jane	11	F	Unknown	06J102Mr
Betsey	9	F	Child	06J102Mr
Sarah	7	F	Child	06J102Mr
James	6	M	Child	06J102Mr
Price	4	M	Child	06J102Mr
John	2	M	Child	06J102Mr
BARKER, Thomas	24	M	Unknown	06J102Mr
MALLEY, Margaret	20	F	Unknown	06J102Mr
WHITE, Wm.	23	M	Unknown	06J102Mr
FALEY, Thomas	20	M	Unknown	06J102Mr
TRACY, Catherine	16	F	Unknown	06J102Mr
BLAKE, Mary	16	F	Unknown	06J102Mr
CARROLL, Henry	50	M	Unknown	06J102Mr
Catherine	45	F	Unknown	06J102Mr
Wm.	20	M	Unknown	06J102Mr
Mary	18	F	Unknown	06J102Mr
Thomas	16	M	Unknown	06J102Mr
Denis	11	M	Unknown	06J102Mr
Ellen	9	F	Child	06J102Mr
Honora	7	F	Child	06J102Mr
Harry	5	M	Child	06J102Mr
FARLY, Catherine	25	F	Unknown	06J102Mr
WADE, Pat	28	M	Unknown	06J102Mr
CAIRN, Thomas	22	M	Unknown	06J102Mr
Eliza	23	F	Unknown	06J102Mr
MCDEIRINS, Henry	20	M	Unknown	06J102Mr
THOMPSON, Arthur	48	M	Unknown	06J102Mr
MCCANN, Geo.	52	M	Unknown	06J102Mr
John	19	M	Unknown	06J102Mr
PADDEN, John	40	M	Unknown	06J102Mr
GREFFITH, Daniel	25	M	Unknown	06J102Mr
Michael	19	M	Unknown	06J102Mr
Honora	22	F	Unknown	06J102Mr
Marg.	20	F	Unknown	06J102Mr
B.	18	F	Unknown	06J102Mr
KENNEY, Mary	19	F	Unknown	06J102Mr
John	26	M	Unknown	06J102Mr
Honora	26	F	Unknown	06J102Mr
Richd.	.00	M	Infant	06J102Mr
DANEY, Bess	20	F	Unknown	06J102Mr
Sara	20	F	Unknown	06J102Mr
MCAULIFF, John	28	M	Unknown	06J102Mr
FALVEY, James	24	M	Unknown	06J102Mr
BRADY, John	20	M	Unknown	06J102Mr

NAMES OF PASSENGERS	AGE	SEX	OCCUPATIONS	DATE PORT SHIP
KEAF, Edwd.	25	M	Unknown	06J102Mr
LARKIN, Joseph	23	M	Unknown	06J102Mr
MOORECROFT, Chas.	25	M	Unknown	06J102Mr
Elizabeth	25	F	Unknown	06J102Mr
William	3	M	Child	06J102Mr
Herbert	1	M	Child	06J102Mr
DALY, John Died-At-Sea	20	M	Unknown	06J102Mr
RAKINS, James	23	M	Unknown	06J102Mr
Margt.	20	F	Unknown	06J102Mr
BURON, Joseph	20	M	Unknown	06J102Mr
REILY, John	25	M	Unknown	06J102Mr
BORNLAN, Thos.	26	M	Unknown	06J102Mr
MCCARTY, U-Mrs.	50	F	Unknown	06J102Mr
U-Miss	24	F	Unknown	06J102Mr
MORRIS, Thos.	30	M	Unknown	06J102Mr
BIRMINGHAM, Garet	22	M	Unknown	06J102Mr
Edwd.	25	M	Unknown	06J102Mr
Bridget	21	F	Unknown	06J102Mr
Mary	24	F	Unknown	06J102Mr
Anne	3	F	Child	06J102Mr
MCDONALD, Cath.	40	F	Unknown	06J102Mr
WARD, Laurence	00	M	Unknown	06J102Mr
LEARY, Daniel	00	M	Unknown	06J102Mr
FITZPATRICK, James	00	M	Unknown	06J102Mr
BODEN, Barnard	00	M	Unknown	06J102Mr

ALEXINA 06 JULY 1849

From Limerick

NAMES OF PASSENGERS	AGE	SEX	OCCUPATIONS	DATE PORT SHIP
FROSTE, James	50	M	Farmer	06J135Lx
Ann (W)	50	F	Wife	06J135Lx
Bridgett	20	F	Spinster	06J135Lx
Mary	19	F	Spinster	06J135Lx
Kate	15	F	Spinster	06J135Lx
Ann	5	F	Child	06J135Lx
Wm.	15	M	Unknown	06J135Lx
Patt	12	M	Unknown	06J135Lx
James	9	M	Child	06J135Lx
John	7	M	Child	06J135Lx
FOLEY, Mary	23	F	Spinster	06J135Lx
CONNERS, Bridgett	20	F	Spinster	06J135Lx
Catherine	16	F	Spinster	06J135Lx
WHELAN, Patt	50	M	Farmer	06J135Lx
Bridgett	15	F	Spinster	06J135Lx
LYNCH, Bridgett	18	F	Spinster	06J135L
MCMAHON, Margaret	18	F	Spinster	06J135Lx
Winifred	23	F	Spinster	06J135L
KILFOYLE, John	30	M	Teacher	06J135L
MCMAHON, Patt	20	M	Laborer	06J135L
KILFOYLE, Annastatias	20	F	Spinster	06J135L
MCNAMARA, John	45	M	Smith	06J135L
U (W)	30	F	Wife	06J135L
Ellen	10	F	Unknown	06J135L
Patt	7	M	Child	06J135L
John	5	M	Child	06J135L
Danl.	3	M	Child	06J135L
Willm.	.00	M	Infant	06J135L
KILLEEN, Ellen	40	F	Matron	06J135L
GONLEE, Margt.	20	F	Spinster	06J135L
RIORDAN, Mich.	20	M	Laborer	06J135L
BOLAND, Mary	20	F	Spinster	06J135L
Catherine	18	F	Spinster	06J135L
Ellen	16	F	Spinster	06J135L
BURNS, Thomas	20	M	Farmer	06J135L
Ann (W)	18	F	Wife	06J135L
MELODY, John	20	M	Farmer	06J135L
VAUGHAN, Catherine	18	F	Spinster	06J135L

NAMES OF PASSENGERS	AGE	SEX	OCCUPATIONS	DATE PORT SHIP
MCMAHON, Bryan	14	M	Unknown	06J135Lx
KELLY, Patt	28	M	Farmer	06J135Lx
Margt. (W)	24	F	Wife	06J135Lx
COGHLAN, Sarah	25	F	Spinster	06J135Lx
Bridgett	3	F	Child	06J135Lx
MACK, Michl.	24	M	Laborer	06J135Lx
SULLIVAN, James	48	M	Farmer	06J135Lx
Ellen (W)	40	F	Wife	06J135Lx
Barry	16	M	Laborer	06J135Lx
Mary	14	F	Unknown	06J135Lx
Thady	12	M	Unknown	06J135Lx
Richd.	10	M	Unknown	06J135Lx
Maurice	8	M	Child	06J135Lx
Catherine	6	F	Child	06J135Lx
James	.06	M	Infant	06J135Lx
OBRIEN, Connor	48	M	Laborer	06J135Lx
HARTE, Patt	35	M	Laborer	06J135Lx
RYAN, Michl.	53	M	Laborer	06J135Lx
U (W)	45	F	Wife	06J135Lx
Catherine	25	F	Spinster	06J135Lx
Michl.	13	M	Unknown	06J135Lx
Ellen	12	F	Unknown	06J135Lx
BOURKE, Thos.	48	M	Farmer	06J135Lx
Johana (W)	38	F	Wife	06J135Lx
John	28	M	Farmer	06J135Lx
Ellen (W)	28	F	Wife	06J135Lx
Michl.	38	M	Laborer	06J135Lx
Patt	12	M	Unknown	06J135Lx
Wm.	10	M	Unknown	06J135Lx
James	8	M	Child	06J135Lx
John	6	M	Child	06J135Lx
Maurice	4	M	Child	06J135Lx
SMITH, Denis	26	M	Farmer	06J135Lx
Michl.	18	M	Farmer	06J135Lx
HATLY, James	26	M	Farmer	06J135Lx
Bridgett (W)	24	F	Wife	06J135Lx
KEYS, James	4	M	Child	06J135Lx
RALEIGH, Bridgett	20	F	Spinster	06J135Lx
GLEASON, Thomas	22	M	Farmer	06J135Lx
COLEMAN, Bridgett	48	F	Matron	06J135Lx
QUINN, Norry	22	F	Spinster	06J135Lx
OBRIEN, James	24	M	Farmer	06J135Lx
RYAN, James	3	M	Child	06J135Lx
BEAN, Eliza	43	F	Matron	06J135Lx
GUBBINS, Michl.	13	M	Laborer	06J135Lx
MORAN, James	26	M	Laborer	06J135Lx
MCGRATH, Thos.	38	M	Laborer	06J135Lx
Peter	13	M	Unknown	06J135Lx
ODEA, Patt	24	M	Laborer	06J135Lx
ENRIGHT, Thos.	20	M	Laborer	06J135Lx
HAYES, Norry	26	F	Spinster	06J135Lx
RYAN, James	20	M	Farmer	06J135Lx
FLANNERY, Denis	30	M	Farmer	06J135Lx
Mary (W)	26	F	Wife	06J135Lx
Winfred	3	M	Child	06J135Lx
Ellen	.04	F	Infant	06J135Lx
MURRAY, James	25	M	Farmer	06J135Lx
GLEESON, Anne	20	F	Spinster	06J135Lx
SKENE, Thos.	22	M	Laborer	06J135Lx
MURPHY, Cornl.	45	M	Laborer	06J135Lx
Mary (W)	30	F	Wife	06J135Lx
MCNAMARA, Catherine	60	F	Matron	06J135Lx
MACK, Ellen	22	F	Spinster	06J135Lx
Michl.	18	M	Laborer	06J135Lx
MULQUEEN, John	28	M	Laborer	06J135Lx
CARROLL, John	24	M	Laborer	06J135Lx
SHEA, John	20	M	Laborer	06J135Lx
CORREEN, Thos.	18	M	Laborer	06J135Lx
SHANNON, James	35	M	Laborer	06J135Lx
Ellen (W)	27	F	Wife	06J135Lx
Michl.	5	M	Child	06J135Lx
Mary	3	F	Child	06J135Lx
Bridgett	.00	F	Infant	06J135Lx
MCGUIRE, Mary	19	F	Spinster	06J135Lx
OYLE, George	36	M	Laborer	06J135Lx
CARING, Daniel	25	M	Laborer	06J135Lx
SWEENEY, Mary	22	F	Spinster	06J135Lx
Michl.	7	M	Child	06J135Lx
DOHERTY, Mary	21	F	Spinster	06J135Lx
William	25	M	Farmer	06J135Lx
Edwd.	20	M	Farmer	06J135Lx
CONWAY, Edward	26	M	Farmer	06J135Lx
LYNCH, John	43	M	Farmer	06J135Lx
HAROLD, Mich.	20	M	Farmer	06J135Lx
SULLIVAN, Winfred	24	F	Spinster	06J135Lx
NANAN, Mary	19	F	Spinster	06J135Lx
MCINERNEY, Mary	24	F	Spinster	06J135Lx
Catherine	22	F	Spinster	06J135Lx
LUBY, John	25	M	Farmer	06J135Lx
KEARNEY, Lawrence	20	M	Farmer	06J135Lx
RYAN, Patt	18	M	Farmer	06J135Lx
Matt	17	M	Farmer	06J135Lx
Bridgett	21	F	Spinster	06J135Lx
Mary	16	F	Spinster	06J135Lx
John	22	M	Farmer	06J135Lx
HAYES, Nicholas	31	M	Farmer	06J135Lx
Mary (W)	32	F	Wife	06J135Lx
PURCELL, Ellen	21	F	Spinster	06J135Lx
HAYES, Matthew	13	M	Unknown	06J135Lx
Honora	11	F	Unknown	06J135Lx
Michl.	9	M	Child	06J135Lx
Mary	7	F	Child	06J135Lx
Catherine	4	F	Child	06J135Lx
Ellen	.11	F	Infant	06J135Lx
KINNAN, Patt	16	M	Laborer	06J135Lx
Bridgett	21	F	Spinster	06J135Lx
Margt.	17	F	Spinster	06J135Lx
KIRBY, James	19	M	Farmer	06J135Lx
SCANLAN, Thos.	20	M	Farmer	06J135Lx
BARRY, James	20	M	Farmer	06J135Lx
Thos.	24	M	Farmer	06J135Lx
HALLIRAN, Patt	25	M	Farmer	06J135Lx
CONELL, Cath.	28	F	Servant	06J135Lx
OBRIEN, Johanna	30	F	Servant	06J135Lx
NOLAN, Kate	18	F	Servant	06J135Lx
Mary	15	F	Servant	06J135Lx

GERMANIA 06 JULY 1849

From London

NAMES OF PASSENGERS	AGE	SEX	OCCUPATIONS	DATE PORT SHIP
CROCKENDER, William	31	M	Farmer	06J113My
Mary	34	F	None	06J113My
JONES, Enoch	26	M	Shoemaker	06J113My
SAMLER, Catherine	26	F	None	06J113My
Emma	2	F	Child	06J113My
Eliza	5	F	Child	06J113My
CURTIS, James	28	M	Tailor	06J113My
WOODCOCK, Samuel	21	M	Laborer	06J113My
RECKET, George	25	M	Laborer	06J113My
SMITH, James	35	M	Laborer	06J113My
Phoebe	35	F	Laborer	06J113My
John	13	M	Laborer	06J113My
William	11	M	Laborer	06J113My
Charles	10	M	Child	06J113My
Honora	8	F	Child	06J113My
Samuel	6	M	Child	06J113My
Ann	5	F	Child	06J113My
James	.10	M	Infant	06J113My
SCOTT, James	29	M	Shoemaker	06J113My
SLADE, John	30	M	Laborer	06J113My
RAKE, William	44	M	Laborer	06J113My
WRIGHT, Edmund	31	M	Laborer	06J113My
REID, John	33	M	Farmer	06J113My

NAMES OF PASSENGERS	AGE	SEX	OCCUPATIONS	DATE PORT SHIP
REID, Helen	28	F	Farmer	06Jl13My
Edward	29	M	Farmer	06Jl13My
Edward	5	M	Child	06Jl13My
CLANCY, Ian	24	M	Tailor	06Jl13My
William	8	M	Child	06Jl13My
Jarvis	6	M	Child	06Jl13My
SMITH, Henry	37	M	Laborer	06Jl13My
Mary	40	F	Laborer	06Jl13My
Henry	11	M	Laborer	06Jl13My
Mary-Ann	7	F	Child	06Jl13My
GRINONNCAN, James	50	M	Laborer	06Jl13My
Charles	15	M	Laborer	06Jl13My
ALBERS, Henry	25	M	Tailor	06Jl13My
BOOTH, William	29	M	Smith	06Jl13My
Ann	26	F	None	06Jl13My
George	4	M	Child	06Jl13My
Alfred	3	M	Child	06Jl13My
Herbert	.10	M	Infant	06Jl13My
LAW, Thomas	33	M	Laborer	06Jl13My
WILLIAMS, William	30	M	Laborer	06Jl13My
GREGORY, Henry	17	M	Laborer	06Jl13My
FEARY, Louis	24	M	Farmer	06Jl13My
Mathilda	21	F	Farmer	06Jl13My
Lewis	44	M	Farmer	06Jl13My
Susan	44	F	Farmer	06Jl13My
Mary	20	F	Farmer	06Jl13My
John	18	M	Farmer	06Jl13My
Susan	12	M	Farmer	06Jl13My
William	12	M	Farmer	06Jl13My
Jane	11	F	Farmer	06Jl13My
George	9	M	Child	06Jl13My
Frederick	5	M	Child	06Jl13My
Sarah-Jane	5	F	Child	06Jl13My
Charles	.10	M	Infant	06Jl13My
FAITHFUL, Mary	40	F	None	06Jl13My
GILDEN, Ann	44	F	None	06Jl13My
COLLIER, Thomas	36	M	Blacksmith	06Jl13My
ROURK, Mary	42	F	None	06Jl13My
CARTER, Edward	30	M	Laborer	06Jl13My
ELLIS, James	41	M	Laborer	06Jl13My
CARTER, John	30	M	Farmer	06Jl13My
ELLIS, James	15	M	Farmer	06Jl13My
ADAM, Jane	60	F	Farmer	06Jl13My
USHER, Betsey	30	F	None	06Jl13My
CARTER, Mary	27	F	None	06Jl13My
WALLER, Sarah	26	F	None	06Jl13My
ADAM, Fanny	30	F	None	06Jl13My
ELLIS, Sarah	11	F	None	06Jl13My
John	9	M	Child	06Jl13My
Fanny	7	F	Child	06Jl13My
Thomas	5	M	Child	06Jl13My
Mary	3	F	Child	06Jl13My
WALLER, John	5	M	Child	06Jl13My
CHESTER, Joseph	21	M	Farmer	06Jl13My
STANARD, Joseph	28	M	Farmer	06Jl13My
CONNOR, Patrick	28	M	Farmer	06Jl13My
Julia	28	F	Farmer	06Jl13My
BROSNESHEA, Margaret	24	F	Farmer	06Jl13My
HICKY, Jeremiah	28	M	Laborer	06Jl13My
DYSON, John	27	M	Laborer	06Jl13My
CALMAN, Patrick	26	M	Laborer	06Jl13My
Ellen	60	F	Laborer	06Jl13My
Margaret	28	F	Laborer	06Jl13My
HEALEY, James	21	M	Shoemaker	06Jl13My
DOIL, Timothy	35	M	Shoemaker	06Jl13My
AARON, Ellen	22	F	Shoemaker	06Jl13My
CONNOR, John	25	M	Laborer	06Jl13My
HEALY, Francis	21	M	Laborer	06Jl13My
POWELL, Benjamin	45	M	Laborer	06Jl13My
Mary	40	F	Laborer	06Jl13My
Mary	18	F	Laborer	06Jl13My
Elisabeth	17	F	Laborer	06Jl13My
Benjamin	12	M	Laborer	06Jl13My
RICE, Mary	48	F	Laborer	06Jl13My
Rebecca	12	F	Laborer	06Jl13My

NAMES OF PASSENGERS	AGE	SEX	OCCUPATIONS	DATE PORT SHIP
CLARK, Robert	36	M	Farmer	06Jl13My
Charlotte	32	F	Farmer	06Jl13My
FERMIN, John	40	M	Farmer	06Jl13My
Ann	40	F	Farmer	06Jl13My
Ann	.09	F	Infant	06Jl13My
EDWARDS, John	26	M	Laborer	06Jl13My
Ann	26	F	Laborer	06Jl13My
Jane	16	F	Laborer	06Jl13My
Catherine	11	F	Laborer	06Jl13My
John	.08	M	Infant	06Jl13My
ALLINS, James	26	M	Farmer	06Jl13My
HEAVY, John	20	M	Farmer	06Jl13My
SALT, William	33	M	Farmer	06Jl13My
SAWYER, George	31	M	Farmer	06Jl13My
FOLEY, Patrick	34	M	Farmer	06Jl13My
CRADDOCK, John	23	M	Farmer	06Jl13My
TAYLOR, George	26	M	Laborer	06Jl13My
Emma	21	F	None	06Jl13My
ROGERS, Eliza.	52	F	None	06Jl13My
Maria	21	F	None	06Jl13My
FITZGERALD, Laurence	25	M	None	06Jl13My
Patrick	3	M	Child	06Jl13My
Edmund	30	M	Laborer	06Jl13My
WELSH, Edmund	30	M	Laborer	06Jl13My
HANNARN, William	40	M	Laborer	06Jl13My
William	11	M	Laborer	06Jl13My
KIDDLE, Eliza.	20	F	Laborer	06Jl13My
BROSINHIN, Dennis	40	M	Laborer	06Jl13My
MCONORUM, Arthur	35	F	Laborer	06Jl13My
HOWARD, Edward	40	M	Laborer	06Jl13My
Elizabeth	41	F	Laborer	06Jl13My
MERKA, John	25	M	Tailor	06Jl13My
HALL, James	30	M	Tailor	06Jl13My
MAHONEY, Ellen	20	F	None	06Jl13My
MERDON, Patrick	40	M	Laborer	06Jl13My
LAW, Samuel	40	M	Laborer	06Jl13My
SMITH, John	24	M	Laborer	06Jl13My
WATKINS, Frederick	22	M	Laborer	06Jl13My
LODDER, Henry	17	M	Laborer	06Jl13My
DUNN, Michael	30	M	Laborer	06Jl13My
SULLIVAN, Cornelius	26	M	Laborer	06Jl13My
NEWBERY, Thomas	24	M	Laborer	06Jl13My
KENEDY, Tate	28	M	Laborer	06Jl13My
Ellen	27	F	Laborer	06Jl13My
ELLIS, Mary	40	F	Farmer	06Jl13My

CUSHLAMACHREE 06 JULY 1849

From Galway

NAMES OF PASSENGERS	AGE	SEX	OCCUPATIONS	DATE PORT SHIP
KENEDY, Patt.	57	M	Laborer	06Jl06M
Ann	55	F	Wife	06Jl06M
Martin	19	M	Laborer	06Jl06M
Peter	14	M	Laborer	06Jl06M
Bridget	12	F	None	06Jl06M
Eleanor	10	F	None	06Jl06M
SILVER, Martin	41	M	Laborer	06Jl06M
WALL, Thomas	21	M	Laborer	06Jl06M
Died-At-Sea				
MULLIN, Biddy	30	F	Spinster	06Jl06M
Michael	6	M	Child	06Jl06M
ONEAL, Catherine	30	F	Spinster	06Jl06M
NEAL, Michael	10	M	None	06Jl06M
MORRIS, Patt.	20	M	Laborer	06Jl06M
CONNELLY, Martin	42	M	Laborer	06Jl06M
Peggy	35	F	Wife	06Jl06M
NEAGLE, Michael	22	M	Weaver	06Jl06M
Ann	17	F	Spinster	06Jl06M
CONNELLY, Peter	15	M	Laborer	06Jl06M

NAMES OF PASSENGERS	AGE	SEX	OCCUPATIONS	DATE PORT SHIP
DELANE, May	40	F	Spinster	06J106Mt
CONNELLEY, Patt.	5	M	Child	06J106Mt
CARTY, Biddy	40	F	Spinster	06J106Mt
Michael	21	M	Laborer	06J106Mt
Denis	18	M	Laborer	06J106Mt
John	16	M	Laborer	06J106Mt
Mary	12	F	None	06J106Mt
Ellen	15	F	None	06J106Mt
ODEA, John	30	M	Carpenter	06J106Mt
Biddy	25	F	Wife	06J106Mt
LENANE, John	20	M	Laborer	06J106Mt
MURPHY, Biddy	25	F	Spinster	06J106Mt
GORMAN, Patt.	25	M	Laborer	06J106Mt
Mary	18	F	Wife	06J106Mt
NALLY, Edward	50	M	Laborer	06J106Mt
Kitty	45	F	Wife	06J106Mt
Edward	17	M	Laborer	06J106Mt
Mary	12	F	None	06J106Mt
Martin	10	M	None	06J106Mt
Ann	6	F	Child	06J106Mt
FLYNN, Biddy	28	F	Spinster	06J106Mt
MANNION, Judy	28	F	Spinster	06J106Mt
GERATHY, Catherine	25	F	Spinster	06J106Mt
MCDONOGH, Margaret	30	F	Spinster	06J106Mt
CALLAGHAN, Betty	28	F	Spinster	06J106Mt
Honor	.11	F	Infant	06J106Mt
READY, James	25	M	Cobbler	06J106Mt
Sally	16	F	Wife	06J106Mt
FAHERTY, Martin	21	M	Laborer	06J106Mt
ONEAL, Michael	25	M	Laborer	06J106Mt
Celia	37	F	Wife	06J106Mt
Jane	12	F	None	06J106Mt
Celia	11	F	None	06J106Mt
Biddy	10	F	None	06J106Mt
Mary	9	F	Child	06J106Mt
Eliza	7	F	Child	06J106Mt
Ann	5	F	Child	06J106Mt
James	.00	M	Infant	06J106Mt
SWEENEY, Michael	25	M	Laborer	06J106Mt
DONOHUE, Patt.	25	M	Laborer	06J106Mt
TRESSY, Ann	30	F	Spinster	06J106Mt
Patt.	11	M	None	06J106Mt
FAHERTY, Teady	19	M	Weaver	06J106Mt
GLEASON, Michael	22	M	Laborer	06J106Mt
ONEAL, Martin	40	M	Laborer	06J106Mt
DAMELLAN, Stephen	15	M	Laborer	06J106Mt
HARE, Patt.	35	M	Laborer	06J106Mt
Mary	25	F	Wife	06J106Mt
Denis	10	M	None	06J106Mt
Michael	5	M	Child	06J106Mt
Bridget	3	F	Child	06J106Mt
Patt.	.00	M	Infant	06J106Mt
DONOHUE, Ellen	24	F	Spinster	06J106Mt
WARD, Michael	25	M	Laborer	06J106Mt
DONOHUE, Mary	20	F	Spinster	06J106Mt
HUSSY, Patt.	23	M	Laborer	06J106Mt
WALSH, Bridget	18	F	Spinster	06J106Mt
Mathias	13	M	None	06J106Mt
TIERNEY, Denis	23	M	Blacksmith	06J106Mt
Bridget	21	F	Wife	06J106Mt
THINE, Bridget	21	F	Spinster	06J106Mt
GREADY, John	38	M	Laborer	06J106Mt
James	12	M	None	06J106Mt
MORRIS, Patt.	18	M	Laborer	06J106Mt
FYMM, Austin	27	M	Laborer	06J106Mt
Michael	21	M	Laborer	06J106Mt
HILL, Patt.	50	M	Laborer	06J106Mt
Bridget	29	F	Spinster	06J106Mt
Pat.	20	M	Laborer	06J106Mt
Mary	00	F	Unknown	06J106Mt
Timothy	6	M	Child	06J106Mt
John	4	M	Child	06J106Mt
Patt.	.00	M	Infant	06J106Mt
ORMAN, Bridget	25	F	Spinster	06J106Mt
GAN, Honor	13	F	None	06J106Mt
TANIAN, Bridget	35	F	Spinster	06J106Mt
Michael	4	M	Child	06J106Mt
QUIGLY, Patt.	46	M	Laborer	06J106Mt
Nancy	35	F	Wife	06J106Mt
Mary	.00	F	Infant	06J106Mt
Michael	12	M	None	06J106Mt
CARNEY, Stephen	44	M	Laborer	06J106Mt
Hannah	35	F	Wife	06J106Mt
Mary	5	F	Child	06J106Mt
CORRIDINE, Silvester	21	M	Laborer	06J106Mt
HAVERTY, Michael	24	M	Laborer	06J106Mt
OHALLORAN, George	32	M	Laborer	06J106Mt
Margaret	28	F	Spinster	06J106Mt
HOGAN, Catherine	25	F	Spinster	06J106Mt
OHALLORAN, John	.00	M	Infant	06J106Mt
HEHIR, Patt.	35	M	Laborer	06J106Mt
ONARKHAM, Bridget	25	F	Spinster	06J106Mt
TORPEY, Patt.	17	M	Laborer	06J106Mt
HAYES, John	33	M	Laborer	06J106Mt
Ann	35	F	Wife	06J106Mt
FITZGERALD, Mary	28	F	Spinster	06J106Mt
HAYES, Morley	8	F	Child	06J106Mt
Michael	6	M	Child	06J106Mt
George	4	M	Child	06J106Mt
Maria	.00	F	Infant	06J106Mt
Eliza	.10	F	Infant	06J106Mt
Bridget	40	F	Spinster	06J106Mt
WALSH, John	30	M	Laborer	06J106Mt
HAYES, Jeremiah	6	M	Child	06J106Mt
Michael	4	M	Child	06J106Mt
Honor	.10	F	Infant	06J106Mt
CRAVE, Patt.	28	M	Carpenter	06J106Mt
KUFFE, Michael	32	M	Laborer	06J106Mt
OHALLORAN, Terence	21	M	Laborer	06J106Mt
HALLORAN, Jane	24	F	Wife	06J106Mt
Bridget	22	F	Spinster	06J106Mt
MOONEY, Bridget	25	F	Spinster	06J106Mt
HEHIRE, U-Mrs.	36	F	Matron	06J106Mt
Margaret	8	F	Child	06J106Mt
Patt.	7	M	Child	06J106Mt
SAUNDERS, Catherine	25	F	Spinster	06J106Mt
CALLANANE, John	25	M	Laborer	06J106Mt
CATY, Jane-Mrs.	50	F	Matron	06J106Mt
CRAVAN, Biddy	23	F	Spinster	06J106Mt
CUMMINS, Patt.	24	M	Laborer	06J106Mt
HILL, Patt.	00	M	Unknown	06J106Mt
Bridget	00	F	Unknown	06J106Mt
Kate	00	F	Unknown	06J106Mt
GORMAN, U-Miss	00	F	Unknown	06J106Mt

MARIA-BRENNAN 06 JULY 1849

From Limerick

NAMES OF PASSENGERS	AGE	SEX	OCCUPATIONS	DATE PORT SHIP
MADIGAN, John	20	M	Farmer	06J135Mz
Jeremiah	25	M	Farmer	06J135Mz
Cath.	20	F	Unknown	06J135Mz
CASEY, James	21	M	Farmer	06J135Mz
Margt.	24	F	Unknown	06J135Mz
RAIMAN, Pat	24	M	Farmer	06J135Mz
Margt.	21	F	Unknown	06J135Mz
RIERLIHY, Johannah	20	F	Unknown	06J135Mz
Eliza	22	F	Unknown	06J135Mz
ODONNELL, Mich	23	M	Farmer	06J135Mz
IVERS, Mary	26	F	Unknown	06J135Mz
QUIRK, Pat	26	M	Farmer	06J135Mz
HEINS, Michl.	26	M	Farmer	06J135Mz
MOONEY, Margt.	22	F	Unknown	06J135Mz
Bridget	.00	F	Infant	06J135Mz

NAMES OF PASSENGERS	AGE	SEX	OCCUPATIONS	DATE PORT SHIP
CAREY, Timothy	56	M	Farmer	06J135Mz
Alice	50	F	Unknown	06J135Mz
Cornelius	28	M	Farmer	06J135Mz
Catherine	26	F	Unknown	06J135Mz
Ellen	24	F	Unknown	06J135Mz
Margt.	21	F	Unknown	06J135Mz
James	18	M	Farmer	06J135Mz
GLEESON, Mary	36	F	Unknown	06J135Mz
Mich.	27	M	Farmer	06J135Mz
WILSON, Bridget	26	F	Unknown	06J135Mz
SULLIVAN, Margt.	22	F	Unknown	06J135Mz
SWEENEY, Johannah	22	F	Unknown	06J135Mz
GRIFFIN, James	32	M	Farmer	06J135Mz
Mary	30	F	Unknown	06J135Mz
Martin	.00	M	Infant	06J135Mz
OBRIEN, Ellen	21	F	Unknown	06J135Mz
Johannah	3	F	Child	06J135Mz
WOOD, James	20	M	Farmer	06J135Mz
STACK, John	30	M	Farmer	06J135Mz
GALVIN, Pat	20	M	Farmer	06J135Mz
GRIFFIN, Edw.	24	M	Farmer	06J135Mz
HEALY, James	30	M	Farmer	06J135Mz
MANGAN, Danl.	26	M	Farmer	06J135Mz
DESMOND, Ellen	48	F	Unknown	06J135Mz
NAUGH, Patt	35	M	Farmer	06J135Mz
Cath.	30	F	Unknown	06J135Mz
Mary	.00	F	Infant	06J135Mz
NOLAN, Cath.	21	F	Unknown	06J135Mz
CONNOR, Patt	22	M	Laborer	06J135Mz
MARSHALL, Wm.	45	M	Laborer	06J135Mz
MOORE, Michl.	28	M	Laborer	06J135Mz
FORD, Michl.	48	M	Laborer	06J135Mz
Thomas	28	M	Laborer	06J135Mz
Timothy	17	M	Laborer	06J135Mz
Lott	30	M	Laborer	06J135Mz
Ramorah	23	M	Laborer	06J135Mz
Bridget	24	F	Unknown	06J135Mz
MCMAHON, John	26	M	Laborer	06J135Mz
ENRIGHT, Bridget	20	F	Unknown	06J135Mz
MCDONNELL, Mary	21	F	Unknown	06J135Mz
CARROLL, Michael	26	M	Laborer	06J135Mz
Bridget	26	F	Unknown	06J135Mz
Owen	3	M	Child	06J135Mz
Michael	.00	M	Infant	06J135Mz
CARAVANE, Jas.	28	M	Unknown	06J135Mz
Anne	21	F	Unknown	06J135Mz
MOLONEY, Dennis	30	M	Unknown	06J135Mz
David	25	M	Unknown	06J135Mz
MUNGAVIN, James	28	M	Unknown	06J135Mz
OCAIN, Michael	27	M	Unknown	06J135Mz
STAMERS, Martin	35	M	Laborer	06J135Mz
James	22	M	Unknown	06J135Mz
HANLEY, Patt.	26	M	Farmer	06J135Mz
James	26	M	Farmer	06J135Mz
Johannah	19	F	Unknown	06J135Mz
Margaret	13	F	Unknown	06J135Mz
FITZGIBBONS, Jas.	28	M	Farmer	06J135Mz
Bridget	19	F	Unknown	06J135Mz
RUSSEL, Michael	31	M	Farmer	06J135Mz
John	29	M	Farmer	06J135Mz
Thomas	28	M	Farmer	06J135Mz
Catherine	22	F	Unknown	06J135Mz
RARTNEY, William	31	M	Farmer	06J135Mz
MORRISEY, Dennis	21	M	Farmer	06J135Mz
COLLINS, Cath.	22	F	Unknown	06J135Mz
Ellen	17	F	Unknown	06J135Mz
CALLAGHAN, John	25	M	Farmer	06J135Mz
Mary	24	F	Unknown	06J135Mz
John	.00	M	Infant	06J135Mz
CROSS, Margt.	24	F	Unknown	06J135Mz
SPELLENY, James	59	M	Farmer	06J135Mz
James-Jr.	20	M	Unknown	06J135Mz
Patt	19	M	Unknown	06J135Mz
OBRIEN, Michael	23	M	Unknown	06J135Mz
RYAN, Edmond	23	M	Unknown	06J135Mz
JONES, Henry	37	M	Farmer	06J135Mz
Mary	27	F	Unknown	06J135Mz
Thomas	3	M	Child	06J135Mz
Timothy	2	M	Child	06J135Mz
Pat	.00	M	Infant	06J135Mz
STARK, Adam	24	M	Unknown	06J135Mz
OCONNELL, Maurice	30	M	Unknown	06J135Mz
HAYES, John	21	M	Gentleman	06J135Mz
Bridget	21	F	Unknown	06J135Mz
STACK, Andrew	22	M	Gentleman	06J135Mz
Frances	21	F	Unknown	06J135Mz
MCENERNAY, Jas.	21	M	Unknown	06J135Mz

VICTORIA 06 JULY 1849

From Waterford

NAMES OF PASSENGERS	AGE	SEX	OCCUPATIONS	DATE PORT SHIP
WALSH, Margt.	59	F	Unknown	06J115Cl
Richd.	33	M	Unknown	06J115Cl
Alice	25	F	Unknown	06J115Cl
MCCARTHY, Thomas	28	M	Unknown	06J115Cl
Bridget	28	F	Unknown	06J115Cl
Magt.	2	F	Child	06J115Cl
John	.00	M	Infant	06J115Cl
MEEHAN, Dennis	32	M	Unknown	06J115Cl
Magt.	29	F	Unknown	06J115Cl
Patk.	4	M	Child	06J115Cl
Thomas	.00	M	Infant	06J115Cl
CONNORS, Thomas	19	M	Unknown	06J115Cl
ENGLISH, J.	28	M	Unknown	06J115Cl
SWEENY, Thomas	30	M	Unknown	06J115Cl
Mary	30	F	Unknown	06J115Cl
Michael	12	M	Unknown	06J115Cl
DELAHUNTY, Jno.	47	M	Unknown	06J115Cl
HURLEY, Patk.	35	M	Unknown	06J115Cl
Bridget	26	F	Unknown	06J115Cl
MULCAHY, Maria	37	M	Unknown	06J115Cl
Ellen	37	F	Unknown	06J115Cl
Mary	1	F	Child	06J115Cl
M.	.00	M	Infant	06J115Cl
MORGAN, James	37	M	Unknown	06J115Cl
Mary	32	F	Unknown	06J115Cl
Thomas	30	M	Unknown	06J115Cl
John	.00	M	Infant	06J115Cl
CARROLL, Johanna	20	F	Unknown	06J115Cl
FITZHENRY, Thomas	21	M	Unknown	06J115Cl
Mary-Anne	19	F	Unknown	06J115Cl
POWER, Pierce	25	M	Unknown	06J115Cl
Ann	17	F	Unknown	06J115Cl
MAKLEY, John	35	M	Unknown	06J115Cl
TAYLOR, David	30	M	Unknown	06J115Cl
SULLIVAN, Richd.	35	M	Unknown	06J115Cl
Norry	36	F	Unknown	06J115Cl
KAVANAGH, John	30	M	Unknown	06J115Cl
REILLY, Elizth.	40	F	Unknown	06J115Cl
Ann	2	F	Child	06J115Cl
KAVANAGH, Magt.	25	F	Unknown	06J115Cl
SULLIVAN, Ann	20	F	Unknown	06J115Cl
DUGGAN, Edwd.	24	M	Unknown	06J115Cl
Ellen	24	F	Unknown	06J115Cl
COONEY, Wm.	40	M	Unknown	06J115Cl
DALEY, James	36	M	Unknown	06J115Cl
DWYER, Norry	40	F	Unknown	06J115Cl
Philip	36	M	Unknown	06J115Cl
CONNOR, Andrew	21	M	Unknown	06J115Cl
SMITH, Wm.	30	M	Unknown	06J115C
POWER, Richd.	38	M	Unknown	06J115C
FOLEY, Johanna	40	F	Unknown	06J115C
Thomas	20	M	Unknown	06J115C

NAMES OF PASSENGERS	AGE	SEX	OCCUPATIONS	DATE PORT SHIP
COMERFORD, James	29	M	Unknown	06JI15CI
Johanna	28	F	Unknown	06JI15CI
FENNELLY, Ellen	20	F	Unknown	06JI15CI
BRAY, John	23	M	Unknown	06JI15CI
Cath.	26	F	Unknown	06JI15CI
HIAR, John	20	M	Unknown	06JI15CI
WATERS, Mary	35	F	Unknown	06JI15CI
John	2	M	Child	06JI15CI
STRANGE, Cath.	22	F	Unknown	06JI15CI
HEAN, Cath.	22	F	Unknown	06JI15CI
POWER, Patk.	7	M	Child	06JI15CI
Mary	22	F	Unknown	06JI15CI
Cath.	20	F	Unknown	06JI15CI
TOBIN, William	35	M	Unknown	06JI15CI
TROY, Cath.	28	F	Unknown	06JI15CI
DONOHUE, Patk.	34	M	Unknown	06JI15CI
Cath.	30	F	Unknown	06JI15CI
Cath.	8	F	Child	06JI15CI
Mary	4	F	Child	06JI15CI
Richd.	6	M	Child	06JI15CI
RYAN, James	40	M	Unknown	06JI15CI
Mary	30	F	Unknown	06JI15CI
Ellen	10	F	Unknown	06JI15CI
Timothy	4	M	Child	06JI15CI
Cath.	.00	F	Infant	06JI15CI
JACKSON, Eliza	30	F	Unknown	06JI15CI
Johanna	26	F	Unknown	06JI15CI
HAYES, John	30	M	Unknown	06JI15CI
Magt.	24	F	Unknown	06JI15CI

JANE 06 JULY 1849

From Liverpool

NAMES OF PASSENGERS	AGE	SEX	OCCUPATIONS	DATE PORT SHIP
STAPLETON, James	37	M	Farmer	06JI02Ib
Sarah	24	F	Seamstress	06JI02Ib
Matthew	.05	M	Infant	06JI02Ib
MAHON, Michael	18	M	Farmer	06JI02Ib
BUCKLEY, Michael	35	M	Farmer	06JI02Ib
Mary	48	F	Seamstress	06JI02Ib
DUGAN, John	28	M	Laborer	06JI02Ib
KELLY, Thos.	22	M	Farmer	06JI02Ib
DOOLEY, Michael	23	M	Laborer	06JI02Ib
FOX, James	22	M	Farmer	06JI02Ib
WALSH, Matthew	26	M	Laborer	06JI02Ib
Bridget	25	F	Seamstress	06JI02Ib
KILDEA, John	20	M	Laborer	06JI02Ib
WALSH, Catherine	.06	F	Infant	06JI02Ib
HENESSY, Thomas	46	M	Mason	06JI02Ib
MCGOWAN, Jane	20	F	Grocer	06JI02Ib
Anne	22	F	Grocer	06JI02Ib
MCVITY, James	20	M	Tailor	06JI02Ib
SMITH, Patrick	26	M	Laborer	06JI02Ib
COONEY, Matthew	19	M	Farmer	06JI02Ib
Anne	18	F	Spinster	06JI02Ib
DUNN, Anne	15	F	Servant	06JI02Ib
BRADY, John	14	M	Servant	06JI02Ib
GLENN, Patrick	28	M	Laborer	06JI02Ib
HENRY, Charles	31	M	Servant	06JI02Ib
Edward	18	M	Servant	06JI02Ib
WRIGHT, Bridget	18	F	Servant	06JI02Ib
MCELROY, Patrick	15	M	Farmer	06JI02Ib
WALSH, Thomas	38	M	Laborer	06JI02Ib
KELLETT, Richard	23	M	Farmer	06JI02Ib
Laurence	21	M	Sawer	06JI02Ib
SCANTLON, Anne	30	F	Seamstress	06JI02Ib
Margaret	7	F	Child	06JI02Ib
John	2	M	Child	06JI02Ib
John	30	M	Farmer	06JI02Ib
SCANTLON, William	.07	M	Infant	06JI02Ib
Eliza	4	F	Child	06JI02Ib
BREEMAN, Thomas	27	M	Laborer	06JI02Ib
Mary	25	F	Servant	06JI02Ib
James	.08	M	Infant	06JI02Ib
Cath.	3	F	Child	06JI02Ib
BARRY, Michael	28	M	Tobacconist	06JI02Ib
MCGEE, Andrew	25	M	Laborer	06JI02Ib
Patrick	25	M	Farmer	06JI02Ib
BOURKE, Jas.	29	M	Farmer	06JI02Ib
REGAN, John	24	M	Farmer	06JI02Ib
CAHILL, David	20	M	Laborer	06JI02Ib
ROBERTS, Wm.	24	M	Joiner	06JI02Ib
HENRY, Catherine	9	F	Child	06JI02Ib
HENDON, James	43	M	Laborer	06JI02Ib
Eliza	50	F	Seamstress	06JI02Ib
Isabella	17	F	Servant	06JI02Ib
Mary	13	F	None	06JI02Ib
Eliza	11	F	None	06JI02Ib
Maria	9	F	Child	06JI02Ib
JOHNSTON, John	20	M	Saddler	06JI02Ib
SHEHEE, Edward	22	M	Laborer	06JI02Ib
DONAHUE, Mary	49	F	Seamstress	06JI02Ib
Andrew	24	M	Laborer	06JI02Ib
Thomas	14	M	Laborer	06JI02Ib
Margaret	15	F	Servant	06JI02Ib
Eliza	16	F	Servant	06JI02Ib
ERLEY, Patrick	29	M	Hairdresser	06JI02Ib
DONNELLY, Michael	35	M	Laborer	06JI02Ib
KELLY, William	30	M	Laborer	06JI02Ib
DRAYNON, Wm.	28	M	Laborer	06JI02Ib
BOYLE, Osten	32	M	Laborer	06JI02Ib
Mary	28	F	Spinster	06JI02Ib
James	3	M	Child	06JI02Ib
Eliza	5	F	Child	06JI02Ib
HAGAN, John	19	M	Laborer	06JI02Ib
KELLY, Edward	35	M	Laborer	06JI02Ib
GARDNER, John	47	M	Farmer	06JI02Ib
FAUCETT, Robert	53	M	Farmer	06JI02Ib
Anne	21	F	Milliner	06JI02Ib
BARNES, Barbara	58	F	Milliner	06JI02Ib
Mary-Anne	18	F	Milliner	06JI02Ib
NASH, Patrick	28	M	Farmer	06JI02Ib
Johanna	20	F	Servant	06JI02Ib
LYONS, Thomas	18	M	Servant	06JI02Ib
DAILY, Daniel	40	M	Mason	06JI02Ib
DENEHY, Michael	25	M	Joiner	06JI02Ib
SULLIVAN, Daniel	40	M	Laborer	06JI02Ib
LYONS, Patrick	29	M	Laborer	06JI02Ib
HARTNETT, Edward	45	M	Farmer	06JI02Ib
Johanna	42	F	Spinster	06JI02Ib
Laurence	20	M	Farmer	06JI02Ib
Mary	18	F	Seamstress	06JI02Ib
Helen	16	F	Servant	06JI02Ib
Johanna	10	F	Servant	06JI02Ib
Timothy	7	M	Child	06JI02Ib
Patrick	4	M	Child	06JI02Ib
SHEEHAM, Margt.	18	F	Spinster	06JI02Ib
Mary	20	F	Servant	06JI02Ib
MURPHY, James	24	M	Servant	06JI02Ib
RUBY, Wm.	20	M	Saddler	06JI02Ib
CORCORAN, Michael	30	M	Farmer	06JI02Ib
REILLY, Thomas	19	M	Laborer	06JI02Ib
SHUE, Judy	28	F	Seamstress	06JI02Ib
KERMAS, Ellen	20	F	Servant	06JI02Ib
LEARY, Johanna	19	F	Servant	06JI02Ib
MCCARTY, James	22	M	Farmer	06JI02Ib
HAIR, George	25	M	Farmer	06JI02Ib
BLACK, Isabella	24	F	Servant	06JI02Ib
Robt.	20	M	Farmer	06JI02Ib
LEMON, Hugh	50	M	Farmer	06JI02Ib
Margaret	50	F	Seamstress	06JI02Ib
Eliza	20	F	Milliner	06JI02Ib
James	11	M	Farmer	06JI02Ib
DALE, Amelia	19	F	Dressmaker	06JI02Ib

NAMES OF PASSENGERS	AGE	SEX	OCCUPATIONS	DATE PORT SHIP
MCEWIN, John	18	M	Farmer	06J102Ib
STEWART, Alice	22	F	Seamstress	06J102Ib
REILLY, Patrick	30	M	Grocer	06J102Ib
ROSSWELL, John	30	M	Excavator	06J102Ib
BOURKE, James	32	M	Farmer	06J102Ib
Mary	34	F	Spinster	06J102Ib
Michael	36	M	Laborer	06J102Ib
NEAL, Thomas	38	M	Farmer	06J102Ib
FARRILL, Mary	20	F	Servant	06J102Ib
KELLY, James	28	M	Laborer	06J102Ib
COCHLIN, Bridget	45	F	Servant	06J102Ib
Mary	5	F	Child	06J102Ib
Cath.	3	F	Child	06J102Ib
EGAN, Martin	30	M	Joiner	06J102Ib
Mary	25	F	Milliner	06J102Ib
Ellen	5	F	Child	06J102Ib
John	2	M	Child	06J102Ib
Thomas	.07	M	Infant	06J102Ib
OHARE, Andrew	20	M	Laborer	06J102Ib
MAHONY, Edward	30	M	Laborer	06J102Ib
Mary	30	F	Spinster	06J102Ib
Daniel	4	M	Child	06J102Ib
Cornelius	2	M	Child	06J102Ib
Maria	.04	F	Infant	06J102Ib
GUNN, Hugh	38	M	Farmer	06J102Ib
Cath.	35	F	Seamstress	06J102Ib
Andrew	6	M	Child	06J102Ib
MCGRATH, Christy	26	M	Farmer	06J102Ib
Catherine	24	F	Seamstress	06J102Ib
MOLOY, John	20	M	Cooper	06J102Ib
KEENEY, Edwd.	42	M	Farmer	06J102Ib
Matthew	12	M	Farmer	06J102Ib
Mary	17	F	Seamstress	06J102Ib
Lucy	17	F	Seamstress	06J102Ib
NEALON, John	26	M	Servant	06J102Ib
FOY, John	20	M	Clerk	06J102Ib
OBRIEN, Owen	26	M	Farmer	06J102Ib
LYNCH, Joseph	19	M	Farmer	06J102Ib
Mary	22	F	Spinster	06J102Ib
CLARKE, Michael	27	M	Laborer	06J102Ib
Sarah	27	F	Spinster	06J102Ib
Alice	.02	F	Infant	06J102Ib
KELLY, James	21	M	Puddler	06J102Ib
BROWN, Garrett	30	M	Laborer	06J102Ib
James	23	M	Farmer	06J102Ib
GRIFFITH, David	20	M	Blacksmith	06J102Ib
WILLIAMS, John	45	M	Blacksmith	06J102Ib
Anne	26	F	Spinster	06J102Ib
OLIVER, Isaac	37	M	Tailor	06J102Ib
Rachael	40	F	Tailor	06J102Ib
David	13	M	Tailor	06J102Ib
Margaret	11	F	None	06J102Ib
EVANS, Thos.	33	M	Farmer	06J102Ib
DAVIES, David	.09	M	Infant	06J102Ib
JONES, David	20	M	Farmer	06J102Ib
HUGHES, Morgan	30	M	Plasterer	06J102Ib
DAVIES, Mary	32	F	Seamstress	06J102Ib
Mary	8	F	Child	06J102Ib
EDWARDS, David	4	M	Child	06J102Ib
Lewis	30	M	Hawker	06J102Ib
Anne	30	F	Spinster	06J102Ib
BRANIN, Owen	35	M	Laborer	06J102Ib
WILLIAMS, Sarah	20	F	Spinster	06J102Ib

QUEBEC 06 JULY 1849

From Penzance

NAMES OF PASSENGERS	AGE	SEX	OCCUPATIONS	DATE PORT SHIP
BRYANT, Thomas	35	M	Miner	06J120Mv
Tamson	33	M	Unknown	06J120Mv
HICKFORD, James	25	M	Unknown	06J120Mv
Walter	15	M	Unknown	06J120Mv
MURRAY, Emily	28	F	Unknown	06J120Mv
TREGAY, Jno.	60	M	Unknown	06J120Mv
Emma	27	F	Unknown	06J120Mv
MARTIN, Mary	30	F	Unknown	06J120Mv
John	11	M	Unknown	06J120Mv
Mary	9	F	Child	06J120Mv
Rebecca	8	F	Child	06J120Mv
Arthur	4	M	Child	06J120Mv
Jane	.00	F	Infant	06J120Mv
CHEWIDDEN, Thomas	35	M	Unknown	06J120Mv
Pamela	32	F	Unknown	06J120Mv
U	.00	U	Infant	06J120Mv
Elizabeth	10	F	Unknown	06J120Mv
Jane	7	F	Child	06J120Mv
Thomas	9	M	Child	06J120Mv
Eliza	5	F	Child	06J120Mv
MARTIN, Jane	25	F	Unknown	06J120Mv
Thos.	5	M	Child	06J120Mv
James	3	M	Child	06J120Mv
NARSHY, Stephen	21	M	Unknown	06J120Mv
Ann	23	F	Unknown	06J120Mv
HARVEY, Ann	39	F	Unknown	06J120Mv
U	.00	F	Infant	06J120Mv
DENNIS, Mary-Ann	22	F	Unknown	06J120Mv
UREN, Sarah	21	F	Unknown	06J120Mv
Mary	17	F	Unknown	06J120Mv
PENROSE, Isaac	18	F	Unknown	06J120Mv
Wm.	37	M	Unknown	06J120Mv
CARBIS, John	19	M	Unknown	06J120Mv
TRYSHALL, Grace	28	F	Unknown	06J120Mv
U	.00	U	Infant	06J120Mv
Saml.	10	M	Unknown	06J120Mv
John	7	M	Child	06J120Mv
TREMBASH, Sally	5	F	Child	06J120Mv
TRYSHALL, William	3	M	Child	06J120Mv
Mary	21	F	Unknown	06J120Mv
Mary	4	F	Child	06J120Mv
GILL, Joseph	24	M	Unknown	06J120Mv
PASSMORE, William	21	M	Unknown	06J120Mv
WILLIAMS, William	30	M	Unknown	06J120Mv
Jenifer	28	F	Unknown	06J120Mv
REYNOLDS, James	22	M	Unknown	06J120Mv
POOLEY, John	22	M	Unknown	06J120Mv
ROBERTS, Wm.	35	M	Unknown	06J120Mv
Mary	36	F	Unknown	06J120Mv
REYNOLDS, Elizabeth	26	F	Unknown	06J120Mv
Wm.Hy.	7	M	Child	06J120Mv
WILLIAMS, Eliza-Jane	4	F	Child	06J120Mv
EDWARDS, J.	39	M	Unknown	06J120Mv
RICHARDS, Thomas	25	M	Unknown	06J120Mv
SODDY, Henry	23	M	Unknown	06J120Mv
COOK, Richard	32	M	Unknown	06J120Mv
Elizabeth	31	F	Unknown	06J120Mv
U	.00	U	Infant	06J120Mv
William	7	M	Child	06J120Mv
ROBERTS, Mary	12	F	Unknown	06J120Mv
REYNOLDS, Wm.	11	M	Unknown	06J120Mv
ROBERTS, Peter	9	M	Child	06J120Mv
Henry	4	M	Child	06J120Mv
Eliza-Jane	.00	F	Infant	06J120Mv
POLLARD, James	35	M	Unknown	06J120Mv

NAMES OF PASSENGERS	AGE	SEX	OCCUPATIONS	DATE PORT SHIP
POLLARD, Elizabeth	45	F	Unknown	06JI20Mv
Elizb.Ann	22	F	Unknown	06JI20Mv
E.J.	19	M	Unknown	06JI20Mv
Wm.Hy.	12	M	Unknown	06JI20Mv
Phillippa	11	M	Unknown	06JI20Mv
John	9	M	Child	06JI20Mv
Constance	7	F	Child	06JI20Mv
RULE, John	36	M	Unknown	06JI20Mv
Richard	23	M	Unknown	06JI20Mv
NICHOLAS, Susanna	24	F	Unknown	06JI20Mv
Sarah	23	F	Unknown	06JI20Mv
Lydia	22	F	Unknown	06JI20Mv
Jane	21	F	Unknown	06JI20Mv
BENNETT, Robert	30	M	Unknown	06JI20Mv
TRERASKIS, James	32	M	Unknown	06JI20Mv
CURNOW, Matthew	34	M	Unknown	06JI20Mv
SIMONS, William	43	M	Unknown	06JI20Mv
CURNOW, Peter	29	M	Unknown	06JI20Mv
CLARK, John	23	M	Unknown	06JI20Mv
HORE, Francis	23	M	Unknown	06JI20Mv
WINMAN, Harriet	8	F	Child	06JI20Mv
Harriet	23	F	Unknown	06JI20Mv
ROSEVEAR, George	22	M	Unknown	06JI20Mv
TREBILCOCK, Robt.	44	M	Unknown	06JI20Mv
Mary	22	F	Unknown	06JI20Mv
William	17	M	Unknown	06JI20Mv
Thomas	11	M	Unknown	06JI20Mv
MARKS, John	40	M	Unknown	06JI20Mv
Mary	36	F	Unknown	06JI20Mv
U	.00	U	Infant	06JI20Mv
Melinda	11	F	Unknown	06JI20Mv
Frederick	6	M	Child	06JI20Mv
TREMELLYN, John	27	M	Unknown	06JI20Mv
Mary-Ann	24	F	Unknown	06JI20Mv
U	.00	U	Infant	06JI20Mv
HOLMES, William	21	M	Unknown	06JI20Mv
KEMP, James	22	M	Unknown	06JI20Mv
Catherine	24	F	Unknown	06JI20Mv
TRELORN, Thomas	17	M	Unknown	06JI20Mv
TREBILCOCK, James	22	M	Unknown	06JI20Mv

FEROZEPORE 06 JULY 1849

From Liverpool

NAMES OF PASSENGERS	AGE	SEX	OCCUPATIONS	DATE PORT SHIP
CASEY, Danl.	7	M	Child	06JI02Mu
Thomas	5	M	Child	06JI02Mu
James	3	M	Child	06JI02Mu
Jno.	3	M	Child	06JI02Mu
HAYS, Jno.	30	M	Laborer	06JI02Mu
YELLOWBY, Jno.	20	M	Laborer	06JI02Mu
Thomas	20	M	Laborer	06JI02Mu
SHARKEY, Chas.	20	M	Laborer	06JI02Mu
BAYLEY, Jno.	30	M	Laborer	06JI02Mu
U (W)	25	F	Spinster	06JI02Mu
CASEY, Jas.	20	M	Laborer	06JI02Mu
RILEY, Jno.	25	M	Laborer	06JI02Mu
WILSON, Wm.	26	M	Farmer	06JI02Mu
BETTZ, Geo.	29	M	Farmer	06JI02Mu
Astor	27	M	Farmer	06JI02Mu
MADDOCK, Thos.	24	M	Farmer	06JI02Mu
LING, Wm.	43	M	Farmer	06JI02Mu
Mary	39	F	Farmer	06JI02Mu
Mary	14	F	Farmer	06JI02Mu
MEAD, Garret	23	M	Farmer	06JI02Mu
Margt.	30	F	Farmer	06JI02Mu
LING, Thos.	13	M	Farmer	06JI02Mu
Ellen	11	F	Farmer	06JI02Mu
Catherine	9	F	Child	06JI02Mu
LING, Wm.	7	M	Child	06JI02Mu
Johanna	3	F	Child	06JI02Mu
Bridget	4	F	Child	06JI02Mu
FOGARTY, Mich.	20	M	Farmer	06JI02Mu
GRAHAM, Jas.	25	M	Farmer	06JI02Mu
DALY, Wm.	18	M	Farmer	06JI02Mu
HELDEN, Pat	25	M	Farmer	06JI02Mu
Bridget	18	F	Farmer	06JI02Mu
NEAL, Mary	26	F	Farmer	06JI02Mu
WALSH, Jas.	24	M	Farmer	06JI02Mu
DUNN, Alice	30	F	Farmer	06JI02Mu
Alice	13	F	Farmer	06JI02Mu
Betty	11	F	Farmer	06JI02Mu
Jno.	7	M	Child	06JI02Mu
DOWNING, Mich.	18	M	Farmer	06JI02Mu
HOOGAN, Peter	29	M	Farmer	06JI02Mu
SHEEHAN, Thos.	35	M	Farmer	06JI02Mu
CONNELL, Mich.	25	M	Farmer	06JI02Mu
TALEY, Bridget	23	F	Farmer	06JI02Mu
DUMPHY, Nancy	26	F	Farmer	06JI02Mu
JOHNSON, Thos.	28	M	Farmer	06JI02Mu
BURKE, Martha	18	F	Farmer	06JI02Mu
DOUGHANY, Richd.	35	M	Farmer	06JI02Mu
WHITMORE, G.T.	21	M	Farmer	06JI02Mu
GOWAN, Wm.	22	M	Farmer	06JI02Mu
QUINN, And.	30	M	Farmer	06JI02Mu
DALY, Martha	40	F	Farmer	06JI02Mu
Honor	40	F	Farmer	06JI02Mu
Mary	13	F	Farmer	06JI02Mu
Cath.	8	F	Child	06JI02Mu
Margt.	6	F	Child	06JI02Mu
Bridget	4	F	Child	06JI02Mu
DILLON, Mary	20	F	Farmer	06JI02Mu
DARCY, Cath.	23	F	Farmer	06JI02Mu
REEGAN, Bridget	20	F	Laborer	06JI02Mu
MURPHY, Patt	35	F	Laborer	06JI02Mu
Rose	17	F	Laborer	06JI02Mu
Ann	15	F	Laborer	06JI02Mu
SKELLY, July	25	F	Laborer	06JI02Mu
Pat	26	M	Laborer	06JI02Mu
ROSENTER, Stephen	18	M	Laborer	06JI02Mu
Leonard	16	M	Laborer	06JI02Mu
MOON, Maria	25	F	Laborer	06JI02Mu
SANES, Sarah-J.	26	F	Laborer	06JI02Mu
GIBSON, Pat	23	M	Laborer	06JI02Mu
TUITE, Mary	20	F	Laborer	06JI02Mu
Betsey	.00	F	Infant	06JI02Mu
MCCAULEY, Mary	29	F	Laborer	06JI02Mu
RABBIT, Bridget	20	F	Laborer	06JI02Mu
CONNOR, Ann	20	F	Laborer	06JI02Mu
MORAN, Julia	20	F	Laborer	06JI02Mu
BYRNE, Jas.	20	M	Laborer	06JI02Mu
Bridget	18	F	Laborer	06JI02Mu
SARMEN, Ellen	30	F	Laborer	06JI02Mu
Biddy	6	F	Child	06JI02Mu
U, Thos.	.00	M	Infant	06JI02Mu
CUNNINGHAM, Peter	22	M	Laborer	06JI02Mu
Mick	19	M	Laborer	06JI02Mu
FARNAM, Cath.	21	F	Laborer	06JI02Mu
HANLEY, Rich.	25	M	Laborer	06JI02Mu
Judy	27	F	Laborer	06JI02Mu
GALLAGHER, Jas.	30	M	Laborer	06JI02Mu
DIXON, Hugh	21	M	Laborer	06JI02Mu
MARTIN, Thomas	60	M	Laborer	06JI02Mu
ANDREWS, Andrew	35	M	Laborer	06JI02Mu
Julia	25	F	Laborer	06JI02Mu
Mary-Ann	5	F	Child	06JI02Mu
WISLAS, Jas.	9	M	Child	06JI02Mu
SEINNS, Jas.	20	M	Laborer	06JI02Mu
ADAMS, Sam	19	M	Laborer	06JI02Mu
WATKINS, Danl.	34	M	Laborer	06JI02Mu
SEVENS, Mary	60	F	Laborer	06JI02Mu
GERAGHAN, Ca.	15	F	Laborer	06JI02Mu
Thomas	7	M	Child	06JI02Mu
Catherine	6	F	Child	06JI02Mu

NAMES OF PASSENGERS		AGE	SEX	OCCUPATIONS	DATE PORT SHIP
MCKINNEY, Pat		5	M	Child	06J102Mu
Ann		4	F	Child	06J102Mu
Mary		2	F	Child	06J102Mu
MALONE, Bridget		20	F	Laborer	06J102Mu
CURTIS, Mary		20	F	Laborer	06J102Mu
FLANEGAN, Catherine		19	F	Laborer	06J102Mu
SPEAR, Thos.		23	M	Laborer	06J102Mu
TREASEY, Wm.		20	M	Laborer	06J102Mu
KING, Wm.		20	M	Laborer	06J102Mu
MULLONY, Jno.		45	M	Laborer	06J102Mu
U	(W)	46	F	Laborer	06J102Mu
Mary-Anne		13	F	Laborer	06J102Mu
Alice		12	F	Laborer	06J102Mu
Catherine		10	F	Laborer	06J102Mu
Mick		8	M	Child	06J102Mu
Peter		4	M	Child	06J102Mu
Anastasia		1	F	Child	06J102Mu
COLLINS, Mary		30	F	Laborer	06J102Mu
Patt		13	M	Laborer	06J102Mu
Thomas		12	M	Laborer	06J102Mu
MCEVOY, Jno.		20	M	Laborer	06J102Mu
MCDAW, Jno.		26	M	Laborer	06J102Mu
MCGUIRE, Mich.		40	M	Laborer	06J102Mu
Anny		40	F	Laborer	06J102Mu
Margt.		12	F	Laborer	06J102Mu
FARRELL, Owne		40	M	Laborer	06J102Mu
U	(W)	36	F	Laborer	06J102Mu
Patt		12	M	Laborer	06J102Mu
Michl.		8	M	Child	06J102Mu
Easter		10	F	Laborer	06J102Mu
James		6	M	Child	06J102Mu
Christopher		4	M	Child	06J102Mu
Mary		2	F	Child	06J102Mu
Anne		.00	F	Infant	06J102Mu
BYRNE, Patt		24	M	Laborer	06J102Mu
MCELROY, Michl.		40	M	Laborer	06J102Mu
Catherine		10	F	Laborer	06J102Mu
BENDERIDGE, Jno.		30	M	Laborer	06J102Mu
William		26	M	Laborer	06J102Mu
HEPSCUM, Jno.		22	M	Laborer	06J102Mu
MILLAN, Barbara		44	F	Laborer	06J102Mu
MCDONNELLAGH, Michl.		44	M	Laborer	06J102Mu
Timery		20	M	Laborer	06J102Mu
Maria		16	F	Laborer	06J102Mu
Bridget		15	F	Laborer	06J102Mu
COWLEY, Patt		15	M	Laborer	06J102Mu
Bridget		20	F	Laborer	06J102Mu
Bridget		19	F	Laborer	06J102Mu
CASEY, Thos.		30	M	Farmer	06J102Mu
U	(W)	40	F	Farmer	06J102Mu
Bridget		1	F	Child	06J102Mu
BATES, Henry		25	M	Farmer	06J102Mu
U	(W)	25	F	Farmer	06J102Mu
Elizabeth		4	F	Child	06J102Mu
ENNIS, Magt.		52	F	Farmer	06J102Mu
WOODS, Thos.		26	M	Farmer	06J102Mu
MATHEWS, Wm.		26	M	Farmer	06J102Mu
LOVE, Margt.		16	F	Farmer	06J102Mu
Martha		18	F	Farmer	06J102Mu
MCDONOHUE, Danl.		40	M	Farmer	06J102Mu
DAVIS, U-Mrs.		45	F	Farmer	06J102Mu
Mary		14	F	Farmer	06J102Mu
Anne		11	F	Farmer	06J102Mu
Evan		9	M	Child	06J102Mu
Sarah		7	F	Child	06J102Mu
David		6	M	Child	06J102Mu
TACKANNEY, Connor		25	M	Farmer	06J102Mu
U	(W)	25	F	Farmer	06J102Mu
Mary		9	F	Child	06J102Mu
BRADY, Terence		26	M	Farmer	06J102Mu
MAXWELL, Martha		18	F	Farmer	06J102Mu
ATKINSON, H.		20	M	Farmer	06J102Mu
U	(W)	20	F	Farmer	06J102Mu
MATHEWS, Robt.		30	M	Farmer	06J102Mu
Anne		25	F	Farmer	06J102Mu

NAMES OF PASSENGERS		AGE	SEX	OCCUPATIONS	DATE PORT SHIP
HALL, Jno.		39	M	Farmer	06J102Mu
U	(W)	36	F	Farmer	06J102Mu
DONOHUE, Jas.		25	M	Farmer	06J102Mu
HEATHCOT, Geo.		40	M	Farmer	06J102Mu
Mary		36	F	Farmer	06J102Mu
William		20	M	Farmer	06J102Mu
Susannah		19	F	Farmer	06J102Mu
Phebe		17	F	Farmer	06J102Mu
Thos.		11	M	Farmer	06J102Mu
Mary-Anne		10	F	Farmer	06J102Mu
George		8	M	Child	06J102Mu
Walter		5	M	Child	06J102Mu
Louis		3	M	Child	06J102Mu
George		.00	M	Infant	06J102Mu
HICKEY, Jas.		40	M	Farmer	06J102Mu
James		27	M	Farmer	06J102Mu
CLARKE, Rose		40	F	Farmer	06J102Mu
DERMOTT, Jno.		2	M	Child	06J102Mu
SPEAR, Wm.		36	M	Laborer	06J102Mu
Ellen		30	F	Laborer	06J102Mu
MORTAL, Wm.		34	M	Laborer	06J102Mu
MCCARDELL, Peter		21	M	Laborer	06J102Mu
BRADIGAN, M.		30	M	Laborer	06J102Mu
KELLSON, Ellen		16	F	Laborer	06J102Mu
TERRY, Anne		19	F	Laborer	06J102Mu
MCGARRY, Biddy		20	F	Laborer	06J102Mu
ROONEY, U-Mrs.		30	F	Laborer	06J102Mu
Mary		14	F	Laborer	06J102Mu
Jno.		8	M	Child	06J102Mu
Michl.		4	M	Child	06J102Mu
Jas.		18	M	Laborer	06J102Mu
Winfred		16	M	Laborer	06J102Mu
DAVIS, Danl.		64	M	Laborer	06J102Mu
Eliza		31	F	Laborer	06J102Mu
Jane		26	F	Laborer	06J102Mu
Anne		18	F	Laborer	06J102Mu
DOWDE, Owne		30	M	Laborer	06J102Mu
GUNN, Anne		40	F	Laborer	06J102Mu
M.Ann		10	F	Laborer	06J102Mu
Hannah		9	F	Child	06J102Mu
MOHAN, Mary		16	F	Laborer	06J102Mu
MCKERREN, Mary		30	F	Laborer	06J102Mu
John		10	M	Laborer	06J102Mu
Wm.		5	M	Child	06J102Mu
Eliza		8	F	Child	06J102Mu
FENTON, Owen		30	M	Laborer	06J102Mu
CROONAN, F.		46	M	Laborer	06J102Mu
U	(W)	40	F	Laborer	06J102Mu
Honora		20	F	Laborer	06J102Mu
Eliza		18	F	Laborer	06J102Mu
Bridget		16	F	Laborer	06J102Mu
Dennis		17	M	Laborer	06J102Mu
Jno.		12	M	Laborer	06J102Mu
SULLIVAN, Thos.		30	M	Laborer	06J102Mu
AHERN, Thos.		20	M	Laborer	06J102Mu
MEHAN, Jas.		28	M	Laborer	06J102Mu
Bridget		28	F	Laborer	06J102Mu
MCANNS, Mary		50	F	Laborer	06J102Mu
LITTLE, Robt.		17	M	Laborer	06J102Mu
HINES, Mary		30	F	Laborer	06J102Mu
MCDONALD, Owen		17	M	Laborer	06J102Mu
WRIGHT, Wm.		22	M	Laborer	06J102Mu
MCGOULERK, Thos.		21	M	Laborer	06J102Mu
Cath.		40	F	Laborer	06J102Mu
Edwd.		2	M	Child	06J102Mu
James		.00	M	Infant	06J102Mu
BRENNAN, Mary		16	F	Laborer	06J102Mu
MCGARRY, Thos.		22	M	Laborer	06J102Mu
Catherine		15	F	Laborer	06J102Mu
BEST, U-Mrs.		25	F	Laborer	06J102Mu
U		.00	F	Infant	06J102Mu
Mary		30	F	Laborer	06J102Mu
Bridget		20	F	Laborer	06J102Mu
BRENNEAN, Honora		21	F	Laborer	06J102Mu
ONEILL, M.		23	M	Laborer	06J102Mu

NAMES OF PASSENGERS	AGE	SEX	OCCUPATIONS	DATE PORT SHIP
LONG, Nicholas	20	M	Laborer	06JI02Mu
Margt.	20	F	Laborer	06JI02Mu
BOYLL, Jno.	40	M	Laborer	06JI02Mu
U (W)	40	F	Laborer	06JI02Mu
Elizabeth	20	F	Laborer	06JI02Mu
Margt.	17	F	Laborer	06JI02Mu
David	16	M	Laborer	06JI02Mu
Frances	15	F	Laborer	06JI02Mu
Jane	13	F	Laborer	06JI02Mu
Jackey	10	M	Laborer	06JI02Mu
Thomas	20	M	Laborer	06JI02Mu
COTHANS, Jas.	18	M	Laborer	06JI02Mu
CALAGHEN, Owne	50	M	Laborer	06JI02Mu
Jas.	26	M	Laborer	06JI02Mu
Betty	8	F	Child	06JI02Mu
MCSETTUCK, Anne	30	F	Laborer	06JI02Mu
U	.00	F	Infant	06JI02Mu
OGARE, Mary	20	F	Laborer	06JI02Mu
CASSIDY, Jno.	20	M	Laborer	06JI02Mu
Cath.	18	F	Laborer	06JI02Mu
MOYNAHAN, Cath.	20	F	Laborer	06JI02Mu
Bessy	18	F	Laborer	06JI02Mu
TRUION, Cath.	36	F	Laborer	06JI02Mu
MCWILLIAMS, Jas.	40	M	Laborer	06JI02Mu
Sarah	30	F	Laborer	06JI02Mu
ROONEY, Mat.	24	M	Laborer	06JI02Mu
FLANNEGAN, J.	20	M	Laborer	06JI02Mu
Sarah	24	F	Laborer	06JI02Mu
MOTT, Jno.D.	35	M	Laborer	06JI02Mu
CLEARY, Jno.	30	M	Laborer	06JI02Mu
Mooney	30	M	Laborer	06JI02Mu
Mich.	30	M	Laborer	06JI02Mu
MCKINNEY, Jas.	31	M	Laborer	06JI02Mu
Peter	24	M	Laborer	06JI02Mu
John	20	M	Laborer	06JI02Mu
Cath.	27	F	Laborer	06JI02Mu
Mich.	19	M	Laborer	06JI02Mu
Mary	16	F	Laborer	06JI02Mu
Wm.	14	M	Laborer	06JI02Mu
MCCALL, Alice	27	F	Laborer	06JI02Mu
Rich.	18	M	Laborer	06JI02Mu
Ann	16	F	Laborer	06JI02Mu
Bridget	10	F	Laborer	06JI02Mu
Mary	12	F	Laborer	06JI02Mu
Cath.	10	F	Laborer	06JI02Mu
Alice	8	F	Child	06JI02Mu
John	7	M	Child	06JI02Mu
Mary	4	F	Child	06JI02Mu
Anne	11	F	Laborer	06JI02Mu
Joseph	8	M	Child	06JI02Mu
Mary	6	F	Child	06JI02Mu
Margt.	3	F	Child	06JI02Mu
Jno.	.00	M	Infant	06JI02Mu
REILLEY, Mary	30	F	Laborer	06JI02Mu
BURKE, Pat	24	M	Laborer	06JI02Mu
DAVIS, Saml.	23	M	Laborer	06JI02Mu
MARSHALL, Ann	24	F	Laborer	06JI02Mu
CAUGAN, Mathew	35	M	Laborer	06JI02Mu
Margt.	35	F	Laborer	06JI02Mu
Biddy	11	F	Laborer	06JI02Mu
Margt.	.00	F	Infant	06JI02Mu
Mary	10	F	Laborer	06JI02Mu

KATE-HUNTER 07 JULY 1849

From Liverpool

NAMES OF PASSENGERS	AGE	SEX	OCCUPATIONS	DATE PORT SHIP
BOYLE, Mary	20	F	Servant	07JI02Mw
FEENY, Catherine	40	F	Unknown	07JI02Mw
FEENY, Catherine	.07	F	Infant	07JI02Mw
Pat.	9	M	Child	07JI02Mw
Willey	5	M	Child	07JI02Mw
MOARN, Nancy	40	F	Unknown	07JI02Mw
Mathew	5	M	Child	07JI02Mw
John	.03	M	Infant	07JI02Mw
MURPHY, Ellen	18	F	Unknown	07JI02Mw
GOODMAN, Ellen	45	F	Unknown	07JI02Mw
THOMAS, George	35	M	Unknown	07JI02Mw
Sarah	21	F	Unknown	07JI02Mw
John	3	M	Child	07JI02Mw
Robt.	.09	M	Infant	07JI02Mw
ROSE, William	35	M	Laborer	07JI02Mw
CROFT, Hueny	30	M	Unknown	07JI02Mw
HANLEY, Thomas	30	M	Unknown	07JI02Mw
Margret	25	F	Unknown	07JI02Mw
NOLAN, Mary	20	F	Unknown	07JI02Mw
FLANNAGHAN, William	26	M	Servant	07JI02Mw
TOWER, William	25	M	Unknown	07JI02Mw
SHEENY, Mary	20	F	Unknown	07JI02Mw
MATHEWS, Thomas	30	M	Unknown	07JI02Mw
HUNTON, Morris	23	M	Unknown	07JI02Mw
FLOOD, James	31	M	Unknown	07JI02Mw
DEACON, Sarah	30	F	Unknown	07JI02Mw
Edwin	11	M	Unknown	07JI02Mw
Elizabeth	9	F	Child	07JI02Mw
QUINN, Luke	25	M	Laborer	07JI02Mw
ARMSTRONG, John	15	M	Unknown	07JI02Mw
ROBINSON, George	21	M	Unknown	07JI02Mw
ROGERS, Pat.	45	M	Unknown	07JI02Mw
Mary	11	F	Unknown	07JI02Mw
Bridget	8	F	Child	07JI02Mw
Phillip	3	M	Child	07JI02Mw
John	7	M	Child	07JI02Mw
Edward	2	M	Child	07JI02Mw
Catherine	.07	F	Infant	07JI02Mw
BURGESS, Joseph	24	F	Unknown	07JI02Mw
Ann	25	F	Unknown	07JI02Mw
Ann	.06	F	Infant	07JI02Mw
EDWARDS, John	21	M	Unknown	07JI02Mw
JONES, Elizabeth	60	F	Unknown	07JI02Mw
PHILLIPS, Theofilus	25	M	Unknown	07JI02Mw
BASSETT, Wm.	30	M	Unknown	07JI02Mw
MCCANN, Mary	40	F	Servant	07JI02Mw
FAGAN, John	2	M	Child	07JI02Mw
DALY, Alik	27	M	Unknown	07JI02Mw
Catherine	25	F	Unknown	07JI02Mw
Mary-Ann	1	F	Child	07JI02Mw
James	.08	M	Infant	07JI02Mw
TRACEY, Pat.	20	M	Unknown	07JI02Mw
MORRISH, Constantine	21	F	Unknown	07JI02Mw
John	16	M	Unknown	07JI02Mw
Ann	18	F	Unknown	07JI02Mw
MULLIN, Sally	18	F	Farmer	07JI02Mw
DONEWARD, James	21	M	Unknown	07JI02Mw
HARLEY, Margt.	29	F	Unknown	07JI02Mw
MCAVOY, Michl.	50	M	Laborer	07JI02Mw
Catherine	12	F	Unknown	07JI02Mw
LYNCH, Charles	35	M	Unknown	07JI02Mw
FARADAY, John	50	M	Laborer	07JI02Mw
Cath.	20	F	Unknown	07JI02Mw
Pat	16	M	Unknown	07JI02Mw
Thos.	13	M	Unknown	07JI02Mw
Rose	11	F	Unknown	07JI02Mw
Bridget	7	F	Child	07JI02Mw
John	35	M	Mechanic	07JI02Mw
CALDWELL, Thos.	35	M	Unknown	07JI02Mw
HARTZ, Mary	30	F	Unknown	07JI02Mw
KAY, John	20	M	Unknown	07JI02Mw
FAGAN, James	20	M	Unknown	07JI02Mw
FAINAN, Bessy	30	F	Unknown	07JI02Mw
Charles	8	M	Child	07JI02Mw
Billy	4	M	Child	07JI02Mw
Cath.	18	F	Unknown	07JI02Mw
Bridget	.07	F	Infant	07JI02Mw

NAMES OF PASSENGERS	AGE	SEX	OCCUPATIONS	DATE PORT SHIP
MULLIGAN, Rose	40	F	Unknown	07JI02Mw
Margt.	18	F	Servant	07JI02Mw
Mary	20	F	Unknown	07JI02Mw
FLYNN, Terence	20	M	Unknown	07JI02Mw
BRADY, Margt.	18	F	Unknown	07JI02Mw
HUGES, Mary	46	F	Unknown	07JI02Mw
Thos.	8	M	Child	07JI02Mw
Mary	10	F	Unknown	07JI02Mw
COYLE, Pat	40	M	Unknown	07JI02Mw
CREA, Nannis	28	M	Unknown	07JI02Mw
Bessey	18	F	Unknown	07JI02Mw
LOLAHAN, Bessey	20	F	Unknown	07JI02Mw
TOWNNY, Pat	28	M	Unknown	07JI02Mw
FARLEY, Cath.	50	F	Unknown	07JI02Mw
Ellen	21	F	Unknown	07JI02Mw
LORBY, Pat	21	M	Unknown	07JI02Mw
MANGEB, John	44	M	Unknown	07JI02Mw
Ann	34	F	Unknown	07JI02Mw
MCCARTY, Ann	25	F	Unknown	07JI02Mw
MAUGET, Thos.	11	M	Unknown	07JI02Mw
James	10	M	Unknown	07JI02Mw
John	9	M	Child	07JI02Mw
Mary	6	F	Child	07JI02Mw
Ann	.10	F	Infant	07JI02Mw
KEEN, Thos.	50	M	Unknown	07JI02Mw
Robt.	24	M	Laborer	07JI02Mw
Mary	22	F	Unknown	07JI02Mw
CARR, Ann	17	F	Unknown	07JI02Mw
ARMITAGE, Joseph	30	M	Unknown	07JI02Mw
Susan	25	F	Unknown	07JI02Mw
FARRELL, Margt.	29	F	Unknown	07JI02Mw
MATHEWS, Bryant	25	M	Laborer	07JI02Mw
Ann	26	F	Unknown	07JI02Mw
GLEESON, John	21	M	Unknown	07JI02Mw
Mary	20	F	Unknown	07JI02Mw
LEDGWICK, Thos.	21	M	Servant	07JI02Mw
WOODCOCK, Saml.	22	M	Unknown	07JI02Mw
MCCABE, Henery	10	M	Unknown	07JI02Mw
LEONARD, James	43	M	Laborer	07JI02Mw
Ellen	12	F	Laborer	07JI02Mw
GOODWIN, Pat	21	M	Unknown	07JI02Mw
SHARP, Jean	29	F	Unknown	07JI02Mw
Danl.	.10	M	Infant	07JI02Mw
STEPHENS, Mary-Jane	16	F	Servant	07JI02Mw
Fanny	41	F	Unknown	07JI02Mw
WELSH, Anty	20	F	Unknown	07JI02Mw

SALACIA 07 JULY 1849

From Liverpool

NAMES OF PASSENGERS	AGE	SEX	OCCUPATIONS	DATE PORT SHIP
MURRAY, Pat.	40	M	Laborer	07JI02Ms
M.	35	M	Laborer	07JI02Ms
KEMPLOR, James	18	M	Laborer	07JI02Ms
MACKEY, Peter	30	M	Laborer	07JI02Ms
U (W)	28	F	Servant	07JI02Ms
Pat	7	M	Child	07JI02Ms
Susan	.00	F	Infant	07JI02Ms
RAILLY, Mick	45	M	Laborer	07JI02Ms
Mary	40	F	Wife	07JI02Ms
Pat	17	M	Laborer	07JI02Ms
Cath.	14	F	Servant	07JI02Ms
Mary	9	F	Child	07JI02Ms
Mick	5	M	Child	07JI02Ms
GOUGH, Richd.	25	M	Laborer	07JI02Ms
CARRY, Pat	24	M	Laborer	07JI02Ms
CLARK, Pat	24	M	Laborer	07JI02Ms
FLINNE, Cath.	25	F	Servant	07JI02Ms
CULLINS, Biddy	26	F	Servant	07JI02Ms
KURIN, Margt.	25	F	Servant	07JI02Ms
MORIARTY, Tim.	20	M	Laborer	07JI02Ms
DEEN, James	18	M	Laborer	07JI02Ms
Eugene	18	M	Laborer	07JI02Ms
MCMANUS, Mary	17	F	Servant	07JI02Ms
Jane	20	F	Servant	07JI02Ms
MAXWELL, Alick	21	M	Laborer	07JI02Ms
MCLAUGHLIN, Thos.	22	M	Laborer	07JI02Ms
FITZPATRICK, John	13	F	Unknown	07JI02Ms
DISCOL, Margt.	20	F	Laborer	07JI02Ms
GURRIN, Brid.	23	F	Laborer	07JI02Ms
Joseph	10	M	Unknown	07JI02Ms
Joseph	2	M	Child	07JI02Ms
MULROWE, Peter	17	M	Laborer	07JI02Ms
GIBBONS, Patrick	31	M	Laborer	07JI02Ms
Cecily	18	F	Servant	07JI02Ms
MORGAN, Margt.	11	F	Unknown	07JI02Ms
MORAN, W.	10	M	Unknown	07JI02Ms
ROACH, Mary	30	F	Servant	07JI02Ms
WALSH, James	21	M	Laborer	07JI02Ms
BARRY, Eliza	30	F	Servant	07JI02Ms
Mary	10	F	Unknown	07JI02Ms
Edmond	11	M	Laborer	07JI02Ms
Julia	8	F	Child	07JI02Ms
Ellen	5	F	Child	07JI02Ms
SHINY, Brid.	20	F	Servant	07JI02Ms
CONNELL, John	20	M	Laborer	07JI02Ms
HERBERT, James	22	M	Laborer	07JI02Ms
MILES, Mary	40	F	Servant	07JI02Ms
MULICK, Tere.	20	M	Laborer	07JI02Ms
CAINE, Biddy	16	F	Unknown	07JI02Ms
Ann	20	F	Servant	07JI02Ms
ROURKE, Terence	40	M	Laborer	07JI02Ms
DONERELY, John	26	M	Laborer	07JI02Ms
Margt.	24	F	Servant	07JI02Ms
ROBINSON, John	45	M	Laborer	07JI02Ms
MCLAUGHLIN, Jenny	20	F	Servant	07JI02Ms
MORRIS, Cath.	21	F	Servant	07JI02Ms
WINTERS, Honor	22	F	Servant	07JI02Ms
CONWAY, Jenny	16	F	Servant	07JI02Ms
GALLAGHER, Bridt.	18	F	Servant	07JI02Ms
SHINY, Jerem.	30	M	Laborer	07JI02Ms
GULOM, Margt.	22	F	Servant	07JI02Ms
Johanna	24	F	Servant	07JI02Ms
DARCY, Julia	50	F	Servant	07JI02Ms
WALSH, James	18	M	Laborer	07JI02Ms
Johanna	14	F	Servant	07JI02Ms
HARRINGTON, David	19	M	Laborer	07JI02Ms
Johanna	17	F	Servant	07JI02Ms
SUTTON, Thos.	48	M	Laborer	07JI02Ms
U (W)	28	F	Servant	07JI02Ms
Thos.	2	M	Child	07JI02Ms
REILLY, Owen	24	M	Laborer	07JI02Ms
DAM, Cath.	22	F	Servant	07JI02Ms
HOWELL, Patrick	18	M	Laborer	07JI02Ms
Margt.	16	F	Laborer	07JI02Ms
CARROLL, Francis	60	M	Laborer	07JI02Ms
Margt.	58	F	Servant	07JI02Ms
Ellen	9	F	Child	07JI02Ms
KEARNEY, Ann	16	F	Servant	07JI02Ms
CARROL, Celia	5	F	Child	07JI02Ms
LOMEY, Simon	18	M	Laborer	07JI02Ms
SPILLNEY, Thomas	14	M	Laborer	07JI02Ms
Mary	19	F	Servant	07JI02Ms
OROWE, Cath.	28	F	Servant	07JI02Ms
Cath.	.00	F	Infant	07JI02Ms
Peter	3	M	Child	07JI02Ms
BUSLAN, Jos.	17	M	Laborer	07JI02Ms
Bridget	14	F	Servant	07JI02Ms
MCADAMS, Harry	17	M	Laborer	07JI02Ms
KIRK, Thomas	18	M	Laborer	07JI02Ms
MCGAHEY, Allen	19	M	Laborer	07JI02Ms
MCNULLY, John	21	M	Laborer	07JI02Ms
MCGUINNESS, Eliza	20	F	Servant	07JI02Ms
SERINAN, Bridget	20	F	Servant	07JI02Ms

NAMES OF PASSENGERS	AGE	SEX	OCCUPATIONS	DATE PORT SHIP
COLEWICK, Ann	15	F	Servant	07J102Ms
Mary	12	F	Unknown	07J102Ms
CONNELLY, James	19	M	Laborer	07J102Ms
HANLAN, Ellen	18	F	Servant	07J102Ms
MCLARKIN, Michl.	21	M	Laborer	07J102Ms
GENSON, Michl.	21	M	Laborer	07J102Ms
James	20	M	Laborer	07J102Ms
MURKIN, Wm.	21	M	Laborer	07J102Ms
DUFFY, Cath.	19	F	Servant	07J102Ms
KEARNEY, Ann	30	F	Servant	07J102Ms
SHARKEY, Jenny	10	F	Servant	07J102Ms
KEARNEY, Pat	8	M	Child	07J102Ms
Ann	5	F	Child	07J102Ms
John	18	M	Laborer	07J102Ms
BLAKE, Ann	25	F	Servant	07J102Ms
SCULLY, Jane	3	F	Child	07J102Ms
Cath.	40	F	Servant	07J102Ms
GALLAGHER, Loddy	40	M	Laborer	07J102Ms
Rose	11	F	Unknown	07J102Ms
Pat	10	M	Unknown	07J102Ms
Margt.	8	F	Child	07J102Ms
Hugh	50	M	Laborer	07J102Ms
Bridget	25	F	Servant	07J102Ms
ALLEN, Wm.	30	M	Laborer	07J102Ms
LUDLOW, George	6	M	Child	07J102Ms
James	3	M	Child	07J102Ms
Jane	20	F	Laborer	07J102Ms
BROWN, Thomas	33	M	Laborer	07J102Ms
Thomas	25	M	Laborer	07J102Ms
Thomas	35	M	Laborer	07J102Ms
HAMPTON, John	26	M	Laborer	07J102Ms
Cath.	7	F	Child	07J102Ms
Ann	21	F	Servant	07J102Ms
Mich.	6	M	Child	07J102Ms
John	4	M	Child	07J102Ms
Maria	.00	F	Infant	07J102Ms
WALSH, Morris	21	M	Laborer	07J102Ms
Daniel	16	M	Laborer	07J102Ms
WADDLE, Pat	38	M	Laborer	07J102Ms
Ann	37	F	Servant	07J102Ms
Lacey	12	F	Unknown	07J102Ms
John	9	M	Child	07J102Ms
Mary	7	F	Child	07J102Ms
Berd.	5	M	Child	07J102Ms
Edward	3	M	Child	07J102Ms
Pat.	.00	M	Infant	07J102Ms
HANNAH, Eliza	20	F	Servant	07J102Ms
COOGAN, Cath.	20	F	Servant	07J102Ms
Chris.	4	M	Child	07J102Ms
Julia	8	F	Child	07J102Ms
Jane	40	F	Servant	07J102Ms
Thomas	7	M	Child	07J102Ms
Ann	5	F	Child	07J102Ms
SHORT, Pat	29	M	Laborer	07J102Ms
GALLAGHER, Mary	23	F	Servant	07J102Ms
TRAVERS, Jos.	50	M	Laborer	07J102Ms
Mary	45	F	Servant	07J102Ms
John	15	M	Laborer	07J102Ms
Wm.	13	M	Unknown	07J102Ms
Jos.	11	M	Unknown	07J102Ms
Bridget	9	F	Child	07J102Ms
Pat	7	M	Child	07J102Ms
Thomas	5	M	Child	07J102Ms
PETTEL, Edwd.	30	M	Laborer	07J102Ms
BYAM, Eliza	17	F	Servant	07J102Ms
Chas.	14	M	Laborer	07J102Ms
UNION, Wm.	28	M	Laborer	07J102Ms
Mary	27	F	Servant	07J102Ms
Wm.	3	M	Child	07J102Ms
Alfred	2	M	Child	07J102Ms
Eliza	.00	F	Infant	07J102Ms
MEDCALF, Jno.	23	M	Laborer	07J102Ms
Sarah	22	F	Servant	07J102Ms
U	.00	F	Infant	07J102Ms
DANSON, John	35	M	Laborer	07J102Ms
DANSON, Geo.	26	M	Laborer	07J102Ms
Fanny	24	F	Servant	07J102Ms
Eliza	21	F	Servant	07J102Ms
Jane	17	F	Servant	07J102Ms
Jane	.00	F	Infant	07J102Ms
GENLAND, Martha	25	F	Servant	07J102Ms
Jane	27	F	Servant	07J102Ms
John	11	M	Unknown	07J102Ms
Jane	.00	F	Infant	07J102Ms
THOMPSON, Robt.	35	M	Laborer	07J102Ms
JACKSON, Henry	34	M	Laborer	07J102Ms
TENNANT, Chas.	23	M	Laborer	07J102Ms
GODFREY, Robt.	21	M	Laborer	07J102Ms
GEODAN, Robt.	22	M	Laborer	07J102Ms
SEGGETT, Samuel	25	M	Laborer	07J102Ms
U (W)	25	F	Servant	07J102Ms
Mary	.00	F	Infant	07J102Ms
GALAGHER, Pat	30	M	Laborer	07J102Ms
SILIVAN, Mick	41	M	Laborer	07J102Ms
U (W)	50	F	Servant	07J102Ms
Margaret	17	F	Servant	07J102Ms
TENNBE, Thomas	26	M	Laborer	07J102Ms
U (W)	24	F	Servant	07J102Ms
GEFRIS, Geo.	27	M	Laborer	07J102Ms
U (W)	23	F	Servant	07J102Ms
BULL, Geo.	24	M	Laborer	07J102Ms
U (W)	23	F	Servant	07J102Ms
CAULIFFE, Wm.W.	20	M	Laborer	07J102Ms
KENNEDY, Jas.	41	M	Laborer	07J102Ms
U (W)	39	F	Servant	07J102Ms
U-Miss	18	F	Servant	07J102Ms
MCCLINSKEY, Jane	30	F	Servant	07J102Ms
DUFFEY, Robt.	40	M	Laborer	07J102Ms
Margt.	15	F	Servant	07J102Ms
James	10	M	Unknown	07J102Ms
Alice	8	F	Child	07J102Ms
Leblia	5	F	Child	07J102Ms
COUTHBET, Richd.	33	M	Laborer	07J102Ms
U (W)	30	F	Servant	07J102Ms
Nancy	20	F	Servant	07J102Ms
James	17	M	Laborer	07J102Ms
Margt.	11	F	Unknown	07J102Ms
Ralph	10	M	Unknown	07J102Ms
Nance	8	F	Child	07J102Ms
Jane	5	F	Child	07J102Ms
Ann	3	F	Child	07J102Ms
John	.00	M	Infant	07J102Ms
SEAGRAVE, Adam	56	M	Laborer	07J102Ms
U (W)	50	F	Servant	07J102Ms
Adam	21	M	Laborer	07J102Ms
Thomas	19	M	Laborer	07J102Ms
Mary	15	F	Servant	07J102Ms
BAXTER, U	38	M	Laborer	07J102Ms
Hany	34	F	Servant	07J102Ms
Janet	16	F	Servant	07J102Ms
WILSON, James	26	M	Laborer	07J102Ms
HASTINGS, U-Mrs.	30	F	Servant	07J102Ms
Archd.	3	M	Child	07J102Ms
KILSON, Sally	17	F	Servant	07J102Ms
John	13	M	Unknown	07J102Ms
COX, Jenny	25	F	Servant	07J102Ms
VALLIN, Danl.	19	M	Laborer	07J102Ms
PARSIN, Wm.	19	M	Laborer	07J102Ms
KNIGHT, John-M.	21	M	Laborer	07J102Ms
HINES, Thomas	24	M	Laborer	07J102Ms
MCCARR, Eliza	28	F	Servant	07J102Ms
NEWGATE, Thos.	21	M	Laborer	07J102Ms
JOHNSTON, Jos.	20	M	Laborer	07J102Ms
GARNES, Thos.	30	M	Laborer	07J102Ms
U (W)	27	F	Servant	07J102Ms
MURPHY, Jas.	40	M	Laborer	07J102Ms
Anne	40	F	Servant	07J102Ms
Biddy	9	F	Child	07J102Ms
Mary	7	F	Child	07J102Ms
CORMLY, Biddy	30	F	Servant	07J102Ms

NAMES OF PASSENGERS	AGE	SEX	OCCUPATIONS	DATE PORT SHIP
FOX, Cath.	18	F	Servant	07J102Ms
Cath.	13	F	Servant	07J102Ms
POWER, John	28	M	Laborer	07J102Ms
SAWYER, Bernard	25	M	Laborer	07J102Ms
James	25	M	Laborer	07J102Ms
LYNCH, Bridget	18	F	Servant	07J102Ms
DEMPSEY, Cath.	20	F	Servant	07J102Ms
KEEFE, Biddy	18	F	Servant	07J102Ms
STUMP, John	33	M	Laborer	07J102Ms
Jonathan	20	M	Laborer	07J102Ms
Isaac	23	M	Laborer	07J102Ms
BRAZIL, Thos.	30	M	Laborer	07J102Ms
MUNRO, John	28	M	Laborer	07J102Ms
MORGANS, Eliza	20	F	Servant	07J102Ms
LYNCH, Ann	50	F	Servant	07J102Ms
Cath.	13	F	Unknown	07J102Ms
GAWRAIN, Susan	20	F	Servant	07J102Ms
Ann	13	F	Servant	07J102Ms
CARROLL, Mary	50	F	Servant	07J102Ms
MARTIN, Mary	22	F	Servant	07J102Ms
Ellen	28	F	Servant	07J102Ms
U-Miss	8	F	Child	07J102Ms
Cath.	.00	F	Infant	07J102Ms
KENNEDY, Edwd.	60	M	Laborer	07J102Ms
Margt.	60	F	Servant	07J102Ms
Lau.	26	M	Laborer	07J102Ms
DAWSON, Geo.	.00	M	Infant	07J102Ms
DAM, Cath.	17	F	Servant	07J102Ms
CARROLL, Ann	18	F	Servant	07J102Ms

MARY-ANN-HENRY 09 JULY 1849

From Limerick

NAMES OF PASSENGERS	AGE	SEX	OCCUPATIONS	DATE PORT SHIP
REDDEN, Pat	30	M	Laborer	09J135Nb
CUMMINGS, John	30	M	Laborer	09J135Nb
ONIEL, Jas.	25	M	Laborer	09J135Nb
HISHIN, Margaret	20	F	Milliner	09J135Nb
DILLON, Mary	17	F	Servant	09J135Nb
Pat	18	M	Laborer	09J135Nb
SULLIVAN, Timothy	21	M	Laborer	09J135Nb
Mary	27	F	Servant	09J135Nb
Margaret	.06	F	Infant	09J135Nb
COOPER, Wm.	36	M	Laborer	09J135Nb
MOLONY, Jno.	20	M	Laborer	09J135Nb
HISHEN, Pat	18	M	Laborer	09J135Nb
BROWN, Thos.	23	M	Laborer	09J135Nb
BARINT, John	23	M	Laborer	09J135Nb
Kate	1	F	Child	09J135Nb
JOHNSTON, Wm.	35	M	Laborer	09J135Nb
Margaret	35	F	Unknown	09J135Nb
Ellen	6	F	Child	09J135Nb
John	3	M	Child	09J135Nb
William	.06	M	Infant	09J135Nb
MULLALEA, Andrew	30	M	Unknown	09J135Nb
CLEARY, John	30	M	Unknown	09J135Nb
CROUT, Malachy	20	M	Unknown	09J135Nb
CLEARY, Margaret	45	F	Unknown	09J135Nb
HAWISHAR, Pat	23	M	Unknown	09J135Nb
GLEESON, Edward	35	M	Unknown	09J135Nb
Daniel	28	M	Unknown	09J135Nb
CLEARY, Wm.	28	M	Unknown	09J135Nb
Thos.	16	M	Unknown	09J135Nb
Bridget	20	F	Unknown	09J135Nb
GUINIEL, Wm.	21	M	Unknown	09J135Nb
GRIFFIN, Maurice	30	F	Unknown	09J135Nb
Bridget	30	M	Unknown	09J135Nb
John	3	M	Child	09J135Nb
Power	.04	M	Infant	09J135Nb

NAMES OF PASSENGERS	AGE	SEX	OCCUPATIONS	DATE PORT SHIP
GRIFFIN, Patrick	22	M	Unknown	09J135Nb
Ellen	18	F	Unknown	09J135Nb
COMORY, John	24	M	Unknown	09J135Nb
GROGAN, Michael	30	M	Unknown	09J135Nb
COSTOLO, Edward	24	M	Unknown	09J135Nb
Thomas	22	M	Unknown	09J135Nb
KEANE, James	30	M	Unknown	09J135Nb
CONOLY, John	27	M	Unknown	09J135Nb
Mary	22	F	Unknown	09J135Nb
Ellen	19	F	Unknown	09J135Nb
GUINILL, Edward	30	M	Unknown	09J135Nb
WALSH, Michael	25	M	Unknown	09J135Nb
ENRIGHT, John	20	M	Unknown	09J135Nb
MOORE, James	30	M	Unknown	09J135Nb
Mary	30	F	Unknown	09J135Nb
James	3	M	Child	09J135Nb
Margaret	5	F	Child	09J135Nb
Mary	.04	F	Infant	09J135Nb
HUNT, N.	26	M	Unknown	09J135Nb
DELAINEY, Mary	18	F	Unknown	09J135Nb
RYAN, Pat	22	M	Unknown	09J135Nb
BENSON, Wm.	28	M	Unknown	09J135Nb
Eliza	25	F	Unknown	09J135Nb
SHANAHAN, Thos.	30	M	Unknown	09J135Nb
COLLINS, Michael	35	M	Unknown	09J135Nb
TRACEY, Pat	35	M	Unknown	09J135Nb
H.	29	M	Unknown	09J135Nb
Mary	10	F	Unknown	09J135Nb
Wen.	28	M	Unknown	09J135Nb
DELAINEY, Martin	30	M	Unknown	09J135Nb
Margaret	26	F	Unknown	09J135Nb
HOGAN, John	23	M	Unknown	09J135Nb
QUINN, Anthony	18	M	Unknown	09J135Nb
HOGAN, Mary	17	F	Unknown	09J135Nb
Michael	10	M	Unknown	09J135Nb
ODONNELL, Jas.	18	M	Unknown	09J135Nb
HONNAY, Wm.	25	M	Unknown	09J135Nb
BURKE, John	30	M	Unknown	09J135Nb
COLLINS, Sally	20	F	Unknown	09J135Nb
KENNEDY, Margaret	31	F	Unknown	09J135Nb
CLEARY, John	18	M	Unknown	09J135Nb
BYRNES, Ann	16	F	Unknown	09J135Nb
MCMAHON, Ann	25	F	Unknown	09J135Nb
WALCH, Pat	25	M	Unknown	09J135Nb
Thos.	20	M	Unknown	09J135Nb
MCNAMARA, Michael	20	M	Unknown	09J135Nb
MADIGAN, Mathew	20	M	Unknown	09J135Nb
BIRNES, Bernard	25	M	Unknown	09J135Nb
MOLONY, Margaret	22	F	Unknown	09J135Nb
Bridget	.10	F	Infant	09J135Nb
HANLY, Thos.	25	M	Unknown	09J135Nb
DILLON, Thos.	25	M	Unknown	09J135Nb
KEANE, Debora	20	F	Unknown	09J135Nb
MALOOHILL, Thos.	20	M	Unknown	09J135Nb
Mary	22	F	Unknown	09J135Nb
REEVES, Thos.	23	M	Unknown	09J135Nb
HICKEY, John	19	M	Unknown	09J135Nb
GILOOLY, Margaret	25	F	Unknown	09J135Nb
MCMAHON, Alley	12	F	Unknown	09J135Nb
John	9	M	Child	09J135Nb
Margaret	6	F	Child	09J135Nb
HANRATUS, Thos.	36	M	Unknown	09J135Nb
CONSIDEM, John	28	M	Unknown	09J135Nb
SHEA, John	25	M	Unknown	09J135Nb
Michael	17	M	Unknown	09J135Nb
Darby	20	M	Unknown	09J135Nb
Mary	18	F	Unknown	09J135Nb
Biddy	26	F	Unknown	09J135Nb
Noony	22	M	Unknown	09J135Nb
LYNCH, Thos.	30	M	Unknown	09J135Nb
LYONS, James	40	M	Unknown	09J135Nb
KILEY, Daniel	30	M	Unknown	09J135Nb
BRUN, Pat	20	M	Unknown	09J135Nb
CORBITT, Dennis	20	M	Unknown	09J135Nb
Cos--, Catherine	20	F	Unknown	09J135Nb

NAMES OF PASSENGERS	A G E	S E X	OCCUPATIONS	DATE PORT SHIP
KEANE, Pat	17	M	Unknown	09J135Nb
Mary	50	F	Unknown	09J135Nb
Michael	15	M	Unknown	09J135Nb
DOWLING, Margaret	22	F	Unknown	09J135Nb
SCANLAN, Anne	30	F	Unknown	09J135Nb
CONNOLY, Michael	24	M	Unknown	09J135Nb
Anne	25	F	Unknown	09J135Nb
SAQUIX, Mary-Anne	17	F	Unknown	09J135Nb
HAYES, Mary	50	F	Unknown	09J135Nb
MOLONY, Mary	25	F	Unknown	09J135Nb
LITTLETON, Michael	21	M	Unknown	09J135Nb
FITZMAURICE, Pat	18	M	Unknown	09J135Nb
CONNOLY, David	30	M	Unknown	09J135Nb
ONEIL, Mary	12	F	Unknown	09J135Nb
CLARY, Margaret	30	F	Unknown	09J135Nb
Michael	.08	M	Infant	09J135Nb
MOWNYS, Catherine	35	F	Unknown	09J135Nb
Helen	13	F	Unknown	09J135Nb
Davis	9	M	Child	09J135Nb
Bridget	21	F	Unknown	09J135Nb
BIRMINGHAM, John	25	M	Unknown	09J135Nb
CRAUFORD, Ellen	16	F	Unknown	09J135Nb
Ann	13	F	Unknown	09J135Nb
MCAULIFFE, Pat	14	M	Unknown	09J135Nb
GLEESON, Pat	22	M	Unknown	09J135Nb
KINNENANE, Margaret	50	F	Unknown	09J135Nb
James	21	M	Unknown	09J135Nb
Martin	19	M	Unknown	09J135Nb
Mary	15	F	Unknown	09J135Nb
Michael	11	M	Unknown	09J135Nb
Sarah	9	F	Child	09J135Nb
Daniel	7	M	Child	09J135Nb
Pat	4	M	Child	09J135Nb
Margaret	11	F	Unknown	09J135Nb
BENSON, Kate	50	F	Unknown	09J135Nb
WOLFS, John	50	M	Unknown	09J135Nb
Bridget	18	F	Unknown	09J135Nb
Camo--, Thos.	18	M	Unknown	09J135Nb
CONNORS, Wm.	17	M	Unknown	09J135Nb
WOLF, Ellen	14	F	Unknown	09J135Nb
Cate	11	F	Unknown	09J135Nb
Maurice	9	M	Child	09J135Nb
Daniel	7	M	Child	09J135Nb
Johanna	5	F	Child	09J135Nb
Bridget	4	F	Child	09J135Nb
Julia	2	F	Child	09J135Nb
Anne	40	F	Unknown	09J135Nb
QUIN, John	24	M	Unknown	09J135Nb
CADMORE, Pat	30	M	Unknown	09J135Nb
HEALEY, Mary	32	F	Unknown	09J135Nb
Ellen	21	F	Unknown	09J135Nb
KENNEDY, Michael	45	M	Unknown	09J135Nb
CASEY, U-Mrs.	20	F	Unknown	09J135Nb
Biddy	19	F	Unknown	09J135Nb
COLLINS, Sarah	27	F	Unknown	09J135Nb
KENNEDY, Jno.	27	M	Unknown	09J135Nb
MALONE, Daniel	48	M	Unknown	09J135Nb
DWYER, Mary	23	F	Unknown	09J135Nb
Ellen	20	F	Unknown	09J135Nb
ODONNELL, Michael	22	M	Unknown	09J135Nb
KELLY, John	24	M	Unknown	09J135Nb
KENNEDY, Ellen	29	F	Unknown	09J135Nb
HANGTON, Wm.	29	M	Unknown	09J135Nb
GADOR, P.	20	M	Unknown	09J135Nb
Winfield	18	M	Unknown	09J135Nb
MOLONY, Mary-Ann	.03	F	Infant	09J135Nb
DILLON, Mary	22	F	Unknown	09J135Nb

ORION 09 JULY 1849

From Newcastle

NAMES OF PASSENGERS	A G E	S E X	OCCUPATIONS	DATE PORT SHIP
PALFRYMAN, Benjamin	32	M	Machinist	09J118Mx
CHANCE, John	42	M	Machinist	09J118Mx
DEMPSTER, Robert	28	M	Cooper	09J118Mx

OREGON 09 JULY 1849

From London

NAMES OF PASSENGERS	A G E	S E X	OCCUPATIONS	DATE PORT SHIP
DOWLING, Patrick	27	M	Fiddler	09J113Kb
Helena	28	F	Fiddler	09J113Kb
NEVILLE, John	32	M	Bookbinder	09J113Kb
CROWLEY, Ellen	20	F	Spinster	09J113Kb
HALLINAN, Thomas	30	M	Farmer	09J113Kb
Jeremiah	32	M	Farmer	09J113Kb
Catherine	27	F	Farmer	09J113Kb
Mary-Ann	00	F	Unknown	09J113Kb
MADDIGAN, Margaret	24	F	Spinster	09J113Kb
DILLON, Mary	13	F	Spinster	09J113Kb
Johanna	17	F	Spinster	09J113Kb
CARROL, Martin	28	M	Blacksmith	09J113Kb
GROGAN, Mary	26	F	Spinster	09J113Kb
DONGAN, Mary	24	F	Spinster	09J113Kb
CARROL, Elizabeth	34	F	Spinster	09J113Kb
CLIFFORD, Patrick	28	M	Painter	09J113Kb
BRYAN, Margaret	24	F	Spinster	09J113Kb
BROSHANAN, Danl.	23	M	Laborer	09J113Kb
SULLIVAN, Bridget	24	F	Unknown	09J113Kb
MORGAN, George	25	M	Blacksmith	09J113Kb
CONNEL, Ellen	30	F	None	09J113Kb
RAVINE, William	28	M	Blacksmith	09J113Kb
DRISCOLL, James	25	M	Laborer	09J113Kb
SLATER, John	26	M	Farmer	09J113Kb
NOWLAND, James	29	M	Laborer	09J113Kb
BREEN, Mark	26	M	Joiner	09J113Kb
TAYLOR, Thomas	26	M	Laborer	09J113Kb
RILLY, Mary	28	F	Spinster	09J113Kb
MCCABE, John	33	M	Laborer	09J113Kb
James	8	M	Child	09J113Kb
John	7	M	Child	09J113Kb
ALLAN, Bridget	26	F	Spinster	09J113Kb

CHARLOTTE 09 JULY 1849

From Liverpool

NAMES OF PASSENGERS	A G E	S E X	OCCUPATIONS	DATE PORT SHIP
RYFFEN, Robt.	42	M	Merchant	09J102Nc
Jas.	30	M	Merchant	09J102Nc
Mary-Jane	13	F	Spinster	09J102Nc
Richd.	10	M	None	09J102Nc
Eliza	8	F	Child	09J102Nc
Cath.	6	F	Child	09J102Nc
Ellen	4	F	Child	09J102Nc
DUNN, Honora	20	F	Spinster	09J102Nc

NAMES OF PASSENGERS		AGE	SEX	OCCUPATIONS	DATE PORT SHIP
DUNN, Ann		19	F	Spinster	09JI02Nc
RUSSEL, Da.		25	M	Engineer	09JI02Nc
Isabella	(W)	24	F	None	09JI02Nc
KIRKLAN, John		27	M	Mechanic	09JI02Nc
Maria		22	F	Spinster	09JI02Nc
THOMPSON, Margt.		23	F	Spinster	09JI02Nc
KENNEDY, Ellen		18	F	Spinster	09JI02Nc
SMITH, Bartly		31	M	Laborer	09JI02Nc
BOYLE, Owen		30	M	Laborer	09JI02Nc
Magt.	(W)	24	F	None	09JI02Nc
GLYNN, Pat		50	M	Weaver	09JI02Nc
Mary		30	F	Spinster	09JI02Nc
MCCLEARY, W.		45	M	Mechanic	09JI02Nc
Ann-Jane		30	F	Spinster	09JI02Nc
HANLON, Cath.		40	F	Wi	09JI02Nc
Mary		18	F	Spinster	09JI02Nc
Betty		16	F	Spinster	09JI02Nc
CROZER, John		25	M	Unknown	09JI02Nc
Jane	(W)	21	F	None	09JI02Nc
DUFFIE, Joseph		40	M	Laborer	09JI02Nc
Mary-Ann		26	F	Spinster	09JI02Nc
CAMPBELL, Joseph		25	M	Laborer	09JI02Nc
L--, Barnard		22	M	Laborer	09JI02Nc
MURPHY, Mary		18	F	Spinster	09JI02Nc
Cath.		16	F	Spinster	09JI02Nc
ABBOT, Henry		40	M	Laborer	09JI02Nc
MARLEY, Wm.		24	M	Laborer	09JI02Nc
BELL, Arthur		25	M	Cooper	09JI02Nc
OCONNELL, Jas.		23	M	Laborer	09JI02Nc
Charlotte		22	F	Spinster	09JI02Nc
CONNOR, Philip		18	M	Laborer	09JI02Nc
Mary	(W)	40	F	None	09JI02Nc
Terry		13	M	None	09JI02Nc
Eliza		.09	F	Infant	09JI02Nc
RITCHIE, Jas.		25	M	Laborer	09JI02Nc
ROACH, John		22	M	Laborer	09JI02Nc
AHERN, Pat		26	M	Turner	09JI02Nc
WHITE, Mary		20	F	Spinster	09JI02Nc
MCDONAGH, Henry		21	M	Shoemaker	09JI02Nc
MURPHY, John		30	M	Miller	09JI02Nc
HIGGINS, Owen		40	M	Mechanic	09JI02Nc
U	(W)	35	F	None	09JI02Nc
Pat		15	M	None	09JI02Nc
Mary		13	F	Spinster	09JI02Nc
Bridgt.		10	F	Spinster	09JI02Nc
Bariah		3	F	Child	09JI02Nc
MEAPLES, Wm.		25	M	Laborer	09JI02Nc
SMITH, Danl.		39	M	Laborer	09JI02Nc
FINAGAN, Ellen		40	F	Wife	09JI02Nc
CAVANAGH, Judy		40	F	Wife	09JI02Nc
RAFTER, Ann		18	F	Spinster	09JI02Nc
HENRY, John		21	M	Laborer	09JI02Nc
SHORT, James		24	M	Laborer	09JI02Nc
FOGARTY, Mat.		24	M	Laborer	09JI02Nc
CAIN, Stephen		22	M	Laborer	09JI02Nc
CLANCY, Cath.		15	F	Spinster	09JI02Nc
GALAGHER, Jas.		21	M	Laborer	09JI02Nc
CUFF, Ann		21	F	Spinster	09JI02Nc
MCMAREN, Pat		21	M	Laborer	09JI02Nc
CANAT, James		21	M	Laborer	09JI02Nc
TIGHE, Jas.		40	M	Weaver	09JI02Nc
Mary		5	F	Child	09JI02Nc
Bridget		40	F	Wife	09JI02Nc
WHITE, James		50	M	Laborer	09JI02Nc
CONNOR, Bridgt.		20	F	Wife	09JI02Nc
Pat		.06	M	Infant	09JI02Nc
TIGHE, Ann		32	F	Spinster	09JI02Nc
Pat		30	M	Shoemaker	09JI02Nc
CONNER, Mich.		25	M	Laborer	09JI02Nc
MCMANUS, Bridgt.		25	F	Spinster	09JI02Nc
WHITE, Farrel		18	M	Carpenter	09JI02Nc
SCANLON, John		28	M	Carpenter	09JI02Nc
Honora		22	F	Spinster	09JI02Nc
Mary		18	F	Spinster	09JI02Nc
GAFFNEY, Pat		26	M	Laborer	09JI02Nc

NAMES OF PASSENGERS		AGE	SEX	OCCUPATIONS	DATE PORT SHIP
MCCORMICK, Jas.		30	M	Laborer	09JI02Nc
Ellen	(W)	30	F	None	09JI02Nc
Mary		2	F	Child	09JI02Nc
John		.09	M	Infant	09JI02Nc
CARTY, Bernard		18	M	Laborer	09JI02Nc
PADDEN, Mary-Ann		17	F	Spinster	09JI02Nc
LYNCH, Eliza		16	F	Spinster	09JI02Nc
LINN, James		27	M	Laborer	09JI02Nc
HEALEY, Danl.		24	M	Laborer	09JI02Nc
MCGUIRE, Pat		21	M	Laborer	09JI02Nc
Ellen	(W)	21	F	None	09JI02Nc
John		.08	M	Infant	09JI02Nc
MORTIMER, John		31	M	Laborer	09JI02Nc
Mary		18	F	Spinster	09JI02Nc
MURPHY, Pat		20	M	Laborer	09JI02Nc
Mich.		19	M	Laborer	09JI02Nc
Mich.		18	M	Laborer	09JI02Nc
DUNN, Michl.		40	M	Laborer	09JI02Nc
Danl.		35	M	Laborer	09JI02Nc
Ellen		30	F	Spinster	09JI02Nc
QUINN, Pat		17	M	Laborer	09JI02Nc
MCTISE, Cath.		17	F	Spinster	09JI02Nc
MCSWEENY, Bridgt.		28	F	Wife	09JI02Nc
Margt.		.09	F	Infant	09JI02Nc
HUNT, Mary		24	F	Spinster	09JI02Nc
MCGUIRE, M.		20	M	Butler	09JI02Nc
Kem--, Richd.		60	M	Farmer	09JI02Nc
WHITLEY, Will.		35	M	Farmer	09JI02Nc
GILMORE, Ann		18	F	Spinster	09JI02Nc
MOSES, John		17	M	Laborer	09JI02Nc
George		14	M	Laborer	09JI02Nc
Mary		10	F	Spinster	09JI02Nc
WATSON, Edw.		23	M	Laborer	09JI02Nc
RILEY, Ellen		18	F	Spinster	09JI02Nc
COSTELLO, Cath.		20	F	Spinster	09JI02Nc
BROTHERICK, John		30	M	Laborer	09JI02Nc
Thos.		28	M	Laborer	09JI02Nc
CUMINS, Darby		25	M	Laborer	09JI02Nc
DORE, James		25	M	Laborer	09JI02Nc
Died-At-Sea					
Bridgt.		28	F	Wi	09JI02Nc
OLDS, Thos.		22	M	Laborer	09JI02Nc
SEATON, Jane		21	F	Spinster	09JI02Nc
BYRNE, Pat		25	M	Laborer	09JI02Nc
J.		23	U	Unknown	09JI02Nc
ROACH, Danl.		30	M	Laborer	09JI02Nc
Johanna	(W)	30	F	None	09JI02Nc
James		3	M	Child	09JI02Nc
Mary		.06	F	Infant	09JI02Nc
KELLY, Thos.		30	M	Clerk	09JI02Nc
BRIEN, John		50	M	Farmer	09JI02Nc
Honora	(W)	45	F	None	09JI02Nc
Maria		20	F	Spinster	09JI02Nc
Thos.		13	M	None	09JI02Nc
Henry		12	M	None	09JI02Nc
John		8	M	Child	09JI02Nc
Eliza	(D)	9	F	Child	09JI02Nc
Pat		6	M	Child	09JI02Nc
James		4	M	Child	09JI02Nc
Pat		.10	M	Infant	09JI02Nc
DUNN, La.		24	M	Mechanic	09JI02Nc
SCALLY, Michl.		27	M	Laborer	09JI02Nc
QUINN, John		23	M	Laborer	09JI02Nc
Bridg.		25	F	Spinster	09JI02Nc
CULLEN, John		24	M	Laborer	09JI02Nc
TROY, Fras.		22	M	Miner	09JI02Nc
Bridgt.	(W)	20	F	None	09JI02Nc
COLLINS, James		19	M	Miner	09JI02Nc
WILLIAMS, Thos.		11	M	None	09JI02Nc
Eliza		9	F	Child	09JI02Nc
John		7	M	Child	09JI02Nc
Eliza		5	F	Child	09JI02Nc
Cath.		.06	F	Infant	09JI02Nc
CARRY, John		26	M	Laborer	09JI02Nc
CAREY, Honora	(W)	26	F	None	09JI02Nc

NAMES OF PASSENGERS		AGE	SEX	OCCUPATIONS	DATE PORT SHIP
CAREY, Richd.		.08	M	Infant	09JI02Nc
Dan--, Bessy		20	F	Spinster	09JI02Nc
HANLON, Pat		18	M	Laborer	09JI02Nc
BYRNE, Pat		24	M	Laborer	09JI02Nc
Cath.		22	F	Spinster	09JI02Nc
QUINN, John		30	M	Laborer	09JI02Nc
DUNN, La.		40	M	Laborer	09JI02Nc
ANDERSON, Pat		40	M	Laborer	09JI02Nc
MACK, Ca.		50	F	Spinster	09JI02Nc
HALL, Stephen		20	M	Laborer	09JI02Nc
WILKS, Jas.		31	M	Mason	09JI02Nc
HAUGH, Ellen		35	F	Wi	09JI02Nc
Margt.		17	F	Unknown	09JI02Nc
Michl.		15	M	Laborer	09JI02Nc
Pat		13	M	None	09JI02Nc
Mary		11	F	None	09JI02Nc
Ellen		9	F	Child	09JI02Nc
Jenny		7	F	Child	09JI02Nc
Johanna		17	F	None	09JI02Nc
James		40	M	Farmer	09JI02Nc
Mary		18	F	Spinster	09JI02Nc
Ellen		30	F	Wife	09JI02Nc
John		18	M	Farmer	09JI02Nc
Julia		12	F	Spinster	09JI02Nc
Ellen		7	F	Child	09JI02Nc
Edwd.		40	M	Laborer	09JI02Nc
Mary	(W)	40	F	None	09JI02Nc
Margt.		18	F	Spinster	09JI02Nc
Mich.		16	M	None	09JI02Nc
John		11	M	None	09JI02Nc
Edwd.		8	M	Child	09JI02Nc
Wm.		6	M	Child	09JI02Nc
Mary		3	F	Child	09JI02Nc
James		.09	F	Infant	09JI02Nc
BROWN, John		28	M	Laborer	09JI02Nc
Pat		25	M	Laborer	09JI02Nc
BUCKLY, Pat		21	M	Laborer	09JI02Nc
NOONAN, Jas.		17	M	Shoemaker	09JI02Nc
HICKEY, Cath.		30	F	Wi	09JI02Nc
Mary		11	F	Spinster	09JI02Nc
Magt.		9	F	Child	09JI02Nc
Bridg.		6	F	Child	09JI02Nc
SHEATY, John		28	M	Laborer	09JI02Nc
NOONAN, Danl.		18	M	Laborer	09JI02Nc
Johanna		20	F	Spinster	09JI02Nc
SHEEHAN, Michl.		28	M	Laborer	09JI02Nc
DOOLAN, Tim		25	M	Laborer	09JI02Nc
FITZGERALD, Peter		18	M	Laborer	09JI02Nc
WALSH, James		20	M	Laborer	09JI02Nc
GILMOR, Thos.		18	M	Laborer	09JI02Nc
HOY, Peter		50	M	Laborer	09JI02Nc
U	(W)	50	F	None	09JI02Nc
Mary		22	F	Spinster	09JI02Nc
MATTHIS, Thos.		25	M	Mechanic	09JI02Nc
DOOLEY, Pat		20	M	Laborer	09JI02Nc
Barnard		18	M	Laborer	09JI02Nc
WHEATLEY, George		25	M	Laborer	09JI02Nc
U	(W)	25	F	None	09JI02Nc
Thos.		.06	M	Infant	09JI02Nc
MURRAY, James		25	M	Mason	09JI02Nc
Cath.	(W)	23	F	None	09JI02Nc
LANAGHAN, Margt.		21	F	Spinster	09JI02Nc
SAVAGE, Mary		15	F	Spinster	09JI02Nc
MITCHELL, Henry		50	M	Farmer	09JI02Nc
Jane	(W)	45	F	None	09JI02Nc
Mary		18	F	Spinster	09JI02Nc
Robt.		16	M	Laborer	09JI02Nc
Henry		13	M	Laborer	09JI02Nc
PERRY, Wm.		30	M	Laborer	09JI02Nc
MURPHY, Thos.		28	M	Unknown	09JI02Nc
Michl.		25	M	Laborer	09JI02Nc
KEERAN, Cath.		35	F	Wi	09JI02Nc
BARNES, John		28	M	Unknown	09JI02Nc
MOLE, Thomas		25	M	Unknown	09JI02Nc
Ar--, Mary		38	F	Wi	09JI02Nc

NAMES OF PASSENGERS		AGE	SEX	OCCUPATIONS	DATE PORT SHIP
GOODE, John		6	M	Child	09JI02Nc
Michl.		4	M	Child	09JI02Nc
Mullo--, James		30	M	Laborer	09JI02Nc
DONAHUE, Pat		25	M	Laborer	09JI02Nc
HEALEY, Jerry		24	M	Laborer	09JI02Nc
Julia	(W)	18	F	None	09JI02Nc
DONAHUE, Rhoda		29	F	Spinster	09JI02Nc

ST.GEORGE 12 JULY 1849

From Liverpool

NAMES OF PASSENGERS		AGE	SEX	OCCUPATIONS	DATE PORT SHIP
GRANH, John		28	M	Servant	12JI02Na
MCCLEAN, Mathew-Mrs.		22	F	Servant	12JI02Na
FARLEY, Charles		29	M	Wheelwright	12JI02Na
Ann		26	F	Servant	12JI02Na
Philip		.00	M	Infant	12JI02Na
DAILEY, James		19	M	Laborer	12JI02Na
Catharine		23	F	Unknown	12JI02Na
Margaret		12	F	Unknown	12JI02Na
GANNON, Robert		37	M	Mason	12JI02Na
Eliza		22	F	Unknown	12JI02Na
William		.00	M	Infant	12JI02Na
MCARTY, Ellen		35	F	Unknown	12JI02Na
CONDOR, Mary-Ann		19	F	Unknown	12JI02Na
BATTOCSEE, Mary		50	F	Unknown	12JI02Na
HURLEY, Hannah		24	F	Unknown	12JI02Na
Eliza		20	F	Unknown	12JI02Na
DESMOND, Ellen		17	F	Unknown	12JI02Na
DAGNANT, James		24	M	Farmer	12JI02Na
MAHON, Timothy		21	M	Laborer	12JI02Na
LARKINS, Ann		20	F	Unknown	12JI02Na
Stephen		15	M	Unknown	12JI02Na
FLANERY, Catherine		30	F	Servant	12JI02Na
DONNELLY, Pat		7	M	Child	12JI02Na
CARROT, Anna		24	F	Unknown	12JI02Na
SWANLEY, Margaret		25	F	Unknown	12JI02Na
REYNOLDS, Ellen		20	F	Unknown	12JI02Na
CALAHAN, Bridget		20	F	Unknown	12JI02Na
MURPHY, Bernard		40	M	Laborer	12JI02Na
Mary		16	F	Unknown	12JI02Na
NAVIN, John		24	M	Laborer	12JI02Na
CONCION, William		28	M	Laborer	12JI02Na
MALLIN, Thomas		25	M	Laborer	12JI02Na
BUTTERLY, John		14	M	Unknown	12JI02Na
Thomas		34	M	Unknown	12JI02Na
Peter		8	M	Child	12JI02Na
Thomas		2	M	Child	12JI02Na
Ann		30	F	Unknown	12JI02Na
Catharine		10	F	Unknown	12JI02Na
DUNN, Mary		25	F	Unknown	12JI02Na
Joseph		5	M	Child	12JI02Na
Eloise		3	F	Child	12JI02Na
Mary		.00	F	Infant	12JI02Na
REYNOLDS, Sarah		19	F	Unknown	12JI02Na
MARTIN, Edward		27	M	Shoemaker	12JI02Na
WEBB, Mary		30	F	Unknown	12JI02Na
Pat		16	M	Unknown	12JI02Na
Thomas		7	M	Child	12JI02Na
FAGAN, Matthew		18	M	Laborer	12JI02Na
Thomas		14	M	Unknown	12JI02Na
Peter		8	M	Child	12JI02Na
RYAN, Edward		18	M	Laborer	12JI02Na
NULTY, Pat		26	M	Laborer	12JI02Na
BLAKE, Matt		25	M	Laborer	12JI02Na
Johanna		23	F	Servant	12JI02Na
FOGARTY, Pat		23	M	Farmer	12JI02Na
MCCARTY, John		27	M	Farmer	12JI02Na
RICE, Mary		30	F	Unknown	12JI02Na

NAMES OF PASSENGERS	AGE	SEX	OCCUPATIONS	DATE PORT SHIP
RENWICK, Catharine	20	F	Unknown	12J102Na
LARKINS, Catharine	20	F	Unknown	12J102Na
WHITE, Caroline	20	F	Servant	12J102Na
SULLIVAN, Jeremiah	32	M	Weaver	12J102Na
Pat	17	M	Shoemaker	12J102Na
CLIFFORD, Pat	25	M	Laborer	12J102Na
RAHLER, Jeremiah	28	M	Laborer	12J102Na
Matcher	22	M	Laborer	12J102Na
Mary	6	F	Child	12J102Na
HOLLERAN, Abbey	27	F	Servant	12J102Na
GORMAN, Mary	15	F	Servant	12J102Na
CONNOLY, Margaret	30	F	Unknown	12J102Na
Bridget	11	F	Unknown	12J102Na
Jane	8	F	Child	12J102Na
Mary	6	F	Child	12J102Na
Thomas	4	M	Child	12J102Na
Margaret	.00	F	Infant	12J102Na
TESKY, Terssa	24	F	Servant	12J102Na
GARNEY, Maria	30	F	Servant	12J102Na
SULLIVAN, Timothy	24	M	Laborer	12J102Na
Ellen	7	F	Child	12J102Na
Andrew	4	M	Child	12J102Na
James	.00	M	Infant	12J102Na
Died-At-Sea				
DALEY, John	50	M	Laborer	12J102Na
JONES, Richard	30	M	Laborer	12J102Na
Margaret	30	F	Unknown	12J102Na
Johanna	9	F	Child	12J102Na
Margaret	7	F	Child	12J102Na
Richard	5	M	Child	12J102Na
SULLIVAN, Johanna	32	F	Unknown	12J102Na
DOWNEY, Phillip	40	M	Laborer	12J102Na
Catharine	30	F	Unknown	12J102Na
John	.00	M	Infant	12J102Na
MELEY, Bernard	24	M	Laborer	12J102Na
MAHON, Nicholas	19	M	Laborer	12J102Na
MURPHY, Catharine	20	F	Unknown	12J102Na
FAGAN, Margaret	18	F	Unknown	12J102Na
BURKE, Ann	20	F	Unknown	12J102Na
NOWLAN, Andrew	22	M	Laborer	12J102Na
CAFFREY, John	25	M	Laborer	12J102Na
FLAHERTY, Dennis	36	M	Clerk	12J102Na
GEANEY, James	50	M	Laborer	12J102Na
Bridget	40	F	Unknown	12J102Na
John	18	M	Unknown	12J102Na
Mary	16	F	Unknown	12J102Na
Philip	14	M	Unknown	12J102Na
James	12	M	Unknown	12J102Na
Patt	10	M	Unknown	12J102Na
Michael	5	M	Child	12J102Na
Bridget	3	F	Child	12J102Na
GANNON, Eliza	18	F	Servant	12J102Na
Bridget	20	F	Servant	12J102Na
FYRE, John	26	M	Laborer	12J102Na
DOLLARD, Catharine	25	F	Servant	12J102Na
GLENGARRET, Bridget	16	F	Servant	12J102Na
COFFEE, Sarah	18	F	Servant	12J102Na
CORRIGAN, Catharine	20	F	Servant	12J102Na
GEANEY, John	35	M	Servant	12J102Na
FYRE, Con.	35	M	Servant	12J102Na
GILLAN, Patrick	25	M	Laborer	12J102Na
WEST, Thomas	25	M	Laborer	12J102Na
ROACH, James	24	M	Laborer	12J102Na
PERSALL, Anna	23	F	Unknown	12J102Na
STERLING, James	23	M	Engineer	12J102Na
Ann	23	F	Unknown	12J102Na
John	.00	M	Infant	12J102Na
Bridget	55	F	Unknown	12J102Na
MCCANNA, Bridget	10	F	Unknown	12J102Na
KELLY, Bridget	13	F	Unknown	12J102Na
GREENE, Michael	26	M	Laborer	12J102Na
GANNON, Margaret	19	F	Unknown	12J102Na
WEIR, William	24	M	Unknown	12J102Na
HULBERT, Michael	56	M	Currier	12J102Na
MCMAHON, Margaret	24	F	Servant	12J102Na

NAMES OF PASSENGERS	AGE	SEX	OCCUPATIONS	DATE PORT SHIP
DUANE, Michael	40	M	Laborer	12J102Na
KEIRNEY, Bridget	14	F	Unknown	12J102Na
AGAN, John	30	M	Laborer	12J102Na
HOLLERIN, Michael	35	M	Laborer	12J102Na
MCNAMARA, John	45	M	Laborer	12J102Na
RONAN, Patt	30	M	Laborer	12J102Na
MAHON, Denis	40	M	Laborer	12J102Na
MCCORMICK, Margaret	41	F	Unknown	12J102Na
Hellen	8	F	Child	12J102Na
Bridget	10	F	Unknown	12J102Na
James	6	M	Child	12J102Na
Dominick	5	M	Child	12J102Na
Morris	3	M	Child	12J102Na
HOCKTON, Samuel	28	M	Farmer	12J102Na
CURRY, Thomas	24	M	Farmer	12J102Na
MURPHY, Teddy	25	M	Laborer	12J102Na
BORAN, James	24	M	Laborer	12J102Na
HURLEY, Patt	25	M	Laborer	12J102Na
MCMAHON, Pat	18	M	Laborer	12J102Na
Mike	10	M	Unknown	12J102Na
CONLIN, Thomas	14	M	Unknown	12J102Na
MCNAMARA, Mary	20	F	Unknown	12J102Na
Sarah	18	F	Unknown	12J102Na
Margaret	16	F	Unknown	12J102Na
HEADERMAN, Patt	20	M	Laborer	12J102Na
MURPHY, Danl.	21	M	Laborer	12J102Na
Pat	18	M	Laborer	12J102Na
Catharine	16	F	Servant	12J102Na
KALING, Ann	17	F	Servant	12J102Na
BRENDELL, John	24	M	Laborer	12J102Na
NAUGHTON, John	30	M	Laborer	12J102Na
Judy	30	F	Unknown	12J102Na
Michael	3	M	Child	12J102Na
Thomas	.00	M	Infant	12J102Na
COLBERT, Judy	45	F	Unknown	12J102Na
WISEMAN, Edward	22	M	Laborer	12J102Na
Mary	15	F	Unknown	12J102Na
MINAHAN, Thomas	32	M	Laborer	12J102Na
Michael	4	M	Child	12J102Na
Johanna	20	F	Unknown	12J102Na
SULLIVAN, Margaret	25	F	Servant	12J102Na
PATRULLO, Mary	16	F	Servant	12J102Na
KATING, Johanna	30	F	Servant	12J102Na
Catharine	3	F	Child	12J102Na
George	.00	M	Infant	12J102Na
COUGHLIN, Ellen	18	F	Unknown	12J102Na
MCOLIFF, Mary	38	F	Unknown	12J102Na
BRYAN, Lawrence	28	M	Laborer	12J102Na
BRODERICK, Thomas	28	M	Laborer	12J102Na
BORAN, Pat	30	M	Laborer	12J102Na
Mary	28	F	Unknown	12J102Na
Patt	.00	M	Infant	12J102Na
HICKEY, Lawrence	23	M	Unknown	12J102Na
Simeon	20	M	Laborer	12J102Na
Catharine	16	F	Unknown	12J102Na
John	19	M	Clerk	12J102Na
GRIFFIN, Daniel	20	M	Laborer	12J102Na
CONNER, Honora	25	F	Unknown	12J102Na
TYNE, Margaret	20	F	Servant	12J102Na
MURPHY, Johanna	20	F	Servant	12J102Na
HEARY, Charles	45	M	Printer	12J102Na
FALLAN, Michael	35	M	Shoemaker	12J102Na
GRADY, Pat	24	M	Laborer	12J102Na
Mike	22	M	Laborer	12J102Na
TIME, John	34	M	Laborer	12J102Na
DALEY, Honora	26	F	Servant	12J102Na
MCCARTY, Mary	26	F	Servant	12J102Na
KEOGH, Martin	21	M	Carpenter	12J102Na
LYNCH, Mary	14	F	Unknown	12J102Na
Martin	12	M	Unknown	12J102Na
GREERY, Jeremiah	40	M	Laborer	12J102Na
CHERRY, Pat	35	M	Laborer	12J102Na
KEGAN, Lawrence	38	M	Laborer	12J102Na
Judith	30	F	Unknown	12J102Na
Bridget	13	F	Unknown	12J102Na

NAMES OF PASSENGERS	AGE	SEX	OCCUPATIONS	DATE PORT SHIP
KEGAN, Mary-Ann	11	F	Unknown	12J102Na
Rosa	9	F	Child	12J102Na
Mike	5	M	Child	12J102Na
Judy	3	F	Child	12J102Na
Ellen	.00	F	Infant	12J102Na
Bridget	17	F	Unknown	12J102Na
WELSH, John	18	M	Laborer	12J102Na
MILLARD, Mike	21	M	Laborer	12J102Na
Bridget	24	F	Servant	12J102Na
QUILL, John	24	M	Laborer	12J102Na
BRADY, John	18	M	Laborer	12J102Na
GIRTY, James	22	M	Laborer	12J102Na
COOK, Patt	24	M	Laborer	12J102Na
GREENE, John	24	M	Miller	12J102Na
ANDERSON, Robert	45	M	Servant	12J102Na
CONNOLY, John	25	M	Laborer	12J102Na
Judy	20	F	Unknown	12J102Na
HASTINGS, James	24	M	Laborer	12J102Na
Ellen	26	F	Milliner	12J102Na
Jane	3	F	Child	12J102Na
Mary-Ann	.00	F	Infant	12J102Na
CASEY, Mary	45	F	Unknown	12J102Na
GILLAN, John	45	M	Servant	12J102Na
BRAHAN, Mary	13	F	Servant	12J102Na
BROWN, Joseph	18	M	Laborer	12J102Na
Sarah	36	F	Unknown	12J102Na
BURNS, John	30	M	Carpenter	12J102Na
Julia	12	F	Unknown	12J102Na
BUTTERLY, John	50	M	Laborer	12J102Na
John-Jr.	28	M	Unknown	12J102Na
Mary	27	F	Unknown	12J102Na
Mary-Ann	2	F	Child	12J102Na
HARTFORD, Margaret	20	F	Servant	12J102Na
GILLAN, Bridget	36	F	Unknown	12J102Na
BURNS, Edward	12	M	Unknown	12J102Na
KILARNEY, Ann	19	F	Unknown	12J102Na
Lawrence	22	M	Laborer	12J102Na
BARNARD, Sally	20	F	Unknown	12J102Na
STEWART, Margaret-J.	20	F	Unknown	12J102Na
CLARK, Mary-Ann	19	F	Servant	12J102Na
CASSADY, Ann	22	F	Servant	12J102Na
CASSIDY, Peter	14	M	Unknown	12J102Na
CAMPBELL, Dennis	38	M	Laborer	12J102Na
MCGRAGH, Philip	26	M	Laborer	12J102Na
Catharine	22	F	Unknown	12J102Na
Thomas	.00	M	Infant	12J102Na
Judy	21	F	Unknown	12J102Na
MURPHY, John	16	M	Laborer	12J102Na
CROWLEY, Peggy	38	F	Servant	12J102Na
CARTER, Peggy	38	F	Servant	12J102Na
MURPHY, Margaret	14	F	Servant	12J102Na
GOFF, Thomas	50	M	Laborer	12J102Na
MCCABE, Mary	14	F	Unknown	12J102Na
MURPHY, David	25	M	Laborer	12J102Na
DOYLE, Eliza	17	F	Unknown	12J102Na
BARRETT, Ellen	24	F	Unknown	12J102Na
BUTLER, Mary	40	F	Unknown	12J102Na
BARRETT, Thomas	23	M	Tailor	12J102Na
MURPHY, Mike	25	M	Butcher	12J102Na
MCDONOUGH, Mary	35	F	Unknown	12J102Na
John	11	M	None	12J102Na
Catharine	11	F	None	12J102Na
Ann	10	F	None	12J102Na
Thomas	6	M	Child	12J102Na
Pat	4	M	Child	12J102Na
WILLIAMS, John	22	M	Laborer	12J102Na
DUNN, Mary	35	F	Unknown	12J102Na
MURPHY, Ann	40	F	Unknown	12J102Na
BRIDGE, Bridget	45	F	Unknown	12J102Na
MURRAY, David	36	M	Laborer	12J102Na
REIDY, James	21	M	Laborer	12J102Na
CAMPBELL, James	38	M	Printer	12J102Na
CANEAR, Joshua	26	M	Printer	12J102Na
REDFIELD, Isabella	16	F	Unknown	12J102Na
FURLEY, Catharine	17	F	Unknown	12J102Na

NAMES OF PASSENGERS	AGE	SEX	OCCUPATIONS	DATE PORT SHIP
BERRY, John	40	M	Shoemaker	12J102Na
Mary-Ann	42	F	Unknown	12J102Na
Nathaniel	18	M	Unknown	12J102Na
Harriet	16	F	Unknown	12J102Na
HOWE, Thomas	20	M	Servant	12J102Na
GIRON, Armiger	26	M	Servant	12J102Na
DALEY, Barnard	49	M	Rope Maker	12J102Na
Catharine	50	F	Unknown	12J102Na
Thomas	19	M	Weaver	12J102Na
NOWLAN, Lawrence	40	M	Cordwainer	12J102Na
Margaret	28	F	Unknown	12J102Na
William	10	M	None	12J102Na
Jane	8	F	Child	12J102Na
Mary	6	F	Child	12J102Na
Eliza	4	F	Child	12J102Na
John	.00	M	Infant	12J102Na
LUCY, Eliza	50	F	Unknown	12J102Na
CURRIER, Ann	20	F	Unknown	12J102Na
MCCOY, George	40	M	Engineer	12J102Na
GEARY, Wm.S.	23	M	Engraver	12J102Na

GREAT-BRITAIN 12 JULY 1849

From Limerick

NAMES OF PASSENGERS	AGE	SEX	OCCUPATIONS	DATE PORT SHIP
HALPIN, Biddy	21	F	Laborer	12J135Ar
MACKE, Michl.	19	M	Laborer	12J135Ar
CALLIHAN, Jeremiah	20	M	Laborer	12J135Ar
Michl.	17	M	Laborer	12J135Ar
HARTY, Ann	22	F	Laborer	12J135Ar
Margt.	20	F	Laborer	12J135Ar
MCNAMARA, Michl.	25	M	Laborer	12J135Ar
Johanna	26	F	Laborer	12J135Ar
Hanah	24	F	Laborer	12J135Ar
BLAKE, Margt.	24	F	Laborer	12J135Ar
NICHOLAS, Michl.	24	M	Laborer	12J135Ar
CASEY, Mary	25	F	Laborer	12J135Ar
THURMOND, Matt	20	M	Laborer	12J135Ar
BYRNES, Edmund	50	M	Laborer	12J135Ar
Mary	40	F	Laborer	12J135Ar
Michl.	25	M	Laborer	12J135Ar
Edmund	20	M	Laborer	12J135Ar
John	18	M	Laborer	12J135Ar
Johana	18	M	Laborer	12J135Ar
MADDON, Cath.	20	F	Laborer	12J135Ar
QUINN, Mary	25	F	Laborer	12J135Ar
MOLONEY, Ellen	20	F	Laborer	12J135Ar
PUNCH, Richd.	24	M	Laborer	12J135Ar
CORBETT, Martin	18	M	Laborer	12J135Ar
OCONNELL, Daniel	20	M	Laborer	12J135Ar
CONNORS, Winifred	32	M	Laborer	12J135Ar
CASSACK, Martin	15	M	Laborer	12J135Ar
Hannah	17	F	Laborer	12J135Ar
FITZGERALD, James	19	M	Laborer	12J135Ar
MCGUIRE, Mary	18	F	Laborer	12J135Ar
RYAN, Margt.	17	F	Laborer	12J135Ar
Mary	17	F	Laborer	12J135Ar
DOOLEY, Martin	23	M	Laborer	12J135Ar
Honor	20	F	Laborer	12J135Ar
LYONS, Ellen	24	F	Laborer	12J135Ar
MALCULLY, Patt	20	M	Laborer	12J135Ar
BROWNE, Honor	26	F	Laborer	12J135Ar
Ann	20	F	Laborer	12J135Ar
MOORE, Garett	26	M	Laborer	12J135Ar
CONDON, Patt	20	M	Laborer	12J135Ar
John	35	M	Laborer	12J135Ar
Hanah	27	F	Laborer	12J135Ar
Wo., Cath.	2	F	Child	12J135Ar
Mary	.00	F	Infant	12J135Ar

NAMES OF PASSENGERS	AGE	SEX	OCCUPATIONS	DATE PORT SHIP
BENSON, John	30	M	Laborer	12J135Ar
Cath.	30	F	Laborer	12J135Ar
Cath.	2	F	Child	12J135Ar
William	.00	M	Infant	12J135Ar
DILLANE, Mary	30	F	Laborer	12J135Ar
LANLEY, Margt.	30	F	Laborer	12J135Ar
ARMBUSS, John	38	M	Laborer	12J135Ar
Margt.	18	F	Laborer	12J135Ar
James	18	M	Laborer	12J135Ar
M--ULL, Joseph	24	M	Laborer	12J135Ar
RALLAMAN, M.	50	U	Laborer	12J135Ar
John	26	M	Laborer	12J135Ar
WALSH, Mary	40	F	Laborer	12J135Ar
RYAN, Edmund	26	M	Laborer	12J135Ar
BARRY, Rich.	35	M	Laborer	12J135Ar
WALSH, Ellen	40	F	Laborer	12J135Ar
Mary	16	F	Laborer	12J135Ar
Maggy	14	F	Laborer	12J135Ar
Patt	13	M	Laborer	12J135Ar
Biddy	40	F	Laborer	12J135Ar
CONDON, Edmund	26	M	Laborer	12J135Ar
OBRIEN, Jno.	21	M	Laborer	12J135Ar
Wm.	17	M	Laborer	12J135Ar
CALLINAN, Mary	26	F	Laborer	12J135Ar
LAWLER, James	26	M	Laborer	12J135Ar
MCMAHON, James	23	M	Laborer	12J135Ar
Elizath.	19	F	Laborer	12J135Ar
VAUGHAN, Cath.	25	F	Laborer	12J135Ar
CORBETT, John	30	M	Laborer	12J135Ar
DONOGHER, Ellen	29	F	Laborer	12J135Ar
JOYCE, Kitty	25	F	Laborer	12J135Ar
Patt	3	M	Child	12J135Ar
HILL, Patt	28	M	Laborer	12J135Ar
MCNAMARA, Patt	31	M	Laborer	12J135Ar
Michl.	19	M	Laborer	12J135Ar
LALLY, Bridget	18	F	Laborer	12J135Ar
BUTLER, John	19	M	Laborer	12J135Ar
FLANNERY, Michl.	14	M	Laborer	12J135Ar
MEEHAN, Dennis	22	M	Laborer	12J135Ar
LYDON, John	20	M	Laborer	12J135Ar
Bridgt.	17	F	Laborer	12J135Ar
Ellen	14	F	Laborer	12J135Ar
Patt	5	M	Child	12J135Ar
RENN, Honor	16	F	Laborer	12J135Ar
HINDSO, Dennis	21	M	Laborer	12J135Ar
DONOGHUE, Frank	21	M	Laborer	12J135Ar
HENLY, Biddy	20	F	Laborer	12J135Ar
Ann	18	F	Laborer	12J135Ar
GOMAN, Nelly	19	F	Laborer	12J135Ar
HOGAN, John	32	M	Laborer	12J135Ar
DONOGHOE, Eliza	20	F	Laborer	12J135Ar
GLEESON, Michl.	18	M	Laborer	12J135Ar
CONSIDINE, Ann	21	F	Laborer	12J135Ar
BURKE, Patt	30	M	Laborer	12J135Ar
John	3	M	Child	12J135Ar
DENNIS, Joseph	36	M	Laborer	12J135Ar
BREED, Patt	22	M	Laborer	12J135Ar
Cornelius	19	M	Laborer	12J135Ar
Bedilia	17	F	Laborer	12J135Ar
COFFEE, Michl.	27	M	Laborer	12J135Ar
OWENS, Thady	23	M	Laborer	12J135Ar
Ellen	21	F	Laborer	12J135Ar
GONNUN, W.	19	U	Laborer	12J135Ar
Mary	18	F	Laborer	12J135Ar
DENANE, Rich.	18	M	Laborer	12J135Ar
COCHLAN, Owen	27	M	Laborer	12J135Ar
John	20	M	Laborer	12J135Ar
HANTNEY, Mary	18	F	Laborer	12J135Ar
MCMAHON, Ellen	5	F	Child	12J135Ar
SIMONS, Mary	20	F	Laborer	12J135Ar
KEANE, Thos.	34	M	Laborer	12J135Ar
Dennis	25	M	Laborer	12J135Ar
Honora	22	F	Laborer	12J135Ar
Cath.	18	F	Laborer	12J135Ar
PURCELL, Ellen	24	F	Laborer	12J135Ar
BARNEY, Thomas	50	M	Unknown	12J135Ar
Margt.	50	F	Unknown	12J135Ar
Julia	25	F	Unknown	12J135Ar
Mary-Ann	20	F	Unknown	12J135Ar
Bridgt.	15	F	Unknown	12J135Ar
Margt.	14	F	Unknown	12J135Ar
Cath.	17	F	Unknown	12J135Ar
Garrett	11	M	Unknown	12J135Ar
Johanna	6	F	Child	12J135Ar
Terresa	2	F	Child	12J135Ar
Ellen	26	F	Unknown	12J135Ar

TADMOR 16 JULY 1849

From Greenock

NAMES OF PASSENGERS	AGE	SEX	OCCUPATIONS	DATE PORT SHIP
DRUMMOND, George	60	M	Farmer	16J133Kj
U-Mrs.	60	F	Farmer	16J133Kj
Reuben	26	M	Farmer	16J133Kj
Margaret	23	F	None	16J133Kj
Jean	14	F	None	16J133Kj
MILLER, John	28	M	Servant	16J133Kj
U-Mrs.	28	F	None	16J133Kj
Margaret	5	F	Child	16J133Kj
John	3	M	Child	16J133Kj
GALLACHER, George	18	M	Laborer	16J133Kj
MOWBERRY, Thomas	49	M	Laborer	16J133Kj
U-Mrs.	45	F	None	16J133Kj
Alice	22	F	None	16J133Kj
Thomas	20	M	Farmer	16J133Kj
John	17	M	Farmer	16J133Kj
Robert	15	M	Farmer	16J133Kj
Margaret	12	F	None	16J133Kj
Mary	7	F	Child	16J133Kj
James	4	M	Child	16J133Kj
WATSON, Bertram	25	M	Mason	16J133Kj
U-Mrs.	25	F	None	16J133Kj
BISHOP, Archibald	20	M	Farmer	16J133Kj
WILSON, Wm.	35	M	Farmer	16J133Kj
U-Mrs.	40	F	None	16J133Kj
James	3	M	Child	16J133Kj
Thomas	13	M	Farmer	16J133Kj
David	21	M	Printer	16J133Kj
WALLACE, Robert	22	M	Printer	16J133Kj
THORN, John	26	M	Weaver	16J133Kj
U-Mrs.	22	F	None	16J133Kj
Elizabeth	3	F	Child	16J133Kj
HILLIEND, Robert	26	M	Hammer Man	16J133Kj
MCGILL, Margaret	34	F	None	16J133Kj
James	9	M	Child	16J133Kj
Agnes	3	F	Child	16J133Kj
William	.00	M	Infant	16J133Kj
FALLS, Barbara	50	F	None	16J133Kj
RULE, Henry	20	U	None	16J133Kj
BLAIN, George	39	M	Merchant	16J133Kj
Helen	27	F	None	16J133Kj
Christina	9	F	None	16J133Kj
James	7	M	Child	16J133Kj
Margaret	4	F	Child	16J133Kj
PETLIN, Robert	35	M	Unknown	16J133Kj
U-Mrs.	30	F	None	16J133Kj
Margaret	9	F	Child	16J133Kj
Elizabeth	5	F	Child	16J133Kj
HENDERSON, Duncan	28	M	Miller	16J133Kj
U-Mrs.	28	F	None	16J133Kj
Cahterine	45	F	None	16J133Kj
BECHIN, Robert	27	M	Farmer	16J133Kj
U-Mrs.	27	F	None	16J133Kj
Mary	.00	F	Infant	16J133Kj

NAMES OF PASSENGERS	AGE	SEX	OCCUPATIONS	DATE PORT SHIP
OLIVER, William	24	F	Farmer	16J133Kj
U-Mrs.	26	F	None	16J133Kj
FORMAN, James	27	M	Farmer	16J133Kj
U-Mrs.	21	F	None	16J133Kj
BOWNDING, James	31	M	Farmer	16J133Kj
U-Mrs.	38	F	None	16J133Kj
May	10	F	Child	16J133Kj
Helen	.00	F	Infant	16J133Kj
FERGUSON, U-Mrs.	28	F	None	16J133Kj
RENWICK, Francis	27	M	Saddler	16J133Kj
JAMISON, Isabella	24	F	None	16J133Kj
COOPER, John	23	M	Baker	16J133Kj
HUNTER, Mason	27	M	Farmer	16J133Kj
COGHILL, Francis	24	M	Farmer	16J133Kj
TAYLOR, Alen	46	M	Farmer	16J133Kj
U-Mrs.	29	F	None	16J133Kj
Mary	11	F	None	16J133Kj
Marion	9	M	Child	16J133Kj
Agnes	7	F	Child	16J133Kj
Grace	5	F	Child	16J133Kj
James	3	M	Child	16J133Kj
GRAHAM, Charles	28	M	Farmer	16J133Kj
SMITH, John	23	M	Mechanic	16J133Kj
MURPHY, James	25	M	Mechanic	16J133Kj
SMITH, John	20	M	Mechanic	16J133Kj
HINT, Peter	22	M	Mechanic	16J133Kj
TURNER, Alen	.00	M	Infant	16J133Kj
GLENDINNER, David	22	M	Laborer	16J133Kj
DAVIDSON, Agnes	22	F	None	16J133Kj
WILLIAMSON, Henry	38	M	Laborer	16J133Kj
BEN, Walter	24	M	Laborer	16J133Kj
MCKAY, Arthur	26	M	Laborer	16J133Kj
DUNLOP, Andrew	21	M	Laborer	16J133Kj
SMITH, Berand	30	M	Laborer	16J133Kj
SCOTT, James	32	M	Laborer	16J133Kj
U-Mrs.	31	F	None	16J133Kj
James	13	M	None	16J133Kj
George	10	M	Child	16J133Kj
Mary	2	F	Child	16J133Kj
JOHNSTON, Henry	20	M	Laborer	16J133Kj
HIGGINS, Cameron	30	M	Laborer	16J133Kj
BROWN, Hinton	40	M	Laborer	16J133Kj
THOMSON, A.	29	M	Laborer	16J133Kj
Ann	27	F	None	16J133Kj
Helen	1	F	Child	16J133Kj
LYNCH, James	35	M	Laborer	16J133Kj
Margaret	27	F	None	16J133Kj
DUNFRES, Burdet	20	M	Laborer	16J133Kj
EARLON, Betsey	23	F	None	16J133Kj
BUNTON, John	23	M	Laborer	16J133Kj
WILLIS, Robt.	26	M	Laborer	16J133Kj
MCLACHLAN, Hugh	45	M	Laborer	16J133Kj
U-Mrs.	35	F	None	16J133Kj
Hugh	9	M	Child	16J133Kj
Frances	7	F	Child	16J133Kj
Ann-Jane	6	F	Child	16J133Kj
Thomas	5	M	Child	16J133Kj
Margaret	2	F	Child	16J133Kj
WELSH, Ann	22	F	None	16J133Kj
NEELY, Martha	24	F	None	16J133Kj
HOWARD, George	30	M	Laborer	16J133Kj
GREY, Andrew	27	M	Laborer	16J133Kj
Mary	26	F	None	16J133Kj
Alexander	.00	M	Infant	16J133Kj
MCGRUGH, Thomas	22	M	Laborer	16J133Kj
BROOK, Thomas	31	M	Mason	16J133Kj
CRAIG, John	50	M	Farmer	16J133Kj
U-Mrs.	45	F	None	16J133Kj
DALREET, John	25	M	Farmer	16J133Kj
Agnes	14	F	None	16J133Kj
DALNIE, Jas.	21	M	Farmer	16J133Kj
Wm.	19	M	Farmer	16J133Kj
Janet	10	F	Child	16J133Kj
[illegible]OOINN, Francis	40	M	Farmer	16J133Kj
HAMILTON, Geo.	31	M	Farmer	16J133Kj
MCEWIN, Jas.	33	M	Farmer	16J133Kj
CARRICAN, Ann	20	F	None	16J133Kj
MCGOUGH, Bridg.	16	F	None	16J133Kj
DOOLE, D.	35	M	Farmer	16J133Kj
MCGUIN, C.	30	M	Farmer	16J133Kj
LYNCH, Thos.	29	M	Farmer	16J133Kj
U-Mrs.	22	F	None	16J133Kj
Jas.	.11	M	Infant	16J133Kj
DOHERTY, Jno.	26	M	Laborer	16J133Kj
LAVALL, Peter	21	M	Laborer	16J133Kj
LAWSON, Wm.	30	M	Laborer	16J133Kj
BROWN, Jno.	29	M	Laborer	16J133Kj
MARAT, Jno.	28	M	Laborer	16J133Kj
CAMERON, Alan	24	M	Laborer	16J133Kj
U-Mrs.	21	F	None	16J133Kj
MARTIN, Jno.	18	M	Laborer	16J133Kj
FARQUAHAR, F.L.	23	M	Laborer	16J133Kj
KIFF, Jno.	19	M	Laborer	16J133Kj
AMCIN, H.	25	M	Laborer	16J133Kj
LESLIE, Jas.	28	M	Laborer	16J133Kj
Ann	23	F	None	16J133Kj
DONALD, Jas.	33	M	Laborer	16J133Kj
DULTHINE, Eliz.	23	F	None	16J133Kj
DOW, El.	30	M	Laborer	16J133Kj
DONALD, Cath.	5	F	Child	16J133Kj
KEPRIN, Wm.	42	M	Laborer	16J133Kj
U-Mrs.	43	F	None	16J133Kj
David	17	M	Laborer	16J133Kj
Robt.	13	M	Laborer	16J133Kj
Janet	12	F	None	16J133Kj
MAIN, Robt.	50	M	Laborer	16J133Kj
Helen	12	F	None	16J133Kj
David	10	M	Child	16J133Kj
Janet	8	F	Child	16J133Kj
Jno.	20	M	Laborer	16J133Kj
Ann	19	F	None	16J133Kj
TAYLOR, Geo.	45	M	Mechanic	16J133Kj
And.	18	M	None	16J133Kj
POWER, R.	23	M	None	16J133Kj
WALSINGHAM, A.	25	M	None	16J133Kj
KING, Jas.	25	M	None	16J133Kj
WILSON, Jno.	25	M	None	16J133Kj
CURRIN, Jno.	35	M	None	16J133Kj
U-Mrs.	35	F	None	16J133Kj
Cath.	13	F	None	16J133Kj
Margt.	9	F	Child	16J133Kj
ADAMS, Janet	30	F	None	16J133Kj
PIERCE, Alex.	30	M	Mechanic	16J133Kj
ROBINSON, Jas.	29	M	Mechanic	16J133Kj
ROMAGNE, Wm.	25	M	Farmer	16J133Kj
SMITH, Jno.	50	M	Farmer	16J133Kj
SHANLE, Colin	49	M	Farmer	16J133Kj
Jno.	18	M	Farmer	16J133Kj
TALLOCK, Jas.	28	M	Farmer	16J133Kj
Ross	23	M	Farmer	16J133Kj
Agnes	24	F	None	16J133Kj
Janet	29	F	None	16J133Kj
Wm.	9	M	Child	16J133Kj
Wm.	.09	M	Infant	16J133Kj
DICKIE, U	55	M	Laborer	16J133Kj
HOLLAND, U	30	M	Laborer	16J133Kj
U-Mrs.	30	M	Laborer	16J133Kj
Maria	9	F	Child	16J133Kj
Anne	5	F	Child	16J133Kj
Margt.	.06	F	Infant	16J133Kj
YOUNG, Jas.	22	M	Laborer	16J133Kj
BARREL, Ann	23	F	None	16J133Kj
Wm.	3	M	Child	16J133Kj
Fanny	.06	F	Infant	16J133Kj
MCMULLIN, Alen	22	M	Laborer	16J133Kj
U-Mrs.	18	F	None	16J133Kj
HATTIN, U	32	M	Laborer	16J133Kj
U-Mrs.	28	F	None	16J133Kj
Wm.	3	M	Child	16J133Kj
May-A.	1	F	Child	16J133Kj

NAMES OF PASSENGERS		AGE	SEX	OCCUPATIONS	DATE PORT SHIP
HATTIN, Jas.		2	M	Child	16J133Kj
THOMPSON, Jno.		27	M	Laborer	16J133Kj
GRAY, Jas.		20	M	Mechanic	16J133Kj
STEVENS, Jas.		24	M	Mechanic	16J133Kj
U-Mrs.		26	F	None	16J133Kj
SMITH, Wm.		31	M	Mechanic	16J133Kj
CAMPBELL, Jas.		20	M	Mechanic	16J133Kj
HARDEE, Thos.		22	M	Mechanic	16J133Kj
U-Mrs.		22	F	None	16J133Kj
GIBB, Francis		30	M	Mechanic	16J133Kj
U-Mrs.		29	F	None	16J133Kj
Wm.		9	M	Child	16J133Kj
DORAN, Rose		20	F	None	16J133Kj
MARCHE, Jno.		20	M	Laborer	16J133Kj
MURPHY, Hugh		32	M	Laborer	16J133Kj
Francis		25	F	None	16J133Kj
CAMPBELL, Jas.		29	M	Laborer	16J133Kj
MCFARLAN, Hugh		40	M	Laborer	16J133Kj
LUNDIE, Alex.		33	M	Laborer	16J133Kj
BROWN, Danl.		19	M	Laborer	16J133Kj
HAGEN, Ann		25	F	None	16J133Kj
DONNELLY, Cath.		25	F	None	16J133Kj
QUINN, Jas.		29	M	Laborer	16J133Kj
Isabella		20	F	None	16J133Kj
KELLY, Ann		16	F	None	16J133Kj
DOBSIN, Wm.		35	M	Laborer	16J133Kj
Robt.		24	M	Laborer	16J133Kj
SHELLINGTON, Ann		26	F	None	16J133Kj
MCLENNON, Eliz.		21	F	None	16J133Kj
GIBSON, Geo.		50	M	Mechanic	16J133Kj

LIVERPOOL 17 JULY 1849

From Liverpool

NAMES OF PASSENGERS		AGE	SEX	OCCUPATIONS	DATE PORT SHIP
COWER, Ann-Miss		45	F	Lady	17JI02Nd
Mary-Ann-Miss		23	F	Lady	17JI02Nd
WRIGHT, George		5	M	Child	17JI02Nd
Joseph-E.		1	M	Child	17JI02Nd
PATTERSON, Mary		16	F	Servant	17JI02Nd
TEED, U-Mrs.		48	F	Lady	17JI02Nd
John-Mrs.		35	F	Lady	17JI02Nd
MORRISS, John		39	M	Gentleman	17JI02Nd
COLLEY, John		23	M	Gentleman	17JI02Nd
MCCARGILL, Benj.		27	M	Mdsp	17JI02Nd
CONNER, Owen		30	M	Laborer	17JI02Nd
ROURKE, Cathe.		20	F	Servant	17JI02Nd
DONNELLY, John		29	M	Baker	17JI02Nd
MCCOWEN, John-J.		26	M	Sailor	17JI02Nd
Mary		50	F	Dressmaker	17JI02Nd
Rachael		28	F	Dressmaker	17JI02Nd
Mary		20	F	Dressmaker	17JI02Nd
THOMPSON, John		26	M	Paper Maker	17JI02Nd
HARPER, Jas.		23	M	Paper Maker	17JI02Nd
Ellen	(W)	20	F	None	17JI02Nd
Ellen		.03	F	Infant	17JI02Nd
DOOLAN, John		20	M	Farmer	17JI02Nd
Mary	(W)	21	F	None	17JI02Nd
LYONS, Pat		21	M	Laborer	17JI02Nd
KINSELLER, Pat		40	M	Laborer	17JI02Nd
WALSH, Denis		21	M	Laborer	17JI02Nd
ROONEY, Mary		18	F	Servant	17JI02Nd
DOUNEY, Mary		20	F	Servant	17JI02Nd
RAMSEY, Thos.		12	M	Servant	17JI02Nd
John		23	M	Servant	17JI02Nd
DONNELL, Phil		25	M	Laborer	17JI02Nd
FURY, Jane		22	F	Laborer	17JI02Nd
MULLIGAN, Hugh		22	M	Laborer	17JI02Nd
MOORE, Hugh		50	M	Laborer	17JI02Nd
WATTAN, Wm.		18	M	Laborer	17JI02Nd
DUNLOP, Robert		20	M	Laborer	17JI02Nd
STERN, Wm.		16	M	Laborer	17JI02Nd
MCCANN, Jas.		22	M	Nailer	17JI02Nd
RODGERS, Thos.		20	M	Laborer	17JI02Nd
KEEFE, Jere.		25	M	Laborer	17JI02Nd
Ann		20	F	Dressmaker	17JI02Nd
COLLIGAN, John		18	M	Laborer	17JI02Nd
TOWSON, Fras.		60	M	Laborer	17JI02Nd
Martha		25	F	Laborer	17JI02Nd
Ben		22	M	Laborer	17JI02Nd
Mary		19	F	Servant	17JI02Nd
Cathe.		16	F	Servant	17JI02Nd
Wm.		14	M	Servant	17JI02Nd
Hannah		10	F	Servant	17JI02Nd
Mary		.03	F	Infant	17JI02Nd
MILLER, Richd.		30	M	Farmer	17JI02Nd
MCCORMICK, Thos.		27	M	Laborer	17JI02Nd
MILLS, John		20	M	Laborer	17JI02Nd
CANVAN, George		27	M	Printer	17JI02Nd
Eliza	(W)	18	F	None	17JI02Nd
BECK, Willm.		60	M	Carpenter	17JI02Nd
BYRNE, Cathe.		20	F	Servant	17JI02Nd
CAVANAGH, Owen		35	M	Laborer	17JI02Nd
Sarah	(W)	26	F	None	17JI02Nd
Bridget		3	F	Child	17JI02Nd
FLANNERY, Margt.		20	F	Servant	17JI02Nd
FLYNN, Bernd.		40	M	Laborer	17JI02Nd
Margt.		14	F	Servant	17JI02Nd
Eliza		12	F	Servant	17JI02Nd
John		10	M	Servant	17JI02Nd
Jane		8	F	Child	17JI02Nd
MINNOCK, James		41	M	Laborer	17JI02Nd
Mary	(W)	40	F	None	17JI02Nd
Bernd.		11	M	None	17JI02Nd
Bridget		9	F	Child	17JI02Nd
Willm.		7	M	Child	17JI02Nd
Rose		5	F	Child	17JI02Nd
Martin		3	M	Child	17JI02Nd
Ellen		.05	F	Infant	17JI02Nd
COGHLAN, Ann		25	F	Servant	17JI02Nd
KEARN, Pat		20	M	Shoemaker	17JI02Nd
NERLAND, Michl.		45	M	Laborer	17JI02Nd
Bridget		30	F	Servant	17JI02Nd
Cathe.		.04	F	Infant	17JI02Nd
MCDERMOTT, Thos.		50	M	Laborer	17JI02Nd
DOHERTY, Willm.		28	M	Laborer	17JI02Nd
LOWNDES, John		25	M	Laborer	17JI02Nd
Mary		18	F	Servant	17JI02Nd
Betsey		17	F	Servant	17JI02Nd
Ann		16	F	Servant	17JI02Nd
Margt.		15	F	Servant	17JI02Nd
Mary		10	F	Servant	17JI02Nd
MURTAGH, Daniel		43	M	Laborer	17JI02Nd
LYNAN, Laurence		18	M	Laborer	17JI02Nd
COWAN, Jas.		28	M	Laborer	17JI02Nd
COLLAN, Pat		26	M	Miller	17JI02Nd
CASEY, Henry		24	M	Laborer	17JI02Nd
JORDON, Peter		20	M	Laborer	17JI02Nd
LOWTH, John		19	M	Farmer	17JI02Nd
RYAN, John		32	M	Cnf	17JI02Nd
KALLAHAN, John		24	M	Carpenter	17JI02Nd
Mary		28	F	Servant	17JI02Nd
Sarah		26	F	Servant	17JI02Nd
SUMNERS, Thos.		45	M	Laborer	17JI02Nd
KAVANAGH, Mary		35	F	Servant	17JI02Nd
MCDONNELL, Mary		24	F	Servant	17JI02Nd
MULLOY, John		22	M	Laborer	17JI02Nd
FRAZER, John		29	M	Mason	17JI02Nd
HENRY, James		30	M	Saddler	17JI02Nd
BUZZO, Henry		30	M	Miner	17JI02Nd
HOLMES, Mary		33	F	Milliner	17JI02Nd
EGAN, John		20	M	Clerk	17JI02Nd
MULKEARN, Thos.		20	M	Laborer	17JI02N
BRODERICK, M--Ty		20	M	Laborer	17JI02N

NAMES OF PASSENGERS	AGE	SEX	OCCUPATIONS	DATE PORT SHIP
SHERRY, Ned	20	M	Laborer	17J102Nd
LYONS, Honora	20	F	Laborer	17J102Nd
BROGAN, Honora	20	F	Laborer	17J102Nd
KEATING, Bridgt.	10	F	Servant	17J102Nd
CRYN, Thos.	20	M	Servant	17J102Nd
DELANY, Michl.	22	M	Laborer	17J102Nd
KELLEY, Jas.	25	M	Tailor	17J102Nd
WILKIN, Joseph	22	M	Farmer	17J102Nd
MCCOWAN, John	22	M	Tailor	17J102Nd
ADAMS, Hugh	30	M	Laborer	17J102Nd
Mary (W)	30	F	None	17J102Nd
Mary	5	F	Child	17J102Nd
Ann	2	F	Child	17J102Nd
KELLY, Bridgt.	20	F	Servant	17J102Nd
John	28	M	Laborer	17J102Nd
Mary	14	F	Servant	17J102Nd
L.	11	U	Servant	17J102Nd
Cathe.	9	F	Child	17J102Nd
ROBINSON, Ellen	22	F	Servant	17J102Nd
ROURKE, Margt.	18	F	Servant	17J102Nd
MCCOVEY, Thos.	20	M	Laborer	17J102Nd
BLACK, Hugh	25	M	Laborer	17J102Nd
GREER, Susannah	18	F	Servant	17J102Nd
FOX, Sarah	19	F	Servant	17J102Nd
HENRY, Jane	20	F	Servant	17J102Nd
MCCUTCHEN, Rebecca	19	F	Servant	17J102Nd
GILMOR, Mary-A.	19	F	Servant	17J102Nd
DONOHUE, Ally	18	F	Servant	17J102Nd
CONNER, Ann	30	F	Wife	17J102Nd
John	11	M	None	17J102Nd
Cathe.	8	F	Child	17J102Nd
Stephen	3	F	Child	17J102Nd
KILDOYLE, Pat	28	M	Laborer	17J102Nd
Jas.	6	M	Child	17J102Nd
LAWLESS, Margt.	23	F	Servant	17J102Nd
COYLE, Jas.	32	M	Laborer	17J102Nd
CARRIHAN, Ellen	18	F	Servant	17J102Nd
BURKE, John	40	M	Laborer	17J102Nd
Ellen (W)	30	F	None	17J102Nd
DEVINE, John	13	M	Laborer	17J102Nd
CLOGHER, Bridget	25	F	Servant	17J102Nd
LOVETT, Frank	18	M	Servant	17J102Nd
KILDUFF, Ann	20	F	Servant	17J102Nd
MALLOY, Margt.	15	F	Servant	17J102Nd
EGAN, Pat	26	M	Laborer	17J102Nd
Mary (W)	26	F	None	17J102Nd
HENRY, Mary	52	F	Wife	17J102Nd
Willm.	16	M	None	17J102Nd
Mat	13	M	None	17J102Nd
James	10	M	None	17J102Nd
Peggy	8	F	Child	17J102Nd
Alexander	9	M	Child	17J102Nd
FORGERY, Isabella	55	F	Servant	17J102Nd
BARRETT, Margt.	50	F	Wife	17J102Nd
Bridget	23	F	Servant	17J102Nd
BYRNE, Sally	20	F	Servant	17J102Nd
KENNEDY, Pat	46	M	Laborer	17J102Nd
BYRNES, Jane	36	F	Servant	17J102Nd
PENNELL, Esther	26	F	Servant	17J102Nd
John	24	F	Servant	17J102Nd
FENESEY, Michl.	18	M	Carpenter	17J102Nd
DONOHUE, Mary	20	F	Dressmaker	17J102Nd
NORCOTT, John	23	M	Laborer	17J102Nd
ROURKE, Cathe.	26	F	Servant	17J102Nd
Bridget	2	F	Child	17J102Nd
HANLY, Fanny	20	F	Dressmaker	17J102Nd
Margt.	21	F	Dressmaker	17J102Nd
HUGHES, Cathe.	18	F	Dressmaker	17J102Nd
RAWLINGS, Cathe.	21	F	Dressmaker	17J102Nd
MILLS, Mary-A.	18	F	Dressmaker	17J102Nd
BRIEN, John	25	M	Laborer	17J102Nd
Bridget (W)	24	F	None	17J102Nd
Bridget	.04	F	Infant	17J102Nd
WREEN, Mary	26	F	Servant	17J102Nd
RIELLY, Fanny	18	F	Servant	17J102Nd
CAVANAGH, John	28	M	Joiner	17J102Nd
CARNEY, Thos.	45	M	Laborer	17J102Nd
BYRNES, Thos.	26	M	Laborer	17J102Nd
BARRITH, John	28	M	Laborer	17J102Nd
HENESSY, Thos.	45	M	Laborer	17J102Nd
JONES, George	40	M	Farmer	17J102Nd
Susan	18	F	Servant	17J102Nd
TARNON, Martin	27	M	Mason	17J102Nd
BURN, Edward	40	M	Laborer	17J102Nd
Mary (W)	36	F	None	17J102Nd
Ann	25	F	None	17J102Nd
Jas.	7	M	Child	17J102Nd
Ann	5	F	Child	17J102Nd
Mary	3	F	Child	17J102Nd
Thos.	.04	M	Infant	17J102Nd
WHALEN, Thos.	30	M	Laborer	17J102Nd

DAVID-CARMON 18 JULY 1849

From Liverpool

NAMES OF PASSENGERS	AGE	SEX	OCCUPATIONS	DATE PORT SHIP
STEVENSON, Wm.	35	M	Laborer	18J102Kk
WELDON, Martin	31	M	Laborer	18J102Kk
SUGDEN, Geo.	27	M	Laborer	18J102Kk
POTTER, John	23	M	Laborer	18J102Kk
MCGILL, John	18	M	Laborer	18J102Kk
WINTHRUP, John	52	M	Laborer	18J102Kk
Edwd.	28	M	Laborer	18J102Kk
BAFF, John	24	M	Laborer	18J102Kk
GIBSON, Mick.	24	M	Laborer	18J102Kk
EARLEY, Jane	21	F	Laborer	18J102Kk
CURRIN, Margt.	21	F	Laborer	18J102Kk
ROBINSON, John	26	M	Laborer	18J102Kk
MUMB, John	31	M	Laborer	18J102Kk
GLEEN, Php.	35	M	Laborer	18J102Kk
John	25	M	Laborer	18J102Kk
HINKEY, Bryan	50	M	Laborer	18J102Kk
Ellen	50	F	Laborer	18J102Kk
Peter	20	M	Laborer	18J102Kk
John	15	M	Laborer	18J102Kk
Cath.	13	M	Laborer	18J102Kk
Mary	17	F	Laborer	18J102Kk
Bridget	9	F	Child	18J102Kk
CONAN, Moses	30	F	Laborer	18J102Kk
GRADY, Ann	20	F	Laborer	18J102Kk
DELANEY, Margt.	22	F	Laborer	18J102Kk
Ann	20	F	Laborer	18J102Kk
TEHAN, Sarah	20	F	Laborer	18J102Kk
MURRAY, Ellen	40	F	Laborer	18J102Kk
Pat.	9	M	Child	18J102Kk
MASON, Henry	60	M	Laborer	18J102Kk
Mary	25	F	Laborer	18J102Kk
Wm.	20	M	Laborer	18J102Kk
OWENS, Morgan	27	M	Laborer	18J102Kk
WILLIAMS, Wm.	34	M	Laborer	18J102Kk
DAVIS, Evan	40	M	Laborer	18J102Kk
EVANS, Eliz.	18	F	Laborer	18J102Kk
HOGG, Alex.	40	M	Laborer	18J102Kk
KEAGH, Thos.	45	M	Laborer	18J102Kk
Cath.	38	F	Laborer	18J102Kk
TEAGH, Ann	14	F	Laborer	18J102Kk
John	10	M	Child	18J102Kk
Mary	7	F	Child	18J102Kk
Cath.	.00	F	Infant	18J102Kk
Wm.	.00	M	Infant	18J102Kk
BURNS, Wm.	36	M	Laborer	18J102Kk
ROUCH, John	40	M	Laborer	18J102Kk
SMITH, Wm.	20	M	Laborer	18J102Kk
SCOTT, John	20	M	Laborer	18J102Kk

NAMES OF PASSENGERS	AGE	SEX	OCCUPATIONS	DATE PORT SHIP
MORRAN, Martin	25	M	Laborer	18JI02Kk
Ellen	25	F	Laborer	18JI02Kk
SLEVIN, Alice	32	F	Laborer	18JI02Kk
Cath.	7	F	Child	18JI02Kk
Mary-Ann	3	F	Child	18JI02Kk
Rosannah	.00	F	Infant	18JI02Kk
WELSH, Ann	46	F	Laborer	18JI02Kk
ARMSTRONG, Geo.	24	M	Unknown	18JI02Kk
Mrs.	26	F	Unknown	18JI02Kk
Sarah	.00	F	Infant	18JI02Kk
MCFARTHER, Bella	25	F	Laborer	18JI02Kk
FITZPATRICK, Mary	26	F	Laborer	18JI02Kk
BUTLER, Thos.	26	M	Laborer	18JI02Kk
Eliza.	29	F	Laborer	18JI02Kk
Pat.	.00	M	Infant	18JI02Kk
BRITT, John	20	M	Laborer	18JI02Kk
NEILL, Bridget	19	F	Laborer	18JI02Kk
MCLEOUD, Thos.	37	M	Laborer	18JI02Kk
Jane	32	F	Laborer	18JI02Kk
DELANTY, Kate	24	F	Laborer	18JI02Kk
FLEMMING, Eliza.	19	F	Laborer	18JI02Kk
KEEFE, Alice	18	F	Laborer	18JI02Kk
FARRAH, Jas.	20	M	Laborer	18JI02Kk
Mary	20	F	Laborer	18JI02Kk
Wm.	.00	M	Infant	18JI02Kk
Saml.	24	M	Laborer	18JI02Kk
Isabella	17	F	Laborer	18JI02Kk
MANELLY, James	29	M	Laborer	18JI02Kk
Thos.	32	M	Laborer	18JI02Kk
KARNEY, Sarah	32	M	Laborer	18JI02Kk
Cath.	16	F	Laborer	18JI02Kk
DAYTON, Harriet	32	F	Laborer	18JI02Kk
SCOTT, Eliza.	25	F	Laborer	18JI02Kk
DAYTON, Ellen	9	F	Child	18JI02Kk
Jane	5	F	Child	18JI02Kk
QUALTROUGH, Edwd.	25	M	Laborer	18JI02Kk
Eleanor	24	F	Laborer	18JI02Kk
DUKE, Margt.	18	F	Laborer	18JI02Kk
MAXWELL, Mary-E.	17	F	Laborer	18JI02Kk
CORRIN, Edwd.	28	M	Laborer	18JI02Kk
Margt.	22	F	Laborer	18JI02Kk
TUBMAN, Thos.	26	M	Laborer	18JI02Kk
Ann	26	F	Laborer	18JI02Kk
John	.00	M	Infant	18JI02Kk
GOWAN, Cath.	19	F	Laborer	18JI02Kk
SMITH, Henry	28	M	Laborer	18JI02Kk
PADDON, James	34	M	Laborer	18JI02Kk
OBOYLE, Jas.	28	M	Laborer	18JI02Kk
LAND, Matth.Ron.	25	M	Laborer	18JI02Kk
Mary-Ann	45	F	Laborer	18JI02Kk
Cath.	20	F	Laborer	18JI02Kk
TALBOT, John	40	M	Laborer	18JI02Kk
Sarah	36	F	Laborer	18JI02Kk
Francis	14	M	Laborer	18JI02Kk
Lucy	10	F	Child	18JI02Kk
P.	7	M	Child	18JI02Kk
MCKENNAY, Chas.	25	M	Laborer	18JI02Kk
ALLEN, Geo.	32	M	Laborer	18JI02Kk
LOUGHLIN, And.	24	M	Laborer	18JI02Kk
WARD, Geo.	30	M	Laborer	18JI02Kk
WILLCOCK, Elias	25	M	Laborer	18JI02Kk
BAKER, Chas.	21	M	Laborer	18JI02Kk
KENNEDY, Michl.	25	M	Laborer	18JI02Kk
KELLY, Jas.P.	26	M	Laborer	18JI02Kk
Maria	28	F	Laborer	18JI02Kk
MORRIS, Cath.	22	F	Laborer	18JI02Kk
KELLY, Bridget	19	F	Laborer	18JI02Kk
Maria	22	F	Laborer	18JI02Kk
MILLROY, Jas.	23	M	Laborer	18JI02Kk
PHILIPS, Wm.	27	M	Laborer	18JI02Kk
Margt.	23	F	Laborer	18JI02Kk
ALEXANDER, John	33	M	Laborer	18JI02Kk
WHITLOW, Jas.	26	M	Laborer	18JI02Kk
NICKSON, Michl.	24	M	Laborer	18JI02Kk
CLOANEY, Thos.	40	M	Laborer	18JI02Kk
CLOANEY, Margt.	37	F	Laborer	18JI02Kk
Margt.	15	F	Laborer	18JI02Kk
ROUCH, Mary	20	F	Laborer	18JI02Kk
MURPHY, Edwd.	25	M	Laborer	18JI02Kk
BROWN, Thos.	34	M	Laborer	18JI02Kk
Emma	24	F	Laborer	18JI02Kk
Emma	6	F	Child	18JI02Kk
KEEFE, Thomas	38	M	Laborer	18JI02Kk
HOLGATE, John	31	M	Laborer	18JI02Kk
FOX, Wm.	29	M	Laborer	18JI02Kk
WHITEHILL, John	33	M	Laborer	18JI02Kk
HALL, Miles	43	M	Laborer	18JI02Kk
LUPTON, Wm.	25	M	Laborer	18JI02Kk
HOPKIRK, Jas.	22	M	Laborer	18JI02Kk
BEATTIE, Jas.	23	M	Laborer	18JI02Kk
JOHNSON, And.	40	M	Laborer	18JI02Kk
Jane	35	F	Laborer	18JI02Kk
Jane	18	F	Laborer	18JI02Kk
STANTON, Edwd.	22	M	Laborer	18JI02Kk
KELLY, Pat.	21	M	Laborer	18JI02Kk
MEARS, Wm.	34	M	Laborer	18JI02Kk
Jacob	28	M	Laborer	18JI02Kk
DOGERS, Ann	21	F	Laborer	18JI02Kk
Stephen	4	M	Child	18JI02Kk
Louisa	.00	F	Infant	18JI02Kk
MCSHEA, Edwd.	14	M	Laborer	18JI02Kk
Rose	7	F	Child	18JI02Kk
Pat.	5	M	Child	18JI02Kk
Margt.	3	F	Child	18JI02Kk
LENNON, Dennis	17	M	Laborer	18JI02Kk
SMITH, Jas.	35	M	Laborer	18JI02Kk
Ellen	35	F	Laborer	18JI02Kk
Wm.	12	M	Laborer	18JI02Kk
Mary-Ann	10	F	Laborer	18JI02Kk
James	8	M	Child	18JI02Kk
John	6	M	Child	18JI02Kk
GEORGE, Alex.	26	M	Laborer	18JI02Kk
Alex.	5	M	Child	18JI02Kk
Margt.	3	F	Child	18JI02Kk
SMITH, Wm.	31	M	Laborer	18JI02Kk
Jane	32	F	Laborer	18JI02Kk
Sarah	7	F	Child	18JI02Kk
Christopher	5	M	Child	18JI02Kk
Wm.	3	M	Child	18JI02Kk
John	.00	M	Infant	18JI02Kk
CAYAN, Mary	30	F	Laborer	18JI02Kk
Cath.	18	F	Laborer	18JI02Kk
Daniel	6	M	Child	18JI02Kk
Cath.	7	F	Child	18JI02Kk
NORTON, Thos.	23	M	Laborer	18JI02Kk
LAYHEY, Jas.	23	M	Laborer	18JI02Kk
LYNCH, Ann	16	F	Laborer	18JI02Kk
GOLAN, Mary	12	F	Laborer	18JI02Kk
ALEXANDER, Henry	26	M	Laborer	18JI02Kk
TOBIAS, H.	60	M	Laborer	18JI02Kk
OHALLORAN, Pat.	28	M	Laborer	18JI02Kk
Ryne-KYNE, Pat.	28	M	Laborer	18JI02Kk
HARDY, Chris.	20	M	Laborer	18JI02Kk
WINN, Bridget	17	F	Laborer	18JI02Kk
REYNOLDS, Thos.	50	F	Laborer	18JI02Kk
MCCANN, John	28	F	Laborer	18JI02Kk
SHACKLETON, John	22	F	Laborer	18JI02Kk
BRINE, John	23	M	Laborer	18JI02Kk
DUNN, Pat.	26	M	Laborer	18JI02Kk
Maria	21	F	Laborer	18JI02Kk
BROWN, Saml.	25	M	Laborer	18JI02Kk
Janett	26	F	Laborer	18JI02Kk
Margt.	36	F	Laborer	18JI02Kk
Wm.	5	M	Child	18JI02Kk
John	.00	M	Infant	18JI02Kk
James	.00	M	Infant	18JI02Kk
NICHOLS, Thos.	18	M	Laborer	18JI02Kk
BROWN, John	25	M	Laborer	18JI02Kk
THOMAS, Wm.W.	23	M	Laborer	18JI02Kk
CARLYLE, Jas.	24	M	Laborer	18JI02Kk

NAMES OF PASSENGERS	AGE	SEX	OCCUPATIONS	DATE PORT SHIP	NAMES OF PASSENGERS	AGE	SEX	OCCUPATIONS	DATE PORT SHIP
RYAN, Daniel	35	M	Laborer	18JI02Kk	TRAVES, Mick	35	M	Laborer	18JI02Kk
HOLMES, Thos.	21	M	Laborer	18JI02Kk	CLINTON, Pat.	27	M	Laborer	18JI02Kk
MCDONALD, Jas.	35	M	Laborer	18JI02Kk	COHCAN, Mary	26	F	Laborer	18JI02Kk
COWMAN, John	23	M	Laborer	18JI02Kk	Mary	15	F	Laborer	18JI02Kk
CAVENAGH, John	21	M	Laborer	18JI02Kk	SULLIVAN, Julia	22	F	Laborer	18JI02Kk
MURPHY, Edw.	24	M	Laborer	18JI02Kk	LOVETT, Honora	14	F	Laborer	18JI02Kk
CAVANAGH, Jas.	20	M	Laborer	18JI02Kk	MONONGE, Mich.	40	M	Laborer	18JI02Kk
BRANNIN, John	25	M	Laborer	18JI02Kk	Bridget	12	F	Laborer	18JI02Kk
ALLEN, Robt.	26	M	Laborer	18JI02Kk	Pat.	11	M	Laborer	18JI02Kk
MEIGHAN, Pat.	26	M	Laborer	18JI02Kk	BURNS, Hannah	22	F	Laborer	18JI02Kk
Cath.	24	M	Laborer	18JI02Kk	TOBIN, Bridget	26	F	Laborer	18JI02Kk
Bridget	20	F	Laborer	18JI02Kk	BRANNAGHAN, John	40	M	Laborer	18JI02Kk
BURGAN, Peg.	20	M	Laborer	18JI02Kk	BARRON, Thos.	20	M	Laborer	18JI02Kk
FLEMMING, C.	28	M	Laborer	18JI02Kk	HOGAN, Ann	17	F	Laborer	18JI02Kk
RYAN, Thos.	22	M	Laborer	18JI02Kk	HUGHES, Mary	34	F	Laborer	18JI02Kk
CROOKE, Margt.	24	F	Laborer	18JI02Kk	LOYN, Bridget	46	F	Laborer	18JI02Kk
Ellen	20	F	Laborer	18JI02Kk	Mick	17	M	Laborer	18JI02Kk
ROUCH, Mary	20	F	Laborer	18JI02Kk	MALEAKE, Daniel	21	M	Laborer	18JI02Kk
BULGER, Mary	64	F	Laborer	18JI02Kk	WATCHFORD, Pat.	34	M	Laborer	18JI02Kk
Alice	2	F	Child	18JI02Kk	Francis	21	M	Laborer	18JI02Kk
BREEN, Mary	35	F	Child	18JI02Kk	MARLOW, Pat.	14	M	Laborer	18JI02Kk
Ann	12	F	Laborer	18JI02Kk	Ann	18	F	Laborer	18JI02Kk
CLEARY, John	28	M	Laborer	18JI02Kk	CARL, John	14	M	Laborer	18JI02Kk
MCGUIRE, Francis	22	M	Laborer	18JI02Kk	DONLAY, Mary	17	F	Laborer	18JI02Kk
SHEA, Marty	27	F	Laborer	18JI02Kk	CORNAN, Harvey	30	M	Laborer	18JI02Kk
Pat.	10	M	Child	18JI02Kk	MCGOWAN, Ellen	25	F	Laborer	18JI02Kk
SULLIVAN, Dennis	21	M	Laborer	18JI02Kk	AARON, John	25	F	Laborer	18JI02Kk
CAMPBELL, Bridget	29	F	Laborer	18JI02Kk	Mary-A.	18	F	Laborer	18JI02Kk
Ann	13	F	Laborer	18JI02Kk	CONAN, John	30	M	Laborer	18JI02Kk
Pat.	12	M	Laborer	18JI02Kk	Cath.	30	F	Laborer	18JI02Kk
LAYHE, John	28	M	Laborer	18JI02Kk	Dominick	24	M	Laborer	18JI02Kk
CORKEY, Dan.	20	M	Laborer	18JI02Kk	John	.00	M	Infant	18JI02Kk
KEEFE, Dan.	26	M	Laborer	18JI02Kk	DEVANEY, John	18	M	Laborer	18JI02Kk
Margt.	20	F	Laborer	18JI02Kk	MCGOVERN, John	25	M	Laborer	18JI02Kk
STIMSON, Ann	21	F	Laborer	18JI02Kk	GEE, Thos.	21	M	Laborer	18JI02Kk
MCNERICK, Bridget	23	F	Laborer	18JI02Kk	MCDANIEL, Pat.	21	M	Laborer	18JI02Kk
BRANON, Johan	22	F	Laborer	18JI02Kk	BRADY, Owen	23	M	Laborer	18JI02Kk
GALLOVAN, Mary	20	M	Laborer	18JI02Kk	Margt.	18	F	Laborer	18JI02Kk
POWERS, Cath.	25	M	Laborer	18JI02Kk	FOX, Jas.	17	M	Laborer	18JI02Kk
MILLER, Sarah	28	F	Laborer	18JI02Kk	FALLON, Pat.	20	M	Laborer	18JI02Kk
Edw.	3	M	Laborer	18JI02Kk	CASEY, Thos.	17	M	Laborer	18JI02Kk
Charlotte	.00	F	Infant	18JI02Kk	RODGERS, Thos.	22	M	Laborer	18JI02Kk
WELSH, Peggy	25	F	Laborer	18JI02Kk	MCGREEN, Pat.	28	M	Laborer	18JI02Kk
FOX, Cath.	60	F	Laborer	18JI02Kk	Cath.	20	F	Laborer	18JI02Kk
Michl.	17	M	Laborer	18JI02Kk	RODGERS, Mary	20	F	Laborer	18JI02Kk
Margt.	14	F	Laborer	18JI02Kk	CLARKE, Richd.	40	M	Laborer	18JI02Kk
Wm.	.00	M	Infant	18JI02Kk	Ann	60	F	Laborer	18JI02Kk
NOLAN, John	24	M	Laborer	18JI02Kk	John	12	M	Laborer	18JI02Kk
Jas.	22	M	Laborer	18JI02Kk	James	9	M	Child	18JI02Kk
SHEA, Mary	60	F	Laborer	18JI02Kk	CONLIFF, Joseph	30	M	Laborer	18JI02Kk
SULLIVAN, Mary	30	F	Laborer	18JI02Kk	DIFFIL, Ann	19	F	Laborer	18JI02Kk
John	5	M	Child	18JI02Kk	HIGGINS, Mick	24	M	Laborer	18JI02Kk
Peggy	3	M	Child	18JI02Kk	BENNETT, Ann	22	F	Laborer	18JI02Kk
SHEA, Betsey	35	F	Laborer	18JI02Kk	BEATTIE, A.	25	U	Laborer	18JI02Kk
Mary	10	F	Child	18JI02Kk	HUNT, Jas.	4	M	Child	18JI02Kk
John	7	M	Child	18JI02Kk	ALLEN, Robt.	24	M	Laborer	18JI02Kk
Julia	3	F	Child	18JI02Kk	ANDERSON, Margt.	60	F	Laborer	18JI02Kk
MCQUADE, Jas.	16	M	Child	18JI02Kk	MCDONALD, D.	23	M	Laborer	18JI02Kk
SWEENY, Thos.	25	M	Laborer	18JI02Kk	WELSH, Pat.	30	M	Laborer	18JI02Kk
KEEFE, Pat.	45	M	Laborer	18JI02Kk	MCDONALD, Jas.	40	M	Laborer	18JI02Kk
Margt.	40	F	Laborer	18JI02Kk	MULLIGAN, Thos.	56	M	Laborer	18JI02Kk
Pat.	19	M	Laborer	18JI02Kk	Bridget	50	F	Laborer	18JI02Kk
Margt.	17	F	Laborer	18JI02Kk	Cath.	10	F	Child	18JI02Kk
Thos.	14	M	Laborer	18JI02Kk	GILL, Owen	22	M	Laborer	18JI02Kk
Mick	8	M	Laborer	18JI02Kk	Mary	20	F	Laborer	18JI02Kk
FINKENSTONE, Harris	19	M	Laborer	18JI02Kk	MEAHER, Mick	35	M	Laborer	18JI02Kk
GUGAN, Barnett	21	M	Laborer	18JI02Kk	Margt.	23	F	Laborer	18JI02Kk
SWEETINAN, Jacob	30	M	Laborer	18JI02Kk	Philip	24	M	Laborer	18JI02Kk
JACOBS, Isaac	18	M	Laborer	18JI02Kk	Henry	3	M	Child	18JI02Kk
CARLSHIRE, Taly	18	M	Laborer	18JI02Kk	Richd.	4	M	Child	18JI02Kk
JOSEPH, Martin	40	M	Laborer	18JI02Kk	Mary	.00	F	Infant	18JI02Kk
Sarah	30	F	Laborer	18JI02Kk	Campbell	20	M	Laborer	18JI02Kk
Rose-Ann	5	F	Child	18JI02Kk	STEVENSON, Saml.	22	M	Laborer	18JI02Kk
KELLEY, Cisley	26	F	Laborer	18JI02Kk	GEILLY, Cosmor	60	M	Laborer	18JI02Kk
OBRIEN, Mary	26	F	Laborer	18JI02Kk	Cath.	40	F	Laborer	18JI02Kk

NAMES OF PASSENGERS	AGE	SEX	OCCUPATIONS	DATE PORT SHIP
GEILLY, James	20	M	Laborer	18JI02Kk
Ann	17	F	Laborer	18JI02Kk
Phillip	15	M	Laborer	18JI02Kk
Pat.	13	M	Laborer	18JI02Kk
Corn.	.00	M	Infant	18JI02Kk
MCCONNOR, Margt.	35	F	Laborer	18JI02Kk
DALEY, Mary	20	F	Laborer	18JI02Kk
BROWN, Bridget	20	F	Laborer	18JI02Kk
WALL, Philip	30	M	Laborer	18JI02Kk
CARROLL, Pat.	22	M	Laborer	18JI02Kk
KENNAN, Susan	30	F	Laborer	18JI02Kk
MORGAN, Ann	25	F	Laborer	18JI02Kk
CAMPBELL, John	20	M	Laborer	18JI02Kk
WHITE, Ann	20	F	Laborer	18JI02Kk
CARTEY, Mary	43	F	Laborer	18JI02Kk
John	15	M	Laborer	18JI02Kk
James	13	M	Laborer	18JI02Kk
Edward	6	M	Child	18JI02Kk
DOYLE, Pat.	21	M	Laborer	18JI02Kk
Bridget	40	F	Laborer	18JI02Kk
John	14	F	Laborer	18JI02Kk
Danl.	5	M	Child	18JI02Kk
CARTEY, Pat.	27	M	Laborer	18JI02Kk
Rosey	25	F	Laborer	18JI02Kk
GORMLEY, John	25	M	Laborer	18JI02Kk
CARTEY, Mary	9	F	Child	18JI02Kk
Margt.	7	F	Child	18JI02Kk
Cath.	.00	F	Infant	18JI02Kk
MCMAUGHAM, John	37	M	Laborer	18JI02Kk
Peggy	18	F	Laborer	18JI02Kk
GRIFFIN, John	22	M	Laborer	18JI02Kk
ENGLISH, Wm.	24	M	Laborer	18JI02Kk
LINDSAY, John	27	M	Laborer	18JI02Kk
FLUKIN, Pat.	28	M	Laborer	18JI02Kk
Margt.	24	F	Laborer	18JI02Kk
Thomas	35	M	Laborer	18JI02Kk
MEARS, John	26	M	Laborer	18JI02Kk
Matt.	24	M	Laborer	18JI02Kk
OBRIEN, Anty.	28	M	Laborer	18JI02Kk
GRIFFIN, John	25	M	Laborer	18JI02Kk
DILLON, John	35	M	Laborer	18JI02Kk
Bridget	28	F	Laborer	18JI02Kk
Mary	5	F	Child	18JI02Kk
Edmond	.00	M	Infant	18JI02Kk
MEARS, Mary	20	F	Laborer	18JI02Kk
HOWITT, Jno.W.	20	M	Laborer	18JI02Kk
MCCUSHAN, John	22	M	Laborer	18JI02Kk
GILROY, Margt.	20	F	Laborer	18JI02Kk
COOK, Cath.	20	F	Laborer	18JI02Kk
SAUL, James	20	M	Laborer	18JI02Kk
BRASSELL, John	20	M	Laborer	18JI02Kk
HENESSY, John	25	M	Laborer	18JI02Kk
GARCY, Michl.	30	M	Laborer	18JI02Kk
MCCARTEY, Terence	30	M	Laborer	18JI02Kk
Betty	24	F	Laborer	18JI02Kk
MCGUIRE, Betty	30	F	Laborer	18JI02Kk
CAIN, Dennis	42	M	Laborer	18JI02Kk
GRIFFIN, John	27	M	Laborer	18JI02Kk
KENNEDY, Ellen	38	F	Laborer	18JI02Kk
HATNETT, Bridget	30	F	Laborer	18JI02Kk
HENNESSY, Peggy	35	F	Laborer	18JI02Kk
CRONEAN, Connor	30	M	Laborer	18JI02Kk
Cath.	22	F	Laborer	18JI02Kk
MADIGAN, Pat.	40	M	Laborer	18JI02Kk
Ellen	23	F	Laborer	18JI02Kk
ONEILL, Pat.	22	M	Laborer	18JI02Kk
FOX, Pat.	20	M	Laborer	18JI02Kk
DALTON, Pierce	20	M	Laborer	18JI02Kk
BREEN, Pat.	30	M	Laborer	18JI02Kk
HANABURY, Richd.	26	M	Laborer	18JI02Kk
ROURK, John	47	M	Laborer	18JI02Kk
Margt.	27	F	Laborer	18JI02Kk
Wm.	3	M	Child	18JI02Kk
MURRAY, Bridget	26	F	Laborer	18JI02Kk
KELLEY, Michl.	22	M	Laborer	18JI02Kk

NAMES OF PASSENGERS	AGE	SEX	OCCUPATIONS	DATE PORT SHIP
KELLEY, John	24	M	Laborer	18JI02Kk
DUNN, Pat.	36	M	Laborer	18JI02Kk
Cath.	30	F	Laborer	18JI02Kk
Pat.	9	M	Child	18JI02Kk
Dennis	6	M	Child	18JI02Kk
WOLF, Margt.	18	F	Laborer	18JI02Kk
BEAGAN, Mary	20	F	Laborer	18JI02Kk
ROURKE, Mary	16	F	Laborer	18JI02Kk
DOYLE, Bridget	19	F	Laborer	18JI02Kk
ROURKE, Johana	6	F	Child	18JI02Kk
Bridget	3	F	Child	18JI02Kk
GAHALL, Lawr.	30	M	Laborer	18JI02Kk
CASON, Michl.	22	M	Laborer	18JI02Kk
ROWLAND, Ellen	30	F	Laborer	18JI02Kk
ANSTACE, Bridget	22	F	Laborer	18JI02Kk
DORIN, John	29	M	Laborer	18JI02Kk
CORAL, John	46	M	Laborer	18JI02Kk
CONNELLY, John	34	M	Laborer	18JI02Kk
Wm.	30	M	Laborer	18JI02Kk
CONELLY, Wm.	.00	M	Infant	18JI02Kk
PRATT, John	30	M	Unknown	18JI02Kk
CARROLL, Pat.	40	M	Laborer	18JI02Kk
Danl.	18	M	Laborer	18JI02Kk
MARSHALL, Rody	18	M	Laborer	18JI02Kk
KARNES, Alexr.	24	M	Laborer	18JI02Kk
Martha	22	F	Laborer	18JI02Kk
Martha	.00	F	Infant	18JI02Kk
MORLEY, John	31	M	Laborer	18JI02Kk
TALOR, Wm.	39	M	Laborer	18JI02Kk
DYKES, Robt.	40	M	Laborer	18JI02Kk
MCMAHON, John	26	M	Laborer	18JI02Kk
David	25	M	Laborer	18JI02Kk
GINNAMER, Dennis	25	M	Laborer	18JI02Kk
HAWKINS, Cath.	33	F	Laborer	18JI02Kk
Isabella	6	F	Child	18JI02Kk
Henry	.00	M	Infant	18JI02Kk
LEWIS, Sarah-Ann	13	F	Laborer	18JI02Kk
LANNAHAN, Pat.	45	M	Laborer	18JI02Kk
MILLS, Charlotte	.00	F	Infant	18JI02Kk
DILLON, Alice	.00	F	Infant	18JI02Kk
LANAHAN, Margt.	30	F	Laborer	18JI02Kk
FENAH, Wm.	.00	M	Infant	18JI02Kk
MCANLIFFE, Bridget	18	F	Laborer	18JI02Kk
CONNOR, Margt.	28	F	Laborer	18JI02Kk
KEEFE, Ann	.00	F	Infant	18JI02Kk
LANAHAN, Dennis	38	M	Laborer	18JI02Kk
James	23	M	Laborer	18JI02Kk
GAVINS, Thos.	26	M	Laborer	18JI02Kk
ONEILL, Jas.	26	M	Laborer	18JI02Kk
SIMPSON, Rose	20	F	Laborer	18JI02Kk
Emily	.00	F	Infant	18JI02Kk
SHEA, Sarah	21	F	Laborer	18JI02Kk
MCNEILL, Jane	45	F	Laborer	18JI02Kk
KENNADY, Mark	31	M	Laborer	18JI02Kk
Eliza.	30	F	Laborer	18JI02Kk
James	12	M	Laborer	18JI02Kk
John	5	M	Child	18JI02Kk
Joseph	3	M	Child	18JI02Kk
Susan	.00	F	Infant	18JI02Kk
DESMOND, Johana	60	F	Laborer	18JI02Kk
Margt.	24	F	Laborer	18JI02Kk
MCCARTEY, Ann	17	F	Laborer	18JI02Kk
NICHOLSON, Mary	10	F	Child	18JI02Kk
Bridget	12	F	Laborer	18JI02Kk
MCCAFFREY, Mary	20	F	Laborer	18JI02Kk
DONALD, David	42	M	Laborer	18JI02Kk
CONOLLY, Wm.	.00	M	Infant	18JI02Kk
HOPKINS, Margt.	30	F	Laborer	18JI02Kk
Ellen	10	F	Child	18JI02Kk
Mary-Ann	7	F	Child	18JI02Kk
Margt.	4	F	Child	18JI02Kk
Edward	2	M	Child	18JI02Kk
CUMMINS, Cath.	.00	F	Infant	18JI02Kk
DESMOND, Dennis	26	F	Laborer	18JI02Kk
Mary	30	F	Laborer	18JI02Kk

NAMES OF PASSENGERS	AGE	SEX	OCCUPATIONS	DATE PORT SHIP
CALAHAN, Thos.	28	M	Laborer	18Jl02Kk
COCKLIN, Dennis	25	M	Laborer	18Jl02Kk
MCCARTY, Danl.	26	M	Laborer	18Jl02Kk
Jas.	18	M	Laborer	18Jl02Kk
Honora	12	F	Laborer	18Jl02Kk
FITZSIMMONS, Thos.F.	38	M	Laborer	18Jl02Kk
Mary	25	F	Laborer	18Jl02Kk
Mary	4	F	Child	18Jl02Kk
Cath.	2	F	Child	18Jl02Kk
COMMINS, Pat.	28	M	Laborer	18Jl02Kk
Ellen	28	M	Laborer	18Jl02Kk
Thos.	4	M	Child	18Jl02Kk
Cath.	3	F	Child	18Jl02Kk
LANE, Cath.	24	M	Child	18Jl02Kk
WELSH, Johana	17	F	Laborer	18Jl02Kk
HOPKINS, Edwd.	.00	M	Infant	18Jl02Kk
COMINS, Arch.	17	M	Laborer	18Jl02Kk
DOWLIN, Pat.	34	M	Laborer	18Jl02Kk
TOBIN, Peter	30	M	Laborer	18Jl02Kk
CONLAN, Jas.	50	M	Laborer	18Jl02Kk
Julia	42	F	Laborer	18Jl02Kk
Francis	20	M	Laborer	18Jl02Kk
Edwd.	17	M	Laborer	18Jl02Kk
John	15	M	Laborer	18Jl02Kk
Rosey	12	F	Laborer	18Jl02Kk
Cath.	9	F	Child	18Jl02Kk
James	4	M	Child	18Jl02Kk
RYAN, Jerh.	.00	M	Infant	18Jl02Kk
MANSFIELD, John	28	M	Laborer	18Jl02Kk
LENNON, Edwd.	25	M	Laborer	18Jl02Kk
RYAN, Danl.	23	M	Laborer	18Jl02Kk
LENNON, Honora	20	F	Laborer	18Jl02Kk
James	.00	M	Infant	18Jl02Kk
FINN, Margt.	18	F	Laborer	18Jl02Kk
FARLIN, Judy	30	F	Laborer	18Jl02Kk
DELANEY, James	36	M	Laborer	18Jl02Kk
Ann	37	F	Laborer	18Jl02Kk
Thos.	3	M	Child	18Jl02Kk
Susan	.00	F	Infant	18Jl02Kk
WATKINS, Robt.	39	M	Laborer	18Jl02Kk
MCCANN, Pat.	25	M	Laborer	18Jl02Kk
RILEY, Ann	30	F	Laborer	18Jl02Kk
Mary	12	F	Laborer	18Jl02Kk
Bridget	6	F	Child	18Jl02Kk
Ellen	25	F	Laborer	18Jl02Kk
MAHER, Henry	.00	M	Infant	18Jl02Kk
FARLEY, Mary	20	F	Laborer	18Jl02Kk
TRACEY, John	50	M	Laborer	18Jl02Kk
BLESSING, Pat.	25	M	Laborer	18Jl02Kk
SMITH, Pat.	29	M	Laborer	18Jl02Kk
Margt.	30	F	Laborer	18Jl02Kk
Mick	.00	M	Infant	18Jl02Kk
HANLEY, Bridget	25	F	Laborer	18Jl02Kk
RYAN, Jas.	40	M	Laborer	18Jl02Kk
Margt.	30	F	Laborer	18Jl02Kk
Johanna	7	F	Child	18Jl02Kk
Jane	.00	F	Infant	18Jl02Kk
BRASSELL, Margt.	50	F	Laborer	18Jl02Kk
Jerome	17	M	Laborer	18Jl02Kk
John	15	M	Laborer	18Jl02Kk
Johana	12	F	Laborer	18Jl02Kk
Ellen	12	F	Laborer	18Jl02Kk
John	.00	M	Infant	18Jl02Kk
Mary	13	F	Laborer	18Jl02Kk
Thos.	10	M	Child	18Jl02Kk
TRAINOR, Francis	28	F	Laborer	18Jl02Kk
Mary	26	F	Laborer	18Jl02Kk
KILBRIDE, Bess	12	F	Laborer	18Jl02Kk
Pat.	10	M	Child	18Jl02Kk
Ann	7	F	Child	18Jl02Kk
BODEN, Pat.	24	F	Laborer	18Jl02Kk
Eliza.	16	F	Laborer	18Jl02Kk
KELLY, Eliza.	25	F	Laborer	18Jl02Kk
MULLIGAN, Julia	22	F	Laborer	18Jl02Kk
BURNS, Jas.	25	M	Laborer	18Jl02Kk

NAMES OF PASSENGERS	AGE	SEX	OCCUPATIONS	DATE PORT SHIP
MILLER, Hugh	30	M	Laborer	18Jl02Kk
FAGAN, Owen	24	M	Laborer	18Jl02Kk
HARRISON, Wm.	37	M	Laborer	18Jl02Kk
BARRY, Jas.	18	M	Laborer	18Jl02Kk
Mary	25	F	Laborer	18Jl02Kk
Cath.	21	F	Laborer	18Jl02Kk
WISE, Bridget	14	F	Laborer	18Jl02Kk
Cath.	8	F	Child	18Jl02Kk
Dennis	6	M	Child	18Jl02Kk
LANNIGAN, John	25	M	Laborer	18Jl02Kk
MASTERSON, Edwd.	30	M	Laborer	18Jl02Kk
MCCABE, James	50	M	Laborer	18Jl02Kk
Margt.	20	F	Laborer	18Jl02Kk
KELLY, Ann	50	F	Laborer	18Jl02Kk
Mary	8	F	Child	18Jl02Kk
Ann	6	F	Child	18Jl02Kk
Pat.	4	M	Child	18Jl02Kk
MCDONALD, Bess	20	F	Laborer	18Jl02Kk
JUDGE, Margt.	20	F	Laborer	18Jl02Kk
DAYLEY, Martin	23	M	Laborer	18Jl02Kk
Bridget	20	F	Laborer	18Jl02Kk
DOHERTY, Edmond	30	M	Laborer	18Jl02Kk
BURKE, Mat.	30	M	Laborer	18Jl02Kk
MATTHEWS, Michl.	20	M	Laborer	18Jl02Kk
NILAN, Jas.	18	M	Laborer	18Jl02Kk
HESLAND, Nicholas	20	M	Laborer	18Jl02Kk
Rose	18	F	Laborer	18Jl02Kk
BARRY, Hannah	15	F	Laborer	18Jl02Kk
TRASEY, James	24	M	Laborer	18Jl02Kk
BURNS, John	00	M	Unknown	18Jl02Kk
MILLIGAN, John	00	M	Unknown	18Jl02Kk
DELANEY, Pat.	00	M	Unknown	18Jl02Kk
WILLIAMS, John	00	M	Unknown	18Jl02Kk
GEORGE, Jane	30	F	Laborer	18Jl02Kk

SIDDONS 18 JULY 1849

From Liverpool

NAMES OF PASSENGERS	AGE	SEX	OCCUPATIONS	DATE PORT SHIP
MORGAN, Anne	26	F	None	18Jl02Ng
DUNNE, Wm.	41	M	Clcp	18Jl02Ng
Mary	30	F	None	18Jl02Ng
MURPHY, John	35	M	Farmer	18Jl02Ng
Mary	30	F	None	18Jl02Ng
HALL, Michael	48	M	Builder	18Jl02Ng
Michael	21	M	Joiner	18Jl02Ng
Henry	13	M	None	18Jl02Ng
Charles	12	M	None	18Jl02Ng
Catherine	17	F	None	18Jl02Ng
Eleanor	15	F	None	18Jl02Ng
Bridget	10	F	None	18Jl02Ng
Ellen	00	F	Unknown	18Jl02Ng
OCONNELL, Eliza	17	F	None	18Jl02Ng
WILSON, Ralph	32	M	Farmer	18Jl02Ng
MULHALLEN, Frank	30	M	Laborer	18Jl02Ng
KENNY, Owen	32	M	Surveyor	18Jl02Ng
Eliza	27	F	None	18Jl02Ng
Catherine-Anne	2	F	Child	18Jl02Ng
MONK, Thomas	30	M	Laborer	18Jl02Ng
Pat	34	M	Laborer	18Jl02Ng
JONES, Geo.	30	M	Weaver	18Jl02Ng
Margret	25	F	None	18Jl02Ng
Edward	3	M	Child	18Jl02Ng
Sarah	1	F	Child	18Jl02Ng
COLAN, Laurence	52	M	Laborer	18Jl02Ng
Judith	50	F	None	18Jl02Ng
Judith	16	F	None	18Jl02Ng
MORONEY, Pat	30	M	Laborer	18Jl02Ng
DOHENY, James	30	M	Laborer	18Jl02Ng

NAMES OF PASSENGERS	AGE	SEX	OCCUPATIONS	DATE PORT SHIP
DOHENY, Alice	26	F	None	18J102Ng
Catherine	2	F	Child	18J102Ng
John	.11	M	Infant	18J102Ng
DELANY, Mary	24	F	None	18J102Ng
HAWKCETT, Samuel	22	M	Artist	18J102Ng
Mary	18	F	None	18J102Ng
BRIEN, Thomas	19	M	Laborer	18J102Ng
MCGRADE, Pat	30	M	Grocer	18J102Ng
Mary	25	F	None	18J102Ng
BRADY, Pat	30	M	Farmer	18J102Ng
Bridget	28	F	None	18J102Ng
CARROLL, Terence	19	M	Farmer	18J102Ng
MCSHEAN, Edward	30	M	Farmer	18J102Ng
GRAHAM, Andrew	40	M	Farmer	18J102Ng
Eliza-Anne	40	F	None	18J102Ng
Sarah	12	F	None	18J102Ng
Thomas	10	M	None	18J102Ng
Robert	8	M	Child	18J102Ng
HENDERSON, Philip	22	M	Shoemaker	18J102Ng
KELLY, John	23	M	Cooper	18J102Ng
KING, John	19	M	Laborer	18J102Ng
IGOE, John	21	M	Shoemaker	18J102Ng
SHEILS, Thomas	23	M	Laborer	18J102Ng
CROWE, John	25	M	Laborer	18J102Ng
SCHOFIELD, David	24	M	Laborer	18J102Ng
ROE, John	21	M	Laborer	18J102Ng
MURPHY, Pat	28	M	Joiner	18J102Ng
Bridget	21	F	None	18J102Ng
MCMURRELL, Nicholas	40	M	Laborer	18J102Ng
Pat	30	M	Laborer	18J102Ng
James	16	M	Laborer	18J102Ng
Eliza	13	F	None	18J102Ng
Nicholas	11	M	None	18J102Ng
Catherine	8	F	Child	18J102Ng
LENNON, Daniel	40	M	Laborer	18J102Ng
Eliza	35	F	None	18J102Ng
MCSHEAN, Thomas	23	M	Laborer	18J102Ng
RYAN, Wm.	34	M	Laborer	18J102Ng
Anne	35	F	None	18J102Ng
BARKER, Peter	22	M	Laborer	18J102Ng
MCCORMICK, Pat	26	M	Tailor	18J102Ng
LYNCH, Charles	40	M	Carpenter	18J102Ng
TORMEY, Thomas	28	M	Miller	18J102Ng
Mary	21	F	None	18J102Ng
OBRIEN, Frances	18	F	None	18J102Ng
Rhody	21	U	None	18J102Ng
EVANS, Mary	26	F	None	18J102Ng
Alfred	3	M	Child	18J102Ng
John	1	M	Child	18J102Ng
GEOGHEGAN, Philip	40	M	Laborer	18J102Ng
MOLLOY, Bernard	28	M	Farmer	18J102Ng
Mary	23	F	None	18J102Ng
CROPPER, James	25	M	Farmer	18J102Ng
GRAHAM, Pierce	36	M	Farmer	18J102Ng
Margret	26	F	None	18J102Ng
Bridget	22	F	None	18J102Ng
KELLY, Daniel	32	M	Farmer	18J102Ng
GRAY, Eliza	28	F	None	18J102Ng
MAHER, Edward	27	M	Shopkeeper	18J102Ng
HUGHES, Jas.	19	M	Laborer	18J102Ng
BEATTY, Alexr.	26	M	Laborer	18J102Ng
John	24	M	Shoemaker	18J102Ng
HAMILTON, Jos.	22	M	Cbtmkr	18J102Ng
DANIEL, Ellen	22	F	Dressmaker	18J102Ng
EGAN, Mat	25	M	Farmer	18J102Ng
Sarah	27	F	None	18J102Ng
KEANE, John	50	M	Laborer	18J102Ng
SHANAHAN, Pat	28	M	Shoemaker	18J102Ng
Sarah	25	F	None	18J102Ng
Malick	4	M	Child	18J102Ng
Gilbert	2	M	Child	18J102Ng
Mary	1	F	Child	18J102Ng
WITHERELL, Judith	18	F	Dressmaker	18J102Ng
PORTER, Alexr.	21	M	Laborer	18J102Ng
KEANE, Edward	30	M	Laborer	18J102Ng
KEANE, Mat	20	M	Tailor	18J102Ng
KEAN, Mary	15	F	None	18J102Ng
CRUNNY, Bridget	21	F	Bookbinder	18J102Ng
MCPARNELL, Rose	22	F	Servant	18J102Ng
COSGRAVE, Mary-Anne	22	F	Clrwkr	18J102Ng
SHANAHAN, John	40	M	Laborer	18J102Ng
Anne	36	F	None	18J102Ng
Mary	9	F	Child	18J102Ng
Bridget	7	F	Child	18J102Ng
KENNY, James	23	M	Laborer	18J102Ng
Catherine	21	F	Servant	18J102Ng
FOLLIS, Pat	21	M	Laborer	18J102Ng
Catherine	24	F	None	18J102Ng
Michael	10	M	None	18J102Ng
Mary	7	F	Child	18J102Ng
GREEN, Margret	25	F	None	18J102Ng
RYAN, Martin	36	M	Laborer	18J102Ng
Judy	26	F	None	18J102Ng
James	9	M	Child	18J102Ng
Mary	7	F	Child	18J102Ng
Martin	3	M	Child	18J102Ng
Johanna	2	F	Child	18J102Ng
Anne	.01	F	Infant	18J102Ng
MAGEE, Arthur	50	M	Laborer	18J102Ng
DUNNE, Mary	30	F	None	18J102Ng
Margret	7	F	Child	18J102Ng
James	5	M	Child	18J102Ng
MATHEW, Bernard	18	M	Laborer	18J102Ng
MCKEON, John	18	M	Laborer	18J102Ng
CUNNINGHAM, Pat	40	M	Laborer	18J102Ng
Alice	30	F	None	18J102Ng
Owen	13	M	None	18J102Ng
Mary	10	F	None	18J102Ng
Alice	7	F	Child	18J102Ng
CALLAGHAN, James	40	M	Laborer	18J102Ng
Anne	11	F	None	18J102Ng
Catherine	9	F	Child	18J102Ng
Patrick	7	M	Child	18J102Ng
QUINN, Francis	23	M	Shoemaker	18J102Ng
HARVEY, James	22	M	Laborer	18J102Ng
DUFFY, James	18	M	Laborer	18J102Ng
Catherine	16	F	None	18J102Ng
MAHONY, Pat	30	M	Laborer	18J102Ng
CONNOLLY, Thomas	35	M	Laborer	18J102Ng
Pat	8	M	Child	18J102Ng
Judith	6	F	Child	18J102Ng
Anne	4	F	Child	18J102Ng
Peter	3	M	Child	18J102Ng
Thomas	.09	M	Infant	18J102Ng
MATHEWS, Anne	20	F	Servant	18J102Ng
KELLY, Pat	55	M	Laborer	18J102Ng
Margret	50	F	None	18J102Ng
Sarah	20	F	Dressmaker	18J102Ng
ONEILL, Pat	52	M	Laborer	18J102Ng
Mary	40	F	None	18J102Ng
John	12	M	None	18J102Ng
Bridget	9	F	Child	18J102Ng
Owen	7	M	Child	18J102Ng
OSBORNE, Thos.	26	M	Laborer	18J102Ng
Catherine	25	F	None	18J102Ng
COMISKEY, Hugh	17	M	Laborer	18J102Ng
BYRNE, Thos.	24	M	Laborer	18J102Ng
GLANCY, Pat	20	M	Laborer	18J102Ng
SHEA, Bridget	40	F	None	18J102Ng
SMITH, Rose	27	F	None	18J102Ng
DONAGHY, Mark	26	M	Weaver	18J102Ng
Eliza	30	F	None	18J102Ng
MULHOLLAND, Bernard	12	M	Laborer	18J102Ng
MALLEN, Mary	30	F	None	18J102Ng
ONEILL, James	40	M	Laborer	18J102Ng
Honor	19	F	None	18J102Ng
Alice	12	F	None	18J102Ng
Phelix	12	M	None	18J102Ng
Pat	12	M	None	18J102Ng
Catherine	9	F	Child	18J102Ng

NAMES OF PASSENGERS	AGE	SEX	OCCUPATIONS	DATE PORT SHIP
HARKNETT, Pat	40	M	Laborer	18Jl02Ng
Margret	13	F	Laborer	18Jl02Ng
MURPHY, Peter	32	M	Laborer	18Jl02Ng
TROTTER, Thomas	33	M	Clerk	18Jl02Ng
Sarah	33	F	None	18Jl02Ng
Eliza	10	F	None	18Jl02Ng
William	8	M	Child	18Jl02Ng
Sarah	6	F	Child	18Jl02Ng
Rose	4	F	Child	18Jl02Ng
Mary	.10	F	Infant	18Jl02Ng
MARKIN, John	45	M	Laborer	18Jl02Ng
CORBERT, Edmond	19	M	Laborer	18Jl02Ng
SLATTERY, Denis	29	M	Laborer	18Jl02Ng
HAGARTY, Michael	19	M	Clerk	18Jl02Ng
LOGUE, Pat	20	M	Laborer	18Jl02Ng
CAVANAGH, Pat	25	M	Farmer	18Jl02Ng
Mary	50	F	None	18Jl02Ng
Anne	11	F	None	18Jl02Ng
FLANAGAN, Mary	19	F	Servant	18Jl02Ng
MAUNSELL, Eliza	24	F	Servant	18Jl02Ng
KERR, James	24	M	Shoemaker	18Jl02Ng
Lucy	22	F	None	18Jl02Ng
Henry	18	M	None	18Jl02Ng
HAGAN, Owen	20	M	Mason	18Jl02Ng
ROE, Geo.	17	M	Unknown	18Jl02Ng
RING, Thos.	36	M	Laborer	18Jl02Ng
POWER, Johanna	19	F	Servant	18Jl02Ng
Ellen	23	F	Servant	18Jl02Ng
WALSH, Bridget	16	F	Servant	18Jl02Ng
POWER, Bridget	.02	F	Infant	18Jl02Ng
BURNETT, Jane	19	F	Servant	18Jl02Ng
REEDY, Margret	17	F	Servant	18Jl02Ng
Anne	15	F	Servant	18Jl02Ng
ODONNELL, Michael	20	M	Laborer	18Jl02Ng
FINNON, Pat	26	M	Laborer	18Jl02Ng
CURTIS, James	21	M	Laborer	18Jl02Ng
HENRY, Joseph	20	M	Student	18Jl02Ng
REILLY, Thomas	50	M	Laborer	18Jl02Ng
Anne	50	F	None	18Jl02Ng
POWER, Pat	38	M	Dyer	18Jl02Ng
KEARNEY, Mary	22	F	Weaver	18Jl02Ng
BRIDE, Margret	16	F	Servant	18Jl02Ng
SPEEN, Sarah	30	F	Bookbinder	18Jl02Ng
Ellen	12	F	None	18Jl02Ng
RYAN, Fanny	21	F	Servant	18Jl02Ng
WILLIAMSON, Sarah-Jane	21	F	Servant	18Jl02Ng
DOYLE, Mary	15	F	Servant	18Jl02Ng
QUINN, Catherine	20	F	Servant	18Jl02Ng
Bridget	19	F	Servant	18Jl02Ng
ROACH, Bridget	20	F	Servant	18Jl02Ng
Margret	30	F	Servant	18Jl02Ng
Pat	8	M	Child	18Jl02Ng
Andrew	6	M	Child	18Jl02Ng
David	4	M	Child	18Jl02Ng
Anisha	3	F	Child	18Jl02Ng
MADOCK, Mary	10	F	None	18Jl02Ng
Hanola	.10	F	Infant	18Jl02Ng
GAHAN, Anne	25	F	Dressmaker	18Jl02Ng
ODONNELL, John	20	M	Laborer	18Jl02Ng
Ellen	25	F	None	18Jl02Ng
Mary	21	F	None	18Jl02Ng
HERON, Barney	17	M	Laborer	18Jl02Ng
MURPHY, Bridget	28	F	Servant	18Jl02Ng
MARTIN, Fanny	29	F	Servant	18Jl02Ng
Rose	12	F	Servant	18Jl02Ng
Margret	11	F	Servant	18Jl02Ng
George	6	M	Child	18Jl02Ng
DUFFY, Edward	19	M	Laborer	18Jl02Ng
WHITE, Mary	22	F	Servant	18Jl02Ng
BARRELL, Bridget	30	F	Servant	18Jl02Ng
POWER, Mary	16	F	Servant	18Jl02Ng
KEERAN, Bryan	30	M	Laborer	18Jl02Ng
John	23	M	Laborer	18Jl02Ng
KELLY, Michael	25	M	Laborer	18Jl02Ng
IVORS, Gertrude	19	F	Servant	18Jl02Ng

NAMES OF PASSENGERS	AGE	SEX	OCCUPATIONS	DATE PORT SHIP
SMITH, Martin	25	M	Laborer	18Jl02Ng
KELLY, Bridget	30	F	Servant	18Jl02Ng
OCONNOR, Jas.	40	M	Laborer	18Jl02Ng
DOHERTY, Philip	27	M	Laborer	18Jl02Ng
PEPPER, Geo.	20	M	Hrstnr	18Jl02Ng
RICE, Thomas	30	M	Laborer	18Jl02Ng
MULLEN, Anne	17	F	Servant	18Jl02Ng
CONSEDY, Catherine	17	F	Servant	18Jl02Ng
KELLY, Catherine	19	F	Servant	18Jl02Ng
GREEN, Pat	50	M	Laborer	18Jl02Ng
LILLIS, David	4	M	Child	18Jl02Ng
KEARNEY, Thos.	53	M	Millwright	18Jl02Ng
Catherine	44	F	None	18Jl02Ng
Mary	22	F	None	18Jl02Ng
Thos.	20	M	None	18Jl02Ng
Margret	19	F	None	18Jl02Ng
John	17	M	None	18Jl02Ng
Catherine	15	F	None	18Jl02Ng
Julia	10	F	None	18Jl02Ng
Edward	9	M	Child	18Jl02Ng
James	7	M	Child	18Jl02Ng
Maria	5	F	Child	18Jl02Ng
Maurice	2	M	Child	18Jl02Ng
MCEVOY, Anne	20	F	None	18Jl02Ng
DERRITT, Mary	22	F	None	18Jl02Ng
MCEVOY, Pat	30	M	Laborer	18Jl02Ng
FRASER, George	25	M	Clerk	18Jl02Ng
Themison	23	F	None	18Jl02Ng
BELFEKILGHRON, Joseph	22	M	Student	18Jl02Ng
Jas.	17	M	None	18Jl02Ng
MCKENNA, Hugh	20	M	Laborer	18Jl02Ng
RANAHAN, John	21	M	Baker	18Jl02Ng
EGAN, Margret	24	F	Servant	18Jl02Ng
Mary	22	F	Servant	18Jl02Ng
LANE, Geo.	46	M	Farmer	18Jl02Ng
Amelia	34	F	None	18Jl02Ng
Henry-Philip-Delmar	8	M	Child	18Jl02Ng

CORA-LINN 19 JULY 1849

From Glasgow

NAMES OF PASSENGERS	AGE	SEX	OCCUPATIONS	DATE PORT SHIP
MCCRACKEN, Bernard	30	M	Bootmaker	19Jl04Nh
Ellen	26	F	None	19Jl04Nh
Ellen-Ann-Mrs.	60	F	None	19Jl04Nh
Hugh	.11	M	Infant	19Jl04Nh
KERRIGAN, John	28	M	Spinner	19Jl04Nh
Sarah	60	F	None	19Jl04Nh
MCGOWN, Wm.	23	M	Blacksmith	19Jl04Nh
GRAHAM, John	22	M	Unknown	19Jl04Nh
FIELD, Andw.	42	M	Shoemaker	19Jl04Nh
CROSSEN, Hugh	35	M	Iron Maker	19Jl04Nh
Mary	33	F	None	19Jl04Nh
HAGGARTY, Peter	9	M	Child	19Jl04Nh
CROSSEN, Nancy	9	F	Child	19Jl04Nh
Mary	5	F	Child	19Jl04Nh
Sarah	.06	F	Infant	19Jl04Nh
SEVANIE, John	48	M	Farmer	19Jl04Nh
Helen	40	F	None	19Jl04Nh
James	19	M	Farmer	19Jl04Nh
John	16	M	Farmer	19Jl04Nh
Dennis	13	M	Farmer	19Jl04Nh
Francis	12	M	Farmer	19Jl04Nh
Jeanie	10	F	Child	19Jl04Nh
MCDEVITT, Edward	24	M	Farmer	19Jl04Nh
SHIELS, John	16	M	Farmer	19Jl04Nh
KELLY, B.Mrs.	26	F	None	19Jl04Nh
MCCULLOCH, M.Miss	24	F	None	19Jl04Nh
MCDEVITT, Patrick	29	M	Farmer	19Jl04Nh

NAMES OF PASSENGERS	AGE	SEX	OCCUPATIONS	DATE PORT SHIP
MCDEVITT, James	2	M	Child	19Jl04Nh
HAGGERTY, James	30	M	Joiner	19Jl04Nh
MOONEY, Thos.	25	M	Laborer	19Jl04Nh
Anne	25	F	None	19Jl04Nh
Mary-Anne	4	F	Child	19Jl04Nh
BURNS, Patrick	24	M	Laborer	19Jl04Nh
LONG, Matthew	59	M	Laborer	19Jl04Nh
WALLACE, Alex.	21	M	Laborer	19Jl04Nh
MCGOWAN, Peter	23	M	Laborer	19Jl04Nh
COYLE, Catherine	22	F	None	19Jl04Nh
GRAHAM, Margt.	26	F	None	19Jl04Nh
CARVING, Catherine	40	F	None	19Jl04Nh
BROWN, Ann	50	F	None	19Jl04Nh
Mary-Ann	14	F	None	19Jl04Nh
Margt.	12	F	None	19Jl04Nh
Helen	9	F	Child	19Jl04Nh
MORTON, Patrick	30	M	Laborer	19Jl04Nh
MCCAFFERTY, Thos.	22	M	Laborer	19Jl04Nh
GARTLAND, Catherine	20	F	None	19Jl04Nh
MONDAY, James	20	M	None	19Jl04Nh
DEVITT, Mary	25	F	None	19Jl04Nh
LONG, Thomas	20	M	None	19Jl04Nh
U, U	.00	U	Infant	19Jl04Nh
Born-At-Sea				
CHALMERS, Charles	00	M	Unknown	19Jl04Nh
STEEL, Arch.	00	M	Unknown	19Jl04Nh
MCDOUGALL, John	00	M	Unknown	19Jl04Nh
MORRIS, Janet-Miss	00	F	Unknown	19Jl04Nh
CHALMERS, Christina	00	F	Unknown	19Jl04Nh

MONTEZUMA 19 JULY 1849

From Liverpool

NAMES OF PASSENGERS	AGE	SEX	OCCUPATIONS	DATE PORT SHIP
PHILIP, William	30	M	Unknown	19Jl02Ca
PAUL, Robert	55	M	Surgeon	19Jl02Ca
RUSSEL, Thomas	21	M	Farmer	19Jl02Ca
DALTON, Ellen	52	F	Unknown	19Jl02Ca
Rose	27	F	Unknown	19Jl02Ca
Mary	25	F	Unknown	19Jl02Ca
Ellen	21	F	Unknown	19Jl02Ca
Richard	20	M	Farmer	19Jl02Ca
CASEY, Darby	25	M	Farmer	19Jl02Ca
Daniel	20	M	Farmer	19Jl02Ca
John	13	M	Unknown	19Jl02Ca
BABBINGTON, John	30	M	Attorney	19Jl02Ca
Letetia	36	F	Unknown	19Jl02Ca
Mary	34	F	Unknown	19Jl02Ca
MONTFORT, William	24	M	Gentleman	19Jl02Ca
BARRY, James-B.	26	M	Comedian	19Jl02Ca
WALTERS, George	25	M	Comedian	19Jl02Ca
LEE, Patrick	55	M	Farmer	19Jl02Ca
Alice	40	F	Farmer	19Jl02Ca
Patrick	24	M	Unknown	19Jl02Ca
Margaret	21	F	Unknown	19Jl02Ca
Jane	20	F	Unknown	19Jl02Ca
Joanna	17	F	Unknown	19Jl02Ca
Bridget	16	F	Unknown	19Jl02Ca
John	12	M	Unknown	19Jl02Ca
MCELROY, James	32	M	Farmer	19Jl02Ca
Elizabeth	32	F	Unknown	19Jl02Ca
Terence	3	M	Child	19Jl02Ca
John	.00	M	Infant	19Jl02Ca
SMITH, Catharine	22	F	Unknown	19Jl02Ca
SALMON, James	29	M	Mason	19Jl02Ca
Ellen	22	F	Unknown	19Jl02Ca
Josephine	.00	F	Infant	19Jl02Ca
DALTON, William	40	M	Laborer	19Jl02Ca
HARRINGTON, Pat	44	M	Laborer	19Jl02Ca

NAMES OF PASSENGERS	AGE	SEX	OCCUPATIONS	DATE PORT SHIP
MULLIGAN, Judy	21	F	Servant	19Jl02Ca
MCDONNOUGH, Catharine	21	F	Servant	19Jl02Ca
HAGAN, John	40	M	Laborer	19Jl02Ca
Mary	40	F	Unknown	19Jl02Ca
Kearn	.00	M	Infant	19Jl02Ca
Mary	4	F	Child	19Jl02Ca
Ann	2	F	Child	19Jl02Ca
GRIMES, Thomas	26	M	Laborer	19Jl02Ca
MCGUIRE, John	21	M	Laborer	19Jl02Ca
KYLEY, William	28	M	Laborer	19Jl02Ca
Mary	35	F	Unknown	19Jl02Ca
Mary	17	F	Unknown	19Jl02Ca
Dennis	13	M	Unknown	19Jl02Ca
Michael	11	M	Unknown	19Jl02Ca
Catharine	9	F	Child	19Jl02Ca
HACKETT, Martin	42	M	Laborer	19Jl02Ca
Briget	36	F	Unknown	19Jl02Ca
Mary	36	F	Unknown	19Jl02Ca
Martin	4	M	Child	19Jl02Ca
HICKEY, James	25	M	Laborer	19Jl02Ca
John	24	M	Laborer	19Jl02Ca
DAWSON, John	32	M	Laborer	19Jl02Ca
KEANE, Timothy	25	M	Laborer	19Jl02Ca
DAVIS, Robert	26	M	Laborer	19Jl02Ca
Abbey	25	F	Unknown	19Jl02Ca
KEANE, Bridget	17	F	Unknown	19Jl02Ca
DONOHOE, John	00	M	Laborer	19Jl02Ca
Died-At-Sea				
Ann	40	F	Unknown	19Jl02Ca
Ann	.00	F	Infant	19Jl02Ca
Patrick	17	M	Laborer	19Jl02Ca
Bridget	15	F	Unknown	19Jl02Ca
John	12	M	Unknown	19Jl02Ca
Timothy	9	M	Child	19Jl02Ca
Philip	7	M	Child	19Jl02Ca
Mary	4	F	Child	19Jl02Ca
Catharine	2	F	Child	19Jl02Ca
RILEY, Bernard	60	M	Laborer	19Jl02Ca
Catharine	60	F	Unknown	19Jl02Ca
Rose	20	F	Unknown	19Jl02Ca
Michael	18	M	Unknown	19Jl02Ca
FARRELL, Thomas	16	M	Laborer	19Jl02Ca
Catharine	15	F	Unknown	19Jl02Ca
Pat	10	M	Unknown	19Jl02Ca
John	6	M	Child	19Jl02Ca
Maria	4	F	Child	19Jl02Ca
BARRETT, John	25	M	Laborer	19Jl02Ca
James	21	M	Laborer	19Jl02Ca
WALLACE, Robert	22	M	Laborer	19Jl02Ca
ROLSTAIN, Christopher	21	M	Tailor	19Jl02Ca
HAGGEITY, James	40	M	Laborer	19Jl02Ca
CARLTON, Philip	21	M	Laborer	19Jl02Ca
James	20	M	Laborer	19Jl02Ca
RILEY, Pat	18	M	Servant	19Jl02Ca
TOBIN, Edmund	30	M	Laborer	19Jl02Ca
MAHER, Mary	24	F	Servant	19Jl02Ca
HAYES, Margaret	19	F	Servant	19Jl02Ca
DENNY, Ellen	18	F	Servant	19Jl02Ca
FLANIGAN, Thomas	25	M	Carpenter	19Jl02Ca
Catharine	17	F	Servant	19Jl02Ca
Bridget	20	F	Servant	19Jl02Ca
KEHOR, Ann	22	F	Dressmaker	19Jl02Ca
HERBERT, William	20	M	Laborer	19Jl02Ca
MURRY, Michael	21	M	Laborer	19Jl02Ca
BUCKLEY, Daniel	18	M	Laborer	19Jl02Ca
ODONNELL, Edward	22	M	Laborer	19Jl02Ca
KEOGH, Michael	28	M	Laborer	19Jl02Ca
FARRELL, John	45	M	Laborer	19Jl02Ca
Ellen	45	F	Unknown	19Jl02Ca
Dennis	25	M	Unknown	19Jl02Ca
Valentine	20	M	Unknown	19Jl02Ca
Bridget	17	F	Unknown	19Jl02Ca
William	16	F	Unknown	19Jl02Ca
Edmund	9	M	Child	19Jl02Ca
John	9	M	Child	19Jl02Ca

NAMES OF PASSENGERS	AGE	SEX	OCCUPATIONS	DATE PORT SHIP
FARRELL, Catharine	10	F	Unknown	19J102Ca
Johanna	2	F	Child	19J102Ca
DELANY, Joseph	21	M	Laborer	19J102Ca
FITZPATRICK, Pat	25	M	Laborer	19J102Ca
SALMON, Mary	14	F	Servant	19J102Ca
FALON, Ann	19	F	Servant	19J102Ca
FOGARTY, Honora	20	F	Servant	19J102Ca
DAILEY, Pat	28	M	Laborer	19J102Ca
Mary	28	F	Unknown	19J102Ca
Bridget	.00	F	Infant	19J102Ca
CONNELL, Michael	23	M	Laborer	19J102Ca
Thomas	18	M	Laborer	19J102Ca
FLAGGERTY, John	23	M	Blacksmith	19J102Ca
Johanna	25	F	Unknown	19J102Ca
RING, John	35	M	Laborer	19J102Ca
DINNON, Ellen	28	F	Servant	19J102Ca
Margaret	25	F	Servant	19J102Ca
SHANNAHAN, John	22	M	Laborer	19J102Ca
MULLHALL, Pat	56	M	Laborer	19J102Ca
Mary	50	F	Unknown	19J102Ca
Simon	27	M	Unknown	19J102Ca
Michael	26	M	Unknown	19J102Ca
Bridget	24	F	Unknown	19J102Ca
Sally	21	F	Unknown	19J102Ca
Ann	20	F	Unknown	19J102Ca
Mary	18	F	Unknown	19J102Ca
Eliza	17	F	Unknown	19J102Ca
Eliza	15	F	Unknown	19J102Ca
William	13	M	Unknown	19J102Ca
Catharine	9	F	Child	19J102Ca
BURNE, John	28	M	Laborer	19J102Ca
CONOHON, Mary	29	F	Servant	19J102Ca
Catharine	5	F	Child	19J102Ca
MCARTHY, Daniel	32	M	Farmer	19J102Ca
Ellen	32	F	Unknown	19J102Ca
Stephen	.00	M	Infant	19J102Ca
Pat	27	M	Laborer	19J102Ca
Eugene	4	M	Child	19J102Ca
LOVETT, John	27	M	Laborer	19J102Ca
HAGAN, Maurice	23	M	Laborer	19J102Ca
Ellen	20	F	Unknown	19J102Ca
Honora	.00	F	Infant	19J102Ca
BRUSHNAIN, James	23	M	Laborer	19J102Ca
LOVETT, Jeremiah	40	M	Laborer	19J102Ca
John	30	M	Laborer	19J102Ca
HAULEY, Michael	22	M	Laborer	19J102Ca
LOVETT, Catharine	16	F	Servant	19J102Ca
COSTELLO, Catharine	27	F	Servant	19J102Ca
TRANT, Catharine	16	F	Servant	19J102Ca
LAWLER, Jerry	24	M	Carpenter	19J102Ca
John	14	M	Unknown	19J102Ca
Ellen	50	F	Unknown	19J102Ca
MURRY, William	30	M	Laborer	19J102Ca
JOLLEY, Mary-Ann	18	F	Dressmaker	19J102Ca
BARRETT, William	26	M	Shipwright	19J102Ca
PIERCY, Robert	28	M	Coppersmith	19J102Ca
Ann	28	F	Unknown	19J102Ca
Martha	.00	F	Infant	19J102Ca
CORCEROY, Timothy	27	M	Laborer	19J102Ca
Honora	27	F	Unknown	19J102Ca
John	.00	M	Infant	19J102Ca
Mary	25	F	Unknown	19J102Ca
Ellen	22	F	Unknown	19J102Ca
Margaret	18	F	Unknown	19J102Ca
John	20	M	Unknown	19J102Ca
Michael	13	M	Unknown	19J102Ca
Daniel	11	M	Unknown	19J102Ca
Dan	2	M	Child	19J102Ca
CALLAHON, John	28	M	Laborer	19J102Ca
ODONNELL, Margaret	25	F	Servant	19J102Ca
DONOVAN, Mary	25	F	Servant	19J102Ca
COUGHLIN, James	25	M	Laborer	19J102Ca
DALY, John	45	M	Laborer	19J102Ca
Ellen	19	F	Servant	19J102Ca
LYONS, Ellen	25	F	Servant	19J102Ca
FLYNN, Mary	40	F	Servant	19J102Ca
MCARDLE, Mary	28	F	Servant	19J102Ca
HALLERON, James	19	M	Laborer	19J102Ca
CLAY, John	19	M	Laborer	19J102Ca
SMITH, William	21	M	Baker	19J102Ca
FLANNERY, John	21	M	Laborer	19J102Ca
FITZGERALD, Edward	21	M	Laborer	19J102Ca
SLAVEN, Pat	20	M	Farmer	19J102Ca
CARTY, Thomas	22	M	Farmer	19J102Ca
BURKE, Margaret	22	F	Servant	19J102Ca
MCDONNOR, Maria	.00	F	Infant	19J102Ca
DAVIDSON, Bridget	21	F	Servant	19J102Ca
HAGAN, Eliza	37	F	Servant	19J102Ca
James	.00	M	Infant	19J102Ca
Died-At-Sea				
Michael	9	M	Child	19J102Ca
Peter	2	M	Child	19J102Ca
Pat	7	M	Child	19J102Ca
Johnny	5	M	Child	19J102Ca
DOYLE, James	30	M	Maurer	19J102Ca
KIRBY, William	39	M	Miner	19J102Ca
RYAN, William	24	M	Carpenter	19J102Ca
Michael	45	M	Laborer	19J102Ca
Margaret	40	F	Unknown	19J102Ca
Mary	.00	F	Infant	19J102Ca
Lawless	18	M	Unknown	19J102Ca
Stephen	17	M	Unknown	19J102Ca
Ann	14	F	Unknown	19J102Ca
Michael	11	M	Unknown	19J102Ca
Ellen	9	F	Child	19J102Ca
Thomas	21	M	Unknown	19J102Ca
Dan	5	M	Child	19J102Ca
CARROLL, Daniel	46	M	Farmer	19J102Ca
Mary	40	F	Unknown	19J102Ca
Ann	20	F	Unknown	19J102Ca
Mary	21	F	Unknown	19J102Ca
Alley	18	F	Unknown	19J102Ca
Catharine	19	F	Unknown	19J102Ca
Ellen	14	F	Unknown	19J102Ca
Bridget	12	F	Unknown	19J102Ca
Michael	11	M	Unknown	19J102Ca
FARMING, Ellen	18	F	Servant	19J102Ca
Catharine	19	F	Servant	19J102Ca
CARTER, John	27	M	Farmer	19J102Ca
MAGAN, Michael	20	M	Laborer	19J102Ca
Thomas	18	M	Laborer	19J102Ca
KANE, James	21	M	Laborer	19J102Ca
John	12	M	Laborer	19J102Ca
BRYAN, Andrew	55	M	Laborer	19J102Ca
Bridget	50	F	Laborer	19J102Ca
Andey	2	M	Child	19J102Ca
Pat	18	M	Unknown	19J102Ca
Michael	17	M	Unknown	19J102Ca
John	9	M	Child	19J102Ca
Johanna	10	F	Unknown	19J102Ca
Catharine	7	F	Child	19J102Ca
MCBRIDE, James	50	M	Laborer	19J102Ca
HANLON, Thomas	48	M	Laborer	19J102Ca
LYNCH, Bridget	16	F	Servant	19J102Ca
BRADY, Nicholas	39	M	Laborer	19J102Ca
Rose	29	F	Unknown	19J102Ca
Biddy	.00	F	Infant	19J102Ca
Ellen	12	F	Unknown	19J102Ca
John	11	M	Unknown	19J102Ca
Mary	9	F	Child	19J102Ca
FLYNN, Michael	26	M	Laborer	19J102Ca
John	20	M	Laborer	19J102Ca
Rose	22	F	Servant	19J102Ca
Sally	26	F	Servant	19J102Ca
BRADY, James	40	M	Laborer	19J102Ca
MOLLOY, Pat	17	M	Laborer	19J102Ca
Bernard	30	M	Laborer	19J102Ca
Rose	30	F	Unknown	19J102Ca
Margaret	.00	F	Infant	19J102Ca
Keeran	6	M	Child	19J102Ca

NAMES OF PASSENGERS	AGE	SEX	OCCUPATIONS	DATE PORT SHIP
MOLLOY, Bernard	4	M	Child	19J102Ca
MCMASTER, Margaret	30	F	Servant	19J102Ca
HUNT, Bryan	42	M	Laborer	19J102Ca
FITZMORRIS, Martin	24	M	Laborer	19J102Ca
HEALING, John	19	M	Laborer	19J102Ca
ODWYER, Margaret	19	F	Servant	19J102Ca
JOYCE, Patrick	20	M	Farmer	19J102Ca
MACMANS, James	30	M	Laborer	19J102Ca
MCADAM, Frank	27	M	Laborer	19J102Ca
REDMON, John	40	M	Laborer	19J102Ca
CONWAY, Thomas	47	M	Laborer	19J102Ca
James	10	M	Unknown	19J102Ca
Ann	7	F	Child	19J102Ca
FARREL, Daniel	47	M	Laborer	19J102Ca
MANGAN, James	40	M	Laborer	19J102Ca
Peggy	35	F	Unknown	19J102Ca
John	11	M	Unknown	19J102Ca
Margaret	8	F	Child	19J102Ca
Pat	8	M	Child	19J102Ca
SWEENEY, Catharine	18	F	Servant	19J102Ca
BROWN, Agnes	67	F	Unknown	19J102Ca
Andrew	25	M	Laborer	19J102Ca
SULLIVAN, Timothy	35	M	Laborer	19J102Ca
Julia	30	F	Unknown	19J102Ca
WHITE, William	20	M	Laborer	19J102Ca
Michael	19	M	Laborer	19J102Ca
BRIDE, Mary	20	F	Servant	19J102Ca
GILMORE, Margaret	25	F	Servant	19J102Ca
Thomas	.00	M	Infant	19J102Ca
GALLAHAN, Condy	23	M	Laborer	19J102Ca
WOOD, Michael	26	M	Shoemaker	19J102Ca
CLARKE, Eliza	28	F	Servant	19J102Ca
COSTELLO, Bridget	14	F	Servant	19J102Ca
FOX, James	30	M	Laborer	19J102Ca
John	25	M	Laborer	19J102Ca
HANNIGAN, Bridget	24	F	Servant	19J102Ca
HOBLAN, Hannah	16	F	Servant	19J102Ca
KELLY, William	25	M	Laborer	19J102Ca
MCGIBLING, Ann	18	F	Servant	19J102Ca
CONNELL, Jane	29	F	Servant	19J102Ca
Catharine	11	F	Unknown	19J102Ca
Rose	7	F	Child	19J102Ca
HAGGERTY, Barney	20	M	Laborer	19J102Ca
MULLAN, Bridget	16	F	Servant	19J102Ca
Ann	14	F	Servant	19J102Ca
GREEN, Pat	40	M	Laborer	19J102Ca
Thomas	36	M	Laborer	19J102Ca
DALEY, James	10	M	Unknown	19J102Ca
RYAN, Jeremiah	14	M	Laborer	19J102Ca
Ellen	12	F	Unknown	19J102Ca
ONEILL, Con.	26	M	Maurer	19J102Ca
GAITLEY, Hannah	28	F	Servant	19J102Ca
DOYLE, Michael	24	M	Accountant	19J102Ca
CODY, Pat	16	M	Carpenter	19J102Ca
CONORTON, Thomas	45	M	Laborer	19J102Ca
HENNESSY, James	40	M	Laborer	19J102Ca
Catharine	18	F	Unknown	19J102Ca
Pat	12	M	Unknown	19J102Ca
Bridget	10	F	Unknown	19J102Ca
GLANCEY, Mary	27	F	Servant	19J102Ca
MADDEN, Andrew	34	M	Surveyor	19J102Ca
TURNER, Robert	30	M	Laborer	19J102Ca
MILNE, George	22	M	Laborer	19J102Ca
QUIN, Michael	27	M	Laborer	19J102Ca
FITZGERALD, Bridget	17	F	Servant	19J102Ca
SMITH, John	22	M	Laborer	19J102Ca

SUPERB 19 JULY 1849

From Glasgow

NAMES OF PASSENGERS	AGE	SEX	OCCUPATIONS	DATE PORT SHIP
RAE, James	28	M	Farmer	19J104Nj
Margaret	28	F	None	19J104Nj
William	7	M	Child	19J104Nj
Peter	5	M	Child	19J104Nj
Barbara	3	F	Child	19J104Nj
George	.06	M	Infant	19J104Nj
William	60	M	Farmer	19J104Nj
Elizabeth	60	F	None	19J104Nj
Jane	26	F	None	19J104Nj
William-Jr.	30	M	Farmer	19J104Nj
Ann	30	F	None	19J104Nj
Alexander	.06	M	Infant	19J104Nj
BINNIE, Andrew	44	M	Farmer	19J104Nj
Agnes	36	F	None	19J104Nj
Robert	7	M	Child	19J104Nj
John	7	M	Child	19J104Nj
Andrew	5	M	Child	19J104Nj
James	4	M	Child	19J104Nj
Ann	2	F	Child	19J104Nj
LAMB, George	29	M	Farmer	19J104Nj
Jane	25	F	None	19J104Nj
James	2	M	Child	19J104Nj
George	.09	M	Infant	19J104Nj
HAMILTON, James	31	M	Farmer	19J104Nj
Jane	30	F	None	19J104Nj
Jane-Matilda	8	F	Child	19J104Nj
Janet	6	F	Child	19J104Nj
Mary	4	F	Child	19J104Nj
John	2	M	Child	19J104Nj
William	22	M	Farmer	19J104Nj
EWING, Ann	26	F	Weaver	19J104Nj
AIKMAN, James	36	M	Smith	19J104Nj
Janet	11	F	None	19J104Nj
John	39	M	Engineer	19J104Nj
James	15	M	None	19J104Nj
Isabella	36	F	None	19J104Nj
DICK, John	3	M	Child	19J104Nj
AIKMAN, John	6	M	Child	19J104Nj
SCRYMINGER, Joseph	26	M	Farmer	19J104Nj
ADAM, Archibald	30	M	Farmer	19J104Nj
MAILER, Andrew	27	M	Shoemaker	19J104Nj
Barbara	26	F	None	19J104Nj
SPEED, Thomas	28	M	Bootmaker	19J104Nj
Elizabeth	28	F	None	19J104Nj
IMRIE, James	25	M	Shoemaker	19J104Nj
DICK, Peter	26	M	Shoemaker	19J104Nj
Helen	29	F	None	19J104Nj
Agnes	68	F	None	19J104Nj
BERTRAM, Peter	67	M	Laborer	19J104Nj
Elizabeth	67	F	None	19J104Nj
Jean	26	F	Servant	19J104Nj
DARLING, John	49	M	Laborer	19J104Nj
Susan	30	F	None	19J104Nj
John	24	M	Laborer	19J104Nj
James	22	M	Laborer	19J104Nj
Thomas	20	M	Laborer	19J104Nj
Peter	4	M	Child	19J104Nj
David	2	M	Child	19J104Nj
LAIDLAW, John	31	M	Laborer	19J104Nj
Isabella	33	F	None	19J104Nj
Elizabeth	3	F	Child	19J104Nj
Jenie	2	F	Child	19J104Nj
PURVIS, George	38	M	Laborer	19J104Nj
Elizabeth	39	F	None	19J104Nj
William	13	M	None	19J104Nj

NAMES OF PASSENGERS	AGE	SEX	OCCUPATIONS	DATE PORT SHIP
PURVIS, Peter	12	M	None	19J104Nj
John	10	M	None	19J104Nj
Elizabeth	8	F	Child	19J104Nj
George	7	M	Child	19J104Nj
Christina	4	F	Child	19J104Nj
Isabella	.09	F	Infant	19J104Nj
GOW, James	21	M	Laborer	19J104Nj
OWENS, Barbara	32	F	Servant	19J104Nj
Jane	13	F	Servant	19J104Nj
MCCOLL, Muir	25	M	Laborer	19J104Nj
BARRETT, Amos	23	M	Miner	19J104Nj
LAMB, Robert	30	M	Farmer	19J104Nj
ROBERTSON, Peter	40	M	Farmer	19J104Nj
Elizabeth	38	F	None	19J104Nj
Peter	19	M	Farmer	19J104Nj
Catherine	15	F	None	19J104Nj
Mary	13	F	None	19J104Nj
James	11	M	None	19J104Nj
Alexander	4	M	Child	19J104Nj
HARVEY, William	46	M	Farmer	19J104Nj
FARRELL, Lawrence	28	M	Laborer	19J104Nj
WILSON, John	35	M	Plasterer	19J104Nj
Alexr.	27	M	Plasterer	19J104Nj
Jane	23	F	None	19J104Nj
Ann	.10	F	Infant	19J104Nj
ALLAN, Richard	18	M	Engineer	19J104Nj
BEATTIE, Robert	32	M	Engineer	19J104Nj
Elizabeth	34	F	None	19J104Nj
James	12	M	None	19J104Nj
Isabella	10	F	None	19J104Nj
Andrew	8	M	Child	19J104Nj
Mary	5	F	Child	19J104Nj
STEWART, Robert	55	M	Farmer	19J104Nj
Mary	55	F	None	19J104Nj
Duncan	20	M	Farmer	19J104Nj
James	18	M	Farmer	19J104Nj
Alexr.	16	M	Farmer	19J104Nj
Laidlaw	15	M	Farmer	19J104Nj
Robert	13	M	None	19J104Nj
CARR, George	26	M	Laborer	19J104Nj
MITCHELL, William	13	M	None	19J104Nj
PACK, Charles	30	M	Laborer	19J104Nj
Mary	28	F	None	19J104Nj
BRANTON, John	20	M	Laborer	19J104Nj
FORTON, John	24	M	Laborer	19J104Nj
HENDERSON, Ellen	25	F	Servant	19J104Nj
William	.10	M	Infant	19J104Nj
HUNTER, Alexander	21	M	Farmer	19J104Nj
Catherine	22	F	None	19J104Nj
DARNING, J.	33	M	Mason	19J104Nj
ONIELL, James	30	M	Laborer	19J104Nj
DOGGINS, Eliza	36	F	Servant	19J104Nj
BURT, Robert	21	M	Laborer	19J104Nj
Elizabeth	22	F	Servant	19J104Nj
CHRYSTALL, Margaret	30	F	Servant	19J104Nj
Elizabeth	30	F	Servant	19J104Nj
ANDERSON, William	26	M	Toll Keeper	19J104Nj
GILMOUR, James	28	M	Mason	19J104Nj
Sarah	24	F	None	19J104Nj
Alexander	2	M	Child	19J104Nj
MCLEAN, Hector	43	M	Mason	19J104Nj
Mary	43	F	None	19J104Nj
Alexander	17	M	Mason	19J104Nj
John	15	M	Mason	19J104Nj
Duncan	12	M	Mason	19J104Nj
Isabella	9	F	Child	19J104Nj
Hector	7	M	Child	19J104Nj
CAMERON, Eliza	33	F	Nurse	19J104Nj
PENNYCOOK, Mary	24	F	Nurse	19J104Nj
FUNNY, Ann	31	F	Servant	19J104Nj
CAMERON, Colin	37	M	Smith	19J104Nj
MCCRAE, John	26	M	Laborer	19J104Nj
John-Jr.	15	M	Smith	19J104Nj
SMITH, Alexander	20	M	Paper Maker	19J104Nj
LYON, John	30	M	Laborer	19J104Nj
CURRIE, Edward	35	M	Laborer	19J104Nj
MAINS, Charles	24	M	Laborer	19J104Nj
Sarah	24	F	None	19J104Nj
Rose	16	F	Servant	19J104Nj
BENSON, Thomas	18	M	Laborer	19J104Nj
BRADLEY, James	56	M	Laborer	19J104Nj
Mary	54	F	None	19J104Nj
Henry	20	M	Laborer	19J104Nj
James	17	M	Laborer	19J104Nj
Frances	7	F	Child	19J104Nj
DIVINE, Patrick-Jr.	20	M	Laborer	19J104Nj
Catherine	16	F	Servant	19J104Nj
Patrick	40	M	Baker	19J104Nj
FARMER, John	24	M	Farmer	19J104Nj
HARRIOTT, George	25	M	Farmer	19J104Nj
KELLAR, Euphemie	23	F	Servant	19J104Nj
MCKENZIE, John	23	M	Laborer	19J104Nj
Donald	20	M	Laborer	19J104Nj
EDINGTON, Wm.	19	M	Farmer	19J104Nj
HOGG, John	24	M	Farmer	19J104Nj
LEDOTA, John	29	M	Farmer	19J104Nj
LOTHIAN, George	28	M	Farmer	19J104Nj
TORRANCE, William	24	M	Blacksmith	19J104Nj
Jane	21	F	None	19J104Nj
GRANT, James	34	M	Smith	19J104Nj
Margaret	32	F	None	19J104Nj
John	8	M	Child	19J104Nj
WHITE, James	23	M	Joiner	19J104Nj
Elizabeth	23	F	None	19J104Nj
ROBERTSON, William	17	M	Farmer	19J104Nj
SCOTT, James	20	M	Farmer	19J104Nj
DAVIDSON, Donald	67	M	Farmer	19J104Nj
Janet	64	F	None	19J104Nj
Ann	28	F	Servant	19J104Nj
MCPHERSON, Ann	60	F	Servant	19J104Nj
BRUCE, Alexander	22	M	Farmer	19J104Nj
DUNCAN, John-Jr.	31	M	Cooper	19J104Nj
EDGAR, John	30	M	Cooper	19J104Nj
DUNCAN, John-Sr.	60	M	Cooper	19J104Nj
Mary	28	F	None	19J104Nj
Ann	7	F	Child	19J104Nj
Agnes	3	F	Child	19J104Nj
THOMSON, Robert	27	M	Brf	19J104Nj
Mary	27	F	None	19J104Nj
MCINTYRE, Alexander	30	M	Farmer	19J104Nj
GILLIGAN, Catherine	28	F	Servant	19J104Nj
STEWART, Elizabeth	18	F	Servant	19J104Nj
MCKIE, George	25	M	Farmer	19J104Nj
MILLAR, Hugh	30	M	Weaver	19J104Nj
SAMSON, Robert	30	M	Weaver	19J104Nj
Margaret	60	F	None	19J104Nj
Sarah	23	F	Servant	19J104Nj
Nancy	16	F	Servant	19J104Nj
MCCLELLAND, Ellen	25	F	Servant	19J104Nj
Eliza	2	F	Child	19J104Nj
WRIGHT, Matilda	26	F	Servant	19J104Nj
RANKIN, Nancy	24	F	Servant	19J104Nj
TRIMBLE, Sarah	8	F	Child	19J104Nj
TAYLOR, William	20	M	Laborer	19J104Nj
MCKETTRICK, James	20	M	Laborer	19J104Nj
MCCALL, James	35	M	Laborer	19J104Nj
MCKINLAY, Neil	30	M	Laborer	19J104Nj

PREDRAGA 20 JULY 1849

From Nassau

NAMES OF PASSENGERS	AGE	SEX	OCCUPATIONS	DATE PORT SHIP
ELLIS, Francis	30	M	Gentleman	20J170Mo

VANDALIA 21 JULY 1849

From Liverpool

NAMES OF PASSENGERS	AGE	SEX	OCCUPATIONS	DATE PORT SHIP
OCALLAGHAN, William	19	M	Laborer	21J102Nn
Thomas	17	M	Laborer	21J102Nn
SMITH, Sarah	12	F	Servant	21J102Nn
REDDY, Allice	25	F	Seamstress	21J102Nn
MULVEY, Joseph	10	M	Laborer	21J102Nn
Michael	8	M	Child	21J102Nn
MCGINTY, Catharine	19	F	Servant	21J102Nn
LYNCH, Ann	50	F	Servant	21J102Nn
CAYAN, Mary	50	F	Seamstress	21J102Nn
Daniel	16	M	Laborer	21J102Nn
Ellen	14	F	Servant	21J102Nn
Mary	12	F	Servant	21J102Nn
Margaret	10	F	Servant	21J102Nn
James	8	M	Child	21J102Nn
Bridget	35	F	Servant	21J102Nn
Catharine	9	F	Child	21J102Nn
Mary	6	F	Child	21J102Nn
John	4	M	Child	21J102Nn
MCENNEY, Michael	20	M	Laborer	21J102Nn
COLLINS, Thomas	25	M	Laborer	21J102Nn
MACKENZIE, James	19	M	Laborer	21J102Nn
CANTWELL, Edward	28	M	Laborer	21J102Nn
GROGHAN, Bridget	50	F	Nurse	21J102Nn
FLYNN, Bridget	20	F	Nurse	21J102Nn
MILLS, Mary	17	F	Nurse	21J102Nn
KENNEY, Martin	34	M	Laborer	21J102Nn
Margaret	24	F	Servant	21J102Nn
BELUNE, Michael	29	M	Laborer	21J102Nn
Thomas	24	M	Laborer	21J102Nn
CRAW, Ann	19	F	Nurse	21J102Nn
SHUTTLEWORTH, Martha	30	F	Nurse	21J102Nn
Mary	9	F	Child	21J102Nn
EVANS, Mary	28	F	Nurse	21J102Nn
DULLAN, Michael	27	M	Laborer	21J102Nn
THURLBY, Richard	21	M	Laborer	21J102Nn
EDWARDS, William	21	M	Laborer	21J102Nn
Thomas	19	M	Laborer	21J102Nn
TEERDALE, John	20	M	Laborer	21J102Nn
TALLEY, Patrick	30	M	Laborer	21J102Nn
Mary	18	F	Laborer	21J102Nn
HILL, Patrick	40	M	Laborer	21J102Nn
Pattrick	9	M	Child	21J102Nn
KIERNAN, William	15	M	Farmer	21J102Nn
Elizabeth	18	F	Farmer	21J102Nn
ROWLEY, Robert	20	M	Farmer	21J102Nn
EDWARDS, John	30	M	Farmer	21J102Nn
James	22	M	Laborer	21J102Nn
FARRELL, Phill	20	M	Laborer	21J102Nn
PATE, John	32	M	Laborer	21J102Nn
Elizabeth	25	F	Laborer	21J102Nn
MCDONALD, Michael	30	M	Laborer	21J102Nn
DAVIS, Mary	20	F	Nurse	21J102Nn
FINNIE, Joseph	25	M	Laborer	21J102Nn
U-Mrs.	24	F	Laborer	21J102Nn
Mary-Ann	3	F	Child	21J102Nn
Jane	.00	F	Infant	21J102Nn
BRITTLE, Robert	26	M	Laborer	21J102Nn
WALLACE, John	21	M	Laborer	21J102Nn
Mary-Ann	28	F	Laborer	21J102Nn
MALONEY, John	40	M	Laborer	21J102Nn
Ellen	31	F	Laborer	21J102Nn
Mary	.00	F	Infant	21J102Nn
KEEFE, Kearn	24	M	Laborer	21J102Nn
CRUMMING, Mary	42	F	Nurse	21J102Nn
STAIRS, Margaret	19	F	Nurse	21J102Nn
PATTERSON, Isabella	26	F	Nurse	21J102Nn
Jane	.00	F	Infant	21J102Nn
BARCLAY, Sarah	20	F	Nurse	21J102Nn
DONNELLY, Barney	20	M	Laborer	21J102Nn
LYNCH, Catherine	20	F	Nurse	21J102Nn
Elizabeth	18	F	Nurse	21J102Nn
COFFEE, James	25	M	Laborer	21J102Nn

NAPOLEON 21 JULY 1849

From Belfast

NAMES OF PASSENGERS	AGE	SEX	OCCUPATIONS	DATE PORT SHIP
BLAIR, Hugh	53	M	Laborer	21J105Nk
JAMISON, James	58	M	Laborer	21J105Nk
Mary	60	F	Laborer	21J105Nk
Margt.	25	F	Laborer	21J105Nk
Mary	13	F	Laborer	21J105Nk
Jane	11	F	Laborer	21J105Nk
Mary	23	F	Laborer	21J105Nk
REID, James	49	M	Laborer	21J105Nk
ADAMS, John	55	M	Laborer	21J105Nk
Jane	35	F	Laborer	21J105Nk
Joseph	16	M	Laborer	21J105Nk
John	8	M	Child	21J105Nk
Mary	6	F	Child	21J105Nk
Samuel-A.	4	M	Child	21J105Nk
ANDERSON, John	50	M	Laborer	21J105Nk
Mary	49	F	Laborer	21J105Nk
Alexr.	26	M	Laborer	21J105Nk
SMITH, James	25	M	Laborer	21J105Nk
ONEIL, John	22	M	Laborer	21J105Nk
BRIGGS, Margt.	20	F	Laborer	21J105Nk
SIMPSON, John	22	M	Laborer	21J105Nk
REID, William	30	M	Laborer	21J105Nk
Sarah	40	F	Laborer	21J105Nk
OFFICER, William	25	M	Laborer	21J105Nk
James	49	M	Laborer	21J105Nk
STEPHENSON, William	28	M	Laborer	21J105Nk
Isabella	24	F	Laborer	21J105Nk
Jane	.00	F	Infant	21J105Nk
REID, William	22	M	Laborer	21J105Nk
Mary-A.	24	F	Laborer	21J105Nk
Magt.	20	F	Laborer	21J105Nk
Matthew	16	M	Laborer	21J105Nk
John	13	M	Laborer	21J105Nk
AGNEW, Henry	13	M	Laborer	21J105Nk
BOYD, Susan	60	F	Laborer	21J105Nk
Susan	20	F	Laborer	21J105Nk
Agnes	19	F	Laborer	21J105Nk
STRAGHAN, George	30	M	Laborer	21J105Nk
BIGHAM, Saml.	30	M	Laborer	21J105Nk
Elizt.	40	F	Laborer	21J105Nk
Samuel	24	M	Laborer	21J105Nk
MARTIN, Thomas	40	M	Laborer	21J105Nk
Esther	30	F	Laborer	21J105Nk
John	3	M	Child	21J105Nk
William	.00	M	Infant	21J105Nk
KANE, Henry	36	M	Laborer	21J105Nk
MCKENNEDY, U-Mrs.	38	F	Laborer	21J105Nk
Robert	19	M	Laborer	21J105Nk
Philip	16	M	Laborer	21J105Nk
Nancy	11	F	Laborer	21J105Nk
Felix	9	M	Child	21J105Nk
Jane	7	F	Child	21J105Nk
John	5	M	Child	21J105Nk
James	3	M	Child	21J105Nk
Joseph	.00	M	Infant	21J105Nk
CORBIT, Margt.	35	F	Laborer	21J105N
Eliza	18	F	Laborer	21J105N

NAMES OF PASSENGERS	AGE	SEX	OCCUPATIONS	DATE PORT SHIP
CORBIT, Samuel	13	M	Laborer	21J105Nk
Agnes	9	F	Child	21J105Nk
James	7	M	Child	21J105Nk
Robt.	5	M	Child	21J105Nk
MONTGOMERY, William	24	M	Laborer	21J105Nk
WESION, Sarah	19	F	Laborer	21J105Nk
GLASGOW, David	26	M	Laborer	21J105Nk
MCGOUGH, William	40	M	Laborer	21J105Nk
SMITH, James	24	M	Laborer	21J105Nk
Bridgt.	20	F	Laborer	21J105Nk
TRAYNOR, Mary-A.	24	F	Laborer	21J105Nk
MCELROY, Mary	22	F	Laborer	21J105Nk
MCGOREN, James	30	M	Laborer	21J105Nk
WILLIAMS, James	26	M	Laborer	21J105Nk
MCALEAN, Pat.	23	M	Laborer	21J105Nk
MCKENNEDY, Wm.	34	M	Laborer	21J105Nk
Eliza	30	F	Laborer	21J105Nk
Margt.	8	F	Child	21J105Nk
Eliza	5	F	Child	21J105Nk
Mary-A.	.00	F	Infant	21J105Nk
MCALISH, Hannah	30	F	Laborer	21J105Nk
MCKELSO, Mich.	20	M	Laborer	21J105Nk
Mary	18	F	Laborer	21J105Nk
QUINN, Joseph	22	M	Laborer	21J105Nk
Jane	19	F	Laborer	21J105Nk
GARROW, John	18	M	Laborer	21J105Nk
THOMPSON, John	20	M	Laborer	21J105Nk
KING, James	19	M	Laborer	21J105Nk
MURPHY, Jane	22	F	Laborer	21J105Nk
HOLDEN, Isabella	19	F	Laborer	21J105Nk
GORR, Pat	42	M	Laborer	21J105Nk
FARRIS, Ellen	40	F	Laborer	21J105Nk
Thomas	46	M	Laborer	21J105Nk
TRAINOR, James	24	M	Laborer	21J105Nk
SMITH, U-Mrs.	50	F	Laborer	21J105Nk
Mary	18	F	Laborer	21J105Nk
Ellen	16	F	Laborer	21J105Nk
Eliza	13	F	Laborer	21J105Nk
Alex.	11	M	Laborer	21J105Nk
John	7	M	Child	21J105Nk

NO RECORD OF SHIP

From Londonderry

NAMES OF PASSENGERS	AGE	SEX	OCCUPATIONS	DATE PORT SHIP
MEGARRY, Danl.	24	M	Laborer	01

ALLICE-WILSON 21 JULY 1849

From Dublin

NAMES OF PASSENGERS	AGE	SEX	OCCUPATIONS	DATE PORT SHIP
FAGAN, Mary	25	F	Farmer	21JI12NI
GOGARTY, Patt	21	M	Unknown	21JI12NI
DUNNCAN, U-Mrs.	24	F	Unknown	21JI12NI
SLEON, Pat	18	M	Unknown	21JI12NI
BLANCH, James	26	M	Unknown	21JI12NI
Bridget	22	F	Unknown	21JI12NI
Andy	19	M	Unknown	21JI12NI
KEATING, Margt.	20	F	Unknown	21JI12NI
James	.00	M	Infant	21JI12NI
MURRAY, James	31	M	Unknown	21JI12NI
HOCY, Thomas	42	M	Unknown	21JI12NI
DUFFY, Catherine	25	F	Unknown	21JI12NI

NAMES OF PASSENGERS	AGE	SEX	OCCUPATIONS	DATE PORT SHIP
FOX, James	25	M	Unknown	21JI12NI
Margt.	21	F	Unknown	21JI12NI
Mary	.00	F	Infant	21JI12NI
CASSIDY, Sarah	50	F	Unknown	21JI12NI
John	28	M	Unknown	21JI12NI
Martin	26	M	Unknown	21JI12NI
DOYLE, Frederick	20	M	Unknown	21JI12NI
MUTTY, Marton	30	M	Unknown	21JI12NI
BRENNAN, William	22	M	Unknown	21JI12NI
BURKE, Bridget	22	F	Unknown	21JI12NI
PRICE, James	22	M	Unknown	21JI12NI
FLAHERTY, John	50	M	Unknown	21JI12NI
Rebecca	30	F	Unknown	21JI12NI
Andy	12	M	Unknown	21JI12NI
Eliza	2	F	Child	21JI12NI
Rebecca	.00	F	Infant	21JI12NI
DOLLAN, James	40	M	Unknown	21JI12NI
Mary	40	F	Unknown	21JI12NI
Mary	20	F	Unknown	21JI12NI
Kate	17	F	Unknown	21JI12NI
DOLLAND, Zerecca	13	M	Unknown	21JI12NI
John	6	M	Child	21JI12NI
MCDONNALD, Michal	21	M	Unknown	21JI12NI
CONALL, Catherine	34	F	Unknown	21JI12NI
Mary-A.	12	F	Unknown	21JI12NI
CUDDY, Mary	21	F	Unknown	21JI12NI
John	.00	M	Infant	21JI12NI
HARREGAN, Mary	20	F	Unknown	21JI12NI
Mary	20	F	Unknown	21JI12NI
LEONES, Lawrence	18	M	Unknown	21JI12NI
MURPHY, Patt	30	M	Unknown	21JI12NI
WALSH, Mick	18	M	Unknown	21JI12NI
RINSELLA, U-Mrs.	16	F	Unknown	21JI12NI
John	13	M	Unknown	21JI12NI
BROPHY, Richard	17	M	Unknown	21JI12NI
COFFEY, Pat	22	M	Unknown	21JI12NI
LENNOX, U	20	M	Unknown	21JI12NI
U-Mrs.	28	F	Unknown	21JI12NI
SHORT, John	24	M	Unknown	21JI12NI
BRIDE, Jane	22	F	Unknown	21JI12NI
WALSH, Anna	20	F	Unknown	21JI12NI
Catherine	24	F	Unknown	21JI12NI
CINHEOR, Mary	22	F	Unknown	21JI12NI
RELLY, Pat	17	M	Unknown	21JI12NI
Mary	24	F	Unknown	21JI12NI
SCOTT, U	22	M	Unknown	21JI12NI
MOON, James	22	M	Unknown	21JI12NI
SCULLY, Allis	20	F	Unknown	21JI12NI
ARCHY, Mary	23	F	Unknown	21JI12NI
Richard	.00	M	Infant	21JI12NI
ROONEY, Catherine	33	F	Unknown	21JI12NI
Jane	22	F	Unknown	21JI12NI
KEEGAN, Alice	20	F	Unknown	21JI12NI
James	.00	M	Infant	21JI12NI
FITZGERALD, Thomas	25	M	Unknown	21JI12NI
BIRD, U-Mrs.	40	F	Unknown	21JI12NI
U-Miss	20	F	Unknown	21JI12NI
LEE, U	36	M	Unknown	21JI12NI
U-Mrs.	34	F	Unknown	21JI12NI
Patt	16	M	Unknown	21JI12NI
Mary	13	F	Unknown	21JI12NI
Robert	10	M	Child	21JI12NI
Thomas	6	M	Child	21JI12NI
Luke	4	M	Child	21JI12NI
James	.00	M	Infant	21JI12NI
POWER, Edward	15	M	Unknown	21JI12NI
ROONEY, Catherine	19	F	Unknown	21JI12NI
RONNEY, Eliza	18	F	Unknown	21JI12NI
Margt.	16	F	Unknown	21JI12NI
SHAW, Ann	20	F	Unknown	21JI12NI
SCHOLFIELD, Michael	16	M	Unknown	21JI12NI
PALLAN, John	20	M	Unknown	21JI12NI
Catherine	20	F	Unknown	21JI12NI
KEATING, Pat	24	M	Unknown	21JI12NI
Winney	25	M	Unknown	21JI12NI

NAMES OF PASSENGERS	AGE	SEX	OCCUPATIONS	DATE PORT SHIP
HART, Michael	30	M	Unknown	21J112NI
U-Mrs.	25	F	Unknown	21J112NI
James	2	M	Child	21J112NI
Mary	.00	F	Infant	21J112NI
MADDEN, U	16	M	Unknown	21J112NI
Thomas	12	M	Unknown	21J112NI
Mary-A.	20	F	Unknown	21J112NI
MCNALLY, Mary	50	F	Unknown	21J112NI
Margt.	19	F	Unknown	21J112NI
Bridget	12	F	Unknown	21J112NI
James	.00	M	Infant	21J112NI
BURHAN, Eliza	20	F	Unknown	21J112NI
MARKS, Mary	20	F	Unknown	21J112NI
ROCHFORD, Larance	23	M	Unknown	21J112NI
MARK, James	20	M	Unknown	21J112NI
HARMAN, John	20	M	Unknown	21J112NI
DOYLE, U	35	M	Unknown	21J112NI
DEMPSEY, U	25	M	Unknown	21J112NI
DOYLE, U-Mrs.	20	F	Unknown	21J112NI
CULLEN, U-Miss	20	F	Unknown	21J112NI
HAMILTON, Richard	18	M	Unknown	21J112NI
Eliza	22	F	Unknown	21J112NI
CRANNY, John	18	M	Unknown	21J112NI
HOGAN, Pat	20	M	Unknown	21J112NI
CULLEN, Charles	20	M	Unknown	21J112NI
HANLLEN, James	19	M	Unknown	21J112NI
Emily	28	F	Unknown	21J112NI
MURPHY, James	21	M	Unknown	21J112NI
LOLLD, John	37	M	Unknown	21J112NI
WHILOCK, Charles	37	M	Unknown	21J112NI
KEENAN, Michael	20	M	Unknown	21J112NI
LORONY, Pat	20	M	Unknown	21J112NI
PATTEN, John	44	M	Unknown	21J112NI
U-Mrs.	13	F	Unknown	21J112NI
Michael	24	M	Unknown	21J112NI
William	24	M	Unknown	21J112NI
BEHAN, John	20	M	Unknown	21J112NI
DORA, Ellen	20	F	Unknown	21J112NI
Mary	20	F	Unknown	21J112NI
BURTLER, Winney	35	M	Unknown	21J112NI
CEAL, Eliza	26	F	Unknown	21J112NI
MORAN, John	20	M	Unknown	21J112NI
PRICE, William	40	M	Unknown	21J112NI
PURCE, U-Mrs.	38	F	Unknown	21J112NI
Ann	16	F	Unknown	21J112NI
Thomas	13	M	Unknown	21J112NI
Maria	.00	F	Infant	21J112NI
BYRNE, Pat	25	M	Unknown	21J112NI
U-Mrs.	25	F	Unknown	21J112NI
Peter	25	M	Unknown	21J112NI
CLARK, Thomas	23	M	Unknown	21J112NI
SHERRY, U-Mrs.	21	F	Unknown	21J112NI
MARK, Larance	13	M	Unknown	21J112NI
James	10	M	Child	21J112NI
GLAYBROOK, John	30	M	Unknown	21J112NI
WALSH, John	24	M	Unknown	21J112NI
Francis	22	M	Unknown	21J112NI
Mary-Jane	22	F	Unknown	21J112NI
MARTON, William	20	M	Unknown	21J112NI
MOLONE, U-Mrs.	25	F	Unknown	21J112NI
BRAY, U-Mrs.	50	F	Unknown	21J112NI
Edward	18	M	Unknown	21J112NI
U-Miss	24	F	Unknown	21J112NI
Mary	17	F	Unknown	21J112NI
Ellen	16	F	Unknown	21J112NI
Julia	.00	F	Infant	21J112NI
BYRNE, U-Mrs.	24	F	Unknown	21J112NI
Hana	22	F	Unknown	21J112NI
Charles	2	M	Child	21J112NI
Sarah	.00	F	Infant	21J112NI
Ellen	20	F	Unknown	21J112NI
HALL, Mat	20	M	Unknown	21J112NI
KELLY, Tim	20	M	Unknown	21J112NI
JOHNSTON, Sam	22	M	Unknown	21J112NI
BRYAN, Edward	20	M	Unknown	21J112NI

NAMES OF PASSENGERS	AGE	SEX	OCCUPATIONS	DATE PORT SHIP
BRYAN, Ann	20	F	Unknown	21J112NI
Bessy	25	F	Unknown	21J112NI
MADDEN, Francis	20	F	Unknown	21J112NI
MURRAY, Pat	35	M	Unknown	21J112NI
Peggy	30	F	Unknown	21J112NI
Margt.	5	F	Child	21J112NI
Pat	3	M	Child	21J112NI
Murray	.00	F	Infant	21J112NI
KAVANAGH, James	35	M	Unknown	21J112NI
MURPHY, James	38	M	Unknown	21J112NI
CONNELL, Byn	30	M	Unknown	21J112NI
U-Mrs.	28	F	Unknown	21J112NI
Mary	.00	F	Infant	21J112NI
BERUCEK, James	22	M	Unknown	21J112NI
DALEY, John	25	M	Unknown	21J112NI
HIGGANS, Edward	27	M	Unknown	21J112NI
DUNN, Michael	22	M	Unknown	21J112NI
U-Mrs.	18	F	Unknown	21J112NI
CARREGAN, Bridget	30	F	Unknown	21J112NI
DEMPSEY, James	21	M	Unknown	21J112NI
SHORT, Tom	27	M	Unknown	21J112NI
U-Mrs.	26	F	Unknown	21J112NI
Mary	8	F	Child	21J112NI
Bernard	.00	M	Infant	21J112NI
FITZPATRICK, Jane	20	F	Unknown	21J112NI
Bessey	19	F	Unknown	21J112NI
U-Mrs.	20	F	Unknown	21J112NI
GOGARTY, Mary	20	F	Unknown	21J112NI
Fanny	21	F	Unknown	21J112NI
BYRNES, Mary	20	F	Unknown	21J112NI
GACKEN, Owen	30	M	Unknown	21J112NI
Mary	35	F	Unknown	21J112NI
Bess	.00	F	Infant	21J112NI
ESTACA, William	42	M	Unknown	21J112NI
Patt	20	M	Unknown	21J112NI
Ann	10	F	Child	21J112NI
Cath.	7	F	Child	21J112NI
Mary	5	F	Child	21J112NI
William	.00	M	Infant	21J112NI
MCCORMACK, Mary	20	F	Unknown	21J112NI
MURRAY, Eliza	20	F	Unknown	21J112NI
SHERDAN, Margt.	20	F	Unknown	21J112NI
MALLONE, Pat	27	M	Unknown	21J112NI
COUCHOR, Lancan	28	M	Unknown	21J112NI
U-Mrs.	26	F	Unknown	21J112NI
John	.00	M	Infant	21J112NI
KELLY, Philip	26	M	Unknown	21J112NI
DONOHUE, Julia	20	F	Unknown	21J112NI
HAUKINS, Sarah	45	F	Unknown	21J112NI
Thomas	7	M	Child	21J112NI
Peter	28	M	Unknown	21J112NI
MCCANN, Samuel	22	M	Unknown	21J112NI
Julia	20	F	Unknown	21J112NI
SORAHAN, Michal	28	M	Unknown	21J112NI
U-Mrs.	23	F	Unknown	21J112NI
DELAHANT, Math.	45	M	Unknown	21J112NI
U-Mrs.	40	F	Unknown	21J112NI
James	24	M	Unknown	21J112NI
John	20	M	Unknown	21J112NI
Charles	18	M	Unknown	21J112NI
Mary	15	F	Unknown	21J112NI
Hannah	12	F	Unknown	21J112NI
Margt.	9	F	Child	21J112NI
Michal	7	M	Child	21J112NI
Bridget	3	F	Child	21J112NI
Pat	.00	M	Infant	21J112NI
FAGAN, Matt	22	M	Unknown	21J112NI
LANNAN, Thomas	22	M	Unknown	21J112NI
JOHNSON, Ann	20	F	Unknown	21J112NI
WALSH, Pat	21	M	Unknown	21J112NI
CARROLL, Bridget	24	F	Unknown	21J112NI
LAULESS, Bridget	20	F	Unknown	21J112NI
STRONG, Pat	25	M	Unknown	21J112NI
CANNOLL, Charles	50	M	Unknown	21J112NI
U-Mrs.	46	F	Unknown	21J112NI

NAMES OF PASSENGERS	AGE	SEX	OCCUPATIONS	DATE PORT SHIP
CANNOLL, Mary	23	F	Unknown	21JI12NI
Tim	18	M	Unknown	21JI12NI
Margt.	21	F	Unknown	21JI12NI
Honor	15	F	Unknown	21JI12NI
Charles	13	M	Unknown	21JI12NI
John	9	M	Child	21JI12NI
Bridget	7	F	Child	21JI12NI
James	.00	M	Infant	21JI12NI
KINSELLA, William	30	M	Unknown	21JI12NI
U-Mrs.	28	F	Unknown	21JI12NI
Michael	3	M	Child	21JI12NI
Margt.	.00	F	Infant	21JI12NI
BYRNE, Ann	20	F	Unknown	21JI12NI
ONELL, John	24	M	Unknown	21JI12NI
U-Mrs.	24	F	Unknown	21JI12NI
John	.00	M	Infant	21JI12NI
DEMPSEY, Pat	25	M	Unknown	21JI12NI
FLYNN, Pat	22	M	Unknown	21JI12NI
BRANGAN, Peter	23	M	Unknown	21JI12NI
Mary	20	F	Unknown	21JI12NI
BOULGER, U	25	M	Unknown	21JI12NI
WILSON, U	30	M	Unknown	21JI12NI
KELLY, U	17	M	Unknown	21JI12NI
John	12	M	Unknown	21JI12NI
MORRISON, U-Mrs.	12	M	Unknown	21JI12NI
Eliza	10	F	Child	21JI12NI
Lawrence	.00	M	Infant	21JI12NI
Thomas	8	M	Child	21JI12NI
JORDAN, Simon	30	M	Unknown	21JI12NI
BRYAN, James	24	M	Unknown	21JI12NI
ROWLAND, U-Mrs.	22	M	Unknown	21JI12NI
MURRAY, John	20	M	Unknown	21JI12NI
CRUCHLEY, Henry	20	M	Unknown	21JI12NI
MURRAY, Mary	20	F	Unknown	21JI12NI
ALLEN, Ellen	20	F	Unknown	21JI12NI
LODGE, Mary-Ann	20	F	Unknown	21JI12NI
KENNEY, William	40	M	Unknown	21JI12NI
U-Mrs.	30	F	Unknown	21JI12NI
REYNOLD, Mary	18	F	Unknown	21JI12NI
Mary-A.	.00	F	Infant	21JI12NI
GOUGASH, John	20	M	Unknown	21JI12NI
U-Mrs.	26	F	Unknown	21JI12NI
Mary-Ann	13	F	Unknown	21JI12NI
Ann	.00	F	Infant	21JI12NI
RICHFIELD, John	22	M	Unknown	21JI12NI
HAMILTON, Pt.	24	M	Unknown	21JI12NI
HARVEY, Pat	40	M	Unknown	21JI12NI
DUNNE, Ann	24	F	Unknown	21JI12NI
JORDAN, Sarah	20	F	Unknown	21JI12NI
MARK, Ellen	20	F	Unknown	21JI12NI
HARRELL, William	24	M	Unknown	21JI12NI
HEWETT, John	24	M	Unknown	21JI12NI
MAHAN, U-Mrs.	50	F	Unknown	21JI12NI
Eliza	22	F	Unknown	21JI12NI
Charlotte	20	F	Unknown	21JI12NI
Fanny	18	F	Unknown	21JI12NI
James	16	M	Unknown	21JI12NI
Sarah	12	F	Unknown	21JI12NI
William	10	M	Child	21JI12NI
Stephen	7	M	Child	21JI12NI
Samuel	.00	M	Infant	21JI12NI
COUGHLEY, Catherine	20	F	Unknown	21JI12NI
BOLTON, A.	40	M	Unknown	21JI12NI
U-Mrs.	30	F	Unknown	21JI12NI
James	24	M	Unknown	21JI12NI
Samuel	12	M	Unknown	21JI12NI
Susan	8	F	Child	21JI12NI
Kate	6	F	Child	21JI12NI
DALY, U	30	M	Unknown	21JI12NI
MOLLOY, John	22	M	Unknown	21JI12NI
BAKER, Edward	3	M	Child	21JI12NI
U-Mrs.	28	F	Unknown	21JI12NI
U-Miss	21	F	Unknown	21JI12NI
HENRY, James	18	M	Unknown	21JI12NI
BOYLE, U	26	M	Unknown	21JI12NI

BERKENHEAD 23 JULY 1849

From Liverpool And Cork

NAMES OF PASSENGERS	AGE	SEX	OCCUPATIONS	DATE PORT SHIP
ROSS, Sarah	20	F	None	23JI68Np
REGAN, John	24	M	Laborer	23JI68Np
ADAMS, Rodger	20	M	Laborer	23JI68Np
COLLINS, John	40	M	Laborer	23JI68Np
MAYE, Mary	20	F	None	23JI68Np
GEDERS, Sarah	26	F	None	23JI68Np
Sarah	8	F	Child	23JI68Np
Martha	5	F	Child	23JI68Np
Sandy	.00	F	Infant	23JI68Np
MAGNEW, Michl.	21	M	Laborer	23JI68Np
James	17	M	Laborer	23JI68Np
Mary	24	F	None	23JI68Np
STAHAN, Johanna	55	F	None	23JI68Np
BOWEN, Jerry	29	M	Laborer	23JI68Np
LANE, Jane	21	F	None	23JI68Np
Susan	19	F	None	23JI68Np
BROWN, George	54	M	Laborer	23JI68Np
Mary	21	F	None	23JI68Np
Sarah	18	F	None	23JI68Np
WALKER, Mary	50	F	None	23JI68Np
Henry	18	M	Laborer	23JI68Np
RYAN, John	17	M	Laborer	23JI68Np
DORHERTY, James	28	M	Laborer	23JI68Np
KENNEDY, Mary	25	F	None	23JI68Np
CASHMAN, Alice	22	F	None	23JI68Np
DENEEN, Denis	50	M	Laborer	23JI68Np
Honora	40	F	None	23JI68Np
Cathne.	20	F	None	23JI68Np
FLEMING, Ellen	50	F	None	23JI68Np
Pat.	15	M	Laborer	23JI68Np
ROBERTS, Anne	50	F	None	23JI68Np
Eliza	13	F	None	23JI68Np
HOLBERTSON, Jane	45	F	None	23JI68Np
CROWLEY, Jane	17	F	None	23JI68Np
FRIHY, John	24	M	Laborer	23JI68Np
FRILEY, Honora	22	F	None	23JI68Np
BYRNE, Michl.	25	M	Laborer	23JI68Np
CLIFFORD, Wm.	94	M	Laborer	23JI68Np
MORLAN, Wm.	27	M	Laborer	23JI68Np
FENNESSEY, Bridget	25	F	None	23JI68Np
SHEEHAN, Eliza	30	F	None	23JI68Np
ROURKE, Mary	40	F	None	23JI68Np
SULLIVAN, Corns.	24	M	Laborer	23JI68Np
ASHTON, Wm.	24	M	Laborer	23JI68Np
Marsella	26	F	None	23JI68Np
MALONY, Thomas	25	M	Laborer	23JI68Np
HICKEY, Danl.	25	M	Laborer	23JI68Np
HOLLAND, Johanna	22	F	None	23JI68Np
MCAULIFFE, John	24	M	Laborer	23JI68Np
Johan.	30	F	None	23JI68Np
Margt.	16	F	None	23JI68Np
Timy.	14	M	Laborer	23JI68Np
Jerry	13	M	Laborer	23JI68Np
Joha.	9	F	Child	23JI68Np
Cathne.	9	F	Child	23JI68Np
Ellen	7	F	Child	23JI68Np
Mary	5	F	Child	23JI68Np
Danl.	3	M	Child	23JI68Np
TAOMEY, Johanna	20	F	None	23JI68Np
ZUINLAN, Eliza	15	F	None	23JI68Np
Jerry	16	M	Laborer	23JI68Np
LANE, Michl.	12	M	Laborer	23JI68Np
WARREN, Denis	30	M	Laborer	23JI68Np
MCGRATH, Johanna	25	F	None	23JI68Np
Hannah	27	F	None	23JI68Np

NAMES OF PASSENGERS	AGE	SEX	OCCUPATIONS	DATE PORT SHIP
MYLES, Mary	20	F	None	23J168Np
FITZPATRICK, John	35	M	Laborer	23J168Np
GOULDEN, Michl.	26	M	Laborer	23J168Np
CONNOR, Peggy	20	F	None	23J168Np
LOWERY, Isabella	20	F	None	23J168Np
LEHANE, Tim.	40	M	Laborer	23J168Np
Mary	30	F	None	23J168Np
Cathne.	14	F	None	23J168Np
John	12	M	Laborer	23J168Np
Mary	10	F	Child	23J168Np
Nancy	7	F	Child	23J168Np
James	2	M	Child	23J168Np
CONNOLY, Ellen	20	F	None	23J168Np
CRAWLEY, Julia	20	F	None	23J168Np
OCONNOR, Margt.	30	F	None	23J168Np
James	5	M	Child	23J168Np
STANTON, Eliza.	16	F	None	23J168Np
KEEFE, Arthur	25	M	Laborer	23J168Np
DUANE, John	30	M	Laborer	23J168Np
Susan	25	F	None	23J168Np
ROCHE, Bridget	20	F	None	23J168Np
Hannah	.00	F	Infant	23J168Np
WALL, Wm.	30	M	Laborer	23J168Np
James	18	M	Laborer	23J168Np
LANTRY, Margt.	60	F	None	23J168Np
Danl.	25	M	None	23J168Np
GRUEEN, Eliza.	20	F	None	23J168Np
COUGHLAN, James	45	M	Laborer	23J168Np
Honora	45	F	None	23J168Np
FENELY, Mary	26	F	None	23J168Np
GRIFFIN, John	22	M	Laborer	23J168Np
HARZ, Philip	30	M	Laborer	23J168Np
Mary	30	F	None	23J168Np
Thomas	6	M	Child	23J168Np
Mary	.00	F	Infant	23J168Np
Anne	5	F	Child	23J168Np
COLLINS, John	25	M	Laborer	23J168Np
ELLINS, George	24	M	Laborer	23J168Np
ARMSTRONG, Mary	25	F	None	23J168Np
Mary	30	F	None	23J168Np
SULLY, Hester	50	F	None	23J168Np
LAPHAM, Brad.	21	M	Laborer	23J168Np
RIVIDAN, Pierce	24	M	Laborer	23J168Np
DONNELL, Wm.	27	M	Laborer	23J168Np
Julia	20	F	None	23J168Np
HEILEY, Margt.	20	F	None	23J168Np
BURKE, Andw.	20	M	None	23J168Np
Mary	20	F	None	23J168Np
SHEEHAN, Ann	18	F	None	23J168Np
GARVANE, John	25	M	Laborer	23J168Np
GODMATER, Eliza.	20	F	None	23J168Np
LYNCH, Danl.	35	M	Laborer	23J168Np
Cathne.	35	F	None	23J168Np
Mary	9	F	Child	23J168Np
CULLIMAN, Michl.	35	M	Laborer	23J168Np
LYNCH, Tim.	3	M	Child	23J168Np
CULLIMAN, Mary	30	F	None	23J168Np
QUILTY, Bridget	20	F	None	23J168Np
CULLIMAN, Joseph	20	M	Laborer	23J168Np
Wm.	.00	M	Infant	23J168Np
HURRY, Henry	19	M	Laborer	23J168Np
CALLAGHAN, Corns.	20	M	Laborer	23J168Np
MURPHY, John	33	M	Laborer	23J168Np
SHOEMAKER, John	24	M	Laborer	23J168Np
HALLESSEY, Tim.	16	M	Laborer	23J168Np
JONES, John	20	M	Laborer	23J168Np
LINEHAM, Deborah	20	F	None	23J168Np
BLENNAN, John	23	M	Laborer	23J168Np
GRACEY, John	40	M	Laborer	23J168Np
Fanny	35	F	None	23J168Np
MURPHY, Jane	20	F	None	23J168Np
RIORDAN, John	20	M	Laborer	23J168Np
STACK, Michl.	30	M	Laborer	23J168Np
John	28	M	Laborer	23J168Np
Margt.	26	F	None	23J168Np
STACK, Thomas	24	M	Laborer	23J168Np
Cathne.	22	F	None	23J168Np
Johanna	20	F	None	23J168Np
Julia	13	F	None	23J168Np
FITZGERALD, Pat.	20	M	Laborer	23J168Np
SULLIVAN, Bridget	40	F	None	23J168Np
WHITE, Andw.	27	M	Laborer	23J168Np
FENTON, Thomas	22	M	Laborer	23J168Np
WALSH, Bridget	50	F	None	23J168Np
Anne	20	F	None	23J168Np
COTTER, Margt.	21	F	None	23J168Np
FOLEY, John	22	M	Laborer	23J168Np
MURPHY, John	40	M	Laborer	23J168Np
STACK, John	30	M	Laborer	23J168Np
Honora	30	F	None	23J168Np
CONNOR, Margt.	60	F	None	23J168Np
Michl.	17	M	Laborer	23J168Np
Jerry	12	M	Laborer	23J168Np
Tim	9	M	Child	23J168Np
NEILLE, Corns.	26	M	Laborer	23J168Np
Mary	24	F	None	23J168Np
Mary	.00	F	Infant	23J168Np
CRONIN, Daniel	20	M	Laborer	23J168Np
MURPHY, Moses	45	M	Laborer	23J168Np
Cathne.	45	F	None	23J168Np
John	20	M	Laborer	23J168Np
Denis	18	M	Laborer	23J168Np
Cathne.	13	F	None	23J168Np
Mary	11	F	None	23J168Np
Michl.	2	M	Child	23J168Np
Cathne.	20	F	None	23J168Np
CRONIN, Jerry	45	M	Laborer	23J168Np
Stephen	19	M	Laborer	23J168Np
Julia	15	F	None	23J168Np
KEANE, Thomas	21	M	Laborer	23J168Np
DELANEY, Mary	24	F	None	23J168Np
Ellen	25	F	None	23J168Np
Eliza.	18	F	None	23J168Np
OLEARY, Mary-A.	10	F	Child	23J168Np
MORIARTY, Michl.	28	M	Laborer	23J168Np
DONOGHUE, Tim.	10	M	Child	23J168Np
CONNELL, John	30	M	Laborer	23J168Np
WALSH, Pat.	19	M	Laborer	23J168Np
Johanna	20	F	None	23J168Np
CONNELL, Kate	20	F	None	23J168Np
Mary	20	F	None	23J168Np
MORAN, Pat.	4	M	Child	23J168Np
FENTON, Jas.	37	M	Laborer	23J168Np
Honora	30	F	None	23J168Np
CRAWLEY, Mary	24	F	None	23J168Np
Denis	.00	M	Infant	23J168Np
BOURK, Pat	34	M	Laborer	23J168Np
George	22	M	Laborer	23J168Np
CLIFFORD, Mary	25	F	None	23J168Np
James	.00	M	Infant	23J168Np
OGRADY, Thos.	22	M	Laborer	23J168Np
Cathne.	18	F	None	23J168Np
OSULLIVAN, Tim.	17	M	Laborer	23J168Np
SOMERS, Pierce	20	M	Laborer	23J168Np
CONNOR, Ellen	50	F	None	23J168Np
John	18	M	Laborer	23J168Np
CONDON, David	30	M	Laborer	23J168Np
WALSH, Pat.	30	M	Laborer	23J168Np
DELANEY, Cathne.	20	F	None	23J168Np
CASEY, John	45	M	Laborer	23J168Np
Johanna	45	F	None	23J168Np
AHERN, Honora	40	F	None	23J168Np
MILLARD, Mary	24	F	None	23J168Np
AHERN, Cathne.	22	F	None	23J168Np
Eliza.	16	F	None	23J168Np
Honora	13	F	None	23J168Np
MILLER, Richd.	6	M	Child	23J168Np
Thos.	4	M	Child	23J168Np
Robert	2	M	Child	23J168Np
Eliza.	.00	F	Infant	23J168Np

NAMES OF PASSENGERS	AGE	SEX	OCCUPATIONS	DATE PORT SHIP
KEANE, James	50	M	Laborer	23J168Np
Eliza	50	F	None	23J168Np
Sally	16	F	None	23J168Np
Anna	7	F	Child	23J168Np
SULLIVAN, Ellen	20	F	None	23J168Np
MORIARTY, Pat.	28	M	Laborer	23J168Np
DOBBIN, John	30	M	Unknown	23J168Np
Bridget	25	F	None	23J168Np
MCCARTHY, Ellen	19	F	None	23J168Np
BRESNAN, Tim.	30	M	Laborer	23J168Np
Cathne.	35	F	None	23J168Np
Johannah	8	F	Child	23J168Np
Denis	.00	M	Infant	23J168Np
KELCHER, Johanna	20	F	None	23J168Np
Kate	13	F	None	23J168Np
BROSNAN, Corns.	30	M	Laborer	23J168Np
Kate	20	F	None	23J168Np
Hugh	22	M	Laborer	23J168Np
Honora	15	F	None	23J168Np
BROHAN, Eliza.	22	F	None	23J168Np
Wm.	18	M	Laborer	23J168Np
Thomas	26	M	Laborer	23J168Np
BRIEN, Margt.	21	F	None	23J168Np
MOYLAN, Michl.	26	M	Laborer	23J168Np
ROCHE, Bridget	50	F	None	23J168Np
Mary	30	F	None	23J168Np
DALTON, Mary	20	F	None	23J168Np
BYRNE, Mary	18	F	None	23J168Np
FORD, Mary	18	F	None	23J168Np
OBRIEN, James	40	M	Unknown	23J168Np
RYAN, Lawce.	20	M	Unknown	23J168Np
MORIARTY, Owen	34	M	Laborer	23J168Np
SULLIVAN, Owen	32	M	Laborer	23J168Np
Danl.	28	M	Laborer	23J168Np
CROWLEY, Tim.	26	M	Laborer	23J168Np
SNOW, Thomas	20	M	Laborer	23J168Np
REEVES, John	50	M	Laborer	23J168Np
SIMMONS, George	35	M	Laborer	23J168Np
WILTZSHAW, John	19	M	Laborer	23J168Np
SIMMONS, Charlotte	28	F	None	23J168Np
HARRIS, Thomas	29	M	Laborer	23J168Np
DAILEY, Gideon	26	M	Laborer	23J168Np
TRACEY, Thomas	20	M	Laborer	23J168Np
DONOVAN, Pat.	29	M	Laborer	23J168Np
JENKINS, James	00	M	Unknown	23J168Np
DALY, Margt.	20	F	Laborer	23J168Np
BYRNE, Jane	24	F	Laborer	23J168Np
TAYLOR, Jane	27	F	Laborer	23J168Np
BRYNE, Edward	.00	M	Infant	23J168Np

KOREA 23 JULY 1849

From Belfast

NAMES OF PASSENGERS	AGE	SEX	OCCUPATIONS	DATE PORT SHIP
GORDON, Samuel	21	M	Farmer	23J105Ne
BIRNEY, Thos.	60	M	Farmer	23J105Ne
Margaret	30	F	Farmer	23J105Ne
John	10	M	Farmer	23J105Ne
Mary	8	F	Child	23J105Ne
Charlotte	6	F	Child	23J105Ne
WILLIAMSON, John	50	M	Farmer	23J105Ne
Martha	45	F	Farmer	23J105Ne
Isabella	20	F	Farmer	23J105Ne
Lilly	18	F	Farmer	23J105Ne
Martha	16	F	Farmer	23J105Ne
Nancy	14	F	Farmer	23J105Ne
Margaret	10	F	Farmer	23J105Ne
BRADY, Mich.	50	M	Farmer	23J105Ne
Biddy	40	F	Farmer	23J105Ne
BRADY, Biddy	19	F	Farmer	23J105Ne
Mary	17	F	Farmer	23J105Ne
Michl.	15	M	Farmer	23J105Ne
Denis	12	M	Farmer	23J105Ne
Nancy	10	F	Farmer	23J105Ne
Susan	5	F	Child	23J105Ne
James	.00	M	Infant	23J105Ne
KIRNEY, John	50	M	Farmer	23J105Ne
Biddy	40	F	Farmer	23J105Ne
Patrick	20	M	Farmer	23J105Ne
Mary	18	F	Farmer	23J105Ne
Peter	16	M	Farmer	23J105Ne
Biddy	12	F	Farmer	23J105Ne
Owen	10	M	Farmer	23J105Ne
Alice	8	F	Child	23J105Ne
John	6	M	Child	23J105Ne
James	3	M	Child	23J105Ne
Joseph	.00	M	Infant	23J105Ne
Phil.	52	M	Farmer	23J105Ne
Mary	45	F	Farmer	23J105Ne
James	21	M	Farmer	23J105Ne
Patrick	18	M	Farmer	23J105Ne
Biddy	16	F	Farmer	23J105Ne
Mary	12	F	Farmer	23J105Ne
Alice	6	F	Child	23J105Ne
Isabella	.00	F	Infant	23J105Ne
KERR, Sarah	40	F	Farmer	23J105Ne
Michael	.00	M	Infant	23J105Ne
Biddy	12	F	Farmer	23J105Ne
Sarah	9	F	Child	23J105Ne
STEWART, Rose	20	F	Farmer	23J105Ne
ROBINSON, Archi.	25	M	Farmer	23J105Ne
Catherine	35	F	Farmer	23J105Ne
Henry	.00	M	Infant	23J105Ne
Stewart	3	M	Child	23J105Ne
MCKEE, Wm.	25	M	Farmer	23J105Ne
Eliza	24	F	Farmer	23J105Ne
AICKEN, Ann	24	F	Farmer	23J105Ne
Mary	20	F	Farmer	23J105Ne
Jane	60	F	Farmer	23J105Ne
CROLE, Hamilton	21	M	Farmer	23J105Ne
Agnes	18	F	Farmer	23J105Ne
WILSON, William	22	M	Farmer	23J105Ne
Isabella	20	F	Farmer	23J105Ne
TODD, Sarah	18	F	Farmer	23J105Ne
JOHNSON, Sarah	20	F	Farmer	23J105Ne
ANDERSON, Jane	9	F	Child	23J105Ne
Thomas	7	M	Child	23J105Ne
CRAIG, Ann-Maria	26	F	Farmer	23J105Ne
Jane	.00	F	Infant	23J105Ne
DOWNEY, Alex.	35	M	Farmer	23J105Ne
Agnes	34	F	Farmer	23J105Ne
Mary	11	F	Farmer	23J105Ne
Sarah	.00	F	Infant	23J105Ne
DORAN, John	40	M	Farmer	23J105Ne
James	21	M	Farmer	23J105Ne
Mary-Ann	23	F	Farmer	23J105Ne
Ellen	16	F	Farmer	23J105Ne
MCMURTRY, Sam.	27	M	Farmer	23J105Ne
MCROBERTS, Robert	20	M	Farmer	23J105Ne
ALLEN, Cath.	25	F	Farmer	23J105Ne
DEVIN, Sarah	49	F	Farmer	23J105Ne
Mary	19	F	Farmer	23J105Ne
Francis	16	M	Farmer	23J105Ne
Patrick	13	M	Farmer	23J105Ne
Sarah	10	F	Farmer	23J105Ne
Felix	7	M	Child	23J105Ne
Mary	.00	F	Infant	23J105Ne
HILL, John	20	M	Farmer	23J105Ne
Margaret	20	F	Farmer	23J105Ne
HENRY, John	18	M	Farmer	23J105Ne
BEADLEY, John	35	M	Farmer	23J105Ne
MCAULEY, Sam.	25	M	Farmer	23J105Ne
MCMULLEN, Ann	20	F	Farmer	23J105Ne
MARTIN, Jno.	18	M	Farmer	23J105Ne

NAMES OF PASSENGERS	AGE	SEX	OCCUPATIONS	DATE PORT SHIP
MAGEE, Edward	30	M	Farmer	23J105Ne
BELL, David	25	M	Farmer	23J105Ne
SCOHILL, Nancy	30	F	Farmer	23J105Ne
Bessy	16	F	Farmer	23J105Ne
Biddy	13	F	Farmer	23J105Ne
Nancy	11	F	Farmer	23J105Ne
GRAHAM, Rachel	20	F	Farmer	23J105Ne
Mary	18	F	Farmer	23J105Ne
MATHER, Christopher	21	M	Farmer	23J105Ne
SHERIDAN, Thos.	21	M	Farmer	23J105Ne
CAMNER, Robert	35	M	Farmer	23J105Ne
Margaret	30	F	Farmer	23J105Ne
James	3	M	Child	23J105Ne
Samuel	.00	M	Infant	23J105Ne
MCCANMON, James	24	M	Farmer	23J105Ne
MCCAULIFE, Daniel	35	M	Farmer	23J105Ne
LANE, Margaret	40	F	Farmer	23J105Ne
Mary	21	F	Farmer	23J105Ne
MOORE, Catherine	50	F	Farmer	23J105Ne
HAMILTON, Moses	20	M	Farmer	23J105Ne
MULHOLLAND, Daniel	21	M	Farmer	23J105Ne
Alice	20	F	Farmer	23J105Ne
MELIN, Hanna	25	F	Farmer	23J105Ne
OHARA, Mary	20	F	Farmer	23J105Ne
MARKS, Mary-Ann	22	F	Farmer	23J105Ne
DORRANCE, Alex.	30	M	Farmer	23J105Ne
Catherine	30	F	Farmer	23J105Ne
Mary-Ann	.00	F	Infant	23J105Ne
HANNAH, Mary	39	F	Farmer	23J105Ne
TAYLOR, Henry	24	M	Farmer	23J105Ne
MAUGH, Eliza	20	F	Farmer	23J105Ne
BOYD, John	18	M	Farmer	23J105Ne
SALLAN, John	22	M	Farmer	23J105Ne
ORR, John	25	M	Farmer	23J105Ne
Samuel	20	M	Farmer	23J105Ne
NICHOL, John	25	M	Farmer	23J105Ne
MCGILL, Daniel	30	M	Farmer	23J105Ne
COULTER, Ellen	20	F	Farmer	23J105Ne
Martha	18	F	Farmer	23J105Ne
THOMPSON, Alex.	30	M	Farmer	23J105Ne
Eliza	25	F	Farmer	23J105Ne
HENRY, Daniel	40	M	Farmer	23J105Ne
MCCLEHAMOND, John	30	M	Farmer	23J105Ne
JOHNSON, Sophia	26	F	Farmer	23J105Ne
SLOAN, John	25	M	Farmer	23J105Ne
WILSON, Mary	22	F	Farmer	23J105Ne
MCILVENNA, Hugh	20	M	Farmer	23J105Ne
BOYCE, Agnes	30	F	Farmer	23J105Ne
Margaret	9	F	Child	23J105Ne
Martha	7	F	Child	23J105Ne
MCCABE, Agnes	42	F	Farmer	23J105Ne
Hugh	20	M	Farmer	23J105Ne
Richard	14	M	Farmer	23J105Ne
KANE, Patrick	40	M	Farmer	23J105Ne
Catherine	20	F	Farmer	23J105Ne
Jane	18	F	Farmer	23J105Ne
ERWIN, Mary	20	F	Farmer	23J105Ne
MCILROY, James	20	M	Farmer	23J105Ne
Eliza	20	F	Farmer	23J105Ne
FERGUSON, Thos.	25	M	Farmer	23J105Ne
HANNAH, Margt.	48	F	Farmer	23J105Ne
John	16	M	Farmer	23J105Ne
FORSYTH, James	28	M	Farmer	23J105Ne
Mary	26	F	Farmer	23J105Ne
Eliza	2	F	Child	23J105Ne
William	.00	M	Infant	23J105Ne
Margaret	.00	F	Infant	23J105Ne
COLESON, Sarah	20	F	Farmer	23J105Ne
SAWEL, John	20	M	Farmer	23J105Ne
MONAGHAN, Rose	22	F	Farmer	23J105Ne
Catherine	17	F	Farmer	23J105Ne
HAUGHAM, James	20	M	Farmer	23J105Ne
Mary	16	F	Farmer	23J105Ne
STEVENSON, Mary	30	F	Farmer	23J105Ne
Ellen	22	F	Farmer	23J105Ne

NAMES OF PASSENGERS	AGE	SEX	OCCUPATIONS	DATE PORT SHIP
OSWALD, James	28	M	Farmer	23J105Ne
MADIN, Arthur	26	M	Farmer	23J105Ne
MARSHALL, Sarah	22	F	Farmer	23J105Ne
Thomas	21	M	Farmer	23J105Ne
MURPHY, Sarah	19	F	Farmer	23J105Ne
CRAWLEY, Biddy	18	F	Farmer	23J105Ne
SIMPSON, Thomas	20	M	Farmer	23J105Ne
MCJUROR, Wm.	25	M	Farmer	23J105Ne
JOHNSON, Wm.Jno.	30	M	Farmer	23J105Ne
Sarah	25	F	Farmer	23J105Ne
HANNAH, Thomas	20	M	Farmer	23J105Ne
MATHESON, Sam.	25	M	Farmer	23J105Ne
Sarah	20	F	Farmer	23J105Ne
Margaret	18	F	Farmer	23J105Ne
MCCURDY, Robert	20	M	Farmer	23J105Ne
MCGLAUGHLIN, Bernard	21	M	Farmer	23J105Ne
MCMURTRY, Arch.	30	M	Farmer	23J105Ne
Maria	30	F	Farmer	23J105Ne
Mary	18	F	Farmer	23J105Ne
John	16	M	Farmer	23J105Ne
Margaret	14	F	Farmer	23J105Ne
DINSMORE, Sally	30	F	Farmer	23J105Ne
DONALD, Ann	20	F	Farmer	23J105Ne
MCLAMON, Margt.	25	F	Farmer	23J105Ne
LOGAN, James	21	M	Farmer	23J105Ne
DONSMORE, Samson	20	M	Farmer	23J105Ne
SPEAR, William	20	M	Farmer	23J105Ne
Nancy	22	F	Farmer	23J105Ne
LOGAN, Robert	25	M	Farmer	23J105Ne
JONES, Eliza	20	F	Farmer	23J105Ne
DAVINSON, John	24	M	Farmer	23J105Ne
Mary-Jane	21	F	Farmer	23J105Ne
Eliza	23	F	Farmer	23J105Ne
BAXTER, Mary	20	F	Farmer	23J105Ne
KELLY, Mary	20	F	Farmer	23J105Ne
SPEAR, Eliza	20	F	Farmer	23J105Ne
PATTERSON, Alex.	18	M	Farmer	23J105Ne
DONAGAN, Richard	50	M	Farmer	23J105Ne
Margaret	50	F	Farmer	23J105Ne
Michael	22	M	Farmer	23J105Ne
Mary	20	F	Farmer	23J105Ne
Catherine	18	F	Farmer	23J105Ne
Ann	16	F	Farmer	23J105Ne
Rose	15	F	Farmer	23J105Ne
NEIL, Mary	20	F	Farmer	23J105Ne
LOMLEY, Marg.	20	F	Farmer	23J105Ne
DALTON, Joseph	19	M	Farmer	23J105Ne
Nesby	26	M	Farmer	23J105Ne
George	21	M	Farmer	23J105Ne
JOHNSON, William	25	M	Farmer	23J105Ne
DENVIN, James	20	M	Farmer	23J105Ne
KEATING, Susan	47	F	Farmer	23J105Ne
Mary	18	F	Farmer	23J105Ne
JOHNSON, Geo.	25	M	Farmer	23J105Ne
AVILLO, William	25	M	Farmer	23J105Ne
LIVINGSTON, Jane	45	F	Farmer	23J105Ne
Sarah	22	F	Farmer	23J105Ne
William	20	M	Farmer	23J105Ne
John	18	M	Farmer	23J105Ne
Eliza	16	F	Farmer	23J105Ne
David	13	M	Farmer	23J105Ne
James	11	M	Farmer	23J105Ne
Jolten	9	M	Child	23J105Ne
Susanna	7	F	Child	23J105Ne
MCIBORE, Henry	23	M	Farmer	23J105Ne
Hugh	20	M	Farmer	23J105Ne
MCKEOWN, Patt.	20	M	Farmer	23J105Ne
MCGLENCHY, Mary	18	F	Farmer	23J105Ne
ROONEY, Ann	40	F	Farmer	23J105Ne
William	13	M	Farmer	23J105Ne
Toddy	11	M	Farmer	23J105Ne
Bernard	4	M	Child	23J105Ne
MCGORMAN, Billy	25	M	Farmer	23J105Ne
DEASEY, James	30	M	Farmer	23J105Ne
MCVEIGH, Mary	25	F	Farmer	23J105Ne

NAMES OF PASSENGERS	AGE	SEX	OCCUPATIONS	DATE PORT SHIP
NEIL, Nangl.	20	M	Farmer	23Jl05Ne
MCINTOSH, John	54	M	Farmer	23Jl05Ne
John	25	M	Farmer	23Jl05Ne
Elizth.	50	F	Farmer	23Jl05Ne
HERON, Jane	45	F	Farmer	23Jl05Ne

DUKE-OF-WELLINGTON 23 JULY 1849

From Dublin

NAMES OF PASSENGERS	AGE	SEX	OCCUPATIONS	DATE PORT SHIP
FLEMMING, Thomas	21	M	Farmer	23Jl12Nq
REILLY, John	14	M	Unknown	23Jl12Nq
Julia	20	F	Unknown	23Jl12Nq
KELLY, Mary	16	F	Unknown	23Jl12Nq
BLAKE, Mary	21	F	Unknown	23Jl12Nq
BRADY, Cornelius	22	F	Unknown	23Jl12Nq
SHANLEY, John	18	M	Unknown	23Jl12Nq
MAGUIRE, James	37	M	Unknown	23Jl12Nq
RARDON, Michal	26	M	Unknown	23Jl12Nq
Mary	26	M	Unknown	23Jl12Nq
Alice	.00	F	Infant	23Jl12Nq
HARREGAN, Mary	20	F	Unknown	23Jl12Nq
COMERS, Margt.	50	F	Unknown	23Jl12Nq
CASTLE, Mary	29	F	Unknown	23Jl12Nq
Maria	9	F	Child	23Jl12Nq
Jane	7	F	Child	23Jl12Nq
Harriet	5	F	Child	23Jl12Nq
Eliza	.00	F	Infant	23Jl12Nq
GILLIGAN, Thomas	22	M	Unknown	23Jl12Nq
COGHAM, Michal	19	M	Unknown	23Jl12Nq
MCGUNNS, Patrick	45	M	Unknown	23Jl12Nq
CRAYTON, John	20	M	Unknown	23Jl12Nq
LERD, Richard-M.	3	M	Child	23Jl12Nq
BRENNON, Malcolm	24	M	Unknown	23Jl12Nq
Margret	16	F	Unknown	23Jl12Nq
John	14	M	Unknown	23Jl12Nq
James	22	M	Unknown	23Jl12Nq
Mary	18	F	Unknown	23Jl12Nq
KELLY, Nancy	13	F	Unknown	23Jl12Nq
TURNEY, Michal	23	M	Unknown	23Jl12Nq
GROGAN, Patrick	19	M	Unknown	23Jl12Nq
PHILLIPS, John	20	M	Unknown	23Jl12Nq
WHITE, Patrick	21	M	Unknown	23Jl12Nq
BERGAN, Ellen	21	F	Unknown	23Jl12Nq
Fany	19	F	Unknown	23Jl12Nq
Thomas	13	M	Unknown	23Jl12Nq
Michael	22	M	Unknown	23Jl12Nq
James	18	M	Unknown	23Jl12Nq
U-Mrs.	17	F	Unknown	23Jl12Nq
Bridget	45	F	Unknown	23Jl12Nq
Honor	7	F	Child	23Jl12Nq
MCMULLEN, Jas.	21	M	Unknown	23Jl12Nq
REILLY, Thomas	40	M	Unknown	23Jl12Nq
DOILLY, John	23	M	Unknown	23Jl12Nq
RIELLY, John	30	M	Unknown	23Jl12Nq
SMITH, Maria	16	F	Unknown	23Jl12Nq
GABBON, Patrick	8	M	Child	23Jl12Nq
RIELLY, Elizabeth	.00	F	Infant	23Jl12Nq
MURPHY, James	22	M	Unknown	23Jl12Nq
SMITH, Thomas	27	M	Unknown	23Jl12Nq
PRINEFEL, Mathew	24	M	Unknown	23Jl12Nq
DUNCAN, Mary	27	F	Unknown	23Jl12Nq
BRACKAN, Mary	24	F	Unknown	23Jl12Nq
CAHILL, John	28	M	Unknown	23Jl12Nq
PRATT, William	18	M	Unknown	23Jl12Nq
Abon	16	F	Unknown	23Jl12Nq
CUSACK, Michal	23	M	Unknown	23Jl12Nq
Patrick	20	M	Unknown	23Jl12Nq
Thomas	13	M	Unknown	23Jl12Nq

NAMES OF PASSENGERS	AGE	SEX	OCCUPATIONS	DATE PORT SHIP
CONNOR, Patrick	42	M	Unknown	23Jl12Nq
SMITH, Adam	56	M	Unknown	23Jl12Nq
U-Mrs.	56	F	Unknown	23Jl12Nq
Gilbit	18	F	Unknown	23Jl12Nq
Mary	18	F	Unknown	23Jl12Nq
CAMFIELD, Honor	35	F	Unknown	23Jl12Nq
NAGAL, Mary	30	F	Unknown	23Jl12Nq
CAUFIELD, Mary	20	F	Unknown	23Jl12Nq
NUGLE, John	8	M	Child	23Jl12Nq
CULEHILLY, Michl.	38	M	Unknown	23Jl12Nq
Margaret	40	F	Unknown	23Jl12Nq
James	18	M	Unknown	23Jl12Nq
Bridget	10	F	Unknown	23Jl12Nq
Corn.	7	M	Child	23Jl12Nq
Michael	.00	M	Infant	23Jl12Nq
RYELL, Anne	24	F	Unknown	23Jl12Nq
COOLING, Cath.	21	F	Unknown	23Jl12Nq
DENNIS, Ann	24	F	Unknown	23Jl12Nq
CONNELL, Sarah	19	F	Unknown	23Jl12Nq
DOYLE, Michl.	55	M	Unknown	23Jl12Nq
Bridget	54	F	Unknown	23Jl12Nq
Patrick	18	M	Unknown	23Jl12Nq
HYNES, Bridget	18	F	Unknown	23Jl12Nq
KENNY, Bridget	16	F	Unknown	23Jl12Nq
Dolly	23	F	Unknown	23Jl12Nq
GROGAN, Cath.	18	F	Unknown	23Jl12Nq
GAFFNEY, Rose	18	F	Unknown	23Jl12Nq
COEN, Mary	30	F	Unknown	23Jl12Nq
Catharine	21	F	Unknown	23Jl12Nq
TOWNSEND, Geo.	20	M	Unknown	23Jl12Nq
U-Mrs.	37	F	Unknown	23Jl12Nq
MORRIS, John	35	M	Unknown	23Jl12Nq
Samel	54	M	Unknown	23Jl12Nq
John	22	M	Unknown	23Jl12Nq
LAHEY, Bridget	20	F	Unknown	23Jl12Nq
KELLY, Cath.	25	F	Unknown	23Jl12Nq
FLANIGAN, Martin	20	M	Unknown	23Jl12Nq
BANNON, Pat	23	M	Unknown	23Jl12Nq
SCALLY, Pat	20	M	Unknown	23Jl12Nq
FOX, Bridget	40	F	Unknown	23Jl12Nq
Mary	13	F	Unknown	23Jl12Nq
James	9	M	Child	23Jl12Nq
DALEY, Mary	17	F	Unknown	23Jl12Nq
RUDEY, George	45	M	Unknown	23Jl12Nq
William	19	M	Unknown	23Jl12Nq
BLAKE, Edward	25	M	Unknown	23Jl12Nq
GALVIN, Bridget	30	F	Unknown	23Jl12Nq
KELLY, Bridget	13	F	Unknown	23Jl12Nq
HYNES, John	16	M	Unknown	23Jl12Nq
KENNY, James	21	M	Unknown	23Jl12Nq
Patrick	20	M	Unknown	23Jl12Nq
Martin	34	M	Unknown	23Jl12Nq
CONNOR, Ellen	19	F	Unknown	23Jl12Nq
BEHAN, Honor	19	F	Unknown	23Jl12Nq
GALLAGHER, Jas.	32	M	Unknown	23Jl12Nq
Honor	30	F	Unknown	23Jl12Nq
MURRAY, Mathew	00	M	Unknown	23Jl12Nq
Ann	30	F	Unknown	23Jl12Nq
U	.00	U	Infant	23Jl12Nq
CAVANAGH, Alex.	40	M	Unknown	23Jl12Nq
MULDOON, Mary	20	F	Unknown	23Jl12Nq
DOYLE, Wm.	24	M	Unknown	23Jl12Nq
Bridget	18	F	Unknown	23Jl12Nq
Jane	18	F	Unknown	23Jl12Nq
QUIGLEY, Charlott	30	F	Unknown	23Jl12Nq
SMALL, Cath	22	F	Unknown	23Jl12Nq
DALEY, Ann	24	F	Unknown	23Jl12Nq
KENNEY, Jane	22	F	Unknown	23Jl12Nq
HALLEGAN, Pat	24	M	Unknown	23Jl12Nq
STONEHAM, Pat	13	M	Unknown	23Jl12Nq
Elizth.	13	F	Unknown	23Jl12Nq
MEARA, Martin	18	M	Unknown	23Jl12Nq
Mary	20	F	Unknown	23Jl12Nq
BENTON, John	55	M	Unknown	23Jl12Nq
Michael	29	M	Unknown	23Jl12Nq

NAMES OF PASSENGERS	AGE	SEX	OCCUPATIONS	DATE PORT SHIP
BENTON, Jane	25	F	Unknown	23JI12Nq
Robert	26	M	Unknown	23JI12Nq
John	4	M	Child	23JI12Nq
Margaret	2	F	Child	23JI12Nq
Bridget	.00	F	Infant	23JI12Nq
LYNCH, Jas.	18	M	Unknown	23JI12Nq
Julia	16	F	Unknown	23JI12Nq
HUGGUBTHAR, William	31	M	Unknown	23JI12Nq
DICKSON, Edward	27	M	Unknown	23JI12Nq
EVOY, Thomas-M.	24	M	Unknown	23JI12Nq
Ann	24	F	Unknown	23JI12Nq
WALSH, Mary	33	F	Unknown	23JI12Nq
LENARD, John	21	M	Unknown	23JI12Nq
DAVIS, Luou	21	F	Unknown	23JI12Nq
BROWN, Thomas	25	M	Unknown	23JI12Nq
CARPUTE, Rose	19	F	Unknown	23JI12Nq
KEMSSEY, David	35	M	Unknown	23JI12Nq
WILSON, Michl.	00	M	Unknown	23JI12Nq

HELEN 23 JULY 1849

From Belfast

NAMES OF PASSENGERS	AGE	SEX	OCCUPATIONS	DATE PORT SHIP
FLEMING, Pat.	60	M	Laborer	23JI05Ni
Mary	60	F	Laborer	23JI05Ni
DREW, Henry	25	M	Laborer	23JI05Ni
John	16	M	Laborer	23JI05Ni
DONNELLY, Cath.	17	F	Laborer	23JI05Ni
Sarah-Jane	11	F	Laborer	23JI05Ni
MCWEIGH, John	44	M	Laborer	23JI05Ni
MONTGOMERY, Anne	18	F	Laborer	23JI05Ni
MCGURLEY, Mary	22	F	Laborer	23JI05Ni
Margaret	18	F	Laborer	23JI05Ni
MAUGHER, Bridget	18	F	Laborer	23JI05Ni
MCKENNEY, Mary	18	F	Laborer	23JI05Ni
MAUGHAN, Alice	16	F	Laborer	23JI05Ni
WODS, Robert	29	M	Laborer	23JI05Ni
Elaine	19	F	Laborer	23JI05Ni
HILL, Mary	31	F	Laborer	23JI05Ni
Elizabeth	8	F	Child	23JI05Ni
William	5	M	Child	23JI05Ni
John	3	M	Child	23JI05Ni
Jane	.00	F	Infant	23JI05Ni
WILSON, William	31	M	Laborer	23JI05Ni
Jane	29	F	Laborer	23JI05Ni
Margt.	13	F	Laborer	23JI05Ni
Mary	.00	F	Infant	23JI05Ni
CANFIELD, Jane	21	F	Laborer	23JI05Ni
MCWRIGHT, Magt.	30	F	Laborer	23JI05Ni
Hugh	13	M	Laborer	23JI05Ni
Alexr.	10	M	Laborer	23JI05Ni
MOOLAN, Elizabeth	16	F	Laborer	23JI05Ni
LITTLE, Mary	20	F	Laborer	23JI05Ni
Margaret	18	F	Laborer	23JI05Ni
Rebecca	14	F	Laborer	23JI05Ni
CONWAY, Bridget	20	F	Laborer	23JI05Ni
Cath.	18	F	Laborer	23JI05Ni
WHITTER, William	25	M	Laborer	23JI05Ni
Margaret	25	F	Laborer	23JI05Ni
Jane	16	F	Laborer	23JI05Ni
David	9	M	Child	23JI05Ni
Died-At-Sea				
OGAT, Lawrence	18	M	Laborer	23JI05Ni
WHITTAN, John	8	M	Child	23JI05Ni
Henry	6	M	Child	23JI05Ni
CARTWRIGHT, Charles	66	M	Laborer	23JI05Ni
Died-At-Sea				
Mary	37	F	Laborer	23JI05Ni
Mary-Anne	22	F	Laborer	23JI05Ni
WILSON, James	19	M	Laborer	23JI05Ni
BURNSIDE, Anne	19	F	Laborer	23JI05Ni
DUFF, Mary-Anne	26	F	Laborer	23JI05Ni
George	.00	M	Infant	23JI05Ni
WRIGHT, Andrew	20	M	Laborer	23JI05Ni
FENNER, W.S.	25	M	Laborer	23JI05Ni
SAMPSON, Sarah	45	F	Laborer	23JI05Ni
James	18	M	Laborer	23JI05Ni
William	16	M	Laborer	23JI05Ni
KELLY, Eliza	40	F	Laborer	23JI05Ni
HATHORN, Mary	38	F	Laborer	23JI05Ni
LONNY, Sarah	60	F	Laborer	23JI05Ni
Samuel	25	M	Laborer	23JI05Ni
Died-At-Sea				
ELVIN, Samuel	36	M	Laborer	23JI05Ni
Oliver	16	M	Laborer	23JI05Ni
Susan	14	F	Laborer	23JI05Ni
ACKER, George	20	M	Laborer	23JI05Ni
Jane	20	F	Laborer	23JI05Ni
WILEY, David	34	M	Laborer	23JI05Ni
David	11	M	Laborer	23JI05Ni
OMITE, Joseph	28	M	Laborer	23JI05Ni
WILSON, Joseph	58	M	Laborer	23JI05Ni
Margaret	58	F	Laborer	23JI05Ni
Matilda	20	F	Laborer	23JI05Ni
KEAY, Emily	16	F	Laborer	23JI05Ni
MCKEEGAN, James	18	M	Laborer	23JI05Ni
LANE, Mich.	16	M	Laborer	23JI05Ni
MILLIKEN, Sarah	18	F	Laborer	23JI05Ni
KERRCHY, Sarah	16	F	Laborer	23JI05Ni
DONAGHY, Mary	18	F	Laborer	23JI05Ni
QUINN, Margaret	18	F	Laborer	23JI05Ni
DONAGH, John	21	M	Laborer	23JI05Ni
LALLY, Patt.	30	M	Laborer	23JI05Ni
Bridget	25	F	Laborer	23JI05Ni
MINNY, Hugh	60	M	Laborer	23JI05Ni
Margt.	60	F	Laborer	23JI05Ni
James	24	M	Laborer	23JI05Ni
Mary	28	F	Laborer	23JI05Ni
Rose	23	F	Laborer	23JI05Ni
RANN, Bessy	.00	F	Infant	23JI05Ni
MCCUTCHEON, Samuel	30	M	Laborer	23JI05Ni
HIND, Jane	24	F	Laborer	23JI05Ni
Rachael	19	F	Laborer	23JI05Ni
COOK, Peggy-A.	19	F	Laborer	23JI05Ni
MCAULEY, Margt.	21	F	Laborer	23JI05Ni
GEER, Ellen	43	F	Laborer	23JI05Ni
Robert	30	M	Laborer	23JI05Ni
MCAULEY, James	19	M	Laborer	23JI05Ni
Margt.	18	F	Laborer	23JI05Ni
Richard	16	M	Laborer	23JI05Ni
Mary-Jane	14	F	Laborer	23JI05Ni
Ellen	11	F	Laborer	23JI05Ni
George	5	M	Child	23JI05Ni
HENGIN, Mary-Jane	20	F	Laborer	23JI05Ni
HOVEY, John	32	M	Laborer	23JI05Ni
MCRAY, Thomas	29	M	Laborer	23JI05Ni
Mary-Anne	21	F	Laborer	23JI05Ni
James	30	M	Laborer	23JI05Ni
CLARKE, Wini.	18	F	Laborer	23JI05Ni
BLAIR, Thos.	35	M	Laborer	23JI05Ni
COUSINS, John	19	M	Laborer	23JI05Ni
ALLEN, Anne	24	F	Laborer	23JI05Ni
CUNNINGHAM, Mary-Anne	19	F	Laborer	23JI05Ni
HEATHINGTON, Thos.	16	M	Laborer	23JI05Ni
DOHERTY, Wm.	26	M	Laborer	23JI05Ni
CARRY, Wm.	26	M	Laborer	23JI05Ni
WARD, Barbara	25	F	Laborer	23JI05Ni
CULLY, W.L.	9	M	Child	23JI05Ni
Ellen	7	F	Child	23JI05Ni
Andrew	5	M	Child	23JI05Ni
Mary	.00	F	Infant	23JI05Ni
Emily	8	F	Child	23JI05Ni
James	2	M	Child	23JI05Ni
DOENNA, Ellen	18	F	Laborer	23JI05Ni

NAMES OF PASSENGERS		AGE	SEX	OCCUPATIONS	DATE PORT SHIP
BRADELL, Anne		20	F	Laborer	23J105Ni
HILL, William		31	M	Laborer	23J105Ni
NEIL, John		30	M	Laborer	23J105Ni
MCCULLOUGH, John		40	M	Laborer	23J105Ni
ROURKE, Cath.		40	F	Laborer	23J105Ni
ANGHY, Megan		20	F	Laborer	23J105Ni
MORRISON, Anne		22	F	Laborer	23J105Ni
CRAIG, Theresa		22	F	Laborer	23J105Ni
DUFFY, Robert		3	M	Child	23J105Ni
LARKIN, Thomas		25	M	Laborer	23J105Ni
MORAN, Mary-Anne		25	F	Laborer	23J105Ni
James		3	M	Child	23J105Ni
LARKIN, Eleanor		25	F	Laborer	23J105Ni
REID, Mary		31	F	Laborer	23J105Ni
Mary		3	F	Child	23J105Ni
John		17	M	Laborer	23J105Ni

DEVONSHIRE 24 JULY 1849

From London

NAMES OF PASSENGERS		AGE	SEX	OCCUPATIONS	DATE PORT SHIP
THOMAS, William		44	M	Farmer	24J113Nt
ENSOUGHT, Patrick		20	M	Laborer	24J113Nt
ROWEN, Jas.		28	M	Laborer	24J113Nt
Ellen		24	F	None	24J113Nt
SHEEN, Thos.		48	M	Laborer	24J113Nt
Bridget		36	F	None	24J113Nt

EMERALD 24 JULY 1849

From Cork

NAMES OF PASSENGERS		AGE	SEX	OCCUPATIONS	DATE PORT SHIP
WALSH, Mary		40	F	Wi	24J108Nm
Patrick		20	M	Laborer	24J108Nm
Mary		14	F	Spinster	24J108Nm
Bessy		10	F	Spinster	24J108Nm
MCCARTHY, Dennis		50	M	Farmer	24J108Nm
Eliza.		24	F	Spinster	24J108Nm
BENNETT, Ann		20	F	Spinster	24J108Nm
LYONS, Mary		20	F	Spinster	24J108Nm
LEVISON, Thurston		40	M	Farmer	24J108Nm
Robt.		16	M	Farmer	24J108Nm
HULDEN, Johana		20	F	Spinster	24J108Nm
James		18	M	Laborer	24J108Nm
HAUGHY, Mary		56	F	Wi	24J108Nm
MCGILLDAY, Owen		50	M	Farmer	24J108Nm
Mary	(W)	40	F	None	24J108Nm
Thomas		22	M	Laborer	24J108Nm
CRONAN, Wm.		25	M	Laborer	24J108Nm
Ellen		22	F	Spinster	24J108Nm
Honora		20	F	Spinster	24J108Nm
John		25	M	Laborer	24J108Nm
BARRON, John		25	M	Farmer	24J108Nm
Sarah	(W)	23	F	None	24J108Nm
CROWLEY, Michl.		50	M	Farmer	24J108Nm
Mary	(W)	50	F	None	24J108Nm
MURPHY, Mary	(W)	50	F	None	24J108Nm
Danl.		21	M	Laborer	24J108Nm
Terry		13	M	Laborer	24J108Nm
HURLEY, Biddy		16	F	Spinster	24J108Nm
DUGGAN, Corn.		28	M	Laborer	24J108Nm
REGAN, Jerry		26	M	Laborer	24J108Nm
CUHAN, E.		29	M	Laborer	24J108Nm
DALEY, Michl.		20	M	Laborer	24J108Nm
MAHONEY, John		23	M	Laborer	24J108Nm
REGAN, Pat		24	M	Laborer	24J108Nm
Johana		16	F	Spinster	24J108Nm
SULLIVAN, John		28	M	Laborer	24J108Nm
QUIRK, John		30	M	Laborer	24J108Nm
REORDAN, Peter		30	M	Farmer	24J108Nm
Mary	(W)	28	F	None	24J108Nm
Johana		4	F	Child	24J108Nm
RILEY, Maurice		23	M	Laborer	24J108Nm
LEARY, Danl.		20	M	Laborer	24J108Nm
Mary		10	F	Child	24J108Nm
Danl.		17	M	Laborer	24J108Nm
MCCARTHY, James		24	M	Laborer	24J108Nm
SULLIVAN, Jerry		30	M	Laborer	24J108Nm
REGAN, Dennis		30	M	Laborer	24J108Nm
COLLINS, John		25	M	Laborer	24J108Nm
REGAN, Peggy		24	F	Spinster	24J108Nm
SULLIVAN, Julia		21	F	Spinster	24J108Nm
MURPHY, John		19	M	Laborer	24J108Nm
HENLY, John		40	M	Laborer	24J108Nm
BOURK, Richd.		23	M	Laborer	24J108Nm
LANE, John		28	M	Laborer	24J108Nm
Johana		26	F	Spinster	24J108Nm
COLEMAN, John		28	M	Farmer	24J108Nm
Mary	(T)	25	F	None	24J108Nm
BRESNAHAN, Michl.		24	M	Laborer	24J108Nm
MCGUIRE, Hugh		26	M	Laborer	24J108Nm
KELLEHAN, Corn.		20	M	Laborer	24J108Nm
RAHILLY, Michl.		25	M	Laborer	24J108Nm
DOMULLY, Pat.		21	M	Laborer	24J108Nm
CONNOR, Thos.		21	M	Laborer	24J108Nm
FLYNN, John		25	M	Laborer	24J108Nm
DONNOVAN, Randall		40	M	Farmer	24J108Nm
MORGAN, Pat.		21	M	Farmer	24J108Nm
TERHOY, Michl.		30	M	Farmer	24J108Nm
MURPHY, Dennis		26	M	Laborer	24J108Nm
COMONS, Mary-Ann		19	F	Spinster	24J108Nm
SULLIVAN, John		35	M	Laborer	24J108Nm

NO RECORD OF SHIP

From Glasgow

NAMES OF PASSENGERS		AGE	SEX	OCCUPATIONS	DATE PORT SHIP
MADDEN, Janet		32	F	None	24J104
MCDONALD, Thos.		27	M	Grocer	24J104
LYNCH, Wm.		18	M	Porter	24J104
MCLAUCHLIN, Jas.		25	M	Laborer	24J104
COLQUHON, John		25	M	Servant	24J104
CLEARY, Michl.		25	M	Grocer	24J104

EUGENIA 25 JULY 1849

From Vera Cruz

NAMES OF PASSENGERS		AGE	SEX	OCCUPATIONS	DATE PORT SHIP
ERO, Margaret		23	F	Unknown	25J171Mc
Julia		.04	F	Infant	25J171Mc

FAVORITE 26 JULY 1849

From Liverpool

NAMES OF PASSENGERS	AGE	SEX	OCCUPATIONS	DATE PORT SHIP
DENNISON, Phil	45	M	Unknown	26JI02Nf
Cathe.	40	F	Unknown	26JI02Nf
Pat	8	M	Child	26JI02Nf
Eliza	5	F	Child	26JI02Nf
Mary	2	F	Child	26JI02Nf
BRYAN, Mary	28	F	Unknown	26JI02Nf
Ann	24	F	Unknown	26JI02Nf
Cathe.	.00	F	Infant	26JI02Nf
MCMINNION, Jas.	25	M	Unknown	26JI02Nf
Jane	25	F	Unknown	26JI02Nf
BURNS, Anty	56	M	Unknown	26JI02Nf
Hugh	13	M	Unknown	26JI02Nf
QUIRK, Thos.	21	M	Unknown	26JI02Nf
STRALSEY, Hugh	21	M	Unknown	26JI02Nf
MCKENNONA, Wm.	13	M	Unknown	26JI02Nf
DUNNE, Martin	13	M	Unknown	26JI02Nf
KENNA, Jno.	47	M	Unknown	26JI02Nf
PHELAN, Jno.	35	M	Unknown	26JI02Nf
DOOLEY, Wm.	36	M	Unknown	26JI02Nf
MCDEVITT, Dennis	45	M	Unknown	26JI02Nf
CLARKE, Peter	40	M	Unknown	26JI02Nf
Phillip	35	M	Unknown	26JI02Nf
Max	32	M	Unknown	26JI02Nf
MCARDLE, Bernard	34	M	Unknown	26JI02Nf
CLARKE, Judith	30	F	Unknown	26JI02Nf
Judith	11	F	Unknown	26JI02Nf
HATTON, Wm.Hy.	13	M	Unknown	26JI02Nf
DALLAHERTY, Michl.	42	M	Unknown	26JI02Nf
Julia	32	F	Unknown	26JI02Nf
LEANY, Thos.	40	M	Unknown	26JI02Nf
Sally	22	F	Unknown	26JI02Nf
Winnifred	22	F	Unknown	26JI02Nf
James	50	M	Unknown	26JI02Nf
Judy	28	F	Unknown	26JI02Nf
Mary	30	F	Unknown	26JI02Nf
MCMARA, Margaret	25	F	Unknown	26JI02Nf
Sally	.00	F	Infant	26JI02Nf
HALLIGAN, Mic.	20	M	Unknown	26JI02Nf
CONLAN, Pat	30	M	Unknown	26JI02Nf
MAHER, Thos.	24	M	Unknown	26JI02Nf
Jno.	20	M	Unknown	26JI02Nf
Mary	17	F	Unknown	26JI02Nf
Cath.	16	F	Unknown	26JI02Nf
U	13	M	Unknown	26JI02Nf
THOMAS, Mic.	51	M	Unknown	26JI02Nf
Jno.	40	M	Unknown	26JI02Nf
Bridget	35	F	Unknown	26JI02Nf
Robert	13	M	Unknown	26JI02Nf
Josh.	12	M	Unknown	26JI02Nf
Jno.	10	M	Unknown	26JI02Nf
Mary	7	F	Child	26JI02Nf
Ann	5	F	Child	26JI02Nf
James	3	M	Child	26JI02Nf
Wm.	.00	M	Infant	26JI02Nf
BOYLE, Hugh	13	M	Unknown	26JI02Nf
ANGILL, Richd.	27	M	Unknown	26JI02Nf
LECKEY, Ann	20	F	Unknown	26JI02Nf
MCDERMOT, James	24	M	Unknown	26JI02Nf
REGAN, Thos.	28	M	Unknown	26JI02Nf
Honora	16	F	Unknown	26JI02Nf
PARSONS, Wm.	25	M	Unknown	26JI02Nf
OBRIAN, Luke	20	M	Unknown	26JI02Nf
WHEELER, Andrew	30	M	Unknown	26JI02Nf
UPTON, Margt.	27	F	Unknown	26JI02Nf
Mary	21	F	Unknown	26JI02Nf
MCCULLAGH, Wm.	20	M	Unknown	26JI02Nf
Nancy	22	F	Unknown	26JI02Nf
DONKING, Sara	26	F	Unknown	26JI02Nf
CARROLL, Jno.	35	M	Unknown	26JI02Nf
Ann	33	F	Unknown	26JI02Nf
Margt.	5	F	Child	26JI02Nf
Chas.	3	M	Child	26JI02Nf
Honora	.00	F	Infant	26JI02Nf
Richard	30	M	Unknown	26JI02Nf
WARD, Jno.	25	M	Unknown	26JI02Nf
Mary	26	F	Unknown	26JI02Nf
BOLAND, Thos.	20	M	Unknown	26JI02Nf
LEE, Michael	27	M	Unknown	26JI02Nf
KENNOVAN, Jno.	26	M	Unknown	26JI02Nf
RYAN, Jno.	29	M	Unknown	26JI02Nf
BLIGH, Andrew	45	M	Unknown	26JI02Nf
Mary	35	F	Unknown	26JI02Nf
Wm.	13	M	Unknown	26JI02Nf
Saml.	12	M	Unknown	26JI02Nf
Jno.	9	M	Child	26JI02Nf
Andw.	6	M	Child	26JI02Nf
George	4	M	Child	26JI02Nf
MCCARTHY, Jno.	34	M	Unknown	26JI02Nf
FEGAN, Betsy	20	F	Unknown	26JI02Nf
SCANLON, Francis	29	M	Unknown	26JI02Nf
THORPE, Jas.	43	M	Unknown	26JI02Nf
Cath.	40	F	Unknown	26JI02Nf
DATTON, Michl.	13	M	Unknown	26JI02Nf
BRIAN, Mic.	13	M	Unknown	26JI02Nf
THORPE, Jno.	10	M	Unknown	26JI02Nf
Thos.	5	M	Child	26JI02Nf
Ann	.00	F	Infant	26JI02Nf
DOYLE, Mary	43	F	Unknown	26JI02Nf
DOOLAN, Mary	20	F	Unknown	26JI02Nf
FENLON, Michl.	30	M	Unknown	26JI02Nf
SHEEHAN, Mic.	32	M	Unknown	26JI02Nf
Margt.	30	F	Unknown	26JI02Nf
Ann	9	F	Child	26JI02Nf
Richd.	7	M	Child	26JI02Nf
Jno.	5	M	Child	26JI02Nf
Wm.	3	M	Child	26JI02Nf
Pat	2	M	Child	26JI02Nf
Mich.	.00	M	Infant	26JI02Nf
GOLDER, Wm.	40	M	Unknown	26JI02Nf
Bridget	38	F	Unknown	26JI02Nf
CARROLL, Martin	30	M	Unknown	26JI02Nf
MORRISEY, Wm.	27	M	Unknown	26JI02Nf
Mary	25	F	Unknown	26JI02Nf
Wm.	.00	M	Infant	26JI02Nf
CANNON, Dooley	25	M	Unknown	26JI02Nf
NEVELL, Jno.	23	M	Unknown	26JI02Nf
CLEMENTS, Catha.	35	F	Unknown	26JI02Nf
Mary	30	F	Unknown	26JI02Nf
Jane	20	F	Unknown	26JI02Nf
Pat	9	M	Child	26JI02Nf
Arthur	7	M	Child	26JI02Nf
Sara-Ann	6	F	Child	26JI02Nf
Jno.	3	M	Child	26JI02Nf
Edward	.00	M	Infant	26JI02Nf
MURPHY, Tom	28	M	Unknown	26JI02Nf
BURKE, Margt.	35	F	Unknown	26JI02Nf
Johanna	2	F	Child	26JI02Nf
Pat	.00	M	Infant	26JI02Nf
FEHILY, Jno.	20	M	Unknown	26JI02Nf
KERAN, Johanna	17	F	Unknown	26JI02Nf
BURN, Jas.	30	M	Unknown	26JI02Nf
RYAN, John	42	M	Unknown	26JI02Nf
Elizth.	25	F	Unknown	26JI02Nf
Jas.	.00	M	Infant	26JI02Nf
WHITTAKER, Jas.	24	M	Unknown	26JI02Nf
CONNOLLY, Hugh	28	M	Unknown	26JI02Nf
HAVERIE, Cath.	24	F	Unknown	26JI02Nf
POTTER, Chas.	22	M	Unknown	26JI02Nf
POWER, Peter	30	M	Unknown	26JI02Nf
DALY, James	36	M	Unknown	26JI02Nf

NAMES OF PASSENGERS	AGE	SEX	OCCUPATIONS	DATE PORT SHIP
KELLY, John	24	M	Unknown	26J102Nf
THOMPSON, Hugh	17	M	Unknown	26J102Nf
CLARKE, Bridget	45	F	Unknown	26J102Nf
Mary	16	F	Unknown	26J102Nf
Cathe.	15	F	Unknown	26J102Nf
Ellis	11	M	Unknown	26J102Nf
Jno.	15	M	Unknown	26J102Nf
Michl.	8	M	Child	26J102Nf
MCDOWEL, Lawce.	27	M	Unknown	26J102Nf
RILEY, Jas.	13	M	Unknown	26J102Nf
MCKAY, Pat	26	M	Unknown	26J102Nf
DERRITT, Wm.	21	M	Unknown	26J102Nf
Ca--, Jno.	20	M	Unknown	26J102Nf
He--ON, Mary	38	F	Unknown	26J102Nf
HAGGERTY, Mic.	35	M	Unknown	26J102Nf
Owen	12	M	Unknown	26J102Nf
HOOY, Barney	25	M	Unknown	26J102Nf
Margt.	20	F	Unknown	26J102Nf
LYNES, Jas.	48	M	Unknown	26J102Nf
Jno.	35	M	Unknown	26J102Nf
Jas.	10	M	Unknown	26J102Nf
Jno.	8	M	Child	26J102Nf
Bridget	7	F	Child	26J102Nf
CORMICK, Mick	18	M	Unknown	26J102Nf
BIGGS, Thos.	15	M	Unknown	26J102Nf
CORMICK, Thomas	20	M	Unknown	26J102Nf
LOUGHRAN, Pat	20	M	Unknown	26J102Nf
CONLAN, Jno.	50	M	Unknown	26J102Nf
Jno.	26	M	Unknown	26J102Nf
Pat	22	M	Unknown	26J102Nf
Cath.	21	F	Unknown	26J102Nf
Jane	12	F	Unknown	26J102Nf
WELCH, Betty	22	F	Unknown	26J102Nf
DEVINA, Ann	22	F	Unknown	26J102Nf
DANIEL, Jno.	28	M	Unknown	26J102Nf
BLACKFORD, Mic.	25	M	Unknown	26J102Nf
MARIL, Jno.	25	M	Unknown	26J102Nf
AGNEW, Thos.	26	M	Unknown	26J102Nf
LYNES, Jas.	28	M	Unknown	26J102Nf
Maria	26	F	Unknown	26J102Nf
MCVEY, Sara	35	F	Unknown	26J102Nf
JOHNSON, Eliza-Jane	6	F	Child	26J102Nf
SHEEHAN, Wm.	20	M	Unknown	26J102Nf
FEENEY, Rose	20	F	Unknown	26J102Nf
MARTIN, Pat	30	M	Unknown	26J102Nf
CARROLL, Margt.	38	F	Unknown	26J102Nf
TRACY, Mary	27	F	Unknown	26J102Nf
WELDON, Jno.	25	M	Unknown	26J102Nf
DANEGHY, James	18	M	Unknown	26J102Nf
Edward	16	M	Unknown	26J102Nf
MILLER, Bart	18	M	Unknown	26J102Nf
Pat	16	M	Unknown	26J102Nf
MCMAHON, Alex	20	M	Unknown	26J102Nf
ONEILL, Sara-Ann	18	F	Unknown	26J102Nf
HICKEY, Jno.	30	M	Unknown	26J102Nf
POWER, Ellen	20	F	Unknown	26J102Nf
MULLVEY, Wm.	41	M	Unknown	26J102Nf
Betty	30	F	Unknown	26J102Nf
Margt.	11	F	Unknown	26J102Nf
Ann	10	F	Unknown	26J102Nf
Thos.	8	M	Child	26J102Nf
Elizb.	6	F	Child	26J102Nf
Ellen	3	F	Child	26J102Nf
Hance	.00	M	Infant	26J102Nf
MCDERMOTT, Mic.	34	M	Unknown	26J102Nf
Ellen	30	F	Unknown	26J102Nf
BRACKIN, Martin	20	M	Unknown	26J102Nf
CARTER, Biddy	20	F	Unknown	26J102Nf
MURRAY, Thos.	40	M	Unknown	26J102Nf
Bridget	40	F	Unknown	26J102Nf
Eliza	18	F	Unknown	26J102Nf
Cathe.	16	F	Unknown	26J102Nf

BACHE-MCEVERS 26 JULY 1849

From Cork

NAMES OF PASSENGERS	AGE	SEX	OCCUPATIONS	DATE PORT SHIP
DESMOND, Patrick	38	M	Laborer	26J108Ns
Ellen	36	F	Unknown	26J108Ns
John	6	M	Child	26J108Ns
Ellen	16	F	Unknown	26J108Ns
MURRAY, Thomas	24	M	Unknown	26J108Ns
HEALY, Abraham	20	M	Unknown	26J108Ns
COUGHLAN, John	20	M	Unknown	26J108Ns
Mary	24	F	Unknown	26J108Ns
Mary	5	F	Child	26J108Ns
Bess	4	F	Child	26J108Ns
Johanna	.00	F	Infant	26J108Ns
POWER, Jno.	26	M	Unknown	26J108Ns
Abbe	24	F	Unknown	26J108Ns
BUCKLY, Agnes	20	F	Unknown	26J108Ns
POWER, Johanna	20	F	Unknown	26J108Ns
BARY, Ellen	20	F	Unknown	26J108Ns
COGAN, Jas.	20	M	Unknown	26J108Ns
BARRY, Johanna	50	F	Unknown	26J108Ns
FITZGERALD, Bridget	20	F	Unknown	26J108Ns
HEAGARTHY, Catherine	20	F	Unknown	26J108Ns
DODD, Mary	20	F	Unknown	26J108Ns
MURPHY, Jane	26	F	Unknown	26J108Ns
Jane	9	F	Child	26J108Ns
Mary	5	F	Child	26J108Ns
CONNOR, Margt.	14	F	Unknown	26J108Ns
LEARY, Humphrey	15	M	Unknown	26J108Ns
DOE, Jno.	26	M	Unknown	26J108Ns
Jno.	16	M	Unknown	26J108Ns
MAHONEY, Catherine	30	F	Unknown	26J108Ns
BRIEN, Hannah	20	F	Unknown	26J108Ns
CARBERY, Eliza	20	F	Unknown	26J108Ns
ROBINSON, M.Anne	30	F	Unknown	26J108Ns
Anne	16	F	Unknown	26J108Ns
Andrew	12	M	Unknown	26J108Ns
Robt.	8	M	Child	26J108Ns
REORDAN, Jno.	20	M	Unknown	26J108Ns
Hannah	20	F	Unknown	26J108Ns
LONG, Mary	20	F	Unknown	26J108Ns
LOWTON, Matthew	40	M	Unknown	26J108Ns
Ellen	13	F	Unknown	26J108Ns
GLASSIN, Jno.	35	M	Unknown	26J108Ns
BURKE, Michael	20	M	Unknown	26J108Ns
COUGHLAN, Pat	20	M	Unknown	26J108Ns
MOHONEY, Timothy	26	M	Unknown	26J108Ns
RAYCROFT, Richard	20	M	Unknown	26J108Ns
SULLIVAN, Kitty	20	F	Unknown	26J108Ns
MCNAMARA, Kate	6	F	Child	26J108Ns
ROSS, Mary	20	F	Unknown	26J108Ns
RYAN, Catherine	20	F	Unknown	26J108Ns
SULLIVAN, Mary	24	F	Unknown	26J108Ns
Mary	20	F	Unknown	26J108Ns
GRIFFIN, Danl.	20	M	Unknown	26J108Ns
SULLIVAN, Jno.	24	M	Unknown	26J108Ns
Kevin	20	M	Unknown	26J108Ns
DUCAT, Mary	20	F	Unknown	26J108Ns
MANSFIELD, Hannah	26	F	Unknown	26J108Ns
Anne	11	F	Unknown	26J108Ns
Honora	9	F	Child	26J108Ns
Wm.	6	M	Child	26J108Ns
Joseph	4	M	Child	26J108Ns
SULLIVAN, Danl.	26	M	Unknown	26J108Ns
Michael	21	M	Unknown	26J108Ns
LEAN, Ned	10	M	Unknown	26J108Ns
Jead	9	U	Child	26J108Ns
Mary	6	F	Child	26J108Ns

NAMES OF PASSENGERS	AGE	SEX	OCCUPATIONS	DATE PORT SHIP
LEAN, James	3	M	Child	26J108Ns
SULLIVAN, Margt.	28	F	Unknown	26J108Ns
Denis	5	M	Child	26J108Ns
Ellen	.06	F	Infant	26J108Ns
KENNEDY, Alice	20	F	Unknown	26J108Ns
ROBERTS, U-Mrs.	20	F	Unknown	26J108Ns
HICKLY, Michael	20	M	Unknown	26J108Ns
DESMOND, Anne	20	F	Unknown	26J108Ns
RYAN, Patt	.00	M	Infant	26J108Ns
COGAN, Margt.	20	F	Unknown	26J108Ns

LADY-OF-THE-LAKE 26 JULY 1849

From Glasgow

NAMES OF PASSENGERS	AGE	SEX	OCCUPATIONS	DATE PORT SHIP
FRAME, Robert	40	M	Laborer	26J104Nu
Jane	36	F	None	26J104Nu
Agnes	17	F	None	26J104Nu
Robt.	15	M	None	26J104Nu
John	12	M	None	26J104Nu
William	11	M	None	26J104Nu
Jane	9	F	Child	26J104Nu
George	7	M	Child	26J104Nu
Catherine	.00	F	Infant	26J104Nu
THORNTON, Peter	21	M	None	26J104Nu
LAUSON, William	36	M	Engineer	26J104Nu
Agnes	32	F	None	26J104Nu
GRANT, Margaret	26	F	None	26J104Nu
GEDDES, William	45	M	Engineer	26J104Nu
Elizabeth	42	F	None	26J104Nu
Robert	17	M	None	26J104Nu
James	15	M	None	26J104Nu
Elizabeth	17	F	None	26J104Nu
William	19	M	None	26J104Nu
Margaret	5	F	Child	26J104Nu
Ann	.00	F	Infant	26J104Nu
Marion	3	F	Child	26J104Nu
TURNER, Sarah	21	F	None	26J104Nu
BROWN, U-Mrs.	26	F	Spinster	26J104Nu
Janet	6	F	Child	26J104Nu
John	2	M	Child	26J104Nu
CARSWELL, Mary	21	F	None	26J104Nu
MACKIE, John	45	M	None	26J104Nu
Jane	43	F	None	26J104Nu
Agnes	3	F	Child	26J104Nu
John	.00	M	Infant	26J104Nu
Mary	2	F	Child	26J104Nu
MILNE, Peter	26	M	Miller	26J104Nu
Jane	22	F	None	26J104Nu
Peter	4	M	Child	26J104Nu
Mary	6	F	Child	26J104Nu
QUAVIN, Peter	30	M	None	26J104Nu
DOCHERTY, George	21	M	Laborer	26J104Nu
CRENNOND, Margt.	21	F	None	26J104Nu
Mary	21	F	None	26J104Nu
Susan	19	F	None	26J104Nu
CREROND, Ann	15	F	None	26J104Nu
Ann	17	F	None	26J104Nu
DOGERTY, Margt.	21	F	None	26J104Nu
KISON, James	40	M	Cbtmkr	26J104Nu
Isabella	38	F	None	26J104Nu
Hugh	13	M	None	26J104Nu
William	.00	M	Infant	26J104Nu
MUIR, Wm.	21	M	None	26J104Nu
David	19	M	None	26J104Nu
TEMPLETON, Matthew	21	M	Gasfitter	26J104Nu
PLUNKET, Hugh	21	M	None	26J104Nu
MCCLAINE, Jane	35	F	None	26J104Nu
DRUMMOND, Peter	16	M	Farmer	26J104Nu
DRUMMOND, Ann	38	F	None	26J104Nu
Donald	8	M	Child	26J104Nu
John	.00	M	Infant	26J104Nu
MCMURRAY, John	20	M	None	26J104Nu
HANDLEY, Mary	20	F	None	26J104Nu
COLIN, Ann	19	F	None	26J104Nu
LYNCH, Jane	17	F	None	26J104Nu
FLAVIN, Cath.	18	F	None	26J104Nu
Cath.	7	F	Child	26J104Nu
Mcna--, Colina	25	F	None	26J104Nu
HUNTER, Thos.	36	M	Laborer	26J104Nu
Margt.	32	F	None	26J104Nu
Mary	17	F	None	26J104Nu
Grace	15	F	None	26J104Nu
John	12	M	None	26J104Nu
Ellen	10	F	None	26J104Nu
Rachel	8	F	Child	26J104Nu
George	6	M	Child	26J104Nu
John	4	M	Child	26J104Nu
Janet	2	F	Child	26J104Nu
George	.00	M	Infant	26J104Nu
Grace	19	F	None	26J104Nu
Andrew	21	M	None	26J104Nu
MCCULLOUGH, Hugh	30	M	None	26J104Nu
Agnes	28	F	None	26J104Nu
GRIM, George	21	M	None	26J104Nu
Mary	20	F	None	26J104Nu
Agnes	17	F	None	26J104Nu
George	13	M	None	26J104Nu
MORRISON, James	45	M	None	26J104Nu
Janet	40	F	None	26J104Nu
Arch.	6	M	Child	26J104Nu
Thos.	4	M	Child	26J104Nu
Chas.	.00	M	Infant	26J104Nu
Susan	8	F	Child	26J104Nu
COGAN, John	19	M	Laborer	26J104Nu
CUNNINGHAM, James	20	M	None	26J104Nu
CASSIDY, Peter	19	M	None	26J104Nu
MORRISON, Maria	34	F	None	26J104Nu
TAYLOR, Robt.	19	M	None	26J104Nu
CRORBET, James	19	M	None	26J104Nu
Mary	21	F	None	26J104Nu
Susan	19	F	None	26J104Nu
Juan	15	M	None	26J104Nu
CRICHTON, John	21	M	None	26J104Nu
SIM, Dennis	21	M	None	26J104Nu
COLL, Dennis	22	M	None	26J104Nu
ADAMS, Janet	30	F	None	26J104Nu
Helen	13	F	None	26J104Nu
Janet	8	F	Child	26J104Nu
Isabella	.00	F	Infant	26J104Nu
FLEMING, John	21	M	None	26J104Nu
Agnes	19	F	None	26J104Nu
MCCASKER, Michael	26	M	None	26J104Nu
DORONEL, Wm.	19	M	None	26J104Nu
MCKELLAR, Mary	19	F	None	26J104Nu
Patrick	17	M	None	26J104Nu
Barney	10	M	None	26J104Nu
Cath.	6	F	Child	26J104Nu
DUNCAN, Edward	8	M	Child	26J104Nu
MCCELLAR, Francis	21	M	None	26J104Nu
CUNNINGHAM, John	25	M	None	26J104Nu
BROGH, Robt.	23	M	None	26J104Nu
Mary	26	F	None	26J104Nu
WILBORN, Agnes	26	F	None	26J104Nu
BRAHAM, Hugh	29	M	None	26J104Nu
Mary	19	F	None	26J104Nu
SHANNAN, Chas.	18	F	None	26J104Nu
GILSON, Jane	17	F	None	26J104Nu
CARUTHERS, Peter	45	M	None	26J104Nu
Janet	40	F	None	26J104Nu
Janet	14	F	None	26J104Nu
Peter	12	M	None	26J104Nu
Mary	11	F	None	26J104Nu
Euphemia	10	F	None	26J104N

NAMES OF PASSENGERS	AGE	SEX	OCCUPATIONS	DATE PORT SHIP
CARUTHERS, Isabella	7	F	Child	26J104Nu
Margt.	6	F	Child	26J104Nu
Alexander	3	M	Child	26J104Nu
Jane	.00	F	Infant	26J104Nu
SMITH, John	26	M	None	26J104Nu
CASSIDY, Patrick	21	M	None	26J104Nu
SHIELDS, Leslie	19	U	None	26J104Nu
ANDERSON, John	23	M	None	26J104Nu
MCGREGOR, Alexander	30	M	None	26J104Nu
Margt.	27	F	None	26J104Nu
Daneen	5	U	Child	26J104Nu
ROBERTSON, Wm.	22	M	None	26J104Nu
MONDAY, Patrick	19	M	None	26J104Nu
DUNCAN, Margt.	30	F	None	26J104Nu
Janet	27	F	None	26J104Nu
Wm.	10	M	None	26J104Nu
Marion	9	F	Child	26J104Nu
Edward	6	M	Child	26J104Nu
Robt.	.00	M	Infant	26J104Nu
DENNISON, John	26	M	None	26J104Nu
Mary	25	F	None	26J104Nu
John	10	M	None	26J104Nu
Alexander	6	F	Child	26J104Nu
CULLEN, John	30	M	None	26J104Nu
DONNAGHY, Hugh	21	M	None	26J104Nu
Mcmoo--, Mary	21	F	None	26J104Nu
BOWIE, Alexander	24	M	None	26J104Nu
HENRY, John	19	M	None	26J104Nu
ROSS, Hugh	23	M	None	26J104Nu
Jane	21	F	None	26J104Nu
MCCEY, Cath.	17	F	None	26J104Nu
ROSS, George	26	M	None	26J104Nu
SMITH, Alexander	29	M	None	26J104Nu
George	00	M	None	26J104Nu
U	.00	U	Infant	26J104Nu
MCNUTT, James	23	M	None	26J104Nu
SEGGIE, James	19	M	Shoemaker	26J104Nu

VICTORIA 26 JULY 1849

From Liverpool And Cork

NAMES OF PASSENGERS	AGE	SEX	OCCUPATIONS	DATE PORT SHIP
MCMAHEN, Pat	14	M	Laborer	26J168Cl
MCLAULAND, Thos.	22	M	Blacksmith	26J168Cl
FITZPATRICK, John	13	M	Servant	26J168Cl
DRISCOLL, Margt.	20	F	Servant	26J168Cl
Died-At-Sea				
FERGUSON, Julia	38	F	Servant	26J168Cl
Margt.	6	F	Child	26J168Cl
John	4	M	Child	26J168Cl
Robt.	2	M	Child	26J168Cl
James	.06	M	Infant	26J168Cl
Died-At-Sea				
FLYN, Wm.	18	M	Laborer	26J168Cl
MARAN, Wm.	36	M	Carpenter	26J168Cl
Ann	17	F	Unknown	26J168Cl
MCNEILL, Elisa	12	F	Laborer	26J168Cl
MCKEON, Brid.	19	F	Unknown	26J168Cl
BREAKLY, Cath.	35	F	Unknown	26J168Cl
Thos.	9	M	Child	26J168Cl
Jas.	7	M	Child	26J168Cl
BRENEN, Michl.	30	M	Servant	26J168Cl
SEWARD, Bart	33	M	Blacksmith	26J168Cl
DELANY, Jas.	25	M	Laborer	26J168Cl
MONOHAN, John	32	M	Farmer	26J168Cl
Eliz.	22	F	Farmer	26J168Cl
MERIDITH, Elisa	20	F	Unknown	26J168Cl
LAUD, Joshua	35	M	Laborer	26J168Cl
Rebecca	35	F	Unknown	26J168Cl
BARR, Margt.	50	F	Unknown	26J168Cl
RODY, Mary	11	F	Unknown	26J168Cl
AQUIN, Rose	19	F	Unknown	26J168Cl
GALVIN, Murta	22	F	Unknown	26J168Cl
Johana	24	F	Unknown	26J168Cl
EGAN, Mady	35	U	Unknown	26J168Cl
MCMANNUS, Margt.	17	F	Unknown	26J168Cl
Jane	10	F	Unknown	26J168Cl
COLLAGHAN, Ellen	17	F	Unknown	26J168Cl
SPILLACY, Thos.	14	M	Unknown	26J168Cl
Mary	19	F	Unknown	26J168Cl
GRADY, Mary	30	F	Unknown	26J168Cl
John	8	M	Child	26J168Cl
Margt.	.06	F	Infant	26J168Cl
MCLAUGHLIN, John	40	M	Unknown	26J168Cl
Pat	20	M	Unknown	26J168Cl
John	17	M	Unknown	26J168Cl
BONNER, Wm.	26	M	Unknown	26J168Cl
Ann	26	F	Unknown	26J168Cl
Edward	.06	M	Infant	26J168Cl
RILEY, Mary	30	F	Unknown	26J168Cl
Hugh	13	M	Unknown	26J168Cl
Owen	9	M	Child	26J168Cl
NOLAND, Brid.	18	F	Unknown	26J168Cl
REARDEN, Margt.	18	F	Unknown	26J168Cl
CONNER, Carney	55	M	Unknown	26J168Cl
Carney	23	M	Unknown	26J168Cl
John	30	M	Unknown	26J168Cl
Eliza	30	F	Unknown	26J168Cl
Ellen	12	F	Unknown	26J168Cl
SHENEY, Jerry	30	M	Unknown	26J168Cl
HOLLAND, Hyrun	24	M	Unknown	26J168Cl
DELANY, Michl.	24	M	Unknown	26J168Cl
MCALARNY, Pat	27	M	Unknown	26J168Cl
KIEFFE, Elisa	27	F	Unknown	26J168Cl
Elisa	.08	F	Infant	26J168Cl
Danl.	40	M	Unknown	26J168Cl
MARCH, Thos.	20	F	Unknown	26J168Cl
ROURKE, Jas.	35	M	Farmer	26J168Cl
Mary	35	F	Farmer	26J168Cl
Ann	11	F	Unknown	26J168Cl
Michl.	10	M	Unknown	26J168Cl
Bernard	8	M	Child	26J168Cl
Mary	6	F	Child	26J168Cl
Patt	3	M	Child	26J168Cl
HENEY, Bernd.	40	M	Unknown	26J168Cl
Peter	12	M	Unknown	26J168Cl
SWEENEY, Edward	30	M	Laborer	26J168Cl
MCCABE, Thos.	50	M	Farmer	26J168Cl
Phil	24	M	Farmer	26J168Cl
Thos.	21	M	Farmer	26J168Cl
Brid.	23	F	Unknown	26J168Cl
Rose	40	F	Unknown	26J168Cl
ALLAN, Hughue	12	M	Unknown	26J168Cl
MCMAHAN, Cath.	50	F	Laborer	26J168Cl
Lawrence	5	M	Child	26J168Cl
CARROLL, Thos.	40	M	Laborer	26J168Cl
Brid.	40	F	Laborer	26J168Cl
Patt	20	M	Laborer	26J168Cl
Rose	18	F	Laborer	26J168Cl
John	13	M	Laborer	26J168Cl
Thos.	12	M	Laborer	26J168Cl
LOWRY, Thos.	21	M	Laborer	26J168Cl
Mary	23	F	Laborer	26J168Cl
Mary	2	F	Child	26J168Cl
John	.07	M	Infant	26J168Cl
LARKIN, Thos.	30	M	Laborer	26J168Cl
Ann	24	M	Laborer	26J168Cl
Thos.	2	M	Child	26J168Cl
CARROLL, Michl.	25	M	Laborer	26J168Cl
KESBY, Elisabeth	23	F	Laborer	26J168Cl
BERCH, Sarah	30	F	Laborer	26J168Cl
Died-At-Sea				
Mine.	7	U	Child	26J168Cl
Saml.	4	M	Child	26J168Cl

NAMES OF PASSENGERS	AGE	SEX	OCCUPATIONS	DATE PORT SHIP
BERCH, David	2	M	Child	26J168CI
MORAN, Mary	4	F	Child	26J168CI
CONDY, Thos.	22	M	Blacksmith	26J168CI
Lidia	18	F	Unknown	26J168CI
FERRILL, John	35	M	Laborer	26J168CI
DOWLING, Edward	24	M	Servant	26J168CI
HALGRAVES, Ann	25	F	Servant	26J168CI
WHELAN, Mary	28	F	Servant	26J168CI
Brid.	5	F	Child	26J168CI
Michl.	.10	M	Infant	26J168CI
HOSEY, Margt.	22	F	Servant	26J168CI
WHELAN, Mary	20	F	Servant	26J168CI
MCDONNELL, Cath.	30	F	Servant	26J168CI
NEWMAN, Thos.	25	M	Servant	26J168CI
Cath.	22	F	Servant	26J168CI
NEAL, Michl.	26	M	Laborer	26J168CI
Bridget	21	F	Laborer	26J168CI
DONNELLY, John	26	M	Weaver	26J168CI
Margt.	24	F	Weaver	26J168CI
GRIFFIN, Pat	30	M	Laborer	26J168CI
Elly	25	U	Laborer	26J168CI
Jas.	21	M	Laborer	26J168CI
Ann	20	F	Laborer	26J168CI
Died-At-Sea				
Jas.	2	M	Child	26J168CI
Died-At-Sea				
Patt	.09	M	Infant	26J168CI
KEOGH, Wm.	25	M	Surveyor	26J168CI
GETHRAB, Henry	20	M	Carpenter	26J168CI
GILMAN, Pat	23	M	Laborer	26J168CI
LOVE, John	40	M	Laborer	26J168CI
FARLEY, Barney	20	M	Laborer	26J168CI
Ann	20	F	Unknown	26J168CI
MULDOWNY, Brid.	22	F	Laborer	26J168CI
DELANY, Brid.	50	F	Laborer	26J168CI
Brid.	12	F	Laborer	26J168CI
HENLEN, Ellen	21	F	Laborer	26J168CI
MURRAY, Pat	40	M	Miner	26J168CI
Died-At-Sea				
Jerry	35	M	Miner	26J168CI
MULVEY, Mary	40	F	Farmer	26J168CI
FINN, John	22	M	Laborer	26J168CI
DOWDALL, Cath.	40	F	Laborer	26J168CI
BROTHERS, John	16	M	Laborer	26J168CI
Hughue	13	M	Laborer	26J168CI
BUCKLEY, Cath.	18	F	Laborer	26J168CI
AYLWOOD, Edward	32	M	Farmer	26J168CI
Ellen	44	F	Farmer	26J168CI
Elisa	24	F	Farmer	26J168CI
Mary	22	F	Farmer	26J168CI
John	13	M	Farmer	26J168CI
HERRON, Jas.	32	M	Shoemaker	26J168CI
CONNIFF, Michl.	20	M	Laborer	26J168CI
HOWARD, Jas.	25	M	Laborer	26J168CI
Thos.	21	M	Laborer	26J168CI
MCGLIFFE, Jas.	60	M	Laborer	26J168CI
EGAN, Jas.	5	M	Child	26J168CI
DUNN, Ellen	20	F	Laborer	26J168CI
MCAULIFFE, John	45	M	Farmer	26J168CI
Cath.	45	F	Unknown	26J168CI
Tom	17	M	Shoemaker	26J168CI
Dan	13	M	Farmer	26J168CI
Cath.	11	F	Farmer	26J168CI
MULLONE, Danl.	3	M	Child	26J168CI
COLLINS, Betty	26	F	Laborer	26J168CI
KENNEDY, Mary	25	F	Laborer	26J168CI
SHENEY, Cath.	25	F	Laborer	26J168CI
CALWELL, Ann	15	F	Laborer	26J168CI
Mary	12	F	Laborer	26J168CI
KERNON, Brid.	22	F	Laborer	26J168CI
COMMINS, Mary	17	F	Laborer	26J168CI
MCCABE, Peter	26	M	Farmer	26J168CI
MCGRATH, Johanna	40	F	Laborer	26J168CI
John	17	M	Laborer	26J168CI
BAREY, Elisa	30	F	Laborer	26J168CI

NAMES OF PASSENGERS	AGE	SEX	OCCUPATIONS	DATE PORT SHIP
BAREY, Edward	11	M	Unknown	26J168CI
Mary	10	F	Unknown	26J168CI
Julia	8	F	Child	26J168CI
Ellen	5	F	Child	26J168CI
SLANEY, Bridget	20	F	Unknown	26J168CI
WELCH, Jas.	21	M	Laborer	26J168CI
GRANT, Pat	53	M	Laborer	26J168CI
John	22	M	Laborer	26J168CI
GLIN, Cath.	23	F	Laborer	26J168CI
FRANCIS, John	24	M	Miner	26J168CI
FITZGERALD, Michl.	45	M	Farmer	26J168CI
FOLEY, Elisabeth	25	F	Farmer	26J168CI
HIGGINS, Nane	20	U	Farmer	26J168CI
Wm.	19	M	Farmer	26J168CI
SAUNDERS, John	28	M	Farmer	26J168CI
MEAGHERS, Michl.	24	M	Carpenter	26J168CI
MURPHY, Michl.	24	M	Laborer	26J168CI
LANE, David	24	M	Laborer	26J168CI
Mary	20	F	Laborer	26J168CI
John	20	M	Laborer	26J168CI
DONOVAN, Dennis	20	M	Laborer	26J168CI
Nelly	20	F	Laborer	26J168CI
Mary	24	F	Laborer	26J168CI
Tim	24	M	Laborer	26J168CI
MCARTHY, John	20	M	Laborer	26J168CI
Bess	20	M	Laborer	26J168CI
Mary	20	M	Laborer	26J168CI
PIGGOTT, Kate	40	F	Laborer	26J168CI
Eugene	14	M	Laborer	26J168CI
Cath.	3	F	Child	26J168CI
MURPHY, Conn.	20	M	Laborer	26J168CI
Johanna	20	F	Laborer	26J168CI
MAHONY, John	20	M	Laborer	26J168CI
COURNICK, Danl.	20	M	Laborer	26J168CI
CONNELL, Cornelius	20	M	Shoemaker	26J168CI
RIERDEN, Jerry	20	M	Laborer	26J168CI
Corn.	20	M	Laborer	26J168CI
CONNELL, Fanny	20	F	Laborer	26J168CI
Margt.	17	F	Laborer	26J168CI
COLEMAN, Andy	25	M	Laborer	26J168CI
MCCARTHY, Michl.	25	M	Laborer	26J168CI
LUCY, Con.	25	M	Laborer	26J168CI
BARRY, Henry	20	M	Laborer	26J168CI
CAREY, Dennis	21	M	Laborer	26J168CI
BRENAGH, Bridget	20	F	Laborer	26J168CI
ALBERTH, Ellen	20	F	Laborer	26J168CI
ROGERS, Cath.	40	F	Laborer	26J168CI
Elisa	20	F	Laborer	26J168CI
Ellen	13	F	Laborer	26J168CI
John	12	M	Laborer	26J168CI
George	10	M	Laborer	26J168CI
Wm.	9	M	Child	26J168CI
Peter	4	M	Child	26J168CI
Heram	2	U	Child	26J168CI
CONNER, Thos.	26	M	Laborer	26J168CI
LAWLIN, Bridget	15	F	Laborer	26J168CI
Cath.	14	F	Laborer	26J168CI
HANIVAN, Mary	20	F	Laborer	26J168CI
EDWARDS, Patt	20	M	Laborer	26J168CI
MCCARTHY, Ann	18	F	Laborer	26J168CI
MAHONY, Thos.	14	M	Laborer	26J168CI
NEAL, Jas.	35	M	Laborer	26J168CI
Ellen	30	F	Laborer	26J168CI
Patt.	.02	M	Infant	26J168CI
DORAN, Archibald	57	M	Gentleman	26J168CI
CLANCY, Patrick	00	M	Unknown	26J168CI
SHEY, Patrick	00	M	Unknown	26J168CI
BUSTER, Elisa	00	F	Unknown	26J168CI
KIEFF, Elisa	00	F	Unknown	26J168CI

NAMES OF PASSENGERS	AGE	SEX	OCCUPATIONS	DATE PORT SHIP

JULIA-HOWARD 27 JULY 1849

From Liverpool

NAMES OF PASSENGERS	AGE	SEX	OCCUPATIONS	DATE PORT SHIP
MADDEN, Pat	50	M	Joiner	27Jl02Nv
Margt.	50	F	None	27Jl02Nv
Pat	22	M	Laborer	27Jl02Nv
MURPHY, Wm.	27	M	Farmer	27Jl02Nv
PORRES, Bridt.	21	F	None	27Jl02Nv
MCKILLOGOT, Morris	25	M	Laborer	27Jl02Nv
MCMANS, Pat	25	M	Laborer	27Jl02Nv
Michael	18	M	Laborer	27Jl02Nv
FALLAN, Pat	40	M	Laborer	27Jl02Nv
HEFFERAN, Pat	20	M	Laborer	27Jl02Nv
MAHON, Jas.	38	M	Laborer	27Jl02Nv
MURPHY, Jas.	22	M	Student	27Jl02Nv
Judy	18	F	None	27Jl02Nv
BERRY, Pat	26	M	Laborer	27Jl02Nv
Henry	17	M	Laborer	27Jl02Nv
Catharine	16	F	None	27Jl02Nv
Danl.	15	M	Sailor	27Jl02Nv
David	11	M	None	27Jl02Nv
J.	10	M	None	27Jl02Nv
MELODY, Ann	30	F	None	27Jl02Nv
Catharine	16	F	None	27Jl02Nv
Phil	10	M	None	27Jl02Nv
MCHOOYNE, Rose	16	F	None	27Jl02Nv
NEILY, Mary-J.	17	F	None	27Jl02Nv
MURRY, Hannah	16	F	None	27Jl02Nv
MCBRIDE, Elisa	17	F	None	27Jl02Nv
NEDLEY, Michael	22	M	Laborer	27Jl02Nv
KING, Christopher	21	M	Laborer	27Jl02Nv
SHIELDS, Ann	20	F	None	27Jl02Nv
THOMPSON, Mary-A.	22	F	None	27Jl02Nv
DUFFEY, John	33	M	Dealer	27Jl02Nv
MCKENNA, Jas.	27	M	Student	27Jl02Nv
HACKET, Ann	40	F	None	27Jl02Nv
Margaret	13	F	None	27Jl02Nv
John	10	M	None	27Jl02Nv
May	8	F	Child	27Jl02Nv
Ellen	6	F	Child	27Jl02Nv
DORON, May	18	F	None	27Jl02Nv
CARROLL, Edward	22	M	Unknown	27Jl02Nv
COLEMAN, David	24	M	Laborer	27Jl02Nv
KENNIDY, Pat	50	M	Farmer	27Jl02Nv
Betty	50	F	None	27Jl02Nv
Jas.	26	M	Farmer	27Jl02Nv
Mary	17	F	None	27Jl02Nv
Bridt.	14	F	None	27Jl02Nv
DONNEY, Pat	22	M	Herd	27Jl02Nv
HEFFERAN, Edward	32	M	Laborer	27Jl02Nv
CRANFORD, Thos.	65	M	Weaver	27Jl02Nv
Ellen	60	F	None	27Jl02Nv
Mary-A.	30	F	None	27Jl02Nv
Ellen	25	F	None	27Jl02Nv
David	12	M	None	27Jl02Nv
Mary	9	F	Child	27Jl02Nv
Robt.	7	M	Child	27Jl02Nv
MCKENNA, Danl.	42	M	Weaver	27Jl02Nv
Mary	42	F	None	27Jl02Nv
Robt.	20	M	None	27Jl02Nv
Thos.	11	M	None	27Jl02Nv
Danl.	5	M	Child	27Jl02Nv
CUNLISH, Thos.	12	M	None	27Jl02Nv
MADDEN, Richd.	40	M	Laborer	27Jl02Nv
May	40	F	None	27Jl02Nv
MCMANNES, Ricd.	38	M	Laborer	27Jl02Nv
GREY, Ellen	22	F	None	27Jl02Nv
CONROY, John	30	M	Laborer	27Jl02Nv

NAMES OF PASSENGERS	AGE	SEX	OCCUPATIONS	DATE PORT SHIP
DONNAVON, Honor	30	F	None	27Jl02Nv
Teddy	9	M	Child	27Jl02Nv
MCAUDLIFFE, Judy	34	F	None	27Jl02Nv
GALLAGHER, Sabena	30	F	None	27Jl02Nv
TOLAN, Michl.	6	M	Child	27Jl02Nv
Pat	4	M	Child	27Jl02Nv
Jas.	3	M	Child	27Jl02Nv
CARROLL, Peter	23	M	Shoemaker	27Jl02Nv
Catharine	18	F	None	27Jl02Nv
MCDONALD, Mary-A.	5	F	Child	27Jl02Nv
ROAN, Gennet	35	M	Shoemaker	27Jl02Nv
U (W)	26	F	None	27Jl02Nv
Jas.	3	M	Child	27Jl02Nv
HESTER, Owen	30	M	Laborer	27Jl02Nv
MULANY, John	25	M	Laborer	27Jl02Nv
GURGAN, Edward	22	M	Laborer	27Jl02Nv
Jane	12	F	None	27Jl02Nv
Catherine	10	F	None	27Jl02Nv
Michl.	8	M	Child	27Jl02Nv
LYNCH, Pat	30	M	Laborer	27Jl02Nv
Michl.	40	M	Carpenter	27Jl02Nv
Mary	18	F	None	27Jl02Nv
CASEY, Dennis	30	M	Laborer	27Jl02Nv
STANTON, W.	23	M	Carpenter	27Jl02Nv
MOORE, Pat	40	M	Unknown	27Jl02Nv
Died-At-Sea				
RYAN, Tim	20	M	Laborer	27Jl02Nv
PHELAN, Price	32	M	Farmer	27Jl02Nv
GILLESPIE, Pat	20	M	Laborer	27Jl02Nv
COMMONS, John	20	M	Laborer	27Jl02Nv
BLACK, Mary	43	F	None	27Jl02Nv
MCELGIN, John	27	M	Carpenter	27Jl02Nv
U (W)	25	F	None	27Jl02Nv
John	.10	M	Infant	27Jl02Nv
HUNT, Pat	24	M	Laborer	27Jl02Nv
GIBBONS, Pat	40	M	Laborer	27Jl02Nv
MULLONEY, Jas.	40	M	Farmer	27Jl02Nv
Judy	16	F	None	27Jl02Nv
CAIN, John	22	M	Laborer	27Jl02Nv
BROPHY, Thos.	21	M	Laborer	27Jl02Nv
GILLAN, Mich.	20	M	Laborer	27Jl02Nv
DOUD, M.	20	M	Laborer	27Jl02Nv
Mary	45	F	None	27Jl02Nv
GILMARTIN, Michl.	20	M	Laborer	27Jl02Nv
GONAN, Pat	15	M	Laborer	27Jl02Nv
G--, P.	14	F	None	27Jl02Nv
CAVANAH, John	20	M	Laborer	27Jl02Nv
A.	21	U	Unknown	27Jl02Nv
DRUMMOND, Elisabeth	27	F	None	27Jl02Nv
WARD, Michael	25	M	Laborer	27Jl02Nv
Ann	22	F	None	27Jl02Nv
RILEY, Mary	20	F	None	27Jl02Nv
DUNN, Timm	40	M	Laborer	27Jl02Nv
U (W)	40	F	None	27Jl02Nv
Hon.	3	F	Child	27Jl02Nv
Maria	.03	F	Infant	27Jl02Nv
WALLACE, John	25	M	Nail Maker	27Jl02Nv
ALEXANDER, Thos.	42	M	Painter	27Jl02Nv
Emma	40	F	None	27Jl02Nv
HOULEY, John	35	M	Laborer	27Jl02Nv
Jas.	30	M	Laborer	27Jl02Nv
ODONNOLD, John	20	M	Laborer	27Jl02Nv
Pat	25	M	Laborer	27Jl02Nv
HOULEY, Michl.	30	M	Laborer	27Jl02Nv
LANGTRY, Hugh	18	M	Laborer	27Jl02Nv
Richd.	20	M	Weaver	27Jl02Nv
FINLAN, Pat	30	M	Laborer	27Jl02Nv
MCNALLY, Bridt.	20	F	None	27Jl02Nv
FLANGAN, Ann	18	F	None	27Jl02Nv
ROGERS, Mary	50	F	None	27Jl02Nv
GILLESPIE, Ellen	21	F	None	27Jl02Nv
RODGERS, Jane	12	F	None	27Jl02Nv
JUDGE, Michl.	32	M	Weaver	27Jl02Nv
FARRALL, Pat	47	M	Unknown	27Jl02Nv
BULGER, Jas.	51	M	Merchant	27Jl02Nv

NAMES OF PASSENGERS	AGE	SEX	OCCUPATIONS	DATE PORT SHIP
BULGER, Morris	17	M	Merchant	27JI02Nv
DONOHUE, Martin	20	M	Shoemaker	27JI02Nv
TOONEY, Michl.	20	M	Joiner	27JI02Nv
MULDONEY, John	25	M	Laborer	27JI02Nv
MULDOWNEY, Catherine	19	F	None	27JI02Nv
HENNESY, Cath.	22	F	None	27JI02Nv
FIELDHOUSE, Wm.	30	M	Farrier	27JI02Nv
U (W)	33	F	None	27JI02Nv
NIEL, Bernd.	20	M	Laborer	27JI02Nv
RYAN, Bridt.	20	F	None	27JI02Nv
Richd.	24	M	Laborer	27JI02Nv
Mary	22	F	None	27JI02Nv
DOYLE, John	24	M	Laborer	27JI02Nv
PURCELL, Mary	20	F	None	27JI02Nv
MCDONALD, Jas.	21	U	None	27JI02Nv
CARROLL, U	30	M	Merchant	27JI02Nv
U (W)	00	F	None	27JI02Nv
U	.09	U	Infant	27JI02Nv
Maria	4	F	Child	27JI02Nv
Danl.	2	M	Child	27JI02Nv
SHANAHAN, U-Mrs.	28	F	None	27JI02Nv
U	.11	U	Infant	27JI02Nv
MCMILLAN, Wm.	19	M	Laborer	27JI02Nv
TUITE, Michl.	35	M	Victualler	27JI02Nv
Michl.	3	M	Child	27JI02Nv
John	4	M	Child	27JI02Nv
MURPHY, Bridt.	36	F	None	27JI02Nv
MCMAROW, H.	22	M	Laborer	27JI02Nv
MCMORROW, Wm.	26	M	Laborer	27JI02Nv
Jas.	18	M	Laborer	27JI02Nv
HART, Jno.	21	M	Laborer	27JI02Nv
WARD, Jno.	32	M	Laborer	27JI02Nv
MCGUIRE, Owen	21	M	Laborer	27JI02Nv
MCGOVEN, Pat	25	M	Laborer	27JI02Nv
Peter	60	M	Laborer	27JI02Nv
Judy	50	F	None	27JI02Nv
Susan	22	F	None	27JI02Nv
Mary	20	F	None	27JI02Nv
DOOGAN, Peter	30	M	Laborer	27JI02Nv
MCNIFF, Hugh	30	M	Laborer	27JI02Nv
GALLAGHER, Jas.	20	M	Laborer	27JI02Nv
MCGOWN, Jno.	30	M	Laborer	27JI02Nv
WARE, Michl.	24	M	Laborer	27JI02Nv
MCLOUGHLIN, Cath.	20	F	None	27JI02Nv
GALLIGAN, Pat	20	M	Laborer	27JI02Nv
BRADLEY, Michl.	22	M	Laborer	27JI02Nv
CUFFAT, Matilda	25	F	None	27JI02Nv
Phebe	24	F	None	27JI02Nv
KEOUN, Jas.	21	M	Laborer	27JI02Nv
Ann	19	F	None	27JI02Nv
MONAGHAN, Law.	21	M	Tailor	27JI02Nv
DOUGHERTY, Bryan	26	M	Laborer	27JI02Nv
CARY, Ridy	19	M	Laborer	27JI02Nv
FLANIGAN, Peter	35	M	Laborer	27JI02Nv
DAY, Eliza	13	F	None	27JI02Nv
May	20	F	None	27JI02Nv
CARY, Ann	20	F	None	27JI02Nv
RYAN, Brid.	18	F	None	27JI02Nv
CANNON, Jas.	18	M	Laborer	27JI02Nv
Alice	20	F	None	27JI02Nv
BERNE, Thos.	27	M	Laborer	27JI02Nv
DOBSON, John	21	M	Laborer	27JI02Nv
DUNN, W.	27	M	Farmer	27JI02Nv
CALLEY, W.	20	M	Laborer	27JI02Nv
FLENEMENT, N.	40	M	Sawer	27JI02Nv
TOOL, M.	22	M	Laborer	27JI02Nv

JNO.KERR 28 JULY 1849

From Glasgow

NAMES OF PASSENGERS	AGE	SEX	OCCUPATIONS	DATE PORT SHIP
MURPHY, Peter	21	M	Shoemaker	28JI04Nw
Mary	26	F	Matron	28JI04Nw
Corn.	2	M	Child	28JI04Nw
DRAIN, Daniel	35	M	Farmer	28JI04Nw
Patrick	30	M	Farmer	28JI04Nw
Agness	32	F	Matron	28JI04Nw
CARNEY, Robert	22	M	Laborer	28JI04Nw
BARBER, Hugh	55	M	Farmer	28JI04Nw
ONEIL, Daniel	21	M	Weaver	28JI04Nw
DIAMOND, Rose	33	F	Matron	28JI04Nw
SHARKY, Mary	30	F	Matron	28JI04Nw
DIAMOND, James	4	M	Child	28JI04Nw
Eliza.	.00	F	Infant	28JI04Nw
FLAVERN, Barney	25	M	Ctnsp	28JI04Nw
HUGGINS, John	20	M	Laborer	28JI04Nw
HESTON, Michael	27	M	Laborer	28JI04Nw
WATERS, Hugh	26	M	Plasterer	28JI04Nw
MCQUICK, James	30	M	Laborer	28JI04Nw
Ann	30	F	Matron	28JI04Nw
Patrick	.00	M	Infant	28JI04Nw
MCDIBIL, Hannah	18	F	Matron	28JI04Nw
Mary-Anne	.00	F	Infant	28JI04Nw
COGAN, John	26	M	Farmer	28JI04Nw
Mary	26	F	Matron	28JI04Nw
George	3	M	Child	28JI04Nw
Arthur	1	M	Child	28JI04Nw
SPINS, U	16	M	Laborer	28JI04Nw
BROWN, John	40	M	Laborer	28JI04Nw
Mary	38	F	Matron	28JI04Nw
John	27	M	Farmer	28JI04Nw
Isabella	18	F	Spinster	28JI04Nw
Ann	13	F	Child	28JI04Nw
Hugh	8	M	Child	28JI04Nw
Margaret	5	F	Child	28JI04Nw
Mary	3	F	Child	28JI04Nw
MCCLACY, Robt.	24	M	Laborer	28JI04Nw
SCULLION, Edward	21	M	Laborer	28JI04Nw
Agnes	24	F	Matron	28JI04Nw
MCGACHEN, Alice	25	F	Servant	28JI04Nw
GORDON, Robt.	17	M	Laborer	28JI04Nw
ALWILD, Francis	33	M	Laborer	28JI04Nw
KENNAN, James	18	M	Carpenter	28JI04Nw
COGAN, U Born-At-Sea	.00	F	Infant	28JI04Nw
KENNAN, May	40	F	Matron	28JI04Nw
Elizabeth	16	F	Spinster	28JI04Nw
George	28	M	Carpenter	28JI04Nw
Elizabeth	22	F	Matron	28JI04Nw
Maria	15	F	Spinster	28JI04Nw
Francis	8	M	Child	28JI04Nw
REID, Alxd.	25	M	Laborer	28JI04Nw
Elizabeth	23	F	Matron	28JI04Nw
Thomas	2	M	Child	28JI04Nw
James	.00	M	Infant	28JI04Nw
SNOUGH, John	45	M	Laborer	28JI04Nw
Catherine	40	F	Matron	28JI04Nw
John	8	M	Child	28JI04Nw
William	6	M	Child	28JI04Nw
Sarah	.00	F	Infant	28JI04Nw
MCFER, Daniel	19	M	Blacksmith	28JI04Nw
HUGHES, Isabella	24	F	Spinster	28JI04Nw
SNOUGH, Euphemia	6	F	Child	28JI04Nw
MARTIN, Robert	26	M	Laborer	28JI04Nw
BROWN, Robert	32	M	Unknown	28JI04Nw
MCNASH, Archibald	32	M	Unknown	28JI04Nw

ATLAS 28 JULY 1849

From Liverpool

NAMES OF PASSENGERS	AGE	SEX	OCCUPATIONS	DATE PORT SHIP
WILSON, Jeremiah	14	M	Laborer	28JI02Nx
MORGAN, Stephen	24	M	Laborer	28JI02Nx
MCGINN, Catherine	18	F	None	28JI02Nx
TAYLOR, U-Mrs.	21	F	None	28JI02Nx
JOHNSTON, Alexr.M.	16	M	None	28JI02Nx
STEPHENSON, Matthew	24	M	Unknown	28JI02Nx
WILKINSON, John	20	M	Unknown	28JI02Nx
Elizabeth	24	F	None	28JI02Nx
SATTERTHWAITE, Thomas	26	M	Unknown	28JI02Nx
Mary	25	F	None	28JI02Nx
Jane-Ann	5	F	Child	28JI02Nx
MCCLEAN, Mary	44	F	None	28JI02Nx
Rachel	10	F	None	28JI02Nx
REILLY, Terence	40	M	Unknown	28JI02Nx
Ann	35	F	Unknown	28JI02Nx
Margaret	35	F	Unknown	28JI02Nx
Jane	.00	F	Infant	28JI02Nx
SAUNDERS, Alice	40	F	Unknown	28JI02Nx
FAWLY, John	40	M	Musician	28JI02Nx
Mary	40	F	Unknown	28JI02Nx
Margaret	11	F	Unknown	28JI02Nx
George	6	M	Child	28JI02Nx
Mary	36	F	Unknown	28JI02Nx
Ernest	6	M	Child	28JI02Nx
Catherine	15	F	Unknown	28JI02Nx
MCDERMOTT, Owen	24	M	Laborer	28JI02Nx
HOGAN, Thomas	30	M	Laborer	28JI02Nx
HARDMAN, James	26	M	Laborer	28JI02Nx
Margaret	24	F	None	28JI02Nx
James	5	M	Child	28JI02Nx
SMITH, Bridget	18	F	None	28JI02Nx
DOWLING, Thomas	20	M	Laborer	28JI02Nx
Mary	19	M	Laborer	28JI02Nx
CONNELLY, Con	18	M	Laborer	28JI02Nx
CURLEY, Patrick	40	M	Unknown	28JI02Nx
GUMMO, John	22	M	Laborer	28JI02Nx
SCALLY, Hugh	20	M	Laborer	28JI02Nx
Patrick	30	M	Laborer	28JI02Nx
MCHENRY, James	25	M	Laborer	28JI02Nx
RIDDEN, Rory	53	M	Laborer	28JI02Nx
BROGAN, Patrick	18	M	Laborer	28JI02Nx
CLEARY, Mary	18	F	None	28JI02Nx
MCDONALD, Bernard	50	M	Laborer	28JI02Nx
HEALY, Mary	22	F	None	28JI02Nx
Margaret	20	F	None	28JI02Nx
Dennis	12	M	None	28JI02Nx
FAHEY, U	28	M	Laborer	28JI02Nx
U (W)	24	F	None	28JI02Nx
KINNEALY, Dennis	23	M	Laborer	28JI02Nx
AYLETT, John	31	M	Laborer	28JI02Nx
MALINSON, Elizabeth	35	F	None	28JI02Nx
Joseph	12	M	None	28JI02Nx
REECE, William	28	M	Laborer	28JI02Nx
MARSHALL, William	26	M	Laborer	28JI02Nx
Ellen	24	F	None	28JI02Nx
John	.00	M	Infant	28JI02Nx
Bridget	.06	F	Infant	28JI02Nx
WINTER, John	50	M	Laborer	28JI02Nx
HENDLEY, Thomas	35	M	Laborer	28JI02Nx
SHERIDAN, Farrel	40	M	Laborer	28JI02Nx
U	12	M	Laborer	28JI02Nx
RICE, Robert	30	M	Shoemaker	28JI02Nx
COOPER, Benjamin	20	M	Shoemaker	28JI02Nx
Elijah	21	M	Shoemaker	28JI02Nx
SULLIVAN, Corns.	26	M	Shoemaker	28JI02Nx

NAMES OF PASSENGERS	AGE	SEX	OCCUPATIONS	DATE PORT SHIP
NICHOLLS, Susan	39	F	None	28JI02Nx
Eliza	15	F	None	28JI02Nx
Henry	9	M	Child	28JI02Nx
Ann	11	F	None	28JI02Nx
Maria	7	F	Child	28JI02Nx
James	3	M	Child	28JI02Nx
Jane	.07	F	Infant	28JI02Nx
BUTTERS, John	40	M	Shoemaker	28JI02Nx
JORDAN, John	26	M	Laborer	28JI02Nx
GOTT, William	40	M	Laborer	28JI02Nx
Margaret	35	F	None	28JI02Nx
James	16	M	Laborer	28JI02Nx
Ann	11	F	None	28JI02Nx
William	10	M	None	28JI02Nx
Jane	6	F	Child	28JI02Nx
Thomas	4	M	Child	28JI02Nx
John	.09	M	Infant	28JI02Nx
GWIN, Ann	30	F	None	28JI02Nx
DALEY, Michael	30	M	Laborer	28JI02Nx
Bridget	28	F	None	28JI02Nx
Honora	.10	F	Infant	28JI02Nx
Mary-Ann	00	F	Unknown	28JI02Nx
CROKER, John	30	M	Laborer	28JI02Nx
Nancy	28	F	None	28JI02Nx
Mary	4	F	Child	28JI02Nx
Jane	.11	F	Infant	28JI02Nx
COLLINS, Catherine	19	F	Shoemaker	28JI02Nx
RYAN, John	20	M	Shoemaker	28JI02Nx
WALSH, David	35	M	Shoemaker	28JI02Nx
SHIVERS, Anthony	50	M	Shoemaker	28JI02Nx
MCTEAGUE, Peter	22	M	Laborer	28JI02Nx
Alice	21	F	None	28JI02Nx
MCCARTER, Mary	20	F	None	28JI02Nx
MCGORMORA, James	22	M	Laborer	28JI02Nx
Catherine	24	F	None	28JI02Nx
MULLONY, Patrick	35	M	Laborer	28JI02Nx
Margaret	35	F	None	28JI02Nx
Edmond	20	M	Laborer	28JI02Nx
Michael	18	M	Laborer	28JI02Nx
Catherine	16	F	None	28JI02Nx
Mary	15	F	None	28JI02Nx
Bridget	12	F	None	28JI02Nx
John	8	M	Child	28JI02Nx
Margt.	1	F	Child	28JI02Nx
CONNOR, Edmond	24	M	Laborer	28JI02Nx
Johanna	20	F	None	28JI02Nx
Eliza	18	F	None	28JI02Nx
DUNNE, Michael	25	M	Carpenter	28JI02Nx
Eliza	23	F	None	28JI02Nx
Sarah	1	F	Child	28JI02Nx
MURPHY, Joseph	19	M	Carpenter	28JI02Nx
Mary	21	F	None	28JI02Nx
MORGAN, John	19	M	Carpenter	28JI02Nx
DOWLING, Mary	19	F	None	28JI02Nx
QUINN, Catherine	20	F	None	28JI02Nx
Ellen	4	F	Child	28JI02Nx
Patrick	2	M	Child	28JI02Nx
PARKER, Catherine	10	F	None	28JI02Nx
CULLEN, Thomas	26	M	Carpenter	28JI02Nx
Eliza	26	F	None	28JI02Nx
Patrick	4	M	Child	28JI02Nx
Mary	2	F	Child	28JI02Nx
Ann	20	F	None	28JI02Nx
Matthew	27	M	Carpenter	28JI02Nx
Ann	20	F	None	28JI02Nx
James	2	M	Child	28JI02Nx
Ann	1	F	Child	28JI02Nx
WARREN, Edward	44	M	Carpenter	28JI02Nx
James	20	M	Carpenter	28JI02Nx
HUMBLE, Thomas	58	M	Engineer	28JI02Nx
U (W)	56	F	None	28JI02Nx
William	20	M	Engineer	28JI02Nx
Elizabeth	17	F	None	28JI02Nx
STEVENSON, Margaret	24	F	None	28JI02Nx
John	3	M	Child	28JI02Nx

NAMES OF PASSENGERS	AGE	SEX	OCCUPATIONS	DATE PORT SHIP
KELLY, Catherine	35	F	None	28J102Nx
Alice	1	F	Child	28J102Nx
GAERTY, Alice	20	F	None	28J102Nx
Ann	17	F	None	28J102Nx
PRICHARD, James	20	M	Engineer	28J102Nx
CRINIGAN, Honora	18	F	None	28J102Nx
James	50	M	Engineer	28J102Nx
HIGGINS, Ellen	6	F	Child	28J102Nx
BLACKBURN, William	25	M	Engineer	28J102Nx
BOWMAN, John	28	M	Engineer	28J102Nx
WARRING, Henry	40	M	Engineer	28J102Nx
BANCROFT, Peter	40	M	Farmer	28J102Nx
JELLY, James	30	M	Farmer	28J102Nx
Esther	30	F	None	28J102Nx
Sarah	10	F	None	28J102Nx
ROOM, Jane	35	F	None	28J102Nx
LEE, William	26	M	Shoemaker	28J102Nx
Jane	20	F	None	28J102Nx
Jane	1	F	Child	28J102Nx
CALDWELL, Patrick	22	M	Shoemaker	28J102Nx
DAVIS, Ambrose	24	M	Shoemaker	28J102Nx
THORN, Thomas	22	M	Shoemaker	28J102Nx
MCARDLE, Margaret	25	F	None	28J102Nx
ROWLAND, Peter	27	M	Laborer	28J102Nx
Mary	20	F	None	28J102Nx
HERRATY, Matthew	45	M	Laborer	28J102Nx
Mary	45	F	None	28J102Nx
GIBBONS, Mary	10	F	None	28J102Nx
HEGARTY, Dennis	40	M	Laborer	28J102Nx
FAHEY, Wm.	21	M	Laborer	28J102Nx
GRADY, John	22	M	Laborer	28J102Nx
Owen	15	M	Laborer	28J102Nx
GALLAHER, Daniel	30	M	Laborer	28J102Nx
Jane	16	F	None	28J102Nx
Mary	13	F	None	28J102Nx
James	13	M	None	28J102Nx
Alice	10	F	None	28J102Nx
MURRAY, John	34	M	Laborer	28J102Nx
KENNEDY, Dorothy	23	F	None	28J102Nx
Died-At-Sea				
WALSH, Peter	50	M	Laborer	28J102Nx
Margaret	45	F	None	28J102Nx
Died-At-Sea				
Margaret	19	F	None	28J102Nx
Bridget	17	F	None	28J102Nx
Thomas	13	M	None	28J102Nx
Ann	11	F	None	28J102Nx
Walter	9	M	Child	28J102Nx
QUINN, Patrick	44	M	Laborer	28J102Nx
Ellen	13	F	None	28J102Nx
HICKEY, Andrew	25	M	Laborer	28J102Nx
WHELEHAN, Etty	19	F	None	28J102Nx
Honora	17	F	None	28J102Nx
NOWLAN, James	37	M	Laborer	28J102Nx
MCDESMOND, Daniel	30	M	Laborer	28J102Nx
MCSORLEY, Patrick	30	M	Laborer	28J102Nx
Charles	24	M	Laborer	28J102Nx
James	9	M	Child	28J102Nx
MCATEER, Catherine	24	F	None	28J102Nx
MCCAFFREY, John	17	M	Laborer	28J102Nx
MCANELLY, John	23	M	Laborer	28J102Nx
QUINN, Edward	22	M	Laborer	28J102Nx
MCCAIRN, Joseph	20	M	Laborer	28J102Nx
WHITE, Joseph	18	M	Laborer	28J102Nx
HALFPENNY, James	45	M	Laborer	28J102Nx
Catherine	40	F	None	28J102Nx
Betty	19	F	None	28J102Nx
Luke	17	M	Laborer	28J102Nx
John	13	M	None	28J102Nx
Mary-Ann	10	F	None	28J102Nx
Alice	4	F	Child	28J102Nx
DALTON, Jane	50	F	None	28J102Nx
James	22	M	Laborer	28J102Nx
ROGERS, Michael	50	M	Laborer	28J102Nx
FEGAN, Lawrence	22	M	Laborer	28J102Nx
FEGAN, Julia	14	F	None	28J102Nx
DEGNAN, Mary	18	F	None	28J102Nx
FLYNN, Bridget	37	F	None	28J102Nx
Mary	8	F	Child	28J102Nx
Margaret	4	F	Child	28J102Nx
Kate	3	F	Child	28J102Nx
Patrick	20	M	Laborer	28J102Nx
John	12	M	None	28J102Nx
FRECKWELL, Margaret	28	F	None	28J102Nx
SWEENY, James	36	M	Laborer	28J102Nx
REGAN, James	20	M	Laborer	28J102Nx
Miles	22	M	Laborer	28J102Nx
Margaret	18	F	None	28J102Nx
Timothy	18	M	Laborer	28J102Nx
Daniel	16	M	Laborer	28J102Nx
John	24	M	Laborer	28J102Nx
RICHMOND, Jane	23	F	None	28J102Nx
Mary	60	F	None	28J102Nx
BARRY, Ellen	21	F	None	28J102Nx
Margaret	17	F	None	28J102Nx
GAFFNEY, Peter	50	M	Laborer	28J102Nx
Mary	50	F	None	28J102Nx
Margaret	13	F	None	28J102Nx
Elisabeth	17	F	None	28J102Nx
LEONARD, Cath.	16	F	None	28J102Nx
WARD, Mary	30	F	None	28J102Nx
James	8	M	Child	28J102Nx
Mary	6	F	Child	28J102Nx
CANNON, Peter	16	M	Laborer	28J102Nx
NICHOLS, Lucy	5	F	Child	28J102Nx
MOONY, Michael	12	M	None	28J102Nx
CARANAHACH, Rich.	30	M	Unknown	28J102Nx
HARDINGHAM, Rebecca	12	F	None	28J102Nx
BAYLY, Henry	25	M	Unknown	28J102Nx
MCDERMOTT, Ann	21	F	Unknown	28J102Nx

BRITISH-OAK 30 JULY 1849

From Sligo

NAMES OF PASSENGERS	AGE	SEX	OCCUPATIONS	DATE PORT SHIP
FAHANY, Jno.	25	M	Farmer	30J121No
Mary	25	F	Spinster	30J121No
KILLEON, Biddy	26	F	Spinster	30J121No
CURRAD, Mary	18	F	Spinster	30J121No
FANZEY, Bridget	17	F	Spinster	30J121No
TANZY, Mary	14	F	Spinster	30J121No
BOYLE, Susan	16	F	Spinster	30J121No
MULLEN, Mich.	35	M	Farmer	30J121No
Bridget	28	F	Laborer	30J121No
Jas.	6	M	Child	30J121No
REGAN, Jas.	30	M	Laborer	30J121No
Ann	28	F	Spinster	30J121No
Catherine	8	F	Child	30J121No
ARMSTRONG, Margt.	25	F	Spinster	30J121No
Isabella	18	F	Spinster	30J121No
MCINTYRE, Mary	17	F	Spinster	30J121No
WARD, Barry	20	M	Laborer	30J121No
FOLEY, Michl.	20	M	Laborer	30J121No
HEALLY, Ellen	23	F	Spinster	30J121No
FEE, Jane	30	F	Spinster	30J121No
SHENDAN, Marg.	27	F	Spinster	30J121No
MONAGHAN, Henry	28	M	Laborer	30J121No
Wm.	30	M	Laborer	30J121No
BURKE, Nancy	19	F	Spinster	30J121No
KEARY, Wm.	34	M	Tailor	30J121No
Mary-Ann	23	F	Wife	30J121No
GELMAN, Besy	25	F	Spinster	30J121No
BINAN, Mary	30	F	Spinster	30J121No
DORHERTY, Pat	41	M	Laborer	30J121No

NAMES OF PASSENGERS	AGE	SEX	OCCUPATIONS	DATE PORT SHIP
DORHERTY, Ann	35	F	Laborer	30Jl21No
MILMORE, Mary	29	F	Spinster	30Jl21No
MCCORMACK, Jas.	30	M	Laborer	30Jl21No
FOLEY, Thomas	21	M	Farmer	30Jl21No
Mary	60	F	Wife	30Jl21No
MCGOWAN, Pat	21	M	Laborer	30Jl21No
Bridget	31	F	Wife	30Jl21No
OATES, Catherine	41	F	Spinster	30Jl21No
FINAN, Bridget	35	F	Spinster	30Jl21No
KEARENS, Dominick	18	M	Laborer	30Jl21No
HARRISON, Mich.	19	M	Unknown	30Jl21No
BRADY, Henry	20	M	Laborer	30Jl21No
FLANAGHAN, Edward	31	M	Laborer	30Jl21No
ORMSLEY, Mary-A.	37	F	Spinster	30Jl21No
HUNT, Ann	44	F	Spinster	30Jl21No
Patt	20	M	Unknown	30Jl21No
Ellen	17	F	Unknown	30Jl21No
Jas.	8	M	Child	30Jl21No
Mary	6	F	Child	30Jl21No
Jno.	4	M	Child	30Jl21No
MCCANN, Ann	23	F	Spinster	30Jl21No
DOLAN, Pat	27	M	Butler	30Jl21No
GORMAN, Pat	34	M	Laborer	30Jl21No
BYRNES, Ellen-A.	29	F	Spinster	30Jl21No
CLIFFORD, Ballard	30	M	Unknown	30Jl21No
CORNER, Roger	41	M	Laborer	30Jl21No
MCDONAGL, Pat	34	M	Laborer	30Jl21No
SMITH, Wm.	27	M	Laborer	30Jl21No
TOFFEE, Catherine	34	F	Spinster	30Jl21No
KELLY, Jane	21	F	Spinster	30Jl21No
RAWLET, Pegg.	37	F	Spinster	30Jl21No
FLEMING, Pat	42	M	Laborer	30Jl21No
CONNOR, Jas.	21	M	Laborer	30Jl21No
OCONNOR, Ann	30	F	Spinster	30Jl21No
CUNNINGHAM, Michl.	28	M	Laborer	30Jl21No
KILLCULLEN, Rich.	26	M	Laborer	30Jl21No
FEE, Wm.	31	M	Laborer	30Jl21No
KERR, Patt	40	M	Carpenter	30Jl21No
Ann-Jane	37	F	Spinster	30Jl21No
Hannah	16	F	Unknown	30Jl21No
KILLGALLEN, Ellen	24	F	Spinster	30Jl21No
LOFTERS, Wm.	37	M	Unknown	30Jl21No
BURNS, Richard	41	M	Farmer	30Jl21No
GIBBON, Mary	22	F	Spinster	30Jl21No
KAVENY, Dominick	34	M	Saddler	30Jl21No
Margt.	28	F	Wife	30Jl21No
MCDONOGH, Sarah	24	F	Spinster	30Jl21No
MCDERMOTT, Mary	37	F	Spinster	30Jl21No
LOFTERS, Martin	41	M	Laborer	30Jl21No
COGAN, Pat	28	M	Farmer	30Jl21No
GILLEN, Margt.	39	F	Spinster	30Jl21No
FEENY, Margt.	21	F	Spinster	30Jl21No
REED, Maria	30	F	Spinster	30Jl21No
MCCARTY, Catherine	30	F	Spinster	30Jl21No
OMELIA, Rebecca	29	F	Spinster	30Jl21No
GORMAN, Sally	30	F	Spinster	30Jl21No
SCOTT, Ann	20	U	Spinster	30Jl21No
GREAHAM, Ellen	25	F	Spinster	30Jl21No

MARY 31 JULY 1849

From Glasgow

NAMES OF PASSENGERS	AGE	SEX	OCCUPATIONS	DATE PORT SHIP
EDWARDS, Alex	38	M	Laborer	31Jl04Im
Margt.	38	F	None	31Jl04Im
George	9	M	Child	31Jl04Im
Peter	6	M	Child	31Jl04Im
Robert	4	M	Child	31Jl04Im
Allan	29	M	Laborer	31Jl04Im
EDWARDS, Isabella	31	F	None	31Jl04Im
George	9	M	Child	31Jl04Im
William	7	M	Child	31Jl04Im
Robert	4	M	Child	31Jl04Im
Anne	.00	F	Infant	31Jl04Im
WILLIAMSON, George	26	M	Laborer	31Jl04Im
SHAW, William	26	M	Laborer	31Jl04Im
BELL, Agnes	35	F	None	31Jl04Im
Elizabeth	8	F	Child	31Jl04Im
RAE, James	21	M	Laborer	31Jl04Im
BROWN, Henry	28	M	Laborer	31Jl04Im
TOD, Isabella	26	F	None	31Jl04Im
Robert	2	M	Child	31Jl04Im
Margaret	.00	F	Infant	31Jl04Im
HARVEY, Margery	26	M	None	31Jl04Im
MUIR, Alex	24	M	Laborer	31Jl04Im
YOUNG, James	18	M	Laborer	31Jl04Im
MUNRO, Thomas	28	M	Laborer	31Jl04Im
Betsy	27	F	None	31Jl04Im
DAVIDSON, George-P.	45	M	Laborer	31Jl04Im
Martha	40	F	None	31Jl04Im
George	15	M	Laborer	31Jl04Im
John	11	M	Laborer	31Jl04Im
James	9	M	Child	31Jl04Im
Eliz.	7	F	Child	31Jl04Im
William	5	M	Child	31Jl04Im
Robert	4	M	Child	31Jl04Im
DICKIE, William	25	M	Laborer	31Jl04Im
Mary	23	F	None	31Jl04Im
TAYLOR, Andrew	22	M	Laborer	31Jl04Im
BELL, George	26	M	Laborer	31Jl04Im
NICOLL, James	25	M	Laborer	31Jl04Im
MCKENZIE, James	25	M	Laborer	31Jl04Im
Peter	23	M	Laborer	31Jl04Im
James	36	M	Laborer	31Jl04Im
James	20	M	Laborer	31Jl04Im
MORRISON, Robert	10	M	Child	31Jl04Im
LILLBURN, John	28	M	Laborer	31Jl04Im
POTTER, David	30	M	Laborer	31Jl04Im
Elizabeth	25	F	None	31Jl04Im
John	8	M	Child	31Jl04Im
William	6	M	Child	31Jl04Im
COCHRAN, Allan	29	M	Laborer	31Jl04Im
Elizabeth	26	F	None	31Jl04Im
John	.00	M	Infant	31Jl04Im
WILLIAMS, William	40	M	Laborer	31Jl04Im
KNIGHT, Andrew	26	M	Laborer	31Jl04Im
MATHIESON, James	19	M	Laborer	31Jl04Im
CUNNINGHAM, Jean	25	F	None	31Jl04Im
ROSS, William	27	M	Laborer	31Jl04Im
LANDER, John	33	M	Laborer	31Jl04Im
Martha	25	F	None	31Jl04Im
AFFLECH, David	33	M	Laborer	31Jl04Im
Jane	33	F	None	31Jl04Im
James	4	M	Child	31Jl04Im
NIXON, Ann	40	F	None	31Jl04Im
LESLIE, Isabella	63	F	None	31Jl04Im
TUNE, Robert	31	M	Laborer	31Jl04Im
Jane	31	F	None	31Jl04Im
Isabella	10	F	Child	31Jl04Im
Hugh	7	M	Child	31Jl04Im
Jean	6	F	Child	31Jl04Im
James	3	M	Child	31Jl04Im
LIVINGSTON, James	35	M	Laborer	31Jl04Im
MITCHELL, Alex	32	M	Laborer	31Jl04Im
BENNIE, John	30	M	Laborer	31Jl04Im
KERN, Robert-J.	22	M	Laborer	31Jl04Im
CAMERON, John	31	M	Laborer	31Jl04Im
MCDONALD, John	24	M	Laborer	31Jl04Im
MONK, Richard	25	M	Laborer	31Jl04Im
PARKISON, William	23	M	Laborer	31Jl04Im
FALKNER, Betsy	60	F	None	31Jl04Im
Mary-Jane	20	F	None	31Jl04Im
John	18	F	None	31Jl04Im
Hugh	16	M	Laborer	31Jl04Im

NAMES OF PASSENGERS	AGE	SEX	OCCUPATIONS	DATE PORT SHIP
FALKNER, Nancy	12	F	None	31J104Im
Eliza	9	F	Child	31J104Im
GRAHAM, Esther	27	F	None	31J104Im
BLOOMFIELD, Ann-J.	20	F	None	31J104Im
TATE, Alex	18	M	Laborer	31J104Im
WALKER, Joseph	27	M	Laborer	31J104Im
Ellen	26	F	None	31J104Im
Eliza	3	F	Child	31J104Im
Mary-Ann	2	F	Child	31J104Im
James	.00	M	Infant	31J104Im
MONKE, James	26	M	Laborer	31J104Im
Cath.	26	F	None	31J104Im
Margery	18	F	None	31J104Im
BLACK, Eliza	29	M	Laborer	31J104Im
Margaret	4	M	None	31J104Im
James	6	M	Child	31J104Im
John	2	M	Child	31J104Im
William	.00	M	Infant	31J104Im
CONN, Bridget	40	F	None	31J104Im
Hugh	10	M	Child	31J104Im
Michl.	12	M	Laborer	31J104Im
KEANE, Eliza	17	F	None	31J104Im
BONNER, James	10	M	Child	31J104Im
ROHAN, Michael	34	M	Laborer	31J104Im
BALL, Michael	72	M	Unknown	31J104Im

CREMONA 31 JULY 1849

From Galway

NAMES OF PASSENGERS	AGE	SEX	OCCUPATIONS	DATE PORT SHIP
DOWNES, James	26	M	Laborer	31J106Ny
MCCARMACK, Margt.	22	F	Unknown	31J106Ny
Celia	20	F	Unknown	31J106Ny
Pat	.00	M	Infant	31J106Ny
DEVANEY, Pat	30	M	Unknown	31J106Ny
MULLEN, Honor	21	F	Unknown	31J106Ny
DONNELLY, Mary	27	F	Unknown	31J106Ny
MCREON, Terisa	20	F	Unknown	31J106Ny
EARDLEY, Peter	32	M	Unknown	31J106Ny
HART, Thomas	33	M	Unknown	31J106Ny
BURKE, Mary	26	F	Unknown	31J106Ny
EARDLEY, Mary	36	F	Unknown	31J106Ny
MALLY, Charles	30	M	Unknown	31J106Ny
Michael	25	M	Unknown	31J106Ny
SULLIVAN, Michael	20	M	Unknown	31J106Ny
Margret	18	F	Unknown	31J106Ny
MCDONAGH, John	36	M	Unknown	31J106Ny
FLOOD, Margret	18	F	Unknown	31J106Ny
Jane	17	F	Unknown	31J106Ny
KING, John	24	M	Unknown	31J106Ny
BURKE, Bryan	.00	M	Infant	31J106Ny
GANNON, Bridget	26	F	Unknown	31J106Ny
FALLON, Sarah	20	F	Unknown	31J106Ny
BOHAN, Patrick	30	M	Unknown	31J106Ny
Julia	20	F	Unknown	31J106Ny
GILL, Daniel	20	M	Unknown	31J106Ny
MCDONAGH, John	35	M	Unknown	31J106Ny
GREAVEN, Mary	30	F	Unknown	31J106Ny
CREAVAN, Michael	7	M	Child	31J106Ny
Pat	.00	M	Infant	31J106Ny
KELLY, Thomas	25	M	Unknown	31J106Ny
CLANCY, Peter	18	M	Unknown	31J106Ny
POLAM, Mary	24	F	Unknown	31J106Ny
GANNON, James	20	M	Unknown	31J106Ny
MCDONAGH, Subb.	18	F	Unknown	31J106Ny
KING, Bridget	30	F	Unknown	31J106Ny
Bryan	25	M	Unknown	31J106Ny
Pat	.00	M	Infant	31J106Ny
HUGHES, John	24	M	Unknown	31J106Ny
HUGHS, Mary	19	F	Unknown	31J106Ny
MURPHY, Kate	22	F	Unknown	31J106Ny
LEGDON, Michael	50	M	Unknown	31J106Ny
FLANEGAN, Richard	28	M	Unknown	31J106Ny
GORHAM, Barthy	21	M	Unknown	31J106Ny
CONNERLY, U	15	M	Unknown	31J106Ny
FLYNN, Charles	38	M	Unknown	31J106Ny
LYDEN, Thomas	35	M	Unknown	31J106Ny
DOYLE, John	35	M	Unknown	31J106Ny
Mary	35	F	Unknown	31J106Ny
Pat	13	M	Unknown	31J106Ny
John	11	M	Unknown	31J106Ny
Edward	4	M	Child	31J106Ny
Mary	.00	F	Infant	31J106Ny
COONEY, John	28	M	Unknown	31J106Ny
COONY, Winfred	23	M	Unknown	31J106Ny
CONNOR, Anthony	22	M	Unknown	31J106Ny
Mary-Ann	17	F	Unknown	31J106Ny
DERMADDY, Bridget	20	F	Unknown	31J106Ny
GEARY, John	25	M	Unknown	31J106Ny
SCANLAN, Michael	18	M	Unknown	31J106Ny
Thomas	26	M	Unknown	31J106Ny
FINNEGAN, James	22	M	Unknown	31J106Ny
GRACE, John	21	M	Unknown	31J106Ny
COONEY, Margt.	21	F	Unknown	31J106Ny
KELLEAN, Honor	23	F	Unknown	31J106Ny
QUINN, Margt.	22	F	Unknown	31J106Ny
MCMAHAN, Honora	26	F	Unknown	31J106Ny
SLUTTERY, Thomas	24	M	Unknown	31J106Ny
Bridget	22	M	Unknown	31J106Ny
REILLY, Pat	35	M	Unknown	31J106Ny
Michael	22	M	Unknown	31J106Ny
CULLMAN, Michael	21	M	Unknown	31J106Ny
Mary	23	F	Unknown	31J106Ny
KERANAN, Michael	15	M	Unknown	31J106Ny
RIAN, Mary	36	F	Unknown	31J106Ny
OBRIAN, Ellen	48	F	Unknown	31J106Ny
Francis	21	M	Unknown	31J106Ny
Catherine	18	M	Unknown	31J106Ny
Margt.	16	F	Unknown	31J106Ny
Ellen	13	F	Unknown	31J106Ny
Ann	.00	F	Infant	31J106Ny
CALLANAN, Mary	15	F	Unknown	31J106Ny
MONAGHAN, Eliza	22	F	Unknown	31J106Ny
MARY, Thomas	19	M	Unknown	31J106Ny
KING, Patrick	35	M	Unknown	31J106Ny
FAHEY, Ann	40	F	Unknown	31J106Ny
Thomas	16	M	Unknown	31J106Ny
FAHY, Kitty	15	F	Unknown	31J106Ny
Mary	.00	F	Infant	31J106Ny
MACKEN, Margt.	30	F	Unknown	31J106Ny
FERRIS, Thomas	19	M	Unknown	31J106Ny
HOLLAND, James	22	M	Unknown	31J106Ny
KILLEEN, Michael	21	M	Unknown	31J106Ny
Mary	16	F	Unknown	31J106Ny
Ann	15	F	Unknown	31J106Ny
MERIS, Catherine	30	F	Unknown	31J106Ny
PYE, William	32	M	Unknown	31J106Ny
DOYLE, Ann	25	F	Unknown	31J106Ny
BEEGAN, Julia	24	F	Unknown	31J106Ny
Josephina	5	F	Child	31J106Ny
John	.00	M	Infant	31J106Ny
CREAM, Bridget	25	F	Unknown	31J106Ny
GREMEA, Bridget	20	F	Unknown	31J106Ny
FORD, Michael	37	M	Unknown	31J106Ny
MCDONNELL, Michael	13	M	Unknown	31J106Ny
HAVERTY, Catherine	25	F	Unknown	31J106Ny
Bridget	.00	F	Infant	31J106Ny
LARKEN, Thomas	30	M	Unknown	31J106Ny
WARD, Ellen	20	F	Unknown	31J106Ny
KELLY, Patt	24	M	Unknown	31J106Ny
James	20	M	Unknown	31J106Ny
Indy	16	F	Unknown	31J106Ny
Eliza	45	F	Unknown	31J106Ny
CONNELLY, Margt.	28	F	Unknown	31J106Ny

NAMES OF PASSENGERS	AGE	SEX	OCCUPATIONS	DATE PORT SHIP
FLYNN, Patt	38	M	Unknown	31J106Ny
KELLY, Mary	48	F	Unknown	31J106Ny
Ann	26	F	Unknown	31J106Ny
Margt.	18	F	Unknown	31J106Ny
Edward	15	M	Unknown	31J106Ny
Patt	.00	M	Infant	31J106Ny
FORD, Honor	25	F	Unknown	31J106Ny
Bridget	18	F	Unknown	31J106Ny
HANEHAN, Mary	20	F	Unknown	31J106Ny
HENEHAN, Winny	18	M	Unknown	31J106Ny
MCNAMARA, Mary	22	F	Unknown	31J106Ny
CARR, John	45	M	Unknown	31J106Ny
Bridget	40	F	Unknown	31J106Ny
Mary	13	F	Unknown	31J106Ny
John	10	F	Unknown	31J106Ny
Catherine	8	F	Child	31J106Ny
Sarah	6	F	Child	31J106Ny
Margt.	.00	F	Infant	31J106Ny
KANE, Michael	46	M	Unknown	31J106Ny
CANSADINE, John	23	M	Unknown	31J106Ny
CONSADINE, Margt.	18	F	Unknown	31J106Ny
DONOHOE, Bridget	21	F	Unknown	31J106Ny
QUINN, Michael	24	M	Unknown	31J106Ny
Mary	20	F	Unknown	31J106Ny
John	18	M	Unknown	31J106Ny
Patt	13	M	Unknown	31J106Ny
EGAN, Thomas	40	M	Unknown	31J106Ny
Bridget	38	F	Unknown	31J106Ny
Thomas	18	M	Unknown	31J106Ny
KENNY, Mary	21	F	Unknown	31J106Ny
MCTYGHE, Patt	30	M	Unknown	31J106Ny
KANE, Mark	23	M	Unknown	31J106Ny
DAVIS, Michael	20	M	Unknown	31J106Ny
MANNON, John	30	M	Unknown	31J106Ny
MCMAHON, Cath.	25	F	Unknown	31J106Ny
DELANY, Edward	27	M	Unknown	31J106Ny
Mary-Ann	20	F	Unknown	31J106Ny
MCGRATH, Biddy	24	F	Unknown	31J106Ny
CARBETT, John	21	M	Unknown	31J106Ny
Bridget	20	F	Unknown	31J106Ny
Henry	13	M	Unknown	31J106Ny
FLYNN, Patt	25	M	Unknown	31J106Ny
ROURKE, Bridgt.	20	F	Unknown	31J106Ny
MANNON, Bridget	20	F	Unknown	31J106Ny
MORAN, Fanny	.00	F	Infant	31J106Ny
GLYANN, Mary	23	F	Unknown	31J106Ny
DRONEY, John	22	M	Unknown	31J106Ny
KELLY, Edward	30	M	Unknown	31J106Ny
CONOLLY, Cath.	36	F	Unknown	31J106Ny
CARLESS, Thomas	25	M	Unknown	31J106Ny
CORLESS, Mary	40	F	Unknown	31J106Ny
DOOLEY, Catherine	22	F	Unknown	31J106Ny
CORLESS, Bridget	18	F	Unknown	31J106Ny
DOOLEY, Patt	4	M	Child	31J106Ny
Mary	.00	F	Infant	31J106Ny
GILL, Thomas	23	M	Unknown	31J106Ny
SHAUGHNESSY, Cath.	25	F	Unknown	31J106Ny
MORAN, John	19	M	Unknown	31J106Ny
HORAN, Michael	32	M	Unknown	31J106Ny
Mary	25	F	Unknown	31J106Ny
Thomas	7	M	Child	31J106Ny
John	.00	M	Infant	31J106Ny
MCNAMARA, Michael	25	M	Unknown	31J106Ny
RIGEN, Michael	30	M	Unknown	31J106Ny
FAHY, William	28	M	Unknown	31J106Ny
NAGAL, John	40	M	Unknown	31J106Ny
MAHAN, James	28	M	Unknown	31J106Ny
BURKE, Margt.	35	F	Unknown	31J106Ny
John	13	M	Unknown	31J106Ny
Margt.	.00	F	Infant	31J106Ny
BURNS, John	23	M	Unknown	31J106Ny
Norry	22	F	Unknown	31J106Ny
KIARS, Robert	45	M	Unknown	31J106Ny
KAIRS, Margt.	16	F	Unknown	31J106Ny
KARSE, Michael	19	M	Unknown	31J106Ny
KARSE, Thody	17	F	Unknown	31J106Ny
KITTER, Patt	32	M	Unknown	31J106Ny
DOLANGHTY, Michael	22	M	Unknown	31J106Ny
KEATING, Owen	17	M	Unknown	31J106Ny
OBRIAN, D.	32	M	Unknown	31J106Ny
CONWAY, Ellen	23	F	Unknown	31J106Ny
Margt.	19	F	Unknown	31J106Ny
LARKING, Patt	21	M	Unknown	31J106Ny
NOLAN, Patt	28	M	Unknown	31J106Ny
Cath.	25	F	Unknown	31J106Ny
CANNANIN, Thomas	7	M	Child	31J106Ny
NAUGHTON, Biddy	13	F	Child	31J106Ny
Eliza	20	F	Child	31J106Ny
MALLY, D.	16	M	Child	31J106Ny
KELLY, Patt	28	M	Child	31J106Ny
GLYNN, James	30	M	Child	31J106Ny
GANNON, John	24	M	Child	31J106Ny
Mary	20	F	Child	31J106Ny
MOLLAY, Edward	20	M	Child	31J106Ny
QUINN, John	26	M	Child	31J106Ny
MARRAY, Math.	18	M	Child	31J106Ny
MURRAY, Eliza	24	F	Child	31J106Ny
KENN, Mary	12	F	Child	31J106Ny
MARTYN, Catherine	23	F	Child	31J106Ny
Mary	3	F	Child	31J106Ny
DALY, Mary-Ann	21	F	Unknown	31J106Ny
Margt.	17	F	Unknown	31J106Ny
FAHEY, Sarah	26	F	Unknown	31J106Ny
BURK, Patrick	25	M	Unknown	31J106Ny
Jane	22	F	Unknown	31J106Ny
ROCHE, G.W.W.	38	M	Unknown	31J106Ny
G.W.W.	9	M	Child	31J106Ny
LYNCH, James	35	M	Unknown	31J106Ny
Ann-Maria	27	F	Unknown	31J106Ny
FRENCH, Anna	26	F	Unknown	31J106Ny
DALY, Celia	40	F	Unknown	31J106Ny
Jane	15	F	Unknown	31J106Ny
Rose	14	F	Unknown	31J106Ny
Julia	12	F	Unknown	31J106Ny
Ann	.00	F	Infant	31J106Ny
PARKS, Ann	25	F	Unknown	31J106Ny
Flahy--Bbo--, Mary	19	F	Unknown	31J106Ny
KEOGH, Richard	36	M	Unknown	31J106Ny
Ann	32	F	Unknown	31J106Ny
Edward	13	M	Unknown	31J106Ny
Helena	18	F	Unknown	31J106Ny
Ada	4	F	Child	31J106Ny
Richard	.00	M	Infant	31J106Ny
RILLEY, De.	22	M	Unknown	31J106Ny
LEO, Mary	18	F	Unknown	31J106Ny
CRAVEN, Mary	.00	F	Infant	31J106Ny
DALEY, John	24	M	Unknown	31J106Ny

COLUMBIA 01 AUGUST 1849

From Liverpool

NAMES OF PASSENGERS	AGE	SEX	OCCUPATIONS	DATE PORT SHIP
WILLAN, Mary	29	F	Unknown	01Au02ll
James	19	M	Unknown	01Au02ll
Julia	17	F	Unknown	01Au02ll
Peter	12	M	Unknown	01Au02ll
BRADLY, Elizabeth	00	F	Unknown	01Au02ll
Patrick	12	M	Unknown	01Au02ll
Michael	10	M	Child	01Au02ll
Anne	8	F	Child	01Au02ll
Peter	4	F	Child	01Au02ll
DONLAND, Peter	3	M	Child	01Au02ll
REILEY, James	26	M	Unknown	01Au02ll
FARLEY, Thomas	22	M	Unknown	01Au02ll

NAMES OF PASSENGERS	AGE	SEX	OCCUPATIONS	DATE PORT SHIP
BEDDY, Thomas	12	M	Unknown	01Au02II
Danl.	9	M	Child	01Au02II
MCGREGORY, James	22	M	Unknown	01Au02II
U, U	21	U	Unknown	01Au02II
MCGRATH, Ellen	33	F	Unknown	01Au02II
Peter	7	M	Child	01Au02II
Mary	6	M	Child	01Au02II
RINGROSE, Patrick	20	M	Unknown	01Au02II
James	18	M	Unknown	01Au02II
Eliza	11	F	Unknown	01Au02II
BRADLEY, Mary	20	F	Unknown	01Au02II
COMMERFORD, Ellen	19	M	Unknown	01Au02II
MURPHY, James	18	M	Unknown	01Au02II
LOLLY, Michael	41	M	Unknown	01Au02II
BRODERIC, Richard	12	M	Unknown	01Au02II
Mary	14	F	Unknown	01Au02II
HOLLARAN, Peter	26	M	Unknown	01Au02II
Honora	17	F	Unknown	01Au02II
Bridget	16	F	Unknown	01Au02II
COLLINS, James	11	M	Unknown	01Au02II
Joseph	9	M	Child	01Au02II
Anne	6	F	Child	01Au02II
John	4	M	Child	01Au02II
HARE, Ellen	20	F	Unknown	01Au02II
Patrick	16	M	Unknown	01Au02II
Daniel	17	M	Unknown	01Au02II
HALPERN, Sally	24	F	Unknown	01Au02II
Anne	12	F	Unknown	01Au02II
Peter	10	M	Child	01Au02II
Edward	8	M	Child	01Au02II
Jane	9	F	Child	01Au02II
RYAN, Mary	12	F	Unknown	01Au02II
DURMAN, Alice	21	F	Unknown	01Au02II
MCMARMLEY, Mary	19	F	Unknown	01Au02II
MITCHELL, Thomas	12	M	Unknown	01Au02II
Mary	00	F	Unknown	01Au02II
Edward	7	M	Child	01Au02II
MONAGHAN, John	19	M	Unknown	01Au02II
EGAN, Patrick	27	M	Unknown	01Au02II
DEWYER, Mary	29	F	Unknown	01Au02II
GAFNEY, Patrick	30	M	Unknown	01Au02II
Margaret	16	F	Unknown	01Au02II
DOOLAN, Anne	17	F	Unknown	01Au02II
CARNEY, Thomas	14	M	Unknown	01Au02II
MCCORMAC, Anne	17	F	Unknown	01Au02II
DELANEY, James	19	M	Unknown	01Au02II
CONNEL, Stephen	14	M	Unknown	01Au02II
CASSIDY, James	36	M	Unknown	01Au02II
Margret	29	F	Unknown	01Au02II
Rose	18	F	Unknown	01Au02II
John	11	F	Unknown	01Au02II
Henry	11	F	Unknown	01Au02II
Jane	9	M	Child	01Au02II
Anne	7	F	Child	01Au02II
ROBERTS, Susannah	14	F	Unknown	01Au02II
LEWIS, Edwin	16	M	Unknown	01Au02II
MURPHY, Patrick	19	M	Unknown	01Au02II
JONES, James-F.	27	M	Unknown	01Au02II
Emma	20	F	Unknown	01Au02II
U	.00	U	Infant	01Au02II
MURRAY, Thomas	36	M	Unknown	01Au02II
John	40	M	Unknown	01Au02II
John	19	M	Unknown	01Au02II
MCELLIOTT, Anne	11	F	Unknown	01Au02II
KERKINS, Samuel	19	M	Unknown	01Au02II
CONNER, Patrick	17	M	Unknown	01Au02II
OKEEFE, Catharine	17	M	Unknown	01Au02II
KERNEY, John	22	M	Unknown	01Au02II
U	.00	U	Infant	01Au02II
Mary	19	F	Unknown	01Au02II
Ally	10	F	Child	01Au02II
Thomas	11	M	Unknown	01Au02II
FARRELS, Margaret	17	F	Unknown	01Au02II
DOMIRE, Margaret	20	F	Unknown	01Au02II
MASTHERS, John	19	M	Unknown	01Au02II
JONES, Henry	18	M	Unknown	01Au02II
HIGGS, George	16	M	Unknown	01Au02II
MASTHERS, Thomas	22	M	Unknown	01Au02II
TIERMAN, John	21	M	Unknown	01Au02II
BURKE, Mary	19	F	Unknown	01Au02II
FUDGE, Joseph	26	M	Unknown	01Au02II
PARKER, James	20	M	Unknown	01Au02II
CATHCART, James	36	M	Unknown	01Au02II
Allen	27	M	Unknown	01Au02II
HENDERSON, James	24	M	Unknown	01Au02II
ACHESON, Jane	18	F	Unknown	01Au02II
CATHCART, Mary-J.	18	F	Unknown	01Au02II
EAMES, Margret	17	F	Unknown	01Au02II
LANAHAY, Patrick	30	M	Unknown	01Au02II
Patrick	19	M	Unknown	01Au02II
Bryan	18	M	Unknown	01Au02II
John	16	M	Unknown	01Au02II
Catharine	17	F	Unknown	01Au02II
Margaret	26	F	Unknown	01Au02II
U	.00	U	Infant	01Au02II
Anne	21	F	Unknown	01Au02II
MARKEY, John	27	M	Unknown	01Au02II
Margaret	19	F	Unknown	01Au02II
LYNCH, Catharine	19	F	Unknown	01Au02II
WALSH, Catharine	18	F	Unknown	01Au02II
LENAHAY, Bernard	17	M	Unknown	01Au02II
PATTISON, Andrew	22	M	Unknown	01Au02II
REILLEY, Patrick	20	M	Unknown	01Au02II
BRADY, Hugh	16	M	Unknown	01Au02II
LANDERS, Pierce	27	M	Unknown	01Au02II
U-Mrs.	40	F	Unknown	01Au02II
Joseph	9	M	Child	01Au02II
JONES, Thomas	29	M	Unknown	01Au02II
Owen	26	M	Unknown	01Au02II
Eliza	30	F	Unknown	01Au02II
U	.00	U	Infant	01Au02II
Rose	6	F	Child	01Au02II
HARTNELL, Johannah	40	F	Unknown	01Au02II
MCENNERY, Michael	17	M	Unknown	01Au02II
KINSELA, Thomas	18	M	Unknown	01Au02II
WRIGHT, George	24	M	Unknown	01Au02II
U-Mrs.	00	F	Unknown	01Au02II
U	.00	U	Infant	01Au02II
George	4	M	Child	01Au02II
EVANS, Bernard	17	M	Unknown	01Au02II
FEE, Mary	19	F	Unknown	01Au02II
CONROY, Patrick	17	M	Unknown	01Au02II
RYAN, Patrick	19	M	Unknown	01Au02II
DWYER, Mary	22	F	Unknown	01Au02II
RYAN, James	26	M	Unknown	01Au02II
Julia	22	F	Unknown	01Au02II
Nancy	20	F	Unknown	01Au02II
Catharine	18	F	Unknown	01Au02II
MORAN, Henry	29	M	Unknown	01Au02II
U-Mrs.	20	F	Unknown	01Au02II
HERNER, Maria	30	F	Unknown	01Au02II
GAYNOR, Patrick	19	M	Unknown	01Au02II
SMYTH, Mary	18	F	Unknown	01Au02II
Betty	11	F	Unknown	01Au02II
REILY, Catharine	20	F	Unknown	01Au02II
CLANCY, Patrick	29	M	Unknown	01Au02II
FINN, Martin	26	M	Unknown	01Au02II
U-Mrs.	26	F	Unknown	01Au02II
SHANNON, Mary	26	F	Unknown	01Au02II
FALLEN, William	19	M	Unknown	01Au02II
HIGGINS, Edward	17	M	Unknown	01Au02II
DUFFY, Catharine	19	F	Unknown	01Au02II
QUAIL, Charles	22	M	Unknown	01Au02II
LEDDY, Thomas	19	M	Unknown	01Au02II
PRIEST, Julia	6	F	Unknown	01Au02II
ROSBOTTOM, James	29	M	Unknown	01Au02II
Jane	25	F	Unknown	01Au02II
HAILY, James	00	M	Unknown	01Au02II
BRENNAN, Anne	17	F	Unknown	01Au02II
CONNOLY, Bridget	19	F	Unknown	01Au02II

NAMES OF PASSENGERS	AGE	SEX	OCCUPATIONS	DATE PORT SHIP
EGAN, Patrick	20	M	Unknown	01Au02II
CONNORS, Michael	17	M	Unknown	01Au02II
POWER, Thomas	18	M	Unknown	01Au02II
Mary	19	F	Unknown	01Au02II
MONAGHAN, Patrick	00	M	Unknown	01Au02II
DOYLE, Morgan	17	M	Unknown	01Au02II
MCCULLEN, Patrick	16	M	Unknown	01Au02II
LARKIN, Thomas	19	M	Unknown	01Au02II
Winafred	20	F	Unknown	01Au02II
SHELDON, Mary	19	F	Unknown	01Au02II
Margaret	18	F	Unknown	01Au02II
HENNESSY, William	30	M	Unknown	01Au02II
U-Mrs.	25	F	Unknown	01Au02II
BLACK, Betsey	18	F	Unknown	01Au02II
HURLEY, Edward	19	M	Unknown	01Au02II
NAREY, Michael	19	M	Unknown	01Au02II
MAY, Patrick	19	M	Unknown	01Au02II
Judy	17	F	Unknown	01Au02II
HEANEY, Catharine	00	F	Unknown	01Au02II
U	.00	U	Infant	01Au02II
Mary	16	F	Unknown	01Au02II
Michael	7	M	Child	01Au02II
LARRISEY, James	00	M	Unknown	01Au02II
U	.00	U	Infant	01Au02II
Mary	16	F	Unknown	01Au02II
Michael	16	M	Unknown	01Au02II
Bridget	19	F	Unknown	01Au02II
Mary	12	F	Unknown	01Au02II
LAMBERT, Bridget	19	F	Unknown	01Au02II
SHANLEY, Anne	16	F	Unknown	01Au02II
LARVEY, James	17	M	Unknown	01Au02II
Catharine	19	F	Unknown	01Au02II
JONES, Peter	19	M	Unknown	01Au02II
Betsey	19	F	Unknown	01Au02II
LARKIN, Owen	17	M	Unknown	01Au02II
MCGLYNN, James	24	M	Unknown	01Au02II
Francis	20	M	Unknown	01Au02II
David	10	M	Child	01Au02II
REILY, Hugh	17	M	Unknown	01Au02II
DUGGAN, Danl.	40	M	Unknown	01Au02II
NAGLE, George	30	M	Unknown	01Au02II
COLLINGSON, Caroline	00	F	Unknown	01Au02II
U	.00	U	Infant	01Au02II
Mary	2	F	Child	01Au02II
COLENANE, John	29	M	Unknown	01Au02II
U-Mrs.	26	F	Unknown	01Au02II
MCNALEY, John	26	M	Unknown	01Au02II
Margt.	20	F	Unknown	01Au02II
U	.00	U	Infant	01Au02II
HEINZ, Andrew	36	M	Unknown	01Au02II
Winford	32	U	Unknown	01Au02II
U	.00	U	Infant	01Au02II
Thomas	10	M	Child	01Au02II
John	9	M	Child	01Au02II
Terry	6	M	Child	01Au02II
Dennis	5	M	Child	01Au02II
Margaret	2	F	Child	01Au02II
John	30	M	Unknown	01Au02II
Ellen	40	F	Unknown	01Au02II
John	9	M	Unknown	01Au02II
CARNEY, Mary	00	F	Unknown	01Au02II
AGRE, Patrick	19	M	Unknown	01Au02II
Mary	22	F	Unknown	01Au02II
John	18	M	Unknown	01Au02II
WARD, Margaret	00	F	Unknown	01Au02II
REILY, John	12	M	Unknown	01Au02II
Margaret	20	F	Unknown	01Au02II
OCONNOR, William	19	M	Unknown	01Au02II
HOWARD, Francis	20	M	Unknown	01Au02II
Mary	19	F	Unknown	01Au02II
DONAGHUE, Catharine	17	F	Unknown	01Au02II
HOPKINS, Thomas	16	M	Unknown	01Au02II
REYNOLDS, Rose	18	F	Unknown	01Au02II
MURRAY, Julia	20	F	Unknown	01Au02II
MCDERMOTH, James	24	M	Unknown	01Au02II
MCCUE, Anne	20	F	Unknown	01Au02II
CONNEL, John	17	M	Unknown	01Au02II
BARTON, Martin	24	M	Unknown	01Au02II
HOLLERAN, Denis	26	M	Unknown	01Au02II
HALE, Edmund	31	M	Unknown	01Au02II
Patrick	29	M	Unknown	01Au02II
HARTNELL, U-Miss	19	F	Unknown	01Au02II
Mary	16	F	Unknown	01Au02II
Daniel	14	M	Unknown	01Au02II
DWYER, Bridget	17	F	Unknown	01Au02II
Thomas	11	M	Unknown	01Au02II
Margret	4	F	Child	01Au02II
STEPHENS, Robert	22	M	Unknown	01Au02II
LYNCH, Patrick	30	M	Unknown	01Au02II
Bridget	30	F	Unknown	01Au02II
TORNKINS, Nicholas	17	M	Unknown	01Au02II
GARVEY, Patrick	18	M	Unknown	01Au02II
CONNOLY, Bridget	19	F	Unknown	01Au02II
SMYTH, James	20	M	Unknown	01Au02II
FARLEY, Ellen	20	F	Unknown	01Au02II
FARREL, Thomas	19	M	Unknown	01Au02II
CAMPBELL, Alexander	27	M	Unknown	01Au02II
John	19	M	Unknown	01Au02II
MCGILL, William	19	M	Unknown	01Au02II
DALEY, Jane	22	F	Unknown	01Au02II
WILSON, Margaret	20	F	Unknown	01Au02II
CLAVIN, James	19	M	Unknown	01Au02II
CONBOY, James	18	M	Unknown	01Au02II
CARROLL, Alice	19	F	Unknown	01Au02II
SCOTT, Margaret	20	F	Unknown	01Au02II
LENNARD, Bridget	19	F	Unknown	01Au02II
MURTAGH, Nancy	17	F	Unknown	01Au02II
MCMANUS, Michl.	10	M	Child	01Au02II
CRUMLEY, Ellen	17	F	Unknown	01Au02II
John	10	M	Child	01Au02II
Mary	11	F	Unknown	01Au02II
NOWLAN, Patrick	20	M	Unknown	01Au02II
Patrick	13	M	Unknown	01Au02II
Bridget	11	F	Unknown	01Au02II
SHEILAS, Bernard	19	M	Unknown	01Au02II
Anthony	17	M	Unknown	01Au02II
Joseph	16	M	Unknown	01Au02II
Elizabeth	15	F	Unknown	01Au02II
MCPEAKE, Sarah	62	F	Unknown	01Au02II
Sarah	34	F	Unknown	01Au02II
U	.00	U	Infant	01Au02II
Mary	19	F	Unknown	01Au02II
James	7	M	Child	01Au02II
Mary	5	F	Child	01Au02II
BURN, John	11	M	Unknown	01Au02II
James	6	M	Child	01Au02II
QUINN, Hugh	19	M	Unknown	01Au02II
MULLEN, Thomas	19	M	Unknown	01Au02II
EPWORTH, George	18	M	Unknown	01Au02II
CARR, John	22	M	Unknown	01Au02II
Emma	20	F	Unknown	01Au02II
U	.00	U	Infant	01Au02II
SHORT, Thomas	19	M	Unknown	01Au02II
MCCOEN, Alexander	19	M	Unknown	01Au02II
BAXTER, Thomas	18	M	Unknown	01Au02II
CASEY, John	41	M	Unknown	01Au02II
COADY, Francis	24	M	Unknown	01Au02II
HEANY, Margaret	11	F	Unknown	01Au02II
Mary	7	F	Child	01Au02II
SHEA, Margaret	21	F	Unknown	01Au02II
Honora	19	F	Unknown	01Au02II
MCCABE, John	30	M	Unknown	01Au02II
TIERNEY, Michael	20	M	Unknown	01Au02II
PENNY, Thomas	19	M	Unknown	01Au02II
BLACKWELL, Henry	17	M	Unknown	01Au02II
ENWRIGHT, Michael	19	M	Unknown	01Au02II
CORCORAN, Margaret	22	F	Unknown	01Au02II
COLLINS, James	20	M	Unknown	01Au02II
Anne	17	F	Unknown	01Au02II
HANFORD, Ellen	19	F	Unknown	01Au02II

NAMES OF PASSENGERS	AGE	SEX	OCCUPATIONS	DATE PORT SHIP
DONEVAN, John	22	M	Unknown	01Au02II
James	21	M	Unknown	01Au02II
RYAN, Peter	27	M	Unknown	01Au02II
NORMAN, Mary	26	F	Unknown	01Au02II
MAHONEY, Richard	22	M	Unknown	01Au02II
COLLINS, John	19	M	Unknown	01Au02II
DUGGAN, Ellen	18	F	Unknown	01Au02II
Dennis	26	M	Unknown	01Au02II
WILLIAMS, Thomas	17	M	Unknown	01Au02II
MATHEW, George	19	M	Unknown	01Au02II
SHEA, Pat	19	M	Unknown	01Au02II
STEVENS, Charles	18	M	Unknown	01Au02II
FARMER, Kate	12	F	Unknown	01Au02II
MURREY, Mary	19	F	Unknown	01Au02II
REILY, John	17	M	Unknown	01Au02II
Bridget	19	F	Unknown	01Au02II
BRAY, Bridget	17	F	Unknown	01Au02II
Anne	19	F	Unknown	01Au02II
SLOAM, Bessy	16	F	Unknown	01Au02II
GROMAY, Judy	19	F	Unknown	01Au02II
CAFFREY, Bridget	18	F	Unknown	01Au02II
FARREL, Michael	20	M	Unknown	01Au02II
John	19	M	Unknown	01Au02II
KEAN, Mary	17	F	Unknown	01Au02II
U	.00	U	Infant	01Au02II
RITTY, William	19	M	Unknown	01Au02II
SMYTH, Philip	40	M	Unknown	01Au02II
Catharine	58	F	Unknown	01Au02II
Patrick	26	M	Unknown	01Au02II
James	22	M	Unknown	01Au02II
Catharine	19	F	Unknown	01Au02II
John	20	M	Unknown	01Au02II
William	19	M	Unknown	01Au02II
BARRY, Mary	30	F	Unknown	01Au02II
Mary	17	F	Unknown	01Au02II
SPELEAN, Mary	30	F	Unknown	01Au02II
John	13	M	Unknown	01Au02II
Michl.	36	M	Unknown	01Au02II
LUCY, Patrick	19	M	Unknown	01Au02II
BURKE, John	40	M	Unknown	01Au02II
Michl.	39	M	Unknown	01Au02II
Mary	35	F	Unknown	01Au02II
Timothy	60	M	Unknown	01Au02II
Michl.	18	M	Unknown	01Au02II
Danl.	6	M	Child	01Au02II
DONEVAN, Mary	7	F	Child	01Au02II
ODONALD, James	40	M	Unknown	01Au02II
SHEA, Darly	40	F	Unknown	01Au02II
REILY, Eliza	15	F	Unknown	01Au02II
Margaret	13	F	Unknown	01Au02II
CONBOY, Francis	28	M	Unknown	01Au02II
Bessy	20	F	Unknown	01Au02II
MCCRAY, Margaret	16	F	Unknown	01Au02II
COMROR, Thomas	20	M	Unknown	01Au02II
Margaret	19	F	Unknown	01Au02II
DONEVAN, Margaret	17	F	Unknown	01Au02II
WILLINK, Eliza.	30	F	Unknown	01Au02II
Mary	29	F	Unknown	01Au02II
Michl.	4	M	Child	01Au02II
Mary	6	F	Child	01Au02II
COLLINS, Timothy	00	F	Child	01Au02II
Dennis	11	M	Unknown	01Au02II
CONNOR, Mary	30	F	Unknown	01Au02II
CONROE, John	12	M	Unknown	01Au02II
Bridget	16	F	Unknown	01Au02II
LEIMUTH, Catharine	26	F	Unknown	01Au02II
SULLIVAN, Ellen	30	F	Unknown	01Au02II
U	.00	U	Infant	01Au02II
Margaret	41	F	Unknown	01Au02II
MCCLUSKEY, Catharine	19	F	Unknown	01Au02II
MCGILL, James	11	M	Unknown	01Au02II
Mary	9	F	Child	01Au02II
Anne	7	F	Child	01Au02II
WALSH, Margaret	40	F	Unknown	01Au02II
Margaret	24	F	Unknown	01Au02II

NAMES OF PASSENGERS	AGE	SEX	OCCUPATIONS	DATE PORT SHIP
MCDONALD, Anne	20	F	Unknown	01Au02II
SMYTH, Michl.	20	F	Unknown	01Au02II
MILLS, Catharine	17	F	Unknown	01Au02II
HARRIGAN, Mary	40	F	Unknown	01Au02II
John	16	M	Unknown	01Au02II
Rose	10	F	Unknown	01Au02II
Mary	14	F	Unknown	01Au02II
Catharine	10	F	Child	01Au02II
Patt	8	M	Child	01Au02II
BOURDEN, James	41	M	Unknown	01Au02II
NOWLEN, Patrick	30	M	Unknown	01Au02II
SCOTT, Francis	32	M	Unknown	01Au02II
Anne	28	F	Unknown	01Au02II
U	.00	U	Infant	01Au02II
HARRIS, John-T.	16	M	Unknown	01Au02II
E.C.	19	M	Unknown	01Au02II
DESMOND, Ellen	17	F	Unknown	01Au02II
SCOFIELD, Luthbert	36	M	Unknown	01Au02II
MAKIN, Charles	27	M	Unknown	01Au02II
Bessy	17	F	Unknown	01Au02II
Emily	8	F	Child	01Au02II
MCMOLE, John	22	M	Unknown	01Au02II
WILLIAMS, Jane	22	F	Unknown	01Au02II
MOLLY, Margt.	16	F	Unknown	01Au02II
ALLEN, Robt.	22	M	Unknown	01Au02II
MURPHY, Wm.	26	M	Unknown	01Au02II
CORBELL, James	36	M	Unknown	01Au02II
CASEY, William	29	M	Unknown	01Au02II
HART, R.W.	00	M	Unknown	01Au02II
U-Mrs.	00	F	Unknown	01Au02II
U-Miss	00	F	Unknown	01Au02II
MOLSTON, Edwd.	00	M	Unknown	01Au02II
PRATT, John	00	M	Unknown	01Au02II
ADAMSON, U-Rev.	00	M	Unknown	01Au02II
WENSTROW, W.	00	U	Unknown	01Au02II
FINNIGAN, U-Mrs.	00	F	Unknown	01Au02II
U	.00	U	Infant	01Au02II
U-Miss	00	F	Unknown	01Au02II
Mary	00	F	Unknown	01Au02II
James	00	M	Unknown	01Au02II
William	00	M	Unknown	01Au02II
Joseph	00	M	Unknown	01Au02II
BRADLY, U	.00	U	Infant	01Au02II

CANTON 01 AUGUST 1849

From Belfast

NAMES OF PASSENGERS	AGE	SEX	OCCUPATIONS	DATE PORT SHIP
WARD, James	50	M	Farmer	01Au05Ab
Margaret	40	F	Spinster	01Au05Ab
William	16	M	Laborer	01Au05Ab
John	13	M	Laborer	01Au05Ab
Gawn	12	M	None	01Au05Ab
Matthew	10	M	None	01Au05Ab
Thomas	3	M	Child	01Au05Ab
Margaret	18	F	Spinster	01Au05Ab
LINDSAY, Isaac	20	M	Laborer	01Au05Ab
William	18	M	Laborer	01Au05Ab
DAVY, Mary-Ann	21	F	Spinster	01Au05Ab
Henry	19	M	Laborer	01Au05Ab
BAGLEY, John	21	M	Laborer	01Au05Ab
STEWART, James	19	M	Laborer	01Au05Ab
Eyekiel	17	M	Laborer	01Au05Ab
William	16	M	Laborer	01Au05Ab
GORDON, Robert	17	M	Laborer	01Au05Ab
Rachael	15	F	Spinster	01Au05Ab
James	13	M	None	01Au05Ab
Samuel	11	M	None	01Au05Ab
Wm.John	9	M	Child	01Au05Ab

NAMES OF PASSENGERS	AGE	SEX	OCCUPATIONS	DATE PORT SHIP
WALKER, James	26	M	Laborer	01Au05Ab
Hugh	20	M	Laborer	01Au05Ab
EGGLESTON, Margaret	20	F	Spinster	01Au05Ab
DICKS, Samuel	19	M	Laborer	01Au05Ab
Mary	17	F	Spinster	01Au05Ab
Mary-Ann	25	F	Spinster	01Au05Ab
Martha	.00	F	Infant	01Au05Ab
GASCOYNE, Mary	19	F	Spinster	01Au05Ab
HAMILTON, Deborah	18	F	Spinster	01Au05Ab
MOORE, Mary	18	F	Spinster	01Au05Ab
CORRIGAN, Bridget	22	F	Spinster	01Au05Ab
Mary	20	F	Spinster	01Au05Ab
CONN, James	20	M	Farmer	01Au05Ab
Jane	50	F	Spinster	01Au05Ab
Eliza	24	F	Spinster	01Au05Ab
MCKILVEY, Eliza	20	F	Spinster	01Au05Ab
BINGHAM, Robert	16	M	Laborer	01Au05Ab
LINDSAY, John	23	M	Whitesmith	01Au05Ab
James	16	M	Whitesmith	01Au05Ab
HEUROT, David	40	M	Shoemaker	01Au05Ab
Sti--, John	19	M	Laborer	01Au05Ab
NEWELL, William	24	M	Laborer	01Au05Ab
MCILWAINE, Alexander	25	M	Laborer	01Au05Ab
JOHNSTON, Elizabeth	35	F	Spinster	01Au05Ab
Jane	13	F	None	01Au05Ab
CASSIDAY, Peter	18	M	Laborer	01Au05Ab
JOHNSTON, Wm.James	6	M	Child	01Au05Ab
John	4	M	Child	01Au05Ab
Thomas	2	M	Child	01Au05Ab
Andrew	7	M	Child	01Au05Ab
FITZSIMMONS, Garret	55	M	Laborer	01Au05Ab
John	18	M	Laborer	01Au05Ab
Felix	15	M	Laborer	01Au05Ab
WATSON, Robert	25	M	Laborer	01Au05Ab
MCKEE, Robert	20	M	Laborer	01Au05Ab
GARDEN, Andrew	25	M	Laborer	01Au05Ab
Margaret	23	F	Spinster	01Au05Ab
SWEENY, Mary	24	F	Spinster	01Au05Ab
LONG, Elizabeth	24	F	Spinster	01Au05Ab
HAMILL, Joyce	19	F	Spinster	01Au05Ab
DONELLY, Martha	20	F	Spinster	01Au05Ab
MCGAITON, Elizabeth	20	F	Spinster	01Au05Ab
CROSSEN, Margaret	24	F	Spinster	01Au05Ab
DUNLOP, Rachael	19	F	Spinster	01Au05Ab
GILL, Catherine	19	F	Spinster	01Au05Ab
MCARTY, Mary-Ann	24	F	Spinster	01Au05Ab
MCGIRN, Nicholas	38	M	Tailor	01Au05Ab
Mary	30	F	Spinster	01Au05Ab
REYNOLDS, Jayne	23	F	Spinster	01Au05Ab
MCGUIRE, Alice	4	F	Child	01Au05Ab
Margaret	3	F	Child	01Au05Ab
Patrick	.00	M	Infant	01Au05Ab
MCALUTER, Dennis	30	M	Laborer	01Au05Ab
KIRK, Thomas	28	M	Laborer	01Au05Ab
COLLINS, Rose	22	F	Spinster	01Au05Ab
MCGARRY, Isaac	48	M	Laborer	01Au05Ab
POLLICK, Hugh	35	M	Laborer	01Au05Ab
BARRY, Mary-A.	15	F	Spinster	01Au05Ab
HOLLAND, Agnes	22	F	Spinster	01Au05Ab
Margaret	21	F	Spinster	01Au05Ab
MCKETTICE, James	20	M	Laborer	01Au05Ab
Catharine	21	F	Spinster	01Au05Ab
SHEILS, Peter	22	M	Laborer	01Au05Ab
ARMSTRONG, Wm.	20	M	Laborer	01Au05Ab
MCNEIL, Eliza	21	F	Spinster	01Au05Ab
MURPHY, Catherine	20	F	Spinster	01Au05Ab
POTTER, Jane	18	F	Spinster	01Au05Ab
QUIN, Bernard	19	M	Laborer	01Au05Ab
HUGHES, Patrick	24	M	Laborer	01Au05Ab
Patrick	26	M	Laborer	01Au05Ab
Ellen	18	F	Spinster	01Au05Ab
MCDONNEL, Neal	20	M	Laborer	01Au05Ab
Judy	22	F	Spinster	01Au05Ab
Susan	18	F	Spinster	01Au05Ab
LENNER, David	24	M	Laborer	01Au05Ab
HAGAN, Hannah	22	F	Spinster	01Au05Ab
MARTIN, George	21	M	Laborer	01Au05Ab
MCCARTY, John	52	M	Laborer	01Au05Ab
MCAULEY, Samuel	23	M	Laborer	01Au05Ab
MCMERY, David	25	M	Weaver	01Au05Ab
Jane (W)	28	F	Wife	01Au05Ab
Thomas	3	M	Child	01Au05Ab
James	2	M	Child	01Au05Ab
Mary-A.	.00	F	Infant	01Au05Ab
LEMON, James	24	M	Tailor	01Au05Ab
PATTERSON, Alexander	35	M	Farmer	01Au05Ab
Sarah (W)	30	F	Wife	01Au05Ab
Sarah-Jane	3	F	Child	01Au05Ab
James	1	M	Child	01Au05Ab
Harriet	.00	F	Infant	01Au05Ab
RELLINS, Mary-Jane	18	F	Spinster	01Au05Ab
MORGAN, Catherine	9	F	Child	01Au05Ab
Mary	7	F	Child	01Au05Ab
Susanna	5	F	Child	01Au05Ab
MCMAY, Margaret	57	F	Wi	01Au05Ab
MCNAUGHTON, Hugh	25	M	Weaver	01Au05Ab
MCUER, Margaret	16	F	Spinster	01Au05Ab
YOUNG, John	24	M	Laborer	01Au05Ab
Joseph	20	M	Laborer	01Au05Ab
MATHESON, Thos.	22	M	Laborer	01Au05Ab
BURTON, John	50	M	Laborer	01Au05Ab
Rebecca	60	F	Wi	01Au05Ab
BELL, Sarah-J.	25	F	Wi	01Au05Ab
Mary	3	F	Child	01Au05Ab
William	.00	M	Infant	01Au05Ab
MCFERRAN, Robt.	30	M	Tailor	01Au05Ab
MCDORAN, Michael	30	M	Weaver	01Au05Ab
MCFERRAN, Ellen	25	F	Wi	01Au05Ab
Ellen	7	F	Child	01Au05Ab
CHAMBERS, William	30	M	Laborer	01Au05Ab
MAGEE, John	20	M	Laborer	01Au05Ab
CALWELL, Nancy	30	F	Spinster	01Au05Ab
REA, Wm.	32	M	Laborer	01Au05Ab
SCOTT, Joseph-H.	45	M	Farmer	01Au05Ab
Mary (W)	42	F	Wife	01Au05Ab
Sarah-E.	13	F	None	01Au05Ab
Eleanor	12	F	None	01Au05Ab
Josep	10	M	None	01Au05Ab
Mary-Jane	8	F	Child	01Au05Ab
Hugh	7	M	Child	01Au05Ab
Anna-Bella	5	F	Child	01Au05Ab
COWAN, William	27	M	Weaver	01Au05Ab
Mary-A. (W)	30	F	Wife	01Au05Ab
NIBLOCK, James	45	M	Tailor	01Au05Ab
MEENAN, P.	20	M	Tailor	01Au05Ab
CRICKARD, Thomas	26	M	Farmer	01Au05Ab
MCKINLEY, John	32	M	Laborer	01Au05Ab
CUNNINGHAM, Wm.	28	M	Weaver	01Au05Ab
Patrick	22	M	Weaver	01Au05Ab
MCCLURY, Joseph	24	M	Weaver	01Au05Ab
Margaret (W)	29	F	Wife	01Au05Ab
PATTERSON, David	34	M	Laborer	01Au05Ab
Catherine (W)	34	F	Wife	01Au05Ab
FENNING, William	25	M	Farmer	01Au05Ab
Edward	60	M	Farmer	01Au05Ab
FOWLER, Mary	33	F	Wi	01Au05Ab
John (B)	27	M	Brother	01Au05Ab
William	4	M	Child	01Au05Ab
James	.00	M	Infant	01Au05Ab
FERGUSON, George	25	M	Weaver	01Au05Ab
DUNN, John	23	M	Weaver	01Au05Ab
Helen (M)	43	F	Unknown	01Au05Ab
Henry	9	M	Child	01Au05Ab
Sarah	5	F	Child	01Au05Ab
ROBINSON, William	25	M	Laborer	01Au05Ab
GREENON, Sarah	21	F	Spinster	01Au05Ab
MCILROY, Robert	20	M	Weaver	01Au05Ab
MAXWELL, Jane	30	F	Spinster	01Au05Ab
MCDONELL, Ruth	24	F	Spinster	01Au05Ab
Ruth	20	F	Wi	01Au05Ab

NAMES OF PASSENGERS	AGE	SEX	OCCUPATIONS	DATE PORT SHIP
MCDONELL, Fanny	.00	F	Infant	01Au05Ab
DOYLE, Bernard	20	M	Laborer	01Au05Ab
Rose	16	F	Spinster	01Au05Ab
CARR, Mary	19	F	Spinster	01Au05Ab
MCCRACKEN, Eliza	34	F	Wi	01Au05Ab
Ellen	5	F	Child	01Au05Ab
SHARP, Wm.	21	M	Tailor	01Au05Ab
FULTON, Adam	45	M	Unknown	01Au05Ab
U-Mrs.	40	F	Unknown	01Au05Ab
HILL, U	35	F	Unknown	01Au05Ab
BOAL, Mary	20	F	Servant	01Au05Ab
Jane	21	F	Servant	01Au05Ab

AMERICAN-EAGLE 01 AUGUST 1849

From London

NAMES OF PASSENGERS	AGE	SEX	OCCUPATIONS	DATE PORT SHIP
PEACOCK, Jonathan	39	M	Laborer	01Au130o
Sarah	40	F	None	01Au130o
Elizabeth	11	F	None	01Au130o
William	7	M	Child	01Au130o
FROMIN, Joseph	30	M	Carpenter	01Au130o
Susan	29	F	None	01Au130o
Elliott	9	M	Child	01Au130o
Frederick	7	M	Child	01Au130o
John	5	M	Child	01Au130o
James	3	M	Child	01Au130o
Emma	.00	F	Infant	01Au130o
ENGEL, Ann	9	F	Child	01Au130o
LEES, Harriett	29	F	Servant	01Au130o
Sarah	23	F	Servant	01Au130o
DOSSETT, Thomas	20	M	Laborer	01Au130o
SHARP, Samuel	27	M	Laborer	01Au130o
HOCKERDEN, James	47	M	Farmer	01Au130o
Ann	44	F	None	01Au130o
BISHOP, John	17	M	Farmer	01Au130o
Josiah	13	M	None	01Au130o
TRIST, Jane	31	F	None	01Au130o
HUSHAM, Thomas	21	M	None	01Au130o
TRIST, Mary-Ann	6	F	Child	01Au130o
WORTLEY, Daniel	58	M	Farmer	01Au130o
Eliza	28	F	None	01Au130o
Sophia	17	F	None	01Au130o
Died-At-Sea				
DEBOUFER, Charles	22	M	None	01Au130o
Jane	21	F	None	01Au130o
Jane	50	F	None	01Au130o
Elizabeth	5	F	Child	01Au130o
Charles	.00	M	Infant	01Au130o
BARCLAY, Henry	18	M	Carpenter	01Au130o
DAY, John	40	M	Carpenter	01Au130o
Rebecca	50	F	None	01Au130o
Mary	8	F	Child	01Au130o
Samuel	48	M	None	01Au130o
Edward	46	M	None	01Au130o
Joseph	44	M	None	01Au130o
David	30	M	None	01Au130o
TRYON, George	35	M	None	01Au130o
Sophia	34	F	None	01Au130o
George	11	M	None	01Au130o
Edwin	9	M	Child	01Au130o
William	2	M	Child	01Au130o
CLINTON, Richard	25	M	None	01Au130o
DAY, George	38	M	None	01Au130o
CHAFFEY, George	43	M	Joiner	01Au130o
Kate	40	F	None	01Au130o
Frank	17	M	None	01Au130o
Elizabeth	14	F	None	01Au130o
Isabella	11	F	None	01Au130o
CHAFFEY, Ellen	9	F	Child	01Au130o
Ann	7	F	Child	01Au130o
Alice	5	F	Child	01Au130o
WISE, William	32	M	Laborer	01Au130o
Mary	31	F	None	01Au130o
AMOS, William	17	M	None	01Au130o
MORRIS, John	47	M	None	01Au130o
Margaret	35	F	None	01Au130o
Jane	11	F	None	01Au130o
MORGAN, Charles	28	M	Farmer	01Au130o
Elizabeth	28	F	Farmer	01Au130o
Elizabeth	2	F	Child	01Au130o
Charles	.00	M	Infant	01Au130o
HOLLYWELL, John	30	M	Unknown	01Au130o
HENDLEY, Mary	36	F	Laborer	01Au130o
Bridget	9	F	Child	01Au130o
Michael	7	M	Child	01Au130o
Julia	5	F	Child	01Au130o
William	1	M	Child	01Au130o
DAVIS, Evan	30	M	Merchant	01Au130o
MCKAY, James	13	M	None	01Au130o
SCUTTER, James	46	M	Publican	01Au130o
Catharine	47	F	None	01Au130o
Died-At-Sea				
Catharine	14	F	None	01Au130o
Sophia	13	F	None	01Au130o
Died-At-Sea				
Mary	8	F	Child	01Au130o
Thomas	9	M	Child	01Au130o
MILLS, John	26	M	Laborer	01Au130o
Emma	35	F	None	01Au130o
Samuel	11	M	None	01Au130o
MCDONALD, Jane	32	F	None	01Au130o
DAVIS, Griffith	34	M	None	01Au130o
Mary-Ann	28	F	None	01Au130o
BROWN, Moses	00	M	Farmer	01Au130o
Died-At-Sea				
U (W)	00	F	None	01Au130o
Died-At-Sea				
ABBEE, Joseph	48	M	None	01Au130o
CROUCH, James	18	M	None	01Au130o
HARDWICK, Henry	23	M	None	01Au130o
Sarah	22	F	None	01Au130o
JOHNSTON, George	21	M	None	01Au130o
MCCARTHY, Jane	44	F	Laborer	01Au130o
Ellen	44	F	None	01Au130o
Died-At-Sea				
James	25	M	None	01Au130o
James	7	M	Child	01Au130o
HARTIGAN, Michael	24	M	Unknown	01Au130o
MYHILL, William	35	M	None	01Au130o
Phillis	27	F	None	01Au130o
Alfred	4	M	Child	01Au130o
Thomas	.00	M	Infant	01Au130o
ROBERTSON, Margaret	30	F	None	01Au130o
SMITH, George	26	M	None	01Au130o
Martha	28	F	None	01Au130o
PALLEN, Charles	22	M	None	01Au130o
TERRY, George	34	M	None	01Au130o
Elizabeth	29	F	None	01Au130o
George	.00	M	Infant	01Au130o
HELLING, Joseph	41	M	Wheelwright	01Au130o
Elizabeth	19	F	None	01Au130o
Martha	16	F	None	01Au130o
Joseph	13	M	None	01Au130o
ADZE, Alfred	34	M	None	01Au130o
Mary	27	F	None	01Au130o
THOMPSON, George	.00	M	Infant	01Au130o
MARSHALL, Walter	27	M	Carpenter	01Au130o
BING, Edward	24	M	None	01Au130o
DAVIS, Sarah	51	F	None	01Au130o
Mary-Ann	23	F	None	01Au130o
Sarah	20	F	None	01Au130o
Thomas	11	M	None	01Au130o
EVANS, Thomas	33	M	Bootmaker	01Au130o

NAMES OF PASSENGERS	AGE	SEX	OCCUPATIONS	DATE PORT SHIP
EVANS, Elizabeth	33	F	None	01Au130o
STANTON, Michael	26	M	None	01Au130o
FINN, Alfred	19	M	None	01Au130o
HOCKING, Walter	28	M	Blacksmith	01Au130o
JARVIS, William	44	M	Gdnr	01Au130o
DAVIS, William-H.	18	M	Miller	01Au130o
BOURKE, John	26	M	Laborer	01Au130o
WILLIAMS, Thomas	26	M	Laborer	01Au130o
JACKSON, Ann	25	F	None	01Au130o
TAYLOR, John	25	M	Laborer	01Au130o
PALMER, Mary	40	F	None	01Au130o
TERRY, William	37	M	Wheelwright	01Au130o
Charlotte	38	F	None	01Au130o
Charles	11	M	None	01Au130o
Sarah	10	F	None	01Au130o
Amelia	8	F	Child	01Au130o
Samuel	6	M	Child	01Au130o
William	5	M	Child	01Au130o
Charlotte	4	F	Child	01Au130o
Edwin	2	M	Child	01Au130o
RALPH, Richard	21	M	Shoemaker	01Au130o
CLARK, Thomas	12	M	None	01Au130o
THOMPSON, Mary-Ann	26	F	None	01Au130o
ENGLE, James	48	M	Laborer	01Au130o
BINDEN, Thomas	27	M	None	01Au130o
LONG, John	00	M	None	01Au130o
BELCER, Henry	44	M	None	01Au130o
HARRIS, George	30	M	None	01Au130o
CROFT, Benjamin Died-At-Sea	40	M	None	01Au130o
ROTH, Johan	00	M	None	01Au130o
LISSENDEN, Ephraim	29	M	Farmer	01Au130o
Caroline	30	F	None	01Au130o
Thomas	13	M	None	01Au130o
John	11	M	None	01Au130o
Elizabeth	10	F	None	01Au130o
Sarah	9	F	Child	01Au130o
George	7	M	Child	01Au130o
Jane	1	F	Child	01Au130o
CHONNON, Francis	30	M	Miner	01Au130o
Sarah	28	F	None	01Au130o
BASSETT, Maria	30	F	None	01Au130o
KELLY, William	23	M	Farmer	01Au130o
WALL, Patrick	29	M	Farmer	01Au130o

INDIANA 02 SEPTEMBER 1849

From St.Martins

NAMES OF PASSENGERS	AGE	SEX	OCCUPATIONS	DATE PORT SHIP
BAILEY, Charles	27	M	Seaman	02Se19Nz

JOHN-BARING 04 AUGUST 1849

From Liverpool

NAMES OF PASSENGERS	AGE	SEX	OCCUPATIONS	DATE PORT SHIP
BONER, James	35	M	Farmer	04Au020a
MARTIN, Margaret	23	F	Farmer	04Au020a
GARVIN, Patrick	38	M	Farmer	04Au020a
ENGLISH, John	40	M	Farmer	04Au020a
LUNARD, James	40	M	Farmer	04Au020a
John	5	M	Child	04Au020a
Mary-Ann	3	F	Child	04Au020a
CASI, Rose	20	F	Farmer	04Au020a
CIRILLY, James	34	M	Farmer	04Au020a
MCCANELL, Ann	34	F	Farmer	04Au020a
CAHILL, John	23	M	Farmer	04Au020a
FEGAN, Thomas	25	M	Farmer	04Au020a
GAFFNEY, Thomas	20	M	Farmer	04Au020a
KELLEY, Bridget	19	F	Farmer	04Au020a
Elizabeth	21	F	Farmer	04Au020a
HOGAN, John	28	M	Farmer	04Au020a
BURKE, Patk.	14	M	Farmer	04Au020a
PARCEL, Thomas	14	M	Farmer	04Au020a
U-Mrs.	40	F	Farmer	04Au020a
MCMAHON, Margt.	20	F	Farmer	04Au020a
CAREY, Ellen	16	F	Farmer	04Au020a
BYRNES, Margaret	16	F	Farmer	04Au020a
CARY, Peter	19	M	Farmer	04Au020a
WARD, John	22	M	Farmer	04Au020a
MALONEY, John	17	M	Farmer	04Au020a
GAVIN, Jeremiah	24	M	Farmer	04Au020a
Patrick	4	M	Child	04Au020a
MCMAHON, Catherine	9	F	Child	04Au020a
DONALDSON, Judy	50	F	Farmer	04Au020a
James (S)	18	M	Farmer	04Au020a
William (S)	16	M	Farmer	04Au020a
HARAGIN, Pat	30	M	Farmer	04Au020a
CANYON, Thomas	20	M	Farmer	04Au020a

LIVELY 04 AUGUST 1849

From Galway

NAMES OF PASSENGERS	AGE	SEX	OCCUPATIONS	DATE PORT SHIP
OLOUGHLAN, John	30	M	Farmer	04Au060b
Elizabeth	29	F	Farmer	04Au060b
CONNELL, John	27	M	Farmer	04Au060b
OLOUGHLAN, Margt.	17	F	Farmer	04Au060b
Terence	50	M	Farmer	04Au060b
Honora	25	F	Farmer	04Au060b
Terence	.00	M	Infant	04Au060b
MARRINON, Martin	20	M	Farmer	04Au060b
BORN, Biddy	20	F	Farmer	04Au060b
SHOUGHNESSY, John	24	M	Farmer	04Au060b
OBRIAN, Michael	34	M	Farmer	04Au060b
Mary	20	F	Farmer	04Au060b
John	18	M	Farmer	04Au060b
GALVIN, John	40	M	Farmer	04Au060b
CLOHESSY, James	40	M	Farmer	04Au060b
GALVIN, Judy	18	F	Farmer	04Au060b
Ellen	14	F	Farmer	04Au060b
Mary	11	F	Farmer	04Au060b
James	.00	M	Infant	04Au060b
HENNSY, James	26	M	Farmer	04Au060b
John	24	M	Farmer	04Au060b
CROW, Thomas	40	M	Farmer	04Au060b
KEAN, Peter	30	M	Farmer	04Au060b
FLANEGAN, Nancy	24	F	Farmer	04Au060b
Michael	5	M	Child	04Au060b
KEAN, Anthony	.00	M	Infant	04Au060b
CLUNE, Mary	19	F	Farmer	04Au060b
Michael	17	M	Farmer	04Au060b
KENORY, Susan	25	F	Farmer	04Au060b
HOGAN, Hanna	29	F	Farmer	04Au060b
John	26	M	Farmer	04Au060b
Marton	2	M	Child	04Au060b
Patt	.00	M	Infant	04Au060b
MCGATMAN, Michael	24	M	Farmer	04Au060b
MCHUGHS, John	24	M	Farmer	04Au060b
HANNIGAN, Timothy	20	M	Farmer	04Au060b
Bridget	22	F	Farmer	04Au060b
DONAHUE, Mathew	24	M	Farmer	04Au060b
DARCY, John	26	M	Farmer	04Au060b

NAMES OF PASSENGERS	AGE	SEX	OCCUPATIONS	DATE PORT SHIP
DARCY, Bridget	20	F	Farmer	04Au060b
CLARY, James	21	M	Farmer	04Au060b
MURPHY, Patt	40	M	Farmer	04Au060b
LANAN, Mary	50	F	Farmer	04Au060b
MURPHY, Bridget	12	F	Farmer	04Au060b
Tom	6	M	Child	04Au060b
Ann	.00	F	Infant	04Au060b
KEMPEL, Thomas	20	M	Farmer	04Au060b
HYNES, Mary	18	F	Farmer	04Au060b
KEADY, John	27	M	Farmer	04Au060b
Judy	29	F	Farmer	04Au060b
FAHY, Daniel	21	M	Farmer	04Au060b
COUNDY, Marton	19	M	Farmer	04Au060b
GREENE, Ellen	20	F	Farmer	04Au060b
KENNY, Patt	36	M	Farmer	04Au060b
Mary	30	F	Farmer	04Au060b
FORDE, Michael	36	M	Farmer	04Au060b
Biddy	16	F	Farmer	04Au060b
CAUHLAN, Mary	20	F	Farmer	04Au060b
BARRY, Bridget	32	F	Farmer	04Au060b
Pat	3	M	Child	04Au060b
Nicholas	.00	M	Infant	04Au060b
HAGAN, Patt	24	M	Farmer	04Au060b
ROBERTS, Ellen	21	F	Farmer	04Au060b
HILL, Honor	21	F	Farmer	04Au060b
Sabina	14	F	Farmer	04Au060b
CONSDANE, Michael	19	M	Farmer	04Au060b
FURY, James	39	M	Farmer	04Au060b
MAHON, Mary	20	F	Farmer	04Au060b
WILSON, Catherine	37	F	Farmer	04Au060b
WILLSON, Thomas	12	M	Farmer	04Au060b
Alfred	10	M	Child	04Au060b
Henry	8	M	Child	04Au060b
Harriet	6	F	Child	04Au060b
George	.00	M	Infant	04Au060b
MCKENDY, Catherine	38	F	Farmer	04Au060b
Patrick	12	M	Farmer	04Au060b
John	8	M	Child	04Au060b
Hugh	.00	M	Infant	04Au060b
HIGGANS, Martin	28	M	Farmer	04Au060b
FAHERTY, Michael	40	M	Farmer	04Au060b
Bridget	6	F	Child	04Au060b
HARLEY, Catherine	24	F	Farmer	04Au060b
DONNELLAN, Tom	19	M	Farmer	04Au060b
DUFFY, Thomas	29	M	Farmer	04Au060b
CRANE, Mary	.00	F	Infant	04Au060b
MCDONOGH, Michael	28	M	Farmer	04Au060b
Patt	21	M	Farmer	04Au060b
CASY, Peter	24	M	Farmer	04Au060b
WALSH, Cathn.	22	F	Farmer	04Au060b
LIVENNY, John	24	M	Farmer	04Au060b
CONNOR, John	46	M	Farmer	04Au060b
DOOLAN, Thomas	20	M	Farmer	04Au060b
CUSARK, Honor	20	F	Farmer	04Au060b
Bridget	19	F	Farmer	04Au060b
SHAYHESSY, Mary	35	F	Farmer	04Au060b
MADDIN, Thomas	30	M	Farmer	04Au060b
Martin	28	M	Farmer	04Au060b
MCGUIRE, John	26	M	Farmer	04Au060b
MARRAHAN, Patt	25	M	Farmer	04Au060b
CLARY, Peggy	30	F	Farmer	04Au060b
OBRIAN, Mary	19	F	Farmer	04Au060b
CASEY, James	28	M	Unknown	04Au060b
CONNLLY, Margt.	22	F	Unknown	04Au060b
FARLEY, John	24	M	Unknown	04Au060b
GLYNN, Patrick	23	M	Unknown	04Au060b
Mary	18	F	Unknown	04Au060b
COWN, John	33	M	Unknown	04Au060b
QUINN, Mary	16	M	Unknown	04Au060b

ORION 04 AUGUST 1849

From Cork

NAMES OF PASSENGERS	AGE	SEX	OCCUPATIONS	DATE PORT SHIP
MURPH, Catharine	50	F	Farmer	04Au08Mx
Denis	25	M	Farmer	04Au08Mx
Julia	18	F	Farmer	04Au08Mx
CONNORS, Ellen	20	F	Farmer	04Au08Mx
FOLEY, John	28	M	Farmer	04Au08Mx
Catherine	26	F	Farmer	04Au08Mx
SULLIVAN, Catharine	28	F	Farmer	04Au08Mx
MACARTHY, F.	30	F	Farmer	04Au08Mx
ONEILL, Ann	19	F	Farmer	04Au08Mx
CRONEN, Cors.	30	M	Farmer	04Au08Mx
DONOGHUE, Jerry	26	M	Farmer	04Au08Mx
Mary	21	F	Farmer	04Au08Mx
LYNCH, Winey	16	M	Farmer	04Au08Mx
HAYES, Denis	35	M	Farmer	04Au08Mx
THOMPSON, John	35	M	Farmer	04Au08Mx
WHAYTON, John	30	M	Farmer	04Au08Mx
MAHONEY, Jane	24	F	Farmer	04Au08Mx
HARDD, John	40	M	Farmer	04Au08Mx
MCAULIFF, John	26	M	Farmer	04Au08Mx
FITZGERALD, Edward	30	M	Farmer	04Au08Mx
HOOLAHAN, Catherine	22	F	Farmer	04Au08Mx
DESMOND, Daniel	40	M	Farmer	04Au08Mx
LANE, Ellen	50	F	Farmer	04Au08Mx
Jerry	28	M	Farmer	04Au08Mx
Bridget	26	F	Farmer	04Au08Mx
James	22	M	Farmer	04Au08Mx
Margt.	17	F	Farmer	04Au08Mx
Dennis	19	M	Farmer	04Au08Mx
Daniel	.00	M	Infant	04Au08Mx
CALLAHAN, Mary	30	F	Farmer	04Au08Mx
REGAN, Margt.	25	F	Farmer	04Au08Mx
OSULLIVAN, Patt	35	M	Farmer	04Au08Mx
Mary	24	F	Farmer	04Au08Mx
Patt	.00	M	Infant	04Au08Mx
Ann	55	F	Farmer	04Au08Mx
Daniel	15	M	Farmer	04Au08Mx
BRENNAN, James	20	M	Farmer	04Au08Mx
GOSSIN, Richard	30	M	Farmer	04Au08Mx
SULLIVAN, Hanna	18	F	Farmer	04Au08Mx
Margt.	18	F	Farmer	04Au08Mx
COLEMAN, Johannah	30	F	Farmer	04Au08Mx
CRUMAN, Ellen	21	F	Farmer	04Au08Mx
MURPHY, Humphry	21	M	Farmer	04Au08Mx
Mary	18	F	Farmer	04Au08Mx
Mary	.00	F	Infant	04Au08Mx
SULLIVAN, Catherine	17	F	Farmer	04Au08Mx
John	28	M	Farmer	04Au08Mx
MOOR, Charles	30	M	Farmer	04Au08Mx
SULLIVAN, Michael	28	M	Farmer	04Au08Mx
RING, Daniel	26	M	Farmer	04Au08Mx
AHERN, Jerry	40	M	Farmer	04Au08Mx
CONNELL, Marton	22	M	Farmer	04Au08Mx
James	16	M	Farmer	04Au08Mx
CLIFFORD, John	19	M	Farmer	04Au08Mx
MATHEWS, Ann	21	F	Farmer	04Au08Mx
SULLIVAN, Mary	20	F	Farmer	04Au08Mx
John	15	M	Farmer	04Au08Mx
FINN, Daniel	30	M	Farmer	04Au08Mx
HEGARTY, Daniel	16	M	Farmer	04Au08Mx
Ellen	15	F	Farmer	04Au08Mx
DENERTY, Cornelius	22	M	Farmer	04Au08Mx
MCSWEENEY, James	24	M	Farmer	04Au08Mx
HALMAN, Nathaniel	40	M	Farmer	04Au08M
BUTLER, William	22	M	Farmer	04Au08M
LANS, Mary-Ann	28	F	Farmer	04Au08M

NAMES OF PASSENGERS	AGE	SEX	OCCUPATIONS	DATE PORT SHIP
MARIGAN, Thomas	27	M	Farmer	04Au08Mx
LALY, Daniel	20	M	Farmer	04Au08Mx
MCCARTHY, Daniel	25	M	Farmer	04Au08Mx
BRUHAN, Michael	27	M	Farmer	04Au08Mx

ROLLA 04 AUGUST 1849

From London

NAMES OF PASSENGERS	AGE	SEX	OCCUPATIONS	DATE PORT SHIP
GIDDINGS, Ann	30	F	Unknown	04Au13Qc
GRAHAM, John	32	M	Unknown	04Au13Qc
BRAIM, K.	26	M	Unknown	04Au13Qc
CURBY, John	42	M	Unknown	04Au13Qc
LYONS, Ann	33	F	Unknown	04Au13Qc
JACKSON, Thos.	32	M	Unknown	04Au13Qc
Mary	23	F	Unknown	04Au13Qc
ENGLISH, Mary	29	F	Unknown	04Au13Qc
HARLIN, Wm.	34	M	Unknown	04Au13Qc
Harriett	30	F	Unknown	04Au13Qc
Harriett	.11	F	Infant	04Au13Qc
Elizth.	9	F	Child	04Au13Qc
Wm.	6	M	Child	04Au13Qc
Sarah	2	F	Child	04Au13Qc
John	.00	M	Infant	04Au13Qc
CARROLE, Moreton	39	M	Unknown	04Au13Qc
Thomas	13	M	Unknown	04Au13Qc
GOODRICH, Wm.	22	M	Unknown	04Au13Qc
BEDFORD, Wm.	24	M	Unknown	04Au13Qc
PEARCE, Louise	34	F	Unknown	04Au13Qc
George	34	M	Unknown	04Au13Qc
Louise	.00	F	Infant	04Au13Qc
Ann	10	F	Unknown	04Au13Qc
George	8	M	Child	04Au13Qc
Harriett	4	F	Child	04Au13Qc
Richard	2	M	Child	04Au13Qc
Ralph	00	M	Unknown	04Au13Qc
BARNES, John	30	M	Unknown	04Au13Qc
WARD, Thos.	30	M	Unknown	04Au13Qc
HUGES, Martin	20	M	Unknown	04Au13Qc
HARTLEY, Jas.	21	M	Unknown	04Au13Qc
SEETLY, John	22	M	Unknown	04Au13Qc
FLEMMING, John	31	M	Unknown	04Au13Qc
Ellen	30	F	Unknown	04Au13Qc
Mary	7	F	Child	04Au13Qc
Julia	5	F	Child	04Au13Qc
Catherine	.00	F	Infant	04Au13Qc
SMITH, Bridget	00	F	Unknown	04Au13Qc
BLANDRON, John	40	M	Unknown	04Au13Qc
Hannah	39	F	Unknown	04Au13Qc
Henry	13	M	Unknown	04Au13Qc
Elizth.	13	F	Unknown	04Au13Qc
Edwin	12	M	Unknown	04Au13Qc
Emily	10	F	Unknown	04Au13Qc
John	6	M	Child	04Au13Qc
Mathilda	4	F	Child	04Au13Qc
Charles	2	M	Child	04Au13Qc
FLYNN, Patrick	30	M	Unknown	04Au13Qc
SAUNDERS, Wm.	26	M	Unknown	04Au13Qc
RADFORD, Jane	23	F	Unknown	04Au13Qc
DUNN, Andrew	22	M	Unknown	04Au13Qc
COODY, James	35	M	Unknown	04Au13Qc
Mary	34	F	Unknown	04Au13Qc
FERNOR, Jas.	40	M	Unknown	04Au13Qc
KELLY, Jas.	20	M	Unknown	04Au13Qc
Ellen	19	F	Unknown	04Au13Qc
FITZGERALD, Thomas	30	M	Mechanic	04Au13Qc

HERO 04 AUGUST 1849

From PICTOU,N.S.

NAMES OF PASSENGERS	AGE	SEX	OCCUPATIONS	DATE PORT SHIP
GILMORE, Andrew	28	M	Miner	04Au62OI
MCNIEL, L.	24	M	Sailor	04Au62OI

AMERICA 06 AUGUST 1849

From Liverpool

NAMES OF PASSENGERS	AGE	SEX	OCCUPATIONS	DATE PORT SHIP
DRISCOLL, John	22	M	Cbtmkr	06Au02Eb
MCCARTHY, John	24	M	Coachman	06Au02Eb
DEVINE, Thos.	22	M	Laborer	06Au02Eb
HAYES, Dennis	56	M	Gdnr	06Au02Eb
Dennis	18	M	Gdnr	06Au02Eb
Thomas	11	M	Gdnr	06Au02Eb
Charles	9	M	Child	06Au02Eb
Thomas	16	M	Gdnr	06Au02Eb
Fanny	21	F	Gdnr	06Au02Eb
Ann	8	F	Child	06Au02Eb
GRIFFIN, John	26	M	Currier	06Au02Eb
Eliza	26	F	None	06Au02Eb
U	.00	U	Infant	06Au02Eb
Margaret	26	F	None	06Au02Eb
CORMAN, John	30	M	Laborer	06Au02Eb
Catherine	25	F	None	06Au02Eb
BUCKLEY, Patrick	18	M	Student	06Au02Eb
M--, Patrick	23	M	Laborer	06Au02Eb
CARROLL, Mary	16	F	Farmer	06Au02Eb
MCCARTHY, Catherine	18	F	Spinster	06Au02Eb
GRIFFIN, Michael	31	M	Laborer	06Au02Eb
Mary	35	F	None	06Au02Eb
Bridget	6	F	Child	06Au02Eb
Norry	4	F	Child	06Au02Eb
Richard	2	M	Child	06Au02Eb
MCCARTHY, Mary	11	F	Spinster	06Au02Eb
ODEA, Mary	22	F	Spinster	06Au02Eb
BRYEN, Pat	26	M	Laborer	06Au02Eb
MCGUIRE, Richard	35	M	Laborer	06Au02Eb
DONNELL, Edward	21	M	Laborer	06Au02Eb
WALLACE, Stephen	21	M	Laborer	06Au02Eb
John	19	M	Laborer	06Au02Eb
BROWN, David	25	M	Blacksmith	06Au02Eb
CARR, John	18	M	Laborer	06Au02Eb
BARRY, John	57	M	Farmer	06Au02Eb
Mary	48	F	Farmer	06Au02Eb
Michael	25	F	Farmer	06Au02Eb
Richard	6	M	Child	06Au02Eb
James	5	M	Child	06Au02Eb
Michael	16	M	Farmer	06Au02Eb
Mary	11	F	None	06Au02Eb
Kate	25	F	None	06Au02Eb
Abbey	25	F	None	06Au02Eb
Ellen	7	F	Child	06Au02Eb
Mary	5	F	Child	06Au02Eb
Honora	2	F	Child	06Au02Eb
Ellen	16	F	Farmer	06Au02Eb
Abagail	11	F	None	06Au02Eb
Eliza	8	F	Child	06Au02Eb
U-Dr.	28	M	Apothecary	06Au02Eb
LONG, Mick	19	M	Laborer	06Au02Eb
SAMPIER, Ellen	40	F	Spinster	06Au02Eb

NAMES OF PASSENGERS	AGE	SEX	OCCUPATIONS	DATE PORT SHIP
FLANNIGAN, Mick	34	M	Laborer	06Au02Eb
Margaret	26	F	None	06Au02Eb
Honora	4	F	Child	06Au02Eb
Margaret	2	F	Child	06Au02Eb
GIBBONS, Michael	28	M	Shoemaker	06Au02Eb
MCDONNELL, Ann	30	F	Carpenter	06Au02Eb
Ann	11	F	None	06Au02Eb
Ellen	9	F	Child	06Au02Eb
John	7	M	Child	06Au02Eb
Mary	3	F	Child	06Au02Eb
MCCANN, Nicholas	52	M	Farmer	06Au02Eb
Rose	50	F	None	06Au02Eb
Margaret	21	F	None	06Au02Eb
John	20	M	Farmer	06Au02Eb
Patrick	18	M	Farmer	06Au02Eb
Nicholas	16	M	Farmer	06Au02Eb
Rose	14	F	None	06Au02Eb
Catherine	11	F	None	06Au02Eb
Thomas	9	M	Child	06Au02Eb
Mary	50	F	None	06Au02Eb
WELCH, Geo.	21	M	Laborer	06Au02Eb
FLYNN, Andrew	4	M	Child	06Au02Eb
U	.00	U	Infant	06Au02Eb
DALY, Thomas	25	M	Laborer	06Au02Eb
U (W)	25	F	None	06Au02Eb
MURRAY, Mick	20	M	Laborer	06Au02Eb
DONNELLY, Pat	30	M	Laborer	06Au02Eb
NIMOH, Alexander	20	M	Laborer	06Au02Eb
BALL, Mary	20	F	Spinster	06Au02Eb
THOMAS, Holt	20	M	Ctntw	06Au02Eb
HOWLSHAN, Mary	11	F	Spinster	06Au02Eb
JAMES, Thomas	51	M	Farmer	06Au02Eb
Kate	50	F	None	06Au02Eb
Margaret	18	F	None	06Au02Eb
Ally	11	F	None	06Au02Eb
James	9	M	Child	06Au02Eb
Edward	7	M	Child	06Au02Eb
SCANLAN, Catherine	18	F	Spinster	06Au02Eb
BROWN, Thos.	28	M	Laborer	06Au02Eb
HARTLEY, Richard	20	M	Laborer	06Au02Eb
STARK, Darby	40	F	Wi	06Au02Eb
WOLF, Margaret	20	F	Spinster	06Au02Eb
Died-At-Sea				
CARROLL, Richard	45	M	Carpenter	06Au02Eb
STAPLETON, Patrick	25	M	Laborer	06Au02Eb
BURK, Phillip	19	M	Laborer	06Au02Eb
VAUGHAN, Johanna	28	F	Spinster	06Au02Eb
OBRIEN, Mary	29	F	Spinster	06Au02Eb
DONNELLY, James	18	M	Laborer	06Au02Eb
BURKE, Edward-J.	22	M	Student	06Au02Eb
CUMMINS, Eliza	17	F	Spinster	06Au02Eb
Margaret	22	F	Spinster	06Au02Eb
MUIRE, Patrick	26	M	Laborer	06Au02Eb
MCEVOY, Patrick	20	M	Laborer	06Au02Eb
HEIN, Sidney	20	F	Spinster	06Au02Eb
MCVEY, Jas.	47	M	Miner	06Au02Eb
Margaret	47	F	None	06Au02Eb
STANFORD, Michael	42	M	Laborer	06Au02Eb
PEET, Geo.	30	M	Carpenter	06Au02Eb
Mary	30	F	None	06Au02Eb
U	.00	U	Infant	06Au02Eb
David	3	M	Child	06Au02Eb
DICKENSON, William	24	M	Blacksmith	06Au02Eb
RAWLIE, Thomas	24	M	Wool Comber	06Au02Eb
EAST, Edward	23	M	Weaver	06Au02Eb
Died-At-Sea				
MCKENZIE, Alexander	26	M	Laborer	06Au02Eb
BELLOWBY, Thomas	26	M	Engd	06Au02Eb
STANLEY, James	33	M	Engd	06Au02Eb
BELLOWBY, Peter	30	M	Engd	06Au02Eb
MURPHY, Patrick	35	M	Blacksmith	06Au02Eb
Margaret	30	F	None	06Au02Eb
Patrick	8	M	Child	06Au02Eb
HILL, Thos.	40	M	Laborer	06Au02Eb
MCMAHON, John	24	M	Laborer	06Au02Eb
MCMAHON, Ann	19	F	None	06Au02Eb
HALPIN, Ellen	19	F	Spinster	06Au02Eb
FITZGERALD, Pat	28	M	Laborer	06Au02Eb
CARNODY, Gaunt	28	M	Farmer	06Au02Eb
Nancy	16	F	None	06Au02Eb
DORE, Honora	17	F	Spinster	06Au02Eb
SCANLAN, Pat	24	M	Clerk	06Au02Eb
BRESNAHAN, Hugh	25	M	Shoemaker	06Au02Eb
Catherine	35	F	None	06Au02Eb
U	.00	U	Infant	06Au02Eb
James	6	M	Child	06Au02Eb
John	4	M	Child	06Au02Eb
BRADNEY, Cornelius	28	M	Laborer	06Au02Eb
BARRETT, Dennis	26	M	Laborer	06Au02Eb
NAGLE, Edward	26	M	Laborer	06Au02Eb
KELLY, John	26	M	Laborer	06Au02Eb
Sarah	28	F	None	06Au02Eb
FITZGIBBON, Joshua	25	M	Laborer	06Au02Eb
COLEMAN, Thomas	25	M	Laborer	06Au02Eb
MORTELL, Nicholas	40	M	Laborer	06Au02Eb
BUCKLEY, Margaret	28	F	None	06Au02Eb
Nancy	.00	F	Infant	06Au02Eb
LYONS, Margaret	23	F	Spinster	06Au02Eb
OLEARY, Ann	15	F	Spinster	06Au02Eb
LYNCH, Cath.	40	F	Baker	06Au02Eb
Charles	10	M	None	06Au02Eb
QUIGLEY, Timothy	32	M	Clerk	06Au02Eb
COFFREY, Edward	17	M	Laborer	06Au02Eb
WARREN, Valentine	17	M	Clerk	06Au02Eb
LYNCH, Richard	27	M	Laborer	06Au02Eb
HUGHES, Edward	23	M	Laborer	06Au02Eb
SMITHERS, William	36	M	Laborer	06Au02Eb
HORTON, Margaret	30	F	Spinster	06Au02Eb
HICKEY, Margaret	30	F	Spinster	06Au02Eb
BARGEN, Ann	46	F	Spinster	06Au02Eb
MOONEY, Margaret	23	F	Spinster	06Au02Eb
AYLWARD, Mary	18	F	Spinster	06Au02Eb
VALE, Catherine	15	F	Spinster	06Au02Eb
Biddy	11	F	Spinster	06Au02Eb
FLYNN, Andrew	40	M	Miner	06Au02Eb
Margaret	30	F	None	06Au02Eb
Margaret	14	F	None	06Au02Eb
Rose	14	F	None	06Au02Eb
Jane	9	F	Child	06Au02Eb
Eliza	7	F	Child	06Au02Eb
Mary	6	F	Child	06Au02Eb
John	5	M	Child	06Au02Eb
HOLLAND, Mary	20	F	Spinster	06Au02Eb
Margaret	11	F	Spinster	06Au02Eb
DESMOND, Hannah	20	F	Laborer	06Au02Eb
John	4	M	Child	06Au02Eb
FITZGERALD, Mick	30	M	Laborer	06Au02Eb
Michael	5	M	Child	06Au02Eb
BYRNE, Margaret	44	F	Slater	06Au02Eb
James	16	M	Slater	06Au02Eb
Died-At-Sea				
Thomas	11	M	None	06Au02Eb
Ellen	10	F	None	06Au02Eb
Hannah	8	F	Child	06Au02Eb
Died-At-Sea				
Peter	6	M	Child	06Au02Eb
CRAWFORD, John	18	M	Laborer	06Au02Eb
REDMOND, Ann	17	F	Spinster	06Au02Eb
DALY, Michael	11	M	Laborer	06Au02Eb
TAVILL, Mary	60	F	Weaver	06Au02Eb
Rody	27	F	Weaver	06Au02Eb
Ruth	25	F	Weaver	06Au02Eb
Ellen	26	F	Weaver	06Au02Eb
Hannah	17	F	Weaver	06Au02Eb
John	26	M	Weaver	06Au02Eb
Ann	24	F	Weaver	06Au02Eb
Benjamin	6	M	Child	06Au02Eb
George	3	M	Child	06Au02Eb
DONNELL, Mary-Ann	20	F	Spinster	06Au02Eb
SIMMONS, Martha	20	F	Spinster	06Au02Eb

NAMES OF PASSENGERS	AGE	SEX	OCCUPATIONS	DATE PORT SHIP
MURRAY, Thomas	10	M	Tailor	06Au02Eb
MCEVOY, Catherine	50	F	Laborer	06Au02Eb
BLESSING, James	40	M	Laborer	06Au02Eb
Rosanna	11	F	None	06Au02Eb
Catherine	7	F	Child	06Au02Eb
Ellen	4	F	Child	06Au02Eb
CURRAN, Charles	28	M	Musician	06Au02Eb
ROCHFORT, Cath.	30	F	Spinster	06Au02Eb
GRIFFEN, James	24	M	Molder	06Au02Eb
Died-At-Sea				
SLATER, William	33	M	Publican	06Au02Eb
Betty	37	F	None	06Au02Eb
Nancy-H.	.00	F	Infant	06Au02Eb
FAITH, Jas.	38	M	Laborer	06Au02Eb
WOOD, Thomas	38	M	Farmer	06Au02Eb
U (W)	30	F	None	06Au02Eb
Luther	6	M	Child	06Au02Eb
Mary-Ann	5	F	Child	06Au02Eb
George	3	M	Child	06Au02Eb
Thomas	1	M	Child	06Au02Eb
Lucy	.00	F	Infant	06Au02Eb
SAMPSON, Joseph	23	M	Blr	06Au02Eb
MCMAHON, Hugh	20	M	Carpenter	06Au02Eb
QUIN, Mary	2	F	Child	06Au02Eb
Died-At-Sea				
U	.00	U	Infant	06Au02Eb
Died-At-Sea				
HANNAHAN, Sally	22	F	Spinster	06Au02Eb
ROWLEY, Thos.	52	M	Waterman	06Au02Eb
Sarah	47	F	None	06Au02Eb
WALTON, John	26	M	Waterman	06Au02Eb
James	22	M	Waterman	06Au02Eb
ROWLEY, Sarah	20	F	None	06Au02Eb
Elizabeth	.00	F	Infant	06Au02Eb
LAMB, Wm.	30	M	Laborer	06Au02Eb
Jane	30	F	None	06Au02Eb
SHERIDAN, John	35	M	Groom	06Au02Eb
FAGAN, Margt.	25	F	Spinster	06Au02Eb
CONLIN, Peter	20	M	Laborer	06Au02Eb
Margt.	30	F	None	06Au02Eb
LAYDEN, James	18	M	Laborer	06Au02Eb
DOYLE, James	21	M	Laborer	06Au02Eb
LEE, Ann	18	F	Spinster	06Au02Eb
MCCAULY, James	20	M	Laborer	06Au02Eb
POLLOCK, John	30	M	Laborer	06Au02Eb
BURKE, Redmond	16	M	Laborer	06Au02Eb
DURKIN, Wm.	24	M	Laborer	06Au02Eb
MCGLYNN, Eliza	6	F	Child	06Au02Eb
DUNN, Nancy	14	F	Spinster	06Au02Eb
WALLACE, Thos.	00	M	Laborer	06Au02Eb
Catherine	28	F	None	06Au02Eb
Honora	9	F	Child	06Au02Eb
Margaret	4	F	Child	06Au02Eb
Catherine	3	F	Child	06Au02Eb
John	.00	M	Infant	06Au02Eb
RUSH, John	28	M	Blacksmith	06Au02Eb
FITZSIMMONS, Bartley	25	M	Groom	06Au02Eb
NEWALL, Mich.	26	M	Stone Mason	06Au02Eb
DONOVAN, Danl.	27	M	Shoemaker	06Au02Eb
STEWART, James	31	M	Sglnmkr	06Au02Eb
U (W)	24	F	None	06Au02Eb
U	8	M	Child	06Au02Eb
U	6	F	Child	06Au02Eb
U	3	M	Child	06Au02Eb
MURPHY, John	18	M	Laborer	06Au02Eb
QUIN, Pat	32	M	Laborer	06Au02Eb
MCNAMARA, Thos.	42	M	Farmer	06Au02Eb
Ellen	42	F	None	06Au02Eb
CODY, Mary	35	F	Cooper	06Au02Eb
Eliza	19	F	None	06Au02Eb
James	12	M	None	06Au02Eb
LOUGHREA, Bridget	20	F	Spinster	06Au02Eb
NORVILLE, Michl.	45	M	Laborer	06Au02Eb
Mary	16	F	None	06Au02Eb
MONGORAN, Thos.	25	M	Laborer	06Au02Eb

NAMES OF PASSENGERS	AGE	SEX	OCCUPATIONS	DATE PORT SHIP
MONGORAN, James	20	M	Laborer	06Au02Eb
WRIGHT, Geo.	25	M	Butcher	06Au02Eb
HARRISON, James	18	M	Druggist	06Au02Eb
BARTLETT, Thos.	28	M	Laborer	06Au02Eb
LAMBOWM, Thos.	21	M	Laborer	06Au02Eb
MCGOVERN, Michl.	25	M	Weaver	06Au02Eb
LUCAS, Edward	24	M	Laborer	06Au02Eb
Ellen	20	F	None	06Au02Eb
DONOHOE, Jas.	22	M	Laborer	06Au02Eb
Margaret	20	F	None	06Au02Eb
WILSON, Thomas	20	M	Baker	06Au02Eb
JOHNSON, John	30	M	Cutler	06Au02Eb
SALT, Mark-Henry	29	M	Glsbr	06Au02Eb
Elizabeth	25	F	None	06Au02Eb
Died-At-Sea				
John-Harry	3	M	Child	06Au02Eb
Jane-Morris	.00	F	Infant	06Au02Eb
MERRYWEATHER, Charles	34	M	Laborer	06Au02Eb
KEGWORTH, Thos.	21	M	Laborer	06Au02Eb
DAWSON, Arthur	39	M	Laborer	06Au02Eb
SLEIGHTAM, Robt.	25	M	Mason	06Au02Eb
COX, Francis	30	M	Miller	06Au02Eb
HOBBS, Cath.	25	F	Spinster	06Au02Eb
HOLTON, Cath.	20	F	Spinster	06Au02Eb
SHORT, Jas.	17	M	Laborer	06Au02Eb
John	18	M	Laborer	06Au02Eb
MURPHY, Robt.	35	M	Carpenter	06Au02Eb
Bridt.	35	F	None	06Au02Eb
NEWTON, Wm.	36	M	Fitter	06Au02Eb
Margt.	37	F	Dressmaker	06Au02Eb
Mary	16	F	Dressmaker	06Au02Eb
BARKER, Margaret	26	F	Dressmaker	06Au02Eb
GILBERT, John	24	M	Pawn Broker	06Au02Eb
Sam-Mrs.	23	F	None	06Au02Eb
SMITH, George	40	M	Farmer	06Au02Eb
Rachel	35	F	None	06Au02Eb
Mary	8	F	Child	06Au02Eb
Charles	12	M	None	06Au02Eb
Richard	11	M	None	06Au02Eb
U	3	U	Child	06Au02Eb
U	.00	U	Infant	06Au02Eb
DAVIS, David	34	M	Collier	06Au02Eb
Hannah	32	F	None	06Au02Eb
Margt.	9	F	Child	06Au02Eb
John	6	M	Child	06Au02Eb
Willm.	4	M	Child	06Au02Eb
MCGLYNN, Pat	40	M	Laborer	06Au02Eb
HUMPHRIES, John	25	M	Farmer	06Au02Eb
RAY, Richd.	38	M	Laborer	06Au02Eb
Harriet	31	F	None	06Au02Eb
Jane	3	F	Child	06Au02Eb
Sarah	2	F	Child	06Au02Eb
WHITE, Joseph	26	M	Laborer	06Au02Eb
MURRAY, Henry	30	M	Farmer	06Au02Eb
Cath.	24	F	None	06Au02Eb
Robt.	5	M	Child	06Au02Eb
Wm.	3	M	Child	06Au02Eb
Henry	1	M	Child	06Au02Eb
KELLY, Martin	20	M	Farmer	06Au02Eb
ADAMS, Joseph	31	M	Diastr	06Au02Eb
BLAIR, Sam	35	M	Blr	06Au02Eb
Rose	26	F	None	06Au02Eb
EVANS, Evans	24	M	Wheelwright	06Au02Eb
GRAHAM, Mary	30	F	Wi	06Au02Eb
Elizth.	8	F	Child	06Au02Eb
William	6	M	Child	06Au02Eb
Joseph	.00	M	Infant	06Au02Eb
ROBSON, Thos.	25	M	Miller	06Au02Eb
HUMPHRIES, Henry	30	M	Farmer	06Au02Eb
Caroline	25	F	Farmer	06Au02Eb
DAY, Thos.	60	M	Farmer	06Au02Eb
MULLINS, Rebecca	30	F	Tailor	06Au02Eb
Jane	14	F	Tailor	06Au02Eb
Thomas	12	M	None	06Au02Eb
James	7	M	Child	06Au02Eb

NAMES OF PASSENGERS		AGE	SEX	OCCUPATIONS	DATE PORT SHIP
MULLINS, Mary		3	F	Child	06Au02Eb
MCKENNA, Bridget		19	F	Spinster	06Au02Eb
HACKET, Ann		20	F	Spinster	06Au02Eb
HULTRON, Joseph		40	M	Laborer	06Au02Eb
MCCARROLL, Margt.		19	F	Spinster	06Au02Eb
KENNEDY, Joseph		24	M	Laborer	06Au02Eb
FRENCH, James		30	M	Laborer	06Au02Eb
BREEN, Wm.		30	M	Shoemaker	06Au02Eb
Bridget		40	F	None	06Au02Eb
Sarah		13	F	None	06Au02Eb
Patrick		11	M	None	06Au02Eb
Catherine		5	F	Child	06Au02Eb
George		.00	M	Infant	06Au02Eb
RABBETT, Pat		30	M	Laborer	06Au02Eb
Bridgett		26	F	Spinster	06Au02Eb
BUSHELL, Patk.		33	M	Laborer	06Au02Eb
SIVELLANE, Mich.		35	M	Laborer	06Au02Eb
Bridgett		24	F	None	06Au02Eb
Mary		16	F	None	06Au02Eb
Ann		.00	F	Infant	06Au02Eb
QUIN, Phillip		30	M	Shoemaker	06Au02Eb
Michael		34	M	Laborer	06Au02Eb
Honor		34	F	None	06Au02Eb
MONAGHAN, John		18	M	Laborer	06Au02Eb
MCELROY, Chas.		50	M	Laborer	06Au02Eb
Mary		14	F	None	06Au02Eb
William		19	M	Laborer	06Au02Eb
BARRY, Elba		35	M	Clerk	06Au02Eb
John		13	M	None	06Au02Eb
CRONIN, Mary		6	F	Child	06Au02Eb
John		17	M	Laborer	06Au02Eb
SHANNAHAN, Mich.		20	M	Laborer	06Au02Eb
HARE, Eliza		12	F	Spinster	06Au02Eb
SHANNAHAN, Margt.		20	F	Spinster	06Au02Eb
CLARKE, John		18	M	Laborer	06Au02Eb
HAWKS, Henry		24	M	Laborer	06Au02Eb
Lath--, John		30	M	Laborer	06Au02Eb
COOK, John		24	M	Laborer	06Au02Eb
U	(W)	22	F	None	06Au02Eb
LEE, John		30	M	Laborer	06Au02Eb
Lockday		20	M	Laborer	06Au02Eb
ROYLAND, Wm.		31	M	Laborer	06Au02Eb
SMITH, Jacob		55	M	Laborer	06Au02Eb
HAWKES, Wm.		31	M	Gentleman	06Au02Eb
RICHARDS, Joseph		25	M	Molder	06Au02Eb
FARMER, Thos.		28	M	Blacksmith	06Au02Eb
Cornelius		26	M	Blacksmith	06Au02Eb
U	(W)	24	F	None	06Au02Eb
Thomas		4	M	Child	06Au02Eb
MULLIGAN, Cath.		30	F	None	06Au02Eb
Ann		6	F	Child	06Au02Eb
Elizabeth		3	F	Child	06Au02Eb
THOMAS, Rob.		34	M	Farmer	06Au02Eb
Ann		32	F	None	06Au02Eb
Ann		9	F	Child	06Au02Eb
Willm.		7	M	Child	06Au02Eb
U		.00	U	Infant	06Au02Eb
COLLINS, Robt.		34	M	Machinist	06Au02Eb
JOHNSTONE, Mary		26	F	Tailor	06Au02Eb
Saml.		8	M	Child	06Au02Eb
Edward		5	M	Child	06Au02Eb
Robert		3	M	Child	06Au02Eb
HARRIS, Christ.		25	M	Laborer	06Au02Eb
KING, Geo.Johnson		25	M	Gentleman	06Au02Eb
LILLY, Robt.		45	M	Gentleman	06Au02Eb
BARNETT, John		25	M	Gentleman	06Au02Eb
U	(W)	25	F	Lady	06Au02Eb

HUNTRESS 06 AUGUST 1849

From Tortola

NAMES OF PASSENGERS	AGE	SEX	OCCUPATIONS	DATE PORT SHIP
ROGER, Wm.	19	M	Merchant	06Au720d

GROWLER 07 AUGUST 1849

From PICTOU,N.S.

NAMES OF PASSENGERS	AGE	SEX	OCCUPATIONS	DATE PORT SHIP
MCCARTY, Mary	19	F	Dressmaker	07Au620m

PRINCE-ALBERT 08 AUGUST 1849

From London

NAMES OF PASSENGERS	AGE	SEX	OCCUPATIONS	DATE PORT SHIP
FUTEMONCE, Honor	21	F	Milliner	08Au13As
MURPHY, Ellen	27	F	Cook	08Au13As
Henrietta	34	F	None	08Au13As
Minor	32	F	None	08Au13As

COLONIST 09 AUGUST 1849

From Londonderry

NAMES OF PASSENGERS	AGE	SEX	OCCUPATIONS	DATE PORT SHIP
JAMISON, Jas.J.	40	M	Merchant	09Au01Kv
MCDOUGALL, Alex	45	M	Farmer	09Au01Kv
MCDONNELL, Thos.	23	M	None	09Au01Kv
BARRETT, Edwd.	29	M	Merchant	09Au01Kv

WISCONSIN 09 AUGUST 1849

From Liverpool

NAMES OF PASSENGERS	AGE	SEX	OCCUPATIONS	DATE PORT SHIP
CLAZERS, Michael	21	M	Mason	09Au02Aa
FARRALL, Bridget	37	F	Unknown	09Au02Aa
Ann	13	F	Unknown	09Au02Aa
Edward	12	M	Unknown	09Au02Aa
James	11	M	Unknown	09Au02Aa
Kate	11	F	Unknown	09Au02Aa
MALONE, Pierre	40	M	Mason	09Au02Aa
MULLIGAN, George	25	M	Mason	09Au02Aa
LAWLOR, Michael	25	M	Mason	09Au02A
KEEL, William	28	M	Farmer	09Au02A
Hannah	25	F	Unknown	09Au02A

NAMES OF PASSENGERS	AGE	SEX	OCCUPATIONS	DATE PORT SHIP
KIERNAN, Thomas	22	M	Farmer	09Au02Aa
Margaret	22	F	Unknown	09Au02Aa
Ann	20	F	Unknown	09Au02Aa
HEARNE, Patrick	18	M	Laborer	09Au02Aa
FITZGERALD, Mary-Ann	22	F	Servant	09Au02Aa
GLYMN, Mary	18	F	Servant	09Au02Aa
HENNESSEY, Patrick	22	M	Laborer	09Au02Aa
CONNELLY, Danl.	19	M	Laborer	09Au02Aa
OBRIEN, William	60	M	Farmer	09Au02Aa
William	19	M	Unknown	09Au02Aa
James	12	M	Unknown	09Au02Aa
Ann	14	F	Unknown	09Au02Aa
SHEELAY, Thomas	21	M	Laborer	09Au02Aa
FAGAN, John	20	M	Tailor	09Au02Aa
Died-At-Sea				
Mary	20	F	Unknown	09Au02Aa
MORAN, Andrew	28	M	Laborer	09Au02Aa
NEALE, Margaret	28	F	Servant	09Au02Aa
CADDEN, Mary	30	F	Servant	09Au02Aa
Mary	10	F	Unknown	09Au02Aa
Sarah	5	F	Child	09Au02Aa
MCGREEGH, Francis	19	M	Laborer	09Au02Aa
DONOVAN, Charles	22	M	Laborer	09Au02Aa
KEOGH, Bridget	50	F	Servant	09Au02Aa
COONEY, James	20	M	Laborer	09Au02Aa
BLEYARD, John	37	M	Farmer	09Au02Aa
Allice	37	F	Unknown	09Au02Aa
Nancy	11	F	Unknown	09Au02Aa
Betsey	9	F	Child	09Au02Aa
William	7	M	Child	09Au02Aa
MURTHER, Patrick	20	M	Laborer	09Au02Aa
Mary	17	F	Unknown	09Au02Aa
MCWHATEN, Robert	28	M	Laborer	09Au02Aa
MCDERMOTT, John	26	M	Laborer	09Au02Aa
CAFFRA, John	19	M	Laborer	09Au02Aa
MCLUZEE, Charles	18	M	Laborer	09Au02Aa
Ann	12	F	Unknown	09Au02Aa
FEATHERSTONE, Mary	26	F	Unknown	09Au02Aa
Thomas	3	M	Child	09Au02Aa
Jasper	.00	M	Infant	09Au02Aa
GRIFF!TH, Maria	40	F	Unknown	09Au02Aa
John	19	M	Unknown	09Au02Aa
Morris	8	M	Child	09Au02Aa
Evan	5	M	Child	09Au02Aa
MORGAN, Semuel	18	M	Tailor	09Au02Aa
MCLOGHLAN, John	50	M	Laborer	09Au02Aa
QUIN, Patrick	54	M	Farmer	09Au02Aa
Margeret	40	F	Unknown	09Au02Aa
Mary	20	F	Unknown	09Au02Aa
Margeret	18	F	Unknown	09Au02Aa
Jane	10	F	Unknown	09Au02Aa
Catherine	8	F	Child	09Au02Aa
Francis	12	M	Unknown	09Au02Aa
Quin--, Mary	20	F	Servant	09Au02Aa
MURPHY, Patrick	17	M	Laborer	09Au02Aa
DUNNING, James	40	M	Farmer	09Au02Aa
Matilda	27	F	Unknown	09Au02Aa
John	6	M	Child	09Au02Aa
Henry	3	M	Child	09Au02Aa
Eliza	.00	F	Infant	09Au02Aa
COLERALLE, Patrick	36	M	Mason	09Au02Aa
Catherine	30	F	Unknown	09Au02Aa
PARKIN, Matthew	20	M	Mason	09Au02Aa
Anne	18	F	Unknown	09Au02Aa
MCMANUS, James	16	M	Laborer	09Au02Aa
GILLEN, Catherine	40	F	Servant	09Au02Aa
KENRICK, Ellen	24	F	Servant	09Au02Aa
SULLIVAN, Patrick	27	M	Laborer	09Au02Aa
CORRIE, John	60	M	Tailor	09Au02Aa
Ann	50	F	Unknown	09Au02Aa
MCKEE, James	21	M	Farmer	09Au02Aa
Margeret	5	F	Child	09Au02Aa
SHANLEY, Catherine	19	F	Servant	09Au02Aa
DOYLE, William	28	M	Laborer	09Au02Aa
BRADY, Bridget	12	F	Servant	09Au02Aa
LYNCH, James	13	M	Laborer	09Au02Aa
BRADY, John	22	M	Laborer	09Au02Aa
Elizabeth	15	F	Unknown	09Au02Aa
FITZPATRICK, John	18	M	Mason	09Au02Aa
PURTLIN, Miles	17	M	Weaver	09Au02Aa
CAMERON, Ann	18	F	Servant	09Au02Aa
MCGIVERN, Mary	20	F	Servant	09Au02Aa
TURBY, Ann	20	F	Servant	09Au02Aa
DONOHOE, John	23	M	Laborer	09Au02Aa
CARTY, Bridget	18	F	Servant	09Au02Aa
MCGIVERN, Rose	50	F	Unknown	09Au02Aa
Died-At-Sea				
Mary	18	F	Unknown	09Au02Aa
FITZPATRICK, Ann	20	F	Servant	09Au02Aa
GURNEY, Bridget	20	F	Servant	09Au02Aa
MCNAMEE, Ann	26	F	Servant	09Au02Aa
SORT, Samuel	30	M	Tailor	09Au02Aa
TURNER, George	28	M	Mason	09Au02Aa
INNIS, Robert	30	M	Mason	09Au02Aa
CARLIN, Margeret	30	F	Servant	09Au02Aa
MURPHY, Elizabeth	20	F	Servant	09Au02Aa
RAMSAY, Catherine	24	F	Servant	09Au02Aa
Rose	18	F	Servant	09Au02Aa
MCNALLY, Michael	26	M	Laborer	09Au02Aa
KENNY, Michael	22	M	Mason	09Au02Aa
MCCARTY, Peter	15	M	Laborer	09Au02Aa
HUTCHINSON, Biddy	24	F	Servant	09Au02Aa
MCCORMICK, John	28	M	Laborer	09Au02Aa
MOROAN, Betty	22	F	Servant	09Au02Aa
GALLAGHER, Hugh	25	M	Laborer	09Au02Aa
YOUNG, C.R.	5	M	Child	09Au02Aa
Harriet	3	F	Child	09Au02Aa
Robert	.00	M	Infant	09Au02Aa
John	40	M	Doctor	09Au02Aa
Ann	35	F	Unknown	09Au02Aa
Emma	12	F	Unknown	09Au02Aa
Ellen	10	F	Unknown	09Au02Aa
Mary	8	F	Child	09Au02Aa

QUEEN-OF-THE-WEST 10 AUGUST 1849

From Liverpool

NAMES OF PASSENGERS	AGE	SEX	OCCUPATIONS	DATE PORT SHIP
FITZGERALD, Fra.	48	M	Farmer	10Au02Ao
U (W)	46	F	None	10Au02Ao
Henry	16	M	None	10Au02Ao
Isab.	13	F	None	10Au02Ao
Eliza	11	F	None	10Au02Ao
Han.	8	F	Child	10Au02Ao
Charlotte	4	F	Child	10Au02Ao
John	.00	M	Infant	10Au02Ao
MCDONALD, Mat.	30	M	Farmer	10Au02Ao
Eliza	11	F	None	10Au02Ao
HALEY, Judy	28	F	None	10Au02Ao
KELCHER, Margt.	20	F	Servant	10Au02Ao
GEOGHAN, Lucy	29	F	None	10Au02Ao
WASLEY, Mary	30	F	None	10Au02Ao
Ja.H.	10	M	None	10Au02Ao
Mary-A.	.00	F	Infant	10Au02Ao
MOOR, U	4	F	Child	10Au02Ao
U	2	F	Child	10Au02Ao
JOHNSTON, Margt.	16	F	None	10Au02Ao
MATHEWS, Maria	17	F	None	10Au02Ao
Margt.	11	F	None	10Au02Ao
Wm.	13	M	None	10Au02Ao
GRAHAM, Wm.	25	M	None	10Au02Ao
U (W)	25	F	None	10Au02Ao
CASEY, U	27	M	Surveyor	10Au02Ao
Cath.	20	F	None	10Au02Ao

NAMES OF PASSENGERS	AGE	SEX	OCCUPATIONS	DATE PORT SHIP
CASEY, Edwd.	2	M	Child	10Au02Ao
Rose	.00	F	Infant	10Au02Ao
DANIEL, Richd.	24	M	Porter	10Au02Ao
U	20	F	None	10Au02Ao
Mary	.00	F	Infant	10Au02Ao
BURNE, Pat	20	M	Carpenter	10Au02Ao
DWYER, Thos.	25	M	Carpenter	10Au02Ao
CONNOR, J.	20	F	None	10Au02Ao
MURPHY, Ter.	30	M	Saddler	10Au02Ao
Mary	26	F	None	10Au02Ao
Cath.	5	F	Child	10Au02Ao
Honor	.00	F	Infant	10Au02Ao
MANNING, Cath.	22	F	None	10Au02Ao
Mary	30	F	None	10Au02Ao
Wm.	16	M	None	10Au02Ao
Dan.	12	M	None	10Au02Ao
DONOHUE, Thos.	30	M	Shoemaker	10Au02Ao
COCKREL, Pat.	32	M	Farmer	10Au02Ao
CLARKE, Thos.	21	M	Printer	10Au02Ao
Ann	23	F	None	10Au02Ao
GILL, Jas.	20	M	Laborer	10Au02Ao
Brid.	21	F	Laborer	10Au02Ao
Peggy	18	F	Laborer	10Au02Ao
Pat	12	M	Laborer	10Au02Ao
FITZPATRICK, Mary	14	F	None	10Au02Ao
WALSH, Mary	20	F	None	10Au02Ao
Mary	18	F	None	10Au02Ao
Brid.	13	F	None	10Au02Ao
BURKE, Mary	16	F	None	10Au02Ao
HAGAN, Thos.	24	M	Laborer	10Au02Ao
Brid.	20	F	None	10Au02Ao
MCHEON, Dan.	18	M	Laborer	10Au02Ao
FLAHERTY, Honor	18	F	None	10Au02Ao
MAHONEY, Michael	40	M	Laborer	10Au02Ao
BRIEN, John	25	M	Laborer	10Au02Ao
Julia	30	F	None	10Au02Ao
DALY, Jas.	25	M	Laborer	10Au02Ao
WHELELAN, Mat	17	M	Laborer	10Au02Ao
Pat	52	M	Laborer	10Au02Ao
Chas.	23	M	Laborer	10Au02Ao
Bessy	18	F	None	10Au02Ao
STAUNTON, John	20	M	Laborer	10Au02Ao
Margt.	17	F	None	10Au02Ao
MINCHAM, Thos.	23	M	Currier	10Au02Ao
METTAM, Chas.	25	M	Architect	10Au02Ao
Frances	20	F	None	10Au02Ao
Wm.	6	M	Child	10Au02Ao
Louisa	3	F	Child	10Au02Ao
Cath.	.00	F	Infant	10Au02Ao
MCDANIEL, John	16	M	None	10Au02Ao
MAHER, Michael	30	M	Laborer	10Au02Ao
DEE, Julia	60	F	None	10Au02Ao
Julia	24	F	None	10Au02Ao
Mary-A.	5	F	Child	10Au02Ao
MAHONEY, Margt.	60	F	None	10Au02Ao
Honora	15	F	None	10Au02Ao
Pat	27	M	None	10Au02Ao
MULLEN, Ann	22	F	None	10Au02Ao
MCPHILLIP, John	21	M	Carpenter	10Au02Ao
BARRY, Cath.	30	F	None	10Au02Ao
Wm.	10	M	None	10Au02Ao
MARKS, Ellen	28	F	None	10Au02Ao
SULLIVAN, Wm.	4	M	Child	10Au02Ao
DICKEY, Jas.	13	M	None	10Au02Ao
Robt.	11	M	None	10Au02Ao
Ann	8	F	Child	10Au02Ao
CANTY, Johan.	18	F	None	10Au02Ao
GRIFFIN, Mary	18	F	None	10Au02Ao
CONOLLY, Tim	17	M	None	10Au02Ao
MOONEY, Julia	22	F	None	10Au02Ao
DELANEY, Mary	50	F	None	10Au02Ao
Thos.	13	M	None	10Au02Ao
Pat	11	M	None	10Au02Ao
Margt.	8	F	Child	10Au02Ao
Mary	6	F	Child	10Au02Ao
SIMONS, Mary	22	F	None	10Au02Ao
HART, Rose	22	F	None	10Au02Ao
Mary	3	F	Child	10Au02Ao
MCCORMICK, Brid.	18	F	None	10Au02Ao
KILLILEA, John	25	M	Laborer	10Au02Ao
MAHER, Denis	30	M	Farmer	10Au02Ao
Sally	28	F	None	10Au02Ao
Jas.	.00	M	Infant	10Au02Ao
DOOLAN, Pat	24	M	Laborer	10Au02Ao
U (W)	20	F	None	10Au02Ao
DEVYRE, Martin	30	M	Laborer	10Au02Ao
FRANE, Jas.	24	M	Mason	10Au02Ao
FAULS, Melinda	20	F	None	10Au02Ao
WOODS, Mary	20	F	None	10Au02Ao
MCCARTY, David	28	M	Laborer	10Au02Ao
MONOHAN, Thos.	40	M	Tailor	10Au02Ao
Brid.	35	F	None	10Au02Ao
MONAHAN, Mary	8	F	Child	10Au02Ao
Eliza	6	F	Child	10Au02Ao
GRAY, Nancy	16	F	None	10Au02Ao
Ann	11	F	None	10Au02Ao
SIMPSON, James	34	M	Laborer	10Au02Ao
Sam	19	M	Laborer	10Au02Ao
Isab.	20	F	None	10Au02Ao
HANLEY, Mary	30	F	None	10Au02Ao
Pat	8	M	Child	10Au02Ao
Margt.	5	F	Child	10Au02Ao
LARKIN, Thos.	20	M	Laborer	10Au02Ao
Eliza	16	F	None	10Au02Ao
Brid.	13	F	None	10Au02Ao
J.	10	M	None	10Au02Ao
CLARKE, Jas.	19	M	Laborer	10Au02Ao
MOHAN, Phil.	17	M	Laborer	10Au02Ao
REILLY, Rose	18	F	None	10Au02Ao
DONOHUE, Phil.	5	M	Child	10Au02Ao
SOMERVILLE, Alex.	20	M	Laborer	10Au02Ao
CUNNINGHAM, Johan.	17	M	None	10Au02Ao
CLARKE, Pat.	18	M	Laborer	10Au02Ao
NIXON, And.Jas.	23	M	Chandler	10Au02Ao
SMITH, Rose	16	F	None	10Au02Ao
ROBERTS, Sarah	26	F	None	10Au02Ao
PURCEL, Sarah	20	F	None	10Au02Ao
Cath.	25	F	None	10Au02Ao
LAKE, Cath.	28	F	None	10Au02Ao
SUMNERS, Bartly	20	M	Servant	10Au02Ao
FITZGERALD, Henry	27	M	Merchant	10Au02Ao
KELLY, Mary	14	F	None	10Au02Ao
DONNELLY, Mary	20	F	None	10Au02Ao
CALLIN, Ann	18	F	None	10Au02Ao
WALLACE, Mary	20	F	None	10Au02Ao
Rebec.	22	F	None	10Au02Ao
KELLY, Richd.	15	M	None	10Au02Ao
HAMMILL, Ellen	30	F	None	10Au02Ao
Ann	24	F	None	10Au02Ao
GIVAN, Wm.	24	M	Stctr	10Au02Ao
ONEILL, Pat.	26	M	Stctr	10Au02Ao
Ellen	26	F	None	10Au02Ao
BOLAN, Eliza	18	F	None	10Au02Ao
MCGEE, Jas.E.	00	M	Unknown	10Au02Ao
U (W)	00	F	Unknown	10Au02Ao
Mary	00	F	Unknown	10Au02Ao
BODEN, Mary	00	F	Unknown	10Au02Ao
FITZGIBBON, Thos.	00	M	Unknown	10Au02Ao

BROOKSBY 10 AUGUST 1849

From Glasgow

NAMES OF PASSENGERS	AGE	SEX	OCCUPATIONS	DATE PORT SHIP
MULBRINE, Christopher	14	M	None	10Au04Aj

WATERLOO 10 AUGUST 1849

From Liverpool

NAMES OF PASSENGERS	AGE	SEX	OCCUPATIONS	DATE PORT SHIP
BATEMAN, Eliza	27	F	Lady	10Au02Of
GREEN, E.	36	U	Pvmt	10Au02Of
E.	11	U	Unknown	10Au02Of
CAMPBELL, George	28	M	Pvmt	10Au02Of
Harriet	21	F	Unknown	10Au02Of
DOVE, Wm.	22	M	Farmer	10Au02Of
ANDERSON, J.	50	M	Merchant	10Au02Of
DUDLEY, W.R.A.	22	M	None	10Au02Of
ALLEXANDER, Alex.	30	M	Farmer	10Au02Of
Sarah	22	F	Unknown	10Au02Of
Sarah-Jane	.03	F	Infant	10Au02Of
FIRMER, W.	17	U	None	10Au02Of
HAYLEY, C.L.	19	U	Unknown	10Au02Of
KNOX, G.A.	20	U	Unknown	10Au02Of
CHAPMAN, M.A.	45	U	Unknown	10Au02Of
Ellen	16	F	Unknown	10Au02Of
William	11	M	Unknown	10Au02Of
ENTWISTLE, Ellen	24	F	Laborer	10Au02Of
CORMICK, A.	24	U	Unknown	10Au02Of
KEALY, E.	24	U	Unknown	10Au02Of
WOOD, S.	23	U	Unknown	10Au02Of
HARRISON, R.	20	U	Unknown	10Au02Of
HUMPHREYS, W.	23	U	Unknown	10Au02Of
ALEXANDER, J.	30	U	Unknown	10Au02Of
RYAN, T.	50	U	Unknown	10Au02Of
M.	50	U	Unknown	10Au02Of
Margaret	11	F	Unknown	10Au02Of
Edmond	9	M	Child	10Au02Of
Jerry	7	M	Child	10Au02Of
Timothy	3	M	Child	10Au02Of
PIERCE, W.	34	U	Unknown	10Au02Of
William	65	M	Unknown	10Au02Of
FAY, Dennis	25	M	Unknown	10Au02Of
BRANNAN, M.	20	U	Unknown	10Au02Of
MURPHY, J.	35	U	Unknown	10Au02Of
RIORDON, H.	17	U	Unknown	10Au02Of
THORNTON, M.	29	U	Unknown	10Au02Of
MCGARY, M.	32	U	Unknown	10Au02Of
Mariah	25	F	Unknown	10Au02Of
MCDERMOTT, A.	23	U	Unknown	10Au02Of
GETHEN, E.	22	U	Unknown	10Au02Of
ORIORDON, J.	20	U	Unknown	10Au02Of
AYER, D.	20	U	Unknown	10Au02Of
RYAN, Patt	18	M	Unknown	10Au02Of
METAS, John	22	M	Unknown	10Au02Of
CARTER, R.	36	U	Laborer	10Au02Of
DOON, J.	35	U	Laborer	10Au02Of
Catherine	32	F	Unknown	10Au02Of
William	12	M	Unknown	10Au02Of
John	9	M	Child	10Au02Of
Joseph	7	M	Child	10Au02Of
Christian	5	M	Child	10Au02Of
Robert	.10	M	Infant	10Au02Of
JONES, C.	26	U	Unknown	10Au02Of
MURCURDY, J.	20	U	Unknown	10Au02Of
BURK, John	50	M	Unknown	10Au02Of
Emaly	23	F	Unknown	10Au02Of
Eliza	21	F	Unknown	10Au02Of
MCWILLIAMS, J.	35	U	Unknown	10Au02Of
Jessey	34	U	Unknown	10Au02Of
Hugh	11	U	Unknown	10Au02Of
James	8	M	Child	10Au02Of
SCOTT, E.	28	U	Unknown	10Au02Of
GILMARTIN, J.	48	U	Unknown	10Au02Of
John	24	M	Unknown	10Au02Of
Margaret	22	F	Unknown	10Au02Of
Michel	20	M	Unknown	10Au02Of
Mary	18	F	Unknown	10Au02Of
Patrick	13	M	Unknown	10Au02Of
James	12	M	Unknown	10Au02Of
BURK, John	2	M	Child	10Au02Of
RYAN, J.	22	U	Unknown	10Au02Of
Ann	20	F	Unknown	10Au02Of
Margaret	20	F	Unknown	10Au02Of
BUCK, E.	21	U	Unknown	10Au02Of
PADEN, J.	25	U	Unknown	10Au02Of
Hannah	22	F	Unknown	10Au02Of
CRAIG, S.	25	U	Unknown	10Au02Of
DAVIS, R.	39	U	Unknown	10Au02Of
Mary	50	F	Unknown	10Au02Of
Ellen	9	F	Child	10Au02Of
Catherine	6	F	Child	10Au02Of
John	4	M	Child	10Au02Of
ARMITAGE, R.	21	U	Unknown	10Au02Of
TROWN, J.	64	U	Unknown	10Au02Of
MURPHY, P.	30	U	Unknown	10Au02Of
Ellen	34	F	Unknown	10Au02Of
BRENNAN, A.	60	U	Unknown	10Au02Of
Mary	12	F	Unknown	10Au02Of
DUNN, J.	25	U	Unknown	10Au02Of
Margaret	26	F	Unknown	10Au02Of
DORAN, E.	23	F	Unknown	10Au02Of
Ann	20	F	Unknown	10Au02Of
Mary	19	F	Unknown	10Au02Of
CORMAICK, C.	24	U	Unknown	10Au02Of
BRONAN, P.	35	U	Unknown	10Au02Of
CARROLL, C.	26	U	Unknown	10Au02Of
FIGIN, A.	48	U	Unknown	10Au02Of
Owin	28	U	Unknown	10Au02Of
LAXTON, J.	49	U	Unknown	10Au02Of
Rebecha	48	F	Unknown	10Au02Of
RIGHT, W.	34	U	Unknown	10Au02Of
TODD, Sarah	28	F	Laborer	10Au02Of
William	26	M	Unknown	10Au02Of
Edward	18	M	Unknown	10Au02Of
LAPTHORNE, W.	29	M	Unknown	10Au02Of
Hannah	24	F	Unknown	10Au02Of
BECHET, J.	26	U	Unknown	10Au02Of
MURPHY, A.	19	U	Unknown	10Au02Of
John	17	M	Unknown	10Au02Of
KINLAND, Hugh	26	M	Unknown	10Au02Of
MANGAN, P.	30	U	Unknown	10Au02Of
DADSON, J.	44	U	Unknown	10Au02Of
STANWAT, S.	50	U	Unknown	10Au02Of
BUCK, J.	50	U	Unknown	10Au02Of
William	25	M	Unknown	10Au02Of
Thomas	20	M	Unknown	10Au02Of
Catherine	18	F	Unknown	10Au02Of
Mary	16	F	Unknown	10Au02Of
Edmond	12	M	Unknown	10Au02Of
James	10	M	Unknown	10Au02Of
MARTIN, W.	18	U	Unknown	10Au02Of
EVANS, S.	24	U	Unknown	10Au02Of
John	24	M	Unknown	10Au02Of
John	2	M	Unknown	10Au02Of
COCHS, R.	18	U	Unknown	10Au02Of
CAHILL, P.	30	U	Unknown	10Au02Of
Mary	28	F	Unknown	10Au02Of

NAMES OF PASSENGERS	AGE	SEX	OCCUPATIONS	DATE PORT SHIP
CAHILL, Margaret	4	M	Child	10Au020f
Thomas	.10	M	Infant	10Au020f
HANLEY, P.	30	U	Unknown	10Au020f
LEACY, P.	20	U	Unknown	10Au020f
MURRAY, P.	30	U	Unknown	10Au020f
CHRISTY, J.	22	U	Unknown	10Au020f
BOYL, E.	20	U	Unknown	10Au020f
LAMBERT, M.	23	U	Unknown	10Au020f
Hellina	24	F	Unknown	10Au020f
BOYL, M.	18	U	Unknown	10Au020f
COOK, W.	10	U	Unknown	10Au020f
MYRES, E.	23	U	Unknown	10Au020f
MARTHA, W.	13	U	Unknown	10Au020f
DILLON, W.	60	U	Unknown	10Au020f
Mary	54	F	Unknown	10Au020f
Maria	25	F	Unknown	10Au020f
Ellen	13	F	Unknown	10Au020f
MURPHY, M.	58	U	Unknown	10Au020f
M.A.	20	U	Unknown	10Au020f
FINLEY, C.	23	U	Unknown	10Au020f
COSTELLO, R.	32	U	Unknown	10Au020f
NOLAND, T.	30	U	Unknown	10Au020f
DUNN, J.	13	U	Unknown	10Au020f
KINDER, J.	39	U	Unknown	10Au020f
Isabella	8	F	Child	10Au020f
LEONARD, P.	26	U	Unknown	10Au020f
Bridget	20	F	Unknown	10Au020f
John	28	M	Unknown	10Au020f
HOWARD, T.	20	U	Unknown	10Au020f
BROWN, G.	27	U	Unknown	10Au020f
FOOLEY, P.	28	U	Unknown	10Au020f
Allice	27	F	Unknown	10Au020f
MARTHA, C.	11	U	Laborer	10Au020f
FITZPATRICK, J.	34	U	Unknown	10Au020f
Catherine	18	F	Unknown	10Au020f
PEARS, John	28	M	Unknown	10Au020f
Ellen	26	F	Unknown	10Au020f
William	7	M	Child	10Au020f
Dorothy	3	F	Child	10Au020f
SHERDAN, W.	35	U	Unknown	10Au020f
HART, J.	23	U	Unknown	10Au020f
LAWRA, J.	33	U	Unknown	10Au020f
Patt	12	M	Unknown	10Au020f
DONAHOE, M.	30	U	Unknown	10Au020f
MORTON, J.	18	U	Unknown	10Au020f
EMMETT, P.	28	U	Unknown	10Au020f
SMITH, J.	39	U	Unknown	10Au020f
Lidia	29	F	Unknown	10Au020f
Fanny	2	F	Child	10Au020f
F.	26	U	Unknown	10Au020f
MILISH, G.	21	U	Unknown	10Au020f
FULAHOUSE, R.	19	U	Unknown	10Au020f
Amelia	14	F	Unknown	10Au020f
CODD, P.	38	U	Unknown	10Au020f
Ellen	25	F	Unknown	10Au020f
MULVAHELE, J.	22	U	Unknown	10Au020f
BINN, J.	14	U	Unknown	10Au020f
GODSEFT, E.	28	U	Unknown	10Au020f
COLLIER, D.	50	U	Unknown	10Au020f
GAGG, J.	33	U	Unknown	10Au020f
Ann	2	F	Child	10Au020f
J.	.07	U	Infant	10Au020f
ADAMS, A.	50	U	Unknown	10Au020f
Maud	20	F	Unknown	10Au020f
Mary	13	F	Unknown	10Au020f
GAGG, W.	29	U	Unknown	10Au020f
MCDONALD, T.	23	U	Unknown	10Au020f
REYNOLDS, P.	30	U	Unknown	10Au020f
Catherine	28	F	Unknown	10Au020f
Mary	26	F	Unknown	10Au020f
Mary	.10	F	Infant	10Au020f
SMITH, B.	26	U	Unknown	10Au020f
GUIN, C.	21	U	Unknown	10Au020f
FLANNIGAN, J.	28	U	Unknown	10Au020f
Allice	23	F	Unknown	10Au020f
FLANNIGAN, Rose	22	F	Unknown	10Au020f
Rose	8	F	Child	10Au020f
Biddy	5	F	Child	10Au020f
William	3	M	Child	10Au020f
RATICAN, H.	36	U	Unknown	10Au020f
Dennis	38	M	Unknown	10Au020f
BEACHEN, J.P.	58	U	Unknown	10Au020f
THOMAS, H.	21	U	Unknown	10Au020f
HAYS, J.	21	U	Unknown	10Au020f
BIRCH, J.	19	U	Unknown	10Au020f
A.	21	U	Unknown	10Au020f
Margaret	10	F	Unknown	10Au020f
Ann	21	F	Unknown	10Au020f
HIGGINS, P.T.	36	U	Laborer	10Au020f
WALKER, W.	20	U	Laborer	10Au020f
G.	17	U	Unknown	10Au020f
JONES, H.	22	U	Unknown	10Au020f
HAMBLETON, C.	8	U	Child	10Au020f
ROUNDTON, M.	24	U	Unknown	10Au020f
PEEL, H.	19	U	Unknown	10Au020f
Thomas	24	M	Unknown	10Au020f
John	19	M	Unknown	10Au020f
MURRY, W.	24	U	Unknown	10Au020f
WAKEFIELD, T.	26	U	Unknown	10Au020f
Elizabeth	26	F	Unknown	10Au020f
James	7	M	Child	10Au020f
GOOLDING, W.	15	U	Unknown	10Au020f
DUNKINSON, R.	28	U	Unknown	10Au020f
MULLER, M.J.	20	U	Unknown	10Au020f
Mary	17	F	Unknown	10Au020f
FORD, R.	30	U	Unknown	10Au020f
COLBERT, R.	20	U	Unknown	10Au020f
LYNES, L.	25	U	Unknown	10Au020f
CONNIS, M.	25	U	Unknown	10Au020f
FOOT, W.	50	U	Unknown	10Au020f
William	23	M	Unknown	10Au020f
NORTHCOAT, H.	30	U	Unknown	10Au020f
Mary-Ann	30	F	Unknown	10Au020f
ONEAL, P.	34	U	Unknown	10Au020f
Edward	15	M	Unknown	10Au020f
WHYSELE, G.	38	U	Unknown	10Au020f
MONARCH, J.	40	U	Unknown	10Au020f
Bridget	40	F	Unknown	10Au020f
John	14	M	Unknown	10Au020f
Mary	12	F	Unknown	10Au020f
Rose	10	F	Unknown	10Au020f
Thomas	4	M	Child	10Au020f
LEONARD, M.	24	U	Unknown	10Au020f
ROSE, G.	25	U	Unknown	10Au020f
WILL, S.	45	U	Unknown	10Au020f
M.	45	U	Unknown	10Au020f
CRIBBIN, J.	24	U	Unknown	10Au020f
LOCHRAN, M.	40	U	Unknown	10Au020f
Rose	18	F	Unknown	10Au020f
Mary	13	F	Unknown	10Au020f
MONAHAN, P.	50	U	Unknown	10Au020f
NOLAN, Ann	21	F	Unknown	10Au020f
NORMAN, P.	31	U	Unknown	10Au020f
BATCHELOR, J.	50	U	Unknown	10Au020f
CORR, L.	33	U	Unknown	10Au020f
Mary	18	F	Unknown	10Au020f
REVILE, J.	31	U	Unknown	10Au020f
HILL, J.	29	U	Unknown	10Au020f
ONEAL, J.	19	U	Unknown	10Au020f
BARRY, J.	23	U	Unknown	10Au020f
SMITH, M.	30	U	Unknown	10Au020f
CORDY, M.	15	U	Unknown	10Au020f
WHITE, T.	50	U	Unknown	10Au020
Ellen	17	F	Laborer	10Au020
Michel	15	M	Unknown	10Au020
James	10	M	Unknown	10Au020
ORANGE, W.	30	U	Unknown	10Au020
ONEAL, T.	20	U	Unknown	10Au020
OBRIAN, M.	20	U	Unknown	10Au020
MORAN, M.	19	U	Unknown	10Au020

NAMES OF PASSENGERS	AGE	SEX	OCCUPATIONS	DATE PORT SHIP
ARMSTRONG, J.	22	U	Unknown	10Au020f
RAYNOR, J.	26	U	Unknown	10Au020f
TRAYNOR, A.	20	U	Unknown	10Au020f
MCPAIK, J.	19	U	Unknown	10Au020f
DWIER, T.	17	U	Unknown	10Au020f
MOONEY, P.	18	U	Unknown	10Au020f
Ann	34	F	Unknown	10Au020f
QUIGLEY, M.	30	U	Unknown	10Au020f
MORAN, M.	40	U	Unknown	10Au020f
Ann	22	F	Unknown	10Au020f
JOHNSON, J.	20	F	Unknown	10Au020f
TREHEY, B.	17	U	Unknown	10Au020f
COHEN, M.	30	U	Unknown	10Au020f
Ellen	27	F	Unknown	10Au020f
J.	5	U	Child	10Au020f
COCHNAN, H.	15	U	Unknown	10Au020f
MURPHY, C.	40	U	Unknown	10Au020f
Michel	7	M	Child	10Au020f
Francis	4	M	Child	10Au020f
HARAN, M.	18	U	Unknown	10Au020f

PILGRIM 11 AUGUST 1849

From Glasgow

NAMES OF PASSENGERS	AGE	SEX	OCCUPATIONS	DATE PORT SHIP
JAMIESON, Alex.	45	M	Merchant	11Au040g
U-Mrs.	40	F	Unknown	11Au040g
Robert	29	M	Unknown	11Au040g
Wm.	25	M	Unknown	11Au040g
Margt.	23	F	Unknown	11Au040g
Elizabeth	20	F	Unknown	11Au040g
David	17	M	Unknown	11Au040g
Wilson	13	M	Unknown	11Au040g
John	10	M	Unknown	11Au040g
MCCALLUM, Arch.	32	M	Miner	11Au040g
U-Mrs.	26	F	Unknown	11Au040g
Arch.	4	M	Child	11Au040g
Margt.	2	F	Child	11Au040g
Mary	.09	F	Infant	11Au040g
BROWN, James	33	M	Unknown	11Au040g
LEVIE, John	22	M	Blacksmith	11Au040g
U-Mrs.	24	F	Unknown	11Au040g
MILLER, Wm.	24	M	Blr	11Au040g
GALLACHER, Neill	45	M	Shoemaker	11Au040g
DOUNER, James	25	M	Weaver	11Au040g
OAKLY, George	35	M	Unknown	11Au040g
POWERS, James	24	M	Unknown	11Au040g
HEYENS, Robert	35	M	Unknown	11Au040g
LOCKENT, Wm.	23	M	Unknown	11Au040g
ALEXANDER, Rober.	26	M	Gdnr	11Au040g
U-Mrs.	25	F	Unknown	11Au040g
MORRIS, Alex.	20	M	Weaver	11Au040g
MCFURGUSON, John	17	M	Unknown	11Au040g
PATERSON, George	25	M	Unknown	11Au040g
MORTON, Hugh	26	M	Unknown	11Au040g
U-Mrs.	25	F	Unknown	11Au040g
RUSSEL, Alex.	26	M	Unknown	11Au040g
HERUN, Isabela	30	F	Unknown	11Au040g
William	20	M	Unknown	11Au040g
WILD, Wm.R.	25	M	Unknown	11Au040g
CLOUDE, Peter	27	M	Unknown	11Au040g
HUNTER, John	24	M	Unknown	11Au040g
OURIE, Wm.	30	M	Shopman	11Au040g
U-Mrs.	28	F	Unknown	11Au040g
U-Mrs.Sr.	60	F	Unknown	11Au040g
Wm.	4	M	Child	11Au040g
MCKERNON, Jane	24	F	Unknown	11Au040g
ROBERTSON, John	30	M	Merchant	11Au040g
INGLIS, Wm.	21	M	Brf	11Au040g
WILSON, Thomas-A.	24	M	Unknown	11Au040g
HEFFIE, Wm.	27	M	Unknown	11Au040g
MALON, Duncan	32	M	Unknown	11Au040g
MCGILL, Thomas	23	M	Unknown	11Au040g
TAILOR, James	26	M	Carpenter	11Au040g
MCGREGOR, Charles	27	M	Unknown	11Au040g
MACKIE, Alex.	32	M	Unknown	11Au040g
U-Mrs.	31	F	Unknown	11Au040g
FRASER, U-Mrs.	70	F	Unknown	11Au040g
ROSS, Cath.	38	F	Unknown	11Au040g
MACKIE, John	6	M	Child	11Au040g
James	.09	M	Infant	11Au040g
MCLELLAN, John	40	M	Unknown	11Au040g

BROTHERS 10 AUGUST 1849

From Glasgow

NAMES OF PASSENGERS	AGE	SEX	OCCUPATIONS	DATE PORT SHIP
REMOR, Robert	49	M	Farmer	10Au04Hd
LONG, Mary	30	F	Servant	10Au04Hd
WATERS, James	50	M	Laborer	10Au04Hd
U-Mrs.	49	F	None	10Au04Hd
Samuel	19	M	None	10Au04Hd
Ann	14	F	None	10Au04Hd
MCCUE, Malcolm	21	M	Laborer	10Au04Hd
MARSHALL, Joshua	51	M	Farmer	10Au04Hd
U-Mrs.	50	F	None	10Au04Hd
Matilda	15	F	None	10Au04Hd
Sarah	13	F	None	10Au04Hd
Joseph	11	M	None	10Au04Hd
John	7	M	Child	10Au04Hd
HARVEY, John	29	M	None	10Au04Hd
U-Mrs.	28	F	None	10Au04Hd
Patrick	00	M	None	10Au04Hd
Catherine	18	F	None	10Au04Hd

AMERICA 10 AUGUST 1849

From Liverpool

NAMES OF PASSENGERS	AGE	SEX	OCCUPATIONS	DATE PORT SHIP
KINGSTON, Arth.M.	54	M	Gentleman	10Au02Eb
GAMBLE, R.A.	35	M	Merchant	10Au02Eb

MARMION 10 AUGUST 1849

From Liverpool

NAMES OF PASSENGERS	AGE	SEX	OCCUPATIONS	DATE PORT SHIP
CONROY, Mary	18	F	Servant	10Au02Cw
Elisa	14	F	Servant	10Au02Cw
Andrew	11	M	Servant	10Au02Cw
HENNESSY, James	30	M	Laborer	10Au02Cw
JORDAN, Celia	20	F	Servant	10Au02Cw
WAX, Patrick	30	M	Laborer	10Au02Cw
KARN, Jane	40	F	None	10Au02Cw
Mary	00	F	None	10Au02Cw
Ann	00	F	None	10Au02Cw
Agnes	00	F	None	10Au02Cw

NAMES OF PASSENGERS	AGE	SEX	OCCUPATIONS	DATE PORT SHIP
SMITH, Thomas	16	M	Tailor	10Au02Cw
KELLY, Ann	20	M	Farmer	10Au02Cw
DUNN, William	26	M	Maurer	10Au02Cw
REDMOND, Cath.	42	F	None	10Au02Cw
Bridget	20	F	Servant	10Au02Cw
GAIN, Bridget	25	F	Servant	10Au02Cw
RILEY, Edward	36	M	Laborer	10Au02Cw
MCDONNELL, Edwd.	22	M	Laborer	10Au02Cw
ROURKE, Christopher	26	M	Farmer	10Au02Cw
FLANNIGAN, Michael	23	M	Farmer	10Au02Cw
WALSH, John	25	M	Laborer	10Au02Cw
Ann	25	F	None	10Au02Cw
HANNIGAN, William	30	M	Laborer	10Au02Cw
RYAN, Matt	48	M	Farmer	10Au02Cw
GARRETT, Ellen	25	F	Servant	10Au02Cw
DALEY, Hugh	20	M	Shoemaker	10Au02Cw
ELLIS, Hannah	18	F	Servant	10Au02Cw
CROWE, Patt	25	M	Laborer	10Au02Cw
William	20	M	Laborer	10Au02Cw
Michl.	18	M	Laborer	10Au02Cw
Bridget	21	F	None	10Au02Cw
Winnefred	19	F	None	10Au02Cw
Ann	19	F	None	10Au02Cw
Ellen	16	F	None	10Au02Cw
Amy	14	F	None	10Au02Cw
Margaret	15	F	None	10Au02Cw
EAGAN, Thos.	20	M	Laborer	10Au02Cw
HOGAN, James	30	M	Miller	10Au02Cw
Julia	21	F	None	10Au02Cw
WODRIK, Morgan	21	M	Laborer	10Au02Cw
FITZGERALD, Thos.	26	M	Servant	10Au02Cw
HENESSY, Marg.	20	F	None	10Au02Cw
Michael	7	M	Child	10Au02Cw
FITZGERALD, Maria	20	F	Servant	10Au02Cw
FITZPATRICK, William	00	M	Laborer	10Au02Cw
DURK, Michael	31	M	Laborer	10Au02Cw
MATTIGAN, Patty	29	M	Laborer	10Au02Cw
Thomas	9	M	Child	10Au02Cw
Honora	6	F	Child	10Au02Cw
MCMAHON, Margt.	58	F	None	10Au02Cw
Bernard	30	M	Stone Mason	10Au02Cw
Hugh	20	M	Stone Mason	10Au02Cw
GANLEY, John	20	M	Shoemaker	10Au02Cw
DONNELLY, Elizabeth	20	F	Servant	10Au02Cw
DEADY, John	50	M	Farrier	10Au02Cw
Thos.	18	M	Laborer	10Au02Cw
Edmd.	16	M	Laborer	10Au02Cw
Michael	15	M	Laborer	10Au02Cw
Margaret	25	F	Servant	10Au02Cw
DUNN, John	30	M	Laborer	10Au02Cw
Catherine	24	F	None	10Au02Cw
Died-At-Sea				
Bridget	.00	F	Infant	10Au02Cw
RICE, John	65	M	Farmer	10Au02Cw
Margaret	18	F	None	10Au02Cw
Mary	16	F	None	10Au02Cw
Judy	15	F	None	10Au02Cw
Catherine	22	F	None	10Au02Cw
MCGRATT, John	22	M	Laborer	10Au02Cw
May	24	F	None	10Au02Cw
Ellen	20	F	None	10Au02Cw
Catherine	24	F	None	10Au02Cw
SMITH, Henry	21	M	Laborer	10Au02Cw
BRINE, John	29	M	Laborer	10Au02Cw
STEWART, Robert	19	M	Chandler	10Au02Cw
DELANEY, John	24	M	Laborer	10Au02Cw
REILY, Michael	24	M	Servant	10Au02Cw
Rose	24	F	Servant	10Au02Cw
MORGAN, John	28	M	Clerk	10Au02Cw
HENNABY, Michael	21	M	Laborer	10Au02Cw
CONWAY, Johanna	30	F	None	10Au02Cw
Michael	2	M	Child	10Au02Cw
KELLY, Eliza.	20	F	Servant	10Au02Cw
QUINN, Henry	18	M	Flaxdr	10Au02Cw
MCSHANE, William	18	M	Servant	10Au02Cw
MANGAN, Julia	35	M	Servant	10Au02Cw
SULLIVAN, Michael	30	M	Laborer	10Au02Cw
Michael	29	M	Laborer	10Au02Cw
Michael	6	M	Child	10Au02Cw
BANNETT, Thos.	26	M	Laborer	10Au02Cw
DRISCOLL, William	25	M	Laborer	10Au02Cw
CARROLL, John	21	M	Laborer	10Au02Cw
Patt	26	M	Laborer	10Au02Cw
BRENNAN, Marg.	20	F	Servant	10Au02Cw
Mary	21	F	Servant	10Au02Cw
KING, Honoria	19	F	Servant	10Au02Cw
HENNESSY, Ellen	20	F	Servant	10Au02Cw
GRADY, Elizabeth	21	F	Servant	10Au02Cw
EARLEY, Patk.	27	M	Crpw	10Au02Cw
RYAN, Jane	20	F	Servant	10Au02Cw
MCANLIFFE, Jeremiah	29	M	Laborer	10Au02Cw
Johanna	29	F	Laborer	10Au02Cw
TAYLOR, Richard	39	M	Shoemaker	10Au02Cw
George	20	M	Laborer	10Au02Cw
MCMAHON, Cath.	25	F	None	10Au02Cw
Bernard	.00	M	Infant	10Au02Cw
CARRELL, Dennis	35	M	Machinist	10Au02Cw
FLYNN, Michael	40	M	Laborer	10Au02Cw
Johanna	37	F	None	10Au02Cw
OBRIEN, Humphrey	50	M	Blacksmith	10Au02Cw
Ellen	17	F	None	10Au02Cw
Ellen	2	F	Child	10Au02Cw
Humphrey	16	M	None	10Au02Cw
Catherine	12	F	None	10Au02Cw
MCQUIN, Timothy	20	M	Laborer	10Au02Cw
SHEA, Johanna	5	F	Child	10Au02Cw
JOHNSTON, Bridget	40	F	None	10Au02Cw
Francis	21	M	Seaman	10Au02Cw
James	12	M	None	10Au02Cw
Mary-Ann	10	F	Child	10Au02Cw
Robert	8	M	Child	10Au02Cw
Henry	8	M	Child	10Au02Cw
PARRETT, Mary	20	F	Servant	10Au02Cw
FITZGERALD, Maurice	43	M	Laborer	10Au02Cw
Michael	8	M	Child	10Au02Cw
NOLAN, Jeremiah	21	M	Laborer	10Au02Cw
Margaret	20	F	Servant	10Au02Cw
Nancy	18	F	Servant	10Au02Cw
RIORDAN, Ellen	21	F	Servant	10Au02Cw
CONNOR, Simon	45	M	Farmer	10Au02Cw
Catherine	35	F	None	10Au02Cw
Barbara	12	F	None	10Au02Cw
DWYER, Richard	26	M	Groom	10Au02Cw
HERBERT, Marg.	40	F	Dressmaker	10Au02Cw
DONOVAN, Cath.	21	F	Servant	10Au02Cw
CURTIN, John	19	M	Laborer	10Au02Cw
DONOLAN, Michael	25	M	Laborer	10Au02Cw
OBREIN, Cath.	22	F	Servant	10Au02Cw
BURKE, Bridget	21	F	Servant	10Au02Cw
Bridget	.00	F	Infant	10Au02Cw
OCONNOR, Michael	20	M	Laborer	10Au02Cw
WALSH, David	24	M	Laborer	10Au02Cw
MORONEY, John	21	M	Laborer	10Au02Cw
BUNCE, Mary	14	F	Servant	10Au02Cw
FLYNN, John	45	M	Servant	10Au02Cw
SLEHAN, Thomas	22	M	Laborer	10Au02Cw
BURKLEY, James	19	M	Laborer	10Au02Cw
HENESSY, Michl.	35	M	Laborer	10Au02Cw
William	33	M	Laborer	10Au02Cw
PHILLIPS, Ann	26	F	Servant	10Au02Cw
GRAY, Matthew	25	M	Laborer	10Au02Cw
LYNCH, Owen	40	M	Laborer	10Au02Cw
BYRNE, Thomas	31	M	Shoemaker	10Au02Cw
DALTON, Edward	30	M	Laborer	10Au02Cw
Mary	50	F	Laborer	10Au02Cw
CARR, Chrles	21	M	Sawer	10Au02Cw
MURPHY, Cornelius	22	M	Laborer	10Au02Cw
KENNA, Michael	22	M	Laborer	10Au02Cw
BUTLER, Mary	18	F	Servant	10Au02Cw
RYAN, Phillip	24	M	Laborer	10Au02C

NAMES OF PASSENGERS	AGE	SEX	OCCUPATIONS	DATE PORT SHIP
HALLIAN, Patk.	30	M	Clerk	10Au02Cw
FILAN, James	30	M	Weaver	10Au02Cw
FOGARTY, Margt.	19	F	Servant	10Au02Cw
Nancy	20	F	Servant	10Au02Cw
CROSS, Marg.	17	F	Servant	10Au02Cw
TULLY, Andrew	30	M	Laborer	10Au02Cw
REILLY, Owen	30	M	Laborer	10Au02Cw
DELANY, Michael	45	M	Farmer	10Au02Cw
John	14	M	Farmer	10Au02Cw
Mary	10	F	Child	10Au02Cw
DUFFEY, Mary	30	F	Servant	10Au02Cw
BRADY, Mary	19	F	Servant	10Au02Cw
CORRIGAN, Cath.	20	F	Servant	10Au02Cw
FITZGERALD, Thos.	29	M	Carpenter	10Au02Cw
HALLEY, William	22	M	Laborer	10Au02Cw
MORISSY, John	30	M	Shoemaker	10Au02Cw
DUFFEY, Honora	20	F	Servant	10Au02Cw
HORN, Eliza.	24	F	Servant	10Au02Cw
COURTENAY, Martha	29	F	None	10Au02Cw
John	29	M	Farmer	10Au02Cw
CUNNINGHAM, Patk.	30	M	Maurer	10Au02Cw
Rose	30	F	None	10Au02Cw
Cath.	20	F	None	10Au02Cw
May	16	F	None	10Au02Cw
RUDDY, Patk.	20	M	Rope Maker	10Au02Cw
CAFFRAY, Michael	38	M	Plumber	10Au02Cw
SHEA, Bridget	18	F	Servant	10Au02Cw
CONROY, Jane	55	F	Servant	10Au02Cw
John	26	M	Laborer	10Au02Cw
Patrick	23	M	Laborer	10Au02Cw
ONEILL, Patrick	24	M	Clerk	10Au02Cw
Charles	2	M	Child	10Au02Cw
CASSERLY, Ann	20	F	Servant	10Au02Cw
Michael	15	M	None	10Au02Cw
MCCABE, Patrick	19	M	Laborer	10Au02Cw
GRAY, Elizabeth	19	F	Servant	10Au02Cw
BYRNE, James	19	M	Laborer	10Au02Cw
GANLEY, Michael	20	M	Laborer	10Au02Cw
Winnefred	18	F	Servant	10Au02Cw
DUNIGAN, Cath.	60	F	None	10Au02Cw
Margt.	11	F	None	10Au02Cw
GRAHAM, Margt.	2	F	Child	10Au02Cw
BOWKER, Marg.	23	F	None	10Au02Cw
Alfred	4	M	Child	10Au02Cw
Ann	.00	F	Infant	10Au02Cw
EARLEY, Ann	70	F	None	10Au02Cw
FORRESTER, Michl.	21	M	Carpenter	10Au02Cw
HAYE, Patrick	30	M	Weaver	10Au02Cw
BARTLE, John	20	M	Farmer	10Au02Cw
WALKER, Daniel	18	M	Farmer	10Au02Cw

NEW-YORK 11 AUGUST 1849

From Liverpool

NAMES OF PASSENGERS	AGE	SEX	OCCUPATIONS	DATE PORT SHIP
STANTON, Thomas	28	M	Laborer	11Au02Ax
Michael	6	M	Child	11Au02Ax
KELLY, Silina	18	F	Spinster	11Au02Ax
MURPHY, Mary	23	F	Spinster	11Au02Ax
GILDER, Hannah	41	F	Seamstress	11Au02Ax
U	.00	F	Infant	11Au02Ax
MECHAN, John	52	M	Laborer	11Au02Ax
DURNAM, Bridget	29	F	Spinster	11Au02Ax
MCDERMOTT, Owen	22	M	Laborer	11Au02Ax
LARENS, George	24	M	Laborer	11Au02Ax
ROGAN, Patk.	24	M	Laborer	11Au02Ax
CARLEY, Patk.	29	M	Laborer	11Au02Ax
FLYNN, James	44	M	Laborer	11Au02Ax
WILLIAMS, John	22	M	Laborer	11Au02Ax
FADEN, George	30	M	Laborer	11Au02Ax
KELLY, Mary	17	F	Spinster	11Au02Ax
HANLY, Manus	55	M	Laborer	11Au02Ax
Ellen	18	F	Spinster	11Au02Ax
Mary	16	F	Spinster	11Au02Ax
SLAVIN, Christn.	34	M	Laborer	11Au02Ax
CONNOLLY, Patk.	30	M	Laborer	11Au02Ax
Elizabeth	25	F	Unknown	11Au02Ax
MURTAGH, Henry	40	M	Mechanic	11Au02Ax
BYRNE, John	28	M	Laborer	11Au02Ax
AGNEW, Lawrence	25	M	Mechanic	11Au02Ax
Jane	24	F	Unknown	11Au02Ax
U	.00	M	Infant	11Au02Ax
John	3	M	Child	11Au02Ax
Henrietta	1	F	Child	11Au02Ax
COMISKY, John	51	M	Laborer	11Au02Ax
SLAVIN, Timothy	19	M	Laborer	11Au02Ax
MOLINE, John	28	M	Laborer	11Au02Ax
U-Mrs.	27	F	Unknown	11Au02Ax
BYRNE, George	26	M	Laborer	11Au02Ax
GRANT, Michl.	31	M	Laborer	11Au02Ax
Patk.	3	M	Child	11Au02Ax
Margt.	23	F	Unknown	11Au02Ax
Michl.	2	M	Child	11Au02Ax
DEMPSEY, Peter	16	M	Laborer	11Au02Ax
DALY, U-Mrs.	32	F	Unknown	11Au02Ax
John	45	M	Laborer	11Au02Ax
U	.08	F	Infant	11Au02Ax
Margt.	7	F	Child	11Au02Ax
SHARMAN, Sarah	20	F	Spinster	11Au02Ax
ONEIL, Patk.	52	M	Laborer	11Au02Ax
U-Mrs.	50	F	Laborer	11Au02Ax
HOOLAHANE, John	46	M	Laborer	11Au02Ax
NAGLE, John	30	M	Laborer	11Au02Ax
GRIFFIN, James	42	M	Laborer	11Au02Ax
BATES, William	4	M	Child	11Au02Ax
EVANS, David	48	M	Laborer	11Au02Ax
Eliza	52	F	Unknown	11Au02Ax
Mary	12	F	Unknown	11Au02Ax
Jane	16	F	Unknown	11Au02Ax
GLOVER, Cath.	8	F	Child	11Au02Ax
KENNEDY, Thos.	40	M	Laborer	11Au02Ax
Died-At-Sea				
MAHER, Ed.	27	M	Laborer	11Au02Ax
BALES, Henry	31	M	Engraver	11Au02Ax
Mary	31	F	Unknown	11Au02Ax
U	.08	F	Infant	11Au02Ax
Died-At-Sea				
Matilda	5	F	Child	11Au02Ax
Died-At-Sea				
KENIGHAM, Jas.	24	M	Laborer	11Au02Ax
KERIGAN, Mathew	30	M	Laborer	11Au02Ax
MCELLISTON, Philip	37	M	Laborer	11Au02Ax
Maria	17	F	Spinster	11Au02Ax
Cath.	12	F	Unknown	11Au02Ax
Thomas	10	M	Unknown	11Au02Ax
MOYNAHAN, Mary	30	F	Spinster	11Au02Ax
NAGLE, James	19	M	Laborer	11Au02Ax
CARTY, Mary	19	F	Spinster	11Au02Ax
MURPHY, Mary	19	F	Spinster	11Au02Ax
James	19	M	Laborer	11Au02Ax
JONES, Isac	40	M	Laborer	11Au02Ax
FAHEY, Anne	20	F	Spinster	11Au02Ax
DUANE, Patk.	40	M	Laborer	11Au02Ax
Died-At-Sea				
Margt.	35	F	Unknown	11Au02Ax
Johan	12	F	Unknown	11Au02Ax
Died-At-Sea				
Ellen	8	F	Child	11Au02Ax
William	5	M	Child	11Au02Ax
HERLIHY, Winny	5	F	Child	11Au02Ax
John	2	M	Child	11Au02Ax
HONIKAN, Fredk.	30	M	Laborer	11Au02Ax
MULLINS, Mary	12	F	Unknown	11Au02Ax

NAMES OF PASSENGERS	AGE	SEX	OCCUPATIONS	DATE PORT SHIP
TEENEHY, James	40	M	Laborer	11Au02Ax
Died-At-Sea				
TEENEHY, John	7	M	Child	11Au02Ax
LYONS, Margt.	22	F	Spinster	11Au02Ax
CROWLY, Danl.	26	M	Laborer	11Au02Ax
Michl.	30	M	Laborer	11Au02Ax
SULLIVAN, Jerry	12	M	Unknown	11Au02Ax
NORTHINGS, Nat	21	M	Laborer	11Au02Ax
NORTRIDGE, John	35	M	Laborer	11Au02Ax
William	20	M	Laborer	11Au02Ax
BUCKLEY, Joha.	23	F	Spinster	11Au02Ax
MCGRATH, Darby	40	M	Laborer	11Au02Ax
Died-At-Sea				
HERNABERY, Willm.	38	M	Laborer	11Au02Ax
Ellen	32	F	Unknown	11Au02Ax
U	.07	F	Infant	11Au02Ax
John	15	M	Unknown	11Au02Ax
James	8	M	Child	11Au02Ax
John	6	M	Child	11Au02Ax
Patk.	3	M	Child	11Au02Ax
GIBSON, Jane	21	F	Spinster	11Au02Ax
KILLEHER, Michl.	30	M	Laborer	11Au02Ax
MURPHY, Patk.	28	M	Laborer	11Au02Ax
Ellen	20	F	Unknown	11Au02Ax
KELLEHER, Mary	17	F	Spinster	11Au02Ax
REARDON, Mary	26	F	Spinster	11Au02Ax
Honora	20	F	Spinster	11Au02Ax
MURPHY, Thomas	25	M	Laborer	11Au02Ax
SULLIVAN, Denis	18	M	Laborer	11Au02Ax
LOONEY, Jerry	19	M	Laborer	11Au02Ax
HALEY, Redmond	16	M	Laborer	11Au02Ax
RYAN, John	38	M	Laborer	11Au02Ax
GORDAN, John	45	M	Laborer	11Au02Ax
Mary	39	F	Unknown	11Au02Ax
Eliza	18	F	Spinster	11Au02Ax
Joseph	16	M	Unknown	11Au02Ax
Willm.	12	M	Unknown	11Au02Ax
George	11	M	Unknown	11Au02Ax
Mary-Ann	9	F	Child	11Au02Ax
Dorah	7	F	Child	11Au02Ax
CORCORAN, Amelia	2	F	Child	11Au02Ax
Cath.	11	F	Unknown	11Au02Ax
Cath.	30	F	Seamstress	11Au02Ax
BYRNES, Richd.	40	M	Laborer	11Au02Ax
MARKY, Mary	26	F	Spinster	11Au02Ax
CROSBY, Rose	23	F	Spinster	11Au02Ax
COLEMAN, Con.	29	M	Laborer	11Au02Ax
GUINEEN, Timothy	28	M	Laborer	11Au02Ax
U-Mrs.	22	F	Unknown	11Au02Ax
Margt.	6	F	Child	11Au02Ax
FLYNN, Maria	22	F	Spinster	11Au02Ax
SCULLY, U-Miss	21	F	Spinster	11Au02Ax
CALLAGHAN, John	42	M	Laborer	11Au02Ax
STEREN, James	28	M	Laborer	11Au02Ax
Eliza	17	F	Unknown	11Au02Ax
RIERDAN, David	40	M	Laborer	11Au02Ax
John	28	M	Laborer	11Au02Ax
FOLEY, John	20	M	Laborer	11Au02Ax
RIERDAN, Joha.	12	F	Unknown	11Au02Ax
Kitty	10	F	Unknown	11Au02Ax
Mary	8	F	Child	11Au02Ax
Norry	6	F	Child	11Au02Ax
BYRNE, Denis	40	M	Laborer	11Au02Ax
Margt.	30	F	Unknown	11Au02Ax
GRAHAM, Lewis	20	M	Laborer	11Au02Ax
Martha	25	F	Unknown	11Au02Ax
Willm.	18	M	Mechanic	11Au02Ax
REDMOND, Margt.	20	F	Spinster	11Au02Ax
Cath.	21	F	Spinster	11Au02Ax
KEARNS, Mary	20	F	Spinster	11Au02Ax
DOOLEY, Sarah	40	F	Seamstress	11Au02Ax
U	.08	F	Infant	11Au02Ax
Died-At-Sea				
WINTERS, Margt.	18	F	Spinster	11Au02Ax
BUTLER, Cath.	25	F	Seamstress	11Au02Ax

NAMES OF PASSENGERS	AGE	SEX	OCCUPATIONS	DATE PORT SHIP
BUTLER, U	.06	M	Infant	11Au02Ax
MURPHY, Mary	30	F	Seamstress	11Au02Ax
Ellen	4	F	Child	11Au02Ax
Willm.	3	M	Child	11Au02Ax
KENNY, Jane	30	F	Seamstress	11Au02Ax
U	.07	M	Infant	11Au02Ax
DOWNES, Patk.	41	M	Laborer	11Au02Ax
Mary-Ann	16	F	Unknown	11Au02Ax
Agnes	13	F	Unknown	11Au02Ax
DOLAN, Willm.	28	M	Laborer	11Au02Ax
STAMDEN, George	36	M	Laborer	11Au02Ax
LYNAM, Owen	25	M	Laborer	11Au02Ax
Mary	12	F	Unknown	11Au02Ax
DOYLE, Michl.	22	M	Laborer	11Au02Ax
CARROLL, James	20	M	Laborer	11Au02Ax
Betty	38	F	Unknown	11Au02Ax
CUNNINGHAM, John	25	M	Laborer	11Au02Ax
Biddy	17	F	Unknown	11Au02Ax
CARROLL, John	12	M	Laborer	11Au02Ax
COOK, James	36	M	Laborer	11Au02Ax
KIRBY, Margt.	50	F	Unknown	11Au02Ax
Conner	13	M	Unknown	11Au02Ax
Jane	11	F	Unknown	11Au02Ax
Ellen	21	F	Spinster	11Au02Ax
FITZSIMMONS, Hugh	40	M	Laborer	11Au02Ax
Bridget	42	F	Unknown	11Au02Ax
Rose	13	F	Unknown	11Au02Ax
Bridgt.	12	F	Unknown	11Au02Ax
Mathew	10	M	Unknown	11Au02Ax
Mary	30	F	Unknown	11Au02Ax
U	.04	F	Infant	11Au02Ax
LYNCH, Cath.	30	F	Unknown	11Au02Ax
U	.05	F	Infant	11Au02Ax
SMITH, Cath.	13	F	Seamstress	11Au02Ax
Peter	12	M	Unknown	11Au02Ax
HOPE, James	35	M	Mechanic	11Au02Ax
BENNETT, Willm.	25	M	Laborer	11Au02Ax
MURTHA, Timothy	22	M	Laborer	11Au02Ax
SCULLY, Cath.	22	F	Spinster	11Au02Ax
HALLON, Biddy	18	F	Spinster	11Au02Ax
John	18	M	Laborer	11Au02Ax
Patk.	20	M	Laborer	11Au02Ax
DIFFNEY, Mary	17	F	Spinster	11Au02Ax
MULHOLLAND, Joseph	25	M	Laborer	11Au02Ax
Anne	25	F	Unknown	11Au02Ax
GAFFNEY, Anne	29	F	Seamstress	11Au02Ax
Eliza	16	F	Unknown	11Au02Ax
U	.09	F	Infant	11Au02Ax
Patk.	7	M	Child	11Au02Ax
Eliza	2	F	Child	11Au02Ax
MCDONNELL, Willm.	32	M	Laborer	11Au02Ax
FITZPATRICK, Thos.	20	M	Laborer	11Au02Ax
CARTY, Barney	25	M	Laborer	11Au02Ax
CONROY, Michl.	30	M	Laborer	11Au02Ax
COWAN, Willm.	21	M	Laborer	11Au02Ax
BELL, Thomas	21	M	Mechanic	11Au02Ax
MEREDITH, Bernard	21	M	Laborer	11Au02Ax
BRIEN, Bridgt.	22	F	Spinster	11Au02Ax
Timothy	6	M	Child	11Au02Ax
MURPHY, Bridget	60	F	Unknown	11Au02Ax
BROWNE, Henry	19	M	Laborer	11Au02Ax
TURNER, James	28	M	Mechanic	11Au02Ax
Barbara	28	F	Unknown	11Au02Ax
U	.09	F	Infant	11Au02Ax
CURTIS, James	22	M	Mechanic	11Au02Ax
CARTY, Thos.	48	M	Laborer	11Au02Ax
Mary	22	F	Unknown	11Au02Ax
KENNY, Aley	20	M	Spinster	11Au02Ax
SMITH, U-Mrs.	25	F	Seamstress	11Au02Ax
U	.06	F	Infant	11Au02Ax
Agnes	5	F	Child	11Au02Ax
Cath.	3	F	Child	11Au02Ax
BARNWELL, Richd.	30	M	Mechanic	11Au02Ax
GREY, Chas.	22	M	Mechanic	11Au02Ax
Cath.	19	F	Unknown	11Au02Ax

NAMES OF PASSENGERS	AGE	SEX	OCCUPATIONS	DATE PORT SHIP
CROWLY, Eugene	38	M	Laborer	11Au02Ax
BARRETT, Richard	20	M	Laborer	11Au02Ax
DUGGAN, Margt.	24	F	Spinster	11Au02Ax
MCHALE, John	25	M	Mechanic	11Au02Ax
SULLIVAN, Owen	31	M	Laborer	11Au02Ax
INGHAM, Thomas	22	M	Laborer	11Au02Ax
MCCARTY, Thomas	19	M	Laborer	11Au02Ax
LYONS, Margt.	22	F	Spinster	11Au02Ax
EARLY, Willm.	44	M	Laborer	11Au02Ax
TIMMONS, Anne	28	F	Spinster	11Au02Ax
BRENAN, Mary	50	F	Spinster	11Au02Ax
MURPHY, Mathew	27	M	Laborer	11Au02Ax
KELLY, Thomas	36	M	Laborer	11Au02Ax
GILLIS, David	35	M	Mechanic	11Au02Ax
Judy	40	F	Unknown	11Au02Ax
Anne	12	F	Unknown	11Au02Ax
Ellen	8	F	Child	11Au02Ax
CALLAGHAN, Alice	28	F	Seamstress	11Au02Ax
Mary	8	F	Child	11Au02Ax
Patk.	6	M	Child	11Au02Ax
Eliza	2	F	Child	11Au02Ax
CONLIN, Larry	28	M	Laborer	11Au02Ax
Anne	1	F	Child	11Au02Ax
Died-At-Sea				
FITZSIMONS, Bridgt.	20	F	Spinster	11Au02Ax
REILY, Farrel	28	M	Laborer	11Au02Ax
WATERS, Mary	24	F	Spinster	11Au02Ax
MURPHY, Julia	55	F	Spinster	11Au02Ax
John	21	M	Laborer	11Au02Ax
Bridgt.	36	F	Unknown	11Au02Ax
REILY, James	34	M	Laborer	11Au02Ax
MCCLUSKY, Mary	28	F	Spinster	11Au02Ax
TANNER, Cath.	40	F	Spinster	11Au02Ax
John	7	M	Child	11Au02Ax
Patk.	6	M	Child	11Au02Ax
Mary	4	F	Child	11Au02Ax
MILES, Andrew	35	M	Mechanic	11Au02Ax
Bridgt.	33	F	Unknown	11Au02Ax
Patk.	.05	M	Infant	11Au02Ax
Thomas	6	M	Child	11Au02Ax
John	4	M	Child	11Au02Ax
Rose	2	F	Child	11Au02Ax
CORDON, John	17	M	Laborer	11Au02Ax
Martin	16	M	Laborer	11Au02Ax
DUGGAN, Mathew	13	M	Laborer	11Au02Ax
MEEHAN, Rose	21	F	Spinster	11Au02Ax
HARTLEY, Jane	24	F	Spinster	11Au02Ax
CARROLL, Margt.	22	F	Spinster	11Au02Ax
KEATING, Edw.	22	M	Laborer	11Au02Ax
FITZSIMONS, Cath.	30	F	Unknown	11Au02Ax
Eliza	5	F	Child	11Au02Ax
FARRELL, Fredk.	42	M	Laborer	11Au02Ax
GARRY, Patk.	70	M	Laborer	11Au02Ax
Bridgt.	62	F	Unknown	11Au02Ax
Mary	18	F	Spinster	11Au02Ax
FAGAN, Mary	34	F	Spinster	11Au02Ax
MCDERMOTT, Hugh	21	M	Laborer	11Au02Ax
DOHERTY, Suzan	32	F	Spinster	11Au02Ax
Anne	14	F	Unknown	11Au02Ax
Rose	3	F	Child	11Au02Ax
MOONEY, Neil	73	M	Laborer	11Au02Ax
Anne	30	F	Spinster	11Au02Ax
DURR, Bridgt.	22	F	Spinster	11Au02Ax
MULLOHILL, Thos.	4	M	Child	11Au02Ax
SULLIVAN, Margt.	19	F	Spinster	11Au02Ax
RUDDY, Patk.	26	M	Mechanic	11Au02Ax
MORRISSON, Benjn.	20	M	Mechanic	11Au02Ax
Silly-Anne	32	F	Spinster	11Au02Ax
KELLY, Anne	30	F	Spinster	11Au02Ax
MCCORMACK, John	3	M	Child	11Au02Ax
MCCOPLEY, Eliza	19	F	Unknown	11Au02Ax
HANLAN, Sarah	16	F	Unknown	11Au02Ax
Phillip	11	M	Unknown	11Au02Ax
RYAN, Cath.	24	F	Spinster	11Au02Ax
TOOMY, Thomas	21	M	Laborer	11Au02Ax
KEARNY, U-Mrs.	22	F	Unknown	11Au02Ax
U	.08	F	Infant	11Au02Ax
Died-At-Sea				
Mary-A.	4	F	Child	11Au02Ax
Ellen	6	F	Child	11Au02Ax
STOLEY, Tracey	17	M	Mechanic	11Au02Ax
MATHEWS, George	21	M	Mechanic	11Au02Ax
Mary-A.	24	F	Unknown	11Au02Ax
DRANEY, John	25	M	Laborer	11Au02Ax
DOOLEY, Martin	36	M	Laborer	11Au02Ax
WOGAN, Martin	30	M	Mechanic	11Au02Ax
CANTWELL, Walter	48	M	Clergyman	11Au02Ax
HAWKSHAW, Henry	32	M	Gentleman	11Au02Ax
D.Mrs.	21	F	Unknown	11Au02Ax

WESTMINSTER 11 AUGUST 1849

From London

NAMES OF PASSENGERS	AGE	SEX	OCCUPATIONS	DATE PORT SHIP
CURLEY, John	37	M	Laborer	11Au13Bd

PIONEER 10 AUGUST 1849

From London

NAMES OF PASSENGERS	AGE	SEX	OCCUPATIONS	DATE PORT SHIP
SCLATER, Emma	19	F	Servant	10Au13Oh
MAYNARD, Thomas	42	M	Unknown	10Au13Oh
Sarah	17	F	Unknown	10Au13Oh
Thomas	13	M	Unknown	10Au13Oh
Harriet	12	F	Unknown	10Au13Oh
William	10	M	Unknown	10Au13Oh
John	8	M	Child	10Au13Oh
Sophia	7	F	Child	10Au13Oh
Charles	5	M	Child	10Au13Oh
Ephraim	4	M	Child	10Au13Oh
MARTIN, John	49	M	Smith	10Au13Oh
Mary	52	F	Unknown	10Au13Oh
Catherine	13	F	Unknown	10Au13Oh
WALKER, John	55	M	Laborer	10Au13Oh
Ann	53	F	Unknown	10Au13Oh
James	22	M	Unknown	10Au13Oh
John	18	M	Unknown	10Au13Oh
William	15	M	Unknown	10Au13Oh
Alice	11	F	Unknown	10Au13Oh
Sarah	25	F	Unknown	10Au13Oh
CORNWELL, William	27	M	Unknown	10Au13Oh
Mary	42	F	Unknown	10Au13Oh
John	14	M	Unknown	10Au13Oh
MONK, Francis	25	M	Unknown	10Au13Oh
NASH, William	33	M	Laborer	10Au13Oh
Theodosia	33	F	Unknown	10Au13Oh
U	.00	U	Infant	10Au13Oh
George	7	M	Child	10Au13Oh
John	6	M	Child	10Au13Oh
TUPP, Jane	40	F	Unknown	10Au13Oh
CRAIGIN, Peter	28	M	Smith	10Au13Oh
NOTT, Michael	28	M	Clock Maker	10Au13Oh
BESHETT, Thomas	27	M	Joiner	10Au13Oh
PEARSON, Robert	23	M	Unknown	10Au13Oh
WALKER, Abraham	30	M	Laborer	10Au13Oh
Mary	28	F	Unknown	10Au13Oh
William	3	M	Child	10Au13Oh
MODELL, Joachim	33	M	Laborer	10Au13Oh

NAMES OF PASSENGERS		AGE	SEX	OCCUPATIONS	DATE PORT SHIP
MODELL, Maria		25	F	Unknown	10Au13Oh
SEATON, Thomas		26	M	Unknown	10Au13Oh
FRANKLIN, Thomas		25	M	Engineer	10Au13Oh
FOLEY, Mary		16	F	Servant	10Au13Oh
HAGARTY, Mary		42	F	Unknown	10Au13Oh
Margaret		13	F	Unknown	10Au13Oh
John		11	M	Unknown	10Au13Oh
Ann		6	F	Child	10Au13Oh
Michael		4	M	Child	10Au13Oh
SYMONS, Helen		17	F	Unknown	10Au13Oh
KENZIE, John-M.		40	M	Unknown	10Au13Oh
SARGRANT, Thomas		39	M	Laborer	10Au13Oh
FRASER, William		25	M	Fitter	10Au13Oh
ALDINE, James		31	M	Unknown	10Au13Oh
Sarah		35	F	Unknown	10Au13Oh
LAWERENCE, John		24	M	Carpenter	10Au13Oh
Jane		24	F	Unknown	10Au13Oh
STEVENS, John		29	M	Joiner	10Au13Oh
Mary-Anne		29	F	Unknown	10Au13Oh
Mary-Anne		8	F	Child	10Au13Oh
Ellen		6	F	Child	10Au13Oh
Emily		4	F	Child	10Au13Oh
Bessio		2	F	Child	10Au13Oh
HERTY, Hannah		32	F	Unknown	10Au13Oh
Rosa		8	F	Child	10Au13Oh
Minna		6	F	Child	10Au13Oh
Rinour		4	F	Child	10Au13Oh
WALKIM, Edward		28	M	Rope Maker	10Au13Oh
Anna		26	F	Unknown	10Au13Oh
CANAGHAN, Thomas-M.		36	M	Unknown	10Au13Oh
JONES, John		18	M	Unknown	10Au13Oh
DAVIS, John		23	M	Cbtmkr	10Au13Oh
Mary		24	F	Unknown	10Au13Oh
ROBINS, Edward		24	M	Tailor	10Au13Oh
Amelia		24	F	Unknown	10Au13Oh
BRADFORD, U		45	M	Unknown	10Au13Oh
U-Mrs.		45	F	Unknown	10Au13Oh
U	(S)	19	M	Son	10Au13Oh
U	(D)	17	F	Daughter	10Au13Oh
MAYNARD, U-Mrs.		38	F	Unknown	10Au13Oh
U		.00	U	Infant	10Au13Oh
U, U		00	F	Servant	10Au13Oh
STEELE, Richard		21	M	Unknown	10Au13Oh

HYNDEFORD 11 AUGUST 1849

From Glasgow

NAMES OF PASSENGERS		AGE	SEX	OCCUPATIONS	DATE PORT SHIP
LAURIE, James		24	M	Laborer	11Au04Bo
MULHOLLAND, Elizabeth		60	F	Unknown	11Au04Bo
MCFARLANE, Duncan		60	M	Farmer	11Au04Bo
U-Mrs.	(W)	60	F	Wife	11Au04Bo
John		35	M	Farmer	11Au04Bo
Betsey	(W)	35	F	Wife	11Au04Bo
Janet		2	F	Child	11Au04Bo
Isabella		.01	F	Infant	11Au04Bo
George		30	M	Relative	11Au04Bo
MCNAB, Isabella		30	F	Unknown	11Au04Bo
John		28	M	Farmer	11Au04Bo
Archd.		20	M	Farmer	11Au04Bo
Peter		18	M	Farmer	11Au04Bo
GALE, James		43	M	Agent	11Au04Bo
U-Mrs.	(W)	40	F	Wife	11Au04Bo
Mary		14	F	Relative	11Au04Bo
Willm.		10	M	Relative	11Au04Bo
James		7	M	Child	11Au04Bo
KINCAID, Robt.		64	M	Weaver	11Au04Bo
Elizabeth	(W)	64	F	Wife	11Au04Bo
Robert		3	M	Child	11Au04Bo
KINCAID, Agness		.10	F	Infant	11Au04Bo
Catherine		25	F	Relative	11Au04Bo
HARKNESS, Sarah		26	F	Unknown	11Au04Bo
Alex.		.09	M	Infant	11Au04Bo
PATTERSON, John		33	M	Laborer	11Au04Bo
CALDWELL, Margt.		40	M	Wife	11Au04Bo
Jane		7	F	Child	11Au04Bo
Agness		5	F	Child	11Au04Bo
MCLEAN, Grace		20	F	Unknown	11Au04Bo
Grace		.08	F	Infant	11Au04Bo
MORRISON, Donald		43	M	Farmer	11Au04Bo
Mary		30	F	Relative	11Au04Bo
Archd.		45	M	Relative	11Au04Bo
Catherine		9	F	Child	11Au04Bo
John		7	M	Child	11Au04Bo
Archd.		5	M	Child	11Au04Bo
Donald		3	M	Child	11Au04Bo
Mary		.09	F	Infant	11Au04Bo
MCLAREN, Ronald		24	M	Farmer	11Au04Bo
Isabella		55	F	Relative	11Au04Bo
Agness		26	F	Relative	11Au04Bo
SHEPPARD, Janet		50	F	Spinster	11Au04Bo
WHEELER, Thos.		24	M	Laborer	11Au04Bo
MONAGHAN, Dennis		31	M	Laborer	11Au04Bo
Martha	(W)	30	F	Wife	11Au04Bo
HUGHES, Peter		40	M	Laborer	11Au04Bo
Elizabeth	(W)	40	F	Wife	11Au04Bo
Catherine		9	F	Child	11Au04Bo
Susan		7	F	Child	11Au04Bo
Henry		5	M	Child	11Au04Bo
Elizabeth		1	F	Child	11Au04Bo
MCCANN, James		40	M	Laborer	11Au04Bo
Margt.		40	F	Relative	11Au04Bo
Catherine		9	F	Child	11Au04Bo
Susana		6	F	Child	11Au04Bo
HUGHES, Catherine		60	F	Unknown	11Au04Bo
James		30	M	Unknown	11Au04Bo
MCGILP, Archd.		21	M	Laborer	11Au04Bo
WHESTON, James		54	M	Blacksmith	11Au04Bo
FRIER, Adam		53	M	Blacksmith	11Au04Bo
RENNIE, Rachel		28	F	Wife	11Au04Bo
James		9	M	Child	11Au04Bo
GALLAGHER, Cecilea		38	F	Unknown	11Au04Bo
John		12	M	Relative	11Au04Bo
Helen		8	F	Child	11Au04Bo
Willm.		6	M	Child	11Au04Bo
Hugh		4	M	Child	11Au04Bo
Andrew		3	M	Child	11Au04Bo
MCGLUSKIE, Patk.		26	M	Laborer	11Au04Bo
Ann	(W)	22	F	Wife	11Au04Bo
CARSON, Willm.		24	M	Laborer	11Au04Bo
CARNIE, Edwd.		33	M	Laborer	11Au04Bo
Catherine		29	F	Relative	11Au04Bo
Catherine		6	F	Child	11Au04Bo
Margaret		.10	F	Infant	11Au04Bo
PRENTICE, Ann		20	F	Spinster	11Au04Bo
MCFARLANE, Archd.		23	M	Laborer	11Au04Bo
Margt.		18	F	Unknown	11Au04Bo
LANGE, James		19	M	Unknown	11Au04Bo
GALLOCHER, Hugh		33	M	Unknown	11Au04Bo
GEMMEL, Alex.		13	M	Unknown	11Au04Bo
THOMSON, Isabella		20	F	Spinster	11Au04Bo
MCCRAIG, Willm.		19	M	Laborer	11Au04Bo
DUFFY, Patk.		21	M	Laborer	11Au04Bo
ADAIR, Peter		30	M	Laborer	11Au04Bo
MCFAYDEN, Jas.		24	M	Laborer	11Au04Bo
MURPHY, Margt.		35	F	Wife	11Au04Bo
Bernard		7	M	Child	11Au04Bo
Mary		5	F	Child	11Au04Bo
Margt.		3	F	Child	11Au04Bo
GALBRAITH, Angus		55	M	Farmer	11Au04Bo
Catherine		50	F	Relative	11Au04Bo
Donald		24	M	Relative	11Au04Bo
Angus		18	M	Relative	11Au04Bo
Lucy		13	F	Relative	11Au04Bo

NAMES OF PASSENGERS	AGE	SEX	OCCUPATIONS	DATE PORT SHIP
GALBRAITH, Archd.	13	M	Farmer	11Au04Bo
Malcolm	22	M	Farmer	11Au04Bo
Alex.	7	M	Child	11Au04Bo
MCNEIL, Donald	55	M	Farmer	11Au04Bo
Flora	54	F	Unknown	11Au04Bo
Flora	22	F	Unknown	11Au04Bo
Donald	20	M	Unknown	11Au04Bo
Catherine	18	F	Unknown	11Au04Bo
Daniel	40	M	Unknown	11Au04Bo
Archd.	38	M	Unknown	11Au04Bo
Malcolm	3	M	Child	11Au04Bo
MCMILLAN, James	30	M	Farmer	11Au04Bo
Sally	2	F	Child	11Au04Bo
Roger	.11	M	Infant	11Au04Bo
MCNEIL, Donald	36	M	Farmer	11Au04Bo
Sally	30	F	Relative	11Au04Bo
Ann	3	F	Child	11Au04Bo
Marion	.08	F	Infant	11Au04Bo
BROWN, Donald	24	M	Farmer	11Au04Bo
MCNEIL, John	24	M	Farmer	11Au04Bo
MCEUCHEN, Malcolm	32	M	Farmer	11Au04Bo
Mary	28	F	Relative	11Au04Bo
Donald	7	M	Child	11Au04Bo
Angus	3	M	Child	11Au04Bo
Esther	2	F	Child	11Au04Bo
BUCHANAN, Neil	24	M	Farmer	11Au04Bo
Catherine (W)	23	F	Wife	11Au04Bo
Duncan	.03	M	Infant	11Au04Bo
GALBRAITH, Jno.	30	M	Farmer	11Au04Bo
MCMILLAN, Alex.	35	M	Farmer	11Au04Bo
Mary	33	F	Relative	11Au04Bo
John	4	M	Child	11Au04Bo
Malcolm	3	M	Child	11Au04Bo
Catherine	6	F	Child	11Au04Bo
Mary	.03	F	Infant	11Au04Bo
Margt.	25	F	Relative	11Au04Bo
CAMPBELL, U-Mrs.	50	F	Wife	11Au04Bo
BLUE, Barbara	20	F	Unknown	11Au04Bo
GRAHAM, John	30	M	Laborer	11Au04Bo
GALBRAITH, Jas.	26	M	Laborer	11Au04Bo
DOWAL, Jno.	30	M	Laborer	11Au04Bo
DRUMMOND, Thos.	25	M	Laborer	11Au04Bo
MURRAY, Alex.	22	M	Laborer	11Au04Bo
MCCABE, Ann	29	F	Wife	11Au04Bo
Mary	8	F	Child	11Au04Bo
James	6	M	Child	11Au04Bo
Susan	.08	F	Infant	11Au04Bo
DONELLY, Tobias	21	M	Laborer	11Au04Bo
MCEVAN, Jno.	20	M	Laborer	11Au04Bo
BLACK, Robt.	30	M	Unknown	11Au04Bo
MCGREGOR, Wm.	40	M	Shoemaker	11Au04Bo
Jane (W)	30	F	Wife	11Au04Bo
ROBERTSON, Margaret	30	F	Spinster	11Au04Bo
MCGLEASHEN, Henry	30	M	Laborer	11Au04Bo
GARRITY, Catherine	30	F	Servant	11Au04Bo
MCGACE, Catherine	50	F	Wife	11Au04Bo
Mary-Ann	11	F	Unknown	11Au04Bo
GORDON, Wm.	29	M	Laborer	11Au04Bo
MCNEIL, James	3	M	Child	11Au04Bo

CONSTITUTION 11 AUGUST 1849

From Liverpool

NAMES OF PASSENGERS	AGE	SEX	OCCUPATIONS	DATE PORT SHIP
MCKENTY, Samuel	19	M	Farmer	11Au02Dp
BRUCE, Robert	20	M	Unknown	11Au02Dp
BOGAN, John	15	M	Unknown	11Au02Dp
DOYLE, James	20	M	Unknown	11Au02Dp
CUMMIN, Francis	21	M	Unknown	11Au02Dp
MCMINANY, Abby	30	F	Unknown	11Au02Dp
William	.00	M	Infant	11Au02Dp
KERR, William-J.	21	M	Unknown	11Au02Dp
MOORE, Sarah	33	F	Unknown	11Au02Dp
Jane	32	F	Unknown	11Au02Dp
FARR, George	23	M	Unknown	11Au02Dp
OBRIEN, James	28	M	Unknown	11Au02Dp
HART, Samuel	18	M	Unknown	11Au02Dp
LOUGHRAN, Hanna	20	F	Unknown	11Au02Dp
May	18	F	Unknown	11Au02Dp
WILSON, Elizabeth	17	F	Unknown	11Au02Dp
Jane	12	F	Unknown	11Au02Dp
VALENTINE, Rosanna	25	F	Unknown	11Au02Dp
James	15	M	Unknown	11Au02Dp
ARMSTRONG, Robert	28	M	Unknown	11Au02Dp
FRIZEL, Ann	15	F	Unknown	11Au02Dp
CONWAY, Mary	.00	F	Infant	11Au02Dp
CONNELL, Mary	18	F	Unknown	11Au02Dp
MCCAME, Elizabeth	60	F	Unknown	11Au02Dp
MCNAALL, John	30	M	Unknown	11Au02Dp
DENNING, Elizabeth	20	F	Unknown	11Au02Dp
CONNELLY, Edward	30	M	Unknown	11Au02Dp
CONAN, James	20	M	Unknown	11Au02Dp
WOODS, Mary	20	F	Unknown	11Au02Dp
HUGHES, Margaret	18	F	Unknown	11Au02Dp
MCCREAT, Sarah	30	F	Unknown	11Au02Dp
ROBINSON, John	16	M	Unknown	11Au02Dp
EDGAR, James	22	M	Unknown	11Au02Dp
COLGAN, Terance	22	M	Unknown	11Au02Dp
BROWN, Jane	55	F	Unknown	11Au02Dp
HANNA, Richard	29	M	Unknown	11Au02Dp
ANGLE, Samuel	25	M	Unknown	11Au02Dp
Mary-Ann	22	F	Unknown	11Au02Dp
LONERTY, Patk.	48	M	Unknown	11Au02Dp
Mary	48	F	Unknown	11Au02Dp
Owne	21	M	Unknown	11Au02Dp
Henry	20	M	Unknown	11Au02Dp
James	18	M	Unknown	11Au02Dp
Anne	16	F	Unknown	11Au02Dp
Mary	14	F	Unknown	11Au02Dp
MCKENNA, Rosanna	48	F	Unknown	11Au02Dp
Mary	12	F	Unknown	11Au02Dp
John	10	M	Unknown	11Au02Dp
CORRIGAN, Pat	48	M	Unknown	11Au02Dp
Ellenor	40	F	Unknown	11Au02Dp
John	16	M	Unknown	11Au02Dp
James	14	M	Unknown	11Au02Dp
Mary	12	F	Unknown	11Au02Dp
Patrick	10	M	Unknown	11Au02Dp
Ellenor	8	F	Child	11Au02Dp
Daniel	6	M	Child	11Au02Dp
GRAHAM, Ann	24	F	Unknown	11Au02Dp
Fanny-Maria	11	F	Unknown	11Au02Dp
Mary-Isabella	.00	F	Infant	11Au02Dp
MCLOUGHLIN, David	11	M	Unknown	11Au02Dp
MURRAY, Jane	35	F	Unknown	11Au02Dp
Mark	12	M	Unknown	11Au02Dp
James	9	M	Child	11Au02Dp
Joseph	17	M	Unknown	11Au02Dp
Patrick	.00	M	Infant	11Au02Dp
HYNES, James	24	M	Unknown	11Au02Dp
DAVIS, Robert	24	M	Unknown	11Au02Dp
Anne	23	F	Unknown	11Au02Dp
CONWAY, Thomas	50	M	Unknown	11Au02Dp
James	32	M	Unknown	11Au02Dp
Hugh	14	M	Unknown	11Au02Dp
REID, James	23	M	Unknown	11Au02Dp
CONWAY, Elizabeth	50	F	Unknown	11Au02Dp
Grace	25	F	Unknown	11Au02Dp
Elizabeth	23	F	Unknown	11Au02Dp
Elizabeth	6	F	Child	11Au02Dp
Grace	3	F	Child	11Au02Dp
Anne	.00	F	Infant	11Au02Dp
QUIN, Mary	50	F	Unknown	11Au02Dp
BURNS, Jane	26	F	Unknown	11Au02Dp

NAMES OF PASSENGERS	AGE	SEX	OCCUPATIONS	DATE PORT SHIP
BURNS, Wm.Robt.	2	M	Child	11Au02Dp
Thos.Benj.	.00	M	Infant	11Au02Dp
CAMPBELL, Sarah	15	F	Unknown	11Au02Dp
DONAGHEY, Anne	26	F	Unknown	11Au02Dp
QUIN, Anne	20	F	Unknown	11Au02Dp
MALLEN, Isabella	25	F	Unknown	11Au02Dp
BANE, Sarah-Anne	24	F	Unknown	11Au02Dp
Anne	.00	F	Infant	11Au02Dp
GRAHAM, Robert	40	M	Unknown	11Au02Dp
Roseanna	40	F	Unknown	11Au02Dp
Elenor	17	F	Unknown	11Au02Dp
Henry	14	M	Unknown	11Au02Dp
Anne	9	F	Child	11Au02Dp
HADDOCK, John	50	M	Unknown	11Au02Dp
William	18	M	Unknown	11Au02Dp
Mary	15	F	Unknown	11Au02Dp
CAMPBELL, Robert	30	M	Unknown	11Au02Dp
OLIVER, Mary	45	F	Unknown	11Au02Dp
Sarah	18	F	Unknown	11Au02Dp
Samuel	15	M	Unknown	11Au02Dp
James	13	M	Unknown	11Au02Dp
Robert	11	M	Unknown	11Au02Dp
Mary-Jane	8	F	Child	11Au02Dp
Martha	6	F	Child	11Au02Dp
Eliza	.00	F	Infant	11Au02Dp
BOYD, Samuel	20	M	Unknown	11Au02Dp
WALLACE, Margt.	24	F	Unknown	11Au02Dp
R.Thomas	4	M	Child	11Au02Dp
Carolina	.00	F	Infant	11Au02Dp
JACKSON, Henry	23	M	Unknown	11Au02Dp
Margaret	20	F	Unknown	11Au02Dp
CUNANS, Thomas	18	M	Unknown	11Au02Dp
Jane	14	M	Unknown	11Au02Dp
MCNALL, Bernard	20	M	Unknown	11Au02Dp
GANETT, James	18	M	Unknown	11Au02Dp
ROSBOTTAM, Robert	42	M	Unknown	11Au02Dp
BOYD, Catherine	18	F	Unknown	11Au02Dp
HAMMELL, Henry	23	M	Unknown	11Au02Dp
HUNTER, Isaac	26	M	Unknown	11Au02Dp
Jane	24	F	Unknown	11Au02Dp
GRAHAMS, Patrick	35	M	Unknown	11Au02Dp
Margt.	20	F	Unknown	11Au02Dp
Jane	18	F	Unknown	11Au02Dp
MCCRIGHAM, Catherine	30	F	Unknown	11Au02Dp
FISHER, John	55	M	Unknown	11Au02Dp
Jane	55	F	Unknown	11Au02Dp
Rachel	20	F	Unknown	11Au02Dp
Jane	22	F	Unknown	11Au02Dp
ROBINSON, Robert	23	M	Unknown	11Au02Dp
MCGOHICK, John	35	M	Unknown	11Au02Dp
TRANE, Bernard	28	M	Unknown	11Au02Dp
WARNICK, Wm.	18	M	Unknown	11Au02Dp
WILTON, Mary	30	M	Unknown	11Au02Dp
John	8	M	Child	11Au02Dp
MCMAGHAN, Alice	38	F	Unknown	11Au02Dp
William	30	M	Unknown	11Au02Dp
Eliza	17	F	Unknown	11Au02Dp
Alice	12	F	Unknown	11Au02Dp
Patrick	10	M	Unknown	11Au02Dp
Rose	17	F	Unknown	11Au02Dp
HARRISON, John	25	M	Unknown	11Au02Dp
PATTERSON, John	22	M	Unknown	11Au02Dp
MCGEE, Ann	24	F	Unknown	11Au02Dp
J.Alex.	.00	M	Infant	11Au02Dp
William	4	M	Child	11Au02Dp
DARLY, Ellen	24	F	Unknown	11Au02Dp
Mary-Ann	22	F	Unknown	11Au02Dp
RILEY, Mary	50	F	Unknown	11Au02Dp
Anne	16	F	Unknown	11Au02Dp
Hulda	21	F	Unknown	11Au02Dp
PALMER, William	25	M	Unknown	11Au02Dp
ANDERSON, Joseph	20	M	Unknown	11Au02Dp
Mary	20	F	Unknown	11Au02Dp
Jane	.00	F	Infant	11Au02Dp
KERNAGHAN, James	20	M	Unknown	11Au02Dp
MCCULLOUGH, John	18	M	Unknown	11Au02Dp
NULLY, Wm.Joh.	35	M	Unknown	11Au02Dp
Eliza	30	F	Unknown	11Au02Dp
Eliza	6	F	Child	11Au02Dp
Martha	3	F	Child	11Au02Dp
Robt.	.00	M	Infant	11Au02Dp
JOHNSTON, John	56	M	Unknown	11Au02Dp
Mary	40	F	Unknown	11Au02Dp
MCCLOY, Nancy	19	F	Unknown	11Au02Dp
PALMER, Wm.	20	M	Unknown	11Au02Dp
JACKSON, Martha-Ann	21	F	Unknown	11Au02Dp
TRAINOR, Thomas-John	34	M	Unknown	11Au02Dp
Hanna	21	F	Unknown	11Au02Dp
CUNNINGHAM, Sally	50	F	Unknown	11Au02Dp
Edward	20	M	Unknown	11Au02Dp
GERVIN, Charles	23	M	Unknown	11Au02Dp
Letitia	20	F	Unknown	11Au02Dp
Mcre--, Mary	10	F	Unknown	11Au02Dp
MARTIN, Hugh	22	M	Unknown	11Au02Dp
Jane	21	F	Unknown	11Au02Dp
MCCREEDY, Robt.	47	M	Unknown	11Au02Dp
Jane	51	F	Unknown	11Au02Dp
Mary	6	F	Child	11Au02Dp
Robt.	4	M	Child	11Au02Dp
Eliza	3	F	Child	11Au02Dp
Ann	.00	F	Infant	11Au02Dp
ELLIS, Edward	15	M	Unknown	11Au02Dp
CAMERON, Nancy	40	F	Unknown	11Au02Dp
SCOTT, James	28	M	Unknown	11Au02Dp
BUSBY, Margt.	17	F	Unknown	11Au02Dp
COURT, Robt.	20	M	Unknown	11Au02Dp
Eliza	18	F	Unknown	11Au02Dp
MCCANE, Mary	39	F	Unknown	11Au02Dp
MCMAHON, U	18	M	Unknown	11Au02Dp
FLYNN, Edward	40	M	Unknown	11Au02Dp
Eliza	40	F	Unknown	11Au02Dp
Elizabeth	20	F	Unknown	11Au02Dp
Mary	13	F	Unknown	11Au02Dp
Geo.	11	M	Unknown	11Au02Dp
James	9	M	Child	11Au02Dp
William	7	M	Child	11Au02Dp
Sally	.00	F	Infant	11Au02Dp
PATTERSON, Matilda	30	F	Unknown	11Au02Dp
Mary	9	F	Child	11Au02Dp
Margt.	6	F	Child	11Au02Dp
William	4	M	Child	11Au02Dp
M.	.00	F	Infant	11Au02Dp
MCBLAIN, Mary	00	F	Unknown	11Au02Dp
Nancy	00	F	Unknown	11Au02Dp
BEATTY, Margt.	00	F	Unknown	11Au02Dp

L.Z. 11 AUGUST 1849

From Liverpool

NAMES OF PASSENGERS	AGE	SEX	OCCUPATIONS	DATE PORT SHIP
SHEEHEY, Phillipp	18	M	Laborer	11Au02Bb
BOND, John	31	M	Millwright	11Au02Bb
U (W)	31	F	Seamstress	11Au02Bb
Betty	6	F	Child	11Au02Bb
George	4	M	Child	11Au02Bb
Matthew	.00	M	Infant	11Au02Bb
Died-At-Sea				
MCBRIGHT, John	24	M	Laborer	11Au02Bb
FEARN, Michael	21	M	Laborer	11Au02Bb
MCDONNELL, Henry	20	M	Carter	11Au02Bb
MAHER, John	20	M	Carter	11Au02Bb
MCDONNELL, Michael	30	M	Carter	11Au02Bb
Mary	28	F	Servant	11Au02Bb
Eliza	24	F	Servant	11Au02Bb

NAMES OF PASSENGERS		AGE	SEX	OCCUPATIONS	DATE PORT SHIP
RILEY, Phillipp		30	M	Laborer	11Au02Bb
Rose		30	F	Servant	11Au02Bb
Mary		6	F	Child	11Au02Bb
Phillipp		4	M	Child	11Au02Bb
Thomas		2	M	Child	11Au02Bb
Ann		.00	F	Infant	11Au02Bb
Died-At-Sea					
ONEILL, John		12	M	Laborer	11Au02Bb
SCUDDER, Pat		22	M	Laborer	11Au02Bb
BIHAN, John		24	M	Laborer	11Au02Bb
SULLIVAN, Matthew		36	M	Laborer	11Au02Bb
U	(W)	36	F	Servant	11Au02Bb
Ann		16	F	Servant	11Au02Bb
Daniel		13	M	Servant	11Au02Bb
Michael		11	M	Servant	11Au02Bb
Margarett		9	F	Child	11Au02Bb
Mary		7	F	Child	11Au02Bb
Catharine		5	F	Child	11Au02Bb
Richard		.00	M	Infant	11Au02Bb
MALONEY, Pat		40	M	Farmer	11Au02Bb
DOONEY, Pat		35	M	Laborer	11Au02Bb
MORRIS, Peggy		26	F	Servant	11Au02Bb
WEBB, John		22	M	Cutler	11Au02Bb
SEEL, Honora		18	F	Lad	11Au02Bb
MCGUIRE, Pat		50	M	Laborer	11Au02Bb
U	(W)	35	F	Servant	11Au02Bb
Thomas		2	M	Child	11Au02Bb
COLLINS, James		20	M	Laborer	11Au02Bb
DEVINE, James		25	M	Farmer	11Au02Bb
U	(W)	20	F	Seamstress	11Au02Bb
RYAN, Pat		30	M	Laborer	11Au02Bb
Mary		24	F	Servant	11Au02Bb
CONNELLY, Eliza		23	F	Servant	11Au02Bb
DURKAM, Mattw.		27	M	Laborer	11Au02Bb
Mary		25	F	Servant	11Au02Bb
MCNAREN, Peter		22	M	Laborer	11Au02Bb
Eliza		20	F	Servant	11Au02Bb
BEVANS, Ann		35	F	Servant	11Au02Bb
Ann		30	F	Servant	11Au02Bb
Mary		11	F	Servant	11Au02Bb
Ann		5	F	Child	11Au02Bb
William		2	M	Child	11Au02Bb
BREELLY, Bridget		23	F	Servant	11Au02Bb
MURPHY, Pat		20	M	Laborer	11Au02Bb
Margarett		21	F	Servant	11Au02Bb
DANAHOE, John		28	M	Laborer	11Au02Bb
Ann		25	F	Servant	11Au02Bb
DOYLE, Bridget		22	F	Servant	11Au02Bb
GORMAN, Bridget		22	F	Servant	11Au02Bb
FOGARTY, Daniel		22	M	Farmer	11Au02Bb
CROUGH, John		20	M	Farmer	11Au02Bb
GRACE, James		22	M	Farmer	11Au02Bb
Catharine		20	F	Servant	11Au02Bb
REGAN, Mary		30	F	Servant	11Au02Bb
CAAR, Jim		24	M	Laborer	11Au02Bb
CASEY, Christopher		50	M	Laborer	11Au02Bb
Catherine		50	F	Servant	11Au02Bb
James		12	M	Servant	11Au02Bb
CALLY, Mary		18	F	Servant	11Au02Bb
MCCADE, Edward		21	M	Laborer	11Au02Bb
CONNER, John		19	F	Laborer	11Au02Bb
KENELLY, James		25	M	Miner	11Au02Bb
HENEVAN, Ellen		17	F	Servant	11Au02Bb
CARTY, Pat		34	M	Laborer	11Au02Bb
Michael		4	M	Child	11Au02Bb
John		2	M	Child	11Au02Bb
MCGARRY, Ann		18	F	Servant	11Au02Bb
BUTLER, Bridget		25	F	Servant	11Au02Bb
LEARY, Peter		25	M	Laborer	11Au02Bb
DONNELY, Catherine		18	F	Servant	11Au02Bb
STEELE, Isabella		60	F	Servant	11Au02Bb
Eliza		17	F	Servant	11Au02Bb
DUFFY, John		25	M	Laborer	11Au02Bb
FLANAGAN, Marcella		16	F	Laborer	11Au02Bb
LEONARD, Bessey		18	F	Servant	11Au02Bb
COSTELLO, Judy		20	F	Servant	11Au02Bb
MCKEON, Teddy		22	M	Laborer	11Au02Bb
LASTHY, Betty		33	F	Servant	11Au02Bb
MCCANTEY, Mary		28	F	Spinster	11Au02Bb
CASEY, Catherine		18	F	Spinster	11Au02Bb
KIRLAHAN, Ann		20	F	Spinster	11Au02Bb
MCGIVEN, Cathe.		25	F	Spinster	11Au02Bb
Honora		.00	F	Infant	11Au02Bb
Died-At-Sea					
KITTLE, Pat		18	M	Laborer	11Au02Bb
LYNCH, Pat		30	M	Laborer	11Au02Bb
BUNTLEY, U		20	U	Milliner	11Au02Bb
QUINAN, James		30	M	Laborer	11Au02Bb
LESLEY, Bessey		18	F	Servant	11Au02Bb
CARROLL, John		24	M	Laborer	11Au02Bb
OBRIEN, Margarett		25	F	Servant	11Au02Bb
WALDRON, Pat		28	M	Laborer	11Au02Bb
CERNAN, Catherine		30	F	Servant	11Au02Bb
Elizabeth		20	F	Servant	11Au02Bb
Francis		18	F	Servant	11Au02Bb
Rosa		22	F	Servant	11Au02Bb
Thomas		2	M	Child	11Au02Bb
KENAN, Pat		4	M	Child	11Au02Bb
DENNY, Peggy		30	F	Servant	11Au02Bb
ROANE, Ann		18	F	Servant	11Au02Bb
FAHEY, Bridget		23	F	Servant	11Au02Bb
MCNALLY, Pat		20	M	Laborer	11Au02Bb
LYNCH, Matthew		20	M	Laborer	11Au02Bb
MONAGMAN, Edward		25	M	Laborer	11Au02Bb
Rosey		20	F	Servant	11Au02Bb
REGAN, Simon		30	M	Laborer	11Au02Bb
GILEGAN, Pat		27	M	Laborer	11Au02Bb
CRAWAY, Catharine		20	F	Servant	11Au02Bb
LYONS, Peter		20	M	Laborer	11Au02Bb
TOOHEY, Thomas		20	M	Laborer	11Au02Bb
TANNEY, James		20	M	Laborer	11Au02Bb
KEOGH, Felix		22	M	Laborer	11Au02Bb
BRADY, Pat		20	M	Laborer	11Au02Bb
LAURENCE, Thomas		20	M	Laborer	11Au02Bb
CASEY, Mary		18	M	Servant	11Au02Bb
DENEHY, Catharine		18	M	Servant	11Au02Bb
KELLEY, James		38	M	Laborer	11Au02Bb
CARLY, Mary		18	F	Servant	11Au02Bb
REGAN, William		19	M	Farmer	11Au02Bb
CONNELL, Sarah-Ann		19	F	Servant	11Au02Bb
DRISCOLL, Margarett		30	F	Milliner	11Au02Bb
STEWART, Mary		30	F	Milliner	11Au02Bb
Miney		20	F	Milliner	11Au02Bb
William		4	M	Child	11Au02Bb
BRENAN, Andrew		25	M	Servant	11Au02Bb
Mary		25	F	Seamstress	11Au02Bb
Ann		6	F	Child	11Au02Bb
Pat		4	M	Child	11Au02Bb
Jenny		2	F	Child	11Au02Bb
OCONNER, James		42	M	Merchant	11Au02Bb
U	(W)	37	F	None	11Au02Bb
Eliza		20	F	None	11Au02Bb
Jane		18	F	None	11Au02Bb
Mary		13	F	None	11Au02Bb
James		12	M	None	11Au02Bb
William		9	M	Child	11Au02Bb
Charles		6	M	Child	11Au02Bb
Edward		6	M	Child	11Au02Bb

M.HAWES 11 AUGUST 1849

From London And Plymouth

NAMES OF PASSENGERS	AGE	SEX	OCCUPATIONS	DATE PORT SHIP
RINEY, Wm.	35	M	Farmer	11Au54Kc
Ellen	33	F	Unknown	11Au54Kc
Mary	6	F	Child	11Au54Kc
Bridget	8	F	Child	11Au54Kc
POWER, Patk.	23	M	Carpenter	11Au54Kc
LEAVE, Thomas	24	M	Shoemaker	11Au54Kc
Mary	38	F	Unknown	11Au54Kc
Caroline	8	F	Child	11Au54Kc
Clara	6	F	Child	11Au54Kc
Heratio	4	M	Child	11Au54Kc
HALLOWEN, Francis	34	M	Clerk	11Au54Kc
Bridget	24	F	Unknown	11Au54Kc
Maurice	.00	M	Infant	11Au54Kc
LOAG, James	50	M	Baker	11Au54Kc
Sarah	50	F	Unknown	11Au54Kc
Henry	18	M	Unknown	11Au54Kc
David	45	M	Unknown	11Au54Kc
WALKER, Abraham	22	M	Laborer	11Au54Kc
DAVIS, John	26	M	Carpenter	11Au54Kc
CHAPMAN, James	34	M	Carpenter	11Au54Kc
Jane	32	F	Unknown	11Au54Kc
LAWKE, John	19	M	Laborer	11Au54Kc
CHAPMAN, Julia	3	F	Child	11Au54Kc
James	.00	M	Infant	11Au54Kc
REID, John	13	M	Unknown	11Au54Kc
BARRFIELD, H.	30	M	Farmer	11Au54Kc
Frs.	30	M	Farmer	11Au54Kc
H.	6	U	Child	11Au54Kc
M.	3	U	Child	11Au54Kc
Blanch	.00	F	Infant	11Au54Kc
GILLER, Geo.	24	M	Silversmith	11Au54Kc
CHAPMAN, John	29	M	Carpenter	11Au54Kc
BRIAN, Jas.	52	M	Unknown	11Au54Kc
Mary	41	F	Unknown	11Au54Kc
Ellen	16	F	Unknown	11Au54Kc
Thaddeus	13	M	Unknown	11Au54Kc
Mary-Ann	4	F	Child	11Au54Kc
OLEARY, Ellen	62	F	Laborer	11Au54Kc
HUGH, Patrack	24	M	Laborer	11Au54Kc
WARD, Mary-Ann	24	F	Unknown	11Au54Kc
Mary-Ann	.00	F	Infant	11Au54Kc
NEALLY, Michael	30	M	Laborer	11Au54Kc
EDWARD, Schorhan	20	U	Laborer	11Au54Kc
GALVIN, Mary-Ann	20	F	Unknown	11Au54Kc
BELBEE, Carl	29	M	Silversmith	11Au54Kc
DEPPERAMRY, E.	33	U	Carpenter	11Au54Kc
KING, C.	37	M	Servant	11Au54Kc
ROFF, Jos.	24	M	Laborer	11Au54Kc
SCHLERFE, Benedier	30	U	Laborer	11Au54Kc
GODFRIEND, Leonard	34	M	Laborer	11Au54Kc
PRISCLIND, Caroline	27	F	Unknown	11Au54Kc
GABRIEL, Mich.	34	M	Unknown	11Au54Kc
MULCHANSON, U	39	U	Unknown	11Au54Kc
Lewis	26	M	Unknown	11Au54Kc
BERRSIVAY, S.	19	U	Unknown	11Au54Kc
WEIL, Thos.	18	M	Unknown	11Au54Kc
PFAIRLANCH, Jos.	22	M	Shoemaker	11Au54Kc
GOETZ, Jacob	20	M	Laborer	11Au54Kc
JOSEPH, Samuel	11	M	Unknown	11Au54Kc
SLEYMAN, Francis	21	M	Unknown	11Au54Kc
HEYMAN, R.	20	U	Unknown	11Au54Kc
GANDELFINGER, F.	20	M	Merchant	11Au54Kc
KOOP, L.	19	M	Merchant	11Au54Kc
JSCUEYER, U	28	M	Shoemaker	11Au54Kc
LEOPOLD, Lar.	23	M	Laborer	11Au54Kc
SCHOWBERN, A.	18	M	Miner	11Au54Kc
ANDREWS, U	38	M	Engineer	11Au54Kc
A.M.	36	M	Engineer	11Au54Kc
Catherine	10	F	Unknown	11Au54Kc
Jacobin	2	M	Child	11Au54Kc
TREBARN, Jacob	23	M	Farmer	11Au54Kc
MAISS, Margaret	18	F	Unknown	11Au54Kc
REISS, Eliza	26	F	Unknown	11Au54Kc
ASCHEIVER, Isaac	18	M	Farmer	11Au54Kc
ROSAFLEUGER, Henry	22	M	Unknown	11Au54Kc
GUTMAN, C.	16	U	Unknown	11Au54Kc
SCHIVERNT, C.	32	U	Servant	11Au54Kc
BARROCH, B.	26	M	Farmer	11Au54Kc
CALIN, Jonas	30	M	Laborer	11Au54Kc
ALTIN, B.	24	M	Laborer	11Au54Kc
STRAWS, Rosin	24	U	Unknown	11Au54Kc
Kalchin	24	U	Unknown	11Au54Kc
WESTHEIN, Z.	24	M	Laborer	11Au54Kc
ROSENTHAL, B.	26	M	Shoemaker	11Au54Kc
HARWICK, K.	22	M	Shoemaker	11Au54Kc
KACHERN, P.	32	M	Millwright	11Au54Kc
ROTHS, Lewis	16	M	Farmer	11Au54Kc
Fredk.	15	M	Farmer	11Au54Kc
M.	27	U	Farmer	11Au54Kc
MOLLERS, Sophia	33	F	Midwife	11Au54Kc
BAPPER, G.	26	M	Farmer	11Au54Kc
Ann	4	F	Child	11Au54Kc
J.	4	U	Child	11Au54Kc
Gustin	2	U	Child	11Au54Kc
HOLSHEIM, Regin	28	U	Farmer	11Au54Kc
BEERNEN, Catherine	35	F	Unknown	11Au54Kc
Theresa	2	F	Child	11Au54Kc
KURSH, Lawson	19	M	Farmer	11Au54Kc
MARIE, Serot	37	U	Unknown	11Au54Kc
OBEYLEAN, Lothan	35	M	Laborer	11Au54Kc
SCHWARTZ, J.	63	M	Farmer	11Au54Kc
GUTERAN, Joel	19	M	Unknown	11Au54Kc
DUKE, Johanna	21	M	Unknown	11Au54Kc
KOCH, L.	19	U	Unknown	11Au54Kc
BARTLEN, Mary-Ann	33	F	Unknown	11Au54Kc
GEAHE, Thos.	22	M	Farmer	11Au54Kc
PETERS, John	33	M	Farmer	11Au54Kc
Mary	26	F	Unknown	11Au54Kc
Elizabeth	2	F	Child	11Au54Kc
RUNDLE, John	23	M	Laborer	11Au54Kc
James	25	M	Unknown	11Au54Kc
HAMEFORD, Peter	35	M	Shoemaker	11Au54Kc
Mary	35	F	Unknown	11Au54Kc
M.H.	.00	U	Infant	11Au54Kc
M.Harrold	4	M	Child	11Au54Kc
John	3	M	Child	11Au54Kc
MARTIN, Chas.	26	M	Farmer	11Au54Kc
Ann-C.	27	F	Unknown	11Au54Kc
Chas.H.	.00	M	Infant	11Au54Kc
WALTERS, John	23	M	Laborer	11Au54Kc
James	21	M	Unknown	11Au54Kc
MOYLE, Elizabeth	40	F	Unknown	11Au54Kc
Jane	12	F	Unknown	11Au54Kc
Henry	6	M	Child	11Au54Kc
Mary	3	F	Child	11Au54Kc
FOOT, Henry	38	M	Farmer	11Au54Kc
Maria	31	F	Unknown	11Au54Kc
Ann-Marie	8	F	Child	11Au54Kc
Anna	6	F	Child	11Au54Kc
Fredk.	2	M	Child	11Au54Kc
HADDY, John	17	M	Farmer	11Au54Kc
SULLIVAN, Pat	21	M	Laborer	11Au54Kc
CLEAN, Thos.	60	M	Laborer	11Au54Kc
Catherine	53	F	Unknown	11Au54Kc
Anne	21	F	Unknown	11Au54Kc
Arthur	21	M	Unknown	11Au54Kc
Thos.	10	M	Unknown	11Au54Kc
DAREY, Josh	23	M	Laborer	11Au54Kc
FOOT, Ellen-L.	.00	F	Infant	11Au54Kc
OPIE, Jas.	31	M	Farmer	11Au54Kc

NAMES OF PASSENGERS	AGE	SEX	OCCUPATIONS	DATE PORT SHIP
DURGEN, John	35	M	Farmer	11Au54Kc
Elizabeth	28	F	Unknown	11Au54Kc
Jane	7	F	Child	11Au54Kc
E.Ann	3	F	Child	11Au54Kc
DWYER, Millen	3	M	Child	11Au54Kc
BONE, Mary-Ann	1	F	Child	11Au54Kc
SOLOMON, Abras.	45	M	Farmer	11Au54Kc
Maria	38	F	Unknown	11Au54Kc
VISTER, John	45	M	Weaver	11Au54Kc
CREBBIN, Saml.	30	M	Weaver	11Au54Kc
Jane	28	F	Unknown	11Au54Kc
Mary-Jane	9	F	Child	11Au54Kc
PHILLIPS, M.	22	M	Farmer	11Au54Kc
MITCHEN, Mary-Ann	21	F	Unknown	11Au54Kc
THORN, Henry	29	M	Farmer	11Au54Kc
Jesse	22	M	Unknown	11Au54Kc
GEORGE, M.	30	U	Unknown	11Au54Kc
Mary-Ann	23	F	Unknown	11Au54Kc
Wilber	.00	M	Infant	11Au54Kc
DAWS, Mary	31	F	Unknown	11Au54Kc
OBRYAN, Wm.	71	M	Weaver	11Au54Kc
THORNE, T.	15	M	Unknown	11Au54Kc
HENE, John	40	M	Laborer	11Au54Kc
CLEARY, Catherine	25	F	Unknown	11Au54Kc
BARTLER, John	.00	M	Infant	11Au54Kc
DOLTON, William	30	M	None	11Au54Kc
Anna	25	F	None	11Au54Kc
Anna	1	F	Child	11Au54Kc
CROCHMAN, E.	21	U	Servant	11Au54Kc

GREAT-WESTERN 11 AUGUST 1849

From Bermuda

NAMES OF PASSENGERS	AGE	SEX	OCCUPATIONS	DATE PORT SHIP
MOORE, U	45	M	Merchant	11Au29Iz
HIGGINS, U	30	M	Planter	11Au29Iz
U-Mrs.	24	F	Unknown	11Au29Iz
J.	5	F	Child	11Au29Iz
W.	.09	F	Infant	11Au29Iz
STONE, M.	40	M	Clergyman	11Au29Iz
JONES, Jane	19	F	Servant	11Au29Iz
FOWKE, U-Lieut.	26	M	Military	11Au29Iz
U-Mrs.	25	F	Unknown	11Au29Iz
U, Maryann	19	F	Servant	11Au29Iz
FOWKE, U	.09	F	Infant	11Au29Iz

JUNIATA 11 AUGUST 1849

From London

NAMES OF PASSENGERS	AGE	SEX	OCCUPATIONS	DATE PORT SHIP
SULLIVAN, Patrick	30	M	Laborer	11Au13Me
Ellen	18	F	Laborer	11Au13Me
Ellen	9	F	Child	11Au13Me
YOUNG, Richard	30	M	Laborer	11Au13Me
Mary	23	F	Laborer	11Au13Me
Rebecca	3	F	Child	11Au13Me
George	2	M	Child	11Au13Me
BATEMAN, Charles	41	M	Farmer	11Au13Me
James	12	M	Farmer	11Au13Me
WALKER, Charles	27	M	Cbtmkr	11Au13Me
COLLINS, Florenzo	40	M	Shoemaker	11Au13Me
Ellen	18	F	None	11Au13Me
Mary	12	F	None	11Au13Me
MCDONNELL, William	32	M	Laborer	11Au13Me
HAYS, Jeremiah	33	M	Laborer	11Au13Me
Johanna	36	F	None	11Au13Me
Julia	6	F	Child	11Au13Me
MCCARTHY, John	36	M	Laborer	11Au13Me
Mary	30	F	None	11Au13Me
SULLIVAN, Patrick	52	M	Laborer	11Au13Me
Jeremiah	10	M	None	11Au13Me
DENIN, John	17	M	Shoemaker	11Au13Me
DONOHUE, Catherine	30	F	Domestic	11Au13Me
Mary	22	F	Domestic	11Au13Me
KING, David	27	M	Laborer	11Au13Me
QUIRK, James	48	M	Laborer	11Au13Me
Bridget	40	F	None	11Au13Me
James	20	M	Laborer	11Au13Me
CONNELL, William	35	M	Laborer	11Au13Me
DAGERTY, Barbary	31	F	Wife	11Au13Me
Michael	9	M	Child	11Au13Me
Mary	5	F	Child	11Au13Me
Honora	4	F	Child	11Au13Me
John	3	M	Child	11Au13Me
MAHONY, Michael	27	M	Laborer	11Au13Me
DONOVAN, Jeremiah	28	M	Laborer	11Au13Me
John	23	M	Laborer	11Au13Me
John	27	M	Porter	11Au13Me
BURK, James	32	M	Laborer	11Au13Me
COLLINS, John	30	M	Laborer	11Au13Me
Margaret	30	F	None	11Au13Me
HORAN, Michael	60	M	Laborer	11Au13Me
Bridget	38	F	None	11Au13Me
KEEFE, Ellen	25	F	None	11Au13Me
John	4	M	Child	11Au13Me
Joseph	.11	M	Infant	11Au13Me
SARSFIELD, Patrick	27	M	Laborer	11Au13Me
Mary	54	F	None	11Au13Me
GARRETT, Patrick	34	M	Laborer	11Au13Me
Mary	30	F	None	11Au13Me
Martin	13	M	None	11Au13Me
Sarah	12	F	None	11Au13Me
Mary-Ann	9	F	Child	11Au13Me
DAVIS, Jane	32	F	None	11Au13Me
Emma	17	F	None	11Au13Me
Richard	9	M	Child	11Au13Me
David	7	M	Child	11Au13Me
Jane	3	F	Child	11Au13Me
William	.09	M	Infant	11Au13Me
KINLEY, Edward	45	M	Business	11Au13Me
RIELY, Michael	34	M	Carpenter	11Au13Me
Mary	52	F	None	11Au13Me
Elizabeth	5	F	Child	11Au13Me
MACK, Jeremiah	40	M	None	11Au13Me
KEEFE, Michael Died-At-Sea	27	M	Laborer	11Au13Me
GARRETT, Thomas Died-At-Sea	6	M	Child	11Au13Me
Catherine Died-At-Sea	.06	F	Infant	11Au13Me
KEMPSTON, John	32	M	Unknown	11Au13Me
Mary-Adelaide	22	F	None	11Au13Me

ANN-DASHWOOD 13 AUGUST 1849

From Liverpool

NAMES OF PASSENGERS	AGE	SEX	OCCUPATIONS	DATE PORT SHIP
CANAVAN, Pat	18	M	Surveyor	13Au02Md
OATES, Bridget	18	F	Spinster	13Au02Md
DAGNAN, Cath.	18	F	Spinster	13Au02Md
BRITT, James	29	M	Tailor	13Au02Md
Margaret (W)	22	F	Wife	13Au02Md

NAMES OF PASSENGERS		AGE	SEX	OCCUPATIONS	DATE PORT SHIP	NAMES OF PASSENGERS		AGE	SEX	OCCUPATIONS	DATE PORT SHIP
TAFE, Francis		25	M	Shoemaker	13Au02Md	MILAN, James		24	M	Laborer	13Au02Md
Eliza		16	F	Spinster	13Au02Md	MADDEN, John		20	M	Laborer	13Au02Md
CARROLL, Daniel		30	M	Tailor	13Au02Md	STAUNTON, Mary		24	F	Spinster	13Au02Md
WARD, Mary		19	F	Spinster	13Au02Md	MCALPINE, Cath.		26	F	Wife	13Au02Md
TOSNEY, Bridget		10	F	Spinster	13Au02Md	GAVIN, John		23	M	Laborer	13Au02Md
MCSTEIN, John		18	M	Laborer	13Au02Md	SHEAN, John		25	M	Laborer	13Au02Md
SAVAGE, Mary		60	F	Wife	13Au02Md	RYAN, Mc.		35	M	Laborer	13Au02Md
WELSH, Thos.		11	M	None	13Au02Md	Mary	(W)	22	F	Wife	13Au02Md
BYRNE, George		22	M	Farmer	13Au02Md	GREENAN, Joseph		20	M	Laborer	13Au02Md
Mic.		21	M	Farmer	13Au02Md	Mary		60	F	Wi	13Au02Md
Magt.		20	F	Spinster	13Au02Md	MECHAN, Andrew		60	M	Laborer	13Au02Md
MCNAMARA, Mary		20	F	Spinster	13Au02Md	CORREGAN, Ed		28	M	Laborer	13Au02Md
John		19	M	Farmer	13Au02Md	MORNEY, Pat		55	M	Laborer	13Au02Md
Ann		8	F	Child	13Au02Md	Pat-Jr.		19	M	Laborer	13Au02Md
MORROW, John		50	M	Farmer	13Au02Md	Maria		17	F	Spinster	13Au02Md
Ann	(W)	48	F	Wife	13Au02Md	Cath.		15	F	Spinster	13Au02Md
John		25	M	Farmer	13Au02Md	BURKE, Sarah		24	F	Spinster	13Au02Md
Robert		22	M	Farmer	13Au02Md	CASTER, Wm.		24	M	Laborer	13Au02Md
James		18	M	Farmer	13Au02Md	MCQUEENHY, Dan.		26	M	Laborer	13Au02Md
Thomas		14	M	None	13Au02Md	Mary	(W)	20	F	Wife	13Au02Md
Mary-Anne		11	F	None	13Au02Md	Bernard		2	M	Child	13Au02Md
Eliza		9	F	Child	13Au02Md	Maria		.03	F	Infant	13Au02Md
William		5	M	Child	13Au02Md	HELY, Cath.		22	F	Spinster	13Au02Md
Jane		2	F	Child	13Au02Md	KENDY, John		25	M	Laborer	13Au02Md
DOWNIE, Peter		24	M	Laborer	13Au02Md	Helen	(W)	25	F	Wife	13Au02Md
VALLELY, Mary		18	F	Spinster	13Au02Md	John		1	M	Child	13Au02Md
JOHNSTONE, George		45	M	Laborer	13Au02Md	Ann		1	F	Child	13Au02Md
Elizth.	(W)	45	F	Wife	13Au02Md	MCNAMARA, Mic.		25	M	Laborer	13Au02Md
Mary-Jane		14	F	None	13Au02Md	PERRY, Joseph		60	M	Tailor	13Au02Md
DUNN, Patk.		25	M	Shoemaker	13Au02Md	Died-At-Sea					
Wm.		20	M	Laborer	13Au02Md	Mary-Ann		16	F	Spinster	13Au02Md
KEARNAN, Michael		17	M	Laborer	13Au02Md	BLAKE, James		30	M	Mason	13Au02Md
Mary		34	F	Wife	13Au02Md	RATCLIFFE, Thomas		60	M	Farmer	13Au02Md
Anne		16	F	Spinster	13Au02Md	U-Mrs.	(W)	52	F	Wife	13Au02Md
Cath.		15	F	None	13Au02Md	Thos.		26	M	Farmer	13Au02Md
Susan		12	F	None	13Au02Md	J.T.		18	M	Farmer	13Au02Md
Thos.		9	M	Child	13Au02Md	MULLALLY, Mic.		30	M	Servant	13Au02Md
BRESAN, Mary		14	F	None	13Au02Md	OLDFIELD, Wm.		40	M	Optician	13Au02Md
GILSHIGAN, Ann		13	F	None	13Au02Md	WILSON, Thos.D.		20	M	Iron Monger	13Au02Md
FYNN, Ann		16	F	None	13Au02Md	HAYDEN, Mic.		17	M	None	13Au02Md
RILEY, Helen		18	F	None	13Au02Md	KIRVAN, Thos.		50	M	Laborer	13Au02Md
WELSH, James		5	M	Child	13Au02Md	Philip		21	M	Laborer	13Au02Md
OHARA, Jas.		32	M	Shoemaker	13Au02Md	Mary		14	F	None	13Au02Md
FERGUSSON, Cath.		35	F	Wife	13Au02Md	Margaret		12	F	None	13Au02Md
John		18	M	None	13Au02Md	Bridget		6	F	Child	13Au02Md
Hugh		16	M	None	13Au02Md	HORN, John		40	M	Laborer	13Au02Md
Cath.		13	F	None	13Au02Md	Tim		15	M	None	13Au02Md
NANGLE, Michael		24	M	Mason	13Au02Md	Bridget		13	F	None	13Au02Md
Joanne	(W)	22	F	Wife	13Au02Md	Pat		11	M	None	13Au02Md
Edward		1	M	Child	13Au02Md	MALONE, Wm.		45	M	Farmer	13Au02Md
BURKE, Edward		22	M	Mason	13Au02Md	Honor	(W)	40	F	Wife	13Au02Md
DONOVAN, William		25	M	Farmer	13Au02Md	BRADY, W.F.		24	M	Mariner	13Au02Md
Denis		23	M	Farmer	13Au02Md	Archd.		13	M	None	13Au02Md
Bernard		22	M	Farmer	13Au02Md	KELLY, James		18	M	Laborer	13Au02Md
Michael		18	M	Farmer	13Au02Md	FIGHT, John		22	M	Laborer	13Au02Md
Pat		16	M	None	13Au02Md	FAHEY, Tho.		18	M	Laborer	13Au02Md
Thomas		14	M	None	13Au02Md	GLYNN, Pat		23	M	Laborer	13Au02Md
Morris		12	M	None	13Au02Md	BOHANA, Bridget		35	F	Wife	13Au02Md
Maria		16	F	Spinster	13Au02Md	Thomas		9	M	Child	13Au02Md
Marcella		15	F	Spinster	13Au02Md	John		7	M	Child	13Au02Md
Margaret		24	F	Spinster	13Au02Md	Mary		5	F	Child	13Au02Md
Catherine		10	F	None	13Au02Md	OBRIEN, Mic.		40	M	Mason	13Au02Md
WALLACE, Ann		16	F	Spinster	13Au02Md	LAMBERT, James		40	M	Farmer	13Au02Md
SMITH, Wm.		19	M	Watchmaker	13Au02Md	Margt.	(W)	36	F	Wife	13Au02Md
FITZGERALD, Robert		27	M	Farmer	13Au02Md	Pat		11	M	None	13Au02Md
CUTHBERT, John		35	M	Clcp	13Au02Md	Rose		9	F	Child	13Au02Md
MCWILLIAMS, John		21	M	Bootmaker	13Au02Md	Mary		5	F	Child	13Au02Md
THOMAS, Mary-Jane		30	F	Spinster	13Au02Md	Kitty		3	F	Child	13Au02Md
IRVINE, Margaret		28	F	Spinster	13Au02Md	MERNAGH, Edward		43	M	Farmer	13Au02Md
DUNN, Winifred		12	F	None	13Au02Md	MCLAUCHLAN, Helen		19	F	Spinster	13Au02Md
Judith		10	F	None	13Au02Md	NAIL, Moses		26	M	Laborer	13Au02Md
James		8	M	Child	13Au02Md	Pat		22	M	Laborer	13Au02Md
Eleanor		4	F	Child	13Au02Md	Wm.		18	M	Laborer	13Au02Md
Margt.		6	F	Child	13Au02Md	RYAN, Thos.		20	M	Sawer	13Au02Md
Anne		2	F	Child	13Au02Md	BERRY, John		26	M	Shopkeeper	13Au02Md

NAMES OF PASSENGERS		AGE	SEX	OCCUPATIONS	DATE PORT SHIP
NAIL, Sally		50	F	Wi	13Au02Md
Margaret		24	F	Spinster	13Au02Md
DUN, Pat		40	M	Farmer	13Au02Md
Mary	(W)	35	F	Wife	13Au02Md
Anstey		18	F	Spinster	13Au02Md
Cath.		16	F	Spinster	13Au02Md
Mary		15	F	None	13Au02Md
LEADER, John		21	M	Laborer	13Au02Md
OSHEA, Dan.		20	M	Laborer	13Au02Md
RAXTON, Cath.		27	F	Wife	13Au02Md
Thos.		6	M	Child	13Au02Md
Helen		4	F	Child	13Au02Md
MOFFAT, Pat		21	M	Laborer	13Au02Md
Mary		8	F	Child	13Au02Md
Michael		6	M	Child	13Au02Md
BRUNWIG, Joanna		30	F	Wife	13Au02Md
BRYAN, Bridget		26	F	Spinster	13Au02Md
Mary		6	F	Child	13Au02Md
Donald		4	M	Child	13Au02Md
BRAKEN, Mic.		19	M	Laborer	13Au02Md
MITCHELL, Bridget		15	F	Spinster	13Au02Md
KILLIAN, John		17	M	Laborer	13Au02Md
Thomas		18	M	Laborer	13Au02Md
James		20	M	Laborer	13Au02Md
NEWMAN, And.		27	M	Laborer	13Au02Md
LACHLAN, James		20	M	Laborer	13Au02Md
FAGAN, Mary		22	F	Spinster	13Au02Md
CURRAN, Bridget		18	F	Spinster	13Au02Md
SHORT, Helen		16	F	Spinster	13Au02Md
MARSHALL, William		27	M	Blacksmith	13Au02Md
FING, John		21	M	Mason	13Au02Md
SHORT, Henry		17	M	Joiner	13Au02Md
MURRAY, Pat		16	M	Joiner	13Au02Md
James		45	M	Joiner	13Au02Md
BOYHAN, Patk.		22	M	Blacksmith	13Au02Md
Eliza		22	M	Blacksmith	13Au02Md
MARA, Dennis		14	M	None	13Au02Md
John		12	M	None	13Au02Md
MUCKATEE, Rosa		40	F	Wife	13Au02Md
Mary		8	F	Child	13Au02Md
John		10	M	None	13Au02Md
SHERIDAN, Elizth.		24	F	Wife	13Au02Md
CONOLLY, Mary		14	F	None	13Au02Md
SCHOLAR, Thos.		24	M	Laborer	13Au02Md
CARROLL, Peggy		18	F	Spinster	13Au02Md
Cath.		16	F	Spinster	13Au02Md
RILEY, Mic.		27	M	Laborer	13Au02Md
GRIFFIN, Gil.		27	M	Laborer	13Au02Md
MONAGHAN, Pat		28	M	Laborer	13Au02Md
MCKENNA, Thos.		45	M	Laborer	13Au02Md
Cath.		30	F	Wife	13Au02Md
Felix		5	M	Child	13Au02Md
Thomas		2	M	Child	13Au02Md
GING, James		20	M	Laborer	13Au02Md
RILEY, Lawrence		22	M	Laborer	13Au02Md
CONNOR, Pat		20	M	Laborer	13Au02Md
FOX, Mic.		20	M	Laborer	13Au02Md
MOULAN, Mic.		30	M	Laborer	13Au02Md
FITZSIMMONS, Mary		30	F	Wife	13Au02Md
Joseph		12	M	None	13Au02Md
Cath.		11	F	None	13Au02Md
MURRAY, John		20	M	Laborer	13Au02Md
Mary		18	F	Spinster	13Au02Md
James		16	M	None	13Au02Md
Judy		10	F	None	13Au02Md
Karne		9	M	Child	13Au02Md
LENNAN, Wm.		18	M	Laborer	13Au02Md
LYNCH, Cornelius		45	M	Shopkeeper	13Au02Md
Mary	(W)	40	F	Wife	13Au02Md
Corn-Jr.		8	M	Child	13Au02Md
John		4	M	Child	13Au02Md
HUGHES, Mathew		46	M	Farmer	13Au02Md
Eliza	(W)	40	F	Wife	13Au02Md
Bridget		18	F	Spinster	13Au02Md
Ann		16	F	Spinster	13Au02Md
HUGHES, John		13	M	None	13Au02Md
Cath.		12	F	None	13Au02Md
Mic.		9	M	Child	13Au02Md
Elizth.		7	F	Child	13Au02Md
Margt.		5	F	Child	13Au02Md
BRENNAN, Bridget		18	F	Spinster	13Au02Md
FARLEY, Thos.		21	M	Laborer	13Au02Md
BRADY, Phil		21	M	Laborer	13Au02Md
MURRAY, Tim		28	M	Carpenter	13Au02Md
MYERS, Mic.		21	M	Carpenter	13Au02Md
HAGNEY, James		20	M	Tailor	13Au02Md
HYNDES, Mic.		18	M	Laborer	13Au02Md
RYAN, Helen		24	F	Spinster	13Au02Md
HAYDEN, John		50	M	Laborer	13Au02Md
Mary	(W)	48	F	Wife	13Au02Md
Helen		25	F	Spinster	13Au02Md
Sally		19	F	Spinster	13Au02Md
MORROW, Sarah		7	F	Child	13Au02Md

GENERAL-GREENE 13 AUGUST 1849

From Dublin

NAMES OF PASSENGERS	AGE	SEX	OCCUPATIONS	DATE PORT SHIP
WALSH, U-Mrs.	40	F	Farmer	13Au12Ap
U	.10	U	Infant	13Au12Ap
Mary	13	F	Farmer	13Au12Ap
Edward	12	M	Farmer	13Au12Ap
Jno.	10	M	Farmer	13Au12Ap
Eliza	6	F	Child	13Au12Ap
BYRNE, Thomas	40	M	Farmer	13Au12Ap
Mary	30	F	Farmer	13Au12Ap
Ann	15	F	Farmer	13Au12Ap
EGAN, Ann	20	F	Farmer	13Au12Ap
KELLY, Elizabeth	50	F	Farmer	13Au12Ap
MURPHY, Wm.	18	M	Farmer	13Au12Ap
MOUGHTON, Catherine	20	F	Farmer	13Au12Ap
GRAHAM, Josh.	30	M	Farmer	13Au12Ap
BENNETT, Michl.	35	M	Farmer	13Au12Ap
MARTIN, Mary-J.	17	F	Farmer	13Au12Ap
Jas.	8	M	Child	13Au12Ap
OCONNOR, Thos.	17	M	Farmer	13Au12Ap
LARKIN, Bridget	50	F	Farmer	13Au12Ap
ELWOOD, Jno.	33	M	Farmer	13Au12Ap
CONNOLY, Jno.	20	M	Farmer	13Au12Ap
BYRNE, Mary-A.	24	F	Farmer	13Au12Ap
Teressa	23	F	Farmer	13Au12Ap
Mary	23	F	Farmer	13Au12Ap
BROWN, Mary-A.	34	F	Farmer	13Au12Ap
Wm.	18	M	Farmer	13Au12Ap
James	16	M	Farmer	13Au12Ap
DEVERALL, Master	28	M	Farmer	13Au12Ap
RILEY, Teressa	25	F	Farmer	13Au12Ap
MEIGHAN, Ellen	25	F	Farmer	13Au12Ap
U	.06	U	Infant	13Au12Ap
Mary	3	F	Child	13Au12Ap
Wm.	2	M	Child	13Au12Ap
BETOGH, James	20	M	Farmer	13Au12Ap
RYSE, Susan	27	F	Farmer	13Au12Ap
GLEASON, Wm.	20	M	Farmer	13Au12Ap
KENDY, S.	40	M	Farmer	13Au12Ap
HOGAN, Peter	25	M	Farmer	13Au12Ap
Mary	27	F	Farmer	13Au12Ap
STATLERY, Jno.	34	M	Farmer	13Au12Ap
Stephan	20	M	Farmer	13Au12Ap
RYAN, Margaret	22	F	Farmer	13Au12Ap
U	.11	U	Infant	13Au12Ap
WALSH, Jno.	38	M	Farmer	13Au12Ap
Wm.	30	M	Farmer	13Au12Ap
Thos.	12	M	Farmer	13Au12Ap

NAMES OF PASSENGERS	AGE	SEX	OCCUPATIONS	DATE PORT SHIP
WALSH, Jns.	7	M	Child	13Au12Ap
QUADE, Pat	26	M	Farmer	13Au12Ap
DUNARVAN, Michl.Mrs.	30	F	Farmer	13Au12Ap
TYRELL, Garrett	40	M	Farmer	13Au12Ap
SMYTH, Mat	19	M	Farmer	13Au12Ap
SLEVIN, Mary-A.	20	F	Farmer	13Au12Ap
KEARY, Andy	28	M	Farmer	13Au12Ap
Mary	28	F	Farmer	13Au12Ap
DUNLEVY, Maty	20	M	Farmer	13Au12Ap
KEARY, U	.03	U	Infant	13Au12Ap
MCDONNELL, Julia	25	F	Farmer	13Au12Ap
KELLETT, John	26	M	Farmer	13Au12Ap
Mary	27	F	Farmer	13Au12Ap
U	.10	U	Infant	13Au12Ap
SOLAN, Bernard	18	M	Farmer	13Au12Ap
KEVILL, Peter	42	M	Farmer	13Au12Ap
Betty	39	F	Farmer	13Au12Ap
Thos.	10	M	Child	13Au12Ap
Mary	7	F	Child	13Au12Ap
Jane	4	F	Child	13Au12Ap
WALSH, Jno.	36	M	Farmer	13Au12Ap
HAYS, Eliza	40	F	Farmer	13Au12Ap
U	.05	U	Infant	13Au12Ap
Ann	17	F	Farmer	13Au12Ap
Thos.	7	M	Child	13Au12Ap
KELLS, Martha	20	F	Farmer	13Au12Ap
HOWARD, Peggy	40	F	Farmer	13Au12Ap
BRIEN, Jno.	50	M	Farmer	13Au12Ap
Eliza.	45	F	Farmer	13Au12Ap
Alice	18	F	Farmer	13Au12Ap
Mary	15	F	Farmer	13Au12Ap
Wm.	7	M	Child	13Au12Ap
KERANAUGH, Mary	50	F	Farmer	13Au12Ap
MERCEN, Henry	36	M	Farmer	13Au12Ap
Alicia	40	F	Farmer	13Au12Ap
Robert	30	M	Farmer	13Au12Ap
DORKEN, Ellen	50	F	Farmer	13Au12Ap
MEIGHAN, Ann	25	F	Farmer	13Au12Ap
Josh.	25	M	Farmer	13Au12Ap
GANNON, Alice	20	F	Farmer	13Au12Ap
SMYTH, Ann	21	F	Farmer	13Au12Ap
KINSELLA, Wm.	24	M	Farmer	13Au12Ap
JACKSON, Allice	27	F	Farmer	13Au12Ap
WHITEHEAD, Jno.	17	M	Farmer	13Au12Ap
MADDEN, Wm.	35	M	Farmer	13Au12Ap
MULLERRY, Margt.	20	F	Farmer	13Au12Ap
GURREN, Mary	21	F	Farmer	13Au12Ap
DUFFY, James	24	M	Farmer	13Au12Ap
LITTLE, Martha	29	F	Farmer	13Au12Ap
NEARY, Thos.	20	M	Farmer	13Au12Ap
DUNN, Eliza	20	F	Farmer	13Au12Ap
FLEMING, Eliza	38	F	Farmer	13Au12Ap
U	.09	U	Infant	13Au12Ap
Mary	9	F	Child	13Au12Ap
Bridget	30	F	Farmer	13Au12Ap
CULLEN, Pat.	25	M	Farmer	13Au12Ap
EMERSON, Mary	23	F	Farmer	13Au12Ap
CORBALLY, Cathn.	23	F	Farmer	13Au12Ap
FURNEY, James	20	M	Farmer	13Au12Ap
MITCHEL, Thos.	30	M	Farmer	13Au12Ap
MCNAMARA, Martha	23	F	Farmer	13Au12Ap
U	.07	F	Infant	13Au12Ap
DOYLE, James	30	M	Farmer	13Au12Ap
U-Mrs.	28	F	Farmer	13Au12Ap
U	.11	U	Infant	13Au12Ap
Jno.	3	M	Child	13Au12Ap
Larry	20	M	Farmer	13Au12Ap
SHAILY, Terrens	20	M	Farmer	13Au12Ap
BRENNAN, Catherine	20	F	Farmer	13Au12Ap
BRIEN, Wm.	24	M	Farmer	13Au12Ap
Isabella	20	F	Farmer	13Au12Ap
MCGRATH, James	24	M	Farmer	13Au12Ap
Mary	20	F	Farmer	13Au12Ap
DOYLE, Bridget	20	F	Farmer	13Au12Ap
MCMILLY, Jane	30	F	Farmer	13Au12Ap

NAMES OF PASSENGERS	AGE	SEX	OCCUPATIONS	DATE PORT SHIP
COY, Mary	19	F	Farmer	13Au12Ap
HUGHS, Ester	19	F	Farmer	13Au12Ap
MURPHY, Mary	22	F	Farmer	13Au12Ap

CALLENDAR 14 AUGUST 1849

From Liverpool

NAMES OF PASSENGERS	AGE	SEX	OCCUPATIONS	DATE PORT SHIP
SHELBY, Mary	21	F	Servant	14Au020I
John	20	M	Laborer	14Au020I
Jas.	13	M	Laborer	14Au020I
HAWLEY, John	28	M	Laborer	14Au020I
CAVENAGH, Mick	40	M	Laborer	14Au020I
HORNE, Josh	22	M	Laborer	14Au020I
CALLAN, Pat	35	M	Laborer	14Au020I
Sarah	30	F	Spinster	14Au020I
MCRAY, Francis	24	M	Laborer	14Au020I
Eliza	26	F	Servant	14Au020I
MCMANUS, Josh.	37	M	Servant	14Au020I
Mary	37	F	Servant	14Au020I
John	8	M	Child	14Au020I
Jas.	6	M	Child	14Au020I
Pat	3	M	Child	14Au020I
Michael	2	M	Child	14Au020I
Wm.	.00	M	Infant	14Au020I
FERRIS, John	50	M	Laborer	14Au020I
Mary	50	F	Servant	14Au020I
Elizah.	25	F	Servant	14Au020I
Martha	23	F	Servant	14Au020I
John	21	M	Servant	14Au020I
Mary	19	F	Servant	14Au020I
Jas.	13	M	Laborer	14Au020I
PEBLES, John	20	M	Laborer	14Au020I
WHITTENGTON, Eliza	23	F	Servant	14Au020I
CLIGON, Michl.	18	M	Laborer	14Au020I
DUNWEDY, Jane	30	F	Laborer	14Au020I
Ellen	9	F	Child	14Au020I
Sarah	7	F	Child	14Au020I
Cath.	5	F	Child	14Au020I
Petra	.00	M	Infant	14Au020I
LEARY, Edward	36	M	Laborer	14Au020I
Margaret	26	F	Spinster	14Au020I
PEARSON, John	30	M	Spinster	14Au020I
COUPLAND, Wm.	38	M	Unknown	14Au020I
Sarah	37	F	Servant	14Au020I
Wm.	14	M	Laborer	14Au020I
Thos.	12	M	Laborer	14Au020I
John	8	M	Child	14Au020I
Sarah	6	F	Child	14Au020I
Jedeh	4	F	Child	14Au020I
Robt.	2	M	Child	14Au020I
Harris	.00	M	Infant	14Au020I
HAYES, Edmond	24	M	Laborer	14Au020I
GALLEHER, Susan	21	F	Servant	14Au020I
Kate	18	F	Servant	14Au020I
MALONEY, Margt.	20	F	Servant	14Au020I
BLIDDON, Thos.	27	M	Laborer	14Au020I
Caroline	28	F	Spinster	14Au020I
Wm.	14	M	Laborer	14Au020I
Ellen	2	F	Child	14Au020I
Caroline	.00	F	Infant	14Au020I
BURNS, Jane	30	F	Servant	14Au020I
DOUGHERTY, Wm.	35	M	Servant	14Au020I
Cath.	30	F	Servant	14Au020I
Thos.	13	M	Laborer	14Au020I
Haria	11	M	Laborer	14Au020I
Pat	8	M	Child	14Au020I
Wm.	4	M	Child	14Au020I
Cath.	.00	F	Infant	14Au020I

NAMES OF PASSENGERS	AGE	SEX	OCCUPATIONS	DATE PORT SHIP
BANNON, Jas.	25	M	Laborer	14Au020I
DUNN, Judy	20	F	Spinster	14Au020I
MCCLARON, Michl.	27	M	Laborer	14Au020I
MURPHY, Hugh	35	M	Laborer	14Au020I
Bridget	50	F	Servant	14Au020I
Pat	18	M	Laborer	14Au020I
MCGLAVON, Thos.	7	M	Laborer	14Au020I
Philippe	7	M	Laborer	14Au020I
John	3	M	Laborer	14Au020I
POWER, John	22	M	Laborer	14Au020I
LYONS, Mary	19	F	Servant	14Au020I
HOGAN, John	25	M	Servant	14Au020I
COWFIELD, Thos.	50	M	Servant	14Au020I
BESTICK, Ellen	20	F	Servant	14Au020I
DIXSON, Wm.	40	M	Laborer	14Au020I
Ann	35	F	Servant	14Au020I
Chris	15	M	Servant	14Au020I
Eliza	13	F	Servant	14Au020I
Thos.	9	M	Child	14Au020I
Wm.	.00	M	Infant	14Au020I
CONLON, Margaret	17	F	Servant	14Au020I
HACKETT, Michl.	21	M	Laborer	14Au020I
HONOPHAN, Mat	25	M	Laborer	14Au020I
Mary	30	F	Servant	14Au020I
MALONEY, Pat	30	M	Laborer	14Au020I
Mary	22	F	Servant	14Au020I
Honora	.00	F	Infant	14Au020I
OHANA, Mary	25	F	Servant	14Au020I
HACKETT, John	34	M	Laborer	14Au020I
GLEESON, Cath.	38	F	Servant	14Au020I
ROGERS, Thos.	30	M	Farmer	14Au020I
DEMPSEY, Jas.	22	M	Farmer	14Au020I
Ann	23	F	Servant	14Au020I
RALLEY, Stephen	28	M	Laborer	14Au020I
Bridget	34	F	Servant	14Au020I
John	9	M	Child	14Au020I
Peter	7	M	Child	14Au020I
GREEN, Edward	20	M	Servant	14Au020I
MCDARNELL, Mariah	16	F	Servant	14Au020I
Dora	14	F	Servant	14Au020I
CANNON, Wm.	35	M	Laborer	14Au020I
Sarah	32	F	Servant	14Au020I
Bridget	3	F	Child	14Au020I
Norry	.00	F	Infant	14Au020I
COLLINS, Pat	35	M	Laborer	14Au020I
KELLY, John	35	M	Laborer	14Au020I
Michael	25	M	Laborer	14Au020I
Martin	32	M	Laborer	14Au020I
SHELLY, Michael	35	M	Laborer	14Au020I
DOWLING, Henry	28	M	Laborer	14Au020I
Eliza	54	F	Servant	14Au020I
Chas.	25	M	Laborer	14Au020I
DOLAN, John	25	M	Laborer	14Au020I
Kate	17	F	Servant	14Au020I
DOLLAHAN, John	23	M	Laborer	14Au020I
CASEY, Anthony	26	M	Laborer	14Au020I
GLEESON, Honora	20	F	Spinster	14Au020I
HIGGANS, Biddy	40	F	Spinster	14Au020I
John	40	M	Laborer	14Au020I
Margaret	18	F	Servant	14Au020I
John	16	M	Laborer	14Au020I
Pat	13	M	Laborer	14Au020I
Alice	9	F	Child	14Au020I
Edmond	6	M	Servant	14Au020I
Martin	18	M	Servant	14Au020I
BREMAN, John	35	M	Laborer	14Au020I
MOLEY, John	17	M	Laborer	14Au020I
CONDELLY, Peter	18	M	Laborer	14Au020I
Mary	40	F	Servant	14Au020I
MORRIS, Mary	20	F	Servant	14Au020I
WARD, Mathew	46	M	Servant	14Au020I
MCGLOUGHLIN, Peter	20	M	Laborer	14Au020I
FARRADY, Job	24	M	Laborer	14Au020I
STEELE, Thos.	20	M	Laborer	14Au020I
Mary	18	F	Servant	14Au020I
MCMANELLE, Thos.	19	M	Servant	14Au020I
Mary	20	F	Servant	14Au020I
SHORT, Thos.	25	M	Laborer	14Au020I
Bridget	40	F	Servant	14Au020I
Bridget	21	F	Servant	14Au020I
MCGRULLON, Mary	20	F	Servant	14Au020I
CURSEN, Mary	40	F	Servant	14Au020I
John	19	M	Servant	14Au020I
BENNILL, Offit	37	M	Servant	14Au020I
Jane	32	F	Servant	14Au020I
Mary	.00	F	Infant	14Au020I
GORMAN, Walter	30	M	Laborer	14Au020I
Richard	24	M	Laborer	14Au020I
WELSH, Johannah	5	F	Child	14Au020I
Mary	2	F	Child	14Au020I
GALLIGAN, Ann	23	F	Servant	14Au020I
FLYNN, Pat	20	M	Laborer	14Au020I
FOLEY, Michael	30	M	Laborer	14Au020I
Mary	24	F	Servant	14Au020I
Jas.	.00	M	Infant	14Au020I
SLACKER, Michael	26	M	Laborer	14Au020I
REILEY, Thos.	23	M	Laborer	14Au020I
Bridget	23	M	Spinster	14Au020I
Jas.	.00	M	Infant	14Au020I
RUSSELL, Judith	20	F	Servant	14Au020I
LYNCH, Bridget	20	F	Servant	14Au020I
BURNES, Honora	20	F	Servant	14Au020I
SMITH, Pat	20	M	Laborer	14Au020I
Rose	32	F	Servant	14Au020I
MAKIN, Eliza	56	F	Servant	14Au020I
HUGHES, Pat	38	M	Laborer	14Au020I
MURPHY, Mary	22	F	Servant	14Au020I
SIXSMITHS, Cath.	26	F	Servant	14Au020I
MAULDALL, Mary	20	F	Servant	14Au020I
Margaret	14	F	Servant	14Au020I
MURPHY, Edward	18	M	Laborer	14Au020I
WHITLOW, John	17	M	Laborer	14Au020I
DELANEY, Wm.	25	M	Laborer	14Au020I
MURANE, Bridget	22	F	Servant	14Au020I
KELLEY, John	36	M	Laborer	14Au020I
WARD, Eliza	18	F	Spinster	14Au020I
RYAN, John	26	M	Servant	14Au020I
BITTS, Thos.	26	M	Servant	14Au020I
SCULLY, Ann	27	F	Spinster	14Au020I
GORDON, Cath.	18	F	Spinster	14Au020I
MCMAURIS, Naly	16	F	Spinster	14Au020I
Abby	12	F	Spinster	14Au020I
CHANA, Francis	35	M	Laborer	14Au020I
GALEHAN, Bridget	30	F	Servant	14Au020I
Honora	35	F	Servant	14Au020I
WALKER, Rebecca	24	F	Servant	14Au020I
DARLIN, Peter	24	M	Laborer	14Au020I
TRACY, Hugh	21	M	Laborer	14Au020I
KENEDY, John	45	M	Laborer	14Au020I
HOFFERTY, Ben.	33	M	Laborer	14Au020I
MCANLIFFE, Con.	28	M	Laborer	14Au020I
HALL, Mary-Ann	19	F	Servant	14Au020I
MCLOULUANN, Mary	30	F	Servant	14Au020I
John	6	M	Child	14Au020I
Bernard	.00	M	Infant	14Au020I
CLARK, Bridget	22	F	Servant	14Au020I
RORMAN, Ann	18	F	Servant	14Au020I
CASEY, Margaret	25	F	Servant	14Au020I
MCGUIRE, Con.	17	F	Servant	14Au020I
Edward	10	M	Laborer	14Au020I
MURPHY, Michael	40	M	Laborer	14Au020I
Mary	35	F	Servant	14Au020I
Mary	10	F	Servant	14Au020I
Danl.	2	M	Child	14Au020I
Elizabeth	.00	F	Infant	14Au020I
SWEENEY, Eugene	30	M	Servant	14Au020I
BARNES, Julia	17	F	Servant	14Au020I
BRIAN, Ann	23	F	Servant	14Au020I
MORNSON, Wm.	20	M	Laborer	14Au020I
DIXON, Nicholas	17	M	Laborer	14Au020I

NAMES OF PASSENGERS	AGE	SEX	OCCUPATIONS	DATE PORT SHIP
BLANK, Pat	17	M	Laborer	14Au020i
MCLOULUANN, Ben.	35	M	Laborer	14Au020i

SIR-WILLIAM-MOLESWORTH 14 AUGUST 1849

From Glasgow

NAMES OF PASSENGERS	AGE	SEX	OCCUPATIONS	DATE PORT SHIP
MCLACHLIN, Colin	26	M	Farmer	14Au040j
Jane (W)	26	F	None	14Au040j
GING, George	28	M	Laborer	14Au040j
MULLEN, Mary	20	F	Spinster	14Au040j
Catherine	17	F	Spinster	14Au040j
Nancy	15	F	Spinster	14Au040j
MCLARN, Abigal	36	F	Wife	14Au040j
Jane	13	F	Relative	14Au040j
William	11	M	Relative	14Au040j
Thomas	.09	M	Infant	14Au040j
Elizabeth	6	F	Child	14Au040j
John	9	M	Child	14Au040j
MCMURRAY, Thos.	45	M	Farmer	14Au040j
TORRENCE, U-Mrs.	40	F	Wife	14Au040j
Isabella	13	F	Relative	14Au040j
John	11	M	Relative	14Au040j
Archibald	11	M	Relative	14Au040j
David	8	M	Child	14Au040j
James	9	M	Child	14Au040j
MCLEAN, Jane	18	F	Spinster	14Au040j
MULLEN, Biddy	18	F	Spinster	14Au040j
Ann	16	F	Spinster	14Au040j
DOCHANTY, Jane	40	F	Spinster	14Au040j
HIGGERTY, Wm.	25	M	Farmer	14Au040j
ODAIR, John	21	M	Farmer	14Au040j
Mary	22	F	Farmer	14Au040j
WILSON, John	22	M	Farmer	14Au040j
HART, Sally	18	F	Spinster	14Au040j
DIVINE, Alice	25	F	Spinster	14Au040j
MITCHELL, Isabella	22	F	Spinster	14Au040j
Isabella	.10	F	Infant	14Au040j
HENDERSON, Margaret	45	F	Wife	14Au040j
Margaret	10	F	Relative	14Au040j
PHILIP, Isadore	16	M	Clerk	14Au040j
MCKAY, James	25	M	Clerk	14Au040j
James	.09	M	Infant	14Au040j
Eliza	26	F	None	14Au040j

NIAGARA 14 AUGUST 1849

From Liverpool

NAMES OF PASSENGERS	AGE	SEX	OCCUPATIONS	DATE PORT SHIP
FOWLER, John	27	M	Farmer	14Au021g
Jane	25	F	None	14Au021g
Jane	2	F	Child	14Au021g
KNUDSON, Matthias	41	M	Merchant	14Au021g
MADSEN, Gustav	30	M	Merchant	14Au021g
GODFREY, H.M.	27	M	Doctor	14Au021g
CLEMENTS, Arabella	33	F	None	14Au021g
Lydia	2	F	Child	14Au021g
HOESLEY, Wm.	40	M	None	14Au021g
LUTHBERY, Ellen	11	F	None	14Au021g
Fanny	12	F	None	14Au021g
BURLEY, Edw.	28	M	Mechanic	14Au021g
MCPHERSON, Jane	33	F	None	14Au021g
DIXON, Margt.	34	F	None	14Au021g
DIXON, Agnes	4	F	Child	14Au021g
Chas.	2	M	Child	14Au021g
Margaret	.06	F	Infant	14Au021g
CANRAN, Ann	45	F	None	14Au021g
Margt.	27	F	None	14Au021g
Martin	20	M	Mechanic	14Au021g
Ann	18	F	None	14Au021g
Cath.	16	F	None	14Au021g
Bartholomew	14	M	None	14Au021g
Ellen	13	F	None	14Au021g
John	6	M	Child	14Au021g
CLARKE, John	25	M	Farmer	14Au021g
FORD, Cath.	22	F	None	14Au021g
SMITH, Cath.	27	F	None	14Au021g
Johan	14	M	None	14Au021g
Honora	11	F	None	14Au021g
Ann	9	F	Child	14Au021g
Patrick	7	M	Child	14Au021g
Francis	7	M	Child	14Au021g
Honora	4	F	Child	14Au021g
PRUNTY, James	28	M	Mechanic	14Au021g
LAIN, Cons.	39	F	Seamstress	14Au021g
Hannah	19	F	None	14Au021g
NAMAN, Philip	32	M	Laborer	14Au021g
CALANON, Pat	24	M	None	14Au021g
GUNOT, Geo.	37	M	Clergyman	14Au021g
GILLESPIE, Cath.	16	F	Servant	14Au021g
MCCALL, Hannah	13	F	Servant	14Au021g
LEACH, Sarah	47	F	Nurse	14Au021g
SUGONE, Mary	21	F	None	14Au021g
Cath.	19	F	None	14Au021g
John	17	M	None	14Au021g
Eugene	15	M	None	14Au021g
Michael	10	M	None	14Au021g
Ellen	.00	F	Infant	14Au021g
John	.00	M	Infant	14Au021g
Margt.	1	F	Child	14Au021g
CULLOLLY, James	30	M	Farmer	14Au021g
Cath.	30	F	None	14Au021g
Ellen	12	F	None	14Au021g
John	5	M	Child	14Au021g
Wa.	3	F	Child	14Au021g
DONOHUE, Pat	23	M	Laborer	14Au021g
WELSCH, J.	23	M	Laborer	14Au021g
Julia	.00	F	Infant	14Au021g
Cath.	5	F	Child	14Au021g
MOLONEY, Peggy	22	F	None	14Au021g
LEND, Solomon	22	M	None	14Au021g
MOSELEY, Samuel	26	M	Laborer	14Au021g
SOAPER, Wm.	57	M	Farmer	14Au021g
Geo.	26	M	Mechanic	14Au021g
FAYHEY, Ellen	19	F	Servant	14Au021g
Eliza	20	F	None	14Au021g
GINLIN, Cath.	11	F	None	14Au021g
Bridget	.00	F	Infant	14Au021g
FAGAN, James	26	M	Mechanic	14Au021g
Sarah	27	F	None	14Au021g
William	.00	M	Infant	14Au021g
Mary-Jane	4	F	Child	14Au021g
MURPHY, Thomas	18	M	Laborer	14Au021g
Ellen	12	F	Servant	14Au021g
OLIVER, Joseph	50	M	Mechanic	14Au021g
Mary	55	F	None	14Au021g
Joseph	14	M	None	14Au021g
MUNGOIS, Peter	20	M	Servant	14Au021g
MCMEEHAN, John	22	M	Servant	14Au021g
RYAN, Andrew	22	M	Servant	14Au021g
DRISCOLL, Ellen	40	F	None	14Au021g
Cath.	12	F	None	14Au021g
Mary	11	F	None	14Au021g
John	.00	M	Infant	14Au021g
HARRIS, John	22	M	Farmer	14Au021g
MCCONAL, Condy	21	M	Farmer	14Au021g
DEAN, Edwd.	22	M	Farmer	14Au021g
HEANEY, Pat	14	M	Farmer	14Au021g

NAMES OF PASSENGERS	AGE	SEX	OCCUPATIONS	DATE PORT SHIP
DUFFY, Richd.	25	M	Farmer	14Au02Ig
SPRATT, John	48	M	Farmer	14Au02Ig
Ann	17	F	Farmer	14Au02Ig
GARVIN, Ann	22	F	Farmer	14Au02Ig
MCMAHON, Ann	22	F	Farmer	14Au02Ig
DUFFEY, Margt.	22	F	Farmer	14Au02Ig
AVERY, Cath.	30	F	Farmer	14Au02Ig
MCCORMACK, Chas.	29	M	Laborer	14Au02Ig
Ann	60	F	Laborer	14Au02Ig
MCGUIN, Sarah	18	F	Laborer	14Au02Ig
HARD, Bridget	60	F	Laborer	14Au02Ig
HARPIE, James	39	M	Laborer	14Au02Ig
Ann	36	F	Laborer	14Au02Ig
Mary	9	F	Child	14Au02Ig
Margt.	5	F	Child	14Au02Ig
Sarah	3	F	Child	14Au02Ig
Eliza	.00	F	Infant	14Au02Ig
COSTELLO, John	20	M	Attorney	14Au02Ig
COLLIS, U	19	M	Mechanic	14Au02Ig
MASON, Thos.	30	M	Mechanic	14Au02Ig
Adeline	30	F	None	14Au02Ig
PICKERING, Caroline	28	F	None	14Au02Ig
Amelia	8	F	Child	14Au02Ig
Emma	5	F	Child	14Au02Ig
Lucy	3	F	Child	14Au02Ig
Marion	.00	U	Infant	14Au02Ig
SWIFT, Cornelius	24	M	Unknown	14Au02Ig
Caroline	25	F	Unknown	14Au02Ig
Sarah	.00	F	Infant	14Au02Ig
ELLIOT, George	46	M	Merchant	14Au02Ig
Miriam	20	F	None	14Au02Ig
Eliza	18	F	None	14Au02Ig
Martha	15	F	None	14Au02Ig
COPELAND, Eliza	18	F	None	14Au02Ig
MONTCRAFT, Betsey	18	F	None	14Au02Ig
HONNESSY, Michael	25	M	Farmer	14Au02Ig
NORRIS, Alice	18	F	None	14Au02Ig
WATT, Richard	20	M	Butcher	14Au02Ig
Jesey	21	F	None	14Au02Ig
HEOLD, Merry	23	F	None	14Au02Ig
LYNDER, Julia	10	F	None	14Au02Ig
Catherine	8	F	Child	14Au02Ig
LENYIN, Patrick	50	M	Farmer	14Au02Ig
Bridget	55	F	None	14Au02Ig
Alibia	26	F	None	14Au02Ig
Patrk.	.00	M	Infant	14Au02Ig
SHARKEY, Hone	38	F	None	14Au02Ig
Ann	28	F	None	14Au02Ig
Ann	.00	F	Infant	14Au02Ig
DONALD, John	22	M	Farmer	14Au02Ig
Ellen	18	F	None	14Au02Ig
POWER, Michl.	35	M	Farmer	14Au02Ig
FANSON, Nelly	42	F	None	14Au02Ig
Thos.	16	M	None	14Au02Ig
Margt.	15	F	None	14Au02Ig
Jno.	12	M	None	14Au02Ig
Richd.	10	M	None	14Au02Ig
Wm.	7	M	Child	14Au02Ig
Mary-Ann	.00	F	Infant	14Au02Ig
ENGLAND, Geo.	14	M	None	14Au02Ig
PATEIZE, Geo.	21	M	None	14Au02Ig
DEINT, Wm.	28	M	None	14Au02Ig
PENGALLY, Thos.	27	M	None	14Au02Ig
MCCABE, Bridget	16	F	None	14Au02Ig
ODONALD, Mathw.	30	M	Laborer	14Au02Ig
John	26	M	None	14Au02Ig
Wm.	14	M	None	14Au02Ig
John	.00	M	Infant	14Au02Ig
MCCARTY, Mary	12	F	None	14Au02Ig
DONALD, Cathe.	5	F	Child	14Au02Ig
BEAMAN, Michael	45	M	Farmer	14Au02Ig
Susan	25	F	None	14Au02Ig
John	12	M	None	14Au02Ig
Andrew	.00	M	Infant	14Au02Ig
SUGONS, Thos.	51	M	Farmer	14Au02Ig
SUGONS, Johanna	54	F	None	14Au02Ig
Sally	27	F	None	14Au02Ig
James	25	M	None	14Au02Ig
Ann	23	F	None	14Au02Ig
DEAN, Sarah	70	F	None	14Au02Ig
Hannah	41	F	None	14Au02Ig
Sarah-Ann	21	F	None	14Au02Ig
Maria	18	F	None	14Au02Ig
Emma	15	F	None	14Au02Ig
Frances	12	F	None	14Au02Ig
Richard	10	M	None	14Au02Ig
Thos.	8	M	Child	14Au02Ig
George	6	M	Child	14Au02Ig
Anthony	.00	M	Infant	14Au02Ig
RICHARDSON, Francis	24	M	Mechanic	14Au02Ig
Hannah	26	F	None	14Au02Ig
DEIHERST, Harriet	32	F	None	14Au02Ig
Joseph	8	M	Child	14Au02Ig
Edward	2	M	Child	14Au02Ig
REY, John	25	M	Farmer	14Au02Ig
DENT, Saml.	26	M	Farmer	14Au02Ig
Wm.	20	M	None	14Au02Ig
Emma	.00	F	Infant	14Au02Ig
SOPER, Wm.	29	M	Mechanic	14Au02Ig
Matilda	27	F	None	14Au02Ig
RYATT, Richd.	54	M	Farmer	14Au02Ig
Theobold	49	M	Farmer	14Au02Ig
Maria	21	F	None	14Au02Ig
Elijah	27	M	None	14Au02Ig
Sarah	26	F	None	14Au02Ig
Wm.	5	M	Child	14Au02Ig
Ann	3	F	Child	14Au02Ig
Eliza	.00	F	Infant	14Au02Ig
COULSON, Chas.	27	M	None	14Au02Ig
Ann	23	F	None	14Au02Ig
SCOTT, U	22	M	Mechanic	14Au02Ig
ASHTON, Joseph	35	M	Farmer	14Au02Ig
DOBSON, Henry	18	M	Farmer	14Au02Ig
DORMAR, Peter	27	M	Farmer	14Au02Ig
BEHEN, Jno.	21	M	Mechanic	14Au02Ig
CARROLL, Ellen	32	F	None	14Au02Ig
DAVIS, Jas.	66	M	Mechanic	14Au02Ig
Cathe.	65	F	None	14Au02Ig
Elizabeth	35	F	None	14Au02Ig
Mary	33	F	None	14Au02Ig
MORGAN, Hannah	31	F	None	14Au02Ig
DAVIS, Elinore	28	F	None	14Au02Ig
Catherine	26	F	None	14Au02Ig
Sarah	25	F	None	14Au02Ig
MORGAN, Jane	7	F	Child	14Au02Ig
Cathe.	5	F	Child	14Au02Ig
Maria	.00	F	Infant	14Au02Ig
MOORE, Henry	34	M	Mechanic	14Au02Ig
Sarah	34	F	None	14Au02Ig
Philip	9	M	Child	14Au02Ig
GARTLEDGE, Jno.	24	M	Farmer	14Au02Ig
Robt.	21	M	None	14Au02Ig
BUTLER, Chas.	24	M	Farmer	14Au02Ig
Wm.	23	M	Farmer	14Au02Ig
Joseph	18	M	None	14Au02Ig
Murphy	36	M	Miner	14Au02Ig
Sarah	50	F	None	14Au02Ig
Caroline	8	F	Child	14Au02Ig
Eliza	.00	F	Infant	14Au02Ig
Mary-A.	12	F	None	14Au02Ig
ROBINSON, Saml.	13	M	None	14Au02Ig
HAYES, John	30	M	Mechanic	14Au02Ig

ANDREW-FOSTER 14 AUGUST 1849

From Liverpool

NAMES OF PASSENGERS	AGE	SEX	OCCUPATIONS	DATE PORT SHIP
MADDEN, Michael	45	M	Laborer	14Au02Du
Mary	24	F	None	14Au02Du
Johannah	20	F	None	14Au02Du
John	17	M	Laborer	14Au02Du
Michl.	14	M	Laborer	14Au02Du
MCCLUIR, John	8	M	Child	14Au02Du
SCULLY, Ellen	26	F	None	14Au02Du
Edward	22	M	Laborer	14Au02Du
Mary	14	F	None	14Au02Du
MARKAM, Daniel	37	M	Laborer	14Au02Du
Samuel	30	M	Laborer	14Au02Du
COMOO, Daniel	44	M	Laborer	14Au02Du
MADDEN, Catherine	20	F	None	14Au02Du
FLAHERTY, Daniel	28	M	Laborer	14Au02Du
WALPELL, Wm.	26	M	Laborer	14Au02Du
Honora	19	F	None	14Au02Du
MCANLIFFE, Luisa	22	F	None	14Au02Du
Ann	24	F	None	14Au02Du
Catherine	3	F	Child	14Au02Du
NILE, John	50	M	Laborer	14Au02Du
BAILEY, Catherine	20	F	None	14Au02Du
Catherine	.06	F	Infant	14Au02Du
RYAN, Thos.	19	M	Laborer	14Au02Du
REGAN, Thos.	12	M	Laborer	14Au02Du
KIEFFE, Patrick	11	M	Laborer	14Au02Du
Margt.	20	F	None	14Au02Du
DOOGAN, Mary	21	F	None	14Au02Du
Mary	.04	F	Infant	14Au02Du
CORDOW, John	28	M	Laborer	14Au02Du
Judy	24	F	None	14Au02Du
Patrick	.03	M	Infant	14Au02Du
READY, Ellen	40	F	None	14Au02Du
Mary	17	F	None	14Au02Du
Margt.	15	F	None	14Au02Du
Thadius	14	M	Laborer	14Au02Du
Martin	11	M	Child	14Au02Du
Levy	10	M	Child	14Au02Du
MAHONY, Mary	40	F	None	14Au02Du
FOLEY, Patrick	20	M	Laborer	14Au02Du
WALCH, Lewis	45	M	Laborer	14Au02Du
Joseph	11	M	Laborer	14Au02Du
MCANLIFFE, Jerry	27	M	Laborer	14Au02Du
KEPPLE, Richard	40	M	Laborer	14Au02Du
Johanna	40	F	None	14Au02Du
Honoria	7	F	Child	14Au02Du
Jane	.06	F	Infant	14Au02Du
Michael	2	M	Child	14Au02Du
BYRNE, Joseph	22	M	Laborer	14Au02Du
Mary	20	F	None	14Au02Du
NEVIN, Mary	18	F	None	14Au02Du
GLESON, Mike	50	M	Laborer	14Au02Du
BRYAN, Ellen	50	F	None	14Au02Du
COLERANE, Ellen	20	F	None	14Au02Du
DOYLE, Ann	40	F	None	14Au02Du
Ann	.02	F	Infant	14Au02Du
Peter	8	M	Child	14Au02Du
LEVEY, Anne	24	F	None	14Au02Du
OBRIEN, Nelle	22	M	Laborer	14Au02Du
BURKE, James	14	M	Laborer	14Au02Du
NEVIN, Catherine	19	F	None	14Au02Du
DOYLE, Anne	6	F	Child	14Au02Du
HEALY, Julia	23	F	None	14Au02Du
ENNIS, Mary	23	F	None	14Au02Du
HEAGH, Pat	23	M	None	14Au02Du
DEVOY, Jane	20	F	None	14Au02Du
ELLIOT, Catherine	50	F	None	14Au02Du
SULLIVAN, Richard	30	M	Laborer	14Au02Du
CONNOR, Thos.	46	M	Laborer	14Au02Du
Margt.	45	F	None	14Au02Du
Margt.	17	F	None	14Au02Du
Richard	16	M	Laborer	14Au02Du
Maurice	10	M	Child	14Au02Du
John	8	M	Child	14Au02Du
WHEELEN, Michael	22	M	Laborer	14Au02Du
KELLY, Edward	22	M	Laborer	14Au02Du
DOLEY, Pat.	22	M	Laborer	14Au02Du
HEYDEN, John	20	M	Laborer	14Au02Du
BOYDE, Biddy	19	F	None	14Au02Du
DONOVAN, Jane	24	M	Laborer	14Au02Du
KEENAN, John	21	M	Unknown	14Au02Du
HORAN, Mary	30	F	None	14Au02Du
MOONEY, Pat.	21	M	None	14Au02Du
MCKENSEY, Edward	21	M	None	14Au02Du
Etty	25	F	None	14Au02Du
TOOLE, Pat.	20	M	None	14Au02Du
DALEY, Lawrence	30	M	None	14Au02Du
Bridget	26	F	None	14Au02Du
Ann	20	F	None	14Au02Du
MELIN, Mary	30	F	None	14Au02Du
GUION, Wm.	18	M	Carpenter	14Au02Du
JOYCE, Ann	30	F	None	14Au02Du
Thos.	7	M	Child	14Au02Du
CONNORTON, Ann	7	F	Child	14Au02Du
Bridget	.03	F	Infant	14Au02Du
Thos.	6	M	Child	14Au02Du
Bridget	2	F	Child	14Au02Du
Jas.	3	M	Child	14Au02Du
WHEELAN, Thos.	24	M	Laborer	14Au02Du
Judy	20	F	None	14Au02Du
BRIEN, Michael	24	M	Laborer	14Au02Du
BURKE, Henry	20	M	Laborer	14Au02Du
MCVIEW, Jas.	40	M	Laborer	14Au02Du
HARPER, Robert	27	M	Laborer	14Au02Du
RYAN, Michael	50	M	Laborer	14Au02Du
Dennis	20	M	Laborer	14Au02Du
SCOTT, Mary	35	F	None	14Au02Du
Patrick	20	M	Laborer	14Au02Du
James	9	M	Child	14Au02Du
Ann	13	F	None	14Au02Du
MULLEN, John	40	M	Laborer	14Au02Du
Mary	38	F	None	14Au02Du
Jas.	11	M	Laborer	14Au02Du
MATHEWS, Wm.	45	M	Laborer	14Au02Du
DOWNEY, Thos.	30	M	Laborer	14Au02Du
CONNER, Pat	30	M	Laborer	14Au02Du
Bridget	26	F	None	14Au02Du
MELAN, Jas.	25	M	Laborer	14Au02Du
TROLE, Rody	19	M	Laborer	14Au02Du
HALFPENNY, Wm.	36	M	Seaman	14Au02Du
Wm.	20	M	Laborer	14Au02Du
Catherine	30	F	None	14Au02Du
Mary	9	F	Child	14Au02Du
Anne	8	F	Child	14Au02Du
Conner	22	M	Tailor	14Au02Du
COOK, Jas.	26	M	Laborer	14Au02Du
KEGAN, Chas.	20	M	Laborer	14Au02Du
SHARKY, Mary	9	F	Laborer	14Au02Du
MCCLUSKY, Owen	27	M	Laborer	14Au02Du
Catherine	24	F	None	14Au02Du
FLYMAN, Thos.	20	M	Laborer	14Au02Du
FITZPATRICK, Michael	11	M	Carpenter	14Au02Du
WHELAN, Wm.	30	M	Laborer	14Au02Du
Anne	23	F	None	14Au02Du
MULLAHY, John	20	M	Laborer	14Au02Du
MORRIS, John	24	M	Laborer	14Au02Du
JONES, Celia	24	F	None	14Au02Du
WALCH, Martin	34	M	Laborer	14Au02Du
CANA, John	30	M	Laborer	14Au02Du
FLYNN, Ellen	18	F	None	14Au02Du
Bridget	16	F	None	14Au02Du

NAMES OF PASSENGERS	AGE	SEX	OCCUPATIONS	DATE PORT SHIP
KEOW, Anastia	17	F	None	14Au02Du
DALEY, Mary	24	F	None	14Au02Du
GRIMES, Mary	21	F	Tailor	14Au02Du
Mary	60	F	None	14Au02Du
FARRELL, Pat	30	M	Laborer	14Au02Du
Mary	24	F	Laborer	14Au02Du
REGAN, Dennis	21	M	Laborer	14Au02Du
Amelia	19	F	None	14Au02Du
CALLIGHAN, Daniel	20	M	Laborer	14Au02Du
DONOVAN, Thos.	24	M	Laborer	14Au02Du
MORRIS, Hannah	26	F	None	14Au02Du
NOWLAND, Pat	26	M	Laborer	14Au02Du
CASEY, Michael	8	M	Child	14Au02Du
WHEELAN, Judy	20	F	None	14Au02Du
CALLERTON, Catherine	30	F	None	14Au02Du
GILLIOT, Thos.	27	M	Laborer	14Au02Du
LAUGH, Mary	27	M	Laborer	14Au02Du
Peter	24	M	Laborer	14Au02Du
FITZPATRICK, Catherine	21	F	None	14Au02Du
GILLELAN, Peter	26	M	None	14Au02Du
Mary	26	F	None	14Au02Du
Patrick	7	M	Child	14Au02Du
FLAHERTY, Michael	26	M	Laborer	14Au02Du
CROSBIE, Anne	17	F	None	14Au02Du
COOLEY, Francis	14	M	Laborer	14Au02Du
GILLAN, Margaret	18	F	None	14Au02Du
BUTLER, Mary	24	F	None	14Au02Du
BURKE, Thos.	18	M	Laborer	14Au02Du
KENNEY, James	30	M	Laborer	14Au02Du
GORMAN, Jas.	26	M	Laborer	14Au02Du
MACKAY, Mark	27	M	Laborer	14Au02Du
DOUGHERTY, Mary	16	F	None	14Au02Du
LYNCH, Geo.	27	M	Laborer	14Au02Du
Mary	25	F	None	14Au02Du
Margt.	14	F	None	14Au02Du
MCNAMARA, Bridget	50	F	None	14Au02Du
ALMION, Bridget	64	F	None	14Au02Du
Michael	4	M	Child	14Au02Du
FITZGERALD, Edward	40	M	Laborer	14Au02Du
QUILLAN, Mary	16	F	None	14Au02Du
James	13	M	Laborer	14Au02Du
Johanna	8	F	Child	14Au02Du
RYAN, Thos.	24	M	Laborer	14Au02Du
DOYLE, Catherine	19	F	None	14Au02Du
MURPHY, Julia	26	F	None	14Au02Du
CASSIDAY, Mary	55	F	None	14Au02Du
Died-At-Sea				
BURNS, Wm.	21	M	Unknown	14Au02Du
MCKAY, Thos.	18	M	Laborer	14Au02Du
LONGTON, Thos.M.	20	M	Laborer	14Au02Du
BARNES, John	25	M	Carpenter	14Au02Du
Wm.	46	M	Carpenter	14Au02Du
DUNCAN, John	26	M	Clergyman	14Au02Du
CLAIR, John	35	M	Laborer	14Au02Du
Eliza.	35	M	Laborer	14Au02Du
Bridget	7	F	Child	14Au02Du
Daniel	3	M	Child	14Au02Du
GLASON, Dennis	28	M	Farmer	14Au02Du
MCGUINESS, Hannah	32	F	None	14Au02Du
GELMARTIN, Mary	22	F	None	14Au02Du
MCCABE, Sarah	40	F	None	14Au02Du
Ann	24	F	None	14Au02Du
Mary	30	F	None	14Au02Du
BURKE, John	25	M	Laborer	14Au02Du
Patrick	23	M	Laborer	14Au02Du
DONOHUE, John	22	M	Laborer	14Au02Du
COONEY, Bridget	24	F	None	14Au02Du
FITZGERALD, Jas.	19	M	Laborer	14Au02Du
Bridget	19	F	None	14Au02Du
RYAN, Simon	35	M	Laborer	14Au02Du
KELSEY, Robert	30	M	Laborer	14Au02Du
Ann	25	F	None	14Au02Du
MORIARTY, July	25	F	None	14Au02Du
HANLON, Margt.	25	F	None	14Au02Du
MURPHY, Timothy	45	M	Laborer	14Au02Du
OKEEFE, Joseph	28	M	Laborer	14Au02Du
FLAERTY, Pat	27	M	Laborer	14Au02Du
DONOVAN, John	27	M	Laborer	14Au02Du
BAY, Pat	18	M	Laborer	14Au02Du
CONSIDEN, Margt.	40	F	None	14Au02Du
AKIN, Robert	16	M	Laborer	14Au02Du
FITZGERALD, John	21	M	Farmer	14Au02Du
Patrick	18	M	Farmer	14Au02Du
Jane	17	F	None	14Au02Du
Margt.	16	F	None	14Au02Du
Ellen	4	F	Child	14Au02Du
Ann	45	F	None	14Au02Du
LYSITH, Ann	21	F	None	14Au02Du
BRADY, Bridget	21	F	None	14Au02Du
MCNAMAR, Mary	21	F	None	14Au02Du
MOONEY, James	46	M	Laborer	14Au02Du
Patrick	21	M	Laborer	14Au02Du
CONNELL, Mary	24	F	None	14Au02Du
Bridget	21	F	None	14Au02Du
BIDDLE, Wm.	15	M	None	14Au02Du
GIBBON, Edward	38	M	Laborer	14Au02Du
Thos.	15	M	Laborer	14Au02Du
CLARY, Thos.	22	M	Laborer	14Au02Du
MARTHER, John	22	M	Laborer	14Au02Du
BAGAN, Joseph	28	M	Laborer	14Au02Du
EVANS, Edwin	20	M	Laborer	14Au02Du
SULLIVAN, John	32	M	Laborer	14Au02Du
Mary	25	F	None	14Au02Du
BYRNE, Mathew	40	M	Laborer	14Au02Du
Catherine	20	F	None	14Au02Du
FLINN, Mathew	20	M	Laborer	14Au02Du
REILLY, John	30	M	Laborer	14Au02Du
RAPE, Ewd.	21	M	Laborer	14Au02Du
Anthony	23	M	Laborer	14Au02Du
Biddy	50	F	None	14Au02Du
RUDDY, Sally	21	F	None	14Au02Du
Mary	11	F	None	14Au02Du
LAWLER, Wm.	26	M	Laborer	14Au02Du
DUNN, Mary	22	F	None	14Au02Du
MCCARTH, Michl.	24	M	Laborer	14Au02Du
DILLON, John	24	M	Laborer	14Au02Du
DOYLE, Sarah	24	F	None	14Au02Du
Ann	5	F	Child	14Au02Du
MCLAUGHLIN, John	17	M	Laborer	14Au02Du
Ellen	15	F	None	14Au02Du
ALWELL, Jas.	23	M	Laborer	14Au02Du
Mary	20	F	None	14Au02Du
CASTLES, Ann	20	F	None	14Au02Du
KEENAN, Catherine	18	F	None	14Au02Du
KENNEDY, Margt.	25	F	None	14Au02Du
FALLIN, Jas.	20	M	Laborer	14Au02Du
KENNAN, Ellen	24	F	None	14Au02Du
MCGEE, Patrick	35	M	Laborer	14Au02Du
BURKE, Bridget	50	F	None	14Au02Du
GALLAGHER, John	35	M	Laborer	14Au02Du
Bridget	37	F	None	14Au02Du
Ann	8	F	Child	14Au02Du
Dennis	6	M	Child	14Au02Du
FANNIGAN, Barry	44	M	Laborer	14Au02Du
BELL, Jane	24	F	None	14Au02Du
MULLIHILL, Julia	16	F	None	14Au02Du
BUDGET, Bridgt.	38	F	None	14Au02Du
Eliza	26	F	None	14Au02Du
Patrick	11	M	None	14Au02Du
Mary	6	F	Child	14Au02Du
RULLY, James	25	M	None	14Au02Du
DONNELY, Wm.	28	M	Laborer	14Au02Du
MCNAMAR, Ann	40	F	None	14Au02Du
SHEA, Catherine	27	F	None	14Au02Du
CONNELLY, Ann	18	F	None	14Au02Du
HARA, Ann	19	F	None	14Au02Du
RILLY, Biddy	14	F	None	14Au02Du
Died-At-Sea				
CLEARY, John	27	M	Laborer	14Au02Du
MCCAULY, John	18	M	Laborer	14Au02Du

NAMES OF PASSENGERS	AGE	SEX	OCCUPATIONS	DATE PORT SHIP
HAYDEN, Michl.	22	M	Laborer	14Au02Du
GALLAGHER, Rose	18	F	None	14Au02Du
Catherine	20	F	None	14Au02Du
MONTGOMERY, Bridget	18	F	None	14Au02Du
BRADY, Jas.	24	M	Farmer	14Au02Du
FARRELL, John	25	M	Laborer	14Au02Du
GLYNN, Mary	18	F	None	14Au02Du
BRADY, Hugh	26	M	Laborer	14Au02Du
MCDONALD, John	35	M	Laborer	14Au02Du
BURGEN, Bridgt.	21	F	None	14Au02Du
DALEY, Mary	60	F	None	14Au02Du
DELANY, John	21	M	Laborer	14Au02Du
MCNAMAR, Thos.	21	M	Laborer	14Au02Du
CATELLE, Jerry	35	M	Laborer	14Au02Du
MALLANOY, Hugh	30	M	Laborer	14Au02Du
SCOTT, Jas.	21	M	Laborer	14Au02Du
Catherine	20	F	None	14Au02Du
Mary	25	F	None	14Au02Du
BAGAN, Daniel	27	M	Laborer	14Au02Du
QUIGLEY, John	15	M	Laborer	14Au02Du
Patrick	10	M	Child	14Au02Du
FLINN, John	17	M	Laborer	14Au02Du
Peter	16	M	Laborer	14Au02Du
CLARK, Rose	19	F	None	14Au02Du
Rose	.04	F	Infant	14Au02Du
CASSIDY, Hugh	24	M	Laborer	14Au02Du
Ann	22	F	None	14Au02Du
LOURY, Martin	25	M	Laborer	14Au02Du
Mary	24	F	None	14Au02Du
MARREN, Margaret	24	F	None	14Au02Du
GIBBINS, Peter	20	M	Laborer	14Au02Du
BLOWNEY, Mary-Jane	18	F	None	14Au02Du
ODONNELL, Minty	17	F	None	14Au02Du
Ann	16	F	None	14Au02Du
Biddy	18	F	None	14Au02Du
Unity	19	F	None	14Au02Du
LADDIN, Catherine	23	F	None	14Au02Du
BEATY, Mary	30	F	None	14Au02Du
BLOWNEY, Benjn.	16	M	Laborer	14Au02Du
CONLEY, Mary	50	F	None	14Au02Du
MCCORMICK, Eliza	20	F	None	14Au02Du
FITZGERRALD, Ellen	20	F	None	14Au02Du
SMITH, Ann	20	F	None	14Au02Du
Thos.	16	M	None	14Au02Du
Jas.	14	M	None	14Au02Du
Judith	12	F	None	14Au02Du
LIVESAY, Ann	30	F	None	14Au02Du
James	6	M	Child	14Au02Du
Starkey	5	M	Child	14Au02Du
Jane	2	F	Child	14Au02Du
CURTIS, Wm.	20	M	Farmer	14Au02Du
KENNEDY, Ellen	18	F	None	14Au02Du
MCINTIRE, Ellen	20	F	None	14Au02Du
MCGARTH, Bridget	4	F	Child	14Au02Du
HEWIT, Wm.	25	M	Farmer	14Au02Du
TRETON, James	12	M	None	14Au02Du
Thos.	14	F	None	14Au02Du
HEWIT, Mary	22	F	None	14Au02Du
Sarah	.02	F	Infant	14Au02Du
RAY, Wm.	25	M	Laborer	14Au02Du
KING, Robert	20	M	Laborer	14Au02Du
ANTONIA, Francis	19	M	Laborer	14Au02Du
KILGORE, John	27	M	Seaman	14Au02Du
GAULD, Geo.	18	M	Smith	14Au02Du
MILLER, Peter	30	F	Farmer	14Au02Du
PARROT, Chas.	19	M	Farmer	14Au02Du
BAKER, Michl.	22	M	Farmer	14Au02Du
Mary	19	F	None	14Au02Du
MURPHY, Michl.	31	M	Laborer	14Au02Du
WATKINS, Phillip	33	M	Seaman	14Au02Du
WHEELAN, Francis	30	M	Carpenter	14Au02Du

JESSICA 14 AUGUST 1849

From Liverpool

NAMES OF PASSENGERS	AGE	SEX	OCCUPATIONS	DATE PORT SHIP
GLANCEY, Brigt.	20	F	Laborer	14Au020k
FLANNAGAN, Jno.	20	M	Unknown	14Au020k
Margt.	21	F	Unknown	14Au020k
FITZPATRICK, Thos.	35	M	Unknown	14Au020k
Helen	32	F	Unknown	14Au020k
U	.00	U	Infant	14Au020k
ROECK, Jno.	20	M	Unknown	14Au020k
JORDAN, Mary	18	F	Unknown	14Au020k
MCCARTHY, Hugh	21	M	Unknown	14Au020k
THOMPSON, Alex.	19	M	Unknown	14Au020k
BYRNE, Jno.	29	M	Unknown	14Au020k
Margt.	28	F	Unknown	14Au020k
Mary	8	F	Child	14Au020k
Johanna	6	F	Child	14Au020k
Magt.	.00	F	Infant	14Au020k
MCKEELAN, Mick	25	M	Unknown	14Au020k
U-Mrs.	25	F	Unknown	14Au020k
POWERS, Wm.	20	M	Unknown	14Au020k
Math.	.00	F	Infant	14Au020k
Cath.	.00	F	Infant	14Au020k
GLEESON, Thos.	18	M	Unknown	14Au020k
FEELAN, Patt.	20	M	Unknown	14Au020k
CUNNINGHAM, Peter	30	M	Unknown	14Au020k
Brigt.	21	F	Unknown	14Au020k
HASSAN, Jenny	20	F	Unknown	14Au020k
HORMAN, Phillip	25	M	Unknown	14Au020k
BRADLEY, Wm.	33	M	Unknown	14Au020k
Thos.	12	M	Unknown	14Au020k
SMITH, Thos.	30	M	Unknown	14Au020k
Chas.	26	M	Unknown	14Au020k
GILMORE, Thos.	24	M	Unknown	14Au020k
MONAHAN, Mary	21	F	Unknown	14Au020k
Honor	30	F	Unknown	14Au020k
Thos.	5	M	Child	14Au020k
UNWINN, Jno.	19	M	Unknown	14Au020k
FALLON, Nick.	38	M	Unknown	14Au020k
ALLEN, Bryon	40	M	Unknown	14Au020k
LOWRY, Henry	28	M	Unknown	14Au020k
KAVANAGH, Arthur	28	M	Unknown	14Au020k
SHALLON, Patt	45	M	Unknown	14Au020k
Mary	45	F	Laborer	14Au020k
Judas	41	M	Unknown	14Au020k
Jno.	13	M	Unknown	14Au020k
Helen	12	F	Unknown	14Au020k
Cath.	9	F	Child	14Au020k
Margt.	7	F	Child	14Au020k
NALLY, Patt	3	M	Child	14Au020k
Cath	50	F	Unknown	14Au020k
MCMAHON, James	50	M	Unknown	14Au020k
U-Mrs.	30	F	Unknown	14Au020k
U	.00	U	Infant	14Au020k
U	.00	U	Infant	14Au020k
U	.00	U	Infant	14Au020k
RUDDER, Teddy	25	M	Unknown	14Au020k
STERLING, Thos.	30	M	Unknown	14Au020k
MARTIN, Jas.	40	M	Unknown	14Au020k
YOUNG, Jno.	28	M	Unknown	14Au020k
NOX, Hugh	24	M	Unknown	14Au020k
HANSON, Henry	26	M	Unknown	14Au020k
U-Mrs.	26	F	Unknown	14Au020k
HENRY, Walter	.00	M	Infant	14Au020k
BAGSHAW, Jno.	24	M	Unknown	14Au020k
U	23	F	Unknown	14Au020k
U	.00	U	Infant	14Au020k
MURPHY, Andrew	22	M	Unknown	14Au020k

NAMES OF PASSENGERS	AGE	SEX	OCCUPATIONS	DATE PORT SHIP
MURPHY, U-Mrs.	20	F	Unknown	14Au020k
U	.00	U	Infant	14Au020k
BLACK, Chas.	35	M	Unknown	14Au020k
U-Mrs.	30	F	Unknown	14Au020k
QUIN, Arthur	24	M	Unknown	14Au020k
MCKIERNAN, Martin	27	M	Unknown	14Au020k
CHARLTON, Jno.	27	M	Unknown	14Au020k
MCKERNON, Mary	24	F	Unknown	14Au020k
KERNS, Peter	13	M	Unknown	14Au020k
HAYS, Rich.	36	M	Unknown	14Au020k
Mary	36	F	Unknown	14Au020k
Johanna	36	F	Unknown	14Au020k
TOOLEY, Wm.	50	M	Unknown	14Au020k
Brigt.	45	F	Unknown	14Au020k
Anne	20	F	Unknown	14Au020k
Mary	18	F	Unknown	14Au020k
Magt.	16	F	Unknown	14Au020k
Anty	13	F	Unknown	14Au020k
Thos.	13	F	Unknown	14Au020k
Jas.	9	M	Child	14Au020k
Judith	5	F	Child	14Au020k
MURPHY, Michl.	21	M	Unknown	14Au020k
MCGOLVERK, Jas.	30	M	Unknown	14Au020k
Jas.	80	M	Unknown	14Au020k
BRIEN, Jno.	23	M	Unknown	14Au020k
Thos.	20	M	Unknown	14Au020k
Con.	18	M	Unknown	14Au020k
Kitty	56	F	Unknown	14Au020k
Died-At-Sea				
CALLAGHAN, Andrew	18	M	Laborer	14Au020k
DALEY, Bridt.	20	F	Unknown	14Au020k
RYAN, Margt.	45	F	Unknown	14Au020k
Maria	18	F	Unknown	14Au020k
Jno.	10	M	Unknown	14Au020k
LINKEY, Patt	80	M	Unknown	14Au020k
RAFFTY, Thos.	35	M	Unknown	14Au020k
PENDER, Mary	40	F	Unknown	14Au020k
Peggy	20	F	Unknown	14Au020k
U	.00	F	Infant	14Au020k
BEARDSLEY, Jno.	30	M	Unknown	14Au020k
Magt.	27	F	Unknown	14Au020k
RORKE, Johanna	6	F	Child	14Au020k
Died-At-Sea				
Wm.	6	M	Child	14Au020k
Mary	.00	F	Infant	14Au020k
Eliza	40	F	Unknown	14Au020k
NELSON, Andrew	30	M	Unknown	14Au020k
U-Mrs.	27	F	Unknown	14Au020k
Mary	9	F	Child	14Au020k
Andrew	7	M	Child	14Au020k
Jas.	21	M	Unknown	14Au020k
HONNICK, Anne	19	F	Unknown	14Au020k
CLAY, Jno.	21	M	Unknown	14Au020k
Anne	6	F	Child	14Au020k
Rich	4	M	Child	14Au020k
Henry	.00	M	Infant	14Au020k
Died-At-Sea				
Johan	.00	F	Infant	14Au020k
Died-At-Sea				
CONNER, Jno.	20	M	Unknown	14Au020k
Died-At-Sea				
RAUR, Helen	21	F	Unknown	14Au020k
RYAN, Mick	29	M	Unknown	14Au020k
JACKS, John	26	M	Unknown	14Au020k
HUGHS, James	21	M	Unknown	14Au020k
MURPHY, Bridgt.	49	F	Unknown	14Au020k
CONNER, Thos.	30	M	Unknown	14Au020k
Brigt.	24	F	Unknown	14Au020k
Jas.	.00	M	Infant	14Au020k
COWAY, Patt	20	M	Unknown	14Au020k
MCGALEY, Wm.	19	M	Unknown	14Au020k
Margt.	18	F	Unknown	14Au020k
DOLEN, Anne	30	F	Unknown	14Au020k
GARRIGAN, Ed.	24	M	Unknown	14Au020k
Anne	21	F	Unknown	14Au020k
WAKIN, Jno.	21	M	Unknown	14Au020k
KELESIDE, U-Miss	20	F	Unknown	14Au020k
Charlotte	19	F	Unknown	14Au020k
EGAN, Thos.	24	M	Unknown	14Au020k
TOOL, Jas.	24	M	Unknown	14Au020k
U-Mrs.	30	F	Unknown	14Au020k
Margt.	.00	F	Infant	14Au020k
Nickl.	30	M	Unknown	14Au020k
ROOKE, Robt.	31	M	Unknown	14Au020k
Died-At-Sea				
KAVANAH, Thos.	30	M	Unknown	14Au020k
U-Mrs.	30	F	Unknown	14Au020k
Mary	25	F	Unknown	14Au020k
BURNS, Luke	29	M	Laborer	14Au020k
U-Mrs.	29	F	Unknown	14Au020k
BULGER, Jno.	29	M	Unknown	14Au020k
U-Mrs.	22	F	Unknown	14Au020k
BAKER, U-Mrs.	29	F	Unknown	14Au020k
U	29	M	Unknown	14Au020k
BILLER, Jas.	20	M	Unknown	14Au020k
U-Mrs.	29	F	Unknown	14Au020k
DOYLE, Thos.	29	M	Unknown	14Au020k
MCMANUS, Neill	20	M	Unknown	14Au020k
MCMILLEN, Mich.	29	M	Unknown	14Au020k
DONOUHUE, Byrone	30	M	Unknown	14Au020k
U-Mrs.	30	F	Unknown	14Au020k
U	.10	U	Infant	14Au020k
Michl.	7	M	Child	14Au020k
Biddy	4	F	Child	14Au020k
Patt	2	M	Child	14Au020k
James	1	M	Child	14Au020k
SHERIDAN, Jno.	21	M	Unknown	14Au020k
CONVEN, Joseph	18	M	Unknown	14Au020k
POWER, Luke	40	M	Unknown	14Au020k
U-Mrs.	40	F	Unknown	14Au020k
FEINLEY, Jno.	28	M	Unknown	14Au020k
Mary	32	F	Unknown	14Au020k
POWER, Mary	32	F	Unknown	14Au020k
Michl.	12	M	Unknown	14Au020k
Judy	10	F	Unknown	14Au020k
Cath.	7	F	Child	14Au020k
Helen	4	F	Child	14Au020k
Died-At-Sea				
Patt	.00	M	Infant	14Au020k
Rick	34	M	Unknown	14Au020k
Died-At-Sea				
MURPHY, Cath.	50	F	Unknown	14Au020k
POWER, Mary	13	F	Unknown	14Au020k
Michl.	11	M	Unknown	14Au020k
Cath.	8	F	Child	14Au020k
Died-At-Sea				
Biddy	6	F	Child	14Au020k
Wm.	.00	M	Infant	14Au020k
Walter	28	M	Unknown	14Au020k
BUTTON, Nicholas	21	M	Unknown	14Au020k
Luke	28	M	Unknown	14Au020k
Michl.	8	M	Child	14Au020k
DENBY, Thos.	24	M	Unknown	14Au020k
U-Mrs.	21	F	Unknown	14Au020k
BYRON, Patt	24	M	Unknown	14Au020k
CANDES, U	24	M	Unknown	14Au020k
CODEY, Cath.	22	F	Unknown	14Au020k
THOMPSON, Dorah	24	F	Unknown	14Au020k
CAKILL, Cath.	10	F	Unknown	14Au020k
SHEA, Cath.	22	F	Unknown	14Au020k
MCMANUS, Jno.	21	M	Unknown	14Au020k
BURNS, Luke	28	M	Laborer	14Au020k
LEACY, Jas.	59	M	Unknown	14Au020k
Mick	20	M	Unknown	14Au020k
Mary	27	F	Unknown	14Au020k
KEATING, Jas.	20	M	Unknown	14Au020k
WALSH, Wm.	35	M	Unknown	14Au020k
Patt	18	M	Unknown	14Au020k
DUFFY, Owen	24	M	Unknown	14Au020k
MCMAHON, Jno.	22	M	Unknown	14Au020k

NAMES OF PASSENGERS	AGE	SEX	OCCUPATIONS	DATE PORT SHIP
NEILL, Anne	25	F	Unknown	14Au020k
STANLEY, W.J.	21	M	Unknown	14Au020k
ARMSTRONG, Robt.	37	M	Unknown	14Au020k
U-Mrs.	24	F	Unknown	14Au020k
Jane	9	F	Child	14Au020k
Died-At-Sea				
BOLAN, Dennis	25	M	Unknown	14Au020k
JOIEL, Barter	15	M	Unknown	14Au020k
HICKEY, Mary	60	F	Unknown	14Au020k
Mrgt.	22	F	Unknown	14Au020k
Brigt.	20	F	Unknown	14Au020k
Mary	16	F	Unknown	14Au020k
Catherine	13	F	Unknown	14Au020k
Hannah	15	F	Unknown	14Au020k
Steph.	11	M	Unknown	14Au020k
Richd.	9	M	Child	14Au020k
Maurice	7	M	Child	14Au020k
HAYS, Brigt.	30	F	Unknown	14Au020k
Jno.	32	M	Unknown	14Au020k
U	.00	U	Infant	14Au020k
Died-At-Sea				
MCGIVIRN, Jas.	20	M	Unknown	14Au020k
Thos.	21	M	Unknown	14Au020k
HYLAND, Htos.	21	M	Unknown	14Au020k
Richd.	18	M	Unknown	14Au020k
Maria	26	F	Unknown	14Au020k
William	21	M	Unknown	14Au020k
U-Mrs.	29	F	Unknown	14Au020k
CARROLL, Brigt.	21	F	Unknown	14Au020k
SAXTON, Cath.	28	F	Unknown	14Au020k
BRENNON, Ed	18	M	Unknown	14Au020k
KENNA, James	12	M	Unknown	14Au020k
DOHERTY, Magt.	30	F	Unknown	14Au020k
COCKTON, Ally	20	F	Unknown	14Au020k
GAHAGAN, Mary	20	F	Unknown	14Au020k
DOYLE, Anne	30	F	Unknown	14Au020k
Mary	20	F	Unknown	14Au020k
Died-At-Sea				
Fras.	13	F	Unknown	14Au020k
U	9	F	Child	14Au020k
Anthony	6	M	Child	14Au020k
Bair	5	M	Child	14Au020k
SHARK, Marth.	40	F	Unknown	14Au020k
DUNN, James	20	M	Unknown	14Au020k
MARTHA, Jno.	34	M	Unknown	14Au020k
CLARY, Wm.	21	M	Unknown	14Au020k
Died-At-Sea				
ROWN, Patt	21	M	Laborer	14Au020k
OBRIEN, Edw.	20	M	Unknown	14Au020k
SULLIVAN, Ely	28	M	Unknown	14Au020k
CONROY, Jno.	31	M	Unknown	14Au020k
WHEELER, Michl.	33	M	Unknown	14Au020k
Judy	33	F	Unknown	14Au020k
ROACH, Patt	22	M	Unknown	14Au020k
CUNNINGHAM, Patt	26	M	Unknown	14Au020k
PHEALAN, Michl.	24	M	Unknown	14Au020k
CAUPHEN, Mary	20	F	Unknown	14Au020k
GORMAN, Jno.	12	M	Unknown	14Au020k
KENNELLY, Magt.	21	F	Unknown	14Au020k
HENDY, James	26	M	Unknown	14Au020k
Tom	29	M	Unknown	14Au020k
Toby	30	M	Unknown	14Au020k
FOURD, Patt	50	M	Unknown	14Au020k
BREMON, Patt	50	M	Unknown	14Au020k
Died-At-Sea				
Andrew	26	M	Unknown	14Au020k
David	18	M	Unknown	14Au020k
Brigt.	22	F	Unknown	14Au020k
MAYO, Frederick	30	M	Unknown	14Au020k
LUSSY, Wm.	30	M	Unknown	14Au020k
Eliza	47	F	Unknown	14Au020k
Dalby	25	M	Unknown	14Au020k
Cath.	23	F	Unknown	14Au020k
DAMON, Patt	30	M	Unknown	14Au020k
GILLEGAN, Brigt.	21	F	Unknown	14Au020k
JUDGE, Arthur	21	M	Unknown	14Au020k
LENOX, Thomas	29	M	Unknown	14Au020k
CULIMAN, Patt	20	M	Unknown	14Au020k
MULROY, Thos.	30	M	Unknown	14Au020k
CONNER, Andrew	26	M	Unknown	14Au020k
RYAN, John	30	M	Unknown	14Au020k
Anne	26	F	Unknown	14Au020k
KELLY, Anne	19	F	Unknown	14Au020k
GRIMS, James	20	M	Unknown	14Au020k
JONES, Robt.	24	M	Unknown	14Au020k
IRVIN, Georg	23	M	Unknown	14Au020k
MATHEWS, Thomas	22	M	Unknown	14Au020k
MCALESTER, Chas.	40	M	Unknown	14Au020k
Frans.	5	F	Child	14Au020k
Alex.	2	M	Child	14Au020k
Elizth.	40	F	Unknown	14Au020k
Frans.	17	F	Unknown	14Au020k
Hannah	7	F	Child	14Au020k
GAITLAND, Rose	24	F	Unknown	14Au020k
SPENCER, Will.	30	M	Unknown	14Au020k
PARKS, Jno.	30	M	Unknown	14Au020k
CULLEN, Gerald	20	M	Unknown	14Au020k
RARRELL, Patt	30	M	Unknown	14Au020k
Cath.	24	F	Unknown	14Au020k
Maria	17	F	Unknown	14Au020k
CURRAN, Jno.	14	M	Unknown	14Au020k
Anne	40	F	Unknown	14Au020k
CASSIDY, Mary	20	F	Laborer	14Au020k
MCCABE, Cath.	16	F	Unknown	14Au020k
Biddy	14	F	Unknown	14Au020k
RIELY, Mary	40	F	Unknown	14Au020k
BLUMBERG, Theo.	24	M	Unknown	14Au020k
BELL, Will.	50	M	Unknown	14Au020k
Died-At-Sea				
James	16	M	Unknown	14Au020k
Agnes	14	F	Unknown	14Au020k
Wm.	12	M	Unknown	14Au020k
BREDLEY, Jas.	26	M	Unknown	14Au020k
Wm.	30	M	Unknown	14Au020k
Henry	22	M	Unknown	14Au020k
Michl.	20	M	Unknown	14Au020k
Margt.	24	F	Unknown	14Au020k
Brigt.	45	F	Unknown	14Au020k
FEAHAM, Sally	22	F	Unknown	14Au020k
TOWSEND, Henry	20	M	Unknown	14Au020k
LOWN, Margt.	25	M	Unknown	14Au020k
EAGAN, Judy	26	M	Unknown	14Au020k
MALTREN, Edw.	46	M	Unknown	14Au020k
Anne	8	F	Child	14Au020k
CUNNINGHAM, Wm.	25	M	Unknown	14Au020k
Andrew	35	M	Unknown	14Au020k
DOOLEY, Jno.	26	M	Unknown	14Au020k
Eliza	30	F	Unknown	14Au020k
Sarah	3	F	Child	14Au020k
CUNNINGHAM, Danl.	20	M	Unknown	14Au020k
FEEHAN, Jno.	20	M	Unknown	14Au020k
BATTY, Jas.	36	M	Unknown	14Au020k
Jno.	26	M	Unknown	14Au020k
BENNETT, Wm.	36	M	Unknown	14Au020k
HALVEY, Jno.	24	M	Unknown	14Au020k
JOICE, Patt	20	M	Unknown	14Au020k
BLANDER, Will.	19	M	Unknown	14Au020k
Geo.	25	M	Unknown	14Au020k
Jno.	31	M	Unknown	14Au020k
Charlotte	24	F	Unknown	14Au020k
CONNER, Thos.	28	M	Unknown	14Au020k
CASH, Patt	26	M	Unknown	14Au020k
Biddy	50	F	Unknown	14Au020k
NOLAN, Richd.	30	M	Unknown	14Au020k
Cathn.	30	F	Unknown	14Au020k
Thos.	5	M	Child	14Au020k
CASH, Mary	45	F	Unknown	14Au020k
Biddy	18	F	Unknown	14Au020k
FLETCHER, Isaac	25	M	Unknown	14Au020k
WHITE, Edw.	25	M	Unknown	14Au020k

NAMES OF PASSENGERS		AGE	SEX	OCCUPATIONS	DATE PORT SHIP
WHITE, Rosella		48	F	Unknown	14Au020k
FINNERTY, Biddy		16	F	Unknown	14Au020k
MCGIVERN, Michl.		18	M	Unknown	14Au020k
CLEARY, Michael		3	M	Child	14Au020k
GRAY, Bryan		28	M	Unknown	14Au020k
Biddy		22	F	Unknown	14Au020k
Jno.		8	M	Child	14Au020k
KING, Martha		16	F	Unknown	14Au020k
Mary		13	F	Unknown	14Au020k
OWEN, Mary		13	F	Unknown	14Au020k
KINSELLA, Cath.		19	F	Unknown	14Au020k

MARCHIONESS-OF-BUTE 15 AUGUST 1849

From Newry

NAMES OF PASSENGERS		AGE	SEX	OCCUPATIONS	DATE PORT SHIP
SANDFORD, Edward		20	M	Farmer	15Au110p
Ann		24	F	Spinster	15Au110p
BELL, Martha		18	F	Spinster	15Au110p
MORISON, Mary-Ann		18	F	Servant	15Au110p
CAHILL, Joseph		30	M	Farmer	15Au110p
Jane	(W)	21	F	Wife	15Au110p
Jane		.05	F	Infant	15Au110p
ARMSTRONG, Margaret		26	F	Spinster	15Au110p
ATCHINSON, Ann		20	F	Spinster	15Au110p
Grace		14	F	Spinster	15Au110p
HAGAN, John		26	M	Blacksmith	15Au110p
MOORE, Mary		40	F	Spinster	15Au110p
Rose		24	F	Servant	15Au110p
Francis		22	M	Relative	15Au110p
Alice		14	F	Relative	15Au110p
Mary		12	F	Relative	15Au110p
Michael		9	M	Child	15Au110p
SHERNY, Margaret		20	F	Servant	15Au110p
QUIGLEY, James		27	M	Laborer	15Au110p
Mary-Ann	(W)	22	F	Wife	15Au110p
Patrick		2	M	Child	15Au110p
MCMAHAON, Catherine		25	F	Haberdasher	15Au110p
MADRION, Mary-Ann		25	F	Bomkr	15Au110p
OHEAR, Sarah		16	F	Spinster	15Au110p
FLEET, Sarah-J.		17	F	Spinster	15Au110p
DOWNEY, Rose		25	F	Spinster	15Au110p
MCALEARY, Mary		34	F	Servant	15Au110p
Margaret		8	F	Child	15Au110p
DONALDSON, John		15	M	Tailor	15Au110p
Margaret		17	F	Spinster	15Au110p
DONAGHAY, Peter		30	M	Ploughman	15Au110p
EAGAN, Thomas		35	M	Farmer	15Au110p
KERR, Catherine		20	F	Spinster	15Au110p
Bridget		20	F	Spinster	15Au110p
GLASSY, William		22	M	Baker	15Au110p
MCCULLOUGH, Jane		30	F	Spinster	15Au110p
REILLY, James		30	M	Ploughman	15Au110p
SCANLIN, Charles		22	M	Watchmaker	15Au110p
TUFTS, William		38	M	Gdnr	15Au110p
Margaret	(W)	34	F	Wife	15Au110p
HAGAN, Lawrence		26	M	Wood Ranger	15Au110p
MCPAITLAND, Thomas		22	M	Florist	15Au110p
CASSIDY, John		19	M	Ploughman	15Au110p
DUFFY, Mary		30	F	Milliner	15Au110p
Catherine		9	F	Child	15Au110p
Thomas		7	M	Child	15Au110p
MCKEE, Catherine		30	F	Spinster	15Au110p
Ellen		22	F	Milliner	15Au110p
Jane		24	F	Servant	15Au110p
Sally		20	F	Servant	15Au110p
MAGUIRE, Edward		26	M	Blacksmith	15Au110p
CALLANS, Patrick		35	M	Farmer	15Au110p
DONNELLY, Biddy		20	F	Spinster	15Au110p

NAMES OF PASSENGERS		AGE	SEX	OCCUPATIONS	DATE PORT SHIP
TAYLOR, Johannah		20	F	Spinster	15Au110p
MCKINLEY, Alexander		39	M	Laborer	15Au110p
GOLLOGLY, Bridget		24	F	Servant	15Au110p
MALLEN, Thomas		20	M	Farmer	15Au110p
WOODS, Elizabeth		22	F	Servant	15Au110p
MASTERSON, Bridget		20	F	Servant	15Au110p
COULTER, William		28	M	Ploughman	15Au110p
SHIERAN, John		22	M	Shoemaker	15Au110p
HURNALTY, Mary		4	F	Child	15Au110p
CUNNINGHAM, James		11	M	Servant	15Au110p
SMITH, Charles		17	M	Servant	15Au110p
CONNOLLY, Bridget		36	F	Spinster	15Au110p
Mary		15	F	None	15Au110p
Bernard		8	M	Child	15Au110p
GORDEN, Mary		17	F	Servant	15Au110p
ARMSTRONG, Mary		.00	F	Infant	15Au110p
SMITH, James		30	M	Laborer	15Au110p
Margaret	(W)	30	F	Wife	15Au110p
Philip		9	M	Child	15Au110p
James		7	M	Child	15Au110p
Patt		5	M	Child	15Au110p
John		2	M	Child	15Au110p
MCCORMACK, Betty		21	F	Servant	15Au110p
SMITH, John		18	M	Laborer	15Au110p
WILSON, Mathew		35	M	Ploughman	15Au110p
CARAHER, James		20	M	Farmer	15Au110p
MARTIN, John		22	M	Laborer	15Au110p
MARVERY, Thomas		20	M	Waiter	15Au110p
ONEILL, Patrick		50	M	Laborer	15Au110p
Jane	(W)	50	F	Wife	15Au110p
FEGAN, Catherine		22	F	Spinster	15Au110p
MCCANN, Patrick		2	M	Clerk	15Au110p
Bridget	(W)	24	F	Wife	15Au110p
FEGAN, Michael		24	M	Mason	15Au110p
MCGIVERN, William		18	M	Servant	15Au110p
MCDONALD, Patrick		25	M	Laborer	15Au110p
GORDAN, Luke		22	M	Farmer	15Au110p
DOLLAN, Mary		17	F	Spinster	15Au110p
HUNRALTY, Ann		35	F	Servant	15Au110p
AGNEW, Mary		50	F	Spinster	15Au110p
John		20	M	Relative	15Au110p
Peter		16	M	Relative	15Au110p
Mary		22	F	Relative	15Au110p
TREANOR, Anne		36	F	Servant	15Au110p
BYRNE, Catherine		23	F	Spinster	15Au110p
Henry		25	M	Laborer	15Au110p
MCCABE, John		20	M	Farmer	15Au110p
Mary	(W)	18	F	Wife	15Au110p
MCENEARY, Patrick		20	M	Servant	15Au110p
Ann		17	F	Spinster	15Au110p
CULLAN, Patrick		30	M	Farmer	15Au110p
Jane	(W)	35	F	Wife	15Au110p
MCSHANE, Richard		40	M	Mason	15Au110p
Catherine	(W)	22	F	Wife	15Au110p
FINNEGAN, Patt		20	M	Servant	15Au110p
Phill.		14	M	Servant	15Au110p
Felix		.09	M	Infant	15Au110p
MCDANIEL, Peter		50	M	Laborer	15Au110p
Catherine	(W)	37	F	Wife	15Au110p
Patt		17	M	Relative	15Au110p
Anne		13	F	Relative	15Au110p
Judy		8	F	Child	15Au110p
Catherine		6	F	Child	15Au110p
MCKENNA, Thomas		50	M	Farmer	15Au110p
James		15	M	None	15Au110p
Margaret	(W)	45	F	Wife	15Au110p
FINNEGAN, Owen		20	M	Laborer	15Au110p
Rose		22	F	Servant	15Au110p
WARD, James		25	M	Laborer	15Au110p
Mary	(W)	26	F	Wife	15Au110p
Rose		2	F	Child	15Au110p
Eleanor		.00	F	Infant	15Au110p
CASEY, Rose		50	F	Spinster	15Au110p
CALLAN, Margaret		26	F	Spinster	15Au110p
MURPHY, John		14	M	Servant	15Au110p

NAMES OF PASSENGERS		AGE	SEX	OCCUPATIONS	DATE PORT SHIP
MURPHY, Philip		12	M	Servant	15Au110p
MCDANIEL, Peter		21	M	Ploughman	15Au110p
Mary		22	F	Spinster	15Au110p
MCARDLE, Mary		21	F	Servant	15Au110p
Betty		16	F	Servant	15Au110p
Catherine		14	F	Servant	15Au110p
WOODS, Owen		36	M	Laborer	15Au110p
Catherine	(W)	45	F	Wife	15Au110p
Thomas		12	M	None	15Au110p
Alice		10	F	None	15Au110p
BISHOP, Mary		19	F	Servant	15Au110p
JONES, William		50	M	Farmer	15Au110p
Mary	(W)	44	F	Wife	15Au110p
Edward		9	M	Child	15Au110p
Patt		7	M	Child	15Au110p
John		3	M	Child	15Au110p
Died-At-Sea					
Mary		.00	F	Infant	15Au110p
DONNELLY, Mary		20	F	Spinster	15Au110p
CUNNINGHAM, Elizabeth		38	F	Servant	15Au110p
BOTHWELL, Margaret		16	F	Bomkr	15Au110p
MARRON, James		50	M	Farmer	15Au110p
Died-At-Sea					
Margaret		40	F	Servant	15Au110p
Edward		22	M	Relative	15Au110p
Stephen		16	M	Relative	15Au110p
Michael		13	M	Relative	15Au110p
SMITH, Thomas		26	M	Farmer	15Au110p
Catherine	(W)	24	F	Wife	15Au110p
CONNOLLY, Felix		40	M	Ploughman	15Au110p
Rose	(W)	33	F	Wife	15Au110p
Mary		12	F	Relative	15Au110p
Biddy		9	F	Child	15Au110p
Sally		7	F	Child	15Au110p
Michael		4	M	Child	15Au110p
Catherine		2	F	Child	15Au110p
GRIMES, John		50	M	Servant	15Au110p
Patt		20	M	Servant	15Au110p
Catherine		16	F	Spinster	15Au110p
Edward		7	M	Child	15Au110p
REILLY, John		45	M	Butcher	15Au110p
Catharine	(W)	40	F	Wife	15Au110p
Biddy		13	F	Relative	15Au110p
Alice		10	F	Relative	15Au110p
Michael		8	M	Child	15Au110p
John		5	M	Child	15Au110p
SHEVLIN, Ann		40	F	Spinster	15Au110p
Mary		19	F	Relative	15Au110p
Ann		11	F	Relative	15Au110p
Judith		9	F	Child	15Au110p
Betty		6	F	Child	15Au110p
Bridget		16	F	Relative	15Au110p
Catherine		.00	F	Infant	15Au110p
BYRNE, John		50	M	Farmer	15Au110p
Mary	(W)	35	F	Wife	15Au110p
Biddy		10	F	Relative	15Au110p
Patt		6	M	Child	15Au110p
MCAROLE, Catherine		12	F	Spinster	15Au110p
James	(B)	17	M	Brother	15Au110p
Mary		20	F	Spinster	15Au110p
Bernard		27	M	Laborer	15Au110p
CARROLL, Edward		55	M	Ploughman	15Au110p
Biddy		16	F	Spinster	15Au110p
GAITLAND, Daniel		45	M	Ploughman	15Au110p
Alice	(W)	35	F	Wife	15Au110p
Thomas		9	M	Child	15Au110p
John		7	M	Child	15Au110p
Hugh		5	M	Child	15Au110p
Daniel		3	M	Child	15Au110p
Peter		.00	M	Infant	15Au110p
REILLY, Owen		50	M	Farmer	15Au110p
Mary	(W)	30	F	Wife	15Au110p
Hugh		22	M	Relative	15Au110p
Michael		18	M	Relative	15Au110p
Ann		2	F	Child	15Au110p
QUINN, Bridget		50	F	Spinster	15Au110p
MCCOMT, John		25	M	Ploughman	15Au110p
SINART, Mary		35	F	Spinster	15Au110p
Nancy		7	F	Child	15Au110p
William		4	M	Child	15Au110p
MCQUILLEN, William		22	M	Tailor	15Au110p
KEENAN, Ann		26	F	Servant	15Au110p
ROLSON, Mary-Jane		38	F	Spinster	15Au110p
Margaret		7	F	Child	15Au110p
James		5	M	Child	15Au110p
William		3	M	Child	15Au110p
Mary-Jane		3	F	Child	15Au110p
Richard		.00	M	Infant	15Au110p
BOYCE, James		23	M	Laborer	15Au110p
Jane	(W)	19	F	Wife	15Au110p
John		.00	M	Infant	15Au110p
EAGAN, Joseph		20	M	Millwright	15Au110p
MCCONNELL, Sarah		20	F	Milliner	15Au110p
HUGHES, Sarah		18	F	Spinster	15Au110p
CUNNINGHAM, Catherine		37	F	Spinster	15Au110p
Mary-Ann		13	F	Relative	15Au110p
Peter		9	M	Child	15Au110p
Eliza		7	F	Child	15Au110p
Margaret		5	F	Child	15Au110p
John		2	M	Child	15Au110p
BOYLE, Richard		27	M	Farmer	15Au110p
QUIGLEY, John		50	M	Laborer	15Au110p
John		19	M	Servant	15Au110p
Catherine		17	F	Spinster	15Au110p
Anne		15	F	Spinster	15Au110p
Peter		13	M	Servant	15Au110p
SCOTT, George		35	M	Butcher	15Au110p
GILLESPIE, Thomas		26	M	Carpenter	15Au110p
Mary	(W)	2	F	Wife	15Au110p
CORVAN, Philip		34	M	Farmer	15Au110p
James		10	M	Farmer	15Au110p
Margaret		7	F	Child	15Au110p
Catherine		5	F	Child	15Au110p
Thomas		3	M	Child	15Au110p
MCKENNA, Patrick		25	M	Machinist	15Au110p
Ann	(W)	20	F	Wife	15Au110p
Michael		15	M	Brother	15Au110p
MCCROWN, George		21	M	Laborer	15Au110p
KELLY, Patrick		30	M	Shoemaker	15Au110p
MURPHY, Michael		20	M	Smith	15Au110p
Mary	(W)	19	F	Wife	15Au110p
LINCH, Thomas		28	M	Currier	15Au110p
Ann	(W)	23	F	Wife	15Au110p
Thomas		.00	M	Infant	15Au110p
Died-At-Sea					
HENRY, Eliza		20	F	Spinster	15Au110p
Mary		18	F	Relative	15Au110p
Alexander		15	M	Relative	15Au110p
Richard		12	M	Relative	15Au110p
James		8	M	Child	15Au110p
Joseph		6	M	Child	15Au110p
Andrew		2	M	Child	15Au110p
Alexander		50	M	Relative	15Au110p
Margaret		45	F	Relative	15Au110p
WOODS, Michael		35	M	Laborer	15Au110p
DONNELLY, Patrick		28	M	Farmer	15Au110p
RUDDY, Patrick		20	M	Butcher	15Au110p
LARKIN, Patrick		24	M	Servant	15Au110p
HANLON, Thomas		40	M	Farmer	15Au110p
Hugh		44	M	Farmer	15Au110p
Alice	(W)	45	F	Wife	15Au110p
Thomas	(S)	12	M	Son	15Au110p
MCKEOWN, Mary		19	F	Spinster	15Au110p
James		17	M	Shoemaker	15Au110p
MORGAN, Thomas		22	M	Saddler	15Au110p
Ann	(W)	22	F	Wife	15Au110p
MCKEOWN, Patt		35	M	Tailor	15Au110p
Ann	(W)	35	F	Wife	15Au110p
Mary-Jane		9	F	Child	15Au110p
Sarah		5	F	Child	15Au110p

NAMES OF PASSENGERS		AGE	SEX	OCCUPATIONS	DATE PORT SHIP
MCKEOWN, Margaret		.00	F	Infant	15Au110p
MCALEROY, John		8	M	Child	15Au110p
DONNELLY, Betty		14	F	Spinster	15Au110p
Margaret		12	F	Spinster	15Au110p
Patrick	(B)	6	M	Child	15Au110p
SMITH, Mary		40	F	Spinster	15Au110p
KEENAN, James		40	M	Laborer	15Au110p
HANLON, Hugh		.00	M	Infant	15Au110p
MARKS, Mary		26	F	Spinster	15Au110p
MCCORMICK, John		24	M	Farmer	15Au110p
LONGHEAD, Joseph		50	M	Merchant	15Au110p
Catharine	(W)	50	F	Wife	15Au110p
Mary		17	F	Relative	15Au110p
Sarah		15	F	Relative	15Au110p
Anne		13	F	Relative	15Au110p
Elizabeth		11	F	Relative	15Au110p
Jane		9	F	Child	15Au110p
Martha		5	F	Child	15Au110p
BLAKE, Alice		22	F	Governess	15Au110p
RANSON, Samuel		38	M	Gentleman	15Au110p
MCKENNA, U-Mrs.		22	F	Servant	15Au110p
Charlotte		.03	F	Infant	15Au110p

CALEB-GRIMSHAW 15 AUGUST 1849

From Liverpool

NAMES OF PASSENGERS		AGE	SEX	OCCUPATIONS	DATE PORT SHIP
ROYNAN, John		28	M	Farmer	15Au02Ej
FEENEY, Thos.		24	M	Farmer	15Au02Ej
BRISLAM, Jas.		23	M	Laborer	15Au02Ej
REYNOLDS, Thos.		24	M	Laborer	15Au02Ej
THOMAS, Wm.		40	M	Laborer	15Au02Ej
ALLEN, Wm.		27	M	Laborer	15Au02Ej
U	(W)	20	F	None	15Au02Ej
John		.00	M	Infant	15Au02Ej
WHITESIDE, John		28	M	Laborer	15Au02Ej
Hannah		18	F	None	15Au02Ej
Jane		3	F	Child	15Au02Ej
Ellen		2	F	Child	15Au02Ej
SMITH, Mary		30	F	None	15Au02Ej
BRADY, Biddy		30	F	None	15Au02Ej
CONNOLLY, Ann		25	F	Servant	15Au02Ej
MURPHY, John		34	M	None	15Au02Ej
EVANS, David		47	M	Miner	15Au02Ej
Mary		45	F	None	15Au02Ej
Mary		9	F	Child	15Au02Ej
Ann		6	F	Child	15Au02Ej
Elizh.		3	F	Child	15Au02Ej
RYAN, Wm.		20	M	Laborer	15Au02Ej
BRADY, Bdgt.		17	F	Dressmaker	15Au02Ej
WOODHOUSE, Saml.		27	M	Farmer	15Au02Ej
KELLY, Michl.		20	M	Farmer	15Au02Ej
TRACY, Maria		20	F	None	15Au02Ej
BIRMINGHAM, John		40	M	Miner	15Au02Ej
Pat		50	M	None	15Au02Ej
CRADDOCK, Jas.		34	M	Carpenter	15Au02Ej
Nichs.		27	M	Carpenter	15Au02Ej
BROHAN, Ellen		14	F	None	15Au02Ej
GARVEY, Ann		55	F	WI	15Au02Ej
Mary		30	F	None	15Au02Ej
Died-At-Sea					
GALLAGHER, Luke		32	M	Carpenter	15Au02Ej
Pat		30	M	None	15Au02Ej
MAHER, John		40	M	Carpenter	15Au02Ej
Died-At-Sea					
Margt.		14	F	None	15Au02Ej
Died-At-Sea					
MCKENNA, Sarah		40	F	None	15Au02Ej
Died-At-Sea					
MCKENNA, Mary		11	F	None	15Au02Ej
BURKE, John		22	M	Laborer	15Au02Ej
MCGRATH, Michl.		27	M	None	15Au02Ej
WELSH, John		30	M	None	15Au02Ej
MOHANY, John		27	M	None	15Au02Ej
GORDON, Danl.		30	M	None	15Au02Ej
MAHANY, Honora		25	F	None	15Au02Ej
Ellen		24	F	None	15Au02Ej
QUINN, Mary		40	F	None	15Au02Ej
Mary		7	F	Child	15Au02Ej
James		6	M	Child	15Au02Ej
John		2	M	Child	15Au02Ej
Died-At-Sea					
MCCARTHY, Danl.		33	M	None	15Au02Ej
DALY, John		26	M	Laborer	15Au02Ej
MULCAHY, Mary		14	F	None	15Au02Ej
Michl.		14	M	None	15Au02Ej
WEST, Robt.		25	M	None	15Au02Ej
LEA, John		19	M	None	15Au02Ej
ROARKE, Cath.		17	F	Laborer	15Au02Ej
GIBNEY, Michl.		17	M	None	15Au02Ej
HENNESSY, Mary		27	F	Servant	15Au02Ej
PENDERGAST, Edward		25	M	Laborer	15Au02Ej
RAFTER, Mary		5	F	Child	15Au02Ej
CAIN, Rosey		.00	F	Infant	15Au02Ej
SHAW, John		28	M	None	15Au02Ej
REYNOLDS, Pat		24	M	Servant	15Au02Ej
WALKER, Benj.		22	M	Servant	15Au02Ej
MCMANUS, Jas.		30	M	None	15Au02Ej
Danl.		20	M	None	15Au02Ej
PARNTON, Elizh.		26	F	Servant	15Au02Ej
Thos.		17	M	None	15Au02Ej
Wm.		16	M	None	15Au02Ej
Died-At-Sea					
Elizh.		16	F	None	15Au02Ej
Died-At-Sea					
Harriet		8	F	Child	15Au02Ej
Geo.		6	F	Child	15Au02Ej
Mary-Ann		2	F	Child	15Au02Ej
SPEAKE, Elizh.		25	F	None	15Au02Ej
JONES, J.H.		30	M	Unknown	15Au02Ej
Died-At-Sea					
Mary		25	F	None	15Au02Ej
Charles		.00	M	Infant	15Au02Ej
Wm.		20	M	None	15Au02Ej
Evan		27	M	None	15Au02Ej
Mary		20	F	None	15Au02Ej
PARNTON, Wm.		10	M	None	15Au02Ej
SWIFT, John		50	M	Farmer	15Au02Ej
Died-At-Sea					
Mary		45	F	None	15Au02Ej
Pat		12	M	None	15Au02Ej
Margt.		10	F	None	15Au02Ej
Fras.		8	M	Child	15Au02Ej
Mary		6	F	Child	15Au02Ej
Judy		3	F	Child	15Au02Ej
Jas.		.00	M	Infant	15Au02Ej
DORSEY, Wm.		27	M	None	15Au02Ej
DAGGAN, Francis		30	M	None	15Au02Ej
BRIERLY, Saml.		22	M	None	15Au02Ej
Mary		21	F	None	15Au02Ej
KEENAN, Terence		22	M	None	15Au02Ej
Edward		23	M	None	15Au02Ej
HAMILTON, Thos.		30	M	None	15Au02Ej
U	(W)	29	F	None	15Au02Ej
Died-At-Sea					
U-Mrs.		28	F	None	15Au02Ej
Adam		15	M	None	15Au02Ej
Jas.		13	M	None	15Au02Ej
Jane		10	F	None	15Au02Ej
Mary-A.		8	F	Child	15Au02Ej
Margt.		6	F	Child	15Au02Ej
Lilly		3	F	Child	15Au02Ej
Robt.		.00	M	Infant	15Au02Ej
TAZELL, Jas.		30	M	None	15Au02Ej

NAMES OF PASSENGERS	AGE	SEX	OCCUPATIONS	DATE PORT SHIP
ARMSTRONG, Julia	34	F	None	15Au02Ej
Susan-Jane	14	F	None	15Au02Ej
Edwd.Thos.	9	M	Child	15Au02Ej
Geo.	3	M	Child	15Au02Ej
Died-At-Sea				
DAVISON, Ellen	32	F	None	15Au02Ej
MERLEY, Jas.	17	M	None	15Au02Ej
MCCANN, Telford	10	M	None	15Au02Ej

BOADICEA 15 AUGUST 1849

From Liverpool

NAMES OF PASSENGERS	AGE	SEX	OCCUPATIONS	DATE PORT SHIP
LETT, Charles	18	M	Surgeon	15Au020s
MCLEAN, Ann	25	F	None	15Au020s
BRADY, Mary	36	F	None	15Au020s
Eugene	36	M	Farmer	15Au020s
OREILLY, Elizabeth	40	F	None	15Au020s
Caroline	18	F	None	15Au020s
CUNNEY, Michael	30	M	Laborer	15Au020s
MCEVOY, Michael	51	M	Farmer	15Au020s
GRAHAM, Mary-Ann	16	F	None	15Au020s
PERKINS, Ellen	25	F	None	15Au020s
WYNNE, Patrick	28	M	Laborer	15Au020s
HOAY, Catherine	16	F	Servant	15Au020s
GRAHAM, James	21	M	Mariner	15Au020s
DONNELLY, John	26	M	Laborer	15Au020s
DELAHUNTY, Mary	20	F	None	15Au020s
POWER, Ellen	16	F	Servant	15Au020s
FRIERY, Catherine	16	F	Servant	15Au020s
MCNELLIS, William	18	M	Laborer	15Au020s
SWAN, Ann	40	F	Wet-Nurse	15Au020s
Thomas	12	M	None	15Au020s
John	10	M	None	15Au020s
James	8	M	Child	15Au020s
William	6	M	Child	15Au020s
Patrick	4	M	Child	15Au020s
Mary	1	F	Child	15Au020s
DOYLE, Patrick	30	M	Laborer	15Au020s
Eliza	25	F	Servant	15Au020s
KENNEY, Thomas	26	M	Tailor	15Au020s
Catherine	23	F	Servant	15Au020s
DOYLE, Ann	.10	F	Infant	15Au020s
Simon	.10	M	Infant	15Au020s
MCNAMARA, Martin	25	M	Laborer	15Au020s
Bridget	20	F	Servant	15Au020s
Boadicea	.01	F	Infant	15Au020s
Born-At-Sea				
MOLOWNEY, John	35	M	Miner	15Au020s
GORMAN, Patrick	28	M	Laborer	15Au020s
MOLOWNEY, Mary	35	F	Servant	15Au020s
KINELLY, Mark	45	M	Laborer	15Au020s
KANE, Margaret	61	F	None	15Au020s
Daniel	24	M	Farmer	15Au020s
Ann	22	F	Milliner	15Au020s
Grace	11	F	None	15Au020s
Margaret	7	F	Child	15Au020s
SAUNDERS, Daniel	25	M	Bootmaker	15Au020s
SHANAHAN, William	22	M	Laborer	15Au020s
Mary	20	F	Servant	15Au020s
Margaret	20	F	Servant	15Au020s
MCNEARY, Margaret	20	F	Servant	15Au020s
Johanna	21	F	Unknown	15Au020s
MCCORMICK, John	40	M	Farmer	15Au020s
John	16	M	Farmer	15Au020s
OGRADY, James	23	M	Laborer	15Au020s
Patrick	24	M	Laborer	15Au020s
MACARTNEY, Eliza	30	F	Servant	15Au020s
PRESTON, Eliza	20	F	Servant	15Au020s
MORDAUNT, Peter	45	M	Laborer	15Au020s
Mary	22	F	Servant	15Au020s
Catherine	18	F	Servant	15Au020s
Michael	13	M	Servant	15Au020s
STAKIN, James	30	M	Soldier	15Au020s
MCLAUGHLIN, Margaret	19	F	Nurse	15Au020s
JOHNSTONE, Eliza	30	F	Milliner	15Au020s
MCNAMARA, Thomas	23	M	Farmer	15Au020s
NEARY, Edward	56	M	Farmer	15Au020s
Esther	56	F	None	15Au020s
HONAHAN, William	23	M	Groom	15Au020s
WALL, Martin	25	M	Laborer	15Au020s
ALLEN, James	40	M	Scriviner	15Au020s
Martin	19	M	Clerk	15Au020s
BOWES, Robert	57	M	Painter	15Au020s
Robert	19	M	Painter	15Au020s
OSHAUGHNESSY, Caleman	40	M	Joiner	15Au020s
READY, William	21	M	Farmer	15Au020s
Maria	21	F	Servant	15Au020s
Ellen	11	F	None	15Au020s
MUNGAVIN, John	40	M	Laborer	15Au020s
RYAN, Hannah	25	M	Servant	15Au020s
GRIFFIN, William	20	M	Laborer	15Au020s
James	21	M	Laborer	15Au020s
BROWN, Timothy	20	M	Laborer	15Au020s
DELANEY, John	27	M	Smith	15Au020s
Ellen	16	F	Milliner	15Au020s
FISHER, William	22	M	Farmer	15Au020s
VALENTINE, Peter	30	M	Farmer	15Au020s
DELAHUNTY, Richard	40	M	Farmer	15Au020s
Richard	36	M	Farmer	15Au020s
Allice	30	F	Dairymaid	15Au020s
Johanna	30	F	Dairymaid	15Au020s
Catherine	26	F	Dressmaker	15Au020s
Anty	.09	F	Infant	15Au020s
MULVANEY, Christopher	40	M	Groom	15Au020s
DANN, Sarah	30	F	Servant	15Au020s
CROAK, William	25	M	Laborer	15Au020s
Catherine	23	F	Servant	15Au020s
DOULING, Arthur	20	M	Laborer	15Au020s
ROURKE, Eliza	20	F	Dressmaker	15Au020s
JACKSON, Margaret	38	F	Servant	15Au020s
James	9	M	Child	15Au020s
Neptune	.01	M	Infant	15Au020s
Born-At-Sea				
MAXWELL, James	21	M	None	15Au020s
ANGLINE, Jerry	24	M	Laborer	15Au020s
FRASEY, Ellen	30	F	None	15Au020s
Catherine	20	F	None	15Au020s
GROGAN, William	34	M	Laborer	15Au020s
OMARA, Maria	10	F	None	15Au020s
MURRAY, Michael	26	M	Laborer	15Au020s
U-Mrs.	25	F	Servant	15Au020s
DONOHOE, Michael	40	M	Laborer	15Au020s
BRADY, Terence	13	M	None	15Au020s
John	12	M	None	15Au020s
HUGHES, Joseph	18	M	None	15Au020s
HAYES, Michael	21	M	Laborer	15Au020s
BYRNES, William	21	M	Laborer	15Au020s
LARKIN, Michael	40	M	Farmer	15Au020s
KELLY, Nancy	40	F	None	15Au020s
Peggy	18	F	None	15Au020s
MCDONNELL, Catherine	14	F	Servant	15Au020s
DALEY, James	27	M	Policeman	15Au020s
Bridget	20	F	None	15Au020s
BRYAN, Martin	25	M	Laborer	15Au020s
MURPHY, Bridget	30	F	None	15Au020s
MCMAHON, William	30	M	Tailor	15Au020s
GRANT, Thomas	30	M	Laborer	15Au020s
MCSHEAN, Rosa	35	F	Servant	15Au020s
MOORE, Margaret	30	F	Servant	15Au020s
CROWLEY, Catherine	30	F	Servant	15Au020s
DRISCOLL, Margaret	40	F	Housekeeper	15Au020s
John	21	M	Tailor	15Au020s
MCNULTY, Ann	40	F	Servant	15Au020s

NAMES OF PASSENGERS	AGE	SEX	OCCUPATIONS	DATE PORT SHIP
HAGGERTY, Andrew	48	M	Gdnr	15Au020s
Catherine	40	F	None	15Au020s
MCCARTY, John	25	M	None	15Au020s
MCGINLEY, Bridget	12	F	None	15Au020s
Mary-Ann	10	F	None	15Au020s
MULLIN, John	49	M	None	15Au020s
Esther	40	F	None	15Au020s
Isabella	19	F	None	15Au020s
ALCORN, Elizabeth	40	F	None	15Au020s
James	.11	M	Infant	15Au020s
Esther	10	F	None	15Au020s
Jemima	7	F	Child	15Au020s
John	5	M	Child	15Au020s
William	3	M	Child	15Au020s
MCNUTT, Robert	22	M	Laborer	15Au020s
Catherine	20	F	None	15Au020s
RYAN, Lawrence	30	M	Laborer	15Au020s
Michael	30	M	Laborer	15Au020s
Mary	27	F	None	15Au020s
Ann	20	F	None	15Au020s
Mary	8	F	Child	15Au020s
Rody	1	M	Child	15Au020s
BRUCE, William	24	M	None	15Au020s
Jane	23	F	None	15Au020s
MCCAFFREY, Patrick	23	M	Laborer	15Au020s
DOHERTY, Rosa	16	F	None	15Au020s
MCCAFFREY, Rosa	23	F	Dressmaker	15Au020s
SCULLY, John	27	M	Laborer	15Au020s
MCCAIN, Bridget	20	F	None	15Au020s
CAHILL, John	18	M	Clerk	15Au020s
CONLAN, John	40	M	Laborer	15Au020s
Eliza	40	F	Servant	15Au020s
SCOTT, Jerold	20	M	Mariner	15Au020s
BOYD, Henry	20	M	None	15Au020s
HOLMES, Margaret	21	F	Servant	15Au020s
MCKIM, Phillip	23	M	Farmer	15Au020s
Helena	40	F	None	15Au020s
John	21	M	None	15Au020s
Patrick	8	M	Child	15Au020s
Catherine	20	F	None	15Au020s
Isabella	15	F	None	15Au020s
GANNON, Lawrence	25	M	Servant	15Au020s
Ann	21	F	Servant	15Au020s
MADDEN, James	24	M	Servant	15Au020s
DONELLY, Sarah	50	F	None	15Au020s
Hugh	18	M	Weaver	15Au020s
Mary	16	F	None	15Au020s
Charles	14	M	None	15Au020s
Catherine	12	F	None	15Au020s
KENNEY, Patrick	20	M	Laborer	15Au020s
MCGOWAN, Patrick	18	M	Laborer	15Au020s
GALLIGAN, Peter	30	M	Fireman	15Au020s
Mary	24	F	Servant	15Au020s
Hannah	21	F	Dressmaker	15Au020s
MCDONNELL, Phillip	25	M	Farmer	15Au020s
Bridget	18	F	None	15Au020s
MEEHAN, Sarah	20	F	None	15Au020s
WELSH, Mary	40	F	None	15Au020s
BOLAND, Patrick	20	M	Tailor	15Au020s
REGAN, Daniel	21	M	Laborer	15Au020s
MCCUE, Ann	40	F	None	15Au020s
Mary	25	F	None	15Au020s
Patrick	20	M	Laborer	15Au020s
JORDAN, Bridget	40	F	None	15Au020s
WELSH, Anthony	23	M	Laborer	15Au020s
Brdget	22	F	None	15Au020s
WHITE, Catherine	30	F	None	15Au020s
PLUNKETT, John	20	M	Laborer	15Au020s
Ann	16	F	None	15Au020s
GRADY, Mary	18	F	None	15Au020s
REYNOLDS, Thomas	50	M	Laborer	15Au020s
Michael	10	M	None	15Au020s
James	8	M	Child	15Au020s
Bridget	6	F	Child	15Au020s
Judy	5	F	Child	15Au020s

NAMES OF PASSENGERS	AGE	SEX	OCCUPATIONS	DATE PORT SHIP
HANNAH, William	40	M	Laborer	15Au020s
CUNLISH, Sarah	20	F	Servant	15Au020s
DOHERTY, Bridget	14	F	Servant	15Au020s
MURRAY, James	20	M	Shoemaker	15Au020s
Ann	20	F	Servant	15Au020s
SHORT, Mary	13	F	Servant	15Au020s
CUFF, Henry	25	M	None	15Au020s
Emma	25	F	None	15Au020s
KENNEY, James	21	M	None	15Au020s
HALLORAN, Mary	35	F	None	15Au020s
Maria	25	F	None	15Au020s
Michael	12	M	None	15Au020s
John	10	M	None	15Au020s
DOBSON, Charles	11	M	None	15Au020s
Jane	3	F	Child	15Au020s
ENNIS, Winne	20	U	None	15Au020s
MOLOWNEY, John	40	M	Laborer	15Au020s
Johanna	30	F	Nurse	15Au020s
Mary	15	F	Nurse	15Au020s
ELEHER, Mary	22	F	Servant	15Au020s
KENNEDY, Mary	13	F	Servant	15Au020s
CONNER, Francis	20	M	Laborer	15Au020s
FAY, Elizabeth	17	F	Servant	15Au020s
DIXON, John	20	M	Laborer	15Au020s
Ellen	3	F	Child	15Au020s
Bridget	5	F	Child	15Au020s
DEVON, Thomas	24	M	Carpenter	15Au020s
LONG, Edward	18	M	Carpenter	15Au020s
MITCHELL, James	50	M	Mason	15Au020s
Bridget	40	F	None	15Au020s
Martin	15	M	None	15Au020s
Catherine	1	F	Child	15Au020s
KELLEY, Patrick	20	M	Laborer	15Au020s
MCDERMOTT, Catherine	18	F	Servant	15Au020s
ROURK, Michael	20	M	Laborer	15Au020s
Patrick	5	M	Child	15Au020s
ROCHE, John	20	M	Laborer	15Au020s
LANAHAN, Patrick	40	M	Clerk	15Au020s
LEWIS, Sarah	22	F	Dressmaker	15Au020s
SHARPLEY, Mary-Ann	22	F	Dressmaker	15Au020s
FRENEY, Mary	30	F	None	15Au020s
FLOYD, James	21	M	Mariner	15Au020s
CARLEY, Andy	40	M	Laborer	15Au020s
WELSH, Isaac	.01	M	Infant	15Au020s
Born-At-Sea				
MURPHY, William	23	M	Unknown	15Au020s
WHITE, James	25	M	Laborer	15Au020s

EL-DORADO 15 AUGUST 1849

From Londonderry

NAMES OF PASSENGERS	AGE	SEX	OCCUPATIONS	DATE PORT SHIP
SWEENY, Cornelius	35	M	Laborer	15Au01Es
FERRY, James	23	M	Laborer	15Au01Es
Mary	16	F	None	15Au01Es
CAMPBELL, Margaret	16	F	None	15Au01Es
MCDAID, George	17	M	Laborer	15Au01Es
BOYLE, Patrick	29	M	Laborer	15Au01Es
MCCREVAND, Margaret	21	F	Laborer	15Au01Es
MADDEN, John	34	M	Laborer	15Au01Es
Sarah	28	F	Laborer	15Au01Es
Sarah	14	F	None	15Au01Es
DOOJUN, Matilda	14	F	None	15Au01Es
James	2	M	Child	15Au01Es
CAULFIELD, Jane	1	F	Child	15Au01Es
MCBRIDE, Daniel	19	M	Laborer	15Au01Es
Catherine	17	F	None	15Au01Es
Margaret	19	F	None	15Au01Es
HURT, Hannah	18	F	None	15Au01Es

NAMES OF PASSENGERS	AGE	SEX	OCCUPATIONS	DATE PORT SHIP
HURT, Marg.	18	F	None	15Au01Es
MCLAUGHLIN, Elizabeth	19	F	None	15Au01Es
MULLIN, Andrew	25	M	Laborer	15Au01Es
Patrick	23	M	Laborer	15Au01Es
Ellen	19	F	None	15Au01Es
CARLIN, Bridget	16	F	None	15Au01Es
MORRIS, Peter	22	M	Laborer	15Au01Es
MCBRIDE, James	22	M	Laborer	15Au01Es
Bridget	20	F	Laborer	15Au01Es
MCCORKEL, Margaret	15	F	None	15Au01Es
Archibald	19	M	Laborer	15Au01Es
John-Joseph	26	M	Laborer	15Au01Es
MAGUIRE, Henry	32	M	Laborer	15Au01Es
Mary	27	F	Laborer	15Au01Es
PERRY, Samuel	18	M	Baker	15Au01Es
Samuel	23	M	Baker	15Au01Es
Margaret	25	F	Spinster	15Au01Es
John	34	M	Laborer	15Au01Es
MCLAUGHLIN, Peter	27	M	Laborer	15Au01Es
LOGEN, Jane	16	F	None	15Au01Es
TREARTY, Hannah	15	F	None	15Au01Es
Mary	17	F	None	15Au01Es
ODONNELL, Ellen	19	F	None	15Au01Es
KEOGH, John	19	M	Laborer	15Au01Es
MCCOOLGEN, Bridget	29	F	Laborer	15Au01Es
ODONNELL, William	27	M	Laborer	15Au01Es
COYLE, Jane	17	F	None	15Au01Es
John	21	M	Laborer	15Au01Es
GINLEY, Ellen	27	F	Laborer	15Au01Es
BROGAN, Margaret	16	F	None	15Au01Es
KAIN, James	29	M	Laborer	15Au01Es
LAUGHRY, James	35	M	Laborer	15Au01Es
ALKERSON, William	17	M	Laborer	15Au01Es
Thomas	19	M	Laborer	15Au01Es
MAGUIRE, James	27	F	Laborer	15Au01Es
MCCOURT, David	16	M	None	15Au01Es
CARLIN, Mary	16	F	None	15Au01Es
CROSSON, Mary-Ann	24	F	Laborer	15Au01Es
EATEN, Matthew	23	M	Laborer	15Au01Es
Rebecca	20	F	Laborer	15Au01Es
COYLE, Ames	16	M	None	15Au01Es
HONE, Christopher	21	M	Printer	15Au01Es
BARR, Michael	31	M	Laborer	15Au01Es
CURRAN, Rose	17	F	None	15Au01Es
GALLAGHER, Jane	21	F	Laborer	15Au01Es
MCCLEMENTS, Elizabeth	21	F	Laborer	15Au01Es
GALLAGHER, Charles	19	M	Laborer	15Au01Es
ODONNELL, Mary	18	F	None	15Au01Es
MCCORKEL, Margaret	23	F	Laborer	15Au01Es
ROSBOROUGH, Sarah	26	F	Laborer	15Au01Es
DOHERTY, John	28	M	Laborer	15Au01Es
MCCOOL, Nancy	15	F	None	15Au01Es
John	17	M	Laborer	15Au01Es
Mary	14	F	None	15Au01Es
Mary	6	F	Child	15Au01Es
FRELL, Mary	4	F	Child	15Au01Es
FOY, John	29	M	Laborer	15Au01Es
MULLIN, Ann-J.	32	M	Laborer	15Au01Es
MCCULLION, Rose	29	F	Laborer	15Au01Es
MULDOON, Patrick	31	M	Laborer	15Au01Es
Patrick	23	M	Laborer	15Au01Es
MCLAUGHLIN, Patrick	29	M	Laborer	15Au01Es
BYRONE, Hugh	27	M	Laborer	15Au01Es
CAMPBELL, John	23	M	Laborer	15Au01Es
MCGINNESS, Peter	23	M	Laborer	15Au01Es
ODONNELL, Mary-J.	12	F	None	15Au01Es
FENNIS, John	19	M	Laborer	15Au01Es
Ann	16	F	None	15Au01Es
Isabella	8	F	Child	15Au01Es
GALLAGHER, Susan	6	F	Child	15Au01Es
MULLIN, Sarah	10	F	None	15Au01Es
MCGOWAN, Robert	27	M	Laborer	15Au01Es
MCCULGAN, Eleanor	19	F	None	15Au01Es
PORTER, Catherine	20	F	Laborer	15Au01Es
ORR, Jane	32	F	Laborer	15Au01Es

NAMES OF PASSENGERS	AGE	SEX	OCCUPATIONS	DATE PORT SHIP
DOHENY, Catherine	17	F	None	15Au01Es
GINNIS, Catherine	21	F	Laborer	15Au01Es
EAVENS, Sarah	17	F	None	15Au01Es
MCSORLEY, Bridget	17	F	None	15Au01Es
KAIN, John	22	M	Shipsmith	15Au01Es
LYNCH, Catherine	24	F	Laborer	15Au01Es
Ann	11	F	None	15Au01Es
Sarah	8	F	Child	15Au01Es
John	5	M	Child	15Au01Es
BROGAN, Hugh	19	M	Laborer	15Au01Es
MCKENNEY, Mary	21	F	Laborer	15Au01Es
Ellen	17	F	None	15Au01Es
Catherine	14	F	None	15Au01Es
MCCLOSKEY, James	24	M	Laborer	15Au01Es
EATEN, William	23	M	Laborer	15Au01Es
DOHERTY, James	31	M	Laborer	15Au01Es
Eliza	23	F	Laborer	15Au01Es
SWEENEY, Sarah	19	F	None	15Au01Es
MILLS, Mathew	13	M	None	15Au01Es
Elizabeth	17	F	None	15Au01Es
Easter	15	F	None	15Au01Es
MCFARLIN, Robert	27	M	Laborer	15Au01Es
Sarah	23	F	Laborer	15Au01Es
Margaret	17	F	None	15Au01Es
Margaret	.00	F	Infant	15Au01Es
MCCLAIN, Alexander	21	M	Laborer	15Au01Es
Eliza	18	F	None	15Au01Es
BORLAND, John	27	M	Laborer	15Au01Es
BLACK, James	34	M	Laborer	15Au01Es
Henry	32	M	Laborer	15Au01Es
GALLAGHER, Nancy	19	F	None	15Au01Es
James	15	M	None	15Au01Es
Margaret	10	F	None	15Au01Es
Eleanor	6	F	Child	15Au01Es
HUMPHRIES, Ann	3	F	Child	15Au01Es
SWEENEY, Bridget	17	F	None	15Au01Es
ODONNELL, David	26	M	Laborer	15Au01Es
MCGITTIGANE, Michl.	32	M	Laborer	15Au01Es
CUTLIP, Jane	16	F	None	15Au01Es
KELLY, John	16	M	None	15Au01Es
GRIEVE, Elizabeth	21	F	Laborer	15Au01Es
FARDEN, Jane	20	F	Laborer	15Au01Es
MURPHY, William	18	M	Laborer	15Au01Es
GALLAGHER, Charles	18	M	Laborer	15Au01Es
Rosey	15	F	None	15Au01Es
HIGGINS, Ellen	19	F	None	15Au01Es
Hannah	4	F	Child	15Au01Es
Steven	.00	M	Infant	15Au01Es
BRANDON, William	27	M	Laborer	15Au01Es
SHANNON, Hugh	19	M	Laborer	15Au01Es
HEGARTY, Hugh	19	M	Laborer	15Au01Es
GALLAGHER, Daniel	33	M	Laborer	15Au01Es
EAKIN, Mathew	21	M	Laborer	15Au01Es
GAMBLE, Thomas	18	M	Laborer	15Au01Es
MCHUGH, Sarah	18	F	None	15Au01Es
MCCORMICK, Ann	17	F	None	15Au01Es
COULTON, Michl.	16	M	None	15Au01Es
IRWIN, Eliza	17	F	None	15Au01Es
MCGINN, Barthm.	19	M	Laborer	15Au01Es
CURRY, Patrick	29	M	Laborer	15Au01Es
MCGLINN, Patrick	28	M	Laborer	15Au01Es
MCELDUFF, James	27	M	Laborer	15Au01Es
RAND, Cormick	24	M	Laborer	15Au01Es
OBRIEN, James	31	M	Laborer	15Au01Es
AKIN, Nancy	24	F	Laborer	15Au01Es
Eliza	21	F	Laborer	15Au01Es
MCHENRY, Patrick	28	M	Laborer	15Au01Es
MURPHY, Pat	19	M	Laborer	15Au01Es
DEVLIN, Hannah	16	F	None	15Au01Es
MOONEY, Nancy	23	F	Laborer	15Au01Es
NUGENT, Hugh	26	M	Laborer	15Au01Es
RHYNES, Mary	24	F	Laborer	15Au01Es
TAGGART, Margaret	19	F	None	15Au01Es
BRIGGS, James	17	M	Laborer	15Au01Es
MCCONNOMY, Mag.	21	F	Laborer	15Au01Es

NAMES OF PASSENGERS	AGE	SEX	OCCUPATIONS	DATE PORT SHIP
MCCLOSKEY, Ellen	21	F	Laborer	15Au01Es
GILLINA, William	27	M	Laborer	15Au01Es
Rose	22	F	Laborer	15Au01Es
MCGOWEN, Ellen	21	F	Laborer	15Au01Es
DOUGLAS, Patrick	27	M	Laborer	15Au01Es
BOYLE, Barny	24	M	Laborer	15Au01Es
DOHERTY, Neil	32	M	Laborer	15Au01Es
Maria	27	F	Laborer	15Au01Es
Neil	.00	M	Infant	15Au01Es
DOLLIS, Margaret	11	F	None	15Au01Es
James	9	M	Child	15Au01Es
Joseph	00	M	Unknown	15Au01Es
COLLINS, Ellen	5	F	Child	15Au01Es
DILLIN, Michael	27	M	Laborer	15Au01Es
MARTIN, Pat	22	M	Laborer	15Au01Es
BRADLEY, Mary	19	F	None	15Au01Es
DOHERTY, Con	27	M	Laborer	15Au01Es
FINLEY, Robert	30	M	Laborer	15Au01Es
Emley	26	F	Laborer	15Au01Es
MCFETUS, Mary-Ann	30	F	Laborer	15Au01Es
William	13	M	None	15Au01Es
Margaret	10	F	None	15Au01Es
John	7	M	Child	15Au01Es
Matilda	4	F	Child	15Au01Es
STEWART, Rebeca	19	F	None	15Au01Es
DOHERTY, James	22	M	Laborer	15Au01Es
WATSON, Eliza	17	F	None	15Au01Es
REILLY, Jane	16	F	None	15Au01Es
LYNCH, John	19	M	Laborer	15Au01Es
Biddy	14	F	None	15Au01Es
CONOLEY, Henry	29	M	Laborer	15Au01Es
DOAL, Fanny	26	F	Laborer	15Au01Es
Betsey	.00	F	Infant	15Au01Es
QUINN, Charles	29	M	Laborer	15Au01Es
Mary	24	F	Laborer	15Au01Es
MCBRIDE, Betty	31	F	Laborer	15Au01Es
Mary	8	F	Child	15Au01Es
Thomas	12	M	None	15Au01Es
Margaret	14	F	None	15Au01Es
John	5	M	Child	15Au01Es
Pat	2	M	Child	15Au01Es
DIVER, Robert	23	M	Laborer	15Au01Es
Lak--, Isabella	22	F	Laborer	15Au01Es
KEENAN, Mary	19	F	None	15Au01Es
John	14	M	None	15Au01Es
MITCHELL, Elizabeth	16	F	None	15Au01Es
BLACK, Jane	18	F	None	15Au01Es
Robert	14	M	None	15Au01Es
VARTICE, Thomas	33	M	Laborer	15Au01Es
FAIRMAN, James	30	M	Laborer	15Au01Es
Eliza	25	F	Laborer	15Au01Es
MCADOO, Nancy	17	F	None	15Au01Es
GREEN, Geo.	38	M	Laborer	15Au01Es
Win.John	30	M	Laborer	15Au01Es
James	27	M	Laborer	15Au01Es
MCCLOSKEY, James	24	M	Laborer	15Au01Es
BRADY, Nancy	24	F	Laborer	15Au01Es
SMITH, Bridget	13	F	None	15Au01Es
Patrick	21	M	Laborer	15Au01Es
Catharine	15	F	None	15Au01Es
Mary-Ann	12	F	None	15Au01Es
Ellen	8	F	Child	15Au01Es
BRADLEY, Mary	26	F	Laborer	15Au01Es
MURRY, Mary	17	F	None	15Au01Es
MCSWIGGAN, Ann	17	F	None	15Au01Es
SWANSTON, James	22	M	Laborer	15Au01Es
Ann	19	F	None	15Au01Es
BELL, Ann	33	F	Laborer	15Au01Es
John	40	M	Laborer	15Au01Es
Walter	21	M	Laborer	15Au01Es
GEORGE, Mary-Ann	47	F	Laborer	15Au01Es
William	10	M	None	15Au01Es
James	7	M	Child	15Au01Es
Eliza-Jane	3	F	Child	15Au01Es
Mary-Ann	11	F	None	15Au01Es
CHRISTY, Catherine	17	F	None	15Au01Es
James	12	M	None	15Au01Es
John	10	M	None	15Au01Es
Mary-Jane	4	F	Child	15Au01Es
LOGAN, James	40	M	Laborer	15Au01Es
MCWILLIAMS, Michael	38	M	Laborer	15Au01Es
Mary	33	F	Laborer	15Au01Es
MCDONALD, Sarah	19	F	None	15Au01Es
BRADLEY, Mary	17	F	None	15Au01Es
MCMILLAN, Jane	17	F	None	15Au01Es
KENNEDY, Catherine	27	F	Laborer	15Au01Es
GLENN, Thomas	30	M	Laborer	15Au01Es
SAUNDERS, John	26	M	Laborer	15Au01Es
BAXTER, Eliza	17	F	None	15Au01Es
MCCARTHEY, Mary-Ann	19	F	None	15Au01Es
Jane	13	F	None	15Au01Es
John	9	M	Child	15Au01Es
OLIVER, Henry	30	M	Laborer	15Au01Es
Elizabeth	27	F	Laborer	15Au01Es
MCNULTY, Ellen	28	F	Laborer	15Au01Es
Hannah	4	F	Child	15Au01Es
Mary	2	F	Child	15Au01Es
BLEAR, James	42	M	Laborer	15Au01Es
GREGG, David	40	M	Laborer	15Au01Es
MCSWIGGAN, Bridget	27	F	Laborer	15Au01Es
HOHNES, Mary-Ann	29	F	Laborer	15Au01Es
SHIELDS, Sarah	24	F	Laborer	15Au01Es
MULLAN, Hugh	29	M	Laborer	15Au01Es
STEWART, Elizabeth	21	F	Laborer	15Au01Es
MCCONABRY, Robert	31	M	Laborer	15Au01Es
BUCHANAN, Patrick	30	M	Laborer	15Au01Es
DUGGAN, Pat	19	M	Laborer	15Au01Es
FLETCHER, Robert	19	M	Laborer	15Au01Es
MCCOURT, Michael	17	M	Laborer	15Au01Es
CHRISTY, Eliza	11	F	None	15Au01Es
MADDEN, Henry	34	M	Laborer	15Au01Es
MCCONOLOGUE, Thomas	27	M	Unknown	15Au01Es
FLEMMING, Margaret-Mis	22	F	Unknown	15Au01Es
Elizabeth-Miss	19	F	Unknown	15Au01Es
YOUNG, U-Miss	17	F	Unknown	15Au01Es
HAMILTON, Patrick	28	M	Unknown	15Au01Es
MCMORRIS, John	32	M	Unknown	15Au01Es
HUTTON, Rose-Ann	17	F	Unknown	15Au01Es
HOLLAND, Charles	38	M	Unknown	15Au01Es
Eleanor	35	F	Unknown	15Au01Es
MCGOBRICK, Ann	32	F	Unknown	15Au01Es
BEATTY, John	28	M	Unknown	15Au01Es
Sarah	18	F	Unknown	15Au01Es
JOHNSTONE, Alexander	29	M	Unknown	15Au01Es
CLEGG, Francis	30	M	Unknown	15Au01Es
REYNOLDS, Owen	32	M	Unknown	15Au01Es
FISHER, Margaret	46	F	Unknown	15Au01Es
MCALEER, Mary	19	F	Unknown	15Au01Es
Ann	10	F	Unknown	15Au01Es
John	5	M	Child	15Au01Es
MCCAFFERY, James	29	M	Unknown	15Au01Es
Ellen	31	F	Unknown	15Au01Es
Joseph	29	M	Unknown	15Au01Es
Margaret	27	F	Unknown	15Au01Es
John	10	M	Unknown	15Au01Es
CLANNAHAN, Patrick	41	M	Unknown	15Au01Es
STEVENSON, Robert	24	M	Unknown	15Au01Es
BANKS, U-Mrs.	40	F	Unknown	15Au01Es
U-Miss	17	F	Unknown	15Au01Es
SPRATT, U	55	M	Minister	15Au01Es
MCCARRON, U-Mrs.	68	F	Lady	15Au01Es
MCNULTY, Elizabeth-Mis	34	F	Dressmaker	15Au01Es
THOMPSON, U-Mrs.	20	F	Wife	15Au01Es
MCAVOY, Ann-Miss	19	F	Servant	15Au01Es
WALLACE, Margaret-Miss	17	F	Lady	15Au01Es

HARTFORD 15 AUGUST 1849

From Liverpool

NAMES OF PASSENGERS	AGE	SEX	OCCUPATIONS	DATE PORT SHIP
ELLIOTT, Judith	42	F	None	15Au020u
Mary	21	F	None	15Au020u
FORBELL, Susan	17	F	None	15Au020u
MILLICK, William	40	M	Laborer	15Au020u
Mary	40	F	None	15Au020u
John	14	M	None	15Au020u
Thomas	12	M	None	15Au020u
William	10	M	None	15Au020u
Mary	8	F	Child	15Au020u
MCHALL, Mary	20	F	Spinster	15Au020u
ROCH, Pat	21	M	Farmer	15Au020u
MCINNIS, P.	58	M	Farmer	15Au020u
Judith	48	F	None	15Au020u
Michael	14	M	None	15Au020u
Rich	12	M	None	15Au020u
Judith	10	F	None	15Au020u
Robt.	8	M	Child	15Au020u
Pat	6	M	Child	15Au020u
Mary	4	F	Child	15Au020u
GENNES, Pat	38	M	Farmer	15Au020u
Mary	23	F	None	15Au020u
Catrine	00	U	Unknown	15Au020u
Walter	.00	M	Infant	15Au020u
WHELSTADE, Pat	42	M	Baker	15Au020u
BLAKE, W.G.	35	M	Laborer	15Au020u
KALGRIFF, James	18	M	Butcher	15Au020u
HOWARD, Thos.	27	M	Laborer	15Au020u
BURK, John	40	M	Laborer	15Au020u
GIBBONS, Frank	13	M	Laborer	15Au020u
MENIGHAN, Patk.	35	M	None	15Au020u
NOON, Brigett	14	F	None	15Au020u
LAVELLE, Ann	20	F	None	15Au020u
Peter	12	M	None	15Au020u
NOLLIN, Brigett	18	F	None	15Au020u
SALE, Thomas	27	M	Mechanic	15Au020u
LAVINS, James	39	M	Mechanic	15Au020u
GRADY, James	25	M	Laborer	15Au020u
SHANAHAN, Daniel	26	M	Laborer	15Au020u
MANGAN, Bryan	40	M	Laborer	15Au020u
TONLEY, Mary	26	F	None	15Au020u
John	4	M	Child	15Au020u
William	.00	M	Infant	15Au020u
SHIEL, Amos	30	M	Farmer	15Au020u
Mary	30	F	None	15Au020u
COOK, Benj.	27	M	Saddler	15Au020u
Arch.	25	M	Saddler	15Au020u
MCKENNA, Pat	22	M	Laborer	15Au020u
HUGHES, Mary	18	F	None	15Au020u
VIENNA, Moriah	25	F	None	15Au020u
Peter	26	M	None	15Au020u
WRIGHT, Lann	30	F	None	15Au020u
TRAINER, Rose	22	F	None	15Au020u
REILLY, Ann	34	F	None	15Au020u
MONIGHAN, John	20	M	None	15Au020u
Ann	13	F	None	15Au020u
BRUCE, Ralph	20	M	Mechanic	15Au020u
FARLEY, Pat	20	M	Laborer	15Au020u
Cat.	18	F	None	15Au020u
Margt.	7	F	Child	15Au020u
GILSHANNA, Philip	20	M	None	15Au020u
LYNCH, Cat.	17	F	None	15Au020u
Frank	18	M	None	15Au020u
MAHON, John	29	M	Farmer	15Au020u
FLOOD, John	18	M	Laborer	15Au020u
DWYRE, Daniel	22	M	Farmer	15Au020u
DWYRE, Rich.	26	M	None	15Au020u
Pat	18	M	None	15Au020u
REDFORD, John	30	M	Mechanic	15Au020u
ELLIOT, John	30	M	Laborer	15Au020u
Hannah	00	F	Spinster	15Au020u
GUNEL, John	48	M	Mechanic	15Au020u
GRIFFIN, Mich.	22	M	None	15Au020u
MCGOTHAN, John	27	M	Farmer	15Au020u
Ann	27	F	None	15Au020u
OBRIEN, James	40	M	Farmer	15Au020u
HADNER, Mary	22	F	Spinster	15Au020u
FADDEN, Ann	20	F	Spinster	15Au020u
CARR, Mary	20	F	Spinster	15Au020u
Bridgett	18	F	None	15Au020u
LYON, Unity	20	F	Spinster	15Au020u
LOOBY, Michael	12	M	None	15Au020u
Lorry	10	M	None	15Au020u
ESKINE, James	21	M	Farmer	15Au020u
Margaret	22	F	Spinster	15Au020u
COWLIN, Ann	27	F	Spinster	15Au020u
HUGHES, Ann	20	F	Spinster	15Au020u
Bridgett	18	F	None	15Au020u
TOWNSEND, James	21	M	Laborer	15Au020u
Joseph	18	M	Laborer	15Au020u
RAFFERTY, James	60	M	Laborer	15Au020u
COFFE, Bridgett	35	F	Spinster	15Au020u
MURPHY, Michael	26	M	Laborer	15Au020u
MILLIGHAN, Mary	60	F	Spinster	15Au020u
HASKITT, Matthew	20	M	Laborer	15Au020u
Peter	12	M	None	15Au020u
HAMILL, Celia	24	F	Spinster	15Au020u
DWYER, Mary	50	F	Spinster	15Au020u
Mary	10	F	None	15Au020u
Ned	9	M	Child	15Au020u
HOLLAND, Margaret	25	F	Spinster	15Au020u
HAMILL, Pat	21	M	Laborer	15Au020u
REILLY, Pat	28	M	Laborer	15Au020u
Ann	35	F	Spinster	15Au020u
Wm.	10	M	None	15Au020u
John	8	M	Child	15Au020u
Mary	6	F	Child	15Au020u
Ann	4	F	Child	15Au020u
Margaret	3	F	Child	15Au020u
INGOLSEBY, Catharine	21	F	Spinster	15Au020u
LITTLE, Mary	40	F	None	15Au020u
Mary	10	F	None	15Au020u
Bryan	13	M	None	15Au020u
WARD, Peter	40	M	Laborer	15Au020u
MARTIN, Rose	14	F	Spinster	15Au020u
LYNCH, Bridgett	18	F	Spinster	15Au020u
HIGGINS, Pat	26	M	Laborer	15Au020u
REILLEY, James	46	M	Laborer	15Au020u
MCCHARTY, Dennis	28	M	Laborer	15Au020u
CORKERY, John	30	M	Laborer	15Au020u
Ellen	26	F	Spinster	15Au020u
BURKE, Edward	30	M	Laborer	15Au020u
SULLIVAN, Dan	26	M	Laborer	15Au020u
MCGOWEN, Pat-S.	60	M	Laborer	15Au020u
Ellen	12	F	None	15Au020u
BURKE, Mary	24	F	None	15Au020u
FITZGERALD, Thomas	50	M	Laborer	15Au020u
TRACY, John	29	M	Laborer	15Au020u
MCFARRELL, John	55	M	Laborer	15Au020u
Bridgett	15	F	Spinster	15Au020u
FORSYTH, Isabella	50	F	None	15Au020u
Andrew	18	M	None	15Au020u
Esther	9	F	Child	15Au020u
Isabella	6	F	Child	15Au020u
JOHNSON, Thomas	20	M	Laborer	15Au020u
MINER, James	25	M	Laborer	15Au020u
HUGHES, Betty	12	F	None	15Au020u
FLAGHARTY, Sarah	25	F	Spinster	15Au020u
Isabella	6	F	Child	15Au020u
James	7	M	Child	15Au020u
REILLEY, Margeret	30	F	Spinster	15Au020u

NAMES OF PASSENGERS	AGE	SEX	OCCUPATIONS	DATE PORT SHIP
REILLEY, Margeret	5	F	Child	15Au02Ou
SALTER, Ann	36	F	Spinster	15Au02Ou
Eleanor	15	F	Spinster	15Au02Ou
Thomas	10	M	None	15Au02Ou
Namman	6	M	Child	15Au02Ou
Robert-H.	.00	M	Infant	15Au02Ou
COOPER, James	17	M	None	15Au02Ou
ROBSON, John	28	M	Miner	15Au02Ou
Doretha	25	F	None	15Au02Ou
Jane	.00	F	Infant	15Au02Ou
JANKS, Thomas	22	M	Miner	15Au02Ou
ROSE, John	35	M	Miner	15Au02Ou
DIGNAL, Pat	23	M	Laborer	15Au02Ou
LAWLESS, Robt.	24	M	Baker	15Au02Ou
Honor	22	F	None	15Au02Ou
Mary	5	F	Child	15Au02Ou
Margaret	3	F	Child	15Au02Ou
MCGOWAN, Jane	20	F	None	15Au02Ou
PANTERY, Simeon	21	M	Laborer	15Au02Ou
BYRNELL, Pat	23	M	None	15Au02Ou
Mcfo--, Brigett	27	F	None	15Au02Ou
Honor	.00	F	Infant	15Au02Ou
WOODS, John	23	M	Laborer	15Au02Ou
KING, Chas.	27	M	Laborer	15Au02Ou
Marg.	26	F	None	15Au02Ou
MILLS, U	18	M	None	15Au02Ou
COOK, Margt.	18	F	None	15Au02Ou
WOODS, David	42	M	Laborer	15Au02Ou
MCFRAY, Thos.	23	M	None	15Au02Ou
SKINNER, Thos.	25	M	Joiner	15Au02Ou
Braind--, Mary	16	F	None	15Au02Ou
EGLIN, Richard	30	M	Laborer	15Au02Ou
Susan	30	F	None	15Au02Ou
CROW, William	45	M	Mechanic	15Au02Ou
TOBIN, James	25	M	Laborer	15Au02Ou
NEWSCOMBE, Pat	19	M	Laborer	15Au02Ou
CONFREY, Pat	24	M	None	15Au02Ou
KENNAN, Bessy	30	F	None	15Au02Ou
SHELLAM, Brigett	16	F	None	15Au02Ou
KENNAN, Mary	20	F	None	15Au02Ou
GEAKEY, George	22	M	None	15Au02Ou
KENNER, Pat	17	M	None	15Au02Ou
GALLAGHER, Con	20	M	None	15Au02Ou
John	9	M	Child	15Au02Ou
HAYS, Daniel	23	M	None	15Au02Ou
COOGAN, Hugh	40	M	None	15Au02Ou
Brigett	16	F	None	15Au02Ou
Ann	10	F	None	15Au02Ou
Kitty	8	F	Child	15Au02Ou
Honor	7	F	Child	15Au02Ou
SEDEL, Ralph	26	M	Mechanic	15Au02Ou
STONE, Daniel	28	M	Mechanic	15Au02Ou
WALSH, Matilda	21	F	None	15Au02Ou
WILSON, Jane	50	F	None	15Au02Ou
James	28	M	Laborer	15Au02Ou
CORCORAN, Pat	30	M	Laborer	15Au02Ou
Allice	30	F	None	15Au02Ou
James	6	M	Child	15Au02Ou
HOLLMER, Mary	17	F	None	15Au02Ou
MCGOWEN, Pat	22	M	None	15Au02Ou
Margt.	13	F	None	15Au02Ou
REILLY, Thos.	12	M	None	15Au02Ou
LEE, Owen	34	M	None	15Au02Ou

SHERIDAN 16 AUGUST 1849

From Liverpool

NAMES OF PASSENGERS	AGE	SEX	OCCUPATIONS	DATE PORT SHIP
BEATTEY, Archibald	39	M	Gentleman	16Au02Bx
U-Mrs.	37	F	Lady	16Au02Bx
John	13	M	Gentleman	16Au02Bx
Archbd.	9	M	Child	16Au02Bx
Thos.	5	M	Child	16Au02Bx
Betsey	5	F	Child	16Au02Bx
HUGHES, Harriet	11	F	None	16Au02Bx
STACK, Thos.	26	M	Carpenter	16Au02Bx
BANNEN, Ellen	40	F	Servant	16Au02Bx
MURRAY, Susan	20	F	Servant	16Au02Bx
FARRADY, Margt.	20	F	Servant	16Au02Bx
U	.00	U	Infant	16Au02Bx
CROOKS, John	20	M	Baker	16Au02Bx
DOYLE, Patt	40	M	Paper Maker	16Au02Bx
DALTON, Francis	50	M	Laborer	16Au02Bx
Died-At-Sea				
Ann	44	F	None	16Au02Bx
Michl.	21	M	Laborer	16Au02Bx
Columbia	18	F	None	16Au02Bx
Thos.	11	M	None	16Au02Bx
Wm.	8	M	Child	16Au02Bx
Mary	10	F	Child	16Au02Bx
Ellen	.00	F	Infant	16Au02Bx
Died-At-Sea				
MCDERMOTT, Danl.	50	M	Laborer	16Au02Bx
Thomas	40	M	Laborer	16Au02Bx
Wm.	18	M	Laborer	16Au02Bx
Marcella	7	F	Child	16Au02Bx
POLE, Honora	11	F	None	16Au02Bx
DUFFEY, Patk.	30	M	Laborer	16Au02Bx
John	22	M	Laborer	16Au02Bx
BOWE, Michl.	24	M	Laborer	16Au02Bx
HOGAN, Ann	21	F	Laborer	16Au02Bx
JORDAN, Edwd.	35	M	Laborer	16Au02Bx
Cathn.	40	M	Laborer	16Au02Bx
Michl.	30	M	Laborer	16Au02Bx
Bridget	26	M	Laborer	16Au02Bx
John	8	M	Child	16Au02Bx
KAVANAGH, Joseph	24	M	Laborer	16Au02Bx
Died-At-Sea				
MCCORMICK, Alice	18	F	Laborer	16Au02Bx
NUGENT, Wm.	40	M	Tailor	16Au02Bx
MCCOY, Michl.	38	M	Laborer	16Au02Bx
GLANCEY, Danl.	21	M	Unknown	16Au02Bx
DIGNAN, Cathn.	17	F	None	16Au02Bx
BRAGAN, Eliza.	18	F	Servant	16Au02Bx
MAINING, Mary	30	F	Servant	16Au02Bx
CORSORAN, Bridt.	30	F	Servant	16Au02Bx
QUIGLEY, Mary	18	F	Servant	16Au02Bx
NOWLAN, John	30	M	Laborer	16Au02Bx
KEHOE, Bridget	22	F	Servant	16Au(2Bx
SMITH, Jas.	20	F	Servant	16Au02Bx
CALLAHAN, Honora	18	F	Servant	16Au02Bx
DIVYAN, Bridget	18	F	Servant	16Au02Bx
MCCALL, Thos.	20	M	Weaver	16Au02Bx
Essy	18	F	Weaver	16Au02Bx
Margt.	11	F	None	16Au02Bx
MCKENNA, Judith	20	F	Servant	16Au02Bx
MCCARTHY, Ellen	18	F	Servant	16Au02Bx
HEMISON, James	22	M	Draper	16Au02Bx
BARRY, Cathn.	40	F	Housekeeper	16Au02Bx
Margt.	18	F	Housekeeper	16Au02Bx
Mary-Ann	.00	F	Infant	16Au02Bx
Cahtn.	16	F	None	16Au02Bx
DOLAN, Ann	20	F	Servant	16Au02Bx

NAMES OF PASSENGERS	AGE	SEX	OCCUPATIONS	DATE PORT SHIP
COLEMAN, Patk.	44	M	Farmer	16Au02Bx
DILL, Peter	29	M	Farmer	16Au02Bx
BARRY, Cathn.	21	F	Dressmaker	16Au02Bx
Ellen	17	F	Dressmaker	16Au02Bx
MORRISEY, Michl.	28	M	Shoemaker	16Au02Bx
GERMAN, Timothy	35	M	Blacksmith	16Au02Bx
JOHNSTON, Jane	40	F	Servant	16Au02Bx
QUINN, Ann	23	F	Servant	16Au02Bx
ARTHUR, David	23	M	Laborer	16Au02Bx
FLYNN, Philip	30	M	Chandler	16Au02Bx
Patt	21	M	Tailor	16Au02Bx
MADDEN, Michl.	28	M	Laborer	16Au02Bx
Mary	26	F	Servant	16Au02Bx
KELLAHAN, Charles	24	M	Laborer	16Au02Bx
COGHLIN, Jas.	21	M	Laborer	16Au02Bx
Sarah	15	F	Dressmaker	16Au02Bx
Ellen	13	F	Dressmaker	16Au02Bx
DOWLING, Michael	28	M	Shoemaker	16Au02Bx
BROPHY, Michl.	20	M	Laborer	16Au02Bx
DOYLE, John	28	M	Shoemaker	16Au02Bx
BRYAN, Jas.	34	M	Laborer	16Au02Bx
Biddy	30	M	Laborer	16Au02Bx
James	6	M	Child	16Au02Bx
Bridget	4	F	Child	16Au02Bx
SMITH, Thos.	24	M	Laborer	16Au02Bx
Peter	22	M	Baker	16Au02Bx
CAVANAH, Christopher	28	M	Laborer	16Au02Bx
DOYLE, Cathne.	30	F	Housekeeper	16Au02Bx
Died-At-Sea				
Judy	11	F	None	16Au02Bx
Mary	8	F	Child	16Au02Bx
Cathn.	5	F	Child	16Au02Bx
Michl.	23	F	Child	16Au02Bx
DALTON, John	18	M	Cloth Maker	16Au02Bx
FREENEY, Johanna	31	F	Saddler	16Au02Bx
REILEY, Mary	16	F	Servant	16Au02Bx
FLINN, Michl.	22	M	Laborer	16Au02Bx
James	7	M	Child	16Au02Bx
MCCARTHY, Danl.	21	M	Shoemaker	16Au02Bx
Ellen	18	F	None	16Au02Bx
PARKS, Margt.	21	F	Servant	16Au02Bx
TAYLOR, James	17	M	Weaver	16Au02Bx
Oliver	15	M	Laborer	16Au02Bx
Wm.John	13	M	Laborer	16Au02Bx
Letitia	10	F	Child	16Au02Bx
SANDS, Sarah	40	F	Child	16Au02Bx
QUAIL, Mary	20	F	Milliner	16Au02Bx
MCEVANS, Mary	50	F	Housekeeper	16Au02Bx
Owen	19	F	Housekeeper	16Au02Bx
Ann	15	F	Housekeeper	16Au02Bx
CROPAN, Patk.	16	M	None	16Au02Bx
Owen	12	M	None	16Au02Bx
HEARY, Jospeh	20	M	Laborer	16Au02Bx
ANDERSON, Dorothea	45	F	Housekeeper	16Au02Bx
Agnes	26	F	Housekeeper	16Au02Bx
Eliza.	24	F	Housekeeper	16Au02Bx
Margt.	21	F	Housekeeper	16Au02Bx
David	19	F	Housekeeper	16Au02Bx
Andrew	16	M	None	16Au02Bx
Mariana	17	F	None	16Au02Bx
Sarah	14	F	None	16Au02Bx
Jane	12	F	None	16Au02Bx
JACKSON, Robt.	19	M	None	16Au02Bx
LEARY, Michl.	25	M	Draper	16Au02Bx
DUFF, Owen	40	M	Laborer	16Au02Bx
Jane	23	F	Laborer	16Au02Bx
Thos.	.00	M	Infant	16Au02Bx
DENNIELLE, Michl.	20	M	Shoemaker	16Au02Bx
MORRIS, Michl.	36	M	Brazier	16Au02Bx
MAXWELL, John	44	M	Laborer	16Au02Bx
Kitty	35	F	None	16Au02Bx
Ann	.00	F	Infant	16Au02Bx
MONK, Thos.	25	M	Laborer	16Au02Bx
COX, Winifer	28	F	None	16Au02Bx
BREIGHAN, Ellen	30	F	Servant	16Au02Bx

NAMES OF PASSENGERS	AGE	SEX	OCCUPATIONS	DATE PORT SHIP
KELLY, Felix	29	M	Smith	16Au02Bx
OBRIEN, Joseph	40	M	Smith	16Au02Bx
SHANNON, John	56	M	Laborer	16Au02Bx
Died-At-Sea				
ROONEY, John	36	M	Laborer	16Au02Bx
SHANNON, Mary	56	F	None	16Au02Bx
CARROLL, Corns.	20	M	Clerk	16Au02Bx
CORMAN, Ann	18	F	Domestic	16Au02Bx
DARGAN, Ellen	23	F	Domestic	16Au02Bx
CORMAC, Thos.	22	M	Laborer	16Au02Bx
MAHON, Mary	27	F	Servant	16Au02Bx
QUINLAN, Patk.	36	M	Laborer	16Au02Bx
BRIEN, Michl.	35	M	Laborer	16Au02Bx
Died-At-Sea				
CORMAC, Richd.	20	M	Laborer	16Au02Bx
CLANCY, Mary	40	F	Housekeeper	16Au02Bx
Bridget	5	F	Child	16Au02Bx
MCKEAMA, Ann	22	F	Servant	16Au02Bx
MCILROY, John	52	M	Laborer	16Au02Bx
MITCHELL, Margt.	20	F	Laborer	16Au02Bx
Wm.	20	M	Laborer	16Au02Bx
Eliza.	12	F	None	16Au02Bx
KELLAHAN, Ellen	20	F	Servant	16Au02Bx
CLINE, Ann	16	F	Servant	16Au02Bx
COSTELLE, Mary	25	F	Servant	16Au02Bx
CARROLL, Michl.	21	M	Clerk	16Au02Bx
Wm.	21	M	Carpenter	16Au02Bx
JOHNSON, Henry	26	M	Laborer	16Au02Bx
MCMAHON, Thos.	19	M	Laborer	16Au02Bx
OHARA, Peter	24	M	Engineer	16Au02Bx
Alice	20	F	None	16Au02Bx
LENNON, Patt	20	M	Laborer	16Au02Bx
DALTON, James	13	M	Laborer	16Au02Bx
MARNION, Edwd.	26	M	Laborer	16Au02Bx
MAGEE, Haugh	22	M	Laborer	16Au02Bx
FLYNN, Patt	22	M	Shoemaker	16Au02Bx
REILLEY, Charles	25	M	Laborer	16Au02Bx
KELLY, P.O.	25	M	Laborer	16Au02Bx
MCDONNAGH, Patt	20	M	Ctnsp	16Au02Bx
HADEN, John	16	M	Unknown	16Au02Bx
GUINES, Mary	19	F	Housekeeper	16Au02Bx
Bridget	8	F	Child	16Au02Bx
John	18	M	Unknown	16Au02Bx
Died-At-Sea				
FEENES, Mathew	22	F	Laborer	16Au02Bx
MAHON, Thos.	26	M	Tailor	16Au02Bx
JOHNSTON, Jas.	30	M	Laborer	16Au02Bx
U-Mrs.	28	F	None	16Au02Bx
FARRELL, Mathew	21	M	Laborer	16Au02Bx
Died-At-Sea				
DARCY, Francis	22	M	Laborer	16Au02Bx
KELLEY, Matt	23	M	Laborer	16Au02Bx
Bridget	19	F	None	16Au02Bx
Patt	18	M	Laborer	16Au02Bx
SCAUFF, Ann	33	F	Housekeeper	16Au02Bx
Cathn.	13	F	Housekeeper	16Au02Bx
Wm.	8	M	Child	16Au02Bx
Joseph	6	M	Child	16Au02Bx
MCLAVERTY, John	28	M	Painter	16Au02Bx
GLACKEN, Wm.	35	M	Laborer	16Au02Bx
James	13	M	Laborer	16Au02Bx
John	11	M	Laborer	16Au02Bx
Elizth.	9	F	Child	16Au02Bx
Margt.	6	F	Child	16Au02Bx
David	4	M	Child	16Au02Bx
Joseph	2	M	Child	16Au02Bx
Hugh	.00	M	Infant	16Au02Bx
MAHER, Ann	30	F	Servant	16Au02Bx
FITZPATRICK, Florence	28	F	Laborer	16Au02Bx
THOMPSON, Wm.	20	M	Butcher	16Au02Bx
KELLY, Ellen	20	F	Servant	16Au02Bx
BURNES, Mary-A.	20	F	Servant	16Au02Bx
MINTON, Wm.	15	M	Servant	16Au02Bx
Robt.	11	M	Servant	16Au02Bx
MONAGHAN, Bridget	25	F	Housekeeper	16Au02Bx

NAMES OF PASSENGERS	AGE	SEX	OCCUPATIONS	DATE PORT SHIP
MONAGHAN, John	2	M	Child	16Au02Bx
Michl.	.00	M	Infant	16Au02Bx
GARERTHY, Mary	14	F	Servant	16Au02Bx
DOWDE, Francis	50	M	Laborer	16Au02Bx
John	3	M	Child	16Au02Bx
CONWAS, David	25	M	Laborer	16Au02Bx
SMITH, Jas.	40	M	Farmer	16Au02Bx
U-Mrs.	30	F	Farmer	16Au02Bx
George	7	M	Child	16Au02Bx
Bachen	4	U	Child	16Au02Bx
Joseph	2	M	Child	16Au02Bx
Died-At-Sea				
Richd.	.00	M	Infant	16Au02Bx
Died-At-Sea				
GREEN, George	46	M	Laborer	16Au02Bx
U-Mrs.	40	F	None	16Au02Bx
Wm.	25	M	Laborer	16Au02Bx
Clare	21	F	None	16Au02Bx
Morris	19	M	Laborer	16Au02Bx
Ann	17	F	None	16Au02Bx
Sarah	7	F	Child	16Au02Bx
STONE, Jas.	30	M	Laborer	16Au02Bx
KELLY, Thos.	14	M	Laborer	16Au02Bx
LEMON, Mary	21	F	Servant	16Au02Bx
CONN, Mary	18	F	Servant	16Au02Bx
MILLIGAN, Wm.	17	M	Laborer	16Au02Bx
Margt.	7	F	Child	16Au02Bx
WHITE, John	44	M	Laborer	16Au02Bx
HALL, Edwd.	28	M	Laborer	16Au02Bx
MCCALLES, John	24	M	Laborer	16Au02Bx
HICKEY, John	20	M	Laborer	16Au02Bx
GRASON, Rose	40	F	Housekeeper	16Au02Bx
Francis	20	M	Housekeeper	16Au02Bx
DIXON, Cathn.	16	F	Housekeeper	16Au02Bx
Eliza.	14	F	Housekeeper	16Au02Bx
COOPER, Henry	29	M	Tailor	16Au02Bx
U-Mrs.	24	F	None	16Au02Bx
LYNCH, John	20	M	Baker	16Au02Bx
CONNELL, Cathn.	16	F	Servant	16Au02Bx
DAILEY, Wm.	25	M	Merchant	16Au02Bx
U-Mrs.	18	F	None	16Au02Bx
RICHARDSON, Mary-Ann	24	F	None	16Au02Bx
BURKE, Slier	20	M	Soldier	16Au02Bx
Annette	16	F	None	16Au02Bx
HOUGHTON, Thos.	18	M	Unknown	16Au02Bx
KELLY, Richd.	56	M	Stationer	16Au02Bx
Michl.	18	M	Stationer	16Au02Bx
Stephen	16	M	Stationer	16Au02Bx
ASPINELL, Alfred	28	M	Unknown	16Au02Bx
Ann	31	F	None	16Au02Bx
MORRONES, Ann	18	F	None	16Au02Bx
SINGLETON, Eliza	30	F	None	16Au02Bx
MCKANNA, Richd.	17	M	None	16Au02Bx
AUSTIN, John	30	M	None	16Au02Bx
Susanna	26	F	None	16Au02Bx
BEATTEY, Isabella	7	F	Child	16Au02Bx

ODESSA 17 AUGUST 1849

From Dublin

NAMES OF PASSENGERS	AGE	SEX	OCCUPATIONS	DATE PORT SHIP
WALSH, Lawrence	30	M	Laborer	17Au12Or
COLLINS, Martha	21	F	Unknown	17Au12Or
GALLAGHER, Patrk.	19	M	Unknown	17Au12Or
MANGAN, Jno.	34	M	Unknown	17Au12Or
Christy	11	F	Unknown	17Au12Or
Lawrence	8	M	Child	17Au12Or
SHERIDAN, Cath.	20	F	Unknown	17Au12Or
DONNELLY, Mary-A.	20	F	Unknown	17Au12Or
SOMERS, Cath.	24	F	Unknown	17Au12Or
Margt.	10	F	Unknown	17Au12Or
Margt.	.00	F	Infant	17Au12Or
MCDERMOTT, T.	24	M	Unknown	17Au12Or
CARTON, Fras.	23	M	Unknown	17Au12Or
MEEHAN, Mary	40	F	Unknown	17Au12Or
Eliza	12	F	Unknown	17Au12Or
DOYLE, Rebecca	24	F	Unknown	17Au12Or
Eliza	.00	F	Infant	17Au12Or
COONEY, Patk.	20	M	Unknown	17Au12Or
COURTNEY, Bridgt.	18	F	Unknown	17Au12Or
MAHER, Cornelius	25	M	Unknown	17Au12Or
U-Mrs.	24	F	Unknown	17Au12Or
GANLY, Margt.	24	F	Unknown	17Au12Or
Ann	24	F	Unknown	17Au12Or
CULLEN, Teresa	18	F	Unknown	17Au12Or
FEGAN, James	32	M	Unknown	17Au12Or
U-Mrs.	32	F	Unknown	17Au12Or
Thomas	9	M	Child	17Au12Or
Rosana	9	F	Child	17Au12Or
Mary	7	F	Child	17Au12Or
John	5	M	Child	17Au12Or
James	3	M	Child	17Au12Or
Joseph	.00	M	Infant	17Au12Or
DUNIC, Biddy	20	F	Unknown	17Au12Or
KEENAN, Pat	30	M	Unknown	17Au12Or
Ellen	30	F	Unknown	17Au12Or
James	7	M	Child	17Au12Or
Maria	5	F	Child	17Au12Or
Essy	3	F	Child	17Au12Or
Patk.	.00	M	Infant	17Au12Or
COONEY, Edward	60	M	Unknown	17Au12Or
Died-At-Sea				
Wm.	40	M	Unknown	17Au12Or
Margt.	38	F	Laborer	17Au12Or
Michl.	22	M	Unknown	17Au12Or
Patk.	20	M	Unknown	17Au12Or
Ann	18	F	Unknown	17Au12Or
Edward	16	M	Unknown	17Au12Or
Mary	14	F	Unknown	17Au12Or
Margt.	16	F	Unknown	17Au12Or
Bridget	7	F	Child	17Au12Or
Eleanor	3	F	Child	17Au12Or
KELLY, Mathew	30	M	Unknown	17Au12Or
MITCHELL, Cath.	20	F	Unknown	17Au12Or
DUNNE, Ryan	50	M	Unknown	17Au12Or
Christian	45	M	Unknown	17Au12Or
Eleanor	24	F	Unknown	17Au12Or
Cath.	22	F	Unknown	17Au12Or
Christian	26	M	Unknown	17Au12Or
Bryan	18	M	Unknown	17Au12Or
HUGHES, Michl.	55	M	Unknown	17Au12Or
Died-At-Sea				
Mary	45	F	Unknown	17Au12Or
Peter	14	M	Unknown	17Au12Or
John	12	M	Unknown	17Au12Or
Mary	12	F	Unknown	17Au12Or
Wm.	8	M	Child	17Au12Or
Patk.	6	M	Child	17Au12Or
Anne	4	F	Child	17Au12Or
Michl.	2	M	Child	17Au12Or
DIGNON, James	40	M	Unknown	17Au12Or
LAPPAN, John	45	M	Unknown	17Au12Or
Mary	40	F	Unknown	17Au12Or
Elizabeth	16	F	Unknown	17Au12Or
Patk.	14	M	Unknown	17Au12Or
Mary	12	F	Unknown	17Au12Or
John	10	M	Unknown	17Au12Or
Phillip	8	M	Child	17Au12Or
James	6	M	Child	17Au12Or
Sally	4	F	Child	17Au12Or
Hannah	2	F	Child	17Au12Or
Wm.Scott	21	M	Unknown	17Au12Or
FITZGERALD, Mathew	50	M	Unknown	17Au12Or
Eleanor	50	F	Unknown	17Au12Or

NAMES OF PASSENGERS	AGE	SEX	OCCUPATIONS	DATE PORT SHIP
FITZGERALD, Judith	25	F	Unknown	17Au120r
Eleanor	22	F	Unknown	17Au120r
Bridget	15	F	Unknown	17Au120r
John	20	M	Unknown	17Au120r
Wm.	18	M	Unknown	17Au120r
Mathew	14	M	Unknown	17Au120r
Michael	12	M	Unknown	17Au120r
HAMMEL, Mary	15	F	Unknown	17Au120r
FOX, Joseph	30	M	Unknown	17Au120r
GALLAGHER, Thomas	32	M	Unknown	17Au120r
Michael	28	M	Unknown	17Au120r
Richard	26	M	Unknown	17Au120r
SMITH, U-Miss	21	F	Laborer	17Au120r
DODD, James	24	M	Unknown	17Au120r
JONES, Peter	20	M	Unknown	17Au120r
MCEVOY, Thomas	31	M	Unknown	17Au120r
FENNELLE, Cath.	21	F	Unknown	17Au120r
HUGHES, Ann-Miss	21	F	Unknown	17Au120r
DILLAN, U-Mrs.	21	F	Unknown	17Au120r
MCCORMACK, James	30	M	Unknown	17Au120r
Died-At-Sea				
LEE, Cath.	20	F	Unknown	17Au120r
DUFFY, Thomas	21	M	Unknown	17Au120r
FOGGART, Mary	20	F	Unknown	17Au120r
CAULFIELD, John	25	M	Unknown	17Au120r
Michl.	20	M	Unknown	17Au120r
Ann	21	F	Unknown	17Au120r
Eliza	19	F	Unknown	17Au120r
Anne	.00	F	Infant	17Au120r
GULLAN, Christy	45	M	Unknown	17Au120r
Mary	45	F	Unknown	17Au120r
REILLY, Mary	76	F	Unknown	17Au120r
GULTAN, Edwd.	7	M	Child	17Au120r
GITROSS, Wm.	40	M	Unknown	17Au120r
ROURKE, James	20	M	Unknown	17Au120r
CORRIGAN, Ann	25	F	Unknown	17Au120r
BORMINGHAM, U-Mrs.	40	F	Unknown	17Au120r
Mary-A.	17	F	Unknown	17Au120r
Wm.	12	M	Unknown	17Au120r
DURGENAM, Christy	30	M	Unknown	17Au120r
Eliza	22	F	Unknown	17Au120r
Cath.	20	F	Unknown	17Au120r
MORTON, Celia	50	F	Unknown	17Au120r
James	15	M	Unknown	17Au120r
Mary	22	M	Unknown	17Au120r
John	13	M	Unknown	17Au120r
Thos.	11	M	Unknown	17Au120r
GALLAGHER, Edward	30	M	Unknown	17Au120r
MURRAY, Rachael	26	F	Unknown	17Au120r
Julia	20	F	Unknown	17Au120r
SMITH, U	38	M	Unknown	17Au120r
MERIDAN, Margt.	26	F	Unknown	17Au120r
Ann	27	F	Unknown	17Au120r
Mary	19	F	Unknown	17Au120r
Margt.	18	F	Unknown	17Au120r

HARRIET-AND-AUGUSTA 17 AUGUST 1849

From Liverpool

NAMES OF PASSENGERS	AGE	SEX	OCCUPATIONS	DATE PORT SHIP
RYLEY, Pat.	20	M	Laborer	17Au020q
RYAN, Joanna	20	F	Laborer	17Au020q
Se--Y	.00	F	Infant	17Au020q
MCCARRALL, Ellen	30	F	None	17Au020q
THOMPSON, John	25	M	None	17Au020q
Bridget	28	F	None	17Au020q
HOLLAND, Bridget	21	F	None	17Au020q
OLIVERSON, John	26	M	Shoemaker	17Au020q
Ann	49	F	None	17Au020q
OLIVERSON, John	23	M	Laborer	17Au020q
Thomas	19	M	Laborer	17Au020q
Esther	18	F	Laborer	17Au020q
Joseph	17	M	Laborer	17Au020q
Richard	12	M	None	17Au020q
WATERS, John	20	M	Laborer	17Au020q
Mary	22	F	Laborer	17Au020q
Ann	16	F	Laborer	17Au020q
LING, John	50	M	Laborer	17Au020q
Elizabeth	45	F	Laborer	17Au020q
GRIMES, Lawrence	21	M	Painter	17Au020q
CARROLL, Andrew	27	M	Laborer	17Au020q
Jane	26	F	Laborer	17Au020q
MONTGOMERY, Henry	26	M	Seaman	17Au020q
Mary	28	F	None	17Au020q
CAWEN, Pat	22	M	Laborer	17Au020q
Bridget	20	F	Laborer	17Au020q
Thomas	6	M	Child	17Au020q
Catherine	.00	F	Infant	17Au020q
DEVON, Chas.	19	M	Laborer	17Au020q
CASSIDY, Andrew	26	M	Laborer	17Au020q
Mary	20	F	Laborer	17Au020q
BEIRNE, George	27	M	Laborer	17Au020q
Ann	25	F	Laborer	17Au020q
Mary-Jane	3	F	Child	17Au020q
Ellen	.00	F	Infant	17Au020q
MURPHY, John	33	M	Laborer	17Au020q
KELLEY, Ann	21	F	Laborer	17Au020q
Catherine	20	F	Laborer	17Au020q
FARRELL, James	20	M	Laborer	17Au020q
FLYNN, Michael	20	M	Laborer	17Au020q
FARRELL, Thomas	22	M	Laborer	17Au020q
Ellen	18	F	Laborer	17Au020q
CUMMINS, Richard	38	M	Laborer	17Au020q
William	31	M	Laborer	17Au020q
Mary-Ann	21	F	Laborer	17Au020q
Bridget	19	F	Laborer	17Au020q
Ellen	21	F	None	17Au020q
Richard	.00	M	Infant	17Au020q
Died-At-Sea				
MCDONNELL, Michael	30	M	Laborer	17Au020q
Mary	25	F	Laborer	17Au020q
Henry	11	M	None	17Au020q
Queen	2	F	Child	17Au020q
Peter	.00	M	Infant	17Au020q
MCGWINN, Peter	25	M	Laborer	17Au020q
Mary	22	F	None	17Au020q
DAVIN, Patt	20	M	Laborer	17Au020q
HACKETT, L.	22	M	Hrsm	17Au020q
VEALE, Patrick	23	M	Laborer	17Au020q
HACKETT, Michael	28	M	Smith	17Au020q
COLLINS, John	25	M	Laborer	17Au020q
NEWMAN, Michael	23	M	Laborer	17Au020q
COLLINS, Joanna	23	F	None	17Au020q
Mary	23	F	None	17Au020q
KELLY, Bridget	31	F	None	17Au020q
Jane	3	F	Child	17Au020q
Mary	.00	F	Infant	17Au020q
SILK, Thomas	46	M	Hrsm	17Au020q
Elizabeth	50	F	None	17Au020q
Catherine	18	F	None	17Au020q
BIGGS, John	24	M	Tailor	17Au020q
CABE, Daniel	20	M	None	17Au020q
Ann	30	F	None	17Au020q
CARROLL, Michael	30	M	Shoemaker	17Au020q
RYAN, M.	30	M	Laborer	17Au020q
Michael	28	M	Laborer	17Au020q
Catherine	25	F	Laborer	17Au020q
Bridget	24	F	Laborer	17Au020q
MANLEY, John	31	M	Laborer	17Au020q
HAMESON, John	30	M	Carpenter	17Au020q
MOORE, George	25	M	Laborer	17Au020q
LINTON, Mary	30	M	Laborer	17Au020q
James	6	M	Child	17Au020q
CANTWELL, Thomas	24	M	Laborer	17Au020q

NAMES OF PASSENGERS	AGE	SEX	OCCUPATIONS	DATE PORT SHIP
GRENT, John	25	M	Laborer	17Au020q
MURRONY, Edwd.	30	M	Laborer	17Au020q
Mary	50	F	Laborer	17Au020q
Edward	23	M	Laborer	17Au020q
MARLEE, Mary	20	F	Laborer	17Au020q
RILEY, Daniel	31	M	Tailor	17Au020q
BURKE, Thomas	50	M	Laborer	17Au020q
Margaret	50	F	Laborer	17Au020q
William	16	M	Laborer	17Au020q
ROURKE, Bryan	25	M	Laborer	17Au020q
BLACK, Charles	24	M	Laborer	17Au020q
HALL, Michael	18	M	Laborer	17Au020q
DENNY, Martin	20	M	Laborer	17Au020q
DALEY, Thomas	40	M	Laborer	17Au020q
U (W)	20	F	Laborer	17Au020q
KILBURN, Thomas	18	M	Laborer	17Au020q
Mary	12	F	None	17Au020q
Bridget	19	F	None	17Au020q
REWIT, Thomas	36	M	Unknown	17Au020q
U (W)	30	F	None	17Au020q
Patrick Died-At-Sea	.00	M	Infant	17Au020q
FISHER, Edward	60	M	Seaman	17Au020q
U (W)	40	F	None	17Au020q
LYONS, John	24	F	None	17Au020q
ENNIS, Michael-G.	60	M	Laborer	17Au020q
GRAY, John	00	M	Surveyor	17Au020q
J. (W)	26	F	None	17Au020q
GERVING, James	18	M	Laborer	17Au020q
SHERIDAN, Bridget	18	F	None	17Au020q
WHITE, Thomas	21	M	Laborer	17Au020q
COMFORT, James	25	M	Laborer	17Au020q
GRAY, Timothy	18	M	Shoemaker	17Au020q
MCGERVIN, Patty	40	F	None	17Au020q
EGAN, Pat	25	M	Laborer	17Au020q
Mcc--K, Pat	25	M	Unknown	17Au020q
Bryan	20	M	Unknown	17Au020q
WHITE, Margaret	20	F	Unknown	17Au020q
Catherine	10	F	None	17Au020q
MILLEY, Walter	20	F	None	17Au020q
CANNAN, Philip	00	M	Mason	17Au020q
FEGAN, Daniel	40	M	Laborer	17Au020q
FITZGERALD, Michael	30	M	Laborer	17Au020q
CONNETT, George	23	M	Unknown	17Au020q
CUMMIN, Mary	22	F	None	17Au020q
CRONIN, Thomas	5	M	Child	17Au020q
Ellen	2	F	Child	17Au020q
CLARY, James	49	M	Laborer	17Au020q
U (W)	36	F	None	17Au020q
John	9	M	Child	17Au020q
Ellen	7	F	Child	17Au020q
Mary	5	F	Child	17Au020q
Joanna	3	F	Child	17Au020q
Ann	.00	F	Infant	17Au020q
Pat	32	M	Shoemaker	17Au020q
Catharine	30	F	None	17Au020q
MEARLUCH, Patt	18	M	Laborer	17Au020q
James	18	M	Laborer	17Au020q
GERVIN, Honora	25	F	Laborer	17Au020q
RI--, Sally	28	F	Laborer	17Au020q
RYAN, C.	15	F	Laborer	17Au020q
PAYLEY, Bridget	20	F	Laborer	17Au020q
FARRELL, Michael	20	M	Tailor	17Au020q
LOWLY, Bridget	12	F	None	17Au020q
MUNROE, Aaron	20	M	Laborer	17Au020q
MISCALL, Marg.	20	F	Laborer	17Au020q
FISH, Bern.	26	M	Laborer	17Au020q
GAFFNEY, Patrick	20	M	Laborer	17Au020q
MCCOUL, Andrew	31	M	Laborer	17Au020q
CULL, Catharine	22	F	None	17Au020q
MILLAN, Margaret	55	F	None	17Au020q
Peter	13	M	None	17Au020q
GANYAN, Betsey	25	F	None	17Au020q
DONOVAN, Daniel	00	M	Seaman	17Au020q
GARRETY, Margaret	40	F	None	17Au020q

NAMES OF PASSENGERS	AGE	SEX	OCCUPATIONS	DATE PORT SHIP
GARRETY, John	15	M	None	17Au020q
Richard	12	M	None	17Au020q
Rose	00	F	Unknown	17Au020q
Maria	5	F	Child	17Au020q
RAPE, Christopher	33	M	Miller	17Au020q
WALLACE, Catharine	24	F	None	17Au020q
CARTING, Jerry	46	M	Laborer	17Au020q
U (W)	30	F	Laborer	17Au020q
Helen	7	F	Child	17Au020q
Mary	5	F	Child	17Au020q
Catharine	.00	M	Infant	17Au020q
Joanna	27	F	None	17Au020q
Catherine	25	F	None	17Au020q
CUNNINGHAM, Catherine	25	F	None	17Au020q
MADDEN, Michael	21	M	Tailor	17Au020q
HAYS, Ellen	30	F	None	17Au020q
BIGGIN, Mary	15	F	None	17Au020q
Matthew	10	M	None	17Au020q
Catharine	14	F	None	17Au020q
BAWLER, John	44	M	Laborer	17Au020q
BURKE, John	8	M	Child	17Au020q

OREGON 17 AUGUST 1849

From Penzance

NAMES OF PASSENGERS	AGE	SEX	OCCUPATIONS	DATE PORT SHIP
SIMMONS, Joseph	50	M	Farmer	17Au20Kb
Joseph	20	M	Farmer	17Au20Kb
SOPER, Ann	47	F	Wife	17Au20Kb
Elizabeth (D)	16	F	None	17Au20Kb
William (S)	12	M	None	17Au20Kb
Richard (S)	11	M	None	17Au20Kb
BENNETTS, James	22	M	Smith	17Au20Kb
PEARCE, Wm.	27	M	Smith	17Au20Kb
Sarah	27	F	Dressmaker	17Au20Kb
Alexander	22	M	Smith	17Au20Kb
Joseph	16	M	Smith	17Au20Kb
MARTIN, Wm.	22	M	Miner	17Au20Kb
John	18	M	Miner	17Au20Kb
Mary	17	F	Servant	17Au20Kb
Benjamin	13	M	Miner	17Au20Kb
BOWDEN, Joseph	44	M	Molder	17Au20Kb
WILLIAMS, John	35	M	Miner	17Au20Kb
SPRAGUE, Thomas	48	M	Unknown	17Au20Kb
DENNIS, John	42	M	Miner	17Au20Kb
DUNN, James	35	M	Miner	17Au20Kb
SWARNE, Elizabeth	40	F	Innkeeper	17Au20Kb
GRIBBLE, Joseph	24	M	Painter	17Au20Kb
Elizabeth	19	F	Spinster	17Au20Kb
Helen	13	F	None	17Au20Kb
Mary	11	F	None	17Au20Kb
JOLLY, James	22	M	Painter	17Au20Kb
PERRY, Richard	20	M	Miner	17Au20Kb
HOLLOW, Stephen	21	M	Mason	17Au20Kb
HALL, George	18	M	Farmer	17Au20Kb
Edward	14	M	Farmer	17Au20Kb
Wm.	12	M	Farmer	17Au20Kb
DALE, Mary	49	F	Tailor	17Au20Kb
WELLS, Anne	21	F	Dressmaker	17Au20Kb
NICHOLLS, John	32	M	Farmer	17Au20Kb
Mary	32	F	Spinster	17Au20Kb
ROGERS, John	27	M	Miner	17Au20Kb
Betsey	31	F	Tailor	17Au20Kb
John	5	M	Child	17Au20Kb
Mary	3	F	Child	17Au20Kb
TREWBAD, Thomas	54	M	Painter	17Au20Kb
Elizabeth	53	F	Dressmaker	17Au20Kb
Wm.	16	M	Miner	17Au20Kb
Richd.	13	M	Farmer	17Au20Kb

NAMES OF PASSENGERS		AGE	SEX	OCCUPATIONS	DATE PORT SHIP
TREWBAD, Elizabeth		25	F	Unknown	17Au20Kb
SAUNDRY, Sarah		22	F	Unknown	17Au20Kb
HACKET, Thos.		30	M	Miner	17Au20Kb
HOSKING, Edw.		25	M	Miner	17Au20Kb
Elizabeth		28	F	Dressmaker	17Au20Kb
MARKET, Thomas		6	M	Child	17Au20Kb
U		3	U	Child	17Au20Kb
HOSKING, Jane		26	F	Servant	17Au20Kb
LOCKETT, George		28	M	Smith	17Au20Kb
TREMBALT, U		46	F	Wife	17Au20Kb
U		50	U	Unknown	17Au20Kb
U		19	F	Wife	17Au20Kb
Richd.		18	M	Miner	17Au20Kb
Wm.		12	M	None	17Au20Kb
Elisabeth		59	F	Spinster	17Au20Kb
TRETHEWAY, Samuel		26	M	Miner	17Au20Kb
May	(W)	27	F	None	17Au20Kb
U		.00	U	Infant	17Au20Kb
TRETEN, Samuel		2	M	Child	17Au20Kb
WILLIAMS, Zenefe		26	F	Wife	17Au20Kb
Elizabeth		3	F	Child	17Au20Kb
John		1	M	Child	17Au20Kb
ALLEN, Wm.		24	M	Miner	17Au20Kb
PERRYMAN, Robert		23	M	Miller	17Au20Kb
TRETHEWAY, Louisa		12	F	Servant	17Au20Kb
HENWOOD, Emma		48	F	Wife	17Au20Kb
Martha		16	F	None	17Au20Kb
Bessy		11	F	None	17Au20Kb
Edw.		15	M	None	17Au20Kb
Harold		13	M	None	17Au20Kb
VIVIAN, Henry		28	M	Unknown	17Au20Kb
Jane		20	F	Unknown	17Au20Kb
Cath.		5	F	Child	17Au20Kb
Martha		4	F	Child	17Au20Kb
MAY, Wm.		12	M	Unknown	17Au20Kb
TYACKE, Margt.		25	F	Unknown	17Au20Kb
Edwd.		1	M	Child	17Au20Kb

JOHN-FULDEN 18 AUGUST 1849

From Liverpool

NAMES OF PASSENGERS		AGE	SEX	OCCUPATIONS	DATE PORT SHIP
HOPKINS, Martin		20	M	Laborer	18Au020w
MCANANY, Cath.		16	F	Dressmaker	18Au020w
POWER, James		32	M	Carpenter	18Au020w
Sarah	(W)	28	F	None	18Au020w
Henry		28	M	Joiner	18Au020w
Catherine		20	F	Servant	18Au020w
HOGAN, Mary		20	F	Servant	18Au020w
RYAN, Thomas		30	M	Laborer	18Au020w
WALLER, Eliza		30	F	Servant	18Au020w
MAKAN, Nichel		30	M	Laborer	18Au020w
FEHNE, Frank.		36	M	Laborer	18Au020w
BURNS, Saml.		29	M	Laborer	18Au020w
DANE, John		22	M	Laborer	18Au020w
FOGERTY, John		27	M	Laborer	18Au020w
DUNN, Johannah		25	F	Servant	18Au020w
DIVINE, Magt.		50	F	Servant	18Au020w
Johanah		14	F	Servant	18Au020w
Margaret		22	F	Servant	18Au020w
Tim		25	M	Laborer	18Au020w
TAYLOR, Rody		25	M	Weaver	18Au020w
SCANLON, Dennis		30	M	Laborer	18Au020w
James		32	M	Laborer	18Au020w
TRACEY, Larry		30	M	Unknown	18Au020w
SCANLON, Judy		30	F	Unknown	18Au020w
Mary		4	F	Child	18Au020w
Ellen		.00	F	Infant	18Au020w
FALEY, Rose		20	F	Unknown	18Au020w

NAMES OF PASSENGERS		AGE	SEX	OCCUPATIONS	DATE PORT SHIP
LONG, Frank		40	M	Unknown	18Au020w
JONES, Wm.		25	M	Unknown	18Au020w
CAFFRAY, Thos.		28	M	Unknown	18Au020w
SWEENEY, Edwd.		25	M	Unknown	18Au020w
SCANLON, Richd.		6	M	Child	18Au020w
SWEENEY, Owen		18	M	Unknown	18Au020w
MCDONALD, James		25	M	Farmer	18Au020w
ROACH, David		25	M	Laborer	18Au020w
SHEHAN, John		28	M	Laborer	18Au020w
BURKE, Wm.		28	M	Servant	18Au020w
WALL, Martin		20	M	Laborer	18Au020w
Margt.	(W)	20	F	None	18Au020w
RYAN, Stephen		25	M	Farmer	18Au020w
Martha	(W)	25	F	None	18Au020w
James		56	M	Farmer	18Au020w
Judy		23	F	Servant	18Au020w
Mary		23	F	Servant	18Au020w
Julia		.00	F	Infant	18Au020w
Margt.		.00	F	Infant	18Au020w
SULLIVAN, Danl.		45	M	Laborer	18Au020w
EBIT, Josh.		45	M	Farmer	18Au020w
Eliz.		43	M	Farmer	18Au020w
Rebecca		22	F	Farmer	18Au020w
Wm.		18	M	Farmer	18Au020w
Josh.		17	M	Farmer	18Au020w
Jemima		15	F	Farmer	18Au020w
Eliza-Jane		14	F	Farmer	18Au020w
Letitia		10	F	Farmer	18Au020w
Ralph		9	M	Child	18Au020w
James		7	M	Child	18Au020w
Joshua		4	M	Child	18Au020w
ARMSTRONG, U-Miss		23	F	None	18Au020w
MANN, Jno.		30	M	Laborer	18Au020w
GOMERY, James		20	M	Laborer	18Au020w
DEVINE, Mich.		23	M	Laborer	18Au020w
Kate		40	F	Servant	18Au020w
LINDSAY, John		45	M	Brick Maker	18Au020w
Mary-Ann	(D)	17	F	None	18Au020w
Marg.	(W)	40	F	None	18Au020w
Mary	(D)	13	F	None	18Au020w
Sarah	(D)	10	F	None	18Au020w
Catherine	(D)	7	F	Child	18Au020w
Judy	(D)	5	F	Child	18Au020w
Ellen	(D)	3	F	Child	18Au020w
DICKINSON, Thomas		40	M	Baker	18Au020w
REEDEN, Rose		18	F	Servant	18Au020w
MCGEE, Margaret		18	F	Servant	18Au020w
KELLY, Pat		23	M	Laborer	18Au020w
RYAN, James		22	M	Carpenter	18Au020w
FITZSIMMONS, Thomas		18	M	Laborer	18Au020w
MCKENNA, Wm.		18	M	Laborer	18Au020w
HUGHS, Johannah		21	F	None	18Au020w
GORMAN, Matthew		28	M	Laborer	18Au020w
Jane		21	F	Servant	18Au020w
DELLEHANTY, Mary		27	F	Servant	18Au020w
QUIN, John		50	M	Butcher	18Au020w
DELLEHANTY, Thos.		5	M	Child	18Au020w
Johannah		6	F	Child	18Au020w
James		.00	M	Infant	18Au020w
OHARA, Pat		35	M	Tinman	18Au020w
Ann	(W)	30	F	None	18Au020w
Jane		11	F	Relative	18Au020w
John		.00	M	Infant	18Au020w
WARD, Dorothea		18	F	Servant	18Au020w
DELANY, John		20	M	Servant	18Au020w
HUSTANG, John		20	M	Servant	18Au020w
FOLEY, John		32	M	Servant	18Au020w
OHARA, Bryan		30	M	Laborer	18Au020w
MULLKURTHY, Pat		18	M	Laborer	18Au020w
OHARA, Ellen		18	F	Servant	18Au020w
FORD, Augustus		20	M	Tailor	18Au020w
MCARTHUR, Pat		20	M	Laborer	18Au020w
ROONEY, Bridget		18	F	Servant	18Au020w
MULLARTY, Bridget		44	F	Servant	18Au020w
MCMALLAN, Mary		40	F	Servant	18Au020w

NAMES OF PASSENGERS		AGE	SEX	OCCUPATIONS	DATE PORT SHIP
MCMALLAN, James		12	M	Servant	18Au020w
John		10	M	Servant	18Au020w
Frank		8	M	Child	18Au020w
MAHOON, Pat		5	M	Child	18Au020w
MULLARTY, Mary		20	F	Servant	18Au020w
CARROL, Martin		30	M	Shoemaker	18Au020w
Honora	(W)	28	F	None	18Au020w
John	(S)	6	M	Child	18Au020w
Ellen	(D)	3	F	Child	18Au020w
Kat.	(D)	.00	F	Infant	18Au020w
HENRY, Bartlet		40	M	Laborer	18Au020w
KENNEDY, Joseph		56	M	Laborer	18Au020w
Bridget		20	F	Servant	18Au020w
Eliza		18	F	Servant	18Au020w
MANYON, Pat		22	M	Laborer	18Au020w
John		30	M	Laborer	18Au020w
WAIT, James		35	M	Laborer	18Au020w
MOONEY, Mary		17	F	Servant	18Au020w
FALY, Peter		32	M	Laborer	18Au020w
NOWLAN, Peter		28	M	Wheelwright	18Au020w
Alley	(W)	28	F	None	18Au020w
James		.00	M	Infant	18Au020w
ROSE, Martha		20	F	Servant	18Au020w
DUFFY, Alley		19	M	Servant	18Au020w
MCDANIELL, Sarah		24	F	Servant	18Au020w
RYLEY, Cathr.		22	F	Servant	18Au020w
NOWLAN, James		18	M	Laborer	18Au020w
FIRMINGHAM, James		25	M	Laborer	18Au020w
BURNS, Ann		19	F	Laborer	18Au020w
MCCAFFERY, John		18	M	Laborer	18Au020w
ANNUSON, James		18	M	Laborer	18Au020w
FAGAN, Pat		26	M	Laborer	18Au020w
DORAN, John		28	M	Laborer	18Au020w
SCALLY, Richd.		21	M	Laborer	18Au020w
William		20	M	Laborer	18Au020w
WILWOOD, William		45	M	Laborer	18Au020w
Sarah	(D)	14	F	None	18Au020w
KENNA, Bridget		45	F	Servant	18Au020w
Mary		23	F	Servant	18Au020w
GORCY, Wm.		30	M	Servant	18Au020w
Judith	(W)	23	F	None	18Au020w
DORAN, Andy		30	M	Carpenter	18Au020w
Eliz.	(W)	25	F	None	18Au020w
Ann		26	F	Servant	18Au020w
ROURKE, Margt.		25	F	Servant	18Au020w
GOURIE, Pat		43	M	Laborer	18Au020w
DEANE, James		15	M	Laborer	18Au020w
KERAN, Ellan		18	F	Servant	18Au020w
FARRELL, Pat		21	M	Laborer	18Au020w
MOONEY, Andy		20	M	Laborer	18Au020w
WELCH, Thos.		24	M	Carpenter	18Au020w
LUNT, Josh.		40	M	Engineer	18Au020w
Richd.		20	M	Plumber	18Au020w
Ann		18	F	Milliner	18Au020w
Martha		12	F	None	18Au020w
Susan		6	F	Child	18Au020w
DALY, Ambrose		30	M	Laborer	18Au020w
PURCE, Wm.		26	M	Laborer	18Au020w
Margt.	(W)	24	F	None	18Au020w
BURNS, Michl.		27	M	Laborer	18Au020w
Ellen	(W)	20	F	None	18Au020w
FARRINGDON, Julia		46	F	Farmer	18Au020w
Ann		21	F	Farmer	18Au020w
Theresa		16	F	Farmer	18Au020w
John		15	M	Farmer	18Au020w
Kate		14	F	Farmer	18Au020w
GOURIE, Chrs.		23	M	Laborer	18Au020w
BURNS, Mary		12	F	Servant	18Au020w
SULLIVAN, Pat		40	M	Blacksmith	18Au020w
U	(S)	17	M	Blacksmith	18Au020w
DUFFY, Owen		25	M	Laborer	18Au020w
HANEY, Peter		30	M	Laborer	18Au020w
Sarah	(W)	36	F	None	18Au020w
FLEMING, John		21	M	Laborer	18Au020w
CANTWELL, James		26	M	Servant	18Au020w
CANTWELL, Mary		18	F	Servant	18Au020w
MILCH, Mary		18	F	Servant	18Au020w
LEVEY, Bridget		32	F	Servant	18Au020w
LUCY, Wm.		24	M	Laborer	18Au020w
BRENNON, Cath.		50	F	Servant	18Au020w
OWEN, Mary		19	F	Servant	18Au020w
BRENNAN, Mary		15	F	Servant	18Au020w
DIVINE, Kate		30	F	Servant	18Au020w
HAND, Pat		25	M	Laborer	18Au020w
BRANNAN, Henry		45	M	Laborer	18Au020w
MCCANNA, Owen		60	M	Laborer	18Au020w
Ann	(W)	60	F	None	18Au020w
Ellen		18	F	Relative	18Au020w
Owen		13	M	Relative	18Au020w
IGO, Catherine		35	F	Wife	18Au020w
Mary	(D)	16	F	None	18Au020w
Ann	(D)	10	F	None	18Au020w
Bridget	(D)	8	F	Child	18Au020w
John	(S)	6	M	Child	18Au020w
Catherine	(D)	4	F	Child	18Au020w
CLEARY, John		38	M	Laborer	18Au020w
SMITH, John		25	M	Laborer	18Au020w
Ellen	(W)	22	F	None	18Au020w
RILEY, Pat		23	M	Laborer	18Au020w
ONEAL, Francis		24	M	Mason	18Au020w
HAGAN, John		17	M	Worm Cutter	18Au020w
TALBOT, Chas.		48	M	Blacksmith	18Au020w
RILEY, Peter		48	M	Laborer	18Au020w
Peggy		16	F	Wife	18Au020w
MCNALLAN, Watt.		7	M	Child	18Au020w
CARNEY, Jer.		40	M	Unknown	18Au020w
Died-At-Sea					
FARRINGTON, Jane		.00	F	Infant	18Au020w
Died-At-Sea					
WOOD, Thomas		45	M	Unknown	18Au020w
Died-At-Sea					
REED, Paul		25	M	Unknown	18Au020w
Died-At-Sea					
WARD, Mg.		40	F	Unknown	18Au020w
Died-At-Sea					
SHOCK, J.		.00	F	Infant	18Au020w
Died-At-Sea					
WILLIAMS, U		00	M	Unknown	18Au020w
Died-At-Sea					
KELLY, John		30	M	Unknown	18Au020w
Died-At-Sea					
FARRINGTON, U		22	F	Unknown	18Au020w
Died-At-Sea					
LEWIS, Dan.		25	M	Unknown	18Au020w
Died-At-Sea					
MANLEY, William		21	M	Bookkeeper	18Au020w

NORTHUMBERLAND 18 AUGUST 1849

From London

NAMES OF PASSENGERS		AGE	SEX	OCCUPATIONS	DATE PORT SHIP
BALIN, Thomas		32	M	Painter	18Au13Ds
Sophia		30	F	None	18Au13Ds
Edward		10	M	None	18Au13Ds
James		7	M	Child	18Au13Ds
Emily		5	F	Child	18Au13Ds
Edith		3	F	Child	18Au13Ds
PAGE, Ann		24	F	None	18Au13Ds
Mary		.07	F	Infant	18Au13Ds
BARRETT, William-Major		38	M	Merchant	18Au13Ds
GRETTON, Henry		55	M	Unknown	18Au13Ds
Mary-Elizabeth		38	F	Unknown	18Au13Ds
Henry		27	M	Unknown	18Au13Ds
Edwin-Wallace		1	M	Child	18Au13Ds

NAMES OF PASSENGERS	AGE	SEX	OCCUPATIONS	DATE PORT SHIP
STEWART, Charles	23	M	Surveyor	18Au13Ds
WHALE, Henry	23	M	Clerk	18Au13Ds
HILL, Samuel	27	M	Cver	18Au13Ds
HUGGINS, Hester	25	F	None	18Au13Ds
CORDWILL, Eliza	23	F	None	18Au13Ds
MILLS, Eliza	21	F	None	18Au13Ds
WHITE, Edward	29	M	Farmer	18Au13Ds
Sarah	29	F	None	18Au13Ds
Edward	2	M	Child	18Au13Ds
Fanny	.04	F	Infant	18Au13Ds
HENNESEY, Timothy	32	M	Laborer	18Au13Ds
Julia	28	F	None	18Au13Ds
HILL, Martin	28	M	Laborer	18Au13Ds
GOFF, Elizabeth	49	F	None	18Au13Ds
Anna	22	F	None	18Au13Ds
Henry	12	M	None	18Au13Ds
Elizabeth	10	F	None	18Au13Ds
CROFTS, John	32	M	Laborer	18Au13Ds
Sarah	30	F	None	18Au13Ds
SMITH, John-B.	35	M	Laborer	18Au13Ds
COOPER, Edward	32	M	Laborer	18Au13Ds
GIBBS, Richard	32	M	Laborer	18Au13Ds
Rebecca	28	F	None	18Au13Ds
UNCLES, Thomas	60	M	Shoemaker	18Au13Ds
BENTLEY, Thomas	45	M	Laborer	18Au13Ds
Eliza	36	F	None	18Au13Ds
Thomas	20	M	Laborer	18Au13Ds
James	35	M	Laborer	18Au13Ds
Sarah	21	F	None	18Au13Ds
Fanny	12	F	None	18Au13Ds
Alice	5	F	Child	18Au13Ds
Henry	.00	M	Infant	18Au13Ds
BROWN, William	23	M	Laborer	18Au13Ds
HOUGH, Mary-Ann	21	F	None	18Au13Ds
Eliza	17	F	None	18Au13Ds
SABINE, Alfred	26	M	Laborer	18Au13Ds
Mary-Ann	23	F	None	18Au13Ds
Daniel	.00	M	Infant	18Au13Ds
FAHY, Edward	40	M	Laborer	18Au13Ds
Mary	40	F	None	18Au13Ds
Nerah	3	F	Child	18Au13Ds
MURPHY, Mary	46	F	None	18Au13Ds
THOMPSON, James	30	M	Laborer	18Au13Ds
Ann	31	F	None	18Au13Ds
Ann	.00	F	Infant	18Au13Ds
PHILLIPS, Thomas	27	M	Laborer	18Au13Ds
Margaret	25	F	None	18Au13Ds
Mary	5	F	Child	18Au13Ds
KEELEY, Elizabeth	30	F	None	18Au13Ds
Mary	.00	F	Infant	18Au13Ds
George	3	M	Child	18Au13Ds
EDWARDS, Eliza	32	F	None	18Au13Ds
Robert	10	M	None	18Au13Ds
Eliza	9	F	Child	18Au13Ds
BEARD, Thomas	17	M	Baker	18Au13Ds
STEERS, Henry	23	M	Grocer	18Au13Ds
MCGUIRE, Mary	35	F	None	18Au13Ds
WILLS, Wilhelm	45	M	Laborer	18Au13Ds
Mary	49	F	None	18Au13Ds
Mary	66	F	None	18Au13Ds
Margaret	20	F	None	18Au13Ds
Garret-H.	20	M	Laborer	18Au13Ds
Charles	17	M	Laborer	18Au13Ds
Elizabeth	13	F	None	18Au13Ds
William	21	M	Laborer	18Au13Ds
CALSTON, James	37	M	Bookkeeper	18Au13Ds
EHRAN, John	19	M	Bookkeeper	18Au13Ds
RICKMAN, Arthur	7	M	Child	18Au13Ds
Edwin	43	M	Farmer	18Au13Ds
John	8	M	Child	18Au13Ds
HOLTMAN, Caroline	24	F	None	18Au13Ds
Ann	4	F	Child	18Au13Ds
William	.00	M	Infant	18Au13Ds
GREENBAND, Susan	28	F	None	18Au13Ds
SOMERS, Sarah	19	F	None	18Au13Ds
MORIATY, John	27	M	Laborer	18Au13Ds
Mary	24	F	None	18Au13Ds
LIDGOLD, Thomas	29	M	Gdnr	18Au13Ds
Sophia	34	F	None	18Au13Ds
YOUNG, James	24	M	Brfhr	18Au13Ds
BARWELL, William	22	M	Clerk	18Au13Ds
HENRY, William	34	M	Laborer	18Au13Ds
Ellen	32	F	None	18Au13Ds
Mary-Ann	11	F	None	18Au13Ds
Eugene	9	M	Child	18Au13Ds
Amelia	7	F	Child	18Au13Ds
Thomas	5	M	Child	18Au13Ds
Catherine	.00	F	Infant	18Au13Ds
TUMEY, Jeremiah	45	M	Laborer	18Au13Ds
Jane	46	F	None	18Au13Ds
Michael	18	M	None	18Au13Ds
Mary	16	F	None	18Au13Ds
Margaret	14	F	None	18Au13Ds
Jeremiah	11	M	None	18Au13Ds
Ellen	.00	F	Infant	18Au13Ds
STONE, John	51	M	Laborer	18Au13Ds
SMITH, Bartlet	21	M	Clerk	18Au13Ds
BURNHAN, Henry	20	M	Laborer	18Au13Ds
MORTIMER, John	61	M	Laborer	18Au13Ds
Jane	52	F	None	18Au13Ds
RYDEN, Mary	46	F	None	18Au13Ds
MORTIMER, Susan	15	F	None	18Au13Ds
ACKRELL, John	5	M	Child	18Au13Ds
TERRY, Christopher	26	M	Laborer	18Au13Ds
Jane	27	F	None	18Au13Ds
DOWNEY, Julia	30	F	None	18Au13Ds
FORELANDER, Richard	29	M	Laborer	18Au13Ds
ROWLAND, Richard	21	M	Cigar Maker	18Au13Ds
BOYLE, Thomas	28	M	Seaman	18Au13Ds
Hannah	28	F	None	18Au13Ds
Ann	6	F	Child	18Au13Ds
Catherine	5	F	Child	18Au13Ds
CANTON, Henry	21	M	Laborer	18Au13Ds
NORTH, William	44	M	Tailor	18Au13Ds
Harriett	36	F	None	18Au13Ds
BARNETT, Helen	25	F	None	18Au13Ds
EGAN, Harriett	26	F	None	18Au13Ds
Alice	2	F	Child	18Au13Ds
BALLARD, Morris	21	M	Laborer	18Au13Ds
JAMES, Jesse	27	M	Laborer	18Au13Ds
Charlotte	21	F	None	18Au13Ds
Joseph	2	M	Child	18Au13Ds
MCCARTY, Patrick	34	M	Laborer	18Au13Ds
KNATCHBULL, Robert	32	M	Clerk	18Au13Ds
Mary	32	F	None	18Au13Ds
Robert	4	M	Child	18Au13Ds
Elizabeth	2	F	Child	18Au13Ds
Alfred	.00	M	Infant	18Au13Ds
WEST, Susan	30	F	None	18Au13Ds
Sarah	7	F	Child	18Au13Ds
Jane	5	F	Child	18Au13Ds
SMITH, William	41	M	Laborer	18Au13Ds
Sophia	41	F	None	18Au13Ds
Fra.	16	F	None	18Au13Ds
HORSEPOOL, John	30	M	Laborer	18Au13Ds
SAUNTY, William	20	M	Laborer	18Au13Ds
BILLING, Thomas	19	M	Laborer	18Au13Ds
GUNTON, James	19	M	Laborer	18Au13Ds
MUDD, Frederick	20	M	Laborer	18Au13Ds
SCHOLER, John	30	M	Miller	18Au13Ds
Mary	28	F	None	18Au13Ds
Arthur	6	M	Child	18Au13Ds
GOLDSMITH, Woolf	25	M	Merchant	18Au13Ds
KENYON, Thomas	37	M	Laborer	18Au13Ds
Susanah	34	F	None	18Au13Ds
William	10	M	None	18Au13Ds
COX, Richard	37	M	Clerk	18Au13Ds
BENNETT, James	31	M	Clerk	18Au13Ds
GRAVELY, Samuel	36	M	Clerk	18Au13Ds
ROSE, Ambrose	20	M	Laborer	18Au13Ds

NAMES OF PASSENGERS	AGE	SEX	OCCUPATIONS	DATE PORT SHIP
MOBBS, George	24	M	Laborer	18Au13Ds
EMMERSON, John	30	M	Farmer	18Au13Ds
Mary	24	F	None	18Au13Ds
WILKINSON, John	38	M	Laborer	18Au13Ds
MCKAY, Margaret	40	F	None	18Au13Ds
Thomas	11	M	None	18Au13Ds
SCUDDER, James	16	M	Laborer	18Au13Ds
PAICE, James	36	M	Mechanic	18Au13Ds
Euphemia	36	F	None	18Au13Ds
James	5	M	Child	18Au13Ds
William	3	M	Child	18Au13Ds
John	2	M	Child	18Au13Ds
George	.07	M	Infant	18Au13Ds
DUNDEN, Mary	40	F	None	18Au13Ds
Eliza	3	F	Child	18Au13Ds
TROUGH, Edward	22	M	Laborer	18Au13Ds
BUTLER, George	26	M	Laborer	18Au13Ds
Alice	26	F	None	18Au13Ds
George	6	M	Child	18Au13Ds
SOLOMAN, Blumer	45	F	None	18Au13Ds
Mary-Ann	21	F	None	18Au13Ds
Rose	17	F	None	18Au13Ds
Leon	4	M	Child	18Au13Ds
Simon	3	M	Child	18Au13Ds
KLUSSMAN, Henry	47	M	Musician	18Au13Ds
H.	30	F	None	18Au13Ds
Dorothy	10	F	None	18Au13Ds
Ellen	8	F	Child	18Au13Ds
Kate	7	F	Child	18Au13Ds
Elizabeth	5	F	Child	18Au13Ds
Henry	3	M	Child	18Au13Ds
Garrett	1	M	Child	18Au13Ds
DUNN, Elizabeth	20	F	None	18Au13Ds
SAIN, John	32	M	Draper	18Au13Ds
PHILLIPS, Frederick	20	M	Laborer	18Au13Ds
THOMPSON, Henry	31	M	Laborer	18Au13Ds
HANSARD, George	19	M	Laborer	18Au13Ds

LAUREL 18 AUGUST 1849

From Londonderry

NAMES OF PASSENGERS	AGE	SEX	OCCUPATIONS	DATE PORT SHIP
CRENFORD, Eliza	30	F	Unknown	18Au01Ov
KERR, Molly	20	F	Unknown	18Au01Ov
IRVINE, Robert	18	M	Unknown	18Au01Ov
MCCLEON, James	74	M	Unknown	18Au01Ov
Died-At-Sea				
Mary	72	F	Unknown	18Au01Ov
James	33	M	Unknown	18Au01Ov
Sarah	29	F	Unknown	18Au01Ov
Mary	8	F	Child	18Au01Ov
Robert	6	M	Child	18Au01Ov
David	3	M	Child	18Au01Ov
Ellen-Jane	1	F	Child	18Au01Ov
BIGS, James	13	M	Unknown	18Au01Ov
HIGINS, Francis	52	M	Unknown	18Au01Ov
Sarah	52	F	Unknown	18Au01Ov
James	20	M	Unknown	18Au01Ov
John	13	M	Unknown	18Au01Ov
DICKENS, Bell-M.	20	F	Unknown	18Au01Ov
NICKLE, Eliza	22	F	Unknown	18Au01Ov
LICKEY, Eliza	20	F	Unknown	18Au01Ov
BOYD, Eliza	20	F	Unknown	18Au01Ov
MCKINLEY, Samuel	40	M	Unknown	18Au01Ov
NICKLE, Thomas	34	M	Unknown	18Au01Ov
LOUGHNEY, James	18	M	Unknown	18Au01Ov
ANDERSON, Wm.	18	M	Unknown	18Au01Ov
Robert	18	M	Unknown	18Au01Ov
MCKERNON, Mary	20	F	Unknown	18Au01Ov
EWIN, Ann	25	F	Unknown	18Au01Ov
HAMILTON, Margret	30	F	Unknown	18Au01Ov
MORROW, Peggy	20	F	Unknown	18Au01Ov
ANDREWS, William	18	M	Unknown	18Au01Ov
BOSLAND, Joseph	16	M	Unknown	18Au01Ov
QUINN, Michael	20	M	Unknown	18Au01Ov
BOYD, Richard	30	M	Unknown	18Au01Ov
Richard	30	M	Unknown	18Au01Ov
John	80	M	Unknown	18Au01Ov
WINDLE, Ellen	18	F	Unknown	18Au01Ov
Eliza	16	F	Unknown	18Au01Ov
BACON, Christopher	25	M	Unknown	18Au01Ov
CAMPBELL, John	24	M	Unknown	18Au01Ov
LURURN, Ann	16	F	Unknown	18Au01Ov
MASON, Martha	18	F	Unknown	18Au01Ov
Jane	20	F	Unknown	18Au01Ov
STEWART, William	25	M	Unknown	18Au01Ov
Ann	30	F	Unknown	18Au01Ov
MILLER, Martha-J.	16	F	Unknown	18Au01Ov
Nancy	15	F	Unknown	18Au01Ov
MCGILL, Edward	18	M	Unknown	18Au01Ov
MCCOWEY, Catherine	20	F	Unknown	18Au01Ov
RUSSEL, Robert	25	M	Unknown	18Au01Ov
MCWILLIAMS, Pat	18	M	Unknown	18Au01Ov
BROWN, John	22	M	Unknown	18Au01Ov
FREIL, Ann	19	F	Unknown	18Au01Ov
Daniel	20	M	Unknown	18Au01Ov
TAYLOR, Mary	20	F	Unknown	18Au01Ov
COWAN, Eliza	50	F	Unknown	18Au01Ov
MONTGOMERY, James	28	M	Unknown	18Au01Ov
Eliza	12	F	Unknown	18Au01Ov
George	10	M	Unknown	18Au01Ov
COLBEOIN, Wm.	20	M	Unknown	18Au01Ov
Eliza	18	F	Unknown	18Au01Ov
MOYNE, Saml.J.	44	M	Unknown	18Au01Ov
CAMERON, Owen	35	M	Unknown	18Au01Ov
JACKSON, Samuel	18	M	Unknown	18Au01Ov
MURPHY, Eliza	18	F	Unknown	18Au01Ov
Margret	12	F	Unknown	18Au01Ov
GORMLEY, Sarah	16	F	Unknown	18Au01Ov
Jane	18	F	Unknown	18Au01Ov
Pat	20	M	Unknown	18Au01Ov
Margt.	.00	F	Infant	18Au01Ov
GRAHAM, Arthur	40	M	Unknown	18Au01Ov
Jane	35	F	Unknown	18Au01Ov
MCCLEAN, Simpson	25	M	Unknown	18Au01Ov
U	.00	U	Infant	18Au01Ov
BOYLE, Bernard	26	M	Unknown	18Au01Ov
HUTCHINSON, Margt.	50	F	Unknown	18Au01Ov
Ellen	27	F	Unknown	18Au01Ov
Alex.	25	M	Unknown	18Au01Ov
Mary	18	F	Unknown	18Au01Ov
ARMSTRONG, Martha	7	F	Child	18Au01Ov
HANLY, Thomas	25	M	Unknown	18Au01Ov
Wm.	20	M	Unknown	18Au01Ov
MULLEN, Hannah	18	F	Unknown	18Au01Ov
MCDADE, John	19	M	Unknown	18Au01Ov
IRVINE, Sarah	20	F	Unknown	18Au01Ov
DOWBY, Joseph	25	M	Unknown	18Au01Ov
Mary	20	F	Unknown	18Au01Ov
Sarah	19	F	Unknown	18Au01Ov
Hugh	18	M	Unknown	18Au01Ov
Robert	16	M	Unknown	18Au01Ov
Mary	18	F	Unknown	18Au01Ov
MCLAUGHLIN, Wm.	20	M	Unknown	18Au01Ov
YOUNG, Eliza	25	F	Unknown	18Au01Ov
James	30	M	Unknown	18Au01Ov
FORREST, Mary	60	F	Unknown	18Au01Ov
STILLEY, John	25	M	Unknown	18Au01Ov
QUINN, James	19	M	Unknown	18Au01Ov
Mary	18	F	Unknown	18Au01Ov
Mary	.00	F	Infant	18Au01Ov
BOYD, John	19	M	Unknown	18Au01Ov
MULLEN, James	18	M	Unknown	18Au01Ov
Jane	50	F	Unknown	18Au01Ov

NAMES OF PASSENGERS	AGE	SEX	OCCUPATIONS	DATE PORT SHIP
MULLEN, Robert	13	F	Unknown	18Au010v
Sarah	7	F	Child	18Au010v
CASFRER, James	22	M	Unknown	18Au010v
HENRY, Isaac	19	M	Unknown	18Au010v
HALL, Mary	26	F	Unknown	18Au010v
HART, Mary	16	F	Unknown	18Au010v
CRESWELL, Richard	54	M	Unknown	18Au010v
R.	30	M	Unknown	18Au010v
Mary	19	F	Unknown	18Au010v
MCGOWAN, Mirty	35	F	Unknown	18Au010v
Elizth.	12	F	Unknown	18Au010v
Jane	10	F	Unknown	18Au010v
Mary	8	F	Child	18Au010v
Thomas	6	M	Child	18Au010v
Bartley	4	M	Child	18Au010v
Ellen	.00	F	Infant	18Au010v
GRAHAM, Thomas	30	M	Unknown	18Au010v
GOUBIN, Chas.	28	M	Unknown	18Au010v
Ann	30	F	Unknown	18Au010v
Crestian	19	F	Unknown	18Au010v
Fred	20	M	Unknown	18Au010v
Mary	18	F	Unknown	18Au010v
James	16	M	Unknown	18Au010v
William	14	M	Unknown	18Au010v
Thomas	12	M	Unknown	18Au010v
Arthur	.00	M	Infant	18Au010v
GREY, William	25	M	Unknown	18Au010v
GREEN, Ellen	20	F	Unknown	18Au010v
MOORE, Nancy	60	F	Unknown	18Au010v
NEILY, William	30	M	Unknown	18Au010v
DOHERTY, Catherine	42	F	Unknown	18Au010v
Rosa	18	F	Unknown	18Au010v
Daniel	12	M	Unknown	18Au010v
Biddy	9	F	Child	18Au010v
Phil	6	M	Child	18Au010v
John	4	M	Child	18Au010v
Mary	2	F	Child	18Au010v
Catherine	14	F	Unknown	18Au010v
COVEY, Charles	25	M	Unknown	18Au010v
COYLE, Margret	30	F	Unknown	18Au010v
Daniel	20	M	Unknown	18Au010v
James	18	M	Unknown	18Au010v
Ellen	16	F	Unknown	18Au010v
LINSEY, Allen	14	M	Unknown	18Au010v
Mary	25	F	Unknown	18Au010v
MCMOWELL, James	30	M	Unknown	18Au010v
KELLOGH, William	18	M	Unknown	18Au010v
Catherine	20	F	Unknown	18Au010v
MCALEESE, James	25	M	Unknown	18Au010v
Jane	28	F	Unknown	18Au010v
Ann	18	F	Unknown	18Au010v
MCKOWEN, John	19	M	Unknown	18Au010v
Nancy	16	F	Unknown	18Au010v
William	18	M	Unknown	18Au010v
Mary	20	F	Unknown	18Au010v
John	16	M	Unknown	18Au010v
MCCLEON, John	14	M	Unknown	18Au010v
Hannah	12	F	Unknown	18Au010v
W.J.	12	M	Unknown	18Au010v
KEARNEY, Eliza	20	F	Unknown	18Au010v
CASSIDY, Peter	18	M	Unknown	18Au010v
CAMPBELL, John	25	M	Unknown	18Au010v
MONOGHAN, Allice	25	F	Unknown	18Au010v
CAMPBELL, Mary	19	F	Unknown	18Au010v
Wm.	16	M	Unknown	18Au010v
Jane	6	F	Child	18Au010v
Robert	9	M	Child	18Au010v
James	11	M	Child	18Au010v
Mary	44	F	Unknown	18Au010v
MULHOLLAND, A.	30	F	Unknown	18Au010v
HOGAN, Jane	20	F	Unknown	18Au010v
MCCAULEY, James	19	M	Unknown	18Au010v
GALLOUGHER, Catherine	22	F	Unknown	18Au010v
Bridget	20	F	Unknown	18Au010v
OBRIAN, Robert	28	M	Unknown	18Au010v
OBRIAN, Mary	27	F	Unknown	18Au010v
U	.00	U	Infant	18Au010v
JOHNSTON, Margret	17	F	Unknown	18Au010v
RAGESS, John	22	M	Unknown	18Au010v
MCNEIL, John	22	M	Unknown	18Au010v
JOHNSTON, Mathew	38	M	Unknown	18Au010v
MCCLEON, Wm.	25	M	Unknown	18Au010v
DUNLOP, John	25	M	Unknown	18Au010v
BROWN, Phebe	30	F	Unknown	18Au010v
BLACK, Robert	25	M	Unknown	18Au010v
REYDON, James	19	M	Unknown	18Au010v
JOHNSTON, Wm.	20	M	Unknown	18Au010v
DIXON, Mary-J.	20	F	Unknown	18Au010v
Ann	20	F	Unknown	18Au010v
GALLAGHER, Pat	20	M	Unknown	18Au010v
WINTER, Ellen	40	F	Unknown	18Au010v
John	45	M	Unknown	18Au010v
James	22	M	Unknown	18Au010v
Monah	19	M	Unknown	18Au010v
Biddy	16	F	Unknown	18Au010v
John	14	M	Unknown	18Au010v
Ann	12	M	Unknown	18Au010v
James	8	M	Child	18Au010v
MCLESLEY, Charles	30	M	Unknown	18Au010v
Biddy	35	F	Unknown	18Au010v
John	28	M	Unknown	18Au010v
Nam.	19	M	Unknown	18Au010v
Michael	14	M	Unknown	18Au010v
Mary	12	F	Unknown	18Au010v
BARTON, Eliza	12	F	Unknown	18Au010v
Margret	20	F	Unknown	18Au010v
LYNCH, Ellen	18	F	Unknown	18Au010v
CAVANOUGH, James	26	M	Unknown	18Au010v
Mary	27	F	Unknown	18Au010v
Pat	.00	M	Infant	18Au010v
Hugh	2	M	Child	18Au010v
GAMBLE, David	35	M	Unknown	18Au010v
Charlotte	32	F	Unknown	18Au010v
Jane	2	F	Child	18Au010v
Robert	.00	M	Infant	18Au010v
RAMSEY, Mary	4	F	Child	18Au010v
Robert	8	M	Child	18Au010v
DOHERTY, Henry	40	M	Unknown	18Au010v
U	15	F	Unknown	18Au010v
ALLISON, John	26	M	Unknown	18Au010v
CUNNINGHAM, B.	30	M	Unknown	18Au010v
NICKLE, Samuel	28	M	Unknown	18Au010v
CAMPBELL, Wm.	20	M	Unknown	18Au010v
FARREN, Francis	19	M	Unknown	18Au010v
Margt.	18	F	Unknown	18Au010v
Catherine	16	F	Unknown	18Au010v
Ann	15	F	Unknown	18Au010v
Ennis	12	F	Unknown	18Au010v
MILLER, James	20	M	Unknown	18Au010v
RORTY, Ann	22	F	Unknown	18Au010v
LILLY, Joseph	19	M	Unknown	18Au010v
MCELLROY, Joseph	20	M	Unknown	18Au010v
MCGOLDRICK, Margt.	18	F	Unknown	18Au010v
KENNEDY, Margt.	18	F	Unknown	18Au010v
MCDADE, Thomas	20	M	Unknown	18Au010v
Hanah	18	F	Unknown	18Au010v
Jane	12	F	Unknown	18Au010v
BROWN, Charles	16	M	Unknown	18Au010v
James	20	M	Unknown	18Au010v
STEWART, Mary	18	F	Unknown	18Au010v
U	20	F	Unknown	18Au010v
CRAWFORD, Saml.	18	M	Unknown	18Au010v
MCLAUGHLIN, Jas.	30	M	Unknown	18Au010v
Catherine	20	F	Unknown	18Au010v
Wm.	18	M	Unknown	18Au010v
WATSON, Charles	19	M	Unknown	18Au010v
CRAWDER, U	25	M	Unknown	18Au010v
U	20	M	Unknown	18Au010v
MCGOWAN, Rosey	22	F	Unknown	18Au010v
MULLEN, Mary	16	F	Unknown	18Au010v

NAMES OF PASSENGERS	AGE	SEX	OCCUPATIONS	DATE PORT SHIP
GORMLEY, Ellen	.00	F	Infant	18Au01Ov
MOORE, Mary-L.	00	F	Unknown	18Au01Ov
John	00	M	Unknown	18Au01Ov
Charles	00	M	Unknown	18Au01Ov
Robert	00	M	Unknown	18Au01Ov
MCCUTCHEON, James	00	M	Unknown	18Au01Ov
PHILSON, Joseph-B.	00	M	Unknown	18Au01Ov
Sophia-C.	00	F	Unknown	18Au01Ov
Martha	00	F	Unknown	18Au01Ov
Eliza-B.	00	F	Unknown	18Au01Ov

HENRY-CLAY 18 AUGUST 1849

From Liverpool

NAMES OF PASSENGERS	AGE	SEX	OCCUPATIONS	DATE PORT SHIP
CLAREY, John	24	M	Farmer	18Au02Co
PAMHAM, John	24	M	Farmer	18Au02Co
COONEY, James	50	M	Laborer	18Au02Co
CASLEY, John	17	M	Laborer	18Au02Co
Patrick	11	M	Laborer	18Au02Co
MULENCY, Michael	23	M	Mechanic	18Au02Co
CARRELL, John	21	M	Mechanic	18Au02Co
MCCLARAN, Janet	42	F	Unknown	18Au02Co
William	42	M	Laborer	18Au02Co
Ellen	13	F	Unknown	18Au02Co
Mary	12	F	Unknown	18Au02Co
Jane	10	F	Unknown	18Au02Co
Flemina	8	F	Child	18Au02Co
Elizabeth	6	F	Child	18Au02Co
Diana	.00	F	Infant	18Au02Co
Margaret	.00	F	Infant	18Au02Co
COOLEY, Mary	33	F	Unknown	18Au02Co
Mary	.00	F	Infant	18Au02Co
MURRAY, Ellen	17	F	Unknown	18Au02Co
ROYLEY, Ann	14	F	Unknown	18Au02Co
BATES, Fredk.	19	M	Mechanic	18Au02Co
MACASSHNY, John	18	M	Laborer	18Au02Co
CRAWLEY, Timothy	24	M	Seaman	18Au02Co
HERRAN, John	22	M	Farmer	18Au02Co
Eugene	20	M	Farmer	18Au02Co
SHERIDAN, Mary	20	M	Unknown	18Au02Co
HENRY, Mc.	28	M	Mechanic	18Au02Co
BELL, John	29	M	Mechanic	18Au02Co
U-Mrs.	30	F	Unknown	18Au02Co
WILSON, Eliza	28	F	Unknown	18Au02Co
Elizabeth	.00	F	Infant	18Au02Co
KIPPAR, Maria	30	F	Unknown	18Au02Co
Matthew	.00	M	Infant	18Au02Co
HILL, Anna	26	F	Unknown	18Au02Co
Margaret	.00	F	Infant	18Au02Co
SMITH, Margaret	50	F	Unknown	18Au02Co
MURPHY, Margaret	25	F	Unknown	18Au02Co
HURRELL, John	36	M	Laborer	18Au02Co
Thomas	32	M	Laborer	18Au02Co
Mary	38	F	Unknown	18Au02Co
MEALBY, Thomas	32	M	Laborer	18Au02Co
CORLAY, Mary	14	F	Unknown	18Au02Co
HALLERGAN, John	16	M	Unknown	18Au02Co
KOUGH, Valentine	50	M	Farmer	18Au02Co
Anthony	10	M	Unknown	18Au02Co
HUSSAN, Michael	20	M	Laborer	18Au02Co
RERINGTON, William	44	M	Clerk	18Au02Co
Susan	36	F	Unknown	18Au02Co
Mary	17	F	Unknown	18Au02Co
Sarah	11	F	Unknown	18Au02Co
Jane	6	F	Child	18Au02Co
William	.00	M	Infant	18Au02Co
John	.00	M	Infant	18Au02Co
LUTTRELL, Alexander	40	M	Mechanic	18Au02Co

NAMES OF PASSENGERS	AGE	SEX	OCCUPATIONS	DATE PORT SHIP
LUTTRELL, Mary-Ann	35	F	Unknown	18Au02Co
Theopas	19	M	Unknown	18Au02Co
Emily	18	F	Unknown	18Au02Co
Alexd.	12	M	Unknown	18Au02Co
John	9	M	Child	18Au02Co
Jane	8	F	Child	18Au02Co
Louisa	6	F	Child	18Au02Co
Henry	.00	M	Infant	18Au02Co
Eliza	.00	F	Infant	18Au02Co
MOORE, Eliza	25	F	Unknown	18Au02Co
DELANEY, John	30	M	Laborer	18Au02Co
DYNAR, William	21	M	Laborer	18Au02Co
SHANNON, John	30	M	Laborer	18Au02Co
HERN, James	30	M	Mechanic	18Au02Co
LINDSAY, David	46	M	Mechanic	18Au02Co
ALEXANDER, John	30	M	Farmer	18Au02Co
KEANE, Mary	16	F	Unknown	18Au02Co
MCCABE, Bridget	17	F	Unknown	18Au02Co
LEWIS, John	20	M	Mechanic	18Au02Co
BENTLEY, Robt.	34	M	Mechanic	18Au02Co
PRENDERGRASS, Thomas	45	M	Mechanic	18Au02Co
Mary	30	F	Unknown	18Au02Co
MCCARTHY, Peter	23	M	Mechanic	18Au02Co
BOYD, Peter	24	M	Farmer	18Au02Co
Ellen	22	F	Unknown	18Au02Co
BROGAN, Mary	22	F	Unknown	18Au02Co
KNOWLAN, William	40	M	Laborer	18Au02Co
MAGRATH, Murty	20	M	Laborer	18Au02Co
CURRAN, James	18	M	Laborer	18Au02Co
OBRIAN, Timothy	33	M	Laborer	18Au02Co
Mary	35	F	Unknown	18Au02Co
Margt.	25	F	Unknown	18Au02Co
NOWLAN, David	25	M	Mechanic	18Au02Co
KENNAN, Mary	20	F	Unknown	18Au02Co
REYNOLDS, John	40	M	Mechanic	18Au02Co
LAMIE, Frederick	22	M	Mechanic	18Au02Co
MURRAY, Francis	21	M	Farmer	18Au02Co
SHERIDAN, John	18	M	Clerk	18Au02Co
JONES, Mark	35	M	Farmer	18Au02Co
TOYNE, Garrett	30	M	Laborer	18Au02Co
HOGERTY, Mary	40	F	Unknown	18Au02Co
Ellen	.00	F	Infant	18Au02Co
BROWN, Ellen	18	F	Unknown	18Au02Co
CLARK, Matthew	40	M	Mechanic	18Au02Co
Elizabeth	40	F	Unknown	18Au02Co
CARROLL, Catherine	30	F	Unknown	18Au02Co
John	.00	M	Infant	18Au02Co
HINES, Jacob	30	M	Mechanic	18Au02Co
BROWN, Eliza	20	F	Unknown	18Au02Co
Julia	19	F	Unknown	18Au02Co
Emma	16	F	Unknown	18Au02Co
James	14	M	Unknown	18Au02Co
Thomas	12	M	Unknown	18Au02Co
Nancy	10	F	Unknown	18Au02Co
Clementena	7	F	Child	18Au02Co
William	.00	M	Infant	18Au02Co
Louisa	.00	F	Infant	18Au02Co
HIGGINS, Peter	33	M	Laborer	18Au02Co
Sarah	33	F	Unknown	18Au02Co
William	.00	M	Infant	18Au02Co
Sarah	.00	F	Infant	18Au02Co
RYLEY, Patrick	35	M	Unknown	18Au02Co
SHANE, Patrick	19	M	Unknown	18Au02Co
CLARKE, Henry	21	M	Mechanic	18Au02Co
PERNALL, Henry	30	M	Laborer	18Au02Co
NUGENT, George	24	M	Mechanic	18Au02Co
CROOKES, George	21	M	Farmer	18Au02Co
Eliza	23	F	Unknown	18Au02Co
PHILIPS, Elizabeth	40	F	Unknown	18Au02Co
NEWPORT, Fanny	30	F	Unknown	18Au02Co
James	7	M	Child	18Au02Co
Thomas	.00	M	Infant	18Au02Co
ORAFFEY, Ellen	20	F	Unknown	18Au02Co
MCKONAR, Jas.	50	M	Laborer	18Au02Co
Mary-Eliza	17	F	Unknown	18Au02Co

NAMES OF PASSENGERS	AGE	SEX	OCCUPATIONS	DATE PORT SHIP
MCKONAR, Richard	00	M	Unknown	18Au02Co
CONNELL, John	70	M	Farmer	18Au02Co
John-Jr.	20	M	Farmer	18Au02Co
LEA, John	20	M	Farmer	18Au02Co
Margaret	28	F	Unknown	18Au02Co
MURPHY, Alexander	23	M	Laborer	18Au02Co
DODD, Paul	21	M	Laborer	18Au02Co
FLANAGAN, Peter	45	M	Laborer	18Au02Co
BRIAN, James	40	M	Farmer	18Au02Co
Robt.	11	M	Unknown	18Au02Co
BARRETT, Charles	18	M	Farmer	18Au02Co
Margaret	25	F	Unknown	18Au02Co
Daniel	60	M	Mechanic	18Au02Co
ALLEN, Michael	32	M	Mechanic	18Au02Co
Mary-Anna	28	F	Unknown	18Au02Co
FLINN, Katherine	23	F	Unknown	18Au02Co
THOMPSON, William	20	M	Farmer	18Au02Co
KARRELL, Eliza	20	F	Unknown	18Au02Co
CAVANOCK, Nancy	20	F	Unknown	18Au02Co
BRIAN, Margaret	25	F	Unknown	18Au02Co
REID, Ann	30	F	Unknown	18Au02Co
Maurice	13	M	Unknown	18Au02Co
Phil.	12	M	Unknown	18Au02Co
RYAN, Mary	24	F	Unknown	18Au02Co
BANN, Thomas	16	M	Mechanic	18Au02Co
MCCON, John	28	M	Laborer	18Au02Co
CLAREY, Katherine	21	F	Unknown	18Au02Co
HYLAND, Patrick	35	M	Farmer	18Au02Co
Mary	35	F	Unknown	18Au02Co
Katherine	15	F	Unknown	18Au02Co
Margaret	13	F	Unknown	18Au02Co
John	11	M	Unknown	18Au02Co
Hinson	8	M	Child	18Au02Co
Patrick	.00	M	Infant	18Au02Co
HARLEY, Patrick	31	M	Laborer	18Au02Co
NEAGLE, Wm.	42	M	Farmer	18Au02Co
Edward	18	M	Unknown	18Au02Co
Richard	17	M	Unknown	18Au02Co
William	15	M	Unknown	18Au02Co
CRON, Catherine	60	F	Unknown	18Au02Co
Thomas	70	M	Farmer	18Au02Co
Patrick	30	M	Farmer	18Au02Co
HOGAN, Margaret	29	F	Unknown	18Au02Co
Patrick	24	M	Laborer	18Au02Co
James	22	M	Laborer	18Au02Co
WARD, Catherine	20	F	Unknown	18Au02Co
JACKMAN, William	50	M	Mechanic	18Au02Co
Mary-Ann	50	F	Unknown	18Au02Co
Mary	46	F	Unknown	18Au02Co
James	17	M	Unknown	18Au02Co
Thomas	46	M	Unknown	18Au02Co
Martin	7	M	Child	18Au02Co
Thomas	22	M	Unknown	18Au02Co
William	28	M	Unknown	18Au02Co
CAMARPRO, James	32	M	Mechanic	18Au02Co
Sarah	27	F	Unknown	18Au02Co
Mary	.00	M	Infant	18Au02Co
CONNER, John	36	M	Farmer	18Au02Co
Johanna	36	F	Unknown	18Au02Co
Ellen	13	F	Unknown	18Au02Co
Mary	11	F	Unknown	18Au02Co
John	8	M	Child	18Au02Co
Margaret	25	F	Unknown	18Au02Co
READY, John	38	M	Laborer	18Au02Co
Rosa	35	F	Unknown	18Au02Co
Catherine	7	F	Child	18Au02Co
James	.00	M	Infant	18Au02Co
FITZGERALD, Christophe	50	M	Unknown	18Au02Co
Peggy	50	F	Unknown	18Au02Co
Catherine	18	F	Unknown	18Au02Co
Mary	16	F	Unknown	18Au02Co
HOGAN, Ellen	34	F	Unknown	18Au02Co
BAKER, Stephen	35	M	Mechanic	18Au02Co
MERISSEY, Jane	20	F	Unknown	18Au02Co
KELLY, John	22	M	Laborer	18Au02Co
MERISSAY, Jane	20	F	Unknown	18Au02Co
KELLY, John	22	M	Laborer	18Au02Co
Ellen	20	F	Unknown	18Au02Co
AMETT, Timothy	35	M	Laborer	18Au02Co
Mary	35	F	Unknown	18Au02Co
Johanna	.00	F	Infant	18Au02Co
BRIDGES, Edward	60	M	Mechanic	18Au02Co
MULLEN, Catherine	34	F	Unknown	18Au02Co
KELLY, Catherine	18	F	Unknown	18Au02Co
BOYLIN, Patrick	20	M	Mechanic	18Au02Co
KAYLEY, Margaret	60	F	Unknown	18Au02Co
PORTELL, Mary	30	F	Unknown	18Au02Co
AGNEW, William	28	M	Sailor	18Au02Co
HODGERS, Saml.	28	M	Mechanic	18Au02Co
DONAKEY, Thomas	22	M	Laborer	18Au02Co
GERMAN, Wm.	20	M	Laborer	18Au02Co
HOGDEN, Saml.	60	M	Mechanic	18Au02Co
Rebecca	50	F	Unknown	18Au02Co
JONES, Richard	22	M	Farmer	18Au02Co
HANAGAN, John	20	M	Laborer	18Au02Co
KELLY, Margaret	30	F	Unknown	18Au02Co
Thomas	.00	M	Infant	18Au02Co
Marsellas	50	F	Unknown	18Au02Co
Ellen	20	F	Unknown	18Au02Co
SMITH, Michael	23	M	Laborer	18Au02Co
Betsey	21	F	Unknown	18Au02Co
COLLINS, Anna	26	F	Unknown	18Au02Co
Michael	16	M	Laborer	18Au02Co
CLAREY, Ellen	22	F	Laborer	18Au02Co
DORSEY, Ann	20	F	Unknown	18Au02Co
BARRY, Garrett	50	M	Mechanic	18Au02Co
Mary-Ann	18	F	Unknown	18Au02Co
Michael	22	M	Mechanic	18Au02Co
Catherine	18	F	Unknown	18Au02Co
GREEN, Margaret	18	F	Unknown	18Au02Co
COCKLIN, Michael	18	M	Laborer	18Au02Co
DOYLE, Michael	28	M	Farmer	18Au02Co
BRENN, John	30	M	Farmer	18Au02Co
BARRETT, Eliza	17	F	Unknown	18Au02Co
MURPHY, Timothy	36	M	Unknown	18Au02Co
HELLANEY, Ellen	26	F	Unknown	18Au02Co
Margaret	24	F	Unknown	18Au02Co
CUSHEN, Ellen	20	F	Unknown	18Au02Co
DYNAR, Denis	23	M	Laborer	18Au02Co
DEAN, Mary	20	F	Unknown	18Au02Co
Michael	10	M	Unknown	18Au02Co
Anthony	8	M	Child	18Au02Co
CLARK, Biddy	20	F	Unknown	18Au02Co
Kitty	21	F	Unknown	18Au02Co
THOMPSON, Mary	19	F	Unknown	18Au02Co
REYNOLDS, Michael	14	M	Unknown	18Au02Co
John	12	M	Unknown	18Au02Co
BRANNAN, Rose	57	F	Unknown	18Au02Co
Bridget	20	F	Unknown	18Au02Co
James	11	M	Unknown	18Au02Co
Thomas	.00	M	Infant	18Au02Co
CONNELL, James	50	M	Farmer	18Au02Co
John	40	M	Unknown	18Au02Co
James	36	M	Unknown	18Au02Co
Eliza	30	F	Unknown	18Au02Co
Bridget	20	F	Unknown	18Au02Co
HARMAN, Ellen	15	F	Unknown	18Au02Co
CONNELL, Ellen	11	F	Unknown	18Au02Co
MAGRATH, Michael	30	M	Farmer	18Au02Co
Margaret	20	F	Unknown	18Au02Co
Ann	.00	F	Infant	18Au02Co
John	6	M	Child	18Au02Co
Nicholas	.00	M	Infant	18Au02Co
MURTAUGH, Mary-Ann	16	F	Unknown	18Au02Co
DONOVAN, Ann	17	F	Unknown	18Au02Co
RYAN, Lawrence	22	M	Unknown	18Au02Co
MOONEY, William	28	M	Unknown	18Au02Co
DAVIER, James	30	M	Mechanic	18Au02Co
Sarah	21	F	Unknown	18Au02Co
SMITH, Sarah	27	F	Unknown	18Au02Co

NAMES OF PASSENGERS	AGE	SEX	OCCUPATIONS	DATE PORT SHIP
HALEY, John	60	M	Farmer	18Au02Co
Michael	25	M	Farmer	18Au02Co
Michael	6	M	Child	18Au02Co
Tracey	28	U	Unknown	18Au02Co
Patrick	27	M	Unknown	18Au02Co
Patrick	.00	M	Infant	18Au02Co
Margaret	28	F	Unknown	18Au02Co
Died-At-Sea				
Catherine	.00	M	Infant	18Au02Co
Margaret	.00	M	Infant	18Au02Co
TOMART, Patrick	17	M	Laborer	18Au02Co
Bridget	20	F	Unknown	18Au02Co
KELLY, Patrick	28	M	Mechanic	18Au02Co
OBRIAN, John	28	M	Mechanic	18Au02Co
Fanny	30	F	Unknown	18Au02Co
Honoria	.00	F	Infant	18Au02Co
BERNARD, Margaret	23	F	Unknown	18Au02Co
Emma	.00	F	Infant	18Au02Co
DINLEY, Margaret	25	F	Unknown	18Au02Co
CONNER, James	25	M	Mechanic	18Au02Co
MCHENRY, John	40	M	Mechanic	18Au02Co
CASLEY, Ann	50	F	Unknown	18Au02Co
Died-At-Sea				
FITZPATRICK, Michael	31	M	Laborer	18Au02Co
Died-At-Sea				
Cath.	33	F	Unknown	18Au02Co
Died-At-Sea				
GUTHRIDGE, Margt.	65	F	Unknown	18Au02Co
Died-At-Sea				
BRENN, U	45	M	Mechanic	18Au02Co
Died-At-Sea				
HARLEY, U-Mrs.	22	F	Unknown	18Au02Co
Died-At-Sea				
OCONNER, Anthony	46	M	Laborer	18Au02Co
Died-At-Sea				
CONNOR, Biddy	24	F	Unknown	18Au02Co
Died-At-Sea				
SMITH, Bridget	.00	F	Infant	18Au02Co
Died-At-Sea				

MONUMENT 18 AUGUST 1849

From Liverpool

NAMES OF PASSENGERS	AGE	SEX	OCCUPATIONS	DATE PORT SHIP
HAGAN, Ann	35	F	None	18Au020x
William	14	M	None	18Au020x
Edmund	12	M	None	18Au020x
Mary	10	F	Child	18Au020x
Fanny	8	F	Child	18Au020x
John	2	M	Child	18Au020x
MCROY, Math.	33	M	Shopkeeper	18Au020x
RAY, William	60	M	Musician	18Au020x
Charles	24	M	Druggist	18Au020x
FORBES, Arthur	38	M	Shoemaker	18Au020x
Jane	34	F	None	18Au020x
William	11	M	None	18Au020x
Margaret	9	F	Child	18Au020x
Arthur	7	M	Child	18Au020x
George	5	M	Child	18Au020x
Jane	.00	F	Infant	18Au020x
Ann	34	F	None	18Au020x
HOWARD, Bridget	25	F	None	18Au020x
GRIFFITH, Ann	20	F	House Maid	18Au020x
TRACY, Bridget	25	F	Cook	18Au020x
MCGILLIAN, Bridget	35	F	Cook	18Au020x
WHILAN, Ellen	19	F	House Maid	18Au020x
RHINER, Mary	38	F	None	18Au020x
BROPHY, John	33	M	Blacksmith	18Au020x
Charles	31	M	Blacksmith	18Au020x
FINN, Edmond	18	M	Tailor	18Au020x
STERLING, Rose	18	F	House Maid	18Au020x

HUMPHREY-PURINTON 20 AUGUST 1849

From Liverpool

NAMES OF PASSENGERS	AGE	SEX	OCCUPATIONS	DATE PORT SHIP
MCKILLOP, James	36	M	Laborer	20Au020y
Mary	36	F	Unknown	20Au020y
Mary-Ann	8	F	Child	20Au020y
Jane	3	F	Child	20Au020y
Margaret	3	F	Child	20Au020y
Samuel	11	M	Unknown	20Au020y
GIDDES, Elizabeth	24	F	Unknown	20Au020y
HUTCHINSON, Matthew	25	M	Unknown	20Au020y
SIMPSON, Alexander	45	M	Unknown	20Au020y
COURTNEY, Jane	22	F	Unknown	20Au020y
BRIEN, Jeffrey	26	M	Unknown	20Au020y
POWER, Patrick	23	M	Unknown	20Au020y
SEXTON, Mary	21	F	Unknown	20Au020y
KAYE, Ellen	25	F	Unknown	20Au020y
SHANAHAN, Dennis	26	M	Unknown	20Au020y
CREED, Thomas	20	M	Unknown	20Au020y
HAYES, Joseph	30	M	Unknown	20Au020y
COSTIGAN, Patrick	24	M	Unknown	20Au020y
Mary	21	F	Unknown	20Au020y
FITZPATRICK, Dennis	20	M	Unknown	20Au020y
MARA, Margaret	22	F	Unknown	20Au020y
HOGAN, Sally	20	F	Unknown	20Au020y
HULSE, Charles	30	M	Unknown	20Au020y
Charles	13	M	Unknown	20Au020y
George	9	M	Child	20Au020y
KERSEY, Richard	25	M	Unknown	20Au020y
CONLAN, William	20	M	Unknown	20Au020y
Michael	26	M	Unknown	20Au020y
WALKER, William	30	M	Unknown	20Au020y
DOYLE, Charles	26	M	Unknown	20Au020y
LONIGAN, James	30	M	Unknown	20Au020y
OHALLORAN, John	25	M	Unknown	20Au020y
FLYNN, Catherine	46	F	Unknown	20Au020y
Catherine	18	F	Unknown	20Au020y
COLCLOUGH, William	24	M	Unknown	20Au020y
SYNNOT, Ann	22	F	Unknown	20Au020y
RODGERS, John	24	M	Unknown	20Au020y
Mary-Ann	17	F	Unknown	20Au020y
DOYLE, Patrick	40	M	Unknown	20Au020y
KIRWIN, Patrick	34	M	Unknown	20Au020y
William	16	M	Unknown	20Au020y
TROYCROSS, Joseph	30	M	Unknown	20Au020y
Emma	23	F	Unknown	20Au020y
Joseph	9	M	Child	20Au020y
Emma	.00	F	Infant	20Au020y
Mcma--, James	35	M	Unknown	20Au020y
MURPHY, Peter	26	M	Unknown	20Au020y
U (W)	24	F	Unknown	20Au020y
SHERIDAN, Matthew	24	M	Unknown	20Au020y
Mary-Ann	20	F	Unknown	20Au020y
COLLINS, Michael	30	M	Unknown	20Au020y
Ellen	25	F	Unknown	20Au020y
John	.00	M	Infant	20Au020y
WHITE, Mary	30	F	Unknown	20Au020y
James	9	M	Child	20Au020y
Johanna	7	F	Child	20Au020y
Joseph	4	M	Child	20Au020y
WEST, John	40	M	Unknown	20Au020y
HALLIGAN, Nancy	28	F	Unknown	20Au020y
Patrick	19	M	Unknown	20Au020y
CLIFFORD, William	30	M	Unknown	20Au020y
Mary	30	F	Unknown	20Au020y

NAMES OF PASSENGERS	AGE	SEX	OCCUPATIONS	DATE PORT SHIP
CLIFFORD, Ellen	24	F	Unknown	20Au020y
Margaret	5	F	Child	20Au020y
MCCARTY, Charles	20	M	Unknown	20Au020y
FULLER, Robert	40	M	Unknown	20Au020y
Johanna	55	F	Unknown	20Au020y
John	11	M	Unknown	20Au020y
Mary	9	F	Child	20Au020y
Robert	4	M	Child	20Au020y
RIAL, Patrick	23	M	Unknown	20Au020y
Johanna	54	F	Unknown	20Au020y
Garret	11	M	Unknown	20Au020y
GREEN, Biddy	17	F	Unknown	20Au020y
LENNARD, Patk.	24	M	Unknown	20Au020y
HIGGINS, Patrick	36	M	Unknown	20Au020y
TOBIN, Richard	30	M	Unknown	20Au020y
GRADY, Michael	22	M	Unknown	20Au020y
CONNERS, John	30	M	Unknown	20Au020y
WRIGHT, Peter	35	M	Unknown	20Au020y
Honora	25	F	Unknown	20Au020y
OSHEA, John	25	M	Unknown	20Au020y
Bridget	25	F	Unknown	20Au020y
SULLIVAN, Honora	29	F	Unknown	20Au020y
Margaret	23	F	Unknown	20Au020y
MCGRATH, Daniel	24	M	Unknown	20Au020y
BATEMAN, John	24	M	Unknown	20Au020y
STACK, Ellen	25	F	Unknown	20Au020y
OLEARY, Margaret	25	F	Unknown	20Au020y
NORMELL, Nicholas	30	M	Unknown	20Au020y
Catharine	26	F	Unknown	20Au020y
Catharine	12	F	Unknown	20Au020y
Mary	4	F	Child	20Au020y
Dennis	3	M	Child	20Au020y
CREGAN, Martin	30	M	Unknown	20Au020y
Johanna	26	F	Unknown	20Au020y
Anne	3	F	Child	20Au020y
Elizabeth	13	F	Unknown	20Au020y
Mary	.00	F	Infant	20Au020y
Died-At-Sea				
Dennis	35	M	Unknown	20Au020y
Hannah	9	F	Child	20Au020y
GOULDING, Patrick	24	M	Unknown	20Au020y
MCKESSEY, John	22	M	Unknown	20Au020y
Johanna	20	F	Unknown	20Au020y
VAUHAN, Catharine	50	F	Unknown	20Au020y
Mary	22	F	Unknown	20Au020y
Mary	.00	F	Infant	20Au020y
DUANE, Margaret	28	F	Unknown	20Au020y
BOURKE, Thomas	24	M	Unknown	20Au020y
Mary	24	F	Unknown	20Au020y
BROWNE, Mary	21	F	Unknown	20Au020y
MOONY, Thomas	30	M	Unknown	20Au020y
Johanna	27	F	Unknown	20Au020y
MURPHEY, Patrick	24	M	Unknown	20Au020y
RYAN, James	35	M	Unknown	20Au020y
COLLINS, Darby	24	M	Unknown	20Au020y
MCCARTY, Dennis	50	M	Unknown	20Au020y
Catherine	40	F	Unknown	20Au020y
Daniel	24	M	Unknown	20Au020y
DESMOND, Michael	24	M	Unknown	20Au020y
COTTER, Catharine	22	F	Unknown	20Au020y
HAYES, Catharine	20	F	Unknown	20Au020y
Patrick	11	M	Unknown	20Au020y
KIRBY, John	24	M	Unknown	20Au020y
Margaret	18	F	Unknown	20Au020y
DEE, John	50	M	Unknown	20Au020y
HOURIGAN, Honora	34	F	Unknown	20Au020y
COLLINS, Bridget	10	F	Unknown	20Au020y
SHEHAN, John	30	M	Unknown	20Au020y
FENTON, Johanna	25	F	Unknown	20Au020y
Ellen	23	F	Unknown	20Au020y
FOREST, Honora	22	F	Unknown	20Au020y
SULLIVAN, Elizabeth	22	F	Unknown	20Au020y
BOWEN, Benjamin	2	M	Child	20Au020y
DORHERTY, Benjamin	35	M	Unknown	20Au020y
MORGAN, Margaret	17	F	Unknown	20Au020y
MULLEN, Thomas	25	M	Unknown	20Au020y
REILLY, Catharine	23	F	Unknown	20Au020y
MCCABE, Ellen	24	F	Unknown	20Au020y
HUGHS, Michael	50	M	Unknown	20Au020y
John	23	M	Unknown	20Au020y
CRAWFORD, David	25	M	Unknown	20Au020y
Joseph	24	F	Unknown	20Au020y
Anne	2	F	Child	20Au020y
Joseph	.00	M	Infant	20Au020y
SEYMORE, Elizabeth	22	F	Unknown	20Au020y
CRAWFORD, Hugh	20	M	Unknown	20Au020y
MURRAY, William	30	M	Unknown	20Au020y
MAHONY, Timothy	10	M	Unknown	20Au020y
Michael	30	M	Unknown	20Au020y
Fanny	8	F	Child	20Au020y
Eliza	6	F	Child	20Au020y
LUPPEN, Ellen	45	F	Unknown	20Au020y
James	14	M	Unknown	20Au020y
Catherine	10	F	Unknown	20Au020y
Elizabeth	2	F	Child	20Au020y
ROACH, Mary	21	F	Unknown	20Au020y
MURPHEY, Mary	16	F	Unknown	20Au020y
LYNCH, Peter	3	M	Child	20Au020y
MADDEN, Thomas	10	M	Unknown	20Au020y
Michael	6	M	Child	20Au020y
Patrick	5	M	Child	20Au020y
DAWSON, Thomas	22	M	Unknown	20Au020y
MOONY, Sarah	22	F	Unknown	20Au020y
BRACKEN, Michael	29	M	Unknown	20Au020y
Bridget	6	F	Child	20Au020y
MCBRIDE, James	20	M	Unknown	20Au020y
ONEIL, Barnard	35	M	Unknown	20Au020y
Bridget	34	F	Unknown	20Au020y
Thomas	10	M	Unknown	20Au020y
Ellen	7	F	Child	20Au020y
Mary	3	F	Child	20Au020y
Sarah	2	F	Child	20Au020y
MCGRATH, Mary	24	F	Unknown	20Au020y
MCSWEENEY, Edward	25	M	Unknown	20Au020y

WM.HITCHCOCK 20 AUGUST 1849

From Glasgow

NAMES OF PASSENGERS	AGE	SEX	OCCUPATIONS	DATE PORT SHIP
BYRON, Patrick	26	M	Laborer	20Au040z
C.	24	U	Unknown	20Au040z
Ann	40	F	Spinster	20Au040z
Rossel	.09	U	Infant	20Au040z
ALISON, Jane	24	F	Spinster	20Au040z
GIRDLE, James	18	M	Laborer	20Au040z

SOLON 20 AUGUST 1849

From Liverpool

NAMES OF PASSENGERS	AGE	SEX	OCCUPATIONS	DATE PORT SHIP
HUTCHINGS, Thomas	27	M	Carpenter	20Au02Pa
MCCONNELL, Andrew	20	M	Laborer	20Au02Pa
Mary	18	F	None	20Au02Pa
Wm.	19	M	None	20Au02Pa
Mrgtt.	.00	F	Infant	20Au02Pa
SMITH, Geo.	50	M	Mason	20Au02Pa
Sarah	48	F	None	20Au02Pa
Pat	15	M	None	20Au02Pa

NAMES OF PASSENGERS	AGE	SEX	OCCUPATIONS	DATE PORT SHIP
SMITH, James	12	M	None	20Au02Pa
Mary	9	F	Child	20Au02Pa
Elenor	24	F	None	20Au02Pa
Rosanna	3	F	Child	20Au02Pa
Sarah	2	F	Child	20Au02Pa
Mary	.00	F	Infant	20Au02Pa
KELLY, Ann	20	F	None	20Au02Pa
HENRY, Edwd.	25	M	Laborer	20Au02Pa
James	22	M	Laborer	20Au02Pa
Thomas	25	M	Laborer	20Au02Pa
Wm.	23	M	Laborer	20Au02Pa
HILDEN, James	40	M	Mason	20Au02Pa
RYAN, Dennis	30	M	Carpenter	20Au02Pa
CONWAY, Pat	30	M	Laborer	20Au02Pa
MCNAMARA, Mary	20	F	None	20Au02Pa
SMITH, James	32	M	Farmer	20Au02Pa
Jane	23	F	None	20Au02Pa
James	.00	M	Infant	20Au02Pa
PIERCE, Saml.	30	M	Smith	20Au02Pa
SLATERY, Rory	30	M	Laborer	20Au02Pa
Sarah	25	F	None	20Au02Pa
Kate	3	F	None	20Au02Pa
Timothy	.00	M	Infant	20Au02Pa
WHITE, Ellen	21	F	None	20Au02Pa
Aurora	.00	F	Infant	20Au02Pa
MCDOUGAL, John	27	M	Carpenter	20Au02Pa
WALKER, George	24	M	Laborer	20Au02Pa
LAWLER, Mary	26	F	None	20Au02Pa
MOORE, Ann	20	F	None	20Au02Pa
MCCABE, James	16	M	Laborer	20Au02Pa
Ann	14	F	None	20Au02Pa
CRADEN, Edwd.	40	M	Laborer	20Au02Pa
JONES, Wm.	26	M	Laborer	20Au02Pa

JERSEY 21 AUGUST 1849

From Liverpool

NAMES OF PASSENGERS	AGE	SEX	OCCUPATIONS	DATE PORT SHIP
RIORDAN, Denis	25	M	Shoemaker	21Au02Pg
Elizabeth	50	F	Unknown	21Au02Pg
Anne	16	F	Unknown	21Au02Pg
Eliza	13	F	Unknown	21Au02Pg
LEELY, Ellen	50	F	Unknown	21Au02Pg
MCCARTHY, Mary	25	F	Unknown	21Au02Pg
KIDNEY, Hannah	28	F	Unknown	21Au02Pg
Mary	3	F	Child	21Au02Pg
Mary	24	F	Unknown	21Au02Pg
Cath.	20	F	Unknown	21Au02Pg
MURPHY, Denis	50	M	Laborer	21Au02Pg
MORE, And.	45	M	Collier	21Au02Pg
Margt.	40	F	Unknown	21Au02Pg
John	23	M	Unknown	21Au02Pg
CRONIN, Ellen	18	F	Unknown	21Au02Pg
SULLIVAN, John	22	M	Laborer	21Au02Pg
OLEARY, Patt	52	M	Hatter	21Au02Pg
CULLIVAN, Cornelius	20	M	Laborer	21Au02Pg
SHEA, Pat	15	M	Laborer	21Au02Pg
STACK, Garrett	29	M	Laborer	21Au02Pg
Mary	29	F	Laborer	21Au02Pg
John	.00	M	Infant	21Au02Pg
Patt	18	M	Unknown	21Au02Pg
Died-At-Sea				
OCOOHOHAN, Cornelius	20	M	Unknown	21Au02Pg
VINE, John	13	M	Unknown	21Au02Pg
DONOHOE, Florence	20	F	Unknown	21Au02Pg
Ellen	26	F	Unknown	21Au02Pg
Mary	1	F	Child	21Au02Pg
John	.00	M	Infant	21Au02Pg
Michl.	22	M	Unknown	21Au02Pg
SULLIVAN, John	22	M	Laborer	21Au02Pg
DONAVAN, Patt	18	M	Laborer	21Au02Pg
WHOLEHAN, Patt	21	M	Laborer	21Au02Pg
Died-At-Sea				
SHERNEY, Jerry	45	M	Laborer	21Au02Pg
COOKLEY, Michl.	22	M	Miner	21Au02Pg
WALPOOL, U-Mrs.	40	F	Unknown	21Au02Pg
Nina	16	F	Unknown	21Au02Pg
Margt.	14	F	Unknown	21Au02Pg
Jane	13	F	Unknown	21Au02Pg
Eliza	10	F	Unknown	21Au02Pg
Ellen	8	F	Child	21Au02Pg
Cath.	6	F	Child	21Au02Pg
James	3	M	Child	21Au02Pg
GAYHAJER, John	29	M	Laborer	21Au02Pg
FERGUSON, Owen	20	M	Laborer	21Au02Pg
Thoms.	16	M	Laborer	21Au02Pg
QUINE, Mckl.	25	M	Laborer	21Au02Pg
Wm.	24	M	Laborer	21Au02Pg
U-Mrs.	24	F	Unknown	21Au02Pg
Michl.	.00	M	Infant	21Au02Pg
SMYTH, Cath.	20	F	Unknown	21Au02Pg
Owin	.00	M	Infant	21Au02Pg
SHERON, Thomas	45	M	Unknown	21Au02Pg
STEWART, George	20	M	Laborer	21Au02Pg
Mary-Jane	9	F	Child	21Au02Pg
DILLON, James	50	M	Laborer	21Au02Pg
DONALLY, Thomas	21	M	Laborer	21Au02Pg
WALSH, James	20	M	Laborer	21Au02Pg
WARD, Michl.	28	M	Laborer	21Au02Pg
HOWE, John	25	M	Laborer	21Au02Pg
RYAN, James	20	M	Farmer	21Au02Pg
Johanna	20	F	Unknown	21Au02Pg
FREIL, John	20	M	Tinker	21Au02Pg
HIGLAND, Magt.	25	F	Unknown	21Au02Pg
DUGAN, John	50	M	Laborer	21Au02Pg
FELAS, Patt	25	M	Laborer	21Au02Pg
WHELAN, Edw.	20	M	Laborer	21Au02Pg
ELLETT, Michl.	25	M	Laborer	21Au02Pg
TOWNEY, George	28	M	Blacksmith	21Au02Pg
U-Mrs.	29	F	Unknown	21Au02Pg
Lenard	3	M	Child	21Au02Pg
FITZGERALD, Wm.	25	M	Laborer	21Au02Pg
George	10	M	Unknown	21Au02Pg
Mary	25	F	Unknown	21Au02Pg
Mary-Jane	3	F	Child	21Au02Pg
ROICK, Mary	17	F	Unknown	21Au02Pg
TUITE, Michl.	24	M	Unknown	21Au02Pg
HEATHSTONE, John	40	M	Laborer	21Au02Pg
MCNAMARA, Mich.	27	M	Laborer	21Au02Pg
CONNER, Chas.	29	M	Laborer	21Au02Pg
LEONARD, Richd.	25	M	Shoemaker	21Au02Pg
TOKER, Biddy	17	F	Unknown	21Au02Pg
WHITSON, George	28	M	Collier	21Au02Pg
ROBINSON, Anthy	25	M	Collier	21Au02Pg
KELLY, Mary	16	F	Unknown	21Au02Pg
Mary	18	F	Unknown	21Au02Pg
FITZPATTRICK, Margt.	18	F	Unknown	21Au02Pg
WALLS, Anne	20	F	Unknown	21Au02Pg
COYNE, Patt	30	M	Laborer	21Au02Pg
KELCHER, Felix	30	M	Laborer	21Au02Pg
PARSON, Wm.	31	M	Gdnr	21Au02Pg
U-Mrs.	26	F	Unknown	21Au02Pg
UPTON, Mark	28	M	Collier	21Au02Pg
WEAMOUTH, Thoms.	21	M	Collier	21Au02Pg
PIERSONS, Eliza	2	F	Child	21Au02Pg
Wm.	.00	M	Infant	21Au02Pg
MCGILL, James	20	M	Mason	21Au02Pg
HAMON, John	20	M	Mason	21Au02Pg
RILEY, Mary-Ann	35	F	Unknown	21Au02Pg
Eliza	12	F	Unknown	21Au02Pg
KING, Biddy	28	F	Unknown	21Au02Pg
WALSH, James	45	M	Farmer	21Au02Pg
Bridget	44	F	Unknown	21Au02Pg
Henry	21	M	Unknown	21Au02Pg

NAMES OF PASSENGERS	AGE	SEX	OCCUPATIONS	DATE PORT SHIP
WALSH, James	11	M	Unknown	21Au02Pg
Peggy	23	F	Unknown	21Au02Pg
PARKER, John	00	M	Unknown	21Au02Pg
MOYER, William	00	M	Unknown	21Au02Pg
KUOCK, Michl.	00	M	Unknown	21Au02Pg
LARKER, James	41	M	Mason	21Au02Pg
COFFEE, John	00	M	Unknown	21Au02Pg
U, Jane	39	F	Unknown	21Au02Pg
Henry	21	M	Unknown	21Au02Pg
Stephen	19	M	Unknown	21Au02Pg
Jane	16	F	Unknown	21Au02Pg
James	13	M	Unknown	21Au02Pg
Mary	11	F	Unknown	21Au02Pg
Andrew	7	M	Child	21Au02Pg
Richard	4	M	Child	21Au02Pg
Joseph	.00	M	Infant	21Au02Pg
HOGARTY, Michael	24	M	Mason	21Au02Pg
HORE, Michael	21	M	Mason	21Au02Pg
SMITH, Bryan	34	M	Laborer	21Au02Pg
Patrick	.00	M	Infant	21Au02Pg
MORAN, Edward	24	M	Laborer	21Au02Pg
GANNON, Honora	16	F	Unknown	21Au02Pg
SEXTON, Mich.	26	M	Turner	21Au02Pg
SHULLEFF, Josh.	50	M	Shoemaker	21Au02Pg
U-Mrs.	48	F	Unknown	21Au02Pg
Catherine	19	F	Unknown	21Au02Pg
William	17	M	Cbtmkr	21Au02Pg
Robert	14	M	Unknown	21Au02Pg
Thomas	11	M	Unknown	21Au02Pg
BRIEN, Margt.	20	F	Unknown	21Au02Pg
TUNNE, Cath.	14	F	Unknown	21Au02Pg
HOGAN, Mary	24	F	Unknown	21Au02Pg
Died-At-Sea				
Ellen	25	F	Unknown	21Au02Pg
DOYLE, Saml.	38	M	Mason	21Au02Pg
U-Mrs.	34	F	Unknown	21Au02Pg
Cath.	13	F	Unknown	21Au02Pg
William	11	M	Unknown	21Au02Pg
Rachel	5	F	Child	21Au02Pg
CORRY, Daniel	30	M	Laborer	21Au02Pg
BYRNE, James	18	M	Laborer	21Au02Pg
OCONNELL, John	35	M	Unknown	21Au02Pg
Eliza	24	F	Collier	21Au02Pg
WILSON, Thom.	25	M	Laborer	21Au02Pg
DOOLAN, John	28	M	Farmer	21Au02Pg
Dorah	27	F	Unknown	21Au02Pg
Mich.	10	M	Unknown	21Au02Pg
Margt.	6	F	Child	21Au02Pg
Martin	.00	M	Infant	21Au02Pg
KEOUGH, Michl.	23	M	Laborer	21Au02Pg
LYONS, Cath.	22	F	Unknown	21Au02Pg
MORAN, Eliza	21	F	Unknown	21Au02Pg
COYNE, John	35	M	Laborer	21Au02Pg
BRENNAN, Pat	23	M	Laborer	21Au02Pg
Edward	7	M	Child	21Au02Pg
BROWNELL, Thom.	28	M	Laborer	21Au02Pg
MCCURDEN, James	26	M	Laborer	21Au02Pg
BARRETT, Peter	25	M	Laborer	21Au02Pg
SAVAN, Dominick	15	M	Laborer	21Au02Pg
PARKER, Thom.	16	M	Laborer	21Au02Pg
MCKIERNAN, Farrel	21	M	Laborer	21Au02Pg
BYRNE, Andrew	30	M	Laborer	21Au02Pg
WHALAN, Bridget	27	F	Unknown	21Au02Pg
Johanna	.00	F	Infant	21Au02Pg
Died-At-Sea				
CARLEY, Winefred	19	U	Unknown	21Au02Pg
MCKELLOP, Anne	40	F	Unknown	21Au02Pg
ONEILL, Cornl.	28	M	Mason	21Au02Pg
Bridget	26	F	Unknown	21Au02Pg
MURRAY, Bridget	19	F	Unknown	21Au02Pg
SHERIDAN, Rose	30	F	Unknown	21Au02Pg
Ellen	12	F	Unknown	21Au02Pg
ALEXANDER, Jane	22	F	Unknown	21Au02Pg
CULLEN, Mary	28	F	Unknown	21Au02Pg
Catherine	5	F	Child	21Au02Pg
CULLEN, Eliza	3	F	Child	21Au02Pg
Died-At-Sea				
GREENE, Mary	50	F	Unknown	21Au02Pg
Died-At-Sea				
MCMANUS, Thomas	20	M	Laborer	21Au02Pg
Died-At-Sea				
FINAN, Luke	25	M	Laborer	21Au02Pg
FOUL, Bidy	20	F	Unknown	21Au02Pg
Mich.	20	M	Laborer	21Au02Pg
CONNELL, Ellen	20	F	Laborer	21Au02Pg

OXFORD 21 AUGUST 1849

From Liverpool

NAMES OF PASSENGERS	AGE	SEX	OCCUPATIONS	DATE PORT SHIP
SISSON, Edmond-J.	28	M	Gentleman	21Au02Do
Mary	20	F	Unknown	21Au02Do
FLEMING, Pierce	28	M	Clerk	21Au02Do
Kate	28	F	Unknown	21Au02Do
CONLON, Eliza	18	F	Servant	21Au02Do
CONNOR, Matthew	20	M	Currier	21Au02Do
MURTAGH, Mary	37	F	Servant	21Au02Do
OCONNOR, Jane	26	F	Servant	21Au02Do
BIRNE, Hannah	25	F	Servant	21Au02Do
WOODS, Eliza	16	F	Servant	21Au02Do
Michael	14	M	Servant	21Au02Do
TOOHIGHE, Patrick	32	M	Clerk	21Au02Do
BURK, Catherine	19	F	Servant	21Au02Do
Margaret	3	F	Child	21Au02Do
MAHER, Nancy	50	F	Servant	21Au02Do
Died-At-Sea				
Mary	20	F	Servant	21Au02Do
Died-At-Sea				
Norry	15	U	Servant	21Au02Do
Thomas	10	M	Servant	21Au02Do
BRIEN, Richard	16	M	Laborer	21Au02Do
CASEY, Patrick	60	M	Weaver	21Au02Do
Died-At-Sea				
HIGGINS, Ellen	45	F	Servant	21Au02Do
Died-At-Sea				
John	23	M	Farmer	21Au02Do
DAGNAN, John	20	M	Laborer	21Au02Do
DOUGHERTY, Patrick	18	M	Blacksmith	21Au02Do
CLARK, John	24	M	Laborer	21Au02Do
DUNNE, John	11	M	Laborer	21Au02Do
Sarah	24	F	Laborer	21Au02Do
DOYLE, Bridget	23	F	Servant	21Au02Do
POINTON, Elizabeth	29	F	Servant	21Au02Do
DOUGLAS, John	27	M	Mechanic	21Au02Do
FINNAGAN, Ann	20	F	Unknown	21Au02Do
MCGUIRE, William	30	M	Servant	21Au02Do
SMITH, Catherine	34	F	Servant	21Au02Do
Ann	22	F	Servant	21Au02Do
John	4	M	Child	21Au02Do
James	6	M	Child	21Au02Do
Amelia	5	F	Child	21Au02Do
MCCORMICK, Catherine	20	F	Servant	21Au02Do
Michael	7	M	Child	21Au02Do
ROGERS, Catherine	26	F	Child	21Au02Do
CULLEN, Daniel	24	M	Laborer	21Au02Do
HEYDEN, Peter	18	M	Laborer	21Au02Do
CARTEY, Kate	18	F	Servant	21Au02Do
LINNEN, Catherine	18	F	Servant	21Au02Do
MCLAUGHLIN, Eliza	25	F	Servant	21Au02Do
Ann	.00	F	Infant	21Au02Do
Died-At-Sea				
HART, James	60	M	Laborer	21Au02Do
EYERS, William	55	M	Laborer	21Au02Do
HART, Dennis	16	M	Laborer	21Au02Do

NAMES OF PASSENGERS	AGE	SEX	OCCUPATIONS	DATE PORT SHIP
GILLROY, Patrick	23	M	Laborer	21Au02Do
Died-At-Sea				
COWLEY, Anthony	17	M	Carpenter	21Au02Do
MORAN, Martin	35	M	Laborer	21Au02Do
CONNORS, Eliza	32	F	W-Labr	21Au02Do
Mary	.00	F	Infant	21Au02Do
Margaret	3	F	Child	21Au02Do
James	2	M	Child	21Au02Do
William	4	M	Child	21Au02Do
MCGARTLAND, Edward	40	M	Laborer	21Au02Do
HEFFERNAN, Anne	17	F	Servant	21Au02Do
MCANULTY, Matilda	16	F	Servant	21Au02Do
FAMINE, John	23	M	Laborer	21Au02Do
Catherine	16	F	Unknown	21Au02Do
Patrick	28	M	Laborer	21Au02Do
Margaret	17	F	Laborer	21Au02Do
PLANT, Mary	50	F	Laborer	21Au02Do
Nancy	22	F	W-Labr	21Au02Do
Hannah	18	F	W-Labr	21Au02Do
Peter	.00	M	Infant	21Au02Do
WILSON, Jane	36	F	Unknown	21Au02Do
William	10	M	Unknown	21Au02Do
Charles	4	M	Child	21Au02Do
Eliza-Ann	3	F	Child	21Au02Do
John	2	M	Child	21Au02Do
LESLIE, Jane	23	F	Servant	21Au02Do
Sarah	3	F	Child	21Au02Do
James	2	M	Child	21Au02Do
SCALLY, Bridget	17	F	Servant	21Au02Do
CAREY, John	40	M	Laborer	21Au02Do
Died-At-Sea				
TOOMEY, Cornelius	28	M	Laborer	21Au02Do
GORMLY, Catherine	16	F	Servant	21Au02Do
KELLY, Mary	16	F	Servant	21Au02Do
WATERS, Mary	20	F	Servant	21Au02Do
FITZPATRICK, Bridget	28	F	Servant	21Au02Do
MEE, Mary	18	F	Servant	21Au02Do
CROULD, James	18	M	Laborer	21Au02Do
PLUNKET, James	24	M	Servant	21Au02Do
NIXON, Margaret	19	F	Servant	21Au02Do
James	21	M	Servant	21Au02Do
WARD, Michael	21	M	Laborer	21Au02Do
CONNON, Edward	24	M	Laborer	21Au02Do
BOYLE, Mary	50	F	Unknown	21Au02Do
RILEY, John	6	M	Child	21Au02Do
GREEN, Margaret	40	F	Unknown	21Au02Do
BRADLEY, James	26	M	Laborer	21Au02Do
MCLAUGHLIN, Patrick	19	M	Laborer	21Au02Do
MCANULTY, Martin	21	M	Laborer	21Au02Do
BRIDGE, John	21	M	Laborer	21Au02Do
MURPHY, Patrick	24	M	Laborer	21Au02Do
MEALY, Brien	25	M	Laborer	21Au02Do
OBRIEN, Michael	25	M	Laborer	21Au02Do
DAGNON, James	27	M	Carpenter	21Au02Do
RIELY, Patrick	26	M	Surveyor	21Au02Do
CLARKE, Margaret	17	F	Servant	21Au02Do
BRADLEY, Eliza	19	F	Servant	21Au02Do
HOGAN, Thomas	21	M	Laborer	21Au02Do
Jane	20	F	Unknown	21Au02Do
FITZPATRICK, Michael	20	M	Baker	21Au02Do
Catherine	18	F	Servant	21Au02Do
Died-At-Sea				
BOWERS, Jane	28	F	Servant	21Au02Do
DONNELY, Mary-Ann	23	F	Servant	21Au02Do
DALEY, James	21	M	Servant	21Au02Do
Margaret	19	F	Servant	21Au02Do
FISHER, Jane	45	F	Servant	21Au02Do
MCGRATH, Pat	20	M	Laborer	21Au02Do
FISHER, Mary-Jane	12	F	Servant	21Au02Do
HAGARTHY, Timothy	40	M	Laborer	21Au02Do
DOUGLASS, Charlotte	30	F	Servant	21Au02Do
DOYLE, Margaret	19	F	Servant	21Au02Do
RYAN, Patrick	20	M	Servant	21Au02Do
FLYNN, Christopher	17	M	Servant	21Au02Do
REGAN, John	25	M	Shoemaker	21Au02Do
BRADY, Charles	40	M	Laborer	21Au02Do
RILEY, Ellen	30	F	Servant	21Au02Do
MALOY, Margaret	30	F	Servant	21Au02Do
SHERIDAN, Margaret	50	F	Servant	21Au02Do
MELADY, Catherine	16	F	Servant	21Au02Do
REYNOLDS, Patrick	30	M	Laborer	21Au02Do
Died-At-Sea				
KELLY, Catherine	17	F	Servant	21Au02Do
John	14	M	Servant	21Au02Do
REYNOLDS, John	4	M	Child	21Au02Do
Died-At-Sea				
DOWNEY, Patrick	24	M	Laborer	21Au02Do
Margaret	18	F	Servant	21Au02Do
KELLY, Mary	66	F	W-Labr	21Au02Do
Died-At-Sea				
FALLON, Owen	35	M	Laborer	21Au02Do
Biddy	35	F	Servant	21Au02Do
Peter	7	M	Child	21Au02Do
John	5	M	Child	21Au02Do
KELLY, Michael	20	M	Laborer	21Au02Do
DOWNEY, John	20	M	Laborer	21Au02Do
KENNEFIE, Mary	23	F	Servant	21Au02Do
Edward	4	M	Child	21Au02Do
Nancy	2	F	Child	21Au02Do
Died-At-Sea				
Bridget	7	F	Child	21Au02Do
SULLIVAN, Mary	20	F	Servant	21Au02Do
MAHONY, William	36	M	Laborer	21Au02Do
Died-At-Sea				
Mary	31	F	Servant	21Au02Do
Ellen	2	F	Child	21Au02Do
James	4	M	Child	21Au02Do
TAYLOR, Margaret	38	F	Servant	21Au02Do
Agnes	14	F	Servant	21Au02Do
Philip	6	M	Child	21Au02Do
Robt.	7	M	Child	21Au02Do
BRIEN, William	21	M	Laborer	21Au02Do
ROACH, John	40	M	Laborer	21Au02Do
KYLEY, Mary	18	F	Servant	21Au02Do
CONNOR, Harly	22	M	Laborer	21Au02Do
GLAVIN, Michael	16	M	Cooper	21Au02Do
SCANLON, Maurice	30	M	Laborer	21Au02Do
DOUGLAS, Maria	.00	F	Infant	21Au02Do
GAVIN, Betty	30	F	Servant	21Au02Do
Michael	10	M	Servant	21Au02Do
John	8	M	Child	21Au02Do
Bridget	6	F	Child	21Au02Do
Died-At-Sea				
SWEENEY, Michael	16	M	Blacksmith	21Au02Do
William	12	M	Shoemaker	21Au02Do
BRYAN, Patrick	16	M	Laborer	21Au02Do
Jerry	40	M	Laborer	21Au02Do
WALLACE, Ellen	23	F	Dressmaker	21Au02Do
LEHANE, Ellen	.00	F	Infant	21Au02Do
FALVEY, Patrick	16	M	Laborer	21Au02Do
HORAN, John	22	M	Farmer	21Au02Do
CUFFIE, Thomas	20	M	Farmer	21Au02Do
KINSELLA, Thomas	26	M	Farmer	21Au02Do
CROSBIE, John	25	M	Farmer	21Au02Do
TYRELL, John	26	M	Farmer	21Au02Do
Margaret	20	F	W-Fmr	21Au02Do
RILEY, Edward	35	M	Laborer	21Au02Do
FOX, Timothy	23	M	Laborer	21Au02Do
MURTHA, Michael	16	M	Laborer	21Au02Do
ADAMS, Judy	20	F	Servant	21Au02Do
Ann	22	F	Servant	21Au02Do
Died-At-Sea				
BRENNAN, Thomas	24	M	Laborer	21Au02Do
SMITH, Margaret	18	F	Servant	21Au02Do
FITZPATRICK, Margaret	20	F	Servant	21Au02Do
CUDDY, Henry	26	M	Servant	21Au02Do
MURRAY, Ellen	24	F	Servant	21Au02Do
Patrick	14	M	Gdnr	21Au02Do
BYRNE, George	50	M	Laborer	21Au02Do
DOUGHERTY, William	24	M	Laborer	21Au02Do

NAMES OF PASSENGERS	AGE	SEX	OCCUPATIONS	DATE PORT SHIP
BURK, James	34	M	Laborer	21Au02Do
LEDWORTH, Patrick	33	M	Laborer	21Au02Do
MURPHY, Bartle	33	M	Laborer	21Au02Do
SCALLY, Edward	26	M	Laborer	21Au02Do
Mary	22	F	Unknown	21Au02Do
RAFFERTY, John	25	M	Laborer	21Au02Do
DELANY, Cornelius	20	M	Laborer	21Au02Do
BLAKE, Anthony	50	M	Laborer	21Au02Do
Patrick	50	M	Laborer	21Au02Do
Catherine	16	F	Servant	21Au02Do
DELANY, Ally	20	F	Servant	21Au02Do
BRIDGE, Ann	24	F	Servant	21Au02Do
RIELY, Margaret	26	F	Servant	21Au02Do
DARDIS, William	45	M	Farmer	21Au02Do
Mary	50	F	Unknown	21Au02Do
Died-At-Sea				
SMITH, Lawrence	50	M	Gdnr	21Au02Do
James	24	M	Gdnr	21Au02Do
Rose	24	F	Unknown	21Au02Do
Thomas	17	M	Unknown	21Au02Do
Rose	19	F	Unknown	21Au02Do
MCMANUS, Mary	56	F	Unknown	21Au02Do
CRONIN, Michael	16	M	Grocer	21Au02Do
MAULIGHAN, Patrick	21	M	Tailor	21Au02Do

R.A.PARK 21 AUGUST 1849

From Galway

NAMES OF PASSENGERS	AGE	SEX	OCCUPATIONS	DATE PORT SHIP
CUNNINGHAM, Mathias	50	M	Laborer	21Au06Pc
Mary	40	F	Unknown	21Au06Pc
Mary	30	F	Unknown	21Au06Pc
Pat	14	M	Unknown	21Au06Pc
Jno.	10	M	Unknown	21Au06Pc
Wm.	7	M	Child	21Au06Pc
Margt.	3	F	Child	21Au06Pc
Thomas	2	M	Child	21Au06Pc
MACK, Bridget	20	F	Unknown	21Au06Pc
RYAN, Mary	6	F	Child	21Au06Pc
Bridget	4	F	Child	21Au06Pc
COSTELLO, Mary	22	F	Unknown	21Au06Pc
TYNE, Laurence	25	M	Unknown	21Au06Pc
MAHON, Mary	15	F	Unknown	21Au06Pc
BRODUCK, Catherine	26	F	Unknown	21Au06Pc
Bridget	.00	F	Infant	21Au06Pc
Jno.	1	M	Child	21Au06Pc
Bridget	24	F	Unknown	21Au06Pc
Jas.	3	M	Child	21Au06Pc
Michael	2	M	Child	21Au06Pc
MURPHY, Margt.	19	F	Unknown	21Au06Pc
ROONAN, Thos	00	M	Unknown	21Au06Pc
NEVIL, Bridget	12	F	Unknown	21Au06Pc
RUSSELL, Jas.	30	M	Unknown	21Au06Pc
KEARNS, Jas.	27	M	Unknown	21Au06Pc
SHAUGHNESSEY, Mary	21	F	Unknown	21Au06Pc
Jas.	18	M	Unknown	21Au06Pc
KENNEDY, Rebecca	46	F	Unknown	21Au06Pc
Nelly	30	F	Unknown	21Au06Pc
DAVERN, Catherine	24	F	Unknown	21Au06Pc
Jno.	.00	M	Infant	21Au06Pc
Eliza	1	F	Child	21Au06Pc
MAHON, Chas.	17	M	Unknown	21Au06Pc
Jno.	30	F	Unknown	21Au06Pc
OLOUGHLIN, M.	35	M	Unknown	21Au06Pc
Martin	14	M	Unknown	21Au06Pc
Jane	9	F	Child	21Au06Pc
KILKELLY, Edward	18	M	Unknown	21Au06Pc
Mary	20	F	Unknown	21Au06Pc
Bridget	21	F	Unknown	21Au06Pc

NAMES OF PASSENGERS	AGE	SEX	OCCUPATIONS	DATE PORT SHIP
CONEY, Jno.	28	M	Unknown	21Au06Pc
MOREI, Thomas	27	M	Unknown	21Au06Pc
DRISCOLL, Thomas	27	M	Unknown	21Au06Pc
HYNES, Catherine	25	F	Unknown	21Au06Pc
GRADY, Mary	22	F	Unknown	21Au06Pc
Tom	2	M	Child	21Au06Pc
ROONN, Ellen	22	F	Unknown	21Au06Pc
Pat	5	M	Unknown	21Au06Pc
GREARY, Pat	16	M	Unknown	21Au06Pc
CAREEN, M.	21	M	Unknown	21Au06Pc
BROUGHAM, M.	32	M	Unknown	21Au06Pc
John	36	M	Unknown	21Au06Pc
Mary	22	F	Unknown	21Au06Pc
Margt.	20	F	Unknown	21Au06Pc
FLAHERTY, Tim	15	M	Unknown	21Au06Pc
HOWARD, Jno.	34	M	Unknown	21Au06Pc
JENNINGS, Jno.	50	M	Unknown	21Au06Pc
MCAULIFFE, Mary	26	F	Unknown	21Au06Pc
DOHE, Joseph	20	M	Unknown	21Au06Pc
OKEEFFE, Patt	34	M	Unknown	21Au06Pc
Catherine	30	F	Unknown	21Au06Pc
Danl.	1	M	Child	21Au06Pc
BORKE, Jno.	20	M	Unknown	21Au06Pc
REDDING, Jno.	12	M	Unknown	21Au06Pc
KEAN, Patt	20	M	Unknown	21Au06Pc
Ellen	22	F	Unknown	21Au06Pc
GILLIGHAN, Dennis	21	M	Unknown	21Au06Pc
DALY, Jno.	40	M	Unknown	21Au06Pc
Francis	15	M	Unknown	21Au06Pc
DILLON, Pat	40	M	Unknown	21Au06Pc
GARWAY, Peggy	17	F	Unknown	21Au06Pc
SHEA, Bridget	17	F	Unknown	21Au06Pc
LYDON, Ellen	32	F	Unknown	21Au06Pc
HAOERN, M.	50	M	Unknown	21Au06Pc
Emma	35	F	Unknown	21Au06Pc
Michl.	14	M	Unknown	21Au06Pc
Mary	7	F	Child	21Au06Pc
Tom	4	M	Child	21Au06Pc
Ann	.04	F	Infant	21Au06Pc
SHAUGHNESSY, Tom	20	M	Unknown	21Au06Pc
FLANIGAN, Thomas	36	M	Unknown	21Au06Pc
Margt.	24	F	Unknown	21Au06Pc
GARWEY, Mary	15	F	Unknown	21Au06Pc
FLANEGAN, Jno.	.00	M	Infant	21Au06Pc
TALLY, Coleman	20	M	Unknown	21Au06Pc
LEAREY, Martin	25	M	Unknown	21Au06Pc
HYNES, Catherine	18	F	Unknown	21Au06Pc
LUCAS, Jno.	00	M	Unknown	21Au06Pc
Bridget	28	F	Unknown	21Au06Pc
HOGAN, Susan	26	F	Unknown	21Au06Pc
KELLY, Biddy	26	F	Unknown	21Au06Pc
CARTY, Jno.	20	M	Unknown	21Au06Pc
LYASKEY, Judy	20	F	Unknown	21Au06Pc
Patt	14	M	Unknown	21Au06Pc
Tom	4	M	Child	21Au06Pc
Kitty	2	F	Child	21Au06Pc
TEENEY, Ann	20	F	Unknown	21Au06Pc
Bridget	30	F	Unknown	21Au06Pc
CONNOR, Michl.	20	M	Unknown	21Au06Pc
MCTYNE, Pat	24	M	Unknown	21Au06Pc
COOK, Mary	7	F	Child	21Au06Pc
BOUGHAN, Pat	20	M	Unknown	21Au06Pc
Dennis	17	M	Unknown	21Au06Pc
Michl.	14	M	Unknown	21Au06Pc
LYNCH, Jas.	50	M	Unknown	21Au06Pc
Ann	12	F	Unknown	21Au06Pc
BARRY, Phillip	25	M	Unknown	21Au06Pc
MCMAHON, U	39	M	Unknown	21Au06Pc
LYNCH, Jno.	21	M	Unknown	21Au06Pc
GORHAM, Pat	28	M	Unknown	21Au06Pc
HAYNES, Jno.	38	M	Unknown	21Au06Pc
KEAN, Tom	30	M	Unknown	21Au06Pc
Honor	27	F	Unknown	21Au06Pc
Mary	6	F	Child	21Au06Pc
Michl.	4	M	Child	21Au06Pc

NAMES OF PASSENGERS	AGE	SEX	OCCUPATIONS	DATE PORT SHIP
KEAN, Frank	2	M	Child	21Au06Pc
BATLER, T.	30	M	Unknown	21Au06Pc
KEAN, Stephen	20	M	Unknown	21Au06Pc
HULAND, Jno.	23	M	Unknown	21Au06Pc
MCLOUGHLIN, Ann	25	F	Unknown	21Au06Pc
Mich.	21	M	Unknown	21Au06Pc
Died-At-Sea				
Mary	.00	F	Infant	21Au06Pc
RONEY, Thomas	35	M	Unknown	21Au06Pc
MCDONNELL, Jno.	15	M	Unknown	21Au06Pc
Thomas	13	M	Unknown	21Au06Pc
GAVIN, Mary	14	F	Unknown	21Au06Pc
Jas.	13	M	Unknown	21Au06Pc
CONEWAY, Jas.	35	M	Unknown	21Au06Pc
TATTY, Mary	13	F	Unknown	21Au06Pc
CARREEN, Cathe.	35	F	Unknown	21Au06Pc
HYLAND, Peggy	16	F	Unknown	21Au06Pc
MCCARTY, Edward	3	M	Child	21Au06Pc
OLOUGHLIN, Eliza	19	F	Unknown	21Au06Pc
NALLY, U-Mrs.	30	F	Unknown	21Au06Pc
Catherine	10	F	Unknown	21Au06Pc
Michl.	9	M	Child	21Au06Pc
Ellen	9	F	Child	21Au06Pc
Esther	.00	F	Infant	21Au06Pc
CAMRON, Jno.	30	M	Unknown	21Au06Pc
Mary	24	F	Unknown	21Au06Pc
KYANEY, Winney	14	F	Unknown	21Au06Pc
GAHAN, Danl.	26	M	Unknown	21Au06Pc
TIMOTHY, U	28	M	Unknown	21Au06Pc
KYNE, Jno.	16	M	Unknown	21Au06Pc
FLAHERTY, Sally	20	F	Unknown	21Au06Pc
TIMOTHY, U-Mrs.	21	F	Unknown	21Au06Pc
GLYNE, Mary	25	F	Unknown	21Au06Pc
CAHON, Mary	31	F	Unknown	21Au06Pc
MOLONEY, Mary	24	F	Unknown	21Au06Pc
GREALY, Jno.	24	M	Unknown	21Au06Pc
GORMAN, Daniel	33	M	Unknown	21Au06Pc

CANADA 21 AUGUST 1849

From Liverpool

NAMES OF PASSENGERS	AGE	SEX	OCCUPATIONS	DATE PORT SHIP
CONNLER, I.	50	M	Merchant	21Au02Fy
HAIGH, W.R.	32	M	Merchant	21Au02Fy
Ellen	25	F	Merchant	21Au02Fy
COCHRANE, S.A.	23	M	Merchant	21Au02Fy
MELLER, R.	32	M	Merchant	21Au02Fy
MIDDLEBROOK, S.	39	M	Merchant	21Au02Fy
U (W)	29	F	Unknown	21Au02Fy
HOLMES, G.	30	M	Merchant	21Au02Fy
DAY, H.S.	34	M	Merchant	21Au02Fy
AITKEN, S.M.	27	M	Merchant	21Au02Fy
MACFARLANE, U-Mrs.	61	F	Unknown	21Au02Fy
U-Miss	25	F	Unknown	21Au02Fy
J.	20	F	Unknown	21Au02Fy
GRIEG, B.	23	M	Unknown	21Au02Fy
FISKEN, Jno.	31	M	Merchant	21Au02Fy
COHEN, J.	40	M	Merchant	21Au02Fy
U-Miss	25	F	Unknown	21Au02Fy
HIGGINS, U-Mrs.	30	F	Unknown	21Au02Fy
GARRETT, E.	26	M	Merchant	21Au02Fy
SANDFORD, J.	40	M	Merchant	21Au02Fy
STEWART, A.T.	30	M	Merchant	21Au02Fy
SPEW, Henry	36	M	Merchant	21Au02Fy
SANDERSON, W.	25	M	Merchant	21Au02Fy
HEENIAS, R.	21	M	Merchant	21Au02Fy
GOODWIN, Henry	29	M	Merchant	21Au02Fy
U (W)	20	F	Unknown	21Au02Fy
OULD, J.	25	M	Merchant	21Au02Fy
FENWICK, Jno.	30	M	Merchant	21Au02Fy
NOLAN, John	24	M	Merchant	21Au02Fy
EDWARDS, Thos.	40	M	None	21Au02Fy
BEANE, Edward	32	M	Engineer	21Au02Fy
CAMERON, John	67	M	Engineer	21Au02Fy
MCKENZIE, R.	42	M	Baker	21Au02Fy
HAY, J.B.	38	M	Molder	21Au02Fy
MAYNARD, T.	28	M	Soap Maker	21Au02Fy
THORNE, Jno.	39	M	Soap Maker	21Au02Fy
U (W)	42	F	Unknown	21Au02Fy
BULT, Jno.E.	45	M	Farmer	21Au02Fy
U (W)	46	F	Unknown	21Au02Fy
Jno.	4	M	Child	21Au02Fy
Jane	2	F	Child	21Au02Fy
TAVENDER, J.	29	M	Chandler	21Au02Fy
U (W)	20	F	Unknown	21Au02Fy
SAMSON, A.	41	M	Merchant	21Au02Fy

HUGUENOT 22 AUGUST 1849

From Liverpool

NAMES OF PASSENGERS	AGE	SEX	OCCUPATIONS	DATE PORT SHIP
HENERY, Nancy	36	F	Farmer	22Au02Pd
Mary	15	F	Farmer	22Au02Pd
Dennis	9	M	Child	22Au02Pd
Hannah	7	F	Child	22Au02Pd
Peggy	6	F	Child	22Au02Pd
Bridget	8	F	Child	22Au02Pd
James	.00	M	Infant	22Au02Pd
BOYLAN, John	40	M	Tanner	22Au02Pd
DOONAN, Pat	27	M	Laborer	22Au02Pd
HACKER, Cathe.	30	F	None	22Au02Pd
MULKATEN, Pat	32	M	Farmer	22Au02Pd
WILLIAMS, Griffith	30	M	Laborer	22Au02Pd
RYAN, Wm.	30	M	Laborer	22Au02Pd
Stephen	22	M	Laborer	22Au02Pd
MARTIN, Thos.	15	M	None	22Au02Pd
Pat	14	M	None	22Au02Pd
KELLY, Jane	16	F	Unknown	22Au02Pd
CAMPBELL, Ellen	18	F	Unknown	22Au02Pd
Cathe.	20	F	Unknown	22Au02Pd
BELLANE, Bessey	18	F	Seamstress	22Au02Pd
MCELLBERN, Ann	20	M	Laborer	22Au02Pd
CONNELLY, Sally	25	F	None	22Au02Pd
MAHONEY, Jno.	35	M	None	22Au02Pd
SMITH, Catherine	30	F	None	22Au02Pd
Augustus	12	M	None	22Au02Pd
Jno.	.00	F	Infant	22Au02Pd
WARD, Pat	45	M	Mason	22Au02Pd
Died-At-Sea				
Pat	18	M	Mason	22Au02Pd
Larry	22	M	Mason	22Au02Pd
CORIGAN, Alice	16	F	Seamstress	22Au02Pd
HUGHES, Henry	30	M	Mason	22Au02Pd
MEE, Winney	44	F	Seamstress	22Au02Pd
NEVILLE, Bridget	17	F	Seamstress	22Au02Pd
GALLAGHAN, Pat	35	M	Laborer	22Au02Pd
CURRAN, Edwd.	21	M	Laborer	22Au02Pd
FARRELL, Mary	17	F	Unknown	22Au02Pd
OGALLAGHER, John	50	M	Laborer	22Au02Pd
Julia	45	F	None	22Au02Pd
Charles	13	M	None	22Au02Pd
GILLON, Ann	17	F	Unknown	22Au02Pd
MCNEIL, Mary	30	F	Seamstress	22Au02Pd
Jno.	7	M	Child	22Au02Pd
CUISSEY, Pat	25	M	Laborer	22Au02Pd
Mary-A.	24	F	None	22Au02Pd
WHITE, Julia	25	M	Unknown	22Au02Pd
Patt	7	M	Child	22Au02Pd

NAMES OF PASSENGERS	AGE	SEX	OCCUPATIONS	DATE PORT SHIP
MCCANN, Michael	32	M	Laborer	22Au02Pd
Died-At-Sea				
NOWLAND, U-Mrs.	26	F	None	22Au02Pd
Died-At-Sea				
KINSLY, Mary	22	F	None	22Au02Pd

HEATHER-BELL 22 AUGUST 1849

From Limerick

NAMES OF PASSENGERS	AGE	SEX	OCCUPATIONS	DATE PORT SHIP
OKEEFFE, Patrick	20	M	Farmer	22Au35Fa
HAYSE, Magt.	20	F	Spinster	22Au35Fa
STEVENS, Michl.	16	M	Farmer	22Au35Fa
Denis	21	M	Farmer	22Au35Fa
ONEILL, Bridget	30	F	Spinster	22Au35Fa
Peggy	20	F	Spinster	22Au35Fa
Bridget	8	F	Child	22Au35Fa
Mary	6	F	Child	22Au35Fa
Patt	.00	M	Infant	22Au35Fa
HENNESSY, Catharine	20	F	Spinster	22Au35Fa
OKEEFFE, Michael	26	M	Farmer	22Au35Fa
SULLIVAN, John	22	M	Farmer	22Au35Fa
Michael	30	M	Farmer	22Au35Fa
Mary	30	F	Spinster	22Au35Fa
Catharine	2	F	Child	22Au35Fa
William	.00	M	Infant	22Au35Fa
MANNING, John	30	M	Farmer	22Au35Fa
COSTELLOE, Denis	20	M	Farmer	22Au35Fa
EDWARDS, Patt	24	M	Farmer	22Au35Fa
SHAUGHNESSY, Bridget	20	F	Spinster	22Au35Fa
DILLON, Hannah	22	F	Spinster	22Au35Fa
KENNEDY, William	14	M	Farmer	22Au35Fa
Johannah	18	F	Spinster	22Au35Fa
RYAN, Patt	24	M	Farmer	22Au35Fa
GORMAN, John	20	M	Farmer	22Au35Fa
MURRAY, Kitty	14	F	Spinster	22Au35Fa
Thomas	12	M	None	22Au35Fa
HARTIGAN, Thomas	20	M	Farmer	22Au35Fa
DUNNIGAN, Catharine	55	F	Matron	22Au35Fa
Edmond	19	M	None	22Au35Fa
Thomas	16	M	None	22Au35Fa
Ellen	.00	F	Infant	22Au35Fa
COLLIGAN, Michael	22	M	Farmer	22Au35Fa
Michael	.00	M	Infant	22Au35Fa
HAWKINS, Michael	40	M	Farmer	22Au35Fa
LYONS, John	15	M	Farmer	22Au35Fa
HUMES, Michael	15	M	Farmer	22Au35Fa
SULLIVAN, Maria	20	F	Spinster	22Au35Fa
KITTSON, Mary	24	F	Spinster	22Au35Fa
KERRIN, Susan	19	F	Spinster	22Au35Fa
MCMAHON, Johannah	20	F	Spinster	22Au35Fa
Michael	.00	M	Infant	22Au35Fa
Died-At-Sea				
HOGLIN, Martin	30	M	Farmer	22Au35Fa
MCINERNEY, Thomas	17	M	Farmer	22Au35Fa
WHELAN, Mary	20	F	Spinster	22Au35Fa
Biddy	20	F	Spinster	22Au35Fa
OCONNOR, Patrick	22	M	Farmer	22Au35Fa
HALLORAN, Eliza	28	F	Spinster	22Au35Fa
Marry	5	F	Child	22Au35Fa
Stephen	.00	M	Infant	22Au35Fa
ORGAN, Biddy	28	F	None	22Au35Fa
Mary	10	F	None	22Au35Fa
LOWRY, Hanorah	21	F	Spinster	22Au35Fa
STAUNTON, Michael	22	M	Farmer	22Au35Fa
SHAUGHNESSY, Ellen	36	F	Spinster	22Au35Fa
TUOHY, Patt	30	M	Farmer	22Au35Fa
Hanorah	28	F	Spinster	22Au35Fa
Patt	2	M	Child	22Au35Fa
TUOHY, Mary	.00	F	Infant	22Au35Fa
SHANKE, Catharine	18	F	Spinster	22Au35Fa
HOWARD, Mary	19	F	Spinster	22Au35Fa
TUOHY, Biddy	18	F	Spinster	22Au35Fa
TOBIN, Michael	20	M	Farmer	22Au35Fa
CLEARY, Denis	30	M	Farmer	22Au35Fa
DONNELLAN, Thomas	20	M	Farmer	22Au35Fa
Catharine	25	F	Matron	22Au35Fa
GRIFFY, John	.00	M	Infant	22Au35Fa
CALLAGHAN, Mary	40	F	Matron	22Au35Fa
John	10	M	None	22Au35Fa
NEVYLON, Thomas	16	M	Farmer	22Au35Fa
CARMODY, Denis	23	M	Farmer	22Au35Fa
DALY, Mary	21	F	None	22Au35Fa
STACKPOOL, Agness	22	F	None	22Au35Fa
Maria	20	F	None	22Au35Fa
Catharine	19	F	None	22Au35Fa
Thomas	24	M	None	22Au35Fa
MALQUANY, Patt	19	M	Farmer	22Au35Fa
Ellen	19	F	Spinster	22Au35Fa
MULVILIDE, Martin	24	M	Farmer	22Au35Fa
SHEAHAN, Ellen	47	F	None	22Au35Fa
Bridget	17	F	None	22Au35Fa
Patt	.00	M	Infant	22Au35Fa
FITZMAURICE, Mary	21	F	Spinster	22Au35Fa
OBRINE, Mary	24	F	Spinster	22Au35Fa
HANNIGAN, Ellen	19	F	Spinster	22Au35Fa
HIGGINS, Bridget	17	F	Spinster	22Au35Fa
Catharine	20	F	Spinster	22Au35Fa
SHAHY, Fanny	18	F	Spinster	22Au35Fa
John	.00	M	Infant	22Au35Fa
FLYNN, William	40	M	Farmer	22Au35Fa
MOLONEY, Margaret	30	F	Spinster	22Au35Fa
LYONS, Margaret	20	F	Spinster	22Au35Fa
Margaret	.00	F	Infant	22Au35Fa
HENLLEY, Bridget	25	F	Spinster	22Au35Fa
BURDAN, Mary	19	F	Spinster	22Au35Fa
PARNELL, Biddy	19	F	Spinster	22Au35Fa
Mary	.00	F	Infant	22Au35Fa
CULLIGAN, John	16	M	Farmer	22Au35Fa
BURNES, Edmond	18	M	Farmer	22Au35Fa
RODEN, Bridget	16	F	Spinster	22Au35Fa
Margaret	.00	F	Infant	22Au35Fa
CORNEY, Mary	30	F	Spinster	22Au35Fa
MCDARNAN, Patt	6	M	Child	22Au35Fa
MEADE, Bridget	18	F	Spinster	22Au35Fa
MULLINS, Mary	20	F	Spinster	22Au35Fa
CORBETT, Mary	25	F	Spinster	22Au35Fa
RYANE, Stephen	52	M	Farmer	22Au35Fa
Eliza	45	F	Farmer	22Au35Fa
Michael	19	M	None	22Au35Fa
Patt	11	M	None	22Au35Fa
James	7	M	Child	22Au35Fa
Martin	.00	M	Infant	22Au35Fa
MCMAHON, Michael	26	M	None	22Au35Fa
Magt.	20	F	None	22Au35Fa
CONWALL, Mary	25	F	Spinster	22Au35Fa
COLLINS, James	22	M	Farmer	22Au35Fa
HEALY, John	33	M	Farmer	22Au35Fa
ODONNELL, James	20	M	Farmer	22Au35Fa
RYAN, Mary	28	F	Spinster	22Au35Fa
GLEESON, Patt	30	M	Farmer	22Au35Fa
Mary	21	F	Spinster	22Au35Fa
CORTELL, Bridget	22	F	Spinster	22Au35Fa
ROWAN, Margarett	34	F	Spinster	22Au35Fa
DONNELLY, Charles	26	M	Unknown	22Au35Fa
KNOX, John-E.	22	M	Unknown	22Au35Fa
LYNCH, Michael	26	M	Unknown	22Au35Fa
Patt	23	M	Unknown	22Au35Fa
James	22	M	Unknown	22Au35Fa
Magt.	19	F	Unknown	22Au35Fa
KERIN, Susan	19	F	Unknown	22Au35Fa
CARY, Catharine	22	F	Unknown	22Au35Fa
OBRINE, Margaret	20	F	Unknown	22Au35Fa
OSHEA, Eliza	21	F	Unknown	22Au35Fa

NAMES OF PASSENGERS	AGE	SEX	OCCUPATIONS	DATE PORT SHIP
OBRINE, John	25	M	Unknown	22Au35Fa
CARROL, Patrick	14	M	Unknown	22Au35Fa
GRACE, Bridget	18	F	Unknown	22Au35Fa
SARSFIELD, Kitty	25	F	Servant	22Au35Fa

ELSINOR 22 AUGUST 1849

From Liverpool

NAMES OF PASSENGERS	AGE	SEX	OCCUPATIONS	DATE PORT SHIP
WILLIAMS, John	43	M	Laborer	22Au02Au
HAVARD, Sol.	18	M	Unknown	22Au02Au
Evan	24	M	Unknown	22Au02Au
Mary	22	F	Unknown	22Au02Au
Thomas	.00	M	Infant	22Au02Au
BROWN, Wm.	31	M	Unknown	22Au02Au
U (W)	20	F	Unknown	22Au02Au
WATSON, Richd.	55	M	Unknown	22Au02Au
U (W)	34	F	Unknown	22Au02Au
ELLIOTT, George	25	M	Unknown	22Au02Au
Susan	24	F	Unknown	22Au02Au
John-Wilson	18	M	Unknown	22Au02Au
James	16	M	Unknown	22Au02Au
DOOLEY, James	50	M	Unknown	22Au02Au
Porb--, Mary	20	F	Unknown	22Au02Au
COSTELLO, Bridget	40	F	Unknown	22Au02Au
Paul	13	M	Unknown	22Au02Au
RUSSELL, U-Mrs.	21	F	Unknown	22Au02Au
DUNNE, Wm.	21	M	Unknown	22Au02Au
HOWE, James	21	M	Unknown	22Au02Au
STOULDING, Mary	40	F	Unknown	22Au02Au
George	27	M	Unknown	22Au02Au
John	23	M	Unknown	22Au02Au
William	19	M	Unknown	22Au02Au
Robert	16	M	Unknown	22Au02Au
Eleanor	21	F	Unknown	22Au02Au
Sophia	19	F	Unknown	22Au02Au
CADE, Zach.	22	M	Unknown	22Au02Au
KELLY, Cath.	18	F	Unknown	22Au02Au
SHURENS, Edw.	22	M	Unknown	22Au02Au
POHL, Anthy.	23	M	Unknown	22Au02Au
COOK, Wm.	21	M	Unknown	22Au02Au
Chas.	20	M	Unknown	22Au02Au
Mary	20	F	Unknown	22Au02Au
Mary	24	F	Unknown	22Au02Au
John	.00	M	Infant	22Au02Au
MCCANN, James	22	M	Unknown	22Au02Au
Mary	20	F	Unknown	22Au02Au
Cathe.	.00	F	Infant	22Au02Au
BROWN, James	21	M	Unknown	22Au02Au
RICE, John	22	M	Unknown	22Au02Au
CUNNINGHAM, Jas.	21	M	Laborer	22Au02Au
DIXON, Wm.	24	M	Unknown	22Au02Au
HOPEWELL, H.	22	M	Unknown	22Au02Au
CRAPPER, Jonan.	23	M	Unknown	22Au02Au
LEERY, Thos.	24	M	Unknown	22Au02Au
Louisa	24	F	Unknown	22Au02Au
Mary	5	F	Child	22Au02Au
CONNOR, Tim.	35	M	Unknown	22Au02Au
Mary	40	F	Unknown	22Au02Au
Mary	20	F	Unknown	22Au02Au
MOORE, Jas.	24	M	Unknown	22Au02Au
Jane	22	F	Unknown	22Au02Au
SHIELDS, Isaac	24	M	Unknown	22Au02Au
RATCLIFFE, H.	24	M	Unknown	22Au02Au
HETHERTON, Jas.	24	M	Unknown	22Au02Au
RATCLIFFE, Anth.	28	M	Unknown	22Au02Au
Jane	65	F	Unknown	22Au02Au
POTTS, Mary	19	F	Unknown	22Au02Au
Joseph-J.	21	M	Unknown	22Au02Au
HARE, Joseph	24	M	Unknown	22Au02Au
DELANY, John	30	M	Unknown	22Au02Au
Mary	20	F	Unknown	22Au02Au
AVERY, Joseph	36	M	Unknown	22Au02Au
Wm.	40	M	Unknown	22Au02Au
LAWS, Matthw.	27	M	Unknown	22Au02Au
Eliz.	25	F	Unknown	22Au02Au
Mag.	.00	F	Infant	22Au02Au
Anne	.00	F	Infant	22Au02Au
RYLAND, Wm.	45	M	Unknown	22Au02Au
DIXON, Chas.	26	M	Unknown	22Au02Au
Emma	24	F	Unknown	22Au02Au
Thos.	.00	M	Infant	22Au02Au
CHAPMAN, Saml.	29	M	Unknown	22Au02Au
MCDONNELL, Chas.	21	M	Unknown	22Au02Au
PARY, Wm.	22	M	Unknown	22Au02Au
TENNANT, Wm.	24	M	Unknown	22Au02Au
Laurence	20	M	Unknown	22Au02Au
CLUDEY, Thos.	26	M	Unknown	22Au02Au
JENNINGS, Mich.	40	M	Unknown	22Au02Au
BARNETT, Chas.	64	M	Unknown	22Au02Au
Eliz.	62	F	Unknown	22Au02Au
FEENY, Jane	20	F	Unknown	22Au02Au
GEORGE, Thos.	32	M	Unknown	22Au02Au
CHRISTMAS, H.	30	M	Unknown	22Au02Au
RIORDAN, John	30	M	Unknown	22Au02Au
JAMES, Richd.	27	M	Unknown	22Au02Au
Anne	40	F	Unknown	22Au02Au
MORGAN, Jane	27	F	Unknown	22Au02Au
CAHILL, John	35	M	Unknown	22Au02Au
Magt.	30	F	Unknown	22Au02Au
Cath.	.00	F	Infant	22Au02Au
PIPLON, Henry	26	M	Laborer	22Au02Au
SYKES, George	24	M	Unknown	22Au02Au
ONEILL, John	20	M	Unknown	22Au02Au
MCGUIRE, Wm.	25	M	Unknown	22Au02Au
LAWLER, James	37	M	Unknown	22Au02Au
Anne	21	F	Unknown	22Au02Au
KELLY, Mary	20	F	Unknown	22Au02Au
Bridget	18	F	Unknown	22Au02Au
KENNY, Thos.	24	M	Unknown	22Au02Au
James	18	M	Unknown	22Au02Au
GANNON, Mary	28	F	Unknown	22Au02Au
TRUMBULL, Thos.	21	M	Unknown	22Au02Au
John	19	M	Unknown	22Au02Au
SCALLY, Pat	21	M	Unknown	22Au02Au
CARSEN, Matt	20	M	Unknown	22Au02Au
OBERTON, Mary	21	F	Unknown	22Au02Au
GRAHAM, Jane	20	F	Unknown	22Au02Au
CORSWHITE, John	22	M	Unknown	22Au02Au
SPENCER, Gilead	24	M	Unknown	22Au02Au
GRIFFITH, Wm.	30	M	Unknown	22Au02Au
BURNETT, Henry	35	M	Unknown	22Au02Au
Joseph	39	M	Unknown	22Au02Au
WALTHEN, John	22	M	Unknown	22Au02Au
PATE, John	23	M	Unknown	22Au02Au
ROTHWELL, Henry	30	M	Unknown	22Au02Au
JONES, David	44	M	Unknown	22Au02Au
GILLEICE, Rose	20	F	Unknown	22Au02Au
STONE, Bridget	50	F	Unknown	22Au02Au
Thomas	21	M	Unknown	22Au02Au
Cath.	18	F	Unknown	22Au02Au
John	17	M	Unknown	22Au02Au
An.	16	F	Unknown	22Au02Au
Edmund	13	M	Unknown	22Au02Au
Judith	12	F	Unknown	22Au02Au
CASHIN, John	42	M	Unknown	22Au02Au
RYAN, Michael	35	M	Unknown	22Au02Au
U (W)	30	F	Unknown	22Au02Au
WEEKS, Wm.	21	M	Unknown	22Au02Au
GUNKIN, Sarah	22	F	Unknown	22Au02Au
Honora	.00	F	Infant	22Au02Au
CAFFREY, Thos.	26	M	Unknown	22Au02Au
COX, Jane	27	M	Unknown	22Au02Au
DONNELLY, Peter	27	M	Unknown	22Au02Au

NAMES OF PASSENGERS	AGE	SEX	OCCUPATIONS	DATE PORT SHIP
DONNELLY, Anne	23	F	Unknown	22Au02Au
John	.00	M	Infant	22Au02Au
COMMONS, Terence	32	M	Unknown	22Au02Au
Mc--GGAN, Cath.	18	F	Unknown	22Au02Au
REILLY, Hugh	23	M	Unknown	22Au02Au
LEGG, Anne	19	F	Unknown	22Au02Au
MCCABE, Hannah	17	F	Unknown	22Au02Au
MCCAFFREY, Matilda	20	F	Unknown	22Au02Au
MULLEN, Mary	20	F	Laborer	22Au02Au
Rose	18	F	Unknown	22Au02Au
SMITH, Anne	25	F	Unknown	22Au02Au
MCMANNUS, Cath.	30	F	Unknown	22Au02Au
Cath.	7	F	Child	22Au02Au
Owen	3	M	Child	22Au02Au
U	.00	U	Infant	22Au02Au
GRAY, James	25	M	Unknown	22Au02Au
DWYER, Tim	63	M	Unknown	22Au02Au
Eleanor	60	F	Unknown	22Au02Au
Eleanor	10	F	Unknown	22Au02Au
BRICKLY, Patk.	18	M	Unknown	22Au02Au
CUNNIFF, Mich.	58	M	Unknown	22Au02Au
CURLEY, Danl.	24	M	Unknown	22Au02Au
Thos.	9	M	Child	22Au02Au
Bridget	50	F	Unknown	22Au02Au
HICKEY, Wm.	25	M	Unknown	22Au02Au
Mary	19	F	Unknown	22Au02Au
FITZSIMMONS, Matthew	18	M	Unknown	22Au02Au
POTTERS, Wm.	20	M	Unknown	22Au02Au
DALY, Margt.	30	F	Unknown	22Au02Au
Honora	5	F	Child	22Au02Au
FOLEY, Daniel	21	M	Unknown	22Au02Au
ONEILL, Ellen	25	F	Unknown	22Au02Au
James	13	M	Unknown	22Au02Au
Patrick	12	M	Unknown	22Au02Au
GRENNAN, Mary	20	F	Unknown	22Au02Au
Eliza	15	F	Unknown	22Au02Au
COREY, Mary	30	F	Unknown	22Au02Au
FARREN, Danl.	18	M	Unknown	22Au02Au
BREEN, Rose	18	F	Unknown	22Au02Au
GILLESPIE, John	20	M	Unknown	22Au02Au
MEYHAN, Cornelius	25	M	Unknown	22Au02Au
U (W)	25	F	Unknown	22Au02Au
BRADY, John	23	M	Unknown	22Au02Au
MCKENNA, U-Mrs.	23	F	Unknown	22Au02Au
Mary	3	F	Child	22Au02Au
U	.00	U	Infant	22Au02Au
Michael	21	M	Unknown	22Au02Au
Peter	8	M	Child	22Au02Au
REILLY, Owen	35	M	Unknown	22Au02Au
WALL, Patk.	18	M	Unknown	22Au02Au
CALLAGHAN, Thos.	35	M	Unknown	22Au02Au
Mary	35	F	Unknown	22Au02Au
Hugh	4	M	Child	22Au02Au
GILLEICE, Pat	20	M	Unknown	22Au02Au
Bridget	30	F	Unknown	22Au02Au
John	40	M	Unknown	22Au02Au
Cathn.	30	F	Unknown	22Au02Au
Thomas	5	M	Child	22Au02Au
Biddy	.00	F	Infant	22Au02Au
MCGORHICK, Anne	17	F	Unknown	22Au02Au
MCBRIDE, Peter	19	M	Laborer	22Au02Au
MCHUGH, Anne	17	F	Unknown	22Au02Au
DUNN, Bridget	18	F	Unknown	22Au02Au
MATTHEWS, Cath.	16	F	Unknown	22Au02Au
DAN, Mich.	25	M	Unknown	22Au02Au
Mary	5	F	Child	22Au02Au
HENRY, James	43	M	Unknown	22Au02Au
Cath.	30	F	Unknown	22Au02Au
Mary	16	F	Unknown	22Au02Au
Bryan	13	F	Unknown	22Au02Au
Cathn.	5	F	Child	22Au02Au
ROGERS, John	27	M	Unknown	22Au02Au
MCGUIRE, Mary	35	F	Unknown	22Au02Au
Anne	6	F	Child	22Au02Au
Teresa	3	F	Child	22Au02Au
MCGUIRE, Laurence	.00	M	Infant	22Au02Au
SHEAN, Rich.	25	M	Unknown	22Au02Au
RIGNEY, Rich.	22	M	Unknown	22Au02Au
FRIEL, Mich.	20	M	Unknown	22Au02Au
Biddy	18	F	Unknown	22Au02Au
SCARY, Mich.	35	M	Unknown	22Au02Au
Johanna	30	F	Unknown	22Au02Au
Mary	10	F	Unknown	22Au02Au
REDMOND, James	21	M	Unknown	22Au02Au
CONNELL, Maurice	20	M	Unknown	22Au02Au
Honora	20	F	Unknown	22Au02Au
Cath.	.00	F	Infant	22Au02Au
DOYLE, Pat	16	M	Unknown	22Au02Au
KELLY, M.	22	M	Unknown	22Au02Au
CONNER, James	32	M	Unknown	22Au02Au
Nancy	30	F	Unknown	22Au02Au
Philip	2	M	Child	22Au02Au
Terry	.00	M	Infant	22Au02Au
SULLIVAN, Jera.	36	M	Unknown	22Au02Au
SHAUGHNESSY, Mary	20	F	Unknown	22Au02Au
WHELAN, John	23	M	Unknown	22Au02Au
FLYNN, Thos.	24	M	Unknown	22Au02Au
Mich.	16	M	Unknown	22Au02Au
MURPHY, Julia	25	F	Unknown	22Au02Au
Maurice	7	M	Child	22Au02Au
SULLIVAN, Cath.	20	F	Unknown	22Au02Au
Mary-Anne	18	F	Unknown	22Au02Au
Honora	3	F	Child	22Au02Au
Honora	.00	F	Infant	22Au02Au
REILLY, Bernard	30	M	Unknown	22Au02Au
Mary	10	F	Unknown	22Au02Au
John	8	M	Child	22Au02Au
Francis	6	M	Child	22Au02Au
Michael	12	M	Unknown	22Au02Au
Betsey	24	F	Unknown	22Au02Au
HARTLEY, Jane	16	F	Unknown	22Au02Au
MCAULEY, Joseph	19	M	Unknown	22Au02Au
DEANE, Honora	20	F	Unknown	22Au02Au
PORTER, Elizh.	35	F	Unknown	22Au02Au
Robert	11	M	Unknown	22Au02Au
Wm.	10	M	Unknown	22Au02Au
Eliza	7	F	Child	22Au02Au
John	2	M	Child	22Au02Au
Samuel	2	M	Child	22Au02Au
Sarah	.00	F	Infant	22Au02Au
MONKS, Christ.	18	M	Unknown	22Au02Au
BRADLEY, James	22	M	Unknown	22Au02Au
BRENNAN, Thos.	20	M	Unknown	22Au02Au

BOMBAY 22 AUGUST 1849

From Liverpool

NAMES OF PASSENGERS	AGE	SEX	OCCUPATIONS	DATE PORT SHIP
MORTON, James	25	M	Laborer	22Au02Pe
Judy	24	F	Servant	22Au02Pe
Bridget	20	F	Servant	22Au02Pe
COMMONS, Mary	45	F	Servant	22Au02Pe
Hannah	25	F	Servant	22Au02Pe
BURN, Francis	28	M	Laborer	22Au02Pe
Mary	24	F	Servant	22Au02Pe
HENERSON, Rose	30	F	None	22Au02Pe
MCNALLY, Ann	28	F	None	22Au02Pe
Peter	14	M	Laborer	22Au02Pe
FALLAN, Wm.	22	M	Laborer	22Au02Pe
CONLON, Francis	19	M	Laborer	22Au02Pe
Isa.	25	F	Servant	22Au02Pe
Anna	8	F	Child	22Au02Pe
MCFARLAND, Michael	26	M	Laborer	22Au02Pe
WOODS, John	46	M	Farmer	22Au02Pe

NAMES OF PASSENGERS	AGE	SEX	OCCUPATIONS	DATE PORT SHIP
WOODS, Jane	40	F	Servant	22Au02Pe
Mary	14	F	None	22Au02Pe
Catherine	12	F	None	22Au02Pe
Francis	8	M	Child	22Au02Pe
CONWAY, Pat	18	M	Laborer	22Au02Pe
FINLEY, Catherine	3	F	Child	22Au02Pe
Peter	1	M	Child	22Au02Pe
GORREY, Mosell	17	F	Servant	22Au02Pe
MORRISON, Pat	20	M	Blacksmith	22Au02Pe
MARRAH, Kenan	31	M	Farmer	22Au02Pe
Judy	27	F	Servant	22Au02Pe
CARROL, Geo.	35	M	Miller	22Au02Pe
LAMB, John	40	M	Farmer	22Au02Pe
James	23	M	Farmer	22Au02Pe
Mary	24	F	Servant	22Au02Pe
Catherine	19	F	Servant	22Au02Pe
Margt.	.00	F	Infant	22Au02Pe
SWEENEY, James	19	M	Laborer	22Au02Pe
DUNN, Phillip	34	M	Farmer	22Au02Pe
Mary	14	F	Servant	22Au02Pe
Ellen	11	F	None	22Au02Pe
Rodey	9	F	Child	22Au02Pe
RYAN, Pat	25	M	Farmer	22Au02Pe
Mary	22	F	Servant	22Au02Pe
Timothy	.00	M	Infant	22Au02Pe
Ann	19	F	Servant	22Au02Pe
Mat	20	M	Farmer	22Au02Pe
Michael	17	M	Farmer	22Au02Pe
SANDFORD, Eliza	23	F	Servant	22Au02Pe
DOHERTY, Mat	40	M	Farmer	22Au02Pe
Margt.	35	F	Servant	22Au02Pe
Mary	13	F	None	22Au02Pe
Catherine	11	F	None	22Au02Pe
Pat	9	M	Child	22Au02Pe
Wm.	6	M	Child	22Au02Pe
MAHAH, Thos.	28	M	Laborer	22Au02Pe
CARROLL, Bridget	25	F	Servant	22Au02Pe
GLEASON, Ellen	24	F	Servant	22Au02Pe
MAHAH, Nancy	26	F	Servant	22Au02Pe
Thos.	2	M	Child	22Au02Pe
GLEASON, Mary	4	F	Child	22Au02Pe
RYLEY, Rose	18	F	Servant	22Au02Pe
MCCLANE, Catherine	18	F	Servant	22Au02Pe
Bridget	16	F	Servant	22Au02Pe
DOOLEY, Bridget	38	F	Servant	22Au02Pe
Pat	18	M	Laborer	22Au02Pe
Ann	16	F	Servant	22Au02Pe
MCCOY, Robert	16	M	Farmer	22Au02Pe
CASSIDY, Srah	50	F	Servant	22Au02Pe
BRADY, Rose	18	F	Servant	22Au02Pe
Ann	20	F	Servant	22Au02Pe
MALONEY, John	22	M	Laborer	22Au02Pe
LOGLAN, Pat	35	M	Laborer	22Au02Pe
GORRY, John	40	M	Farmer	22Au02Pe
Ellen	35	F	Servant	22Au02Pe
Pat	9	M	Child	22Au02Pe
Eliza	7	F	Child	22Au02Pe
GOWAN, Teresa	16	F	Dressmaker	22Au02Pe
Mary	18	F	Dressmaker	22Au02Pe
Sarah	24	F	Servant	22Au02Pe
DURWIN, Catherine	30	F	Servant	22Au02Pe
Ann	5	F	Child	22Au02Pe
Michl.	2	M	Child	22Au02Pe
OHARRA, Michl.	25	M	Laborer	22Au02Pe
HICKEY, Mary	19	F	Servant	22Au02Pe
MCNACHS, Mary	17	F	Servant	22Au02Pe
FLOOD, Anne	17	F	Milliner	22Au02Pe
CASNE, Thos.	24	M	Plasterer	22Au02Pe
FITZPATRICK, John	23	M	Laborer	22Au02Pe
MARRAH, John	46	M	Farmer	22Au02Pe
Margt.	17	F	Servant	22Au02Pe
Mary	15	F	None	22Au02Pe
Duin	11	M	None	22Au02Pe
WELSH, Margt.	45	F	Servant	22Au02Pe
ATKINSON, John	20	M	Laborer	22Au02Pe
DALTON, John	15	M	Farmer	22Au02Pe
Margt.	25	F	Servant	22Au02Pe
John	.00	M	Infant	22Au02Pe
CARROL, Pat	40	M	Laborer	22Au02Pe
KELLY, Thos.	27	M	Laborer	22Au02Pe
MARRAH, Margt.	14	F	Servant	22Au02Pe
Michl.	25	M	Laborer	22Au02Pe
HEYMAN, Mary	35	F	Servant	22Au02Pe
MCCALLISTER, Michl.	28	M	Farmer	22Au02Pe
BRODWICK, Johannah	18	F	Servant	22Au02Pe
CAVANAGH, John	20	M	Laborer	22Au02Pe
Edwd.	24	M	Farmer	22Au02Pe
CYROCK, John	26	M	Carpenter	22Au02Pe
DUNICAN, James	23	M	Shoemaker	22Au02Pe
DALLARD, Bridget	20	F	Servant	22Au02Pe
TURNER, Peter	20	M	Laborer	22Au02Pe
FITZPATRICK, James	17	M	Laborer	22Au02Pe
KEFFE, Michl.	25	M	Farmer	22Au02Pe
Bridget	23	F	Servant	22Au02Pe
KEEFE, Barnard	.00	M	Infant	22Au02Pe
FARMER, Margt.	13	F	None	22Au02Pe
Bridget	14	F	None	22Au02Pe
HOWARD, Ann	20	F	Servant	22Au02Pe
FEE, Catherine	18	F	Servant	22Au02Pe
MCGORAN, Ellen	30	F	Servant	22Au02Pe
KENNON, Margt.	30	F	Servant	22Au02Pe
Anty.	8	M	Child	22Au02Pe
John	6	M	Child	22Au02Pe
Michl.	37	M	Farmer	22Au02Pe
BURK, Catherine	34	F	Servant	22Au02Pe
RYAN, Richd.	25	F	Laborer	22Au02Pe
BURK, Michl.	38	M	Farmer	22Au02Pe
Mary	32	F	Matron	22Au02Pe
Mary	12	F	Child	22Au02Pe
Catherine	9	F	Child	22Au02Pe
Don	6	M	Child	22Au02Pe
Billy	5	M	Child	22Au02Pe
Thomas	.00	M	Infant	22Au02Pe
HACKET, Mary	14	M	Child	22Au02Pe
CONWAY, Jno.	30	M	Farmer	22Au02Pe
Pat	5	M	Child	22Au02Pe
Wm.	.00	M	Infant	22Au02Pe
CLARY, Catherine	20	F	Servant	22Au02Pe
Richd.	18	M	Carpenter	22Au02Pe
MCCURON, Alex.	20	M	Laborer	22Au02Pe
BYRON, Pat	34	M	Baker	22Au02Pe
Ellen	34	F	Servant	22Au02Pe
OKELLY, Dan	24	M	Shopkeeper	22Au02Pe
CUSAC, Jas.	40	M	Weaver	22Au02Pe
MCDERMOT, Dom.	35	M	Laborer	22Au02Pe
MCTHIERRY, Edw.	28	M	Groom	22Au02Pe
Mary	39	F	Servant	22Au02Pe
MCGUINES, Jos.	19	M	Shopkeeper	22Au02Pe
HICKEY, Cun.	25	M	Laborer	22Au02Pe
Bridt.	22	F	Servant	22Au02Pe
REILLY, Thos.	26	M	Laborer	22Au02Pe
Pat.	32	M	Laborer	22Au02Pe
Mary	20	F	Servant	22Au02Pe
Ellen	6	F	Child	22Au02Pe
Edwd.	.00	M	Infant	22Au02Pe
BLAKE, John	36	M	Farmer	22Au02Pe
Mary	35	F	Servant	22Au02Pe
Edwd.	15	M	Laborer	22Au02Pe
MCCULLOUGH, John	21	M	Laborer	22Au02Pe
MULANY, Cornls.	21	M	Farmer	22Au02Pe
CHAMBERS, Alxr.	60	M	Laborer	22Au02Pe
Anne	56	F	Servant	22Au02Pe
WILKINSON, Eliza	15	F	Servant	22Au02Pe
JORDAN, John	26	M	Laborer	22Au02Pe
Isabella	20	F	Servant	22Au02Pe
Marian	5	F	Child	22Au02Pe
Eliza.Jane	2	F	Child	22Au02Pe
CURRY, James	40	M	Mason	22Au02Pe
Terence	14	M	Laborer	22Au02Pe
KERNAN, Brian	25	M	Laborer	22Au02Pe

NAMES OF PASSENGERS	AGE	SEX	OCCUPATIONS	DATE PORT SHIP
CULLEN, Francis	20	M	Laborer	22Au02Pe
CONNER, Pat	20	M	Laborer	22Au02Pe
FITZGERALD, Thos.	45	F	Farmer	22Au02Pe
GRIFFITH, Martha	26	F	Servant	22Au02Pe
Isabella	23	F	Servant	22Au02Pe
HENWRIGHT, John	23	F	Servant	22Au02Pe
Catherine	20	F	Servant	22Au02Pe
Catherine	50	F	Servant	22Au02Pe
GWEN, James	24	M	Shoemaker	22Au02Pe
HEYNES, Michl.	19	M	Laborer	22Au02Pe
James	20	M	Laborer	22Au02Pe
MCFRY, James	23	M	Laborer	22Au02Pe
TIMBERMAID, Pat	24	M	Laborer	22Au02Pe
MURPHY, John	22	M	Laborer	22Au02Pe
KEHOL, John	24	M	Laborer	22Au02Pe
FIELD, Thos.	35	M	Laborer	22Au02Pe
Marsella	25	F	Servant	22Au02Pe
COATUS, Daniel	18	M	Laborer	22Au02Pe
MAHONEY, Jerry	25	M	Laborer	22Au02Pe
SLATTERY, Michl.	25	M	Laborer	22Au02Pe
COCHRANE, Mary	12	F	None	22Au02Pe
Elizth.	10	F	Child	22Au02Pe
Anthony	3	M	Child	22Au02Pe
Teresa	8	F	Child	22Au02Pe
WINTERS, Mary	18	F	Servant	22Au02Pe
SUMMERS, Cath.	20	F	Servant	22Au02Pe
CARWAN, Judy	17	F	Servant	22Au02Pe
CONNOR, Matthew	16	M	Servant	22Au02Pe
MURPHY, Mary	26	F	Servant	22Au02Pe
RYAN, Francis	24	M	Laborer	22Au02Pe
SULLIVAN, Michl.	17	M	Laborer	22Au02Pe
MURPHY, Chas.	50	M	Joiner	22Au02Pe
MCMINNS, Peter	24	M	Accountant	22Au02Pe
Mary	24	F	Servant	22Au02Pe
HOGAN, Patrick	35	M	Laborer	22Au02Pe
SENNOYN, John	36	M	Laborer	22Au02Pe
Margt.J.	34	F	Servant	22Au02Pe
James	.00	M	Infant	22Au02Pe
BRADY, Francis	22	M	Laborer	22Au02Pe
MURPHY, Michl.	28	M	Carpenter	22Au02Pe
GROGAN, Francis	25	M	Laborer	22Au02Pe
MCGLUIN, Patrick	45	M	Laborer	22Au02Pe
Died-At-Sea				
LIVINGSTON, U	.00	M	Infant	22Au02Pe
Died-At-Sea				
HANNIGAN, Mary	50	F	None	22Au02Pe
Died-At-Sea				
HAYNE, U	.00	M	Infant	22Au02Pe
Died-At-Sea				
VENES, U	.00	M	Infant	22Au02Pe
DOTHUNDER, U	.00	F	Infant	22Au02Pe
CURDY, Nancy	17	F	Servant	22Au02Pe
BARR, Bitty	30	F	Servant	22Au02Pe
Median	7	F	Child	22Au02Pe
Eliza	4	F	Child	22Au02Pe
Robt.	.00	M	Infant	22Au02Pe
REILY, John	18	M	Laborer	22Au02Pe
FOGERTY, Mary	15	F	Servant	22Au02Pe
CARROLL, M.C.	28	F	Servant	22Au02Pe
HENNIGAN, Ann	18	F	Servant	22Au02Pe
MORGAN, Bridget	35	F	Servant	22Au02Pe
Maureen	13	F	Servant	22Au02Pe
Martha	8	F	Child	22Au02Pe
MCNICHOLS, Sarah	18	F	Servant	22Au02Pe
SKINNER, Mary	16	F	Servant	22Au02Pe
DOW, Mary	30	F	Servant	22Au02Pe
KENNEDY, Tom	8	M	Child	22Au02Pe
DONNE, Mary	6	F	Child	22Au02Pe
CRUM, Peter	25	M	Laborer	22Au02Pe
BRAND, Henry	40	M	Laborer	22Au02Pe
MCCARGHAN, Alxr.	18	M	Laborer	22Au02Pe
HERNAN, Richd.	22	M	Laborer	22Au02Pe
DUFFY, James	30	M	Mason	22Au02Pe
FURIE, Sarah	30	F	Servant	22Au02Pe
CASTLE, Lawrence	21	M	Unknown	22Au02Pe
SCOTT, Wm.	33	M	Laborer	22Au02Pe
Eliz.	48	F	Servant	22Au02Pe
Geo.	4	M	Child	22Au02Pe
R.	3	M	Child	22Au02Pe
Margt.	.00	F	Infant	22Au02Pe
BLACKBURN, Wm.	25	M	Farmer	22Au02Pe
Eliz.	20	F	Servant	22Au02Pe
FERGUSON, James	14	F	Servant	22Au02Pe
MCCORMACK, Ed.	30	M	Laborer	22Au02Pe
Mary	25	F	Matron	22Au02Pe
FERGUSON, John	12	M	Child	22Au02Pe
CONNER, Farrel	22	M	Laborer	22Au02Pe
GEHAN, Mary	36	F	Servant	22Au02Pe
COPELLA, Jacob	20	M	Miner	22Au02Pe
Agnes	27	F	Servant	22Au02Pe
ENGHBERT, George	30	M	Painter	22Au02Pe
DIX, Connie	28	M	Painter	22Au02Pe
ENGHINEN, Peter	26	M	Physician	22Au02Pe
STIFFLELAUB, Paul	19	M	Teacher	22Au02Pe
RIDER, Christopher	26	M	Merchant	22Au02Pe
SMITH, John	53	M	Miner	22Au02Pe
Henrietta	52	F	Matron	22Au02Pe
CLEARY, Ann	18	F	Servant	22Au02Pe

POLANDER 22 AUGUST 1849

From London

NAMES OF PASSENGERS	AGE	SEX	OCCUPATIONS	DATE PORT SHIP
TARREN, Mary	37	F	Unknown	22Au13Pf
John	13	M	Unknown	22Au13Pf
Wm.	12	M	Unknown	22Au13Pf
Jas.	10	M	Unknown	22Au13Pf
Michael	4	M	Child	22Au13Pf
CURLIN, Jas.	26	M	Unknown	22Au13Pf
Mary	24	F	Unknown	22Au13Pf
TASKAR, Henry	23	M	Unknown	22Au13Pf
Anna	24	F	Unknown	22Au13Pf
Died-At-Sea				
FITZGERALD, Thos.	28	M	Unknown	22Au13Pf
Mary	28	F	Unknown	22Au13Pf
SULIVAN, Jos.	30	M	Unknown	22Au13Pf
LEONARD, Jno.	48	M	Unknown	22Au13Pf
WIDGNEY, Wm.	32	M	Unknown	22Au13Pf
WILD, Isabella	36	F	Unknown	22Au13Pf
Esther	19	F	Unknown	22Au13Pf
Eleanor	18	F	Unknown	22Au13Pf
Jane	17	F	Unknown	22Au13Pf
Eliza	16	F	Unknown	22Au13Pf
Sarah	12	F	Unknown	22Au13Pf
Wm.	11	M	Unknown	22Au13Pf
Chs.	10	M	Unknown	22Au13Pf
Emily	7	F	Child	22Au13Pf
Clara	5	F	Child	22Au13Pf
Died-At-Sea				
Louisa	2	F	Child	22Au13Pf
KELLY, John	21	M	Unknown	22Au13Pf
DAWSON, Mary	35	F	Unknown	22Au13Pf
PLACE, George	20	M	Unknown	22Au13Pf
TURNER, Geo.	36	M	Unknown	22Au13Pf
Mary	35	F	Unknown	22Au13Pf
Geo.	2	M	Child	22Au13Pf
FICKLEY, Henry	33	M	Unknown	22Au13Pf
CONCAVE, John	23	M	Unknown	22Au13Pf
COLLET, John	32	M	Unknown	22Au13Pf
Elizabeth	46	F	Unknown	22Au13Pf
JARVIS, Francis	20	M	Unknown	22Au13Pf
MURPHY, Jeremiah	22	M	Unknown	22Au13Pf
REYNOLDS, W.	60	M	Unknown	22Au13Pf
Matilda	16	F	Unknown	22Au13Pf

NAMES OF PASSENGERS		AGE	SEX	OCCUPATIONS	DATE PORT SHIP
MILLER, John		30	M	Unknown	22Au13Pf
HALLEY, Mary		30	F	Unknown	22Au13Pf
HILL, John		19	M	Unknown	22Au13Pf
CAMERON, John		29	M	Unknown	22Au13Pf
READING, Timothy		29	M	Unknown	22Au13Pf
Betsey		25	F	Unknown	22Au13Pf
HOLEY, Jeremiah		24	M	Unknown	22Au13Pf
ELLIS, Benj.		34	M	Unknown	22Au13Pf
Eliza		32	F	Unknown	22Au13Pf
SMITH, James		25	M	Unknown	22Au13Pf
JONES, John		35	M	Unknown	22Au13Pf
WATKINSON, W.		22	M	Unknown	22Au13Pf
GAFFREY, Margt.		10	F	Child	23Au02Ph
Ellen		7	F	Child	23Au02Ph
Maria		5	F	Child	23Au02Ph
James		3	M	Child	23Au02Ph
BERYN, U		50	M	Farmer	23Au02Ph
Ann	(W)	48	F	None	23Au02Ph
Mary		20	F	Dressmaker	23Au02Ph
Wm.		18	M	Farmer	23Au02Ph
John		16	M	Farmer	23Au02Ph
Thos.		12	M	Farmer	23Au02Ph

ROSALINDA 23 AUGUST 1849

From Liverpool

NAMES OF PASSENGERS		AGE	SEX	OCCUPATIONS	DATE PORT SHIP
COSTELLO, John		22	M	Farmer	23Au02Ph
DURHAN, Michl.		35	M	Baker	23Au02Ph
Mary		30	F	Dressmaker	23Au02Ph
John		5	M	Child	23Au02Ph
Ann		2	F	Child	23Au02Ph
Ellen		.06	F	Infant	23Au02Ph
SPURSUND, Ann		20	F	Servant	23Au02Ph
TOONEY, Wm.		30	M	Farmer	23Au02Ph
Mary	(W)	30	F	None	23Au02Ph
Thomas		12	M	None	23Au02Ph
Jeremiah		9	M	Child	23Au02Ph
Mary		3	F	Child	23Au02Ph
Charles		.09	M	Infant	23Au02Ph
SULLIVAN, Mary		15	F	Spinster	23Au02Ph
OBRIAN, John		50	M	Farmer	23Au02Ph
Bridget	(W)	30	F	None	23Au02Ph
Mary		5	F	Child	23Au02Ph
Jane		3	F	Child	23Au02Ph
Margt.		.08	F	Infant	23Au02Ph
SHORTELL, Mary		22	F	Servant	23Au02Ph
PATTERSON, Arnold		40	M	Farmer	23Au02Ph
Isabella	(W)	34	F	None	23Au02Ph
Cath.		35	F	Spinster	23Au02Ph
Cath.		13	F	Spinster	23Au02Ph
Thos.		11	M	None	23Au02Ph
Chas.		9	M	Child	23Au02Ph
James		6	M	Husband	23Au02Ph
Mary		.06	F	Infant	23Au02Ph
Died-At-Sea					
MURPHY, Thos.		25	M	Laborer	23Au02Ph
SHETLAN, Thos.		19	M	Surveyor	23Au02Ph
MCNEARY, Danl.		18	M	Laborer	23Au02Ph
SCHOOLS, U		25	M	Shopkeeper	23Au02Ph
Robt.		21	M	Shopkeeper	23Au02Ph
Oliver		30	M	Shopkeeper	23Au02Ph
Emily		28	F	Spinster	23Au02Ph
JACKSON, Henry		22	M	Chemist	23Au02Ph
David		20	M	Chemist	23Au02Ph
PEDRON, Cath.		48	F	Servant	23Au02Ph
Ellen		10	F	Child	23Au02Ph
Mary		8	F	Child	23Au02Ph
Cath.		6	F	Child	23Au02Ph
Luke		4	M	Child	23Au02Ph
MITCHELL, John		30	M	Laborer	23Au02Ph
Barbara	(W)	25	F	None	23Au02Ph
John		3	M	Child	23Au02Ph
Bridgt.		.10	F	Infant	23Au02Ph
MCLEAN, Wm.		12	M	Laborer	23Au02Ph
GAFFREY, John		41	M	Coach Maker	23Au02Ph
Julia	(W)	40	F	None	23Au02Ph
Joseph		16	M	Coach Maker	23Au02Ph
KINSELL, Sarah		25	F	Spinster	23Au02Ph

LADY-OF-THE-LAKE 23 AUGUST 1849

From HAMILTON, Bermuda

NAMES OF PASSENGERS		AGE	SEX	OCCUPATIONS	DATE PORT SHIP
TOBIAS, John		46	M	None	23Au60Nu
BAXTER, Ann		15	F	None	23Au60Nu
MCKEDRICH, James		30	M	None	23Au60Nu
BIZZARD, Fras.		20	M	None	23Au60Nu
PENNY, Ann		22	F	None	23Au60Nu
DUBSON, James		30	M	None	23Au60Nu
BIZZARD, Thos.		1	M	Child	23Au60Nu

FANNY 23 AUGUST 1849

From Londonderry

NAMES OF PASSENGERS		AGE	SEX	OCCUPATIONS	DATE PORT SHIP
MCCLOSKY, Ann		24	F	Servant	23Au01Dk
MCLAUGHLIN, Wm.		29	M	Laborer	23Au01Dk
MCALINNER, Alexander		60	M	Laborer	23Au01Dk
Catherine		19	F	Servant	23Au01Dk
MCCLOSKY, Mary		40	F	Servant	23Au01Dk
Arthur		10	M	Unknown	23Au01Dk
James		5	M	Child	23Au01Dk
HARLEY, Mary-Ann		50	F	Servant	23Au01Dk
Susan		13	F	None	23Au01Dk
ELLIS, Mary		20	F	Servant	23Au01Dk
WILEY, Sarah		20	F	Servant	23Au01Dk
Thomas		1	M	Child	23Au01Dk
CURRY, Robert		32	M	Laborer	23Au01Dk
Jane		28	F	Servant	23Au01Dk
Michael		10	M	Unknown	23Au01Dk
Jane		6	F	Child	23Au01Dk
Mary		4	F	Child	23Au01Dk
Unity		.02	F	Infant	23Au01Dk
CARLAND, Biddy		18	F	Servant	23Au01Dk
MCNALLY, Mark		20	M	Laborer	23Au01Dk
LOGAN, John		23	M	Laborer	23Au01Dk
MARTIN, Bernard		19	M	Laborer	23Au01Dk
QUINN, Michael		8	M	Child	23Au01Dk
ROLESTONE, James		18	M	Laborer	23Au01Dk
GILLESPIE, Catherine		17	F	Servant	23Au01Dk
BOVIARD, Ann		40	F	Servant	23Au01Dk
DOUGHERTY, Alexander		18	M	Laborer	23Au01Dk
HAUGHEY, Ann		24	F	Servant	23Au01Dk
NORRY, Margaret		23	F	Servant	23Au01Dk
MCGLEIN, Ann		19	F	Servant	23Au01Dk
MCCARTER, John		19	M	Laborer	23Au01Dk
WRIGHT, John		32	M	Laborer	23Au01Dk
Margaret		34	F	Servant	23Au01Dk
CHRISTIE, Ann		24	F	Servant	23Au01Dk
Margaret		2	F	Child	23Au01Dk
PAUL, Mary-A.		19	F	Servant	23Au01Dk

NAMES OF PASSENGERS		AGE	SEX	OCCUPATIONS	DATE PORT SHIP
SAWYER, John		28	M	Laborer	23Au01Dk
ANDREWS, Margaret		22	F	Servant	23Au01Dk
MCLAUGHLIN, Biddy		26	F	Servant	23Au01Dk
BONAN, Bitty		12	F	None	23Au01Dk
MCELHILL, Pat		16	M	Laborer	23Au01Dk
FERGUSON, Robert		30	M	Laborer	23Au01Dk
Sarah	(W)	35	F	None	23Au01Dk
Matilda	(D)	10	F	Unknown	23Au01Dk
Robert	(S)	7	M	Child	23Au01Dk
James	(S)	5	M	Child	23Au01Dk
John	(S)	3	M	Child	23Au01Dk
Mathew	(S)	1	M	Child	23Au01Dk
ODONNELL, Thomas		21	M	Laborer	23Au01Dk
MCGINNIS, Joseph		15	M	Laborer	23Au01Dk
BONAN, John		25	M	Laborer	23Au01Dk
BREESLAND, Ann		19	F	Servant	23Au01Dk
GALLAGHER, Mary		18	F	Servant	23Au01Dk
BOGH, Mary		14	F	None	23Au01Dk
KERR, Ann		25	F	Servant	23Au01Dk
Ann		2	F	Child	23Au01Dk
Wm.		1	M	Child	23Au01Dk
MCCANN, James		20	M	Unknown	23Au01Dk
MCCONOLOGUE, Biddy		26	F	Servant	23Au01Dk
Magry		27	F	Servant	23Au01Dk
BREESLAND, Marg.		26	F	Servant	23Au01Dk
MCLAUGHLIN, Michael		29	M	Laborer	23Au01Dk
MCAULEY, Marg.		21	F	Servant	23Au01Dk
MCGITTIGAN, Marg.		27	F	Servant	23Au01Dk
HUGHES, Stephen		27	M	Laborer	23Au01Dk
FERGUSON, Thos.		21	M	Unknown	23Au01Dk
HYNES, Elizabeth		60	F	Servant	23Au01Dk
KELLY, Ann		12	F	Unknown	23Au01Dk
MCDONALD, James		50	M	Laborer	23Au01Dk
Ann		5	F	Child	23Au01Dk
MONTGOMERY, John		14	M	Unknown	23Au01Dk
MCGINLEY, Mary		21	F	Servant	23Au01Dk
HARKIN, John		22	M	Laborer	23Au01Dk
Marg.	(W)	20	F	None	23Au01Dk
KERRIGAN, Terence		30	M	Laborer	23Au01Dk
Mary		18	F	Servant	23Au01Dk
GALLAGHER, John		30	M	Laborer	23Au01Dk
Wm.		26	M	Laborer	23Au01Dk
MCCAFFERTY, Wm.		25	M	Laborer	23Au01Dk
GALLAGHER, Sarah		25	F	Servant	23Au01Dk
REILLY, Charles		12	M	None	23Au01Dk
SWEENY, John		40	M	Ngtwtch	23Au01Dk
QUIGLEY, Ann		25	F	Servant	23Au01Dk
Wm.		20	M	Laborer	23Au01Dk
HART, Wm.		13	M	None	23Au01Dk
ELLISON, Samuel		14	M	Nephew	23Au01Dk
CAIN, Mary		58	F	Servant	23Au01Dk
BLAIR, Ellen		21	F	Servant	23Au01Dk
CAMPBELL, Wm.P.		21	M	Laborer	23Au01Dk
BOGGS, Mary-A.		22	F	Milliner	23Au01Dk
Catherine		20	F	Milliner	23Au01Dk
MCGILL, James		37	M	Laborer	23Au01Dk
John		18	M	Laborer	23Au01Dk
GUNN, James		21	M	Laborer	23Au01Dk
COOL, Hugh		25	M	Laborer	23Au01Dk
CLARKE, Charles		25	M	Laborer	23Au01Dk
DOHERTY, James		38	M	Laborer	23Au01Dk
MCELHILL, James		45	M	Laborer	23Au01Dk
Ann	(W)	41	F	None	23Au01Dk
Mary	(D)	17	F	None	23Au01Dk
Catherine	(D)	19	F	None	23Au01Dk
Edward	(S)	14	M	None	23Au01Dk
James	(S)	11	M	None	23Au01Dk
Ellenor	(D)	8	F	Child	23Au01Dk
Bridget	(D)	2	F	Child	23Au01Dk
Teresa	(M)	80	F	None	23Au01Dk
DONAGHY, John		40	M	Laborer	23Au01Dk
Sarah	(W)	40	F	None	23Au01Dk
DONNELLY, Pat		35	M	Laborer	23Au01Dk
COLLINS, Pat		35	M	Laborer	23Au01Dk
GANN, Catherine		21	F	Servant	23Au01Dk
MCCOLGAN, Mary		9	F	Child	23Au01Dk
John		4	M	Child	23Au01Dk
LITTA, Bitty		40	F	Servant	23Au01Dk
James		6	M	Child	23Au01Dk
PORTIFF, Humphrey		24	M	Laborer	23Au01Dk
Ellenor		17	F	Servant	23Au01Dk
MCDAID, Hugh		20	M	Laborer	23Au01Dk
Ellenor	(M)	40	F	None	23Au01Dk
Mary	(T)	14	F	None	23Au01Dk
GALLAGHER, James		35	M	Laborer	23Au01Dk
GORMAN, Judy		35	F	Servant	23Au01Dk
Rebecca		30	F	Servant	23Au01Dk
MCCOOL, Barry		70	M	Farmer	23Au01Dk
Barry	(S)	35	M	Farmer	23Au01Dk
Fanny	(D)	46	F	None	23Au01Dk
MCCOLGAN, Bitty		35	F	Servant	23Au01Dk
Phillip		3	M	Child	23Au01Dk
Elizabeth		.10	F	Infant	23Au01Dk
MCLAUGHLIN, Mary		21	F	Servant	23Au01Dk
MCCONNELL, Mary		20	F	Servant	23Au01Dk

NEW-HAMPSHIRE 23 AUGUST 1849

From Liverpool

NAMES OF PASSENGERS		AGE	SEX	OCCUPATIONS	DATE PORT SHIP
BENNETT, Pat		25	M	Unknown	23Au02Pi
Bridget		22	F	Unknown	23Au02Pi
GOLDING, Pat		20	M	Unknown	23Au02Pi
REDDING, Rose		40	F	Unknown	23Au02Pi
Mary		3	F	Child	23Au02Pi
Ellen		.06	F	Infant	23Au02Pi
KENDRICK, Solomon		35	M	Unknown	23Au02Pi
NEAL, Michael		40	M	Unknown	23Au02Pi
QUINLAN, Philip		40	M	Unknown	23Au02Pi
U-Mrs.		40	F	Unknown	23Au02Pi
Maria		16	F	Unknown	23Au02Pi
Mary-A.		14	F	Unknown	23Au02Pi
Ellen		12	F	Unknown	23Au02Pi
John		10	M	Unknown	23Au02Pi
Margaret		7	F	Child	23Au02Pi
Philip		4	M	Child	23Au02Pi
Pat		00	M	Child	23Au02Pi
Michael		.08	M	Infant	23Au02Pi
RYAN, Mary		17	F	Unknown	23Au02Pi
FLOOD, Catherine		20	F	Unknown	23Au02Pi
FEGAN, Mary		40	F	Unknown	23Au02Pi
CAREY, Thomas		25	M	Unknown	23Au02Pi
MEEHAN, Daniel		22	M	Unknown	23Au02Pi
BRIAN, Pat		22	M	Unknown	23Au02Pi
U-Mrs.		20	F	Unknown	23Au02Pi
Margarett		.06	F	Infant	23Au02Pi
GLEESON, Wm.		22	M	Unknown	23Au02Pi
Honor		18	F	Unknown	23Au02Pi
Judy		20	F	Unknown	23Au02Pi
MCCORLY, James		24	M	Unknown	23Au02Pi
FEALY, Pat		20	M	Unknown	23Au02Pi
CODY, Mary		24	F	Unknown	23Au02Pi
BRITTON, Elison		30	F	Unknown	23Au02Pi
Elison		10	F	Child	23Au02Pi
SILK, John		23	M	Unknown	23Au02Pi
U-Mrs.		23	F	Unknown	23Au02Pi
Mark		3	F	Child	23Au02Pi
Bridgett		1	F	Child	23Au02Pi
MCPHERY, Michael		30	M	Unknown	23Au02Pi
U-Mrs.		30	F	Unknown	23Au02Pi
MCHOWARD, Pat		20	M	Unknown	23Au02Pi
MOSS, Henry		26	M	Unknown	23Au02Pi
BREMON, John		22	M	Unknown	23Au02Pi
HURLEY, Edmond		42	M	Unknown	23Au02Pi

NAMES OF PASSENGERS	AGE	SEX	OCCUPATIONS	DATE PORT SHIP	NAMES OF PASSENGERS	AGE	SEX	OCCUPATIONS	DATE PORT SHIP
HURLEY, Win.	40	F	Unknown	23Au02Pi	LOONEY, Thomas	15	M	Unknown	23Au02Pi
Pat	8	M	Child	23Au02Pi	MURPHY, Denis	16	M	Unknown	23Au02Pi
OLEARY, Win.	.07	M	Infant	23Au02Pi	Honor	16	F	Unknown	23Au02Pi
MCGRATH, John	25	M	Unknown	23Au02Pi	SHEA, Daniel	20	M	Unknown	23Au02Pi
LYNCH, Edmund	24	M	Unknown	23Au02Pi	DESMOND, John	20	M	Unknown	23Au02Pi
Ned	20	M	Unknown	23Au02Pi	DONOHUE, Catherine	2	F	Child	23Au02Pi
RYAN, Pat	26	M	Unknown	23Au02Pi	LYNCH, Mary	50	F	Unknown	23Au02Pi
GILMARTIN, James	20	M	Unknown	23Au02Pi	Mary	11	F	Unknown	23Au02Pi
DUNN, Martin	20	M	Unknown	23Au02Pi	MCCARTHY, John	36	M	Unknown	23Au02Pi
BREARTON, Edmond	25	M	Unknown	23Au02Pi	HARRINGTON, Mary	45	F	Unknown	23Au02Pi
Nancy	22	F	Unknown	23Au02Pi	SULLIVAN, Samuel	24	M	Unknown	23Au02Pi
Michael	21	M	Unknown	23Au02Pi	HANLEY, Thomas	29	M	Unknown	23Au02Pi
John	16	M	Unknown	23Au02Pi	SHEA, Margaret	20	F	Unknown	23Au02Pi
SMALL, John	27	M	Unknown	23Au02Pi	CONNEW, Catherine	10	F	Child	23Au02Pi
LOUGHNON, Peggy	27	M	Unknown	23Au02Pi	MCCABE, Pat	45	M	Unknown	23Au02Pi
MARTIN, Michael	25	M	Unknown	23Au02Pi	Ann	35	F	Unknown	23Au02Pi
CUNOM, Jno.	20	M	Unknown	23Au02Pi	Mary	6	F	Child	23Au02Pi
MORIARTY, George	65	M	Unknown	23Au02Pi	Alexander	5	M	Child	23Au02Pi
Elisa	19	F	Unknown	23Au02Pi	John	.02	M	Infant	23Au02Pi
Margarett	25	F	Unknown	23Au02Pi	RICHARDSON, Mary	70	F	Unknown	23Au02Pi
WHITE, Jane	9	F	Child	23Au02Pi	Mary	23	F	Unknown	23Au02Pi
MOOREHEAD, Mary	6	F	Child	23Au02Pi	REED, William	22	M	Unknown	23Au02Pi
MANGAN, Malachi	30	M	Unknown	23Au02Pi	Catherine	23	F	Unknown	23Au02Pi
TORN, Catherine	20	F	Unknown	23Au02Pi	Eliza	.07	F	Infant	23Au02Pi
FINNEGAN, Margarett	30	F	Unknown	23Au02Pi	MORIARTY, John	11	M	Unknown	23Au02Pi
HIGGINS, Catherine	20	F	Unknown	23Au02Pi	SHEEHAN, Patt	14	M	Unknown	23Au02Pi
PORE, John	38	M	Unknown	23Au02Pi	CARROLL, Maria	18	F	Unknown	23Au02Pi
Mary	30	F	Unknown	23Au02Pi	EDWARDS, Ann	19	F	Unknown	23Au02Pi
Margarett	22	F	Unknown	23Au02Pi	TOBIN, Ann	16	F	Unknown	23Au02Pi
Pat	22	M	Unknown	23Au02Pi	GARSON, Philip	40	M	Unknown	23Au02Pi
CALLAHAN, Mary	12	F	Unknown	23Au02Pi	MCCABE, Alice	25	F	Unknown	23Au02Pi
MOULTON, Richard	50	M	Unknown	23Au02Pi	MCGUIRE, Margaret	30	F	Unknown	23Au02Pi
Mary	40	F	Unknown	23Au02Pi	CAVANAGH, Thomas	26	M	Unknown	23Au02Pi
Bridget	12	F	Unknown	23Au02Pi	ROURKE, Bridget	17	F	Unknown	23Au02Pi
Margarett	10	F	Child	23Au02Pi	ALMER, Thomas	25	M	Unknown	23Au02Pi
Eliza	8	F	Child	23Au02Pi	U-Mrs.	23	F	Unknown	23Au02Pi
Mary	9	F	Child	23Au02Pi	SCARLON, James	35	M	Unknown	23Au02Pi
Pat	4	M	Child	23Au02Pi	U-Mrs.	30	F	Unknown	23Au02Pi
Eliza	.06	F	Infant	23Au02Pi	John	7	M	Child	23Au02Pi
CAIN, Margarett	30	F	Unknown	23Au02Pi	Michael	5	M	Child	23Au02Pi
Ann	.08	F	Infant	23Au02Pi	Catherine	4	F	Child	23Au02Pi
HANLY, Mary	22	F	Unknown	23Au02Pi	Martin	4	M	Child	23Au02Pi
WERE, James	20	M	Unknown	23Au02Pi	Dan	17	M	Unknown	23Au02Pi
BELL, Henry	33	M	Unknown	23Au02Pi	BRENNAN, James	26	M	Unknown	23Au02Pi
DERNON, Barny	25	M	Unknown	23Au02Pi	HANLEY, William	35	M	Unknown	23Au02Pi
MCCARTNEY, Benjamin	28	M	Unknown	23Au02Pi	Margaret	30	F	Unknown	23Au02Pi
Anner	26	F	Unknown	23Au02Pi	Daniel	18	M	Unknown	23Au02Pi
Sarah	.05	F	Infant	23Au02Pi	Mary	16	F	Unknown	23Au02Pi
MCCARTY, Michael	21	M	Unknown	23Au02Pi	Margaret	13	F	Unknown	23Au02Pi
DOWNEY, John	27	M	Unknown	23Au02Pi	John	10	M	Child	23Au02Pi
TAYNER, John	30	M	Unknown	23Au02Pi	Bessy	8	F	Child	23Au02Pi
MEEGAN, Pat	30	M	Unknown	23Au02Pi	Catherine	8	F	Child	23Au02Pi
TURNER, George	17	M	Unknown	23Au02Pi	HAILEY, Ellen	5	F	Child	23Au02Pi
SIMS, Michael	22	M	Unknown	23Au02Pi	Edmund	11	M	Child	23Au02Pi
DIGNON, James	19	M	Unknown	23Au02Pi	Ann	3	F	Child	23Au02Pi
Mary	20	F	Unknown	23Au02Pi	William	1	M	Child	23Au02Pi
CONNELL, David	46	M	Unknown	23Au02Pi	Bridget	1	F	Child	23Au02Pi
MURPHY, William	13	M	Unknown	23Au02Pi	CREHAN, Philip	45	M	Unknown	23Au02Pi
DELURY, John	21	M	Unknown	23Au02Pi	Margaret	35	F	Unknown	23Au02Pi
GORMAN, Ellen	25	F	Unknown	23Au02Pi	Pat	11	M	Unknown	23Au02Pi
FLYNN, Mary	28	F	Unknown	23Au02Pi	James	10	M	Child	23Au02Pi
MARSHALL, Fanny	22	F	Unknown	23Au02Pi	Mary	8	F	Child	23Au02Pi
MCCRAHAN, Bridget	36	F	Unknown	23Au02Pi	Michael	6	M	Child	23Au02Pi
GILRONON, Mary	16	F	Unknown	23Au02Pi	Mat	2	M	Child	23Au02Pi
MURRY, Henry	20	M	Unknown	23Au02Pi	Catherine	.08	F	Infant	23Au02Pi
FEGAN, James	24	M	Unknown	23Au02Pi	WALSH, Kernon	33	M	Unknown	23Au02Pi
Ellie	20	F	Unknown	23Au02Pi	U-Mrs.	30	F	Unknown	23Au02Pi
Judy	22	F	Unknown	23Au02Pi	TONE, Thomas	25	M	Unknown	23Au02Pi
GIBNEY, John	29	M	Unknown	23Au02Pi	MELANPHY, Barny	19	F	Unknown	23Au02Pi
Pat	20	M	Unknown	23Au02Pi	DOYLE, Mary	28	F	Unknown	23Au02Pi
BYRNE, Philip	20	M	Unknown	23Au02Pi	James	25	M	Unknown	23Au02Pi
MCGRADE, Hugh	30	M	Unknown	23Au02Pi	Charles	11	M	Unknown	23Au02Pi
MCCOOL, Polly	16	F	Unknown	23Au02Pi	Michael	9	M	Child	23Au02Pi
MEERE, Pat	32	M	Unknown	23Au02Pi	John	7	M	Child	23Au02Pi
HOGAN, Pat	25	M	Unknown	23Au02Pi	LONG, James	30	M	Unknown	23Au02Pi

NAMES OF PASSENGERS	AGE	SEX	OCCUPATIONS	DATE PORT SHIP
MCCORMICK, Catherine	6	F	Child	23Au02Pi
WHELON, Edward	40	M	Unknown	23Au02Pi
WHELAN, Mary	36	F	Unknown	23Au02Pi
Margaret	11	F	Unknown	23Au02Pi
Catherine	9	F	Child	23Au02Pi
Maria	7	F	Child	23Au02Pi
John	5	M	Child	23Au02Pi
Judy	3	F	Child	23Au02Pi
Pat	.07	M	Infant	23Au02Pi
BURN, James	26	M	Unknown	23Au02Pi
DOWD, Pat	31	M	Unknown	23Au02Pi
RYAN, Tim	24	M	Unknown	23Au02Pi
Richard	24	M	Unknown	23Au02Pi
BRANNON, Thomas	18	M	Unknown	23Au02Pi
CASE, William	28	M	Unknown	23Au02Pi
Harriett	27	F	Unknown	23Au02Pi
Mary	30	F	Unknown	23Au02Pi
MADA, Alice	40	F	Unknown	23Au02Pi
William	17	M	Unknown	23Au02Pi
Ann	14	F	Unknown	23Au02Pi
Jane	12	F	Unknown	23Au02Pi
John	10	M	Child	23Au02Pi
Pat	4	M	Child	23Au02Pi
Nicholas	2	M	Child	23Au02Pi
DOWLING, Henry	35	M	Unknown	23Au02Pi
Mary	27	F	Unknown	23Au02Pi
GILDING, John	26	M	Unknown	23Au02Pi
COSGROVE, James	32	M	Unknown	23Au02Pi
SHURDIN, Mary	35	F	Unknown	23Au02Pi
CLARK, Mary	25	F	Unknown	23Au02Pi
CULLIN, Ann	40	F	Unknown	23Au02Pi
FARLING, Biddy	25	F	Unknown	23Au02Pi
BLYGH, Mary	22	F	Unknown	23Au02Pi
CLARK, Biddy	25	F	Unknown	23Au02Pi
CORLIN, Ann	.00	F	Infant	23Au02Pi
Born-At-Sea				
MADA, Thomas	7	M	Child	23Au02Pi

RICHARD-COBDEN 24 AUGUST 1849

From Liverpool

NAMES OF PASSENGERS	AGE	SEX	OCCUPATIONS	DATE PORT SHIP
MATHIESON, Ann	23	F	Servant	24Au02Pj
KENNEY, Margaret	20	F	Servant	24Au02Pj
DAMOODY, Hugh	27	M	Mason	24Au02Pj
DOLAN, Peter	14	M	Son	24Au02Pj
Laurence	3	M	Child	24Au02Pj
KENNEY, James	16	M	Laborer	24Au02Pj
Mary	14	F	None	24Au02Pj
Martin	13	M	None	24Au02Pj
Eliza	8	F	Child	24Au02Pj
MURPHY, James	50	M	Laborer	24Au02Pj
Phil	15	M	Laborer	24Au02Pj
SMALL, Thomas	27	M	Laborer	24Au02Pj
Died-At-Sea				
MACNULTY, Susan	40	F	Wife	24Au02Pj
Mary	11	F	None	24Au02Pj
Catherine	9	F	Child	24Au02Pj
CORNELLE, Peggy	20	F	Servant	24Au02Pj
MACCORMICK, Marcella	16	F	Servant	24Au02Pj
NUGENT, Joseph	40	M	Farmer	24Au02Pj
Biddy	40	F	None	24Au02Pj
Andrew	17	M	None	24Au02Pj
Biddy	9	F	Child	24Au02Pj
Ann	6	F	Child	24Au02Pj
Bessey	1	F	Child	24Au02Pj
DORSEY, Henry	30	M	Clerk	24Au02Pj
GOLDEN, Martha	60	F	Unknown	24Au02Pj
CORNIFF, Margaret	18	F	Sister	24Au02Pj
MULDOON, John	20	M	Laborer	24Au02Pj
DUNN, John	25	M	Laborer	24Au02Pj
BRICKLEY, John	30	M	Laborer	24Au02Pj
ADAMS, Margaret	50	F	None	24Au02Pj
Mary	20	F	None	24Au02Pj
John	17	M	None	24Au02Pj
CORLISS, Biddy	30	F	Wife	24Au02Pj
Mary	5	F	Child	24Au02Pj
BROFIELD, Margaret	16	F	Servant	24Au02Pj
DUNMOODY, Bridget	22	F	Servant	24Au02Pj
BUCKLIN, Margaret	36	F	Wife	24Au02Pj
CARROLL, Mary	34	F	Sister	24Au02Pj
Biddy	16	F	None	24Au02Pj
MARLIN, Pat	20	M	Laborer	24Au02Pj
Ann	18	F	None	24Au02Pj
Frank	8	M	Child	24Au02Pj
John	6	M	Child	24Au02Pj
Rundy	4	M	Child	24Au02Pj
MULLIN, James	18	M	Laborer	24Au02Pj
FINN, Margaret	32	F	Wife	24Au02Pj
Mary	9	F	Child	24Au02Pj
Eliza	7	F	Child	24Au02Pj
Bridget	3	F	Child	24Au02Pj
OHARA, Bridget	18	F	Servant	24Au02Pj
SMITH, Biddy	20	F	Servant	24Au02Pj
GUNTHER, Ann	18	F	Servant	24Au02Pj
QUILL, Alice	30	F	Wife	24Au02Pj
Teddy	12	M	None	24Au02Pj
Davy	10	M	None	24Au02Pj
Alice	.10	F	Infant	24Au02Pj
HERSON, Catherine	18	F	Servant	24Au02Pj
KANE, John	25	M	Laborer	24Au02Pj
CONNELL, Patrick	22	M	Laborer	24Au02Pj
Thomas	22	M	Laborer	24Au02Pj
FARRELL, Timothy	25	M	Laborer	24Au02Pj
PERKINS, William	23	M	Laborer	24Au02Pj
WARD, Michael	18	M	Clerk	24Au02Pj
GILMOUR, Archibald	24	M	Imcht	24Au02Pj
SILLER, Joseph	32	M	Shopkeeper	24Au02Pj
Richard	23	M	Miner	24Au02Pj
MAHER, Mary	12	F	None	24Au02Pj
CULLEN, Mary	23	F	Servant	24Au02Pj
BERRY, John	30	M	Farmer	24Au02Pj
BOYLE, Teresa	60	F	Unknown	24Au02Pj
LINES, Mary	50	F	Unknown	24Au02Pj
Sarah	14	F	None	24Au02Pj
John	12	M	None	24Au02Pj
Patrick	7	M	Child	24Au02Pj
HORN, Catherine	14	F	Servant	24Au02Pj
MURPHY, John	28	M	Laborer	24Au02Pj
Died-At-Sea				
Catherine	28	F	Servant	24Au02Pj
KEY, Catherine	23	F	Servant	24Au02Pj
CARROLL, Judy	19	F	Servant	24Au02Pj
LARKIN, Ann	22	F	Servant	24Au02Pj
MACNAMARA, Ellen	24	F	Wife	24Au02Pj
Ann	.03	F	Infant	24Au02Pj
MILLAN, Ann	21	F	Servant	24Au02Pj
GREEN, Michael	20	M	Laborer	24Au02Pj
MACCORMICK, John	25	M	Laborer	24Au02Pj
RYAN, Ann	22	F	Sister	24Au02Pj
CORBITT, Michael	45	M	Laborer	24Au02Pj
Joanna	35	F	None	24Au02Pj
Patrick	12	M	None	24Au02Pj
Mary	10	F	None	24Au02Pj
William	9	M	Child	24Au02Pj
Joanna	8	F	Child	24Au02Pj
Michael	6	M	Child	24Au02Pj
John	5	M	Child	24Au02Pj
Bridget	3	F	Child	24Au02Pj
Martin	.06	M	Infant	24Au02Pj
PIERSALL, John	28	M	Laborer	24Au02Pj
Eliza	26	F	None	24Au02Pj
Catherine	26	F	None	24Au02Pj
William	1	M	Child	24Au02Pj

NAMES OF PASSENGERS	AGE	SEX	OCCUPATIONS	DATE PORT SHIP
BARRON, James	21	M	Laborer	24Au02Pj
KELLY, Phill.	34	M	Laborer	24Au02Pj
CONDON, Luke	19	M	Blacksmith	24Au02Pj
MAHER, Timothy	40	M	Laborer	24Au02Pj
Died-At-Sea				
BUTLER, Ketty	12	F	Servant	24Au02Pj
MACCORMICK, Edward	19	M	Laborer	24Au02Pj
Ann	10	F	None	24Au02Pj
FLAMMERRY, Margaret	20	F	Servant	24Au02Pj
GAFFNEY, Michael	28	M	Laborer	24Au02Pj
Mary	20	F	Servant	24Au02Pj
FARRALL, Patrick	36	M	Laborer	24Au02Pj
Judy	32	F	None	24Au02Pj
Susan	6	F	Child	24Au02Pj
Catherine	4	F	Child	24Au02Pj
Edward	.10	M	Infant	24Au02Pj
CARNEY, John	18	M	Laborer	24Au02Pj
FINNIGAN, Michael	18	M	Laborer	24Au02Pj
GULLOON, Edward	24	M	Laborer	24Au02Pj
MADDEN, Jane	19	F	Servant	24Au02Pj
WARD, Bridget	17	F	Servant	24Au02Pj
DELANEY, Mary	23	F	Servant	24Au02Pj
MACDONALD, Peter	22	M	Laborer	24Au02Pj
Peter	18	M	Laborer	24Au02Pj
CARR, William	22	M	Coachman	24Au02Pj
CLARK, Lawrence	34	M	Laborer	24Au02Pj
GAFNEY, Francis	30	M	Shopkeeper	24Au02Pj
SHORT, Peter	38	M	Laborer	24Au02Pj
Mary	30	F	None	24Au02Pj
LORLER, Mary	45	F	Wife	24Au02Pj
CORNELL, Margaret	20	F	Sister	24Au02Pj
BRYAN, Thomas	25	M	Laborer	24Au02Pj
RYAN, Catherine	60	F	Unknown	24Au02Pj
BRENNAN, Patrick	35	M	Laborer	24Au02Pj
Jane	30	F	None	24Au02Pj
Patrick	8	M	Child	24Au02Pj
GRADY, Nancy	50	F	Unknown	24Au02Pj
CONNOR, Betty	21	F	Servant	24Au02Pj
KELLEY, Michael	22	M	Smith	24Au02Pj
JENKINS, William	22	M	Laborer	24Au02Pj
WHALAN, Jerry	24	M	Laborer	24Au02Pj
BURKE, Mary	32	F	Servant	24Au02Pj
Patrick	14	M	None	24Au02Pj
LENNAN, Bridget	23	F	Servant	24Au02Pj
MANAHAN, John	34	M	Laborer	24Au02Pj
Died-At-Sea				
Bridget	30	F	None	24Au02Pj
Margaret	9	F	Child	24Au02Pj
Thomas	8	M	Child	24Au02Pj
Michael	.11	M	Infant	24Au02Pj
Died-At-Sea				
MOONEY, William	22	M	Laborer	24Au02Pj
MANHERRIN, Pat	20	M	Baker	24Au02Pj
HARPER, John	22	M	Laborer	24Au02Pj
DONELLAN, Catherine	18	F	Servant	24Au02Pj
WARD, Eliza	21	F	Servant	24Au02Pj
COOLAN, Mary	14	F	Servant	24Au02Pj
Phil	18	M	Laborer	24Au02Pj
Edward	22	M	Laborer	24Au02Pj
John	20	M	Laborer	24Au02Pj
DENNISSEY, Michael	22	M	Laborer	24Au02Pj
REYNOLDS, Mary	33	F	Wife	24Au02Pj
Mary	10	F	None	24Au02Pj
Ann	6	F	Child	24Au02Pj
Thomas	13	M	None	24Au02Pj

SARAH-SANDS 25 AUGUST 1849

From Liverpool

NAMES OF PASSENGERS	AGE	SEX	OCCUPATIONS	DATE PORT SHIP
WALMSLEY, John	18	M	Gentleman	25Au02Dm
WOOD, Fanny	50	F	Unknown	25Au02Dm
Ann	20	F	Unknown	25Au02Dm
STEVENSON, Andrew-Thos	21	M	Gentleman	25Au02Dm
LOWRY, Joseph	30	M	Merchant	25Au02Dm
MCNEALE, Neil	24	M	Cver	25Au02Dm
MCNAMARA, James	40	M	Gentleman	25Au02Dm
BRABAZON, Timothy	38	M	Trader	25Au02Dm
George	3	M	Child	25Au02Dm
WILLIAMS, John	21	M	Farmer	25Au02Dm
MCCAW, John	24	M	Farmer	25Au02Dm
MILLS, James	32	M	Gentleman	25Au02Dm
HANSON, James	30	M	Spinner	25Au02Dm
WARD, Elizabeth	38	F	None	25Au02Dm
Ann	31	F	None	25Au02Dm
Mary	19	F	None	25Au02Dm
Henry	9	M	Child	25Au02Dm
Joseph	7	M	Child	25Au02Dm
James	5	M	Child	25Au02Dm
Thomas	2	M	Child	25Au02Dm
MCCABE, Catherine	22	F	None	25Au02Dm
LYNCH, Catherine	18	F	None	25Au02Dm
GIBSON, Eliza	32	F	None	25Au02Dm
Joseph	6	M	Child	25Au02Dm
Mary	4	F	Child	25Au02Dm
Jno.	3	M	Child	25Au02Dm
Catherine	2	F	Child	25Au02Dm
RUTHERFORD, Joseph	22	M	Farmer	25Au02Dm
HEADON, Michael	24	M	Smith	25Au02Dm
BURKE, John	32	M	Farmer	25Au02Dm
NOONEY, James	27	M	Laborer	25Au02Dm
SMITH, John	19	M	Btnm	25Au02Dm
MARKLEW, Sarah	19	F	None	25Au02Dm
DAVIS, Jane	28	F	None	25Au02Dm
Julia	4	F	Child	25Au02Dm
GARLAND, Edwd.A.	30	M	Painter	25Au02Dm
ARTHURS, Nancy	20	F	None	25Au02Dm

LINDEN 25 AUGUST 1849

From Sligo

NAMES OF PASSENGERS	AGE	SEX	OCCUPATIONS	DATE PORT SHIP
MCGOWAN, Jean	19	F	Spinster	25Au21Eo
RUANE, Ann	24	F	Spinster	25Au21Eo
MCMORD, Pat	18	M	Laborer	25Au21Eo
John	.02	M	Infant	25Au21Eo
Mary	22	F	Spinster	25Au21Eo
BRENAN, Mary	20	F	Spinster	25Au21Eo
BREHENY, Mary	19	F	Spinster	25Au21Eo
HOY, Catheren	22	F	Spinster	25Au21Eo
BOID, Rose-A.	19	F	Spinster	25Au21Eo
Catherine	12	F	Spinster	25Au21Eo
OATS, Pat	40	M	Laborer	25Au21Eo
WALSH, Antony	40	M	Laborer	25Au21Eo
DERAM, Richard	50	M	Shopkeeper	25Au21Eo
MCMORD, Barney	25	M	Laborer	25Au21Eo
Mary	21	F	Spinster	25Au21Eo
PALMOR, Bridget	16	F	Spinster	25Au21Eo
Mary	18	F	Unknown	25Au21Eo

NAMES OF PASSENGERS		AGE	SEX	OCCUPATIONS	DATE PORT SHIP
BANKS, John		25	M	Laborer	25Au21Eo
GALLAGHER, Catherine		20	F	Spinster	25Au21Eo
BLACK, James		25	M	Laborer	25Au21Eo
Elisa.		23	F	Matron	25Au21Eo
Daniel		5	M	Child	25Au21Eo
Mary-L.		2	F	Child	25Au21Eo
William-L.		.11	M	Infant	25Au21Eo
Hana		.01	F	Infant	25Au21Eo
BARRET, Mary		30	F	Matron	25Au21Eo
Honor		50	F	Matron	25Au21Eo
Bridget		3	F	Child	25Au21Eo
HEGGINS, Bess		18	F	Spinster	25Au21Eo
GAHAGAN, Charles		14	M	Laborer	25Au21Eo
CONNEL, Pat		5	M	Child	25Au21Eo
Michael		4	M	Child	25Au21Eo
Henry		.11	M	Infant	25Au21Eo
DEVIT, Pat		20	M	Laborer	25Au21Eo
Margret		15	F	Spinster	25Au21Eo
SWEENY, Bernard		18	M	Laborer	25Au21Eo
HENEGHAN, Michael		18	M	Laborer	25Au21Eo
MCCERRICK, Bridget		18	F	Spinster	25Au21Eo
RILLEY, Jean		16	F	Spinster	25Au21Eo
Jean		19	F	Spinster	25Au21Eo
Charles		24	M	Hatter	25Au21Eo
CRYSTER, Margret		19	F	Spinster	25Au21Eo
BURNE, Pat		17	M	Laborer	25Au21Eo
BURK, Pat		55	M	Shopkeeper	25Au21Eo
Mary-A.		54	F	Wife	25Au21Eo
BARRET, Frances		20	M	Laborer	25Au21Eo
Mary		14	F	Spinster	25Au21Eo
LANGAN, Michael		17	M	Laborer	25Au21Eo
ANDERSON, Bess		17	F	Spinster	25Au21Eo
Stephen		15	M	Laborer	25Au21Eo
DIXON, Bridget		41	F	Matron	25Au21Eo
Jas.		11	M	Unknown	25Au21Eo
Mary		9	F	Child	25Au21Eo
Pat		7	M	Child	25Au21Eo
Catherine		2	F	Child	25Au21Eo
Thos.		1	M	Child	25Au21Eo
GORMAN, Richard		16	M	Laborer	25Au21Eo
CONNELLY, Jean		13	F	Spinster	25Au21Eo
HIGGINS, Ann		10	F	Spinster	25Au21Eo
KEAVENY, Thos.		18	M	Laborer	25Au21Eo
FALK, Thos.		28	M	Shoemaker	25Au21Eo
OBRIAN, John		20	M	Laborer	25Au21Eo
HIGGINS, Michael		24	M	Laborer	25Au21Eo
MCGUIRE, Hugh		25	M	Shopkeeper	25Au21Eo
Catherine		25	F	Wife	25Au21Eo
Honor	(D)	10	F	None	25Au21Eo
Pat	(S)	8	M	Child	25Au21Eo
Charles	(S)	2	M	Child	25Au21Eo
Charles		22	M	Laborer	25Au21Eo
DINISON, Barthly		30	M	Laborer	25Au21Eo
Margaret		25	F	Matron	25Au21Eo
Ann	(D)	3	F	Child	25Au21Eo
CREAN, Mary		40	F	Matron	25Au21Eo
TIMLIN, Charlet		20	F	Spinster	25Au21Eo
SAYNY, Celia		20	F	Spinster	25Au21Eo
Esibela		22	F	Spinster	25Au21Eo
EVANS, Maria		19	F	Spinster	25Au21Eo
HEALY, Mary		19	F	Spinster	25Au21Eo
FLYN, Ann		6	F	Child	25Au21Eo
OHARA, Bridget		24	F	Spinster	25Au21Eo
Elenor		16	F	Spinster	25Au21Eo
GILLMARTIN, Daniel		56	M	Farmer	25Au21Eo
Mary		21	F	Spinster	25Au21Eo
Bridget		19	F	Spinster	25Au21Eo
Ann		13	F	None	25Au21Eo
BRADLY, Mary		20	F	Spinster	25Au21Eo
SYNN, Pat		29	M	Smith	25Au21Eo
Mary	(W)	29	F	None	25Au21Eo
Winifred	(D)	6	F	Child	25Au21Eo
Michael	(S)	3	M	Child	25Au21Eo
Bridget	(D)	00	F	Unknown	25Au21Eo
CALLAGHAN, Ann		15	F	Spinster	25Au21Eo
BURK, Richard		37	M	Mason	25Au21Eo
Bridget		22	F	Wife	25Au21Eo
Margaret		.11	F	Infant	25Au21Eo
FLYN, Pat		24	M	Clerk	25Au21Eo
MCENTIRE, Owen		40	M	Laborer	25Au21Eo
BLACK, Thos.		24	M	Laborer	25Au21Eo
MCGOWAN, Bridget		21	F	Spinster	25Au21Eo
CAVAND, Honor		28	F	Spinster	25Au21Eo
COSGROVE, Sarah		23	F	Spinster	25Au21Eo
BELGY, Mary		.02	F	Infant	25Au21Eo
REED, George		19	M	Laborer	25Au21Eo
MCGUIRE, Ann		25	F	Spinster	25Au21Eo
Thos.		21	M	Laborer	25Au21Eo
Pat		19	M	Laborer	25Au21Eo
Jas.		17	M	Laborer	25Au21Eo
SLEVIN, Mary		20	F	Spinster	25Au21Eo
HUGHES, Mary		22	F	Spinster	25Au21Eo
Pat		20	M	Unknown	25Au21Eo
CONLAN, Ann		20	F	Spinster	25Au21Eo
Honor		22	F	Spinster	25Au21Eo
PALMOR, Margret		23	F	Spinster	25Au21Eo
BLACK, Sarah		26	F	Spinster	25Au21Eo
Catherine	(D)	10	F	None	25Au21Eo
CONLAN, Frances		2	M	Child	25Au21Eo
MCGLOUGHLIN, Thos.		40	M	Laborer	25Au21Eo
GILLON, Catherine		18	F	Spinster	25Au21Eo
CONNOR, Bridget		12	F	Spinster	25Au21Eo
RYAN, Bridget		22	F	Spinster	25Au21Eo
BEGLING, Arthur		40	M	Laborer	25Au21Eo
FEENY, Margret		20	F	Spinster	25Au21Eo
BROWN, Thos.		40	M	Laborer	25Au21Eo
SMITH, Martin		22	M	Laborer	25Au21Eo
Catherine		60	F	Matron	25Au21Eo
Honor		20	F	Spinster	25Au21Eo
GRIMES, Ann		20	F	Spinster	25Au21Eo
HENRY, Andrew		33	M	Farmer	25Au21Eo
CAR, Robert		33	M	Carpenter	25Au21Eo
IRWIN, Mary		23	F	Spinster	25Au21Eo
DIXON, Daniel		18	M	Laborer	25Au21Eo
HUNT, Winifred		50	F	Matron	25Au21Eo
Winifred	(D)	12	F	None	25Au21Eo
CARMICK, Edward		48	M	Unknown	25Au21Eo
Elenor		40	F	Unknown	25Au21Eo
Bridget		8	F	Child	25Au21Eo
Mary-A.		6	F	Child	25Au21Eo
Patk.		5	M	Child	25Au21Eo
John		.10	M	Infant	25Au21Eo
Edmond		.10	M	Infant	25Au21Eo
MCGLOUGHLIN, Pat		19	M	Unknown	25Au21Eo
Maria		20	F	Unknown	25Au21Eo
CORMICK, Mary		17	F	Unknown	25Au21Eo
PHIBBS, Thos.		67	M	Unknown	25Au21Eo
GAHAGAN, Letty		30	F	Matron	25Au21Eo

HALCYON 25 AUGUST 1849

From Liverpool

NAMES OF PASSENGERS	AGE	SEX	OCCUPATIONS	DATE PORT SHIP
ANDERSON, John	29	M	Surgeon	25Au02P
U-Mrs.	27	F	Unknown	25Au02P
Elizabeth	8	F	Child	25Au02P
Maria	6	F	Child	25Au02P
William	.07	M	Infant	25Au02P
JORDAN, William	38	M	Clerk	25Au02P
Sarah	39	F	Housekeeper	25Au02P
FORD, Thomas	18	M	Stableman	25Au02P
FANNAHAN, James	17	M	Tailor	25Au02P
CASSIDY, Henry	45	M	Unknown	25Au02P
MCCULLOGH, Brig.	18	F	Servant	25Au02P

NAMES OF PASSENGERS		AGE	SEX	OCCUPATIONS	DATE PORT SHIP
ROURKE, Patk.		27	M	Sawer	25Au02Pk
HACKET, Margaret		20	F	Servant	25Au02Pk
GOLDILZER, Francis		35	M	Clock Maker	25Au02Pk
DONELLY, Mary		15	F	Servant	25Au02Pk
MALOY, Bart.		32	M	Carpenter	25Au02Pk
PERCY, Alex.		34	M	Laborer	25Au02Pk
MCCANN, Pat.		20	M	Laborer	25Au02Pk
FITZSIMMONS, Catharine		19	F	Servant	25Au02Pk
ARNOLS, James		00	M	Unknown	25Au02Pk
IGO, Patk.		19	M	Laborer	25Au02Pk
Honora		17	F	Shoemaker	25Au02Pk
SOMMERS, Bernard		24	M	Shoemaker	25Au02Pk
KELLY, Sarah		23	F	Housekeeper	25Au02Pk
DEWINE, Bernard		30	M	Laborer	25Au02Pk
Mary		23	F	Wife	25Au02Pk
Mich.		17	M	Laborer	25Au02Pk
Catharine		3	F	Child	25Au02Pk
Pat		2	M	Child	25Au02Pk
John		.00	M	Infant	25Au02Pk
Jno.		17	M	Unknown	25Au02Pk
BYRNE, Eleanor		17	F	Unknown	25Au02Pk
GRUNDY, Jno.		25	M	Painter	25Au02Pk
LAWLER, James		24	M	Laborer	25Au02Pk
Mary		27	F	Unknown	25Au02Pk
Judy		22	F	Unknown	25Au02Pk
Judy		3	F	Child	25Au02Pk
OATES, Barney		26	M	Laborer	25Au02Pk
LEE, Peter		22	M	Laborer	25Au02Pk
HUNT, Mary		25	F	Weaver	25Au02Pk
LEYLAND, Mary		36	F	Seamstress	25Au02Pk
CARROL, Margaret		23	F	Car Driver	25Au02Pk
SHARKETT, Ann		30	F	Seamstress	25Au02Pk
Margaret		6	F	Child	25Au02Pk
MALLON, Charles		34	M	Laborer	25Au02Pk
Ann		30	F	Housewife	25Au02Pk
Ann		13	F	None	25Au02Pk
Maria		10	F	None	25Au02Pk
Margaret		4	F	Child	25Au02Pk
James		3	M	Child	25Au02Pk
Elizabeth		.03	F	Infant	25Au02Pk
MCGUIRE, Michael		18	M	Laborer	25Au02Pk
CULLEN, Michael		18	M	Clerk	25Au02Pk
ENGLAND, James		30	M	Mason	25Au02Pk
Wm.		28	M	Mason	25Au02Pk
SAWYERS, James		30	M	Carpenter	25Au02Pk
BURKE, Wm.		40	M	Laborer	25Au02Pk
Catharine		32	F	Housekeeper	25Au02Pk
Jno.		13	M	Housekeeper	25Au02Pk
Julia		11	F	Housekeeper	25Au02Pk
Anna		9	F	Child	25Au02Pk
Margaret		6	F	Child	25Au02Pk
Mary		3	F	Child	25Au02Pk
Thos.		.11	M	Infant	25Au02Pk
ROWLY, James		34	M	Scholar	25Au02Pk
RYAN, Mary		40	F	Housekeeper	25Au02Pk
LANE, Steven		22	M	Laborer	25Au02Pk
U-Mrs.		21	F	Laborer	25Au02Pk
John		.11	M	Infant	25Au02Pk
MCGRAIL, Paul		24	M	Laborer	25Au02Pk
COSTELLO, Mary		18	F	Servant	25Au02Pk
BIGLEY, Bridget		20	F	Servant	25Au02Pk
HOGAN, Jno.		18	M	Laborer	25Au02Pk
Bridget		18	F	Servant	25Au02Pk
HAYES, Eawd.		17	M	Servant	25Au02Pk
ROLAN, Jno.		17	M	Servant	25Au02Pk
MCGRATH, John		35	M	Clerk	25Au02Pk
U-Mrs.	(W)	30	F	Housekeeper	25Au02Pk
RAHALY, Michl.	(W)	22	M	Laborer	25Au02Pk
RAILLY, Peter	(W)	23	M	Laborer	25Au02Pk
Bridget	(W)	25	F	Servant	25Au02Pk
WALLINGHAM, James	(W)	25	M	Laborer	25Au02Pk
WATERS, Ann	(W)	29	F	Servant	25Au02Pk
CHAPPELL, Ann	(W)	40	F	Housekeeper	25Au02Pk
Danl.	(W)	20	M	Printer	25Au02Pk
Lewis	(W)	12	M	Unknown	25Au02Pk
CHAPPELL, Edwd.	(W)	7	M	Child	25Au02Pk
John	(W)	3	M	Child	25Au02Pk
ONEAL, John	(W)	28	M	Millwright	25Au02Pk
Ann		21	F	Housekeeper	25Au02Pk
Eliza.		.09	F	Infant	25Au02Pk
POWER, Sarah		30	F	Dressmaker	25Au02Pk
PERCY, James		24	M	Laborer	25Au02Pk
GOLDEN, James		19	M	Laborer	25Au02Pk
QUIRK, Judith		54	F	Servant	25Au02Pk
KEATENS, Jean		19	F	Servant	25Au02Pk
HUGGARD, Jane		20	F	Housekeeper	25Au02Pk
Barbara		18	F	Housekeeper	25Au02Pk
Ann		17	F	Housekeeper	25Au02Pk
CURTIN, David		27	M	Servant	25Au02Pk
CRONIN, Elen		17	F	Servant	25Au02Pk
Pat.		13	M	Servant	25Au02Pk
BUCKLEY, Dennis		24	M	Paper Maker	25Au02Pk
MURPHY, Maurice		19	M	Paper Maker	25Au02Pk
FOX, Michael		34	M	Clock Maker	25Au02Pk
Mary-J.		17	F	Unknown	25Au02Pk
LYONS, Bridget		26	F	Housekeeper	25Au02Pk
Pat		5	M	Child	25Au02Pk
TRACY, Pat		19	M	Servant	25Au02Pk
Jane		30	F	Servant	25Au02Pk
MCGARITY, Sarah		30	F	Servant	25Au02Pk
Sarah		2	F	Child	25Au02Pk
MCKINNA, James		17	M	Servant	25Au02Pk
MCCUE, Sarah		18	F	Servant	25Au02Pk
KEAN, Mary		17	F	Servant	25Au02Pk
BRADY, Mary		60	F	Servant	25Au02Pk
Jams		25	M	Laborer	25Au02Pk
BIRMINGHAM, Mary-A.		35	F	Dressmaker	25Au02Pk
William		00	M	Servant	25Au02Pk
KEENAN, Mary		40	F	Housekeeper	25Au02Pk
Mary		13	F	Housekeeper	25Au02Pk
Lawrence		9	M	Child	25Au02Pk
Felix		6	M	Child	25Au02Pk
MCNEAL, James		9	M	Child	25Au02Pk
DONNELLY, Mary		20	F	Servant	25Au02Pk
MCGUIRE, Martin		26	M	Laborer	25Au02Pk
LANGAN, Mary-A.		12	F	Unknown	25Au02Pk
Bridget		8	F	Child	25Au02Pk
Michl.		6	M	Child	25Au02Pk
John		4	M	Child	25Au02Pk
Catharine		2	F	Child	25Au02Pk
LENNET, Cecilia		17	F	Servant	25Au02Pk
GILSHENNON, Michael		12	M	Servant	25Au02Pk
LAYNG, Jane		20	F	Milliner	25Au02Pk
DUFFY, James		20	M	Coachman	25Au02Pk
MCMERCHEN, Bernard		11	M	Servant	25Au02Pk
MCMERKEN, Mary		10	F	Servant	25Au02Pk
MCARDLE, Mary-A.		14	F	Servant	25Au02Pk
Rachel		16	F	Servant	25Au02Pk
Catharine		11	F	Servant	25Au02Pk
GANNON, Bridget		12	F	Servant	25Au02Pk
Margaret		10	F	Servant	25Au02Pk
CHUTE, Margaret		16	F	Servant	25Au02Pk
Mary		30	F	Servant	25Au02Pk
LYNCH, Ann		6	F	Child	25Au02Pk
KELLY, Bridget		16	F	Servant	25Au02Pk
HOLOHAN, Thomas		26	M	Stctr	25Au02Pk
OROURKE, Danl.		27	M	Stctr	25Au02Pk
MCHALE, James		18	M	Servant	25Au02Pk
WALLACE, John		18	M	Servant	25Au02Pk
FISHER, Ellen-S.		18	F	Servant	25Au02Pk
Peggy		13	F	Servant	25Au02Pk
DANIEL, Ann		24	F	Bomkr	25Au02Pk
William		.11	M	Infant	25Au02Pk
Bridget		36	F	Unknown	25Au02Pk
MANIX, Dennis		20	M	Laborer	25Au02Pk
Michl.		7	M	Child	25Au02Pk
CONNELL, Pat		19	M	Laborer	25Au02Pk
M---CY, Bridget		7	F	Child	25Au02Pk
FLOOD, Michl.		22	M	Child	25Au02Pk
Pat		23	M	Laborer	25Au02Pk

NAMES OF PASSENGERS	AGE	SEX	OCCUPATIONS	DATE PORT SHIP
SULLIVAN, Dennis	15	M	Laborer	25Au02Pk
CUNNINGHAM, James	25	M	Laborer	25Au02Pk
SMITH, Mary	13	F	Servant	25Au02Pk
DUNN, Susan	30	F	Weaver	25Au02Pk
Pat	18	M	Weaver	25Au02Pk
Anty	11	F	Weaver	25Au02Pk
FEALY, Mary	28	F	Servant	25Au02Pk
MCGEE, Thomas	26	M	Servant	25Au02Pk
TROY, Pat	16	M	Servant	25Au02Pk
SLATTERY, Bridget	20	F	Servant	25Au02Pk
KELLY, Ann	16	F	Servant	25Au02Pk
MEAGHER, Kate	22	F	Servant	25Au02Pk
BRADSHAW, Bridget	18	F	Servant	25Au02Pk
Wm.	27	M	Laborer	25Au02Pk
CONNER, Catharine	14	F	Laborer	25Au02Pk
RILEY, Pat	18	M	Laborer	25Au02Pk
GRIMES, Felix	24	M	Laborer	25Au02Pk
TYRRELL, Eawd.	25	M	Laborer	25Au02Pk
QUINN, Wm.	19	M	Laborer	25Au02Pk
SHAUGHNESSY, Pat	20	M	Laborer	25Au02Pk
BLAIR, Jane	25	F	Servant	25Au02Pk
Martha	3	F	Child	25Au02Pk
Sarah	.07	F	Infant	25Au02Pk
RAGAN, Mary-A.	50	F	Servant	25Au02Pk
Sarah	5	F	Child	25Au02Pk
Maria	3	F	Child	25Au02Pk
DALTON, John	24	M	Carpenter	25Au02Pk
RICE, Alice	30	F	Housekeeper	25Au02Pk
Edwd.	8	M	Child	25Au02Pk
Michael	6	M	Child	25Au02Pk
Mary	2	F	Child	25Au02Pk
MULLEN, William	16	M	Servant	25Au02Pk
CARR, Margaret	30	F	Servant	25Au02Pk
MCGINNISS, Pat	25	M	Laborer	25Au02Pk
KEEFE, Wm.	17	M	Laborer	25Au02Pk
DUKE, Martha	15	M	Laborer	25Au02Pk
KANE, Pat	34	M	Laborer	25Au02Pk
COGLIN, Martin	45	M	Weaver	25Au02Pk
CASH, Jere.	29	M	Laborer	25Au02Pk
DELANY, Edwd.	44	M	Weigher	25Au02Pk
DEVON, Edwd.	30	M	Laborer	25Au02Pk
WALCH, Thomas	30	M	Laborer	25Au02Pk
DILLON, John	28	M	Laborer	25Au02Pk
BURKE, William	50	M	Laborer	25Au02Pk
U-Mrs.	50	F	Laborer	25Au02Pk
FLINN, Pat	3	M	Child	25Au02Pk
MAHER, William	22	M	Laborer	25Au02Pk
DOYLE, John	22	M	Laborer	25Au02Pk
SHERLOCK, Margaret	28	M	Laborer	25Au02Pk
Margaret	79	F	Unknown	25Au02Pk
Pat	12	M	Laborer	25Au02Pk
KELLY, Jane	40	F	Laborer	25Au02Pk
STEWART, Catharine	30	F	Laborer	25Au02Pk
MCCOY, William	16	M	Laborer	25Au02Pk
MCKELLOPP, John	18	M	Laborer	25Au02Pk
ROBINSON, Robert	16	M	Laborer	25Au02Pk
MORGAN, John	19	M	Laborer	25Au02Pk
BANNON, Peter	20	M	Laborer	25Au02Pk
GIBBON, Peter	24	M	Carter	25Au02Pk
MALONY, Michael	18	M	Grocer	25Au02Pk
STOKES, Michael	30	M	Laborer	25Au02Pk
RILEY, Winnie	20	F	Laborer	25Au02Pk
ROANEY, Bridget	19	F	Laborer	25Au02Pk
GILNOE, Michael	21	M	Laborer	25Au02Pk
SHELLY, Mary	52	F	Laborer	25Au02Pk
Margaret	12	F	Unknown	25Au02Pk
DONALD, James	19	M	Laborer	25Au02Pk
FENAGHTY, Steven	20	M	Laborer	25Au02Pk
HOGAN, Dan	28	M	Laborer	25Au02Pk
MAGUIRE, Margaret	60	F	Laborer	25Au02Pk
ANDERSON, U	.00	U	Infant	25Au02Pk
Born-At-Sea				

ERIN-GO-BRAGH 25 AUGUST 1849

From Liverpool

NAMES OF PASSENGERS	AGE	SEX	OCCUPATIONS	DATE PORT SHIP
EGAN, Pat	30	M	Laborer	25Au02Pl
LONG, Edwd.	37	M	Laborer	25Au02Pl
MCNAMARA, James	30	M	Laborer	25Au02Pl
FLEMING, Mich.	28	M	Laborer	25Au02Pl
BANNER, Mary	55	F	Matron	25Au02Pl
Peggy	13	F	None	25Au02Pl
Mary	6	F	Child	25Au02Pl
Ellen	4	F	Child	25Au02Pl
Jno.	.00	M	Infant	25Au02Pl
KEEFE, Johno	30	M	Laborer	25Au02Pl
HOUGHTON, Pat	30	M	Laborer	25Au02Pl
CARAN, Arthur	20	M	Laborer	25Au02Pl
GLASGOW, John	30	M	Laborer	25Au02Pl
Margt.	28	F	Matron	25Au02Pl
John	.00	M	Infant	25Au02Pl
SINNOTT, Martin	50	M	Laborer	25Au02Pl
Pat	25	M	Laborer	25Au02Pl
Ned	23	M	Laborer	25Au02Pl
Michl.	20	M	Laborer	25Au02Pl
RUSH, Ann	20	F	Servant	25Au02Pl
FENNON, Rose	25	F	Servant	25Au02Pl
CAMPBELL, John	20	M	Laborer	25Au02Pl
MCKEOWN, Francis	25	M	Laborer	25Au02Pl
SHANNON, Cath.	18	F	Servant	25Au02Pl
CROOTY, John	25	M	Laborer	25Au02Pl
Ellen	19	F	Matron	25Au02Pl
DELANE, John	30	M	Laborer	25Au02Pl
KELLY, James	27	M	Laborer	25Au02Pl
John	.00	M	Infant	25Au02Pl
Bridget	24	F	Matron	25Au02Pl
James	3	M	Child	25Au02Pl
MCMAHON, Pat	50	M	Laborer	25Au02Pl
Mary	30	F	Matron	25Au02Pl
Jane	20	F	Servant	25Au02Pl
Phillip	13	M	None	25Au02Pl
Pat	11	M	None	25Au02Pl
Betsy	8	F	Child	25Au02Pl
Alice	.00	F	Infant	25Au02Pl
KERSELN, Thos.	20	M	None	25Au02Pl
MCGRATH, John	40	M	Laborer	25Au02Pl
MONAHAN, Ann	18	F	Servant	25Au02Pl
Brid.	20	F	Servant	25Au02Pl
S--ION, David	25	M	Laborer	25Au02Pl
Mary	20	F	Matron	25Au02Pl
Mary	.00	F	Infant	25Au02Pl
BARNES, Thomas	32	M	Laborer	25Au02Pl
DARDIN, Jos.	30	M	Laborer	25Au02Pl
Mary	30	F	Servant	25Au02Pl
James	.00	M	Infant	25Au02Pl
JONES, Francis	31	M	Laborer	25Au02Pl
ENGLISH, Mary	40	F	Servant	25Au02Pl
Margt.	13	F	None	25Au02Pl
HOGARTY, James	45	M	Laborer	25Au02Pl
Judith	30	F	Matron	25Au02Pl
CONNOLLY, Brid.	28	F	Servant	25Au02Pl
HEGGARTY, James	11	M	None	25Au02Pl
Peter	9	M	Child	25Au02Pl
Ann	7	F	Child	25Au02Pl
John	6	M	Child	25Au02Pl
Michl.	4	M	Child	25Au02Pl
Thos.	.00	M	Infant	25Au02Pl
DORAN, Michl.	50	M	Laborer	25Au02Pl
Cath.	50	F	Matron	25Au02Pl
Ellen	27	F	Servant	25Au02Pl
Mary	25	F	Servant	25Au02Pl

NAMES OF PASSENGERS	AGE	SEX	OCCUPATIONS	DATE PORT SHIP
DORAN, Robert	22	M	Laborer	25Au02Pl
Edwd.	18	M	Laborer	25Au02Pl
Ally	15	F	Servant	25Au02Pl
Cath.	13	F	None	25Au02Pl
Wm.	11	M	None	25Au02Pl
TYNE, U	21	M	Laborer	25Au02Pl
BRAUGHN, Thos.	26	M	Laborer	25Au02Pl
Margt.	26	F	Servant	25Au02Pl
HAROLD, James	26	M	Laborer	25Au02Pl
MCCOURT, Edwd.	40	M	Laborer	25Au02Pl
GALLAGHER, John	27	M	Laborer	25Au02Pl
Jane	25	F	Matron	25Au02Pl
Susan	.00	F	Infant	25Au02Pl
Palla--, Mary	13	F	None	25Au02Pl
C--NE, Mary-A.	16	F	Servant	25Au02Pl
PRIOR, Pat	16	M	Laborer	25Au02Pl
STACK, Garritt	35	M	Laborer	25Au02Pl
Cath.	30	F	Matron	25Au02Pl
Pat	12	M	None	25Au02Pl
James	9	M	Child	25Au02Pl
John	6	M	Child	25Au02Pl
U	3	M	Child	25Au02Pl
Wm.	.00	M	Infant	25Au02Pl
Thos.	33	M	Laborer	25Au02Pl
SAVAGE, Mic.	36	M	Laborer	25Au02Pl
SMITH, Jos.	20	M	Laborer	25Au02Pl
Mary	40	F	Matron	25Au02Pl
GUY, Ed.	30	M	Laborer	25Au02Pl
BINN, Michl.	30	M	Laborer	25Au02Pl
MCDONALD, Mary	22	F	Servant	25Au02Pl
OBRIEN, Hugh	18	M	Laborer	25Au02Pl
KELLY, Thos.	35	M	Laborer	25Au02Pl
U (W)	35	F	None	25Au02Pl
MCKENNA, John	24	M	Laborer	25Au02Pl
MCHUGH, Ann	25	F	Servant	25Au02Pl
RYAN, Pat	13	M	None	25Au02Pl
LENARD, Thos.	17	M	Laborer	25Au02Pl
Elias	18	M	Laborer	25Au02Pl
OMEARA, Pat	19	M	Laborer	25Au02Pl
Eliz.	13	F	None	25Au02Pl
Agnes	.00	F	Infant	25Au02Pl
BUTLER, Barnard	40	M	Laborer	25Au02Pl
Ann (W)	35	F	None	25Au02Pl
John	2	M	Child	25Au02Pl
Margt.	.00	F	Infant	25Au02Pl
WHELAN, Mary	35	F	Servant	25Au02Pl
FITZPATRICK, Margt.	28	F	Servant	25Au02Pl
DOWLING, John	30	M	Laborer	25Au02Pl
KAVANNAH, Ellen	55	F	Matron	25Au02Pl
Ann	30	F	Servant	25Au02Pl
ANDERSON, Thos.	22	M	Laborer	25Au02Pl
MCLAUGLIN, Jas.	20	M	Laborer	25Au02Pl
CARPENTER, Jas.	35	M	Laborer	25Au02Pl
OBRIEN, Corne.	26	M	Laborer	25Au02Pl
SULLIVAN, Corn.	20	M	Laborer	25Au02Pl
STOCKS, John	18	M	Laborer	25Au02Pl
HONNAN, Dan	30	M	Laborer	25Au02Pl
CONNELL, Nancy	20	F	Servant	25Au02Pl
HIGGINSON, Jas.	18	M	Laborer	25Au02Pl
BANNON, Thos.	30	M	Laborer	25Au02Pl
MOLON, Mich.	30	M	Laborer	25Au02Pl
OBRIEN, Pat	26	M	Laborer	25Au02Pl
RYAN, Mary	24	F	Servant	25Au02Pl
MORAN, Betty	20	F	Servant	25Au02Pl
Fe--E, Judy	20	F	Servant	25Au02Pl
Sa--, Pat	20	M	Laborer	25Au02Pl
SANDERS, John	20	M	Laborer	25Au02Pl
CROWLEY, Pat	20	M	Laborer	25Au02Pl
ROONEY, Pat	29	M	Laborer	25Au02Pl
HANLAN, John	25	M	Laborer	25Au02Pl
HANS, J.	30	M	Laborer	25Au02Pl
C--FF, Jos.	35	M	Laborer	25Au02Pl
MCGOWNE, Alice	30	F	Servant	25Au02Pl
MACKIE, Thos.	26	M	Laborer	25Au02Pl
Ann	23	F	Servant	25Au02Pl
MCCLUNE, Chas.	22	M	Laborer	25Au02Pl
GEARING, Timo.	20	M	Laborer	25Au02Pl
MCLEOD, John	22	M	Laborer	25Au02Pl
LONGHAN, Ellen	35	F	Matron	25Au02Pl
Mary	4	F	Child	25Au02Pl
Brid.	9	F	Child	25Au02Pl
Margt.	.00	F	Infant	25Au02Pl
ROUGHAN, Edwd.	32	M	Laborer	25Au02Pl
Bird.	32	F	Servant	25Au02Pl
Mary	20	F	Servant	25Au02Pl
Ne--M, Wm.	21	M	Laborer	25Au02Pl
HART, Peter	33	M	Laborer	25Au02Pl
Ann	30	F	Matron	25Au02Pl
Mary	5	F	Child	25Au02Pl
Michl.	.00	M	Infant	25Au02Pl
ROBINSON, J.	20	F	Servant	25Au02Pl
DONOGHOE, Cal.	30	M	Laborer	25Au02Pl
DALY, John	40	M	Laborer	25Au02Pl
Margt.	38	F	Matron	25Au02Pl
Died-At-Sea				
Ann	11	F	None	25Au02Pl
Dan	.00	M	Infant	25Au02Pl
James	4	M	Child	25Au02Pl
PEPPER, Pat	39	M	Laborer	25Au02Pl
Bridget	39	F	Matron	25Au02Pl
B.	5	F	Child	25Au02Pl
Mich.	.00	M	Infant	25Au02Pl
ONEILL, T.	30	M	Laborer	25Au02Pl
MARKEY, J.	29	M	Laborer	25Au02Pl
GILL, J.	27	M	Laborer	25Au02Pl
BORSH, J.	28	M	Laborer	25Au02Pl
GILMOUR, J.	30	M	Laborer	25Au02Pl
KELLY, John	31	M	Laborer	25Au02Pl
Ann	27	F	Matron	25Au02Pl
Wm.	.00	M	Infant	25Au02Pl
HARON, John	25	M	Laborer	25Au02Pl
CRARY, John	35	M	Laborer	25Au02Pl
Ann	35	F	Matron	25Au02Pl
Jenny	5	F	Child	25Au02Pl
Ann	.00	F	Infant	25Au02Pl
Biddy	4	F	Child	25Au02Pl
GORE, John	47	M	Laborer	25Au02Pl
HART, Thomas	19	M	Laborer	25Au02Pl
U, James-Erin	.00	M	Infant	25Au02Pl
Born-At-Sea				

FANCHON 25 AUGUST 1849

From Liverpool

NAMES OF PASSENGERS	AGE	SEX	OCCUPATIONS	DATE PORT SHIP
HANNA, Thomas	23	M	Gentleman	25Au02Pm
GRAHAM, Margaret	21	F	Stewardess	25Au02Pm
James	50	M	Cbtmkr	25Au02Pm
GALLAGHER, Dennis	30	M	Carpenter	25Au02Pm
Pat	25	M	Laborer	25Au02Pm
GIBLIN, Thomas	25	M	Mason	25Au02Pm
MCGARITY, Bridget	20	F	Servant	25Au02Pm
GARA, Bridget	40	F	None	25Au02Pm
Died-At-Sea				
Bridget	17	F	None	25Au02Pm
John	8	M	Child	25Au02Pm
Bridget	2	F	Child	25Au02Pm
HAUGHEY, John	40	M	Laborer	25Au02Pm
BOYLE, Ellen	40	F	None	25Au02Pm
Rose	12	F	None	25Au02Pm
Bridget	10	F	None	25Au02Pm
Patrick	9	M	Child	25Au02Pm
James	7	M	Child	25Au02Pm
John	4	M	Child	25Au02Pm

NAMES OF PASSENGERS	AGE	SEX	OCCUPATIONS	DATE PORT SHIP
BOYLE, Miles	.04	M	Infant	25Au02Pm
MCKEORON, Philip	20	M	Nailer	25Au02Pm
Barney	25	M	Nailer	25Au02Pm
Died-At-Sea				
HOLLAND, John	19	M	Laborer	25Au02Pm
SHEEHAN, John	17	M	Laborer	25Au02Pm
HICKEY, Mary	40	F	None	25Au02Pm
Joanna	19	F	Servant	25Au02Pm
Bridgett	16	F	Servant	25Au02Pm
Michael	12	M	None	25Au02Pm
John	10	M	None	25Au02Pm
FITZGERALD, Anna	50	F	None	25Au02Pm
Michael	18	M	Mechanic	25Au02Pm
William	13	M	None	25Au02Pm
Francis	12	M	None	25Au02Pm
Margaret	9	F	Child	25Au02Pm
OBRIEN, Margaret	28	F	Servant	25Au02Pm
Mat	60	M	Mason	25Au02Pm
CASSIDY, Ellen	25	F	Servant	25Au02Pm
DONOHUE, James	24	M	Laborer	25Au02Pm
LAWSON, William	26	M	Clerk	25Au02Pm
KEEFE, Margaret	33	F	Servant	25Au02Pm
Betsey	15	F	Servant	25Au02Pm
LANG, John	19	M	Laborer	25Au02Pm
MCDOUGAL, John	20	M	Engineer	25Au02Pm
SOMMERVILLE, John	18	M	Laborer	25Au02Pm
COWELL, John	22	M	Laborer	25Au02Pm
Eliza	17	F	None	25Au02Pm
NAW, William	25	M	Teamster	25Au02Pm
Catharine	23	F	None	25Au02Pm
William	2	M	Child	25Au02Pm
Judy	22	F	Servant	25Au02Pm
FLANNERY, Thomas	17	M	Servant	25Au02Pm
NELSON, John	23	M	Miner	25Au02Pm
GARVEY, Peter	22	M	Laborer	25Au02Pm
LEVELLE, Patrick	22	M	Joiner	25Au02Pm
RILEY, Bernard	28	M	Laborer	25Au02Pm
BYRNES, Mary	20	F	Servant	25Au02Pm
ROONEY, Thomas	18	M	Laborer	25Au02Pm
Mary	22	F	Servant	25Au02Pm
HOWLAND, Pat	40	M	Laborer	25Au02Pm
DOYLE, Thomas	45	M	Laborer	25Au02Pm
FERGUSON, Eliza	20	F	Servant	25Au02Pm
LEARY, Margaret	22	F	Servant	25Au02Pm
MCMANN, James	18	M	Servant	25Au02Pm
Ann	20	F	Servant	25Au02Pm
MCANNESTRY, Bridget	18	F	Servant	25Au02Pm
CONROY, Rosey	15	F	Servant	25Au02Pm
MARTIN, John	20	M	Laborer	25Au02Pm
DOONEGAN, Bryan	40	M	Laborer	25Au02Pm
MCCORMICK, Thomas	26	M	Weaver	25Au02Pm
MULDOON, Julia	18	F	Servant	25Au02Pm
MCCLUSKEY, James	4	M	Child	25Au02Pm
MCKERNAN, Michael	22	M	Laborer	25Au02Pm
Patrick	18	M	Laborer	25Au02Pm
Philip	8	M	Child	25Au02Pm
PARKER, Ellen	20	F	Servant	25Au02Pm
ROACH, Judah	20	F	Servant	25Au02Pm
BRONEYNE, Judith	25	F	Servant	25Au02Pm
ELLIGATE, Patrick	30	M	Laborer	25Au02Pm
Michael	28	M	Laborer	25Au02Pm
GLEESON, Con.	22	M	Laborer	25Au02Pm
Bridget	16	F	Servant	25Au02Pm
LYNCH, Con.	22	M	Laborer	25Au02Pm
MCDONALD, Bridgett	24	F	Servant	25Au02Pm
Died-At-Sea				
HORREGAN, Margaret	22	F	Servant	25Au02Pm
MURPHY, Mary	16	F	Servant	25Au02Pm
SULLIVAN, Ellen	20	F	Servant	25Au02Pm
HARLOW, Michael	20	M	Laborer	25Au02Pm
Bridgett	18	F	Servant	25Au02Pm
MADDEN, Mary	20	F	Servant	25Au02Pm
TRAINER, Pat	50	M	Cooper	25Au02Pm
Nancy	50	F	None	25Au02Pm
Pat	12	M	None	25Au02Pm
RAFFERTY, Alice	14	F	None	25Au02Pm
DAYLEY, James	18	M	Laborer	25Au02Pm
SLACK, Joseph	50	M	Tailor	25Au02Pm
William	25	M	Tailor	25Au02Pm
THOMPSON, James	28	M	Laborer	25Au02Pm
CORR, Peter	35	M	Laborer	25Au02Pm

ABBY-PRATT 25 AUGUST 1849

From Liverpool

NAMES OF PASSENGERS	AGE	SEX	OCCUPATIONS	DATE PORT SHIP
MILLER, Bess	24	F	Servant	25Au02Pn
Mary	22	F	Servant	25Au02Pn
FARLEY, Owen	50	M	Laborer	25Au02Pn
Owen	56	M	Laborer	25Au02Pn
Died-At-Sea				
MCGAVIN, Bernard	37	M	Laborer	25Au02Pn
Ellen	16	F	Laborer	25Au02Pn
RILEY, Catherine	34	F	Milliner	25Au02Pn
FOLEY, James	22	M	Laborer	25Au02Pn
James	9	M	Child	25Au02Pn
GLARKIN, Mary	34	F	Laborer	25Au02Pn
MARTIN, Lawrence	40	M	Laborer	25Au02Pn
CAMPBELL, Terence	41	M	Weaver	25Au02Pn
Catherine	35	F	None	25Au02Pn
Patrick	3	M	Child	25Au02Pn
Terence	.10	M	Infant	25Au02Pn
QUINN, Bridget	18	F	Servant	25Au02Pn
CURRY, James	36	M	Servant	25Au02Pn
Ellen	36	F	Servant	25Au02Pn
Edmund	3	M	Child	25Au02Pn
Thaddy	.11	M	Infant	25Au02Pn
MACK, Ellen	76	F	Servant	25Au02Pn
REIVES, William	40	M	Servant	25Au02Pn
Bridget	40	F	Servant	25Au02Pn
Mary	9	F	Child	25Au02Pn
Ellen	2	F	Child	25Au02Pn
BRODRICK, James	24	M	Servant	25Au02Pn
Judy	20	F	Servant	25Au02Pn
HINCHEY, Pat	28	M	Carpenter	25Au02Pn
CALLEN, Ann	18	F	Servant	25Au02Pn
CLARKE, James	40	M	Laborer	25Au02Pn
WHALANT, Chas.	40	M	Laborer	25Au02Pn
MCMAHON, Thos.	21	M	Laborer	25Au02Pn
Jas.	16	M	Laborer	25Au02Pn
HALESON, Michael	30	M	Laborer	25Au02Pn
Mary	28	F	Laborer	25Au02Pn
HOULIHAN, Judy	26	F	Laborer	25Au02Pn
MALONY, Mary	21	F	Laborer	25Au02Pn
FINN, Bridget	20	F	Laborer	25Au02Pn
NAUGHTON, Catherine	24	F	Servant	25Au02Pn
HERA, Catherine	20	F	Servant	25Au02Pn
DEMPSEY, Mary	48	F	Servant	25Au02Pn
Ann	24	F	Servant	25Au02Pn
KENNEDY, Mary	48	F	Servant	25Au02Pn
Betsy	7	F	Child	25Au02Pn
Mary	12	F	Servant	25Au02Pn
Sarah	8	F	Child	25Au02Pn
William	6	M	Child	25Au02Pn
SHANNON, Ann	24	F	Servant	25Au02Pn
CARLETON, Samuel	14	F	Servant	25Au02Pn
MONAHAN, Mary	17	F	Servant	25Au02Pn
MCGOVERN, Biddy	28	F	Servant	25Au02Pn
MCGUIRE, Jas.	11	M	Servant	25Au02Pn
Thos.	10	M	Child	25Au02Pn
FARREY, Edward	78	M	Weaver	25Au02Pn
Bridget	23	F	Weaver	25Au02Pn
Ann	19	F	Weaver	25Au02Pn
HAGGERTY, Matt	26	M	Laborer	25Au02Pn

NAMES OF PASSENGERS	AGE	SEX	OCCUPATIONS	DATE PORT SHIP
DOUGHERTY, Ellen	25	F	Laborer	25Au02Pn
Nancy	.11	F	Infant	25Au02Pn
Died-At-Sea				
MCDEVITT, Margaret	26	F	Servant	25Au02Pn
Hannah	4	F	Child	25Au02Pn
MCGARVEY, James	20	M	Laborer	25Au02Pn
DOWLING, Anne	30	F	Laborer	25Au02Pn
Marcella	4	F	Child	25Au02Pn
Peter	.11	M	Infant	25Au02Pn
FLINN, William	35	M	Laborer	25Au02Pn
Catherine	18	F	Laborer	25Au02Pn
GORMAN, John	30	M	Tailor	25Au02Pn
FEALY, Connor	30	M	Laborer	25Au02Pn
Ally	24	F	Laborer	25Au02Pn
MURRAY, John	36	M	Laborer	25Au02Pn
Ann	22	F	Laborer	25Au02Pn
CASSIDY, Mary	30	F	Laborer	25Au02Pn
DUFFY, Mary	22	F	Laborer	25Au02Pn
HUGHES, Sarah	26	F	Servant	25Au02Pn
FRAZER, James	24	M	Laborer	25Au02Pn
Ellen	19	F	Laborer	25Au02Pn
MALONE, Michael	21	M	Laborer	25Au02Pn
MCDONAGH, Winifred	16	F	Servant	25Au02Pn
MOONEY, Catherine	19	F	Servant	25Au02Pn
LEARY, Mary	55	F	Servant	25Au02Pn
Mary-Ann	12	F	Servant	25Au02Pn
William	28	M	Servant	25Au02Pn
Thomas	26	M	Servant	25Au02Pn
Catherine	26	F	Servant	25Au02Pn
Bridget	2	F	Child	25Au02Pn
Mary	.02	F	Infant	25Au02Pn
HEART, Bryan	20	M	Gasfitter	25Au02Pn
KELLY, Anne	30	F	Servant	25Au02Pn
Died-At-Sea				
BYRNES, Catherine	24	F	Servant	25Au02Pn
Died-At-Sea				
Bridget	20	F	Servant	25Au02Pn
Died-At-Sea				
KELLY, John	35	M	Stone Mason	25Au02Pn
CARROLL, William	34	M	Laborer	25Au02Pn
FARRELL, Dennis	22	M	Laborer	25Au02Pn
BRYAN, Biddy	19	F	Laborer	25Au02Pn
KIRWIN, Peter	30	M	Laborer	25Au02Pn
Mary	24	F	Laborer	25Au02Pn
WELSH, Edward	26	M	Laborer	25Au02Pn
SAVAGE, Lawrence	30	M	Laborer	25Au02Pn
STEVENS, Margaret	24	F	Laborer	25Au02Pn
Pat	10	M	Child	25Au02Pn
Stephen	.10	M	Infant	25Au02Pn
PIERCE, Michael	30	M	Stone Mason	25Au02Pn
Catherine	25	F	None	25Au02Pn
Joanna	3	F	Child	25Au02Pn
Mary	.02	F	Infant	25Au02Pn
Thomas	2	M	Child	25Au02Pn
CONNOR, John	27	M	Laborer	25Au02Pn
HUGHES, Pat	23	M	Laborer	25Au02Pn
MCDERMITT, John	37	M	Laborer	25Au02Pn
RENOLDS, Ann	17	F	Laborer	25Au02Pn
HALLORAN, Jas.	28	M	Laborer	25Au02Pn
ROONEY, Susan	30	F	Laborer	25Au02Pn
Pat	.04	M	Infant	25Au02Pn
DORAN, James	22	M	Laborer	25Au02Pn
REILLEY, Pat	20	M	Baker	25Au02Pn
HARRAGAN, Pat	20	M	Blacksmith	25Au02Pn
BOYLE, Patrick	30	M	Blacksmith	25Au02Pn
Jane	22	F	None	25Au02Pn
Henry	.05	M	Infant	25Au02Pn
HAY, Laughlin	40	M	Laborer	25Au02Pn
MCENERNEY, Michael	34	M	Laborer	25Au02Pn
REILLEY, John	35	M	Laborer	25Au02Pn
SHANLEY, Ellen	27	F	Laborer	25Au02Pn
HOGG, Thos.	28	M	Whitesmith	25Au02Pn
FAIRLEY, Elizth.	21	F	Servant	25Au02Pn
GROGAN, Matilda	18	F	Servant	25Au02Pn
MCCABE, Mary	25	F	Laborer	25Au02Pn

NAMES OF PASSENGERS	AGE	SEX	OCCUPATIONS	DATE PORT SHIP
MCCABE, Catherine	.03	F	Infant	25Au02Pn
STEWART, Hugh-K.	22	M	Farmer	25Au02Pn
Eliza.Jane	18	F	None	25Au02Pn
MCMURRAY, Matthew	20	M	Laborer	25Au02Pn
GEORGE, John	20	M	Laborer	25Au02Pn
GROGAN, Michael	43	M	Japanner	25Au02Pn
MAXWELL, Christopher	20	M	Laborer	25Au02Pn
Richard	18	M	Laborer	25Au02Pn
RILEY, Patt	22	M	Laborer	25Au02Pn
LAWLESS, James	50	M	Laborer	25Au02Pn
Ellen	46	F	None	25Au02Pn
Lucy	13	F	None	25Au02Pn
Ellen	11	F	None	25Au02Pn
Joseph	8	M	Child	25Au02Pn
Augustine	3	M	Child	25Au02Pn
SHORT, Anne	25	F	Servant	25Au02Pn
Catherine	22	F	Servant	25Au02Pn
SHARKEY, James	50	M	Laborer	25Au02Pn
Mary	17	F	None	25Au02Pn
Joseph	12	M	None	25Au02Pn
MCKANNA, Mary	20	F	None	25Au02Pn
OLIVER, John	25	M	None	25Au02Pn
HODGINS, Thomas	22	M	Shoemaker	25Au02Pn
SMITH, Michael	46	M	Laborer	25Au02Pn
Patt	8	M	Child	25Au02Pn
Michael	7	M	Child	25Au02Pn
EUTAW, Bridget	72	F	None	25Au02Pn
Died-At-Sea				
CAVANAGH, Peter	28	M	Laborer	25Au02Pn
Ann	24	F	None	25Au02Pn
SHORT, Michael	28	M	None	25Au02Pn
MORAN, Catherine	30	F	None	25Au02Pn
Mary	10	F	Child	25Au02Pn
Catherine	8	F	Child	25Au02Pn
Patrick	.11	M	Infant	25Au02Pn
Died-At-Sea				
SINGLETON, John	25	M	Laborer	25Au02Pn
Died-At-Sea				
Jane	23	F	None	25Au02Pn
Catherine	.11	F	Infant	25Au02Pn
CONALLY, Margaret	18	F	None	25Au02Pn
WINTERS, James	32	M	Shoemaker	25Au02Pn
HURHERSON, Robert	45	M	Farmer	25Au02Pn
Mary	42	F	None	25Au02Pn
Jane	19	F	None	25Au02Pn
Hugh	17	M	None	25Au02Pn
William	15	M	None	25Au02Pn
Alexander	8	M	Child	25Au02Pn
Elizabeth	5	F	Child	25Au02Pn
Robert	2	M	Child	25Au02Pn
CAREY, Richard	27	M	Baker	25Au02Pn
MCCORMACK, James	22	M	Baker	25Au02Pn
Ann	19	F	None	25Au02Pn
MANIFOLD, Margaret	56	F	None	25Au02Pn
Sarah	17	F	None	25Au02Pn
RODGERS, Andrew	25	M	Laborer	25Au02Pn
Ellen	20	F	None	25Au02Pn
MALONEY, Patrick	59	M	None	25Au02Pn
Bridget	40	F	None	25Au02Pn
Maria	20	F	None	25Au02Pn
RYAN, John	40	M	Tailor	25Au02Pn
FLEMING, James	32	M	Peddler	25Au02Pn
CARR, Esther	30	F	None	25Au02Pn
Eliza	.10	F	Infant	25Au02Pn
Died-At-Sea				
WATERS, Bridget	15	F	None	25Au02Pn
Michael	12	M	None	25Au02Pn
GILLESPIE, Jane	21	F	None	25Au02Pn
CLARK, John	18	M	Lrdrs	25Au02Pn
HAGAN, Michael	32	M	Laborer	25Au02Pn
BRYAN, Dennis	39	M	Farmer	25Au02Pn
TROY, Fanny	20	F	None	25Au02Pn
William	14	M	None	25Au02Pn
MCCALLEN, Mary	19	F	None	25Au02Pn
FURBER, Mary	40	F	None	25Au02Pn

NAMES OF PASSENGERS		AGE	SEX	OCCUPATIONS	DATE PORT SHIP
SMITH, William		26	M	Gunsmith	25Au02Pn
ROSS, Margaret		30	F	Servant	25Au02Pn
Died-At-Sea					

JOHN-R.SKIDDY 27 AUGUST 1849

From Liverpool

NAMES OF PASSENGERS		AGE	SEX	OCCUPATIONS	DATE PORT SHIP
HEWSON, William		30	M	Unknown	27Au02Ei
Sarah	(W)	24	F	Wife	27Au02Ei
SWAN, Jane		21	F	None	27Au02Ei
WRIGHT, Richard		20	M	Bootmaker	27Au02Ei
CHAMBERS, Bridget		20	F	Nurse	27Au02Ei
BURKE, Margaret		22	F	Nurse	27Au02Ei
MCGAUREY, Rose		19	F	Servant	27Au02Ei
ADAMS, Ellen		24	F	Servant	27Au02Ei
Bridget		19	F	Servant	27Au02Ei
Anne		14	F	Servant	27Au02Ei
Johanna		9	F	Child	27Au02Ei
QUINLAN, Andrew		35	M	Laborer	27Au02Ei
Mary	(W)	24	F	Wife	27Au02Ei
CONLAN, Lawrence		30	M	Laborer	27Au02Ei
HAFER, Moses		40	M	Laborer	27Au02Ei
KEARNEY, James		26	M	Laborer	27Au02Ei
DONLAN, Thomas		30	M	Groom	27Au02Ei
TOOLE, Peter		35	M	Laborer	27Au02Ei
KELLY, Michael		25	M	Laborer	27Au02Ei
DEVON, Edmund		26	M	Laborer	27Au02Ei
GALLIGAN, Charles		48	M	Laborer	27Au02Ei
GIRVIN, Richard		28	M	Laborer	27Au02Ei
Ellen		30	F	Servant	27Au02Ei
James		7	M	Child	27Au02Ei
Margaret		5	F	Child	27Au02Ei
Johanna		4	F	Child	27Au02Ei
William		1	M	Child	27Au02Ei
Mary		21	F	Servant	27Au02Ei
Bridget		19	F	Servant	27Au02Ei
CALLAGHAN, Thomas		21	M	Grocer	27Au02Ei
MCCOMB, Charles		35	M	Laborer	27Au02Ei
Jane	(W)	36	F	Wife	27Au02Ei
Mary-Jane		8	F	Child	27Au02Ei
Willm.John		5	M	Child	27Au02Ei
Sarah		3	F	Child	27Au02Ei
MARTIN, Samuel		17	M	Laborer	27Au02Ei
CUNLAN, Catherine		24	F	Servant	27Au02Ei
Mary		4	F	Child	27Au02Ei
Ellen		3	F	Child	27Au02Ei
Pat		.00	M	Infant	27Au02Ei
KESAR, Juda		31	M	Servant	27Au02Ei
WARD, Bridget		17	F	Servant	27Au02Ei
FIGH, Mary		24	F	Servant	27Au02Ei
GRADY, Michael		28	M	Laborer	27Au02Ei
MURPHY, James		20	M	Laborer	27Au02Ei
GRUICA, John		26	M	Sail Maker	27Au02Ei
Anne	(W)	26	F	Wife	27Au02Ei
GIBNEY, Thomas		25	M	Gdnr	27Au02Ei
MCKERNAN, James		34	M	Maurer	27Au02Ei
Anne	(W)	28	F	Wife	27Au02Ei
CONNOR, Brian		19	M	Mason	27Au02Ei
FLINN, Mathew		38	M	Laborer	27Au02Ei
LOWE, James		38	M	Flaxdr	27Au02Ei
GILLESPIE, Isabella		30	F	Servant	27Au02Ei
SAYRES, Margaret		17	F	Servant	27Au02Ei
GRADY, Mary-Anne		18	F	Servant	27Au02Ei
Anne		17	F	Servant	27Au02Ei
MALBY, Nancy		59	F	None	27Au02Ei
MACAULEY, Anne		66	F	None	27Au02Ei
FARROR, Catherine		39	F	Servant	27Au02Ei
Eliza		13	F	None	27Au02Ei
FARROR, Margaret		11	F	None	27Au02Ei
Richard		.00	M	Infant	27Au02Ei
KEARNEY, John		13	M	Laborer	27Au02Ei
Bridget		11	F	None	27Au02Ei
Thomas		10	M	None	27Au02Ei
Ellen		8	F	Child	27Au02Ei
Brownrigg-SOMMERS, Mor		28	M	Laborer	27Au02Ei
MORRISON, John		60	M	Farmer	27Au02Ei
WALSH, Martin		28	M	Mason	27Au02Ei
Maria	(W)	38	F	Wife	27Au02Ei
Ann	(W)	30	F	Servant	27Au02Ei
DANIEL, Catherine		20	F	Servant	27Au02Ei
RILEY, Kitty		21	F	Servant	27Au02Ei
MCPHILLIPS, Patrick		60	M	Laborer	27Au02Ei
FITZSIMONS, Owen		30	M	Laborer	27Au02Ei
CONNOLLY, Rosa		20	F	Servant	27Au02Ei
KENNEY, Ann		20	F	Milliner	27Au02Ei
John		18	M	Laborer	27Au02Ei
LANGSHAW, Dolly		40	F	Servant	27Au02Ei
Harry		16	M	Laborer	27Au02Ei
John		6	M	Child	27Au02Ei
Mary		4	F	Child	27Au02Ei
James		3	M	Child	27Au02Ei
HARLEY, Juda		17	M	Servant	27Au02Ei
QUAYLAND, James		26	M	Laborer	27Au02Ei
HILL, Francis		13	M	None	27Au02Ei
Barney		11	M	None	27Au02Ei
CONNOLLY, Mary-Ann	(W)	21	F	Wife	27Au02Ei
Catherine		3	F	Child	27Au02Ei
Edward		.00	M	Infant	27Au02Ei
GILLIGAN, Susan	(W)	20	F	Wife	27Au02Ei
Michael		24	M	Stone Mason	27Au02Ei
Mary		3	F	Child	27Au02Ei
Jane		.00	F	Infant	27Au02Ei
HINDS, Ann		24	F	Servant	27Au02Ei
Mary-Jane		.00	F	Infant	27Au02Ei
JELLEY, Henry		19	M	Laborer	27Au02Ei
TIERNON, Pat		32	M	Laborer	27Au02Ei
HYLAND, Thomas		27	M	Laborer	27Au02Ei
NOYLAND, Catherine		20	F	Servant	27Au02Ei
RYAN, John		42	M	Laborer	27Au02Ei
Bridget		18	F	Servant	27Au02Ei
MCULLOCH, David		38	M	Mariner	27Au02Ei
Isabella	(W)	30	F	Wife	27Au02Ei
James		3	M	Child	27Au02Ei
SHEAHAN, Andrew		28	M	Storekeeper	27Au02Ei
Margaret	(W)	27	F	Wife	27Au02Ei
Johanna		5	F	Child	27Au02Ei
Michael		3	M	Child	27Au02Ei
Bridget		.00	F	Infant	27Au02Ei
WALKER, Ann		20	F	Servant	27Au02Ei
MURPHY, Timothy		60	M	Farmer	27Au02Ei
Mary	(W)	58	F	Wife	27Au02Ei
GOLDING, Ellen		29	F	Servant	27Au02Ei
Ellen		.00	F	Infant	27Au02Ei
Died-At-Sea					
TAYLOR, William		50	M	Gcr-Agr	27Au02Ei
Jane	(W)	43	F	Wife	27Au02Ei
Ansalam		12	M	None	27Au02Ei
Mary-Ann		11	F	None	27Au02Ei
Edward		9	M	Child	27Au02Ei
CONNELL, Mary		20	F	None	27Au02Ei
THORNEY, Pat		30	M	Laborer	27Au02Ei
NOLAND, Sarah		28	F	Housekeeper	27Au02Ei
STEWART, William		24	M	Lnwvr	27Au02Ei
LOUD, Lawrence		63	M	Laborer	27Au02Ei
MULDOON, Arthur		18	M	Laborer	27Au02Ei
MCCARTY, Lawrence		34	M	Farmer	27Au02Ei
Caroline		5	F	Child	27Au02Ei
Timothy		3	M	Child	27Au02Ei
MONAGHAN, James		32	M	Laborer	27Au02Ei
LYNCH, John		25	M	Shoemaker	27Au02Ei
DUNN, John		45	M	Shoemaker	27Au02Ei
HYLAND, Thomas		25	M	Shoemaker	27Au02Ei
WALSH, Ellen		26	M	Servant	27Au02Ei

NAMES OF PASSENGERS	AGE	SEX	OCCUPATIONS	DATE PORT SHIP
WALSH, Bridget	24	M	Servant	27Au02Ei
Mary	22	M	Servant	27Au02Ei
KEARN, Darby	23	M	Laborer	27Au02Ei
MCGUIRE, James	20	M	Carpenter	27Au02Ei
Pat	22	M	Carpenter	27Au02Ei
COUPLAND, Jane	21	F	Servant	27Au02Ei
SMITH, Catherine	30	F	Servant	27Au02Ei
BRENNAN, Martin	22	M	Laborer	27Au02Ei
DOYLE, John	23	M	Carpenter	27Au02Ei
ROUTH, John	40	M	Farmer	27Au02Ei
Pat	18	M	Servant	27Au02Ei
Lawrence	17	M	None	27Au02Ei
Mary	13	F	None	27Au02Ei
FENNELLY, Thomas	23	M	Draper	27Au02Ei
NOLAND, James	20	M	Grocer	27Au02Ei
CONWAY, Patrick	22	M	Farmer	27Au02Ei
MCGINNIS, Bernard	15	M	Laborer	27Au02Ei
CLÉAR, James	29	M	Farmer	27Au02Ei
WALTON, Daniel	32	M	Farmer	27Au02Ei
BROCK, Pat	21	M	Laborer	27Au02Ei
STAFFORD, Catherine	20	F	Boot Closer	27Au02Ei
ONEILL, Mary	30	F	Housekeeper	27Au02Ei
BREEN, Ann	22	F	Housekeeper	27Au02Ei
Isabella	20	F	Milliner	27Au02Ei
BURNES, Mary	25	F	Servant	27Au02Ei
ARMSTRONG, Edward	30	M	Laborer	27Au02Ei
MALONEY, Charlotte	17	F	Servant	27Au02Ei
Florence	53	F	Laborer	27Au02Ei
GRAHAM, Patrick	28	M	Plumber	27Au02Ei
CORKIN, Mary-Jane	25	F	Dressmaker	27Au02Ei
Mary-Ann	3	F	Child	27Au02Ei
William-James	2	M	Child	27Au02Ei
CRICKARD, Robert	22	M	Tailor	27Au02Ei
Margaret	20	F	Dressmaker	27Au02Ei
OCONNOR, Rose	22	F	None	27Au02Ei
Eliza	20	F	None	27Au02Ei
DONOVAN, Hannah	19	F	None	27Au02Ei
HASKEN, Jane	38	F	None	27Au02Ei
MCBRIDE, Margaret	25	F	Housekeeper	27Au02Ei
KERRIGAN, James	26	M	Laborer	27Au02Ei
Died-At-Sea				
FARRELL, Kate	2	F	Child	27Au02Ei
BRYSON, William	31	M	Cver	27Au02Ei
Julia (W)	33	F	Wife	27Au02Ei
Isabella	9	F	Child	27Au02Ei
Emma	5	F	Child	27Au02Ei
William	4	M	Child	27Au02Ei
GOODWIN, Hannah	20	F	None	27Au02Ei
EAGER, Richard	22	M	None	27Au02Ei
GILES, Jno.	24	M	Clerk	27Au02Ei

ST.LAWRENCE 27 AUGUST 1849

From Belfast

NAMES OF PASSENGERS	AGE	SEX	OCCUPATIONS	DATE PORT SHIP
KERR, Cath.	40	F	Laborer	27Au05Bh
Mary	20	F	Unknown	27Au05Bh
Jno.	11	M	Unknown	27Au05Bh
FOSTER, Nicolas	20	M	Unknown	27Au05Bh
COCHRAN, Sarah	20	F	Unknown	27Au05Bh
HAY, Robt.	20	M	Unknown	27Au05Bh
James	18	M	Unknown	27Au05Bh
MCGALPIN, Nancy	24	F	Unknown	27Au05Bh
MONEY, Jane	27	F	Unknown	27Au05Bh
GILCHRIST, Margt.	25	F	Unknown	27Au05Bh
Margt.	2	F	Child	27Au05Bh
Jane	.00	F	Infant	27Au05Bh
BLACK, Henry	25	M	Unknown	27Au05Bh
MCKEAVER, Jane	24	F	Unknown	27Au05Bh
BOSTON, Thomas	25	M	Unknown	27Au05Bh
TURKENTON, Eliza	22	F	Unknown	27Au05Bh
CONWAY, Mary	35	F	Unknown	27Au05Bh
Jas.	10	M	Child	27Au05Bh
Mary	8	F	Child	27Au05Bh
Thomas	6	M	Child	27Au05Bh
Biddy	3	F	Child	27Au05Bh
BOYNTIN, Edwd.	26	M	Unknown	27Au05Bh
MCBYRINE, Ann	25	F	Unknown	27Au05Bh
Jno.	15	M	Unknown	27Au05Bh
CASSIDY, Michl.	19	M	Unknown	27Au05Bh
SCULLIN, Henry	19	M	Unknown	27Au05Bh
Died-At-Sea				
MULLIN, Mary	24	F	Unknown	27Au05Bh
Sarah	20	F	Unknown	27Au05Bh
TOGHEL, Jno.	24	M	Unknown	27Au05Bh
Mary	18	F	Unknown	27Au05Bh
BOYLE, Margt.	22	F	Unknown	27Au05Bh
James	18	M	Unknown	27Au05Bh
HANNAH, James	40	M	Unknown	27Au05Bh
Patk.	22	M	Unknown	27Au05Bh
BLEAKLY, James	20	M	Unknown	27Au05Bh
Margret	18	F	Unknown	27Au05Bh
MCCURRY, Nancy	25	F	Unknown	27Au05Bh
BAMBER, Jno.	20	M	Unknown	27Au05Bh
SMITH, Martha	25	F	Unknown	27Au05Bh
LOGAN, Biddy	50	F	Unknown	27Au05Bh
Cath.	19	F	Unknown	27Au05Bh
FERGUSON, James	25	M	Laborer	27Au05Bh
LEE, Wm.	45	M	Unknown	27Au05Bh
ALEXANDER, Wm.	22	M	Unknown	27Au05Bh
LENDRUM, Mathew	26	M	Unknown	27Au05Bh
Andrew	24	M	Unknown	27Au05Bh
BAMBER, Nancy	40	F	Unknown	27Au05Bh
COHRILLE, Sophia	27	F	Unknown	27Au05Bh
Robt.	7	M	Child	27Au05Bh
KNOX, James	50	M	Unknown	27Au05Bh
Jane	50	F	Unknown	27Au05Bh
Mary-J.	15	F	Unknown	27Au05Bh
Eliza	13	F	Unknown	27Au05Bh
Ann	9	F	Child	27Au05Bh
MCCARTNAY, Margt.	18	F	Unknown	27Au05Bh
MCKUGAN, Jane	30	F	Unknown	27Au05Bh
MCCORMACK, Mary	60	F	Unknown	27Au05Bh
MCKUGAN, Hugh	40	M	Unknown	27Au05Bh
Jno.	.00	M	Infant	27Au05Bh
LAVERTY, Patk.	20	M	Unknown	27Au05Bh
Peggy-Jane	18	F	Unknown	27Au05Bh
CONLEY, Jno.	18	M	Unknown	27Au05Bh
JAMESON, James	18	M	Unknown	27Au05Bh
POLLOCK, James	20	M	Unknown	27Au05Bh
Robt.	13	M	Unknown	27Au05Bh
James	11	M	Unknown	27Au05Bh
MCCORMACK, John	22	M	Unknown	27Au05Bh
MCVEY, Saml.	23	M	Unknown	27Au05Bh
WALLACE, Ann	18	F	Unknown	27Au05Bh
Francis	15	M	Unknown	27Au05Bh
MCELRA, Ann	18	M	Unknown	27Au05Bh
KIRKLAND, James	26	M	Unknown	27Au05Bh
MCCANN, John	21	M	Unknown	27Au05Bh
MCCRANE, John	18	M	Unknown	27Au05Bh
Mary-J.	16	F	Unknown	27Au05Bh
Wm.	13	M	Unknown	27Au05Bh
KEEVENAGH, James	28	M	Unknown	27Au05Bh
RADLEY, Mary	30	F	Unknown	27Au05Bh
GRAHAM, James	56	M	Unknown	27Au05Bh
Mary	57	F	Unknown	27Au05Bh
LIPSEY, Thomas	45	M	Unknown	27Au05Bh
Maria	00	F	Unknown	27Au05Bh
Ann	00	F	Unknown	27Au05Bh
Robt.	00	M	Unknown	27Au05Bh
Wm.J.	00	M	Unknown	27Au05Bh
GLASS, Ann	00	F	Unknown	27Au05Bh
MCNEILL, Jane	00	F	Unknown	27Au05Bh
FULLERTON, Mary-A.	00	F	Unknown	27Au05Bh

NAMES OF PASSENGERS	AGE	SEX	OCCUPATIONS	DATE PORT SHIP
FULLERTON, John	00	M	Unknown	27Au05Bh
COURTLAND, Mary-M.	00	F	Unknown	27Au05Bh
KENNEDY, Robt.	23	M	Unknown	27Au05Bh
GIBSON, Thomas	32	M	Unknown	27Au05Bh
DUNCAN, James-A.	20	M	Unknown	27Au05Bh

REPUBLIC 27 AUGUST 1849

From Liverpool

NAMES OF PASSENGERS	AGE	SEX	OCCUPATIONS	DATE PORT SHIP
PIERCE, Richard	40	M	Laborer	27Au02Po
Ellen	35	F	Unknown	27Au02Po
Jane	12	F	Unknown	27Au02Po
Mary	10	F	Child	27Au02Po
Ellen	7	F	Child	27Au02Po
Hugh	5	M	Child	27Au02Po
Margt.	1	F	Child	27Au02Po
GRIFFITH, Richd.	42	M	Unknown	27Au02Po
WILLIAMS, Griffith	20	M	Unknown	27Au02Po
Mary	60	F	Unknown	27Au02Po
JONES, Gaynor	25	M	Unknown	27Au02Po
Hannah	20	F	Unknown	27Au02Po
WILLIAMS, Hannah	25	F	Unknown	27Au02Po
CALLAHAN, Terrence	32	M	Unknown	27Au02Po
MOORE, James	40	M	Unknown	27Au02Po
LYONS, Michl.	25	M	Unknown	27Au02Po
John	23	M	Unknown	27Au02Po
Bridget	56	F	Unknown	27Au02Po
CASTELLO, Cath.	20	F	Unknown	27Au02Po
WARD, Pat	8	M	Child	27Au02Po
GLYNN, Mary	6	F	Child	27Au02Po
FINNALY, Jno.	32	M	Unknown	27Au02Po
Bridget	22	F	Unknown	27Au02Po
HUGHS, Peter	28	M	Unknown	27Au02Po
Mary	25	F	Unknown	27Au02Po
SANDERSON, John	52	M	Unknown	27Au02Po
GALLIOT, Francis	28	M	Unknown	27Au02Po
PACKSON, Richd.	24	M	Unknown	27Au02Po
U-Mrs.	21	F	Unknown	27Au02Po
CORE, Ann	20	F	Unknown	27Au02Po
SIMPSON, Wm.	25	M	Unknown	27Au02Po
MILLER, Isaac	18	M	Unknown	27Au02Po
THOMAS, John	27	M	Unknown	27Au02Po
REILY, M.A.	34	F	Unknown	27Au02Po
Thomas	12	M	Unknown	27Au02Po
Edward	10	M	Child	27Au02Po
James	7	M	Child	27Au02Po
Beman	5	M	Child	27Au02Po
Jane	3	F	Child	27Au02Po
Cath.	60	F	Unknown	27Au02Po
CLEARY, Pat	22	M	Unknown	27Au02Po
CARTHEY, Jno.	22	M	Unknown	27Au02Po
CAIN, Bridget	20	F	Unknown	27Au02Po
LOYD, Maurice	18	M	Unknown	27Au02Po
REED, Mary	19	F	Unknown	27Au02Po
James	20	M	Laborer	27Au02Po
DONNODY, Martin	22	M	Laborer	27Au02Po
QUICK, Joseph	32	M	Laborer	27Au02Po
Mgt.	32	F	Laborer	27Au02Po
Elizh.	9	F	Child	27Au02Po
Mary	8	F	Child	27Au02Po
Richard	5	M	Child	27Au02Po
Joseph	3	M	Child	27Au02Po
James	.01	M	Infant	27Au02Po
HAMINS, Ellen	76	F	Unknown	27Au02Po
HODGES, Hugh	23	M	Unknown	27Au02Po
DENBLUNST, Richd.	22	M	Unknown	27Au02Po
Betsy	22	F	Unknown	27Au02Po
Thomas	.01	M	Infant	27Au02Po

NAMES OF PASSENGERS	AGE	SEX	OCCUPATIONS	DATE PORT SHIP
PHILIPS, M.A.	31	F	Unknown	27Au02Po
Wm.	6	M	Child	27Au02Po
MCCABE, Ann	20	F	Unknown	27Au02Po
Rosy	18	F	Unknown	27Au02Po
WRIGHT, Wm.	21	M	Unknown	27Au02Po
CONNOR, Thomas	42	M	Unknown	27Au02Po
MURRAY, U-Mrs.	40	F	Unknown	27Au02Po
John	.05	M	Infant	27Au02Po
Laurence	33	M	Unknown	27Au02Po
RYAN, John	40	M	Unknown	27Au02Po
LAWYER, Mary	20	F	Unknown	27Au02Po
MURRAY, James	.03	M	Infant	27Au02Po
KEHOE, U-Miss	18	F	Unknown	27Au02Po
U-Miss	20	F	Unknown	27Au02Po
CACEY, Edward	30	M	Unknown	27Au02Po
FLANIGAN, Maria	17	F	Unknown	27Au02Po
BYRNE, Johanna	25	F	Unknown	27Au02Po
MURPHY, Pat	27	M	Unknown	27Au02Po
RICHARDS, Saml.	33	M	Unknown	27Au02Po
Sarah	33	F	Unknown	27Au02Po
Ann	12	F	Unknown	27Au02Po
Ben	10	M	Child	27Au02Po
Kitty	7	F	Child	27Au02Po
Mary	5	F	Child	27Au02Po
Anna	2	F	Child	27Au02Po
ATTY, Ew.	22	M	Unknown	27Au02Po
EVINS, Richd.	50	M	Unknown	27Au02Po
DUFF, Henry	26	M	Unknown	27Au02Po
MURPHY, Thomas	30	M	Unknown	27Au02Po
DOYLE, Thomas	36	M	Unknown	27Au02Po
MAILER, John	34	M	Unknown	27Au02Po
Margt.	30	F	Unknown	27Au02Po
Dennis	5	M	Child	27Au02Po
Richard	3	M	Child	27Au02Po
TRAINER, Mary	30	F	Unknown	27Au02Po
GRANT, Thomas	35	M	Unknown	27Au02Po
JONES, John	27	M	Unknown	27Au02Po
WILLIAMS, Cath.	23	F	Unknown	27Au02Po
EUSTICE, James	26	M	Unknown	27Au02Po
LARKIN, Peter	22	M	Unknown	27Au02Po
CARROLL, Cath.	18	F	Unknown	27Au02Po
SCOTT, Thomas	28	M	Unknown	27Au02Po
GEE, Thomas	31	M	Laborer	27Au02Po
U	30	F	Unknown	27Au02Po
BELL, John	23	M	Unknown	27Au02Po
LYNCH, Danl.	26	M	Unknown	27Au02Po
MARVIN, Peter	24	M	Unknown	27Au02Po
KEHOE, Ellen	35	F	Unknown	27Au02Po
Eliza	7	F	Child	27Au02Po
OBRIEN, Jno.	21	M	Unknown	27Au02Po
MCAULIFF, Jno.	26	M	Unknown	27Au02Po
TAYLOR, Thomas	21	M	Unknown	27Au02Po
DENANNY, Ann	21	F	Unknown	27Au02Po
KING, Cath.	24	F	Unknown	27Au02Po
KILLY, Ann	24	F	Unknown	27Au02Po
CANNON, Bridget	22	F	Unknown	27Au02Po
MURPHY, Edward	50	M	Unknown	27Au02Po
U-Mrs.	48	F	Unknown	27Au02Po
Hugh	24	M	Unknown	27Au02Po
Jno.	20	M	Unknown	27Au02Po
Michl.	18	M	Unknown	27Au02Po
Edward	10	M	Unknown	27Au02Po
Owen	3	M	Child	27Au02Po
BARTHY, Francis	26	M	Unknown	27Au02Po
Mary	20	F	Unknown	27Au02Po
Jno.	1	F	Unknown	27Au02Po
CAMPBELL, Henry	22	F	Unknown	27Au02Po
HAYNES, Edwd.	26	F	Unknown	27Au02Po
CALLANY, Michael	22	M	Unknown	27Au02Po
CRAGAN, Laurence	25	M	Unknown	27Au02Po
Margt.	22	F	Unknown	27Au02Po
Bridget	13	F	Unknown	27Au02Po
SMITH, Thomas	21	M	Unknown	27Au02Po
SPENCE, George	64	M	Unknown	27Au02Po
Mary	50	F	Unknown	27Au02Po

NAMES OF PASSENGERS	AGE	SEX	OCCUPATIONS	DATE PORT SHIP	NAMES OF PASSENGERS	AGE	SEX	OCCUPATIONS	DATE PORT SHIP
SPENCE, Jane	11	F	Unknown	27Au02Po	BONNER, Rebecca	6	F	Child	27Au02Po
JAMESON, Mary	20	F	Unknown	27Au02Po	John	4	M	Child	27Au02Po
WRIGLEY, Wm.	30	M	Unknown	27Au02Po	Fanny	2	F	Child	27Au02Po
READY, Honor	20	F	Unknown	27Au02Po	Mary	1	F	Child	27Au02Po
GOODING, Ann	23	F	Unknown	27Au02Po	HAWKINS, Sarah	16	F	Unknown	27Au02Po
Thomas	1	M	Child	27Au02Po	George	20	M	Laborer	27Au02Po
ETHINGTON, John	31	M	Unknown	27Au02Po	SHEARON, Mary	25	F	Unknown	27Au02Po
Elizh.	27	F	Unknown	27Au02Po	MCSWIFFINS, Dennis	19	M	Unknown	27Au02Po
Maria	4	F	Child	27Au02Po	DILLINS, Pat	27	M	Unknown	27Au02Po
Wm.	2	M	Child	27Au02Po	HEALEY, Wm.	24	M	Unknown	27Au02Po
Elizh.	.01	F	Infant	27Au02Po	BROWN, Jane	17	F	Unknown	27Au02Po
MCDONALD, Geo.	41	M	Unknown	27Au02Po	HUGHES, James	40	M	Unknown	27Au02Po
TAYLOR, Mark	36	M	Unknown	27Au02Po	Wm.	16	M	Unknown	27Au02Po
Hannah	36	F	Unknown	27Au02Po	Patrick	12	M	Unknown	27Au02Po
Mary	18	F	Unknown	27Au02Po	DOTTOM, Patrick	18	M	Unknown	27Au02Po
Sarah	7	F	Child	27Au02Po	SWEENEY, Margt.	25	F	Unknown	27Au02Po
Ann	6	F	Child	27Au02Po	LUCEY, Thomas	40	M	Unknown	27Au02Po
WARD, Joseph	40	M	Unknown	27Au02Po	John	13	M	Unknown	27Au02Po
Herbert	21	M	Unknown	27Au02Po	SWORLEN, Mary	40	F	Unknown	27Au02Po
Jno.	18	M	Unknown	27Au02Po	Charles	18	M	Unknown	27Au02Po
MARTIN, Thos.	38	M	Unknown	27Au02Po	Sarah	16	F	Unknown	27Au02Po
Eliza	34	F	Unknown	27Au02Po	HARRIS, John	26	M	Unknown	27Au02Po
IRONMONGER, James	26	M	Unknown	27Au02Po	KNIGHTLY, James	23	M	Unknown	27Au02Po
Charlotte	26	F	Unknown	27Au02Po	SMITH, John	22	M	Unknown	27Au02Po
EVANS, Thomas	30	M	Unknown	27Au02Po	KNIGHT, Wm.	21	M	Unknown	27Au02Po
Mary	26	F	Unknown	27Au02Po	THOMPSON, Robert	30	M	Unknown	27Au02Po
SMITH, U	26	M	Unknown	27Au02Po	DONNA, Pat	23	M	Unknown	27Au02Po
Mary	26	F	Unknown	27Au02Po	Mary	20	F	Unknown	27Au02Po
NEVYTON, Joseph	24	M	Laborer	27Au02Po	Michl.	28	M	Unknown	27Au02Po
MCKENNA, Francis	28	M	Unknown	27Au02Po	Judy	27	F	Unknown	27Au02Po
Bridget	23	F	Unknown	27Au02Po	Ann	1	F	Child	27Au02Po
LAMB, Peter	27	M	Unknown	27Au02Po	CONNOR, Andrew	30	M	Unknown	27Au02Po
FANNELL, Bridget	30	F	Unknown	27Au02Po	SHERIDAN, Ann	35	F	Unknown	27Au02Po
CASSIDY, Edward	26	M	Unknown	27Au02Po	Edward	12	M	Unknown	27Au02Po
MURPHY, Cath.	28	F	Unknown	27Au02Po	MCCOOL, Alex	48	M	Unknown	27Au02Po
Bernard	1	M	Child	27Au02Po	DOODY, Cath.	40	F	Unknown	27Au02Po
CAWAN, Wm.	30	M	Unknown	27Au02Po	SMITH, Bridget	34	F	Unknown	27Au02Po
MURRAY, Barth.	25	M	Unknown	27Au02Po	DOODY, Pat	11	M	Unknown	27Au02Po
Mary	45	M	Unknown	27Au02Po	Thomas	9	M	Child	27Au02Po
BASHELL, John	40	M	Unknown	27Au02Po	Michl.	7	M	Child	27Au02Po
Michael	20	M	Unknown	27Au02Po	Mary-Ann	1	F	Child	27Au02Po
CASEY, Cath.	20	F	Unknown	27Au02Po	CONWAY, Thomas	24	M	Unknown	27Au02Po
MCMANNUS, Mary	30	F	Unknown	27Au02Po	MOORE, Wm.	17	M	Unknown	27Au02Po
Ann	6	F	Child	27Au02Po	MAKER, John	18	M	Unknown	27Au02Po
John	4	M	Child	27Au02Po	CONDOR, Jno.	22	M	Unknown	27Au02Po
Mary	1	F	Child	27Au02Po	LINEGAN, James	23	M	Unknown	27Au02Po
CONNOLY, James	40	M	Unknown	27Au02Po	CONNELL, Ann	24	F	Unknown	27Au02Po
John	12	M	Unknown	27Au02Po	Margt.	1	F	Child	27Au02Po
BARK, Edwd.	21	M	Unknown	27Au02Po	PERKINS, Jno.	13	M	Child	27Au02Po
Samuel	12	M	Unknown	27Au02Po	Cath.	6	F	Child	27Au02Po
Thomas	10	M	Child	27Au02Po	Mary-Anne	35	F	Unknown	27Au02Po
Ann	7	F	Child	27Au02Po	BARNES, Jno.	20	M	Unknown	27Au02Po
James	5	M	Child	27Au02Po	OSHER, Pat	12	M	Unknown	27Au02Po
READY, Cath.	20	F	Unknown	27Au02Po	Pat	35	M	Unknown	27Au02Po
CALLIHAN, Mary	19	F	Unknown	27Au02Po	CURTAIN, Kate	13	F	Unknown	27Au02Po
STRINGER, John	24	M	Unknown	27Au02Po	Mick	22	M	Unknown	27Au02Po
BARKE, Margt.	14	F	Unknown	27Au02Po	QUINN, Margt.	26	F	Unknown	27Au02Po
Patrick	16	M	Unknown	27Au02Po	BEGADE, Michael	24	M	Unknown	27Au02Po
MARRON, Alice	19	F	Unknown	27Au02Po	MCCARNS, Mary	32	F	Laborer	27Au02Po
Bryan	20	M	Unknown	27Au02Po	CRONIN, Dennis	33	M	Unknown	27Au02Po
DOLAN, James	16	M	Unknown	27Au02Po	U-Mrs.	32	F	Unknown	27Au02Po
COOK, Jno.	28	M	Unknown	27Au02Po	Jno.	2	M	Child	27Au02Po
Elizabeth	3	F	Child	27Au02Po	Thaddy	2	M	Child	27Au02Po
Danny	.01	M	Infant	27Au02Po	DUGGAN, Julia	18	F	Unknown	27Au02Po
MCGUIRE, Pat	38	M	Unknown	27Au02Po	GRIFFITH, Jerry	50	M	Unknown	27Au02Po
Mary	34	F	Unknown	27Au02Po	Nony	50	M	Unknown	27Au02Po
ROURKE, John	30	M	Unknown	27Au02Po	RYAN, Pat	24	M	Unknown	27Au02Po
KENNY, Mary	30	F	Unknown	27Au02Po	DOUGHERTY, John	29	M	Unknown	27Au02Po
REYNOLDS, Cath.	20	F	Unknown	27Au02Po	KERDAN, Bernard	20	M	Unknown	27Au02Po
BONNER, Joseph	40	M	Unknown	27Au02Po	CARTER, David	24	M	Unknown	27Au02Po
Mary	35	F	Unknown	27Au02Po	PHELAN, Jas.	21	M	Unknown	27Au02Po
Margt.	15	F	Unknown	27Au02Po	GEARTY, Cath.	19	F	Unknown	27Au02Po
Andrew	13	M	Unknown	27Au02Po	POOL, Jno.	40	M	Unknown	27Au02Po
Eliza.	10	F	Child	27Au02Po	WALSH, Jno.	45	M	Unknown	27Au02Po
Tom	8	M	Child	27Au02Po	U-Mrs.	44	F	Unknown	27Au02Po

NAMES OF PASSENGERS	AGE	SEX	OCCUPATIONS	DATE PORT SHIP
WALSH, Edwd.	14	M	Unknown	27Au02Po
Eliza.	17	F	Unknown	27Au02Po
Ellen	15	F	Unknown	27Au02Po
Mary	12	F	Unknown	27Au02Po
Laurence	10	M	Child	27Au02Po
Andrew	8	M	Child	27Au02Po
Michl.	6	M	Child	27Au02Po
Pat	4	M	Child	27Au02Po
BRIEN, Pat	25	M	Unknown	27Au02Po
BELL, Jno.	28	M	Unknown	27Au02Po
YOUNG, Thos.	30	M	Unknown	27Au02Po
MOORE, Thos.	27	M	Unknown	27Au02Po
PLATT, Alex	26	M	Unknown	27Au02Po
GASGOGAN, Jas.	41	M	Unknown	27Au02Po
George	23	M	Unknown	27Au02Po
HUMBLE, Ann	26	F	Unknown	27Au02Po
Margt.	6	F	Child	27Au02Po
Benj.	4	M	Child	27Au02Po
Michl.	3	M	Child	27Au02Po
Mary	1	F	Child	27Au02Po
CARLTON, Wm.	20	M	Unknown	27Au02Po
KANE, Thomas	18	M	Unknown	27Au02Po
EUBBING, Thos.	20	M	Unknown	27Au02Po
Ellen	40	F	Unknown	27Au02Po
Mary	16	F	Unknown	27Au02Po
MITCHELL, Hugh	17	M	Unknown	27Au02Po
MINSKIP, Thos.	30	M	Unknown	27Au02Po
ROBINSON, Jas.	5	M	Child	27Au02Po
HIGGINS, Cath.	45	F	Unknown	27Au02Po
Mary	20	F	Unknown	27Au02Po
Barney	10	M	Child	27Au02Po
BEARTON, James	30	M	Unknown	27Au02Po
CASSOCK, Jno.	21	M	Unknown	27Au02Po
LYNN, Henry	18	M	Unknown	27Au02Po
EAGAN, Thomas	23	M	Laborer	27Au02Po
U-Mrs.	21	F	Unknown	27Au02Po
KNIFFLEBREN, Timy.	26	M	Unknown	27Au02Po
MURPHY, Jas.	40	M	Unknown	27Au02Po
CARLEY, Thomas	19	M	Unknown	27Au02Po
WALSH, Alley	21	M	Unknown	27Au02Po
BULGER, Joseph	26	M	Unknown	27Au02Po
MAHON, Eliza.	45	F	Unknown	27Au02Po
Mary	25	F	Unknown	27Au02Po
KANE, Philip	21	M	Unknown	27Au02Po
SMALL, Bernard	46	M	Unknown	27Au02Po
ROONEY, Thos.	26	M	Unknown	27Au02Po
MCGRATH, U-Mrs.	22	F	Unknown	27Au02Po
Jno.	.00	M	Infant	27Au02Po
COMEFORD, Honora	26	F	Unknown	27Au02Po
MALONEY, Bridget	36	F	Unknown	27Au02Po
Stephen	6	M	Child	27Au02Po
BUCKLEY, Ann	16	F	Unknown	27Au02Po
BURKE, John	21	M	Unknown	27Au02Po
LYMAN, Margt.	20	F	Unknown	27Au02Po
WALSH, Thomas	24	M	Unknown	27Au02Po
FITZPATRICK, Margt.	20	F	Unknown	27Au02Po
MCMANNA, Mary	20	F	Unknown	27Au02Po
Pam	26	F	Unknown	27Au02Po
SWEANNY, James	21	M	Unknown	27Au02Po
HAYES, Dennis	30	M	Unknown	27Au02Po
BLAKE, James	55	M	Unknown	27Au02Po
CANDLAN, John	26	M	Unknown	27Au02Po
FAHEY, Jas.	19	M	Unknown	27Au02Po
Edward	22	M	Unknown	27Au02Po
KILLY, Ann	20	F	Unknown	27Au02Po
CARROLL, Ellen	21	F	Unknown	27Au02Po
SYMS, Math.	40	M	Unknown	27Au02Po
James	19	M	Unknown	27Au02Po
Samuel	16	M	Unknown	27Au02Po
Mary	22	F	Unknown	27Au02Po
U-Mrs.	37	F	Unknown	27Au02Po
THOMPSON, James	40	M	Unknown	27Au02Po
DUFFY, Pat	17	M	Unknown	27Au02Po
MONHAHAN, Jas.	35	M	Unknown	27Au02Po
PETREE, Jas.	17	M	Unknown	27Au02Po

NAMES OF PASSENGERS	AGE	SEX	OCCUPATIONS	DATE PORT SHIP
PETREE, Wm.	15	M	Unknown	27Au02Po
SMITH, U	25	M	Unknown	27Au02Po
Died-At-Sea				
Mary	25	F	Unknown	27Au02Po
Died-At-Sea				
U, U	00	M	Unknown	27Au02Po
Died-At-Sea				
U	00	M	Unknown	27Au02Po
Died-At-Sea				
PARKS, Robert	25	M	Unknown	27Au02Po
WILLINS, Thos.	21	M	Unknown	27Au02Po
WILLSON, U-Mrs.	50	F	Unknown	27Au02Po
OGORMEN, U-Dr.	30	M	Unknown	27Au02Po

CLARENCE 27 AUGUST 1849

From Galway

NAMES OF PASSENGERS	AGE	SEX	OCCUPATIONS	DATE PORT SHIP
DALY, Catherine	35	F	None	27Au06Pq
Catherine	9	F	Child	27Au06Pq
Eliza	7	F	Child	27Au06Pq
FLAHERTY, Mary	50	F	Unknown	27Au06Pq
Mary	30	F	Domestic	27Au06Pq
CONNELE, Patt	12	M	Servant	27Au06Pq
FLAHERTY, Thos.	18	M	Laborer	27Au06Pq
Jas.	15	M	Laborer	27Au06Pq
CRADICK, Jane	25	F	Domestic	27Au06Pq
KOONE, Michl.	17	M	Laborer	27Au06Pq
WALSH, Bridget	18	F	Domestic	27Au06Pq
DUANE, Mary	17	F	Servant	27Au06Pq
Margt.	11	F	Servant	27Au06Pq
MCMAHON, Bridget	16	F	Servant	27Au06Pq
Sally	6	F	Child	27Au06Pq
Bridgt.	21	F	Spinster	27Au06Pq
Mary	3	F	Child	27Au06Pq
FLEMING, Honor	19	F	Spinster	27Au06Pq
FLANAGAN, Jno.	40	M	Unknown	27Au06Pq
FLAHERTY, Patt	20	M	Shoemaker	27Au06Pq
NEALAN, Margt.	22	F	Servant	27Au06Pq
HURT, Thos.	17	M	Laborer	27Au06Pq
KEOGH, Thos.	20	M	Unknown	27Au06Pq
Mary	21	F	Unknown	27Au06Pq
MALLONY, Honor	25	F	Unknown	27Au06Pq
KEEF, Biddy	21	F	Unknown	27Au06Pq
MCDONOUGH, Kitty	19	F	Unknown	27Au06Pq
CONNOLY, Patt	45	M	Unknown	27Au06Pq
FRENCH, Wm.C.	16	M	Unknown	27Au06Pq
STUART, Henry	32	M	Unknown	27Au06Pq
KEALAHAN, Jno.	27	M	Shoemaker	27Au06Pq
Marg.	26	F	Unknown	27Au06Pq
Maria	4	F	Child	27Au06Pq
MCHUGH, Mary	25	F	Unknown	27Au06Pq
Mary	23	F	Unknown	27Au06Pq
OFLANAGAN, Honor	10	F	Child	27Au06Pq
WALSH, John	24	M	Unknown	27Au06Pq
CALETTO, Catherine	20	F	Unknown	27Au06Pq
MURRY, Mary	18	F	Unknown	27Au06Pq
KENNEDY, James	15	M	Unknown	27Au06Pq
COHEN, Wm.	24	M	Unknown	27Au06Pq
MURPHY, Jno.	18	M	Unknown	27Au06Pq
Thos.	15	M	Unknown	27Au06Pq
MULLINS, Michl.	24	M	Tailor	27Au06Pq
FAHEY, Mary	18	F	Unknown	27Au06Pq
CONELLY, Sarah	15	F	Unknown	27Au06Pq
BUTLER, Winifred	20	F	Unknown	27Au06Pq
Patt	26	M	Unknown	27Au06Pq
REILLY, Margt.	4	F	Child	27Au06Pq
Bidilia	1	F	Child	27Au06Pq
SHAUGNISSY, Bridgt.	25	F	Child	27Au06Pq

NAMES OF PASSENGERS	AGE	SEX	OCCUPATIONS	DATE PORT SHIP
VOUSDEN, Thos.	50	M	Unknown	27Au06Pq
Ths.	16	M	Unknown	27Au06Pq
John	19	M	Unknown	27Au06Pq
Anne	50	F	Unknown	27Au06Pq
CONALLY, Sally	20	F	Unknown	27Au06Pq
MCDONOUGH, Ellen	40	F	Unknown	27Au06Pq
Susan	9	F	Child	27Au06Pq
MULKEIN, Michl.	3	M	Child	27Au06Pq
Barbara	25	F	Unknown	27Au06Pq
FLEMING, Catherine	22	F	Unknown	27Au06Pq
EGAN, Michl.	19	M	Unknown	27Au06Pq
HARDING, Mary-Ann	20	F	Unknown	27Au06Pq
SHIELDS, Mary	30	F	Unknown	27Au06Pq
DUGGAN, Margt.	20	F	Unknown	27Au06Pq
SLATTERY, Winny	40	F	Unknown	27Au06Pq
DAVEY, Thos.	21	M	Unknown	27Au06Pq
JOINER, Ellen	26	F	Unknown	27Au06Pq
COY, Honor	23	F	Unknown	27Au06Pq
WHEALAN, Jas.	19	M	Unknown	27Au06Pq
MCGLYNN, Michl.	19	M	Unknown	27Au06Pq
CANAVAN, Michl.	19	M	Unknown	27Au06Pq
COY, Judy	25	F	Unknown	27Au06Pq
RAFERTY, Maria	22	F	Unknown	27Au06Pq
HYNES, Mary	20	F	Unknown	27Au06Pq
DEMPSEY, James	18	M	Shoemaker	27Au06Pq
ELLWOOD, James	30	M	Unknown	27Au06Pq
CANAVAN, Thos.	22	M	Unknown	27Au06Pq
WORK, Margt.	20	F	Unknown	27Au06Pq
MCGOWN, Margt.	20	F	Unknown	27Au06Pq
CALAGHAN, Patt	00	M	Unknown	27Au06Pq
GALLAGHER, Rosy	00	F	Unknown	27Au06Pq
SEACOCK, Sarah	00	F	Unknown	27Au06Pq
Eliza.	00	F	Unknown	27Au06Pq
DANSIN, Peggy	00	F	Unknown	27Au06Pq
SEACOCK, Wm.	00	M	Unknown	27Au06Pq
Peggy	00	F	Unknown	27Au06Pq
FINLEY, Eliza	00	F	Unknown	27Au06Pq
REID, Margt.	00	F	Unknown	27Au06Pq
KELLY, Ann	00	F	Unknown	27Au06Pq
MCCARVELL, Jno.	00	M	Unknown	27Au06Pq
ROBERTS, Margt.	00	F	Unknown	27Au06Pq
KINNISTER, Mary	00	F	Unknown	27Au06Pq
SWEENEY, Jas.	00	M	Unknown	27Au06Pq
Peggy	00	F	Unknown	27Au06Pq
CROSSET, Jas.	60	M	Unknown	27Au06Pq
Thos.	20	M	Unknown	27Au06Pq
WILLIAMS, Monica	23	F	Unknown	27Au06Pq
Catherine	3	F	Child	27Au06Pq
GROSS, George	00	M	Unknown	27Au06Pq
ODONOUGH, T.T.	00	M	Unknown	27Au06Pq
WELSH, Margt.	00	F	Unknown	27Au06Pq
MCMAHON, Thos.	00	F	Unknown	27Au06Pq
Bridget	00	F	Unknown	27Au06Pq
Ellen	00	F	Unknown	27Au06Pq

LAURA 28 AUGUST 1849

From Limerick

NAMES OF PASSENGERS	AGE	SEX	OCCUPATIONS	DATE PORT SHIP
GLEESON, Mary	19	F	Farmer	28Au35Pr
WALSH, Thomas	21	M	Unknown	28Au35Pr
Patrick	23	M	Unknown	28Au35Pr
OSHEA, Ellen	24	F	Unknown	28Au35Pr
Margaret	20	F	Unknown	28Au35Pr
Michael	18	M	Unknown	28Au35Pr
TAYLOR, Wm.Alex.	35	M	Unknown	28Au35Pr
Robert	11	M	Unknown	28Au35Pr
POWELL, Mary	15	F	Unknown	28Au35Pr
MESKELL, Michl.	55	M	Unknown	28Au35Pr
MESKELL, Pat	.00	M	Infant	28Au35Pr
ONEILL, Honor	16	F	Unknown	28Au35Pr
MORGAN, Ellen	18	F	Unknown	28Au35Pr
DILLON, Bridget	24	F	Unknown	28Au35Pr
Peter	21	M	Unknown	28Au35Pr
MOYNIHAN, Pat	13	M	Unknown	28Au35Pr
HOGAN, Mary	30	F	Unknown	28Au35Pr
Patrick	8	M	Child	28Au35Pr
Margaret	.00	F	Infant	28Au35Pr
BOUGHAN, Mary	19	F	Unknown	28Au35Pr
WALSH, Patt	23	M	Unknown	28Au35Pr
William	18	M	Unknown	28Au35Pr
BEWES, Luke	23	M	Unknown	28Au35Pr
MCNAMARA, Denis	30	M	Unknown	28Au35Pr
Patt	24	M	Unknown	28Au35Pr
BRITT, Cornelius	25	M	Unknown	28Au35Pr
HANDAHAN, Marg.	20	F	Unknown	28Au35Pr
BURKE, Michl.	20	M	Unknown	28Au35Pr
F--NAN, Margt.	22	F	Unknown	28Au35Pr
HANRAHAN, Bridget	21	F	Unknown	28Au35Pr
MCINEREY, Mich.	30	M	Unknown	28Au35Pr
LYNCH, Michael	22	M	Unknown	28Au35Pr
CRADON, Teresa	24	F	Unknown	28Au35Pr
Mary	.00	F	Infant	28Au35Pr
BOURKE, John	28	M	Unknown	28Au35Pr
NASH, Catherine	25	F	Unknown	28Au35Pr
GUERIN, Catharine	33	F	Unknown	28Au35Pr
DUMES, Patt	50	M	Unknown	28Au35Pr
Bridget	18	F	Unknown	28Au35Pr
Ellen	17	F	Unknown	28Au35Pr
FLANIGAN, Michael	35	M	Unknown	28Au35Pr
BARAGRIE, Thos.	19	M	Unknown	28Au35Pr
HARTIGAN, John	22	M	Unknown	28Au35Pr
Michael	20	M	Unknown	28Au35Pr
ODONNELL, Cath.	20	F	Unknown	28Au35Pr
MCMAHON, Ellen	25	F	Unknown	28Au35Pr
DONOGHUE, Mary	30	F	Unknown	28Au35Pr
BOING, Patt	30	M	Unknown	28Au35Pr
YERAULEY, John	26	M	Unknown	28Au35Pr
Margaret	46	F	Unknown	28Au35Pr
HENNERRY, Biddy	22	F	Unknown	28Au35Pr
KELLY, Thomas	24	M	Unknown	28Au35Pr
Terence	24	M	Unknown	28Au35Pr
CAREY, Stephen	16	M	Unknown	28Au35Pr
KELEERY, Patt	13	M	Unknown	28Au35Pr
COTTER, Edmond	21	M	Unknown	28Au35Pr
GILLIGOTT, John	50	M	Unknown	28Au35Pr
OSHAUGHNESSY, Jas.	23	M	Unknown	28Au35Pr
ARTTO, Ellen	27	F	Unknown	28Au35Pr
PROYSER, William	24	M	Unknown	28Au35Pr
H--RDY, Catherine	16	F	Unknown	28Au35Pr
FITZGERALD, Margret	51	F	Unknown	28Au35Pr
Catherine	26	F	Unknown	28Au35Pr
John	24	M	Unknown	28Au35Pr
Norry	21	M	Unknown	28Au35Pr
Bridget	18	F	Unknown	28Au35Pr
James	.00	M	Infant	28Au35Pr
MCMAHN, Patt	3	M	Child	28Au35Pr
SURTTER, Amos	26	M	Unknown	28Au35Pr
BUCKLEY, Nancy	30	F	Unknown	28Au35Pr
Larry	31	M	Unknown	28Au35Pr
OBRIEN, Helen-Miss	22	F	Unknown	28Au35Pr
Mary	19	F	Unknown	28Au35Pr
OCONNOR, Ann-Mrs.	35	F	Unknown	28Au35Pr
Mary-Miss	8	F	Child	28Au35Pr
OGRADY, Dy.	22	M	Unknown	28Au35Pr
QUINN, James	24	M	Unknown	28Au35Pr
DONOFIN, Rodger	32	M	Unknown	28Au35Pr
CONNELL, Patrick	20	M	Unknown	28Au35Pr
S--CANY, John	40	M	Unknown	28Au35Pr
DONOHUE, Allis	6	F	Child	28Au35Pr
FITZGIBONS, Bridget	20	F	Unknown	28Au35Pr

JENNY-LIND 28 AUGUST 1849

From Belfast

NAMES OF PASSENGERS		AGE	SEX	OCCUPATIONS	DATE PORT SHIP
RIGHT, William		18	M	Laborer	28Au05Ps
MCGILLODING, Mary		20	F	Laborer	28Au05Ps
LITTLE, Easy		40	F	Seamstress	28Au05Ps
BUSTARD, Bessy		21	F	Seamstress	28Au05Ps
LITTLE, Bessy		18	F	Seamstress	28Au05Ps
HALL, Jane		20	F	Seamstress	28Au05Ps
BEAGHAN, Hessy		30	F	Seamstress	28Au05Ps
Charles		12	M	Unknown	28Au05Ps
RICHARDSON, Joseph		18	M	Laborer	28Au05Ps
CRAIG, Ellenor		15	F	Spinster	28Au05Ps
James		30	M	Laborer	28Au05Ps
Mary		00	F	Unknown	28Au05Ps
Sarah		20	F	Unknown	28Au05Ps
FERGUS, James		23	M	Unknown	28Au05Ps
CARLIN, James		38	M	Unknown	28Au05Ps
BOGAN, Edward		27	M	Unknown	28Au05Ps
PARR, Charles		35	M	Farmer	28Au05Ps
MCAULEY, Elizabeth		26	F	Wife	28Au05Ps
John		3	M	Child	28Au05Ps
Bernard		.00	M	Infant	28Au05Ps
MCCAFFERTY, Ann		19	F	Spinster	28Au05Ps
ORAM, Margaret		25	F	Spinster	28Au05Ps
STITT, John		25	M	Laborer	28Au05Ps
MCCHENERY, Chas.		19	M	Farmer	28Au05Ps
Margaret	(M)	40	F	None	28Au05Ps
CACEY, Thomas		26	M	Farmer	28Au05Ps
Mary	(W)	28	F	None	28Au05Ps
Matilda	(T)	16	F	None	28Au05Ps
MCCAYD, Jas.		20	M	Servant	28Au05Ps
THOMPSON, Richard		18	M	Servant	28Au05Ps
SAMPLE, Henry		22	M	Servant	28Au05Ps
TOTTEN, Eliza		16	F	Servant	28Au05Ps
Margaret		14	F	Servant	28Au05Ps
FALOON, Rodgers		23	M	Farmer	28Au05Ps
MCALASTER, Jas.		22	M	Farmer	28Au05Ps
Elizabeth	(W)	21	F	Unknown	28Au05Ps
Letitia	(T)	19	F	None	28Au05Ps
William	(S)	8	M	Child	28Au05Ps
John	(S)	.00	M	Infant	28Au05Ps
KEYLAND, James		40	M	Farmer	28Au05Ps
John		26	M	Farmer	28Au05Ps
BLACK, Margaret		30	F	Seamstress	28Au05Ps
Catherine		10	F	Child	28Au05Ps
John		8	M	Child	28Au05Ps
Andrew		6	M	Child	28Au05Ps
James		4	M	Child	28Au05Ps
YOUNG, Sam		19	M	Tailor	28Au05Ps
MILEY, Robt.		35	M	Farmer	28Au05Ps
FERGUSON, James		17	M	Farmer	28Au05Ps
MCFENAN, Patrick		35	M	Farmer	28Au05Ps
Mary	(W)	26	F	None	28Au05Ps
Dennis		.00	M	Infant	28Au05Ps
OKEANE, Daniel		30	M	Servant	28Au05Ps
BLESSING, John		45	M	Servant	28Au05Ps
Jane		45	F	Servant	28Au05Ps
Jane		15	F	Servant	28Au05Ps
JOHNSTON, Mary-Ann		26	F	Seamstress	28Au05Ps
Emily		2	F	Child	28Au05Ps
FORBES, Alexander		40	M	Farmer	28Au05Ps
Mary	(W)	40	F	None	28Au05Ps
Alexander		2	M	Child	28Au05Ps
BRYERS, Patrick		18	M	Servant	28Au05Ps
LAVINY, John		20	M	Servant	28Au05Ps
MEALEY, Wm.		19	M	Servant	28Au05Ps
ESKIN, Joseph		13	M	Child	28Au05Ps
ESKIN, Sarah		12	F	Child	28Au05Ps
Eliza		10	F	Child	28Au05Ps
FORSYTHE, Wm.		30	M	Farmer	28Au05Ps
Saml.		27	M	Farmer	28Au05Ps
ANDREWS, Osley		30	F	Seamstress	28Au05Ps
Sarah-E.		28	F	Seamstress	28Au05Ps
MCGROMY, Jas.		24	M	Servant	28Au05Ps
CORLETT, John		19	M	Servant	28Au05Ps
DEMPSTER, Sarah		22	F	Servant	28Au05Ps
GLASS, Jas.		23	M	Farmer	28Au05Ps
MCCAULEY, Edward		45	M	Farmer	28Au05Ps
Mary	(W)	36	F	None	28Au05Ps
Charlotte	(D)	18	F	None	28Au05Ps
Eassy	(D)	13	F	None	28Au05Ps
Elizabeth	(D)	10	F	Child	28Au05Ps
ALMAN, Pheanox		28	U	Servant	28Au05Ps
KEARNEY, Bridget		20	F	Seamstress	28Au05Ps
CARR, James		50	M	Servant	28Au05Ps
Isabella	(D)	12	F	None	28Au05Ps
Anne	(D)	10	F	Child	28Au05Ps
MCILHOME, Jno.		25	M	Servant	28Au05Ps
Felix		22	M	Servant	28Au05Ps
ALAN, Anne		30	F	Servant	28Au05Ps
PATTERSON, Robt.		18	M	Servant	28Au05Ps
TODD, Saml.		23	M	Servant	28Au05Ps
Robt.		18	M	Servant	28Au05Ps
LAMOM, James		24	M	Farmer	28Au05Ps
Anne	(W)	26	F	None	28Au05Ps
SIMPSON, Wm.		29	M	Farmer	28Au05Ps
ARNOLD, Mary		25	F	Servant	28Au05Ps
CONNERY, Michael		25	M	Servant	28Au05Ps
Sarah	(W)	25	F	None	28Au05Ps
John		.00	M	Infant	28Au05Ps
MCDONALD, Alex		23	F	Servant	28Au05Ps
Hugh		24	F	Servant	28Au05Ps
SMITH, Wm.		25	F	Servant	28Au05Ps
MANSON, Jas.		24	M	Servant	28Au05Ps
Anne	(W)	27	F	None	28Au05Ps
MILLER, David		28	M	Servant	28Au05Ps
HANNAH, Jane		60	F	Wife	28Au05Ps
Jane	(T)	25	F	None	28Au05Ps
Mary-E.	(T)	22	F	None	28Au05Ps
Isabella		7	F	Child	28Au05Ps
BAYDEN, Wm.		21	M	Servant	28Au05Ps
MCGOWAN, Jas.		18	M	Servant	28Au05Ps
KERR, Jno.		26	M	Servant	28Au05Ps
Mary		32	F	Servant	28Au05Ps
James		5	M	Child	28Au05Ps
John		3	M	Child	28Au05Ps
JACK, Alice		38	F	Servant	28Au05Ps
Ready		20	U	Servant	28Au05Ps
Thomas		14	U	Servant	28Au05Ps
John		10	M	Child	28Au05Ps
Charles		8	M	Child	28Au05Ps
Alexander		7	M	Child	28Au05Ps
Rebca.		.00	F	Infant	28Au05Ps
SMITH, Wm.		25	M	Farmer	28Au05Ps
Anne	(W)	20	F	None	28Au05Ps
William		.00	M	Infant	28Au05Ps
REA, Margaret		31	F	Farmer	28Au05Ps
Isabella		11	F	Child	28Au05Ps
Martha		9	F	Child	28Au05Ps
Mary		7	F	Child	28Au05Ps
Wm.		5	M	Child	28Au05Ps
George		3	M	Child	28Au05Ps
Saml.		2	M	Child	28Au05Ps
Agnes		.00	F	Infant	28Au05Ps
MCCOEY, Jas.		40	M	Servant	28Au05Ps
Ellen	(W)	35	F	None	28Au05Ps
Ellen		12	F	Child	28Au05Ps
Dorothea		10	F	Child	28Au05Ps
Alice		.00	F	Infant	28Au05Ps
TAYLOR, Wm.		27	M	Servant	28Au05Ps
MCGLINN, Jno.		27	M	Servant	28Au05Ps
Margt.		60	F	Servant	28Au05Ps

NAMES OF PASSENGERS	AGE	SEX	OCCUPATIONS	DATE PORT SHIP
MCCLELLAND, Saml.	49	M	Servant	28Au05Ps
TODD, Abraham	27	M	Servant	28Au05Ps
SIMMS, Chas.	48	M	Farmer	28Au05Ps
Isabella (W)	40	F	None	28Au05Ps
Eliza.	12	F	Child	28Au05Ps
Jno.	10	M	Child	28Au05Ps
Mary	4	F	Child	28Au05Ps
Andrew	.00	M	Infant	28Au05Ps
CRAWFORD, Catherine	16	F	Servant	28Au05Ps
MCGAUGHER, Jno.	27	M	Farmer	28Au05Ps
MCCONNELL, Margt.	19	F	Spinster	28Au05Ps
Catherine	20	F	Spinster	28Au05Ps
KEANE, Isabella	20	F	Spinster	28Au05Ps
Henry	8	M	Child	28Au05Ps
MCCARTIN, Jas.	38	M	Laborer	28Au05Ps
MCCORY, Jas.	10	M	Child	28Au05Ps
RAFERTY, Ann	20	F	Spinster	28Au05Ps
CASEY, Jas.	00	M	Unknown	28Au05Ps
ONEIL, Chas.	00	M	Unknown	28Au05Ps
TOWNLEY, Mary	00	F	Unknown	28Au05Ps
U, U Born-At-Sea	.00	U	Infant	28Au05Ps

CAROLINE-READ 29 AUGUST 1849

From Liverpool

NAMES OF PASSENGERS	AGE	SEX	OCCUPATIONS	DATE PORT SHIP
ROGERS, William	26	M	Laborer	29Au02Ct
James	20	M	Laborer	29Au02Ct
KELLY, Patrick	28	M	Laborer	29Au02Ct
AHERN, Daniel	26	M	Laborer	29Au02Ct
HEFFERMAN, Daniel	20	M	Laborer	29Au02Ct
BRYAN, Mary	18	F	Servant	29Au02Ct
LYNSE, Charles	29	M	Cooper	29Au02Ct
Anna	27	F	Servant	29Au02Ct
James	9	M	Child	29Au02Ct
John	6	M	Child	29Au02Ct
Anna	.00	F	Infant	29Au02Ct
BROWN, James	19	M	Laborer	29Au02Ct
LYNCH, Richard	22	M	Laborer	29Au02Ct
JONES, Thomas-H.	30	M	Laborer	29Au02Ct
FITZGERALD, Edward	26	M	Blacksmith	29Au02Ct
Mary	24	F	None	29Au02Ct
GORMAN, Richard	25	M	Laborer	29Au02Ct
KEALEY, Martin	23	M	Laborer	29Au02Ct
MCBRIDE, Patrick	32	M	Weaver	29Au02Ct
BRIMFORD, Ellen	24	F	Servant	29Au02Ct
Jeremiah	.00	M	Infant	29Au02Ct
Margaret	33	F	None	29Au02Ct
LEGG, John	40	M	Laborer	29Au02Ct
MCDONALD, John	20	M	Laborer	29Au02Ct
HAMILL, Henry	40	M	Maurer	29Au02Ct
Mary	28	F	None	29Au02Ct
Paul	9	M	Child	29Au02Ct
Daniel	5	M	Child	29Au02Ct
BYRNE, Peter	22	M	Laborer	29Au02Ct
MORIS, Bernard	30	M	Tailor	29Au02Ct
Mary	28	F	None	29Au02Ct
Bridget	3	F	Child	29Au02Ct
John	6	M	Child	29Au02Ct
James	.00	M	Infant	29Au02Ct
BARRON, Ann	20	F	Servant	29Au02Ct
ROSS, John	26	M	Laborer	29Au02Ct
MCLOUGHLIN, Denis	21	M	Laborer	29Au02Ct
Horace	24	M	Laborer	29Au02Ct
MCMAHON, Mathew	23	M	Laborer	29Au02Ct
Ellen	34	F	Laborer	29Au02Ct
CLARK, William	23	M	Laborer	29Au02Ct
KELLY, Patrick	46	M	Laborer	29Au02Ct
DOHERTY, Mary	26	F	Farmer	29Au02Ct
Hugh	5	M	Child	29Au02Ct
Rose	3	F	Child	29Au02Ct
DINNEN, Mathew	13	M	Laborer	29Au02Ct
Dorothy	26	F	None	29Au02Ct
John	26	M	None	29Au02Ct
William	6	M	Child	29Au02Ct
Eliza-Jane	.00	F	Infant	29Au02Ct
BRUNT, James	20	M	None	29Au02Ct
Anne	17	F	None	29Au02Ct
FREEMAN, William	26	M	Laborer	29Au02Ct
CREDDER, Biddy	24	F	None	29Au02Ct
MCLARKER, Owen	16	M	Laborer	29Au02Ct
Sophia	32	F	None	29Au02Ct
HEALY, Ann	24	F	None	29Au02Ct
HEFFERAN, Ellen	28	F	None	29Au02Ct
LYNCH, Daniel	30	M	Laborer	29Au02Ct
LEARY, Julia	14	F	None	29Au02Ct
DEMPSEY, William	36	M	Laborer	29Au02Ct
Mary	30	F	None	29Au02Ct
LANE, John	50	M	Laborer	29Au02Ct
BRIEN, Margaret	21	F	Servant	29Au02Ct
Eliza	19	F	Servant	29Au02Ct
STELLGY, Christopher	20	M	Laborer	29Au02Ct
HALTERY, Denis	40	M	Laborer	29Au02Ct
SLATTERY, Margaret	40	F	Laborer	29Au02Ct
MALVENELL, Judy	30	F	Laborer	29Au02Ct
Mary	23	F	Laborer	29Au02Ct
FLYNNE, Bertha	32	F	Laborer	29Au02Ct
CONNOR, Thomas	20	M	Laborer	29Au02Ct
Deborah	15	F	None	29Au02Ct
SULLIVAN, Mary	20	F	None	29Au02Ct
MCGLEN, Michael	30	M	Laborer	29Au02Ct
HANNEGAN, Ellen	22	F	Laborer	29Au02Ct
DOOLAN, Thomas	22	M	Laborer	29Au02Ct
LEAHY, Bridget	22	F	Laborer	29Au02Ct
DOOLAN, Pat	12	M	None	29Au02Ct
GRIFFIN, Thomas	2	M	Child	29Au02Ct
DOOLAN, Eliza	18	F	Servant	29Au02Ct
HAYS, Thomas	24	M	Laborer	29Au02Ct
HORE, John	45	M	Laborer	29Au02Ct
Michael	18	M	Laborer	29Au02Ct
FARRELL, Ellen	15	F	None	29Au02Ct
HOWARD, Simeon	21	F	None	29Au02Ct
Margaret	20	F	None	29Au02Ct
John	18	M	Laborer	29Au02Ct
BEEHAN, Bridget	20	F	Laborer	29Au02Ct
DOWLING, Edward	30	M	Laborer	29Au02Ct
KELLY, Patrick	24	M	Laborer	29Au02Ct
HENRY, Mary	22	F	Laborer	29Au02Ct
POWER, James	22	M	Laborer	29Au02Ct
Dan.	22	M	Laborer	29Au02Ct
HEAPHY, Mary	50	F	None	29Au02Ct
PATTERSON, Jane	32	F	None	29Au02Ct
Catherine	12	F	None	29Au02Ct
William	7	M	Child	29Au02Ct
John	5	M	Child	29Au02Ct
DONALDON, Margaret	18	F	Servant	29Au02Ct
DOOLY, Michael	50	M	Laborer	29Au02Ct
Catherine	45	F	Laborer	29Au02Ct
John	14	M	None	29Au02Ct
SALINGER, Margaret	21	F	None	29Au02Ct
MURAN, Patrick	24	M	Laborer	29Au02Ct
LANERY, Margaret	28	F	Laborer	29Au02Ct
OBRIEN, William	25	M	Laborer	29Au02Ct
MURPHY, Catherine	43	F	Laborer	29Au02Ct
Patrick	12	M	None	29Au02Ct
Margaret	9	F	Child	29Au02Ct
Edward	5	M	Child	29Au02Ct
KELLY, Arthur	35	M	Laborer	29Au02Ct
Anne	7	F	Child	29Au02Ct
Margaret	.00	F	Infant	29Au02Ct
SAVAGE, Michael	24	M	Laborer	29Au02Ct
DOWLING, Walter	13	M	Laborer	29Au02Ct
FAME, Mary	17	F	None	29Au02Ct

NAMES OF PASSENGERS	AGE	SEX	OCCUPATIONS	DATE PORT SHIP
FITZGERALD, Mary	28	F	None	29Au02Ct
GORMAN, Ellen	22	F	None	29Au02Ct
MCGRATHER, Mary	30	F	None	29Au02Ct
Bridget	36	F	None	29Au02Ct
Margt.	.00	F	Infant	29Au02Ct
FITZGIBBON, Alice	15	F	None	29Au02Ct
CONDOR, Thomas	27	M	Laborer	29Au02Ct
DUCKNEY, Margaret	40	F	Servant	29Au02Ct
Ellen	20	F	Servant	29Au02Ct
Michael	9	M	Child	29Au02Ct
Thomas	7	M	Child	29Au02Ct
FITZSIMON, Margaret	19	F	None	29Au02Ct
HEALEY, Laurence	30	M	Laborer	29Au02Ct
HEAPHY, Michael	36	M	Laborer	29Au02Ct
Daniel	30	M	Laborer	29Au02Ct
FLYN, Honora	16	F	None	29Au02Ct
DOWNS, Andrew	19	M	Laborer	29Au02Ct
Margaret	21	F	Servant	29Au02Ct
MALLIGAN, John	11	M	Laborer	29Au02Ct
OLWELL, Catherine	56	F	Laborer	29Au02Ct
Catherine	00	F	Laborer	29Au02Ct
William	18	M	Laborer	29Au02Ct
Patrick	13	M	Farmer	29Au02Ct
Mary	12	F	Farmer	29Au02Ct
Margaret	8	F	Child	29Au02Ct
John	6	M	Child	29Au02Ct
Eliza	5	F	Child	29Au02Ct
MULERY, Anna	21	F	None	29Au02Ct
GRAD, James	21	M	Laborer	29Au02Ct
BRACKNEY, Bridget	11	F	None	29Au02Ct
MCGOWN, Philip	30	M	Laborer	29Au02Ct
EAGAN, Catherine	18	F	None	29Au02Ct
DAVIS, Mary-Anne	16	F	None	29Au02Ct
Bridget	15	F	None	29Au02Ct

TERRA-NOVA 29 AUGUST 1849

From PICTOU,N.S.

NAMES OF PASSENGERS	AGE	SEX	OCCUPATIONS	DATE PORT SHIP
MURPHY, James	30	M	Merchant	29Au62Pv

HOLYOKE 29 AUGUST 1849

From Liverpool

NAMES OF PASSENGERS	AGE	SEX	OCCUPATIONS	DATE PORT SHIP
WALPOYLE, Samuel	50	M	Unknown	29Au02Pt
WALPOLYE, Dorcas (W)	50	F	None	29Au02Pt
Samuel	21	M	Draper	29Au02Pt
WALPOYLE, Daniel	19	M	Draper	29Au02Pt
John	18	M	Draper	29Au02Pt
WALPOLYE, James	11	M	None	29Au02Pt
Jane	20	F	Dressmaker	29Au02Pt
Charlotte	14	F	None	29Au02Pt
HOLLINS, Bass	25	F	None	29Au02Pt
RYOYN, Henry	45	M	Gentleman	29Au02Pt
HOGAN, Thomas	40	M	Farmer	29Au02Pt
Cath.	14	F	None	29Au02Pt
BHOLON, Bridget	30	F	Housekeeper	29Au02Pt
HOWE, Thomas	20	M	Laborer	29Au02Pt
ORORKE, Michael	22	M	Laborer	29Au02Pt
LAWLER, Mary	21	F	Dressmaker	29Au02Pt
CARLEN, Mary	23	F	Dressmaker	29Au02Pt

PRINCE-OF-WALES 29 AUGUST 1849

From Liverpool

NAMES OF PASSENGERS	AGE	SEX	OCCUPATIONS	DATE PORT SHIP
DESMOND, Patt	20	M	Laborer	29Au02Pu
BARRY, U-Mrs.	50	F	Matron	29Au02Pu
Mary	15	F	Servant	29Au02Pu
AMBROSE, Mary	20	F	Servant	29Au02Pu
MADDEN, John	40	M	Blacksmith	29Au02Pu
John	5	M	Child	29Au02Pu
MAHER, Wm.	25	M	Laborer	29Au02Pu
MURPHY, Margt.	20	F	Servant	29Au02Pu
WALSH, Jas.	25	M	Laborer	29Au02Pu
LANNEGAN, Margt.	45	F	Servant	29Au02Pu
David	12	M	None	29Au02Pu
John	6	M	Child	29Au02Pu
FITZGERALD, Margt.	20	F	Dressmaker	29Au02Pu
FINLEY, John	25	M	Servant	29Au02Pu
BURNAN, Michl.	19	M	Laborer	29Au02Pu
Honora	17	F	Servant	29Au02Pu
CONNORS, Chas.	40	M	Laborer	29Au02Pu
NAUGHTON, Ellen	26	F	Servant	29Au02Pu
Anne	20	F	Servant	29Au02Pu
RYAN, Bridget	8	F	Child	29Au02Pu
BROWN, Jane	26	F	Servant	29Au02Pu
DARR, John	34	M	Laborer	29Au02Pu
Patt	5	M	Child	29Au02Pu
CUDMORE, Anne	25	F	Laborer	29Au02Pu
MCLONE, Johanna	28	F	Servant	29Au02Pu
PHILLIPS, Thos.	27	M	Laborer	29Au02Pu
HOGAN, Patt	15	M	None	29Au02Pu
MONKEY, Anne	20	F	Servant	29Au02Pu
SULLIVAN, Denis	21	M	Laborer	29Au02Pu
MCCARTHY, John	24	M	Laborer	29Au02Pu
OSULLIVAN, Peggy	20	F	Servant	29Au02Pu
CONNOR, Peggy	20	F	Servant	29Au02Pu
SULLIVAN, Mary	22	F	Servant	29Au02Pu
MURPHY, Julia	19	F	Dressmaker	29Au02Pu
FLYN, John	15	M	Laborer	29Au02Pu
KER, Alice	15	F	Servant	29Au02Pu
Margaret	37	F	Servant	29Au02Pu
William	1	M	Child	29Au02Pu
Biddy	13	F	Servant	29Au02Pu
John	7	M	Child	29Au02Pu
LYNE, Patt	26	M	Laborer	29Au02Pu
Ellen	25	F	Servant	29Au02Pu
Jerry	.00	M	Infant	29Au02Pu
RYAN, Mary	19	F	Servant	29Au02Pu
CREENEY, Guy-C.	18	M	Laborer	29Au02Pu
MARTIN, Catherine	30	F	Servant	29Au02Pu
Sarah	10	F	None	29Au02Pu
Mary-Anne	12	F	None	29Au02Pu
Elizabeth	6	F	Child	29Au02Pu
Ellen	8	F	Child	29Au02Pu
James	3	M	Child	29Au02Pu
Anthony	.00	M	Infant	29Au02Pu
MULAY, Elizabeth	24	F	Servant	29Au02Pu
FARRELL, James	20	M	Laborer	29Au02Pu
CORHALY, U-Miss	22	F	Spinster	29Au02Pu
Peter	19	M	Laborer	29Au02Pu
KEOUGH, Anthony	18	M	Laborer	29Au02Pu
STAFFORD, Thos.	21	M	Laborer	29Au02Pu
FORD, Patt	20	M	Laborer	29Au02Pu
STAFFORD, Mary	20	F	Servant	29Au02Pu
Margt.	21	F	Servant	29Au02Pu
Bridget	12	F	None	29Au02Pu
TYNAN, Peter	28	M	Laborer	29Au02Pu
KENNEY, M.Fred	30	M	Laborer	29Au02Pu
THOMPSON, Edwd.	36	M	Miller	29Au02Pu

NAMES OF PASSENGERS		AGE	SEX	OCCUPATIONS	DATE PORT SHIP
THOMPSON, U	(W)	30	F	Matron	29Au02Pu
Edmond-Thomas		6	M	Child	29Au02Pu
John-Henry		4	M	Child	29Au02Pu
George		.00	M	Infant	29Au02Pu
MARKEY, Owen		30	M	Laborer	29Au02Pu
Mick		15	M	None	29Au02Pu
Catherine		10	F	None	29Au02Pu
James		8	M	Child	29Au02Pu
Patt		6	M	Child	29Au02Pu
HARRIS, Francis		25	M	Cooper	29Au02Pu
MCINTYRE, John		20	M	Laborer	29Au02Pu
KELEHER, James		25	M	Laborer	29Au02Pu
BYLAND, Eliza		23	F	Servant	29Au02Pu
KERNEY, Dan		20	M	Laborer	29Au02Pu
MALONEY, William		19	M	Laborer	29Au02Pu
KENNEDY, Patt		21	M	Laborer	29Au02Pu
CAVANAGH, Mary		22	F	Servant	29Au02Pu
LYNCH, Thos.		35	M	Laborer	29Au02Pu
CURRACK, Jane		22	F	Servant	29Au02Pu
LITTLE, Anne		20	F	Servant	29Au02Pu
Jane		20	F	Servant	29Au02Pu
CLERKIN, Cathe.		25	F	Servant	29Au02Pu
HOUGH, John		20	M	Laborer	29Au02Pu
SMITH, John		20	M	Laborer	29Au02Pu
MULLEN, John		26	M	Sailor	29Au02Pu
GOLDING, John		26	M	Mason	29Au02Pu
Mary		10	F	None	29Au02Pu
GI--M, Bridget		17	F	Servant	29Au02Pu
GUCHAN, Cath.		18	F	Dressmaker	29Au02Pu
LINCKEY, Mary		18	F	Dressmaker	29Au02Pu
FANSTON, Simon		30	M	Laborer	29Au02Pu
Jane		18	F	Matron	29Au02Pu
BAILEY, C.		27	F	Servant	29Au02Pu
JOHNSON, Sarah		27	F	Servant	29Au02Pu
S--R--TON, Martin		23	M	Laborer	29Au02Pu
U	(W)	23	F	Servant	29Au02Pu
HAGAN, Thos.		23	M	Laborer	29Au02Pu
Mcguine--, Sam		20	M	Laborer	29Au02Pu
WHITT, James		23	M	Laborer	29Au02Pu
MCCARTHEY, Dan		30	M	Tinker	29Au02Pu
HEDDEN, Patt		21	M	Laborer	29Au02Pu
HART, Patt		22	M	Laborer	29Au02Pu
DUFFY, Hugh		22	M	Laborer	29Au02Pu
LAINCEY, Cathn.		25	F	Servant	29Au02Pu
James		2	M	Child	29Au02Pu
WHITE, Mary		16	F	Servant	29Au02Pu
MAHER, Thos.		18	M	Laborer	29Au02Pu
FAULKNER, Wm.		42	M	Laborer	29Au02Pu
Mary		40	F	Matron	29Au02Pu
Ellen		11	F	None	29Au02Pu
Willm.		9	M	Child	29Au02Pu
Edward		7	M	Child	29Au02Pu
Henry		.00	M	Infant	29Au02Pu
CORRIGAN, Wm.		22	M	Laborer	29Au02Pu
PERDIN, Maria		21	F	Servant	29Au02Pu
MORRIS, John		20	M	Laborer	29Au02Pu
CONROY, Mich.		30	M	Laborer	29Au02Pu
KERLEY, Bernard		25	M	Laborer	29Au02Pu
HINES, John		45	M	Laborer	29Au02Pu
John		12	M	None	29Au02Pu
BOWER, Jeffrey		27	M	Laborer	29Au02Pu
Cathne.		22	F	Servant	29Au02Pu
SLATTERY, Kyran		26	M	Laborer	29Au02Pu
MALONEY, James		25	M	Laborer	29Au02Pu
COOK, Mich.		24	M	Laborer	29Au02Pu
PURCELL, John		23	M	Laborer	29Au02Pu
BROWN, Mary		28	F	Servant	29Au02Pu
CALDWELL, John		34	M	Laborer	29Au02Pu
Cathne.		34	F	Matron	29Au02Pu
Margt.		6	F	Child	29Au02Pu
John		5	M	Child	29Au02Pu
Bridget		.00	F	Infant	29Au02Pu
SCULLY, Patrick		17	M	Laborer	29Au02Pu
Thomas		13	M	Laborer	29Au02Pu
CORCORAN, James		27	M	Laborer	29Au02Pu

NAMES OF PASSENGERS	AGE	SEX	OCCUPATIONS	DATE PORT SHIP
CORCORAN, Lawrence	20	M	Laborer	29Au02Pu
DILLON, Mary	22	F	Servant	29Au02Pu
SHEW, John	25	M	Laborer	29Au02Pu
Betty	25	F	Servant	29Au02Pu
KELLY, John	42	M	Laborer	29Au02Pu
Bridget	42	F	Matron	29Au02Pu
Michl.	8	M	Child	29Au02Pu
William	4	M	Child	29Au02Pu
Mary	.00	F	Infant	29Au02Pu
SHEW, Bridget	.00	F	Infant	29Au02Pu
MCCARTHY, Eliza	28	F	Servant	29Au02Pu
MADDEN, Michl.	28	M	Laborer	29Au02Pu
Mary	26	F	Servant	29Au02Pu
OBRIEN, Pat	26	M	Laborer	29Au02Pu
DALY, Ann	40	F	Matron	29Au02Pu
William	40	M	Laborer	29Au02Pu
Thomas	25	M	Laborer	29Au02Pu
Ann	20	F	Servant	29Au02Pu
Ellen	20	F	Servant	29Au02Pu
Mary	16	F	Servant	29Au02Pu
Eliza	14	F	Servant	29Au02Pu
GEOGHEGAN, Ann	20	F	Servant	29Au02Pu
STONES, Mary	25	F	Servant	29Au02Pu
John	20	M	Laborer	29Au02Pu
James	20	M	Laborer	29Au02Pu
Mary	16	F	Servant	29Au02Pu
Patrick	14	M	Laborer	29Au02Pu
Andrew	12	M	None	29Au02Pu
Lawrence	10	M	None	29Au02Pu
Mary	6	F	Child	29Au02Pu
Catherine	3	F	Child	29Au02Pu
DALY, Mary	2	F	Child	29Au02Pu
SCOTT, Edwd.	25	M	Carpenter	29Au02Pu
FINNEGAN, Owen	22	M	Laborer	29Au02Pu
SULLIVAN, James	22	M	Laborer	29Au02Pu
GUIRIN, Hartwell	18	M	Laborer	29Au02Pu
MORAN, Pat	19	M	Carpenter	29Au02Pu
Eliza	20	F	Servant	29Au02Pu
CORMICK, Philip	35	M	Laborer	29Au02Pu
Honor	30	F	Matron	29Au02Pu
Alice	8	F	Child	29Au02Pu
Lawrence	.00	M	Infant	29Au02Pu
MEADE, Philip	24	M	Laborer	29Au02Pu
Bridget	22	F	Servant	29Au02Pu
Ann	50	F	Matron	29Au02Pu
James	18	M	Laborer	29Au02Pu
Mary	17	F	Servant	29Au02Pu
Betsy	20	F	Servant	29Au02Pu
James	.00	M	Infant	29Au02Pu
Francis	35	M	Laborer	29Au02Pu
Cath.	25	F	Servant	29Au02Pu
Pat	7	M	Child	29Au02Pu
CONNERS, Pat	25	M	Laborer	29Au02Pu
GILLSTON, Mary	30	F	Servant	29Au02Pu
Joseph	20	M	Laborer	29Au02Pu
HAYES, Margt.	23	F	Servant	29Au02Pu
CONNER, Thos.	25	M	Servant	29Au02Pu
Bridget	20	F	Matron	29Au02Pu
WALL, Johanna	20	F	Servant	29Au02Pu
Johanna	18	F	Servant	29Au02Pu
FARRELL, Edwd.	20	M	Laborer	29Au02Pu
COLEMAN, Deborah	18	F	Servant	29Au02Pu
HENESEY, John	38	M	Laborer	29Au02Pu
BRYAN, James	36	M	Blacksmith	29Au02Pu
LYNCH, Pat	40	M	Laborer	29Au02Pu
Catherine	40	F	Servant	29Au02Pu
DONNELAN, Tim	30	M	Laborer	29Au02Pu
DOWD, James	35	M	Laborer	29Au02Pu
MANON, John	50	M	Laborer	29Au02Pu
CARROLL, Michl.	21	M	Laborer	29Au02Pu
FERGUSON, Hugh	21	M	Laborer	29Au02Pu
Catharine	23	F	Matron	29Au02Pu
WELSH, John	25	M	Laborer	29Au02Pu
DIXON, Peggy	15	F	Servant	29Au02Pu
LAHY, John	30	M	Laborer	29Au02Pu

NAMES OF PASSENGERS		AGE	SEX	OCCUPATIONS	DATE PORT SHIP
REGAN, John		20	M	Laborer	29Au02Pu
CLARKE, Danl.		45	M	Laborer	29Au02Pu
JONES, Robt.		26	M	Laborer	29Au02Pu
SHEILL, Andw.		25	M	Laborer	29Au02Pu
RICHARDSON, Wm.		28	M	Laborer	29Au02Pu
FORDE, John		25	M	Laborer	29Au02Pu
DILLON, John		25	M	Laborer	29Au02Pu
LEHR, Philip		30	M	Laborer	29Au02Pu
MORAN, Edmond		40	M	Laborer	29Au02Pu
Cath.		30	F	Matron	29Au02Pu
Thomas		2	M	Child	29Au02Pu
Jane		.00	F	Infant	29Au02Pu
Margaret		22	F	Servant	29Au02Pu
LARNEY, Mary		25	F	Servant	29Au02Pu
BURK, Mich.		30	M	Laborer	29Au02Pu
YORKEN, James		26	M	Laborer	29Au02Pu
Owen		24	M	Laborer	29Au02Pu
Patrick		.00	M	Infant	29Au02Pu
Died-At-Sea					
CONWAY, Pat		28	M	Clerk	29Au02Pu
AYRE, Peter		20	M	Laborer	29Au02Pu
GREELY, Mich.		30	M	Laborer	29Au02Pu
U	(W)	30	F	Matron	29Au02Pu
John		28	M	Laborer	29Au02Pu
Mary		12	F	None	29Au02Pu
Ellen		6	F	Child	29Au02Pu
Bridget		2	F	Child	29Au02Pu
COFFREY, Catherine		25	F	Servant	29Au02Pu
CONLAN, James		10	M	None	29Au02Pu
LARKIN, Denis		20	M	Laborer	29Au02Pu
LEARY, Jerry		24	M	Laborer	29Au02Pu
U	(W)	20	F	Servant	29Au02Pu
CORCORAN, U		.00	F	Infant	29Au02Pu
Born-At-Sea					

BARBARA 30 AUGUST 1849

From Dublin

NAMES OF PASSENGERS		AGE	SEX	OCCUPATIONS	DATE PORT SHIP
BURKE, Catherin		21	F	Spinster	30Au12Jb
DOHERTY, Fred.		31	M	Laborer	30Au12Jb
Cathn.		60	F	Matron	30Au12Jb
S--LINVAN, Timy.		42	M	Laborer	30Au12Jb
Robt.		26	M	Laborer	30Au12Jb
GAHAN, Maria		20	F	Spinster	30Au12Jb
CLANCY, Cathn.		30	F	Spinster	30Au12Jb
JUNKINS, Ellen		19	F	Spinster	30Au12Jb
MCGUIRE, U-Mrs.		40	F	Matron	30Au12Jb
POWER, Wm.		50	M	Laborer	30Au12Jb
Teresa		21	F	Spinster	30Au12Jb
Lucy		20	F	Spinster	30Au12Jb
BENNETT, Robt.		22	M	Farmer	30Au12Jb
Maria		24	F	Matron	30Au12Jb
MOLAN, Jas.		24	M	Farmer	30Au12Jb
FULLERTON, William		40	M	Farmer	30Au12Jb
John		12	M	Unknown	30Au12Jb
U		.00	U	Infant	30Au12Jb
FARRELL, Margaret		18	F	Spinster	30Au12Jb
Winfield		16	M	Laborer	30Au12Jb
DAY, John		29	M	Laborer	30Au12Jb
COYKELY, Eliza		20	F	Spinster	30Au12Jb
U		.00	U	Infant	30Au12Jb
Jas.		12	M	Unknown	30Au12Jb
Ann		2	F	Child	30Au12Jb
CONNOLLY, Patk.		29	M	Laborer	30Au12Jb
U	(W)	25	F	Matron	30Au12Jb
Mary		6	F	Child	30Au12Jb
Thomas		4	M	Child	30Au12Jb
Patk.		2	M	Child	30Au12Jb
CONNOLLY, U		.00	U	Infant	30Au12Jb
GRATTAN, Catherin		50	F	Matron	30Au12Jb
CUNNINGHAM, Thos.		12	M	Unknown	30Au12Jb
COSGROVE, Peter		30	M	Laborer	30Au12Jb
Eliza		23	F	Matron	30Au12Jb
U		.00	U	Infant	30Au12Jb
BRISCOE, Daniel		26	M	Farmer	30Au12Jb
U	(W)	20	F	Matron	30Au12Jb
DELANEY, Jane		10	F	Unknown	30Au12Jb
WHITE, Frances		12	F	Unknown	30Au12Jb
GALLILEE, Michael		45	M	Laborer	30Au12Jb
Mary		45	F	Matron	30Au12Jb
Mary-Anne		5	F	Child	30Au12Jb
U		.00	U	Infant	30Au12Jb
SCULLY, Thomas		13	M	Unknown	30Au12Jb
RORKE, Miles		28	M	Laborer	30Au12Jb
Jane		25	F	Spinster	30Au12Jb
BYRNE, Edwd.		20	M	Laborer	30Au12Jb
U	(W)	24	F	Laborer	30Au12Jb
FLEMING, Thos.		50	M	Laborer	30Au12Jb
Jane		30	F	Dressmaker	30Au12Jb
Ellen		10	F	Unknown	30Au12Jb
Edwd.		9	M	Child	30Au12Jb
Christy		7	U	Child	30Au12Jb
DANIEL, U-Mr.		33	M	Draper	30Au12Jb
U-Miss		28	F	Spinster	30Au12Jb
GRAYDEN, T.Miss		12	F	Unknown	30Au12Jb
DERMODY, Philip		19	M	Laborer	30Au12Jb
James		4	M	Child	30Au12Jb
HEWITT, Bridget		32	F	Spinster	30Au12Jb
Susan		6	F	Child	30Au12Jb
Mary-Ann		4	F	Child	30Au12Jb
U		.00	U	Infant	30Au12Jb
CREIGHTON, Eliza		40	F	Spinster	30Au12Jb
U		8	U	Child	30Au12Jb
U		6	U	Child	30Au12Jb
FLETCHER, U-Mr.		30	M	Farmer	30Au12Jb
U	(W)	30	F	Matron	30Au12Jb
U	(S)	17	M	Farmer	30Au12Jb
LUCAS, Mary		18	F	Spinster	30Au12Jb
KNAGGS, Robt.		24	M	Laborer	30Au12Jb
Ann		55	F	Matron	30Au12Jb
James		9	M	Child	30Au12Jb
MELVILL, Ann		22	F	Spinster	30Au12Jb
FINLAW, Patk.		40	M	Laborer	30Au12Jb
U	(W)	40	F	Matron	30Au12Jb
Mary-A.		8	F	Child	30Au12Jb
U		.00	U	Infant	30Au12Jb
SPUNK, Alexr.		24	M	Farmer	30Au12Jb
BATES, Jas.J.		29	M	Farmer	30Au12Jb
DONNELLY, Ann		28	F	Matron	30Au12Jb
Mary-A.		8	F	Child	30Au12Jb
Esther		5	F	Child	30Au12Jb
Ellen		3	F	Child	30Au12Jb
Cathn.		20	F	Spinster	30Au12Jb
U		.00	U	Infant	30Au12Jb
HOEY, Richd.		20	M	Farmer	30Au12Jb
MURRANE, Thos.		20	M	Farmer	30Au12Jb
DRUM, Charles		22	M	Shopkeeper	30Au12Jb
MASON, James		25	M	Shopkeeper	30Au12Jb
Cathn.		8	F	Child	30Au12Jb
FLAHERTY, James		23	M	Farmer	30Au12Jb
FLANAGAN, Biddy		9	F	Child	30Au12Jb
MOREE, Mary		11	F	Unknown	30Au12Jb
HACKETT, Rozanna		16	F	Spinster	30Au12Jb
CAHILL, Johanna		20	M	Spinster	30Au12Jb
WALLACE, William		12	M	Unknown	30Au12Jb
GIL, John		30	M	Farmer	30Au12Jb
GAINFORD, Jane		40	F	Matron	30Au12Jb
Eliza		3	F	Child	30Au12Jb
ASKEW, Wm.		39	M	Farmer	30Au12Jb
MATTHEWS, Rose		50	F	Matron	30Au12Jb
Jas.		12	M	Unknown	30Au12Jb
CLARK, James		30	M	Farmer	30Au12Jb
Bridget		30	F	Matron	30Au12Jb

NAMES OF PASSENGERS	AGE	SEX	OCCUPATIONS	DATE PORT SHIP
BLIGHE, Jane	12	F	Unknown	30Au12Jb
MCCABE, Peter	10	M	Unknown	30Au12Jb
GAINFORD, U	.00	U	Infant	30Au12Jb
MCCABE, Ann	6	F	Child	30Au12Jb
CLARK, Mary	20	F	Spinster	30Au12Jb
BELL, Eliza	13	F	Unknown	30Au12Jb
Teressa	18	F	Spinster	30Au12Jb
DALY, Dermod	20	M	Laborer	30Au12Jb
LYNCH, James	25	M	Laborer	30Au12Jb
U (W)	25	F	Matron	30Au12Jb
BANNON, Julia	23	F	Matron	30Au12Jb
MURRAY, Margt.	23	F	Matron	30Au12Jb
Philip	4	M	Child	30Au12Jb
RYAN, Mary	28	F	Spinster	30Au12Jb
Sarah	18	F	Spinster	30Au12Jb
Bridget	16	F	Spinster	30Au12Jb
MURRAY, Con	8	M	Child	30Au12Jb
GLEESON, Margt.	22	F	Spinster	30Au12Jb
MCDERMOTT, Dennis	20	M	Laborer	30Au12Jb
U (W)	20	F	Matron	30Au12Jb
KELLY, Isabella	15	F	Spinster	30Au12Jb
HOWARD, Ellen	19	F	Spinster	30Au12Jb
BURKE, John	45	M	Farmer	30Au12Jb
PURCELL, George	50	M	Farmer	30Au12Jb
Cathn.	50	F	Matron	30Au12Jb
Jane	12	F	Unknown	30Au12Jb
Ann	20	F	Matron	30Au12Jb
Martin	13	M	Unknown	30Au12Jb
DONOHOE, John	10	M	Unknown	30Au12Jb
Bridget	25	F	Spinster	30Au12Jb
Ann	2	F	Child	30Au12Jb
Patrick	12	M	Unknown	30Au12Jb
RYAN, Michael	40	M	Farmer	30Au12Jb
Mary	18	F	Wife	30Au12Jb
PURCELL, Patk.	30	M	Farmer	30Au12Jb
Mary	30	F	Wife	30Au12Jb
John	10	M	Unknown	30Au12Jb
COSTELLOW, Eliza	20	F	Spinster	30Au12Jb
Ellen	20	F	Spinster	30Au12Jb
ENRIGHT, Thomas	20	M	Shoemaker	30Au12Jb
PURCELL, John	30	M	Shoemaker	30Au12Jb
DOSTAN, Patk.	20	M	Weaver	30Au12Jb
KEOGH, Ambrose	20	M	Farmer	30Au12Jb
WALSH, John	30	M	Farmer	30Au12Jb
DOYLE, Marty	30	M	Farmer	30Au12Jb
Mary	26	F	Matron	30Au12Jb
Kitty	26	F	Matron	30Au12Jb
GREEN, Eliza	21	F	Matron	30Au12Jb
BRIEN, Ann	29	F	Matron	30Au12Jb
WALSH, Magt.	20	F	Spinster	30Au12Jb
HUGHES, Robt.	26	M	Unknown	30Au12Jb
PURCELL, U	.00	U	Infant	30Au12Jb
CRAWFORD, James	30	M	Unknown	30Au12Jb
MCSWEENEY, J.	35	M	Unknown	30Au12Jb

JESSORE 01 SEPTEMBER 1849

From Liverpool

NAMES OF PASSENGERS	AGE	SEX	OCCUPATIONS	DATE PORT SHIP
DALY, Thomas	23	M	Laborer	01Se02Py
CORLAND, Anthony	56	M	Laborer	01Se02Py
Anthony-Jr.	22	M	Laborer	01Se02Py
Catharine	18	F	None	01Se02Py
HALPIN, John	24	M	Blacksmith	01Se02Py
Daniel	26	M	Shoemaker	01Se02Py
ROWARTH, Margaret	18	F	None	01Se02Py
SCANLON, Alice	25	F	None	01Se02Py
DONAVAN, John	22	M	Laborer	01Se02Py
SHEIL, John	00	M	Tailor	01Se02Py
FLANAGAN, J.	35	M	Unknown	01Se02Py
HICKEY, John	18	M	Unknown	01Se02Py
MCLAUGHTON, Peter	23	M	Unknown	01Se02Py
EYRES, Catherine	40	F	None	01Se02Py
Winifred	11	F	None	01Se02Py
Lawrence	14	M	Laborer	01Se02Py
Patrick	8	M	Child	01Se02Py
John	5	M	Child	01Se02Py
RYAN, Edward	40	M	Farmer	01Se02Py
James	23	M	Baker	01Se02Py
MCCARTHY, Margaret	28	F	None	01Se02Py
Bridget	4	F	Child	01Se02Py
Mary Died-At-Sea	.00	F	Infant	01Se02Py
DELAHANTY, Pat.	23	M	Tailor	01Se02Py
BRADY, John	17	M	Laborer	01Se02Py
MAHER, Bridget	55	F	None	01Se02Py
SHELLY, Marg.	23	F	None	01Se02Py
MAHER, Patr.	16	M	Laborer	01Se02Py
MOGAN, Thomas	50	M	Farmer	01Se02Py
SWINN, John	28	M	Painter	01Se02Py
SEXTON, Patrick	24	M	Laborer	01Se02Py
LYNCH, Timothy	30	M	Footman	01Se02Py
CONNOR, John	18	M	Cbtmkr	01Se02Py
COONEY, Edmond	40	M	Laborer	01Se02Py
FAGAN, Ann	40	F	None	01Se02Py
DUNN, Mary	19	F	None	01Se02Py
FARRELL, Bridget	18	F	None	01Se02Py
TUITE, Maria	18	F	None	01Se02Py
BURNS, Mary	22	F	None	01Se02Py
DOHERTY, John	35	M	Laborer	01Se02Py
WELSH, Edmund	21	M	Unknown	01Se02Py
FAHEY, Timothy	32	M	Laborer	01Se02Py
SEARY, Mary	20	F	None	01Se02Py
HARRINGTON, Catherine	22	F	None	01Se02Py
MCDONOUGH, Isabella	16	F	None	01Se02Py
DEVANNAH, Ann	16	F	None	01Se02Py
Margaret	22	F	None	01Se02Py
FOGARTY, Ellen	18	F	None	01Se02Py
FARRELL, Bridget	17	F	None	01Se02Py
KELLY, John	20	M	Laborer	01Se02Py
MEARNS, John	22	M	Farmer	01Se02Py
HEARLEY, Daniel	18	M	Laborer	01Se02Py
DAGANON, Ann	12	F	None	01Se02Py
HEARLEY, Ann	14	F	None	01Se02Py
REYNOLDS, Ann	25	F	None	01Se02Py
KENNY, Patrick	12	M	None	01Se02Py
MCGHEE, Peterson	23	M	Baker	01Se02Py
MONEY, Phillip	31	M	Shoemaker	01Se02Py
GOULD, Jane	17	F	None	01Se02Py
HADDAFID, Robert	32	M	Shoemaker	01Se02Py
Elizabeth	28	F	None	01Se02Py
Robert	2	M	Child	01Se02Py
Jane	5	F	Child	01Se02Py
MCVAGH, Edward	42	M	Dealer	01Se02Py
Ellen	43	F	None	01Se02Py
Elizabeth	10	F	None	01Se02Py
HEALEY, Michael	53	M	Mason	01Se02Py
Margeret	53	F	None	01Se02Py
Catherine	20	F	None	01Se02Py
FERGUSON, James	47	M	Farmer	01Se02Py
Harriett	40	F	None	01Se02Py
John	19	M	None	01Se02Py
Selina	21	F	None	01Se02Py
Mary	17	F	None	01Se02Py
Margaret	16	F	None	01Se02Py
Harriett	15	F	None	01Se02Py
Emily	13	F	None	01Se02Py
Charlotte	7	F	Child	01Se02Py
Olivia	5	F	Child	01Se02Py
HARRISON, Sarah	24	F	None	01Se02Py
MANSFIELD, Ralph	36	M	Farmer	01Se02Py
HARVEY, Alice	35	F	None	01Se02Py
Rose	13	F	None	01Se02Py
Sarah	6	F	Child	01Se02Py

NAMES OF PASSENGERS	AGE	SEX	OCCUPATIONS	DATE PORT SHIP
HARVEY, Alice	2	F	Child	01Se02Py
REARDON, Andrew	56	M	Cbtmkr	01Se02Py
WILSON, James	21	M	Laborer	01Se02Py
CALLAHA, Timothy	34	M	Laborer	01Se02Py
MCCARTHY, Catherine	22	F	None	01Se02Py
GORMAN, Margaret	25	F	None	01Se02Py
LYNCH, Mary	20	F	None	01Se02Py
CONDRUN, Margaret	18	F	None	01Se02Py
JACKSON, Miles	28	M	Chtmr	01Se02Py
FLANIGAN, Thomas	40	M	None	01Se02Py
Honor	21	F	None	01Se02Py
GAUGHAN, Betty	21	F	None	01Se02Py
WELSH, James	28	M	Farmer	01Se02Py
George	25	M	Farmer	01Se02Py
Mary-Ann	22	F	None	01Se02Py
Lucy	25	F	None	01Se02Py
KARRAGH, Ann	18	F	None	01Se02Py
HOGAN, Mary	17	F	None	01Se02Py
MATTHEWS, Honoria	18	F	None	01Se02Py
HINDS, Stephen	24	M	Laborer	01Se02Py
GLEESON, Michael	30	M	Laborer	01Se02Py
COYLE, Peter	40	M	Weaver	01Se02Py
John	27	M	Laborer	01Se02Py
Thomas	38	M	Laborer	01Se02Py
CLARK, Charles	47	M	Joiner	01Se02Py
KEYNS, Michael	24	M	Laborer	01Se02Py
VICTORY, John	46	M	Farmer	01Se02Py
Catherine	18	F	None	01Se02Py
FOY, Farrell	20	M	Laborer	01Se02Py
MCDONALD, John	20	M	Shoemaker	01Se02Py
Peter	17	M	Laborer	01Se02Py
FITZGERALD, Maurice	44	M	Farmer	01Se02Py
DONOHUE, John	16	M	Mason	01Se02Py
FITZGERALD, Mary	12	F	None	01Se02Py
WOOD, Thomas	60	M	Farmer	01Se02Py
Patrick	14	M	None	01Se02Py
Mary	12	F	None	01Se02Py
Margeret	11	F	None	01Se02Py
Catherine	10	F	None	01Se02Py
Peter	8	M	Child	01Se02Py
Jemmy	7	M	Child	01Se02Py
Thomas	5	M	Child	01Se02Py
John	.00	M	Infant	01Se02Py
RING, Richard	18	M	Cook	01Se02Py
Elizabeth	49	F	None	01Se02Py
MOLOY, Catherine	40	F	None	01Se02Py
Peter	7	F	Child	01Se02Py
Sarah	.00	F	Infant	01Se02Py
KEATING, William	24	M	Painter	01Se02Py
James	9	M	Child	01Se02Py
SHANNON, Catherine	28	F	None	01Se02Py
CROFTON, John	11	M	Laborer	01Se02Py
MCKAIG, James	30	M	Laborer	01Se02Py
HINES, Lawrence	20	M	Laborer	01Se02Py
KILLEEN, Thos.	19	M	Laborer	01Se02Py
CANNON, Michael	42	M	Laborer	01Se02Py
Mary	8	F	Child	01Se02Py
Patrick	6	M	Child	01Se02Py
BURKE, Mary	10	F	None	01Se02Py
ABBOTT, Terence	30	M	Laborer	01Se02Py
Catherine	18	F	None	01Se02Py
DAXON, Edward	28	M	Groom	01Se02Py
OKEEFE, Mary	30	F	Dairymaid	01Se02Py
ROCHE, Peggy	24	F	Dairymaid	01Se02Py
LATIMER, Jane	18	F	Dairymaid	01Se02Py
DELAHANTY, Margeret	23	F	Dairymaid	01Se02Py
KILLIFY, Patrick	25	M	Laborer	01Se02Py
TOUHEY, Nancy	22	F	None	01Se02Py
WELSH, Winifred	20	F	None	01Se02Py
TOUHEY, John	22	M	None	01Se02Py
KENNEDY, Thomas	20	M	None	01Se02Py
COONEY, John	18	M	None	01Se02Py
TOUHEY, Martin	18	M	None	01Se02Py
COMINGS, James	15	M	None	01Se02Py
MORAN, Michael	23	M	Laborer	01Se02Py

NAMES OF PASSENGERS	AGE	SEX	OCCUPATIONS	DATE PORT SHIP
MORAN, Mary	20	F	Laborer	01Se02Py
LUNDRIGAN, James	27	M	Laborer	01Se02Py
BURKE, William	26	M	Laborer	01Se02Py
FOORD, Martin	20	M	Laborer	01Se02Py
KERNEY, William	26	M	Shoemaker	01Se02Py
Honoria	25	F	None	01Se02Py
Thos.Francis	.11	M	Infant	01Se02Py
KEITH, Michael	30	M	Laborer	01Se02Py
KELLY, Thomas	40	M	Laborer	01Se02Py
HARRIGAN, Cornelius	40	M	Laborer	01Se02Py
James	6	M	Child	01Se02Py
Johanna	4	F	Child	01Se02Py

CAMBRIDGE 01 SEPTEMBER 1849

From Liverpool

NAMES OF PASSENGERS	AGE	SEX	OCCUPATIONS	DATE PORT SHIP
PHILLIPS, Geo.	35	M	Merchant	01Se02Gk
Rosanna	30	F	None	01Se02Gk
Richd.	11	M	None	01Se02Gk
George	6	M	Child	01Se02Gk
William	4	M	Child	01Se02Gk
Joseph	2	M	Child	01Se02Gk
HUGHES, Joannah	14	F	None	01Se02Gk
BREWER, Thomas	35	M	Farmer	01Se02Gk
Jane	28	F	None	01Se02Gk
DESMOND, John	28	M	Cooper	01Se02Gk
Julia	21	F	None	01Se02Gk
CLINTON, Richard	30	M	Farmer	01Se02Gk
Margaret	30	F	None	01Se02Gk
Margaret	.00	F	Infant	01Se02Gk
EGAN, William	60	M	Laborer	01Se02Gk
HAMILTON, Sally	64	F	None	01Se02Gk
RADDICAN, Bridget	50	F	Servant	01Se02Gk
Peter	21	M	Servant	01Se02Gk
Ellen	22	F	Servant	01Se02Gk
FITSPATRICK, Margt.	60	F	Servant	01Se02Gk
FELTS, Pat.	18	M	Laborer	01Se02Gk
BRUDEN, Bridget	45	F	Servant	01Se02Gk
Mary	13	F	Servant	01Se02Gk
Sarah	10	F	Child	01Se02Gk
Pat	8	M	Child	01Se02Gk
CARR, Bridget	40	F	Servant	01Se02Gk
Winny	60	F	Servant	01Se02Gk
CARNAY, Bridget	6	F	Child	01Se02Gk
RAHOLLY, Margt.	60	F	Servant	01Se02Gk
MURPHEY, Tim	20	M	Laborer	01Se02Gk
GLENNON, James	23	M	Laborer	01Se02Gk
CULLARTY, Daily	20	M	Laborer	01Se02Gk
MCSWAINEY, Ellen	22	F	Servant	01Se02Gk
Cath.	4	F	Child	01Se02Gk
RAHOLY, Margt.	10	F	Child	01Se02Gk
PRENNABLE, Cath.	7	F	Child	01Se02Gk
FLEMMERY, John	25	M	Laborer	01Se02Gk
KELLY, Jer.	23	M	Laborer	01Se02Gk
Thomas	17	M	Laborer	01Se02Gk
CURRAN, James	30	M	Laborer	01Se02Gk
BURKE, Walter	25	M	Laborer	01Se02Gk
RYAN, Ellen	18	F	Servant	01Se02Gk
Mary	16	F	Servant	01Se02Gk
CULLAN, Bridget	22	F	Servant	01Se02Gk
FLAMMERY, Jerh.	10	M	Laborer	01Se02Gk
PARKINSON, Robt.	60	M	Laborer	01Se02Gk
CRYNE, Margt.	30	F	Servant	01Se02Gk
OWENS, John	45	M	Laborer	01Se02Gk
DOONEY, Martin	45	M	Laborer	01Se02Gk
Connor	19	M	Servant	01Se02Gk
FLOOD, Ann	55	F	Servant	01Se02Gk
Eliza	20	F	Servant	01Se02Gk

NAMES OF PASSENGERS	AGE	SEX	OCCUPATIONS	DATE PORT SHIP
FARRELL, Cath.	35	F	Servant	01Se02Gk
MAHON, James	30	M	Laborer	01Se02Gk
MCGUIRE, Mary	34	F	Servant	01Se02Gk
Pat	6	M	Child	01Se02Gk
Mary	7	F	Child	01Se02Gk
Michael	.00	M	Infant	01Se02Gk
DWIRE, Mary	30	F	Servant	01Se02Gk
Ann	10	F	Child	01Se02Gk
Cath.	8	F	Child	01Se02Gk
Mary	7	F	Child	01Se02Gk
John	4	M	Child	01Se02Gk
WALSH, Bartley	68	M	Shoemaker	01Se02Gk
HOPKINS, Michael	17	M	Laborer	01Se02Gk
Raley	15	M	Laborer	01Se02Gk
Pat	12	M	Laborer	01Se02Gk
CUNNINGHAM, John	30	M	Laborer	01Se02Gk
SHEA, Thos.	30	M	Laborer	01Se02Gk
FARRELL, John	50	M	Laborer	01Se02Gk
DWIRE, Thomas	14	M	Servant	01Se02Gk
MULRAY, James	30	M	Laborer	01Se02Gk
Mary	40	F	Servant	01Se02Gk
MCCABE, Barnard	18	M	Laborer	01Se02Gk
Peter	11	M	Laborer	01Se02Gk
BONDIDEN, Mary	18	F	Servant	01Se02Gk
SCULLIN, Henry	21	M	Laborer	01Se02Gk
EGAN, John	18	M	Laborer	01Se02Gk
MCNULTY, James	18	M	Laborer	01Se02Gk
FENNELL, Cath.	29	F	Servant	01Se02Gk
MCCAFFERTY, Pat	20	M	Laborer	01Se02Gk
MCNAMINY, James	23	M	Laborer	01Se02Gk
CRAWLEY, Thos.	40	M	Laborer	01Se02Gk
HUGHES, Henry	12	M	Laborer	01Se02Gk
CASSIDY, Cath.	28	F	Vintner	01Se02Gk
Mary	6	F	Child	01Se02Gk
Nancy	4	F	Child	01Se02Gk
James	2	M	Child	01Se02Gk
ONEIL, John	36	M	Shoemaker	01Se02Gk
FARVIN, Simeon	25	M	Laborer	01Se02Gk
SULIVAN, Bart.	19	M	Laborer	01Se02Gk
MURPHY, David	56	M	Laborer	01Se02Gk
KILDUFF, Mary	22	F	Servant	01Se02Gk
Betsey	.00	F	Infant	01Se02Gk
BRADLEY, Mary	18	F	Servant	01Se02Gk
KANE, Bridget	4	F	Child	01Se02Gk
CROMPTON, Rachael	23	F	Servant	01Se02Gk
Eliza	2	F	Child	01Se02Gk
Martha	.00	F	Infant	01Se02Gk
GILROY, Terrell	21	M	Laborer	01Se02Gk
HARTNETT, James	20	M	Servant	01Se02Gk
DOGHERTY, John	16	M	Laborer	01Se02Gk
LENNARD, Mary	22	F	Dressmaker	01Se02Gk
SHELLY, Bridget	22	F	Dressmaker	01Se02Gk
Mary	20	F	Dressmaker	01Se02Gk
MASON, John	19	M	Gdnr	01Se02Gk
MCDONNALD, Alexr.	22	M	Cooper	01Se02Gk
STEWART, John	22	M	Laborer	01Se02Gk
SILL, Eliza	22	F	Servant	01Se02Gk
James	4	M	Child	01Se02Gk
MORRISON, Edmund	40	M	Laborer	01Se02Gk
BRIDEN, Ellen	15	F	Servant	01Se02Gk
John	10	M	Child	01Se02Gk
Cath.	7	F	Child	01Se02Gk
PENDIN, Mary	21	F	Servant	01Se02Gk
Joannah	13	F	Servant	01Se02Gk
DREWS, John	22	M	Laborer	01Se02Gk
STEKELAND, Pat	40	M	Laborer	01Se02Gk
DICKSON, Hugh	24	M	Laborer	01Se02Gk
BROWN, Julia	60	F	None	01Se02Gk
Jerh.	19	M	Waiter	01Se02Gk
Thomas	10	M	Child	01Se02Gk
Valentine	15	M	None	01Se02Gk
Julia	17	F	None	01Se02Gk
HUGHES, Geo.	13	M	None	01Se02Gk
BURSTON, Mary	24	F	Servant	01Se02Gk
CUSSLEY, Ann	45	F	Servant	01Se02Gk
DARVIL, James	23	M	Grinder	01Se02Gk
HAMILTON, Thos.	40	M	Laborer	01Se02Gk
Isab.	25	F	None	01Se02Gk
DUVAN, Martin	22	M	Laborer	01Se02Gk
KELLY, John	45	M	Laborer	01Se02Gk
Maria	45	F	None	01Se02Gk
Mary	16	F	None	01Se02Gk
Alice	10	F	Child	01Se02Gk
Catherine	4	F	Child	01Se02Gk
DUFFY, Mary-A.	16	F	Servant	01Se02Gk
KELLY, Mary	15	F	Servant	01Se02Gk
CLARKE, Peter	21	M	Blacksmith	01Se02Gk
RUTFORD, James	27	M	Laborer	01Se02Gk
Cath.	18	F	Unknown	01Se02Gk
POLLARD, Ellen	24	F	Servant	01Se02Gk
RIDNEY, Rebecca	19	F	Servant	01Se02Gk
FENNELL, Eliza	24	F	Servant	01Se02Gk
BERRY, Maria	17	F	Servant	01Se02Gk
HARRIS, Mary-A.	19	F	Servant	01Se02Gk
BRANNAGAN, Hugh	50	M	Weaver	01Se02Gk
HENRY, Susan	20	F	None	01Se02Gk
DELANEY, Daniel	31	M	Wagon Maker	01Se02Gk
MCGONNELL, Ann	18	F	Servant	01Se02Gk
GAFFNEY, Mary	38	F	Servant	01Se02Gk
SILK, John	25	M	Painter	01Se02Gk
SHERRAN, Jane	30	F	Servant	01Se02Gk
GARRITY, Rose	26	F	Servant	01Se02Gk
ROGAN, Daniel	28	M	Cooper	01Se02Gk
MCCALLEY, Geo.	21	M	Laborer	01Se02Gk
Hariet	21	F	Housekeeper	01Se02Gk
LIEWS, Nancy-J.	20	F	Servant	01Se02Gk
FLOOD, John	30	M	Laborer	01Se02Gk
HUGHES, Michael	17	M	Laborer	01Se02Gk
BURNS, Pat	21	M	Laborer	01Se02Gk
Alice	20	F	Laborer	01Se02Gk
ROHAN, Edmund	17	M	Laborer	01Se02Gk
Honorah	18	F	Servant	01Se02Gk
MCKENNAN, Betsey	18	F	Servant	01Se02Gk
MURTHAN, Wm.	17	M	Laborer	01Se02Gk
MORRISON, Dan.K.	18	M	Laborer	01Se02Gk
SMYTH, John	21	M	Laborer	01Se02Gk
FERRALL, Margaret	40	F	Servant	01Se02Gk
Wynett	8	F	Child	01Se02Gk
Mary	6	F	Child	01Se02Gk
HUGHES, John	28	M	Laborer	01Se02Gk
Ann	20	F	Housekeeper	01Se02Gk
Ann	11	F	Housekeeper	01Se02Gk
KELLY, James	25	M	Laborer	01Se02Gk
MCGOWAN, Rose	28	F	Servant	01Se02Gk
RAFFER, Thomas	23	M	Laborer	01Se02Gk
Nancy	21	F	Housekeeper	01Se02Gk
St.JOHN, Cath.	20	F	Servant	01Se02Gk
MCDONNELLY, Mary	50	F	Servant	01Se02Gk
John	4	M	Child	01Se02Gk
Cath.	.00	F	Infant	01Se02Gk
Mary	3	F	Child	01Se02Gk
BOYD, Mary	27	F	Servant	01Se02Gk
Samuel	3	M	Child	01Se02Gk
BUSKETT, Michael	20	M	Clerk	01Se02Gk
NOTTON, Mary	20	F	Servant	01Se02Gk
FLANNAGAN, Catherine	17	F	Servant	01Se02Gk
EGAN, Bridgt.	30	F	Servant	01Se02Gk
Christopher	14	M	Servant	01Se02Gk
Pat	9	M	Child	01Se02Gk
James	7	M	Child	01Se02Gk
Thos.	4	M	Child	01Se02Gk
Eliza.	2	F	Child	01Se02Gk
Marsella	12	F	None	01Se02Gk
GRADY, Alice	40	F	Housekeeper	01Se02Gk
Judy	.00	M	Infant	01Se02Gk
Pat	6	M	Child	01Se02Gk
Mary	7	F	Child	01Se02Gk
OBRIEN, Michael	40	M	Laborer	01Se02Gk
Ellen	35	F	Housekeeper	01Se02Gk
Margt.	.00	F	Infant	01Se02Gk

NAMES OF PASSENGERS	AGE	SEX	OCCUPATIONS	DATE PORT SHIP
OBRIEN, Thos.	9	M	Child	01Se02Gk
Pat	6	M	Child	01Se02Gk
Judy	5	F	Child	01Se02Gk
Nancy	4	F	Child	01Se02Gk
GONNIN, Dennis	19	M	Laborer	01Se02Gk
SHERIDAN, Bridget	40	F	Servant	01Se02Gk
Mich.	9	M	Child	01Se02Gk
CULLIHAN, Jerh.	11	M	Laborer	01Se02Gk
ODONNELL, Biddy	28	F	Servant	01Se02Gk
Nathan	2	M	Child	01Se02Gk
RYAN, Mullekey	18	M	Laborer	01Se02Gk
Thos.	20	M	Laborer	01Se02Gk
BROWN, Wm.	25	M	Laborer	01Se02Gk
Michael	18	M	Laborer	01Se02Gk
Deborah	18	F	Servant	01Se02Gk
GORMAN, Conn	35	M	Laborer	01Se02Gk
CARR, John	25	M	Laborer	01Se02Gk
RONNALDS, Margt.	25	F	Servant	01Se02Gk
MCCLEAN, Michl.	45	M	Laborer	01Se02Gk
Cath.	35	F	Housekeeper	01Se02Gk
Ellen	12	F	None	01Se02Gk
John	10	M	Child	01Se02Gk
Thos.	8	M	Child	01Se02Gk
Michl.	2	M	Child	01Se02Gk
Joannah	.00	F	Infant	01Se02Gk
RYAN, James	21	M	Laborer	01Se02Gk
MCCLEAN, Mary	5	F	Child	01Se02Gk
MCBUSH, Sarah	38	F	Servant	01Se02Gk
OWENS, Margt.	20	F	Servant	01Se02Gk
Cath.	18	F	Servant	01Se02Gk
FEGAN, Biddy	27	F	Servant	01Se02Gk
GULL, Christopher	40	M	Shoemaker	01Se02Gk
CAPHLAN, Robt.	30	M	Laborer	01Se02Gk
DAOLAN, Pat	27	M	Laborer	01Se02Gk
ROBINSON, Rosey	20	F	Dressmaker	01Se02Gk
LOWE, Ann	20	F	Dressmaker	01Se02Gk
TROONEY, Hugh	35	M	Laborer	01Se02Gk
MARTIN, Pat	28	M	Laborer	01Se02Gk
DOONEY, Eliza	25	F	Servant	01Se02Gk
PARKS, Arthur	56	M	Laborer	01Se02Gk
Thos.	30	M	Laborer	01Se02Gk
Eliza	14	F	Servant	01Se02Gk
Arthur	12	M	None	01Se02Gk
Wm.	10	M	Child	01Se02Gk
John	24	M	Laborer	01Se02Gk
HENDERSON, Joseph	18	M	Laborer	01Se02Gk
SETTON, Jane	21	F	Servant	01Se02Gk
HARVEY, John	30	M	Farmer	01Se02Gk
Mary	18	F	None	01Se02Gk
Pat	3	M	Child	01Se02Gk
CARSON, James	40	M	Laborer	01Se02Gk
Hugh	18	M	Laborer	01Se02Gk
GULTON, Neil	18	M	Laborer	01Se02Gk
KELLY, James	21	M	Laborer	01Se02Gk
CONNOR, Eliza	16	F	Servant	01Se02Gk
HAYLES, Daniel	18	M	Laborer	01Se02Gk
CLARKE, James	23	M	Laborer	01Se02Gk
MARKEY, Hugh	23	M	Laborer	01Se02Gk
WILLIAMS, Michl.	29	M	Maurer	01Se02Gk
Mary	29	F	Housekeeper	01Se02Gk
Ann	4	F	Child	01Se02Gk
John	.00	M	Infant	01Se02Gk
CASSOCK, John	19	M	Laborer	01Se02Gk
HERGAN, Michael	60	M	Laborer	01Se02Gk
Mary	60	F	Servant	01Se02Gk
KERNON, Stephen	60	M	Servant	01Se02Gk
BAGAN, Sarah	20	F	Dressmaker	01Se02Gk
Mary	30	F	Dressmaker	01Se02Gk
HIGHLAND, Mary	20	F	Servant	01Se02Gk
MCCURDAY, Alex.	22	M	Laborer	01Se02Gk
TOUR, James	20	M	Unknown	01Se02Gk
Bridget	22	F	Servant	01Se02Gk
Bridget	20	F	Dressmaker	01Se02Gk
DUSKILL, Judy	35	F	Servant	01Se02Gk
WHALEN, Michl.	10	M	Child	01Se02Gk
MCKERVEN, John	40	M	Shepherd	01Se02Gk
MCSWENEY, Margt.	28	F	Servant	01Se02Gk
HUGHES, Ann	20	F	Servant	01Se02Gk
DOGHERTY, Cath.	20	F	Servant	01Se02Gk
Biddy	29	F	Servant	01Se02Gk
MCCURLEY, Eliza	25	F	Servant	01Se02Gk
ANGELICO, Jacob	18	M	Mariner	01Se02Gk

FAIRFIELD 03 SEPTEMBER 1849

From Liverpool

NAMES OF PASSENGERS	AGE	SEX	OCCUPATIONS	DATE PORT SHIP
MAWDSLEY, Evan-C.	24	M	Gentleman	03Se02Pz
U (W)	23	F	Lady	03Se02Pz
Ann-Mrs.	50	F	Lady	03Se02Pz
FARRY, Mary	30	F	Spinster	03Se02Pz
HAGAN, Mary	19	F	Spinster	03Se02Pz
ROWBOTTOM, Jno.	13	M	Laborer	03Se02Pz
MULDOON, Pat	18	M	Laborer	03Se02Pz
DIVINE, Pat	18	M	Laborer	03Se02Pz
DILWORTH, Jno.	40	M	Farmer	03Se02Pz
MCCARR, Denis	40	M	Farmer	03Se02Pz
Bridget	35	F	Spinster	03Se02Pz
Anne	6	F	Child	03Se02Pz
James	4	M	Child	03Se02Pz
Rose	.09	F	Infant	03Se02Pz
SMITH, Mary	24	F	Spinster	03Se02Pz
WALSH, Jas.	33	M	Farmer	03Se02Pz
Elizabeth (W)	34	F	None	03Se02Pz
Mary-A	14	F	Spinster	03Se02Pz
John	12	M	Farmer	03Se02Pz
Thomas	9	M	Child	03Se02Pz
Jas.Jr.	7	M	Child	03Se02Pz
Isabella	5	F	Child	03Se02Pz
Joseph	4	M	Child	03Se02Pz
Elizabeth	.07	F	Infant	03Se02Pz
MORRIS, Wm.	34	M	Laborer	03Se02Pz
CLEARY, Jas.	36	M	Laborer	03Se02Pz
OBRIEN, Lawrence	22	M	Laborer	03Se02Pz
Eleanor	20	F	Spinster	03Se02Pz
FOLBOYS, Ann	34	F	Spinster	03Se02Pz
Bery	15	M	None	03Se02Pz
Jane	13	F	Spinster	03Se02Pz
Charlotte	10	F	Child	03Se02Pz
Robert	8	M	Child	03Se02Pz
Mary-Ann	6	F	Child	03Se02Pz
PARKINS, Eliza	33	F	Spinster	03Se02Pz
Eliza	1	F	Child	03Se02Pz
Manuel	8	M	Child	03Se02Pz
Chas.	3	M	Child	03Se02Pz
NEWTON, Sarah	28	F	Spinster	03Se02Pz
Sarah	.03	F	Infant	03Se02Pz
John	5	M	Child	03Se02Pz
Thos.	1	M	Child	03Se02Pz
FRADDER, Barney	17	M	Laborer	03Se02Pz
HIGGINS, Ann	17	F	Spinster	03Se02Pz
MALONE, Esther	15	F	Spinster	03Se02Pz
MCKENNA, Patk.	18	M	Laborer	03Se02Pz
MURPHY, Johanna	11	F	Spinster	03Se02Pz
Catherine	10	F	Child	03Se02Pz
FEENY, Pat	48	M	Laborer	03Se02Pz
Thomas	.02	M	Infant	03Se02Pz
VOSE, Elizabeth	54	F	Spinster	03Se02Pz
Henry	18	M	Laborer	03Se02Pz
QUINN, Pat	20	M	Mechanic	03Se02Pz
GAYNER, Jas.	27	M	Mechanic	03Se02Pz
CONNEL, Daniel	15	M	Laborer	03Se02Pz
Thos.	.05	M	Infant	03Se02Pz
HAYES, And.	18	M	Laborer	03Se02Pz

NAMES OF PASSENGERS	AGE	SEX	OCCUPATIONS	DATE PORT SHIP
CONNEL, Eleanor	22	F	Spinster	03Se02Pz
KEARNEY, Edmond	45	M	Farmer	03Se02Pz
Mary	34	F	Spinster	03Se02Pz
CALLAHAN, Mary	18	F	Spinster	03Se02Pz
KEARNEY, Pat	13	M	None	03Se02Pz
Mag	11	F	Spinster	03Se02Pz
Ellen	9	F	Child	03Se02Pz
Edmond	7	M	Child	03Se02Pz
Mary	2	F	Child	03Se02Pz
CONNEL, Jas.	28	M	Laborer	03Se02Pz
DOYLE, Pat	35	M	Laborer	03Se02Pz
RICHARD, John	25	M	Laborer	03Se02Pz
MCCONNEL, Mag	20	F	Spinster	03Se02Pz
BUCKLEY, Tim	50	M	Laborer	03Se02Pz
Mary	50	F	Spinster	03Se02Pz
Mich.	18	M	Unknown	03Se02Pz
Tim-Jr.	13	M	Unknown	03Se02Pz
Mary	9	F	Child	03Se02Pz
GETTANGS, Isabel	50	F	Spinster	03Se02Pz
QUINN, Alex	17	M	Laborer	03Se02Pz
WALSH, Wm.	35	M	Laborer	03Se02Pz
Sarah	28	F	Spinster	03Se02Pz
Pat	10	M	Child	03Se02Pz
Bridget	8	F	Child	03Se02Pz
Mich.	5	M	Child	03Se02Pz
MCGOVERN, Mich.	21	M	Laborer	03Se02Pz
KELLY, Pat	26	M	Laborer	03Se02Pz
Ellen	21	F	Spinster	03Se02Pz
KILEHAN, Peter	35	M	Laborer	03Se02Pz
GIRTY, Ellen	16	F	Spinster	03Se02Pz
Elisa	8	F	Child	03Se02Pz
DILLON, Jas.	50	M	Laborer	03Se02Pz
CARTER, Wm.	30	M	Laborer	03Se02Pz
Bridget	28	F	Spinster	03Se02Pz
OBRIEN, Jno.	40	M	Unknown	03Se02Pz
CARTER, Mich.	4	M	Infant	03Se02Pz
Jho.	2	M	Child	03Se02Pz
Mary-Ann	.03	F	Infant	03Se02Pz
CONNOR, Ann	50	F	None	03Se02Pz
BREWS, Henry	25	M	Unknown	03Se02Pz
CALLAHAN, Jno.	20	M	Unknown	03Se02Pz
THOMAS, Jas.	29	M	Laborer	03Se02Pz
GAFFNEY, Jno.	27	M	Laborer	03Se02Pz
HIGGINS, Wm.	30	M	Laborer	03Se02Pz
GAFFNEY, Jane	29	F	Spinster	03Se02Pz
Mich.	5	M	Child	03Se02Pz
Richd.	00	M	Unknown	03Se02Pz
Died-At-Sea				
Mag	.00	F	Infant	03Se02Pz
HENNING, Eleanor	20	F	Spinster	03Se02Pz
MCKURWIN, Mary	24	F	Spinster	03Se02Pz
And.	25	M	Laborer	03Se02Pz
CROTHERS, Wm.	24	M	Laborer	03Se02Pz
Martha	24	F	Spinster	03Se02Pz
FAGAN, Mary	33	F	Spinster	03Se02Pz
Matilda	3	F	Child	03Se02Pz
MCLAUGHLIN, Francis	50	M	Laborer	03Se02Pz
CONNEL, Pat	24	M	Laborer	03Se02Pz
Alice	24	F	Spinster	03Se02Pz
MCGILL, Jane	20	F	Spinster	03Se02Pz
EGAN, John	20	M	Laborer	03Se02Pz
SCALLY, Edwd.	19	M	Laborer	03Se02Pz
RILEY, Jas.	32	M	Laborer	03Se02Pz
Essy	32	M	Laborer	03Se02Pz
Anne	.00	F	Infant	03Se02Pz
Essy	4	F	Child	03Se02Pz
Lawrence	2	M	Child	03Se02Pz
GREENSMITH, Elisa	30	F	Spinster	03Se02Pz
Wm.	40	F	Spinster	03Se02Pz
CONNER, Mag	55	F	Spinster	03Se02Pz
John	7	M	Child	03Se02Pz
MCKENNA, Jno.	50	M	Laborer	03Se02Pz
RILEY, Jno.	20	M	Laborer	03Se02Pz
MILLABY, Pat	22	M	Laborer	03Se02Pz
ROONEY, Mag	30	F	None	03Se02Pz
ROONEY, Mag	.03	F	Infant	03Se02Pz
PRIOR, Thos.	16	M	Laborer	03Se02Pz
EGAN, Mark	32	M	Mechanic	03Se02Pz
Ann	32	F	Mechanic	03Se02Pz
Jno.	27	F	Mechanic	03Se02Pz
Mary	20	F	None	03Se02Pz
Brian	.00	M	Infant	03Se02Pz
Nath.	39	M	Mechanic	03Se02Pz
LOVELAND, A.C.	00	F	Cptw	03Se02Pz
Jno.H. (S)	00	M	Unknown	03Se02Pz

ST.PATRICK 03 SEPTEMBER 1849

From Liverpool

NAMES OF PASSENGERS	AGE	SEX	OCCUPATIONS	DATE PORT SHIP
MCGARRY, Catherine	24	F	Wife	03Se02Ha
LYNCH, Julia	18	F	Spinster	03Se02Ha
CULLEN, Mary	20	F	Spinster	03Se02Ha
MURRAY, Mary	20	F	Spinster	03Se02Ha
JENKINS, Eliza	19	F	Spinster	03Se02Ha
RONAMER, Mary	22	F	Spinster	03Se02Ha
DYOTT, Robert	60	M	Quarryman	03Se02Ha
LYNCH, John	28	M	Farmer	03Se02Ha
Thomas	20	M	Farmer	03Se02Ha
Margt.	22	F	Spinster	03Se02Ha
FLANAGAN, Martha	21	F	Laborer	03Se02Ha
Ann	20	F	Spinster	03Se02Ha
MCKOUGAN, James	30	M	Cooper	03Se02Ha
MURPHY, John	20	M	Laborer	03Se02Ha
MCKOUGAN, Mary	20	F	Spinster	03Se02Ha
Catharine	20	F	Spinster	03Se02Ha
HUGHES, Catharine	18	F	Spinster	03Se02Ha
COWLINGS, James	40	M	Laborer	03Se02Ha
EGAN, Ma.	21	M	Tailor	03Se02Ha
Died-At-Sea				
Thomas	23	M	Laborer	03Se02Ha
FLANAGAN, Ellen	26	F	Spinster	03Se02Ha
QUIN, Catharine	21	F	Spinster	03Se02Ha
SEERY, John	50	M	Tailor	03Se02Ha
Bridget (W)	44	F	None	03Se02Ha
Edward	17	M	Laborer	03Se02Ha
Maria	14	F	Spinster	03Se02Ha
Cathr.	9	F	Child	03Se02Ha
Eliza	7	F	Child	03Se02Ha
Joseph	5	M	Child	03Se02Ha
Patrick	2	M	Child	03Se02Ha
KENNEDY, Ann	20	F	Wi	03Se02Ha
MASON, Thomas	18	M	Laborer	03Se02Ha
MITTY, Patrick	18	M	Carpenter	03Se02Ha
Mary	17	F	Spinster	03Se02Ha
DROUGHT, William	50	F	Servant	03Se02Ha
Thomas	17	F	Servant	03Se02Ha
ANDERSON, Robert	26	M	Boatman	03Se02Ha
BRANAGAN, Owen	17	M	Butler	03Se02Ha
KILCHER, Bridget	20	F	Spinster	03Se02Ha
LYNCH, Mary	9	F	Child	03Se02Ha
MCCONNELL, Ann	22	F	Spinster	03Se02Ha
DYOTT, Hugh	30	M	Laborer	03Se02Ha
MCANDRAN, William	18	M	Laborer	03Se02Ha
ELLIOTT, John	20	M	Laborer	03Se02Ha
Cath.	18	F	Spinster	03Se02Ha
MONAGHAN, Catherine	20	F	Spinster	03Se02Ha
BRANAGAN, Jno.Mrs.	60	F	Wi	03Se02Ha
MCGUIRE, William	19	M	Tailor	03Se02Ha
KENNEDY, Margt.	40	F	Wife	03Se02Ha
Jane	18	F	Spinster	03Se02Ha
HOGAN, Ann	18	F	Spinster	03Se02Ha
MORRISS, Patrick	32	M	Mason	03Se02Ha
MULLIDY, John	22	M	Servant	03Se02Ha

NAMES OF PASSENGERS	AGE	SEX	OCCUPATIONS	DATE PORT SHIP
OBRIEN, Margt.Mrs.	45	F	Wi	03Se02Ha
COWLING, Mary	12	F	Spinster	03Se02Ha
Mary	28	F	Spinster	03Se02Ha
KILLY, Mary-Ann	18	F	Spinster	03Se02Ha
James	8	M	Child	03Se02Ha
GALLIVAN, Patrick	25	M	Laborer	03Se02Ha
BROCK, Mary	60	F	Wi	03Se02Ha
Margt.	30	F	Spinster	03Se02Ha
Catharine	28	F	Spinster	03Se02Ha
FARRELL, Thomas	22	M	Clerk	03Se02Ha
KERNAHAN, Bridget	38	F	Wi	03Se02Ha
DUFFY, Bridget	11	F	None	03Se02Ha
KERNAGHAN, Thomas	8	M	Child	03Se02Ha
MCAULIFF, Michl.	27	M	Laborer	03Se02Ha
Ellen	20	F	Spinster	03Se02Ha
MEEHAN, Ann	35	F	Wi	03Se02Ha
James	12	M	None	03Se02Ha
REILLY, James	13	M	None	03Se02Ha
MCINTYRE, Mary	26	F	Wife	03Se02Ha
Cath.	9	F	Child	03Se02Ha
Margt.	5	F	Child	03Se02Ha
Rosa	3	F	Child	03Se02Ha
HENERTY, Michl.	25	M	Laborer	03Se02Ha
MCNULTY, Agnes	22	F	Spinster	03Se02Ha
OHARA, Mary	17	F	Spinster	03Se02Ha
Honor	15	F	Spinster	03Se02Ha
BOURKE, Edmund	18	M	Laborer	03Se02Ha
TINNEY, William	24	M	Laborer	03Se02Ha
DRUNY, Ann	21	F	Spinster	03Se02Ha
SMITH, Patrick	20	M	Laborer	03Se02Ha
TIGHE, Patrick	30	M	Laborer	03Se02Ha
Owen	16	M	Laborer	03Se02Ha
Rose	10	F	Spinster	03Se02Ha
Eliza	8	F	Child	03Se02Ha
CLARKE, Joseph	24	M	Laborer	03Se02Ha
MOORE, Mary	18	F	Spinster	03Se02Ha
FARLEY, Catharine	17	F	Spinster	03Se02Ha
MCARUNEY, Cornelius	40	M	Carpenter	03Se02Ha
Bridget (W)	40	F	None	03Se02Ha
Mary	11	F	None	03Se02Ha
Francis	9	M	Child	03Se02Ha
Bridget	4	F	Child	03Se02Ha
HOUSTON, Robert	27	M	Shoemaker	03Se02Ha
U (W)	22	F	None	03Se02Ha
James	4	M	Child	03Se02Ha
Agnes	2	F	Child	03Se02Ha
U	.00	F	Infant	03Se02Ha
MOORE, Ann	20	F	Spinster	03Se02Ha
DUFFY, Rose	20	F	Spinster	03Se02Ha
HOGG, Matilda	21	F	Spinster	03Se02Ha
HART, Peter	27	M	Laborer	03Se02Ha
OCONNER, John	20	M	Clerk	03Se02Ha
MAGUEN, John	26	M	Shopman	03Se02Ha
COX, Thomas	22	M	Laborer	03Se02Ha
DEVLIN, Mary	23	F	Spinster	03Se02Ha
ROCK, Catherine	14	F	Spinster	03Se02Ha
MCCANN, Ann-Ellen	14	F	Spinster	03Se02Ha
MALONE, William	35	M	Laborer	03Se02Ha
Joseph	10	M	None	03Se02Ha
Ellen	40	F	Wife	03Se02Ha
LENNON, Rose	42	F	Wi	03Se02Ha
Alley	10	F	None	03Se02Ha
Mary	8	F	Child	03Se02Ha
Ellen	6	F	Child	03Se02Ha
Elizabeth	3	F	Child	03Se02Ha
Susan	20	F	None	03Se02Ha
DUKE, Thomas	20	M	Laborer	03Se02Ha
Ann	40	F	Wife	03Se02Ha
LYON, Te.	40	M	Ostler	03Se02Ha
FORMAN, Laughlin	30	M	Laborer	03Se02Ha
DOONAN, Barney	40	M	Laborer	03Se02Ha
G--LDEN, Thomas	29	M	Miner	03Se02Ha
LENIGAN, Michl.	26	M	Shearer	03Se02Ha
Ellen	00	F	Unknown	03Se02Ha
Mary	00	F	Unknown	03Se02Ha
LENIGAN, Cath. Died-At-Sea	.00	F	Infant	03Se02Ha
HAMMOND, John	40	M	Laborer	03Se02Ha
CARR, Mark	40	M	Mason	03Se02Ha
GOLDEN, Hugh	20	M	Miner	03Se02Ha
CUSSWELL, James	20	M	Laborer	03Se02Ha
HEGARTY, Mich.	20	M	Laborer	03Se02Ha
CULLEN, Cath.	20	F	Wife	03Se02Ha
MCGOWAN, Bernard	20	M	Laborer	03Se02Ha
ADAIR, William	30	M	Engineer	03Se02Ha
NOBLE, John	26	M	Farmer	03Se02Ha
MCKENNA, Thomas	25	M	Laborer	03Se02Ha
RUSH, M.	26	M	Laborer	03Se02Ha
JOHNSON, Joseph	21	M	Servant	03Se02Ha
MCGREEGAN, Mary	30	F	Spinster	03Se02Ha
KELLEY, Bridget	25	F	Wife	03Se02Ha
CORNELL, Margt.	30	F	Spinster	03Se02Ha
LOFTIS, Ann	23	F	Spinster	03Se02Ha
WITTY, Francis	23	F	Unknown	03Se02Ha
DALEY, Bridget	40	F	Wi	03Se02Ha
Mary	17	F	Spinster	03Se02Ha

SILAS-GREENMAN 03 SEPTEMBER 1849

From Liverpool

NAMES OF PASSENGERS	AGE	SEX	OCCUPATIONS	DATE PORT SHIP
CAUGHLIN, James	20	M	Farmer	03Se02Et
Margaret	19	F	Farmer	03Se02Et
DAWLING, Patrick	26	M	Farmer	03Se02Et
BRENNAN, Mathew	30	M	Farmer	03Se02Et
DALY, Nicholas	30	M	Farmer	03Se02Et
Ellen-Mrs.	29	F	Farmer	03Se02Et
JOYCE, Michael	23	M	Carpenter	03Se02Et
John	20	M	Carpenter	03Se02Et
OMARA, Jeremiah	19	M	Carpenter	03Se02Et
LORKIN, Edward	30	M	Carpenter	03Se02Et
Ellen-Mrs.	28	F	Carpenter	03Se02Et
HALFFRENNY, Cath.	18	F	Unknown	03Se02Et
ROSS, Morris	54	M	Shoemaker	03Se02Et
Anne-Mrs.	50	F	None	03Se02Et
MOREHEAD, Hubert	30	M	Farmer	03Se02Et
FOLEY, Anne	19	F	None	03Se02Et
CRAIG, Anne	30	F	Farmer	03Se02Et
Margt.	.00	F	Infant	03Se02Et
KEELBY, Laurence	18	M	Farmer	03Se02Et
CAMERFORD, Richard	19	M	Farmer	03Se02Et
BRITTON, William	20	M	Farmer	03Se02Et
RYAN, John	40	M	Farmer	03Se02Et
Patrick	38	M	Farmer	03Se02Et
LOUGHLIN, John	14	M	Farmer	03Se02Et
MACKIN, Mary	18	F	Farmer	03Se02Et
MULLEN, Biddy	24	F	Farmer	03Se02Et
Benard	3	M	Child	03Se02Et
WALSH, Mathew	19	M	Farmer	03Se02Et
HAYES, Margt.	50	F	Farmer	03Se02Et
BILTON, Thomas	21	M	Farmer	03Se02Et
DEERY, Ellen	20	F	Farmer	03Se02Et
DUFFY, Ellen	20	F	Farmer	03Se02Et
Bridget	19	F	Farmer	03Se02Et
Anne	17	F	Farmer	03Se02Et
KELLY, Margt.	22	F	Farmer	03Se02Et
PORTERS, Simon	27	M	Farmer	03Se02Et
Anne	27	F	Farmer	03Se02Et
William	8	M	Child	03Se02Et
Ellen	5	F	Child	03Se02Et
James	1	M	Child	03Se02Et
BULFIELD, Edmund	30	M	Farmer	03Se02Et
FORAN, Ellen	21	F	Farmer	03Se02Et
MCCARTNEY, James	24	M	Farmer	03Se02Et

NAMES OF PASSENGERS	AGE	SEX	OCCUPATIONS	DATE PORT SHIP
MCCAFFREY, Cath.	19	F	Farmer	03Se02Et
GORMAN, Edmond	22	M	Farmer	03Se02Et
HUNNISSY, John	23	M	Farmer	03Se02Et
MURNA, Ellen	20	F	Farmer	03Se02Et
John	20	M	Farmer	03Se02Et
Mary	16	F	Farmer	03Se02Et
MURPHY, Thomas	26	M	Farmer	03Se02Et
Rose	50	F	None	03Se02Et
GRACE, James	43	M	Blacksmith	03Se02Et
Jeremiah	18	M	Blacksmith	03Se02Et
FLEMING, Michl.	38	M	Laborer	03Se02Et
Honora	36	F	Unknown	03Se02Et
KENEDY, Honora	18	F	Unknown	03Se02Et
FLEMING, Thomas	2	M	Child	03Se02Et
Biddy	.00	F	Infant	03Se02Et
HOGAN, James	25	M	Farmer	03Se02Et
MURRAY, Michael	22	M	Farmer	03Se02Et
HEFFERNAN, Mary	32	F	Farmer	03Se02Et
William	10	M	Farmer	03Se02Et
CONNELL, Stephen	26	M	Farmer	03Se02Et
FLANNAGAN, William	21	M	Farmer	03Se02Et
HIGGINS, William	24	M	Farmer	03Se02Et
LENNON, James	20	M	Farmer	03Se02Et
Peggy	28	F	Farmer	03Se02Et
Catharine	.00	F	Infant	03Se02Et
KELLY, U-Mrs.	40	F	Unknown	03Se02Et
Michael	17	M	Unknown	03Se02Et
BUCKLEY, Johanna	26	F	Farmer	03Se02Et
MEANY, Patrick	24	M	Farmer	03Se02Et
CAVEY, William	35	M	Farmer	03Se02Et
SHEEHAN, Jerry	25	M	Farmer	03Se02Et
FITZGERALD, Michl.	23	M	Farmer	03Se02Et
GARVEY, Patrick	26	M	Farmer	03Se02Et
MCGORNAN, James	48	M	Farmer	03Se02Et
Agnes	40	F	Farmer	03Se02Et
Margaret	5	F	Child	03Se02Et
Mary-Anne	2	F	Child	03Se02Et
REA, Richd.	35	M	Farmer	03Se02Et
DAWSON, John	24	M	Farmer	03Se02Et
BERIGAN, William	20	M	Farmer	03Se02Et
Patrick	17	M	Farmer	03Se02Et
BERGIN, Daniel	22	M	Farmer	03Se02Et
CLARKE, Mary-A.	19	F	Farmer	03Se02Et
Francis	17	F	Farmer	03Se02Et
BROWNE, Thomas	21	M	Farmer	03Se02Et
HOWARD, Robert	27	M	Farmer	03Se02Et
HUGHES, Nancy	17	F	Farmer	03Se02Et
CASSIDY, James	10	M	Farmer	03Se02Et
HUGHES, Susan	22	F	Farmer	03Se02Et
MULVEHELL, Margt.	28	F	Farmer	03Se02Et
Thomas	5	M	Child	03Se02Et
John	3	M	Child	03Se02Et
Michael	.00	M	Infant	03Se02Et
ODONALD, Bryan	25	M	Farmer	03Se02Et
MCGURE, James	26	M	Farmer	03Se02Et
WILERY, Sampson	28	F	Farmer	03Se02Et
Margt.	22	F	Farmer	03Se02Et
Anne-Jane	.00	F	Infant	03Se02Et
HUGIN, Peter	4	M	Child	03Se02Et
Bridget	16	F	Unknown	03Se02Et
Patrick	12	M	Unknown	03Se02Et
John	9	M	Child	03Se02Et
BIGLEY, Jane	26	F	Unknown	03Se02Et
Margt.	26	F	Unknown	03Se02Et
CODY, Judy	27	F	Unknown	03Se02Et
Patrick	4	M	Child	03Se02Et
BYRNE, Mary	18	F	Unknown	03Se02Et
KELLY, Edward	19	M	Unknown	03Se02Et
John	17	M	Unknown	03Se02Et
BYRNE, Patrick	20	M	Farmer	03Se02Et

EMPIRE-STATE 03 SEPTEMBER 1849

From Liverpool

NAMES OF PASSENGERS	AGE	SEX	OCCUPATIONS	DATE PORT SHIP
WARD, Maurice	16	M	Unknown	03Se02Qe
HENRY, Chas.	24	M	Laborer	03Se02Qe
Ellen	22	F	Unknown	03Se02Qe
Cath.	.07	F	Infant	03Se02Qe
BRADLY, Pat	35	M	Mason	03Se02Qe
Mary	26	F	Unknown	03Se02Qe
Died-At-Sea				
Ann	20	F	Mason	03Se02Qe
Ann	.10	F	Infant	03Se02Qe
Died-At-Sea				
MCANN, Pat	31	M	Farmer	03Se02Qe
Cath.	26	F	Farmer	03Se02Qe
Died-At-Sea				
Margt.	4	F	Child	03Se02Qe
CROWLEY, Barth.	19	M	Farmer	03Se02Qe
MCINNERNEY, Johanna	18	F	Servant	03Se02Qe

WM.CHASE 04 SEPTEMBER 1849

From Londonderry

NAMES OF PASSENGERS	AGE	SEX	OCCUPATIONS	DATE PORT SHIP
EATON, Thomas	60	M	Laborer	04Se01Qa
Ellen	58	F	Unknown	04Se01Qa
Margt.	18	F	Unknown	04Se01Qa
Matilda	16	F	Unknown	04Se01Qa
BELLINGHAM, James	27	M	Unknown	04Se01Qa
HAYNEY, Mary	25	F	Unknown	04Se01Qa
Alice	13	F	Unknown	04Se01Qa
Peter	17	M	Unknown	04Se01Qa
KARNE, John	18	M	Unknown	04Se01Qa
MCCLARY, Fanny	44	F	Unknown	04Se01Qa
Wm.	18	M	Unknown	04Se01Qa
Rebecca	14	F	Unknown	04Se01Qa
Fanny	12	F	Unknown	04Se01Qa
FANE, Ann	7	F	Child	04Se01Qa
MCCLARY, Mary	.00	F	Infant	04Se01Qa
MCMINAMUS, John	70	M	Unknown	04Se01Qa
COLLIER, Margt.	35	F	Unknown	04Se01Qa
MCMINIMER, Bridget	13	F	Unknown	04Se01Qa
COLLIER, John	9	M	Child	04Se01Qa
Patk.	7	M	Child	04Se01Qa
COLLINS, Sarah	4	F	Child	04Se01Qa
Mary	2	F	Child	04Se01Qa
MCANALL, Mary	44	F	Unknown	04Se01Qa
Margt.	11	F	Unknown	04Se01Qa
Sarah	9	F	Child	04Se01Qa
MCADEN, Mary	19	F	Unknown	04Se01Qa
MOORHEAD, Jane	32	F	Unknown	04Se01Qa
James	8	M	Child	04Se01Qa
Jacob	6	M	Child	04Se01Qa
Mary-Ann	3	F	Child	04Se01Qa
John	2	M	Child	04Se01Qa
STERLING, Elizabeth	26	F	Unknown	04Se01Qa
WHITE, Matilda	18	F	Unknown	04Se01Qa
SHARP, Ann	18	F	Unknown	04Se01Qa
MOORE, Ann	20	F	Unknown	04Se01Qa
SPEER, Elizabeth	20	F	Unknown	04Se01Qa
LOGAN, James	15	M	Unknown	04Se01Qa
MARSHALL, Thos.	23	M	Unknown	04Se01Qa

NAMES OF PASSENGERS	AGE	SEX	OCCUPATIONS	DATE PORT SHIP
FANE, Wm.	35	M	Unknown	04Se01Qa
DERMITT, Wm.	23	M	Unknown	04Se01Qa
BERRY, John-B.	28	M	Unknown	04Se01Qa
SHARP, Henry	18	M	Unknown	04Se01Qa
DOHERTY, Stephen	25	M	Unknown	04Se01Qa
CURRAN, Hugh	18	M	Unknown	04Se01Qa
Cath.	24	F	Unknown	04Se01Qa
FLAHERTY, Elizabeth	18	F	Unknown	04Se01Qa
SHARKY, Patk.	40	M	Unknown	04Se01Qa
Susannah	29	F	Unknown	04Se01Qa
Eliza	4	F	Child	04Se01Qa
MCLAUGHLIN, Jane	14	F	Unknown	04Se01Qa
DEANY, John	17	M	Unknown	04Se01Qa
MCGINTY, Patk.	20	M	Unknown	04Se01Qa
CUNNINGHAM, Thomas	18	M	Unknown	04Se01Qa
John	24	M	Unknown	04Se01Qa
CREENAN, Margt.	24	F	Unknown	04Se01Qa
DAVIS, Cath.	50	F	Unknown	04Se01Qa
MCALEY, Noel	19	M	Unknown	04Se01Qa
Elizabeth	55	F	Unknown	04Se01Qa
Stephen	50	M	Unknown	04Se01Qa
Sally	26	F	Unknown	04Se01Qa
Margt.	16	F	Unknown	04Se01Qa
James	.00	M	Infant	04Se01Qa
WALLACE, Thos.	20	M	Unknown	04Se01Qa
MCCORMACK, John	56	M	Unknown	04Se01Qa
FITZPATRICK, James	35	M	Unknown	04Se01Qa
Susan	40	F	Unknown	04Se01Qa
Wm.	8	M	Child	04Se01Qa
James	6	M	Child	04Se01Qa
MOOR, Ann	18	F	Unknown	04Se01Qa
YOUNG, James	50	M	Unknown	04Se01Qa
ROBB, James	35	M	Unknown	04Se01Qa
DOUGHERTY, M.	40	M	Unknown	04Se01Qa
Mary	35	F	Unknown	04Se01Qa
Thomas	11	M	Unknown	04Se01Qa
Nancy	10	F	Child	04Se01Qa
John	7	M	Child	04Se01Qa
James	3	M	Child	04Se01Qa
WILSON, Henry	23	M	Unknown	04Se01Qa
ODONALD, John	21	M	Unknown	04Se01Qa
Mary	18	F	Unknown	04Se01Qa
Elizabeth	19	F	Unknown	04Se01Qa
COIL, James	30	M	Unknown	04Se01Qa
MCELDWER, Wm.	45	M	Unknown	04Se01Qa
Chas.	24	M	Unknown	04Se01Qa
Biddy	18	F	Unknown	04Se01Qa
Biddy	18	F	Unknown	04Se01Qa
GRAY, Elizabeth	17	F	Unknown	04Se01Qa
BERTZ, Robert	32	M	Unknown	04Se01Qa
MOORE, Mary-Ann	23	F	Unknown	04Se01Qa
James	3	M	Child	04Se01Qa
Mary-Ann	.00	F	Infant	04Se01Qa
MCRUTH, Mary	17	F	Unknown	04Se01Qa
MCLAUGHLIN, Mary	17	F	Unknown	04Se01Qa
DINVER, Elizabeth	16	F	Unknown	04Se01Qa
Mary-Ann	14	F	Unknown	04Se01Qa
BARNARD, Mary	14	F	Unknown	04Se01Qa
KILGORE, Elizabeth	18	F	Unknown	04Se01Qa
CURREN, Mary	19	F	Unknown	04Se01Qa
GALLACHER, Mary	24	F	Unknown	04Se01Qa
Margt.	5	F	Child	04Se01Qa
Mary-Jane	.00	F	Infant	04Se01Qa
MCBRAIN, Jas.	20	M	Unknown	04Se01Qa
ERVIN, Sarah	16	F	Unknown	04Se01Qa
WIGGINS, Ann	20	F	Unknown	04Se01Qa
Thos.	.00	M	Infant	04Se01Qa
LOGUE, Mary	18	F	Unknown	04Se01Qa
MINNERY, Mary	18	F	Unknown	04Se01Qa
ROLSTON, Jannet	25	F	Unknown	04Se01Qa
COCKBURN, James	35	M	Unknown	04Se01Qa
COTH, Fanny	18	F	Unknown	04Se01Qa
JOHNSTON, Fanny	17	F	Unknown	04Se01Qa
MCDAVETH, Biddy	23	F	Unknown	04Se01Qa
Daniel	5	M	Child	04Se01Qa
MCDAVETH, John	2	M	Child	04Se01Qa
QUIEELY, Susan	19	F	Unknown	04Se01Qa
CARLIN, Ellen	19	F	Unknown	04Se01Qa
Mary	13	F	Unknown	04Se01Qa
Anna	11	F	Unknown	04Se01Qa

CONSTITUTION 05 SEPTEMBER 1849

From Liverpool

NAMES OF PASSENGERS	AGE	SEX	OCCUPATIONS	DATE PORT SHIP
CARTWRIGHT, Chas.	22	M	Tailor	05Se02Dp
MORAN, John	24	M	Laborer	05Se02Dp
CRANSHAW, Thos.	30	M	Laborer	05Se02Dp
DEVIDEN, Wm.	29	M	Laborer	05Se02Dp
PRATT, Mary	40	F	None	05Se02Dp
Jas.	13	M	None	05Se02Dp
Mary	12	F	None	05Se02Dp
Selina	00	F	None	05Se02Dp
Thos.	8	M	Child	05Se02Dp
Jno.	2	M	Child	05Se02Dp
CRYER, Robt.	19	M	Farmer	05Se02Dp
ASHLEY, Wm.	32	M	Farmer	05Se02Dp
Mary	32	F	None	05Se02Dp
Anne	6	F	Child	05Se02Dp
Mary	3	F	Child	05Se02Dp
Hy.	25	M	None	05Se02Dp
Mary	27	F	None	05Se02Dp
MCGOVERN, Pat.	20	M	Laborer	05Se02Dp
KING, Wm.	20	M	Laborer	05Se02Dp
LEVER, Thos.	25	M	Laborer	05Se02Dp
MCLURE, Jas.	28	M	Laborer	05Se02Dp
JONES, Thos.	24	M	Farmer	05Se02Dp
BUCK, Jno.	23	M	Blacksmith	05Se02Dp
HATERSBY, Jno.	26	M	Blacksmith	05Se02Dp
BRUDLAND, Jno.	37	M	Merchant	05Se02Dp
Pauline	38	F	None	05Se02Dp
Cornelia	16	F	None	05Se02Dp
Ellen	11	M	None	05Se02Dp
Wm.	8	M	Child	05Se02Dp
BOSWORTH, Wm.	23	M	Farmer	05Se02Dp
U-Mrs.	23	F	Farmer	05Se02Dp
BARKER, Chas.	50	M	Unknown	05Se02Dp
U-Mrs.	50	F	None	05Se02Dp
Harriett	11	F	None	05Se02Dp
Alfred	7	M	Child	05Se02Dp
HAWLEY, Edwd.	25	M	Merchant	05Se02Dp
BORSLAY, Dan.	25	M	Tailor	05Se02Dp
ROBINSON, Thos.	23	M	Farmer	05Se02Dp
CARROLL, Wm.	24	M	Farmer	05Se02Dp
FLYNN, Jas.	32	M	Farmer	05Se02Dp
GEE, Thos.	24	M	Farmer	05Se02Dp
TRUKILL, Jno.	24	M	Farmer	05Se02Dp
HINDLER, Sam.	28	M	Tailor	05Se02Dp
Mgt.	21	F	Tailor	05Se02Dp
Eliza.	.00	F	Infant	05Se02Dp
SOMSLEY, Martha	57	F	None	05Se02Dp
Ann	8	F	Child	05Se02Dp
BROOKS, Richd.	20	M	Unknown	05Se02Dp
CARMICHAEL, Hugh	20	M	Laborer	05Se02Dp
HAWKINS, Jno.	50	M	Carpenter	05Se02Dp
Jno.	21	M	Carpenter	05Se02Dp
Eliza	18	F	None	05Se02Dp
NEVILLE, Michl.	36	M	Shoemaker	05Se02Dp
U-Mrs.	36	F	None	05Se02Dp
Mary	3	F	Child	05Se02Dp
BRYAN, Jno.	30	M	Laborer	05Se02Dp
FEDRICK, David	22	M	Laborer	05Se02Dp
Peter	24	M	Laborer	05Se02Dp
Michl.	18	M	Laborer	05Se02Dp

NAMES OF PASSENGERS	AGE	SEX	OCCUPATIONS	DATE PORT SHIP
FEDRICK, Dan.	20	M	Laborer	05Se02Dp
RYAN, Thos.	21	M	Laborer	05Se02Dp
Jno.	19	M	Laborer	05Se02Dp
ROBERT, Wm.	21	M	Farmer	05Se02Dp
CONNER, Nancy	32	F	None	05Se02Dp
FROST, Geo.	35	M	Carpenter	05Se02Dp
GILBERT, Jno.	28	M	Carpenter	05Se02Dp
WELCH, Winnie	20	F	None	05Se02Dp
HAMPSHIRE, U-Miss	20	F	None	05Se02Dp
FARRELL, Ben-B.	40	M	Laborer	05Se02Dp
JONES, Thos.	21	M	Miller	05Se02Dp
GRAHAM, Sally	20	F	None	05Se02Dp
MURRAY, Susan	50	F	None	05Se02Dp
Edwd.	14	M	None	05Se02Dp
MCVEE, Mary	34	F	None	05Se02Dp
LAMBERT, Mary-A.	26	F	None	05Se02Dp
Jno.	24	M	Surveyor	05Se02Dp
SMITH, Mary-A.	11	F	None	05Se02Dp
MCHIGH, Cath.	19	F	None	05Se02Dp
ARMSTRONG, Phoebe	14	F	None	05Se02Dp
MCGLUE, Jas.	22	M	Laborer	05Se02Dp
Luke	20	M	Laborer	05Se02Dp
PLUNKET, Fanny	6	F	Laborer	05Se02Dp
Thos.	5	M	Child	05Se02Dp
WESTLAKE, Geo.	30	M	Carpenter	05Se02Dp
Jane	25	F	None	05Se02Dp
DRAKE, Jno.	31	M	None	05Se02Dp
MATTHEWS, Thos.	25	M	Farmer	05Se02Dp
DUNLOP, Dan	37	M	Farmer	05Se02Dp
U-Mrs.	37	F	None	05Se02Dp
Eliza	15	F	None	05Se02Dp
Mary	11	F	Child	05Se02Dp
Dan	7	M	Child	05Se02Dp
Jane	2	F	Child	05Se02Dp
MCADAM, Jno.	40	M	Merchant	05Se02Dp
Eliz.	17	F	None	05Se02Dp
GORDON, Mary	16	F	None	05Se02Dp
FIELDS, U	40	U	Unknown	05Se02Dp
U-Mrs.	40	F	Unknown	05Se02Dp
Emily	1	F	None	05Se02Dp
HODGSON, Jno.	30	M	Tailor	05Se02Dp
U-Mrs.	30	F	None	05Se02Dp
FITZPATRICK, Betsey	20	F	None	05Se02Dp
ROBERTSON, U	29	M	Farmer	05Se02Dp
GALLAGHER, Sarah	36	F	None	05Se02Dp
Ellen	42	F	None	05Se02Dp
Frank	16	M	None	05Se02Dp
Dan	13	M	None	05Se02Dp
Mary	12	F	None	05Se02Dp
Ann	10	F	Child	05Se02Dp
Grace	5	F	Child	05Se02Dp
Brid.	8	F	Child	05Se02Dp
Isab.	3	F	Child	05Se02Dp
CORLAN, Andy	16	M	Unknown	05Se02Dp
FLANAGAN, Wm.	30	M	Laborer	05Se02Dp
Pat	32	M	Laborer	05Se02Dp
Peter	28	M	Laborer	05Se02Dp
Maria	28	F	None	05Se02Dp
JULIAN, Jas.	31	M	Tailor	05Se02Dp
U-Mrs.	30	F	None	05Se02Dp
Charlotte	4	F	Child	05Se02Dp
ROACH, Thos.	20	M	Jeweller	05Se02Dp
Wm.	40	M	Jeweller	05Se02Dp
Mary	38	F	None	05Se02Dp
Agnes	12	F	None	05Se02Dp
Susan	8	F	Child	05Se02Dp
Wm.	8	M	Child	05Se02Dp
Mary	3	F	Child	05Se02Dp
Richd.	2	M	Child	05Se02Dp
LAPTON, Jay-S.	27	M	Farmer	05Se02Dp
Sarah	23	F	None	05Se02Dp
Emily	.00	F	Infant	05Se02Dp
MCPHARLAN, Mary	12	F	None	05Se02Dp
THOMAS, Saml.	50	M	Plumber	05Se02Dp
Sarah	17	F	None	05Se02Dp
THOMAS, Hannah	.00	F	Infant	05Se02Dp
Geo.	21	M	Unknown	05Se02Dp
Wm.	27	M	Unknown	05Se02Dp
STEAK, Jas.	40	M	Farmer	05Se02Dp
U-Mrs.	24	F	None	05Se02Dp
GARDNER, Edwd.	36	M	Unknown	05Se02Dp
Fred	19	M	Unknown	05Se02Dp
Mgt.	40	F	None	05Se02Dp
RADNER, Hannah	26	M	None	05Se02Dp
Sarah	3	F	Child	05Se02Dp
WILLIAMSON, Thos.	22	M	Merchant	05Se02Dp
DILLON, Mary	50	F	None	05Se02Dp
QUINN, Jas.	30	M	Laborer	05Se02Dp
MURPHY, Geo.	30	M	Laborer	05Se02Dp
TAYLOR, Hy.	40	M	Laborer	05Se02Dp
GUEST, Robt.	33	M	Farmer	05Se02Dp
Mary	25	F	None	05Se02Dp
WILKINSON, Geo.	24	M	Farmer	05Se02Dp
Mary-A.	28	F	None	05Se02Dp
Wm.	5	M	Child	05Se02Dp
LUCAS, Sam.	24	M	Carpenter	05Se02Dp
Alex.	19	M	Carpenter	05Se02Dp
HUDSON, Robt.	28	M	Farmer	05Se02Dp
Eliza	22	F	Farmer	05Se02Dp
Jane	.00	F	Infant	05Se02Dp
Margt.	2	F	Child	05Se02Dp
TEASDALE, Thos.	35	M	Tailor	05Se02Dp
Hannah	31	F	None	05Se02Dp
Jno.	2	M	Child	05Se02Dp
Wm.	.00	M	Infant	05Se02Dp
CALVERT, Jno.	21	M	Unknown	05Se02Dp
WILD, Jas.	20	M	Shoemaker	05Se02Dp
SELICK, Andw.	30	M	Farmer	05Se02Dp
MULLIGAN, Richd.	19	M	Farmer	05Se02Dp
GATH, Mary-A.	26	F	None	05Se02Dp
Sarah	4	F	Child	05Se02Dp
Eliza	50	F	None	05Se02Dp
Susannah	.00	F	Infant	05Se02Dp
JOYCE, Pat	50	M	None	05Se02Dp
Cath.	50	F	None	05Se02Dp
Dennis	26	M	Servant	05Se02Dp
Pat	24	M	Servant	05Se02Dp
Mgt.	20	F	None	05Se02Dp
Jno.	16	M	Unknown	05Se02Dp
Lucia	11	F	None	05Se02Dp
HAND, Jno.	22	M	Farmer	05Se02Dp
SCOTT, Jno.	22	M	Farmer	05Se02Dp
DILLON, Eliza	20	F	None	05Se02Dp
GARNETT, Mgt.	20	F	None	05Se02Dp
BARKER, Brid.	20	F	None	05Se02Dp
ROURK, Brid.	20	F	None	05Se02Dp
BURNS, Jno.	22	M	Unknown	05Se02Dp
MAHON, Pat	20	M	Laborer	05Se02Dp
LYNCH, Brid.	24	F	None	05Se02Dp
PRICE, Jane	20	F	None	05Se02Dp
DALY, Cath.	10	F	Child	05Se02Dp
BROPHY, Robert	31	M	Unknown	05Se02Dp
Eliza	24	F	None	05Se02Dp
LEXTON, Michl.	20	M	Unknown	05Se02Dp
FLANAGAN, Ellen	21	F	None	05Se02Dp
KING, Pat	30	M	Unknown	05Se02Dp
HENRY, Jno.	30	M	Unknown	05Se02Dp
Mary	28	F	None	05Se02Dp
Jas.	2	M	Child	05Se02Dp
Pat	.00	M	Infant	05Se02Dp
KANE, Edwd.	28	M	Unknown	05Se02Dp
Pat	40	M	Unknown	05Se02Dp
KEATING, Michl.	65	M	Unknown	05Se02Dp
Honora	40	F	None	05Se02Dp
Mary	30	F	None	05Se02Dp
Jno.	28	M	Unknown	05Se02Dp
Cath.	23	F	Unknown	05Se02Dp
Alice	21	F	Unknown	05Se02Dp
Michl.	21	M	Unknown	05Se02Dp
MONAGAN, Mich.	18	M	Unknown	05Se02Dp

NAMES OF PASSENGERS	AGE	SEX	OCCUPATIONS	DATE PORT SHIP
HICKY, Pat	18	M	Unknown	05Se02Dp
GERICK, Pat	16	M	Unknown	05Se02Dp
Thos.	8	M	Child	05Se02Dp
FENTON, Edwd.	19	M	Unknown	05Se02Dp
TRAPP, Cath.	19	F	Unknown	05Se02Dp
MCCORMACK, Mary (F)	23	F	Unknown	05Se02Dp
COLLINS, Johan.	23	F	Unknown	05Se02Dp
KEHANE, Mary	7	F	Child	05Se02Dp
TALBOTT, Eliza	25	F	Unknown	05Se02Dp
RALPH, Jno.	21	M	Farmer	05Se02Dp
Brid.	23	F	Unknown	05Se02Dp
BONNEY, Pat	19	M	Laborer	05Se02Dp
Mich.	11	M	Unknown	05Se02Dp
AGNEW, Ned	50	M	Unknown	05Se02Dp
Robt.	20	M	Unknown	05Se02Dp
BADGER, Danl.	28	M	Unknown	05Se02Dp
Hannah	21	F	None	05Se02Dp
Thos.	2	M	Child	05Se02Dp
WEST, Wm.	30	M	Farmer	05Se02Dp
MCCORMACK, Ellen	16	F	Unknown	05Se02Dp
BRONEY, Sophia	26	F	Unknown	05Se02Dp
GALLAGHER, Rosanna	22	F	Unknown	05Se02Dp
CAVANNAGH, Jas.	13	M	Laborer	05Se02Dp
ADAIR, Mary	24	F	None	05Se02Dp
PHILAN, Thos.	24	M	Unknown	05Se02Dp
PURCELL, Brid.	30	F	Unknown	05Se02Dp
MUNDY, Brid.	17	F	Unknown	05Se02Dp
CUNNINGHAM, Pat	25	M	Tailor	05Se02Dp
HAWKINS, Maria	6	F	Child	05Se02Dp
TIGHE, Eliza	18	F	Unknown	05Se02Dp
CUMMINGS, Geo.	30	M	Unknown	05Se02Dp
MURPHY, Mary	30	F	Unknown	05Se02Dp
Ellen	00	F	Unknown	05Se02Dp
FOX, Ann	50	F	Unknown	05Se02Dp
Died-At-Sea				
SMITH, Jas.	25	M	Laborer	05Se02Dp
HUGHES, Mgt.	25	F	Unknown	05Se02Dp
Ann	25	F	Unknown	05Se02Dp
Mgt.	5	F	Child	05Se02Dp
Pat	2	M	Child	05Se02Dp
Died-At-Sea				
JUNIPER, Wm.	49	M	Farmer	05Se02Dp
Susan	45	F	Unknown	05Se02Dp
Eliza	10	F	Child	05Se02Dp
Sarah	8	F	Child	05Se02Dp
Mary	5	F	Child	05Se02Dp
HENDERSON, Jno.	21	M	Carpenter	05Se02Dp
Mgt.	24	F	Unknown	05Se02Dp
Jno.	1	M	Child	05Se02Dp
Martha	40	F	Unknown	05Se02Dp
BROWN, Eliza-J.	18	F	Unknown	05Se02Dp
Tho.	16	M	Unknown	05Se02Dp
FEGAN, Brid.	20	F	Unknown	05Se02Dp
MCNAMARA, Hetty	30	F	Unknown	05Se02Dp
KERRICK, Mary	8	F	Child	05Se02Dp
Ann	4	F	Child	05Se02Dp
DARLEN, Brid.	19	F	Unknown	05Se02Dp
HEALY, Mary	20	F	Unknown	05Se02Dp
CLEAR, Mgt.	20	F	Unknown	05Se02Dp
MCCARTHY, Jas.	25	M	Laborer	05Se02Dp
Ann	25	F	Laborer	05Se02Dp
Mary	12	F	None	05Se02Dp
KEAN, Mary	13	F	None	05Se02Dp
HENRY, Hannah	19	F	None	05Se02Dp
Ann	18	F	None	05Se02Dp
Mary	20	F	None	05Se02Dp
BOWDEN, Fran.	45	M	Laborer	05Se02Dp
Geo.	16	M	Laborer	05Se02Dp
RILEY, Farrel	25	M	Laborer	05Se02Dp
KELLY, Wm.	40	M	Farmer	05Se02Dp
Georgina	18	F	None	05Se02Dp
Thos.	10	M	None	05Se02Dp
Mary-A.	8	F	Child	05Se02Dp
Richd.	5	M	Child	05Se02Dp
Anna-Maria	4	F	Child	05Se02Dp

NAMES OF PASSENGERS	AGE	SEX	OCCUPATIONS	DATE PORT SHIP
PERT, Robt.	20	M	Laborer	05Se02Dp
Carter	18	M	Laborer	05Se02Dp
MCCUE, Mary	18	F	Unknown	05Se02Dp
BRALY, Ann	18	F	Unknown	05Se02Dp
WILD, Thos.	28	M	Tailor	05Se02Dp
HALL, Richard	14	M	Shoemaker	05Se02Dp
MCCARTY, U-Mrs.	25	F	None	05Se02Dp
PRESTON, Mgt.	18	F	None	05Se02Dp
Cathe.	9	F	Child	05Se02Dp
MURDOCK, Wm.	32	M	Farmer	05Se02Dp
U-Mrs.	30	F	None	05Se02Dp
Wm.	7	M	Child	05Se02Dp
Jno.	3	M	Child	05Se02Dp
DWANE, Phil.	22	M	Laborer	05Se02Dp
RUSSELL, Jno.	21	M	Clerk	05Se02Dp
WHITE, Watson	18	M	Clerk	05Se02Dp
HAWKERIDGE, Sarah	25	F	None	05Se02Dp
Harriett	4	F	Child	05Se02Dp
Jas.	2	M	Child	05Se02Dp
REGAN, Mich.	20	M	Laborer	05Se02Dp
CUSHING, Jno.	20	M	Laborer	05Se02Dp
HACKERAY, Pat	17	M	Laborer	05Se02Dp
Ann	16	F	None	05Se02Dp
MURTHA, Mary	20	F	None	05Se02Dp
HANNIGAN, Ann	20	F	None	05Se02Dp
FLYNN, Honor	24	F	None	05Se02Dp
SULLIVAN, Wm.	50	M	Laborer	05Se02Dp
Mary	40	F	None	05Se02Dp
HASLOF, Cath.	20	F	None	05Se02Dp
SHEA, Mary	18	F	None	05Se02Dp
HILLIARD, Jas.	27	M	Farmer	05Se02Dp
U-Mrs.	24	F	None	05Se02Dp
Ellen	1	F	Child	05Se02Dp
CREARY, Jas.	35	M	Laborer	05Se02Dp
Wm.	37	M	Laborer	05Se02Dp
U-Mrs.	37	F	Laborer	05Se02Dp
Isab.	9	F	Child	05Se02Dp
Jane	7	F	Child	05Se02Dp
Wm.	5	M	Child	05Se02Dp
Jno.	2	M	Child	05Se02Dp
HAINSLEY, Wm.	32	M	Farmer	05Se02Dp
U-Mrs.	30	F	None	05Se02Dp
Eliza	2	F	Child	05Se02Dp
ATKINSON, Jno.	31	M	Unknown	05Se02Dp
BLOOMFIELD, Pat	21	M	Laborer	05Se02Dp
GERATY, Jane	20	F	None	05Se02Dp
CREELY, Pat	40	M	Laborer	05Se02Dp
U-Mrs.	40	F	None	05Se02Dp
Mich.	11	M	None	05Se02Dp
Brid.	20	F	None	05Se02Dp
CHALLENGER, Emily	34	M	None	05Se02Dp
CHATTERTON, Geo.	36	M	None	05Se02Dp
U-Mrs.	34	F	None	05Se02Dp
Olive	7	M	Child	05Se02Dp
Henry	.00	M	Infant	05Se02Dp
OLTIER, Jno.	.00	M	Infant	05Se02Dp
Mary	25	F	None	05Se02Dp
BATTLE, Jno.	29	M	Unknown	05Se02Dp
Ann	25	F	None	05Se02Dp
Jas.	1	M	Child	05Se02Dp
BENT, Frank	40	M	Brush Maker	05Se02Dp
QUINLAN, Jo.	21	M	Unknown	05Se02Dp
SHORT, Chas.	24	M	Unknown	05Se02Dp
ROWLEY, Peter	16	M	Unknown	05Se02Dp
CURTIN, Mgt.	24	F	None	05Se02Dp
COGHLIN, Eliza	16	F	None	05Se02Dp
MCGOWERS, Ann	15	F	None	05Se02Dp
HALLAHAN, Dan	24	M	Laborer	05Se02Dp
COLLIVAN, Chas.	23	M	Laborer	05Se02Dp
DACY, Jno.	35	M	Laborer	05Se02Dp
LENAHAN, Mich.	28	M	Laborer	05Se02Dp
LYNCH, Dan	23	M	Laborer	05Se02Dp
CRAVEN, Hugh	26	M	Laborer	05Se02Dp
COYLE, Cath.	12	F	None	05Se02Dp
BURNS, Jas.	19	M	Laborer	05Se02Dp

NAMES OF PASSENGERS	AGE	SEX	OCCUPATIONS	DATE PORT SHIP
SMITH, Mary	50	F	None	05Se02Dp
HASSETT, Wm.	20	M	Laborer	05Se02Dp
SULLIVAN, Dan	40	M	Laborer	05Se02Dp
COLLINS, Mgt.	32	F	None	05Se02Dp
CATH.	7	F	CHILD	05SE02DP
Mich.	4	M	Child	05Se02Dp
NEWMAN, Jno.	35	M	Laborer	05Se02Dp
WALSH, Brid.	45	F	None	05Se02Dp
Ann	5	F	Child	05Se02Dp
HUGHES, Ally	50	F	None	05Se02Dp
BRAY, Cath.	21	F	None	05Se02Dp
DIXON, Jno.	25	M	Carpenter	05Se02Dp
MORRIS, Rich.	50	M	Farmer	05Se02Dp
U-Mrs.	50	F	None	05Se02Dp
Wm.	27	M	Farmer	05Se02Dp
Anna	3	F	Child	05Se02Dp
Robt.	21	M	Farmer	05Se02Dp
Sam	18	M	Farmer	05Se02Dp
Fanny	18	F	None	05Se02Dp
BURNE, Chris	21	M	Farmer	05Se02Dp
BRODRICK, Jno.	23	M	Farmer	05Se02Dp
RUSHTON, Abel	27	M	Farmer	05Se02Dp
WHALAN, N.	26	F	None	05Se02Dp
Susannah	28	F	None	05Se02Dp
Bernd.	35	M	None	05Se02Dp
U-Mrs.	35	M	None	05Se02Dp
MAHAN, Dan	16	M	Laborer	05Se02Dp
BURKE, Jas.	44	M	Laborer	05Se02Dp
SULLIVAN, Mary	20	F	None	05Se02Dp
MORAN, Maria	20	F	None	05Se02Dp
Cathe.	18	F	None	05Se02Dp
PEYTON, Brid.	12	F	None	05Se02Dp
SULLIVAN, Jno.	22	M	Laborer	05Se02Dp
KIRBY, Jas.	30	M	Laborer	05Se02Dp
MAHONNY, Thos.	19	M	Laborer	05Se02Dp
SACKETT, Wm.	23	M	Merchant	05Se02Dp
BENT, Maria	20	F	None	05Se02Dp
COFFEY, Peter	20	M	Laborer	05Se02Dp
MALONY, Mgt.	25	F	None	05Se02Dp
KINSETTA, Jno.	50	M	Laborer	05Se02Dp
MULHALL, Pat	50	M	Laborer	05Se02Dp
Died-At-Sea				
Mgt.	26	F	None	05Se02Dp
WARD, Mary	45	F	None	05Se02Dp
Julia	15	F	None	05Se02Dp
Edwd.	9	M	Child	05Se02Dp
WOODMAN, U-Mrs.	20	F	None	05Se02Dp
HAMPSON, Fanny	36	F	None	05Se02Dp
Mary-A.	11	F	None	05Se02Dp
Martha	9	F	Child	05Se02Dp
Sarah	71	M	None	05Se02Dp
Eliza	6	F	Child	05Se02Dp
Charlotte	4	F	Child	05Se02Dp
Thos.	1	M	Child	05Se02Dp
BROWN, Eliza	30	F	None	05Se02Dp
Ellen	12	F	None	05Se02Dp
Jno.	10	M	Child	05Se02Dp
Robt.	8	M	Child	05Se02Dp
Ann	4	F	Child	05Se02Dp
COX, Christ.	24	M	Saddler	05Se02Dp
Christ.	22	M	Saddler	05Se02Dp
Sarah	17	F	None	05Se02Dp
LYONS, J.	33	F	Farmer	05Se02Dp
MCCARDY, Bernd.	30	M	Laborer	05Se02Dp
BUCKLEY, Jonathan	40	M	Farmer	05Se02Dp
CADERGAN, Sam.	24	M	Laborer	05Se02Dp
Mgt.	22	F	None	05Se02Dp
LYNCH, Jno.Rev.	40	M	Dd	05Se02Dp
NOBLE, Chas.	31	M	Merchant	05Se02Dp
PASSARANT, C.	30	M	Engineer	05Se02Dp
BARNETT, B.	17	M	Gentleman	05Se02Dp
THOMAS, Brid.	19	F	Unknown	05Se02Dp
STEAK, Hannah	7	F	Child	05Se02Dp

Swan 05 September 1849

From Cork

NAMES OF PASSENGERS	AGE	SEX	OCCUPATIONS	DATE PORT SHIP
AHERN, Elizabeth	26	F	Laborer	05Se08Cx
Mary	24	F	Laborer	05Se08Cx
John	2	M	Child	05Se08Cx
HALLIHAN, Patrick	50	M	Laborer	05Se08Cx
Mary	40	F	Laborer	05Se08Cx
Thomas	20	M	Laborer	05Se08Cx
Patrick	18	M	Laborer	05Se08Cx
John	13	M	Laborer	05Se08Cx
Bridget	8	F	Child	05Se08Cx
Mary	4	F	Child	05Se08Cx
Nany	4	F	Child	05Se08Cx
Michael	1	M	Child	05Se08Cx
KENNEDY, Michael	40	M	Laborer	05Se08Cx
Jas.	40	M	Laborer	05Se08Cx
HANLON, Maurice	10	M	Laborer	05Se08Cx
CONROY, Johannah	20	F	Laborer	05Se08Cx
COLBERT, John	22	M	Laborer	05Se08Cx
David	26	M	Laborer	05Se08Cx
MOHONEY, Mary	26	F	Laborer	05Se08Cx
CRENIN, Daniel	35	M	Laborer	05Se08Cx
Johannah	30	F	Laborer	05Se08Cx
Bridget	10	F	Laborer	05Se08Cx
Mary	8	F	Child	05Se08Cx
Ellen	4	F	Child	05Se08Cx
MAGILLACUDDY, Timothy	20	M	Laborer	05Se08Cx
GRANT, Jas.	30	M	Laborer	05Se08Cx
DORGAN, Thomas	40	M	Laborer	05Se08Cx
Margt.	36	F	Laborer	05Se08Cx
FARETZ, Edward	18	M	Laborer	05Se08Cx
DORGAN, Maurice	11	M	Laborer	05Se08Cx
Thomas	9	M	Child	05Se08Cx
Margt.	4	F	Child	05Se08Cx
Johanna	.09	F	Infant	05Se08Cx
CONTILLION, Thomas	30	M	Laborer	05Se08Cx
Bridget	26	F	Laborer	05Se08Cx
Bridget	5	F	Child	05Se08Cx
Mary	3	F	Child	05Se08Cx
John	.07	M	Infant	05Se08Cx
CONNOR, Michael	30	M	Laborer	05Se08Cx
Johannah	24	F	Laborer	05Se08Cx
Peter	16	M	Laborer	05Se08Cx
Ellen	13	F	Laborer	05Se08Cx
Jeremiah	10	M	Laborer	05Se08Cx
Mary	6	F	Child	05Se08Cx
Nanna	3	F	Child	05Se08Cx
Bridget	.01	F	Infant	05Se08Cx
MCCARTHY, Jno.	20	M	Laborer	05Se08Cx
FINNE, Bridget	20	F	Laborer	05Se08Cx
Mary	10	F	Laborer	05Se08Cx
Ellen	8	F	Child	05Se08Cx
FERETER, Nany	18	F	Laborer	05Se08Cx
MORIARTY, Michael	10	M	Laborer	05Se08Cx
John	7	M	Child	05Se08Cx
Thomas	4	M	Child	05Se08Cx
MOHONEY, Thomas	30	M	Laborer	05Se08Cx
Mary	26	F	Laborer	05Se08Cx
Ellen	18	F	Laborer	05Se08Cx
Patt	31	M	Laborer	05Se08Cx
Barry	26	M	Laborer	05Se08Cx
Bridget	6	F	Child	05Se08Cx
Johannah	.11	F	Infant	05Se08Cx
WALSH, Mary	60	F	Laborer	05Se08Cx
Mary	45	F	Laborer	05Se08Cx
Michael	10	M	Laborer	05Se08Cx
QUIRK, Patt	16	M	Laborer	05Se08Cx

NAMES OF PASSENGERS	AGE	SEX	OCCUPATIONS	DATE PORT SHIP
SMITH, William	30	M	Laborer	05Se08Cx
Anne	28	F	Laborer	05Se08Cx
CAHILL, Jno.	30	M	Laborer	05Se08Cx
CROWLEY, Pat	20	M	Laborer	05Se08Cx
VIEL, Michael	25	M	Laborer	05Se08Cx
CRONIN, Julia	20	F	Laborer	05Se08Cx
MURPHY, Michael	18	M	Laborer	05Se08Cx
Jno.	16	M	Laborer	05Se08Cx
SULLIVAN, Honora	30	F	Laborer	05Se08Cx
Bridget	20	F	Laborer	05Se08Cx
Ellen	1	F	Child	05Se08Cx
BROWN, Bridget	25	F	Laborer	05Se08Cx
MCAULIFFE, Michael	24	M	Laborer	05Se08Cx
CRONIN, Frederick	16	M	Laborer	05Se08Cx
Ellen	10	F	Laborer	05Se08Cx
MOHONEY, Mary	4	F	Child	05Se08Cx
MURPHY, Bridget	20	F	Laborer	05Se08Cx
Jno.	20	M	Laborer	05Se08Cx
RILEY, Honora	30	F	Laborer	05Se08Cx
Anne	21	F	Laborer	05Se08Cx
CONDON, Mary	20	F	Laborer	05Se08Cx
FITZGERALD, Pat	25	M	Laborer	05Se08Cx
KELLY, William	22	M	Laborer	05Se08Cx
SULLIVAN, James	23	M	Laborer	05Se08Cx
FITZGERALD, Michael	20	M	Laborer	05Se08Cx
REGAN, Jno.	14	M	Laborer	05Se08Cx
Margt.	18	F	Laborer	05Se08Cx
Kate	12	F	Laborer	05Se08Cx
RIORDAN, Hannah	20	F	Laborer	05Se08Cx
CAHILL, Julia	6	F	Child	05Se08Cx
ADAMS, Jno.	20	M	Laborer	05Se08Cx
MCCARTHY, Ellen	40	F	Laborer	05Se08Cx
MCCORMACK, Michl.	20	M	Laborer	05Se08Cx
DRAKE, Patt	26	M	Laborer	05Se08Cx
Jno.	16	M	Laborer	05Se08Cx

SCHOODIAC 07 SEPTEMBER 1849

From Liverpool

NAMES OF PASSENGERS	AGE	SEX	OCCUPATIONS	DATE PORT SHIP
FURGUSON, Jas.	20	M	Unknown	07Se02Qf
MCCABE, Jno.	45	M	Unknown	07Se02Qf
FURGUSON, Jno.	50	M	Unknown	07Se02Qf
MARTIN, Thos.	40	M	Unknown	07Se02Qf
Died-At-Sea				
Anne	29	F	Unknown	07Se02Qf
Elizab.	11	F	Unknown	07Se02Qf
Anne	9	F	Child	07Se02Qf
Herbert	9	M	Child	07Se02Qf
Maria	.00	F	Infant	07Se02Qf
FACULSKY, Hyam	40	M	Unknown	07Se02Qf
Mean	40	M	Unknown	07Se02Qf
Rebecca	12	F	Unknown	07Se02Qf
Shepsel	3	M	Child	07Se02Qf
Alfred	.00	M	Infant	07Se02Qf
PINDER, Jas.	15	M	Unknown	07Se02Qf
DORREN, Danl.	25	M	Unknown	07Se02Qf
U, Margt.	17	M	Unknown	07Se02Qf
CARLESK, Pat	29	M	Unknown	07Se02Qf
Sarah	21	F	Unknown	07Se02Qf
James	4	M	Child	07Se02Qf
Pather--, Cath.	.00	F	Infant	07Se02Qf
FINLAN, Ann	22	F	Unknown	07Se02Qf
BRIEN, Ann	22	F	Unknown	07Se02Qf
FINLAN, Margt.	10	F	Unknown	07Se02Qf
MCNAMARA, Brien	40	M	Unknown	07Se02Qf
ROSE, Jas.	28	M	Unknown	07Se02Qf
CHARLESWORTH, Jas.	22	M	Unknown	07Se02Qf
PRICE, Thos.	40	M	Unknown	07Se02Qf
PRICE, Judy	40	F	Unknown	07Se02Qf
Judy	.00	F	Infant	07Se02Qf
Cath.	9	F	Child	07Se02Qf
Pat	.00	M	Infant	07Se02Qf
Died-At-Sea				
MCCLOGHEY, Anne	50	F	Unknown	07Se02Qf
Mary	22	F	Unknown	07Se02Qf
MCCLOSKEY, Jas.	20	M	Unknown	07Se02Qf
QUILLON, Anne	25	M	Unknown	07Se02Qf
KEELEY, Mary	20	F	Unknown	07Se02Qf
Car--EL, Luke	25	M	Unknown	07Se02Qf
NELIGORN, David	38	M	Unknown	07Se02Qf
U (W)	25	F	Unknown	07Se02Qf
REARDON, Mich.	21	M	Unknown	07Se02Qf
U (W)	16	F	Unknown	07Se02Qf
CONLIN, Ed.	32	M	Unknown	07Se02Qf
COULTER, Pat	35	M	Unknown	07Se02Qf
MCCALL, Pat	20	M	Unknown	07Se02Qf
SMITH, Terence	17	M	Unknown	07Se02Qf
AHERN, Jno.	22	M	Unknown	07Se02Qf
LANGTON, Wm.	20	M	Unknown	07Se02Qf
MULLIN, Wm.	30	M	Unknown	07Se02Qf
DAVIS, Wm.	29	M	Unknown	07Se02Qf
JOICE, Wm.	25	M	Unknown	07Se02Qf
MARTIN, U-Mrs.	22	F	Unknown	07Se02Qf
LYONS, U-Mrs.	30	F	Unknown	07Se02Qf
CASEY, Ferugus	36	M	Unknown	07Se02Qf
MAHONE, Ann	21	F	Unknown	07Se02Qf
Ellen	20	F	Unknown	07Se02Qf
MURPHY, Ann	30	F	Unknown	07Se02Qf
Ellen	15	F	Unknown	07Se02Qf
BRULY, John	28	M	Unknown	07Se02Qf
Died-At-Sea				
U (W)	26	F	Unknown	07Se02Qf
Edwd.	.00	M	Infant	07Se02Qf
JONES, Johannah	22	F	Unknown	07Se02Qf
BURKE, Martha	30	F	Unknown	07Se02Qf
Jas.	9	M	Child	07Se02Qf
Wm.	9	M	Child	07Se02Qf
Michl.	.00	M	Infant	07Se02Qf
WHELAN, Margt.	50	F	Unknown	07Se02Qf
BUTLER, Margt.	45	F	Unknown	07Se02Qf
Honor	11	F	Unknown	07Se02Qf
BROPHY, Margt.	44	F	Unknown	07Se02Qf
HATS, Jacob	25	M	Unknown	07Se02Qf
Morris	27	M	Unknown	07Se02Qf
DOWLIN, Danes	28	M	Unknown	07Se02Qf
REILLY, Henry	40	M	Unknown	07Se02Qf
Bridget	30	F	Unknown	07Se02Qf
Jas.	18	M	Unknown	07Se02Qf
Michl.	10	M	Unknown	07Se02Qf
Pat	.00	M	Infant	07Se02Qf
Died-At-Sea				
Elizab.	.00	F	Infant	07Se02Qf
CLAYTON, Jno.	24	M	Unknown	07Se02Qf
BOLAN, Mich.	29	M	Unknown	07Se02Qf
KILLILEA, Jno.	30	M	Unknown	07Se02Qf
Bridget	30	F	Unknown	07Se02Qf
KENNEY, Honor	24	F	Unknown	07Se02Qf
FLANIGAN, Margt.	21	F	Unknown	07Se02Qf
HEYDEN, Eliza	22	F	Unknown	07Se02Qf
KENNEY, Pat	21	M	Unknown	07Se02Qf
MURRAY, Mich.	22	M	Unknown	07Se02Qf
CLUNE, Mary	30	F	Unknown	07Se02Qf
CARROLL, Wm.	23	M	Unknown	07Se02Qf
WARREN, Jas.	32	M	Unknown	07Se02Qf
FAGGOT, Jno.	22	M	Unknown	07Se02Qf
U (W)	20	F	Unknown	07Se02Qf
ONEIL, Owen	36	M	Unknown	07Se02Qf
Betty	18	F	Unknown	07Se02Qf
POSENGER, Jas.	26	M	Unknown	07Se02Qf
GROVER, Robt.	22	M	Unknown	07Se02Qf
WOOD, Jas.	30	M	Unknown	07Se02Qf
CARROLL, Thos.	24	M	Unknown	07Se02Qf

NAMES OF PASSENGERS	AGE	SEX	OCCUPATIONS	DATE PORT SHIP
Margt.	21	F	Unknown	07Se02Qf
Died-At-Sea				
BENSON, John	29	M	Unknown	07Se02Qf
KELLY, Michl.	22	M	Unknown	07Se02Qf
HANOHAN, Mich.	20	M	Unknown	07Se02Qf
HOGAN, Stephen	20	M	Unknown	07Se02Qf
KELLY, Cath.	21	F	Unknown	07Se02Qf
BENSON, Biddy	30	F	Unknown	07Se02Qf
GANN, Jno.	30	M	Unknown	07Se02Qf
Bridget	30	F	Unknown	07Se02Qf
GALLIGHAN, Pat	40	M	Unknown	07Se02Qf
Michl.	26	M	Unknown	07Se02Qf
Jno.	24	M	Unknown	07Se02Qf
Thomas	25	M	Unknown	07Se02Qf
Mary	21	F	Unknown	07Se02Qf
Ann	18	F	Unknown	07Se02Qf
Betsy	12	F	Unknown	07Se02Qf
Jane	10	F	Unknown	07Se02Qf
Betty	40	F	Unknown	07Se02Qf
MCDONALD, Mary	29	F	Unknown	07Se02Qf
Martha	.00	F	Infant	07Se02Qf
DONOVAN, Anne	20	F	Unknown	07Se02Qf
Pat	.00	M	Infant	07Se02Qf
Died-At-Sea				
COLSTER, U	28	M	Unknown	07Se02Qf
Elizab.	.00	F	Infant	07Se02Qf
Rosannah	.00	F	Infant	07Se02Qf
MCCARTHY, Carl	30	M	Unknown	07Se02Qf
Jno.	16	M	Unknown	07Se02Qf
LENNON, Luke	30	M	Unknown	07Se02Qf
FARREL, Cath.	25	F	Unknown	07Se02Qf
MULHOLLEN, Jno.	30	M	Unknown	07Se02Qf
Died-At-Sea				
MCCARTHY, Jno.	30	M	Unknown	07Se02Qf
CARTON, Jas.	31	M	Unknown	07Se02Qf
CLINCH, Jas.	37	M	Unknown	07Se02Qf
HEWETT, U	39	M	Unknown	07Se02Qf
SCOTT, Wm.	21	M	Unknown	07Se02Qf
WHEALON, Danl.	22	M	Unknown	07Se02Qf
Cath.	24	F	Unknown	07Se02Qf
Ann	17	F	Unknown	07Se02Qf
Ann	24	F	Unknown	07Se02Qf
HIGGINS, Margt.	30	F	Unknown	07Se02Qf
Thos.	18	M	Unknown	07Se02Qf
Danl.	13	M	Unknown	07Se02Qf
John	9	M	Child	07Se02Qf
Jas.	40	M	Unknown	07Se02Qf
MULLAND, Philip	20	M	Unknown	07Se02Qf
Mary	18	F	Unknown	07Se02Qf
MULLANO, Margaret	13	F	Unknown	07Se02Qf
PARRIS, Simon	16	M	Unknown	07Se02Qf
ARMSTRONG, Wm.	30	M	Unknown	07Se02Qf
LYMAN, Mary	40	F	Unknown	07Se02Qf
Martin	15	M	Unknown	07Se02Qf
DEALLY, Mary	20	F	Unknown	07Se02Qf
SPALLIN, Pat	20	M	Unknown	07Se02Qf
RATICAN, Pat	21	M	Unknown	07Se02Qf
EVANS, Jno.	21	M	Unknown	07Se02Qf
KINCHEDA, Dennis	40	M	Unknown	07Se02Qf
Mary	36	F	Unknown	07Se02Qf
Anne	10	F	Unknown	07Se02Qf
Jno.	5	M	Child	07Se02Qf
Michl.	.00	M	Infant	07Se02Qf
Fanny	.00	F	Infant	07Se02Qf
GIBNEY, Thomas	28	M	Unknown	07Se02Qf
Ann	17	F	Unknown	07Se02Qf
SMYTH, Michl.	24	M	Unknown	07Se02Qf
SHERRINTON, Joseph	28	M	Unknown	07Se02Qf
Lucy	30	F	Unknown	07Se02Qf
Lucy	.00	F	Infant	07Se02Qf
BROLAN, Cath.	23	F	Unknown	07Se02Qf
Andrew	.00	M	Infant	07Se02Qf
Thomas	.00	M	Infant	07Se02Qf
LINDIN, Elizab.	29	F	Unknown	07Se02Qf
John	.00	M	Infant	07Se02Qf
LINDIN, Mary-Ann	.00	F	Infant	07Se02Qf
GARRIGAN, Pat	47	M	Unknown	07Se02Qf
Died-At-Sea				
Judy	47	F	Unknown	07Se02Qf
Died-At-Sea				
Pat	7	M	Child	07Se02Qf
MCGUIRE, Edwd.	11	M	Unknown	07Se02Qf
Jas.	13	M	Unknown	07Se02Qf
SCHONETAG, Ger.	20	M	Unknown	07Se02Qf
Ellen	20	F	Unknown	07Se02Qf
COWEN, Phil.	21	M	Unknown	07Se02Qf
SENNADON, Henry	20	M	Unknown	07Se02Qf
Alex	21	M	Unknown	07Se02Qf
BOURKE, John	20	M	Unknown	07Se02Qf
CARTER, Mary	40	F	Unknown	07Se02Qf
Died-At-Sea				
Thos.	12	M	Unknown	07Se02Qf
Jas.	11	M	Unknown	07Se02Qf
CORNISH, Phil.	25	M	Unknown	07Se02Qf
SMITH, Wm.	26	M	Unknown	07Se02Qf
Harriett	20	F	Unknown	07Se02Qf
MCCASHEY, Bridget	25	F	Unknown	07Se02Qf
BERRY, Anne	18	F	Unknown	07Se02Qf
MCCABE, Helen	16	F	Unknown	07Se02Qf
Bridget	14	F	Unknown	07Se02Qf
MCDONALD, Helen	18	F	Unknown	07Se02Qf
MORRIS, Saml.	26	M	Unknown	07Se02Qf
Simeon	20	M	Unknown	07Se02Qf
SHANE, Pat	26	M	Unknown	07Se02Qf
MALONE, Mary	40	F	Unknown	07Se02Qf
Mary-Ann	8	F	Child	07Se02Qf
Pat	6	M	Child	07Se02Qf
Martha	.00	F	Infant	07Se02Qf
Jno.	.00	M	Infant	07Se02Qf
MCALROY, Mary	20	F	Unknown	07Se02Qf
IGO, Cath.	29	F	Unknown	07Se02Qf
Cath.	14	F	Unknown	07Se02Qf
Ann	6	F	Child	07Se02Qf
Pat	15	M	Unknown	07Se02Qf
MARKS, Lewis	28	M	Unknown	07Se02Qf
DELANEY, Bridget	32	F	Unknown	07Se02Qf
MORRISSEY, Michl.	20	M	Unknown	07Se02Qf
SWEENY, Pat	28	M	Unknown	07Se02Qf
KENNEDY, Pat	28	M	Unknown	07Se02Qf
LEVI, Jas.	24	M	Unknown	07Se02Qf
Sarah	40	F	Unknown	07Se02Qf
Esther	19	F	Unknown	07Se02Qf
Diana	36	F	Unknown	07Se02Qf
Lee	36	M	Unknown	07Se02Qf
Ras.	6	M	Child	07Se02Qf
Levi	.00	M	Infant	07Se02Qf
CAFFNY, Math.	40	M	Unknown	07Se02Qf
Died-At-Sea				
Mary	40	F	Unknown	07Se02Qf
Michl.	18	M	Unknown	07Se02Qf
Bessy	21	F	Unknown	07Se02Qf
James	14	M	Unknown	07Se02Qf
Math.	8	M	Child	07Se02Qf
Pat	.00	M	Infant	07Se02Qf
Bridget	12	F	Unknown	07Se02Qf
Mary	11	F	Unknown	07Se02Qf
GRATEL, Mary	19	F	Unknown	07Se02Qf
KERIGAN, Rose	17	F	Unknown	07Se02Qf
GALAGHER, Michl.	29	M	Unknown	07Se02Qf
Henry	21	M	Unknown	07Se02Qf
CLARKIN, Terence	39	M	Unknown	07Se02Qf
CRAHEN, Cath.	22	F	Unknown	07Se02Qf
MCCUSKER, Helen	20	F	Unknown	07Se02Qf
HESSETT, Jno.	22	M	Unknown	07Se02Qf
CUMMING, Ann	20	F	Unknown	07Se02Qf
BEAN, Mary	20	F	Unknown	07Se02Qf
DONOVAN, Jno.	45	M	Unknown	07Se02Qf
Died-At-Sea				
MCNAMARA, Jno.	45	M	Unknown	07Se02Qf
Ann	19	F	Unknown	07Se02Qf

NAMES OF PASSENGERS	A G E	S E X	OCCUPATIONS	DATE PORT SHIP
HAROLY, Owen	32	M	Unknown	07Se02Qf
FOLEY, Thos.	25	M	Unknown	07Se02Qf
Bridget	23	F	Unknown	07Se02Qf
BEALE, John	29	M	Unknown	07Se02Qf
MAHER, Math.	25	M	Unknown	07Se02Qf
RYAN, Biddy	20	F	Unknown	07Se02Qf
HUGH, James	40	M	Unknown	07Se02Qf
Anne	16	F	Unknown	07Se02Qf
ONEIL, Fras.	20	M	Unknown	07Se02Qf
CADDEN, Matthew	21	M	Unknown	07Se02Qf
RYAN, Robt.	28	M	Unknown	07Se02Qf
Margt.	.00	F	Infant	07Se02Qf
Died-At-Sea				
MAHONE, Heliger	18	M	Unknown	07Se02Qf
Died-At-Sea				
FREDERICK, Will	25	M	Unknown	07Se02Qf
CROSBY, Geo.	28	M	Unknown	07Se02Qf
KEALY, Maria	19	F	Unknown	07Se02Qf
CARRIGAN, Eliza	20	F	Unknown	07Se02Qf
FINNIHER, Thos.	23	M	Unknown	07Se02Qf
WALSH, Dar.	22	M	Unknown	07Se02Qf
CRATER, Dar.	40	M	Unknown	07Se02Qf
REYNOLDS, Edw.	38	M	Unknown	07Se02Qf
Cath.	38	F	Unknown	07Se02Qf
MCGAN, Dennis	24	M	Unknown	07Se02Qf
Jno.	36	M	Unknown	07Se02Qf
FULLWOOD, Jno.	27	M	Unknown	07Se02Qf
COLLIGHAN, Bridget	20	F	Unknown	07Se02Qf
Jno.	19	M	Unknown	07Se02Qf
THOMSON, Jas.	26	M	Unknown	07Se02Qf
FOX, Helen	30	F	Unknown	07Se02Qf
Margt.	.00	F	Infant	07Se02Qf
Maria	.00	F	Infant	07Se02Qf
BOHAN, Honor	30	F	Unknown	07Se02Qf
REILLY, Mary	20	F	Unknown	07Se02Qf
FARMAN, Pat	40	M	Unknown	07Se02Qf
DONEHONEY, Margt.	30	F	Unknown	07Se02Qf
FLYNN, Margt.	17	F	Unknown	07Se02Qf
JAFFE, John	36	M	Unknown	07Se02Qf
Anne	30	F	Unknown	07Se02Qf
Sarah	3	F	Child	07Se02Qf
Cath.	.00	F	Infant	07Se02Qf
DONALD, Henry-A.	25	M	Unknown	07Se02Qf
Ann	23	F	Unknown	07Se02Qf
Hugh	.00	M	Infant	07Se02Qf
FARREL, Jno.	7	M	Child	07Se02Qf
TONER, Jas.	22	M	Unknown	07Se02Qf
KELLY, Berrey	25	F	Unknown	07Se02Qf
Ann	.00	F	Infant	07Se02Qf
REILLY, Hugh	20	M	Unknown	07Se02Qf
COLLAN, M.	22	M	Unknown	07Se02Qf
HINDES, Ellen	21	F	Unknown	07Se02Qf
BROWN, W.	24	M	Unknown	07Se02Qf
HEGAN, M.	32	M	Unknown	07Se02Qf
Anne	33	F	Unknown	07Se02Qf
MCGRATH, P.	29	M	Unknown	07Se02Qf
WELSH, P.	23	M	Unknown	07Se02Qf
C.	23	M	Unknown	07Se02Qf
WILSON, T.	30	M	Unknown	07Se02Qf
ROWLAND, D.	30	M	Unknown	07Se02Qf
DAVIS, Geo.	47	M	Unknown	07Se02Qf
Emma	46	F	Unknown	07Se02Qf
William-Geo.	17	M	Unknown	07Se02Qf
Jane-Oliver	17	F	Unknown	07Se02Qf
SPEIGELSTINE, A.	17	F	Unknown	07Se02Qf
U	.00	U	Infant	07Se02Qf
HAYLO, Thos.	30	M	Unknown	07Se02Qf
RYDER, Mary	78	F	Unknown	07Se02Qf
Died-At-Sea				
CARROLL, Pat	.00	M	Infant	07Se02Qf
Died-At-Sea				
FARMER, Mary	27	F	Unknown	07Se02Qf
Died-At-Sea				
CUMMING, Pat	55	M	Unknown	07Se02Qf
Died-At-Sea				

NIAGARA 07 SEPTEMBER 1849

From Liverpool

NAMES OF PASSENGERS	A G E	S E X	OCCUPATIONS	DATE PORT SHIP
MOORE, W.	30	M	Merchant	07Se02lg
U-Mrs.	28	F	Lady	07Se02lg
U-Miss.	9	F	Child	07Se02lg
MCMASTER, J.	40	M	Merchant	07Se02lg
MCKEE, Jas.	30	M	Merchant	07Se02lg
COCHEAN, Jas.	37	M	Merchant	07Se02lg

INDUSTRY 07 SEPTEMBER 1849

From Dublin

NAMES OF PASSENGERS	A G E	S E X	OCCUPATIONS	DATE PORT SHIP
CLAREY, U-Mrs.	30	F	Farmer	07Se12Cc
Mary	8	F	Child	07Se12Cc
John	3	M	Child	07Se12Cc
Denny	.00	M	Infant	07Se12Cc
MULLALLY, U-Mrs.	45	F	Unknown	07Se12Cc
U-Miss	22	F	Unknown	07Se12Cc
MAUD, U	18	F	Unknown	07Se12Cc
BULGER, Eliza	20	F	Unknown	07Se12Cc
HIGGINSON, Michael	18	M	Unknown	07Se12Cc
MCPROUD, U-Miss	20	F	Unknown	07Se12Cc
Margaret	18	F	Unknown	07Se12Cc
MOULT, Sarah	20	F	Unknown	07Se12Cc
MORRISON, U-Miss	20	F	Unknown	07Se12Cc
MCLAUGHLAN, Thos.	20	M	Unknown	07Se12Cc
WALSH, Thos.	14	F	Unknown	07Se12Cc
CREAMAN, E.Mrs.	20	F	Unknown	07Se12Cc
LEONARD, John	23	M	Unknown	07Se12Cc
TRACY, W.	20	M	Unknown	07Se12Cc
KEAN, Owen	20	M	Unknown	07Se12Cc
FARRELL, U-Mrs.	35	F	Unknown	07Se12Cc
Hanah	20	F	Unknown	07Se12Cc
Ellen	18	M	Unknown	07Se12Cc
LYON, William	9	M	Child	07Se12Cc
James	11	M	Unknown	07Se12Cc
WHITE, Matt	18	M	Unknown	07Se12Cc
Catherine	25	F	Unknown	07Se12Cc
KELLY, U-Mrs.	25	F	Unknown	07Se12Cc
Edward	2	M	Child	07Se12Cc
John	.00	M	Infant	07Se12Cc
GALVIN, Patt	28	M	Unknown	07Se12Cc
MATHEWS, Simon	35	M	Unknown	07Se12Cc
U (W)	34	F	Unknown	07Se12Cc
Mary	16	F	Unknown	07Se12Cc
Patt	13	M	Unknown	07Se12Cc
John	11	M	Unknown	07Se12Cc
Catherine	.00	F	Infant	07Se12Cc
Patt	30	M	Unknown	07Se12Cc
NOULAN, M.	25	M	Unknown	07Se12Cc
Margret	24	F	Unknown	07Se12Cc
HORAN, Maria	20	F	Unknown	07Se12Cc
DUNN, James	11	M	Unknown	07Se12Cc
MCKENNA, John	20	M	Unknown	07Se12Cc
MORRIGAN, Rose	30	F	Unknown	07Se12Cc
BRADY, Margret	20	F	Unknown	07Se12Cc
SMITH, P.	29	M	Unknown	07Se12Cc
CODY, M.Mrs.	21	F	Unknown	07Se12Cc
James	.00	M	Infant	07Se12Cc
PLANT, William	16	M	Unknown	07Se12Cc

NAMES OF PASSENGERS		AGE	SEX	OCCUPATIONS	DATE PORT SHIP
OBRIAN, Pat		36	M	Unknown	07Se12Cc
U	(W)	25	F	Unknown	07Se12Cc
Michael		4	M	Child	07Se12Cc
Mary		.00	F	Infant	07Se12Cc
LAUGHLAN, Hugh		45	M	Unknown	07Se12Cc
U	(W)	25	F	Unknown	07Se12Cc
Mary		5	F	Child	07Se12Cc
MORAN, Thomas		28	M	Unknown	07Se12Cc
U	(W)	22	F	Unknown	07Se12Cc
Catherine		18	F	Unknown	07Se12Cc
John		4	M	Child	07Se12Cc
GOULDING, M.A.Mrs.		25	M	Unknown	07Se12Cc
George		.00	M	Infant	07Se12Cc
GERRARD, James		19	M	Unknown	07Se12Cc
MERCER, Catherine		26	F	Unknown	07Se12Cc
ELTON, Jane		24	M	Unknown	07Se12Cc
Ann		20	F	Unknown	07Se12Cc
Joseph		.00	M	Infant	07Se12Cc
MARSER, George		14	M	Unknown	07Se12Cc
Mary-Ann		.00	F	Infant	07Se12Cc
BRADY, Andy		21	M	Unknown	07Se12Cc
LOOBY, Thomas		20	M	Unknown	07Se12Cc
CARROLL, James		21	M	Unknown	07Se12Cc
ARMSTRONG, James		24	M	Unknown	07Se12Cc
BYAN, Bridget		40	F	Unknown	07Se12Cc
Biddy		22	F	Unknown	07Se12Cc
Michael		16	M	Unknown	07Se12Cc
BYREN, Judy		35	F	Unknown	07Se12Cc
David		6	M	Child	07Se12Cc
Joseph		3	M	Child	07Se12Cc
DONLEY, Peter		24	M	Unknown	07Se12Cc
Ann		20	F	Unknown	07Se12Cc
RICHMOND, U-Miss		20	F	Unknown	07Se12Cc
SAVAGE, Patt		20	M	Unknown	07Se12Cc
CARTY, John		26	M	Unknown	07Se12Cc
DOORLEY, Margret		35	F	Unknown	07Se12Cc
Anne		12	F	Unknown	07Se12Cc
BRYAN, George		20	M	Unknown	07Se12Cc
COFFEY, Edward		42	M	Unknown	07Se12Cc
Christy		20	M	Unknown	07Se12Cc
Margret		40	F	Unknown	07Se12Cc
Rose		20	F	Unknown	07Se12Cc
HURST, U-Mrs.		50	F	Unknown	07Se12Cc
Jane		17	F	Unknown	07Se12Cc
CAREY, Michael		21	M	Unknown	07Se12Cc
GIBSON, George		20	M	Unknown	07Se12Cc
HOME, U-Mrs.		36	F	Unknown	07Se12Cc
Matilda		10	F	Unknown	07Se12Cc
William		8	M	Child	07Se12Cc
Samuel		6	M	Child	07Se12Cc
John		4	M	Child	07Se12Cc
Robert		.00	M	Infant	07Se12Cc
BELTON, Jane		20	F	Unknown	07Se12Cc
William		21	M	Unknown	07Se12Cc
BEAVER, Bernard		20	M	Unknown	07Se12Cc
CAREY, Catherine		20	F	Unknown	07Se12Cc
CLOOWAN, Mary		20	F	Unknown	07Se12Cc
POWER, Ann		30	F	Unknown	07Se12Cc
Eliza		22	F	Unknown	07Se12Cc
HORAHAN, Margret		20	F	Unknown	07Se12Cc
ARNOLD, James		20	M	Unknown	07Se12Cc
Mary-A.		30	F	Unknown	07Se12Cc
BROWN, Allis		25	F	Unknown	07Se12Cc
ARNOLD, Peter		5	M	Child	07Se12Cc
James		2	M	Child	07Se12Cc
BOWON, Patt		.00	M	Infant	07Se12Cc
Margret		45	F	Unknown	07Se12Cc
Mary		34	F	Unknown	07Se12Cc
Thomas		5	M	Child	07Se12Cc
Bridget		3	F	Child	07Se12Cc
George		.00	M	Infant	07Se12Cc
BRADY, Catherine		22	F	Unknown	07Se12Cc
CAREY, Edward		20	M	Unknown	07Se12Cc
NOWLAN, Bridget		20	F	Unknown	07Se12Cc
PURCELL, James		40	M	Unknown	07Se12Cc
Sh--AN, Anty.		25	F	Unknown	07Se12Cc
Thomas		10	M	Unknown	07Se12Cc
BOLGER, John		27	M	Unknown	07Se12Cc
Catherine		15	F	Unknown	07Se12Cc
Mary		10	F	Unknown	07Se12Cc
James		.00	M	Infant	07Se12Cc
FLOOD, Mary		26	F	Unknown	07Se12Cc
TUSHER, Jane		25	F	Unknown	07Se12Cc
JOWERS, Owen		23	M	Unknown	07Se12Cc
CAMPTON, Mary		35	F	Unknown	07Se12Cc
Thomas		3	M	Child	07Se12Cc
DOYLE, Margret		25	F	Unknown	07Se12Cc
NOWLAN, Nancy		42	F	Unknown	07Se12Cc
Bridget		16	F	Unknown	07Se12Cc
Marton		12	M	Unknown	07Se12Cc
William		9	M	Child	07Se12Cc
LEFROY, Catherine		28	F	Unknown	07Se12Cc
HOLLAND, Patt		40	M	Unknown	07Se12Cc
HANY, Patt		26	M	Unknown	07Se12Cc
Judy		30	F	Unknown	07Se12Cc
HENEY, Mary		24	F	Unknown	07Se12Cc
WALSH, Margret		20	F	Unknown	07Se12Cc
FLETCHER, Joseph		35	M	Unknown	07Se12Cc
Sarah		60	F	Unknown	07Se12Cc
Dorah		40	F	Unknown	07Se12Cc
Joseph		7	M	Child	07Se12Cc
QUIRK, John		22	M	Unknown	07Se12Cc
Patt		25	M	Unknown	07Se12Cc
CASSIDY, Biddy		20	F	Unknown	07Se12Cc
DALEY, Margret		17	F	Unknown	07Se12Cc
RICHFORD, John		66	M	Unknown	07Se12Cc
U	(W)	50	F	Unknown	07Se12Cc
BYRNE, Michael		20	M	Unknown	07Se12Cc
HENRICK, Julia		20	F	Unknown	07Se12Cc
DALEY, Michael		60	M	Unknown	07Se12Cc
James		34	M	Unknown	07Se12Cc
Larance		29	M	Unknown	07Se12Cc
Edward		26	M	Unknown	07Se12Cc
John		18	M	Unknown	07Se12Cc
Michael		.00	M	Infant	07Se12Cc
Ann		24	F	Unknown	07Se12Cc
Sally		20	F	Unknown	07Se12Cc
Mary		13	F	Unknown	07Se12Cc
LALOR, Rose		26	F	Unknown	07Se12Cc
FARRELL, Michael		20	M	Unknown	07Se12Cc
MOONY, Margret		20	F	Unknown	07Se12Cc
OLDAN, U		24	M	Unknown	07Se12Cc
GOOD, Edward		20	M	Unknown	07Se12Cc
KEALY, Ellen		20	F	Unknown	07Se12Cc
DALEY, Peter		20	M	Unknown	07Se12Cc
Mu--LY, James		20	M	Unknown	07Se12Cc
DELANY, Patt		21	M	Unknown	07Se12Cc
RELLEY, William		21	M	Unknown	07Se12Cc
KEGAN, James		20	M	Unknown	07Se12Cc
STONES, Edward		20	M	Unknown	07Se12Cc
SHEA, Ann		20	F	Unknown	07Se12Cc
KENNEDY, Rose		20	F	Unknown	07Se12Cc
HANNAN, Michael		30	M	Unknown	07Se12Cc
Betty		30	F	Unknown	07Se12Cc
MCCORMACK, James		20	M	Unknown	07Se12Cc
DWYRE, William		26	M	Unknown	07Se12Cc
HANNAGHTY, Ann		22	F	Unknown	07Se12Cc
MCGOVERNAN, Thomas		51	M	Unknown	07Se12Cc
Maria		45	F	Unknown	07Se12Cc
Easter		22	F	Unknown	07Se12Cc
Betty		20	F	Unknown	07Se12Cc
Judy		16	F	Unknown	07Se12Cc
Edward		8	M	Child	07Se12Cc
Mary		5	F	Child	07Se12Cc
LAUGHLAN, Patt		35	M	Unknown	07Se12Cc
Judy		35	F	Unknown	07Se12Cc
James		15	M	Unknown	07Se12Cc
Patt		8	M	Child	07Se12Cc
Mary		6	F	Child	07Se12Cc
Thomas		.00	M	Infant	07Se12Cc

NAMES OF PASSENGERS		AGE	SEX	OCCUPATIONS	DATE PORT SHIP
KELLY, James		30	M	Unknown	07Se12Cc
CAREY, Michael		22	M	Unknown	07Se12Cc
GOGAN, Michael		22	M	Unknown	07Se12Cc
DOORLEY, Michael		21	M	Unknown	07Se12Cc
THOMPSON, U-Mrs.		35	F	Unknown	07Se12Cc
Margaret		13	F	Unknown	07Se12Cc
DOHENY, Mary		20	F	Unknown	07Se12Cc
SALMAN, Margret		20	F	Unknown	07Se12Cc
FITZPATRICK, Dan.		12	M	Unknown	07Se12Cc
THOMPSON, Sarah		5	F	Child	07Se12Cc
MCENTIRE, Margret		20	F	Unknown	07Se12Cc
JERRY, Michael		21	M	Unknown	07Se12Cc
BRADY, Mary		22	F	Unknown	07Se12Cc
Catherine		20	F	Unknown	07Se12Cc
MCMAHAN, U-Miss		16	F	Unknown	07Se12Cc
ODWYER, U		20	M	Unknown	07Se12Cc
MADDEN, U-Miss		17	F	Unknown	07Se12Cc
BAKER, U		22	M	Unknown	07Se12Cc
MORTH, U		19	M	Unknown	07Se12Cc
EDEN, U-Miss		16	F	Unknown	07Se12Cc
WELL, W.H.Mrs.		20	F	Unknown	07Se12Cc
PRIDE, U-Miss		16	F	Unknown	07Se12Cc

ABERDEEN 07 SEPTEMBER 1849

From Liverpool

NAMES OF PASSENGERS		AGE	SEX	OCCUPATIONS	DATE PORT SHIP
SWINOCOR, Mary-Ann		40	F	Lady	07Se02Gu
Henry		18	M	Son	07Se02Gu
Harriet		14	F	Daughter	07Se02Gu
Amanda		10	F	Daughter	07Se02Gu
George		8	M	Child	07Se02Gu
Alfreda		1	F	Child	07Se02Gu
HOUSE, David		36	M	Farmer	07Se02Gu
U	(W)	34	F	Wife	07Se02Gu
James		12	M	Son	07Se02Gu
Nathaniel		10	M	Son	07Se02Gu
Emma		8	F	Child	07Se02Gu
John		7	M	Child	07Se02Gu
William		2	M	Child	07Se02Gu
MAYTON, Henry		27	M	Mechanic	07Se02Gu
U	(W)	26	F	Wife	07Se02Gu
Elizabeth		.00	F	Infant	07Se02Gu
HAM, Thomas		28	M	Comedian	07Se02Gu
Edward		.00	M	Infant	07Se02Gu
KNIGHT, John		31	M	Mechanic	07Se02Gu
CHARD, Charles		27	M	Mechanic	07Se02Gu
IRERD, Thomas		47	M	Mechanic	07Se02Gu
GREENE, Edward		49	M	Mechanic	07Se02Gu
Joseph		45	M	Mechanic	07Se02Gu
SCOTT, Jonathan		28	M	Mechanic	07Se02Gu
U	(W)	28	F	Wife	07Se02Gu
Charles		5	M	Child	07Se02Gu
George		3	M	Child	07Se02Gu
Eliza		6	F	Child	07Se02Gu
Anne		11	F	Child	07Se02Gu
HARDCASTLE, Edward		29	M	Mechanic	07Se02Gu
HOPWOOD, William		43	M	Mechanic	07Se02Gu
Hannah		43	F	Mechanic	07Se02Gu
Emma		16	F	Daughter	07Se02Gu
Elizabeth		13	F	Daughter	07Se02Gu
John		10	M	Son	07Se02Gu
George		7	M	Child	07Se02Gu
Elijah		4	M	Child	07Se02Gu
HENDERSON, David		33	M	Mechanic	07Se02Gu
U	(W)	28	F	Wife	07Se02Gu
James		8	M	Child	07Se02Gu
Mary-Ann		6	F	Child	07Se02Gu
Janet		4	F	Child	07Se02Gu

NAMES OF PASSENGERS		AGE	SEX	OCCUPATIONS	DATE PORT SHIP
HENDERSON, David		.00	M	Infant	07Se02Gu
MCSARTY, Malcolm		50	M	Mechanic	07Se02Gu
FARRELL, Henry		13	M	Mechanic	07Se02Gu
Margaret		12	F	Sister	07Se02Gu
NOBLE, Richard		37	M	Mechanic	07Se02Gu
Jane		21	F	Wife	07Se02Gu
John		4	M	Child	07Se02Gu
Mary-Ann		.00	F	Infant	07Se02Gu
KIRKHAM, James		27	M	Mechanic	07Se02Gu
U	(W)	24	F	Wife	07Se02Gu
Frederick		2	M	Child	07Se02Gu
Mary		.00	F	Infant	07Se02Gu
TILL, Caleb		45	M	Mechanic	07Se02Gu
Henry		13	M	Nephew	07Se02Gu
SKINNER, Ann		22	F	Unknown	07Se02Gu
Elizabeth		2	F	Child	07Se02Gu
Mary-Ann		.00	F	Infant	07Se02Gu
MOFFAT, Frances		24	M	Cnf	07Se02Gu
Mary		3	F	Child	07Se02Gu
RUSH, Catherine		22	F	Servant	07Se02Gu
STANTON, Henry-C.		35	M	Mechanic	07Se02Gu
U	(W)	35	F	Wife	07Se02Gu
Lucy		12	F	Daughter	07Se02Gu
Mary-Ann		9	F	Child	07Se02Gu
Catherine		7	F	Child	07Se02Gu
Ellen		5	F	Child	07Se02Gu
David		3	M	Child	07Se02Gu
Edwin		.00	M	Infant	07Se02Gu
HOLT, John		36	M	Laborer	07Se02Gu
CHAPMAN, John		45	M	Mechanic	07Se02Gu
Ellen		16	F	Daughter	07Se02Gu
John		11	M	Son	07Se02Gu
NOWLAN, Robert		24	M	Mechanic	07Se02Gu
DUDD, Thomas		17	M	Mechanic	07Se02Gu
STEELE, Samuel		25	M	Laborer	07Se02Gu
BARRETT, George		22	M	Mechanic	07Se02Gu
U	(W)	23	F	Wife	07Se02Gu
MYERS, Robt.		26	M	Mechanic	07Se02Gu
HILL, Stephen		29	M	Mechanic	07Se02Gu
U	(W)	29	F	Wife	07Se02Gu
Stephen		2	M	Child	07Se02Gu
Sarah-Anne		.00	F	Infant	07Se02Gu
WINTERBOTTOM, John		23	M	Mechanic	07Se02Gu
WITTELZ, Henry		28	M	Mechanic	07Se02Gu
John		31	M	Mechanic	07Se02Gu
CARPENTER, John		55	M	Mechanic	07Se02Gu
SCOTT, Charles		25	M	Mechanic	07Se02Gu
HAND, Uriel		55	M	Mechanic	07Se02Gu
Cyrus	(S)	22	M	Son	07Se02Gu
MASON, John		23	M	Mechanic	07Se02Gu
CALCUT, William		24	M	Mechanic	07Se02Gu
ALBERT, Samuel		35	M	Mechanic	07Se02Gu
U	(W)	29	F	Wife	07Se02Gu
U	(W)	29	F	Wife	07Se02Gu
MACHIN, Samuel		36	M	Mechanic	07Se02Gu
Jane	(W)	35	F	Wife	07Se02Gu
William		13	M	Son	07Se02Gu
Lucy		6	F	Child	07Se02Gu
Mary		.00	F	Infant	07Se02Gu
HASLEM, Alfred		37	M	Mechanic	07Se02Gu
Eliza		14	F	Daughter	07Se02Gu
Emma		10	F	Daughter	07Se02Gu
Selina		6	F	Child	07Se02Gu
BRIGGS, Moses		32	M	Mechanic	07Se02Gu
Alice		28	F	Wife	07Se02Gu
Edmund		11	M	Son	07Se02Gu
Anne		8	F	Child	07Se02Gu
BETTS, William		50	M	Laborer	07Se02Gu
Hannah		48	F	Wife	07Se02Gu
Thomas		19	M	Son	07Se02Gu
Charles		13	M	Son	07Se02Gu
Anne		11	F	Daughter	07Se02Gu
Henry		9	M	Child	07Se02Gu
Maria		7	F	Child	07Se02Gu
Frederick		2	M	Child	07Se02Gu

NAMES OF PASSENGERS		AGE	SEX	OCCUPATIONS	DATE PORT SHIP
BETTS, John		4	M	Child	07Se02Gu
ELKES, Paul		42	M	Mechanic	07Se02Gu
U	(W)	38	F	Wife	07Se02Gu
HICKS, William		28	M	Laborer	07Se02Gu
Mark		24	M	Laborer	07Se02Gu
WALKER, Jabez		16	M	Laborer	07Se02Gu
UNDY, Charlotte		36	F	Unknown	07Se02Gu
Anne		16	F	Daughter	07Se02Gu
Fanny		12	F	Daughter	07Se02Gu
Walker	(S)	5	M	Child	07Se02Gu
HICKMAN, Peter		30	M	Mechanic	07Se02Gu
U	(W)	26	F	Wife	07Se02Gu
Henry	(S)	3	M	Child	07Se02Gu
Hannah	(D)	.00	F	Infant	07Se02Gu
PARKS, Frederick		39	M	Mechanic	07Se02Gu
CLIVE, John		50	M	Laborer	07Se02Gu
Richard		23	M	Druggist	07Se02Gu
PHILIPS, Benjamin		21	M	Farmer	07Se02Gu
THOMAS, Price		20	M	Laborer	07Se02Gu
PHILIPS, Benjamin		20	M	Laborer	07Se02Gu
RICHARDS, John		22	M	Mechanic	07Se02Gu
PROCTOR, John		25	M	Mechanic	07Se02Gu
WINTERBOTTOM, James		30	M	Mechanic	07Se02Gu
BAMFORTH, John		25	M	Mechanic	07Se02Gu
COUGHLIN, John		24	M	Laborer	07Se02Gu
BRIEN, Hannah		22	F	None	07Se02Gu
BIRMINGHAM, Bridget		28	F	None	07Se02Gu
CARNEY, Martin		33	M	None	07Se02Gu
FITZGERALD, John		24	M	Fisherman	07Se02Gu
GLEESON, Darby		32	M	Laborer	07Se02Gu
COONEY, Nelly		24	F	Laborer	07Se02Gu
AMBLER, David		25	M	Laborer	07Se02Gu
Mary	(W)	22	F	Wife	07Se02Gu
George	(S)	5	M	Child	07Se02Gu
Thomas	(S)	4	M	Child	07Se02Gu
Elizabeth	(D)	3	F	Child	07Se02Gu
John	(S)	.00	M	Infant	07Se02Gu
Ralph		24	M	Mechanic	07Se02Gu
Charlotte		26	F	Wife	07Se02Gu
Elizabeth	(D)	3	F	Child	07Se02Gu
John	(S)	.00	M	Infant	07Se02Gu
SADLER, Michael		20	M	Laborer	07Se02Gu
WADE, John		21	M	Laborer	07Se02Gu
CASS, William		75	M	Surgeon	07Se02Gu
U	(W)	60	F	Wife	07Se02Gu
U-Miss		20	F	Daughter	07Se02Gu
WRIGHT, U-Mrs.		30	F	None	07Se02Gu
Thomas	(S)	8	M	Child	07Se02Gu
Mary-Anne	(D)	7	F	Child	07Se02Gu
Lorenzo	(S)	5	M	Infant	07Se02Gu
Walter	(S)	3	M	Child	07Se02Gu
John	(S)	.00	M	Infant	07Se02Gu
BYRNE, Mary		26	F	Unknown	07Se02Gu
Catherine	(D)	4	F	Child	07Se02Gu
BROWN, William		27	M	Merchant	07Se02Gu
U	(W)	28	F	Wife	07Se02Gu
Catherine	(D)	.00	F	Infant	07Se02Gu
COLEMAN, Maria		23	F	Servant	07Se02Gu
CONLAN, Daniel		23	M	Farmer	07Se02Gu
PHILIPS, Patrick		45	M	Laborer	07Se02Gu
Catherine		18	F	Daughter	07Se02Gu
SKEIN, Ellen		35	F	Unknown	07Se02Gu
Paul		14	M	Son	07Se02Gu
John		12	M	Son	07Se02Gu
Margaret		10	F	Daughter	07Se02Gu
Michael	(S)	8	M	Child	07Se02Gu
Catherine	(D)	6	F	Child	07Se02Gu
Mary	(D)	3	F	Child	07Se02Gu
William	(S)	.00	M	Infant	07Se02Gu
CARRIGAN, Peter		20	M	Laborer	07Se02Gu
MORRISON, William		18	M	Clerk	07Se02Gu
QUINN, Thos.		40	M	Mechanic	07Se02Gu
Patrick		14	M	Son	07Se02Gu
Thomas		12	M	Son	07Se02Gu
James		10	M	Son	07Se02Gu
QUINN, Mary-Anne	(D)	4	F	Child	07Se02Gu
Charles	(S)	2	M	Child	07Se02Gu
PINDAR, Margarett		18	F	Laborer	07Se02Gu
Maria		18	F	Cousin	07Se02Gu
GLYNNE, Catherine		20	F	Laborer	07Se02Gu
CRAMER, James		20	M	Laborer	07Se02Gu
DOOLAN, John		22	M	Laborer	07Se02Gu
BYRNE, Francis		22	M	Laborer	07Se02Gu
GRANT, Robert		21	M	Laborer	07Se02Gu
ROONEY, John		44	M	Laborer	07Se02Gu
Catherine		17	F	Daughter	07Se02Gu
MCKINNA, Sarah		28	F	Unknown	07Se02Gu
TONA, Catherine		20	F	Laborer	07Se02Gu
DURMIN, Margaret		30	F	None	07Se02Gu
WALKER, James		40	M	Porter	07Se02Gu
U	(W)	30	F	Wife	07Se02Gu
RYAN, John		33	M	Laborer	07Se02Gu
Ellen		20	F	Laborer	07Se02Gu
GLEESON, Thomas		22	M	Laborer	07Se02Gu
HENNESSY, James		22	M	Laborer	07Se02Gu
HEALY, Stephen		20	M	Laborer	07Se02Gu
HICKY, U-Mrs.		35	F	Laborer	07Se02Gu
RUDDEN, Philip		28	M	Laborer	07Se02Gu
MCANERNY, Bridget		50	F	Unknown	07Se02Gu
STOTT, William		21	M	Mechanic	07Se02Gu
CLIFFORD, Jerry		20	M	Laborer	07Se02Gu
SWEENEY, Michael		21	M	Laborer	07Se02Gu
HAGGERTY, Julia		24	F	Servant	07Se02Gu
MCCAMMOND, Robert		20	M	Chemist	07Se02Gu
TOWNLEY, Joseph		36	M	Chemist	07Se02Gu
MCGUIN, Eliza		44	F	Unknown	07Se02Gu
BYRNE, Michael		27	M	Fireman	07Se02Gu
Daniel		24	M	Mariner	07Se02Gu
TAYLOR, Joseph		48	M	Unknown	07Se02Gu
Charles		13	M	Son	07Se02Gu
MARTIN, John		25	M	Mechanic	07Se02Gu
MILLS, Thomas		51	M	Laborer	07Se02Gu
Anne		53	F	Wife	07Se02Gu
Sarah		18	F	Daughter	07Se02Gu
Thomas		15	M	Son	07Se02Gu
Jane		10	F	Daughter	07Se02Gu
SLATER, Ainsworth		38	M	Mechanic	07Se02Gu
Mary		38	F	Wife	07Se02Gu
Elizabeth-Anne		10	F	Daughter	07Se02Gu
COUNTY, Denis		40	M	Mechanic	07Se02Gu
KENNEDY, Patrick		30	M	Servant	07Se02Gu
CHILD, Sarah		28	F	Lady	07Se02Gu
COOK, John		16	M	Servant	07Se02Gu
CARSON, Mary-Ann		20	F	None	07Se02Gu
WRIGHT, Rachael		18	F	Unknown	07Se02Gu
William		10	M	None	07Se02Gu
MCKOWN, Alexander		20	M	Laborer	07Se02Gu
MCTAGERT, Brita		20	F	None	07Se02Gu
DUFFIN, Mary-Ann		20	F	None	07Se02Gu
WARDELL, Nancy		20	F	None	07Se02Gu
MURPHY, Jane		18	F	None	07Se02Gu
MORRISON, Margaret		50	F	Unknown	07Se02Gu
Mary-Anne		12	F	Daughter	07Se02Gu
Fanny		11	F	Daughter	07Se02Gu
QUINN, James		18	M	Laborer	07Se02Gu
FINNEGAN, Bridget		18	M	None	07Se02Gu
MAHONEY, John		22	M	Laborer	07Se02Gu
MOORE, Catherine		25	F	None	07Se02Gu
FLAHERTY, Bridget		24	F	None	07Se02Gu
LYONS, William		23	M	Mechanic	07Se02Gu
Mary		21	F	Wife	07Se02Gu
Ellen		.00	F	Infant	07Se02Gu
WALSH, Margaret		46	F	Unknown	07Se02Gu
Patrick		20	M	Son	07Se02Gu
Johanna		15	F	Daughter	07Se02Gu
Thomas		11	M	Son	07Se02Gu
Ellen		12	F	Daughter	07Se02Gu
FLYNNE, John		47	M	Laborer	07Se02Gu
Ellen		46	F	Wife	07Se02Gu
Thomas		12	M	Son	07Se02Gu

NAMES OF PASSENGERS	AGE	SEX	OCCUPATIONS	DATE PORT SHIP
FLYNNE, Johanna	9	F	Child	07Se02Gu
PERKINS, Hugh	21	M	Clerk	07Se02Gu
CASS, Lorenzo	3	M	Child	07Se02Gu
MULLIGAN, Margaret	25	F	Unknown	07Se02Gu
Elizabeth	16	F	Sister	07Se02Gu
William	3	M	Child	07Se02Gu
Sarah-Jane	2	F	Child	07Se02Gu
MILLS, Thomas	21	M	Laborer	07Se02Gu
GRAHAM, Rebecca	20	F	None	07Se02Gu
QUINLAN, John	24	M	None	07Se02Gu

DEVONSHIRE 10 SEPTEMBER 1849

From Liverpool

NAMES OF PASSENGERS	AGE	SEX	OCCUPATIONS	DATE PORT SHIP
GRETY, Emma	40	F	Servant	10Se02Nt
Pat	11	M	Servant	10Se02Nt
Winifred	9	F	Child	10Se02Nt
Mary	9	F	Child	10Se02Nt
Daniel	5	M	Child	10Se02Nt
Henry	3	M	Child	10Se02Nt
John	1	M	Child	10Se02Nt
DERVIN, Ann	17	F	Servant	10Se02Nt
GUNTY, Bridget	5	F	Child	10Se02Nt
Daniel	3	M	Child	10Se02Nt
BOYL, Ellen	21	F	Servant	10Se02Nt
LENARD, John	22	M	Carpenter	10Se02Nt
U (W)	18	F	Carpenter	10Se02Nt
DUNN, Eliza	24	F	Servant	10Se02Nt
MELOND, Catherine	20	F	Milliner	10Se02Nt
HARSIN, Margaret	15	F	Servant	10Se02Nt
Isabella	17	F	Servant	10Se02Nt
CONEY, William	50	M	Farmer	10Se02Nt
Catherine	13	F	Farmer	10Se02Nt
Michael	8	M	Child	10Se02Nt
Johanna	10	F	Farmer	10Se02Nt
Mary	5	F	Child	10Se02Nt
Thomas	30	M	Farmer	10Se02Nt
Mary	30	F	Farmer	10Se02Nt
Mary	5	F	Child	10Se02Nt
BOYLE, Pat	20	M	Farmer	10Se02Nt
KELLEY, John	50	M	Farmer	10Se02Nt
Margaret	16	F	Farmer	10Se02Nt
MARAHY, Michael	18	M	Farmer	10Se02Nt
CUSICK, Daniel	24	M	Farmer	10Se02Nt
CALY, Margaret	24	F	Farmer	10Se02Nt
BRADY, James	28	M	Servant	10Se02Nt
MELOND, Edward	20	M	Servant	10Se02Nt
CURRAN, Michael	27	M	Servant	10Se02Nt
HORAN, Margaret	35	F	Servant	10Se02Nt
RILY, Sarah	28	F	Servant	10Se02Nt
MEONTS, John	25	M	Merchant	10Se02Nt
MURPHY, John	26	M	Laborer	10Se02Nt
U (W)	20	F	Laborer	10Se02Nt
DOYL, James	30	M	Laborer	10Se02Nt
MCDONAL, Martin	21	M	Tailor	10Se02Nt
U (W)	20	F	Tailor	10Se02Nt
WHALER, John	40	M	Laborer	10Se02Nt
U (W)	40	F	Laborer	10Se02Nt
Patrick	14	M	Laborer	10Se02Nt
Bridget	8	F	Child	10Se02Nt
MOON, Patrick	16	M	Laborer	10Se02Nt
Margaret	18	F	Laborer	10Se02Nt
KELLY, Ann	21	F	Servant	10Se02Nt
William	19	M	Servant	10Se02Nt
COLLOHY, Cornelius	21	M	Laborer	10Se02Nt
GRUMSAIN, Michael	30	M	Laborer	10Se02Nt
FAYS, Michael	23	M	Laborer	10Se02Nt
FAIN, Ellen	22	F	Servant	10Se02Nt
MEGNIN, James	20	F	Servant	10Se02Nt
MURPHY, John	19	M	Baker	10Se02Nt
DALBONE, Margaret	22	F	Servant	10Se02Nt
RYON, Margaret	50	F	Servant	10Se02Nt
Elizabeth	16	F	Servant	10Se02Nt
BERNINGHAM, Margaret	30	F	Servant	10Se02Nt
Megan	10	F	Servant	10Se02Nt
James	.00	M	Infant	10Se02Nt
CASEY, Margaret	13	F	Servant	10Se02Nt
BRODRICK, Pat	30	M	Laborer	10Se02Nt
U (W)	30	F	Laborer	10Se02Nt
Michael	6	M	Child	10Se02Nt
John	.00	M	Infant	10Se02Nt
LARRY, John	28	M	Laborer	10Se02Nt
Jeremiah	20	M	Laborer	10Se02Nt
WHELER, Ann	30	F	Laborer	10Se02Nt
James	.00	M	Infant	10Se02Nt
Matilda	5	F	Child	10Se02Nt
John	3	M	Child	10Se02Nt
LANTHEY, Thomas	30	M	Laborer	10Se02Nt
CONNER, Pat	38	M	Laborer	10Se02Nt
Catherine	3	F	Child	10Se02Nt
MEHAN, Luke	26	M	Blacksmith	10Se02Nt
MCGALDRICK, Biddy	18	F	Servant	10Se02Nt
Ellen	20	F	Servant	10Se02Nt
MEVEY, Mary	23	F	Servant	10Se02Nt
BROWN, Thomas	25	M	Servant	10Se02Nt
U (W)	25	M	Servant	10Se02Nt
Jesse	.00	M	Infant	10Se02Nt
ATKINS, William	22	M	Farmer	10Se02Nt
DUGON, Thomas	17	M	Servant	10Se02Nt
Ellen	22	F	Servant	10Se02Nt
CONNER, Matthew	50	M	Laborer	10Se02Nt
Patrick	30	M	Laborer	10Se02Nt
U (W)	25	F	Laborer	10Se02Nt
John	3	M	Child	10Se02Nt
Matthew	.00	M	Infant	10Se02Nt
MORISON, Patrick	50	M	Laborer	10Se02Nt
Catherine	25	F	Laborer	10Se02Nt
Bessy	4	F	Child	10Se02Nt
James	3	M	Child	10Se02Nt
Mary	2	F	Child	10Se02Nt
Catherine	.00	F	Infant	10Se02Nt
HANKET, Margaret	22	F	Servant	10Se02Nt
JOHNSON, John	24	M	Carpenter	10Se02Nt
U (W)	20	F	Carpenter	10Se02Nt
SHELLY, Daniel	28	M	Laborer	10Se02Nt
U (W)	26	F	Laborer	10Se02Nt
Bessy	6	F	Child	10Se02Nt
Mary	2	F	Child	10Se02Nt
Winny	.00	F	Infant	10Se02Nt
LEACH, John	25	M	Shoemaker	10Se02Nt
ROKE, Mary	20	F	Servant	10Se02Nt
Patrick	13	M	Servant	10Se02Nt
MARNE, Bridy	22	F	Servant	10Se02Nt
MACKORMIK, William	17	M	Servant	10Se02Nt
QUIN, Sarah	59	F	Servant	10Se02Nt
NORGIN, Catherine	24	F	Servant	10Se02Nt
ROBERTSON, Thomas	18	M	Servant	10Se02Nt
Robert	13	M	Servant	10Se02Nt
CORN, Peter	25	M	Tailor	10Se02Nt
U (W)	18	F	Tailor	10Se02Nt
QUIN, Robert	12	M	Servant	10Se02Nt
Bess	20	F	Servant	10Se02Nt
MILLS, James	31	M	Tailor	10Se02Nt
U (W)	29	F	Tailor	10Se02Nt
ARCHIBALD, James	31	M	Tailor	10Se02Nt
Samuel	.00	M	Infant	10Se02Nt
DAUGHITY, Peter	45	M	Laborer	10Se02Nt
Mary	40	F	Laborer	10Se02Nt
Peter	11	M	Laborer	10Se02Nt
James	6	M	Child	10Se02Nt
CALIHAN, Bridget	17	F	Servant	10Se02Nt
Mary	20	F	Servant	10Se02Nt
Johanna	18	F	Servant	10Se02Nt

NAMES OF PASSENGERS	AGE	SEX	OCCUPATIONS	DATE PORT SHIP
CUNNAN, Puda	20	U	Servant	10Se02Nt
RYAN, Mary	16	F	Servant	10Se02Nt
CAIN, Mary	17	F	Servant	10Se02Nt
Bridget	10	F	Servant	10Se02Nt
MANNING, Mary	14	F	Servant	10Se02Nt
Johana	7	F	Child	10Se02Nt
BERNHAM, Mathew	16	M	Laborer	10Se02Nt
AVINS, Thomas	20	M	Mason	10Se02Nt
DAUGHITY, Mary	20	F	Servant	10Se02Nt
SWINEY, Ann	20	F	Servant	10Se02Nt
BATES, Eliza	30	F	Servant	10Se02Nt
Mary	8	F	Child	10Se02Nt
LINCH, Catherine	30	F	Servant	10Se02Nt
Bridget	9	F	Child	10Se02Nt
Judah	6	M	Child	10Se02Nt
Elisa	4	F	Child	10Se02Nt
Ann	2	F	Child	10Se02Nt
CONLEY, Andrew	30	M	Laborer	10Se02Nt
Ann	10	F	Laborer	10Se02Nt
Mary	8	F	Child	10Se02Nt
Betsey	4	F	Child	10Se02Nt
BRADY, Francis	18	M	Servant	10Se02Nt
Alice	20	F	Servant	10Se02Nt
MAGUIRE, Pat	40	M	Farmer	10Se02Nt
BYRNES, Catherine	20	F	Servant	10Se02Nt
MCEVOY, John	20	M	Laborer	10Se02Nt
MURY, Michael	40	M	Laborer	10Se02Nt
BURS, John	25	M	Mason	10Se02Nt
AHERN, Bat	25	M	Laborer	10Se02Nt
SHURDY, John	23	M	Laborer	10Se02Nt
Amy	30	F	Laborer	10Se02Nt
Michael	14	M	Servant	10Se02Nt
MACOLOM, Andrew	23	M	Servant	10Se02Nt
BRENNAN, John	25	M	Servant	10Se02Nt
SHANNON, James	23	M	Servant	10Se02Nt
FAGAN, John	25	M	Merchant	10Se02Nt
Juliet	25	F	Merchant	10Se02Nt
FARINTON, Bridey	20	F	Servant	10Se02Nt
John	25	M	Servant	10Se02Nt
MARSHALL, James	28	M	Merchant	10Se02Nt
James	28	M	Servant	10Se02Nt
CAROLINE, Catherine	18	F	Servant	10Se02Nt
REGIN, James	26	M	Laborer	10Se02Nt
Bridget	17	F	Laborer	10Se02Nt
CRUMLE, William	50	M	Miner	10Se02Nt
Isabella	50	F	Miner	10Se02Nt
Margaret	20	F	Miner	10Se02Nt
John	13	M	Miner	10Se02Nt
Robert	11	M	Miner	10Se02Nt
Mary	9	F	Child	10Se02Nt
CALIHAN, Denney	19	M	Laborer	10Se02Nt
COOLEY, Ellen	19	F	Laborer	10Se02Nt
Margaret	17	F	Laborer	10Se02Nt
JOHNSON, John	34	M	Confessor	10Se02Nt
TAYLOR, James	34	M	Mason	10Se02Nt
WONTY, Peter	17	M	Laborer	10Se02Nt
MCANLLY, Neil	20	M	Laborer	10Se02Nt
ARND, Thomas	27	M	Laborer	10Se02Nt
GALLIGAN, John	30	M	Laborer	10Se02Nt
LOLLY, Margaret	21	F	Servant	10Se02Nt
COUSLINE, Bridy	18	F	Servant	10Se02Nt
MAKEY, James	48	M	Laborer	10Se02Nt
John	40	M	Laborer	10Se02Nt
COLLIN, James	23	M	Farmer	10Se02Nt
BYRNES, Ann	18	F	Servant	10Se02Nt
Rose	17	F	Servant	10Se02Nt
WOOLLY, Ann	15	F	Servant	10Se02Nt
FRANE, Bridget	16	F	Servant	10Se02Nt
THOMPSON, Thomas	20	M	Farmer	10Se02Nt
RILEY, John	25	M	Farmer	10Se02Nt
BONIGAN, Pat	31	M	Farmer	10Se02Nt
MARLIN, Matilda	18	F	Servant	10Se02Nt
MACROY, Mathew	30	M	Servant	10Se02Nt
DANY, Bess	20	F	Servant	10Se02Nt
TANER, William	30	M	Merchant	10Se02Nt
TANER, Margaret	8	F	Child	10Se02Nt
Mary	5	F	Child	10Se02Nt
MCARTHUR, James	20	M	Laborer	10Se02Nt
SMITH, Alexander	45	M	Laborer	10Se02Nt
Eliza	36	F	Laborer	10Se02Nt
MURPHY, Catherine	18	F	Servant	10Se02Nt
REDMANS, Bardy	19	M	Servant	10Se02Nt
Margaret	22	F	Servant	10Se02Nt
FARLE, Michael	25	M	Tailor	10Se02Nt
Eliza	25	F	Tailor	10Se02Nt
DANSON, Dennis	25	M	Tailor	10Se02Nt
Catherine	25	F	Tailor	10Se02Nt
Ellen	10	F	Tailor	10Se02Nt
Edward	12	M	Tailor	10Se02Nt
CASSIDY, David	24	M	Druggist	10Se02Nt
CUNNINGHAM, Thomas	24	M	Laborer	10Se02Nt
CAIN, John	25	M	Farmer	10Se02Nt
Kate	25	F	Farmer	10Se02Nt
RICE, Mary	18	F	Servant	10Se02Nt
FLEMMING, Janet	50	F	Servant	10Se02Nt
Bridget	24	F	Servant	10Se02Nt
DELAN, Mary	12	F	Servant	10Se02Nt
HAMMOND, William	25	M	Miller	10Se02Nt
CLARK, Eliza	18	F	Servant	10Se02Nt
ROY, Ann	22	F	Servant	10Se02Nt
Emma	27	F	Servant	10Se02Nt
HORUKS, Margaret	27	F	Servant	10Se02Nt
Ellen	6	F	Child	10Se02Nt
James	4	M	Child	10Se02Nt
Mary	3	F	Child	10Se02Nt
Eliza	.11	F	Infant	10Se02Nt
PECOK, Thomas	30	M	Merchant	10Se02Nt
HALL, William	24	M	Collier	10Se02Nt
PERRY, Joseph	24	M	Collier	10Se02Nt
Margaret	24	F	Collier	10Se02Nt
Catherine	.00	F	Infant	10Se02Nt
WALLACE, George	24	M	Collier	10Se02Nt
Mary	24	F	Collier	10Se02Nt
MCANIS, Thomas	28	M	Collier	10Se02Nt
U (W)	28	F	Collier	10Se02Nt
Jane	3	F	Child	10Se02Nt
Elisa	3	F	Child	10Se02Nt
George	.00	M	Infant	10Se02Nt
BALE, John	24	M	Collier	10Se02Nt
KYLE, George	21	M	Collier	10Se02Nt
OGILVIE, Francis	28	M	Collier	10Se02Nt
HILL, Robert	24	M	Collier	10Se02Nt
OCONNOR, John	25	M	Baker	10Se02Nt
MILBURN, Edward	40	M	Miner	10Se02Nt
U (W)	40	F	Miner	10Se02Nt
William	19	M	Miner	10Se02Nt
HALL, Peter	71	M	Miner	10Se02Nt
U (W)	66	F	Miner	10Se02Nt
Ann	30	F	Miner	10Se02Nt
Margaret	22	F	Miner	10Se02Nt
MORGAN, George	33	M	Miner	10Se02Nt
U (W)	33	F	Miner	10Se02Nt
Lydia	6	F	Child	10Se02Nt
Benjamin	3	M	Child	10Se02Nt
Lian	.00	M	Infant	10Se02Nt
James	37	M	Miner	10Se02Nt
U (W)	37	F	Miner	10Se02Nt
HALE, Henry	23	M	Miner	10Se02Nt
U (W)	23	F	Miner	10Se02Nt
KEAN, George	20	M	Miner	10Se02Nt
KELLEY, James	40	M	Farmer	10Se02Nt
U (W)	34	F	Farmer	10Se02Nt
James	16	M	Farmer	10Se02Nt
Ann	14	F	Farmer	10Se02Nt
Thomas	11	M	Farmer	10Se02Nt
Henry	9	M	Child	10Se02Nt
Mary	4	F	Child	10Se02Nt
Daniel	1	M	Child	10Se02Nt
JONES, Isaac	22	M	Draper	10Se02Nt
U (W)	22	F	Draper	10Se02Nt

NAMES OF PASSENGERS	AGE	SEX	OCCUPATIONS	DATE PORT SHIP
CARDIFF, James	31	M	Potter	10Se02Nt
U (W)	21	F	Potter	10Se02Nt
LEVINS, Mathew	27	M	Farmer	10Se02Nt
U-Mrs.	50	F	Farmer	10Se02Nt
Ann	35	F	Farmer	10Se02Nt
Margaret	3	F	Child	10Se02Nt
JONES, William	22	M	Farmer	10Se02Nt
Andrew	22	M	Farmer	10Se02Nt
MEGUIRE, George	25	M	Farmer	10Se02Nt
REDKIND, Robert	25	M	Farmer	10Se02Nt
STORY, John	30	M	Maurer	10Se02Nt
MCGARRY, James	21	M	Laborer	10Se02Nt
Julie	21	F	Laborer	10Se02Nt
BURK, Mary	50	F	Midwife	10Se02Nt
RIVIN, Daniel	27	M	Farmer	10Se02Nt
Margaret	47	F	Farmer	10Se02Nt
John	25	M	Farmer	10Se02Nt
Mary	20	F	Farmer	10Se02Nt
ROKE, Bryan	22	M	Farmer	10Se02Nt
MCTURN, Bridget	13	F	Servant	10Se02Nt
DUNGHLY, Bridget	13	F	Servant	10Se02Nt
CONNOR, Maria	14	F	Servant	10Se02Nt
Bridget	3	F	Child	10Se02Nt
WEATCH, Kate	30	F	Servant	10Se02Nt
LALEY, John	35	M	Laborer	10Se02Nt
Mary	30	F	Laborer	10Se02Nt
James	4	M	Child	10Se02Nt
Maria	2	F	Child	10Se02Nt
John	.00	M	Infant	10Se02Nt
MAYLOR, James	40	M	Shepherd	10Se02Nt
Annie	40	F	Shepherd	10Se02Nt
Catherine	16	F	Shepherd	10Se02Nt
Mary	12	F	Shepherd	10Se02Nt
Thomas	10	M	Shepherd	10Se02Nt
Martin	9	M	Child	10Se02Nt
Peggy	8	F	Child	10Se02Nt
SULIVAN, Barthy	20	M	Servant	10Se02Nt
DOLMAN, Joseph	32	M	Plasterer	10Se02Nt
GUNNTAND, Charlotte	22	F	Servant	10Se02Nt
CARNE, Catherine	22	F	Servant	10Se02Nt
LAMNOR, Sarah	24	F	Servant	10Se02Nt
Susan	8	F	Child	10Se02Nt
LEONARD, Anty.	25	M	Carpenter	10Se02Nt
U (W)	22	F	Carpenter	10Se02Nt
STRAVER, William	28	M	Laborer	10Se02Nt
LANDRUM, Antonia	28	F	Laborer	10Se02Nt
BARLOW, Emma	36	F	Dressmaker	10Se02Nt
Lydia	9	F	Child	10Se02Nt
Henry	6	M	Child	10Se02Nt
Lucy	.00	F	Infant	10Se02Nt
SIKER, John	39	M	Carpenter	10Se02Nt
Bridget	30	F	Carpenter	10Se02Nt
John	5	M	Child	10Se02Nt
WATSON, James	21	M	Farmer	10Se02Nt
David	24	M	Farmer	10Se02Nt
Ann	30	F	Farmer	10Se02Nt
Margaret	17	F	Farmer	10Se02Nt
Mary	15	F	Farmer	10Se02Nt
JAMES, U-Mrs.	20	F	Farmer	10Se02Nt
ANSON, George	22	M	Merchant	10Se02Nt
U (W)	20	F	Merchant	10Se02Nt
EDWARDS, Thomas	23	M	Merchant	10Se02Nt
U (W)	20	F	Merchant	10Se02Nt
BRAWNT, Richard	22	M	Merchant	10Se02Nt
Margaret	48	F	Merchant	10Se02Nt
Ellen	25	F	Merchant	10Se02Nt

YORKTOWN 12 SEPTEMBER 1849

From London

NAMES OF PASSENGERS	AGE	SEX	OCCUPATIONS	DATE PORT SHIP
BESTON, Edward	23	M	Laborer	12Se13Hs
Josephine	24	F	Unknown	12Se13Hs
BROWN, Elizabeth	23	F	Unknown	12Se13Hs
ARJOZ, Julias	25	M	Unknown	12Se13Hs
BESWICK, Thomas	56	M	Watchmaker	12Se13Hs
Elizabeth	43	F	Unknown	12Se13Hs
Thomas	11	M	Unknown	12Se13Hs
Samuel	10	M	Unknown	12Se13Hs
James	8	M	Child	12Se13Hs
John	6	M	Child	12Se13Hs
Matilda	2	F	Child	12Se13Hs
JUKES, Henry-Jacob	21	M	Unknown	12Se13Hs
Daniel	55	M	Unknown	12Se13Hs
HOLMES, William	35	M	Unknown	12Se13Hs
Henrietta	51	F	Unknown	12Se13Hs
Henrietta	10	F	Unknown	12Se13Hs
HAWKSWORTH, Hannah	30	F	Unknown	12Se13Hs
PAYNE, Ann	20	F	Unknown	12Se13Hs
BOOTH, Harriet	40	F	Unknown	12Se13Hs
COOK, Sarah	20	F	Unknown	12Se13Hs
BRANCH, George	22	M	Unknown	12Se13Hs
LEDDER, Samuel	23	M	Unknown	12Se13Hs
Mary	22	F	Unknown	12Se13Hs
WATERMAN, Richard	43	M	Unknown	12Se13Hs
Maria	53	F	Unknown	12Se13Hs
LECOMBE, Edward	26	M	Unknown	12Se13Hs
Mary-Ann	25	F	Unknown	12Se13Hs
Edward	4	M	Child	12Se13Hs
Mary-Ann	2	F	Child	12Se13Hs
QUINLAN, James	26	M	Unknown	12Se13Hs
HURLEY, Catharine	14	F	Unknown	12Se13Hs
MACCANEY, John	35	M	Unknown	12Se13Hs
MCMANN, Michael	35	M	Unknown	12Se13Hs
Johanna	36	F	Unknown	12Se13Hs
BRUSFIELD, William	16	M	Unknown	12Se13Hs
LANGSTON, Thomas	20	M	Unknown	12Se13Hs
AUSTIN, William	38	M	Unknown	12Se13Hs
HANNINGTON, Robert	56	M	Merchant	12Se13Hs
Julia	35	F	Unknown	12Se13Hs
Julia	15	F	Unknown	12Se13Hs
Robert	11	M	Unknown	12Se13Hs
Ellen	10	F	Unknown	12Se13Hs
COX, William	51	M	Farmer	12Se13Hs
Elizabeth	54	F	Unknown	12Se13Hs
Mary	26	F	Unknown	12Se13Hs
William	.00	M	Infant	12Se13Hs
BROWN, Henry	25	M	Carpenter	12Se13Hs
Isabella	25	F	Unknown	12Se13Hs
Isabella	1	F	Child	12Se13Hs
Charlotte	.00	F	Infant	12Se13Hs
HART, Cornelius	21	M	Laborer	12Se13Hs
KELLY, Margaret	26	F	Unknown	12Se13Hs
HALEY, Mary	21	F	Unknown	12Se13Hs
ADAMS, James-W.	27	M	Sailor	12Se13Hs
RUSSELL, Betsy	30	M	Unknown	12Se13Hs
Elizabeth	60	F	Unknown	12Se13Hs
Ann	24	F	Unknown	12Se13Hs
PALYER, William	26	M	Laborer	12Se13Hs
Martha	26	F	Unknown	12Se13Hs
PLAYER, William	3	M	Child	12Se13Hs
ADAMS, Lucian	26	M	Sailor	12Se13Hs
Charlotte	25	F	Unknown	12Se13Hs
LYNCH, Ann	30	F	Unknown	12Se13Hs
Eliza	8	F	Child	12Se13Hs
Julia	3	F	Child	12Se13Hs

NAMES OF PASSENGERS	AGE	SEX	OCCUPATIONS	DATE PORT SHIP
LYNCH, Frederick	.00	M	Infant	12Se13Hs
MEARS, Morris	37	M	Unknown	12Se13Hs
Elizabeth	37	F	Unknown	12Se13Hs
ARNOLD, Joseph	23	M	Unknown	12Se13Hs
June	28	F	Unknown	12Se13Hs
COADICK, James	38	M	Unknown	12Se13Hs
Agnes	33	F	Unknown	12Se13Hs
Pheobe	4	F	Child	12Se13Hs
James	.00	M	Infant	12Se13Hs
HIGGS, Richard	25	M	Plasterer	12Se13Hs
YOUNG, William	26	M	Unknown	12Se13Hs
Elizabeth	25	F	Unknown	12Se13Hs
Elizabeth	4	F	Child	12Se13Hs
ROOFE, George	30	M	Laborer	12Se13Hs
MCNAMARA, John	24	M	Unknown	12Se13Hs
NALLY, John	50	M	Unknown	12Se13Hs
Bridget	46	F	Unknown	12Se13Hs
Bridget	13	F	Unknown	12Se13Hs
Ellen	11	F	Unknown	12Se13Hs
John	9	M	Child	12Se13Hs
Michael	6	M	Child	12Se13Hs
CRAWLEY, Daniel	35	M	Baker	12Se13Hs
HINTON, James	21	M	Unknown	12Se13Hs
COCKLIN, Margaret	28	F	Unknown	12Se13Hs
ROLPH, John	29	M	Unknown	12Se13Hs
MALLARKY, Mary	30	F	Unknown	12Se13Hs
Elizabeth	5	F	Child	12Se13Hs
EUSON, John	35	M	Unknown	12Se13Hs
Sarah	36	F	Unknown	12Se13Hs
John	10	M	Unknown	12Se13Hs
William	8	M	Child	12Se13Hs
Sarah	7	F	Child	12Se13Hs
Susanna	6	F	Child	12Se13Hs
Henry	1	M	Child	12Se13Hs
James	.00	M	Infant	12Se13Hs
GURLEY, John	26	M	Unknown	12Se13Hs
Ann	27	F	Unknown	12Se13Hs
LOVERIDGE, Seth	35	M	Printer	12Se13Hs
Mary-Ann	37	F	Printer	12Se13Hs
BROOKS, Ebenezer	28	M	Unknown	12Se13Hs
HUSCEY, Catharine	25	F	Unknown	12Se13Hs
Edward	17	M	Unknown	12Se13Hs
LARDNER, Sarah	25	F	Unknown	12Se13Hs
PERRY, Charles	42	M	Unknown	12Se13Hs
Mary-Ann	42	F	Unknown	12Se13Hs
George	11	M	Unknown	12Se13Hs
Emily	.00	F	Infant	12Se13Hs
ROWLEY, Thomas	26	M	Unknown	12Se13Hs
CARTER, James	40	M	Unknown	12Se13Hs
ROWLEY, Ellen	20	F	Unknown	12Se13Hs
SOMERTON, Thomas	17	M	Unknown	12Se13Hs
WILDBONE, Mary	32	F	Unknown	12Se13Hs
Ellen	2	F	Child	12Se13Hs
James	3	M	Child	12Se13Hs
CARROLL, William	34	M	Unknown	12Se13Hs
Ellen	32	F	Unknown	12Se13Hs
John	5	M	Child	12Se13Hs
Henry	2	M	Child	12Se13Hs
William	.00	M	Infant	12Se13Hs
FISHER, George	23	M	Unknown	12Se13Hs
HALL, Samuel	33	M	Unknown	12Se13Hs
Elizabeth	23	F	Unknown	12Se13Hs
Thomas	2	M	Child	12Se13Hs
STELL, Thomas	35	M	Unknown	12Se13Hs
Julia	21	F	Unknown	12Se13Hs
HICKS, William	17	M	Unknown	12Se13Hs
OFFARD, William	46	M	Unknown	12Se13Hs
HAYNES, John	19	M	Unknown	12Se13Hs
MCMANN, John	24	M	Unknown	12Se13Hs
LAWRENCE, William	23	M	Laborer	12Se13Hs
NEWMAN, John	25	M	Unknown	12Se13Hs
MARIETT, Ann	43	F	Unknown	12Se13Hs
TICKEN, Henry	23	M	Unknown	12Se13Hs
COURT, William	15	M	Unknown	12Se13Hs
BENNETT, Sarah	21	F	Unknown	12Se13Hs
BENNETT, Samuel	7	M	Child	12Se13Hs
BREWER, Elizabeth	45	F	Unknown	12Se13Hs
Emily	21	F	Unknown	12Se13Hs
Charles	7	M	Child	12Se13Hs
Julia	3	F	Child	12Se13Hs
Alfred	.00	M	Infant	12Se13Hs
ROUND, George	44	M	Unknown	12Se13Hs
CHAPMAN, William	24	M	Unknown	12Se13Hs
CHARTIES, Margaret	40	F	Unknown	12Se13Hs
William	11	M	Unknown	12Se13Hs
Hannah	18	F	Unknown	12Se13Hs
SHARP, William	32	M	Unknown	12Se13Hs
Lella	27	F	Unknown	12Se13Hs
John	.00	M	Infant	12Se13Hs
MARTEN, James	20	M	Unknown	12Se13Hs
BOYLE, Grace	26	F	Unknown	12Se13Hs
BOON, Gordon	4	M	Child	12Se13Hs
STRIDWICK, Mary	38	F	Unknown	12Se13Hs
Maria	15	F	Unknown	12Se13Hs
Alfred	11	M	Unknown	12Se13Hs
James	9	M	Child	12Se13Hs
George	5	M	Child	12Se13Hs
BELAND, Charles	25	M	Unknown	12Se13Hs
CLARKE, John	52	M	Unknown	12Se13Hs
Rosetta	45	F	Unknown	12Se13Hs
John	16	M	Unknown	12Se13Hs
James	9	M	Child	12Se13Hs
Grace	7	F	Child	12Se13Hs
Eliza	5	F	Child	12Se13Hs
GRANT, Jerimia	42	M	Unknown	12Se13Hs
CLEAL, Catharine	46	F	Unknown	12Se13Hs
LOAT, Thomas	37	M	Unknown	12Se13Hs
Jane	24	F	Unknown	12Se13Hs
Mary	3	F	Child	12Se13Hs
Sarah	.00	F	Infant	12Se13Hs
BARNWELL, Thomas	40	M	Unknown	12Se13Hs
Thomas	13	M	Unknown	12Se13Hs
PARKER, Francis	28	M	Unknown	12Se13Hs
SERJEANT, William	45	M	Unknown	12Se13Hs
FORD, Mary	33	F	Unknown	12Se13Hs
Mary	68	F	Unknown	12Se13Hs
Mary	.00	F	Infant	12Se13Hs
VERE, Charles	44	M	Unknown	12Se13Hs
Maria	46	F	Unknown	12Se13Hs
Charles	17	M	Unknown	12Se13Hs
Walter	15	M	Unknown	12Se13Hs
Sara-Ann	19	F	Unknown	12Se13Hs
Layrius	13	F	Unknown	12Se13Hs
Frederick	10	M	Unknown	12Se13Hs
BRAUM, Johann	16	M	Farmer	12Se13Hs
WINZ, Peter	29	M	Unknown	12Se13Hs
SHAPPERT, Anton	27	M	Unknown	12Se13Hs
Jacob	30	M	Unknown	12Se13Hs
HANSSACKER, Christiana	39	F	Unknown	12Se13Hs
JULI, Adam	34	M	Unknown	12Se13Hs
BECKER, Fabian	20	M	Merchant	12Se13Hs
ERKSTEIN, Christiana	22	F	Unknown	12Se13Hs
OCHS, Helena	28	F	Unknown	12Se13Hs
COHEN, Albert	20	M	Merchant	12Se13Hs
BRECKHEIMER, Wm.	39	M	Brewer	12Se13Hs
SCHMITH, Peter	54	M	Farmer	12Se13Hs
Elizabeth	49	F	Farmer	12Se13Hs
Henrick	20	M	Farmer	12Se13Hs
Peter	15	M	Farmer	12Se13Hs
Maria	8	F	Child	12Se13Hs
Phillip	5	M	Child	12Se13Hs
PLOTT, Jacob	24	M	Unknown	12Se13Hs
LINNEL, F.G.	31	U	Unknown	12Se13Hs
Elizabeth	25	F	Unknown	12Se13Hs
FRITZGEN, Conrad	62	M	Unknown	12Se13Hs
Elizabeth	5	F	Child	12Se13Hs
Conrad	2	M	Child	12Se13Hs
WOUND, Henrick	34	M	Unknown	12Se13Hs
Catharine	23	F	Unknown	12Se13Hs
UNVERZAG, Joham	29	U	Unknown	12Se13Hs

NAMES OF PASSENGERS	AGE	SEX	OCCUPATIONS	DATE PORT SHIP
REPP, Helena	21	F	Unknown	12Se13Hs
HESS, Joseph	22	M	Unknown	12Se13Hs
DETRITCH, Peter	21	M	Unknown	12Se13Hs
BORNET, F.	29	U	Unknown	12Se13Hs
OPPERMAYER, Louis	40	M	Unknown	12Se13Hs
MULLER, Carl	19	M	Unknown	12Se13Hs
KUCHLER, Ernt.	18	U	Unknown	12Se13Hs
BECKER, U	44	U	Unknown	12Se13Hs
U	15	U	Unknown	12Se13Hs
U	10	U	Unknown	12Se13Hs
U	.00	U	Infant	12Se13Hs
MCDERMOTT, John	25	M	Unknown	12Se13Hs
ODONNEL, Timothy	20	M	Unknown	12Se13Hs
HAYNES, Frederick	30	M	Unknown	12Se13Hs
NICHOLS, Frederick	28	M	Unknown	12Se13Hs
Esther	26	F	Unknown	12Se13Hs
MOTT, Ann	27	F	Unknown	12Se13Hs
WATTS, U	38	U	Unknown	12Se13Hs
U	36	U	Unknown	12Se13Hs
SMITH, Mary	40	F	Unknown	12Se13Hs
JONES, Edward	39	M	Unknown	12Se13Hs
LYNOMS, James	28	M	Unknown	12Se13Hs
ROUND, George	40	M	Unknown	12Se13Hs
CHAPMAN, Julia	19	M	Unknown	12Se13Hs
SIEGFRIED, U	25	U	Unknown	12Se13Hs
HUNT, Charles-B.	28	M	Unknown	12Se13Hs
HENSHAW, Julius	28	M	Unknown	12Se13Hs
GRAM, Henry	30	M	Unknown	12Se13Hs
LAWRENCE, James	21	M	Unknown	12Se13Hs
SIMMONS, James	28	M	Unknown	12Se13Hs

GARRICK 12 SEPTEMBER 1849

From Liverpool

NAMES OF PASSENGERS	AGE	SEX	OCCUPATIONS	DATE PORT SHIP
DALY, William	15	M	Laborer	12Se02Hh
John	23	M	Laborer	12Se02Hh
QUIGLEY, Ellen	25	F	None	12Se02Hh
KEIWARD, Catherine	30	F	None	12Se02Hh
CARR, Isabella	18	F	None	12Se02Hh
REYNOLDS, Peter	25	M	Laborer	12Se02Hh
BREEZE, Ellen	40	F	Laborer	12Se02Hh
MCWHALE, Hugh	30	M	Laborer	12Se02Hh
KENNY, Ann	25	F	None	12Se02Hh
DONOHUE, Catherine	30	F	None	12Se02Hh
Mary	10	F	Child	12Se02Hh
Margaret	8	F	Child	12Se02Hh
Pat	00	M	Child	12Se02Hh
CAFFREY, Peter	7	M	Child	12Se02Hh
DONEGAN, Elizabeth	19	F	Laborer	12Se02Hh
HOLEHAM, Catherine	23	F	Servant	12Se02Hh
HEERY, Frances	18	F	Servant	12Se02Hh
MCCANN, Michl.	25	M	Laborer	12Se02Hh
LAWLOR, James	45	M	Laborer	12Se02Hh
Julia	20	F	Laborer	12Se02Hh
PRIMES, Mary	13	F	None	12Se02Hh
PEOPLES, James	25	M	Laborer	12Se02Hh
BAXTER, Nancy	40	F	None	12Se02Hh
Jane	7	F	Child	12Se02Hh
Mary	5	F	Child	12Se02Hh
Matilda	3	F	Child	12Se02Hh
LONNON, Nancy	19	F	None	12Se02Hh
Thos.	12	M	None	12Se02Hh
Wm.J.	10	M	Child	12Se02Hh
GRIMES, Robert	14	M	None	12Se02Hh
HENRY, Barb.Jane	24	F	None	12Se02Hh
SMITH, Patk.	50	M	Laborer	12Se02Hh
WHELAN, Mich.	28	M	Mason	12Se02Hh
Thos.	20	M	Mason	12Se02Hh
CASEY, Mary	19	F	Servant	12Se02Hh
TRACY, Bridget	50	F	Servant	12Se02Hh
BRENAN, Cath.	19	F	Servant	12Se02Hh
MANLEY, Wm.	50	M	Farmer	12Se02Hh
U-Mrs.	36	F	None	12Se02Hh
Sarah	15	F	None	12Se02Hh
Winslow	14	M	None	12Se02Hh
Margaret	12	F	None	12Se02Hh
Joseph	10	M	Child	12Se02Hh
Joshua	9	M	Child	12Se02Hh
Hubert	8	M	Child	12Se02Hh
Redmond	7	M	Child	12Se02Hh
Charles	5	M	Child	12Se02Hh
FARLANE, Jos.	42	M	Mason	12Se02Hh
RYAN, Nancy	24	F	None	12Se02Hh
GLESON, Ony	21	F	Dressmaker	12Se02Hh
BEGAL, Pat.	26	M	Laborer	12Se02Hh
MCWHALE, Ann	20	F	None	12Se02Hh
HEFFEREN, Dennis	44	M	Farmer	12Se02Hh
Michl.	38	M	Farmer	12Se02Hh
Mary	12	F	None	12Se02Hh
Ellen	9	F	Child	12Se02Hh
KERBY, Edwd.	20	M	Carpenter	12Se02Hh
HEFFEREN, Wm.	12	M	None	12Se02Hh
KEEF, Jeremiah	24	M	Blacksmith	12Se02Hh
Sarah	26	F	None	12Se02Hh
HENRY, Robt.	21	M	Weaver	12Se02Hh
HARPER, Margt.J.	19	F	None	12Se02Hh
JEPPON, U	36	M	Mason	12Se02Hh
LACKEY, John	25	M	Servant	12Se02Hh
MURRY, Wm.	30	M	Sailor	12Se02Hh
RIHAN, John	20	M	Carpenter	12Se02Hh
FITZPATRICK, Bernd.	50	M	Dop	12Se02Hh
Ann	40	F	Nurse	12Se02Hh
Eliza	20	F	Nurse	12Se02Hh
Ann	18	F	Nurse	12Se02Hh
WEST, Mark	35	M	Laborer	12Se02Hh
Ann	30	F	None	12Se02Hh
Maria	13	F	None	12Se02Hh
Jane	11	F	None	12Se02Hh
Thos.	10	M	Child	12Se02Hh
Susan	7	F	Child	12Se02Hh
Ann	5	F	Child	12Se02Hh
Ellen	3	F	Child	12Se02Hh
Elizabeth	.00	F	Infant	12Se02Hh
MOFFATT, James	28	M	Laborer	12Se02Hh
Matilda	17	F	None	12Se02Hh
DELANY, Cath.	24	F	None	12Se02Hh
MCCUSKY, U-Mrs.	30	F	None	12Se02Hh
BUTLER, Richd.	23	M	Unknown	12Se02Hh
DONNELLY, Mary	20	F	None	12Se02Hh
Pat	23	M	Laborer	12Se02Hh
CUNNIGNHAM, James	23	M	Laborer	12Se02Hh
HAYES, John	21	M	Laborer	12Se02Hh
MCQUAY, Thos.	32	M	Laborer	12Se02Hh
DOURGHTY, Hugh	35	M	Laborer	12Se02Hh
DAILLY, John	20	M	Laborer	12Se02Hh
BURNE, James	21	M	Laborer	12Se02Hh
HEART, Ann	21	F	None	12Se02Hh
Ellen	20	F	None	12Se02Hh
DOUGHT, Mary	30	F	None	12Se02Hh
John	5	M	Child	12Se02Hh
Jane	1	F	Child	12Se02Hh
SMITH, John	20	M	Laborer	12Se02Hh
BURNE, Judy	22	F	Servant	12Se02Hh
OATS, Peggy	22	F	Servant	12Se02Hh
BROWN, John	30	M	Gdnr	12Se02Hh
KING, Emily	21	F	Servant	12Se02Hh
MCQUIRE, Eliza	28	F	Dressmaker	12Se02Hh
FEANY, Cath.	30	F	None	12Se02Hh
Cath.	16	F	None	12Se02Hh
REILLY, Rosa	18	F	None	12Se02Hh
CONOUGHT, Judy	18	F	None	12Se02Hh
CAREY, Mick	10	M	Child	12Se02Hh
MAHAN, Mick	30	M	Laborer	12Se02Hh

NAMES OF PASSENGERS	AGE	SEX	OCCUPATIONS	DATE PORT SHIP
STACY, Ann	30	F	None	12Se02Hh
Eliza	1	F	Child	12Se02Hh
John	.00	M	Infant	12Se02Hh
MCCULLEN, John	26	M	Plasterer	12Se02Hh
DUNN, John	24	M	Laborer	12Se02Hh
LIBERTY, Ann	20	F	Servant	12Se02Hh
OREAGAN, John	18	M	Eccl	12Se02Hh
FAREHER, James	20	M	Laborer	12Se02Hh
MURPHY, Cath.	18	F	Servant	12Se02Hh
TART, Thos.	35	M	Tailor	12Se02Hh
U-Mrs.	35	F	None	12Se02Hh
Jane	11	F	None	12Se02Hh
George	10	M	Child	12Se02Hh
Hannah	7	F	Child	12Se02Hh
BAILEY, Wm.S.	27	M	Clerk	12Se02Hh
U-Mrs.	25	F	Milliner	12Se02Hh
EARLE, Danl.	40	M	Coachman	12Se02Hh
U-Mrs.	40	F	None	12Se02Hh
Mary	12	F	None	12Se02Hh
Margt.	10	F	Child	12Se02Hh
Wm.	8	M	Child	12Se02Hh
Cath.	6	F	Child	12Se02Hh
Eliza	4	F	Child	12Se02Hh
Julia	22	F	None	12Se02Hh
CUPPAGE, Wm.	15	F	Farmer	12Se02Hh
BRIDGET, Henry	50	M	Laborer	12Se02Hh
ROURKE, John	30	M	Laborer	12Se02Hh
Mary (W)	20	F	None	12Se02Hh
Eliza	23	F	None	12Se02Hh
Mary	20	F	None	12Se02Hh
DAY, John	30	M	Laborer	12Se02Hh
KELLY, Pat	30	M	Laborer	12Se02Hh
OATES, Mick	40	M	Laborer	12Se02Hh
Thos.	30	M	Laborer	12Se02Hh
MULHERIN, Bridgt.	40	F	None	12Se02Hh
Thos.	15	M	None	12Se02Hh
MINER, Bridgt.	30	F	None	12Se02Hh
Denis	16	M	Printer	12Se02Hh
KEEGAN, Cath.	30	F	Servant	12Se02Hh
CALWELL, Brid.	18	F	Servant	12Se02Hh
Michl.	.00	M	Infant	12Se02Hh
BYRNE, Pat	28	M	Joiner	12Se02Hh
GILLEGAN, Owen	46	M	Laborer	12Se02Hh
Brid.	36	F	None	12Se02Hh
Cath.	17	F	None	12Se02Hh
James	15	M	None	12Se02Hh
Wm.	12	M	None	12Se02Hh
Mary	10	F	Child	12Se02Hh
John	8	M	Child	12Se02Hh
Brid.	3	F	Child	12Se02Hh
Edwd.	.00	M	Infant	12Se02Hh
ROURKE, Garrett	20	M	Clerk	12Se02Hh
Mich.	20	M	Clerk	12Se02Hh
HICKEY, Pat	25	M	Laborer	12Se02Hh
CARTY, Margt.	20	F	Servant	12Se02Hh
MCGUINESS, Julia	29	F	Servant	12Se02Hh
Ann	4	F	Child	12Se02Hh
TRACY, Wm.	30	M	Laborer	12Se02Hh
BRESLON, Mary	40	F	None	12Se02Hh
Jane	9	F	Child	12Se02Hh
Michl.	7	M	Child	12Se02Hh
Martha	4	F	Child	12Se02Hh
MURPHY, John	40	M	Tailor	12Se02Hh
CROWLEY, Eugene	28	M	Laborer	12Se02Hh
CONFREY, Ellen	30	F	None	12Se02Hh
Michl.	6	M	Child	12Se02Hh
HIGGINS, Biddy	18	F	Servant	12Se02Hh
FALLAN, John	40	M	Laborer	12Se02Hh
MURRAY, Mich.	20	M	Laborer	12Se02Hh
FALLAN, Mich.	20	M	Laborer	12Se02Hh
GREER, Pat	18	M	Laborer	12Se02Hh
FALLAN, Cath.	20	F	Servant	12Se02Hh
Rich.	30	M	Laborer	12Se02Hh
MURRAY, Margt.	30	F	None	12Se02Hh
Mary	26	F	Servant	12Se02Hh
GREEN, Bridgt.	18	F	Servant	12Se02Hh
Ellen	17	F	Servant	12Se02Hh
HINDS, Cath.	15	F	Servant	12Se02Hh
GREEN, Mary	.00	F	Infant	12Se02Hh
BOWDEN, John	28	M	Farmer	12Se02Hh
U-Mrs.	20	F	None	12Se02Hh
John-Jr.	.00	M	Infant	12Se02Hh
COLEMAN, Math.	18	F	Servant	12Se02Hh
MURPHY, Peter	18	M	Laborer	12Se02Hh
Mich.	16	M	Laborer	12Se02Hh
Maria	14	F	Servant	12Se02Hh
Julia	12	F	Servant	12Se02Hh
DOLAN, Ann	14	F	Servant	12Se02Hh
TULLY, Margt.	20	F	Servant	12Se02Hh
STEWART, Wm.	34	M	Tailor	12Se02Hh
LEPHAM, U-Mrs.	26	F	None	12Se02Hh
STAPLETON, James	25	M	Shoemaker	12Se02Hh
Mary	23	F	None	12Se02Hh
Daniel	.00	M	Infant	12Se02Hh
MCGUIRE, Mary	16	F	Lad	12Se02Hh
SMITH, Mary	20	F	None	12Se02Hh
KELLY, Ann	36	F	None	12Se02Hh
Cath.	9	F	Child	12Se02Hh
Ann	3	F	Child	12Se02Hh
Bridgt.	2	F	Child	12Se02Hh
WHITE, Richd.	48	M	Laborer	12Se02Hh
Mary	34	F	None	12Se02Hh
Alice	50	F	None	12Se02Hh
Peter	11	M	None	12Se02Hh
Bridget	9	F	Child	12Se02Hh
Richd.Jr.	7	M	Child	12Se02Hh
Michl.	5	M	Child	12Se02Hh
Eliza	2	F	Child	12Se02Hh
Ann	.00	F	Infant	12Se02Hh
CAFREY, Ellen	36	F	None	12Se02Hh
Michl.	6	M	Child	12Se02Hh
CROWLEY, Johanna	30	F	Servant	12Se02Hh
HALE, Jonathan	29	M	Clerk	12Se02Hh
WHITE, Margaret	18	F	None	12Se02Hh

MINERVA 12 SEPTEMBER 1849

From Halifax

NAMES OF PASSENGERS	AGE	SEX	OCCUPATIONS	DATE PORT SHIP
MUMFORD, Wm.	25	M	Merchant	12Se43Px
KEITH, John	45	M	Merchant	12Se43Px
WALL, Elizabeth	45	F	Unknown	12Se43Px
U	15	U	Child	12Se43Px
U	00	U	Child	12Se43Px
U	00	U	Child	12Se43Px
U	00	U	Child	12Se43Px
U	5	U	Child	12Se43Px

LIBERTY 13 SEPTEMBER 1849

From Liverpool

NAMES OF PASSENGERS	AGE	SEX	OCCUPATIONS	DATE PORT SHIP
HALLAN, Thomas	50	M	Builder	13Se02Gf
Jane	50	F	Builder	13Se02Gf
BURKE, John	35	M	Laborer	13Se02Gf
Bridget	32	F	Laborer	13Se02Gf
Patrick	11	M	Laborer	13Se02Gf
John	8	M	Child	13Se02Gf

NAMES OF PASSENGERS	AGE	SEX	OCCUPATIONS	DATE PORT SHIP
BURKE, Richd	4	M	Child	13Se02Gf
Thomas	2	M	Child	13Se02Gf
RYAN, Anne	17	F	Spinster	13Se02Gf
FISHER, John	15	M	Laborer	13Se02Gf
COLAHAN, John	20	M	Laborer	13Se02Gf
CORNELL, Mary	15	F	Laborer	13Se02Gf
DENEHY, James	28	M	Servant	13Se02Gf
NEAL, Michl.	45	M	Servant	13Se02Gf
Michl.	19	M	Servant	13Se02Gf
DOODY, Nelly	46	F	Servant	13Se02Gf
KEELING, U-Mrs.	25	F	Servant	13Se02Gf
QUIN, Biddy	20	F	Servant	13Se02Gf
ABRAM, Thos.	25	M	Servant	13Se02Gf
WILLIAMS, George	25	M	Tinman	13Se02Gf
BRAMLEY, Thos.	28	M	Tinman	13Se02Gf
HEALY, Michael	25	M	Tinman	13Se02Gf
Died-At-Sea				
GADDS, James	20	M	Servant	13Se02Gf
REILLY, Johanna	25	F	Servant	13Se02Gf
LYNCH, Luke	32	M	Servant	13Se02Gf
BURGESS, Cicily	21	F	Servant	13Se02Gf
ROURKE, Rose	21	F	Servant	13Se02Gf
Mary	11	F	Servant	13Se02Gf
Anne	9	F	Child	13Se02Gf
Margt.	6	F	Child	13Se02Gf
Bridget	4	F	Child	13Se02Gf
Catharine	2	F	Child	13Se02Gf
CREAMER, Wm.	28	M	Laborer	13Se02Gf
FOLEY, John	31	M	Laborer	13Se02Gf
GAFFREY, Catharine	19	F	Laborer	13Se02Gf
Roseyt	20	F	Laborer	13Se02Gf
FAGAN, Mary	13	F	Laborer	13Se02Gf
MCCABE, Margt.	15	F	Laborer	13Se02Gf
RYAN, Bridget	18	F	Laborer	13Se02Gf
CORCORAN, James	50	M	Laborer	13Se02Gf
Cath.	50	F	Laborer	13Se02Gf
James	25	M	Laborer	13Se02Gf
Timothy	20	M	Laborer	13Se02Gf
Anne	18	F	Laborer	13Se02Gf
Mary	16	F	Laborer	13Se02Gf
BOYLE, John	50	M	Laborer	13Se02Gf
Mary	28	F	Laborer	13Se02Gf
Sally	20	F	Laborer	13Se02Gf
Anne	12	F	Laborer	13Se02Gf
Judy	10	F	Laborer	13Se02Gf
John	8	M	Child	13Se02Gf
DARCY, Aney	20	M	Laborer	13Se02Gf
LEECH, John	60	M	Laborer	13Se02Gf
Cath.	60	F	Laborer	13Se02Gf
Redmond	19	M	Laborer	13Se02Gf
Martin	13	M	Laborer	13Se02Gf
MCEVERY, Margt.	24	F	Spinster	13Se02Gf
LOWETH, Chas.	40	M	None	13Se02Gf
U-Mrs.	35	F	None	13Se02Gf
Ebenezar	5	M	Child	13Se02Gf
Amy	2	F	Child	13Se02Gf
CONNELL, Rose	20	F	Child	13Se02Gf
HILLER, Thompson	27	M	Child	13Se02Gf
Sarah	25	F	Fiddler	13Se02Gf
CONNELLY, James	30	M	Laborer	13Se02Gf
SPRATT, James	21	M	Laborer	13Se02Gf
BRADLEY, Mary	20	F	Servant	13Se02Gf
ONEILL, Mary	40	F	Servant	13Se02Gf
Edward	15	M	Servant	13Se02Gf
Denis	31	M	Laborer	13Se02Gf
Anne	21	F	Laborer	13Se02Gf
James	8	M	Child	13Se02Gf
Wm.	2	M	Child	13Se02Gf
BYRON, Bridget	18	F	Servant	13Se02Gf
RHODEN, Mark	20	M	Laborer	13Se02Gf
HOPKINS, John	26	M	Soldier	13Se02Gf
Jane	25	F	None	13Se02Gf
CARTER, Alfred	16	M	Carpenter	13Se02Gf
MCDONALD, James	22	M	Turf Cutter	13Se02Gf
Michael	21	M	Turf Cutter	13Se02Gf
GAVAN, John	27	M	Turf Cutter	13Se02Gf
MILLARICK, Mary	17	F	Turf Cutter	13Se02Gf
Ellen	15	F	Turf Cutter	13Se02Gf
John	7	M	Child	13Se02Gf
KEEFE, Cath.	21	F	Servant	13Se02Gf
ONEILL, Honora	10	F	Servant	13Se02Gf
SAWTON, Margt.	20	F	Servant	13Se02Gf
MCKEOWN, Mary	30	F	Servant	13Se02Gf
SHANNON, C.	39	M	Minister	13Se02Gf
HOMAN, Jane	20	F	Spinster	13Se02Gf
GLINMAN, Ann	15	F	Spinster	13Se02Gf
SAZOW, Wm.	23	M	Laborer	13Se02Gf
DOUGLAS, Mary-Ann	23	F	Servant	13Se02Gf

CALCUTTA 13 SEPTEMBER 1849

From Liverpool

NAMES OF PASSENGERS	AGE	SEX	OCCUPATIONS	DATE PORT SHIP
WILLIAMS, Wm.	10	M	Laborer	13Se02Qg
OWENS, John	20	M	Laborer	13Se02Qg
MORLEY, Henry	27	M	Laborer	13Se02Qg
HUNT, Wm.	17	M	Laborer	13Se02Qg
JUDGE, Mary	50	M	Servant	13Se02Qg
OHAID, Honor	63	F	Servant	13Se02Qg
HARRIS, Edwd.	29	M	Servant	13Se02Qg
GUY, Wm.	20	M	Servant	13Se02Qg
Rose	26	F	Servant	13Se02Qg
SCULLIVE, Jno.	40	M	Laborer	13Se02Qg
Pat	30	M	Laborer	13Se02Qg
OFFITT, Sarah	26	F	Servant	13Se02Qg
WHITEHEAD, Chris	38	M	Servant	13Se02Qg
Peter	21	M	Servant	13Se02Qg
BARRINGTON, Thos.	24	M	Laborer	13Se02Qg
WHITE, Jno.	22	M	Laborer	13Se02Qg
WHILIAR, Hny.	12	M	Laborer	13Se02Qg
Wm.	8	M	Child	13Se02Qg
SURAYHAN, Saml.	40	M	Laborer	13Se02Qg
Mary	17	F	Laborer	13Se02Qg
Bridget	12	F	Laborer	13Se02Qg
Saml.	13	M	Laborer	13Se02Qg
Cathne.	18	F	Laborer	13Se02Qg
ENGLISH, Jno.	50	M	Laborer	13Se02Qg
Cath.	40	F	Laborer	13Se02Qg
NAYLOR, Mary	14	F	Laborer	13Se02Qg
John	13	M	Laborer	13Se02Qg
Pat	12	M	Laborer	13Se02Qg
GARDMEN, Robt.	30	M	Ditcher	13Se02Qg
Bridget	30	F	None	13Se02Qg
John	1	M	Child	13Se02Qg
WOODHOUSE, Henry	26	M	Laborer	13Se02Qg
Elizabeth	24	F	Servant	13Se02Qg
DAVIS, Jas.	24	M	Laborer	13Se02Qg
MURPHY, Jno.	35	M	Laborer	13Se02Qg
Thos.	40	M	Laborer	13Se02Qg
Jno.	35	M	Laborer	13Se02Qg
HANEY, Percy	27	M	Laborer	13Se02Qg
MURPHY, Mary	35	M	Servant	13Se02Qg
Bridget	.00	F	Infant	13Se02Qg
MULTY, Matt	26	M	Laborer	13Se02Qg
Jno.	20	M	Laborer	13Se02Qg
SMITH, George	26	M	Laborer	13Se02Qg
PROBIT, Hannah	25	F	None	13Se02Qg
LOVETT, Bartle	13	M	Laborer	13Se02Qg
MULLENS, Ellen	28	F	Servant	13Se02Qg
MALONEY, Mary	30	F	Servant	13Se02Qg
Danl.	11	M	Servant	13Se02Qg
MAGINES, Thos.	26	M	Servant	13Se02Qg
Ann	21	F	Servant	13Se02Qg
MCDANIEL, Miles	31	M	Laborer	13Se02Qg

NAMES OF PASSENGERS	AGE	SEX	OCCUPATIONS	DATE PORT SHIP
MORBY, Ebenezer	50	M	Laborer	13Se02Qg
CHARTON, Robt.	27	M	Laborer	13Se02Qg
STEVENSON, Jno.G.	26	M	Laborer	13Se02Qg
WESTMORELAND, Mat.	22	M	Laborer	13Se02Qg
Jos.	28	M	Laborer	13Se02Qg
BRYERS, Robt.	49	M	Laborer	13Se02Qg
HANLONE, Mary-C.	50	F	Laborer	13Se02Qg
DONALD, Michl.	36	M	Laborer	13Se02Qg
BUNYAN, Wm.	22	M	Laborer	13Se02Qg
Tobias	28	M	Servant	13Se02Qg
HARDIN, Ann	50	F	Servant	13Se02Qg
Eliza	18	F	Servant	13Se02Qg
Ann	15	F	Servant	13Se02Qg
Jno.	13	M	Servant	13Se02Qg
HART, Pat	16	M	Servant	13Se02Qg
HARRICK, Saml.	22	M	Laborer	13Se02Qg
SCHOFIELD, Jas.	21	M	Laborer	13Se02Qg
TAYLOR, Thos.	21	M	Laborer	13Se02Qg
MURRAY, Denis	30	M	Laborer	13Se02Qg
Ann	27	F	Servant	13Se02Qg
Margt.	.00	F	Infant	13Se02Qg
KELLY, Thos.	26	M	Laborer	13Se02Qg
Cathne.	22	F	Servant	13Se02Qg
CORYNE, James	36	M	Laborer	13Se02Qg
Mary	32	F	Servant	13Se02Qg
Mary-Ann	12	F	Servant	13Se02Qg
Julia	10	F	Child	13Se02Qg
Eliza	8	F	Child	13Se02Qg
Joseph	7	M	Child	13Se02Qg
Margt.	6	F	Child	13Se02Qg
Thomas	.00	M	Infant	13Se02Qg
REDDAN, Mary	30	F	Servant	13Se02Qg
MUHAN, Mary	13	F	Servant	13Se02Qg
KEGAN, Michl.	50	M	Servant	13Se02Qg
HASSETT, Margt.	40	F	Servant	13Se02Qg
Cath.	13	F	Servant	13Se02Qg
Martin	11	M	Servant	13Se02Qg
Mary	9	F	Child	13Se02Qg
Elizb.	5	F	Child	13Se02Qg
Johannah	7	F	Child	13Se02Qg
CORMICK, Mary	17	F	Servant	13Se02Qg
BAYGUTT, Edwd.	25	M	Laborer	13Se02Qg
QUADE, Martin	25	M	Laborer	13Se02Qg
LYONS, Margt.	30	F	Servant	13Se02Qg
BROWN, Michl.	22	M	Laborer	13Se02Qg
CONNER, Philip	29	M	Laborer	13Se02Qg
SHEEHAN, Wm.	24	M	Laborer	13Se02Qg
DOUGHERTY, James	22	M	Laborer	13Se02Qg
GRIFFITH, Derrick	24	M	Laborer	13Se02Qg
DORAN, Eliza	20	F	Laborer	13Se02Qg
WILLIAMS, Morris	20	M	Laborer	13Se02Qg
OLIVE, Wm.	20	M	Laborer	13Se02Qg
KELLY, John	33	M	Laborer	13Se02Qg
TOOLE, Chas.	24	M	Servant	13Se02Qg
FLEMING, John	22	M	Laborer	13Se02Qg
MAHON, Patrick	18	M	Laborer	13Se02Qg
COLLINS, Pat	26	M	Laborer	13Se02Qg
Cath.	26	F	Servant	13Se02Qg
James	2	M	Child	13Se02Qg
Cath.	.00	F	Infant	13Se02Qg
DORMAN, Mgt.	21	F	Servant	13Se02Qg
MURPHY, James	22	M	Laborer	13Se02Qg
MACHNAMMON, Jn.	24	M	Laborer	13Se02Qg
FINCH, Eliza	23	F	Servant	13Se02Qg
MALONE, Jno.	18	M	Laborer	13Se02Qg
BOYLE, Michl.	20	M	Laborer	13Se02Qg
Arthur	20	M	Laborer	13Se02Qg
HUNTER, Math.	26	M	Laborer	13Se02Qg
BYRNES, Mary	30	F	Servant	13Se02Qg
RYAN, Judy	27	F	Servant	13Se02Qg
Ellen	3	F	Child	13Se02Qg
GALWAY, Mary	30	F	Servant	13Se02Qg
Jno.	7	M	Child	13Se02Qg
DIXON, Thomas	25	M	Laborer	13Se02Qg
DAVIS, Margaret	29	F	Laborer	13Se02Qg
DONELY, Agnes	20	F	Laborer	13Se02Qg
KELLY, Mary	26	F	Servant	13Se02Qg
MAGEE, John	30	M	Servant	13Se02Qg
DORAN, Thomas	15	M	Servant	13Se02Qg
MAGEE, Margaret	28	F	Servant	13Se02Qg
FITZPATRICK, Bary	32	M	Servant	13Se02Qg
MAGEE, Jno.	.00	M	Infant	13Se02Qg
DUNDASS, Phillip	68	M	Laborer	13Se02Qg
Jane	40	F	Laborer	13Se02Qg
ROBINSON, James	23	M	Laborer	13Se02Qg
Maria	25	F	Servant	13Se02Qg
Mary-Jane	.00	F	Infant	13Se02Qg
KIRVAN, Mary	40	F	Servant	13Se02Qg
John	4	M	Child	13Se02Qg
FARRELL, Elizb.	28	F	Servant	13Se02Qg
Mary	2	F	Child	13Se02Qg
MCGILLIS, U	18	M	Servant	13Se02Qg
MCALEAR, Martha	40	F	Servant	13Se02Qg
Catherine	40	F	Servant	13Se02Qg
Biddy	28	F	Servant	13Se02Qg
Martha	18	F	Servant	13Se02Qg
Kate	11	F	Servant	13Se02Qg
James	8	M	Child	13Se02Qg
Kate	10	F	Child	13Se02Qg
Bridget	.00	F	Infant	13Se02Qg
OHARE, Ann	9	F	Child	13Se02Qg
Elizabeth	30	F	Servant	13Se02Qg
MCALEAR, Christ.	40	M	Laborer	13Se02Qg
Mary	40	F	Laborer	13Se02Qg
John	.00	M	Infant	13Se02Qg
WILSON, Jane	23	F	Servant	13Se02Qg
Robt.	25	M	Laborer	13Se02Qg
Sarah	20	F	Laborer	13Se02Qg
CAROL, Mary	16	F	Laborer	13Se02Qg
Pat	12	M	Laborer	13Se02Qg
RIGGINS, Peter	36	M	Laborer	13Se02Qg
LOY, Peter	30	M	Laborer	13Se02Qg
BARRETT, Allen	30	M	Laborer	13Se02Qg
RENNOLDS, Bran	32	M	Laborer	13Se02Qg
Pat	10	M	Child	13Se02Qg
Cathne.	8	F	Child	13Se02Qg
MCLAUGHLIN, James	25	M	Laborer	13Se02Qg
U-Mrs.	23	F	Servant	13Se02Qg
PERGIS, Jane	18	F	Servant	13Se02Qg
SEARS, John	21	M	Laborer	13Se02Qg
Mary	20	F	Laborer	13Se02Qg
MURPHY, Pat	50	M	Laborer	13Se02Qg
CORRIGAN, Thos.	25	M	Laborer	13Se02Qg
CASEY, Elizth.	30	F	Servant	13Se02Qg
Mary	5	F	Child	13Se02Qg
HEGORITY, Jno.	23	M	Laborer	13Se02Qg
BRIEN, Michl.	27	M	Laborer	13Se02Qg
SHIGRY, Jno.	22	M	Laborer	13Se02Qg
Cathn.	22	F	Servant	13Se02Qg
SMITH, Bert.	18	M	Servant	13Se02Qg
WALDON, Elizab.	35	F	Servant	13Se02Qg
Isaac	5	M	Child	13Se02Qg
Jacob	3	M	Child	13Se02Qg
LYNCH, Richd.	55	M	Laborer	13Se02Qg
Mary	50	F	Laborer	13Se02Qg
David	25	M	Laborer	13Se02Qg
Jno.	23	M	Laborer	13Se02Qg
Sarah	22	F	Servant	13Se02Qg
Bridget	20	F	Servant	13Se02Qg
Cathn.	18	F	Servant	13Se02Qg
Jno.	16	M	Servant	13Se02Qg
Domik.	9	M	Child	13Se02Qg
Richd.	4	M	Child	13Se02Qg
MCMULY, Jno.	24	M	Servant	13Se02Qg
Jane	22	F	Servant	13Se02Qg

NAMES OF PASSENGERS		AGE	SEX	OCCUPATIONS	DATE PORT SHIP

CATHERINE 13 SEPTEMBER 1849

From Dublin

NAMES OF PASSENGERS		AGE	SEX	OCCUPATIONS	DATE PORT SHIP
SMITH, George		40	M	Unknown	13Se12Hn
U	(W)	40	F	Unknown	13Se12Hn
James		16	M	Unknown	13Se12Hn
JENNINGS, Bridget		21	F	Unknown	13Se12Hn
HICKEY, U-Mrs.		26	F	Unknown	13Se12Hn
Emma		8	F	Child	13Se12Hn
William		7	M	Child	13Se12Hn
George		5	M	Child	13Se12Hn
Henry		3	M	Child	13Se12Hn
M.		20	F	Unknown	13Se12Hn
CASEY, U-Mrs.		40	F	Unknown	13Se12Hn
John		18	M	Unknown	13Se12Hn
Patt		16	M	Unknown	13Se12Hn
Mary		13	F	Unknown	13Se12Hn
Marcella		11	F	Unknown	13Se12Hn
Jerrard		10	M	Unknown	13Se12Hn
Nicholas		8	M	Child	13Se12Hn
Ann		6	F	Child	13Se12Hn
B--OW, Wm.		30	M	Unknown	13Se12Hn
U	(W)	28	F	Unknown	13Se12Hn
David		4	M	Child	13Se12Hn
Johanna		2	F	Child	13Se12Hn
Patt		.00	M	Infant	13Se12Hn
David		32	M	Unknown	13Se12Hn
Matthew		20	M	Unknown	13Se12Hn
SMITH, Andrew		20	M	Unknown	13Se12Hn
HOAR, Margt.		20	F	Unknown	13Se12Hn
DELAHUNT, Margt.		30	F	Unknown	13Se12Hn
Margt.		8	F	Child	13Se12Hn
George		6	M	Child	13Se12Hn
James		4	M	Child	13Se12Hn
Thos.		.00	M	Infant	13Se12Hn
MUNCEY, Al.		23	M	Unknown	13Se12Hn
U	(W)	20	F	Unknown	13Se12Hn
Wm.		.00	M	Infant	13Se12Hn
GALLAGHER, John		22	M	Unknown	13Se12Hn
CARIGAN, Jas.		20	M	Unknown	13Se12Hn
Died-At-Sea					
EARLEY, Thos.		20	M	Unknown	13Se12Hn
BENNY, Ellen		20	F	Unknown	13Se12Hn
ENNIS, Thos.		40	M	Unknown	13Se12Hn
U	(W)	35	F	Unknown	13Se12Hn
Peter		17	M	Unknown	13Se12Hn
John		13	M	Unknown	13Se12Hn
Anne		11	F	Unknown	13Se12Hn
Mary		9	F	Child	13Se12Hn
Eliza		7	F	Child	13Se12Hn
Kate		5	F	Child	13Se12Hn
Thos.		3	M	Child	13Se12Hn
CAROLINE, Patt		21	M	Unknown	13Se12Hn
GRADY, Judy		20	F	Unknown	13Se12Hn
PURCELL, Margt.		21	F	Unknown	13Se12Hn
DELANY, U-Mrs.		40	F	Unknown	13Se12Hn
George		24	M	Unknown	13Se12Hn
Catharine		18	F	Unknown	13Se12Hn
John		20	M	Unknown	13Se12Hn
WHITNEY, Mary		30	F	Unknown	13Se12Hn
MCKENNA, Rosanna		20	F	Unknown	13Se12Hn
DOONEY, Michl.		30	M	Unknown	13Se12Hn
MCDONAGH, John		30	M	Unknown	13Se12Hn
CONNOR, James		26	M	Unknown	13Se12Hn
U	(W)	24	F	Unknown	13Se12Hn
Kate		5	F	Child	13Se12Hn
Joe		.00	M	Infant	13Se12Hn
HARDREY, W.H.		20	M	Unknown	13Se12Hn
POWER, U-Mrs.		40	F	Unknown	13Se12Hn
U-Miss		20	F	Unknown	13Se12Hn
Eliza		20	F	Unknown	13Se12Hn
FLYNN, John		20	M	Unknown	13Se12Hn
BUTLER, Mary		20	F	Unknown	13Se12Hn
MASON, Garrett		50	M	Unknown	13Se12Hn
U	(W)	40	F	Unknown	13Se12Hn
Patt		24	M	Unknown	13Se12Hn
Michl.		22	M	Unknown	13Se12Hn
Mary		20	F	Unknown	13Se12Hn
Eliza		16	F	Unknown	13Se12Hn
Thos.		12	M	Unknown	13Se12Hn
Kate		10	F	Unknown	13Se12Hn
BATTERLY, Thos.		20	M	Unknown	13Se12Hn
BECK, John-F.		30	M	Unknown	13Se12Hn
WHITE, Pierce		20	M	Unknown	13Se12Hn
U	(W)	20	F	Unknown	13Se12Hn
EGGLESON, Wm.		30	M	Unknown	13Se12Hn
Died-At-Sea					
J.		28	F	Unknown	13Se12Hn
Mary		10	F	Unknown	13Se12Hn
Peter		8	M	Child	13Se12Hn
Margt.		6	F	Child	13Se12Hn
Catharine		4	F	Child	13Se12Hn
Anne		.00	F	Infant	13Se12Hn
BOWEN, Hugh		30	M	Unknown	13Se12Hn
U	(W)	29	F	Unknown	13Se12Hn
WHITLEY, John		22	M	Unknown	13Se12Hn
WALSH, Patt		20	M	Unknown	13Se12Hn
DWYRE, James		24	M	Unknown	13Se12Hn
Anne		20	F	Unknown	13Se12Hn
RICHARDSON, Wm.		60	M	Unknown	13Se12Hn
Died-At-Sea					
Mary		50	F	Unknown	13Se12Hn
Edwd.		30	M	Unknown	13Se12Hn
RUSCULL, Eliza		22	F	Unknown	13Se12Hn
Edwd.		23	M	Unknown	13Se12Hn
RICHARDSON, Sam		13	M	Unknown	13Se12Hn
Mary		17	F	Unknown	13Se12Hn
LANGAN, Cathe.		22	F	Unknown	13Se12Hn
FINNEY, Bernard		22	M	Unknown	13Se12Hn
John		24	M	Unknown	13Se12Hn
KINSELLA, Wm.		24	M	Unknown	13Se12Hn
MCDONNELL, Mary		34	F	Unknown	13Se12Hn
OFARRELL, Hugh		40	M	Unknown	13Se12Hn
U	(W)	35	F	Unknown	13Se12Hn
Edwd.		14	M	Unknown	13Se12Hn
Cath.		10	F	Unknown	13Se12Hn
Mary		7	F	Child	13Se12Hn
Bridget		5	F	Child	13Se12Hn
Anne		5	F	Child	13Se12Hn
U		.00	U	Infant	13Se12Hn
WALSH, Alexander		28	M	Unknown	13Se12Hn
ROE, John		25	M	Unknown	13Se12Hn
U	(W)	22	F	Unknown	13Se12Hn
CAULFIELD, P.		32	M	Unknown	13Se12Hn
U	(W)	30	F	Unknown	13Se12Hn
Mary-A.		11	F	Unknown	13Se12Hn
Catherine		9	F	Child	13Se12Hn
William		7	M	Child	13Se12Hn
Died-At-Sea					
James		6	M	Child	13Se12Hn
Alban		4	M	Child	13Se12Hn
Teresa		3	F	Child	13Se12Hn
Emma		.00	F	Infant	13Se12Hn
MANAN, Michl.		20	M	Unknown	13Se12Hn
MOLLY, James		20	M	Unknown	13Se12Hn
Kate		20	F	Unknown	13Se12Hn
Bridget		18	F	Unknown	13Se12Hn
MOLLOY, Michl.		36	M	Unknown	13Se12Hn
Margt.		35	F	Unknown	13Se12Hn
Eliza		13	F	Unknown	13Se12Hn
Mary		11	F	Unknown	13Se12Hn
Margt.		9	F	Child	13Se12Hn
Ellen		4	F	Child	13Se12Hn

NAMES OF PASSENGERS		AGE	SEX	OCCUPATIONS	DATE PORT SHIP
MOLLOY, Bridget		.00	F	Infant	13Se12Hn
KANE, Patt		20	M	Unknown	13Se12Hn
Bridget		25	F	Unknown	13Se12Hn
ROURKE, Wm.		48	M	Unknown	13Se12Hn
Anne		30	F	Unknown	13Se12Hn
Julia		20	F	Unknown	13Se12Hn
John		16	M	Unknown	13Se12Hn
Wm.		14	M	Unknown	13Se12Hn
Michl.		12	M	Unknown	13Se12Hn
James		7	M	Child	13Se12Hn
Patt		5	M	Child	13Se12Hn
Jem		2	M	Child	13Se12Hn
RYAN, Peter		30	M	Unknown	13Se12Hn
SMITH, Francis		22	M	Unknown	13Se12Hn
U	(W)	20	F	Unknown	13Se12Hn
Died-At-Sea					
MATTHEWS, Geo.		17	M	Unknown	13Se12Hn
DWYRE, Julia		30	F	Unknown	13Se12Hn
KELLY, Thos.		24	M	Unknown	13Se12Hn
U	(W)	21	F	Unknown	13Se12Hn
Died-At-Sea					
BOHAN, Marg.		40	F	Unknown	13Se12Hn
Died-At-Sea					
Marg.		20	F	Unknown	13Se12Hn
Patt		20	M	Unknown	13Se12Hn
Died-At-Sea					
PAINE, Cathe.		20	F	Unknown	13Se12Hn
HANNAN, W.		40	M	Unknown	13Se12Hn
U	(W)	40	F	Unknown	13Se12Hn
Margt.		11	F	Unknown	13Se12Hn
Mary		8	F	Child	13Se12Hn
Patt		6	M	Child	13Se12Hn
Biddy		5	F	Child	13Se12Hn
Died-At-Sea					
Cathe.		2	F	Child	13Se12Hn
Died-At-Sea					
Ellen		2	F	Child	13Se12Hn
Died-At-Sea					
Tom		.00	M	Infant	13Se12Hn
Died-At-Sea					
CURSELL, Ellen		20	F	Unknown	13Se12Hn
MORRIS, John		20	M	Unknown	13Se12Hn
CASSIDY, John		21	M	Unknown	13Se12Hn
Died-At-Sea					
NEWMAN, James		21	M	Unknown	13Se12Hn
DEMPSEY, Margt.		21	F	Unknown	13Se12Hn
HENNESSEY, Cathe.		36	F	Unknown	13Se12Hn
HORAHAN, Margt.		30	F	Unknown	13Se12Hn
HENNESSY, Wm.		11	M	Unknown	13Se12Hn
Eliza		5	F	Child	13Se12Hn
MARKS, U-Mrs.		32	F	Unknown	13Se12Hn
Wm.		32	F	Unknown	13Se12Hn
Francis		13	M	Unknown	13Se12Hn
Louisa		11	F	Unknown	13Se12Hn
Eliza		7	F	Child	13Se12Hn
Peter		5	M	Child	13Se12Hn
Peter		40	M	Unknown	13Se12Hn
HUGHES, Thos.		50	M	Unknown	13Se12Hn
Biddy		44	F	Unknown	13Se12Hn
Died-At-Sea					
Peter		19	M	Unknown	13Se12Hn
Died-At-Sea					
Wm.		17	M	Unknown	13Se12Hn
Mary		14	F	Unknown	13Se12Hn
Ann		13	F	Unknown	13Se12Hn
Cathe.		10	F	Unknown	13Se12Hn
Died-At-Sea					
Jas.		3	M	Child	13Se12Hn
Died-At-Sea					
Tom		.00	M	Infant	13Se12Hn
Died-At-Sea					
CARNEY, Teresa		20	F	Unknown	13Se12Hn
HYLAND, Catharine		20	F	Unknown	13Se12Hn
Died-At-Sea					
SCULLY, John		16	M	Unknown	13Se12Hn

NAMES OF PASSENGERS		AGE	SEX	OCCUPATIONS	DATE PORT SHIP
CLOONEY, John		20	M	Unknown	13Se12Hn
LYNCH, Thos.		35	M	Unknown	13Se12Hn
John		16	M	Unknown	13Se12Hn
LESTRANGE, Eliza		20	F	Unknown	13Se12Hn
LERNORE, Henry		28	M	Unknown	13Se12Hn
CRAVEN, John		21	M	Unknown	13Se12Hn
BYRNE, Eliza		23	F	Unknown	13Se12Hn
Mary		24	F	Unknown	13Se12Hn
Cathe.		25	F	Unknown	13Se12Hn
BESTON, Jas.		50	M	Unknown	13Se12Hn
Biddy		40	F	Unknown	13Se12Hn
Margt.		13	F	Unknown	13Se12Hn
Thomas		11	M	Unknown	13Se12Hn
Patt		9	M	Child	13Se12Hn
Mary		7	F	Child	13Se12Hn
Simon		4	M	Child	13Se12Hn
Died-At-Sea					
MURRAY, Patt		20	M	Unknown	13Se12Hn
MURPHY, Thomas		20	M	Unknown	13Se12Hn
COUSIN, Margt.		46	F	Unknown	13Se12Hn
Tom		21	M	Unknown	13Se12Hn
Sarah		46	F	Unknown	13Se12Hn
Patt		21	M	Unknown	13Se12Hn
Margt.		20	F	Unknown	13Se12Hn
Edwd.		17	M	Unknown	13Se12Hn
Died-At-Sea					
GIBBON, U		12	M	Unknown	13Se12Hn
TRACY, Jas.		10	M	Unknown	13Se12Hn
Ellen		29	F	Unknown	13Se12Hn
John		45	M	Unknown	13Se12Hn
Johanna		45	F	Unknown	13Se12Hn
Edwd.		27	M	Unknown	13Se12Hn
Martin		24	M	Unknown	13Se12Hn
Michl.		22	M	Unknown	13Se12Hn
Jas.		20	M	Unknown	13Se12Hn
Catharine		18	F	Unknown	13Se12Hn
TRAHEY, John		20	M	Unknown	13Se12Hn
Mary		21	F	Unknown	13Se12Hn
Dan		22	M	Unknown	13Se12Hn
Dan		22	M	Unknown	13Se12Hn
CARNACK, Thos.		20	M	Unknown	13Se12Hn
Mary		21	F	Unknown	13Se12Hn
LAHEY, Judith		22	F	Unknown	13Se12Hn
TORNEY, Sally		30	F	Unknown	13Se12Hn
Mary		30	F	Unknown	13Se12Hn
KELLY, Mary		55	F	Unknown	13Se12Hn
Anne		28	F	Unknown	13Se12Hn
Marcella		26	F	Unknown	13Se12Hn
Terence		24	M	Unknown	13Se12Hn
Catharine		22	F	Unknown	13Se12Hn
Mary		20	F	Unknown	13Se12Hn
Margt.		18	F	Unknown	13Se12Hn
Denis		13	M	Unknown	13Se12Hn
Patt		11	M	Unknown	13Se12Hn
Died-At-Sea					
DELANEY, Cathe.		20	F	Unknown	13Se12Hn
DUNNE, Jas.		35	M	Unknown	13Se12Hn
Mary		30	F	Unknown	13Se12Hn
WALSH, Henry		30	M	Unknown	13Se12Hn
Catharine		30	F	Unknown	13Se12Hn
Henry		8	M	Child	13Se12Hn
Thomas		5	M	Child	13Se12Hn
James		3	M	Child	13Se12Hn
Catharine		.00	F	Infant	13Se12Hn
BRIEN, Patt		34	M	Unknown	13Se12Hn
U	(W)	30	F	Unknown	13Se12Hn
Mary		.00	F	Infant	13Se12Hn
MORRIS, John		30	M	Unknown	13Se12Hn
MURRAY, Ellen		30	F	Unknown	13Se12Hn
John		20	M	Unknown	13Se12Hn
Jane		11	F	Unknown	13Se12Hn
CARTER, U		40	M	Unknown	13Se12Hn
James		30	M	Unknown	13Se12Hn
MORRIS, John		46	M	Unknown	13Se12Hn

HYPERION 14 SEPTEMBER 1849

From Glasgow

NAMES OF PASSENGERS	AGE	SEX	OCCUPATIONS	DATE PORT SHIP
HARVEY, Nathl.	30	M	Tailor	14Se04Kt
GRAHAM, Thos.	20	M	Laborer	14Se04Kt
MCALTON, John	26	M	Laborer	14Se04Kt
WALTON, Saml.	17	M	Coach Maker	14Se04Kt
CHURCH, Thos.	44	M	Mariner	14Se04Kt
Elisabeth	27	F	Unknown	14Se04Kt
FON, John	27	M	Mason	14Se04Kt
CARD, Peter	32	M	Molder	14Se04Kt
RIDGEHUB, Henry	23	M	Clerk	14Se04Kt
CARD, Eliza	34	F	Molder	14Se04Kt
Andrew	9	M	Child	14Se04Kt
Robert	8	M	Child	14Se04Kt
Margaret	7	F	Child	14Se04Kt
Rebecca	2	F	Child	14Se04Kt
ROBERTSON, John	31	M	Grocer	14Se04Kt
Catherine	31	F	Unknown	14Se04Kt
PASCOE, Jesse	30	M	Miner	14Se04Kt
Archd.	1	M	Child	14Se04Kt
YOUNG, Edward	33	M	Molder	14Se04Kt
Eliza	19	F	Unknown	14Se04Kt
Andrew	30	M	Joiner	14Se04Kt
Agnes	30	F	Unknown	14Se04Kt
Engwith	3	M	Child	14Se04Kt
Charlotte	1	F	Child	14Se04Kt
BLAIR, Robert	35	M	Grocer	14Se04Kt
Marian	24	F	Unknown	14Se04Kt
Mary-Anne	7	F	Child	14Se04Kt
Margaret	5	F	Child	14Se04Kt
DOUGHERTY, John	26	M	Chemist	14Se04Kt
Rose	50	F	Unknown	14Se04Kt
HUME, Margaret	16	F	Servant	14Se04Kt
WARD, Catherine	25	F	Milliner	14Se04Kt
PHILLIPS, Agnes	29	F	Molder	14Se04Kt
Jane	3	F	Child	14Se04Kt
MAGREGOR, Thos.	26	M	Laborer	14Se04Kt
John	24	M	Laborer	14Se04Kt
James	33	M	Laborer	14Se04Kt
Catherine	24	F	Unknown	14Se04Kt
Michael	9	M	Child	14Se04Kt
James	7	M	Child	14Se04Kt
LAWRIE, James	19	M	Tailor	14Se04Kt
Jannet	50	F	Unknown	14Se04Kt
Christiana	26	F	Servant	14Se04Kt
Thomas	12	M	Unknown	14Se04Kt
STEWART, Jannet	3	F	Child	14Se04Kt
Mary	.04	F	Infant	14Se04Kt
MCMANUS, William	26	M	Laborer	14Se04Kt
Ellen	24	F	Unknown	14Se04Kt
MCSINOLD, Ellen	23	F	Servant	14Se04Kt
HUGHES, Margaret	69	F	Weaver	14Se04Kt
Mary	25	F	Weaver	14Se04Kt
CLARK, Mary	36	F	Servant	14Se04Kt
DOIG, Robert	27	M	Farmer	14Se04Kt
Jane	22	F	Unknown	14Se04Kt
John	6	M	Child	14Se04Kt
Agnes	4	F	Child	14Se04Kt
JERKINS, Elizabeth	30	F	Servant	14Se04Kt
CHRISTIE, George	29	M	Currier	14Se04Kt
Alexander	26	M	Mason	14Se04Kt
INNES, Wm.	27	M	Mason	14Se04Kt
ROBERTSON, Mary	44	F	Cook	14Se04Kt
Elizabeth	20	F	Cook	14Se04Kt
Maria	9	F	Child	14Se04Kt
MCCARRA, Judith	48	F	Servant	14Se04Kt
Mary	16	F	Servant	14Se04Kt

NAMES OF PASSENGERS	AGE	SEX	OCCUPATIONS	DATE PORT SHIP
MCCARRA, John	10	M	Unknown	14Se04Kt
Hugh	9	M	Child	14Se04Kt
Catherine	6	F	Child	14Se04Kt
DOUGHERTY, Bridget	19	F	Servant	14Se04Kt
SLEVIN, Jane	26	F	Seamstress	14Se04Kt
Hugh	7	M	Child	14Se04Kt
Mary	5	F	Child	14Se04Kt
Margaret	3	F	Child	14Se04Kt
JACKSON, Jane	22	M	Weaver	14Se04Kt
Elisabeth	1	F	Child	14Se04Kt
DAVIDSON, Elisabeth	12	F	Unknown	14Se04Kt
MCWILLIAMS, Ellen	20	F	Bleacher	14Se04Kt
SMITH, Margaret	24	F	Cook	14Se04Kt
Margaret	5	F	Child	14Se04Kt
Agnes	3	F	Child	14Se04Kt
Mary	1	F	Child	14Se04Kt
MCDOUGULL, Alexander	54	M	Miner	14Se04Kt
Jannet	8	F	Child	14Se04Kt
KEY, Alexander	44	M	Paper Maker	14Se04Kt
Elizabeth	33	F	Unknown	14Se04Kt
William	10	M	Unknown	14Se04Kt
Sarah	8	F	Child	14Se04Kt
Robert	5	M	Child	14Se04Kt
SELKIRK, Agnes	29	F	Servant	14Se04Kt
John	5	M	Child	14Se04Kt
Catherine	3	F	Child	14Se04Kt
CARROL, Mary	26	F	Servant	14Se04Kt
John	2	M	Child	14Se04Kt
MCWILLIAMS, Mary	19	F	Servant	14Se04Kt
MCCARRULL, Ellen	22	F	Servant	14Se04Kt
Frances	4	F	Child	14Se04Kt
Rose	2	F	Child	14Se04Kt
THOMPSON, James	21	M	Butcher	14Se04Kt
Alexander	11	M	Unknown	14Se04Kt
MILLER, Patrick	32	M	Laborer	14Se04Kt
MCKINNON, Christine	40	F	Servant	14Se04Kt
John	17	M	Unknown	14Se04Kt
SOMERONIL, Agnes	39	F	Servant	14Se04Kt
Mary	7	F	Child	14Se04Kt
John	8	M	Child	14Se04Kt
Susan	6	F	Child	14Se04Kt
HORTON, David	28	M	Farmer	14Se04Kt
Elizabeth	28	F	Unknown	14Se04Kt
CUNADU, Henry	26	M	Mariner	14Se04Kt
Sarah	25	F	Unknown	14Se04Kt
William	.08	M	Infant	14Se04Kt
MORE, Hugh	20	M	Laborer	14Se04Kt
GREEN, George	32	M	Farmer	14Se04Kt
Eliza	32	F	Unknown	14Se04Kt
Robert	8	M	Child	14Se04Kt
Thomas	6	M	Child	14Se04Kt
Eliza	4	F	Child	14Se04Kt
Maria	.08	F	Infant	14Se04Kt
MURPHY, Catherine	20	F	Servant	14Se04Kt
HORTON, Esther	24	F	Servant	14Se04Kt
VOAK, Sydney	18	M	Tailor	14Se04Kt
Rachel	16	F	Milliner	14Se04Kt
GREEN, Adam	48	M	Farmer	14Se04Kt
John	4	M	Child	14Se04Kt
DALEY, Peter	19	M	Laborer	14Se04Kt
Mary	18	F	Servant	14Se04Kt
MCGREGAIN, Patrick	20	M	Laborer	14Se04Kt
HARVEY, William	19	M	Laborer	14Se04Kt
DYNAN, James	23	M	Laborer	14Se04Kt
Bridget	22	F	Servant	14Se04Kt
STORY, Thomas	36	M	Laborer	14Se04Kt
Catherine	28	F	Unknown	14Se04Kt
Peter	9	M	Child	14Se04Kt
Ann	7	F	Child	14Se04Kt
DOUGHERTY, John	51	M	Laborer	14Se04Kt
John	17	M	Bleacher	14Se04Kt
STEWART, Alexander	40	M	Shoemaker	14Se04Kt
Ann	31	F	Unknown	14Se04Kt
Ann-S.	5	F	Child	14Se04Kt
Charlotte	4	F	Child	14Se04Kt

NAMES OF PASSENGERS	AGE	SEX	OCCUPATIONS	DATE PORT SHIP
SMALL, Mary	1	F	Child	14Se04Kt
ANDERSON, Isabella	38	F	Tailor	14Se04Kt
SWINNEY, Ellen	20	F	Servant	14Se04Kt
DOUGHERTY, Mary	30	F	Bleacher	14Se04Kt
MURRAY, Isabella	23	F	Brf	14Se04Kt
SMALL, Jessie	23	F	Unknown	14Se04Kt
MURRAY, John	.05	M	Infant	14Se04Kt
TURNER, William	35	M	Engineer	14Se04Kt
Jannet	40	F	Unknown	14Se04Kt
George	10	M	Unknown	14Se04Kt
Jannet	8	F	Child	14Se04Kt
Ann	6	F	Child	14Se04Kt
James	5	M	Child	14Se04Kt
Margaret	4	F	Child	14Se04Kt
Mary	3	F	Child	14Se04Kt
Elizabeth	2	F	Child	14Se04Kt
BEVIN, Edward	23	M	Plumber	14Se04Kt
THOMSON, Jannet	30	F	Servant	14Se04Kt
David	8	M	Child	14Se04Kt
Mary	3	F	Child	14Se04Kt
Ellen	5	F	Child	14Se04Kt
John	2	M	Child	14Se04Kt
CRAWFORD, William	30	M	Tailor	14Se04Kt
HIGGINBOTHAM, Robt.	18	M	Carter	14Se04Kt
SLOOAN, Mary	40	F	Servant	14Se04Kt
John	18	M	Unknown	14Se04Kt
Barney	12	M	Unknown	14Se04Kt
James	10	M	Unknown	14Se04Kt
SHULAN, Henry	17	M	Miner	14Se04Kt
MORE, John	20	M	Miner	14Se04Kt
HARRIS, William	53	M	Clerk	14Se04Kt
BUCHANAN, Duncan	29	M	Carder	14Se04Kt
CARROLL, David	26	M	Unknown	14Se04Kt
Catherine	64	F	Unknown	14Se04Kt
Mary	34	F	Weaver	14Se04Kt
WILLIS, James	40	M	Blr	14Se04Kt
STEED, William	32	M	Blr	14Se04Kt
CRAWFORD, John	30	M	Printer	14Se04Kt
BLACK, Ann	30	F	Servant	14Se04Kt
William	4	M	Child	14Se04Kt
THOMPSON, William	10	M	Unknown	14Se04Kt
NESMITH, U-Mrs.	00	F	Unknown	14Se04Kt
U	.00	U	Infant	14Se04Kt
MCKENZIE, U	00	M	Unknown	14Se04Kt
FORBES, U	00	M	Unknown	14Se04Kt

A.Z. 15 SEPTEMBER 1849

From Liverpool

NAMES OF PASSENGERS	AGE	SEX	OCCUPATIONS	DATE PORT SHIP
CONELLY, Mich.	9	M	Unknown	15Se02Ip
Arthur	2	M	Unknown	15Se02Ip
WHITE, Mary	25	F	Servant	15Se02Ip
KEAGAN, Cath.	19	F	Servant	15Se02Ip
KING, Mary-A.	19	F	Servant	15Se02Ip
Ann	21	F	Servant	15Se02Ip
LEPANE, Jolen	30	M	Tailor	15Se02Ip
CREEDEN, Dan	26	M	Laborer	15Se02Ip
ROACH, Cath.	22	F	Servant	15Se02Ip
DONEGAN, Ellen	22	F	Servant	15Se02Ip
MULLIN, Mary	28	F	Servant	15Se02Ip
KELLY, Thomas	45	M	Brewer	15Se02Ip
U-Mrs. Died-At-Sea	30	F	Unknown	15Se02Ip
Margt. Died-At-Sea	8	F	Child	15Se02Ip
Mary Died-At-Sea	6	F	Child	15Se02Ip
Cath. Died-At-Sea	.00	F	Infant	15Se02Ip
QUINLAN, Dennis	45	M	Grocer	15Se02Ip
John	47	M	Grocer	15Se02Ip
CONARAY, Cath.	40	F	Grocer	15Se02Ip
CARR, Charles	23	M	Glass Maker	15Se02Ip
U-Mrs. Died-At-Sea	19	F	Unknown	15Se02Ip
Mary Died-At-Sea	.00	F	Infant	15Se02Ip
CORORAN, Mary	20	F	Servant	15Se02Ip
DEVINE, Mary	28	F	Servant	15Se02Ip
REILLY, Mary	19	F	Servant	15Se02Ip
SHERIDAN, Bridg.	26	F	Servant	15Se02Ip
DUFFEY, Luke	37	M	Laborer	15Se02Ip
Sarah	3	F	Child	15Se02Ip
MCCAHEY, Bridg.	31	F	Servant	15Se02Ip
DEACON, Bridg.	40	F	Lad	15Se02Ip
Margt.	2	F	Child	15Se02Ip
Mary	12	F	Lad	15Se02Ip
KENNEY, Bridg.	20	F	Servant	15Se02Ip
Cath.	14	F	Servant	15Se02Ip
CUNNINGHAM, Mick	22	M	Laborer	15Se02Ip
MCNORMEE, Terance	18	M	Laborer	15Se02Ip
Mary	18	F	Servant	15Se02Ip
KELLY, Sally	17	F	Servant	15Se02Ip
COYLE, Mary	20	F	Servant	15Se02Ip
ROSSETER, Peggy	51	F	Servant	15Se02Ip
LONGHMAN, Pat	40	M	Laborer	15Se02Ip
MULLIGAN, Ann	25	F	Servant	15Se02Ip
OBRIAN, Mary	40	F	Servant	15Se02Ip
CHURCHILL, Glen	16	M	Laborer	15Se02Ip
Phil	14	M	Laborer	15Se02Ip
Bridg	11	F	Laborer	15Se02Ip
MORNGAN, Mary	18	F	Servant	15Se02Ip
TOUEL, Jolen	18	M	Weaver	15Se02Ip
MCGARREY, William	25	M	Dresser	15Se02Ip
Cath.	20	F	Dresser	15Se02Ip
James	.00	M	Infant	15Se02Ip
ROAN, James	35	M	Laborer	15Se02Ip
Brid.	30	F	Laborer	15Se02Ip
BRACKIN, Dennis	35	M	Laborer	15Se02Ip
May	21	F	Laborer	15Se02Ip
CARR, Patt	15	M	Weaver	15Se02Ip
Cath.	15	F	Weaver	15Se02Ip
WADE, Dan	19	M	Laborer	15Se02Ip
Michel	18	M	Laborer	15Se02Ip
HERON, Jolen	20	M	Laborer	15Se02Ip
Pat	11	M	Laborer	15Se02Ip
Mary	9	F	Child	15Se02Ip
Anne Died-At-Sea	7	F	Child	15Se02Ip
KELLY, Pat	22	M	Laborer	15Se02Ip
MCCAULIFFE, Thomas	32	M	Laborer	15Se02Ip
Johanna	5	F	Child	15Se02Ip
Cath. Died-At-Sea	32	F	Laborer	15Se02Ip
May Died-At-Sea	7	F	Child	15Se02Ip
Cath. Died-At-Sea	2	F	Child	15Se02Ip
Brid.	.00	F	Infant	15Se02Ip
KENNELLY, Jolen	25	M	Laborer	15Se02Ip
FITZGERALD, Mary	35	F	Laborer	15Se02Ip
Pat	10	M	Laborer	15Se02Ip
James	8	M	Child	15Se02Ip
BROWN, Will.	15	M	Painter	15Se02Ip
MCMULLEN, Pat	20	M	Weaver	15Se02Ip
BUTLER, Margt.	18	F	Servant	15Se02Ip
RYAN, Phil	20	M	Stctr	15Se02Ip
CAVANAGH, Julia	20	F	Servant	15Se02Ip
WILLIAMSON, James	33	M	Laborer	15Se02Ip
HANES, Jolen	19	M	Laborer	15Se02Ip
KELLY, James	50	M	Laborer	15Se02Ip
Peter	26	M	Laborer	15Se02Ip

NAMES OF PASSENGERS	AGE	SEX	OCCUPATIONS	DATE PORT SHIP
KELLY, Thomas	24	M	Laborer	15Se02Ip
Pat	22	M	Laborer	15Se02Ip
Brennan	18	M	Laborer	15Se02Ip
Cath	19	F	Laborer	15Se02Ip
Ann	17	F	Laborer	15Se02Ip
MCANALLY, James	22	M	Laborer	15Se02Ip
Terence	10	M	Laborer	15Se02Ip
Margt.	17	F	Laborer	15Se02Ip
Rose	14	F	Laborer	15Se02Ip
BURNE, Thomas	45	M	Farmer	15Se02Ip
U-Mrs.	45	F	Farmer	15Se02Ip
Pat	16	M	Farmer	15Se02Ip
Thomas	13	M	Farmer	15Se02Ip
James	11	M	Farmer	15Se02Ip
Hugh	6	M	Child	15Se02Ip
Bernard	.00	M	Infant	15Se02Ip
May	7	F	Child	15Se02Ip
Died-At-Sea				
Bridg.	4	F	Child	15Se02Ip
MCGINNISS, Margt.	45	F	None	15Se02Ip
Betty	15	F	None	15Se02Ip
Pat	17	M	None	15Se02Ip
Died-At-Sea				
Jolen	13	M	Unknown	15Se02Ip
MCGUIRE, Theo.	50	M	Farmer	15Se02Ip
U-Mrs.	45	F	Farmer	15Se02Ip
Jolen	16	M	Farmer	15Se02Ip
Henry	14	M	Farmer	15Se02Ip
Alice	12	F	Farmer	15Se02Ip
Mary	10	F	Farmer	15Se02Ip
Cath.	8	F	Child	15Se02Ip
Ann	4	F	Child	15Se02Ip
Fred	6	M	Child	15Se02Ip
Pat	2	M	Child	15Se02Ip
MCCIVE, Thomas	20	M	Laborer	15Se02Ip
CAVANAGH, Mary	15	F	Servant	15Se02Ip
FEGAN, Henry	40	M	Farmer	15Se02Ip
Jolen	30	M	Farmer	15Se02Ip
Thomas	32	M	Farmer	15Se02Ip
Margt.	35	F	Farmer	15Se02Ip
REILLY, William	26	M	Dresser	15Se02Ip
Ellen	25	F	Dresser	15Se02Ip
ODONNELL, Edmond	26	M	Laborer	15Se02Ip
PURDEN, Thomas	19	M	Laborer	15Se02Ip
DIXON, Jolen	20	M	Laborer	15Se02Ip
BURNE, Pat	22	M	Laborer	15Se02Ip
Adam	22	M	Laborer	15Se02Ip
JENNINGS, Margt.	18	F	Servant	15Se02Ip
Cath.	16	F	Servant	15Se02Ip
STRAYER, Thomas	50	M	None	15Se02Ip
Cath.	36	F	None	15Se02Ip
Edmond	13	M	None	15Se02Ip
May	11	F	None	15Se02Ip
HEENAN, Tim	48	M	Farmer	15Se02Ip
Died-At-Sea				
Cath.	35	F	Farmer	15Se02Ip
John	56	M	Farmer	15Se02Ip
Died-At-Sea				
Edward	18	M	Farmer	15Se02Ip
Margt.	15	F	Farmer	15Se02Ip
Cath.	12	F	Farmer	15Se02Ip
John	10	M	Farmer	15Se02Ip
Tim	7	M	Child	15Se02Ip
William	6	M	Child	15Se02Ip
Pat	3	M	Child	15Se02Ip
Died-At-Sea				
Mat	.00	M	Infant	15Se02Ip
BERGIN, Judy	50	F	Servant	15Se02Ip
Andy	12	M	Servant	15Se02Ip
BRINE, John	16	M	Laborer	15Se02Ip
CONIGAN, Law.	24	M	Laborer	15Se02Ip
Cath.	22	F	Servant	15Se02Ip
MCNANGHT, June	24	F	Servant	15Se02Ip
MCCLOSKEY, May	20	F	Servant	15Se02Ip
MCDONOUGH, Mary	32	F	Servant	15Se02Ip
MCDONOUGH, George	7	M	Child	15Se02Ip
John	5	M	Child	15Se02Ip
CONNORTON, Michel	30	M	Laborer	15Se02Ip
BENSON, Thomas	20	M	Nail Maker	15Se02Ip
SCANLOAN, Tim	20	M	Laborer	15Se02Ip
MULVEY, Pat	20	M	Laborer	15Se02Ip
MCKENNA, Rose	24	F	Servant	15Se02Ip
SHERIDAN, Cath.	16	F	Servant	15Se02Ip
FOLEY, James	30	M	Blacksmith	15Se02Ip
SHERIDAN, Con.	18	M	Farmer	15Se02Ip
MEARTIN, Mary	30	F	Servant	15Se02Ip
CANFIELD, Bridg.	50	F	Servant	15Se02Ip
Ann	12	F	Servant	15Se02Ip
Mary	11	F	Servant	15Se02Ip
MCGUINNEY, Thomas	9	M	Child	15Se02Ip
DAVID, Walter	30	M	Agrc	15Se02Ip
MULLAHAN, Mat	22	M	Laborer	15Se02Ip
TERRANCE, Owen	20	M	Laborer	15Se02Ip
CURREN, Ellen	22	F	Servant	15Se02Ip
OMULLEN, Elizth.	27	F	Servant	15Se02Ip
HEENAN, Ellen	4	F	Child	15Se02Ip

CHRISTIAN 17 SEPTEMBER 1849

From Glasgow

NAMES OF PASSENGERS	AGE	SEX	OCCUPATIONS	DATE PORT SHIP
MCLACHLAND, James	47	M	Tanner	17Se04Jg
Mary	5	F	Child	17Se04Jg
James	3	M	Child	17Se04Jg
Catherine	3	F	Child	17Se04Jg
Sarah	00	F	Child	17Se04Jg
Elizabeth	00	F	Unknown	17Se04Jg
CAINE, Helen	33	F	Spinster	17Se04Jg
ROWAN, Dennis	33	M	Bleacher	17Se04Jg
MCILROY, Margaret	27	F	Unknown	17Se04Jg
MCCAIB, Elizabeth	19	F	House Maid	17Se04Jg
RUTHERFORD, James	20	M	Sawer	17Se04Jg
DOCHERTY, Betty	20	F	None	17Se04Jg
MCMONIGLE, Ann	30	F	Spinster	17Se04Jg
Mary	9	F	Child	17Se04Jg
MORRISON, William	28	M	Collier	17Se04Jg
TRACY, John	21	M	Laborer	17Se04Jg
MCGUIGAN, Robert	34	M	Minister	17Se04Jg
WINNING, William	27	M	Solicitor	17Se04Jg
U-Mrs.	25	F	None	17Se04Jg
Ann	.06	F	Infant	17Se04Jg
Died-At-Sea				

JAMESTOWN 17 SEPTEMBER 1849

From Liverpool

NAMES OF PASSENGERS	AGE	SEX	OCCUPATIONS	DATE PORT SHIP
CORNELLY, Jane	21	F	None	17Se02Jf
DALY, Mary	22	F	None	17Se02Jf
SMITH, Jane	18	F	None	17Se02Jf
NEENAN, Patrick	20	M	Laborer	17Se02Jf
MARMION, Jane	21	F	None	17Se02Jf
MCLAUGHLIN, James	24	M	Mechanic	17Se02Jf
MANLEY, William	40	M	Publican	17Se02Jf
Elizabeth	40	F	None	17Se02Jf
MARTIN, William	34	M	Mechanic	17Se02Jf
Mary	40	F	None	17Se02Jf
M--, Edwin	9	M	Child	17Se02Jf

NAMES OF PASSENGERS	AGE	SEX	OCCUPATIONS	DATE PORT SHIP
MANLEY, Sarah	11	F	None	17Se02Jf
TETLEY, John	39	M	Laborer	17Se02Jf
Mary	40	F	None	17Se02Jf
Joseph	12	M	Laborer	17Se02Jf
Maria	10	F	None	17Se02Jf
Eliza	8	F	Child	17Se02Jf
William	6	M	Child	17Se02Jf
Sarah	4	F	Child	17Se02Jf
John	.00	M	Infant	17Se02Jf
MULLIGAN, John	24	M	Laborer	17Se02Jf
CARBURY, Andrew	23	M	Laborer	17Se02Jf
DONAHUE, Mary	20	F	None	17Se02Jf
Margaret	14	F	None	17Se02Jf
MCCANN, Rose	13	F	None	17Se02Jf
RITCHIE, Robert	24	M	Laborer	17Se02Jf
BLAKE, William	35	M	Laborer	17Se02Jf
Hannah	30	F	None	17Se02Jf
STUART, Daniel	45	M	Laborer	17Se02Jf
HUESTON, Robert	19	M	Laborer	17Se02Jf
MCGOVERN, John	40	M	Laborer	17Se02Jf
Mary	35	F	None	17Se02Jf
CAILLAHER, Rose	18	F	None	17Se02Jf
ROURKE, Bridget	20	F	None	17Se02Jf
PETIT, Thomas	20	M	Laborer	17Se02Jf
DORAN, Peter	26	M	Laborer	17Se02Jf
Mary	24	F	None	17Se02Jf
CARLISLE, John	23	M	Laborer	17Se02Jf
Mary	20	F	None	17Se02Jf
FREEHILL, Frances	20	F	None	17Se02Jf
RUDDEN, Patt	20	M	Laborer	17Se02Jf
TOOLE, Mary	18	F	None	17Se02Jf
REGAN, Catherine	20	F	None	17Se02Jf
REILLEY, Matthew	20	M	Laborer	17Se02Jf
WALSH, Mary	20	F	None	17Se02Jf
Catherine	18	F	None	17Se02Jf
BUTLER, Mary	22	F	None	17Se02Jf
William	.00	M	Infant	17Se02Jf
LARGAY, James	28	M	Mechanic	17Se02Jf
MARTIN, Margaret	28	F	None	17Se02Jf
Elizabeth	.00	F	Infant	17Se02Jf
HART, Thomas	25	M	Mechanic	17Se02Jf
SCULLY, John	27	M	Mechanic	17Se02Jf
COURTNAY, Edward	25	M	Mechanic	17Se02Jf
Ellen	20	F	None	17Se02Jf
HART, Eliza	22	F	None	17Se02Jf
MCENTEE, Bridget	24	F	None	17Se02Jf
CROWE, John	30	M	Laborer	17Se02Jf
Margaret	25	F	None	17Se02Jf
Bridget	.00	F	Infant	17Se02Jf
RYAN, Denis	28	M	Laborer	17Se02Jf
Winifred	20	F	None	17Se02Jf
SHERRY, Patt	25	M	Laborer	17Se02Jf
MACKEN, Thomas	20	M	Mechanic	17Se02Jf
MOORE, Sir-John	30	M	Mechanic	17Se02Jf
FORTESQUE, Peter	21	M	Mechanic	17Se02Jf
KELLY, Catherine	20	F	None	17Se02Jf
LAWLER, John	20	M	Laborer	17Se02Jf
MAHER, John	20	M	Mechanic	17Se02Jf
FLANNERY, Hugh	20	M	Laborer	17Se02Jf
DUNNE, Michael	30	M	Mechanic	17Se02Jf
Catherine	25	F	None	17Se02Jf
Biddy	9	F	Child	17Se02Jf
Thomas	6	M	Child	17Se02Jf
William	3	M	Child	17Se02Jf
DOYLE, Denis	25	M	Laborer	17Se02Jf
Bridget	22	F	None	17Se02Jf
POLLARD, Nicholas	28	M	Laborer	17Se02Jf
Anne	22	F	None	17Se02Jf
SUFFRIN, Jane	19	F	None	17Se02Jf
DUNNE, Laurence	24	M	Mechanic	17Se02Jf
CARROLL, Edward	24	M	Mechanic	17Se02Jf
QUINN, Patrick	24	M	Laborer	17Se02Jf
Mary	23	F	None	17Se02Jf
HYNES, John	24	M	Laborer	17Se02Jf
Mary	19	F	None	17Se02Jf

NAMES OF PASSENGERS	AGE	SEX	OCCUPATIONS	DATE PORT SHIP
CARROLL, Betty	20	F	None	17Se02Jf
MCANENY, Thomas	19	M	Laborer	17Se02Jf
MCMAHON, Patt	28	M	Mechanic	17Se02Jf
WARD, Bridget	20	F	None	17Se02Jf
VAUGHAN, Bridget	20	F	None	17Se02Jf
LONG, John	22	M	Laborer	17Se02Jf
CLARKE, John	40	M	Laborer	17Se02Jf
SHEEHAN, John	21	M	Clerk	17Se02Jf
CLEARY, Daniel	22	M	Laborer	17Se02Jf
Ellen	18	F	None	17Se02Jf
MURPHY, Ellen	11	F	None	17Se02Jf
HIGGINS, Thomas	50	M	Mechanic	17Se02Jf
MCGUIRE, Rose	30	F	None	17Se02Jf
KINNEALY, Biddy	30	F	None	17Se02Jf
GRADY, James	30	M	Laborer	17Se02Jf
Jeremiah	23	M	Laborer	17Se02Jf
CRONIN, John	26	M	Laborer	17Se02Jf
Johanna	21	F	None	17Se02Jf
LYNCH, Mathew	25	M	Laborer	17Se02Jf
Bridget	23	F	None	17Se02Jf
GANNON, James	23	M	Farmer	17Se02Jf
John	20	M	Farmer	17Se02Jf
HARPER, William	55	M	Mechanic	17Se02Jf
Catherine	50	F	None	17Se02Jf
Jane	26	F	None	17Se02Jf
Robert	24	M	Laborer	17Se02Jf
Mary-Anne	20	F	None	17Se02Jf
James	18	M	Mechanic	17Se02Jf
FITZSIMMONS, Mary	35	F	None	17Se02Jf
Philip	18	M	Laborer	17Se02Jf
James	12	M	None	17Se02Jf
Philip	10	M	None	17Se02Jf
Ellen	8	F	None	17Se02Jf
Bryan	6	M	None	17Se02Jf
Anne	4	M	None	17Se02Jf
MARTIN, Thomas	24	M	Laborer	17Se02Jf
FARRELL, Mary	20	F	None	17Se02Jf
MASTERSON, Catherine	19	F	None	17Se02Jf
MADDEN, William	26	M	Laborer	17Se02Jf
Mary	25	F	None	17Se02Jf
Mary	2	F	Child	17Se02Jf
POLLARD, Patrick	30	M	Laborer	17Se02Jf
Mary	23	F	None	17Se02Jf
Mary	30	F	None	17Se02Jf
Margaret	1	F	Child	17Se02Jf
James	.00	M	Infant	17Se02Jf
John	9	M	Child	17Se02Jf
MCGUIRE, Jane	25	F	None	17Se02Jf
BURKE, Michael	35	M	Mechanic	17Se02Jf
CONNELL, James	18	M	Laborer	17Se02Jf
HURLEY, Eliza	35	F	None	17Se02Jf
James	4	M	Child	17Se02Jf
Mary	8	F	Child	17Se02Jf
Michael	6	M	Child	17Se02Jf
DESMOND, Eliza	16	F	None	17Se02Jf
Daniel	21	M	Mechanic	17Se02Jf
Daniel	.00	M	Infant	17Se02Jf
COLEMAN, John	30	M	Mechanic	17Se02Jf
Mary-Anne	30	F	None	17Se02Jf
Anne	.00	F	Infant	17Se02Jf
LEAHY, Mary	30	F	None	17Se02Jf
Mary	50	F	None	17Se02Jf
Ellen	8	F	Child	17Se02Jf
Thomas	7	M	Child	17Se02Jf
John	5	M	Child	17Se02Jf
Daniel	.00	M	Infant	17Se02Jf
CAVANAGH, Hannah	15	F	None	17Se02Jf
FITZGIBBON, Johanna	33	F	None	17Se02Jf
Michael	6	M	Child	17Se02Jf
Robert	4	M	Child	17Se02Jf
OBRIEN, Daniel	25	M	Mechanic	17Se02Jf
GWINN, Ellen	50	F	None	17Se02Jf
Ellen	20	F	None	17Se02Jf
RYAN, John	4	M	Child	17Se02Jf
BASTABLE, Bartholomew	55	M	Laborer	17Se02Jf

NAMES OF PASSENGERS	AGE	SEX	OCCUPATIONS	DATE PORT SHIP
DONNELLY, Mary	20	F	None	17Se02Jf
DALEY, William	16	M	Laborer	17Se02Jf
Maurice	12	M	None	17Se02Jf
Mory	9	U	Child	17Se02Jf
Patrick	7	M	Child	17Se02Jf
MCELLIGOT, Margeret	20	F	None	17Se02Jf
FALVEY, Honora	26	F	None	17Se02Jf
CONNELL, John	20	M	Laborer	17Se02Jf
REGAN, James	25	M	Laborer	17Se02Jf
Catherine	22	F	None	17Se02Jf
HIGGINS, Johanna	40	F	None	17Se02Jf
Mary	30	F	None	17Se02Jf
Eliza	20	F	None	17Se02Jf
EARS, James	36	M	Laborer	17Se02Jf
DAVIES, William	29	M	Mechanic	17Se02Jf
MADDEN, Timothy	28	M	Laborer	17Se02Jf
WALL, Julia	45	F	None	17Se02Jf
LAWLESS, Denis	13	M	Laborer	17Se02Jf
WARD, Mathew	20	M	Laborer	17Se02Jf
GILBRIDE, Mary	24	F	None	17Se02Jf
MARKHAM, John	50	M	Mechanic	17Se02Jf
BOYCE, Margeret	19	F	None	17Se02Jf
KELLY, Margeret	20	F	None	17Se02Jf
MCALEER, Anne	30	F	None	17Se02Jf
MURPHY, Anne	25	F	None	17Se02Jf
BERRIN, Luke	35	M	Laborer	17Se02Jf
KELLY, John	12	M	Laborer	17Se02Jf
Catherine	9	F	Child	17Se02Jf
Margaret	7	F	Child	17Se02Jf
MCGUIRE, Martin	30	M	Laborer	17Se02Jf
HYLAND, Michael	30	M	Laborer	17Se02Jf
CONNELL, Catherine	10	F	None	17Se02Jf
Mary	8	F	Child	17Se02Jf
GALLAHER, John	47	M	Laborer	17Se02Jf
LAWN, Bernard	24	M	Laborer	17Se02Jf
WALSH, Mary	20	F	None	17Se02Jf
ODONNELL, Hannah	25	F	None	17Se02Jf
Mary	3	F	Child	17Se02Jf
Mary	.00	F	Infant	17Se02Jf
CALLAHAN, Sarah	40	F	None	17Se02Jf
Nancy	18	F	None	17Se02Jf
BOYLE, Michael	18	M	None	17Se02Jf
WRIGHT, David	30	M	Mechanic	17Se02Jf
John	12	M	None	17Se02Jf
KANE, Grey	26	M	Laborer	17Se02Jf
GORDON, James	15	M	Laborer	17Se02Jf
ROONEY, John	24	M	Mechanic	17Se02Jf
WALKER, James	45	M	Laborer	17Se02Jf
MCCLUSKEY, Thomas	28	M	Laborer	17Se02Jf
SMITH, William	17	M	Laborer	17Se02Jf
CASEY, Michael	15	M	Laborer	17Se02Jf
Mary	18	F	None	17Se02Jf
LASUNN, Michael	24	M	Laborer	17Se02Jf
KELLY, John	19	M	Laborer	17Se02Jf
Anne	20	F	None	17Se02Jf
Mary	18	F	None	17Se02Jf
Ellen	13	F	None	17Se02Jf
HART, Patrick	18	M	Laborer	17Se02Jf
HANLEY, Joseph	21	M	Laborer	17Se02Jf
BROOSHER, Catherine	3	F	Child	17Se02Jf
FLYNNE, Thomas	20	M	Laborer	17Se02Jf
WREN, Daniel	26	M	Laborer	17Se02Jf
BROODER, Ellen	24	F	None	17Se02Jf
HARTNETT, Patt	26	M	Laborer	17Se02Jf
Ellen	27	F	None	17Se02Jf
ODONNELL, Thomas	25	M	Laborer	17Se02Jf
CONNOR, Margaret	22	F	None	17Se02Jf
FITZGERALD, John	26	M	Laborer	17Se02Jf
OBRIEN, Patrick	19	M	Mechanic	17Se02Jf
PRENDERGAST, Catherine	25	F	None	17Se02Jf
FLOOD, Michael	30	M	Laborer	17Se02Jf
Anne	28	F	None	17Se02Jf
John	7	M	Child	17Se02Jf
Mary	3	F	Child	17Se02Jf
James	.00	M	Infant	17Se02Jf
CARNEY, Ambrose	33	M	Mechanic	17Se02Jf
MCMAHON, Patrick	45	M	Laborer	17Se02Jf
TIERNAN, Bridget	22	F	None	17Se02Jf
Elizabeth	9	F	Child	17Se02Jf
CULLEN, Edward	16	M	Laborer	17Se02Jf
CARBURY, John	40	M	Laborer	17Se02Jf
BANNON, Anne	37	F	None	17Se02Jf
Patrick	16	M	Laborer	17Se02Jf
Mary	14	F	None	17Se02Jf
Catherine	10	F	None	17Se02Jf
Anne	8	F	Child	17Se02Jf
MURTAGH, Peter	13	M	Laborer	17Se02Jf
GRIMES, James	20	M	Laborer	17Se02Jf
CREAMER, Margaret	30	F	None	17Se02Jf
Bridget	10	F	None	17Se02Jf
Mary	6	F	Child	17Se02Jf
Anne	4	F	Child	17Se02Jf
Margaret	2	F	Child	17Se02Jf
MORAN, Ellen	17	F	None	17Se02Jf
MURROUGH, Dominick	25	M	Mechanic	17Se02Jf
JUDGE, James	16	M	Laborer	17Se02Jf
Hannah	10	F	None	17Se02Jf
John	6	M	Child	17Se02Jf
Mary-Anne	4	F	Child	17Se02Jf

MARGARET 17 SEPTEMBER 1849

From Greenock

NAMES OF PASSENGERS	AGE	SEX	OCCUPATIONS	DATE PORT SHIP
MORE, Janet	42	F	Unknown	17Se33Cs
Catherine	13	F	Unknown	17Se33Cs
Agnes	11	F	Unknown	17Se33Cs
Janet	9	F	Child	17Se33Cs
Robert	7	M	Child	17Se33Cs
CAMPBELL, Wilson	34	M	Rope Maker	17Se33Cs
CONNOR, Dennis	22	M	Tailor	17Se33Cs
Janet	20	F	Unknown	17Se33Cs
Janet	.08	F	Infant	17Se33Cs
WYLIE, Janet	26	F	Unknown	17Se33Cs
Eliza	4	F	Child	17Se33Cs
Agnes	2	F	Child	17Se33Cs
THOMSON, John	20	M	Laborer	17Se33Cs
MCKINSROW, John	24	M	Laborer	17Se33Cs
MCDOUGALL, John	16	M	Clerk	17Se33Cs
MURPHY, James	25	M	Laborer	17Se33Cs
ELLIOTT, James	38	M	Officer	17Se33Cs
Isabella	30	F	Unknown	17Se33Cs
MCMAIN, Robert	40	M	Engineer	17Se33Cs
HUTCHINSON, A.	39	M	Merchant	17Se33Cs
Helen	35	F	Unknown	17Se33Cs
William	9	M	Child	17Se33Cs
Christian	7	F	Child	17Se33Cs
George	5	M	Child	17Se33Cs
FRAIL, Margaret	20	F	Servant	17Se33Cs
MCKENZIE, Janet	26	M	Laborer	17Se33Cs
FARGAHAN, John-W.	26	M	Laborer	17Se33Cs
CAMPBELL, Jeamie	20	F	Servant	17Se33Cs
GILCHRISH, Margaret	18	F	Servant	17Se33Cs
MCCULLOCK, John-W.	21	M	Clerk	17Se33Cs
URGUHART, Alex.	21	M	Tailor	17Se33Cs
LANG, Robert	19	M	Joiner	17Se33Cs
ROBERTSON, George	20	M	Gdnr	17Se33Cs
SCOTT, John	32	M	Gdnr	17Se33Cs
SHAW, J.B.	30	M	Merchant	17Se33Cs
Eliza	28	F	Unknown	17Se33Cs
MCKRURY, Bridget	19	F	Servant	17Se33Cs
Marg.Jane	7	F	Child	17Se33Cs
MORISON, David	45	M	Shoemaker	17Se33Cs
WRIGHT, Archa.	20	M	Shoemaker	17Se33Cs

NAMES OF PASSENGERS	AGE	SEX	OCCUPATIONS	DATE PORT SHIP
ROBERTSON, William	54	M	Weaver	17Se33Cs
Christina	42	F	Unknown	17Se33Cs
Robert	.06	M	Infant	17Se33Cs
HUME, James	30	M	Shoemaker	17Se33Cs
MONAGHAN, John	26	M	Shoemaker	17Se33Cs
DUGAN, Bernard	34	M	Shoemaker	17Se33Cs
PRAY, John	15	M	Shoemaker	17Se33Cs
WELSH, John	33	M	Laborer	17Se33Cs
ADAMS, Isabella	22	F	Servant	17Se33Cs
AITKEN, John	20	M	Gdnr	17Se33Cs
HAY, Walter	22	M	Laborer	17Se33Cs
CONNARBY, Henry	22	M	Laborer	17Se33Cs
SMITH, Philip	22	M	Laborer	17Se33Cs
WILSON, Andrew	32	M	Laborer	17Se33Cs
KER, John	31	M	Laborer	17Se33Cs
DOHERTY, Peter	31	M	Laborer	17Se33Cs
GILLESPIE, John	21	M	Laborer	17Se33Cs
MCOWON, Hugh	19	M	Laborer	17Se33Cs
MURRAY, Edward	32	M	Laborer	17Se33Cs
CAMION, Bridget	32	F	Servant	17Se33Cs
DAILEY, William	34	M	Printer	17Se33Cs
LLOYD, John	20	M	Laborer	17Se33Cs
ANDERSON, William	24	M	Weaver	17Se33Cs
WARRINGTON, John	41	M	Laborer	17Se33Cs
Gran-, Andrew	23	M	Laborer	17Se33Cs
NOBLE, William	21	M	Gilder	17Se33Cs
Marg.	21	F	Servant	17Se33Cs
LOWRY, Andrew	28	M	Laborer	17Se33Cs
Mary	28	F	Unknown	17Se33Cs
Eliza	6	F	Child	17Se33Cs
Mary-Ann	4	F	Child	17Se33Cs
MCSHERE, Mary-Jane	16	F	Servant	17Se33Cs
SPALLION, Mary	16	F	Servant	17Se33Cs
MARTIN, Samuel	18	M	Laborer	17Se33Cs
BRAXLEY, John	24	M	Laborer	17Se33Cs
WHITESIDE, Robert	25	M	Laborer	17Se33Cs
Mary	40	F	Unknown	17Se33Cs
MORROW, John	30	M	Laborer	17Se33Cs
CLARK, William	27	M	Baker	17Se33Cs
Thomas	18	M	Baker	17Se33Cs
KERR, Alex.	29	M	Rope Maker	17Se33Cs
STEWART, Rob	40	M	Spinner	17Se33Cs
GRAY, Robert	22	M	Smith	17Se33Cs
MICHELE, Andrew	27	M	Cbtmkr	17Se33Cs
KERR, Henry	25	M	Porter	17Se33Cs
Henry	4	M	Child	17Se33Cs
FITZGERALD, Patk.	20	M	Laborer	17Se33Cs
NOBLE, William	2	M	Child	17Se33Cs
RAWLEY, Prudence	30	F	Unknown	17Se33Cs
GIBSON, William	28	M	Unknown	17Se33Cs
KELLY, Patrick	26	M	Unknown	17Se33Cs
HAMILTON, John	23	M	Laborer	17Se33Cs
NICHOLE, Adam	65	M	Merchant	17Se33Cs

FOREST-KING 17 SEPTEMBER 1849

From Liverpool

NAMES OF PASSENGERS	AGE	SEX	OCCUPATIONS	DATE PORT SHIP
REILEY, Margaret	18	F	None	17Se02LI
BRADY, Beranrd	26	M	Laborer	17Se02LI
KELLY, Christ.	30	M	Laborer	17Se02LI
U-Mrs.	24	F	None	17Se02LI
Wm.	9	M	Child	17Se02LI
KENERDY, Honora	30	F	None	17Se02LI
Edward	8	M	Child	17Se02LI
Thomas	6	M	Child	17Se02LI
Margaret	5	F	Child	17Se02LI
Maria	1	F	Child	17Se02LI
MCGIRCK, James	24	M	Laborer	17Se02LI
BRENNAN, Michael	40	F	Farmer	17Se02LI
HEVNEY, Michael	24	F	Farmer	17Se02LI
MCMARON, Mary	20	F	None	17Se02LI
James	.00	M	Infant	17Se02LI
BRENNON, Daniel	30	M	Grocer	17Se02LI
U-Mrs.	28	F	None	17Se02LI
Daniel	6	M	Child	17Se02LI
Thomas	5	M	Child	17Se02LI
Mary-Ann	3	F	Child	17Se02LI
John	.00	M	Infant	17Se02LI
John	19	M	Laborer	17Se02LI
LATHY, Celia	22	F	None	17Se02LI
DONOVAN, James	26	M	Gdnr	17Se02LI
LANAGAN, James	29	M	Laborer	17Se02LI
Anty	25	F	None	17Se02LI
James	4	M	Child	17Se02LI
Thomas	3	M	Child	17Se02LI
John	.00	M	Infant	17Se02LI
WHELAN, Michael	27	M	Laborer	17Se02LI
NORTON, Daniel	37	M	Laborer	17Se02LI
SHANNARAN, Danl.	26	M	Laborer	17Se02LI
HICKEY, Daniel	28	M	Laborer	17Se02LI
WALSH, Margaret	22	F	None	17Se02LI
LEWES, U-Mrs.	24	F	None	17Se02LI
HICKEY, Thomas	6	M	Child	17Se02LI
RYAN, James	22	M	Miner	17Se02LI
Bridget	23	F	None	17Se02LI
CONNELL, James	18	M	Miner	17Se02LI
Eliza	20	F	None	17Se02LI
Anne	15	F	None	17Se02LI
Daniel	12	M	None	17Se02LI
OBRIEN, James	22	M	Shoemaker	17Se02LI
MCCARATH, Michael	40	M	Hawker	17Se02LI
OHARA, Jane	30	F	None	17Se02LI
MCCARROT, Anne	50	F	None	17Se02LI
Thomas	5	M	Child	17Se02LI
Alice	4	F	Child	17Se02LI
Jane	2	F	Child	17Se02LI
CORTOHE, Mary	17	F	None	17Se02LI
KENEDY, Mary-Ann	24	F	None	17Se02LI
John	.00	M	Infant	17Se02LI
ODONNELL, Maria	15	F	None	17Se02LI
Elizabeth	13	F	None	17Se02LI
MONTFORD, U	18	M	Unknown	17Se02LI
MCCOSERT, Ann	21	F	None	17Se02LI
GARNER, James	32	M	Laborer	17Se02LI
Agnes	27	F	None	17Se02LI
Agnes	3	F	Child	17Se02LI
Anne-Jane	6	F	Child	17Se02LI
Sarah	.00	F	Infant	17Se02LI
MCCARNEY, Catherine	22	F	None	17Se02LI
MARRON, Francis	22	M	Laborer	17Se02LI
Catherine	28	F	None	17Se02LI
LEMON, Catherine	18	F	None	17Se02LI
DONOHUE, Ellen	18	F	None	17Se02LI
MCMARRON, Mary	19	F	None	17Se02LI
MURPHY, John	40	M	Laborer	17Se02LI
DAY, Wm.	20	M	Laborer	17Se02LI
GROMLEY, Margaret	16	F	None	17Se02LI
FARRAL, John	20	M	Laborer	17Se02LI
MORRIS, Rita	20	F	None	17Se02LI
DEVENEY, Jane	20	F	None	17Se02LI
KELLEY, Marcella	20	F	Laborer	17Se02LI
MURTAGH, Hugh	40	M	Laborer	17Se02LI
Rose	20	F	None	17Se02LI
MANAFRY, James	21	M	Laborer	17Se02LI
ENNIS, Patrick	30	M	Laborer	17Se02LI
John	4	M	Child	17Se02LI
U-Mrs.	25	F	None	17Se02LI
Thomas	3	M	Child	17Se02LI
James	.00	M	Infant	17Se02LI
MCMARON, Anne	18	F	None	17Se02LI
Rose	16	F	None	17Se02LI
HUGHES, Edward	19	M	Laborer	17Se02LI
MCCLARREN, James	37	M	Laborer	17Se02LI

NAMES OF PASSENGERS	AGE	SEX	OCCUPATIONS	DATE PORT SHIP
MCCLARREN, James	5	M	Child	17Se02LI
James	10	M	Child	17Se02LI
Mary	30	F	None	17Se02LI
RINGWOOD, Mary	28	F	None	17Se02LI
Joseph	.00	M	Infant	17Se02LI
SPLANE, Morgan	22	M	Laborer	17Se02LI
James	18	M	Laborer	17Se02LI
John	18	M	Laborer	17Se02LI
Alice	20	F	None	17Se02LI
BRADY, John	19	M	Laborer	17Se02LI
CARTY, Patrick	22	M	Laborer	17Se02LI
Catherine	21	F	None	17Se02LI
ROMNEY, Patrick	35	M	Mason	17Se02LI
Hugh	22	M	Miner	17Se02LI
ADAMS, Jones	25	M	Laborer	17Se02LI
GLEISON, Bridget	15	F	None	17Se02LI
DONNEGAN, Eugene	22	M	Laborer	17Se02LI
Ellen	20	F	Laborer	17Se02LI
LAW, Eliza	23	F	Laborer	17Se02LI
Eliza	6	F	Child	17Se02LI
GAWRAN, James	45	M	Laborer	17Se02LI
Jane	38	F	None	17Se02LI
Biddy	20	F	None	17Se02LI
Michael	17	M	Laborer	17Se02LI
Mary	15	F	None	17Se02LI
Eliza	13	F	None	17Se02LI
Barnard	11	M	None	17Se02LI
James	9	M	Child	17Se02LI
Anne	7	F	Child	17Se02LI
Matt.	2	F	Child	17Se02LI
CALBERT, John	20	M	Laborer	17Se02LI
Bridget	23	F	None	17Se02LI
DUNPHY, John	28	M	Farmer	17Se02LI
HANLEY, Bridget	23	F	None	17Se02LI
Patrick	.00	M	Infant	17Se02LI
FOLEY, Patt	22	M	Clerk	17Se02LI
HEANEY, Michael	30	M	Weaver	17Se02LI
MACGRATH, Edward	54	M	Weaver	17Se02LI
Rose	49	F	None	17Se02LI
DOWD, Joseph	24	M	Laborer	17Se02LI
BRISLAHAN, Ellen	20	F	Shoemaker	17Se02LI
CRONAN, Edmund	30	M	Laborer	17Se02LI
HOWARD, Mary	22	F	None	17Se02LI
DESMOND, Mary	24	F	None	17Se02LI
HURLEHY, James	18	M	Laborer	17Se02LI
Ann	22	F	None	17Se02LI
KENNEDY, Patt	33	M	Carpenter	17Se02LI
MURPHY, U-Mrs.	25	F	None	17Se02LI
SHERIDAN, Thos.	35	M	Gdnr·	17Se02LI
Hugh	34	M	Gdnr	17Se02LI
OHARA, Johanna	24	F	None	17Se02LI
GLEESON, Mary	11	F	None	17Se02LI
Cornelius	13	M	None	17Se02LI
TIERNAN, Patrick	34	M	Laborer	17Se02LI
MURPHY, Daniel	24	M	Laborer	17Se02LI
CAHILL, Lawrence	40	M	Laborer	17Se02LI
MURPHY, Thomas	22	M	Laborer	17Se02LI
MCCARTNEY, Elizabeth	41	F	None	17Se02LI
William	6	F	Child	17Se02LI
CORNELL, Johanna	17	F	None	17Se02LI
PENDERGAST, Wm.	20	M	Laborer	17Se02LI
Thos.	5	M	Child	17Se02LI
Anne	4	F	Laborer	17Se02LI
DUNPHY, Catherine	20	F	None	17Se02LI
BURKE, Patt	26	M	Laborer	17Se02LI
BRISLAHAN, Michael	30	M	Laborer	17Se02LI
ROBINSON, D.	00	M	Unknown	17Se02LI
U (W)	00	F	Unknown	17Se02LI
U	.00	U	Infant	17Se02LI

KINGSTON 18 SEPTEMBER 1849

From Liverpool

NAMES OF PASSENGERS	AGE	SEX	OCCUPATIONS	DATE PORT SHIP
CAMPBELL, John	20	M	Unknown	18Se02Pp
DORMBY, Susan	20	F	Servant	18Se02Pp
LINDSAY, Hugh	11	M	Child	18Se02Pp
Morris	11	M	Child	18Se02Pp
OSULLIVAN, Michl.	23	M	Laborer	18Se02Pp
FITZGERALD, Pat	40	M	Laborer	18Se02Pp
PARTY, Morgan	36	M	Laborer	18Se02Pp
DONOVAN, Wm.	36	M	Laborer	18Se02Pp
MALONEY, Rodger	34	M	Laborer	18Se02Pp
LYNCH, John	22	M	Tailor	18Se02Pp
DANIEL, Thos.	24	M	Laborer	18Se02Pp
EGON, Bridget	25	F	Servant	18Se02Pp
KEATING, John	50	M	Laborer	18Se02Pp
U-Mrs.	50	F	None	18Se02Pp
Catherine	10	F	Child	18Se02Pp
Michael	7	M	Child	18Se02Pp
HINDS, Richd.	26	M	Laborer	18Se02Pp
Anasterak	16	F	Servant	18Se02Pp
CAINON, Jane	50	F	Wi	18Se02Pp
OCONNOR, Philip	24	M	Laborer	18Se02Pp
Johanna	21	F	Servant	18Se02Pp
Thomas	18	M	Servant	18Se02Pp
Maurice	27	M	Carpenter	18Se02Pp
MURPHY, John	60	M	Unknown	18Se02Pp
Eliza	30	F	Servant	18Se02Pp
KEARNEY, Bridget	8	F	Child	18Se02Pp
SLAVEN, Andrew	27	M	Laborer	18Se02Pp
MCCABE, Barry	43	M	Laborer	18Se02Pp
KARLING, Philip	20	M	Laborer	18Se02Pp
BURNS, John	25	M	Carpenter	18Se02Pp
KEARNS, Wm.	24	M	Laborer	18Se02Pp
ROACH, Anthony	17	M	Laborer	18Se02Pp
STEIN, John	20	M	Carpenter	18Se02Pp
CAMPBELL, Robt.	21	M	Laborer	18Se02Pp
MCADEN, Robt.	22	M	Laborer	18Se02Pp
BOYLE, Wm.	19	M	Saddler	18Se02Pp
Danl.	18	M	Saddler	18Se02Pp
DOUGHERTY, Mary-Ann	21	F	Servant	18Se02Pp
BOYLE, Rosanna	19	F	Servant	18Se02Pp
HAGGERTY, Betty	18	F	Servant	18Se02Pp
CUNNINGHAM, Thomas	38	M	Laborer	18Se02Pp
KELLY, Peter	36	M	Laborer	18Se02Pp
MCCABE, John	19	M	Laborer	18Se02Pp
MANSFIELD, Mary-Ann	22	F	Servant	18Se02Pp
GREEN, Ann	20	F	Dressmaker	18Se02Pp
CURRIE, Eliza	15	F	Servant	18Se02Pp
GILL, Adm.	44	M	Unknown	18Se02Pp
DONNELLY, Ann	22	F	Servant	18Se02Pp
DEULIN, Terry	47	M	Laborer	18Se02Pp
CURTIN, Thomas	22	M	Laborer	18Se02Pp
MCGALLIGAN, Michael	30	M	Laborer	18Se02Pp
CADMAN, Philip	26	M	Laborer	18Se02Pp
HALE, Bridget	40	F	Wife	18Se02Pp
David	12	M	Child	18Se02Pp
Michael	10	M	Child	18Se02Pp
Mary	6	F	Child	18Se02Pp
OBRIEN, Jacob	30	M	Laborer	18Se02Pp
George	13	M	Child	18Se02Pp
Robert	.00	M	Infant	18Se02Pp
Hester	30	F	Servant	18Se02Pp
Nancy	10	F	Child	18Se02Pp
Hannah	9	F	Child	18Se02Pp
MAHON, Mathew	15	M	Laborer	18Se02Pp
Thos.	11	M	Child	18Se02Pp
Patrick	10	M	Child	18Se02Pp

NAMES OF PASSENGERS	AGE	SEX	OCCUPATIONS	DATE PORT SHIP
MAHON, Eliza	9	F	Child	18Se02Pp
Ann	14	F	Child	18Se02Pp
BURCHEN, Johanna	22	F	Dressmaker	18Se02Pp
LYNCH, Ann	19	F	Servant	18Se02Pp
WELCH, Mary-Ann	21	F	Dressmaker	18Se02Pp
NEALE, Mary	30	F	Servant	18Se02Pp
LUSH, Margaret	42	F	Wi	18Se02Pp
Maria	16	F	Child	18Se02Pp
Eliza	13	F	Child	18Se02Pp
Ann	10	F	Child	18Se02Pp
MARDISH, Eliza	52	F	Wife	18Se02Pp
GLENTON, Wm.	19	M	Clerk	18Se02Pp
Mary-Ann	23	F	Wife	18Se02Pp
VERNON, John	33	M	Shoemaker	18Se02Pp
Ann	62	F	Wi	18Se02Pp
STERLING, John	4	M	Child	18Se02Pp
Alexr.	12	M	Child	18Se02Pp
LANNANGAN, Thos.	30	M	Gdnr	18Se02Pp
MAHER, Margaret	24	F	Servant	18Se02Pp
DOYLE, Mary	28	F	Servant	18Se02Pp
NEILL, Catherine	22	F	Servant	18Se02Pp
BOGAN, Jas.	23	M	Laborer	18Se02Pp
Eliza	24	F	Servant	18Se02Pp
KINGHTEN, Robt.	40	M	Laborer	18Se02Pp
GALLIGAN, Margaret	20	F	Wife	18Se02Pp
Grace	4	F	Child	18Se02Pp
HUNT, Wm.	42	M	Laborer	18Se02Pp
U-Mrs.	42	F	Wife	18Se02Pp
Luke	19	M	Laborer	18Se02Pp
William	17	M	Laborer	18Se02Pp
Mary	10	F	Child	18Se02Pp
Elizabeth	5	F	Child	18Se02Pp
SULLIVAN, Cornelius	5	M	Child	18Se02Pp
SINGHTER, Johanna	25	F	Servant	18Se02Pp
GRIPPEN, James	40	M	Laborer	18Se02Pp
CASHAN, Pat	30	M	Laborer	18Se02Pp
RIDDEN, John	20	M	Smith	18Se02Pp
LANNAGAN, Pat	20	M	Laborer	18Se02Pp
CALLIGIN, Dennis	32	M	Laborer	18Se02Pp
ENRIGHT, Bridget	20	F	Servant	18Se02Pp
John	36	M	Laborer	18Se02Pp
Margaret	36	F	Wife	18Se02Pp
Mary	2	F	Child	18Se02Pp
GEELY, Mary	22	F	Servant	18Se02Pp
LANDERS, Mary	21	F	Wife	18Se02Pp
ALEVIGAN, Margaret	21	F	Servant	18Se02Pp
Johanna	17	F	Servant	18Se02Pp
HENRIGHT, John	28	M	Laborer	18Se02Pp
Margaret	28	F	Wife	18Se02Pp
Bridget	2	F	Child	18Se02Pp
James	7	M	Child	18Se02Pp
KANNADY, John	25	M	Laborer	18Se02Pp
CAUNE, Michael	47	M	Laborer	18Se02Pp
CARLE, Jas.	14	M	Child	18Se02Pp
Patty	34	F	Wi	18Se02Pp
Eliza	11	F	Child	18Se02Pp
Daniel	7	M	Child	18Se02Pp
James	.00	M	Infant	18Se02Pp
MURPHY, Margaret	59	F	Servant	18Se02Pp
NEVIN, John	20	M	Tailor	18Se02Pp
Hugh	9	M	Child	18Se02Pp
Catherine	8	F	Child	18Se02Pp
JOHNSTON, Wm.	16	M	Laborer	18Se02Pp
JOHNSON, Jas.	14	M	Child	18Se02Pp
Robt.	12	M	Child	18Se02Pp
Mary-Ann	15	F	Child	18Se02Pp
Mary	8	F	Child	18Se02Pp
HUGHES, John	23	M	Laborer	18Se02Pp
DILLON, John	23	M	None	18Se02Pp
HUGHES, John	21	M	Miner	18Se02Pp
MCBRIDE, John	23	M	Miner	18Se02Pp
FRUSE, Margaret	21	F	Dressmaker	18Se02Pp
MORNE, Sarah	26	F	Wi	18Se02Pp
Jas.	5	M	Child	18Se02Pp
Sarah-Frances	22	F	Servant	18Se02Pp

NAMES OF PASSENGERS		AGE	SEX	OCCUPATIONS	DATE PORT SHIP
KELLY, Margaret		45	F	Wife	18Se02Pp
Bridget		5	F	Child	18Se02Pp
WELSH, Bridget		21	F	Servant	18Se02Pp
BURNS, Chs.		35	M	Laborer	18Se02Pp
Catherine		33	F	Wife	18Se02Pp
Edward		.00	M	Infant	18Se02Pp
GOOD, James		60	M	Laborer	18Se02Pp
Jane		50	F	Wife	18Se02Pp
Thos.		14	M	Child	18Se02Pp
John		22	M	Laborer	18Se02Pp
Margaret		10	F	Child	18Se02Pp
CONNELL, Daniel		20	M	Laborer	18Se02Pp
Mary		20	F	Servant	18Se02Pp
CONOR, Ann		20	F	Servant	18Se02Pp
Mary		7	F	Child	18Se02Pp
Margaret		5	F	Child	18Se02Pp
Johanna		.00	F	Infant	18Se02Pp
GILLIGAN, John		45	M	Laborer	18Se02Pp
Mary		40	F	Wife	18Se02Pp
Alice		18	F	None	18Se02Pp
MOORE, Susan		35	F	Wife	18Se02Pp
Ann-Jane		4	F	Child	18Se02Pp
Eliza		2	F	Child	18Se02Pp
U		.00	U	Infant	18Se02Pp
GILLIGAN, Mary		17	F	Servant	18Se02Pp
Annen		12	M	Child	18Se02Pp
Joseph		7	M	Child	18Se02Pp
BURNS, Francis		18	M	Laborer	18Se02Pp
Bridget		50	F	Wi	18Se02Pp
BYRON, Thos.		44	M	Laborer	18Se02Pp
John		20	M	Laborer	18Se02Pp
Dennis		14	M	Laborer	18Se02Pp
Sally		40	F	Wife	18Se02Pp
Charles		7	M	Child	18Se02Pp
MAHAN, Mary		40	F	Servant	18Se02Pp
SEYMOUR, Wm.		22	M	Clerk	18Se02Pp
Agnes		20	F	Wife	18Se02Pp
BROWNING, James		22	M	Clerk	18Se02Pp
BLAKE, Margaret		45	F	Wi	18Se02Pp
Henrietta	(D)	15	F	None	18Se02Pp
COLLUM, Ann		18	F	Servant	18Se02Pp
HAMMILL, Richard		20	M	Laborer	18Se02Pp
ALLEN, Andrew		21	M	Laborer	18Se02Pp
MCCODMICK, Alice		13	M	Servant	18Se02Pp
BYRNE, Peter		27	M	Laborer	18Se02Pp
Bridget		9	F	Child	18Se02Pp

SUSAN 19 SEPTEMBER 1849

From Glasgow

NAMES OF PASSENGERS		AGE	SEX	OCCUPATIONS	DATE PORT SHIP
CAMERON, William		25	M	Laborer	19Se04Oc
DUNCAN, Mary		40	F	Wife	19Se04Oc
James		21	M	Miner	19Se04Oc
John		14	M	Miner	19Se04Oc
George		12	M	Miner	19Se04Oc
CAIRNS, Elizabeth		19	F	None	19Se04Oc
ADAMS, John		25	M	Tailor	19Se04Oc
QUINN, Peter		25	M	Tailor	19Se04Oc
WADDELL, John		24	M	Farmer	19Se04Oc
U	(W)	23	F	None	19Se04Oc
Clementina	(D)	5	F	Child	19Se04Oc
Isabella	(D)	4	F	Child	19Se04Oc
George	(S)	13	M	None	19Se04Oc
James	(S)	.11	M	Infant	19Se04Oc
U, Judy-Mrs.		60	F	None	19Se04Oc
POLLOCK, Isabella		32	F	Wife	19Se04Oc
Agnes	(D)	18	F	None	19Se04Oc
Isabella	(D)	8	F	Child	19Se04Oc

NAMES OF PASSENGERS		AGE	SEX	OCCUPATIONS	DATE PORT SHIP
POLLOCK, Samuel	(S)	6	M	Child	19Se040c
Mary	(D)	2	F	Child	19Se040c
CARRIGAN, James		30	M	Plasterer	19Se040c
WHEELER, Margt.Mrs.		30	F	None	19Se040c
CARRIGAN, Andrew		25	M	Laborer	19Se040c
MURRAY, Rose		24	F	Wife	19Se040c
Mary-Jane	(D)	3	F	Wife	19Se040c
Theresa	(D)	.10	F	Infant	19Se040c
FRASER, U-Mrs.		40	F	Wife	19Se040c
MCMURRY, John		24	F	Weaver	19Se040c
PRENTICE, Margt.		22	F	Wife	19Se040c
James	(S)	2	M	Child	19Se040c
MAXWELL, Archibald		19	M	Laborer	19Se040c
SNEDDIN, Janet		18	F	None	19Se040c
BERRIE, John		30	M	Engineer	19Se040c
FRELTON, Mary		3	F	Daughter	19Se040c
DUNNING, Peter		30	F	Tailor	19Se040c
Elizabeth	(W)	24	F	None	19Se040c
FULTON, David		53	M	Miner	19Se040c
Catherine	(W)	55	F	None	19Se040c
David		25	M	Miner	19Se040c
Mary	(W)	25	F	None	19Se040c
Alexander		20	M	None	19Se040c
WATT, Barbara		28	F	Wife	19Se040c
James	(S)	5	M	Child	19Se040c
William	(S)	3	M	Child	19Se040c
LOVE, David		20	M	Farmer	19Se040c
WHITE, Thomas		24	M	Merchant	19Se040c
BLACK, James		18	M	Joiner	19Se040c
LONG, William		28	M	Bleacher	19Se040c
PATTERSON, James		27	M	Engineer	19Se040c
Margaret	(W)	27	F	None	19Se040c
Margaret	(D)	5	F	Child	19Se040c
Jane	(D)	.10	F	Infant	19Se040c
CALDER, John		22	M	Engineer	19Se040c
PHILLIPS, John		24	M	Laborer	19Se040c
BORLAND, Mary		34	M	Wife	19Se040c
Agnes	(D)	12	F	None	19Se040c
James	(S)	10	M	Child	19Se040c
George	(S)	8	M	Child	19Se040c
Euphemia	(D)	6	F	Child	19Se040c
Archibald	(S)	1	M	Child	19Se040c
MCKENZIE, Robert-G.		24	M	Merchant	19Se040c
U-Mrs.		20	F	None	19Se040c
FILMOUR, Janet		20	F	None	19Se040c
NICHOLSON, John		28	M	Joiner	19Se040c
MAY, Michael		28	M	Laborer	19Se040c
WHITE, Catherine		24	F	Wife	19Se040c
FULTON, Catherine		1	F	Daughter	19Se040c
WATT, Peter		.11	M	Infant	19Se040c

LONDON 19 SEPTEMBER 1849

From St.JOHNS,N.B.

NAMES OF PASSENGERS	AGE	SEX	OCCUPATIONS	DATE PORT SHIP
DUGAN, Bryan	30	M	Mchtcl	19Se61Ju
Jane	25	F	None	19Se61Ju
John	7	M	Child	19Se61Ju
Margaret	5	F	Child	19Se61Ju

OHIO 20 SEPTEMBER 1849

From Galway

NAMES OF PASSENGERS	AGE	SEX	OCCUPATIONS	DATE PORT SHIP
STOUNTON, Margaret	30	F	Unknown	20Se06Pw
Bridget	13	F	Unknown	20Se06Pw
Andrew	12	M	Unknown	20Se06Pw
FALRY, Catherine	24	F	Unknown	20Se06Pw
BURK, Catherine	25	F	Unknown	20Se06Pw
QUIRK, Ann	18	F	Unknown	20Se06Pw
GORMAN, Harriet	14	F	Unknown	20Se06Pw
Celia	13	F	Unknown	20Se06Pw
GRIFFIN, Kitty	24	F	Unknown	20Se06Pw
Thomas	3	M	Child	20Se06Pw
FLYNN, Catherine	35	F	Unknown	20Se06Pw
HIGHLAND, Connor	6	M	Child	20Se06Pw
Bridget	4	F	Child	20Se06Pw
Mary	2	F	Child	20Se06Pw
CORR, John	17	M	Tailor	20Se06Pw
Patt	16	M	Shoemaker	20Se06Pw
COFFEE, Patt	18	M	Laborer	20Se06Pw
MORRISSON, Bridget	30	F	Unknown	20Se06Pw
DAVERN, Julia	22	F	Unknown	20Se06Pw
LYNCH, Martin	24	M	Laborer	20Se06Pw
HAWKINS, Peter	30	M	Laborer	20Se06Pw
KELLY, Maria	15	F	Unknown	20Se06Pw
Catherine	12	F	Unknown	20Se06Pw
KESSION, Maria	69	F	Unknown	20Se06Pw
MULHOLLEN, Ellen	25	F	Unknown	20Se06Pw
JORDAN, Biddy	35	F	Unknown	20Se06Pw
Pat	8	M	Child	20Se06Pw
QUINN, Mary	22	F	Unknown	20Se06Pw
HUSSION, Bridget	15	F	Unknown	20Se06Pw
CASSIDY, John	33	M	Laborer	20Se06Pw
CONWAY, Bridget	24	F	Unknown	20Se06Pw
MANIN, Michael	23	M	Laborer	20Se06Pw
OLOUGHLIN, Lawrence	30	M	Laborer	20Se06Pw
MONNION, Catherine	23	F	Unknown	20Se06Pw
MURPHY, Honour	40	F	Unknown	20Se06Pw
Bridget	20	F	Unknown	20Se06Pw
Catherine	18	F	Unknown	20Se06Pw
Margt.	14	F	Unknown	20Se06Pw
Patt	13	M	Unknown	20Se06Pw
Mary	12	F	Unknown	20Se06Pw
MONNION, Margt.	19	F	Unknown	20Se06Pw
HART, Ellen	30	F	Unknown	20Se06Pw
Bridget	19	F	Unknown	20Se06Pw
DEVINE, Honour	22	F	Unknown	20Se06Pw
KELLY, William	30	M	Unknown	20Se06Pw
BURK, John	26	M	Laborer	20Se06Pw
FAHEY, Thomas	20	M	Shopman	20Se06Pw
CAHILL, Honoria	30	F	Unknown	20Se06Pw
JENNINGS, Ellen	49	F	Unknown	20Se06Pw
GREEN, Bridget	20	F	Unknown	20Se06Pw
MADDEN, Margt.	49	F	Unknown	20Se06Pw
LAWRENCE, William	27	M	Laborer	20Se06Pw
GERAGHTY, Catherine	23	F	Unknown	20Se06Pw
LAMON, Catherine	28	F	Unknown	20Se06Pw
SHEAY, Michael	20	M	Laborer	20Se06Pw
MCGUIRE, Mary	21	F	Unknown	20Se06Pw
HALLORAN, Bridget	22	F	Unknown	20Se06Pw
MELEN, John	30	M	Laborer	20Se06Pw
CONOLLY, Maria	18	F	Unknown	20Se06Pw
WALSH, Francis	18	M	Laborer	20Se06Pw
COYNE, Thomas	34	M	Victualler	20Se06Pw
MOONEY, Anne	18	F	Unknown	20Se06Pw
Bridget	12	F	Unknown	20Se06Pw
KEOGH, Mary-Ann	12	F	Unknown	20Se06Pw
GILL, Catherine	18	F	Unknown	20Se06Pw

NAMES OF PASSENGERS	AGE	SEX	OCCUPATIONS	DATE PORT SHIP
HAMFY, Catherine	38	F	Unknown	20Se06Pw
DOOLEY, Mary	24	F	Unknown	20Se06Pw
DEVINE, Timothy	29	M	Laborer	20Se06Pw
Catherine	29	F	Unknown	20Se06Pw
ROBIT, Patt	22	M	Laborer	20Se06Pw
MAHON, Patt	24	M	Laborer	20Se06Pw
HAIRE, Anne	20	F	Unknown	20Se06Pw
MULLIN, Mary	26	F	Unknown	20Se06Pw
Biddy	18	F	Unknown	20Se06Pw
Richard	15	M	Unknown	20Se06Pw
BURK, Mary	30	F	Unknown	20Se06Pw
HYNES, Bertho	23	M	Laborer	20Se06Pw
REGAN, Sally	17	F	Unknown	20Se06Pw
LEONARD, Mary	22	F	Unknown	20Se06Pw
BRYON, Honour	23	F	Unknown	20Se06Pw
FAHY, Wm.	26	M	Laborer	20Se06Pw
FARRELL, John	23	M	Laborer	20Se06Pw
HYNES, Biddy	20	F	Unknown	20Se06Pw
LINSKEY, Agnes	21	F	Unknown	20Se06Pw
CLOONAN, Mary	20	F	Unknown	20Se06Pw
MCDONALD, Mary	34	F	Unknown	20Se06Pw
LOFTUS, Michael	7	M	Child	20Se06Pw
MCDONNELL, Patt	.10	M	Infant	20Se06Pw
SPELLMAN, Mary	25	F	Unknown	20Se06Pw
John	7	M	Child	20Se06Pw
KELLEY, Sabina	20	F	Unknown	20Se06Pw
FREEMAN, Biddy	26	F	Unknown	20Se06Pw
BARRETT, Bridget	30	F	Unknown	20Se06Pw
MORGAN, Patt	27	M	Laborer	20Se06Pw
MORAN, James	8	M	Child	20Se06Pw
SULLIVAN, Margt.	22	F	Unknown	20Se06Pw
DOLEY, Ellen	20	F	Unknown	20Se06Pw
COMMONS, Bridget	28	F	Unknown	20Se06Pw
MCDONOUGH, John	4	M	Child	20Se06Pw
KELLY, Honour	18	F	Unknown	20Se06Pw
WELDON, Anne	57	F	Unknown	20Se06Pw
Catherine	26	F	Unknown	20Se06Pw
Anne	10	F	Unknown	20Se06Pw
OMALLEY, Patt	20	M	Tailor	20Se06Pw
WALSH, Margt.	19	F	Unknown	20Se06Pw

PRINCETON 20 SEPTEMBER 1849

From Liverpool

NAMES OF PASSENGERS	AGE	SEX	OCCUPATIONS	DATE PORT SHIP
TAYLOR, James	24	M	Laborer	20Se020e
HOGAN, John	43	M	Laborer	20Se020e
MCGINLEY, Dennis	23	M	Laborer	20Se020e
DONOUGH, Maria	17	M	Domestic	20Se020e
Patrick	13	M	Domestic	20Se020e
MCDONALD, Wm.	27	M	Stctr	20Se020e
Julia	25	F	Cook	20Se020e
LAFFEY, Michael	48	M	Sawer	20Se020e
COTTER, James	30	M	Laborer	20Se020e
Margaret	50	F	Domestic	20Se020e
GAREY, Patrick	50	M	Laborer	20Se020e
BROGAN, Michael	40	M	Laborer	20Se020e
Bridget	40	F	Wife	20Se020e
Maria	9	F	Child	20Se020e
Edward	7	M	Child	20Se020e
Bridget	20	F	Domestic	20Se020e
GALLAGHAN, Thos.	30	M	Clerk	20Se020e
Mary	18	F	Dressmaker	20Se020e
Mary	17	F	Domestic	20Se020e
GERATY, Patrick	20	M	Farmer	20Se020e
REILLY, Philip	20	M	Laborer	20Se020e
DONALLY, Michl.	16	M	Carpenter	20Se020e
John	9	M	Child	20Se020e
EDWARDS, Keron	42	M	Laborer	20Se020e
LEONARD, James	27	M	Laborer	20Se020e
POTTS, Mary	20	F	Domestic	20Se020e
BURKE, Alice	45	F	Wife	20Se020e
GLANCY, Mary	14	F	Domestic	20Se020e
MCKEIVAN, Elizth.	20	F	Domestic	20Se020e
NAUGHTON, Wm.	28	M	Carpenter	20Se020e
GALVIN, James	22	M	Laborer	20Se020e
DONAHU, Danl.	30	M	Laborer	20Se020e
Owen	18	M	Laborer	20Se020e
SCOTT, Wm.	40	M	Laborer	20Se020e
CLARK, Owen	38	M	Laborer	20Se020e
BOYLE, Mary	32	F	Wife	20Se020e
Thomas	9	M	Child	20Se020e
Mary	7	F	Child	20Se020e
Timothy	3	M	Child	20Se020e
GALVIN, Ann	24	F	Domestic	20Se020e
Mary	24	F	Domestic	20Se020e
NAUGHTON, Mary	18	F	Domestic	20Se020e
REYNOLDS, Thomas	30	M	Laborer	20Se020e
CAREN, Mary	19	F	Laborer	20Se020e
HUGHES, Mary	17	F	Wife	20Se020e
WHEELAHAN, Mathew	54	M	Carpenter	20Se020e
Margaret	34	F	Carpenter	20Se020e
Charles	48	M	Laborer	20Se020e
Patrick	8	M	Child	20Se020e
James	6	M	Child	20Se020e
Julia	14	F	Domestic	20Se020e
Ann	4	F	Child	20Se020e
Bridget	2	F	Child	20Se020e
HYNES, Patrick	19	M	Waiter	20Se020e
FOX, Martin	30	M	Laborer	20Se020e
DUFFY, Michael	18	M	Laborer	20Se020e
MCDONALD, Peter	30	M	Farmer	20Se020e
Mary	24	F	Wife	20Se020e
HUGHES, Margaret	23	F	Domestic	20Se020e
MCDONALD, Patrick	.08	M	Infant	20Se020e
WEST, Mary	28	F	Wife	20Se020e
DWYER, Mary	49	F	Domestic	20Se020e
David	32	M	Clerk	20Se020e
CAMMESKEY, Bridget	48	F	Cook	20Se020e
MCMAHON, Tim.	46	M	Maurer	20Se020e
Mary	36	F	Wife	20Se020e
Patrick	17	M	Maurer	20Se020e
Michl.	13	M	Maurer	20Se020e
Lena	1	F	Child	20Se020e
GANLY, Patrick	18	M	Laborer	20Se020e
Thos.	12	M	Laborer	20Se020e
ONEIL, Mary	20	F	Unknown	20Se020e
BURKE, Daniel	20	M	Laborer	20Se020e
HOLLIAN, Sally	13	F	Spinster	20Se020e
Patrick	11	M	None	20Se020e
Luke	9	M	Child	20Se020e
WALKER, Charles	55	M	Farmer	20Se020e
QUINN, Catherine	40	F	Wife	20Se020e
Died-At-Sea				
Mary	10	F	None	20Se020e
Ann	8	F	Child	20Se020e
Catherine	6	F	Child	20Se020e
Patrick	6	M	Child	20Se020e
Francis	3	M	Child	20Se020e
Theresa	.06	F	Infant	20Se020e
TAYLOR, Francis	40	M	Blacksmith	20Se020e
Ann	30	F	Wife	20Se020e
Thomas	13	M	None	20Se020e
Died-At-Sea				
Mary-Ann	8	F	Child	20Se020e
Sarah	6	F	Child	20Se020e
Jane	4	F	Child	20Se020e
Died-At-Sea				
Richard	4	M	Child	20Se020e
TEINEY, Michael	20	M	Laborer	20Se020e
OREILLY, Andrew	15	M	None	20Se020e
Robert	12	M	None	20Se020e
ONEIL, Margaret	12	F	None	20Se020e
TURNER, Sally	15	F	Domestic	20Se020e

NAMES OF PASSENGERS	AGE	SEX	OCCUPATIONS	DATE PORT SHIP
TURNER, Jane	10	F	Domestic	20Se020e
FLANNAGAN, Mary	17	F	Domestic	20Se020e
MCNALLY, Ann	19	F	Domestic	20Se020e
Peter	12	M	Laborer	20Se020e
COVICE, Catherine	19	F	Domestic	20Se020e
MCELROY, Mary	20	F	Domestic	20Se020e
ONEIL, Rose	20	F	Weaver	20Se020e
HORAN, Michael	60	M	Laborer	20Se020e
Died-At-Sea				
BARTON, Michael	34	M	Laborer	20Se020e
Died-At-Sea				
BRIEN, Corndia	30	F	Domestic	20Se020e
GRIFFIN, Ellen	30	F	Wife	20Se020e
Nancy	9	F	Child	20Se020e
Thomas	7	M	Child	20Se020e
John	5	M	Child	20Se020e
Daniel	2	M	Child	20Se020e
GARVIN, Johana	14	F	Spinster	20Se020e
ROARKE, Margaret	60	F	Wife	20Se020e
Died-At-Sea				
Catherine	23	F	Spinster	20Se020e
Died-At-Sea				
MONAGHAN, Patrick	15	M	Laborer	20Se020e
Bridget	14	F	Domestic	20Se020e
MANGAN, Mary	13	F	Domestic	20Se020e
DANKIN, Mark	14	M	Laborer	20Se020e
John	11	M	None	20Se020e
WALSH, Ann	16	F	Domestic	20Se020e
MCANLIFFE, Anthony	21	M	Laborer	20Se020e
KILDERRY, Dennis	20	M	Laborer	20Se020e
HORAN, Patrick	16	M	Laborer	20Se020e
WOOLF, Mary	40	F	Cook	20Se020e
MCGRA, Mary	20	F	Domestic	20Se020e
SULLIVAN, Ellen	22	F	Domestic	20Se020e
CASEY, Biddy	15	F	Domestic	20Se020e
Ellen	19	F	Domestic	20Se020e
HANLEY, Biddy	17	F	Domestic	20Se020e
Ellen	14	F	Domestic	20Se020e
MURRAY, Betty	50	F	Wife	20Se020e
MANAHAN, Lewis	27	M	Shoemaker	20Se020e
HAYES, Maurice	18	M	Butcher	20Se020e
CONNOR, Patrick	21	M	Laborer	20Se020e
GERRY, William	20	M	Wheelwright	20Se020e
Died-At-Sea				
RYAN, Mary	22	F	Domestic	20Se020e
Catherine	18	F	Domestic	20Se020e
GORMAN, Bridget	60	F	Housekeeper	20Se020e
FOLEY, James	27	M	Laborer	20Se020e
GORMAN, Charles	17	M	Coppersmith	20Se020e
Wm.	25	M	Coach Maker	20Se020e
ORRE, Wm.	18	M	Laborer	20Se020e
ADAMS, Ann	18	F	Domestic	20Se020e
KENEDY, Margaret	17	F	Domestic	20Se020e
CALAHAN, Margaret	30	F	Tailor	20Se020e
DOONAN, Catherine	16	F	Domestic	20Se020e
COVLEY, Bridget	15	F	Domestic	20Se020e
Margaret	10	F	None	20Se020e
MOORE, Eliza	23	F	Domestic	20Se020e
MULCAHEY, Patk.	25	M	Laborer	20Se020e
MURPHY, Edward	50	M	Carpenter	20Se020e
John	17	M	Carpenter	20Se020e
KEATING, Mary	43	F	Farmer	20Se020e
Richard	19	M	Farmer	20Se020e
DOYLE, Alice	16	F	Domestic	20Se020e
MCANN, Elizabeth	16	F	Domestic	20Se020e
BROWN, John	56	M	Blacksmith	20Se020e
Julia	28	F	Domestic	20Se020e
John	20	M	Blacksmith	20Se020e
Michael	16	M	Blacksmith	20Se020e
DENNON, Patrick	45	M	Laborer	20Se020e
Ellen	40	F	Domestic	20Se020e
John	14	M	Laborer	20Se020e
Jude	10	M	Laborer	20Se020e
MCCARTY, Mary	40	F	Housekeeper	20Se020e
Gobby	9	F	Child	20Se020e

NAMES OF PASSENGERS	AGE	SEX	OCCUPATIONS	DATE PORT SHIP
MCCARTY, Owen	7	M	Child	20Se020e
Lady	5	F	Child	20Se020e
Died-At-Sea				
GALVIN, Nancy	19	M	Domestic	20Se020e
SCOTT, Timothy	44	M	Laborer	20Se020e
Mary	40	F	Laborer	20Se020e
John	14	M	Laborer	20Se020e
Ellen	10	F	None	20Se020e
Mary	9	F	Child	20Se020e
James	5	M	Child	20Se020e
MURPHY, Michael	50	M	Tailor	20Se020e
Mary	45	F	Tailor	20Se020e
Margaret	20	F	Tailor	20Se020e
Thomas	17	M	Laborer	20Se020e
QUINLAN, Morris	50	M	Laborer	20Se020e
Julia	50	M	Domestic	20Se020e
Michael	19	M	Laborer	20Se020e
Mary	15	F	Domestic	20Se020e
Larry	13	M	Domestic	20Se020e
MOORE, Edwin	50	M	Quarryman	20Se020e
Edwin	22	M	Quarryman	20Se020e
Ellen	53	F	Wife	20Se020e
Biddy	21	F	Domestic	20Se020e
MORRE, John	18	M	Laborer	20Se020e
Jerry	16	M	Laborer	20Se020e
Ellen	14	F	Domestic	20Se020e
SULLIVAN, John	40	M	Laborer	20Se020e
Owen	35	M	Laborer	20Se020e
Catherine	16	F	Domestic	20Se020e
Dennis	10	M	None	20Se020e
John	7	M	Child	20Se020e
Daniel	2	M	Child	20Se020e
SHEA, John	22	M	Laborer	20Se020e
Mary	50	F	Housekeeper	20Se020e
Owen	24	M	Laborer	20Se020e
Biddy	22	F	Domestic	20Se020e
Daniel	19	M	Tailor	20Se020e
John	17	M	Laborer	20Se020e
Catherine	45	F	Housekeeper	20Se020e
John	7	M	Child	20Se020e
Johana	4	F	Child	20Se020e
QUIRK, Michael	46	M	Laborer	20Se020e
Johana	40	F	Wife	20Se020e
Julia	19	F	Spinster	20Se020e
Thomas	17	M	Laborer	20Se020e
John	14	M	Laborer	20Se020e
Johana	11	F	None	20Se020e
Michael	7	M	Child	20Se020e
Catherine	5	F	Child	20Se020e
REILLY, Patrick	18	M	Laborer	20Se020e
SMITH, Brian	18	M	Laborer	20Se020e
Biddy	30	F	Wife	20Se020e
Ann	1	F	Child	20Se020e
COSGROVE, Bridget	28	F	Domestic	20Se020e
MCGOVERN, Biddy	16	F	Domestic	20Se020e
SMITH, Mary	30	F	Wife	20Se020e
Ann	12	F	None	20Se020e
Thomas	10	M	None	20Se020e
LEARY, John	50	M	Laborer	20Se020e
Mary	15	F	Domestic	20Se020e
Daniel	12	M	None	20Se020e
Biddy	10	F	None	20Se020e
Mary	23	F	Domestic	20Se020e
COONAN, Catherine	50	F	Housekeeper	20Se020e
Sally	34	F	Domestic	20Se020e
Catherine	20	F	Domestic	20Se020e
Michael	18	M	Laborer	20Se020e
WALSH, Catherine	20	F	Domestic	20Se020e
SHEA, Daniel	40	M	Laborer	20Se020e
Died-At-Sea				
MCCANN, Thos.	20	M	Shoemaker	20Se020e
Died-At-Sea				
GREEN, Wm.	26	M	Gentleman	20Se020e
MURTAGH, Thomas	16	M	Laborer	20Se020e
WILLIS, Ann	19	F	Domestic	20Se020e

NAMES OF PASSENGERS		AGE	SEX	OCCUPATIONS	DATE PORT SHIP
CALAGHAN, James		6	M	Child	20Se02Oe

ELIJAH-SWIFT 20 SEPTEMBER 1849

From Glasgow

NAMES OF PASSENGERS		AGE	SEX	OCCUPATIONS	DATE PORT SHIP
MCGROSTY, Ann		21	F	Servant	20Se04Gs
CHRISTY, Thos.		35	M	Tailor	20Se04Gs
Agnes		25	F	None	20Se04Gs
Jane		.03	F	Infant	20Se04Gs
DUFFY, Mary		20	F	Servant	20Se04Gs
Charles		19	M	Unknown	20Se04Gs
CRUMPSTON, Eliza		18	F	None	20Se04Gs
Robert		13	M	Unknown	20Se04Gs
Agnes		11	F	None	20Se04Gs
Sarah		8	F	Child	20Se04Gs
William		11	M	None	20Se04Gs
MCCORMICK, Wm.G.		18	M	Servant	20Se04Gs
HIRD, James		23	M	Builder	20Se04Gs
GILLIGAN, Pat		24	M	Servant	20Se04Gs
MCCLURE, Wm.		38	M	Unknown	20Se04Gs
BARCLAY, Jas.		22	M	Unknown	20Se04Gs
Mary		20	F	None	20Se04Gs
Katherine		.11	F	Infant	20Se04Gs

NEW-WORLD 21 SEPTEMBER 1849

From Liverpool

NAMES OF PASSENGERS		AGE	SEX	OCCUPATIONS	DATE PORT SHIP
BRACKEN, Eliza		21	F	Servant	21Se02Hg
Jane		20	F	Servant	21Se02Hg
ONEILL, Chris.		57	M	Servant	21Se02Hg
Julia	(W)	26	F	None	21Se02Hg
FARRELL, James		50	M	Laborer	21Se02Hg
James		30	M	Laborer	21Se02Hg
Christopher		18	M	Laborer	21Se02Hg
MCCALUM, Cathn.		31	F	Wife	21Se02Hg
James		10	M	Child	21Se02Hg
Edward	(S)	5	M	Child	21Se02Hg
LEONARD, James		36	M	Laborer	21Se02Hg
EGAN, Pat		40	M	Laborer	21Se02Hg
James		13	M	Laborer	21Se02Hg
John		11	M	Laborer	21Se02Hg
Eliza		9	F	Child	21Se02Hg
Ellen		7	F	Child	21Se02Hg
Mary		4	F	Child	21Se02Hg
Bernard		1	M	Child	21Se02Hg
DURKIN, Barthm.		50	M	Laborer	21Se02Hg
Mary		40	F	Wife	21Se02Hg
U		.00	U	Infant	21Se02Hg
ROBINSON, Danl.		22	M	Laborer	21Se02Hg
CROW, Bridget		22	F	Servant	21Se02Hg
GLEESON, Wm.		28	M	Laborer	21Se02Hg
CAREY, James		27	M	Laborer	21Se02Hg
Died-At-Sea					
POWELL, Philip		20	M	Laborer	21Se02Hg
CAREY, John		23	M	Gdnr	21Se02Hg
WHELAN, Thos.		20	M	Laborer	21Se02Hg
BRADY, William		16	M	Laborer	21Se02Hg
DONOGHLY, Mary		20	F	Servant	21Se02Hg
PHILLIPS, Thos.		20	M	Laborer	21Se02Hg
GAHAN, Cathn.		22	F	Servant	21Se02Hg
WOODRUFF, John		21	M	Gdnr	21Se02Hg
SLATER, Cathne.		25	F	Servant	21Se02Hg
Ann		23	F	Servant	21Se02Hg
MCCONVILLE, Mary		34	F	Servant	21Se02Hg
ELLIOTT, Ellen		60	F	Unknown	21Se02Hg
MULLIGAN, Ellen		16	F	Servant	21Se02Hg
Cathn.		4	F	Child	21Se02Hg
MCINROE, Ann		3	F	Child	21Se02Hg
MCMANUS, Mary		30	F	Wife	21Se02Hg
Mary	(D)	11	F	None	21Se02Hg
James	(S)	9	M	Child	21Se02Hg
WILSON, Sarah-Ann		44	F	Wife	21Se02Hg
Rebecca	(D)	17	F	None	21Se02Hg
Wm.John	(S)	15	M	None	21Se02Hg
Richard	(S)	11	M	None	21Se02Hg
Sarah	(D)	9	F	Child	21Se02Hg
Eliza-Jane	(D)	6	F	Child	21Se02Hg
Martha	(D)	4	F	Child	21Se02Hg
Marianne	(D)	2	F	Child	21Se02Hg
KENNY, Margt.		23	F	Servant	21Se02Hg
WILLIAMS, Jas.		26	M	Laborer	21Se02Hg
JONES, Thos.		21	M	Blacksmith	21Se02Hg
WILLIAMSON, John		50	M	Clerk	21Se02Hg
Mary	(W)	40	F	None	21Se02Hg
John-George	(S)	11	M	None	21Se02Hg
Robt.Jas.	(S)	10	M	Child	21Se02Hg
SMITH, Margt.		18	F	Servant	21Se02Hg
DOUGHERTY, Mary		40	F	Wife	21Se02Hg
Thos.	(S)	14	M	None	21Se02Hg
BRADY, Cathn.		15	F	Servant	21Se02Hg
DELANY, Michael		20	M	Laborer	21Se02Hg
DOWD, Bridget		20	F	Servant	21Se02Hg
DOYLE, Mary		19	F	Servant	21Se02Hg
TIERNEY, Mary		18	F	Servant	21Se02Hg
HAZLETON, Simon		50	M	Physician	21Se02Hg
Abm.		21	M	Clerk	21Se02Hg
Ann	(D)	24	F	None	21Se02Hg
LYONS, Margt.		21	F	Servant	21Se02Hg
BRODELIN, Mary		25	F	Servant	21Se02Hg
NICHOLS, Adam		20	M	Laborer	21Se02Hg
REID, Philip		20	M	Laborer	21Se02Hg
SYKS, Chas.		25	M	Stctr	21Se02Hg
KEALY, Dennis		27	M	Carpenter	21Se02Hg
Mary		25	F	None	21Se02Hg
BRIEN, Thos.		22	M	Laborer	21Se02Hg
LAWLOR, Elizth.		24	F	Servant	21Se02Hg
FITZPATRICK, Cathn.		24	F	Servant	21Se02Hg
PURCELL, Mary		25	F	Wife	21Se02Hg
John	(S)	11	M	None	21Se02Hg
Richd.	(S)	6	M	Child	21Se02Hg
Bridget	(D)	8	F	Child	21Se02Hg
Ellen	(D)	7	F	Child	21Se02Hg
OHARE, Margt.		25	F	Wife	21Se02Hg
William	(S)	.00	M	Infant	21Se02Hg
CALLEN, U-Mrs.		28	F	Wife	21Se02Hg
HOGAN, Johanna		26	F	Servant	21Se02Hg
CANE, Patrick		22	M	Laborer	21Se02Hg
John		30	M	Laborer	21Se02Hg
Honora	(W)	24	F	None	21Se02Hg
Mary		54	F	None	21Se02Hg
Nichs.	(S)	.00	M	Infant	21Se02Hg
Danl.	(S)	3	M	Child	21Se02Hg
DILLON, Michael		30	M	Shoemaker	21Se02Hg
Margt.	(W)	26	F	None	21Se02Hg
Richard	(S)	3	M	Child	21Se02Hg
Mary	(D)	.00	F	Infant	21Se02Hg
LIDDON, Jim		24	M	Shoemaker	21Se02Hg
CARR, Ann		24	F	Servant	21Se02Hg
DILLON, Honora		24	F	Servant	21Se02Hg
Mary		20	F	Servant	21Se02Hg
CLEARRY, Sarah		20	F	Servant	21Se02Hg
Agnes		18	F	Servant	21Se02Hg
Margt.		16	F	Servant	21Se02Hg
HOLT, John		9	M	Child	21Se02Hg
Fanny		7	F	Child	21Se02Hg
HIGGINS, John		24	M	Maurer	21Se02Hg

NAMES OF PASSENGERS		AGE	SEX	OCCUPATIONS	DATE PORT SHIP
DREW, Michl.		21	M	Maurer	21Se02Hg
CAREY, John		24	M	Laborer	21Se02Hg
MCNALLY, Jas.		26	M	Maurer	21Se02Hg
Ellen	(W)	20	F	None	21Se02Hg
Henry	(S)	.00	M	Infant	21Se02Hg
MCILROY, Chas.		40	M	Chandler	21Se02Hg
Mary	(W)	40	F	None	21Se02Hg
Margt.	(D)	18	F	None	21Se02Hg
MCCARTHY, John		26	M	Laborer	21Se02Hg
GRIBBEN, Ellen		30	F	Servant	21Se02Hg
CUMMINGS, James		45	M	Grocer	21Se02Hg
Fanny	(W)	44	M	None	21Se02Hg
Patrick	(S)	16	M	None	21Se02Hg
Essy	(D)	16	F	None	21Se02Hg
KINAHAN, Ann		14	F	Servant	21Se02Hg
FAGARTY, Margt.		24	F	Servant	21Se02Hg
COYLE, Edward		18	M	Blacksmith	21Se02Hg
GRAHAM, Mary		28	F	Servant	21Se02Hg
Honora		18	F	Servant	21Se02Hg
COAKLEY, Mary		40	F	Servant	21Se02Hg
GERMAN, Maria		21	F	Laborer	21Se02Hg
Timothy		19	M	Laborer	21Se02Hg
DOYLE, U		60	F	Wi	21Se02Hg
SPELLMAN, Jerh.		8	M	Child	21Se02Hg
COSTELLO, Teresa		00	F	Servant	21Se02Hg
WALSH, Michael		21	M	Laborer	21Se02Hg
DONAGHY, Mary-Jane		18	F	Servant	21Se02Hg
Sarah		22	F	Servant	21Se02Hg
MILLER, Sarah		19	F	Servant	21Se02Hg
CLARKE, Ann		20	F	Servant	21Se02Hg
REILLY, James		38	M	Laborer	21Se02Hg
CLAIR, Margt.		12	F	Servant	21Se02Hg
MCENTEGART, Ann		20	F	Servant	21Se02Hg
SMYTH, John		60	M	Coach Maker	21Se02Hg
Margt.	(W)	40	F	None	21Se02Hg
Ellen	(D)	20	F	None	21Se02Hg
Robt.	(S)	19	M	None	21Se02Hg
Joseph	(S)	18	M	None	21Se02Hg
Francis	(S)	16	M	None	21Se02Hg
Margt.	(D)	16	M	None	21Se02Hg
Mary	(D)	10	F	Child	21Se02Hg
Elizth.	(D)	1	F	Child	21Se02Hg
BARKER, Martha		18	F	Servant	21Se02Hg
HOGAN, Sarah-Ann		21	F	Servant	21Se02Hg
LEES, Ann		31	F	Wife	21Se02Hg
Joseph	(S)	7	M	Child	21Se02Hg
Betty	(D)	4	F	Child	21Se02Hg
FARRELL, James		25	M	Painter	21Se02Hg
NOWLAN, James		19	M	Miller	21Se02Hg
ABERNATHY, Richd.		28	M	Shoemaker	21Se02Hg
Eliza	(W)	20	F	None	21Se02Hg
SMYTH, Frank		20	M	Laborer	21Se02Hg
MURPHY, Martin		26	M	Ccmcht	21Se02Hg
HYNES, Michl.		23	M	Baker	21Se02Hg
TULLY, John		19	M	Laborer	21Se02Hg
NOWLAN, Bryan		32	M	Groom	21Se02Hg
TULIAN, John		19	M	Laborer	21Se02Hg
CAREY, Thos.		28	M	Laborer	21Se02Hg
DOOGAN, Michl.		20	M	Laborer	21Se02Hg
MAHER, Jas.		30	M	Laborer	21Se02Hg
Ellen		24	F	Servant	21Se02Hg
Mary		20	F	Servant	21Se02Hg
MCCOY, Andrew		25	M	Gentleman	21Se02Hg
Catherine	(W)	23	F	None	21Se02Hg
Mary	(D)	1	F	Child	21Se02Hg
Ann	(D)	.00	F	Infant	21Se02Hg
MCCALEE, Thos.		21	M	Laborer	21Se02Hg
James		26	M	Laborer	21Se02Hg
MCCARDLE, Ann		40	F	Wife	21Se02Hg
Mary-Ann	(D)	13	F	None	21Se02Hg
Henry	(S)	11	M	None	21Se02Hg
LYNCH, Mary		13	F	Servant	21Se02Hg
GAIGARD, Margt.		25	F	None	21Se02Hg
DENNIGAN, John		25	M	Carpenter	21Se02Hg
GAIGAN, Pat		24	M	Laborer	21Se02Hg
CALLENY, Pat		36	M	Laborer	21Se02Hg
WYLIE, James		20	M	Laborer	21Se02Hg
Mary-Ann	(W)	18	F	None	21Se02Hg
CAREY, Betsey		25	F	Servant	21Se02Hg
MURPHY, James		40	M	Mariner	21Se02Hg
LEONARD, Edwd.		20	M	Laborer	21Se02Hg
WALES, Ann		22	F	Servant	21Se02Hg
MCKEEVER, Mary		17	F	Servant	21Se02Hg
CONNORS, Wm.		45	M	Laborer	21Se02Hg
CORBOY, Ann		24	F	Servant	21Se02Hg
QUIN, Ann		20	F	Servant	21Se02Hg
BUTLER, William		28	M	Baker	21Se02Hg
FAGARTY, Thos.B.		21	M	Laborer	21Se02Hg
PHILAN, Mary-Ann		17	F	Servant	21Se02Hg
DAWSON, Martha		18	F	Servant	21Se02Hg
DONALDSON, Sarah		28	F	Servant	21Se02Hg
MCCOLLUM, Wm.		21	M	Laborer	21Se02Hg
Edwd.		15	M	Laborer	21Se02Hg
STEWART, U-Mrs.		25	F	Wife	21Se02Hg
NEWBURN, Mary		30	F	Wife	21Se02Hg
Margt.	(D)	10	F	Child	21Se02Hg
SANDS, Matilda		26	F	Servant	21Se02Hg
GILMORE, Dennis		21	M	Draper	21Se02Hg
BROWNE, Mary		30	F	Servant	21Se02Hg
ARMSTRONG, George		00	M	Laborer	21Se02Hg
HUGHES, James		40	M	Laborer	21Se02Hg
Nancy		50	F	Wife	21Se02Hg
CASSIDY, Ann		18	F	Servant	21Se02Hg
BRUKE, Pat		6	M	Child	21Se02Hg
Ann		5	F	Child	21Se02Hg
MURPHY, Ann		24	F	Servant	21Se02Hg
QUILT, Ann		36	F	Servant	21Se02Hg
BERRIGAN, Robert		30	M	Laborer	21Se02Hg
RYAN, Bridget		18	F	Servant	21Se02Hg
TIERNEY, Bridget		9	F	Child	21Se02Hg
BOOTH, At		12	M	Laborer	21Se02Hg
COLLINS, Pat		42	M	Farmer	21Se02Hg
Cathn.	(D)	11	F	None	21Se02Hg
Pat	(D)	9	M	Child	21Se02Hg
BARRY, Michael		21	M	Servant	21Se02Hg
Mary		18	F	Servant	21Se02Hg
RYAN, Cathn.		16	F	Servant	21Se02Hg
MCCREIGHT, Honora		18	F	Servant	21Se02Hg
STONE, Henry		22	M	Shoemaker	21Se02Hg
Edward		18	M	Shoemaker	21Se02Hg
MCCANN, Hugh		30	M	Laborer	21Se02Hg
ROURKE, Pat		35	M	Laborer	21Se02Hg
MCGARRY, Thos.		25	M	Laborer	21Se02Hg
Tim		22	M	Laborer	21Se02Hg
Ellen		20	F	Servant	21Se02Hg
Ellen	(D)	10	F	Child	21Se02Hg
DOYLE, James		23	M	Laborer	21Se02Hg
BYRNE, Cathn.		23	F	Laborer	21Se02Hg
EAGAN, John		23	F	Laborer	21Se02Hg
HIGGINS, Mary		18	F	Servant	21Se02Hg
LEONARD, Cathn.		24	F	Laborer	21Se02Hg
OSTENIN, William		30	M	Spinner	21Se02Hg
COWLEY, John		30	M	Mason	21Se02Hg
MCCULLOUGH, John		50	M	Laborer	21Se02Hg
WADE, John		22	M	Laborer	21Se02Hg
Mary	(W)	20	F	None	21Se02Hg
MOORE, Michl.		18	M	Laborer	21Se02Hg
DELAHUNT, Ary		19	F	Servant	21Se02Hg
CALLAHAN, Cornl.		22	F	Servant	21Se02Hg
Margt.	(W)	27	F	None	21Se02Hg
WATSON, Susan		.00	F	Infant	21Se02Hg
Died-At-Sea					
DOYLE, Esther		30	F	Wife	21Se02Hg
Eliza		7	F	Child	21Se02Hg
Cathn.		5	F	Child	21Se02Hg
Joseph		.00	M	Infant	21Se02Hg
DOBBINS, Fanny		25	F	Servant	21Se02Hg
CONNOR, Margt.		25	F	Servant	21Se02Hg
MCMANUS, Cathn.		15	F	Servant	21Se02Hg
NORRIS, John		40	M	Laborer	21Se02Hg

NAMES OF PASSENGERS		AGE	SEX	OCCUPATIONS	DATE PORT SHIP
NORRIS, Cathn.		8	F	Child	21Se02Hg
FOX, Pat		16	M	Laborer	21Se02Hg
BOYLE, Mary		16	F	Servant	21Se02Hg
MULLIGAN, Pat		8	M	Child	21Se02Hg
Peter		4	M	Child	21Se02Hg
KILBRIDGE, John		30	M	Laborer	21Se02Hg
Johanna		9	F	Child	21Se02Hg
Mary		6	F	Child	21Se02Hg
SMITH, Luke		30	M	Shoemaker	21Se02Hg
MALONE, Bridget		30	F	Servant	21Se02Hg
PENCELL, John		10	M	Child	21Se02Hg
KILLEDAY, Margt.		20	F	Servant	21Se02Hg
COFFEE, Margt.		17	F	Servant	21Se02Hg
Michl.		10	M	Unknown	21Se02Hg
Pat		8	M	Child	21Se02Hg
MCCOWEN, Esther		40	F	Wife	21Se02Hg
James	(S)	17	M	None	21Se02Hg
Hughes	(S)	14	M	None	21Se02Hg
Robert	(S)	2	M	Child	21Se02Hg
Margt.	(D)	10	F	Unknown	21Se02Hg
SWORDS, Michl.		23	M	Laborer	21Se02Hg
Bridget		22	F	Laborer	21Se02Hg
HERLEHY, Honor		20	F	Servant	21Se02Hg
JUDGE, Chrsn.		45	M	Laborer	21Se02Hg
Nicholas		18	M	Laborer	21Se02Hg
Ann		14	F	Servant	21Se02Hg
Cathn.		11	F	Servant	21Se02Hg
ROGERS, Wm.		40	M	Farmer	21Se02Hg
U-Mrs.		40	F	Wife	21Se02Hg
Mary		18	F	Wife	21Se02Hg
Eliza		11	F	Wife	21Se02Hg
Charlotte		9	F	Child	21Se02Hg
Louisa		9	F	Child	21Se02Hg
MCBRINE, Margery		25	F	Servant	21Se02Hg
RULLY, Eliza		12	F	Servant	21Se02Hg
OSHIA, Bernd.		20	M	Laborer	21Se02Hg
WELBY, Margt.		27	F	Servant	21Se02Hg
SWEENY, Wm.		25	M	Laborer	21Se02Hg
MCMAHON, Thos.		12	M	None	21Se02Hg
PLUNKETT, Charlotte		20	F	Servant	21Se02Hg
DOGHERTY, Edwd.		25	M	Laborer	21Se02Hg
MCAREE, Arthur		28	M	Laborer	21Se02Hg
MCCARRON, Mary		22	F	Servant	21Se02Hg
MINER, Mary		30	F	Wife	21Se02Hg
John		10	M	Child	21Se02Hg
Mary		5	F	Child	21Se02Hg
James		2	M	Child	21Se02Hg
Cathn.		7	F	Child	21Se02Hg
GRADY, Bridget		20	F	Servant	21Se02Hg
MARTIN, Pat		24	F	Laborer	21Se02Hg
BURKE, Richd.		20	M	Laborer	21Se02Hg
GRADY, Jim		20	M	Laborer	21Se02Hg
POWER, Honor		20	F	Wife	21Se02Hg
Alice	(D)	4	F	Child	21Se02Hg
MALUNM, Pat		20	M	Fiddler	21Se02Hg
Bridget		50	F	Wife	21Se02Hg
Bridget	(D)	20	F	None	21Se02Hg
MAHEN, James		20	M	Laborer	21Se02Hg
MCARDLE, John		25	M	Tailor	21Se02Hg
Jane	(W)	25	F	None	21Se02Hg
James		.00	M	Infant	21Se02Hg
MCCLOSKEY, Mary		25	F	Wife	21Se02Hg
Peter		.00	M	Infant	21Se02Hg
Bridget		4	F	Child	21Se02Hg
Ann		2	F	Child	21Se02Hg
Patrick		2	M	Child	21Se02Hg
TIERNEY, William		23	M	Blacksmith	21Se02Hg
Pat		20	M	Blacksmith	21Se02Hg
LUSK, Betty		40	F	Wife	21Se02Hg
Bridget		9	F	Child	21Se02Hg
Luke		6	M	Child	21Se02Hg
Philip		4	M	Child	21Se02Hg
Peter		3	M	Child	21Se02Hg
CONLON, Felix		26	M	Laborer	21Se02Hg
Ellen		5	F	Child	21Se02Hg
HEAVY, Margt.		30	F	Wife	21Se02Hg
Mick		4	M	Child	21Se02Hg
Mary		.00	F	Infant	21Se02Hg
QUIGLEY, Margt.		20	F	Wife	21Se02Hg
Maria		2	F	Child	21Se02Hg
DYMON, John		20	M	Laborer	21Se02Hg
BULGER, Ann		22	F	Servant	21Se02Hg
Cathn.		22	F	Wife	21Se02Hg
Margt.		2	F	Child	21Se02Hg
GLEASON, Ann		50	F	Wife	21Se02Hg
CAULTIN, Cathn.		12	F	Unknown	21Se02Hg
DUNN, Mary		20	F	Servant	21Se02Hg
QUIN, Thomas		43	M	Shoemaker	21Se02Hg
MCCANN, Pat		18	M	Laborer	21Se02Hg
BURNE, Mary		20	F	Servant	21Se02Hg
LEAHILL, Judy		17	F	Servant	21Se02Hg
LIDDY, Jeremiah		19	M	Servant	21Se02Hg
KEENAN, Mary		15	F	Servant	21Se02Hg
RIDLEY, Joseph		50	M	Farmer	21Se02Hg
Mary		40	F	Wife	21Se02Hg
Mary		.00	F	Infant	21Se02Hg
Mary		7	F	Child	21Se02Hg
Cathn.		5	F	Child	21Se02Hg
Edwd.		3	M	Child	21Se02Hg
MCGUIRE, Sally		20	F	Servant	21Se02Hg
PLUNKETT, Bridget		18	F	Servant	21Se02Hg
CULLEN, Ann		8	F	Child	21Se02Hg
Mary		5	F	Child	21Se02Hg
CROWIN, Tim		20	M	Laborer	21Se02Hg
MCDONALD, Janet		17	F	Wife	21Se02Hg
GIBBON, Martin		24	M	Laborer	21Se02Hg
Ellen		18	F	Wife	21Se02Hg
GEWOGAN, Daniel		32	M	Mechanic	21Se02Hg
U		22	F	None	21Se02Hg
Maria		10	F	Unknown	21Se02Hg
Cathn.		8	F	Child	21Se02Hg
Margt.		2	F	Child	21Se02Hg
CLUSY, Michael		22	M	Shoemaker	21Se02Hg
Edward		25	M	Shoemaker	21Se02Hg
NOONAN, James		26	M	Clerk	21Se02Hg
Pat		36	M	Cbtmkr	21Se02Hg
KUON, Bridget		22	F	Servant	21Se02Hg
Cathn.		20	F	Servant	21Se02Hg
Anthony		.00	M	Infant	21Se02Hg
Died-At-Sea					
OFERRAL, Richard		20	M	Blacksmith	21Se02Hg
Wu		20	F	None	21Se02Hg
MCGLUCKAN, Michl.		18	M	Mason	21Se02Hg
OWENS, Nathan		21	M	Farmer	21Se02Hg
Mary		40	F	Unknown	21Se02Hg
DOGHERTY, Bridget		22	F	Servant	21Se02Hg
MCGARY, Cathn.		19	F	Servant	21Se02Hg
MURPHY, Lucy		25	F	Servant	21Se02Hg
BYRNE, Bridget		20	F	Servant	21Se02Hg
MYRES, Honor		40	F	Servant	21Se02Hg
SWEENY, John		00	M	Farmer	21Se02Hg
LYNCH, Pat		22	M	Saddler	21Se02Hg
HASSETT, Honor		20	F	Servant	21Se02Hg
BARRY, Mary		20	F	Servant	21Se02Hg
KELLY, Mary		20	F	Servant	21Se02Hg
KENNADY, Michael		56	M	Laborer	21Se02Hg
ODEA, Martin		25	M	Laborer	21Se02Hg
VAUGHAN, Honor		18	F	Servant	21Se02Hg
Darley		13	F	Servant	21Se02Hg
DOLAN, Mary		22	F	Servant	21Se02Hg
FAHY, Bridget		32	F	Wife	21Se02Hg
CULLEN, Michael		40	M	Laborer	21Se02Hg
WALPOOL, James		20	F	Carver	21Se02Hg
KEEFE, Thomas		35	M	Butcher	21Se02Hg
GRIOMK, Nichs.		26	M	Shoemaker	21Se02Hg
BROPHY, Pat		24	M	Laborer	21Se02Hg
BRENNAN, Mary		18	F	Servant	21Se02Hg
COYLE, Edwd.		24	M	Laborer	21Se02Hg
KENNEDY, Wm.		29	M	Blacksmith	21Se02Hg
GIBBIN, Wm.		22	M	Blacksmith	21Se02Hg

NAMES OF PASSENGERS	AGE	SEX	OCCUPATIONS	DATE PORT SHIP
Mah--, Cath.	35	F	Laborer	21Se02Hg
FERGUSON, A.E.	24	U	Servant	21Se02Hg

SENATOR 22 SEPTEMBER 1849

From Liverpool

NAMES OF PASSENGERS	AGE	SEX	OCCUPATIONS	DATE PORT SHIP
DOHERTY, John	46	M	Farmer	22Se02Ir
Mary	50	F	None	22Se02Ir
Johanna	24	F	None	22Se02Ir
Margaret	23	F	Farmer	22Se02Ir
Richard	21	M	Farmer	22Se02Ir
Mary	19	F	Farmer	22Se02Ir
John	16	M	Farmer	22Se02Ir
Caniel	14	U	Farmer	22Se02Ir
James	10	M	Farmer	22Se02Ir
HICKEY, John	26	M	Laborer	22Se02Ir
SHELLEY, Pat	25	M	Servant	22Se02Ir
LAULER, Catherine	34	F	Servant	22Se02Ir
Wm.	8	M	Child	22Se02Ir
MCMANNS, Charles	25	M	Tailor	22Se02Ir
QUINN, Eliza	50	F	Spinster	22Se02Ir
Eliza	14	F	None	22Se02Ir
Kate	10	F	None	22Se02Ir
Sarah	8	F	Child	22Se02Ir
James	7	M	Child	22Se02Ir
Ellen	3	F	Child	22Se02Ir
HANLEY, John	25	M	Draper	22Se02Ir
MARA, Patrick	20	M	Grocer	22Se02Ir
Mary (W)	26	F	None	22Se02Ir
Maria	6	F	Child	22Se02Ir
Margaret	4	F	Child	22Se02Ir
John	.06	M	Infant	22Se02Ir
BURKE, Bridgt.	40	F	Servant	22Se02Ir
Patrick	.06	M	Infant	22Se02Ir
MCCONNELL, James	32	M	Laborer	22Se02Ir
MCCORMICK, Martin	28	M	Laborer	22Se02Ir
Michael	25	M	Shoemaker	22Se02Ir
CONNELLY, Stephen	30	M	Unknown	22Se02Ir
MCADAMS, Mary	30	F	Servant	22Se02Ir
MOONEY, Thomas	35	M	Laborer	22Se02Ir
CUNNINGHAM, James	25	M	Laborer	22Se02Ir
SHEEHY, John	30	M	Laborer	22Se02Ir
Bridgt. (W)	30	F	None	22Se02Ir
Roger	4	M	Child	22Se02Ir
Bridgt.	2	F	Child	22Se02Ir
STACK, Margaret	20	F	Spinster	22Se02Ir
SULLIVAN, Johanna	20	F	Spinster	22Se02Ir
MULVY, Bartholemeu	.06	M	Infant	22Se02Ir
Cornelius	35	M	Laborer	22Se02Ir
FLAGHIRN, Michael	24	M	Laborer	22Se02Ir
BROWN, Thomas	25	M	Laborer	22Se02Ir
LAGNEY, Elizabeth	23	F	Wife	22Se02Ir
Bartholemeu	.09	M	Infant	22Se02Ir
Died-At-Sea				
MOLONEY, Honoria	21	F	Spinster	22Se02Ir
WHITE, Patrick	22	M	Mason	22Se02Ir
MINOR, Mary	40	F	Spinster	22Se02Ir
NELLIGAN, Maurice	60	M	Cooper	22Se02Ir
Margaret (W)	50	F	None	22Se02Ir
Maurice	14	M	Child	22Se02Ir
LEAKY, Margt.	22	F	Spinster	22Se02Ir
Joh.	23	M	Laborer	22Se02Ir
LYNCH, Margaret	18	F	Spinster	22Se02Ir
MCMAHR, Winifred	20	F	Spinster	22Se02Ir
FREEHILY, Patrick	39	M	Cooper	22Se02Ir
Thomas	15	M	None	22Se02Ir
Matthew	11	M	None	22Se02Ir
Eliza	9	F	Child	22Se02Ir
FREEHILY, Catherine	7	F	Child	22Se02Ir
WINTERS, John	36	M	Clerk	22Se02Ir
COWNEY, John	24	M	Clerk	22Se02Ir
CAMPBELL, John	30	M	Carter	22Se02Ir
Mary (W)	20	F	None	22Se02Ir
HYNES, Rachel	20	F	Servant	22Se02Ir
LYONS, Thomas	25	M	Shoemaker	22Se02Ir
TIERNEY, Jane	25	F	Milliner	22Se02Ir
MURPHY, Michael	28	M	Tailor	22Se02Ir
GROGAN, John	24	M	Tailor	22Se02Ir
WALSH, Sarah	22	F	Weaver	22Se02Ir
DOWNS, Peter	26	M	Weaver	22Se02Ir
SHERRY, Pat	27	M	Laborer	22Se02Ir
Pat	15	M	Laborer	22Se02Ir
FEE, Mary	19	F	Servant	22Se02Ir
DONOVAN, Anne	20	F	Servant	22Se02Ir
Jane	19	F	Servant	22Se02Ir
FIZARD, Bridgt.	33	F	Wife	22Se02Ir
CAVANAGH, Edwd.	30	M	Laborer	22Se02Ir
FOLEY, Anty	26	M	Laborer	22Se02Ir
KEELY, Anne	20	F	Spinster	22Se02Ir
Bridgt.	18	F	Spinster	22Se02Ir
Margt.	16	F	Spinster	22Se02Ir
HYNES, John	33	M	Laborer	22Se02Ir
MATHEWS, Alice	50	F	Milliner	22Se02Ir
Ellen	18	F	Milliner	22Se02Ir
NIDDLETON, Mary-Anne	18	F	Milliner	22Se02Ir
CANAVAN, Richard	33	M	Vsgn	22Se02Ir
Winifred (W)	25	F	None	22Se02Ir
DOYLE, Andrew	26	M	Hatter	22Se02Ir
LUDLOW, Margaret	18	F	Servant	22Se02Ir
WOLFE, Maurice	44	M	Tailor	22Se02Ir
Johanne (W)	35	F	None	22Se02Ir
Richd.	18	M	None	22Se02Ir
Margaret	20	F	None	22Se02Ir
James	11	M	None	22Se02Ir
Johanna	9	F	Child	22Se02Ir
Catherine	7	F	Child	22Se02Ir
Maurice	.11	M	Infant	22Se02Ir
BROWN, William	52	M	Servant	22Se02Ir
FALEY, Denis	25	M	Servant	22Se02Ir
Died-At-Sea				
MAGHER, Margt.	20	F	Spinster	22Se02Ir
NEAL, Mary	26	F	Spinster	22Se02Ir
MCGELLETRAND, Catherin	22	F	Spinster	22Se02Ir
COOR, John	45	M	Laborer	22Se02Ir
STACK, Thomas	25	M	Laborer	22Se02Ir
LYONS, Michael	20	M	Laborer	22Se02Ir
John	23	M	Sailor	22Se02Ir
MCEVAN, John	29	M	Farmer	22Se02Ir
Anne (W)	24	F	None	22Se02Ir
BURKE, Mary	60	F	Wife	22Se02Ir
Martin	20	M	Laborer	22Se02Ir
Pat	14	M	Laborer	22Se02Ir
John	11	M	Laborer	22Se02Ir
MOOR, John	32	M	Farmer	22Se02Ir
Mary-Anne (W)	30	F	None	22Se02Ir
Emily	8	F	Child	22Se02Ir
Ellen	7	F	Child	22Se02Ir
Elizabeth	5	F	Child	22Se02Ir
George	3	M	Child	22Se02Ir
John	2	M	Child	22Se02Ir
Alexander	.04	M	Infant	22Se02Ir
GRATHON, Jack	40	M	Servant	22Se02Ir
ESFEY, Eliza	21	F	Servant	22Se02Ir
KELLY, John	22	M	Clerk	22Se02Ir
CREED, James	27	M	Clerk	22Se02Ir
DONNELAN, Patrick	18	M	Laborer	22Se02Ir
BUTLER, Columb	25	M	Laborer	22Se02Ir
Anne (W)	21	F	None	22Se02Ir
TROY, Pat	23	F	Shoemaker	22Se02Ir
BYRNE, Jeremiah	45	M	Carpenter	22Se02Ir
Catherine (W)	40	F	None	22Se02Ir
John	19	M	None	22Se02Ir
Mary	17	F	None	22Se02Ir

NAMES OF PASSENGERS		AGE	SEX	OCCUPATIONS	DATE PORT SHIP
BYRNE, Judy		11	F	None	22Se02Ir
DUNNE, James		24	M	Laborer	22Se02Ir
Mary	(W)	25	F	None	22Se02Ir
MCPHILLIPS, John		18	M	Laborer	22Se02Ir
FLAHERTY, William		27	M	Laborer	22Se02Ir
SHEHAN, John		25	M	Maurer	22Se02Ir
LEAKY, John		27	M	Carpenter	22Se02Ir
Patrick		25	M	Laborer	22Se02Ir
James		19	M	Laborer	22Se02Ir
Bridget		23	F	Spinster	22Se02Ir
ELLIS, William		22	M	Laborer	22Se02Ir
Mary	(W)	20	F	None	22Se02Ir
Margaret		.03	F	Infant	22Se02Ir
OBRIEN, William		26	M	Unknown	22Se02Ir
Mary	(W)	20	F	None	22Se02Ir
CARROL, Thomas		26	M	Hawker	22Se02Ir
EGAN, Michael		19	M	Glazier	22Se02Ir
MCDERMOTT, Peter		31	M	Miner	22Se02Ir
Mary	(W)	30	F	None	22Se02Ir
Hugh		1	M	Child	22Se02Ir
Ann		.02	F	Infant	22Se02Ir
WALSH, Jeremiah		25	M	Laborer	22Se02Ir
DONOVAN, Denis		20	M	Laborer	22Se02Ir
LANNON, Bridgt.		17	F	Spinster	22Se02Ir
LAWLER, James		64	M	Locksmith	22Se02Ir
Charlotte	(W)	57	F	None	22Se02Ir
Lau.		12	M	None	22Se02Ir
HARDING, William		57	M	Servant	22Se02Ir
MULLOY, Mary		46	F	Wi	22Se02Ir
Robt.		16	M	None	22Se02Ir
RYAN, Michael		21	M	Laborer	22Se02Ir
SMITH, Peter		24	M	Baker	22Se02Ir
MCLOUGHLIN, Edwd.		25	M	Joiner	22Se02Ir
WALKER, James		30	M	Laborer	22Se02Ir
Mary	(W)	25	F	None	22Se02Ir
Mary		5	F	Child	22Se02Ir
Anne		4	F	Child	22Se02Ir
James		.09	M	Infant	22Se02Ir
BLOOMER, Effice		20	F	Spinster	22Se02Ir
DOYLE, John		26	M	Hatter	22Se02Ir
MURPHY, George		13	M	None	22Se02Ir
KELLY, Catherine		25	F	Servant	22Se02Ir
EDGEWORTH, Maria		16	F	Dressmaker	22Se02Ir
MCGAN, Mary		40	F	Wi	22Se02Ir
Peter		14	M	None	22Se02Ir
Joseph		12	M	None	22Se02Ir
Mary		11	F	None	22Se02Ir
James		9	M	Child	22Se02Ir
CASEY, Anne		32	F	Wi	22Se02Ir
Rose		12	F	None	22Se02Ir
Eliza		19	F	None	22Se02Ir
SWEENY, Catherine		18	F	Servant	22Se02Ir
CASEY, James		9	M	Child	22Se02Ir
MURPHY, Margaret		20	F	Spinster	22Se02Ir
John		6	M	Child	22Se02Ir
Ellen		.10	F	Infant	22Se02Ir
SULLIVAN, Margaret		40	F	Wife	22Se02Ir
Eliza		2	F	Child	22Se02Ir
CONNOR, Michael		26	M	Laborer	22Se02Ir
OSULLIVAN, Mary		20	F	Spinster	22Se02Ir
CAHIL, Johanna		20	F	Spinster	22Se02Ir
RYAN, Mary		16	F	Spinster	22Se02Ir
H--IKE, James		16	M	Laborer	22Se02Ir
Mary		15	F	Spinster	22Se02Ir
OBRIEN, Mary		22	F	Spinster	22Se02Ir
MURRAY, John		27	M	Laborer	22Se02Ir
CROUDY, John		22	M	Laborer	22Se02Ir
CHAMBERS, John		25	M	Sawer	22Se02Ir
Anne	(W)	22	F	None	22Se02Ir
Anne		.04	F	Infant	22Se02Ir
WALSH, Honor		19	F	Spinster	22Se02Ir
OBRIEN, Jeremiah		55	M	Laborer	22Se02Ir
Margaret	(W)	52	F	None	22Se02Ir
Michael		20	M	None	22Se02Ir
William		18	M	None	22Se02Ir

NAMES OF PASSENGERS		AGE	SEX	OCCUPATIONS	DATE PORT SHIP
OBRIEN, Margaret		15	F	None	22Se02Ir
Paddy		13	M	None	22Se02Ir
Nancy		12	F	None	22Se02Ir
CRAWLY, Timothy		35	M	Laborer	22Se02Ir
HALPIN, Bridget		21	F	Servant	22Se02Ir
John		18	M	Laborer	22Se02Ir
CROKER, Thomas		22	M	Laborer	22Se02Ir
COSTELLO, James		20	M	Laborer	22Se02Ir
CONNELLY, Peter		20	M	Laborer	22Se02Ir
KEIBY, Laurence		25	M	Laborer	22Se02Ir
MURPHY, Catherine		18	F	Servant	22Se02Ir
MCGUIN, Rose		21	F	Servant	22Se02Ir
CONNOIR, Elizabeth		19	F	Servant	22Se02Ir
CONNOR, John		35	M	Unknown	22Se02Ir
REGAN, Charles		25	M	Laborer	22Se02Ir
FERRILLLY, Thomas		18	M	Laborer	22Se02Ir
John		13	M	Laborer	22Se02Ir
DONNEY, James		24	M	Laborer	22Se02Ir
ONEIL, Francis		22	M	Laborer	22Se02Ir
HALL, Mary		16	F	Spinster	22Se02Ir
TURNER, Margaret		35	F	Wi	22Se02Ir
BUTLER, Anne		.02	F	Infant	22Se02Ir

WEST-POINT 22 SEPTEMBER 1849

From Liverpool

NAMES OF PASSENGERS		AGE	SEX	OCCUPATIONS	DATE PORT SHIP
NORRIS, C.N.		25	M	Gentleman	22Se02Hl
DREW, N.H.Dr.		35	M	Surgeon	22Se02Hl
Mary-Miss		30	F	Lady	22Se02Hl
GANNON, Mary		21	F	None	22Se02Hl
CRUSE, James		20	M	Laborer	22Se02Hl
WATSON, Jos.		22	M	Laborer	22Se02Hl
U	(W)	22	F	Wife	22Se02Hl
Mary		.00	F	Infant	22Se02Hl
DOHERTY, Jno.		30	M	Brf	22Se02Hl
Ann		30	F	Wife	22Se02Hl
GALLAGHER, Tim		19	M	Laborer	22Se02Hl
KELLY, James		19	M	Tailor	22Se02Hl
HILL, Mary		18	F	Servant	22Se02Hl
Maria		21	F	Servant	22Se02Hl
CORNELL, Mary		18	F	Servant	22Se02Hl
CAHILL, Cath.		20	F	Servant	22Se02Hl
REILEY, Pat		17	M	Servant	22Se02Hl
SMITH, Bridget		18	F	Servant	22Se02Hl
Bernard		13	M	Servant	22Se02Hl
KENNEDY, Bridget		21	F	Servant	22Se02Hl
BUTLER, John		45	M	Farmer	22Se02Hl
U	(W)	35	F	Wife	22Se02Hl
Maria		17	F	Daughter	22Se02Hl
Alice		15	F	Daughter	22Se02Hl
James		13	M	Son	22Se02Hl
Richard		9	M	Child	22Se02Hl
John		6	M	Child	22Se02Hl
Robert		4	M	Child	22Se02Hl
Andrew		2	M	Child	22Se02Hl
Ann		.00	F	Infant	22Se02Hl
MORRIS, William		30	M	Farmer	22Se02Hl
U	(W)	30	F	Wife	22Se02Hl
Alicia		4	F	Child	22Se02Hl
Ann		2	F	Child	22Se02Hl
MURRY, John		22	M	Relative	22Se02Hl
U-Miss		25	F	Relative	22Se02Hl
MAHON, Harriett		29	F	Relative	22Se02Hl
GILL, Bridget		25	F	Servant	22Se02Hl
Edward		5	M	Child	22Se02Hl
Pat		4	M	Child	22Se02Hl
Mary		2	F	Child	22Se02Hl
Berey		.00	M	Infant	22Se02Hl

NAMES OF PASSENGERS	AGE	SEX	OCCUPATIONS	DATE PORT SHIP
ROUKE, Thomas	30	M	Stone Mason	22Se02HI
HORACE, Dennis	20	M	Relative	22Se02HI
ROUKE, Ellen	24	F	Relative	22Se02HI
LAWLER, John	26	M	Relative	22Se02HI
KELLY, William	23	M	Relative	22Se02HI
CLARKE, Simon	24	M	Relative	22Se02HI
TOOLEY, James	30	M	Tailor	22Se02HI
U (W)	30	F	Wife	22Se02HI
Maria	2	F	Child	22Se02HI
SMITH, Francis	32	M	Relative	22Se02HI
GLOVER, James	30	M	Relative	22Se02HI
TOOLEY, U	.00	U	Infant	22Se02HI
STURK, Henry	26	M	Laborer	22Se02HI
KELLY, Ellen	30	F	Relative	22Se02HI
Mary	12	F	Relative	22Se02HI
Mary	9	F	Child	22Se02HI
Edward	7	M	Child	22Se02HI
Ira	5	M	Child	22Se02HI
Daniel	1	M	Child	22Se02HI
SULLIVAN, John	18	M	Servant	22Se02HI
NEIL, John	17	M	Servant	22Se02HI
HOLMES, James	30	M	Laborer	22Se02HI
U (W)	30	F	Wife	22Se02HI
LEARY, Silvest.	26	M	Farmer	22Se02HI
REDMON, Alice	26	F	Servant	22Se02HI
FARRELL, Mary	17	F	Servant	22Se02HI
FALEN, Mary	28	F	Servant	22Se02HI
ROUKE, Alice	23	F	Servant	22Se02HI
REYNOLDS, U-Mrs.	29	F	Servant	22Se02HI
U-Miss	20	F	Servant	22Se02HI
U	.00	F	Infant	22Se02HI
MITCHELL, Jim	21	M	Servant	22Se02HI
HOOD, William	40	M	Servant	22Se02HI
MCCORMACK, Stephen	21	M	Printer	22Se02HI
U-Mrs.	18	F	Relative	22Se02HI
MCKAY, H.R.	18	M	Printer	22Se02HI
Robt.	17	M	Porter	22Se02HI
BATTLE, Mary	25	F	Farmer	22Se02HI
Mary-A.	4	F	Child	22Se02HI
Elizabeth	3	F	Child	22Se02HI
Michael	2	M	Child	22Se02HI
Jno.	.00	M	Infant	22Se02HI
Died-At-Sea				
BRADY, Mary	18	F	Servant	22Se02HI
DAILEY, Cath.	8	F	Child	22Se02HI
Bernard	6	M	Child	22Se02HI
REILLY, Mary	19	F	Servant	22Se02HI
JORDAN, Margt.	16	F	Servant	22Se02HI
MURY, Biddy	18	F	Servant	22Se02HI
KRATER, Bernard	17	M	Servant	22Se02HI
HENDERSON, Alexander	20	M	Cooper	22Se02HI
PERCIVAL, William	20	M	Draper	22Se02HI
CROFORD, Dennis	30	M	Laborer	22Se02HI
MCQUILLAN, James	38	M	Laborer	22Se02HI
U (W)	40	F	Unknown	22Se02HI
FARLEY, Catherine	24	F	Servant	22Se02HI
STEVENS, Samuel	25	M	Brwkr	22Se02HI
MCGOVERN, Pat	14	M	Servant	22Se02HI
SHERIDAN, Margaret	20	F	Servant	22Se02HI
CAMPBELL, John	22	M	Laborer	22Se02HI
FISHER, Cyn	26	M	Laborer	22Se02HI
MCNALLIS, Pat	20	M	Tailor	22Se02HI
HAGERTY, Morris	18	M	Laborer	22Se02HI
CUNNINGHAM, Mary	20	F	Servant	22Se02HI
FAGAN, Pat	25	M	Relative	22Se02HI
Hannah	16	F	Relative	22Se02HI
DUNLAVY, Frn.	20	M	Relative	22Se02HI
Anty.	9	M	Child	22Se02HI
CORR, Christ.	20	M	Relative	22Se02HI
Peggy	9	F	Child	22Se02HI
REYNOLDS, Elizabeth	16	F	Relative	22Se02HI
REILLY, Ann	20	F	Servant	22Se02HI
Died-At-Sea				
Cath.	00	F	Unknown	22Se02HI
Died-At-Sea				

NAMES OF PASSENGERS	AGE	SEX	OCCUPATIONS	DATE PORT SHIP
MCMAHON, Mary	30	F	Servant	22Se02HI
John	7	M	Child	22Se02HI
Daniel	20	M	Servant	22Se02HI
LEARY, Mary	23	F	Servant	22Se02HI
HARNEY, Pat	9	M	Child	22Se02HI
Margaret	12	F	Servant	22Se02HI
Died-At-Sea				
REILLY, Johan	13	M	Servant	22Se02HI
Mary	9	F	Child	22Se02HI
Dennis	7	M	Child	22Se02HI
MCGOWAN, Catherine	40	F	Relative	22Se02HI
Hugh	13	M	Relative	22Se02HI
Biddy	9	F	Child	22Se02HI
Catherine	6	F	Child	22Se02HI
Ann	3	F	Child	22Se02HI
Died-At-Sea				
WALSH, Ann	25	F	Relative	22Se02HI
Catherine	12	F	Relative	22Se02HI
James	.00	M	Infant	22Se02HI
HEFFERSON, Simon	20	M	Unknown	22Se02HI
INGOLDSBY, Ann	18	F	Unknown	22Se02HI
FINN, Mary	20	F	Unknown	22Se02HI
FINLAN, Mary	60	F	Unknown	22Se02HI
BARRY, Margt.	20	F	Unknown	22Se02HI
MCSWEENEY, Dan	23	M	Unknown	22Se02HI
COKELY, Timy.	23	M	Unknown	22Se02HI
MURPHY, Mary	23	F	Unknown	22Se02HI
SMITH, Ann	18	F	Unknown	22Se02HI
DILLON, Dan	48	M	Unknown	22Se02HI
MYRES, Mary	40	F	Unknown	22Se02HI
HASEY, Pat	20	M	Unknown	22Se02HI
DUNN, Henry	23	M	Unknown	22Se02HI
CARTY, Dennis	19	M	Unknown	22Se02HI
REILLY, Cath.	7	F	Child	22Se02HI
CUMMINS, Thomas	28	M	Unknown	22Se02HI
HARTWELL, Lawrence	28	M	Unknown	22Se02HI
HAYES, Thomas	30	M	Unknown	22Se02HI
RYAN, John	22	M	Unknown	22Se02HI
MCNAMARA, Bridget	17	F	Unknown	22Se02HI
WHITE, Mary	25	F	Unknown	22Se02HI
Sarah	18	F	Unknown	22Se02HI
CARLEY, Bridget	16	F	Unknown	22Se02HI
Mary	18	F	Unknown	22Se02HI
COLLINS, Catherine	18	F	Unknown	22Se02HI
SMITH, James	44	M	Laborer	22Se02HI
Died-At-Sea				
Elizabeth	18	F	Relative	22Se02HI
Maria	7	F	Child	22Se02HI
Peter	5	M	Child	22Se02HI
RATCHFORD, Thomas	20	M	Laborer	22Se02HI
Mary	30	F	Relative	22Se02HI
Died-At-Sea				
Rose	10	F	Unknown	22Se02HI
Thomas	8	M	Child	22Se02HI
Died-At-Sea				
Michael	6	M	Child	22Se02HI
Catherine	4	F	Child	22Se02HI
Died-At-Sea				
John	.00	M	Infant	22Se02HI
DARBY, Terence	25	M	Laborer	22Se02HI
Mary	28	F	Wife	22Se02HI
Ellen	8	F	Child	22Se02HI
Mary	6	F	Child	22Se02HI
Ann	2	F	Child	22Se02HI
Died-At-Sea				
Cath	.00	F	Infant	22Se02HI
Died-At-Sea				
BAILEY, James	19	M	Relative	22Se02HI
KEENE, James	28	M	Shoemaker	22Se02HI
HANRAHAN, Bridget	.00	F	Infant	22Se02HI
Michael	20	M	Relative	22Se02HI
Kate	23	F	Relative	22Se02HI
MAHON, Dennis	23	M	Relative	22Se02HI
HANRAHAN, Bridget	.00	F	Infant	22Se02HI
BURNS, John	27	M	Laborer	22Se02HI

NAMES OF PASSENGERS	AGE	SEX	OCCUPATIONS	DATE PORT SHIP
BURNS, Margt.	25	F	Relative	22Se02HI
FITZPATRICK, John	25	M	Laborer	22Se02HI
Pat	20	M	Relative	22Se02HI
HAILEY, Pat	24	F	Relative	22Se02HI
Ann	2	F	Child	22Se02HI
Cath.	.00	F	Infant	22Se02HI
MATHER, Hugh	20	M	Relative	22Se02HI
MARTIN, Mary	20	F	Relative	22Se02HI
Cath.	18	F	Relative	22Se02HI
FARRELL, John	24	M	Farmer	22Se02HI
KELLY, Michael	50	M	Relative	22Se02HI
U (W)	45	F	Relative	22Se02HI
BRADY, Pat	15	M	Relative	22Se02HI
Thomas	12	M	Relative	22Se02HI
FARRELL, Bridget	20	F	Relative	22Se02HI
REARDON, John	13	M	Relative	22Se02HI
DONOVAN, Ellen	20	F	Servant	22Se02HI
HAILEY, Ann	24	F	Farmer	22Se02HI
BIRD, Margt.	16	F	Relative	22Se02HI
MCCORRIGAN, Ann	17	F	Relative	22Se02HI
DIMOND, Pat	30	M	Farmer	22Se02HI
U (W)	30	F	Wife	22Se02HI
GALLAGHER, Mary	20	F	Relative	22Se02HI
Sabina	40	F	Relative	22Se02HI
Died-At-Sea				
MALONY, William	30	M	Grocer	22Se02HI
KERNAN, Jane	24	F	Servant	22Se02HI
QUINN, Ann	25	F	Servant	22Se02HI
PALMER, Jane	21	F	Servant	22Se02HI
PHILLIPS, Benj.M.	50	M	Farmer	22Se02HI
NORTON, Thos.	22	M	Laborer	22Se02HI
Maria	26	F	Servant	22Se02HI

NAMES OF PASSENGERS	AGE	SEX	OCCUPATIONS	DATE PORT SHIP
EDWARDS, Henry	00	M	Unknown	22Se13Cz
U	00	F	Lady	22Se13Cz
U	00	U	Child	22Se13Cz
U	00	U	Child	22Se13Cz
U	00	U	Child	22Se13Cz
U	00	U	Child	22Se13Cz
BARWICK, Eliza	00	F	Unknown	22Se13Cz
U	00	U	Child	22Se13Cz
U	00	U	Child	22Se13Cz
U	00	U	Child	22Se13Cz
U	00	U	Child	22Se13Cz
U	00	U	Child	22Se13Cz
BROWN, Thomas	00	M	Unknown	22Se13Cz
HIGHAM, Samuel	00	M	Unknown	22Se13Cz
U	00	F	Lady	22Se13Cz
U	00	U	Child	22Se13Cz
U	00	U	Child	22Se13Cz
U	00	U	Child	22Se13Cz
U	00	U	Child	22Se13Cz
U	00	U	Child	22Se13Cz
U, U	00	U	Servant	22Se13Cz
GRUBB, Laphia	00	F	Unknown	22Se13Cz
LOUIS, U-Mrs	00	F	Unknown	22Se13Cz
BRAHAW, Wm.	00	M	Unknown	22Se13Cz
Valthaniel	00	M	Unknown	22Se13Cz
BURBANK, John	00	M	Unknown	22Se13Cz
LLOYD, Jane	00	F	Unknown	22Se13Cz
U	00	U	Child	22Se13Cz
U	00	U	Child	22Se13Cz
U	00	U	Child	22Se13Cz
U	00	U	Child	22Se13Cz
U	00	U	Child	22Se13Cz
WHEELWRIGHT, George	00	M	Unknown	22Se13Cz
DICKINS, Susan	00	F	Unknown	22Se13Cz

INDEPENDENCE 22 SEPTEMBER 1849

From London

NAMES OF PASSENGERS	AGE	SEX	OCCUPATIONS	DATE PORT SHIP
MCGARN, Thomas	40	M	Wheelwright	22Se13Cz
Ann	35	F	Unknown	22Se13Cz
COWAN, Margaret	18	F	Unknown	22Se13Cz
MCGRANE, Samuel	1	M	Child	22Se13Cz
Thomas	.00	M	Infant	22Se13Cz
STEPHENS, Kezia	24	M	Sailor	22Se13Cz
WELKS, William	27	M	Stone Mason	22Se13Cz
Sarah	23	F	Stone Mason	22Se13Cz
WEBSTER, John	26	M	Cbtmkr	22Se13Cz
STIOTOLPH, Henry	26	M	Cvr-Gldr	22Se13Cz
Jane	23	F	Unknown	22Se13Cz
LYONS, Morris	23	M	Sailor	22Se13Cz
MARNEY, Jeremiah	40	M	Laborer	22Se13Cz
SMITH, Sabine	48	F	Tailor	22Se13Cz
DAVIES, John	63	M	Tailor	22Se13Cz
BAYLEY, U	30	U	Tailor	22Se13Cz
LEADER, John	35	M	Unknown	22Se13Cz
MERRITT, William	23	M	Unknown	22Se13Cz
DALEY, Mary	26	F	Unknown	22Se13Cz
REINHARD, Ludwig	19	M	Saddler	22Se13Cz
GAUZ, Margt.	20	F	Saddler	22Se13Cz
BALZHAUDER, Joh	24	M	Unknown	22Se13Cz
WANNER, Sophie	35	F	Unknown	22Se13Cz
Adolf	14	M	Unknown	22Se13Cz
HAAS, Michl.	19	M	Farmer	22Se13Cz
Christiana	56	F	Unknown	22Se13Cz
JUCHS, Frederick	24	M	Laborer	22Se13Cz
HELD, Jacob	29	M	Laborer	22Se13Cz
WINSWERBER, Carl	24	M	Laborer	22Se13Cz
STERNER, Anna	18	F	Laborer	22Se13Cz
FELTMUNGER, B.	25	U	Laborer	22Se13Cz
SHAW, Jacob	19	M	Laborer	22Se13Cz

REINZI 22 SEPTEMBER 1849

From Belfast

NAMES OF PASSENGERS	AGE	SEX	OCCUPATIONS	DATE PORT SHIP
MCAULEY, George	20	M	Farmer	22Se05Iq
MONTGOMERY, Susannah	19	F	Seamstress	22Se05Iq
Margaret	16	F	Servant	22Se05Iq
James	2	M	Child	22Se05Iq
MCAULEY, Mary-Jane	15	F	Servant	22Se05Iq
MCATEE, Elizebeth	30	F	Wife	22Se05Iq
Margaret	18	F	Spinster	22Se05Iq
HARE, Elizabeth	20	F	Spinster	22Se05Iq
John	00	M	Servant	22Se05Iq
Matilda	16	F	Servant	22Se05Iq
Mary-Jane	13	F	None	22Se05Iq
FOSTER, Antony	26	M	Servant	22Se05Iq
MAGILL, Andrew	33	M	Farmer	22Se05Iq
Mary (W)	31	F	None	22Se05Iq
Mary-Margaret	8	F	Child	22Se05Iq
David	6	M	Child	22Se05Iq
James	3	M	Child	22Se05Iq
Thomas	.00	M	Infant	22Se05Iq
WARNOCK, Hugh	24	M	Farmer	22Se05Iq
Martha (W)	24	F	None	22Se05Iq
RYANS, Fanny	26	F	Seamstress	22Se05Iq
Patrick	21	M	Clerk	22Se05Iq
Catherine	16	F	Servant	22Se05Iq
Fanny	2	F	Child	22Se05Iq
Patrick	.00	M	Infant	22Se05Iq
Ellen	.00	F	Infant	22Se05Iq
Ann	17	F	Wife	22Se05Iq
MCNALLY, Ann	18	F	Servant	22Se05Iq
DEUWIR, Elizabeth	18	F	Servant	22Se05Iq
ATKINSON, James	25	M	Laborer	22Se05Iq

NAMES OF PASSENGERS		AGE	SEX	OCCUPATIONS	DATE PORT SHIP
ATKINSON, Jane	(W)	21	F	None	22Se05lq
HENNING, Robert		25	M	Laborer	22Se05lq
MCMANUS, Mary-Ann		25	F	Servant	22Se05lq
CUNNINGHAM, Susanna		25	F	Seamstress	22Se05lq
THOMPSON, Mary-J.		19	F	Seamstress	22Se05lq
Eliza		17	F	Seamstress	22Se05lq
YOUNG, James		30	M	Laborer	22Se05lq
Jane	(W)	30	F	None	22Se05lq
James		4	M	Child	22Se05lq
Cath.Ann		2	F	Child	22Se05lq
EWING, George		25	M	Farmer	22Se05lq
Ann	(W)	29	F	None	22Se05lq
THOMPSON, U-Mrs.		30	F	Wife	22Se05lq
MCCORMAC, Thomas		40	M	Farmer	22Se05lq
Lea	(W)	40	F	None	22Se05lq
BURR, Arthur		24	M	Farmer	22Se05lq
Sarah-Jane	(W)	23	F	None	22Se05lq
MCCORMAC, John		27	M	Farmer	22Se05lq
Margaret		25	F	Servant	22Se05lq
Wm.		26	M	Servant	22Se05lq
Lea		23	F	Servant	22Se05lq
Eliza		21	F	Servant	22Se05lq
Nancy		19	F	Servant	22Se05lq
GIBSON, Robt.John		20	M	Servant	22Se05lq
GORMAN, John		25	M	Laborer	22Se05lq
WHITE, William		32	M	Laborer	22Se05lq
Jane	(W)	30	F	None	22Se05lq
Anne		6	F	Child	22Se05lq
BERNARD, Margt.		20	F	Servant	22Se05lq
WRIGHT, James		26	M	Servant	22Se05lq
DELARGY, Peggy		20	F	Servant	22Se05lq
Cath.		00	F	None	22Se05lq
MCCLUSKEY, Mary		26	F	Servant	22Se05lq
BURNS, Anne		18	F	Servant	22Se05lq
Bridget		20	F	Servant	22Se05lq
SMITH, Mary		20	F	Servant	22Se05lq
MCKERNEY, Mary-A.		19	F	Servant	22Se05lq
MCAULEY, Jane		19	F	Servant	22Se05lq
BROWN, Mary-Jane		22	F	Servant	22Se05lq
MCGILLIAM, Patrick		25	M	Servant	22Se05lq
Died-At-Sea					
Elizabeth		22	F	Servant	22Se05lq
HUME, Anne		20	F	Servant	22Se05lq
WALLACE, Mary		35	F	Servant	22Se05lq
STEPHENSON, Jas.		13	M	None	22Se05lq
GOARAN, Margt.		45	F	Wife	22Se05lq
Jane		12	F	None	22Se05lq
John		8	M	Child	22Se05lq
DARRAGH, Neal		25	M	Servant	22Se05lq
Died-At-Sea					
Roxanna		22	F	Servant	22Se05lq
Mary		.00	F	Infant	22Se05lq
JENKINS, Willm.		28	M	Farmer	22Se05lq
Cath.	(W)	29	F	None	22Se05lq
Ellen		.00	F	Infant	22Se05lq
Died-At-Sea					
BOYD, William		28	M	Servant	22Se05lq
ASTIN, John		52	M	Farmer	22Se05lq
Mary	(W)	42	F	None	22Se05lq
Agnes		21	F	Servant	22Se05lq
Savage		16	M	Servant	22Se05lq
Mary		14	F	Servant	22Se05lq
Thomas		12	M	None	22Se05lq
Martha		9	F	Child	22Se05lq
Robert		6	M	Child	22Se05lq
John		4	M	Child	22Se05lq
Samuel		3	M	Child	22Se05lq
HENDRISON, Richd.		26	M	Farmer	22Se05lq
Margt.	(W)	26	F	None	22Se05lq
Robert		.00	M	Infant	22Se05lq
MAGNE, Grace		32	F	Seamstress	22Se05lq
CLARK, Susanna		18	F	Seamstress	22Se05lq
GRAHAM, Willm.		22	M	Farmer	22Se05lq
HARTE, Jas.		26	M	Farmer	22Se05lq
SHAW, Jas.		21	M	Farmer	22Se05lq

NAMES OF PASSENGERS		AGE	SEX	OCCUPATIONS	DATE PORT SHIP
SMITH, Daniel		38	M	Farmer	22Se05lq
MUIRE, John		24	M	Farmer	22Se05lq
JORDAN, Henry		24	M	Farmer	22Se05lq
RIED, John		18	M	Farmer	22Se05lq
DEVLIN, Margt.		22	F	Seamstress	22Se05lq
MACKILL, Mary		18	F	Seamstress	22Se05lq
BIGGERSTAFF, Willm.		50	M	Farmer	22Se05lq
Agnes	(W)	50	F	None	22Se05lq
Mary	(D)	25	F	None	22Se05lq
Samuel	(S)	23	M	None	22Se05lq
James	(S)	19	M	None	22Se05lq
William	(S)	13	M	None	22Se05lq
John	(S)	11	M	None	22Se05lq
SMITH, Margret		26	F	Seamstress	22Se05lq
Edward		5	M	Child	22Se05lq
Cath.		3	F	Child	22Se05lq
Anne		1	F	Child	22Se05lq
MAGUIRE, Bridget		20	F	Servant	22Se05lq
CAVERT, Jane		59	F	Wife	22Se05lq
Died-At-Sea					
Margt.		28	F	Seamstress	22Se05lq
Died-At-Sea					
COATS, Eliza		26	F	Seamstress	22Se05lq
Theodocia		.00	F	Infant	22Se05lq
BROWN, Thos.		19	M	Farmer	22Se05lq
SMITH, Alexr.		20	M	Farmer	22Se05lq
DALEY, Jas.		21	M	Farmer	22Se05lq
Margt.	(W)	21	F	None	22Se05lq
DONAGHUE, Jas.		30	M	Farmer	22Se05lq
Elizabeth	(W)	22	F	None	22Se05lq
Edward		.00	M	Infant	22Se05lq
SIMMS, Robt.		39	M	Farmer	22Se05lq
Mary-Jane	(W)	27	F	None	22Se05lq
Abigail		4	F	Child	22Se05lq
Samuel		2	M	Child	22Se05lq
Susannah		.00	F	Infant	22Se05lq
MCCLURE, Mary		19	F	Seamstress	22Se05lq
CHAMBERS, U-Mrs.		40	F	Wife	22Se05lq
Matilda		9	F	Child	22Se05lq
Andrew		4	M	Child	22Se05lq
IRELAND, Alexr.		30	M	Laborer	22Se05lq
SHAW, William		21	M	Laborer	22Se05lq
HARVEY, Willm.		26	M	Farmer	22Se05lq
Samuel		28	M	Farmer	22Se05lq
James		23	M	Farmer	22Se05lq
BIRKMYRE, James		28	M	Farmer	22Se05lq
FARREN, Henry		28	M	Seaman	22Se05lq
SOFTLY, Sarah		19	F	Servant	22Se05lq
MAGILL, Arthur		28	M	Servant	22Se05lq
MADILL, Thos.		30	M	Clerk	22Se05lq
IRWING, Jane		50	F	Seamstress	22Se05lq
LOGAN, Michl.		22	M	Laborer	22Se05lq
MCKENNA, Sarah		16	F	Spinster	22Se05lq
KENNEY, Nancy		14	F	Servant	22Se05lq
COMENY, Mauris		20	F	Servant	22Se05lq
Bridget		22	F	Servant	22Se05lq
KENNEDY, Mary		21	F	Servant	22Se05lq
James		.00	M	Infant	22Se05lq
MCCLELLAND, Mary		24	F	Servant	22Se05lq
MCFADDEN, Jas.		60	M	Farmer	22Se05lq
Ellen	(W)	62	F	None	22Se05lq
Died-At-Sea					
Elizabeth		22	F	Seamstress	22Se05lq
Ellen		20	F	Seamstress	22Se05lq
HARBISON, John		20	M	Servant	22Se05lq
BOYD, Isabella		17	F	Servant	22Se05lq
TRAINOR, Cathe.		20	F	Servant	22Se05lq
SIMINGTON, Sophia		20	F	Servant	22Se05lq
Sally		3	F	Child	22Se05lq
ABRAHAM, Letitia		13	F	None	22Se05lq
CONNOR, Jane		50	F	Wife	22Se05lq
Sarah		25	F	Seamstress	22Se05lq
Margt.		20	F	Seamstress	22Se05lq
MCQUE, Wm.		20	M	Laborer	22Se05lq
LINCH, Mary		19	F	Servant	22Se05lq

NAMES OF PASSENGERS	AGE	SEX	OCCUPATIONS	DATE PORT SHIP
LINCH, Patrick	.00	M	Infant	22Se05Iq
BLAKELY, Jane	16	F	Servant	22Se05Iq
Jane	13	F	None	22Se05Iq
HARBISON, Jane	20	F	Servant	22Se05Iq
BALLENTINE, Sarah	20	F	Servant	22Se05Iq
COLLINS, George	22	M	Servant	22Se05Iq
James	20	M	Servant	22Se05Iq
STOREY, Robert	25	M	Farmer	22Se05Iq
BOOMER, James	32	M	Farmer	22Se05Iq
WILSON, Mary	30	F	Spinster	22Se05Iq
WHITE, Wm.	4	M	Child	22Se05Iq
Anne	2	F	Child	22Se05Iq
SPENCE, Andrew	35	M	Pvmt	22Se05Iq
Ann (W)	27	F	None	22Se05Iq
Andrew	4	M	Child	22Se05Iq
John	1	M	Child	22Se05Iq
MCDOWALL, Wm.J. (N)	13	M	None	22Se05Iq
KEENIN, Mary-J. (N)	20	F	None	22Se05Iq
MCATEE, John	18	M	Seaman	22Se05Iq
DIGBY, Jane-Mrs.	00	F	Unknown	22Se05Iq
Margt.	00	F	Unknown	22Se05Iq
MCCOLLOUGH, Ellen	00	F	Unknown	22Se05Iq

CAMBRIA 22 SEPTEMBER 1849

From Liverpool

NAMES OF PASSENGERS	AGE	SEX	OCCUPATIONS	DATE PORT SHIP
EVANS, F.	29	M	Merchant	22Se02Jj

ELVIRA 23 SEPTEMBER 1849

From Fortune Island

NAMES OF PASSENGERS	AGE	SEX	OCCUPATIONS	DATE PORT SHIP
WOOLMSSTRY, James-H.	35	M	Captain	23Se59Qh

SIR-HARRY-SMITH 24 SEPTEMBER 1849

From Liverpool

NAMES OF PASSENGERS	AGE	SEX	OCCUPATIONS	DATE PORT SHIP
GRACE, Thomas	20	M	Shop Boy	24Se02Qb
CARSON, Andrew	40	M	Farmer	24Se02Qb
Sarah	30	F	Farmer	24Se02Qb
James	20	M	Farmer	24Se02Qb
Anderson	18	M	Farmer	24Se02Qb
Margaret	16	F	Unknown	24Se02Qb
Jane	12	F	Unknown	24Se02Qb
Moses	5	M	Child	24Se02Qb
Sarah	10	F	Unknown	24Se02Qb
Mary-Ann	5	F	Child	24Se02Qb
ATKINSON, Thomas	20	M	Farmer	24Se02Qb
CARSON, James	20	M	Tailor	24Se02Qb
Ann	22	F	Unknown	24Se02Qb
HANLY, Richard	31	M	Laborer	24Se02Qb
Ann	28	F	Unknown	24Se02Qb
JACKSON, James	45	M	Farmer	24Se02Qb
Margaret	37	F	Farmer	24Se02Qb
Jane	15	F	Farmer	24Se02Qb
JACKSON, Henry	12	M	Farmer	24Se02Qb
Samuel	11	M	Farmer	24Se02Qb
Richard	7	M	Child	24Se02Qb
Charles	5	M	Child	24Se02Qb
James	5	M	Child	24Se02Qb
Ann	3	F	Child	24Se02Qb
Bend.	.00	M	Infant	24Se02Qb
MCMILLEN, Eliza	.00	F	Infant	24Se02Qb
John	4	M	Child	24Se02Qb
MCGIVERN, Michael	40	M	Farmer	24Se02Qb
Catherine	40	F	Unknown	24Se02Qb
Rosana	.00	F	Infant	24Se02Qb
XXXXXXXXX, James	20	M	Carpenter	24Se02Qb
MARCH, Peter	11	M	Unknown	24Se02Qb
Maria	10	F	Unknown	24Se02Qb
BURN, Ann	30	F	Unknown	24Se02Qb
HEALEY, Catherine	22	F	Unknown	24Se02Qb
BURN, James	11	M	Unknown	24Se02Qb
JACKSON, John	.00	M	Infant	24Se02Qb
BULGER, Elcia	24	F	Servant	24Se02Qb
BAGGS, Mary	35	F	Unknown	24Se02Qb
Mary	11	F	Unknown	24Se02Qb
MCBRIDE, James	22	M	Laborer	24Se02Qb
B---, William	18	M	Laborer	24Se02Qb
OCONNOR, John	35	M	Victualler	24Se02Qb
Catherine	42	F	Unknown	24Se02Qb
John	14	M	Unknown	24Se02Qb
Michael	21	M	Gdnr	24Se02Qb
Peter	9	M	Child	24Se02Qb
SMITH, Mary-A.	22	F	Dressmaker	24Se02Qb
BUCHANAN, John	20	M	Laborer	24Se02Qb
MCGLAUGHLIN, Mary	22	F	Weaver	24Se02Qb
Catherine	20	F	Weaver	24Se02Qb
HENRY, John	18	M	Laborer	24Se02Qb
JOHNSON, James	27	M	Shoemaker	24Se02Qb
WALIS, Margaret	18	F	Servant	24Se02Qb
MCGERRY, Michael	27	M	Shoemaker	24Se02Qb
Fanny	27	F	Unknown	24Se02Qb
Mary-Ann	.00	F	Infant	24Se02Qb
HAWKINMS, John	35	M	Miller	24Se02Qb
OHARA, Patrick	30	M	Surveyor	24Se02Qb
Sarah	58	F	Unknown	24Se02Qb
DOWLING, James	27	M	Weaver	24Se02Qb
GAFFNEY, Jane	20	F	Unknown	24Se02Qb
CONLIN, Bridget	18	F	Unknown	24Se02Qb
BATERBY, Thomas	33	M	Farmer	24Se02Qb
Died-At-Sea				
Sarah	32	F	Farmer	24Se02Qb
Thomas	9	M	Child	24Se02Qb
Died-At-Sea				
Ellen	8	F	Child	24Se02Qb
William	6	M	Child	24Se02Qb
Died-At-Sea				
Isabella	.00	F	Infant	24Se02Qb
Caroline	.00	F	Infant	24Se02Qb
Died-At-Sea				
CAHILL, Ally	22	F	Unknown	24Se02Qb
SANDS, Eliza	20	F	Unknown	24Se02Qb
BELL, Mary	27	F	Unknown	24Se02Qb
MCMILLEN, Mary-I.	12	F	Unknown	24Se02Qb
Fanny	8	F	Child	24Se02Qb
BURN, Charlotte	18	F	Unknown	24Se02Qb
Patrick	4	M	Child	24Se02Qb
GULLIN, Elizabeth	16	F	Unknown	24Se02Qb
BOYCE, Joseph	22	M	Weaver	24Se02Qb
KIRTH, Esther	20	F	Unknown	24Se02Qb
DONNELLY, James	22	M	Weaver	24Se02Qb
BRANNON, John	40	M	Servant	24Se02Qb
Mary	35	F	Unknown	24Se02Qb
Dolly	35	F	Unknown	24Se02Qb
Patrick	15	M	Unknown	24Se02Qb
Catherine	13	F	Unknown	24Se02Qb
James	8	M	Child	24Se02Qb
BRIGGS, John	22	M	Unknown	24Se02Qb
CONNOLLY, Patt	50	M	Tailor	24Se02Qb

NAMES OF PASSENGERS	AGE	SEX	OCCUPATIONS	DATE PORT SHIP
CONNOLLY, Ellen	48	F	Unknown	24Se02Qb
Patt	27	M	Unknown	24Se02Qb
James	21	M	Unknown	24Se02Qb
Ellen	22	F	Unknown	24Se02Qb
Mary	34	F	Unknown	24Se02Qb
CAREY, Thomas	40	M	Gdnr	24Se02Qb
LENAT, Patt	10	M	Unknown	24Se02Qb
NOLAN, Patt	34	M	Chemist	24Se02Qb
CURTIS, Richard	30	M	Farmer	24Se02Qb
STANNGLE, John	48	M	Baker	24Se02Qb
Caroline	30	F	Unknown	24Se02Qb
Samuel	16	M	Unknown	24Se02Qb
Ann-Maria	10	F	Unknown	24Se02Qb
William	7	M	Child	24Se02Qb
Ellen	.00	F	Infant	24Se02Qb
Died-At-Sea				
MILLICHAUT, Edward	45	M	Cbtmkr	24Se02Qb
Ann	40	F	Unknown	24Se02Qb
William	24	M	Unknown	24Se02Qb
Anne	21	F	Unknown	24Se02Qb
David	19	M	Unknown	24Se02Qb
Died-At-Sea				
Joseph	15	M	Unknown	24Se02Qb
Rachael	13	F	Unknown	24Se02Qb
Elizabeth	11	F	Unknown	24Se02Qb
SMITH, Peter	35	M	Laborer	24Se02Qb
Ann	30	F	Unknown	24Se02Qb
Catherine	9	F	Child	24Se02Qb
Margaret	6	F	Child	24Se02Qb
John	.00	M	Infant	24Se02Qb
MCCABE, Felix	20	M	Maurer	24Se02Qb
SMITH, Patt	20	M	Maurer	24Se02Qb
CAMPBELL, Anne	18	F	Dressmaker	24Se02Qb
CLAIN, Charles	22	M	Mason	24Se02Qb
DOIL, Brian	50	M	Shoemaker	24Se02Qb
James	29	M	Shoemaker	24Se02Qb
Margaret	30	F	Unknown	24Se02Qb
WALSH, John	37	M	Laborer	24Se02Qb
U-Mrs	30	F	Wife	24Se02Qb
WALLACE, U-Mrs.	50	F	Wife	24Se02Qb
Died-At-Sea				
HAYES, Thomas	25	M	Laborer	24Se02Qb
Ellen	20	F	Unknown	24Se02Qb
MAGNER, Richard	34	M	Laborer	24Se02Qb
WALSH, Margaret	8	F	Child	24Se02Qb
Patrick	3	M	Child	24Se02Qb
Anastasia	5	F	Child	24Se02Qb
Michael	.00	M	Infant	24Se02Qb
FERMILLY, Patt	40	M	Servant	24Se02Qb
PAIVER, Patt	30	M	Unknown	24Se02Qb
WISE, Henry	18	M	Laborer	24Se02Qb
DERRY, Mathew	30	M	Laborer	24Se02Qb
DALY, John	37	M	Laborer	24Se02Qb
Bridget	30	F	Unknown	24Se02Qb
Susan	.00	F	Infant	24Se02Qb
BRANNON, Bridget	6	F	Child	24Se02Qb
Mary	.00	F	Infant	24Se02Qb
SWEENY, U-Mrs.	35	F	Lady'S Maid	24Se02Qb
CLARKE, U-Mrs.	37	F	Wife	24Se02Qb
Mary	4	F	Child	24Se02Qb
WOODS, Bartly	30	M	Tailor	24Se02Qb
Mary	28	F	Unknown	24Se02Qb
Arthur	16	M	Laborer	24Se02Qb
Bartley	18	M	Laborer	24Se02Qb
WALLIS, James	20	M	Unknown	24Se02Qb
DOLIN, Ann	20	F	Unknown	24Se02Qb
LAWLISS, Caroline	30	F	House Maid	24Se02Qb
MOONEY, Catherine	41	F	Unknown	24Se02Qb
SCULLEN, Peter	25	M	Weaver	24Se02Qb
DALY, Mary	32	F	Servant	24Se02Qb
Ellen	19	F	Servant	24Se02Qb
Henry	17	M	Laborer	24Se02Qb
Susan	26	F	Servant	24Se02Qb
MCINTOSH, Darby	28	M	Unknown	24Se02Qb
MACKIN, Pat	19	M	Laborer	24Se02Qb
FLEMMING, Joseph	24	M	Laborer	24Se02Qb
PEEL, Thomas	60	M	Laborer	24Se02Qb
U-Mrs. (W)	60	F	Unknown	24Se02Qb
Thomas	40	M	Laborer	24Se02Qb
U-Mrs. (W)	35	F	Unknown	24Se02Qb
Thomas	7	M	Child	24Se02Qb
Ellen	4	F	Child	24Se02Qb
Emme	.00	F	Infant	24Se02Qb
STEWART, Wm.	40	M	Laborer	24Se02Qb
U-Mrs. (W)	36	F	Unknown	24Se02Qb
Mary-Anne	13	F	Unknown	24Se02Qb
John	9	M	Child	24Se02Qb
Susan	7	F	Child	24Se02Qb
Elize	.00	F	Infant	24Se02Qb
PEEL, George	20	M	Unknown	24Se02Qb
MCCULLOUGH, Jane	30	F	Unknown	24Se02Qb
BOWLAN, John	48	M	Shoemaker	24Se02Qb
BLANNIK, U-Mrs.	25	F	Nurse	24Se02Qb
Ed.D.	9	M	Child	24Se02Qb
FLOOD, Mary	20	F	Dressmaker	24Se02Qb
Biddy	13	F	Unknown	24Se02Qb
KELLY, Pat	23	M	Laborer	24Se02Qb
RINSHULA, Ellen	30	F	Unknown	24Se02Qb
John	9	M	Child	24Se02Qb
Margaret	7	F	Child	24Se02Qb
Alice	4	F	Child	24Se02Qb
Elize	.00	F	Infant	24Se02Qb
BROWN, Ellen	30	F	House Maid	24Se02Qb
Mary	.00	F	Infant	24Se02Qb
COONEY, George	40	F	Turner	24Se02Qb
U-Mrs. (W)	40	F	Unknown	24Se02Qb
Mary	11	F	Unknown	24Se02Qb
Anthony	9	M	Child	24Se02Qb
John	7	M	Child	24Se02Qb
BROWNE, Pat	21	M	Baker	24Se02Qb
Mary	20	F	Unknown	24Se02Qb
DUNNE, Francis	35	M	Farmer	24Se02Qb
Jane	16	F	Unknown	24Se02Qb
HEETKEY, John	18	M	Laborer	24Se02Qb
FERGUSON, Bridget	17	F	Servant	24Se02Qb
HUGHES, David	24	M	Farmer	24Se02Qb
Harriet	21	F	Unknown	24Se02Qb
DALY, Edward	50	M	Laborer	24Se02Qb
SHEA, John	30	M	Laborer	24Se02Qb
FOSTER, George	25	M	Farmer	24Se02Qb
COLOTHY, Mary	24	F	Servant	24Se02Qb
CUNNINGHAM, Hugh	28	M	Farmer	24Se02Qb
SULLIVAN, Ellen	32	F	Unknown	24Se02Qb
Corn.	.00	M	Infant	24Se02Qb
BUTLER, Margaret	35	F	Unknown	24Se02Qb
John	6	M	Child	24Se02Qb
OCONNELL, Michael	28	M	Laborer	24Se02Qb
HAYS, Margaret	4	F	Child	24Se02Qb
Catherine	18	F	Unknown	24Se02Qb
Died-At-Sea				
DONOHOE, Mary	20	F	Servant	24Se02Qb
Catherine	11	F	Unknown	24Se02Qb
HAYS, Maryanne	5	F	Child	24Se02Qb
Died-At-Sea				
DRISCOLL, Mary	18	F	Servant	24Se02Qb
DONNELLY, John	25	M	Gdnr	24Se02Qb
Cath.	22	F	Unknown	24Se02Qb
DALY, Susan	16	F	Unknown	24Se02Qb
Robt.	20	M	Laborer	24Se02Qb
William	18	M	Unknown	24Se02Qb
Peter	16	M	Unknown	24Se02Qb
HENDERSON, John	35	M	Mariner	24Se02Qb
Mary-Ann	30	F	Unknown	24Se02Qb
Francis	8	M	Child	24Se02Qb
Margaret	6	F	Child	24Se02Qb
HIGGINS, Charles	23	M	Laborer	24Se02Qb
Jane	21	F	Unknown	24Se02Qb
Elizabeth	50	F	Unknown	24Se02Qb
JEFFERS, Mary	20	F	Unknown	24Se02Qb
QUILLAN, Ann	20	F	Servant	24Se02Qb

NAMES OF PASSENGERS	AGE	SEX	OCCUPATIONS	DATE PORT SHIP
QUILLAN, Betsy	.00	F	Infant	24Se02Qb
CONWAY, Catherine	18	F	Servant	24Se02Qb
SPRUCE, William	20	M	Laborer	24Se02Qb
Sarah	20	F	Unknown	24Se02Qb
John	.00	M	Infant	24Se02Qb
WHELAN, Martin	23	M	Laborer	24Se02Qb
Eliza	21	F	Laborer	24Se02Qb
MONOGAN, Betsy	20	F	Servant	24Se02Qb
BUTLER, Jerry	16	M	Laborer	24Se02Qb
KILLAN, John	21	M	Engineer	24Se02Qb
Mary	21	F	Unknown	24Se02Qb
LIN, Ellen Died-At-Sea	20	F	Unknown	24Se02Qb

JAMES-H.SHEPHERD 25 SEPTEMBER 1849

From Liverpool

NAMES OF PASSENGERS	AGE	SEX	OCCUPATIONS	DATE PORT SHIP
DUFFER, Margt.	20	F	Miner	25Se02Jo
TOLEMAN, James	20	M	Laborer	25Se02Jo
CARY, John	7	M	Child	25Se02Jo
James	11	M	Laborer	25Se02Jo
MULLEN, Pat	37	M	Tailor	25Se02Jo
Ann	28	F	Tailor	25Se02Jo
Betsy	2	F	Child	25Se02Jo
Cath.	1	F	Child	25Se02Jo
FLYNN, Maria	12	F	Unknown	25Se02Jo
PENDERGRASS, Pat	35	M	Laborer	25Se02Jo
MCCARTNEY, Mary	27	F	Servant	25Se02Jo
Mgt.	45	F	Servant	25Se02Jo
Ann	4	F	Child	25Se02Jo
QUIGLEY, John	34	M	Gdnr	25Se02Jo
HALEY, Honor	24	F	Servant	25Se02Jo
WADE, Ellen	40	F	Servant	25Se02Jo
Maria	12	F	Servant	25Se02Jo
Thos.	10	M	Unknown	25Se02Jo
Wm.	8	M	Child	25Se02Jo
RYAN, Ellen	18	F	Unknown	25Se02Jo
COX, John	20	M	Laborer	25Se02Jo
WALSH, P.	23	M	Laborer	25Se02Jo
DAILEY, James	24	M	Laborer	25Se02Jo
Mgt.	26	F	Laborer	25Se02Jo
Mgt.	.07	F	Infant	25Se02Jo
COATS, Julia	20	F	Unknown	25Se02Jo
WOVEN, Pat	46	M	Laborer	25Se02Jo
Mary	46	F	Unknown	25Se02Jo
Pat.	8	M	Child	25Se02Jo
Cath.	5	F	Child	25Se02Jo
Michl.	.00	M	Infant	25Se02Jo
MCGRATH, Ann	20	F	Laborer	25Se02Jo
KELLY, Ann	20	F	Laborer	25Se02Jo
DONLY, Matilda	9	F	Child	25Se02Jo
HEUITH, Mary	35	F	Unknown	25Se02Jo
Robt.	9	M	Child	25Se02Jo
Thos.	7	M	Child	25Se02Jo
Dutton	6	M	Child	25Se02Jo
KEVIN, Mary	16	F	Unknown	25Se02Jo
CONNELLY, Owen	30	M	Putter	25Se02Jo
Cath.	30	F	Unknown	25Se02Jo
CLAFFEY, Pat	20	M	Laborer	25Se02Jo
MCDOWNY, Owen	36	M	Tailor	25Se02Jo
BUCKLY, James	36	M	Tailor	25Se02Jo
Betty	16	F	Unknown	25Se02Jo
Mary	12	F	Unknown	25Se02Jo
FITZGERALD, U-Mrs.	45	F	Unknown	25Se02Jo
RYAN, Cath.	20	F	Unknown	25Se02Jo
TUTTLE, Rosan	18	F	Unknown	25Se02Jo
REILLY, Ellen	20	F	Unknown	25Se02Jo
KING, Mary	18	F	Unknown	25Se02Jo
RIELLY, Ellen	6	F	Child	25Se02Jo
MARKY, Pat	28	M	Shoemaker	25Se02Jo
COUGAN, Martha	20	F	Unknown	25Se02Jo
HEFFENER, James	16	M	Unknown	25Se02Jo
PATTERSON, Wm.	20	M	Laborer	25Se02Jo
Saml.	15	M	Unknown	25Se02Jo
CONNELY, Ann-J.	24	F	Unknown	25Se02Jo
M.J.	3	F	Child	25Se02Jo
NEAGLE, Cath.	52	F	Unknown	25Se02Jo
Mgt.	17	F	Unknown	25Se02Jo
MCCLUSKY, Mgt.	20	F	Servant	25Se02Jo
MCCAHILL, John	5	M	Child	25Se02Jo
REDDINGTON, Michl.	19	M	Laborer	25Se02Jo
Bridget	10	F	Unknown	25Se02Jo
SILL, John	6	M	Child	25Se02Jo
HONOUGHAD, Brdgt. Died-At-Sea	30	F	Unknown	25Se02Jo
Mary	5	F	Child	25Se02Jo
BOURK, Wm.	26	M	Laborer	25Se02Jo
CARREN, Mary	16	F	Servant	25Se02Jo
FLYNN, Pat	18	F	Servant	25Se02Jo
Edwd.	17	M	Unknown	25Se02Jo
Maria	12	F	Unknown	25Se02Jo
LALLY, Eliz.	18	F	Unknown	25Se02Jo
RUNIG, Michl.	19	M	Laborer	25Se02Jo
BRADY, Ann	18	F	Unknown	25Se02Jo
SHERIDAN, Areth.	19	F	Laborer	25Se02Jo
CAAHAN, John	50	M	Laborer	25Se02Jo
Mary	12	F	Unknown	25Se02Jo
Michl.	10	M	Unknown	25Se02Jo
CUMMINGS, Allice	30	F	Servant	25Se02Jo
Pat	4	M	Child	25Se02Jo
JOHNSON, Brdgt.	40	F	Unknown	25Se02Jo
ROGERSON, James	19	M	Laborer	25Se02Jo
GALLEGHER, Brdgt.	26	F	Servant	25Se02Jo
HORE, James	13	M	Unknown	25Se02Jo
ONEILL, Thos.	19	F	Servant	25Se02Jo
BARRY, Honora	50	F	Unknown	25Se02Jo
Thos.	8	M	Child	25Se02Jo
Ellen	7	F	Child	25Se02Jo
BRIEN, Jane	17	F	Unknown	25Se02Jo
DENNELLY, Mary	50	F	Unknown	25Se02Jo
SULLIVAN, Julia	27	F	Unknown	25Se02Jo
CONNOR, Eliz.	20	F	Unknown	25Se02Jo
MOFFATT, Mgt.	5	F	Child	25Se02Jo
TEENY, Cath.	25	F	Unknown	25Se02Jo
Michl.	.00	M	Infant	25Se02Jo
Mary	6	F	Child	25Se02Jo
Ellen	3	F	Child	25Se02Jo
MONAGHAN, Peggy	25	F	Unknown	25Se02Jo
John	7	M	Child	25Se02Jo
DRISCOLL, Cornelus.	20	M	Founder	25Se02Jo
MOON, Bart.	35	M	Laborer	25Se02Jo
WELSH, Honor	17	F	Servant	25Se02Jo
HELLORD, Brdgt.	20	F	Servant	25Se02Jo
Serien	12	M	Servant	25Se02Jo
Thos.	8	M	Child	25Se02Jo
MULAN, Brdgt.	21	F	Servant	25Se02Jo
CLAUSKY, James	20	M	Laborer	25Se02Jo
Cath.	18	F	Unknown	25Se02Jo
HICKEY, Edwd.	21	M	Teacher	25Se02Jo
BRANFTON, Allice	20	F	Servant	25Se02Jo
ROONEY, Cath.	17	F	Servant	25Se02Jo
GOODWIN, James	12	M	Unknown	25Se02Jo
HAMILTON, Charlotte	32	F	Unknown	25Se02Jo
Elizabeth	8	F	Child	25Se02Jo
Joseph	6	M	Child	25Se02Jo
William	4	M	Child	25Se02Jo
Thomas	2	M	Child	25Se02Jo
CEILY, Pat	50	M	Miner	25Se02Jo
John	16	M	Unknown	25Se02Jo
Julia	18	F	Unknown	25Se02Jo
BRANNUN, Agnes	19	F	Unknown	25Se02Jo
WHITLEY, Agnes	14	F	Servant	25Se02Jo
Eliz.	14	F	Unknown	25Se02Jo

NAMES OF PASSENGERS	AGE	SEX	OCCUPATIONS	DATE PORT SHIP
DALTON, Mary	22	F	Servant	25Se02Jo
PETERS, Ann	19	F	Servant	25Se02Jo
SMITH, Mary	33	F	Unknown	25Se02Jo
REARDON, Simon	59	M	Unknown	25Se02Jo
Ann	50	F	Unknown	25Se02Jo
REID, Wm.	18	M	Laborer	25Se02Jo
KEATING, Dan	28	M	Laborer	25Se02Jo
Mary	28	F	Unknown	25Se02Jo
Dennis	5	M	Child	25Se02Jo
Mary	3	F	Child	25Se02Jo
KADY, Brdgt.	20	F	Servant	25Se02Jo
OHEARN, John	26	M	Tailor	25Se02Jo
DELLAHUNT, Betty	12	F	Unknown	25Se02Jo
Ellen	8	F	Child	25Se02Jo
HUDSON, Richd.	21	M	Laborer	25Se02Jo
FITZGERALD, John	24	M	Laborer	25Se02Jo
SHEEHAN, Maurice	25	M	Laborer	25Se02Jo
ODONNELL, Mgt.	20	F	Laborer	25Se02Jo
KERWAN, Mary	17	F	Servant	25Se02Jo
SHERIDAN, Mary	19	F	Servant	25Se02Jo
JOHNSON, Juliana	19	F	Servant	25Se02Jo
KERWAN, Mgt.	20	F	Servant	25Se02Jo

E.Z. 25 SEPTEMBER 1849

From Liverpool

NAMES OF PASSENGERS	AGE	SEX	OCCUPATIONS	DATE PORT SHIP
CLEAR, Mary	18	F	Seamstress	25Se02Ky
DELANY, John	21	M	Laborer	25Se02Ky
THORNTON, Wm.	30	M	Laborer	25Se02Ky
M. (W)	23	F	Laborer	25Se02Ky
MORRAN, Edwd.	12	M	Laborer	25Se02Ky
COSGROUGH, John	40	M	Farmer	25Se02Ky
William	30	M	Farmer	25Se02Ky
Fanny	28	F	Farmer	25Se02Ky
John	22	M	Farmer	25Se02Ky
Ann	24	F	Farmer	25Se02Ky
Ann	20	F	Farmer	25Se02Ky
Rich.	24	M	Farmer	25Se02Ky
MCCLUR, John	26	M	Laborer	25Se02Ky
Cath.	19	F	Laborer	25Se02Ky
Ann	20	F	Laborer	25Se02Ky
MULLIGAN, Biddy	22	F	Laborer	25Se02Ky
DONNELL, John	30	M	Laborer	25Se02Ky
RUSH, Tho.	40	M	Farmer	25Se02Ky
Ellen	35	F	Farmer	25Se02Ky
Mary	14	F	Farmer	25Se02Ky
Thoms.	10	M	Farmer	25Se02Ky
Ann	7	F	Child	25Se02Ky
John	5	M	Child	25Se02Ky
Mary	5	F	Child	25Se02Ky
HIGGINS, Jams.	13	M	Farmer	25Se02Ky
MITCHELL, Ann	20	F	Farmer	25Se02Ky
DANLEY, Cath.	40	F	Farmer	25Se02Ky
John	20	M	Farmer	25Se02Ky
Ann	18	F	Farmer	25Se02Ky
Cathn.	15	F	Farmer	25Se02Ky
Michl.	12	M	Farmer	25Se02Ky
Mary	10	F	Farmer	25Se02Ky
Magt.	6	F	Child	25Se02Ky
Sarah	4	F	Child	25Se02Ky
Bridt.	2	F	Child	25Se02Ky
FINEGAN, John	2	M	Child	25Se02Ky
BREEN, Bridt.	18	F	Seamstress	25Se02Ky
Cath.	26	F	Seamstress	25Se02Ky
Ann	20	F	Seamstress	25Se02Ky
MARLIN, Jane	40	F	Seamstress	25Se02Ky
WOODS, Micl.	12	M	Unknown	25Se02Ky
CLAFFEY, Ann	20	F	Seamstress	25Se02Ky
CLAFFEY, Cath.	18	F	Seamstress	25Se02Ky
MCLAUGHLIN, Cath.	18	F	Servant	25Se02Ky
HOGAN, Cath.	31	F	Servant	25Se02Ky
Cath.	5	F	Child	25Se02Ky
John	5	M	Child	25Se02Ky
COSGROVE, Ann	11	F	Servant	25Se02Ky
CARNTON, Henry	22	M	Servant	25Se02Ky
KEIFFE, Robt.	20	M	Servant	25Se02Ky
TIBBONS, John	20	M	Farmer	25Se02Ky
U	27	F	Farmer	25Se02Ky
Mary	26	F	Farmer	25Se02Ky
George	2	M	Child	25Se02Ky
GRUMLY, Cath.	20	F	Laborer	25Se02Ky
MCVEY, Michl.	20	M	Laborer	25Se02Ky
SAMUEL, Joseph	30	M	Laborer	25Se02Ky
MAHAN, Thos.	25	M	Laborer	25Se02Ky
MULLIGAN, Martin	26	M	Laborer	25Se02Ky
PATCHETT, John	34	M	Farmer	25Se02Ky
Lucy	37	F	Farmer	25Se02Ky
Eliza	9	F	Child	25Se02Ky
Bridget	7	F	Child	25Se02Ky
John	5	M	Child	25Se02Ky
Saml.	.00	M	Infant	25Se02Ky
PEPPER, George	19	M	Farmer	25Se02Ky
KNOWLE, Ann	30	F	Farmer	25Se02Ky
Mary	11	F	Farmer	25Se02Ky
Sarah	9	F	Child	25Se02Ky
Jessy	7	F	Child	25Se02Ky
GABIN, Cath.	30	F	Laborer	25Se02Ky
CONN, Brid.	19	F	Laborer	25Se02Ky
MULIGAN, Michl.	48	M	Laborer	25Se02Ky
DALEY, Cath.	16	F	Laborer	25Se02Ky
CLYNE, Ann	18	F	Laborer	25Se02Ky
MCGRATH, Mary	21	F	Laborer	25Se02Ky
MEHAN, Anty	18	F	Laborer	25Se02Ky
KIRK, George	24	M	Laborer	25Se02Ky
GILLEN, Francis	22	M	Laborer	25Se02Ky
WHITE, James	21	M	Laborer	25Se02Ky
BYRON, James	30	M	Laborer	25Se02Ky
KEIFFE, Cath.	24	F	Laborer	25Se02Ky
FARRELL, Roger	26	M	Carpenter	25Se02Ky
HAY, Timothy	26	M	Farmer	25Se02Ky
JOHNSON, Mary	21	F	Farmer	25Se02Ky
MADDEN, Eleanor	30	F	Farmer	25Se02Ky
HARRIGAN, Patk.	18	M	Farmer	25Se02Ky
NOLAN, Mary	40	F	Farmer	25Se02Ky
SAUL, Brid.	17	F	Farmer	25Se02Ky
SHEHAN, Cath.	50	F	Farmer	25Se02Ky
Mary	20	F	Farmer	25Se02Ky
Thos.	2	M	Child	25Se02Ky
Mary	.00	F	Infant	25Se02Ky
LADEN, Mary	20	F	Seamstress	25Se02Ky
DOYLE, Jane	28	F	Laborer	25Se02Ky
MADDEN, John	24	M	Laborer	25Se02Ky
REILLY, Jerome	28	M	Laborer	25Se02Ky
Eliza	24	F	Laborer	25Se02Ky
Ann	12	F	Laborer	25Se02Ky
Biddy	9	F	Child	25Se02Ky
Patt.	8	M	Child	25Se02Ky
Margt.	3	F	Child	25Se02Ky
John	.00	M	Infant	25Se02Ky
CONNOR, Mary	20	F	Laborer	25Se02Ky
LAVIN, Cath.	30	F	Laborer	25Se02Ky
Mary	18	F	Laborer	25Se02Ky
Edw.	19	M	Laborer	25Se02Ky
Thos.	9	M	Child	25Se02Ky
Patt	12	M	Laborer	25Se02Ky
Bridget	16	F	Laborer	25Se02Ky
CONNOR, Ann	18	F	Laborer	25Se02Ky
Stephen	16	M	Laborer	25Se02Ky
MULLIGAN, Patk.	16	M	Laborer	25Se02Ky
COYLE, John	17	M	Laborer	25Se02Ky
CRAWLEY, Michl.	27	M	Laborer	25Se02Ky
PHILLIPS, Patt	13	M	Laborer	25Se02Ky
DELANY, Mary	11	F	Laborer	25Se02Ky

NAMES OF PASSENGERS	AGE	SEX	OCCUPATIONS	DATE PORT SHIP
DELANY, Bridget	13	F	Laborer	25Se02Ky
STAPLETON, John	25	M	Shoemaker	25Se02Ky
DUNN, Biddy	19	F	Shoemaker	25Se02Ky
Eliza	17	F	Shoemaker	25Se02Ky
FARRELL, John	21	M	Shoemaker	25Se02Ky
MCCARNEY, John	21	M	Shoemaker	25Se02Ky
Cath.	19	F	Shoemaker	25Se02Ky
DUNN, Eliza	30	F	Shoemaker	25Se02Ky
Mary	8	F	Child	25Se02Ky
Cath.	6	F	Child	25Se02Ky
John	5	M	Child	25Se02Ky
Patt	3	M	Child	25Se02Ky
Ann	1	F	Child	25Se02Ky
FARRELL, Mary	31	F	Laborer	25Se02Ky
MCGOWER, Owen	20	M	Laborer	25Se02Ky
Cath.	4	F	Child	25Se02Ky
BALISTER, John	65	M	Laborer	25Se02Ky
LINDSAY, Alex.	20	M	Laborer	25Se02Ky
MCHENRY, John	30	M	Laborer	25Se02Ky
SHEHAN, Dan	24	M	Laborer	25Se02Ky
SHENTA, John	24	M	Laborer	25Se02Ky
YATES, John	36	M	Farmer	25Se02Ky
Eliza	13	F	Farmer	25Se02Ky
John	6	M	Child	25Se02Ky
Richd.	3	M	Child	25Se02Ky
MCINTIRE, Mary	20	F	Farmer	25Se02Ky
MCGINLEY, Ann	20	F	Farmer	25Se02Ky
MCCOLGIN, Robt.	20	M	Farmer	25Se02Ky
HAINES, Thomas	26	M	Farmer	25Se02Ky
James	22	M	Farmer	25Se02Ky
MCPECK, Ellen	18	F	Farmer	25Se02Ky
GALAGHER, Ann	19	F	Farmer	25Se02Ky
Hugh	14	M	Farmer	25Se02Ky
Henry	11	M	Farmer	25Se02Ky
Peggy	18	F	Farmer	25Se02Ky
Edw.	15	M	Farmer	25Se02Ky
HENRY, A.Mrs.	27	F	Farmer	25Se02Ky
FARRELL, Cath.	5	F	Child	25Se02Ky
THORNTON, James	12	M	Farmer	25Se02Ky
COLEMAN, John	42	M	Farmer	25Se02Ky
Margt.	30	F	Farmer	25Se02Ky
Rose	13	F	Farmer	25Se02Ky
Patt	11	M	Farmer	25Se02Ky
Brid.	4	F	Child	25Se02Ky
Ann	2	F	Child	25Se02Ky
John	.00	M	Infant	25Se02Ky
Thos.	22	M	Farmer	25Se02Ky
John	20	M	Farmer	25Se02Ky
Judy	12	F	Farmer	25Se02Ky
MCKERRY, Mary	22	F	Farmer	25Se02Ky
STEPHENSON, Sarah	40	F	Farmer	25Se02Ky
Vincent	18	M	Laborer	25Se02Ky
BURNE, Thos.	42	M	Laborer	25Se02Ky
Ann	35	F	Laborer	25Se02Ky
TRANTIE, James	40	M	Laborer	25Se02Ky
GATTNEY, Ewd.	30	M	Laborer	25Se02Ky
RYAN, U-Mrs.	40	F	Laborer	25Se02Ky
KELLY, Ed.	25	M	Laborer	25Se02Ky
Cath.	22	F	Shoemaker	25Se02Ky
Cath.	20	F	Shoemaker	25Se02Ky
Ellen	20	F	Shoemaker	25Se02Ky
CORCORAN, Mary	20	F	Shoemaker	25Se02Ky
LOCKE, Patt	20	M	Laborer	25Se02Ky
WARD, Bridt.	22	F	Laborer	25Se02Ky
Wm.	4	M	Child	25Se02Ky
REILLY, Patt	18	M	Laborer	25Se02Ky
Ann	18	F	Laborer	25Se02Ky
CUNNINGHAM, Mary	18	F	Laborer	25Se02Ky
CLAFFEY, Mary	29	F	Laborer	25Se02Ky
HAINES, Mary	20	F	Laborer	25Se02Ky
GILROY, Cath.	15	F	Laborer	25Se02Ky
Ann	26	F	Laborer	25Se02Ky
Ewd.	.00	M	Infant	25Se02Ky
MCGUIRE, Thos.	18	M	Laborer	25Se02Ky
NAREN, Ann	15	F	Laborer	25Se02Ky
CONERTY, Thos.	19	M	Laborer	25Se02Ky
Ellen	15	F	Laborer	25Se02Ky
SMITH, Rose	16	F	Laborer	25Se02Ky
MORRIS, Cath.	40	F	Laborer	25Se02Ky
BRADY, Julia	40	F	Seamstress	25Se02Ky
Ann	17	F	Seamstress	25Se02Ky
GIBSON, Rose	16	F	Seamstress	25Se02Ky
MORRIS, Mary	18	F	Laborer	25Se02Ky
MALROY, Mary	1	F	Child	25Se02Ky
MEEHAN, Ann	4	F	Child	25Se02Ky
MULROY, Jams.	.00	M	Infant	25Se02Ky
HIGGINS, Henry	15	M	Laborer	25Se02Ky
MORRISON, Patt	22	M	Laborer	25Se02Ky
HIGGINS, Mary	12	F	Laborer	25Se02Ky
Dennis	10	M	Laborer	25Se02Ky
Bridg.	7	F	Child	25Se02Ky
BRADLEY, Bridgt.	12	F	Laborer	25Se02Ky
SHEHAN, James	54	M	Farmer	25Se02Ky
LINTON, Alex.	21	M	Farmer	25Se02Ky
SHEEHAN, John	24	M	Farmer	25Se02Ky
Zachr.	22	M	Farmer	25Se02Ky
LEPREL, Mary	30	F	Farmer	25Se02Ky
LINTON, Mary	50	F	Farmer	25Se02Ky
TYRREL, John	.00	M	Infant	25Se02Ky
MCCEERY, Patt	12	M	Farmer	25Se02Ky
SESSTA, Wm.	34	M	Farmer	25Se02Ky
CONNERTY, Mary	22	F	Farmer	25Se02Ky
FLYNN, Saml.	25	M	Farmer	25Se02Ky
Magt.	23	F	Farmer	25Se02Ky
BURKE, John	30	M	Farmer	25Se02Ky
FLYNN, James	.00	M	Infant	25Se02Ky
JOHNSON, Ann	24	F	Farmer	25Se02Ky
BRENNAN, Margt.	26	F	Farmer	25Se02Ky
GARVIN, Wm.	18	M	Farmer	25Se02Ky

NOEMIE 25 SEPTEMBER 1849

From Liverpool

NAMES OF PASSENGERS	AGE	SEX	OCCUPATIONS	DATE PORT SHIP
KEARNS, Thos.	35	M	Farmer	25Se02Ec
THOMAS, Catherine	20	F	Spinster	25Se02Ec
DONOHUE, Thomas	12	M	Farmer	25Se02Ec
William	10	M	Farmer	25Se02Ec
Bridget	8	F	Child	25Se02Ec
Mary	6	F	Child	25Se02Ec
Patrick	.00	M	Infant	25Se02Ec
JENNINGS, Alley	21	F	Spinster	25Se02Ec
GAVIN, Margt.	6	F	Child	25Se02Ec
SPEAR, William	28	M	Farmer	25Se02Ec
EGAN, Mary	21	F	Farmer	25Se02Ec
FITZPATRICK, Sarah	65	F	Farmer	25Se02Ec
CUNNINGHAM, Bridget	60	F	Farmer	25Se02Ec
Margaret	20	F	Farmer	25Se02Ec
GALLAHER, Bridget	20	F	Farmer	25Se02Ec
MERAIN, John	19	M	Farmer	25Se02Ec
MURPHY, Patrick	34	M	Farmer	25Se02Ec
WALLACE, Ann	25	F	Farmer	25Se02Ec
COOPER, Martha	22	F	Farmer	25Se02Ec
GILLER, Mary	10	F	Farmer	25Se02Ec
LYNCH, Patrick	20	M	Farmer	25Se02Ec
Margaret	28	F	Farmer	25Se02Ec
FARREL, Cathrine	40	F	Farmer	25Se02Ec
Ann	10	F	Farmer	25Se02Ec
MCCUE, Biddy	12	F	Farmer	25Se02Ec
RILEY, Mary	20	F	Farmer	25Se02Ec
Ann	10	F	Farmer	25Se02Ec
WALLACE, Ann	25	F	Farmer	25Se02Ec
FITZPATRICK, Martin	28	M	Farmer	25Se02Ec
GILMORE, Honor	35	F	Farmer	25Se02Ec

NAMES OF PASSENGERS	AGE	SEX	OCCUPATIONS	DATE PORT SHIP
GILMORE, Dominick	11	M	Farmer	25Se02Ec
John	9	M	Child	25Se02Ec
Catherine	7	F	Child	25Se02Ec
Mary	5	F	Child	25Se02Ec
Jane	3	F	Child	25Se02Ec
Honor	.06	F	Infant	25Se02Ec
FLYNN, John	13	M	Farmer	25Se02Ec
MCCARRY, James	20	M	Farmer	25Se02Ec
MCKENDRIE, James	18	M	Farmer	25Se02Ec
SMITH, John	30	M	Farmer	25Se02Ec
DELANY, Michael	19	M	Farmer	25Se02Ec
FOSTER, James	52	M	Farmer	25Se02Ec
Mary	50	F	Farmer	25Se02Ec
Margaret	16	F	Farmer	25Se02Ec
RYAN, Alice	19	F	Farmer	25Se02Ec
WALSH, Mary	26	F	Farmer	25Se02Ec
Catherine	3	F	Child	25Se02Ec
Michl.	.08	M	Infant	25Se02Ec
HANNAH, Margaret	45	F	Farmer	25Se02Ec
DUGGAN, Bridget	23	F	Farmer	25Se02Ec
CARR, Patrick	20	M	Farmer	25Se02Ec
GLOVER, Robert	27	M	Farmer	25Se02Ec
DELANY, Bridget	20	F	Farmer	25Se02Ec
CUNNINGHAM, Esther	20	F	Farmer	25Se02Ec
MCHAB, Mary	23	F	Farmer	25Se02Ec
CONNERTY, Jane	22	F	Farmer	25Se02Ec
Rose	17	F	Farmer	25Se02Ec
KELLY, Biddy	23	F	Farmer	25Se02Ec
MCQUAID, Catherine	7	F	Child	25Se02Ec
GORE, Isabella	23	F	Farmer	25Se02Ec
RILEY, Patrick	13	M	Farmer	25Se02Ec
SHEA, John	23	M	Farmer	25Se02Ec
BROWN, Jane	20	F	Farmer	25Se02Ec
LYNCH, Edward	28	M	Farmer	25Se02Ec
DONGAN, Nancy	40	F	Farmer	25Se02Ec
Catherine	18	F	Farmer	25Se02Ec
Andrew	12	M	Farmer	25Se02Ec
Francis	5	F	Child	25Se02Ec
Patrick	2	M	Child	25Se02Ec
Peter	.06	M	Infant	25Se02Ec
FORTER, Maria	12	F	Farmer	25Se02Ec
LOCKMAN, John	19	M	Farmer	25Se02Ec
Ellen	27	F	Farmer	25Se02Ec
Cathrine	17	F	Farmer	25Se02Ec
HARTNEY, Ellen	24	F	Farmer	25Se02Ec
WALL, Mary	36	F	Farmer	25Se02Ec
Emelina	11	F	Farmer	25Se02Ec
COLLMAN, James	14	M	Farmer	25Se02Ec
MCDONNELL, Mary	30	F	Farmer	25Se02Ec
Dennis	9	M	Child	25Se02Ec
Catherine	.06	F	Infant	25Se02Ec
OBRIEN, William	16	M	Farmer	25Se02Ec
Sarah	9	F	Child	25Se02Ec
Elisabeth	6	F	Child	25Se02Ec
CONKIN, Hugh	20	M	Farmer	25Se02Ec
BROWN, William	25	M	Farmer	25Se02Ec
SCHWARTS, Hepiah	30	F	Farmer	25Se02Ec
Rifga	9	F	Child	25Se02Ec
Malca	4	M	Child	25Se02Ec
Risa	.10	F	Infant	25Se02Ec
WORD, Roger	32	M	Farmer	25Se02Ec
RICE, Andrew	24	M	Farmer	25Se02Ec
COOPER, William	26	M	Farmer	25Se02Ec
CONROY, Biddy	40	F	Farmer	25Se02Ec
CONEY, Catherine	33	F	Farmer	25Se02Ec
Patrick	4	M	Child	25Se02Ec
DICKER, Mary	20	F	Farmer	25Se02Ec
CORMICK, William	26	M	Farmer	25Se02Ec
Phillip	20	M	Farmer	25Se02Ec
DORLAN, William	21	M	Farmer	25Se02Ec
Allice	26	F	Farmer	25Se02Ec
HAYNES, Mary	40	F	Farmer	25Se02Ec
CRAWLEY, Daniel	23	M	Farmer	25Se02Ec
HENAPHAN, John	21	M	Farmer	25Se02Ec
KING, John	50	M	Farmer	25Se02Ec
WYNAN, Honor	23	F	Farmer	25Se02Ec
James	.01	M	Infant	25Se02Ec
EVANS, Ann	20	F	Farmer	25Se02Ec
MORAIN, James	17	M	Farmer	25Se02Ec
Bernard	12	M	Farmer	25Se02Ec
Bridget	10	F	Farmer	25Se02Ec
Ellen	8	F	Child	25Se02Ec
CRACORE, Morris	18	M	Farmer	25Se02Ec
RUBAN, Nahan	20	U	Farmer	25Se02Ec
EPHRON, Catherine	37	F	Farmer	25Se02Ec
FARRELY, Mary	20	F	Farmer	25Se02Ec
POWELL, Catherine	40	F	Farmer	25Se02Ec
Kernan	5	M	Child	25Se02Ec
Patrick	.07	M	Infant	25Se02Ec
ROGERS, Thomas	33	M	Farmer	25Se02Ec
James	21	M	Farmer	25Se02Ec
Mary	21	F	Farmer	25Se02Ec
HASLINE, John	20	M	Farmer	25Se02Ec
SHAIN, Robt.	25	M	Farmer	25Se02Ec
CLYNE, Margaret	20	F	Farmer	25Se02Ec
MCMANUS, John	20	M	Farmer	25Se02Ec
TOWNEY, Catherine	13	F	Farmer	25Se02Ec
ONEIL, Richard	20	M	Farmer	25Se02Ec
WHELPLEY, Mary	22	F	Farmer	25Se02Ec
ODRISCOLL, Mary	20	F	Farmer	25Se02Ec
MCDONALD, Robt.	20	M	Farmer	25Se02Ec
LOWE, Catherine	22	F	Farmer	25Se02Ec
BUTLER, Edward	.10	M	Infant	25Se02Ec
SHILLAN, Catherine	24	F	Farmer	25Se02Ec
RYAN, Thomas	29	M	Farmer	25Se02Ec
Kate	23	F	Farmer	25Se02Ec
SLATERY, James	18	M	Farmer	25Se02Ec
KERBY, James	22	M	Farmer	25Se02Ec
Mary	20	F	Farmer	25Se02Ec
FARREL, Bridget	40	F	Farmer	25Se02Ec
Peggy	14	F	Farmer	25Se02Ec
Patrick	12	M	Farmer	25Se02Ec
Fanny	10	F	Farmer	25Se02Ec
Catherine	5	F	Child	25Se02Ec
Biddy	2	F	Child	25Se02Ec
Ann	.06	F	Infant	25Se02Ec
ALLISON, John	42	M	Farmer	25Se02Ec
FERGUS, James	49	M	Farmer	25Se02Ec
Alexander	14	M	Farmer	25Se02Ec
LEE, Margaret	20	F	Farmer	25Se02Ec
DIGNAN, Mary	21	F	Farmer	25Se02Ec
Bridget	20	F	Farmer	25Se02Ec
MURPHY, Patrick	21	M	Farmer	25Se02Ec
BARNS, Ellen	21	F	Farmer	25Se02Ec
LINHAHAN, Ann	30	F	Farmer	25Se02Ec
FARREL, Jane	17	F	Farmer	25Se02Ec
Andrew	19	F	Farmer	25Se02Ec
CASTIGAN, John	22	M	Farmer	25Se02Ec
POGUIN, Johnson	60	M	Farmer	25Se02Ec
HIGGINGS, Ann	27	F	Farmer	25Se02Ec
BRUNLAN, John	42	M	Farmer	25Se02Ec
RYAN, George	20	M	Farmer	25Se02Ec
COLLINS, Mary	20	F	Farmer	25Se02Ec
QUINLAN, Honora	16	F	Farmer	25Se02Ec
Mary	8	F	Child	25Se02Ec
HENLAHAN, Michael	25	M	Farmer	25Se02Ec
BURK, Edward	27	M	Farmer	25Se02Ec
BUCKLY, Michael	25	M	Farmer	25Se02Ec
MCCARTHY, Michael	23	M	Farmer	25Se02Ec
DARRELY, John	10	M	Farmer	25Se02Ec
HARTIGAN, Patrick	23	M	Farmer	25Se02Ec
DONOHUE, Maurice	24	M	Farmer	25Se02Ec
SCOTT, Patrick	23	M	Farmer	25Se02Ec
Mary	13	F	Farmer	25Se02Ec
MCCARTHY, Patrick	24	M	Unknown	25Se02Ec
HANLIN, Julia	28	F	Unknown	25Se02Ec
Johanna	.07	F	Infant	25Se02Ec
CHADWICK, Samuel	41	M	Unknown	25Se02Ec
James	16	M	Unknown	25Se02Ec
BRENNAN, James	16	M	Unknown	25Se02Ec

NAMES OF PASSENGERS	AGE	SEX	OCCUPATIONS	DATE PORT SHIP
COX, James	27	M	Unknown	25Se02Ec
ROACH, John	22	M	Unknown	25Se02Ec
James	20	M	Unknown	25Se02Ec
Margaret	26	F	Unknown	25Se02Ec
Ann	24	F	Unknown	25Se02Ec
FLINN, John	45	M	Unknown	25Se02Ec
Michael	10	M	Unknown	25Se02Ec
CONNERTRI, Catherine	20	F	Unknown	25Se02Ec
DORAN, Margaret	13	F	Unknown	25Se02Ec
SKEFFINGTON, Catherine	16	F	Unknown	25Se02Ec
LYONS, Michael	23	M	Unknown	25Se02Ec
REILLY, Patrick	30	M	Unknown	25Se02Ec
Mary	21	F	Unknown	25Se02Ec
NAVAN, John	26	M	Unknown	25Se02Ec
Mary	26	F	Unknown	25Se02Ec
Daniel	.05	M	Infant	25Se02Ec
MORRIS, Winifred	18	F	Unknown	25Se02Ec
MULLEN, Margaret	20	F	Unknown	25Se02Ec
CATHY, John	30	M	Unknown	25Se02Ec
Martha	23	F	Unknown	25Se02Ec
NUNCRAFT, Alexander	23	M	Unknown	25Se02Ec
CRAWFORD, John	20	M	Unknown	25Se02Ec
MURRY, Ann	20	F	Unknown	25Se02Ec
MCILVOY, Patrick	23	M	Unknown	25Se02Ec
WHELAN, Richard	19	M	Unknown	25Se02Ec
CRONAN, Martin	38	M	Unknown	25Se02Ec
WALKER, Thomas	25	M	Unknown	25Se02Ec
George	.10	M	Infant	25Se02Ec
Mary	30	F	Unknown	25Se02Ec
Mary	.06	F	Infant	25Se02Ec
FLINN, Bridget	50	F	Unknown	25Se02Ec
GOLLICK, Patrick	23	M	Unknown	25Se02Ec
LENNON, John	22	M	Unknown	25Se02Ec
Margaret	17	F	Unknown	25Se02Ec
Catherin	24	F	Unknown	25Se02Ec
James	16	M	Unknown	25Se02Ec
James	.08	M	Infant	25Se02Ec
HOLLAND, Michael	18	M	Unknown	25Se02Ec
MULCHENOCK, William-P.	29	M	Gentleman	25Se02Ec
Allice	24	F	Unknown	25Se02Ec
Allice	.11	F	Infant	25Se02Ec
WHITAKER, Robt.H.	30	M	Infant	25Se02Ec
BURKE, Mary	50	F	Unknown	25Se02Ec
Elisabeth	23	F	Unknown	25Se02Ec
C.R.L.W.	20	F	Unknown	25Se02Ec

SHANNON 26 SEPTEMBER 1849

From Liverpool

NAMES OF PASSENGERS	AGE	SEX	OCCUPATIONS	DATE PORT SHIP
CROWLEY, Dennis	40	M	Laborer	26Se02Id
WALSH, Lawrence	25	M	Laborer	26Se02Id
DUGAN, Michl.	36	M	Musician	26Se02Id
Winifred	30	F	Spinster	26Se02Id
Margaret	.07	F	Infant	26Se02Id
GLEESON, Margaret	20	F	Spinster	26Se02Id
BRENNAN, Michl.	20	M	Laborer	26Se02Id
Mary	24	F	Laborer	26Se02Id
FARRINGTON, Armesly	24	M	Grocer	26Se02Id
U-Mrs.	23	F	Grocer	26Se02Id
ARMSTRONG, Samuel	24	M	Grocer	26Se02Id
John	22	M	Grocer	26Se02Id
U-Mrs.	21	F	Grocer	26Se02Id
BURKE, Robert	26	M	Laborer	26Se02Id
Ruth	24	F	Laborer	26Se02Id
NAGLE, Mary	45	F	Spinster	26Se02Id
CONNELL, Johana	26	F	Spinster	26Se02Id
Patrick	9	M	Child	26Se02Id
SULLIVAN, Margaret	26	F	Child	26Se02Id
CONNELL, Mary	24	F	Child	26Se02Id
Mary	25	F	Spinster	26Se02Id
REILLY, John	24	M	Laborer	26Se02Id
HILL, John	26	M	Laborer	26Se02Id
CROWLEY, Julia	20	F	Spinster	26Se02Id
CUNNINGHAM, John	25	M	Laborer	26Se02Id
GARVEY, Michl.	20	M	Laborer	26Se02Id
FEE, Ellen	20	F	Laborer	26Se02Id
GILMORE, Allice	35	F	Laborer	26Se02Id
Sally	16	F	Laborer	26Se02Id
CONNOR, Mary	19	F	Laborer	26Se02Id
REILLY, Allice	30	F	Laborer	26Se02Id
Peter	11	M	Laborer	26Se02Id
Bonner	10	M	Laborer	26Se02Id
Margaret	4	F	Child	26Se02Id
GILMORE, Patt	24	M	Laborer	26Se02Id
QUIGLEY, Cath.	14	F	Spinster	26Se02Id
MACKIN, Anne	22	F	Spinster	26Se02Id
DONNELLY, Mary	28	F	Spinster	26Se02Id
MCKUSKIR, Sarah	14	F	Spinster	26Se02Id
Hugh	11	M	Spinster	26Se02Id
Mary	4	F	Child	26Se02Id
HUGHES, Catharine	20	F	Spinster	26Se02Id
MCQUADE, William	26	M	Laborer	26Se02Id
Died-At-Sea				
Edwd.	21	M	Laborer	26Se02Id
RIELLY, Elizabeth	35	F	Spinster	26Se02Id
DRURY, Michl.	22	M	Laborer	26Se02Id
ROONEY, Michl.	25	M	Laborer	26Se02Id
Patrick	38	M	Laborer	26Se02Id
FORD, Patrick	22	M	Laborer	26Se02Id
DUFFY, James	24	M	Laborer	26Se02Id
Anne	18	F	Laborer	26Se02Id
Rielly	28	F	Spinster	26Se02Id
Margt.	6	F	Child	26Se02Id
Ellen	4	F	Child	26Se02Id
William	2	M	Child	26Se02Id
Died-At-Sea				
John	.09	M	Infant	26Se02Id
LAMB, Bernard	22	M	Laborer	26Se02Id
MCEVEY, John	24	M	Laborer	26Se02Id
DONOHUE, Owen	30	M	Laborer	26Se02Id
Allice	25	F	Laborer	26Se02Id
Mary	2	F	Child	26Se02Id
GAFFNEY, Hugh	20	M	Laborer	26Se02Id
Died-At-Sea				
FLYNN, Stephen	30	M	Bootmaker	26Se02Id
Mary	30	F	Bootmaker	26Se02Id
Bridget	15	F	Bootmaker	26Se02Id
Stephen	11	M	Bootmaker	26Se02Id
Thomas	9	M	Child	26Se02Id
Mary	7	F	Child	26Se02Id
Jane	5	F	Child	26Se02Id
William	2	M	Child	26Se02Id
Ellen	.08	F	Infant	26Se02Id
FORKNER, Henry	30	M	Bootmaker	26Se02Id
Sophia	26	F	Bootmaker	26Se02Id
Sophia	9	F	Child	26Se02Id
Elizabeth	6	F	Child	26Se02Id
HEALY, Luke	30	M	Laborer	26Se02Id
KENEDY, Timothy	30	M	Laborer	26Se02Id
DOONER, Michael	16	M	Laborer	26Se02Id
REILLY, Thomas	28	M	Mason	26Se02Id
Catharine	25	F	Mason	26Se02Id
Mary-Anne	00	F	Mason	26Se02Id
BRAY, Stephen	30	M	Laborer	26Se02Id
Margaret	26	F	Laborer	26Se02Id
John	5	M	Child	26Se02Id
Michl.	3	M	Child	26Se02Id
Norry	1	F	Child	26Se02Id
James	22	M	Laborer	26Se02Id
ROACH, John	22	M	Laborer	26Se02Id
BRAY, Cath.	40	F	Laborer	26Se02Id
Cath.	14	F	Laborer	26Se02Id
Winifred	11	F	Laborer	26Se02Id

NAMES OF PASSENGERS	AGE	SEX	OCCUPATIONS	DATE PORT SHIP
DOWNS, Betsey	35	F	Spinster	26Se02Id
Anne	12	F	Spinster	26Se02Id
Agnes	10	F	Spinster	26Se02Id
Michael	8	M	Child	26Se02Id
Elizabeth	6	F	Child	26Se02Id
Robert	4	M	Child	26Se02Id
Elizabeth	00	F	Unknown	26Se02Id
MCAULLFFE, Bridget	20	F	Spinster	26Se02Id
MITCHAEL, George	21	M	Laborer	26Se02Id
CORNEY, James	24	M	Laborer	26Se02Id
DONOHUE, Eugine	35	M	Laborer	26Se02Id
James	25	M	Laborer	26Se02Id
BRIERLY, Mary	55	F	Spinster	26Se02Id
Abel	16	M	Laborer	26Se02Id
MCGUCKIN, John	26	M	Storekeeper	26Se02Id
CAHEY, Mary	30	F	Spinster	26Se02Id
MCGUCKIN, Mary	30	F	Spinster	26Se02Id
ARMESLY, Robert	30	M	Farmer	26Se02Id
Anne	25	F	Farmer	26Se02Id
Robert	.11	M	Infant	26Se02Id
Mary	1	F	Child	26Se02Id
GITTHORP, Mary	20	F	Farmer	26Se02Id
PALFRY, Mary	20	F	Spinster	26Se02Id
MCKINLY, Eliza	20	F	Spinster	26Se02Id
Margaret	18	F	Spinster	26Se02Id
CLYNCH, Margaret	19	F	Spinster	26Se02Id
EGAN, Cath.	30	F	Spinster	26Se02Id
FIFE, U-Miss	22	F	Spinster	26Se02Id
HILLARD, Maria	19	F	Spinster	26Se02Id
KEER, Michl.	19	M	Laborer	26Se02Id
KEEGAN, Garrett	40	M	Laborer	26Se02Id
ROSS, Matilda	13	F	Spinster	26Se02Id
Robert	11	M	Spinster	26Se02Id
SCALLY, Biddy	12	F	Spinster	26Se02Id
DEACON, Thomas	10	M	Spinster	26Se02Id
Alexander	9	M	Child	26Se02Id
CONNOR, Margt.	22	F	Spinster	26Se02Id
MCELHATTON, Michael	30	M	Laborer	26Se02Id
Anne	30	F	Laborer	26Se02Id
Maria	4	F	Child	26Se02Id
FLEMING, Catharine	40	F	Unknown	26Se02Id
John	26	M	Farmer	26Se02Id
Laughlin	18	M	Farmer	26Se02Id
Mary	16	F	Farmer	26Se02Id
Anne	13	F	Farmer	26Se02Id
Sarah	11	F	Farmer	26Se02Id
Patrick	9	M	Child	26Se02Id
Bridget	7	F	Child	26Se02Id
William	5	M	Child	26Se02Id
MULLAY, Robert	24	M	Laborer	26Se02Id
GILLAN, Mary	20	F	Spinster	26Se02Id
SENEHAN, Lucy	19	F	Spinster	26Se02Id
THOMPSON, James	30	M	Laborer	26Se02Id
ROONEY, Anne	18	F	Spinster	26Se02Id
ROSS, Eliza	16	F	Spinster	26Se02Id
MCCABE, Thomas	17	M	Laborer	26Se02Id
LANGLEY, James	18	M	Laborer	26Se02Id
LEE, James	29	M	Laborer	26Se02Id
JOHNSTON, William	20	M	Laborer	26Se02Id
CROSS, Sarah	34	F	Spinster	26Se02Id
REDDINGTON, Bridget	25	F	Spinster	26Se02Id
CARROLL, Mary	30	F	Spinster	26Se02Id
CORMACK, Mary	25	F	Spinster	26Se02Id
WOOD, John	18	M	Laborer	26Se02Id
POWER, Richard	20	M	Laborer	26Se02Id
BOHAN, Margaret	30	F	Spinster	26Se02Id
Terry	3	M	Child	26Se02Id
Dennis	.09	M	Infant	26Se02Id
Died-At-Sea				
DALY, John	20	M	Laborer	26Se02Id
MCCARTY, Florence	25	F	Spinster	26Se02Id
RODDY, Allice	25	F	Spinster	26Se02Id
KING, Margaret	16	F	Spinster	26Se02Id
SHED, Mary	20	F	Spinster	26Se02Id
DOODS, Patt	21	M	Laborer	26Se02Id

NAMES OF PASSENGERS	AGE	SEX	OCCUPATIONS	DATE PORT SHIP
SULLIVAN, Honora	20	F	Spinster	26Se02Id
ALBRIDGE, Mary	22	F	Spinster	26Se02Id
DUGGAN, Charles	50	M	Laborer	26Se02Id
Johana	50	F	Laborer	26Se02Id
ROACH, Terry	30	M	Laborer	26Se02Id
DALY, Charles	40	M	Laborer	26Se02Id
John	20	M	Laborer	26Se02Id
Ellen	18	F	Laborer	26Se02Id
FITZGERALD, Honora	18	F	Spinster	26Se02Id
Honora	7	F	Child	26Se02Id
Hannah	5	F	Child	26Se02Id
Abegal	3	M	Child	26Se02Id
TOBIN, Richd.	40	M	Laborer	26Se02Id
WALSH, Catharine	30	F	Spinster	26Se02Id
DOODY, Mary	21	F	Spinster	26Se02Id
FITZGERALD, Ellen	21	F	Spinster	26Se02Id
PRENDERVILLE, Mary	30	F	Spinster	26Se02Id
William	10	M	Laborer	26Se02Id
CULLIMAN, Mathew	40	M	Laborer	26Se02Id
Thos.	6	M	Child	26Se02Id
BERRETT, Margaret	30	F	Laborer	26Se02Id
Henrietta	00	F	Laborer	26Se02Id
PATTERSON, James	25	M	Farmer	26Se02Id
U-Mrs.	21	F	Farmer	26Se02Id
PRITCHARD, Thomas	24	M	Laborer	26Se02Id
BYRNE, Phillip	22	M	Laborer	26Se02Id
U-Mrs.	20	F	Laborer	26Se02Id
CALLENY, Mary	50	F	Spinster	26Se02Id
MCKIE, Thos.	23	M	Farmer	26Se02Id
John	20	M	Farmer	26Se02Id
Patrick	14	M	Farmer	26Se02Id
Ellen	18	F	Farmer	26Se02Id
Catharine	22	F	Farmer	26Se02Id
DURY, John	20	M	Farmer	26Se02Id
James	28	M	Farmer	26Se02Id
HERMAN, John	30	M	Millwright	26Se02Id
U-Mrs.	25	F	Millwright	26Se02Id
Mary	9	F	Child	26Se02Id
MORRIS, Peter	18	M	Laborer	26Se02Id
FITZPATRICK, Margaret	16	F	Spinster	26Se02Id
GUNN, Mary	50	F	Spinster	26Se02Id
James	24	M	Laborer	26Se02Id
DOHERTY, Daniel	30	M	Laborer	26Se02Id
SCALLY, Owen	9	M	Child	26Se02Id
CLYNE, Thos.	19	M	Laborer	26Se02Id
FITZPATRICK, Elizabeth	6	F	Child	26Se02Id
FARRELL, Mary	20	F	Laborer	26Se02Id
Anne	18	F	Laborer	26Se02Id
John	12	M	Laborer	26Se02Id
TOBIAS, William	30	M	Laborer	26Se02Id
U-Mrs.	30	F	Laborer	26Se02Id
William	5	M	Child	26Se02Id
Mary	3	F	Child	26Se02Id
Anne-Jane	00	F	Laborer	26Se02Id
COUGHLAN, Mary	40	F	Spinster	26Se02Id
PAIN, Richd.	35	M	Laborer	26Se02Id
SULLIVA, Daniel	33	M	Laborer	26Se02Id
Mary	32	F	Laborer	26Se02Id
SULLIVAN, William	12	M	Laborer	26Se02Id
John	8	M	Child	26Se02Id
Mary	10	F	Child	26Se02Id
Bridget	6	F	Child	26Se02Id
James	4	M	Child	26Se02Id
John	2	M	Child	26Se02Id
COURNANE, Nancy	30	F	Spinster	26Se02Id
Bridget	9	F	Child	26Se02Id
Kate	5	F	Child	26Se02Id
Johana	3	F	Child	26Se02Id
Patrick	.07	M	Infant	26Se02Id
Died-At-Sea				
KELLY, Judy	40	F	Spinster	26Se02Id
Died-At-Sea				
Margaret	18	F	Spinster	26Se02Id
KING, John	28	M	Laborer	26Se02Id
Died-At-Sea				

NAMES OF PASSENGERS	AGE	SEX	OCCUPATIONS	DATE PORT SHIP
FITZPATRICK, Catharine	30	F	Spinster	26Se02Id
Died-At-Sea				
Honora	27	F	Spinster	26Se02Id
FITZGERALD, Anne	17	F	Spinster	26Se02Id
Patrick	.10	M	Infant	26Se02Id
Died-At-Sea				
Bridget	12	F	Spinster	26Se02Id
BOURK, Mary	22	F	Spinster	26Se02Id
MOUNT, John	30	M	Laborer	26Se02Id
MCGOWAN, Samuel	20	M	Laborer	26Se02Id
CONLAN, Peter	25	M	Laborer	26Se02Id
DOYLE, Wm.	40	M	Farmer	26Se02Id
YOUNG, Joseph	17	M	Farmer	26Se02Id
CONNORS, John	30	M	Laborer	26Se02Id
MCDONNELL, Bridget	22	F	Spinster	26Se02Id
KELTON, Maria-S.	23	F	Spinster	26Se02Id
BYRNS, Maria	21	F	Spinster	26Se02Id
NOWLAN, Maria	24	F	Spinster	26Se02Id
GENDER, William	28	M	Laborer	26Se02Id
Mary	22	F	Laborer	26Se02Id
Michl.	00	M	Laborer	26Se02Id
FARRELL, Rosana	20	F	Spinster	26Se02Id
MONHAN, Peter	45	M	Laborer	26Se02Id
U-Mrs.	45	F	Laborer	26Se02Id
John	17	M	Laborer	26Se02Id
Sarah	13	F	Laborer	26Se02Id
Hannah	15	F	Laborer	26Se02Id
Frances	11	F	Laborer	26Se02Id
Elizabeth	4	F	Child	26Se02Id
CARTAN, Cath.	15	F	Spinster	26Se02Id
Margt.	20	F	Spinster	26Se02Id
CALLAHAN, Mary	18	F	Spinster	26Se02Id
Bridget	13	F	Spinster	26Se02Id
KELLY, Ellen	20	F	Spinster	26Se02Id
NEWBERRY, U	50	M	Unknown	26Se02Id
U	45	F	Lady	26Se02Id
BEAL, T.	30	U	Unknown	26Se02Id
GOWAN, C.	25	M	Unknown	26Se02Id

BURLINGTON 26 SEPTEMBER 1849

From Liverpool

NAMES OF PASSENGERS	AGE	SEX	OCCUPATIONS	DATE PORT SHIP
RILEY, Ann	12	F	None	26Se02Ci
MORRIS, Martha	60	F	Dairymaid	26Se02Ci
DILLON, Richd.	17	M	Clerk	26Se02Ci
Sarah	13	F	None	26Se02Ci
CLANCY, Mary-Ann	26	F	Wife	26Se02Ci
John	3	M	Child	26Se02Ci
HOGAN, Mary	00	F	Unknown	26Se02Ci
OCONNOR, Bridget	30	F	Wife	26Se02Ci
Mary	7	F	Child	26Se02Ci
Bridget	5	F	Child	26Se02Ci
Kate	.09	F	Infant	26Se02Ci
SULLIVAN, John	16	M	Clerk	26Se02Ci
Mary	12	F	None	26Se02Ci
SWEENY, Margt.	25	F	Servant	26Se02Ci
FOLEY, Ellen	22	F	Servant	26Se02Ci
SULLIVAN, Ellen	24	F	Servant	26Se02Ci
BROPHY, Margt.	22	F	Servant	26Se02Ci
ROCK, Margt.	30	F	Wife	26Se02Ci
David	13	M	None	26Se02Ci
Margt.	11	F	None	26Se02Ci
Elline	8	F	Child	26Se02Ci
Peter	4	M	Child	26Se02Ci
Margt.	2	F	Child	26Se02Ci
BAKER, Mary-S.	26	F	Wife	26Se02Ci
James	2	M	Child	26Se02Ci
MAHONY, Hannah	18	F	Servant	26Se02Ci
SHEA, Tim	27	M	Coachman	26Se02Ci
OCONNOR, Ann	25	F	Servant	26Se02Ci
GRIFFIN, Honora	30	F	Servant	26Se02Ci
DONOHUE, Jerry	22	M	Butler	26Se02Ci
SULLIVAN, Steph.	20	M	Tailor	26Se02Ci
Mary	22	F	Servant	26Se02Ci
Ellen	24	F	Servant	26Se02Ci
MCEVOY, James	40	M	Laborer	26Se02Ci
ARMSTRONG, John	3	M	Child	26Se02Ci
MCCARTY, Jane	29	F	Schms	26Se02Ci
FEENY, Pat	16	M	None	26Se02Ci
Ann	12	F	None	26Se02Ci
MCCARY, John	15	M	None	26Se02Ci
MURRAHAN, Mary	25	F	Servant	26Se02Ci
GRIFFEN, Bridget	18	F	Servant	26Se02Ci
COLLINS, Lawrence	19	M	Laborer	26Se02Ci
Thomas	35	M	Laborer	26Se02Ci
TAULPY, Jas.	25	M	Laborer	26Se02Ci
Anthony	26	M	Laborer	26Se02Ci
EGAN, Ellen	18	F	Servant	26Se02Ci
KENNEDY, John	30	M	Clerk	26Se02Ci
LEARY, James	26	M	Laborer	26Se02Ci
U (W)	24	F	None	26Se02Ci
CHAMBERS, Ann	22	F	Servant	26Se02Ci
DOLAN, Winney	19	F	Servant	26Se02Ci
Mary	10	F	None	26Se02Ci
OBRIAN, Cath.	22	F	Mtmkr	26Se02Ci
BELL, Susannah	20	F	Mtmkr	26Se02Ci
CONLY, Adam	25	M	Laborer	26Se02Ci
DONOVAN, Mary	28	F	Servant	26Se02Ci
Edmund	19	M	Baker	26Se02Ci
EVANS, Mary	18	F	Dressmaker	26Se02Ci
GALLEGHAND, John	25	M	Tailor	26Se02Ci
CAROLINE, Margt.	44	F	Servant	26Se02Ci
DONNELLY, Mick	20	M	Laborer	26Se02Ci
MORROW, Mary	19	F	Servant	26Se02Ci
FITZPATRICK, Mary	9	F	Child	26Se02Ci
MAXWELL, Bridget	14	F	None	26Se02Ci
COGAND, Thomas	40	M	Tailor	26Se02Ci
QUINN, Margt.	40	F	Wife	26Se02Ci
Anne	12	F	None	26Se02Ci
Henry	6	M	Child	26Se02Ci
FARRALY, Pat	14	M	None	26Se02Ci
Sarah	9	F	Child	26Se02Ci
MURRAY, Mick	40	M	Weaver	26Se02Ci
GORMLEY, John	6	M	Child	26Se02Ci
Pat	4	M	Child	26Se02Ci
STRATTON, Joseph	25	M	Cooper	26Se02Ci
DONNELEAN, Bridget	18	F	Servant	26Se02Ci
ALLEN, William	29	M	Unknown	26Se02Ci
OROURK, Perry	20	M	Laborer	26Se02Ci
MULLOY, Rose	25	F	Wife	26Se02Ci
Cath.	4	F	Child	26Se02Ci
GAFFREY, Mick	25	M	Laborer	26Se02Ci
Mary	45	F	Servant	26Se02Ci
CAMERON, Margt.	25	F	Servant	26Se02Ci
MOORE, Eliza	12	F	None	26Se02Ci
RAFFERTY, Mary	18	F	Servant	26Se02Ci
MCGLEN, Julia	8	F	Child	26Se02Ci
Julia	9	F	Child	26Se02Ci
FOGARTY, Mick	12	M	None	26Se02Ci
Martin	10	M	None	26Se02Ci
MATHEWS, Will	19	M	Laborer	26Se02Ci
GERAGHTY, Will	15	M	None	26Se02Ci
MCCORMAL, Jas.	15	M	None	26Se02Ci
Margt.	17	F	Servant	26Se02Ci
BRADY, Honora	18	F	Servant	26Se02Ci
LAMB, Cornelius	15	M	None	26Se02Ci
Betty	12	F	None	26Se02Ci
WILLIAMS, Bridget	16	F	None	26Se02Ci
VENABOLD, Eliz.	52	F	Wife	26Se02Ci
Mary-Ann	17	F	Servant	26Se02Ci
CARVER, David	20	M	Laborer	26Se02Ci
RYAN, William	20	M	Laborer	26Se02Ci
BORMAN, Bridget	20	F	Wife	26Se02Ci

NAMES OF PASSENGERS		AGE	SEX	OCCUPATIONS	DATE PORT SHIP
BORMAN, Ellen		4	F	Child	26Se02Ci
KEOUGH, John		40	M	Mason	26Se02Ci
Mary	(W)	38	F	None	26Se02Ci
Jas.		26	M	Mason	26Se02Ci
Ellen		10	F	None	26Se02Ci
John		6	M	Child	26Se02Ci
Eliz.		3	F	Child	26Se02Ci
Died-At-Sea					
MURRAY, Mary		20	F	Servant	26Se02Ci
RILEY, Chas.		14	M	None	26Se02Ci
ROCK, Margt.		12	F	None	26Se02Ci
OBRIEN, Pat		23	M	Laborer	26Se02Ci
RAY, Mary		40	F	Wife	26Se02Ci
Child		.10	F	Infant	26Se02Ci
Honora		5	F	Child	26Se02Ci
MCDERMOTT, Edwd.		20	M	Laborer	26Se02Ci
MCKERNARN, Susan		26	F	Servant	26Se02Ci
CADMAN, Thomas		15	M	None	26Se02Ci
KELLY, Jas.		25	M	Carpenter	26Se02Ci
Dennis		26	M	Carpenter	26Se02Ci
U-Mrs.	(W)	25	F	None	26Se02Ci
HAWLEY, Martin		30	M	Laborer	26Se02Ci
SULLIVAN, Pat		46	M	Farmer	26Se02Ci
Mary	(W)	48	F	None	26Se02Ci
Mary		14	F	None	26Se02Ci
Andrew		13	M	None	26Se02Ci
James		9	M	Child	26Se02Ci
KER, Cornelius		60	M	Farmer	26Se02Ci
Maggy	(W)	65	F	None	26Se02Ci
BROWN, John		18	M	Laborer	26Se02Ci
CARROL, Phil		18	M	Laborer	26Se02Ci
RODGERS, Cath.		12	F	None	26Se02Ci
MCNAMARA, Jane		15	F	None	26Se02Ci
REYNOLDS, Eliza		16	F	Dressmaker	26Se02Ci
NELSON, Ellen		17	F	Dressmaker	26Se02Ci
MULLEN, Margt.		19	F	Dressmaker	26Se02Ci
FLANAGAN, Francis		20	M	Laborer	26Se02Ci
DICKSON, William		17	M	Laborer	26Se02Ci
LEONARD, Margt.		18	F	Servant	26Se02Ci
MATTHEWS, Will		24	M	Carpenter	26Se02Ci
WARD, Richd.		22	M	Farmer	26Se02Ci
Sarah	(W)	30	F	None	26Se02Ci
BRICH, Robt.		21	M	Carpenter	26Se02Ci
GUINEA, William		26	M	Farmer	26Se02Ci
Ti--Y		26	M	Farmer	26Se02Ci
John		9	M	Child	26Se02Ci
ROBERTSON, William		22	M	Laborer	26Se02Ci
Andrew		14	M	None	26Se02Ci
Jane		12	F	None	26Se02Ci
YANDLE, Will		16	M	None	26Se02Ci
FLOOD, Johanna		20	F	Servant	26Se02Ci
Martha		18	F	Servant	26Se02Ci
ROCK, Ellen		29	F	Wife	26Se02Ci
Margt.		21	F	Servant	26Se02Ci
Kate		18	F	None	26Se02Ci
Hannah		5	F	Child	26Se02Ci
FLYNN, Edwd.		28	M	Laborer	26Se02Ci
ODONNELL, Cath.		23	F	Servant	26Se02Ci
BARRY, Lawrence		20	M	Laborer	26Se02Ci
Peggy		17	F	Servant	26Se02Ci
U-Mrs.		25	F	Wife	26Se02Ci
Ann		7	F	Child	26Se02Ci
Margt.		5	F	Child	26Se02Ci
GALLAGHER, Mick		22	M	Laborer	26Se02Ci
HANNON, Bridget		14	F	None	26Se02Ci
LAWLESS, James		25	M	Laborer	26Se02Ci
Ellen		23	F	Servant	26Se02Ci
GRIFFEN, Ann		20	F	Servant	26Se02Ci
SAUNDERS, Mary		19	F	Servant	26Se02Ci
DONOHUE, Cornelius		24	M	Shoemaker	26Se02Ci
CANDLERS, Jane		19	F	Servant	26Se02Ci
BUTLER, Ellen		30	F	Wife	26Se02Ci
William		6	M	Child	26Se02Ci
Mary		.07	F	Infant	26Se02Ci
James		1	M	Child	26Se02Ci

CRESCENT-CITY 27 SEPTEMBER 1849

From Chagres And Jamaica

NAMES OF PASSENGERS	AGE	SEX	OCCUPATIONS	DATE PORT SHIP
Moult--E, Chas.	37	M	Merchant	27Se58Bi
PALACHI, Gilbert	30	M	Merchant	27Se58Bi
CONDOR, John	25	M	Merchant	27Se58Bi
RENNIE, Mary	25	F	Missionary	27Se58Bi

ISAAC-WRIGHT 27 SEPTEMBER 1849

From Liverpool

NAMES OF PASSENGERS	AGE	SEX	OCCUPATIONS	DATE PORT SHIP
CORCORAN, Pat	18	M	Unknown	27Se02Km
MCCARTHY, John	18	M	Laborer	27Se02Km
LEARY, Pat	30	M	Laborer	27Se02Km
HORAN, Nancy	30	F	Unknown	27Se02Km
Michl.	15	M	Laborer	27Se02Km
John	20	M	Laborer	27Se02Km
Pat	11	M	Unknown	27Se02Km
John	6	M	Child	27Se02Km
Jas.	7	M	Child	27Se02Km
ROWLEY, Cath.	18	F	Spinster	27Se02Km
JOHNSTON, Cath.	22	F	Spinster	27Se02Km
HENESSY, Pat	25	M	Shoemaker	27Se02Km
FITZGERALD, Mary	18	F	Spinster	27Se02Km
COX, Darby	20	M	Laborer	27Se02Km
Maria	10	F	Unknown	27Se02Km
Died-At-Sea				
GILLIGAN, Margt.	19	F	Spinster	27Se02Km
MOONEY, Mary	20	F	Spinster	27Se02Km
LENOARD, Patt	20	M	Laborer	27Se02Km
DUNN, Ann	20	F	Spinster	27Se02Km
GILES, Mary	18	F	Spinster	27Se02Km
KELLY, Betty	30	F	Spinster	27Se02Km
GILES, Cath.	20	F	Spinster	27Se02Km
MCCANN, Mary	20	F	Spinster	27Se02Km
WALKER, Ann	20	F	Spinster	27Se02Km
MAHONY, Jno.	30	M	Carpenter	27Se02Km
Jno.	11	M	Carpenter	27Se02Km
Elandor	9	M	Child	27Se02Km
Fanny	7	F	Child	27Se02Km
FOLLIS, Geo.	18	M	Mason	27Se02Km
HALLIGAN, A-Mrs.	50	F	Unknown	27Se02Km
Ann	24	F	Unknown	27Se02Km
Brid.	22	F	Unknown	27Se02Km
Jis.	21	F	Unknown	27Se02Km
Ellen	18	F	Unknown	27Se02Km
YONGER, A-Mrs.	50	F	Unknown	27Se02Km
Maria	17	F	Unknown	27Se02Km
Cath.	15	F	Unknown	27Se02Km
Tho.	13	M	Unknown	27Se02Km
Jas.	11	M	Unknown	27Se02Km
MCQUADE, Jas.	30	M	Carpenter	27Se02Km
MORAN, U-Miss.	17	F	Unknown	27Se02Km
Mary	18	F	Unknown	27Se02Km
WARD, Cath.	8	F	Child	27Se02Km
John	11	M	Unknown	27Se02Km
Eliza	5	F	Child	27Se02Km
RILEY, Ann	50	F	Unknown	27Se02Km
Margt.A.	4	F	Child	27Se02Km
Died-At-Sea				
Tho.	29	M	Unknown	27Se02Km

NAMES OF PASSENGERS	AGE	SEX	OCCUPATIONS	DATE PORT SHIP
RILEY, Bernd.	27	M	Unknown	27Se02Km
Edward	20	M	Unknown	27Se02Km
LEE, Julia-Mrs.	26	F	Spinster	27Se02Km
HANDRAHAM, Mary	18	F	Spinster	27Se02Km
WHELAN, Cath.	26	F	Spinster	27Se02Km
DONLIN, Ellen	25	F	Spinster	27Se02Km
MADDEN, Wm.	21	M	Laborer	27Se02Km
KELLY, Ann	19	F	Unknown	27Se02Km
AUSTIN, Martin	24	M	Laborer	27Se02Km
FLOOD, Edwd.	25	M	Laborer	27Se02Km
BIGGERS, Nancy	11	F	Spinster	27Se02Km
MCGENA, Jas.	50	M	Laborer	27Se02Km
MCGLOUGHLIN, Dennis	50	M	Weaver	27Se02Km
Mary	50	F	Unknown	27Se02Km
Died-At-Sea				
Jno.	24	M	Weaver	27Se02Km
MCANNERY, Alice	20	F	Spinster	27Se02Km
CALLON, Brid.	9	F	Child	27Se02Km
Jas.	6	M	Child	27Se02Km
Died-At-Sea				
Ann	3	F	Child	27Se02Km
MALROY, Mary	28	F	Spinster	27Se02Km
Mary	.11	F	Infant	27Se02Km
TILDING, Ester	25	F	Spinster	27Se02Km
Ester	.00	F	Infant	27Se02Km
MCCABE, Mary	18	F	Spinster	27Se02Km
SULLIVAN, Cath.	19	F	Spinster	27Se02Km
GREENAN, Jas.	23	M	Laborer	27Se02Km
SWINGS, Eliza	22	F	Spinster	27Se02Km
MARTIN, Cath.	30	F	Unknown	27Se02Km
Brid.	14	F	Unknown	27Se02Km
Jno.	7	M	Child	27Se02Km
Ann	5	F	Child	27Se02Km
DUFFY, Tho.	23	M	Carpenter	27Se02Km
HAYES, Ann	20	F	Spinster	27Se02Km
BYRNE, Longhling	35	M	Mason	27Se02Km
CARDELL, Ellen	27	F	Spinster	27Se02Km
DRAWNEAR, Sarah	20	F	Spinster	27Se02Km
OWENS, Michl.	25	M	Laborer	27Se02Km
RILEY, Michl.	20	M	Tailor	27Se02Km
SHERIDAN, Margt.	24	F	Spinster	27Se02Km
CANARAN, Margt.	22	F	Spinster	27Se02Km
GILLIGAN, Mart.	30	F	Spinster	27Se02Km
GILL, Jno.	19	M	Laborer	27Se02Km
HOWARD, Jas.	25	M	Laborer	27Se02Km
MADDEN, Thos.	24	M	Laborer	27Se02Km
MURRY, Ann	20	F	Spinster	27Se02Km
DUNN, Cath.	18	F	Spinster	27Se02Km
HAVEN, Larr.	20	F	Spinster	27Se02Km
KANE, Ann	40	F	Spinster	27Se02Km
FLOOD, Pat	10	M	Laborer	27Se02Km
Died-At-Sea				
ONIEL, Wm.	30	M	Laborer	27Se02Km
RAIL, Pat	18	M	Laborer	27Se02Km
FINNELL, Mary	22	F	Spinster	27Se02Km
DORDEN, Ann	20	F	Spinster	27Se02Km
CONNADER, Jas.	30	M	Unknown	27Se02Km
U-Mrs.	28	F	Unknown	27Se02Km
Tho.	11	M	Unknown	27Se02Km
Jas.	10	M	Unknown	27Se02Km
Tho.	7	M	Child	27Se02Km
CANE, Ann	24	F	Unknown	27Se02Km
John	.00	M	Infant	27Se02Km
Dennis	20	M	Unknown	27Se02Km
CARTY, Ann	25	F	Unknown	27Se02Km
CARR, Wm.	30	M	Pressman	27Se02Km
BUTERWORTH, Tho.	32	M	Weaver	27Se02Km
MOONEY, Ann	45	F	Unknown	27Se02Km
NULTY, Ally	21	F	Spinster	27Se02Km
SMITH, Cath.	17	F	Spinster	27Se02Km
KANE, Cath.	21	F	Spinster	27Se02Km
WHITE, U-Mrs.	40	F	Unknown	27Se02Km
John	16	M	Unknown	27Se02Km
Alice	13	F	Unknown	27Se02Km
Margt.	10	F	Unknown	27Se02Km

NAMES OF PASSENGERS	AGE	SEX	OCCUPATIONS	DATE PORT SHIP
WHITE, Harriet	11	F	Unknown	27Se02Km
Caroline	.00	F	Infant	27Se02Km
MCNAMARA, Malaclin	25	M	Laborer	27Se02Km
U-Mrs.	22	F	Unknown	27Se02Km
Brid.	.00	F	Infant	27Se02Km
FRILDERY, Samuel	25	M	Unknown	27Se02Km
U-Mrs.	22	F	Unknown	27Se02Km
Mary	2	F	Child	27Se02Km
RYAN, Alice	40	F	Spinster	27Se02Km
CARPENTER, Mary	26	F	Spinster	27Se02Km
KING, Ann	25	F	Spinster	27Se02Km
WALSH, Mary	25	F	Spinster	27Se02Km
Cath.	.00	F	Infant	27Se02Km
Cath.	24	F	Unknown	27Se02Km
BURKE, Edwd.	23	M	Laborer	27Se02Km
Jno.	21	M	Laborer	27Se02Km
DONOHOE, Michl.	45	M	Laborer	27Se02Km
FLANAGAN, Charles	21	M	Unknown	27Se02Km
MEARY, Hannah	23	F	Unknown	27Se02Km
HOWELLS, John	25	M	Unknown	27Se02Km
Eliza	23	F	Unknown	27Se02Km
FLYNN, Pat	24	M	Unknown	27Se02Km
Died-At-Sea				
MCNAMARRA, Ester	40	F	Unknown	27Se02Km
Tho.	23	M	Laborer	27Se02Km
Brid.	27	F	Unknown	27Se02Km
CONNELL, Ellen	60	F	Spinster	27Se02Km
Margt.	25	F	Spinster	27Se02Km
GILMARTIN, Ann	20	F	Spinster	27Se02Km
FITZPATRICK, Margt.	40	F	Unknown	27Se02Km
Mary	20	F	Unknown	27Se02Km
Ann	18	F	Unknown	27Se02Km
Sarah	16	F	Unknown	27Se02Km
Kate	12	F	Unknown	27Se02Km
Margt.	12	F	Unknown	27Se02Km
Tho.	11	M	Unknown	27Se02Km
Rich.	7	M	Child	27Se02Km
Pat	2	M	Child	27Se02Km
Brid.	4	F	Child	27Se02Km
TRULY, Judy	29	F	Unknown	27Se02Km
CONNOR, Ann	20	F	Unknown	27Se02Km
MCTUSTED, Mary	40	F	Unknown	27Se02Km
Died-At-Sea				
COLEMAN, Pat	30	M	Laborer	27Se02Km
Judy	30	F	Laborer	27Se02Km
BURNS, Honor	20	F	Unknown	27Se02Km
Maria	18	F	Unknown	27Se02Km
MULROY, Jas.	22	M	Unknown	27Se02Km
KEELAN, Larr	22	M	Unknown	27Se02Km
DEVINE, Wm.	50	M	Master	27Se02Km
Mary	8	F	Child	27Se02Km
MCNAMARIS, Cath.	14	F	Spinster	27Se02Km
Pat	18	M	Unknown	27Se02Km
GLYNN, Mary	19	F	Unknown	27Se02Km
Margt.	16	F	Unknown	27Se02Km
Michl.	16	F	Unknown	27Se02Km
QUIRK, Michl.	18	F	Laborer	27Se02Km
DOUGHERTY, Pat	8	M	Child	27Se02Km
HOUGHTON, Jas.	45	M	Laborer	27Se02Km
KYLE, Sarah	18	F	Spinster	27Se02Km
CONGHLIN, Margt.	21	F	Spinster	27Se02Km
CLEMENTS, Rose	24	F	Spinster	27Se02Km
DUFFY, Ellen	18	F	Spinster	27Se02Km
Died-At-Sea				
CUMMERS, Thom.	28	M	Laborer	27Se02Km
RYAN, Gho.	30	M	Shoemaker	27Se02Km
Hugh	20	M	Laborer	27Se02Km
PARREN, Pat	26	M	Laborer	27Se02Km
Brid.	25	F	Unknown	27Se02Km
NULTY, Cath.	50	F	Unknown	27Se02Km
Rosan	3	F	Child	27Se02Km
HACKETT, Mary	50	F	Unknown	27Se02Km
Cath.	28	F	Unknown	27Se02Km
Jas.	3	M	Child	27Se02Km
Win.	1	M	Child	27Se02Km

NAMES OF PASSENGERS	AGE	SEX	OCCUPATIONS	DATE PORT SHIP
DONOHOE, Dan.	20	M	Tailor	27Se02Km
DUGAN, Anty.	20	F	Spinster	27Se02Km
WELHERS, Gho.	23	M	Laborer	27Se02Km
KELLY, Michl.	40	M	Laborer	27Se02Km
Jno.	6	M	Child	27Se02Km
Cath.	4	F	Child	27Se02Km
MCCORMICK, Mary	17	F	Spinster	27Se02Km
MULHALY, Cath.	20	F	Spinster	27Se02Km
KENNEDY, Anty	40	F	Unknown	27Se02Km
Alice	17	F	Unknown	27Se02Km
Jas.	12	M	Unknown	27Se02Km
Edwd.	10	M	Unknown	27Se02Km
Margt.	4	F	Child	27Se02Km
Mary	4	F	Child	27Se02Km
KEATING, Mary	40	F	Unknown	27Se02Km
FLANIGAN, Wm.	9	M	Child	27Se02Km
DONOHOE, Rose Died-At-Sea	20	F	Spinster	27Se02Km
CALLAHAN, Rose Died-At-Sea	8	F	Child	27Se02Km
John	6	M	Child	27Se02Km
Tho. Died-At-Sea	4	M	Child	27Se02Km
CALLON, Ann	11	F	Unknown	27Se02Km
Phil. Died-At-Sea	6	M	Child	27Se02Km
Peter	4	M	Child	27Se02Km
MCGUIRE, Michl.	13	M	Unknown	27Se02Km
Owen	11	M	Unknown	27Se02Km
RIELY, Nancy	17	F	Unknown	27Se02Km
HOLLAND, Edward	21	M	Carpenter	27Se02Km
SWALLOW, Jno.	24	M	Plasterer	27Se02Km
U-Mrs.	28	F	Unknown	27Se02Km
Ann	4	F	Child	27Se02Km
CONNALL, Margt.	30	F	Unknown	27Se02Km
Ann	9	F	Child	27Se02Km
Brid.	5	F	Child	27Se02Km
Cath. Died-At-Sea	2	F	Child	27Se02Km
SIMMONS, Mary Died-At-Sea	50	F	Unknown	27Se02Km
Ann	19	F	Unknown	27Se02Km
Margt.	22	F	Unknown	27Se02Km
Honor	8	F	Child	27Se02Km
DOUGHERTY, Hugh	12	M	Unknown	27Se02Km
BURK, Wm.	24	M	Laborer	27Se02Km
LODEN, Martin	25	M	Shoemaker	27Se02Km
SAMMONS, Honora	30	F	Unknown	27Se02Km
Ann	7	F	Child	27Se02Km
Mary	3	F	Child	27Se02Km
Jas.	2	M	Child	27Se02Km
DEVENIE, Alex.	20	M	Laborer	27Se02Km
MCCABE, Ann	11	F	Unknown	27Se02Km
HINES, Wid.	40	F	Unknown	27Se02Km
Ann	19	F	Unknown	27Se02Km
WARD, U-Mrs.	36	F	Unknown	27Se02Km
Mary	10	F	Unknown	27Se02Km
Pat	8	M	Child	27Se02Km
Tho.	5	M	Child	27Se02Km
MALONY, Michl.	25	M	Unknown	27Se02Km
DUGAN, Mary	25	F	Unknown	27Se02Km
Phil.	8	M	Child	27Se02Km
MORAN, Brid.	30	F	Spinster	27Se02Km
Mary	8	F	Child	27Se02Km
MCCANLEY, Pat	8	M	Child	27Se02Km
Ann	5	F	Child	27Se02Km
FARRELL, Peter	20	M	Laborer	27Se02Km
KNOX, Jane	19	F	Spinster	27Se02Km
Jas.	7	M	Child	27Se02Km
Wm.	5	M	Child	27Se02Km
MCGRERR, Betty-Ann	16	F	Spinster	27Se02Km
John	11	M	Unknown	27Se02Km
Jas.	9	M	Child	27Se02Km
WILSON, Cath.	20	F	Spinster	27Se02Km
Cath.	9	F	Child	27Se02Km

NAMES OF PASSENGERS	AGE	SEX	OCCUPATIONS	DATE PORT SHIP
WILSON, Mary-J.	7	F	Child	27Se02Km
GRAHAM, Jane	20	F	Spinster	27Se02Km
REYNOLDS, Sarah	30	F	Unknown	27Se02Km
Ben.	20	M	Unknown	27Se02Km
Peter	8	M	Child	27Se02Km
MARTIN, Ann	20	F	Unknown	27Se02Km
ABRAHAM, John	27	M	Shoemaker	27Se02Km
GOWNLEY, Pat	22	M	Laborer	27Se02Km
PHILIPS, Jas.	21	M	Mason	27Se02Km
TULLY, Jas.	21	M	Mason	27Se02Km
NEVEN, U-Miss.	20	F	Unknown	27Se02Km
BAXTER, Jno.	29	M	Laborer	27Se02Km
Mary	25	F	Unknown	27Se02Km
Margt.	2	F	Child	27Se02Km
Cath.	.00	F	Infant	27Se02Km
DRISCOLL, Brid.	23	F	Unknown	27Se02Km
Ben.	23	M	Laborer	27Se02Km
HORREN, Cath.	22	F	Unknown	27Se02Km
Jas.	2	M	Child	27Se02Km
MCGUINN, Manus	30	M	Joiner	27Se02Km
RILY, Mary	20	F	Unknown	27Se02Km
Ellen	19	F	Unknown	27Se02Km
KELLY, Brid.	20	F	Unknown	27Se02Km
MULLEN, Michl.	40	M	Scholar	27Se02Km
PLUNKET, Cath.	10	F	Unknown	27Se02Km
CAREY, Michl.	18	M	Laborer	27Se02Km
BRADY, Pat	20	M	Turner	27Se02Km
BRADLEY, Eliza	40	F	Spinster	27Se02Km
MCMULLEN, Richd.	24	M	Laborer	27Se02Km
CURTIS, Nich.	35	M	Laborer	27Se02Km
RONE, Ellen	17	F	Unknown	27Se02Km
CONLEY, Mary	17	F	Unknown	27Se02Km
NOLAN, Hugh	23	M	Laborer	27Se02Km
Cath.	22	F	Unknown	27Se02Km
OCALLAGHAN, Edwd.	22	M	Turner	27Se02Km
BROPHY, Mary	30	F	Spinster	27Se02Km
DOHENY, Mary	26	F	Spinster	27Se02Km
Pat	5	M	Child	27Se02Km
FLOOD, Stew	49	M	Unknown	27Se02Km
FITZGIBBONS, Pat	40	M	Unknown	27Se02Km
Elandor	38	M	Unknown	27Se02Km
Mary Died-At-Sea	9	F	Child	27Se02Km
Ellen	7	F	Child	27Se02Km
Michl.	5	M	Child	27Se02Km
Honora	3	F	Child	27Se02Km
Brid.	.00	F	Infant	27Se02Km
CAMUDY, George	35	M	Unknown	27Se02Km
DOYLE, Mary	28	F	Unknown	27Se02Km
Jno.	8	M	Child	27Se02Km
Andrew Died-At-Sea	4	M	Child	27Se02Km
Brid.	6	F	Child	27Se02Km
Hugh	22	M	Unknown	27Se02Km
Brid.	20	F	Unknown	27Se02Km
DUFFY, Cath.	18	F	Unknown	27Se02Km
WALKER, Jno.	44	M	Unknown	27Se02Km
WAITE, George	22	M	Unknown	27Se02Km
RIELY, John	12	M	Unknown	27Se02Km

N.H.WOLFE 28 SEPTEMBER 1849

From Liverpool

NAMES OF PASSENGERS	AGE	SEX	OCCUPATIONS	DATE PORT SHIP
ROWAN, James	27	M	Laborer	28Se02Gd
MCNALLY, Mary	26	F	Unknown	28Se02Gd
NAYLER, Mary	22	F	Unknown	28Se02Gd
MCMAHEN, Philip	50	M	Unknown	28Se02Gd
James	33	M	Unknown	28Se02Gd

NAMES OF PASSENGERS	AGE	SEX	OCCUPATIONS	DATE PORT SHIP
MCMAHEN, Philip	9	M	Child	28Se02Gd
Michael	6	M	Child	28Se02Gd
MCFOUGHEL, Hugh	20	M	Unknown	28Se02Gd
BROWN, William	20	M	Unknown	28Se02Gd
CARR, Ann	18	F	Unknown	28Se02Gd
ONEIL, Patrick	32	M	Unknown	28Se02Gd
KILEY, Eliza	24	F	Unknown	28Se02Gd
COOK, Robert	34	M	Unknown	28Se02Gd
REGAN, Betsey	26	F	Unknown	28Se02Gd
CUNNINGHAM, Bridget	26	F	Unknown	28Se02Gd
Eliza	26	F	Unknown	28Se02Gd
CLARKE, Mary	38	F	Unknown	28Se02Gd
Nicholas	20	M	Unknown	28Se02Gd
MCNALLY, Eugene	20	M	Unknown	28Se02Gd
MCGOWAN, Ann	17	F	Unknown	28Se02Gd
KING, Margaret	16	F	Unknown	28Se02Gd
KNOWLES, George	26	M	Unknown	28Se02Gd
Jane	23	F	Unknown	28Se02Gd
WHELAN, Peter	17	M	Unknown	28Se02Gd
MURPHY, Martin	18	M	Unknown	28Se02Gd
Died-At-Sea				
GLEASON, Daniel	40	M	Unknown	28Se02Gd
BRIEN, Ellen	50	F	Unknown	28Se02Gd
BUCKLEY, Ellen	3	F	Child	28Se02Gd
Died-At-Sea				
CALINE, John	40	M	Unknown	28Se02Gd
Mary	30	F	Unknown	28Se02Gd
KANYLE, John	32	M	Unknown	28Se02Gd
Died-At-Sea				
CASTEN, John	3	M	Child	28Se02Gd
RYAN, Mi.	20	M	Unknown	28Se02Gd
SULLIVAN, Michael	20	M	Unknown	28Se02Gd
U-Mrs.	20	F	Unknown	28Se02Gd
RYAN, John	30	M	Unknown	28Se02Gd
Ellen	25	F	Unknown	28Se02Gd
SPEARS, John	50	M	Unknown	28Se02Gd
Mary-Jane	19	F	Unknown	28Se02Gd
Mary	36	F	Unknown	28Se02Gd
Solomon	8	M	Child	28Se02Gd
William	7	M	Child	28Se02Gd
John	11	M	Laborer	28Se02Gd
Ann	4	F	Child	28Se02Gd
Edward	.00	M	Infant	28Se02Gd
CONNER, James	28	M	Unknown	28Se02Gd
Eliza	28	F	Unknown	28Se02Gd
Margaret	5	F	Child	28Se02Gd
Susan	4	F	Child	28Se02Gd
James	.00	M	Infant	28Se02Gd
Died-At-Sea				
MARTINSON, Bridget	30	F	Unknown	28Se02Gd
Mary	6	F	Child	28Se02Gd
Ann	4	F	Child	28Se02Gd
Patrick	2	M	Child	28Se02Gd
JENKINS, John	18	M	Unknown	28Se02Gd
COFFER, John	5	M	Child	28Se02Gd
DOWLING, John	21	M	Unknown	28Se02Gd
Mary	17	F	Unknown	28Se02Gd
RIELEY, Mary	30	F	Unknown	28Se02Gd
HORAN, Charles	28	M	Unknown	28Se02Gd
Mary	28	F	Unknown	28Se02Gd
SULLIVAN, Honora	20	F	Unknown	28Se02Gd
DOLTEN, Ellen	20	F	Unknown	28Se02Gd
BUCHANON, Johanna	18	F	Unknown	28Se02Gd
LEARY, Honora	20	F	Unknown	28Se02Gd
HORAN, Edward	4	M	Child	28Se02Gd
SMITH, Barbara	40	F	Unknown	28Se02Gd
Frank	12	M	Unknown	28Se02Gd
John	8	M	Child	28Se02Gd
PARKINS, Esther	23	F	Unknown	28Se02Gd
GREEN, John	26	M	Laborer	28Se02Gd
Julia	22	F	Unknown	28Se02Gd
Michael	5	M	Child	28Se02Gd
Judy	.00	F	Infant	28Se02Gd
KENNEDY, Michael	2	M	Child	28Se02Gd
COULBERT, Mary	34	F	Unknown	28Se02Gd
COULBERT, Michael	25	M	Unknown	28Se02Gd
ONIEL, Thomas	23	M	Unknown	28Se02Gd
OWENS, Susan	19	F	Unknown	28Se02Gd
Mary	10	F	Unknown	28Se02Gd
BURNS, Patrick	13	M	Unknown	28Se02Gd
RIELY, Bridget	45	F	Unknown	28Se02Gd
Emelia	46	F	Unknown	28Se02Gd
MCDERMOT, Michael	17	M	Unknown	28Se02Gd
KELLEY, Ann	15	F	Unknown	28Se02Gd
Mary-Ann	10	F	Unknown	28Se02Gd
Febry	12	F	Unknown	28Se02Gd
Martha	19	F	Unknown	28Se02Gd
Ellen	22	F	Unknown	28Se02Gd
HOLAN, John	24	M	Unknown	28Se02Gd
Died-At-Sea				
SUTTON, Patrick	35	M	Unknown	28Se02Gd
FLEMAN, Thos.	34	M	Unknown	28Se02Gd
BURRY, Richard	35	M	Unknown	28Se02Gd
BURNS, James	34	M	Laborer	28Se02Gd
Ann	36	F	Unknown	28Se02Gd
Margaret	25	F	Unknown	28Se02Gd
Mary	5	F	Child	28Se02Gd
Harvey	2	M	Child	28Se02Gd
Elizabeth	.00	F	Infant	28Se02Gd
Died-At-Sea				
Margaret	22	F	Unknown	28Se02Gd
Nancy	.02	F	Infant	28Se02Gd
WILLIAMS, Thomas	20	M	Unknown	28Se02Gd
Died-At-Sea				
CARTER, J.H.	20	M	Unknown	28Se02Gd
NOLAN, Michael	63	M	Unknown	28Se02Gd
Ellen	60	F	Unknown	28Se02Gd
Mary	25	F	Unknown	28Se02Gd
James	.00	M	Infant	28Se02Gd
BRIAN, Patrick	40	M	Unknown	28Se02Gd
Mary	40	F	Unknown	28Se02Gd
Thomas	17	M	Unknown	28Se02Gd
Michael	13	M	Unknown	28Se02Gd
Mary	11	F	Unknown	28Se02Gd
John	9	M	Child	28Se02Gd
Margaret	7	F	Child	28Se02Gd
Christopher	5	M	Child	28Se02Gd
MULLAN, Ann	24	F	Unknown	28Se02Gd
BURK, Oliver	25	M	Unknown	28Se02Gd
DOHERTY, Mary	38	F	Unknown	28Se02Gd
DANDER, Michael	34	M	Unknown	28Se02Gd
Judith	20	F	Unknown	28Se02Gd
THORPE, Mary	30	F	Unknown	28Se02Gd
Died-At-Sea				
John-C.	5	M	Child	28Se02Gd
Thomas	4	M	Child	28Se02Gd
Died-At-Sea				
Edward	1	M	Child	28Se02Gd
Died-At-Sea				
COOK, Mary	69	F	Unknown	28Se02Gd
Died-At-Sea				
MULHOLLAND, Francis	35	M	Unknown	28Se02Gd
Margaret	30	F	Unknown	28Se02Gd
Patrick	3	M	Child	28Se02Gd
MCKEY, Edward	35	M	Unknown	28Se02Gd
READY, William	25	M	Unknown	28Se02Gd
Margaret	22	F	Unknown	28Se02Gd
MORRISON, Mary	45	F	Unknown	28Se02Gd
George	25	M	Unknown	28Se02Gd
Thomas	21	M	Unknown	28Se02Gd
Wm.	15	M	Unknown	28Se02Gd
Eliza	17	F	Unknown	28Se02Gd
Jane	17	F	Unknown	28Se02Gd
Eliza	26	F	Unknown	28Se02Gd
Arthur	.00	M	Infant	28Se02Gd
BOKER, Robert	50	M	Unknown	28Se02Gd
Ann	50	F	Unknown	28Se02Gd
Jane	20	F	Unknown	28Se02Gd
FLINN, Honora	8	F	Child	28Se02Gd
Robert	10	M	Child	28Se02Gd

NAMES OF PASSENGERS	AGE	SEX	OCCUPATIONS	DATE PORT SHIP
COUGHLIN, Margaret	22	F	Unknown	28Se02Gd
COLCLOUGH, Bridget	28	F	Unknown	28Se02Gd
DOWDALL, William	22	M	Unknown	28Se02Gd
Margaret	22	F	Unknown	28Se02Gd
Maria	.00	F	Infant	28Se02Gd
HONRAN, Thomas	25	M	Unknown	28Se02Gd
Margaret	26	F	Unknown	28Se02Gd
Isabella	10	F	Unknown	28Se02Gd
Othwell	3	M	Child	28Se02Gd
William	.00	M	Infant	28Se02Gd
MURPHY, Ron	25	M	Unknown	28Se02Gd
And.	25	M	Unknown	28Se02Gd
KEARNEN, James	22	M	Unknown	28Se02Gd
MCLEON, Ann	40	F	Unknown	28Se02Gd
Margaret	24	F	Unknown	28Se02Gd
SHANNON, John	11	M	Unknown	28Se02Gd
Ellen	29	F	Unknown	28Se02Gd
Mary	34	F	Unknown	28Se02Gd
OWENS, John	35	M	Unknown	28Se02Gd
MORGAN, Henry	23	M	Unknown	28Se02Gd
U	28	F	Unknown	28Se02Gd
Henry-Jr.	26	M	Unknown	28Se02Gd
ROBISON, John	23	M	Unknown	28Se02Gd
Jane	26	F	Unknown	28Se02Gd
Mary-Ann Died-At-Sea	3	F	Child	28Se02Gd
Eliza Died-At-Sea	.00	F	Infant	28Se02Gd
CONWELL, Martin	25	M	Unknown	28Se02Gd
WOODS, Thomas	22	M	Unknown	28Se02Gd
CONWELL, Mary	60	F	Unknown	28Se02Gd
MCMAHON, John	21	M	Unknown	28Se02Gd
GREEN, Ellen	14	F	Unknown	28Se02Gd
Mary	17	F	Unknown	28Se02Gd
FENNING, Thomas	25	M	Unknown	28Se02Gd
NIEL, Margaret	35	F	Unknown	28Se02Gd
Mary	21	F	Unknown	28Se02Gd
MCMAHON, Andrew	35	M	Unknown	28Se02Gd
Mary	25	F	Unknown	28Se02Gd
SAWYER, William	30	M	Unknown	28Se02Gd
Johanna	26	F	Unknown	28Se02Gd
James	26	M	Unknown	28Se02Gd
Mary	2	F	Child	28Se02Gd
John	.00	M	Infant	28Se02Gd
Bridget	3	F	Child	28Se02Gd
LAMBERT, Robert	23	M	Unknown	28Se02Gd
CONWAY, Charles	35	M	Unknown	28Se02Gd
SIMPSON, George	23	M	Unknown	28Se02Gd
HANOVER, Solomen	35	M	Unknown	28Se02Gd
Eliza	27	F	Unknown	28Se02Gd
Francis	4	M	Child	28Se02Gd
Sarah	.00	F	Infant	28Se02Gd
CONNOR, Mary	40	F	Unknown	28Se02Gd
Thomas	20	M	Unknown	28Se02Gd
Bridget	18	F	Unknown	28Se02Gd
SANDLER, Margaret	16	F	Unknown	28Se02Gd
WALSH, Alex	17	M	Unknown	28Se02Gd
KERBY, Winch	20	M	Unknown	28Se02Gd
DALEY, James	24	M	Unknown	28Se02Gd
KENNEDY, John	20	M	Unknown	28Se02Gd

LADY-OF-THE-LAKE 28 SEPTEMBER 1849

From Bermuda

NAMES OF PASSENGERS	AGE	SEX	OCCUPATIONS	DATE PORT SHIP
THOMAS, John	40	M	Baker	28Se29Nu
Sally	35	F	Baker	28Se29Nu
GIBSON, John	18	M	Maurer	28Se29Nu

JOHN-HANCOCK 28 SEPTEMBER 1849

From Liverpool

NAMES OF PASSENGERS	AGE	SEX	OCCUPATIONS	DATE PORT SHIP
CRONIN, Dennis	35	M	Laborer	28Se02Jt
Margaret	35	F	Unknown	28Se02Jt
LANNON, John	12	M	Unknown	28Se02Jt
Ann	11	F	Unknown	28Se02Jt
Timothy	7	M	Child	28Se02Jt
LOAGHEAD, Anne	40	F	Unknown	28Se02Jt
William	13	M	Unknown	28Se02Jt
Anne	9	F	Child	28Se02Jt
Eliza	5	F	Child	28Se02Jt
Cecilia	3	F	Child	28Se02Jt
BODY, Robert	32	M	Unknown	28Se02Jt
ROACH, John	21	M	Unknown	28Se02Jt
Eliza	19	F	Unknown	28Se02Jt
ASPDEN, U-Mrs.	40	F	Unknown	28Se02Jt
Sera	19	F	Unknown	28Se02Jt
Alice	16	F	Unknown	28Se02Jt
Mary-Anne	14	F	Unknown	28Se02Jt
Henry	11	M	Unknown	28Se02Jt
James	9	M	Child	28Se02Jt
Ellen	6	F	Child	28Se02Jt
Joseph	3	M	Child	28Se02Jt
JUDGE, Thomas	26	M	Unknown	28Se02Jt
Bridget	25	F	Unknown	28Se02Jt
Anne	00	F	Unknown	28Se02Jt
GORDON, Anthony	18	M	Unknown	28Se02Jt
Mary	50	F	Unknown	28Se02Jt
SWEENY, Jedy	23	F	Unknown	28Se02Jt
GALAGHER, John	20	M	Unknown	28Se02Jt
GLASSBROOK, Joseph	28	M	Unknown	28Se02Jt
Mary	26	F	Unknown	28Se02Jt
MAHONY, Narry	20	M	Unknown	28Se02Jt
GLASSBROOK, Thomas	7	M	Child	28Se02Jt
Eliza	5	F	Child	28Se02Jt
Timothy	3	M	Child	28Se02Jt
Margaret	.00	F	Infant	28Se02Jt
COULBERT, John	24	M	Unknown	28Se02Jt
COLLINS, Mary	20	F	Unknown	28Se02Jt
JONES, Edward	25	M	Unknown	28Se02Jt
Elenor	23	F	Unknown	28Se02Jt
Mary	2	F	Child	28Se02Jt
FARRELL, Daniel	29	M	Unknown	28Se02Jt
Mary	18	F	Unknown	28Se02Jt
DURKIN, Ellen	30	F	Unknown	28Se02Jt
MCDONALD, Rosana	16	F	Unknown	28Se02Jt
ONEILL, James	21	M	Unknown	28Se02Jt
Mary	23	F	Unknown	28Se02Jt
Anne	30	F	Unknown	28Se02Jt
James	7	M	Child	28Se02Jt
Betsey	5	F	Child	28Se02Jt
John	3	M	Child	28Se02Jt
HIGGINS, Michael	22	M	Unknown	28Se02Jt
TWOHY, Alice	22	F	Unknown	28Se02Jt
Patrick	2	M	Child	28Se02Jt
Sera	.09	F	Infant	28Se02Jt
MURPHY, Charles	40	M	Unknown	28Se02Jt
Mary	35	F	Unknown	28Se02Jt
Nicholas	19	M	Unknown	28Se02Jt
Moses	16	M	Unknown	28Se02Jt
HUGHY, Myles	30	M	Unknown	28Se02Jt
Penelope	28	F	Unknown	28Se02Jt
Catherine	2	F	Child	28Se02Jt
Margaret	.00	F	Infant	28Se02Jt
SANDEY, U-Mrs.	28	F	Unknown	28Se02Jt
Wm.	24	M	Unknown	28Se02Jt
MURRAY, Ellen	32	F	Unknown	28Se02Jt

NAMES OF PASSENGERS	A G E	S E X	OCCUPATIONS	DATE PORT SHIP
LYNCH, Bridget	22	F	Unknown	28Se02Jt
RYAN, Stephen	30	M	Unknown	28Se02Jt
GARGAN, Henry	27	M	Unknown	28Se02Jt
Esther	30	F	Unknown	28Se02Jt
CAROLIN, Catherine	18	F	Unknown	28Se02Jt
SMITH, Betsy	18	F	Unknown	28Se02Jt
CAROLIN, Mary	19	F	Unknown	28Se02Jt
Philip	7	M	Child	28Se02Jt
Francis	7	M	Child	28Se02Jt
Mary	3	F	Child	28Se02Jt
MCCABE, Henry	22	M	Unknown	28Se02Jt
SARLCIN, Larry	34	M	Unknown	28Se02Jt
DWYER, Malach	23	M	Unknown	28Se02Jt
COLLINS, Thomas	30	M	Unknown	28Se02Jt
Margaret	28	F	Unknown	28Se02Jt
Bridget	26	F	Unknown	28Se02Jt
Ellen	9	F	Child	28Se02Jt
Thomas	8	M	Child	28Se02Jt
Eliza	6	F	Child	28Se02Jt
Bridget	3	F	Child	28Se02Jt
Margaret	3	F	Child	28Se02Jt
Owen	.00	M	Infant	28Se02Jt
FARLEY, Bridget	20	F	Unknown	28Se02Jt
Tyresa	17	F	Unknown	28Se02Jt
HENDERSON, Joseph	28	M	Unknown	28Se02Jt
Mary	27	F	Unknown	28Se02Jt
BRENNAN, Benard	20	M	Unknown	28Se02Jt
HIGGINS, Pat	35	M	Unknown	28Se02Jt
Martin	35	M	Unknown	28Se02Jt
OKES, Ann	20	F	Unknown	28Se02Jt
Margaret	18	F	Unknown	28Se02Jt
DUFFY, Susanna	19	F	Unknown	28Se02Jt
FITZPATRICK, Margt.	50	F	Unknown	28Se02Jt
DUBBIN, Mary	25	F	Unknown	28Se02Jt
MURPHY, Patrick	22	M	Unknown	28Se02Jt
Ellen	23	F	Unknown	28Se02Jt
Ellen	20	F	Unknown	28Se02Jt
Mary	5	F	Child	28Se02Jt
SOUTHWELL, Mary	30	F	Child	28Se02Jt
BIGLEY, Mary-Ann	30	F	Child	28Se02Jt
MCCANN, James	25	M	Unknown	28Se02Jt
Mary	23	F	Unknown	28Se02Jt
HADDEN, John	32	M	Unknown	28Se02Jt
Jane	55	F	Unknown	28Se02Jt
Anne	26	F	Unknown	28Se02Jt
GILLOWS, Edwd.	22	M	Unknown	28Se02Jt
WARD, William	26	M	Unknown	28Se02Jt
Michael	21	M	Unknown	28Se02Jt
GRADY, Patrick	18	M	Unknown	28Se02Jt
CUDDY, Michael	20	M	Unknown	28Se02Jt
STANLEY, Sera	20	F	Unknown	28Se02Jt
CASEY, John	23	M	Unknown	28Se02Jt
HUGHES, Walter	45	M	Unknown	28Se02Jt
Mary	23	F	Unknown	28Se02Jt
Prisella	18	F	Unknown	28Se02Jt
MOORE, Catherine	20	F	Unknown	28Se02Jt
HICKEY, William	30	M	Unknown	28Se02Jt
FALLUM, Mary	45	F	Unknown	28Se02Jt
Mary	11	F	Unknown	28Se02Jt
Bridget	8	F	Child	28Se02Jt
Margaret	7	F	Unknown	28Se02Jt
IRWIN, John	25	M	Unknown	28Se02Jt
SHINLE, James	19	M	Unknown	28Se02Jt
TYSON, William	24	M	Unknown	28Se02Jt
Elenor	23	F	Unknown	28Se02Jt
DEERY, Patrick	46	M	Unknown	28Se02Jt
CONNOR, Ellen	60	F	Unknown	28Se02Jt
ODEA, Sylvia	35	F	Unknown	28Se02Jt
John	35	M	Unknown	28Se02Jt
Biddy	6	F	Child	28Se02Jt
Biddy	50	F	Unknown	28Se02Jt
MORONEY, Eliza	18	F	Unknown	28Se02Jt
GLASS, Mabe	18	F	Unknown	28Se02Jt
BRODY, Mabe	17	F	Unknown	28Se02Jt
HOGAN, John	20	M	Unknown	28Se02Jt
HOGAN, Ellen	22	F	Unknown	28Se02Jt
OCONNOR, Bridget	20	F	Unknown	28Se02Jt
GRIFFIN, Biddy	30	F	Unknown	28Se02Jt
OCONNOR, Biddy	3	F	Child	28Se02Jt
SPRAIGHT, John	29	M	Unknown	28Se02Jt
James	24	M	Unknown	28Se02Jt
Margt.	24	F	Unknown	28Se02Jt
MATHEWS, James	20	M	Unknown	28Se02Jt
MCSOUGHLIN, Bernard	20	M	Unknown	28Se02Jt
GALVICH, Laurence	25	M	Unknown	28Se02Jt
MURPHY, Patrick	17	M	Unknown	28Se02Jt
Margt.	25	F	Unknown	28Se02Jt
WALSH, Mary	20	F	Unknown	28Se02Jt
REGAN, Michael	21	M	Unknown	28Se02Jt
REYNOLT, Martha	16	F	Unknown	28Se02Jt
James	13	M	Unknown	28Se02Jt
DRISCOLL, Timothy	18	M	Unknown	28Se02Jt
MARTIN, Bridget	20	F	Unknown	28Se02Jt
MURPHY, Ellen	16	F	Unknown	28Se02Jt
REARD, Honora	19	F	Unknown	28Se02Jt
Richard	.00	M	Infant	28Se02Jt
ROUCER, James	29	M	Unknown	28Se02Jt
James	70	M	Unknown	28Se02Jt
Catherine	60	F	Unknown	28Se02Jt
Bridget	21	F	Unknown	28Se02Jt
Catherine	18	F	Unknown	28Se02Jt
Margt.	19	F	Unknown	28Se02Jt
Bridget	16	F	Unknown	28Se02Jt
Mary	17	F	Unknown	28Se02Jt
HIGGINS, Michael	40	M	Unknown	28Se02Jt
Catherine	32	F	Unknown	28Se02Jt
Maria	3	F	Child	28Se02Jt
Patrick	.00	M	Infant	28Se02Jt
CONNOR, Johanna	50	F	Unknown	28Se02Jt
NILBOY, Ellen	8	F	Child	28Se02Jt
William	5	M	Child	28Se02Jt
QUINN, Rose	30	F	Unknown	28Se02Jt
Bridget	6	F	Child	28Se02Jt
Mary-Ann	3	F	Child	28Se02Jt
Mary	20	F	Unknown	28Se02Jt
James	.00	M	Infant	28Se02Jt
QUIGLY, William	29	M	Unknown	28Se02Jt
Margt.	25	F	Unknown	28Se02Jt
John	2	M	Child	28Se02Jt
Mary	.00	F	Infant	28Se02Jt
FINTON, James	23	M	Unknown	28Se02Jt
CROGHAM, John	16	M	Unknown	28Se02Jt
JOHNSON, John	36	M	Unknown	28Se02Jt
CURTIN, Patrick	27	M	Unknown	28Se02Jt
Mary	23	F	Unknown	28Se02Jt
William	.00	M	Infant	28Se02Jt
MCGUIRE, Patrick	19	M	Unknown	28Se02Jt
HALM, Michael	21	M	Unknown	28Se02Jt
REARDON, John	27	M	Unknown	28Se02Jt
MAHON, Peter	20	M	Unknown	28Se02Jt
Anne	18	F	Unknown	28Se02Jt
ROGERS, Patrick	20	M	Unknown	28Se02Jt
Bridget	16	F	Unknown	28Se02Jt
Maria	10	F	Unknown	28Se02Jt
CLANCY, Alley	30	F	Unknown	28Se02Jt
COWAN, Wilfred	16	M	Unknown	28Se02Jt
LYNCH, John	22	M	Unknown	28Se02Jt
MCCONNELL, Elizabeth	34	F	Unknown	28Se02Jt
BRADY, Ellen	20	F	Unknown	28Se02Jt
FLEMING, Margt.	22	F	Unknown	28Se02Jt
Anne	25	F	Unknown	28Se02Jt
MCGOVERN, Thomas	30	U	Unknown	28Se02Jt
Ellen	25	F	Unknown	28Se02Jt
Owen	.00	M	Infant	28Se02Jt
ROURKE, Michael	30	M	Unknown	28Se02Jt
TALBOT, Joseph	31	M	Unknown	28Se02Jt
NUGENT, Margt.	43	F	Unknown	28Se02Jt
Susan	25	F	Unknown	28Se02Jt
Margt.	23	F	Unknown	28Se02Jt
Elenor	19	F	Unknown	28Se02Jt

NAMES OF PASSENGERS	AGE	SEX	OCCUPATIONS	DATE PORT SHIP
NUGENT, Richard	17	M	Unknown	28Se02Jt
Alice	13	F	Unknown	28Se02Jt
Charles	9	M	Child	28Se02Jt
Margt.	25	F	Unknown	28Se02Jt
MCENEVY, Mary	20	F	Unknown	28Se02Jt
Patrick	15	M	Unknown	28Se02Jt
BRADY, Bernard	21	M	Unknown	28Se02Jt
MCENEVY, Elenor	17	F	Unknown	28Se02Jt
MCDONNELL, Rose	21	F	Unknown	28Se02Jt
BYRNE, Anne	24	F	Unknown	28Se02Jt
CASTLES, Elizabeth	24	F	Unknown	28Se02Jt
Richard	7	M	Child	28Se02Jt
Anne	3	F	Child	28Se02Jt
CAMERON, Wm.	23	M	Unknown	28Se02Jt
JARRETT, Benjamin	28	M	Unknown	28Se02Jt
Anne	25	F	Unknown	28Se02Jt
Stephen	2	M	Child	28Se02Jt
Edward	.00	M	Infant	28Se02Jt
CARVIN, Michael	30	M	Unknown	28Se02Jt
Anne	26	F	Unknown	28Se02Jt
Mary	.00	F	Infant	28Se02Jt
ANDERSON, Margt.	34	F	Unknown	28Se02Jt
Jane	14	F	Unknown	28Se02Jt
HOLLAND, John	23	M	Unknown	28Se02Jt
CAHILL, Johanna	40	F	Unknown	28Se02Jt
LITTLE, Susan	30	F	Unknown	28Se02Jt
GROGHAN, Lawrence	44	M	Unknown	28Se02Jt
FLAHERTY, William	5	M	Child	28Se02Jt
CONOLLY, Thomas	28	M	Unknown	28Se02Jt
Patrick	25	M	Unknown	28Se02Jt
MCDONNELL, Alex	23	M	Unknown	28Se02Jt
BRODIGAN, Wm.	24	M	Unknown	28Se02Jt
MARTIN, Margaret	39	F	Unknown	28Se02Jt
Bridget	12	F	Unknown	28Se02Jt
Elenor	10	F	Unknown	28Se02Jt
Alice	8	F	Child	28Se02Jt
Ann	5	F	Child	28Se02Jt
DEANE, Thomas	27	M	Unknown	28Se02Jt
U-Mrs.	24	F	Unknown	28Se02Jt
WILLIAMS, John	36	M	Unknown	28Se02Jt
BYRNE, John	30	M	Unknown	28Se02Jt
Bridget	25	F	Unknown	28Se02Jt
Mary	.00	F	Infant	28Se02Jt
Died-At-Sea				
CONDIFF, Jeremiah	57	M	Unknown	28Se02Jt
Julia	30	F	Unknown	28Se02Jt
Honora	17	F	Unknown	28Se02Jt
Timothy	12	M	Unknown	28Se02Jt
Johanna	11	F	Unknown	28Se02Jt
SHEA, Johanna	30	F	Unknown	28Se02Jt
BUSHELL, Richard	47	M	Unknown	28Se02Jt
MCKEVER, Ann	18	F	Unknown	28Se02Jt
Bridget	16	F	Unknown	28Se02Jt
Mary	40	F	Unknown	28Se02Jt
HARRATTY, Ann	50	F	Unknown	28Se02Jt
MCKEVER, Mary	13	F	Unknown	28Se02Jt
Jane	12	F	Unknown	28Se02Jt
John	9	M	Child	28Se02Jt
James	11	M	Unknown	28Se02Jt
Brien	6	M	Child	28Se02Jt
CLEAVY, John	27	M	Unknown	28Se02Jt
MCCORMICK, James	50	M	Unknown	28Se02Jt
Brien	20	M	Unknown	28Se02Jt
BENSON, Catherine	23	F	Unknown	28Se02Jt
Ann	19	F	Unknown	28Se02Jt
WARRIN, James	25	M	Unknown	28Se02Jt
STANLEY, Mary	21	F	Unknown	28Se02Jt
FOX, Mary	22	F	Unknown	28Se02Jt
READY, John	30	M	Unknown	28Se02Jt
WALSH, Thomas	32	M	Unknown	28Se02Jt
MCCAFFRE, John	18	M	Unknown	28Se02Jt
BLIGHT, Thomas	20	M	Unknown	28Se02Jt
BARRY, James	15	M	Unknown	28Se02Jt
JORDAN, Barth.	26	M	Unknown	28Se02Jt
Mary	24	F	Unknown	28Se02Jt
LENANE, Winiford	25	M	Unknown	28Se02Jt
CUNNINGHAM, Edward	20	M	Unknown	28Se02Jt
DRAKE, Raphael	26	M	Unknown	28Se02Jt
MCLILLAN, Brien	00	M	Unknown	28Se02Jt
WOODS, James	45	M	Farmer	28Se02Jt
Ellen	16	F	Farmer	28Se02Jt
BRICE, William	38	M	Farmer	28Se02Jt
Sarah	34	F	Unknown	28Se02Jt
Sarah	12	F	Unknown	28Se02Jt
William	10	M	Unknown	28Se02Jt
Charlotte	8	F	Child	28Se02Jt
Louis-K.	7	M	Child	28Se02Jt
Margaret	6	F	Unknown	28Se02Jt
Charles	.00	M	Infant	28Se02Jt
SUTHERLAND, James	26	M	Unknown	28Se02Jt
WILSON, Thomas	24	M	Unknown	28Se02Jt
BYRNES, Mary	33	F	Unknown	28Se02Jt
LLOYD, Thomas	34	M	Unknown	28Se02Jt
Hannah	33	F	Unknown	28Se02Jt
Margaret-Ann	3	F	Child	28Se02Jt
TROFANT, Emma	.00	F	Infant	28Se02Jt
CONOLLY, Michael	22	M	Unknown	28Se02Jt
WILKINSON, Thomas	21	M	Laborer	28Se02Jt

ANN-HARLEY 28 SEPTEMBER 1849

From Glasgow

NAMES OF PASSENGERS		AGE	SEX	OCCUPATIONS	DATE PORT SHIP
CONNOLLY, James		35	M	Laborer	28Se04Hj
Jane	(W)	40	F	Wife	28Se04Hj
HAVLIN, Sarah		45	F	Wife	28Se04Hj
Patrick		10	M	Unknown	28Se04Hj
Thomas		8	M	Child	28Se04Hj
MURRAY, William		32	M	Farmer	28Se04Hj
Hugh		9	M	Child	28Se04Hj
John		30	M	Farmer	28Se04Hj
Patrick		25	M	Farmer	28Se04Hj
Catherine		22	F	Spinster	28Se04Hj
Ann		21	F	Spinster	28Se04Hj
GARVEY, John		27	M	Laborer	28Se04Hj
Owen		21	M	Laborer	28Se04Hj
DILLON, Edward		24	M	Laborer	28Se04Hj
Helen	(W)	18	F	Wife	28Se04Hj
MCCENNAY, Eliza		24	F	Spinster	28Se04Hj
DOYLE, Mary		28	F	Spinster	28Se04Hj
MURPHY, Margaret		00	F	Unknown	28Se04Hj

WYANDOTTE 29 SEPTEMBER 1849

From Limerick

NAMES OF PASSENGERS		AGE	SEX	OCCUPATIONS	DATE PORT SHIP
CURTIN, Patt		24	M	Farmer	29Se35Qi
Mary	(W)	27	F	None	29Se35Qi
FITZGERALD, David		18	M	Farmer	29Se35Qi
MCCARTHY, Mary		30	F	Spinster	29Se35Qi
NASH, Francis		20	M	Laborer	29Se35Qi
Bridget		24	F	Spinster	29Se35Qi
Betsy		22	F	Spinster	29Se35Qi
OSHANNESSY, William		56	M	Farmer	29Se35Qi
Sarah	(W)	49	F	None	29Se35Qi
Sarah		16	F	None	29Se35Qi
William		12	M	None	29Se35Qi
Mary-Ann		10	F	None	29Se35Qi

NAMES OF PASSENGERS	AGE	SEX	OCCUPATIONS	DATE PORT SHIP
OSHANNESSY, John	6	M	Child	29Se35Qi
CONNORS, Garry	44	M	Farmer	29Se35Qi
Ellen (W)	40	F	None	29Se35Qi
Thomas	21	M	Farmer	29Se35Qi
Mary	18	F	None	29Se35Qi
Patt	5	M	Child	29Se35Qi
Johanna	3	F	Child	29Se35Qi
Bridget	.05	F	Infant	29Se35Qi
Died-At-Sea				
OSHEA, Mary-Ann	17	F	Spinster	29Se35Qi
HALVEY, Ellen	26	F	Spinster	29Se35Qi
FARREL, Thomas	20	M	Laborer	29Se35Qi
CONNELLY, Andrew-J.	22	M	Clerk	29Se35Qi
CORBETT, Thomas	17	M	Laborer	29Se35Qi
ODEA, Margaret	20	F	Spinster	29Se35Qi
MULVAHILL, Michael	21	M	Laborer	29Se35Qi
FITZGERALD, John	37	M	Laborer	29Se35Qi
CANNODY, Mary	22	F	Spinster	29Se35Qi
Johanna	20	F	Spinster	29Se35Qi
CANBOY, Dennis	22	M	Laborer	29Se35Qi
William	25	M	Laborer	29Se35Qi
U, U	00	U	Unknown	29Se35Qi
William	18	M	Unknown	29Se35Qi
POWER, Thomas	18	M	Unknown	29Se35Qi
Catherine	21	F	Spinster	29Se35Qi
FLEMING, Ellen	30	F	Spinster	29Se35Qi
CARROLL, Anty	30	M	Spinster	29Se35Qi
MORRITY, Michael	40	M	Farmer	29Se35Qi
MCMAHON, Thomas	20	M	Farmer	29Se35Qi
VERNON, Catherine	18	F	Spinster	29Se35Qi
LEONARD, Catherine	18	F	Spinster	29Se35Qi
Catherine	.07	F	Infant	29Se35Qi
HONERBY, James	22	M	Farmer	29Se35Qi
Johanna	19	F	Spinster	29Se35Qi
NEALON, Mary	20	F	Spinster	29Se35Qi
COSGRIFF, Michael	23	M	Laborer	29Se35Qi
OKEAF, John	21	M	Laborer	29Se35Qi
HANLEY, Cornelius	40	M	Laborer	29Se35Qi
HARNETT, John	24	M	Laborer	29Se35Qi
Catherine (W)	21	F	None	29Se35Qi
STUBBINS, Michael	30	M	Laborer	29Se35Qi
Ellen (W)	22	F	None	29Se35Qi
Mary	4	F	Child	29Se35Qi
John	6	M	Child	29Se35Qi
Michael	2	M	Child	29Se35Qi
WHITAKER, John	40	M	Laborer	29Se35Qi
NEWMAN, Thomas	13	M	Laborer	29Se35Qi
Mary	11	F	Unknown	29Se35Qi
DOOLING, Alice	22	F	Spinster	29Se35Qi
OKEEF, Patt	20	M	Farmer	29Se35Qi
CONNOLLY, Winfred	40	M	Farmer	29Se35Qi
Mary	14	F	None	29Se35Qi
Julia	12	F	None	29Se35Qi
John	10	M	None	29Se35Qi
Dorah	8	F	Child	29Se35Qi
Maurice	6	M	Child	29Se35Qi
Ann	4	F	Child	29Se35Qi
Thomas	.01	M	Infant	29Se35Qi
OBRIEN, Michael	44	M	Laborer	29Se35Qi
Ellen (W)	25	F	None	29Se35Qi
BOLAND, John	30	M	Laborer	29Se35Qi
KENNAN, Michael	32	M	Laborer	29Se35Qi
Catherine (W)	32	F	None	29Se35Qi
LAFFEN, William	25	M	Farmer	29Se35Qi
Richard	20	M	Farmer	29Se35Qi
HAYES, Dennis	24	M	Farmer	29Se35Qi
MCINERNEY, James	20	M	Farmer	29Se35Qi
HAYES, Bridget	24	F	Wife	29Se35Qi
MCINERNEY, Ann	20	F	Wife	29Se35Qi
OBRIEN, John	34	M	Farmer	29Se35Qi
Bridget	20	F	Spinster	29Se35Qi
Mary	18	F	Spinster	29Se35Qi
KENNEDY, Michael	30	M	Farmer	29Se35Qi
LAVY, Mary	20	F	Spinster	29Se35Qi
Mary	18	F	Spinster	29Se35Qi
SHANNON, Magt.	18	F	Spinster	29Se35Qi
FORAN, Mary-Bounce	40	F	Spinster	29Se35Qi
Susan	8	F	Child	29Se35Qi
Mary	6	F	Child	29Se35Qi
CURTIN, Bridget	20	F	Spinster	29Se35Qi
ODEA, Catherine	18	F	Spinster	29Se35Qi
HANDBY, Cathe.	19	F	Spinster	29Se35Qi
ONEILL, Honora	20	F	Spinster	29Se35Qi
OBRIEN, Ellen	22	F	Spinster	29Se35Qi
CROW, Ellen	20	F	Spinster	29Se35Qi
KELLY, Winfred	26	M	Spinster	29Se35Qi
HEALY, John	12	M	None	29Se35Qi
TARRY, Johanna	30	F	Spinster	29Se35Qi
MILLINS, John	32	M	Unknown	29Se35Qi
Patt	17	M	Unknown	29Se35Qi
BURK, Bridget	18	F	Unknown	29Se35Qi
BOLAND, Catherine	16	F	Unknown	29Se35Qi
CURRY, Bridget	20	F	Unknown	29Se35Qi
BOUNCE, Michl.	36	M	Farmer	29Se35Qi
COLLINS, Mary	18	F	Unknown	29Se35Qi
Nitty	16	F	Unknown	29Se35Qi
FLANIGAN, Jeremiah	20	M	Laborer	29Se35Qi
DRISCOTT, John	25	M	Unknown	29Se35Qi
GALVIN, Mary	38	F	Unknown	29Se35Qi
Patt	.11	M	Infant	29Se35Qi
DUNNE, Bridget	50	F	Unknown	29Se35Qi
Eliza	22	F	Unknown	29Se35Qi
Mary-Ann	20	F	Unknown	29Se35Qi
SULLIVAN, Michael	18	M	Farmer	29Se35Qi
RYAN, Thomas	22	M	Farmer	29Se35Qi
HUNT, Garret	36	M	Farmer	29Se35Qi
WESTROFS, John	36	M	Farmer	29Se35Qi
GRIFFIN, Thomas	24	M	Farmer	29Se35Qi
Gerald	20	M	Farmer	29Se35Qi
FITZGERALD, Ann	16	F	Unknown	29Se35Qi
Maria	12	F	Unknown	29Se35Qi
HINCHEY, Bridget	18	F	Unknown	29Se35Qi
MULLY, U-Mrs.	28	F	Unknown	29Se35Qi
Johanna	.09	F	Infant	29Se35Qi
CONNORS, Ellen	13	F	Unknown	29Se35Qi

ELIZABETH 29 SEPTEMBER 1849

From Dublin

NAMES OF PASSENGERS	AGE	SEX	OCCUPATIONS	DATE PORT SHIP
WILSON, John	22	M	Laborer	29Se12Bk
ELLISON, Edward	21	M	Laborer	29Se12Bk
MORAN, Michael	45	M	Laborer	29Se12Bk
HADDIGAN, Patt	20	M	Laborer	29Se12Bk
CONNOLLY, Michl.	20	M	Laborer	29Se12Bk
HESLIT, Bridget	20	F	Spinster	29Se12Bk
CAVANNAGH, Owen	40	M	Laborer	29Se12Bk
Catherine	36	F	Unknown	29Se12Bk
FARRELL, Mary	20	F	Unknown	29Se12Bk
GRAY, John	16	M	Unknown	29Se12Bk
BRIDE, Ellen	26	F	Unknown	29Se12Bk
George	1	M	Child	29Se12Bk
CUDDY, Richard	22	M	Laborer	29Se12Bk
OLAUGHLIN, Thos.	40	M	Laborer	29Se12Bk
U-Mrs.	36	F	Unknown	29Se12Bk
Mary	18	F	Unknown	29Se12Bk
Biddy	16	F	Unknown	29Se12Bk
Catherine	13	F	Unknown	29Se12Bk
Joe	9	M	Child	29Se12Bk
Anne	6	M	Child	29Se12Bk
Thomas	4	M	Child	29Se12Bk
HAVERTY, Anne	20	F	Spinster	29Se12Bk
STANTON, Mary	20	F	Spinster	29Se12Bk
CRAWLEY, Michael	30	M	Blacksmith	29Se12Bk

NAMES OF PASSENGERS	AGE	SEX	OCCUPATIONS	DATE PORT SHIP
LYNCH, Mary	21	F	Spinster	29Se12Bk
BRAY, Jas.	24	M	Cartwright	29Se12Bk
CORMACK, Anne	14	F	Unknown	29Se12Bk
Mary	11	F	Unknown	29Se12Bk
Catherine	9	F	Child	29Se12Bk
MCCARTY, U-Mrs.	22	F	Unknown	29Se12Bk
SHANLEY, Mrs.	30	F	Unknown	29Se12Bk
Edwd.	8	M	Child	29Se12Bk
Patt	2	M	Child	29Se12Bk
Mary	5	F	Child	29Se12Bk
Wm.	16	M	Unknown	29Se12Bk
Peter	18	M	Unknown	29Se12Bk
JORDAN, Thos.	30	M	Shoemaker	29Se12Bk
MELCONNELL, Susan	20	F	Unknown	29Se12Bk
BOYLAN, Anne	18	F	Unknown	29Se12Bk
WHELAN, Michael	21	M	Laborer	29Se12Bk
HAYES, Abbin	26	M	Laborer	29Se12Bk
BRENNAN, Eliza	16	F	Unknown	29Se12Bk
Margaret	20	F	Unknown	29Se12Bk
John	22	M	Unknown	29Se12Bk
Bridget	24	F	Unknown	29Se12Bk
CREGAN, Mary	20	F	Unknown	29Se12Bk
MAGUIRE, Martin	20	M	Laborer	29Se12Bk
Mary	20	F	Unknown	29Se12Bk
Bridget	27	F	Unknown	29Se12Bk
WHITE, Ellen	22	F	Unknown	29Se12Bk
GOVERN, M.	20	M	Cbtmkr	29Se12Bk
COFFEY, Michael	46	M	Laborer	29Se12Bk
Mary	46	F	Unknown	29Se12Bk
HAYS, John	22	M	Blacksmith	29Se12Bk
MURRAN, Patt	23	M	Blacksmith	29Se12Bk
Bridget	20	F	Unknown	29Se12Bk
CAVANNAGH, Henry	13	M	Unknown	29Se12Bk
LYNCH, J.P.	40	M	Laborer	29Se12Bk
MASON, Isabella	22	F	Unknown	29Se12Bk
Ellen	20	F	Unknown	29Se12Bk
Eliza	21	F	Unknown	29Se12Bk
NIELLY, Christn.-O.	20	M	Laborer	29Se12Bk
FENLAN, U-Miss.	21	F	Unknown	29Se12Bk
Ellen	19	F	Unknown	29Se12Bk
HICKEY, Thos.	35	M	Wheelwright	29Se12Bk
U-Mrs.	30	F	Unknown	29Se12Bk
PARKINSON, Michael	40	M	Laborer	29Se12Bk
GREGGORY, Geo.	28	M	Laborer	29Se12Bk
EUSTOW, Jno.	24	M	Laborer	29Se12Bk
WILLIS, Jno.	22	M	Laborer	29Se12Bk
WHITE, Jas.	27	M	Laborer	29Se12Bk
CARVY, Wm.	25	M	Laborer	29Se12Bk
OSGOOD, Geo.	23	M	Laborer	29Se12Bk
CARROLL, Wm.	21	M	Laborer	29Se12Bk
DOYLE, Mary	20	F	Unknown	29Se12Bk
BATES, Jno.	35	M	Gentleman	29Se12Bk
WILSON, Thos.	26	M	Laborer	29Se12Bk

INDEX

Wol
Wol
C